LUTHERAN
CYCLOPEDIA

LUTHERAN CYCLOPEDIA

ERWIN L. LUEKER
Editor in Chief

CONCORDIA   PUBLISHING   HOUSE
SAINT LOUIS, MISSOURI

Editor's Preface

The LUTHERAN CYCLOPEDIA treats important aspects of the thought and life of the Church since the days of the Apostles. It includes the following areas:

Bible Interpretation (e. g., introduction to the Bible, commentaries, dictionaries and encyclopedias, canon, translations, higher and textual criticism, and other areas).

Systematized Theology (dogmatics, symbolical books, confessions and confessional statements, church bodies, philosophy, ethics, apologetics, terminology, polemics, and other areas).

Church History (church history from the time of the Apostles to modern times, history of doctrine, biography, archaeology, geography, patristics, movements in the Church, movements which have affected the Church, special emphasis on Lutheranism in America and other areas).

Life and Worship in the Church (pastoral theology, church polity, Christian education, homiletics, missions, diaconics, liturgics, music, art, architecture, hymnology, church organizations, publicity, social work, and other areas).

The LUTHERAN CYCLOPEDIA was written under the auspices of the General Literature Board of The Lutheran Church — Missouri Synod (Alfred Doerffler, Otto Nieting, Walter E. Hohenstein, William H. Eifert, William A. Kramer, Otto A. Dorn). This board considered policy, read the manuscript, and made suggestions to the editor.

William F. Arndt, Richard R. Caemmerer, Otto A. Dorn, and Frederick E. Mayer were requested to serve as editorial advisers. Frederick E. Mayer gave the editor suggestions he had gathered and then concentrated his attention on religious bodies. The other three advisers participated in the work as a whole until it reached the page-proof stage.

Arthur C. Repp and Richard R. Caemmerer read the final draft of the entire manuscript and gave suggestions for its improvement.

The following served as departmental consultants: William F. Arndt (New Testament); Walter A. Baepler (History; Ethics); Paul M. Bretscher (Philosophy); Walter E. Buszin (Church Music); Richard R. Caemmerer (Homiletics; other areas); John H. C. Fritz (Homiletics; Pastoral Theology); Theodore Graebner (Secret Societies; other areas); Theodore Hoyer (Reformation History); John T. Mueller (Apologetics; Dogmatics); Jaroslav Pelikan (General Church History); William G. Polack (Lutheran Church in America; Hymnology); George V. Schick (Old Testament; Ethnic Religions); Otto H. Schmidt (Missions); Lewis W. Spitz (General Church History); August R. Suelflow (Lutheran Church in America — served in this area after the death of William G. Polack); John M. Weiden-

PREFACE

schilling (Ethical Terms of the Bible); Emil C. Weis (General English Literature); Henry F. Wind (Social Work). The Board for Parish Education and Arthur C. Repp served as consultants in the area of Christian Education. Edward J. Saleska (librarian, Concordia Seminary, St. Louis), Lando C. Otto (librarian, St. Paul's College, Concordia, Mo.), and their staffs assisted the editor in the use of the libraries. Changes, additions, and short contributions by the above men were not initialed. Also longer articles which represent the work of several men are not initialed.

Basic articles were prepared by scholars in many fields. Their names are given under *Initials of Contributors*.

The following supplied information and material, gave suggestions, or assisted the editor in other ways: John Bajus; Emil M. Biegener; Lorenz Blankenbuehler; T. O. Burntvedt; George Dolak; Elmer E. Foelber; William Graumann; Herman Harms; R. W. Heikkinen; Fred Hortig; Alfred Jensen; Hans C. Jersild; Julia Koenig; Herman H. Koppelmann; Karl Kretzmann; Robert Lange; P. G. Lindhardt; Anna Marie Lueker; Carl E. Lund-Quist; Enok Mortensen; Martin J. Neeb; Paul C. Nyholm; Arthur C. Piepkorn; F. Eppling Reinartz; John Wargelin; Gilbert K. Wenger; Walter F. Wolbrecht; Leonhard C. Wuerffel; A. A. Uppala; Elmer C. Zimmermann; the editorial department of Concordia Publishing House; members of the board, faculty, and student body of St. Paul's College, Concordia, Mo.; members of the seminary faculties at St. Louis, Mo., and Springfield, Ill.

Materials from *Concordia Cyclopedia* (CPH, 1927) were adapted and used. Theodore Graebner first suggested and outlined this work and served as a member of the Editorial Board until 1923. Ludwig Fuerbringer and Theodore Engelder served as editors from the beginning, and Paul E. Kretzmann replaced Theodore Graebner. The associate editors were: Frederick Brand, William Dallmann, John H. C. Fritz, Theodore Graebner, Adolph Haentzschel, Edward Koehler, Karl Kretzmann, George W. Mueller, John T. Mueller, H. C. F. Otte, Theodore H. Schroedel, Franz C. Verwiebe. Some articles were written by John S. Bradac, Carl J. A. Hoffmann, J. A. Moldstad, H. K. Moussa, William H. Behrens, Frederick Wenger. Notes with varied suggestions by Ludwig Fuerbringer and other editors of *Concordia Cyclopedia* were made available to the editor.

With the permission of the publisher or author some materials, including articles in *Abiding Word* (Theodore Laetsch, editor), were condensed for LUTHERAN CYCLOPEDIA. The original author is indicated (with an asterisk in the list), but the editor alone is responsible for the condensation.

While it is not the function of a cyclopedia to serve as a book of current statistical information, the editor felt that figures near the middle of the 20th century would give some idea of the size or scope and also serve as a basis for future comparisons. In some instances, especially in the case of foreign countries, statistics are approximations by experts. The editor endeavored to secure the latest statistics available at the time the galleys were returned to the publisher. The reader who is interested in the latest current statistics is referred to the article *Statistics*.

PREFACE

The editor sought to adhere to the following principles:

1. Unless required by the specific nature of the subject matter, the treatment is factual and/or historical.
2. Statements which could be regarded as polemical and propagandic are avoided.

All contributions were subject to change as demanded by the size and scope of the cyclopedia.

In making a list of biographies it was considered best, especially in the case of Lutheranism in America, to follow the practice which places contemporary men into works like *Who's Who* rather than cyclopedias.

May the Lord of the Church find use for the efforts which men who love Him have given to this work.

St. Paul's College, Concordia, Mo.

February 1, 1954   ERWIN L. LUEKER

Editorial Staff

Abbreviations

Most of the abbreviations used in this volume are standard and may be found in standard dictionaries. The following is a list of some which are not well known or have a special meaning in this work.

* Person or thing thus starred in the body of the cyclopedia is separately listed; in the *Initials of Contributors* asterisks indicate authors of material which was condensed.

ABCFM American Board of Commissioners for Foreign Missions

AC Augsburg Confession

ACCC American Council of Christian Churches

ad. addition(s)

ALC American Lutheran Church

AP Apology of the Augsburg Confession

Ar. Arabic

art. article(s)

ATS American Tract Society

Aug. Augustana Evangelical Lutheran Church

b. born

bd. board

c. century; copyright

Cat. Catechism

cf. confer

c. f. condensed from

ch. church; chapter

CHIQ *Concordia Historical Institute Quarterly*

chrm. chairman

CIM China Inland Mission

CMS Church Missionary Society

coll. college

com. commission; committee

Conc. Concordia

cp. compare

CPH Concordia Publishing House

CTM *Concordia Theological Monthly*

d. died

Dan. Danish Lutheran

dist. district

ed. edition; editor

EKID Evangelische Kirche in Deutschland

ELC Evangelical Lutheran Church

em. emeritus

ev. evangelical

Ev. Rev. Evangelical Review

ex. executive; extrasynodical

FCCCA Federal Council of Churches of Christ in America

FMCNA Foreign Missions Conference of North America

F. of C. Formula of Concord

G. Greek

Ger. German

grad. graduate(d)

H. Hebrew

hist. history

int. intersynodical

L. Latin

LB Lutheran Brethren

LF Lutheran Free Church

LMS London Missionary Society

LQ Lutheran Quarterly

Luth. Lutheran; *Lutheraner*

L. u. W. Lehre und Wehre

Macm. Macmillan

mem. member

Mo. Missouri; Lutheran Church—Missouri Synod

NAE National Association of Evangelicals for United Action

n. d. no date

n. p. name of publisher or printer not given

NT New Testament

Norw. Norwegian

O. F. Old French

OT Old Testament

pub. publishing; publication

R. C. Roman Catholic

SC Synodical Conference

SELC Slovak Evangelical Lutheran Church

sem. seminary

Slov. Slovak Synod

soc. society

SPCK Society for Promoting Christian Knowledge

SPG Society for the Propagation of the Gospel

St. L. ed. Concordia (St. Louis) edition of Luther's Works

SVM Student Volunteer Movement

syn. synod

theol. theological

Thor. Decl. Thorough Declaration of the Formula of Concord

TQ Theological Quarterly

TQS Theologische Quartalschrift

Trigl. Triglot; Triglotta

UE United Evangelical Lutheran Church

ULC(A) United Lutheran Church in America

univ. (U.) university

VELKD Vereinigte Evangelisch-Lutherische Kirche in Deutschland

INITIALS OF CONTRIBUTORS

ACM	Arnold C. Mueller	JK *	John W. Klotz
ACR	Arthur C. Repp	JMJ	John M. Jensen
ACS	August C. Stellhorn	JMW	John M. Weidenschilling
AFK	Arnold F. Krentz	JP	Jaroslav Pelikan
AHG *	Arnold H. Grumm	JSB	John S. Bradac
AHN	Allen H. Nauss	JTM	John T. Mueller
AHS	Alfred H. Schwermann	KK	Karl Kurth
AJCM	Albert J. C. Moeller	LCW	Leonhard C. Wuerffel
ALA	Arthur L. Amt	LER *	Louis E. Roehm
ALG	August L. Graebner	LFW	Lorenz F. Wahlers
ALM	Arthur L. Miller	LJS	Louis J. Sieck
AlS	Alfred Schmieding	LW *	Lorenz Wunderlich
AMR	Alfred M. Rehwinkel	LWS	Lewis W. Spitz
ARS	August R. Suelflow	MHF	Martin H. Franzmann
AS	Armin Schroeder	MS	Martin H. Scharlemann
AWG	Arthur W. Gross	NG	Norman F. Gienapp
CaB	Carl Bergen	OAD	Otto A. Dorn
CAB *	Charles A. Behnke	OCH	Oswald C. J. Hoffmann
CAH	C. August Hardt	OEF	Oscar E. Feucht
CB	Conrad Bergendoff	OES.	Otto E. Sohn
CCS *	Curtis C. Stephan	OGM	O. G. Malmin
CK	Clarence E. Krumbholz	OHS	Otto H. Schmidt
CP	Clarence Peters	OTW	Oscar T. Walle
ECW	Emil C. Weis	PFB *	Paul F. Bente
ECZ	Elmer C. Zimmermann	PFS *	Paul F. Siegel
EER	Edward E. Ryden	PLD	Paul L. Dannenfeldt
EEY	Ernest E. Yunghans	PR	Paul H. Riedel
EGS	Ernest G. Schwiebert	RGL	Robert G. Lange
EHK	Erich H. Kiehl	RH *	Rudolf Herrmann
EJS	Edward J. Saleska	RHL	Ralph H. Long
EL	Erwin L. Lueker	RL	Richard H. Luecke
ELW *	Edwin L. Wilson	RLS *	Roger L. Sommer
EM	Elmer Maschoff	RRC	Richard R. Caemmerer
EMP *	Emil M. Plass	RWH	Reuben W. Hahn
ER	Edmund C. Reim	SCY	Sigurd C. Ylvisaker
ERB	Eugene R. Bertermann	SFR	Sadie Fulk Roehrs
EWG	Egon W. Gebauer	TC	Thomas Coates
FCS	Frank C. Streufert	TDM	Theodore D. Martens
FEM	Frederick E. Mayer	TG	Theodore Graebner
FK *	Fred Kramer	TGE	Theodore G. Eggers
FRW	Frederick R. Webber	TGS	Theodore G. Stelzer
GAA	Gustaf A. Aho	TGT	Theodore G. Tappert
GM	Gerhardt Mahler	TH	Theodore Hoyer
GVS	George V. Schick	WA	William F. Arndt
HAP	Herman A. Preus	WAB	Walter A. Baepler
HFW	Henry F. Wind	WAK	William A. Kramer
HH	Henry P. Hamann	WB	Walter E. Bauer
HHH	Herman H. Hohenstein	WEB	Walter E. Buszin
HHK	Herman H. Koppelmann	WFG *	Walter F. Geihsler
HLY	Harold L. Yochum	WFW *	Walter F. Wolbrecht
HM	Herman A. Mayer	WGP	William G. Polack
HS *	Henry P. Studtmann	WHM *	Wallace H. McLaughlin
HT	Harry A. Timm	WHW *	Walter H. Wente
HWG	Herman W. Gockel	WR	Walter R. Roehrs
JD	John Daniel, Jr.	WS	William Schaller
JHCF	John H. C. Fritz	WT	Wilfried Tappert

LUTHERAN CYCLOPEDIA

tinians; a forceful preacher, appealing to popular fancy; among his writings *Auf, auf, ihr Christen* (against Turks), *Judas der Erzschelm* (an imaginary autobiography), *Grammatica Religiosa* (compend of moral theology).

Abraham, Testament of. See *Apocrypha*, A 4.

Abrahamson, L. G. Pastor of the Augustana Synod and editor of its Swedish organ, *Augustana;* b. in Sweden, Mar. 2, 1856, and came to the United States, Jamestown, N. Y. Ordained in Des Moines, Iowa, on June 20, 1880; pastor at Altona and Wataga, Ill., 1880 to 1886; at Salem Church, Chicago, Ill., 1886—1908, when he was elected editor of *Augustana* by his synod. This position he held for over thirty years, retiring in 1940, continuing as "Editor Emeritus" until the time of his death on Nov. 3, 1946, at his home in Rock Island.

Abreaction. See *Psychology*, J 7.

Abrenunciation. The formal repudiation or utter renunciation of the devil and all his works and all his pomp, as practiced in the Church since ancient times in connection with the vow of Baptism. See *Exorcism.*

Absolute (L. "set free," "complete"). That which is self-sufficient. Philosophers used the term in various ways, Hegel, for example, applying it to the totality of the real. In cosmogony it is applied to the First Cause. Christians have applied the term to God.

Absolution. See *Keys, Office of.*

Absolution (Liturgical). The term is used in the Lutheran Church in a twofold sense. In the wider sense it refers to the so-called General Absolution which many church orders of the 16th century included in the regular service on Sunday morning, the pastor being required to read a general confession of sins after the sermon, followed by an absolution to the entire congregation. There were objections to this custom and several orders placed the General Absolution at the beginning of worship, where it was also placed by the Common Service. It is a declaration of the grace of God to repentant sinners. In a more restricted sense the term *absolution* refers to the public declaration of God's grace and mercy following the General Confession in the special preparatory service before the celebration of the Holy Communion. The communicants, hav-

ing had the Word of God applied to themselves in admonition and promise, make public confession of their sins, also of their faith in the forgiveness, state their willingness henceforth to amend their sinful lives, and are thereupon given the assurance of the grace of God in the simple and stately words of the formula of absolution. It is immaterial whether this proclamation be termed "Declaration of Grace" or "Absolution." In either case the forgiveness of sins declared in the Gospel is actually transmitted to all believers. See *Liturgics.*

Absolution (R. C.). See *Keys, Office of*, 8 b.

Absolutism. A theological term to designate the view held by exponents of an unconditional predestination,* that is, that God by an absolute decree destined certain men to eternal damnation.

Abstinence. Refraining from indulgence in food, wine, and pleasure. Examples of abstinence in the OT are: blood (Lev. 3:17), meats (Lev. 11), parts sacred to the altar (Lev. 3:9-17), meats consecrated to idols (Ex. 34:15), special (Lev. 9:10; Num. 6:5). The NT gives everyone liberty according to the dictates of conscience* and love regarding abstinence in adiaphora* (Rom. 14:1-3; 1 Cor. 8; Acts 15), condemns legalistic sects (1 Tim. 4:3, 4), and enjoins abstinence from all that has the appearance of evil (1 Thess. 5:22). See *Asceticism, Monasticism, Adiaphora.*

Abu Hanifa (d. 767). Persian Moslem; founder of Sunnite school of jurisprudence; liberal in interpretation of Koran.

Abuna. See *Abyssinia.*

Abyssinia. Located in East Africa, near the Red Sea, part of ancient Ethiopia. Population 15,000,000 (1947), chiefly Semitic Abyssinians, Somali Negroes, and Felashas of Jewish faith. Gained prominence in World War II through the attack of Italy, with the tragic figure of its emperor, Hailie Selassie, "the Lion of Judah," unable to find any help or comfort from the rest of the nations. Christianity came about 320, through two young captives, one of whom, Frumentius, later became the first bishop. Since the 6th century Monophysitism gained great influence. Has Coptic* form of Christianity (the chief priest called *abuna, i. e., father,* nomi-

A

Aarhus, Rasmus Jensen of. See *Canada, Lutheranism in,* 1.

Abbess. In many monastic communities of women, the superior, whose position corresponds to that of an abbot, except that she has no spiritual jurisdiction.

Abbey. A monastic house governed by an abbot or an abbess. In the Middle Ages the living quarters of the monastics were usually built in connection with the abbey church.

Abbo, Abbot of Fleury (ca. 945 to 1004). French scholar; during the decay of Anglo-Saxon culture he kept alive intellectual pursuits and, by emphasizing dialectics, directed theology toward scholasticism; his writings are source material on the Papacy during the reign of Robert II.

Abbot (from Syrian *abba,* father). The superior in certain communities of monks, especially Benedictines. Abbots must be priests and are usually elected for life by the members of the community. They are exempt from the jurisdiction of the bishop, administer the property of their abbey, maintain discipline, absolve, and, in certain cases, dispense. Some abbots, in the Middle Ages, held high rank and wielded great power.

Abbot, Ezra (1819—84). Unitarian; professor of NT criticism at Harvard; probably his most important work is *The Authorship of the Fourth Gospel,* in which he defends the Johannine authorship and shows the relation of Justin Martyr to this Gospel; textual critic.

Abbot, George (1562—1633). Archbishop of Canterbury; opposed Laud; supported Puritanism; one of those who prepared the King James Version.

Abbott, Lyman (1835—1922). Congregationalist clergyman and writer; editor of *Outlook;* wrote exegetical and practical treatises which emphasized social reform and the liberal "New Theology."

Abdas. Bishop of Susa; in 414 destroyed a heathen temple and caused a persecution against Christians during the reign of Yazdegerd I.

Abelard, Peter (1079—1142; Pierre de Palais). Studied under Roscellinus (leading nominalist), William of Champeaux (outstanding realist), Anselm of Laon and others; lectured at Corbeil and Paris; known because of his romance with Heloise; used the method of logical analysis to arrive at religious realities, thus contributing to the flowering of scholasticism; in his *Sic et Non* he showed the fathers to be contradictory, ambiguous, or both, thus arousing a critical attitude; in his Christology he emphasized the exemplary love manifested in Christ's death. Important works: *Logica Ingredientibus, Theologia Christiana, Sic et Non, Historia Calamitatum.*

J. G. Sikes, *Peter Abaelard,* Cambridge, 1932; E. C. Moore, *The Story of Instruction,* Macm. 1938 (pp. 301 to 381).

Abeokuta. A mission station of the Methodist Church on the Ogun River in West Africa, inhabited almost entirely by members of the Egba tribe, who fled before the Mohammedan invasion and united, in 1829, in a sort of nation. The work of the Methodists (1841) was followed by that of the Anglican Church (1845), which labored with conspicuous success. See *Crowther, Samuel; Missions, Bibliography.*

Abhiseka. 1) The Vedic rite of sprinkling rulers and officials. 2) The tenth Buddhic stage of perfection. 3) Hindu ceremonial bathing.

Ability, Child. See *Christian Teaching,* L.

Abjuration. 1) R. C., renunciation of apostasy, heresy, or schism by oath. 2) An oath ordained by Charles II of England abjuring doctrines of the Church of Rome.

Ablution. Water and wine with which Roman priests wash their fingers after Communion to preserve particles that may adhere to them. The priests drink the ablution.

Abraham a Sancta Clara. Monastic name of German preacher Ulrich Megerle (1644—1709); educated by Jesuits and Benedictines; held high positions in order of barefooted Augus-

nated by the patriarch of Cairo, whom the Copts acknowledge as their spiritual father). Abyssinia is called a Christian island in a sea of Mohammedanism,* though its Christianity is tainted by Jewish customs (circumcision, abstaining from certain foods as unclean, observance of Saturday as well as Sunday). Interminable and bitter disunity is present in Abyssinia because of disputes in respect to the unction of Christ. The language of the Church is Geez, though the language of the people is Amharic, in which tongue a translation of the Scriptures was prepared by Peter Heiling of Luebeck, who essayed missionary work there in 1834. In 1830 the Church Mission Society sent Samuel Gobat (1799—1879; after missionary efforts, bishop in Jerusalem) and others, who were expelled after ten years of missionary effort. Later, missionary attempts were made by Spittler (Chrischona), 1856; Dr. Stern, 1860, sent by the London Jews' Society; the American United Presbyterians, 1861; the Swedish Evangeliska Fosterlands Stiftelsen (1861, in Eritrea). Unsuccessful attempts were made by the Jesuits to attach the Abyssinian Church to Rome in the 16th, 17th, and 18th centuries. In 1947 there were 8,500,000 Christians, 2,500,000 Mohammedans, and 4,000,000 pagans in Abyssinia (estimated). See *Missions, Bibliography.* OHS

Abyssos. See *Hereafter,* C 6.

Acacians. Followers of Acacius of Caesarea (d. 366), a fragment of whose *Adversum Marcellum* is preserved by Epiphanius. Held the Son is like the Father in will only.

Accentus. The individual chanting of the service by the officiating priest, found chiefly in the Roman Church, seven accents being distinguished in liturgiology, namely, *medius, gravis, moderatus, acutus, interrogativus, immutabilis,* and *finalis.*

Acceptilation. A theological term first applied in the Middle Ages to denote the acceptance by God of an atonement, not because it is in itself an equivalent, but because God determines to accept it as such.

Accident. That which does not exist by itself essentially, but subsists in another self-existent essence, *e. g.,* original sin. In the Roman Catholic doctrine of transubstantiation bread and wine are defined as accidents, since the essence of bread and wine is said to be withdrawn after the consecration.

Accident Theory. See *Atonement, Theories of,* 1.

Accidie. Indifference or repugnance to worship (ennui), which is considered by Roman Catholics as one of the seven deadly sins.

Accommodation. 1. Term early used by mystical interpreters of Scripture to indicate that certain passages of Scripture conveyed higher thoughts than implicit in the words. 2. Socinian writers used it to denote the equivocal character supposed to inhere in sacred writers. 3. In more recent times it was applied to OT quotations in the NT which seemed quoted out of context (*e. g.,* Matt. 13:35; 8:17; 2:17, 18, *et al.*). 4. It also designates a rationalistic theory according to which Christ (in the Bible) accommodated Himself to mental conditions and errors of the times. 5. In the Catholic Church the *Accommodation Controversy* raged in the 17th and 18th centuries because Jesuits had permitted Chinese converts to pray to Confucius, continue ancestor worship, and call God *Tien* (Sky), claiming these to be harmless accommodations. 6. In evolutionary hypotheses it is applied to the adjustments which an organism is held to achieve or perfect in the lifetime of an individual.

Achenbach, Wilhelm. B. in Darmstadt, Hessen, Oct. 6, 1831, graduate of Concordia Seminary, St. Louis, ordained and installed as pastor in Grand Rapids, Mich., 1859; professor at Fort Wayne 1863 (senior asst.); pastor at Venedy, Ill. (1871), and St. Louis (Carondelet), Mo. (1883); d. Feb. 24, 1899.

Achrenius, Abraham. See *Finland, Lutheranism in,* 4.

Ackermann, Carl. B. Sept. 12, 1858; studied at Capital U. and Theol. Sem.; held various pastorates in Ohio; president Lima (Ohio) College, later professor; president Pacific Sem., Olympia, Wash.; professor at Capital University. D. June 7, 1943.

Acoemetae (G. "sleepless"). An Eastern order of monks (5th c.), which divided into choirs and celebrated services without intermission.

Acolyte. See *Hierarchy; Clergy.*

Acosmism. See *Pantheism.*

Acrelius, Israel (1714—1800). Born and trained in Sweden. Provost of the Swedish churches along the Delaware and pastor at Fort Christina (Wilmington, Del.), 1749—56. Recalled to Sweden, pastor at Fellensboro in the diocese of Westeras. Wrote *Description of the Former and Present Condition of the Swedish Churches in What Was Called New Sweden*, Stockholm, 1759. He was a friend of the patriarch Muhlenberg and defended him and his co-workers in his writings.

Acrostics. See *Symbolism, Christian*.

Act (Judicial). See *Justification*.

Act of Assembly. See *Presbyterian Bodies*, 1.

Act of Toleration. An act passed by the English Parliament under William and Mary (1689) relieving the legal disabilities of Protestant dissenters and protecting their worship. It restricted the laws passed under Elizabeth, James I, Charles I, and Charles II. Papists and anti-Trinitarians were excepted from the act.

Act of Uniformity. See *Congregational and Christian Churches*, A 1.

Acta Apocrypha. See *Apocrypha*, B 3.

Acta Apostolicae Sedis. Official periodical of the papal see, established Jan. 1, 1909, by Pius X.

Acta Facientes. See *Persecutions of Christians*, 4.

Acta Historico-Ecclesiasta. Journal published at Weimar (1734—1756) which gives information on contemporary Lutheran beginnings in America.

Acta Martyrum. Accounts of the trials of early martyrs which were circulated and often read on their birthdays. Important early *Acta* are: *Martyrium Polycarpi* (ca. 157), *Acta Justini et sociorum* (after 165), *Acta martyrum Scilitanorum* (ca. 185), *Passio Felicitatis et Perpetuae* (ca. 202). Beginning with the fourth century the *Acta* were gathered in special books (*Martyrologia* or *Calendaria*) which came to be used in commemorative feasts in the Roman Church. The accounts of the trials and deaths of martyrs were collected by Jesuits at Antwerp (1643 to 1910) with the title *Acta Sanctorum*. The company of Jesuits especially devoted to this task were called Bollandists after Jan Bolland.

O. v. Gebhardt, *Acta Martyrum Selecta*, Berlin, 1903. A. Harnack, *Gesch. der altchr. Litt. bis Euseb.*, Berlin, 1894 (pp. 807—834).

Acta Sanctorum. See *Acta Martyrum*.

Action Sermon. The pre-Communion sermon in Scottish Presbyterian churches, the Lord's Supper being termed the *action*.

Acts of 1905. See *Presbyterian Bodies*, 1.

Acts of John (of Paul, Peter, Thomas, etc.) See *Apocrypha*, B 3.

Adalbert (ca. 1000—1072). Archbishop of Hamburg and Bremen; through the favor of Henry III became archbishop and planned to unite Northern Europe under himself; this plan was frustrated by the Papacy.

Adalbert of Prague (ca. 956—997). Apostle of Bohemians and Prussians; as bishop of Prague he sought to remove heathen customs and institute moral reforms; repulsed, he devoted himself to mission work in Germany and Poland; baptized Stephen of Hungary; slain by heathen priest.

H. G. Voigt, *Adalbert von Prag*, Berlin, 1898.

Adam of Bremen (d. ca. 1076). Wrote *Gesta Hammenburgensis ecclesiae pontificum*, important source for northern European church history (788 to 1072).

Adamites. A sect in North Africa (2d—3d c.) which claimed the primitive innocence of Adam, met naked in its meetings (*"paradeises"*), and condemned marriage. Similar sect in Bohemia (15th—18th c.).

Adamnan (ca. 624—704). Irish monk; wrote *Life of St. Columba, de locis sanctis, Cain Adamnain* (?); upheld Roman date of Easter.

Adapa. Mythical Babylonian hero.

Addison, Joseph (1672—1719). B. May 1, 1672, at Milston, Wiltshire, England, son of the Rev. Lancelot Addison, sometime Dean of Litchfield. He was educated at Oxford and gave himself to the study of law and politics. He held some very important posts, e. g., Chief Secretary for Ireland. In 1716 he married the Dowager Charlotte, Countess of Warwick. Joseph Addison is particularly known for his contributions to *The Spectator*. Not only the leading literary light of his time, but also a devout Christian, he used his talents for hymn writing. Five of his hymns appeared in *The Spectator* in 1712.

Adelard of Bath (12th c.). English philosopher, theologian, astronomer, natural scientist; wrote *Per difficiles* *quaestiones naturales* (seeks to prove existence of God on basis of motion) and *De eodem et Diverso* (doctrine of indifference; unity of Plato and Aristotle).

Adelberg, R. (1835—1911). Educated at Hartwick Seminary; pastor at Albany and vice-president of New York Ministerium, 1859; joined Wisconsin Synod, 1869; pastor at Watertown and Milwaukee; synodical treasurer, editor *Gemeindeblatt,* assistant professor at seminary.

Adelophagi (G. "eat in secret"). A sect (4th c.) holding that Christians should eat in secret as prophets supposedly did.

Adeste, Fideles. Christmas hymn whose authorship has been ascribed to Bonaventura, also to Bishop Borderies, since it is apparently of seventeenth or eighteenth century origin; translations: "Come Hither, Ye Faithful," credited to Charles Porterfield Krauth; "Oh, Come, All Ye Faithful" by Edward Caswall and altered by Philip Schaff.

Adiaphora (G. "indifferent," "*Mitteldinge,*" "middle-matters"). The Lutheran Confessions speak of adiaphora as "church rites which are neither commanded nor forbidden in the Word of God." There is a definite province of activity which is not specifically covered by either God's command or God's prohibition. In the Old Dispensation, lives of believers were far more constricted than is the case today. Under the New Covenant God has lifted this yoke from us, and has not framed all human activity with His commands and prohibitions, but has consigned many acts to the discretion and judgment of the Christian (1 Cor. 6:12; 10:23; Rom. 14:3, 6; Col. 2:16, 17). While God has removed some matters from the domain of divine Law to the domain of adiaphora, it should, however, be noted that adiaphora (*in abstracto*) may cease to be adiaphora (*in concreto*) under certain circumstances (*e. g.,* when holding a life insurance policy springs from lack of trust in God; when smoking injures health; when drinking exceeds moderation; when immersion in Baptism is defended as the only correct mode; when cremation is an expression of atheism).

Pietists, in harmony with their doctrine of rebirth (*theologia regenitorum:* one reborn and having attained full spiritual manhood is free from sin), denied the existence of adiaphora,

quoting such passages as 1 Cor. 10:31; Col. 3:17; Rom. 14:23. They, however, confused the action itself with the life consecrated to God.

Adiaphora lie within the domain of Christian liberty, which may be defined as consisting of the freedom of believers from the curse (Gal. 3:13) and coercion (Rom. 6:14) of the Law, from Levitical ceremonies, and from human ordinances (Matt. 23:8-10; Luke 22:26; Rev. 5:10; 1 Pet. 2:8). This liberty is the direct result of justification (1 Tim. 1:9; Rom. 10:4; John 8:31,32,36). Adiaphora, however, are not a part of justifying faith, for they are not a product of that faith, they do not impose guilt (1 Cor. 7:36, 37), they do not effect a different relation between God and the sinner (1 Cor. 8:8; Rom. 14), they are not to be regarded as worship.

The doctrine of adiaphora is abused when it is made a springboard for loose living (Gal. 5:13). Another abuse results from any attempt to make adiaphora a matter of conscience for others (Matt. 23:4-8; Matt. 20:25, 26; 1 Cor. 3:5; 1 Pet. 5:3). Lutheran principles differ widely from those of Catholicism and many representatives of Protestantism, who claim for the Church the right to command or forbid things neither commanded nor forbidden by God. To be sure, church officials, boards, teachers, and pastors can effect desirable changes in the field of *Mitteldinge,* but it should be done by instruction and advice. Another abuse of this doctrine results when the question of offense to a weak brother is not taken into consideration (Rom. 14:1, 2; 15:1; 1 Cor. 8:8, 11; 9:22). The guiding principle here as always must be love toward the weak (Rom. 13:10; 1 Cor. 16:14; 9:19), without, however, bolstering weakness or covering malice and stubbornness (Gal. 2:5). C. f. LW, *Abiding Word,* II, 686—708.

J. Schiller, *Probleme der christl. Ethik,* Berlin, 1888; Th. Graebner, *The Borderland of Right and Wrong,* CPH, 1951; Synodical Reports: Central, 1859; Eastern, 1857; Nebraska, 1912, 1913; Northern, 1859; Western, 1856. *Protokoll ueber die Verhandlungen des Colloquiums in Buffalo, N. Y.,* 1866, 23 ff.

Adiaphoristic Controversy. Caused by the Augsburg Interim, forced on the prostrate Lutherans in 1548 by the victorious emperor, which conceded the cup and clerical marriage, but demanded the restoration of the Mass, the seven sacraments, the authority of the

Pope and bishops, etc., till matters might be finally adjusted. Melanchthon and others in the Leipzig Interim submitted and said these Romish ceremonies might be observed as matters indifferent in themselves. Professor Flacius of Wittenberg, only twenty-eight, at the risk of losing his position, attacked the Interim, seconded by Wigand, Gallus, Brenz, and others. They held it wrong to observe even indifferent ceremonies when a false impression is thereby created. "Nothing is an adiaphoron when confession and offense are involved." The Passau Treaty of 1552 and the Augsburg Religious Peace of 1555 removed the cause; yet the controversy went on because the Adiaphorists continued to defend their position. Art. X of the Formula of Concord settled the controversy.

Joachim Westphal, *Luthers Meinung von den Mitteldingen*, 1550; Joh. G. Walch, *Historische u. Theologische Einleitung in die Religionsstreitigkeiten unserer Kirche v. d. Reformation bis auf jetzige Zeiten*, 1730; Standard histories; W. Richard, *Philip Melanchthon, Protestant Preceptor of Germany*, 1907 (ch. 28).

Adjuration. The act whereby one person imposes upon another the obligation of speaking as under oath (Josh. 6:26; 1 Sam. 14:24; 1 Kings 22:16; 2 Chron. 18:15; Matt. 26:63; Acts 19:13).

Adler, Alfred (1870—1937). Austrian psychologist ("individual psychology"). Opposed his teacher Freud's emphasis on sex and substituted man's "will to power." Emphasized the role inferiority feelings play in human action. Wrote: *Study of Organ Inferiority and Its Psychical Compensation; Social Interest; et al.*

Adler, Felix. See *Ethical Culture.*

Admadija. A Moslem sect founded when Mirza Admad offered himself as the Mahdi or last Imam (1879).

Administration, Educational. See *Parish Education, K.*

Admonition. 1) The duty of admonishing is taught repeatedly in the NT (Matt. 18:15-17; Rom. 15:14; 1 Cor. 4:14; Eph. 6:4; Col. 3:16; Titus 3:10; 1 Thess. 5:14). The early Church frequently practiced admonition: privately, in private offenses; publicly, in public offenses. See, *Keys, Office of.* 2) R. C., a secret rebuke of a cleric by a prelate.

Adolescence. The period of transition in a person's life between childhood and adulthood, beginning with the advent of puberty and ending with the full maturity of the individual. The female sex enters the period of adolescence approximately one and one-half to two years before the male, and it is commonly held that the mental development of young women is somewhat more rapid in the early teens than that of boys of the same age. Adolescence may be divided into early adolescence, in which the physical changes tending toward adulthood are most apparent, middle adolescence, in which the mental changes (with a strong growth of skepticism and romanticism) are most strongly in evidence, and late adolescence, during which maturation should reach a state of stable equilibrium. It is particularly in middle and late adolescence that the religious educator must be alert, both for evidences of religious skepticism and of youthful eagerness to grow in knowledge.

Adonai Shomo Community. See *Communistic Societies.*

Adoptionism. The view that Christ according to His humanity is the Son of God by adoption only. Its first exponent was Theodotus the Fuller, who came to Rome from Byzantium about 190, teaching that Jesus was a mere man, whose deity was only a miraculous power which as Christ or the Holy Spirit (identifying the two) came upon Him at His Baptism. Paul of Samosata held similar views, declaring that Jesus was a mere man who, inspired by the *Logos* (Word), gradually acquired a divine dignity which eventually merited the designation "God" (260—272). In the days of Charlemagne, an Adoptionist Controversy was stirred up in Spain by Elipandus, bishop of Toledo, and Felix, bishop of Urgel, who contended that Christ as the second Person of the Trinity is the only-begotten Son of the Father, but as the Son of Mary He is the adopted Son of God. They were opposed by Beatus, a priest, and Heterius of Libana, a monk (785), who emphasized the divine Christ made man for us. Alcuin wrote his *Seven Books Against Felix.* The Frankish Synods at Regensburg (792), Frankfort (794), and Aachen (794) condemned the teachings of these Spanish theologians, as did Popes Hadrian I and Leo III. A similar controversy again arose in the twelfth century, when

Bishop Eberhard of Bamberg defended Adoptionist views, accusing his opponents of Eutychianism.

See references to historical treatments under *Dogmatics;* A. Harnack, *Lehrbuch der Dogmengeschichte,* Freiburg, 1890; J. Bach, *Dogmengeschichte des Mittelalters,* Vienna, 1873—1875.

Adoration. Primarily, worship directed to God in His majesty, but also performed to idols and men. The OT forms of worship varied (*e. g.,* Ex. 3:5; Josh. 5:15; Ps. 2:12; Job 31:26-28). In Roman Catholicism the term is applied to the erroneous worship of Jesus in the Eucharist, for which a ritual drawn up by Thomas Aquinas is still used.

Adrian IV. See *Popes,* 8.

Adult Education. Adult education is as old as civilization. Christ dealt chiefly with adults. The letters of the NT are lessons for adult Christians. However, the Christian Church limited in the main its formal education to children and youth. The Scriptures impose no such limitation. The beginnings of adult education, as it is thought of, go back to the Birmingham Sunday Society of 1789, Great Britain's labor colleges, Grundtvig's adult schools in Denmark; to lyceums, chautauquas, correspondence courses, university extension work; to Bible study groups, adult Sunday schools, and missionary societies. The modern adult education movement is traceable to E. L. Thorndike's research into adult learning (ca. 1925), which reversed popular opinion that adults do not learn well, and to the organization of the American Association of Adult Education (1926). The Protestant churches of America, especially through the United Christian Adult Movement (1936) initiated by the International Council of Religious Education, spearheaded the development of religious adult education. Areas for study were set up, and "learning for life" courses developed. Textbooks were written for leadership training in the adult field. Steady progress has been made. Emphasis was placed on the young adult, family life training, the community, and the older adult. The churches discovered that people "learn as long as they live," that the church *is* a school, that Christian discipleship is lifelong growth in understanding, skills, and attitudes, and that it is the adult who sets the pattern of spiritual life for this generation and the next. Adults are the church's most influential teachers,

its "living examples of Christian thought and practice."

Attention to adults does not lessen the needs of children and youth, but simply recognizes the central role which adults play in our world. Adult education in the church is based on the doctrine of the priesthood of all believers and on the conviction that every Christian has a mission in life to fulfill. Adults learn through all that happens in them, to them, and around them. Their whole environment is a part of their education. In the churches, adult education is carried on in the church service, congregational assemblies, through committees, projects, and activities, Bible classes, classes in Christian doctrine for adults, fellowship gatherings, organizations and groups within the parish; and in conventions, institutes, and the like outside the local church. Christian adult education should foster growth in eight areas: Bible knowledge and skills, Christian doctrine and life, worship and the arts, Christian education, Christian family life, the Christian in society and the Church in the world (history), Evangelism and missions, and Christian stewardship. Adult education in the church is strategic, because it (1) helps adults grow spiritually (Col. 1:9, 10), (2) helps them face life victoriously with Jesus (1 John 5:4), (3) strengthens Christian elementary education and makes it pay larger dividends, because children follow adults (Matt. 18:6), (4) builds stronger Christian homes (Luke 10:38-42), (5) provides more lay workers for the church (Luke 10:1), (6) lifts consecration and stewardship performance for the church's work at home and abroad (Matt. 25:14-30), (7) helps to prevent spiritual indifference, nominal Christianity, and the loss of souls (John 15:2, 6), and (8) helps to stem the new secularism (Ps. 10:4). What the home, the church, and the nation are, and what these will be in the future, depends, under God, largely on the understanding, attitudes, skills, and spiritual responsiveness of the adult.

OEF

Yeaxlee, *Spiritual Values in Adult Education,* Oxford Press, 1925; Westphal, *The Church's Opportunity in Adult Education,* Westminster Press, 1941; Knowles, *Informal Adult Education,* Association Press, 1950.

Adultery. The illicit sexual intercourse between a man and a woman, either of whom is married to another. Under the ancient ecclesiastical law it was immaterial which party was married, the man or the woman, or whether both were married and both were guilty. An essential factor of the sin is the meeting of wills on both sides, even though this be due to persuasion, Deut. 22:22; for where this element is absent, it is a case of humbling or forcing, Ezek. 22:11; Deut. 22:24; 2 Sam. 13:12. The sin of adultery is condemned in the strongest terms throughout the Bible; it was punished with death in the Old Testament, Deut. 22:22; Lev. 20:10, and in the New Testament we find it listed with the open sins of the flesh, Gal. 5:19. While Scripture nowhere states that adultery dissolves the marital union, Christ names fornication as the one and only exception to the absolute prohibition of divorcing one's spouse. It is clear that adultery is the extreme and deliberate setting aside of that marital faithfulness demanded in holy wedlock according to God's institution, Gen. 2:24, whence it is but natural that the Lord names this sin as the one which at once grants to the innocent party the right to put away his spouse. Matt. 19:9. If both parties to a marriage become guilty of adultery, the guilt on either side equalizes the transgression, and neither party is entitled to a divorce. The same holds true in the case of connivance or collusion, also in instances of condonation, if the parties live together subsequently with full knowledge of the adultery on the part of the one who is innocent. Such condonation may be the result of Christian forgiveness; for the Lord does not command a divorce on account of adultery, but merely grants it. See *Marriage*.

Advent. See *Church Year*.

Advent Christian Church. See *Adventist Bodies*, 3.

Advent of Christ. The Church speaks of a threefold coming of Christ: 1) The lowly coming in the flesh (Zech. 9:9; Matt. 21:4; see *Incarnation*); 2) His spiritual coming in the hearts of the pious and His constant presence in the Church (John 14:18, 23; see *Mystical Union*); 3) His return to Judgment (Matt. 24:30; see *Last Things*).

Adventist Bodies. 1. Adventism is the belief that the second coming of Christ is imminent and that the central feature of this event is the establishment of the millennial reign. While Adventism has been existent throughout the history of the Church, especially in times of unusual stress, the most significant Adventist movement of modern times originated with William Miller (1782—1849). An uneducated farmer, a Baptist licentiate, and an ardent student of the "chronological portions" of the prophetic writings of the Bible, Miller believed that the date for all important events in sacred history has been fixed in prophecy. Since the exact dates of the Flood, the sojourn of Israel in Egypt, the destruction of the Canaanites, the duration of the Exile, had been foretold, the exact date of Christ's second coming must also have been prophesied. Miller believed that he found the date of Christ's second coming in Dan. 8:13, 14, which speaks of 2,300 days until the cleansing of the sanctuary. He fixed the date of the beginning of this period in 457 B.C., the year in which the command to rebuild Jerusalem was given, Dan. 9:25, and following the practice of most time setters that according to Num. 14:34 a day in prophecy denotes a year, he proclaimed that the cleansing of the sanctuary would occur within a year after Mar. 21, 1843. The seventy weeks of Dan. 9:24, totaling 490 years and ending A. D. 33, would constitute the first part of the 2,300 "days," and the 1,335 days of Dan. 12:12 would constitute the second part of this period and would end in 1843. Miller held that the cleansing of the sanctuary was figurative language denoting the personal return of Christ to cleanse the world of all its pride and power, pomp and vanity, and to establish the peaceful kingdom of the Messiah in place of the kingdoms of this world. In 1831 Miller opened a vigorous campaign to gain adherents for his views, and by 1843 his followers numbered fifty thousand. When Mar. 21, 1844, passed without the Lord's visible return, there was keen disappointment, and Miller published his mistake. However, several prominent leaders believed that the coming of the Lord was to occur on the Festival of the Atonement, Oct. 22, 1844, and not on the Jewish New Year, as Miller had predicted. This encouraged the Adventists, and they made extensive preparations for the Lord's glorious appearance, only to be bitterly disappointed again.

2. The belief that Christ would appear at an early date to establish His millennial reign persisted, and in 1845 the Adventists met at Albany, N. Y., to define their position and to adopt principles embodying the views of Miller concerning the character of Christ's sec-

ond advent, the resurrection, and the renewal of the earth. The salient points agreed upon at Albany are as follows: 1) The present world is to be destroyed by fire, and a new earth is to be created for the believers. 2) There are only two advents of Christ, both visible and personal. 3) The second advent is imminent. 4) The condition of sharing in the millennial reign of Christ is repentance and faith, a godly and watchful life. 5) There are two resurrections, that of the believers at Christ's second coming and that of the unbelievers after the millenium. 6) The departed saints do not enter Paradise in soul and spirit until the final blessedness of the everlasting kingdom will be revealed at Christ's second coming. However, differences arose within the group concerning the nature of Christ's coming, the immortality of the soul, the condition of the dead in the intermediate state, and the observance of the Sabbath. Controversies on these points led to the organization of various groups of Adventist bodies, the largest being the Seventh-Day Adventist denomination, next in numerical strength the Advent Christian Church, and three bodies numbering only a few congregations.

3. *Advent Christian Church.* After the disappointment of 1844, Jon. Cummings and others predicted that the Lord would come in 1853 or 1854. This caused a division among Adventists. When the prophecy remained unfulfilled, Cummings admitted his mistake and advised his adherents to re-unite with the parent body. However, during the years of separation from the main body the followers of Cummings had developed ideas on the immortality of the soul which were at variance with the views of the majority. For this reason they organized a separate body in 1861 and have since then been known as the Advent Christian Church. With other evangelical Christians they accept the Bible as the only divinely revealed truth, thus repudiating the so-called inspired writings of Mrs. Ellen White (1827 to 1915); and they confess the doctrine of the Trinity. Their distinctive tenet is the theory that man, who was created for immortality, forfeited his divine birthright through sin and that only believers in Christ will receive immortality. They believe that death is the state of unconsciousness and that all men will remain in this "soul sleep" until the second coming of Christ, when the righteous will receive everlasting life, while the wicked will be annihilated. In common with other Adventists they believe that Christ will return visibly and rule personally in this world, which will be rejuvenated as the eternal home of the redeemed. They observe Sunday as the proper Sabbath and refuse to bear arms.

4. *Seventh-Day Adventists.* The movement which resulted in the organization of the Seventh-Day Adventist denomination originated with those Adventist leaders who believed that the date of the cleansing of the sanctuary had been fixed correctly by Wm. Miller, but who differed from him in interpreting the nature of this event. They held that the cleansing of the sanctuary did not refer to the rejuvenating of the world, as Miller had believed, but to Christ's "investigative judgment" in the sanctuary of heaven. According to this view Christ began in the fall of 1844 to judge the conduct of His chosen people according to the standard of the Decalog. In the meantime a congregation connected with the Adventist movement had come into contact with Seventh-Day Baptists, and this group insisted that the keeping of the Old Testament Sabbath was God's everlasting commandment. Gradually an increasing number of Adventists held that Christ was cleansing the sanctuary according "to the fourth principle of the Decalog," that is, judging people as to their attitude over against the commandment to observe the Sabbath according to the Mosaic Law. These views were generally accepted by Adventists, when Mrs. Ellen White claimed to have had visions in support of this doctrine. In one vision she saw two angels standing by the heavenly ark of the covenant in the "sanctuary" and Jesus raising the cover of the ark containing the Ten Commandments, the "fourth" being surrounded by a halo. In another vision she was informed that the third angel's message, Rev. 14:9-12, referred to the Papacy, and that according to Dan. 7:25 the great antichristian sin is the changing of the Old Testament Sabbath into Sunday. The Seventh-Day Adventists believe that at the conclusion of His investigative judgment, begun in 1844 and based on man's attitude over against the Sabbath, Christ will return to this world, resurrect and translate all the just who have observed the Sabbath, consume the unjust who have kept the Sunday, remove the just from this world, and leave the world desolate for a thousand years. After the thousand years Christ and

the saints will return to this world, the unjust will be raised, be granted a period of probation, and, if found unworthy, be annihilated with Satan. This earth will then become the rejuvenated home of the redeemed race of Adam. The Seventh-Day Adventists believe that it is their work to announce to all nations that the keeping of the Sabbath is man's only hope of preparing for the Lord's second coming. In the interest of this central doctrine the Seventh-Day Adventists have developed their entire theology. 1) While they claim to accept the Holy Scriptures as the only source of faith and practice, they actually base their central doctrine on the visions and revelations of Mrs. Ellen White, whom they consider to have been an inspired prophetess. 2) On the one hand the Seventh-Day Adventists confess with evangelical Christians that the sinner is "justified by the Savior's grace, who cleanses from sin," but on the other hand they subscribe to Mrs. White's doctrine that the work of Christ consisted largely in showing that the Law of God could be kept by man. Obedience to such commandments as keeping the Sabbath, contributing the tithe, abstaining from pork, intoxicants, wearing modest clothes, occupies a prominent place in their scheme of salvation. 3) In the doctrine of Christ's sacerdotal office the Seventh-Day Adventists differ fundamentally from historic evangelical doctrine. On the basis of Heb. 8:1, 2 and similar passages they teach that the priestly office of Christ consists of two phases, the first extending from His ascension until 1844, and the second inaugurated in the fall of 1844. The theory of the Atonement is as follows: As the Old Testament high priest pleaded for the congregation in the Holy of the Temple throughout the year, so Christ interceded for His people during the New Testament period; and as the high priest entered the Holy of Holies once a year and placed the sins of the congregation on the scapegoat, thus cleansing the sanctuary, so Christ entered the heavenly sanctuary in 1844 and is now placing the sins of His people on the devil. 4) Since the Atonement is not completed until the sins have been removed from the sanctuary, the fate of the departed cannot be determined until Christ's second coming. In the interest of this theory they hold that all the dead, good and evil, are in a state of unconsciousness in the intermediate state. This is in line with their view that man is by nature mortal, that immortality will be given only to the believers, whereas all wicked men will be entirely annihilated. When the world is rejuvenated, there will be no hell. — The Seventh-Day Adventists are a militantly aggressive denomination, claim to work in 375 countries, their missionaries employing almost 400 different languages and dialects.

5. *Church of God* (Adventist). This small denomination agrees substantially with the doctrine of the Seventh-Day Adventists except that they reject the inspiration of the alleged visions of Mrs. White.

6. *Church of God* (Oregon, Ill.). A millennialistic denomination whose tenets agree in general with those of the Adventists.

7. *Life and Advent Union.* A small denomination of Adventists, which teaches that there will be no resurrection of the wicked. Total Adventist membership in the U. S.: 596,340 (1952). See *Religious Bodies (U. S.), Bibliography.* FEM

Advocatus Dei, Advocatus Diaboli. See *Canonization.*

Advowson. The right of presentation to an ecclesiastical benefice, first mentioned in 441 (Council of Orange). In a presentative advowson a patron presents a candidate for the bishop's endorsement; in a collative advowson the bishop himself is the patron.

Aelfric (ca. 955—1020). English abbot; compiled grammar (hence called "The Grammarian"); translated parts of OT; wrote homilies ("Lives of the Saints" most important); denied the Immaculate Conception.*

Aemilie Juliane (1637—1706), Countess of Schwarzburg-Rudolstadt. Born at Heidecksburg, Schwarzburg-Rudolstadt, Germany; orphaned at five, she was adopted by her aunt and educated in music and poetry. She was the most productive of German female hymn writers, some 600 hymns being attributed to her. Her hymns are full of a deep love for her Savior.

Aeons. See *Gnosticism,* 5.

Aerius. Presbyter and director of an asylum or hospital at Sebaste in Pontus in the fourth century; an opponent of strong hierarchical tendencies and of prayers for the dead; the "Aerians" named after him.

Aesthetics. The philosophical study of beauty as applied to art and nature. Plato and Aristotle regarded beauty as identical with order and proportion. Neoplatonism regarded beauty as belonging to all that exists as such. In the Middle Ages the transition to the modern theories of beauty took place. While clinging to its objective nature, the element of feeling evoked or pleasure experienced was added. The modern trend is to study aesthetics entirely from the subjective or psychological point of view. Thus Kant, in accordance with his system, did not regard beauty as adhering objectively in the object, but only in the perception of the object. *Aestheticism* is a term applied to the theory which fails to distinguish between the beautiful and the good (true, to a certain extent, of the Greeks). While the Bible frequently uses connotations of beauty in describing the good (Eph. 5:27; Ps. 149:4; Is. 28:1; Rev. 21; and others), it carefully distinguishes between external beauty and moral uprightness (1 Pet. 3:3 f.; Prov. 11:22). See *Architecture, Art, Music*. EL

Aeterni Patris Unigenitus Filius (bull). See *Roman Catholic Confessions*, E 1.

Aetius (d. 367). Native of Antioch, bishop without a see; first to return to pure Arianism after 350; wrote *On God Unengendered and on That Which Is Engendered.*

Affirmation. See *Brief Statement.*

Afghanistan. In central Asia, bordering on Baluchistan, India, Persia, Soviet Russia. Area, about 245,000 square miles. Population, about 12 million. Languages, Persian and Pushtov. People are of mixed races, some Jewish traces. Religion, Animistic and Mohammedan. Early attempts of Christian mission work (424). Carey translated the Bible into the Pushtov language in 1825; translation revised in 1886. Apparently no Christian mission work of note at the present time, the fanaticism of the inhabitants permitting no mission work by Christian forces. See *Missions, Bibliography.*

Africa. Africa, with 11,500,000 square miles and 198,000,000 (estimated, 1951) people, is still roughly one half pagan (58 per cent). The diversified forms of paganism, developed strongly especially along the West Coast, usually embody three points: a belief in a supreme being; a belief in survival after death; a belief in mana-sorcery. Fetishism is a form of spirit worship connected with the use of fetishes. There are animism, spiritism, dynamism, fears and superstitions connected with their belief in spirits and their conviction that objects are endowed with mysterious qualities by means of magical rites and substances. Ancestors are revered, consulted, and honored. Amulets are used extensively. But paganism is in a state of decay.

Mohammedanism, with 36 per cent of the population, rules almost absolutely in the north and is making progress towards the south. It has become indigenous, is to a certain degree a civilizing influence, and has been difficult to Christianize.

Other elements are the Copts (750,000), a mixture with Judaistic elements, and the Abyssinian Christians, carrying over from the early Christian era. The Roman Catholics are represented with about 1⅖ per cent of the population, and the Greek Orthodox in about similar strength. Protestants comprise about 2 per cent of the population, and Jews about 3/10 of 1 per cent. There are some 800 dialects, with the Bible or parts of it translated into one hundred of them.

Northern Africa early came under the influence of Christianity, perhaps at the end of the first century. Christianity here developed a vigor and growth unrivaled elsewhere in the Roman Empire except in Asia Minor. But Arian vandalism and Moslem fanaticism turned it into a religious wilderness.

Christian missions have done much work in Central and South Africa, the Moravians beginning in 1792. The Synodical Conference entered the field in 1936, in Nigeria, and in 1951 was serving some 163 stations, with 7,428 communicant members, under the care of 20 American missionaries and two native pastors, plus 459 native teachers. In 1952, 5 missionaries and 8 native pastors were added. For other missions active in Africa, see the several countries.

There is still much unoccupied territory in Africa as far as mission work is concerned. The climate, tropical diseases, the low level of education, the political complexion, the many different governments, the difficulty of transportation and communication, all combine to make mission work difficult.

In 1947 there were (estimated) in Africa: 15,517,025 Christians (of whom

4,422,777 were Protestant); Mohammedans: 55,538,211; Jewish: 542,869; Primitive: 76,301,961. See *Missions, Bibliography.* OHS

African Methodist Episcopal Church. This church body began when Negroes under the leadership of Richard Allen, William White, and Absalom Jones withdrew from St. George's Church, Philadelphia, because of attempted racial segregation. In 1816 the Negroes withdrew from the Methodist Episcopal Church and organized the church for the colored. The church has a seminary and college at Wilberforce, Ohio. Membership: 1,057,951 (1952). See *Religious Bodies* (U.S.), *Bibliography.*

African Methodist Episcopal Zion Church. See *Methodist Bodies,* 4 c.

African Orthodox Church. This is a body of Negro Episcopalians organized independently of the Protestant Episcopalian Church. In doctrine it follows quite closely the High Church party in the Anglican Church. Membership: about 2,000.

African Union Methodist Protestant Church. See *Methodist Bodies.*

Agape. (Love feasts.) In the early Church (cf. Acts 2:42) simple meals partaken of in common by the assembled congregation as an expression of brotherly love. Connected at first with the celebration of the Eucharist, they were separated from the latter already in the second century. In course of time the abuses attending these feasts (already censured by Paul; cf. 1 Cor. 11:20) led to their total abolition. See *Charities, Christian.*

Agapetae (G. "beloved"). In the early centuries, virgins who lived with men in a so-called state of spiritual love. Abuses led to condemnation at Ancyra (314). Later a Gnostic sect was known by the same name (395).

Agatha, St. A Sicilian noblewoman martyred by Quintianus, governor of Sicily, A.D. 251.

Age (ages). See *Time.*

Age, Canonical. The age at which the Roman Church admits its subjects to various obligations and privileges. A child, upon attaining the "age of reason," about the seventh year, is held capable of mortal sin and of receiving the sacraments of penance and extreme unction, becomes subject to the law of the Church, and can contract an en-

gagement of marriage. Shortly after, confirmation and Communion are administered. Girls may contract marriage at twelve, boys at fourteen. The obligation of fasting begins at twenty-one and ends at sixty. A deacon must be twenty-two years old; a priest, twenty-four; a bishop, thirty.

Aged and Infirm, Lutheran Homes for (by States with affiliation given: ALC — within American Lutheran Church; Aug — within Augustana Synod; Dan — within Danish Church; ELC — within Evangelical Lutheran Church; Ex — Extrasynodical; Int — Intersynodical; LB — Lutheran Brethren; LF — within Lutheran Free Church; Mo — within Missouri Synod; SC — within Synodical Conference; Slov — within Slovak Church; Wis — within Wisconsin Synod; ULC — within United Lutheran Church; UE — within United Evangelical Church). Statistics compiled in 1948.

California: California Lutheran Home, 2500 S. Fremont, Alhambra (ULC); Lutheran Home Association of California, Anaheim (Mo); Solheim Home for the Aged, 2236 Merton, Los Angeles (ELC); Salem Lutheran Home for the Aged, 2361 E. 29th St., Oakland (Ex); Bethel Home, R. 1, Box 258, Selma (UE).

Colorado: Eben-Ezer Mercy Institute, Brush (Int); Bethpage Rest Home, 404 N. Spruce, Colo. Springs (Ex); Bonell Memorial Home, 2208 8th Ave., Greeley (Ex).

Connecticut: Lutheran Home for the Aged, Southbury (Ex).

District of Columbia: Nat. Luth. Home for the Aged, 18th and Douglas Sts., Washington (ULC).

Florida: The Lutheran Haven, Slavia (Slov).

Idaho: Coeur d'Alene Homes for the Aged, Coeur d'Alene (ELC).

Illinois: Lutheran Home and Service for the Aged, 508 Northwest Hwy., Arlington Heights (SC); Augustana Home for the Aged, 7540 Stony Island Ave., Chicago (Aug); Norw. Luth. Bethesda Home, 2833 N. Nordica Ave., Chicago (ELC); Norw. Old People's Home, 6016 Nina Ave., Chicago (ELC); Pleasant View Luther Home, 555 Pleasant Ave., Ottawa (ELC); Salem Home for the Aged, 1313 S. Rowell Ave., Joliet (Aug).

Indiana: Luth. Old People's Home, 612 E. Mitchell St., Kendallville (Mo); Mulberry Luth. Home for the Aged, Mulberry (ULC).

Iowa: Aase Haugen Home for the Aged, Decorah (ELC); Danish Old People's Home, 1101 Grand View Ave., Des Moines (Dan); Salem Luth. Old People's Home, Elk Horn (Ex); Iowa Luth. Home for the Aged, Madrid (Aug); Luth. Homes, Muscatine (ALC); Story City Old People's Home, Story City (ELC); Luth. Home for the Aged, Strawberry Point (Ex); Home for the Aged, Vinton (Mo).

Kansas: Ev. Luth. Bethany Home for the Aged, 321 N. Chestnut, Lindsborg (Aug).

Kentucky: Louisville Luth. Home, Jeffersontown (ULC).

Maryland: Augsburg Luth. Home, Pikesville (Baltimore) (Mo).

Massachusetts: Luth. Home for the Aged, 26 Harvard St., Worcester (Aug).

Michigan: Edmore Old People's Home, Edmore (Ex); Luth. Home for the Aged, 1706 S. Division Ave., Grand Rapids (Aug); Ev. Luth. Old Folks' Home, Monroe (SC).

Minnesota: Bethany Home, Alexandria (Aug); Knute Nelson Memorial Home, Alexandria (ELC); Luth. Home for the Aged, Belle Plaine (Wis); Bethesda Old People's Home, Chicago City (Aug); Lakeshore Luth. Home, 4002 London Rd., Duluth (Aug); Pioneer Memorial Home, Fergus Falls (ELC); Luth. Old People's Home, Madison (ELC); Mankato Luth. Home, 718 Mound Ave., Mankato (Aug); Augustana Home for the Aged, 1405 10th Ave., S. Minneapolis (Aug); Danebo Old People's Home, 3030 W. River Rd., Minneapolis (Ex); Ebenezer Home for the Aged, 2545 Portland Ave., Minneapolis (Ex); Red Wing Seminary Mem. Homes, 906 College Ave., Red Wing (ELC); Sarepta Home for the Aged, Sauk Center (LB); St. John's Old Folks' Home, Springfield (ALC); Luth. Memorial Home, Twin Valley (ELC); Tyler Old People's Home, Tyler (Dan); Bethesda Homes, Willmar (LF).

Missouri: Salem Luth. Home for the Aged, 3008 Baltimore, Kansas City (Aug); Luth. Altenheim Soc. of Mo., 8721 Halls Ferry Rd., St. Louis (SC); Luth. Boarding Home for the Aged, 3652 S. Jefferson Ave., St. Louis (SC).

Nebraska: Good Shepherd Luth. Home, Blair (UE); Luth. Home for the Aged, Fremont (Ex); Tabitha Home, 4720 Randolph, Lincoln (ULC); Bethany Old People's Home, Minden (UE); Immanuel Home for the Aged, 34th and Fowler Aves., Omaha (Aug); Luth. Old People's Home, 1240 S. 10th St., Omaha (SC).

New Jersey: Kinderfreund Old Folks' Home, 93 Nelson Ave., Jersey City (Ex); Morristown Luth. Home, Morristown (ULC).

New York: Luth. Home for the Aged, 688 Madison Ave., Albany (Ex); Swedish Augustana Home for the Aged, 1680 60th St., Brooklyn (Aug); Wartburg Luth. Home for the Aged and Infirm, 2598 Fulton St., Brooklyn (Mo); Luth. Church Home, 217 E. Delavan Ave., Buffalo (Ex); The Luth. Hospice, 117 Glenwood Ave., Buffalo (SC); Luth. Church Home for Aged, Clinton (Ex); Luth. Home for Aged, 715 Falconer St., Jamestown (Aug); Marie Louise Heins Home, c/o Wartburg, Mt. Vernon (Ex); Eger Norw. Luth. Home for Aged, Meisner and Rockland, New Drop (ELC).

North Dakota: Good Samaritan Home, Arthur (Ex); Luth. Home for Aged, Fargo (Ex); G. F. Home for the Aged, 1023 Almonte Ave., Grand Forks (Ex); Luth. Home for Aged, Jamestown (Ex); Northwood Old People's Home, Northwood (Ex); Luth. Home for the Aged, Valley City (Ex).

Ohio: Luth. Home for the Aged, R. 7, Box 285, Dayton (Ex); Feghtly Luth. Home, Tipp City (ULC); Luth. Old Folks' Home, 2465 Seaman St., Toledo (ALC); Cleveland Luth. Home for the Aged, 2116 Dover Rd., Westlake (SC).

Oregon: Sunset Home, 172 W. 12th Ave., Eugene (Ex).

Pennsylvania: Good Shepherd Home, 6th and St. John Sts., Allentown (ULC); Artman Home for Lutherans, Ambler (Ex); Concordia Luth. Home, R. 1, Cabot (SC); Luth. Home for the Aged, 2201 Sassafras St., Erie (Ex); St. John's Luth. Home, Mars (ALC); Luth. Home for Orphans and Aged, 6950 Germantown Ave., Philadelphia (ULC); Mary J. Drexel Home, 2100 S. College, Philadelphia (ULC); Luth. Home at Topton, Topton (ULC); Old People's Home, Zelienople (ULC).

South Carolina: Jacob Washington Franke Home, 261 Calhoun St., Charlestown (Ex); Lowman Home for Aged and Helpless, White Rock (ULC).

South Dakota: Bethesda Home for Aged, Beresford (ELC); Luth. Home for the Aged, Eureka (Ex); Luth. Hospital for Old People, Hot Springs (Ex); Luth. Home for the Aged, 400 W. 3d, Sioux Falls (Ex).

Texas: Trinity Luth. Old Folks' Home, Round Rock (Ex).

Washington: Bethany Home for the Aged, 3322 Broadway, Everett (Ex); Ebenezer Home, Poulsbo (LF); Luth. Home, Puyallup (Ex); Columbia Conf. Home for Aged, 405 N. 48th St., Seattle (Aug); L. C. Foss Sunset Home, 10529 Ashworth, Seattle (Ex); Josephine Sunset Home, Stanwood (ELC).

Wisconsin: Luth. Home for Aged, 244 N. Macy, Fond du Lac (ALC); Luther Home for Aged, Marinette (Aug); Skaalen Home for the Aged, Stoughton (ELC); Home for Aged Lutherans (Altenheim), 7500 W. Worth Ave., Wauwatosa (SC); Homme Home for the Aged, Wittenberg (ELC).

Canada: Bethany Sunset Home, Alta., Bawlf (ELC); Canada Conference Home for the Aged, Wetaskiwin, Alta. (Aug); Bethel Old Folks' Home, Gimli, Manitoba (ULC); St. Paul's Luth. Old Folks' Home, Melville, Sask. (ALC). (Information gathered by the National Lutheran Council, Division of Public Relations. Ad. by AS). HFW-CK

Agencies, Educational. See *Christian Teaching,* O; *Parish Education.*

Agenda. A book containing directions for, and exact forms of, all the sacred acts performed in the liturgical worship of the Church, both public and private. The derivation of the word is most probably to be found in the *missas agere* of the Western Church, the word "agenda" (neutr. plur.) thus designating that which was to be performed by the officiating clergyman (priest or pastor) in administering the means of grace. The use of written forms has been traced back to the fifth century, the texts before that time having been preserved chiefly by oral tradition. The Roman Church eventually had a great number of service books, all coming under the general name *Rituale,* while the Lutheran Church early adopted the name *Agenda.* At the present time a distinction is being observed, the acts of public worship, including all prayers, collects, and lessons, being spoken of as the Liturgy, and all special acts of the pastor, particularly Baptisms, marriages, the Communion of the sick, and funerals, being included in the *Agenda* proper. — The history of the Lutheran books of worship may be said to have begun with the publication of Luther's *Formula Missae et Communionis pro Ecclesia Wittenbergensi,* in November, 1523,

followed, a little more than two years later, by his *German Mass and Order of Services,* which, as Luther expressly stated, was not intended to supersede or change the *Formula Missae.* As far as occasional sacred acts are concerned, the influence of Luther's *Taufbuechlein* of 1523 and of his *Traubuechlein* of 1534 may be traced to the present day. Many of the Lutheran church orders of the sixteenth century, indeed, gave only the order of the parts of service, without the texts, referring, at the same time, to the versions of Luther; but others offered a complete liturgical apparatus. The liturgical books of the latter part of the sixteenth century may roughly be divided into three classes. The first of these groups includes the forms that were most conservative, following, in general, the traditional uses, among these being the Brandenburg of 1540, the Pfalz-Neuburg of 1543, and the Austrian of 1571. To the second group belong all the church orders of the Saxon-Lutheran type, based upon Luther's work, such as the Prussian of 1525 and the Pomeranian of 1535. The third group includes the so-called mediating type, mediating between the Lutheran and the Reformed service. The beginning of this type was made by Bucer, Capito, and Hedio, in 1525, and it persisted chiefly in Southern Germany. The tendency in the Lutheran Church of America is to return to the best development of the Lutheran spirit in the sixteenth century, both in the liturgy used in public worship and in the forms employed for the special sacred acts. See *Liturgics.*

Agenda Controversy. A controversy in Prussia occasioned by the attempts of Frederick William III of Prussia to introduce the so-called "Prussian Liturgy." Some churches petitioned that the agenda be amended as early as 1787. In 1816 a liturgy for the Court and Garrison Church appeared without the author's name, but championed by the king. Opposition to this and other attempts to introduce a uniform agenda was led by Schleiermacher, who upheld the right to vary from the agenda.

Agiographa. See *Apocrypha,* A 2.

Agnes, St. Martyr mentioned by numerous early Fathers. Worshiped in Eastern and Western Catholic churches as a model of purity.

Agni. See *Brahmanism,* 2.

Agnoetae (G. "be ignorant of"). 1) A sect of the 4th century which denied the omniscience of God. 2) A sect of the 6th century maintaining there were things which Christ did not know.

Agnosticism (G. "not know"). A word first used by Huxley (1869) and applied to the belief that certain knowledge in a particular field (*e. g.,* religion) or in general has not been attained. In religion, agnosticism holds that certain knowledge of the existence and nature of God and of the supernatural world in general has not been reached. It differs from skepticism in that agnosticism usually grants the possibility of attaining knowledge in the future.

Agnus Dei. A liturgical prayer used in the service of the Holy Communion, transplanted from the Greek Church into the Western Church. It was formerly spoken or chanted by the priest or the choir, but in the Lutheran Church it is sung by the people just before the Distribution.

Agobard of Lyons. Prominent theologian of Gallican Church; b. in Spain, 779; d. in Saintonge, Western France, in 840. Trained by Leidrad, archbishop of Lyons, whose successor he became; one of the bishops who forced Louis le Debonnaire to his humiliating penance at Soissons; wrote theological treatises against Adoptionism, etc.

Agrapha. A technical term for supposed sayings of Jesus which were handed down through oral tradition.
M. R. James, *The Apocryphal New Testament,* Clerendon, Oxford, 1924.

Agricola (Schnitter), **John.** B. 1492 at Eisleben, studied at Wittenberg, kept minutes of the Leipzig Debate in 1519, sent by Luther to reform Frankfurt, pastor at Eisleben, at University of Wittenberg, 1537, court preacher at Brandenburg, 1540, one of the authors of the Augsburg Interim in 1548, d. 1566. See *Antinomian Controversy.*
G. Kawerau, *Joh. Agricola v. Eisleben,* Berlin, 1881.

Agricola, Martin (?—1556). Kantor at cathedral school of Magdeburg; wrote works important for the history of music during the Reformation period.

Agricola, Michael. See *Finland, Lutheranism in,* 2.

Agricola, Rudolf. See *Humanism, 16th c.; Reformed Church,* 2.

Agricola, Stephen (1486?—1547). Accepted Reformation at Augsburg; on Luther's side at Marburg Colloquy; signed Luther's Smalcald Articles (1537); introduced Reformation in Upper Palatinate.

Ahlberg, P. A. B. in Sweden, 1823, d. 1887; trained many young men for the ministry of the Augustana Synod; earnest, evangelical, popular preacher.

Ahlbrand, Albert H. Buggy manufacturer; b. Seymour, Ind., Apr. 27, 1872; Concordia College, Fort Wayne, Ind., 1886; Financial Secretary, Central District, Mo. Synod; member of Board of Directors, 1923; d. Apr. 29, 1946.

Ahle, Johann Rudolf (1625—73). Like his contemporary Andreas Hammerschmidt, Ahle wrote vocal and choral sacred dialogs which helped prepare the way for the church cantatas written by the Lutheran composers of later generations. Ahle makes frequent use of the aria and of the ritornel, and his compositions distinguish themselves through their simplicity.

Ahlfeld, Johann Friedrich (1810 to 1884). Lutheran clergyman; in 1847 succeeded rationalist Wislicenus at Halle; in 1851 successor to Adolph von Harless as pastor of St. Nicolai, Leipzig, till 1881; lectured in Homiletics and Pastoral Theology to theological candidates in Leipzig.

Ahlwardt, Peter (?—1791). Professor of Logic at Greifswald; treated Christian truths in terms of Wolffian philosophy.

Ahriman. See *Zoroastrianism.*

Ahura Mazda. See *Zoroastrianism.*

Aichinger, Gregor (1564—1628). German composer of the Roman Catholic Church, whom Ambros considers the superior to Handl (Gallus). Like his contemporary Hans Leo Hassler, he was a product of the Venetian School and served as organist of the Fugger family. In his last years he served as a priest in the church at Regensburg.

Aims, Educational. See *Christian Education,* G.

Ainsworth, Henry (1571—1623). Learned champion of English Separatists; b. near Norwich; fled to Amsterdam, 1593; teacher there of Separatists till his death. Hebraist; controversialist.

Ainus. Aboriginal people in northern Japan, about 20,000 strong, prehistoric religion. In 1620 Jesuit Hieronymus de Angelis paid them a visit and wrote a description. Religion apparently originally monotheistic, now polytheistic (animism, goddess of fire, ancestor worship). See *Missions, Bibliography.*

Aionios. See *Hereafter,* B 6.

Ajivikas. A Hindu sect, similar to Jainism, with humanistic tendencies founded in 6th century.

Akbar (1542—1605). Mogul emperor of India, Moslem by birth, known for his tolerance and the interreligion discussions which he conducted. Founder of "Divine Faith," an eclectic religion.

Akiba ("Father of Rabbinic Judaism"; ca. 50—135). Systematized the Halakah and evolved new principles of interpretation; increased the range of the Halakah. His influence was also felt in philosophy, politics, and haggadah.

Akron Rule. See *Galesburg Rule.*

A Lasco, Johannes (1499—1560). Polish nobleman; Calvinistic theologian; b. Warsaw; d. Pirchow. Reared in the Roman Catholic Church, but turned Protestant and left Poland with recommendations of Polish king; superintendent of East Frisia, of Church of Foreign Protestants, London, and of Reformed churches, Poland; failed to reconcile Reformed and Lutherans; prepared, with seventeen others, the Polish version of the Bible.

Alaska. Acquired from Russia by the United States in 1867, with 590,000 square miles, and a population of 72,524, of whom about 29,000 are whites, 40 per cent of the rest Indians, the others Eskimos. The Missouri Synod has been active there since 1937, with two pastors, two congregations, 134 communicants (1951). The Greek Orthodox Church has had mission stations in the Aleutians since 1793. Protestant missions are conducted at about 30 places among Indians or Eskimo tribes. Protestant churches at work in Alaska are the American Presbyterians, the Moravians, the Protestant Episcopal Church, the Baptists, the Congregationalists, Lutherans (Missouri Synod and ELC), the Methodist Episcopal Church, the Church Missionary Society, and the Evangelical Mission Covenant Church of America. Whereas the native population has been going down, the work of the missions has shown that this trend can be reversed. See *Missions, Biliography.*

Alb. See *Vestments, Clerical.*

Alba. See *Bible Societies,* 6.

Albania. A small country along the Adriatic Sea, bounded by Jugoslavia and Greece. Population, about 1,135,000; mostly Mohammedan, although the Greek Orthodox Church is still strong. See *Missions, Bibliography.*

Albanian Orthodox Church. See *Eastern Orthodox Churches.*

Albert of Brandenburg (1490 to 1545). Archbishop and Elector of Mainz. Luther made his famous protest against the sale of indulgences granted to Albert by the Pope.

Albert, Heinrich (1604—51). A cousin and pupil of Heinrich Schuetz who excelled as a composer of sacred and secular songs and arias, one of which, "God, Who Madest Earth and Heaven," became a popular chorale, finding its way into practically all Lutheran hymnals.

Alberta. See *Canada.*

Alberti, Johann Friedrich (1642 to 1710). An eminent Lutheran organist who devoted his earlier years to the study of theology and jurisprudence. As an organist he brought fame to Merseburg and was rivaled in his day only by Johann Christian Bach.

Alberti, Valentin (1635—1697). Lutheran theologian; lecturer at Leipzig; opposed Pietism and Catholicism.

Albertus Magnus (1193—1280). Founder of the most flourishing period of scholasticism; b. at Lauingen, Bavaria; studied at Padua, where he entered the Dominican order, served as lector of convent schools of his order in Germany; became general of his order for Germany after studying theology at Paris; later bishop of Regensburg for two years; many-sided author, which gave him the title of "Doctor Universalis"; wrote a commentary on the *Sententiae* of Peter Lombard and a *Summum Theologiae;* prepared way for modern conflict between theology and false science.

Alberus, Erasmus (1500—53). One of the Prussian reformers, a pupil of Luther, at first schoolmaster in Frankfurt on the Main and in Heldenbergen, then pastor at Berlin, at Magedeburg, and elsewhere, finally General Superintendent in Mecklenburg; prominent hymn writer, the ruggedness of whose poetry has been compared with that of Luther; wrote: "Gott hat das Evangelium"; "Ihr lieben Christen, freut euch nun"; "Nun freut euch, Gottes Kinder all'."

Alberus, Matthew (1495—1570). "Luther of Swabia"; pastor of Reutlingen, which he won for the Reformation; abolished Latin Mass; introduced use of native language in service; opposed images; did not accept Real Presence.

Albigenses. A branch of the Cathari* found chiefly in Northern Italy and Southern France. They developed a New Manichaeism, believing in a god of light and a prince of this world. The angels were "the lost sheep of the house of Israel," and Jesus' death was only apparent (see Docetism). Their anticlerical criticisms led to crusades against them by the Inquisition (1181 to 1182; 1208—29). Some of them held out in spite of reverses and cruel treatment, and they did not disappear until the middle of the 14th century. Their teaching of salvation is found in the hymn "Eternal Light, Eternal Light."

C. G. Coulton, *Inquisition and Liberty*, Heinemann, London, 1938; C. Schmidt, *Histoire de la secte des Cathares ou Albigeois*, 1849; F. W. Buckler, "Albigenses," in V. Ferm, *Encyclopedia of Religion and Ethics.*

Albinus, Johann Georg (1624 to 1679). B. at Unter-Nessa, Saxony; orphaned at eleven, he was adopted by a cousin, Lucas Pollio, diaconus at St. Nicholas Church in Leipzig, where he was educated. Later he became pastor in Naumburg. His poems are forceful; his hymns are pervaded by a deep religious spirit.

Albo, Joseph (1380—1444). Defended Judaism against Christianity (*Book of Principles*). Religion, he held, is based upon three facts: existence of God; revelation; reward and punishment, in the hereafter. Last of Jewish medieval philosophers.

Albrecht, Christian Johann (1847 to 1924). B. at Echenau, Wuerttemberg; educated at St. Crischona; came to Minnesota, 1872; pastor Greenwood; New Ulm, since 1882. President of Minnesota Synod, 1883—1894; father of the college and practical seminary at New Ulm (1884); acted as first director

and taught some branches under Director Hoyer as long as New Ulm remained a theological seminary (1893). Active in forming Joint Synod of Wisconsin and Other States; president of China Mission Society, which sent first missionary (E. L. Arndt).

Albrecht, Margrave of Brandenburg-Culmbach (1522—57). The Younger, Evangelical prince, daring in his youth, one of the Prussian reformers; wrote "Was mein Gott will, das g'scheh' allzeit."

Albrecht, Max John Frederick. B. Mar. 10, 1861, at Gross-Polzin, Germany; graduated St. Louis 1883; pastor at Lebanon, Wis., 1883—88; at Janesville, Wis., 1888—91; at Fort Wayne, Ind. (Emmanuel), 1891—93; president of Concordia College, Milwaukee, Wis., 1893—1921; professor there 1921—37; retired; d. Oct. 25, 1943.

Albrecht of Prussia, Margrave of Brandenburg-Ansbach. B. 1490; Grand Master of the German Order when only twenty-one. His "father in God" was Osiander of Nuernberg. In 1523 Luther encouraged him to marry and secularize his order, which he did. Introduced the Reformation; founded the University of Koenigsberg in 1544. The Osiandrian controversy embittered his last years. The labors of Chemnitz and Moerlin in 1567 brought peace, and Albrecht died in 1568, praying, "Lord, into Thy hands I commend my spirit."

Albrechtsberger, Johann Georg (1736—1809). Contrapuntist and composer; a teacher of Beethoven and Hummel; based 279 compositions on liturgical texts.

Albrechtsbrueder. See *Evangelical Church.*

Albright, Jacob. See *Evangelical Church.*

Albright Methodists. See *Evangelical Church.*

Alcuin (735—804). Educated in cathedral school of York, England; head of the court school of Charlemagne; revised the Vulgate; sought to convert invaders by the Gospel, not force; opposed Adoptionism; greatest scholar of his age.

Aldhelm, St.* (ca. 640—709). Bishop and scholar in England; founded centers of learning; introduced Benedictine rules; wrote extensively (101 riddles in Latin hexameter).

Alemannians. Also known as Suevi, a Germanic tribe, conquered by Chlodwig in 496 and supplied with the Gospel early in the sixth century by Fridolin (d. 530), an Irish monk. In the seventh century Columbanus and Gallus labored among them, and still later Pirmin.

Alesius (Alane), Alexander (1500 to 1565). Converted by Patrick Hamilton; fled from prison to Wittenberg; took Melanchthon's *Loci* to King Henry VIII of England; professor at Frankfurt; took part in many religious conferences in England under Edward VI; twice rector of the Leipzig University.

Aleutian Islands. Part of the territory of Alaska (U.S.), a string of islands along the coast and pointing towards Asia. Two of the islands invaded by Japan during World War II, the only points of North America to come under enemy invasion. Thinly populated, mostly by people of Kamchatkan stock. Some mission stations by Greek Catholic Church. See *Alaska.* See *Missions, Bibliography.*

Alexander, Bishop of Alexandria (ca. 273—326). Active leader on the positive side of the Arian controversy. Two of his epistles extant (Socrates, *Hist. Ecc.*, I, 6; Theodoret, *Hist. Ecc.* I, 4). See *Arianism.*

Alexander III. See *Popes,* 9.

Alexander VI. See *Popes,* 18.

Alexander of Hales (*Doctor Irrefragabilis; Theologorum monarcha;* d. ca. 1245). Educated at Hales; lectured at Paris; entered order of St. Francis (1222). His great work *Summa Universae Theologiae* teaches the *character indelebilis* * and is a handbook of dialectic theology. He perfected the triple division of questions into *pro, contra,* and *resolutio,* which was adopted by scholasticism. Also the author of the *Treasury of Merits,* which is the basis of the entire indulgence theory.

Alexander, Samuel (1859—1938). Drew a distinction between deity and God in which deity is considered the aspiration of an emerging order and God the objective character of the universe.

Alexander, William (1824—1911). Anglican Primate of All Ireland; wrote *Witness of Psalms to Christ;* contributor to *Speaker's Commentary,* etc.

Alexandria, School of. See *Exegesis,* 3; *Schools, Early Christian,* 1.

Alexandrinus, Codex. See *Manuscripts of the Bible.*

Alexians. A R. C. religious order of laymen originating from laymen who served during the "Black Death" (15th c.), named after Alexius (5th c.) who had served in hospitals in Syria. They have several hospitals in the U. S.

Al-Farabi. See *Arabic Philosophy.*

Alford, Henry (1810—71). B. Oct. 7, 1810, in London; educated at Cambridge; held numerous important positions, such as Fellow of Trinity, Hulsean lecturer, and Dean of Canterbury. While still young, he wrote several Latin odes, a history of the Jews, and a series of homiletic outlines. His noblest undertaking was his commentary of the Greek Testament, the result of twenty years of labor. His hymnological and poetical works were numerous, *e. g.,* "Ten Thousand Times Ten Thousand."

Alfred the Great (849—899). King of England; founder of Oxford; gathered scholars and translated portions of Bible and Fathers (Boethius, Bede, Gregory the Great) into Saxon.

Algeria and Tunis. French colony in Northern Africa. Area, 847,818 square miles. Population, 8,676,016 (1948), native Berbers predominating; also many Bedouins (Arabs, mostly nomads); probably 65,000 Jews. Islam the dominant religion. The Methodist Episcopal Church of North America (chiefly among the Kabyles), the British and Foreign Bible Society, the North Africa Mission, the Foereningen Kvinnliga Missions Arbetare, and the Algiers Mission Band carry on some mission work, with 44 foreign men and 38 native workers (in 1949) and 1,575 baptized members. See *Missions, Bibliography.*

Al-Ghazali. See *Arabic Philosophy.*

Al-Jahiz. See *Arabic Philosophy.*

Al-Kindi. See *Arabic Philosophy.*

All Saints' Day. See *Church Year.*

All Souls' Day. See *Church Year.*

Allah. See *Mohammedanism.*

Allatu. See *Babylonians, Religion of,* 5.

Allegheny Synod. Organized Sept. 9, 1842, in Hollidaysburg, Pa., by 12 pastors and 10 lay delegates. Territory: western slope of the Allegheny Mountains in Pennsylvania. Belonged to the

General Synod and entered the United Lutheran Church with it in 1918. Joined with two other synods to form the Central Pennsylvania Synod in 1938.

Allegorical Interpretation. See *Exegesis*, 3, 5.

Allegorizing. See *Preaching, Christian*, etc.

Allegory. See *Exegesis*, 3 ff.

Allegri, Gregorio (1582—1652). Composer of Latin church music; priest at the cathedral at Fermo, where his instrumental compositions attracted the attention of Pope Urban, who appointed him to the choir of the Sistine Chapel. He is best known for a *Miserere* for two choirs, of subtle and delicate sadness, traditionally sung in Rome during Holy Week. See *Music, Christian*.

Allen, Oswald (1816—1878). B. at Kirkby-Lonsdale, Westmoreland, England, he was an invalid all his life, suffering from a diseased spine. In the course of time he became manager of his father's bank and a philanthropist. During the severe winter of 1859—1860 he composed his work *Hymns of the Christian Life*, containing 148 hymns, all from his own pen. His hymn: "To-day Thy Mercy Calls Us" is still in use.

Allen, R. See *Methodist Bodies*, 4 c.

Allendorf, Johann Ludwig Conrad (1693—1773). Court preacher of Koethen; pastor in Wernigerode and Halle; hymn writer of Pietistic School.

Allgemeine Evangelisch-Lutherische Konferenz. An organization consisting of representatives of the various Lutheran bodies of Germany, which has met since 1868 as need required. The first president was Harless, who was followed by Kliefoth. The official organ of the *Konferenz* is the *Allgemeine Evangelisch-Lutherische Kirchenzeitung*, edited for many years by Luthardt, and later by W. Laible. With it is connected the *Theologisches Literaturblatt*. Some of the leaders of the organization were connected also with the Eisenach Conference and with the *Lutherische Gotteskasten*.

Alliance of the Reformed Churches Throughout the World Holding the Presbyterian System. Organized in London, 1875; general councils meet every four years; eastern and western sections meet annually.

Allied American Veterans. See *Veterans Organizations*.

Allis, Oswald Thompson. See *Higher Criticism*, 19.

Allocution. A solemn address delivered by the Pope to the cardinals gathered in secret consistory, usually published later, to present the Pope's position on some matter.

Alloiosis. A figure of speech by which Zwingli construed all those passages of Scripture in which anything is ascribed to the divine nature of Christ or to the entire Christ which properly is the property of the human nature. The purpose of the *Alloiosis*, as used by Zwingli, was the denial of the communication of attributes. He also used it in the doctrine of absolution. Thus, when it is said: "Ought not Christ to have suffered these things and to enter into His glory?" (Luke 24:28) Zwingli declared that the term "Christ" in this passage referred only to His human nature, since it is a mere figure of speech if the suffering and death of our Lord is ascribed to His divine nature.

Luther, *Large Confession Concerning the Lord's Supper* (St. L. Ed., XX; 894—1105); Formula of Concord, Thor. Decl., VIII: 39 ff.

Allwardt, H. A. B. Mar. 2, 1840, at Wachendorf, Mecklenburg-Schwerin; to America, 1853; educated Concordia College, Fort Wayne, 1858, Concordia Seminary, St. Louis, Mo.; pastor, Crystal Lake, Wis., 1865—73; Lebanon, Wis., 1874—1910. One of C. F. W. Walther's opponents in the Predestinarian Controversy; suspended by Missouri Synod, 1881; joined Ohio Synod with others 1881; president of Ohio Synod's Northeastern District until 1899; president of the Board of Luther Seminary, Afton, later St. Paul, Minn., 1884—1910. D. D. from Capital University 1898. D. Apr. 9, 1910.

Alms (G. *eleemosyne*, mercifulness, act of charity). Matt. 6:1-4; Luke 11:41; 12:23; Acts 3:2, 3, 10; 10:2, 4, 31; 24:17. The word "alms" means gifts to the poor and indigent, although in some sectors of the early Church, so-called "alms" were divided into four equal parts: for the bishop, priests, deacons and subdeacons, the poor. Almsgiving occupies an important place in some primitive cultures (Aleuts, Eskimos, Egyptians, Sioux and Muskogee Indians) and has religious significance in Buddhism and Mohammedanism. In the

OT the facts that all things belong to God and that the rule of conduct is: "Thou shalt love thy neighbor as thyself," are stressed (Lev. 19:18, 34; cf. Ex. 23:11; Lev. 23:22; 25:25 ff.; Deut. 15:9-11; Amos; Prov. 14:20, 21; 21:13; 28:8). After the return from Captivity the increasing need caused increasing stress to be laid on almsgiving. The Apocrypha* made almsgiving a meritorious act and even an atonement for sin (Tob. 12:8 ff.; Sir. 3:30). The NT opposes this apocryphal teaching (Matt. 6) and emphasizes that man is saved by faith alone (Eph. 2:8 ff.). In view of the fact that works are the fruits and evidences of faith (Matt. 7:15 ff.; James 2), the NT speaks of rewards (Matt. 6:4; 19:21; Matt. 25:34-40; Luke 14:14; Gal. 6:9).

The Christian Church from its very beginning emphasized almsgiving (Acts 4:34, 35; 1 Cor. 16:1 ff.). The apocryphal idea of the efficaciousness of almsgiving crept into the Church and is found in such early writers as Polycarp (*Ep.* X), Hermas (*Simil.*, II), II Clement, XVI, Cyprian (*De opere et eleem.*), Tertullian (*De poen.*), and Augustine (*De fide et opere*, XXVI). These aberrations ultimately grew into the medieval system of almsgiving.

Luther restored almsgiving to its NT status, namely, that it is a pleasing work of the new life created through faith (St. L. Ed., XIII:813; VII:492 ff.; Large Cat., Seventh Commandment, 247). This teaching is also in the Confessions (AC, VI; *Ap.*, III; VI:42; and elsewhere). See *Charities, Christian.* EL

Alogi. See *Monarchism,* A 1.

Alpha Synod. Of the Ev. Luth. Church of Freedmen in America, organized May 8, 1889, by four pastors who had been ordained by the North Carolina Synod, David Koonts, president, W. Philo Phifer, secretary, Sam Holt, Nathan Clapp. When Koonts died, the synod died with him. Phifer, in the name of the other two pastors, wrote to President Schwan of the Missouri Synod. The result was that the Synodical Conference took up the work among the colored people in North Carolina.

Alt, Heinrich (1811—93). Educated in Berlin under Neander; teacher and preacher at the Charité Hospital. Wrote *Der christliche Kultus.*

Altar. In the Lutheran Church, a table for the celebration of the Lord's Supper and the place where the liturgical part of the service centers. The altar is often richly ornamented, also with a retabulum, or reredos, but it is in no sense representative of a sepulcher or sarcophagus.

Altar Bread. Bread especially prepared for the Lord's Supper,* unleavened in the Western and Armenian Church, leavened in Eastern.

Altar Cards (R. C.). Three cards, containing parts of the ritual of the Mass, which are placed on the altar, under the crucifix, at the celebration of the Mass. They are used by the officiant in case of lapse of memory.

Altar Fellowship. The practice of communing at the same altar, which, in the Lutheran Church, is a correlate of Close Communion, according to which only those who hold the same faith and confession are permitted to partake of the Lord's Supper at the same altar. The Lutheran Church early adopted the practice of Close Communion as a testimony of the unity of faith and a protest against errors, especially those of Zwingli and Calvin. The practice was followed until the establishment of the Prussian Union (1817). Lutheran State Churches continued to observe Close Communion after 1817, though Reformed were more and more admitted to their Lord's Supper. Among early Lutherans in America altar fellowship with Reformed was widely practiced. Reactions to the Prussian Union as well as the emigration of strict Lutherans, especially in the 19th century, led to a more conservative practice. Close Communion was practiced by the Joint Synod of Ohio, German Synod of Iowa, Synodical Conference, and Scandinavian synods. The General Council expressed its position in the famous Galesburg Rule.* The General Synod, believing "that the unity of the Church must be outwardly expressed," adhered "to the practice which marked the prevalent sentiment in America from the beginning, opening the privilege of the Lord's Supper to members, in good and regular standing, of other orthodox churches." Generally speaking, men prominent in the struggle for confessionalism also advocated Close Communion (C. P. Krauth, C. F. Walther, S. Fritschel), and the rising emphasis on Lutheran Confessionalism was marked by a stricter altar practice. For additional information and bibliography see *Fellowship; Lutheran Confessions.*

Altenburg Colloquy. Held at Altenburg (Oct. 20, 1568—Mar. 9, 1569) between the Wittenberg theologians (Eber, Cruciger, and others) and the Jena theologians (Wigand, Coelestin, Kirchner, and others). The Philippists (Wittenberg) defended the Augsburg Confession of 1540. Subjects discussed were: justification, free will, and adiaphora. The Colloquy led to no results.

Altenburg Debate and Theses. A debate or disputation held at Altenburg, Mo., between Pastor C. F. W. Walther and Adolf Marbach, a Lutheran lawyer, in April, 1841. See *CTM*, XII: 161 ff. The theses, here given, successfully defended by Pastor Walther, saved the Saxon Lutherans from disorganization: 1. The true Church, in the most perfect sense, is the totality [*Gesamtheit*] of all true believers, who from the begining to the end of the world, from among all peoples and tongues, have been called and sanctified by the Spirit through the Word. And since God alone knows these true believers (2 Tim. 2:19), the Church is also called invisible. No one belongs to this true Church who is not spiritually united with Christ, for it is the spiritual body of Jesus Christ. 2. The name of the true Church also belongs to all those visible societies in whose midst the Word of God is purely taught and the holy Sacraments are administered according to the institution of Christ. True, in this Church there are also godless men, hypocrites, and heretics, but they are not true members of the Church, nor do they constitute the Church. 3. The name *Church,* and in a certain sense the name *real Church,* also belongs to such visible societies as are united in the confession of a falsified faith and therefore are guilty of a partial falling away from the truth, provided they retain its purity so much of the Word of God and the holy Sacraments as is necessary that children of God may thereby be born. When such societies are called true Churches, the intention is not to state that they are faithful, but merely that they are real Churches, as opposed to secular organizations [*Gemeinschaften*]. 4. It is not improper to apply the name *Church* to heterodox societies, since that is in accord with the manner of speech of the Word of God itself. And it is not immaterial that this high name is granted to such societies, for from this follows: (1) That members also of such societies may be saved; for outside the Church there is no salvation. 5. (2) That the outward separation of a heterodox society from the orthodox Church is not necessarily a separation from the universal Christian Church or a relapse into heathenism and does not yet deprive that society of the name *Church.* 6. (3) Even heterodox societies have church power; even among them the treasures of the Church may be validly dispensed, the ministry established, the Sacraments validly administered, and the keys of the kingdom of heaven exercised. 7. Even heterodox societies are not to be dissolved, but reformed. 8. The orthodox Church is to be judged principally by the common, orthodox, and public confession to which the members acknowledge themselves to have been pledged and which they profess. See bibliography under *Lutheran Church — Missouri Synod.*

Altenburg, Johann Michael (1584 to 1640). A contemporary of Schein, Scheidt, and Schuetz who wrote motets, the excellency of which prompted a contemporary to refer to him as the Lassus of Thuringia. However, many of his day considered his compositions outmoded. In 1609 he entered the Lutheran ministry, and later the ravages of the Thirty Years' War brought much unhappiness into his life.

Altenburger Bibelwerk. Not a commentary, but the Bible reprinted with Luther's prefaces and marginal notes, summaries by Vitus Dietrich, prefaces and prayers by Franciscus Vierling, for devotional purposes. (3 vols.)

Altenburger Religionsgespraech. See *Altenburg Colloquy.*

Altenheim. See *Aged and Infirm, Lutheran Homes for.*

Althamer, Andreas (1500—39). Lutheran Reformer. B. at Brenz in Wuerttemberg; d. at Ansbach. Studied at Leipzig and Tuebingen. Priest at Schwaebisch-Gmuend, 1524; fled to Wittenberg, 1525; went to Nuremberg, 1526; pastor at Eltersdorf, 1527; deacon at St. Sebaldus', Nuremberg, 1528; called to Ansbach to aid the Reformation in Brandenburg, 1528. His *Catechism in Question and Answer,* 1528, was the first writing of that kind to be called a catechism. His selection of collects was widely used in Southern Germany.

T. Kolde, *Andreas Althamer, der Humanist und Reformator in Brandenburg-Ansbach, Erlangen,* 1895.

Althaus, Paul (1861—1925). Educated at Erlangen and Goettingen, held several pastorates from 1887 to 1897, later professor at Goettingen; wrote: *Die historische und dogmatische Grundlage der lutherischen Taufliturgie, Die Heilsbedeutung der Taufe im Neuen Testament,* etc.

Alting, Johann Heinrich (1583 to 1644). Reformed theologian. B. at Emden, East Frisia; d. at Groningen. Professor of dogmatics at Heidelberg, 1613; director of the seminary in the *Collegium Sapientiae,* 1616; professor at Groningen, 1627; a delegate from the Palatinate to the Synod of Dort, 1618 to 1619; collaborated on the Dutch Bible version. His *Theologia historica,* published by his son in 1664, is an early attempt at the history of doctrine.

Altlutheraner. See *Old Lutherans.*

Altnikol, Johann Christoph (1719 to 1759). A pupil and son-in-law of J. S. Bach, whose compositions show the unmistakable stamp of his mentor. He was privileged to be at the deathbed of Bach, who had become blind and who dictated to Altnikol his last composition.

Altruism. Term invented by Comte (French philosopher, 1798—1857) to denote unselfish regard for the welfare of others, opposed to egoism, and considered by him to be the only moral principle of life.

Altruist Community. See *Communistic Societies.*

Amana Society, or *Community of True Inspiration,* or *Inspirationists.* A German communistic religious society in Iowa. It traces its origin back to 1714, when separatists in Northern and Western Germany, stimulated by the preaching of the French Camisard prophets, under the leadership of Eberhard Gruber and Johann Rock, organized *Inspirationsgemeinden.* The movement flourished for a generation, then declined almost completely, but was revived, 1817 and the following years, in Hesse, the Palatinate, and Alsace, through the influence of the new *Werkzeuge* Michael Krausert, Barbara Heinemann, an illiterate Alsatian peasant girl, and Christian Metz. When they refused to send their children to the state schools, swear allegiance, and bear arms, the government used repressive measures, as a result of which they began to emigrate to America, 1842. They first settled near Buffalo and or-

ganized under the name of Ebenezer Society, 1843. In 1855 they removed to Iowa Co., Iowa, where they bought 26,000 acres of land, laid out seven villages, of which the principal one is Amana, and incorporated as Amana Society 1859 until 1932. The community was primarily religious, and their communism, which at first was incidental, was made to serve this primary purpose. They held all property in common and carried on agriculture, manufacture, and trade. The entire government was vested in thirteen trustees. "In 1932 communism was abolished, and according to the incorporation papers of May 18, 1932, all civil affairs were taken over by a corporation known as the Amana Society, while all ecclesiastical matters are in the hands of the Amana Church Society. This change has not affected the religious tenets of the society." Religiously the society was divided into three *Abteilungen,* or classes, graded according to their piety. Their main religious tenets, as contained in *Glaubensbekenntnis der wahren Inspirationsgemeinde* and *Katechetischer Unterricht von der Lehre des Heils,* included, besides the fundamental doctrine of present-day inspiration, belief in the Trinity, in the resurrection of the dead, and in the Judgment, but also in justification through forgiveness of sins and holy life, perfectionism, and millenarianism. The Sacraments are not means of grace. Baptism is rejected, and the Lord's Supper, or *Liebesmahl,* is celebrated whenever the Spirit prompts them, that is, about every two years, when the highest *Abteilung* also practices the rite of foot washing. There is a possibility of salvation after death, and the wicked are not punished eternally. Oaths are forbidden. Prominent in their religious life is an annual *Untersuchung,* or examination, of the spiritual condition of each member. See *Religious Bodies (U.S.), Bibliography.*

FEM

Amandus. See *Germany, 1.*

Amandus, John (d. 1530). Pastor at Altstadt; first greeted by Luther as friend, but discarded as a "turbulent spirit"; raised riot against monks; inveighed against civil authorities. Citizens finally rose against him, causing him to flee. D. while Superintendent of Churches in Goslar.

Amaterasu. The sun goddess of primitive Shinto, supposed to have been born from the left eye of Izanagi, the creator; from her is descended Jimmu Tenno, the first human ruler of Japan, 660 B. C. See also *Shinto*.

Ambo. See *Architecture, Ecclesiastical*, 3 ff.

Ambrose. Noted leader and teacher of the Western Church; b. Treves, 340; d. Milan, 397. Educated in Rome for a legal career; appointed consular prefect for Upper Italy; took up his residence in Milan about 370. After death of Bishop Auxentius a dispute between the orthodox and Arian parties caused a severe quarrel which threatened the peace of the city. Ambrose, as magistrate, was present to maintain order, when the people, suddenly turning to him as a new candidate, transferred him from his official position to the episcopate. Since he was still a catechumen, he was baptized at once, and eight days later, in 374, he was consecrated bishop. Ambrose was distinguished for his defense of the orthodox faith and for his firm stand in all matters revealed in Scripture, opposing both paganism and heresy with equal zeal. He did not hesitate to rebuke even the emperor when he permitted himself to become guilty of a massacre. As a teacher of the Church, Ambrose was concerned more with the practical and ethical side of Christianity than with the scientifically theological; among his works are *De Officiis Ministrorum* (Of the Offices of Christian Ministers), *De Virginibus* (Of Virgins), and others. Toward the end of his life he exhibited a stronger tendency toward asceticism, for he emphasized the supposed value of celibacy, of voluntary poverty, and of the martyr's death. He did much for the reform and development of church music, not only in hymns, but also in the liturgy which is associated with his name. See *Ambrosian Chant*.

Th. Forster, *Ambrosius, Bischof v. Mailand*, Halle, 1884; Bibliography under *Patristics*.

Ambrosian Chant. The mode of singing or chanting in the form of a lively, rhythmical, congregational singing, based upon the ancient Greek musical system in four modes (Dorian, in d; Phrygian, in e; Aeolian, in f; Mixolydian, in g), introduced by St. Ambrose in the Cathedral in Milan, whence it rapidly spread throughout the Occident. Later condemned by Gregory the Great.

Ambrosian Liturgy. See *Ambrose*.

Ambrosians. 1) Religious brotherhoods, owing little to St. Ambrose, which were founded in the region of Milan after the 14th century. Dissolved (1650) by Innocent X. 2) An Anabaptist sect which denied the need of Bible or priests and claimed direct communication of the Spirit (John 1:9).

Ambrosiaster. The name usually given the author of the *Commentarii in XIII Epistolas B. Pauli* (4th c.).

Amen. A liturgical term derived from the Hebrew, its root meaning "certainty." It signifies assent, confidence: "Verily," or, as Luther puts it: "Yea, yea; it shall be so."

Amen, Jacob. See *Mennonite Bodies*, 3.

American Association of Social Workers. This is the name of the chief and most comprehensive organization of professional social workers. It grew out of the first and foremost of all conferences in the field of social work, the National Conference of Social Work (founded as the National Conference of Charities and Correction in 1873). The need of a placement service for social workers led to the organization of the National Social Workers' Exchange in 1916, which in 1921 was transformed into the American Association of Social Workers.

The Association stated its purpose in 1939 as "an association of social workers meeting qualifications of training and experience, working in the area of human relationships, interested in advancing the quality of social service by means of individual and collective action in defining, promoting, and protecting social work concepts and principles in the following areas: social work practice and the advancing body of knowledge and skills required in practice; personnel standards, including professional education; standards of organization and administration affecting practice; and social problems observed in social work practice." (By-Laws, Art. II.)

Membership requirements are on the basis of education as a measurement of professional competence. Forty-seven graduate schools of social work are approved by the American Association of Schools of Social Work. Practitioners in various fields of social work have also formed associations of their own. Among them are the American Association of Medical Social Workers (1918), the American Association of

School Social Workers (1919), and the American Association of Psychiatric Social Workers (1926).

Membership in the parent organization in 1952 was 13,500. The Association publishes *The Compass* as its house organ. See *Social Work.*

American Association of Theological Schools. See *Ministry, Ed. of,* VI B.

American Baptist Association. See *Baptist Bodies,* 14.

American Bible Society. See *Bible Societies,* 5.

American Bible Union. See *Bible Societies,* 5.

American Board of Commissioners for Foreign Missions. Founded Sept. 5, 1810, by the General Association of Congregational Churches of Massachusetts, at Bradford, Mass. First missionaries sent out were Adoniram Judson, Samuel Newell, Samuel Nott, and others, 1812, to India. In 1812 the Presbyterian churches resolved to work through the American Board; in 1814 the Associate Reform Church joined; in 1816 the Dutch Reformed Church; later again the German Reformed Church. In 1825 the Presbyterian United Foreign Missions Society, formed for work among the Indians, by resolution turned over its work to the American Board. A separation of the Old-school people took place in 1837. The New-school Presbyterians continued the relation until 1870 and then withdrew to join the reunited Presbyterian Board. In 1857 the Reformed Dutch withdrew to organize their own Foreign Missions Board. They were followed in quick succession by the Associate Reformed Presbyterians and the German Reformed Church. Since 1870 the American Board represents practically only Congregational churches.

There is no purely American society that has engaged more extensively in foreign mission work than the American Board. Associated with it are several women's societies. Fields: Asia: Japan, Korea (Chosen), China, Philippine Islands, India, Ceylon, Transcaucasia, Asiatic Turkey, Syria; Africa: Angola, Union of South Africa, Southern Rhodesia, Portuguese East Africa; Oceania: Micronesia; North America: Mexico; Europe: Turkey, Bulgaria, Czechoslovakia, Spain.

American Catholic Church. See *Old Catholics,* 4.

American Christian Convention. See *Congregational and Christian Churches,* B.

American Council of Christian Churches. See *Union Movements,* 11.

American Ethical Culture Union. See *Ethical Culture.*

American and Foreign Bible Society. See *Bible Societies,* 5.

American Holy Orthodox Catholic Eastern Church. See *Eastern Orthodox Churches.*

American Legion. See *Veterans Organizations.*

American Lutheran Church, The. The American Lutheran Church is a merger of three independent synods, generally known by the names "Buffalo," * "Iowa," * and "Ohio" * which formed an organic union on Aug. 11, 1930, incorporated under the laws of the State of Illinois.

Each body brought to this union an interesting background and history, a significant contribution of distinctive spirit and heritage. All three had experienced internal as well as intersynodical controversies and had maintained a conservative position in doctrine and practice. Efforts on the part of the Ohio and Iowa Synods to reach an understanding resulted in the *Toledo Theses* * of 1909, on the basis of which fellowship was established in 1918. Continued negotiations on the part of all three bodies during the ensuing years led to the consummation of the merger in 1930.

From the beginning it was made clear that the merger should be complete, the new body thoroughly unified. It was divided into thirteen districts on a geographical basis; the districts are not incorporated, do not hold property; educational institutions, missions, etc., are synodical rather than district projects.

The synod meets biennially with a lay delegate and a pastoral delegate from each precinct of eighteen parishes, elected at district conventions. The district conventions are held annually; all active pastors are delegates; each parish is entitled to one lay delegate. "The Church being an advisory body, any local congregation connected with the Church remains its own highest authority in all matters, subject to the Word of God, and does not in any degree surrender ownership or control of its property. The local congregation, however, voluntarily obligates itself to co-operate in the work of the Church and in the maintenance of the regulations of the Church." (Constitution, Art. V, Sect. 3.)

In its "Confession of Faith" (Constitution, Art. II) the American Lutheran Church declares:

"The Church accepts the Canonical Books of the Old and New Testaments as the inspired Word of God and the only infallible authority in all matters of faith and life.

"The Church also accepts each and all of the Symbolical Books of the Evangelical Lutheran Church as the true exposition and presentation of the faith once for all delivered unto the saints, to wit: The three Ecumenical Creeds, viz.: The Apostles', the Nicene, and the Athanasian Creeds; the Unaltered Augsburg Confession and its Apology; the Smalcald Articles; the Large and Small Catechisms of Luther; and the Formula of Concord.

"The Church regards unity in doctrine and practice as the necessary prerequisites for church fellowship and therefore adheres to the rule: Lutheran pulpits for Lutheran pastors only, and Lutheran altars for Lutheran communicants only, and rejects unionism in all its forms.

"The Church is earnestly opposed to all organizations or societies, secret or open, which, without confessing faith in the Triune God and in Jesus Christ as the eternal Son of the eternal God, incarnate in order to be our only Savior from sin, are avowedly religious or practice forms of religion, teaching salvation by works. It declares such organizations and societies to be anti-Christian and rejects any fellowship with them." (Quoted entire.)

The history of the American Lutheran Church has been characterized by efforts to solve internal problems, remove pre-merger indebtedness, weather the depression of the thirties, reorganize its program of higher education, expand its home and foreign missions, promote spirituality, evangelism, and stewardship. At the same time it has manifested great interest in external relationships, co-operating in the National Lutheran Council,* and participating actively in the American Lutheran Conference * and the Lutheran World Convention,* devoted to the promotion of intersynodical fellowship and unity.

Since the three merging synods had previously engaged in negotiations with Scandinavian synods and had with them accepted the *Minneapolis Theses*,* it was logical that the newly organized American Lutheran Church should participate in the formation of the American Lutheran Conference later in the fall of 1930. Negotiations were begun with the United Lutheran Church in America and with the Missouri Synod in the hope that agreement and fellowship might be established. In 1938 the *Brief Statement* * of the Missouri Synod was adopted by the American Lutheran Church with an accompanying *Declaration*. In 1940 both the American Lutheran Church and the United Lutheran Church * in America adopted the *Pittsburgh Agreement*.* Feeling that "obstacles" still stood in the way of complete fellowship with either body, the A. L. C. at its 1946 convention adopted a resolution authorizing a "selective fellowship" * with such pastors and parishes of other Lutheran synods as agree in doctrine and practice with the declarations made in the confessional paragraph of the Constitution (quoted above); it continues to seek complete agreement and fellowship with all Lutherans.

At its 1950 convention the American Lutheran Church resolved "to adopt the Common Confession * as submitted by our Committee on Fellowship and the Committee on Doctrinal Unity of The Lutheran Church — Missouri Synod as a correct and concise statement of our faith in the doctrines herein confessed. We rejoice that agreement has been attained therein regarding doctrines that have been in controversy between our Church and The Lutheran Church — Missouri Synod." It voted in favor of a merger with the United Evangelical Lutheran Church * and the Evangelical Lutheran Church.* The Augustana Evangelical Lutheran Church * and the Lutheran Free Church * were to be invited "to participate in negotiations toward organic union." Concerning a closer approach to the United Lutheran Church in America * the convention stated: "Any negotiations for organic union must begin with discussion of doctrine and practice."

Delegates were sent to the convention of the Lutheran World Federation at Lund, Sweden, in 1947, and to previous meetings of that body. Membership in the World Council of Churches * was authorized at the 1944 convention and approved in 1946.

Recognizing problems arising from the expansion of its work and changing conditions, the synod at its 1946 convention set up a committee to restudy its organizational structure and functional procedures.

The following statistics are as of 1950:

Confirmed membership, 510,536; baptized membership, 737,653; 1,999 churches; 1,807 ordained pastors. In the 1,976 Sunday schools there are 231,009 pupils enrolled; in the 42 Christian day schools, approximately 3,100. In 30 per cent of the churches some German services are conducted. In 1952 the communicant membership reached 715,885.

During the year a grand total of $18,400,000 was given for local expenditures, including improvements and retirement of debts: over $4,700,000 was given for synodically budgeted benevolences. The total property valuation of all parishes was $95,688,748.

The American Lutheran Church is active in home mission work in the States, including some Mexican and Negro missions. In 1952 it had 12 ordained, 1 medical, and 7 lay workers in India; 20 ordained, 6 medical, and 20 lay workers in New Guinea.

Two senior colleges are maintained, Capital at Columbus, Ohio, and Wartburg at Waverly, Iowa. Texas Lutheran at Seguin is being developed into a senior college. A junior college is located at Regina, Sask. Pacific Lutheran College at Parkland, Wash., and the seminary at Saskatoon, Sask., are maintained jointly with other Lutheran synods. Two seminaries are maintained, one at Columbus, Ohio, and the other at Dubuque, Iowa. Student service at non-Lutheran schools is provided by the National Lutheran Council. (See *Ministry, Education of,* VIII, XIC; *Students, Spiritual Care of,* B.)

Church-owned charitable institutions are located at Mars, Pa.; Melville, Sask.; Richmond, Ind.; Springfield, Minn.; and San Antonio, Tex. Church-related institutions are at Muscatine, Iowa; Toledo, Ohio; Waverly, Iowa. The Church recognizes institutions at Sterling, Nebr.; Williston, Ohio; and Round Rock, Tex.; as well as non-synodical agencies of charity and welfare in most large cities. A deaconess motherhouse is located at Milwaukee, Wis. (See *Charities, Christian,* and the references given.)

A Board of Pensions provides for the retirement and aid of aged pastors.

The publication house, the Wartburg Press, is located at Columbus, Ohio; it publishes Sunday school materials, theological and devotional literature, and the official papers. The *Lutheran Standard* has a circulation of some 90,000; the *Kirchenblatt,* of 5,500; the *Lutheran Youth,* of 24,000; *The Child's Paper,* of 11,000; *the Women's Missionary Outlook,* of 45,000 (1952 statistics).

Synodically fostered organizations are the *Luther League,** the *Women's Missionary Federation,** and the *Brotherhood.**

The Church offices are located at 57 E. Main St., Columbus, Ohio. Presidents: Carl Christian Hein, 1930—37; Em. Poppen, 1937—50; Henry F. Schuh, 1950—. HLY

E. J. Wolf, *The Lutherans in America,* J. A. Hill & Co., New York, 1889; J. L. Neve, *History of the Lutheran Church in America,* Luth. Lit. Bd., Burlington, Iowa, 1934; *Constitution of the American Luth. Church, Convention Minutes of the American Luth. Church; Statistical Tables of the American Luth. Church.*

American Lutheran Conference, The. 1. A recognition of unity and a sense of fellowship transcending nationalistic lines were expressed in the formation of a federation of five synodical bodies in 1930. Designated "The American Lutheran Conference," this new organization has its strength in the upper Mississippi Valley, second- and third-generation descendants of Norwegian, German, Swedish, and Danish immigrants. The constituent synodical bodies are: American Lutheran Church, Augustana Evangelical Lutheran Church, Evangelical Lutheran Church, Lutheran Free Church, and United Evangelical Lutheran Church in America.

2. The doctrinal basis of this federation is a document known as the *Minneapolis Theses,** drawn up in 1925 by synodical representatives at a colloquium in Minneapolis and submitted for adoption to the bodies designated above. Incorporated into this document are eight points of doctrine quoted from the *Chicago Theses* * of 1919, adopted by some of the bodies in 1920. On this basis these bodies voted to establish pulpit and altar fellowship with one another, individually adopted the proposed Constitution of the American Lutheran Conference, and through their delegates organized as The American

Lutheran Conference on Oct. 29—31, 1930, at Minneapolis, Minn. (The documents named are in the January, 1941, issue of the *Journal of Theology* of the American Lutheran Conference.)

3. The spirit and purpose of those who fostered this organization is expressed in the following quotation from the preamble of the Constitution: "In the providence of God the time appears to have come when Lutheran church bodies in America that are one in faith and that have declared pulpit and altar fellowship with one another should manifest their oneness by seeking to foster fraternal relations and by cooperating in the extension of the Kingdom of Christ. These church bodies believe that it is conducive to the attainment of these objectives to enter into an organization." Objectives are stated in the Constitution as follows: "Mutual counsel concerning the faith, life, and work of the Church. Cooperation in matters of common interest and responsibility. . . ." Power is limited, each constituent body retaining its autonomy; only such functions as are specifically assigned to the Conference by its constituent bodies may be exercised by it. Conventions are held every two years, with representation based on communicant members and consisting of an equal number of pastors and laymen. Most of the work between conventions is done by commissions under the direction of the Executive Committee.

4. Perhaps the most tangible project sponsored by the Conference has been Student Service. A careful co-ordination of the efforts in this field conducted by constituent bodies led to a growing unification of the work and consultation with the Board of Education of the United Lutheran Church in America. In 1944 the Conference authorized the unification of this enterprise and the transfer of its direction to the National Lutheran Council.

5. A Commission on Lutheran Unity has studied intersynodical relations and has sought both to strengthen internal ties and to facilitate closer relationships with other Lutheran bodies. An effort in this direction was the *Overture for Lutheran Unity* * published in January, 1944.

6. The Conference has sponsored all-Lutheran seminars which have brought together pastors of Lutheran bodies generally in selected key cities; these seminars are held biennially.

7. Current social problems are studied and pertinent statements are formulated by the Commission on Social Relations.

8. The Commissions on Christian Higher Education, Elementary or Parish Education, and Youth Work have enabled the constituent bodies to share research and promotion and to coordinate their activities in these fields.

9. In the work of the Commission on Common Liturgy, efforts have been made to achieve uniformity of forms of public worship and a common hymnal.

10. The official publication of the Conference is the *Lutheran Outlook*, formerly the *Theological Journal*. It seeks to reflect current thinking and action of interest to all Lutherans, particularly striving to promote Lutheran unity.

11. The total baptized membership of the synodical bodies comprising the American Lutheran Conference is 2,153,350 (1952), very nearly the same as the membership of the United Lutheran Church in America and the Synodical Conference respectively. Presidents: Otto Mees, 1930—34; T. F. Gullixson, 1934—38; E. E. Ryden, 1938 to 1942; Harold Yochum, 1942—46; L. M. Stavig, 1946—50; Oscar A. Benson, 1950 to 1952; S. E. Engstrom, 1952—. HLY

Journal of Theology of the American Lutheran Conference; Lutheran Outlook; Lutheran World Almanac (1937).

American Lutheran Publicity Bureau. Owing to the fact that the Lutheran Church was little known by the American people, and also much misunderstood, and being therefore convinced that the Lutheran Church, its doctrines, and its work, ought to be given more publicity, the American Lutheran Publicity Bureau was organized in New York City in 1913 (1914). The constitution adopted October 26, 1920, being essentially the same as that adopted at the organization, says that the object of the A. L. P. B. shall be "to make known the teachings, principles, practice, and history of the Lutheran Church by spreading proper literature, by lecture courses, through the public press, and by means of other publicity methods." "Any communicant member of a congregation connected with the Synodical Conference or of a congregation in doctrinal affiliation with the Synodical Conference, or a society connected with such a congregation, or such a congregation may become a member of the American Lutheran Publicity Bureau on payment of at least one dollar annual dues." The Bureau has a Free Tract Fund and a Free Bible Fund. Its official magazine is the *American Lutheran*. The work is supported by the annual dues and by voluntary contributions. A board of directors, consisting of the officers and an even number of pastors and laymen, the total membership not exceeding twenty-four, conducts the Bureau's business in the intervals between the meetings of the general body.

American Lutheranism. A movement fathered by S. S. Schmucker, B. Kurtz, S. Sprecher, and other leaders of the General Synod about the middle of the nineteenth century. It was "essentially Calvinistic, Methodistic, Puritanic, indifferentistic, and unionistic, hence anything but truly Lutheran; denied and assailed every doctrine distinctive of Lutheranism . . .; attacked what was most sacred to Luther and most prominent in the Lutheran Confessions." It was sponsored by B. Kurtz in the *Observer*, by Weyl in *Luth. Hirtenstimme*, and later by the *American Lutheran* (1865). The promoters of this movement called the champions of the Lutheran Confessions "Symbolists" and pictured them as "extremists of the most dangerous sort." American Lutheranism was the result of fraternizing with the sects, of the influence of the Prussian Union, and of the Methodistic revivals. Though decrying the Lutheran Confessions, the leaders of the movement proposed a "Definite Platform" * as a confession of faith on which they hoped to unite the Lutheran Church of America. The movement played a part in the disruption of the General Synod in 1866. Thereafter the General Synod gradually moved toward a more confessional basis.

S. S. Schmucker, *Elements of Popular Theology*, Miles, Phila., 1845; S. Sprecher, *A System of Ev. Luth. Theology*, Luth. Pub. Soc., Phila., 1879; V. Firm, *The Crisis in Am. Luth. Theology*, Century, New York, 1927; C. Mauelshagen, *American Lutheranism Surrenders to Forces of Conservatism*, University of Georgia, Division of Publications, 1936.

American Old Catholic Church. See *Old Catholics*, 4.

American Order of Patriots. See *Veterans Organizations*.

American Protective Association. See *Lodges*.

American Rescue Workers. This branch of the Salvation Army originated in 1882, when Thomas E. Moore, who had come to America to superintend the work here, withdrew from the organization because of differences between himself and General Booth in regard to the financial administration and began independent work. This movement was incorporated in 1884, and in 1885 an amended charter was granted to it under the name of "Salvation Army of America." Subsequent changes in the Salvation Army in the United States resulted in the return of a considerable number of officers to that organization, but about 25 posts refused to return, and these reorganized under the name of "American Salvation Army." In 1913 the name was changed to "American Rescue Workers." In its general doctrine and polity this body is very similar to the older one, except that it is a Christian Church, with the usual Sacraments of Baptism and the Lord's Supper, rather than an evangelistic or philanthropic organization. However, the organization does general philanthropic work.

American Rite. See *Freemasonry*.

American Sunday School Union. "The First Day or Sunday School Society," organized in Philadelphia, January 11, 1791, composed of members of different denominations, including the Society of Friends, was the first general Sunday school organization. The teachers were paid for their services. The New York Sunday School Union was organized in 1816; the Philadelphia Sunday and Adult School Union in 1817. The last-named organization was in 1824 merged in the American Sunday School Union. It is composed of members belonging to different denominations, publishes Sunday school literature, founds Sunday schools, and distributes Bibles and tracts.

American Theology. See *New England Theology*, 2.

American Tract Society. See *Religious Tract Movement*.

American Unitarian Association. See *Unitarians*.

Americanism. A term used by Leo XIII (1899, *Testem Benevolentiae*) in a pronouncement addressed to Cardinal Gibbons, condemning a tendency supposedly exalting natural virtues above passive obedience. The letter was indirectly aimed at the attempt to introduce American ideals regarding the relationship between Church and State into Europe.

Ames, Edward Scribner (1870—). Professor at Butler U. and Chicago U.; professor and dean Disciples of Christ Divinity House, Chicago; liberal theologian.

Amesha Spentas. A specific class of beings in Zoroastrianism which corresponds roughly to archangels.

Amiatinus, Codex. The Latin manuscript of the Vulgate which was written in England (ca. 700) and used in the preparation of the Sistine edition.

Amice. See *Vestments, Clerical.*

Amish, The. See *Mennonite Bodies,* 3.

Amling, Wolfgang (1542—1606). Protestant theologian of Germany, known for his opposition to the Formula of Concord and for winning a large portion of Anhalt to the Reformed Church. Author of the *Confessio Anhaldina.*

Ammon, Christoph Friedrich von. B. 1766, d. 1850 at Dresden as court preacher and vice-president of the consistory; considered the most skillful defender of popular rationalism.

Amora. Title of a teacher of the Mishnah.

Amorc. See *Rosicrucians.*

Ampullae. In ancient times, vases for oil and perfumes; in Catholicism, a vessel containing oil consecrated for ritual use.

Amsdorf, Nicholas von (1483—1565). One of first students at Wittenberg in 1502; professor; intimate with Luther; went with him to Worms without a safe conduct. In 1542 Luther consecrated him Bishop of Naumburg; ousted after Battle of Muehlberg. Opposed Interim. Faithful to the captive John Frederick. After 1552 at Eisenach, without office, but actually at head of church affairs. "Good works were harmful to salvation," he said against Major's "Good works are necessary to salvation."

M. Meurer, *Das Leben der Altvaeter d. Luth. Kirche,* Leipzig, 1863 (III, 108—267).

Amulets. Objects, or charms, which are believed to have magic powers to bring their wearer good fortune or protect him from harm. Their use has been almost universal among pagans at all times. The semipagan influence of the fourth century brought them into the

Christian Church, where they were denounced as a species of idolatry. The increasing degeneracy of the Church, however, permitted them to survive under a Christian coloring. Relics enclosed in costly cases, called phylacteries, were worn as potent protectors; holy water, blessed salt, and consecrated wafers were carried on the person. Contact with the East during the Crusades multiplied the talismans and charms of the superstitious Middle Ages. Roman Catholic writers strongly denounce the use of amulets, but it is not easy to see wherein these differ from the objects worn by devout Romanists — the endless variety of scapulars,* crosses, medals, and medallions, all blessed or consecrated by contact with relics, and supposed, for that reason, to have definite power of protecting the wearers. Rome seems, by such objects, to foster among her adherents reliance in a kind of ecclesiastical magic.

Amusements. The Bible does not endorse a pietistic attitude toward amusements as such, but mentions innocent and wholesome amusements for old and young in a favorable light (Zech. 8:5; Luke 15:22 f.; Eccl. 11:9). The time for recreation and amusements, however, is a time when a person is free from his regular occupation, and its purpose is recreation or relaxation from work. A Christian should shun sinful amusements, since all pastimes and amusements are judged by God's Word: "Know thou that for all these things God will bring thee into judgment" (Eccl. 11:9).

Reu-Buehring, "Social Intercourse," *Christian Ethics,* Luth. Book Concern, 1935 (368—372); *Walther League Manual.*

Amyraldians. See *Cameron, John.*

Amyrault, Amyraldus Moses. Pastor, later professor at Saumur, France (d. 1664), notable Bible commentator and preacher, author of a book on Christian ethics. In the doctrine of predestination he tried to harmonize universalism with particularism.

Anabaptist Creeds. See *Democratic Declarations,* 1.

Anabaptists. See *Mennonite Bodies; Baptist Bodies,* 2.

Anacletus. After Linus, the second successor of Peter as bishop of Rome according to Catholic tradition.

Anagogical Interpretation. See *Exegesis,* 5.

Anahita. Ancient Persian goddess of fertility.

Analogy. The analogy of Scripture is that quality of Holy Writ according to which all its statements are in harmonious relation to one another, so that they mutually clarify and expound the doctrines concerned.

Analogy of Faith. See *Hermeneutics.*

Anaphora (Greek Catholic). Part of service which includes consecration of elements.

Anarchism (G. "without rule"). A theory which regards government as the source of social evils and would substitute spontaneous co-operation for political rule.

Anathema. Used in New Testament and terminology of the Church (like the OT "accursed"; cf. P. Kretzmann, *Pop. Com.,* OT, II, 725) as a solemn curse pronounced in God's name upon heretics and ungodly (Gal. 1:8, 9; 1 Cor. 16:22). Generally designates eternal separation from God (Rom. 9:3); also used as a formula for sinful cursing, 1 Cor. 12:3; Acts 23:14. See *Blessing and Cursing.*

Anatolia. The extreme western section of Asia, bordering Turkey. Part of the Turkish Empire. About 199,272 square miles. Population, about 10 million, chiefly Turks of Mohammedan faith. Modern missions: the American Board of Commissioners for Foreign Missions and Church Missionary Society. See *Missions, Bibliography.*

Anaxagoras (ca. 500—430 B. C.). Author of *peri phuseos;* brought philosophy from Ionia to Athens; influenced Periclean age. Held that mind was an abstract being which arranged all. Explained and investigated many natural phenomena.

Ancestor Worship. Worship directed to deceased parents or forefathers. The cult is one of the most ancient and is encountered in all parts of the globe. It still survives where Christianity, Judaism, and Mohammedanism have not exerted their influence, as in the South Pacific Islands, India, Southern and Western Africa, North and South America. It plays a prominent role in the religious life of China and Japan and among the ancients was practiced by the Babylonians and especially by the Romans. The cult is based on the universal belief in the existence of an immaterial part of man which leaves the body at death (see *Animism*). The deceased, furthermore, is believed to have the same kindly interest in the affairs of the living as when alive and to interfere in the course of events for the welfare of the family or clan. He is able to protect his relatives, help them in war, give them success in their undertakings, and therefore demands their continued service, reverence, and sacrifices; or he may bring diseases, storms, or other misfortunes upon them, if his worship is neglected. The motive behind ancestor worship is therefore not only filial piety, but frequently also fear, often a mixture of both. With the ancient Romans, ancestor worship was a sort of family religion. Masks or images, embodying the *manes,* i. e., the spirits of the deceased, who had become gods of the lower world, were set up in the homes, altars erected, sacrifices made, and prayers offered to them in the same manner as to the *penates,* the protecting spirits of the household. The Hindus bring sacrifices to the *pitris* (*patres*), the divine spirits of deceased ancestors, and implore them for assistance. In China, ancestor worship is universal. Tablets of wood bearing the name and date of birth and death of the deceased are found in most homes, and incense and spirit money are burned before them. Often an entire room is set aside for this purpose, and a rich family will erect a separate building. The oldest son especially is obligated to perform this worship, from which fact comes the great desire for male offspring and the little regard paid to girl babies. In the first part of April a general worship of ancestors is observed with sacrifices, libations, burning of candles, incense, and paper. From China, ancestor worship passed to Japan, where, too, it became firmly established.

Besides actual worship of the spirits of the deceased there has been prevalent among many races the custom of supplying the dead with things which they enjoyed while alive, under the assumption that they needed them as much in the other world as in the present. Food, clothing, utensils, and weapons were placed in the tomb, as was done by the ancient Egyptians. Among some savage races the dead man's wife, servants, and favorite animals were killed or buried alive with their former master. However, as this was done to minister to his needs, not to implore him for help, such practices alone are not ancestor worship in the strict sense.

Associated with ancestor worship is the belief in the possibility of communicating with the spirits of the dead and obtaining their counsel and assistance in times of danger and misfortune through the agency of medicine men, wizards, or seers (see *Spiritism*). There is also a widely prevalent belief that ancestors are reincarnated in newborn children, for which see *Transmigration.* Ancestor worship has in some cases developed into idol worship, and the Roman worship of the *manes* was the substructure upon which developed the worship of saints in the Roman Catholic Church. See *Religion, Comparative, Bibliography.*

Anchorites. See *Hermits.*

Anderson, Lars. See *Andreae, Laurentius.*

Anderson, Paul (1821—92). B. in Norway; came to America in 1843; educated at Beloit College, Beloit, Wis.; ordained by the Frankean Synod in 1848; was the first Scandinavian Lutheran minister in America to hold regular English services and to establish a Sunday school; organized First Norwegian Lutheran Church in Chicago; was elected president of the Northern Illinois Synod, 1857; was prominent in organizing the Scandinavian Augustana Synod in 1860, also in organizing the Norwegian Augustana Synod in 1870; was pastor in Milwaukee, Wis., 1876—1883.

Andover Controversy. A controversy in the Congregational Church (1886—93), which arose when a committee of the American Board for Foreign Missions refused to sanction missionaries who held the opinion of some Andover professors that heathen who had died without hearing the Gospel would have a second chance.

Andover Theology. See *New England Theology.*

Andreae, Jakob (1528—90). Studied at Tuebingen; at eighteen preacher at Stuttgart; chancellor of Tuebingen; active reformer in all Southern Germany; confessed his faith before King Antony of Navarre at Paris and discussed it with Patriarch Jeremiah of Constantinople; failed to unite the Flacians and Philippists at Zerbst in 1570; preached six sermons on the disputed points; revised again and again the basis of the Formula of Concord; the Church owes the Formula, next to Chemnitz, to him.

Johann V. Andreae, *Fama Andreana reflorescens,* Strasbourg, 1630.

Andreae, Johann Valentin (1586 to 1654). Grandson of above; studied at Tuebingen; insisted on pure morals as well as pure doctrine; called to Calv in 1620; pioneer in Inner Mission work; called to Stuttgart in 1639 as court preacher; labored to educate ministers and to introduce church discipline.

Andreae, Laurentius (1470—1552). Swedish archdeacon won by Olavus Petri * for the Reformation; church diplomat and politician, chancellor to Gustavus Vasa * 1529, arranging the first reformed polity of the Swedish church; with Olavus Petri condemned to death for resistance to presbyterian system (1541) but reprieved.

Andreen, Gustav Albert. Educator, college president; b. 1864 in Porter, Ind.; educated chiefly at Augustana College, Rock Island, Ill., and Yale; instructor at Augustana College, 1882—84; professor of languages at Bethany College, Kansas, 1884—94; professor at Yale, 1894—1901; president of Augustana College, 1901—35; author of *Det Svenska Spraeket i Amerika, Studies in the German Idyl, History of the Educational Work of the Augustana Synod, The Early Missionary Work of the Augustana Synod in New York City, L. P. Fabjoern and the Pioneers of 1849, History of Augustana College at Its 75th Anniversary.* D. Oct. 1, 1940.

Andrew of Crete (660—732). Deacon of Constantinople, archbishop of Crete, vigorous opponent of the Monothelites. Hymns still sung in Greek churches.

Anerio, Felice (1560—1614). The successor of Palestrina as composer of the papal chapel, who also served as maestro at the English College in Rome and helped edit the *Editio Medicea* (1614) of Gregorian chant, which exerted a great influence, but which fell into disrepute in the 19th century because of its untrustworthiness.

Angel of the Lord. The special, uncreated Angel of the Old Testament, the Son of God as He appeared to the believers of the Old Testament upon various occasions. The Angel of the Lord, we are told, appeared to Hagar in the wilderness, Gen. 16:7 ff.; later again, Gen. 21:17; in company with two created angels He visits Abraham in Mamre,

Gen. 18; He appears to Abraham as he is about to sacrifice Isaac, Gen. 22:11; to Jacob at Bethel, Gen. 31:11-13; cf. 28: 10 ff.; Jacob wrestles with Him at Peniel, Gen. 32:24 (cf. Hos. 12:3-5); Jacob asks Him to bless the sons of Joseph, Gen. 48:16; He appears to Moses in the burning bush, Ex. 3; goes before the camp of Israel, Ex. 14:19; God warns Israel not to provoke Him, Ex. 23:20 f.; is again promised to Israel after they had committed idolatry with the golden calf, Ex. 32:34; 33:1-12; leads them to Kadesh, Num. 20:16; appears to Balaam, Num. 22:22 ff.; appears to Joshua as the Captain of the Lord's host, Josh. 5:13—6:2; comes to Bochim, Judg. 2: 1-4; tells Israel to curse Meroz, Judg. 5:23; appears to Gideon, Judg. 6:11; to Manoah and his wife, Judg. 13:2 ff.; His name is used in a proverbial expression, 1 Sam. 29:9; 2 Sam. 14:17, 20; 19:27; when David had numbered Israel, the Angel of the Lord stretched His hand over Jerusalem to destroy it, 2 Sam. 24:16 ff.; 1 Chron. 22:15-30; He appears to Elijah under the juniper tree, 1 Kings 19:5-7; sends Elijah to Ahaziah, 2 Kings 1:1-3; smites 185,000 Assyrians, 2 Kings 19:35; 2 Chron. 32:21; Is. 37:36; David mentions Him, Ps. 34:7; 35:5, 6; Isaiah calls Him the Angel of God's presence, Is. 63:9; He appears to Zechariah, who mentions His name, 1:8 ff.; 3:1 ff.; 12:8; and Malachi calls Him the Messenger, or Angel, of the Covenant, Mal. 3:1.

E. W. Hengstenberg, *Christologie des Alten Testaments,* Ludwig Oehmigke, Berlin, 1829.

Angelicals, Order of. An order of Augustinian nuns, founded at Milan about 1530, now extinct for nearly a century. Every member adopted the name "Angelica."

Angelico, Fra (1387—1455). Pious and spiritual artist, most famous works in Chapel of Nicholas V.

Angelicus, Doctor. See *Aquinas, Thomas.*

Angelolatry. That angelolatry, the worshiping of angels, was practiced very early is evident from the condemnation voiced in Col. 2:18. This passage, together with Rev. 22:8, 9, long kept this unscriptural cult in check. Eusebius, Augustine, and even Pope Gregory the Great reproved it, and the Council of Laodicea called it disguised idolatry. With the increasing veneration of images * and saints,* the invocation of angels also gained vogue, was sanc-

tioned by the Second Council of Nicaea (787), and has since been practiced in the Roman and Greek Churches. The *Catechismus Romanus* (III, 2, 8) says: "That also must carefully be taught in the explanation of this Commandment [the First], that the veneration and invocation of the holy angels . . . is not contrary to this law. For though the Christians are said to adore the angels, according to the example of the saints of the Old Testament [!], they nevertheless do not show them that veneration which they give God." See *Latria.*

Angels, the Evil. See *Devil.*

Angels, the Good. The word "angel" literally means a messenger and is so translated Luke 7:24, etc. It generally stands for the messengers of God, the unseen citizens of heaven, who are continually doing the bidding of the Most High. Ps. 104:4; Matt. 4:6; Heb. 2:7. The "angels of the seven churches" in Revelation are evidently the pastors of these churches. "Angel of the Lord" is an Old Testament term for the Second Person of the Holy Trinity. See article on *Angel of the Lord.*

According to their nature the angels are creatures, Col. 1:16, and are members of the great family of God under the Head, Jesus Christ, Eph. 1:10; 3:15. Their characteristic is spirituality. Heb. 1:14. They are personal, conscious, intelligent beings, who differ from men in the completeness of their spiritual nature, which does not require a body in order to constitute a personality. The angels are endowed with knowledge, power, and the ability of free locomotion. They recognize the depth and glory of the divine counsels, but grow in their knowledge of God's plan of salvation as they see it in process of completion. Matt. 24:36; 1 Pet. 1:12; Eph. 3:10. By reason of their great power — evidenced in mighty acts of judgment, Gen. 19; 2 Kings 19:35; Matt. 13:49, 50; they "excel in strength," Ps. 103:20, 21 — they are given tremendous titles: Thrones, Principalities, Powers, etc., Rom. 8:38; Eph. 1:21; 3:10; Col. 2:10; 1:16; 1 Pet. 3:22; 2 Pet. 2:10. Their power is employed in the preservation of the faithful. Dan. 3:25; Acts 5:19; 12:7.

In numbers the angels are so great that the word "hosts" is characteristic of them. There are "many thousands," myriads, multitudes of them. Deut. 33:2; Dan. 7:10. As such they were created, since their multiplication by natural increase is excluded. Matt. 22:30.

While some of the angels fell (see article *Devil*), the rest have been confirmed in their state of innocency. Hence theirs is not only an ability not to sin, but an inability to sin, Matt. 18:10; and they are for this reason called the Holy Ones of God, Ps. 89:7; Luke 9:26, and elsewhere. The passage Job 4:18 marks the difference between the absolute holiness of God and the sinlessness of the angels. The knowledge of their presence should fill us with holy dread. 1 Cor. 11:10.

Whenever angels have been made manifest to man, it has always been in human form. Gen. 18 and 19; Luke 24:4; Acts 1:10; etc. Of what these bodies in which they were clothed for association with man consisted is a question unanswered in Scripture. Whenever they appeared in human form, it was in order to bring a message or perform some service among men as agents of God's providence. The operation of natural forces is sometimes described as fulfilling the will of God under angelic guidance, as in the case of pestilence. Ex. 12:23; Heb. 11:28; 1 Cor. 10:10; 2 Sam. 24:16. The plagues which cut off the army of Sennacherib, 2 Kings 19:35, and which ended the career of Herod, Acts 12:23, are plainly attributed to the work of an angel. — But by far the most numerous appearances of angels are those connected with the scheme of redemption and the sanctification of man. The angels mingled with, and watched over, the family of Abraham. Angelic guidance was withheld when the prophetic office began with Samuel, except when needed by the Prophets themselves. 1 Kings 19:5; 2 Kings 6:17. But during and after the Babylonian Captivity, angels are again announced to Daniel and Zechariah as watching over the national life of Israel.

In the New Testament age the angels are revealed as ministering spirits to each individual member of Christ. While their visible appearances are infrequent after the Incarnation, their presence and their aid are referred to familiarly almost as a thing of course. They watch over Christ's little ones, Matt. 18:10; they rejoice over penitent sinners, Luke 15:10; they attend the worship of Christians, 1 Cor. 11:10; they bear the souls of the redeemed into Paradise, Luke 16:22. In all these employments the angels do not act independently, but as the instruments of God and by His command.

Of the angels, several are mentioned by name. Gabriel was the messenger sent to Daniel, to the father of John the Baptist, and to the mother of our Lord. The name means "champion of God." Michael ("Who is like God?"), another of the archangels or angels of higher rank, is described in Daniel as having special charge of the Israelites and in Jude as disputing with Satan about the body of Moses. The nature and method of his war against Satan are not revealed to us. See also under *Cherubim* and *Seraphim*.

A. C. Gaebelein, *The Angels of God*, 1924; *L. u. W.*, XXII:273—77; XXIII: 273—76; references under *Dogmatics*.

Angelus. A prayer repeated by Roman Catholics three times a day, at morning, noon, and night, when the bells sound three times three strokes, with intervals between. It ordinarily consists of three "Hail, Marys!" with versicles and a prayer; in paschal time a hymn to the Virgin (*Regina Coeli*) is substituted. An indulgence of a hundred days is gained for each recitation, with a plenary indulgence once a month.

Angelus Temple. The central church of the International Church of the Foursquare Gospel.* It is located in Los Angeles, Calif.

Anglican Catechism. See *Anglican Confessions*, 9.

Anglican Church. See *England*.

Anglican Confessions. 1. The *Ten Articles* were issued by Henry VIII (1536) to define necessary beliefs concerning salvation and ceremonies (five articles on each). This confession held that Holy Scripture and three Creeds (also first four Councils and traditions not contrary to Scripture) are bases for Christian living; that men are justified through the merits of Christ (good works, however, necessary); that Baptism is necessary for regeneration; the *Articles* retained transubstantiation, use of images, prayers to saints, purgatory, auricular confession.

2. The *Articles* were supplanted by the *Bishop's Book* (1537; called *Institute of a Christian Man*; exposition of the Creed, Lord's Prayer, seven sacraments, Commandments, justification, and purgatory), and the *King's Book* (1543; added matters on free will, good works, justification, predestination, purgatory).

3. In 1538 English and German scholars drafted *Thirteen Articles* on the basis of the Augsburg Confession. Though never published, these became the bases for the *Forty-Two Articles*.

4. The following year (1539), Henry VIII reacted to the Reformation and enacted the *Six Articles* which provided the death penalty for the rejection of transubstantiation, auricular confession, celibacy, Communion in one kind; monastic vows; private masses.

5. Cranmer continued to work for a Protestant creed, and in 1549 an Act of Parliament authorized King Edward VI to appoint 32 persons (among those appointed were Cranmer, Ridley, Hooper, Coverdale, Peter Martyr, and Justis Hales) to draw up ecclesiastical laws. These drew up the *Forty-Two Articles* (1553) which were issued without the formal authorization. Soon after their publication Edward VI died, and Cranmer and Ridley were burned under Mary.

6. After the death of Mary, Elizabeth gave Matthew Parker (1504—1575) the task of recasting the *Forty-Two Articles*. Using the Augsburg Confession and other Lutheran and Reformed formulations, he revised the *Forty-Two* into the *Thirty-Nine Articles*, which received final revision by the Convocation of 1571. In the same year an act was passed requiring subscription to them. The *Articles* give prominence to those tenets which separate Anglicans from Rome (supremacy of the Pope; enforced celibacy; denial of the cup to the laity; transubstantiation; sacraments; purgatory; relics; images; works of supererogation). They often lack clarity because of efforts at compromise between Lutheran and Reformed theology. The theological affinity of their article on predestination has been much disputed; on the Lord's Supper they are definitely Reformed. The separation of the American colonies from England made changes necessary in the *Articles*. The General Convention at Trenton (1801) adopted the *Thirty-Nine Articles* but omitted the Athanasian Creed and made other changes necessitated by changed political conditions.

7. *Lambeth Articles*. After the adoption of the *Thirty-Nine Articles*, Calvinism gained strength in England. The *Lambeth Articles* (Nov. 20, 1595) are a strong enunciation of Calvin's predestinarian system but never attained to symbolical authority.

8. *Irish Articles*. Drawn up chiefly by James Ussher and approved at the Convocation of Dublin (1615). These articles (104) revised the *Thirty-Nine Articles* in a strongly Calvinistic direction (absolute predestination and perseverance, Pope is Antichrist, Puritan view of Sabbath, no mention of episcopal ordination) and became a basis for the Westminster Confession.

9. *Other Confessions*. In addition to the above, the Anglican Catechisms must be considered. Henry VII published a *Primer* based on 15th-century *Prymer* (Lord's Prayer, Creed, Ten Commandments) with some additions. Cranmer's catechism was drawn from Lutheran sources (1548). In the Prayer Books of Edward VI a catechism for children was included which underwent frequent alterations and is still used. See also *Book of Common Prayer*. See *Reformed Episcopal Church*, England.

EL

P. Schaff, *Creeds of Christendom*, Harpers, 1899 (3 vols.); H. E. Jacobs, *The Luth. Movements in England During the Reigns of Henry VIII and Edward VI*, General Council Pub. House, Phila., 1908; E. J. Bicknell, *A Theological Introduction to the Thirty-Nine Articles of the Church of England*, Longmans, Green, 1925; E. G. Rupp, *Studies in the Making of the English Protestant Tradition*, Cambridge, 1947.

Anglo-Catholics. A term applied to the Church of England in the 17th century. Later the term was more specifically applied to the Oxford Group, to those emphasizing ritual, and to High-churchmen generally.

Anglo-Israelism. The theory that the inhabitants of England are the descendants of the lost Ten Tribes of Israel. The theory was first advanced by John Sadler (1649) and later developed by Richard Brothers (1757 to 1824). It is not in agreement with historical facts as known.

Anglo-Saxon Religious Poetry. After the second Christianizing of Britain, following the Anglo-Saxon conquest, a good deal of religious poetry was produced, such as Caedmon's paraphrases of Sacred History, Cynewulf's *Crist*, and many shorter poems.

Anglo-Saxons, Conversion of. When the Angles and their confederates, under Hengist and Horsa, conquered England, beginning with 449, they almost eradicated Christianity, which had been established several centuries before. But at the end of the next century King Ethelbert of Kent (560—616) married a Christian princess, Bertha of Paris, who brought with her a Christian chaplain, Liudhard. The first obstacles having thus been removed, the emissary of Gregory the Great, Augustine of Canterbury, was able, in 596, to establish Christianity in Kent, whence, in spite of various reverses, it spread to Northumbria, Wessex, and the other parts of England. Toward the end of the sixth century the Culdees, or Irish missionaries, came to the northern part of England, so that, until the Council of Whitby (662) there were two Christian Churches in England.

Angola. Portuguese Southwest Africa; 481,351 square miles, population 4,111,796 (1950). Ten societies carrying on mission work there; about 50,000 communicants; 56 ordained, 2,111 not ordained native workers; 167 foreign missionary workers; includes Island of Sao Tome. Most rapid growth of any African Protestant church in the 13 years before 1938. See *Missions, Bibliography.*

Angra-Mainyn. See *Zoroastrianism, 3.*

Animatism. The belief in *mana* (Melanesian term), a vague, impersonal, supernatural power by which things were believed created, preserved, and replenished. This power was not individualized or personalized. Similar to *mana* was the power worshiped as *manitou* (Algonquin Indians), *orenda* (Iroquois), *wakan* (Sioux), and others.

Animism. Belief in, and worship of, spirits. Found among all primitive peoples and survives also in many superstitions and in the folklore of civilized groups. It seems to owe its origin to the belief that the human being has a soul which is separable from the body and can exist alone. Next, souls were attributed to other living things, as animals and plants, and even to inanimate objects, as the heavenly bodies, springs, rocks, and tools. In the end developed the belief in spirits which are completely without bodies. These latter were largely regarded as malevolent, causing illness and bringing on misfortune. Where animism holds sway, the life of people is filled with dread of these invisible forces, which men then seek to control by magic or sorcery. Belief that an independent spirit may enter a material object and through it exert an influence leads to fetishism.* Belief in separable human souls and their complete departure from the body at death and their subsequent intervention in the affairs of the living furnishes the basis of ancestor worship * and spiritism.* While Scripture (Rom. 1:18-25) declares that the heathen animistic and polytheistic conceptions are due to a perverted view of God's manifestations in nature, evolutionistic science of religion assumes that animism is the lowest, or one of the lowest, stages in the upward development of religion. See *Religion, Comparative, Bibliography.*

Annates. A fee collected by the Pope from persons appointed to bishoprics and (later) lower officials.

Annihilationism. The belief that the unrighteous pass out of existence after death. Some adherents of this belief hold that such annihilation is the result of the gradual disintegration occasioned by sin. Others hold that the wicked will suffer after death in expiation of their sins, but that such suffering is followed by complete cessation of being. The origin of such teachings is to be found in the natural horror which men feel when confronted with the idea of eternal punishment. For the Scriptural doctrine opposing annihilationism see *Eschatology* and *Hereafter.*
D. M. Gilbert, "The Annihilation Theory Briefly Examined," *L. Q.,* IX, 613 to 648.

Annunciation. A festival commemorating the tidings brought Mary by Gabriel celebrated on March 25 by Greek, Roman, and Anglican churches.

Annunciation, Orders of. Those orders (R. C.), founded under the patronage of Mary: 1. *Annunciade,* founded at Bourges (1501) by Jeanne of France; also known as the Nuns of Ten Virtues. 2. *Celestines,* founded by Maria Victoria Fornari (1604). 3. *Annunziata,* founded by Count Amadeus (15th c.). 4. *Annunciates,* founded under the direction of Beccaria (1408). 5. *Servites,* founded 1239 and devoted to missions and teaching in secondary schools. 6. *Archconfraternity of the Annunciation,* devoted to providing dowries for poor girls.

Anomoians. Arians who denied the likeness of the Son to the Father; distinguished from the semi-Arians, who only denied the consubstantiality. See *Arianism, 1.*

Anselm of Canterbury (1033 to 1109). Succeeded Lanfranc of Bec as prior (1063) and as archbishop of Canterbury, England. Studied Augustine extensively and lived himself into his spirit. In his *Cur Deus Homo* he subjected the doctrine of the atonement to dialectical investigation and vindication. In the *Monologium* he developed his ontological argument for God. Had many difficulties with the king of England over rights and privileges. In character he was humble, kind of heart, and charitable. Father of medieval scholasticism.

A. C. Welch, *Anselm and His Work*, London, 1901; *CTM*, XIV: 673 ff. M. Grabmann, *Geschichte der scholastischen Methode*, Freiburg, 1909 (vol. 1); J. M. Rigg, *Anselm of Canterbury*, Methuen, London, 1896.

Ansgar (801—865). The "Apostle of the North"; first archbishop of Hamburg; missionary to Denmark at the request of King Harold, and to Sweden. Thereafter given the bishopric of Hamburg with the right to send missionaries to all northern lands.

Antediluvians. A name applied to people who lived before the Flood.

Ante-Nicene Fathers. See *Patristics*.

Anthem. A sacred choral work whose text, though taken from the Bible, is non-liturgical. While 17th-century anthems were usually sung without accompaniment, modern anthems include an instrumental accompaniment. Excellent anthems were written by English master composers in the 17th and 18th centuries. The use of the anthem declined in some areas toward the middle of the 20th century.

Anthony of Padua. See *Preaching, Christian, History of*, 8.

Anthony, St. The father of Christian monasticism; b. ca. 251 in Egypt; d. 356. Said to have lived as a hermit for eighty years. He organized hermit colonies in which monks lived separately, but met for religious services. Anthony left no written rule.

Anthony, St., Orders of. Religious orders which claimed St. Anthony as their patron (Antonians, Hospital Brothers of St. Anthony, Armenian Antonians, Congregation of St. Anthony, Chaldean Antonians).

Anthropology. That part of Christian dogmatics, or doctrinal theology, referring to man's creation, essential parts, fall, and subsequent sinfulness. Man was originally created in God's image, *i. e.*, in concreate wisdom, holiness, and righteousness (Col. 3:10; Eph. 4:24). Although positively good both in body and soul (Gen. 1:31), man yet could fall (Gen. 2:17), though the question as to how this could be, belongs to the mystery of the origin of sin. Man's fall was voluntary, for though Eve was deceived by the devil (1 Tim. 2:14), she and Adam sinned against their better knowledge (Gen. 3:1 ff.). While the Fall was foreseen by God, it was not willed by Him (Ps. 5:4, 5). Scripture rejects all forms of determinism * and fatalism.* After the Fall, man still retains a free will,* not only inasmuch as he is endowed with the faculty to will, but also as he can exercise his free will in worldly affairs and in civil matters. But he has no free will in spiritual matters, *i. e.*, he cannot by his own reason or strength believe in Jesus Christ and thus convert himself (John 1:14, 15; 3:9; John 3:5, 6; Col. 2:13). The Moral Law was originally written in the human heart (according to one interpretation of Rom. 2:14, 15; 1:19 ff.), so that in the state of innocence Adam knew God's will even without special revelation (Gen. 2:20 ff.). After the Fall, man still retains the knowledge of God's Law and will, though it is obscured by sin (Rom. 1:32). Conscience * is man's moral faculty which, on the basis of the natural law, judges between right and wrong. Since the Fall has obscured the natural law and also weakened man's moral judgment, his opinions of moral and spiritual matters are often wrong, and conscience, therefore, is no longer a safe guide in doctrine and life, but must be normed according to Scripture, which is the only source and rule of faith and life (cf. *Dogmatics*). JTM

Anthropomorphism (G. *anthropos*, "man," and *morphe*, "form"). The Scriptural mode of speech by which the possession of human sense, limbs, and organs is attributed to God. God is spoken of as having a face, eyes, ears, nose, heart, arm, hand, finger (Gen. 3:8; Ex. 6:6; 7:4; 13:3; Ps. 11:4; 18:8; 10:17; 34:16; 63:8; 95:4; 139:16; Is. 52:10; 62:8; Jer. 27:5; Luke 11:20). Since God is not composed of material, but is simply spirit, complete in His spiritual nature, the Bible, when it speaks of God as possessing human parts or affections (*anthropopathism*, G. "human feeling"), purposes to convey to the human mind some notion of the ways of God in His universe (cf. Is. 55:8 f.; Rom. 11:33 ff.).

The term anthropomorphism is applied to heretical teachings which attribute an actual body and human emotions to God. Thus Latter-Day Saints * hold that God is a material being, with human passions, who created man as men beget children. Those who thus ascribe human parts, attributes, and passions to God are called *anthropomorphites*.

Anthropopathism. See *Anthropomorphism*.

Antichrist. 1. A term used in the NT of (1) all false teachers (1 John 2:18; 4:3) and (2) of one outstanding adversary of Christ (1 John 2:18). The characteristics of Antichrist are taken from Dan. 7; 8; 11:31-35; Rev. 10; 13; 17; 18; writings of John; and especially 2 Thess. 2:3-12. His habitation is between the seas (Dan. 11:45) and on seven hills (Rev. 17:9-18); his power is growing already in the time of the Apostles (1 John 2:18; 2 Thess. 2:8); he works with all power and signs and lying wonders (2 Thess. 2:9); a "falling away" precedes his coming (2 Thess. 2:3); he sits in the temple of God (2 Thess. 2:4); he exalts himself above God and shows himself as God (2 Thess. 2:4); is a mystery of iniquity (2 Thess. 2:7, 8); restrained in Apostolic times (2 Thess. 2:7; "Roman Empire" — Bousset).

2. The word ἀντίχριστος occurs for the first time in the NT, and there only in the writings of John. The idea, however, is previously mentioned in the NT, and the roots go back into OT prophecy. Vain attempts have been made to seek the origin of the idea in heathen lands (*e. g.*, battle of Ahura Mazda and Angra Mainyu-Bousset). Antiochus IV was the first historical figure to whom the prophecies of Daniel (7:8, 19-25; 8:9-12; 11:21-45) were applied. Later they were applied to Pompey, Herod, and Caligula.

3. The passages which are generally applied to Antichrist were correlated early in the Christian era. Polycarp (VII) quotes 1 John 4:3 in connection with those who do not confess the testimony of the Cross; the *Didache* (XVI:4) speaks of the Antichrist as the world deceiver who is to come; Ps. Barnabas (IV) speaks of the "beast" as the wicked one yet to come. Irenaeus (*Haer.* VI:31; 3 ff.; V:29 ff.) applies Jer. 8:16; Dan. 8:8 ff.; 2 Thess. 2; *et al.* to Antichrist. Hippolytus (*De antichr.*) quotes Gen. 49:16, 17; Deut. 33:22; Dan. 11:31; 12:11, 12; Rev. 7; Matt. 24:15-22; 2 Thess. 2; *et al.* as pertaining to Antichrist.

4. In early Christian times Antichrist was connected with the expected return of Nero (Irenaeus, *Haer.*, V; Hippolytus,

De antichr. Cf. Suetonius, *Nero,* 57; Tacitus, *Hist.*, II:8). In the succeeding centuries the predictions of Antichrist and his characteristics remain relatively the same, but the external application changes. In the fourth century predictions of a "last Roman Emperor before Antichrist" became prominent. In the age of Islam, Antichrist apocalypses flourished (*e. g.*, Ps. Methodius) and developed intensity during the Crusades. The time came when people saw Antichrist in every political, national, social, or ecclesiastical opponent.

5. The Franciscans of the opposition assiduously held that the Pope is Antichrist. The Bohemians Millic of Kremsier and Matthias of Janow followed this view. Wyclif and Purvey as well as Huss were firmly convinced that the Pope is the Antichrist.

6. Luther regarded the Pope as the Antichrist chiefly because the Papacy substituted work-righteousness for grace in Christ (St. L. Ed., IX:14, 35, 243, 1556; X:2098; *et al.*). The Reformer also mentions the following: The Papacy substitutes man-made rules for the divine Law (IV:778; IX:342); forbids marriage and foods (XIV:408); usurps power (IV:512, 770 ff.; XXII: 875, 900; XIII:1186); usurps position of Christ (I:1063; VI:1110; XII:1301; XIII: 323; XIV:372); sits in the temple (IV: 2106; IX:44); exalts himself above God (III:1422; XIV:372); falsifies God's Word (XIV:481); *et al.* Luther also spoke of the Turk (together with the Pope) as Antichrist (I:1062. Cf. XV: 2430).

7. The Augsburg Confession does not speak of the Pope as the Antichrist, but indicates that the subscribers are willing to continue in the Catholic system provided that abuses are corrected (which included matters. pertaining to temporal power, abuse of power, supremacy of councils, etc. — XXVIII: 28 ff.). The Apology shows that the Papacy has the marks of the Antichrist as depicted by Daniel (Art. IV:24; VIII:19; XI:25; XII:51) and by Paul (IV:4). It speaks of the Papacy as a part of the kingdom of the Antichrist (VIII:18). The Smalcald Articles hold that the Pope by his doctrine and practice has clearly shown himself the Antichrist since he exceeds even Turks and Tartars in keeping people from their Savior (*Haec doctrina praeclare ostendit papam esse ipsum verum antichristum.* — II:iv, and throughout, especially in appended Treatise). The

Formula of Concord quotes the Smalcald Articles on Antichrist.

8. Lutheran dogmaticians (Quenstedt, Baier, and others, including Walther) regarded the teaching of the Antichrist as a non-fundamental doctrine. At the same time, however, they warn in strong language against ignoring plain statements of Scripture against one's better judgment and conscience (*Luth.*, XXI: 113—15).

9. Lutherans in America generally follow the Confessions and hold that the claims and characteristics of the Papacy necessarily lead to its identification with the Antichrist. Some, however, distinguish between Scriptural teachings and historical applications. EL

Nicolaus Hunnius, *Demonstratio theologica, ostendens quod papa Romanus sit universalis ecclesiae seductor, quodve Lutherus illum . . . iure, optimo et spiritu divino adortus fuerit,* 1618; Tobias, Hermann, *"De Antichristo,"* in *Disputationes Bellarmino oppositae,* Jena, 1620 (p. 97 ff.); C. J. H. Fick, *Das Geheimnis der Bosheit im roemischen Papsttum,* 1873; Heinrich R. G. Ebel, *Der Widerchrist im Lichte Heiliger Schrift,* 1875; W. Dallmann, "The Rise of Antichrist," *TQ,* XIV: 208—242; W. Hoenecke, "Vom Antichrist," *TQS.,* XL: 166—188; XLI: 32—55, 91—109; P. E. Kretzmann, *"Papam esse verum Antichristum,"* CTM, IV: 424 ff.; Th. Graebner, *War in the Light of Prophecy,* CPH, 1942 (51—57); W. Bousset in *Hastings' Encyclopedia of Religion and Ethics* (Religionsgeschichtlich); *L. u. W.,* XIII: 297—308, 325—347; XIX: 97—106; XXIII: 145—152; XV: 39—44. For an Anglican view see George Milligan, *St. Paul's Epistles to the Thessalonians,* Macm., 1908 (158—165).

Antilegomena. Literally, "spoken against, questioned by some," certain books of the New Testament concerning which there was no unanimity, or at least some degree of uncertainty in the early Church with regard to their canonicity.* They are distinguished from *homologoumena,* or universally accepted books. Due to the fact that certain false teachers and other unauthorized persons tried to have their writings introduced into the Christian congregations (cp. 2 Thess. 2:2; Luke 1:1-3), it was necessary that the Christians watched with the greatest care, lest false gospels or letters be acknowledged, especially by being ascribed to true Apostles or disciples of these Apostles. It was due chiefly to this special vigilance that the following

books were not accepted by the Church everywhere before the latter part of the fourth century: James, Jude, 2 and 3 John, 2 Peter, Hebrews, and the Apocalypse. This was due partly to conditions under which the writings went out, partly to a degree of uncertainty concerning their authorship. Thus the author of Hebrews is not definitely known; the identity of the James who is the author of the letter was not altogether certain, and the content of the letter was misunderstood; 2 and 3 John are addressed to private persons and were not made accessible to larger circles; 2 Peter was most likely written shortly before the death of the author and had no definite addressees; Jude is very short and has a very circumscribed message; and the Apocalypse was under suspicion on account of its nature. Over against these objections it is to be noted that all of these books are mentioned at a very early date, some of them are referred to as early as the beginning of the second century as Apostolic writings, and all of them were finally accepted by the Church in the course of the fourth century. While doubts have been expressed regarding the one or the other of these books even by orthodox Lutheran teachers, it may be said that, in almost every case, the clear Apostolic doctrine, the depth of the admonitions and of the entire presentation, and the high prophetic insight into events of the future almost compel one to acknowledge them. Most of the objections voiced in recent centuries have been satisfactorily met by earnest searchers after the truth.

For general information see references under *Canon, Bible;* for position of Luth. dogmaticians see C. F. Walther, "Ist derjenige fuer einen Ketzer oder gefaehrlichen Irrlehrer zu erklaeren, welcher nicht alle in dem Convolut des Neuen Testaments befindlichen Buecher fuer kanonisch haelt und erklaert?" *L. u. W.,* II: 204—223.

Antilles. Two groups of islands in the Caribbean Sea, virtually all except the Bahamas. The Greater Antilles (see Cuba, Haiti, Jamaica, Puerto Rico) have a population of about 10,884,901 (1947). The Lesser Antilles (the Virgin Islands, the Caribbee Islands, Barbados, the South American islands) have a population of 1,500,000. Great Britain, France, Holland, and the United States are represented in this group. The colored race predominates. In the Lesser Antilles, mission work is carried on by the Apostolic Holiness Union, the Presbyterian Church in Canada, the National Baptist Convention, the African M. E. Church, the Christian Mission in Many Lands, the United Free Church of Scotland, the Seventh-Day Adventists, the Society for the Propagation of the Gospel, the Wesleyan Methodist Missionary Society, the Moravian Church, the Baptist Church in Trinidad. Members, baptized 269,866; 97,546 communicants. See *Missions, Bibliography.*

Anti-Missourian Brotherhood. This body was organized in 1887 by a group of ministers of the Norwegian Synod under the leadership of the Rev. F. A. Schmidt, Norwegian professor at Concordia Seminary, St. Louis, 1872—1876. In 1890 it became part of the United Norwegian Lutheran Church in America. See *Evangelical Lutheran Church,* 10.

Anti-National Religious Organization Movement. An antimissionary antibenevolent movement which arose in the early 19th century and was supported by Baptists (John Taylor, Daniel Parker, Alexander Campbell), Freethinkers, Universalists, Reformed Methodists, Unitarians, and others. The basic motive for the movement was the fear that religious authority would be concentrated as a result of the various undenominational benevolent associations and thus the separation of Church and State be obliterated.

See article "Antimissionary Movement in the U. S." in Vergilius Ferm, *An Encyclopedia of Religion.*

Antinomian Controversy. Begun in 1527 by Melanchthon's urging the Law to prevent the abuse of free grace, Agricola of Eisleben holding the Law had no place at all in the Church; the knowledge of sin and contrition to be wrought, not by the Law, but by the Gospel. Luther made peace between the two. Professor at Wittenberg in 1536 through Luther's influence, Agricola spread his error in sermons and these to Brandenburg, Frankfurt, and especially in Freiberg, through Jacob Schenk. Luther stopped him from lecturing and printing. Agricola recanted and was reconciled in 1538. But he kept on in his evil course, and Luther repeatedly wrote *Against the Antinomians,* "these disputations ranking among the very best of his writings." Agricola attacked Luther and escaped trial by breaking his parole and fleeing to Berlin, where he again recanted, in 1541, and again kept on spreading his error.

In the Second Antinomistic Controversy the main issue was the Third Use of the Law. Poach, Otto, and others denied that, with respect to good works, the Law was of any service whatever to Christians. Theses such as these were defended: "The Law does not teach good works. Evangelical preachers are to preach the Gospel only and no Law." (*Conc. Trigl.,* Introd.) — Finally, following Melanchthon, the Philippists taught: "The Gospel alone is expressly and particularly, truly and properly, a preaching and a voice of repentance, or conversion," revealing the baseness of sin (Paul Crell), which is exactly what the arch-antinomian Agricola had said.

The Formula of Concord settled the matter by recognizing the triple use of the Law — 1) for outward decency, 2) for revealing sin, 3) for the rule of life to the regenerate, who need it on account of their Old Adam. These controversies served to bring out with yet greater clearness the distinction between the Law and the Gospel, justification and sanctification.

Antioch, Councils of. Councils * held regarding Arianism * (340).

Antioch, School of Interpretation. See *Exegesis,* 4 ff.; *Schools, Early Chr.*

Antiochene Rite. The collection of rules, liturgies, and traditions of the early church of Antioch from which the rites of the Monophysite Church are derived.

Anti-organ. See *Disciples,* 2 e.

Antiphon. A response, or versicle, sung before a Psalm, a lesson, or a collect, the pastor intoning the versicle by chanting the first line and the congregation answering by chanting its second half.

Antiphonary. A book of antiphons.

Antipope. See *Papacy.*

Anti-Semitism. See *Judaism.*

Anti-tactae. See *Gnosticism,* 7 j.

Antitrinitarianism. See *Unitarianism.*

Anton, Paul (1661—1730). Protestant theologian of Germany; one of the founders of the Pietistic school at Halle; most important writing: *Collegium Antitheticum.*

Antoninus Pius. See *Persecutions of Christians,* 3.

Antonius. See *Norway, Luth. in,* 1.

Antwerp Polyglot. See *Polyglot Bibles.*

Antwerp, Synod of (1563). See *Reformed Church,* 2.

Aphraates (4th c.). "The Persian Sage"; probably born of heathen parents; wrote 23 homilies on Christian doctrine and practice (337—345); important in the study of the Syriac text tradition because of his many quotations; seems at some time in his life to have taken the name "Jacob," which later caused confusion in his identification.

Apocalypse of Paul, Peter, etc. See *Apocrypha,* B 5.

Apocalypticism (G. "to uncover" or "reveal"). A word applied to Scriptural writings (*e. g.,* Daniel, Revelation) which reveal events of the last times, the Judgment, and the hereafter. It also applies to non-canonical literature which flourished in late Judaism and early Christianity (*Enoch, Baruch, Apocalypse of Peter, Ascension of Isaiah, Assumption of Moses, Book of Jubilees, Shepherd of Hermas*). See *Apocrypha.*

Apocatastasis. See *Restitution.*

Apocrypha (G. *Apokruphos,* "hidden"), a term applied in patristic literature to writings that were esoteric or otherwise obscure and to books whose authorship was unknown (extended to mean "spurious"). Gradually the word came to be used synonymously with the Hebrew *sepharim hitsonim* ("outside books," *i. e.,* outside the canon; "apocrypha" so used by Cyril of Jerusalem, Jerome). Scholars of the Reformation period narrowed the usage of "apocrypha" to the uncanonical books in the Vulgate (thence extended again to books of the NT period). The other "outside books" of the Jews and early Christians were then designated by the unsatisfactory term *pseudepigrapha* (J. A. Fabricius, *Codex pseudepigraphus,* 1722).

A. 1. *Old Testament.* The Jews at an early date (2 Esdras 14:6; 12:37 f.; 14:45 ff.) distinguished between the canonical books for general use and others reserved ("hidden," hence "apocrypha") for the wise (cf. Josephus, *Apion* 1:8; *Antiq.,* XI: 1—5; 6:6 ff.). The destruction of Jerusalem and the circulation of Christian literature led to the suppression of Jewish "outside books." The Hellenistic Jews, however, preserved these books in translations from which they passed into Christian usage and were gradually assimilated at various places in the OT canon. Alleged NT quotations from the Apocrypha have not been established (Matt. 23:34, 35; Luke 11:49 f.; Jude 14 f.; 1 Cor. 2:9; *et al.*); similarities, however, are noticeable (Jude 6, 9, 14—16; 2 Peter 2:4; James 1, 19; Heb. 11:34 ff.; *et al.*). Already among the earliest Fathers (*I Clem.* 5, 5; *Barnab.* 19:9; *Polycarp* 10) the Apocrypha are quoted, and they continued to be used in spite of the fact that their spuriousness was attested (Melito of Sardis, Jerome).

2. Karlstadt (*Libellus de canonicis scripturis,* 1520) separated the Apocrypha from the canon, named a number of them *libri agiographa* (following Jerome: Wisdom, Sirach, Judith, Tobit, 1 and 2 Maccabees) and pronounced the rest unworthy of Christian use. Luther's edition (1534) placed all the Apocrypha after the OT with the remark: "Apocrypha: Das sind Buecher, so nicht der Heiligen Schrift gleichgehalten und doch nuetzlich und gut zu lesen sind." A movement in England (19th c.) led to their exclusion from English Bibles.

3. In familiar usage fourteen books (found in LXX and Vulgate) are included in the OT Apocrypha: 1) *1 Esdras* (a compilation largely from Ezra); 2) *2 Esdras* (Esdras receives information about future events from an angel); 3) *Additions to Esther* (dream of Mordecai, edict of Artaxerxes, etc.); 4) *Song of the Three Children* (sung by Hananiah, Mishael, and Azariah after their deliverance), including the "Prayer of Azariah"; 5) *History of Susannah* (a pious woman freed from an adultery charge by Daniel); 6) *Bel and the Dragon* (Daniel shows the falseness of two idols); 7) *Prayer of Manasses* (cf. 2 Chron. 33:18 f.); 8) *Baruch and the Epistles of Jeremiah* (history and exhortations from Babylonian Captivity period); 9) *Tobit* (Jew and Jewess aided by Raphael during Assyrian Captivity); 10) *Judith* (a pious Jewess slays Holofernes and frees besieged "Bethulia"); 11) *1 Maccabees* (Jewish struggles for freedom under the Hasmonean brothers' leadership); 12) *2 Maccabees*; 13) *Ecclesiasticus,* or *Wisdom of Sirach* (practical philosophy); 14) *Wisdom of Solomon* (discussion of God-centered wisdom).

4. The Council of Trent (1546) reaffirmed the canonicity of all the above except *1* and *2 Esdras* and the *Prayer*

of Manasses. Catholics call the Apocrypha "deuterocanonical" and reserve the word "apocrypha" for "outside books" not in the Vulgate (usually called "pseudepigrapha"). The most important of the latter are: *4 Maccabees; Psalms of Solomon; Sibylline Books; Enoch; Assumption of Moses; Apocalypse of Baruch; Book of Jubilees; Testament of the Twelve Patriarchs; Book of Adam and Eve; Martyrdom of Isaiah; Lives of the Prophets; Testament of Job; Testament of Abraham.*

B. 1. *New Testament.* Here the terms "apocrypha" and "pseudepigrapha" are usually used interchangeably and include all those writings which claimed to be a part of the canon but were rejected or never considered. Some were a pious fraud, but others were written to disseminate false doctrines. The NT Apocrypha may be divided into four groups:

2. The Gospels were usually written to cover *lacunae* in the life of Christ and advance private doctrines. They contain pure fiction, development of Gospel statements, words of Jesus translated into action, traditions, parallels to OT miracles, literal fulfillment of prophecies. The most important are: *Gospel according to the Egyptians* (ca. A. D. 130; Encratite and ascetic); *Gospel according to the Hebrews* (ca. 130; many of the sayings, *logia,* of Jesus found at Oxyrhynchus seem derived from this Gospel); *British Museum Gospel* (ca. 135; condenses the four Gospels into one); *Gospel according to Peter* (ca. 130; Docetic); *Gospel of Thomas* (the lost original was Gnostic; others by the same name are probably condensations); *Traditions of Matthias* (ca. 185; philosophical); *Gospel of the Ebionites* (ca. 200; Ebionite, opposed animal sacrifice, advocated vegetarianism); *Gospel of James* (ca. 200; perpetual virginity). Lesser Gospels are those of *Pseudo-Matthew, of the Infancy, of Basilides, of Judas, of Truth, of Philip, of Nicodemus (Acts of Pilate), of Bartholomew, of Andrew, of Barnabas.*

3. The apocryphal *Acts* were evidently used most extensively for the propagation of false views. The most important are: *Acts of Paul* (ca. 160; extends history of Acts; Tekla story; opposes marriage and antifeminism); *Acts of John* (ca. 180; Docetic); *Acts of Peter* (ca. 210; glorification of Peter, step in growing importance of Roman bishop); *Acts of Thomas* (ca. 220; ascetic); *Acts of Andrew* (ca. 250; ascetic).

4. Among the *Epistles* are chiefly those ascribed to Christ (correspondence of Abgar and Christ), Mary (to Ignatius and Florentinus), and the Apostles (correspondence of Peter and James, Paul and Seneca, *Epistle of Barnabas,* etc.). Prominent are letters purporting to be those alluded to in the NT (1 Cor. 5:9).

5. The NT *Apocalyptic* literature includes such writings as the *Shepherd of Hermas* (ca. 95; no repentance for serious sins after Baptism); *Apocalypse of Peter* (ca. 130; influenced Dante); *Sibylline Oracles* (2d—3d c.; pagan, Jewish, Christian); *Pistis Sophia* (ca. 250; Gnostic); *Apocalypse of Paul* (cf. 2 Cor. 12:2 ff.). Others are the *Apocalypse of Bartholomew, of Mary, of Thomas.* EL

E. J. Goodspeed, *The Apocrypha,* University of Chicago Press, 1938; M. R. James, *The Apocryphal New Testament,* Clarendon P., Oxford, 1924; Charles Cutler Torrey, *The Apocryphal Literature,* Yale University Press, ca. 1945; R. H. Charles, *The Apocrypha and Pseudepigrapha of the Old Testament in English,* Clarendon P., Oxford, 1913 (2 vols.); A. Hauck, *Realencyklopaedie,* Hinrich, Leipzig, 1896 (I: 622—670).

Apollinaris of Laodicea (d. 390). Opposed Arius; fell, however, into the error of teaching that Christ did not have a human soul, but the Logos in its stead; this teaching was condemned as Docetism (381). When Julian forbade the Christians to teach the classics, Apollinaris produced Sacred Scriptures in classical form.

Appollonius Tyaneus (3 B. C.—A. D. 96). Neo-Pythagorean soothsayer and magician. His biography, written by Philostratus about A. D. 20, is an idealizing romance with the polemical aim, it would seem, of denying the exclusive claims of Christianity. Apollonius is pictured as a great worker of miracles, who cast out demons, possessed the knowledge of all languages, raised the dead; in fine, as a pagan Messiah.

Apologetics (Christian). 1. *Definition of Apologetics.* Christian Apologetics is the scientific vindication of the truth and absoluteness of the Christian religion against unbelief. The expression "Christian Evidence" more properly denotes the scientific proof of the divine authority of Christianity. The term "Apology" denotes an argument in defense of a doctrine that has been attacked.

2. *Relation to Other Branches of Theology.* Apologetics is a branch of Systematic Theology. While Christian Dogmatics sets forth and expounds the Christian religion on the basis of Scripture, Apologetics vindicates its truth on the grounds of reason, showing the unreasonableness of infidelity. Apologetics concerns itself with errorists outside the Church, Polemics with errorists within Christendom.

3. *History of Apologetics.* * The history of Apologetics may be divided as follows: 1. the Apologetic Period, A. D. 70—350; 2. the Polemic Period, 250—730; 3. the Medieval Period, 730—1517; 4. the Modern Period, 1517 to date.

4. *Methodology of Apologetics.* The Apologetic method may be either historical or philosophical, or it may combine both approaches. The first vindicates Christianity chiefly by defending Scripture, its fact and importance in human history, and the value of its teachings in human society. The philosophical approach vindicates such fundamentals of Christianity as the doctrine of God, of man's ethical obligation, and the like, on the basis of pure reason. A simple, but very practical grouping is the following: Fundamental, Historical, and Philosophical Apologetics.

I. *Fundamental Apologetics.* A. *Being and Nature of God.* Christianity proclaims and defends the existence and rule of a divine, infinite, spiritual Being, absolutely one in essence, but three in Persons, endowed with all divine attributes properly belonging to such a perfect, personal Spirit-Being against such anti-Christian theories as: 1. Atheism,* 2. Materialism,* 3. Pantheism,* 4. Deism,* 5. Rationalism,* 6. Idealism,* 7. Positivism,* 8. Agnosticism,* 9. Monism,* 10. Pluralism,* 11. Pessimism,* 12. Modernism,* teaching that deity is finite, 13. Natural Theology,* 14. Polytheism,* 15. Judaism,* and other forms of unbelief that deny that God is the first and ultimate and only divinely efficient Cause. God's existence is demonstrated not only by the specifically Biblical proofs, but also by corroborative arguments of sound reasoning, e. g., the theological, cosmological, teleological, moral, aesthetic, and ontological.

B. *The Cosmological Problem.* 1. Christianity confesses and defends the creation * of all things by the Triune God within six natural days, to His glory and man's good. The doctrine of creation embraces three facts in agreement with reason and experience: a.

Matter is not infinite, but finite; b. All things outside God were called into being out of nothing at the beginning of time by the omnipotent and all-wise Creator; c. Creatures are propagated according to fixed laws ("propagation after his kind"). 2. The doctrine of creation is denied by both atheistic and theistic evolution.* 3. Teleology * definitely supports the doctrine of creation. 4. Science and the Bible * are not in conflict with each other, although scientists and defenders of the Bible have been in conflict. Many conflicts have been caused by inaccurate perceptions or false conclusions based on the categories of science (*i. e.,* the sense world) on the one hand or by erroneous interpretations of the Bible on the other.

C. *The Anthropological Problem.* 1. Christianity declares that man is a personal, moral, free being, originally created in the divine image, which he has now lost through the Fall, by which he was deprived of his concreate wisdom, holiness, and righteousness, having become a sinner both as to original and actual sin. 2. With the brutes he has a certain relationship in physical things, but though fallen, he is still endowed with intelligence and free will.* He is not a development from brutes, but the lord or ruler of all things under God. 3. While he has lost his power of free will in spiritual things, he still retains it in earthly matters and the area of civil righteousness and so remains a free moral agent, though after the Fall, he cannot do otherwise than sin. 4. Man is a religious being and seeks to worship higher beings or powers Acts 17:26, 27), though, unless converted, in a perverted form (Rom. 1: 21-23). Such worship distinguishes man from the brutes as also does intelligence and will. 5. The doctrine of man, as proclaimed by Christianity, satisfies man's striving and furnishes him a goal for his efforts, while evolution also here proves itself an unsatisfactory and fruitless hypothesis.

D. *The Ethical Problem.* 1. Christianity teaches that at the creation of man God wrote the Moral Law * into the human heart, which, though obscured by sin, still is a criterion for conscience.* Through the Moral Law God rules man both individually and collectively as a society. Ethical norms are not mere conventions, but laws of God innate in man. 2. The universe is not ruled by chance, but by Law under Moral Government. 3. Christianity neither ignores sin nor attempts to explain its origin, but declares that God is not its author or abettor, but rather forbids it, often prevents it, and where He permits it to occur, it becomes the cause of its own destruction and cannot do lasting harm to believers. 4. Prompted by His goodness, God from eternity decreed to redeem sinful man through the vicarious active and passive obedience of His incarnate Son, whom He made man's Substitute and Redeemer. (See *Christ Jesus; Atonement.*) The denial of redemption contradicts the innate redemptive idea in man (as expressed, in corrupt form, in their traditions regarding "Champions" or "Saviors" of humanity).

E. *The Problem of Man's Immortality.* 1. Christianity teaches that man, redeemed by Christ and born again through the Holy Spirit, shall live with God throughout eternity in perfect happiness. 2. All who deny man's immortality do so contrary to all rational grounds and arguments (*e. g.,* the metaphysical, teleological, ethical, historical) and the widespread belief in immortality.

II. *Historical Apologetics.* A. *The Supernatural in History.* 1. Christianity holds that since God is the merciful Creator and hourly Benefactor of man, in whom man has his being (Acts 17:28; Col. 1:17), it is reasonable for Him to reveal Himself to man (Acts 17:25, 26). 2. The necessity of the supernatural is grounded in man's need of God, its possibility in God's omnipotence, its reality in God's saving love, its purpose in God's desire to draw man to Himself. 3. The manifestation of the supernatural in history assumes the forms of revelation,* miracles,* and inspiration,* the latter especially in Scripture.

B. *The Bible in History.* 1. The Bible * is a special divine revelation, both possible and necessary. 2. It was given by divine inspiration,* and attests itself as God's Word by its authority,* efficacy, sufficiency, and perspicuity, an altogether unique Book. 3. It is further witnessed to as the divine truth by its internal and external proofs, its profound, convincing doctrines,* its noble ethics,* its unity and consistency, its historical character, its complete body of doctrines, its soberness of teaching, its wonderful Redeemer, its dependable writers, its spiritual appeal, its miraculous preservation, its prophecy and fulfillment, its remarkable attestation by archaeology.* 4. To these evidences must be appended its amazing miracles * (Christ, the Miracle of the ages, Paul's

conversion *), its uplifting influences, its superiority over man-made religions (Confucianism,* Taoism,* Brahmanism,* Buddhism,* Greek systems of philosophy, *e. g.,* Stoicism,* Epicureanism,* and the like, Persian Dualism,* Mohammedanism,* modern cults, all of which have failed to supply man's spiritual needs).

C. *Christ in History.* 1. His wonderful incarnation *; 2. His amazing Person; His ethical purity, spiritual insight, divine love, patience, etc.; His marvelous claims, His unique redemption; His compassion upon lost sinners, His transformed Apostles; 3. As there is but one Holy Bible, so there is also only one divine Christ.

D. *The Church in History.* 1. Its supernatural origin; 2. its divine preservation in the midst of tribulation; 3. its glorious victories over its enemies; 4. its absolute religion, offering to men both the perfect truth and a perfect salvation *; 5. its manifold blessings to the world.

III. *Philosophical Apologetics.* A. *Definition and Scope of Philosophical Apologetics.* Philosophical Apologetics draws its material in the main from 1. the philosophy of religion; 2. the philosophy of history; 3. the psychology of religion; 4. the facts of Christianity itself. While Fundamental Apologetics deals with the problems belonging to natural theology, and Historical Apologetics presents the evidences showing Christianity to be divine in its origin and existence, Philosophical Apologetics seeks its proofs from the very essence of religion itself.

B. *Philosophy of Religion.* The philosophy of religion inquires into the general subject of religion from the philosophical point of view, that is, it employs critical analysis and evaluation for the defense of Christianity, treating such points as the nature, function, and value of religion; the nature of evil; the problem of human spirit and its destiny; the relation of the human to the divine with special regard to the freedom and responsibility of the individual; the meaning of human existence; the nature of belief, and the like.

C. *Philosophy of History.* The philosophy of history, in its stricter sense, denotes the explanation, from philosophical principles, of historical phenomena in general or of the entire course of historical development, treating as such also the origin, rise, and spread of Christianity and its influence in the world. Its value for Apologetics is therefore apparent, as it shows Christianity to be a mighty dynamic contributing toward the world's well-being.

D. *Psychology of Religion.* The psychology of religion is concerned with man's religious consciousness, in particular, with beliefs as developments of human experience. While in itself it does not favor Christianity, it supplies valuable data used by the apologist for the defense of religious truth.

E. *The Facts of Christianity.* Christianity being factual and dynamic, it represents religious phenomena which may be evaluated for its own defense, e. g., the existence and nature of God, the immortality of the soul, the reality and objectivity of truth, the categorical nature of duty, the imperative of unselfish love, and the like. Christianity thus becomes its own best apology.

JTM

Adama, J. M., *Ancient Records and the Bible,* 1946; Barton, G. A., *Archaeology and the Bible,* 1937; Carrington, P., *Christian Apologetics in the Second Century,* 1921; Cobern, C. M., *The New Archaeological Discoveries and Their Bearing on the New Testament,* 1917; Dallmann, W., *The Battle of the Bible with the "Bibles,"* 1926; Fairbairn, A. M., *The Grounds of Theistic and Christian Belief,* 1911; Finegan, J., *Light from the Ancient Past,* 1946; Graebner, T., *Evolution: An Investigation and a Criticism,* 1926; Keyser, L. S., *A System of Christian Evidence,* 1939; Machen, J. G., *The Origin of Paul's Religion,* 1921; Marston, C., *New Bible Evidence,* 1934; Nelson, D., *The Cause and Cure of Infidelity,* 1926; Orr, J., *Revelation and Inspiration,* 1910; Sheldon, H. C., *Unbelief in the Nineteenth Century,* 1917; Wells, A. R., *Why We Believe in the Bible,* 1910; Wilson, R. D., *A Scientific Investigation of the Old Testament,* 1923.

Apologists. See *Doctrine, Christian, History of,* 2; *Patristics; Apologetics,* 3.

Apology of the Augsburg Confession. See *Lutheran Confessions,* A 3.

Apostasy (G., "from" — "standing"). A total lapsing from principles or faith. The NT mentions as causes of apostasy: the putting away of faith and a good conscience (1 Tim. 1:19 f.); listening to seducing spirits and doctrines of devils (1 Tim. 4:1; 2 Tim. 4:4); shallowness (Luke 8:13); lack of spiritual insight (John 6:63 ff.); love of the world (2 Tim. 4:10; Matt. 19:22). The OT gives, among others, the following reasons: absence of spiritual leaders (Ex. 32:1); evil

company (1 Kings 11:4); worldly success (Ps. 78:57; Hos. 6:4; Zeph. 1:6).

Apostles' Creed. See *Ecumenical Creeds,* A.

Apostolic Canon. See *Apostolic Constitution.*

Apostolic Christian Church (Nazarene). See *Holiness Bodies,* 2.

Apostolic Christian Organization. See *Evangelistic Associations,* 2.

Apostolic Church. See *Evangelistic Associations,* 1.

Apostolic Church Directory. 35 articles pertaining to church morals and discipline written in the 4th century but ascribed to the Apostles.

Apostolic Constitutions (and Canons). An ancient collection of ecclesiastical precepts, ostensibly regulations for the organization and government of the Church put out by the Apostles themselves. Some of the older sections may go back to the fourth century and even beyond, but the present form goes back to about the eighth century. There are eight books of the *Constitutions* and eighty-five *Canons,* the latter going back to a greater antiquity than the *Constitutions* and being possibly based upon traditions handed down from the early second century. The collection is interesting not only on account of the regulations it contains, but especially for the list of canonical books which it offers.

Roberts & Donaldson, *Ante-Nicene Fathers,* Chr. Lit. Co., Buffalo, 1886 (vii, 387 ff.).

Apostolic Delegate. See *Legates.*

Apostolic Episcopal Church (The Holy Eastern Catholic and Apostolic Orthodox Church). See *Eastern Orthodox Churches.*

Apostolic Faith Mission. See *Evangelistic Associations; Holiness Bodies,* 2.

Apostolic Fathers. This title is ascribed to those writers of the Early Church who are claimed to have been associated with the Apostles. Although the listing varies, the following are usually included:

1. *Clement of Rome.* A disciple of Peter and Paul; bishop of Rome, 92 to 101 (Eusebius); first of the "Apostolic Fathers." Many things of a legendary character are written about him (consecrated by Peter; Clement of Phil. 4:3; *Martyrium Clementis*). Of the many writings ascribed to him, only the first

to the Corinthians (in which he seeks to settle disturbances between clerics and laics) is considered authentic (A. D. 96). He was well read in the Scriptures and more than other early fathers showed a comprehension of Pauline theology.

2. *Ignatius of Antioch.* Third bishop of Antioch; martyred, according to tradition (Eusebius, iii, 36), under Trajan in 107. On his journey to Rome he wrote seven letters (to the Ephesians, Magnesians, Trallians, Philadelphians, Smyrneans, Polycarp, and the Romans) in which he stressed respect for bishops and opposition to Docetism. The letter to the Romans pleads with the Christians there not to prevent his martyrdom. The integrity of the epistles (of which there are various recensions) has been attacked. If genuine, they show early traces of the "monarchical episcopate."

3. *Polycarp* (ca. 69—156). Bishop of Smyrna; disciple of John and friend of Ignatius; supported the Asiatic view of the celebration of Easter at Rome; burned at the stake during the persecution under Antoninus Pius; man of piety and zeal. His one surviving work is a letter to the Philippians covering the Epistles of Ignatius. His martyrdom is described in a letter by the Smyrneans to the church of Philomelium.

4. *Papias* (ca. 150). Bishop of Hierapolis; disciple of John (?) and friend of Polycarp; Eusebius accuses him of chiliasm and other "strange sayings." He wrote *Exposition of the Lord's Oracles,* of which fragments remain. In this work he treats the origin of Matthew and Mark. His statement concerning "presbyter John" occupies a prominent place in the isagogical discussion of the Fourth Gospel.

5. *Shepherd of Hermas.* According to ancient tradition written A. D. 140 (but probably of earlier date) by a Roman Christian, Hermas. Nothing certain is known about the author. It contains five visions, twelve mandates, and ten similitudes. The central thought is exhortation to repentance in view of the impending *parousia.* It assures a second repentance for sins after Baptism. Though of slight literary merit, it was highly esteemed in the Early Church and included at times in the canon.

6. *Barnabas, Epistle of.* Originated in Egypt, ca. A. D. 130. It is characterized by allegorizing and at times cabalistic interpretation. Written to Christians who were in danger of lapsing into Judaism. The ascription to the Barnabas of the NT is considered false by modern scholars.

7. *Epistle to Diognetus.* Written in a beautiful style, this epistle has been assigned to the 2d, 3d, and even 4th century. It is addressed to Diognetus, perhaps the teacher of Marcus Aurelius. The last two chapters are by another hand (Hippolytus?). It compares the Christians' relation to the world with that of the soul to the body.

8. *The Didache (Teaching of the Twelve Apostles).* Written about A. D. 150, the *Didache* was intended to be used in the instruction preliminary to Baptism. The first part (1—6) presents under the image of the two ways of life and death moral precepts with which the catechumen was to be acquainted before Baptism. The second part (perhaps for after Baptism) gives instructions regarding Baptism, fasts, prayers, Eucharist, and "offices" in the church. The use of a somewhat different document in *Barnabas* and variant recensions indicate that the source for the *Didache* was some early Christian document for converts (perhaps based on a manual for Jewish proselytes). EL

J. B. Lightfoot, *Apostolic Fathers,* Macm., 1926; Kirsopp Lake, *Apostolic Fathers,* Putnam's, 1917 (Loeb ed.); Glim, Marique, Walsh, *Fathers of the Church,* Cima Pub. House, N. Y., 1947 (vol. 1); see bibliography under *Patristics.*

Apostolic Lutherans. See *Finland, Lutheranism in,* 8.

Apostolic Methodist Church. A small Holiness * body numbering 60 members.

Apostolic Overcoming Holy Church of God. See *Holiness Bodies,* 2.

Apostolic See (Holy See). The diocese of the Pope (also applied to the Pope or his authority).

Apostolic Succession. By this term is understood the claim made by most episcopally ordained clergymen and bishops (Anglican, Far Eastern, and Catholic) that they constitute links in an uninterrupted chain of similarly ordained persons, the first of whom were ordained by the Apostles themselves. With this opinion is combined the view that only clergymen who are in the line of this spiritual succession are entitled to a pastoral office in the Christian Church, and that all others usurp the functions of the ministry. In other words, the apostolic succession, it is held, is the continuation of the ministerial commission and authority conferred by Christ upon the Apostles by means of a regular chain of successive ordinations. This view presupposes the founding by the Savior of the visible Church on earth, the purpose of which was to carry on His work through the testimony of the Gospel. Out of the general company of the disciples, the adherents of apostolic succession maintain, Christ chose the Twelve to be with Him and afterwards to go forth in His name. Having prepared these Twelve by a trial mission during His own earthly ministry, He, when leaving the earth, gave them the commission to represent Him in His visible kingdom, which they were to found in the world. Matt. 28:18, 19; John 20:21-23. Thus the twelve Apostles constituted a distinct company within the general society of the Church, with divine functions not to be changed at will, and with commissions subject to no limitations. Their authority, it is held, was from above and not merely deputed from below. This authoritative pastorate, or episcopacy, was intended by Christ to be perpetuated in every generation; and hence the authoritatively commissioned ministry is the proper divine instrumentality through which Christ, the exalted invisible Head of the Church, who works by the Holy Spirit, communicates to His people His promised gifts of grace. Accordingly, the apostolic succession is the guarantee of Christ's presence and His divine work in the visible Church; and the episcopate, with its chain of successions, is the link of historical continuity which is needed in a universal spiritual society.

Opponents of the apostolic succession maintain that this view is based upon a misunderstanding of Christ's commission, of the adherent power and efficacy of the Word, of the nature and character of the Church, of the Office of the Keys, and the spiritual priesthood of all Christians. They further maintain that Christ, by commissioning His Apostles, did not create a distinct body within the Church, vested with inalienable authority, but merely charged them with the preaching of the Gospel and the administration of the Sacraments, which Christ has laid upon the whole Church of believers as their duty and function. Hence ministers of the Church perform their public and official functions not by right of apostolic succession, but by reason of their call, through which the rights, privileges, and duties which

Christ has given to all Christians are delegated to them for official execution in the name of the Church. See *Ministerial Office*, 1.

Apotelesmata. All functions which Christ as the Savior of all men performed in the State of Humiliation and still performs in His State of Exaltation, such as dying for the sins of the world, destroying the works of the devil, being present with, and ruling and protecting, His Church, etc.

Apotheosis. The elevation of human beings to the rank of gods. Instances of this practice are found among the Assyrians, Egyptians, and Persians in antiquity. The ancient Greeks deified their mythical heroes, such as Hercules. The Romans for a long period accorded this token of respect to Romulus, the founder of their city, alone; but in later times the emperor, *e. g.*, Caesar, Augustus, and even women of the imperial court, were given divine status by decree of the senate.

Apperceptive Background. See *Christian Teaching*, C.

Apportionment. See *Finances in the Church*.

Appreciation. See *Christian Teaching*, L 2.

Approbation. The formal judgment of a Roman prelate declaring a priest fit to hear confession. Without it the absolution of a secular priest is held invalid.

Apse. See *Architecture, Ecclesiastical*, 1 ff.; 7.

Aquila, Caspar (1488—1560). B. at Augsburg; d. at Saalfeld. Studied at Leipzig, 1515; Wittenberg, after 1513. Chaplain under Sickingen, 1515; pastor at Jengen, near Augsburg, 1516, where Luther's writings drew him to the Reformation; helped Luther translate the OT, 1524; pastor, 1527, and superintendent, 1528, in Saalfeld; dean of the Collegiate Institute at Smalcald, 1550. He engaged in controversy with Agricola, Osiander, and Major.

Aquinas, Thomas (ca. 1224—74). Doctor Angelicus; b. near Aquino, Italy, he became a member of the Dominican order in 1243, studied under Albertus Magnus at Cologne, and was appointed instructor there in 1248. He now began to publish his first works, commentaries on the ethics and the philosophy of Aristotle. In 1252 he was sent to Paris, where he and his friend the Franciscan Bonaventura obtained their degrees of

Doctor. In 1261 Urban IV called him to Italy to teach in Rome, Bologna, and Pisa. Until his death Aquinas enjoyed the highest esteem in the Church. His pupils called him the "Angelic Doctor," and the Dominicans were zealous in the defense of his doctrines. He wrote extensively on Catholic doctrine and morals, and his works enjoyed a high reputation for clearness and completeness. His *Summa Theologiae* remains to this day the standard authority in the Roman Church, opposed only by the Scotists of the Franciscan order and by a school of Jesuit theology. Death came suddenly to Aquinas while he was on the way to a council at Lyons (1274). He was canonized in 1323 and proclaimed a "Doctor of the Church" in 1567.

Martin Grabmann, *Thomas Aquinas*, Longmans, 1928; Martin Grabmann, *Die echten Schriften des hl. Thomas v. Aquin*, Muenster, 1920; Anton C. Pegis, *Basic Writings of St. Thomas Aquinas*, N. Y., 1945; Hugo Meyer, *The Philosophy of St. Thomas Aquinas*, Herder, St. Louis, rev. 1945.

Arabia. Large peninsula of Southwestern Asia, between the Persian Gulf, the Indian Ocean, and the Red Sea, about 1,350,000 square miles, with about 10,000,000 (1952) people. Language, Arabic. Religion, Mohammedan. Christianity never made much progress in these vast regions, though it was not unrepresented in the early centuries of our era. The destruction of Jerusalem and the Roman persecutions probably drove many Christians into the peninsula. Petra, in the fourth century, was the seat of a metropolitan bishop whose diocese included several Christian bishoprics. The Hinyarite king of Yemen, Abd-Kelal (A. D. 275), was a Christian. During the reign of his son Marthad (330—350) Emperor Constantius sent an embassy to the Hinyarite court and secured certain privileges for the professors of the Christian faith in Yemen. The cruel persecution of Dzu-Nowas (490—525), who had embraced the Jewish faith, resulted in the invasion and subjection of Yemen by the Nestorian prince of Abyssinia. Two successive Abyssinian viceroys made vigorous efforts to establish Christianity in the land. With a view to diverting the Arab tribes from Mecca, a magnificent cathedral was built at Sana. But this hope was doomed to disappointment. Abraha, the second of the above-mentioned princes, then conceived the plan to destroy the Kaaba itself. The expedition failed, and its leader perished (A. D. 570, the year of Mohammed's birth). Also the tribes of the Arabia Deserta had in part embraced Christianity during the third and fourth centuries. It remains to add that the Christianity of Arabia was mostly corrupt and heretical.

Because of determined Islamic opposition, Christian missions have found practically no footing. Attempts were made by Ian Keith-Falconer in 1885 at Aden; in 1891 by Bishop French of the Church Missionary Society; since 1894 by the Dutch Reformed Church in America, of which Dr. S. M. Zwemer was a missionary; the Danish Church Mission in Arabia. The Roman Catholic Church is attempting mission work in Arabia from the Persian Gulf. 100 communicants; 13 ordained, 11 not ordained foreign missionaries (1952). See *Missions, Bibliography*. OHS

Arabic Bible Versions. See *Bible Versions, F.*

Arabic Philosophy. Arabic philosophy originated in Bagdad and is, in part, a synthesis of Hellenic and Oriental philosophies. Hellenic and Oriental writings were translated into Arabic between A. D. 762 and 900 (the Greek under Nestorian influence). The House of Wisdom was erected (832) under enlightened caliphs and had as its first famous scholar Hunain ibn Ishaq (Johannitus, 809—877). This revived learning came to Christians through Muslims in Sicily and Spain. Among the outstanding Arabic philosophers were:

Al-Farabi (d. 950) sought to support Mohammedan mysticism with Neo-Platonism (soul is light emanating from divine intelligence); wrote *De Ortu Scientarum*.

Avicenna (Ibn-Sina; 980—1037) is chiefly famous as a physician, but his metaphysical writings were also widely read in the Middle Ages.

Averroes (1126—1198) denied freedom of the will and immortality. His commentary on Aristotle was widely read by Christian scholars in spite of Roman Catholic opposition. Followed Al-Farabi's theory of the soul.

Al-Kindi (d. 870) considered science and logic as basic to theology.

Al-Ghazali (1058—1109), "the Muslim Aquinas"; greatest theologian of Mohammedanism.

Al-Jahiz (d. 869) wrote a large encyclopedia in which he tried to show the import in theology of natural phenomena.

Arabic philosophy influenced not

only Jewish thinkers (Avicebron; Maimonides), but also Christian and contributed to the rise of scholasticism.*

D. B. Macdonald, *Development of Muslim Theology, Jurisprudence and Constitutional Theory*, London, 1903; DeL. E. O'Leary, *Arabic Thought and Its Place in History*, Dutton, 1920.

Arcade. See *Architecture, Ecclesiastical, 3.*

Arcani Disciplina. Literally, "instruction in the secret," or initiation into the mystery, a term applied to the peculiar withholding of information concerning the Christian mysteries, especially the Sacraments and the fundamental confessions, the baptismal formula, the Lord's Prayer, and the Creed, from non-members. The practice was probably based upon a good intention (cp. Matt. 7:6), but it led to much misunderstanding on the part of outsiders and served no real purpose. See *Ecumenical Creeds.*

Th. Harnack, "Ursprung und Entstehung der Arcani Disciplina," in *Der christliche Gemeindegottesdienst im Apostolischen und alt-katholischen Zeitalter*, Blaesing, Erlangen, 1854.

Archaeological Periods. See *Time.*

Archaeology, Biblical and Christian (G. *archaios*, "ancient"; *logos*, "word," "discussion," "discourse"). Archaeology has been defined as the systematic study of the material remains of the past. Biblical and Christian archaeology is concerned with the study of the remains in Palestine, those ancient countries with which the Hebrews came into contact, and those places to which early Christianity was brought. Its work includes the scientific excavation of sites (often mounds, or "tells," with which ancient cities were covered in the process of time), the decipherment of inscriptions, and the study of remains (including documents) of all kinds.

Little archaeological interest was evidenced in ancient times. Ashurbanipal (7th c. B.C.) of Assyria collected ancient documents for his library at Nineveh; Nabonidus (6th c. B.C.) made some excavations and restorations on the ziggurat at Ur; Setna-Khaemuast, son of Ptolemy II, sought certain papyri. The Greeks did not interest themselves especially in archaeology, though a scholar like Pausanias might describe monuments which he saw. The Romans were still less interested.

Although there had been previous interest in museums and archaeology in England, the beginnings of modern archaeology are usually traced to Napoleon's expedition to Egypt, on which about a hundred scholars and artists accompanied him to study the monuments (1798). C. J. Rich of the East India Company in Bagdad made the first excavations in Mesopotamia. Edward Robinson of Union Theological Seminary, New York, made extensive observations in Palestine (1838, 1852). His work led to the organization of the Palestine Exploration Fund in London (1865). From these beginnings archaeology developed into its modern proportions.

While the earlier excavators (ca. 1800—1890) were chiefly interested in finding objects of interest, the scientific aspects of archaeology soon developed (1890—1915), and excavations are made with great care. Where layers of ruins are found, the excavators seek to establish chronological tables and carefully map and study everything pertaining to the site.

The excavations in Mesopotamia have shown that the story of the patriarchs in the OT fit into the historical setting of the period in which they lived. Special interest has been centered on evidence of great floods (such evidence found at Ur, Shuruppak, and Kish). The Babylonian flood and creation accounts go back to Sumerian times. While there are some similarities between the Babylonian flood story and the sacred record, the content and spirit of the Gilgamesh epic, especially the creation story, is unlike that of Genesis. The Laws of Hammurabi (found by Jacques de Morgan, Dec., 1901—Jan., 1902) have often been compared with the laws of the OT. Scholars, however, have pointed out that, while similar environmental factors would lead to related legal problems, the solution often differs, and a large portion of the Code of Hammurabi has no parallel in the OT, and hence the latter cannot be proved to have derived from the laws of Hammurabi.

The excavations in Egypt have provided no direct evidence regarding the sojourn of the Israelites there or of the Exodus. Archaeology has, however, given historical credibility to the Biblical narrative of the sojourn. Of special interest are the Tell El-Amarna Tablets (which mention Palestine and Jerusalem, and in which the name Habiru has been taken to refer to the Hebrews of the OT, but not necessarily so) and the Merneptah Stela (which mentions a defeat of Israel). The most important archaeological contributions of Egypt are the papyri (see *Manuscripts*) which survived in the hot, dry climate.

The discovery of the civilization of the Hittites (whose existence had been denied) is a triumph of archaeology. The remains (Boghaz-keui; Carchemish) show the nature of a civilization with which the Israelites came into contact when they entered Palestine. Excavations in Crete and Philistia also provide historical background for Biblical narrative.

The tablets found at Ras Shamra in Syria, in addition to revealing the earliest alphabet in wedge-shaped signs, are important because they contain evidence regarding the religion of the Canaanites with whom the Israelites came into contact (El, Baal, Aliyan, Mot, Dagon).

The archaeological records of Assyria provide historical background, confirm the Biblical description of the cruelty of Assyrian rulers (*e. g.*, the annals of Ashur-nasir-pal II) and substantiate, or complement, OT records (*e. g.*, Shalmaneser III as shown in Black Obelisk, annals of Tiglath-pileser III, Sargon II, Sennacherib). Complementary evidence has also been found from the time of the New Babylonian Empire and Persian Empire. Especially noteworthy are the Elephantine papyri, which show that the Persian kings took an interest in the religion of their subjects and mention Sanballat and Johanan by name (see *Nehemiah*).

To archaeologists the results of excavations in Palestine appear disappointing. This is due to the fact that Palestine was frequently plundered. Important discoveries, however, were made in various places. Among the most interesting, perhaps, are the fallen walls of Jericho, the ancient synagog of Capernaum, the Lachish Letters and the "Tell Duweir (Lachish) ewer," which has been dated in the first quarter of the 13th century and contains Phoenician or proto-Hebrew characters of the alphabet.

Biblical archaeology has also concerned itself with the places visited by Paul and the other Apostles. Much of this work, like that in Palestine, has been topographical (see *Geography, Christian*).

The catacombs * from the early Christian era, as well as sarcophagi (sculptured stone coffins), churches, and Christian sites offer material for archaeological investigation.

Among the more prominent finds of Biblical archaeology might be mentioned: extensive background material for Biblical narrative; early alphabet writings; manuscripts * of the Bible.

Some of the results are: 1) interest in inner meaning of the sacred text has to some extent replaced interest in literary criticism; 2) the trustworthiness of the sacred text as found in the best manuscripts * has been demonstrated; 3) it has been demonstrated that the Biblical narrative fits the period which it claims for itself; 4) the superiority of the Bible over other ancient religious literature is shown; 5) fallacies of reconstructions of OT history as those of the Graf-Wellhausen school are revealed; 6) finally, archaeology itself is shown to be an aid which is very useful in certain areas, but cannot be applied to all problems of Biblical knowledge.

EL

Frederic Kenyon, *The Bible and Archaeology*, Harper, N. Y., 1940; Elihu Grant (editor), *The Haverford Symposium on Archaeology and the Bible*, American Schools of Oriental Research, New Haven, Conn., 1938; Jack Finegan, *Light from the Ancient Past — The Archaeological Background of the Hebrew Christian Religion*, Princeton U. Press, 1946; G. A. Barton, *Archaeology and the Bible*, American Sunday School Union, Philadelphia, 1937 (7th ed.); W. F. Albright, *The Archaeology of Palestine and the Bible*, Fleming H. Revell, 1932 (later important work by same author: *From the Old Stone Age to Christianity*, 1940); Stephen L. Caiger, *Bible and Spade*, Oxford U. Press, 1932; works by Deissmann, especially, *Light from the Ancient East* (tr. by L. R. M. Strachan); M. Burrows, *What Mean These Stones?* 1941; the *Biblical Archaeologist*, a journal published by American Schools of Oriental Research; the above general works give references to publications covering certain areas of archaeology, e. g., A. Heidel, *The Babylonian Genesis* (by same author: *Gilgamesh Epic and Old Testament Parallels*).

Archbishop (or *Metropolitan*). A Roman Catholic bishop who not only has charge of his own diocese (called the archdiocese), but also has a certain oversight and precedence over a number of other bishops (the suffragan bishops) whose dioceses, together with his own, form the archepiscopal province. The powers of archbishops have declined since the Middle Ages. They now have the right of compelling the suffragans to assemble in provincial council every three years, of admonishing them to discharge their duties faithfully, of judging them in civil causes, and of receiving appeals from the courts of the suffragans (see *Courts, Spiritual*). They have no direct jurisdiction over the subjects of the suffragans and can visit suffragan dioceses only with the approval of the provincial council. If a suffragan disobeys or disregards his archbishop, the latter has no recourse but to report to Rome. Even these rights, however, are rarely used nowadays, and archbishops are chiefly distinguished by being accorded certain honors and a superior dignity. There were 27 archdioceses in the U. S. in 1952.

Archdeacon. An official who was formerly chief confidant, assistant, and, frequently, representative of a bishop. A similar position is now usually held by the vicar-general.

Archdiocese. See *Archbishop*.

Archer, Frederick (1838—1901). Born in England, studied in London and Leipzig; organist in London and, 1881, in New York; conductor of the Boston Oratorio Society and of the Pittsburgh Orchestra; showed great interest in liturgics and hymnology.

Architecture, Ecclesiastical. 1. That branch of Christian art which deals with the history of the church buildings of the Christians and lays down the principles for their construction. The development of Christian architecture probably took place in this way, that the form of the ancient Roman dwelling was used for the ground plan, its peristyle, or atrium, together with the tablinum (in Roman houses, the alae) being changed by a colonnade surrounding the impluvium, an open court with a water basin, which permitted the introduction of clerestory windows. The result was an ideal hall for the Christian assembly, the tablinum serving as the apse, the alae as the transepts. Somewhat later, in the fourth and fifth centuries, the size of the congregation made the basilica form of church possible, a rectangular structure with a semicircular apse, this modification, together with certain other changes, distinguishing the Christian church building from the public or forensic basilica.

2. In the Orient a central type of church building was a little more prevalent, in the form of a round or polygonal structure, whose heavy dome construction required a very solid supporting wall, which, however, was often broken or relieved by a series of niches, partly for artistic considerations, but also for economy in the use of building material. These churches, as a rule, had semi-circular apses. From this central type of church building the so-called Byzantine style of church architecture was developed. In this form or style we distinguish the narthex, or entrance hall, the nave, or church proper, sometimes broken into aisles in order to bring out the principle of length, and the sanctuary, or apse, with its side chapels. The structure proper is crowned with the cupola, or dome, which in various forms became characteristic of the Byzantine style as it has persisted, with slight modifications, to the present day. The most noted monument of the early Byzantine is the Hagia Sofia at Constantinople, and of the second period, St. Mark of Venice. The most modern example of Byzantine is the Hagia Sophia of Los Angeles, dedicated in 1952.

3. Meanwhile in the entire West, and wherever its influence was potent enough, the basilica in its Christian form became the model for all church buildings. It consisted of three main parts. In front of the entrance was the atrium, or forecourt, an open space surrounded by a covered arcade, portico, or cloister, with a fountain or basin of pure water, the cantharus, in its center. The church proper usually had the form of a rectangle, known as the body, or nave, the principle of length being always observed. The width of the church hall was commonly broken by either three or five aisles. The roof of the central aisle, or nave proper, was generally raised above the outer aisles, thus forming clerestory walls with windows. In the east end of the nave was the place for the choir, sometimes on a level with the nave, then again elevated to the level of the apse, and usually enclosed by a balustrade. There was an *ambo*, or reading pulpit, on either side of the choir, the one on the south side for the Epistles, that on the north side for the Gospels. Even in the early days, but oftener after the coalition of the Gallican Church with that of Rome, the transept was added in the eastern end of the nave, thus giving to the church the shape of a cross. The apse, altar space, or chancel, was a round or polygonal extension on the eastern end of the church building, in line with

the nave. There are some few buildings of this type extant, and some art critics favor its introduction at the present time, but in a modified form, on account of the difficulties of the flat roof construction.

4. From the basilica there was developed the Romanesque, or round-arched, style of Western Europe, especially among the Germanic peoples, the Lombard, Rhenish, Romance, Norman, Tuscan, and Sicilian subdivisions being distinguished. In the churches of this type the ground plan of the basilica was retained, in smaller churches without aisle divisions, in larger structures with three or five aisles. The cruciform plan was common; additional apses were frequently built at either end of the transept, also at the western end of the church, as well as a second transept, narrower and shorter than the first. Extensions of the cross have formed an ambulatory around the sanctuary with the high altar. In the earlier part of this period the walls and columns were very heavy. Objections to the flat roof resulted in the adoption of round vaulting, which became the distinguishing characteristic of the Romanesque style. Another feature was the barrel vaulting of the ceiling, which afterwards was modified to cross vaulting, in order to distribute the thrust of the arches upon pillars and pilasters, the latter being reinforced by buttresses strengthening the walls where they were placed on the inside. The severely plain appearance of the exterior of the church was relieved by breaking up and diversifying the façades or western walls of the churches, where the main entrance was, by the application of appropriate ornamentation, both in the frieze and in the arches. It also became the custom to place a large circular window over the main portal. The tower, originally an independent structure, especially where it served as campanile or baptistery, became an integral part of the church structure.

5. The Gothic style is a sequel and outgrowth of the Romanesque, but the pointed arch, its most characteristic feature, changed both structure and symbolism of the church building entirely. The pointed arch resulted in concentrating the strains of the roof upon isolated points of support by groined instead of barrel or simple cross vaults, the ribbed vaulting of many churches being carried to the very limit of graceful endeavor and its thrust being re-

ceived by the flagrantly flaunted device of the flying buttress reinforcing both the pilaster in the outside wall and the pillar bearing the clerestory. The Gothic style lifted up highly pitched roofs and gables to heights never dreamed of in earlier times and crowned the entire edifice with slender spires and pinnacles, growing ever more decorative and ever pointing upward in joyful ecstasy until the whole building seems a splendid symphony in stone. The Cathedral of Amiens in France and that of York in England represent this type in the acme of its perfection.

6. When ostentation and playfulness became the prime object in building, a decline set in from which ecclesiastical art has not yet fully recovered. This period is commonly called the *Baroque*. Although critics have now become charitable enough to find some admirable traits in certain works of art which have been preserved from this period, it remains true, nevertheless, that arbitrariness and license characterize all its achievements, all the principles of construction being sacrificed for the sake of pictorial effect. The final decline set in with the period of the *Rococo*, when all pretense of definite architectural laws was given up, when the basic forms in construction were so completely covered that only a disharmonious conglomeration of strange combinations remained in view, the result often being a veritable nightmare of fantastic and bizarre construction.

7. The following definitions of the chief parts of a church building may assist in understanding the principles of architecture. The *façade* is the front of the church. It is sometimes ornamented with decorative frieze, with sculpture work, and with the rose window over the main entrance. The *atrium,* or *narthex,* has become the entrance hall, or vestibule, of the modern church. The *clerestory* is the upper part of the church, its walls being set back the width of the outer aisle, usually with many window openings. The *nave* is the *auditorium,* or body of the church, in which the principle of length must not be missing, the axis of the church running down the main aisle from the main entrance to the *apse,* on whose elevated platform the altar is situated. The *transepts,* or cross arms, of the church should not be too deep, nor the chancel; for the pastor, in the performance of his official acts, should always be in full view of the congregation. *Galleries* are permissible

only at the western end of the church building and in the transepts, if used at all. The best plan is to have the *balcony* above the vestibule reserved for the choir alone, with the organ (organ loft), in order to have the congregation present a compact body. The tower, with its surmounting steeple or spire, should be an integral part of the church building. The *triumphal arch* forming the entrance to the apse, as well as all pillars and pilasters, with their capitals, should conform to the style of the church. See also *Cathedral*.

E. H. Short, *A History of Religious Architecture*, Macm., 1936; F. R. Webber, *The Small Church*, Jansen, Cleveland, 1937; P. E. Kretzmann, *Christian Art in the Place and in the Form of Luth. Worship*, CPH, 1921; R. Sturgis, *Dictionary of Architecture and Building*, 1901—1902; W. H. Leach, *Protestant Church Building*. See *Symbolism*.

Archives. Unless we today properly collect and preserve our official church records under efficient supervision, the danger of their destruction as time advances is very great. The accessibility of such archives also greatly increases their value. Lutheran archives, open to students of church history, are located at the various theological seminaries. The official archives of the American Lutheran Church are located at Wartburg Seminary, Dubuque, Iowa. Quite an amount of original source material pertaining especially to the history of the Joint Synod of Ohio is deposited at Capital University, Columbus, Ohio. The *Historical Society of the American Lutheran Church* supports this work. The Augustana Synod has its archives located in the Augustana College Library, Rock Island, Ill. A historical society has also been organized, called the *Augustana Historical Society*. The Lutheran Church — Missouri Synod designated as its official historical depository the *Concordia Historical Institute*, founded in 1927 and located on the campus of Concordia Seminary, St. Louis. A wealth of material pertaining especially to the Missouri Synod and to the Lutheran Church of America is deposited here. The United Lutheran Church has one of its archives at Lutheran Theological Seminary, Mount Airy, Pa. The archives of the Pennsylvania Ministerium are also located there. Another is located at Lutheran Theological Seminary, Gettysburg, Pa. In connection with the Gettysburg archives, the *Historical Society of the*

United Lutheran Church in America was organized in 1843. ARS

Arensius, Bernard. One of the earliest Luth. clergymen in New York City; successor of Jacob Fabritius as pastor of Trinity Luth. Church, Broadway and Rector St.; Arensius directed the building of a second church, the first, erected 1671, having been demolished (1673) by the Dutch; his gentle character contrasted favorably with the despotic tendencies of Fabritius.

Arensky, Anton (1861 — 1906). A Russian composer whose compositions, sacred as well as secular, are often catchy and pretty rather than virile and strong.

Argentina. The second largest country in South America, area: 1,078,278 square miles. It lies largely within the Temperate Zone. There is, however, prolonged heat in the north and continual snow and ice in the deep south. 8,517,000 of the approximately 16,000,000 inhabitants live in the central plains, the Pampas. Here is not only the bulk of the fertile and productive lands with cattle and sheep raising, and dairy products, but also the foremost metropolitan city of South America, Buenos Aires, which has a population of over 2,982,580 (1952). It is the center of culture and the heart of manufacturing industries.

The People. A few Indian tribes are still in existence, especially in the Chaco area; the majority are scattered and intermingled with other races that came to possess the land. Of the present 16,000,000 inhabitants 88 per cent are of European extraction, the Italians leading with 6,000,000 and the Germans claiming 2,000,000 descendants. About 80 per cent of the population live in larger urban centers.

The Church. The Constitution of Argentina gives the Roman Catholic Church first and foremost rights, recognizing it as the official Church and insisting that President and Vice-President are adherents of the same. Religious liberty, however, is guaranteed to all. Missions are conducted by a large number of churches and societies (1949: 146 ordained men; 140 laymen; 111 women), including The Lutheran Church — Missouri Synod and the United Lutheran Church. Ninety per cent of the population claim membership at least nominally with the Roman Catholic Church. A law has been enacted which demands that the State religion be taught in all public schools, colleges, normal schools, and universities of the State. If parents will not have their children instructed in the Roman Catholic religion, they must so express their desire in writing to the school authorities. Such children will then receive a course in morals. A law requires all Protestant churches to register with the government.

The Lutheran Church — Missouri Synod. In 1905 a colony of German-Russian immigrants asked for the services of a Lutheran pastor in a letter addressed to the President of the Brazil District of the Missouri Synod, Dr. W. Mahler, by Pastor P. von Matthesius. Pastor H. Wittrock, the first missionary sent, settled in a newly established colony at Rincao do Valles, about 60 km. from Cruz Alta. He was followed by J. H. Meyer and others.

Christian Education. Parochial schools were conducted for a number of years, but owing to unfavorable school laws and adverse propaganda the schools were gradually closed until only one, in a faraway area, was left. To offset this problem, weekday religious instruction is given wherever possible before or after the regular hours set for the public schools. Attendance at public schools or authorized private schools is obligatory.

Training a Native Ministry. In 1922 a tract of land was purchased at Crespo for a preparatory school. Necessary buildings and residences were gradually erected. In 1936 the entire property was presented to The Lutheran Church — Missouri Synod. Until 1942 the graduates at Crespo completed their studies at Concordia Seminary, Porto Alegre, Brazil. Changing world conditions and difference in language in Brazil and in Argentina made it impossible to continue this arrangement. In March, 1942, the Theological Seminary was opened at Buenos Aires, Argentina. Director Albert Lehenbauer of Crespo was called as the first theological professor. A new plant for the seminary was erected at Villa Ballester, a suburb of Buenos Aires, and dedicated in February, 1948.

Expansion Program. While work for many years concentrated on rural areas, heeding the call of the immigrants that had come from European countries and settled in colonies and sparsely settled communities, since 1937 the mission activity expanded to larger cities. The work was extended in metropolitan Buenos Aires, population 3,633,256, and to Bahia Blanca, population 94,500 (1951). This is the southernmost mission field of the Missouri Synod and is conducted exclusively in the Spanish language. Later the work of the Missouri Synod advanced to Mar del Plata, 140,000, largest summer resort in Argentina with ocean front, to Villa Ballester and Lanus, suburbs of Buenos Aires, to Rosario, 521,210 (1951), to Santa Fe, Parana, Formosa, Concordia, and others. Each of these places has a population of over 60,000. In 1927 the Argentine District of The Lutheran Church — Missouri Synod was organized.

Periodicals. The District publishes two church papers. The *Ev. Lutherische Kirchen-Bote* and *El Luterano,* with a combined circulation of 3,500.

Statistics (1951): 36 pastors, 90 congregations, 14,949 baptized members, 7,986 communicants. See also *South America.* FCS

Argula von Stauff (von Grumbach). B. before 1490, d. 1554, first authoress of the German Reformation, friend of Luther, zealous student of the Bible, fearless in denouncing attacks on Lutheranism.

Arianism. 1. The heresy which began with Arius (256—336; pupil of Lucian * and follower of Paul of Samosata *) and continued for decades after its condemnation at Nicaea (325). Arius sought to combine the monarchianism * and adoptianism of Paul of Samosata with Greek ideas of the transcendence and utter inaccessibility of God, which led to the denial of the co-eternity and co-essentiality of Christ with God, the Father. God is an abstract "monad," alone unbegotten, without equal, eternal, unchangeable, ineffable, transcendental, and removed from the world by an impassable gulf. He could not create the world directly because of the total transcendence and inaccessibility of God. To bridge the chasm, Arius held that God created out of nothing, "before all times and aeons," an intermediate being, exalted above other creatures, through whom He made the world and all things. This being is called the Son of God, *Logos,* but is not true God, true power (*dynamis*), "not eternal," but "dissimilar" (*anomoios*) in all respects from the essence of the Father. He is a perfect creature, yet not inherently sinless, but capable of moral progress, choosing the good and continuing therein. He does not "fully know the Father nor his own nature." In time this imaginary being assumed a human body, but not a human soul and redeemed humanity by showing how, as free moral agents, men might choose the good and become sons of God.

2. Alexander, bishop of Alexandria, called a council which deposed and excommunicated Arius. The latter continued propagating his views and found some powerful adherents (Eusebius of Nicomedia * and Eusebius of Caesarea *). Constantine advised the disputants to overlook trivialities inasmuch as there was agreement on fundamentals. When this advice failed of its object, the Emperor submitted the matter to a council (Nicaea, 325). The formula of faith proposed by the Arians under the leadership of Eusebius of Nicomedia (hence *Eusebians*) was summarily rejected. A second form, submitted by Eusebius of Caesarea, the leader of the mediating party, while approaching the orthodox position, avoided the *homo-ousia* (Christ of the *same* substance as the Father) and admitted an Arian or semi-Arian interpretation. Under the leadership of Athanasius,* the orthodox party won the day for *homo-ousianism*. The second formula (Eusebian) was revised and purged of all Arian tendencies (see *Nicene Creed*).

3. After Nicaea, the Arian and semi-Arian (Christ is co-eternal; not of the same, *homo-ousios*, essence as the Father, but only of *like* essence, *homoi-ousios*) reaction came (325—361). Under imperial protection, *homoi-ousianism* gained the ascendancy in the Roman Empire, and Constantine tried to force on the Church the compromising formula which used the term *homoios* (Christ is *like* the Father) and avoided *ousios* (essence) altogether. After the death of Constantius (361) Arianism declined, and orthodoxy under the championship of the three Cappadocians,* Ambrose of Milan, and Athanasius gained strength. The Council of Constantinople (381) reaffirmed the Nicene faith. Arianism, however, continued among the Teutonic invaders, who had embraced Christianity during the Arian ascendancy (Goths, Suevi, Burgundians, Lombards, Vandals).

C. J. Hefele, *Conciliengeschichte*, 1873—1880 (English translation by W. R. Clark published by T. & T. Clark); J. H. Newman, *The Arians of the Fourth Century*, 1833; H. M. Gwatkin, *Studies in Arianism*, Deighton Bell, Cambridge, 1882.

Aristides. Christian apologist who addressed his *Apology* to Hadrian, according to Eusebius (generally considered, however, as addressed to Antoninus). The idea of God and the moral superiority of Christians forms the basis of his apology. See bibliography under *Patristics*.

Aristotle (384/3—322 B.C.). 1. Aristotle was born in the Greek colony of Stagira on the Macedonian peninsula Chalcidice, the son of Nicomachus, court physician to Amyntas II, king of Macedon and father of Philip the Great. In his eighteenth year Aristotle was sent to Athens, where he remained in close association with the Academy for twenty years, until the death of Plato in 348/7. Leaving Athens, Aristotle resided with friends of the Academy first at Atarneus, in the Troad, and then at Mitylene, on the island of Lesbos, where he doubtless engaged in biological research. Invited by Philip to take charge of his son's education, Aristotle became tutor to Alexander, probably for the years just preceding Alexander's appointment as regent for his father. In 335/4, Aristotle returned to Athens, where he labored for twelve years in the establishment of the Lyceum, instituting and pursuing a program of investigation in almost every branch of human knowledge, and composing at least the more scientific portions of his now extant writings. An outburst of anti-Macedonian feeling at Athens in 323 precipitated Aristotle's flight — lest the Athenians should "sin twice against philosophy" — to Chalcis in Euboea, where he died in 322, within a little more than a year of the deaths of Alexander and Demosthenes.

2. The Aristotelian corpus, excluding doubtful and spurious works, includes 1) the logical treatises of the *Organon: Categories, De Interpretatione, Prior Analytics, Posterior Analytics, Topics,* and *Sophistici Elenchi;* 2) the treatises on natural science now distinguished as a) physical science: *Physics, De Coelo, De Generatione et Corruptione,* and *Meteorologica;* b) psychology: *De Anima* and a collection of shorter works known as *Parva Naturalia;* c) biology: *Historia Animalium, De Partibus Animalium, De Motu* and *De Incessu Animalium,* and *De Generatione Animalium;* and d) *Problemata;* 3) First Philosophy or *Metaphysics;* 4) the treatises on practical science distinguished as a) ethics: *Nicomachean* and *Eudemian Ethics;* and b) politics: *Politics,* and *Constitution of Athens;*

5) the treatises on productive science: two works dealing with literary arts, *Rhetoric* and *Poetics*. The standard edition of the Greek text is that of Bekker (Berlin Academy, 1831—1870). A complete English translation of the works included in the Berlin edition has been prepared under the editorship of W. D. Ross (Oxford, 1908—1931).

3. The logic of Aristotle, by him called "analytic," is a discipline prior to all others, setting forth the requirements of scientific inquiry and proof. Science, in the strict sense, is demonstrated knowledge of the causes of things. Such demonstrated knowledge is obtained by syllogistic deduction from premises in themselves certain — thus science differs from dialectic, which employs probable premises, and from eristic, which aims not at truth, but at forensic victory. The Aristotelian logic of terms, propositions, and syllogisms depends, then, not merely on the formal relations exemplified in the statement of proof, but on the possibility of discovering principles, *i. e.*, universals and causes, which are true of nature. Thus Aristotle is fond of tracing the transition in knowledge from the particulars of sense experience (the things more knowable to us) to the universals present in an inchoate way in sensation but grasped by intuitive reason or *nous* (the things more knowable in themselves). Thus Aristotle claims to have accounted for human science without reducing knowledge to the motion of atoms, as had Democritus, or transforming things into ideas, as he thought Plato did.

4. The causes, which can be stated as connectives among terms because they are links among the phenomena of nature, are of four sorts: material (the stuff of which a thing is made), formal (its essence or nature, *what* it is), efficient (the agency which brings it into being), and final (its end, or that for the sake of which it exists). Thus for Aristotle every sensible object is a union of two principles, matter and form — the matter in every case regarded as potentiality for the form which actualizes it. The fact of motion or change is then accounted for as a process by which potential being passes over, through form, into actual being. This analysis Aristotle regards as a triumph over Platonism, which, appealing only to form, left motion unintelligible as a passage from non-being to being, and over Democritean atomism, which, reducing scientific ex-

planation to the discovery of material parts, simply assumed motion as a principle.

5. Aristotle proceeds, on the basis of the causes, to divide the sciences into the theoretic, the practical, and the productive. The theoretic sciences have as their end simply to know, as their subject matter "substances," things possessing an internal principle of motion or rest; as their form strict demonstration or necessity; as their agency the "intellectual virtues of "intuitive reason" and "science" (combined in "philosophic wisdom"), the capacities of grasping first principles and demonstrating from them. The special theoretic sciences are differentiated according to differences found in their subject matters. Physics deals with "common sensible matter," with kinds of sensible natural objects — its subject matter is never purely formal, but always includes matter and motion. Mathematics treats of "intelligent matter," of numbers, points, lines, surfaces, volumes, which cannot exist apart from bodies, yet are abstracted in thought and treated separately in this science. Metaphysics, the science of "being qua being," investigates the first principles and causes which are assumed in the separate sciences, and therefore it treats of a substance which not only can be known apart, but which also exists apart from matter and motion, whose existence is established in the famous proof of the necessity of an unmoved mover as the cause of existence and motion. For if there were no separated substance, all sciences would be reduced to physics; and if forms and numbers existed separately, all philosophy would be reduced to mathematics.

6. The practical and productive sciences have as their end action (*i. e.*, doing and making, respectively) rather than knowledge; as their subject matter things done and things made, whose principle of motion is in an external agent and which have no natural definitions; their principles are established dialectically, hence their conclusions are only probable; and the virtues required to pursue these sciences are "practical wisdom" and "art." The practical sciences are differentiated as ethics, which treats of individual action, and politics, which treats of forms of community. In his ethics, Aristotle dialectically determines the good for man as the actualization or exercise of his distinctive faculty, reason, in the habitual subordination of appetite to rational

principle — it is here that particular moral virtues are defined as means between extremes — and in the search for and contemplation of truth. In the *Politics*, concerned with constitutions and forms of human associations which again have no natural definitions, a basis for proportional rules is found in the needs and interdependences of man for the ends of living and of living well — it is in this sense that man is by nature a "political animal." The productive sciences, finally, are differentiated according to their products, and the kinds of art according to the object, means, and manner of their imitation of nature. Thus in the Poetics, tragedy is distinguished by isolating its means of imitation, and the "liberal arts" are distinguished by their educative influence in preparing men for freedom.

7. The influence of Aristotle on subsequent philosophy and science is incalculably extensive. This influence is rendered intricate by the fact that he has been read in widely different ways and adapted to modes of thought to which he explicitly opposed his own. During the Hellenistic period, when nearly all the philosophies reflected the impress of his thought, Aristotle was regarded as merely the most eminent of Plato's disciples, and "peripatetic" signified a specialist in science rather than a philosopher. In the early Middle Ages there was slight direct contact with his writings, and infiltrations of Greek thought into Christian philosophy was rather Neo-platonic than Aristotelian. In the twelfth and thirteenth centuries, however, all the works of Aristotle were translated into Latin and were made the object of intense study and voluminous commentaries. The revolt of Renaissance philosophers against Aristotle was probably as much against this scholastic mode of discussion as against Aristotle's doctrine. A renaissance of Aristotelian studies in recent decades has been a result of the modern edition of his works by the Berlin Academy and of the papal blessing of the work of Thomas Aquinas. Aristotle is alive today in Neo-scholasticism, in behaviorist psychology, in the vitalism and dynamism of such thinkers as Bergson, and in much of the technical vocabulary, if not in the spirit, of modern science and philosophy. See also *Psychology*, C 3. RL

Arles, Synod of (314). Called by Constantine; first synod of the West; its 22 canons condemned Donatism.

Armed Forces, Spiritual Care of. See *Armed Services Commission.*

Armed Services Commission. Was called into being by the action of the synodical convention of the Evangelical Lutheran Synod of Missouri, Ohio, and Other States, assembled in Cleveland in June, 1935. Its organization was effected on February 13, 1936. The chief duties of the Commission are to give ecclesiastical endorsement to qualified pastors for a commission as chaplains in the military service, to counsel chaplains, and to provide for and give spiritual guidance and help to those serving in the Armed Forces and to those in Veterans Hospitals. The scope and the volume of the Commission's work increased greatly when the numerical strength of the Armed Forces of the United States was raised through the Selective Service Act in 1940, and it took on global aspects when World War II swept over the nations. Executive offices were established in Chicago, Ill., late in 1940 and still later a branch service office in Winnipeg, Canada. When the United States became involved in the war, a most comprehensive and far-flung program of spiritual ministry to those in the Armed Forces was developed and put into action under the slogan "They shall not march alone." A unique feature of the Commission's program was and still is a complete and constantly up-to-date mailing list of all men and women of the Missouri Synod serving in the Armed Forces. The names and addresses of such members were and are forwarded to chaplains, service pastors, or key pastors, who in turn contact the individual members. Every name on the mailing list receives the *Loyalty — Christ and Country* magazine monthly with its short order of service and a sermon. *At Ease,* a pamphlet written in a lighter vein, was mailed with the *Loyalty* magazine during the war years. *The Lutheran Chaplain,* a monthly professional magazine, was sent to every chaplain and pastor of Synod and continues to appear every three months. Other publications are such as *Service Manual for Chaplains, Service Prayer Book, Let Us Reason Together,* for instructing catechumens, *Loyalty News,* informative booklets on the Commission's program, and *Double Time,* sent out at intervals. Tracts and other small publications include *A Prayer for You, Your Orders, Church Call, Stirring Scenes of Holy Baptism, Arise and Be Baptized, Purity of Thought, On Using*

Profanity, If You Are in a Hospital, Directory of Key Pastors and Service Centers, Altar Prayers, Memorial Services, Calendars, Identification Tags.

A total of 253 pastors of Synod served as chaplains in World War II, five of these with the Canadian forces, and seven of the chaplains passed away while on duty. Quite a number of the chaplains had very responsible positions. In addition to the regimental duties the chaplains embraced the opportunities to conduct special Lutheran services, and it was not uncommon for them to have from 40 to 79 divine services per month along the battle lines and at numerous small installations. The public and private Gospel ministry of the chaplains received a response from the men in the service such as was never before attained in any previous war or other time of emergency in the history of our nation.

By the close of the war a total of 47 Service Centers and 44 Parish Centers were being operated either alone or jointly with the National Lutheran Council, and later were under the auspices of the Lutheran Service Commission. Service Centers outside of the Continental United States included Honolulu, London, Paris, Kunming, Alaska, Australia, Frankfurt, Canal Zone, Manila. The Service Centers were staffed by service pastors and were "Homes Away from Home." The Centers provided opportunities for divine worship, Holy Communion, Bible classes, fellowship with Christians, social and recreational pastimes. The attendance figures per month ran from 3,000 to 50,000 at the separate centers.

More than 70 contact key pastors performed an extensive ministry of love to Lutheran service personnel at neighboring camps, air bases, naval stations and schools.

In addition to an executive secretary the office had a director of publications and at the peak of activity 50 full-time employees, 43 part-time employees, and at the time of large mailings additional volunteer help. Total pieces of mail sent out to service men and women were approximately twenty million; sent in quantity shipments to chaplains and pastors, etc., approximately sixty million; total number of *Service Prayer Books,* 435,613.

Official acts by chaplains and service pastors: Baptisms, 2,569; confirmations, 921; marriages, 4,937; number communed, 281,978; sermons delivered, 96,675.

The names of approximately 135,000 men and women of Synod serving in the Armed Forces were on file in the office, not including 4,000 such names in the Winnipeg office. The supreme sacrifice was made by 3,738. The total number of changes of address received from the beginning of 1943 to the close of 1946 was 555,250.

The total cost of the program from January 1, 1941, to December 31, 1946, amounted to about $2,250,000. See *National Lutheran Council.* PLD

Armenia. In Western Asia, bordering on Asia Minor, between the Black and the Caspian Sea and the Taurus and Caucasus Mountains, mainly high tableland. In 1918 the Republic of Armenia (Erivan) was founded, with recognition in 1920 by the United States, which country, however, did not accept the mandate for this new republic. In 1922 part of it, with Azerbaijan and Georgia, was incorporated with the Soviet States, but much of former Armenia is now a part of Turkey. Population of this area, in 1951, about 2,000,000, of whom 85 per cent were Armenians. Religion originally much like that of Persia, sun and moon revered, male and female temple prostitutes. Christianity penetrated into this country early, probably from Antioch. Through the efforts of Gregory the Illuminator, Christianity replaced paganism as the national church. About the year 420 the Bible was translated into the language of the Armenians. They maintained their religion despite strenuous efforts of Zoroastrians and later the Turks to impose their beliefs, these efforts often accompanied by unspeakable persecutions, even in recent times. Some differences from orthodox beliefs, for instance, that the Armenians accept a strict Monophysitic doctrine.* Head of the Armenian Church is the catholicos or supreme patriarch, elected by national council, residing at Echmiadzin; two lower patriarchs at Jerusalem and Constantinople. Colonies of Armenians are found in most larger cities of the world, and usually these people remain faithful to their religion. Many emigrated to America, especially after the Turkish massacres near the beginning of this century, settling largely in the San Joaquin Valley in California. See *Armenians.*

Protestant mission work was begun in Armenia in 1820 by the American Board of Commissioners. The Presbyterian Church followed in 1870. Robert College at Constantinople was a famed institution, and a girls' school was conducted at Scutari. See *Missions, Bibliography.* OHS

Armenian Bible Versions. See *Bible Versions, G.*

Armenians. (*Church of Armenia in America.*) They are related to the Eastern Catholics in doctrine, liturgy, and church government. Owing to their Monophysite views they have separated from the other Eastern churches since Chalcedon. Turkish persecution in 1894 brought large numbers to America, especially to New England, New York, and California. While some have joined Protestant denominations, the majority is attempting to perpetuate the native language, customs, and religious views, and has organized the Church of Armenia in America. Membership: 200,000 (1952).

Arminianism. The term "Arminianism" embraces, in general, the teachings of Arminius, or James Harmensen (Jacob Hermanas; 1560—1609; minister in Amsterdam, afterwards professor of theology at Leyden). The theological views of Arminius and his followers were summed up in five points, which may be briefly stated thus: 1. God from all eternity predestinated to eternal life those of whom He foresaw that they would remain steadfast in faith unto their end. 2. Christ died for all mankind, not simply for the elect. 3. Man co-operates in his conversion by free will. 4. Man may resist divine grace. 5. Man may fall from divine grace. This last tenet was at first held but doubtfully; ultimately, however, it was firmly accepted. The Synod of Dort (1618—1619) condemned the Arminian doctrines, and the civil powers, as was the general practice of the age, enforced the decrees of the council by pains and penalties. Nevertheless, the new view spread rapidly. In 1621 Episcopius (b. at Amsterdam, Jan. 8, 1583; d. there Apr. 4, 1643), at the request of the leading Remonstrants (Arminians), drew up a formula of faith in twenty-five chapters, which was widely circulated and subscribed by the most eminent men in Holland and France, such as Grotius; Limborch (Philip van Limborch, Dutch Remonstrant theologian; b. Amsterdam, June 19, 1633; d. there Apr. 30, 1712); Le Clerc (Clericus, a learned theologian; b. Geneva, Mar. 19, 1657; d. Jan. 8, 1736); and Wetstein (Johann Jakob Wetstein, New Testament scholar; b. Basel, Mar.

5, 1693; d. Amsterdam, Mar. 9, 1754). In France the effect of the controversy appeared in the modified Calvinism of Amyraldus (see *Amyrault*). Archbishop Laud introduced Arminianism into the Church of England, where it was adopted by such men as Cudworth, Pierce, Jeremy Taylor, Tillotson, Chillingworth, Pearson, Whitby, etc. Arminianism in the Church of England at last became a negative term, implying the negation of Calvinism rather than any exact system of theology whatever. Much of what passed for Arminianism was in fact Pelagianism, synergism in some form. A modified Arminianism arose again in England in the great Wesleyan Reformation of the seventeenth century, and its ablest expositions may be found in the writings of John Wesley, John Fletcher, and Richard Watson, while the remainder of English conformists and the Presbyterians in Scotland and elsewhere continued to be mainly Calvinists. See *Methodist Church* (2); *Baptist Bodies* (2); *Holiness Bodies.* FEM

Armsdorf, Andreas (1670—99). A pupil of Johann Pachelbel, whose compositions for the organ reflect the influence of Pachelbel. Many short chorale fugues were written by Armsdorf.

Arnauld, Antoine. Most illustrious of a famous French family; b. Paris, 1612; d. Brussels, 1694; noted for his defense of Jansenism and for his attacks on the Jesuits.

Arndt, Edward L. (Dec. 19, 1864, to Apr. 17, 1929). B. at Bukowni, Pomerania; graduated St. Louis, 1885; pastor at Saginaw, Mich., 1885—97; professor at Concordia College, St. Paul, Minn., 1897—1910; organized Ev. Luth. Mission for China May 1, 1912; commissioned by society as missionary to China July 12, 1912. Arrived Shanghai, Feb. 25, 1913; established missions and schools in Hankow territory. Mo. Synod took over mission in 1917. Wrote: *Our Task in China;* edited *Missionsbriefe;* translated hymns and sermons into Chinese. Died Apr. 17, 1929; buried in International Cemetery, Hankow.

Arndt, Ernst Moritz (1769—1860). Historian and hymnologist; b. on island of Ruegen, d. Bonn; professor of history at Bonn 1818—20 and after 1840; wrote a treatise *Von dem Worte und dem Kirchenlied* (Of the Word and the Church Hymn) and a number of hymns.

Arndt (Arnd), Johann (1555—1621). Devotional writer; 1583 pastor in Badeborn, Anhalt, 1590 in Quedlinburg, 1599 in Brunswick, 1611 court preacher and general superintendent in Celle. His fame rests chiefly on his *True Christianity*, translated into almost all European languages, which in some parts, however, is drawn from medieval writers like Tauler and not always sound.

Arnobius (d. 327?). Teacher of rhetoric at Sicca, Numidia; first a pagan and opponent of Christianity; after his conversion he wrote his *Adversus Nationes* as a public avowal of his sincerity (reveals great familiarity with the classics, but deficient in Biblical and Christian knowledge). See bibliography under *Patristics*.

Arnold, Gottfried (1666—1714). Protestant, whose *Die erste Liebe zu Christo* received renewed emphasis through Leo Tolstoy. His *Unparteiische Kirchen- und Ketzerhistorie* reveals an attempt to understand the psychological and thought factors of heresy.

Arnold, Matthew (1822—1888). English poet, critic, and essayist; was known best as "the great English apostle of culture." He was born at Laleham, Middlesex, the son of Dr. Thomas Arnold of Rugby; educated at Winchester, Rugby, and Oxford. He was private secretary to Lord Lansdowne, 1847 to 1851; appointed inspector of schools, 1851; professor of poetry at Oxford, 1857—1867. As literary critic, Arnold propounded the need of maintaining the neglected qualities of dignity, harmony, and simplicity. Chief works: *On Translating Homer; Essays in Criticism* (first series, 1865); *Essays in Criticism* (second series, 1888); *Culture and Anarchy; St. Paul and Protestantism; Literature and Dogma; God and the Bible; Last Essays on Church and Religion; A Friend of God. Poems: Resignation; Self-Dependence; The Scholar Gypsy; Requiescat; Sohrab and Rustum; Dover Beach; Thyrsis; The Last Word; Rugby Chapel.*

Arnold, Thomas (1795—1842). Broad Churchman; b. West Cowes; priest, 1828; headmaster (famous for his stimulative influence) Rugby, 1828; Professor of Modern History, Oxford, 1841; d. Rugby. Wrote *History of Rome.*

Arrogance, Spiritual. See *Pride.*

Ars Moriendi ("art of dying"). Book written to guide priests in their ministrations at deathbeds.

Art, Ecclesiastical and Religious. 1. That branch of art in general which, while employing the principles of art as basic for all productions coming under this division of esthetics, makes the special applications of these fundamental rules to the Christian church building and its decoration, as well as to those productions which tend to the edification of the individual Christian or of the Christian family in the home. The earliest examples of Christian art, whether in the form of church buildings or in the expression of the artistic mind in painting or sculpture, are placed by critics in the third century. The catacombs furnish examples not only of fresco paintings, some of which show a high degree of excellence, but also of designs and figures carved in the stone slabs of the sarcophagi. Wood- and ivory-carving in pieces of furniture, in diptychs, in ivory coverings for gospels, church books, and the like, in pyxes, patens, ampullas, vases of gold and silver, eucharistic doves, altar fronts, and ciboria, all indicate that the Church did not reject artistic work as incompatible with the Christian doctrine. Between the fourth and the eleventh century, sculpture work in the Church hardly rose above the level of industrial carving, although there are individual examples of unusual work. With the great era of church-building, which began in the eleventh century, the plastic arts were given due attention, the result being found in the many beautiful portals, columns, buttresses, pillars, and tympanums of the late medieval period. The façades of many cathedrals erected during this time show individual as well as ensemble work which ranks with the finest productions of the sculptor's art of all times. Beginning with the thirteenth century, the Italian schools flourished, at Pisa, at Florence, at Siena, at Naples. At this time, sculptured altar pieces, pulpits, choirs, galleries, fonts, ciboria, tabernacles, candelabra, single statues of saints and angels, crucifixes, madonnas, large groups of statues, begin to appear in endless variety. Names like that of Ghiberti, Donatello, and Michelangelo stand out most prominently at this time. There was a golden period of the plastic arts in Germany in the fifteenth century, the names of Peter Vischer, of Michael Wohlgemuth, of Veit Stoss, and of Adam Kraft standing out above the rest. Since the Renaissance little work has been done in Christian sculpture except by Stone in England and by Thorwaldsen in Denmark. Among the German sculptors of the last century Rauch and Rietschel deserve mention. Among modern American sculptors of the Lutheran Church we have Oskar J. W. Hansen of Virginia; Arnold Flaten of St. Olaf; George Loeber of New York; Palmer Eide of Sioux Falls, S. Dak., Roger Sogge of South Dakota; and Ernest Amundson of Teaneck, N. J.

2. The history of Christian painting offers a few more pages of interest. The pictures of the catacombs are well worth the study which they have received in the last decades. The mosaic work of the early Christian centuries stands in a class by itself, some of its productions, both in geometrical designs and in figures, being unsurpassed to this day, such as those of the baptistery of San Giovanni in Fonte and of San Apollinare Nuovo, both of Ravenna. The use of mosaic work for floors has continued to this day, but wall mosaics are now rarely used except in the apse, where also the finest examples of the early Middle Ages are found. Unique, too, is the art of the iconographer, whose products are highly venerated in the Eastern churches. The most famous painter was Andrew Ruble (1370—1430). His best-known work is "The Old Testament Trinity." The art of Christian painting was naturally influenced by the iconoclastic disturbances, but the revival came with Charlemagne, both in mosaics and in frescoes. But the full awakening did not occur till the middle of the thirteenth century. There was a school of Cologne, noted for mural paintings, but the impetus was caught up in Italy, and the development was rapid. Here we find the names of Brunelleschi, Lippi, the Bellinis. Later came Leonardo da Vinci and after him Michelangelo, Raphael, and Correggio. The later Venetian school produced two great artists, Titian, the color genius, and Tintoretto, on the threshold of the Baroque. In Spain there was Velasquez, master technician, and also Murillo, expressive of religious charm and fervor. In the Flemish school of the Netherlands Rubens stands supreme, in spite of his sensual art, while in Holland Rembrandt easily surpasses all other painters. In England very few artists of the first rank outside of the Preraffaelites produced religious pictures of note, and in France the situation is the same, though one might mention Poussin and Doré. In Ger-

many there was the Nuremberg school, with Duerer as the greatest master, the Swabian school, with Hans Burgkmaier, and the modern school with its various tendencies, as represented by Overbeck, Schnorr von Carolsfeld, Richter, Hofmann, Plockhorst, Thoma, Gebhardt, Steinhausen, and Uhde, though others might be named. Some of the more notable American artists of the Lutheran Church are Siegfried Reinhardt of St. Louis; R. Brownell McGrew of Los Angeles; Ellen Florence Roeder Hatter of Bronxville, N. Y.; Wilbert Seidel of Northwestern University; Charles Baum of Sellersville, Pa.; and Elsa Kesatie of Suomi College, Hancock, Mich.

3. So far as art windows are concerned, their "golden age" began with the wide introduction of the Gothic style in France, England, and Germany; for every device was employed to make the large expanses of windows works of the highest art in themselves and to have them serve for enhancing the total effect of the interior by proper gradations in color. During the earlier period the mosaic effect was used extensively; later came colored figure work, combined with grisaille, and finally followed the decline with the introduction of the flamboyant and the abandonment of the natural form in ornament. Modern American artists in the Lutheran Church include Robert Berg of St. James kiln in St. Paul and Milton Frenzel of Ironton, Mo.

4. Book art had two great periods, the earlier being that asociated with the practice of illuminating the manuscripts, which was carried to the greatest heights of artistic endeavor. Since the invention of the printing press much attention has been given to fine illustrations as well as elaborate ornamentation of covers, particularly in gift books and in altar Bibles, the art of the silversmith having been engaged in producing bindings whose artistic value is evident at first glance. Of important art centers Constantinople, Ravenna, and Florence may be named for the earlier period, and Munich, Duesseldorf, Paris, London, and New York for the present time. See also *Hymns, Church Music, Cathedral.*

C. R. Morey, *Christian Art,* Longmans, 1935; Josef Strzyowski, *Origin of Christian Church Art,* Oxford Press, 1923; P. E. Kretzmann, *Art in the Place and in the Form of Luth. Worship,* CPH, 1921; see references under *Symbolism, Christian.* A. C. Piepkorn, "The

Church of the Augsburg Confession and the Fine Arts," *Lutheran Scholar*, October, 1952.

Artemonites. See *Monarchianism*, A 3.

Articles of Faith. See *Fundamental Doctrines*.

Articles of Faith (1611). See *Baptist Bodies*, 2.

Articles of Polity of the Church. See *Calvin, John*, 3.

Articles of Religion (25). See *Democratic Declarations*, 6.

Articles of Visitation. In order to crush Crypto-Calvinism, which under Chancellor Nicholas Crell was again rearing its head in Electoral Saxony, a general visitation of churches and schools was ordered at Torgau in 1592, to be conducted according to the Articles of Visitation, drawn up under the lead of Aegidius Hunnius in 1593. Four articles treat the Lord's Supper, the Person of Christ, Holy Baptism, and the Election of Grace, each in from four to six terse, canonlike sentences in substantial agreement with the Formula of Concord. To these are added just as terse statements of the errors of the Calvinists on these points. These Articles had to be confessed by all preachers and teachers and for a long time had a confessional character, especially in Saxony.

Artman, Horace G. B. (Sept. 23, 1857—Sept. 18, 1884). B. at Zionsville, Lehigh Co., Pa. Graduate of Lutheran Theological Seminary, Philadelphia; ordained at Lancaster, Pa., May, 1880, for mission work in India; arrived at Rajahmundry July 7, 1880; became headmaster of the mission schools; also started a high school for Brahmin and Mohammedan boys, the management of which broke his health. He died soon after at Rajahmundry.

Artopaeus, Peter (1491—1563). Lutheran theologian whose friendly attitude toward Osiander caused his deposition; wrote *scholia* on parts of OT and NT.

Arya Samaj. See *Hinduism*.

Asbury, Francis (1745—1816). Sent by Wesley as missionary to America; first bishop of Methodist Episcopal Church ordained in America; his *Journals* reveal his zeal and wide missionary activity.

Ascension. The name applied to that event in which the risen Christ removed His visible presence from the society of men and passed into the heavens. The doctrine of the Ascension is based on Acts 1:1-12; Mark 16:19; and Luke 24:49-51 (which narrate the event); John 6:62; 20:17 (which look forward to it); Eph. 4:8-10; 1 Tim. 3:16; 1 Pet. 3:22; Heb. 4:14 (which imply it). The Ascension is also implied in the references of Acts, the Epistles, and Revelation to Christ's being "seated at the right hand of God." Acts 2:33; 3:21; 5:31; 7:56; 13:35-37; Phil. 2:9; Heb. 1:3; 2:9; 12:2; Rev. 1:13; 5:6; etc. Throughout the Apostolic Age the Ascension is assumed as a fact among the other facts of Christ's life, as consistent with them and as real.

The Ascension marks, for the Savior, the highest degree of exaltation, as it implies His session at the right hand of God, His entering upon the full use, according to His human nature, of the divine attributes, of which He relinquished the full, continued, and unintermittent use and enjoyment during His State of Humiliation.

To the Christian the doctrine of the Ascension has manifold comforts. In the knowledge that our Brother, Christ, is ascended on high and now is ever and everywhere present also according to His human nature with, and governs, His Church on earth, our faith and hope for the future of God's kingdom rest secure. There is to be "a redemption of our body," Rom. 8:23; there is "an image of the heavenly," 1 Cor. 15:49, we shall bear; a "spiritual body," v. 44, the "body of glory," Phil. 3:21, that will be raised; "our mortal bodies" are to be "quickened," Rom. 8:11. The future life is not to be one of pure spirit; it is to be "clothed upon." 2 Cor. 5:2. And, best of all, we shall "see Him as He is."

Ascension, Feast of. See *Church Year*, 5.

Ascension of Isaiah. See *Apocalypticism*.

Asceticism (G. "exercise," "practice," a term used by Greek philosophers to denote moral discipline). Asceticism was practiced by Essenes, Pythagoreans, Therapeutae, and other religious and philosophical cults in pre-Christian times. It is found in varying degrees in almost all religions.

Outward asceticism was seldom practiced in OT times (cf., however, Nazarenes: Num. 6:2, 3, 13; Judg. 13:5; 1 Sam. 1:11; Lam. 4:7; Amos 2:11). In later Judaism it became a frequent practice (Tobit 12:8; Matt. 6:16; 9:14; Luke 18:22). The NT opposes work-righteous asceticism (Col. 2:16-23; 1 Tim. 4:1-3), but mentions fasting as an auxiliary to prayer (Matt. 17:21). It speaks of true asceticism (1 Tim. 4:7,8), namely, that the Christian should be willing to take up the cross, that is, exercise watchfulness, patience, sobriety, self-control, in order to be able to bear suffering and perform the tasks which come to him (Matt. 10:38; 16:24; Mark 10:21; Luke 14:26; Rom. 8:13; Gal. 5:24).

Asceticism was practiced by Gnosticism and Manichaeism, which sought to free individuals from matter regarded as evil. From these and other Hellenistic and Jewish influences asceticism entered the Early Church. Thus there were fixed times for fasting, fixed hours for prayer, regulations regarding food, abstinence from marriage, withdrawal from the world, and similar ascetic practices (Clement A., *Strom.*, VI:12; Irenaeus, *Haer.* III:xi:9). Asceticism continued to grow until the time of the Reformation and emphasized the following notions: 1) the body's enjoyment of material things is evil; 2) the individual's duty is to gain his own blessedness; 3) penance is accomplished through ascetic practices; 4) it is a God-pleasing work to imitate the suffering of Christ.

Luther in his *Freedom of the Christian Man* struck at the very heart of asceticism by showing that works cannot justify and that the Christian can use all God's creatures but must obey the Moral Law. In addition, Luther frequently censures monks for their work-righteousness (St. L. Ed., IX:526), for considering their mode of life higher than that of others (V:1152, 1375; VII: 2266; VIII:635; IX:673), for leaving the difficulties and duties of normal life for an invented mode of existence (IV: 1920; IX:284). The Lutheran Confessions oppose asceticism because its works were not commanded by God (AC, XXVI:8, 18; 23:6 ff.; *et al.*) and opposed righteousness by faith (AC, XX:8, 18; 23:6 ff.; *et al.*). They emphasize obedience to the Moral Law (AC, XXVI:8 ff.) and teach a true asceticism which consists in rendering the moral and natural powers instruments of righteousness for God and man (AC, XXVI:31 ff.).

O. Zoeckler, *Askese u. Moenchtum*, 1897; H. C. Lea, *History of Sacerdotal Celibacy in the Latin Church*, Macm., 1907 (2 vols.); O. Hardman, *The Ideals of Asceticism*, Macm., 1924; "Monasticism" in Cambridge Medieval History (vol. I, ch. 18). EL

Ash Wednesday. See *Church Year*, 4.

Asia. The largest continent, of 16,188,200 square miles, with about 1,150,000,000 population, with all the great religions of the world represented and large sections still without knowledge of Christianity. Siberia and adjacent areas would nominally be under the Greek Catholic faith. Tibet and areas about it have their own religion. In China, Japan, India, Burma, Indo-China, Buddhism would be found; also Confucianism, Taoism, Animism. Turkey, Persia, Afghanistan, Arabia, and most of West Asia almost entirely under the influence of Islam. Judaism and Zoroastrianism and other religions are also represented. See the various countries for further descriptions. See *Missions, Bibliography*.

Asia Minor. The extreme western section of Asia, recently called Anatolia.*

Asoka. See *Buddhism*.

Asperges (R. C.). The ceremony of sprinkling people with holy water before Mass.

Assassins (Ar., *hashashin*, "hashish eaters"). Secret politico-religious Shiite sect (Mohammedan of the baser kind), founded in 1090 and flourishing in Syria and Persia until suppressed in 13th century. Became terror of their neighbors by practicing "assassination." Their head, known as "Old Man of the Mountain," had the "assassins" drugged with *hashish* (an extract of hemp; intoxicating) before sending them on their murderous missions.

Assemblies of God. See *Holiness Bodies*, 2.

Assemblies of God, General Council. This denomination had its origin in the revival movement of 1906 and is typically Pentecostal in doctrine and church polity. They believe that entire sanctification must be the goal of all believers, that the gifts of speaking in tongues and divine healing must be present today, that the second coming of Christ is imminent and will be premillennial, that Christians cannot participate in war. While at first opposed to every type of denominational organization, the church polity now is a combination of the Congregational and Presbyterian form of church government. See also *Holiness Bodies.*

Assig, Hans von (1650—94). Silesian nobleman, high official at Schwiebus in the Electorate of Brandenburg; hymn writer.

Assignment Board. See *Teachers,* A 6.

Associate Reformed Church. Organized in 1743 by Presbyterians who traced their origin to the secessionists in Scotland (1733) and Reformed Presbyterians. Later this group joined with descendants of the dissenters of 1782 to form the *United Presbyterian Church in North America.*

Associate Synod. See *Presbyterian Bodies,* 1.

Associated Lutheran Charities Within the Evangelical Lutheran Synodical Conference of North America. A. *Early History.* — 1. Known popularly as Associated Lutheran Charities, this association of charitable agencies was founded in 1901 in Chicago by three pioneers in city or institutional mission work, the Rev. F. W. Herzberger of St. Louis, the Rev. August Schlechte of Chicago, and the Rev. F. T. Ruhland of Buffalo. Men prominent in the movement in later years included the Rev. Carl Eissfeldt of Milwaukee, a worker in the field of child welfare, the Rev. Philip Wambsganss of Fort Wayne, whose interest was centered in hospitals and child welfare agencies, and the Rev. Enno Duemling, long-time institutional missionary in Milwaukee. In the early days of the organization an annual conference for mutual instruction and encouragement was the sole objective; other objectives were added to the program in later years.

2. When Associated Lutheran Charities came into being, the charitable endeavors conducted by societies and agencies within The Lutheran Church — Missouri Synod were already well developed. The first charitable agency within this Synod was the Lutheran Hospital of St. Louis, founded in 1858 by the Rev. Johann Friedrich Buenger, pastor of Immanuel Lutheran Church. Ten years later, in 1868, Pastor Buenger established the first orphanage within the bounds of Synod in Des Peres, Mo., near St. Louis. The first Home for the Aged was opened in 1875 in Brooklyn, N. Y.

3. In 1896 a significant development occurred in the founding of the first Children's Friend Society within the Missouri Synod. After the founding of the Des Peres Orphanage seven other orphanages had become established in rapid succession in various sections of the country. Now the building of orphan homes ceased, and agencies for foster-home placement of dependent children took their place. 1896 marked the establishment of the Children's Friend Society of Wisconsin, and this was followed by the establishment of ten additional agencies for foster-home care within the next decade. Foster-home care is now generally recognized by all child welfare agencies as the ideal method of care for dependent children.

4. Associated Lutheran Charities was instrumental in the establishment of Bethesda Lutheran Home for feeble-minded and epileptic children in 1903. This large institution is located at Watertown, Wis. It also provided the impetus for the foundation of the Deaconess Society in 1920.

B. *Present Constituency.* — Associated Lutheran Charities, although a voluntary association of agencies and purely advisory in character, today (1953) includes almost all of the charitable and so-called "inner mission" agencies within the Synodical Conference. The 121 member agencies are classified in four groupings: 1. City and Institutional Missions; 2. Family and Child Care; 3. Care of the Aged; 4. Health and Hospitals. Four standing committees, each made up of representative workers in these fields, are in charge of the work of these departments. There is also a case-work section, in which professionally trained social case workers hold membership. Other active committees are: Recruitment and Training, Service, and Membership. An Executive Board of nine elected members conducts the affairs of the organization. Officers include a president, first and second vice-presidents, secretary, treasurer, statistician, and business manager.

C. *Program of Activities.* — 1. The association sponsors a biennial national convention of three and one-half days. Business is transacted, and essays on subjects in the fields of missionary and social work are delivered in general meetings held in the forenoon of each day. Afternoon sessions are devoted to meetings of agency representatives grouped according to their interests and fields of work. Evening meetings feature forums and discussions of timely subjects of especial interest.

2. The association also sponsors regional meetings, conducted each year in strategically located centers. Such meetings have been held in New York, Baltimore, Chicago, St. Louis, Fort Wayne, Minneapolis-St. Paul, Seattle, San Francisco. Institutes and seminars in social and missionary work are featured at the regional meetings.

3. At the request of member agencies, area surveys as well as surveys of individual agencies are conducted. A counseling service is also maintained. The association was successful in promoting the creation of a synodical Department of Social Welfare in 1950.

D. *Publications.* — *The Proceedings,* an annual, containing the membership roster, reports, and papers delivered at the annual convention.

The Good News, a religious monthly of four pages intended for distribution in hospitals and other institutions by pastors and missionaries.

Numerous pamphlets and monographs on various subjects have also been published by the association. See *Charities, Christian; Social Work.* HFW

Association of Lutheran Brotherhoods. See *Laymen's Activity in the Luth. Church.*

Associations and Institutions (Ed.). See *Christian Teaching,* B; *Parish Education.*

Assumption, Feast of (R. C. and Eastern Orthodox). Aug. 15, celebrated in memory of the resurrection and ascension of Mary, a fiction traced to *De Transitu Mariae* and other apocrypha. *Assumption of Mary.* See *Bulls; Mariolatry.*

Assumption of Moses. See *Apocrypha,* A 4.

Assurance. The firm persuasion of being in a state of grace. Whereas the Council of Trent laid its anathema upon the doctrine that a Christian may be sure of his salvation, the Church of the Reformation upheld it. It is not denied that the Christian during his entire life will be cast about with many a conflict, many a doubt. He is to work out his salvation with fear and trembling. Yet he knows, being made divinely sure by the Holy Spirit, that "He which hath begun a good work in him will perform it," the gift of the Spirit through the means of grace being an earnest of the inheritance laid up in heaven. By this assurance the Christian is upheld in

tribulation and often rescued from utter despair. As Christians we have "full assurance of understanding," that is, a perfect knowledge and entire persuasion of the truth of the doctrine of Christ. The "assurance of faith," Heb. 9:22, is trust in the sacrifice and priestly office of Christ. The "assurance of hope," mentioned Heb. 6:11, relates to the heavenly inheritance and must necessarily imply a full persuasion that we are the children of God and therefore heirs of His glory; and from this passage it must certainly be concluded that such an assurance is what every Christian ought to aim at, and that it is attainable.

In a sense, assurance is the very essence of Christian faith. It expresses itself in such Scriptural terms as: "There is now no condemnation to them which are in Christ Jesus"; "Being justified by faith, we have peace with God"; "Ye have received ... the Spirit of adoption, whereby we cry, Abba Father." Compare the many passages expressive of the confidence and the joy of Christians, their union with God, and their assurance that sins are forgiven and the ground of fear of future punishment taken away.

The Lutheran Confessions throughout agree with the Formula of Concord, Art. IV:12: "[Justifying] faith is a living bold [firm] trust in God's grace, so certain that a man would die a thousand times for it [rather than suffer this truth to be wrested from him]." See *Certainty.*

Assyria, Religion of. See *Babylonians, Religion of.*

Astrology. See *Psychology,* E 3 ff.

Astruc, Jean (1684—1766). French physician and Biblical scholar; called the father of the documentary hypothesis because he was the first to hold that the use of Jahveh and Elohim in the OT indicated different writers or sources (views published in *Conjectures sur les memoirs originaux* . . .).

Astrup, Hans Joergen S. B. Aug. 30, 1852, at Grue, Soloer, Norway. Attended Trondhjem Cathedral School, 1865—1870; Christiania Univ., 1870 to 1876; Leipzig Univ., 1875—76, 1883 to 1884, 1892—93. Pastor, S. Aurdal, 1878 to 1880; Jevnaker, 1880; S. Land, 1881 to 1884. Missionary (Schreuder Mission), Entumeni, Zulu, S. Africa, 1884 to 1892; on furlough, Norway and U. S., 1892—93; Entumeni, 1893—1913; U. S.

1913—14; returned to Entumeni, 1914. Author, *Adolf Hammer,* 1911; *Blik paa amerikanske forholde,* 1893; *Kristus i det gamle testamente,* 1898; *Den hellige skrifts inspiration,* 1913; *Tilbake til skriften,* 1924; several schoolbooks in Zulu. He was ordained in 1878. Married Wilhelmina Margrethe Aabel, 1881 (died 1883); Thekla Elise Mathilde Breder, 1887 (died 1920); Anna Sophie Stenberg, 1924. He died in 1939.

Astrup, Johannes. Nephew of Hans. Missionary among Zulus, South Africa; b. Kristiania, Norway, Dec. 3, 1872.

Athanasian Creed. See *Ecumenical Creeds,* C.

Athanasius (ca. 296—373). "The Father of Orthodoxy" and one of the most imposing figures in the history of the Church. His life's history shows great heroism, fortitude, and faith. It was his great mission to vindicate against Arianism and Semi-Arianism the true deity of Christ and thus to safeguard the Christian faith against pagan dissolution. "*Athanasius contra mundum et mundus contra Athanasium.*" (A. against the world, and the world against A.) well illustrates the commanding position which he held in the controversies of his times. To him, more than to any other, is due the triumph of the Nicene Creed over a view which would have made of Christianity a thinly veneered paganism. His *Against the Gentiles* and *On the Incarnation* reveal his outstanding ability before the Arian controversy. His eminent gifts attracted the notice of Bishop Alexander, who appointed him deacon (319). In 325 he accompanied his bishop to the Council of Nicaea, where it was chiefly due to his dialectic skill and fearless testimony that the Arian heresy was condemned. The decisive terms, which came from the West, he more and more made his own. In 328 he became bishop of Alexandria, and continued the defense of the Nicene faith. Five times he was banished; twenty years he spent in exile. He died in 373, before the conclusion of the Arian controversy, but with the final victory of orthodoxy in sight. Additional important writings: *An Encyclical Letter to All Bishops* (341); *On the Decrees of the Council of Nicaea* (352); *On the Opinion of Dionysius of Alexandria* (352); *An Epistle to the Bishops of Egypt and Libya* (356); *Four Orations Against the Arians* (358); *An Apology Against the*

Arians. His commentary on the Psalter is marred by allegorizing.

A. Robertson's introduction to the works of Athanasius in the *Nicene and post-Nicene Fathers.* See bibliography under *Patristics.*

Atheism. Denial of the existence of God, a term which has been used in a variety of senses, depending upon the definition of God. The pagans applied the term to the early Christians because they rejected heathen idolatry. In the theological controversies of the early Christian Church the contending parties not uncommonly called each other atheists, and the Roman Church justified the burning of heretics by applying this epithet to them. — Aside from this improper usage the term has been variously used in scientific literature. In its widest sense it denotes the antithesis of theism and includes pantheism and deism. In a more restricted sense it denotes the denial of the Deity above and outside of the physical universe. In the most commonly accepted sense it is a positive dogmatic denial of anything that may be called God. The term is also used to express a merely negative attitude on the question of the existence of God, such as agnosticism (*q. v.*) and the so-called "practical atheism," which is not based on scientific reasoning, but is merely a refusal to worship any deity.

The materialism of the 18th and 19th centuries and biological evolution have given a strong impetus to atheistic trend of thought. In France the 18th century produced many antitheistic writers, among them the Encyclopedists * Diderot, Holbach, and Lamettrie. Voltaire called Holbach's *Système de la Nature* the Bible of atheism. German materialists of the 19th century: Feuerbach,* D. Fr. Strauss,* Vogt,* Buechner,* Haeckel,* were equally outspoken, Comte's Positivism,* English Secularism, whose two main exponents are Holyoake and Bradlaugh, and continental Socialism are essentially atheistic. Of the great religions of the world, Buddhism,* Jainism,* and the Sankhya system of Brahmanic philosophy (see *Brahmanism*) deny either positively or practically the existence of God.

The question as to whether it is really possible for a man to be an atheist in the commonly accepted sense, in his innermost conviction, must be answered in the negative. No amount of reasoning will eradicate from the human heart the God-given conviction that there is a Superior Being, and those who theoretically deny God's existence set up something else to take His place. Likewise, no people has ever been found entirely devoid of religious belief. The difficulties which atheism involves are expressed by Bacon: "I had rather believe all the fabulous tales in the Talmud and the Koran than that the universal frame is without mind." The hopelessness of antitheism is apparent in the confession of Romanes, who speaks of "the appalling contrast between the hallowed glory of that creed which once was mine and the lonely existence as now I find it."

Th. Graebner, *God and the Cosmos*, Eerdmans, Grand Rapids, Mich., 1932 (1st ed.).

Athenagoras. Athenian Christian apologist of the 2d century; wrote *Appeal on Behalf of Christians* to Marcus Aurelius and *On the Resurrection of the Dead;* sought a rational demonstration of the unity of God and the Trinity.

Atonement, The. According to the doctrine of both Old and New Testament Scriptures the salvation of the world was to be accomplished through the Messiah's substitutionary, sacrificial death. By making His soul and life an offering for sin, the Savior was to fulfill not only what was foreshadowed in the redemption of Israel from Egypt, but also in the redemptions of the Ceremonial Law and what was clearly foretold in prophecy. Mark 10:45; Matt. 20:28; 1 Tim. 2:6; Titus 2:14; 1 Pet. 1:18; Is. 53:10. Cf. 2 Sam. 7:23; Ex. 13:13; Num. 18:15. The Atonement, then, is the reconciling work of Jesus Christ, by which He, through the voluntary sacrifice of Himself on the cross once and for all on behalf and instead of sinful man, made satisfaction for the sins of the world and restored communion between God and man.

Over against various false and inadequate theories of the Atonement we hold firmly to the truth that the New Testament consistently represents the work of Christ as arising in the gracious will of the Father (2 Cor. 5:18, 19; Rom. 5:8; 8:32; Col. 1:19, 20; Eph. 1:9, 10; 1 Thess. 5:9; Titus 3:4; cf. 1 Pet. 1:3; John 3:16, and *passim,* 1 John 3:1), yet invariably regards it as the loving act (2 Cor. 5:14; 8:9; Gal. 1:4; 2:20; Rom. 8:37; Eph. 5:2; cf. John 10:11; Rev. 1:5) of a Mediator (1 Tim. 2:5, 6; cf. Heb. 9:15), producing

in the first instance a change in God's attitude towards the sinner (2 Thess. 1: 8, 9; Rom. 8:1; cf. vv. 7, 8), turning away wrath (1 Thess. 1:10; Rom. 5:9), removing trespasses (2 Cor. 5:19), and "providing a channel through which God might forgive sins as an act not only of mercy, but of justice (Rom. 3:26)."

No doubt is left in Scripture as to the objective character of the Atonement. It is not an act which depends for its completeness on some work of man. It stands complete before the preaching enters whereby comes hearing and faith. "When we were enemies, we were reconciled to God by the death of His Son." Rom. 5:10; cf. vv. 6, 8, 9; Col. 1:21, 22.

The doctrine is, then, securely founded in the Scriptures; indeed, it is the very heart of the Christian message, being the essential element in the ideas of reconciliation, propitiation, redemption, and salvation. Reconciliation and Atonement are everywhere, except Heb. 2:17, translations of the same Greek word, meaning the state of friendship and acceptance into which the Gospel introduces us. "Reconciliation" in the sense of Heb. 2:17 and atonement in the uniform sense of the Old Testament, as well as propitiation and expiation, are all different renderings of the same Hebrew and Greek words meaning "to appease" and also "to clear from guilt." The central thought in the divine work described by these terms is "substitution." Apart from the particular prepositions in the texts quoted ("on behalf of," "for," and "instead") three sets of phrases clearly teach this doctrine. 1. Christ was made a curse for us. Gal. 3:13; a similar phrase 2 Cor. 5:21. 2. He gave Himself as a sacrifice for our sins. 1 Cor. 15:3; 1 Tim. 2:6, 14; Heb. 7:27; 5:1, 3; 10:12; Rom. 5:6, 7; 1 Cor. 1:13; 5:7; 11:24; 1 Pet. 3:18; 4:1. 3. Christ gave His life for our life, or, we live by His death. Gal. 2:20; Rom. 14:15; 2 Cor. 5:15. The idea of substitution is in all these passages, and the term ("substitution," "vicarious atonement"), though not found in Scripture, is a convenient summary of them all.

Through the vicarious suffering of Christ, God and the entire human race are reconciled. In the resurrection of Christ we find the last answer to our doubts regarding salvation. By raising His Son from the dead, God has pronounced absolution upon the entire race. Cf. Rom. 5:6: justifying the ungodly; Rom. 3:23. The universality of the Atonement is emphasized 2 Cor. 5:14; 1 John 2:2; John 1:29. Through the means of grace the benefits of the Atonement are conferred upon the individual believers. 2 Cor. 5:18, 19.

The relation of faith to the Atonement is stated by the Augsburg Confession as follows (Apology, III, 40): "Trusting in our own fulfillment of the Law is sheer idolatry and blaspheming Christ, and in the end it collapses and causes our consciences to despair. Therefore this foundation shall stand forever, namely, that for Christ's sake we are accepted with God and justified by faith, not on account of our love and works. This we shall make so plain and certain that anybody may grasp it. As long as the heart is not at peace with God, it cannot be righteous; for it flees from the wrath of God, despairs, and would have God not to judge it. Therefore the heart cannot be righteous and accepted with God while it is not at peace with God. Now, faith alone makes the heart to be content and obtains peace and life, Rom. 5:1, because it confidently and frankly relies on the promise of God for Christ's sake. But our works do not make the heart content, for we always find that they are not pure. Therefore it must follow that we are accepted with God and justified by faith alone when in our hearts we conclude that God desires to be gracious unto us, not on account of our good works and fulfillment of the Law, but from pure grace, for Christ's sake."

The literature on this topic is immense. The Atonement occupies a prominent place in dogmatical works (see references under *Dogmatics*). Among the older works may be mentioned: Anselm, *Cur Deus Homo?* Baier, *Lehre v. d. Versoehnung;* Thomasius, *Christi Person und Werk,* Philippi, *Der taetige Gehorsam Christi.* Other literature: J. Schaller, "Die stellvertretende Versoehnung," *Theol. Quartalschrift,* VI:259 ff.; P. E. Kretzmann, *For Us,* CPH, 1939; L. S. Keyser, "The Lutheran View of the Atonement," *Luth. Quart.,* April, 1916; Thomas Coates, *The Vicarious Atonement in the Sacrificial Ritual of the Old Testament,* Concordia Seminary, St. Louis, 1942 (unpublished S. T. M. thesis); "Die stellvertretende Versoehnung," *Quartalschrift,* VII:1-29; 83—102. See references, *Atonement, Theories of; Grace.*

Atonement, Day of. See *Judaism.*

Atonement, Theories of. Among the theories of atonement, which objectors to the Scriptural doctrine of the vicarious atonement of Christ offer as substitutes, the following may be noted: 1. The *Accident Theory:* Christ's death was an accident, as unforeseen and unexpected as that of any other victim of man's hatred (Modernists); 2. The *Martyr Theory:* Christ gave up His life for a principle of truth which was opposed to the spirit of His day (Modernists); 3. The *Declaratory Theory:* Christ died to show men how greatly God loves them (Ritschl); 4. The *Moral-Example Theory (Moral-Influence Theory; Moral-Power View of the Atonement):* Christ died to influence mankind toward moral improvement (Socinians, Horace Bushnell); 5. The *Governmental Theory:* God made Christ an example of suffering to exhibit to erring man that sin is displeasing to Him; or: God's government of the world made it necessary for Him to evince His wrath against sin in Christ (Hugo Grotius; New England Theology); 6. The *Guaranty Theory:* Reconciliation is based not on Christ's expiation of sin, but on His guaranty to win followers and thus conquer human sinfulness (Schleiermacher, Kirn, Hofmann). All these and other man-made theories of the Atonement deny Christ's vicarious satisfaction and are based on the same leading thought: salvation by works, or salvation through personal sanctification, stimulated by Christ's death. JTM

R. S. Franks, *A History of the Doctrine of the Work of Christ in Its Ecclesiastical Development,* Hodder and Stoughton, 1918 (2 vols.).

Atrium. See *Architecture, Ecclesiastical,* 1, 7.

Atterbury, Francis (1662—1732). Anglican prelate; b. Bedford; ordained 1687; Bishop of Rochester 1713; banished as Jacobite 1723; d. Paris. Preacher; controversialist; politician.

Attitudes. See *Christian Teaching,* L 2.

Attributes of God. See *God.*

Attrition. A term used by Roman Catholic theologians. They call a hatred of sin arising from love of the offended God, perfect contrition; arising from other motives (fear of hell and of punishment, realization of the heinousness of sin), attrition. They teach that attrition alone does not justify, but that "by it the penitent, being assisted, prepares a way for himself unto justice" (Council of Trent, Sess. XIV, chap. 4), and that if, with attrition, he properly receives the Sacrament of Penance, he is justified. This teaching, taken in connection with the doctrine of *opus operatum* and the fact that true faith in Christ is demanded neither in attrition nor in the Sacrament of Penance (*Catechismus Romanus*, II, 5, 5), opens the way to a mechanical justification without Christ, partly through the acts of the penitent, partly through those of the priest. (See *Opus Operatum.*)

Attwood, Thomas (1765—1838). Mozart thought highly of Attwood, his pupil, who was organist of St. Paul's Cathedral for thirty years and among the first in England to recognize the genius of Mendelssohn. His compositions are surpassed by those of other English masters.

Auberlen, Karl August (1824—1864). B. at Fellbach; professor of theology at Basel; exponent of the Suabian theology of Bengel, Roos, and Rieger; wrote *The Prophet Daniel and the Apocalypse of John, Divine Revelation.*

Auburn Affirmation. A document signed by almost 1,300 ministers of the Northern Presbyterian Church as a protest against the Five Points adopted by the General Convention in 1923 against Modernism, namely: the inerrant inspiration of the Bible; the virgin birth of Christ; the atoning sacrifice of Christ; the resurrection, ascension, and intercession of Christ; and miracles. The Affirmation contended that the General Assembly could not constitutionally commit the Church to any "theories" concerning these five points and claimed, furthermore, that fellowship must be maintained with Modernists who employ various theories to explain these essential points.

Auburn Declaration. A declaration adopted by the New School Presbyterians in 1838, both as a protest against the Plan of Union, an instrument to foster interdenominational mission work, and as a re-statement of Calvinism against the charge of Arminianism.

Audians. A sect of anthropomorphites, the followers of a certain Audius, a Mesopotamian of the time of Arius, who founded this sect in protest against the worldly conduct of the clergy. It labored principally among the Goths.

Audientes. See *Catechetics*, 3.

Audio-visual. See *Christian Teaching*, D b.

Aufklaerung. See *Enlightenment.*

Augsburg Confession. See *Lutheran Confessions*, A.

Augsburg Diet. See *Lutheran Confessions*, A.

Augsburg Interim. See *Lutheran Confessions*, C 1.

Augsburg Publishing House. See *Publication Houses, Lutheran.*

Augsburg Religious Peace. Diet, 1555, a peace between the Emperor and the Protestant princes of Germany. The Emperor (Charles V) threatened war at Augsburg in 1530 and began the Smalcald War in 1546, held captive the Elector John Frederick of Saxony and the Landgrave Philip of Hesse, and would force the intolerable Augsburg Interim on the helpless Lutherans. The Elector Maurice of Saxony gathered an army to punish the Lutheran city of Magdeburg and then suddenly treacherously turned on the Emperor at Innsbruck and in 1552 wrung from him the Treaty of Passau, ratified in 1555 by the Augsburg Religious Peace. The princes of the Church were to tolerate their Lutheran subjects; the temporal princes might uphold their own religion in their own territories; if the subjects did not agree, they could emigrate; if a spiritual prince should turn Lutheran, the *reservatum ecclesiasticum* forced him to give up his office. The last two provisions caused the Thirty Years' War. The Augsburg Religious Peace established the break in the unity of the faith in Germany and accordingly granted religious liberty to the governments. The Lutherans could have secured a more favorable peace if they had had stronger leaders, because the Lutherans had a greater number of adherents. The arrangement whereby Catholic princes who became Protestant forfeited their estates lamed the Protestants' power of expansion.

Augsburg Seminary. See *Ministry, Education of*, XI G.

Augsburg Synod. A Lutheran synod of the Mississippi Valley. The German Augsburg Synod of the Ev. Luth. Church was organized May 5, 1876. It consisted largely of people who did not feel at home among the liberal men of the General Synod. It had congregations in Ohio, Illinois, Pennsylvania, Missouri, Indiana, Iowa, Wisconsin, Michigan, Maryland, Arkansas, and Tennessee. Its organ was *Der Sendbote von Augsburg*. In 1897 the Augsburg

Synod united with the Michigan Synod after the latter's withdrawal from the Synodical Conference. But in 1900 the two synods separated again on account of doctrinal differences, and in 1900 the Augsburg Synod joined the General Synod. In 1902 the Augsburg Synod was dissolved; many of its members entered the Ohio Synod.

August, Elector of Saxony (1526 to 1586) succeeded his brother Maurice in 1553; staunch Lutheran, but, hood-winked by the Crypto-Calvinists, he deposed the true Lutherans who opposed the Calvinizing Wittenberg Cate-chism and the Dresden Consensus. When, however, the Exegesis Perspicua appeared in 1574, which actually attacked the Lutheran doctrine of the Lord's Supper, he imprisoned the deceivers and spent 80,000 Taler to bring about the *Book of Concord* of 1580. For the success of this work "Father August" and his godly wife, "Mother Anna," prayed on bended knees.

Augustana. See *Lutheran Confessions,* A.

Augustana Book Concern. See *Publication Houses, Lutheran.*

Augustana Evangelical Lutheran Church. 1. Although the Augustana Lutheran Church did not come into being until the year 1860, it had its congregational beginnings more than a decade earlier.

2. In 1845 a small body of Swedish immigrants arrived in the Mississippi Valley and settled in Jefferson Co., Iowa. They called their community "New Sweden." In January, 1848, they organized a congregation. Because no ordained pastor was available, they called one of their own number to preach the Word and administer the Sacraments. His name was Magnus F. Hokanson, a shoemaker who once had planned to become a missionary to the Laplanders. Though lacking in theological education and somewhat vacillating in his doctrinal position, he was a fluent preacher. From the very beginning the New Sweden congregation was beset by proselytizers who attempted to unsettle the convictions of Hokanson and to disrupt the little flock. Only the timely arrival of stronger spiritual leaders from Sweden saved a remnant, and thus New Sweden became the starting point of the future Augustana Lutheran Church.

3. The first ordained Swedish Lutheran pastor to come to the Middle West was the Rev. Lars P. Esbjorn. Strongly pietistic, Esbjorn, like many other clergymen in Sweden, felt deeply distressed over the low state of morals and spirituality in the Established Church of his day. Wesleyan influences, emanating from England, to some extent affected his thinking, although he was thoroughly loyal to the Lutheran Confessions. Moved by reports of the spiritual destitution of his countrymen who had migrated in large numbers to America, he determined to cast his lot with them. Together with 146 emigrants, many of whom were from his own parish of Ostervola, in northern Sweden, Esbjorn, accompanied by his wife and six small children, sailed from Gävle on June 29, 1849.

4. Before they reached their destination at Andover, Ill., three months later, many of the party had succumbed to cholera and other diseases. Among the victims were two of Esbjorn's children. Esbjorn himself was stricken with cholera in Chicago, but recovered. When he finally reached Andover, he found his party disintegrating. Some had moved to other places, while others had deserted to sects. So hostile was the attitude of many Swedish immigrants toward the State Church of Sweden that Esbjorn was constrained to lay aside his clerical garb and use of liturgy. His bitter experiences with the sects, however, caused him to lose all enthusiasm for Wesleyanism. In his first published appeal to Scandinavians he warned them against proselytizers and exhorted them to remain loyal to the Augsburg Confession and Luther's Small Catechism. It was not until March 18, 1850, that he was able to effect the organization of a Lutheran congregation, and even then only ten persons were willing to become charter members. Andover thus became the first congregation of the future Augustana Synod to be organized and served by an ordained pastor.

5. Esbjorn's field of labor was soon extended to Moline, Rock Island, Galesburg, Princeton, Swedona, and other places. He also visited New Sweden, Iowa, where he gave encouragement to Hokanson. Beset by poverty and hardships, he made an extended trip in 1851 to Lutheran centers in the East to collect money for his missionary work. He obtained $2,200, of which $1,500 was given by Jenny Lind, the "Swedish Nightingale," then touring America. **This money helped to build small**

church structures at Andover, Moline, and New Sweden.

6. When the Evangelical Lutheran Synod of Northern Illinois * was organized in September, 1851, Esbjorn became a member, but only after taking exception to the doctrinal basis of the new body, which grudgingly acknowledged the Augsburg Confession as "mainly correct." Upon Esbjorn's request it was entered into the minutes of the Synod that his congregations had written into their constitutions "that the Symbolical Books of the Lutheran Church contain a correct summary and exposition of the divine Word; wherefore we declare and adopt them as the foundation of our faith and doctrine, next to the Holy Scriptures." Esbjorn's correspondence from this period reveals his hope that with the arrival of more Scandinavian Lutherans in the Middle West there would be a rising tide of confessional Lutheranism, and that the General Synod,* of which the Synod of Northern Illinois became a part, would eventually become dominated by the conservative element.

7. When immigration began to reach flood tide, Esbjorn wrote urgent appeals to the pietist leaders in the homeland, Peter Fjellstedt and Peter Wieselgren, asking them to send help. In response to these appeals the Rev. Tuve N. Hasselquist arrived in Galesburg, Ill., in 1852. This man was destined to become the leader of the future Augustana Synod as pastor, editor, college president, and head of the Church. Others who responded to the call were Erland Carlsson, who arrived in Chicago in 1853; Jonas Swensson, who came to Sugar Grove, Pa., and Jamestown, N. Y., in 1856, and O. C. T. Andren, who arrived at Moline, Ill., in the same year. Among theological students from Sweden who also answered the call were Eric Norelius, future historian of the Synod; Andrew Andreen, P. A. Cederstam, and Peter Sjoblom, all of whom were subsequently ordained by the Synod of Northern Illinois.

8. With the arrival of additional pastors from Sweden and Norway the conservative Scandinavian elements soon dominated the Synod of Northern Illinois. Within the Synod were a number of Norwegian congregations; these were organized as the Chicago Conference. The Swedes formed the Mississippi Conference. Friction, however, began to develop between the Scandinavians and the "New Lutherans." In 1852 the Synod of Northern Illinois had established an institution known as Illinois State University at Springfield, and in 1858 Esbjorn had become a professor at this institution. He soon found himself in conflict with the Neo-Lutheran elements, however, and on March 31, 1860, tendered his resignation, advised the Scandinavian students to go home, and left forthwith for Chicago. At a meeting of the two Scandinavian Conferences, held in Chicago, April 23, 1860, Esbjorn's action was endorsed, and initial steps were taken to organize an independent synod. This plan was consummated at Jefferson Prairie, Rock County, Wis., June 5—11, 1860, when representatives of the Swedish and Norwegian churches voted unanimously to found the *Scandinavian Evangelical Lutheran Augustana Synod in North America*. The constitution acknowledged the Holy Scriptures as "the revealed Word of God" and "the only infallible rule and standard of faith and practice," accepted the Apostolic, Nicene, and Athanasian Creeds, and declared adherence to "the unaltered Augsburg Confession as a short and correct summary of the principal Christian doctrines, understood as developed and explained in the other Symbolical Books of the Lutheran Church."

9. Hasselquist was elected president of the Synod. Augustana Seminary was established at Chicago, with Esbjorn as its head. Ten years later, in 1870, the Norwegians withdrew peaceably from the Synod, leaving the Swedish Lutherans to work out their own destiny.

10. The formation of the Augustana Synod was regarded by many as presaging the breakup of the General Synod, due to doctrinal laxity, and this occurred in 1867, when the General Council was formed. Delegates from the Augustana Synod attended meetings of the Council from the very beginning, and in 1870, the year of the Norwegian withdrawal, the Synod formally affiliated with the Council. However, when the General Council merged with the General Synod and the United Synod of the South in 1918 to form the United Lutheran Church in America, the Augustana Synod voted not to become a part of the new union. In 1930 it participated with four other Lutheran bodies in the formation of the American Lutheran Conference.* It was also one of the original founders of the National Lutheran Council.* It is a member of the Lutheran World Federation and of the World Council of Churches. In

1948 the Synod adopted a new constitution, changing its name to *Augustana Evangelical Lutheran Church*.

11. While other Lutherans in America of European origins have been split into various segments, the Augustana Lutheran Church is unique in that it is the only Lutheran general body in this country or Canada of Swedish origin. It has never experienced a schism. The Evangelical Mission Covenant Church of America, although it had its roots in the "free church" movement in Sweden and has many congregations, pastors, and members who have regarded themselves as Lutherans, has never been a confessional Lutheran Church. Bitter theological controversies with this group regarding the doctrine of the Atonement marked the early history of the Augustana Church.

12. In its home mission outreach the Augustana Church has extended its activities from the Atlantic to the Pacific as well as into Canada. Its congregations are found in thirty-five States and the District of Columbia as well as five Canadian provinces. The Church's major divisions are known as Conferences, thirteen in number, and these in turn are divided into Districts. With the organization in 1938 of the synodical Board of Home Missions (Board of American Missions since 1949) home missions activities were transferred from the various Conferences to the Church as a whole. This marked an important step in a strong centralization trend which has been noted toward the middle of the 20th century.

13. As early as 1862 the Augustana Synod contributed funds to the Swedish Missionary Society in Stockholm and the Hermannsburg Mission to help spread the Gospel to pagan lands. When the Synod became a part of the General Council in 1870, it shared in the mission work of that body in India. It has also co-operated in Puerto Rico, where the Lutheran Church was planted by an Augustana pastor. A China mission movement, launched in Minnesota in 1902, was officially taken over by the Church in 1908. The Synod's field is in Honan Province, but, as a result of the Japanese invasion and subsequent Communist revolution, the Augustana Mission has spread its activities to other parts of China. In 1922 the Synod took over the Leipzig Mission in Tanganyika, Africa, from which German missionaries had been expelled in World War I. When these returned in 1924, the Augustana Mission opened a new field among the Iramba people in the same territory. Three large German missions again became orphaned with the outbreak of World War II, whereupon the Augustana Mission cared for them under the jurisdiction of the Lutheran World Federation.

14. The Augustana Lutheran Church and its Conferences maintain a theological seminary, four liberal arts colleges, and a junior college. Augustana College and Theological Seminary, which came into being with the organization of the Synod in 1860, was moved from Chicago to Paxton, Ill., in 1863. Twelve years later it found a permanent location in Rock Island, Ill. The seminary became a separate entity in 1948. Gustavus Adolphus College had its beginnings in Red Wing, Minn., in 1862, was subsequently moved to East Union, Carver County, Minn., where it bore the name St. Ansgar's Academy, and in 1876 was permanently located in St. Peter, Minn. It is owned and controlled by the Minnesota Conference. Bethany College, noted for its "Messiah" festivals, had its beginnings in 1881 at Lindsborg, Kans., as an academy. The Kansas Conference assumed jurisdiction over the school in 1884. Upsala College, owned and supported by the New York and New England Conferences, was founded in 1893. First housed in Brooklyn churches, it was moved to Kenilworth, N. J., in 1898, and finally found a home in East Orange, N. J. Luther College, Wahoo, Nebr., an academy and junior college, opened its doors in 1883. It is owned by the Nebraska Conference. In addition to these institutions, the Augustana Lutheran Church co-operates with other Lutheran bodies in maintaining a theological seminary at Saskatoon, Sask., for the training of a Canadian ministry and in support of Pacific Lutheran College, Parkland, Wash., and Texas Lutheran College, Seguin, Tex.

15. Eleemosynary work is conducted by the Church and its Conferences in various areas. Immanuel Deaconess Institute, where the Synod trains a female diaconate, is virtually a colony of mercy. Hospitals throughout the country number 11; homes for the aged, 17; children's homes, 10. There are also 10 hospices and inner mission homes for young women, and two immigrant and seamen's homes.

16. The first publication venture in the Augustana Synod occurred in 1855, when Hasselquist, in Galesburg, Ill., began printing a newspaper known as

The Homeland: the Old and the New.
A year later he started an exclusively
religious publication known as *The True
Homeland.* This became the forerunner
of *Augustana,* the Church's official
Swedish publication. The Synod's Eng-
lish publication, *The Lutheran Com-
panion,* which was launched as the
Alumnus in 1892, was merged with
Augustana to form *The Augustana Lu-
theran* on January 1, 1950. Augustana
Book Concern, located in Rock Island,
Ill., is the Church's publishing house.
Founded originally as a private corpo-
ration, it was taken over by the Synod
in 1889.

17. Auxiliary organizations include
the Women's Missionary Society, which
has given strong support to the missionary program of the Church; the
Augustana Brotherhood, a laymen's
group; and the Augustana Luther
League, the youth organization of the
Church.

18. While the Augustana Lutheran
Church in polity and practice is theoretically congregational, it has carried
over from the State Church of Sweden
a concept of the Church as something
more than the sum total of its local
congregations. It has, however, not
adopted the episcopal form of government, as the Church of Sweden has.
All candidates for the ministry are ordained by the president of the Church
at synodical meetings. While a call
from a congregation is essential for
ordination, the pastor through ordination becomes a minister of the Church.
The constitution of the Church explicitly states that the Church "shall
consist of all pastors and congregations
regularly connected with it."

19. Services in Swedish are a thing
of the past, except in rare instances.
However, much of the rich hymn heritage of the Church of Sweden, as well
as its order of worship, has been preserved in translated form. Use of the
Common Service was also authorized
when the present *Hymnal* was published
in 1925. Church headquarters are at
2445 Park Ave., Minneapolis, Minn. EER

The presidents of the Augustana
Synod have been: T. N. Hasselquist,
1860—1870; Jonas Swensson, 1870—1873;
Eric Norelius, 1874—1881; Erland Carlsson, 1881—1888; S. P. A. Lindahl, 1888
to 1891; P. J. Sward, 1891—1899; Eric
Norelius, 1899—1911; L. A. Johnston,
1911—1918; G. A. Brandelle, 1918—1935;
P. O. Bersell, 1935—51; Oscar A.
Benson, 1951—. The interest of
the Augustana Synod in Lutheran

mergers and union and also in inter-
church agencies was shown by the
following resolutions of the 1950 convention: to become a charter member
of the National Council of Churches of
Christ in the United States of America;
to approve the merger plan affecting
the participating bodies in the National
Lutheran Council. The Synod is a
member of the Lutheran World Federation. Baptized membership: 459,363
(1950).

Eric Norelius, *De Svenska Luterska
Församlingarnas Historia i Amerika,*
Augustana Book Concern; George M.
Stephenson, *The Religious Aspects of
Swedish Immigration,* Univ. of Minne-
sota Press; *The American Origin of the
Augustana Synod,* from Contemporary
Lutheran Periodicals, 1851—1860, Au-
gustana Historical Publication, IX, by
O. Fridtjof Ander and Oscar L. Nord-
strom; *Century of Life and Growth,*
1848—1948, Augustana Book Concern;
Abdel Ross Wentz, *The Lutheran
Church in American History;* O. N.
Olson, "The Augustana Lutheran
Church in America," vol. 1, *Pioneer
Period,* Rock Island, 1950.

Augustana Historical Society. See
Archives.

Augustana Theological Seminary.
See *Ministry, Education of,* XI E.

Augusti, Johann C. W. (1771—1841).
B. at Eschenberga; d. at Coblenz. Studied theology at Jena. Professor of
philosophy there, 1800, and of Oriental
languages, 1823; of theology at Breslau,
1812; at Bonn, 1819; counselor of the
consistory at Coblenz, 1828; its president, 1835. He wrote in the field of
archaeology, history of dogma, and introduction to the OT.

Augustine. One of the greatest of
the Latin Church Fathers and one of
the outstanding figures of all ages;
b. Tagaste, 354; d. at Hippo Regius, 430,
both in Africa. His father, Patricius,
although a member of the council of his
home town, was not particularly distinguished for either learning or wealth
and remained hostile to the Christian
Church until shortly before his death,
in 371, when he received Baptism. His
mother, Monica, on the other hand, was
a consecrated, self-sacrificing, honorable woman, whose Christian virtues
her illustrious son rightly extolled in
his writings. Augustine received the
rudiments of his education at Tagaste
and was there also enrolled as catechumen, even being near Baptism. On

account of the fine progress which he made in his studies, his father sent him first to Madaura, and then to Carthage. At the latter city he was drawn into the moral rottenness of the day, with some degree of sexual excesses, also living in common-law relation with a woman, by whom he had a son, Adeodatus, in 372. He studied rhetoric and philosophy and once more showed a strong inclination toward Christianity, but came under Manichaean * influence, holding to their doctrines for nine years, although he did not become a formal convert to the sect. After he had finished his studies, he became a teacher of grammar at Tagaste, returning to Carthage a year later as a teacher of rhetoric. It was in 385 that he was sent to Milan, Italy, as teacher of rhetoric, and this proved to be the turning point in his career, for here he came under the influence of Ambrose.* At first he was attracted only by the great bishop's eloquence, and for a while Neo-Platonism * exerted a counterinfluence upon him, but finally he was induced to take up the Epistles of St. Paul, and the study of Romans resulted in his conversion in the summer of 386. He returned to Africa about two years after his Baptism, which took place at Milan in 387. About the year 391 he sold his inheritance at Hippo and was ordained presbyter. He founded a monastery with a clerical school and entered into a controversy with the Manichaeans. In 395 he was consecrated as coadjutor to Bishop Valerius of Hippo and very soon succeeded to the office.

For more than thirty years Augustine was the leading theologian and leader of the Church in Africa, his influence at the various synods and councils being decisive. As a defender of the orthodox faith he stands head and shoulders above his contemporaries, although in some points he did not reach the clearness in the doctrine of sin and grace which is found in the later writings of Luther. But he fought the Pelagian heresy * consistently, chiefly in the interest of letting the grace of God stand forth in the fullness of its beauty over against man. Among his chief writings are: De Gratia et Libero Arbitrio (Of Grace and of Free Will), De Catechizandis Rudibus (a treatise on the art of catechizing), De Doctrina Christiana (Of the Christian Doctrine), De Civitate Dei (Of the City of God), and his Confessions.

The individual books on Augustine number in the hundreds, a large number being of recent date. Much was written on the fifteen-hundredth anniversary of his death (1930). Many phases of his life and theology are treated in separate volumes. For references consult the general works under Patristics. The first outstanding edition of his works was produced by J. Amerbach, Basel, 1506 (reprint, Paris, 1515). His works are given in J. P. Migne, Patrologia, and the Viennese Corpus Scriptorum Ecclesiasticorum Latinorum. For Augustine's influence on Luther: Adolf Hamel, Der junge Luther und Augustin, Bertelsmann, Guetersloh, rev. 1935.

Augustine of Canterbury (d. 604). Arrived in England in 597 with Frankish clergy and after converting Ethelbert, king of Kent, converted and baptized many Anglo-Saxons. Thereupon the Pope made him the first archbishop of Canterbury.

Augustinian Monks (Hermits of St. Augustine, Augustinian Friars; to be distinguished from Augustinian Canons, for which see Canon, Regular). This order was formed in 1265 by Pope Alexander IV by means of a merger of several small hermit bodies. It was intended as a counterpoise to the growing power of the older mendicant orders (Franciscans and Dominicans) and was linked more closely to the Papacy than they. The so-called Augustinian Rule furnished the basis of its rather strict regulations. Soon the hermit character was exchanged for that of mendicancy, and the Augustinians became known as the fourth of the great mendicant orders (see Mendicant Monks). The order spread rapidly and in its prime had no fewer than 2,000 monasteries and 30,000 members. In the fourteenth century a decline in discipline led to reforms, as a result of which part of the order became barefooted monks.* The German "congregation" of the order was divided into four provinces. Into the monastery at Erfurt, in the Saxon province, Martin Luther entered in 1505, tortured himself with rigorous privations of every kind, and went about with a sack as a mendicant, or beggar. The provincial, John von Staupitz, referred him to Christ and encouraged him to study the Scriptures, caused him to be called to the University of Wittenberg, and remained his friend though he himself continued in the Roman Church. So many other Augustinians, however, including Staupitz's successor, accepted Luther's doctrine that the German congregation of the order ceased to exist as early as 1526 and was re-established, as a province, only in 1895. The Augustinians have been active chiefly as teachers and writers, but also as missionaries. They were the missionary pioneers in the Philippines. The motherhouse in the United States is at Villanova, Pa.

Augustinianism. Augustine was bishop of Hippo, North Africa, and died A. D. 430. Augustinianism is the theological system of Augustine. It involves the following points of doctrine: 1. Infant Baptism. Children are by original sin under the power of the devil, from which they are freed by Baptism. 2. Original sin, by which the entire human nature has become physically and morally corrupt. 3. Free will. In man's present depraved state the freedom of the will has been entirely lost; man can will and do only evil. 4. Grace. If man is converted, it is the result of the operation of divine grace. Man can do nothing without grace nor anything against it; it is irresistible. 5. Predestination. Of the corrupt mass of humanity God decreed from eternity to save a few. To those destined for salvation He gives effective means of grace. On the rest merited destruction falls. Christ came into the world and died only for the elect. The predestinarian teaching of Augustine is in a narrower sense called Augustinianism. Calvin went beyond Augustine by maintaining that the fall of man was itself predestinated by God (supralapsarianism).

Aulén, Gustav. See *Sweden, Lutheran Church in,* 6.

Auricular Confession. See *Confession.*

Aurifaber, Andreas (1514—59). B. in Breslau; d. at Koenigsberg. Studied at Wittenberg and Padua. Rector in Danzig and Elbing; professor of physics and medicine in Koenigsberg; son-in-law of Andreas Osiander and active member of his party. Opposed by Flacius.

Aurifaber, Johann (1517—68), brother of Andreas. Studied at Wittenberg and Magdeburg, like Andreas a friend of Melanchthon. Rector in Breslau; professor at Rostock; chief author of the church order of Mecklenburg, 1551—1552; professor at Koenigsberg, 1554; helped to draw up the Prussian

church order; tried to mediate in the Osiandrian controversy; pastor and school inspector at Breslau, 1567, where he died.

Aurifaber, Johann (1519—75). Studied at Wittenberg, 1537. Tutor to the count of Mansfeld, 1540—44; Luther's famulus, 1545; witnessed Luther's death, 1546; court preacher at Weimar, 1550; went to Eisleben, 1561; pastor at Erfurt, 1566. He was a co-editor of the Jena edition of Luther's works, editor of a volume of Luther's Latin letters, and of the *Tischreden.* He died at Erfurt.

Aurogallus (Goldhahn), Matthaeus (1490—1543). B. in Bohemia; professor of Hebrew in Wittenberg, 1521; his Hebrew Grammar came out in 1525 and 1539; aided Luther in the translation of the Old Testament, especially in the revision of 1540.

Aurora Community. See *Communistic Societies.*

Austin Agreement (Settlement). See *Madison Agreement.*

Australia, Lutheranism in. The history of Lutheranism in Australia dates back to 1836, when Pastor August Ludwig Christian Kavel (1796 to 1860), of Klemzig, near Frankfurt on the Oder, Prussia, went to London for the purpose of making arrangements for an entire congregation to emigrate to America or Australia. The reason for the contemplated emigration was the manner in which the Prussian Union was being forced on confessional-minded Lutherans. Emigration agents in London persuaded Kavel to take his flock to South Australia. The emigrants arrived at Port Adelaide in November, 1838, and formed a short-lived settlement which they called Klemzig, a few miles from what is now the center of Adelaide. In 1839 another colony of several hundred souls was planted at Hahndorf; and in 1841 Pastor Gotthold Daniel Fritzsche (1797—1863) led another band of emigrants who founded Bethany and Lobethal. Other congregations were founded. Being filled with great zeal for the true worship of God and its perpetuation, these Lutherans had established a synod soon after their arrival. However, the young Church was soon disrupted by doctrinal controversies. Pastor Kavel's chiliastic teachings, his attitude toward the Lutheran Confessions, and his views on church government led to a rupture in 1846. Henceforth the followers of

Fritzsche and of Kavel pursued separate ways. In 1864, after both leaders had died, there was a brief *rapprochement;* but this "Confessional Union" did not lead to synodical reunion and was dissolved ten years later on the question of calling pastors from seminaries not genuinely Lutheran (Basel). The followers of Kavel were now known as the Immanuel Synod. The antichiliastic party became the Ev. Luth. Synod of South Australia; then, after the organization of other districts, the Ev. Luth. Synod in Australia; finally, since 1941, the Ev. Luth. Church of Australia.

A. 1. The body now known as the *Ev. Luth. Church of Australia* (E. L. C. A.) developed along sound, conservative Lutheran lines and shows a steady, if slow, growth externally. Pastor Fritzsche had founded a college and seminary as early as 1845 (Lobethal); but the doctrinal controversies then raging, as well as many other labors that claimed his time, caused the closing of the school in 1855 after it had furnished three pastors. A number of missionaries sent by the Dresden Mission Society, 1838—1840 (Teichelmann, Schuermann, Meyer, Klose), increased the numbers of the ministry; later the Church depended on Hermannsburg, Germany, for ministers. In 1876, a private academy at Hahndorf was taken over by the synod. It turned out some good parish school teachers, but was closed owing to lack of support (1885).

2. With this decade began the "Missourian" influence in the history of the E. L. C. A. Pastor Ernst Homann, having become acquainted with "Missouri" through *Lehre u. Wehre,* sought counsel from Dr. Walther. He became an enthusiastic "Missourian" and convinced others of the correctness of the position upheld by that Church. In 1881 Pastor Caspar E. Dorsch came as the first emissary of the St. Louis Seminary and took charge of Bethlehem Church in Adelaide. Other men followed; but far greater was the number of young Australian Lutherans who received or completed their theological training at various schools of the Missouri Synod: Fort Wayne, St. Louis, Springfield. This movement was most pronounced at the turn of the century, when the third attempt to found a college and seminary (at Murtoa, Victoria, 1890) had not yet led to the inception of seminary classes nor of the higher preparatory classes. The abandonment of the Murtoa College was staved off by

the advice of Dr. A. L. Graebner, who visited Australia at the request of Pres. Ernst Homann (d. 1915) in 1902. Next year the Rev. C. F. Graebner, who had been called as principal of the college, arrived and began his work. In 1905 the college and seminary was removed to Unley, a suburb of Adelaide. For the next 25 years all regularly called teachers (G. Koch, M. T. Winkler, Wm. Zscheh, H. Hamann) were graduates of the St. Louis Seminary. The institution is co-educational since 1927. Since 1912 Concordia College (as it is called) has regularly supplied the Church with theological graduates (117 up to 1947). Concordia College has also furnished most of the parish school teachers. In 1946 the Queensland Concordia College at Toowomba, Queensland, was launched. This school (co-educational and numbering about 40 pupils) is designed as a secondary school, but will also offer training to pretheological students.

3. The parish school system, which was maintained from the organization of the Church, suffered greatly during World War I, when all schools in South Australia were closed by the government. Rehabilitation has been slow, but the cause is still ardently championed.

4. The official organ is *The Australian Lutheran,* published since 1913; the *Kirchenbote,* founded 1873, succumbed some years ago owing to lack of readers.

5. Home mission work, which languished for many years because practically all the old settlers lived in the country, has been more energetically pursued in the last twenty years. A mission station for work among aboriginals is maintained at Koonibba, on the so-called West Coast of South Australia (native congregation, school, children's home, hospital) since 1901, when Rev. C. A. Wiebusch (St. Louis graduate) became the first missionary in charge. After supporting the work of the Missouri Synod in China and India with means and a few men, the Church acquired a foreign mission field of its own in 1935: the Rooke-Siassi group of islands northeast of New Guinea. This enterprise suffered much from the Japanese invasion in World War II; but the work of restoration has been going on rapidly. In 1951 the work was extended to the mainland of New Guinea.

6. *Statistics:* The E. L. C. A. is organized in five districts: South Australia (107 congregations), Victoria (52), New South Wales (27), Queensland (44), New Zealand (8), Western Australia,

which belongs to the South Australia District (9).

B. 1. *The United Ev. Luth. Church in Australia* (U. E. L. C. A.) came into being in 1921 after a checkered history of secessions and reunions, of the affiliation and re-affiliation of various synods. The branch which followed Pastor Kavel experienced a secession movement (1860, the year of Kavel's death); the seceders linked up with the *Ev. Luth. Synod of Victoria* (founded 1856 by Pastor Matthias Goethe). Goethe worked energetically among the many Germans who had come to Victoria, though not from the religious reasons that had prompted the first immigration into South Australia. Full Lutheran conviction was lacking; and through Goethe's successor in leadership, Pastor Herman Herlitz, the influence of the "United" *(unierte)* Basel Missionary Institute, as well as "United" influence in general, became more pronounced. Hence the union of the Ev. Luth. Victoria Synod with the Kavel branch, which took the name of Ev. Luth. Immanuel Synod, was the signal for the dissolution of the "Confessional Union" (1874). The affiliation of the Immanuel Synod and the Victoria Synod, known as the Ev. Luth. General Synod, endured for ten years. The separation (1884) was caused by the same circumstance that had led the conservative Lutherans (later E. L. C. A.) to part from Immanuel ten years earlier: the determination of the Victoria Synod to continue calling *unierte* pastors from Basel. With the Victoria Synod went a part of the Immanuel Synod that called itself the Immanuel Synod *auf alter Grundlage* (a. a. G.). Continuing under the name of *Ev. Luth. General Synod*, these two were joined in 1889 by the laxer of the two Lutheran Churches that had been organized (1885) in distant Queensland, where missionaries and lay helpers sent by "Father" Gossner had operated since 1837 and where a heavy German immigration had set in subsequently: the *Ev. Luth. Synod of Queensland*. The more confessional-minded pastors (mostly Hermannsburg men), who had given their organization the name of United German-Scandinavian Ev. Luth. Synod of Queensland, joined the Immanuel Synod in 1910 to form the Ev. Luth. Church Union (*Kirchenbund*). This body continued its connection with Neuendettelsau and Hermannsburg, whence it drew its supply of ministers. Finally, owing, no doubt, in part to experiences during

World War I, the General Synod joined with the *Kirchenbund*, and the U. E. L. C. A. was organized at Ebenezer, South Australia (Mar. 8, 1921). One small body that had separated from the E. L. C. A. in 1902 was for a number of years a district of the Ohio Synod (U. S.) but joined the U. E. L. C. A. in 1926. One reason for the merger was the situation in the field of foreign missions; for the Immanuel Synod together with the Iowa Synod (U. S.) had long supported the work of the Neuendettelsau Mission Society in what was the German New Guinea. After World War I this territory was mandated to Australia, which was to dispose of the German mission. Since the government would not give the mission to a Church outside Australia, the bodies mentioned formed a merger strong enough to handle the matter. In this they were supported by the Iowa Synod, which sent its president, Dr. Fr. Richter, to advise the Australian Lutherans. When German missionaries were permitted to return later, the field was divided between the German mission and the Iowa Synod (subsequently the American Luth. Church), the U. E. L. C. A. taking an active part in the work under the leadership of their Missions Director, the Rev. F. O. Thiele. The partnership with the American Lutheran Church continued through and after World War II. Thus the U. E. L. C. A. is practically in fellowship with the American Luth. Church, without, however, necessarily sharing its doctrinal position altogether. It has in the past maintained connections with various Lutheran churches in Germany. In its constitution it declares its acceptance of the Scriptures "as the revealed Word of God and the sole rule and norm of faith and living," and of all Confessions of the Lutheran Church "as the pure, unadulterated exposition and explanation of the divine Word and will." At its organization theologically heterogeneous, it is safe to say that the body as a whole has progressed toward sound confessional Lutheranism.

2. A college was opened at Point Pass, South Australia (1895), remained small, and was devoted chiefly to the training of parish school teachers. As late as 1919 young men went to Neuendettelsau and to Dubuque, Iowa, for theological training. The formation of the U. E. L. C. A. led to the founding of a small seminary at Tanunda, South Australia; but in 1923 college and seminary were moved to North Adelaide

(where Angas College had been purchased). Wartime difficulties led to the acquisition of extensive properties in North Walkerville, a suburb of Adelaide, where the co-educational high school classes are now quartered and taught; the "pro-seminary" and theological classes are lodged in the North Adelaide property. In 1945 a college was opened at Brisbane, Queensland; in 1948 a boarding school with elementary and secondary classes was launched at Walla Walla, New South Wales. Of late there has been a slow revival of the parish school, which had disappeared; five such schools were in existence in 1948.

3. The Church not only actively supports the New Guinea mission, but also maintains two mission stations for aborigines (at Hermannsburg, Central Australia, and Hope Valley, Queensland).

4. The U. E. L. C. A. has 4 districts (1946). The official organ is *The Lutheran Herald.*

5. Metropolitan congregations in Sydney and Melbourne left the U. E. L. C. A. in 1923 and 1934, respectively; their confessional status is sufficiently characterized by the fact that they joined the then German *Reichskirche* in 1929 and 1934. HH

C. *Statistics.* An important factor in the Lutheran statistics of Australia is the immigration wave from Europe after World War II. In 1946 the E. L. C. A. numbered 101 pastors in charge of congregations, 247 congregations, 152 preaching stations, 29,026 souls, 19,753 communicants. The U. E. L. C. A. numbered 96 pastors (including teachers at the seminary and 11 retired pastors), 29,681 baptized members and 20,645 communicant members. The official census of 1947 listed the total Lutheran community in Australia as numbering 66,891, exclusive of aboriginals. By 1950 the E. L. C. A. and U. E. L. C. A. had made arrangements to care for 20,000 anticipated Lutheran immigrants.

Australia (Missions). 1. The mission work among the Australian aborigines has met with indifferent success. The original Australians are a dying race (estimated between 300,000 and 350,000 in 1788; 1944 census: 47,014 full-blooded natives, 24,881 half-caste). The inveterate nomadic habits of these people were formidable obstacles in the way of Christian evangelists. Missionary endeavors almost invariably took the form of the mission station with church, school, children's home, hospitals, and cottages for those who cared to stay. Men and women who cannot remain at the station are followed up by the missionaries at their places of work or cared for by the nearest resident pastor. So far it has not been found possible to create a real community and community life for the natives apart from the mission station and supervised government camps. Yet the mission stations have had good success in evangelizing the people as well as in lifting them to a higher level socially and economically.

2. History. In 1823 the Society for the Propagation of the Gospel expressed its willingness to assist in establishing a mission in New South Wales, but met with no success. In 1825 the London Missionary Society made an attempt near Lake Macquarie, in the vicinity of Sydney, to win the aborigines for Christ, but also with no success. In 1830 the Church Missionary Society opened a station at Wellington Bay, some 200 miles from Sydney. The mission was discontinued in 1842. Missionaries sent by the Dresden Mission Society came out in 1838 and 1840; but they were compelled to relinquish their work and joined the ranks of the Lutheran ministry. In 1840 the Gossner Mission began to operate at Moreton Bay and at Keppel Bay (Queensland), but without lasting success. In 1851 the Society for the Propagation of the Gospel opened stations in South Australia at Povindie on the Spencer Gulf, with some degree of success. The Moravians began a mission (1859) in the Wimmera District of Victoria. In the course of the following years, work was taken up by the Anglican Church, the Presbyterians, the *Gesellschaft fuer innere und aeussere Mission im Sinne der lutherischen Kirche*, various Lutheran bodies, the Interdenominational Mission Society, the New South Wales Aborigines' Mission. In some cases stations had to be given up because of drought, illness, the trekking off or the dying out of natives. Of other non-European peoples there are very few in Australia: Chinese, Hindus, Indians, Japanese, Malays, South Sea Islanders, and others. The "White Australian Policy" excludes them, except for special cases. Mission work on a limited scale carried out among them by various religious bodies was not entirely without success. Of the excluded Kanakas not a few had become Christians and returned to their native islands as witnesses for Christ.

Comprehensive statistics are not available. The Koonibba Mission Station (E. L. C. A.) numbered 500 souls in 1948; the reports on the two mission stations of the U. E. L. C. A. show a total of 576 souls (1946). HH

Australia, Evangelical Lutheran Church of. See *Australia, A.*

Australia, United Evangelical Lutheran Church in. See *Australia, B.*

Australian Lutheran. See *Australia, A 4.*

Austria. Since World War I, constituted as the Republic of Austria, with an area of some 32,360 square miles, and a population of 6,760,000, with Upper and Lower Austria, Styria, Salzburg, Carinthia, Tyrol, and Vorarlberg. The territory included in this country was originally Christianized at the time of Charlemagne, who defeated the Avari and placed their land in charge of a margrave, calling it the Ostmark. The name Austria was first officially given in 996, and the main object of this territory was to act as a buffer country against the barbarians of the Hungarian plains. The Benedictines, who were chiefly instrumental in evangelizing the country, founded elaborate monasteries and established the Christian Church (Catholicism). Between 1483 and 1804 Austria, under the Hapsburgs, was most intimately concerned in all the fortunes of the German Empire. Maximilian I really established the empire and incidentally fixed its relation to the Pope, especially by uniting Spain and the Netherlands under his dominion, so that as a result Philip II became one of the most powerful Catholic monarchs the world has ever seen. At the time of Charles V the Reformation gained a foothold in Austria, and its influence became a very strong factor, in spite of the efforts of the Catholic hierarchy to stem its progress until the Counter-Reformation,* when 450 families of Protestant ministers were driven out of the country. It seems that about two thirds of the inhabitants had become friends of the evangelical truth. But the cause of Protestantism received a severe setback by the Edict of Restitution of Ferdinand II, in 1629, so that the Evangelical congregations had to fight for their very existence. So severe did the persecutions of the Protestants become that large areas of the country were almost depopulated by the zealotism of their rulers, as in the case of the

Salzburgers. (See *Salzburgers.*) Since the beginning of the eighteenth century, Protestantism has existed within the area of Austria with varying fortunes. The greatest victory for the hierarchy was the Concordat of 1855, which practically made the Pope the ruler of the country. But six years later the Evangelicals again won a pronounced success, and the Patent guaranteeing them religious liberty and ecclesiastical independence was followed by the recall of the Concordat, in 1870. The situation has not been materially changed by the First World War, and the Evangelical Church enjoys a nominal equality, chief difficulty being the establishment of religious schools.

The Catholic Church is both numerically and politically by far the strongest church body in the Republic of Austria. There are two archbishoprics and a corresponding number of episcopal sees in the country. Of its population, which numbers somewhat more than six millions, about four fifths are Roman Catholic. It has countless Roman Catholic societies, institutions, and foundations. In almost every parish there are brotherhoods and societies for prayer, associations of both sexes and of all ages, societies of priests, congregations of Mary, Franciscan Tertiaries, and the Society of the Holy Family. Children and the youth are cared for in protectories and kindergartens, orphan asylums, refectories, boarding schools, refuges, training schools for apprentices, and the like.

The Protestant, or Evangelical, churches of Austria are not strong at present, the total number of their adherents being about 250,000. The movement away from Rome has gained some force in the German sections of Steiermark. Among the institutions of the inner mission of the Evangelical Church the Deaconess Mother House of Gallneukirchen is important, since it has now been established for more than seventy-five years. There is another Deaconess Mother House at Graz, and the number of orphanages, refuges, and asylums has increased during the last few years.

Other church organizations that have some adherents in Austria are the Greek Catholics, the Armenians, the Old Catholics, the Anglicans, and the Mennonites. The Jews are strong in Lower Austria, and there are some followers of Islam in Vienna and in Styria. Some work has been done in recent years by English and American denominations, but they have been regarded as undenominational before the law and were allowed to worship only in private.

Authenticity. See *Isagogics.*

Authority. As in all spheres of human endeavor that impose or involve responsibilities, privileges, obligations, and duties, there is and must be authority, so there is authority also in the Church. This authority was bought and established by the blood of Christ and is given to the Church by Him, to be exercised by the Church as such or conferred by the Church on its individual members. Authority in the Church, then, is an authority of the Word of Christ, which must always be the *norma normans* in confessing, teaching, and living. Authority must be in perfect accord with the Christian liberty which is ours through the redemption in Christ Jesus. Since authority is given by the Scriptures to the spiritual priesthood of all believers (see *Keys, Office of*), of which, in fact, delegated authority is an emanation, those who have been given authority cannot lord it over the Christian congregation. They are stewards rather than masters, servants rather than lords, and accountable to their God in their respective congregations, which, though it consist of only two or three members, has all rights and spiritual powers. Those who exercise these powers for the congregation must administer such authority (1) in the fear of God, (2) for the welfare of the Church, (3) in the interest of their fellow men, and (4) unto the glory of God. C. f. HS, *Abiding Word*, I: 410—441.

Dist. Reports: Canada, 1900; Central, 1859; Northern, 1859; Western, 1883, 1885; Wisconsin, 1892, 1894. Conrad Bergendoff, *Christ as Authority*, Augustana Book Concern, 1948.

Authorized Version. See *Bible Versions,* L 10.

Auto-da-fé (Portuguese: "act of faith"). The ceremony attending the official final sentence of the Inquisition, especially in Spain. It included the procession to the place of condemnation, the preaching of the sermon, reconciliation or sentence of condemnation, the handing over of recalcitrants to civil authority.

Auto-Redemption. A term used to describe the belief (held by Unitarians, Modernists, and similar groups) that man must save himself.

Avatars. See *Hinduism,* 4.

Ave Maria (Hail, Mary). A R. C. prayer to Mary consisting of Luke 1: 28, 42 and a precatory sentence ("Holy Mary, mother of God, pray for us sinners now and in the hour of our death") added in the 15th century. Pius V ordered its daily use (1568). With the *Credo* and *Pater Noster* it has long been popular and is the repeated prayer of the Rosary * and the Angelus.*

Averroes. See *Arabic Philosophy.*

Avesta. See *Zend-Avesta.*

Avicenna. See *Arabic Philosophy.*

Avignon and the *"Babylonian Captivity."* The city is the capital of the Department of Vaucluse, in Southern France, about 50 miles north of Marseilles. It became the home of certain Popes between 1309 and 1377, namely, of Clement V, John XXII, Benedict XII, Clement VI, Innocent VI, Urban V, and Gregory XI. During this so-called Babylonian Captivity, when antipopes held the throne at Rome, Avignon was a gay and corrupt city. The antipopes Clement VII and Benedict XIII continued to reside there, the latter till 1408, when he fled to Aragon. It is not a flattering chapter in the history of the Papacy. See *Schism, Papal.*

Awakening of Confessional Lutheranism. See *Lutheran Confessions,* A 6.

Awakening, Great. See *Great Awakening.*

Axiology (G. "worthy thought"). A theory of values which holds that the results of psychology, religion, logic, philosophy, metaphysics, etc., are to be correlated.

Axiom (G. "worthy"). A statement regarded as self-evident and accepted without proof. The modern tendency is to doubt axiomatic propositions. The existence of God is often treated as axiomatic in the Bible (John 14:1; Heb. 11:6) though evidences are also treated.

Aztecs, Religion of. The Aztecs, the capital of whose empire was Tenochtitlan (Mexico City), were polytheists. Chief gods in their religious system were Uitzilopochtli (originally the god of war), Tezcatlipoca (the creator and god of the sky), and Quetzalcoatl (the god of arts and crafts, of the calendar, and of culture). The first of these was ultimately associated with the sun and rose to the position of the most important god in the Aztec pantheon. Other gods were: Tlaloc, the rain-god; Chalchiulicue, the goddess of flowing waters; Xipe Totec, the god of young vegetation; and the awe-inspiring Mictlanteculli, the skeleton god of death. The religious rites included human sacrifice on a large scale, the essential feature of which was the offering of the human heart torn from the breast. Records indicate that at the dedication of the great sacred pyramid in Tenochtitlan 20,000 victims were slaughtered. On the other hand, the liturgies and rituals are in some instances on a higher plane than generally found among pagan religions. The explanation is that the fierce and warlike Aztecs conquered nations which had a more refined form of religion and from them adopted the milder elements into their own more barbarous religious system. Thus no human sacrifice was offered to Quetzalcoatl, known originally to have been a god of the Mayas, whom the Aztecs subjugated. See *Religion, Comparative, Bibliography.*

Azymite Controversy. The name *azymitai,* "users of unleavened bread," was given by the Greek Church to the Latin Church from the eleventh century, because the latter used unleavened bread in the Lord's Supper, whereas the Greek Orthodox Church insists upon leavened bread. The Western Church maintained that it was immaterial whether the one or the other kind of bread was used. The Council of Florence (1439) decided that each Church was to follow its own custom.

B

Baader, Franz von (1765—1841). Catholic, deeply interested in Eckhardt, Martin, and Boehme; left engineering profession to teach philosophical theology at Munich. Considered God an everlasting process of activity, ethics the realization of divine life, and history the unfolding of God's redeeming love.

Babists. The followers of Mirza Ali Mohammed of Shiraz, Persia, who, assuming the title Bab (Gate), in 1844 proclaimed himself the reformer of Islam. Exposing the hypocrisy of the Mohammedan clergy and declaring his revelation superior to that of Mohammed, he gained many disciples. The Persian government imprisoned the Bab and executed him in 1850. When some of his followers, in 1852, attempted to assassinate the Shah, a bloody persecution followed, in which 20,000 Babists are said to have perished. Such as escaped sought refuge in Turkish territory. For the subsequent history of the movement see *Bahaism.*

Babylonian Captivity of the Popes. See *Avignon.*

Babylonians, Religion of the. 1. A composite polytheistic form of religion in which the religious ideas current in the area of the city of Babylon were ultimately merged with those prevailing in the city-states of the lower Tigris-Euphrates valley, when the latter were gradually absorbed into the Babylonian Empire under the first dynasty of Babylon (ca. 1800 B.C.). Marduk (Bel, *i. e.,* Lord), chief deity of Babylon, the victorious city, emerged as the head of the empire's pantheon. But homage was paid also to the gods of the conquered cities, chief among them Nabu (the god of wisdom and of writing) of Borsippa, Shamash (the sun god) of Larsa and Sippar, Sin (the moon god) of Ur, Ishtar (the mother goddess) of Uruk, Ea (the god of the watery deep) of Eridu, Enlil (the storm god) of Nippur. As the names indicate, the arising religion included elements of Sumerian and Semitic origin. Worship of these gods included votive offerings, prayers which voiced the worshiper's praise of the respective god or presented petitions to him, the recitation of psalms of repentance, and, at the time of the spring equinox, the great ceremonial procession in connection with the New Year festival. On the latter occasion the king of Babylon took the hands of Marduk, a symbolic action to express that he was the god's adopted son.

2. The Babylonians further recognized the existence of a large number of demons, depicted in frightful form, which plagued mankind with disease and a host of other evils. To ward these off, the religious Babylonian wore amulets and resorted to incantations, the chanting of which was a specialty of a certain class of priests. There was, however, also a belief that there were beneficent genii, and each Babylonian was thought to have his particular patron god or goddess to whom he could appeal for help and protection and who would intercede in his behalf before the great gods. Witches and the evil eye were greatly feared.

3. The religious cult was in charge of a numerous priesthood grouped in many classes and ranks. Besides being in charge of the temple worship carried on in the sanctuaries of the various gods, the priests were the recognized authorities in the field of divination carried on by inspecting sheep's livers (hepatoscopy), reading the future in the stars (astrology), and interpreting dreams and omens of a wide variety (abnormalities of newborn children and animals; the shape assumed by a drop of sesame oil on water). The priests, however, were also the learned men of their time and devoted themselves to the preservation of religious and other literature, copying it for use in the temple libraries.

4. Imposing temples housed the images of the many gods, and kings considered it of special merit to erect such sanctuaries in the centers where each god was worshiped. A special feature in connection with some of these structures was the *ziggurat*, a square tower of as many as seven stories of decreasing size, with a ramp running around the outside and serving as a staircase leading to the top. Famous is the temple-tower at Borsippa, forming part of the temple of Nabu. Today a large mound, known as Birs Nimrud (Tower of Nimrod) marks the location.

5. Death to the Babylonian meant the separation of the soul from the body, the former entering the realm of the dead to continue a cheerless and shadowy existence in dark surroundings. Rulers of this nether world were the goddess Allatu, or Ereshkigal, and her husband Nergal, or Ninazu. In order that the soul might come to rest it was essential that the body be properly interred and not be disturbed in the grave.

6. Among the abundant remains of the religious literature of the Babylonians two are the most important: an epic glorifying Marduk and the so-called Gilgamesh epic. The former relates how the gods, the universe, and the human race came into being, and how Marduk attained the position of leadership among the gods. The latter epic contains an account of the Flood, which in many respects closely parallels the Biblical story.

7. The religious beliefs of the Assyrians were essentially the same as those of the Babylonians, with the exception that their chief god was Ashur. With the fall of Nineveh (612 B.C.) and the capture of Babylon by Cyrus (539 B. C.) the religion of the Babylonians and Assyrians fell into disuse.

GVS

M. Zastrow, *The Religion of Babylonia and Assyria*, Ginn and Co., Boston, 1898; R. W. Rogers, *The Religion of Babylonia and Assyria*, New York, 1908. For individual items consult the larger encyclopedias.

Bach, Carl Philipp Emanuel (1714 to 1788). Son of J. S. Bach, who serves as an important link between J. S. Bach and Jos. Haydn. He associated with Klopstock and was for a time in the service of Frederick the Great. His *Versuch ueber die wahre Art Klavier zu spielen* was the first well-organized treatise on playing keyboard instruments. It is a standard work to this day and has been translated into English by Wm. J. Mitchell (Norton, N. Y., 1948). His compositions often lack depth and show the influence of the Rationalistic Era; his "Fantasy and Fugue in C Minor" for organ represents him at his best.

Bach, Johann Christian (1735 to 1782). Regarded the most highly talented son of J. S. Bach; the first Bach to study in Italy, where he became a pupil of Padre Martini, became organist of the Milan Cathedral, and joined the Roman Catholic Church. Later went to London and became a friend of Mozart, whom he influenced greatly as a composer.

Bach, Johann Christoph (1642 to 1703). Uncle of J. S. Bach, who exerted a wholesome influence on Pachelbel. His *44 Choraele zum Praeambulieren* are gems in miniature and his *Ich lasse dich nicht* is a motet which his nephew would have been proud to claim as his own composition.

Bach, Johann Michael (1649—94). Father of the first wife of J. S. Bach and a writer of chorale preludes of the *cantus firmus* type.

Bach, Johann Sebastian (1685 to 1750). B. in Eisenach, Mar. 21, the son of Johann Ambrosius Bach and his wife, Elisabeth, nee Laemmerhirt. His parents died before the end of his tenth year; he then lived with an older brother, Johann Christoph, a former pupil of Pachelbel. At the age of 15 he became a chorister at Lueneburg for the Michaeliskirche, where he remained for three years and studied organ, clavichord, violin, and composition and was a pupil of Georg Boehm, the organist of the Johanniskirche, who developed in his pupil a love for French music. In 1703 Bach became organist in Arnstadt, after having spent some time in Weimar. During his tenure here (1705) he was granted a month's leave of absence to become acquainted with Buxtehude and his work in Luebeck. Bach overstayed his leave by three months, thus incurring the displeasure of the Arnstadt people. However, his contacts with Buxtehude proved to be of great benefit to Bach and to posterity. He soon left Arnstadt for Muehlhausen (1707), became organist and choirmaster of St. Blasius Church, married Maria Barbara Bach, and became a devoted husband and father. Maria Barbara bore him seven children, including two talented sons, Wilhelm Friedemann and Carl Philipp Emanuel. Bach remained in Muehlhausen for only one year; intense strife had developed there between orthodox Lutherans and the Pietists. Bach was a profound believer in confessional Lutheran orthodoxy, but had friends among the Pietists; a number of embarrassing situations developed which soon prompted him to leave the service of the Church (1708) to become a musician at the court of Duke Wilhelm of Saxe-Weimar, a profoundly religious man, whose motto was "Alles mit Gott" and who was very devoted to his subjects. Bach wrote much organ music at Weimar, likewise many cantatas. Here he matured as a composer and wrote much music which today enjoys wide popularity. Having been unduly slighted on several occasions by the Duke, Bach left Weimar in 1717 to become *Kapellmeister* of Prince Leopold of Coethen. Here Maria Barbara died in 1720 during Bach's absence from Coethen; he later married Anna Magdalena Wuelkens, who possessed a beautiful soprano voice and likewise a genuine appreciation of her husband's musical genius. In Coethen, Bach composed his Brandenburg Concertos and much music for the clavichord, violin, and other instruments, also some church music. Desiring again to compose more church and organ music, desiring also to send his older sons to a university, Bach left Coethen in 1723 for Leipzig to become Cantor of the School of St. Thomas and director of music at the St. Thomaskirche and Nikolaikirche. Here, despite many adversities and lack of appreciation and understanding on the part of his townspeople, he wrote much of his greatest music, including several cycles of church cantatas, his greatest organ music, the *Passions According to St. Matthew* and *St. John*, the *Christmas Oratorio*, several motets, his *B Minor Mass*, the *Musical Offering*, and *The Art of Fugue*. In his own fields Bach has never been excelled or even equaled. Contrapuntal music found in him its greatest master; coupled with his skill and artistry one soon discovers a Lutheran religiosity and theological acumen which are astounding and which manifest themselves particularly in his music based on texts of the Bible, of Lutheran chorales, and of Christian liturgies. Though at times the musicians' musician, Bach is today regarded as one of the great musicians of the people; he enjoys a popularity which surpasses that of any other great composer. He became blind in 1749, but lived until July 28, 1750. His greatness was not appreciated fully until more than a century had elapsed after his death. Bach is one of the most outstanding geniuses of Lutheranism, and his work, like that of Luther, is universal and timeless. WEB

David-Mendel, *The Bach Reader*, W. W. Norton, New York, 1945; W. Gurlitt, *Johann Sebastian Bach, Der Meister und sein Werk*, Ernst Reinhardt Verlag, Basel, 1946; Fr. Hasshagen, *Johann Seb. Bach als Saenger und Musiker des Evangeliums und der lutherischen Reformation*, Evangel. Buchhandlung, Emmishofen (Schweiz), 1925; Gerhard Herz, *Johann Seb. Bach im Zeitalter des Rationalismus und der Fruehromantik*, Paul Haupt Verlag, Bern-Leipzig, 1936; Hermann Kretzschmar, *Bach Kolleg*, Breitkopf & Haertel, Leipzig, 1922; C. Hubert Parry, *Johann Sebastian Bach*, Putnam's Sons, New York, 1910; Albert Schweitzer, *Johann Sebastian Bach*, Breitkopf & Haertel, Leipzig, 1930; Philipp Spitta, *Johann Sebastian Bach*, Breitkopf

& Haertel, Leipzig, 1930; Charles Sanford Terry, *Bach, A Biography,* Oxford University Press, London, 1928; Phil. Wolfrum, *Johann Sebastian Bach,* Breitkopf & Haertel, Leipzig, 1910; Friedrich Blume, *Two Centuries of Bach,* Oxford University Press, 1950; Friedrich Blume, *Die Musik in Geschichte und Gegenwart,* Bärenreiter Verlag, Kassel, 1951; Fred Hamel, *Johann Seb. Bach — Geistige Welt,* Deuerlichsche Verlagsbuchhandlung, Goettingen, 1951; Friedrich Smend, *Bach in Koethen,* Christlicher Zeitschriftenverlag, Berlin, 1951.

Bach, Wilhelm Friedemann (1710 to 1784). Oldest son of J. S. Bach, excelled his brothers in originality. His organ works bespeak the talent he inherited from his father.

Bachman, John. B. at Rhinebeck, N. Y., Feb. 4, 1790; d. Charleston, S. C., Feb. 24, 1874. Educated at Williams College, honorary M. A.; taught at Frankfurt and Philadelphia. His theological instructors were Dr. Quitman and Dr. P. F. Mayer. Pastor at Gilead, N. Y., 1813; ordained by N. Y. Ministerium; at St. John's, Charleston, for 53 years; joined S. C. Synod, also pres. Helped to establish Theological Seminary at Lexington, S. C., and later Newberry College. Helped to establish General Synod (pres., 1835, 1837); afterwards he belonged to General Synod South; helped in adoption of Book of Worship; sympathized with Southerners during Civil War; collaborated with Audubon in *Birds of America,* and in the *Quadrupeds;* D. D. from Pennsylvania College, 1835; Ph. D., Univ. of Berlin; LL. D., 1848; professor of natural history in college of Charleston. Wrote: *Unity of the Human Race* and *A Defense of Luther.*

Bachmann, Johannes F. J. B. in Berlin, Feb. 24, 1832; pupil of Tholuck and Hengstenberg; taught at Berlin, 1856; professor and university preacher at Rostock, 1858; noted for his thorough work on the festival laws of the Pentateuch; also wrote *Commentary on Judges, Life of Hengstenberg;* was well versed in Lutheran hymnology. D. Apr. 28, 1888.

Bachmann, Philip (1864—1931). B. at Geislingen; educated at Erlangen and Muenchen; Professor of Systematic Theology at Erlangen, 1902; collaborator on Th. Zahn's New Testament Commentary; Lutheran theologian.

Backhaus, J. L. B. in Amsterdam, Holland, Aug. 1, 1842; educated at Teachers' Seminary, Fort Wayne, Ind.; teacher in Readfield, Wis., 1864; Bloomington, Ill., 1865—66; Venedy, Ill., 1867 to 1882; St. Matthew's School, Chicago, 1883—84; professor at Teachers' Seminary, Addison, Ill., 1884—1915 (when he resigned); contributed articles to *Lutheraner* on education and schools. D. Mar. 11, 1919.

Backslide. The falling away in religion; apostasy. Acts 21:21; 2 Thess. 2:3; 1 Tim. 4:1. It must be distinguished from hypocrisy, as it may sometimes occur unintentionally, while hypocrisy is intentional fraud. According to the Scriptures, backsliding is caused by cares of the world, evil company, and pride. It is manifested by indifference to prayer and to the means of grace, sometimes by gross immorality. Notable instances are Saul, Judas, and Demas.

Backus, Isaac (1724—1806). Originally Congregationalist; joined Baptists with his congregation at Middleborough, Mass.; trustee of Brown University; known for his *History of New England with Special Reference to the Baptists.* See *Baptist Bodies,* 22.

Bacmeister, Luke (1530—1608). B. at Lueneburg; professor at Rostock; superintendent at Rostock; wrote *Vom christlichen Bann, kurzer und gruendlicher Bericht aus Gottes Wort und aus Lutheri Schriften;* a history of the churches of Rostock.

Bacmeister, Luke (1570—1638). Son of preceding; professor at Wittenberg; superintendent at Rostock and Gustrow; wrote *Disputationes contra Decreta Concilii Tridentini, Tractatus de Lege, Disputationes de S. Trinitate;* author of German hymns.

Bacon, Benjamin Wisner (1860 to 1932). Congregationalist; professor of NT criticism at Yale; wrote numerous works on introduction and exegesis.

Bacon, Francis (1561—1626). English statesman and philosopher. Entered Parliament, became Lord Chancellor, raised to peerage. Charged with taking bribes, found guilty. Paved way for modern philosophy by criticizing Scholastics for neglect of natural sciences and by advocating inductive (empirical) method. In *Novum Organum* separated spheres of faith (theology) and knowledge (philosophy). Revelation sole source of faith. Experience source of knowledge.

Thomas Fowler, *Novum Organum,* Clarendon Press, 1889; R. W. Church, *Francis Bacon,* Macm., 1908; G. W. Steeves, *Francis Bacon,* Methuen & Co., 1910.

Bacon, Roger (1214—94). Perhaps the most learned man of the Middle Ages, *Doctor Mirabilis* or *Profundus;* of Oxford. Opposing Scholasticism, he insisted on the supreme authority of the Scriptures in theology, the right of the laity to the Bible, the importance of its study in the original languages, and fearlessly castigated the corruption of the priests and monks. His knowledge of physics, chemistry, and astronomy, gained by researches and experiments, placed him far ahead of his times. He did not escape the charge of sorcery and heresy; his order, the Franciscans, at one time forbade his lectures and twice had him imprisoned for ten and fourteen years, respectively. H. O. Taylor, *The Medieval Mind,* Macm., 1925; E. P. Cheyney, *The Dawn of a New Era, 1250—1453,* Harper, 1936.

Bade, Wm. Frederic (1871—1936). Professor of OT subjects at Moravian College and Pacific School of Religion; wrote *Old Testament in the Light of Today* and other works; led archaeological expeditions to Palestine.

Baden, J. H. (Dec. 20, 1823, to July 10, 1897). B. at Westeresch, Hannover. Studied theology at the University of Berlin. Came to America; was assistant to Dr. Stohlmann, New York; organized Lutheran congregations at Mount Vernon and Hastings, N. Y., also St. Luke's German Evangelical Lutheran Church at Brooklyn, which he served for 24 years; became editor of the *Herold,* organ of the New York Ministerium in 1879; elected president of the Ministerium in 1881; active in establishing a Lutheran Home for Immigrants in New York; pres. of the Lutheran Theological Seminary in Philadelphia; on Board of Trustees of Wartburg Orphans' Home.

Baden, Laurids (1618—89). Danish theologian; pastor at Horson; known for his devotional book *Himmelstige.*

Bading, Johann. B. 1824, Rixdorf, near Berlin. Studied in Gossner's school for African Missions, 1846; in Hermannsburg, 1848. Deciding to go to America, he went to Barmen, 1852; was sent to Wisconsin by the Langenberg Society, 1853. Held pastorates at Calumet, Theresa, Watertown, Milwaukee (St. John's), Wis. His energy made him a leader from the beginning. Was most active in redeeming Wisconsin Synod for sound Lutheranism. Chiefly instrumental in locating Northwestern College at Watertown rather than in Milwaukee. President of the Wisconsin Synod, 1860—89, excepting 1864—67. Journeyed through Germany and Russia, raising funds to finance Northwestern, 1863—64. Though closely related to German missionary societies, he did not hesitate to sever connections with them when it became necessary, forfeiting the fruits of his collection tour. Was one of chief negotiators with Missouri in forming the Synodical Conference, 1872, of which he was president 1882—1912. Resigned pastorate, 1908, but remained assistant until his death in 1913. President of board of trustees of Northwestern, 1865—1912.

Baepler, Andrew. B. July 28, 1850, at Baltimore, Md., graduated St. Louis 1874; pastor at Dallas, Tex., 1874—75; near Cole Camp, Mo., 1875—79; at Mobile, Ala., 1879—82; English missionary for the Western District, 1882—84; professor at St. Paul's College, Concordia, Mo., 1884—87 and 1899—1925; president of Concordia College, Fort Wayne, Ind., 1888—94; pastor at Little Rock, Ark., 1894—99; D. D. (St. Louis); retired 1925; d. Oct. 10, 1927.

Baetis, William. B. 1777; d. Aug. 17, 1867. Member of the Pennsylvania Ministerium; pastor at Cohenzy, N. J., and several congregations in Lebanon Co., Pa., from 1810 to 1836, when he became pastor of Zion Lutheran Church, Lancaster, and also Senior of the Pennsylvania Ministerium.

Baetyl. Sacred rock (often meteor) used in heathen worship.

Bager, John George (1725—94). Early American Lutheran pastor; came from Germany to America in 1752; served German Christ Church, New York City, Zion Church, Baltimore, Md., and also charges in Lebanon and York Counties, Pa.

Bagster's Polyglot. See *Polyglot Bibles.*

Bahaism. With the death of Ali Mohammed (see *Babists*) the movement which he inaugurated did not terminate. In 1863 Baha'-u'llah (Splendor of God), a follower of the Bab, proceeded to formulate the sect's teachings while confined in Palestine by the Turkish government. After Baha'-u'llah's death in 1892 his oldest son, Abdul Baha, a Turkish prisoner till 1908, carried on. He visited the United States in 1912 and died at Haifa, Palestine, in 1921.

The present leader is Shoghi Effendi. There are over five hundred constituted local assemblies in Persia, and assemblies are found in many other countries. The cult is represented in America since the Chicago World's Fair of 1893. A magnificent temple, Mashrak-el-Azkar ("The Dawning Point of the Commemorations" of God), was erected at Willmette, Ill.; designed by Louis J. Bourgeois; is nine-sided, with intricate ornamentation of exquisite beauty, was dedicated in 1942, and is open to the nine great religions.

Bahaism has "no professional clergy, no ritualistic service"; proclaims itself a call to religious unity; and sets up as basic Bahai teachings: the oneness of mankind, independent investigation of truth, equality of men and women, universal peace, universal education, spiritual solution of the economic problem, a universal language, an international tribunal, but knows of no Savior from sin or of hope beyond the grave. See *Religion, Comparative, Bibliography*.

Baha'-u'llah. See *Bahaism*.

Bahnmaier, Jonathan Friedrich (1774—1841). B. near Marbach; professor at Tuebingen; wrote *De Miraculis NT Meletemata* and some sermons and works on asceticism; wrote hymns including "Walte, walte, nah und fern."

Bahya, Ben Joseph (11th c.). Jewish rabbinical judge at Saragossa, Spain; wrote *Guide to the Duties of the Heart*, first systematic Jewish ethics.

Baier, Johann Wilhelm (1647—95). Prof. at Jena, rector of the University of Halle, general superintendent, court preacher, and city pastor at Weimar; d. there. His chief work is *Compendium Theologiae Positivae*, which shows the great influence Johann Musaeus, his teacher and father-in-law, had upon him (synergism). This work passed through many editions, latest by Dr. Walther, St. Louis, Mo., 1879, with a rich collection of extracts from earlier Lutheran theologians.

An exact list of Baier's writings in G. A. Will, *Nuernbergisches Gelehrtenlexikon*, Nuernberg, 1755; J. J. Beyer, *Alte und neue Geschichte der Halle-* *schen Gelehrten* (vol. I), Halle, 1739. See references under *Dogmatics* and *Doctrine*.

Baierlein, Edward R. B. April 24, 1819; d. Oct. 12, 1901, in Germany. Lutheran missionary among the Chippewa Indians near Frankenmuth, Mich. (Station Bethany, St. Louis, Mich.), 1847—1853; missionary to India in service of the Lutheran Leipzig Mission until 1886. Returned to Germany and engaged in literary work.

E. R. Baierlein, *Nach und aus Indien*, J. Naumann, Leipzig, 1873; E. R. Baierlein, *Im Urwalde*, J. Naumann, Dresden, 1889.

Baius, Michael (1513—89). Belgian Catholic theologian; forerunner of Jansen; had conflict with popes on questions of grace, free will, and sin; fused Catholicism with elements of Protestantism.

Bake, Reinhard (1587—1657). Pastor of Cathedral Church of Magdeburg; remained staunch Lutheran in spite of Jesuit attempts to convert him; met Tilly at the church portal with quotation from Vergil.

Baker, George. See *Father Divine*.

Baker, Henry Williams (1821—77). B. in London, educated at Cambridge. Ordained a priest, he became the Vicar of Monkland, Herefordshire. He is best known as editor of *Hymns Ancient and Modern* (first ed., 1861). He wrote thirty-three hymns. One of the best known is his paraphrase of Psalm 23, "The King of Love My Shepherd Is."

Baker, John Christopher (1792 to 1859). Member of Pennsylvania Ministerium; held three pastorates, the last at St. Luke's, Philadelphia; able preacher and pastor.

Balder. In Norse mythology, son of Odin and Frigga; personification of sun's brightness; killed through treachery of Loki.

Balduin, Friedrich (1575—1627). Poet laureate, 1597; 1601, member of the philosophical faculty at Wittenberg; 1602, preacher at Freiberg; 1603, superintendent at Oelsnitz; 1604, professor of theology at Wittenberg; 1607, also superintendent. Among his numerous books is a Latin commentary on all the Epistles of St. Paul, a classical work in Lutheran exegetical literature. His *Tractatus de Casibus Conscientiae* was published after his death.

Balkan Churches. See *Eastern Orthodox Churches.*

Balle, Nicolai. See *Denmark, Lutheranism in,* 7.

Ballou, Hosea (1771—1852). Often called "Father of Universalism." Differed from John Murray in his thoroughgoing anti-Calvinism. Most important work: *Examination of the Doctrine of Future Retribution.*

Baltic States. See *Esthonia; Latvia; Lithuania.*

Baltimore Catechism. See *Catechetics,* 14.

Baltimore, Councils of. See *Councils and Synods,* 6.

Bambino. In art, name given to Jesus in swaddling clothes.

Ban. 1) The declaration of excommunication (see *Keys, Office of*); 2) a fine imposed for sacrilege.

Bangor. An abbey in Ulster, Ireland, established about 555 by Comgall, the teacher of Columba, who became one of the great missionaries to the Continent; said to have sheltered 4,000 monks.

Banks, A. A. See *Baptist Bodies,* 29.

Banns. See *Marriage.*

Baptism. See *Grace, Means of,* III.

Baptism for the Dead. Practiced by the Mormons for the salvation of others as an ordinance instituted by God from eternity. But the Biblical way of salvation rules out vicarious Baptism, salvation being by personal faith and personal Baptism, Heb. 2:4; Mark 16:15, 16; Acts 2:38; Matt. 28: 19, 20. Moreover, Heb. 9:27 denies the possibility of salvation after death. Therefore 1 Cor. 15:29 cannot be quoted in favor of vicarious Baptism. The Greek preposition *hyper* here may mean *over* or *with reference to,* the Baptism of the early adult Christians thus being a confession of their hope of the resurrection of the body to eternal life. The Catholic Apostolic Church also practices baptism for the dead. See Lenski's Commentary on 1 Cor. 15:29.

Baptism, Lay. See *Grace, Means of; Keys, Office of.*

Baptism, Liturgical. The ritual of Baptism, as developed to the time of Gregory the Great, remained practically unchanged throughout the Middle Ages. According to the *Agenda Moguntinensis* of 1513 the following parts belonged to the Order of Baptizing Children (*Ordo ad baptizandum pueros*): I. Introduction (at the doors of the church): Inquiry after Name, Sign of Cross and Prayer, Tasting of Salt, and Greeting of Peace with Prayer, Great Exorcism, the Lesson, the Lord's Prayer with Ave Maria and Apostolic Creed, Ephphatha Ceremony, Entrance into Church; II. Rite of Baptism: Renunciation, the Creed, Anointing (on the breast and between the shoulder blades, in the form of a cross), Admonition to Sponsors, the Act of Baptism (performed with child's head pointing to east, north, and south, respectively, at the three infusions), Prayer of Thanksgiving, Clothing in Chrisom, or White Robe. Other ceremonies prescribed by some church orders were the Kiss of Brotherhood or Peace, the Placing of a Lighted Taper into the Hand of the Child, and others. The ceremonies of the two exorcisms, the *gustus salis* (placing a little salt in the mouth or on the tongue of the child), and the act of anointing were those whose significance was emphasized so strongly as to cause these ceremonies to obscure the rite of Baptism itself. In spite of this fact, however, Luther retained the ceremonies in his first compilation of the Order of Baptism, since they were not essentially wrong or to be condemned. His first attempt in this line was his *Taufbuechlein verdeutscht* of 1523. It was in substance nothing but a translation of the liturgy of Baptism as then in use in Wittenberg. It contained the Small Exorcism, Signum Crucis with Prayers, the Tasting of Salt with the "Flood" Prayer, the Great Exorcism with Prayer and Greeting of Peace, Lesson (Mark 10), the Lord's Prayer, the Ephphatha Ceremony, Ingression; Renunciation, Creed, Act of Baptism, Anointing (cross on head only), Clothing with Chrisom, Placing of Taper in Hand of the Child. After Luther had issued a second order or outline of a liturgy for Baptism, omitting some of the ceremonies upon which the papists had laid so much stress, he came out in 1526 with an order which discarded all the usages which were in any way connected with superstition. But he retained the division into two parts. Most of the Lutheran church orders adopted the form of 1526, many of them, however, preferring to omit the exsufflation (the same as the Small **Ex-**

orcism above), the signation, and the exorcism. They all agree in retaining the division of the act into two parts, and the most prominent church orders have the admonition to the sponsors at the end, since it is not an integral part of the ceremony. The questions are usually addressed to the child, the sponsors being expressly asked to answer in the name of the infant. The tendency in our days is toward abbreviation of the formula of Baptism. See *Liturgics.*

Baptism, *Roman Catholic Doctrine.* The Roman Church teaches that Baptism indeed remits all sin, both original and actual, of which the recipient stands guilty at the moment of Baptism, including the deserved punishment. It denies, however, that through repentance and faith the efficacy of baptismal grace is continued and renewed for sins committed after Baptism. Titus 3:5-7; 2 Tim. 2:13; Gal. 3:24-27. For the removal of these sins it demands submission to the so-called Sacrament of Penance * with its works of satisfaction. Rome further denies that infants themselves have the faith required in Baptism and teaches that they believe through the faith of their parents or of the whole Church (*Catechismus Romanus,* II, 2, 32), a vicarious arrangement of which the Scriptures know nothing. Nor is there any Scriptural warrant for the doctrine that Baptism imprints an indelible mark (see *Character Indelebilis*), which makes the recipient capable of receiving the other sacraments and subjects him of right, even though "heretically" baptized, to the canon law and the Pope. — Among the ceremonies of Roman Baptism are the following: The priest breathes on the candidate and exorcises the devil; puts salt in his mouth; anoints his ears and nostrils with spittle, his breast and back with oil, and the crown of his head with chrism (see *Oil, Holy*); finally he places a lighted candle in his hand. Protestants properly baptized are subject to the Pope according to the Catholic theory of *Invincible Ignorance.* (Regarding unbaptized infants see *Limbo;* see also *Opus Operatum.*)

Baptismal Font. See *Church Furniture,* 1.

Baptismal Formula. See *Ecumenical Creeds,* A.

Baptismal Regeneration. See *Grace, Means of,* III.

Baptismal Vow. A promise (made immediately before Baptism) to live according to the Christian faith and to avoid evil.

Baptist Bodies. 1. The basic principle on which Baptists all over the world are agreed is "liberty of conscience." This principle manifests itself negatively in this, that Baptists reject subscription to human creeds, establishment of ecclesiastical organizations, and the teaching of any form of sacramentalism and sacerdotalism; and positively in this, that Baptists are enthusiastic, lay great emphasis on the competence and the responsibility of each individual soul in spiritual matters, accept only "believer's Baptism," and vigorously maintain the absolute separation of Church and State. Baptists do not consider creeds as tests of orthodoxy, but as evidences of unanimity. Since it is the inalienable right of the individual to formulate his own creed, there can be, strictly speaking, no heresy in Baptist bodies. See *Democratic Declaration,* 3. Nevertheless, historically the Baptists are divided theologically into two large families, the General and the Particular Baptists, the former being Arminian and believing in universal salvation, the latter being Calvinistic and subscribing to the theory of a limited atonement.

2. The *General Baptists* are the spiritual descendants of the Anabaptists,* who misinterpreted the Reformation principle of the priesthood of all believers by making it applicable also to the political and social spheres. After the collapse of the Anabaptist movement in 1535, the scattered remnants of these re-baptizers were gathered by Menno Simons and organized as the Mennonites.* The theology of the Mennonites was Pelagian since its beginning and stressed such errors as freedom of the will, a false enthusiasm, or mysticism, asceticism, and extreme literalism. The Mennonites placed great emphasis on the outward purity of the Church and held that the restoration of Apostolic Christianity must include Baptism by immersion. Anabaptists came to England as early as 1534, but were unable to gain a foothold because of the bitter persecutions resulting from the Act of Uniformity of 1559, which disenfranchised all religious non-conformists. John Smith (Smyth), who had spent some time at Amsterdam and there

with Thomas Helwys had organized a Baptist congregation, returned to England in 1611 and established the first English Baptist church. Owing to Dutch Mennonite influence, these early English Baptists were Arminian and became known as General Baptists. However, the distinctive principle of all Baptists, "liberty of conscience," was clearly enunciated in the Articles of Faith adopted about 1611: "The magistrate is not by virtue of his office to meddle with religious or matters of conscience, or compel men to this or that form of religion, for Christ only is King and Lawgiver of the Church and conscience." The *Particular*, or *Calvinistic*, Baptists trace their origin in part to the Separatist Movement in England during the 16th century. Two groups of English Protestants, the Puritans and the Separatists, opposed the Romanizing tendencies of the Established, or the Anglican, Church, the former holding that the reformation of the Anglican Church must be accomplished by remaining within the Established Church, the latter by complete separation. Both the Puritans and the Separatists, also known as Non-Conformists or Congregationalists, were agreed on the principles of Calvinism. They differed only in matters of church polity, the Puritans favoring Presbyterianism, the Separatists, however, believing that the "Church should be a congregation of free men, founded after the pattern of the Apostolic Church, governing itself, not according to the laws of the State, but according to the Bible." In the course of time some of the Separatists adopted the view that only "believer's Baptism" by immersion was a valid Baptism, and in 1639 they organized the first Baptist Separatist congregation. In theology these early Calvinistic, or Particular, Baptists were in full accord with the Presbyterians and the Congregationalists, except on doctrines of the Church and the Sacraments. Charles H. Spurgeon is the outstanding English Calvinistic Baptist, and John Bunyan the best-known English General Baptist. Since 1891 the distinction between the General and Particular Baptists no longer applies in England, since both groups have united on the following basic principles of Baptist theology: the supreme authority of Scripture, a regenerate membership, a democratic church government, and believer's Baptism by immersion. On all other points great latitude of opinion is permitted.

3. The *American Baptist Churches* owe their origin very largely to the work of Roger Williams (ca. 1600—83), successively an Anglican, Puritan, Separatist, Baptist, Seeker. Coming to Massachusetts in 1631, he was for a short season assistant pastor at Plymouth and then, in 1635, was ordained pastor of the Salem church. His Separatist views, however, went far beyond those of the Salem Separatists and precipitated a bitter conflict with the ecclesiastical and secular authorities. Being an "archindividualist," he maintained that the colonists had trespassed upon the rights of the Indians in acquiring the respective land charters. This interest in civil and individual liberty helped to crystallize his views concerning religious liberty. He was bitterly opposed to the theocratic form of government in the Puritan colonies, denied the magistrates jurisdiction over matters of conscience and religion, and contended for the liberty of conscience, for the separation of Church and State, and for the right of the people to choose their own rulers. This led to Williams' banishment from the colony and to the founding of the colony at Providence, R. I., in 1635, where "the Apostle of Liberty" put into practice the principles of civil and religious liberty which he later on defended in his *Bloody Tenent of Persecution for the Cause of Conscience*. In 1638 he and his followers adopted Baptism by immersion, and the Providence church may therefore rightly be called the oldest Baptist church in America. The distinctive tenet of this group was the rigid individualism, which manifested itself chiefly in stressing the inner religious experience of the individual and showing little, if any, interest in the visible Church and considering all ecclesiastical organizations on a par with secular institutions. The Providence Baptists were in principle opposed to the adoption of any creedal statements and granted equal rights to members of Calvinistic and Arminian convictions. The Arminian group at Providence held that the "six principles" of Heb. 6:1, 2 included the laying on of hands as a divine ordinance, and in the subsequent controversy on this point the views of the Arminian Baptists, later known as General Six-Principle Baptists, gained general acceptance by 1652. While the Providence church is the oldest Baptist church in

America, the distinction of being the first Calvinist Baptist church in America is usually given to the Newport, R. I., church, founded by John Clarke in 1641. The Baptists in the New England States were Calvinists, while the majority of the early Baptists in the Southern Colonies favored Arminianism. The Arminian, or General, Baptists, however, failed to gain a foothold, because the majority of the early colonists were reared in the tradition of Calvinism. The Calvinistic, or Particular, Baptists laid greater emphasis on a trained ministry and were able to develop greater denominational consciousness than the General Baptists.

4. The Baptists developed their greatest strength in the Middle Colonies, owing largely to the influence of the Philadelphia Association, which adopted the Philadelphia Confession in 1742. This is a Calvinistic standard identical with the Confession adopted by London Baptists in 1677, which in turn is in full agreement with the Westminster Confession of 1644 (Presbyterian) and the Savoy Declaration of 1658 (Congregational) except in the statements concerning the Sacraments and the Church. It is therefore correct to state that the theological antecedents of the vast majority of American Baptists are rooted in Calvinistic theology, and this accounts for the fact that formerly all and today many Particular Baptists subscribe to such doctrines as the total depravity of man, the necessity and sufficiency of Christ's atonement, limited, however, to the elect, and unconditional election. Historians are agreed that the Baptist agitation for the separation of Church and State played a prominent part in the adoption of the First Amendment of our Federal Constitution. The great period of expansion of the Baptist Church began about 1800. The vast majority of Baptists are known simply as Baptists, sometimes also as "Regular Baptists," and have organized the Northern, Southern, and Negro Baptist Conventions, comprising about eight million members. Some Baptist bodies use a descriptive adjective, as "Primitive," "Six-Principle," "Regular," "General," "Two-Seed-in-the-Spirit." There are eighteen such smaller bodies comprising less than one half million members.

5. *Doctrine.* "It is a distinct principle with Baptists that they acknowledge no human founder, recognize no human authority, and subscribe to no human creed." "Absolute liberty of conscience under Christ has always been the distinguishing tenet of Baptists." (A. H. Strong.) The competency of the individual soul under God is said to eliminate every extraneous thing to stand between the soul and God, such as ecclesiastical or civil order, ordinances, sacraments, preacher, or priest. Strictly speaking, there can be no heresy trial in the Baptist Church, because there is no creed subscription; there is no creed subscription, because it is the inalienable right of every individual to form his own creed. This basic principle — in many points similar to that of the Congregational churches — is largely responsible for the fact that the Baptists, especially those of the Northern Convention, grant equal rights to both the Modernists and the Fundamentalists. The Conservatives, who still hold to the principles of the Philadelphia and New Hampshire Confessions, and the Liberals, who have accepted the theories of Higher Criticism, divine immanence, and the social gospel, must recognize each other's views according to the basic Baptist principle. The essentially distinctive feature of the Baptists is not their practice of immersion nor their rejection of infant Baptism, but their insistence upon the right and competence of every individual without the intervention of any outside agency to acknowledge by faith the lordship of Christ and to profess such faith by immersion. The *Census Report of Religious Bodies* (1936) summarizes the principles which distinguish Baptists from other Reformed denominations as follows: 1. Independence of the local church; 2. separation of Church and State; 3. religious liberty an inalienable and inherent right of the soul; 4. the local church is a body of regenerated people, Baptism being the outward profession of their personal faith; 5. infant Baptism is fatal to the spirituality of the Church; 6. immersion (a dramatic proclamation of the believer's spiritual death and resurrection); 7. the Scriptural church officers are pastors and deacons; 8. the Lord's Supper is observed in commemoration of Christ's death. The controversial points which originally separated Particular and General Baptists are no longer an issue among the "Regular" Baptists, though they are still a live issue in some of the smaller Baptist bodies. (See below.)

6. *Polity.* In accord with its basic theological principle, Baptist church

polity is congregational, the local congregation being absolutely autonomous in fixing its own doctrinal platform, discipline, and worship. All members have equal voting rights. Baptists are opposed in principle to every kind of ecclesiastical organization. This anti-clericalism accounts in a large measure for the aggressive lay participation in church activities. Ordinarily Baptist churches unite as associations or State conventions; these bodies, however, have no legislative, judicial, nor executive powers. Formerly the missionary and educational activities of the Baptists were carried on by various societies whose membership was not identical with the Baptist congregations, but was made up of those individuals who regularly contribute toward the respective society. Toward the close of the eighteenth century a number of such societies were founded for the purpose of spreading Baptist ideas and succeeded in establishing Baptist churches in the territories which were opened after the Revolutionary War. In 1814 the Baptists organized a society for foreign missions; in 1824 the American Baptist Publication Society; in 1832 the Home Missions Society. These societies were entirely independent of ecclesiastical control and were responsible to their membership alone. The various activities of the Northern Baptists have been reorganized somewhat along denominational lines in the hope that this move will eliminate duplication and work for greater efficiency.

7. **The Particular Baptists (8—17).** These bodies originally followed and to some extent still follow Calvinistic rather than Arminian theology. The Northern and Southern Conventions and the Negro Baptists constitute the vast majority of so-called Particular Baptists. These three large bodies are agreed in doctrine and polity, but each group has retained its denominational identity for purposes of more efficient administration.

8. *The American Baptist Convention.* The history of this body until 1844 is described in the previous general statement. In that year the State conventions of the North and those of the South separated on the question whether a slaveholding Baptist could be appointed as a foreign missionary. It must also be noted that the Northern Baptists were more willing to recognize the desirability of ecclesiastical organizations for more effective and systematic church work. This resulted in

organizing the Northern Baptist Convention as a corporation in 1907, so that all churches, while retaining their local autonomy and independence of every other church and the Convention itself, nevertheless are united in carrying out the various Baptist activities. By uniting and co-ordinating the work of the many Baptist societies and boards, each working independently prior to 1907, the Northern Baptists have been able to expand their missionary, educational, and philanthropic work considerably. In doctrine the Northern Baptists have become increasingly liberalistic. Their disregard for creeds and opposition to "regimentation of thought" has made it possible that without public censure such theological schools as Rochester-Colgate (Wm. N. Clarke and W. Rauschenbusch) and the Divinity School of the University of Chicago (Shailer Mathews) introduced liberal theology with its Higher Criticism, the theories of evolution and divine immanence, and the social gospel. The Northern Baptists adopted the name American Baptist Convention in 1950.

9. *Southern Baptist Convention.* The center of activity of the early Baptists was in the New England and the Atlantic Seaboard States. When Baptist churches were planted in the South after the Revolutionary War by missionaries from the North, it was only natural that the Southern Baptists united with Northern Baptists in such activities as foreign missions. The agency for this phase of Baptist work was the Missionary Convention for Foreign Missions, organized in 1814, with headquarters at Boston. This society was antislavery and refused to approve the appointing of a candidate for foreign mission work who was a slaveholder. Thereupon the State Associations in the South withdrew from the Northern Convention and in 1845 organized the Southern Baptist Convention at Augusta, Ga. In doctrine the Southern Baptists are much more conservative than the Northern, and generally adhere to the Calvinistic New Hampshire Confession. Many of their churches practice close Communion. The seminaries, Southern Baptist at Louisville, Ky., Southwestern at Fort Worth, Tex., and Baptist Bible School at New Orleans are fundamentalistic. The Southern Baptist Convention has repeatedly voted against membership in the Federal Council of Churches. But the basic principle of all Baptists,

namely, the right of the individual in all matters of conscience, permits the conservative Southern Baptists to interchange membership and ministry on terms of perfect equality with Northern Baptists. The reason for the continued separation of the two bodies is not doctrinal, but purely administrative. Five denominational boards have charge respectively of home missions, foreign missions, Sunday school work, educational institutions, and ministerial relief.

10. National Baptist Convention. This is the largest Baptist convention, comprising virtually all Negro Baptists. In the fifteen years after the Civil War the Baptists claim to have gained approximately 1,000,000 adherents among the Negroes. The rapid expansion of the Baptist Church among the freed slaves is due in part to the Baptist principle of individual liberty, to the ease with which local churches could be formed, and to the low standard of indoctrination required. In 1886 the Negro Baptist churches organized the National Baptist Convention at St. Louis. The Negro Baptists are in general agreement with the Northern and especially the Southern Convention in doctrine and polity, though the lack of ecclesiastical organization has resulted in many separations and reunions among the Negroes. Seven boards have charge of the denominational activities, home and foreign missions, education, Sunday school work, women's and young people's work, and ministerial relief.

11. Primitive Baptists. Following the Baptist principle that Christians must turn to the New Testament not only for doctrine but also for practice, including ceremonies and church rites, the Primitive Baptists hold that every form of ecclesiastical organization is sinful if not expressly prescribed in the New Testament. Since no missionary societies with a "money basis" are mentioned in the New Testament, a number of Baptist associations denounced the formation of all mission societies and the publications of educational boards as contrary to the New Testament. In protest against what they viewed as anti-Scriptural ecclesiasticism, a number of associations, local groups of Baptist congregations, announced that they would no longer maintain fellowship with those associations which had "united themselves with the world" and by supporting benevolent societies through payment of membership dues "were preaching

a different Gospel." These associations are in principle opposed to every form of denominational organization, to State or national conventions. The only bond uniting the various associations is the exchange of the annual minutes. Any association whose minutes are not approved is dropped from fellowship. Since there is no denominational organization, these Baptists have no official distinctive name and have been known as "Antimission," "Hard Shell," "Old School," and most commonly as "Primitive" Baptists. In polity these Baptists are extremely congregational. Theological training for pastors is not required; mission work is not on an organized basis; instrumental music in the service, Sunday schools, and secret societies are not authorized. In theology the "Primitive" Baptists are strictly Calvinistic.

12. Colored Primitive Baptists. The principles of this group agree with those described above.

13. Two-Seed-in-the-Spirit Predestinarian Baptists. This body is diminishing rapidly and is of interest only because of its extreme views on predestination, essentially a form of dualistic Gnosticism. Owing in part to the Baptists' original aversion to all church organizations, in part to the opposition to an educated ministry, and in part to the extreme Calvinism of some Baptists, a strong antimission movement developed among the Baptists of the Southeast in the early decades of the nineteenth century. This antimission spirit, prevalent among the Primitive Baptists, reached its climax in the formation of the Two-Seed Predestinarians, based upon the principles proclaimed by Daniel Parker in 1826. His views have been summarized as follows: "The essence of good is God; the essence of evil is the devil. Good angels are emanations from, or particles of, God; evil angels are particles of the devil. When God created Adam and Eve, they were endowed with an emanation from Himself, or particles of God were included in their constitution. Satan, however, infused into them particles of his essence, by which they were corrupted. In the beginning God had appointed that Eve should bring forth only a certain number of offspring; the same provision applied to each of her daughters. But when the particles of evil essence had been infused by Satan, the conception of Eve and of her daughters was increased. They were now required to bear the original number, who were styled the seed of God, and an additional number, who were called the seed of the Serpent. The seed of God constituted a part of the body of Christ. For them the Atonement was absolute; they would all be saved. The seed of the Serpent did not partake of the benefits of the Atonement and would all be lost. All the manifestations of good or evil in men are but displays of the essence that has been infused into them. The Christian warfare is a conflict between these essences." This group still holds that as seed must produce after its kind, either wheat or tares, so neither the origin nor the destiny of man can be changed from that which God had decreed at the beginning. They believe that Jesus is a full and complete Savior and will finish the work of salvation without the help of ministers. The Two-Seed Baptists have often been identified with the Primitive Baptists and are popularly known as "Hard Shell" Baptists.

14. *American Baptist Association.* A separate group of Baptists who withdrew from the various conventions, because they considered the organization of such conventions or denominations as contrary to the letter and spirit of the New Testament. Believing that their churches alone are true churches, they claim to be "the divine custodians of the truth, and that they only have the right of carrying out the Great Commission, of executing the laws of the Kingdom, and of administering the ordinances of the Gospel." This association is a co-operation of local congregations for the purpose of joint work, but its constituent members are so averse to ecclesiastical organizations and so zealous in preserving the rights of local congregations, that the annual meetings are called "the meeting of the messengers [delegates] composing the American Baptist Association." In doctrine they are in harmony with the New Hampshire Confession, but interpret Article XVIII concerning Christ's second coming according to modern premillennialism. This group of Baptists is represented chiefly in the South and Southwest.

15. *General Association of Regular Baptists.* This group is very similar to the American Baptist Association in its theology and polity. Its churches are found chiefly in the North Central States.

16. *Seventh-Day Baptists.* The first Seventh-Day Baptist church was or-

ganized in London probably as early as 1617. Some members in both the Providence and Newport, R. I., Baptist churches shared the views of this London Baptist church and maintained fellowship with other Baptists until 1671, when Stephen Mumford organized the first American Seventh-Day Baptist church. The Sabbatarian Baptists have been unable to gain a large following in their denomination. They have, however, been a large factor in determining the views of the Seventh-Day Adventists * and the German Seventh-Day Baptists (see below). In church polity the Seventh-Day Baptists agree fully with all Baptists, being thoroughly congregationalistic and uniting for joint work on a purely voluntary basis. In doctrine they follow the Calvinistic Baptists, except in their view that the Sabbath was instituted at man's creation and sanctioned by Christ and the Apostles. However, their latitudinarianism permits them to fellowship with all immersionists.

17. *Seventh-Day Baptists (German, 1728).* This is the group of German Brethren organized by Conrad Beissel in 1732 as a communistic and celibate society at Ephrata, Pa. An extreme form of pietism, mysticism, and legalism characterized this group. After a brief period of success as a monastic community with its flourishing industries, school, and printing press, the denomination is represented by three small congregations. In theology and practice they agree with the Brethren.*

18. **General Baptists (19—29).** These are the groups whose doctrinal position is closely related to that of the Anabaptists or who in the course of time adopted Arminian theology. In contrast to the Particular Baptists they emphasize such doctrines as the universal Atonement and human responsibility. Many of the General Baptists practice foot washing, observe close Communion, and in general may be said to be legalistic, pietistic, and given to enthusiastic expressionism. They are opposed to denominational and organized church work, the majority of the General Baptists being united in associations or local federations for purposes of fellowship. Fellowship between the various associations is established and maintained by exchanging the annual minutes. The Arminian Baptists were unable to gain a large following, owing, no doubt, to the fact that they were opposed to the organization of denominations and

93

therefore lacked denominational consciousness and primarily that they did not believe in a trained ministry, whereas the Particular Baptists did. Many Arminian Baptists have affiliated with the Calvinistic Baptists.

19. *General Six-Principle Baptists.* The Arminian group in the Providence church (see above) held that the laying on of hands was not only a ceremony, but one of the six principles which according to Heb. 6:1, 2 is as essential as the other five, namely, repentance, faith, Baptism, resurrection, judgment. By 1652 the Six-Principle Baptists had gained the majority of the Providence church and made the laying on of hands immediately after Baptism the sign of the reception of the Holy Ghost and an indispensable condition for church membership. Though the General Six-Principle Baptists claim to be the original Baptist Church, founded by Williams, they are rapidly disappearing.

20. *General Baptists.* While all those Baptist bodies which reject the Calvinism of the Particular Baptists are called General Baptists (see general statement above), there is also a separate branch by this name. The origin of this group is probably due to the work of Robert Nordin and Thos. White, who were sent to the Arminian Baptists in Virginia by the London General Baptists in 1714. It was not until 1823, however, that General Baptists appear as a separate group. In recent years this branch has attempted to unite with other Baptist bodies and in 1915 formed a co-operative union with the Northern Convention.

21. *Regular Baptists.* While the term Regular Baptists is often used to denote the Particular Baptists in the three large conventions, there are also a number of smaller associations who claim to represent the original English Baptist principles before a distinction was made between Particular and General Baptists. They are similar to Duck River Association Baptists and are found in the South Atlantic States. In doctrine they are generally Arminian, practice foot washing, observe close Communion, reject creeds and denominational organizations, and establish fellowship with like-minded associations.

22. *Separate Baptists.* The origin of the Separate movement may be traced to the Whitefield revival, which caused the "New" and "Old Light" controversy among Congregationalists, Presbyterians, and Baptists, the "New Lights" overemphasizing the spiritual qualifications of the ministry. Under the leadership of the outstanding Baptist theologian Isaac Backus, who occupied a mediating position between Calvinism and Arminianism, many New England Baptist churches withdrew from fellowship with the Regular Baptists. This breach is now healed in New England and practically so in Virginia. In 1754 New England Separate Baptists under S. Stearns settled in North Carolina and spread westward, organizing several associations in the South Central States. These Separate Baptists are anti-Calvinistic, rejecting the limited Atonement and the double predestination, and lean toward Arminianism. In polity they follow the strict Baptist principles and are opposed to all ecclesiastical organizations.

23. *Duck River and Kindred Associations of Baptists.* As a protest against the theory of a limited Atonement a number of Baptist churches withdrew from the strictly Calvinistic Elk River (Tenn.) Association and in 1825 organized the Duck River Association. This association and smaller associations in the mountains of Tennessee occupy a mediating position between Calvinism and Arminianism, and are closely related to the Separate, United, and Regular Baptists. These associations frown upon every form of denominational organization and have no missionary or benevolent societies.

24. *Freewill Baptists.* The history of the so-called Freewill Baptists is difficult to trace, because these Baptists developed no real denominational consciousness and had no interest in organizing as a denomination. The earliest group of Arminian Baptists known as Freewill Baptists was gathered by Paul Palmer in North Carolina in 1727. But subsequently the Philadelphia Association exerted its Calvinistic influence, and during the eighteenth century the Freewill Baptists all but disappeared. Toward the close of this century John Randall, a Congregationalist, who had embraced Arminian and Baptist views, was denied fellowship with the Regular Baptists in New England and sought fellowship with the Freewill Baptists of the Middle and South Atlantic States. This and other support from Northern Freewill Baptists enabled the Southern "Freewillers" to re-organize and gradually to expand their work considerably. In the course of time the Free-

will Baptists of New England, also known as Free Baptists, lost heavily to the Adventist movement, and the remnant united with the Northern Convention of Baptists and are no longer a separate group. In doctrine the Freewill Baptists accept the "Five Points" of Arminianism, stressing particularly free will, stating that "all men, at one time or another, are found in such capacity as that, through the grace of God, they may be eternally saved."

25. *United American Freewill Baptist Church.* This is the colored Church corresponding in doctrine to the Freewill Baptists. In polity this group grants greater authority to the association or conference than most Arminian Baptists.

26. *United Baptists.* The origin of this group of Baptists is similar to that of Regular Baptists, ignoring the distinction between Calvinistic and Arminian views. In recent years many United Baptist churches, while retaining their historic name and affiliation with their respective associations, are also enrolled with the Northern or Southern Baptist Conventions.

27. *Christian Unity Baptist Association.* A small group of Arminian Baptists in North Carolina, which separated from the Regular Baptists in 1909.

28. *Independent Baptist Church of America.* A small group of Swedish Baptist churches following the Six-Principle Baptists. They are conscientious objectors to war.

29. *National Baptist Evangelical Life and Soul Saving Assembly of the U. S. A.* Founded by A. A. Banks in 1925 in Kansas City.

30. The total Baptist membership in the U. S. (1952): 17,500,734. See *Religious Bodies (U. S.), Bibliography.*

FEM

Baptist Brethren. See *Brethren* (*Dunkers*, etc.).

Baptist Student Union. See *Students, Spiritual Care of,* A.

Baptist World Alliance. See *Union Movements,* 10 ff.

Baptist Young People's Union. See *Young People's Organizations,* IV, 1—3.

Baraita. A Jewish book containing teachings of Tanna not included in the Mishna.

Barat, Ste.* Madeleine (1779—1865). French nun; founder of the Society of the Sacred Heart.

Barclay, Robert. See *Friends, Society of.*

Bardesanes. See *Gnosticism,* 7 h.

Barefooted Monks (and Nuns). The popular name for members of various orders who wear no footcovering whatever or only sandals. They are also known as "discalced" (*e. g.,* discalced Carmelites), though this term is properly applied only to those who wear sandals. The custom was introduced in the West by St. Francis,* probably with reference to Matt. 10:10. It has been followed by the stricter branches of many orders, among others by Capuchins, Poor Clares, Augustinians, Carmelites, Servites, and Passionists.

Baring-Gould, Sabine (1834—1924). Educated at Cambridge; held a number of positions as clergyman, last in Devonshire; wrote *Lives of the Saints* and numerous other works; best-known hymn: "Onward, Christian Soldiers."

Bar Kokba. See *Christs, False.*

Barmen Theses. In harmony with the basic principle of the National Socialism* of Germany, an attempt was made by the so-called *Deutsche Christen* to make the people's state central in religion. ("The social work of the German Evangelical Church endorses the social miracle of the *Volkswerden* in the national socialistic revolution; it aims to fill the newly awakened and newly developing German people with the Spirit of the Word of God in order that a new national and social 'Christ-striving' might find expression in the united people's community.") The basic principle of the movement, *"die Volkskirche bekennt sich zu Blut und Rasse,"* was stated in the first of the *Twenty-Eight Theses* of the *Braune Synode* held in Saxony (prepared by Walter Grundmann-Dresden and others, 1933).

Various opposition fronts developed (*e. g.,* Notbund of Niemoeller). The most important were the opposition *Bekenntnissynoden.* On Jan. 3 and 4, 1934, 320 pastors gathered at Barmen-Gemarke. There Barth's *Bekenntnis der freien Kirchensynode* was accepted as an answer to the *Twenty-Eight Theses.* In five parts (I. The Church in the Present Time; II. The Church under the Word of God; III. The Church in the World; IV. The Message of the Church; V. The Power of the Church) this confession fought against the aggrandizement of humanity in the Church and stressed the

95

need of submission to, and dependence on, God. Similar synods were held in various places in Germany, and Barth became a prominent leader among German opponents of the *Deutsche Christen* until stopped by Hitler. EL

Kurt Dietrich Schmidt, *Die Bekenntnisse und grundsaetzlichen Aeusserungen zur Kirchenfrage des Jahres 1933*, Vandenhoek u. Ruprecht, Goettingen, 1934 (*Bd. II: Das Jahr 1934* was published 1935 and contains the Barmen Theses); Stuart Herman, *It's Your Souls We Want*, Harper, c. 1943. For leaders on both sides as well as additional information see articles by W. Oesch, *CTM*, V:683—707; VI:594 to 600; 732—39; 835—48; 892—902. Discussion of principles in Theo. Engelder, "Kirche, Staat, Obrigkeit, Volk, Rasse, Familie — und Gottes Wort," *CTM*, VI:881—88; Hans Asmussen, "Barmen", *Theologische Existenz heute*, 24.

Bar Mitzvah (H. "son" of "duty"). A term applied to a Jewish boy when he has reached the age of thirteen; also the ceremony which solemnizes the fact that the boy has reached the age of duty.

Barnabas, Epistle of. See *Apostolic Fathers*, 6.

Barnabites, Order of. A religious order of secular clergy, established at Milan in 1533 and properly called Regular Clerks of the Congregation of Saint Paul.

Barnardo, Thomas John (1845 to 1905). B. in Dublin, Ireland; d. in London; founded "Barnardo Homes" for waifs and stray children; these homes cared for 60,000 up to the time of Barnardo's death; the homes trained the children in the religion of their parents.

Barnby, Joseph (1838—96). Composer of several hundred hymn tunes and of sacred choral music; editor of five hymnbooks; successful English organist and choirmaster; arranged for and conducted many English performances of the works of J. S. Bach. Barnby's compositions no longer enjoy their former popularity on account of their obsolete and saccharine character.

Barnes, Albert (1798—1870). Presbyterian theologian; b. at Rome, N.Y.; pastor at Philadelphia; leader of Liberals at the disruption (1837) of Presbyterian Church (reunited 1870); d. at Philadelphia; exegetical writer.

Barnes, Robert (1495—1540). Prior of Augustinians at Cambridge in 1523; converted by Luther's writings; fled to Wittenberg about 1528; published *Sentences* and a *History of the Popes*; frequent messenger between Henry VIII and Luther when the former was trying to arrange for his divorce; arranged meeting of the English divines with the Wittenbergers in 1536 and that of the Lutherans with the English at Lambeth in 1538; had a part in arranging the marriage of the king with Anne of Cleves; burned July 30, 1540, after a good confession, which Luther published in memory of "our good, pious table companion and guest of our home, this holy martyr St. Robertus."

Wm. Dallmann, *Robert Barnes, Luther's English Friend*, CPH, n. d.; "History of Robert Barnes," *British Reformers* (vol. 2), Presbyterian Bd. of Publication, Philadelphia, 1842.

Baronius, Caesar (1538—1607). Roman Catholic theologian; studied theology and law at Veroli and Naples; living in the Congregation of the Oratory at Rome, he spent thirty years gathering unpublished material in the Vatican archives for his *Annales Ecclesiastici*, which begin with the birth of Christ and go down to 1198, in chronicle form.

Baroque. See *Architecture, Ecclesiastical*, 6.

Barrow, Isaac (1630—77). Anglican theologian, mathematician. Londoner; ordained 1659; professor of mathematics at Cambridge, 1663 (resigned in favor of his pupil Isaac Newton); vice-chancellor, Cambridge, 1675. *Sermons; Pope's Supremacy;* etc.

Barsom. A number of small wire rods bound together and used as a sacred object by the Parsees (followers of Zoroaster) in their sacrificial ceremonies.

Barth, Christian Gottlob. B. July 13, 1799, Stuttgart; d. Nov. 12, 1862, Calv. Pastor at Moettlingen, 1824. Retiring from the ministry, 1838, he devoted his life to missions in connection with the Basel Missions. Founder of the Missionary Society of Wuerttemberg; edited *Calwer Missionsblatt*.

Barth, Karl. B. May 10, 1886, at Basel, Switzerland, son of Fritz Barth, mediating Reformed professor; pastor in Safenwyl, 1921; professor at Goettingen, 1921, Muenster, 1925, and Bonn,

1930; exiled by Nazis, 1935; professor at Basel, 1935; in his earlier years he was under the influence of Kierkegaard, neo-Kantianism, and the religious socialism of Ragaz; his *Roemerbrief* inaugurated the first phase of the Barthian movement, namely, a criticism of everything human in view of the "wholly Other"; the second phase began ca. 1925 and emphasized the formula *deus dixit* from a Calvinistic point of view. Works: *Credo, Roemerbrief, Das Wort Gottes und die Theologie, Die christliche Dogmatik im Entwurf, Die Lehre vom Wort Gottes, Prolegomena zur kirchlichen Dogmatik, Die kirchliche Dogmatik, Zwischen den Zeiten, Theologische Existenz heute,* and others. For discussion of his theology see *Switzerland, Contemporary Theology in.*

J. T. Mueller, "Karl Barth," *CTM,* XV:361—84 (extensive bibliography).

Barthel, Friedrich Wilhelm. B. Apr. 2, 1791, at Rosswein, Saxony; d. Feb. 12, 1857. One of the few who in that rationalistic age retained the old faith, he still held an influential government position at Leipzig, and his home became a center of true piety and Biblical Christianity, especially for the serious-minded among the students of the university. Emigrated with Stephan in 1838. First treasurer of the Missouri Synod.

Bartholomew, St., Massacre of. After the third religious war in France, which ended with the peace of St. Germain, the Protestants, called Huguenots, enjoyed freedom of conscience and worship and had three cities of safety. But this state of affairs was distasteful to the queen dowager of France, Catherine de Medici. Margaret of Valois, sister of King Charles IX, had married Henry of Navarre, the Huguenot leader, and this marriage was generally regarded as favorable to the Protestant cause. Catherine de Medici, nevertheless, sought to assassinate Admiral Gaspard de Coligny, a Huguenot leader who was in favor with the King. When her plot failed, she resolved to massacre all the Huguenots. She gained the support of Roman Catholic leaders and persuaded the King that the massacre was necessary for public safety. After gaining the King's authorization, the anti-Huguenot elements in the populace were turned against the Huguenots. The massacre began at four o'clock on Sunday, Aug. 24, 1572, St. Bartholo-

mew's Day. Coligny was first to fall before his enemies' treachery. From Paris the massacre spread throughout France; neither age, sex, rank, nor learning being spared. The number of victims is estimated between 25,000 and 100,000. Pope Gregory XIII had a solemn *Te Deum* sung at the Vatican, and a medal was struck commemorating the slaughter of the Protestants.

Bartolus of Sassoferrato (1314—57). Famous Italian jurist; reformed dialectical method (already used by Odofredus); wrote famous *Commentary on the Code of Justinian;* held Church and State to be equal in authority; defended the principle *rex in regno suo est imperator regni sui.*

Barton, Elizabeth. A noted impostor at the time of Henry VIII, who made use of a nervous disorder to simulate inspired possession, especially in the interest of hindering the progress of the Reformation in England; confessed to fraud and was beheaded in London, Apr. 20, 1534.

Barton, James Levi, D. D. B. Sept. 23, 1855, Charlotte, Vt.; ordained to Congregational ministry, 1885; missionary of American Board (Congregational) at Harpoot, Turkey, 1885—92; professor at Theological Seminary; 1888—92 in field; Foreign Secretary of American Board from 1894. D. 1936.

Baruch. See *Apocrypha,* A 3.

Bascom, John (1827—1911). American philosophical writer; pres. of U. of Wis.; professor at Williams; among his works: *Aesthetics, The New Theology, God and His Goodness.*

Basedow, Johann Heinrich (1724 to 1790). Educational reformer who advocated the preparation of special textbooks and literature for children; emphasized pleasurable interest in teaching, object teaching, nature study, physical training. In his Philanthropinum at Dessau he was given opportunity to put his reform ideas into practice. Wrote: *Methodenbuch; Elementarwerk.*

Basel Bible Society. See *Bible Societies,* 2.

Basel, Confession of. See *Reformed Confessions,* A 5.

Basel, Council of (1431—48). The last of the three Reform Councils (see *Councils,* 7). The objectives of the Council as stated in the first session were: 1) extirpation of heresy; 2) reunion of all Christians; 3) make provision for instruction in the faith; 4) settle disputes between Christian princes; 5) reformation of the Church in head and members; 6) re-establishment of discipline. The Council reaffirmed the Constance * doctrine of the supremacy of the council over the Pope. It granted the Hussites the right to give the cup to the laity. In 1433 Pope Eugenius IV, who had been summoned to appear before the Council, issued a bull annulling all the decrees of the Council passed against himself (this bull was later retracted). In 1437 Eugenius ordered the Council to reconvene at Ferrara. The remnant which remained at Basel deposed Eugenius and chose Felix V as pope (1439). In 1448 the rump council moved to Lausanne. After the death of Eugenius, Nicholas V was chosen pope and generally recognized. Felix thereupon abdicated (1449). Thus the schism came to an end, and the conciliar theory suffered a defeat.

J. H. von Wessenberg, *Die Grossen Kirchenversammlungen des 15. und 16. Jahrhunderts,* Constance, 1840.

Basel Evangelical Missionary Society. One of the oldest missionary societies, an offshoot of the *Deutsche Christentumsgesellschaft.* Founders: C. F. Spittler, Nicolaus von Brunn, Friedrich Steinkopf. Organized May 25, 1815; Christian Gottlieb Blumhardt, formerly secretary of the Christian Society, was first inspector, or manager. The society began sending out missionaries in 1822; missions were opened in Southern Russia, Liberia, the Gold Coast, South India, Kamerun, and China. The society is unionistic. Inspector Joseph Josenhans (1850—79) did much in systematizing and industrializing the work in the fields. Under his supervision the *Missionshaus* at Basel was erected. Female and medical missionaries were first sent out during the term of Inspector Otto Schott (1879—84). The missions in India and Africa suffered greatly during World War I. — Fields: Asia: China, British Malaya, Netherlands Indies; Africa: Gold Coast, Togoland, English and French Mandates in Kamerun. All work in India has been transferred to other organizations; also that in Africa.

Basil of Caesarea (the Great, 330? to 379). One of the "Three Great Cappadocians"; received Christian training from his mother, Emmelia, and his grandmother, Macrina; taught philosophy and other subjects in Caesarea,

Cappadocia; baptized and appointed lector; established a cloister in Pontus which became a pattern for Eastern monasteries; presbyter in Caesarea, 364; bishop, 370. Champion of orthodoxy in the Trinitarian controversies. The Church owed the final suppression of Arianism and semi-Arianism to Athanasius and the three Cappadocians. Basil thoroughly instructed and established his own congregation in the Scriptural truth, influenced others by his writings and wise counsels, and checked the persecution of the Arian Emperor Valens by his manly resistance. His work in the field of liturgics (the Byzantine Liturgy) and hymnology was also valuable. His practical Christianity is attested by the Basilians, an institution for the care of travelers, poor, and sick, to which he devoted all his revenues, himself living in the humblest manner. He left a great number of important books, among them the three books against Eunomius, the leader of the extreme Arians, and his work on *The Procession of the Holy Ghost,* against the Pneumatomachians.

W. K. L. Clarke, *St. Basil the Great,* Cambridge, 1913.

Basilians. 1. Monks or nuns following the rule of St. Basil; therefore, often, simply monks of the Greek Church. Basilian monasteries acknowledging the Pope are found in Sicily and Slavonian countries. 2. Priests of St. Basil. A society founded in France in 1800 for the training of priests. It has no connection with the rule of Basil or its monks. The society has a total of 188 Fathers and 107 professed clerics.

Basilica. See *Architecture,* 1 ff.

Basilides. See *Gnosticism,* 7e.

Bassler, Gottlieb (Dec. 10, 1813, to Oct. 3, 1868). B. at Langenthal, Switzerland; came to America at the age of 4; first served as printer and at 23 attended Pennsylvania College and the Lutheran Theological Seminary at Gettysburg, Pa. Active as teacher, missionary, pastor, and director. Licensed by the West Pennsylvania Synod, 1842; founded several Lutheran congregations; was secretary of the convention of the meeting that founded the Pittsburgh Synod, January, 1845; president of the Pittsburgh Synod, 1848—50, 1856—58, 1865—67. He was director of the Orphans' Farm School at Zelienople, Ohio, 1854—68, and first president of the General Council of the Evangelical Lutheran Church in North America, 1867—68.

Basutoland. British crown colony in South Africa (1884). Area, 11,716 square miles; population, 562,000. The Basutos are allied to the Bechuanos and of the same stock as the Kaffirs (superior to them in intelligence, inferior in bodily development); they engage in cattle raising; they permit no white settlements. Missions by the *Societe des Missions Evangeliques* since 1825, the Anglican Church, the Society for the Propagation of the Gospel. The Roman Catholic Church also carries on some mission work. See *Missions, Bibliography.*

Bataks (also Batta). Natives of Sumatra, East Indies. Speak a Malay dialect. The American Board made unsuccessful mission attempts among them (1834). The Rhenish Missionary Society was more successful, chiefly through L. Nommensen (d. 1918). They had, as of 1952, a membership of 600,000. In 1952 the Batak Christian Protestant Church became a member of the Lutheran World Federation. See *Missions, Bibliography.*

Bates, William (1625—99). The silver-tongued divine. Londoner; pastor (Presbyterian), London; ejected for non-conformity, 1662; failed in all efforts to bring about settlement between bishops and Dissenters. Wrote *Harmony of the Divine Attributes.*

Battle-Axe Experiment. See *Gates, Theophilus.*

Bauer, Bruno (1809—82). New Testament rational critic; taught at Berlin until his *Kritik der evangelischen Geschichte des Johannes* and *Kritik der evangelischen Geschichte der Synoptiker* brought about the revocation of his license.

Bauer, Friedrich (1812—74). Active with Wm. Loehe at Neuendettelsau, assisting him in training young men for Lutheran church work in the Middle West of the U. S. Author of a German grammar (15 editions published).

Bauernkrieg. See *Peasants' War.*

Baugher, Henry Lewis, Sr. (1803 to 1868). B. in Adams Co., Pa.; educated at Dickinson College and at the Princeton and Gettysburg seminaries. Pastor in Boonsboro, Md.; teacher at Gettysburg College, 1831; professor of Greek at Pennsylvania College, 1832 to 1850; second president of the last-mentioned institution, which position he held until his death. In 1844 he was a member of the committee which formed an "Abstract of the Doctrines and Practice of the Evangelical Lutheran Synod of Maryland," which omitted or rejected all distinctively Lutheran doctrines.

Baugher, Henry Lewis, Jr. B. 1840 at Gettysburg, Pa.; educated at Pennsylvania College and at the seminaries at Gettysburg, Pa., and Andover, Mass. He held pastorates at Wheeling, W. Va., Norristown, Pa., Indianapolis, Ind., and Omaha, Nebr.; served as professor of Greek in Pennsylvania College for 24 years and for a short time in Howard College, Washington, D. C.; president of the General Synod of the Lutheran Church, 1895—97; thereafter (1898) elected professor of theology for the United Synod of the South. D. Feb. 11, 1899.

Baumgarten, Michael (1812—89). German theologian; moved to religious life by Claus Harms; follower of Hengstenberg; then influenced by Schleiermacher and von Hofmann; deposed at Rostock for his utterances and publications without having been given permission to defend himself and without having Scriptural evidence cited against him; this procedure was later severely criticized even by staunch Lutherans.

Baumgarten, Sigismund Jacob (1706—57). Professor at Halle; introduced the philosophical methods of Chr. Wolff into theology, which marked the transition from Pietism to Rationalism.

Baumgarten-Crusius, Ludwig Friedrich Otto (1788—1842). B. at Merseburg; d. at Jena. Studied theology and philology at Leipzig. Professor there, 1810; at Jena, 1812; lectured on all branches of theology except church history; interested chiefly in history of dogma. Advocate of rational supernaturalism; opposed vulgar rationalism, but also the ninety-five theses of Klaus Harms.*

Baur, Ferdinand Christian (1792 to 1860). Founder and chief representative of the later Tuebingen school of theology; became professor of theology at Tuebingen in 1826; applied Hegel's principles and methods of philosophy to theology. The real essence of the Christian religion is to him the strictly ethical content of the teaching of Jesus, to the exclusion of the miraculous element. Peter represents the particularistic Jewish, Paul, the universalistic heathen-Christian viewpoint of Christ's teaching — both antagonistic to each other. Later, in the second century, these teachings were gradually brought into agreement. Thus the Christian religion has a perfectly natural historical development. Of St. Paul's Epistles only those to the Romans, Corinthians, and Galatians are genuine; all the rest, because of their conciliatory tendency, are considered spurious. See *Exegesis*.

Baur, Gustav Ad. L. (1816—89). Professor at Giessen and Leipzig; "combined broad culture and mild Lutheranism in teaching OT exegesis and practical theology."

Bauslin, David H. B. at Winchester, Va., Jan. 21, 1852; educated at Wittenberg College; ordained 1878; received D. D. from Wittenberg, 1890, and LL. D. from Lenoir College, 1920; pastor at Tippecanoe City, Bucyrus, Springfield, and Canton, Ohio; professor of historical and practical theology at Hamma Divinity School, Springfield, Ohio, 1896 to 1922; dean of the seminary, 1911—22. Editor of the *Lutheran World*, 1901 to 1912; president of General Synod, 1905 to 1907; author of *Lutheran Movement of the 16th Century; Is the Ministry an Attractive Vocation?* Active in organization of the United Lutheran Church of America, 1918. D. Mar. 3, 1922, at Bucyrus, Ohio.

Bautain, Louis, Abbe (1796—1867). French philosophical theologian; following Kant, he rejected rational theistic arguments but was required to sign statements upholding the rationality of the existence of God, immortality, and revelation.

Bavarian Foreign Mission Society. See *Neuendettelsau Missionary Society.*

Baxter, Richard (1615—91). Educated at Wroxeter School; held chaplaincy to Cromwell, later to Charles II; refused bishopric of Hereford; afterwards took out license as Nonconformist minister; published *Saints' Everlasting Rest;* did much work in early English hymnody and the English Psalters; wrote: "Lord, It Belongs Not to My Care."

Bayle, Pierre (1647—1706). French philosopher; professor at Sedan and Rotterdam; skeptic; considered faith and reason exclusive realms; emphasized freedom of thought and toleration; d. in exile. Wrote: *Pensées diverses sur la comete de 1680; Critique Générale de l'Histoire du Calvinisme de Maimbourg; Dictionnaire historique et critique.*

Bazaars. See *Finances in the Church,* 5.

Beadle. 1. A mace-bearer attendant upon ecclesiastical dignitaries. 2. An inferior parish officer with various minor duties connected with a church or vestry (chiefly in England).

Beads, Use of. See *Rosary.*

Beatific Vision. See *Glory.*

Beatification. See *Canonization.*

Beaufort, Pierre de. See *Popes,* 14.

Bec. A monastery in Normandy made famous by Anselm and Lanfranc.

Bechuanas. Kaffir natives of Bechuanaland (275,000 square miles) in Transvaal, Africa. Under British sovereignty. They number approximately 294,000. Amenable to civilization. Seem to have had little of heathen religion or practice. Missions by the London Mission Society (Livingstone, Robert Moffat), the Anglican Church, the Wesleyan Mission Society, the Adventists, the Nederduits-Gereformeerde Kerk, and the Ev. Luth. Hermannsburg Mission, the United Free Church of Scotland. See *Missions, Bibliography.*

Beck, Johann Tobias (1804—78). B. in Balingen; pastor at Waldthann near Crailsheim, and Mergentheim; prof. at Basel, 1836, and Tuebingen, 1843. Opponent of the critico-historical method as developed by Strauss and Baur; emphasized return to the Bible and Biblical truth. He sought to build his system of doctrine on the Bible alone, avoiding historical theological terms and holding that even the Confessions were significant only because they performed a significant task in history. He held that inspiration was the living, dynamic union and interpenetration of the human and divine spirit (three levels of *theopneustia;* errors and contradictions in "irrelevant" matters in Scripture). The kingdom of God, he taught, was the supermundane economy of spirit and life (the heavenly reality), which was brought and revealed to man through Christ. The ethical or moral is the first and essential mark of the Christian. The above formal and material principles led to departures from Lutheran orthodoxy in Beck's theological system (emphasis on the psychological in his doctrine of justification rather than on the objective act, seeing the saving hand of love rather than the majestic pronouncement of the Judge; faith, construed as the active ethical grasp of Christ — a dynamic gift producing personal righteousness — is the cause of justification).

Beck, Vilhelm. See *Denmark, Lutheranism in,* 10.

Becker, Albert Ernst Anton (1834 to 1899). Conductor of the Berlin Cathedral Choir; composer of orchestral and choral music. His *Reformation Cantata* won for him a much-coveted prize in 1883 and is a work deserving of the recognition it has enjoyed.

Becker, Cornelius (1561—1604). Hymn writer who vainly prepared the Psalter in hymn form so as to offset the influence of Ambrosius Lobwasser. Though used by Seth Calvisius and Heinrich Schuetz, Becker's texts lacked the popular appeal of the texts prepared by Ludwig Helmbold.

Becket, Thomas à (1118—70). As chancellor of England (1157), an ardent supporter of King Henry II in his endeavor to obtain absolute mastery in State and Church; as archbishop of Canterbury (1162) he sought to free the Church from all civil jurisdiction; his refusal to sign the "Constitution of Clarendon" made it necessary for him to flee to France; the Pope succeeded in forcing a reconciliation, and he returned to England; new difficulties ensued, and Becket was murdered by four retainers of Henry; within three years after his death, Becket was canonized by Alexander III; his burial place was a shrine until Becket was stigmatized as a traitor by Henry VIII; his feast is celebrated on Dec. 29.

Beckman, And. Fredrik (1812—94). Professor of theology at Upsala, Sweden; played an important part in swaying the faculty of Upsala from neology (see *Sweden, Luth. Ch. in,* 3 f.) to evangelical theology by his defense of the deity of Christ.

Beddome, Benjamin (1717—95). At first Anglican; joined Baptist Church; from 1740 till his death, minister at Bourton-on-the-Water, Gloucestershire; wrote: "When Israel Through the Desert Passed" and many other hymns.

Bede (673—735; "the Venerable"). B. in Northumbria; studied and taught at Jarrow; wrote scientific and theological treatises, among these 24 commentaries (allegorical), two books of hymns and epigrams, and his famous *Church History of the Angles.* Though

many of his pupils occupied prominent positions, he remained a simple monk. His influence spread through Europe, and he is often called "the Teacher of the Middle Ages." He dictated the last part of his Anglo-Saxon translation of John on his deathbed. See bibliography under *Saints.*

Bedlam (corruption of Bethlehem). Institution originally founded in 1247 for housing visiting bishops and canons of St. Mary of Bethlehem; given by Henry VIII to the city of London as a hospital for lunatics, 1547; in later years it became known for its brutal treatment of insane people.

Beecher, Henry Ward (1813—87). Famous orator; b. Litchfield, Conn.; son of Lyman Beecher; minister (Presbyterian at Lawrenceburg and Indianapolis, Ind., and at Plymouth Church (Congregational), Brooklyn, N. Y., 1847; issued hymnal; made antislavery speeches; lecturer; accepted evolution and Higher Criticism; was sued for adultery, but acquitted; withdrew, with his church, from Congregational Association 1882; d. Brooklyn. Author.

Beecher, Lyman (1775—1863). Noted clergyman; b. New Haven, Conn.; pastor (Congregational) at Litchfield, Conn., and Boston; pastor (Presbyterian) at Cincinnati and president there of Lane Theological Seminary; father of Harriet Beecher Stowe; d. Brooklyn, N. Y. Author.

Beethoven, Ludwig van (1770 to 1827). The master in whose hands the classical temper in music reached its highest development and who went beyond the bounds of classicism and helped bring on the advent of Romanticism. Born at Bonn, he was the son of an irrational father who foolishly wanted to force Ludwig to become a child prodigy like the young Mozart that he, the father, might live in financial security. However, Beethoven's profound talent developed more slowly than that of the more brilliant Mozart. Beethoven later studied with Haydn, who proved to be unsatisfactory as a teacher. Albrechtsberger was then approached, and Beethoven found him to be an outstanding pedagog. In Vienna, the music capital of his day, Beethoven soon won acclaim for his ability as a pianist; he was respected as a composer, but not understood, not even by Haydn. His deafness of later years troubled him a great deal, though for posterity it proved to be a blessing in disguise since it caused him to withdraw from others and concentrate on his inner self. His works include nine symphonies, five piano concertos, one violin concerto, thirty-two piano sonatas, nine sonatas for violin and piano, seventeen string quartets, a large number of shorter works, the oratorio *Christus am Oelberg*, and the *Missa Solemnis*. Beethoven may hardly be called a church composer; even his *Missa Solemnis* was intended for the concert stage and not for the church.

Paul Bekker, *Beethoven*, London, 1925; John N. Burk, *The Life and Work of Beethoven*, New York, 1943; A. Kalischer, *Beethoven und seine Zeitgenossen*, Leipzig, 1910; W. Riezler, *Beethoven*, New York, 1938; Alexander W. Thayer, *The Life of Ludwig van Beethoven* (English ed. by H. E. Krehbiel), Beethoven Assn., New York, 1921.

Beghards, Beguins. Semimonastic communities of Western Europe, from the 12th century on, the sisterhood of the Beguins the original order; celibacy required as long as one remained a member; supporting themselves by manual labor, they devoted themselves to devotional exercises and deaconess work. Already in the 13th century the second stage of monasticism set in: corruption, worldliness, immorality. Persecuted for heresy and prosecuted for concubinage, etc., many joined the Tertiaries of the mendicant orders. The few Beguinages remaining in the Netherlands serve for the maintenance of unmarried women.

Behavior. See *Christian Teaching*, 1 ff.

Behaviorism. See *Psychology*, A, J 4.

Behm, Martin. B. Sept. 16, 1557, in Lauban, Silesia. After serving as private tutor in Vienna, he studied at the University of Strassburg, and later became diaconus and eventually chief pastor at Lauban, Silesia. A renowned preacher and faithful pastor in times of trouble (famine — pestilence — war), he likewise became a prolific author and hymn writer. He wrote some 480 hymns, which emphasize especially the Passion of our Lord. D. 1622.

Behrens, Wm. Henry. B. Dec. 6, 1870, at St. Louis, Mo.; graduated at St. Louis, 1893; pastor at Salt Lake City, Utah, 1893—94; at Tacoma, Wash. (doing mission work in practically the entire State), 1894—98; at Portland, Oreg., 1898—1909; at Chester, Ill., 1909

to 1924; professor at Concordia Seminary, Springfield, Ill., 1924—43; d. Mar. 29, 1943; Vice-President of the Oregon and Washington District, 1899 to 1906; President, 1906—09.

Beichtvesper. See *Confession*.

Beissel, Conrad (1690—1768). German mystic; emigrated to Pennsylvania; established Seventh-Day Baptists; wrote earliest volume of German poetry in America: *Goettliche Liebestoene.* See *Baptist Bodies*, 17; *Brethren, Dunkers*, 1; *Communistic Societies*, 5.

Bekenntnissynoden (1933—34). See *Barmen Theses.*

Bel and the Dragon. See *Apocrypha*, A 3.

Belgian Congo. See *Congo*.

Belgic Confession. See *Reformed Confessions*, C 1.

Belgium. A small country north of France, formerly a part of the Netherlands, but since 1830 a separate country, the northern portion of which is Flemish and the southern Walloon. Area: 11,752 square miles; population, 8,361,220. The country was evangelized at the time when northern France was gained for the Gospel and, in part, when the lowlands of Holland were Christianized. The country became very strongly Catholic and has remained so to the present day, the Protestant communions being represented only sparingly by immigrants from Germany, Sweden, and by Anglicans and Methodists (who report 1,850 members as of 1952). The Swedish Lutherans have churches in Brussels and Antwerp. In 1952 only one half of one per cent of the population was Protestant, with approximately 125 stations. A strong Protestant organization is the Union of Evangelical Protestant Churches of Belgium, with French, Dutch, and formerly German congregations, the strongest stations being Liége, Verviers, Seraing, Brussels, Antwerp, Ghent, La Bouverie, Dour, Paturages, Jolimont, and Tournai. In addition to this body there is the Evangelical Society or the Belgian Christian Missionary Church, which is a free Church, made up of converts from Roman Catholicism or their children. It has its greatest strength in the Walloon districts. There are English churches at Antwerp, Bruges, Brussels, and Ostend. There is also a Protestant society for carrying on mission work in the Belgian Congo. The Ev. Luth. Free

Church of Belgium (2 pastors, 1952) is affiliated with the Synodical Conference. The Roman Catholic Church of Belgium was formally organized in 1561, this date also indicating the cessation of foreign authority. After Belgium became an independent country, an adjustment of boundaries was made to arrange for the new situation. The priests are educated at episcopal seminaries and at the University of Louvain. The Roman Catholic Church receives a direct sum of money from the state, although it does not enjoy any particular legal prerogative. The archdiocese of Mechlin, which is co-extensive with Belgium, was created by the Pope in 1559, and the most important bishoprics are those of Bruges, Ghent, Liége, Namur, and Tournai. See *Missions, Bibliography; Reformed Confessions.* OHS

Believers. See *Brethren, Plymouth.*

Believer's Baptism. See *Baptist Bodies,* 1.

Bell, Book, and Candle. An expression referring to symbolic actions formerly used in excommunication: shutting the book after pronouncing the curse, extinguishing a candle, and tolling the bell as for the dead. "Bell, book, and candle — candle, book, and bell, forward and backward to curse Faustus to hell" (Marlowe).

Bellamy, Joseph. See *New England Theology,* 3.

Bellarmine (Bellarmino, Roberto Francesco Romolo). Roman Catholic theologian; b. in Tuscany, 1542; d. at Rome, 1621. Showed brilliant gifts early in life; his mother's wish that he become a Jesuit carried out; studied theology at Padua and Louvain, beginning with 1567; ordained priest at Ghent, 1570; knew both Greek and Hebrew; his chief writing the celebrated *Disputationes de Controversiis Christianae Fidei,* in four volumes, the first treating of the Word of God, of Christ, and of the Pope, the second of the authority of the councils and of the Church, the third of the Sacraments, and the fourth of grace, free will, justification, and good works, a systematic presentation of the doctrines promulgated by the Council of Trent, to which J. Gerhard,* in his *Loci,* gave the proper answer.

Bells, Church. In the early Christian Church the faithful were summoned to worship by word of mouth; at a later date, trumpets were used, also large hammers, struck against wooden or iron instruments. Bells were introduced in the ninth century, suspended at first in special bell towers, or campaniles, later in the spires of the churches themselves, their use meeting with great favor almost everywhere.

Belot, Gustave (1859—1930). French philosopher; opposed the science of morals because he held that metaphysics could not be used to establish morality; held that morality, like culture, is a development or growth.

Beltane. The spring religious festival of Christian Celtic peoples.

Bender, William (1845—1901). Professor at Bonn; added the illusionistic critique to Ritschlian thought.

Benedicite. See *Canticles.*

Benedict, St.* See *Benedictines.*

Benedict XIV. See *Popes,* 24.

Benedict XV. See *Popes,* 31.

Benedict of Aniane (751—821). A Visigothic monastic reformer supported by Charlemagne; writer in Adoptionist controversy; compiler of monastic rules; general supervisor of Frankish monasteries.

Benedict of Nursia (ca. 480 to ca. 543). Founder of Monte Cassino (ca. 530); using earlier writings (of Basil, Cassian, and others), he worked out the Rule of 529, which was almost universally adopted in the Middle Ages by Western monasteries. The rule shows excellence in organizing the worship, reading, and laboring activities of monks.

Benedictines. The monastic order founded on the Rule of Benedict of Nursia, the father of Western monasticism. This rule was based on earlier rules, and while strict in some respects, was, in general, quite moderate. In addition to the three usual obligations of poverty, celibacy, and obedience it required manual labor of the monks, but also provided for daily reading and for the establishment of convent libraries. Favored by Rome, the Benedictines absorbed the adherents of rival rules, and by 811 only traces of the rivals remained. Thereafter, for centuries, the Benedictine remained the normal monastic type. During the palmy days of the order (821—1200) its influence controlled the civilization of the entire Christian West. The Benedictines repaid with usury the favor extended them by the Papacy. The riches gathered by the monasteries, however, brought widespread corruption and immorality into the order, which were only partly and temporarily checked by the Cluniac, the Cistercian, and other reforms. Inner decline and attacks from without reduced the 37,000 Benedictine houses of the 14th century to only 50 in the early 19th century. There are approximately 550 Benedictine priests in the U. S., 130 clerics and several hundred lay brothers (1950).

Benedict's sister, Scholastica, established a convent, but it is doubtful whether that was the beginning of the Benedictine nuns. Certainly many women early adopted Benedict's rule, though they were not strictly enclosed. Benedictine nuns came to Germany with Boniface.

Benedictions. The Aaronic benediction, Num. 6:24-26, was in use throughout the Old Testament period, not as a mere utterance of a pious wish, but the offering of the grace of God, to be re-received unto salvation by faith. The position of the Aaronic benediction, both in the Temple services and in synagog worship, was at the end of the liturgical part of the service. This benediction was in use in the early Church, as a passage in the *Apostolic Constitutions* (II, 57) shows, and was retained by Luther in his orders of service as the only one commanded by God. It conveys to the assembled congregation, which has accepted the salvation of God in the means of grace, the blessing of the Triune God. The Apostolic benediction, 2 Cor. 13:14, is customarily used only in the minor services, at the same place in the order of worship which is set aside for the Aaronic benediction in the morning worship.

Benedictus. See *Canticles.*

Benefice. The right, granted to a cleric, of receiving the income from lands or other church property in return for the performance of spiritual duties. The value of benefices led to many abuses and much controversy in the Middle Ages. (See *Simony.*) Benefices are almost unknown in the United States.

Beneficence. See *Benevolence.*

Beneficiary Education. A term applied to the systematic assistance given to young men in their preparation for the ministry.

Benefit of Clergy. See *Clergy.*

Benevolence. See *Alms; Charities, Christian; Social Work; Inner Missions; Deaconesses.*

Benevolent Societies. See *Aged, Homes for; Hospitals,* etc.; *Child Care and Child-Placing Agencies.*

Bengel, Johann Albrecht (1687 to 1752). Foremost theologian of the post-Reformation period in Wuerttemberg; studied at Tuebingen; professor of the *Klosterschule* at Denkendorf and (1713) pastor of the village congregation; in 1741 appointed "prelate" at Herbrechtingen, in 1749 at Alpirsbach and Consistorial Counselor, with residence at Stuttgart. Bengel was a man of eminent piety and of vast and sound learning. In 1734 he published an edition of the New Testament with an *apparatus criticus,* based on a careful study of the text in various manuscripts. His greatest work — most valuable even to this day — is *Gnomon Novi Testamenti* (1742). He taught Chiliasm and predicted the millennium for the year 1837.

O. Waechter, *J. A. Bengel, Lebensabriss,* Stuttgart, 1865.

Ben Hur Life Association. Formerly *Supreme Tribe of Ben Hur,* an order which operates on the lodge system, but provides for insurance members, of whom no initiation or attendance at meetings is required.

Bennett, John Coleman. B. July 22, 1902; studied Williams College, Oxford Univ., Union Theol. Seminary; professor Auburn Theol. Sem., then Pacific School of Religion, at Union Theol. Seminary since 1943; liberal in theology, author of noted books.

Bennett, Sir William Sterndale (1816—75). Received his musical training in England and Germany (Leipzig). Robert Schumann and F. Mendelssohn-Bartholdy were among his personal friends and admirers. His ability as a performer, conductor, and composer were recognized in Germany (Gewandhaus concerts) before they were recognized in his native land. The Victorian character of his music relegates it more to the background, also in the field of church music.

Benson, Louis Fitz-Gerald (1855 to 1930). B. in Philadelphia; educated at the University of Pennsylvania; practiced law for seven years. Then entered upon and completed the theological course at Princeton Theological Seminary and was ordained to the Presbyterian ministry in 1886. After a pastorate of six years he took up his lifework, that of hymnody and liturgics. He edited a series of hymnbooks for his Church and wrote a number of works, chief among them: *The English Hymnal, The Hymnody of the Christian Church, Studies of Familiar Hymns* (2 vol.).

Bente, G. Friedrich. B. Jan. 22, 1858, at Wimmer, Hanover; graduated St. Louis 1881; pastor at Humberstone, Stonebridge, and Jordan, Ontario, 1882 to 1893; vice-president of Canada (now Ontario) District 1885, president 1887 to 1893; professor at Concordia Seminary, St. Louis, Mo., 1893—1926; D. D. (Adelaide); for years editor of *Lehre und Wehre;* wrote: *Was steht der Vereinigung der lutherischen Synoden Amerikas im Wege? Gesetz und Evangelium; Amerikanisches Luthertum; American Lutheranism;* edited *Concordia Triglotta* (English text conjointly with Dr. Dau). D. Dec. 15, 1930, at Redwood City, Calif.; buried, St. Louis, Mo., Dec. 22, 1930.

J. Bente, *Dr. Friedrich Bente,* CPH, 1936; L. Fuerbringer, "F. Bente als Theolog," *CTM,* II: 416 ff.

Bentham, Jeremy (1748 — 1 8 3 2). English philosophical jurist; especially through his *Introduction to Principles of Morals and Legislation* he influenced thinking on government, social and prison reform.

Bentley, Richard (1662 — 1742). Founder of historical philology; b. near Wakefield; priest 1692; master of Trinity College, Cambridge, and later professor of divinity; d. there. Philological works; proposed critical edition of New Testament; *Lectures Against Atheism.*

Benze, Chas. Theo. B. Sept. 19, 1865; ordained 1897; pastor: Beaver Falls, Pa., 1897—98; Erie, Pa., 1898—1908; pres. of Pittsburgh Synod (General Council), 1908—10; pres. of Thiel College, 1909—13; American professor at Kropp Seminary, Germany, 1913—15; professor at Mt. Airy, Pa., 1915—36; sent by General Council as commissioner to its mission field in India, 1918; vice-president of Board of Foreign Missions (U. L. C.), 1918; sent by National Lutheran Council to Russia, 1922, to establish relief work; contributor to the *Lutheran, Lutheran Quarterly,* etc.; author, together with T. E. Schmauk, of *The Confessional Principle of the Lutheran Church.* D. July 3, 1936, at Philadelphia.

Benzelius Family. See *Sweden, Church of,* 2.

Berdyaev, Nikolai Alexandrovich (1874—1948). B. at Kiev. Studied there. Russian philosopher, at first a Marxist, later leaning to Neo-Kantianism. Banished from Russia, he continued his activity in Berlin and Paris, where he founded religio-philosophical academies. Man is the center of his teaching: human liberty and creativity.

Berean Bands. In the year 1909 Charles J. G. Hensman of London, England, founded an international and interdenominational movement to encourage the habit of memorizing Scripture and named it Berean Band Movement. Gradually the movement spread over England and in America. Berean Bands are numerous in Great Britain, with memberships running from six or more to many hundreds. That of the Metropolitan Tabernacle, London, has 800 members. The sole obligation of membership is to learn one Bible verse every week, with the suggestion that this be called to mind at least once every day until the first Lord's day of the month following. The membership fee is only five cents annually, and a list of verses for the year is furnished without charge. These are carefully chosen, with a definite subject each month and, as far as possible, a completeness of subjects in each year. The Moody Bible Institute of Chicago is now the American representative of the movement.

Berengar of Tours. B. early in the 11th century at Tours, canon of the cathedral there and head of its school; d. 1088. The important facts of his life are connected with the second Eucharistic controversy.* This controversy with Lanfranc ushered in the period of Scholasticism.*

Berg Bible Society. See *Bible Societies,* 2.

Berg, Frederick. B. Mar. 20, 1856, Logansport, Ind.; educated at Concordia College, Fort Wayne, and Concordia Seminary, St. Louis; commissioned (1878) as first resident missionary and pastor of the Negro Lutheran church, Little Rock, Ark.; pastor: Decatur, Ind., 1881—91; Beardstown, Ill., 1891—1911; professor at Immanuel Luth. College, Greensboro, N. C., 1911—36. Received honorary D. D. from Concordia Seminary, St. Louis, 1936. D. Mar. 9, 1939.

Bergemann, Gustav Ernst. B. Aug. 9, 1862, Hustisford, Wis., educated at Northwestern College, Watertown, and the Milwaukee Seminary of the Wis. Synod; pastor: Bay City, Mich., 1887 to 1892; Tomah, Wis., 1892—99; Fond du Lac, Wis., since 1899; member of Indian Missions Board, 1903—17; pres. of old Wis. Synod, 1908—17; then pres. of the new Joint Synod 1917—33.

Bergh, Johan A. B. Jan. 12, 1847, at Odemark, Norway; came to America in 1860; grad., Augustana Coll., 1869; Augsburg Sem., 1871; pastorates at Fergus Falls, Minn., 1871—77; Waterloo Ridge, Iowa, 1877—82; Luther Valley, Wis., 1882—1912; Elliott, Ill., 1912 to 1916; hospital missionary, St. Paul, Minn., 1916—; supt., Chicago Dist. Norw. Luth. Conf., 1883—90; chrm., Madison Circuit, United Norw. Luth. Ch., 1897—1912. Author: *Gammel og my retning; Hans Egede; Livsbilleder fra Kirken i Norden; Underfuld boenhoerelse; I sidste oieblik; I ledige stunder; Slaveristriden; Den norsk lutherske kirke i Amerika; Den norsk lutherske kirkes historie i Amerika; Se, det Guds lam.* Editor: *Ugeblad for kirken og hjemmet; Vort blad; Kirken og hjemmet.* D. Feb. 5, 1927.

Bergic Book. See *Lutheran Confessions,* C 2.

Bergmann, Christopher (1793 to 1832). B. at Ebenezer, Ga.; studied under his father, John E. Bergmann; pastor at Ebenezer; member of Synod of South Carolina and secretary, 1825 to 1832. Influenced by Dr. John Bachmann to become Lutheran minister; ordained 1824; succeeded his father at Ebenezer; held Salzburger churches together and brought them into connection with the South Carolina Synod.

Bergmann, John Ernest. Last of the ministers sent to the Salzburgers in Georgia by Dr. S. Samuel Urlsperger of Augsburg; labored in Georgia from 1785 to the time of his death, 1824.

Bergson, Henri (1859—1941). French Jew; philosopher; b. at Paris, professor at College de France; recipient of Nobel prize. In his philosophy, Bergson conceived of a Vital Impulse which is basic to all activity and the creative spirit of world-process. This god is itself not complete, but grows in goodness, knowledge, power, etc. He stressed the reality of time and the importance of change and evolution more than Hegel. Consciousness is

continuous knowledge of the past and survives after death. Intuition was to him the highest source of truth, and in accordance with that view he took a special interest in mystics. Wrote *Essay on Immediate Data of Consciousness; Matter and Memory; Creative Evolution; Spiritual Energy; Two Sources of Morality and Religion;* and others.

Berkeley, Dean. See *Protestant Episcopal Church,* 1.

Berkeley, George (1685 — 1753). English philosopher; lecturer at Dublin; lived for a while in America; spent last years in retirement at Oxford. The philosophy of Berkeley champions idealism. Beginning with the observation that all our knowledge comes to us through sense impressions, he sought to reduce matter to a complex of impressions and thus deny the existence of material substance. He believed, however, in the reality of spiritual being. Wrote *Essay Towards a New Theory of Vision* and *A Treatise Concerning the Principles of Human Knowledge.*

Berkemeier, Gottlieb C. L. (1855 to 1924). For many years German secretary of General Council; director of Wartburg Orphans' Home, Mount Vernon, N. Y.; author, poet; editor of *Der deutsche Lutheraner.*

Berkemeier, W. C. (1820—99). Came from Germany to America 1847; attended Gettysburg 1849—51; pastor at Pittsburgh, Pa., Wheeling, W. Va., and Mt. Vernon, N. Y.; associated with R. Neumann in pioneer Emigrant Mission work.

Berkenmeyer, Wm. C. (1686—1751). B. in Lueneburg; became successor to Falckner in Hudson Valley churches, 1725. During his pastorate in New York a substantial stone church was built in 1729. In 1731 he moved to Loonenburg, in the northern part of his extended parish. Representing the orthodox school of Lutheranism in America, he became the leader of the pastors in the Hudson Valley. A *Kerck-Ordinantie,* drafted by him, bound the Dutch and German churches of New York and New Jersey together in a synod as early as 1735, which had only one meeting as far as the records show. Berkenmeyer in his work and writings sought to advance pure Lutheranism and prevent the ecclesiastical mingling of Lutherans and Reformed. Married Benigna

Sibylla Kocherthal in 1727. His journal, written in Dutch, German, and Latin, contains much valuable historical material.

Berkshire Theology. See *New England Theology*, 2.

Berlin Missionary Society I (*Gesellschaft zur Befoerderung der evangelischen Missionen unter den Heiden*). Originated by "Father" Jaenicke (1748 to 1827) in Berlin, 1800, when he founded a training school for missionaries; organized in 1824 by Neander, Tholuck, von Gerlach, and others. 1834 the society sent out its own missionaries. The character of the society is unionistic. It is well organized, having many branches throughout Germany. A large training school is maintained at Berlin. On the field industrial work is fostered. Fields: Africa, East Indies, China. In common with all German missions in Africa the mission work was disorganized by World War II.

Berlin Missionary Society II. See *Gossner Missionary Society*.

Bernard of Clairvaux, St. (1091 to 1153). The most influential man of his day; an upright monk (Cistercian), spending himself in ascetic practices. His wise rule as first and lifelong abbot of the newly founded cloister at Clairvaux, France (1115), served to extend the order (now also called Bernardines) throughout Europe, and the influence of his eloquence and personality gave a new impetus to monasticism. He ended the papal schism in favor of Innocent II. In his controversy with Abelard, the rationalist (1140), he stood for the equally false principle of mysticism. He preached the Second Crusade (1146), which, contrary to his prophecy, did not sweep back the Mohammedans, but swept Eugene III into office. He was an eloquent preacher, an able writer of theological treatises, a composer of beautiful hymns, a universal mediator, the adviser of pope and king and of the common man. Despite his exaltation of monachism as the ideal of Christianity, his excessive glorification of Mary (whose "immaculate conception," however, he opposed), and his enthusiastic support of the Papacy as the highest authority in the Church, he was a sincerely pious, a truly humble Christian, and he was that because he loved the Bible and because he believed in justification by faith, deploring on his deathbed, as throughout his life, the sinfulness of his life (*Perdite vixi*), and

imploring the mercy of God for the sake of the righteousness gained by Christ — a psychological enigma indeed. Luther says: "When Bernard is speaking of Christ, it is a pleasure indeed to listen to him; but when he leaves that subject and discourses on rules and works, it is no longer St. Bernard." Aug. Neander, *Der heilige Bernhard und sein Zeitalter*, F. & A. Perthes, Hamburg & Gotha, 1848 (English trans. by Mathilda Wrench); J. C. Morison, *Life and Times of St. Bernard*, Macm., 1863; A. Harnack, *Dogmengeschichte* (vol. III), Mohr, Tuebingen, 1905; T. Dierks, "The Doctrine of Justification According to Bernard," *CTM*, VIII: 748—53.

Bernard of Morlaix or of *Cluny*. Lived in twelfth century; entered Abbey of Cluny, afterwards becoming abbot, while the monastery was at the height of wealth and fame; composed *De contemptu mundi*, from which the hymns "Jerusalem the Golden," "Brief Life Is Here Our Portion," "For Thee, O Dear, Dear Country," and "The World Is Very Evil" are taken.

Bernard Sylvestris (12th c.). Medieval Platonist; expositor of the macrocosm-microcosm fantasy; wrote *De mundi universitate*.

Bernardine Monks. See *Bernard of Clairvaux; Cistercians*.

Bernhard, Christoph (1627—92). The last and most important pupil of Heinrich Schuetz, served as *Kapellmeister* in Dresden, where Schuetz had been active. He studied also with Carissimi and was active for a time in Hamburg. Bernhard's works reveal his skill as a composer and contrapuntist.

Bernheim, Gotthardt D. B. Nov. 8, 1827, at Iserlohn, Prussia; came to America 1831; grad., Luth. Sem., Lexington, S. C., 1849; pastorates at: Charleston, S. C., 1850—58; near Concord, N. C., 1858—60; Phillipsburg, N. J., 1883—93; Wilmington, N. C., 1893—95; organized the later Mont Amoena Female Seminary at Mt. Pleasant, N. C.; instructor at Elizabeth Coll., Mt. Pleasant, N. C. Author: *The Success of God's Work; History of the German Settlements and of the Lutheran Church of North and South Carolina; Localities of the Reformation; The First Twenty Years of the History of St. Paul's Church, Wilmington;* Editor: *At Home and Abroad,* 1881—88. D. Oct. 25, 1916.

Bertha of Kent. Franconian princess; in 596 married Ethelbert of Kent, the most important of the seven small monarchies of England; instrumental in reintroducing Christianity in England, in 597. See *Augustine of Canterbury*.

Berthold of Regensburg. See *Preaching, Christian, History of*, 8.

Bertling, Ernst August (1721—69). German theologian; studied law; then theology; professor at Helmstedt (1748 to 1753); rector of *Gymnasium* at Danzig; wrote: *Disputatio de Gradibus Prohibitis Secundum Jus Naturae, Disputatio de Jure Gentium Voluntario*, and other works which show the influence of his legal training.

Bes. Egyptian god of dancing and pleasure whose image the Gnostics adopted as an amulet.

Besant, Annie (1847—1933). British theosophist; first loyal Episcopalian; later worked with Charles Bradlaugh in Free Thought movements; became pupil of Mme. Blavatsky; pres. of Theosophical Society (1907); traveled widely in its interest, especially in India; founded two schools for Hindus in Benares; established Indian Home Rule League; vacillated in her support of nationalist position; traveled in England and America with J. Krishnamurti, the "new world teacher," and founded new Order of the Star.

Besold, Hieronymus (d. 1562). Friend of Luther, Melanchthon, and Veit Dietrich; edited *Enarrationes Lutheri in Genesin*.

Bessarion (1395—1472). Patriarch of Constantinople; archbishop of Nicaea; sought to reconcile Eastern and Western churches; friend of Eugenius IV, who made him cardinal; greatest scholar of his day, he extended speculative thought in theology by his defense of Plato: *In Calumniatorem Platonis*.

Besser, Wilhelm Friedrich (1816 to 1884). Educated at Halle (Tholuck) and Berlin (Hengstenberg); opposed Prussian Union; served as pastor of Lutheran churches in Pomerania and Silesia; member of Breslau Synod and its ruling board; wrote *Bibelstunden*, a work passing through many editions.

Bestiares. Description of animals (real and imaginary) originating from Greek sources; influenced moral teaching and art in the Middle Ages.

Beta Sigma Psi. See *Students, Spiritual Care of*, A.

Beth, Karl (1872—). Professor in Vienna; interpreter of Christianity and other religions in terms of philosophy, sociology, and psychology; in conflict with Freud and Karl Barth.

Bethany Lutheran Seminary. See *Ministry, Education of*, XI, A 3.

Bethel Community. See *Communistic Societies*, 5.

Bethesda Lutheran Home for the Feeble-Minded. See *Associated Luth. Charities*, A 4.

Bethlehemites. 1) An order of monks who settled in England, 1257; 2) An order of monks established by Pedro de Bethencourt in Guatemala; 3) Followers of Huss, so-called from the name of the church in which he preached.

Bethune, George Washington (1805 to 1862). Studied at Dickinson and Princeton; pastor of Reformed Dutch Church in various cities; wrote original hymns and translated Malan's "It Is Not Death to Die."

Betrothal. See *Marriage*.

Bettex, Friedrich (1837—1916). B. in Switzerland; d. in Wuerttemberg, Germany; of Catholic parentage, but strongly Protestant in later life. Wrote forceful apologetical works: *Glaube und Kritik, Das erste Blatt der Bibel, Das Lied von der Schoepfung, Die Bibel — Gottes Wort, Naturstudium und Christentum*, and *Israels Geschichte*.

Beweis des Glaubens. A well-known German religious monthly, founded in 1867 for the "establishment and defense of Christian truth."

Beyer, Hartmann (1516—77). Studied at Wittenberg; friend of Melanchthon, Bugenhagen, Jonas, Brenz, Andreae, Dietrich, Major, Wigand, and other prominent Lutherans with whom he carried on continuous correspondence; called to Frankfurt, where he zealously opposed the Augsburg Interim and checked the advance of Calvinism. Beyer wrote two works against Catholicism (under the pseudonyms Sigismund Cephalus and Andreas Epitimius) and a mathematical treatise (*De Sphaera*). His sermons were preserved in manuscript form.

Beyer, Johann Paul. Clergyman; b. at Reinwarzhofen, Bavaria, 1832; attended Concordia College, Fort Wayne, and Concordia Seminary, St. Louis, 1855; pastor at Memphis, Tenn.; Altenburg, Mo.; Chicago, Ill.; Pittsburgh, Pa.; and Brooklyn, N. Y.; Vice-President of Missouri Synod 1893—99; President of Eastern District 1875—88; founder and editor of *Kinder- und Jugendblatt;* author of *Der Brief an die Epheser in Predigten;* d. at Brooklyn, N. Y., 1905.

Beyschlag, Willibald (1823—1900). Professor at Halle 1860; leader of the so-called *Mittelpartei,* mediating between Confessionals and Liberals; opposed Ultramontanism in Germany.

Beza, Theodore (1519—1605). French humanist, Reformed leader. B. at Vézelay, France; renounced Catholicism at Geneva, 1548; professor of Greek at Lausanne; professor and pastor at Geneva; defended burning of Servetus; Calvin's second self and successor; strongly opposed the Lutheran doctrines of the Eucharist and of the person of Christ; a power among the Huguenots; real originator of *Textus Receptus* (the Greek text used for several centuries); presented Cambridge with Codex D (an ancient copy of the New Testament); d. at Geneva. *Translation of New Testament into Latin with Annotations; Ecclesiastical History; Life of Calvin;* and other works.

G. Friedlaender, *Beitraege zur Reformationsgeschichte* (vol. VIII), Mueller, Berlin, 1837; H. Heppe, "Theodor Beza," in *Leben und ausgewaehlte Schriften der Vaeter und Begruender der reformierten Kirche,* Friedrichs, Elberfeld, 1861.

Bezae, Codex. See *Manuscripts,* 3.

Bhagavad-Gita. A section of the *Mahabharata* (Sanskrit) which depicts the meeting of Arjuna with Krishna, who reveals himself as Lord of Creation. Confuses pantheism with monism, but still the greatest product of Hindu philosophy.

Bhakti. See *Hinduism.*

Bhikkus. See *Buddhism,* 4.

Bibelstunden (Bible Hours). Devotional services, often informal, in which longer sections of Scripture are explained usually in the form of a homily. Such devotional services were common in the Lutheran Church in Germany (*e. g.,* those by Louis Harms) and in America.

Bible (cf. *Apologetics*). While the Bible as the Word of God attests itself in the heart of the believer as the divine truth through the witness of the Holy Spirit, indissolubly connected with the Word, the Christian apologist is in the fortunate position to show by *internal* and *external* proofs that the Bible is *the* divine Book, in a class by itself. To the internal proofs belong the following: its deep and amazing doctrines of divine love, goodness, and salvation, not found in any book of religion written by men; the purity of its ethics, anchored in love toward God and the neighbor; the unity and consistency of its teachings, though the various Bible books were written by various authors in different lands during a period of fifteen hundred years; the soberness and all-sidedness of its teachings which are relevant to man's needs; the wonderful Christ, of whom only the Bible speaks; the reliable witness of its writers in both the Old and the New Testament; the fact of Christ's resurrection and His appearance to His Apostles; the marvelous conversion and work of St. Paul, the foremost missionary among the Gentiles and the greatest theologian, next to Christ Himself, in the New Testament. Among the external proofs for the divine authority of the Bible we may mention the following: the universal experience of the truth of the Bible by the Christian Church; the salutary influences of its teachings in all lands; the multitudinous proofs from archaeology; the wonderful preservation of the Bible in a world of bitter enemies; the superhuman power of the Bible as a moral and spiritual corrective and as the world's greatest blessing in every way. See *Grace, Means of; Inspiration.*

Bible Belt. A term applied to Southern States because the South, as a whole, was more conservative and less devastated by Modernism and liberalism.

Bible, Canon of. See *Canon, Bible.*

Bible Churchman's Missionary Society. An organization formed in England in the third decade of the 20th century by conservative evangelicals when the largest society, the Church Missionary Society (1799), became predominantly liberal.

Bible Classes. See *Adult Education; Bible Study; Parish Education.*

Bible in Education. See *Christian Education,* D 4 ff.

Bible History. Often differentiated from Biblical history,* Bible history emphasizes the use of the Bible story for instructional and religious values. In the NT, knowledge of the OT was communicated at home (2 Tim. 3:15) or at public services (1 Tim. 4:13). In the primitive Church, home reading, private instruction, and public services provided knowledge of Bible history (Eusebius, *Hist. ecc.*, vi:2; Chrysostom on Eph. 4:4; Cyril, *Catech.*, iv:35). Instruction in Bible history was almost forgotten during the Middle Ages (lack of common schools, cost of Bibles, dearth of Bibles in vernacular). Luther and Melanchthon stressed the use of Bible history. Otto Braunfels sought to introduce Bible history in his Latin school (*Heldenbuechlein*). Luther's *Passionale* (1529; 11 OT, 38 NT pictures with explanatory notes) has been called the first Bible history for the home. With the establishment of Christian common schools, instruction in Bible history came into its own. Noted early texts were Justus Gesenius, *Biblische Historien* (1656), and Johann Huebner, *Zweimal 52 auserlesene biblische Historien* (1714). Since these were published, the use of the Bible story for instruction has been greatly expanded (core of Sunday school training; special Bible histories for different ages; pictorial presentations of the Bible stories; films and slides; prominent in Saturday schools, summer schools, etc.).

J. M. Reu, *Quellen zur Geschichte des biblischen Unterrichts*, Guetersloh, 1906; M. Reu, *Catechetics*, Wartburg, Chicago, 1931.

Bible, Inspiration of. See *Inspiration*.

Bible Institutes. See *Parish Education; Adult Education.*

Bible Manuscripts. See *Manuscripts of the Bible.*

Bible, Poor Man's. See *Biblia Pauperum.*

Bible Presbyterian Church. See *Presbyterian Bodies.*

Bible and Psychology. See *Psychology*, D.

Bible Reading. The Bible, being the inspired Word of God, furnishes absolutely reliable information as to the origin, the fall, the redemption, and the eternal destiny of man and therefore should be the most interesting book, which is to be diligently read and studied by every human being. Among the early Christians this was done. Acts 17:11; Col. 4:16. The Bible being the basic source of religious information, the reading of the sacred writings formed an essential part of the instruction communicated by pastors to their congregations and their catechumens. Chrysostom (d. 407) and Augustine (d. 430) continually reminded their hearers that private reading and study of the Bible should follow attendance at public worship. But in 1080 Gregory VII ordered that Latin should be the universal language of Catholic worship and, consequently, excluded all vernacular reading of the Scriptures in church services. Innocent III, in 1199, prohibited the private possession and reading of the Bible. The Council of Trent, 1546, made the Vulgate Latin Version the sole authoritative source of quotation and condemned those who dared to interpret the Bible contrary to the accepted sense given by the Fathers. Translations of the Bible other than those approved by the Roman hierarchy were put on the index of forbidden books, which also enjoined the necessity of obtaining written permission from the bishop before a lay person was permitted to read the Bible in the vernacular. As late as 1864 Pius IX, in his *Syllabus of Errors*, condemned Bible societies, because they published the Bible "without [Catholic] note and comment." In an encyclical of Leo XIII (*Officiorum et Munerum*, Jan. 25, 1897) the rule is laid down (ch. 3, 7) that "all versions in the vernacular, even by Catholics, are altogether prohibited, unless approved by the Holy See, or published under the vigilant care of the bishops, with annotations from the Fathers of the Church and learned Catholic writers." So Roman laymen may now read "properly annotated" versions without special permission, but they are carefully taught not to permit themselves to understand anything in the Bible otherwise than the Church tells them to understand it. It is both natural and illuminating that recent Popes have bitterly condemned Bible societies, which make it their object to spread the simple Bible text, as "a pest." Pius IX (*Qui Pluribus*) laments: "Thus the divine traditions, the teachings of the Fathers, and the authority of the Catholic Church are rejected, and everyone in his own way interprets the words of the Lord and distorts their meaning, thereby falling into miserable errors." Toward the middle of the 20th century, however, the Roman Catholic Church encouraged some Bible reading in some countries. The Reformation wrought a change. Luther himself read and studied the Bible diligently, and he wanted others to do the same. His masterly and hitherto unsurpassed classical translation of the Bible from the Hebrew and Greek texts into German (1534), the English Authorized, or King James, Version (1611), and many others make it possible for the laity to read the Word of God in the vernacular. Since then the Bible or parts of it have been printed and published into over a thousand languages and dialects, and Bible societies continue to translate and spread the Sacred Scriptures, so that they are within the reach of everybody. It is of paramount importance that the Word of God be read. God wants us to read the Book (John 5:39) and promises great benefit from the study of it (2 Tim. 3:15). It should not be read as the word of man, but as the Word of God (1 Thess. 2:13). The proper attitude, when reading the Bible, is one of awe and reverence (Is. 66:2). Hence we should read attentively (Matt. 24:15) in faith and obedience, keeping what we have read in an honest and good heart and bringing forth fruit with patience (Luke 8:15). See *Bible Study; Bible Societies.*

Bible Revision. See *Bible Versions.*

Bible, Rules for. See *Hermeneutics.*

Bible Societies. 1. The Formal Principle * of the Lutheran Reformation brought about a renewed emphasis on Bible study, and the Protestant mission activities of the 17th and 18th centuries brought a philanthropic element into the distribution of Bibles which led to the organization of Bible societies in the 18th and 19th centuries. 2. *Germany.* Baron Karl Hildebrand von Canstein (1667—1719) felt that the low spirituality of his times revealed a need for a Bible in every home. The funds which he received as a result of his pleas made it possible for him to establish the *Canstein Bible Institute* (1710), the earliest organization created for the distribution of Bibles. The *Nuremberg Bible Society* (1804; moved to *Basel,* 1806) was founded with aid from the British and Foreign Bible Society. The *Berlin Bible Society* was organized through the efforts of J. Jaenicke (1806) for the purpose of providing Bibles for Bohemians in Berlin. Later it was expanded and

called the *Prussian Bible Society* (1814). The *Wuerttemberg Bible Society* was organized through the efforts of Dr. Steinkopf and others (1812). Additional societies arose: *Bible Society of Saxony* (1813), *Bible Society of Schleswig-Holstein* (1826), *Berg Bible Society* (1814), and others.

3. *England.* Various Christian organizations, which included Bible distribution on their program, arose out of the Evangelical movements of the 17th and 18th centuries. Among these were: *Society for the Promotion of Christian Knowledge* (1698; worked especially in India); *Society for the Propagation of the Gospel in Foreign Parts* (1701; worked, among other places, in the American colonies; oldest missionary organization of the Anglican Church); the *Scottish Society for Promoting Christian Knowledge* (1709; worked in Scotland and America); *Society for Promoting Christian Knowledge Among the Poor* (1750); *Naval and Military Bible Society* (1780; originally called *Bible Society*); *French Bible Society* (1792).

The *British and Foreign Bible Society,* the most important in England, was founded at the London Tavern (1804; 300 persons of various denominations present) after a speech by Jos. Hughes. Its object was "to promote the circulation of Holy Scriptures, without note or comment, both at home and in foreign lands." The first goal was to provide Wales with Bibles, but the Society soon extended its activities to Europe, Asia, Africa, South America, Canada, and elsewhere. It assisted in the establishment of Bible societies in Germany, Scandinavia, and other countries (often as branches). The controversy regarding the Apocrypha caused the Society much difficulty, and when it decided to discontinue the printing of the Apocrypha (1826), more than fifty branch organizations severed connections with it.

4. *Other European Countries.* In *Scotland,* the *Edinburgh Bible Society* (1809) and the *Glasgow Bible Society* (1812) withdrew from the *British and Foreign Bible Society* as a result of the Apocrypha controversy and united to form the *National Bible Society of Scotland* (1861). In *Ireland* the *Hibernian Bible Society* was organized (1806). The most important societies of *France* are: *Bible Society of France* (*Societe biblique de France,* 1864) and the *Bible Society of Paris* (*Societe biblique de Paris,* 1818). The *Bible Society*

Bible Societies (handwritten annotation)

‑landsch
tained a
‑ganized
Sweden
listribu‑
ing be‑
h Bible
ble So‑
14; the
gian in
e Malta
an im‑
Society
Catho‑
imperial
ppressed
Society

idelphia
in 1808
it, Mas‑
nd New
. Many
of these
ning.
ty was
) by 60
societies
to the
he Bible
ggestion

of Samuel J. Mills (1815). The first president was Elias Boudinot (1740 to 1821; lawyer, philanthropist, statesman, author). The object of the society was "the circulation of the Holy Scriptures in the commonly received version (AV) without note or comment." In 1822 the Bible House on Nassau Street was erected and in 1852 the Bible House on Astor Place. In 1835 Baptist missionaries translated *baptismos* and *baptizo* with Burmese words meaning "to immerse." When the A. B. S. refused to print the version, the *American and Foreign Bible Society* (Baptist) was organized (1837). When this society agreed to use the commonly received version in English, seceders organized the *American Bible Union* (1850).

The *Christian Commercial Travelers' Association of America (Gideons;* organized 1899; headquarters: Chicago) supplies hotel and hospital rooms with Bibles.

The *United Bible Society (Sociedades Biblicas Unidas;* offices in Buenos Aires, Bogota, Cristobal, Havana, Lima, London, Mexico, New York, Rio de Janeiro, Santiago) works in Latin American languages.

6. The Catholic Church took a negative attitude toward Bible Societies (see *Bible Reading*). The *Pious Society of St. Jerome, Society of Cardinal Ferrari,* and the *Alba* operate in Italy with papal approval.

7. Bible societies aid translators, publish and distribute Bibles. In the homeland the societies are interested in distributing Bibles to the needy, the unconverted, and prisoners. Bibles are distributed to soldiers and prisoners of war. Special books and phonograph records are made for the blind. Colporteurs and missionaries distribute Bibles in mission countries. Bible societies and related agencies distribute about 25,000,000 Bibles or parts thereof annually. The *American Bible Society* has home offices in New York, Chicago, San Francisco, Philadelphia, Washington, Richmond, Dallas, Denver, and Cincinnati. EL

C. Breest, "Bibelgesellschaften," in Herzog-Hauck, *Realencyklopaedie fuer Protestantische Theologie und Kirche,* Hinrichs, Leipzig, 1897; Eric M. North, *The Bible in a Thousand Tongues,* publ. by Harper for Am. Bible Society, 1938; O. M. Norlie, *The Bible in a Thousand Tongues,* Augsburg Publ. House, 1935; Reports of Societies.

Bible Study. Bible study is that activity by which a person comes to an understanding of the Bible text and its relation to Christ and personally reflects on the words he has read for a fuller application of God's will to his life. It comes to its climax when it is translated into daily living. Bible study is not an end in itself, but a means used by the Holy Spirit to create and sustain faith in Christ. It equips the man of God to fulfill his mission in life. It is the means by which he develops into a mature Christian. True Bible study penetrates into whole divisions, periods, books, chapters as well as the individual verses and words of the Holy Scriptures.

Meditating on the words of Scripture was the immediate rule of life for every Jew (Deut. 6:32; Joshua 1; 2 Chron. 34; Neh. 8; 1 Macc. 1:67). Bible reading and study is the normal expression of intelligent Christian discipleship. This is clear from many passages of the New Testament and from the practice of the early Church (John 5:39; Luke 24:27; Acts 17:11; 18:24-28; 2 Tim. 3:14-17; Heb. 5:12-14; 2 Pet. 1:19-21; 3:2).

The apostolic fathers and the early apologists are united in the belief "that the regular way to become a convinced

Christian was to read the Holy Scriptures." Justin, Irenaeus, Tertullian, and Origen expected Bible study, not only of adults, but of children. The Bible was to them "the great public book of Christendom, to which all men must be introduced," so that they might feed their souls "from every Scripture of the Lord." Polycarp writes to the Philippian church: "I trust that ye are well exercised in the Holy Scriptures and that nothing is there hidden from you." This implies personal study. Chrysostom commended private Bible study classes. Like Augustine, he knew that the Bible is the Church's best missionary.

Bible study declined, however, with the growing institutionalization of the Church. As time went on, the laity made less and less use of its right to a firsthand approach to Scripture. When in the twelfth century the Waldenses came forth with a Christianity growing out of private Bible study, it was too late. A church based on priesthood and mystery had not only crushed the development of Bible study, but had practically withdrawn the Book from the common people. This happened despite Jerome's warning: "Ignorance of the Scripture is ignorance of Christ."

With the Reformation a new day dawned for Scripture study. Luther appealed from the dicta of the Church to the naked truth of Scripture alone. This renascence of Bible study was greatly aided by the invention of printing and Bibles in the vernacular. Adolf Harnack rightly says: ". . . the Reformation by placing the Bible into the hands of the layman has only returned to the simple confidence of the early Church."

One of the basic assumptions of the Protestant faith is that those who embrace it will be able to read and interpret the Bible for themselves (the right of private judgment). But not always and not fully did the Protestant churches carry out the principles of the Reformation. Often there was too much study "about" the Bible and too little "in" the Bible. Bible histories, catechisms, and lesson materials have often supplanted personal Bible use. Strange as it may seem, the Bible has had to struggle to be received up to the present moment. Century after century it was put down to second place by ecclesiasticism and clericalism of various forms and degrees.

Modern Bible study received a strong impetus from Pietism, particularly the popular Bible expositions of August Hermann Francke, which met the common need. Since 1685 Bible study has won a leading place within all Protestant denominations. Other factors contributing greatly to Bible study were the organization of the Bible societies and the development of the Sunday school with classes for young people and adults devoted chiefly to Bible study. A revival of interest in the Bible at the beginning of the twentieth century suffered reverses at the hands of modern liberalism and higher criticism. Two world wars, the failure of materialism, and advances in general adult education stimulated various efforts to call the people of the disordered world back to God through Bible study.

Some Bible study was carried on in the earlier days of the Missouri Synod chiefly through *Bibelstunden* and young people's societies. The first regularly issued Bible study materials appeared in 1912. Bible study classes were put on a firmer footing when they were received into the Sunday school structure. A new advance in Bible study came with the Centennial Bible Study Program initiated by the Board for Parish Education in 1947, and from the rise of Bible Institutes.

Bible study is essential for the vitality of the Church and for the preservation of human freedom. Through Bible study, privately and in a class, the Scriptures become "the Book to live by."

There are five essentials of good method in Bible study: (1) Good motivation; (2) the intensive and repeated reading of the Bible text itself; (3) observing exactly what the text says; (4) finding Christ and doctrinal content; (5) assimilation through meditation. OEF

Adolph Harnack, *Bible Reading in the Early Church*, Engl. Ed., 1923; F. Pieper, "De Scriptura Sacra," *Christian Dogmatics*, CPH, 1950 (Engl. Ed.); John T. McFarland *et al.*, *The Encyclopedia of Sunday Schools and Religious Education*.

Bible Versions. A. *Septuagint.* 1. The earliest attempt to translate the Scriptures is represented by the Greek version of the Old Testament commonly known as the Septuagint (LXX). It owes its name to the story (now discredited) that it is the work of seventy-two translators, six from each tribe of Israel, who at the instance of

King Ptolemy Philadelphus II (285 to 247 B.C.) were deputed to Egypt by the high priest Eleazar to prepare a version of the Jewish Law for the royal library at Alexandria. While there is doubtless a kernel of truth in this story and the bare fact of a translation of the Law in the days of Ptolemy need not be questioned, the Septuagint as a whole exhibits such varying degrees of skill and accuracy that it can be neither the product of a single body of translators acting in unison nor even the product of a single age. The translation of the Pentateuch, for example, is pretty well done; that of Daniel is exceedingly poor (the early Christian Church from about A.D. 200 on employed the Greek version of Theodotion in its stead); while the rendering of Ecclesiastes is so slavishly literal that it is little more than Grecized Hebrew. The most that can be said as to the origin of the Septuagint is that it was begun about 285 B.C. and completed before 132 B.C. (Cf. the Prolog of Ecclesiasticus.) The Septuagint differs strongly from the Hebrew in content and arrangement (Job, for instance, is some 400 lines shorter in the Greek, while the Greek Jeremiah differs from the Hebrew by addition, omission, and transposition) and presents also in its renderings innumerable divergences from our present Masoretic text. This is due in part, no doubt, to the arbitrary procedure of the translators, but also in some cases to the fact that the Hebrew original differed from the text we possess today. This fact makes the Septuagint an invaluable aid, though to be used with caution, in the textual criticism of the Old Testament.

2. The Septuagint was adopted by the Greek-speaking Jews, was used, as a rule, by the writers of the New Testament in citing the Old, and was regarded as authoritative, even inspired, by the early Christian Fathers. The constant appeal to it on the part of the leaders of the Church to prove the Messiahship of Jesus aroused the antagonism of the Jews and gave rise, in the second century, to three rival translations: the strictly literal version of Aquila; the revision of the Septuagint by Theodotion; and the elegantly periphrastic version of Symmachus. These versions have been preserved only in isolated fragments.

B. *Targums.* The *Targums,* or Aramaic paraphrases, arose from the oral interpretation of the Old Testament Scriptures which had become necessary since the days of the Exile, when Aramaic became the language of common intercourse in Palestine. These oral paraphrases were, in course of time, reduced to writing. The most important Targums are the Targum of Onkelos (first or second century) on the Pentateuch, which received its present form about the third century after Christ, and the Targum of Jonathan ben Uzziel on the Prophets: Jonathan was a pupil of Hillel and lived in the first century after Christ, but the Targum associated with his name did not receive its final form until about the fifth century. The Targums are of value to the scholar in helping to determine the Hebrew text employed in the early Synagog as well as in determining what interpretation the Jews gave to difficult passages.

C. *Syriac.* 1. For the Old Testament, the oldest and most important version is the Peshitta. Whether this translation is of Jewish or of Christian origin remains uncertain; at any rate, it was used early by the Syriac-speaking Church and has remained the chief version of the Syriac Old Testament. It is by various hands, though in fairly uniform style, and was made directly from the Hebrew. There are, however, traces of Septuagint influence.

2. Two later versions of the Old Testament, that by Philoxenus of Mabbogh (A. D. 508) and that by Paul of Tella (A. D. 616), were based on the Septuagint. Neither succeeded in displacing the Peshitta in common use.

3. Of the oldest Syriac translation of the New Testament, dating from the second century, only the Gospels have been preserved. This old Syriac version is of the highest importance for the textual criticism of the Gospels, representing as it does a textual tradition independent of the two great branches of the textual tradition represented by the manuscripts B and D.

4. However, the version destined to become the Authorized Version of the New Testament for the Syriac-speaking Church was the Peshitta, a complete revision of the New Testament undertaken at the beginning of the fifth century by Rabbula, Bishop of Edessa. "Its style is beautifully smooth and clear, and it can claim to be one of the great literary achievements of the Eastern Church." (T. H. Robinson.)

5. Two later versions, or better, revisions, deserve notice because they contain those portions of the New

Testament originally omitted from the Syriac Canon (2 Peter, 2 and 3 John, Jude, Apocalypse). That of Philoxenus of Mabbogh (A. D. 508) first included the five disputed books; it has hardly survived except for the four catholic Epistles, which are usually printed from this version. Similarly, the version by Thomas of Harkel, the New Testament counterpart to the Old Testament Version by Paul of Tella and of about the same date (A. D. 616), is used in Syriac Bibles only for the Apocalypse, although it is extant in its entirety.

D. *Egyptian.* There were three Egyptian, or Coptic (the word is a corruption of *Aigyptios*) versions: the Sahidic, the dialect of Upper (southern) Egypt; the Bohairic, the speech of the western delta; and the Fayumic of Central Egypt (this last of the New Testament only). Very little is known of the Fayumic at present. The Sahidic is the earlier of the two complete versions, having originated in the second or third century after Christ. The Bohairic, now in ecclesiastical use among all Egyptian Christians, is considerably later, being dated about A. D. 600. Both the Sahidic and the Bohairic are important for the textual criticism of the New Testament; the earlier Sahidic shows both "Neutral" and "Western" affinities, while the later Bohairic is more pronouncedly "Neutral." The Old Testament portion of both these versions is based on the Septuagint, not on the original Hebrew.

E. *Ethiopic.* The *Ethiopic* version, still used by the Abyssinians although Ethiopic has long ceased to be spoken, possibly dates from the fourth century. In the Old Testament the translation was made from the Septuagint, though it contains many variations from the Greek, the text in some of the manuscripts having been corrected from the Hebrew.

F. *Arabic.* Among the *Arabic* versions of the Old Testament that of Saadia ben Joseph, an Egyptian Jew (d. A. D. 942), was made directly from the Hebrew text. It won great popularity among the Jews and was publicly read in the synagogs alongside of the Hebrew text. However, only the Pentateuch, Isaiah, Canticles, Proverbs, and Job have been printed. The complete text of the Old Testament in Arabic appeared in the Paris and London polyglots of the seventeenth century; but it is of composite origin. The Pentateuch is the translation of

Saadia. Joshua, though also derived from the Hebrew, is by another hand. Judges, Samuel, Kings, Chronicles, and Job are based on the Peshitta, while the Prophets, Psalms, and Proverbs are made from the Septuagint. As to the New Testament, Arabic versions have been made from the Greek, from the Peshitta, and from the Latin. The current Arabic New Testament is a translation, in the main, from the Bohairic dialect, with corrections and additions from the Greek and Syriac.

G. *Armenian.* The *Armenian* version is ascribed by a fifth-century Armenian writer, Moses of Chorene, to the patriarch Sahak (patriarch A. D. 390—428); his version was made from a Syriac text. Koriun, also of the fifth century, is authority for the statement that Mesrop (inventor of the Armenian alphabet) had by 411 translated the entire Bible from the Greek. He is said to have begun with Proverbs; this may indicate that the earlier books had been translated previously by unknown hands. Sahak and Mesrop later (after A. D. 431) revised the Armenian Bible on the basis of a Greek Bible brought from Constantinople.

H. *Slavonic.* The *Old Slavonic* version, dating from the middle of the ninth century, is generally attributed to Cyril and Methodius, the apostles of the Slavs. The Old Testament translation is based on the Septuagint, that of the New Testament on the Greek. Except for fragments which survive in the official Slavonic Bible, the old version has been lost.

I. *Gothic.* The *Gothic* version is the work of Ulfilas (d. A. D. 381 or 388), Bishop of the West Goths. Of the Old Testament, which was based on the Septuagint, only the most meager fragments remain. Most of the New Testament, a literally faithful version, is preserved in various manuscripts, preeminent among which is the superb Codex Argenteus. The story that Ulfilas omitted from the translation of the Old Testament the Books of Kings for fear of exciting the warlike passions of the Goths is unworthy of credence, since such considerations would have barred Joshua and Judges as well. The probability is that Ulfilas did not live to finish the translation.

J. *Latin.* 1. *Latin* versions antedating the work of Jerome (A. D. 340? to 420) are now commonly designated as the Old Latin. The term "Itala" formerly used and applied by Augustine to one of these versions is rightly avoided. The term Old Latin designates a number of versions rather than *a* version, for if there was a single early version at all (and there is some evidence which points in that direction), it was probably not the work of one man, but rather the result of a process of accretion and revision, book being added to book and the resulting whole subjected to constant revision in various localities to meet local standards and needs. The Old Latin versions probably originated in Africa, since Tertullian of Carthage (ca. A. D. 150—220) is the first to mention a Latin version and his younger contemporary Cyprian (A. D. 200—258) cites Scripture in a form that is identical with the oldest type of Old Latin text found in existing manuscripts. The version, or versions, date from the second century onward and are, therefore, valuable in textual criticism, since they enable the scholar to tap the stream of textual tradition at a point several centuries earlier than that of most extant Greek manuscripts.

2. By the fourth century there was such a welter of Latin versions that Pope Damasus in 382 called upon Jerome to produce the much-needed revision of the Old Latin Bible. By 405 Jerome had completed the stupendous task. "The New Testament," he writes, "I have restored to the true Greek form; the Old I have rendered from the Hebrew." He began by translating the Old Testament from the Septuagint; the Gallican Psalter, which is the version included in the modern Vulgate, represents this rendering from the Greek. But Jerome became convinced as he proceeded that a satisfactory version could be made only from the Hebrew directly, and the rest of the Old Testament books in the Vulgate are a direct rendering of the original. Jerome's revisions of the Gospels appeared in 383, and it is possible that the rest of the New Testament was also revised at this time. But there is some doubt as to the extent of Jerome's revision of the New Testament outside the Gospels. Jerome himself does not cite the Epistles, for instance, in the present Vulgate form — and Augustine, though he shows knowledge of the Vulgate Gospels and Old Testament, seems not to have known the Epistles in their revised form. Jerome's new translation encountered stubborn opposition, and it was not until the sixth or seventh century that it won general acceptance in the Church. From the thirteenth century onward it is known as the *Vulgata,* a name which had formerly been applied to the Septuagint. In 1546 the Council of Trent decreed that it be used exclusively, and from that time on it has been the official Bible of the Roman Catholic Church.

K. Of the hundreds of modern versions only a few of the most important can be mentioned here. Since the Reformation the Bible has been translated into all the languages and many of the dialects of Europe. Among the *French* versions that of Lefevre d' Etaples (first printed completely in Antwerp, 1530), of Olivetan (Neuchatel, 1535), and especially the Geneva Bible, a revision of Olivetan's work made by pastors of Geneva with the assistance of Beza and others, deserve particular notice. The latter version, having undergone numerous revisions, still holds its place, though there are more recent translations. The principal *Dutch* version is the so-called States Bible (because authorized by the States General in 1594), published with the sanction of the Council of Dort in 1637. It is still in use.

L. *English.* 1. Although portions of the Bible had been translated into the vernacular in Anglo-Saxon times, and also after the Norman Conquest, the translation known as Wyclif's (1320 to 1384) was the first complete English version. It was based on the Vulgate and appeared in 1382—1384. It is uncertain how much of the work is actually Wyclif's. The greater part of the Old Testament is probably the work of Nicholas Hereford. The New Testament is attributed to Wyclif himself, but even this attribution is not beyond doubt. A revision of Wyclif's Bible, probably made by John Purvey, one of Wyclif's followers, appeared not long after Wyclif's death. This second version remained in common use until the beginning of the sixteenth century, when it was displaced by the work of William Tyndale.

2. The first Englishman to translate the New Testament from the original Greek was William Tyndale. His translation appeared on the Continent in two editions (3,000 copies each) before 1526. In 1530 Tyndale published his version of the Pentateuch and in the following year the Book of Jonah. In the Old Testament, too, Tyndale worked from the original, using Luther and the Vulgate as aids.

3. In 1535 Miles Coverdale published at Zurich his translation of the whole Bible "out of the Douche and Latin" (*i. e.,* the German of Luther and the Zurich Bible, and the Vulgate). This was the first complete printed Bible in English and the first complete translation by a single hand.

4. The so-called Matthew's Bible, essentially a compilation from Tyndale and Coverdale, prepared by John Rogers, appeared in 1537 and was dedicated to "The most noble and gracyous Prynce Kyng Henry the Eyght and Queen Jane." Since it bore on its title page the inscription "Set forth with the Kinges most gracyous lycense," it may be considered the first English authorized version.

5. Because of the deficiencies of both the Coverdale and the Matthew version, Coverdale, at the instance of Thomas Cromwell, undertook a fresh revision, which appeared in 1539; because of the splendid proportions of the book (it measured ten by fifteen inches), it was known as the Great Bible.

6. Richard Taverner's version, a revision of Matthew's, which appeared in the same year as the Great Bible, 1539, never became very popular.

7. During the persecution under Mary Tudor some of the English reformers found refuge in Geneva. It was here that Whittingham, a brother-in-law of Calvin, and his associates undertook a revision of Tyndale, collated with the Great Bible. Their work resulted in what is known as the Geneva Bible, which was completed in 1560 and ranks as the most scholarly of the early English versions. It won immediate popularity (this was the Bible that Shakespeare knew and used), no fewer than one hundred and twenty editions appearing up to the year 1611. It did not, however, at once displace the Great Bible, but was used side by side with it until the appearance of the Bishops' Bible in 1568 displaced the Great Bible from public use.

8. The Bishops' Bible is a revision of the Great Bible and owes its name to the fact that most of the revisers were bishops. The revision was an attempt to counteract the popularity of the Geneva Bible, with its "pestilent glosses" or comments, often caustic. The Bishops' Bible, though never quite popular, passed through twenty editions, the last appearing in 1606. This version is important historically, since the improved and revised edition of

1572 is the basis of the revision that led to the Authorized Version of 1611.

9. At this point mention must be made of the Roman Catholic version published at Rheims (New Testament, 1582) and at Douai (Old Testament, 1609—10). It is, of course, based on the Vulgate and is literal to the point of obscurity.

10. The Authorized Version of 1611 owes its inception to a suggestion made by Dr. John Reynolds, the Puritan president of Corpus Christi College, at the Hampton Court Conference held by James in 1604, for the purpose of arranging differences between the Puritan and Anglican elements in the Church. "He moved his Majestie, that there might be a newe translation of the Bible, because those which were allowed in the raignes of Henrie the eight and Edward the sixt, were corrupt and not aunswerabel to the truth of the Originall." King James, who took a lively interest in theology, took up the suggestion eagerly and on February 10, 1604, ordained "that a translation be made of the whole Bible, as consonant as can be to the original Hebrew and Greek . . . and only to be used in all Churches of England." To insure accuracy, the translators (fifty-four were appointed, but only about fifty of them can be identified) were bound to observe no fewer than fifteen specific rules in the prosecution of their task. In particular, it was provided that the entire body of translators, who were divided into six companies, should pass upon the work of every man in the company. The version is essentially a revision of the Bishops' Bible of 1572 which was "to be followed and as little altered as the truth of the original will permit."

11. The new version, appearing under royal authority and commended by the best scholarship of the age, though bitterly criticized in some quarters, soon won general favor. For three centuries it has held its place as the Bible of the English-speaking world. The rare beauty and purity of its diction, its dignified and elegant simplicity, its reverential spirit and attitude have endeared it to millions of hearts and made it the most popular book in the English tongue.

12. *The Revised Version.* The discovery and collation of numerous Biblical manuscripts in the first half of the nineteenth century, as well as the advances made in Greek and Hebrew scholarship, revealed some of the in-

accuracies of the Authorized Version and started the movement for revision, a movement that began to take definite shape about 1855. In 1870 a committee representing nearly all the evangelical bodies in England (no Roman Catholics were included) was entrusted with the work of preparing a revised version. The New Testament company began its work on June 22, 1870, and the Old Testament company on June 30. In response to an invitation on the part of the British revisers to participate in the task, an American revision committee was organized toward the close of the following year. The details of the plan of co-operation were, however, not fully arranged until 1875. The English committee promised to give due consideration to all the American suggestions and renderings before the conclusion of its own labors and to permit the publication, in an appendix, of all important differences of rendering and reading which the British reviewers should decline to accept. On the other hand, the American committee was to give its moral support to the British editions "with a view to their freest circulation within the United States, and not to issue an edition of its own for a term of fourteen years." On May 17, 1881, the English revised New Testament was put on sale in England and three days later in the United States. In both countries the demand was enormous, about three million copies being sold within one year of publication. The Old Testament revision was completed in 1884, and the entire Revised Version, bound in one volume, appeared in the following year. The American Standard Version, which embodied not only the readings which had appeared in the appendix to the English Revised Version, but also others which had been adopted by the American revisers later, appeared in 1901. Neither the British Revised nor the American Standard Version achieved the widespread acceptance that had been anticipated for them. The Authorized Version has remained the English Bible.

13. Of the many private versions that have appeared since 1901, the scholarly renderings of Ferrar Fenton (1903), R. F. Weymouth (New Testament only, 1902), James Moffatt (New Testament 1913; Old Testament 1924), E. J. Goodspeed (New Testament, 1923), E. J. Goodspeed and J. M. Powis Smith, with the assistance of other scholars (Old and New Testaments, 1935, Apocrypha, 1938), deserve mention.

14. The most important version of the twentieth century thus far is the Revised Standard Version, of which the New Testament was published in 1946 and the Old Testament in 1952. This version is officially a revision of the American Standard Version of 1901, "designed for use in public and private worship, and to be in the direction of the simple, classic style of the King James Version." The reception accorded the work has not been unmixed but seems to be preponderantly favorable. How widely the revision will establish itself in public and private use remains to be seen.

M. *German.* The Bible was translated into *German* as early as the fourteenth century. This translation follows the Vulgate. After the invention of printing it appeared (1466 to 1521) in no fewer than eighteen editions, fourteen in the High and four — according to some, five — in the Low German dialect. The origin of the pre-Lutheran German Bible is still uncertain. That Luther was acquainted with it and made use of it has been established. Luther's version was made from the Hebrew and Greek and everywhere bears the stamp of originality. Its merits are well known. Schaff calls it "a wonderful monument of genius, learning, and piety." Its homely simplicity and rugged vigor, its idiomatic diction and rhythmic flow of language, its happily alliterative phrases (*Stecken und Stab, Dornen und Disteln, matt und muede,* etc.), and its freedom from all pedantic restraint have assured it a permanent place in the hearts of the German people. Luther began his work on the New Testament in November, or early in December, 1521, and completed it in the following March before he left the Wartburg. The translation was published in September, 1522. In the greater and more difficult task of translating the Old Testament, begun in 1522, Luther had the assistance of Melanchthon, Bugenhagen, Cruciger, and others. The work was completed in 1534, but Luther continued to improve his translation with every new edition, especially on the linguistic side. Luther's version not only formed the basis of several other versions (Danish, Swedish, Icelandic, Dutch), but naturally gave rise to counterversions by the Catholics (Emser, 1527; Dietenberger, 1534; Eck, 1537). The translation of Dietenberger, as revised by Ulenberg in 1630 and by the clergy of Mainz in 1662, became known as the "Catholic Bible." A revision of Luther's version known as the "Revidierte Bibel", appeared in 1892 but has not met with general favor. Finally, several scholarly translations deserve mention, notably that of Kautzsch (Old Testament) and Weizsaecker (New Testament), which have also been published together in one volume, DeWette, J. Fr. Meier, and others. Among twentieth-century German versions, those of Schlachter and Menge deserve special mention. MHF

Biblia Pauperum. A Poor Man's Bible, a Picture Bible, prepared in the Middle Ages for the children of the poor. It consisted of forty to fifty pictures from the life of Christ and some Old Testament events; each picture was accompanied by an illustrative text or sentence in Latin. A similar work was called *Speculum Humanae Salvationis.* Before the Reformation these two books were the principal text used by monks in preaching. After the invention of printing the *Biblia Pauperum* was perhaps the first book printed in the Netherlands and Germany. — The name *Biblia Pauperum* was also given to an entirely different work, that of Bonaventura, in which the Biblical events were alphabetically arranged and accompanied by notes for the purpose of relieving the intellectual shortcomings of the preachers.

Biblical and Christian Archaeology. See *Archaeology.*

Biblical Canonics. That part of Biblical Introduction which deals with the historical side of the aim to determine what books constitute the Bible. See *Canon, Bible.*

Biblical Criticism. See *Higher Criticism; Textual Criticism.*

Biblical Geography. See *Geography, Christian.*

Biblical Hermeneutics. See *Hermeneutics.*

Biblical History. Biblical history follows the Bible in its chronology and treats the Jewish dispensation, life of Christ, life of the Apostles, and the founding of the Church to the end of the first century. The chief sources are the Bible, Apocryphal books, Philo, Josephus, some classical authors (Herodotus, Ctesias, Polybius, Diodorus Siculus, Strabo, Plutarch, Livy,

Tacitus), archaeological discoveries, patristic writings, papyri, and other manuscript discoveries. Biblical history treats all phases (political, economic, social, religious) of the sacred narrative. Noted histories of the OT: A. Edersheim, *Bible History;* J. H. Kurtz, *History of the Old Covenant;* E. W. Hengstenberg, *History of the Kingdom of God;* S. Koehler, *Lehrbuch der Geschichte des A. T.;* J. Robertson, *Early Religion of Israel.* For NT see *Christ, Lives of; Paul, Lives of.*

A select bibliography in R. F. Weidner, *Theological Encyclopedia,* Wartburg, Chicago, 1910, pp. 28—34.

Biblical Isagogics. See *Isagogics.*

Biblical Philology. The study of the original languages of the Bible, of both the Old and the New Testament, together with the linguistic peculiarities, historical development and tradition concerning the text, also all auxiliary factors necessary for the understanding of the inspired writings. The Old Testament is written in Hebrew (with the exception of a few passages in Daniel and Ezra), the New Testament in the Greek language as it was spoken at the time of Christ and as it was used in ordinary intercourse, also among the unlearned. This language is known as the *koine.* The style of several New Testament writers was influenced to some extent by the Septuagint, the Greek version of the Old Testament.

Biblical Psychology. See *Psychology, D.*

Biblical Textual Criticism. See *Textual Criticism.*

Biblical Theology. The orderly presentation of the doctrinal contents of Holy Scripture in a manner which is midway between exegesis * and dogmatics.*

Bibliography, Theological. That branch of the preliminary work in the field of theology which pertains to the actual books recommended for use in each department of theology. See *Theological Encyclopedia.*

Bibliolatry (G. "book worship"). A term applied, usually in reproach, to those who are regarded as giving too much reverence to the letter of the Scriptures. While there are instances in which erroneous views were held regarding the significance of a particular translation, version, text tradition, and other elements subject to human influence and error, the term itself is a misnomer in most instances, especially when it is intended to convey implications of superstitious idolatry bordering on fetishism (as when the word is applied with such connotations to those who hold that the Bible was divinely inspired and hence the only infallible norm of church doctrine and practice). The term has a negative effect when it detracts from the reverence due the Word of God.

Bibliology. That part of dogmatics or doctrinal theology which deals with the essence and attributes of the Holy Scriptures in their relation to mankind.

Bickell, Johann Wilhelm (1799 to 1848). Authority on canon law. B. at Marburg; d. at Cassel. Studied law at Marburg and Goettingen. Professor of jurisprudence at Marburg, 1824—34; president of the supreme court of Hesse-Cassel, 1841, and minister of state, 1846. He upheld the necessity of the subscription of pastors to the Confessions.

Bickersteth, Edward Henry (1825 to 1906). Educated at Cambridge; held a number of charges in the Established Church; successful editor of hymnals; wrote, among others: "Stand, Soldier of the Cross."

Bidding Prayer. An ancient prayer, appointed especially for Good Friday, with intercessions for the various classes of men both in the Church and without, so called because the deacon bids the people pray and mentions the things to be prayed for.

Biddle, John (1615—62). Founder of English Unitarianism; imprisoned several times for the anti-Trinitarian views expressed in *Twelve Arguments* and *Confession of Faith Concerning the Holy Trinity.* D. a martyr to his views.

Bidembach, Balthasar (1533—78). Doctor of theology; provost at Stuttgart; wrote: *Homiliae in Libros Priores Regum* and sermons on Romans.

Biedermann, Alois Emil (1819—85). B. in Switzerland; d. at Zurich; dogmatician of Free Protestantism; Hegelian pantheist; held that spirituality and infinity were central in the idea of God; from 1850 to his death professor at Zurich.

Biedermann, Richard D. B. in New Wells, Mo., Oct. 6, 1864; educated at Concordia College, Fort Wayne, and Concordia Seminary, St. Louis; graduated 1885; pastor in St. Paul, Minn.;

Mobile, Ala.; Kendallville and Indianapolis, Ind.; president of Concordia Seminary, Springfield, Ill., 1914—21; secretary of the Missouri Synod for fifteen years; d. Mar. 8, 1921.

Biel, Gabriel (d. 1495). German scholastic philosopher, a nominalist, teacher at Tuebingen; faithful exponent of Catholic theology, he stood for pronounced Semi-Pelagianism, the mechanical theory of the Sacraments, and the "mighty dignity" of the priest; advocated the Immaculate Conception; his position on church polity was that of the Council of Constance. Wrote commentary on *Sentences* of Peter Lombard. His writings were among the first theological works read by Luther.

Bielefeld. See *Bodelschwingh.*

Bienemann, Kaspar (*Melissander*) (1540—91). General superintendent of Pfalz-Neuburg, later tutor at ducal court, Jena, then pastor at Altenburg; wrote: "Herr, wie du willst, so schick's mit mir" ("Lord, as Thou Wilt, Deal Thou with Me").

Biewend, Adolph Friedrich Theodor. B. May 6, 1816, Rothehuette, Hannover; educated at Goettingen; tutor 1838—41. F. K. D. Wyneken induced him to come to America; pastor, Washington, D. C., 1843—47; teacher of sciences and ancient languages at Columbian College of that city till 1849. Succeeded C. L. A. Wolter at the Practical Seminary, Fort Wayne, Ind.; professor at Concordia Seminary and College, St. Louis, 1850; director of the college department 1856; representative of Mo. Synod at conventions of the Norwegian and Tennessee Synods. D. Apr. 10, 1858.

H. C. Wyneken, *Adolph F. T. Biewend,* CPH, 1896.

Bigamy. The formal entering into of a marriage while a former one remains undissolved. The normal form of marriage as instituted by God (Gen. 1:27) and acknowledged and reaffirmed by Christ (Matt. 19:4-6) is monogamy. Bigamy, accordingly, is a corruption of the original institution of marriage and is tolerated neither by the Church nor, as a rule, by the State.

Billicanus (Gernolt), Theobald. German theologian who first favored Luther, then Zwingli, and finally returned to Roman Catholicism. He died as professor of rhetoric at Marburg in 1554.

Billing, Einar Magnus (1871 to 1939). Professor at Upsala 1900—20, thereafter bishop of Vaesteras; interpreted Christianity as force in conflict with evil; active in Swedish religious education. See *Sweden, Luth. Church in.*

Bilney, Theodore (1495—1531). English martyr. Converted by perusal of Erasmus' New Testament and Luther's works; preached against Rome; submitted; preached again; was burned in London at Wolsey's command.

Bilocation. The term is used to denote the power to be in two places at the same time. In theology, bilocation receives consideration in the doctrine of Christology, for while the Son of Man (Christ's human nature) was on earth, He was at the same time also in heaven (John 3:13), a truth which Calvinism denies on the ground that nothing can be ascribed to Christ's human nature which must be denied to human nature in general.

Biltz, F. J. B. July 24, 1825, in Mittel-Frohna, Saxony; came over with the Saxons led by Stephan, an orphan of 13 years; one of the first students at Concordia College, Altenburg; ordained Mar. 12, 1848; served in Dessin, Cape Girardeau Co., Mo., Cumberland, Md., and Concordia, Mo. Missionary among German immigrants; President of the Western District of the Missouri Synod; member of Electoral College; instrumental in founding St. Paul's College, Concordia, Mo. D. Nov. 19, 1908.

Bimeler, Joseph. See *Communistic Societies,* 5.

Bination (L. "twice"). The offering of Mass twice on the same day by the same person.

Bindemann, F. W. See *Canada, Lutheranism in,* 6.

Bingham, Joseph (1668—1723). Archaeologist. B. Wakefield; rector near Winchester, Havant (d. there). *Origines Ecclesiasticae,* or *Antiquities of the Christian Church* (Anglican point of view).

Binney, Joseph Getschall (1807 to 1877). Pastor of Baptist Church; American Board (Congregationalist) missionary to Karens in Burma, 1844 to 1850, and Rangoon, Burma, 1858—76.

Biography (Bibliography). I. *General.* **Biographical Encyclopedia of the World,** Institute for Research in Biography, N. Y., 1946; *Biographical Encyclopedia of America,* Biographical

Encyclopedia of America, Ind., N. Y., 1940; Allen Johnson (American Council of Learned Societies), *American Biography,* Scribner, H, ca. 1928—37 (22 vols.). For contemporary men consult the *Who's Who in America,* the A. N. Marquis Company, Chicago, Ill. (published since 1899); *Who Was Who in America,* the A. N. Marquis Co., Chicago, Ill. Biographies and bibliographies are also given in encyclopedias.*

II. *Biblical.* Outstanding biographical material is given in Bible dictionaries * as well as in encyclopedias *; Morton, *Women of the Bible,* Dodd & Mead, N. Y., 1941; Ludwig Wangemann, *Biblische Biographien und Monographien,* George Reichardt, Leipzig, 1899; Hunter, H., *Sacred Biography* (6 vols.), Manning & Loring, Boston, 1794; Wenger, R., *Die Frauen des Neuen Testaments,* Calwer Vereinsbuchhandlung, Stuttgart, 1927; Hastings, James, *Greater Men and Women of the Bible,* Scribner's, 1913—16 (6 vols.).

III. *Early Christianity.* See references under *Patristics;* Saints, see references under *Saints;* Popes, see references under *Popes;* Rudelbach, A. G., *Biographien von Zeugen der christlichen Kirche,* Doerffling u. Franke, Leipzig, 1850.

IV. *Christian (General).* Smith, Wm.-Wace, Henry, *Dictionary of Christian Biography,* Murray, London, 1877 to 1887 (4 vols.); Meurer, M., *Das Leben der Altvaeter d. Luth. Kirche,* Leipzig u. Dresden, vol. I—IV, 1861 to 1864; Adam, M., *Vitae Germanorum Theologorum,* 1620; Rudelbach, A. G., *Biographien von Zeugen der Christlichen Kirche,* 1850; Rudelbach, A. G., *Christliche Biographien,* 1850; Schwarz, J. C., *Religious Leaders of America,* N. Y., 1941—42; Sample, R. F., *Beacon Lights of the Reformation,* Presbyterian Board of Publication and Sabbath School Work, Philadelphia, 1889; Harrison, E. M., *Heroes of Faith on Pioneer Trails,* Moody Press, Chicago, Ill., 1945; Hagenbach, K. R., *Leben und Auserwaehlte Schriften der Vaeter und Begruender der Reformierten Kirche* (10 vols.), R. L. Friedrichs, Elberfeld, 1859—62. Good sources and bibliographies can be found in religious encyclopedias.*

V. *American Lutheran.* Richards, J. W., *Penn's Lutheran Forerunners and Friends,* Lutheran Book Concern, Columbus, Ohio, 1926; Fuerbringer, L., *Persons and Events,* Concordia Publishing House, St. Louis, Mo., 1947; Hay, C. A., *Memoirs of J. Goering;* G.

Lochmann; B. Kurtz, Lutheran Publication Society, Philadelphia, 1887; Nothstein, I. O., *Lutheran Makers of America,* United Lutheran Publication House, Philadelphia, 1930; Wentz, A. R., *History of Gettysburg Theological Seminary,* United Lutheran Publication House, Philadelphia, Pa., 1926; Finch, W. J., *Lutheran Landmarks and Pioneers in America,* General Council Publication House, Philadelphia, 1913; *Lutheran World Almanac,* published since 1921 by the National Lutheran Council; *Concordia Historical Institute Quarterly,* published since 1928 by Concordia Historical Institute; Jacobs, H. E.-Haas, J. A. W., *The Lutheran Cyclopedia,* Charles Scribner's Sons, New York, 1899; Jensson, J. C., *American Lutheran Biographies,* Press of Houtkamp & Son, Milwaukee, 1890; Morris, J. G., *Fifty Years in the Lutheran Ministry,* James Young, Baltimore, 1878; Norlie, O. M., *Prominent Personalities,* Northfield, Minn., 1942; Norlie, O. M., *School Calendar, 1824—1924,* Augsburg Publishing House, Minneapolis, 1924; W. B. Sprague, *Annals of the American Lutheran Pulpit,* Carter, New York, 1869; *American Lutheran Church Histories* (Graebner, Jacobs, Fritschel, Bente, Neve, Wentz, Wolf, and others). ARS

Biran, Maine de (1766—1824). Outstanding French psychologist; defender of French spiritualism; regarded religion as a matter of emotion rather than belief.

Biretta. A square cap with three or four projecting prominences and a tassel, worn by priests when approaching the altar for Mass, and in choir, etc. A cardinal's biretta is red, a bishop's purple, that of other clerics black.

Birgitta. See *Bridget, St.*

Birkedal, Schoeller P. W. (1809—92). Graduated from University of Copenhagen; pastor at Omme and Ryslinge, Denmark; propagated the theology of Grundtvig; established a free congregation, which, after 1868, functioned under the care of the bishop of the established church.

Birken (Betulius), Siegmund von (1626—81). B. at Wildstein, Bohemia, May 5, 1626; his family, because of religious persecution, fled to Nuernberg, where he started his schooling. He studied law and theology at the University of Jena. By virtue of his poetical gifts he was admitted as a member of the Pegnitz Shepherd and Flower Order. He was appointed tutor at Wolfenbuettel to the princes of Brunswick-Lueneburg, at which time he was crowned as a poet. He was tutor at various courts. He wrote 52 hymns, of which "Jesus, I will Ponder Now" and "Let Us Ever Walk with Jesus" are best known.

Birkner, Henry Philip Ludwig. B. Feb. 26, 1857, at Brooklyn, N. Y.; graduated at St. Louis 1878; New York University 1878—79; pastor at Gordonville, Mo., 1879—86; at St. Louis, Mo., 1886—90; at Boston, Mass., from 1890 on; vice-president of Atlantic District 1915 to 1918; president 1918—30; d. Nov. 7, 1937.

Bischoff, Rudolf Adam. Clergyman and educator; b. St. Louis, Mo., 1847, attended Concordia College, Fort Wayne, Ind., and Concordia Seminary, St. Louis, Mo., 1870; pastor at Alexandria, Va., professor at Concordia College, Fort Wayne, 1872—82; president 1882—86; pastor at Bingen, Ind., again professor at Fort Wayne, 1889—1904; edited *Lutheran Pioneer* 1879—1912; d. Bingen, Ind., 1916.

Bishop. The New Testament recognizes no superiority of bishops (overseers) over the pastors (elders) of congregations (Acts 20:17, 28; Titus 1:5, 7). The Roman Church, however, teaches that bishops are of divine right, superior to simple priests (see *Hierarchy; Ordination*), and that they alone have the power of administering ordination and confirmation, blessing holy oils, churches, etc. A bishop is responsible only to the Pope, and, except as he is limited by the canon law or the papal will, is supreme in his diocese over both clergy and laity. He makes laws, abrogates them, and dispenses from them; he exercises judicial power (see *Courts, Spiritual*), pronounces sentence, inflicts penalties, excommunicates, and suspends; he erects and suppresses parishes, assigns charges to the clergy, and superintends financial affairs. Since the bishop cannot do all these things in person, he is assisted by various officials, chiefly his vicar-general.* Bishops are elected in various ways, but must always be confirmed by the Pope. They must visit Rome at stated intervals, varying with the distance, to report on their dioceses (from the U. S., every 10 years), and they can be removed only by the Pope. "Titular" bishops are those who bear the titles of extinct dioceses (*e. g.*, in Mohammedan lands) and whose office is therefore chiefly honorary. (See also *Ordinary; Diocese.*)

Since bishops existed when the Reformation started, the conservative reformers at the beginning favored the retention of bishops. It was, however, repeatedly emphasized that bishops and pastors were one and the same thing (Luther, St. L. Ed., IV:1126; IX:1098, 1101; XII:564; XVI:2026; XVII:1047; XX:1101; *et al.* See also Treatise on Bishops added to the Smalcald Art.). Luther repeatedly censures Roman Catholic bishops for seeking worldly glory and especially for not preaching the Gospel (*e. g.*, St. L. Ed., IV:407, 431; V:58; VII:1109; IX:71) and emphasizes that succession does not make a bishop (XIV:600). Up to the year 1545 the chief question which concerned the Evangelicals was under what conditions they could submit to bishops (so in the *Wittenberg Reformation* published 1545). The Confessions recognize only the pastoral office of the bishop as existing *iure divino* (AC XXVIII; Apology XV:12 ff.). All the powers which the bishops had attained aside from the pastoral, they possessed *iure humano*, and the Reformers were ready to concede them such powers as soon as they acknowledged the Gospel (AC XXV; Apology XIV). This happened in some instances (*e. g.*, George of Polentz, Prussia, 1523), and some Lutheran bishops were also created (*e. g.*, Amsdorf). In Sweden the line of bishops was continued through Laurentius Petri; Denmark received bishops through the ordination of Bugenhagen; in Norway, Bishop Geble Peddersen introduced the Lutheran Reformation. In Germany the supervising functionaries were soon designated by other titles inasmuch as they were no longer "bishops" in the sense developed under Roman Catholicism. In American Lutheranism the ideal of church government is democracy, the functionaries being designated by the name "president." See also *Polity, Ecclesiastical*, 6 (and bibliography).

Bishop Hill Colony. See *Communistic Societies*, 5.

Bishop Lucas. See *Bohemian Moravian Brethren*.

Bishops' Bible. See *Bible Versions*, L 7.

Bishop's Book. See *Anglican Confessions*, 2.

Bismarck Archipelago. Renamed New Britain Archipelago. A group of islands in the S. Pacific off the coast of New Guinea, before World War I a German protectorate, since then taken over by Australia. Area: 19,660 sq. mi. Population: 247,780, mostly Papuan. New Pomerania (New Britain) has a population of about 190,000. Missions have been conducted by the Australian Wesleyans since 1875, mainly under Dr. George Brown. Roman Catholic countermissions 1889. See also *Melanesia*.

Bismillah. Arabic for "in the name of God." A formula appearing at the beginning of each sura (chapter) of the Mohammedan Koran and commonly used by Moslems as a pious expletive.

Bittle, David Frederick (1811—76). After several pastorates became first president of Roanoke College, Va., from 1855 till his death.

Bjarnason, John. See *Canada, Lutheranism in*, 13.

Bjoerling, Carl O. (1804—84). Swedish theologian; studied at Upsala; bishop of Westeras; author of a Christian dogmatics and other works which show his loyalty to the Augsburg Confession.

Bjork, Eric Tobias. B. in Westmanland, Sweden; came to America with Andrew Rudman, after ordination at Upsala in 1697, to serve the Swedish churches along the Delaware. He and Rudman divided the field between themselves, and Gloria Dei Church was built at Wicaco, Pa., and Trinity (Old Swedes Church) at Wilmington, Del. In 1713 he was recalled to Sweden, where he died in 1740.

Black Art. See *Witchcraft*.

Black Fast. A fast during Lent and before ordination practiced up to the tenth century. Not only was the food restricted on such fast days, but it was also stipulated that the food must be eaten in the evening.

Black Fathers and Sisters. Name given those canons and canonesses * who follow the rule of St. Augustine.

Black Friars. Name given Dominican Friars in England.

Black Jews. See *Church of God and Saints of Christ*.

Black Monks. A name given to Benedictine monks in England because of their black attire.

Black Rubric. A name applied by High-churchmen to the rubric printed in black in the Prayer Book (1552) at the insistence of Knox. It explained that kneeling at Communion was not to be considered idolatrous worship of the elements.

Black Week. See *Church Year.*

Blahoslaw, John. See *Bohemian-Moravian Brethren.*

Blair, James. See *Protestant Episcopal Church,* 1.

Blake, William (1757—1827). A visionary, mystic, poet, artist, and philosophical anarchist. Best-known works: *Songs of Innocence; Songs of Experience; The Everlasting Gospel; The Marriage of Heaven and Hell; The Four Zoas; Jerusalem, the Emancipation of the Giant Albion; The Ghost of Abel.*

Blanchard, Charles Albert. B. Galesburg, Ill., Nov. 8, 1848. Congregationalist. Educated Wheaton College and Chicago Theological Seminary, 1875; D.D. from Monmouth College, 1896; agent and lecturer for Nat'l Christian Ass'n, 1870—72; principal, Preparatory Dept., Wheaton College, 1872—74; professor in various subjects until he became pres. in 1882; pres., college section, Ill. State Teachers Ass'n, 1894; pres., Nat'l Christian Ass'n, 1903 to 1904. Wrote: *Modern Secret Societies; Light on the Last Days; Getting Things for God; Visions and Voices.* D. Dec. 20, 1925.

Blandina. A young female slave martyr, renowned for her steadfastness and endurance while being tormented to death during the persecution at Lyons, 177.

Blaues Kreuz. A society organized by Pastor Rochat in Geneva for the purpose of organized effort against drunkenness, 1877. It demands abstinence on the part of its members but does not disapprove of a moderate use of intoxicating drinks on the part of non-members.

Blaurer, Ambrosius (1492—1564). Studied in Tuebingen, joined the Lutheran movement, but was later induced to side with Zwingli, whose extreme position on the Lord's Supper, however, he did not share; was instrumental with Bucer in preparing the *Confessio Tetrapolitana;* in 1534 called to organize the Reformation in southern Wuerttemberg, continued in his mediating tendency, spent the last years of his life in Switzerland.

Blavatsky, Mme. Helena Petrovna. Theosophist; b. 1831, Russia; d. 1891, London. Traveled extensively, especially in America and India. Studied spiritism, occult and cabalistic literature, sacred writings of India. With H. Olcott founded the Theosophical Society in New York, 1875. Claimed miraculous powers, which were proved impostures. Wrote *Isis Unveiled,* 1877 (textbook of Theosophists), *Secret Doctrine,* 1888, *Key to Theosophy,* 1889.

Bleek, Friedrich. B. 1793; d. 1859 as professor at Bonn; mediating theologian; of Schleiermacher's school; wrote introduction to the Old and New Testaments; moderate critic.

Blessedness. State of bliss of the believers, veiled and imperfect in this life, perfect and eternal in heaven (Kingdom of Grace and Kingdom of Glory *). Effected and sealed by the Gospel, appropriated and enjoyed by faith. Consists in spiritual joy, happiness, peace, hope, restoration of divine image in man, eternal glory (1 Cor. 2:9; Matt. 5:3-12; Rom. 4:6-8; Ps. 16:11; 17:15; 23; 92:12-14; 128; Job 36:11; Deut. 28:1-14; Eph. 1:3; 2 Pet. 1:2-4; Rev. 14:13; 1 John 3:2). Cp. Luther IX:997, 1157; XII:136 ff.; P. Kretzmann, *Pop. Com.,* OT. II, 725; NT II, 659; Walther, *Law and Gospel,* 180; Reu-Buehring, *Christian Ethics,* chap. LIII. See *Hereafter.*

Blessing and Cursing. Blessing (benedictions) and cursing are both used effectively in Christ's kingdom, as will be evident on the Last Day, Matt. 25:31, 41; 1 Cor. 16:22. God blesses by bestowing temporal and spiritual benefits upon men, Num. 6: 22-27 (cp. Fritz, *Preacher's Manual,* 157 ff.); Gen. 1:22; 2:3; 9:1-7; Ps. 103:3 ff. Men bless God by praising and thanking Him, Ps. 103, they bless their fellow men by invoking God's favor upon them, Gen. 27:27-29; 48; 49; Deut. 33; Ps. 129:8. Cp. Luther IV:515. See Davis, *Dictionary of Bible* ("Bless and Blessing").

Cursing is solely a prerogative of God. See *Anathema.* God's curse rests upon the transgressors of His Law until they possess His forgiveness, Deut. 27: 15-26. All cursing by men, except their pronouncement of God's curse upon sin and unbelief, is sinful and forbidden.

In the Bible, cursing means an expressed wish or prayer for evil (an imprecation). Cp. Luther XII:350 ff. Cursing, profanity, proceeding from an evil heart, involves a misuse of God's name (Second Commandment). Cp. Kretzmann, *Pop. Com.*, OT, I, 150; II, 175, 258, 728 (Profanity); *Concordia Pulpit*, 1936, Vol. VII, 322, 282. See James 3:10; Rom. 12:14. JMW

Blomfield, Dorothy (Mrs. Gurney) (1858—1932). Wrote a wedding hymn of great poetic beauty for the marriage of her sister in 1883, namely: "O Perfect Love, All Human Thought Transcending!"

Blondus, Flavius (1392—1463). Humanist; secretary to popes; important in the development of modern history.

Blood Relationship. See *Impediments of Marriage, Scriptural and Natural.*

Bloody Tenent of Persecution for the Cause of Conscience. See *Baptist Bodies,* 3.

Blumhardt, Christian Gottlieb. B. Apr. 29, 1779, Stuttgart; d. Dec. 19, 1838, at Basel. He was one of the Basel Missionary Society founders, 1804; inspector Basel Missionary School, 1816.

Blumhardt, Johann Christoph. B. at Stuttgart, July 16, 1805; d. at Boll, Feb. 25, 1880. Studied at Tuebingen. Became teacher at the missionary institution at Basel, 1830, pastor at Moettlingen, 1838. Gained great fame as one who could cure by prayer. His first reported cure was that of a demoniac girl. In 1853 he bought the royal watering place Boll (*Bad Boll*), to which place all kinds of sufferers from all ranks of society and from all countries flocked to be cured by Blumhardt. In 1869 and 1872 he was joined in the work by his sons. The work is continued by Stanger in Moettlingen up to the present day.

B'nai B'rith. See *Students, Spiritual Care of,* A.

Board for Parish Education. See *Christian Education,* E 13; *Parish Education,* M.

Board of Christian Education. See *Parish Education,* K 3.

Boccaccio, Giovanni (1313—75). Friend of Petrarch; humanist; pupil of Dante; because of his *Decameron* often considered the first modern novelist.

Bodelschwingh, Friedrich von (1831 to 1910). German pastor; established charitable institutions such as the Epileptic Institute at Bielefeld (1867; included institutions for training deacons and deaconesses) and the first *Arbeiterkolonie* at Wilhelmsdorf, which through work and spiritual training sought to rehabilitate vagabonds. See *Charities, Christian.*

Bodenschatz, Erhard (d. 1636). A Lutheran editor and composer of church music, whose *Florilegium Portense* (Anthology of Pforta) enjoyed wide use within Lutheran circles in the 17th and 18th centuries. This collection included 265 motets written by 93 composers of Italy, Germany, the Netherlands, and France. It was used by Bach in his Leipzig days.

Boe, Lars Wilhelm. B. Dec. 27, 1875, Calumet, Mich.; educated St. Ansgar Seminary, 1890—93; United Church Seminary, 1893—94; St. Olaf College, 1894—98; and United Church Theol. Seminary, 1898—1901; pastor at Lawler, Iowa, 1901—04; first pres. of Waldorf College at Forest City, 1904—15; pastor at Forest City during that time; became interested in politics; member of House in Iowa Legislature, 1909—11, and Senator, 1913—15; resigned as pres. of Waldorf College, 1915; ex. sec'y. Bd. of Trustees and Bd. of Education in United Church; pres. of St. Olaf College, 1918—42; vice-pres. Southern Minn. Dist.; commissioner of Nat'l Luth. Council and American member of Luth. World Convention; D.D. Roanoke College, 1921; LL.D. Wittenberg College. King Haakon made him Knight of the Order of St. Olav in 1926 and commander of same order in 1940. D. Dec. 27, 1942.

Boeckh, Christian Frederick von (1795—1875). Pastor at Nuremberg and Munich; eminent in liturgic researches; published *Der Agendenkern fuer die ev. Luth. Kirche in Bayern* (1856), *Ev. Luth. Agende* (1870).

Boeckman, Markus Olaus. B. Jan. 9, 1849, at Langesund, Norway; educated in Norway, Egersund High School; Aars and Voss Latin School, University of Christiania; emigrated 1875; asst. pastor near Kenyon, Minn., 1875—80; served parish consisting of Gol and Moland Congs. near Kenyon, 1880—88; at St. Olaf College, 1886; Augsburg Seminary, 1890—93; pres. of United Norwegian Church Seminary, 1893—1917; pres. Luther Theol. Seminary, 1917—30, professor until 1937 and retired. Knighted by King Haakon VII, 1912. D. July 21, 1942.

Boecler, Otto Carl August. B. Nov. 3, 1875, at Memphis, Tenn.; graduated St. Louis 1898; pastor Ludington, Mich., 1898—1906; Grand Rapids, Mich., 1906—09; Chicago, Ill., 1917—25; professor Concordia Seminary, Springfield, Ill., 1909—17; professor Concordia Seminar, St. Louis, Mo., 1925; managing editor *Homiletic Magazine;* pastor Des Plaines, Ill., 1929—42; served on various boards; in 1935 made survey of missionary opportunities in Nigeria, Africa, for the Synodical Conference. D. Sept. 13, 1942.

Boehm, Georg (1661—1733). Lutheran composer of organ music who was organist of the Johanniskirche in Lueneberg; taught J. S. Bach and exerted a great influence on him, exposing him to French music and prevailing upon him to visit such music centers as Celle (French music) and Hamburg (Reinken). The influence of Boehm may be seen clearly in Bach's chorale partitas and in his *Orgelbuechlein.* Friedrich Blume, *Ev. Kirchenmusik,* Potsdam, 1931; Gotthold Frotscher, *Geschichte des Orgelspiels und der Orgelkomposition,* Berlin, 1936; Hans J. Moser, *Geschichte der deutschen Musik,* Stuttgart, 1928—30; F. Blume, *Musik in Geschichte und Gegenwart,* Baerenreiter Verlag, Kassel, 1952.

Boehm, Martin. See *United Brethren,* 1.

Boehme, A. W. (1673—1722). Lutheran theologian; studied at Halle; went to England, 1701; court preacher of George of Denmark and Anne and George I; wrote *Duty of the Reformation; First Principles of Practical Christianity.*

Boehme, Jacob (1575—1624). German theosophist and mystic; b. near Goerlitz; shoemaker in Goerlitz; d. *ibid.* Called *Philosophus Teutonicus.* His theosophy attempts to explain origin of evil. God contains conflicting elements in His nature, harmoniously united, while in the universe, which is an emanation of God, these conflicting elements separated, but can be harmoniously reunited through regeneration in Christ. Profoundly influenced greater minds than his own (Hegel, Schelling), and influence spread to England, where a disciple, Jane Lead, founded the Philadelphians. Believed in Trinity, Incarnation, Atonement. Died after having subscribed to Lutheran Confessions. Wrote *Aurora oder die Morgenroete im Aufgang, Mysterium Magnum, Der Weg zu Christo.*

Boehmer, Heinrich (1869—1927). Professor at Bonn, Marburg, and Leipzig; led studies in history of Reformation and life of Martin Luther; his *Der junge Luther* (1925) issued in translation as *Road to Reformation* (tr. Doberstein and Tappert, Philadelphia, 1946).

Boehne, John William. Manufacturer; b. Vanderburgh Co., Ind., Oct. 28, 1856; attended Commercial College; held offices of city councilman at large, mayor of Evansville, Ind.; member of 60th and 61st Congress U. S. A.; held position as member of Board of Directors, Missouri Synod; active in organizing Luth. Laymen's League; d. Dec. 27, 1947.

Boehringer, Georg Friedrich. B. Maulbronn, 1812; d. Basel, 1879. Reformed theologian, author of *Die Kirche Christi und ihre Zeugen* (24 vols.).

Boethius (ca. 480—524). Christian statesman, writer, philosopher; influenced Theodoric toward a benevolent rule; enemies at court finally brought about his downfall and ruin; sought to translate Greek classics into Latin and thereby assure their accessibility, a plan cut short by his early death; his best-known work, *On the Consolation of Philosophy,* written while awaiting execution, develops the theme that God is good and happiness consists in harmony with Him. Influential also in the field of music. His five books *De Musica* represent the end of antique musical science in the Western world. However, with Boethius, Cassiodorus, and Isidore of Seville began also the medieval science of music. The medieval idea, that music constitutes a unit of mathematical science, may be traced back to Boethius. He also insisted that music is imbued with moral and ethical proclivities.

Bogatzky, Carl Heinrich von. B. at Militsch in Silesia, Sept. 7, 1690; d. 1774. Attended the universities of Jena and Halle, studying first law, then theology under Francke. Unable to take up the active work of the Church on account of poor health, he devoted himself to religious authorship instead and thus spent most of his life in literary pursuits. The last twenty-eight years of his life were spent at Halle at the orphanage, where G. A. Francke gave him a room. His *The Golden Treasury*, done into English by John Berridge, was long a favorite book of devotion in Great Britain. His *Meditations* appeared in seven volumes. His missionary hymn, "Awake, Thou Spirit Who Didst Fire" is widely used.

Bogomiles. A branch of the Cathari, numerous in the twelfth century in Bulgaria and Constantinople. Their theology was a conglomerate of the wildest dualistic-gnostic fancies; they rejected Baptism and the Lord's Supper, shunned the churches as seats of evil spirits, and practiced much praying and strict asceticism. They survived a number of severe persecutions and found adherents in the Western Church.

Bohairic Bible Versions. See *Bible Versions, D.*

Bohemia, Lutheran Theology in.
1. The movement inaugurated by John Hus (d. 1415) did not immediately issue in any definitive theological formulation. In fact, the leadership of the chief Hussite group, the Unity of Bohemian Brethren (founded 1459), expressly directed its members "to let the Law of God suffice and believe it purely, forsaking all other writings." Thus, when Martin Luther challenged the authority of the Roman Church, the Hussites were ready for a theology.

2. Jan Lukáš (d. 1528), bishop of the Unity, was also its doctrinal leader. His spiritualistic conception of the Lord's Supper clashed with that of Luther, and until Lukáš' death the Unity was torn between the two. It was in this connection that Luther composed his treatise of 1523 "On the Adoration of the Sacrament." When Lukáš died, however, the Lutheran teaching prevailed in the Unity, and after several consultations, Luther expressed his approval of their position.

3. That position was expressed in the Bohemian Confession of 1535. Despite certain differences in terminology and emphasis, this Confession is strongly Lutheran, and from it we may date the half century or so of the official predominance of Lutheran theology in Bohemian Protestantism. In their doctrine of the Lord's Supper the Brethren accepted the true presence of Christ, but insisted on an interpretation of Christ's sitting on the right hand of the Father that differed from Luther's; they were also at variance

with his view of the Communion of the unworthy. But Luther was willing to overlook these differences, and in 1538 he published the Bohemian Confession with his preface and endorsement.

4. In the latter part of the sixteenth century the Unity of Bohemian Brethren reaffirmed its stand in the Bohemian Confession of 1575. Largely for political reasons, this statement of faith is even more Lutheran than the earlier one; for the Unity, combined with the new Utraquists, was seeking legal recognition and could secure it only as a Lutheran communion. The Bohemian Confession, therefore, is not an accurate representation of the actual theological situation in the Unity.

5. Alienated by both Philippism and Gnesio-Lutheranism and attracted by John Calvin's emphasis upon discipline, the Unity had begun to switch its theological orientation from Wittenberg to Geneva. This can be seen in the thought and activity of its last bishop, John Amos Comenius (Komenský, 1592—1670), who quite consistently supported Reformed against Lutheran theology.

Whatever chance there may have been for a rebirth of Lutheran theology in Bohemia was crushed by the Battle of White Hill (1620) and the consequent victory of the Counter-Reformation. JP

Georg Loesche, *Luther, Melanchthon und Calvin in Oesterreich-Ungarn* (Tuebingen, 1909); Erhard Peschke, *Die Theologie der Boehmischen Brueder in ihrer Fruehzeit, I, Das Abendmahl, 1. Studien* (Stuttgart, 1935).

Bohemia (Missions). See *Czecho-Slovakia.*

Bohemian Confessions. See *Bohemia, Lutheran Theology in, 3; Reformed Confessions, E 2, 3.*

Bohemian-Moravian Brethren. The *Unitas Fratrum* (Community, or Assembly, of Brethren) was founded by Utraquists (see *Hus*) under Gregor and Peter Chelczich and his followers in Kumwald, Bohemia, 1457, some Waldensians joining, and chose priests of their own at Shotka in 1467, Matthias being consecrated bishop by a Waldensian. Owing to the simplicity of their worship (some of their hymns have found their way into the Lutheran Church), their strict discipline, and their fervid brotherly love, they had a considerable growth under Bishop Lucas, numbering despite severe persecutions 300 to 400 congregations in Bohemia and Moravia in 1500. They refused to join Luther because of the Lutheran doctrines particularly of the Lord's Supper and of justification by faith alone. A second Lutheranizing movement was halted by John Blahoslaw, who stood for Calvinism. (His Bohemian translation of the New Testament is a masterpiece; d. 1574.) The Utraquists or Calixtenes were the Hussite faction that was satisfied with the concessions offered by the Council of Basel; the members of the dissatisfied faction, who were then defeated by Catholics and Utraquists at Boemishbrod and whose remnants founded the *Unitas Fratrum* were the Taborites. Discipline relaxed, great numbers were absorbed by the Reformed Church, and during the Thirty Years' War the society as such was wiped out in Bohemia. Bishop Amos Comenius being among those who were exiled, but survived for some time in Poland and Hungary; a scanty remnant still existing in Posen. See *Moravian Church.*

Bohm, Ed. B. Aug. 30, 1840; assistant pastor of St. Matthew's, New York, 1882, first director of Concordia Institute, Hawthorne, N. Y. (now at Bronxville), 1882; d. Dec. 24, 1895.

Bois, Henri (1862—). Professor at Montaban, France. Holds that God, like man, is endowed with feelings, passions, etc. (personalism).

Bolivia. See *South America.*

Bollandists. See *Acta Martyrum.*

Bolsec, Jerome. See *Reformed Confessions,* A 9.

Bolshevism. See *Socialism.*

Bolzius, John Martin (1703—65). Trained in Halle, selected with the Rev. Israel Christian Gronau to serve the persecuted Salzburgers and to accompany them to America; pastor in the congregation at Ebenezer from 1734 till his death; notable both as preacher and as pastor.

Bonald, Louis (1754—1840). French philosopher; defender of absolutism, papal infallibility, and Jesuitism; in his philosophy he rested upon the divine origin of language which, in his estimation, contained the essence of all truth.

Bonar, Horatius. B. in Edinburgh, Dec. 19, 1808; d. 1889. Six years after his ordination in the Established Church of Scotland he became a founder of the Free Church of Scotland at Kelso. Later he accepted a call to Chalmers Memorial Church in Edinburgh. He was a voluminous writer of sacred poetry. Even before his church authorized hymn singing, he had prepared and published seven tracts of hymns. Among his hymns are "I Heard the Voice of Jesus Say" and "I Lay My Sins on Jesus."

Bonaventura, St. (*Dr. Seraphicus;* 1221—74). Teacher at Paris, later general of the Franciscans, and cardinal; a standard Catholic dogmatician, ranking next to Thomas Aquinas. A schoolman (realist), he attempted to prove that the church doctrine agrees with reason; of the school of mysticism, that mystic contemplation leads to the highest knowledge of God; a poet, he composed *The Mirror of the Blessed Virgin Mary* and *The Psalter of the Blessed Virgin.*

Boniface, St.* (B. before 683; d. 755; Winfrid; "Apostle of the Germans"). After a short stay in Friesland, commissioned by Rome as missionary to Central Germany, 718, and later consecrated bishop. He founded churches in Hessia and Thuringia and organized the province for Rome by establishing sees and monasteries and expelling the anti-Roman Culdees. Although he established four sees in Bavaria, he did not succeed in overcoming the anti-Roman influence exerted by the Culdees. Called by Karlmann and Pepin to regulate the affairs of the Frankish Church, he had the synods pass measures concerning the introduction of Roman laws, doctrines, and customs, the extirpation of the remnants of heathenism, and the "reformation" of the Church. The German National Council, despite opposition from clergy, declared for submission to papal authority and the expulsion of the married clergy, 742. In 747 the majority of the bishops acknowledged the papal supremacy, and the Pope bestowed upon Boniface, the "pillar of papal hierarchy," the see of Mainz. In 744 he founded the monastery of Fulda. In 754 he resigned his office in Mainz to continue work in Friesland, where he met death at the hands of heathen the following year.

Boniface VIII. See *Popes,* 12.

Bonn, Hermann (1504—48). Studied under Luther and Melanchthon; friend of Bugenhagen; father of Low German church song.

Bonosians. Followers of Bonosus (4th c.) who denied the perpetual virginity of Mary.

Bonwetsch, G. Nathanael (1848 to 1925). B. at Nortkaa, Russia, professor at Dorpat; 1891 professor of church history at Goettingen. Wrote books and articles on historical subjects.

Book Art. See *Art, Ecclesiastical*, 4.

Book of Adam and Eve. See *Apocrypha*, A 4.

Book of Changes (of History, of Rites, of Songs). See *Confucianism*.

Book of Common Order. See *Presbyterian Bodies*, 1.

Book of Common Prayer. The only official service book used in the Church of England and its affiliated bodies. It contains in one volume the articles of faith and all the rites, ceremonies, and prescribed forms of the Church of England and is thus not only a prayer book, but a ritual and confession of faith.

In 1549, the First Prayer Book of Edward VI, largely the work of Thomas Cranmer, was confirmed by Parliament. At this time, and subsequently, acceptance of the Prayer Book was made compulsory by the Acts of Uniformity. A great part of it was taken from the old services used before the Reformation, but the labors of Melanchthon and Bucer helped to give the book its Protestant form. Exceptions were taken to some parts of it, and in 1552 Parliament confirmed the second review. This was known as the Second Prayer Book of Edward VI.

The liturgy of Elizabeth (1560) agreed substantially with the Second Prayer Book of Edward VI, with some minor changes.

The official Book of Prayer in the Anglican Church is that of 1662 (revision made to please the Nonconformists). The changes approved by the Church Assembly (1927—28) were not approved by Parliament.

The American Prayer Book is framed closely upon the model of the English book. It was adopted substantially in its present form by the Geneva Convention of 1789, with many variations from the English book, including those rendered necessary by political and local causes. Among the notable variations are the following: the omission of the Athanasian Creed, the Absolution in the Visitation office, the Magnificat and the Nunc Dimittis, the Commination, and the versicles after the Creed; the optional use of the words "He descended into hell" in the Creed, and in many things considerably enlarging the discretional power of the minister; the

addition of a number of prayers; the change of "absolution" into "declaration of absolution," of "verily and indeed taken" into "spiritually taken" (Catechism) and the permission of using an alternative formula instead of "Receive the Holy Ghost," etc. (Ordinal); the introduction of the prayers of invocation and oblation in the Communion office, which was insisted on as rendering the liturgy more in accordance with primitive models.

During the latter part of the 19th century a desire for liturgical enrichment and increased flexibility resulted in the adoption, in 1892, of a considerable number of changes, which brought the book into closer harmony both with the English and with the earlier models. The work of revision is still continuing.

Francis Parker & W. H. Frere, *A History of the Book of Common Prayer*, Macm., 1905; Joseph Ketley, *The Two Liturgies, A. D. 1549 and A. D. 1552, with Other Documents Set Forth by Authority in the Reign of Edward VI*, Oxford U. Press, 1844; Leighton Pullan, *History of the Book of Common Prayer*, Longmans, Green, 1901.

Book of Concord, or *Concordia*. Contains the Confessional Writings of the Lutheran Church, her Symbolical Books. They are the three Ecumenical Creeds — Apostles', Nicene, Athanasian; the Unaltered Augsburg Confession of 1530; its Apology; Luther's Small Catechism and the Large Catechism; Smalcald Articles and Tract; Formula of Concord. Jacob Andreae's German edition appeared officially on June 25, 1580, fifty years after the presentation of the Augsburg Confession; the Latin edition came out in 1584.

For additional information and important editions see *Lutheran Confessions* (especially bibliography).

Book of the Dead. Sacred book of ancient Egypt describing rites and inquisition used in the judgment of the dead.

Book of Discipline. See *Presbyterian Confessions*, 3; *Presbyterian Bodies*, 1.

Book of Homilies. Collection of famous homilies made in England, 1547, and appointed to be read in the churches. See also *Preaching, Christian*.

Book of Mormon. See *Latter-Day Saints*.

Book of Rules and Order. See *Evangelical Ch.*, 3.

Boos, Martin (1762—1825). B. at Huttenried, Bavaria. Roman Catholic priest, whose experiences in asceticism resemble those of Luther and who preached a doctrine resembling the Lutheran. Driven out by the opposition of church authorities, he lived in Austria (1799—1816) until forced to leave that country also and spent his last years at Duesseldorf and Sayn.

Booth, Ballington. See *Volunteers of America.*

Booth, William. See *Salvation Army.*

Bora, Katharina von. See *Luther, Family Life of.*

Boris. See *Bulgaria.*

Borneo, Missions in. One of the largest islands of the world; under British and Dutch government. Area, approximately 200,000 sq. mi. Population, 2,306,000, mostly Mohammedans, with some aboriginal tribes. Malays, Dyaks, Chinese. Islam is very active. Roman attempts at missions in 1687, and the American Board in 1839 and 1850. The Rhenish Mission Society since 1836. The Society for the Propagation of the Gospel also works there, with Sarawak as their center. In a persecution in 1859 four missionaries and families and many native Christians were killed. In 1939 the Anglicans were working in six languages.

Bornhausen, Karl (1882—). Professor in Breslau, Frankfurt; pupil of Troeltsch, advocate of essential Christianity, influenced by classical idealism.

Bornholmers. An organization of Danish Pietists united in "The Lutheran Missionary Society for the Promotion of the Gospel." Though begun in Sweden under Carl Olof Rosenius (1816—68; lay preacher; stressed "life within") in the early nineteenth century, it gained its first strong foothold in Bornholm, Denmark. Here the movement was led by Pastor Trandberg, who left the State Church, organizing a Lutheran Free Church, which also did some mission work. Trandberg came to America in 1882 and later was professor at the (Congregationalist) Chicago Theological Seminary. The movement still continues in Denmark, though its adherents are again more closely associated with the State Church.

Borromeo, Carl (1538—84). B. at Arona; studied law at Pavia; turned to theology upon the accession of his uncle, Pope Pius IV; cardinal and archbishop of Milan, 1560; prominent at Council of Trent; founded seminaries for clergy; severe opponent of heretics; canonized, 1610.

Borthwick, Jane. B. in Edinburgh, Scotland, Apr. 9, 1813; d. 1897. She and her sister, Sarah Findlater, won for themselves a high place among hymn translators. They published *Hymns from the Land of Luther.* Jane also wrote original hymns, many of which were published in *Thoughts for Thoughtful Hours.* Hardly a hymnal has appeared in England or in America without containing some of these hymns.

Bortniansky, Dimitry Spenovich (1751—1825). "Father of Russian church music," despite the fact that his compositions are Italian rather than Russian in character. Catherine the Great sent the young talented Bortniansky to Italy (Venice, Rome, Naples), for expert training in music, that he might return to Russia to effect reform of Russian church music. After having spent eleven years in Italy, Bortniansky returned to his native land, where he dedicated himself to the task which confronted him. Despite adversity, he succeeded remarkably well. Not a few of his compositions have been sung in Lutheran and other Protestant churches.

Bosse, Benjamin. Manufacturer and banker; b. in Scott Township, Ind., 1874; d. at Evansville, Ind., 1922; mayor of Evansville; prominent in Lutheran Laymen's League; member of Missouri Synod's Board of Control and Board of Directors.

Bossuet, Jacques Benigne (1627 to 1704). Roman Catholic preacher; Doctor of Theology, 1652; canon and archdeacon at Metz; bishop of Meaux; tutor of the dauphin of France for some years. Noted as controversialist against Fénelon and separatists among Romanists. His six *Funeral Orations* rank high in the oratory of his Church.

Boston, Declaration of. See *Democratic Declarations, 2.*

Botticelli, Sandro (1447—1510). Italian painter; pupil of Fra Filippo Lippi, whose style, however, he rejected; did some work for the chapel of Sixtus IV at Rome; noted for his "Magnificat" and "The Burial of the Crucified."

Bottome, Marg. See *King's Daughters*.

Bouck, W. C. B. Jan. 7, 1786; Fulton, Schoharie Co., N. Y.; member New York Ministerium; 4 times elected to the Assembly of N. Y.; was state senator; finished a difficult section of the Erie Canal and built 5 other canals; elected governor of N. Y., 1842; appointed Asst. Treas. of the U. S.; participated in the councils of the New York Ministerium. D. Apr. 19, 1859.

Boudinot, Elias. See *Bible Societies, 5*.

Bougle, Celestin Charles Alfred (1870—1940). French scholar; held religion responsible for the caste system in India; held that morality cannot be satisfactory as long as it is dependent on religion.

Bourdaloue, Louis (1632—1704). Often called the founder of French eloquence, Voltaire ranking him above even Bossuet; entered Jesuit order at 16; occupied chairs of rhetoric, philosophy and moral theology; known for piety and honesty.

Bourignon, Mme. Antoinette (1616 to 1680). Quietist who gathered followers in Amsterdam; convent life and efforts at orphans' work failures due to distrust of human nature; attacked religious organizations of every type; denied divine foreknowledge, atonement, need of Scriptures.

Bousset, Johann Franz W. (1865 to 1920). B. at Luebeck; professor of NT exegesis at Goettingen (1896). Protestant theologian of the *religionsgeschichtliche* school. Active in Christian Socialist movement. Wrote *Gnosis; Religion des Judentums im neutestamentlichen Zeitalter;* various studies on the Antichrist; and other works.

Boutroux, Emile (1845—1921). French philosopher; professor at Sorbonne. His earliest work, *De la contingence des lois de la nature,* denied the omnipotence of causality; everything happens freely in accordance with divine intelligence; God is immanent.

Bovon, Jules (1852—1904). Reformed theologian; studied at Lausanne and Berlin; professor of NT on the theological faculty in Lausanne. Described God in a twofold aspect; incomprehensible in His work of creation and preservation; comprehensible in His relation to spiritual life.

Bowne, Borden Parker (1847—1910). Studied at the universities of New York, Halle, Goettingen, and Paris; professor of philosophy at Boston University; wrote on ethics, metaphysics, and personalism.

Bowring, Sir John (1792—1872). B. at Exeter, England, Oct. 17, 1792, he became a great linguist, acquiring, it is said, the mastery of 200 languages and dialects and a speaking knowledge of 100. He served his government in various positions at home and abroad. His extensive writings were published in 36 volumes. As a hymn writer he is known for the hymns "In the Cross of Christ I Glory" and "Watchman, Tell Us of the Night."

Boyce, William (1710—79). English master of church music whose compositions for organ and choir enjoy wide use particularly in Anglican circles.

Boy Scouts of America. Organized first in England by Sir Robert Baden-Powell, the movement was introduced into the United States in 1910. According to the charter granted by Congress, 1916, the purpose of the organization is to "promote, through organization and co-operation with other agencies, the ability of boys to do things for themselves and others, to train them in Scoutcraft, and to teach them patriotism, courage, self-reliance, and kindred virtues, using the methods which are now in common use by Boy Scouts," by placing emphasis upon the Scout Oath or Promise and Law for character development, citizenship training, and physical fitness. Stress is also laid upon the effort made by the organization to further love for outdoor life; for this purpose so-called hikes are made, and some time is spent in summer camps. Such outdoor life is also intended to contribute to health and practical education. The Scout Law, to which obedience must be promised, says that the Scout must be trustworthy, loyal, helpful, friendly, courteous, obedient, cheerful, thrifty, brave, clean, and reverent. Scouts are required to "do a good turn daily." The Scout idea is to instil into the boy love and duty to God, home, and country.

In its initial stages, Scouting could be charged with possessing a religious character but refraining from the use of the Christian Gospel for the building up of a God-pleasing character; that is to say, with seeking to serve God without a true regeneration of the heart and without being guided by the principles of Holy Scripture. Through efforts initiated by the Missouri Synod's committee (1929) for the study of Boy Scouts, Camp Fire Girls, and similar movements, the Boy Scouts of America have given over the entire program of religious instruction and spiritual training to the churches. The organization does maintain that "no boy can grow into the best kind of citizenship without recognizing his obligation to God. . . . The recognition of God as the ruling and leading power in the universe and the grateful acknowledgment of His favors and blessings are necessary to the best type of citizenship, and wholesome precepts in the education of the growing boy." However, while recognizing the religious element in the training of the boy, Scouting refrains from giving religious training or even announcing a program of such training but assigns to the church whatever spiritual guidance and religious instruction the boy is to receive. Various committees of the Missouri Synod at different times made reports on their dealings with Scout authorities and this led to a resolution approving the committee's report in 1944: "Your Committee believes that the matter of Scouting should be left to the individual congregation to decide and that under the circumstances Synod may consider her interests sufficiently protected." (*Proceedings*, page 257.) The official stand of the Scout movement towards religious and moral training is defined as follows: Whatever Scouting has to say about religion refers to "civil righteousness" — termed "character building and citizenship training," "good citizenship through service." The oath: "The Boy Scout 'Pledge' is a promise, not an oath in the Scriptural sense of the term. The upraised hand, with three fingers extended, has reference to the threefold pledge, not to the Trinity." (*Scouting in the Lutheran Church*, copyrighted 1943 by Boy Scouts of America.) "We recognize that there is no Boy Scout authority which supersedes the authority of the local Pastor and the Congregation in any phase of the program affecting the spiritual welfare of Lutheran men and boys in Scouting." (Elbert Fretwell, chief Scout Executive.) TG

Boyle, Robert (1627—91). B. in Ireland; educated in England; devoted to science (Boyle's Law) and theology; founder of Boyle's Lectures, eight lec-tures delivered annually in London against unbelievers; Unitarian.

Bradford, John (ca. 1510—55). Protestant martyr. B. at Manchester, England; prebendary of St. Paul's; chaplain to Edward VI; popular preacher; burned at stake, Smithfield. Many short works.

Bradley, Francis Herbert (1846 to 1924). British philosopher; in his *Ethical Studies* he held that man must first find himself as a whole and then bring himself in line with the universe; in his *Appearance and Reality* he held that the ultimate fact is experience which is unity with the perceived; since, however, absolute spirit is beyond finite minds, judgments err.

Bradwardine, Thomas (ca. 1290 to 1349). *Doctor Profundus;* lecturer at Oxford; fearless confessor of Edward III; archbishop of Canterbury 1349, the year of his death; his *De Causa Dei contra Pelagium* prepared Wyclif for his work.

Braeuniger, Moritz (1836—60). Attended Neuendettelsau; trained by Loehe, and Wartburg Seminary, Dubuque, Iowa; missionary to Upsaroka Indians near Fort Sarpi, Mont., and Cheyenne Indians at Powder River; member Iowa Synod; murdered by a band of Ogallala Indians July 23, 1860, in Montana. His body was never found.

Brahma. See *Brahmanism*.

Brahma-Samaj. See *Hinduism*.

Brahmanaspati. See *Brahmanism, 2.*

Brahmanism. 1. The religion of the Brahmans, the priestly caste in India, particularly its earlier development. Though Brahmanism and Hinduism are sometimes used interchangeably to denote the entire development of orthodox religious thought in India, beginning with the period that follows the composition of the Rig-Veda (see *Veda*) down to modern times, the term Brahmanism is more specifically applied to the earlier form of this development, to ca. 200 B. C., and the term Hinduism to the later with its admixtures of popular beliefs and worship.

2. The earliest religion of the Aryan invaders of India, as we find it portrayed in the Rig-Veda, was, like that of the ancestors of the Persians and that of the Indo-Germanic people in general, a polytheistic nature worship. Chief in the Vedic pantheon is Indra, originally a thunder god, the na-

tional deity, who leads his people in war and brings them to victory. Ranking next are Varuna, the omniscient king of gods and men, who upholds the physical and moral world order, Agni (Lat., *ignis*), a fire god, Soma, originally a sacred intoxicating drink (Iranian, Haoma; see *Zoroastrianism*), Mitra, a sun god (Iranian, Mithra), Dyaus pitar, "Father Heaven" (Gr. Ζεῦς πατήρ, Lat., Diespiter, Jupiter) and his wife, Prithivi matar, "Mother Earth," Ushas, the Dawn, also gods of the storm, wind, rain. Vishnu, a sun god, and Rudra, a malignant storm god, have subordinated positions in the Rig-Veda, but in later centuries rose to supreme importance (see *Hinduism*). The Vedic gods, with the exception of Rudra, were beneficent. Sacrifices of food, particularly of melted butter and soma, were made to them. Their help was implored against the multitudes of demons and evil spirits, which were believed to be the cause of disease and misfortune of all kinds. The Vedic eschatology included belief in heaven and hell, to which, at death, the good and the evildoers pass respectively. In earliest times there were neither temples nor holy places nor priests. But toward the end of the Vedic period a priesthood developed. The power that lay in the priestly sacrifices and prayers was personified in the deity Brahman-aspati, who is also called the creator of heaven and earth, Prajapati, "Lord-of-creatures," or Viçvakarman, "All-worker."

3. There now came a period of transition. The Aryan invaders, who at first had occupied only the north-western part of India, the Punjab, or "five-river" country, moved southward and subjugated the darker-skinned aborigines. A mixture of races resulted, the consequence of which was the beginning of the caste system, which has become such a prominent feature in Hinduism. The four castes are: the Brahman, or priestly caste, which became socially supreme; the Kshatriya, or warrior caste; the Vaisya, or agricultural caste; the Sudra, or servile caste. The literary documents of this transitionary period are the Brahmanas, prose ritualistic commentaries on the Vedic texts, whose composition began ca. 800 B. C. Priestly speculation sought the unity of the godhead, and the prominence now given to the idea of an impersonal deity marks the end of the Vedic period of Indian religious development and the beginning of Brahmanism. During the period that fol-

lowed the main features of the Vedic religion were retained, essentially the same gods were worshiped, and the Veda was regarded as a divine revelation; but the Brahmans gained ever greater importance, until they were regarded as "gods on earth." The priestly speculation which marks this period was a reaction against the sacrifices, which had become more and more numerous, and against the ritual, which, increasingly emphasized, had become an unbearable burden. The essential feature of this speculation, which was philosophical rather than religious, was the belief in an eternal, unchangeable principle, or world soul, the continuation of the Vedic Brahmanaspati. This principle, called Brahman or Atman (*i. e.*, "Self"), lies at the basis of the universe, and all beings are manifestations of it. Man emanated from it and returns to it at death. Salvation is no longer believed to come by works, as during the Vedic period, but through knowledge of, and intellectual absorption in, Brahman-Atman. During this period the doctrine of the transmigration of souls * was also developed. According to this doctrine a man is reincarnated immediately at death, and the deeds in his previous existence determine the character of his rebirth. He is reincarnated in a higher state if his previous deeds were good, but in a lower state, even in animal form, as that of a pig, ass, etc., if his previous deeds were evil. As rebirth meant continued suffering, the great aim was to be released from rebirth. But it was desire that led to rebirth, therefore all desire had to be abolished, and to abolish all desires that fetter the soul to the world and to become one with Brahman-Atman was the great object of human endeavor. This terrible doctrine probably is the result of the fact that life in India had become extremely hard.

4. The Rig-Veda shows that as long as the Aryan invaders were in the Punjab, the joy of living was still theirs; but when they spread over Southern India, the depressing climate changed their outlook upon life. The writings which contain this pantheistic and pessimistic philosophy are the Upanishads, the third group of sacred Indian texts. They date from the 6th century B. C. onward. In the 6th century B. C. the "great heresies," Buddhism * and Jainism,* also arose as revolts from the Brahmanic system.

5. During the centuries in which they flourished six systems of Brahmanic philosophy were developed, which

are based on the Upanishads and are considered orthodox, in distinction from Buddhism and Jainism. Each taught its own way of salvation, *i. e.*, how to be released from rebirth. They are Vedanta, Sankhya, Yoga,* Mimansa, Nyaya, Vaiçeshika. The last three are minor systems. The Sankhya is atheistic and dualistic. It teaches that on the one hand there is the soul, or an infinite plurality of individual souls; on the other, matter. Release from rebirth comes to him who recognizes the complete difference between these two eternal beings. The Vedanta, the most important system, appears in various forms. The most influential school is that of Çankara (ca. A.D. 800). It teaches the identity of the ego with the infinite, unchangeable Brahman. He alone exists, and the multiplicity of phenomena is an illusion. He who attains this knowledge has salvation and is released from rebirth. Opposed to these six systems is that of the Charvakas, the followers of Charvaka, author of a materialistic philosophy which denies the authority of the Vedas, spurns the idea that there is a soul separate from the body, and considers pleasure the only thing worth living for. For the later religious development in India see *Hinduism*. See *Religion, Comparative, Bibliography.*

Brahms, Johannes (1833—1897). With J. S. Bach and Beethoven, is one of the three great B's of the music world. Brahms lived at the close of the Romantic Era and did not fall under the spell of such Romanticists as von Weber, Chopin, Berlioz, Wagner, Liszt, and others; composed in the style of the classical masters, studied the music of Bach assiduously, enriched the classical idiom with a new type of lyricism, originality, and rhythm, and produced such gigantic works as his four symphonies, two piano concertos, his violin concerto, three string quartets, and other outstanding literature. He was an intimate friend of Robert and Clara Schumann and was a member of the Lutheran Church. His *German Requiem*, though concert music, has been called the only great *Lutheran* Requiem Mass. While his motettes reveal the influence of Bach, they likewise reveal the individual style of Brahms himself. His last compositions were a group of eleven organ preludes based on the Lutheran chorale.

Alfred Einstein, *Greatness in Music*, New York, 1941; Alfred Einstein, *Music*

in the Romantic Era, New York, 1947; Karl Geiringer, *Brahms, His Life and Work*, New York, 1936; Walter Nieman, *Brahms* (tr. by Phillips), New York, 1929.

Brainerd, David (1718—47). Ordained by New York Presbytery 1744 for work among Indians; labored successfully in Stockbridge, Mass., Pennsylvania, and New Jersey; made unsuccessful attempt to colonize converts as farmers.

Bramante (*Donato Lazzari*, 1444 to 1514). Planned and executed buildings connecting Belvedere and Vatican in Rome; designed St. Peter's Cathedral, afterward completed by Michelangelo.

Bramhall, John. Anglican prelate. B. near Pontefract, 1594; ordained ca. 1616; bishop of Derry, Ireland, 1634; archbishop of Armagh, 1662 (vacant since Ussher's death); d. at Omagh, 1663. Opposed Hobbes on the freedom of the will.

Brand, Frederick. B. Sept. 9, 1863, at Eden, N. Y.; graduated at St. Louis 1886; pastor at Braddock, Pa., 1886—93; at Pittsburgh, Pa., 1893—1903; at Springfield, Ill., 1903—20; president of Central Illinois District, 1907—17; vice-president of Missouri Synod, 1917—29; director of Foreign Missions since 1920; visited Foreign Mission fields in China and India 1921—22; China 1926; wrote *Our Task in China*, 1922. D. D. (St. Louis) 1927. D. Jan. 1, 1949.

Brand, P. B. Nov. 3, 1839, at Ansbach, Hessen-Nassau; attended college at Cologne; studied theology there and in the seminary at Neuendettelsau; came to America in 1857; missionary at St. Clair, Mich. (Iowa Synod); pastor in Eden Valley, Farnham, and Buffalo (Buffalo Synod); successfully combated the error of Grabau; one of the commissioners at the "Colloquium"; 1869 pastor in Washington, D. C. (Missouri Synod); 1876 of St. Paul's, Pittsburgh (Ohio Synod). Protesting against the stand taken by the Ohio Synod on the doctrines of election and conversion, his congregation with others formed the Concordia Synod and later joined the Missouri Synod. He died as pastor of St. Paul's, Pittsburgh, Jan. 17, 1918. He had been president of the Concordia Synod, president of the Eastern District (1888), vice-president of the General Body (1899), member of the Board for Foreign Missions. He was a wise and fearless leader, a tactful and energetic manager of affairs.

Brandelle, Gust. Alb. B. March 19, 1861, Andover, Ill., educated at Augustana Coll. and Theol. Seminary; grad. 1884; M. A. 1896; D. D. Bethany Coll., Lindsborg, Kans., 1900; LL. D. Augustana Coll.; St. Olaf Coll. 1925; ordained 1884; pastor Denver, Colo., 1884—1918; Grace, Rock Island, Ill., 1918—23; pres. Ev. Luth. Augustana Synod 1918—35; pres. em.; pres. National Luth. Council 8 yrs.; member Bd. of Missions Aug. Synod; editor *Augustana Journal,* 1897 to 1906; delegate Luth. World Convention, Eisenach, Germany, 1923; Copenhagen 1925; d. Jan. 16, 1936.

Brandenburgicum. See *Luth. Confessions,* C 1.

Brandt, Christian Philipp Heinrich (1790—1857). Luth. pastor in Bavaria; defended orthodox faith against rationalism, especially that of Dinter; active in home missions; wrote *Schullehrer-Bibel;* edited *Homiletisch-Liturgisches Korrespondenzblatt.*

Brandt, Nils Olsen. B. in Norway, Jan. 29, 1824; graduate of Kristiania University, 1849; emigrated to America, 1851; pastor in Wisconsin and Iowa; professor at Luther College; co-editor of *Kirketidende;* one of the organizers of the Norwegian Synod and its vice-president, 1857—71; d. 1921.

Brandt, Olaf Elias. B. at Monterey, Wis., Feb. 19, 1862; graduated from Luther College, 1879; Northwestern University, Watertown, Wis., 1880; Concordia Seminary, 1883; pastor at Cleveland, Ohio, 1883—92; Chicago, 1892—97; professor at Luther Seminary, 1897—; member of "The Norwegian Synod" and later of "The Norwegian Lutheran Church of America." D. 1940.

Brant, Sebastian (1458—1521). Professor of jurisprudence at Basel, then city notary for Strassburg; humanist and reformer of morals; most famous work the *Ship of Fools* (*Narrenschiff*), pub. 1494, satire on vices and foibles of age, culturally and poetically most significant.

Brastberger, Immanuel Gottlob (1716—64). *Spezialsuperintendent* at Nuertingen. His sermons on the Gospels, *Evangelische Zeugnisse der Wahrheit,* are very popular; 85th edition in 1883 at Reutlingen.

Bratt, Torbjørn. See *Norway, Lutheranism in,* 3.

Brauer, August G. Manufacturer; b. at Pittsburgh, Pa., May 20, 1857; attended Walther College, St. Louis, Mo.; member Board of Control of Concordia Seminary, St. Louis, Mo. (1893—1932); prominent member of Lutheran Laymen's League of Missouri Synod and first secretary of the organization. D. Sept. 26, 1932.

Brauer, E. A. B. in Northeim, Hannover, Apr. 19, 1819; studied theology at Goettingen and at Berlin. Moved by the appeal of Wyneken, at the advice of Dr. Petri and Pastor Loehe, he came over to America with the Rev. F. Sievers and his company of missionary emigrants and several students in 1847. Rev. Selle in Chicago prevailed upon him to take charge of the newly organized congregation in Addison, Ill. Here he performed pioneer work for ten years; became pastor in Pittsburgh, Pa., 1857; took an active part in the controversy with Grabau; 1863—72 professor of Exegesis, Logic, and Isagogics at Concordia Seminary, St. Louis; 1872—78 pastor of Trinity Church, St. Louis; 1878 pastor in Crete, Ill.; very prolific contributor to *Der Lutheraner* and *Lehre und Wehre;* for a time editor of the latter; wrote a number of tracts; member Electoral College; d. Sept. 29, 1896.
Albert Brauer, *Ernst August Brauer,* CPH, 1898.

Braun, Anton Theodor. B. at Treves; Roman Catholic missionary among the Indians in Canada; convert to Lutheranism, preaching to Lutheran churches in Frontenac and Dundas, Ontario; formally received into Lutheran Church by Dr. J. C. Kunze, Christ Church, New York; ministered to the churches of the Schoharie parish, 1790—93; pastor Ebenezer Church, Albany, 1794—97; from 1798 to 1800 again at Schoharie; 1800—14 served church at Troytown, Guilderland, and New Brunswick, N. Y.; from 1793—97 secretary New York Ministerium; was one of the few conservative men who opposed rationalistic views of Dr. F. H. Quitman. D. March, 1814.

Braune, Karl (1810—79). Pastor near Torgau; general superintendent at Altenburg; active in mission work; wrote *Unsere Zeit und die Innere Mission.*

Bray, Thomas (1656—1730). Educated at Oxford; sent by Bishop Compton to settle church affairs in Maryland; sought to establish parochial libraries in each parish; wrote *Cate-chetical Lectures, Bibliotheca Parochialis, Martyrology*.

Brazil. See *South America*, 4.

Brazil, Lutheranism in. 1. *The country*. Brazil, roughly speaking, occupies the eastern half of the South American continent. It reaches from the temperate zone in the south to far past the equator; from the Atlantic Ocean on the east to a point only 300 miles from the Pacific Ocean on the west. It has an area of 3,275,500 sq. mi. It is larger than the United States without Alaska.

2. The United States has more than 236,000 miles of railroad and several million miles of paved highway. Brazil, however, has only 20,700 miles of railway. Of these 18,000 are in six of the southern states. In other areas there are no rail connections.

3. Brazil's transportation problems are further complicated by the climate, the roughness of the terrain, and by tropical downpours which make dirt roads impassable. Landslides, washouts, lack of bridges add to the transportation difficulties. The cost of paved highways is prohibitive. Then, too, only one out of 1,100 persons owns an auto.

4. *The people*. The typical Brazilian is not of European origin. His attitude, his way of life, his outlook represents a fusion of Indian, Negro, and Portuguese. Brazil has a population of only 40,000,000 plus. Nearly all nations of Europe and some of Asia are represented. Among the immigrants the Italians lead with 1,500,000 and the Germans are second with 500,000. The total number of immigrants is estimated at 4,600,000.

5. *Lutheranism*. In 1899 the Missouri Synod passed the resolution to begin mission work in Brazil, Rev. F. Brutschin having requested Synod to send a pastor to become his successor. Synod sent Rev. C. J. Broders to reconnoiter the field and begin work. He found 25 parishes without an ordained Lutheran pastor. The "pseudo-pastors" who served the churches were usually unscrupulous characters. With the help of a devout Lutheran, who had influence with the better class of people, a congregation was organized in Sao Pedro, Rio Grande do Sul, and in 1901 entrusted to Rev. W. Mahler, the first settled pastor of the Missouri Synod in South America. The same year three candidates of theology went to Brazil

to take charge of some of the parishes which had petitioned Synod to send them pastors.

6. In November, 1903, the first issue of the South American Lutheran church paper, *Das Ev.-Lutherische Kirchenblatt fuer Suedamerika*, made its appearance. In 1917 the *Mensageiro Luterano*, the Portuguese district paper, appeared. It had more than 2,300 subscribers in 1949. Other publications are the *Igreja Luterana*, a monthly for pastors and teachers, *O Jovem Luterano* for the youth, *O Pequeno Luterano* for the children, *O Lar Cristao*, which is the Lutheran Annual for Brazil. The periodicals, together with hymnbooks, tracts, and other Christian literature are printed at the Casa Publicadora, the Concordia Publishing House of Brazil.

7. Severe trials came over the Luth. Church during the days of World War II. War hysteria infuriated mobs in different areas against it. Nineteen of the pastors were jailed for a longer or shorter period of time. One received a prison term of 30 years, another of 20 years. Both, however, after suffering about four years of imprisonment, were released. Fourteen pastors lost their libraries. One church was burned to the ground.

8. One of the greatest hardships during this period was the law which forbade the use of the German language. But this was a blessing in disguise. The use of the Portuguese language in every parish opened wide the door to the millions of "unchurched" living in darkness and superstition. During this period of unrest the parochial schools thrived. The existing schools were filled to capacity "because they had long ago been nationalized."

9. The persecutions against the Church gradually subsided, because it was found that the Missouri Synod Lutherans "had already before 1938 declared in their publications that they were not interested in spreading Americanism or Germanism but solely serving the Christian cause. If the use of the German language became undesirable they would simply preach and teach in Portuguese" (quoted from official document).

10. The official report on the survey made in Brazil referring to an attempt made to unite all Teuto-Brazilians in 1936 definitely states "that the Missouri Synod kept apart from the very be-

ginning. To the great disappointment of the Germans from the Reich it proved impossible even to effect a political synchronization of the Federation."

11. The official document further states that "the churches affiliated with the Missouri Synod and now forming the Synodo Evangelico Luterano do Brasil came from the very beginning into sharp conflict with the German Evangelical Church and this not only due to their rigid creed. The opposition also arose from the fact that the Missouri churches, although their clergymen preached in German, dreaded the anti-assimilation and strongly German nationalist tendencies of the competing synods."

12. *Building an indigenous Church.* Early in 1904 plans were made to open an institution for the education of pastors and teachers in Bom Jesus, in Sao Lourenco, which was later on moved to Porto Alegre, the capital of Rio Grande do Sul, under the name of Concordia Seminary. The enrollment at the Seminary (1949) was approximately 125. Up until 1949, 110 had graduated from this school to work as parish pastors or as teachers in our Christian day schools. Less than 10% of the 1949 clergy were other than nationally trained. Only a scattered few from North America and from Europe remained in the work.

13. *Statistics* (1951): 92 pastors; 333 congregations; 67,926 baptized members; 38,600 communicant members.

FCS

Breckling, Frederick (1629—1711). Lutheran theologian of Denmark; wrote against immoral life of clergy; imprisoned, fled to Hamburg; suspended from office because of difficulties with clergy and chiliastic views; befriended by Spener, Princess Mary, and others.

Breeches Bible. Geneva Bible, so-called because of the translation "made themselves breeches" (Gen. 3:7).

Breithaupt, Joachim Justus (1658 to 1732). Professor at Halle; prominent pietist of Germany.

Breklum Missionary Society. Organized by Pastor Jensen and others, who formerly were in connection with the North German Missionary Society, beginning with a mission institute in 1876 as a Lutheran organization. First missionaries sent out in 1882, to India. Work suffered by World War I. The African mission has been abandoned.

Brentano, Franz (1838—1917). Dominican, liberal Catholic; resigned priesthood; opposed the "content" psychology of Wundt with "act" psychology (all life is action; psychology's task is to find the aim of such action).

Brenz, Johann (1499—1570). Precocious. Saw Luther at Heidelberg in 1518 and became his follower. Suspected and investigated, in 1522, he went to Hall in Suabia and was active there for twenty-four years. In 1525 he, like Luther, told the truth to peasants and princes alike. Oecolampadius' attack on the Lutheran doctrine of the Lord's Supper was repelled in the *Syngramma* of 1925 under the leadership of Brenz. He attended the Marburg Colloquium * in 1529, though without high hopes. He grieved because Hall would not sign the historic Protest at Speyer in 1529. In 1530, at Augsburg, he, like Melanchthon, was timidly willing to concede to the papists the Communion in one kind, priestly vestments, episcopal jurisdiction, and the papal primacy as of human right; he was severely criticized. From the notes for sermons came many commentaries; Amos has a fine introduction by Luther. As early as 1529 Brenz wrote a Small Catechism, followed by a Large Catechism for adults; the order is: Baptism, Creed, Law, Prayer, Lord's Supper, an order still followed in Wuerttemberg. In 1532 he helped Osiander get out the Nuernberg-Brandenburg Order of Service, which influenced others. Exiled since 1519 and returned after the victory of Laufen in 1534, Duke Ulrich of Wuerttemberg used Brenz to carry out the reformation of the country from Stuttgart. Brenz was honored at Schmalkalden in 1537, and he reformed the University of Tuebingen. He was silent at Hagenau and Worms in 1540, seeing no possibility of uniting the devil and Christ, *i. e.*, the Pope and Luther, and he condemned the Interim of Regensburg in 1541. During the Smalcald War, Brenz the "traitor" had to flee to Basel with a price on his head; on his return he was to be taken "dead or alive," and he went into hiding. Duke Christopher, son and successor of Ulrich, called Brenz as his chief adviser, and now Wuerttemberg was thoroughly reformed in Church and State, but with a mixing of the two. Melanchthon faulted Brenz for pacifism in Osiander's doctrine of justification, and Brenz upheld Ubiquity and attacked Melanchthon for departing from the Lutheran doctrine of the Lord's Supper. Brenz was a practical preacher; he refused presents from great lords and lucrative places in Magdeburg, Prussia, and England.

J. Hartmann and K. Jaeger, *Johann Brenz*, Friedrich Perthes, Hamburg, 1840—42 (2 vol.).

Breslau Synod. One of the first independent synods organized by Lutherans in Germany after the decree of Frederick William III, according to which the union Agenda was to be introduced into all the Lutheran and Reformed churches of his kingdom. A persecution of staunch Lutherans followed, which caused a number of those living in Silesia and Saxony to organize and, with the permission of Frederick William IV, in 1841, to form "The Evangelical Lutheran Church in Prussia," with headquarters at Breslau, the general synod assembling there quadrennially. See also *Saxony*.

Brethren, Dunkers, German Baptist Brethren. 1. The German Brethren movement had its origin in the Pietistic revival inaugurated by Philip Jacob Spener during the second half of the seventeenth century. While the majority of the Pietists hoped to reform the Church by retaining their membership in the various state churches, Alexander Mach (1679—1735), a Calvinist, and E. C. Hochmann, a Halle Pietist, believed that a mere protest against the cold formalism of the churches and the laxity of morals was insufficient. In 1708 they withdrew from the state church and organized a separate congregation at Schwarzenau, Westphalia. In line with his Calvinistic and legalistic background, Mach believed that a Christian must enter into a covenant relation with Christ, which is established by triple immersion, hence the names Taeufer, Tunker, Dunker, Dompelaars, German Baptist Brethren. While the Brethren are opposed to the adoption of written creeds, they have worked out a system of doctrine, practice, and church government in line with their enthusiastic, pietistic, mystic, and ascetic views. Like the Quakers and Mennonites, with whom they have often been erroneously identified, they place greater emphasis on the observance of rites and regulations which they find prescribed in the New Testament than upon doctrine, believing that they have re-established the simplicity of life which marked the Apostolic Church. The following rites and practices are

observed by the various groups of Brethren: Baptism by triple forward immersion followed immediately by confirmation while kneeling in the water; the Eucharist, celebrated only in the evening, is preceded by footwashing and the love feast; the "veiling" of women in the public service; the anointing of sick with oil; excommunication according to Matthew 18; total abstinence; non-participation in war; opposition to the use of the oath and civil litigation; simplicity in attire; some also forbid the cutting of the beard. — The movement spread rapidly to various parts of Germany, Holland, and Switzerland. Because of political persecution the Brethren emigrated to Pennsylvania in 1719, and by 1729 practically all the adherents had come to America. Because they at first retained their European customs and dialects, they were considered illiterate by their English neighbors, though the many publications issuing from the presses of Christian Saur at Germantown prove the opposite. A serious defection occurred in 1728 when John Conrad Beissel founded the monastic community at Ephrata, Pa., whose members until recently were classified as Brethren, but are now listed with the Baptists * as Seventh-Day Baptists (German, 1728). In the nineteenth century the Brethren were disturbed by several controversies on matters of church government and practice, and today they are represented by four bodies, though attempts are being made to re-unite these. The total membership of these bodies in the U. S. is approximately 207,900 (1952).

2. *Church of the Brethren (Conservative Dunkers)*. This is the largest group. Its church polity is quasi-presbyterian. Formerly the clergy was largely untrained and was expected to be self-supporting, but in recent years this body has initiated an aggressive program in the fields of education and mission.

3. *Old German Baptist Brethren.* Organized in 1881 as a separate denomination as a protest against the introduction of specially organized missions, Sunday schools, training of ministers, which they consider as being opposed to essential Christianity.

4. *The Brethren Church (Progressive Dunkers)*. Organized in 1882, favor modern methods in church work and the autonomy of the local congregation.

5. *Church of God (New Dunkers)*. A very small group, accepts no de-

nominational name other than "Church. of God." See *Religious Bodies* (*U. S.*), *Bibliography*. FEM

Brethren in Christ. See *Brethren, the River.*

Brethren Church (Progressive Dunkers). See *Brethren, Dunkers.*

Brethren of the Common Life. An association of pious priests and laymen, founded by Gerhard Groot of Deventer, a Carthusian, for a time lay preacher, and Florentius Radewin, not long before the death of Groot in 1384. The Sisters of the Common Life, together with two cloisters for regular canons (see *Clergy; Chapter*), were founded soon afterwards. The theology of the Brethren of the Common Life was that of Mysticism * of the practical type; their object, the furtherance of piety; their occupation, the study of Scripture, the copying and circulating of useful books, manual labor, preaching, and, particularly, popular education. Their organization was of the monastic type, but without the taking of lifelong obligations. The brother house was at Deventer, in the Netherlands. Their spreading of the Scriptures and their piety (commended by Luther) exerted a wholesome influence; but, emphasizing *Christ in us* to the virtual exclusion of *Christ for us*, they were unable to effect a real Reformation. See *Thomas à Kempis.*

Brethren, Plymouth. The Brethren, known popularly as Plymouth Brethren and sometimes as Darbyites, originated in England and Ireland during the second and third decades of the 19th century. Dissatisfied with the schismatic conditions of Christendom and particularly the mingling of Church and State in the Church of England, John Nelson Darby (1800—82) and others held that subscription to creeds, adoption of denominational names, and the setting up of ecclesiastical organizations were inherently sinful. Darby and like-minded people believed that instead of joining organized denominations Christians must follow the pattern of the New Testament Church, gather in local "brotherhoods" to give expression to their "spiritual communion" by the breaking of bread and prayer, await the direction of the Holy Spirit, and listen to anyone who feels called to preach. Rejecting every form of a regular ministry, of creeds and rituals and ecclesiastical organization, they organized

"meetings," the largest being at Plymouth, hence the name Plymouth Brethren, though the members insist on being known by no other names than "Believers," "Christians," "Brethren," or "Saints." Darby was joined by men of outstanding ability, chiefly George Mueller, the father of English orphanages, and S. P. Tregelles, the famous exegete. The theological position of the Brethren is fundamentalistic-literalistic with strong leanings toward Calvinism. Its distinctive doctrine is the belief that the visible Christian Church must be one. They ascribe to the visible Church all the marks which the New Testament predicates of the holy Christian Church and say that membership in a denomination is a denial of the "one body." In line with this false conception of the Church the Brethren hold two major errors: 1) Since only true believers can belong to a "meeting," the Holy Spirit directly governs the assembly when it accepts a member; 2) a person once incorporated into the "visible body of Christ" can never be lost. The Brethren have no regular ministry, frequently not even church buildings. The services are primarily for the purposes of praise and the "breaking of bread" as an act of obedience, of testimony, of fellowship, and of hope. Darby and his co-workers were the forerunners of modern premillennialism. The Brethren came to America about the middle of the 19th century and are now represented by eight groups, all going by the name "Brethren." Instead of presenting a united Christian Church, they have only added to the schisms. The differences are largely concerning matters of discipline, some "meetings" being known as "Open Brethren," others as "Exclusive Brethren," because they exclude from fellowship those with whom they disagree in doctrine or in practice and sometimes even all the members of a "meeting" which had not repudiated an allegedly heterodox "meeting." The total membership of this church in the U. S. is approximately 25,800 (1952). See *Religious Bodies* (*U. S.*), *Bibliography*. FEM

Brethren, The River. The three small denominations *Brethren in Christ, Old Order* or *Yorker Brethren*, and *United Zion's Children*, commonly known as River Brethren, trace their early beginning to Swiss Mennonites who settled in Lancaster County, Pa., in 1752. During the revival of 1770 conducted by Wm. Otterbein and Martin Boehm (see *United Brethren*) and the Engles among Baptists, Lutherans, and Mennonites, differences of opinion arose concerning the mode of Baptism. The groups advocating triple immersion were opposed to formal church organizations and designated their congregations merely as "brotherhoods," each being known by its respective locality. The largest was the "Brotherhood down by the River," the Susquehanna; hence the name River Brethren. The Brethren have not adopted a creed, but follow in general the principles and practices of the Mennonites and the Dunkers. They adhere to a legalistic and literalistic interpretation of such portions of the New Testament as seem important to them, *e. g.*, triple immersion; anointing of the sick; veiling of women in the public service; foot washing, the love feast, and the Eucharist observed in the evening; an unsalaried ministry; nonresistance; non-conformity to the world in dress and social customs. Discussions have arisen in their midst concerning such trivial points as to whether the same person should both wash and dry the feet in the ceremony of foot washing. The Brethren in Christ is the largest and most progressive of the three groups. The total membership of this body in the U. S. is approximately 6,500 (1952). See *Religious Bodies (U. S.)*, *Bibliography*.

Brethren, United. See *United Brethren*.

Bretschneider, Karl Gottlieb (1776 to 1848). General superintendent at Gotha; rational supranaturalist; wrote in the field of dogmatics and prepared a lexicon on the New Testament.

Breve. A papal decree or order in a shorter form, particularly in matters of minor importance as compared with questions of dogma and general church practice; as part of the papal constitutions, sources of ecclesiastical order in the Roman Catholic Church. See also *Bulls*.

Breviary. The book containing the "divine office" which every cleric of the Church of Rome, from subdeacon upward, is bound to recite daily under pain of mortal sin. It is written in Latin and is divided into four parts, corresponding approximately to the four seasons, an "office" being provided for each day. The contents consist of extracts from Scripture, the Church Fathers, and Roman theologians, of prayers, hymns, antiphons, and collects. The book

abounds in legends which are part of the required recitation. See *Canonical Hours*.

Brevis Confessio. See *Mennonite Bodies*, 2.

Brewster, William (1560—1644). Regarded by many as the outstanding leader of the Pilgrims; organized Separatist Church of Scrooby; removed to Holland 1608; came to America on *Mayflower* and served as ruling elder until Ralph Smith arrived.

Bridaine, Jacques (1701—1767). Famous French preacher, educated at the Jesuits' College, Avignon, and Congregation of the Missions of Sainte-Croix; his *Cantiques Spirituels* were often printed; five volumes of his *Sermons* were also published.

Bridel, Philippe (1852—). Swiss theologian; held that God is personal and revealed in Jesus Christ; in harmony with Swiss theology in his emphasis on the inadequacy of terminology in describing God.

Bridges, Matthew (1800—94). Educated in Church of England; joined Roman Catholic Church; published a number of prose productions, also *Hymns of the Heart*; wrote: "Crown Him with Many Crowns," and others.

Bridget, St.* (452—523). Patron saint of Ireland; child of a bondmaid and a prince of Ulster; freed from parental control by the King of Ulster, she founded Kildare and three other monasteries; remains placed beside those of St. Patrick and St. Columba; her feast is Feb. 1.

Bridget, St. (1303—73). See *Brigittines*.

Bridgewater Treatise. A set of eight celebrated works *On the Power, Wisdom, and Goodness of God as Manifested in the Creation*, written by eight authors (Chalmers, Prout, Kirby, Buckland, Bell, Kidd, Whewell, Roget) eminent in their departments and published (1833—40) under a bequest of the last Earl of Bridgewater.

Brief Statement. In its report, which advocated that the *Chicago Theses ** be not accepted in the form submitted, the Committee on Intersynodical Matters at the River Forest convention of the Missouri Synod (June 19—28, 1929) recommended the creation of a committee which was "to formulate theses, which, beginning with the *status controversiae*, are to present the doctrines of Scripture and the Lutheran Confessions in the shortest and simplest manner." The committee appointed by Pres. F. Pfotenhauer (F. Pieper, W. Wenger, E. A. Mayer, L. A. Heerboth, Th. Engelder) issued the *Brief Statement of the Doctrinal Position of the Missouri Synod* in 1931. This document treated Holy Scripture, God, Creation, Man and Sin, Redemption, Faith in Christ, Conversion, Justification, Good Works, Means of Grace, Church, Public Ministry, Church and State, Election of Grace, Sunday, Millennium, Antichrist, Open Questions, Symbols of the Church. This *Brief Statement* was adopted by the Missouri Synod in 1932. Efforts toward unity with the American Lutheran Church continued and, in 1938, the Missouri Synod accepted the *Brief Statement*, the *Declaration* (prepared by the ALC commissioners) and the entire report of the Floor Committee of the Convention as a basis for future fellowship with the American Lutheran Church. In the same year the American Lutheran Church adopted the *Brief Statement* and the *Declaration*. The Missouri Synod Convention at Fort Wayne, 1941, felt that the American Lutheran Church had not done everything possible to carry out the 1938 resolutions (especially in view of the Sandusky Resolutions,* Pittsburgh Agreement,* and the failure to persuade the American Lutheran Conference); the Missouri Synod had, also, been informed that its own sister synods were not yet favorable to active fellowship and, therefore (at the request of synods of the Synodical Conference, 1940) instructed the committee to formulate one document in which "we do not mean to dispense with any doctrinal statement made in our *Brief Statement.*" Three years later this one document (called the *Doctrinal Affirmation*) was in the stages of preparation, 1944. It was presented to the American Lutheran Church in 1946 and declared unsatisfactory. A similar position was taken by the Missouri Synod 1947. The Missouri Synod also reaffirmed the *Brief Statement,* 1947, but declared that the 1938 Resolutions be no longer considered a basis for establishing fellowship. At the same time it instructed its committee to continue discussion with the American Lutheran Church, using the *Brief Statement* and other existing documents (and documents to be formulated) and thus seek to arrive

at one document. See *Common Confession.* EL

Proceedings of the Missouri Synod, 1929: 113; 1932: 154, 155; 1938: 221—233 (contains *Declaration*); 1941:277—304 (contains *Sandusky Resolutions*); 1944: 228 ff. (contains *Mendota Resolutions*); 1947:476—515 (contains *Brief Statement*); *CTM,* II:321—336 (official *Brief Statement* in German), 401—416 (English); *Reports* of the *American Lutheran Church Conventions,* 1938; 1940; *Luth. Standard,* Dec. 7, 1940; *Luth. Companion,* Nov. 28, 1940; *Proceedings of the Synodical Conference,* 1940:81 to 88. An analysis of the situation as it obtained after the Fort Wayne Synod 1941 is given by M. Reu in *Kirchliche Zeitschrift* (Oct., 1941); *Doctrinal Declarations,* CPH, n. d.; *CTM,* XVI: 1—5, 265, 787—88.

Briefs. Papal letters, subscribed by the secretary of briefs, sealed with red wax and the fishermen's ring, written in Roman characters on white skins, and beginning with the issuing pope's name. Simpler and less formal than the bull.

Brieger, Theodor (1842—1915). Ev. theologian; professor at Halle, Marburg, and Leipzig; pupil of Ritschl; scholar of Reformation history.

Briesmann, Johann (1488—1549). Monk at Wittenberg; won for Luther by the disputation at Leipzig; spread the Gospel in Riga and other cities of Livonia; returned to Koenigsberg. "The first disseminator of the pure doctrine in Prussia."

Briggs, Charles Augustus (1841 to 1913). Biblical scholar. B. and d. at New York City; Presbyterian minister; professor of Hebrew, then of Biblical Theology, in Union Theological Seminary; suspended from the ministry by General Assembly, 1893, for entertaining liberal views on place of reason in religion; joined Episcopal Church; exponent of Higher Criticism. Joint editor of *International Critical Commentary,* etc.

Brigittines. An order founded in Sweden by St. Bridget (1303—73; St. Bridget claimed to have had visions and wrote *Revelations* which contain evangelical tendencies) in 1346 as an instrument to spread the Kingdom of God on earth. The monasteries were double, one portion for monks, the other for nuns. The order contributed to the civilization of the North, but was nearly obliterated by the Reformation.

Brilioth, Yngre. See *Sweden, Lutheran Church in,* 6.

Brinck, Sven Dideriksen (1665 to 1728). Educated at Christiania, Upsala, and Copenhagen; army chaplain; pastor of the first Danish-Norwegian Luth. church in London 1692; later returned to Denmark 1702.

Brinckerinck, Jan (1359—1419). Popular preacher of the *Brethren and Sisters of the Common Life;* ordained priest in 1393; introduced discipline for the house for women founded at Deventer by Groote.

British and Foreign Bible Societies. See *Bible Societies,* 3.

British Columbia. Westernmost province of the Dominion of Canada; climate tempered by Japan Stream. Jagged coast line. Some of first Missouri Synod workers in B. C. were the Rev. Ed. Brandt in Vancouver 1911, the Rev. J. E. Herzer in Vernon 1912. Formed a synodical District together with Alberta in 1921. See *Missions, Bibliography.*

British Council of Churches. Formed in 1942 by Protestant churches in Britain and Ireland for the purpose of discussion and joint action.

British Guiana. See *South America.*

British Honduras. See *Central America.*

British Museum Gospel. See *Apocrypha,* B 2.

British West Africa. Consists of the colony and protectorate of Nigeria; the Gambia Colony and Protectorate; the Gold Coast Colony with Ashanti and Northern Territories; and the Sierra Leone Colony and Protectorate; parts of Togoland and the Cameroons (formerly German). Area, approximately 332,000 sq. mi. Population, about 17,500,000. Mohammedanism and paganism dominate. Some Christian missions. See constituent states.

Brito-Pictish Church. See *Celtic Church,* 12.

Broadcasting. See *Radio Stations.*

Broad Church. See *Protestant Episcopal Church,* 7.

Broadus, John Albert (1827—95). Baptist; b. in Virginia; professor at University of Virginia and pastor at Charlottesville; professor, then president, at Southern Baptist Seminary, Louisville, Ky.; wrote: *Preparation and Delivery of Sermons* and other works; gave Lyman Beecher Lectures at Yale.

Brobst, Samuel Kistler. B. Nov. 16, 1822, in Albany Township, Berks Co., Pa., of an old German family, which had come to Pennsylvania at the end of the 17th cent.; became agent for American Sunday School Union; ordained by Ministerium of Pa. in 1847. Editor of periodicals: *Jugend-Freund, Lutherische Zeitschrift,* and *Theologische Monatshefte.* He helped establish the theological seminary in Philadelphia and Muhlenberg College; started *Lutherische Kalender;* pastor at Allentown, Pa., 1869—1876. D. Dec. 23, 1876.

Brochmand, Jaspar Rasmussen. B. 1585; d. at Copenhagen, 1652, as bishop of Zeeland; author of *Systema Universae Theologiae,* very highly esteemed, also of polemic and devotional works, one of which is still in use in Denmark.

Brockmann, J. H. (1833—1904). Graduate of Hermannsburg, 1862; immediately came to Wisconsin Synod; pastor at Algoma, Mosel, Fort Atkinson, Watertown; active member of Northwestern and Indian Mission boards.

Broemel, Albert Robert (1815—85). B. at Teichel, Schwarzburg, 1815; supt. of the duchy of Lauenburg, 1854, and from 1865 member of Lutheran consistory at Kiel. Wrote: *Was heisst Katholisch?* and *Homiletische Charakterbilder.*

Brohm, Theodore. B. Apr. 10, 1846, in New York City; educated Conc. Coll., St. Louis, later Fort Wayne; graduated Concordia Seminary, St. Louis, 1866; post-graduate work New York University; pastor at Immanuel, East Boston, 1869; called to Northwestern College, Watertown, Wis., in 1871; professor at Addison Seminary 1879—1913, when he retired; director of Addison 1906—13; served California Conc. Coll., Oakland, as instructor till 1925. D. Apr. 27, 1926.

Brohm, Theodore Julius. B. Sept. 12, 1808, in Oberwinkel, near Waldenburg, Saxony; studied theology in Leipzig, 1827—32; after graduating, became attached to Pastor Stephan and refused to accept a position in the State Church; emigrated with Stephan to America; his private secretary; co-founder, Concordia Coll., Altenburg, Mo.; instructor until 1843; pastor of Trinity Congregation,

New York; 1858 pastor of Holy Cross Church, St. Louis; resigned 1878; d. Sept. 24, 1881.

Brommer, Carl Fred. B. Mar. 30, 1870, in Wuerttemberg, Germany; graduated St. Louis, 1891; pastor at Tampa, Fla., 1891—96; at Houston, Tex., 1896 to 1901; at Cheyenne, Wyo., 1902—4; at Beatrice, Nebr., 1904—11; at Hampton, Nebr., 1911—24; president of Nebraska District, 1915—22, of Southern Nebraska District 1922—4; president of Concordia Teachers College, Seward, Nebr., 1924 to 1941. D. D. St. Louis. D. at San Diego, Cal., Oct. 19, 1949.

Bronxville Collegiate Institute. See *Ministry, Education of,* IX.

Brook Farm. See *Communistic Societies,* 5.

Brooke, Stopford Augusta (1832 to 1916). Irish preacher; priest in Church of England; seceded and became an independent clergyman with Unitarian inclinations; wrote histories of literature, studies of authors and plays, and other works.

Brooks, Charles Timothy (1813—83). Educated at Harvard and at Cambridge; Unitarian minister in several cities, at last in Newport; wrote the well-known hymn "God Bless Our Native Land."

Brooks, Phillips. B. in Boston, Dec. 13, 1835; studied at Harvard. A failure at teaching, he studied at the Episcopal Theological Seminary at Alexandria, Va., and became rector of the Church of the Advent, Philadelphia, and finally became rector of the famous Trinity Church, Boston, and bishop of Massachusetts. He was one of the most renowned American preachers. He wrote: "O Little Town of Bethlehem." D. 1893.

Brorson, Hans Adolph (1694—1764). Outstanding Danish hymn writer; ordained 1722; bishop of Ribe 1741; popular preacher; his simple and sincere hymns were his greatest contribution to the Danish Church.

Brotherhood of St. Andrew. An organization of laymen in the Protestant Episcopal Church in the United States, in the Church of England, and in their branches. The purpose of the society is "the spread of Christ's kingdom among men, especially young men." Organized in St. James' Church, Chicago, on St. Andrew's Day, 1883, under the leadership of James L. Houghteling. Two rules were adopted: 1. "To pray daily for the spread of Christ's kingdom among men"; 2. "to make an earnest effort each week to bring at least one young man within the hearing of the Gospel of Jesus Christ as set forth in the services of the church and in young men's Bible classes." A junior department for work among boys admits to membership boys twelve years old. There are no amusements or attractions of any kind. No chapter of the brotherhood may be organized without the written consent of the rector in charge of the church. A monthly magazine is published, *St. Andrew's Cross.*

Brotherhoods. See *Laymen's Activity in the Luth. Church.*

Brotherhoods and Sisterhoods. Such organizations as the World Brotherhood Federation (London), which seeks to interpret brotherhood in the light of the life and principles of Jesus and to organize brotherhood societies in various countries; the Brotherhood of Andrew and Philip (Philadelphia), an interdenominational organization of Christian men for the purpose of advancing the kingdom of Christ; Big Brother and Big Sister Federation (New York City), which is devoted to a personal effort of caring for wayward children; and similar organizations.

Brothers Marists (*Little Brothers of Mary*). A Catholic religious institute founded in France in 1817, doing only educational work in parochial and boarding schools, orphanages, etc. The brotherhood developed rapidly in the last seventy years and has over 6,000 members in all parts of the world. It entered North America in 1885.

Brothers of Christ. See *Christadelphians.*

Brown, Abel (1816—94). Professor in Greenville College, Tenn.; principal of Blountville Academy; leader in Tennessee Synod; one of founders of Holston Synod; author.

Brown, Charles Lafayette. B. Dec. 3, 1873, in Iredell Co., N. C.; educated Roanoke College 1895; M. A. 1907; D. D. Lenoir Rhyne College 1907; Roanoke College 1916; ordained 1898; missionary to Japan 1898—1918; teacher at Kyusku Gakuin, Japan, 1912—16; sec. Bd. of Foreign Missions, United Synod of South, 1918—19; ULC 1920—21. Wrote *Japan for Christ;* contributed to pamphlets and Lutheran church papers; advisory Japanese labor delegate, International Labor Conference, 1919. D. Dec. 5, 1921, Liberia, Africa.

Brown, Ford Madox (1821—93). English painter; studied at Bruges, Ghent, Antwerp, and Paris; associated with the Pre-Raphaelite Brotherhood; worked chiefly in the secular field.

Brown, James Allen. B. 1821 in Lancaster Co., Pa., of Quaker lineage; educated at Gettysburg (Pa.) College; baptized in Presbyterian Church; graduated 1842; studied theology privately; licensed in 1845 by Maryland Synod; pastor Baltimore, Md.; Zion, York, Pa.; St. Matthew, Reading, Pa.; professor Newberry College, S. C., and pres. 1860. Left for North because of union sentiments; chaplain of 87th Pa. Regiment as S. S. Schmucker's successor; pres. of General Synod 1866; editor of *Luth. Quarterly* 1871; disabled by paralysis 1879 and resigned. D. 1882.

Brown, John (1722—87). Scottish clergyman and commentator. B. at Carpow; taught himself Latin, Greek, and Hebrew while herdboy to a shepherd; peddler; soldier; schoolmaster; preacher at Haddington during entire ministry; professor of theology. *Self-interpreting Bible*, etc.

Brown, John Newton (1803—68). American Baptist preacher and theological professor, editorial secretary of the American Baptist Publication Society, 1849 to his death; most important literary work the *Encyclopedia of Religious Knowledge*.

Brown, William Adams (1865 to 1944). Studied at Yale, Union Theol. Seminary, Berlin Univ., Univ. of St. Andrews, Scotland; instructor, then professor Union Theol. Seminary, from 1892; author; liberal theologian.

Browne, Robert. See *Congregational and Christian Churches,* A 1.

Browne, Sir Thomas (1605—82). Well-known English author. B. at London; practiced medicine at Norwich (d. there). *Religio Medici* (blending religious feeling and skepticism), *Urn Burial,* etc.

Browning, Robert (1812—99). B. at Camberwell, Surrey; considered the most intellectual and erudite of the Victorian poets. The son of a London banker, received main training under private tutors; read voluminously. Interested in music, painting, sculpture, and poetry; never unsympathetic with

people, but essentially was analytical in his attitudes. In his poems he sought to express the spiritual values in dogmas and contemporary philosophy and emphasized the soul and the future life especially. Chief works: *Paracelsus; Sordello; Pippa Passes; A Blot in the 'Scutcheon; A Soul's Tragedy; My Last Duchess; The Pied Piper of Hamelin; How They Brought the Good News from Ghent to Aix; The Lost Leader; The Bishop Orders His Tomb; The Confessional; The Glove; Fra Lippo Lippi; Saul; Rabbi Ben Ezra; Caliban upon Setrebos, or, Natural Theology in the Island; Prospice; The Ring and the Book.*

Brownists. See *Congregational and Christian Churches,* A 1.

Brownson, Orestes Augustus (1803 to 1876). B. at Stockbridge, Vt.; brought up a Presbyterian; preacher (Universalist, Unitarian, Society of Christian Progress); Catholic, 1844; Catholic apologist; d. at Detroit. Editor, author.

Brueck, Georg (also *Gregor v.;* ca. 1484—1557). Family name Heinse. Studied at Wittenberg and Frankfort on the Oder; famous jurist; elector councilor of Frederick the Wise; later chancellor; greatest services to Lutheranism at the Diet of Augsburg; died at Jena.

Bruckner, Anton (1824—1896). Outstanding composer of the 19th century, though his fame did not spread until 30 years after his death. Wrote only symphonies (9) and religious choral works and was an outstanding organist. An admirer of Richard Wagner, and the relations between Bruckner and Brahms were notoriously hostile. In youth he had grown up in Catholic surroundings and remained a devout Catholic throughout life. Bruckner today regarded by many as the last of the great composers of Roman Catholic church music. His setting of the *Te Deum* enjoys wide popularity.

Paul Henry Lang, *Music in Western Civilization,* New York, 1941; Hugo Leichtentritt, *Music, History and Ideas,* Cambridge, Mass., 1938; Werner Wolff, *Anton Bruckner, Rustic Genius,* New York, 1942.

Brueckner, Benno Bruno (1824 to 1905). Educated at Leipzig; pastor at Hamburg; pastor and professor at Leipzig; canon at Meissen; consistorial counselor of Prussia; chief interest in church government.

Bruederhof Communities. See *Communistic Societies.*

Brumder, George. B. in Strassburg, 1839; came to Milwaukee at age of sixteen; publisher of German newspapers, *Germania* (now *Amerika*), *Rundschau*, etc.; first publisher of Wisconsin German hymnal, which he turned over to that synod before original agreement matured; d. at Milwaukee, 1910.

Brun, Johan Nordal. See *Norway, Lutheranism in,* 10.

Brunelleschi (Brunellesco), **Filippo** (1379—1446). Artist, chiefly architect; solved the problem of a central building over polygonal foundation; builder of the Cathedral of Florence; developed the classical Renaissance in architecture.

Brunn, Arthur J. B. July 10, 1880, in Chicago, Ill., son of the Rev. Friedrich Brunn, Chicago; grandson of the Rev. F. Brunn of Steeden, Germany; grad. of Concordia College, Fort Wayne, Ind., 1900; Concordia Seminary, St. Louis, 1903; pastor at Emmaus Church, Brooklyn, N. Y. 1903—04; of St. Peter's Church, Brooklyn, N. Y., 1904 to 1949; member of Army and Navy Commission during World War I; pres. of the Atlantic District, Missouri Synod, 1930—41; vice-pres., The Lutheran Church — Missouri Synod, 1941 to 1949; member Bd. of Directors of American Luth. Publicity Bureau; associate editor, *The American Lutheran*; exec.-sec., Wartburg Luth. Home for the Aged, Brooklyn; member, Bd. of Directors, Bethlehem Luth. Children's Home, Staten Island; member Bd. of Trustees, Concordia Collegiate Institute, Bronxville, N. Y.; honorary D. D., Concordia Seminary, St. Louis, and Hartwick Seminary. D. Aug. 27, 1949.

Brunn, Friedrich. B. 1819 in the Castle Schaumburg, Duchy of Nassau; studied at Leipzig, Bonn, and the theological seminary at Herborn; entered the ministry in 1842; severed his connections with the State Church of Nassau in 1846 and with 26 families organized an independent congregation at Steeden; 1846 to 1860 years of development; result: break with the Breslau Synod in 1865, with the Immanuel Synod in 1870, and with the Lutheran State Church in 1875. First meeting of the Ev. Luth. Free Church of Saxony, which Brunn joined, was held in 1877. Brunn's first contact with the Missourians dates back to probably 1858, when he was in correspondence with Professor Craemer. Walther's visit to Germany in 1860 gave the impetus to the opening of the preparatory institution at Steeden in 1861, which furnished the Missouri Synod about 250 men. Brunn d. in 1894.

Brunner, Emil. B. 1889; educated in Switzerland; taught in boys' school in England; held pastorate in Switzerland for six years; visiting fellow at Union Theol. Seminary (N. Y.); instructor (1922), then professor (1924) at Univ. of Zurich; lecturer in America, guest professor at Princeton Theol. Seminary 1938—39; returned to Zurich. See *Switzerland, Contemporary Theology in.*

Brunnholz, Peter (d. 1757). Native of Schleswig, a Dane; trained at Halle; came to assist H. M. Muhlenberg, serving at Philadelphia and Germantown, 1745—51; at Philadelphia alone 1751 to 1757; co-founder Pennsylvania Ministerium; a zealous worker, but suffered from poor health.

Bruno of Cologne (925—65). Youngest son of Emperor Henry I (the Fowler); under the reign of his brother, Otto I, chancellor 940, archbishop of Cologne 953, regent in Germany 961; promoted a closer alliance between episcopate and crown.

Bruno, Giordano (1548—1600). Italian philosopher; put to death by the Inquisition for his cosmological theories based on Copernicus; opposed Aristotelianism; held theory of animate monads; taught relativity of space, time, and motion; influenced Boehme, Spinoza, Leibnitz, Descartes, Schelling, Hegel.

Bruno of Prussia. Saxon nobleman, ordained 996 in Rome; sent by Pope Sylvester II as missionary to the Slavs (Poland) and Prussians, among whom he suffered martyrdom 1009.

Brunswick, Confession of. See *Lutheran Confessions,* C 1.

Bryan, William Jennings (1860 to 1925). Prominent as statesman and orator, in wide demand as Chautauqua lecturer; strong advocate of Fundamentalism in religion, speaking and writing in its favor with great earnestness; died at the conclusion of the Scopes trial in Tennessee, at which he defended the truth of revealed religion against attacks of evolutionism.

Bryant, William Cullen (1794—1878). First of the great American poets; educated at Williams College; practiced law for only ten years, after which he followed literary pursuits; general poetical works are well known; among hymns, written at intervals during his life: "Look from Thy Sphere of Endless Day. "

Bryzelius, Paul. See, *Canada, Lutheranism in,* 2.

Bucer, or *Butzer* (Kuhhorn), **Martin.** B. at Schlettstadt, 1491; entered the order of Dominicans; studied theology, Greek, and Hebrew at Heidelberg. The works of Erasmus inclined him towards Protestantism, and his views were confirmed by the influence of Luther at the disputation in Heidelberg, 1518. In 1523 he introduced the Reformation at Strassburg. To avoid theological divisions, he advocated compromises and employed dubious expressions. In the disputes between Luther and Zwingli he adopted a middle course, endeavoring to reconcile both; but his views of the Sacrament, approaching those of Zwingli, exposed him to Luther's criticism and reprobation. At Augsburg, 1530, he generally accorded with the Lutheran views, but declined to subscribe to the Augsburg Confession and later drew up the *Confessio Tetrapolitana* (Strassburg, Constance, Memmingen, Lindau). At the Diet of Ratisbon he also tried to unite Protestants and Catholics. Refusing to sign the *Interim,* he accepted an invitation of Archbishop Cranmer to teach theology at Cambridge and to assist in furthering the Reformation in England. D. at Cambridge, 1551.

Buchholz, Andrew Hy. (1607—71). German divine; wrote *Hercules and Valiska,* which was very popular.

Buchman, Frank N. D. See *Buchmanism.*

Buchmanism (*Oxford Group Movement, First Century Christian Fellowship, Moral Re-Armament*). Founded by Rev. Dr. Frank N. D. Buchman (b. 1878), a graduate of Mount Airy Lutheran Theological Seminary (U. L. C. A.) and member of the Ministerium of Pennsylvania, who between 1907 and 1909 was moved by the English Keswick Movement to a "new career of service," emphasizing "absolute honesty," "absolute purity," "absolute unselfishness," and "absolute love." According to Buchmanism, the barrier of sin is removed by "sharing" (complete confession of all sins and witnessing this confession before others), "surrender," "restitution," and receiving and following immediate "guidance" from God. Thus Buchmanism seeks to "revitalize" Christianity and supply men with

"moral rearmament," though it does not confess the fundamentals of the Christian faith and is unionistic and indifferentistic regarding doctrine.

G. C. Gast, *Oxford Group Movement,* Luth. Book Concern, Columbus, Ohio, rev. 1934; W. G. Schwehn, *What is Buchmanism?* CPH; C. I. Benson, *The Eight Points of the Oxford Group,* 1936; A. W. Eister, *Drawing Room Conversion,* 1950.

Buchner, Charles. B. 1842 at Irwinhill, Jamaica; d. 1907. Moravian missionary, 1879; director of Teachers Seminary at Niesky, 1880—1907; member of Mission Board, Berthelsdorf.

Buchrucker, Karl von (1827—99). Leading Lutheran clergyman in Bavaria; supt. in Munich; Consistorial Counselor 1885; founded *Neue Kirchliche Zeitschrift;* edited catechism which became official in the General Synod of Bavaria.

Buck, Dudley (1839—1909). Studied chiefly at Leipzig and Dresden; held positions as organist in Chicago, Boston, Brooklyn, and New York; wrote a number of cantatas and some excellent church music, both for liturgical and choir use.

Buckley, James Monroe (1836 to 1916). Methodist Episcopal author and influential clergyman; edited *New York Christian Advocate,* 1880—1912.

Budde, Karl (1850—1935). German Protestant theologian; professor at Marburg; outstanding Biblical scholar and orientalist.

Buddeus, Johann F. (1667—1729). Professor at Wittenberg and Jena; mediated between orthodox Lutheranism and Pietism; was considered the most accomplished theologian of his time; several times rector of Jena University. His *Institutiones Theologiae Dogmaticae,* based on Baier, and *Isagoge Historico-Theologica ad Theologiam Universam* were highly esteemed.

Buddha, Gotama. See *Buddhism.*

Buddhism. 1. The religious system founded by Gotama Siddhartha, called the Buddha, *i. e.,* "the Enlightened One," in the 6th century B. C., in northern India, as a revolt against Brahmanism.* It denies the authority of the Vedas, rejects the Brahmanic caste system, ritual, and philosophic speculations, and offers a new way to salvation. For the life of the founder see *Gotama.* (The spelling *Gotama,* preferred by some oriental scholars, is from the Pali;

the spelling *Gautama,* preferred by some lexicographers, is from the Sanskrit.)

2. The texts upon which our knowledge of early Buddhism is based are sacred books found in Ceylon and written in the Pali language, called the *Pitakas.* The most important of these contain the *Jatakas,* wonderful stories of Buddha's birth and previous existence. Other books come from Nepal, written in Sanskrit, and from China and Tibet, written in the languages of these countries. Strictly speaking, Gotama's doctrine is not a religion, but a practical atheism. Of the five requisites of religion: "the belief in a divine power, the acknowledgment of sin, the habit of prayer, the desire to offer sacrifice, and the hope of a future life" (Max Mueller), not one is found in Gotama's system. Though he did not deny the existence of the traditional gods, yet he held that prayer and sacrifice to them were of no avail, as they, like men, were subject to death and rebirth and in rebirth might sink to the level of inferior beings, while men in rebirth might rise to the level of gods. Gotama likewise denied the existence of the soul (see *Transmigration*). However, he held in common with Brahmanism the pessimistic view that life was not worth living; that man was subject to a continuous round of rebirths; that a man's *karma, i. e.,* his acts in one existence, determined his lot in future existences; that salvation consisted (not in escape from sin and hell, as Indian philosophies do not recognize these two factors, but) in obtaining freedom from rebirths; and that ignorance is the cause of the whole evil. But as he rejected the Vedas and taught a new way of destroying ignorance and obtaining freedom from rebirth, his doctrine, like Jainism,* was considered a heresy by the Brahmans.

3. Buddha's entire doctrine is based on the so-called "four noble truths," which speak 1) of the universality of suffering, 2) of the causes of suffering, 3) of the abolition of suffering, 4) of the path that leads to the abolition of suffering. All conscious existence, birth, growth, illness, death, separation from what we love, contact with what we hate, not to attain what we desire, in short, all human life, is suffering and sorrow. This suffering is caused by "thirst," *i. e.,* a craving for life and its pleasures, and this attachment causes rebirth and continued misery. Freedom from rebirth and

consequently from suffering can be obtained if this craving is completely destroyed. The path that leads to this end is the "noble eightfold path," namely, "right belief, right aspirations, right speech, right conduct, right means of subsistence, right effort, right mindfulness, right meditation." This path is called the "middle path," as it is removed from the two extremes of a sensuous life and of asceticism. He who follows this path to its end becomes an *arhat,* or saint. He has destroyed his ignorance, become perfect by knowledge, and broken the fetters that bind him to the wheel of life. The supreme and final goal of this spiritual discipline is *nirvana,* literally, a "blowing out," namely, of the desires and passions that lead to rebirth. As the old *karma* is exhausted and no new *karma* is added, the round of rebirths ceases and ends in an unconscious state. Whether this is equivalent to the annihilation of personality was not stated by Gotama, but many Buddhist texts interpret it in this sense. *Nirvana* may in a certain sense be obtained in this life by the *arhat,* but it is entered upon completely only at death.

4. The followers of Gotama soon were organized into a mendicant order, which was open to all men over twenty years who were physically and legally fit, without caste distinction. The monks, called *bhikkus, i. e.,* "beggars," obligated themselves to keep ten commandments, which forbade 1) the taking of life, 2) theft, 3) sexual impurity, 4) lying, 5) the use of intoxicating liquors, 6) eating at forbidden times, *i. e.,* between noon and the following morning, 7) taking part in dancing, singing, music, the theater, 8) using ornaments and perfumes, 9) sleeping on beds raised from the floor, 10) receiving gold or silver. Every monk had to take the vow of absolute celibacy and poverty. Great stress was laid on the virtues of benevolence — even to animals — patience, and humility. Twice a month he had to confess his faults before the assembled brethren. He had to dress only in rags, beg his food, with the alms-bowl in his hand, live much of the time in forests, and spend many hours in contemplation. Thus an elaborate system of rules governed his entire life. Subordinated to the monks were the nuns, whom Gotama, according to tradition, admitted to the order only with great reluctance. Beside this monastic order also a lay membership was organized. The rules for the lay

members, however, were far less strict. They were obligated to observe only the first five of the ten commandments mentioned above, and they must at all times practice benevolence and charity. As Buddhism is atheistic in principle, it makes no provision for a cult or priesthood. Wherever these are found in modern forms of Buddhism, they are a later development.

5. Little is known of the history of Buddhism during the first two centuries. Tradition relates that the movement suffered numerous schisms and that two councils were held to fix the canon of sacred books, one shortly after Gotama's death, the other a hundred years later at Vaisali. Assured historical knowledge of the progress of Buddhism begins with the reign of Asoka, king of Magadha, in the third century B. C., who became a convert to the new religion and its first royal champion. He convened a third council and proclaimed Buddhism the state religion of his kingdom. Another great name in its history is that of the Indo-Scythian king Kanishka, in the first and second centuries A. D., who also convened a council. A great missionary activity set in during the reign of Asoka. Buddhism spread to practically all India and to Ceylon. It reached Tibet and China about the beginning of our era and spread from China to Korea and Japan. Still later it spread to Burma and Siam.

6. The later history of Indian Buddhism is marked by the great conflict between the two schools called *Hinayana*, "Little Vessel," and *Mahayana*, "Great Vessel." This led to a permanent division into two great sects. The *Hinayana* is the conservative system. It holds to the original teachings of Buddhism, regards Gotama as a mere man, and teaches that salvation can be obtained by only few mortals. It maintained itself in the southern part of the Buddhist sphere, Ceylon, Burma, Siam. *Mahayana* Buddhism, on the other hand, called so because it claimed to be the better vessel to take man across the stream of existence to *nirvana*, transformed Gotama into a god or an incarnation of the Absolute. It is the northern form of Buddhism and is found in Tibet, China, Korea, and Japan. The peculiar hierarchical form into which it developed in Tibet is called Lamaism.* The last phase of decadent Indian Buddhism is that influenced by Tantric Hinduism, beginning with ca. the 7th century

and marked by the crassest superstitions and magic. Gradually Buddhism lost its foothold in India, yielding mainly to Hinduism, later in certain sections to Mohammedanism, and by the 13th century it had become practically extinct in the land of its origin. (See also *Yoga*.)

7. Regarding the number of Buddhists in the world today, it is impossible to give even approximate figures. Some scholars estimate their number at 500,000.000, or one fourth of the human race; but this estimate includes as Buddhists practically all Chinese and Japanese, an unwarranted assumption. In China, Buddhism is intertwined with Confucianism and in Japan with Shintoism, so that it is impossible to ascertain the number of adherents of each religion. As to the question of the relationship between Christianity and Buddhism, some scholars have maintained that Christianity borrowed from Buddhism; others, that Buddhism borrowed from Christianity. But aside from the impossibility of admitting the first assumption from the Christian point of view, the consensus of conservative scholars is that neither hypothesis has any foundation in fact. See *Religion, Comparative, Bibliography.*

Budget. See *Finances of the Church,* 3.

Buechner, Gottfried (1701—1780). B. at Riedersdorf, Bohemia; educated at Jena; rector at Querfurt, Saxony; wrote *Biblische Real- und Verbal-Hand-Concordanz* (published in America by Huebner and Spaeth).

Buechsel, Karl Albert Ludwig (1803 to 1889). Preacher at Berlin, 1846; 1853—84 general superintendent and court preacher; a very influential positive theologian in the Prussian Union, with Lutheran leanings.

Buehler, Jacob Matthias. The pioneer pastor of the Missouri Synod on the Pacific Coast. B. Aug. 8, 1837, in Baltimore, Md.; attended Concordia College and Seminary at St. Louis, graduating 1860; pastor in San Francisco same year. Because of his firm stand for confessional Lutheranism a split ensued, and St. Paulus was organized 1867, the mother church on the Pacific Coast. He organized a day school in 1872, of which Teacher Hargens was in charge for over forty years. California and Oregon District organized in 1887; Buehler president till his death. An excellent preacher, a wise counselor, an ardent lover of the Lord, a friend of the children, a splendid organizer. D. Sept., 1901. J. H. and S. W. Theiss, G. M. *Buehler*, Lutherischer Botschafter, Oakland, Calif., 1902.

Buenger, Johann Friedrich. B. Jan. 2, 1810, at Rosswein, Saxony; scion of a family of clerics reaching back to the Reformation. As student of theology at Leipzig he came under the influence of Candidate Kuehn; acted as private tutor in Dresden; became adherent of Stephan and was one of the immigrants. Of a practical turn of mind, he was of great assistance to the colonists in Perry Co., Mo., being one of the founders of the college at Altenburg. Teacher of Trinity School in St. Louis 1841; assistant pastor of Trinity 1844; pastor of Immanuel 1847. Walther called him the American Lutheran Valerius Herberger. His practical nature was exemplified in his pastoral work. President of Western District of Missouri Synod 1863—74. A friend of missions; "Father" of our Negro Missions. Founder of the Lutheran Hospital of St. Louis, the Orphans' Home, and the Old Folks' Home; d. Jan. 23, 1882.

Buenger, Theodore Henry Carl. B. April 29, 1860, Chicago, Ill.; graduated St. Louis, 1882; home missionary (29 stations) in N. W. Wisconsin 1882—84; pastor at Tinley Park and Orland, Ill., 1884—91; at St. Paul, Minn., 1891—93; professor at Concordia College, St. Paul, Minn., 1893—96, president 1893—1927, then again professor 1927—43; D. D. (St. Louis); d. Sept. 9, 1943.

Buerger, Ernst Moritz. One of the Saxon pioneers; b. 1809 in Saxony, Germany; pastor at Lunzenau; joined the emigrants under Stephan; charter member of the Missouri Synod; pastor at Buffalo, later at West Seneca, N. Y.; then at Washington, D. C.; finally at Winona, Minn.; d. Mar. 22, 1890.

Buffalo Declaration. See *Washington Declaration of the ULC*.

Buffalo Synod. Until 1886 officially called "The Synod of the Lutheran Church Emigrated from Prussia." Originally composed of congregations from different parts of Germany which emigrated to America in 1839 under the leadership of J. A. A. Grabau and settled in and near Buffalo, N. Y., and in Wisconsin, while some remained in New York and, through Grabau, called Rev. Theo. Brohm in 1842 and afterwards

joined the Missouri Synod. The original immigrants were strengthened by later arrivals under Kindermann and Ehrenstroem. The latter became the victim of strange hallucinations and was excommunicated by Grabau. In 1845, in a meeting held at Freistadt, June 3—19, and in Milwaukee, Wis., June 23 and 25, Grabau, together with Pastors H. von Rohr, Leberecht Krause, and G. A. Kindermann, and 18 lay delegates, organized the Buffalo Synod. Grabau remained the dominating spirit till his death in 1879. At first there were high hopes of combining Grabau's adherents with the Saxon immigrants of 1839 and the Loehe emissaries, because, in opposition to other Lutheran synods of that day, they were all unequivocally committed to the Lutheran Confessions; but a *Pastoral Letter* which Grabau issued to the churches under his influence, warning them against preachers who in his opinion were not properly ordained, caused them to remain separate. This *Letter*, which was sent to the Saxons in Missouri for criticism, precipitated the conflict between Grabau and Walther, and, later, between the Buffalo and the Missouri Synods. The strife continued for many years with much bitterness, especially since Missouri felt bound to give pastoral care to such as were unjustly excommunicated by Grabau. In 1853 Grabau visited Germany in the hope of winning friends for his cause. All efforts of the Missouri Synod to bring about a reconciliation by an amicable discussion of the differences were frustrated by Grabau's unwillingness to submit his orthodoxy to a test. His hierarchical action drove some of the best congregations of the Buffalo Synod into the fold of Missouri. Another appeal for reconciliation was answered by Grabau in 1859 with a formal "excommunication" pronounced upon the whole Missouri Synod (over 200 congregations). But as many of the pastors and congregations of the Buffalo Synod were getting tired of Grabau's arbitrary rule, the synod was divided into two camps, headed by Grabau and von Rohr, respectively. The latter group held a colloquium with the Missouri Synod in November, 1866, which resulted in the admission of Rev. Chr. Hochstetter and eleven other pastors into the latter synod. The von Rohr party continued to exist until 1877, when some of the pastors returned to the Grabau group, while others entered other synods. As early as 1840 the

Martin Luther College had been established at Buffalo, with Grabau as its head. Grabau, as "Senior Ministerii," also edited the *Informatorium*. The official organ of the synod was *Die Wachende Kirche*, founded in 1866. In 1886 the constitution was revised, and many of its earlier peculiarities were quietly set aside. The congregations of the former Buffalo Synod are still strict in doctrine and practice. Private absolution is the rule, but public absolution is permitted since 1891. No member is allowed to belong to a secret order. In 1925 the Buffalo Synod numbered 35 pastors, 44 churches, and 6,806 communicants. This synod was merged with the Ohio Synod into the American Lutheran Church in 1930.

J. F. Koestering, "Der Lehrstreit mit der Buffalo Synode," in *Auswanderung der saechsischen Lutheraner im Jahre 1838*, 1867; A. Suelflow, *The Relations of the Missouri with the Buffalo Synod up to 1866*, unpublished S. T. M. Thesis, Concordia Seminary, St. Louis, 1945; *Protokoll ueber d. Verhandlungen des Colloquiums in Buffalo, N. Y., 20. Nov.—5. Dez., 1866*. A complete history of the Buffalo Synod is found in *Wachende Kirche*, 1920—29.

Bugenhagen, Johannes. B. 1485 on the island of Wollin, belonging to Pomerania; talented and studious; rector of the Latin school at Treptow and lecturer on the Bible in the cloister. In 1520 he read Luther's *Babylonian Captivity*. — "The whole world is blind and in great darkness; this is the only man that sees the truth." He came to Wittenberg in 1521, lectured on the Psalms, was made pastor of the City Church in 1522, held out during the plague in 1527, helped Luther in the translation of the Bible, the publication of which he celebrated every year with a festival in his home. His great talent for organizing the Church was called into use in 1528 in Brunswick and Hamburg, in 1530 in Luebeck, in 1534 in Pomerania, in 1537 in Denmark, in 1542 again in Brunswick and in Hildesheim. After declining three bishoprics and other calls, he was made General Superintendent of Electoral Saxony. Luther's death broke Bugenhagen's heart, and he aged rapidly. During the siege of Wittenberg he was told that the Emperor would persecute him, but he remained. After the surrender he preached on the differences between the Lutherans and the Romanists in the presence of many courtiers. Perhaps the surprising mildness of the emperor made Bugenhagen judge the *Interim* with such surprising mildness. His life's motto was: "If you know Christ well, it is enough, even if you know nothing else; if you do not know Christ, it is nothing, even if you learn all else." D. 1558.

Herman Hering, *Doktor Pomeranus, Johannes Bugenhagen*, Verein fuer Reformationsgeschichte, Halle, 1888; L. W. Graepp, *Johannes Bugenhagen*, Guetersloh, 1897.

Bugge, Wilhelm K. (1838—96). Norwegian theologian; professor at Christiana (1870—93); bishop of Christiana (1893—96); one of revisers of Norwegian Bible; wrote especially in the field of Isagogics.

Bulgaria. One of the Balkan countries, west of Black Sea. 42,814 sq. mi.; population 7,022,206 (1946); 75% Greek Orthodox; about 12—14% Mohammedans; rest divided among Roman Catholics (56,000), Armenians, and Protestants (24,627). Won for Christianity chiefly by Cyrillus and Methodius of the Greek Church, under Prince Boris, in about 864; placed, ecclesiastically, by King Boris under the jurisdiction of Rome (a contributing cause of the great schism), and returned to the allegiance of Constantinople in 869. The Bulgarian Church restored in 1870—72, with an exarch in Constantinople. Methodist mission work begun in 1857; the American Board began work later. The Armenians have their own bishop.

Bulgarian National Church. See *Bulgaria; Eastern Orthodox Churches.*

Bull, John (ca. 1562—1628). English composer of the Madrigalian Era who wrote much church music. Though not the equal of Gibbons, Byrd, and others, Bull enjoys a fame which puts him above the rank and file of English composers.

Bullaria. Collections of bulls.* The *Bullarium Romanum Magnum* was a collection begun by Cherubini (1586) and continued by various editors (Maynardus, Cocquelines, Barberi, Tomassetti).

Bullinger, Heinrich (1504—1575). Swiss Reformed leader. B. Bremgarten; left Catholic Church 1522; Zwingli's successor at Zurich 1531; d. at Zurich. Part author of *First Helvetic Confession;* sole author of *Second Helvetic Confession, History of the Reformation;* etc.

Bulls. Documents authenticated by appended (usually leaden) seals (bullae). The name is now applied only to documents issued in the name of the Pope. Less formal papal letters, known as briefs, are sealed on the document itself. On one side of the leaden seal are the heads of Peter and Paul, on the other the Pope's name. All bulls are written on parchment and begin with the name of the Pope, followed by the title *Servus servorum Dei* (Servant of the servants of God). Some bear the Pope's signature; some, that of cardinals and other officials. Bulls and other papal documents are designated by their first words. Among the most famous bulls are the following: *Unam Sanctam* (Boniface VIII, 1302), containing the most sweeping claims ever advanced by the Papacy; *In Coena Domini* (Urban V, 1362), excommunicating heretics, etc., by name — published, with additions, every Maundy Thursday till 1773; *Exsurge, Domine* (Leo X, June 15, 1520), the bull which Luther burned; *Decet Romanum Pontificem* (January 3, 1521), excommunicating Luther; *Dominus ac Redemptor Noster* (Clement XIV, 1773), abolishing the Jesuits, and *Sollicitudo Omnium* (Pius VII, 1814), re-establishing them; *Ineffabilis* (Pius IX, 1854), proclaiming the dogma of the Immaculate Conception; *Pastor Aeternus* (Pius IX, 1870), defining papal infallibility; *Rerum novarum* (Leo XIII, 1891), on social problems; *Quadragesimo Anno* (Pius XI, 1931), on the reconstruction of the social order. The Assumption of Mary was promulgated in a bull on Nov. 1, 1950.

Bultmann, Rudolf (1884—). Professor at Breslau, Giessen and Marburg; dialectical theologian; adherent of the *Formgeschichtliche* school. In 1941 he published *Offenbarung und Heilsgeschichte*, in which the theory known as *Entmythologisierung* (demythologizing) was propounded. This theory holds that there is mythology in the Bible which must be detected by the theologian and given proper evaluation in view of its existential significance. Other works by Bultmann are: *Geschichte der synoptischen Tradition* (1921), *Jesus* (1926, English title: *Jesus and the Word*), commentary on John (1941), *Theologie des Neuen Testaments* (1948).

Bunsen, Baron Christian K. J. von (1791—1861). German scholar and diplomat; friend of Frederick William III and IV of Prussia; assisted in preparation of Prussian *Unionsagende;* edited a hymnbook and wrote on theological and philosophical themes.

Bunyan, John (1628—88). Preacher and religious prose writer; in 1653 joined non-conformist church in Bedford, where he soon took to preaching; came into religious conflict with George Fox and Quakers; at the Restoration, Bunyan ordered to stop preaching, and upon refusal thrown into Bedford jail, where he remained almost 12 years; while in prison wrote most of his great works: *Grace Abounding to the Chief of Sinners; The Life and Death of Mr. Badman; The Losing and Taking Again of the Town of Mansoul* (the theme is the fall and the redemption of mankind); *The Heavenly Footman;* later, *Pilgrim's Progress* (a dream allegory; cf. *Piers Plowman*).

Buonarroti. See *Michelangelo.*

Burchard of Worms (ca. 965—1025). Author of *Decretum,* important collection of canons.

Burchard, Samuel Dickinson (1812 to 1891). Presbyterian clergyman in New York; his derogatory remarks concerning the opponents of Blaine probably caused the latter to lose New York's votes.

Bure, Idelette de. See *Calvin, John,* 4.

Burger, Karl H. A. (1805—84). Member of the Higher Consistory in Munich; supporter of the reforms of Harless; wrote *Bibelstunden;* one of the compilers of the *Bavarian Hymnbook.*

Burial. 1. The usual mode of the disposal of the bodies of the dead, according to Bible accounts. Thus we read that Abraham bought a sepulcher from the Hittites for the burial of Sarah, and that subsequently he himself was buried there, as well as Isaac and Rebekah, his wife; later also Leah and Jacob. Gen. 49:29-32. This burial place was a crypt in an underground tomb, and it is still shown. Rachel was buried "in the way to Ephrath, which is Bethlehem." Gen. 35:19. The two forms of tombs in the Old Testament were cave sepulchers, either in natural cavities in the rock or hewn into the side of a rocky hill, and graves dug in the ground. The idea of cremation seems to have been repugnant to the Jews from the beginning; that which took place in the case of Saul and his sons was probably done on account of the defilement attending their being mutilated by the Philistines. 1 Sam. 31:12; 1 Chron. 10:12. In the case of criminals this mode of disposing of the bodies was used, but not at other times. Gen. 38:24; Lev. 20:14; 21:9; Is. 66:24. There was no change in the form of burial in New Testament times, for we have a reference to whited sepulchers, or graves which were treated with a coat of whitewash to make them conspicuous even at night, Matt. 23:27; we read of the grave of Lazarus as being a cave, or opening in the ground, with a stone upon it, John 11:38; and we have the description of Christ's tomb as being hewn in stone, with a low entrance closed by a stone which could be rolled in place. Luke 23:53; 24:2; John 20:1, 5. — Regarding the preparation for burial, the embalming, of which we read in the case of Jacob and Joseph, was merely in line with Egyptian custom, Gen. 50:2, 26, and has no significance with reference to Jewish usage. In the time of Christ the body was washed, anointed with fragrant spices, such as myrrh and aloes, and more or less completely wrapped in linen cloths, a sudary being spread over the face. Mark 16:1; John 11:44; 20:5, 7; Acts 9:37.

2. One of the principles stated by the reformers of the 16th century was this, that every Christian was entitled to an honorable burial, that is, that ordinarily the pastor of the congregation should conduct the funeral, in the name of the entire congregation. The idea underlying this principle was the manifestation of the fellowship of the believers both in this world and in the world to come, and to make open confession of the church's doctrine of the resurrection (hence non-members, excommunicated persons, suicides, and impenitents in general, were, as a rule, not given Christian burial). There is little uniformity in the church orders of the various countries relative to burial, the act of commitment being omitted in most of them. In the Lutheran Church in America the division of the funeral ceremonies into three parts is commonly observed. The service at the house usually includes the singing of a hymn, together with Scripture lesson and prayer. The service in the church is an act of preaching and prayer, the essential constituents being the lessons, the sermon, and the prayers, the object

being to teach, to console, and to admonish. At the cemetery, commitment follows the singing of a hymn and prayer, and the service is concluded with the blessing upon the assembly (not the dead). On the Sunday following the death or the funeral, mention is made of the departed in the church service, thanks being returned to God for the blessings bestowed upon the departed, prayer for the undisturbed rest of the body in the grave, and intercession made on behalf of the family and friends. See *Cemeteries; Cremation; Dead, Prayers for.* Justin A. Petersen, "Christian Burial," *CTM,* V:509—519. See also J. H. C. Fritz, *Pastoral Theology.*

Buridan, Jean (d. ca. 1360). French scholastic philosopher; pupil of William of Occam; held that the will and intellect are essentially identical; reputed (perhaps erroneously) to have been the author of the dilemma known as "Buridan's Ass"; wrote *Compendium Logicae.*

Burk, Philip David (1714—70). Son-in-law of Bengel; his OT *Gnomon* incomplete. His son, Mark Philip (1755 to 1815), founded the first private schoolteachers' seminary in Wuerttemberg.

Burma. Country in Asia, east of India, south of China. Became independent Jan. 4, 1948. 233,492 sq. mi. Population, 17,000,000 (1947 est.). A stronghold of Buddhism, which reached Burma from India in force in 1057. There are a great many temples and shrines; monasteries are well organized and serve as village schools; by good works people try to acquire merit for the next reincarnation; theoretically every boy at school becomes a monk. The people are tolerant and free from fanaticism. Approximately 83% of the population are Buddhists, 4.9% profess animism (nat-worship, a nat being a supernatural being); 3.9% Moslems; 3.8% Hindus; 3.9% Christians (1941). In 1950 there were 132,000 Roman Catholics and 589,877 other Christians in Burma. Two thirds of the Christians are of the Karen groups, where Christianity made rapid progress, while there was very slow progress among other groups. The Karens comprise 9% of the population, and 13% of them are Christians. Backward hill tribes were made into a strong, self-sufficient church.

Among Protestant groups, the Baptists were the first in Burma, Chater and Mardon of the Baptist Missionary Society of England reaching Rangoon in 1807; Felix Carey came in 1814. The first permanent mission was established by the American Baptist Missionary Union in 1813. Adoniram Judson was the great missionary for them, translating the Bible into Burmese, baptizing his first convert after six years of labor. The first converts among the Karens were baptized in 1828. Self-support was made quite a feature of the work among them, and they evidenced a good deal of missionary spirit themselves. An independent evangelistic movement was started under Ko San Ye. Baptists comprise about 64% of the Christians in Burma. They had 708 schools in 1939. The Anglicans have about 25,000 members and wield a good deal of influence. The Methodists came in 1879 under Bishop Thoburn; they have some schools and also work among the Chinese in Burma. The Wesleyan M. E. Church came in 1889. The Adventists, the Salvation Army, and Christian Scientists also have some work in Burma. Bengalis, Telugus, Tamils, Sikhs, and others conduct schools and try to perpetuate their language and religion, and these efforts are tolerated. The Roman Catholic Church came to Burma about 1700 and established schools in 1721, and next to the Baptists they seem to have been the most successful of the Christian groups. See *Missions (Bibliography)*.

OHS

Burnet, Gilbert (1643—1715). Anglican. B. at Edinburgh; professor of divinity at Glasgow; preacher at London 1674; bishop of Salisbury 1689; d. in London. Wrote: *History of the Reformation; History of My Own Time.*

Burning Bush. See *Evangelistic Associations*, 10.

Burton, Ernest DeWitt (1856 to 1925). Baptist theologian and educator; president of Chicago University (1923 to 1925); wrote *Syntax of the Moods and Tenses in the Greek New Testament;* edited *Biblical World, American Journal of Theology.*

Buruss, K. H. See *Churches of God, Holiness.*

Busenbaum, Hermann (1600—68). German Jesuit theologian; teacher at Cologne; rector at Hildesheim and Muenster; his Jesuit moral theology embodied in *Medulla Theologiae Moralis.*

Bushido. The Japanese code of honor requiring extreme loyalty towards superiors, simplicity of life combined with dignity, and complete indifference towards suffering and even death. It approved of suicide as an escape from disgrace.

Bushnell, Albert (1818—79; "Patriarch of West African Missions"). Went to Africa as missionary of American Board 1844; stationed at Gaboon, Africa. Returned to U. S. five times because of health, always again returning to his African field; d. at Sierre Leone, Africa.

Bushnell, Horace (1802—76). Congregational pastor at Hartford (1833 to 1859; resigned because of ill health). In his *Christian Nurture* he criticized revivals with their emphasis on definite knowledge of the moment of conversion and held that the child should be trained as a Christian from the very beginning. His other prominent works are: *God in Christ, Christ in Theology, Dissertation on Language as Related to Thought and Spirit, Nature and the Supernatural, Law and Forgiveness, Vicarious Sacrifice.*
"Horace Bushnell and Christian Nurture," *Luth. Education,* April, 1948, 486 ff.; *CTM,* XV: 654 ff.

Buskirk, Jacob von. B. Feb. 11, 1739, Hackensack, N. J.; trained in theology under J. A. Weygandt, at Princeton College, and under H. M. Muhlenberg; served churches in Pa. at New Hanover, Germantown, Macungie, and Upper Milford, Saucon, and Salsburg, 1763—69; Allentown, 1769—78; Gwynedd, Whitpain, and Upper Dublin, 1793—95, adding Macungie Church in that year. Probably first American-born Lutheran minister in U. S.; helped to bring about better relations between Netherlanders in N. J. and Germans in Pa.; member of Board of Trustees of Franklin College, Lancaster, Pa. D. Aug. 5, 1800.

Buskirk, Lawrence van (1755—97). Studied at Columbia College, N. Y.; at the time of his death six of his sermons were published, probably the first English Luth. sermons printed in America.

Butler, John George (1754—1816). One of the pioneer pastors of the Pennsylvania Ministerium.

Butler, Dr. John G. (1826—1909). Pastor of Luther Place Church, Washington, D. C., 1848—1909; chaplain in army during Civil War; later, chaplain of Congress; editor of *Lutheran Evangelist.*

Butler, Joseph (1692—1752). Anglican. B. at Wantage; bishop of Bristol 1738, poorest see in England; of Durham 1750, richest see; d. at Bath. His *Analogy of Religion, Natural and Revealed*, ingenious, but inconclusive.

Buttlar Group. A viciously lascivious group headed by Eva von Buttlar, b. 1670 in Eschwege, Hessia; operated under guise of religion; Eva claimed to be the mother of us all, the divine wisdom (sophia) come from heaven and the Holy Ghost.

Buxtehude, Dietrich (1637—1707). Likely not of Danish, but of German ancestry. In 1668 he became organist and *Werkmeister* (general overseer) of the Marienkirche at Luebeck succeeding Franz Tunder, his father-in-law. It was probably Tunder who had introduced the famous *Abendmusiken* in Luebeck; these were evening concerts presented each year following the afternoon services on the last two Sundays of the Trinity season, and on the second, third, and fourth Sundays in Advent. Through Buxtehude these *Abendmusiken* became famous, attracting even young J. S. Bach, who thus became also a pupil of Buxtehude. Many of Buxtehude's cantatas and much of his organ music were written for these concerts. Buxtehude's greatness comes to light particularly in his organ works, though his cantatas are by no means insignificant. His works are imbued with the spirit of Lutheranism, as well as with the spirit of the North and of the Baroque Era. Buxtehude may be regarded as the most typical representative of the great North German School of Lutheran organists.

Bukofzer, Manfred, *Music in the Baroque Era*, New York, 1947; Buszin, W. E., "Dietrich Buxtehude," *Musical Quarterly*, New York, October, 1937; Lang, Paul Henry, *Music in Western Civilization*, New York, 1941.

Buxtorf (Buxtorff), **Johann** (The Elder. 1564—1629). "Master of the Rabbins." B. at Camen, Westphalia; professor of Hebrew at Basel 1591 (d. there) *Lexicon Chaldaicum, Talmudicum e. Rabbinicum;* etc. — Johann Buxtorf the Younger. 1599—1664. Son of preceding; like father, noted Orientalist; professor at Lausanne; successor to father at Basel. — Both maintained divine inspiration of Hebrew vowel points.

Byrd, William (1542 or 1543—1623). Most typical composer of the English Madrigalian Era (1575—ca. 1625). He was a Roman Catholic who suffered persecution because of his religious convictions. Byrd was a great polyphonist; his music is characterized by a wide variety of expression, by grace as well as by massiveness, and by shifting tone colors. He and Orlando Gibbons were the musical giants of England in their days.

Fellowes, E. H., *William Byrd; A Short Account of His Life*, London, 1923; Walker, Ernest, *A History of Music in England*, London, 1924.

Byzantine Church. See *Eastern Orthodox Church*.

Byzantine Style. See *Architecture, Ecclesiastical, 2.*

C

Caaba. See *Kaaba*.

Cabala. See *Kabbala*.

Cabet, Etienne (1788—1856). French socialist; views on taxation, compulsory labor, old-age pension treated in his *Voyage en Icarie* (connects socialism with religion); bought land for a communistic settlement in Texas, but later moved the settlement to Nauvoo, Ill.

Cadman, Samuel Parks (1864—1936). Studied at Wesleyan (Conn.); held honorary doctorates from nine universities; held pastorates in New York City and in Brooklyn; was president of Federal Council of Churches of Christ in America; held various important positions, ecclesiastical and secular; radio preacher (1928—36); wrote *Charles Darwin and Other English Thinkers, Christianity and the State, Imagination and Religion, Pursuit of Happiness*, and other works; liberal theologian.

Caedmon. A Christian poet of England, living in the seventh century, who, according to the testimony of the Venerable Bede, composed the first version of the Bible story in Old English alliterative verse.

Caerularius, Michael. Patriarch of Constantinople (1043—59); brought to completion the schism between the Roman and the Greek Church (1054); excommunicated by Leo IX (1054); exiled by Emperor Isaac Comnenus (1059) to Praeconnesus, where he died.

Caesarean School. See *Schools, Early Christian.*

Caesarius of Arles (ca. 470—543). Catholic saint; served in monastery at Lerins; bishop of Arles (502); he presided at the Council of Orange (as also at several others), which defended Augustine's doctrines against semi-Pelagianism; wrote a *Rule* for monks, and one for nuns; founded monasteries.

Caesarius of Heisterbach (ca. 1170 to 1240). Preacher at Cologne; author of *Dialog of Visions and Miracles, Eight Books of Miracles, Life of St. Engelbert.*

Caesaropapism. The theory that the civil government holds the highest authority in matters pertaining to the Church. The theory was developed in the early centuries of the Christian Church, when the Roman emperor regarded himself as the ruler and arbiter in the affairs of the Church, frequently interfering with its work. During the period of the Reformation the phrase was coined: *Cuius regio, eius religio,* that is, The ruler in charge of a country is by virtue of that fact the highest authority in the Church, and all citizens are guided in their religious tenets by his will. The condition of Caesaropapism obtains in certain countries to this day, where there is either a Roman Catholic or a Protestant state religion. In the hands of an irresponsible monarch this may easily result in harm to the churches of the country.

Cainnech, St. See *Celtic Church,* 6.

Caird, Edward (1835—1908). Scottish professor of moral philosophy at Glasgow. Founded a school of Neo-Hegelianism with T. Green.

Caird, John (1820—98). Brother of Edward; Scottish theologian and philosopher; vice-chancellor of Glasgow; held thought to be the reality; wrote *Introduction to the Philosophy of Religion.*

Cajetan, Thomas (1469—1534). Italian cardinal; member of Dominican order; legate at Diet of Augsburg, 1518; was in charge of first trial of Luther, at Augsburg.

Calas, Jean (1698—1762). French Protestant; falsely accused of murdering son because the latter intended to embrace Catholicism; died on wheel, goods confiscated; later decision reversed, property restored.

Calendar, Ecclesiastical. See *Church Year.*

Calendaria. See *Acta Martyrum.*

California, Concordia College. See *Ministry, Education of,* IX.

California, Synod of. The General Synod started work in California in 1886 through Rev. O. C. Miller. The California Synod was organized in San Francisco, April 2, 1891, by eight pastors and four lay delegates, representing six congregations. The German pastors at first contemplated a separate synod, but afterwards united with the California Synod. With the General Synod it joined the United Lutheran Church in 1918. See *United Lutheran Church, Synods of,* 1.

Caliph. Arabic for "representative." Technically the term is used to designate the representative and successor of Mohammed as head of the Moslem empire and church. See also *Mohammedanism.*

Calisius, Johann Heinrich (1653 to 1698). Hymn writer of the Nuernberg Circle.

Calixt, Georg. Foremost champion of so-called "syncretism" and representative of Melanchthonian theology; b. 1586 in Medelbye, Schleswig; d. 1656. Studied at Helmstedt, where a somewhat liberal tendency in theology prevailed; from 1609 to 1613 he traveled through Germany, Belgium, England, and France; professor of theology at Helmstedt. His main idea was that the prime object of theology was not so much purity of doctrine as a Christian life; hence his unionistic tendency towards the Catholic and Reformed Churches. At the Convention of Thorn he sided with the Reformed delegates, where also, as before, he advocated, as a basis for union, the teachings of the Church in the first five centuries (*Consensus Quinquesaecularis*). — He held that only the doctrinal matter of Scripture was inspired, while in other matters the writers had been merely governed and kept from error by the Spirit. — He introduced the analytic method into dogmatics.

Calixtus II (pope). See *Concordat.*

Calixtines. See *Hussites.*

Call. See *Ministerial Office,* 5; *Conversion,* II, 1.

Call of Teachers. See *Teachers,* A 1 a, A 3.

Callenberg, Johann Heinrich (1694 to 1760). Professor at Halle; known for the extensive mission work among Jews and Mohammedans which he inaugurated.

Calov, Abraham. B. 1612; studied in Koenigsberg and Rostock; 1643 rector of the *Gymnasium* and pastor in Danzig; took part in the Colloquy of Thorn in 1645, where he opposed Georg Calixt. Elector John George I called him in 1650 as theological professor to Wittenberg, where he was also made *Pastor Primarius* and General Superintendent of the district. In all these offices he was eminently successful, drawing many students to Wittenberg. He was the staunchest champion of strict Lutheranism of his age, against Romanism, Calvinism, and syncretism. The number of his writings is almost incredible. Foremost of his works is his *Biblia Illustrata,* 4 vols., in refutation of the commentaries of Grotius. Other works are: *Systema Locorum Theologicorum,* 12 vols.; *Consensus Repetitus Fidei Verae Lutheranae.* D. of apoplexy at Wittenberg, 1686. See references under *Dogmatics.*

Calvary Pentecostal Church. See *Pentecostalism.*

Calvin, John. 1. John Calvin was born in Picardy on July 10, 1509, the son of a fiscal official employed by the local bishop. As a young man he began his studies for the priesthood at Paris, but soon transferred to the law, studying at Orleans and Bourges. He early came in contact both with Humanism and with the evangelical movement initiated by Luther. The exact details of Calvin's conversion to Protestantism are absent from his writings, but it is apparent that this occurred no later than 1533. As a result of espousing the Protestant cause, he fled France in 1534, going to Basel, where he planned to devote himself to scholarship.

2. Aroused by the persecution of the Protestants in France, he wrote, in 1536, a treatise in their behalf, addressed to Francis I. This was the famous *Institutes of the Christian Religion,* the classic exposition of Calvin's theology. A second edition appeared in 1539, and the first French edition in 1540. The *Institutes,* which show a close dependence on Luther, present Calvin's theology in lucid, systematic, and exhaustive form. His *magnum opus,* at the age of 27, established him as a theologian of the first rank.

3. While passing through Geneva in 1536, Calvin was prevailed upon by the local Protestant leader Farel to remain there in order to promote the Evangelical cause. In Geneva his first major accomplishment was the *Articles of Polity of the Church,* in 1537. He also provided the first Genevan Catechism and Creed, demanding a confession of faith from every citizen. This created wide resentment, and Calvin was forced to leave Geneva when the city council turned against him. He planned to return to Basel, but at the insistence of Bucer he went instead to Strasbourg.

4. Calvin was impressed by Bucer's emphasis on the community character of the Church in Strasbourg. Under Bucer's influence, too, his doctrinal views concerning predestination and church order came to maturity during his Strasbourg sojourn. There, too, in 1541, he married a widow, Idelette de Bure, whom he called "the excellent companion of his life." Always sickly, she died in 1549, leaving Calvin to rear two unruly stepsons. Calvin's natural austerity was accentuated by his domestic troubles.

5. Meanwhile, in 1541, Calvin was called back to Geneva, where Farel's Protestant party had succeeded in regaining control of political affairs. As a condition of his return, Calvin insisted on complete authority as leader of the Genevan "theocracy." Under him Geneva became the "city of God."

6. At Calvin's direction, four clerical orders were established: Ministers, elders, teachers, deacons. The former two constituted the ecclesiastical consistory, with full power of church discipline. Calvin was unyielding in his efforts to extirpate heresy; in a notable case, the city council in 1553, at Calvin's insistence, executed on charges of atheism a refugee Spanish physician, Michael Servetus, who had fled to Geneva to escape the Inquisition.

7. Calvin's authority in Geneva was now unquestioned, and his influence spread throughout Europe. Though subject to chronic illness, his output of work was prodigious. He lectured and preached several times a week; wrote

exegetical and homiletical commentaries, in addition to innumerable theological tracts and opinions; carried on a voluminous correspondence; and supervised successive editions of the *Institutes*. In 1555 he founded the Geneva Academy, which attracted thousands of students from all parts of Europe. Always frugal and plain in his manner of life, he never slept more than four hours a night. He died on May 27, 1564, in the arms of his friend Beza.

8. Calvin was a systematic theologian, and the *Institutes* bear the impress of his logical and comprehensive theological method. This work contained four main chapters: the Commandments, the Creed, Prayer, and the Sacraments. To this he later added chapters on False Sacraments, Christian Liberty, the Church, and the Power of the State.

9. His theological orientation is consistently Biblical, and Luther's influence upon his doctrinal formulations is undeniable. There existed, nevertheless, a distinct difference between the two reformers, characterized by Calvin's predominantly formal and legalistic approach to Christianity in contrast to Luther's warm and evangelical spirit. "Luther stresses the glory of God's love; Calvin stresses God's love of glory."

10. The idea of the sovereignty, honor, and glory of God is paramount in Calvin's system. He emphasizes God's love of "docility" and speaks of Him as "spiritual legislator." In the doctrine of justification, Calvin is close to Luther, although his approach is more intellectual and judicial. The Bible he accepts as the sole and infallible source of divine truth. Man, since the fall of Adam, is totally depraved and is redeemed only by the blood of Christ, whom he must accept through faith engendered by the Holy Spirit. He conceives of the Church as the total number of the elect, and insists upon the four orders of church government (see 6 above; *Polity, Ecclesiastical*, 7). To the Sacraments he attaches only a spiritual and symbolical meaning. The State is God's instrument, subject to His sovereignty, and its laws must conform to His; thus Calvin regards every member of the State as also under the discipline of the Church.

11. In his doctrine of Predestination, the "horrible decree," Calvin is swayed by logic: Since only some are elect, he deduces that the others must be reprobate. The Scripture passages on universal grace he applies only to the elect. Concerning this doctrine he asserts that "God will be glorified in His own way."

12. The influence of Calvin spread throughout Switzerland, and in 1549 the "Consensus Tigurinus" provided a doctrinal basis for the unification of Zwinglians and Calvinists in that country. From Geneva, too, Calvinism branched out into all parts of Europe, and gave rise to the French Huguenots, the Dutch Reformed, the Scotch Presbyterians, and the English Puritans. TC

Th. Beza, *Vie de Calvin*, 1564; John Calvin, *Institutes of the Christian Religion* (tr. by John Allen), Presbyterian Bd. of Publications, Philadelphia, 1813 (2 vols.); Williston Walker, *John Calvin*; J. Mackinnon, *Calvin and the Reformation*; Georgia Harkness, *John Calvin — The Man and His Ethics*, Holt, N. Y., 1931.

Calvinism. The term, derived from the name of John Calvin, is currently employed in two or three senses, denoting the individual teachings of John Calvin, the doctrinal system confessed by the body of Protestant churches known as "Reformed Churches," or "Calvinistic Churches," and, lastly, the entire body of conceptions, theological, ethical, philosophical, social, and political, which owe their origin to Calvin. Sometimes also the term Calvinism comprehends his views regarding both theological doctrine and ecclesiastical polity, and at other times it is limited to the former, especially to his views on the doctrine of grace. These views are sometimes called the Five Points of Calvinism, or simply the Five Points: 1. Particular election (supralapsarianism); 2. particular redemption; 3. moral inability in the fallen state; 4. irresistible grace; 5. final perseverance. These Five Points of Calvinism were opposed by the rival system of Arminianism,* which was presented by the Remonstrants at the Synod of Dort. In 1618 and 1619 the Synod of Dort condemned the Arminian doctrines, enforcing the decrees of the council by pains and penalty. In addition to what may be called the doctrines of grace (in which he never reached the right Biblical understanding), Calvin held the spiritual presence of Christ in the Holy Eucharist, but not the doctrine of the real presence of Christ's body in the

Sacrament. All of Calvin's theological views are conditioned by the basic principle of his system, the absolute sovereignty of God. Calvin's views of church government were essentially such as are now called Presbyterian. Holding that the Church should be spiritually independent of the State, he, nevertheless, was willing that the discipline of the Church should be carried out by the civil magistrates. This last opinion involved him in heavy responsibility for the death of his Socinian opponent, Michael Servetus.

The work which first made Calvinism prominent in the world was Calvin's *Institutes of the Christian Religion*, published in 1536. Various Protestant churches adopted Calvin's theological views, together with his ecclesiastical polity. Thus Knox carried both Calvin's theology and polity to Scotland, where the first Presbyterian General Assembly was held in 1560. The early reformers of the English Church mostly held Calvin's views of the doctrines of grace, which prevailed to the end of Queen Elizabeth's reign. When the rival system of Arminius was brought to trial at the Synod of Dort in Holland, in 1618, the English clerical representatives gave Calvinistic votes. In spite of this, Arminianism took deep root in the English as in various other churches. Archbishop Laud was its warm friend and advocate, as were the High Church party generally, while Low Churchmen continued Calvinistic. The ecclesiastical polity of Calvin was embraced by the Puritan party, but never enjoyed the favor of the majority of the English people. Most of the clergymen whom the passing of the Act of Uniformity, in 1662, dissevered from the Church were Calvinists. Of the two great English revivalists of the eighteenth century, Whitefield was Calvinistic (Calvinistic Methodists) and Wesley Arminian (Wesleyan Methodists). The majority of English Baptists are Calvinistic. The theological tenets and the ecclesiastical polity of Calvin have nearly always been dominant in Scotland, though the sterner features of both have almost imperceptibly been softened down.

John Calvin, *Institutes of the Christian Religion* (tr. by John Allen), Presbyterian Bd. of Publications, Philadelphia, 1813 (2 vols.); Williston Walker, *A History of the Christian Church*, Scribner's, 1918; E. F. K. Mueller, *Die Bekenntnisschriften der Reformierten Kirche*, Deichert, Leipzig, 1903.

Calvinism and the Means of Grace. See *Grace, Means of,* 17.

Calvinistic Methodism. George Whitefield * separated from John Wesley, with whom he had been associated in the great revival of England, on the question of predestination and free will, Wesley being Arminian and Whitefield a Calvinist. The Countess of Huntingdon, interested in the religious revival of Methodism, took Whitefield under her special patronage and became responsible for organizing the Calvinistic Methodists, also known as Lady Huntingdon's Connection. Calvinistic Methodism is represented chiefly in Wales, where it is known as Welsh Methodism.

Calvinizing Churches. This term includes all those churches which have more or less come under the influence of Calvinistic views and tenets, such as the Calvinistic Baptists, Calvinistic Methodists, Congregationalists, the Evangelical churches, the German Reformed Church, the Presbyterian bodies, various Calvinistic tendencies within the Lutheran Church, etc., though in most of these churches strict Calvinism was replaced by moderate Calvinistic views. See *Calvinism*.

Calvisius, Seth (Jakob Kallwitz; 1556—1615). The first cantor of St. Thomas in Leipzig to enjoy wide fame; a versatile scholar who excelled in music, mathematics, chronology, astrology, linguistics, and musicology. Selneccer called attention to Calvisius' outstanding talents and leadership ability. Calvisius fostered simple music, notably through his *Harmonia Cantionum Ecclesiasticarum* of 1597. In 1596 Calvisius published a Lutheran hymnal which was based largely on Luther's hymns and was to be sung in four-part harmony. Active in disposing the youth of the Church to good music. F. Blume, *Die ev. Kirchenmusik*, Potsdam, 1931; E. Koch, *Geschichte des Kirchenliedes und Kirchengesanges*, Stuttgart, 1866—76; Sal. Kuemmerle, *Enzyklopaedie der ev. Kirchenmusik*, Guetersloh, 1888; Carl von Winterfeld, *Der ev. Kirchengesang*, Leipzig, 1843 to 1847.

Calvoer, Kaspar (1650—1725). Learned theologian of the school of Calixt; interested in liturgics; among his writings: *Rituale Ecclesiasticum*, the homiletical part of which is of interest even today.

Camaldules. A strict monastic order, originally eremitical, later partly cenobitic, founded by Romuald, about 1018. It now has 24 houses, all but one in Italy, with fewer than 400 inmates.

Cambridge Arminians. See *Latitudinarians.*

Cambridge Platform. See *Congregational and Christian Churches,* A 2; *Democratic Declarations,* 2.

Cambridge Platonists. A latitudinarian school * founded by Whichcote in the 17th century which sought to reconcile reason and religion; believed that good and evil existed apart from God; views led to mysticism and transcendentalism.

Camera. See *Curia.*

Camerarius, Joachim (1500—74). Studied at Leipzig and Erfurt; professor at Nuernberg, Tuebingen, and Leipzig; Greek classicist; friend of Melanchthon and staunch supporter of Luther, especially at Augsburg (1530), where he assisted Melanchthon in preparing the material for the *Apology* *; favored the Leipzig Interim; present at the Religious Peace of Augsburg and the Diet of Regensburg; wrote a biography of Melanchthon and also of Eoban Hesse.

Cameron, John (ca. 1579—1625). Founder of the "moderate" school of Calvinism in France; studied at Paris, Geneva, Heidelberg; pastor at Bordeaux; professor at Saumur and Glasgow; in his theology he opposed the imputation of Christ's active righteousness; no divine decree excludes any man from the benefit of Christ; while God denies none the power to believe, He does not grant all assistance to use the power to eternal salvation. Followers were called Amyraldians.

Cameronians. A group of Scotch Presbyterians among whom Richard Cameron (d. 1680) was a prominent leader. These Presbyterians held that the Solemn League and Covenant was perpetually binding and opposed efforts of Charles II to enforce the Episcopal form of government.

Cameroons (Kameroons). 166,489 sq. mi.; population 2,619,508. Territory on the west coast of Africa. Formerly German colony. English Baptists carried on mission work since 1845, especially under Alfred Saker, who came 1850 (d. 1880); their work turned over to the Basel Mission in 1885. Later the Gossner Mission and the German Baptists started work there; also the Brethren have a small mission there. The Presbyterians in the U. S. A. and the Paris Ev. Missionary Society began work there, taking over when the German missionaries were expelled during the First World War. In 1949 there were 153 foreign workers and 1,865 native workers. See *French Equatorial Africa; Missions, Bibliography.*

Camisards (O. F. *camisade,* "a night attack," from It. *camicia,* "a shirt." Worn over armor to distinguish friend from foe). A French Protestant sect which, secure in mountains of Cevenne, preserved its religious heritage (also called Barbets, Assemblers, Children of God, Fanatics). The movement had fanatical aspects, such as ecstatic prophecies, preternatural lights, and prodigies. Severe persecutions started against them after the revocation of the Edict of Nantes (1685). The assassination of one of the persecutors, Abbe du Chayla (July 23, 1702), marks the beginning of the War of Cevennes, in which Jean Cavalier, teen-age leader of the Camisards, became famous for military skill. The Crusade of Clement XI accomplished little against the Camisards, who had friends everywhere and were aided by Protestant lands. The Camisards were defeated in 1705 and the remnants ruthlessly suppressed.

Campanella, Tommaso (1568—1639). Italian philosopher; joined the Dominican Order (1594); after the publication of his first book, *Philosophia sensibus demonstrata,* he was opposed by Schoolmen and monks; persecuted by Spaniards and imprisoned (1598); freed by Urban VIII; wrote many books of which two important ones are: *Prodromus Philosophiae Instaurandae, seu de Natura Rerum* and *De Sensu Rerum et Magia Libri IV.* He sought to create a philosophy based on experience, but at the same time he held that sense impressions do not reveal external reality, but are merely subjective perceptions (thus anticipating Hobbes and Kant). His best known work is *Civitas Solis.*

Campanile (L. *campana,* bell). Name for a bell tower, usually applied to those of Italy. These were usually detached from the church tower (Florence, Cremona, Bologna, and Pisa).

Campanius, John (1601—83). A native of Stockholm; came to New Sweden with Governor Printz, Feb. 15, 1643, and ministered to the Swedes on the Delaware until 1648. He was chaplain to the governor on Tinicum Island, just below Philadelphia, where the first Lutheran church building in America was dedicated, Sept. 4, 1646. He also translated Luther's Small Catechism into the language of the Indians (fifteen years before Eliot's Indian Bible appeared). Author of *Description of the Province of New Sweden.* Returned to Sweden in 1648.

Campanus, Johannes. Anti-Trinitarian and Anabaptist of the 16th century. B. in bishopric of Liége; d. ca. 1575. Held that Holy Spirit is not divine; Son not co-eternal with God the Father. Imprisoned last twenty years.

Campbell, Alexander. See *Disciples of Christ, 2.*

Campbell, John McLeod (1800—72). Taught that Christ was representative of humanity in repentance rather than substitute under penalty of its sin; in 1830 excluded from Presbyterian General Assembly.

Campbell, Reginald John (1867—). Famous English Congregational, later Anglican, preacher. His book *New Theology,** which attempted to harmonize Christian beliefs with modern critical views, gained wide attention. Other books: *A Faith for Today; Problems of Life; The Peace of God.*

Campbell, Robert (1814—68). Studied at Glasgow and Edinburgh; advocate at law; joined Episcopal Church of Scotland, later the Roman Catholic Church; among his translations: "Christians, Come, in Sweetest Measures."

Campbell, Thomas. See *Disciples of Christ, 2.*

Campbellites. See *Disciples of Christ.*

Camp Fire Girls. The organization was founded to take care of the out-of-school time of the adolescent girls, beginning with the age of eleven years, by "providing activities of natural interest to girls, intelligent appreciation of the beauties of nature, and building up an awareness of their position and responsibility in the community." There is an honor and award system for a great variety of crafts, classified under the general headings Home, Health, Camp, Hand, Nature, Business, Citizenship. Guardians are provided for, aged 18 years and upwards. Regarding "Camp Fire Girls and the Protestant Church" the official literature says: "If a Camp Fire group is organized and sponsored by a church, its activities should be closely integrated with the local church program. The minister is the spiritual leader of the group. Special church services or vesper services are often arranged for the Camp Fire groups. The girls are awarded honors for service to the church. In these groups, Camp Fire leaders work in close collaboration with the ministers and other church leaders."

Canada, Catholic Church in. Since the territory now included in the Dominion of Canada was largely settled by pioneers of the Roman Catholic persuasion, the entire eastern section of the country is to this day predominantly Roman Catholic. It was the Frenchman Cartier who, in 1534, took possession of the Labrador region in the name of France and, in 1535—36, ascended the St. Lawrence as far as Montreal. When the first permanent settlement was made at Quebec, in 1608, under the leadership of Champlain, the settlement with its outposts was strongly Catholic from the beginning; and the Catholic religious history of the Dominion may properly be said to begin with the year 1625, when the Jesuits arrived, immediately beginning their educational and missionary endeavors. For a while, after the country had come under English control in 1763, the number of Protestants increased fairly rapidly in the eastern part of the Dominion, but during the eighteenth century the immigration from Ireland was steady, while the French Catholic population was increased after the Franco-Prussian War by a number of Alsatians. There is no state church in the Dominion of Canada, but the Roman Catholics of Quebec are guaranteed the privileges which they enjoyed before the English became masters of the country, and the Roman Catholic schools have always received recognition before the law, while private schools conducted by Protestant bodies have often been conducted under a handicap which wrought much harm. Over the period from 1871 to 1941 approximately 40 per cent of the population of Canada has been of the Roman Catholic faith. The 1952 percentage was approximately 40 (6,069,496) of the total population of 14,009,429, the percentage being highest in Quebec. The Dominion has an apostolic delegate, who resides at Ottawa. AHS

Canada, Lutheranism in. 1. The first clergyman to conduct a Lutheran service on Canadian soil was the Rev. Rasmus Jensen of Aarhus (d. 1619; first Lutheran pastor in America), chaplain of an expedition sent out by King Christian IV of Denmark, which entered Hudson Bay and landed at the mouth of the Churchill River on September 7, 1619. In 1749 a wave of immigrants, among them many German Lutherans, landed at Halifax, and the first documentary evidence of the existence of a congregation there bears the date of October 12, 1752. Here was erected in 1755 the first Lutheran church on Canadian soil, known as St. George Church. Not until 1783 did these Lutherans obtain their own pastor in the person of Rev. B. M. Houseal (Hausihl; 1727—99), being served in the meantime by a pious layman and later occasionally by an Anglican rector, Dr. Breynton. Rev. Houseal, whose house and church in New York City were burned to the ground in 1776, was an ardent Loyalist and came to Halifax as a man able to minister to the Lutherans in their mother tongue. A year after his arrival he sailed for England to receive re-ordination from the Bishop of London. Upon his return he ministered for 16 years, but gradually led the congregation into the Church of England.

2. With the arrival, on June 7, 1753, of an expedition containing many German Lutherans, the town of Lunenberg, Nova Scotia, was founded. According to Andreas Jung, the historian of the period, Rev. Paul Bryzelius (1713 to 1773), a German-Swede of Moravian leanings, began to serve these Lutherans in 1765. In 1768 they applied to the Rev. H. M. Muhlenberg of Philadelphia for a pastor, but received no answer. Their appeal to the Rev. J. S. Gerock, pastor of Christ Evangelical Church of New York City, resulted in the arrival of the Rev. Frederick Schultz at Lunenberg in 1772. The same year he dedicated Zion Lutheran Church in a congregation which in 1775 had 185 families and which has the longest continuous history of any Lutheran congregation in Canada.

3. The Nova Scotia Conference of the Pittsburgh Synod was organized in 1876 and the Ev. Luth. Synod of Nova Scotia in 1903 (member of General Council, 1903; ULC, 1918). 1952: 32 congregations, 7,084 souls, 14 pastors.

4. Forty German Lutheran families joined other Loyalists in leaving the Mohawk Valley and emigrating to the neighborhood of Kingston, Ontario, where in 1783 two congregations were organized, one at Bath and the other at Ernesttown. Barrenness of soil caused the entire community to move and establish themselves near the present town of Morrisburg, where in 1789 they completed Zion Lutheran Church at Riverside, the first Lutheran church in Ontario, which was dedicated by the Rev. Samuel Schwerdfeger, newly called pastor of Albany, N. Y., and former member of the Ministerium of Pennsylvania, who had taken up residence at Williamsburg, Dundas County, Ontario. Later many of these St. Lawrence Lutherans were lost to the Anglican and Methodist denominations and to pseudo-Lutheran preachers. New life was brought into this rapidly disintegrating community when Prof. Herman Hayunga (d. 1872) of Hartwick Seminary resigned his chair and accepted in 1826 a call to the St. Lawrence Lutherans, where during a ministry of 46 years he gathered a sizable congregation at St. John's, Riverside, and established St. Peter's at North Williamsburg. These congregations and those in York County had joined the Canada Synod but later severed their connections to join the Synods of New York and New England, from which the English-speaking congregations again withdrew to form a church body known as "The Ev. Luth. Synod of Central Canada," later a member of the General Council and in 1918 of the United Lutheran Church in America.

5. Another group of some sixty German Lutheran families moved from the Genesee Valley in New York and settled in Markham Township, about 20 miles north of Toronto, in 1793. According to the record in the National Archives and Library at Ottawa (No. 3987), congregations were organized at Unionville and Buttonville in 1794, and their first pastor was the Rev. Geo. Liebig. After a vacancy of nearly 16 years, an aged Christian, Adam Keffer, traveled 500 miles, mostly on foot, to Klecknerville, Pa., to plead with the Pittsburgh Synod for a pastor. His first visit brought no permanent results other than a visit by the president of the synod, Rev. G. Bassler (1849). But when in the following year Mr. Keffer appeared for the second time with more insistent pleas, the mission committee issued a call to Rev. C. F. Diehl, and he took charge of the congregations in

the townships of Markham and Vaughan that same year, in September, 1850.

6. Lutherans from Hesse, Alsace, and Wuerttemberg began to settle in Waterloo County of western Ontario the early part of the 19th century and were for some 30 years served by the aggressive missionary Rev. F. W. Bindemann (1790—1865), reformed in name and liberal in doctrine. Bindemann organized many congregations; but many of the more conservative Lutherans gradually refused his ministrations; and after a visit by the Rev. J. H. Bernheim in Kitchener in 1836 missionaries were sent from the Pittsburgh Synod and the Ministerium of Pennsylvania.

7. In 1853 the Canada Conference of the Pittsburgh Synod was organized, which in turn became the Ev. Luth. Canada Synod (General Synod) in 1861. It was one of the synods forming the General Council (1867); joined ULC (1918).

8. St. Matthew's Church, Kitchener, founded in 1904, with its 3,200 souls, is the largest congregation in the Canada Synod, and in the entire Dominion.

9. The Canada Synod opened the Waterloo Seminary on October 30, 1911, and in 1924 the Lutheran College, which is affiliated with the University of Western Ontario. 1952: 118 congregations, 45,905 souls, 93 pastors.

10. At a time when the Missouri Synod was still divided into the Northern, Eastern, Western, and Central Districts, the Eastern District began to work in Ontario through the Rev. John Adam Ernst (d. 1895; Loehe missionary; Ohio Synod, 1842—45; active in founding Mo. Synod), the "father of Missouri Lutheranism in Canada," who made mission journeys into the Rhineland and Fisherville area from his home in Eden, N. Y., and organized congregations at the former place in February, 1854, and at the latter in May, 1854. Thus the Rhineland congregation became the mother church of the Missouri Synod in Canada; in the year 1854 it also obtained official membership in this synod. After an enforced resignation from his charge in New York, caused by illness, Pastor Ernst accepted a call in 1862 to the Floradale-Elmira parish, where for 18 years he had a successful pastorate, organizing, together with Pastors Roeder and Sprengeler, many congregations in the Waterloo area. When the Canada District of the Missouri Synod was formed

in 1879, he became its first president. In 1923 the name of this District was changed to Ontario District.

11. Under the direction of its Minnesota District, the Missouri Synod began to work in western Canada in 1879. In that year the Rev. E. Rolf of St. Paul, Minn., came to serve Lutherans at Berlin (Ossowo), Manitoba. Candidate H. Buegel was called to Winnipeg in 1891, and he became the first resident missionary. In Alberta Candidate Emil Eberhardt began the work of pioneering at Stony Plain in 1894, after Rev. F. Eggers from Great Falls, Mont., had explored the territory. The congregations of the two western provinces were organized into the Alberta and British Columbia District in 1921, and the Manitoba and Saskatchewan District was formed in 1922. Since 1921 the Missouri Synod maintains Concordia College at Edmonton, a residential high school and junior college. — The International Lutheran Hour is heard weekly over 51 radio stations in the Dominion (1947).

12. The activity of the Wisconsin Synod in Canada was confined to the work of one man, Rev. Ewald Herrmann. He left the State Church of Hanover, Germany, in 1896 and came to Saskatchewan (Assiniboia) as a member of the General Council, serving congregations at Neudorf, Wellesley, and Josephsburg. While here, he was colloquized by Dr. F. Pfotenhauer and became a member of the Missouri Synod. In 1906 he accepted a call to Wisconsin and joined the Wisconsin Synod but was called back to Regina in 1910; and with the support of the Wisconsin Synod he remained there as pastor of Grace Lutheran Church until 1924, when he resigned because of advancing age and his congregation accepted the service of the Missouri Synod. 1951: Ontario District: 53 congregations, 22,446 souls, 46 pastors, 3 parochial schools. Manitoba and Saskatchewan District: 78 congregations, 15,310 souls, 39 pastors. Alberta and British Columbia District: 74 congregations, 15,272 souls, 49 pastors, 3 parochial schools. In addition there were 80 preaching stations and 64 congregations not yet affiliated with The Lutheran Church — Missouri Synod.

13. Icelanders arrived at Gimli, Manitoba, in October, 1875, and the first Icelandic service in Canada was conducted in their midst in August, 1876, by the Rev. Paul Thorlaksson (1849 to 1882), a graduate of Concordia Semi-

nary, St. Louis, who in October, 1877, accepted the call to three congregations comprising about 120 families. His conservative theology did not find favor with five other congregations of 130 families; these five called the Rev. Jon Bjarnason (1845—1914), also in 1877. This latter group adopted the name The Icelandic Synod of America, while the former were known as The Icelandic Congregation in New Iceland. In 1855 Icelandic congregations on both sides of the international boundary formally organized The Evangelical Lutheran Icelandic Synod of America. In 1913 the Jon Bjarnason Academy was established in Winnipeg and operated continuously up to 1940, when a change in the educational policy of the province brought its existence to a close. Most of the Icelandic pastors received their theological training in ULC seminaries. An Old Folks' Home is maintained at Gimli, Manitoba. 1952: 25 congregations, 5,298 souls.

14. With the advent of the transcontinental railroad in 1885 large numbers of Lutherans arrived in western Canada, principally from Bucovina, Rumania, Galicia, the western provinces of Russia, and some from Germany. In 1888 forty German Lutherans of Winnipeg addressed a request for help to the Canada Synod. President F. Veit visited them and organized Trinity German Ev. Luth. Congregation in Winnipeg on December 16, 1888. Rev. Heinrich C. Schmieder, assistant pastor at St. Paul's Church in Philadelphia and graduate of Kropp Seminary in Germany, accepted the call as first pastor in 1889. The long distance from the Canada Synod in Ontario made the founding of a separate synod in Western Canada imperative; and so four pastors met on July 22, 1897, in Winnipeg to organize the German Ev. Luth. Synod of Manitoba and the Northwest Territories (entered ULC, 1918), which in 1947 was changed to the Ev. Luth. Synod of Western Canada. The General Council, to which the Manitoba Synod belonged, was not able to supply a sufficient number of missionaries for the rapidly growing mission field, and so an agreement was made between the General Council and Pastor Paulsen's Seminary at Kropp, Germany, whereby the latter institution furnished a large number of pastors for the work of the Manitoba Synod. — In 1912 Spruce Grove, Alberta, became the birthplace of the Lutheran College and Seminary. In this year several young

men received some preliminary training in the home of Rev. Juergen Goos. In 1913 the institution was removed to South Edmonton and in 1915 transferred to its permanent home in Saskatoon. Its theological department was added in 1919, and the college section was discontinued in 1933. This Lutheran Seminary is affiliated with the University of Saskatchewan. 1952: 121 congregations, 18,089 souls, 60 pastors.

15. The work of the National Ev. Luth. Church (Finnish), affiliated with the Synodical Conference, dates back to 1895. In this year Rev. Juho Heimonen began to preach at Fort William, Ontario. As first missionary and first resident pastor he organized in 1896 First Lutheran Church in Fort William, and the following year another congregation in Port Arthur, extending his activities also into Saskatchewan. 1952: 7 congregations, 1,087 souls, 3 pastors, 8 preaching stations.

16. The Finnish Suomi Synod, with its headquarters in Hancock, Mich., has been interested in the spiritual welfare of the Finns in Canada ever since its founding in 1890; but its work has always been handicapped by a shortage of ministers. Hence it sought assistance from the United Lutheran Church in America. A plan of co-operation was approved by both churches which lasted from 1921 to 1930. Beginning with 1930, the Synod authorized the ULCA to send and support men to work among the Finns in Canada. In 1931 all Finnish work of this synod became definitely affiliated with the Canadian synods of the ULCA.

17. First English Lutheran Church in Winnipeg is the only Canadian congregation of the English Ev. Luth. Synod of the Northwest (ULCA). 1952: 401 souls.

18. The Pacific Synod (ULCA) has two congregations in British Columbia. 1952: 503 souls. The Slovak-Zion Synod has 2 congregations with 329 souls in Canada.

19. The Joint Synod of Ohio began its work in Canada when part of a former congregation of the Manitoba Synod in Winnipeg appealed to Dr. H. Ernst, then president of the Minnesota District of the Ohio Synod, to supply them with a pastor. It was the Rev. G. Gehrke, later president and mission superintendent, who accepted this call to Winnipeg in 1905. Already in the fall of 1906 there were fourteen pastors who ministered to many mission parishes throughout the prairie

provinces, and these formed the Canada Conference, which in 1908 was organized into the Canada District of the Ohio Synod (ALC). — In 1913 an Academy was erected at Melville, Sask., which in 1926 transferred its location to Regina. This school, known as Luther College, includes in its curriculum all the grades from nine to second-year university and is affiliated with the University of Saskatchewan. A home for orphans and old people is maintained in Melville, Sask. — In 1840 the Buffalo Synod entered Ontario and organized St. John's Congregation at Gas Line. Later this body joined the American Lutheran Church, and its parishes in Ontario (561 souls) are now members of the Eastern District of the ALC. 1951: 131 congregations, 22,610 souls, 56 pastors.

20. The first beginnings of Norwegian Lutheran church work in Canada were made at Parry Sound, Ontario, in 1876, when the Jarlsberg congregation was organized; and in 1889 mission work was begun in Vancouver and New Westminster. With the exception of some work done by the Norwegian Synod in Manitoba as early as 1876, aggressive work was started in 1895. Work had been carried on independently by the Norwegian Synod, the United Norwegian Lutheran Church, and the Hauge Norwegian Ev. Luth. Church. In 1917 the parishes of these three bodies were organized into the Canada District of the Norwegian Lutheran Church in America, and in 1922 this District was incorporated by an Act of Parliament under the name The Norwegian Lutheran Church of Canada. This body has three institutions of higher learning in Canada: Camrose Lutheran College in Alberta, opened in 1911 and offering high school as well as commercial courses; Outlook College in Saskatchewan, organized in 1916, closed in 1936 because of drought conditions and the depression, but reopened in 1939 under the name The Saskatchewan Lutheran Bible Institute and operating since then as a high school and a three-year Bible school; and Luther Theological Seminary in Saskatoon, conducted co-operatively with the Lutheran College and Seminary of the Manitoba Synod since 1939. The church maintains an Old People's Home at Bawlf, Alberta, since 1922. 1951: 216 congregations, 17,864 souls, 53 pastors.

21. In 1885 the Minnesota Conference of the Augustana Synod resolved to begin home mission work in Canada. At Stockholm, Sask., the first congregation was organized in 1889. In 1913 the Canada Conference of the Ev. Luth. Augustana Synod was formed. A school for the training of future ministers was opened in 1912 at Percival, Sask., but was closed again several years later because of financial difficulties. In 1943 an Old Folks' Home was established in Wetaskiwin, Alberta. 1951: 42 congregations, 4,684 souls, 8 pastors.

22. The work of the United Ev. Luth. Church (Danish) was begun in 1904 at Dickson, Alberta, by Rev. J. G. Gundeson, and is organized under the West Canada District of the United Danish Lutheran Church. This body maintains Dane High School at Calgary, Alberta; it is also active in conjunction with Augustana, Norwegian, and Lutheran Free Church members in the Canadian Lutheran Bible Institute at Camrose, Alberta (organized 1932). Another institution is Dana Young People's Home in Calgary, designed chiefly for the purpose of assisting new settlers to become established. 1952: 17 congregations, 2,570 souls, 14 pastors.

23. The Danish Evangelical Lutheran Church has several congregations and is supported by the Danish Church in Foreign Lands. It maintains the Danish Old People's Home in Vancouver. 1952: 2 congregations, 189 souls, 2 pastors.

24. The Lutheran Free Church has been active in Canada since 1895. In that year the Rev. Christian Sangstad, with a group of some eighty Norwegians from Crookston, Minn., went to Bella Coola, British Columbia, where he founded a congregation. In 1903 work was begun in Alberta and in 1904 in Saskatchewan. 1950: 10 congregations, 939 souls, 6 pastors (one of these ELC).

25. In 1928 the Rev. John Horarik of the Slovak Ev. Luth. Church began to minister to Slovak people in Montreal, Toronto, Hamilton, and Oshawa. The original number has increased to four parishes in 1951, numbering 522 souls and 3 pastors, and 4 mission stations.

26. The 1951 census lists the following totals for the 6 major denominations: Roman Catholic, 6,069,496; United Church of Canada, 2,867,271; Anglican, 2,060.720; Presbyterian, 781,747; Baptist, 519,585; Lutheran 444.923. AHS

Valdimar J. Eylands, *Lutherans in Canada;* Ernst George Goos, *Pioneering for Christ in Western Canada;* K.

K. Olafson, *The Icelandic Lutheran Synod, Survey and Interpretation;* John Woelfle, *History of Lutheranism in Ontario;* John E. Herzer, *Homesteading for God;* D. Luther Roth, *Acadie and the Acadiens,* Luth. Pub. Soc., Philadelphia, 1898; Heinz-Lehmann, *Das Deutschtum in West Canada,* Junker und Duemhaupt, Berlin, 1939.

Canada, Protestantism in. (See preceding article for Lutheranism in Canada.)

While the Roman Catholic Church is the dominant church in Quebec and eastern Canada, Protestantism, represented chiefly by the Anglican, the Presbyterian, the Methodist, and the Congregational Churches, has the larger number of adherents in the West and Middle West.

As far back as the close of the 19th century repeated attempts were made to unite the various Protestant denominations which stem from England into one strong Canadian Church. In sparsely settled areas many considered denominationalism unnecessary and wasteful. In 1904 a Joint Committee on Church Union was appointed by the Congregational, Methodist, and Presbyterian Churches to work toward the amalgamation of these three denominations. Doctrinal controversies and theological issues were avoided as "irrelevant and secondary in the face of the practical problems" pressing upon the Church. After much deliberation a Basis of Union was drawn up "in which the two streams of Protestantism were able to merge." This Basis of Union was adopted by the three negotiating bodies, and the United Church of Canada became a reality on June 10, 1925.

While the Basis of Union had guaranteed that there should be no disturbance of the local church in its freedom of action and form of government, the consummation of Union led to upheavals in almost every community. Methodists were not prepared to accept Presbyterian ministers, Presbyterians were not ready to sing out of Congregational hymnals, and so on.

Eventually all Methodist and Congregational churches, with isolated exceptions, joined the United Church of Canada and thus ceased to exist as denominations in Canada. Many Presbyterian churches, however, were divided and declined to join the merger. Comparatively few Presbyterian churches, except in the West, escaped disruption.

According to the 1951 census the leading religious denominations in Canada are: Roman Catholic, 6,069,496; United Church of Canada, 2,867,271; Church of England, 2,060,720; Presbyterian, 781,747; Baptist, 519,585; Lutheran, 444,923; Jewish, 204,836; Ukrainian Catholic, 190,831; Greek Orthodox, 172,271; Mennonite, 125,938. HM

Canada Synod. See *Canada, Lutheranism in,* 7 ff.; *United Lutheran Church, Synods of,* 2.

Cancelli. In the ancient Christian basilica, barriers between the nave with its lay church attendants, and the chancel (and choir) with its clergy. The railing sometimes, as in San Clemente in Rome, enclosed the seats of the lower clergy as well as the ambos (reading desks). The cancelli, in the Eastern Orthodox Church, developed into the iconostasis, or screen hiding the high altar. The rood screen of the medieval churches shows another form of the development. In the West the epistle ambo was moved back (toward the east) into the rood screen, and preaching was done from there. This is the origin of the German word *Kanzel,* now used for the pulpit alone.

Candelabra. See *Church Furniture,* 2.

Candida Casa. See *Celtic Church,* 3.

Candidate. A person who is proposed or offers himself as an aspirant for office. In the Lutheran Church the term is applied to a person who has graduated from a theological school but has not yet been installed as a pastor.

Candidus, Pantaleon (1540—1608). B. in Austria; fled to Germany; city pastor and general supt. at Zweibruecken (1571); published *Dialog on the Two Natures* (1583), an attack on the Torgau Book; with Schwebel led Zweibruecken back to a decided Reformed position.

Candlemas. See *Church Year,* 13.

Candler, David (d. 1744). An early Luth. pastor in Maryland and Pennsylvania, whose activities extended from the Susquehanna to the Potomac.

Candles. The Lutheran Church has renounced all superstitious use of candles, as practiced in the Roman Church, and has returned to the simple ceremonial employment of candles or lights, two candles being commonly lighted during service time.

Canisius, Petrus (1521—67). Prominent Jesuit of Germany; studied at Cologne, where he founded the first Jesuit colony, the order spreading rapidly through Germany; noted for Catechism.

Canitz, Friedrich Rudolph (1654 to 1699). German statesman, pietist, and poet. Studied at Leyden and Leipzig; traveled in England, Holland, Italy, and France. Close friend of Spener. Wrote hymns, one of which, "Come, My Soul, Awake, 'Tis Morning," was translated by Catherine Winkworth.

Cankara. See *Brahmanism, 5.*

Canon and Canoness (*Augustinian Canon*). Canons are men who live under the same rule and often bind themselves by simple or solemn vows. Their duties are neither those of the monastic life nor of the parish priest, but are concerned only with the sacred mysteries. Their monastic basis was established by Chrodegang (8th century), although they claim to have originated with Augustine and usually follow his rule. Such are the Premonstratensian and Trinitarian orders. The canonesses were under the spiritual direction of the canons. Irregularities were frequent among both canons and canonesses. The Reformation in Germany changed many houses of canonesses into asylums for unmarried daughters of the nobility.

Canon, Bible. 1. *Canon* is a Greek word meaning "rule." Canonical, then, means "forming a rule." It has come to mean "inspired," "divine." The word is used to describe the collection of inspired books of the Bible.

2. The Canon of the OT (39 books) has stood unchanged for 2,300 years, after its growth had extended through a full thousand years previous to its completion in Malachi (last of the Prophets: Mal. 3:1; 4:5; 1 Macc. 4:46; 9:27). As God had commanded to put the words of the OT in writing, so He also attended to their collection and preservation (Deut. 31:9, 24-26; Joshua 24:26; 1 Sam. 10:25; 2 Kings 22:8; 2 Chron. 34:15). Thus the preservation of these books was the task of the Jewish people (Rom. 3:2) from the moment that Moses committed to the priests the Book of the Law which he had written to be placed inside of the Ark of the Covenant. That the sacred writings were collected is shown by the fact that later writers were acquainted with those of their predecessors. After the Jewish nation had returned from the Exile, the necessity of a complete and definitive collection of the existing sacred writings was felt for various reasons (repentance of the nation; cessation of prophecy). This collection was undoubtedly accomplished during the time of Ezra and Nehemiah (Ezra 7:6, 12; Neh. 5:14. Cf. Josephus, *Contra Apionem*, I:8; 1 Macc. 12:9; 2 Macc. 2:13-15). This collection was thereafter regarded as sacred and kept separate from other books. It is frequently quoted in the NT ("the Law," "the Scriptures," "the Holy Scriptures," "the Old Testament"). See also *Apocrypha.*

3. The Canon of 27 books in the NT was fixed gradually. It took some time before all the NT books were universally known and recognized as inspired. The Church proceeded cautiously, always asking whether a certain writing came from an Apostle (apostolicity).

4. By the year 100 all books of the NT had been written. Apostolic writings were looked upon at once as divine and were gathered into collections (2 Pet. 3:16; Col. 4:16; 1 Thess. 5:27; 2 Thess. 2:15). Clement of Rome (A.D. 96) mentions 1 Corinthians and has many allusions to Hebrews. In the other Apostolic Fathers there are allusions and reminiscences in regard to a number of NT books. The early apologists frequently refer to, and quote, the NT. Marcion * made a collection of NT books ca. 140. Justin speaks of the memoirs of the Apostles, referring to the four Gospels (ca. 150). The Muratorian Canon was written ca. 160. Toward the end of the second century, Irenaeus, Tertullian, and Clement of Alexandria agree that the four Gospels, Acts, 13 letters of Paul, 1 Peter, 1 John, and Revelation are Apostolic and divine.

5. In the third century, Origen accepts all of our NT books as divine. He mentions that there was doubt as to the Apostolic origin of 2 Peter, 2 and 3 John, Hebrews, Jude, and James. Eusebius (d. 340) submits a special chapter on the inspired books of the NT. (*Hist. Ecc.*, III:25). He makes four classes: 1) *Homologoumena* (universally recognized); 2) *Antilegomena* * (genuineness doubted by some); 3) Books that are not genuine (Acts of Paul, Revelation of Peter, etc.); 4) Worthless books (Acts of Andrew and of John and similar works). About Revelation he is not sure whether it should be in the first or third class. In the second half of the fourth century all our books are regarded as Apostolic and canonical. Athanasius (d. 373), as far as we know, was the first one to issue a list in which all our 27 books and none others are declared to be divine. The first council to publish the list was that of Laodicea (360).

6. Throughout the Middle Ages there was no doubt as to the divine character of any book of the NT. Luther again pointed to the distinction between *homologoumena* and *antilegomena* * (followed by Chemnitz and Flacius). The later dogmaticians let this distinction recede into the background. Instead of antilegomena they use the term *deutero-canonical*. Rationalists use the term canon in the sense of list. Lutherans in America followed Luther and held that the distinction between *homologoumena* and *antilegomena* must not be suppressed. Caution, however, must be exercised not to exaggerate the distinction. See *Isagogics, Higher Criticism.* WA

Books on Introduction (see *Isagogics*) usually contain a section on the history of the Canon. K. F. Keil, *Manual of Historico-Critical Introduction to the Canonical Scriptures of the Old Testament,* T. & T. Clark, Edinburgh, 1868; E. Sellin, *Einleitung in das Alte Testament,* Quelle, Leipzig, 1925; Weber-Deinzer, *Einleitung,* Beck, Muenchen, 1897 (11th ed., 1902); L. Fuerbringer, *Einleitung in das A. T.* and *Einleitung in das N. T.* (printed in Mss.); Th. Zahn, *Einleitung in das Neue Testament,* Deichert, Leipzig, 1924 (2 vols. See also his *Geschichte des N. T. Kanons*); E. J. Goodspeed, *Formation of the New Testament,* University of Chicago Press, 1926; B. F. Westcott, *A General Survey of the History of the Canon of the New Testament,* 1870; Alexander Souter, *The Text and Canon of the New Testament,* Scribner, 1924.

Canon of Hippo Rhegius. See *Hippo Rhegius, Canon of.*

Canon Law. "Canon law is the assemblage of rules or laws relating to faith, morals, and discipline, prescribed or propounded by ecclesiastical authority." The term usually refers to the body of laws governing the Roman Church. The chief repository of canon law has been the *Corpus Iuris Canonici,* consisting of the *Decretum Gratiani,* a compilation and annotation of canons of councils, decrees of Popes, etc., made by Gratian, a monk of Bologna (1151), five books of decretals published by Gregory IX (1234), one by Boniface VIII (1298), the *Clementines* of Clement V (1316), and two books of *Extravagantes,* containing decretals down to 1484. To these must be added the *Ius Novissimum,* consisting of the canons of the Council of Trent, papal decretals, decisions of Roman Congregations, concordats, etc. During the Middle Ages the canon law ruled in all countries subject to the spiritual jurisdiction of Rome, not only in ecclesiastical affairs, but in many matters relating to the civil sphere. For six centuries the stupendous forgeries known as the *False Decretals* were accepted as law, and even when they were rejected, they had ineradicably stamped their spirit on the Roman Church and its discipline. Because many provisions of the canon law were unscriptural, and because Rome declared its man-made precepts binding on the consciences, Luther emphatically repudiated it. On Dec. 10, 1520, together with the papal bull of excommunication, he burned the *Corpus Iuris.* A new codification of the canon law, begun by Pius X, was promulgated by Benedict XV (1917). See *Courts, Spiritual.*

Canonical Age. See *Age, Canonical.*

Canonical Hours. Hours of special prayer and devotions growing out of the custom of the primitive Church, as based on suggestions in the Psalter and in Acts 3:1; 10:9. The Apostolic Constitutions name the third, the sixth, and the ninth hours of the morning, the evening, and at cockcrowing. The rule of Benedict of Nursia included the following hours: 2:00 A. M., Vigils; at dawn, Matins; 6:00 A. M., Prime; 9:00 A. M., Tierce; 12:00 M., Sext; 3:00 P. M., Nones; 6:00 P. M., Vespers; 9:00 P. M., Compline; later one Nocturn was added, and the Matin service on certain days is divided into three Nocturns. Although Luther was very conservative in advocating the retention of hours of devotion, the Lutheran Church now observes only Matins, as an early morning service (especially on great festival days and in colleges), Vespers, as a late afternoon or early evening service, and, in certain instances, Compline, as a late evening service.

Canonicity. See *Canon, Bible.*

Canonics. See *Biblical Canonics.*

Canonization. The process by which the Roman Church declares a person a saint and admits him to the honors accorded saints. The first stage of this long and complicated process determines whether the candidate for sainthood has shown "heroic" virtue during life and can duly be credited with miracles. The inquiry is begun by a bishop and is then transferred to Rome, where it passes through various steps, the *postulator* (*advocatus Dei,* "God's advocate") urging the claims of the candidate, the *promotor fidei* (also called *advocatus diaboli,* "devil's advocate") raising objections. If the inquiry turns out favorably, the Pope issues a decree of beatification. This confers the title of *beatus* ("blessed") on the successful one and permits his limited and partial veneration (in certain districts, orders, etc.). — The process may end here or may, at a later date, be followed by a similar procedure, designed to examine the contention that at least two miracles have been wrought by the intercession of the *beatus* since his beatification. If this contention is upheld, canonization follows. The Pope solemnly pronounces that the person in question shall be inscribed on the register of saints (*Canon Sanctorum*). Henceforth he is venerated throughout the Church, a certain day is set apart for his memory, his relics are exhibited, indulgences are granted for visiting his tomb — in short, he is a full-fledged saint. Ordinarily, proceedings for beatification cannot be started till fifty years after death.

Canons of the Church of England. In England, even before the Reformation, canon laws had little force if they were opposed to the prerogatives of the king or the laws of the land. Some general canons, however, obtained general approbation and became law (*ius canonicum*). These laws were augmented by legative constitutions enacted in national synods (1220, 1268) and provincial constitutions by provincial synods. Henry VIII, at the time of the Reformation, ordered a review of the canons and by the "Act of Submission" made all canons dependent on the king's assent. The revision was never completed, but a collection was published by Parker and others (1571), and 141 canons were gathered and published in 1604 by the Convocations. A legal decision (1736) decided that the Convocation could not bind the laity. Anglican churches outside of England adopt their own canons, and the collections referred to above are little more than precedents.

Canstein, Baron Karl Hildebrand. See *Bible Societies,* 2.

Canstein Bible Society. See *Bible Societies,* 2.

Cantata. While, in the early history of the Lutheran Church, the mass, passion, and motet continued to play the important part they had played in church music of pre-Reformation days, the cantata began to flourish as Lutheran worship music during the Baroque Era (ca. 1625—1750). The cantata is a composite form which may include an instrumental prelude or overture, recitatives, arias, duets, and choruses. Cantatas are usually accompanied by an organ or orchestra, they may be lyrical or dramatic, secular (*cantata da camera*) or sacred (*cantata da chiesa*). The Lutheran cantata, which differs from the Roman Catholic cantatas of Italy and France and from the Anglican and Reformed types of England and America, became an integral part of Lutheran worship in the 17th and 18th centuries. It was not only sung between the Epistle and Gospel of the day, but was related directly to the same, presenting and interpreting the texts of the lections, and of chorales, and thus becoming a service in itself. In these same years the more frequently used liturgical texts of former years were neglected to such an extent that often only the Kyrie and Gloria remained. Not a few cantatas were based on Lutheran chorales and were known as *chorale cantatas;* while cantatas of this type were written largely by such masters as Franz Tunder, Joh. Ph. Krieger, Johann Kuhnau, and particularly by J. S. Bach, Dietrich Buxtehude preferred to base his cantatas on free poetic texts and relate them to the Italian baroque style. However, Buxtehude by no means ignored the chorale. Bach wrote no fewer than five cycles of cantatas (ca. 300) for the church year; of these about 195 have been preserved. Among the Lutheran antecedents of the Lutheran Church cantata we find the *Gespraeche zwischen Gott und einer glaeubigen Seele* of Andreas Hammerschmidt, the *Biblical Scenes* and numerous other works by Heinrich Schuetz, notably his *Symphoniae sacrae* of 1629. After Bach, the cantata was practically absorbed by the oratorio; cantatas of some sort were written by the masters of the Classical and Romantic Eras, also by English and American composers. WEB

G. Adler, *Handbuch der Musikgeschichte*, Frankfurt, 1924; W. Apel, *Harvard Dictionary of Music*, Cambridge, Mass., 1944; F. Blume, *Die ev. Kirchenmusik*, Potsdam, 1931; Grove's *Dictionary of Music and Musicians*, Philadelphia, 1926; H. Kretzschmar, *Fuehrer durch den Konzertsaal*, Leipzig, 1898; Sal. Kuemmerle, *Enzyklopaedie der ev. Kirchenmusik*, Guetersloh, 1888; H. S. Moser, *Geschichte der deutschen Musik*, Stuttgart, 1928—30.

Canterbury. Metropolitan see of England; headquarters of Augustine's missionary work among Anglo-Saxons (596); its primacy in England established by Pope Vitalian and confirmed by Pope Alexander III (1159—81).

Canterbury Club. See *Students, Spiritual Care of*, A.

Canticles. Non-metrical spiritual songs, Psalms, or hymns, taken directly from Scriptures and used in the Church from the earliest times, usually chanted at the prescribed place in the services. In some instances the Bible text has been paraphrased to some extent; in others it has been retained practically unchanged. The canticles which are in use in the Church at this time are the following: the *Gloria Patri:* "Glory be to the Father," etc., based on the baptismal formula Matt. 28:19, a paraphrase in use since the first century, also known as the Lesser Doxology; the *Gloria in Excelsis*, or song of the angels, Luke 2:14, enlarged into a hymn of adoration celebrating the glory and majesty of God as manifested in the merciful gift of His Son; the *Tersanctus*, or *Sanctus*, "Holy, Holy, Holy," at the service of celebration of the Holy Supper, a combination of the hymn of the seraphim before the throne of God, Is. 6:2,3, and of the song of the multitudes as they went forth to meet Christ at the time of His triumphal entry into Jerusalem, Matt. 21:9, the section chanted by the people being taken from the great Hallel of the Jewish festival season, Ps. 118: 25, 26; the *Nunc Dimittis* of the aged Simeon, Luke 2:29-32, his joyful thanksgiving for the salvation manifested and bestowed in Christ Jesus, sung at the close of the Communion service as well as at vespers; the *Te Deum Laudamus*, a hymn of praise, whose authorship is ascribed to either Athanasius or Am-

brosius, including praise, confession of faith, and petition, sung in the morning service, or matins; the *Benedicite*, beginning, "O all ye works of the Lord, bless ye the Lord," from the "Song of the Three Holy Children," in the Apocrypha; the *Magnificat*, beginning, "My soul doth magnify the Lord," the song of praise of the Virgin Mary, Luke 1: 46-55, used in vespers since the earliest times; the *Benedictus*, beginning, "Blessed be the Lord God of Israel," the song of praise intoned by the aged Zacharias after the birth and circumcision of John the Baptist, Luke 1:68-79, used in festival services, especially at Christmastide.

Cantionale. A collection of ecclesiastical or sacred chants or hymns for liturgical use, either in the chief service of the day or in the form of choruses appointed for Sundays and holidays and arranged in the order of the church year. Some of the best examples are the collections by Spangenberg, Lossius, Keuchenthal, Ludecus, and Helder.

Cantor. The precentor, or chief singer, of the one section of the choir in an Anglican church; more loosely applied to an organist and choirmaster in German churches, also in synagogs.

Cantus, Cantus Choralis, Cantus Firmus. See *Gregorian Music*.

Canvass, Every-Member. See *Finances of the Church*, 3.

Canzona or **canzone.** (1) Serious lyrical poems of Italy of the 13th to 17th centuries. (2) Lyrical songs of the 18th and 19th centuries or instrumental music of a simple character. (3) A forerunner of the fugue; at times, notably among the Germans, the term was synonymous with *fugue*. Cf. Bach's *Organ Canzona in D Minor*.

Caodaism. Name of a new religious organization originating in French Indo-China, offering a strongly syncretistic combination of Chinese Buddhism, Taoism, Spiritism, and Theosophy, with certain Christian features. The high altar of one of the largest temples shows the figures of Buddha, Confucius, Christ, Laotse, and the symbol of Caodai, a globe with an eye. "Here the entire unredeemed poverty of the modern form of Buddhism appears, as it grew up on the basis of European Catholic influences in the colonies, a religion which, like Buddhism itself, remains hopelessly subjected to pantheism and an externally pious, but humanly immanent mysticism."

Cape of Good Hope. Formerly *Cape Colony*, a province in the Union of South Africa. Area, 276,966 sq. mi. Population, about 2,600,000, of whom 600,000 are Europeans. The native colored races are chiefly Kaffirs, Bechuanas, Hottentots, and Basutos. In 1737 the Moravian George Schmidt began mission work there, the Dutch having done no spiritual work among the natives. They were followed by the South African Society for Promoting the Extension of Christ's Kingdom (Van der Kemp and Voss); the L. M. S., the Primitive Methodist Society, the Scottish Presbyterians, the Anglican Church, the Berliner Missionsgesellschaft (I), the Barmer Mission. Large native churches have been formed. For latest mission statistics see *Missions, Bibliography*.

Capernaitic Eating. See *Grace, Means of*, IV 4.

Capital and Labor. Name for the problems resulting from the industrial revolution and the development of the modern capitalistic system, between the owners and financiers of industrial enterprises and those carrying out the actual production. The problems are complicated on the level of capital by the fact that those financing the operations are frequently concerned only by way of investment and return of interest or dividends, while the management of the operations is entrusted to employees; and on the level of labor by the modern organization of labor into unions, headed by professional leaders, who bargain with the management for the most advantageous wage and working conditions and enforce their demands by strikes. — The Christian is concerned with these problems on two levels. On the first level he is mindful of the behavior of the Christian who is himself an owner or stockholder in industry, a unit in the management, or a worker. That behavior will be conditioned by Christian love. The Holy Spirit at work in the Christian because of the redemption of Jesus Christ will actuate in him the readiness to be for the other person at the expense of personal sacrifice, if need be, and to look at his relationship as a field of calling in which he can glorify God through his acts of love. In these situations the Christian confronts reactions of his own flesh and patterns of selfishness in the world around him, in which disregard for the interests of the other party is rationalized. Since folkways of be-

havior and attitudes of class consciousness are deeply rooted, it behooves the Christian to be doubly alert and sober in maintaining the watchfulness of love, and in carrying out the principles of love (Eph. 6:5-9; Col. 3:22-24).

On the second level the Christian is concerned for the welfare also of those who do not profess the Christian religion, and for his fellow Christians under the influence of those who are not Christians. That means that he will be interested in the leadership of corporations, the techniques of management and labor relations, and the operations of labor unions. He will be anxious to have Christians be influential in their direction. He will be interested in the part which his government will play in the conciliation of labor disputes, the regulation of securities, the supervision of labor unions. He will be anxious that the right ethical guidance will be imparted in the schools and universities of the land. — Christians recognize that capital property is not in itself a sin, but are aware of the Savior's warnings that it can become a snare for the soul (Mark 10:23-31; cf. 1 Tim. 6:17). On the other hand, while understanding that the drudgery of labor is one of the curses of sin, they are aware of the dignity of work and put the capacity of the spiritual man to work in a zestful carrying out of the opportunities of labor (Eph. 4:28). RRC

John Daniel, *The Church and Labor Management Problems of Our Day*, Bethlehem, Pa., 1947; *Christianity and Property* (ed. by Joseph F. Fletcher), Philadelphia, 1947.

Capital University. See *Ministry, Education of*, VI C.

Capito (Koepflin), Wolfgang (1478 to 1541). Received degree in medicine at University of Freiburg; turned to law, then to theology. In 1515 made Cathedral preacher at Basel; then preacher at Mainz; also attended Diet at Worms, 1521. Espousing the Reformation doctrines, his position at Mainz became intolerable; in 1523 he left for Strassburg, where he was chief preacher of the Church of St. Thomas. Was instrumental in drawing up Tetrapolitan Confession. Helped with Wittenberg Concordia in 1536, achieving agreement with Lutheran party.

Cappa. Originally the wide upper garment in the habit of monks, but in particular also the hood attached to a monk's vestment.

Cappadocian Theologians. Name applied to three great teachers of the Church who worked in Cappadocia, namely, Basil the Great, Gregory of Nazianz, and Gregory of Nyssa. Their influence shaped a large part of the theology of the Eastern Church in the fourth century and later.

Cappel, Louis. See *Reformed Confessions*, A 10.

Capuchins. A branch of the Franciscan order, founded in Italy, in 1528, with the purpose of restoring the original simplicity of the Franciscan Rule. It became independent in 1619. Its members are bound to observe silence all day except during two hours, to practice flagellation, to beg only enough for each day, to take no compensation for masses, and never to touch money. They wear coarse brown habits, long beards, and pointed hoods (*capuches*). The defection of their third general, Ochino of Siena, to Protestantism (1542) nearly destroyed the order, which then renounced all independent judgment in matters of faith and doctrine. Rapid growth came in the 16th century.

Cardinal Virtues. Plato (*Rep.* iv: 427) considered prudence, fortitude, temperance, and justice the chief virtues. Ambrose, according to tradition, adopted these into the Christian system. The "theological" virtues were added by the Church (faith, hope, charity; especially emphasized in the Orthodox Church).

Cardinals. Dignitaries of the Roman Church who rank immediately after the Pope and are his chief counselors. Their number, since 1586, is limited to 70, in three ranks: cardinal bishops (6), cardinal priests (50), and cardinal deacons (14). The places are rarely all filled. Together they form the Sacred College, over whose meetings (consistories) the Pope presides. Cardinals are created by the Pope, and while all nations are supposed to be considered, more cardinals are from Italy than from any other country. Though the Pope is not bound to ask or accept their advice, he consults them in all important matters, both in consistory and otherwise. The cardinals take an active part in the government of the Roman Church through the offices which they hold in the Curia * and various commissions. They frequently serve as legates. Since the 11th century the cardinals elect new Popes (see *Conclave*). Though in theory anyone, even a layman, is eligible to the papal chair, none who was not previously a cardinal has been elected since Urban VI (1378). Cardinals wear red birettas and robes, are styled Your Eminences, and claim the right of addressing emperors and kings as "brothers."

Carey, Felix. See *Burma*.

Carey, William (1761—1834). The pathfinder in England for modern missions. A shoemaker by trade, early interested in missions, studied theology, was pastor of Baptist churches, gave impetus to the founding of Baptist Missionary Society, Oct. 2, 1792. In 1793 he was sent to India. Finding English doors closed to him, he went to Serampore, Danish India, and with Marshman and Ward founded a press. He translated the Bible into six, the New Testament into 21, languages and dialects, and parts of the Bible into seven more dialects.

Caribbean Synod. See *United Lutheran Church, Synods of*, 3.

Carlsson, Erland. B. Aug. 24, 1822, Smaland, Sweden; graduated Univ. of Lund, 1848; served church in Vexio, Sweden, 1849—53; in Chicago and St. Charles, Ill., 1853—75; at Andover, Ill., 1875—87; business manager Augustana College 1887—89; president Augustana Synod 1881—88 and one of the directors of Augustana College from its founding to 1889; for many years editor of *Missionaeren*. D. Oct. 19, 1893, Lindsborg, Kans.

Carlstadt. See *Karlstadt*.

Carlyle, Thomas (1795—1881). B. at Ecclefechan, Dumfrieshire; attended University of Edinburgh; taught mathematics, then devoted himself to the study of German and worked his own way through an extensive reading course in history, poetry, romance, and other fields. His works may be divided into three main groups: I. Literary Criticism. A. German: *The Life of Frederick Schiller; William Meister's Apprenticeship on Travels; German Romance*. B. English: *Essay on Burns; Boswell's Life of Johnson; Sir Walter Scott*. II. Philosophical and Social Writings: *Sartor Resartus* (which depicts his spiritual struggle and is most representative of his genius); *The Life and Opinions of Herr Teufelsdroeckh* (the *Tailor Retailored* contains the famous chapters on "The Everlasting No," "Center of Indifference," and "The

Everlasting Yea"); *Chartism; On Heroes, Hero Worship, and the Heroic in History* (with the famous essay on Luther; advances Carlyle's doctrine that human affairs are shaped by great leaders); *Past and Present* (like *Chartism*, an attack on *laissez faire* and advocates governmental directives for both capital and labor, profit sharing, and educational legislation). III. Historical Writings: *The French Revolution: A History; Oliver Cromwell's Letters and Speeches; History of Frederick II of Prussia.* ECW

Carmelites. This order was founded as a hermit colony on Mount Carmel, in Palestine, during the 12th century. Violent persecution by Saracens later drove it to Europe, where it became a mendicant order. The Carmelites were protagonists of Mariolatry and introduced the scapular of Our Lady. Before the Reformation the order declined, but later became more ascetic and grew rapidly, reaching its zenith in the 17th century. The Carmelites have concocted some of the wildest pieces of ecclesiastical fiction. Their arrogant enumeration of all Prophets and Apostles among their ancient membership led to an acrimonious controversy with the Jesuits, which was ended only by papal command. A portion of the Carmelites are barefoot, and these eat no meat, sleep on a board, and live a highly ascetic life.

Carnival (from *carne vale*, farewell, O flesh). Applied to the period just preceding Lent (during which season the eating of meat is prohibited in the Roman Church), the period being characterized in many countries and districts by festivals of a more or less exuberant nature.

Caro, Joseph (1488—1575). Spanish Jew; wrote *Shulhan Aruk*, authoritative work on Jewish laws and ceremonies.

Carol. A popular spiritual song for festival occasions, particularly a spiritual folk song for the Christmas season, the best ones having come into vogue in Germany, England, and France during the Middle Ages and after the Reformation.

Caroline Books. Books ascribed to Charlemagne opposing decrees of the Second Council of Nicaea.

Caroline Islands. A large archipelago in the western Pacific Ocean, containing about 525 coral islands. Area, 560 sq. mi. Population, 140,000 Micronesians.

Formerly belonged to Germany; from 1914 to 1947 a Japanese mandate; since 1947 a U. S. trusteeship. Missions by the American Board of Commissioners for Foreign Missions; Liebenzeller Mission (before World War I). The Roman Catholic Church is also active. See also *Polynesia*.

Carpenter, William (1762—1833). Lutheran pastor; b. near Madison, Va.; soldier in Revolutionary War; held charges in Madison County, Va., and Boone County, Ky.

Carpov, Jakob (1699—1768). Lecturer at Jena and Weimar on Wolffian philosophy; sought to demonstrate dogmatics by mathematical method; wrote *Theologia Revelata Dogmatica Methodo Scientifica Adornata.*

Carpzov. Renowned family of lawyers and theologians. *Benedikt* (1595 to 1666). Professor and judge at Leipzig; in his *Iurisprudentia Ecclesiastica* he established scientifically the "episcopal system" of church polity. — *Johann Benedikt the Elder,* his brother (1607 to 1657). Professor at Leipzig; wrote best commentary on the Symbolical Books, *Isagoge in Libros Symbolicos.* — *Johann Benedikt the Younger,* son of the preceding (1639—99). Professor and pastor at Leipzig; opponent of Pietism, especially of Spener. — *Samuel Benedikt,* brother of preceding (1647—1707). Spener's successor as court preacher at Dresden. — *Johann Gottlob,* son of preceding (1679—1767). Superintendent at Luebeck; very learned and author of *Introductio in Libros Veteris Testamenti* and of treatises against Pietists and Moravians. — *Johann Benedikt,* grandson of Johann Benedikt the Younger (1720—1803). Professor at Leipzig and Helmstedt; opponent of Rationalism.

Cartesianism. The philosophic views of Descartes, especially his dualism and occasionalism.

Carthage, Canon of. A resolution or canon of the Council of Carthage, held in the year 397. This canon (No. 39) lists the books of the New Testament as we now have it: four Gospels, the Book of the Acts of the Apostles, thirteen Epistles of the Apostle Paul, the Epistle to the Hebrews, two Epistles of Peter, three Epistles of John, the Epistle of James, the Epistle of Jude, the Revelation of John.

Carthage, Synods and Councils * of Since Carthage was, for several centuries, the center of North African

Christianity, many important meetings were held there. Even in the third century, particularly about the middle of the century, at the time of Cyprian and afterward, synods were held there at which as many as seventy-one bishops were in attendance. Some of the chief resolutions at this time concerned the form of penance. During the fourth and at the beginning of the fifth century a number of councils were held there, most of which were held on account of the Donatist controversy. At this time also were held the councils of Carthage: the First Council of Carthage, between 345 and 348, which was attended by fifty bishops, and the Second Council of Carthage, in 390, at which sixty bishops were present. A general African council was held at Hippo, near Carthage, in 393. This is notable for its complete list of the New Testament books. During the time when Augustine * was a bishop, a number of synods were held in connection with the Pelagian controversy. Among the last important synods held at Carthage was that of 419, attended by 217 bishops, and that of 422, both of them showing that a certain feeling of independence, which had always been noticeable in North Africa, was still in evidence. For references see *Councils*.

Carthusians. A monastic order, noted for the uncommon severity of its practices. Disheartened with the degeneracy of the Church in his time, Bruno of Cologne, about 1086, formed a colony of hermits in the lofty Valley of Cartusia (Chartreuse), near Grenoble, France. He did not intend to found an order and wrote no rule; nevertheless, the Carthusian order grew from his example and was officially recognized in 1170. The boast of Carthusians is that they alone among monastics have never required reforms. The rule prescribes practical isolation, not only from the world, but also from brother monks. Each has his own cell. Manual labor, study, prayer, and contemplation follow in prescribed order. The smallest details of life are regulated. Not even the sick receive meat. The order, never very large, has about 26 monasteries.

Cartwright, Peter (1785—1872). Methodist preacher; little formal education; licensed exhorter (1802); deacon (1806); presiding elder (1812); moved from Kentucky to Illinois (1823); known for vigorous sermons and "muscular" Christianity.

Cartwright, Thomas (1535—1603). Puritan. B. at Hertfordshire, England; professor at Cambridge; attacked prelacy, presently to be defended by Hooker; championed Presbyterian polity; drew up *Holy Discipline* for Presbyterian congregations; d. at Warwick.

Carus, Paul (1852—1919). German-American editor and author; edited *The Open Court, The Monist;* in his religious (especially Oriental) and philosophical writings he held that religion must be purified by scientific criticism.

Cary, Lott. First American Negro missionary to Africa. B. 1780 in Virginia as a slave; converted 1807; bought his freedom; founded Richmond Foreign Missions Society, 1813, and the Richmond African Baptist Missionary Society, 1815, by which Cary and Collin Teague were sent to Liberia, 1822. Cary was later Governor of Liberia. D. in Africa, 1828.

Cary, Phoebe (1824—71). Sister of Alice Cary, with whom she moved from her home in Ohio to New York, N. Y., their mutual affection attracting much interest; poetical gift of both of about equal merit, both contributing some hymns; the most popular hymn of Phoebe Cary: "One Sweetly Solemn Thought."

Casas, Bartolomé de las (1474 to 1566). Spanish priest and missionary; became acquainted with the natives of the West Indies and Mexico and was formally declared their protector; hostility of the conquistadores put many obstructions in his way, but he continued his work; bishop of Ciapa, Mexico (1544—47 or 51); wrote *General History of the Indies.*

Casaubon, Isaac (1559—1614). Famous French classicist, ranking immediately after Scaliger. Reformed theologian. Born at Geneva; professor of Greek there, then at Montpellier; royal librarian at Paris; prebendary of Canterbury, Westminster.

Case, Shirley Jackson (1872—1947). Studied at Acadia (N. B., Canada) Univ., Yale Univ., Univ. of Marburg; taught at Yale Divinity School, at Cobb Divinity School; from 1933 dean of Divinity School, Univ. of Chicago, editor *Journal of Religion;* author and lecturer, ordained Baptist, liberal.

Caspari, Carl Paul (1815—92). B. at Dessau of Jewish parents; d. at Christiania; baptized, 1838; studied at Leipzig, called as lector to Christiania in 1847, in 1857 full professor. He was a strict orthodox Lutheran and exerted great influence in Norway.

Caspari, Karl Heinrich. Lutheran. B. 1815 at Eschau; d. 1861 as pastor in Muenchen; wrote *Geistliches und Weltliches*, *Der Schulmeister und sein Sohn;* also on the Catechism.

Caspari, Walter. B. 1847; till 1885 pastor, then professor of practical theology and university preacher at Erlangen. Contributed many articles to reviews and cyclopedias.

Cassel Colloquy. An earlier discussion on the doctrine of the Lord's Supper took place, in 1534, between Bucer (Butzer) and Melanchthon. A more solemn and official colloquy at Cassel, at the instigation of Landgrave William IV, in 1661, was held between the Lutheran theologians Peter Musaeus and John Hennichen and the Reformed theologians Sebastian Curtius and John Hein. The doctrines of the Lord's Supper, of predestination, of the relation of the two natures in Christ, and of Baptism were discussed. The plan of the meeting was to determine the consensus first and then to make an attempt to overcome the dissensus. The Lutherans made such significant concessions that the advantage clearly lay on the Reformed side.

Cassian, John (ca. 360—ca. 435). Monk and theologian; ordained a deacon by Chrysostom; lived among monks of Egypt for a time; founded monastery at Marseilles; among his writings: *De Institutis Coenobiorum* (introduced monastic ideals of East in the West), *Collationes Patrum*, and *De Incarnatione Christi;* opposed Augustine's view of predestination on the one hand, and Pelagianism on the other.

Cassiodorus (ca. 490—580). An early contemporary of Boethius who excelled as a writer and scholar. Cassiodorus founded a monastery for the purpose of perpetuating early Greek culture and wrote a number of treatises and books on the liberal arts and on music in which he ascribed to music various moral potentialities and effects.

Cassock. See *Vestments, Clerical.*

Castalio (Castellio), **Sebastian** (1515 to 1563). B. at Savoy; French Reformed; rector of Latin School at Geneva; professor of Greek at Basel; advocated religious toleration (opposed burying of Servetus); Latin and French translations of Bible; d. at Basel.

Caste. See *Brahmanism*, 3; *Hinduism*, 3.

Castigationes Paternae. Chastisements of God, which flow not from wrath, but from love (Ps. 94:12; Heb. 12:6; Rev. 3:19).

Casuistics. See *Casuistry.*

Casuistry. A branch of theological knowledge related to pastoral theology, although usually regarded as a branch of ethics, dealing with the solution of doubtful cases of conscience or questions of right and wrong according to Scripture. Casuistics, as it is also called, must not sink to a mere outward legalism, but should be based at all times upon the evangelical understanding of norm of human conduct taught in the Bible, with the law of love as the governing principle.

The Jewish *Talmud* shows the absurdities to which casuistry may attain. The Roman Catholic system of penance and absolution led to the writing of books on casuistry which listed sins and weighed circumstances with dialectical skill. One of the earliest of such works is Pennaforti's *Summa de Casibus Poenitentialibus.* Others followed (*Astenana, Angelica, Pisana, Bartholina, Pacifica, Rosella*). The Jesuits introduced the word *Moral Theology* for casuistry (e. g., Ligoro, *Theologia Moralis*, Paris, 1852). Luther's *De Libertate Christiana* struck at the very roots of Catholic casuistry by emphasizing that the individual must stand or fall by himself. Melanchthon's *Consilia* is an example of early Lutheran casuistry. Other Lutherans who wrote on casuistry: Balduin, Koenig, Osiander, Olearius, Dannhauer. Early Reformed work: Perkins, *The Whole Treatises of Cases of Conscience, Distinguished into Three Books*, London, 1602, 1606. Modern Lutheran treatments of casuistry are to be sought in books on Pastoral Theology,* Ethics,* and works treating phases of Christian Life.

Caswall, Edward (1814—78). Educated at Oxford; in office near Salisbury; joined Roman Church in 1850, lived at Oratory, Edgbaston, rest of his life; among his hymns: "O Jesus, King Most Wonderful."

Catacombs. Caverns, grottoes, and subterranean passages, partly natural, partly enlarged by excavating the tufa and sandstone beneath and near certain cities, chiefly in the countries bordering on the Mediterranean Sea, many of them having their origin in quarries. There are catacombs in Syria, Persia, and among the Oriental nations. Those of Upper Egypt are notable for their extent. At Gela, Agrigentum, and Syracuse, in Sicily, there are caverns which rank with the principal monuments of this kind, as well from their extent and depth, as from their architectural ornaments and from historical recollections attached to them. The catacombs in the tufa mountains of Capo di Monte, near Naples, were explored thoroughly by Celano in the middle of the seventeenth century. They consist of subterranean galleries, halls, rooms, basilicas, and rotundas, which extend to the distance of two Italian miles. But the most noted catacombs are those of Rome, along the Via Appia, especially those of Balbina and of Calixtus, that of Domitilla, on the Via Ardeatina, and that of Lucina on the Via Ostiensis. These and other catacombs are composed of practically interminable subterranean galleries, extending beneath the city itself as well as the neighboring country for 526 miles, in six stories of passageways. Along the corridors are horizontal excavations in the walls, which are often widened out into cells or small rooms. Here the dead were deposited, usually in sarcophagi, their total number being estimated at six million. The larger chambers, including the tombs of martyrs, were called *cryptae;* ordinary chambers, *cubicula;* the horizontal tombs, *sepulcra* or *loca.* However, while the catacombs were primarily burial places, being used as such also by the Christians (frequently during persecutions), some of whom, in fact, constructed such galleries for their own use and that of their brethren, some of the crypts were expressly designed for Christian worship, as, for example, that of Miltiades in S. Calixtus. A still larger chapel is a crypt in the Ostrian cemetery, which is divided into nave, presbytery, and apse. Still another very interesting place of worship is the Capella Graeca in S. Priscilla, especially on account of its beautiful decorations. After the year 410, in which the invasion of Alaric took place, the catacombs were no longer used as burial places, and a few centuries later even the crypts of the martyrs were abandoned, their bones having meanwhile, in most cases, been removed to the altar crypts of various churches which bore their names. During the siege of Rome by the Lombards the catacombs were in part destroyed and soon after became entirely inacces-

sible, so that they were practically forgotten, the first excavations in recent times having been made in the sixteenth century. The catacombs are of particular significance today because of the samples they contain of early Christian frescoes, such as that of the Good Shepherd and The Madonna with Child, both dating from the 3d century.

Walter Lowrie, *Monuments of the Early Church*, Macm., 1923.

Catechetical Schools. See *Schools, Early Christian.*

Catechetics. 1. That branch of religious education dealing with the theory and method of teaching Christian doctrine, particularly to children and to such adults as are candidates for church membership. The term is derived from κατηχέω, meaning "to instruct by word of mouth," hence it referred more particularly to oral instruction, usually of an informal type. But by the thirteenth century catechetics had acquired the connotation of instruction in the form of questions and answers. However, not until Luther was the word *catechismus* applied to a book. Luther used the term because he felt such a book would meet the needs of oral instruction though he had no thought of standardizing or systematizing the type of instruction. In the course of time, catechetics has become associated with a systematic questioning on the basis of a catechism.

2. Since the essence of Christianity is based on a faith grounded on knowledge and since Christ commanded His followers to build the Church by teaching and baptizing, it was self-evident from the time of its founding that instruction in doctrine be a most important consideration of the Church. In the Apostolic Church there were two patterns of education, one for the Jewish converts and one for Gentiles. The former was quite simple. The pattern for the Jews had two phases, the one that they recognize Jesus as the promised Messiah and the other that they understand the place of the Law in the New Testament Church. Traces of a pattern for Gentile converts can be seen in the writings of Paul, where we find references to instruction in the Christian faith (Rom. 16:7; 1 Cor. 15: 3-5) and morals (Rom. 6:17; Eph. 4:20).

3. Up to the time of the persecutions (ca. A. D. 200) the type of instruction seems to have been of a more informal nature, though the earlier writings show that the Church Fathers attempt-

ed to systematize the doctrines. With the persecutions the Church became more cautious in the reception of new members. There was now a longer period of probation and preparation, which practice led to a distinct classification called the catechumenate. While the practice was far from uniform, there was a semblance of a pattern. One of the clearest is that given by Origen of Alexandria (d. 254). He tells us that there were three distinct stages in the catechumenate period already in his time. In the first stage there was a preliminary inquiry concerning the individual's character and occupation. This was followed by a brief private instruction. The second stage began with the admission of the candidate as one of the *audientes*. He was now permitted to attend the first part of the public service (*missa catechumenorum*) and sometimes was instructed further privately. After a period of probation, lasting sometimes as long as three years, the individual became a *competent*. There was further inquiry whether the candidate was still fit morally. This was followed by some immediate instruction for Baptism, after which he was admitted into the *missa fidelium*, where the Lord's Supper was celebrated. After the period of the persecutions the catechumenate declined for many reasons, chief of which was the large number of persons who wanted to become Christians because it was the popular thing to do. This made thorough instruction impossible.

4. From the seventh to the twelfth century religious education waned. Mass Baptisms and group decisions made it practically impossible to carry on a systematic form of catechetics. There were a few voices in the wilderness which protested this state of affairs. Men like Pirmin (d. 753), Alcuin (d. 804), together with Charlemagne and Rhabanus Maurus (d. 856), drew up instructions for the training of the members of the Church, but the influence of these men and others was limited.

5. Catechetical works in the stricter sense, though not yet called catechisms, date back to about 840, when Otfried, a monk in the cloister of Weissenburg in Alsatia, wrote a kind of catechism explaining the mortal sins, the Apostles' Creed, the Athanasian Creed, the Lord's Prayer, and the Gloria in Excelsis. The first catechism in the form of questions and answers was written by Bruno, bishop of Wuerzburg (d. 1045).

6. Among the pre-Reformation sects the Waldensians, the Moravians, the Hussites, and the Wycliffites prepared catechisms in the form of questions and answers. They consisted chiefly of three parts explaining the Ten Commandments, the Creed, and the Lord's Prayer, while the Roman Catholic catechism in the Middle Ages had as a rule two divisions, the Lord's Prayer and the Creed.

7. With the Reformation many catechisms came on the scene. Bugenhagen, Melanchthon, Brenz are a few of the many who published various types of catechisms, some for the people and others for the clergy. Luther's *Small Catechism*, published in 1529, is the oldest catechism of the Church still in use. It was the culmination of several series of sermons beginning in 1516. Though only one of the many catechisms coming from this period, it soon outstripped others in its influence and importance and enjoyed translations in practically all the European languages. Its deeply evangelical note, which was not satisfied with a simple historic faith but emphasized a functional living Christianity, is undoubtedly the basis of its popularity. Luther's *Large Catechism* appeared in book form a few months earlier than the *Small Catechism*.

8. Through the action of the Council of Trent, Pope Pius IV in 1556 appointed four theologians to draw up a catechism to serve chiefly as a manual for catechists and preachers. The result of their effort is the *Roman Catechism* of 1566, which is still recommended for the clergy.

9. In the post-Reformation period throughout the Lutheran countries the catechism either by Luther or by one of the other reformers became an important element in the family worship and in the curriculum of the church and schools. In spite of earnest endeavors a tendency grew in many sections of the Church to allow the catechetical instruction to degenerate into mere rote learning of the chief parts of the catechism. When Pietism entered the German Church, notably through Spener, particular measures were taken to avoid this intellectualism. But the Rationalism which followed this period blighted the Church in Europe. The theory of the rationalists was that instruction in religion should not concern itself so much with imparting truths, but should follow the Socratic method of drawing the needed truths

out of the child. They failed to see that a Christian teacher was dealing not simply with reason and experience, but with revelation, which truths must be imparted. They also overlooked the fact that they were not dealing with mature minds, but with children. By the middle of the nineteenth century Luther's catechism was welcomed back into the schools of the greater part of Germany. In the Scandinavian churches Luther's catechisms never lost their hold and are still in use in the upper grades of the public elementary and secondary schools.

10. The Roman Catholic Church also felt the impact of Rationalism. Criticisms were heard that its catechisms "were too dry, too impractical, too scholastic, and not Christian enough." The dissatisfaction with the catechisms culminated in a series of attempts to produce more satisfactory texts, the majority of which bore the mark of Rationalism. As a reaction to this trend a spirit of Romanticism came into the Catholic Church which showed respect "amounting almost to fanaticism" to antiquity and especially to the Middle Ages.

11. When the Lutherans came to America, it was natural that they at first used the catechisms of their native land. Yet, American editions appeared at an early date. In fact, the very first book ever translated into the language of the American Indian was Luther's *Small Catechism*, which was translated by John Campanius in 1646, although it was not printed until 1696. Another early edition of the catechism came from the press of Benjamin Franklin in 1749. That year both the German and English edition appeared. Since then many hundreds of editions have been published in America in nearly all the languages spoken in the country. Among those which have had an important influence were the *Dresden Cross Catechism* and the explanation based on Conrad Dietrich, which was revised and published in St. Louis. Catechisms by Wm. Loehe, J. Stump, J. M. Reu, H. J. Schuh, and C. Gausewitz are among the older explanations of Luther's catechism. Among the Norwegians, Pontoppidan's and the Lund edition of Sverdup's have been preferred. The H. C. Schwan edition was popular in the Missouri Synod until a new synodical catechism appeared in 1943.

12. The catechism enjoyed a prominent position also in the Reformed branches of the Protestant Church. For example, in Scotland Calvin's catechism of 1545 held a dominant place. This was supplanted by an act of Parliament in 1648 by the shorter *Westminster Catechism*, which is still in use in the Presbyterian Church of Great Britain. In Holland and in the Palatinate of Germany, where the Dutch Reformed and German Reformed were prominent, the *Heidelberg Catechism* was used.

13. When the members of these various denominations came to America, they also brought with them the catechisms which they used in the homeland. In time, however, they were supplemented by the writings of Cotton, Harris, and Watts. Much of Cotton's catechism was incorporated in the well-known *New England Primer*.

14. The outstanding catechism of the Roman Catholic Church in America is without question the so-called *Baltimore Catechism*, which appeared in 1885. A Committee of Bishops has now revised this catechism, although various other catechisms are in use in the different dioceses.

15. While catechetics has disappeared in many sections of the Christian Church, it still holds an important place among the Lutherans and the Roman Catholics of today. Efforts are being made to keep abreast with the recent findings in the field of education and apply them also to catechetics.

16. Some of the more important trends in the Lutheran Church are evident in the publications of H. J. Boettcher, J. A. Dell, Henry P. Grimsby, O. F. Nolde, and Jacob Tanner. A distinctive characteristic of these studies is to break away from the formal system of questioning and to return to the original concept of catechetics, which combines the discussion and the expository method in a manner that the doctrine becomes personal and functional in the lives of the children. Pupil activity is emphasized. In line with this trend a committee representing several Lutheran synods is now (1948) producing a series of filmstrips visualizing the catechism. ACR

I. *Historical Studies.* F. Bente, "Historical Introductions to the Symbolical Books of the Evangelical Lutheran Church," in *Concordia Triglotta*, CPH, 1921; Th. Graebner, *History of the Catechism*, CPH, 1928; J. M. Reu, *Catechetics or Theory and Practice of Religious Instruction*, Chicago, 1927; J. M. Reu, *Quellen zur Geschichte des kirchlichen Unterrichts in der evangelischen Kirche Deutschlands zwischen 1530 und 1600;* J. M. Reu, *Luther's Small Catechism;* L. J. Sherrill, *The Rise of Christian Education,* New York, 1944.

II. *Theory of Teaching.* 1) Lutheran. References above; G. H. Gerberding, *The Lutheran Catechist,* Philadelphia, 1910; J. E. Herzer, *Evangelisch-lutherische Katechetik,* CPH, 1911. 2) Catholic. W. Faerber, *Catechism for the Catholic Parochial School of the United States,* St. Louis, 1937. A. N. Fuerst, *The Systematic Teaching of Religion,* New York, 1939; J. A. Weigand, *The Catechist and the Catechumen,* New York, 1924.

III. *Recent Lutheran Studies.* H. J. Boettcher, *Instructor's Manual for Luther's Small Catechism,* CPH, 1946; J. A. Dell, *Senior Catechism,* Columbus, 1939; H. P. Grimsby, *An Explanation of the Catechism,* Minneapolis, 1941; E. Kurth, *Catechetical Helps,* Brooklyn, 1935; O. F. Nolde, *Guidebook in Catechetical Instruction,* Philadelphia, 1929; J. Tanner, *The Junior Confirmation Book,* Minneapolis, 1943; J. Tanner, *The Senior Confirmation Book,* Minneapolis, 1941.

Catechisms. See *Catechetics.*

Catechisms, Luther's. Two books of religious instruction written by Luther for the use of old and young. Beginning with 1516, when Luther preached a series of sermons on the Ten Commandments, he did further preaching and writing on the Lord's Prayer (1517), again on the Ten Commandments (1518), which was followed during the next ten years by many studies in the Catechism and related subjects. Visiting Saxon churches, Luther found the people sunk in superstition and the pastors in ignorance and immorality, and in order to raise the standard, he preached a course of sermons in 1528 on the fundamentals of Christianity and used this material in writing his Catechisms, which were published in 1529. The two Catechisms were prepared simultaneously, but the *Small Catechism* appeared prior to the *Large Catechism.* The *Small Catechism,* in the form in which we have it now, dates from 1531 to 42. The parts on Confession and the Office of the Keys were added later. It is not yet certain whether Luther or his friend John Lang of Erfurt wrote "The Christian Questions."
— The Christian faith is not only to be learned, but also to be lived; how it is to be lived by everyone in the various walks and stations of life is plainly shown in the "Table of Duties," which was probably suggested by John Gerson's *Mode of Living for All the Faithful,* reprinted at Wittenberg in 1513. Probably Luther is not responsible for "What the Hearers Owe to Their Pastors" and "What Subjects Owe to Their Government."

The transcendent merits of both Catechisms gained for them an instant entrance into the home, the school, and the church, and they were soon confessed "as the Bible of the laity, wherein everything is comprised which is treated at greater length in Holy Scripture and is necessary for a Christian man to know for his salvation," as the Epitome of the *Formula of Concord* has it. The *Small Catechism* is undoubtedly the greatest book of instruction ever written, and the explanation of the Second Article is the greatest sentence from a pen not inspired. It is a confession of faith, and it can be prayed. The great historian von Ranke says: "Blessed is he that nourishes his soul with it, that holds fast to it! He possesses an imperishable comfort in every moment, under a thin shell the kernel of truth that will satisfy the wisest of the wise." McGiffert calls it "the gem of the Reformation."

The *Large Catechism* was written to aid pastors and fathers in teaching. It is practical, popular, and, at the same time, deep — an incomparable book. Von Zezschwitz cannot name many other writings that, next to the Bible itself, can more further a Christian and teacher in true faith and sound doctrine. In the Decalog we come to the knowledge of our sins, in the Creed to justification by faith in Christ, and in the Lord's Prayer is manifested the new life in the Spirit. The *Small Catechism* was soon translated into other languages, and for four hundred years it has been in constant use to train the young. The claim has been made that it has a wider circulation than any other book, the Bible alone excepted.

See references under *Catechetics;* Carl Bornhaeuser, *Der Ursinn des Kleinen Katechismus,* Bertelsmann, Guetersloh, rev. 1934; L. H. Koehler, "Luther's Catechism," *Abiding Word,* CPH.

Catechismus Romanus. See *Roman Catholic Confessions,* A 3.

Catechization. See *Catechetics.*

Catechumenate. See *Catechetics;* Christian Education, E 10.

Categorical Imperative. Term used by Kant to denote highest moral law, in so far as it demands absolute obedience, regardless of any possible advantage or pleasure, and by him stated thus: "Handle so, dass die Maxime deines Willens jederzeit zugleich als Prinzip einer allgemeinen Gesetzgebung gelten koenne" ("Act so that the maxim of thy will may at any time be adopted as a universal law"). Opposed to eudemonism.*

Catena (chain). A commentary composed of extracts from different authors elucidating a text, especially the Bible. Their composition dates from the fourth century to the close of the Middle Ages. Many extracts of otherwise unknown works have thus been preserved.

Cathari *(Catharists).* A Manichean sect practically identical with the Albigenses, found in various countries of western Europe, in northern Italy, in France, in Germany, and in Flanders. They were not sound in the doctrine of the Trinity, believed in a baptism of the Spirit in a very peculiar sense connected with ordination, but claimed to have a perfect degree of purity in doctrine and life. They flourished chiefly in the eleventh and twelfth centuries. The Pope proclaimed a crusade against them, but they flourished under persecution.

Catharina, Santa (Parana, and Other States), **Synod of.** An Evangelical Lutheran synod in Brazil, founded 1898, affiliated with the American Lutheran Church.

Catharsis, Mental. See *Psychology,* J 7.

Cathedral. The chief church of a diocese, containing the *cathedra,* or official throne, of the bishop of the diocese. Connected with a cathedral are a bishop, a dean and chapter, and various other dignitaries. There are many notable examples of superb art, both in architecture and in decoration, among the cathedrals of Europe, and their fame has extended throughout the world. Even in the Byzantine style there are some cathedral churches of unusual size and beauty. The most perfect church embodying the ideas and characteristics of the Byzantine style is the Hagia Sofia of Constantinople, which was built by Emperor Justinian from 532 to 537, after the destruction of the first Church of the Holy Wisdom. At the time of its completion it was considered the most gorgeous church in the world, and even today it ranks with the most beautiful edifices of its kind. It served as the see of the Eastern Patriarch. — The most majestic church of the second period of the Byzantine style is San Marco of Venice, built as a shrine for the relics of St. Mark, which were brought from Alexandria to Venice in 828. After the first structure had burned down, the present building was erected, the dedication taking place in 1094. It is an imposing structure, and many critics, including Ruskin, have almost exhausted the English language in describing its beauties. It is built according to the cruciform plan. "St. Mark's of Venice rivals St. Sophia in exquisite beauty of interior and excels it in ornate richness of the exterior." — Among other isolated instances of Byzantine influence in the West might be noted the Cathedral of Pisa with its tower. This cathedral has the basilican principle of length and peristyle and the regular cruciform shape, but its principal and most conspicuous feature is its Byzantine dome, this characteristic being found also in Ravenna and Aachen.

Among the cathedrals of the Romanesque period those of Tournay, Angouleme, Angiers, and Poitiers are masterpieces, the beauty of their façades being fully equaled by the disposition and ornamentation of the interior. The Minster of Cluny prepared the way for the transition to the late Romanesque. Its nave had barrel vaulting, the transepts cross-vaulting. The pilasters and pillars were constructed with the greatest technical skill to counteract the thrust of the arches. — Of the Norman cathedrals of England which have not been reconstructed in the Gothic style is the Cathedral of Durham. Here the flying buttress is employed to rest against the wall of the clerestory and to counteract the thrust of the main roof. The same principle is applied in the transept of the Cathedral of Ely. — In Sicily and southern Italy, where the Romanesque type was introduced during the Norman occupation, there are several monuments which are notable, especially the cathedrals of Palermo and Cefalu. A peculiarity in this entire part of Sicily is the use of Saracenic ornamentation. The Romanesque churches of Germany show a regular, rhythmic, consistent development of the fundamental ideas of the style. The steady progress of architecture was especially notable along the Rhine, the distinctive characteristic of the German Romanesque being the cube capital. The Cathedral of Speyer was rebuilt twice, because of floods and faults in the vaulting. In its final form it presented a three-aisled vaulted basilica with single transept and semicircular apse. The Cathedral of Mainz was modeled after that of Speyer, with minor changes, such as the omission of the ornamental half-column in the case of pilasters that received no thrust. The third cathedral belonging to this group is that of Worms. The round towers of this church flanking both the eastern and the western choir and the octagonal towers over the cross-vaulting of the transept and over the eastern apse are especially noteworthy. The Cathedral of Limburg is an example of the transition from the Romanesque to the Gothic, the round arches of its windows being very agreeably offset by the pointed arches of the inside wall and over the aisles. The same feature is found in the Cathedral of Magdeburg, one of the fine examples of German architecture during this period.

The birthplace of the Gothic style is the Isle de France, where the magnificent Cathedral of Notre Dame was erected between 1163 and 1235. The western façade was the last to be built, the towers being carried up to their present height, but no spires added. Although the unity of the original five-aisled plan has suffered somewhat on account of restorations and changes, the simple beauty of the structure appeals to every visitor. With the increasing floridity in style came a lighter construction of Gothic cathedrals. The Cathedral of Chartres (1195—1260) in its every line expresses daring and pride, mixed with sternness. The apse received an addition of three cells, or niches; nave and transept were three-aisled and of the same width. No less stately and beautiful was the Cathedral of Rheims (1211—95), whose appeal was enhanced by its historical associations. This church belongs to the period of the best development in France, everything being designed to assist the idea of length and growth. The Cathedral of Amiens (1220—88), in many respects the most gorgeous of all French churches, marks the turning point of Gothic art in France. It is 521 feet long, and its vault rises in a tapering arch to a height of 140 feet. But the excellent proportions of its construction are made secondary to the elaborate decoration of its arches and tympanum, with Scriptural reliefs, figures of saints, apostles, martyrs, and angels.

In England, national characteristics and racial development combined in impressing upon the Gothic style a peculiar dignified and challenging stateliness, without the softening features of freedom and grace, while at the same time the English cathedrals generally surpass their Continental rivals in beauty of detail and elegance of proportion, chiefly because the English were the first to grasp the decorative side of the Gothic style. Among the earlier structures, which also exhibit the features of successive periods, are the Cathedral of Canterbury, that of Lincoln, and that of Salisbury. Although Gothic features preponderate in these churches, yet the other characteristics are strong enough to stamp their peculiarity upon them. Next in order we have the Minster of Beverly, the Cathedral of Wells, and parts of the cathedrals of Rochester, Lincoln, Peterborough, and Ely. In all these churches the length of the choir becomes abnormally great, terminating invariably in a straight wall. Examples of the decorated style in England are the cathedrals of Exeter (1280—1370), Lichfield (1296—1420), York (1291—1388), and Wells. Of these, the Cathedral of York is considered by many critics the best exponent of the Gothic style in England, magnificent stateliness being expressed in almost every line of the building. Its façade is the most beautiful in England, although the enormous windows seem out of proportion.

In the countries of the Continent outside France, Italy has the Cathedral of Milan, the one true representative of Gothic art beyond the Alps; Spain has the Cathedral of Burgos, designed after that of Paris. Germany has several notable examples of Gothic art. Churches of the first rank are the Minster of Ulm and the Cathedral of Strassburg, the latter being notable for its single spire. Among the fine churches of Nuremberg that of St. Lorenz, a Lutheran cathedral, with its beautiful façade, is rightly given the first place. — Among the churches which have been erected since the force of the Gothic in Europe spent itself is St. Peter's of Rome, begun by Bramante, continued by Michelangelo, and finished by Fontana, its dome presenting the most beautiful and exalted outline of any edifice in the world. There is also St. Paul's of London, built by Sir Christopher Wren (1675—1710). It has the proportions of a Gothic cathedral, with rotunda and dome, the latter reaching the magnificent height of 360 feet. The best-known cathedral in America is St. John the Divine, New York. This church, 601 ft. in length, was begun in 1892, and is still unfinished. When complete it will be the third largest cathedral in the world. St. Peter's in Rome has an area of 227,069 sq. ft., Seville Cathedral 128,570, while St. John the Divine has an area of 109,082 sq. ft.

Like St. John the Divine, the Washington Cathedral is an Anglican church. The latter was begun in 1907 but is only partially completed. It is the only building entitled to the name of Washington Cathedral, as stipulated by an act of Congress passed in 1907.

There are a number of other cathedrals in America, and while each is a true cathederal — for instance, St. Patrick's of New York — yet the buildings themselves, in size and arrangement, frequently are but large parish churches serving the purpose of a cathedral.

Some of the more notable Lutheran cathedrals are located in Uppsala, Sweden; Oslo, Norway; Copenhagen, Denmark; Helsinki, Finland; and Rejkjavik, Iceland. There are none in the Western Hemisphere.

Catherine of Alexander, St. A royal virgin who confessed Christ at a feast of Maximinus and, according to tradition, was beheaded after the spiked wheel broke at her touch. All information regarding her is legendary.

Catherine de Medici (1519—89). French queen; three of her four sons were rulers of France and through them her influence was felt. Her unscrupulousness is shown by the manner in which she played one side against the other in the religious wars and her responsibility for the massacre of St. Bartholomew.

Catholic. This word, taken from the Greek and meaning "universal," was first applied to the Christian Church as a whole in a letter of St. Ignatius (ca. 110): "Where Christ is, there is the Catholic Church." It was later applied to the true Church in distinction from heretical sects. The word made its appearance in the Third Article of the Apostles' Creed in the fourth century. When the Eastern and Western Churches separated, the former called itself the Orthodox, the latter the Catholic Church. Since the Reformation the word has become an appellative for the papal Church, often with the prefix "Roman" (though also Greek Catholic, Anglo-Catholic). Some Protestants have tried to rescue the term, but as it is not of Biblical origin, no more principle is involved than in the analogous restriction of the term "American."

Catholic Action. See *Roman Catholic Church.*

Catholic Apostolic Church. 1. This denomination, sometimes known as Irvingites, originated under the preaching of the famous Scotch-Presbyterian pulpit orator Edward Irving (1792—1834). The social, political, and religious upheavals of the years 1790 to 1820 in Europe, particularly the French Revolution and the Napoleonic wars, led many people to look for the immediate return of Christ. However, these people felt that the Church was not ready for the Lord's second coming, because the Church was not in possession of the New Testament charismatic gifts. Irving believed that the return of Christ was dependent upon the presence of a living and active apostolate. He held that the premillennial coming of Christ was impossible as long as the Church continued in the crime of neglecting to re-establish the fivefold office of apostles, prophets, evangelists, pastors, and teachers according to Eph. 4:11. He interpreted Acts 1:11 to mean that there must be twelve apostles at Christ's return as there were twelve at His ascension. In 1830 a number of individuals claimed to have received the apostolic charismatic gifts, such as speaking in tongues, the gift of prophecy, and divine healing, and this raised the hope that soon also twelve apostles would be appointed by the Holy Spirit. Another strong supporter of the movement was Thomas Carlyle. On July 14, 1835, twelve men who claimed to have been appointed as apostles were commissioned to inaugurate the real apostolic mission to the Gentiles, of which St. Paul, as one born out of due time, 1 Cor. 15:8, had only barely made the beginning. Seven congregations in London were organized according to the pattern of the seven Asiatic congregations, a manifesto was issued by the hierarchy to the heads of the European states to prepare for the Lord's imminent coming and the establishment of the millennium by accepting the decrees of this newly formed hierarchy and submitting to the "holy sealing" by the apostles as a condition of salvation. Romanizing trends were introduced in the cultus (elaborate vestments), in doctrine (the Lord's Supper a sacrifice, transubstantiation), and in church government (a hierarchy with presumptuous claims). The movement spread to Continental Europe, particularly to Germany. But when one after the other of the "twelve apostles" died before the Lord's return, a sharp division of opinion arose as to the number of apostles, some contending that as there were only twelve in the New Testament Church, so that there can be no more nor fewer than twelve in the end period. This party believed that as the first apostolate was unable to prepare the world for the millennium, so also the apostolate of the 19th century was unable to cope with the wickedness of the world. This party, now known as the Catholic Apostolic Church, has no "living apostles," the last having died in 1901, and no ordinations to the priesthood or the episcopate are possible today. The local churches are governed by "angels" and "priests," and the members await patiently and inactively the Lord's further directions.

2. In Germany, however, Bishop Schwarz headed a group which contended that as Apostles were added to the original twelve, such as Paul, Barnabas, and Silas, so the Holy Spirit may at any time inspire new selections "through the spirit of prophecy." A priest named Preuss was thus selected in 1862. Later Schwarz, Krebs, Niehaus, and others in Saxony, and John Erb of Chicago were selected as apostles. This group, organized as the New Apostolic Church in 1906, is the more active of the two. The theology of both groups centers in the belief that an apostolate is essential to the Church. The apostles are viewed as the spiritual canals who supplement the Bible with their teaching; complete the work of the Atonement; govern the Church; give efficacy to the sacraments; impose the tithe as due Christ the High Priest and Chief Apostle; and through the laying on of hands, the "holy sealing," prepare men for Christ's second coming. See *Religious Bodies* (U. S.), *Bibliography*. FEM

Catholic Church. See *Roman Catholic Church.*

Catholic Church, Liberal. See *Liberal Catholic Church.*

Catholic Clubs. See *Students, Spiritual Care of, A.*

Catholic Directory. Published annually by P. J. Kennedy and Sons, New York, this large volume gives information on the hierarchy and the various activities and institutions of the Roman Catholic Church.

Catholic Education in the United States. See *Roman Catholic Education in the United States.*

Catholic Emancipation Act. British act (1829) repealing laws placing civil strictures on Roman Catholics.

Catholic Lay Societies, Religious Orders, etc. See *Roman Catholic Lay Societies; Orders in the United States.*

Catholicos. The official title of certain Oriental prelates, especially Nestorian and Armenian patriarchs.

Causae Secundae. A term used to denote the secondary causes which God uses to preserve and direct the things which He has made (Ps. 127:1). In the divine act of concurrence both God works and the means work. To emphasize this truth, Lutheran dogmaticians have said that the divine concurrence is not previous (*actio praevia*), but the operation of God and that of the means is numerically one (*una numero actio*).

Causative Authority. A term used in describing the power of the Bible of attesting itself as the divine truth, independently of any external proof (1 Cor. 2:4, 5; 1 Thess. 2:13, 14; 1 Cor. 1:5, 6; John 7:17).

Caux, Bernard de. See *Inquisition, 5.*

Cavaselas, Nickalaos (d. 1371). Archbishop of Thessalonica; supported Greek rights and independence against Roman Church; wrote books with a strong mystic trend, e. g., *Exposition of the Greek Liturgy, The Union of Man with Jesus Christ.*

Cave, William (1637—1713). Anglican patristic scholar. B. at Pickwell; rector at London; canon of Windsor; vicar of Isleworth; d. at Windsor; wrote *Lives of the Fathers;* etc.

Cawood, John (1775—1852). Educated at Oxford; held various positions as clergyman, the last as incumbent at Bewdley, Worcestershire; among his hymns: "Hark! What Mean Those Holy Voices"; "Almighty God, Thy Word Is Cast."

Cazalla, Augustino (1510—59). Spanish martyr. Accompanied Charles V to Smalkald War; lost faith in Catholicism; arraigned by Inquisition and executed as a Lutheran heretic in first auto-da-fé.

Cecilia, Saint. A Christian martyr who died about A. D. 230, her feast day in the calendar being November 22. Considered the patron saint of music, in particular of church music, she is credited by legend with having invented the organ.

Celano, Thomas a. Hymn writer of the 13th century, born in Italy, later a pupil of Francis of Assisi, whose biography he wrote; joined the Franciscan order when it was founded; subsequently custodian of the convents of Worms and Cologne and afterwards of the Rhine districts; composed sequences: "Fregit Victor Virtualis" and "Sanctitatis Nova Signa," but above all the world-renowned "Dies Irae, Dies Illa" ("Day of Wrath, That Day of Mourning").

Celebes. An island of Dutch East Indies. Area, 71,150 sq. mi.; population, estimated at 2,000,000; mostly Malays and Indonesians. Islam and Hinduism are reigning religions. Missions: The Netherlands Missionary Society, active for more than ninety years, established a strong native Christian Church among the Alifurs, whole districts being Christianized.

Celestines. The name of two minor monastic societies, both long extinct, which owed their origin to Pope Celestine V.

Celibacy. Celibacy, the renunciation of marriage, is required in the Roman Church of all who enter major orders, therefore of subdeacons, deacons, priests, and bishops. A married man can be ordained only if he separates from his wife with her consent.

The idea that the single state was more perfect and holy than the married may have been influenced by Jewish (Essenes, Therapeutae) and pagan conceptions. The notion is present in the apocryphal *Acts of Paul and Tekla.* Many Christians soon looked for this "perfection" in their shepherds and gave preference to unmarried pastors. The Synod of Nicaea (325) was asked to prohibit the marriage of clergy and, although the arguments urged by Romanists today were presented. it refused to take such a stand. The Synod of Gangra (355?) found it necessary to raise its voice

against those who refused to accept the ministrations of married clerics. Pope Siricius, however, forbade the marriage of priests (386), claiming that they could not properly perform their spiritual duties if hindered by "obscene desires." Later popes confirmed this edict, and the synods of the West issued canons in the same spirit. For six hundred years the priesthood struggled openly and in secret against the tyranny. Wives were considered concubines and children bastards by Rome. The Synods of Pavia (1018) and Amalfi (1189) adjudged them to actual slavery. Gregory VII decided the struggle for the Papacy. He renewed enactments according to which a married priest who said Mass and a layman who took Communion at his hands were both excommunicated. When married priests opposed Gregory's enactments, he incited the nobility and people against them. Every species of brutality, including mutilation, torture, and death, was visited on the priests and their families. Thus the yoke of celibacy was fixed on the Roman clergy, and though their struggles continued long after Gregory's time, the issue was never again in doubt.

The Reformation called attention to the vicious results of the institution, which were evident on every hand (see Art. XXIII of the Augsburg Confession and the Apology). Emperor Ferdinand and the sovereigns of France, Bavaria, and Poland asked the Council of Trent to consider the repeal of celibacy, but the Council decreed: "If anyone saith that clerics constituted in sacred orders . . . are able to contract marriage and that, being contracted, it is valid . . . let him be accursed." (Sess. XXIV, can. 9.) "If anyone saith that it is not better and more blessed to remain in virginity or in celibacy than to be united in matrimony, let him be accursed." (*Ibid.,* can. 10.) Rome knew too well the advantages of having at the disposal of the hierarchy a priesthood free from every ordinary tie and attachment. Yet the Council found it necessary to make special provisions regarding the "illegitimate sons of clerics." (Sess. XXV, chap. 15.) — Romanists draw specious arguments from such passages as Matt. 19:12; 1 Cor. 7:8, 32, 33, passages which refer to voluntary continence and cannot be applied to enforced celibacy (see 1 Cor. 7:7, 9). The position of the Apostles appears from 1 Cor. 9:5; 1 Tim. 3:2; Titus 1:6; the mark of Antichrist is foretold 1 Tim. 4:3. By making celibacy obligatory, Rome imposes a tyrannous yoke on many who have not received the gift of virginity from God (1 Cor. 7:7), exposes them to temptation, and opens the door to gross immorality and unnatural vices. See *Marriage.*

H. C. Lea, *History of Sacerdotal Celibacy,* Macm., 1907 (2 vols.); O. Hardman, *The Ideals of Asceticism,* Macm., 1924; "Monasticism" in *Cambridge Medieval History,* vol. I, ch. 18; A. Karlstadt, *Super coelibatu monachatu et viduitatate Axiomata perpensa Vittembergae,* Wittemberg, 1521. See also *Asceticism.*

Cellarius, John (1496—1542). Professor of Hebrew at Heidelberg, Leipzig, and Wittenberg, introduced the Lord's Supper celebration in the German language at Frankfurt; staunch supporter of the Luth. Reformation.

Cellarius, Martin (1497 — 1564). Studied under Eck; friend of Melanchthon; won for Reformation by Luther's *On the Liberty of a Christian Man;* spoke and wrote against Anabaptists, but finally joined them; later gave up his enthusiasm and went to Basel, becoming a professor of rhetoric in 1536 and of theology in 1544.

Celsus. Pagan philosopher, second century; first known literary opponent of Christianity. Wrote *Logos Alethes,* A.D. 178, which was lost, but known to us through Origen's reply *Kata Kelsou,* A.D. 248. First attacks Christianity from Jewish viewpoint, then attacks Judaism and Christianity from pagan viewpoint. Christianity is height of nonsense, Christ a mere juggler.

Celtic Church, The. 1. Many facts have been brought to light within the past fifty years in regard to the Celtic Church. Once looked upon as a half-mythical organization, whose true history was obscured by a heavy veneer of traditions and contradictions, careful historical research has revealed a religious organization of great influence and of almost unmatched missionary achievement. It played an important part in the evangelization not only of the British Isles, but of Gaul, Switzerland, and even Italy and the Germanic lands.

2. Among the founders of the Celtic Church was Martin of Tours, a Celtic church leader who had little sympathy with Latin Christianity. He established his training center at Tours, and his organization was Celtic rather than Roman. It was a missionary training school and not a monastery, and its head was given the Syrian name of *ab* and not abbot. Martin of Tours was a great opponent of the Arians and was scourged by that heretical sect because of his fearless testimony in defense of the Second Article of the Nicene Creed. His missionary training center was called *Logo-Tigiac,* or the "bright white house."

3. One of Martin's most famous pupils was Ninian, a native of what was then known as Pictland and which we call Scotland. Ninian was educated at Tours and sent by St. Martin to Pictland to evangelize the northern lands. About the year 397 Ninian established a great missionary training school, known by the Celts as a *muinntir,* at Whithorn in southwestern Scotland. He named it *Candida Casa,* or the "bright white hut." There he trained hundreds of missionaries who went throughout the British Isles, preaching to the pagan Picts.

4. The next famous Celtic pioneer was Piran, an Irish Pict. His true period seems to have been between ca. A. D. 352 and 430, although some historians have placed him a century later. He established a training center at Perranzabuloe in Cornwall, where he trained men who were sent on preaching tours throughout the West of England and Cornwall. The ruins of his little church at Perranzabuloe were discovered in 1835 and exist to this day.

5. Piran was followed by the famous St. Patrick, who was born about the year 389 and died in 461. His work in Ireland is well known, although it is not correct to say that he was the first missionary there. St. Ninian's missionaries had done much to prepare the ground for Patrick in Ireland. St. Patrick was of the Celtic Church, and at no time was he in communion with the Latin Church.

6. St. Finbar (ca. 490—578), with his great *muinntir,* or training school, at Maghbile in Ulster, trained men and directed an important missionary movement in Pictland, or Scotland. St. Cainnech (516—600), an Irish Pict, labored among the western Picts and in Pictland of Alba, establishing training centers in Pictland, and later the noted Achadh-Bo in Ireland. One of his distinguished pupils was Ferghil, an early missionary to Salzburg. St. Kentigern, or Mungo (ca. 518—603), was

not only a preacher of matchless eloquence, but a great pioneer in missionary expansion. One of his most important training centers was at Glasgow. St. Petrock, who flourished about the year 550, worked with conspicuous success in Cornwall and Devon.

7. One of the most eminent Celtic leaders was St. Columba the Gaidheal (521—597), who established a famous school on the Island of Hy, now called Iona. Here he trained hundreds, if not thousands, of missionaries who ranged throughout the British Isles and Continental Europe. Until fifty years ago it was assumed by many historians that Columba was responsible for the evangelization of Britain and much of the north part of Continental Europe. Careful research has dimmed his missionary achievements somewhat by revealing the fact that careless historians in ancient times gave Columba credit for much of the work really accomplished by Ninian, Piran, Patrick, Finbar, Cainnech, Kentigern, and scores of other earlier missionaries and contemporaries.

8. St. Comgall the Great (ca. 525 to 602) was a famous preacher as well as the founder of an influential training center at Bangor of the Ards in Ulster. The educational standards of his school were high. One of his pupils was Columbanus, who became a famous missionary in Gaul, Switzerland, Italy, and South Germany, and whose most famous school was Bobbio, noted for its fine library. Yet another pupil was St. Gall, founder of the great training center in Switzerland, which was taken over in 748 by the Latin Church.

9. Other famous Celtic leaders were Moluag, Aidan, Maelrubha, Kilian, Drostan and Dewi. Kilian became a noted missionary to Wuerzburg and Heilbronn. Dewi, now called David, was the great missionary to Wales.

10. The Celtic Church flourished from A. D. 420 to 890, a period of 470 years. It antedated the Latin Church in northern Europe by 177 years and was a powerful rival of Rome in the North. In almost all respects it differed widely from Rome. Its date of Easter Day was different, it rejected the Roman type of tonsure, it knew nothing of bishops as the Latin Church understood them, it rejected the jurisdiction of the Pope, and it knew nothing of the worship of the Virgin Mary, the intercession of the saints, purgatory, transubstantiation, Communion in one kind, and other typical Roman traditions.

11. Perhaps the most notable characteristic of the Celtic Church was its fiery missionary zeal. It maintained a far-flung chain of *muinntirs*, which were missionary training schools. Here the men were trained who made their way throughout the British Isles and to the European continent, reaching places as far away as Austria, South Germany, Switzerland, and Italy. These men were missioners, not pastors. They made little attempt to found permanent congregations, but were content to be "awakeners," going two and two on lengthy preaching tours. Each great training center maintained a dozen or more communities where a "family" of preachers lived and from which they went out on their preaching missions. They established preaching stations rather than congregations as we understand them today.

12. The Celtic Church has a multitude of "saints," but in the old Celtic languages this word means merely "cleric" or "missionary" and nothing more. The Celts did not canonize their noted men, neither did they dedicate their churches to apostles, martyrs, or noted leaders. The Celtic Church, like the larger denominations of today, was composed of several divisions, the more important of which were the Brito-Pictish Church, the Iro-Pictish Church, and the Church of the Gaidheals. The Picts and the Gaidheals had neither pulpit nor altar fellowship, and each looked upon the other as an erring group.

13. The older accounts of the Celtic Church are a network of contradictions and anachronisms, which led many writers to declare that its true history was lost beyond recovery. However, owing to the laborious research of a group of careful historians, considerable progress has been made. Special mention should be made of Dr. Alexander Macbain, Dr. W. Douglas Simpson, Dr. A. R. MacEwen, and especially Mr. Archibald B. Scott. Mr. Scott has published several books of great importance, the most notable of which is his *The Pictish Nation, Its People and Its Church* (Edinburgh, 1917). These men and others of their school have made available an abundance of material on the Celtic Church and have done much to purge it of the thick veneer of legend, idle speculation, and deliberately garbled history that until recently obscured its true history. The bound volumes of the *Transactions* of the Gaelic Society of Inverness will also

furnish much material for those interested.

14. The Celtic Church is important both for its great missionary achievements and its evangelical character, and because of the fact that its true history fills in what was once a strange gap of 450 years between the end of the Apostolic and Patristic Era and the time of the rise in influence of the Roman Church. Many famous manuscripts of the New Testament were due to the industry of scribes of the Celtic Church, and today we owe to the Celts the preservation of such treasures as the *Muratorian Fragment*, the *Codex Boernerianus*, and the *Codex San-Gallensis*. FRW

Archibald B. Scott, *The Pictish Nation, Its People and Its Church*, Edinburgh, 1917; Archibald B. Scott, *St. Ninian and the Founding of the Celtic Church Among Britons and Picts*, Edinburgh, 1916; W. Douglas Simpson, *St. Ninian and the Origins of the Church in Scotland*, Edinburgh, 1940; W. Douglas Simpson, *The Historical St. Columba*, Aberdeen, 1927; W. Douglas Simpson, *The Celtic Church in Scotland*, Aberdeen, 1935; *Transactions* of the *Gaelic Society of Inverness*.

Cemeteries. According to the etymology of the word (*Coemeterium — koimeterion*), sleeping places; according to Christian use, the final resting places of those who die in the faith. A beautiful sentiment is expressed in the ancient designation "God's acre." The name cemeteries was applied, since ancient days, to special plots set apart for the purpose of burying the dead; but it received a new significance in connection with the catacombs,* the subterranean assembly places and burial grounds of the Christians, chiefly during persecutions. See also *Burial; Catacombs.*

Central America, Missions in. 1. *Guatemala*, the northernmost state. Area, 48,290 sq. mi.; population according to 1940 census, 3,280,000, 55% of whom are pure-blooded Indians. Capital, Guatemala City. Prevailing religion, Roman Catholic, with assured toleration. Language, Spanish. Missions: Presbyterians have been active since 1865; Central American Mission; Church of the Nazarene; Friends' Church of California; Primitive Methodist Church; Seventh-Day Adventists; United Free Gospel and Missionary Society; Church of England. According to latest survey of World Mission (1940): Foreign staff, 108; Protestant Christian community,

62,928; communicants, 21,233. In 1946 The Lutheran Church — Missouri Synod investigated opportunities for mission work in Guatemala City, Zacapa and environs, and Puerto Barrios. The Rev. Robert F. Gussick was sent in August, 1947, as the first missionary. By December 31, 1952, there were five ordained missionaries.

2. *Nicaragua.* Central American republic on the isthmus. Area, 57,150 sq. mi.; population, 1,172,000 (1940 census), Spaniards and Indian mixture. Natives, Mosquito Indians. Language, Spanish. Roman Catholicism is state religion, with toleration. Missions among Mosquitos since 1741 by Society for Propagation of Gospel. Other missions: American Baptist Home Mission Society; Central American Mission; Unitas Fratrum (Moravians); Seventh-Day Adventists; Assemblies of God; Church of the Nazarene; Northern Baptist Convention. Foreign staff, 64; Protestant Christian communicants, 10,598.

3. *Honduras.* 44,480 sq. mi. in area, lies southeast of Guatemala and northeast of Nicaragua and has a front of 350 miles on the Caribbean and 80 miles on the Pacific. Like all Central American countries, the Catholic Church dominates the thinking of the people, but Protestant missions are tolerated. The following Protestant groups are working in Honduras: Central American Mission, Evangelical and Reformed Church, Friends Church, S. P. G., Christian Missions in Many Lands, Methodists, Moravians, Assemblies of God, United Brethren in Christ, National Holiness Missionary Society, Seventh-Day Adventists. Foreign staff: 104; Protestant Christian community, 14,931; communicants, 5,615.

4. *El Salvador.* With its 13,173 square miles and approximately 2,018,845 inhabitants (1946) is the smallest and the most densely populated of the Central American republics. The name of the country and the name of its capital city, San Salvador, indicate the strong Catholic influence, although there is religious liberty. Foreign staff, 38; Protestant Christian communicants, 8,723.

5. *Costa Rica.* Comprises 23,000 square miles of tropical coast land, fertile valleys, and high ranges. Population, 746,535. The Catholic Church, as in all other Latin countries, has its churches in the most prominent locations of the cities. Protestant denominations have been active in Costa Rica

since the middle of the 19th century; Central American Mission, Seventh-Day Adventists, Latin American Mission-Methodists. Foreign staff, 77; Protestant Christian communicants, 2,775.

6. *Panama.* Republic of the isthmus. Area, 32,380 sq. mi.; population, exclusive of Canal Zone, which belongs to the United States, approximately 622,535, of Spanish, Indian, and Negro descent. Language, Spanish. Religion, Roman Catholic, with toleration. Missions (Canal Zone included): American Bible Society; Free Methodist Church; Methodist Episcopal Church; Protestant Episcopal Church; Seventh-Day Adventists; Southern Baptist Convention; Salvation Army; Wesleyan Missionary Society; Jamaica Baptist Missionary Society; International Church of the Four Square Gospel; Independent. Foreign staff, 100; Protestant Christian communicants, 12,776 (1949).

During the Second World War the Armed Services Commission of The Lutheran Church — Missouri Synod ministered to the spiritual needs of servicemen stationed in the Canal Zone. This work developed into a congregation in Balboa, where a Lutheran church and service center was erected in 1948. Services are also being conducted at Cristobal-Colon. HM

Cenobite (Gr. *koinos-bios*, "common life"). Monks living together under a common rule (distinguished from anchorites).

Censor. See *Index of Prohibited Books.*

Central Canada, Synod of. See *Canada, Lutheranism in,* 4.

Central Conference of Mennonites. See *Mennonite Bodies,* 3.

Central Evangelical Holiness Association. See *Church of the Nazarene.*

Central Illinois Synod. See *Illinois, Ev. Luth. Synod of Central.*

Central and Southern Illinois Synod. See *Illinois, Ev. Luth. Synod of Central and Southern.*

Central Pennsylvania Synod. See *United Luth. Church, Synods of,* 25.

Central Schools. See *Parish Education,* I.

Centuries, Magdeburg. A church history published at Magdeburg, each of the 13 volumes covering a century, projected by Flacius in 1553, helped by Wigand, Judex, Faber, Corvinus, Amsdorf, Veltbeck, Holthuter, and Alemann, 1560—74. The monumental work proves Lutheranism to stand on apostolic ground. Caesar Baronius opposed it with his *Annals,* 1588—1607.

Ceremonial Law. See *Grace, Means of,* II 2.

Ceremonies in the Lutheran Church. See *Adiaphora; Adiaphoristic Controversy; Agenda; Liturgics;* articles on individual liturgical acts (*e. g., Baptism, Lord's Supper*).

Cerinthus. See *Gnosticism,* 7 b.

Certainty, Religious. The Bible is the only source of religious truth, because it is God's Word to man (2 Peter 2:19-21); hence it alone can speak with certainty about God and man's relations to Him. Only a true believer can be certain of his salvation. The faith that justifies is itself a certainty of salvation; its essence is "a being sure of God's grace in Christ Jesus" ((*fiducia cordis*), Heb. 11:1; John 3:36; Rom. 4:20, 21; Eph. 2:5; 4:30; 2 Tim. 1:12. Luther (in his Introduction to Romans) defines faith as "a living, moving confidence in God's grace — so certain that for it one could die a thousand deaths." (St. L. XIV:99, 17.) It is an indication of a weak faith when a Christian has doubts and feels uncertain that he is in a state of grace and will be saved. Cp. Luther, IX:1271 ff.; XII:210; XXII:478 ff.; *Trigl.,* p. 1250 (certainty); F. Pieper, *Chr. Dog.* I:123 f.; II:484 ff.; G. Stoeckhardt, *Roemerbrief,* p. 232; Laetsch, *The Abiding Word,* I, 221 ff.; Oregon and Washington District Reports, 1904—1909; Walther, *Law and Gospel,* 139, 391. Note also 2 Cor. 1:20; Rom. 8:31-39; Phil. 1:6; 1 Peter 1:5-9; Heb. 13:9; *Trigl.,* p. 135, 48.

Alfred Kurz, *Die Heilsgewiszheit bei Luther,* Bertelsmann, Guetersloh, 1933; J. T. Mueller, "Die Heilsgewiszheit nach der Konkordienformel," *CTM,* V: 172—178.

Certosa. In reality a Carthusian monastery, but applied also to a secondary, or side, church connected with the cathedral, the special form having been developed at Florence.

Ceylon. Island south of India, British crown colony. Area, 25,332 sq. mi.; population, 7,500,000 (estimated, 1950), mostly native Singhalese, ca. 800,000 Tamils. Religions: Buddhism, Hinduism, Mohammedanism, Christian. — *Missions:* American Board; Seventh-Day Adventists; British: Baptist Missionary Society; British and Foreign Bible Society. Ceylon and India General Mission: Church Missionary Society; Church of England Zenana Missionary Society; Salvation Army; Heneratgoda Village Mission; India Christian Mission, Independent. Protestants, 82,571 baptized members; Roman Catholic, 507,418 members. The Lutheran Church — Missouri Synod has a small mission here.

Chafer, Lewis Sperry. B. Feb. 27, 1871; studied at Oberlin College, later at Wheaton College; ordained in Presbyterian Church; founder and president of Evangelical Theol. College, Dallas, Tex., 1924; dept. editor *Bibliotheca Sacra;* author, conservative in theology.

Chair of St. Peter. See *Papacy.*

Chalcedon, Council of. The Fourth Ecumenical Council was held at Chalcedon, a city in Bithynia, on the Bosporus, opposite Constantinople, in 451. It was occasioned by the Eutychian controversy, which, in turn, was brought about by the rival spirit between the patriarchs of Antioch, Alexandria, and Constantinople. The question centered in the point that the two natures of Christ were included in His one person, not parted or divided into two persons. Leo the Great had already expressed himself on the disputed point with great emphasis, and his exposition was followed by the Council when it declared: "Following the holy fathers, we all with one voice teach men to confess that the Son and our Lord Jesus Christ is one and the same, that He is perfect in Godhead and perfect in manhood, truly God and truly man, of a reasonable soul and body, consubstantial with His Father as touching His Godhead and consubstantial with us as to His manhood, in all things like unto us, without sin; begotten of His Father before all worlds according to His Godhead; but in these last days for us and for our salvation of the Virgin Mary, the Theotokos, according to His manhood [humanity], one and the same Christ, Son, Lord, only-begotten Son, in two natures, unconfusedly, immutably, indivisibly, inseparably; the distinction of natures being preserved and concurring in one person and hypostasis, not separated or divided into two persons, but one and the same Son and Only-begotten, God the Word, the Lord Jesus Christ, as the Prophets from the beginning have spoken concerning Him."

Chaldean Christians. See *Nestorianism.*

Chalice. The vessel containing wine at the celebration of the Lord's Supper. The chalices are of two kinds: the greater, containing a large amount of wine; the less, from which the communicants drink the wine. See *Church Furniture,* 3.

Chalmers, James. B. at Ardishaig, Scotland, 1841; d. in company with Oliver Tomkins, at the hands of cannibals on Goaribari Islands, in the South Pacific, Apr. 8, 1901. Sent by London Missionary Society to Rarotonga, 1866, where he trained many native evangelists; later transferred to New Guinea.

Chalmers, Thomas (1780—1847). First leader of Free Church of Scotland. B. at Anstruther; minister at Kilmany, 1803, interest centering in mathematics and chemistry; pastor at Glasgow, 1815 to 1823, combating vice and pauperism and establishing schools while in charge of St. John's; professor at St. Andrew's, 1823; at Edinburgh, 1828; also member of Church Extension Committee, helping to build 220 new churches. The General Assembly refusing to grant the parishes veto power upon nomination of obnoxious ministers, 471 clergymen left the Establishment and founded the Free Church of Scotland under the moderatorship of Chalmers, 1843. D. as principal of Free Church Divinity School, Edinburgh. Prolific author (refuted Hume's objection to truth of miracles).

F. R. Webber, "Thomas Chalmers, the Walther of Scotland," *CTM,* XVIII: 411—29.

Chalons. A town on the Saone in France. Several important provincial councils were held there in the Middle Ages, the most prominent being the one ordered by Charlemagne (813). Its sixty-six canons ordered the priests to read the Bible, councils, and pastoral of Gregory; commanded preaching and the establishing of schools; held that almsgiving frees only from venial sins; ordered prayers for the dead; condemned pilgrimages made for remission of sins.

Chancel. In liturgical churches a special section of the building elevated several feet above the nave and set apart by the triumphal arch which spans this sanctuary. The chief appointment of the chancel is the altar,* which serves as the table for the celebration of the Lord's Supper and whose platform is the place for liturgical prayers in the Lutheran Church. The baptismal font should have its position at or near the entrance to the chancel, and pulpit and lectern may also be brought into juxtaposition with the chancel. See *Architecture, Ecclesiastical*, 7.

Chancery, Apostolic. Papal office which issues important documents, such as those which create bishops or new dioceses.

Chandler, John. B. at Witley, Surrey, England, June 16, 1806; educated at Corpus Christi College, Oxford; ordained deacon and priest. In 1837 he succeeded his father as vicar of Witley and was afterwards appointed Rural Dean. He wrote numerous sermons and tracts. Chandler was one of the early and successful modern translators, especially of Latin hymns. D. 1876.

Changes, Book of. See *Confucianism*.

Channing, William Ellery. Foremost American Unitarian theologian. B. 1780 at Newport, R. I.; d. 1842 at Bennington, Vt. Pastor in Boston, 1803. Rejected Biblical doctrines of inspiration, Trinity, atonement, total depravity, devil, but accepted Christ's sinlessness, miracles, resurrection. His creed is embodied in the famous Baltimore Sermon, preached at the installation of Rev. Jared Sparks in 1819. See *Unitarianism*.

Chant (L. *cantus*, a song). The word "chant" was used in the early Church to designate the singing of the congregation. The term was later applied to tunes adapted to prose (see *Ambrosian Chant; Gregorian Music*). In the Roman Catholic Church the chant is regularly called Gregorian. The Anglican chant is somewhat more elaborate. In modern liturgical worship generally, the word designates the musical setting and the proper inflections for the liturgical part of the church services, including those for the collects, versicles, prefaces, responses, lections, etc., the Psalm tones, and the whole body of original music for the antiphons, introits, graduals, and the festival norms of the Kyrie, Gloria, Tersanctus, Agnus Dei, and many hymns, based upon the Gregorian music, as modified by the motet.

Chapel. Originally the sanctuary in which was preserved the *cappa*, or cope, of St. Martin of Tours, then expanded to designate any sanctuary containing relics. Many of these being the private or court churches of rulers and princes,

the name was chiefly applied to such sanctuaries. At present the name is used for special compartments or recesses in cathedral churches, usually bearing a special name, and for churches of any denomination.

Chaplain. A clergyman, usually with special, limited functions, as one employed in a private chapel to read the lessons and to preach; used in America especially of men opening or conducting religious services in an assembly of a public or semipublic nature, as in legislative assemblies, in public institutions, and in the Armed Services.*

Chaplet (rosary beads). A string of beads used by Roman Catholics in counting prayers (usually ten *aves* and five *paters*).

Chapter (of a cathedral). The canons * and other dignitaries of an Anglican cathedral church, who together form a kind of diocesan senate and assist the bishop in various ways. The bishop is required to have their counsel for some administrative acts and their consent for others.

Chapters and Verses of the Bible. Before the time of Christ the Jews divided the OT into *parashas* and *haphtoras* for reading in the synagog on the Sabbath. The NT books were also divided at an early date into *titles* and *chapters*. Stephen Langton is generally considered as having introduced the present chapter divisions into the Vulgate (13th c.). Verse divisions were first indicated by Robert Estienne (Stephanus) in his fourth edition of the NT (1551). Verse divisions were introduced a few years later in the whole Bible (Geneva Bible; Antwerp Polyglot).

Character Indelebilis. A term used in Roman Catholic theology to denote a certain spiritual mark which is said to be impressed on the recipients of certain sacraments. "If anyone saith that in the three Sacraments, to wit, Baptism, Confirmation, and Order [ordination], there is not imprinted in the soul a character, that is, a certain spiritual and indelible sign on account of which they cannot be repeated: let him be accursed." (Council of Trent, Sess. VII, can. 9.) The "character" of Baptism is said to distinguish the baptized (including Protestants) as soldiers of Christ and to subject them to the Pope and the canon law, while the "character" of Order sets apart the clergy from the laity. This curious doctrine is one of several which were spawned in the speculations of the scholastics and ended by being solemnly proclaimed Roman doctrine, with a curse for gainsayers attached. The whole fanciful structure is built on three Bible passages which speak of being sealed with the Holy Spirit.

Charismata. A Biblical term, designating extraordinary "spiritual gifts" bestowed by the Holy Spirit upon certain individuals, such gifts as the ability to perform miracles, to speak in languages they had not learned, to foretell future events. These special gifts are clearly distinguished from faith, love, knowledge, and Christian virtues, gifts which the Holy Spirit gives to all believers. 1 Cor. 12—14 treat of charismatic gifts. Cp. also Matt. 10:1, 8; Mark 16:17, 18; Luke 10:1, 9, 17, 19; Acts 2:4; 10:44-46; 1 Cor. 7:7; 2 Cor. 1:11; Rom. 1:11; 5:15; 6:23; 11:29. See J. H. C. Fritz, *The Preacher's Manual*, 187 ff.; *Conc. Trigl.*, 1261 (Gifts of the Holy Ghost); P. Kretzmann, *Pop. Com.*, N. T. II, p. 661 (Gifts, spiritual); Lenski's Commentary on 1 Cor. 12.

Charities, Christian. 1. *The Term.* Charity (plural, charities) — from L. *caritas*. *Caritas* was used by St. Jerome in his translation of the Greek term ἀγάπη (*agápē*) when he translated the New Testament into Latin (Vulgate — 4th c.). 'Αγάπη is almost exclusively a Biblical term and is translated "love." In the Authorized Version of the Bible, however, the Anglicized version of *caritas*, charity, is occasionally used when ἀγάπη indicates the love of man for his fellow men (1 Cor. 13). It denotes not primarily the outward evidences of love, such as almsgiving, but love itself, an inner principle or attitude, a motive which determines man's relation to his fellow man and bestows a peculiar value upon all his activities. Thus 1 Cor. 13 describes it as the greatest and most enduring of Christian virtues.

2. *Later Usage.* As the Church lapsed into legalism and as monastic ideals of morality developed, *caritas*, or charity, gradually assumed a meaning just the opposite of ἀγάπη. In the Middle Ages it meant simply "the giving of goods to feed the poor," which "profiteth nothing" without the motive of Christian love (1 Cor. 13). In present usage the word charity means: 1. An attitude of sympathy toward those who are suffering from misfortune. 2. Liberality in caring for the poor and handicapped. 3. Tolerance in judging the actions of others. It has in our day even acquired in the popular mind an obnoxious connotation of paternalistic benevolence with doubtful motivation and purpose. It is primarily because of these implications that modern revisers of the New Testament have substituted the term "love" for "charity" in the translation of ἀγάπη.

3. *Institutional Use.* A "charity" in present-day usage denotes an eleemosynary institution or agency, founded and operated to assist the poor, sick, handicapped, orphaned, etc., without charge. In the nineteenth century the concept of "charities" was broadened, and particular emphasis was laid upon the natural "right" of the individual to benefit by the bounty of his fellow men. It was out of this enlarged concept, which includes justice, that the Charity Organization Society movement was born in London in 1869. This movement came to the United States when the first Charity Organization Society was founded in Buffalo in 1877. Much of modern social work has developed from this source. The term "charity," used in an institution or agency sense, has now practically disappeared from the vocabulary of secular social work, largely being replaced by the term "service," as being more nearly expressive of the motivation and methods employed in our age in assisting those in distress. (See *Social Service.*) The term is still being used, although with diminishing emphasis, by Church-sponsored organizations for social service, such as Catholic Charities, Associated Lutheran Charities, and others.

4. *Historical Development.* In the Old Testament the "charity" to be practiced by God's children was prescribed in many laws and ordinances. With the coming of Christ these rules were abrogated. The virtue of love for the neighbor was enjoined in the New Testament, but the expression of this attitude in deeds of love became a matter of Christian liberty. In the Apostolic Age, Christians used the method of oblations. Besides the bread and wine used for the celebration of the Lord's Supper, Christians brought to the altar products of every kind to be distributed among the poor. About A. D. 550 the oblations were restricted for the use of the clergy, and gifts for the poor were deposited in a special place. With the disintegration of morals

attendant upon the collapse of the Roman Empire and the economic crises into which society was plunged, the masses became pauperized, and monasteries and charitable institutions, such as hospitals, became central points in the dispensing of charity. Rules and regulations were gradually established. Approximately one fourth of the income of the Church was set aside for charity in the early centuries. While the amount and character of charity dispensed by the Church in the subsequent centuries varied, it remains true that throughout the Middle Ages the Church remained as the only friend and benefactor of the poor and the handicapped. Sad to relate, however, the practice of charity gradually came to be regarded as a meritorious service which would be rewarded by God by the bestowal of special favors. Thus the close of the Middle Ages witnessed the degeneration of Christian charity into the crassest form of work-righteousness. With the coming of the Reformation a new day dawned also for Christian charity. Luther once more championed the liberty of a Christian under God to express his Christian love in conformity with Gal. 6:9-10. Christians were again enjoined to practice charity as an expression of their love to God and to their fellow men and as evidence of their gratitude for the unmerited grace bestowed upon them through Jesus Christ.

5. The nineteenth century particularly witnessed a tremendous expansion of the work of organized Christian charity, originated and conducted largely through the efforts of Lutherans. Deaconess work was begun in Kaiserswerth, Germany, in 1833, largely through the efforts of Pastor Theodore Fliedner, and Kaiserswerth in turn produced numberless agencies and institutions of charity, aiding the sick, the forsaken, the fallen, the orphaned, and the aged in almost every country of Europe. The same year witnessed also the establishment of "Das Rauhe Haus" in Hamburg, a great center of charitable work, which was founded by Johann Heinrich Wichern, the father of the well-known German Inner Mission movement. The great orphanage at Halle, founded by Pastor August Hermann Francke, and the extensive colony for epileptics at Bielefeld, founded by Pastor von Bodelschwingh, deserve special mention among the thousands of agencies and institutions founded by Lutheran Christians in Germany in the nineteenth century. In England the names of Lord Shaftesbury, Dr. Barnardo, and George Mueller are symbolical of great charitable enterprises. Denmark, Norway, Sweden, and other Protestant countries all shared in this development of organized Christian charity, the greatest since the days of the Early Church.

6. The early history of the Lutheran Church in the United States includes reports on the charitable work of the only Lutheran church in New York in 1674, which, together with items of similar nature during the following years, reveal the fact that Lutheran congregations in the early days of our country did not shirk their charitable obligations. In those days congregational action for the relief of the poor seems to have been the universal custom, since the simple economy of life in a new country did not call for large, specialized agencies of charity. With the tremendous increase in the population in the eighteenth and nineteenth centuries, however, such agencies were gradually established. The name of William Alfred Passavant deserves special mention in this connection. He introduced the Kaiserswerth system of diaconics in America and was instrumental in the founding of more than a score of hospitals, orphanages, and other charitable institutions. In the charitable endeavors of the early days of the Missouri Synod the Rev. Johann Friedrich Buenger was prominent. (See *Associated Lutheran Charities*.) In 1947 almost 500 agencies and institutions of mercy conducted under Lutheran auspices testify to the living charity of God's children. See *Aged and Infirm, Homes for; Child Care and Child-Placing Agencies; Hospitals, Sanatoria, Homes for Convalescents and Chronically Ill; Associated Lutheran Charities; Inner Mission; Social Work.*

HFW

Charity, Brothers of. A name common to several benevolent orders of the Roman Church, among them an order founded by John of God in 1540, which is probably the most important male order devoted to the care of the sick. A flourishing order of the same name was founded in Belgium early in this century and has extended its work to America.

Charity Organization Society. See *Charities, Christian, 3.*

Charity Organizations. See *Charities, Christian; Aged and Infirm, Homes for; Child Care and Child-Placing Agencies; Hospitals, Sanatoria, Homes for Convalescents and Chronically Ill.*

Charity, Sisters of. See *Sisters of Charity.*

Charlemagne (*Charles the Great*). Founder of the Holy Roman Empire. B. 742, son of Pepin of the Carolingian line; d. at Aachen, 814. He was anointed (together with his father and his brother Karlman) king of the Franks by Pope Stephen II in 754 and crowned emperor of the Romans by Pope Leo III on Christmas Day, 800. He carried forward the policies of his father and strongly supported the Roman Pontiff throughout his reign, recognizing the Pope's headship and undertaking to deliver the papal territory from Lombard oppression. He conducted five campaigns against the Lombards, the final result being the inclusion of their territory in his own domain. He undertook eighteen expeditions against the Saxons, which had the object of bringing Christianity to this part of Germany and of establishing Frankish rule. Whenever he extended the boundaries of his realm, he provided for the speedy Christianization of the territory acquired by covering the country with Christian institutions and by forcing the people to submit to Baptism and to a full agreement with the cultus of the Roman Church; for the conversion of the entire population in this sense he considered essential to the attainment of his political ends. — There can be no doubt that Charlemagne's services to learning are a prominent feature of his history. He succeeded in gaining some of the most eminent educators of Britain and Italy for this work, among whom Alcuin is particularly notable. Through the monasteries and churches the emperor sought to spread civilization and learning throughout his realm, also in the matter of church music, a field which at that time was still seriously neglected in Germany. He took a decidedly negative stand in the Iconoclastic Controversy, and it was largely due to his influence that there was a revival of Christian art in Germany. At the same time he condemned the adoration and service of images. Altogether, Charlemagne was one of the most outstanding figures of the Middle Ages.

Charles V (1500—58). Emperor of Germany and King of Spain; greatest ruler of the House of Hapsburg; staunch Roman Catholic. His treatment of the Reformers was conditioned by his political and military needs in the struggle with the French and the Turks. He condemned Luther in the Edict of Worms (1521), but was tolerant towards the Lutherans at Speyer in 1526 because the League of Cognac and the menace of the Turks created an unfavorable situation for him. He took a firmer stand at Speyer in 1529 because he felt his position strengthened by the Peace of Cambray. At the time of the Augsburg Diet (1530), Charles needed the support of the German princes against the Turks and thus could not crush Lutheranism. The Religious Peace of Nuernberg (1532) gave the Lutherans religious liberty for a year. The alliance between the Turks and the French undoubtedly motivated the Emperor to make additional concessions to the Lutherans at Speyer in 1541 and 1544. He crushed the Smalcald League in 1547, but through the efforts of Maurice of Saxony he was constrained to sign the Passau Treaty (1552). He permitted the passage of the Religious Peace of Augsburg (1555). He resigned the following year and spent his remaining days in the cloister of St. Just in Spain.

Charles the Bald. See *Inquisition*, 2.

Charles, Elizabeth (nee Rundle) (1828—96). Author of popular works on various periods of church history, also of simple hymns intended principally for children.

Charles of Sweden (X, XI, XII). See *Sweden, Lutheran Church in.*

Charms and Amulets. See *Amulets.*

Charnock, Stephan (1628—80). Puritan; Londoner; proctor at Oxford; chaplain in Ireland; beginning with 1660, preacher without regular charge; joint pastor of Presbyterian congregation, London. Wrote *Existence and Attributes of God;* etc.

Charterhouse (corruption of Chartreuse). A chapel, schoolhouse, and hospital established in London by Sir Thomas Sutton (1611).

Chartres, School of. A school of the seven liberal arts and classical learning founded by Fulbert (ca. 960—1028, French ecclesiastic). Important leaders of the school: Bernard (d. ca. 1125), Thierry (d. ca. 1150), Walter of Mortagne (d. 1174), and John of Salisbury (1110—80).

Charvakas. See *Brahmanism*, 5.

Chastity. In its more general signification the state of physical and moral purity in sexual relations and the proper attitude of positive aloofness from unpermitted sexual desires. Strictly speaking, it involves the complete control of the sexual tendency in the unmarried and the proper governing of this tendency within the married state. While the sexual instinct in itself is not sinful, every transgression of its lawful expression is unchastity, whether in thought (Matt. 5:28), in word (Eph. 5: 3, 12), or in deed (1 Cor. 6:15).

Chasuble. See *Vestments, Clerical.*

Chautauqua. The methods and ideas of the Chautauqua movement are traceable to the Chautauqua Sunday School Assembly, which held its first ten-day session on the shores of Chautauqua Lake, N. Y., in 1874. Since then the scope of the work was enlarged, including all branches of popular education, offering a variety of courses, lectures, religious addresses, entertainments, and concerts. Chautauquas are held in various parts of the United States; they are a unique feature of American life and a factor in the educational system of America. While formerly, on the whole, centers from which stimulating suggestions, important information, and wholesome entertainment were distributed, the chautauquas have largely deteriorated to the level of entertainment bureaus and are falling into disuse.

Chelczich, Gregor and Peter. See *Bohemian-Moravian Brethren.*

Chemnitz Conference. A conference formed in Chemnitz, Saxony (1878), by Lutherans who upheld the Confessions and opposed the Prussian Union, sects, and separatists.

Chemnitz, Martin (1522—86). Lutheran theologian. B. of an impoverished noble family; worked his way through school; studied at Wittenberg in 1545, befriended by Melanchthon; missed some of Luther's lectures on account of philology and astrology; was appointed librarian to Albrecht of Prussia at Koenigsberg in 1550 and studied theology to his heart's content; attacked Osiander's false doctrine of justification and, when Moerlin was deposed, returned to Wittenberg in 1553, Melanchthon's guest and pupil, and substituted for him in lecturing on his *Loci;* Moerlin's coadjutor in Brunswick in 1554, ordained by Bugenhagen; present, in 1557, at Wittenberg at the conference between the true Lutherans and the Philippists and at the religious conference between the Lutherans and the Romanists at Worms, where he saw the need of a united front against Rome. When Moerlin became bishop at Koenigsberg in 1567, Chemnitz was made superintendent of the city of Brunswick, which paid the expenses of his doctorate at Rostock. He successfully upheld a form of true Lutheranism against Philippism in 1570. He helped Duke Julius organize the University of Helmstedt in 1575 and dedicated it. He took the leading part in getting out the Formula of Concord, and the Catalog of Testimonies which is appended to the Symbolical Books is essentially his work. When Duke Julius consecrated one son Bishop of Halberstadt according to the Roman ritual and tonsured two others, Chemnitz criticized him and was deposed as counselor, and the Formula of Concord was denied symbolic recognition in Brunswick, though before Julius had spent money for the good work. Together with Selnecker and Kirchner, Chemnitz, in 1582, published an *Apology of the Book of Concord.* He defended the Lutheran doctrine of the Lord's Supper in 1561, 1569, and 1570. His *Chief Chapters of Jesuit Theology* appeared in 1562 and his monumental *Examen* of the Council of Trent, directed chiefly against the Roman theologian Bellarmine, in four volumes, 1565—73. His *Gospel Harmony* came out in 1593 (continued by Polycarp Leyser and finished by John Gerhard), the greatest work of this kind until that time. His *Loci* were published by Leyser in 1591. Failing health forced him to resign in 1584. The most learned theologian of his time, he was mourned by the whole Lutheran Church; his importance is seen in the Catholic saying that if Chemnitz had not come, Luther had not stood.

The best source of Chemnitz's life is P. J. Rehtmeyer, *Antiquitates Ecclesiasticae inclutae urbis Brusvigae (Der beruehmten Stadt Braunschweig Kirchen-Historie)*, Friedrich Zilligers, Braunschweig, 1707—10 (vol. III: 273 ff.).

Cherubim. The plural form of cherub, a name applied to a certain rank of angels. They are mentioned for the first time in Gen. 3: 24. Cherubim are especially prominent in the visions of Ezekiel (chap. 10). What form they were given in the embellishment of the

Ark of the Covenant in the Tabernacle is a mystery which may never be solved, since we have no description, neither in the Old Testament nor in Jewish tradition, of these figures. In the vision of John the cherubim are evidently a type, no longer of vengeance, but of forgiveness, since they appear in the same choir with the redeemed multitudes (Rev. 4:7; 5:13), no longer armed with flaming swords, but joining in the new song of the Church Triumphant. See commentaries on Gen. 3:24.

Cherubini, Luigi (1760—1842). Italian composer of opera and sacred music, whose childhood genius was recognized in his composition of three masses, an oratorio, three cantatas, and several smaller works in the style of Palestrina, before the age of 16. In his second period of composition he wrote numerous operas, which are seldom performed on the modern stage. Later, upon appointment to the Chapelle Royal in 1816, he turned to the composition of sacred music and produced his greatest works, including additional masses and two requiems, of which the one in C minor is generally considered his greatest achievement.

Chesterton, Gilbert Keith (1874 to 1936). English author; joined the Roman Catholic Church and wrote many works in its defense; mystical in his approach to religious thought.

Cheyne, Thomas Kelly (1841—1915). Anglican; radical critic. B. in London; priest in 1865; Oriel Professor of Interpretation of Scripture at Oxford, 1885; member of Old Testament Revision Company; d. at Oxford. Commentaries and many other publications.

Chicago Luth. Theological Seminary. See *Ministry, Education of,* XI B.

Chicago School of Theology. An approach to theology developed at Chicago University under the leadership of men like Shailer Mathews and Shirley Jackson Case. It made social experience central and basic to all theological systems.

Chicago Synod (formerly *Synod of Indiana*). Belonging to the General Council, so called since 1895, embraced congregations in Indiana, Illinois, Ohio, and Michigan. It maintained Weidner Institute in Mulberry, Ind., established at Colburn, Ind., in 1903. In 1918 the Chicago Synod joined the United Lutheran Church. In 1920 it was divided into three parts, one helping to form the

Illinois Synod (II), one the Indiana Synod (III), and one the Michigan Synod (III) of the U.L.C.A. At the time of its division it numbered 44 pastors, 41 congregations, and 6,485 communicants. See also *Synods, Extinct.*

M. L. Wagner, *The Chicago Synod and Its Antecedents,* Wartburg, Waverly, Iowa, 1909.

Chicago Theses (American Lutheran Conference). Theses adopted on March 11, 1919, by representatives of the Augustana Synod, the Iowa Synod, the Joint Synod of Ohio, the Lutheran Free Church, the Norwegian Church of America, the United Danish Church, and the United Lutheran Church. The theses were later re-examined and incorporated as Sec. IV in the *Minneapolis Theses.* * For text see *CTM,* I:688 ff.; XV:196—97; *Journal of Theology,* Jan., 1941.

Chicago Theses (Intersynodical). After the failure of the intersynodical conferences (1903—07, held at Watertown, Milwaukee, Detroit, and Fort Wayne) to solve the differences on predestination and conversion, the Iowa Synod offered general and open conferences for the discussion of the points at issue (1913). Pastors from the disputing synods signed the so-called *St. Paul Theses* and demanded that the matter be taken up officially. Thus a colloquy started (1917) with representatives of the synods concerned participating. As a result the *Chicago Theses on Conversion, Predestination, and Other Doctrines* were unanimously adopted by representatives of the Buffalo, Iowa, Missouri, Ohio, and Wisconsin Synods on April 15, 1925, at Chicago. "The agreement on the article of Predestination was brought about by Dr. George Fritschel, who, accepting Dr. Stoeckhardt's exegesis of the Epistle to the Romans, succeeded in convincing others that Stoeckhardt had the correct Biblical doctrine" (*CTM,* VI:476). In the fall of the same year, representatives of the Ohio, Iowa, and Buffalo Synods adopted the *Minneapolis Theses* * with representatives of the Norwegian Lutheran Church (Nov. 18, 1925). The *Chicago Theses* were revised and brought before the Missouri Synod at River Forest, 1929. The Missouri members of the Intersynodical Committee acknowledged that fraternal relations were "at present excluded by the connections into which . . . these synods have entered," but urged, at the same time, that action be taken on the *Theses*. An examining committee had recommended that the *Theses* be rejected. The Committee on Intersynodical Matters recommended that the *Theses* be not accepted "in their present form" and that Synod instruct a committee to formulate *Theses*. The Synod adopted the report (see *Brief Statement*).

Chicago Thesen ueber die Bekehrung, Praedestination und andere Lehren, angenommen von Vertretern der Synoden von Buffalo, Iowa, Missouri, Ohio und Wisconsin, Im Verlag des Komitees, n. p., 1925; *Chicagoer Thesen ueber Bekehrung, Praedestination und andere Lehren,* CPH, n. d.; English translation of the theses in *Theologische Quartalschrift,* Oct. 1929; A. C. Haase (secretary of Intersynodical Committee), "Schluszbericht des Intersyn. Komitees," *TQS,* XXV: 266 ff.; *Proceedings* of the Missouri Synod (especially 1929: 113 ff.). EL

Child Care and Child - Placing Agencies and Institutions (by States with affiliation given: ALC — within the American Lutheran Church; Aug — within the Augustana Synod; Dan — within the Danish Luth. Ch.; EVL — within the Ev. Luth. Church; Ex — Extrasynodical; Int — Intersynodical; LB — within Luth. Brethren; LF — within Luth. Free Church; Mo — within Missouri Synod; SC — within Synodical Conf.; ULC — within United Luth. Church; UE — within United Ev. Luth. Church). Compiled 1948.

California: Luth. Children's Friend Soc. of Calif., 969 Eddy St., San Francisco (Mo).

Illinois: Luth. Child Welfare Assn., Addison (SC); Luth. Home for Children and Farm School, Andover (Lynn Center) (Aug); Augustana Nursery, 2042 N. Orleans St., Chicago (Aug); Danish Luth. Children's Home, 3320 Evergreen Ave., Chicago (Dan); Luth. Deaconess Day Nursery, 1808 N. Fairfield Ave., Chicago (EVL); Luth. Home-Finding Soc. of Ill., 4840 Byron St., Chicago (Int); Norw. Luth. Children's Home, 6000 Canfield Ave., Chicago (Ex); Luth. Home for Children, 1323 S. Rowell Ave., Joliet (Aug); Children's Receiving Home, 809 Madison St., Maywood (Ex); Nachusa Luth. Home for Children, Nachusa (ULC).

Indiana: Luth. Child Welfare Assn. of Ind., 3310 E. Washington St., Indianapolis (Mo); Wernle Children's Home, Richmond (ALC).

Iowa: Beloit Luth. Children's Home, Ames (EVL); Luth. Welfare Society of Iowa, 423 Grand Ave., Des Moines (Ex); Elim Luth. Home, Elk Horn (UE); Luth. Home-Finding Soc. of Iowa, 234 N. 9th Ave., Fort Dodge (Mo); Luth. Homes, Muscatine (ALC); Luth. Children's Home, Waverly (ALC).

Kansas: Mariadahl Children's Home, Cleburne (Aug); Luth. Children's Friend Soc., 411 Park, Winfield (Mo).

Louisiana: Bethlehem Orphan Home, 5413 N. Peters St., New Orleans (Mo).

Maryland: Augsburg Home, Pikesville (Balt.) (Mo).

Massachusetts: Luth. Children's Home, 60—70 Main St., Avon (Aug); Luth. Assn. for Works of Mercy, 670 Baker St., W. Roxbury (Mo).

Michigan: Luth. Children's Friend Soc. of Mich., 302 Tuscola Rd., Bay City (SC); Luth. Charities Child Welfare Dept., 414 E. Grand Blvd., Detroit (Ex).

Minnesota: Bethany Children's Home, Alexandria (Aug); Bethany Children's Home, 40th Ave., N., Duluth (Aug); Lake Park Children's Home, Lake Park (EVL); Augustana Children's Home, 1009 E. 14th St., Minneapolis (Aug); Luth. Children's Friend Soc., 3606 Edmund Blvd., Minneapolis (SC); Luth. Welfare Society, 2110 1st Ave., Minneapolis (Ex); Vasa Children's Home, Red Wing (Aug); Bd. of Christian Service, 254 E. 10th St., St. Paul (Aug); Luth. Children's Receiving Home, 1245 N. Hamline, St. Paul (Aug); Tyler Children's Home, Tyler (Dan).

Missouri: Luth. Orphans' Home, 12325 Manchester Rd., St. Louis 22 (SC); Luth. Children's Friend Soc., 2848 a N. Grand Ave., St. Louis 7 (SC).

Nebraska: Tabitha Home, Lincoln (ULC); Immanuel Children's Homes, 34th and Fowler Ave., Omaha (Aug); Luth. Children's Home Soc., 408 Karmach Block, Omaha (SC); Martin Luther Home, Sterling (Ex).

New Jersey: Kinderfreund Orphans' Home, 93 Nelson Ave., Jersey City (Ex).

New York: Children's Home, 564 2nd St., Brooklyn (Ex); Luth. Inner Mission Soc., 525 Clinton Ave., Brooklyn (Ex); Norw. Children's Home, 1355 84th St., Brooklyn (Ex); Ev. Luth. St. John's Orphan Home, Mineral Spring Rd., Buffalo (Ex); Luth. Service Soc. of New York, 115—117 Glenwood Ave., Buffalo (Mo); Gustavus Adolphus Children's Home, 705 Falconer, Jamestown (Aug); Wartburg Orphans' Farm

School, Bradley Ave., Mt. Vernon (Ex); Luth. Welfare Council, 105 E. 22nd St., New York (Ex); Bethlehem Luth. Children's Home, 375 Fingerboard Rd., Staten Island (Mo).
North Carolina: Sipes Orchard Home, R. 1, Conover (Ex).
North Dakota: Luth. Welfare Soc. of N. Dak., 23½ Broadway, Fargo (Ex); Crippled Children's School, Jamestown (Ex).
Ohio: Luth. Children's Aid Soc., 4106 Frank Blvd., Cleveland (SC); Osterlen Home for Children, R. 3, Springfield (ULC); Luth. Orphans' Home, 2411 Seaman St., Toledo (ALC); Luth. Welfare Service of N. W. Ohio, 210 Summit St., Toledo (Ex).
Oklahoma: Cherokee Mission Home, Oaks (UE).
Pennsylvania: Good Shepherd Home, 6th & St. John Sts., Allentown (Ex); Ev. Luth. Concordia Home, Butler Co., Cabot (SC); Tabor Home for Children, Doylestown (Ex); Tressler Orphans' Home, Loysville (ULC); St. John's Luth. Home, Mars (ALC); Bethesda Home for Children, R. 3, Meadville (ULC); Emmaus Orphan Home, Middletown (Ex); Luth. Children's Bureau, 1228 Spruce St., Philadelphia (ULC); Luth. Home for Orphans and Aged, 6950 Germantown Ave., Philadelphia (ULC); Luth. Inner Mission Soc. of Pittsburgh, 533 Wabash Bldg., Pittsburgh (Ex); Luth. Home at Topton, Topton (ULC); Orphans' Home and Farm School, Box 298, Zelienople (ULC).
South Dakota: Bethesda Children's Home, Beresford (EVL); Luth. Welfare Soc. of S. Dak., 327 S. Duluth Ave., Sioux Falls (EVL); Luth. Benevolent Association, 1509 Mulberry, Yankton, S. Dak. (Mo).
Tennessee: Williams-Hensson Home for Boys, R. 3, Knoxville (ULC).
Texas: Trinity Luth. Homes, Round Rock (Ex).
Virginia: Luth. Orphan Home of the South, B. 151, Salem (ULC).
Washington: Parkland Children's Home, Everett (EVL); Martha and Mary Children's Home, Poulsbo (LF); Associated Luth. Welfare, 307 Medical Arts Bldg., Seattle (Ex).
Wisconsin: Luth. Welfare Soc. of Wis., 3005 W. Kilbourn, Milwaukee (Ex); Martin Luther Children's Home, Stoughton (Ex); Bethany Children's Home, Waupaca (Ex); Luth. Children's Friend Soc. of Wis., 8138 Harwood Ave., Wauwatosa (SC); Homme Children's Home, Wittenberg (Ex).

(Information gathered by the National Lutheran Council, Division of Public Relations. Ad. by AS.)

HFW-CK

Child Welfare Associations. See *Child Care and Child-Placing Agencies.*

Children, Dependent, Care and Training of. See *Charities, Christian; Child Care and Child-Placing Agencies.*

Children of the Light (or Truth). See *Friends, Society of.*

Children's Crusade. See *Crusades.*

Children's Friend Society. See *Associated Lutheran Charities, A 3.*

Children's Services. A form of public worship in which hymns and other songs sung by children are the outstanding feature, supplemented by readings, recitations, and catechizations bringing out the special purpose of the day and its service. They are commonly held at Christmas, Easter, on Reformation Day, at Pentecost, and on Rally Day. Often they are liturgical in character.

Chile. See *South America.*

Chiliasm. *See Millennium.*

Chillingworth, William (1602—44). Anglican. B. at Oxford; Catholic, 1630; Anglican again, 1634; chancellor of Salisbury, 1638; chaplain of royal army; prisoner of "rebels"; d. at Chichester. Wrote *Religion of Protestants a Safe Way to Salvation* (1637) in which he vindicated the sole authority of the Bible and the individual's right to study it.

China. The Sinae or Seres of the ancient world, Cathay of the medieval, a republic since 1911, embraces a vast territory in the eastern part of Asia, some 3,422,350 sq. mi., with an estimated population of 469,000,000. The Chinese call it "The Middle Kingdom." The country is divided into provinces, such as Chekiang, Chili, Fukien, Honan, Hopeh, Hunan, Hupeh, Kansu, Kiangsi, Kiangsu, Kwangsi, Kwangtung, Kweichow, Anwhei, Shansi, Shantung, Shensi, Szechuan, Yunnan, Sikang, Sinkiang, Manchuria, Chahar, Suiyuan, Minghsia. The latitude is about the same as that of North American countries (stretching comparatively from Hudson Bay to Nicaragua and from Portland, Me., to San Francisco), and the climate is similar to that of the North American continent. The greater part of the country is mountainous, but there are large tracts of fertile soil, chiefly on the Great Plains and in the valleys of the great rivers. The most important rivers are the Yangtze, 3,000 miles long; the Hwang-Ho or Yellow River, 2,600 miles; the West River, 1,250 miles; the Amur. The Grand Canal (650 miles) connects the Yangtze and the Hwang-Ho. The Chinese belong to the Mongolian type of the human race, some sixty tribes being represented. Civilization early reached a high stage of development in China, but then remained at a standstill for centuries, with the country closed to foreign influences. Education was held in highest esteem, though it was not common. Rigorous examinations in the classical literature of the country were required for political preferment. A great change in educational methods was brought about after the revolution of 1911, common schools rapidly increasing in number and opened to "Western" methods. The early history of the Chinese people, while highly elaborated and embellished by Chinese historians, is hidden in darkness. Dynasty after dynasty is recorded of which no tangible trace appears. But China was a civilized nation when all European nations were steeped in barbarism. Its culture unquestionably antedates that of the Greeks and Romans. The oldest dynasty bordering on historical domain appears to be the Chow dynasty, founded by Wu Wang, and lasting from 1122 B. C. to 255 B. C. During this dynasty Confucius, the great teacher (551 B. C.), and other prominent men, whose writings are still extant, flourished. The religion of China is eclectic, a mixture of Confucianism, Taoism, and Buddhism. All over China there is a multitude of temples, large and small, elaborate and mean, in a good state of preservation and dilapidated and crumbling, and an endless number of ritualistic acts is performed by the generally densely ignorant priests and monks. The average Chinese lives in constant dread of evil spirits, whose malicious intentions he must thwart, whose anger he must appease. Ancestor worship is an outstanding feature of the Chinese cultus. The worship of Heaven, the Earth, the Sun, in short, natural forces, is elementary with Confucianism. Mohammedanism claims some 15 million adherents. Buddhism in China, having come in from India in the first century, is of later origin than Confucianism. Its most prominent feature is the countless "births" through which each individual must pass before entering into "salvation." In the early history of Christianity religious Christian thought appears to have penetrated to China. Some Buddhist sects have distinct reflexes of Biblical truth derived from tracts like *The Awakening of Faith,* and *The Lotus Scripture,* which date back to the third century A. D. (cf. *The Creed of Half Japan,* by Arthur Lloyd). Manichaeism unquestionably had found an entrance into China long before A. D. 800 (cf. "An Ancient Chinese Christian Document" in the *Church Missionary Review,* October, 1912). Nestorianism in China is historical through the remarkable "Nestorian Tablet," which dates from the eighth century and was discovered at Hsianfu in 1625, and through the records of persecutions contained in Chinese literature, had gained a foothold (there is record, for instance, of a bishop, David) before the Mohammedans came in the tenth century. The Popes at Rome, during the centuries antedating the Reformation, made repeated attempts to introduce the Roman faith into China, but only with passing success and with no lasting results. Marco Polo, famed ancient traveler (13th century) mentions Christian churches. John of Monte Corvino wrote in 1305 that he had had no news of Europe in 12 years. In the 16th century new Roman Catholic attempts were made by Francis Xavier (d. Dec. 2, 1552, on Shang Ch'uan Shan, near Macao) and Ricci, a Jesuit (d. 1610). In 1631 the Dominicans arrived. These were followed by the Franciscans in 1633. These two orders protested violently to Rome against the Jesuitic accommodation to paganism, and finally Pope Innocent issued a bull against the Jesuits (1645), which was annulled by Pope Alexander VII (1656), but virtually renewed by Clement XI (1704). In 1692 Kanghsi, the Chinese emperor, who had been educated by the Jesuits, legalized the dissemination of the Christian religion throughout the empire. His successor, Yung-cheng (1736), inaugurated persecutions against the Romish Church, which continued for many years. Many laws were promulgated against popery. Later, popery and the French colonial policy formed an alliance, which led to a renaissance of the Catholic Church in China, but because of its political intrigues also served to make not only it, but all mission work obnoxious. Only the Protestant missions, with their positive stand against court cases, served to remove some of the odium resting upon their work.

Protestant missions, due to the Chinese policy of hermetic exclusion of all foreigners, did not enter China until the middle of the 19th century. Robert Morrison, sent by the L. M. S., came to China, Sept. 7, 1807, followed by Mr. and Mrs. Milne in 1813, who lived in Macao, Malacca, and secretly in Canton, doing valuable linguistic work. In 1813 Morrison published a translation of the whole New Testament. In 1830 the American Board sent Bridgman to Canton. Guetzlaff, a missionary of Father Jaenicke's Seminary in Berlin, reached China in 1831, doing independent missionary work, but only on the border of China. After the notorious Opium War between England and China (1842), China was forced to open the five port cities: Shanghai, Ningpo, Fuchow, Amoy, and Canton, and as a result a new era for commercial and missionary endeavor was ushered in. Later wars opened new ports, but also increased the Chinese opposition to foreign commercial and religious contact, which resulted in frequent persecutions and culminated in the Boxer outbreak of 1900, in which some two hundred missionary folk and thousands of Christians lost their lives. Although American, Canadian, and continental missionary societies of all descriptions have done religious work in China, there are still many districts populated by millions that have not seen a single bearer of the message of Christ Jesus. Since 1835 missions were opened in China by a great number of organizations in Europe, America, and Australia, and by the international China Inland Mission. In addition, 18 China agencies are engaged in some form of mission endeavor. The Missouri Synod entered the field in 1913. Though it appeared that China offered excellent opportunities for mission endeavor after World War II, the coming to power of the People's Government in 1948 forced the withdrawal of mission personnel. By the close of 1952 only about 30 Protestant missionaries were known to be in China. The last Missouri Synod worker came out in June, 1952. Many missionaries once assigned to China have opened new areas occupied heavily by Chinese, especially Malaya, Indonesia, and Formosa (Taiwan). See also Luth. Church — Mo. Syn.; Missions, Bibliography. OHS

China Inland Mission. Founded by the Rev. James Hudson Taylor in 1865, began working about 1854. Interdenominational and international, receiving many of its workers from Europe and Australia, as well as from Canada and the United States. Separate schools for training male and female workers have been established in the field. American headquarters are in Philadelphia. It started with the plan of placing two missionaries in every province. No mission society has penetrated China like the C. I. M., with 1,325 foreign workers in 1938. A so-called faith mission; its workers are promised no fixed salary; it will not go into debt; it depends upon freewill offerings.

China, Religions of. See Buddhism; Confucianism; Taoism.

Chiniqui, Charles Paschal Telesphore. Controversial writer; b. in Canada, 1809; d. at Montreal, 1899; Roman Catholic priest 1833 to 1858, "Apostle of Temperance of Canada"; left Church of Rome and joined Canadian Presbyterians; lectured extensively, also in England and Canada; wrote tracts on temperance and books bitterly hostile to Roman Church.

Choir, Chorister. Although hymns and antiphonal psalms and songs were in use in the Christian Church since earliest times, the choir as a separate organization does not appear until the establishment of Christianity as the state religion, in the fourth century. At that time the choir members, all of them male voices, as a matter of course, were reckoned as members of the lower clergy, their position in the church being next to the apse, in the east end of the nave, between the two ambos. During the medieval period, when the choir took the place of the congregation in the entire liturgical service, its position was shifted to the organ loft, opposite the altar. Since the Reformation three tendencies are to be noted. In the Anglican Church the choir is divided into two sets of voices, the one sitting on the north and the other on the south side of the chancel, the one set being known as the *cantores*, from their position near the *cantor* or *precentor*, the other as the *decani*, from their nearness to the *decanus*, or dean. The *decani* usually have the best voices and sing the solos and the first choir in eight-part music. The choristers in the Church of England are vested and are considered members of the lower clergy. The Anglican idea has influenced many other Reformed bodies, which have either adopted it as a whole or adapted it in some form, since it agrees with their notion of prayer as a means of grace. Luther, by restoring liturgical response and hymn singing to the congregation, did not seek to abolish the choir. The choir is, however, co-operative with the congregation as a whole and does not have a position above it. While it alternates with the congregation in order to beautify the service, it, according to Lutheran custom, does not take the place of the congregation to the latter's exclusion from active participation in the worship.

Choral, Chorale. The choral was developed from the *cantus choralis,* or choral chant, the plain chant introduced at the time of Gregory the Great. It was really structurally monotonic, in part mere musically graduated, stereotyped recitative, the rise and fall of the vocal tone, the choice of intervals, the tonic measure, being determined not with reference to the rhythm of the words or to grace and expression of melody, but simply by the textual notation. To carry out his ideas, Gregory made use of his *schola cantorum* in Rome and ordered that no man was to be ordained priest unless he was thoroughly acquainted with singing. From Rome, choral singing of this form spread to England and to the empire of Charlemagne, the latter being very active in founding schools for singing north of the Alps, the most renowned being that of Metz, under the management of Rhabanus Maurus. The noble simplicity of the Gregorian choral was continued in the Lutheran chorale, as introduced by Luther and his co-workers; the reformers, however, possessed the necessary insight into the circumstances of their times, which prompted them to embody in the choral tunes the elements of the religious folk song, making the Lutheran chorale a metrically coherent, rhythmically expressive, sonorously emotional unit, well adapted for the stately beauty as well as for the delicate shadings of the hymns which were composed in the century of the Reformation. Although the word *chorale* is used variously and is often used to indicate vocal and instrumental music of breadth and majesty, the word is most commonly used to identify and distinguish the hymns of the Lutheran Church, regardless of nationality, time, and spirit. There thus exists a wide variety of chorale types. According to common present day practice the letter *e* is added at the end to distinguish the word from *choral* in meaning and accent, but the final *e* is silent. The word is not capitalized.

Choral Cantata. See *Cantata.*

Chorale Prelude. The chorale prelude is an organ composition based on a chorale. Hymn preludes began to play a very important part in Lutheran services of worship shortly after 1597, the year in which the theological faculty at Wittenberg officially documented its approval of the use of the organ in the Lutheran church service. Although the Thirty Years' War (1618 to 1648) brought a halt to most organ building in Germany, it was during these years that the chorale prelude was born. Although Samuel Scheidt is regarded as "the father of the chorale prelude," the chorale fantasies of Michael Praetorius as well as the chorale variations of the composers of northern Germany helped bring the chorale prelude into existence. By and large, the Lutheran masters, notably of north and central Germany, were at their best in the field of organ composition when writing their chorale preludes. This was due in no small measure to the fact that the chorale was to them a vital part of their worship life. The chorale preludes of men like J. G. Walther, Buxtehude, Pachelbel, and the Bachs are among the finest gems of all organ literature.

Chorister. See *Choir.*

Chosen. See *Korea.*

Chrischona (St. Crischona). Pilgrim Mission (Pilgermission von St. Chrischona bei Basel); founded by Pastor C. F. Spittler of St. Chrischona, 1840, as a mission school; expanded 1860 for mission work in Abyssinia, which, however, was unsuccessful and therefore was soon abandoned; since 1895 in connection with the China Inland Mission. The society also sent missionaries to Lutherans in America.

Chrism. The oil used for certain rites of anointing in the Greek and the Roman Catholic churches, especially in Baptism, confirmation, ordination, and extreme unction. The blessing of this sacramental oil takes place annually, on Maundy Thursday.

Chrismon. A monogram made of the first two Greek letters of *Christos* (XP).

"Christ, Benefits of." The title of a famous evangelical treatise attributed by some, though without sufficient evidence, to the Italian reformer and martyr Aonio Paleario. The book was circulated in thousands of copies, but was suppressed by the Inquisition.

Christ Jesus. The Son of God who became man, being incarnate by the Holy Ghost of the Virgin Mary, suffered and died for the sins of the world. He arose again from the dead, ascended into heaven, sits at the right hand of God, and will return to judge the world. All who believe in Him and accept Him as their Savior are the children of God and receive eternal life.

Christ is referred to by many different names in the Bible. These names are not mere titles, but accurate descriptions of His person. The name Jesus is Hebrew and means Savior (Matt. 1:21. Cf. Acts 4:12). The other name, Christ (Christos), is Greek, and means Anointed. Jesus was anointed with the Holy Spirit at His Baptism (John 1:32, 33; Is. 11:2). The word Messiah is the designation the Jews used after the Babylonian Captivity when they referred to the Savior who was to come (John 4:25; 1:41).

I. Person of Christ. Christ Jesus is true God, begotten of the Father from eternity, and also true man, conceived by the Holy Ghost and born of the Virgin Mary.

A. Deity. So completely is the doctrine of Jesus' deity the foundation of the Christian religion that Jesus recognizes only that faith which acknowledges Him as the Son of God (Matt. 16). Jesus appears as God on the pages of the OT and there reveals Himself by such titles as Angel of the Lord,* Jehovah, Lord (the latter used preeminently in the Old Testament of Christ), etc. (compare 1 Cor. 10:3, 4 with Ex. 13:21; 14:19; John 12:41 with Is. 6:1-5; Heb. 12:18-26 with Ps. 68:7, 8, 17, 18). The NT naturally provides clearer evidence of the deity of Christ. Thus the Gospel of John was written "that ye might believe that Jesus is the Christ, the Son of God" (John 20:31). Because of the unity of His essence with the Father, Jesus could say: "I and My Father are one" (John 10:30; cf. John 14:9).

Christ is begotten or born of the Father from eternity (John 1:14, 18; Rom. 1:3; 8:32; 1 John 1:7; 1 Pet. 1:3; 1 Thess. 1:1; Heb. 1:5; Micah 5:2; Ps. 2:7). The words "this day" in the second Psalm refer to the eternal day of the Father. In His eternal life the Father has generated the Son, who is as old and as eternal as the Father Himself.

Those who deny the deity of Christ (Cerinthus, Arius, modern theologians) reject the foundation of the Christian religion.

B. Humanity. Jesus was conceived by the Holy Ghost and born of the Virgin Mary (Luke 1:35 ff.; Heb. 2:14; Matt. 1:16). He was miraculously (Luke 1:37) made of a woman (Gal. 4:4) as had been prophesied (Gen. 3:15). The conception of Jesus was a sinless conception (Luke 1:35). That Mary remained a virgin until the birth of Christ is shown by Is. 7:14 and Matt. 1:23. The question of how a sinless nature could originate out of the sinful blood of Mary caused Roman Catholics to evolve the doctrine of the immaculate conception of Mary and others to hold that God preserved a sinless flesh from the time of Adam (both ideas are contrary to Scripture, John 3:6; Rom. 5:18). Chemnitz states: "In the article of redemption the Scriptures testify mightily that the Son of God assumed our human nature, which in conception was cleansed from sin." (Cf. Luther, St. Louis Ed., II:1171 f.)

By His birth Jesus became a man in the full sense of the word. He took part of the flesh and blood of children (Heb. 2:14; Rom. 9:5; John 1:14), had a real body and soul and a human will, ate, drank, grew weary, and died a real death (cf. Luther, XIII: 490 f.). Only in one respect did Jesus differ from His brethren: He was without sin (original as well as actual, Heb. 7:26; Rom. 5: 18, 19; 2 Cor. 5:21) and hence free from the germ of death (Rom. 6:23; John 10:18). The humanity of Christ is essential for our salvation, for the Redeemer of the world had to assume the guilt and penalty of the Law which was binding on all men, and this was possible only if He became like us in all things, in a perfect human nature (Gal. 4:4).

Though otherwise a human nature is also a person, it is peculiar to the human nature of Christ that it does not constitute a separate being (enhypostasia) and never existed by itself. The human nature did not receive the divine, but the divine assumed the human.

C. Jesus Christ is true God and true man in one person (John 1:14; 1 Tim. 2:5), in which person the human nature and the divine nature are united in the most intimate communion (1 Tim. 3:16; Rom. 1:3, 4). In this unique union the divine nature is in the human nature and *vice versa*. This uniting of God and man in one being is called the personal union (*unio personalis*) and is expressed in the axiom: Neither is the flesh without the Word, nor the Word without the flesh.

Despite the intimacy of the union of the two natures in Christ, however, each nature remains intact, just as soul and body remain what they are, though united in one person (Col. 2:9). There is no commingling of the natures. By the union of God and man in Christ there did not originate a third nature, the divine-human nature. Because the two natures are so closely conjoined in Christ, the dogmaticians speak of *propositiones personales* (personal statements). Thus one can say on the basis of Scripture: this man is God; and: this God is man (Luke 1:31, 32; 2:11; Gal. 4:4; Acts 20:28; Rom. 5:10). C.f. LER, *Abiding Word*, I:18–38.

D. *Communication of Attributes.* Though in the person of Jesus Christ each nature retains its essential attributes unchanged and undiminished in kind and number, yet each nature also communicates its attributes to the other in the personal union, so that the divine nature participates in properties of the human nature and *vice versa*. Three kinds of statements of Scripture teaching this communication of attributes (*communicatio idiomatum*) have been distinguished. These three kinds of communications have been called *genus idiomaticum, genus maiestaticum, genus apotelesmaticum* (*F. of C.*).

1. Scripture passages classified as statements of the *genus idiomaticum* * are those whereby attributes of either nature are ascribed to the entire person of Christ, *divine* attributes are ascribed to the concrete of His human nature, and *human* attributes are ascribed to the concrete of His divine nature, for instance, Heb. 13:8 and John 21:17; Matt. 9:6 and Gal. 4:4.

2. Propositions of the second group (*genus maiestaticum*), the genus of glory, deal with the divine attributes showing forth the glory of the Only-begotten of the Father. Though the human nature of the person of Christ remains truly human, yet all the divine properties and perfections and the honor and glory pertaining to this divine nature are as truly communicated to His human nature, so that the divine

perfections which the divine nature has as essential attributes, the human nature has as communicated attributes. In Christ dwelleth all the fullness of the Godhead bodily (Col. 2:9; Heb. 1:3). By virtue of the personal union the Son of Man, while He walked on earth and was closeted with Nicodemus, was also in heaven (John 3:13), even as now, being ascended into heaven, He, the Son of Man, is with His Church on earth even unto the end of the world (Matt. 28:20). By the direct communication of the operative attributes, Jesus was constituted an omnipotent man; in the man Christ Jesus there dwelt, through and with the operative attributes, eternal life, infinite wisdom, immutable holiness and righteousness, boundless power, love indivisible and everlasting as God Himself. Although the human nature in Christ remained truly human and as such could be, and was, exposed to temptation, this human nature, by this communicated holiness, was not only sinless, but absolutely impeccable.

3. The third group of Scripture texts concerning the communion of attributes in Christ classifies as the *genus apotelesmaticum*. The term is derived from the Greek word for the performance of a task. Scripture texts under this head assert a union by which in official acts each nature performs what is peculiar to itself with the participation of the other. Not only did the entire person, Christ, die for our sins (1 Cor. 15:3), but we were reconciled to God by the death of His Son (Rom. 5:10). Thus also the obedience of the child Jesus was a fulfillment of the Fourth Commandment rendered by the Son of God. And when He died on the cross, such suffering of body and soul was undergone by that human nature to which alone it was proper to suffer and die, but with the concurrence of the divine nature personally united with the human nature. The third genus, particularly, might appear as an unnecessary burdening of Christian dogmatics. It is, like the Lutheran treatment of Christology in general, occasioned by the Reformed opposition. Reformed theology to the present day strenuously demands the separation of Christ's actions as man from His actions as the Son of God. For instance, Hodge: "Omnipresence and omniscience are not attributes of which a creature can be made the organ." "The human nature of Christ is no more omniscient or almighty than the worker of a miracle is

omnipotent." "A human soul which is omniscient is not a human soul." As a matter of fact even the Reformed Christian will not hesitate to accept 1 John 1:7. But by accepting this text, he subscribes to the three genera of the communion of attributes: for he believes 1) that the blood of Christ, which was the blood of a human being, was the blood of God's Son; 2) that divine power, the cleansing of sin, is to be ascribed to the blood of the man Christ; and 3) that both natures co-operate in a human-divine act.

II. 1. *The States of Humiliation and Exaltation.* For the work of redemption Christ, the God-Man, humiliated Himself (Phil. 2:6). To humble oneself is to forego prerogatives which one might rightfully claim. That nature according to which Christ humbled Himself was the human nature, the divine nature as such being not capable of humiliation or exaltation or any other change of state or condition. Yet it was not the man Christ, independent of the Logos, who humiliated Himself — for thus the man Christ never existed — but the indivisible person Jesus Christ. This humiliation did not consist in the assumption of the human nature by the divine nature, for then His exaltation must have consisted in an abandonment of the human nature by the divine nature and a dissolution of the personal union — the error of the Gnostics * of old — and in this case the Son of Man would not now sit at the right hand of the Father Almighty. The humiliation of the God-Man rather was that self-denial by which He forebore using and enjoying constantly what He might rightfully have used and enjoyed. When He might have deported Himself as the Lord of Lords, He took upon Himself the humble form of a servant. Being rich, He took upon Himself poverty. He who fed the thousands by the lakeside suffered hunger in the desert and thirst on the cross. It was the Lord of Glory who was crucified; the Prince of Life was killed. Lastly, the body of the Holy One of God was laid low in another man's grave. Of course, what Christ did willingly and obediently forego was not the possession, but the full and constant use, of the divine majesty communicated to His human nature. Through all the years of His humiliation, from the night of His nativity to the night which shrouded Golgotha in darkness at midday, rays and flashes of the glory bore the Only-Begotten of the Father bore

witness to the majesty of the Son of Man. He knew what was in Nathanael's heart, read the past history of the Samaritan woman, and saw the thoughts of the disciples as well as of His enemies. He was in heaven while He taught Nicodemus by night. — The purpose of this humiliation of the God-Man was the redemption of the world. The Holy One of God humiliated Himself and became obedient unto death to make atonement for our rebellious disobedience. God in His righteousness demanded that man should fulfill the Law in perfect love toward God and toward his neighbor. And hence man's Substitute was "made under the Law." But as the continued use of His divine majesty would have placed Jesus beyond the power of His human enemies, it was necessary that He should forego such full and constant use of His divine power and majesty, in order that the work of redemption might be performed and the Scriptures might be fulfilled (Matt. 28:19, 20).

2. The resumption and continuation of such full and constant use of His divine attributes according to His human nature was and is the exaltation of Christ, the God-Man. The God-Man was exalted, according to the same nature which alone could be humbled and which alone could be exalted (Eph. 4:8; Heb. 2:7). Before coming forth from the tomb He, according to His human nature, descended to hell and manifested His glory to the spirits condemned because of their unbelief (1 Pet. 3:18 ff. See *Descent into Hell*). Christ's resurrection was the public proclamation of His victory over sin and death. By His ascension He visibly entered according to His human nature into His heavenly kingdom. And now, sitting at the right hand of Power, He exercises dominion also according to His human nature over all creatures and especially over His Church. Thus the form of a servant has been forever put away, and when His exaltation will culminate, He will come again, indeed, as the Son of Man, but He will come and appear in His glory and sit upon the throne of His majesty with power and great glory (Matt. 25:31; Luke 21:27).

III. *The Office of Christ.* The name Christ, strictly speaking, is not a proper name but a designation of office. It signifies a person set apart for a purpose, one anointed to a task, and, in the case of our Lord, "the Anointed One," who functioned and functions in an absolutely unique sense as Prophet, Priest, and King. While Luther, Melanchthon, and the other early Lutheran theologians do not use this distinction technically, it appears even in Eusebius. It was introduced into Lutheran theology by Gerhard. — Anointed, then, means that Jesus was appointed, qualified, commissioned, and accredited to be the Savior of men. He was divinely appointed to the office which He filled (Heb. 5:4). He was qualified in that He received the Spirit "without measure." He was divinely commissioned — the Father sent Him; cf. also Is. 49:6. He is divinely accredited (Acts 2:22). Such is the intensive force of the term Christ. It is summed up in Acts 10:38: "God anointed Him with the Holy Ghost and with power."

1. *Prophet*.* Jesus is the great Revealer of divine Truth, both in His own person and by His Word; the Logos of God to man, revealing to lost mankind the holiness, but above all the mercy and love of God.

2. *Priest*.* By His spotless, all-perfect obedience, obedience unto death, He propitiated, in the place of all mankind, the offended majesty of God. "Himself the Victim and Himself the Priest," He has by His vicarious life and suffering fulfilled all righteousness and atoned for all sin. See *Atonement; Faith; Justification*.

3. *King*.* Possessed of "all power in heaven and on earth," Jesus, also according to His human nature, is now "Lord of all," so that all external events in the world of man and of nature and all spiritual influences are equally under His control. As King He carries into full effect the great purpose of His revelations as Prophet and of His atoning sacrifice as High Priest. Particularly, He exercises dominion over the Church He has redeemed, through the Gospel and the holy ministry, in which and for which Church He now reigns over heaven and earth.

See also *Ascension; Descent into Hell; Last Things*.

The doctrine of Christ is central in Christian dogmatic works (see references under *Dogmatics*); see also references in article *Christ, Lives of;* Louis E. Roehm, "The Person of Christ," *Abiding Word*, CPH, 1946 (I:18—38, see also the bibliography); C. J. Hoffmann, "Office, or Work of Christ," *Abiding Word*, 1947 (II:112—144, see also bibliography); John Schaller, *Biblical Christology*, Northwestern Publishing House, Milwaukee, 1919; Werner Elert, *Morphologie des Luthertums*, Beck,

Munich, 1931 (later ed.); J. Bodensieck, "The Person and the Work of Christ," *What Lutherans Are Thinking*, Wartburg Press, Columbus, 1947; Thomas S. Kepler, *Contemporary Thinking About Jesus*, Nashville, 1944; references to *Synodical Reports* and other literature are given in the articles above quoted from *Abiding Word*.

Christ, Lives of. Since about 1775 an immense literature has grown up which concerns itself with the Life of Christ. A brilliant survey chiefly of the critical, negative works of this nature is furnished in the book of Albert Schweitzer, first issued 1906 under the title *Von Reimarus zu Wrede* and published in a second edition 1913 as *Geschichte der Leben-Jesu-Forschung*. The work was translated into English and entitled *The Quest of the Historical Jesus*. A similar book bringing Schweitzer up to date and introducing several new viewpoints appeared in America, *The Search for the Real Jesus*, by Chester Charlton McCown (1940). Like the work of Schweitzer, it is written from the point of view of the negative critic, but it is valuable because it acquaints one with the productions of radical and skeptical scholarship in this field. The chief phenomena only can be noted. One group of scholars denies that Jesus ever lived; they speak of the story of His life as the Christ-myth (Bruno Bauer, J. M. Robertson, W. B. Smith, A. Kalthoff, P. Jensen, A. Drews, and others). They were decisively refuted by an American scholar, who himself rejects conservative views, S. J. Case, in his book *The Historicity of Jesus*. D. F. Strauss * advocated the so-called mythical theory, that while Jesus was a historical person, we know but few real facts of His life, and that the Gospel accounts are due to mythical development; Renan * wrote a sentimental Life of Jesus in which he treated historical facts more like a novelist than a historian. The so-called "liberal" portrait of Jesus was drawn by scholars who held that Jesus taught chiefly the Fatherhood of God, the brotherhood of man, and the value of human personality (O. Holtzmann, Bousset, Harnack, Frenssen). The "eschatological" Jesus, that is, the view that Jesus very definitely taught that the end of the world was coming soon, probably in a year or two, and that in the catastrophe He would be revealed as the Messiah, was the conception of Albert Schweitzer and J. Weiss. Against all the vagaries, errors, and superficialities of the attackers, Bible scholars like A. Edersheim, F. W. Farrar, J. Stalker, J. Ylvisaker, and more recently A. Fahling, have in large and learned works upheld the Scriptural presentation of the life of the Savior. WA C. C. McCown, *The Search for the Real Jesus*, 1940; "Jesus, Son of Man — A Survey of Recent Discussion," *The Journal of Religion*, Jan., 1948.

"Christ-Myth." See *Christ, Lives of.*

Christadelphians. This small anti-Trinitarian sect was organized by John Thomas (1805—71) at the time of the Civil War. His early affiliation with the Disciples of Christ is evident in his rejection of creeds, the doctrine of the Trinity, and denominational names. He claimed that the existing denominations were apostate and that the churches must return to primitive Christianity in doctrine and practice as defined in the Bible. Though he claimed to accept the inspiration of the Bible, he denied the cardinal doctrines of the Bible, especially 1) the doctrine of the Trinity, teaching a dynamic Monarchianism; 2) the immortality of man, teaching that men are dead in the intermediate state, that the unrighteous will be annihilated, while immortality will be bestowed only upon the righteous; 3) the Scriptural doctrine concerning the Second Coming of Christ, teaching that Israel will be restored in Palestine during a millennium, which will be preceded by the resurrection of the "responsibles" and followed by the Judgment, the just receiving immortality and the unjust to be destroyed; 4) the doctrines of the devil and hell. During the Civil War the followers, being compelled to adopt a name in order to secure exemption from military service, selected the name Christadelphians, "Brothers of Christ." See *(U. S.), Religious Bodies, Bibliography.*

Christaller, Gottlieb. B. at Winnenden, Wuerttemberg; d. at Stuttgart, Dec. 16, 1895. Missionary of Basel Missionary Society to West Africa; made researches into Sudan languages; translated Bible into Tzi (Tschi) and G-a languages.

Christening. See *Grace, Means of; Baptism.*

Christenlehre. See *Parish Education*, F 6.

Christentumsgesellschaft. Founded Aug. 30, 1780, as "Deutsche Gesellschaft thaetiger Befoerderer reiner Lehre und wahrer Gottseligkeit" through the efforts of Joh. Aug. Urlsperger,* Werner Herzog, and others. Its headquarters were at Basel. Originally organized to oppose attacks on the Bible, it soon devoted its energies to missions, charities, and pietistic endeavors.

Christian I (d. 1591). Elector of Saxony; supported Calvinistic party in Saxony; instrumental in the publication of the *Kursaechsische Gebetbuch.*

Christian III. See *Denmark, Lutheranism in*, 2; *Norway, Lutheranism in*, 2.

Christian Alliance. See *Evangelistic Associations*, 5.

Christian and Missionary Alliance. See *Evangelistic Associations*, 5.

Christian Art. See *Art, Ecclesiastical.*

Christian Beacon. See *Union Movements*, 11.

Christian Brotherhood of War Veterans. See *Veterans Organizations.*

Christian Brothers (Brethren of the Christian Schools). Noted and influential Roman Catholic educational brotherhood, founded at Rheims in 1680 by Jean Baptiste de la Salle. The members take the three simple vows,* are pledged to teach without compensation, and wear a special habit. They dare not teach Latin, nor may priests with theological training become members. Except in the United States, they are engaged exclusively in elementary education. Their organization and discipline recall that of the Jesuits, though they have no official connection with that order.

Christian Catholic Apostolic Church in Zion. See *Dowieites.*

Christian Church, History of. Jesus Christ is the central figure in all history. The time preceding His birth was one of preparation for His coming; the time following it is one of planting and growth in His Kingdom of Grace. Church history is the record of this planting and growth, sometimes in the face of great obstacles. The history of the New Testament Church may be roughly divided into three periods: ancient (1—590), medieval (590—1517), and modern (1517—).

I. *Ancient.* 1. *The Apostolic Era.* The disciples of Jesus, the Founder and Head of the Christian Church, were witnesses unto Him in Jerusalem, and in all Judea, and in Samaria, and unto the uttermost part of the earth (Acts

1:8). During the first century there were three great centers in Asia: Jerusalem (30—44), Antioch in Syria (44 to 68), Ephesus (68—100). At Jerusalem was the mother church, which was dispersed before the destruction of Jerusalem (70), many members finding refuge at Pella, in Decapolis. Antioch became the center of Gentile Christianity (disciples first called Christians there, Acts 11:26) and the home base for missions (Acts 13:2). The church at Ephesus, founded by Paul, continued to flourish under John, who went there from Jerusalem when the Jewish War broke out in 66. Before the passing of the Apostolic Era, the Church was firmly planted in the West, e.g., in Rome, where Peter is said to have been crucified in 64, and Paul beheaded in 66.

2. *The Post-Apostolic Era* (100 to 170). In this period were produced the *Writings of the Apostolic Fathers: The First Epistle of Clement* (ca. 97), *The Shepherd of Hermas* (ca. 140—45), *The Epistle of Barnabas* (between 70 and 138), *Seven Epistles of Ignatius* (ca. 110), *Epistle of Polycarp* (ca. 112—18), Papias' *The Exposition of the Oracles of the Lord* (ca. 125), *The Didache* (ca. 100—65), *The Second Epistle of Clement* (ca. 150), and the *Praedicatio Petri* 110—30). To this era also belong the Greek Apologists, who had to defend the Christian faith against the assaults of paganism and Judaism from without and against those of Gnosticism from within. The *Epistle to Diognetus* (ca. 150) is one of the earliest apologies, by an anonymous writer. Among the Greek apologists are the following: Quadratus (Apology to Hadrian, ca. 125), Aristides (Apology to Hadrian or Antoninus Pius), Melito (Apology to Marcus Aurelius), Claudius Apollinaris (Apology to Marcus Aurelius), Miltiades (Apology probably to Marcus Aurelius and Lucius Verus), Athenagoras (Apology to Marcus Aurelius, ca. 177), Theophilus of Antioch (d. about 181; *To Autolycus*), Tatian (Address to the Greeks), Flavius Justinus (2 apologies and Dialog with the Jew Trypho).

Perverters of Christianity: Ebionites,* Elkesaites,* Gnostics* (Simon Magus, Menander, Saturninus, Basilides, Valentinus); Encratites* (Tatian); Ophites or Naaseni. These were opposed by Irenaeus, Tertullian, and Hippolytus (anti-Gnostic Fathers). Marcion (Antithesis: antagonism between the Old and the New Testament). Montanus

(appeared as a prophet and reformer ca. 157). Opponents of the Montanists *: the so-called Alogi.* Against the Montanists the church declares that revelation was closed; the New Testament canon was fixed.

3. *The Ante-Nicene Era* (170—325). Emphasis on the uninterrupted succession of the bishops: to secure the valid transmission of the apostolic tradition, the unity of the episcopacy, and the unity of the church. The church recognized a fixed canon of both the OT (according to the Jewish Synod at Jamnia, ca. A. D. 90) and the NT, a rule of faith, a creed, the Old Roman Symbol. A beginning of scientific theology was made in the Alexandrian Catechetical school (Pantaenus, ca. 185; Clement; Origen, d. 254). The great leaders in the West were Tertullian, Cyprian, Irenaeus, and Hippolytus.

Various heresies threatened the church. Monarchianism *: Dynamic or Adoptionist Monarchianism (Theodotus, the fuller, ca. 190; Theodotus, the money changer, ca. 210; Paul of Samosata); Modalistic Monarchianism (Praxeas, ca. 190). Patripassianism (Noetus, ca. 215). Sabellianism.* Tertullian and others opposing Monarchianism fell into the subordinationist * error. Arianism * (Arius, presbyter and teacher in Alexandria, d. 336) denied that the Son is of one and the same essence as the Father (*homoousios* vs. *homoiousios*). It was opposed by Alexander, Athanasius (d. 373), Gregory of Nazianzus, Basil the Great, Gregory of Nyssa, and Hilary of Poitiers, and condemned by the Council of Nicea (325).

4. *The Post-Nicene Era* (325—590). This era marks new conquests for Christianity and additional formation of doctrine. In 392 Theodosius I forbade all heathen sacrifices; in 529 Justinian I closed the school of philosophy in Athens. A number of barbaric kingdoms, planted on the soil of the decrepit Roman Empire, turned to Christianity. Heresies were combated. Arianism continued to trouble the church. Semi-Arianism (Eusebius of Nicomedia and Theognis of Nicea) was finally defeated at the Council of Constantinople (II), which approved the Nicene Creed, 381. This council also condemned the Macedonians or Pneumatomachians,* who denied that the Holy Spirit was of an essence equal to that of the Father and of the Son, and Apollinarianism (Apollinaris). Nestorianism * (Nestorius), almost converting the two na-

tures of Christ into two persons, was
condemned by the Council of Ephesus
in 431. Monophysitism * (Christ has
only one nature — Eutyches) was condemned at Chalcedon in 451; Constantinople (II, 553), forcibly suppressed it.
Monotheletism * (Christ has only a
divine will) was condemned at Constantinople (III, 680). Donatism *
(Donatus, character of a minister af-
fects his official acts) was opposed by
Augustine, who also combated Pelagianism * (Pelagius, no original sin;
an entirely sinless life is possible).
Pelagianism was condemned at Ephesus (431).

5. Eminent writers of this period:
Ambrose (340—97), Chrysostom (347
to 407), Augustine (354—430), Jerome
(343—420, the Vulgate). Towards the
close of this era there was a great
change in church organization. The
clergy became a special order, economically independent and exempt from
the jurisdiction of the secular courts.
Canon laws and traditions began to
be codified. The power and prestige of
the Bishop of Rome increased. Monasticism * continued to develop (St. Anthony, Symeon Stylites, St. Benedict of
Nursia). But spiritual life deteriorated
(the Dark Ages).

II. The Medieval Period (590—1517).
This period may be divided according
to the fortunes of the Papacy *: its rise
(Gregory I to Gregory VII), its supreme
power (Gregory VII to Boniface VIII),
its decline (Boniface VIII to Leo X).

1. 590—1050. The Eastern Church
suffered tremendous losses to Islam
(Asia overrun). Also the Western
Church (North Africa, Spain), lost
territory, but Islam was turned back
at Tours (732). For the West, however, the period from 590—1050 was
one of great missionary expansion.
St. Patrick had paved the way in Ireland (378—460), Columba (521—97),
Columbanus (543—615), Augustine (d.
604), Willibrord (657—739), Boniface
(672?—755), Ansgar (801—65). Cyrillus and Methodius were missionaries
to the Slavs in Moravia. Vladimir the
Great (d. 1015) Christianized Russia.
The iconoclastic controversy created
much disturbance in the East (Leo the
Isaurian) and was a contributory factor leading to the Great Schism between
the Eastern and the Western churches
(1054). The spurious Donations of
Constantine * pretended to justify the
Pope's temporal power (ca. 751—74),
first established by Pepin III (756).

The Pseudo-Isidorian Decretals * further strengthened the papal power.

Doctrinal Development. The Council of Nicea (787), defining the theory
of image worship, terminated the doctrinal development in the Orthodox
Eastern Church. In the West, the Third
Council of Toledo (589) added the
filioque (and the Son) to the Nicene
Creed. Gregory I defined: the sacrifice
of the Mass, purgatory, intercession of
angels and saints, efficacy of relics,
worship of images, and declared pictures to be the books of the uneducated.
Doctrinal controversies were concerned
with adoptionism * (Elipandus of Toledo and Felix of Urgellis), Gottschalk's
two-fold predestination, and Berengar's
opposition to the doctrine of transubstantiation. Odo of Cluny (942) gave
a new impetus to monasticism and
aimed to reform the church on the
basis of Canon Law. Latin hymnists of
this period: Gregory the Great, Venantius Fortunatus (d. 609), the Venerable
Bede (d. 735), Notker of St. Gall (d.
912), and Peter Damian (d. 1072).

2. 1050—1294. This age includes the
great Investiture conflict * (Gregory
VII vs. Henry IV); the crusades (1096
to 1270); the rise of the military orders *
(Hospitalers or Order of the Knights
of St. John, Knights Templars, the German or Teutonic Knights); the founding of the Mendicant Orders * (the
Dominicans and the Franciscans);
Scholasticism * (realism, nominalism,
conceptualism); the rise of the universities.

3. 1294—1517. Boniface VIII (1294
to 1303) in the bull Unam sanctam
reached the peak of the papal claim to
world supremacy and failed. Pope
Clement V (1304—14) transferred the
papal Curia to Avignon, beginning the
Babylonian Captivity * (1309—77),
which, in turn, resulted in the papal
schism * (1378—1417), ended by the
Council of Constance * (1414—18). The
conciliar movement (Reform Councils:
Pisa, 1409; Constance, 1414—18; Basel,
1431—49). Reformers appeared: Marsilius of Padua (Defensor pacis); William of Occam (1280—1349); John
Gerson (1363—1429); Nicholas of Cusa
(1400—64); the mystics Meister Eckhart (1260—1327) and John Tauler
(1290—1361). Greater than these were:
John Wiclif (1320—84), John Hus
(1369—1415), and Girolamo Savonarola (1452—98).

III. The Modern Period (1517—).
1. The Reformation. Martin Luther
(1483—1546). Leo X (1513—21) ap-

pointed Albert of Brandenburg as chief manager in one district of Germany for the sale of indulgences (John Tetzel, indulgence seller). October 31, 1517, Luther nailed the 95 Theses to a door of the Castle Church in Wittenberg. Luther before Cajetan at the Diet of Augsburg * (1518). The Leipzig Disputation * (1519). Bull of excommunication burned (1520). Luther at the Diet of Worms,* 1521. Translation of the New Testament, 1522. The Peasant Revolt,* 1525. Diet of Spires,* 1526 and 1529 (Protestant). Marburg Colloquy,* 1529. Catechisms, 1529. Diet of Augsburg (Augsburg Confession), 1530. Bible, 1534. Controversies within the German Lutheran churches, 1548—77. Formula of Concord, 1577. Book of Concord published in 1580.

2. Ulrich Zwingli (1484—1531). Zwingli's protest against indulgences preached by Sampson (1519). Zwingli's breach with Rome (1522). Zwingli abolishes mass (1525). Zwingli's death (battle of Kappel, 1531). Zwinglianism is absorbed by Calvinism.

3. John Calvin (1509—64). Calvin's first stay at Geneva (1536—38). *Institutes of the Christian Religion* published (1536). Calvin's second stay at Geneva (1541—64). Cardinal principles of the Reformation: the absolute supremacy of the Bible as the norm for life and doctrine; justification by faith in Jesus Christ; the universal priesthood of all believers.

4. The Lutheran Reformation outside of Germany. Denmark. Frederick I (1523—33) favored Lutheranism. Hans Tausen, "the Danish Luther." Diet of Odense (1527). The *Confessio Haffnica,* Copenhagen (1530). Christian III made Lutheranism the religion of Denmark and of Norway. Diet of Copenhagen legalized the Reformation (1536). The Reformation was introduced in Iceland by Gissur Einarson (1540). Lutheranism was planted in Sweden by Olavus Petri (1493—1552) and his brother Laurentius (1499 to 1573). Gustavus Vasa, elected king of Sweden (1523), favored the Reformation. The Diet of Vesteras (1527) marked its legal introduction. The Reformation was introduced in Finland by Michael Agricola.

5. The Reformation spread rapidly in Poland, but was crushed by Sigismund III. In Bohemia and Moravia Catholicism was upheld by the Jesuits. The Catholic Counter Reformation curbed the spread of the Reformation in Croatia and Slavonia and in Italy.

6. The Swiss reformation spread to nearly all countries of Europe. The first Protestant synod was held in Paris in 1559 (*Confessio Gallicana*). The Protestants in France were called Huguenots. Calvinism became dominant also in the Netherlands. Scotland turned to Calvinism, largely under the leadership of John Knox. The Scottish parliament (1560) officially proclaimed the Reformed faith the religion of Scotland.

7. In England, William Tyndale's (1484—1536) English New Testament (1526) prepared the way for Protestantism. The marital troubles of Henry VIII (1509—47) caused the break with Rome. Thomas Cranmer, the first Protestant archbishop of Canterbury, produced the Ten Articles (1536). The Six Articles constituted a reaction to Protestantism. During the reign of Edward VI (1547—53) Protestantism of the Reformed type was firmly planted. The reaction under Queen Mary (1553 to 1558), was not able to uproot it. Under Queen Elizabeth (1558—1603) Puritans * and Independents * multiplied.

8. Various radical groups sprang up in Europe in the days of the Reformation (Anabaptists; Unitarians).

9. The Catholic Counter Reformation. Organizations opposing the Reformation: the Oratory of Divine Love, the Society of Jesus (Jesuits). The Inquisition * was continued. The Council of Trent * (1545—63) formulated Roman Catholic dogma. The Wars of Religion * worked severe hardships on Catholics as well as Protestants, particularly on the latter. In France three wars (1562—63; 1567—68; 1568—70); in the Netherlands (1572—1609); in Germany (1547—55; 1618—48). Frequently disunion within the Protestant ranks aided the Counter Reformation. So in Poland, in Hungary, and, to some extent, in the Netherlands. Arminianism (Jacob Arminius, 1560—1609) opposed strict Calvinism and was condemned at the Synod of Dort (1619).

10. The seventeenth century was the age of orthodoxy. Protestant doctrines were formulated in a more scientific form (John Gerhard, 1583—1637, Lutheran; Gysbert Voetius, 1589—1676, Reformed). Latitudinarianism * and syncretism were a reaction against the spirit of orthodoxy (William Chillingworth, 1602—44, in England; George Calixtus, 1586—1656, in Germany). The same century produced the Quakers * (George Fox, 1624—91) and

other mystical speculations (Theosophy *).

11. The age of orthodoxy was followed by Pietism * (Philip Jacob Spener, 1635—1705; *collegia pietatis;* August Herman Francke, 1663—1727; Hans Adolph Brorson, d. 1764; Erik Pontoppidan, d. 1755). Sweden suppressed Pietism by a royal decree in 1706. Count Nicholas Ludwig von Zinzendorf (1700—60) made Herrnhut the center of the Moravian * fraternity. In England John Wesley, assisted by his brother Charles and by George Whitefield, founded Methodism.*

12. The indifference to doctrine by Pietism merged into the age of Rationalism,* which was introduced from England, partly directly, partly through France. The eighteenth century made human reason the final test of all things. English Deism recognized it as the only source of knowledge. Unitarianism was favored and God's providence ignored. Roman Catholicism was disturbed by Jansenism * and Quietism.* These religious movements of the 17th and early 18th centuries were violently opposed by the Jesuits. But in the second half of the eighteenth century the Jesuit order was itself temporarily suppressed in Catholic countries, only to come back strong in the nineteenth, and to add greatly to the victory of Ultramontanism (Pius IX, 1846—78).

13. The Holy Orthodox Catholic Apostolic Eastern Church was largely left untouched by the stirring events of Western Christendom. Thoroughly conservative in doctrine and cultus, it was influenced largely only by political movements (rise of the Balkan States; political changes in Russia).

14. The nineteenth and twentieth centuries witnessed a number of religious streams flowing side by side or merging. Romanticism * was a reaction against Rationalism. Friedrich Daniel Ernst Schleiermacher (1768—1834) advocated a religious system which made him the father of Modernism.* Lutheran confessionalism opposed the Prussian Church Union * (1817). Claus Harms (1788—1855).

15. The Church of England produced the Oxford movement (John Henry Newman, 1801—90; John Keble, 1792—1866; Edward B. Pusey, 1800—82). Foreign missions and social reforms were pressed. Many missionary societies were organized. Robert Raikes founded the modern Sunday school (1780). In brief, in spite of new anti-Christian forces unleashed in the world (Communism, materialistic Humanism, Evolutionism), the Church moved forward to new spiritual conquests the world over. LWS

G. P. Fisher, *History of the Christian Church,* Scribner's, N. Y., 1946; R. H. Nichols, *The Growth of the Christian Church,* Westminster Press, Philadelphia, 1941; L. P. Qualben, *A History of the Christian Church,* Thomas Nelson and Sons, N. Y., 1942; W. Walker, *A History of the Christian Church,* Scribner's, 1944.

Christian Church, The (*Church of Christ; Christians*). See *Congregational and Christian Churches,* B.

Christian Commercial Travelers' Association. See *Bible Societies,* 5.

Christian Congregation. See *Evangelistic Associations,* 4.

Christian Education. A. *Christian Education Defined.* Christian education is as old as Christianity. It comprises the efforts of Christians to transmit their beliefs and religious practices to the next generation. The term Christian education is used in various meanings. It may cover the entire teaching program of the Church, including preaching and the instruction and training which is given in the Christian home. Thus used, the term Christian education embraces all activity for the conversion and strengthening of souls. In its strict sense, Christian education begins after a person becomes a child of God, either by Baptism or conversion, and it seeks by means of the Word of God to nourish, strengthen, protect, and perfect him. In practical usage, the term Christian education is most commonly applied in describing the work of individuals or organizations that devote themselves to the teaching of the tenets of Christianity. Christian education is the work of man in so far as he teaches and applies the Word of God; it is the work of God in so far as the Holy Spirit alone makes the Word of God effective in the heart of man.

Religious education may or may not be Christian education. The term may be used to describe the educational efforts of any Christian or non-Christian religious group.

B. *Early Christian Education.* The early Christians were faced with the problem of teaching the tenets of their religion in a world in which they were a small and persecuted minority. At first Christian instruction was given individually, with parents, deacons, and other members of the church doing the teaching. Soon, however, catechumen schools were opened. These were in session at stated periods during the week, and in some cases every day. The instruction extended over a period of several years. Instruction in the secular subjects was received from the parents, from private tutors, and in heathen schools. Christian schools in which the entire education was in charge of Christian teachers came later, beginning perhaps at the end of the second century. An effort was made to train teachers in catechetical schools.

C. *Education During the Middle Ages.* Beginning about A. D. 500, formal education deteriorated and almost disappeared. Whatever education remained retired to monasteries. Some of these taught reading and writing, and some provided for the preservation and copying of manuscripts. Judged by modern standards, the educational activities of even the monasteries were extremely meager.

About A. D. 800, Charlemagne sponsored a movement for an improved and more general education. He brought in scholars, including Alcuin from England, to promote and supervise schools. As a result the monastic schools became more numerous and of a better grade. Some of them provided an education also for youths not intended for the monastic life. But there was no general public demand for education, and the Church failed to emphasize its importance.

Beginning with the 12th century, schools became more numerous. The chantry schools were taught by priests. Sometimes only a select group of children were admitted, sometimes all who would come. In some cases the instruction was free, in others a fee was required.

Guild schools were also organized. These were established by merchants or by craft guilds. They were principally for the children of guild members, though others also attended. In many communities these schools gradually became burgher or town schools, supported by the civic authorities. In many cases they were still taught by priests. The subjects were largely reading and writing in the vernacular and Latin, arithmetic, and some geography and history. Much of the teaching consisted of drill work. There were no textbooks, and the teacher generally dictated what the pupils were to learn.

In general, the education was inadequate, and it reached comparatively few people.

Medieval schools emphasized the seven liberal arts, including the *Trivium* and *Quadrivium* (which see).

D. *Luther and Education.* 1. Modern Christian education stems from the Reformation. The people of Luther's day were unschooled and ignorant, the Papacy being interested in education only in so far as it served to produce faithful and obedient subjects of the Church. Luther's proclamation of the Biblical doctrines of justification by faith and of the universal priesthood of believers liberated the individual from the domination of the Church and made him personally responsible for the salvation of his soul. Thus education became an urgent necessity. Luther therefore advocated universal education, that each individual might be prepared for a faithful discharge of his duties toward God and man.

2. Luther's most important educational treatises are his *Letter to the Mayors and Aldermen of All the Cities in Germany in Behalf of Christian Schools* (1524) and his *Sermon on the Duty of Sending Children to School* (1530). In these and in other writings Luther insisted on an adequate education for all children. He encouraged education on the lower and higher levels. He emphasized *Christian* education throughout and said: "Where the Holy Scriptures do not rule, I certainly advise no one to send his child." He accepted the union of Church and State of his day as a matter of expedience, urging the State both to carry on and to enforce a program of general education. At the same time he continually reminded the parents and the Church of their duties in child training.

3. Luther's educational principles may be summarized briefly as follows: Parents are primarily responsible for the education of their children; universal education is a right and a necessity; it is the duty of the State to establish schools and require regular attendance; the foundation of all school instruction is the Christian religion, but in addition children need to learn Latin, Greek, history, mathematics, singing, physical training, and the practical duties of life; the boys should learn a trade, the girls, housework; children should be taught according to the laws of learning — for example, the knowledge of a thing should precede its name; the teacher must be properly

trained; parents and children owe the teacher due respect, and he should be duly remunerated; the teacher, in turn, should by precept and example show himself worthy of respect; pastors need pedagogical training and teaching experience before entering upon a pastorate, because they are responsible for their congregation's school; every school should have a library.

4. For the study in religion, Luther helped to provide the textbooks. Chief among these was the *Small Catechism* (1529), which already in its first edition recognized the value of visual education in that it included a number of illustrations. Luther's translation of the Bible into the vernacular made also its use possible in the schools. He urged the use of the Bible as "the chief and the most frequently used reading book both in primary and in high schools." The very young were to be "kept in the Gospels." Luther's hymns were also used in the schools.

5. At the request of the Duke of Mansfeld, Luther took an active part in the establishment of two schools in his native town of Eisleben, one for primary, the other for secondary instruction. Both in their courses of study and in their methods, these schools became models for others. The great organizers of Lutheran schools were Luther's co-workers Melanchthon and Bugenhagen. Melanchthon worked especially in the interest of secondary education in central and southern Germany and Bugenhagen (father of Volksschule) in northern Germany and in Denmark. Both were guided by Luther's spirit and principles.

6. Wherever the Reformation spread, education was a part of it, and thus Luther exerted a great influence upon the parochial, private, and public schools of all Protestant countries. He likewise gave impetus to education in the Roman Catholic Church, inasmuch as the Reformation forced the Roman Church to engage in general education as a measure of self-defense.

E. *Lutheran Education since the Reformation.* 1. Since the Reformation, Lutheran schools have followed Lutheranism the world over. Before World War II they were found in Austria, Hungary, Sweden, Norway, Denmark, Russia, Finland, Iceland, Australia, Canada, the United States, and South America, and in Lutheran foreign mission fields in India, China, Africa, and elsewhere.

2. In countries where the Lutheran Church is the state church, as, for example, Norway and Sweden, the teaching of Lutheran doctrine may be carried on in the public schools. In other countries schools are maintained independently by Lutheran congregations, as in the United States and Canada.

3. The first known Lutheran school on American soil was Swedish (1638). When the Salzburgers came to Georgia (1734), they immediately established a school for their children and in time built up a system of Lutheran schools. John Adam Treutlen, the first governor of Georgia, was a product of one of these schools. Henry Melchior Muhlenberg, the "patriarch of the Lutheran Church in America," who arrived in Pennsylvania in 1742, was instrumental in organizing many churches and schools. Lutheran schools of Scandinavian, German, and Dutch origin flourished in New York, Pennsylvania, Delaware, New Jersey, Maryland, the Carolinas, Virginia, and Georgia in early American history.

4. The schools of the Missouri Synod date back to the decade between 1830 and 1840. Among the older of these schools are Immanuel, Cole Camp, Mo. (1834); Zion, Addison (Bensenville), Ill. (1837); St. Paul's, Fort Wayne, Ind. (1837); St. John's, Marysville, Ohio (1839); the schools established by the Saxon immigrants in St. Louis and Perry County, Mo. (1839); and those established by the Bavarian Lutherans in the Saginaw Valley in Michigan (1845). The oldest school in the Missouri Synod is that of St. Matthew's, New York, which has been maintained uninterruptedly since 1753.

5. Early Lutheran schools were often taught in the parsonages by the pastors and were in session only three or four days per week, because of other demands upon the pastors' time. As congregations became more stable and stronger financially, school buildings were erected and full-time teachers called in most instances.

6. In the course of time some Lutheran groups discontinued their schools. Today there are wide differences in the emphasis placed upon Christian education in the various Lutheran church bodies, and upon the agencies and means whereby Christian education is to be achieved. Apart from the Sunday schools and vacation Bible schools, some Lutheran bodies maintain practically no schools, except for

ministerial training schools and foreign mission schools. Others emphasize a complete system of Lutheran education, including elementary schools, high schools, and colleges.

7. Lutheran elementary schools are usually maintained by individual congregations, though some are interparish schools. Lutheran high schools are generally maintained by associations of congregations, because they require a larger constituency. The seminaries, teachers' colleges, and preparatory schools are maintained by Synod, and the Lutheran university at Valparaiso, Ind., is maintained by an association of individuals.

8. The teachers for the Missouri Synod schools are trained at Concordia Teachers College, River Forest, Ill., and at Concordia Teachers College, Seward Nebr. Both train men and women, but the majority of graduates are men who have chosen teaching as their lifework. Also the theological students in the seminaries at St. Louis, Mo., and Springfield, Ill., receive some pedagogical training, because ministerial students and candidates often serve temporarily as supply teachers, and some of the pastors in small parishes are called upon to teach the parochial schools of their congregations. Besides the Missouri Synod, the Joint Synod of Wisconsin maintains a separate teachers' college, Dr. Martin Luther College, New Ulm, Minn.

9. All Lutheran church bodies in the United States maintain Sunday schools, vacation Bible schools, released-time classes, Saturday schools, or other types of classes. The Sunday school is the most popular of these. It was introduced early in the Lutheran bodies that discontinued their parochial schools, but eventually in all Lutheran synods. The Sunday school usually provides a program of Christian education for all ages, from the pre-school age to the adult class. Teacher training departments are conducted in connection with most Lutheran Sunday schools.

10. The Lutheran pastor is held to provide a special course of instruction prior to confirmation, which, normally, occurs at about the age of thirteen or fourteen, but which may occur also at any time during adulthood. Those enrolled in a class that is being prepared for confirmation are called catechumens. Confirmation admits the individual to communicant membership in the Church, but it is not to mark the end of Christian instruction.

11. The various Lutheran church schools are frequently called agencies of Christian education. In most cases these agencies are made to serve the twofold purpose of instruction for the members of the congregation and the winning of the unchurched in the community.

12. The administration and supervision of Christian education rests chiefly in the local congregation. The congregation commonly elects a board of education, which carries on its work under regulations contained in the constitution of the congregation or set up in greater detail apart from the constitution. As a rule, the regulations make the board responsible for the organization, management, and supervision of all educational agencies and activities in the congregation; for increasing enrollments both of members and non-members; for executing resolutions of the congregation in educational matters; for reporting regularly to the congregation; and for proposing changes and improvements in the congregational program of Christian education.

13. The congregational boards and committees of education are aided by official synodical and District boards whose duty is the general supervision and promotion of parish education. Most of the synodical boards of parish education have staffs of full-time workers who counsel congregations in the promotion and improvement of their agencies and who prepare study materials for the various types of schools. They engage in research in Christian education and make their findings available, seeking to establish sound principles and policies of Christian education. In the Missouri Synod the Board for Parish Education is responsible for the larger program of parish education, dealing only indirectly with the individual congregations, though it publishes and promotes most of the educational and promotional publications that serve the local congregation. The District Boards for Parish Education serve in specified geographical areas of the Synod and are closely in touch with the work of the individual congregations. Some Districts have superintendents who visit and counsel the congregations in the parish education efforts.

F. *Statistics on Lutheran Education.*
1. In 1952 Lutheran bodies in the United

States and Canada maintained approximately 27,000 church schools of various kinds. Officers and teachers in these schools numbered 225,000, and the enrollment totaled 2,500,000. The total enrollment in the United Lutheran Church was 900,000, in the American Lutheran Conference, 800,000, and in the Synodical Conference, 800,000.

2. The greater part of the total is accounted for by the Sunday school enrollment, which includes nursery schools and Bible classes. For example: The American Lutheran Church in 1952 had about 275,000 enrolled in its Sunday schools and 54,533 in weekday classes, including 3,119 pupils in its 44 parochial schools.

The strong emphasis on Christian education in the Synodical Conference is evident in the statistics of the bodies belonging to it. In the Missouri Synod, the Sunday school enrollment in 1952 was 525,000, while 104,000 were enrolled in more than 1,000 elementary schools, 14,000 in Saturday schools, 150,000 in vacation Bible schools, and 14,000 in released-time classes, a total of 178,000 enrolled in weekday classes outside of the parochial schools, or a total of 282,000 in all types of weekday schools. Over 4,000 were enrolled in Missouri Synod high schools, and several thousand in church-operated schools of higher education. A somewhat similar ratio prevailed in other bodies belonging to the Synodical Conference.

3. The enrollment in Lutheran elementary schools in America was about 120,000 in 1952. Except for some 3,000 pupils in the schools of the American Lutheran Church, practically all of this enrollment was accounted for by the schools of Synodical Conference churches.

G. *Philosophy of Lutheran Education.* 1. Philosophies of education have their source in the view which men hold of God, of the origin, nature, and destiny of man, of truth, of the Church and of the State, and of other related factors. Thus a philosophy of education forms a pattern whereby those who are engaged in education seek to pass on to future generations a particular set of beliefs and a program of life consistent with these beliefs. Any philosophy of Christian education is so closely articulated with theology that the theology outranks scientific investigation and the postulates of reason as a determinant of the philosophy.

2. Thus the Lutheran philosophy of education is rooted in divine revelation. It gives place to the findings of science and to the postulates of reason which are not at variance with divine revelation. For example: Educational principles and practices that grow out of the origin and destiny of man are derived from revelation, which is divine and irrevocable truth to the Lutheran educator. Principles and practices that grow out of the nature of man are derived in part from revelation, *viz.*, the fact that man is a sinful being; and in part from reason or experience, *viz.*, certain facts which deal with the physical and psychological make-up of man.

3. The Lutheran philosophy of education recognizes the need of consistency in education and the desirability of education in non-conflicting environments, particularly in the case of the young. That is the reason for its insistence on Lutheran schools for Lutherans who engage in formal education (Lutheran elementary schools, Lutheran high schools, and Lutheran colleges and universities), schools that foster the same educational ideals as the Christian home. The Lutheran philosophy holds that the home and the Church have rights and responsibilities in education which are prior to those of the State.

4. On the basis of revelation, Lutheran educators hold that there is one Triune God, who has created man and the universe; that man, rational and distinct from the animals, has a body and soul and has the commission to "subdue the earth," that is, to make it useful for his own good and the good of his fellow men; that Adam and Eve, the first human beings, were created perfectly holy and righteous; that Adam and Eve sinned and that through their disobedience all mankind has become sinful; that the gracious God sacrificed His own Son Jesus Christ for the sins of mankind; that the believer in Christ's redemptive work has pardon for his sins and is saved and will finally go to heaven; that the believer, being a new creature in Christ and the dwelling-place of God's Holy Spirit, loves God and serves Him by prayer and worship, by hearing and reading God's Word, and by living and working in accordance with it; and that in Scripture God has established absolute standards of right and wrong. The Lutheran educator's philosophy revolves about God's grace, Christ's redemptive work, the faith of the believer, and eternal salvation.

5. At the same time Lutheran education recognizes that the Christian

lives in the world and faces such practical problems as making a living, discharging the duties of family life, getting along socially with his fellow men, keeping himself healthy, using his powers for the good of society, and living a satisfying cultural life. The Lutheran philosophy of education therefore provides not only for teaching the way to salvation, but also for teaching the common requirements of life which are inherent in man's physical, social, economic, cultural, and charitable duties and privileges. This calls for attitudes and skills which cover the entire range of man's intellectual, physical, emotional, and volitional life, and Lutheran education seeks to train for these necessary attitudes and skills.

6. Due to its grounding in revelation, Lutheran education is conservative and not easily swayed by new theories of thought. For example: Though it has recognized the contributions of "progressive education" in the field of methods and techniques, it has never accepted its underlying and motivating theory of the natural goodness of man and the perfectibility of man by human means. Because this theory is anti-Scriptural and anti-Christian, Lutheran education rejects it.

7. Lutheran education places a high value upon the individual in accordance with the Biblical doctrine of the universal priesthood. Direct responsibility of the individual to God for his conduct and direct access to God without a priest or other intermediary imply the democratic ideal of education for everyone.

8. While the philosophy of Lutheran education calls for Lutheran schools for all Lutherans who engage in the pursuits of formal education (elementary schools, high schools, colleges, and universities), the practice has not been everywhere consistent with the ideal. Insufficient concentration of Lutheran population in a given area, unsatisfactory economic circumstances of the Lutheran constituency, or other factors have made the ideal impossible of attainment in many communities. It stands nevertheless as an ideal and as a goal, at least in the Lutheran bodies that maintain a system of complete church schools on all levels.

9. The Sunday schools, vacation Bible schools, released-time classes, Bible classes, and other church schools and classes are part of the larger educational program of the Church, and they are being maintained and promoted to achieve those aims and objectives of Lutheran education which can be achieved by these means, as well as to reach those members of the Church and those in the community who cannot be reached by any other means. As to these agencies, the Lutheran Church holds that people of all ages are in need of Christian education, that they might "grow in grace and in the knowledge of their Lord and Savior Jesus Christ" (2 Peter 3:18). For that reason classes are maintained for all age levels, from nursery age to adulthood.

H. *Aims and Objectives of Christian Education.* 1. The ultimate aim of Christian education is the perfect restoration of the image of God which was lost in the fall of man. This aim is achieved partially when man comes to faith in Christ, and it will be fully achieved when the believer enters heaven through a blissful death. All intermediate aims of Christian education center about the ultimate aim. The purpose of Christian education for the life on earth is to restore the Christian to his former blessed state as completely as possible; it is to train men and women who know God as well as He can be known by sinful man, men and women who are sure of their faith in Jesus Christ and of their salvation, and who find their greatest joy in serving God and their fellow men. In short, the aim is an ever-increasing degree of sanctification, which C. F. W. Walther (*Hausandacht,* p. 146) describes as follows: "1. An ever-increasing *enlightenment of the mind;* 2. an ever-increasing *cleanness and renewal of the heart;* 3. an ever-increasing *eagerness in a life of good works.*"

2. Thus the purpose of Christian education and training is to guide, direct, preserve, and strengthen the learner, all in keeping with the Word and will of God; to help him develop a Christian life view; to prepare him for service in home, church, country, and occupation; and to strengthen all other Christian virtues in him. Christian education seeks to develop the individual so that he may become an effective priest for his own person and his own household, as well as an effective witness to the unbelievers about him.

3. Statements of the objectives of Christian education, organized system-

atically and set forth in varying degrees of detail, are found scattered through the publications of the Church. Most of these statements agree in the fundamentals, though they vary greatly in form and in organization. Briefly, they emphasize knowledge of Scriptural truths and the application of these truths to daily living; preparation for worthy membership in the Christian home and family; active and intelligent church membership; active participation in the evangelization of the unchurched community; and the application of Christian principles to the social, economic, and political problems of the community and nation.

I. *Teaching Materials.* 1. The Bible is basic in any program of Christian education, and its content and teaching are emphasized in the teaching materials, though the Bible itself may not always be used by the class. In Lutheran parochial schools, Luther's *Small Catechism* is commonly used for systematic instruction in doctrine. This *Catechism* and its exposition contain a summary of the chief Bible doctrines. A shorter or longer Bible History containing selections from the Bible, usually in Bible language, may be used to teach the most important Biblical historical data in chronological order. Additional Bible reading or Bible study is carried on. In confirmation instruction, Luther's *Catechism* is the basic textbook. Lutheran schools use other modern materials in their religion classes, including workbooks, films, pictures, and similar materials. If a trend can be noted, it is in the direction of more direct study of the Bible itself.

2. Due to varying conditions (length of school term, length of instruction period, different types of students) in the separate agencies, most larger church bodies provide materials that meet as nearly as possible the distinctive needs of the various agencies, such as the parochial school, the Sunday school, the vacation Bible school, released-time classes, or Bible classes. This condition poses difficult problems of co-ordination of materials, because many pupils are enrolled in two or more agencies.

3. The preparation of materials for parochial schools presents the greatest problem, because the parochial school is more than a school to which a course in religion has been added; it is a school in which the Word of God runs like a golden thread through everything that is taught and learned. This is especially true in such subjects as history, geography, civics, literature, sociology, art, and science.

4. The Missouri Synod publishes materials for the religion classes of its parochial schools, a general course of study, curricula for all school subjects, a church history textbook, a reading series, an art series, a textbook in physical education, a music reader and music collections, record forms, and other materials, besides a number of professional books for the teacher.

J. *Legislation Pertaining to Christian Education.* 1. Even in a country that maintains the separation of Church and State, such as the United States, there are a number of areas in the field of Christian education where the interests of Church and State meet, and where legislation is necessary to clarify issues, to insure justice, and to assure an orderly procedure. This legislation deals chiefly with educational standards and supervision, and with provisions for needed social services.

2. There have been times when unfavorable legislation threatened the existence of parochial schools in a number of States. During and after World War I, private and parochial schools on the elementary level were opposed by some as un-American, partly because of foreign languages taught in some of them. A number of schools were closed unlawfully by violence. After this war, the opponents sought to close them by legal means. A number of States passed laws to prohibit the use of any but the English language in the elementary school grades. All such laws were declared unconstitutional when the United States Supreme Court (1923) ruled against the Reed-Norvall foreign-language law of Nebraska, and similar laws of other States. Oregon (1922) passed a law outlawing all private and parochial schools on the elementary level. In 1925 also this law was declared unconstitutional by the United States Supreme Court. The unconstitutionality of the various laws was found chiefly in their restriction of the rights of parents to choose the school and the education for their children. Unfavorable legislation which appeared in Canada, notably in the province of Alberta, during the same period, was later likewise repealed.

3. Legislation pertaining to standards of buildings, equipment, and the school subjects outside of religion in many cases has been a means of improving

the educational program of the parochial schools.

4. In the social service field there exists a wide variety of legislation in the various States. Health service is provided in many communities from State, county, or city funds. Some States or communities furnish bus service or library service for parochial school children. School lunches are generally made available on identical terms to parochial schools and public schools. The Roman Catholic Church demands these services as its right, and in a number of instances the instructional program of the Roman Catholic schools is supported by State funds. The Missouri Synod has tentatively ruled (*Proceedings of Twenty-Fourth Delegate Synod*, Saginaw, Mich., 1944, and *Proceedings of the Twenty-Fifth Delegate Synod*, Chicago, Ill., 1947) that the Church may accept aid for its social service program. Aid to parochial schools is opposed by many American taxpayers, who hold that it violates the principles of the separation of Church and State and that it jeopardizes the welfare of the public schools.

5. State laws and local ordinances frequently authorize or forbid Bible reading in public schools, authorize periods of religious instruction under public school auspices, or permit the release of public school pupils to the church of their choice for religious instruction. The public school authorities in many communities are glad to offer school time particularly for released-time instruction. The management of released-time classes is the responsibility of the church which sponsors them. However, the school as a rule makes three requirements of a church which conducts the classes: 1. That the parents request in writing the release of their children for a specified time; 2. That the church conducting the classes furnish the school with enrollment and attendance reports; 3. That the teachers instructing the released-time classes be qualified to teach. These requirements deal with standards and with the maintenance of good order and are not designed to control the educational program of the participating church.

K. *Judging the Results of Christian Education.* 1. Judging the results of Christian education in terms of doctrinal knowledge and other subject matter presents no great problem, but Christianity deals ultimately with attitudes and beliefs, with such elements

as spiritual advancement, faith, and Christian life. These are difficult, if not impossible, to judge scientifically by existing measuring instruments.

2. To some extent, the results of Christian education may be judged by observation. The strengths and weaknesses of a church body mirror to a large extent its educational system. The behavior of the pupils in a school, the attitude of the individual toward sin, his attitude when he has committed a wrong, his willingness to confess his Savior by word and deed, his trust in God in the time of trouble and need, his prayer life, his love toward God and His Word, his desire to lead a godly life — these are to a certain degree measurable elements for the observant educator. In the case of adults the observer may, in addition, judge on the basis of faithfulness in hearing God's Word and partaking of the Sacrament, active participation in church work, contributions in money and service, the quality of home life, zeal in witness bearing, and similar evidences that the Christian instruction has been effective.

3. In all these judgments it must be kept in mind that the final aim for the Christian is eternal life, that also the weak faith saves, and that the Old Adam at times creates embarrassing situations for even the best of Christians. Viewed in this light, Christian education is seen in terms of souls won for Christ, each single one of which is worth more than all the riches of the world.

4. In general, Christian educators take for granted that the results of Christian education correspond largely to the quantity and quality of the Christian education received. Earnest Christian homes, Christian churches that cling firmly to the Word of God, and schools in which the Word of God runs like a golden thread through all that is taught, ordinarily combine, by the grace of God, to develop strong Christians, willing witnesses for God, loyal members of the home, faithful church members, and good citizens. See bibliography under *Catechetics.*

WAK

W. H. Beck, *Lutheran Elementary Schools in the United States*, CPH, St. Louis, 1939; Paul Bretscher, "Toward a Lutheran Philosophy of Education," *CTM*, XIV: 8—33, 81—95; *General Course of Study for Lutheran Elementary Schools*, CPH, 1943; A. W. C. Guebert, "Luther's Contribution to Modern Elementary Education," *Luth. School*

Journal, 1938, 100 ff.; E. W. A. Koehler, *A Christian Pedagogy,* CPH, 1930; E. A. W. Krauss, "The Missouri Synod and Its Parochial School System," *Ebenezer,* CPH, 1922, 208—228; O. P. Kretzmann, "A Church-Wide Program of Christian Higher Education," *Luth. School Journal,* 1947, 438—444; P. E. Kretzmann, "The Aims of Christian Education," *CTM,* VIII: 842—848; P. E. Kretzmann, *A Brief History of Education,* CPH, n. d.; J. C. W. Lindemann, "Luther als Reformator des deutschen Schulwesens," *Ev.-Luth. Schulblatt,* 1866: 129 ff., 161 ff., 193 ff., 225 ff., 257 ff., 289 ff., 321 ff., 353 ff.; 1867: 129 ff., 161 ff., 193 ff., 257 ff., 289 ff., 321 ff., 353 ff.; Lutheran Education Association, *One Hundred Years of Christian Education,* River Forest, Ill., 1947; F. V. N. Painter, *Luther on Education,* CPH, 1928; David C. Schilke, "The Christian Philosophy of Education," *Luth. School Journal,* 1937, 439—444; A. C. Stellhorn, *The Meaning of Lutheran Education,* CPH, 1928; Herman C. Theiss, "Distinctive Lutheran Ideals in the Field of Education," *American Lutheran,* Dec., 1940, 7, 8; A. Gordon Melvin, *Education* (A History), John A. Day, N. Y., 1946 (pp. 108—40); Wm. A. Kramer (ed.), *The Lutheran One-Teacher School,* CPH, 1949; Wm. A. Kramer (ed.), *Religion in Lutheran Schools,* CPH, 1949; A. C. Mueller, "The Call to Teach Secular Subjects," *Lutheran Education,* Oct., 1952; other histories of education.

Christian Endeavor Society. Officially known as "The Young People's Society of Christian Endeavor." Founded Feb. 2, 1881, by the Rev. Francis E. Clark in the Williston Congregational Church, Portland, Me. The organization was not long confined to America, but spread to all parts of the world. At the world convention at Geneva (1906), a platform of principles was adopted by the representatives of all the great nations and many Protestant denominations, from which the following is quoted: Its covenant for active members demands faith in Christ, open acknowledgment of Christ, service for Christ, and loyalty to Christ's Church. Its activities are as wide as the needs of mankind, and they are directed by the churches of which the societies are an integral part. Its ideals are spirituality, sanity, enthusiasm, loyalty, fellowship, thorough organization, and consecrated devotion. Christian Endeavor stands for spirituality and catholicity, for loyalty and fellowship, for Christian missions and all wise philanthropies at home and abroad, for good citizenship, for peace and good will among men, for beneficence and generous giving, for high intellectual attainments, high devotional attainments, and for pure home life, honest business life, loyal church life, patriotic national life, joyous social life, and brotherhood with all mankind. Being interdenominational in character, this organization is unionistic and not conservative in doctrine.

Christian Ethics. See *Ethics* (Theistic).

Christian Fundamental League. See *Fundamentalism.*

Christian Geography. See *Geography, Christian.*

Christian Missions. See *Missions;* see also names of various countries.

Christian Nation Church. See *Holiness Bodies,* 2.

Christian Reformed Church. See *Reformed Church,* 4 c.

Christian Science. See *Church of Christ, Scientist.*

Christian Social Union. A society founded in England by Westcott, Holland, and Gore (1889), for the purpose of making the Anglican Church more conscious of its social obligations. Although it soon disintegrated, it nevertheless influenced the rise of social thought movements in various churches.

Christian Socialism. This term was first given to a movement inaugurated in 1848 by three Englishmen, Ch. Kingsley (1819—75), J. F. Maurice (1805 to 1872), and J. M. F. Ludlow (1821 to 1911). Their object was to relieve the unfortunate lot of the poorer classes through an organized effort of instruction and general improvement of living and working conditions. In modern usage the term designates a movement which seeks to compromise between the principles of economic Socialism and Christian ethics. Modernism with its "social gospel" substitutes social improvement for the chief object of the Christian Church as clearly described in Scripture, namely, the preaching of Christ Crucified for the spiritual and eternal salvation of man (1 Cor. 1 and 2; Matt. 28: 19, 20; Mark 16: 15). This Gospel has regenerative power and makes the Christian eager and willing to do the will of God, which includes the performance of all his social duties as outlined in such passages as Matt. 5: 7; 25: 34-46; Rom. 12: 13; Gal. 6: 9, 10; Eph. 5, 6; Col. 3, 4; Heb. 13; James 1—5. It is the

Church's duty to exhort the individual Christian to be instrumental in the establishment of social justice and equity, to use his influence, his money and talents in the amelioration of inadequate social conditions.

Christian Symbolism. See *Symbolism, Christian.*

Christian Teaching. A. The term *teaching* implies a necessity and ability. Teaching is necessary because of the fall of man (Gen. 3), through which his capabilities were dulled and his tendencies misdirected. Teaching is possible because life implies the ability to learn [1] (Gen. 3; Deut. 6), and gives the opportunity to alter or direct human behavior. *Christian* teaching, though employing the normal psychological paths, has its specific focal objectives (Deut. 18:19; Ps. 78:1-7; John 5:39). See *Christian Education,* A, H.

B. Teaching also implies learning.[2] Learning utilizes the sensory, neural, muscular, and glandular equipment of the living organism at the time when it is ready to react (compare: Rom. 10:14; Ex. 12:26, 27; Deut. 6:20, 21; Josh. 4: 6-21; Luke 2:46,47).[3] Thus a sensation results from the inner or external stimulation of a sense organ (receptor). As meaning attaches to this sensation, a *percept* (*i. e.,* a meaningful knowledge or impression gained from the senses) develops as an interpretation or understanding of the sensation. The generalization of a *concept* drawn from a number of percepts calls for guidance and teaching in order to avoid errors (Acts 1:6, 7). Christian teaching provides for the proper sensations to be interpreted correctly as true percepts from which clear and correct concepts result. These acquisitions are caused to be associated with each other, with Bible stories, church history, and life situations, in order to achieve the mature ability of judgment (Phil. 1:9), which implies *creative imagination.* Thus a chain of associations is established with which the problems of life are interpreted, judged, and solved (Gen. 39 ff., Joseph). Test: a) accuracy of sensation; b) correct interpretation.

C. *Individual differences* must be recognized. They exist because of varying native capacities and differentiated acquired abilities or apperceptive background (Ex. 35:25, women that were wise hearted; Ex. 36:1, Bezaleel; Dan. 1; Matt. 25:15). Christian teaching recognizes this organismic-environmental differentiation or growth [4] by

adjusting the learning situation to the ability and maturity of the learner at whatever age or level he may be (Luke 18:15-17, children; John 3, teacher; Mark 7:32-35, deaf; Luke 15, the self-righteous; Luke 15, the sinners).

D. *Types of learning* may be distinguished as emanating from the principles stated and should be respected in the teaching process.[2] *Perceptual* (ideational) learning implies a sensation and an interpretation of the learner. It is present in all other types. Teachers must assure themselves that the learner a) actually receives the sensation, and b) interprets it correctly in terms of our best knowledges and understandings. This calls for care in sensory stimulation. Sensory acuity is necessary. Therefore, tests in vision, hearing, and reaction-time are given, and records are preserved for consultation and guidance. Equipment for audio-visual aids is necessary for the greatest clarity in presenting the sensory stimulation. Trained teachers and well-edited texts are needed, that the proper interpretation and meaning may be associated with the given sensation in agreement with the learner's maturity, readiness, and mind-set or motivation. Christian teaching recognizes that perceptual learning is a fundamental type, furnishing a cumulative mass of pyramided abilities for a permanent apperceptive background.

E. *Memorization* utilizes the two steps of perceptual learning and adds a third, *viz.,* drill, or the committing to memory. Notwithstanding popular notions, memorization is not a laborious cramming process, but rather a very orderly sequence of activities, each contributing in direct proportion to successful retention, recognition, and recall. The more clearly the sensation has been received, the more likely will it be retained. The more adequately the sensation has been understood and associated with the total pattern of life, the greater is the chance for retention. The more purposefully and frequently the materials are used, the more permanent will be the memory thereof. Hence it is an error in Christian teaching to expect anyone to remember what he has not adequately sensed, interpreted, or integrated into life situations. Therefore, Christian teaching calls for animated presentation of materials, thoroughly interpreted, understood, integrated, and appreciated before memorization is expected. The result is greater abundance of mastered materials, coupled with maximal precision, retention, joy, and functional value. Tests: a) recognition; b) recall (free association or controlled association tests).

F. *Emotional learning,* or appreciation, is, likewise, based upon perceptual learning.[5] Whatever is to be appreciated or to affect the emotions must be sensed and interpreted. We must not expect the learner to adopt an attitude of appreciation when he has neither sensed the object of appreciation nor been led to interpret or understand it as worthy of high regard. In this respect the process is largely perceptual learning. The third factor, the truly emotional or spiritual level, is attained only through a stimulus or situation which will cause a glandular response or will touch the heart. It is a process which moves the learner, requiring greatest skill on the part of the trained teacher. (Ex. 42:7-20, to see his brothers is a situation charged with some emotion for Joseph. Ex. 43:29-31, as he sees Benjamin, the situation is increased in emotional content, Ex. 44:18-34, to hear Judah, who had suggested to sell him, Gen. 37:27, become surety for Benjamin caused the situation to reach its climax, Ex. 45:1-3. Note also how Paul, in the book of Philemon, mildly, yet persistently builds an emotional appeal for Onesimus.)

G. *Sensori-motor learning,* although concerned with manipulative motor skills, is nevertheless based upon adequate perceptual learning. The skill to be learned must be sensed and correctly interpreted or understood before it can be profitably practiced. Therefore we present a model of what is to be mastered. This involves trained judgment in the choice of procedure: speed of presentation, whole or part method, visual, auditory, or tactual means, and size of class for adequate sensation. Then follow imitation and self-criticism until correct responses are achieved. All this must precede drill or prolonged practice unto mastery. Some phases of Christian teaching require the sensori-motor process. Speech defects are thus corrected. The rote song is taught by this procedure. Penmanship, drawing, and handicraft require it. Many acts of worship are thus acquired. Applied music technique and physical education, dramatization, and games require patient application of this type of learning in addition to others. Test: performance.

H. *Problem solving* may be called the highest type of learning. It uses perceptual learning inasmuch as it senses a difficulty and locates or interprets it. Judgment is required in delimiting the problem. Christian teaching can do much in training for the suspending of judgment until adequate data are at hand. The problem-solving technique suggests inspection through the gathering and classification of data pertaining to a problem. It calls for tentative inferences or suggested hypotheses and probable solutions. The final verification assumes that all data point to a satisfactory conclusion. As the Christian matures, the problem-solving technique can contribute much toward fruitful Bible study and the solution of social problems (John 5:39). Test: a) to state a problem; b) to solve a problem.

I. *Methods and devices* enter into the administration of these types. Moreover, aims and objectives, emanating from an understanding of the learner and of the subject matter, will largely determine the choice of method. (Compare John 3:1-21 and John 19:39 with John 4:6-26 and note that Jesus uses approaches suitable to each case.) Though the method might be classified as conversational, discussion, question, problem, and telling, yet each personality was treated differently. Nicodemus took the initiative, while Jesus countered to correct a mistaken view by leading to a correct concept of Christ. At Sychar, Jesus took the lead, while the woman at first evaded the issue. In both cases the end result was an unequivocal testimony of Himself as the Messiah, the Savior of the world. Furthermore, with reference to teaching, Jesus enjoins upon us (Matt. 28: 19, 20) a) "to teach all nations," *i. e.,* to make disciples, to save souls; and b) to "teach them to observe all things," *i. e.,* purity of doctrine and life in the furthering of His kingdom; He stresses information, attitude, and behavior (Ps. 78:1-7).[6]

J. The extremists in *progressive education* follow *naturalists* in trying to allow expression and development of innate desires, interests, and abilities.[7][8] Christian teaching does it more effectively by adding deliberate planning, indoctrination, direction, and guidance (Gen. 18:19. The effect is seen in Gen. 16:13; 21:17; 24). The true socialized encouraging the child-question (*Kinderfrage*) situation is well emphasized, Gen. 22:7, 8, where Isaac's childlike question is answered with all the wisdom, consideration, and faith of a loving father. The child question as a springboard for teaching is also recognized (Ex. 12:26, 27; Deut. 6:20, 21; Josh. 4:6-21; Luke 2:46,47). It is evident that God suggests methods which imply readiness in a learning situation growing out of a social setting with resulting purposeful answers. Christian teaching employs motivation as well as readiness. It utilizes method as an orderly procedure toward a purpose or goal.

K. *Methods* may be classified in terms of the sensory approach used. While many receptors supplement each other in most situations, certain methods are directed predominantly toward specific senses or mental functions. The eye perceives showing, dramatization, and the written question; the ear notes the topical report, conversation, discussion, the story, outright telling, the lecture, and the oral question; touch and manipulation are largely employed in laboratory experiments and the project; while reason, recall, and judgment are exercised in the developmental method, the problem (inductive and deductive), and most techniques involving group planning.[9][10] The basic principles of learning must be observed in the employment of any method. If the showing of objects, pictures, or procedures is to result in learning, we must provide light conditions favorable to vision. The speed must be adjusted to the reaction-time of the learner. The use of the *discovery method* may require special training in efficient *silent reading* and in keeping the problem in mind. The use of *dramatization* requires histrionic ability, great care and wisdom in portraying facts, situations, and attitudes truthfully and acceptably. Similarly, all methods directed to the ear must be checked for audibility, articulation, pleasantness of tone, and comprehension of vocabulary. The *story* must be organized so as to catch and maintain interest. Imagery must be carefully developed and fostered so the child actually visualizes the scene as it is being related. In *problem solving* it is important that the problem be kept in mind and that sufficient data be assembled and evaluated. Of particular importance is the clear distinction between inductive and deductive procedure. *Inductive reasoning* proceeds from the inspection and study of a number of cases or situations to

the formation of a principle or rule. The *deductive movement of thought* first states the rule and then applies it to cases. Obviously, in the training of children, it is wise to let them observe, hear, and read cases or stories which illustrate a general principle. As the generalization becomes apparent and is clarified, it may be deductively applied to new situations. Thus children are led to independent and efficient habits of study. The selection of materials in inductive reasoning is valuable training in the organization of lesson notes. The most effective application of method consummates in a blend of many methods applied to group techniques. Through such methods the real needs are brought to light and are satisfied by a democratic process in the spirit of the doctrine of the royal priesthood of all believers. However, the selection of materials and the choice of procedures in Christian teaching gain in clarity and purpose by the construction of a psychological learning chart, the curricular syllabus.

L. *A curricular syllabus* can help to make Christian teaching more effective if it meets the following provisions:

1) The curricular syllabus states, as the major aim or objective, the ability to be developed. Thus it helps to keep the primary goal constantly in mind even though it permits and prescribes attention to detail.

2) The curricular syllabus analyzes this ability or breaks it down into its constituent abilities in terms of a) knowledge, information, or understandings; b) attitudes, appreciations, or ideals; c) skills, habits of conduct, or behavior patterns.

This analysis has remarkable possibilities for clearing up our thinking and for giving direction to our procedures in teaching and testing. The breaking down of the constitution of these several abilities into their fundamental components calls for understanding, and it encourages developmental, purposive teaching. Once enumerated and located, these abilities will appear as part of a total pattern and will permit careful examination for integration, overlapping or emphasis, supplementing or complementing, and correlation or transfer between courses, fields, or learning situations.

3) The curricular syllabus provides for appropriate learning activities for each ability to be developed. It recognizes the types of learning best suited,

the present status of the learner, and the motivation needed to secure a favorable mind-set. It calls for subject matter with which the pupil must be brought into contact, as well as the manner and extent of presentation.

Since, according to point 2, we know which abilities we wish to develop, we may the more wisely choose the activities needed to achieve the results. Thus our planned procedures will differ in terms of the outcome desired. This tends to reduce aimless teaching to a minimum. It furthermore permits purposive planning in conjunction with the learner, thus allowing for constant revision of objectives in terms of needs and new developments in curricular and extracurricular activities.

4) The curricular syllabus, finally, provides for the measurement of outcomes through the most effective selection of test items to sample the mastery of abilities taught. This is made possible by the procedure under points 1, 2, and 3. Thus testing is articulated with teaching, giving direction to any further remedial procedures necessary to achieve aims. Furthermore, the type of test is best determined by the type of ability to be measured. Certain items lend themselves readily to objective tests, viz., true-false, completion, multiple-choice, and matching, or to the short answer or essay type.[16]

M. Grading is greatly facilitated by the use of raw scores secured from a series of tests based upon known objectives. Objectively scored, these tests will tend to classify the learners according to the degree of mastery of the scheduled abilities. A fairly simple statistical treatment showing the medium and quartile deviation includes the following steps: 1) Tabulate the raw scores from high to low; 2) locate the 25th centile (Q 1), the 50th centile (median), and the 75th centile (Q 3) by counting up to one fourth, one half, and three fourths of the number of cases, respectively; 3) find Q (quartile deviation) by subtracting the score located at Q 1 from the score located at Q 3 and divide the remainder by 2. This is Q. 4) Find the difference between each score and the median, and divide the remainder by the value of Q, resulting in zero for scores at the median, plus values for those above, and minus quantities for those below the median. This gives the Q-position for each score. 5) Assign grades according to this distribution on the basis of the Q-position: A, those above plus

2.1; B, those from plus 1.1 to plus 2; C, those between minus 1 and plus 1; D, those from minus 1.1 to minus 2; E (conditioned), those from minus 2.1 to minus 3; F (failure), those below minus 3.

N. Christian teaching can profit greatly by this systematic curricular syllabus and its associated testing and grading program because the entire educational plan, the curricular and extra-curricular activities, can be charted. This planning can be extended to cover the span from the cradle to the grave. Moreover, it enables us to exercise good stewardship by differentiating the requirements to meet the several abilities of the learners and the needs of the individual, the church, and the community.

O. This purposive planning, to be effective in Christian teaching, is intended to be co-operative and complete. The home, the part-time agencies, school, church, clubs, and recreational activities — all contribute toward the development of a total personality. A proper adjustment and integration is mandatory for the attainment of the most wholesome results. Christian teaching may not shirk its responsibility by pleading lack of jurisdiction. The outstanding characteristics of Christian teaching are wise guidance, direction, salesmanship, and leadership, rather than authority and power. The Christian home is recognized as developing many of the fundamental abilities of the completed chart. The various agencies of religious education contribute their part as does the church with its services and activities. The limited sphere of child society must be recognized, as well as the mature associations in later life. Christian teaching, therefore, recognizes man as a living, growing organism whose behavior is limited by innate capacities, which can, however, be developed, guided, and modified by an environment of proper teaching materials and procedures. Though conceived and born in sin, the redeemed child of God can be trained to bring forth much fruit in service to God and man (John 15).

P. Courses of study are normal outcomes of curricular planning. The course of study is an orderly presentation of the materials to be mastered in a given agency of instruction in a specified time. The various state departments of public instruction issue their courses of study and administer them through the county superintendents. Lutheran courses of study have been prepared by various local schools, conferences, and synodical Districts. In 1943 a *General Course of Study for Lutheran Elementary Schools* was published (CPH, St. Louis) under the auspices of the Board of Christian Education, The Lutheran Church — Missouri Synod. It espouses Christian pedagogy throughout, covering the branches commonly taught, and is a helpful source for all curricular planning.[11]

Q. Textbooks are a source of much concern in Christian teaching. Since they furnish most of the printed data, they exercise a very intimate influence upon the child's thoughts. This is not a mere matter of indifference, but vital to the teaching process. All learning must glorify God: science and mathematics, because they show forth the marvelous handiwork of His creation; the social studies, since they tell His providence and government; psychology, because it attempts to fathom the abilities of man; literature and all the arts, because they are the product of a dynamic mind created by God; religion, because it establishes the proper relation between man and God through the only reliable source (2 Pet. 1:19). As the twentieth century began, Missouri Synod Lutheran schools, with few exceptions, used texts published by Concordia Publishing House. In the next two decades came an emphasis upon wider contacts, resulting in an all but complete reversal in the use of secular books of other publishers. At the close of the third decade cognizance was taken of the dangers inherent in using texts which were in opposition to Christianity. Therefore, a number of revisions were attempted. In the fifth decade, a staff of competent writers was engaged to complete or produce texts which are adequate in subject-matter and mechanical make-up as well as acceptable and helpful to Christian teaching. The adequacy of materials for agencies of religious education in general is increasingly apparent.[12] The literature produced for the Sunday school excels or compares favorably with other similar publications, while in 1910 it was necessary to patronize private publishers. The materials for Bible study and educational topics were greatly enriched through the fervent activities of the International Walther League.[13]

R. *Teaching standards* have risen with advanced requirements in teacher training. Three years of college work became the minimum standard for a Lutheran Teachers Diploma in 1935, and a four-year program has become the trend since 1938. The intensive summer school program for teachers in service gained constantly in impetus since 1933 in the teachers' colleges at River Forest, Ill., and Seward, Nebr. The type of training, while maintaining the Christian emphasis in subject matter and practice, expanded, particularly in the areas of the natural and the social sciences, and, generally, conforms to the higher national standards for teacher training. As a result, Lutheran teachers continue to be favorably regarded in their communities as leaders, adequately trained and competent in the forward movement of education. Also, the Sunday school teacher training program has gained since the development of the Teacher Training Series.[12]

S. The Lutheran Church — Missouri Synod has, since its organization in 1847, regarded Christian teaching as a primary function of the office of the ministry.* The command in Matt. 28:19, 20 urged pastors to teach confirmation classes, a practice observed throughout the century. Day schools were opened for the children. With the ensuing missionary expansion, the teaching function was constantly maintained.[14] The number of parish schools increased, but the ratio to the number of congregations declined. In 1947 approximately 30 per cent of the congregations maintained parish schools, but the synodical resolution to attempt to raise the enrollment of children in these schools to 50 per cent during the next quarter of a century is evidence of the continued and growing interest and effort in Christian training. Other agencies of religious education have, likewise, received careful study and support. The statistics for 1947 show considerable increase in attendance in Sunday schools, released-time classes, and, particularly, in vacation Bible schools.

T. Other Lutheran bodies have maintained the practice of training their children in part-time agencies even though their parish schools declined.[15] The American Lutheran Church, in particular, has succeeded in maintaining a number of flourishing parish schools. In matters of general equipment and aggressive expansion, however, much may be learned from other denominations which expend much money and labor in reaching and teaching the lambs of their flocks.

U. *Child accounting* has, therefore, become a focal point of interest in congregational statistics. In order to Christianize the flock, the children especially must be accounted for. The cradle roll has been of some assistance, as has the kindergarten. Nevertheless, for effective Christian teaching, every child born, baptized, or brought into a congregation should at once be card-catalogued and dated, so that it may be enrolled in its proper place and time in an appropriate agency upon solicitation by the director of religious education. Likewise, any child moving to another community should be released, transferred, and commended to the care of a sister congregation. It is important that the vital statistics be kept and, when necessary, transcribed and forwarded. Furthermore, these records should be maintained and kept up-to-date throughout life. Christian teaching, just as other educational experience, deserves to be recorded permanently for all persons contacted. This is increasingly facilitated by the organization and intercommunication of boards for parish education and Lutheran superintendents of schools in the Districts.

V. *Records and reports* tend to bring about orderly procedures. As in child accounting, so in the progress of any agency of Christian education a careful system of records and reports should be maintained. The dates of birth, eligibility as prospects, enrollment, attendance and promotion, graduation or transfer should be preserved. The subject matter covered while in attendance and the grade of work done should be recorded. Parents deserve to be informed on the success of their children. Local customs may determine whether a report card should carry marks in per cent, number, or letter, or whether some written remark would be more effective. The church assumes a portion of the responsibility of the parent in Christian teaching and, therefore, owes in return a civil report. Care must be exercised to be polite, considerate, Christian, so that the total effort be a blessed experience. See also *Christian Education, Parish Education, Teachers*.

W. *The Bible is the source book* for Christian teaching. The Holy Spirit works through the Word. Christians must be taught, and teaching can be Christian. TGS

1 E. L. Thorndike, *Briefer Course;* 2 W. H. Burton, *The Nature and Direction of Learning,* Appleton, N. Y.; 8 Douglas & Holland, *Fundamentals of Educational Psychology,* Macm., N. Y.; 4 Roger M. Bellows, "Condition of Learning," *Psychological Review,* March, 1933; 5 T. G. Stelzer, "Appreciation of Music in Lutheran Children," *Lutheran Education,* Dec., 1947; 6 "Aims in Christian Education," *Lutheran School Journal,* April, 1942, p. 242 ff.; 7 J. J. Rousseau, *Emile;* 8 M. P. Porter, *The Teacher in the New School,* World Book Co., Yonkers-on-Hudson, N. Y.; 9 J. Avent, *Beginning Teaching,* Knoxville, Tenn.; 10 A. Schmieding, *Teaching the Bible Story,* CPH, St. Louis; 11 E. W. A. Koehler, *A Christian Pedagogy,* CPH, St. Louis; 12 see material in *Catalog,* CPH, St. Louis; 13 see *ABC of Youth Work,* Walther League, Chicago, Ill.; 14 "One Hundred Years of Christian Education," *Yearbook,* 1947, Luth. Ed. Association; 15 W. H. Beck, *Lutheran Elementary Schools in the United States,* CPH, St. Louis; 16 G. M. Ruch, *The Objective or New-Type Examination,* Scott, Foresman & Co., Chicago.

Christian Union. The early history of this group is identical with that of the Churches of Christ and Disciples of Christ.* When controversial questions of the Civil War period were introduced in some of the pulpits of "Christian Churches," which in principle are opposed to all doctrinal discussions, the Revs. J. V. B. Flack of Missouri and J. F. Given of Ohio organized Christian Union in 1864, maintaining that the discussion of political as well as doctrinal issues disrupted Christian unity. This group grants every individual "the right to his own interpretation of the Bible without controversy on disputed theological questions." Baptism in any form, the Lord's Supper, and, in some instances, foot washing, are observed. Christian character is made the only test of fellowship. This group has remained relatively small. See *Religious Bodies, (U. S.), Bibliography.*

Christian Union (Tenn.). See *Church of God, 2.*

Christian Unity. See *Altar Fellowship; Fellowship, Church; Union Movements.*

Christian Unity Baptist Association. See *Baptist Bodies, 27.*

Christian Unity Science Church, Inc. The name selected in Sept., 1951, by the group formerly known as the Unity Spiritual Science Church. It stresses spiritual healing and ontology. Its headquarters are in Oklahoma City, Okla.

Christian, Wm. See *Churches of the Living God.*

Christianity. See *Christian Church, History of; Church.*

Christians of the Universal Brotherhood. See *Doukhobors.*

Christina, Fort. A settlement of Swedish Lutherans made in 1638 on the Delaware River. When Pastor Reorus Torkillus arrived, in 1640, services were held at the fort until a chapel was built a year or two later.

Christina, Queen of Sweden (1626 to 1689). Daughter of Gustavus Adolphus, who was killed at Luetzen when she was only six years old. She was trained by Oxenstierna to become the ruler of her country. She became queen in 1644 and abdicated ten years later. In 1655 she openly joined the Roman Catholic Church. She died in Rome.

Christlieb, Theodor. B. at Birkenfeld, Wuerttemberg, March 7, 1833; d. at Bonn, Aug. 15. 1889. Founder of Evangelistic Union, of a training school for evangelists, which later was removed to Barmen, and, together with Warneck, of the *Allgemeine Missionszeitschrift* (1874).

Christmas and Christmas Customs. The celebration of Christmas as the birthday of our Lord goes back to the middle of the fourth century, when Pope Julius I (336—52) had the imperial archives of Rome searched for the exact date. Pope Liberius fixed the celebration of Christmas for Dec. 25, in the year 354. From that time on there are numerous records of its celebration. — The customs connected with the Christmas festival are, for the most part, borrowed from pagan sources. The Roman Saturnalia, marking the return of the sun, with the practice of giving and receiving presents, as well as the Yuletide customs of the people of northern Europe, left their mark on the outward observance of Christmas. There is a possibility that the use of evergreens, of holly, ivy, and mistletoe, also of rosemary, was suggested by non-Christian customs, although they soon received a Christian significance. The burning of the Yule log was an important part of the Christmas festivities in England. The domestic Christmas tree first appeared in Germany toward the end of the sixteenth century. One was set up in Windsor Castle in 1841, and the custom came to America shortly afterward. Santa Claus is a combination of Roman Catholic saint

and pagan god. The use of lights and bells accords well with the spirit of the festival. See *Church Year.*

Christological Controversies. A series of controversies in the Early Church pertaining to the Scriptural doctrine concerning the person and the work of Christ. The first was the Arian Controversy, so named after Arius, a presbyter of Alexandria, who denied the true deity of Jesus Christ and His coequality with the Father. This was settled at the Council of Nicea (A. D. 325). The second controversy concerned the Apollinarian and Macedonian heresies, which grew out of the Arian views, the former stating that the Son of God in His incarnation took only the body and the animal soul of man and that the divine person supplied the place of the rational soul; and the latter, while apparently acknowledging the Godhead of the Son, continuing to deny the personality and co-equal Godhead of the Holy Spirit. This controversy was settled at the First Council of Constantinople (381). The third was the Nestorian Controversy, which claimed, in effect, that there were two persons in Christ. This question was settled at the Council of Ephesus (431). The fourth was the Monophysite, or Eutychean, Controversy, when the abbot Eutyches of Alexandria taught that there was only one nature in Christ. This matter was settled at the Council of Chalcedon (451). The fifth was the so-called Controversy of the Three Chapters. The designation was applied to the works of three teachers of the Church, Theodore of Mopsuestia, Theodoret, and Ibas, who were suspected of Nestorianism in a modified form. The fifth general council, which was the second of Constantinople (553), condemned the Three Chapters and specifically Theodore of Mopsuestia. The sixth controversy was that concerning the Monothelite heresy, namely, that in Christ there is only one will and one operation. This teaching was condemned in the sixth general council, which was the Third Council of Constantinople (680 and 681). See references under *Councils and Synods; Doctrine, History of; Dogmatics.*

Christology. That part of dogmatics, or doctrinal theology, which treats of the person of Jesus Christ as the God-Man, with the human nature and the divine nature included in one person. See *Christ Jesus.*

Christopher, St. One of the most popular saints in both East and West; probably a martyr of the third century. He is the subject of many fantastic tales. A legend refers his name of Christopher (Christ-bearer) to his carrying of Jesus, in the form of a child, over a swollen river.

Christotokos. See *Nestorianism.*

Christs, False. The Greek term is pseudo-Christs. The people so designated make the false claim of being the promised Christ or Messiah. Jesus prophesied that deceivers of that kind would appear (Matt. 24: 5, 23 f.; Mark 13: 22). Men of this nature before the destruction of Jerusalem were possibly Simon the sorcerer (Acts 8: 9), Theudas, mentioned in Josephus as causing trouble in the days of Governor Fadus (*Antiquities,* XX, 5, 1), the Egyptian mentioned Acts 21: 38, and Dositheus and Menander, whose names are reported by somewhat later writers. In the second century appeared the arch-false Messiah, *Bar Kokba,* who was a leader of the Jews in the disastrous insurrection of 132—35. Persons whose exaggerated claims remind us of this category were Montanus (around 150), Manes (around 200), Mohammed, the Pope with his infallibility claims, Mrs. Eddy, Dowie — people who maintain that they are in a special way the inspired mouthpieces of God. See commentaries on the Gospel references cited above.

Christ's Sanctified Holy Church. A small Holiness body.*

Christ's Sanctuary Holy Church. See *Holiness Bodies,* 2.

Chrodegang of Metz. B. early in eighth century; d. 766; followed in the footsteps of Boniface in attempting to effect a closer relationship between the Gallican Church and Rome; worked in behalf of ecclesiastical discipline and morals, especially by a strict enforcement of the rule of Benedict of Nursia; did much to diffuse Roman customs throughout Germany.

Chronology, Biblical and Ecclesiastical. The special branch of church history which pertains to the fixing of dates and the chronological sequence of events in sacred and ecclesiastical history. See *Time.*

Chrysostom, John. Patriarch of Constantinople; b. 345 or 347; d. 407. His name "Golden-mouthed" was not applied to him till after his death. Member of a rich patrician family, he studied rhetoric and philosophy, intended to follow law, but turned to the Scriptures instead, leading the life of a strict ascetic in the first years after his baptism; labored as priest in Antioch for twelve years; became patriarch of Constantinople in 398. He immediately inaugurated certain needed reforms and laid the foundation for systematic charitable work. But his position became increasingly insecure on account of the enemies which he made by his rigorous rules and by his fearless attacks on the luxury of his day. Theophilus of Alexandria finally succeeded in having a synod called under the auspices of Empress Eudocia, the Synod ad Quercum, in 403, by which Chrysostom was deposed and banished. After his recall a second synod, held in Constantinople, once more condemned him, whereupon, yielding only to force, he was banished to Asia Minor. The hardships of the last journeys were too great for him, and he died before reaching his final destination, at Comana, Asia Minor. — The writings of Chrysostom cover a large field, but may be divided chiefly into homilies, treatises, and letters. He wrote *On the Priesthood, On Penance,* and *On Celibacy.* His fame rests chiefly on his sermons, in which he reached a height of oratory unsurpassed in the early days of Christianity. His position was unscriptural in a number of doctrines, notably that of the Eucharist and the free will.

C. Baur, *Der heilige Johannes Chrysostomus und seine Zeit,* 2 vols., Muenchen, 1929—30 (Catholic); August Neander, *Der heilige Johannes Chrysostomus und die Kirche,* 2 vols., Berlin, 1858 (Lutheran); William R. W. Stephens, *Saint Chrysostom, His Life and Times,* London, 1883 (Anglican).

Church. 1. The word *church* is derived from the Greek *kyriake,* meaning the Lord's house or assembly. In the Old Testament two words were used to express the idea of assembly: *edhah* and *kahal* (Lev. 4: 13, 14). In the New Testament the idea is designated by *ekklesia,* from *ekkalein,* signifying the assembly that has been summoned forth by an authoritative call of the leader. (Matt. 16: 18; 18: 17; 1 Cor. 10: 32; Eph. 1: 22; 5: 25-27.) The word, derived from a root which means to call, would thus designate those who have been called together by Christ, or the whole company of God's elect. The term *church* is commonly applied to the whole number of true believers, the communion of saints, the invisible

Church of Christ; any particular denomination of Christian people; particular congregations of any Christian denomination; the religious establishment of any particular nation or government (Church of England); the sum total of the various Christian denominations in a country (as, the Church in Australia); and the houses of Christian worship.

2. *The Idea of a Church.* The characteristics of the members of the Church as described in the New Testament are indicated by faith and its immediate effects, or regeneration, justification, and sanctification (Col. 1:2; Eph. 2:19; 1 Pet. 2:9). The indispensable requisite for membership in the Church is regeneration through faith; hence such terms as the believers, the righteous, the children of God, etc., are synonymous with the Church, expressing the relation of its members to God. The idea of union is expressed by such figurative terms as commonwealth, family, flock. The Church, then, may be defined as the community, or union, of believers. The Church, therefore, is a spiritual body and hence cannot be located geographically (Luke 17:20, 21). Although individual congregations or churches (that is, a number of those who profess the Christian faith and are gathered about God's Word at a certain place) can be locally defined ("the church at Philippi," Phil. 1:1), yet the true Church of Christ cannot be exhibited to the eye because faith alone makes a person a member of the Church. To the Lord, however, the Church is always visible (2 Tim. 2:19). He knows who are His, and they are built upon the true doctrine of salvation, the foundation of the Apostles and Prophets (Eph. 2:20). The relation of this Church to Christ is figuratively described: a) It is compared to a body, whose Head is Christ (Eph.1:22, 23); b) It is compared to a temple, with Christ its Foundation and Cornerstone (Eph. 2:20-22). Christ is the Head of the Church, since He is the Author and Ruler of His spiritual body, whose will the body readily obeys. Christ is the Foundation of the Church; first, because of His Word, or teaching; secondly, because of His work of atonement; thirdly, because of His example. Thus the members of the Church, as living stones, are built upon Him by faith, which accepts His teaching, appropriates His merits, and regards, and looks up to, His life as a pattern of holiness. Being built upon Christ, the Church is indestructible. Its foundation is sure, having been laid by the merciful counsel of God in eternity (1 Pet. 2:6); and built upon a rock (Christ), which no enemy shall subvert (John 10:28; Matt. 28:20). Built upon Christ, its purposes are to proclaim the saving message of His work of redemption (1 Pet. 2:9), and provide fellowship and mutual edification for its members (Eph. 4:1 ff.; 1 Cor. 12). Opposed to this definition of the word *church* is the Romanist view (and also the Greek and High Anglican), which assumes that the Church is a form of organic life imposed upon Christian society in a sort of outward way. This Romanist view makes the outward form of a church essential and regards the internal nature as derivative. Since faith in Christ, wrought by the Holy Ghost through the preaching of the Gospel, determines the membership in Christ's Church, the Church, or the communion of saints, properly speaking, will always be invisible to man. Nevertheless we may rightly speak of a visible Church, or churches, by which are meant all those who have and hear the Gospel, profess faith in Christ Jesus, and are thus professed believers. However, if we apply to the entire visible organization of believers the name Church, we do this by a common figure of speech, naming the whole for its chief and noblest part. In this sense we speak of a universal visible Church and of particular visible churches (Gal. 1:2), composed of true Christians, or true believers, and also hypocrites (Revelation 2 and 3). The local church in NT language comprises the believers in that place.

3. *The Marks of a Church.* The invisible Church, or the community of the regenerate, has no existence except through the means of grace, by which regeneration is effected through faith; These means, the Gospel and the Sacraments, are therefore the marks of the Church (Mark 16:15, 16; Matt. 28:19, 20). Moreover, these are the *only* marks of the Church, not the unbroken succession of believing bishops, nor any special illuminations, prophetic utterances, and the manifestation of miraculous powers, nor an organized and graded priesthood with a vicegerent, or vicar, of Christ as its head, since these do not effect justifying and saving faith.

4. *Orthodox Church.* The true and unfailing marks of the Church are not exhibited with the same degree of clearness and exactness in all places and at all times. While the Gospel and the Sac-

raments of Christ remain the same always and everywhere, they are not everywhere understood, interpreted, and publicly professed and administered in the meaning which Christ attached to them.

5. *Rights of the Church; Where Vested.* The Church, the whole number of believers, is compared by Paul to a commonwealth and a household (Eph. 2:19), a community, a society, governed by rules and ordinances. Accordingly, the Church possesses authority (Matt. 16:19; 18:18; 1 Pet. 2:9; 1 Cor. 3:21-23). This authority was transferred to the whole Church (Matt. 18:18-20; 16:19) by the Head of the Church, Christ, who holds all power in heaven and earth (Matt. 28:18). This grant constitutes the Church a sovereign body, a royal priesthood (1 Pet. 2:9; 1 Cor. 3:21-23). This authority is, however, entirely spiritual, extending only to the consciences of men. See *Keys, Office of.*

The doctrine of the Church is extensively treated in dogmatic works (see references under *Dogmatics*); L. W. Spitz, "The Holy Christian Church," *Abiding Word*, CPH, 1946 (I:267—289); P. F. Koehneke, "The Ev. Luth. Church, the True Visible Church of God," *Abiding Word*, CPH, 1946 (I:209—320); H. A. Preus, *The Communion of Saints. A Study of the Origin and Development of Luther's Doctrine of the Church*, Augsburg Publishing House, Minneapolis, 1948; E. H. Wahlstrom, "The Church," *What Lutherans Are Thinking*, Wartburg Press, Columbus, 1947; B. M. Christensen, "Church and Family," *What Lutherans Are Thinking*; C. F. W. Walther, *Die Stimme unserer Kirche in der Frage von Kirche und Amt*, Johannes Herrman, Zwickau, 1894; W. Arndt, "The Ev. Luth. Church the True Visible Church on Earth," *CTM*, VI:801—816; M. Reu, *Die Vollendung der Gottesgemeinschaft*, 1926; Werner Elert, "Die Kirche," *Morphologie des Luthertums*, Beck, Munich, 1931 (later ed.); Paul Althaus, *Communio Sanctorum*, Munich, 1929; Karl Holl, *Gesammelte Aufsaetze zur Kirchengeschichte*, Tuebingen, 1932 (I. Luther, *Die Entstehung von Luthers Kirchenbegriff*, Luther und das landesherrliche Kirchenregiment); J. P. Kirsch, *Die Lehre von der Gemeinschaft der Heiligen*, Mainz, 1900; F. Kattenbusch, *Die Doppelschichtigkeit in Luther's Kirchenbegriff*, Gotha, 1928; Julius Koestlin, *Das Wesen der Kirche beleuchtet nach der Lehre und Geschichte des NT's, in vornehmlicher Ruecksicht auf*

die Streitfrage zwischen Protestantismus und Katholizismus, 1854; J. P. Bang, *The Nature and the Function of the Church*, Danish Book Concern, Cedar Falls, Iowa, 1940; H. N. Bate, "The Nature of the Church," *Faith and Order; Proceedings of the World Conference*, Lausanne, August, 1927. References to synodical reports and essays in *Abiding Word*.

Church Advertising. See *Publicity, Church.*

Church of the Air. See *Radio Evangelism,* 3.

Church Architecture. See *Architecture, Ecclesiastical.*

Church of the Brethren (*Conservative Dunkers*). See *Brethren, Dunkers,* 2.

Church Buildings. See *Architecture, Ecclesiastical.*

Church of Christ (Holiness), U. S. A. Organized by a colored Baptist preacher in 1894, this small denomination emphasizes the views of Holiness bodies.*

Church of Christ, Scientist. 1. A pseudophilosophical system, with a veneer of Christian terms, or according to the Standard Dictionary, "a system of moral and religious instruction founded upon principles formulated by Mary Baker G. Eddy and combined with a method of treating diseases mentally." — *History.* Mrs. Mary Baker G. Eddy, founder of the strange cult which pretends to combine Christianity and science. B. Concord, N. H., 1821, d. Chestnut Hill, Mass., 1910. Even in her youth she had a peculiar tendency toward the occult and the mysterious, spending much time with mesmerism, magnetism, spiritism, hypnotism, and similar subjects. She was married three times: to Major George W. Glover of Charleston, S. C., who died after a few years; to Daniel Patterson, from whom she was divorced; and to Gilbert A. Eddy, who also died after some years. While still a young woman, Mary Baker spent some time in studying homeopathy, her studies convincing her that all causation is mental. Of her peculiar system she writes herself, in *Retrospection and Introspection:* "It was in Massachusetts, in February, 1866, that I discovered the science of divine metaphysical healing, which I afterwards named Christian Science. The discovery came to pass in this way. During twenty years prior to my discovery I had been trying to trace all physical effects to a mental cause, and in the latter part of 1866 I gained the scientific certainty that all causation was mind and every effect a mental phenomenon." The next nine years were spent in retirement and in preliminary work, the result being the strange book *Science and Health with Key to the Scriptures,* which was published in 1875. This book is the bible of the organization founded in Boston, Mass., in 1879.

2. Later investigations have shown that Mrs. Eddy based her strange conclusions on a metaphysical method of healing discovered by a certain Doctor Quimby, who is known as the "parent mental healer" of America. The ideas of Quimby may be summarized as follows: 1) Sickness is unreal, does not really exist, but is present only in the imagination of man. 2) The object of healing is to take away the belief in the existence of sickness in the patient through the "truth," namely, that God Himself is perfect health, and that man lives and is in God. Mrs. Eddy's connection with Dr. Quimby has been established on the basis of her own reports, as published in the *Portland* (Me.) *Courier.* At the same time an examination of Mrs. Eddy's doctrines show that she was dependent, not only upon Dr. Quimby's teaching, but also on the tenets of various heathen religions and philosophical systems, particularly Brahmanism, Buddhism, Manichaeism, Neoplatonism, Mysticism and Gnosticism.

3. *Tenets.* The fundamental principles of Christian Science are given in *Science and Health* in the following four sentences: "1) God is all in all. 2) God is good, God is mind. 3) God, Spirit, being all, nothing is matter. 4) Life, God, omnipotent Good, deny death, evil, sin, disease. — Disease, sin, evil, death, deny Good, omnipotent God, Life" (p. 7). Since every thought or philosophy that claims to be a religious system must be tested by its idea of God, the sentences given above will give a fairly accurate idea of the confusion that existed in the mind of the writer. The following sentences, taken from the official publications of Mrs. Eddy, show the hopeless confusion concerning the idea of God: "God is divine principle. . . . In Christian Science we learn that God is infinitely individual and not personal. . . . God is all-inclusive and is reflected by everything, real and eternal. He fills all space, and it is impossible to conceive of such omnipresence and individuality except as Mind. All is spirit and spiritual. Life, Truth, and Love constitute the triune God, or triply divine Principle." The system identifies the existence of God with the existence of man as a spiritual being. It says: "Man is co-existent with God." Mrs. Eddy, at the same time, uses such a vague phraseology that many of her sentences, taken by themselves, seem to be acceptable to the evangelical Christian as well as to the atheist. But the personality of God is denied by Mrs. Eddy, for the god of this system has no existence apart from the mind or life that thinks god. Christian Science speaks of a trinity, but it is not the Holy Trinity, the Triune God of the Bible. Life, truth, and love are supposed to represent the Triune God, and of them *Science and Health* states: "They represent a trinity in unity, three in one — the same in essence, though multiform in office: God the Father; Christ the type of sonship; Divine Science, or the Holy Comforter. These three express the threefold, essential nature of the Infinite."

4. Every doctrine of the Christian faith is flatly denied by Mrs. Eddy and her system. Instead of accepting the true human nature of Christ, the statement is made: "Mary's conception of Him [Jesus Christ] was spiritual." Christ is identified with Christian Science when it is said: "There is but one way to heaven and harmony, and Christ, Divine Science, shows us that way." Since there is no trinity in the Biblical sense in Christian Science, the Holy Ghost can, of course, not be a person within the Godhead. *Science and Health* states: "The theory of three persons in one God suggests heathen gods, rather than one present I Am." The Third Person of the Godhead is defined: "Holy Ghost, Divine Science; the development of eternal Life, Truth, and Love." Mrs. Eddy also denies the existence of sin, declaring that "man is incapable of sin, sickness, and death, inasmuch as he derives his essence from God and does not derive a single original or underived power. . . . Evil is but an illusion, and error has no real basis; it is a false belief. . . . Evil has no reality. It is neither person [hence there is no devil, the idea is pure delusion] nor place [hence there is no hell] nor thing [hence there is no accountability], but it is simply belief, an illusion of material self." Of course, under such circumstances, Christian Science denies the reality of the suffering of Christ, calling His death "the great illusion." The reconciliation of man with God through the

expiatory work of Christ is weakened to the inane statement that Jesus aided in reconciling man to God "only by giving man a true sense of love." In short, Christian Science is opposed to the great fundamental Christian doctrines (cf. 2 Thess. 2:11; 1 Tim. 6:10). — The total number of Christian Science adherents is in excess of 250,000. See *Religious Bodies (U. S.), Bibliography.*

FEM

Church, Christian *(Apologetics).* The Christian Church claims to be a divine institution, and in its pure, Scriptural form, apart from accidental imperfections or even wrongs, it supplies for this claim rational proofs, as for example 1) its blessings conferred upon individual representatives (St. Paul, Polycarp, etc.); 2) its elevating influences on entire communities or states (transformations wrought through mission work, institutions of education and benevolence, *e. g.,* there having been no hospital in Japan when Dr. Hepburn arrived there in 1859, but there were more than a thousand when he left); 3) the testimony of its enemies, or non-members, in general, who by word and deed acknowledge its benefits and benevolences; 4) its amazing origin, its cornerstone being the crucified Christ and its main propagators humble fishermen and a converted Pharisee; 5) its wonderful gift of a free salvation through faith in Christ Jesus, which is in opposition to all human ways of salvation by works; 6) its perseverance in unspeakable tribulation, as for example during the three centuries of dreadful persecution; 7) its moral truths which go beyond the shallow ethical codes found in ethnic religions and are anchored in true love toward God and one's neighbor; 8) its universal human appeal, there being converts wherever it preaches the Gospel of Christ; 9) its simple, but powerful means of propagation, namely, the Gospel of Christ, which is a stumbling block and foolishness to men, and yet the power of God unto salvation; 10) its absolute otherness from all man-made churches in doctrine, in aim, in solving the problems of men, etc., there being a difference, not merely of degree, but one of kind, the Church itself, in its teaching and work, being its best apologist. All these and many other evidences go far to support its claim, on grounds of rational consideration, that the Christian Church truly is what it claims to be, a divine institution. See *Apologetics.* JTM

Church Congress. This term was first applied to meetings of lay and clerical delegates of the Church of England (the first such congress was held in 1852). The term has been appropriated by other church bodies.

Church of Daniel's Band. See *Evangelistic Associations,* 6; *Holiness Bodies,* 2.

Church of Disciples. See *Disciples of Christ.*

Church of England. See *England, Reformation in.*

Church Extension Fund. See *Finances of the Church,* 7.

Church Festivals. See *Church Year.*

Church of the Full Gospel, Inc. See *Holiness Bodies,* 2.

Church Furniture. 1. In the furniture of the chancel * the altar * stands first, not because a special intrinsic value attaches to it, but because it is the place of prayer and the table for the distribution of the Lord's Supper (1 Cor. 10:21. In the Eastern Orthodox and Anglican liturgies, the altar is called the "Lord's Table," a usage occasionally found in general Protestant circles). Its antecedents were the altars for sacrifice and the tables for incense. Altars are usually constructed of costly stone or hardwood. The *mensa* * (plate or top of the altar) is used for service books and the Communion vessels, a special shelf usually serving to hold the cross * and candelabra (see 2). The *reredos* is the screen or partition wall behind the altar and is often elaborate with ornament and religious symbolism, usually triptych (*i. e.,* in three compartments side by side) in form. Altar paintings or statues are usually placed high so as not to interfere with the cross. The *pulpit* (elevated preaching stand) is located, as a rule, on the Gospel side of the chancel (formerly in the center in many Protestant churches) and often agrees with the altar in style, materials, and construction, its form usually being octagonal. While some Protestant churches used merely a desk on a raised platform, the more formal churches built pulpits which rise from a single shaft or stem and which are richly decorated. The panels of the railing may be carved in very rich effects or constructed in the form of niches, with statues of the four evangelists or four major prophets. The *baptismal font* should have a definite, permanent position in the church, either in a special baptismal chapel or at the entrance of the sanctuary, but not so as to interfere with the movement of the communicants. Baptismal fonts are constructed of metal, stone, beautifully carved wood, or cast in other beautiful material. Some fonts are sculptured of marble with a cover of like material or of ebony wood. The simplest fonts consist of a pedestal and basin holder; others, however, are elaborate with sculpture work, agreeing with other pieces of furniture in the chancel. The *lectern* (reading desk from which the Scripture lessons are read) takes the place of the ancient *ambo* (an elevated, large pulpit in early Christian churches; frequently there were two, one for the reading of the Gospel and one for the Epistle lesson) and harmonizes in material and workmanship with the other pieces in the apse (see *Architecture, Ecclesiastical*, 1 ff., 7). Many lecterns in the form of ordinary reading desks are very effective on account of their simplicity. More elaborate ones are carved from marble or cast in other material, a favorite form being that of the eagle, with wings partly extended, the emblem of the Evangelist John.

2. While the mensa of the altar is reserved for the service books and the Communion vessels, the lowest shelf of the reredos is constructed for the purpose of holding the cross * or crucifix (a cross with the corpus or sculptured figure of Christ) and candelabra. The corpus was hardly known before the ninth century and even then used almost entirely for processional crucifixes. While the Lutheran Church defended the crucifix against iconoclastic tendencies, many of its members have advocated the return to the plain cross. The *candelabra* (ornamented branched candlesticks), with one, three, five or seven lights, should agree in style, materials, and construction with the cross or crucifix and harmonize with other appointments. The same is true of the three-light vesper candlesticks, used at evening services.

3. The pieces of a regular Communion set are the chalice or cups for distributing the wine, the flagon for receiving the wine to be used during the celebration, the paten (or plate) for the wafers, and the *ciborium** (or receptacle) for containing the wafers not in actual use. See *Architecture, Ecclesiastical; Symbolism*.

Paul Zeller Strodach, *A Manual of Worship*, Muhlenberg Press, Philadelphia, 1946; Ernest Geldart, *A Manual of Church Decoration and Symbolism*, London, 1899.

Church of God. 1. There are five groups of perfectionists which for various reasons reject the use of denominational creeds and names, and on the basis of such passages as 1 Cor. 1:2 insist on being known merely as the "Church of God at ——." These bodies have nothing in common with the Church of Christ (Campbellites). For purposes of identification each of the five groups is designated according to the presiding elder or the city where its headquarters are located. They are agreed in their opposition to all forms of ecclesiasticism and in their insistence upon re-establishing the so-called apostolic church order, believing that the Holy Spirit must govern the Church as He did in the days of the Apostles, and are inclined toward a theocratic form of church government. These groups originated with the Holiness Movement of the last two decades of the nineteenth century and advocate tenets common to all the Holiness bodies, stressing such fundamental doctrines as the inspiration of the Bible, the deity of Christ, the vicarious atonement, the resurrection of the body. However, they also teach entire sanctification as an instantaneous experience different from, and subsequent to, conversion, the presence of charismatic gifts (unusual preternatural powers, *e. g.*, speaking in tongues), faith healing, the imminent and pre-millennial reign of Christ. While they reject creeds and claim to go directly to the Bible, they are inclined toward a legalistic and literalistic interpretation of the Bible. Membership (1952): 318,510. See *Holiness Bodies; Divine Healing; Perfectionism; Millennium*, 7.

2. **Church of God** (Cleveland, Tenn.). This group, organized as "Christian Union" in 1886, then known as "Holiness Church," has adopted the name "Church of God," with international headquarters at Cleveland, Tenn. Its church polity is "theocratical," meaning that they claim to decide every question solely by the Word of God. The theology is that of the typical Holiness bodies, with the emphasis on entire sanctification, divine healing, forbidding participation in war, and many matters of indifference, such as the non-wearing of jewelry.

3. **Church of God** (Anderson, Ind.). This body was founded about 1880 by D. W. Warner, formerly connected with the General Eldership of the Churches of God (Winebrennerians). This group

is opposed to every form of ecclesiastical organization and hopes to obtain the high ideal of the New Testament Church, "as the concrete embodiment of the spiritual body of Christ." The Protestant Reformation is said to have restored the New Testament purity of doctrine, while the Church of God is now restoring the New Testament form of church government. This group ascribes the marks of the invisible church to the visible church, which must be spirit-filled and spirit-directed. To this end the Holy Spirit will restore the gifts of the early church, such as prophecy, baptism with the Holy Ghost, divine healing. This denomination has developed an active missionary program with a large publishing house at Anderson, Ind.

4. The (Original) Church of God (Chattanooga, Tenn.). This group claims to be the first to be organized as a church of God according to the pattern of the New Testament.

5. Church of God (Salem, W. Va.). This body, organized in 1933, while agreeing with the preceding groups on basic principles, has carried its views on the theocracy or the "apostolic organization" of the church to its logical conclusions. For example, they advocate the government of the church by twelve apostles, seventy elders, seven business stewards. They consider Jerusalem the international headquarters; believe in the re-establishment of David's throne; advocate the observance of the Sabbath and the celebration of the Lord's Supper on the fourteenth of Nisan.

6. (Tomlinson) Church of God. Organized by A. J. Tomlinson in 1922, this group claims to prepare the world for Christ's second coming by establishing the church along the lines of the "apostolic" pattern. FEM

7. For other bodies under the name "Church of God" see Adventist Bodies; Brethren, Dunkers; Holiness Bodies; Pentecostalism. See Religious Bodies, (U. S.), Bibliography.

Church of God in Christ. Founded in 1897 by C. H. Mason, a Negro. This colored denomination stresses the typical tenets of Pentecostal * churches. See also Holiness Bodies.

Church of God in Christ (Mennonite). See Mennonite Bodies, 3.

Church of God in Christ (Pentecostal). See Pentecostalism.

Church of God as Organized by Christ. See Evangelistic Associations, 7; Holiness Bodies, 2.

Church of God and Saints of Christ. A colored church, sometimes known as Black Jews, organized by Wm. S. Crowdy at Lawrence, Kans., 1896, which holds that the Negro race is descended from the lost ten tribes of Israel. Crowdy and his successors are accepted as prophets divinely called and in true communication with God. This group claims to follow the Bible rigidly. However, they observe such Old Testament customs as seem important to them, particularly the Jewish calendar, the Sabbath, Old Testament festival days, tithing, marriage within their own group. The cult also observes baptism by immersion, the Lord's Supper, and the washing of feet. See British Israelism; Religious Bodies, (U. S.), Bibliography.

Church Government. See Polity, Ecclesiastical.

Church History. See Christian Church, History of.

Church, Institutional. See Institutional Church.

Church of Jesus Christ. See Latter Day Saints, 5.

Church Law of 1686 (Sweden). See Sweden, Luth. Church in, 2.

Church of Living God — Christian Workers of Fellowship. See Holiness Bodies, 2.

Church of the Living God — Pillar and Ground of Truth. See Holiness Bodies, 2.

Church Membership. See Church.

Church Missionary Society for Africa and the East. Founded at London, April 12, 1799, within the Anglican Church "for sending missionaries to the continent of Africa and other parts of the heathen world"; but not officially recognized until 1819. In 1882 the medical mission department was organized. In 1895 the woman's department was fully organized. Fields: Asia: Japan, China (9 provinces), India (15 states), Ceylon, Iran, Palestine; Africa: Egypt, Anglo-Egyptian Sudan, Sierra Leone, Nigeria, Tanganyika Territory, Kenya Colony, Uganda.

Church Modes (ecclesiastical modes; or simply, modes; German: Kirchentoene; Kirchentonarten). These are the medieval parent scales of our major and minor scales (sacred and secular).

They were used quite commonly until about 1600, though employed also by later composers. Many modern composers are again using them, since they offer a larger variety of melodic, harmonic, and contrapuntal treatment than do major and minor keys. In their order, the so-called authentic modes are the following: Dorian, Phrygian, Lydian, Mixolydian, Aeolian, Ionian. The Ionian mode is identical with a major scale. The octave range of the individual modes may be related to any major scale; however, they are most commonly related to C major. Since C major has no sharps or flats, one can easily determine the character of the individual modes at a keyboard instrument by using only the white keys in order to play the following octaves, ascending or descending: Dorian (D—D), Phrygian (E—E), Lydian (F—F; helped pave the way for F major by using B flat instead of B natural to avoid the use of the tritone), Mixolydian (G—G), Aeolian (A—A; same as a pure minor scale), Ionian (C—C). No mode began on the seventh degree, or leading tone of the scale, since this tone leans too heavily on the first degree of the scale. By relating to other major keys, one must use their key signature. To obtain modes with a range wider than the octave, the plagal modes were introduced; they began half an octave lower (G. "hypo") than the authentic modes and thus extended the range to twelve notes. A large percentage of the classical chorales of the 16th and 17th centuries are modal hymns. The majority are in the very masculine Dorian and Phrygian modes, the soft Lydian mode being avoided. Luther's chorale version of the Creed (*The Lutheran Hymnal*, 251, second tune) is in the Dorian mode; his "From Depths of Woe I Cry to Thee" is in the Phrygian mode; his "A Mighty Fortress" is in the Ionian mode. WEB

Church Music. See *Music, Church.*

Church of the Nazarene. This is the largest denomination among the Holiness Bodies. As a result of the emphasis given to "holiness" preaching in the National Holiness Movement, Methodists in New England, New York, Texas, and California, independently of each other, urged a return to the Wesleyan doctrine of perfectionism, stressing particularly that "entire sanctification," an instantaneous experience distinct from, and subsequent to, con-

version, must constitute the heart of Christian preaching. This led to the founding of the Central Evangelical Holiness Association (Rock, Mass.), the Association of Pentecostal Churches of America (Brooklyn, N. Y.), and the Church of the Nazarene (Los Angeles, Calif.) in 1895. These three groups formed the Pentecostal Church of the Nazarene in 1907. Subsequently a number of similar Holiness groups in Texas, Arkansas, and Tennessee, and a laymen's Holiness organization in Minnesota, the Dakotas, and Montana united with the Church of the Nazarene. In doctrine this denomination is Arminian and in common with all Holiness bodies accepts the fundamental Biblical truths of Verbal Inspiration, the virgin birth of Christ, the deity of Christ, the vicarious atonement, the depravity of man, the resurrection of the body. Its distinctive doctrines besides "entire sanctification" are the pre-millennial coming of Christ and divine healing. The term "Pentecostal," usually associated with churches of the "Holy Roller" type, is no longer used in the official title of this denomination, because it never countenanced the doctrine that speaking in tongues is a manifestation of the baptism with the Holy Spirit. Its church polity is patterned after that of the Methodist Church. Membership (1952): 235,670. See *Religious Bodies, (U. S.), Bibliography.*

Church of the New Jerusalem. See *Swedenborgians.*

Church Orders (*Kirchenordnungen*). Regulations, under the general ecclesiastical constitution of a state, by means of which the canonical church forms that had previously prevailed in a land or city were modified in agreement with directions drawn up by men representing the Reformation, while the newly developing church system became progressively established. Those of the sixteenth century are the most important. They usually open with a statement of the doctrinal position of the country or state or city, followed by regulations concerning the liturgy, the appointment of church officers, and the whole administration of the various congregations included in the respective jurisdiction. Since later compilations frequently made use of earlier, acknowledged forms, the orders are grouped in families, by countries or districts.

Luther D. Reed, *The Lutheran Liturgy*, Muhlenberg Press, 1947; Walter

C. Daib, "Church Order and the Confession," *CTM*, XVII: 128—38; studies of certain periods (*e.g.*, v. Lehling, *Ev. Kirchenordnungen d. 16. Jahrhunderts*, Leipzig).

Church Polity. See *Polity, Ecclesiastical.*

Church of Revelation. A small sect organized by Janet Stine Lewis at Long Beach, Calif. (1930). Practices various forms of healing.

Church, Roman Catholic Doctrine of. See *Church; Church and State; Papacy; Polity, Ecclesiastical; Roman Catholic Church.*

Church School. See *Parish Education.*

Church Society for Inner Missions, See *Denmark, Lutheranism in*, 10.

Church and State. The idea of strict separation of the church from the state, and *vice versa,* though clearly taught in the Scriptures, has been realized only in extremely modern times. As soon as the Christian Church was persecuted by the pagan government of Rome, separation of church and state was practiced.

When in the fourth century the Christian religion was established as the official religion of the Roman Empire, the union of church and state became the ideal in Christian lands until modern times, though the principle of the distinction between the two realms was never completely lost sight of. In general it may be said that to the ninth century, the end of the reign of Charlemagne, the state, *i. e.,* the Emperor, was the external head of the church, the title *Pontifex Maximus* being retained for a time as a carryover from the heathen days, and the state included laws for the church in its legislative enactments. At the same time the right of the church to legislate on its own behalf (in synods and church councils) was not abrogated. Church leaders, like Hosius, Ambrose, Jerome, etc., did not hesitate to caution the emperors not to infringe upon the rights of the church. The ideal of Charlemagne was an equal and mutually profitable partnership between church and state. During the latter centuries of the Middle Ages the efforts of the church to dominate the state increased, mainly through the activity of such popes as Gregory VII, Innocent III, and Boniface VIII (cf. the bull *Unam Sanctam*). In the German and French lands

princes began to dominate the church through the rights of patronage and protection (*Eigenkirche*). Martin Luther clearly upheld the theory that church and state should be separate. That the Lutheran Church did become closely linked with the state, even in Luther's day, was due largely to the fact that the idea of the union of church and state was too deeply imbedded in the mind of the age, and with the support of Protestant leaders like Zwingli and Calvin state-churchism became the rule in Protestant lands.

The assumption that the churches, as a part of the state organism, were as absolutely subject to the government of every territory as the civil administration began in the 15th century. Thus arose the territorial system, when the states, confused with the church, organically became universal rulers of the church. This system was vitally changed through the French Revolution of 1789, the Napoleonic reign, and the conquerors of Vienna in 1815. The relation of the Roman Catholic Church in the various countries to the Pope was regulated by concordats, conventions which stipulated what right the state government should allow the Pope to exercise over against the church of a particular country and what influence the state governments should exercise upon the management of the church. In the seventeenth and eighteenth centuries there arose at the same time in the Protestant churches a consciousness of the unworthy servitude into which the church had been forced, and the demand grew stronger and stronger to have at least a part of the self-government of the churches restored to them. Especially in England, where the nonconformists gained greater strength and influence than any dissenters on the continent of Europe, this movement gained in power. In America, church and state were more or less united in most colonies until after the Revolutionary War, and it was only through the adoption of the Constitution that the separation of church and state and the legal equality of all forms of belief were established. The rapid growth of the free American churches had a decided influence upon opinion in the Old World, where in most countries there arose a strong demand for complete separation of church and state, which, however, has been only partially realized, as, to some extent, in France. Nevertheless, the union of state and church, even in those countries where state-churchism exists, has been loosened, and in some countries of Europe the free churches have been reorganized as independent organizations, enjoying the same protection as the state churches. In the first half of the 20th century, due in part to the political changes brought on by World Wars I and II, there have been steady advances in some European lands, such as Germany, Poland, and France, toward a clearer understanding of the principle of the separation of church and state.

WGP

A. Werminghoff, *Verfassungsgeschichte d. deutschen Kirche im Mittelalter*, Leipzig, 1913; Karl Holl, *Gesammelte Aufsaetze*, Tuebingen, 1932;. Karl Mueller, *Kirche, Gemeinde u. Obrigkeit nach Luther*, Tuebingen, 1910; E. Berggrav, *Man and State*, Philadelphia, 1951.

Church Student Movements. See *Students, Spiritual Care of.*

Church Triumphant. See *Hereafter.*

Church Tunes (*Kirchentoene*). See *Church Modes.*

Church of the United Brethren. See *United Brethren.*

Church Usages. See *Adiaphora; Adiaphoristic Controversy; Agenda; Confession; Liturgics;* articles on individual items (*e. g., Baptism, Lord's Supper*).

Church Year. 1. The church year may be divided into the following cycles. It opens with the season of Advent, the period of preparation for the Christmas Festival. The early part of this division is devoted to the discussion of eschatological subjects, not only in the lessons, but also in the liturgy. In the latter part of this season, especially on and after the Fourth Sunday in Advent, the Christmas theme is brought into the foreground. The Christmas Festival is the first of the primary festivals; it has two and even three days of celebration. The Feast of the Innocents falls within the octave, or week, of Christmas, the services of the octave, according to ancient custom, serving to echo the message of the festival itself.

2. In the case of Christmas, its octave is the Festival of the Circumcision, which concurs with the New Year's Day of the civil year. The festival of Epiphany, on Jan. 6, ushers in the story of Christ in the glory of His childhood and early ministry.

3. The season of Septuagesima, or pre-Lent, follows after that of Epiphany. It is devoted to the ministry of Christ in its Sunday services and to the Old Testament story in its secondary services. Quinquagesima Sunday opens the series of lessons treating of the later ministry of Christ, including the last journey to Jerusalem.

4. The season of Lent, beginning with Ash Wednesday, is devoted to an intensive study of the Passion of Christ, this feature becoming unusually pronounced in Holy Week, with the culmination in the great happening of Good Friday, in the death and burial of Christ.

5. The Easter season is ushered in with Easter Sunday, two or three days being devoted to the contemplation of the resurrection of the Lord, and the period extending to Ascension Day. The Easter season merges into that of Pentecost, Exaudi Sunday, however, serving as a special day of preparation for this third great festival of the Church, with its two or even three festival days.

6. In the second part of the church year, beginning with Trinity or, more exactly, the Sunday after Trinity, there are no festivals of the first rank.

7. Most of the festivals referred to in this description were celebrated in the Christian Church from very early times. The celebration of Easter extends back to the time of the Apostles (1 Cor. 5:8). So far as extant documents show, there never was any question as to the celebration, but only as to the date of the celebration, the controversy concerning this question being finally settled by the Council of Nicea (325), which decreed that Easter be celebrated on the first Sunday following the spring equinox. Today it is celebrated following the first full moon after the spring equinox.

8. From very early days Easter was preceded by a special period of preparation, called the Lenten season. The custom of fasting during this time was general at a very early date, but the length of the fast varied, eight days being customary at first, but the time being extended to forty days, after the analogy of the period included in the Lord's temptation, Matt. 4:2. Gregory II (715—731) is said to have fixed the Wednesday now known as Ash Wednesday (from the custom of daubing the foreheads of the worshipers on that day with the ashes of last year's palms, in token of mourning) as the first day of Lent in order to secure uniformity

of observance throughout the Church. The season of preparation for Easter closed with the Great or Black Week, also known as the Holy Week. The Thursday of Holy Week commemorated the institution of the Holy Supper. Since the Gospel of the day was John 13:1-15, the day was also known as the Day of Foot Washing. Its present English name of Maundy Thursday is derived either from the words of the Gospel lesson: *"Mandatum novum do vobis,"* or from the custom of carrying gifts to the poor in maund (y) baskets on that day. Good Friday, almost from the first, was the Day of the Cross, a day of deepest mourning, with a complete fast till 3 or 6 o'clock in the afternoon. In some churches no form of service was prescribed, the faithful merely coming together for silent prayer.

9. Within the fifty days of rejoicing following Easter came the Festival of the Ascension, which is mentioned by Eusebius and may have been celebrated at the end of the third century.

10. Pentecost may also be of very ancient date, perhaps going back to the time of the Apostles and celebrated as the birthday of the church. It is known also as Whitsunday (very likely from the white garments worn on that day), especially in England. Tertullian calls the whole time from Easter to Pentecost by the latter name and gives to each day of the entire period the importance and dignity of a Sunday.

11. In the Early Church less stress was laid upon the birthday of the Lord than upon the fact that the Son of God actually became man (John 1:14). Accordingly we find a festival celebrating this fact as early as the time of Clement of Alexandria, at the beginning of the third century. The 6th of January was the accepted date for this Festival of Epiphany, or the Manifestation of the Lord, at the end of the third century. It commemorated not only the birth of Christ, but also His baptism and, in some cases, His first miracle, thus expressing very well the general idea of the revelation and manifestation of the divinity of Christ in His humanity. The celebration of Christmas as the birthday of our Lord on Dec. 25 goes back to the middle of the fourth century. Tradition has it that Pope Julius I (336—352) had the imperial archives of Rome searched for the exact date of the birth of Christ and found that this was the correct day, according to the tax lists. It has now been established beyond a doubt that Pope Liberius, in 354, fixed the celebration of the Lord's nativity for Dec. 25. There is a record from the year 360 showing that it was celebrated at that time.

12. Just as Easter had its special season of preparation, so a similar period was set aside before Christmas. The length of the Advent season varied according to the ancient *Comites,* Milan observing five Sundays, Rome only four. Finally the custom of having four Sundays was generally accepted, because this agreed with the four millenniums preceding the birth of Christ.

13. After the fifth century the number of festivals in the church increased very rapidly. With the increasing veneration of Mary her festivals gained ground. The Annunciation of Mary, celebrating the conception of the Lord, was fixed for March 25, and that of the Purification of Mary properly followed Christmas, on Feb. 2. Since the special ceremony of this day, in Roman circles, is the benediction of candles, their distribution to the people, and the solemn procession with the lighted tapers, the festival is known in English as Candlemas, in German as *Lichtmess.*

14. Naturally, the feasts of Apostles and Evangelists were soon celebrated, especially those of Peter and Paul, although those of John and James were also favorites. With the rising tide during the Middle Ages came the many saints' and martyrs' days, beginning with that of Stephen, but later including one for all martyrs, as well as All Saints' Day, Nov. 1, when they were commemorated in one total sum, and All Souls' Day, Nov. 2, when there was a concentration of efforts in behalf of the departed souls. Many of the Sundays of the church year were known by special names, usually after the first words of their respective introits, the names of the Sundays in Lent being: Invocavit, Ps. 91:15; Reminiscere, Ps. 25:6; Oculi, Ps. 25:15; Laetare, Is. 66:1; and Judica, Ps. 43:1. The name Palm Sunday is derived not only from the Gospel of the day, Matt. 21:8, but also from the fact that the blessing of the palms formerly took place on that day. The Sundays after Easter are: Quasimodogeniti, or Dominica in Albis (1 Pet. 2:2); Misericordias Domini (Ps. 89:2); Jubilate (Ps. 66:1); Cantate (Ps. 98:1); Rogate (Matt. 7:7); and Exaudi (Ps. 27:7).

15. The reformers of the 16th century, under the leadership of Luther, retained the ancient festivals in honor

of Christ and the Triune God as a matter of course, preferring also to regard Annunciation and Purification as Christ festivals. As for the other festivals, they were careful to keep all such as had any value for the devotion and edification of the Christian congregation, while they eliminated all festivals, or at least all parts and references in the celebration of all festivals, which savored of Romish idolatry. The Festival of the Reformation on Oct. 31 was soon introduced, not on account of any superstitious and idolatrous veneration for the person of Martin Luther, but to commemorate the wonderful blessings which came to the Church in consequence of Luther's courageous stand. In the American Lutheran Church, Thanksgiving Day is celebrated very generally, sometimes in addition to a Harvest Home Festival, for which the church is appropriately decorated and the virtue of Christian charity is emphasized.

16. The church calendar, as in use in the Lutheran Church today, may be said to include the following festivals: A. *Movable Festivals.* Septuagesima, Sexagesima, Quinquagesima (or Esto Mihi), Ash Wednesday, Invocavit, Reminiscere, Oculi, Laetare, Judica, Palmarum, Dies Viridium (or Maundy Thursday), Good Friday, Easter, Quasimodogeniti, Misericordias Domini, Jubilate, Cantate, Rogate, Ascension, Exaudi, Pentecost (or Whitsunday), Trinity. B. *Fixed Festivals.* Circumcision, Jan. 1; Epiphany, Jan. 6; Conversion of St. Paul, Jan. 25; Purification, Feb. 2; St. Matthias, Feb. 24; Annunciation, March 25; SS. Philip and James, May 1; Birth of John the Baptist, June 24; SS. Peter and Paul, June 29; Visitation of Mary, July 2; Mary Magdalene, July 22; St. James the Elder, July 25; St. Lawrence, Aug. 10; St. Bartholomew, Aug. 24; St. Matthew, Sept. 21; Michaelmas, Sept. 29; SS. Simon and Jude, Oct. 28; All Saints', Nov. 1; St. Andrew, Nov. 30; Saint Thomas, Dec. 21; Christmas, Dec. 25; St. Stephen, Dec. 26; St. John the Evangelist, Dec. 27; Innocents' Day, Dec. 28.

Churches of Christ. A denomination which traces its history to the Great Revival following the Revolutionary War under Barton Stone and others who were opposed to every form of denominationalism and "ecclesiasticism." The congregations banded together as the Churches of Christ must be viewed

less as a denomination, but rather as an association of congregations. The movement received further impetus through the work of Thos: and Alexander Campbell, who maintained that denominational names and creeds were the real cause of spiritual and moral decline in Christendom. Originally the names *Churches of Christ* and *Disciples of Christ* * were used interchangeably by congregations believing that nothing may be tolerated in the New Testament churches unless it is expressly sanctioned in the Bible. Claiming to follow the example of the primitive Church, they rejected the use of denominational names, creeds, ecclesiastical terminology, church government. Each local congregation is considered autonomous, and ecclesiastical government or supervision is viewed as contrary to the New Testament. When missionary societies were organized on a "money basis," *i. e.*, with membership on the basis of fixed annual contributions, when some of the churches introduced instrumental music and others adopted "unscriptural means of raising money," the Conservatives gradually separated from the Progressives, until at present there is a clear line of demarcation between the Disciples of Christ ("Progressives," modernistic) and the Churches of Christ ("Conservatives," fundamentalistic). The latter group is particularly strong in the Southern States. Membership (1952): 1,100,000. See *Religious Bodies, U. S. (Bibliography).*

Churches of Christ in Christian Union in Ohio. A group which was formerly united with Christian Union.* In 1909 a number of churches in Ohio separated from the parent body on such fundamentalistic Holiness doctrines as entire sanctification as a second experience distinct from regeneration, divine healing, and the premillennial coming of Christ.

Churches of God in Christ Jesus. In 1921 the name of this Adventist body was changed to Church of God, with headquarters at Oregon, Ill. See *Adventist Bodies.*

Churches of God, Holiness. K. H. Buruss organized this body in the interest of Holiness doctrines at Atlanta, Ga., in 1914. See *Holiness Bodies.*

Churches of God in Jesus Christ. An organization of independent churches formed at Philadelphia (1888). It holds all the general Adventist * doctrines.

Churches of God in North America (*Winebrennerians*).

This body was organized in 1830 by John Winebrenner, former pastor of the German Reformed Church in Harrisburg, Pa., who in 1828 was expelled from the German Reformed Church on account of doctrinal differences. At the meeting held in October, 1830, an "eldership," consisting of an equal number of teaching and ruling elders, was organized, which, to distinguish it from the local church eldership, was called "General Eldership of the Church of God." On May 26, 1845, delegates from three elderships met at Pittsburgh, Pa., and organized the "General Eldership of the Church of God in North America," which name was changed in 1896 to the "General Eldership of the Churches of God in North America." In doctrine the Churches of God are Arminian rather than Calvinistic. They hold as distinctive views that sectarianism is antiscriptural; that each local church is a church of God and should be so called; that, in general, Bible things, as church offices and customs, should be known by Bible names; that there are three ordinances: Baptism, the Lord's Supper, and the religious washing of the saints' feet. The only mode of baptism recognized is the immersion of believers. They have no written creed, but accept the Word of God as their only rule of faith. Their doctrines are set forth in *Declaration of Views of the Church of God*. See *Religious (U. S.) Bodies, Bibliography*.

Churches of the Living God.

Two small Negro denominations are known by this name. The first, organized by Wm. Christian in 1889, has adopted the subtitle "Christian Workers for Fellowship," while the seceding group has added to its denominational name the designation "Pillar and Ground of Truth." The difference between the two groups is largely concerning management. Wm. Christian claimed to have been divinely called as chief in order to institute "freemason religion as the true mode of religion." The first three "corporeal degrees of this operative machinery are Baptism, Holy Supper, and feet washing." Tithing, anointing of the sick, the use of water in the Lord's Supper, are additional distinctive characteristics.

Churches of the New Jerusalem.

See *Swedenborgians*.

Churching of Women.

The custom of offering a special prayer of thanksgiving (with or without the mention of names) for women able to attend divine worship again after childbirth. The custom is probably based upon the Old Testament rite of purification, which declared a woman unclean for forty days in the case of a son and eighty in the case of a daughter and required a special offering of atonement before the woman was admitted to public worship again (Lev. 12).

Churchwarden.

A layman appointed in the Anglican Church to assist in managing the temporal affairs of the church.

Chytraeus (Kochhafe), David

(1531 to 1600). Luther's pupil; lectured in 1548; went to Rostock in 1551; pillar of the university. Commentaries on most books of the Bible; theological oracle of his time; influential in Austria, Sweden, etc.; one of the authors of the Formula of Concord. The last of the "Fathers of the Lutheran Church."

Ciborium

(G. *kiborion*, cup-shaped seed vessel of the Egyptian lily). Originally a canopy over the altar from which the container for the consecrated host was hung. Later the name was applied to the receptacle itself. See *Church Furniture*, 3.

Cincture.

See *Vestments, Clerical or Priestly*.

Circuit Visitor and Education.

See *Parish Education*, L 3.

Circumambulation.

The practice of walking around a person or an object for the purpose of exerting an influence upon it. Examples of it are found among people of Indo-European origin. Keeping the object on the right hand side during the procedure was believed to produce a beneficial effect upon it, while keeping it on the left was thought to have the opposite result.

Cistercians.

This monastic order was founded by a certain Robert, in 1098, at Citeaux in Burgundy, to counteract the laxity which had overtaken the Cluniac reform. It represented a return to a strict observance of the Benedictine Rule and insisted on simplicity, even poverty, of life. In 1112 the great Bernard of Clairvaux, with thirty young noblemen, entered the order, and under his influence and prestige it enjoyed a remarkable development. He was so closely identified with it that Cistercians are often called Bernardines. The Cistercians exemplified the Benedictine policy of work by colonizing northeastern Germany and other waste districts. They took pride in agriculture and cattle raising; but their industry made them too wealthy for their own good. "Religion brought forth riches; riches destroyed religion." The decline was aided by internal dissensions. The most important of various reform movements was the Trappist reform. (See *Trappists*.)

City Missions. The effort put forth by the church, either by preaching or by personal approach, or by both, to reach with the Gospel message the unchurched in our larger cities who live in the poorer sections and in the slum districts; also those who are confined to public institutions, permanently or for a time, as hospitals, institutions for the treatment of mental disorders, penal institutions, etc. This work is usually in charge of one or more city missionaries and, perhaps, deaconesses and social workers, engaged and supported by and under the supervision of the churches (Lutheran, for instance) of a particular city.

Civil Constitution of the Clergy. See *France, 2.*

Civil Government. Civil government is a divine institution comprising the whole number of those persons through whom by divine ordinance the legislative, judicial, and executive powers necessary for the governing of a commonwealth are administered in accordance with the form of government obtaining within that commonwealth (Gen. 9:6; Ex. 3:1-22; Num. 27: 15-23; Josh. 1:1-9; 1 Sam. 9:16; 1 Kings 19:15; 2 Kings 8:13; Dan. 2:21, 37; 4:17; John 19:10; Rom. 13:1 ff.). The duties of civil government are: to promote the general welfare of its people by protecting the individuals and groups in their civil rights and to defend the state against dangers from within and without (1 Tim. 2:2; Gen. 9:6; Matt. 26:52; Rom. 13:4). Hence the power of the church and the civil power must not be confounded (John 18:36; Matt. 22:21; Acts 18:12-17. Cf. *AC*, art. XXVIII). In the administration of its duties government must make use of all ways and means necessary and suitable for the proper discharge of its obligations. In carrying out its legislative, judicial, and executive functions government must follow the Natural Law as it is still inscribed in the hearts of natural man, and the dictates of reason, experience, and common sense. The relation of the members of a commonwealth to their government is that of subjects to a superior authority. As subjects of their government they are to render for conscience' sake due honor, obedience, and service to their government as far as this can be done without violating God's Law. C. f. PFS in: *Abiding Word* (I: 508—521). See *Church and State.*

Clairvoyance. See *Psychical Research.*

Clandestinity. See *Marriage.*

Clare, Nuns of St. This female branch of the Franciscans was founded by Clare of Assisi, about 1213. Its members are dedicated to a life of penance and contemplation. See *Franciscans.*

Clarendon Constitutions (1164). Sixteen chapters drawn up by advisers of Henry II to which Thomas à Becket, moved by threats and entreaties, agreed. They gave the King of England much authority in matters of patronage, crimes of clergymen, ecclesiastical trials, ecclesiastical property, the election of higher clergy, and other matters. The Pope condemned ten of the propositions and tolerated six others.

Clarke, Adam (ca. 1762—1832). English Methodist. B. in Ireland; studied in England; Methodist, 1778; sent out as preacher, 1782; traveled throughout Great Britain; for a time denied "the eternal sonship" of Christ; thrice president of British Conference; scholar of comprehensive attainments; d. in London. Assisted in preparing *Arabic Bible;* published *Commentary on the Bible* (8 vols.).

Clarke, James Freeman (1810—88). Unitarian; graduate of Harvard; leader in the organization of the Church of Disciples which emphasized application of religion to social problems, especially slavery; secretary of Unitarian Association; professor of Christian doctrine at Harvard; wrote *Ten Great Religions, Orthodoxy.* Edited *Western Messenger.*

Clarke, John. See *Baptist Bodies, 3.*

Clarke, Samuel. A well-known English divine and metaphysician; born at Norwich, Oct. 11, 1675; died suddenly, May, 1729. His principal work, translated into German by Semper, prepared the way for German rationalism.

Among other things, he published a *Paraphrase on the Four Gospels.* The Lower House of Convocation, in 1714, complained to the bishops of the heterodox and dangerous tendencies of the Arian tenets advanced by Clarke.

Clarke, William Newton (1841 to 1912). American Baptist clergyman; professor of theology at Colgate University, Hamilton, N. Y. (1890—1908), of Christian ethics (1908—1912); wrote *Outline of Theology* (1897), *The Christian Doctrine of God* (1905), etc.; was responsible for the popularity of Modernism in American theological seminaries; a disciple of Albrecht Ritschl and strong exponent of the theology of experience.

Class Meeting. A distinctive feature of Methodism, introduced by Wesley in London about 1742. The congregation is divided into classes, over each of which the pastor appoints a class leader, whose duties are as follows: 1. To see each person in his class at the appointed meeting place in order to inquire concerning his soul's welfare and to advise, reprove, comfort, or exhort, as may be necessary; also to receive contributions towards the support of the preachers, the church, and the poor. 2. To meet the ministers and the stewards once a week in order to inform the minister of any that are sick, or of disorderly members who will not be reproved, and to pay the stewards the contributions which they have received from the classes each week. See *Methodist Bodies.*

Classis. In Reformed polity (*e.g.,* the Reformed Church in America) a judicatory body corresponding to the presbytery.*

Claude, Jean (1619—87). Leader of French Reformed Church. Born in southwestern France; pastor at Nimes, Montauban, Paris; controversialist; d. at The Hague. Wrote: *On Composition of a Sermon;* etc.

Claudius, Matthias (1740—1815). Layman, sincere believer in, and defender of, Bible faith in the age of Rationalism; also hymn writer; editor of the *Wandsbecker Bote.*

Claudius of Turin. Statesman-bishop under Charlemagne and Louis the Pious; born latter half of eighth century; d. before 832; rendered much service against the Mohammedan Moors; wrote a number of commentaries; opposed the Church in a num-

ber of views, notably that of the power of Peter, and showed iconoclastic tendencies.

Clausen, Claus Lauritz. B. in Denmark, Nov. 3, 1820; teacher, lay preacher; to Norway, 1841; to America, 1843, to work among the Norwegians; ordained, 1843; pastor in Wisconsin and Iowa; member of Iowa Legislature; Commissioner of Immigration; army chaplain; pastor. One of three pastors who, 1851, organized "The Norwegian Evangelical Lutheran Church in America"; its president. One of the organizers of "The Norwegian Synod," 1853 (its vice-president), and of "The Norwegian-Danish Conference," 1870 (its president). Editor and author. D. Feb. 20, 1892. See *Evangelical Lutheran Church,* 7.

O. M. Norlie, *Prominent Personalities,* Northfield, Minn., 1942 (p. 14 ff.).

Clausen, Henrik (1793—1877). Graduate of University of Copenhagen; studied in Germany; instructor in theology at Copenhagen. His rationalism is shown in his *Catholicism and Protestantism,* which led to a controversy with Grundtvig.

Clausnitzer, Tobias (1618—1684). Chaplain of a Swedish regiment; later pastor and inspector at Weiden; wrote: "Jesu, dein betruebtes Leiden"; "Liebster Jesu, wir sind hier"; "Wir glauben all' an einen Gott."

Clay, Albert Tobias. B. Hanover, Pa., Dec. 4, 1866; educated at Franklin and Marshall College, 1889; grad. Mt. Airy Seminary, 1892; Ph. D. Univ. of Pa., 1894; honorary M. A. Yale, 1910; LL. D. Pa. College, 1913; Litt. D. Muhlenberg College, 1918; Assyrian fellow, 1892—93; instr. U. of Pa., 1892—95; Chicago Luth. Seminary, 1895—99; Mt. Airy Theol. Seminary, 1905—10; ass't prof. and prof. at Univ. of Pa., 1899 to 1910; Laffan prof., Yale, 1910—25; Curator, Yale Babylonian Collection, 1912 to 1925; Reinicker lecturer, Episcopal Theol. Seminary, Alexandria, Va., 1908; annual prof. American School of Oriental Research in Jerusalem, 1919—20. Author: *Business Documents of Murashu Sons; Documents from Temple Archives of Nippur Dated in the Region of Cassite Ruler; Legal and Commercial Transactions Dated in the Assyrian and Neo-Babylonian and Persian Periods; Aramaic Endorsements, O. T. and Semitic Studies, in Memory of W. R. Harper; Amurru, the Home of the Northern Semites; Personal Names of the*

Cassite Period; Business Transactions of the First Millennium B. C.; Legal Documents from Erech, Seleucid Era, Epics, Hymns, Omens and Other Texts; Miscellaneous Inscriptions in the Yale Babylonian Collection; The Empire of the Amorites; Neo-Babylonian Letters from Erech; A Hebrew Deluge Story in Cuneiform; The Origin of Biblical Traditions; also (with H. V. Hilprecht) *Business Documents of Murashu Sons of Nippur,* dated in the reign of Artaxerxes I; (with Morris Jastrow, Jr.). *An Old Babylonian Version of the Gilgamesh Epic.* Died Sept. 14, 1925.

Cleanthes (3d c. B. C.). Greek Stoic philosopher, successor of Zeno.

Clement XI. See *Unigenitus.*

Clement XIV. See *Popes,* 25.

Clement of Rome. See *Apostolic Fathers,* 1.

Clement, Titus Flavius (of Alexandria; ca. 150—213). Born of heathen parents (Athens?); studied in Italy, Syria, Palestine; went to Egypt and came into contact with Pantaenus (*Strom.* I: 11: 1); later head of the Alexandrian School (Eusebius, *Hist.,* VI: 6); during the persecution of Septimius Severus he left Alexandria (ca. 203). Under his leadership and that of his pupil Origen, the school of Alexandria became one of the most famous centers of Christian learning. He is an important witness for the early formation of the NT canon. Held that as the Law brought the Jews to God, so Christian philosophy brought the Greeks to Christ. His system centers in the *Logos* by which God enters into relationship with created things. His extensive quotations were probably derived from anthologies. Principal works: *Exhortation to the Heathen, Instructor,* and *Stromata.*

R. B. Tollington, *Clement of Alexandria,* 1914.

Clementines. A series of writings (*Ep. to the Corinthians, 1 and 2; To the Unmarried; Homilies; Apostolic Constitutions; Liturgy; Canons*) ascribed to Clement of Rome. Only the 1st letter to the Corinthians is considered authentic.

Clerestory. See *Architecture, Ecclesiastical,* 3 ff.

Clergy. The term applied to those separated to the work of the Christian ministry. The Apostolic Church knew of no ranks in the clergy. See Acts 20: 17: "elders" identified with "bishops" (overseers), v. 28. From the time of Cyprian (d. 258), the father of the hierarchical system, the distinction of clergy (from laity) as an order in the church and of ranks within the clergy became universal. In the Roman Church the clergy became not only a separate order of Christians, but were regarded as a priesthood with the office of mediatorship between God and men. To the distinction of presbyters (elders) and bishops, as differentiated in rank, was added, in course of time, the distinction of various classes of the (sacerdotal) clergy — the higher (subdeacon, deacon, priest, bishop, metropolitan, patriarch, pope) and the lower (doorkeepers, readers, exorcists, acolytes) clergy. In the later Middle Ages the regular clergy were the members of monastic orders (those under a *regula*), and the term "secular clergy" was applied to those who had charge of parishes. "Benefit" of clergy was the privilege by which clergymen were exempted from trial in the civil courts and by which consecrated places gave asylum against criminal arrest. In Protestantism in America the clergy are generally not considered a separate caste. See *Ministerial Office.*

Clericalism. 1) A principle or policy which gives the clergy of any denomination control over the affairs of the state, education, marriage laws, public charities, or the like. 2) Championing the church in conflicts with the state, as France, Germany, Italy, or elsewhere. 3) The assumption by the clergy for its exclusive right of certain functions which belong to the universal priesthood.

Clericis Laicos. Bull of Boniface VIII (1296) threatening French and English kings with excommunication because of high taxation which the kings imposed.

Clerks, Regular. In Roman Catholicism, men who combine secular duties with the vows of monks (*e. g.,* Jesuits).

Cloeter, O. E. B. in Bayreuth, Bavaria, Apr. 25, 1825; studied in Erlangen and Leipzig; one of Loehe's missioners; pastor in Saginaw, Mich., 1849—1856; Indian missionary in Minnesota at Mille Lac. His mission station was laid waste during the Indian War of 1862. After the war he was missionary at Crow Wing; 1868 pastor in Afton, Minn.; d. Mar. 17, 1897.

Cloister. See *Architecture, Ecclesiastical,* 3.

Close Communion. See *Altar Fellowship; Fellowship.*

Closed Season (*Tempus Clausum*). The entire Lenten season, beginning with Ash Wednesday and closing with the Great Sabbath, as well as the Advent season, beginning with the First Sunday in Advent and ending with Christmas Eve, comes under this heading; the word "closed" having reference to the fact that all open and noisy festivities, including public wedding celebrations, were not permitted during these two periods of the year. The custom is not obligatory in the Lutheran Church, though still observed and to be recommended.

Clovis (ca. 466—511). King of Salian Franks; founder of Frankish monarchy; influenced by wife (Clotilda) to be baptized (496); built Church of Holy Apostles (St. Genevieve) at Paris; convoked Council of Orleans (511). See *France,* 1.

Cluniac Monks. The Cluniacs were not properly a distinct order, but were Benedictines remodeled by the great reform movement issuing from the abbey of Cluny, in France, during the 10th century. This reform purposed to restore the original strictness of Benedict's rule, but it also introduced the correctional principle into monasticism. Till then each monastery was an independent unit; the houses affiliated with Cluny, however, were absolutely subject to its abbot. The famous Pope Gregory VII used the Cluniac movement in forcing celibacy on the clergy and in his struggles against the secular rulers. By the 12th century, the Cluniac movement was spent and was itself in need of reforms, which the Cistercians sought to apply.

Cluny. A monastery in France founded by the Benedictines (10 c.), famous for its scholars (*e.g.,* Gregory VII).

Clutz, Jacob Abraham. B. Adams Co., Pa., Jan. 5, 1848; educated Pa. College, 1869; grad. of Luth. Theol. Seminary, Gettysburg, Pa., 1872; D.D. Pa. College, 1889; LL.D. Midland College, Fremont, Nebr., 1920; pastor at Newville, Pa., and Baltimore, Md., 1872—83; (General Synod) gen. sec'y, Bd. of Home Missions 1883—89; pres. Midland College, Atchison, Kans., 1889—1904; prof. at Western Theol. Seminary, Atchison,

1894—1909; Luth. Theol. Seminary, Gettysburg, 1909—25; sec'y, Bd. Foreign Missions, 1877—83; pres., Gen. Synod 1891; treas., Bd. of Home Missions 1905—13, pres. of same, 1913—15; sec'y, Ways and Means Committee to effect merger of Luth. Gen. Synod, Gen. Council, and United Synod in South, 1917—18; member, Ex. Bd. U. L. C. 1918—24; trustee, Pa. College, 1908—25; co-editor *Lutheran Quarterly* from 1909. Died Sept. 7, 1925.

Co-Adamites. Human beings believed by some opponents of the Scriptural account of creation to have been contemporaries of Adam and Eve, although of a different origin, the theory being related to the suppositions of evolutionism. See also *Pre-adamites.*

Coadjutor. An assistant to a cleric, especially a bishop, who is unable to perform his official duties because of old age, blindness, insanity, etc.

Cobham, Lord (Sir John Oldcastle). English reformer of fourteenth century; strong adherent of Wyclif, whose works he collected, transcribed, and distributed among the people; condemned as heretic and committed to Tower; escaped, but was retaken and burned alive, December, 1417.

Cocceius (Koch), **Johannes** (1603 to 1669). Dutch Reformed. B. at Bremen; professor of theology at Franeker 1643; at Leyden 1650 (d. there). Founder of federal theology (covenant of works before man's fall, of grace after man's fall, latter subdivided into the antelegal, the legal, and the postlegal dispensation); allegorizing and mysterizing exegete; author of first tolerably complete Hebrew dictionary.

Cochlaeus, Johannes (Dobneck, Wendelstinus; 1479—1552). Catholic controversialist; studied at Cologne and in Italy; friend of Miltitz and Aleander; wrote bitter polemical tracts against Luther and the Reformation; found little recognition, even in his own circles.

Codex. See *Manuscripts of the Bible,* 3.

Coena Domini, In (Bull). See *In Coena Domini.*

Coffin, Henry Sloane. B. Jan. 5, 1877; studied at Yale Univ., New College, Edinburgh, Univ. of Marburg, Union Theol. Sem., New York Univ., Harvard Univ.; held pastorates in New York City; professor, and (1926—45)

president of Union Theol. Seminary, New York City; liberal Presbyterian; author.

Cogito, ergo sum. See *Descartes.*

Cohen, Hermann (1842—1918). German philosopher; prof. at Marburg. The idea of God (with ethical connotations) forms the center of his neo-Kantianism.

Colegio Concordia. See *South America, Lutheranism in.*

Colenso, John William (1814—83). Anglican prelate. B. at Cornwall; rector; bishop of Natal, South Africa; denied inspiration of Old Testament; was deposed; deposition not sustained by home government; new see being erected in place of Natal, Colenso was thereafter a schismatic; d. at Durban. Wrote commentaries, etc.; translated New Testament into Zulu.

Coleridge, Samuel Taylor. English poet, critic, philosopher; b. near Exeter, 1772; d. in London, 1834. Passed through stages of rationalism, Unitarianism, pantheism. Rejected Christ's vicarious atonement and objective redemption. Emphasized ethical side of Christianity. Gave impetus to liberal movement in Anglican Church (Broad Church).

Colet, John (ca. 1466—1519). English theologian; studied at Oxford, met Erasmus there, becoming his intimate friend; dean of St. Paul's in 1504; founded St. Paul's School; wrote a devotional book, *Right Fruitful Admonition.*

Coligny, Gaspard de (1517—1572). Celebrated French admiral; defended St. Quentin for seventeen days against superior force of Philip II of Spain (1557) but was finally forced to surrender. Adopted Reformed faith during subsequent imprisonment (1557) and became joint leader with Prince de Condé of the Huguenot party; made several attempts (through Ribault 1562, Laudonniere 1564) to plant colonies in America as an asylum for his persecuted co-religionists; fell first victim of the Massacre of St. Bartholomew's.

Collect. A terse, comprehensive prayer which has a trinitarian ending. The wording of the ending is determined by the person of the Trinity addressed at the beginning. The name *Collect,* derived from the Latin *collecta,* indicates that the needs of the Church are collected and assembled in this prayer; however, the great classic collects of the Church usually include only one petition. Several collects, usually an odd number, were offered rather than include two or more petitions in one Collect.

The Collect is a product of the Western Church. The golden age of the Collect extended from the fourth to the seventh century. These early Collects of the Church are still unsurpassed as far as content, beauty, and structure are concerned. The complete Collect consists of five parts: the address; the reason, usually a relative clause; the petition; the blessing prayed for; the termination or ending. While new parts should never be added, one or two parts may be omitted. Collects in which parts are omitted are known as "thin" Collects. Luther did not reject the Collects which had become a part of the liturgical heritage of the Church, but modified them when necessary. Many of the English translations of ancient Collects were prepared by Thomas Cranmer.

In the Lutheran service the Collect is used before the Epistle and at the close of Communion. In Matins and Vespers it follows the Lord's Prayer. Since the Collect is a prayer of the Church and not of an individual, it is usually read from official publications.

Collections in Churches. See *Finances in the Church.*

College Apostolic. Term applied by Roman Catholics to the body of apostles under the supposed primacy of Peter.

College of Cardinals. See *Cardinals.*

Colleges. See *Ministry, Education of,* VI A; VII.

Colleges, Lutheran. See *Ministry, Education of,* VII ff.

Collegiate System. A term describing the relation of church and state as understood in some parts of Protestantism during the seventeenth and eighteenth centuries. The churches were regarded as legal corporations (*collegia licita*), concerning which the state had a double power: that of superintendence and patronage (*ius circa sacra*), and also certain rights in the internal affairs of the church (*ius in sacris*), transferred to the secular government as the representative of the congregations. Especially during the period of rationalism, princes and statesmen regarded the churches as part of the state organism, absolutely subject to the government. The system led to violation of elementary rights of conscience, and only in the nineteenth century gave way to views of state and church which concede to the latter a greater opportunity to manage its own affairs.

Collin, Nicholas (d. 1831). Swedish pastor; came to America and served at Raccoon, Pennswick (N. J.), and Wicacoa (Gloria Dei, Philadelphia).

Collins, Anthony. See *Deism*, III, 4.

Colloquy. In the Polity of the French Reformed Church a body corresponding to the presbytery.* — The name given to a formal theological discussion.

Collyer, William Bengo (1782 to 1854). B. at Blackheath, England, April 14, 1782, and educated at Homerton College and at twenty began his ministry at the Congregational Church at Peckham. Arian preaching and administration had depleted the churches of England. Now with Collyer's Trinitarian preaching the people came back to church. Collyer compiled a hymnbook primarily for his own congregation, including 57 of his own hymns. He died Jan. 8, 1854.

Colombia. See *South America*, 6.

Colored Cumberland Presbyterian Church. See *Presbyterian Bodies*, 4.

Colored Methodist Episcopal Church. See *Methodist Bodies*, 4 c.

Colored Missions. See *Missions, Lutheran Negro*.

Colored Primitive Baptists. See *Baptist Bodies*, 12.

Colors, Liturgical. On account of the many references in the Book of Revelation to the saints dressed in white, this color was in general use in the church from the earliest times. So far as other colors are concerned, comparatively little is known of their use, although veils, tapestries, and coverings are mentioned at an early date. In the twelfth century, Innocent III authorized the use of four colors: black, scarlet, white, and green; in a very short time, however, the fifth color, violet, was added. William Durandus, in his *Rationale Divinorum Officiorum*, discusses the liturgical colors at length, and the *Missale Romanum* has regulations agreeing almost exactly with his. The colors have been retained in the Anglican and in the Lutheran Church, both on account of their significance and because they serve to emphasize the course of the church year.

White symbolizes innocence and holiness, majesty and glory; red, the color of dominion, joy, light-giving doctrine, fire of the Holy Ghost, blood and martyrdom, symbolizes the love of the Bride, the Church, to Christ, the Bridegroom; green symbolizes hope, peace, and victory; violet is the color of penitence, mourning, humility, concentration, and prayerful self-communion; black symbolizes humiliation, sadness, and deep mourning.

Although there is some difference of opinion in detail, the following are generally regarded the ecclesiastical colors: Advent to Christmas Eve, violet; Christmas Eve (inclusive) to Septuagesima Sunday, white; Septuagesima Sunday (inclusive) to Ash Wednesday, green; Ash Wednesday (inclusive) to Wednesday of Holy Week, violet; Wednesday of Holy Week and Maundy Thursday, white; Good Friday, black; Saturday of Holy Week, violet; Easter to Eve of Pentecost, white; Eve of Pentecost (inclusive) to Trinity Sunday, red; Trinity Sunday to Sunday after Trinity, white; Monday after Sunday after Trinity to Advent, green; minor church festivals, red.

Colportage. The free distribution or sale (usually at low rates) of Bibles and other religious publications to the general public, especially in heathen lands, by colporteurs.

Columba. See *Celtic Church*, 7.

Columbanus (559—615). A scholarly Irish monk, who preached in Burgundy and subsequently in what is now Switzerland, along the upper Rhine. His last years were spent in Northern Italy, where he founded the monastery of Bobbio. See *Franks, Saxons, and Other Germanic Nations*, 2.

Come-Outists. Name given to the Church of God (Anderson, Ind.) founded by Daniel S. Warner (ca. 1880).

Comenius, John Amos (1592—1670). Pastor of the Moravian church at Fulneck; driven from there during the Thirty Years' War, he settled at Leszno. There he became famous as an educational reformer. His complete educational system is published in his *The Great Didactic*, which established his fame as the pioneer of modern educational science. In the field of religion he labored for the union of all Christians. See *Bohemia, Luth. Theology in*, 5; *Moravian Church*.

Comes (Liturgical). An epistolary or lectionary fixing the readings for all the Sundays of the church year, as well as for the festivals and ferial services. See also *Pericope.*

Comgall, St.* See *Celtic Church*, 8.

Commandments of the Church. Certain rules of the Roman Catholic Church (concerning attendance at Mass, fasts, paying salaries of priests, and others) which have often been considered as obligatory as the Decalog.

Commandments, Ten. See *Decalog.*

Commendation of the Dying. Name often given to the prayer spoken at the bedside of a dying person. Lutheran *agendas* contain prayers which usually ask God to forgive the sins of the departing one and receive him or her into heaven.

Commentaries, Biblical. A commentary is an exposition of the Bible or of any book or part of the Bible, the fundamental requirements for sound exegetical work being the agreement with all parts of Scripture, a sound philological and grammatical exposition, a proper consideration of the historical (archaeological, economic) background, and an understanding of the purpose of the writing concerned. Critical commentaries are such as are not only based upon, but directly employ the original Hebrew (Aramaic) and Greek text. Popular commentaries are those which present in untechnical phraseology the results of scholarly research. Homiletical commentaries are those that particularly aim to supply material for sermon making.

Important early commentaries professedly covering the whole Bible were those of Origen and Augustine. Early *scholia* and glosses developed into the *catenae,* which are collections of patristic utterances on individual passages. The *Glossa* of Walafrid Strabo is of this nature. For extensive lists of older commentaries see the *Cyclopedia* of McClintock and Strong (III: 432 and under Old and New Testament). Consult also the *International Standard Bible Encyclopedia* (p. 680 ff.) and the literature references added to the articles on the individual books of the Bible. A partial list of commentaries that served past generations and that may still be consulted with profit follows:

The exegetical work of Luther is paramount. Not only his *Genesis* and

his two expositions of *Galatians,* but also his other exegetical works deserve diligent study.

John Calvin, *Commentarii* (English transl. 52 vols.). Acute, but by no means exegetically sound; its interpretations are from the Calvinistic point of view.

Poole's (Poli) *Synopsis Criticorum* (1669). The annotations of a great number of exegetes collected and condensed. Uncritical, but valuable as an immense collection of opinions.

Starck's *Synopsis,* although by no means profound and exhaustive, is by an orthodox theologian and contains homiletical material.

Matthew Henry, *Exposition* (1704). Little exposition, but *voluminous* sermonizing. Prolix. Generally termed "orthodox," from the Reformed standpoint.

Adam Clarke, *Commentary* (1810). Methodist. Varied, but not always accurate learning. Quotes much from ancients and the Orientals.

Heinrich Olshausen, *Biblischer Commentar* (1837), continued by Ebrard, tr. into English in Clark's Library, Edinburgh. An example of German learning and astuteness still in great part free from Higher Criticism.

Hengstenberg. The commentaries of this great German scholar are fundamental in modern exegetical work of the conservative type. The places in which allegory and fancy are prominent will readily be discovered by the careful reader.

A. Barnes, *Notes on the New Testament* (1850). Simple, lucid, practical, and strikes the dominant note of evangelical passages.

Bengel, *Gnomon of the New Testament.* A series of analytical, philological and expository notes, illuminating the text "in flashes."

Henry Alford's *Greek Testament with Critical Apparatus and Notes,* in 4 vols., has served as a model for The *Expositor's Greek Testament,* in 5 volumes. The Greek text, with commentary and textual criticism in footnotes. Its introductory material often reflects the New Theology, but the notes generally excellent in their treatment of grammatical and syntactical points. Useful especially for quick reference.

H. A. W. Meyer, *Kritisch-exegetischer Kommentar zum Neuen Testament.* Shows penetration, grammatical mastery, and cohesion. The later editions almost complete reworkings of

Meyer's handbooks and generally under the influence of the Higher Criticism. The American revision of the English translation is the best edition of Meyer.

Daechsel's Bibelwerk. A German popular commentary of the entire Bible which, though brief, offers much excellent material for quick orientation.

J. P. Lange, *Bibelwerk.* Summarizes much of the older scholarship and contains much homiletical and devotional material. Published in English translation by Clark, Edinburgh, and considerably reworked in Lange-Schaff, *Commentary.*

Keil-Delitzsch, *Kommentar zum Alten Testament.* The greatest exposition of the Old Testament books ever published. Tr. in the Clark Library, Edinburgh. Although Delitzsch later modified some sections of his work (notably Psalms) in the interest of a more liberal interpretation, Keil's work has remained throughout a monument of evangelical scholarship.

Jamieson, Fausset, and Brown, *One-Volume Commentary on the Bible.* Frequently preferred among one-volume commentaries.

The *Popular Commentary* of P. E. Kretzmann and the scholarly and critical commentary (*Interpretations*) of R. C. H. Lenski, as well as commentaries on individual books (*e. g.,* Stoeckhardt, *Roemerbrief,* Aug. Pieper, *Jesaias II,* T. Laetsch, *Jeremiah*), may be mentioned as part of American Lutherans' contribution to Biblical exegesis.

Commission, The Biblical. Established by Leo XIII (1902); consists of five cardinals and additional consultants; it defends Roman beliefs in Biblical matters; studies progress in interpretation and recent discoveries; acts as judge in controversies.

Commissions, Ecclesiastical. 1) In the Anglican Church, officers who fill the bishop's place in exercising ecclesiastical authority in places so far distant that people cannot be called to the consistory. 2) In the Church of Rome, dignitaries deputed to exercise functions properly belonging to the Pope.

Commistio (or Commixtio). The placing of a portion of the host into the chalice during the celebration of the Roman Mass. It probably symbolizes reunion of Christ's body and blood at His resurrection. It is connected with the Roman denial of the cup to the laity.

Committee on Life and Work of the Churches. See *Union Movements,* 15.

Commodianus (3d c.). Little known of his life; Christian Latin poet; his *Instructiones* (apologetic and hortatory work), *adversus Gentium Deos* (against heathen gods), and *Carmen Apologeticum* (doctrine in verse) are extant.

Common Confession. After The Lutheran Church — Missouri Synod passed the 1938 resolutions regarding fellowship with the American Lutheran Church (see *Brief Statement*) attempts were made to unite the contents of the *Brief Statement* and *Declaration.* The resulting document, *Doctrinal Affirmation,* was adopted by neither of the above-mentioned bodies. The Missouri Synod convention (July 20—29, 1947) instructed its Committee on Doctrinal Unity "to make every effort to arrive ultimately at one document which is Scriptural, clear, concise, and unequivocal."

After a meeting with the synods of the Synodical Conference, the Committee on Doctrinal Unity met with the Fellowship Commission of the American Lutheran Church (May 17, 1948). Subcommittees were selected to draw up the doctrinal theses. After lengthy study and criticism of the preliminary drafts, a plenary session of the committees of the two bodies was held and the theses unanimously approved (Dec. 5, 6, 1949). The Common Confession was accepted by The Lutheran Church — Missouri Synod (June 21—30, 1950) and the American Lutheran Church (October, 1950).

The twelve topics of the *Common Confession* treat the doctrines of God, man, redemption, election, means of grace, justification, conversion, sanctification, the church, the ministry, the Lutheran confessions, the last things.

The *Common Confession* was distributed in pamphlet form prior to the conventions mentioned above; an official copy is found in the *Proceedings of the Forty-First Regular Convention of The Lutheran Church — Missouri Synod;* see also the *Proceedings* of 1947 and minutes of the American Lutheran Church; articles in church papers of the two bodies (1950).

On Feb. 9, 1953, Part II of the *Common Confession* was unanimously adopted by the official committees of the American Lutheran Church and The Lutheran Church — Missouri Synod at a joint meeting held in Chicago, Ill. The purpose of Part II was to supplement and clarify Part I. Under the general heading "The Church in the World" it treats the following topics: i. The Church's Mission; ii. The Church's Resources; iii. The Church and Its Ministrations; iv. The Church and the Home; v. The Church and Vocation; vi. The Church and Education; vii. The Church and Government; viii. The Church and Church Fellowship; ix. The Church and Anti-Christian Organizations; x. The Church and the World to Come. This Part II was published in pamphlet form and in some official publications. EL

Common Grace (*gratia communis*). According to Reformed doctrine (Calvinistic), the elect are converted and preserved in the state of faith and salvation by special or irresistible grace, while to all others the sovereign God grants only common grace, which is resistible. While, according to Reformed theology, common grace does not save, it should be used by men to the glory of God, and its rightful use is rewarded with temporal blessings. The doctrine is not in accord with Scripture, which teaches that divine grace is both universal (John 3:16; 1 Tim. 2:4) and resistible (Matt. 23:37). The distinction between common and irresistible grace should answer the question why, though all men by nature are in the same guilt, and grace alone saves men (Rom. 2:28), some are saved and others are not. To explain this mystery, Calvinism denies universal grace, while synergism (Arminianism, Semi-Pelagianism) denies that grace alone saves (*sola gratia*). Scripture does not solve the problem beyond the information that those who are saved, are saved by grace (Eph. 2:8,9), while those who are lost, are lost through their own unbelief (Hos. 13:9; Rom. 11:20).

Common Law Marriage. See *Marriage*.

Common Prayer, Book of. See *Book of Common Prayer*.

Common Service, Order of. See *Order of Worship; Liturgics*.

Communicatio Idiomatum. See *Idiomatum; Christ Jesus, D*.

Communication of Attributes. See *Christ Jesus, I D; Idiomatum*.

Communio Naturarum. See *Idiomatum*.

Communion. See *Grace, Means of, IV*.

Communion of Saints. See *Church*, 1 ff.

Communion Service. See *Lord's Supper (Liturgical)*.

Communion Set. See *Church Furniture*, 3.

Communion Tokens. Small disks of metal or pieces of paper given to members of a church entitled to partake of Holy Communion, a custom dating back to the early Christian centuries, to protect the faithful from traitors and informers and to serve as testimonials to their good standing. The custom of giving them has now generally fallen into disuse. However, the practice of giving a communion card, introducing a traveling visitor as a member in good standing in his own church and entitling him to commune at the altar of a sister church, is observed.

Communism. See *Socialism*.

Communist Manifesto. See *Marx, Karl*.

Communistic Societies. 1. Religious groups which sought to organize their life and property according to collective ideals were in existence in Palestine (Essenes), Egypt (Therapeutae), and other lands at the time of Christ. The collectivism practiced in the early church at Jerusalem was not an absolute, total, or compulsory community of goods. The individuality of each member was guarded (Acts 5:4) and love was the only law by which each was bound.

2. In the early days of Christianity, the Manichaeans practiced a type of communism associated with their asceticism.* Later, Benedictine * monks introduced communistic ideals within Roman Catholic monasticism.* In the pre-Reformation period, groups which opposed the Papacy often organized on a collective basis (Cathari,* Albigenses,* Waldenses,* Beghards,* Lollards,* Taborites,* Moravian Brethren*).

3. Few religious communistic groups existed in the modern period in Europe (Babeuf in France during the Revolution; Robert Owen * in England). America, however, has seen more than 200 such experiments, some being primarily religious, others only social and economic. Most of the largest and most successful were of German origin. Though a few existed for over a century, many dissolved for various reasons (failure to solve the problem of

family life, the injunction of celibacy, secession of the young, lack of personal liberty, killing individual initiative and endeavor, etc.).

4. The first communistic organization in America was formed by the *Labadists* (followers of John Labadie *) who settled at Elkton, Md., but soon sacrificed their religious convictions to the profit motive. Somewhat later John Kelpius (1673—1708) led the followers of Johann J. Zimmermann to Philadelphia to form the society known as the *Society of the Woman in the Wilderness* (Rev. 12:1 ff.).

5. The more important American societies are the following: *Amana Society,* * *House of David,* * *Oneida Community,* * *Rappists,* * and *Shakers.* * The *Ephrata Community,* near Reading, Pa., was founded (1733) by John Conrad Beissel (1690—1768; influenced by Kelpius) of Eberbach, Germany. It dissolved in 1814, the remaining members incorporating as *German Seventh-Day Baptists* (still extant). *Icaria* was founded by French settlers in Texas (1848), later moved to Illinois, then to Iowa, but was of short duration and its offshoot, *New Icaria,* dissolved in 1895. The *Zoar Separatists,* founded in Wuerttemberg, Germany, by dissenters from the Lutheran State Church under the leadership of the mystic Barbara Grubermann, moved to Ohio (1817; led by Joseph Michael Bimeler, 1778—1853, after the death of Barbara Grubermann), and dissolved in 1898. The *Bethel* and *Aurora* communities, founded in Missouri by William Keil of Nordhausen, dissolved in 1877 and 1881, respectively. Many communistic societies resulted from, or were influenced by, Charles Fourier (1772—1837; French Socialist), of which the best known are: *Brook Farm,* near West Roxbury, Mass. (1841—47; noted for its literary associations: Emerson, Hawthorne, Greeley, and others); The *North American Phalanx* in New Jersey (1843—54); the *Altruist Community,* near St. Louis. The Adventist *Adonai Shomo Community* was organized in Massachusetts in 1876 and dissolved in 1896. The *Bishop Hill Colony* was founded in Illinois by Swedes from Helsingland, Sweden, under the leadership of Eric Janson (who claimed he was the reincarnated Christ) and dissolved in 1862. The *Bruederhof* communities (founded in the 16th century by Jacob Huter, a Mennonite) settled at Wolf Creek and Bon Homme, S. Dak. (1874), at Elm Spring (1877). The *Church*

Triumphant or *Koreshanity,* organized at Chicago (1886), removed to Estero, Florida (1903).

Community of Brethren. See *Bohemian-Moravian Brethren.*

Community Chests. See *Social Work,* D 3.

Community Churches. As a rule a community church is an independent, undenominational, or interdenominational congregation, representing the union of several small or weak denominational churches. The community church ordinarily has no creedal platform. The program of church work is chiefly this-worldly and varies to meet the social and cultural interests of the respective constituency.

Community Social Work. See *Social Work,* C 1.

Commutation of Penance. In the Roman Catholic Church, a change made in the penance * which has been prescribed, usually with relaxation.

Comnena, Anna (1083—1148). The daughter of Alexius Comnenus I, Byzantine emperor; failed in her endeavor to secure the empire for her husband, Nicephorus Briennius; her *Alexias* (history of her father's reign) is principal source for Byzantine history at time of first crusade.

Compactata of Prague. See *Hussites.*

Comparative Religion. See *Religion, Comparative.*

Comparative Symbolics. See *Symbolics.*

Competent. See *Catechetics,* 3.

Compline. See *Canonical Hours.*

Complutensian Polyglot. See *Polyglot Bibles.*

Compostella, Order of. A Spanish military order, with mild Augustinian rule, founded in 1161. It assisted in expelling the Moslems and became extinct in 1835.

Comte, Auguste (1798—1857). French philosopher and mathematician; founder of positivism * (all knowledge must be scientifically verifiable); in his *Positive Philosophy* he sought to establish three stages of mental evolution (theological, metaphysical, and scientific); he sought to remove the supernatural from religion and make it a force for secular and social reforms; died insane.

Concentus. The portion of the church service in the ancient and medieval church sung by the whole choir, characterized by more melismatic *Accentus,** particularly in the Alleluias, Graduals, and other parts of the liturgical service.

Concept. See *Christian Teaching,* B.

Conception, Immaculate. See *Roman Catholic Confessions,* C; *Mariolatry.*

Conceptualism. A theory in logic first expounded by Abelard, as a mediating position between nominalism and realism, and postulating that the concepts in the mind are the instruments of knowledge.

Conciliarism. See *Councils and Synods,* 7.

Conclave. The place where the cardinals assemble for the election of a new Pope (see *Pope*), also, the assembly itself. After a Pope's death, a large part of the Vatican is walled off and divided, by wooden partitions, into cells for the cardinals, two or three to each. Here the cardinals gather on the tenth day, and all entrances are closed, except one, not to be opened till an election is made. Each cardinal may take with him a secretary and a servant (conclavists), sworn to secrecy. The food supply is restricted after three days.

Concordances. Books containing the words of Holy Scripture in alphabetical order with their context usually given and references by chapter and verse. The first concordances were of the Vulgate. Tradition ascribes the first concordance *(Concordantiae Morales)* to Anthony of Padua (1195—1231). Hugh of St. Cher (1200—63) prepared the first authentic concordance with the aid of 500 monks. The first Hebrew concordance was that of Rabbi Isaac Nathan *(Meir Natib,* 1445); the first Greek, that of Xystus Betulius (1500 to 1554), published in 1546. Erasmus Schmid published his *Tameion* in 1638. Conrad Kircher published *A Concordance to the Septuagint* (1602). This work was much improved in the concordance of Abraham Tromm (1718). The earliest English concordance was published without date (before 1540) by Thomas Gybson (NT only); the earliest English concordance of the entire Bible was that of John Marbeck (1550). The concordance of Alexander Cruden (1737) was remarkable for its

exactness and has been excelled only by adding new features (*e. g.,* Greek and Hebrew). The earliest German concordance was by Conrad Agricola (1609). Later concordances can, in most instances, be traced to these earlier works.

For a complete list of the older concordances see "Concordance," McClintock and Strong, *Cyclopedia of Biblical, Theological, and Ecclesiastical Literature.* The following are prominent works usually available in libraries: Alexander Cruden, *A Complete Concordance to the Holy Scriptures of the Old and New Testament,* 1737 (many later editions); J. B. R. Walker, *The Comprehensive Concordance to the Holy Scriptures,* Pilgrim Press, Boston, 1894; James Strong, *The Exhaustive Concordance of the Bible,* Methodist Book Concern, N. Y., 1890; Robert Young, *Analytical Concordance to the Bible,* Funk & Wagnalls, 1920; F. P. Duptripon, *Concordantiae Bibliorum Sacrorum* (Vulgate), Belin-Mandar, Paris, 1838; W. F. Moulton and A. S. Geden, *A Concordance to the Greek Testament,* Edinburgh, 1899; O. Schmoller, *Handkonkordanz zum griechischen Neuen Testament* (6th ed. by Alfred Schmoller), Wuerttembergische Bibelanstalt, 1931; Solomon Mandelkern, *Veteris Testamenti Concordantiae Hebraicae atque Chaldaicae,* Veit, Leipzig, 1896 (2 vol.); Edwin Hatch and H. A. Redpath, *A Concordance to the Septuagint and the Other Greek Versions of the Old Testament Including the Apocryphal Books,* Clarendon Press, Oxford, 1897—1900. EL

Concordat. An agreement, or a treaty, made between the Pope and the civil government of a country to regulate the affairs of the Roman Church in that country, to settle disagreements, or to prevent future difficulties. Bishops formerly made concordats, but the power is now reserved to the Pope. Concordats deal with such matters as the appointment of bishops, public education, marriage, taxation of church property, financial support of the church by the state, and the legal status of the church. Romanists deplore these treaties as unavoidable evils because they hold that the Pope should authoritatively regulate all such matters according to his good pleasure instead of being compelled, by the fear of greater evils, to haggle and compromise with civil authorities (see *Church and State*). Concordats, on publication, become part of the canon law and of the civil law of the respective state. There are three theories regarding the nature of concordats: 1. The legal theory, holding that by concordats the state, as the superior of the church, grants it certain privileges which are, like other laws, revocable at will; 2. the compact theory, holding that concordats are compacts between equals and can, therefore, be broken only by mutual consent; 3. the privilege theory, holding that in concordats the state acknowledges duties already incumbent on it and is granted concessions and indults by the Pope on other duties, such indults being revocable. The first concordat was that of Worms (1122), made between Pope Calixtus II and Emperor Henry V to terminate the investiture quarrel. Concordats became more frequent during the eighteenth century, and still more so during the nineteenth. The most famous concordat is that of 1801, made between Pius VII and Napoleon, then First Consul. By it Catholicism, proscribed during the Revolution, was re-established in France, not, however, as the state religion, but as "the religion of the great majority of Frenchmen." It provided for maintenance of the clergy by the state and for relinquishment by Rome of church property sold during the Revolution. This concordat remained in force until Dec. 9, 1905, when it was abrogated by the French government through its law on the separation of church and state. A famous concordat of recent times is that of 1929 between the Pope and Italy ending the Roman Question.

Concordia. See *Book of Concord.*

Concordia Academy. See *Ministry, Education of,* IX.

Concordia College (Edmonton, Fort Wayne, Milwaukee, St. Paul). See *Ministry, Education of,* IX.

Concordia Collegiate Institute. See *Ministry, Education of,* IX.

Concordia Historical Institute. See *Archives.*

Concordia Publishing House. See *Publication Houses.*

Concordia Seminary (St. Louis, Springfield). See *Ministry, Education of,* XI A 1.

Concordia Synod of Pennsylvania and Other States. Organized June 7, 1882, by 14 pastors, 6 lay delegates, and 1 teacher, who had withdrawn from the Ohio Synod because of its stand in the controversy on election and conversion. Rev. P. Brand of Pittsburgh was made president, the *Lutheran Witness* and the *Lutheraner* the official organs. The synod became a member of the Synodical Conference at the next meeting of that body. The church at Coyner's Store, Va., Rev. F. Kuegele, pastor, which already in 1884 had suggested the founding of an English synod within the bounds of the Synodical Conference, joined the English Missouri Synod in 1888; the other members joined the Missouri Synod.

Concordia Synod of Virginia. Founded in 1868. The official name chosen at its organization was Evangelical Lutheran Concordia Synod of Virginia. Rev. G. Schmucker was elected president. Clergymen present were G. Schmucker, J. E. Seneker, and H. Wetzel, also six laymen. *The Lutheran* and *Missionary* were recommended as reading matter to the members of the congregations. In 1877 it became the Concordia District of the Joint Synod of Ohio. It brought with it 17 congregations and nine mission stations. In 1918 it merged with the Eastern District of the Ohio Synod.

Concordia Synod of the West. Organized in 1862 by F. W. Wier, a former member of the Buffalo Synod, of Washington, Minn., L. F. E. Krause, of Winona, Minn., D. J. Warns, of Bethalto, Ill., and C. F. Junck, of New Oregon, Ia. In its meeting of 1863 it liberally engaged in criticism of J. C. F. Heyer and G. Fachtman. The next year the small synod applied for membership in the Joint Synod of Ohio as a branch synod. This, however, was denied them since the Ohio Synod did not see any need for a branch synod in the West. Later Krause and Warns individually joined the Ohio Synod, and the Concordia Synod died. By 1869 Wier rejoined the Buffalo Synod.

Concordia Teachers College (River Forest, Seward). See *Teachers,* A 5.

Concupiscence. A word used in the *AC* (Art. II) in the definition of original sin.* The German version translates "voll boeser Lust und Neigung." Following Augustine (also Bonaventura, Hugo, and others) the *Apology* (Art. II) interprets concupiscence as the loving of, and seeking after, carnal things (not only pleasure of the body, but also carnal wisdom and righteousness) showing ignorance of God, contempt for God, a being destitute of fear and confidence in God, anger toward God, despair of grace, and (positively) trust in present things (Rom. 7:7, 23; 1 Cor. 2:14). The Luth. Confessions reject the Roman Catholic contention that concupiscence is a penalty and not a sin.

Werner Elert, "Suende" in *Morphologie des Luthertums*, Beck, Munich, 1931 (later ed.).

Concursus. A term in dogmatics describing God's gracious co-operation in all that occurs (Acts 17:28). See *Causae Secundae.*

Conder, Josiah (1789—1855). B. in London, Sept. 17, 1789, became editor and author, publishing numerous prose and poetical works. In 1812 he contributed three hymns to Dr. Collyer's collection, and in 1836 he edited the *Congregational Hymn-Book.* In the year after his death, his poems and all his hymns were published under the title of *Hymns of Praise.*

Condignity. See *Merit.*

Conduct. See *Christian Teaching,* 1 ff.

Conference of the Defenseless Mennonites. See *Mennonite Bodies,* 3.

Conferences (L. *confero,* "bring together." Used by some classical authors of public conferences and discussions. Early used in connection with religious discussions. Cf. Gal. 2:6). Beginning in the 11th century, meetings (often called *Calendae,* because held on the first of the month) of priests were held for the purpose of discussing religious topics, perhaps because the diocese as such had become too large for frequent meetings of all its members. Such meetings of priests declined in the 13th century and have never been fully revived in the Roman Catholic Church although officially endorsed.

In the Protestant Church no fixed meaning attaches to the word "conference" (cf. *Methodist Bodies,* 3; in Congregationalism it designates the voluntary organization of churches in a district). The term has been variously used within the Lutheran Church in America. In the earliest days it was applied to the meetings of synods themselves, as well as to less formal gatherings. Pastoral conferences have been frequently held in Protestant churches of Europe and America. The first pastoral conference in the Lutheran Church of America was held at New Holland (1771). The practice of celebrating Communion at such conferences

soon developed, and the conferences themselves became an institution in American Lutheranism. The Missouri Synod, for example, encourages its Districts to arrange pastoral, teachers', joint (pastors and teachers), and intersynodical conferences for the spiritual and professional growth of the members (*By-Laws,* IV F). See *Teachers,* A 10.

Confessio Pentapolitana. See *Lutheran Confessions,* A 5.

Confession. This specifically Lutheran service is at times held either on Saturday evening or on some evening during the week, when it is known as *Beichtvesper,* or on Sunday morning just before morning worship, its purpose being to prepare the communicants of the day for a worthy reception of the Lord's Supper. Besides a confessional address, the singing of hymns, and the saying of prayer, the general confession of sins is made and the absolution is pronounced. The Confession is often included in the Communion service. *Private confession,* as practiced for several centuries, is still in use in some congregations and is not to be confounded with auricular confession as practiced in the Roman Church.

Auricular confession is a prescribed part of the Roman Sacrament of Penance * and is declared by the Church of Rome to be "of divine right necessary for all who have fallen after baptism." (Council of Trent, *Sess.* XIV, ch. 5.) The basic idea is that, in confession, the sinner, forced by his conscience, accuses himself, and the priest acts as a judge, in Christ's stead. "Christ . . . left priests His own vicars, as presidents and judges, unto whom all the mortal crimes, into which the faithful of Christ may have fallen, should be carried, in order that . . . they may pronounce the sentence of forgiveness or retention of sins." (Council of Trent, *Sess.* XIV, ch. 5.) That the priest may judge accurately and properly assess the satisfaction required (see *Penance*), every mortal sin * must be separately confessed with its circumstances. Venial sins * usually are, but need not be, confessed. A mortal sin deliberately held back is unforgiven and vitiates the absolution for all the other sins at that confession, so that a new confession and absolution is required. Sins overlooked, in spite of careful self-examination, are forgiven, but must be mentioned at a later confession if recalled. The priest, who has been carefully trained in the grading and classification of sins, assists the penitent with questions. He is forbidden, under the severest penalties, to reveal anything confided to him in the confessional.

Every member of the Church who has arrived at years of discretion is bound to confess at least once a year, during Lent. The age of discretion, for this purpose, is held to be about seven years. After the confession is completed, the priest, if he judges the confession and the penitent's state of mind satisfactory, imposes works of satisfaction on the penitent and pronounces absolution.* For some sins, accounted especially grave, an ordinary priest cannot give absolution, but they must be absolved by the bishop or even the Pope (see Reserved Cases). In this manner, the power of absolution, which Jesus gave to His Church, that through it the comfort of His Gospel might be applied to terrified sinners, is turned into a burdensome mechanism. Instead of the minister of Christ, dispensing the free grace of God in Jesus to those who trust in Him, there sits the priest of Rome, a solemn judge, who imposes punishments and penance in the same breath with the absolution and makes that absolution dependent on the fulfillment of his commands. Faith in the atoning sacrifice of Christ is expressly ruled out of the sacrament: "Faith can in no way be rightly called a part of penance." (Catechismus Romanus, II, 5.5.) It is stipulated only as a necessary antecedent to the necessary sorrow of contrition * which leads to confession and satisfaction. Here, as in the other sacraments, the efficacy is said to be ex opere operato (see Opus Operatum).

The Bible clearly enjoins confession of sin to God, 1 John 1:8, 9, and to brethren who have been sinned against, James 5:16. Private confession to pastors, with private absolution, is recommended as desirable, but by no means insisted on as obligatory. JHCF

"Lutherworte von der Beichte," Lutherhefte, Hermann, Zwickau, 1914 (vol. 67.68); AC and Ap, Art. XI; G. E. Westburg, "Private Confession in the Lutheran Church," Augustana Quarterly, XXIV:138—162; A. C. Wedeking, "Augsburg Confession, Article XI," Quarterly Review, VI:485—510; references under Pastoral Theology; Henry Charles Lea, History of Auricular Confession and Indulgences in the Latin Church, Lea Brothers, Philadelphia, 1896 (3 vols.).

Confession of Faith. See Creeds and Confessions.

Confession of Faith to Charles V. See Reformed Confessions, A 3.

Confession of Faith (Moravian). See Moravian Church, 1.

Confessional Lutheranism, Awakening of. See Lutheran Confessions; Luther Renaissance.

Confessions. See Creeds and Confessions.

Confessor. 1) A martyr in the early Church. 2) A person who lived or died under the reputation of sanctity. 3) Clergy who hear confessions * and pronounce the absolution.*

Configuration. See Psychology, J 5.

Confirmation. In the Lutheran Church the rite by which baptized persons after having received a course of instruction make a public confession of their faith and give evidence that they can examine themselves and be admitted to the Lord's Supper (1 Cor. 11:28). They also publicly renew their baptismal vow. Confirmation is considered a sacrament in the Roman and Greek Catholic churches. In the Greek Church it is administered at the same time with, or as soon as possible after, baptism, even in the case of infants. For the Roman Church, the Council of Trent appointed the age of seven to twelve as the age of confirmation (Firmelung, Ger.). In the Anglican (Protestant Episcopal) Church, it is a formal rite administered by the bishop, the High Church party looking upon it as something like a sacramental rite conveying the gift of the Holy Ghost, while the Low Church regards it as being essentially a personal renewal of the promises made in the name of the subject by others in baptism. In conformity with their Romanizing tendency, the High Church Anglicans urge an earlier (five or six years) and the Low Church a later age (fourteen to sixteen) for the performance of confirmation. The Council of Trent calls confirmation "a true and proper sacrament" (Sess. VII, can. 1), and the Catechismus Romanus says: "It must be explained by the pastors that Christ the Lord was not only its author, but that He also, as the holy Roman Pope Fabian testifies, ordered the use of holy oil and the words which the Catholic Church uses in its administration" (II:3, 6). Ordinarily, only the bishop can confirm. He lays his hands on the candidates, traces the sign of the cross on their foreheads with chrism,* or holy oil, and says, "I sign thee with the sign of the cross and confirm thee with the chrism of salvation, in the name of the Father," etc. He then gives them a light blow on the cheek as a sign that they must be ready to suffer for Christ. Rome teaches that by confirmation the new life implanted in baptism is fortified, that particularly the grace to confess the faith is conferred (*Catechismus Romanus*, II:3,5), and that a seal is set on the soul (see *Character Indelebilis*). — All this lacks foundation in Scripture, for Jesus neither instituted such a rite nor supplied it with any promise of grace. See *Catechetics; Parish Education,* F 2.

The early articles of visitation and agendas of the Lutheran Church considered catechization the important element of confirmation and stress the need for examination before admission to the Lord's Supper. The transition to formal confirmation occurred when provisions were made for public examinations. The renewal of the baptismal vow became an important feature of the act. In America, Lutheran children are publicly examined and confirmed when they are 13 or 14 years old (after completing the eighth grade), such confirmations usually taking place on Palm Sunday. Adults are often privately catechized (in an informal, conversational manner) and publicly confirmed. See the articles by F. Kraus, "Salbung," *Kirchenlexikon* and *Realencyklopaedie;* W. Caspari, "Konfirmation," *Realencyklopaedie* (also wrote *Die Ev. Konfirmation, vornaemlich in der Luth. Kirche*); P. Bergstresser, "Catechization and Confirmation in the Lutheran Church," *Luth. Quarterly,* XXI:515—24; references under *Pastoral Theology* and *Catechetics* (especially M. Reu's works).

Confirmation (liturgical). To Luther, confirmation was at first an abomination, because it was declared to be a sacrament by the Romanists. His opposition to it, as voiced in his book *Of the Babylonian Captivity of the Church,* influenced also his co-workers and is found in the Lutheran Confessions. Luther, therefore, did not compile a formula for confirmation, and most of the early church orders omit the rite entirely. At the Ratisbon Colloquium, Melanchthon, Bucer, and Pistorius proposed the rite as a good observance. In the General Articles for Electoral Saxony only the thorough indoctrination of the children is urged

before admitting them to the Lord's Supper. The Wittenberg Reformation of 1545 advocated an evangelical use of the ceremony, mentioning the following parts: 1. indoctrination; 2. admonition, renunciation, and confession of faith; 3. personal profession of doctrine of faith by catechumens; 4. thorough examination; 5. admonition that this implies dissent from all false teaching; 6. exhortation to persevere; 7. public prayer. The Lutheran Church has adhered to these principles, dividing the act of confirmation into three parts: 1. examination; 2. profession and vow; 3. prayer with imposition of hands.

Confirmation Instruction. See *Parish Education,* F 2.

Confiteor. In the Roman Catholic service of the Mass the confession of sins as made by the priest, a significant feature of this part of the introductory service being that at the words *Mea culpa,* "my guilt," the attendant strikes the bell, and the congregation sinks to the knees. In the Lutheran liturgy the confession of sins of the congregation (with the pastor) is often called the Confiteor.

Confraternity (or Sodality). An association among Roman Catholics, usually the laity, for the promotion of definite works of charity or devotion. There have been such associations since the ninth century, but their greatest development has come in recent times. Each local association is under the guidance of a priest. The regulations prescribe devotional practices and frequent attendance at mass and Communion. Each member receives a blessed medal and liberal indulgences. The most ancient confraternity is that of the Children of Mary. The best known in America are the Confraternity of the Blessed Sacrament and the Confraternity of Christian Doctrine. Others are the archconfraternities of the Holy Family, of the Immaculate Heart of Mary, of the Scapular, and of the Assumption. Confraternities are closely related to pious associations, such as the League of the Sacred Heart (see *Sacred Heart of Jesus*), and have many points of contact with third orders (see *Tertiaries*). The membership of these various societies aggregates tens of millions.

Confucianism. 1. The ancient state religion of China, consisting of the old animistic, polydemonistic beliefs and cults upon which were grafted the moral, social, and political teachings of Confucius (Latinized from K'ung-fu-tse, "Master K'ung"), famous Chinese sage, b. 551 B. C. in the ancient kingdom of Lu, now part of Shantung, d. there, 478 B. C.

2. The sacred books upon which the state religion is based are five in number, called *Ching*, viz., *Book of History, Book of Songs, Book of Changes, Spring and Autumn, Book of Rites*. The first four were compiled by Confucius. To these are added four books called *Shu*, compiled by the disciples of Confucius, including the works of Mencius (372? to 289 B. C.), his greatest disciple and expounder.

3. As the modern, so the ancient Chinese believed in the existence of innumerable spirits (see *Animism*) that fill the world in great swarms and inhabit the air and all material objects. These spirits, some good, some evil, have their origin in the *Yang* and the *Yin*, the two world souls, or breaths, which are at the basis of the whole universe. The *Yang* represents the male part of the world, also heat and light, and is divided into innumerable *shen*, or good spirits, to which sacrifices are made, and which make their abode in natural objects, such as sun, moon, stars, rivers, mountains, lakes, rocks, the earth, fire, clouds, rain. The *Yin* represents the female part of the world, also cold and darkness, and is divided into innumerable *kwei*, or evil spirits, which harass men, but may be driven off by lighted torches, gongs, and drums. In addition to the *shen*, the souls of the dead, especially of one's ancestors, are worshiped. At the head of all the spirits is *T'ien*, Heaven, also called *Shang-ti*.

4. Until the fall of the empire, 1912, the emperor, who was believed to be a son of heaven, was the religious head of the people, and the welfare of the nation depended upon his properly observing the religious rites, especially the worship of heaven and earth at the winter and summer solstices, respectively, at the great altars situated on the south and north of Peking. At these occasions the emperor also sacrificed to the tablets of his ancestors and to the sun, moon, stars, winds, rain, clouds, thunder. Other gods in the pantheon of the state religion are the corn spirits, various mountains and streams throughout China, the four seas, famous men and women of antiquity, as Confucius and his disciples, the emperor who taught his people agriculture, the first breeder of silkworms, and the planet Jupiter. These gods were worshiped by the emperor or his proxy and since 1915 by the president or his representative. Still other gods are worshiped by the mandarins and the authorities in the provinces, as the physicians of ancient times, a star which is regarded as the patron of classical studies, the gods and goddesses of walls and moats, cannons, water, rain, architecture, kilns, storehouses, and others. These gods have numerous temples throughout the empire, and although there is no priesthood, the religious observances are thoroughly ritualistic and attended by great pomp. The sacrifices consist of swine, cattle, goats, and silks.

5. To sum up, the state religion consists of nature and ancestor worship. The common people were at first permitted to worship only their ancestors (for which see *Ancestor Worship*), but in the course of time their worship was extended to many of the Confucian deities above mentioned, and everywhere in China there are temples and shrines with innumerable idols and tablets, before which offerings are made.

6. The influence of Confucius upon the ancient religion was conservative rather than reformatory. He looked toward the golden past, endeavoring to preserve the good traditions of antiquity. His highest goal was the welfare of the state, and he believed that this could be obtained, if the sacredness of the five primary relationships, ruler and subject, father and son, husband and wife, elder and younger brother, friend and friend, be kept inviolate. He furthermore stressed the virtues of sincerity, benevolence, and filial love and gave expression to what is called the negative form of the Golden Rule: "Do not to others what you do not want done to yourself." However, he produced neither a philosophical nor a theological system. In fact, his teachings were entirely of an ethical nature, and he refrained from speaking of the deity and of immortality. He does not dwell on the subject of sin, nor does he have any remedy for it. Punishment for wrongdoing is confined to this world, and salvation comes by effort. His teachings met with little success during his lifetime, and in the third century B. C. a systematic attempt was made by a hostile emperor to eradicate Confucianism. After that, however, it gained in influence, and Confucius rose higher and higher in

the estimation of the Chinese, until he was raised to the highest rank of worship. Since A. D. 57 sacrifices have been offered to him. See *Taoism* and *Buddhism* for the other two of the three great religions in China. As most Chinese profess and practice all three religions, it is impossible to give statistics regarding the adherents of each. See *Religion, Comparative, Bibliography*.

Confutatio Pontificia. See *Lutheran Confessions*, A 3.

Congo. Formerly Congo Free State, annexed by Belgium in 1907. Area, 904,751 sq. miles; population, 11,390,950 (1950). The inhabitants are adherents of gross fetishism. Various American, British, and Scandinavian societies are working in that field (over 50 societies in 1952). The leading American missions are by: Presbyterian Church in the U. S.; United Christian Missionary Society; Seventh-Day Adventists; American Baptist Foreign Mission Society; Christian and Missionary Alliance; Assemblies of God; Methodist Church. The total Protestant membership in 1952 was over 1,000,000. The Roman Catholics claimed 2,555,000. See *Missions, Bibliography*.

Congregation. See *Authority; Church; Keys, Office of; Lutheran Congregation; Polity, Ecclesiastical.*

Congregation of the Index. See *Index of Prohibited Books.*

Congregation, Powers of. See *Keys, Office of; Authority; Polity, Ecclesiastical.*

Congregational and Christian Churches. In 1931 the National Council of Congregational Churches and the General Conference of Christian Churches united to form one body known as the General Council of Congregational and Christian Churches. In many localities, however, the congregations of this merger still function either as a Congregational or a Christian Church, and it will be necessary to present the history of each branch separately.

A. *The Congregational Church.* 1. One of the questions which agitated many English Protestants during the 16th century was whether the Established Church of England, the Anglican Church, with its hierarchical tendencies and Romanizing cultus, could still be considered a Christian Church in which a Christian could hold membership.

The Puritans believed that the Anglican Church was essentially still a Christian Church and that Christians should remain in the church in order to help in purifying the church of its papal elements. Others, under the leadership of Robert Browne (ca. 1550 to 1633; followers called "Brownists"), John Robinson, and others, held that the Anglican Church was anti-Christian and that separation from it was necessary. The adherents of this view were known as Separatists, Independents, or Congregationalists. They believed that a Christian congregation must be entirely free and independent of all ecclesiastical and political domination. After the passage of the Act of Uniformity (1559) many fled to Holland. However, they considered themselves strangers and pilgrims in a land whose language and culture were different from those of England. In 1620, 120 Pilgrim Fathers established the colony at Plymouth, Mass., where they could be entirely free and independent of all "clergy rule" and at the same time rear their children in the English tradition. In 1629 a group of Puritans established the near-by Massachusetts Bay Colony.

2. Doctrinally these two groups were agreed, both being strict Calvinists. The difference consisted only in their divergent views concerning the church government: the Separatists denouncing the Anglican Church, the Puritans still considering themselves members of the church. The Puritans were won over to the Congregationalists' ideal especially through the physician Dr. S. Fuller of Plymouth, and Congregationalism was established in Massachusetts in 1646 by the adoption of the Cambridge Platform. The theology on which these two groups united is the same as that contained in the Westminster Confession. (See *Presbyterian Confessions*, 3.) The church government was determined in accordance with their ideal of independency. They established "a church without a bishop and a state without a king." Contrary to their basic principle, however, the early Congregationalists became extremely intolerant. This religious intolerance seems to have originated not among the Plymouth Separatists, but rather among the Massachusetts Bay Puritans. They believed in uniformity of religion, that is, every citizen of the community must conform to the rules laid down by the congregation, which was considered supreme

in every area of human life, religious and political. They favored the complete mingling of state and church, which characterized the New England States. In the public square of New England the courthouse stood next to the church. Only members of the congregation were given suffrage. Heresy and witchcraft were treated as crimes both against the church and the state, and were punished by execution. These undemocratic and intolerant principles, however, gradually gave way to the ideals of the Plymouth Congregationalists. The Pilgrim Fathers had been Separatists in England and therefore believed that absolute freedom from any authority must be granted to every congregation. And this ideal of freedom has been the distinctive mark of Congregationalism. At the same time this principle has become the cause of disastrous results. There can be no doctrinal discipline under the Congregational system. True, Congregationalism has formulated creeds, notably the Savoy Declaration, prepared by English Congregationalists, and adopted by the American Congregationalists in 1680. But since every congregation is autonomous, it may or it may not adopt creeds. Creeds are not accepted as tests of doctrines, but merely as testimonies. Every congregation may determine its own creed according to its "measure of light." It must grant every other congregation the same freedom of religious thought. All congregations which subscribe to this principle are invited to join in an association of independent congregations for purposes of fellowship.

3. This principle explains the fact that Congregationalism has furnished an unusually large number of liberal theologians. Beginning with Jonathan Edwards * and the New England Theology,* the advance guard of rationalistic theologians was Congregational. Unitarianism * and Modernism * were the fruit in a large measure of Congregationalism's indifference to doctrine and insistence upon the right of self-expression without ecclesiastical interference. By 1800 twelve of Boston's fourteen Congregational churches had become Unitarian without any serious controversy; Harvard University likewise was lost to Unitarianism. Modernism entered the Protestant Church chiefly through Congregationalist leaders, particularly Horace Bushnell, Henry Ward Beecher, Lyman Abbott, Washington Gladden. The indifference to doctrine

was also manifest in the Plan of Union of 1801, which virtually erased all denominational lines between Congregationalism and Presbyterianism. This plan was abrogated in 1852, when for a season Congregational consciousness was awakened. The doctrinal position of the Congregational Church is so latitudinarian that the liberal and the conservative can fellowship. Practically the only points of agreement among Congregationalists are: "Freedom of the individual and the right of private judgment; autonomy of the local congregation; fellowship of the churches for counsel and co-operation in matters of common concern" (Kansas City Platform, adopted 1913). This broad principle permits Congregationalists to unite with any church body which subscribes to the platform of independency and fellowship, thereby permitting its members to hold whatsoever views they desire.

B. *The Christian Church.* This group of churches, known also as "Christians," "Christian Church" (American Christian Convention), and "General Convention of the Christian Church," came into being as a result of the protest of James O'Kelly against the episcopal government of the Methodist Episcopal Church. In his protest against every form of ecclesiastical church government he and his adherents went as far as condemning even the use of denominational names and creeds; they wanted to be known merely as Christians who accepted the Bible as their only guide. During the Great Revival of 1800 O'Kelly was joined by Abner Jones, a Baptist, and Burton Stone, a Presbyterian. During this revival all denominational lines were erased, and the autonomy and independence of the local congregation was overemphasized. This resulted in the formation of such groups as the "Churches of Christ" and "Christian Union." A little later the Campbellites united with these "Christians." Many of these "Christians" in their opposition to creeds were opposed to the use of all dogmatical terminology. Ultimately they rejected not only the word "Trinity" as unbiblical, but the doctrine as well. (See *Disciples.*) Throughout its history the Christian Church granted absolute liberty to its members in their interpretation of the Bible. Christian character was the only test for membership. This denomination has always been considered as a Unitarian body, and justly so. Baptism is optional.

C. *The Congregational and Christian Churches.* The two groups which constitute the merger have always emphasized the autonomy of the congregation and the liberty of the individual to interpret the Bible. There is no ecclesiastical organization, no creed, no doctrinal discipline. No one is invested with ecclesiastical authority. The local churches set apart certain officers, the pastor, the deacons, the clerk, for orderly worship and effective administration. The various local congregations gather in associations for fellowship, mutual assistance, and common Christian work. The missionary and educational activities of this group of churches are conducted through two national organizations. Membership in these organizations is not by congregations, but by individual members. The Congregational and Christian Church is committed to the social gospel program of Modernism.

The Congregational and Christian Church worked toward a merger with the Evangelical and Reformed churches* for a number of years. In February, 1949, The General Council of the Congregational Church, holding that the percentage (72.6%) of Congregational Christian churches favoring the merger warranted the action, voted overwhelmingly in favor of the merger with the Evangelical and Reformed Church. Membership (1952): 1,241,477. See *Religious Bodies (U.S.), Bibliography.*

FEM

Congregational Christian Student Fellowship. See *Students, Spiritual Care of,* A 3.

Congregational Holiness Church. This Holiness body * separated from the Pentecostal Holiness Church in 1921 in protest against the episcopal form of church government.

Congregational Independency. See *Polity, Ecclesiastical,* 3, 4.

Congregational Methodist Church. See *Methodist Bodies,* 4 b.

Congregations, Roman. See *Roman Congregations.*

Congress, Church. See *Church Congress.*

Congruity. See *Merit.*

Conrad, Frederick William. B. at Pine Grove, Schuylkill Co., Pa., Jan. 3, 1816; educated at Gettysburg Seminary 1837—40; pastor of churches at Waynesboro, Franklin Co., Pa., 1841—44; St.

John's, Hagerstown, Md., 1844—50; professor at Wittenberg College, Springfield, O., 1850—55; pastor at Dayton, O., 1855—62; Trinity, Lancaster, Pa., 1862 to 64; Chambersburg, Pa., 1864. In 1863 he became part owner and editor of *Lutheran Observer* at Baltimore, in 1866 chief editor till his death; "was prominent in all the work of the General Synod." He contributed to periodicals and put out an edition of Luther's Catechism; joint author of *Lutheran Manual and Guide.* Died Apr. 10, 1898.

Conrad of Gelnhausen. See *Councils and Synods,* 7.

Consalvi, Ercole (1757—1824). Italian cardinal; opponent of French Revolution; chief negotiator of Concordat with Napoleon.

Consanguinity. See *Impediments of Marriage, Scriptural and Natural.*

Conscience. In general usage the term applies to the moral feeling, the urge to do the right thing. Figuratively the word is employed loosely to denote man's intuition of right or wrong; or the sensitiveness of the individual or of groups to moral right or wrong. In general literature the term has a usage which is far from standard or uniform. — The New Testament employs a standard word for conscience, *syneidesis;* despite variations in New Testament authorship, a unified pattern of meaning emerges. In two instances (1 Pet. 2:19; Rom. 13:5) the term seems to imply in more general fashion man's moral conscience toward God, the realization that God is concerned for the goodness of man's actions. In most instances, however, the word is given a more specialized significance. Peter, the writer to the Hebrews, and particularly Paul refer frequently to "the good conscience." By this they imply the awareness, satisfying in feeling, of the rectitude of one's conduct and intimate that conscience involves or presupposes a recognition of a standard. Conversely the writer to the Hebrews and St. Paul speak of a bad conscience, namely, one aware of a moral lapse and offense against an acknowledged standard. This process of recognizing a standard and comparing the action with it is explicit and central in St. Paul's use of the term in the epistles to the Corinthians (1 Cor. 10:25-29; 2 Cor. 1:12; 5:11). There St. Paul describes the results of this process of judgment as being imperfect and unhappy where the standard of judgment is faulty. He speaks of the "weak" conscience (1 Cor. 8:10, 12) as one which is not feeble or sluggish in its activity, but hampered by a faulty norm. Interesting is the word "seared" (1 Tim. 4:2) which some have imagined to mean "calloused" or "insensitive"; but which more consistently implies "branded," in the sense of permanently harmed. St. Paul speaks of conscience serving as a witness (Rom. 2:15; 9:1), namely, to the recognition of moral responsibility. — The purpose of conscience in general usage varies from the complete and potent supply of moral insight and motive, or synonym for overpowering prejudice, to a vagrant and shadowy recognition of duty. In Lutheran literature much has been made of the "terrors of conscience," induced by the indictment of the Law of God, as the indispensable prerequisite and preparation for the Gospel — a synonym for contrition.* The Biblical concept appears to be more limited to the intellectual and emotional reflex accompanying particularly such actions that are consciously contrary to standard. The New Testament, furthermore, with the term conscience, emphasizes man's behavior as lived with the recognition of responsibility toward God, the Giver of the standard and of the task. In the cure of souls, the Christian is interested in removing the tensions of the evil conscience with the guarantee of the good conscience, namely, forgiveness in Christ Jesus, and in equipping the individual with that vitality for living which fosters the good conscience, namely, the life of the Spirit through Jesus Christ. RRC

Charles Scaer, *A Treatise on Conscience*, Stratford, Boston, 1927; E. W. A. Koehler, "Conscience," *CTM*, XIII: 337 to 364.

Consecration of the Elements. See *Lord's Supper (Liturgical).*

Consensus. A term applied to the agreement or promise which establishes with the knowledge of the parents the essence of a valid betrothal. See *Marriage.*

Consensus Gentium (unanimity of the races). A term often used in apologetics,* especially in connection with the doctrine of God and immorality. Thus the general belief in a supreme being is held to demonstrate the reasonableness of belief in the existence of God.

Consensus Patrum. Unanimity of the Church Fathers on a matter of faith

or morals; considered by Romanists as decisive in doctrine.

Consensus of Sandomierz. See *Poland, Lutheranism in,* 3.

Consensus Tigurinus. See *Calvin, John,* 12.

Conservative Amish Mennonites. See *Mennonite Bodies,* 3.

Conservative Dunkers. See *Brethren, Dunkers,* 2.

Consilia Evangelica. The Roman Church teaches that the New Testament, in addition to the rules of life and conduct which it makes binding on all Christians, contains certain evangelical counsels, or counsels of perfection, for those who wish to do more than is strictly necessary and want to travel the shortest road to heaven. As the three evangelical counsels, Rome names voluntary poverty, celibacy, and obedience, claiming that Matt. 19:21 and 1 Cor. 7:8 are intended to convey a permanent counsel and to indicate to Christians the "surest and quickest way to obtain everlasting life." It is evident that these three "counsels" coincide with the three monastic vows. The idea of doing more than God really demands (see Luke 17:10) underlies monasticism and the doctrine of *opera supererogationis.* Here also the pagan doctrine of the merit of works (see *Works, Merit of*) is most strongly entrenched. Article 27 of the Apology of the Augsburg Confession enters on this matter at length.

Consistory. The assemblage of the cardinals in council, usually under the presidency of the Pope, to deliberate on, and transact, important ecclesiastical business. Since the institution of the Roman Congregations,* consistories have diminished in importance and are held less frequently. They may be public, semipublic, or secret. In many Lutheran bodies of Germany the Consistory is an administrative board consisting of members of the higher clergy. A similar arrangement is found in some Reformed bodies.

Consolamentum. The ceremony of the imposition of the hands by which "spirit-baptism" was administered, "Apostolic Succession" conferred, and reception into the ranks of the "perfect" achieved by the Cathari.*

Consolation. 1) Alleviation of sorrow. 2) Evening meal of monks.

Constance, Council of. The second of three councils of the fifteenth century which were intended to bring about a reformation of the Church, held under Pope John XXIII and Emperor Sigismund, 1414—18. The council was unusually well attended, the lowest estimate of strangers in Constance being given at 50,000. The most influential members of the session were Pierre d'Ailly* and Jean Gerson.* Three objects awaited the action of the council. With regard to the great papal schism, the matter was settled by deposing John XXIII and Benedict XIII, while Gregory XII voluntarily abdicated. A new Pope, Martin V, was elected, thus concluding the chapter of the schism. The matter of Johann Hus and his adherents was treated with great thoroughness. He was induced to attend by a promise of safe-conduct, but the emperor's word proved unreliable, and so he was burned on July 6, 1415. His friend Jerome of Prague followed him in a martyr's death on May 30, 1416. The final business before the council was that of certain reforms in the Church, which were loudly urged by a dissatisfied minority, consisting chiefly of the lower clergy, the monks, the doctors and professors, led by d'Ailly and Gerson. But these were unable to reach a full agreement among themselves, and so the agitation, in the end, practically came to naught, especially since the abuses concerned such matters as papal procedures, the administration and income of vacant positions in the Church, simony, indulgences, and dispensations, from which the Pope received much of his income.

See references under *Councils;* Starcke, "Kritische Eroerterung der Frage ueber das dem Joh. Huss gegebene u. gebrochene Geleit," *Ztschr. f. hist. Theol.* (XLIV: 43—71).

Constancy. See *Patience.*

Constantine ("the Great"; 274—337). Roman emperor (312—337), son of Constantius Chlorus and Helena. From 292 to 305 he was kept at the court of Diocletian. After the abdication of Diocletian (305), the rule of the western half of the empire fell to Constantius Chlorus. At the death of Constantius (306), Constantine was proclaimed emperor at York in Britain (through the will of his father and the army). When the heathen usurper Maxentius assumed the title of Augustus and seized the government in Italy and Africa, Constantine crossed the Alps at the head of a large army and inflicted upon his rival a crushing defeat at the Milvian Bridge near Rome (312). On his journey to Rome had occurred the vision of the cross in the sky with the Greek monogram of Christ with the inscription Τούτῳ νίκα ("by this, conquer"), which Constantine wrought into the Roman standard, the *labarum* (the alleged appearance of the sign has occasioned much controversy). The following year (313), Constantine, together with Licinius, published the Edict of Toleration at Milan, which lifted the ban of persecution and granted freedom of worship to Christian and heathen alike. The triumph of Christianity was complete when in 324 Constantine defeated Licinius, who in the meantime had espoused the cause of the heathen party, at Adrianople and Chalcedon and issued a decree of universal toleration. The following year (325) he convened the famous council of Nicea (see *Arianism; Councils and Synods,* 4; *Nicea*). One of the most important acts of his reign was the transfer of the seat of government from Rome to Byzantium (323), which he rebuilt with great magnificence (predominantly Christian in aspect) and inaugurated and named "Constantinople" after himself (330). In 326 Constantine executed Crispus (his oldest son by a former marriage) on charges by Fausta, his wife, and soon thereafter is said to have ordered Fausta suffocated in a heated bath because the charges were false. He was baptized shortly before his death (337) by the Semi-Arian bishop Eusebius of Nicomedia. The Eastern Church soon enrolled him among the saints and to this day declares him the "equal of the Apostles" *(Isapostolos),* while the Western Church honors him with the title of "the Great."

On Constantine's personal relations to Christianity and the motives that governed his imperial policy the most diverse opinions have been held. The one extreme is represented by the Greek Church, referred to above, the other sees in Constantine nothing but a shrewd, calculating politician, who allied himself with the new religion in order to realize his imperial ambitions. That his conduct upon the whole was determined rather by policy than by principle is unquestionable. That his tolerant attitude toward paganism was not merely the result of calculating expediency, but, to some degree, of sympathy with the old faith (at least until quite late in life) seems equally assured. On the other hand, there can be no doubt that his preference for Christianity was not merely a prudential, but, in part at least, a real personal matter. And though the life of Constantine is stained with foul crimes even subsequent to his conversion, the softening and humanizing effects of Christianity are plainly seen in his legislation. His concern for the unity of the Church, threatened with division through Arianism, was probably subordinate to the higher concern for the unity of the empire. Abundance of evidence can be produced in illustration of both sides of his conduct, such as the equivocal use of the word "deity" (*divinitas*), the vague "*Quidquid illud est divinum ac coeleste numen*" (practically an "unknown God") of the Edict of Milan; the injunction, as late as 321, to consult the soothsayers in times of public calamity; the retention of the title Pontifex Maximus to the end of his life, etc. On the other hand, he ascribes his victory over Maxentius to the "saving sign" of the cross (the triumphal arch erected three years later contains the ambiguous *instinctu Divinitatis*, attributing the victory to the "*impulse of the Deity*," a vague and indefinite expression, which both pagans and Christians could interpret in their own way); he exempted the clergy from military and municipal duties; he abolished rites offensive to public morality; he prohibited infanticide and the exposure of children; he mitigated the slave laws; he issued rigorous laws against adultery and placed strong restrictions on the facility of divorce, etc. "Now let us cast away all duplicity," said Constantine, when on his deathbed he received Christian Baptism, honestly admitting that in his private and public life he had been swayed by two conflicting motives — a character, as Stanley says, "not to be imitated or admired, but much to be remembered and deeply to be studied."

Constantine, Donation of. See *Pseudo-Isidorian Decretals*, 2.

Constantinople, Councils of. Three councils, considered as ecumenical, met at Constantinople:

1. The Second Ecumenical Council was called by Emperor Theodosius I in 381, chiefly to confirm the Nicene Creed and to take up other matters relating to the Arian Controversy and to the succession of bishops in the see of Constantinople. Meletius of Antioch, Gregory Nazianzen, and Nectarius successively presided at the meetings of the Council. Gregory Nazianzen was made Patriarch of Constantinople, but was forced to resign, Nectarius being put in his place. When it became apparent that the acceptance of the Nicene faith was an issue at the Council, the thirty-six Macedonian representatives withdrew. Their opinion concerning the inferior position of the Holy Ghost in the Trinity was condemned by the Council, likewise the teaching of Apollinaris concerning the nature of Christ. The Council enacted seven canons, four doctrinal, of which only the first three are of general application and three disciplinary. The Nicene faith was expanded into the form in use at the present time and declared to be dominant. All heretics were anathematized; the bishops were ordered to remain within their own dioceses in their jurisdiction, unless they were invited to officiate elsewhere; the Bishop of Constantinople was given the prerogative of honor after the Bishop of Rome. The Council also addressed a letter to the emperor, which illustrates the relation of the councils to the imperial authority, the ratification of the emperor being requested by the ecclesiastical authorities.

2. The Fifth Ecumenical Council was called in 553 by Justinian I to condemn the so-called three chapters. The proceedings were dominated by the emperor. See *Three Chapters, Controversy of*.

3. The Sixth Ecumenical Council was called by Constantine IV, Pogonatus, in 680. This Council condemned the opinions of the Monothelites * (one-will theory) and anathematized Pope Honorius of Rome. See *Arian Controversy; Councils and Synods*, 4; *Eastern Orthodox Confessions*, A 3; *Ecumenical Creeds*, Bibliography.

Constantinopolitan Creed. See *Ecumenical Creeds*, B.

Constitutions, Congregational. See *Polity, Ecclesiastical*.

Constitutions (R. C.). Decrees by the Pope in matters of doctrine or discipline, used since 1911 in establishing or altering dioceses. In France the word is applied to the bull *Unigenitus*.

Constitutions on the Catholic Faith. See *Roman Catholic Confessions*, E 2.

Consubstantiation. See *Grace, Means of*, IV 3.

Continence (L. *continentia*). The Greek word for "continence" is ἐγκράτεια (ἐγκρατεύομαι; ἐγκρατής; neg.: ἀκρασία). This original word is usually translated by "temperance" and designates the virtue of one who is able to govern self, that is, master and control his desires and passions (1 Cor. 9:25; Acts 24:25; Gal. 5:23; Titus 1:8; 2 Pet. 1:6). Such temperance is enjoined and spoken of as a gift of the Spirit (Gal. 5:23). The English word "continence" is applied to the animal appetites (cf. "abstain from fleshly lusts," 1 Pet. 2:11), especially to the sex urge (1 Cor. 7:5, 9). The latter is not in itself evil, but a gift of God for holy matrimony (Prov. 18:22; 1 Tim. 3:12; 1 Tim. 5:14; Heb. 13:4), and especially the incontinent are enjoined to marry (1 Cor. 7). The Bible opposes all legalistic human continence ordinances (Col. 2:16-23; 1 Tim. 4:1-3), upholds Christian liberty ·(1 Cor. 6:12; 10:23) and considers the practice of continence a voluntary act in harmony with circumstances (1 Cor. 7:1-5, 26), individual gifts (1 Cor. 7:6-9), and Christian vocation (1 Cor. 9:1-6). See *Asceticism*.

Contributions. See *Finances in the Church*.

Contrition. A movement of the heart prior to conversion, namely, "that the heart perceive sin, [and] dread God's wrath" (*F. of C., Thor. Decl.*, II:70). Before the time of Luther, teachings pertaining to contrition were admittedly confused (*AP*, XII [V]:4). In Judaism, repentance (*teshuba*, "return") was man's self-redemption from the thralldom of sin. The Roman Catholic Church teaches that "perfect contrition justifies the sinner without the sacrament of penance" ("attrition" in *Cat. Ency.* Cf. *C. of Trent*, Sess. XIV, can. 4). By "perfect contrition" Romanists mean detestation of sin which arises from love of God. That which arises from any other motive (fear, loss of salvation, etc.) is considered attrition.* In rationalism contrition is the first step toward self-improvement, which it regards the essence of salvation. In many Protestant circles the view prevails, either that contrition procures forgiveness of sins, or, in a milder form, that contrition has an influence on God, moving Him to forgive.

Two truths are taught in Scripture regarding contrition: 1) The non-existence of conversion where contrition has not preceded (*F. of C., Thor. Decl.*, II:70). Contrition is the indispensable

preparation for conversion. In every instance fear of God's wrath and damnation preceded the coming to faith (Acts 16:29; 2:37; Luke 18:13; 15:18; Mark 1:15; Luke 24:47; Joel 2:12; *F. of C., Thor. Decl.*, II:54, 70). The person who does not experience such anguish of conscience (*terrores conscientiae*, the reflex resulting from the sinner's awareness of God's holy Law), despises the grace of God (Luke 5:31 ff.; Luther, St. L. Ed., IX:411; *Ap.*, XII (V):51; III:21; *AC*, XII). From this, however, is not to be concluded that contrition is a cause of forgiveness (Rom. 3:28). 2) Contrition in no way brings about, implements, or occasions justification through faith (Luther, XIX:84; XIII:546, 1953; *F. of C., Thor. Decl.*, III:30 f.). Good works do not justify (Eph. 2:8), and the contrition of the unconverted person is not even a good work, since it is bound together with hatred toward God (God justifies the ungodly, Rom. 4:5). As soon as a person longs for divine grace, faith exists in the heart (Is. 42:3; Mark 9:24. Cf. *F. of C., Thor. Decl.*, II:14). Faith is engendered by the Holy Spirit through the Word (see *Conversion*, 2).

EL

T. Engelder, "Zur Lehre von der Reue," *CTM*, V:218—27, 369—82, 445 to 55, 497—509, 584—96, 657—68; Werner Elert, "Angst," *Morphologie des Luthertums*, Beck, Munich, 1931 (later ed.)

Controversy of the Three Chapters. See *Three Chapters, Controversy of*.

Convalescents, Lutheran Homes for. See *Hospitals, Sanatoria*, etc.

Convent. 1) A name given in monasteries to the assembly of all voting members. 2) The building housing a religious community (in modern usage usually restricted to nunneries).

Conventicle. In the early Christian Church, a house of prayer. Later, a cabal of monks to secure the election of a favorite superior. In England, applied to Wyclif's followers, and, contemptuously, to meetings of Dissenters.

Conventicle Act. See *Presbyterian Bodies*, 2.

Conventuals. A branch of the Friars Minor following a rule less strict than the primitive rule.

Conversion. The doctrine of conversion is of paramount importance in the total body of Scriptural teaching and Christian belief, since it shows how the

salvation won for us by Christ is
brought into the possession of the individual sinner for his soul's eternal
salvation.

I. *Necessity of Conversion.* While it
is God's good and gracious will that
every human being shall be saved
(1 Tim. 2:4; Titus 2:11; John 3:16) and
Jesus fulfilled the Law in our stead
and provided a sufficient ransom from
sin, death, and the devil (John 1:29), it
is, nevertheless, not within the power
of anyone to take for himself the fruits
of Christ's redemption. Faith in Christ,
deliverance from the power of darkness,
and translation into the kingdom of the
Son cannot be achieved by any human
being for himself (Eph. 2:1). The first
disobedience brought dire consequences
to the entire human race. Man lost his
perfect knowledge of God (1 Cor. 13:
9, 10; 2:7-9). While man, after the
Fall, is still a rational being with understanding and a will, thus being able
to acquire intellectual knowledge of the
truths of the Gospel, he cannot of himself acquire the spiritual grasp that accepts, believes, and trusts in what has
been heard and learned (1 Cor. 1:23;
2:14). While man's will is free in
worldly affairs (*AP*, XVIII:76), there is
nothing in the mind and heart of the
natural man that could incline his will
toward God (John 6:44; Gen. 8:21; Rom.
8:5). This corruption of the mind and
will is not merely a relative loss of
righteousness, but natural, unconverted
man no longer possesses a remnant of
the divine image or of his original powers (Eph. 2:12; Mark 16:16; John 8:34;
Eph. 2:1, 2; 2 Tim. 2:26; 2 Cor. 3:5;
Rom. 3:12; John 8:37; John 1:5; 1 Cor.
2:14; Rom. 8:7; John 15:5; Phil. 2:13.
F. of C., Thor. Decl., II:7, 12—14, 20, 21).

II. *Nature of Conversion.* 1. The
word *conversion (epistrophe, epistre-
phein)* is taken from the Scriptures
(Acts 3:19; Ps. 51:13; Is. 60:5; James
5:19, 20. Sometimes translated *turn:*
Acts 11:21; 9:35; 14:15; 26:18; 2 Cor.
3:16; 1 Pet. 2:25). Luther commonly
translates it with *bekehren, Bekehrung.*
Various synonyms are used in Scripture
(*regeneration, awakening, illumination,
call, repentance,* etc.), all, however, designating the act of divine grace by
which the sinner is delivered from the
power of darkness and translated into
the kingdom of Christ (Col. 1:13).

2. The word *conversion* is used in
Scripture in a wider and a narrower
sense. In the wider sense it designates
the entire process whereby man is
transferred from his carnal state into

a spiritual state of faith and grace and
then enters upon, and under the continued influence of the Holy Spirit continues in, a state of faith and spiritual
life.

3. Conversion in the narrower sense
is essentially the bestowal of faith in
God's promise of salvation for Christ's
sake *(donatio fidei).* It takes place in
the heart and consists in this, that the
heart which is broken and contrite because of sin comes to faith in Christ
and trusts in Christ for grace and forgiveness (Acts 11:21). It takes place
when the Holy Spirit engenders faith
in the hearts of penitents through the
Word of God (both Law and Gospel)
and the Sacraments (Rom. 10:17; John
6:63; Rom. 1:16; Is. 55:10, 11. Cf. also
John 1:45-50; Acts 8:34-38; 16:13-34.
Luther, *Large Cat.,* 3d Com.; F. Pieper,
Christliche Dogmatik, II:545 ff.; J. T.
Mueller, *Christian Dogmatics,* 337).

4. Although conversion is a divine
miracle which cannot be understood
through psychological observation and
introspection, Scripture does speak of
distinct "motions" in the heart *(motus
interni, quibus conversio absolvitur),*
namely, contrition and faith. When,
however, contrition and faith are present in the heart, conversion has already
taken place (cf. Mark 9:24; Is. 42:3).
Contrition itself does not form a beginning of, or half of, conversion, nor
does it in itself produce a better spiritual condition in the sinner, since it
of itself can only lead to despair (2 Cor.
7:10); but it is the indispensable preparation for conversion. The converted
person may be sure of his conversion
(2 Cor. 13:5; 1 John 3:14).

5. Conversion is sometimes spoken
of as being gradual; but in that case
the term is used in a wider sense to
include certain outward acts which
commonly precede conversion and only
prepare for conversion. Conversion
proper is the matter of an instant, the
moment when the Holy Spirit through
the means of grace engenders faith in
the contrite heart.

6. Since God's mighty power (Eph.
1:19; 2 Cor. 4:6) works through means
in conversion, it can be resisted (Matt.
23:37; Acts 7:51; 1 Tim. 2:4; Phil. 2:13).

7. Concerning the fact that some
passages of Scripture speak of God's
converting man, and others of man's
converting himself (Jer. 31:18; 24:7;
Acts 3:19), Baier says: "The word
conversion is taken in a double sense
in the Scriptures, inasmuch as at one
time God is said to convert man and,

at another, that man is said to convert himself, although as to the thing itself the action is one and the same."

8. Men may fall from grace after conversion (David, Peter, Hymenaeus, Alexander). Unless the sin against the Holy Ghost has been committed, they may again be converted ("reiterated conversion"; David, Peter; Ezek. 18:23 to 32; 3:16-21).

III. *Effects of Conversion.* Through conversion and faith the believer is made a child of God (Gal. 3:26); enters the kingdom of God; is, for Christ's sake, declared just and absolved from all guilt and punishment (Rom. 3:28; 8:33); has peace, boldness, confidence, comfort (Rom. 5:3-5), and hope of eternal life (Rom. 5:21; 8:30). The Holy Spirit, who creates justifying faith in the heart of the sinner, also from the moment that this faith has been wrought, sets in motion the divine work of sanctification * (Rom. 6:16; 13:10; 8:14) until in the Church Triumphant the divine image of perfect righteousness will be completely restored (Heb. 12:23). See *Contrition; Faith; Justification.* C. f. WHW, "Conversion," *Abiding Word* (I:168—187).

A. L. Graebner, "Conversion" in Jacobs-Haas, *Lutheran Cyclopedia* (see also Graebner's article in *Theological Quarterly*, V:134 f.); *District Reports: Canada*, 1882; *Central*, 1906; *Eastern*, 1882; *Nebraska*, 1883; *Northern*, 1866 (C. F. W. Walther); *Oregon*, 1901; *Southern*, 1882 (F. Pieper); *Southern*, 1884 (A. Graebner); *Texas*, 1919; F. Pieper, *Conversion and Election, A Plea for a United Lutheranism in America*, CPH, 1913; F. Pieper, "Eine deutschlaendische Disputation ueber die Lehre von der Bekehrung," *L. u. W.*, XLVIII: 289—98, 327—33 (see also Pieper's evaluation of theses published in the *Lutherische Herold, L. u. W.*, XLV: 313, 314); Th. Engelder, "Let Us Get Together on the Doctrines of Conversion and Election," *CTM*, VI:539—43; C. G. Carlfelt, "The Work of the Holy Spirit," in *What Lutherans are Thinking*, Wartburg Press, 1947; O. Hallesby, *Infant Baptism and Adult Conversion*, Lutheran Free Ch. Pub. Co., Minneapolis, 1924; L. S. Keyser, *Election and Conversion*, Burlington, 1914. As a result of the controversy on election and conversion a large literature is extant on this subject. There are many articles in *L. u. W., Theol. Zeitblaetter*, and *Theol. Magazine*. A large number of pamphlets are bound together in the Concordia Seminary Library, St. Louis. F. Pieper's *Die*

Grunddifferenz (1903), *Zur Einigung* (1913), F. W. Stellhorn's *Tractatus* (1881), *The Error of Missouri* (published by E. L. S. Tressel, Luth. Book Concern, 1897), Geo. J. Fritschel's *Die Schriftlehre von der Gnadenwahl* (1906) are often referred to. A view of conversion which is widely discussed among Protestants is Emil Brunner's *The Divine Human Encounter*, Westminster Press, 1943.

Conviction of Sin. See *Contrition.*

Cook Islands, New Zealand, a Polynesian island group within the British Empire. Area, 280 sq. mi. Population, 16,350. Discovered by James Cook, 1773—77; annexed to New Zealand, 1901. John Williams was pioneer missionary in Rarotonga. Missions throughout the group by the L. M. S. Many converts have been zealous as evangelists, even as far as the Loyalty Islands (South Pacific Ocean). The Roman Catholic Church has established counter missions. See *Missions, Bibliography.*

Cooke, Henry. See *Presbyterian Bodies, 3.*

Cooper, Anthony Ashley. See *Deism, III, 4.*

Co-operation in Conversion. See *Contrition; Conversion; Synergism.*

Cope. See *Vestments, Clerical.*

Copernicus, Nicolaus (1473—1543). Polish astronomer; educated at Cracow, Bologna, Ferrara, Padua; lectured on astronomy at Rome; bishop of Ermeland. In his *De Revolutionibus Orbium Coelestium* he exchanged the positions of the earth and the sun in the celestial scheme, keeping, however, the chief notions of Hellenic celestial mechanics. His work moved Giordano Bruno to deny a fixed center in the universe and assert the relativity of space, time, and motion. Newton later denied the centrality of the solar system.

Coptic Church (contraction from Greek *Aigyptos*, meaning Egypt).

1. Tradition traces the foundation of this body to the time when St. Mark, shortly after the ascension of Christ, came to Egypt and A. D. 40 gained as his first convert Hananias, who became the next archbishop. The break with Rome came in 451 at the Council of Chalcedon. The Copts denied the Biblical doctrine of the two natures of Christ, "the properties of each nature being preserved and united in one person and one mode of being," and main-

tained that there was only one nature, the divine, or a single compounded nature. Dioscurus, then archbishop, was excommunicated by Rome, and Proterius was elected Patriarch. The Egyptians murdered him and elected Timothy II who had Monophysitic tendencies. In 567 two lines of patriarchs were definitely established: the orthodox Catholic, whose following consisted of a foreign minority, and the Egyptian Monophysites, or the Coptic Church. The seat of the Patriarch, which had been at Alexandria, was moved to Cairo in 1045.

2. The Coptic Church has never been reunited with Rome. The numbers of the Coptic Church were reduced by internal troubles as well as by Catholic persecution and the Persian uprising from 616 to 628. In 640 they sought the refuge of the invading Arabs, but during the massacres of 832 their numbers were cut down considerably. For the next two hundred years the control of Egypt passed between Arabs, Turks, and Syrians, until in 1164, when Saladin became Sultan of Egypt. During the Crusades the Copts were again persecuted by the Mohammedans. The Turks regained power in 1515 and remained until they were overcome by Napoleon. The Copts again suffered at the beginning of the nineteenth century when the English and the French battled in Egypt. After the English victory Mohammed Ali became ruler, under whose reign the Copts attained peace. In 1926 the Coptic Church had 859,670 members. The doctrine of the Copts is in some respects similar to that of Rome, but it is not identical. The primary difference concerns the two natures of Christ, the Copts still maintaining Monophysite views. They also deny transubstantiation and give both kinds to laity and priests. They deny purgatory and, while believing in the sinlessness of Mary, they reject the term "Immaculate Conception" because of its association with Rome. The Church Missionary Society of England attempted work among the Copts in 1839, but turned over their missions to the United Presbyterian Church. Attempts at reform have been made, but have not been altogether successful. A branch of the Coptic Church of Alexandria is the *Ethiopian Church,* founded by Frumentius in 330. He was appointed by Athanasius, then Patriarch of the Coptic Church, to be the first archbishop of Ethiopia. The Ethiopians, also Monophysites, are dominated by the Copts, whose most powerful check against independence is the appointment of the Abuna, or archbishop, by the Patriarch. ECZ

Corbinian. An eighth-century Frankish missionary, one of the predecessors of Boniface; consecrated as bishop by Pope Gregory II; settled at Freising and did mission work in Bavaria and Southern Tyrol.

Cordatus, Konrad (1475—1546). Became interested in the Reformation and visited Wittenberg; pastor in Zwickau, in Niemegk, and finally in Eisleben; introduced the Reformation in Brandenburg; was involved in the Synergistic Controversy with Cruciger, who suggested the co-operation of man in the obedience of sanctification to the point of making repentance a condition of man's justification; friend of Luther.

Cordes, Johann Heinrich Karl. B. Mar. 21, 1813, at Betzendorf, near Lueneburg; entered Dresden Lutheran Mission Seminary, 1837; missionary to India, 1840; Tranquebar, 1841; instrumental in securing the former Danish-Halle Mission remnants and property for the Leipzig Mission; Senior of Missionary Council, 1858; member of Mission Board, Leipzig, 1872; retired, 1887; d. near the end of the century.

Cornelius a Lapide (van den Steen; 1567—1637). Exegete of Roman Church; became Jesuit in 1597; lecturer on the Bible and Hebrew at Louvain, 1596 to 1616, after that at college of Rome; used principle of fourfold exegesis — allegorical, symbolical, typological, and true.

Cornelius, Peter (1783—1867). Painter, idealist of the new German school; did his chief work under the direction of Crown Prince Ludwig of Bavaria in Munich: The Creation, The Redemption Through Christ, The Last Judgment; spent several years in Berlin; planned and made sketches for a series, the so-called Campo Santo pictures, to set forth sin and grace; a master of style, interpreter of his age.

Cornerstone. The stone placed in the most prominent corner of a building, usually with a cavity containing documents of historic interest and current coins.

Cornerus (Korner), Christoph (1518 to 1594). B. in Franconia. Professor of theology in Frankfort-on-the-Oder; general superintendent of Brandenburg at the time of his death. He helped to draw up the *Formula of Concord.*

Corporal. The linen cloth on which the Communion vessels rest. Also the cloth with which the vessels are covered. It was originally intended to represent the cloth in which the body *(corpus)* of Christ was wrapped (Luke 23:53). In the Roman Catholic Church it is applied to the host until just before Communion.

Corporation Act of 1661. An act passed in England under Charles II, excluding Puritans and other Dissenters from various types of corporations in England.

Corpus Catholicorum. Collective name for Roman Catholic States in Germany, to distinguish them from the Protestant *Corpus Evangelicorum.**

Corpus Christi. A festival of the Roman Catholic Church, in honor of the local presence of Christ in the host, celebrated on Thursday after Trinity Sunday. The nun Juliana (ca. 1230), in a vision, saw the Church as a full moon with one dark spot — the lack of such a festival. At her request, Urban IV established the festival with indulgences. John XXII (1316—1334) added a procession in which the host, in a monstrance, a special vessel containing the host, was carried through the streets. Other Popes increased the indulgences. The processions soon became sumptuous exhibitions of ecclesiastical pomp and worldly splendor. Miracle plays and mysteries were given after the procession. Luther considered this the most harmful of medieval festivals, while the Council of Trent gloried in it as a "triumph over heresy." Since the Reformation, Corpus Christi processions have been forbidden in various countries, including some where Romanism preponderates.

Corpus Doctrinae. This term denotes a systematized body of doctrine, the term "body" in this expression meaning, in general, a complete collection of writings on any subject. While the term is not always used in precisely the same sense, it stands, in general, for doctrinal standards accepted either by special denominations or by the whole Christian Church. The ecumenical creeds thus supply a *corpus doctrinae* for the whole Christian Church. The Book of Concord furnishes a *corpus doctrinae* for the Lutheran Church, since it contains the specific Confessions universally recognized as Lutheran. A popular though not orthodox *corpus doctrinae* was the *Corpus Philippicum,*

published in 1560, which contained the three ecumenical creeds, the Altered Augsburg Confession, the Apology, Melanchthon's *Loci,* and other writings of his. The complete expression is *corpus doctrinae Christianae.*

Corpus Evangelicorum. The corporation of evangelicals in Germany. The first league was made between Saxony and Hesse (1528), and later at Spires (1529) the *Corpus Evangelicorum* was organized. It was presided over by Saxony and ended with the German Empire (1806). The name was often used as a collective name for the Protestant states of Germany.

Corpus Evangelicum. See *United Lutheran Church, Synods of,* 29.

Corpus Juris Canonici. See *Canon Law.*

Corpus Lutheranorum. See *Union Movements,* 8.

Correggio, Antonio Allegri da (1494 to 1534). Italian painter of the Renaissance; master of delicacy and of light and shadows; "Ecce Homo," dome frescoes at Parma, and "Holy Night" are characteristic of his art.

Correlation. See *Christian Teaching,* L.

Correspondence Course. See *Parish Education,* E 8.

Corvinus, Antonius (1501—53). Expelled from cloister because of his Lutheranism (1522); preacher in Hessen (1538); advanced the work of the Reformation in Goettingen, Nordheim, Hildesheim, Calenberg; opposed Interim; imprisoned (1549—52); his Sermons on the Gospels and Epistles became popular.

Cosmic Intelligence. See *Rosicrucians.*

Cosmogony (G. *kosmos,* "world"; *gonos,* "generation"). Strictly speaking, the word means the science of the origin of the world. It is usually applied, however, to the study of the various theories regarding the beginning of the world (and also to the theories themselves) as well as to the account of Scripture.

The conception of a creation out of nothing *(ex nihilo)* was practically unknown in early heathen cosmogonies (held to a greater or lesser degree by Etruscans, Druids, Brahmins). By far the majority of the early cosmogonies consider *matter* eternal and attribute the *form* to the activity of a deity. Others regarded both matter and form eternal (Ocellus Lucanus, Ammonius, and others). To this group belong also those who identify deity and matter (Parmenides, Xenophanes, Zeno, and others, including moderns). The Scriptures attribute both matter and form to the Creator (see *Creation*).

Cosmological Arguments. See *God, Arguments for Existence of.*

Cosmology. That part of dogmatics,* or doctrinal theology, which deals with the creation and preservation of the world and of all the creatures of the universe, especially in the relation to man.

Costa Rica. See *Central America, Missions in.*

Cotta, Ursula (d. 1511). Wife of Conrad Cotta of Eisenach. She is remembered for her kindness and charity toward Luther during the latter's student days.

Cotton, John (1585—1652). Patriarch of New England. B. at Derby; pastor of Puritan tendencies, Boston, England; fled to America 1633; "teacher" of First Church, Boston (died there). Published fifty volumes of theological books.

Council of Church Boards of Education. See *Union Movements*, 13.

Council of Reformed Churches. See *Union Movements*, 5.

Councils and Synods. 1. Ecclesiastical assemblies convened for the joint discussion and settlement of questions affecting the faith and discipline of the church. The words "council" and "synod" were at first used interchangeably (as in this item). Later the word "council" was applied to the ecumenical conventions, while the word "synod" was given to councils representing smaller areas. Councils have been distinguished as follows: *diocesan* (embracing the clergy and bishops of a diocese); *provincial* (metropolitan and bishops of his province); *patriarchal* (all of the bishops of a patriarchal district); *national* (applied to the councils of the early Middle Ages which were largely controlled by secular rulers); *ecumenical* (representing the entire Christian world). In Protestantism the word "synod" has various techincal meanings.

2. Attempts to trace the later councils directly to the first council of Chris-

tians (Acts 15) have proved futile. The later synods were of a different nature, one striking similarity, however, being the preface to decrees: "It hath seemed good to the Holy Ghost and to us." It seems that the early synods developed out of enlarged congregational meetings (in earliest times delegates were sent from one congregation to another: *I Clement*, LXIII; *Ignatius, ad Phil.*, X; *ad Smyrn.*, XI; *ad. Polyc.*, VII) or were called into being by some difficult and widespread problem. The earliest councils of which we have record are those held in Asia Minor in connection with the Montanist controversy (ca. 160—175) and those held in connection with the Easter controversy (ca. 190—200). In connection with the Montanist controversy, meetings were held at which numerous "believers" (undoubtedly laymen as well as clergy) deliberated (Eusebius, *Hist.*, V: 16: 10).

3. *Provincial Councils.* The bishops, as the teaching of apostolic succession became prominent, usurped authority which was not originally theirs. In the third century clerics (bishops, presbyters, and deacons) attended synods, and the responsibility for decisions gravitated to the bishops. Such provincial councils became fixed institutions when regular meetings were established (which occurred in the 3d century, but were universally fixed by Canon V of the Council of Nicea) with the metropolitan at the head. The hierarchical tendency is shown by the fact that the bishops acted, not as representatives of the churches, but as successors of the apostles.

4. *Ecumenical Councils.* The ecumenical councils did not develop out of the provincial councils or synods, but were created by Constantine. He called a commission of bishops to Rome in connection with the Donatist controversy, and later a larger council at Arles. In the case of these councils, as well as that of Nicea, Constantine determined the place and time, summoned the bishops, paid expenses, and gave the decisions binding force (Eusebius, *Hist.*, X: 5: 20). Thus the real power in the early ecumenical councils did not stem from bishops as apostolic successors, but from a secular ruler. The following are usually regarded as ecumenical councils (Protestants usually do not consider those after Chalcedon ecumenical): Nicea I * (A. D. 325), Constantinople I * (381), Ephesus * (431), Chalcedon * (451), Constantinople II * (553), Constantinople III * (680—81),

Nicea II * (787), Constantinople IV * (869). The Roman Church, holding that its councils are essentially head-and-members (pope-in-council) adds the following: first five Lateran (1123, 1139, 1179, 1215, 1512—17), Lyons I and II (1245, 1274), Vienna (1311—13), Constance (1414—18, only in part), Basel-Ferrara-Florence (1431—39, only in part).

5. National Councils. During the early Middle Ages the church of the Germanic nations functioned on a national basis. The provincial synods, under the metropolitan or archbishop, met rarely. The national ruler occupied a prominent position in church affairs. The kings usually called the synods and reserved the right to alter or set aside decisions. In the 7th century, the kings or delegates attended synods, and influential men of the state were members. Such a development was especially seen in France. In Spain, under Arian influence, the provincial synods continued longer than elsewhere. Within the framework of the national church the bishoprics changed from city-centered to territorial with diocesan meetings.

6. Roman Catholic Synods. At an early date bishops at Rome, maintaining that they had the primacy in the church, sought to extend the jurisdiction of their provincial synods to the entire church. Thus Julius I invited oriental bishops to a synod at Rome (341), and Gallic bishops attended the synod of Damasus (369). Whether attended by foreign bishops or not, the Roman pontiffs soon insisted that the decisions of their synods were binding because the popes were Peter's successors. The prestige of the papal synods was somewhat lessened by the recognition given the state synods of Otto I and III, and Henry II and III, and Conrad II.

With the ascendancy of papal power under Leo IX, the papal synods increased in prestige and were considered ecumenical by the hierarchy (see 4). They were, however, essentially different from the early ecumenical councils which were controlled by secular power. The popes sought to bring the councils completely under their domination and held that papal authority confirmed the decisions of councils.

The Reform Councils and the Reformation caused the papacy to view councils with distrust. Only the pressing need of a counter-reformation led to the convening of the Council of

Trent.* The Papacy sought to establish the essence of the council along the lines developed before the Reform Councils, with only the higher clergy as members and with control securely in papal hands. Finally, at the Vatican Council, the Papacy obtained absolute primacy in the decree of Infallibility (see Roman Catholic Confessions).

In America the Roman Catholic Church has held provincial councils (1829, 1833, 1837, 1840, 1843, 1849) and national (1852, 1866, 1884) councils at Baltimore, Md. The archbishop of Baltimore presided at all the synods. The national councils were attended by bishops from the entire United States, and its decisions, as sanctioned by the Pope, were binding for Roman Catholics in the nation.

7. Reform Councils. John of Paris (d. 1306) in his De potestate regia et papali advocated conciliarism (the view that the church should be governed by councils and that councils are superior to the pope). Marsilius of Padua (d. 1343) held that councils were representative of the totality of Christendom and were, therefore, of the highest authority and should be composed of clergy and laymen. When the papal schism occurred (1378), a solution to this problem of the church was sought in the views of John and Marsilius; and Conrad of Gelnhausen (1320—1390; prof. at Paris; wrote Epistola Concordiae), Henry of Langenstein (1340 to 1397; prof. at Paris; wrote Epistola Concilii Pacis), Pierre D'Ailly * and John Gerson * led the movement for Reform Councils. The Council of Pisa * failed to end the schism. The Council of Constance * sought to establish universal councils as the highest authority in the church and to have such councils meet regularly. Although endorsed at Basel, the Constance plan failed because of the opposition of the Papacy.

8. Luther on Councils. Luther subordinated councils to the Word of God, which is self-sufficient (St. L. Ed. XIV: 393. Cf. XVI: 2258). The truth of the Gospel cannot be established by councils (XXII: 644), and the Holy Spirit is not bound by conciliar decisions (XIX: 1768; VIII: 1004). Since articles of faith, doctrine, and works existed before councils, the latter cannot establish or decree doctrine, but, as all men, must show that what they say is in harmony with God's Word (XI: 1076; XXII: 1354 ff.) and if their pronouncements show such harmony, they are accepted for the Word's sake (XI: 460, 1398; XVI:

2247, 2262, 2189; XVIII: 1082; XIX: 1769). As individual men, so also councils erred (XV: 1298 ff.; XVIII: 825, 1985).

Taking his stand on the NT (and earliest councils), Luther pointed out that the Holy Spirit dwells in the hearts of believers (XVI: 2291 ff.) and if council members are selected *aus dem Volke Gottes* (from the people of God, including laymen, XVI: 2291) then there is a true council ruled by the Spirit. Luther favored a free (XVII: 1021), Christian (XVI: 2029; XVII: 1027) council (XIII: 386; XV: 2203; XVI: 1972 ff.; XVII: 1022 ff.; VII: 2008). Such a true council, then, is a gathering of pious people for the preservation among them of the pure Word (XVII: 1357). The duty of judging doctrine is a matter for all Christians (XII: 1540), and hence councils of such Christians also judge doctrine and works and arrange externals (XXII: 1349 ff.). Thus Luther opposed the "pope-in-council" ("head and members") idea of Romanists (XVI: 1856 ff.; XVII: 1021 ff.; XIII: 386; XVI: 2036 ff.). Luther regarded the first four councils listed under 4 above (Nicea, Constantinople, Ephesus, and Chalcedon) as ecumenical (XVII: 1038; XXII: 1358). He held that the councils up to the time of Gregory I, were still somewhat pure; from Gregory I to Charles the Great the Pope was a spiritual lord and introduced superstitions; the councils thereafter were the worst because the Pope had usurped the two swords (XXII: 1356).

9. *Protestant Synods.* In Germany the control of churches remained under secular rulers (consistory). The synodical arrangement advocated by Schleiermacher (composed of clergy only) everywhere developed as a representative organ of the church over against the state, and its authority was limited. Calvin, in harmony with his emphasis on Christian association, laid the groundwork for a Presbyterian system (based on representative government — clergy and laymen — originating in the congregation) which was developed in France and spread through Reformed churches. In England the Episcopal state church developed. H. M. Muhlenberg indicated the direction in which Lutheranism in America would go by stressing congregational organization. The first Lutheran synod in America (Philadelphia, 1748) was attended by more lay delegates than clergy. The general tendency in American Lutheranism has been to regard synodical organizations as advisory to the local congregation (for details on this entire paragraph see *Polity, Ecclesiastical*). See also *Church; Keys, Office of; Priesthood of Believers.* EL

C. J. von Hefele, *Conciliengeschichte,* 1873—80 (English translation by W. R. Clark published by T. & T. Clark, Edinburgh, 1894—96); E. H. Landon, *Manual of the Councils of the Catholic Church,* J. Grant, Edinburgh, 1909 (2 vols); W. Bright, *Notes on the Canons of the First Four Councils,* Clarendon Press, Oxford, 1882; Luther, "Von den Consiliis und Kirchen," St. L. Ed., XVI: 2144—2302; "Ausschreibung eines heiligen freien christlichen Concils," XIX: 1762—66; "Von den Concilien," XXII: 1349—70; "Disputation, was ein Concilium fuer Macht und Gewalt habe," XIX: 1766—69 (see also appended references to Walch edition); *AP,* VI: 70; XVIII: 6; *Treatise* appended to *Sm. Art.;* Melanchthon, *Corpus Reformatorum,* III: 468 ff.; "Luther on the Council and the Churches," in *Works of Luther,* Holman Co. & Castle Press, Philadelphia, 1931.

Counselor in Parish Education. See *Parish Education,* L 4.

Counter Reformation. 1. A movement in the Roman Catholic Church intended to counteract the results of the Protestant Reformation. The bases of the Counter Reformation were:

a) A re-definition of the Roman scholastic doctrines and the rejection of Protestant tenets by which the schism between Romanism and Protestantism was made complete. This statement of doctrines of the Council of Trent was chiefly the work of the Jesuits Diego Laynez (1512—65; Spaniard; later general of the Jesuit order) and Alphonsus Salmeron (1515—85; Spaniard, author of NT commentaries). While some Catholic leaders (*e. g.,* Contarini) favored an irenic attitude toward Humanism and Protestantism, their influence did not prevail. Attempts at harmonizing the differences between Romanism and Protestantism were crushed.

b) Concentration of power in the Papacy, thereby making it a more powerful fighting force.

c) The revival of the Inquisition for the suppression of opponents. The Inquisition had been revived in Spain on Nov. 1, 1477. On July 21, 1542, the Papacy provided itself with a more centralized machinery under its own domination through the creation of the

Holy Office of the Universal Church (July 21, 1542).

d) Moral reforms were championed especially by the *Oratory of Divine Love* founded at Rome toward the end of the rule of Leo X. This group did not achieve its full purpose at Trent.

2. A complex of movements led to the Counter Reformation. The reason for the growth of the movement is to be sought partly in the factions which rent the Protestant Church, partly in the outward reform and revival in the Roman Church, which was caused by the work of Luther and his colaborers and other reformers. The reformation of the Church, as understood by theologians of the Counter Reformation, included a measure of secular control, a revival and enforcement of all canonical laws framed to purify the morals of the clergy, a certain accommodation to the ideals of the Humanists, a steady adherence to the main doctrines of the scholastic theology, the preservation of the hierarchical system in its entirety, the retention of the rites and usages of the Medieval Church, and a ruthless suppression of heresy from the standpoint of the Roman Church. In Spain the reorganization of the Catholic sect began under Cardinal Ximenes, who re-established monastic discipline in its most rigid form, put the morals of the secular clergy to a rigid test, and otherwise instituted an outward reform, which some three decades later stood the forces of Catholicism in good stead when the representatives of the empire met at Worms, in 1521, and at Augsburg, in 1530. It was chiefly due to this activity of Ximenes that the anti-Lutheran movement so rapidly checked the advance of the Reformation on the Iberian Peninsula. In Italy it was chiefly a small society of pious laymen and prelates, who met in the little church of Santi Silvestro et Dorotea in the Trastevere (a section of the city west of the Tiber) in Rome, who counteracted the moral corruption of the Church to such an extent as to prepare the way for the Counter Reformation. Among the men at the head of the Italian movement were Contarini, Caraffa, and Cortese. Among the women who worked along similar lines may be mentioned Renée of Ferrara and Vittoria Colonna.

3. After the Council of Trent the Counter Reformation moved forward. The Inquisition held especially Spain and Italy for Romanism. The Roman Missal and Breviary were reformed and the Tridentine Catechism introduced. The Jesuits intensified their educational program. Roman theological colleges were established. The Curia at Rome was reorganized and other reforms were pressed by religious orders. A new Index of Prohibited Books * was published. Mission work was intensified through the creation of the Congregation of the Propaganda.* The centralization of power in the Papacy was fostered until the infallibility of the Pope was declared. See *Roman Catholic Church; Inquisition; Jesuits; Roman Catholic Confessions; Papacy.*

Course of Study. See *Christian Teaching,* L.

Courts, Spiritual (or *Ecclesiastical*). Since the Roman Church claims the right of legislating for its "subjects," it consistently claims also the judicial powers necessary to enforce the laws and to exact penalties from transgressors. These powers are exercised through spiritual courts. The blending of church and state, inaugurated by Constantine, developed such courts and enabled them gradually to enlarge their jurisdiction. Eventually not only all matters with even a remote bearing on the church or religion were taken from the civil courts, but clerics of every degree were exempted from civil jurisdiction, and all cases to which a cleric was a party were tried in spiritual courts, for "it would be utterly unbecoming for persons of superior dignity [clerics] to submit themselves to their inferiors [laymen] for judgment" (*Catholic Encyclopedia*). Spiritual courts formerly inflicted also such temporal punishments as scourging and imprisonment. Three courts of judgement are recognized: that of the bishop or his vicar-general, that of the metropolitan (archbishop), and that of the Pope. Appeal may be taken from the lower courts to the higher. Some cases, however, are in the first instance reserved for the Pope or the various Roman Congregations. Ecclesiastical courts have been shorn of their powers, even in Roman Catholic countries, and with their jurisdiction their importance has dwindled. (See also *Church and State.*)

Cousin, Victor (1792—1867). French philosopher; opposed materialism of eighteenth century; founded school of eclectic philosophy based on Germanic philosophy and Cartesian thought.

Covenant Church of America. See *Evangelical Mission Covenant Church of America.*

Covenant Theology. See *Presbyterian Confessions,* 3 b.

Covenanters. See *Presbyterian Bodies; Presbyterian Confessions,* 1.

Coverdale, Miles (1488—1569). Educated at Cambridge; associated with Tyndale and various continental reformers; his translation of the Bible published in 1535 and the second version of the New Testament in 1538; later, in 1545, pastor of a Lutheran congregation at Bergzabern in Germany; notable work in hymnody is his *Goostly Psalmes,* 1531—39, which contained 41 Lutheran hymns, 22 by Luther, done into metrical verse.

Covetousness. A vice which is forbidden in the Ninth and the Tenth Commandment, being directed against the neighbor's possessions. It is essentially the eager desire to gain some possession on which the heart is set, to the neighbor's impoverishment. It is distinguished from avarice in this, that the latter is bent upon an undue retention of possessions already gained, while covetousness deals only with personal property and other possessions of the neighbor in so far as the covetous person unduly desires them, bending his efforts toward getting them by a show of right or by false and sinful means directly applied. Even obtaining other people's property by legal means may be an act of covetousness, namely, when it is done with the idea of enriching oneself at the expense of the neighbor or of heaping up riches and possessions in order to have a great deal of property. The warnings of Scripture with regard to this sin are found throughout the Bible, their substance being found in the admonition to hate covetousness (Ex. 18:21), not to incline the heart to covetousness (Ps. 119:36), not to be given to covetousness (Jer. 6:13), to be aware of covetousness (Luke 12:15), not to let covetousness be named (Eph. 5:3), to mortify covetousness (Col. 3:5), to let the entire conduct be without covetousness (Heb. 13:5). In addition, the Bible describes some warning examples of covetousness, as when Ahab desired the vineyard of Naboth (1 Kings 21), and committed murder through the hands of his wife, Jezebel; when Jesus calls down the punishment of God upon the scribes and Pharisees in one of His terrible cries of woe upon them (Matt. 23:14); and when the Prophet, in a similar strain, describes those who join house to house and lay field to field, till there be no place left, that they may be placed alone in the midst of the earth (Is. 5:8). Covetousness, together with the love of money shown in avarice, is truly one of the roots of all evil and an enemy of faith (1 Tim. 6:10).

Cowl. A kind of hood worn since ancient times by members of some monastic orders.

Cowper, William (1731—1800). A pre-Romanticist, deeply religious, and given to attacks of melancholy. During his years at Olney he wrote *The Olney Hymns:* "Oh for a Closer Walk with God"; "There Is a Fountain Filled with Blood"; "Hark, My Soul, It Is the Lord"; "God Moves in a Mysterious Way." Another of his better works is *The Task and Other Poems.*

Cox, Frances Elizabeth (1812—1897). B. at Oxford; a very successful translator of hymns from the German; her book in two editions; two of her best: "Jesus Lives! No Longer Now"; "Who Are These Like Stars Appearing."

Coxe, Arthur Cleveland (1818 to 1896). Educated at Univ. of New York; held a number of positions in the Episcopal Church; last, bishop of the Western Diocese of New York; wrote "Savior, Sprinkle Many Nations."

Cradle Roll. See *Parish Education,* B 3.

Craemer, Friedrich August. B. in Klein-Langheim, Bavaria, May 26, 1812; studied theology in Erlangen, 1830 to 1832; member of a Patriotic Students' Society (*Burschenschaft*), he was sentenced to imprisonment following the Frankfort Insurrection of 1833; proved innocent in 1839, but remained under police surveillance; studied Old and Modern Greek, Old and Middle High German, French, and English; in Munich, later, again theology; particularly the Formula of Concord; 1841 tutor to the son of Count Carl von Einsiedel; after two years tutor of the children of Lord and Lady Lovelace in England, the latter a daughter of Lord Byron; tutor of German language and literature at Oxford. The university being dominated by the Tractarians, he severed his connection with it. The *Notruf* of Wyneken took him to Pastor Loehe, who found him to be the man needed as leader of the men he was on the point of sending to America to found a mission colony there. He traveled through northern Germany in the interest of this work; was ordained by Dr. Kliefoth in the cathedral of Schwerin, Apr. 4, 1845. Founded the mission colony at Frankenmuth, Mich., labored for five years as pastor and Indian missionary; upon the advice of Loehe he identified himself with the founders of the Missouri Synod. On the death of Prof. A. Wolter he became president and professor of the Practical Seminary at Fort Wayne, most of whose twenty pupils had been sent over by Loehe. When the seminary was combined with the Theoretical Seminary at St. Louis, in 1861, Professor Walther and he, for a while, constituted the whole faculty. For the sake of the large number of Norwegian students enrolled he took up the study of their language. In 1875 he went with the Practical Seminary to Springfield, Ill., as president and chief instructor. Craemer was an indefatigable worker; enjoyed giving twenty-three lectures a week besides performing the duties connected with the presidency and directorate; during the vacation months he frequently managed to put in his time preparing emergency classes; and, besides assisting the local pastors, he took charge of missions — while in Fort Wayne, at Cedar Creek; in St. Louis, at Minerstown; in Springfield, at Chatham. His labors of forty-one years in the seminary were highly successful, for he knew how to instill, by word and example, his burning zeal into the large classes that sat at his feet. D. May 3, 1891.

L. Fuerbringer, "Friedrich August Craemer," *L. u. W.*, LXVIII: 1 ff.; 33 ff.

Cranach, Lucas (1473—1553). Court painter of the Elector Frederick the Wise in Wittenberg, "painter of the Reformation"; extremely productive; during the earlier period of his life a somewhat romantic strain, during later period dogmatico-symbolical representations; painted several pictures of Luther and his co-workers, also of Catharina of Bora and of Luther's daughter Magdalena.

Cranmer, Thomas (1489—1556). First Protestant Primate of All England; b. at Nottingham; obtained the favor of Henry VIII by advising him to refer his divorce case to the universities, 1529; received appointment to Canterbury see and promptly declared Henry's marriage to Anne Boleyn valid, 1533;

acquiesced in the same year in the burning of Frith, who had denied transubstantiation and purgatory; opposed the enactment of the Six Articles (Bloody Bill) and promoted the circulation of the Bible (Great), 1539; was the chief author of the *First Prayer Book of Edward*, 1549, and of the *Forty-two Articles of Religion*, 1553; vainly signed seven "recantations" on being thrown into prison by Bloody Mary and suffered martyrdom at Oxford. Thrusting his hand into the flames, he repeatedly cried, "That unworthy _ hand!" alternating, as he breathed his last, this exclamation with the prayer: "Lord Jesus, receive my spirit."

Crashaw, Richard (1613?—1649). The son of a Puritan clergyman, turned Catholic shortly before his death. Crashaw, one of the metaphysical poets, often displays great poetic genius in the treatment of religious subjects in spite of the excessive use of figures of speech called "conceits." His most important works: *Epigrammatum Sacrorum Liber; Steps to the Temple; The Flaming Heart; Hymn to St. Theresa; The Weeper.*

Crasselius, Bartholomaeus (1667 to 1724). Pastor at Nidda and at Duesseldorf; hymns full of force and beauty; wrote: "Dir, dir, Jehovah, will ich singen"; "Erwach, o Mensch, erwache!"

Crato, John (1519—85). B. in Breslau; studied at Wittenberg (1534—44); collected the material for the *Table Talk of Luther* at whose house he lived during the six years at Wittenberg; advised by Luther to give up theology and study medicine because of his feeble health; became famous as physician of Breslau during plague of 1553; made *Comes Palatinus* at the court of Maximilian II, he became influential in the cause of Protestantism in Austria; first a Lutheran of the Melanchthonian type, he later became Reformed.

Creation, the Work of (*Hexaemeron*). The divine act by which all objects were brought into being. The objective world, or universe, the things animate and inanimate, which have their existence by virtue of this act, are called "heaven and earth" in the Old and usually in the New Testament, which latter also uses the terms *kosmos* and *aion*. God alone has brought all things into being (Heb. 1:2, 11; 9:3; 3:4; Acts 17:24; 14:15; Ps. 33:6) according to the mode and process of a divine fiat as described in the Genesis record of the "six days' work," or hexaemeron. It was by the Logos, or Word, the Second Person of the Trinity, that all things were made (John 1:3). And it was an act of almighty power by which the Father, as Creator, called into existence that which was non-existent (Rom. 4:17). The wisdom of God is discernible in all His works (Jer. 10:12). All that was done in the creation of the world was done by God's volition alone, and not by virtue of any blind necessity (Rev. 4:11).

The term used for "create" in the Genesis account, *bara*, does not denote the conformation, elaboration, or ordering of a thing, but a new production, as a glance at the texts referred to under *bara* in Gesenius proves. The opening clause of this account sets forth the world as first created out of nothing, and this in a rude, "chaotic" state, while the remainder of the chapter exhibits the elaboration, by successive divine acts, of the recently created mass.

The creation of the world was not by external necessity, but by an interior impulse of the divine nature to manifest itself. Nor was the aim of God, in fashioning the universe, exclusively His own glory; He was impelled by eternal love, desiring the good of His creatures. Their nature is so constituted that they are permeated by God's goodness (Ps. 33:5). Creation reached its culmination in the beings endowed with spirit — the angels and man. — The time occupied by the creative acts is in Genesis called six days, the work of each day being stated separately. While it is true that the word "day" is sometimes used in Scripture in an indefinite period — "the day of vengeance," "the night is far spent, the day is at hand" — the meanings do not apply in Genesis 1. The several days are consecutively numbered, making an exact week, and the alternations of light and darkness are called "night" and "day." This points, together with the text, to the "evening" and "morning" of the text, to a period of six natural days.

While there is progress and order in the acts recorded Genesis 1, the narrative excludes evolution as the method by which things took their present form. The higher forms of life were not evolved out of the lower forms, but were created by a divine fiat for each group of beings. These, moreover, were created as species; for the repeated phrase "after his kind" can be understood in no other way. From this we conclude that the great orders of animal and plant life stood out as separate beings on the third, fifth, and sixth days of the hexaemeron. Moreover, man was not created as a species of animal, but in the image of God. The idea of an evolution of living forms is therefore excluded by the Biblical account. The universe as we see it has not come into being by the action of forces resident in eternal matter, but the very matter of which it is made and the forces with which matter is endowed are products of a sovereign Will and Intelligence, of a personal Power (Jer. 10:12), in which God needed no assistance of means or modes, but by which He was able to create what He desired (Ps. 115:3; 135:6). See also *Evolution*.

G. Viehweg, "The Doctrine of Creation," *Abiding Word*, CPH, 1946 (I:1 to 17 and the extensive references given in the bibliography, p. 583); George McCready Price, "New Proofs of an Original Creation," *CTM*, VI:931—36; L. Franklin Gruber, *The Six Creative Days*, Lutheran Literary Bd., Burlington, Iowa, rev. 1944; C. W. Hale Amos, *The Vital Challenge of Biblical Certitude*, Zondervan, Grand Rapids, Mich., rev. 1935; A. Heidel, *Babylonian Genesis*, University of Chicago Press, 1942.

Creationism. A theory concerning the origin of the human soul. Creationism assumes that not only the soul of Adam, but every human soul, is to be derived from a direct creative act of God. For criticism of this view see *Traducianism*.

Credner, Karl August (1797—1857). Professor of church history and exegesis at Giessen; rationalist New Testament scholar; his chief work is the unfinished *Einleitung in das Neue Testament*.

Credo. See *Creeds*.

Creeds and Confessions. A creed (*credo*, σύμβολον, *regula fidei*) is a confession of faith for public use or a form of words setting forth with authority certain articles of belief. Creeds do not precede faith, but follow it, expressing the convictions of the believer toward Christ and His Word (Schaff). Confession is, then, the outward manifestation of a deed and gift of God. A confession is subjective inasmuch as faith springs from the heart and objective inasmuch as such a faith can be characterized only by its foundation and content.

Creeds were used as summaries of doctrine, bonds of union, safeguards against error, and means of instruction. Creeds have, to a remarkable degree, incorporated the basic principles of their confessors, and an understanding of creeds is indispensable in the study of church cultures. In the Catholic Church creeds are absolute and infallible in authority. In Protestant Churches creeds (norma normata) are relative to the Bible (norma normans). As instruments, creeds have been nobly used (in proclaiming, teaching, defending, preserving the truth) but also abused (compulsion, persecution, suppression, misdirection).

Creeds arose from the general church (e. g., Apostles' Creed), from councils (Nicene Creed), from synods (Westminster Confession), from committees (Formula of Concord), from an individual (Luther's Catechism) or from an individual acting for a group (Augsburg Confession). They developed from precedents beginning with NT confessions (see Ecumenical Creeds). In their history may be traced the unfolding of Scriptural thought (not a development of Scriptural doctrine, but, as Luther said in speaking of the Apostles' Creed, honey gathered from many flowers) as well as the development of false religious premises. In their stress creeds bear the impress of their age and purpose. Though they may not give the Bible's answer to unforeseen crises at all times, their history is a demonstration of the fact that they contain basic principles from which new formulations continually proceed. Thus ecumenical creeds (one or more) are usually considered basic by Christian churches, and later creeds extend or explain them.

After the ecumenical creeds * (the term indicates co-extension with the visible church, but the three creeds have not been equally received in all Christendom) had been written, few creeds were written until the Reformation era. The creeds of that era incorporated the principles which were developed in the succeeding age. The creeds of the 16th century bore the impress of the profound theological controversies. When such controversies subsided, a climax in creed making had been reached, and a reaction is indicated in the brief, popular, and practical creeds of the succeeding ages.

Many platforms and statements are formulated in modern times, though none has attained paramount importance. One trend is indicated by statements which seek to reunite Christ-

tendom on the simplest formulations. Diametrically opposed to such statements are attempts to develop creeds in greater detail in whole or part. In the late nineteenth and the early twentieth century there was a trend away from creedal subscription in some churches. This trend reversed itself by the middle of the twentieth century and a new interest in creeds and confessions became evident.

Creeds have been classified as Ecumenical, Eastern Catholic, Western Catholic, Provincial Church, Confessional Protestant, Democratic Declarations, American Protestant sects and cults. In this volume they are grouped under the following heads: Ecumenical, Eastern Orthodox, Roman Catholic, Lutheran, Reformed, Anglican, Presbyterian, Democratic Declarations, and American sects and cults (the last to be sought under the separate groups).
EL

See bibliography under groups given above; Philip Schaff, Creeds of Christendom, Harpers, 1899—1905 (3 vols.); Werner Elert, "Die Rezeption der Alten Symbole," Morphologie des Luthertums, Beck, Munich, 1931 (later ed.); H. Heppe, Bekenntnisschriften der altprotestantischen Kirche Deutschlands zur Zeit des Augsburgischen Religionsfriedens, 1855; W. A. Curtis, "Confessions," Hastings Encyclopedia of Religion and Ethics; F. W. Bodemann, Vergleichende Darstellung der Unterscheidungslehren der vier christlichen Hauptkonfessionen, Vandenhoeck u. Ruprecht, Goettingen, 1869; Abraham Kuyper, The Implications of Public Confessions, Zondervan, Grand Rapids, Mich., 1934; T. G. Tappert, "The Symbols of the Church," What Lutherans Are Thinking, Wartburg Press, Columbus, Ohio, 1947.

Creed of Pius IV. See Roman Catholic Confessions, 2.

Crell, Nikolaus (1550—1601). Chancellor to Electors of Saxony, leader of the Crypto-Calvinistic and Philippistic parties; under Christian I succeeded in removing oath of obligation to Formula of Concord; at prince's death swept aside by orthodox reaction, tried by imperial court at Prague, and beheaded 1601. See Crypto-Calvinistic Controversy.

Crell, Paul (1531—1579). Successor of Melanchthon at Wittenberg. With Paul Eber, he rejected the ubiquity of Christ. He, however, taught the real presence.

Cremation. The practice of burning corpses, either in such a way as to preserve the bones and the ashes of the flesh, as was the heathen custom, or of having the bones consumed with the flesh, as is the modern custom. Cremation was practiced extensively among the Greeks and Romans. In India it is in use to a limited extent, but only among the Hindus, since the Parsees and Mohammedans are opposed to the practice. An attempt was made to introduce the custom in England in 1873, but there was so much opposition to it that it made little progress there. About the beginning of the 20th century, however, public sentiment has turned in favor of cremation, and there are crematories in practically every large city of Europe, both in England and on the Continent. The first crematory in the United States was established in Washington, Pa., in 1876, and the first person for whom it was used was the Baron de Palm, in December of that year. The movement has spread more or less rapidly throughout the country, most of the larger cities having one or more crematories, as Detroit, St. Louis, Los Angeles, San Francisco, Baltimore, Pittsburgh, Cincinnati, Buffalo, Chicago, together with many smaller cities. — The attitude of the church with regard to cremation has not, on the whole, been favorable. The Roman Catholic Church has been very strict in its prohibition of cremation. Most of the Protestant churches have taken no definite stand, although sentiment among the more conservative bodies is still very strong against the custom. The chief objections consist in this, that cremation was originally a heathen custom, that it is not in line with Bible custom, especially with the burial of Jesus, and that it savors of the unbelief which denies the resurrection of the body. Two reasons advanced in its favor are that cremation is more sanitary than burial and in many instances is less costly than the modern mode of interment. See also *Burial.*

Cremer, August Hermann (1834 to 1903). Pastor in 1859; professor at Greifswald in 1870; conservative Lutheran theologian and prolific author; his best-known work, *Biblisch-theologisches Woerterbuch der neu-testamentlichen Graezitaet,* has passed through many editions.

Crisis Theology. See *Switzerland, Contemporary Theology in.*

Critical Realism. A term used in epistemology to define a position opposite to that of naive realism. Critical realists agree that there is a difference between an object and the perception of an object. There is, however, wide disagreement as to the nature of the datum, *i. e.,* the third essence between the perceiving subject and the object perceived.

Critical Review. See *Literature, Lutheran,* 7.

Criticism, Higher. See *Higher Criticism.*

Criticism, Textual. See *Textual Criticism.*

Critopulus, Metrophanes. See *Eastern Orthodox Confessions,* B 2.

Croft, William (1678—1727). A pupil of John Blow, whom he succeeded as organist of Westminster Abbey, and composer to the Chapel Royal. Most of his finest works are contained in a collection published in 1724, bearing the title *Musica Sacra;* this collection is said to be the earliest example of ecclesiastical music engraved in score on plates. Croft is a noteworthy composer of English church music.

Cromlech. A large flat stone supported by stone pillars, thus forming a chamber and regarded either as an altar or a tomb. The word is also applied to the circle of monoliths which surrounded the altar or tomb. Many cromlechs have been found in Ireland and are regarded as Druidic altars.

Cromwell, Oliver (1599—1658). Early distinguished himself as an austere Puritan and lover of justice and liberty; joined Parliamentary army and commanded the "Ironsides," all God-fearing men; was one of the judges who condemned Charles I to death; controlled affairs in the Commonwealth 1649; appointed Lord Protector 1653; gave to England a vigorous, but tolerant rule.

Cromwell, Thomas (1485?—1540). Chief adviser (with Thomas Cranmer) of Henry VIII in the matter of his divorce and the organization of a new Church in England; after the Act of Supremacy was passed, he became the king's viceregent in church affairs; as such he carried out the suppression of the monasteries; engineered negotiations with Smalcaldic League, in the course of which he promoted the marriage of Henry to Anne of Cleve, but lost his position and his head when

Henry lost interest in the League and in his new marriage after Cromwell had obligated him to it. Able, cunning, unscrupulous, tyrannical; whatever religious sympathies he had probably inclined toward Protestantism; but all his activity was motivated by servile catering to the king's whims.

Cronenwett, Emanuel. Son of the Rev. George Cronenwett and Magdalene, nee Knapp; born near Ann Arbor, Mich., Feb. 22, 1841; educated for the Lutheran ministry at Capital University, Columbus, Ohio; after his ordination at Woodville, Ohio, served at Carrollton, where he ministered to seven congregations in four counties; then at Waynesburg, Ohio, at Wooster, Ohio, at Delaware, Ohio, and the last fifty-four years of his long ministry at Butler, Pa. The degree of D. D. was conferred on him by Grove City (Pa.) College. A volume of his hymns and poems was published in 1926. He died at Butler, Pa., March 9, 1931. "Lord God, We All to Thee Give Praise" (Tr.); "We Have a Sure Prophetic Word"; "Lord Jesus Christ, Thou Hast Prepared" (Tr.); "Invited, Lord, by Boundless Grace"; "Lord, as Thou Wilt, Deal Thou with Me" (Tr.).

Crosby, Fanny (Frances Jane Van Alstyne, 1820—1915). Blind from infancy, yet well educated, taught at New York Institute for the Blind; wrote more than 3,000 hymns, among which: "Pass Me Not, O Gentle Savior"; "Sweet Hour of Prayer."

Crosier (OF crocier from crosse, shepherd's staff). The shepherd's staff early became the symbol of the pastoral office. The archbishop's staff has a floriated cross at the top. The bishop's staff ends in a crook or a circular head. In the Roman Catholic Church the crosier is carried before archbishops, bishops, abbots, and abbesses as a symbol of office.

Cross. 1. In NT times the cross was an instrument used to torture and kill. It is used figuratively in the NT for suffering (Matt. 10:38; Mark 8:34; 10:21; Luke 9:23; 14:27). By Christ's death on the cross, it became a symbol of that great act of atonement (e.g., 1 Cor. 1:17; Gal. 6:12, 14; Eph. 2:16; Phil. 3:18; Heb. 12:2).

2. Four types of crosses are usually distinguished: crux simplex ("simple cross," one stake without cross-bar); crux decussata (St. Andrew's cross, shaped like the letter "X"); crux com-missa (St. Anthony's cross, shaped like the letter "T"; the crux ansata, "cross with circles at the top" is a variation of the crux commissa); crux immissa (Latin cross, shaped like the symbol "+").

3. In Roman Catholic churches, Good Friday is marked by the "adoration of the cross." The worshipers approach with deep genuflections and kiss the feet of the crucifix, clerics removing their shoes before they perform the ceremony. In old England, custom required "creeping to the cross." Thomas Aquinas taught that the cross is to be adored with latria,* and that is still the common opinion among Romanists.

4. The practice of making the sign of the cross may be traced back at least to the time of Tertullian, who writes of it as being a custom of the Christians everywhere, to remind them of the crucified Savior upon all occasions of their life. At a later day a most extravagant and superstitious use was made of the sign of the cross, supernatural powers being ascribed to it during the Middle Ages. The Lutheran Church condemned the superstitious abuse of the symbolic act, but retained it in its proper use in various parts of public worship, e. g., in Baptism and at the benediction. Luther, in his Small Catechism, recommends the ancient use of the sign of the cross in connection with the morning and evening prayer of the individual believer. The Luth. Large Catechism instructs children to cross themselves with the words "In the name, etc." and at the closing clause of the creed. The cross is also found in Christian art, as the most significant and eloquent symbol of Christianity. In some church bodies it lies flat on the altar or is suspended from the ceiling of the apse. In the Luth. Church a crucifix may stand on a shelf provided for that purpose just above the mensa of the altar. A cross may also be used as an ornament in various other pieces of furniture and on the church buildings.

Crotch, William (1775—1847). An English composer who, in his youth, was one of the most unusual infant prodigies ever known. At the age of four he gave a series of public recitals in London. His chief works were the oratorios Palestine and The Captivity of Judah.

Crowdy, Wm. S. See Church of God and Saints of Christ.

Crowther, Samuel Adjai (ca. 1810 to 1891). First native Bishop of Africa. A one-time slave, Crowther became a student at Bathurst, Sierra Leone; later the first enrolled student at Fourah Bay College; ordained in 1843, consecrated bishop of the Niger Country, 1864, in Canterbury Cathedral; made several journeys into the Niger Territory (1859, 1872). One of his most important mission stations was Abeokuta.

Crucifix. A cross with the figure, or corpus, of the Savior attached to it, usually in an attitude of deepest suffering. This form of the cross is found since the seventh century, but came into general use about the ninth century, when it was carried about in the many processions * which were then in general favor. The Lord may also be represented on a crucifix in royal garb (*Christus Rex, Victor, Triumphator*) or in Eucharistic vestments and a crown (Prophet-King).

Cruciger, Caspar (1504—48). Prof. at Wittenberg, 1528; helped Luther translate the Bible; "the Stenographer of the Reformation"; helped reform Leipzig; leaned towards Melanchthon; wavered on the Interim; published many sermons of Luther and, with Roerer, edited the first volumes of the Wittenberg edition of Luther's works.

Cruciger, Elisabeth (*nee* von Meseritz). Married to Caspar Cruciger in 1524, d. 1535; wrote: "Herr Christ, der einig' Gott's Sohn," rugged, but sublime, in the style of the great Reformer.

Crueger, Johannes (1598—1662). Received thorough musical training at Ratisbon under Paulus Homburger; for forty years organist of the St. Nicolai Church in Berlin; wrote many fine chorals, such as "Jesus, meine Zuversicht," adapted "Nun danket alle Gott," set a large number of Paul Gerhardt's hymns to music, published *Geistliche Lieder und Psalmen, Praxis Pietatis Melica, Geistliche Kirchenmelodien,* and other works.

Crull, August (1845—1923). B. at Rostock, Germany; studied at the *Gymnasium* of his home town and, after his emigration to America, at Concordia College and Concordia Seminary, Saint Louis, Mo., graduating in 1865; assistant pastor in Milwaukee; then director of a high school; pastor of the Lutheran congregation in Grand Rapids, Mich.; called to Concordia College, Fort Wayne, Ind., as professor of the German language and literature; distinguished in hymnology, translations of some of the best German hymns appearing in the *Hymn-Book* of Decorah, in *Hymns of the Lutheran Church,* in *Evangelical Lutheran Hymn-Book,* and in the *Lutheran Hymnal;* published also a collection of lyrics, *Gott segne dich,* followed by *Gott troeste dich;* an able theologian and preacher; edited *Das walte Gott,* a book of daily devotions from C. F. W. Walther's sermons; an excellent teacher, whose *Lehrbuch der deutschen Sprache* and *Gestenlehre* were standards for many years, and his lectures on German literature most instructive and stimulating; lived in Milwaukee after his retirement.

Crusades. A number of military expeditions against heathen, Mohammendans. and heretics under the auspices of the church. As first instituted, they were a part of the thousand years' conflict between Christianity and Islam, and they came at a time when the first violent aggression of the Mohammedan leaders had given way to a rather quiet pursuit of worldly interest. During the latter half of the eleventh century, Gregory VII (see *Popes*) had planned a war against the infidels, but his ideas did not mature on account of his difficulties with the emperor. At the end of the century, however, under Urban II, the time seemed more propitious, and so, in 1095, he preached the crusade against the Mohammedans, his appeal stirring the multitudes assembled for the Council of Clermont to a frenzy of enthusiasm, which was further fanned by the fanaticism of Peter the Hermit (Peter of Amiens). Peasants, lower clergy, runaway monks, women and children joined the movement and gave the advance guard of the crusading army the character of a mob.

When the crusading armies set out, in 1096, they included the brothers Godfrey, Eustace, and Baldwin of Bouillon with the men of Lorraine, Robert of Normandy with the men of northern France, Raymond of Toulouse with the men of the Provence, Bohemund and Tancred with the Normans of Italy. Although the crusading armies suffered somewhat from lack of unanimity, the expedition was on the whole, successful. Nicea, in northwestern Asia Minor, was taken; the Sultan of Iconium was defeated shortly afterwards; Antioch of Syria was captured and held against the enemy in June, 1098; and on July 15, 1099, the city of Jerusalem fell into the hands of the Christian invaders. Godfrey of Bouillon was made Protector of the Sepulcher. He died the next year, and his successors were, in turn, Baldwin I (d. 1118), Baldwin II (d. 1131), and Fulk (d. 1143). Meanwhile the increasing prosperity of the armies of occupation and the merchants who settled in Syrian ports led to a weakening and to internal strife, which had disastrous consequences. The frontier fortress of Edessa was captured by the Mohammedan Emir of Mosul on Christmas Day, 1144, and the spirit of battle and conquest was decidedly quenched.

A second crusade was organized in 1147, the leaders in this instance being Louis VII of France and Conrad III of Germany; but the spirit of enthusiasm, in spite of the entreaties of Bernard of Clairvaux, did not rise to the white heat of the first crusade. The lack of harmony among the leaders also became evident very soon. The German army, while on its march through Asia Minor during the winter of 1147—48, was almost totally destroyed, and the other army shared its fate, partly due to the climate and similar factors. Baldwin III of Jerusalem, in 1153 seized Askalon, thereby bringing Egypt into the conflict. When the great champion Saladin, in 1169, became ruler of that country, he made it the object of his life to drive the Christian power out of Palestine. He succeeded, in 1187, in taking the Holy City, and the Christian power was restricted to Antioch, Tripoli, Tyre, and Margat. The news of the fall of Jerusalem caused the greatest consternation in the West, and a third crusade was immediately organized, with Frederick Barbarossa of Germany, Richard I of England, and Philip Augustus of France as the leaders. But Frederick was accidentally drowned in a small river at Salef in Pisidia, in 1190, and after Acre was taken by Richard and Philip, the two kings quarreled, the result being that Philip retired, Richard retiring soon after (in 1192), having gained only this much, that pilgrims might visit the Holy Sepulcher in small bands and unarmed. The crusade was emphatically a failure.

The real crusading spirit was now dead, and the remaining expeditions were more in the nature of papal efforts to divert the rising secular power into channels where it would not harm the Papacy. The fourth crusade occurred between 1202 and 1204. It had been the chief aim of Pope Innocent III's reign to collect a strong army; but the astute Venetians, under the leadership of their doge, Enrico Dandalo, succeeded in turning the crusade to their own purpose, namely, the conquest of Zara, a town which had been taken from them by the King of Hungary. Later, Constantinople was taken and sacked, the empire being apportioned between Venice and the Christian leaders. Shortly afterward, in 1212, an outburst of fanatical enthusiasm led to the Children's Crusade, which brought destruction upon thousands of children. During the next years sporadic attempts were made to rouse the former spirit; however, nothing came of it but defeat and ignominy. The last crusades took place between 1228 and 1270. In the former year Emperor Frederick II sailed for Syria, and his diplomacy achieved unexpected success. The cities of Jerusalem, Bethlehem, and Nazareth were delivered to the Christians for a period of ten years. The episode closed in 1244, when the Mohammedans stormed Jerusalem. The last efforts of Christian monarchs to gain control of the Holy Land are seen in the expeditions sent out by Louis IX of France, the first one against Cyprus, Egypt, and Syria, 1248 to 1254, and the second against Tunis, in 1270. Shortly afterwards the cities of Antioch, Tripoli, and Acre were retaken by the Mohammedans, and the Christian occupation of the Orient ceased.

Some of the results of the crusades were the increase of papal power, on account of the leading role played by the Popes in inauguarating these expeditions, and the spirit of intolerance which manifested itself. It was this spirit which afterward appeared in the Inquisition and in the crusades against heretics in the West. The Fourth Lateran Council, in 1215, especially charged the bishops with the duty of ferreting out and punishing heretics. In 1229 the Council of Toulouse organized this episcopal inquisition along even stricter lines. In 1232 and the following year the work was entrusted to monks of the Dominican order. The crusades which were subsequently organized were directed against the Utraquists, or Calixtines, and the Taborites in Bohemia, and against the Albigenses, the Catharists, and the Bogomiles in other parts of Europe. The force of the crusader spirit in connection with inquisitorial measures abated only gradually.

R. Roehnert, *Geschichte des ersten Kreuz.*, Innsbruck, 1901; Dana C. Munro, *The Kingdom of the Crusades,*

Appleton-Century, N. Y., 1935; *Cambridge Medieval History* (vol. 5); T. A. Archer, *The Crusade of Richard I*, London, 1912.

Crusius, Christian August (1715 to 1775). Professor at Leipzig; worked in the spirit of Bengel; opponent of Wolff's philosophy; sought to prove that positive revelation harmonizes with reason.

Crusius, Martin (d. 1607). Prof. of Latin and Greek at Tuebingen; sought through David of Ungnad (imperial ambassador) and Stephen Gerlach, to lead Jeremiah II, patriarch of Constantinople, to an acceptance of the Lutheran faith; the effort ended in failure. See *Eastern Orthodox Confessions*, A 5.

Crux ansata. "The cross with a handle," *i. e.*, a cross shaped like our English capital T, with a loop added above the horizontal bar at the point where it makes contact with the perpendicular line. The figure symbolizes life on ancient Egyptian sculptures.

Crypt. Originally a vault beneath the apse and the high altar of a church, containing the bones of the martyr after whom the church was named; at present the burial vault of some parish churches and cathedrals, or the basement.

Cryptist-Kenotist Controversy. 1619 to 1627. Mentzer of Giessen, writing against the Reformed, made the statement that omnipresence was not "simple nearness presence," but always "operative presence," and that consequently omnipresence was not to be predicated of the human nature of Christ in the State of Humiliation. M. Hafenreffer, of Tuebingen, appealed to by Mentzer, disapproved of his position, and soon Tuebingen and Giessen were engaged in a public controversy. The question at issue was on the use made by Christ in His human nature of the divine majesty communicated to it in the personal union. The theologians of Giessen (Mentzer and J. Feuerborn) asserted, as did also the Saxon theologians in their *Decisio*, that the human nature of Christ in the State of Humiliation was not present with all creatures, and they were inclined to exclude it from the work of preservation and government of the universe, Christ having thus emptied Himself (Phil. 2:7) as to His human nature of this much of the divine majesty. Hence they were called Kenotists. (They did not hold with the modern Kenotists that Christ emp-

tied Himself of, renounced, the *possession* of certain divine attributes.) Their position is not tenable (John 5:17). They did not, however, go so far as to teach an absolute renunciation of the use of the divine majesty, but freely admitted this use in the case of the miracles of Christ. The Tuebingen theologians (L. Osiander, M. Nicolai, Th. Thummius) ascribed to the human nature of Christ, in the State of Humiliation, the sitting at the right hand of the Father, Christ having thus made the full use, in this respect, of the divine majesty, though in a hidden way (*krypsis* — hence called Kryptists). Their position is untenable in the light of the Scripture passages which ascribe the sitting at the right hand of God to the State of Exaltation. They did admit, however, that Christ, in His sacerdotal office, in His suffering and dying, renounced the full use of the divine majesty communicated to His human nature. During the turbulent times of the Thirty Years' War the controversy soon subsided.

F. Pieper, "Der Kryptisch-kenotische Streit," in *Christliche Dogmatik*, CPH, 1917 (II: 337—58).

Crypto-Calvinistic Controversy. Called forth by Melanchthon's vacillating position on the true doctrine regarding the Lord's Supper. His disciples endeavored to displace Luther and on the basis of Melanchthon's errors unite with the Calvinists while all the time masquerading as good Lutherans. G. Major, P. Eber, P. Crell, and others at Wittenberg were assisted by Caspar Peucer, Melanchthon's son-in-law and physician of the Elector August. Joachim Westphal, of Hamburg, saw the menace and gave a warning in his *Farrago* of 1552. He was aided by John Timann of Bremen, Schnepf, Gallus Flacius, Brenz, Andreae, Chemnitz, and others. The Elector August was influenced by his advisers to fill all positions with Philippists. He gave legal authority to a collection of Melanchthon's writings, the *Corpus Doctrinae*, or *Misnicum*, or *Philippicum*, in 1560, which contained the altered Augsburg Confession, the altered Apology, the new *Loci* of Melanchthon. All loyal Lutheran pastors refusing subscription were deposed, jailed, or banished (Tettelbach, Herbst, Graf, Schade, *et al.*). In 1573 Duke John William died, and August became ruler of Ducal Saxony and deposed such Lutheran champions as Wigand and Hesshusius and banished more than a hundred true Lutheran pastors. The Philippists in the same year published the anonymous *Exegesis Perspicua* with its Sacramentarian errors. When the Elector saw that he, too, was to be drawn into the Calvinistic camp, he drove the Philippists from power and jailed and banished their leaders. True Lutheranism was restored by the *Brief Confession and Articles,* or *Torgau Confession,* of 1574. The unmasking of the Philippists led to the adoption of the *Maulbronn Formula,* parts of which were embodied in the *Formula of Concord.*

Second stage. After the death of August in 1586, Christian I made Nicholas Crell chancellor in 1589, who put Calvinists into places of power. No religious books could be published without his *placet,* which meant the suppression of Lutheran books; but a new Catechism was Calvinistic, and exorcism was abolished in 1591 on pain of deposition. Theologians like Selnecker and Leyser were persecuted, and many pastors were jailed or banished. On the death of Christian I in 1591, the administrator, Duke Frederick William, suppressed Calvinism and re-established true Lutheranism by the *Visitation Articles* of 1593, written by Aegidius Hunnius, Martin Mirus, and George Mylius.

Cuba, Missions in. Cuba is the largest and most fertile island of the Antilles, directly south of Florida. Area, 44,206 sq. mi.; population, 5,348,000 (1950 est.). It is autonomous. Cuba was discovered by Columbus, Oct. 28, 1492. The large native Indian population was gradually exterminated by the Spaniards, and Negro slavery introduced, which in 1880 was finally abolished. For many years the Roman Catholic Church was intolerant of all other churches, practically prohibiting all missionary efforts. In 1871 Bishop Whipple was instrumental in bringing an American clergyman to Havana. Since then quite a number of churches have been active: American Baptist Home Mission Society, American Friends, Assemblies of God, Berean Mission, Church of God, Methodists, Pilgrim Holiness Church, Presbyterian Church in U. S. A., Protestant Episcopal Church in U. S. A., Seventh-Day Adventist, Southern Baptist Convention, The Lutheran Church — Missouri Synod, and others. Protestant Christian community (1952), approximately 166,000.

The Lutheran Church — Missouri Synod has been working in Havana only since 1946. However, on the Isle of Pines, an island about 30 miles south of the mainland of Cuba, work has been carried on since 1912. At one time The Lutheran Church — Missouri Synod had two Christian day schools on the island, and preaching services were held in many communities. It still owns two churches. Because of repeated hurricanes the island has lost much of its attraction, and the work is now being carried on by one pastor who conducts regular services in Nueva Gerona, Palm Grove, and on the South Coast in Jacksonville. A Christian day school has recently been revived in Jacksonville. HM

Cudworth, Ralph (1617—88). The Christian Plato; b. at Somersetshire, England; professor at Cambridge; rector at Ashwell; prebendary of Gloucester; advanced a Platonizing doctrine of philosophy; author. Died at Cambridge.

Culdees. (Probably an abbreviation and corruption of the Latin word *cultus,* worshiper, or from *gille De,* servants of God, or from *cuildich,* a secluded corner.) This name seems originally to have been given to certain Christians who in the early centuries fled from persecution in those districts of Scotland which were beyond the limits of the Roman Empire. One of their number, Columba, who is said to have been from Ireland and of royal extraction, founded the monastery, or abbey, of Iona, ca. A. D. 563. They also founded other semimonastic houses at Dunkeld, Abernathy, Arbroath, Breehin, St. Andrews, etc., each establishment having twelve monks with a president. In the time of keeping Easter they followed the Eastern and not the Western Church until the Synod of Whitby, A. D. 662, when the Culdees, in essential matters, conformed to the Church of Rome. In 1176 the Culdees placed themselves under the Roman Pontiff. Even after Romanism had become established, Culdeeism, with its simple and powerful Gospel influence, continued to live in the hearts of the people long after its form and public administrations had been buried beneath the finery of triumphant Romanism.

Cult. 1) A form of religious worship or devotion, as distinguished from the teaching or creed of a religious organization, a system of religious rites and observances, such as the cult of Mary

277

or the saints, in the Roman Catholic Church. 2) The term is often used as a synonym of "sect" (always in a derogatory sense). Thus it is applied by various Protestant churches to smaller religious groups, especially those which emphasize a peculiar tenet.

Cultus. See *Worship.*

Cumberland Presbyterian Church. See *Presbyterian Bodies*, 4.

Cummings, Jon. See *Adventist Bodies*, 3.

Cummins, George David. See *Reformed Episcopal Church.*

Cupola. See *Architecture, Ecclesiastical*, 2.

Curaeus, Joachim (1532—73). Studied at Wittenberg; friend of Melanchthon; court physician of Duke George; influential on the Philippist side of the controversy regarding the Lord's Supper.

Curate. (L. *cura*, "care"). The Roman Catholic Church originally used this title for assistants and vicars appointed by the bishop. In the Anglican Church it is used for the lowest ranking clergy.

Cure of Souls *(Seelsorge).* See *Ministerial Office.*

Curfew. The practice of calling people, particularly children and young people, off the streets and other public places at a certain hour of the night, in the interest of decency and the public welfare. Curfew in our country was observed particularly under the New England blue laws.

Curia, Roman. The collective name for the various departments of the papal administration at Rome. They are the Roman Congregations, three tribunals (Penitentiaria, Rota, Segnatura), and five curial offices (Chancery, Dataria, Camera, Secretariate of State, Secretariate of Briefs). Roughly speaking, the Congregations exercise administrative, the tribunals judicial, the offices executive powers. The Penitentiaria has jurisdiction in matters of conscience and grants absolutions, dispensations, releases from vows, and the like. The Rota, formerly the supreme ecclesiastical court, now tries cases that are brought to the judgment of the Popes and decides appeals from lower courts (see *Courts Spiritual*). The Segnatura (six cardinals) acts as a court of appeal from the decisions of the Rota and

judges officials of the Rota. The Chancery drafts and expedites bulls. The Dataria administers the benefices reserved to the Pope. The Camera, formerly the central board of finance, has little to do except to administer the papal property during a vacancy. The Secretariate of State has charge of the political affairs of the Papacy; it deals with secular governments, directs the activities of legates, and grants papal orders and patents of nobility. The cardinal Secretary of State is the Pope's confidential assistant. The Secretariate of Briefs prepares allocutions, encyclicals, and apostolic letters.

Curricula. See *Parish Education,* D 5.

Curricular Syllabus. See *Christian Teaching*, L.

Cursing. See *Blessing and Cursing.*

Cursives. See *Manuscripts of the Bible*, 3.

Cuyler, Theodore Ledyard (1822 to 1909). Presbyterian divine, studied theology at Princeton Seminary. Voluminous religious writer.

Cybele. A Phrygian goddess, symbol of the fruitful earth, whose cult was attended with wild ceremonies, some of which were included in the mystery religions.

Cycles of Time. See *Time.*

Cynicism. The philosophy of the Cynics, so called from Cynosarges, the gymnasium in Athens where Antisthenes, the founder of the school, taught, though the name was soon associated with the unconventional, "doglike" habits of the adherents of the sect. Diogenes, the most familiar representative, proudly called himself ὁ κύων, "the dog." Cynicism is a "caricature of the ascetic and unconventional side of Socrates." It teaches as follows: Virtue is the supreme good. It consists in the renunciation of all pleasures and the suppression of desires. The wise man is sufficient unto himself. Pharisaic pride and a snarling contempt for all the amenities and, sometimes, even the decencies of life were marked characteristics of the Cynics.

Cyprian. Bishop of Carthage, b. ca. 200, became a teacher of rhetoric; converted to Christianity ca. 245; raised by popular acclamation to the bishopric of Carthage (248); fled during the Decian persecution to escape the fury of the mob (*"Cyprianum ad leones!"*); condemned and beheaded under the Emperor Valerian (258). Cyprian is the great High Churchman of the ante-Nicene period. His views on the clergy may be summarized as follows: the bishops are the successors of the Apostles and, like them, specially endowed with the Holy Spirit. They rule the *laici*, or the *plebs*, by divine authority. The episcopate is a unity, each individual bishop representing in himself the whole office. From the unity of the episcopate springs the unity of the church, by which Cyprian means an empirical, outward organization. Outside of this there is no salvation. Cyprian's conception of the church makes every schismatic also a heretic. Regarding the Papacy, Cyprian recognized the primacy of Peter. not, however, of authority and jurisdiction, but merely as representing the unity of the church. The Roman bishops are indeed the successors of Peter, but Cyprian addresses the Pope as "brother" and "colleague."

See bibliography under *Patristics;* J. Fichter (S. J.), *Saint Cecil Cyprian,* Herder, St. Louis, 1942.

Cyprian, Ernst Salomon (1673 to 1745). Director and professor of theology at the Casimir College at Coburg and member of the consistory; staunchly opposed and frustrated the plan of uniting the Lutheran and Reformed churches advocated by Friedrich Wilhelm I of Prussia. Wrote the *History of the Augsburg Confession* and other works.

Cyrenaics. Followers of Aristippus (ca. 435—ca. 356 B. C.), who took an opposite view to that of the Cynics,* holding that man can rise above human appetites only by tasting all possible sensual pleasures (hedonism).

Cyril of Alexandria. Prominent theologian of early Eastern Church b. last half of fourth century, d. at Alexandria, 444; successor of his uncle Theophilus as archbishop of Alexandria, 403, at the time when this see was at the height of its power and influence; strong opponent of Nestorius, whose deposition he brought about; prolific writer in dogmatic and exegetical field, especially on the Trinity and on the Christological controversies; his exegesis in the books *On Worship in Spirit and Truth* and in *Elegant Expositions* is strongly allegorical; the final formulation of the doctrine of the Trinity was his work. See *Nestorianism.*

Cyril of Jerusalem (315—368). Prominent theologian of the early Church; bishop of Jerusalem, but deposed and even exiled on two occasions; famous for his twenty-three catechetical lectures on Christian faith and practice. See also *Catechetics.*

Cyrillus and Methodius. The apostles to the Slavs in the ninth century, the former dying in 869, the latter in 885; sons of Drungarius, a military officer at Thessalonica. Cyril began his public life as secretary to the Patriarch of Constantinople, Methodius as abbot of the famous monastery of Polychron. An independent Slavonic principality under Rotislav having been established, Christian teachers were sought at Constantinople, and the task of evangelizing the Slavs was entrusted to Cyril and Methodius. Cyril is said to have invented the Slavonic script, which was first used in Bulgaria. Both brothers also translated large parts of the Bible for the use of the people among whom they labored. Having established their work, they put it under the auspices of the Roman Pontiff. Cyril died shortly afterward. Methodius carried on the work alone, chiefly in Pannonia, becoming archbishop of Sirmium a few years later. There was some trouble with the bishop of Salzburg, who contested the right of Methodius, and the latter was kept a prisoner in Germany for over two years. Returning to Moravia, Methodius labored for a number of years with good success, his work on the Slavonic liturgy being especially notable in this period.

Czecho-Slovakia. The religious history of this country, properly speaking, begins with Cyrillus * and Methodius.* The entire country was under the jurisdiction of the Roman Pope, but in the fifteenth century, after the time of Hus,* the Bohemian Brethren * gained almost the entire western part of the present republic for their views. Luther was in friendly communication with them for a while, but their tendency to remain aloof caused him to withdraw from them in 1524. There were subsequent periods when the Lutheran element became strong in Bohemian Protestantism. The battle of Weissenberg, at the beginning of the Thirty Years' War, destroyed Protestantism in Bohemia and Moravia for more than 150 years. At present there are only a few scanty remnants of the sixteenth century Protestants.

Meanwhile the Roman Catholic

Church regained its ancient strength throughout the present territory of Czecho-Slovakia. As a result of World War I, however, with its arousing of the ancient nationalistic feeling, approximately thirty per cent of the clergy of the country decided to withdraw from the jurisdiction of the Pope and to found a national church. This national church permitted its clergy to marry, stipulated that all services were to be conducted in the national tongue, rejected transubstantiation, and encouraged Bible reading. The Roman Catholic Church, however, held more than half of the population. See *Bohemia, Lutheran Theology in;* items starred above.

D

Dach, Simon (1605—59). Private tutor at Koenigsberg, assistant, conrector, professor, dean, and rector of the university; invalid; leader in Poetical Union of Koenigsberg; hymns, personal and subjective, profound and elegant; wrote: "Ich bin ja, Herr, in deiner Macht"; "O wie selig seid ihr doch, ihr Frommen."

Daechsel, August (1818—1901). Lutheran divine in Steinkirche, Silesia. Wrote a commentary on the whole Bible and Aprocrypha. Bible text written in heavy type, followed by extensive exegetical material compiled from well-known exegetes (7 vols.). Has some chiliastic interpretations in the prophetic sections.

Dahl, Theodor H. B. Apr. 2, 1845, at Baastad, Norway; came to America in 1865; educ. Christiana, Norway; studied theology at Paxton, Ill. (now Augustana Coll.) and theol. sem. at Rock Island, Ill. (D. D. 1905); held pastorates at: Litchfield, Minn., 1868—73; Green Bay, Wis., 1873—81; Stoughton, Wis., 1881—1902; sec., Norw. Danish Conf., 1876—81; pres., 1881—86; vice-pres., United Norw. Luth. Ch., 1902, pres., 1902—17; chrm., Bd. of Regents, Sem., United Norw. Luth. Ch., St. Anthony Park, Minn.; chrm., Bd. of Regents, St. Olaf Coll., Northfield, Minn. Author: *Saloonforretningern* and *Fred og Strid.* D. Jan. 18, 1923.

Dahle, Lars H. (1843—1925). Norwegian Luth. missionary at Antananarivo, Madagascar, where he laid the foundation for training native workers and assisted in the translation of the Bible; after returning home he was leader of the mission society at Stavanger (1889—1920); made noteworthy studies in the language and religion of Madagascar.

D'Ailly, Pierre (1350—1420). Professor and chancellor of University of Paris, bishop, cardinal; prime mover in the "Reformation in the head and members," setting the Bible above the canon law and the Ecumenical Council above the Pope. See *Constance, Council of.*

Dake, Vivian A. See *Evangelistic Associations,* 13.

Dale, Robert William (1829—95). English Congregationalist; noted for his sermons and political and educational activity; his best-known work, *The Atonement,* weakens the doctrine of suffering for guilt.

D'Allemand, Louis (1380—1450). French Roman Catholic cardinal; prominent member of the councils of Constance and of Basel, at the latter of which he opposed Pope Eugenius IV; driven from office, but later restored to dignity and honor; beatified in 1527.

Dallmann, Charles Fred William. B. Dec. 22, 1862, at Neu-Damerow, Pomerania; graduated at Concordia Seminary (St. Louis) 1886; held pastorates at Marshfield, Mo., Baltimore, New York City, Milwaukee; president of English Synod of Missouri 1899—1901; vice-president 1901—09; vice-president of Missouri Synod 1926—30; D. D. (St. Louis); editor of *Lutheran Witness* 1891—95; wrote many biographies of famous characters in church history, such as *John Hus, John Wiclif, William Tyndale, Martin Luther, Catherine Luther;* also *The Christian, The Ten Commandments, The Lord's Prayer, The Battle of the Bible with the "Bibles," The Titles of the Christian in the New Testament, My Life,* lives of *John, Peter, Paul,* etc.; contributor to *Concordia Theological Monthly, American Lutheran,* and other periodicals; retired to Oak Park, Ill.; d. Feb. 2, 1952.

Dalmata, Antonius. Little known of his life; translated the New Testament into Wendish with Primus Truber and Stephen Consul (1553).

Dalmatic. See *Vestments, Clerical.*

Dalmatin, George. Lutheran pastor in Oberkrain in the second half of 16th century; translated the Bible into Slavic (1584).

Damiani, Peter (1007—72). Known for his monkish holiness (self-flagellation); at one time cardinal-bishop of Ostia, he zealously supported the reform party of Cluny (his *Liber Gomorrhianus* describing the indescribable immoralities of the clergy) and the policies of Hildebrand.

Damnation. See *Hereafter*, B.

Dan, Amos. B. Feb. 8, 1848, at Odense, Denmark; sent by Chrischona Missionary Society to the Gallas, East Africa (1869); to the Jews of Khartoum, Egypt, and Palestine (1870—71); came to America (1871); pastor at Racine, Wis. (1871—80); Salinas and San Francisco, Cal. (1880—84); Minneapolis, Minn. (1884—93); Boston, Mass. (1900 to 1902); Chicago, Ill. (1902—26); Clinton, Ia. (1926—31); one of the founders of the Danish Evangelical Lutheran Church in America; president thereof (1872—75; 1912—14); founder and editor of *Kirkelig Samler;* editor of *Dansk Børneblad;* author of novels, poetry, and hymns; knighted by Christian X of Denmark; d. May 6, 1931.

Dance. 1. In the widest use of the word, a springing or leaping in evidence of great emotion, as of joy or elation, or symbolic of stern determination, as in certain war-dances. It is in this sense that the word is used in the Bible of women and children who leaped in joyful steps (Judg. 11:34; 21:21,23; Job 21:11; Matt. 11:17). It is in this meaning, also, that we are told that there is a time to dance (Eccl. 3:4), that is, a time for showing one's joy in measured steps expressive of the inward elation. The Bible also speaks of a formal dancing before the Lord, in token of religious fervor and ecstasy, the rhythmic movements being made in honor of Jehovah (2 Sam. 6:14).

2. The dance plays a prominent part in primitive cultures, where it is often associated with religion or romantic love. The ancient Greeks developed the artistic qualities of the dance, and festive choruses sought to express the beauty of harmony, often, as in their tragedies and comedies, in correlation with poetry and music.

3. The dance in itself is not evil. Thus no fault is found with the Maypole dance, the old-fashioned square dances, and others of a similar nature.

When, however, it becomes a means of expressing lust, it is sinful. That the dance easily becomes such a vehicle is evident from the fact that it became an advertisement of prostitution in the Roman world and also in 18th-century France. The evils of the dance in American society have frequently been pointed out.

4. Since 1918 renewed emphasis has been placed on the purification of the dance and on its recreational and artistic values. The damages to morals and health by much modern social dancing are, however, still generally conceded, and the dance continues to be opposed (or viewed with watchful suspicion) by many religious groups.

5. Luther did not consider dancing a sin or censurable as long as it was chaste, moral, and honorable (St. L. Ed. I:1682; III:379 f.; VII:1030; XI:467 ff.). He, however, pointed out that when dancing goes beyond the limits of decency, it is a temptation to fornication and in itself reveals such sin (III:380, 1310).

6. It is not the public or private nature of the dance which is opposed, but the essential feature of the act, the embrace, which forms the basis of many modern dances. The Bible censures sinful embraces with the words: "Why wilt thou, my son, be ravished with a strange woman, and embrace the bosom of a stranger?" (Prov. 5:20). Whenever a man places his arm about a woman in a close embrace, whether this be done upon the occasion of auto rides, on boat trips, in parks, in the parlor, in public or in private, he is indulging in a familiarity which is not permissible outside legitimate boundaries (Prov. 5: 18—21. See *Marriage*). To this must be added the fact that dances often add to the embrace gestures and acts of indecency which tend to inflame the passions. Moreover, the music which has been invented to accompany dances is often of a nature to stir up the passions. Those who indulge in indecent dances give offense to observers and to their partners in the dance, who are ever in danger of becoming heated in their lusts and to sin in desires and thoughts, if not in words and deeds. The dance of the daughter of Herodias has often been regarded a sensuous dance (Mark 6:22). Such warnings of Scripture as 2 Tim. 2:22; Matt. 5:28; Jer. 17:9; Matt. 15:19; 2 Sam. 11:2-4; James 1:14,15; 1 Cor. 10:12 apply.

Th. Graebner, *The Borderland of Right and Wrong,* pp. 99—117; C. F. W.

Walther, *Tanz und Theaterbesuch*, Luth. Conc. Verlag, St. Louis, 1885; J. T. Crane, *An Essay on Dancing*, Carlton & Phillips, N. Y., 1853; L. Harold DeWolf, "Dancing," in: Vergilius Ferm, *An Encyclopedia of Religion;* Guy A. Lamphear, *The Modern Dance*, Glad Tidings Pub. Co., ca. 1922; C. F. Hafermann, "Evils of Dancing," *Lutheran Standard*, Sept. 28, 1940; numerous tracts published by CPH (Clara J. Jones, Dallmann, and others).

Daniel, Herman Adelbert (1812 to 1871). Most of his life professor and inspector at Halle; author of geographical textbooks; prominent hymnologist and liturgiologist; his chief works in this field: *Thesaurus Hymnologicus*, in five volumes, and *Codex Liturgicus*, offering texts with introductions chiefly from Greek Catholic, Roman Catholic, Lutheran, and Reformed sources.

Danish Free Church. See *Saxony, Lutheran Free Church of.*

Danish-Halle Mission. The first of all Lutheran and Protestant foreign missions, initiated by King Frederick IV of Denmark, advised by Dr. Luetkens, the court preacher, in 1705, in co-operation with August Hermann Francke of Halle, sent out to India Bartholomaeus Ziegenbalg and Heinrich Pluetschau. They landed at Tranquebar, in India, in July, 1706, the first Protestant missionaries to touch the soil of India. The enterprise was fostered by the English Society for the Propagation of Christian Knowledge (founded 1698). After the death of Christian Friedrich Schwartz, possibly the most outstanding missionary of this society (1726—1798), fruits of whose work can still be seen in Tanjoric and Trichinopoly, interest began to decline, and the work in India suffered. In 1847 the buildings and the remaining interests were handed over to the Leipzig Missionary Society.

Danish Lutherans in America. 1. The first Lutheran minister in America was the Danish Pastor Rasmus Jensen, who came to Nova Dania, Hudson Bay (1619), and died there (Feb. 20, 1620). In the course of the following centuries a number of Danish ministers labored in Norwegian, German, and English congregations in America (Peter Brunnholtz, J. C. Leps, H. Hayunga, A. R. Rude, E. Belfour). J. M. Magens, a layman, came to America (1754) and translated Danish sermons on the Augsburg Confession into English. The early Danes were found chiefly among the Dutch in New Netherlands and the

Lutherans and Moravians in Pennsylvania.

2. The chief wave of Danish immigration started about the middle of the 19th century (by the middle of the 20th, there were approximately one-half million Danes in the U. S.). Many of these immigrants were Mormons, others joined Adventist, Baptist, and Methodist churches. The Lutherans joined Norwegian or Swedish churches. The greater number of the immigrants remained unchurched.

3. In 1843 Claus L. Clausen, a Danish student, came to America, was ordained by the Buffalo Synod, worked especially among Norwegian Lutherans, but also organized several Danish congregations. Through his influence *The Society for the Promotion of the Gospel Among the Danes in North America* was organized in Denmark (1869). This organization sent A. C. L. Grove-Rasmussen, A. S. Nielsen, and R. Andersen to America (1871). Clausen had organized the *Norwegian-Danish Conference* (1870) which he hoped the Danes would join. Grove-Rasmussen, who was influenced by Grundtvig (the Apostles' Creed and not the Bible is the formal principle), succeeded in keeping his Danes separate. This group organized *The Missionary Association of the Church* (1872; name later changed to *The Danish Ev. Luth. Church in America*). The official publication of this group is the *Kirkelig Samler*. Later some pastors in this group no longer agreed with its formal principle. A controversy led to the exclusion of 22 pastors from the *Danish Ev. Luth. Church in America*. These 22 pastors organized *The Danish Ev. Luth. Church in North America* (1894). Danes who had affiliated with the Norwegian-Danish Conference organized the Danish Ev. Luth. Association of America (1884). This group united with *The Danish Ev. Luth. Church in North America* in 1896 to form *The United Evangelical Luth. Church in America*. The offices of this synod are located at Blair, Nebr. The official publications are *Luthersk Ugeblad* and *Ansgar Lutheran*.

4. The following have served as presidents of the United Ev. Luth. Church since 1896: G. B. Christiansen (1896—1922), A. N. Andreasen (1922 to 1925), N. C. Carlsen (1925—50), Hans C. Jersild (1950—). Statistics (1951): 193 pastors, 179 congregations, 49,241 baptized members.

5. The following have served as presidents of the Danish Ev. Luth. Church: A. Dan (1872—74), I. A. Hei-

berg (1874—79), A. S. Nielsen (1879 to 1883), T. Helveg (1883—85), A. S. Nielsen (1885—87), J. Pedersen (1887 to 1888), A. L. J. Soholm (1888—91), A. S. Nielsen (1891—93), O. L. Kirkeberg (1893), A. S. Nielsen (1893—94), K. C. Bodholdt (1894—95), P. Kjolhede (1895 to 1903), K. C. Bodholdt (1903—11), N. P. Gravengaard (1911—18), K. C. Bodholdt (1918—20), N. P. Gravengaard (1920—22), S. D. Rodholm (1922—26), H. Jorgensen (1926—36), A. Jensen (1936—). Statistics (1951): 78 pastors, 82 congregations, 19,912 baptized members.
Neve-Allback, *History of the Lutheran Church in America*, Luth. Lit. Bd., Burlington, Ia., 1934 (pp. 325—329; contains bibliography); P. S. Vig, *Dansk Luthersk Mission in America*, Danish Luth. Pub. House, Blair, Nebr., 1917; *Dansk Almanak*, published regularly by Danish Luth. Pub. House; E. Mortensen, *Stories from Our Church*, Luth. Pub. House, Blair, Nebr.

Dankbrand. Chaplain of King Olaf Trygvason, missionary to Iceland 997 to 999; his harsh measures caused resentment, but a compromise made A. D. 1000 resulted in the baptism of the islanders, with certain reservations, which were dropped in 1016 in favor of a full acceptance of Christianity.

Dannhauer, Johann Konrad (1603 to 1666). Precocious, receiving his bachelor's degree at Strassburg in 1619 and his master's in 1621; professor at Strassburg; wrote *Hodosophia Christiana* (doctrinal theology) and *Liber conscientiae* (Christian ethics), also other notable books; pastor at Muenster after 1658, where he issued his sermon collections, especially his *Katechismus-Milch* (explanation of the Catechism).

Dante Alighieri. B. 1265 in Florence; banished in consequence of his antipapal politics; d. in Ravenna, 1321. He was Italy's greatest poet, "the theologian among the poets, the poet of theology" — medieval theology. In the *Divina Comedia* he demands thorough reformation, lashing the moral degeneracy of the time and the corruption of the church and the papal see. In his *De Monarchia* he stresses the co-ordination of Empire and Church; pope and emperor are both vicars of God, thereby denying the Roman claim, promulgated in its crassest form by his contemporary Pope Boniface VIII in the bull *Unam Sanctam*, that the state government receives its power from the church and must therefore be subject to the pope.

Danzig. Free State from 1919 to World War II. Gospel preached there 997 by Adalbert of Prag, the apostle of the Prussians; the Reformation gained entrance (1529) but was checked by the rulers of Poland; annexed to Prussia (1793); population almost equally divided between Evangelicals and Catholics.

Darby, John Nelson. See *Brethren, Plymouth.*

Darkness. See *Light and Darkness.*

Darwin, Charles Robert. English naturalist. B. 1809 at Shrewsbury; d. 1882 at Kent. As young man believer in Christianity, later agnostic. Epochmaking work, *The Origin of Species*, 1859, caused complete revolution and new methods and aims in natural history. Substituted mechanical (natural) for Biblical (supernatural) explanation of origin of varied forms of life. Every species produces many young that do not grow to maturity, those surviving are preserved because of individual differences, which protect them and give them greater ability to obtain food and propagate their kind ("struggle for existence"). The others perish ("survival of the fittest"). These favorable variations are transmitted and intensified from generation to generation by this natural selective process until maximum utility results ("natural selection"). Extended hypothesis also to man in *The Descent of Man*, 1871. Contradicting revelation, his hypothesis caused a storm of protest. Cf. *Evolution.*

Dass, Peter. See *Norway, Lutheranism in*, 7.

D'Astruc, Jean. See *Higher Criticism*, 11.

Dataria. See *Curia.*

Dau, William Herman Theodore. B. Feb. 8, 1864, at Lauenburg, Pomerania; graduated at St. Louis, 1886; pastor at Memphis, Tenn.; professor at Concordia College, Conover, N. C., 1892 to 1899; professor at Concordia Seminary, St. Louis, Mo., 1905—26; vice-president of Central District 1903—05; editor of *Lutheran Witness;* English Department of *Homiletic Magazine;* managing editor of *Theological Quarterly* and *Theological Monthly;* consulting editor of *Alma Mater;* edited: *Four Hundred Years; Ebenezer;* wrote: *At the Tribunal of Caesar; The Great Renunciation; He Loved Me and Gave Himself for Me; The Leipzig Debate in 1519; Luther Examined and Re-exam-*

ined; joint author, with Dr. A. L. Graebner and Dr. L. Wessel, of *Proof-texts of the Catechism, with a Practical Commentary;* joint editor with F. Bente of *Concordia Triglotta;* president of Valparaiso 1926—29; then pres. em.; D. D. from Seminary in Adelaide, Australia, 1923, Concordia Seminary, St. Louis, in 1939; Litt. D. from Valparaiso, 1939. Died Apr. 21, 1944.

D'Aubigne, Merle. See *Merle d'Aubigne.*

Daub, Karl (1752—1836). German Protestant theologian; sought to establish a philosophical reconstruction of orthodoxy; influenced by Kant, Fichte, Schelling, and Hegel.

Davenport Theses. Early in the history of the Iowa Synod controversies arose between it and the Missouri Synod concerning certain points of doctrine and positions to be taken in matters pertaining to the Lutheran Confessions. In 1873 the Northern Iowa Conference requested the Iowa Synod, in session at Davenport, Ia., to state its position toward the Missouri Synod, especially for the sake of those pastors who had recently joined and hence were not acquainted with the course of the controversy. As a result the Iowa Synod adopted 21 theses, which sought to show the status of the controversies at the time by indicating on what points the two synods had approached agreement and on what points there was still divergence. The following doctrines are treated in the theses: *Church and Ministry* (1-5); *Confessions* (6-7); *Antichrist* (8-10); *Chiliasm* (11-15); *Open Questions* (16-21). See also *Iowa Synod; Madison Theses; Toledo Theses.* The theses are printed in full in J. Deindoerfer, *Geschichte der Ev. Luth. Synode von Iowa u. anderen Staaten,* Wartburg, Chicago, 1897; G. J. Fritschel, *Quellen u. Dokumente zur Geschichte und Lehrstellung der Iowa Synode,* Wartburg, Chicago, 1916. See also J. L. Neve, *A Brief History of the Lutheran Church in America,* German Lit. Bd., Burlington, Ia. (1916 ed.) and contemporary periodicals.

David of Dinant (12th—13th century). Belgian scholastic philosopher, who held a materialistic pantheism; wrote *Quaternudi* (condemned at Paris, 1210).

Davidson, Andrew Bruce (1831 to 1902). Scottish divine; professor of oriental languages at New College; member of OT Revision Committee; his commentary on Job was regarded by some as the first scientific commentary on the OT in the English language; wrote other exegetical works and *Introductory Hebrew Grammar.*

Davidson, Samuel (1807—98). English Congregationalist; professor of Biblical literature in Lancashire Independent College, Manchester, 1842 to 1857; later member of the OT Revision Committee; rationalistic in theology; among his books: *An Introduction to the Old Testament, An Introduction to the New Testament, The Canon of the Bible.*

Davies, Samuel. B. 1724, of Welsh parents, in New Castle County, Del.; d. 1761. In 1746 licensed to preach by Presbytery of New Castle. "A preacher of power and genius." A sermon, he said, should be the product of at least four days' hard labor.

Day, David Alexander (1851—97). Pioneer Lutheran missionary in Liberia, where he served for over twenty-three years. The Day Missions Library at Yale University commemorates his work.

Day of Atonement. See *Judaism.*

Dayman, Edward Arthur (1807—90). Educated at Oxford; held a number of positions in the Established Church; worked in Latin hymnology, contributed hymns, among which: "Almighty Father, Heav'n and Earth."

Deaconess Homes. See *Deaconesses.*

Deaconesses. 1. Female servants in the church, unmarried or widows; auxiliary office to the ministry. "Phoebe a deaconess" (Rom. 16:1, *Revised Standard Version*).

2. Their functions in the early church were to instruct female catechumens, to assist at the baptism of women, to care for sick or impoverished women, to minister to women martyrs and confessors in prison, and to act as ushers for women in churches.

3. The 4th century was the Golden Age of the female diaconate. Forty deaconesses served in the congregation of Chrysostom, Constantinople. Noted deaconesses: Olympias and Macrina.

4. Then came the deterioration of the diaconate — looked upon as a meritorious work. The escape sought from a corrupt world resulted in monastic life. By the 12th century the deaconesses had nearly disappeared in the church.

5. Prominent in the restoration of the female diaconate was Th. Fliedner,

Kaiserswerth, Germany (1836), who trained 450 deaconesses. Loehe and others established motherhouses. The diaconate was introduced in England, Denmark, Finland, Norway, Sweden. Noted European motherhouses were established in Kaiserswerth, Bielefeld, Neuendettelsau.

6. Wm. Passavant introduced the diaconate in America. The first Lutheran hospital in America was erected in Pittsburgh (1849). Upon request of Passavant, Fliedner brought over four deaconesses from Germany, who were to constitute the nursing personnel in the "Pittsburgh Infirmary." One of these was Elizabeth Hess, later mother of Pastor Ph. Wambsganss.

7. Another half century elapsed before the Deaconess Movement became firmly established in America. The United Lutheran Church founded a motherhouse in Philadelphia (1884); another in Baltimore (1895); the Augustana Synod in Omaha (1887); the American Lutheran Church in Milwaukee (1893). Other Lutheran deaconess homes are located in Chicago, Minneapolis, Brooklyn, Brush, Colo., and Axtell, Nebr.

8. *Synodical Conference.* Pastor F. W. Herzberger was instrumental in founding the diaconate within the Synodical Conference. He was ably supported by Pastor Ph. Wambsganss, president of the then *Wohltaetigkeitskonferenz.*

9. The Lutheran Deaconess Association within the Synodical Conference was organized Aug. 14, 1919, at Fort Wayne, Ind. Deaconess training was given in connection with the Lutheran Hospital, Fort Wayne. First graduate: Ina Kempff. First deaconess sent to a foreign field: Louise Rathke (1925).

10. Rev. Ph. Wambsganss served as president of the Deaconess Association, 1919—33; Rev. Walter Klausing, 1933—. Superintendents: Rev. Bruno Poch, 1923 to 1932; Rev. H. B. Kohlmeier, 1933—41; Rev. A. Krentz, 1941—. The number of deaconesses trained (1919—48): 141.

11. Deaconess schools: Fort Wayne, 1919—43; Beaver Dam Hospital, Beaver Dam, Wis., 1922—34; Bethesda Lutheran Home, Watertown, Wis., 1925—35; Lutheran Hospital, Hot Springs, S. D., 1924 to 1927(?). In 1935 the Fort Wayne Training School separated from the Lutheran Hospital. The objective at that time was to give an intensive religious education of one year to such students as had previously specialized in nursing, education, or social work.

12. In 1941 the deaconess course was lengthened to two years, which included six months of practical training; courses in sociology and psychology at Indiana University Extension, Fort Wayne.

13. In 1943 the Lutheran Deaconess Association sold its deaconess home on hospital grounds to the Lutheran Hospital Association. Deaconess education was transferred to Valparaiso University, Valparaiso, Ind. In 1946 the deaconess course was lengthened to a four-year college course with a major in Religion leading to a Bachelor's degree. Recent developments include the modernization of the deaconess uniform and full salary for deaconesses (instead of an allowance) with participation in Synod's pension plan. AFK

C. R. Barnes & M. G. Kyle, *The People's Bible Encyclopedia,* People's Pub. Soc., Chicago, Ill., 1924; J. D. Davis, *A Dictionary of the Bible* (4th revised ed.), George H. Doran, New York, N. Y., 1927; Catherine Dentzer, *Deaconess Work,* Luth. Deaconess Motherhouse, Milwaukee, Wis.; F. U. Gift, *The Ministry of Love,* United Luth. Pub. House, Philadelphia, Pa., 1928; H. B. Kohlmeier, *History of the Luth. Deaconess Association* (mimeographed), Fort Wayne, Ind., 1944; P. E. Kretzmann, *A Handbook for the Training of Lutheran Deaconesses,* Young Women's Lutheran Deaconess Assn., St. Louis, Mo.; C. E. Lundquist, *The Statistical Yearbook for the Luth. Churches in America* (mimeographed), New York, N. Y., 1947; Julie Mergner and Mrs. Adolph Spaeth, *The Deaconess and Her Work,* General Council Pub. House, Philadelphia, Pa., 1915; F. Meyer, *Von den Diakonissen und ihrem Beruf,* Beck'sche Verlagsbuchhandlung, Muenchen, 1892; J. F. Ohl, *The Inner Mission,* General Council Pub. House, Philadelphia, Pa., 1913; N. N. Rønning & W. H. Lien, *The Lutheran Deaconess Home and Hospital, Fiftieth Anniversary,* Minneapolis, Minn., 1939; Abdel R. Wentz, *Fliedner the Faithful,* The Bd. of Pub. of the United Luth. Church in America, Philadelphia, Pa., 1936.

Deacons. Officers of the church, particularly of the local congregation, who, according to Apostolic example and precept (Acts 6; 1 Tim. 3:8-13), have charge of certain administrative work, notably that of assisting the servants of the Word in the government of the church, in taking care of its charitable endeavors, and otherwise occupying a leading position of service in the congregation.

Dead, Prayers for. Prayers for the dead can be traced back to early Christian times (Tertullian, *De cor. milit.*, 3; Cyril, *Cat. myst.*, V). Augustine held that the prayers could only help those who had led pious lives before death (*De verbis apostoli serm.*, 32). Prayers for the dead were closely associated with the celebration of the Lord's Supper (*Apost. Const.*, VIII:12). The Roman Catholic doctrine "regarding prayers for the dead is bound up inseparably with the doctrine of purgatory and the more general doctrine of the communion of saints" (*Cat. Encyc.* Cf. C. of Trent, XXV). The Roman Catholic *locus classicus* is 2 Mac. 12:40-46 (cf. 1 Cor. 15:29).

Luther's position is best summarized in the words: "Nothing has been commanded or enjoined upon us concerning the dead. Therefore all this may be safely omitted, even if it were no error and idolatry" (*Smal. Art.*, II:13). He points out that we have no command to pray for the dead, inasmuch as those who are in heaven do not need the prayers, and those who are in hell cannot be helped thereby (St. L. Ed., XI:1206). He admonished Christians of his day (who were accustomed to pray for the dead) to make their prayers conditional (Erlang. ed. XIII:13; XV: 350, 466; XXX:370). The Apology states: "We know that the ancients speak of prayers for the dead, which we do not prohibit" (XXIV:96). Luther and the confessions vigorously oppose purgatory and attempts to gain forgiveness of sins for the dead, especially through masses, almsgiving, etc. (*ex opere operato*). Chemnitz (*Examen*, III) regarded ancient prayers for the dead as exhortations and consolations for the living. The majority of Lutheran theologians regarded prayers for the dead as useless or unpermitted; others emphasized the mystical union of believers and regarded prayers for the dead (though not for their salvation) permissible. Prayers for the salvation of the dead are useless, since it is appointed unto man once to die and after that the judgment (Heb. 9:27; Luke 16:26 ff.).

Smalcald Articles, Part II, Art. II; *Apology*, XXIV (XII); commentaries on 1 Cor. 15:29; L. Dahle, *Das Leben nach dem Tode*, Richter, Leipzig, 1895; J. Stirm, "Darf man fuer die Verstorbenen beten?" *J. D. T.*, VI:278 ff. EL

Death, Temporal. The cessation of natural life; in man, due to the separation of the soul from the body. 2 Pet. 1:

13, 14. It is the effect of sin, Rom. 5:12; and the instrument for bringing it into the world was Satan, Heb. 2:14; John 8:44. Death is but once, Heb. 9:27, and is certain, Job 14:1, 2. The fear of death is a source of anxiety and alarm to a guilty conscience; but Jesus has taken away the sting of death, 1 Cor. 15:56, and has given to His own the assurance that death leads to a state of endless felicity, 2 Cor. 5:8. — That man was not destined for a life which would end in death is clear from the penalty which was to follow transgression. Gen. 2:17. This implies the promise of deathless and incorruptible life so long as the covenant should stand. Man's was the possibility of not sinning, hence of not dying, the *posse non peccare*, which, according to theological statement, based on the analogy of the angels confirmed in holiness, might have led to the *non posse peccare*, the inability to fall into sin, hence also the absolute state of deathlessness. In terms as clear as those of the original covenant of life is the entrance of death and its dominion over man ascribed to the transgression of the Law. Rom. 5:12. As distinguished from spiritual death, the separation of the soul from God, it is called temporal, as superadding exclusion from the things of earth and time to the loss of the life in God. As such it is distinguished from eternal death, or the second death, the complete and final issue of the death process, when the unjust, impenitent, and unbelieving shall awake to the resurrection of damnation. On the other hand, the Scriptures speak of those who have acquired the new spiritual life so that death has no claim on them, but must surrender them on the Last Day to a life glorious and incorruptible.

Death and Funeral Practices. See *Burial*.

DeBres, Guido. See *Reformed Confessions*, C 1.

Decalog. The fundamental Moral Law in the form of "Ten Words" (LXX: *deka logoi*) or sentences. When God created man, He wrote the Law into his heart. Though this Moral Law in man's heart did not disappear entirely with the Fall, it has, nevertheless, been dulled by constant and willful abuse (according to one interpretation of Rom. 2:14, 15. Cf. Gen. 1:27; Eph. 4:24; Lev. 19:2; Gen. 2:25).

In order to make Israel a peculiar treasure above all people unto Himself and make them worship only Him, God gave His holy will in its entirety, speaking the Ten Commandments from Sinai (Ex. 20:1-7; Deut. 5:6-21) and later writing them on two tables (Ex. 31:18; 24:12) which were to be placed into the "Ark of the Testimony" (Ex. 25: 21, 22; Ex. 31:7). Moses broke the first two tables when he came down from the mountain (Ex. 32:19). New tables were then prepared and placed in the "Ark of the Testimony" ("Tabernacle of Testimony"), in which they occupied the most conspicuous place (Ex. 34:1 ff.; Matt. 22:34-40; Heb. 9:1-5; 1 Kings 8: 6-9). The tables may have disappeared at the time when Nebuchadnezzar destroyed the Temple, 2 Kings 25).

Luther stated that the Ten Commandments were given "to the Jews and not to us." That is true of the form in which they were given (Ex. 20: 1-17; Deut. 5:6-21). Luther, following NT precedent (cf. Eph. 6:2-3; Col. 2: 16, 17; Matt. 19:18, 19; Mark 10:19), omitted ceremonial elements ("Sabbath" and ceremonial commands in the 3d Commandment), the prohibition of iconolatry (1st Commandment), the threat attached to the 2d Commandment, and made other changes (NT form of the promise in 4th Commandment; 10th Commandment; position of the Close of the Commandments).

The Ten Commandments tell us in clear language what we are to do and not to do and how we are to be and not to be. Man, however, cannot be saved by the Law (Gal. 2:16) but it does serve him as a curb, a rule, and a mirror (F. C., VI). It serves as a curb "that the unregenerate may be kept under external discipline and thus restrained from outward gross sins" (1 Tim. 1:8-10; Ps. 32:9). It serves as a mirror by showing man what he actually is (Is. 64:6; Rom. 3:20; Rom. 7:7; Gal. 3:24). As a rule it shows what God expects of man.

No man has perfectly fulfilled the Law as demanded by God (Gal. 3:10; Matt. 22:37; James 2:10; 4:17; 1 John 1:8), and all men are, therefore, transgressors and sinners (1 John 3:10; Eph. 2:3; Rom. 3:22, 23) and subject to temporal and eternal punishment (Lev. 26: 14-43; Deut. 28:15-68; Deut. 27:26; Rom. 6:23). Christ, however, fulfilled the Jewish ceremonial and political laws as well as the Moral Law (Luke 2:22-39; Matt. 22:21). In addition He bore the punishment for our transgressions of the Law (1 Cor. 15:3; Gal. 3:13; Rom. 10:4). The redeemed Christian, then, is no longer under the domination of

the Law (Gal. 3:19; 1 Tim. 1:9). C. f. RH, The Abiding Word, I:124—145.

(The Bible gives us no basis for a certain numbering of the Commandments or of determining their respective position. Cp. Matt. 19:18, 19 and Mark 10:19. The Greek and the Reformed Churches make Ex. 20:2, 3 the First, verses 4-6 the Second, verse 17 the Tenth Commandment. The so-called Augustinian division, retained in the Lutheran and Roman Catholic Churches, takes verse 3 (vv. 3-6) as the First Commandment, verse 7 as the Second, and divides verse 17 into the Ninth and the Tenth. Thus the Fourth Commandment of the Lutheran Catechism is the Fifth of the Reformed).

M. Reu, "The Significance of the Law and the Example of Jesus for the Formation of the New Life," Christian Ethics, Luth. Book Concern, Columbus, O., 1935 (114—122 and bibliography); F. W. C. Jesse, Catechetical Preparations, CPH (Part I); Ernst G. W. Keyl, Katechismusauslegung aus Luthers Schriften und den symbolischen Buechern, 1853 (vol. 1); R. Herrmann, "The Decalog and the Close of the Commandments," Abiding Word, CPH, 1946 (pp. 124—145. Extensive bibliography, p. 584).

Decet Romanum (bull). See Reformation, Lutheran, 9.

Decisio Saxonica. A decision rendered in 1624, under the chairmanship of Hoe von Hoenegg, between the theologians of Tuebingen and Giessen. The former held that in Christ's State of Humiliation the God-Man retained both the possession and the use of all His divine attributes, although He applied them only in secret, while the latter held that the Lord had the possession and the functions of His divine attributes, but refrained from using them according to His human nature. The decision declared that in the case of the working of miracles the God-Man temporarily stepped out of His condition of kenosis.

Decius. See Persecutions of Christians, 4.

Decius, Nikolaus. A native of Hof, Upper Franconia, d. 1541; at first monk; joined Reformation movement; schoolteacher in Brunswick; pastor at Saint Nicholas, Stettin; popular preacher, good musician; zealous in introducing the Reformation in Pomerania; wrote: "Allein Gott in der Hoeh' sei Ehr'"; "O Lamm Gottes, unschuldig."

Declaratio Solida. See *Luth. Confessions,* C 2.

Declaration and Address. See *Disciples of Christ,* 2 a.

Declaration of the American Lutheran Church. See *Brief Statement.*

Declaration of 1833. See *Democratic Declarations,* 2.

Declaration of Faith of the Reformed Church in France. See *Reformed Confessions,* B.

Declaratory Act. See *Presbyterian Confessions,* 4.

Declaratory Theory. See *Atonement, Theories of.*

Decoration, Church. See *Art, Ecclesiastical; Church Furniture.*

Decrees of the Council of Trent. See *Roman Catholic Confessions,* A.

Decrees and Decretals. Compilations of decrees or laws, especially of papal laws and decisions, as, for example, those published by authority of Pope Gregory IX in 1234. The term is derived from the Latin *decretalis,* "containing a decree"; cf. the Latin *decretum.* The singular, *decretal,* denotes any authoritative decree or a letter embodying such a decree. Besides the *Decretals of Gregory IX* there are the *Decretals of Gratian,* papal decretals up to Innocent II, published ca. 1150 by Gratian, professor at the University of Bologna; the *Decretals of Boniface VIII,* published in 1298 and containing all decretals since Gregory IX; the *Decretals of Clement V,* published in 1317. Such decretals constitute a part of the canon law (*Corpus Iuris Canonici*). The *Pseudo-Isidorian Decretals,* bearing the signature of Isidore, a Spanish bishop of the sixth century, but being a collection of the ninth century, though professing to be an earlier series from Clement I to Damasus I (384), were regarded as authoritative for 500 years, but are now rejected as forgeries. In the Middle Ages they were widely used to support various papal claims. See also *Canon Law; Bulls.*

Decrees of God. The eternal decrees of Creation, Redemption, and Predestination, or essential acts of God. God decreed to create the world; but, foreseeing that part of the world, possessing a rational nature, would fall from its first estate of innocence, He further-

more decreed to send a Savior to redeem mankind. Again, He decreed to save from sin and the power of Satan and to preserve unto eternal life a certain number of persons through Christ, ordained to be the salvation of all sinners. A decree of God is distinguished from other acts of the divine will in that it is the divine counsel and performance of the thing decreed. The decrees of God cannot be frustrated. The work of creation cannot be frustrated. There was no power to frustrate the decree of redemption. And no one can pluck Christ's elect out of the Father's hand. See *Creation, Election, Redemption.*

Decretals, False. Certain compilations of alleged laws and resolutions of the Roman Church to support false claims, such as the *Pseudo-Isidorian Decretals.*

Decretum Gelasianum. The decree of Pope Gelasius (d. 496), which ordered the celebration of the Lord's Supper under one kind, that is, withdrawing the cup from the laity, a mutilation of the Sacrament, which is condemned in Article 22 of the Augsburg Confession.

Decretum Gratiani. See *Canon Law.*

Dedekennus, Georg (1564—1628). Lutheran; d. as pastor in Hamburg; wrote *Thesaurus Consiliorum et Decisionum* (4 vols., casuistics) and other theological works.

Dedication. The custom of dedicating churches, schools, organs, bells, altars, and other church furniture as well as cemeteries, parish houses, parsonages, etc., is generally retained in the Lutheran Church. While Luther rejected the superstitious elements connected with dedications by the Roman Catholics (St. L. Ed., XVI: 2292 f.; *Smal. Art.,* III: XV), he himself dedicated a church in harmony with the evangelical doctrine (1 Tim. 4: 4, 5) in 1546. The principle which governs every form of dedication is that the use of Scripture in readings, sermons, hymns, and prayers consecrates and hallows all acts of this kind, and that every form of superstition and false doctrine must be kept away from things which are intended for the use of worship in the churches (1 Cor. 14: 26, 40; 1 Tim. 4: 5).

Defectives, Care of. See *Charities, Christian; Hospitals, Sanatoria, Homes for Convalescents and Chronically Ill.*

Defender of the Faith (Fidei Defensor). A title used by sovereigns of England; first conferred on Henry VIII for his treatise against Luther by Leo X (1521).

Defense of Orthodoxy. See *Eastern Orthodox Confessions,* A 2.

"Definite Platform, Doctrinal and Disciplinarian, for Ev. Luth. District Synods, Constructed in Accordance with the Principles of the General Synod." An excrescence of "American Lutheranism" published anonymously in September, 1855, later acknowledged by S. S. Schmucker as his work. According to Schmucker it purported to be the "American Recension of the Augsburg Confession." Its chief object was to obviate the influence of confessional Lutheranism coming from the West, notably from the Missouri Synod. The Definite Platform charges the Augsburg Confession with the following errors: approval of the ceremonies of the Mass, private confession and absolution, denial of the divine obligation of Sunday, baptismal regeneration, the real presence of the body and blood of Christ in the Eucharist. The descent into hell is omitted from the Creed. The Athanasian Creed is eliminated. The rest of the Lutheran symbols are rejected on account of their length and alleged errors.

The Definite Platform, when presented to the constituent synods of the General Synod, was adopted by only three small synods — East Ohio, Wittenberg, and Olive Branch. The other constituent synods either refused to adopt the document or rejected it altogether. The General Synod as such therefore cannot be held responsible for the Definite Platform. It is true, as Neve states, that the mistake (of issuing the Definite Platform) was made by prominent members of the General Synod, but it also is a fact that the popularity of these men suffered greatly after the publication of the document. Dr. Charles Porterfield Krauth wrote that the supporters of the Definite Platform had mistaken a tendency, half devoloped, for a final result (as the widespread opposition proved).

Definite Platform, Doctrinal and Disciplinarian, for Ev. Luth. District Synods, Constructed in Accordance with the Principles of the General Synod, Miller and Burlock, Philadelphia, 1856; E. L. Lueker, "Walther and the Free Lutheran Conferences," *CTM,* XV: 529—63. V. Ferm, *The Crisis in Am.*

Luth. Theology, Century, New York, 1927; C. Mauelshagen, *American Lutheranism Surrenders to Forces of Conservatism,* Univ. of Georgia, Division of Publications, 1936.

Degrees of Glory. See *Hereafter,* A 6.

Degrees, Prohibited, of Marriage. See *Impediments of Marriage, Scriptural and Natural.*

Dei Filius. See *Roman Catholic Confessions,* E 2.

Dei gratia. Latin for "by the grace of God," abbreviated *D. g.* The expression is found in St. Paul's letters, 1 Cor. 1:1 and 2 Cor. 1:1. Since the 5th century high ecclesiastics, and later on also secular rulers, used the expression in connection with their titles to indicate that they held their office by divine will.

Deicide. Literally a slayer of God. The term is sometimes used to designate especially those who took part in the crucifixion of Christ.

Deification. The practice of bestowing upon creatures divine honors and worship.

Deindoerfer, Dr. Johannes (1828 to 1907). An emissary of Loehe; came to Michigan (Frankenhilf), 1851; went with Grossmann to Iowa, 1853; a founder of the Iowa Synod and vice-president from 1854, succeeding Grossmann as president in 1893. Prominent in the opposition of his synod to "Missouri." Author of *Geschichte der Iowasynode* and three *Denkschriften.*

Deinzer, Johannes. B. in Germany, Sept. 2, 1842; successor of Dr. Weber as professor at Neuendettelsau Seminary 1864—72, during this time assistant of Wm. Loehe; inspector 1875—97; came to America in 1879 at the 25th anniversary of the Iowa Synod, representing its friends in Germany; he sent more than 100 missionaries to the Iowa Synod. Wrote *Loehe's Leben,* 3 vols.; edited *Loehe's Agenda,* 3d ed.; also *Loehe's David and Salomo;* Weber's *Einleitung;* editor of *Kirchliche Mitteilungen.* Died Jan. 25, 1897.

Deism. A system of belief which holds either that the universe is a self-sustained mechanism from which God withdrew immediately after creation (Flint), or that God is still active in the universe, but only through natural means.

I. Antecedents. The sources on which deism drew were many, being taken from ancient and later times. 1) Some of the arguments of deists were taken from early opponents of Christianity (Celsus, Porphyry, Philostratus), from statements made in the course of early controversies (Gnostic, Trinitarian and Christological, Pelagian, Arminian, and others), and from pre-Christian philosophers (Socrates, Plato, Democritus, Leucippus, Epicurus, Cicero, Plutarch). 2) The discoveries and explorations of the 15th and 16th centuries brought information to Europe regarding various religions which stimulated the study of comparative religion. 3) Scientific discoveries undermined many views held in the Medieval Church. Newton's "universal laws" led deists to conclude that an observation of the laws established by God was sufficient for religious convictions. 4) Many arguments of deists were taken from contemporary controversies, the Roman Catholics being quoted against Protestants and *vice versa*. 5) The deists criticized abuses in the Church, "lifeless dogmatism," ritualism, and the lack of true spiritual life. 6) While deists criticized the narrow scholasticism of Roman Catholics, they, on the other hand, developed scholastic statements concerning God into a conception of a master mechanic who created the world and then let it operate on its own. 7) The deists drew heavily upon the results of textual criticism as well as upon higher criticism. 8) Dissatisfaction with fanaticism and atrocities ascribed to religous communions prepared the way for many of the deistic arguments. 9) Rationalistic supernaturalists differed from deists in that they did not reject revealed religion entirely, but introduced reason, first as a handmaiden and then as a judge of revelation. The lines between the two are not always sharply drawn.

II. Method. The greater portion of the writings of deists is negative. Inspiration, the Sacred Text, miracles, prophecies, deity of Christ, Biblical characters, ordinances, institutions, rites and doctrines of the Church, the character of the clergy, and other religious matters were subjected to their attacks. The smaller portion of their writings was devoted to the development of a religion of nature.

III. History of Deism. 1. Deism is generally considered as beginning with Lord Herbert of Cherbury (1583—1648; often called "Father of English Deism"; chief work: De Veritate), and ending with Thomas Jefferson (1743—1826), although deism in England declined rapidly after Henry Dodwell (d. 1784).

In so far as Lord Herbert of Cherbury studiously sought to avoid denying the validity of revealed religion, he may be classified as a rationalistic supernaturalist. The ultimate criterion of knowledge for him, however, was based upon the recognition of innate universal characteristics concerning any particular object. He was the author of the so-called five essentials, or "Five Articles," of the English Deists, namely, a belief in the existence of deity, the obligation to reverence such a power as rationally determined, the identification of worship with practical morality, the obligation to repent of sin as not in harmony with the best development of man and to abandon it, and finally, divine recompense in this world and the next. Meanwhile Thomas Hobbes * studied comparative religion and came to the conclusion that all religion is the result of fear. He held that religion is not philosophy but law and as such the creation of the state. While deists disliked Hobbes' intolerance, they were influenced by his rationalism, anticlericalism, and Biblical criticism.

2. Sir Thomas Browne (1605—82) regarded faith and reason as hostile forces, but sought to keep both in separate compartments. He opposed dependence on authority and adherence to antiquity. John Tillotson (1630—94; Archbishop of Canterbury) provided fuel for deists by opposing intolerance and regarding ethics and reason as the chief elements in religion.

3. John Locke (1632—1704), though not a deist, was extensively quoted by deists and gave new directions to deistic thought. His empiricism replaced Cherbury's doctrine of innate ideas as a basis for investigation. His statement that it was difficult to prove the soul immaterial was seized upon by deists, as well as his remark that time weakened the evidence for traditional revelation.

4. Charles Blount (1654—93; wrote Anima Mundi, Two First Books of Apollonius Tyaneous, Oracles of Reason, and Great Is Diana of the Ephesians) marks the transition between Cherbury's doctrine of innate ideas and Locke's empiricism. He opposed revelation by seeking to parallel Biblical narratives with heathen legends and held that what is necessary for salvation must be known to all since there is no special revelation. John Toland (1670—1722; wrote Christianity Not Mysterious, Amyntor, Tetrademus, Pantheisticon) established deism on the

empiricism of Locke, attacked the Scriptural canon, and opposed mysteries in Christianity. Anthony Ashley Cooper (Earl of Shaftesbury; 1671—1713; wrote *Inquiry Concerning Merit; Characteristics of Men, Manners, Opinions, Times; Essay on the Freedom of Wit and Humor*) emphasized ethics and introduced wit and mockery as a mode of attack. William Whiston (1667—1729; wrote *Primitive Christianity Revived, An Essay Towards Restoring the True Text of the New Testament*) directed his attacks against Biblical prophecies, a trend continued by Anthony Collins (1676—1729; wrote *Use of Reason, Discourse on Free Thinking, Inquiry Concerning Human Liberty, Discourse on the Grounds of Reason of the Christian Religion, Scheme of Literal Prophecy Considered*). Peter Annet (1693—1769; wrote *The History of the Man after God's Own Heart, The History and Character of St. Paul, The Resurrection of Jesus Considered*) attacked the trustworthiness of Biblical narratives.

5. Matthew Tindal (1656—1733; the "Great Apostle of Deism"; wrote the "Deistic Bible": *Christianity as Old as Creation, or, The Gospel a Republication of the Religion of Nature*) brought together and enlarged upon all the elements touched by earlier deists. He held that Christ's religion was in harmony with his naturalism. Jesus, according to his view, freed the religion of His day from systematized superstition just as the deists were doing for their times. This thought was followed by such men as Thomas Chubb (1679 to 1746; wrote *Supremacy of the Father Asserted, Discourse Concerning Reason, True Gospel of Jesus Christ Asserted*). Prominent in the deistic movement in England, in addition to the above, were: Bernard de Mandeville (1670—1733), William Wollaston (1659—1724; wrote *Religion of Nature Delineated*), Thomas Woolston (1669—1731), Thomas Morgan (d. 1743; wrote *The Moral Philosopher*), Lord Bolingbroke (1672—1751), Conyers Middleton (1683—1750).

6. Henry Dodwell, Jr. (d. 1784; wrote *Christianity Not Founded on Argument, True Principle of Gospel-Evidence Assigned*), paved the way for the transition from deism to skepticism by denying reason a place in religion. This trend was further augmented by Hume's denial of causality as a force.

IV. The causes of the decline of deism were: Christian apologies (Berkeley, Law, West, Leland, Butler, Paley); differences among deists; exhaustion of

the subject of deism; Methodist * revival; political events.

V. Results. English deism influenced men in France (Rousseau, Voltaire), Germany (Christian Wolff, Johann Conrad Dippel, Moses Mendelssohn, Herman Samuel Reimarus, Gotthold Ephraim Lessing, Immanuel Kant) and America (Benjamin Franklin, Thomas Jefferson, Thomas Paine *). It influenced philosophy during the 19th and 20th centuries, is studied by anti-Christian movements, and many of its thoughts reappeared in the religious movement called *Modernism*. Its influence has also been sought in Freemasonry.* EL

John Orr, *English Deism: Its Roots and Fruits*, Eerdmanns, Grand Rapids, Mich., 1934; S. G. Hefelbower, *The Relation of John Locke to English Deism*, University of Chicago Press, 1918; H. M. Morais, *Deism in Eighteenth Century America*, Columbia University Press, 1934; Leslie Stephen, *History of English Thought in the Eighteenth Century*, Putnam's Sons, 1927.

Deissmann, Gustav Adolf (1866 to 1937). Prof. of NT at Heidelberg and Berlin; pointed out that NT Greek was that of the papyri *(Bibelstudien)*; showed the value of the papyri for NT Greek *(Licht vom Osten)*.

De La Place, Josue. See *Reformed Confessions*, A 10.

Delitzsch, Franz (1813—90). B. and d. at Leipzig; one of the foremost Lutheran theologians of the Erlangen School; *Privatdozent* (lecturer) at Leipzig, 1842; professor at Rostock, at Erlangen, at Leipzig, his special field being exegesis. In earlier life he was intimately associated with the founders of the Missouri Synod and an enthusiastic Lutheran; later on, influenced by modern scientific theology, opposed to the idea "of fencing theology off with the letter of the Formula of Concord." Foremost among his numerous writings are his commentaries on OT books in connection with Keil, especially on Isaiah. He translated the New Testament into Hebrew (1877; 11th edition, 1890).

Delitzsch, Friedrich (1850—1922). B. at Erlangen, d. at Langenschwalbach; son of Franz Delitzsch; professor at Berlin (1899); noted Assyriologist; his lectures *Babel und Bibel*, 1902—93, in which he maintained that OT ideas originated in Babylonia, caused a noted controversy; his opponents showed that, though Israelitish and Babylonian civilizations had points of contact, OT monotheism, sacrifices, and prophetic religion had independent origin; wrote *Assyrische Grammatik, Assyrisches Handwoerterbuch.*

Delivery of Sermon. See *Homiletics.*

Delk, Edwin Heyl. B. Norfolk, Va., Aug. 15, 1859; M.A. Central High School, Philadelphia, Pa., 1880; D.D. Luth. Theol. Seminary, Gettysburg, Pa., 1901; ordained 1882; pastor at Schoharie, N.Y., 1882—85, Hagerstown, Md., 1885 to 1902, Philadelphia, Pa., 1902—29; served on various boards and committees; pres. of Philadelphia Federation of Churches, 1910—14; trustee Lutheran Theol. Seminary and Luth. Deaconess Mother House. Wrote: *Three Vital Problems, The Need of Re-Statement of Theology, Life of Charles S. Albert,* D.D. Died Feb. 8, 1940.

Deluge. See *Flood.*

Demantius, Christoph (1567—1643). A prolific and outstanding Lutheran composer of sacred and secular music, was a native of Bohemia (Reichenberg). His *Passion According to St. John* is of special significance, since it is among the earliest motette passions, different from the recitative passions of Walther and others of earlier times.

Demeter. According to Greek mythology the daughter of Chronos and the sister of Zeus. She was worshiped as the Goddess of Agriculture.

Demetrius, Mysos. A deacon from Constantinople (now Istanbul), who visited Melanchthon in Wittenberg, 1559, and took a Greek translation of the Augsburg Confession with an explanatory writing to the Patriarch Joasaph II, without any apparently favorable results.

Demiurge. See *Gnosticism,* K 7.

Demme, Karl Rudolph. B. 1795 at Muehlhausen, Thueringen; ed. Gymnasium in Altenburg, Univ. of Halle, and Goettingen; to America in 1818; in 1819 licensed by Ministerium of Pa. to serve Hummelstown and Maxe churches; in 1822 called to St. Michael's and Zion Cong. of Philadelphia. Co-editor of the Pennsylvania *Hymnal* of 1849 and *Agenda* of 1855. Published revision of Cotta's and Gfroerer's edition of Flavius Josephus in German. Died 1863.

Democratic Declarations of Faith. Under this head are included those creeds evolved by Protestant denominations after the period of confessional writing based upon involved theological thought had come to an end and are considered exhibitions of unity rather than binding symbols. In general these creeds are less theological, more popular, and leave much room for private judgment. Many of them also are of the nature of a covenant and emphasize voluntary agreement for the achievement of a common purpose.

1. Creeds of this type may be traced to the *Anabaptist* symbol of 1527 which treats baptism, excommunication, Lord's Table, avoidance of evil ministers, cursing, etc. Another prominent creed by the successors of the Anabaptists (Mennonites) was drawn up in 1580 (deals with discipline and interpretation of the words of Jesus).

2. *Congregationalists* weaken general creeds and emphasize particular creeds. Each individual congregation has the right to formulate its own creed. Prominent among their general declarations are: *Savoy Declaration* (1658; explanatory preface and revision of Westminster Confession; emphasizes "mutual indulgence unto saints of all persuasions that keep unto and hold fast the necessary foundations of faith"; the third part defines congregational polity); *Declaration of 1833* (condensation of older confessions). In America the following are noteworthy: *Cambridge Platform* (1648; accepts Westminster Confession except articles on church government and discipline); *Declaration of Synod of Boston* (1680; adopted Savoy Declaration and Cambridge Platform); *Synod of Saybrook* (1708; accepted Heads of Agreement *); National Council of Boston* (1865; endorsed Westminster Confession and Savoy Declaration for substance of doctrine and "the system known as Calvinism").

3. *Baptists* do not consider creeds as a test of orthodoxy, but as a portrayal of unanimity. The Regular Baptists produced the following creeds: *Confession of the Seven Churches in London* (1644; 52 articles replying to Featley's "The Dippers Dipt; or, the Anabaptists Duck'd and Plunged over Head and Ears at a Disputation in Southwark"); *Confession of Somerset* (1656); *Confession of 1688* (Baptist recension of the Westminster Confession; accepted at Philadelphia and hence known as *Philadelphia Confession;* most important). The following declarations are among those of the Arminian Baptists: *A Declaration of Faith of English People Remaining in Amsterdam and Holland*

(1611; election conditioned by fore-known faith; reprobation by fore-known unbelief; perseverance denied); *London Confession* (1660); *Orthodox Creed* (1678; approaches Calvinism with a view to uniting Protestants); *Confession of Faith* prepared by General Conference (1832).

4. The *Quakers* acknowledge no platform or creed. The more conservative follow Robert Barclay's *Apology* (1675) and *Catechism* (1673).

5. *Moravians* have no confession but endorsed the Augsburg Confession. Theology is shown in *Idea Fidei* of Spangenberg.

6. *Methodist* creeds are not logically formulated and allow for development. The Methodists have three classes of standards: a. *Twenty-Five Articles of Religion* (adopted at Baltimore, 1784; prepared by Wesley from *Thirty-Nine Articles*); b. Wesley's *Sermons and Notes on New Testament;* c. *Book of Discipline* and several catechisms (1852, 1868). See individual church bodies. EL

See bibliography under *Creeds and Confessions;* Leonard Hodgson, *Convictions,* Macm., 1934.

De Molay, Order of. See *Freemasonry,* 4.

Demon. The word originally meant "a divinity." In later Greek usage it became a term for a spirit either good or evil. In the New Testament demons are evil spirits or devils.

Demoniacal Possession. The Swiss scholar Maximilian Perty has given us the following description of the outward phenomena which make up the state of being "possessed": "Possession is that awful condition in which a man appears to be seized by a foreign and evil being, which during the attacks controls the body of its victim as if it were its own possession, maltreats and tortures this body in every possible manner, causes the features to become distorted into a ferocious mocking, sometimes diabolical distortion, and — this is characteristic — causes the victim to express disrespect for religion in a bold, cynical manner. The phenomena of bodily possession are so dreadful and at the same time so strong that but a little acuteness of observation is needed in order that the true relation may be recognized and also the unjust diagnosis of abnormal states, as if they represented possession, might be avoided. Possession may be assumed on three grounds: hatred of religion, the power of divining secret things, and psychic phe-

nomena. Persons thus afflicted know about the sins of those present and in the most reckless manner publish such information. They also recognize the spiritual power of their opponents (as in the case of Jesus), know their thoughts, hence are able also to understand unknown tongues and are able even to utter in such tongues some few words or sentences. At the same time the bodies are propelled by invisible forces, and there are phenomena of light and sound. The native of Gadara who was possessed (Luke 8:26-39) shows the characteristic marks of possession: 1. On seeing Jesus he becomes victim of an outburst of rage. He recognizes in Jesus his opponent, but also knows the divine nature and sacred mission of Jesus. 2. He has supernatural strength. He breaks his chains and escapes into the desert. 3. The evil spirits, recognizing that the end of their activities is soon at hand, ask permission to pass into the herd of swine. Jesus permitted this, possibly in order to put an end to their activity so far as human souls are concerned."

The criticism is made that with present advanced knowledge such a story as that recorded by Luke cannot be accepted as actual fact. It is held that Jesus was only humoring a notion of the time in seeming to recognize the existence of such demons and that He only acted a part which was not real in seeming to cast out what was not in. This view has been properly characterized by one of the greatest of expository preachers, Dr. Alexander Maclaren, as "unworthy of the sacred narrative and a reflection on the sincerity of the Teacher before whom we all bow." It would be more candid and more reasonable to say at once that Jesus was mistaken.

The more radical commentaries and works of reference do not hesitate to attribute these struggles between Christ and the evil spirit as due to "the limitations of the knowledge of Jesus." In His diagnosis of these cases He blundered; He misread the facts. The "limitations" of His knowledge made it possible for Him to mistake some ordinary trouble of the brain or of the nerves for a case of satanic possession. As a result Jesus Christ is revealed in the gospel as making Himself ridiculous by going through the form of casting out a devil when no devil existed.

What is evident from the gospel narratives is not only that Christ recognized Satan's power in these cases of possession, but, to quote A. Schlatter, "the evil spirits recognize Jesus as the Son of God, chosen to be the Messiah. . . . Well do they know that on the Day of Judgment they will be irretrievably ruined in hell. But He is not to deliver them over to torment prematurely."

Dr. Miller, the author of *China Inside Out*, comments on these cases: "Unusual manifestations of good often arouse strange activities of evil. When Jesus was upon earth, such cases occurred. The coming of the Christian faith to China has created a somewhat similar situation here, and it is not strange that similar manifestations of malignant possession should be found."

Sometimes these satanic seizures take hold of greater numbers and occasionally rise to the importance of an epidemic. Such was the *bilo* contagion which affected large numbers of heathen inhabitants of Madagascar in 1860 and again in 1910. A writer in the Norwegian paper *Lutheraneren* describes 'the disease as follows:

"The attacks come with great suddenness and cause the afflicted to act like victims of a mania. They leap into the air with wild screams and gesticulations, perform an uncanny dance, sometimes climbing walls and precipices inaccessible under normal conditions; sometimes they utter exclamations which they later explain as the effect of the promptings of spirits. Others again show extreme fright. They run panic-stricken and blindly over the roughest kind of ground, often rushing into water, where they drown if rescuers are not immediately at hand."

Cases of possession are not rare in the history of spiritism and mediumship. One cannot fail to be reminded of the description of the demoniacs by mediumistic seizures or fits as described by the highest authorities such as Sir William Crookes and Mr. Stainton-Moses. The history of Irvingism and the early history of Mormonism are not without examples of demoniacal abuses of human speech. In these and many other cases there are present always the two characteristics of this phenomenon: Those acting under such an impulse are constrained by an inner inexplicable compulsion to speak in short, broken sentences, expressing unmeaning sounds and words. The other characteristic is the rapidity of utterance. There is usually a perfect torrent of words, uttered with an energy that is superhuman. For examples from recent European and American history see the article on "Demoniacal Possession" in the *Concordia Theological Monthly*, 1933, pp. 589—603. TG

Denck, Hans (ca. 1495—1527). One of the ablest leaders of the Anabaptists; befriended by Oecolampadius; scholar of ability and of high personal character; translator of prophetical books; expelled from Nuremberg, Augsburg, Strassburg, and Worms because of his Anabaptist activities.

Denial Week. One week in the year, usually the first of the civil year or Holy Week, set apart by certain religious denominations for sacrifices, when they deny themselves luxuries to which they have become accustomed and which they ordinarily use. The practice is in line with that of the Roman Church in forbidding the eating of meat on Friday and during Lent.

Denicke, David (1603—80). Native of Zittau, Saxony; tutor at Koenigsberg, later at court of Duke George of Brunswick-Lueneburg; member of the consistory at Hannover; edited Hanoverian hymnbooks, 1646—59, together with Justus Gesenius; wrote: "O Herr, dein seligmachend Wort," "Wir Menschen sind zu dem, o Gott," "Kommt, lasst euch den Herren lehren."

Denis, St. (4th century), martyred at Paris, venerated by Roman Catholics on Oct. 9 as patron saint of France.

Denmark. King Harald professed Christianity in 826, but became an apostate in 841. Kaiser Otto I forced Harald Bluetooth to profess Christianity, and the dioceses of Schleswig, Ripen, and Aarhus were founded; Archbishop Unni of Hamburg became the leader. Under Knut the Great, about 1020, Christianity ruled all Denmark. About 1150 the archdiocese of Lund was erected, and the Church became independent of Germany. In 1479 the University of Copenhagen was founded.

Denmark, Lutheranism in. 1. At the beginning of the 16th century the Church of Denmark was in great need of reform. Many of its leaders, bishops and abbots, were worldly and corrupt, not interested in the spiritual life of the people. The Humanistic movement demanded reform, but Paul Helgesen, a gifted and sincere man, was unable to overcome the resistance of the leaders. The church was more independent of Rome than that of many other countries. The king and his councilors appointed Aage Sparre as Archbishop of Lund in 1526, giving Sparre authority to appoint bishops without consulting Rome, but the intention was to remain Roman Catholic.

2. Hans Tausen * began to preach the Lutheran doctrine (1526) at Viborg. King Frederick I, in spite of his pledge to be true to Rome, protected Tausen. Other Lutherans began to preach at various places. After the civil war (1534—36) King Christian III was in financial distress, the Roman churches had great wealth, and the king, who saw that the Reformation was gaining among the people, made the country Lutheran by royal decree in 1536 and confiscated much of the church's wealth.

3. In 1537 John Bugenhagen of Wittenberg was invited to crown the king and ordain seven new bishops. This was a break with the Apostolic succession. The leaders of the Reformation and the men shortly thereafter were strong Lutherans. Calvinistic tendencies were not tolerated. Peder Palladius (d. 1560), one of the most outstanding Danish bishops, had great influence. The Bible was translated into Danish in 1550. A hymnbook was printed, and Tausen published a book of evangelical sermons for pastors.

4. Melanchthonian influence was soon felt. Niels Hemmingsen (d. 1600), "Denmark's Great Teacher," was an outstanding theologian and a follower of "Philippism." His Biblicistic humanism made headway and sought a compromise with Calvinism.

5. After 1600 this humanistic theology was sharply attacked by Lutheran orthodoxy, which dominated the church in the 17th century. Pastors were required to pledge adherence to the Augsburg Confession instead of the former vague promise to "evangelical teaching." The orthodox movement brought new rules and regulations into the church. Pastors were better trained. The family altar was emphasized. But there was a tendency to separate faith and life. Intolerance was prevalent, ignorance and superstition strong. Witches were burned at the stake. In the midst of this was a deep mystic religiosity which found expression in devotional literature and in the emphasis on penitence and prayer. Thomas Kingo (d. 1703) was the great hymn writer of the period.

6. Pietism came to Denmark from Germany in 1703. In 1705 the first Lutheran foreign mission was launched in India by the Danish king in co-operation with the Halle pietists. Pietism gained strength through many small groups, which met for prayer and Bible reading. Orthodox pastors were often worldly men, and all through the 18th century there was a struggle between dead orthodoxy and pietism. But pietistic pastors had great influence. The Danish common school was started with the erection of 240 schools in the land. Children were given a thorough instruction in religion. Confirmation was introduced in 1736. The great hymn writer, H. A. Brorson (d. 1764) was a pietist.

7. The pietistic period was rather short. Its subjective elements quickly melted into the optimistic views of the Enlightenment. Faith in God was replaced by faith in man, and the voice of conscience by reason. Men were not opposed to Christianity, but under the influence of Descartes, Rousseau, and English naturalism the dogmas of the church were discarded and the emphasis was on faith in providence, a demand for a good life, gratitude to God for His gifts, and the hope of eternal life after death. To be a good citizen was sufficient to gain God's favor. The educated classes drifted away from Christianity, church attendance declined, religious indifference was general. A few men tried to stem the tide, among them N. E. Balle (1744—1816), professor and bishop, who stood firm on the Bible. A number of lay people also continued their Bible reading groups.

8. Rationalism held sway at the beginning of the 19th century. N. F. S. Grundtvig (1783—1872), who had his soul deeply rooted in both rationalism and romanticism, took a more orthodox view of the Bible and faith, and confronted with a rationalistic and historic criticism, he sought in the sacraments the clear and unchanging expression of true and pure Christianity as it had come down from Christ Himself through the centuries. By his preaching rationalism began to shake. The Danish Church is greatly influenced by Grundtvig directly and indirectly, not so much by his special theology as by his view of life, by his hymns (about 1500) and the appeal his message had on the popular mind in rural areas (he gained little prestige in the cities). The folk high school movement, even though not directly started by him, owes its existence to the Grundtvigian revival. His great love for Denmark and its history gave his movement a

national spirit, which is still felt. Gradually he reacted against the small, pious Bible reading groups. He maintained that the Bible was a "dead word" over against the "living word" in the Apostolic Confession, and his movement took a more definite national direction with great folk mass meetings, where Christian, national, political, and cultural subjects were discussed. Thus the Grundtvigian view of the Christian faith has become the most liberal in Denmark, but as a whole it has had a beneficial influence by emphasizing congregational life and singing. Grundtvigianism is the term used to describe one of the three main groups within the Danish Church.

9. Otherwise theology after rationalism became ecclesiastical under the influence of J. P. Mynster (1775—1854), bishop of Copenhagen, who turned the educated classes to a confessional form of Christianity. His successor, H. L. Martensen (1808—84), combined Lutheran orthodoxy with Hegelianism and built a vast dogmatic and ethical system on a Christian idealistic philosophy. The influence of these men was in the direction of a churchly view of life. This is represented in the second main trend within the Danish Church by a group known as the "Ecclesiastical Center."

10. When the pious groups in the middle of the 18th century found they could not co-operate with the Grundtvigians because their view of Scripture and their attitude toward the world were so different, a group of lay people organized (1851) a society based on Lutheran confessions with the aim of reviving the life of those "who are sleeping sinners." The society had a slow growth, but in 1861 Pastor Vilhelm Beck (d. 1901) was present at the annual meeting and preached the famous sermon on Peter's Draught of Fishes (fishing by both lay and clergy). He joined the society, the name of which was changed to "Church Society for Inner Missions." Both pastors and laymen were to preach. Mission halls were built in nearly all parishes, in which more informal meetings were held. Beck was the leader of the movement till his death (1901). He was orthodox, but had been stimulated by Soren Kierkegaard's attack on the official church and his demands for a deeper spiritual life. He was eloquent, and great revivals swept the country as a result of his preaching and that of other men of the movement. They de-

manded a Christian life separated from the world. Out of Inner Missions grew a number of activities such as foreign missions, works of charity, and much literary activity. Inner Missions is faithful to the Lutheran doctrine, but it has been influenced by Grundtvig in the high value placed on the sacraments. Baptism is highly esteemed, and the Lord's Supper is celebrated in nearly every church on Sundays. Inner Missions is the third main group within the Danish Church. It represents Christian activity and has learned much from the Anglo-Saxon world.

11. The general secularization of culture in Europe also engulfed Denmark. When positivism and socialism after 1870 made their appearance, the theology of Mynster and Martensen was not strong enough to change the trend. A gap developed between Christianity and modern culture. Secularization became an open fact. The secular and Christian movements divided the people into different groups, but all remained nominal members of the church.

12. Barthianism has had some influence on the pastors of the 20th century, but hardly on the congregations. The most important names in the theological discussions are Barth and Grundtvig, and most of the clergy are influenced by one or both of them. A Swedish high church movement has gained some ground. The theology is more confessional and ecclesiastical. During the last years a renewed study of Luther is gaining momentum. There is hardly any liberalism in theology. The church was in strong opposition to Naziism during the German occupation (1940—45), the most famous opponent being the martyred pastor and writer, Kaj Munk (d. 1944).

13. Soren Kierkegaard's influence was felt only a short time in the middle of the 19th century, but in the 20th century he has been studied a great deal, and his influence has been pronounced in the field of existential theology and philosophy.

14. The Danish Church is governed by parliament. The income of the church is from interest of church property, supplemented by direct taxation. There are nine dioceses with about 1,500 parishes and 2,000 pastors. 98 per cent of the population is Lutheran. The pastors are elected by the congregations and appointed by the king. The symbols of the Danish Church are: the three ecumenical creeds,* the Augsburg Con-

fession, and Luther's Small Catechism (see *Lutheran Confessions*).

15. Danish Lutheranism has had only small influence in America because Danish immigration was small and late, which accounts for the small Lutheran church in America of Danish extraction. H. L. Martensen's systematic theology has been translated into English, and during the 20th century nearly all of Kierkegaard's works have been put into English. A number of Danish hymns have been translated into English. JMJ L. P. Fabricius, *Danmarks Kirkehistorie;* Hal Koch, *Danmarks Kirke.*

Denny, James (1856—1917). Scottish Presbyterian theologian; known for his *The Death of Christ Jesus and the Gospel* in which he tried to adjust Christian doctrines to modernistic views.

De Nobili, Robert (1577—1656). Italian Jesuit missionary who studied and defended Indian culture and social customs.

Dens, Peter (1690—1775). Prominent Belgian Roman Catholic theologian; wrote *Theologia Moralis et Dogmatica,* widely used as textbook in Roman Catholic seminaries.

Deontology. A system of ethics which emphasizes duty rather than right or goodness. The term was the title of a book by Jeremy Bentham.

Departed, Commemoration of. In the early church feasts of apostles and evangelists were soon celebrated, especially those of Peter and Paul, although those of John and James were also favorites. In the Middle Ages saints and martyrs were commemorated on Nov. 1 (All Saints' Day) and on Nov. 2 (All Souls' Day) there was a concentration of prayers in behalf of the departed. In the Greek Church this festival is held on the Saturday before Pentecost or the last Sunday of the Greek church year. In the Moravian Church Easter morning is dedicated to the memory of those who died during the year. In 1816 the last Sunday of the church year was set aside for All Souls' Day by the Ev. Church of Prussia, and this day has been adopted by many Lutherans.

Dependent Children. See *Child Care and Child-Placing Agencies.*

Deposition from Ministerial Office. In the Roman Catholic Church, priests are deposed by bishops and bishops by popes. In the Lutheran Church the act

of deposition is declarative, being a part of the power of the keys (see *Keys, Office of*). In American Lutheranism, synods usually pronounce sentences of deposition against pastors and teachers. In the case of the Missouri Synod, "members who act contrary to the confession laid down in Article II and to the conditions of membership laid down in Article VI or persist in an offensive conduct, shall, after previous futile admonition, be expelled from Synod. Such expulsion is executed, as a rule, by the Districts of Synod; yet those so expelled have the right of appeal to Synod." (*Constitution,* XIII). The congregation which a deposed pastor or teacher served is held to depose him or forfeit its membership in Synod. See *Ministerial Office.*
Handbook of The Lutheran Church — Missouri Synod, CPH, 1949.

Depravity. See *Sin.*

Derschau, Bernhardt von (1591 to 1639). Professor and counselor of the consistory at Koenigsberg; wrote "Herr Jesu, dir sei Preis und Dank."

Dervish (Persian, "beggar," synonymous with Arabic "fakir" *) is the designation for a member of one of the numerous Mohammedan religious orders, whose religious practices include dances and ascetic self-castigation. There are many orders, some of which are housed in monasteries, while the members of others go about ordinary occupations and carry on the practices of their order only on special occasions. The dancing and the howling dervishes are most widely known.

Descant. Originally the name for the highest voice (soprano) in part music. Today it refers to a melody above the regular melody, particularly of a hymn.

Descartes, René (*Renatus Cartesius;* 1596—1650). French philosopher; spent part of life in Holland (1629) and Sweden (1649), died at Stockholm. Trained by Jesuits, he remained all his life in the Catholic Church. His system, however, differs in many respects from Thomism, and he is called "Father of Modern Philosophy" because he broke the sway of Scholasticism (initial doubt, mathematical rationalism, opposition to the Aristotelian method). Held that all knowledge is open to doubt, except reality of self, which he expressed in the maxim "*Cogito, ergo sum*" ("I think, therefore I am"). By his deductive thinking in mathematical terms he envisaged a mechanistic world, from which, however, he exempted the human soul and God (Infinite Substance). Space and motion were ultimate realities. Wrote: *Discourse de la méthode, Meditationes de Prima Philosophia, Principia Philosophiae, Traité des passions de l'ame,* and other works.

Descent into Hell. The doctrine of the descent of Christ into hell is based, primarily, on a passage of Scripture (1 Pet. 3:18 ff.) which has often been considered one of the most difficult texts. Differing interpretations hold that Christ went to the realm of the dead; the place of lost souls; the abode of evil angels (Stoeckhardt held that Christ went to the prison of wicked men and angels). Christ's descent is spoken of as occurring immediately after death (Calvin); immediately after vivification (prominent view among Lutherans). It is regarded as having taken place in the embodied state; in the disembodied state; according to the soul; according to body and soul. It is held that Christ preached to souls who had had no chance in life; to the damned; to the evil angels (Stoeckhardt combines the last two). His preaching is said to have been Gospel; Law and Gospel; a proclamation of victory.

The descent to hell did not take place immediately after death, because the soul of Jesus went to paradise (Luke 23:43). It took place before Christ's coming from the tomb. The word "prison" (Gr. *phulake*) designates the abode of the wicked ones (for *phulake* see Rev. 18:2; 20:7; 1 Pet. 3:18. Cf. Jude 6; 2 Pet. 2:4. It is used many times in NT for earthly prison) to whom Christ proclaimed his victory (Col. 2:15. Cf. Eph. 6:12). Some of these evil ones (so Stoeckhardt, including both angels and the damned) had been disbelieving (*i. e.,* that God would destroy the world) at the time when Noah was preparing the ark.

Luther, "Auslegungen ueber die I. Epistel Petri," *Saemtliche Schriften* (St. L. Ed.), IX:1242—1249; G. Stoeckhardt, *Kommentar ueber den Ersten Brief Petri,* CPH, 1912 (pp. 134—81); F. W. Farrar, *Mercy and Judgment,* Dutton, 1881 (pp. 75—81); John Pearson, *An Exposition of the Creed,* Appleton, N. Y., 1853 (pp. 340—80); J. T. Mueller, "Notes on Christ's Descent to Hell," *CTM,* XVIII:610—17.

Design, Argument from. See *Apologetics.*

Desires. See *Lust.*

Deszler, Wolfgang Christoph (1660 to 1722). Studied theology; amanuensis at Nuernberg; conrector of School of the Holy Ghost; hymns full of depth and fervor; wrote: "Wie wohl ist mir, o Freund der Seelen"; "Ich lass' dich nicht, du musst mein Jesus bleiben."

Determinism. The theory regarding the human will according to which man in his actions is absolutely determined by psychological or other conditions; opposed to indeterminism, which declared man's will to be free. There are various forms of determinism — the theological, as in Calvinism, the mechanical of materialism, which regards man merely as a machine, the fatalistic (see *Fatalism*), and others.

Deuterocanonical. See *Apocrypha,* A 4.

Deuteronomic Code. See *Higher Criticism,* 13.

Deutsche Christen. See *Barmen Theses.*

Deutschmann, John (1625—1706). Son-in-law of Calov; professor at Wittenberg; opposed the syncretism and pietism of Spener.

Devay (Matthias Biro, ca. 1500—45). Originally Catholic; then a strong exponent of Lutheranism ("Ungarischer Luther"); 1539 entered Luther's *Tischkreis;* later went to Geneva and worked for Calvinism.

Developmental Method. See *Christian Teaching,* L.

Devil. A term literally meaning the accuser, 1 Pet. 5:8; in Scripture usually a descriptive name of Satan, also used in the plural for the fallen angels (demons, evil spirits, unclean spirits), the chief of whom, Matt. 12:24, is called Satan by way of eminence. Satan himself, for whose subjugation Christ came, is the originator of all wickedness, Eph. 2:2, an opponent of the kingdom of God. He is the tempter of the faithful, 1 Pet. 5:8 ff., who led Eve into sin and so became the originator and king of death, Heb. 2:14. Originally created good, the evil spirits, through their own fault, fell, 2 Pet. 2:4, and are destined to a future fearful sentence. — That the devil is a personal being is clear from the teaching of the Epistles and no less from the Gospels, being the express teaching of Jesus Christ. Satan enters the heart of Judas. His malign power is evident in many examples of possession. Matt. 12:28, and often. Such texts cannot be explained away on the principle of accommodation to Jewish teaching. Never did Jesus cast suspicion upon this part of the Jewish doctrine. He accepted it without question. Matt. 13; Mark 4:15; Luke 22:31. Again, Jesus sets the seal of His authority upon the doctrine in question by expressly stating that the everlasting punishment to which the unfaithful are condemned was originally "prepared for the devil and his angels" (Matt. 25:41). Finally, He speaks of Satan as the prince of this world and announces as the aim and the certain result of His own work the Judgment and the casting out of Satan and his kingdom (John 12:31).

Devil's Advocate. See *Canonization*.

Devotional Literature. See *Literature, Lutheran,* 3.

DeWette, Wilhelm Martin Leberecht (1780—1849). German theologian; influenced by Paulus and Schleiermacher, professor of Basel; author of OT Introduction, commentaries; edited Luther's works; prepared way for Supplement Theory in OT criticism. See *Higher Criticism,* 13.

Dewi (David). See *Celtic Church,* 9.

Dexter, Henry Martyn (1821—90). Educated at Yale and Andover; Congregational pastor at Manchester and Boston; known as the translator of the hymn: "Shepherd of Tender Youth."

Deyling, Salomo (1677—1755). Lutheran; professor at Leipzig; known for his *Institutiones Prudentiae Pastoralis.*

Diaconate. See *Deacons; Deaconesses.*

Diaconics. That branch of theological knowledge which treats of the history and of the theory of home missions and inner missions, the former dealing with scattered Christians, the latter with the poor, neglected, and wretched, and with criminals.

Dialectic (Gr. *dialegesthai,* to converse). A method of thinking and the things known by such thought. Aristotle held that Zeno discovered the dialectic method. Heraclitus, however, used it long before Zeno. He held that law and harmony in the universe exists as the result of opposites (light — darkness; heat — cold; etc.). Plato was one of the greatest dialecticians, using the method for analyzing ideas in his dia-

logues. Aristotle held that the purpose of dialectics is to examine the bases underlying sciences. As a result of the Stoics' division of dialectics into logic and rhetoric, the Middle Ages regarded the term as synonymous with logic or as a division thereof. Hegel held that all reality is divided into opposite poles and that truth (synthesis) must be sought through antithesis. Karl Marx applied dialectic to social theories, holding, for example, that every class calls into being an opposite class (rulers — subjects; capital — labor) and that progress results from the struggle. Kant used the dialectical method to show that the criteria applied to phenomena cannot be applied to the *Ding an sich.* Karl Barth operates with the dialectical method inasmuch as he shows opposite poles in the "this-side" and the "yon-side" (God — man; eternal — temporal; etc.), but the synthesis in Barth's thinking does not rise *per se* from the opposite poles but must come from the "yon-side."

Diaspora. Denotes, first, the Jews living outside the borders of the Holy Land; later it was used to designate the scattered Christians. Latterly it is applied to Lutherans living among other religionists, chiefly in Roman Catholic countries. The Moravians employed the term to designate the results of their missionary activity among the members of the state churches in Europe.

Diatessaron (Gr. "through four"). A harmony of the Four Gospels written to make one continuous narrative; especially applied to that of Tatian.

Diaz, Juan (d. 1546). Prominent Spanish reformer of the 16th century; studied theology at Paris for thirteen years; brought to the knowledge of evangelical truth by Jaime Enzinas; with Calvin at Geneva and with Bucer at Regensburg; assassinated at the instigation of his brother.

Dibelius, Martin (1883—1947). Professor at Heidelberg (1915); specialist in early Christian history; belongs to the *Formgeschichtliche Schule* (holds, however, that the Passion narrative was essentially a continuous account from earliest times); wrote: *Commentary on James, From Tradition to Gospel, Gospel Criticism and Christology, A Fresh Approach to the New Testament and Early Christian Literature, The Sermon on the Mount, The Message of Jesus,* and others.

Dictatus Papae. Theses on papal rights, formerly ascribed to Gregory VII, but in reality a composition of his followers.

Dictionaries. The earliest important Christian dictionary was the *Onomasticon* of Eusebius, which dealt with Palestinian geography (translated by Jerome). Jerome wrote two works, one on Hebrew proper names (*De Nominibus Hebraicis*) and the other on outstanding Christians (*De Viris Illustris*). Thereafter no important dictionary appeared until the Reformation revived Biblical scholarship. The term *encyclopedia* properly refers in theology to a series of treatises often embracing all theology, with a list of literature. The term *cyclopedia* is also usually used of a work which treats the subject more thoroughly than a dictionary and gives references. This distinction between *cyclopedia* and *dictionary* has practically disappeared in the field of theology. See *Encyclopedia; Lexicon.*

The following list includes the most important works. The latest works are usually by numerous authors whose theological positions are indicated in their contributions. The list gives works called "dictionaries." See *Encyclopedia* for additional titles.

I. *Biblical.* A. Calmet, *Dictionnaire historique, critique, chronologique, geographique, et litterale de la Bible,* Paris, 1722 (2 vols.; 1730 ed., 4 vols.; translation); G. B. Winer, *Biblisches Real-Woerterbuch,* Leipzig, 1820 (2 vols.); Wm. Smith, *Dictionary of the Bible,* London, 1860—64 (3 vols.); John D. Davis, *A Dictionary of the Bible,* The Westminster Press, 1940 (1st ed., 1898. Revised by H. S. Gehman as the *Westminster Dictionary of the Bible*); James Hastings, *Dictionary of the Bible,* Clark, Edinburgh, 1909—14; James Hastings, *Dictionary of the Bible,* Scribner's, 1901—23 (5 vols.); M. W. Jacobs (and others), *A Standard Bible Dictionary,* Funk & Wagnalls, 1909; Th. Graebner, *A Dictionary of Bible Topics,* Zondervan, Grand Rapids, Mich., rev. 1944. See also *Geography.*

II. *Ecclesiastical.* Thomas Broughton, *Bibliotheca Historica Sacra,* London, 1737 (2 vols.); F. Lucius Ferraris, *Prompta Bibliotheca canonica, juridica, moralis, theologica, necnon ascetica, polemica, rubricistica, historica,* Madrid, 1795 (10 vols.; Roman Catholic); Charles Buck, *Unparteiisches Handwoerterbuch der Religion und Kirchengeschichte,*

Schaefer & Konradi, Philadelphia, 1834 (8th ed. copyrighted by Eastern Dist. of Pa.); J. Newton Brown, *Encyclopedia of Religious Knowledge,* or, *Dictionary of the Bible, Theology, Religious Biography, All Religions, Ecclesiastical History and Missions,* Brattleborough, 1835; Wetzer and Welte, *Kirchen-Lexikon,* Freiburg, 1848—56 (12 vols.; Roman Catholic); W. F. Hook, *A Church Dictionary,* London, 1852 (Anglican); John Farrar, *An Ecclesiastical Dictionary,* London, 1853; R. Eden, *The Churchman's Theological Dictionary,* London, 1859 (Anglican); Wm. Smith & Samuel Cheetham, *A Dictionary of Christian Antiquities,* London, 1880; Macaulay Jackson, Talbot Wilson Chambers, Frank Hugh Foster, *Concise Dictionary of Religious Knowledge,* Christian Lit. Co., N. Y., 1891; Carl Meusel, Ernst Haack, B. Lehmann. A. Hofstetter, *Kirchliches Handlexikon,* Naumann, Leipzig, 1887—1902 (7 vols.); Shailer Mathews and Girald Birney Smith, *A Dictionary of Religion and Ethics,* Macm., N. Y., 1921. See references under *Biography.*

III. *Philosophical.* James Mark Baldwin, *Dictionary of Philosophy and Psychology,* Peter Smith, N. Y., 1940 (2 vols.); Dagobert D. Runes, *Dictionary of Philosophy,* Philosophical Library, N. Y., 1942.

Didache. See *Apostolic Fathers, 8.*

Dieckhoff, August Wilhelm (1823 to 1894). Leading confessional Lutheran theologian; 1860 professor at Rostock; wrote against von Hofmann, also against Ritschl; in the controversy on election and conversion he sided with the opponents of the Synodical Conference.

Diedrich, Julius (1819—1899). In 1847 he seceded from the Prussian Union to join the Breslau Synod; there he opposed hierarchical tendencies; 1860 he and six other pastors withdrew from the Breslau Synod and in 1862 formed the Immanuel Synod.

Dieffenbach, Georg Christian (1822 to 1901). Teacher in Schlitz and then in Darmstadt; in 1855 assistant pastor in Schlitz and in 1873 chief pastor; very fruitful in literary labors, especially in liturgical and devotional books, among which are his *Evangelisches Brevier* (for pastors) and *Evangelische Handagende* (for family worship).

Diehl, C. F. See *Canada, Lutheranism in, 5.*

Dies Irae. One of the grandest sequences, or hymns, of the Middle Ages, its author being Thomas of Celano, a pupil of Francis of Assisi, the guiding thought of the poem being taken from Zeph. 1:15 (Vulgate version), but containing the fundamental thought concerning redemption through the atonement of Christ, especially in stanza 10; more than 150 translations.

Diesterweg, Friedrich Adolf Wilhelm (1790—1866). Outstanding German educator of the 19th century; was teacher of the model school at Frankfurt, director of the teachers' seminary at Moors, then of that in Berlin, where through his practice school he revolutionized the methods in the Berlin elementary schools; reduced Pestalozzi's theories to workable methods; an exposition of his ideas is found in his *Wegweiser fuer deutsche Lehrer.*

Diet. Originally the yearly spring meeting of the free Frank warriors. In time the leaders in church and state arrogated powers to themselves and finally became the whole assembly, or Diet. Later on only three ecclesiastical and four lay princes elected the Emperor, and they enlarged their powers by the Capitulations of Election, conditions before election, first sworn to by Charles V. At this time the Diet, or *Reichstag,* consisted of the electors, the princes and nobles, and the representatives of cities.

Diet of Worms. See *Worms, Diet of.*

Dieterich, Konrad. B. Jan. 9, 1575, at Gemuende, Hessen-Cassel; *subdiaconus* at Marburg; deposed and exiled by the Reformed government for his staunch Lutheranism; professor and director at Giessen; superintendent at Ulm, Wuerttemberg, and director of the Gymnasium; wrote a large exposition of Luther's Small Catechism (translated into German by Dr. F. W. A. Notz) and a small one for the schools (translated and edited by authority of the Missouri Synod and was in use in that synod for many years); d. Mar. 22, 1639.

Dietrich of Nieheim (Niem). B. between 1338 and 1348; d. 1418. Jurist; notary of the sacred palace; abbreviator and scriptor in the papal chancery. He is considered one of the greatest publicists at the time of the great schism. As a delegate to the Council of Constance, he listed the misdeeds of Pope John XXIII.

Dietrich, Sixt (1490/95—1548). A Lutheran composer of the Reformation era who lived in Wittenberg (1541—42). A pupil of Heinrich Isaac and a friend of the musicologist Glareanus, who regarded Dietrich as one of the great composers of his day. Seven of his compositions were published by Georg Rhaw; all were based on chorales.

Dietrich, Veit (1506—49). Luther's confidential secretary in 1527; with him at Marburg and the Coburg; preacher in Nuernberg; got out an agenda, Luther's House Postil, and devotional writings, the *Summaries of the Old and the New Testament.* When Nuernberg bowed to the Augsburg Interim, he wished to leave town.

Dietrichson, John W. C. (1815—82). Ordained at Christiania, Norway; came to America (1844) and organized congregations in Wisconsin; returned to Norway (1850).

Diets, Lutheran, in America (1877, 1878, and 1898). These were free assemblies at which clerical and lay Lutherans of various synods met in Philadelphia, Pa., for edification and discussion on doctrinal subjects. At the first two of these about 100 ministers and as many laymen were present, none of whom officially represented his particular Lutheran body. The papers read and discussed were afterwards published in two volumes. The third diet was held from Dec. 27—29, 1898, and was called "The First General Conference of Lutherans in America."

H. E. Jacobs, *First Free Lutheran Diet in America,* J. Frederick Smith, Philadelphia, 1878.

Diffusionist School. In anthropology, a school which opposes the spontaneous, evolutionary development of cultures and holds that cultures developed through borrowing from a few centers (*e. g.,* Babylonia, Egypt, etc.).

Digambara. See *Jainism.*

Diggers, The. A group of revolutionists in the days of Cromwell who advocated communism and adjustment of economic inequalities.

Dilfeld, Konrad Georg (d. 1684). B. and d. in Nordhausen; defender of the Lutheran confessions, especially against pietism; wrote *Theosophia Horbio-Speneriana* against Spener's view that only the converted could teach effectively and administer the sacraments.

Dilherr, Johann Michael (1604—69). Professor at Jena, director of the *Gymnasium*, and later pastor at Nuernberg; one of the most learned men and the greatest preacher of his time; in theology collaborator in the *Weimar Bibelwerk;* deeply interested in poetry; wrote some sixty hymns, among them: "Ermuntre dich, Herz, Mut und Sinn."

Diller (Dilherr), Michael (d. 1570). Little is known about Diller's early youth; b. about 1500; prior of the Augustinian monastery at Spires, he began to preach evangelical sermons in neighboring churches (ca. 1530) without, however, mentioning Luther or the Pope; until 1548 he was protected by the city council against bishops and emperor; went to Basel, but later became court preacher of Ottheinrich of the Palatinate (1553), where, with Johann Brenz, he introduced the Reformation; became court preacher at Heidelberg (1556); participated in the colloquies at Worms (1557) and Maulbronn (1564); throughout the religious controversies he emphasized tolerance; inclined more and more to the Reformed position and finally participated in the introduction of Calvinism.

Dillmann, Christian F. (1823—94). German Lutheran scholar; professor at Tuebingen, Kiel, Giessen, and Berlin; known for his work on the Ethiopic Bible and his commentaries on OT.

Dilthey, William (1833—1911). German philosopher; supporter of positive idealism, regarding the external world as a phenomenon arising out of pure experience.

Ding an sich (thing-in-itself). A term, used by Kant * to denote the real objects which underlie the phenomena and exist outside of our consciousness, in distinction from the phenomena, or appearance, by which they become perceptible to the senses.

Dinsmore, Charles Allen (1860 to 1941). Congregational minister; lecturer at Yale (1920); outstanding American scholar on Dante *(The Teachings of Dante; Aids to the Study of Dante; Life of Dante);* wrote *Atonement in Literature and Life.*

Dinter, Gustav Friedrich (1760 to 1831). Distinguished German clergyman and educator; pastor near Borna; principal of the normal school at Dresden; inspector of schools in the province of Prussia; exerted great influence on the development of German elementary schools, where he first introduced the ideas of the philanthropists and of Pestalozzi; wrote: *Bible for Schoolmasters; Chief Rules of Pedagogy.*

Diocese. The territory administered by a bishop. The diocese of an archbishop is called an archdiocese. The bishop is the ruler of the diocese, but in his administration is bound by the rules of the church. He divides his diocese into parishes and assigns the clergy. Where there are no canons (see Chapter), distinguished members of the diocesan clergy act as consultors, the bishop being held to consult them in important matters. The church where the bishop has his throne *(cathedra)* is the cathedral. After the bishop the principal authority in the diocese is the vicar-general.* The fiscal procurator attends the interests of the diocese in court. A chancellor may be appointed to keep the records; deans, to supervise the clergy of a portion of the diocese. The creation and modification of dioceses is reserved to the Pope. There were 25 archdioceses and 105 dioceses in the U.S. in 1952.

Diocletian (245—313). Roman Emperor (284—305); instituted longest and most severe persecution * of Christians.

Diodati, Giovanni (1576—1649). Genevan of noble Italian family; professor of theology at Geneva; pastor at Nimes; attended Synod of Dort; translated Bible into Italian, 1607; revised French version.

Diodorus (d. before 394). Bishop of Tarsus (378); outstanding leader of the Antiochene school and founder of its dogmatics; fought monophysitism and Arianism; opponent of Alexandrian school; his Christological doctrine condemned as Nestorianism at Ephesus (431).

Diognetus, Epistle to. See *Apostolic Fathers,* 7.

Dionysius of Alexandria (d. 265). B. of heathen parents; pupil of Origen; "teacher of the Catholic Church" (Athanasius); head of catechetical school * at Alexandria (232); banished in reign of Valerian (257); returned (260). Wrote: *De natura* (famous treatise against atomic materialism); *De promissionibus* (opposed Chiliasm of Nepos); *Refutationis et Defensionis* (D. opposed Sabellianism, but is accused by Dionysius of Rome of pluralism and tritheism; prelude to Arian conflict).

Dionysius the Areopagite. Converted by Paul at Athens (Acts 17:34); tradition regards him as the first bishop at Athens; in 6th century certain Neo-Platonic writings were falsely ascribed to him.

Dionysius Exiguus. A monk of the sixth century (d. before 544), who spent much time in computing the probable dates of great events in the history of the world, especially that of the birth of Christ, which he placed on December 25, 754 *a. u. c.* (after the founding of Rome), this being between five and seven years from the correct date. But his computation is the basis of our present chronological reckoning.

Dionysius of Rome. Bishop (259 to 268); reorganized Roman church after Valerian persecution; engaged in doctrinal controversy with Dionysius of Alexandria.

Diplomatics. That part of archaeology which deals with ancient writings, literary and public documents, letters, charters, decrees, etc., especially with regard to their decipherment and dating.

Dippel, Johann Konrad (1866—1933). German physician, alchemist, and Pietist theologian; lived for a time in the Netherlands and Sweden; wrote *Eroeffneter Weg zum Frieden mit Gott und mit allen Kreaturen.*

Diptychs. Lists of names of saints or benefactors which were read from the ambo of the altar during the canon of the mass, thus giving rise to the term "canonization."

Direct Calls. See *Teachers,* A 6.

Director of Christian Education. See *Parish Education,* L 4.

Directory of Church Government. See *Presbyterian Bodies,* 2.

Directory of Worship. See *Norway, Lutheranism in,* 3.

Disabled American Veterans. See *Veterans Organization.*

Discernment of Spirits. A gift possessed in apostolic times whereby the sources of prophets (whether of God, of man, or of demons) were discerned and the secret dispositions of men judged (1 Cor. 12:10; 1 Cor. 14:29; 1 John 5:1). It was a gift needed at a time when many false prophets were in the world (2 John 2:7. Compare Acts 5:39; 8:21; 13:9). Later (Ignatius and the *Didache*) rules for judging prophets were given.

Disciples of Christ. An American religious movement, the original purpose of which was to restore primitive Christianity and to unite all Christians upon the basis of the Bible alone.

1. *Antecedents.* Though the Disciples are an indigenous American church, similar movements antedated it in England. a) John Locke had emphasized that Christians should unite on the basis of such teachings "as the Holy Spirit has in the Holy Scriptures declared, in express words, to be necessary for salvation." b) Eighteenth century Restorationists in England. The *Glassites,* founded by John Glas (1695 to 1773) opposed state connection and sought to conduct affairs of the church after the primitive pattern. This group was also known as Sandemanians (Robert Sandeman; son-in-law of Glas; 1718—1771). A similar movement was started by Robert and James Haldane. The churches of the reformers were usually called "Churches of Christ."

2. *History.* a) Thomas Campbell (1763—1854) gave the initial impulse to the formation of the "Disciples" churches. He was an Irish Seceder Presbyterian minister of Scottish descent who had diligently studied John Locke's *Letters Concerning Toleration* and *Essay on the Human Understanding.* At Rich Hill (near Belfast) he came into contact with the influence of the English Restorationists. He migrated to America (1807) but was soon expelled by the synod which he joined chiefly for practicing open communion and holding that a qualified layman might conduct a service when no pastor was available. Before the final expulsion, Campbell had organized the "Christian Association of Washington, Pa." (1809), for which he wrote the *Declaration and Address* (advocates Christian unity; creeds useful for instruction but not membership tests; New Testament is perfect as a "constitution for worship, discipline, and government"; full knowledge of revealed truth unnecessary for membership; love of brethren only basis for fellowship; rejects all human opinions, deductions, and inferences).

b) Alexander Campbell (son of Thomas, 1788—1866) came to America (1809) and soon became the leader of the new movement. When his first child was born, the Campbells decided that sprinkling of infants was not in harmony with the NT and advocated immersion. Thereupon the "Christian Association of Washington" (known also as "Brush Run Church") applied for membership in the Redstone Baptist Association and from 1813 to 1930 was a reform movement within the Baptist Church. The *Christian Reformer* (1823—29) of Alexander Campbell attacked authority of clergy, synods and church "courts," use of creeds, Bible societies, Sunday schools, etc.

c) The so-called Christian churches, originating in the Cane Ridge Revivals, 1801, adopted principles similar to those of the Campbells (emphasis on primitive Christianity, right of private judgment, local independence). In 1831 the group of these "Christian Churches" under Barton W. Stone merged with the main current of the Disciples.

d) The work of Walter Scott (born Edinburgh, 1796) in the Mahoning Association (Ohio) led to the separation from Baptists. Scott in his "Divinely Authorized Plan of Preaching the Gospel" sought to outline the steps by which a person becomes a Christian: (1) Faith, the persuasion of the mind by rational evidence; (2) Repentance of sins; (3) Baptism; (4) Remission of sins; (5) Gift of the Holy Spirit. The first three steps he regarded as entirely within human power; the last two were God's acts. In 1830 the followers of the Campbells and Scott left the Baptist Church taking many of the latter's members with them (differing doctrines; baptism for remission of sins; faith, baptism, and repentance constitute regeneration; faith, a rational act; Holy Spirit operates through the Word alone; rejection of Calvinistic view of election; rejection of creeds; any believer may administer Sacraments; no sharp distinction between clergy and laity; autonomy of local congregation). Thus began the separate existence of the Disciples. In 1832 a large portion of the group of Christian Churches (especially in Kentucky and Ohio) united with the Disciples. During the ensuing years the Disciples continued to grow (without organization and without headquarters) and developed a sense of unity. Efforts at national organization encountered resistance since the local congregations feared an authoritative body. The first national convention met at Cincinnati (1849) and organized the "American Christian Missionary Society." Most of the missionary work, however, continued to be performed by State and local groups.

e) 1866—1875 is often called "The Period of Controversy" by the Disciples.

Although the group had successfully passed through the Civil War, such questions as open communion, admission of non-immersed as members, use of instrumental music, formulation of creeds, national missionary societies, etc., caused dissension. A group of conservatives withdrew because of their opposition to mission societies and use of instrumental music (anti-organ).

f) Succeeding years were marked by expansion, organization of mission societies (merged, 1920, into the United Christian Missionary Society), and federation.

3. *Doctrine.* Since their fundamental principle is "to restore in faith, spirit, and practice the Christianity of Christ and the Apostles as found in the New Testament," therefore they reject all ecclesiastical terminology, creeds, and denominational names as contrary to the NT. Nevertheless the Disciples have a "distinct message," which is clearly set forth by their representative leaders such as: Thomas Campbell, *Declaration and Address;* Alexander Campbell, *The Christian System;* Peter Ainslee, *The Message of Disciples for Union;* Isaac Errett, *Our Position; A Brief Statement of the Plea for a Return to the Gospel* and *First Principles, or the Elements of the Gospel.* A strong rationalistic trend is evident. Campbell held views, concerning the Trinity which approached Sabellianism, and the Disciples today define the Trinity as "the revelation of God in a threefold personality." They deny total depravity and the election of grace as contrary to reason. Legalism is a characteristic in Disciples' theology: Christ is viewed as King with universal authority and leadership; the distinction between Law and Gospel consists in rejecting the binding character of the Old Testament and making the New Testament the perfect constitution for worship, government, and discipline; baptism, by immersion, is viewed as an act of obedience for the remission of sins; the Lord's Supper is celebrated every Sunday as a memorial feast. In recent years liberalism has gained the upper hand among the Disciples.

4. The polity of the Disciples is congregational. The local church is known as "Church of Christ" or "Christian Church." The churches unite in district and State conventions, but these are advisory in character. A general convention, "The International Convention of the Disciples of Christ," composed of individual members of the

churches, meets annually, but has no jurisdiction over the local churches.

5. The earliest colleges of the Disciples were: Bacon (Lexington, Ky., 1836) and Bethany (Bethany, W. Va., 1841). Today they have 13 colleges and universities, including Butler University. Foundations at state universities were also established.

6. The Disciples have played a prominent role in interdenominational movements. They number 1,945,607 (1952) members in the U. S. Cf. *Congregational and Christian Churches.* See *Religious Bodies (U. S.), Bibliography.*

Disciplina Arcana. See *Ecumenical Creeds,* A 3.

Discipline in General. In its ecclesiastical sense this term denotes actions partly of a penal and partly of a reformatory nature directed against one who has offended against morality or the church law. Discipline existed in the Church in early and medieval times. At the beginning of Lent those convicted of notorious sins were put to open penance for their spiritual benefit as a warning to others. When the Pacacy was at its height, excommunication was a weapon so formidable that even powerful kings quailed at the thought that it might be directed against them. In the Church of England, excommunication has given place to the commination service on Ash Wednesday. In Presbyterian churches, discipline is exercised by the session, an appeal being allowed to the Presbytery and thence to Synod and the General Assembly. In the constitutions of the Reformed churches of America (German and Dutch) the principles and rules of discipline laid down are very similar to those of the Presbyterian Church. In the Lutheran Church, discipline is administered by the local congregation on the basis of the Word of God (Matt. 18). In the Methodist Episcopal Church an accused member is brought to trial before a committee of not less than five, who must not be members of the Quarterly Conference. Appeals are allowed to the Quarterly and Annual Conferences. For information on Scriptural teachings regarding Church Discipline see *Keys, Office of.*

Discipline of 1944. See *Methodist Bodies,* 2.

Discretion, Age of. See *Confession.*

Discussion Method. See *Christian Teaching,* I ff.

Disinterested Benevolence. See *New England Theology,* 3.

Dispensationalism. The Scofield Reference Bible, which advocates dispensationalism, defines a dispensation as a period of time during which man is tested in respect to obedience to some specific revelation of the will of God. Dispensationalists such as Iraeneus, Origen, Tertullian, Montanus, the Shakers, and J. N. Darby have divided the history of the world into three, four, or more dispensations. Modern dispensationalists believe that the history of man will comprise seven dispensations, the last dispensation constituting the millennial reign of Christ on earth. They argue that in previous dispensations God and Christ could not carry out the divine plan for mankind and that for this reason God will test man's obedience in a final dispensation. The pre-millennialists say that because of man's disobedience in general and the Jews' obstinacy in particular, Christ was unable to fulfill the many Messianic prophecies, such as the re-establishment of the' throne of David, the conversion of the Jews, the building of His glorious kingdom. Therefore Christ was satisfied to found only the Kingdom of God, or the Church, during His first coming to the world, and to await the establishment of His own glorious kingdom during His second advent into the world, that is, in the final dispensation. In this final period of God's special revelation the Jewish race will accept Christ as its king, establish a glorious kingdom in Palestine, and rule with Christ for 1,000 years. And all nations will recognize Christ's sovereign rule. In support of these vagaries many premillennialists appeal to the theory that God has and will reveal His will in seven different dispensations. They say that as God created the world in six days and rested on the seventh day, so the history of mankind must also comprise six periods of labor and one period of rest. Prominent dispensationalist writers, *e. g.,* Scofield and Blackstone, see in the number "seven" the sacred rock on which their entire Scripture interpretation seems to be built. The Levitical worship, so they say, revolved about the week. There was a "week of weeks" (seven weeks) between the Passover and the Pentecost festival; a "week of months" (seven months) between the Passover and the atonement; a "week of years," (the sabbatical year); a "week of weeks of years" (the jubilee year after forty-nine years). All millennialists assume that in prophecy 2 Pet. 3:8 (a day is as a thousand years) must apply. The dispensationalists, therefore, claim that each day of the creation week prophetically typifies a corresponding thousand years in the history of the world. The dispensationalists are not agreed in fixing the chronology of the "world-week." Some dispensationalists are time-setters. They divide the history of mankind into seven periods, each lasting exactly 1,000 sun years (?). The year 6,000 since the creation is said to be imminent, and the beginning of the world-Sabbath may be expected momentarily. Some say that each dispensation begins with a catastrophe and ends with a new revelation, even as in Gen. 1, the evening is mentioned before the morning. The majority of the dispensationalists, however, hold that every dispensation begins with a new revelation and ends with a catastrophe, as punishment for man's disobedience, some dispensations being relatively short, others longer. The most popular theory is as follows: 1) The state of innocence ending with the fall. 2) Man is governed by his conscience, proves unfaithful again, and is punished by the Flood. 3) The period of human government, Gen. 9:6, ending with the destruction of Sodom and Gomorrah. 4) God revealed the Messianic promise to the patriarchs. The destruction of Pharaoh shows the inadequacy of this dispensation. 5) In the Mosaic period God revealed Himself as the covenant-God. The crucifixion was the catastrophic ending for this day. 6) We are in the Christian, or the mystery, period in which Christ reveals Himself through the Gospel. This period will end with the great tribulation and the second coming of Christ, the judgment of the nations as to their attitude toward Christ's brethren, the Jews, Matt. 24:31 ff., 40, the destruction of the Antichrist. 7) This is the dispensation of manifestation, the millennium, corresponding to the Sabbath of the creation week, and will last for a thousand years. But even in this period not all will obey, and the world-Sabbath will end with the judgment at the White Throne, the destruction of Satan and the earth. The believers will now enter heaven and the unbelievers eternal destruction.

Pre-millennialists and dispensationalists make much of the "missing week" in Dan. 9:24-27, claiming that this seven-year period will occur immediately prior to Christ's pre-millennial coming. The following events are to occur during the last seven years of our dispensation: Christ's invisible return to resurrect the just and transform the living believers; the ascension of these and the "rapture" of the bride, Eph. 5:25-32; the tribulation over the Jewish people, Matt. 24:21; Christ's visible return to the Mount of Olives; the destruction of the Jews' enemies, the Antichrist; Gog and Magog; conversion of all Jews and their return to Jerusalem; the judgment of the nations; the end of the sixth and the beginning of the seventh dispensation; Christ's rule of equity and universal peace together with His "brethren," the Jews, for 1,000 years.

Dispensationalism is said to be the core and center of the Bible. But this system rests on an arbitrary interpretation of the Bible. In particular the entire system is contrary to the analogy of the Scripture: 1) The distinction between God's kingdom (the Church) and Christ's kingdom (millennium) is without warrant. 2) Throughout the history of the world God deals with men only through the Law and the Gospel. 3) To say that in the period of manifestation the Jews shall be converted by a glorious manifestation of Christ, is the Calvinistic aberration of irresistible grace, and a denial of the efficacy of the means of grace. 4) Scripture nowhere promises that the Church will escape the tribulation during the final period of the world's history. 5) Scripture does not say that the hatred of the Antichrist will be directed primarily against the Jews, the "Lord's brethren," but describes him as the opponent of Christ and His vicarious atonement. The chief characteristic of the Antichrist is his condemnation of the doctrine of justification by faith. 6) The doctrine of the universal conversion of the Jews is not taught in Scriptures. 7) The doctrine of a twofold (or three-fold) resurrection has no foundation in Scripture. 8) The assumption that the resurrected and transformed saints will spend seven years in heaven only to return to this world for a thousand years is unscriptural and unreasonable. 9) And chiefly, the dispensationalists remove soteriology from the center of Christian doctrine and over-emphasize eschatology. In fact, the work of Christ becomes primarily the establishment of a kingdom of peace and prosperity for the present world. His redemption from sin, death, and the devil recedes into the background. — The dispensationalists differ from Jehovah's Witnesses and similar cults whose millennial ideas are based on a different principle. FEM

F. E. Mayer, "Dispensationalism Examined and Found Wanting," *CTM*, XVII: 89—94; O. T. Allis, *Prophecy and the Church*, 1946.

Dispensations. Special relaxations of law in particular cases; usually, licenses granted by Pope or bishop to individuals, suspending for their benefit some law of the Church or relieving them from the normal consequences of transgressing such a law. The supreme dispensing power in the Roman Church is vested in the Pope, and its use is absolutely at his discretion. It is held that he can dispense from all ecclesiastical laws, but not from the divine Law, though, indeed, from obligations to God incurred by a man of his own free will, *i.e.*, by oath or vow. Any limitation, however, must be self-imposed, since the Pope, by virtue of his teaching authority, defines the limits of his own dispensing power. Only the Pope can dispense from universal laws or laws issued by Popes and councils. Bishops can dispense from their own statutes and those of predecessors and are granted additional powers by the Pope. Priests can dispense parishioners from fasting, abstinence, and the like. A large proportion of dispensations are matrimonial dispensations, by which impediments are removed that ordinarily would prohibit or annul a marriage. Such dispensations are granted either to permit an intended marriage or to legitimize one already contracted. If an impediment is admittedly of divine origin, no dispensation can be granted. A bishop can dispense for lighter (prohibitory) impediments; only the Pope, or those empowered by him, for the more serious (diriment) ones. (See *Impediments of Marriage*.) Dispensations which were productive of much revenue in the Middle Ages are now supposed to be gratuitous. The chanceries of bishops are permitted to levy only a single tax. When, however, a request for dispensation must be carried to the Roman Curia, the expenses are considerable. They fall under four heads: expenses of that particular proceeding; a tax for the general administration of dispensations; the componendum, a fine paid to the officials and "applied by them to pious uses" (*Catholic Encyclopedia*); alms distributed by the petitioners. Thus papal indulgences, though gratuitous, still produce some little revenue for application "to pious uses."

Disselhoff, Julius ((1827—96). Ev. theologian; Fliedner's helper at Kaiserswerth; after Fliedner's death, director of the institution.

Dissenter. A term usually applied to those who agree with the Established Church on the most essential doctrines, but differ in some minor points or on questions of church government, relation to the State, rites, etc., as, in England, the Presbyterians, Independents, Baptists, and others.

District Boards of Education. See *Parish Education*, L 2.

District Superintendents. See *Parish Education*, L 4.

Divination. An occult art, practiced extensively by heathen, both ancient and modern, claiming for itself the ability to discover the will of the gods, to forecast the future from certain indications and auguries, and to decide from phenomena of an alleged supernatural kind the correct course of action to be followed in a given instance. The power of divination was often ascribed to persons in an abnormal state of mind, either in a condition of ecstasy or of demoniac possession; but it was usually associated with the office of the priests, who made use of various objects, such as the waves of the sea, twigs of trees, the intestines of animals, the flames of a fire, the motions of stars and planets, the movements of fishes, the casting of lots, and many other things with a strong element of chance associated with them, in order to make known to their followers what they declared to be the will of the gods and the exact unfolding of the future.

Divine Healing. The belief in divine healing, which is considered the normal experience of the "sanctified" believers by some of the Holiness groups, is based on the following false premises:

1) All diseases are the direct result of sin. Sin is removed, therefore sickness also. — But Scripture teaches that sickness is sent also for other reasons, John 9:3; the Book of Job. "Therefore afflictions are not always punishments or signs of wrath." *Apology*, VI: 61.

2) All diseases can be healed by a "complete surrender to Christ." Basing their doctrine on Is. 53:4, the divine healers claim that Christ is man's

"double cure," *viz.*, from sin and from sickness. "When the soul is walking in harmony and obedience, the life of God can fully flow into the body. . . . The living, physical Christ must come into your life, sharing His physical life with you in a union which is nearer than the connubial life, so near that the very life of His veins is transferred into yours." Simpson, *The Fourfold Gospel*, 60, 61. "The sanctified Christian receives the healing in Christ's body by faith and as he abides in Christ's living body," p. 64. — But Scripture shows that Christ's healings were not always conditioned upon the patient's attitude toward Christ, *e. g.*, Luke 22:51. The doctrine of divine healing outlined above is vicious, for Christian sufferers who do not find divine healing (*e. g.*, Job, Epaphroditus, Timothy) must be driven to despair, since according to divine healers "they are holding back part of the full testimony or service to Christ and cannot be helped until this difficulty is removed," p. 60.

3) All who are healed are really healed, no matter what may be the evidence of their senses to the contrary. — This premise is a desperate effort to cover up the many failures of the divine healers; and it is anti-Scriptural, for Christ's healings were instantaneous, and those whom Christ healed knew that they were healed. These people pervert God's order, who commands Christians in time of sickness to do both, to pray for God's help and to use the means which God has appointed, for "creatures are only the hands, channels, and means whereby God gives us everything, . . . neither should we in presumption seek other means than God has commanded." *Large Catechism*, I: 26, 27. — In dealing with divine healers the fact must not be overlooked that medical science and psychology are agreed that strong and persistent impressions and suggestions — such as invariably precede the supposed divine cures — modify the patient's functional disposition. FEM

Divine Nature of Jesus. See *Christ Jesus.*

Divine Office. See *Canonical Hours.*

Divine Plan of the Ages. See *Jehovah's Witnesses.*

Divine Right. An idea of kingship (especially promulgated by the Stuarts in England) according to which the right to rule inheres by divine institution in the person of the king by virtue of his heredity.

Divine Science. A small sect having tenets similar to those of Christian Science, organized by Mrs. Malinda Cramer in California (1885).

Divines. See *Ministerial Office,* 1.

Divorce. See *Marriage.*

Dix, William Chatterton (1837—98). Had only a grammar-school education; contributions to hymnody numerous and very valuable; among his hymns: "Come unto Me, Ye Weary"; "As with Gladness Men of Old."

Doane, George Washington (1799 to 1859). B. at Trenton, N. J., graduated from Union College, Schenectady, N. Y., in 1818, and entered the Episcopalian ministry. He held a number of charges in the Episcopal Church, served as professor at Trinity College, Hartford, Conn.; was made rector of Trinity Church in Boston and at last Bishop of New Jersey. He founded St. Mary's Hall, Burlington, and later Burlington College. He published *Songs by the Way.* He died April 27, 1859.

Docetism. A heretical doctrine found in connection with various sects, although a sect by the name Docetae is mentioned by Clement of Alexandria. The fundamental principle of the heresy is that Christ was only seemingly a human being and not in reality.

Doctor of the Church. Title given to eminent fathers of the Church. The Greek doctors were: Athanasius, Basil the Great, Gregory Nazianzen, and Chrysostom; the Latin: Ambrose, Jerome, Augustine, and Gregory the Great.

Doctrinal Theology. See *Dogmatics.*

Doctrine, Christian, History of. 1. Jesus commanded His disciples to teach all nations to observe all things whatsoever He commanded them (Matt. 28:20). What the disciples taught was Christian doctrine. As long as men teach what Jesus commanded them, they teach the truth; when, however, they teach anything contrary to His commands, they teach error or heresy. The teachers of the Christian Church soon found it necessary to defend the truth of their faith against error within their own midst and against attacks from Jews and pagans without. This made it necessary for them to formulate their doctrine, so that it would be clear to others what they taught. This led to the fixation of dogma. Those who taught error, however, also formulated their doctrine, and as the centuries passed by, error increased in scope and variety. The history of doctrine is the record of the development of doctrine and its fixation as dogma within the Christian Church.

2. The earliest pronouncements of doctrine subsequent to the books of the New Testament may be found in the writings of the Apostolic Fathers.* These were followed by the writings of the so-called Greek Apologists (Epistle to Diognetus, Quadratus, Aristides, Melito, Claudius Apollinaris, Miltiades, Athenagoras, Theophilus of Antioch, Tatian, and Flavius Justinus). These men came to the defense of their faith in an era of persecution, endeavoring to convince their adversaries of the merits of the Christian faith. But in praising Christianity as the highest form of philosophical wisdom and truth, they themselves weakened its power as the only means of salvation. During this same period the Church also had to defend itself against error within its own midst (Ebionites, Elkesaites, Gnostics, Encratites, Ophites, Marcion, Montanus, Alogi). The controversy with these errorists resulted in the declaration that revelation and prophecy had ceased and in the fixation of the New Testament canon. During this time two important schools were founded in the East, marking the beginning of scientific theology (Alexandria: Pantaenus, Clement, Origen; Antioch: Lucian, Diodorus, Theodore of Mopsuestia, John of Antioch, Theodoret). In the West Tertullian by his writings became the father of Latin theology. With Irenaeus and Hippolytus he may be regarded as one of the anti-Gnostic Fathers. The development of scientific theology coincides with serious attacks on fundamental Christian doctrine, but also with the correct formulation of the challenged doctrines and their successful defense. The doctrine of the Trinity was endangered by Dynamic or Adoptionist (the two Theodotuses, Paul of Samosata) and by Modalistic (Praxeas, Sabellius) Monarchianism,* and even more so by Arianism * (Arius, Athanasius, Gregory Nazianzus, Basil the Great, Gregory of Nyssa). This controversy led to the Council of Nicaea (325) and the eventual formulation of the second Ecumenical Creed (the Nicene), which in an amended form has come down to us as the Niceno-Constantinopolitan Creed. This creed also took cognizance of the error of the Macedonians or Pneumatomachians * (Macedonius of Constantinople), who denied the deity of the Holy Ghost. Apollinarianism * (Apollinaris: Logos, the mind of Christ) was condemned by the second ecumenical council at Constantinople (381). Nestorianism * (Nestorius) denied the unity of Christ's person. Cyril of Alexandria brought about the condemnation of Nestorius at the third ecumenical council at Ephesus (431). Eutyches taught that Christ, after the incarnation, had only one nature. The ensuing controversy was settled by the ecumenical council at Chalcedon * (451). The chief ideas of this agreement are to be found in the Athanasian Creed. The Chalcedonian settlement was unsuccessfully challenged by Monophysitism and Monotheletism. Summary: Nicaea (325), Christ is divine; Constantinople (381), Christ is human; Ephesus (431), Christ one in Person; Chalcedon (451), Christ two in nature. A fierce anthropological controversy was stirred up by Pelagius (Pelagianism *; Semi - Pelagianism), who taught freedom of the will in spiritual matters and salvation by works. Augustine was his chief opponent. (Sin and grace; predestination.) The persecutions of the Christians by Decius and Diocletian and the problem of the lapsed gave rise to Novatianism * and Donatism.*

3. The early Middle Ages found the Eastern and the Western Church in controversy regarding the use of images (iconoclastic controversy) and the addition to the Nicene Creed of the words "and the Son" (filioque, adopted by the Third Council of Toledo, 589). The seventh ecumenical synod at Nice (787) virtually closed doctrinal development in the Eastern Church. In the Western Church these doctrinal disputes are to be noted: the adoptionist controversy (Elipandus of Toledo and Felix of Urgellis); controversy on predestination (Gottschalk of Orbais vs. Rhabanus Maurus and Hincmar); on the Lord's Supper (Radbertus vs. Ratramus; later Berengar vs. Lanfranc).

4. In the later Middle Ages, philosophy became the handmaid of theology. The great scholastics aimed to harmonize the various doctrines of the Church with the aid of dialectics. The unscriptural sacramental and the sacerdotal system that had developed in the course of centuries had to be fortified and the supremacy of the Pope explained. The

number of sacraments grew from two to seven. Augustinianism (salvation by grace) gave way to Semi-Pelagianism. The immaculate conception of Mary was still being debated, but the trend was in favor of the dogma, finally proclaimed *ex cathedra* in 1854. The papal victory of the conciliar movement prepared the way for the doctrinal declaration of the Roman Church, the papal infallibility decree (1870). The debates centering around the terms "realism," "nominalism," and "conceptualism" all had their influence on the development of doctrine in the medieval Church. The Council of Trent (1545—63) crystallized Roman dogma.

5. Earlier reformers (Waldo, Wiclif, Huss) had not been able greatly to change the direction in which Romanism was falling away from Biblical truth. The greatest challenge to Roman doctrinal aberrations came with the Protestant Reformation. Protestant doctrinal development is linked with the names of Martin Luther, Ulrich Zwingli, and John Calvin. The name Luther suggests his two catechisms, the Augsburg Confession (Melanchthon), the Smalcald Articles. Zwingli's views are set forth in his Sixty-seven Articles of Belief (1523) and in a modified way in the *Tetrapolitana*. Calvinism gave rise to innumerable symbolical expressions (*e. g.*, the Zuerich Consensus, the *Confessio Gallicana*, the Heidelberg Catechism, the Thirty-nine Articles, the Lambeth Articles). Arminianism (Jacobus Arminius) was a synergistic protest against Calvinism (Remonstrants *vs.* Counter-Remonstrants). Post-reformation controversies in the Lutheran Church (Interimistic or Adiaphoristic, Majoristic, Antinomistic, Osiandristic or Stancarian, Synergistic, Flacian, Crypto-Calvinistic, Descent-into-Hell, Predestination) led to the adoption of the Formula of Concord (1577) and the final adoption of the Book of Concord, containing all Lutheran Confessions (1580). This marks the final dogmatic formulation for the Lutheran Church. For the Reformed (Calvinistic) Church the final dates are 1619 (Synod of Dort) and 1649 (Westminster Assembly). The past two centuries have been as marked by various deviations from the accepted standards of the churches as by faithful adherence to them (Deism,* Rationalism,* Modernism *). Unfaithfulness to the Word of God has led to innumerable doctrinal aberra-

tions and the rise of a multitude of religious sects and cults, each with its own doctrinal idiosyncrasies. But by the grace of God, there is still a host of believers who are faithful to the doctrines of His Word. LWS

E. H. Klotsche-J. T. Mueller, *History of Christian Doctrine,* Luth. Lit. Bd., Burlington, Ia., 1945; J. L. Neve, *History of Christian Thought,* United Luth. Pub. House, Philadelphia, 1943 (vol. II published by Muhlenberg Press, Philadelphia, 1946); Reinhold Seeberg, *Lehrbuch d. Dogmengeschichte,* Scholl, Leipzig, 1913—23 (4 vols.).

Documentary Hypothesis. See *Higher Criticism,* 6.

Doddridge, Philip (1702—51). Studied in the non-conformist seminary at Kibworth; minister at Kibworth, later at Northampton, where he was preceptor; noted for wide range of learning; published the *Family Expositor;* among his hymns: "Hark! the Glad Sound, the Savior Comes."

Dods, Marcus (1834—1909). Scottish Biblical scholar; professor at New College; edited Lange's *Life of Christ,* Augustine's works; author of commentaries on Genesis and 1 Corinthians in *Expositor's Bible;* contributed to *Encyclopedia Britannica* and *Hasting's Dictionary of the Bible.*

Dodwell, Henry. See *Deism,* III, 6.

Doederlein, Johann Christoph (1745 to 1792). Lutheran professor of theology at Altorf and Jena; stood at the point of transition between orthodoxy and rationalism; wrote numerous works of which his *Institutio Theologiae* was most widely used.

Doellinger, Johann Josef Ignaz (1799—1890). Church historian and leader of the Old Catholic movement *; professor at Munich (1826); the break with Rome started on account of the doctrine of the Immaculate Conception; the actual break occurred when the infallibility of the Pope was proclaimed (1870) and Doellinger was formally excommunicated by the Pope; wrote *Past and Present of Catholic Theology, The Reformation, The Pope and the Council.*

Dogma. See *Doctrine, History of; Dogmatics.*

Dogmatic Foundation. See *Fundamental Doctrines.*

Dogmatics. A branch of systematic theology in which the teachings of the Bible concerning God and His work for man and in man are systematically arranged. The Bible was revealed to man in the course of centuries through different penmen, and statements concerning divine truth are found in various parts of the Bible and in various connections. Christian dogmatics seeks to bring all the teachings concerning each divine truth together and to arrange these truths in a systematic way. Thus the truths of the Bible must first be studied and understood (see *Exegesis; Hermeneutics*); then they may be carefully stated and arranged.

I. The word "dogmatics" comes from the Greek word *dogma* (*dokei moi, i. e.*, not only that which seems best and right, but also that which is determined and to be held or believed). The word is used in the Greek translation (LXX) of the Old Testament for decrees and laws (Esther 3:9; Dan. 2:13; 6:8). In the New Testament it is used for the Mosaic Law (Col. 2:14; Eph. 2:15) and for the decisions of the Jerusalem Council (Acts 16:4). In the writings of the Church Fathers the word *dogma* is used for the established truths of Christianity (Ignatius, *ad Magn.*, III; Clement of Alexandria, *Strom.*, VII; and others), but also for teachings which heretics regarded as well-founded and basic (so Origen). For some time after the Reformation the terms *sacra doctrina, theologica* (*loci theologici*) included not only the religious truths taken from the Word of God, but also the systematic discussion and application of ethical principles (*e. g.*, scholastics; Melanchthon). After the moral and ethical (see *Ethics*) had been made a separate theological science (chiefly as the result of the publication of Calixt's *Epitome theologiae moralis*, 1634), the name *dogmatic theology* (*theologica dogmatica*, so Buddeus, 1720; Pfaff, 1723) was given to that part of theological knowledge which presents the doctrines of the Bible in their logical connection and mutual relation.

Particularly after the age of rationalism there was widespread discussion regarding the scope and purpose of dogmatics. The authority of the Church is normative in the Roman Catholic system, although its dogmaticians strive to show that their doctrines are in harmony with Scripture. While Protestants for some time after the Reformation generally held that the Bible is normative, various views have been championed since: a) dogmatics is the systematizing of Biblical doctrine; b) it is the systematizing and evaluation of doctrines held by the Church throughout history; c) it is the systematizing of the creed of a particular church in which the material principle is basic and central; d) it is the systematizing of the doctrines held by a church in a particular period of history; e) it is the systematizing of religious truths as perceived by the individual dogmatician. Other views of the scope of dogmatics, as well as combinations of the above, have been held.

For the Lutheran dogmaticians the principle laid down by Melanchthon in his *Loci* (1521) was formative: *Evangelium est promissio*, not *philosophia coelestis* or *lex Christi*. Melanchthon also emphasized the center of Lutheran dogmatics: God's grace in Christ (*gratia universalis, sola gratia, sola fide*) as revealed in the Word (*sola Scriptura*).

II. History. From earliest times the Church sought to systematize its teachings, although few of the treatments were complete systematizations. Religious, philosophical, and apologetic elements were prominent in the treatises of Clement of Alexandria and Origen. Athanasius, Gregory of Nyssa, and Cyril of Jerusalem made the Trinity and especially christology central in their treatments. John of Damascus was the first to attempt a complete system of dogmatics (I. Trinity; II. Anthropology; III. Christology; IV. Ascension of Christ, Faith, Prayer, Sacraments, Resurrection). Gregory Nazianzen,* Cyprian,* Hilary,* and Augustine * made important contributions to dogmatics.

At the beginning of the Middle Ages, John Scotus Erigena gave to Scholasticism a neo-Platonic character with his translation of the works of Dionysius the Areopagite. Later the influence of Aristotle became prominent. The scholastic movement caused dogmatics to become a logical system of deductions and dialectical elaborations (see *Anselm of Canterbury, Roscellinus, Abelard, Peter Lombard, Alexander of Hales, Albertus Magnus, Thomas Aquinas, Bonaventura, Duns Scotus, Occam, Gabriel Biel*).

As a result of the Lutheran Reformation, anti- and extra-Biblical teachings were separated from Biblical truths, and the latter were stated clearly and convincingly. As a result of their Scriptural learning, accuracy of statement, and devout application, the Lutheran dogmaticians treated Scriptural teachings with greater penetration and understanding than the early Fathers, and the results were judged "more truthful and tenable than those of the scholastics" (Gass). Outstanding dogmaticians of the 16th and 17th centuries were: Luther,* Melanchthon,* Chemnitz,* Hunnius,* Hutter,* Gerhard,* Koenig,* Calov,* Quenstedt,* Hollaz,* Baier.*

This "Age of Orthodoxy" was followed by emphasis on correct living (pietism) to the detriment of correct formulation (Spener, Francke, Freylinghausen). The overemphasis on man led to rationalism, which first sought to explain doctrine rationally, then treated the doctrines themselves rationally (Semler, Michaelis, Doederlein, and others) and finally became completely rationalistic, using Scripture only to corroborate rationalizing deductions (Roehr, Wegscheider). Since this method could not lead to a comprehension of God, Schleiermacher turned the investigation to a consideration of the emotions of man, which, too, proved unsatisfactory. Hegel turned the investigation toward revelation by "seeking a God who seeks to reveal Himself" in man endowed with revelation. This position influenced the dogmaticians known as "mediating theologians," who sought the "Christian Consciousness" for their dogmatic systems. The 19th century produced men with divergent tendencies: Beck,* Hahn,* Nitzsch,* Hase,* Marheineke,* Twesten,* Julius Mueller,* Dorner,* Martensen,* and Kahnis.* More positive still: Sartorius,* Thomasius,* Philippi,* Luthardt,* Schmid,* Frank,* Vilmar,* and Oettingen.* While the influence of Schleiermacher, Ritschl, and similar theologians was pronounced in the second half of the 19th century, nevertheless appreciation of God's revelation in the Scriptures never ceased. More recently the influence of Karl Barth * has been strongly felt, especially in Germany. The most recent trend of theology in central Europe is toward conservatism.

III. The material of dogmatics has been variously arranged. A popular arrangement embraces the following divisions: 1) *Bibliology* (doctrine of the Bible); 2) *Theology* (in the narrow sense: natural knowledge of God, Trinity, God's essence and attributes); 3)

Cosmology (doctrines of creation, preservation, divine providence); 4) *Angelology* (doctrine of angels); 5) *Anthropology* (man in his relation to God, image of God, state of innocence, fall, sin, free-will); 6) *Christology* (Christ's person, state, office); 7) *Soteriology* (doctrine of salvation); 8) *Pneumatology* (doctrine of Holy Spirit and His work); 9) *Sacramentology* (means of grace); 10) *Ecclesiology* (doctrine of the Church); 11) *Eschatology* (doctrine of last things).

For a list of Lutheran dogmaticians as well as non-Lutheran see R. F. Weidner, *Theological Encyclopedia*, Wartburg, Chicago, 1910 (ii, 159 ff. Also wrote *Introduction to Dogmatic Theology*). Historical treatments: E. H. Klotsche-J. T. Mueller, *History of Christian Doctrine*, Luth. Lit. Bd., Burlington, Ia., 1945; J. L. Neve, *History of Christian Thought*, United Luth. Pub. House, Philadelphia, 1943 (vol. II published by the Muhlenberg Press, Philadelphia, 1946); E. C. Fendt, "Lutheran Dogmatics," *JALC*, II, 10 ff.; W. Rohnert, *Die Dogmatik der Ev. Luth. Kirche*, Wollermann, Braunschweig, 1902; R. H. Gruetzmacher, *Textbuch zur systematischen Theologie u. ihrer Geschichte im 16., 17., 18., 19. u. 20. Jahrh.*, Leipzig-Erlangen, 1919; F. Loofs, *Leitfaden zum Studium der Dogmengeschichte*, Niemeyer, Halle, 1906.

Important works published by Lutherans in America: S. S. Schmucker (Gen. Syn.), *Elements of Theology*, Miles, Philadelphia, 1845 (9th ed. enlarged, Smith & English, Philadelphia, 1860); C. Loeber, *Ev. Luth. Dogmatik*, Dette, St. Louis, 1872 (American edition with foreword by C. F. W. Walther); J. G. Baier, *Compendium Theologicae Positivae*, Luth. Concordia Verlag, St. Louis, 1879 (American edition published by C. F. W. Walther); S. Sprecher (Gen. Syn.), *A System of Ev. Luth. Theology*, Luth. Pub. Soc., Philadelphia, 1879; C. P. Krauth (Gen. Council), *The Conservative Reformation and Its Theology*, Lippincott, Philadelphia, 1891; H. E. Jacobs (Gen. Council), *Elements of Religion*, Gen. Council Bd. of Pub., Philadelphia, 1898; Heinrich Schmid, *The Doctrinal Theology of the Ev. Luth. Church* (translated by Hay & Jacobs of the Gen. Council), Luth. Pub. Soc., Philadelphia, 1899; W. Linsemann (Mich. Syn.), *Die Dogmatik der Ev. Luth. Kirche*, Saginaw Pub. House, 1902; H. E. Jacobs (Gen. Council), *A Summary of the Christian Faith*,

United Luth. Pub. House, Philadelphia, 1905; M. Valentine (Gen. Syn.), *Christian Theology*, Luth. Pub. Soc., Philadelphia, 1906 (2 vols.); A. L. Graebner (Mo. Syn.), *Doctrinal Theology*, CPH, 1910 (cf. Dau's mimeographed notes); A. Hoenecke (Wis. Syn.), *Ev. Luth. Dogmatik*, Northwestern Pub. House, Milwaukee, 1909—12; A. G. Voigt (United Syn. South), *Biblical Dogmatics*, Luth. Bd. of Pub., Columbia, S. C., 1917; *The Distinctive Doctrines and Usages of the General Bodies of the Ev. Luth. Church in the United States*, Luth. Pub. Soc., Philadelphia, 1914; John Schaller (Wis. Syn.), *Biblical Christology*, Northwestern Pub. House, 1919; C. E. Lindberg, *Christian Dogmatics and Notes on the History of Dogma* (translated from the Swedish by C. E. Hoffsten, Aug. Syn., revised and enlarged), Augustana Book Concern, Rock Island, Ill., 1922; F. Pieper (Mo. Syn.), *Christliche Dogmatik*, CPH, 1917—24 (3 vols.; special German edition by J. T. Mueller, 1946); F. Pieper (Mo. Syn.), *Christian Dogmatics*, 3 vols., a translation of *Christliche Dogmatik* by Theo. Engelder, W. W. Albrecht, J. T. Mueller, CPH, 1950—53; W. E. Schramm (ALC), *What Lutherans Believe*, Luth. Book Concern, Columbus, O., 1926; G. H. Gerberding (ULC), *Here We Stand*, Augustana Book Concern, Rock Island, Ill., 1925; E. Hove (ELC), *Christian Doctrine*, Augsburg Pub. House, Minneapolis, 1930; P. L. Mellenbruch (ULC), *Doctrines of Christianity*, Fleming H. Revell, N. Y., 1931; Joseph Stump (ULC), *The Christian Faith*, Macm., N. Y., 1932; C. H. Little (ULC), *Disputed Doctrines*, Luth. Lit. Bd., Burlington, Ia., 1933; J. T. Mueller (Mo. Syn.), *Christian Dogmatics*, CPH, 1934; E. C. Fendt (ALC), *Christian Dogmatics*, Luth. Book Concern, Columbus, O., 1938; Herman Sasse (Luth. in Germany), *Here We Stand* (translated by Tappert), Harper, 1938; E. W. A. Koehler (Mo. Syn.), *Summary of Christian Doctrine*, Koehler Pub. House, Chicago, 1938; M. Reu (ALC), *Christian Dogmatics*, 1941—42 (mimeographed notes lack finality of printing); E. Engelder (Mo. Syn.), *Scripture Cannot Be Broken*, CPH, 1944; T. Laetsch (Mo. Syn., editor), *The Abiding Word*, CPH, 1946—47 (2 vols.). EL

Dogmatism. 1) The practice of using the logical-dialectical method incorrectly, often not beginning with the thought matter under consideration, but applying concepts and categories elsewhere derived. 2) A philosophy which assumes certain principles without proof or investigation. 3) In popular usage, any stubborn or arrogant promulgation or defense of an idea which is false or for which there is none or insufficient evidence.

Doles, Johann Friedrich (1715—97). Pupil of Bach while a student of theology at the University of Leipzig and second in line as successor of Bach, serving as cantor at St. Thomas from 1755—89. Though a great admirer of his mentor and respected by musicians of his day as a man and as a composer, it is due largely to Doles that Bach's work as a composer was soon neglected and forgotten. Doles own compositions were superficial, facile, and sensuous and did not measure up to the works of Bach, which they replaced. Doles and Johann Adam Hiller helped bring on the rapid decline of Lutheran church music after the days of Bach.

H. J. Moser, *Geschichte der deutschen Musik*, Stuttgart, 1928—30; P. Spitta, *Johann Seb. Bach*, Leipzig, 1930; B. Helmut, *Johann Friedrich Doles*, Leipzig, 1939.

Domestic and Foreign Missionary Society. See *Protestant Episcopal Church*, 4.

Dominic, St.* See *Dominicans*.

Dominicale. A white linen veil once worn by women to Communion. The term is applied both to the veil worn and the napkin with which women were to receive Communion (perhaps one cloth served both purposes). Still in use in Italy.

Dominican Republic. See *Hispaniola*.

Dominicans (*Ordo Praedicatorum;* Order of Preachers). The Spaniard Domingo, or Dominic (ca. 1170—1221; well educated and became noted for his gravity and austerity), while engaged in efforts to convert the Albigenses of Southern France, conceived the idea of an order of monks living in apostolic poverty, who should combat heresy by preaching. His order was based on the so-called Augustinian Rule and early adopted the mendicant character (see *Mendicant Monks*). Dominic's dying curse on those who should bring temporal possessions into the order was soon disregarded. The order grew rapidly, showed a preference for populous cities, and developed a many-sided activity. Its members preached to the faithful and became missionaries to the heathen, but especially defended the accepted teaching against dissenters (heretics, pagans) by word and book. When gentler arguments failed, they employed the Inquisition, which was in their charge. They preached crusades against Saracens and heretical Christians, earned the eulogies of popes by supporting the Papacy in every way, and even collected papal funds (Tetzel). Matthew of Paris says (1250): "Armed with powers of every kind, they turn all to the profit of the Pope." They likewise fostered learning and produced many eminent scholars (Albertus Magnus, Thomas Aquinas). The order, in the course of time, developed an aristocratic tendency and had frequent quarrels with other orders, especially the Jesuits.

Dominicum. A term used in the early Church to designate the buildings in which the Christian services were held. It was also applied to the celebration of the Lord's Supper.

Domitian. Roman emperor (81—96) who caused a severe persecution * of the Christians.

Dompelaars. See *Brethren, Dunkers.*

Donatello (1386 — 1466). Italian artist in bronze, after the style of Brunnelleschi; his Evangelist John on the façade of the Dome of Florence and his St. George (or San Michele) are his best statues.

Donatio Fidei. See *Conversion,* II, 3.

Donation of Constantine. A forged document of the eighth century, pretending to have been written by Constantine the Great to Pope Sylvester, supporting the papal claims to territory and universal spiritual jurisdiction.

Donatist Schism, The. Substantially of the same character as the Novatian; grew out of the conflict of views as to the discipline called for in the case of the lapsed, now particularly the *traditores* (who had surrendered the sacred books to the persecutors). When on the death of Mensurius, Bishop of Carthage (311), who had frowned upon voluntary martyrdom, the moderate party hastily elected his archdeacon bishop, the rigoristic-fanatical party excommunicated him on the plea that one of

the consecrating bishops was a *traditor* and set up a rival bishop, who, in 313, was succeeded by Donatus the Great. Under his energetic leadership the movement spread through all of North Africa. The Donatists held that the Sacraments administered by one deserving excommunication were invalid, that the Catholic Church, failing to excommunicate such, had ceased to be the true Church, that even its Baptism was invalid, and that they alone, because of their strict discipline and the absolute purity of their members and clergy, were the true bride of Christ. (Cp. Art. 8, Augsb. Conf. and Apology.) When ecclesiastical commissioners and a synod decided against the Donatists, they were subjected to persecution, their churches closed, and their bishops exiled. Since persecution was regarded as a mark of the true Church, their fanaticism only increased, and death met at the hands of the military sent to suppress the revolt to which the *Circumcelliones,* fanatical ascetics allied with the Donatists, had incited the peasants, was regarded as martyrdom. Under Julian the Apostate, who permitted them to take violent revenge upon the Catholics, they flourished, having at that time 400 bishops. Later, severe laws were again passed against them. Inner decay now began to set in, the ostentatious exclusiveness of the extremists caused a schism within the schism, and the twenty years' labor of Augustine won back many of them. At a conference in 411 between 286 Catholic and 279 Donatist bishops the imperial commissioner decided against the Donatists, and they were forbidden to assemble, under pain of death. Augustine justified these coercive measures, appealing, wrongly, to Luke 14:23. The Vandals (429) persecuted Catholics and Donatists alike, and the schism ended in the seventh century with the destruction of the African Church by the Saracens.

Donne, John (1573—1631). Anglican; Londoner; reared a Catholic; turned Protestant; dean of St. Paul's (1621); famous poet and preacher.

Donum Superadditum. A designation of the scholastic doctrine of "superadded grace" given to Adam, in addition to his natural powers, and lost by him through the Fall. Man lived in moral communion with God by virtue of an original righteousness, which exalted him above merely human nature and hence is termed a supernatural gift of grace, superadded to the endowments of nature. The Roman Church teaches that this supernatural presence or likeness of God is restored by Baptism, so that a baptized person stands in the relation of Adam before the Fall.

Dooper. See *Mennonite Bodies.*

Doopsgesind. See *Mennonite Bodies.*

Doorkeeper. See *Hierarchy.*

Dorn, L. W. B. Oct. 15, 1863, in Boeuf Creek, Mo.; graduated from Concordia Seminary, St. Louis, 1885; assistant pastor to his father in Pleasant Ridge, Ill.; pastor at Rockford and later at Belleville, Ill.; 1900, professor of Mathematics and Natural Sciences, later of German and History, in Fort Wayne; editor of the *Kinder- und Jugendblatt* for twenty-two years; contributor to *Homiletisches Magazin* and *Lutheraner;* d. Apr. 4, 1918.

Dorner, August Johann (1846 to 1920). B. at Schiltach. Studied at Goettingen, Tuebingen, and Berlin. *Privatdocent* at Goettingen; professor and co-director at Wittenberg, 1873; professor of systematic theology at Koenigsberg, 1890. His writings reveal him as an exponent of the speculative-critical theology.

Dorner, Isaak August (1809—1884). Mediating theologian, influenced by Schleiermacher; professor at various places, at last in Berlin, 1862—1884; wrote *Die Lehre von der Person Christi.*

Dort Articles of Faith (Mennonite). See *Mennonite Bodies,* 2.

Dort, Synod of. See *Reformed Confessions,* C 2.

Dositheus, Confession of. See *Eastern Orthodox Confessions,* A 2.

Dostoievski, Fyodor Mikhaylovich (1821—1881). Russian novelist; suffered for advocacy of social reform; became opponent of materialism; contributed to reaction in literature and theology against humanism and materialism.

Douai Version. See *Bible Versions,* L 9.

Double Predestination. The belief that God has determined by eternal decree not only who is to be saved but also who is to be damned. See *Presbyterian Confessions,* 3; *Reformed Confessions.*

Double Standard of Morals. A term used to describe the position of those who grant greater license to men in sexual matters than to women. Such a differentiation is not in harmony with Scripture, which demands chaste and decent lives of all.

Doukhobors (Russian "spirit-wrestlers"). Russian sect which in recent years adopted the name of "Christians of the Universal brotherhood." Originated in various parts of Russia and first heard from about the middle of the eighteenth century because of their opposition to the Russian government and the Orthodox Church. The government used repressive measures, but early in the nineteenth century permitted them to congregate in their settlement near the Sea of Azof. Because of crimes committed in their colony they were banished to Transcaucasia, 1841. Continued persecution, due to their refusal to bear arms, internal strife, exile of their leader, Peter Verigin, 1887, prompted the majority, with the assistance of Count Tolstoy * and English Quakers, to emigrate to Canada, 1889, followed by Verigin, 1902. Established settlements in Saskatchewan and British Columbia, with sprinkling in other provinces. They are known to be industrious, abstemious, hospitable, but in dealings with the Canadian government secretive and mendacious. They came into conflict with the authorities through refusal to swear allegiance and obey police regulations and the school laws. As to their religion, they are anti-trinitarians. Christ was a mere man. They reject all church organization, priesthood, sacraments, confession, worship of icons,* marriage ceremony; have no use for the Bible except the Ten Commandments and certain "useful" passages; believe that the Holy Spirit dwells in man's soul and guides him directly. Other tenets are vegetarianism, refusal to kill animals for food or clothing, non-resistance. Their colonies are communistic; all money earned is paid into the central treasury.

Dowieites (*Christian Catholic Apostolic Church in Zion*). Followers of John Alexander Dowie. Dowie was born 1847 at Edinburgh, Scotland; ordained pastor in the Congregational Church, Australia, 1871; established independent church in Melbourne 1882, where he began to practice faith healing; came to America, 1888, first to Pacific Coast, then to Evanston, Ill., 1890; built Zion

Tabernacle in Chicago, 1893, and organized his numerous followers into the "Christian Catholic Church in Zion," 1896, supposedly on the plan of the early Apostolic Church. In 1899 he bought 6,500 acres on Lake Michigan, forty-two miles north of Chicago, and established there a partly religious, partly industrial community, called Zion City, of whose financial and ecclesiastical affairs he had complete control. He established schools and a college and many industries, especially the lace industry, transported bodily from Nottingham, England. He had extraordinary success both as business manager and religious leader, assuming, 1901, the title "Elijah the Restorer" and in 1904 "First Apostle." While he demanded of his followers repentance of sins and faith in Christ, the most prominent religious tenet was that of faith healing, he himself claiming to possess remarkable powers. All diseases are produced by the devil, and as Christ came to destroy the works of the devil, so this power is still bestowed today. Other tenets were Baptism by immersion, millenarianism, abstinence from pork, tobacco, and intoxicating liquors. Dowie established branches in other States and sent missionaries to the Old World. In 1906, the movement had 35 ministers and 5,865 members. After the failure of missionary campaigns in New York City and visits to England, unrest developed and Dowie was accused of immorality and mismanagement and deposed (1906). He died the following year and was succeeded in office by Wilbur Glenn Voliva (former Christian Church minister).

The movement failed to spread, and Zion City ceased to be an exclusive community. Principles were modified and churches and independent businesses welcomed.

Downton, Henry (1818—85). Educated at Cambridge; held a number of positions as clergyman, the last being rector of Hopton; noted as hymn translator; among his hymns: "For Thy Mercy and Thy Grace."

Doxology. A stately and exultant hymn of praise, addressed to the Triune God or to a single person of the Godhead, as in many parts of Paul's letters; in particular, the Greater Doxology (*Gloria in Excelsis*), the Lesser Doxology (*Gloria Patri*), and the longmeter doxology ("Praise God from Whom All Blessings Flow").

Draeseke, Johann Heinrich Bernhard (1774—1849). B. at Brunswick; d. at Potsdam. Studied at Helmstaedt. Pastor at Moelln and Ratzeburg. He was an eminent pulpit orator. Advocating a humanistic Christianity and impressed with the religion of Freemasonry, he found it congenial to work for the conciliation of Pietists and Rationalists.

Dragonades (see *Huguenots*). This word is derived from the French term *dragon*. Dragoons were employed in carrying out the fierce persecutions of the Protestants in France during the reign of Louis XIV.

Drama, Religious. See *Religious Drama*.

Dramatization. See *Christian Teaching,* K.

Dravidian. A non-Aryan people of southern India. Their religion is characterized by a belief in the existence of countless spirits in the world, of which the majority are evil. The religious worship of the Dravidians seeks to appease or ward off these evil spirits so that they will not exercise their malevolent powers on the worshiper and those dear to him.

Dresden Cross Catechism. See *Catechetics,* 11.

Drese, Adam (1620—1701). Musician at the court of Duke Wilhelm of Saxe-Weimar; mayor of Jena; *Kapellmeister* at Arnstadt; strong pietistic tendency; wrote: "Seelenbraeutigam, Jesu, Gottes Lamm."

Dressler, Gallus (1533—after 1580). Composer of Lutheran church music. Dressler succeeded Martin Agricola in Magdeburg and wrote in all about 250 compositions. His *Auserlesene deutsche Lieder zu vier und fuenf Stimmen* contains straightforward polyphonic motets which are based on Bible stories.
S. Kuemmerle, *Enzyklopaedie der ev. Kirchenmusik,* Guetersloh, 1888; Carl von Winterfeld, *Der ev. Kirchengesang,* Leipzig, 1843—47.

Drewes, Christopher Fred John. B. Jan. 12, 1870, at Wolcottsville, N. Y.; graduated at St. Louis, 1892; pastor at Memphis, Tenn., 1892—95; at Hannibal, Mo., 1895—1905; at St. Louis, Mo. (Bethany), 1905—17; member of the Bd. of Negro Missions, 1908—16; director, 1917—31; editor of *Missionstaube* since 1911; of *Concordia Sunday School Lessons;* wrote *Dr. M. Luther's Small Catechism, Explained by Way of Ques-*

tions and Answers; Weissagung und Erfuellung; Half a Century of Lutheranism (Colored Missions). D. March 3, 1931.

Driesch, Hans Adolf (1867—1940). German biologist and philosopher; his experiments led him to a dynamic vitalism, holding that organism possesses a vital entelechy which works with a view to the whole; most important work: *Leib und Seele.*

Drill in Education. See *Christian Teaching, G.*

Driver, Samuel Rolles (1846—1914). Anglican; Bible critic; b. at Southampton, d. at Oxford; successor of Pusey as professor of Hebrew and canon of Christ Church, Oxford, 1883; member of Old Testament Revision Company. Commentaries; *Leviticus* in the *Polychrome Bible;* joint author of *Hebrew and English Lexicon Old Testament;* joint editor of *Hastings' Dictionary of the Bible;* an *Old Testament Introduction;* etc.

Druids. Priests of the Celtic population of ancient Gaul, Britain, and Ireland. Their learning, which was transmitted orally, consisted of a mixture of religion, natural science, medicine, etc. The oak and mistletoe were objects of veneration. The Druids also were prominent politically and socially, but were unable to withstand the advance of Roman civilization in Gaul and Southern Britain, while in Northern Britain and Ireland they later succumbed to the influence of Christianity.

Drummond, Henry (1786—1860). One of the founders of the Catholic Apostolic Church.

Drummond, Henry (1851—97). Scottish scientist and evangelical writer, lecturer at Free Church College; outstanding work: *Natural Law in the Spiritual World.*

Druses. A people believed to be of mixed Aramaic and Arabic origin. Their number is estimated at 100,000 to 150,000, and they inhabit the Lebanon, Anti-Lebanon, and the Hauran. Their religious system, which contains Mohammedan, Christian, and other elements, originated ca. A. D. 1,000, when a certain Hakim declared himself the final incarnation of the divinity. The Druses believe in one God. They also regard holy war as an obligation, and in 1860 their fanaticism led to a massacre of the Christian Maronites (see *Maronites*).

Druthmar, Christian (Grammaticus). Benedictine monk of Corvey, at the beginning of the ninth century, distinguished for his linguistic learning; in 840 Bible expositor at Stablo, near Liége; his *Expositio in Evangelium S. Matthaei* issued in printed form in sixteenth century; emphasized literal sense. See *Eucharistic Controversies.*

Dschagga. An African native tribe near the Kilimanjaro. Mission work was begun by the C. M. S., which in 1893 was taken over by Lutheran Leipzig Mission; since 1922 under the Augustana Lutheran Church.

Dualism. In theology, the assumption of two mutually hostile superior beings, one representing everything morally good and beneficial to man, the other the source of all sin and evil, as in Zoroastrianism * and its modern form, the religion of the Parsees,* and in Gnosticism.* In philosophy the view that in the world there are two principles, or substances, which are wholly independent and totally different from one another, the spiritual and the corporeal, mind and matter, opposed to monism,* which assumes only one primal cause. Theistic (Biblical) dualism, which asserts the essential difference between the Creator and creation, is opposed to pantheism.*

Dubois, Theodore (1837—1924). Taught music at Rheims, later studied at Paris and Rome, held posts as professor of harmony and composition; many secular works; among his oratorios: *The Seven Last Words of Christ.*

Dubourg, Anna. B. 1520 (?). LL. D. Univ. of Orleans; Protestant, 1559; in Parliament pleaded for persecuted Protestants; imprisoned; wrote confession of faith; hanged and burned at Paris, Dec. 23, 1559.

Dubs, R. See *Evangelical Church.*

Dubuque Theses. Theses prepared by S. Fritschel and adopted by the Iowa Synod at Dubuque, Ia., 1882. The seven articles of the statement deal with predestination and conversion. They reject the position that particular election is not the extension of the general decree of grace and salvation to the individual people in whom it attains realization, but an essentially different decree which is the cause of the salvation of the elect. Furthermore, they reject the position that predestination is election "according to the mere pleasure of divine will" without consideration of human behavior, and favor the view that election took place in view of faith.

J. Deindoerfer, *Geschichte der Ev. Luth. Synode von Iowa und anderen Staaten*, Wartburg, Chicago, 1897; Geo. J. Fritschel, *Quellen u. Dokumente*, Wartburg, Chicago, n. d.; *Kirchenblatt*, 1882, 114 ff.

Ducis, Benedict (ca. 1480—1544). Flemish composer of the Reformation era whose name was really Hertoghs or Herzog. He was likely a pupil of Josquin Després. Later an organist at Notre Dame in Antwerp. Perhaps influenced by Walther. Is among the Lutheran composers brought to the fore by Georg Rhaw in his *Neue deutsche geistliche Gesaenge — fuer die gemeinen Schulen.* Wittenberg, 1544, which includes ten compositions by Ducis.

W. Gosslau, *Die religioese Haltung in der Reformationsmusik;* S. Kuemmerle, *Enzyklopaedie der Ev. Kirchenmusik*, Guetersloh, 1888.

Duck River Baptists. See *Baptist Bodies*, 23.

Duemling, Enno A. B. in Fort Wayne, Ind., Jan. 6, 1875, son of Dr. H. and Jenny, *nee* Sulzer; grad. of Con. Col., Fort Wayne, and Con. Sem., St. Louis; pastor, Emmaus Church, Detroit, 1896—1902; organized a mission for the deaf in Detroit, then became institutional missionary of the Synodical Conference in Milwaukee, serving these institutions 44 years until his death. Received honorary appointments from governors of Wisconsin and mayors of Milwaukee. He served as president of Associated Lutheran Charities for 13 years; received honorary D. D. from Concordia Seminary 1942. Married Anna, *nee* Huegli. D. Oct. 22, 1946.

Duemling, H. Educator and writer; b. in Germany, 1845; professor at Teachers' Seminary, Addison, Ill., 1870 to 1874; at Concordia College, Fort Wayne, Ind., 1874—1899; editor of the *Abendschule* for many years; of the *Germania* in Milwaukee, 1899—1913; member of Board of Control of Concordia College of that city; wrote several books on natural history and a series of arithmetics; d. Mar. 11, 1913.

Duerer, Albrecht (1471—1528). Most prominent German painter of the sixteenth century and one of the greatest masters of all time in combining poetry with the art of painting, whose ideas were freely disseminated among the people of his time, also by means of woodcuts and copperplate work; studied under Michael Wohlgemut; made extended trips through Germany and to Italy; issued a number of series, that of the Life of Mary, in which the Flight into Egypt and the Rest in Egypt possess great charm, and the series on the Passion of the Lord, one of twelve and one of sixteen scenes. Of his larger pictures the Adoration of the Three Kings and the Four Apostles are most notable, the latter picture also expressing the artist's position with regard to the Reformation, of which he was an adherent.

Duff, Alexander (1806—78). First missionary of the Church of Scotland to the heathen in India, landing there in 1830. With the assistance of Ram Mohon Roy, the founder of the Brahma Samaj, he founded a school in Calcutta for the higher castes, which at once was successful and exercised a far-reaching influence. Upon the division in the Church of Scotland he went with the Free Church, reorganizing his whole work. Because of ill health he returned to Scotland in 1864, continuing to work for foreign missions until his death.

Duffield, Samuel Willoughby (1843 to 1887). Educated at Yale College; pastor of Presbyterian denomination at Bloomfield, N. J., interested in hymnology; published a *Book of Verse; Laudes Domini; English Hymns, Their Authors and History.*

Duhm, Bernard (1847—1928). German Protestant theologian; professor at Goettingen and Basel; wrote commentaries on Isaiah, Psalms, and Jeremiah; proposed the Trito-Isaiah theory of authorship (ch. 56—66); interested primarily in making the content understandable.

Dulia. See *Latria*.

Dunkers. See *Brethren, Dunkers.*

Duns Scotus, John (ca. 1265—1308). Franciscan teacher at Oxford; doctor of the University of Paris (1304); sent to Cologne, where he died; his system opposes the intellectualistic and deterministic system of Aquinas.

Dunstable, John (ca. 1370—1453). Most important figure in the history of English music of the 16th century. Very little is known of his life; about fifty of his works may be found in vols. VI and XL of the *Denkmaeler der Tonkunst in Oezterreich.* While through Dunstable counterpoint made definite and important steps forward, his music sounds archaic to the modern ear.

Dunstan, St. (ca. 925—88). Abbot of Glastonbury; English archbishop; sought to reform monasticism in accordance with the Benedictine rule and promoted education.

Dupin (Du Pin), Louis Ellies (1657 to 1719). French Roman Catholic historian; received thorough education, becoming a Doctor of the Sorbonne in 1684; voluminous writer; accused of rationalistic tendencies; wrote a treatise on ancient church discipline and edited a library of church authors.

Du Plessis - Mornay (1549—1623). Earnest Protestant Christian, Henry of Navarre's pen and conscience, till Henry turned Catholic; founded the Protestant University of Saumur; "Pope of the Huguenots"; made possible the Edict of Nantes.

Durand, Guillaume (d. 1332; "Doctor Resolutissimus"). French Scholastic theologian; opposed realism of Aquinas and anticipated the terminism of Occam (singularity alone exists); distinguished between realms of reason and faith; opposed Pope in the question of beatific vision.

Durkheim, Emile (1858—1917). French philosopher; held that progress is a mechanical fact; individual's intellectual status comes from his environment and hence education should not only draw out but also fill in.

Dutch Guiana. See *South America*, 13.

Dutch Radicals. A term applied to a school of theologians centering in Holland which held that no NT book antedated the 2d century.

Duties, Table of. See *Haustafel*.

Dwight, John Sullivan (1813—93). B. in Boston, May 13, 1813, educated at Harvard Divinity School, and ordained as pastor of the Unitarian congregation, at Northampton, Mass. After six years of ministerial work he entered the literary field. In 1852 he established *Dwight's Journal of Music*, which he owned and edited for thirty years. He died Sept. 5, 1893.

Dwight, Timothy (1752—1817). Educated at Yale College; after holding several pastorates, president of Yale College; important figure in early American hymnology; wrote: "I Love Thy Kingdom, Lord," and others.

Dwight, Timothy (1828—1916). Congregationalist; grandson of above; b. at Norwich, Conn.; professor of New Testament Greek at Yale; ordained 1861; president of Yale 1886—1899; American Bible reviser; American editor of some of *Meyer's Commentaries*; d. at New Haven.

Dwinell, Israel (1820—90). Professor at Pacific School of Religion; associate editor of *Bibliotheca Sacra*; wrote *Christianity a Religion of Expectancy*.

Dyaus Pitar. See *Erahmanism*, 2.

Dykes, John Bacchus (1823—76). English churchman, known for the composition of many services, anthems, and over 300 hymn tunes, among them many popular melodies.

Dylander, John (1709—41). Native of Sweden; served Swedish churches along the Delaware from 1737—41; preached in English, German, and Swedish; helped organize German congregations at Germantown and Lancaster, Pa.; frequently preached in Episcopalian churches; one of the most influential of Swedish Lutheran ministers in America.

Dynamic Religion. See *Switzerland, Contemporary Theology in*, 3.

Dynamism (Gr. *dynamis*, "power"). This word has been used in various ways: 1) the power of the Gospel to transform lives; 2) Ionic explanation of motion as due to the operation of love and hate; 3) Leibnitz' explanation of substance; 4) Kant's explanation of matter as forces of attraction and repulsion; 5) A. van Gennap's description of the attitude of the savage mind toward the sacred and hidden; 6) the identification of matter and energy in evolutionary theory; 7) Ostwald's monism.

Dyophysites ("two natures"). See *Chalcedon, Council of*.

Dyotheletism (*Diothelism*). The doctrine that in Christ there are two wills, the one divine, the other human. As Christ had a human soul (Matt. 26:38), so also He had a truly human, though sinless will (Matt. 26:42). The doctrine was upheld by orthodox theology against monotheletism, *i. e.*, the doctrine that Christ had but one will. Dyotheletism was adopted officially by the Church at the sixth ecumenical council, held at Constantinople in 680, in the interest of preserving the true human nature of Christ.

E

Ea. See *Babylonians, Religion of,* 1.

Earlier Awakening. See *Finland, Lutheranism in,* 4.

Easter Controversy. It arose from a lack of uniform practice regarding the time of celebrating the Christian Passover. The churches of Asia Minor always celebrated it on the 14th of Nisan, so that the death of Christ might be commemorated on any day of the week. The entire West, on the contrary, uniformly celebrated the death of Christ on a Friday and the resurrection on the Sunday following. This difference, only generally stated here, was already discussed by Polycarp of Smyrna and Anicetus of Rome (ca. 155). Under Victor of Rome, about a generation later, it almost led to a schism. The Council of Nicaea declared itself against the Quartodecimanians (who celebrated Easter on the 14th of Nisan), who were henceforth treated as heretics. See *Quartodeciman Controversy; Church Year,* 5.

Eastern Orthodox Churches. 1. The Holy Eastern Orthodox Church, known also as the Eastern Church, the Greek Catholic Church, Orthodox Church, is represented in Greece, the Balkan States, Russia, Asia Minor, Syria, Egypt, and other Oriental regions and includes the Oriental Church of Greece, the Bulgarian National Church, the Albanian Orthodox Church, the Russian Orthodox Church, and minor branches.

2. *History.* Almost from the beginning a difference of opinion between the eastern and western divisions of the early Church appeared which may, in part, be accounted for by the difference in language and in temperament. Although the eastern section produced the great majority of the most prominent early Fathers, such as Ignatius of Antioch, Polycarp of Smyrna, Papias of Hierapolis, Clement of Alexandria, Origen, Eusebius, Athanasius, Basil, Gregory Nazianzen, Gregory of Nyssa, Chrysostom, Cyril of Jerusalem, and Cyril of Alexandria, and although it had the strong sees of Antioch, Jerusalem, Alexandria, and Constantinople to represent it at the ecumenical councils, seven of which it controlled almost, if not entirely, yet its productive period did not survive the attack of Mohammedanism, and the Western Church, with only one great see, that of Rome, became the more influential in Christendom. Evidences of a difference in spirit appeared even in the Quartodeciman Controversy * and at the Council of Nicaea,* where Hosius of Cordova, a Western theologian, was Emperor Constantine's personal representative; it became more pronounced during the so-called Iconoclastic Controversy,* 726—842; it became more bitter with the Filioque Controversy * and the veiled accusation of heterodoxy attending its discussions; it culminated in the mutual recriminations and condemnations and with the attending declarations of excommunication in 1054. Meanwhile John of Damascus,* the last great theologian of the Greek Church, had summed up the scattered results of the labors of the preceding fathers in a fairly complete system of theology. In the period following the great schism, up to the fall of Constantinople, we have teachers like Theophylact (d. after 1107) and Euthymius Zygabenus (d. after 1118). During this period, in the ninth and tenth centuries, the Greek Church made a great conquest in the conversion of the Slavonians (Bulgarians and Russians), in whose territory she has maintained herself to the present day. The Bolshevist Revolution of 1917 all but liquidated the Orthodox Church in Russia. Since 1945, however, there has been a renascence of the Orthodox Church, and the Soviet State is again tolerating the Church.

3. *Doctrinal Position.* During the period of the seven Ecumenical Councils, that is, till the end of the eighth century, the Eastern Church was orthodox in doctrine, with the exception of her rejection of the procession of the Holy Ghost from the Father *and the Son (Filioque),* which the Western Church had inserted in the Constantinopolitan Creed.* For almost nine centuries after the Second Council of Nicaea (787) the Greek Church accepted no further symbols and made no collection representing her doctrinal position. The chief characteristic of the Orthodox Church has been a tenacious adherence to the old forms, so that innovations were viewed as heresies. No changes in the liturgy, the doctrinal formulations, and church polity were countenanced. This accounts for the fact that the Eastern Churches have not followed the Western Catholic Church in such innova-

tions as the exclusive use of Latin in the Mass, the priestly despotism of the penitential system, the introduction of celibacy, the absolute supremacy and infallibility of the Pope. The Church, according to its system, is the sum total of those divinely called who adhere to the formulated creed. The mysteries are the heritage of Christ, in which a sensual element is always combined with some intelligible factor, by which the soul is sanctified and the body receives its share of the consecration. Christian piety is placed into a scheme, or system, in an altogether mechanical manner, with a catalog of virtues and vices. The use of pictures and icons is justified and encouraged, the intercession of the saints is taught, the proper form of making the cross is transmitted as an essential thing.

4. *Liturgy.* In worship and ritual the Greek Church is much like the Roman, with the sacrifice of the Mass as its center and with an even greater neglect of the sermon, while its worship has become a most elaborate drama, appealing almost entirely to the senses and the imagination, with hardly anything left for the intellect and the heart. There is a most complicated system of ceremonies, with gorgeous and even barbaric display and pomp, with endless changes of sacerdotal dress, crossings, gestures, genuflections, prostrations, washings, processions. The liturgy of St. Chrysostom is used (see *Liturgy*); but there are many later additions, which not only add to the length of the service, but bring in an excess of liturgical refinement and stress the sensuous element.

5. *Polity.* The Greek Church is a patriarchal oligarchy, rather than a monarchy in the Roman sense. The patriarchs of Constantinople, Alexandria, Antioch, and Jerusalem are supposed to be equal in power, but the first has the primacy in honor. The administration of the churches involves, besides the lower clergy, an army of higher and lower ecclesiastical officers.
— *Relation to the Reformation.* The men who were active in the Lutheran Reformation of the sixteenth century did their full duty in trying to bring the truth to the Eastern Church. The Augsburg Confession and the Catechisms of Luther were translated into Greek and sent to Joasaph II, patriarch of Constantinople; David Chytraeus, professor at Rostock, in 1569 published information concerning the Church in Greece; between 1574 and 1581 Martin

Crusius, Jacob Andreae, Lucas Osiander, and Heerbrand corresponded with Patriarch Jeremias II of Constantinople. Later great hopes were placed on Cyril Lucar (1572—1638), who expressed himself as very decidedly in favor of many doctrines taught by the Reformers. But at his death it was found that he had no following, and, what is more, a reaction against Protestantism set in during the latter half of the seventeenth century. Since the middle of the nineteenth century the overtures of the Anglican Church to establish fraternal relations with the Orthodox Churches have broken down in a degree the wall which formerly isolated the Eastern Churches from the Protestant Churches over Europe. The Russians and the Greeks, especially since the First World War, have taken an active part in the World Council on Faith and Order.*

6. *The American Eastern Catholic Churches.* In America the Eastern Church is represented by eleven separate groups, eight of which use the language of their ancestral home and in some instances are still under the spiritual jurisdiction of the mother church: the Albanian, Bulgarian, Greek, Romanian, Russian, Serbian, Syrian, and Ukrainian Orthodox Churches. The American Holy Orthodox Catholic Apostolic Eastern Church, the Apostolic Episcopal Church, and the Holy Orthodox Church in America use English in their services. See *Religious Bodies (U.S.), Bibliography.*

Eastern Orthodox Confessions. The entire Orthodox Church accepts the doctrinal decisions of the seven oldest Ecumenical Councils.* To these is added the Quinisext Council (691) and at times the one held at Constantinople under Photius (879). After these Councils the doctrinal system in the Greek Church remained fixed until a number of manifestoes were evoked against Romanism and Protestantism in the 17th century.

A. 1. *Confessions Formally Endorsed. The Orthodox Confession of the Catholic and Apostolic Eastern Church* was written by Peter Mogilas (1597—1647; patriarch of Jerusalem; metropolitan of Kief) as a catechism for the Russian Church. This Confession, sanctioned at Jerusalem in 1672, was directed especially against Romanism and Protestantism (Cyril Lucar). It treats doctrine under three heads: Faith (Nicene Creed), Hope (Lord's Prayer, Beatitudes), and Love (Decalog and seven virtues).

2. *Decrees of the Synod of Jerusalem and Confession of Dositheus* (1672). This synod is the most important in the history of the Eastern Church and may be compared to the Council of Trent. It issued a new *Defense*, or *Apology*, of the *Greek Orthodoxy* directed chiefly against the Calvinism of Cyril Lucar. It endorsed (in accompanying letter) the answers given by Patriarch Jeremiah to Martin Crusius, sanctioned the confession of Peter Mogilas, and condemned that of Cyril Lucar. Its acts consist of *Six Chapters* and a *Confession of Dositheus*. The latter contains 18 decrees: single procession of the Spirit (I); Scripture not of private, but ecclesiastical interpretation (II); the double election is conditioned on man's use of his free will (III); creation (IV); providence (V); sin, Christ and Mary exempt from sin (VI); incarnation, death, resurrection, ascension, and judgment of Christ (VII); work of Christ — He is the only Mediator, but Mary and saints bring petitions to Him (VIII); faith, which works by love, alone saves (IX); Catholic and Apostolic Church contains all believers — bishops necessary (X); members of the Church are those who hold the faith of Christ, Apostles, and holy synods (XI); the Catholic Church cannot err or be deceived (XII); man justified by faith and works (XIII); in the Fall man did not lose his intellectual and moral nature or free will (XIV); seven sacraments (XV); Baptism — its necessity and effect (XVI); Eucharist both a sacrament and a sacrifice (XVII); souls of dead are either in rest or in torment — those dying in penitence but without satisfaction go to Hades, whence they may be delivered by prayers of priests, alms, unbloody sacrifice of the Mass (XVIII).

3. *Synods of Constantinople* (1672, 1691). The first adopted a brief statement in harmony with the *Confession* of Dositheus; the second condemned Logothete John Caryophylus, who accepted views of Cyril Lucar.

4. *Russian Catechisms.* Platon's (d. 1812; favorite of Catherine II and Paul) Catechism shows a tendency to go directly to the Bible; Philaret's (1782 to 1867; metropolitan of Moscow; learned, eloquent, pious) Catechism was endorsed by all Eastern patriarchs. It is the best summary of Eastern Orthodoxy.

5. *Answers of Jeremiah, Patriarch of Constantinople, to Certain Lutheran Divines.* Melanchthon had sent copies of the Augsburg Confession to Joasaph II without result. When Jacob Andreae and Martin Crusius sent copies to Jeremiah II (1536—95), they received in his *Answers* a rejection of nearly all distinctive Lutheran doctrines.

B. 1. *Private Confessions. Two Confessions of Gennadius* (supporter of the cause of union at Ferrara and Florence; later opposed it) were prepared for the Sultan after the Mohammedan conquest. Philosophical in approach. Authenticity of the second confession often denied.

2. *Confession of Metrophanes Critopulus* (sent by Cyril Lucar to Oxford and Germany; close friend of Calixtus, at whose request he prepared the confession) presents the more liberal and progressive elements of Greek Orthodoxy.

C. *Cyril Lucar* (ca. 1568—1638; became Reformed during travels in Europe; patriarch of Alexandria and Constantinople; strangled by order of Sultan). In his *Confession* he sought to graft Reformed teachings on Orthodox creeds. First eight chapters are Orthodox, remaining ten Reformed in spirit. See also *Ecumenical Creeds; Nestorianism; Monophysite Controversy; Coptic Church; Armenians.* EL.

Philip Schaff, *Creeds of Christendom,* Harpers, 1899—1905; *The General Menaion or the Book of Services,* Davy & Sons, London, 1899; Constantine Callinicos, *A Brief Sketch of Greek Church History* (trans. by Katherine Natzio), Faith Press, London, 1931; Pere Janin, *Separated Eastern Churches,* Herder, St. Louis, 1933.

Eastern Star, Order of. A secret society organized in 1850, closely affiliated with the Masonic Order. As an Adoptive Rite of Freemasonry it stands in the same relation to the basic three degrees (Blue Lodge) as any (American, Scottish Rite, etc.) degrees of the Masonic Order. Membership may be held by Master Masons and their female relatives. Like the Masonic Order it is a system of forms, ceremonies, explanatory lectures, communicated to candidates who pledge secrecy by an oath. Five prominent female characters supply the material for the ritual — Jephthah's daughter, Ruth, Esther, Martha, and "Electa" (2 John 1). The ritual is strongly religious in character, the order being deistic, not Christian. The ritual declares all deceased members to be dwelling in bliss. There is no reference to repentance, faith, and the redemptive work of Christ. Membership, 1949, about 2,000,000.

Eastvold, Carl Johan. B. Mar. 19, 1863, at Stavanger, Norway; came to America in 1880; graduated Red Wing, Minn., Sem., 1891; student Chicago Luth. Sem., 1896—97; held pastorates at Blue Earth, Minn., 1891—96; Faribault Co., Minn., 1896—97; Jewell, Iowa, 1897 to 1913; Dawson, Minn., 1913—17; Volin, S. Dak., 1927—29; vice-pres., Hauge Synod, 1903; pres., 1904—10; re-elected 1917; chrm., joint com. which arranged union of United Church and Norw. Luth. Syn., 1917; pres., South. Minn. Dist. of Norw. Luth. Ch. in America, 1917—27; acting pres., Jewell Luth. Coll., 1911—12; repr. of foreign missions to the church in China, 1916—17; mem. bd. of directors, Norw. Luth. Orient Miss. Soc.; pres., bd. of directors, China Mission, 6 yrs.; pres., Zion Soc. for Israel, 1923—29; pres., "Stavangerlag," 1910—29. D. July 23, 1929.

Ebeling, Johann Georg (1637—76). Born in Lueneburg, in 1662 he became musical director and teacher at St. Nicolai, in Berlin, where Paul Gerhardt then held the office of diaconus, for many of whose hymns he composed the melody. After 1668 he was professor of music at the Gymnasium Carolinum in Stettin. He published *Pauli Gerhardti Geistliche Andachten*, a collection of 120 sacred songs for four voices, two violins, and general bass.

Ebenezer Society. See *Amana Society*.

Eber, Paul (1511—69). Studied at St. Lorenz School in Nuernberg and at Wittenberg under Luther and Melanchthon; Latin professor there in 1544, of Hebrew in 1557; castle preacher; later, city preacher and general superintendent of the electorate; next to Luther, best poet of Wittenberg school; wrote: "Helft mir Gott's Guete preisen"; "Herr Gott, dich loben alle wir"; "Wenn wir in hoechsten Noeten sein"; "Herr Jesu Christ, wahr'r Mensch und Gott."

Eberhardt, Christoph Ludwig. B. 1831 in Lauffen, Wuerttemberg; educated at the Basel Missionary Institute; came to Pastor Schmid, Ann Arbor, 1860; first missionary of Michigan Synod; pastor of St. Paul's, Saginaw, 1861; stood for sound Lutheranism; "Father of Michigan Seminary," contributing liberally and bequeathing a substantial sum; helped found Michigan Synod and remained its leader until his death, 1893.

Eberlin, Johann (ca. 1465—1530). Popular Franciscan preacher in Tuebingen and Ulm; gained for Reformation through Luther's writings; strove for peace and order during Peasants' War; wrote treatises, the best of them being *Wie sich ein Diener Gottes Worts in all seinem Thun halten soll.*

Eberlin, Johann Ernst (1702—62). Contemporary of Bach; composer of organ music which deserves wider recognition. Very little is known of his youth; in his later years he served as organist in Salzburg.

Ebert, Jacob (1549—1614?). Prof. of theology in Frankfurt-on-the-Oder; wrote hymn "Du Friedefuerst, Herr Jesu Christ."

Ebionites (Heb., "poor"). A term probably first applied to Jewish Christians at Jerusalem. Origen uses the word for Judaizing Christians. It was especially applied to an extreme Judaistic sect of the 2d century which adhered to the Torah and practiced asceticism. Jesus was the Messiah but not divine, nor born of a virgin; Paul was rejected; their Gospel either Matthew or the Gospel to Hebrews.

Eccard, Johann (1553—1611). Native of Muehlhausen; outstanding composer of the Lutheran Church. Eccard and Leonhard Lechner were the favorite pupils of di Lasso; their work, though different, reflected the mentor's excellent training. For a time Eccard served as court musician for Jakob Fugger at Augsburg; he was active in Berlin during the last four years of his life. His counterpoint is homophonic in character, and his five-part chorale harmonizations are different from those of his Lutheran contemporaries, serving as a bridge which leads over to the harmonizations of Bach. Eccard fused art music with the chorale. While Winterfeld overestimated the value of Eccard's music, Eccard has been neglected as a church composer.

F. Blume, *Die ev. Kirchenmusik*, Potsdam, 1931; Hans Joachim Moser, *Geschichte der deutschen Musik*, Stuttgart, 1928—30; Carl von Winterfeld, *Der ev. Kirchengesang*, Leipzig, 1843—47.

Ecce Homo (L., "Behold the man"). Name given to representations of the suffering Jesus (John 19:5).

Ecclesia. See *Church,* 1.

Ecclesiastical Center. See *Denmark, Lutheranism in,* 9.

Ecclesiastical Commissions. See *Commissions, Ecclesiastical.*

Ecclesiastical Courts. See *Courts, Spiritual.*

Ecclesiastical Polity. See *Polity, Ecclesiastical.*

Ecclesiasticus. See *Apocrypha,* A 3.

Ecclesiolae. See *Lutheran Theology after 1580,* 6.

Ecclesiology. That part of dogmatics or doctrinal theology which treats of the conception of the Church chiefly according to its internal religious aspect, "the holy Christian Church, the communion of saints."

Eck, Johann (Maier or Mayr; 1486 to 1543). Roman Catholic controversialist; professor and vice-chancellor at the university of Ingolstadt; violent opponent of Luther; semi-Pelagian in his views; attacked Luther in his *Obelisks;* disputation between Eck and Carlstadt at Leipzig (1519), in which Luther was Eck's real opponent; obtained bull *Exsurge, Domine* against Luther (1520); his most popular writing was *Enchiridion adversus Lutherum;* wrote the *Responsio Catholica* at Augsburg, which even the Catholics rejected; issued a version of Emser's translation of the NT.
Theodor Wiedemann, *Dr. Joh. Eck, Prof. d. Theol. a. d. U. Ingolstadt,* Pustet, Regensburg, 1865.

Ecke, Gustav (1855—1920). Ev. theologian at Erfurt; prof. at Koenigsberg (1900) and Bonn (1903). Wrote: *The Theological School of A. Ritschl and the Ev. Church; the Ev. State Church in the 19th Century; Unverrueckbare Grenzsteine (Unmovable Boundary-Stones).*

Eckhardt, Johannes ("Meister"; 1260? to 1327). Father of German speculative mysticism (intuition the highest stage of knowledge); Dominican vicar-general, with power to reform the convents in Bohemia, and teacher of theology in France and Germany (Suso and Tauler his pupils); charged at Cologne with teaching pantheism, which he disclaimed. While his ethical view is of rare purity, he teaches salvation through perfect love for God and self-denial.
Franz Pfeiffer, *Meister Eckhardt*

(trans. by De B. Evans), Watkins, London, 1924; R. B. Blakney, *Meister Eckhardt,* Harper, 1941; H. Bornkamm, "Luther und Meister Eckhardt," *Deutsche Theologie* (vols. 3, 4); W. Ernst, "Die Mystik Meister Eckhardts und der innere Aufbau unsers Volkslebens," *Ztschr. f. sys. Theol.,* XI: 626—62.

Eclecticism. Selecting that which seems best from various systems of religion, philosophy, psychology, etc. In religion it is an attempt to select elements from a number of beliefs, often fixing on those tenets which are common to a number of religions. In the first part of the 20th century eclectics in America stressed mystical and Oriental religions in their selections.

Economy, Divine. See *History, Philosophy of.*

Ecstasy (religious enthusiasm). An abnormal mental condition of exaltation or rapture in which the mind and feelings are absorbed in one dominant idea. Heathen religions used narcotics, intoxicants, and other means to experience the ecstatic state. Christian sects have employed fasting, contemplation, music, psychology, emotional appeals, to produce ecstasy. See *Mysticism.*

Ectoplasm. A term used in *spiritualism* to designate the supposed emanation from the medium.

Ecuador. See *South America,* 7.

Ecumenical Councils. See *Councils and Synods,* 4.

Ecumenical Creeds. The ecumenical creeds (*symbola oecumenica; symbola catholica*) are the three confessions of faith (Apostles' Creed, Nicene Creed, Athanasian Creed) which are used by the Greek, Roman, Lutheran, and some Protestant Churches. The Apostles' Creed is characteristically Western. The Nicene Creed in its original form (without the *filioque* — i. e., the procession of the Spirit from the Father only) is the chief confession in the Eastern Church. The Athanasian Creed was never officially adopted in the Eastern Church (printed as an appendix in its Office Hours). The Lutheran and Anglican Churches have incorporated the three creeds in their Confessions. The Protestant Episcopal Church in the U. S., however, refused to incorporate the Athanasian Creed in its liturgy (1785, 1786). The Reformed bodies, while generally indorsing the Christological doctrines of the Nicene and Athanasian Creeds, adhered chiefly to the Apostles'

Creed and incorporated it in their catechisms. The Christological statements of the Council of Chalcedon * are often included among the ecumenical creeds.

A. 1. *Apostles' Creed.* This creed was not formulated by councils of theologians, but grew spontaneously out of the needs of a living church. Already in the New Testament we have confessions to Jesus (Matt. 16:16; John 1:49; John 6:69; John 11:27; John 20:28; Acts 8:37), of Jesus and the Father (Matt. 10:32, 33; Matt. 16:16; Acts 14:15), and of the Trinity (2 Cor. 13:14; 1 Pet. 1:2). The confession of Peter (Matt. 16:16) and the baptismal formula (Matt. 28:19) undoubtedly influenced the development of the Creed especially.

2. The tradition that the Creed was composed on the day of Pentecost (or shortly thereafter) by the twelve Apostles, each contributing an article, beginning with Peter, is stated by Rufinus in the *Expositio Symboli* (4th c. Rufinus, however, ascribes the theory to ancient tradition), by Ambrose of Milan (*Explanatio symboli ad initiandos*), John Cassian (*De incarnat. Dom.*, vi:3), *et al.* This view, which received ecclesiastical sanction in the *Catechismus Romanus*, prevailed until the 17th c. Luther and Calvin took a neutral position. Some Lutherans (Lessing, Delbrueck, Rudelbach, Grundtvig) defended the tradition. The theory was attacked by Laurentius Valla and Erasmus and proved false by numerous scholars (intrinsic improbability, silence of the Scriptures, silence of ante-Nicene Fathers, various forms extant in early Church, *et al.*).

3. The Creed, then, grew from beginnings made in New Testament times. Early traces of its articles are found in Ignatius (*Ep. ad Tral.*, 9; cf. Justin Martyr's *Apol.*, I:10, 13, 21, 42, 46, 50). Until the Church triumphed in the West, the Creed was usually memorized but not written (*disciplina arcani*). It was explained to the catechumens in the last stages of their preparation. The ante-Nicene Fathers called the early forms of the Creed the "rule of faith" (*regula fidei*), "rule of truth," "apostolic tradition," "apostolic preaching," "symbol of faith." Such "rules of faith" are mentioned by Irenaeus (*Contra haer.*, 10, 1, *et al.*), Tertullian (*De velandis virginibus*, 1), Novatian (*De trin. s. de regula fidei*), Cyprian (*Ep. ad Magnum, et al.*), Origen (*De prin.*, I, 4—10).

4. That the Creed developed independently in different regions is shown by the differences existing among the early creeds (thus an old Roman creed read: "I believe in God the Father Almighty and in Christ Jesus, His Son, our Lord, and in Holy Spirit, Holy Church, and resurrection of the flesh"). A longer form ultimately became standard in the West. Rufinus (390) gives us the complete Latin text and Marcellus of Ancyra, the Greek. Later additions were made ("descended into Hades" from the creed of Aquileja; "catholic" from Oriental creeds; "communion of saints" from Gallican sources; "life everlasting" perhaps from Ravenna and and Antioch) until the present form triumphed in the West (6th—8th c.) owing to the efforts of the Roman Church.

5. Although it occupies a secondary position in the Eastern Church, the Apostles' Creed is the outstanding bond of union between all ages and sections of Christianity. Augustine spoke of it as "a rule of faith both small and great; small in the number of words, but great in the importance of its ideas." Luther said: "Christian truth could not possibly be put into a shorter and clearer statement." Calvin: "We hold this to be beyond controversy that the whole history of our faith is concisely and in distinct order stated in it; on the other hand, it contains nothing which cannot be supported by sound testimonies of the Scriptures." An attack on this Creed is tantamount to an attack on the Scriptures themselves.

B. 1. The *Nicene Creed (Symbolum Nicaeno-Constantinopolitanum)* represents the Eastern development of the baptismal formula and shows directly the results of the Arian Controversy. Three forms may be distinguished:

a. The original Nicene Creed (325) grew out of the immediate necessity of safeguarding the apostolic teaching concerning the deity of Christ against the Arian * heresy. The Creed closed with the words "and in the Holy Ghost" but added an anathema against Arians.

b. The Constantinopolitan Creed is so called because Aetius, when presenting it to the Council of Chalcedon (451), ascribed it to the 150 bishops brought together by Theodosius at Constantinople against the Pneumatomachians (381). It makes minor changes in the original Nicene Creed and extended the third article by asserting the true divinity of the Holy Spirit. The additions bear a marked similarity to the creeds of Epiphanius and Cyril of Jerusalem.

c. The third form differs from the other two by the inclusion of the word *filioque*.* The Greek Church held to the *monarchia* ("sole rule") of the Father and the single procession of the Spirit, which it differentiated from the temporal mission of the Spirit from the Father and the Son. The addition of *filioque* emphasized the procession from the Father and the Son. When the Roman Church in the 11th c. added the word to the Creed, the permanent schism between the Roman Catholic Church and the Eastern Orthodox Communion occurred.

2. The Nicene Creed is more theological and polemical than the Apostles' Creed and echoes the sharp distinctions ("coessential," "coequal," "begotten, not made," *et al.*) drawn by the orthodox against heresies.

C. 1. The *Athanasian Creed (Symbolum Quicunque)* is the third and last of the ecumenical creeds. Its origin is obscure. Since the ninth c. ascribed to Athanasius, this view has been contested since the 17th c. and is today rejected (early councils do not mention the Creed; written in Latin, while Athanasius wrote in Greek; presupposes later heresies: Nestorianism, Eutychianism). It seems to have originated in Gaul or North Africa as a commentary on the first four ecumenical councils. It also seeks to state the doctrine of the Trinity * in Augustinian paradoxes. The ascription to Athanasius, however, brought about its widespread reception.

2. The creed was popular among monks of the Middle Ages who considered it well adapted to meditation and memorizing. In the time of Charlemagne it came to be used as a canticle at Prime. Luther called this Confession the grandest production of the Church since the times of the Apostles. EL

Werner Elert, "Die Rezeption der Alten Symbole," *Morphologie des Luthertums*, Beck, Munich, 1931 (and later edition); Philip Schaff, *Creeds of Christendom*, Harpers, 1899—1905 (3 vols.); Karl Holl, *Gesammelte Aufsaetze*, II: 115—28, Mohr, Tuebingen, 1928; C. H. Moehlmann, "The Origin of the Apostles' Creed," *Journal of Religion*, XIII: 301 to 320; F. Kattenbusch, *Das Apostolische Symbol*, Hinrichs, Leipzig, 1894, 1900 (2 vols.); Hugh M. Scott, *Origin and Development of Nicene Theology*, Chicago Theological Seminary Press, 1896; O. Cullmann, *Die ersten christlichen Glaubensbekenntnisse*, Zurich, 1943.

Ecumenics (G. "inhabited world").

A word applied to the Church in its world-wide aspect (cf. *Ecumenical Creeds*) as a community with various common features and relationships.

Eddas. Two collections of ancient Icelandic literature consisting of mythology and legend.

Eddy, Mary Baker Glover. See *Church of Christ, Scientist.*

Edersheim, Alfred (1825—89). English scholar; b. at Vienna; Jew converted to Christianity; Presbyterian minister, 1846; Anglican curate, 1875; lecturer at Oxford; his *Life and Times of Jesus the Messiah* is an outstanding work on the life of Christ.

Edessa, Conversion of and School at. Edessa, a city in northern Mesopotamia, adopted Christianity before the end of the second century and became the chief seat of Christian life and learning in the East. Its theological school (the *Schola Persica*), established by Ephraem the Syrian ca. 350, after the Persians had destroyed his school at Nisibis, furnished ministers to Mesopotamia and Persia and championed the cause of orthodoxy against Arianism and Nestorianism, until the school itself fell under the charge of the latter and was closed by the bishop (489). In Biblical interpretation the school represented, in the main, the grammatico-historical as opposed to the allegorizing method. See *Exegesis, Schools; Early Christian.*

Edict of Milan. See *Constantine.*

Edict of Nantes. In this edict, Apr. 13, 1598, Henry IV of France granted toleration to his Protestant subjects. It was revoked on Oct. 22, 1685, by Louis XIV, which caused the expatriation of about 50,000 Protestants. See *France*, 6.

Edict of Poitiers. See *France*, 5.

Edict of Toleration (1781). See *Joseph II* and *Josephinism.*

Edict of Toleration (1791). See *Hungary.*

Edict of Worms (1521). The proclamation of the Diet of Worms * putting Luther, his works, and his followers under the ban.

Edinburg Bible Society. See *Bible Societies*, 4.

Edmeston, James. B. at Wapping, London, Sept. 10, 1791, he became a surveyor and architect. Later he moved to Homerton, where he served as churchwarden in the Church of St. Barnabas. He became interested in the London Orphan Asylum. His fondness for children was the source of inspiration for many of his children's hymns. His works include twelve volumes, mostly poems and hymns. D. 1867.

Education, Adult. See *Adult Education.*

Education, Aims and Objectives. See *Christian Education,* H.

Education, Bible in. See *Bible Classes; Christian Education,* G.

Education, Evaluation of. See *Christian Education,* K.

Education, History of. See *Christian Education,* B-E.

Education, Legislation Pertaining to. See *Christian Education,* J.

Education, Methods in. See *Christian Teaching,* I.

Education, Philosophy of Lutheran. See *Christian Education,* G.

Education, Statistics of Lutheran. See *Parish Education,* D 7; E 10; *Christian Education,* F.

Education, Visual. See *Christian Teaching,* D.

Educational Agencies. See *Parish Education,* B ff.

Educational Conferences. See *Teachers,* A 10; *Parish Education,* M.

Educational Journals. See *Teachers,* A 9.

Educational Psychology. A. 1. Man's ordered attempts to control and direct change in behavior are what is called education.

2. Educational psychology is the science that deals with studies and explanations of the processes involved in education. It is not merely a branch of general psychology, but a science in its own right which has already accumulated or developed a vast store of factual knowledge, a system of fundamental principles, and a variety of scientific techniques. It is largely experimental in nature. Its aim is to understand, predict, and control human behavior.

3. Historically the roots of educational psychology lie in associationism. This philosophy, which antedates Aristotle, was formed, reformed, and transformed by a succession of thinkers

even into the present century. Herbart, the first to emphasize the dynamics of learning and apply mathematics to associationism in an attempt to explain learning, is often called the father of educational psychology (five formal steps). Experimentalists, however, of the late 19th and early 20th centuries laid the groundwork for a scientific approach to the study of learning. From their day on research in the field has been abundant.

4. Prominent among the methods of the science are experimentation, controlled observation, rating, testing, measuring, clinical and case study, questionnaire study, and developmental studies. Data obtained by these various research techniques are, when possible, submitted to rigid statistical refinement and interpretation. While much invaluable information has been gleaned from laboratory studies, many investigators in educational psychology prefer to study behavior in actual life situations (e. g., school and classroom).

B. 1. *The Nature of the Human Organism.* The raw material with which the educational psychologist works is the human organism. God so created man that he has a body and a soul. On the basis of Scripture the soul is believed to be a spirit, the real life principle in man, the real self, capable of everlasting existence even outside the body. It inhabits the body during temporal life, expresses itself through the body, and is influenced and restricted in this life by the present assets and limitations of the body. It is believed to be rational, to experience feeling, and to be capable of guidance and development. Though man is structurally dualistic, he is functionally one. While in Christian education concern for the soul is fundamental, understanding and educating the whole man, body and soul, is its goal.

2. Since the soul is beyond the reach of scientific research techniques, it is ignored by most educational psychologists. The Christian, however, considers human behavior the product of the soul's functional unity with the body.

3. Under God, man is the product of two determining forces, heredity and environment. Information on heredity is furnished chiefly by the geneticist, though psychologists frequently investigate its effects. The psychologist concentrates most of his experimentation on the effect of environment on behavior. The question of the effect of

environment on native abilities has provoked animated debate among scientists. For all practical purposes one may operate on the principle that heredity determines the individual's potentials, while the environment determines to what degree his development will approach those potentials in any or all particulars.

4. In the fact that no two persons have both identical heredity and identical environment is found the basis for individual differences. In the understanding of, and in adjusting to, individual differences lies the key to effective education.

5. Christian educators see the hand of God operative through natural laws on finite matter. They cannot, therefore, subscribe to the thought that anyone is what he is solely because of heredity and environment. God's love, wisdom, and power to perform wonders will not be denied.

C. 1. *Psychological Development.* Psychological development includes physical, mental, emotional, social, and spiritual growth and integration. Postnatal growth is a relatively slow process in man. It is continuous, not sporadic, but proceeding at different rates from time to time. The several types of growth do not progress at uniform rates, but may occur in phases which appear quite independent one of another. Growth normally results in changes of behavior, at times sudden.

2. Physical growth begins with conception and continues into maturity, or, in a special sense, in one form or another until death. The stage of physical growth often influences children's abilities, interests, and adjustments. Physical characteristics, appearance, awkwardness, and also physical handicaps and anomalies are significant for personality development to the degree to which the individual maintains an objective attitude toward his assets or his limitations. The Christian child will care for his body and use it as the temple of God.

3. Mental development is very rapid during infancy and the preschool years. It continues at a negatively accelerated rate into the twenties. After some years a gradual recession sets in, but not until one is well past the physiological prime of life does mental ability decrease appreciably. Then factual, technological, or cultural acumen may more than offset the loss in speed of learning. All this augurs well for adult education even in advanced years.

4. Emotions involve the function of the entire system (for either good or bad). The emotional development of the child depends upon both his physiological nature and his past experience. From the infant's original emotional state, best described as excitement, develop varieties of emotional expression related to conditions of distress or delight. These are further specialized by training into definite patterns of likes and dislikes, feelings, attitudes, interests, appreciations, and social attitudes and motives. Emotional balance is intimately associated with feelings of security, acceptance, and personal worth. Successful guidance of the child's development toward emotional maturity requires full co-operation of the parents with the school. Together they endeavor to train the child to control his emotional life and to channel his emotional energies toward the achievement of socially worthy and God-pleasing goals.

5. The newborn child is unsocial and egocentric. His first step toward socialization is the realization of himself as apart from the general confused pattern of persons and things about him. At first he is completely dependent on others. But he becomes an increasingly independent social being as he learns to recognize, to communicate, to co-operate, to follow, and to lead. His personality is turned outward, and he develops interests in others. Such social development is very gradual and often subtle.

6. The exact nature of spiritual growth defies scientific analysis. Spiritual life is a gift of God, a work of the Holy Ghost. It is nourished by Word and Sacrament. Human agencies (parents, pastors, teachers, etc.) are frail implements in the hand of the Spirit as He works in the child faith, justification, and sanctification of life. Without such spiritual growth total development is never achieved. If the child is to mature into a happy and adjusted individual, every aspect of his personality and of his life must be integrated about his spiritual growth, his faith, and his spiritual values. The Christian psychologist acknowledges the significance of spiritual development, and he turns to Scripture for the answer to his questions. [These facts are often quoted by members of The Lutheran Church — Missouri Synod in favor of its system of parochial schools. Ed.]

D. 1. *The Nature of Learning.* When behavior is modified by structural development, maturation has taken place. When change in behavior is correlated with observable activity or with stimuli outside the organism, learning has occurred.

2. Learning may be typed according to the various levels at which it occurs. It may in nature be motor, sensory, emotional, perceptual, verbal, social, or mental and abstract. It may occur on more than one level at a given time. It may be realized because of trial and error, conditioning, insight, rote, drill, imaginary practice, or other causes.

3. Various experimental psychologies have offered explanations of how learning occurs. The first really influential theory was the connectionism of Thorndike and his followers. Repudiating the association of ideas, they postulated a bond between stimulus and response. Three prime laws of learning were formulated (readiness, exercise, and effect). To these laws and their modifications were later added such explanatory terms as belongingness, impressiveness, polarity, identifiability, availability, and mental systems. Connectionism had immediate appeal to educators as a working principle which could readily be taken over into classroom methodology. Readiness, repetition, effect, drill, etc., came to be bywords in the American school.

4. Behaviorism rose as a revolt against structuralism and mentalistic functionalism. Under Watson, its founder, behaviorism was mechanistic. The reflex and its conditioning constituted the complete and final answer to behavior. Even thought was defined in terms of bodily movement. Complex behavior was simply a chain or pattern of many conditioned responses. The laws of conditioning were the laws of learning. Reinforcement insured permanence, and extinction accounted for forgetting. Its influence has been considerable.

5. Koehler and Koffka popularized *Gestaltism.* The *Gestalt* and field theories emphasize the dynamic role of the whole organism reacting not to isolated stimuli, but to whole situations or configurations. For the configurationists, insight, goal consciousness, and goal striving are the cues to the nature of learning. The field theory has also been applied to the study of personality.

6. Among other psychological systems which have influenced American education are functionalism, dynamic psychology, purposivism, and psycho-analysis. The influence of the latter has been most profound for its emphasis on the dynamics of the self and what it consciously or unconsciously brings to the learning situation.

7. Each of the psychologies mentioned has provided helpful facts and theory on the nature of the learning process. No one theory is totally correct and sufficient to the exclusion of others.

E. 1. *Conditions Favorable to Learning.* Educational psychologists have set forth certain principles which may be guides in maintaining conditions favorable to effective learning.

2. The physical nature of the school and the classroom should at least conform with state requirements. The child learns more effectively and enjoys school much more in hygienic and pleasant surroundings conducive to, and convenient for, learning.

3. It appears that, barring excessive fatigue, any hour can be as effective for studies as another.

4. Readiness for school or for any phase of learning is most essential. It may depend upon physical maturation, emotional and social development, general ability, previous experience, information, prerequisite skills, interests, and other factors.

5. The healthy organism profits most in learning. The school should be alert to the health needs of its pupils (illness; handicaps; visual and auditory defects).

6. Adjustment and emotional security influence the effectiveness of learning. The school should study the personality needs of each pupil and, co-operating with the home, strive for conditions of optimal adjustment.

7. Have a learning situation before attempting to teach. Active interest and attention is essential to almost all learning activities in the school.

8. Effective learning depends upon clear initial impressions. The teacher should be definite, clear, concise, patient, and sympathetically understanding and helpful.

9. The teacher should appeal to as many avenues of sense impression as possible (visual and auditory aids; activity programs).

10. Teachers should be guided by psychological considerations rather than logical order and sequence in the presentation of new material.

11. When possible, learning material should be arranged and presented in a form or system. Unit organization is

helpful. It is also applicable to the teaching of religion.

12. Except in the case of very lengthy passages of difficult material, the whole method of memorizing seems better for brighter and experienced pupils. In certain cases the part method may be more effective.

13. Occasionally it may be better to begin with the unknown and proceed to the known, though the opposite procedure has been a good general rule. Frequently spontaneous interest is aroused by the unknown. When ability to recognize or to cope with the unknown depends on previously learned skills or facts, it may be mandatory to proceed from the known to the unknown.

14. Likewise, it may at times be advantageous to begin with the complex and proceed to the simple, though the opposite procedure would generally be indicated.

15. Encourage pupil activity (laboratory exercises; field trips; class discussion; group planning and execution of projects).

16. Active rehearsal of the material to be mastered will facilitate learning and enhance retention. Free and spontaneous class discussion can be one opportunity for active rehearsal.

17. Mastery of techniques is characteristic of certain studies. Meaningful drill based on individual need should precede and accompany the study of subjects which involve the application of definite skills. Practice must be motivated, controlled, and reinforced.

18. Distribution of practice into several short periods is more effective than the same amount of practice confined to one long period. Avoid fatigue.

19. Individual differences among pupils demand adjustment to individual needs, interests, and capacities. Individualized assignments and homogeneous grouping should be used especially in skill subjects. Suitable tests should be used for diagnostic and remedial purposes.

20. Learning is facilitated and made more pleasant when children learn to live together socially. Encourage self-discipline in the interest of the group. Rules should be few, clear, and consistently enforced. Enforced discipline should not be lacking where self-discipline is not forthcoming. Discipline ought always be evangelical.

21. Motivation can hardly be overestimated. Motives initiate, sustain, and direct activity. Intrinsic motivation, derived from pleasure in the task itself, is a powerful, self-sustaining drive to learning. Extrinsic motivation, derived from interest in the goal, in reward, or in any other consequences outside the activity or thing in itself, may also be used. Since motivation involves goal striving, the pupil should be helped to see purpose in his learning activity.

22. Knowledge of one's progress can be an incentive to learning. Children should be trained in objective self-evaluation. If grades are used, they should be given and interpreted objectively.

23. While children should be taught to be realistic and to expect difficulties and frustrations in life, they should, nevertheless, be trained to the habit of success. Children should be taught to view their legitimate mistakes and failures objectively.

24. The effectiveness of rewards and punishment depends upon the situation, the child, and the manner in which the matter is handled. Whenever positive incentives (praise or reward) are used, they should never be allowed to replace the real goal for the child. Neither should children be trained to expect punishment or reward and to live accordingly.

25. The school should not foster individual rivalry between pupils to stimulate learning. Group competition (characterized by fair play and brotherly consideration) and competition with one's own previous achievement are both valuable and stimulating.

26. The Christian child's predominant motive in school and in life generally should be love for God and love for his fellow man.

27. Teach the child how to study. Allow for a good measure of initiative, originality, and freedom in his work.

28. To insure transfer of training in school work or transfer of learning to life the school should teach for transfer. The religious training of the child should be functional and must be taught for transfer.

29. While incidental learning does occur in life, the teacher will not rely on it. It may be the source of spontaneous interest, but also of error, misfortune, bad habit, and later unpleasantness. Learning in school should be purposive, directed activity.

30. The school is becoming the great co-ordinator of various educational forces which beset the modern child. No agency, however, can relieve parents of their God-given responsibilities for the training of their child.

F. *Educational Psychology and the Work of the Church.* The Church has much to gain from encouraging and sponsoring scientific study of teaching, learning, and measurement in the area of religious growth. While no man can directly observe, much less measure, the spiritual life of another, helpful inferences may be drawn from a careful study of what it produces. Faith and newness of life are the work of the Spirit, but there is a human element in religious training. If research helps understand man and more thoroughly eliminate the chance for human error and interference in religious training, it will have been worth while. See also *Psychology; Christian Teaching.* EEY

H. Beaumont and F. G. Macomber, *Psychological Factors in Education,* McGraw-Hill, New York, 1949; W. F. Bruce and Frank S. Freeman, *Development and Learning,* Houghton Mifflin, Boston, 1942; W. H. Burton, *The Guidance of Learning,* Appleton-Century, New York, 1944; W. C. Cruze, *Educational Psychology,* Ronald Press, New York, 1942; M. E. Frampton and H. G. Rowell, *Education of the Handicapped,* World Book Co., Yonkers-on-Hudson, New York, 1938, 1940 (2 vols.); A. I. Gates, A. T. Jersild, T. R. McConnell, R. C. Challman, *Educational Psychology,* Macmillan, New York, 1942; E. R. Guthrie, *The Psychology of Learning,* Harper, New York, 1942; G. W. Hartmann, *Educational Psychology,* American Book Co., New York, 1941; G. Hildreth, *Learning the Three R's,* Educational Publishers, Minneapolis, 1947; E. R. Hilgard, *Theories of Learning,* Appleton-Century-Crofts, New York, 1948; A. M. Jordan, *Educational Psychology,* Henry Holt, New York, 1942; W. A. Kelly, *Educational Psychology,* Bruce Publishing Co., Milwaukee, 1946; W. Koehler, *Gestalt Psychology,* Liveright Publ. Co., New York, 1929; K. Koffka, *Principles of Gestalt Psychology,* Harcourt, Brace, New York, 1935; E. M. Leonard, L. E. Miles, C. S. Van der Kar, *The Child at Home and School,* American Book Co., New York, 1944; J. A. McGeoch, *The Psychology of Human Learning,* Longmans, Green, New York, 1945; W. S. Monroe, *Encyclopedia of Educational Research,* Macmillan, New York, 1941; A. L. Murray, *Psychology for Christian Teachers,* Round Table Press, New York, 1938; J. L. Mursell, *Educational Psychology,* Norton, New York, 1939; National Society for the Study of Education, *The Psychology of Learning,* 41st Yearbook, Part II, Pub-

lic School Publishing Co., Bloomington, Ill., 1942; H. A. Petersen, *Educational Psychology,* Macmillan, 1948; D. A. Prescott, *Emotion and the Educative Process,* American Council on Education, Washington, 1938; S. L. Pressey and F. P. Robinson, *Psychology and the New Education,* Harper, New York, 1944; H. B. Reed, *Psychology of the Elementary School Subjects,* Ginn & Co., New York, 1938; A. Schmieding, *Understanding the Child,* CPH, 1945; R. G. Simpson, *Fundamentals of Educational Psychology,* J. B. Lippincott, Chicago, 1949; C. E. Skinner, *Educational Psychology,* Prentice Hall, New York, 1945; C. E. Skinner (ed.), *Elementary Educational Psychology,* Farrar & Rinehart, New York, 1937; S. Smith (ed.), *An Outline of Educational Psychology,* Barnes & Noble, New York, 1941; H. Sorenson, *Psychology in Education,* McGraw-Hill, New York, 1948; D. Starch, H. M. Stanton, W. Koerth, *Psychology in Education,* Appleton-Century, New York, 1941; J. B. Stroud, *Psychology in Education,* Longmans, Green, New York, 1946; E. J. Swenson *et al.,* *Learning Theory in School Situations,* U. of Minnesota Press, 1949; P. M. Symonds, *Mental Hygiene of the School Child,* Macmillan, New York, 1934; E. L. Thorndike, *Educational Psychology,* Teachers College, Columbia University, New York, 1913—14 (3 vols.); E. L. Thorndike and A. I. Gates, *Elementary Principles of Education,* Macmillan, New York, 1929; E. L. Thorndike *et al.,* *The Fundamentals of Learning,* Teachers College, Columbia University, New York, 1932; J. B. Watson, *Psychology from the Standpoint of a Behaviorist,* J. B. Lippincott, Philadelphia, 1924; R. Wheeler and F. T. Perkins, *Principles of Mental Development,* Crowell, New York, 1932; H. C. Witherington, *Educational Psychology,* Ginn & Co., Boston, 1946; A. D. Woodruff, *The Psychology of Teaching,* Longmans, Green, New York, 1948.

Educational Research, Lutheran. See *Lutheran Education Association; Parish Education.*

Edward VI. See *England, Reformation in,* 4.

Edwardian Theology. See *New England Theology,* 2.

Edwardine Articles. See *Anglican Confessions,* 5.

Edwards, Jonathan (the Elder; 1703 to 1758). The "American Calvin"; b. at

East Windsor, Conn.; pastor at Northampton; two great awakenings, 1734 and 1740; did most of his writing at the Stockton Indian Mission, to which he went, 1751; d. as president of Princeton College. His writings defended Calvinism against Arminianism, opposed the Half-Way Covenant, defended the New England revivals, and paved the way for New England Theology.*
S. E. Dwight, *Life and Works of President Edwards*, 1829 (10 vols.).

Edwards, Jonathan (the Younger, 1745—1801). Son of preceding; pastor; president of Union College, Schenectady, N. Y.; his theory (governmental) of the Atonement was in the main that of Grotius.

Efficacy of the Means of Grace. See *Grace, Means of*, I 5.

Egede, Hans. Lutheran Apostle of Greenland; b. Jan. 31, 1686, Frondenaes, Norway; d. Nov. 5, 1758, at Stubbekjoebing, Denmark. He resigned his pastorate at Vagen to go to Greenland. His heart burned for the people who had once been Christians, but were again steeped in idolatry. After surmounting almost endless difficulties, he finally received permission from Frederick IV of Denmark to engage in this missionary enterprise and set sail May 3, 1721, the whole party numbering 46 people. Landing in Greenland was effected July 3, 1721. After much effort, Egede mastered the Eskimo language, translated Luther's Small Catechism, and began to minister in self-sacrificing manner. The rough climate, indifference of the natives, lack of foodstuffs, enmity of the sorcerers, the offensive life of the Europeans, all tended to increase the difficulties of the work. But the heroic faith of Egede surmounted them all. The Bergen-Greenland Trading Company, organized to assist Egede, proved a failure and was dissolved by the king in 1731. Meanwhile assistance was given him by Pastor Albert Topp and his own son Paul. By their faithful efforts many Greenlanders were converted. In 1736 Egede returned to Copenhagen, where he conducted a seminary for missionaries. Paul Egede translated the New Testament into the Greenland Eskimo language.
J. H. Schneider, *Hans Egede*, Book Concern, Columbus, n. d.

Eglise Reformee Evangelique. See *France*, 7.

Eglises Reformees Unies. See *France*, 7.

Ego. See *Psychology*, J 7.

Egoism. See *Selfishness*.

Egypt. A vast country in northeastern Africa; Constitutional hereditary monarchy. Area (without Sudan), about 383,000 sq. mi. Population in 1949 about 16,000,000. The country is divided into Upper and Lower Egypt. Language, Arabic. Religion, predominantly Mohammedan. Christianity appears to have come to Egypt in the first century. The Bible was translated into three Coptic dialects. Missions conducted by a number of European and American organizations. Statistics: 22 societies were active in Egypt, with 27,865 baptized members, and a total of 408 foreign workers, 53 of them ordained.

Eichelberger, Lewis (1801—59). Luth. pastor at Winchester, Va.; principal for women's seminary there; prof. of theological seminary at Lexington, S. C.

Eichhorn, Joh. Gottfried. See *Higher Criticism*, 12.

Eielsen, Elling. B. Sept. 19, 1804, in Norway; lay preacher in Norway, Sweden, and Denmark, 1832—39; emigrated 1839; ordained 1843, "the first Norwegian Lutheran pastor in America," by the Rev. F. A. Hoffman of near Chicago; organized, 1846, "The Ev. Luth. Church in America" (The Ellingian Synod); its president; d. Jan. 10, 1883. See *Ev. Luth. Church*, 4.

Eielsen Synod. The Evangelical Lutheran Church in America (known as Eielsen Synod) was organized at Jefferson Prairie, Wis., in 1846 by Elling Eielsen and others. The constitution, dictated by Eielsen and accepted April 13 and 14, 1846, made proof of conversion a condition of membership. In 1876 a majority of the clergy, who made acceptance of the Christian faith and moral life the conditions of membership, revised the constitution and chose the name Hauge's Evangelical Lutheran Synod. Eielsen and a minority held to the old constitution and name. Eielsen was president of this group until his death in 1883. Recent presidents (2d quarter of the 20th century): S. M. Stenby, Geo. Bredeson, J. O. Blaness. See references under *Evangelical Lutheran Church*.

Eifrig, Charles William Gustav. B. Sept. 23, 1871, at Doebeln, Saxony;

graduated at St. Louis, 1895; pastor at McKees Rocks, Pa., 1895—99; at Cumberland, Md., 1899—1903; at Ottawa, Can., 1903—09; president of the Canada District, 1906—09; prof. at Concordia Teachers College, River Forest, Ill., 1909—42; Ph. D. from Valparaiso Univ.; wrote: *Our Great Outdoors; Mammals; Reptiles, Amphibia, and Fishes.* D. Nov. 1, 1949.

Eigenkirche. The law of medieval Germany granted the lord who built a church the right to appoint the clergy. The medieval church and the Emperor soon encroached upon, and all but removed, the right. Places where the descendants of lords had the right to approve or veto appointment of clergy still found in the 20th century.

Eilert, Ernst F. B. 1866 in New York; printer and publisher; member of several boards in the United Lutheran Church; treasurer of National Lutheran Council; d. June 26, 1943.

Einarsson, Gizur (1508—48). Studied at Wittenberg; bishop of Skalholt, Iceland; reformed Iceland according to Bugenhagen's Church Order for Denmark.

Eiriksson, Magnus (1806—81). Lived in Copenhagen as tutor and literary man; Unitarian; wrote many bitter polemics especially against Martensen of Denmark.

Eisegesis (opposite of exegesis *). Reading thoughts into a Scripture text rather than drawing thoughts from it.

El Salvador. See *Central America, Missions in.*

Elders. 1. Derived from Old Testament usage, Ex. 3:16, which employs the term *elders* with reference to the chief representatives of the Israelitish tribes, and from the contemporary usage in the synagog, Luke 7:3, the word *presbyter* in the New Testament is a synonym for "pastors," Eph. 4:11; "bishops (overseers)," Acts 22:28 ff.; "leaders" and "rulers," Heb. 13:7; 1 Thess. 5:12; 1 Pet. 5:1-4. Large congregations had a number of presbyters or elders. Acts 11:30; 15:4, 6, 23; 21:18 (Jerusalem); 20:17, 28 (Ephesus); Jas. 5:14, etc. Of these, some served in the teaching office, while others were limited in their functions to the maintenance of Christian discipline and business administration, 1 Tim. 5:17, in which latter function they were evidently associated with the deacons. They appear from the first to have been

elected by the people and, on their being approved by the Apostles or their representatives, to have been inducted into their office by prayer and the laying on of hands. About A. D. 150 differences in rank had been introduced into the offices of the Church, and presbyters thereafter were subordinate to the bishops.

2. In the modern Church, eldership is characteristic of the Presbyterian churches, which derive their name from this institution. Two classes of elders are distinguished, teaching and ruling elders. The former constitute the body of pastors. The latter are laymen, who are set apart as assistants to the ministers in the oversight and ruling of the congregation. Together with the minister they constitute the "session," the lowest among the ruling powers of the Church. *The Form of Government of the Presbyterian Church* contains the following: "Ruling elders are properly the representatives of the people, chosen by them for the purpose of exercising government and discipline, in conjunction with pastors, or ministers." The office is perpetual. One elder from each congregation is a member of the Presbytery and Synod, and one for every twenty-four ministers in each presbytery is sent to the General Assembly, the highest legislative body in the Presbyterian communion.

3. In the Lutheran Church the terms *elder* and *deacon* are used synonymously with reference to the laymen chosen by the congregation annually or for a number of years as assistants to the pastor in the performance of his official duties. Together with the pastor they constitute the Church Board, or Board of Elders, also called Vestry, but with reference to the congregation possess only advisory or executive, not legislative, powers. With the eldership the office of trustee is frequently united, the trusteeship being an office prescribed by law when congregations are incorporated. See also *Clergy.* The duties of trustees concern property management and maintenance.

Th. Graebner, *The Handbook for Congregational Officers,* CPH, 1928.

Eleatics. A school of philosophy at Elea in Asia Minor founded, according to tradition, by Xenophanes (530 B. C.). Parmenides and Zeno were among its famous thinkers. It held that the world was finite and in state of rest so that being, not becoming, is reality.

Election. See *Predestination.*

Eleemosynary Agencies. See *Charities, Christian,* 1 ff.

Elementary Education. See *Parish Education,* C ff.

Elements, Terrestrial. See *Grace, Means of,* IV 4.

Elephantine Papyri. Papyri found at Elephantine, Egypt, in 1901; furnish information on Jewish history.

Elevation of the Host. The Council of Trent says of the Eucharist, without the least Scriptural foundation: "There is no room left for doubt that all the faithful of Christ may render in veneration the worship of latria,* which is due to the true God, to this most holy sacrament." (Sess. XIII, chap. 5.) When the priest, in the Mass, has consecrated the bread, he first adores it himself with bended knee and then elevates it as high as he conveniently can, to be adored by the people. The ringing of a bell gives them notice. In the same manner the chalice is elevated and adored. Elevation was retained in a number of Lutheran rites of the sixteenth century including Luther's *Deutsche Messe.*

Elgar, Sir Edward (1857—1934). English composer of the Roman Catholic persuasion whose compositions reveal outstanding skill and musicianship. Elgar was an aristocrat; this fact is often revealed by the aloofness of many of his compositions, which, despite their expert craftsmanship, too often lack warmth and appeal.
R. J. Buckley, *Sir Edward Elgar,* 1905.

Elias, Levita (ca. 1468—1549). B. near Nuremberg; d. at Venice; his epoch-making works on Hebrew grammar and lexicography were sources from which scholars of the Reformation period gained their knowledge of the Hebrew Bible and its language.

Eliot, John. "Apostle to the Indians" of North America; b. 1604 at Nasing or Widford, near London; d. May 20, 1690, at Roxbury, Mass. A Puritan, he emigrated to America, 1631; became pastor of the Church of Christ, Roxbury, 1632. At the age of forty-two he studied the Indian Mohican tongue, engaged in mission work, amid much opposition and vexation, 1646; translated and published, among other books, the Bible into Mohican, which was the first Bible printed in America. Thirteen churches were founded by him.

Number of converts, in 1674, estimated at 3,600. He educated a large number of native workers, 24 of whom were preachers. Wars seriously impeded and injured his work. Financial assistance was given him by the English "Corporation for Promoting the Gospel among the Indians in New England."

Elipandus. See *Adoptionism.*

Elisabeth of Calenberg. After the death of her husband, Eric I of Brandenburg (1540), played a prominent part in the introduction of the Reformation in Brunswick and Lueneburg.

Elisabeth, St. Wife of the Landgrave of Thuringia; spent her life (1207—1231) in saintly ministrations to the needy and hastened her death by the practice of unnatural asceticism.

Elizabeth. Queen of England 1558 to 1603. Daughter of Henry VIII and Anne Boleyn. Steered middle course in religion and completed establishment of Anglican Church, that is, the fact that it was made the State Church; approved Thirty-Nine Articles (Latin edition) 1563; by destroying the Armada in 1588, foiled Philip of Spain's attempt to re-establish Catholicism in England; was able and accomplished ruler, but cruelly persecuted Nonconformists. See *England, Reformation in,* 6.

Elizabethan Settlement. The English Church as organized under Queen Elizabeth. See *England, Reformation in,* 6, 7.

Elizabethans. A name often given nuns of the third order of St. Francis, who devote themselves to nursing the sick.

Elk River Association. See *Baptist Bodies,* 23.

Elkesaites. See *Gnosticism,* 7 d.

Elks, Benevolent and Protective Order of. Organized in 1866, the Elks lodge originally catered to those in pursuit of social enjoyment, the benevolent and protective features being added to establish the "fraternal" character of the order. Devoted to the pursuit of pleasure, the activities of the Elks have in recent years begun to conform to the standards of polite society, while the religious principles stressed in the ritual have salvation by works as their dominant note. A blessed hereafter is assured to all members in good standing, as such, the burial and memorial rituals stressing "an eternity of bliss" as the "fruition of our Fidelity." In some localities Elks Clubs have been organized which offer some kind of business or social connection without obligating on any ritual. In the absence of initiation or participating in an unchristian ritual, such membership is not equivalent to "lodge membership." Membership (1952) about 1,100,000.

Ellerians (also called Ronsdorf Sect and Zionites). Founded in Elberfeld, Germany, and later removed to Ronsdorf by Elias Eller (1690—1750), whose wife, as the "Mother of Zion," was, a second time, to give birth to the Savior. After Eller's death the sect declined rapidly.

Ellerton, John. B. in London, Dec. 16, 1826, educated at Trinity College, Cambridge; became successively curate of Eastbourne, Sussex, Brighton, and lecturer of St. Peter's and received a number of other appointments. In 1881 he published his *Notes and Illustrations of Church Hymns* in a folio edition. John Ellerton wrote about 50 original hymns and translated some ten from the Latin. D. 1898.

Elliot, Charlotte. B. March 18, 1789, and spent the greater part of her life at Brighton, England. She was unusually well educated, having a passion for music and art. At the age of thirty-two she became an invalid and remained such until her death, in 1871. A member of the Church of England, she wrote a great number of hymns, which have in them a tenderness and sweetness born of much suffering and resignation. She will always be remembered by "Just as I Am, Without One Plea."

Elliot, Julia Anne. Married to the Rev. H. V. Elliot (1833); author of eleven hymns which are in most refined poetical taste; best known: "Father, Who the Light This Day." D. 1841.

Eloheimo, Wm. See *Finnish Lutherans in America*, 1.

Elohists. See *Higher Criticism*, 6.

Elven, Cornelius (1797—1873). For fifty years pastor of a Baptist church in Suffolk; known as the author of a favorite hymn: "With Broken Heart and Contrite Sigh."

Elvira, Synod of (306). Convened after Diocletian persecution to restore order; strongly condemned heathen immoralities; first synod to demand celibacy.

Emanation. A system of Oriental origin holding that all being is derived from God through cosmic processes. See *Gnosticism.*

Ember Days. Days of fasting and prayer in the Roman Church, which approximately mark the beginning of the four seasons. They are the Wednesday, Friday, and Saturday following Ash Wednesday, Pentecost, September 14, and December 13.

Emeritus Pastor or Teacher. A pastor or teacher who is free from duty because of age or disability. Various pension systems are maintained by Lutheran churches for such pastors.

Emerson, Ralph Waldo (1803—82). American poet, essayist, preacher, lecturer, transcendentalist. He helped form the Transcendental Club and contributed importantly to the *Dial,* a paper published by that organization. Main works: *Nature* (shows in compact form his transcendental position); *The American Scholar* ("Men Thinking"; "Our Intellectual Independence" of European thought and culture); *Divinity School Address* (asserts the divinity and the inspiration of man, "Oversoul," and relegates Jesus to a human position); *Essays — First Series:* "Love," "Friendship," "Prudence," "Heroism," "Intellect," "Art," "History," "Self-Reliance" (Trust thyself), "Compensation," "Spiritual Laws," "The Oversoul" (shows especially the mystical side of transcendentalism). *Essays — Second Series:* "The Poet," "Experience," "Nature," "Manners," "Gifts," "Representative Men," "The Conduct of Life." Poetry: Nature Poems; Transcendental; Personal; Public and Patriotic.

Emmons, Nathaniel. See *New England Theology*, 3.

Emory, John (1789—1835). Methodist Episcopal; b. in Queen Anne Co., Md.; studied law; held various pastorates; headed Methodist Book Concern; originated *Methodist Quarterly Review;* bishop 1832; d. near Reisterstown, Md.

Emotional Learning. See *Christian Teaching*, F.

Empirical Theology. A theological system which eliminates all extra-experiential norms. Deity and ethics exist only in experience which is the final criterion of religious value. Different schools of empirical theologians may be distinguished: 1) those who evaluate experience in all fields; 2) those who evaluate experience in the moral field; 3) those who restrict themselves to "religious" experience. Schleiermacher is the father of the last-named school, which includes intuition and mysticism in its category of experience.

Empiricism. The philosophical theory according to which experience is the only source of knowledge. As it denies the possibility of a supernatural source of knowledge, it leads to criticism of Christian ethics and religion. Modern science, being decidedly empirical, is consequently often antagonistic to divine revelation.

Emser, Hieronymus (1478—1527). Bitter controversialist against Luther; studied at Tuebingen and Basel; writings issued by the two principals full of personalities; Emser's translation of the Bible, 1527, a plagiarism of Luther's work.

Emser Punktation. Name applied to a series of twenty-three articles drawn up in 1786 at Ems by the archbishops of Mayence, Treves, Cologne, and Salzburg as a protest against the erection of a papal nuntiature at Munich, an office which the ecclesiastical princes felt to be an infringement upon their rights. The ultimate aim was to establish an independent national church in Germany; but owing to clerical and political opposition the plan failed.

Enckhausen, Heinrich Friedrich (1799—1885). Studied under Aloys Schmitt; organist and director of the *Singakademie;* also court pianist in Hanover; much orchestral and sacred music and standard book of chorals.

Encratites (Abstainers), followers of Tatian, so called from their ascetic life. They abstained from meat, marriage, wine (using water for wine even in the Eucharist).

Encyclicals. Originally circular letters sent by bishops to their people, but now applied almost exclusively to letters addressed by the Pope to all Roman bishops on subjects of general interest (a problem of the times, anniversaries, to promote special devotions). They differ from bulls * and decrees * in being instructional rather than dogmatical. They are originally written in Latin and published in the *Acta Apostolicae Sedis* * and are known by their first words. Some important encyclicals were: *Quanta Cura* (condemning 80

propositions of a theological and philosophical nature); *Rerum Novarum* (against Socialism and Liberalism); *Divini Redemptoris* (against atheistic Communism); *Pascendi* (against Modernism); *Casti Conubii* (marriage and birth control); *Deus Scientarum Dominus* (on education).

Encyclopedia (G. *enkuklopaideia,* "the circle of education"). The Greeks seem to have understood by this word the complete cycle or system of education. This meaning is still preserved in a restricted sense today, namely, when the word "encyclopedia" is applied to the classification of the branches of knowledge. The earliest encyclopedia was Pliny's *Natural History.* This work served as a source for many similar works in the Middle Ages (Isidore, Rhabanus Maurus, etc.). The most famous of the Middle Ages was Beauvais' (1190—1264) *Bibliotheca Mundi.* The first work called "Encyclopedia" was Joachim Fortius Ringelbergius' *Lucubrationes vel potius absolutissima kuklopaideia* (Basel, 1541).

The medieval encyclopedias, as a rule, treated theology together with other knowledge. Encyclopedias for individual branches of knowledge were written as the subject matter increased. While early encyclopedias sought to systematize knowledge and show relationships, modern encyclopedias, as the word is generally understood, give information on items in alphabetical order.

Encyclopedias on individual subjects are listed under the articles (*e. g., Judaism; Roman Catholic Church*). In addition to the references given under *Dictionaries* the following may be noted: J. Newton Brown, *Encyclopedia of Religious Knowledge,* Lippincott, Philadelphia, 1854; Otto Zoeckler, *Handbuch der Theologischen Wissenschaften,* Beck, Noerdlingen, 1885 (4 vols.); John M'Clintock-James Strong, *Cyclopedia of Biblical, Theological, and Ecclesiastical Literature,* Harpers, N. Y., 1891 (12 vols.); Carl Meusel, Ernst Haack, B. Lehmann, *Kirchliches Handlexicon,* Naumann, Leipzig, 1887—1902 (7 vols.); P. Zellner, *Theologisches Handwoerterbuch,* Calwer, Stuttgart, 1891—93 (2 vols.); Samuel Fallows, Andrew Zenos, Herbert Willett, *The Popular and Critical Bible Encyclopedia,* Chicago, 1908 (3 vols.); A. Hauck, *Realencyclopaedie fuer protestantische Theologie und Kirche,* Heinrichs, Leipzig, 1896—1913 (24 vols.); Samuel Macaulay Jackson, *New Schaff-Herzog Encyclopedia of*

Religious Knowledge, Funk-Wagnalls, N. Y., 1909—12 (12 vols.); E. Eckhardt, *Homiletisches Reallexikon nebst Index Rerum,* Success, St. Louis, 1909—17 (8 vols.); James Hastings, *Encyclopedia of Religion and Ethics,* Scribner's, N. Y., 1928 (13 vols.); Herman Gunkel, Leopold Ischarnack, Alfred Bertholet, Herman Faber, Horst Stephan, *Die Religion in Geschichte und Gegenwart,* Mohr, Tuebingen, 1927—32 (6 vols.); James Orr, John L. Nuelsen, Edgar Y. Mullins, Morris O. Evans, Melvin Grove Kyle, *The International Standard Bible Encyclopedia,* Eerdmans, Grand Rapids, Mich., 1943 (5 vols.); Vergilius Ferm, *An Encyclopedia of Religion,* Philosophical Society, N. Y., 1945.

Lutheran in America: Jacobs-Haas, *The Lutheran Cyclopedia,* Scribner's, N. Y., 1899; Fuerbringer-Engelder-Kretzmann, *Concordia Cyclopedia,* CPH, 1927. EL

Encyclopedia, Theological. That part of the preliminary work in the general field of theology which pertains to the general subject matter of theological knowledge with all its divisions. An early Lutheran work on the order of a theological encyclopedia was Abraham Calov's *Encyclopediae disciplinarum realium ideae* (1673). The best-known works were those of the Reformed theologian K. R. Hagenbach and of the Lutheran J. C. K. von Hofmann.

R. F. Weidner, *Theological Encyclopedia,* Fleming H. Revell, 1898; R. Pieper, *Wegweiser durch die Theologischen Disciplinen und deren Literatur,* Germania Publishing House, Milwaukee, 1900 (both Lutheran); George R. Crooks and John F. Hurst, *Library of Biblical and Theological Literature,* Phillips and Hunt, New York, 1884; Abraham Kuyper, *Encyclopedia of Sacred Theology,* Scribner's, N. Y., 1898.

Encyclopedists. Name of editors and collaborators of the epoch-making French *Encyclopedie,* 1751—80, an alphabetically arranged work of reference in 35 volumes, covering the whole field of knowledge and, in a wider sense, all those who shared its philosophical, religious, and political principles. This encyclopedia was edited by Diderot and d'Alembert. Voltaire, Helvetius, Holbach, Rousseau, and Turgot were the most prominent collaborators. It is a product of English deism and French naturalism and exerted a far-reaching destructive influence. It did not openly advocate atheism and materialism, but the fundamental principle is that of skepticism, and it is the most important literary product of the "Enlightenment."

Endogamy. A rule prohibiting the marriage of an individual outside of the social group (as in Hindu society).

Endress, Christian (1755—1827). Pastor at Frankford, Pa., Cohenzy, N. J., Easton, Pa., and Lancaster, Pa.; scholar; active in formation of General Synod.

Engagement. See *Marriage.*

Engelbrecht, Ernest Henry. B. Dec. 23, 1870, at Farmers Retreat, Ind.; graduated at Addison, 1891; teacher at Kendallville, Ind., 1891—1901; in New York City: Immanuel, 1901—11; St. Matthew's, 1911—15; prof. at Concordia Teachers College, River Forest, Ill., 1915 to 1944; field secretary of the Walther League, 1916—41; d. Feb. 28, 1944.

Engelder, Theodore Edward William. B. Jan. 21, 1865, at Olean, N. Y.; ed. at Concordia College, Ft. Wayne, Ind., and Concordia Seminary, St. Louis, Mo. (grad. 1886). He served as pastor at Sugar Grove and Logan, Ohio, 1886 to 1890; Mt. Clemens, Mich., 1890—1914; was professor of Christian Doctrine at Concordia Seminary, Springfield, Ill., 1914—26, and professor of Christian Doctrine at Concordia Seminary, St. Louis, 1926—46. While at Mt. Clemens, Mich., he served the Michigan District of The Lutheran Church — Missouri Synod first as vice-president and then as president. He was a contributor to *Lehre und Wehre, Theological Monthly,* and *Concordia Theological Monthly.* He wrote *Reason or Revelation?* (1941), and *Scriptures Cannot be Broken* (1944). He was a staunch defender of verbal inspiration and molded the thinking of the clergy of the Missouri Synod along dogmatical lines. D. June 23, 1949, at St. Louis, Mo.

Engelhard, George Veit (1791 to 1855). Luth. professor at Erlangen; known for his *Dogmengeschichte.*

Engelhardt, Maurice (1828—81). Professor at Dorpat; wrote monograph on Loescher; defended Schenkel and Strauss; his study on Justin Martyr (in which he advanced the view that Justin was not Christian) answered by Staehlin.

Engelsbrueder. See *Gichtelians.*

England, Early Christianity in. 1. Christianity was introduced into Britain in the third century, or perhaps earlier. The strongest proof for this assumption is the fact that three British bishops attended the conference at Arles A. D. 314. British bishops also attended the councils of Sardica A. D. 347. Pelagianism, at an early date, took root in Britain, which was the native country of Pelagius. By the Saxon invasion (449) the greater part of Britain was again plunged into barbarism, and Christianity maintained an existence only in Wales and Cornwall, where the British rites and usages were preserved until near the end of the seventh century. The monastery of Iona, established about 565 by Columba, became a center of missionary activity not only for Scotland, but also for North Britain.

2. Up to the sixth century, British Christianity was independent of Rome. In 596, however, Augustine, with a number of monks, landed in Britain and converted Ethelbert, King of Kent, and other chieftains of England. In 597 Augustine was consecrated at Arles and became the first Bishop of Canterbury. In 668 Theodore was sent over by the Pope as Primate of England. Under his administration (668—89) the Roman and British Christians were united into one body. From this period up to the time of the Reformation, England was in formal connection with the See of Rome. Among the theologians and missionaries of the early British Church, Bede (735), Alcuin (804), King Alfred (900), are the most prominent.

After the Norman Conquest (1066), the ever-increasing power of the Roman Church gave rise to many struggles between the ecclesiastical and royal powers for supremacy. William the Conqueror refused to acknowledge the Pope as his feudal superior, prohibited the publishing of papal bulls, and deprived the clergy of the right of excommunication without his express permission. The papal encroachments rose to their height during the reign of John, when England was laid under an interdict and the king resigned his crown to the Pope. Edward I gave a check to the power of the clergy, subjected them to taxation. During these centuries few innovations in doctrine were made. However, in 1213 the Council of St. John's Lateran declared transubstantiation to be a tenet of the Church.

3. During the reign of Henry II, in the 12th century, certain German church reformers came to England, preaching the evangelical doctrines in opposition to the Romish Church.

Though bitterly persecuted, their work was not entirely without success. In 1327 John Wyclif was born. As rector of Lutterworth he carried on evangelical work. His translation of the Bible, and his numerous writings made a great impression upon the educated classes, but the work had little effect upon the common people. A small band of his followers in 1400 formed a party called the Lollards, who spread his religious tenets, though they were persecuted and many of them burned for heresy. See *Celtic Church.*

England, Reformation in. 1. The English Reformation is unique among the reform movements of the early sixteenth century. In its beginning it was political, social, and economic rather than religious; for this reason it was never thoroughgoing; gave rise to many sectarian parties; finally resulted in a State Church which is lax in every respect and combines different factions that may even be antagonistic to one another, under the same name, in the same religious body.

2. What is commonly called the English Reformation took place under the auspices chiefly of three English sovereigns: Henry VIII, 1509—47; Edward VI, 1547—53; and Elizabeth, 1558 to 1603. Between the reigns of Edward and Elizabeth there was the brief Catholic reaction under Mary Tudor.

3. The movement under Henry was nothing more than a separation from Rome. The occasion was the annulment of Henry's marriage to Catherine of Aragon; the Pope (Clement VII) would not sanction it, and Henry severed his connection with the Roman Church and organized his own Church. But the English Parliament consented to this; and there was no worth-while opposition on the part of the English people to this change, which entered practically every home in England; this move of Henry, therefore, was possible only because antagonism against the Papacy was so strong in England that the majority of the people welcomed this declaration of independence. The reasons for this antagonism were the state-wide objection to the extortion of money practiced by the Papacy, the antipathy against the moral jurisdiction that the Papacy wielded over the people, prescribing their way of living inside and outside the Church; and on the part of statesmen, the fact that the Church's ownership of a large part of the area of England blocked the Tudor project of centralizing government

authority in the land. The religion of the Church, its doctrine, and its cultus were hardly changed; the king was made "the only supreme head in earth of the Church of England" (Act of Supremacy, 1534). Henry did negotiate with the Lutheran Smalcaldic League * in Germany; but the object was a political alliance against Charles V, the nephew of Catherine of Aragon; while religious discussions were held between committees of both parties, the reason was only that membership in the Smalcaldic League was denied to Henry unless he signed the Augsburg Confession. When the danger of war with the emperor ceased, Henry's interest in Lutheran doctrine also evaporated, and his final confession was the "Six Articles," 1539, which made denial of the chief dogmas of Romanism heresy and felony, to be punished by death. There was an increasing revival of Wycliffism,* later on merging with Lutheranism, in England, but it was not strong enough to exert noticeable influence on the teaching of the new Church.

4. Protestant doctrine entered England under Edward VI. Being a minor, Edward was under a regency committee led by two protectors: John Seymour, Duke of Somerset, 1547—49, and John Dudley, Duke of Northumberland, 1549 to 1553. The Primate of the Church, Thomas Cranmer, Archbishop of Canterbury, leaned more and more toward Calvinism. Both the protectors favored Protestantism. Somerset was moderate, but Northumberland, foreseeing the early death of Edward, attempted more and more radically to make England Protestant (importation of foreign preachers: Bucer, Peter Martyr, Ochino, John á Lasco; Forty-two Articles; *Book of Common Prayer;* Act of Uniformity) before Mary Tudor could succeed to the throne and return England to papal dominion. But even his last desperate plot to substitute Lady Jane Grey, his daughter-in-law, for Mary, failed because of the sudden death of Edward.

5. These violent and obviously selfish measures antagonized the English people; they welcomed Mary and, in a large measure, her efforts to restore the old Church. Had Mary been moderate, the Catholicism of Henry VIII might have become the religion of the State; but Mary, driven by her Catholic advisers and her own conscience, showed even greater fanaticism, viciously persecuted Protestantism (some 400 victims; cause, purely religious). Mary lost the love and support of her people; her fanaticism did more to make the Reformation welcome than all the measures of her predecessor.

6. Under the long reign of Elizabeth the Anglican Reformation was restored and made permanent. While Elizabeth moved cautiously and slowly, she showed preference for Protestantism from the beginning of her reign. While the Roman form of church government (the episcopate) and a great part of the old Church's ritual was retained, a Protestant hierarchy replaced the Roman church officials; the Articles of Religion and the *Common Book of Prayer* of Edward were revised and adopted; the queen refused the title of "Supreme Head," but became the "Supreme Governor" of the Church.

7. The fact that so much of the old church order was retained disappointed the Protestant extremists, particularly those divines who had fled to the continent in the beginning of Mary's reign and had in Geneva, Zurich, Basel, and Frankfurt sat at the feet of Calvinistic teachers and now returned as thorough Calvinists. They formed the backbone of the Puritan Movement,* which began by protesting against the vestments and the ritual of the Anglican Church; demanded more and better preaching in the Church; when the bishops opposed them, they demanded more lay influence and power in the Church; and when the government backed up the bishops (under Charles I) they formed a political party against the king. The Act of Uniformity led to some persecution of Catholics and Dissenters; but usually the laws of the Act were not strictly enforced unless the government appeared to be threatened (persecution and execution of Catholics under Elizabeth and her successors, almost always connected with plots against the crown). When the Stuarts turned extremely High Church (Charles II) and finally Catholic (James II), they were overthrown and William and Mary of Orange invited to take the throne; in 1689 the Act of Toleration gave a moderate religious liberty to all Englishmen. TH

Arthur D. Innes, *England Under the Tudors* (11th ed., revised by J. M. Henderson), Putnam's, N. Y., Methuen, London, 1937; Roland G. Usher, *The Reconstruction of the English Church,* Appleton, New York & London, 1910 (vol. 1 and 2); H. E. Jacobs, *The Lutheran Movement in England During the Reigns of Henry VIII and Edward*

VI, and Its Literary Monuments. General Council Pub. House, Philadelphia, 1916 (revised); George Macaulay Trevelyan, *England Under the Stuarts,* Putnam's, N. Y., Methuen, London, 1938 (17th edition); James Gardner, *The English Church in the Sixteenth Century* from the Accession of Henry VIII to the Death of Mary, in Stephens and Hunt, *A History of the English Church,* Macm., N. Y., London, 1903 (vol. iv); W. H. Frere, *The English Church in the Reigns of Elizabeth and James I* (1558—1625), in Stephens and Hunt, *A History of England,* Macm., 1904 (vol. v).

England, Subsequent History of the Church of. 1. With the accession of William and Mary to the throne of England in 1688 began the movement in favor not only of toleration but of absolute freedom of worship and political equality. Freedom of worship was established by the Act of Toleration, in 1689, and the Test Act was repealed in 1828. In 1829 all disabilities were removed from Roman Catholics, and in 1858 also from the Jews. In the eighteenth century, worldliness and Deism * became rampant. However, this was counteracted by the activity of Whitefield and the Wesleys, and new life sprang up in the Church of England as the result of this revival of practical religion. In consequence of the missionary activity of the Methodists there was an intense interest in missionary activity among the heathen and among the depraved classes at home. In 1780 Robert Raikes of Gloucester organized Sunday schools for the poor, and in 1799 the first missionary society was founded. At this time also a movement was organized toward the abolition of the slave trade. The nineteenth century was characterized particularly by the rise of the Oxford Movement * (Puseyism), through which John Henry Newman, Henry Edward Manning, and other clergymen of note became converts to the Catholic Church. However, this was also characterized by earnest evangelical piety. The British and Foreign Bible Society united both Episcopalians and Dissenters in a common enterprise, while the Evangelical Alliance * in 1846 sought to unify them in spirit and prayer. In the last half of the century Biblical scholarship was developed to a high point by such men as Archbishop Trench, Dean Alford, Bishop Lightfoot, B. F. Westcott, Bishop Ellicott, Dean Stanley, Professors Hatch and Hort, and others. These Bible studies culminated in the movement to revise the English translation of the Bible. (For Established Church see *Elizabeth.*)

2. The High Church party in the Church of England still insists upon its exclusive right to the episcopacy and apostolic succession, upon the ritual, the doctrine of the Real Presence, and baptismal regeneration, and has reintroduced Romanistic practices, such as veneration of the blessed Sacrament, auricular confession, Communion in one kind for the laity, and establishment of monastic orders. The Low Church party represents the evangelical element of the Church; it holds strictly to the natural interpretation of the 39 Articles, denies the episcopal system to be essential to the proper organization of the Church, and denounces all ritualistic practices. The Broad Church party is, to a great extent, composed of latitudinarians, or the liberal element, represented by such men as Arnold, Julius Hare, Kingsley, Stanley, etc. The compulsory church rate Abolition Act (1868) relieved all Dissenters of church taxation and the University Test Act (1871) opened the university to all students, irrespective of creed.

3. The *doctrinal standards* of the Anglican Church are the 39 Articles, and the *Book of Common Prayer,* to which may be added the *Catechism* and the two *Books of Homilies,* issued under Edward VI and sanctioned by the 39 Articles. The worship of the Church of England is liturgical and regulated by the *Book of Common Prayer.* Any departure, even in the smallest detail, from it is illegal. The clergy of the Church of England consists of three orders — deacons, priests (presbyters), and bishops. The canonical age is, respectively, twenty-three, twenty-four, and thirty. The bishop has the exclusive right of ordination and confirmation, and of the consecration of churches. Bishops are appointed by the crown. Deans have charge of cathedral churches and are assisted by canons, the number of whom must not exceed six for any cathedral. The archdeacon assists the bishop in his official duties as superintendent of the diocese, holds synods, delivers charges, and visits parishes. Bishops frequently associate with themselves suffragan bishops. England is divided into the archbishoprics of Canterbury and York. The Irish Church, which was disestablished in 1869, has two archbishops and eleven bishops, while the Scotch Episcopal

Church has seven bishops. The clergy of the Church in priests' orders in England and Wales are called rectors, vicars, or curates. See Hierarchy.

4. The Church of England is one of the estates of the realm, and its relation to the state is one of dependence, the sovereign being the supreme governor and Parliament its highest legislative body. The Archbishop of Canterbury is the first peer in the realm and crowns the king. The bishops have their palaces and seats in the House of Lords. The convocations of Canterbury and York are the two highest official church bodies, the convocations being assembled by the king's writ. Judicial business is transacted in three courts — the lowest, the diocesan, a consistory court, presided over by the bishop's chancellor; the court of arches; and the king in council, or the judicial committee of the privy council. There are three church censures — suspension, deprivation, and degradation. At the first Lambeth Synod, which included the bishops of the Church of England and the colonies as well as all the Protestant Episcopal churches in America, the opposition of a wing of the Low Church party to the Oxford Movement led to the formation of the Free Church of England and to the introduction into England of the Reformed Episcopal Church.

5. The Free Church of England, is a small Protestant organization, which, in 1844, separated from the Church of England on account of the Oxford Movement. It is entirely free from state control and thus claims the right to enter any parish where an advanced ritualism prevails and to establish its own services on the basis of the evangelical party of the Anglican Church. It is governed by its own convocation and by its few bishops, who were consecrated by Bishop Cummins of the American Reformed Episcopal Church. The convocation meets annually in June. It is practically identical with the Reformed Episcopal Church of England, though it refuses to unite with this body on account of differences regarding government and the rights of the laity. See Anglican Confessions; Reformed Episcopal Church; Protestant Episcopal Church.

Stephens and Hunt, A History of the English Church, Macm., 1899—1910 (10 vols.); bibliography under Anglican Confessions; England, Reformation in.

English Synod of Ohio. See United Lutheran Church, Synods of, 21.

Enhypostasia. See Christ Jesus, I B.

Enlightenment (German, Aufklaerung). 1. The subjective and rationalistic spirit of the 18th century which declared its independence of the authority of Biblical revelation, affecting not only theology, but all phases of life, and became the basis of modern culture and history. While in the preceding centuries European life, philosophy, international and national politics, economics, literature, education, were under the domination of the theological spirit, the Enlightenment declared its hostility to the supernaturalism of the Church and its influence on the affairs of the world and in the conflict between reason and faith asserted that man by nature is endowed with sufficient reason to work out every problem that confronts him. While this evolution reached its height in the 18th century, particularly in the second half, which coincides roughly with the reign of Frederick II in Prussia and which Germans call das Zeitalter der Aufklaerung, the beginnings may be traced to the Renaissance.

2. Italian Humanism of the 15th and 16th centuries, which was merely a revival of ancient paganism and fundamentally hostile to Christianity, worked as a leaven throughout Europe. The overwhelming religious interest created by the Reformation repressed its influence for a time, but it came to the surface again, first in Holland in the rationalism of Descartes,* the pantheism and Biblical criticism of Spinoza,* the skepticism of Pierre Bayle,* then in England, where Deism * had taken its rise in the 17th century. The principle of Deism was common sense; it was directed against the supernatural character of Christianity and reduced religion to a system of ethics based on epistemology and psychology. English Deism exerted a great influence on France, where the Enlightenment took a more radical turn. Its development was largely influenced by the conditions created by the reign of Louis XIV — Jesuitic morality, frivolity, bigotry, hypocrisy. A frivolous spirit took possession of the upper classes, to whom Catholicism, Jansenism, and Protestantism were equally ridiculous. The English common sense was changed to a philosophy of esprit, a mere travesty of the former. Its leading exponents were the Encyclopedists,* including the

skeptical Voltaire and the crass materialists Lamettrie and Holbach. It bred an extreme radicalism, which attacked Church, State, and society and reached its climax in the French Revolution with its terrible excesses.

3. German Enlightenment was a product both of the English and the French, aided by the introduction of Freemasonry in 1733 and the popular philosophy of Wolff,* which was based on that of Leibniz.* Prominent factors in the German movement were the influence of the skeptical Frederick II, Nicolai's *Allgemeine Deutsche Bibliothek*, the writings of Moses Mendelssohn, the father of Reform Judaism, Reimarus, and Lessing. Theology became grossly rationalistic. However, the German movement soon sloughed off its vulgar features, mainly through the influence of Goethe and Kant, who, too, were rationalists and products of the Enlightenment, but who criticized its shallowness and led German literature and philosophy to their greatest heights. German Enlightenment was followed by an influential philosophical idealism. Though the Enlightenment in its 18th-century form has passed and a Christian reaction set in in the 19th century, its antichristian influences are still at work in Germany, France, England, America, and were given new impetus and new modes of expression by the theories of biological evolution, which is exerting its influence on every field of human knowledge.

Enlil. See *Babylonians, Religion of*, 1.

Enoch. See *Apocrypha*, A 4.

Enthusiasm. See *Grace, Means of*, I, 5, 7.

Envelope System. See *Finances in the Church*, 3, 4.

Environment. See *Psychology.*

Envy. See *Jealousy.*

Eobanus Hessus. See *Hessus.*

Ephesus, "Robber Synod" of. Held in 449. Dioscorus, through brutality and violence and the support of imperial troops, obtained the temporary restoration of Eutyches and the condemnation of the Antiochene bishops.

Ephesus, Third Ecumenical Council of. The deciding factor in the Nestorian Controversy.* This council was convoked by Theodosius II, who favored Nestorius; met June 22, 431; Cyril, patriarch of Alexandria, the chief opponent of Nestorius, presided. On the same day, refusing to wait any longer for the arrival of the bishops of Syria and the East (the adherents of Nestorius), the bishops present, about 200, condemned the error of Nestorius and deposed and excommunicated him. The decree says: "Mary brought forth, according to the flesh, the Word of God made flesh," bringing out the Scriptural doctrine that God, according to the human nature, was born of the Virgin Mary, that the human nature of Christ is not a separate person, the mere instrument of the divine nature, but that there is one person with the natures indivisibly and inseparably, personally, united. The legates of Celestine of Rome, arriving later, joined in the condemnation of Nestorius, July 11. Closing session, August 31. The judgment, approved by the whole Western Church and the greater part of the East, was confirmed by the Council of Chalcedon. Celestine, appealed to by Cyril, had instructed his legates to utilize the occasion in the interest of the primacy of Rome; God graciously overruled the wiles of Rome, the arrogance of Cyril, and the rivalry between the patriarchates in the interest of the saving doctrine of the person of Christ. — The Council, besides, condemned Pelagianism and the Messalians (Euchites, Eustathians), who made prayer the one means of grace, and on the motion of Cyril refused the bishop of Jerusalem the patriarchal rank. See *Councils and Synods*, 4.

Ephraem the Syrian (d. ca. 378). Most prominent of the Fathers of the Syrian Church in the fourth century, *propheta Syrorum*, its greatest preacher and hymn writer; lived as an anchorite at Edessa, studying and writing, teaching and preaching, and succoring the needy. He wrote commentaries on most books of the Bible. His sermons, combating Arianism and the other heresies of his day, were publicly read in many churches.

Ephraemi, Codex. See *Manuscripts of the Bible*, 3.

Ephrata Community. See *Baptist Bodies*, 17; *Communistic Societies*, 5.

Epiclesis. The liturgical prayer in the Eastern Church by which sacramental elements (water, bread, wine, and oil) are blessed.

Epictetus. Greek philosopher of the first century who emphasized the paternal kinship between God and men.

Epicureanism. The philosophy of Epicurus (341—270 B.C.). It is a combination of the atomism of Democritus with the hedonism of Aristippus. Atomism is as follows: Matter and void are the only real entities, uncreated and eternal. Atoms are the primordial particles of matter, indivisible, invisible, and indestructible, which by fortuitous concourse bring worlds into being. Men and animals are spontaneous products of the earth. The soul, too, is material, made of fine, smooth atoms disseminated through the body and destined to perish. Death ends all. Epicureanism has no room for either theology or teleology. The gods, inconsistently retained in the system, inhabit the placid intermundane spaces and take no part in the government of the world or the affairs of men. This material and mechanical world view, according to Epicurus, is essential to happiness. Indeed, its only purpose is to furnish a physical or philosophic basis for a hedonistic theory of conduct. Pleasure is the highest good, not the fleeting pleasure of the voluptuary, to be sure, but rather an unclouded serenity of mind. To attain this end, religion must be destroyed, since it is the chief cause of mental disquiet and anxiety. Virtue must be preferred, not because it is good in itself, but because it brings peace and contentment. Right and wrong are purely conventional distinctions.

Epileptic Homes. The best-known epileptic home is the one founded by Pastor von Bodelschwingh, "Bethel bei Bielefeld," 1872. Bodelschwingh made the observation that epileptics are best cared for if they are permitted to continue their former occupations and if an institution affords them as much as possible the comforts of home life. Epileptic institutions under Lutheran auspices are maintained at Watertown, Wis. (Synodical Conference), and Rochester, Pa.

Epiphanes. See *Gnosticism,* 7 f.

Epiphanius of Salamis. B. ca. 310; Bishop of Salamis in Cyprus 367; d. 403; highly esteemed for his monastic asceticism, learning, piety, and self-denying care for the poor, and his zeal for orthodoxy; his zeal, however, not always according to knowledge (see *Origen*); noted pulpit orator. His polemical treatises have historical value.

Epiphany. A manifestation of deity, a term applied to the birth, Baptism, appearance of the star, and similar events in Christ's life. It is also applied to Jan. 6, celebrated in commemoration of the visit of the Magi. See *Church Year,* 2.

Episcopacy. In the apostolic age the episcopal office, or office of bishops, was in no wise distinguished from that of eldership, the terms *bishop* (overseer) and *elder* (presbyter) being used synonymously and corresponding to the modern *minister,* or *pastor.* See *Elders, Ministerial Office.*

The Roman Catholic theory of episcopacy is based upon the Roman idea of the Church, which requires an external sacrifice and special priests to perform it. The priest is supposed to receive his internal consecration from God through the external consecration of the Church, and by this is meant the imposition of hands by the bishop. It is held that the episcopate is perpetuated in uninterrupted succession from the Apostles (Apostolic Succession *). The bishops form a perpetual corporation, exercising its powers under a common head, the Pope. The theory that the Pope holds his office as *primus inter pares,* that is, that he is first among equals (Gallican view), and that the bishops rule each by divine right, has gradually yielded to the ultramontane idea of the episcopate, by which the Pope is constituted sole bishop by divine right, all other bishops existing only through him.

The Church of England and the Protestant Episcopal Church in the United States hold that there are three orders of ministers in the Church — bishops, priests, and deacons, and that the bishops are the successors of the Apostles. The High Church (Romanizing) party maintains the divine right of episcopacy and its absolute necessity for the existence of the Church, while the Low Church party denies that episcopacy is of the essence of the Church. In harmony with its view regarding the nature of episcopacy, High Church writers do not regard as a "Church" any denomination which has not the episcopal office by (presumed) apostolic succession. In their opinion the Roman system, the Greek Catholic (Oriental) Church, and the State Church of Sweden, which likewise has bishops, are true churches, while the Methodist, Presbyterian, Lutheran denominations, and Protestant churches generally are not regarded as "churches." The episcopacy of the Anglican Church is diocesan, like that of the Roman Catholic, and the bishops are named from the chief city of the diocese. In the Protestant Episcopal Church (United States) the dioceses are generally co-extensive with the States of the Union, and the bishops are named accordingly. There are no archbishops, but assistant and missionary bishops are authorized.

In the Methodist Episcopal Church the bishops are not regarded as successors to the Apostles, and the New Testament principle that bishops are of no higher rank than other clergy is recognized. Upon the bishops of the Methodist Episcopal Church are devolved certain extraordinary functions, such as ordaining and presiding in assemblies.

Episcopal Inquisition. See *Inquisition*, 3.

Episcopalians. See *Protestant Episcopal Church*.

Episcopius. See *Arminianism*.

Epistemology (G. "theory of knowledge"). A branch of philosophy which investigates the possibility, limits, origin, source, kinds, structure, and other problems of knowledge and seeks to determine the nature of truth. See *Philosophy; Truth*.

Epistle of Barnabas, Peter, etc. See *Apocrypha*, B 4.

Epistolae Obscurorum Virorum. A Humanist attack on Rome by Crotus Rubianus, Hutten, and others (1515; 1517); purported to be written by Dominicans laying absurd problems in scholarship and theology before Professor Ortuin Gratius. The barbaric Latin of the monks is successfully imitated and their ignorance, arrogance, hypocrisy, and licentiousness exposed.

Epitome. See *Lutheran Confessions*, C 2.

Epworth League. An organization for young people in the Methodist churches of America, named after Wesley's birthplace, Epworth, England. Organized at Cleveland, Ohio, 1889, by merging a few young people's societies into one single organization. The purpose of the League is to win young people for Jesus Christ and to train them to serve Him. Weekly devotional meetings are held. Summer institutes for instruction and training in the Christian life have been conducted. Hundreds of volunteers have come from these for the ministry and the mission

fields and other services of the Church. The members of the League contribute liberally to the benevolences of the Church. The *Epworth Herald* is the official paper of the League in the Methodist Episcopal Church, North; the *Epworth Era* is the official paper of the League in the Methodist Episcopal Church, South, and the Methodist Church of Canada.

Equiprobabilism. The theory in ethics which holds that when two divergent judgments are equally defensible, either may be followed.

Equivocation. See *Jesuits and Jesuitism*, 5.

Era. See *Time*.

Erasmus, Desiderius Roterodamus (1466—1536). 1. Dutch Humanist, who also dabbled in theology; b. at Rotterdam, Holland; d. at Basel, Switzerland; received very good education in monastic and semimonastic schools; was admitted to the priesthood, but never exercised its functions; spent much time at learned centers of the Continent; held position of Lady Margaret Professor of Divinity at Cambridge and was offered many other positions of honor, but preferred a life of independent literary activity; noted for his telling Latin style. While in England, Erasmus began a systematic examination of manuscripts of the New Testament in order to prepare a new edition and a Latin translation. This edition was published by Froben of Basel in 1516 and, with its successors, became the basis of the best scientific study of the Bible during the period of the Reformation, Luther making use of an Erasmian edition as the basis of his German translation.

2. When the Reformation began, Erasmus was put to a hard test; he was in sympathy with many points of Luther's writings, especially in the great Reformer's criticism of the external evils of the Church. But he was too strongly settled in his dilatory and vacillating method of thinking, writing, and acting, and his ideas of the reformation of the Church ran along humanistic rather than Biblical lines. The consequence was that, whereas Luther at first expressed his admiration for all that Erasmus had done in the cause of a purer, moral Christianity, he finally, on account of the refusal of Erasmus to commit himself, on account of his dread to suggest any change in the doctrinal position of the Church, and on account

of the treatise *De Libero Arbitrio* (*Of Free Will*) with its equivocal and false theology, was obliged to turn against Erasmus in his noted treatise *De Servo Arbitrio* (*Of the Enslaved Will*). The result of this controversy for Erasmus was that he found himself, at the close of his life, at odds with both parties, the Roman Catholic and the Lutheran, or Protestant. Toward the end of his life he published a book, *Gospel Preacher*, in which he tries to emphasize the importance of preaching in the work of the ministry. He was one of the most learned men of his age, if not of all times, but he did not rise above mediocrity in usefulness, chiefly on account of his vacillating disposition.

Albert Hyma, *Youth of Erasmus*, University of Michigan Press, 1930; Preserved Smith, *Erasmus*, a Study of His Life, Ideals, and Place in History, Harper, 1923.

Erastianism. A view according to which the State is supreme in ecclesiastical causes, the word being derived from Erastus, a Swiss Reformed physician and theologian (d. 1562), who denied that the Church has any power to make laws and decrees and declared that the infliction of penalties, especially such as pertain to the body, belongs to civil magistrates. Erastianism, in its wide application, goes beyond the views held by Erastus.

Erb, John. See *Catholic Apostolic Church*, 2.

Eremites. See *Hermits.*

Erich, Duke of Brunswick (1470 to 1540). Roman Catholic who was impressed by Luther's stand at Worms and sent him refreshments.

Erichsen, Jørgen. See *Norway, Lutheranism in*, 2.

Erigena, John Scotus (815?—77?). B. and probably educated in Ireland; principal of the court school at Paris 847; had a knowledge of Greek exceptional for his days. Though probably neither priest nor monk, he yet discussed theological questions, but from a standpoint of philosophy. His doctrine is the first attempt at a speculative dogmatics in the Occident, and he is the connecting link between Greek and Occidental philosophy, having some influence on Scholasticism.

Erk, Ludwig Christian (1807—83). Trained chiefly by his father and André at Offenbach; music teacher in Moers, then conductor in Berlin; chief work in male choir and in his chorus for mixed voices; in 1857 royal musical director, finally professor; published a number of songbooks for schools, which enjoyed great popularity, and several books of chorals, based upon his studies of the choral in the 16th and 17th centuries.

Erlangen School. Since the reawakening of confessional Lutheranism from rationalism, the University of Erlangen has exerted a far-reaching influence on the Lutheran Church. The leaders of this school have been von Hoffmann and, later, Frank. Other prominent teachers: Harless, Hoefling, Thomasius, Delitzsch, Kahnis, Luthardt, Th. Harnack, Plitt, v. Zezschwitz, Th. Zahn, Ihmels, etc. Its organ was the *Zeitschrift fuer Protestantismus und Kirche*. This school has manfully combated rationalism in its old form, as well as in its modern guise of liberalism, and has made some valuable contributions to Lutheran theology. But, though claiming to represent conservative, confessional Lutheranism, it has forsaken the Lutheran base. It claims the right to develop the doctrines of the Confessions along the lines of a "scientific" theology (*wissenschaftliche Theologie*), has repudiated the principle that Scripture alone is the source of theology (*principium cognoscendi*), and substituted therefor the believing ego, the Christian consciousness, the theologian himself, thus following Schleiermacher rather than Luther. See *Lutheran Theology after 1580*, 11.

Ernest the Confessor. Duke of Brunswick-Lueneburg; b. 1497; nephew of Frederick the Wise; pupil of Luther; reformed his duchy in 1527; signed the Augsburg Confession in 1530; d. 1546.

Ernesti, Johann August. B. 1707; d. 1781 as professor in Leipzig; mediating theologian; trying to hold to the inspiration of the Bible and the Symbolical Books of the Church, he nevertheless made concessions to the rationalistic tendency of his time.

Ernst, Augustus Friedrich. B. June 25, 1841, at Eddesse, Hannover; after graduating from the Celle *Gymnasium*, he studied theology at Goettingen, also philology and philosophy. For one year he instructed at the Clausthal *Gymnasium*, then came to America, 1863, to serve the Lutheran Church. Ordained at Pottstown, Pa., 1864, for a Brooklyn pastorate, which he left, 1868, to go to

Albany. Through the offices of Pastor Adelberg he accepted the call to Northwestern College, Watertown, Wis., as professor and inspector, 1869; two years later he was made president, 1919, from which office he resigned, 1919, remaining as professor; on leave since 1921, when he was incapacitated by illness. It was his task to reconstruct the college (opened 1865); he made of it the American school with Lutheran ideals of the best German traditions that it is today. He could not conceive of a higher ambition than to teach the men who were to teach the Church. He has been called the "Preceptor of the Lutheran Northwest." He was made honorary Ph. D. by Concordia Seminary, St. Louis. Serving his synod in many capacities, he was also the first president of the Joint Synod. The only books this scholar cared to write were textbooks for parish schools, a *Bible History* and a *Reader* (German). D. Aug. 8, 1924.

Ernst, Johann Adam. See *Canada, Lutheranism in,* 10.

Error. See *Fundamental Doctrines; Heresy.*

Erskine, Ebenezer (1680—1754). See *Presbyterian Bodies,* 1.

Erskine, Thomas (1788 — 1870). Scottish theologian; interpreter of the mystical side of Calvinism; wrote: *Essay on Faith; Unconditional Freeness of the Gospel.*

Esbjoern, Lars Paul (1808 — 70). Graduate of Upsala University 1832; pastor in Sweden 1835—49; emigrated 1849; pastor in Illinois 1849—58; Scandinavian professor of theology at Illinois State University 1858—60; president and professor of Augustana Seminary, Chicago, 1860—63; pastor in Sweden 1863—70; author of books and articles. I. O. Nothstein, "The Swedish Missionary Society and Pastor L. P. Esbjoern's Relation to It," *Aug. Quart.,* XXV: 226—41.

Esch, Johann, and **Voes, Heinrich.** Young Augustinians at Antwerp, converted by Luther's writings, firm against Louvain theologians; forced by Hoogstraten to choose between recanting or burning; burned in Brussels market July 1, 1523. Luther celebrated their martyrdom in his first poem and sent a comforting letter to the faithful at Brussels.

"Eschatological" Jesus. See *Christ, Lives of.*

Eschatology. See *Hereafter; Last Things.*

Escobar y Mendoza, Antonio (1589 to 1669). Spanish Jesuit; noted for his asceticism and energy as preacher; wrote extensively in exegesis and moral theology; among his works are commentaries on the gospels and a book of moral theology of the Jesuits (burned by Parlement de Paris, 1761).

Esdras. See *Apocrypha,* A 3.

Espolin, Jon Jonsson (1769—1836). Government official in Iceland; wrote history of Iceland from 1262—1832; wrote a *Commentary on Revelation* which shows familiarity with the work of many exegetes.

Espousal. See *Marriage.*

Essence (L. *essentia* from *esse* "to be"). A term used in philosophy to designate that which underlies all outward manifestations. The term is extensively used in critical realism and is that which lies between the perceiving subject and that which is perceived. Even among critical realists the concept is much controverted.

Essential Foundation. See *Fundamental Doctrines.*

Established Church. See *State Church.*

Esther, Additions to. See *Apocrypha,* A 3.

Esthetic Argument. See *God, Arguments for Existence of.*

Esthonia heard of Christianity in 1190 from Meinhard, "the Apostle of Livonia," and it was forced on the people in 1201 by King Canute VI of Denmark. The Order of Teutonic Knights purchased the country of Waldemar III in 1346 and continued the "missionary" work. In 1521 Walter of Plettenberg, the head of the order, introduced the Reformation. Luther wrote to the Christians of Riga, Reval, capital of Esthonia, and Dorpat in 1523. In these three cities S. Tegetmeier established the Reformation. The Catechism came in 1561, the Bible in 1633. In 1711 Peter the Great took the country. During the nineteenth century the Lutheran Church in the Baltic Provinces suffered much oppression and some losses in consequence of Orthodox propaganda and adverse legislation. — Esthonia, including parts of Livonia (with the island of Oesel) and other territory, became a republic in 1919;

now part of the U. S. S. R. The population was Lutheran to about 80% of its total number; the rest of the people were Greek Orthodox, Roman Catholic, etc. The Esthonians are Finnish in blood and language. The church functioned as a synod, under a bishop.

Estius, Wilhelm (Wilhelm Hessel van Est; 1541—1613). Roman Catholic theologian; rector of seminary at Douay; later chancellor of the university; wrote commentaries on all Pauline letters and annotations of all prooftexts.

Eternal. Existing forever, without beginning or end in time. See *God; Hereafter.*

Eternal Life. The life of the spirit (distinguished from the temporal union of soul and body), which consists of the union of the Christian with God through faith in Christ Jesus, especially the perfect enjoyment thereof in heaven. That eternal life is a present possession of every Christian is clearly taught in Scripture (1 John 5:11; John 3:16). This eternal life, then, commences when it pleases the Father to reveal to us the Son, that we may be enabled to "call Him Lord by the Holy Ghost." Then it is that heaven is opened in the soul, so that the Christian can "rejoice evermore and in all things give thanks." For the future life see *Hereafter.*

Eternal Punishment. See *Hereafter*, B.

Eternally Begotten. A term used to describe the eternal generation of the Son by the Father. See *Christ Jesus.*

Ethelbert. See *England, Early Christianity in, 2.*

Ethical Argument. See *Immortality, Arguments for.*

Ethical Culture. A movement begun in New York (1876) when Felix Adler (1851—1933; b. at Alzey, Germany; son of a Jewish rabbi who emigrated to America in 1857; educated at Columbia College; professor of oriental languages and, later, of philosophy and ethics) founded the New York Society for Ethical Culture, which was designated by him as "the new religion of humanity, whose God is the Good, whose church is the universe, whose heaven is here on earth and not in the clouds." The aim of the society was to bring together the best moral teachings from the earliest times to the present, and

to assert the importance of the application of the ethical factor to all phases of life. The movement declared its independence of all creeds, requiring of its members only the recognition of the ethical aim as the highest goal of life. It welcomes adherents who are theists, or atheists. Each is free to hold his opinions regarding God, immortality, etc. Jesus is regarded as a human teacher who made important contributions to our moral heritage.

Ethical Culture societies were also organized in Chicago (1882), Philadelphia (1885), St. Louis (1886), Brooklyn (1906), and these were united with the New York society into the American Ethical Culture Union (1886). Societies were also established in Germany, France, Italy, England, Austria, Japan, and other countries. An International Ethical Union was organized in 1896, but the movement survived among European nations in England only. The official publication of the society in America is *The Standard.* While the membership of the Ethical Culture Society remained small (ca. 2,500 in U. S.) and embraced chiefly urbane intellectuals, it, nevertheless, exerted an influence on American churches and education.

As great stress is laid on moral instruction of the young, the New York society introduced, besides a Sunday school, an efficient day school (The Ethical Culture School), which emphasizes ethical training at all age levels. The school is open to all regardless of race or social rank. A similar school was opened in Brooklyn (1923). In addition to their educational activities, the Ethical Culture societies have also been active in social reform (child labor, race relations, settlements, refugee work, etc.).

The services are extremely simple, consisting of music, inspirational readings, quiet meditations (instead of prayer), and talks on ethics.

After Adler's death, J. L. Elliot headed the New York group. After the latter's death, it was led by five leaders. The other organizations in the U. S. have individual leaders. See *Religious Bodies (U. S.), Bibliography.*

Ethical Problem. See *Apologetics,* I D.

Ethics (Morals; *Sittenlehre*). Ethics is the science of the moral as it is to be realized first of all in the life of the individual and then also within the community of other personal beings

(Reu). Ethics may be divided into two classes: naturalistic and theistic.

Naturalistic. In its purest form (uninfluenced by Christianity), natural ethics appears among the ancients. While Plato conceived of a metaphysical basis (Shorey: the sanction) for his ethics (the Good), he nevertheless conceives of it in its practical aspects as citizenship guided by wisdom, courage, temperance, and justice. Aristotle was the first among the Greeks to write a treatise on ethics. In it he gives a list of virtues, each of which lies between two opposite vices (moderation). The Epicureans originally advocated a life of refined hedonism. The Stoics favored a life of apathy, affected neither by pleasure or pain. Later Stoics (*e. g.,* Marcus Aurelius) considered each man a part of the whole, related sparks of God, and condemned social distinctions as absurd.

Rousseau held that a man should obey his impulses in a strictly natural environment. Ludwig Feuerbach developed this principle into an egoism, holding that ethics consists in obeying the natural impulse. Ernst Haeckel modified this ethical theory by adding altruism (duty to society) to egoism. Utilitarian ethics (Thomas Hobbes, Bentham) hold that the highest good for the individual must be selected by reason (four sanctions for action: egoistic, social, political, religious). The ethical societies seek to determine the morally good by scientific study of actions and their results. The ethics of evolution is in a continual state of flux. That which is considered ethical today is the result of acts with favorable results in past evolutionary stages, and both past and present are developing toward a future ideal (Herbert Spencer). Elements of naturalism, utilitarianism, and evolutionism are present in empiricism (mechanism, realism, pragmatism, instrumentalism, behaviorism), which occupies a prominent place in contemporary American thought.

Dissatisfied with materialism, Immanuel Kant sought a universal principle for behavior and found it in the superindividual reason which he stated in his categorical imperative: Act according to the rule which you would wish to be a universal law of nature (stated in three formulations). See also *Aesthetics; Schleiermacher.*

Theistic. Religious ethics among heathen claims the sanction of idols for actions. Since attributes of man are attributed to idols, the ethics of idolatry degenerates with social ideals.

Christian ethics is the voluntary acceptance of the divine will as norm by free human personalities and its application in the individual life and social relations. In Roman Catholicism, ethics is a matter of works, each work adding to the building of the morally good person. Romanists also distinguish between a higher and lower ethics, the higher denying the use of the gifts of nature. Reformed theology emphasizes the will of God, making salvation dependent on His decree and regarding the will of God as a law for moral development. Modernism with its emphasis on the Sermon on the Mount is also nomistic. Christian ethics as set forth in Scripture departs radically from these views (as emphasized by Luther) by showing that man does not become good by *doing* good, but, by *being* good, does good. Man is first justified, that is, freed from the rule of sin and brought into the proper relationship to God through faith in Christ, before he does truly good works. Thus he enters into the relationship of love with God and his fellow men ("Love is the fulfilling of the Law."—Rom. 13:10). Christian ethics is not a submission to the will of God, but a harmony with the divine will. Luther described the voluntary and spontaneous nature of good works in the Christian man as follows: "No one bids the sun to shine; it does so of its own accord. No one bids the trees to grow and bring forth fruit; they do so of their own accord. No command is needed to make two and two equal four; they are four. So it is with the justified: he needs no command to produce good works; he does them of his own accord."

Since the regenerate is still in two kingdoms, Law and grace, the Moral Law is not abrogated (for discussion see *Decalog*). See also *Social Ethics.* EL

J. M. Reu-P. H. Buehring, *Christian Ethics,* Luth. Book Concern, Columbus, Ohio, 1935 (contains a select bibliography which is not here given); Richard R. Caemmerer, "The Basic Motives of Christian Ethics in Action," *Lutheran Scholar,* April, 1949; C. C. Rasmussen, "The Lutheran View of Christian Ethics," *What Lutherans Are Thinking,* Wartburg Press, Columbus, 1947; Richard C. Caemmerer, "The Melanchthonian Blight," *CTM,* XVIII: 321 ff.; A. Nygren, *Agape and Eros* (translated by Hebert-Watson, 3 vols.), SPCK, London, 1932, 1938, 1939; L. S. Keyser,

A System of General Ethics, Luth. Lit.
Bd., Burlington, Iowa, 1918; Werner
Betcke, *Luthers Sozialethik,* Bertelsmann, Guetersloh, 1934; H. Preisker,
*Geist und Leben — das Telos — Ethos
des Urchristentums;* O. A. W. Piper,
Grundlagen der Evangelischen Ethik,
1928—30; L. H. Marshall, *The Challenge
of New Testament Ethics,* Macm., 1947;
for ethics of Confucianism, Mohammedanism, etc., see E. H. Sneath, *The
Evolution of Ethics,* Yale University
Press, 1927.

Ethics, Social. See *Social Ethics.*

Ethiopia. See *Abyssinia.*

Ethiopian Church. See *Coptic
Church.*

Ethiopianism. A movement among
the native peoples of central and south
Africa aiming at the dethronement of
white supremacy in that country and at
ultimate expulsion of the white race.
It traces its origin to the past century,
when, about 1892, two native ministers
of the Wesleyan Church defected and
founded the Church of Ethiopia, from
which all whites were to be excluded;
the slogan is, "Africa for the Africans." The African Methodist Episcopal
Church in the United States recognized
Mr. Dwane, one of the founders, and
the Ethiopian Church, as did also the
Anglican Church at Cape Town. In
1898 Bishop Turner of the American
African M. E. Church visited Africa and
ordained many native Kafir ministers.
Later the African Methodist Episcopal
Church delegated Dr. Levi Coppin, of
Philadelphia, as bishop to South Africa,
and he was able to reorganize the natives of the English Methodist missions
in opposition to the Church of Ethiopia.
Much religious and political unrest resulted among the natives from the Ethiopian Movement, such as the Herero
(1904) and the Zulu (1906) uprisings.
Since the end of World War II the
movement has gained momentum.

Ethiopic Bible Version. See *Bible
Versions,* E.

Etiology (G. *aitia,* "cause"). The
science, investigation, or theory of
causes.

Etten, Edwin von. See *Radio Evangelism,* 1.

Eucharist. See *Grace, Means of,* IV.

Eucharist (Liturgical). See *Lord's
Supper* (Liturgical).

Eucharistic Controversies. The theory that during Holy Communion bread
and wine are transformed into the body
and blood of Christ (subsequently
called Transubstantiation) and that the
Mass is a sacrifice, which had been
gaining ground since Gregory I, was
championed in 844 by Paschasius Radbertus, abbot of Corbie, France, who
argued from the authority of the
Fathers and the alleged miraculous
phenomena exhibited by the consecrated bread. Asked for his opinion by
the king, Ratramnus (d. ca. 868), monk
of Corbie, condemned the book of his
abbot, denying, on his part, the real
presence of the body and the blood
and admitting nothing beyond a spiritual eating and drinking — practically
the Reformed doctrine. Rhabanus Maurus (776?—856) and Scotus Erigena
held the same views, Hincmar and
others sided with Radbertus, and Christian Druthmar and others declared for
impanation and consubstantiation, while
the Scriptural doctrine of the real presence, the sacramental, supernatural
union, was entirely lost sight of. The
theory of Radbertus prevailed.—Berengar of Tours, who elaborated the theory
of Ratramnus and denied that the unworthy communicant receives the body
and blood of Christ, was accused of
heresy by Lanfranc, his friend, condemned unheard by a synod in Rome
1050, condemned, while in prison, by a
second synod, which also had the book
of Ratramnus burned, satisfied the papal
legate Hildebrand with an evasive
declaration, was compelled in Rome,
1059, to consign his writings to the fire
and accept an extremely Capernaitic
formula, repudiated his confession and
answered Lanfranc with his chief work,
On the Holy Supper, and was compelled
in 1079, at Rome, by Gregory VII (Hildebrand), who himself did not believe
in transubstantiation, to abjure his view
and accept the popular one. Gregory
prohibited all further controversies, and
transubstantiation came to be universally accepted. 4th Lateran Council
(1215) and Council of Trent. Berengar
retracted his recantation, submitted
after another trial, and died as a solitary penitent.

Luther rejected the Roman Catholic
doctrine of transubstantiation. At the
same time he defended the real presence, which was denied by Zwingli and
Reformed theologians. See *Crypto-Calvinistic Controversy; Grace, Means of,
IV; Lutheran Confessions; Calvinism;
Lord's Supper, Roman Catholic Doctrine.*

Eucharistic Sacrifice. See *Mass.*

Euchites. 1) A sect of Mesopotamia and Syria (4th century) which emphasized mystic experiences and depreciated the means of grace; 2) a Thracian sect (11th century) reviving Manichaeism.

Eucken, Rudolf Christoph (1846 to 1926). Prof. of philosophy at Jena (1874—1920); Nobel prize in literature (1908); exchange prof. at Harvard (1912—13). Wrote numerous works on philosophy and religion. His philosophy was ethical activism, which emphasized the reality of spiritual values and their application in life.

Eudemonism. The ethical theory which makes happiness the highest aim in life. As the sources of happiness vary greatly, we may distinguish gross and fine eudemonism. The former is also called hedonism.* The latter finds happiness in intellectual and aesthetic pursuits. Eudemonism which makes not private, but public welfare or happiness its aim is called utilitarianism. All forms of eudemonism were rejected as immoral by Kant, who, going to the other extreme, established the principle that the good must be done for its own sake.

Eunomius. Bishop of Cyzicus in Mysia; radical Arian, who declared that the Son was unlike (*anomoios*) the Father.

Eusebius of Caesarea (ca. 280—339). Surnamed Pamphili = the friend of Pamphilus, his teacher; imprisoned in Egypt for confessing; bishop of Caesarea soon after 313; enjoyed the confidence of Constantine. He was prominent at Nicea, working for a compromise; he subscribed to the Nicene Creed, but later was at the head of the moderate Semi-Arians and presided at the synod in Tyre, 335, which condemned Athanasius. In the field of Church History he served the Church well, "the Father of Church History," being the first in the field and preserving valuable material for his successors. His *Church History, Chronicle* (a universal history), *Life of Constantine*, etc., are the fruit of most painstaking research. He wrote, besides, apologetic, dogmatic, and exegetic treatises and collaborated with Pamphilus on the *Apology for Origen.*

Eusebius of Nicomedia and Constantinople (d. 341). Strongly Arian in his theology; signed the confession of Nicea after long opposition; later used political power to promote Arianism. See *Arianism* (2).

Eusebius of Samosata (d. ca. 379). Bishop of Samosata (361); opponent of Arianism; killed by a stone thrown by an Arian woman.

Eustathius of Antioch (d. ca. 360). Bishop of Berea and of Antioch; opposed Arians at Nicea; the Arians secured his banishment at the Synod of Antioch (331); his followers refused to recognize another bishop, thus occasioning the *Eustathian* schism; opponent of the school of Origen.

Eustathius of Thessalonica (d. ca. 1193). Bishop of the Greek Church; known for his learning as shown in his commentaries (Homer, Pindar, John of Damascus) and his evangelical feelings.

Eustatius. See *Germany.*

Euthanasia. The intentional cutting short of human life in the case of disease or illness that may be pronounced incurable and is at the same time very painful (mercy killing). The Christian objects to such killing for numerous reasons. It is contrary to the Fifth Commandment. If a man is at all justified in taking life, then specious reasons may also be advanced for infanticide, suicide, killing the aged and those useless in society, etc. Man's life is given him by God (Job 10:8-12; Ps. 139:13-16), and He alone has the right to take it again (Acts 17:26; Job 1:21; 1 John 3:15). Christians do not by wrong means seek to escape the sorrows, tribulations, and trials of life. They know that all trials work for their good (Rom. 8:28) and that suffering serves a purpose (Heb. 12:6, 11; Deut. 8:5; Prov. 13:24; Rom. 5:1-5; John 11:4; Acts 14:22; 2 Cor. 12:7-9; Lev. 26:40-42). J. H. C. Fritz, "Euthanasia," *CTM,* XVIII:94 ff.

Euthymius Zigabenus (12th century). Greek orthodox monk and theologian; wrote *Panoplia Dogmatica* and commentaries.

Eutychianism. A heresy of the fifth century, taking its name from Eutyches, an Alexandrian presbyter and archimandrite, who asserted that there were two natures in Christ before the incarnation. In opposition to Nestorianism, Eutyches taught that the human nature in Christ was absorbed, swallowed up, by the divine nature. Condemned by the Council of Chalcedon.* See *Christological Controversies.*

Evangelical (G. "Gospel"). A term used to denote loyalty to the Gospel of Jesus Christ in contrast to rationalistic and legalistic Christianity. Thus the Lutheran Reformation was "evangelical." In the course of time the term was used to describe those who emphasized the doctrine of atonement for sin and the inerrancy of the Scriptures. Evangelicals are known for activities in mission work, efforts toward personal piety and opposition to ritualism and modernism. In the twentieth century a liberal evangelical movement sought to combine the zeal of evangelicals with liberalism. In England the term is applied to the "Low Church" members.

Evangelical Alliance. Dr. Chalmers (d. 1847), the founder of the Free Church of Scotland, was instrumental in calling, in 1846, a meeting in London of Protestants from all countries, who sought to unite more closely all evangelical Christians, insisted on liberty of conscience and religious tolerance, and were opposed to the Papacy and to Puseyism. Hoffmann of Berlin, Tholuck of Halle, and the Baptist preacher Oncken of Hamburg attended the meeting. They organized and adopted the name *Evangelical Alliance.* All who would accept the following doctrines were to be eligible to membership: 1. the divine inspiration, authority, and sufficiency of the Scriptures; 2. the right and duty of private judgment; 3. the unity of the Godhead and the trinity of the divine persons; 4. the total depravity of human nature as a result of the Fall; 5. the incarnation of the Son of God, His work of redemption for sinful mankind, mediatory intercession, and His kingship; 6. justification only by faith; 7. the work of the Holy Spirit in converting and sanctifying the sinner; 8. the immortality of the soul, the resurrection of the body, the final Judgment by the Savior, receiving the righteous into eternal life and condemning the ungodly to eternal perdition; 9. the divine institution of the office of the ministry and of the Sacraments (Baptism and the Lord's Supper). The Evangelical Alliance did not seek organically to unite the churches, but simply to bring about a closer fellowship of individual Christians. Every member was asked to pray for the common cause on the morning of the first day of every week and during the first week of every year. The *Evangelical Christendom* (founded in London, 1847) and the *Neue evangelische Kirchenzeitung* (founded in Germany, 1859) were the official publications. See also *Union Movements,* 10.

Evangelical Church (Albrights, Albright Methodists, *Albrechtsbrueder*). 1. This denomination was organized by Jacob Albright (orig. Albrecht); b. in Pottstown, Pa., 1759; d. 1808. Under his instruction twenty converts from among the German-speaking people in Pennsylvania united in 1800 to pray with and for each other. Albright did not purpose to found a new church, but the language conditions and the opposition manifested by some Methodists to the modes of worship followed by his converts made a separate ecclesiastical organization necessary. It was not, however, until 1803 that an ecclesiastical organization was effected, at a general assembly held in eastern Pennsylvania, when Albright was set apart as a minister of the Gospel and ordained as an elder. The act of consecration was performed by the laying on of hands in solemn prayer by two of his associates. The first annual conference was held in Lebanon County, Pa., in November, 1807. Albright was elected bishop, and articles of faith and the book of discipline were adopted, but a full form of church government was not devised for some years. The first general conference convened in Buffalo Valley, Center County, Pa., in October, 1816, at which time the denomination adopted the name "Evangelical Association," whereas formerly they were known as Albrights or Albright Methodists. Although in the beginning the activities of the church were carried on in the German language only, the scope was soon widened, and the work was carried on also in English, and of late years English has become the dominant language. The denomination spread into the central and throughout the northern and western States, from New England to the Pacific coast, and north into Canada. For some years the missionary idea, which has always been a dominant purpose of the denomination, found its expression in local work; but in 1839 a General Missionary Society was organized, and a Woman's Society followed in 1883. In 1854 the church first reached out to Europe and began an important work both in Germany and Switzerland. In 1876 work was begun in Japan, and since then missions have been established in China and Russia. As early as 1815 a church publishing house was founded. The official organ, *Der Christliche Botschafter,* was founded in 1836. A division in 1891 resulted in the organization of the United Evangelical Church under

Bishop R. Dubs (Naperville, Ill., 1894). The two bodies reunited in 1922 to form the Evangelical Church. It merged (1947) with the United Brethren to form the Ev. United Brethren Church. Membership (1952) about 730,000.

2. *Doctrine.* In doctrine the church is Arminian, and its articles of faith correspond very closely to those of the Methodist Episcopal Church. Christian perfection is defined as "a state of grace in which Christians are so firmly rooted in God that they have instant victory over every temptation the very moment it presents itself, in which their rest, peace, and joy in God is not interrupted by the vicissitudes of life; in which, in short, sin has lost its power over them, and they rule over the flesh, the world, and Satan, yet in watchfulness." Entire sanctification is the basis of this perfection, which, however, constantly admits of a fuller participation in divine power and a constant expansion in spiritual capacity.

3. *Polity.* Before his death, Albright began a *Book of Rules and Order* which was finished by George Miller (1774 to 1816). A polity was established which was connected in form. Bishops are elected by the General Conference, but not ordained as such. The General Conference has been a delegated body. The annual and quarterly conferences correspond to the smaller bodies in the Methodist Episcopal Church.

4. *Work.* In addition to the work mentioned above, the Evangelical Church established missions in Germany (1850), Japan (1875), China (1900), and also in Africa, United States, and Canada. It has three colleges and two seminaries in the U.S. See *Religious Bodies (U.S.), Bibliography.*

Evangelical Congregational Church. Members of the United Evangelical Church (see *Evangelical Church,* 1) of East Pennsylvania who did not re-enter the union of 1922.

Evangelical Counsels. See *Consilia Evangelica.*

Evangelical Free Church of North America. This body was organized in 1885 by the merger of two Swedish bodies as the Evangelical Mission Covenant Church.* Though of Lutheran origin, it grants its ministers liberty in such fundamental doctrines as the atonement and the Sacraments.

Evangelical Lutheran Church. 1. The Evangelical Lutheran Church (formerly the Norwegian Lutheran Church of America) is the third largest general Lutheran body in America. The following statistical information is current at the close of 1951: baptized membership, 872,813; confirmed membership, 605,151; congregations, 2,717; ordained ministers, 1,780; pastors active in parish work, 1,225; full-time professors, 379; foreign missionaries, 151.

2. The membership of the Evangelical Lutheran Church is distinctly midwestern, more than seventy per cent being concentrated in Wisconsin, Illinois, Minnesota, Iowa, North Dakota, and South Dakota. Smaller concentrations of membership are found in Montana, on the Pacific Coast, in Colorado, in Michigan, on the Atlantic Coast, and in the prairie provinces of Canada.

3. The history of the Evangelical Lutheran Church parallels the history of Norwegian immigration to America and the story of the descendants of those immigrants. While Norwegians came to America in small numbers in the 17th and 18th centuries, immigration is usually considered to have begun in 1825, when the Norwegian sloop, *Restaurationen,* landed in New York. From then on the stream increased until about 1890, then began tapering off until the present, with only a tiny trickle of immigration now continuing. It is very largely from these people and their descendants that the Evangelical Lutheran Church has drawn its strength.

4. Spiritually, several characteristics have been discernible among Norwegian Lutherans in America and their descendants from the beginning of Christian work among them here. First of all has been an unbending loyalty to the Word of God. There has never been any tendency among them to deviate from the conviction that the Word of God is "the sole authority for faith and life." Secondly, Norwegians and their descendants in America have been characterized by a deep-seated piety. The so-called Haugean movement was at its height in Norway during the time of the greatest immigration. Even as this movement came to color the entire spiritual life of Norway, so it has come to color also the spiritual life in America. In the third place, the Lutherans of Norwegian descent in America have always placed a great deal of emphasis upon the *confessional* character of their Lutheranism. While, in the tradition of the motherland, most of the formal confessional statements of

the Church in America have confined themselves to formal adherence to "the Unaltered Augsburg Confession and Luther's Small Catechism," this does not mean that they have rejected the other confessional writings of historic Lutheranism. Norwegian Lutheranism in America has always been distinctly and definitely confessional in type.

5. From the very beginning, and persisting until 1917, two general emphases within the framework of historic Lutheranism may be discerned among the Norwegians in America and their descendants. The one, which may be said to represent the "low church" tendency, stems from the arrival in America in 1839 of the famous layman Elling Eielsen (1804—83). He was a product of the Haugean movement in Norway. However, he was not nearly so sympathetic with the organized church as Hauge and his followers had been. Coming to America, he labored as a layman for some years, but was ordained to the ministry on October 3, 1843, thus being the first Norwegian to be ordained on American soil. The movement of which Pastor Eielsen was the head eventuated, after a number of divisions and unions, in the Hauge Norwegian Evangelical Lutheran Synod, which was reorganized from the Eielsen Synod in 1875. Eielsen opposed this reorganization and continued his own synod, which persists today, with half a dozen pastors and congregations and only a few hundred members.

6. The general characteristics of life within this group among the Norwegians are the following: little emphasis was placed upon the historic liturgy of Norwegian Lutheranism; much emphasis was placed upon the priesthood of believers and upon the development of spiritual gifts among the people; and, although the Hauge Synod always believed in the necessity of training leaders, this was not given as much prominence as was the case in other groups among the Norwegian Lutherans. This, then, is the one trend which characterized Norwegian Lutheranism in America for nearly a hundred years.

7. The other tendency is represented by the leadership of ordained pastors whose training was within the established Church of Norway with its formal liturgy and traditions. C. L. Clausen (a Dane) came as a teacher of Christianity to the Muskego settlement near Milwaukee, Wis., and was ordained to the ministry Oct. 18, 1843. He became the pastor of the first organ-

ized congregation among Norwegians in America, a congregation which still exists, bearing the name "Norway-Muskego Church." This congregation also erected the first church building.

8. Later came pastors such as H. A. Stub, A. C. Preus, Nils Brandt, H. A. Preus, and J. A. Ottesen, all university graduates ordained in Norway. This group, together with Clausen, organized what is best known as the Norwegian Synod in 1853. Its characteristics may be summarized as follows: (1) strict Lutheran orthodoxy; (2) sovereignty of the local congregation; (3) requirement of a congregational call for anyone to preach within a congregation; (4) use of the clerical vestments and liturgy of the Church of Norway.

9. While it may seem like an oversimplification to state that these two directions of thought characterized the entire development in America, it is nevertheless strictly the truth.

10. The Norwegian Synod continued to be the larger and stronger of the two groups for a number of years. However, in the 80's of the last century the so-called predestinarian controversy broke out in the Norwegian Synod, with the result that about one third of the pastors and congregations withdrew and established the "Anti-Missourian Brotherhood" (1887; cf. F. A. Schmidt). They did not organize a new synod, but began negotiations with two other groups which had previously been formed and joined to form the "United Norwegian Lutheran Church of America" in 1890.

11. Not many years after the formation of the United Norwegian Lutheran Church of America, a division took place within that body. Two professors who had been members of one of the merging bodies led a controversy within the United Lutheran Church which did not involve primarily doctrine, but rather a matter of church polity, in the first place, and ownership of certain property in the second place. The result was that a new body was organized, the so-called Lutheran Free Church, which still exists. This was the last important split among Norwegian American Lutherans.

12. The situation at the opening of the 20th century, then, is that the Norwegians were divided into the following bodies: The Norwegian Synod, the Hauge Synod, the United Church, the Lutheran Free Church, and two very small bodies, the so-called Eielsen Synod and the Lutheran Brethren.

13. At no time were the leaders and people of these various bodies happy over the divisions which had been caused and which continued to hamper the work of the church at large. In 1905 the Hauge Synod invited the Norwegian Synod and the United Church to take up discussions with possible union in view. Committees from the three synods went over all controversial points of doctrine and practice very carefully. Little by little, it came to be realized that nothing fundamental divided the major bodies, and the final upshot was that on June 9, 1917, the three large bodies merged, becoming the Norwegian Lutheran Church of America. A small minority of the Norwegian Synod declined to enter the merger and formed a body of their own, the so-called Norwegian Synod, which is today a member of the Synodical Conference. [For the position of this group see *Norwegian Synod of the American Evangelical Lutheran Church*.]

14. The years since 1917 have been years of quiet and steady growth and healthy development for the Church. It was realized for many years that the foreign connotation of the name, "Norwegian Lutheran Church of America," was somewhat unfortunate. However, the roots of the older people were deep in the old tradition, and it was not until 1944 and 1946 that two successive conventions of the Church were able to agree upon amending the constitution in such a way that the name was changed. In 1946, then, the "Norwegian Lutheran Church of America" became "The Evangelical Lutheran Church."

15. In relation to other Lutherans, the Evangelical Lutheran Church has been active in forming such relationships as seem to be for the true welfare of the work of the kingdom of God. It has been a member of the National Lutheran Council since its beginning and became a member of the American Lutheran Conference when it was established in 1930. It has always had an active part in the Lutheran World Convention and, in the summer of 1947, became one of the signatories of the Constitution which established the Lutheran World Convention on a permanent basis, with the title The Lutheran World Federation.* OGM

Chr. Anderson, *The Doctrinal Position of the Norwegian Synod, A Brief Survey of the Position in Doctrine and Practice Held by the Old Norwegian Synod Prior to the Merger of 1917*, Posten Press, Decorah, Iowa, 1927; Con-

stitution of the Norwegian Lutheran Church of America, Augsburg Publ. House, Minneapolis, Minn., 1932; O. M. Norlie, *History of the Norwegian People in America*, Augsburg Publishing House, Minneapolis, Minn., 1925; J. M. Rohne, *Norwegian American Lutheranism up to 1872*, Macm., N. Y., 1926. Presidents of ELC: H. G. Stub, 1917—25; J. A. Aasgaard, 1925—.

Evangelical Lutheran Theological Seminary. See *Ministry, Education of,* XI A; XI C.

Evangelical Lutheran Seminary of Canada. See *Ministry, Education of,* XI B.

Evangelical Mennonite Brethren Conference. See *Mennonite Bodies,* 3.

Evangelical Mission Covenant Church. This body was organized in 1885 by the merger of the Swedish Lutheran Mission Synod and the Swedish Lutheran Ansgarius Synod. These two synods had been founded by Swedish immigrants who in Sweden, though members of the Lutheran state church, were adherents of the Free Church Movement, the result of a pietistic and unionistic religious awakening. These immigrants did not feel at home in the Swedish Augustana Synod, preferring a church body which is strictly congregational and not bound by any creedal statements. Full freedom is given to the congregations in matters of doctrine. See *Augustana Lutheran Church,* 11.

Evangelical Protestant Church of North America. This denomination was formed in Cincinnati (1911), by consolidating the German Evangelical Protestant Ministers' Association and the German Evangelical Ministers' Conference.

Polity and Doctrine. This denomination protests against any compulsion in matters of faith and conscience, and grants to everyone the privilege of individual examination and research. Their doctrinal position is characterized by extreme liberalism, rationalism, and Unitarianism, and they reject all doctrines which transcend reason. See *Free Protestants.*

Evangelical and Reformed Church. This denomination was organized in 1934 by the merger of the Evangelical Synod of North America and the Reformed Church in the United States.

1) *The Reformed Church in the United States* traces its history to the great controversies which disturbed the

Lutheran Church of Germany following the Interim,* especially the controversy on the Lord's Supper. In 1563 the Elector of the Palatinate accepted the Zwinglian and Calvinistic doctrine of the Lord's Supper, and his territory, which had been Lutheran, became Calvinistic or Reformed and adopted the Heidelberg Catechism instead of Luther's Catechism. The Reformed churches of the Palatinate and other German provinces are closely related in doctrine and polity to the Reformed bodies * of Holland and France and the Presbyterians of Scotland. As early as 1683 German Reformed settled in Pennsylvania, but systematic work among these scattered Germans was not begun until 1725. During the early decades of the 18th century the prevalence of mysticism and the woeful lack of ministers were responsible for much dissension among these German Reformed settlers. In 1746 the Reformed Church of Holland commissioned Michael Schlatter as missionary, and he organized the German Reformed congregations as a *coetus* or synod. The great Revival of 1800 deeply affected the German Reformed Church and divided the membership into two parties; the one party emphasized doctrinal orthodoxy and the other the then current pietistic and evangelistic trends. William Philip Otterbein became the leader of the pietistic party and organized the United Brethren Church.* Another controversy which for many years disturbed the church centered about the Mercersburg Theology, advocated by Drs. J. W. Nevin and Philip Schaff of Mercersburg Seminary. Their Calvinistic orthodoxy was challenged, because they advocated views on the Church, the work of Christ, the doctrine of election, the Sacraments, and the liturgy which seemed to indicate a departure from historic Calvinism. The controversy undoubtedly was instrumental in advocating a trend toward liberalism. — During the years of immigration into the central States many Reformed congregations were founded in these States, especially in Ohio. These congregations organized the Western Synod. In 1863, the tercentenary of the Heidelberg Catechism, the Western and Eastern Synods united. While originally a German denomination, its work is now almost exclusively English. In 1924 the Hungarian Reformed Church joined the Reformed Church. The main strength of this body is in Pennsylvania; its chief institution of learning at Lancaster. —

In doctrine this body follows Zwingli and Calvin, and in polity it is Presbyterian.

2) *The Evangelical Synod of North America.* This denomination grew out of the Prussian Union, the union which was foisted upon Lutheran and Reformed churches by Frederick William III of Prussia in 1817. To perpetuate the unionistic principles of the Evangelical State Church of Prussia (*Unierte Kirche*), six ministers formed the Evangelical Union at Gravois Settlement, Mo., in 1840. This was actually only an alliance of ministers. They accepted the Augsburg Confession and Luther's Catechism as well as the Calvinistic Heidelberg Catechism, insofar as they agree. Where they disagree, the evangelical ministers demanded liberty. This made it possible that congregations with Lutheran leanings as well as with Reformed preferences could join the union. In the course of time many German congregations which did not want to be bound by confessions identified themselves with the Evangelical Union and in 1877 organized a denomination known as the German Evangelical Synod of North America. Gradually Reformed theology gained the upper hand, and in recent years the doctrinal indifference has permitted modernism to gain admission into the body. — Its theological seminary is Eden Seminary at Webster Groves, Mo.

3) *The Evangelical and Reformed Church.* The merger of the two bodies was effected in 1934. Luther's Catechism, the Heidelberg Catechism, Melanchthon's altered Augsburg Confession * are accepted as "an authoritative interpretation of the essential truth taught in Holy Scriptures. Wherever they differ, ministers and congregations, in accordance with the liberty of conscience inherent in the Gospel, are allowed to adhere to the interpretation of one of these confessions." In 1944 steps had been taken toward a union of this body with the Congregational and Christian Churches, a denomination which openly advocates Unitarianism. — In church polity the Evangelical and Reformed follow the pattern of the Reformed Church, that is, the presbyterial form of government. — The various educational, missionary, and publishing activities of the two merging bodies are continued under the supervision of the General Synod. At the middle of the twentieth century the Evangelical and Reformed Church was negotiating a merger with the Congre-

gational and Christian Churches. See *Religious Bodies (U. S.), Bibliography.* FEM

Evangelical Society. See *Bible Societies,* 4.

Evangelical Synod of North America. See *Evangelical and Reformed Church,* 2.

Evangelical Union. Founded (1843) in Scotland by pastors expelled from the Evangelical Synod because of their opposition to Calvinistic doctrines. United with Congregational Union (1896).

Evangelical United Brethren Church. The name given the merger of the *Evangelical Church* * and the *United Brethren in Christ* * which was consummated in 1947.

Evangelicals, Anglican. A name given to a movement within the Anglican Church which emphasized Gospel preaching and personal conversion. The move dated from 1750 and had its center at Clapham and Cambridge. The movement led to the organization of the Church Missionary Society (1799). Liberalism within this society led the conservatives to found the Bible Churchmen's Missionary Society.

Evangelische Kirche in Deutschland. See *Union Movements,* 8.

Evangelism. Etymologically, evangelism simply means the spreading of the Gospel. Literally: Gospel-ize; Gospel-ism. It is that activity of the Christian Church by which it seeks to bring unregenerate mankind under the influence of the Gospel message and to win and keep lost souls for Christ.

Historically, the Church began as an evangelistic movement. Acts 8:4. It was the evangelistic fervor of the Early Church, its consuming passion to Gospel-ize the men and women of its day, that enabled it to achieve remarkable success with God's blessing, in the first centuries.

As the Church became more formal in its organization and more institutionalized in its operation, it gradually lost its pristine zeal for evangelistic activity. The lowest ebb of evangelistic fervor was reached by the Church of the Middle Ages, but a revival of the evangelistic spirit was born with the dawn of the Protestant Reformation.

In modern times, especially in the 19th century, and particularly in England and America, the evangelistic program of the Church was given a mighty impetus by such men as George Whitefield, the Wesley brothers, William Booth, Dwight Moody, and Ira Sankey. Large meetings were held in tents or auditoriums or out in the open spaces, to which the general public was invited and at which the unconverted were called to repentance and faith by highly emotional addresses.

It would be historically inaccurate to say that these evangelistic meetings were without their good results. On the contrary, we may say that they were mightily used by God for the accomplishment of His gracious purpose (Is. 55:11). Unfortunately the emotional extravagance and insincere professionalism which characterized many of these meetings brought them into disrepute and subjected the entire movement to the suspicion of spiritual fraud.

In late years, especially since World War II, there has been a remarkable resurgence of the evangelistic spirit throughout American Protestantism. Distinctive of the new evangelism is its departure from the "mass attack" of the previous century and its emphasis on the personal, individual approach. Between 1945 and 1949 almost every major denomination in America launched an intensive program of evangelism. Large segments of the laity were enrolled in training courses with a view to making them more proficient in their daily witness for Christ. Thousands of members were trained in "visitation evangelism," a new term coined to describe the house-to-house visits which members made to the homes of the unchurched. As a result of this accelerated effort, new millions were won for the Church during the early post-war years.

The Lutheran Church — Missouri Synod, while it has frequently avoided the terms "evangelism" and "evangelistic," has been doing what these terms describe. By means of the personal witness of its membership as well as by the use of the radio, the printing press, the motion picture, television, and other modern media, it has made a contribution to the evangelization of America. See also *Evangelical; Scandinavian Countries.* HWG

D. Bryan, *A Handbook of Evangelism for Laymen,* Abingdon-Cokesbury, New York, 1945; L. Meyer (editor), *Your Church at Work,* CPH; S. Powell, *Where Are the People,* Abingdon-Cokesbury, Nashville, 1942; T. B. Kilpatrick, *New Testament Evangelism,* Doran, New York, 1941; D. M. Dawson,

More Power in Soul-Winning, Zondervan, Grand Rapids, 1947; R. A. Torrey, *Personal Work*, Bible Institute Colportage Assn., Chicago, 1901; H. W. Wood, *Winning Men One by One*, Sunday School Times, Philadelphia, 1908; A. W. Blackwood, *Evangelism in the Home Church*, Abingdon - Cokesbury, New York, 1942.

Evangelistic Associations. A group of churches so classified by the census because they are dominated by one general characteristic, namely, the conduct of evangelistic, or missionary, work. Many have holiness leanings or are Methodist. The bodies belonging to this group are as follows:

1. *The Apostolic Church*. A small group organized in Philadelphia, Pa., in 1888 by Albert F. Atwood.

2. *Apostolic Christian Organization*. The Apostolic Christian Church traces its origin to a Swiss (S. H. Froehlich). Its 31 churches number 1,663 members (1952).

3. *The Apostolic Faith Mission*. Originated (1900) at Topeka, Kans., under the leadership of Miss Minnie Hanson and Mrs. M. White. It stands for the "restoration of the faith once delivered to the saints, the old-time religion, camp meetings, revivals, missions, street and prison work, and Christian unity everywhere." Missions in Japan, China, Korea, South America. 17 churches; 2,288 members.

4. *Christian Congregation*. Organized (1887) in Indiana. This church centers its teachings on the "new commandment" of John 13:34, 35 and seeks a non-creedal, non-denominational basis for union. Approximately 5,500 members.

5. *Christian and Missionary Alliance*. This organization originated in the year 1881 through the efforts of A. B. Simpson, pastor of a Presbyterian church in New York City. In 1887 two societies were organized, respectively for home and foreign missionary work, one known as the *Christian Alliance*, for home work among the neglected classes in towns and cities of the U. S., the other, the *International Missionary Alliance*. In 1897 the two societies merged in the Christian and Missionary Alliance. It is non-creedal, but emphasizes sanctification and divine healing. It has no close ecclesiastical organization, though it has organized districts with branches. 891 churches; 57,840 members. Missions in many countries.

6. *Church of Daniel's Band*. Organized (1893) at Marine City, Mich. 4 churches; 131 members.

7. *Church of God as Organized by Christ*. Organized (1896) by P. J. Kaufman, who belonged to the Mennonite Brethren in Christ. It opposes "holyites," "hireling ministry," revivals, creeds, tobacco, lodges, fine clothing, theaters, and other things. Observes Baptism, Communion, foot-washing, but has no binding form for its worship. 14 organizations; 2,192 members.

8. *The Hephzibah Faith Missionary Association*. Under this name a number of independent churches were organized at Glenwood, Iowa, in 1892 for the threefold purpose of preaching the doctrine of holiness, developing missionary work both at home and abroad, and promoting philanthropic work. The missionaries usually support themselves. 20 churches; 700 members.

9. *Lumber River Mission*. A few churches, organized in North Carolina after 1900, were known by this name.

10. *Metropolitan Church Organization* (Burning Bush). An outgrowth of the Metropolitan Methodist Church in Chicago. It has no specific creed, emphasizes "full Gospel," "entire" sanctification, immersion, eradication of original sin. It has no definite form of church organization and does not pay salaries. 21 churches; 961 members.

11. *Missionary Church Association*. Organized at Berne, Ind. (1898), by a number of persons of different denominations for promoting the fuller teaching of the Word of God and for engaging in more aggressive missionary work. It stands for "the evangelical truths of Christendom" with special emphasis on the healing of the body in answer to the prayer of faith, premillennialism, non-resistance, immersion. Claims to be interdenominational. 75 churches and 6,175 members in 1952.

12. *Peniel Missions*. A group organized by T. P. Ferguson in Los Angeles, Calif. (1886).

13. *Missionary Bands of the World*. Grew out of a missionary society of young people formed in the Free Methodist Church by Vivian A. Dake (1885). Became independent (1898) with the name Pentecostal Bands of the World. Present name adopted in 1925. Methodist in character except for stress of holiness. Merged with a Church of God (Holiness) in 1933. 190 members.

14. *Pillar of Fire*. Incorporated as Pentecostal Union Church by Mrs. Alma White (wife of Methodist minister) at Denver, Colo. (1902). Believ-

ing that it was impossible for her to carry out the mission work of the Church in connection with "worldly apostate denominations," and having received a vision of world-wide evangelism, Mrs. White established a number of missions in different cities, and founded a training school at Denver. Headquarters were established at Zarephath, N. J. The name of its publication, *Pillar of Fire*, was adopted by the organization. Doctrinal beliefs include: divine healing, premillennialism, restoration of Jews, eternal punishment, everlasting life. It has around 5,100 members.

15. *Free Christian Zion Church.* Organized by E. D. Brown (colored), at Redemption, Ark. (1905). It claims to agree with non-Episcopal Methodists in doctrine. About 2,500 members.

16. *Apostolic Christian Church of America.* Organized (1847) by a Swiss, Benedict Weyeneth. 56 churches; 7,125 members. See *Pentecostalism; Four Square Gospel; Religious Bodies (U. S.), Bibliography.*

Evangelistics. That branch of theological knowledge which treats of the history and the theory of foreign missions, the extension of Christianity among the heathen.

Evangelization. This is a movement, started by John Hudson Taylor and others, which characterizes the missionary task as consisting in "the evangelization of the world," some adding the words "in this generation." The term evangelization has not been precisely fixed and is often loosely used. Great hosts of evangelists are sent out who give their time almost wholly to preaching and who consider the establishing of organized congregations and Christian schools and also the getting out of Christian literature, to be of secondary importance. The missionary task of the Christian Church, however, is not only to win souls for Christ by preaching the Gospel, but also to gather them into (organized) congregations.

Evans, Christmas (1766 to 1838). "Bunyan of Wales"; b. at Ysgaerwen, d. at Swansea; first, Presbyterian minister, later Baptist; famous for his eloquence.

Evans, James ("Apostle of the North"; 1801—46). B. in England; missionary among Canadian Indians; at St. Clair Indian Mission (1835), Lake Superior regions (1838), and Lake Winnipeg (1840); invented Cree syllabic characters; translated portions of the Bible and hymnbook, assisted by the Wesleyan Missionary Society.

Evensong. English name for Vespers.

Everlasting Life. See *Hereafter, A.*

Evidence, Christian. See *Apologetics.*

Evil. See *Sin.*

Evodius. The first bishop of Antioch according to Eusebius.

Evolution. According to present-day naturalistic philosophy, the process by which the universe in general, but especially our world, together with all the inanimate and animate objects existing thereon, have been evolved or developed, in the course of many millions of years, in accordance with natural laws now existing, from some form of primitive mass which contained the fundamental chemical elements now found in the universe. A distinction may be observed between atheistic evolution, which declares that everything now existing came into being without the power of a supernatural being, and theistic evolution, which is ready to admit that some superior being called the primitive masses into existence and drew up certain fundamental laws of nature. Evolutionists generally are not concerned with origins but only with the development from a simple to a more complex state. Evolutionary theories have been applied to many areas of knowledge. Anthropology, ethnology, sociology, history, comparative religion, metaphysics, and other areas have been permeated by it.

I. *Cosmic Evolution.* Immanuel Kant, influenced by the speculations of Thomas Wright regarding the structure of the universe (published 1750), advocated a nebular hypothesis for the origin of the universe (1755). Pierre Simon de Laplace (1749—1827) set forth a nebular hypothesis, which became popular (*Exposition du Système du Monde*, 1796). Laplace's theory was frequently modified. F. R. Moulton (b. 1872) and T. C. Chamberlin (1843 to 1928) formulated the Planetesimal, or Spiral-Nebula, Hypothesis, according to which the solar system evolved from a spiral nebula caused by the close approach of two stars. Another theory based on the close approach of two stars is the Tidal Theory, formulated by James Jeans (b. 1877) and H. Jeffries (b. 1891). George Darwin's (1845 to 1912) theory of Tidal Evolution, which holds that the earth and moon evolved from a single mass which was disturbed and split by tidal waves caused by the sun, was widely accepted. Evolutionists themselves regard it impossible to prove any theory of cosmic evolution.

II. Biological Evolution. A. The concept of biological evolution was held already by the Greeks and Romans. The Chevalier de Lamarck (Jeanne Baptiste Pierre Antoine de Monet; 1744—1829) was the forerunner of Darwin in modern evolutionary theory. Lamarck advanced the theory of acquired characteristics (Philosophie Zoologique; life by its own efforts tends to increase the volume of every body; formation of new organs is the result of a new need; use determines the extent of development of organs; all changes during life passed on to descendants).

B. Charles Darwin advanced the theory of natural selection (Origin of Species by Means of Natural Selection or the Preservation of Favored Races in the Struggle of Life, 1859). He pointed to the variation in individuals and to the overproduction due to a high birth rate. In the struggle for existence the fittest survive and pass their fitness on to descendants. Thus new species arise by the continued survival and reproduction of individuals best suited to their environment. Objections raised to the theory are the fact that advantageous characteristics are often lost; the existence of structures which do not appear helpful in survival; the small differences which often separate species; and the difficulty of explaining the survival of early steps of a complicated structure such as the eye.

C. Hugo De Vries supplied the mechanism for Darwin's theory. He was impressed by the sudden changes which occur in the Evening Primrose and called these changes mutations (see F).

D. Orthogenesis holds that a developmental principle is at work within the biological species, thus making evolutionary change dependent on certain tendencies in the organism itself and not forced on the organism from without.

E. The following evidence is cited in support of the evolutionary theories:

1. The age of the earth as determined by the uranium time clock. Uranium breaks down through ionium, radium, and radon to lead. This process goes on at a measured rate (1 million grams yield 1/74,000 grams of lead per year) and there is no known means for speeding it up or slowing it down. On the basis of this time clock the world is said to be 2 billion years old. In reply Biblical apologists point out that God put ionium, radium, radon, and lead into rocks at Creation and that conditions may have obtained which speeded up or slowed down the process.

2. Similarity in embryological development is considered evidence of a common descent. Divergence between invertebrates and vertebrates, however, has also led to theories of parallel evolution instead of descent. Furthermore, God in his economy might be expected to use a general plan.

3. It is possible to arrange animals in a family tree in an order of increasing complexity, hence they are held to have evolved from the simple to the complex (taxonomic argument). Evolutionists themselves recognize the weakness of this argument.

4. It is possible to arrange rocks and fossils in a time table of five eras: Archeozoic, Proterozoic, Paleozoic, Mesozoic, and Cenozoic. This is held to support evolutionary theories. This process, however, is often an argument in a circle: fossils date rocks, and rocks date fossils. Furthermore, there are many breaks in the record and some inversions, and at no place is the record complete.

5. Similarity of chemicals found in bodies of organisms indicate that they are related by common descent (physiological evidence). But similarity does not indicate kinship, and the complexity of body physiology actually disproves evolution (blood groups, digestive enzymes, buffer).

6. The fact that flora and fauna of isolated regions are different from those of other areas is considered proof that evolution has taken place. Here again evidence of interrelation by common descent is lacking.

7. Animals have survived due to a color resembling their environment.

8. Males have certain differences which help them win females.

9. An animal which is unpalatable or dangerous in some way advertises this fact (warning coloration).

10. Edible species imitate an inedible one.

In cases 7—10 there is no evidence that any of the changes have occurred in response to need, the desire of the individual, or environmental stimuli. The development of warning or protective characteristics have not been observed either in the laboratory or in nature.

F. The real *crux* in the problem of evolution lies in the genetic approach, since the science of genetics must hold the answer to the mechanism of evolution. Here evolutionists point chiefly to three facts:

1. An infinite number of variations is made possible by recombination of genes already present in the chromosome. It is, however, noteworthy that nothing new is contributed by gene recombinations and that there are definite restrictions on the freedom of assortment.

2. New species have been developed in laboratories as the result of chromosomal aberrations (chromosomes added or subtracted, number doubled or halved; fragments added or subtracted). In this process, however, no new contribution is made but simply a rearrangement of material already present. Furthermore, the addition or subtraction of whole chromosomes is usually harmful and the deletions are usually fatal.

3. Mutations can create varieties, hence it is postulated that they can create species. The cause for natural mutations is not known. Most mutations are either lethal or semilethal (most mutations are recessive and recessives are almost all semilethal). Mutations are never related to environment. Evidence indicates that there are various restrictions on mutations and that reverse mutations to type occur. Finally, evolutionists have not yet shown the development of features by the accumulation and selection of mutants (e. g., hair, feathers, teeth, shells, eyes, etc.), to say nothing of the development of a species as a whole. C.f. JK, "Evolution" (notes for lectures at SPC institute).

III. *Evolution in other fields.* The basic ideas of evolution have been applied to many fields. In the field of metaphysics the theory of Emergent Evolution (associated with the names of L. Morgan and S. Alexander) holds that in the sequence of events levels appear in which something new, which goes beyond the regrouping of previous events, appears. Thus the whole is more than the sum of its separate parts. In the field of comparative religion evolutionary scholars attempt to show that higher forms of religion evolved from lower forms (animism, etc.). Evolutionists in the field of anthropology hold that the psychic unity of mankind leads to independent progress and that all elements of culture must pass through the same stages of development. The dialectical materialism of Marx * and Engel, which holds that everything is made up of opposing factors which occasion internal movement and lead to progress, has had an influence on ethics, sociology, and evolutionary views of history. The ethics of evolutionists is in a continual state of flux. That which is considered ethical today is the result of acts with favorable results in past evolutionary stages. Thus evolutionary theory has made its influence felt in many fields of knowledge.

IV. In addition to the limitations mentioned, evolution fails to account for the origin of life and to evaluate properly the interdependence and balance of organisms. From the philosophical point of view it may be criticized for identifying change with progress.

Ewald, Georg Heinrich August. See *Higher Criticism*, 14.

Ewald, Paul (1857—1911). B. at Leipzig. Studied at Erlangen and Leipzig. *Privatdozent*, 1883, and professor, 1889, at Leipzig; Vienna, 1890; and Erlangen, 1894, where he succeeded Th. Zahn in NT exegesis, 1909.

Exaltation, State of. See *Christ Jesus*, II.

Examinations. See *Christian Teaching*, L 4.

Exarch. A title in the Early Church for the highest clergy; in the Greek Church the exarch is the patriarch's deputy.

Ex Cathedra. See *Roman Catholic Confessions*, E 3.

Exclusive Particles. Words used in Scripture which exclude from conversion and justification every co-operation of unconverted man. The Formula of Concord describes them thus: "Words of the holy Apostle Paul, by which merit of Christ is entirely separated from our works, and the honor given to Christ alone, when the holy Apostle Paul writes: *Of grace, without merit, without Law, without works, not of works.*" (Form. Conc., Epit. III, 7; Conc. Trigl., p. 795.)

Excommunication is the judicial exclusion of unrepentant sinners from the rights and privileges of the communion of saints. According to St. Paul's words in 1 Corinthians 5, this act of exclusion is a duty to be performed by the Christian church when the offender has shown himself unresponsive to admonition, and when properly performed excludes from access to God, from participation in the pardon won by Christ, and from communion with the saints in the life hereafter. Even as the sinner's conversion and his introduction into the Church has been a translation from the kingdom and power of Satan to the kingdom and government of Christ, so by excommunication from the Church the offender is "delivered unto Satan." 1 Tim. 1:19, 20. Cf. Col. 1:13. When the church has declared a member excommunicate, he is to be held a heathen and a publican by the whole multitude of the faithful until he be openly reconciled by penance. Excommunication improperly declared is void, and no repentant and confessing sinner is excluded from the kingdom of God by such a ban. The ultimate purpose of excommunication is not punishment, but the salvation of the offending member, and the removal of offense from the Church. (See *Keys, Office of the.*)

Excommunication, in the Roman Church, cannot be pronounced by congregations or even parish priests, but only by Popes, councils, bishops, and a few other dignitaries. The distinction formerly made between major and minor excommunication was abrogated in 1884. Excommunications are divided into those *ferendae sententiae* (in which a definite sentence of excommunication must be pronounced) and those *latae sententiae* (in which the commission of a stated offense automatically excommunicates the offender). About 50 offenses belong to the latter class. Absolution from some excommunications is reserved to the Pope, from others to the bishop (see *Reserved Cases*); still others are not reserved. Whenever Rome has been able to do so, it has had civil punishments inflicted on the excommunicated; in fact, it has used, and still uses, this power chiefly as a means to beat down opposition and force respect and submission to the hierarchy and the canon law. While such crimes as parricide and incest do not entail excommunication *latae sententiae,* the following do so and are reserved to the Pope: reading heretical books; usurping church property; bringing clerics before civil courts; taking relics from Rome without permission; assaulting, or even slapping, a cleric of any grade. (See *Privilegium Canonis, Keys, Office of the.*)

Execrabilis, Bulla. A notorious bull or official papal document issued Jan. 18, 1460, by Pope Pius II. Even at an assembly of Christian princes held at Mantua, Gregory of Heimburg, the delegate of the Austrian Duke Sigismund, had opposed the crusade proposed by the Pope against the Turks. The result was a quarrel, in the course of which Gregory appealed from the Pope to a general council. But Pius II was clever enough to forestall events which might have turned against him, and so the bull issued by him applied the ban to any appeal of this kind. The logical consequence was a further establishment of the Pope's power.

Exegesis. 1. This Greek word signifies, literally, "leading out" or "leading forth." Generally speaking, every statement has a meaning; and the act or process of setting forth and making clear this meaning is called exegesis. Another term for this process is interpretation. It is true that the Bible is a clear book and that its great truths are expressed in language which everybody can understand; but since it was written in antiquity, many hundred years ago, and since its original languages are not familiar to most readers, and since it does contain a few difficult passages, exegesis is an important branch of theology. While Biblical hermeneutics * lays down the rules for interpreting the Scriptures, Biblical exegesis is the actual practice of interpretation. Its significance becomes evident when one reflects on the vast amount of time and effort given to the explanation of Scripture passages in sermons and catechetical instruction. A good example of exegesis is furnished in the narrative of Philip's exposition of Isaiah 53 to the eunuch of Ethiopia, as reported Acts 8:26-35. Cf. also Luke 24:27, 45; Acts 2:24-32, etc. 2. In the Early Church there soon developed several tendencies in the field of exegesis, of which the chief ones will have to be mentioned. Toward the end of the first century the false teacher Cerinthus interpreted some prophecies in Revelation in a crassly literal way, disregarding the character of the writing he was dealing with, the context, and the parallel passages. It is a tendency which, unfortunately, has persisted to this day. 3. The School of Alexandria, and especially its great scholar Origen (died 254), sponsored what is called allegorical interpretation. It held that the passages of Scripture which relate historical events or speak of earthly things have a deep meaning, different from the literal one. According to his teaching we must distinguish between the literal sense, the allegorical or mystical sense, and the moral sense. The literal sense, so it was maintained, at times is unworthy of the Scriptures; for instance, in the story of Noah's drunkenness; hence we have to assume that a deeper meaning was intended. The existence of a literal sense was not denied, but it was held that this sense often has to be disregarded or discarded.

4. The method of allegorical interpretation was opposed by the School of Antioch, among whose representatives the most famous are Theodore of Mopsuestia (died 428), Theodoret (died 457), and Chrysostom (died 407). These people held that the literal sense is the intended sense and must be adhered to unless it is plain that an allegory is placed before us, as, for instance, in the parables. Regrettably, their sane view did not prevail.

5. In the Middle Ages, up to the days of the Reformation, the allegorical method, generally speaking, was followed and even extended. Scripture passages were declared to have a fourfold meaning: the literal, the allegorical or mystical, the moral, and the anagogic sense (the sense of hope). The Sabbath law, Ex. 20:8, signifies a. the seventh day must be kept as a day of rest; b. Christ rested in the grave; c. the Christian must rest from sin; d. true rest awaits us in heaven. A great deal of ingenuity entered into this kind of exegesis and much nonsense and childishness. The Scriptures were made an obscure book.

6. The age of the Reformation, through the revival of learning and the study of the Hebrew and the Greek languages, introduced a great change in exegetical endeavors. Luther at first was under the spell of allegorical exegesis, but by and by he freed himself of this wrong method and became the mighty interpreter as which he is honored throughout Christendom. Calvin likewise rejected the medieval system and became known as an exegete of extraordinary ability. Through the reformers the principle that the literal, that is, the native, the natural sense, is the sense intended by God, was vindicated and became the directive for Protestant theologians. It was thus that the foundation was laid for the splendid achievements in the exegetical field since the beginning of the 16th century. Cf. commentaries.

7. In later centuries the tendency prevailed for a while to stress typological interpretation, that is, to find types and symbols in nearly everything that the Old Testament relates; the principle that we can with certainty speak of persons or events as being types, that is, as prefiguring persons and events in the New Testament, only where the Bible itself gives us indications to that effect, was disregarded. At the present time a rather common defect of exegetical works is that while they properly stress the linguistic and historical aspects of a text, they ignore its divine origin.

8. While striving to be scholarly and to adhere to what the grammars and lexicons and history say concerning a text, Bible theologians not only always bear in mind that they are dealing with God's Word in their exegetical endeavors, but they realize that to understand the Scriptures properly the gift of the Holy Spirit is required; for the unconverted exegete, be he ever so learned, will in dwelling, for instance, on the spiritual blessings of the children of God, be speaking as a blind man about colors. WA

F. W. Farrar, *History of Interpretation* (8 lectures preached before the U. of Oxford, 1885), Dutton, N.Y., 1886.

Exegetical Preaching. See *Homiletics.*

Exercises, Spiritual. See *Spiritual Exercises.*

Exhorters. A class of lay persons licensed in the Methodist Episcopal Church to exhort, not to preach. The duties of the exhorter are to hold meetings for prayer and exhortation wherever opportunity is afforded. This office is used in developing the talent of persons likely to be called to the ministry.

Existentialism. A theological and philosophical term which owes its origin to Kierkegaard's quest for truth with his total person. For Kierkegaard existentialism implied the whole reaction of becoming on the line of time and eternity. This existentialism accepts by faith the existence of self and God. Its test is dialectical: God meets the individual, and the existence of faith begins. Existentialism is opposed to "detached" religious thought and upholds a faith which involves the whole man. Christianity is personal, "inward," passionate, under tension due to the paradoxes of existence and involves the "leap of faith."

While for Kierkegaard the encounter with despair *(Angst)* was preliminary, it became the chief thing in some later existentialist thinkers. Removing God from their system, they described man as filled with zeal, having freedom unguided by norms, and reaching a crisis of negation without positive solution. J. Pelikan, *From Luther to Kierkegaard,* CPH, 1950; Melville Chaning-Pearce, "Soren Kierkegaard," *Modern Christian Revolutionaries* (D. Attwater, ed.), Devin-Adair, New York, 1947; Helmut Kuhn, *Encounter with Nothingness,* Henry Regnery, Hinsdale, Ill., 1949.

Exogamy. A marriage law compelling people to marry outside of kin or social group.

Ex opere operato. See *Grace, Means of,* I 8.

Exorcism. In connection with the ceremonies of the Christian Church, the rite used in driving out evil spirits, especially in the administration of Holy Baptism, in order to dissever the soul of the candidate from the influence of evil powers, to which he, while in the realm of the world and its wickedness, had been subject. The Greater Exorcism and the Minor Exorcism were distinguished in baptism, but exorcisms were also employed at the dedication of churches and upon other occasions. The exorcism, without its superstitious features, was taken over into the rite of baptism by Luther, but it was rightly spoken of as an indifferent matter and has not been widely used in the Lu-

theran Church since the 17th century. See *Baptism, Liturgical.*

Exorcist. See *Hierarchy.*

Explicit Faith. See *Faith, Explicit and Implicit.*

Exposition. See *Exegesis.*

Exposition of the Christian Faith to Francis I. See *Reformed Confessions,* A 4.

Expository Preaching. See *Homiletics.*

Exsultet (R. C.). "The hymn in praise of the paschal candle sung by the deacon in the liturgy of Holy Saturday" *(Cath. Enc.).*

Exsurge, Domine (bull). See *Reformation,* 9; *Index of Prohibited Books.*

Extravagantes. See *Canon Law.*

Extreme Unction (R. C.). "Extreme Unction is a sacrament of the New Law instituted by Christ to give spiritual aid and comfort and perfect spiritual health, including, if need be, the remission of sins, and also, conditionally, to restore bodily health, to Christians who are seriously ill; it consists essentially in the unction by a priest of the body of the sick person, accompanied by a suitable form of words." *(Cath. Enc.)* (Cf. Council of Trent, Sess. XIV:i). The texts quoted in support of the doctrine are Mark 6:13 and James 5:14, 15. See *Sacraments, Roman Catholic.*

Eyck, van (Hubert, 1370—1426; Jan, 1390—1470; brothers). Artists of the Netherlands, whose most prominent painting is the oil painting of the altar at Ghent, a composite picture, with the lamb in the center.

F

Faber, Basil (1520—75/76). Studied at Wittenberg under Melanchthon; relative of Neander; rector at Nordhausen, Tennstaedt, and Quedlinburg; lost his position for opposing Melanchthonianism; translated Luther's commentary on Genesis into German; collaborator on first four Magdeburg Centuries.

Faber, Ernst. B. at Koburg, Germany, Apr. 15, 1839; d. at Tsingtau, China, 1899; was a Rhenish Mission Society missionary; arrived at Hong Kong, Apr. 25, 1865; resigned from membership of society, 1880, settling in Hong Kong. Joined the Ev. Protestant

Mission Society (Weimar Mission) in 1885, moving to Shanghai; author of renown.

Faber, Frederick William (1814 to 1863). Educated at Oxford; rector of Elton, seceded to Church of Rome in 1846; established the Oratorians, first at London, then at Brompton; wrote: "Sweet Savior, Bless Us ere We Go," and other hymns.

Faber, Jacobus (ca. 1455—1536). Forerunner of French Protestantism; promoted Aristotelian philosophy; translated the Bible; advocated a good system of exegesis. In the introduction to his commentary on Paul's Epistles (1512) he upheld the authority of Scripture, salvation through unmerited grace, opposed merits of good works, *opus operatum*, celibacy, and other Roman doctrines.

Faber, Zachaeus (1583—1632). Superintendent in Chemnitz; wrote "Herr, ich bin ein Gast auf Erden."

Fabricius, Jacob. Chaplain to King Gustavus Adolphus of Sweden and the author of the hymn "Fear Not, O Little Flock, the Foe," written in 1631.

Fabricus, Johann Albert (1668 to 1736). Historian and philologist. B. at Leipzig; d. at Hamburg. Studied at Leipzig. Assistant pastor at Hamburg, 1693; six years later professor of ethics and rhetoric at the gymnasium; rector of the Johanneum, 1708—11. He was a prolific writer. Noteworthy is his *Centifolium Lutheranum*.

Fabricus, Johann Philipp (1711—91). A German Lutheran missionary among the Tamil people of India; retranslated the Ziegenbalg-Schultze Tamil Bible (1758), and issued his own translation of the NT; published a Lutheran hymnbook (1774) and other books; suffered much hardship in the "Thirty Years' War in S. India."

Fabritius, Jacob (d. 1693). Sent by the Lutheran Consistory of Amsterdam to minister to the Lutherans in New York and Albany in 1669; charges were brought against him, and he was banished from Albany; he became pastor of a Swedish church at Wilmington, Del. (1671); pastor at Wicaco (Philadelphia), 1677—93.

Fairbairn, Andrew Martin (1838 to 1912). Congregationalist minister and later principal of Airdale College at Bradford and Mansfield College at Oxford; lectured in American universities; wrote: *Studies in the Life of Christ; Catholicism, Roman and Anglican;* chapter on Calvin and Reformed Church in *Cambridge Modern History.*

Fairbairn, Patrick (1805—74). Scotch Presbyterian; joined Free Church (1843); professor at Free Church College; principal at Glasgow; member of OT revision committee; edited *Imperial Bible Dictionary;* wrote *Typology of Scripture.*

Faith (*fides salvifica; fides justificans*). The active principle by which

the individual enters into that right relation to God which the all-atoning work of Christ has established for the entire world.

The need for a new life through faith is occasioned by man's sin, which separates from God (Rom. 6:6; 7:18; John 3:6; Gen. 8:21). The remedy for sin comes entirely from God (Eph. 2: 5, 8). His gracious plan of salvation is revealed in Scripture and is received by faith (Rom. 4:13, 16).

The Bible uses many images to portray faith (coming to Christ, Luke 14:17; seeing Christ, John 6:40; obedient hearing of Christ, John 10:27, 28; keeping Christ's Word, John 8:51; laying hold of life, 1 Tim. 6:12; winning Christ, Phil. 3:7, 8).

Faith as a soteriological factor (*fides salvifica*) may be defined or described as consisting of knowledge, assent, and confidence. Each of these concepts is a definition of faith if it is understood to imply also the other two.

Faith as *knowledge* is the grasp with the mind, or the mental possession of that which is communicated (Rom. 10: 14, 17; John 17:3; 2 Pet. 1:3; Luke 1:77; 1 Tim. 2:4; John 14:6). This salutary knowledge is not mere intellectual acquaintance (James 2:19) or technical knowledge (1 Cor. 2:14), but a product of divine grace which permeates the entire heart (2 Tim. 1:12; 1 Cor. 2:12; 2 Cor. 4:6).

Faith as *assent* is an act of the will which accepts the exalted phenomena presented to the mind. Hence the preaching of faith is hortatory, pleading, persuasive in its message (Acts 19:18; 26:28; 28:23; and others). Since man is dead in trespasses and sins (Eph. 2:1; 8:7), such turning of the will is the work of God (John 6:29).

Faith as *confidence* means that faith is that certainty, that assurance, which is as great and as firm as though we actually had the things promised in the Sacred Record in our possession, as though we could see, feel, and handle them, as though we had not only the prospect, but the substance of these things (Heb. 11:1). Luther and his followers taught confidence as the great element in saving faith (*Apol.* IV: 48, 60; Gerhard, *Loc.* XVII: 3, 1.81; John 17:8; 1:26; Luke 22:67; Gal. 2:16; 2 Tim. 1:12; Rom. 10:14; 2 Cor. 1:18-20; Rom. 8:24; Titus 3:7; 1 Pet. 1:3, 13; Rom. 4:18; 4:20 ff.; and others).

Faith is also conceived as a *state.* In this respect faith is reviewed as the continued possession of the gifts and blessings of God, in and through Christ, through an enduring, abiding confidence in His all-complete and all-sufficient redemption (2 Cor. 13:5; Col. 2:7; 1 Tim. 4:7; 2 Cor. 10:15; 2 Tim. 4:7; Luke 22:32; Gal. 2:20). Christian faith is capable of increase in intensity (2 Cor. 10:15; Rom. 4:20; 14:1; Matt. 6:30; 8:10; 15:28) and extension (1 Cor. 1:5).

Justification by grace through faith establishes a new relationship between God and man and produces new attitudes, desires, objectives, and ideals (Gal. 2:20; Phil. 4:8; Titus 2:12, 13). True faith, then, is a living, energizing, motivating power, which propels, drives, and urges to action (Matt. 9:23; 17:20; 1 John 5:4). See Ethics; Good Works; Grace, Means of. C. f. ELW, Abiding Word, I:188 ff.

E. L. Wilson, "Faith," Abiding Word, CPH, 1946 (extensive bibliography); J. Gresham Machen, What Is Faith, Eerdmans, Grand Rapids, Mich; references under Dogmatics (especially F. Pieper's Christian Dogmatics).

Faith, Explicit and Implicit. Implicit faith is alleged assent to doctrines by an individual, though they may not be known or thoroughly understood. Explicit faith is the belief in the doctrines of the Church involving the ability to give explanations of details.

Faith, Fathers of (Paccanarists). A society modeled after the Jesuits, founded by Nicolo Paccanari in 1797 to replace the Jesuit order, which had been dissolved by Clement XIV. The life of the society was brief and turbulent, and on the restoration of the Jesuits, in 1814, it disappeared, most of its members joining the restored order.

Faith Healing. See Divine Healing.

Faith, Rule of. The source and criterion of religious truth. According to Lutheran and Protestant doctrine generally, the Scriptures alone are the rule of faith. The Greek and Roman churches and some Anglicans find the rule of faith not only in Scripture, but also in the Church (tradition). The supreme authority in the Roman Church is, indeed, the Pope, as living expounder of religious truth and authorized interpreter of the Bible. The Quakers and many other mystics recognize the "inner light" as the principle of religious knowledge. Rationalism (Modernism) makes reason the final arbiter and the mind of man the measure of truth and thereby destroys the super-

natural in religion and reduces it to a system of morality. See Creeds; Canon.

Fakih. A Moslem teacher of the law.

Fakir. See Dervish.

Falckner, Daniel (1666—ca. 1741). B. at Langen-Reinsdorf, Saxony, where his father, Daniel, was pastor; studied theology in Germany; member of the pietistic circle of A. H. Francke; came to America (1694) and associated with German pietists in Pa.; visited Germany (1698) and returned with his brother Justus and others to Germantown (1700); attorney for Frankfort Land Company; lost all through the intrigues of his partners; in later years he served congregations along the Raritan River in N. J.; 1724—25 he officiated at congregations on the Hudson previously served by Kocherthal; in 1731 he was succeeded by Wolff.

Falckner, Justus. One of the pioneers of Lutheranism in America; b. Nov. 22, 1672, at Langen-Reinsdorf, Saxony, where his father, Daniel, and his grandfather, Christian, had been pastors. He came to America with his brother Daniel in 1700 as a land agent and joined a company of mystics near Philadelphia. In 1703 Rudman persuaded him to accept a call to the Lutheran church in New York. He was ordained in Gloria Dei Church at Wicaco, Nov. 24, 1703 (the first Lutheran ordination of record in America). He took up his work in New York on Dec. 2 and for two decades served a parish extending from Perth Amboy, N. J., in the south, to Albany and the Schoharie Valley in the north. After Kocherthal's death he also served the German colonies bordering on the central part of the Hudson. The records of his ministry, preserved in the archives of St. Matthew Church, New York, show him to have been a devoted pastor, a tireless missionary, and a faithful watchman over his flock. In 1708 he issued his Grondelycke Onderricht, a textbook on Christian doctrine, with special reference to the errors of the Reformed. His hymn "Auf, ihr Christen, Christi Glieder," composed while he was a student at Halle, is found, also in translation, in many hymnals. In 1717 he married Gerritje Hardick of Claverack. D. in 1723.

G. F. Sachse, Justus Falckner, printed by author, Philadelphia, 1903; D. Clark, World of Justus Falckner, Muhlenberg Press, Philadelphia, 1946.

Falk, Johann Daniel (1768—1826). Studied theology at the University of Halle (1792); organized *Gesellschaft der Freunde in der Not* (1813) for the purpose of educating forsaken and neglected children; later, established schools for such children.

Fall of Man. The act of the first parents of our race by which they transgressed the divine command, an act through which, by imputation, all men were constituted sinners (Rom. 5: 12-19) and which had the result that thereby their nature, and the nature of all who are descended from them, became corrupt and subject to sin, having lost the divine image of perfect holiness and true knowledge of God. Man had been placed in a state of probation, possessing the ability not to sin (*posse non peccare*). The test of this probation was obedience to the divine Law. While in this state, man was tempted from without by the enticements of Satan; the temptation appealed to his senses and to his intellect and had accomplished its intent when man first conceived evil lust and then, in the exercise of free will, committed the first forbidden act. The consequence was a separation from God, since man now had become alienated from the life of the Spirit, seeking in self and in the world that whereby he might live. Thus man had been brought to know, though in a different sense from that which he had desired, good and evil. And he had been brought to this state through free choice. Only through the second Adam, Christ, were the ravages of the Fall and its consequences, temporal and eternal death, abundantly made good, and the means of pardon and grace provided for the entire human race. See references under *Dogmatics*.

False Decretals. See *Decretals, False*.

Famiglia. See *Pope*.

Family Life Education. Christian family life education is a term used to describe a program of service to child, youth, and adult which helps to better equip them for living in the Christian family. It aims to enrich the spiritual life of the home, to give parents a better understanding of their children and the skills for their Christian nurture, to make personal and family worship increasingly effective, to supply counsel in problems of family relationships, and to help lift the entire spirit and purpose of the home.

An inclusive program embraces: 1. thorough instruction of young and old in Christian doctrine and ethics; 2. adoption of some type of Christian home standard or charter; 3. giving aid for meaningful family worship, which meets the needs of all age levels and persons in the family; 4. effective and consistent home visitation; 5. pre-marital and post-marital counseling; 6. a practical program of service, especially to new families which move into the parish and to parents after the birth of a child until it is enrolled in a Sunday school class; 7. opportunities to study and discuss marriage preparation, family relations, parent education (reading lists, library, parent-teacher associations, Bible classes, youth, men's, women's, couples' groups); 8. greater home-church co-operation, especially in Christian education; and 9. a family-centered ministry.

God made the home the center of worship and religious training. It conveys not only physical life, but is the primary institution of God to insert the life in Christ into each generation (Gen. 18:19; Deut. 6:6, 7; Eph. 6:1-4). The home is the cradle of personality, the most potent teaching agency, the chief unit in evangelism, the best barrier against evil, the keeper of culture, the bulwark of the Church, and the cornerstone of the nation. The correlation between consistent Christianity and successful marriage is very high. New strains and stresses have been placed on the family by world-shattering changes in society. Modern life has greatly increased the incidence of separation, divorce, broken homes, and child delinquency. Home and Church need each other more than ever before. "The family is one of the most crucial sectors of the battle lines of the Church and the world." Recent research by psychologists, sociologists, and welfare workers has cast new light on family relations. It is logical that the Church should take the lead, because it alone has the regenerating power of the Gospel of Christ, the love and concern of the Good Shepherd, and the teaching facilities and agencies to carry out a balanced program of family life guidance. OEF

W. F. Wolbrecht (ed.), *The Christian Family in the Modern World*, CPH, 1948; O. E. Feucht, *Helping Families Through the Church*, CPH, 1951; Wood, *What the American Family Faces*, Hugh Publishers, 1943.

Family Worship Hour. See *Worship Hour*.

Fanaticism. Irrational zeal (displaying many characteristics of monomania) in behalf of some religious, moral, or philosophical conviction, which prevents deliberation or consideration either on the basis of Scripture or reason (cf. John 19:15; Acts 7:57; 9:1; Luke 9:53).

Fandrey, Gustav Adolf. B. Dec. 20, 1866, in Samter, Posen, Germany; studied at Neuendettelsau Mission School, 1881—4; came to America, 1884; prof. at Wartburg Seminary, Mendota, Ill., 1884—5; pastor at Fort Madison, Iowa, 1883—9; Chicago, Ill., 1889—1930; president of Southern Dist. of the Iowa Synod; vice-pres., then pres. (1927 to 1930) of Iowa Synod; served on many boards and committees; commissioner to Europe for National Lutheran Council, 1919—20; frequently contributed to church papers of his synod; d. July 14, 1930.

Fanon. 1. A shoulder cape worn by the Pope; 2. a napkin used to handle holy vessels at mass.

Farel, Guillaume (1489—1565). French and Swiss reformer; driven from Paris for being a Lutheran (1521); preached at Basel, Neuchatel, Geneva, Metz, Strassburg and other Swiss towns; responsible for the beginning of Calvin's ministry in Geneva. See *Calvin, John.*

Farrant, Richard (1520—80). One of England's foremost composers of sacred choral music. Although his music is not very masculine in character, its tenderness and sensitiveness do not detract from its value. His well-known "Call to Remembrance" is typical of his style and spirit.

Farrar, Frederick William (1831 to 1903). B. in India; canon of Westminster (1876); dean of Canterbury (1895); known for his writings on Biblical times, including a life of Christ, study of the Bible, studies of the Early Church; denied eternal punishment in *Eternal Hope.*

Fasting. Fasting is frequently mentioned in the Old Testament. It was undertaken voluntarily or by public prescription, except on the Day of Atonement, the only fast ordained by the Law (Lev. 16:29). Later, the Pharisees considered fasting a meritorious work (Luke 18:12), their "twice-a-week" being Mondays and Thursdays. Jesus speaks of fasting as a familiar practice, which, in itself, He does not

condemn (Matt. 6:16-18); yet His disciples did not fast (Matt. 9:14), and He nowhere commanded it. The Apostles fasted at times (Acts 13:2; 14:23). In conformity with Jewish custom many in the Early Church fasted twice a week, but, by way of distinction, on Wednesdays and Fridays. Under the influence of monastic ideas the practice gradually lost its voluntary character and was imposed on all Christians as both obligatory and meritorious.

To fast meant, at first, to abstain from all food till evening, when a simple meal of bread, salt, and water was taken. The rigor of this provision was soon relaxed, especially in the West. The Greek Church to the present day keeps its fast with considerable strictness; but the Roman Church, as early as the Middle Ages, permitted fasting to become a very tolerable experience. Its casuists here found a tempting field to exercise their ingenuity. Martin Chemnitz, in the 16th century, pronounced the Romish fasting a mere mockery. Fast days and periods which have commonly been observed in the Roman Catholic Church include: before Communion, Friday (the eating of meat forbidden), all days of Lent, Fridays of Advent, the ember days, and four vigils. Uniformity of fast periods was not observed. Thus Spain and her dominions were granted the privilege of eating meat on Friday by Urban II because that country prevented the Moors from conquering Europe. Efforts were made by Pius XII to rescind this privilege. By the middle of the twentieth century there was some relaxation of fasting regulations.

The manner of keeping these fasts is interesting, as witness the following information: "Fasting essentially consists in eating but one full meal in twenty-four hours, and that about midday." Of course, there must be no meat, but otherwise one may eat as heartily as one pleases. One must be careful that this meal is not broken by a noteworthy interruption (lasting, say, an hour or so); otherwise it will be two meals. Nor should the meal be too long; "ordinarily a duration of more than two hours is considered immoderate in this matter." In addition to this "full meal" a collation of about eight ounces is permitted in the evening, which may include eggs, cheese, butter, milk, and fish ("provided that the fish are small" — *Catholic Dictionary*). "A little tea, coffee, chocolate, or like beverage, with a morsel of bread or a cracker, is now allowed in the morning." Water, lemonade, pop, ginger ale, wine, beer, and similar drinks may be taken outside of mealtimes; honey, soup, and broth are expressly excluded from the list of such interimistic drinks. These provisions are often further relaxed by indult, and "all who cannot comply with the obligation without undergoing more than ordinary hardships are excused." Otherwise the law is binding on all between the ages of twenty-one and sixty. Great stress is laid on the provision that when meat is permitted on a fast-day by indult, fish cannot be eaten at the same meal without sin. "Finally, the Holy See has repeatedly declared that the use of lard, allowed by indult, comprehends butter or the fat of any animal." The mere quotation of these puerilities serves to characterize the Roman boast that its fasting is an aid to devotion and an invaluable means of self-discipline.

There is a far more serious aspect to the matter. These things, which God has not commanded, the Church of Rome binds on the consciences of its adherents under penalty of mortal sin. Thereby it falls under the condemnation of such passages as Gal. 5:1; Matt. 15:9; and Rev. 22:18. Nor does it blush to offer such mummeries to Almighty God as works of merit that have a right to claim every reward at His disposal. The definition of Alexander of Hales, though never officially adopted, embodies the position of the Roman Church: "Fasting is an abstinence from food and drink according to the rule of the Church, which looks to (intuitu) the satisfying for sin and the acquiring of eternal life."

The Lutheran Confessions teach that fasting is useful for keeping the flesh in check; that right fasting is a fruit of repentance commanded by God in the same way as right praying and right alms-giving; and that it is a fine external training in preparation for receiving Holy Communion (Apology, XV: 47; VI: 42, 46; Small Catechism, "Sacrament of the Altar," 10).

Fatalism. The belief that events are inevitably determined, causes or no causes, and hence often spoken of as a blind doctrine. It is decidedly antichristian, denying the possibility of any personal relation between the believer and God, and leads to pessimism. It is a prominent feature of Islam.

Father Divine. George Baker, a religious leader among the Negroes in New York, claims that he is the almighty presence in tangible form, and the "Great Unfoldment" of God in the flesh. He claims to be God in a human body, to have created the world, to bestow physical and spiritual blessings upon his followers, and to control the forces of the universe. Many titles are ascribed to him, such as: Dean of the Universe, the Holy Magnetic Body of God, the Great Tangibilator. Reincarnation or "materialization" of the spirit seems to be a prominent feature of his message. The creation of the world, the incarnation of Christ, and the coming of Father Divine are said to be evidence of the principle of materialization or "tangibilization." By a perfect life, including continence, man can put on the divine mind, overcome sickness, want, and even death, for every man has the "fertile egg," i. e., the Christ within him. Elements of Bahaism, Theosophy, Christian Science, and sheer foolishness make up the strange philosophy of this cultist. His followers are expected to surrender their possessions, and are promised economic security and peace, for "Father Divine, the living tangible god himself, as the highest object of devotion, lives in Harlem."

Father, God the. The term "Father" as used in Scripture ordinarily refers to the God of the Covenant in His relation to the believers and in this sense refers to the Divine Essence without distinction of Persons. See Fatherhood of God. In many texts, however, the Persons are so differentiated as clearly to limit the term Father to the First Person. The Father, personally so named, e. g., John 3:35; 5:20; 15:9; 17 (entire); 20:17; 1 Pet. 1:3, is specifically described as Himself unbegotten, John 5:26, but generating eternally the Son, Ps. 2:7; Acts 13:33; Heb. 1:5, and emitting (spirating) the Holy Spirit, John 15:26; Matt. 10:20; Gal. 4:6. While this act of generation, or begetting, of which the human mind can form no adequate notion, is a true act, yet it is an act which terminates within the Godhead, the Son also being God, of the same one and indivisible essence with the Father, John 10:30. It is therefore called an internal act, performed when nothing existed beside God. Likewise the eternal spiration, performed by the Father and the Son, is an internal act of God. Both the generation and spiration indicate the particular relation existing between Father and Son and between Father, Son, and Spirit and involve no factor of time, as if the Father had existed before the Son was generated, or as if Father and Son had existed before the Holy Ghost proceeded from Them. Even the difference between generation and spiration transcends our comprehension. All we can say is that there is a difference between these two acts. Of the external works of the Deity, two are predicated of the Father. The Father sent His Son to redeem man and gives, or sends, the Holy Spirit. John 3:16, 17; 14:26. Furthermore, there is ascribed to the Father the creation * of the world and its preservation. These works, however, are common to the three Persons, since creation is also predicated of the Son (John 1:3, 10; Colossians 1; 16; Heb. 1:3) and of the Holy Spirit (Ps. 33:6). See *Trinity, Doctrine of; God.*

Fatherhood of God. The term Father is applied to the Triune Divine Essence in Scripture in a twofold sense. God is Father in the sense of Author, Originator, Generator, and Preserver of all things (Ps. 68:5; Is. 64:8). Much more commonly, however, the word Father involves the concepts of love, mercy, and grace, and is equivalent to "God of the covenant." As such He is a Father of those who have entered into covenant relations with Him. The idea of a divine Fatherhood as implying a relation to all mankind in this sense, and apart from the covenant of grace, is foreign to the Scriptures (Rom. 9:8; John 8:44). Its correlated idea is not humanity as such, but mankind redeemed, especially the believers, who have received the blessings of the covenant. In this sense Israel was taught to look upon God as Father (Ex. 4:22; Deut. 32:6; Ps. 89:27 f.; Is. 63:16; John 8:41; 5:45; Jer. 31:9; 2 Cor. 6:18). By adoption (John 1:12, 13) the believers are children of God (John 1:12; Rom. 8:16). In this sense Jesus speaks of God as the Father of believers (Matt. 6:4, 8, 9, 15, 18. See *Father, God the.*

Fathers of the Church. Recognized teachers of the Church from the close of the Apostolic Age down to Pope Gregory (d. 604) and John of Damascus (d. 754), the last Latin and Greek representatives, respectively.

Fauré, Gabriel (1845—1924). French composer of note whose *Requiem Mass* is popular in the U.S. The tender lyricism of his compositions adds to their charm. Fauré has written also much instrumental music. In 1905 he succeeded Theodore Dubois as Director of the Paris Conservatoire.

Fauxbourdon (or Falsobordone). Originally served as the harmonic background of plainchant. Later it was used also by masters like J.S. Bach, notably in chorale preludes (cf. the close of his preludes based on In dulci jubilo and *Wenn wir in hoechsten Noeten sein*). Its harmonies are in the first inversion, at times over a pedal point.

Fawcett, John. B. at Lidget Green, Yorks, England, Jan. 16, 1740. Through George Whitefield's influence he became a Methodist, but changed and was ordained a Baptist minister at Wainsgate, afterwards serving a church at Hebden Bridge, Yorks, till his death, although he had a number of important calls. He was the author of religious prose works, including a devotional commentary on the Bible, and a large amount of sacred poetry. He will always be remembered by the hymns, "Lord, Dismiss Us with Thy Blessing," "How Precious Is the Book Divine," and "Blest Be the Tie That Binds."

Fayyumic Bible Version. See *Bible Versions, D.*

Feast of Asses (Feast of Fools). A festival celebrated on the Continent during the Octave of Epiphany from the 12th to the 16th century, being a burlesque of the ritual by lower clergy (often included election of a "bishop" and leading of an ass into the church); condemned by Huss and others.

Feasts. See *Church Year.*

Febronianism. A name given to a movement in the Catholic Church in Germany (18th century) aiming at the nationalization of the Church. The real power of the Church was to reside in the bishops. Johann Nikolaus, leader of the movement, used the name Justinus Febronius when publishing his work *De statu ecclesiae et legitima potestate Romani pontificis.*

Fechner, Gustav Theodor (1801 to 1887). German psychologist, whose investigations led to the formulation of Fechner's law: "In order that the intensity of a sensation may increase in arithmetic progression, the stimulus must increase in geometrical progression." His philosophy considered God the soul of the universe and natural laws the unfolding of His essence.

Fecht, Johannes (1636—1716). Lutheran theologian and opponent of Pietism. Superintendent in Durlach; after 1690 superintendent and professor at Rostock. Wrote extensively, particularly in dogmatics and polemics.

Federal Council of the Churches of Christ in America. Organized in Philadelphia, Dec., 1908, thirty denominations having been represented. The purpose of the Council, according to its constitution. was: 1. to express the fellowship and catholic unity of the Christian Church; 2. to bring the Christian bodies of America into united service for Christ and the world; 3. to encourage devotional fellowship and mutual counsel concerning the spiritual life and religious activities of the Church; 4. to secure a larger combined influence for the Church of Christ in all matters affecting the moral and social condition of the people, so as to promote the application of the Law of Christ in every relation to human life; 5. to assist in the organization of local branches of the Federal Council, to promote its aim in their communities. It was specifically stated in the constitution that the "Federal Council shall have no authority over the constituent bodies adhering to it. . . . It has no authority to draw up a common creed or form of government or of worship, or in any way to limit the full autonomy of the Christian bodies adhering to it." Most Protestant bodies were members of it (making a combined membership of 25,000,000). Various departments dealt with such phases of its work as missions, research, education, race relations, radio, social service, armed services, prisoners of war, etc. It was absorbed into the National Council of Churches of Christ in the United States of America (1950).

W. Arndt, "Relation Between the U. L. C. A. and the Federal Council," *CTM*, XIII: 874; E. B. Sanford, *Origin and History of the Federal Council of the Churches of Christ in America,* Scranton, Conn., 1916.

Federal Emergency Relief Administration. See *Social Work,* D 1.

Federal Social Security Act. See *Social Work,* D 1.

Federated Churches. See *Community Churches.*

Feet Washing. See *Foot Washing.*

Felicissimus, Schism of. Arose from the hostility of certain presbyters, under the lead of the ecclesiastical demagog Novatus, against Cyprian, Bishop of Carthage, elected 248. Without the consent of the bishop, Novatus ordained the deacon Felicissimus, and when Cyprian, from his retreat during the Decian persecution, ordered a church visitation and a collection for the poor, Felicissimus refused to recognize the bishop's commissioners. The opposition gained ground through the indulgence shown toward the lapsed as compared with the severity of Cyprian. The schismatics were condemned by a council at Carthage (251).

Felix of Urgel. See *Adoptionism.*

Fellowship. A. *Nature of Christian Fellowship.* Christian fellowship is the common sharing in the Gospel (Phil. 1: 5-7), in faith (Philemon 6), and in other spiritual and mutual gifts. It is a creation of God by His calling us into fellowship or partnership with His Son so that we share in all of Christ's works, blessings, glory, and goods (1 Cor. 1: 9; 1 John 1: 3, 6, 7). It is a communion and participation in, and partnership with, all the blessings of Christ and a union with all Christians through the fellowship of the Spirit (2 Cor. 13: 13; 1 John 1: 7; cf. 1 Cor. 10: 16). This communion of believers is a unity or "oneness" in Christ (John 17: 11, 21, 22) which transcends race, social position (Gal. 3: 28; James 2: 1), relationship (1 John 3: 14 ff.; the passages in which non-relatives are called father, mother, brother, sister, son, daughter. Cf. Matt. 12: 49, 50), and death (1 Thess. 4: 13-18; 1 Cor. 15: 6 ff.).

Christian fellowship actuates a participation in the experiences of Christ (Phil. 3: 10; Rom. 14: 8; John 14: 9; Phil. 1: 21; Rom. 6: 1-8) and of one's fellow Christians. Out of the basic communion in the Gospel of Christ comes the communication of spiritual and material gifts (Acts 2: 42-45; Rom. 15: 25; 2 Cor. 8: 4; 9: 13; Heb. 13: 16).

As faith always produces fruit, so the fellowship of the Spirit in Christ manifests itself in action. Christian fellowship is activity in the Gospel (Gal. 2: 9). Its mark is love (1 Pet. 1: 22; 1 John; 1 Cor. 13). Communion of Christians causes them to treat each other as fathers, mothers, brothers, sisters (1 Tim. 5: 1, 2). It is a fellowship of feelings (2 Cor. 11: 29), burdens (Phil. 2: 1; Rom. 15: 1; Gal. 6: 2; Heb. 13: 3), and a communication of help (Acts 20: 35; James 1: 27). The Christian communion is activated by a desire to bring others into its fellowship (1 John 1: 3; Acts 4: 11, 12, 13, 20; 1 Cor. 3: 9) and avoid or heal schism within itself (1 Cor. 1: 11, 12;

3:1-11; Eph. 4:3). A climax is in the Lord's Supper (1 Cor. 10:16).

The ideal of fellowship was portrayed by Christ when He spoke of the Church as one flock under one Shepherd (John 10:16) and of the individual Christians and churches as branches growing from one Vine (John 15:1-6). In His great prayer on the eve of His death the Savior prayed for unity among His followers (John 17:20-23).

The Apostles sought to maintain Christian fellowship (1 Cor. 12:13; Eph. 4:1 ff. Cf. also Rom. 12:5; 1 Cor. 10:17; Gal. 3:28; Eph. 4:13; 1 Cor. 1:10; 2 Cor. 13:11; Phil. 1:27; 1 Pet. 3:8; Acts 2:42; Phil. 1:3; 1 John 1:7), condemned schisms under various leaders (1 Cor. 1:10-17; 3:3-9), and sought to solve difficulties through deliberation and discussion (Acts 15).

B. *Fellowship of Churches.* In the early Church unity was exemplified by fellowship in worship. Pastors in one part of the Church were recognized in other parts, and if present at a service, were invited to take part (compare custom of Judaism in NT times: Matt. 9:35; Luke 4:16 ff.; Acts 13:5, 15; 4:1 ff.; 16:13; 18:24 ff.). The rise of heretics and impostors led to the formulation of rules and safeguards (*Didache; Apostolic Canons.* Cf. Matt. 7:15 ff.; Mark 14:22 ff.; Gal. 1:8; 1 Tim. 1:7; 4:1 ff.; 6:3 ff.; 2 Tim. 4:3 ff.; Titus 1:11; 2 Pet. 2:1). The schismatic spirit, however, continued to be condemned (Cf. *I Ep.* of Clement of Rome) and unity praised (Ignatius in his epistles makes such unity flow from loyalty to the bishop, *e. g., ad Ephesios,* IV; *ad Trallianos,* III; cf. Irenaeus, *Haer,* IV; Clement of Alexander, *Strom.,* VII; Cyprian, *De unitate ecclesiae*).

With the growth of the hierarchical system, fellowship was more and more determined by the hierarchy. Disagreement was revolt and for hundreds of years a capital crime.

The Great Schism (complete, 1054) destroyed fellowship between the East and West Churches which could not be restored at Lyons (1276) and Florence (1439). The Roman Catholic Church makes fellowship dependent on "unity of faith, government, and worship" and will not "seriously entertain" unification with Christian communions "without acknowledgment of the supreme authority of the Roman See."

Luther at first sought to maintain fellowship with the Roman Catholic Church, even though "everything there was in a wretched state." His excommunication made it impossible for him to follow that policy. Nor was fellowship immediately stopped entirely with the Reformed, as is indicated by the fact that the Colloquy at Marburg was opened with a worship service. The ideal of a unified Church is strongly emphasized in the preface to the *Augsburg Confession.* Luther's own efforts for peace are shown in his letter to Cardinal Albrecht of Mainz (St. L. Ed., XVI: 917 ff. Compare XVI: 946 ff.).

The statement of the Augsburg Confession "to the unity of the Church it is enough to agree concerning the doctrine of the Gospel and the administration of the Sacrament" is variously stated in Luther's writings (*e. g.,* unity springs from agreement in Word and doctrine, IX: 831; it springs from the inner spirit, XIX: 345; XIX: 1985; XII: 738 ff.; Sacrament, XIX: 345. Love avails nothing where unity in faith and spirit are lacking, IX: 727 ff.).

After the Diet of Augsburg, Luther held that all who, generally speaking, teach and live in accordance with the *Confession* and its *Apology* must be regarded and treated as brothers (St. L. Ed., XVI: 1538). The Augsburg Confession early became a criterion of fellowship and served as a safeguard against teachings of the Reformed and Roman Catholics. In ensuing years fellowship was usually not denied whole Lutheran state churches which held this confession but did not formally subscribe to the whole Book of Concord (*CTM,* XV: 540). Subsequent efforts at restoring fellowship with the Reformed were unsuccessful (Wittenberg Concord, 1536; Thirteen Articles, 1538; Regensburg Conference, 1541; Interims, 1548; Thorn Conference, 1645; Prussian Union, 1817; Bonn Reunion Conferences, 1874—75; modern movements). The decisions of the Council of Trent completed the breach between Lutherans and Roman Catholics (see *Counter-Reformation*).

Early Lutherans in America had few or no bonds of union, no important rules pertaining to fellowship with other Christians, and were a prey of many religious propagandists. Henry Melchior Muhlenberg * strove to establish a consciousness of Lutheran unity, and loyalty to the Augsburg Confession and "the other Symbolical Books." In this period, however, fellowship with other bodies (especially Episcopalians) continued to be practiced, and confessionalism was not rigidly held. Thereupon followed a period in which confessional distinctions were more and more disregarded and fellowship with other church bodies sought (often following cultural or language lines). Later S. S. Schmucker labored to re-unite Lutherans and to re-introduce a modified loyalty to the Augsburg Confession.

Reactions to the Prussian Union,* the immigration of many Lutherans from Europe, as well as other factors led to the gradual formulation of fellowship rules during the 19th century. The growth of confessional consciousness by the middle of the century is indicated by the widespread opposition to the *Definite Platform*.* At the time of the formation of the General Council, the Missouri Synod, Joint Synod of Ohio, and German Synod of Iowa asked questions regarding fellowship and other matters, which were answered by a committee headed by C. P. Krauth (see *Four Points*). This led to the Pittsburgh Declaration * (1869), Akron Rule * (1872), Galesburg Rule * (1875), and the action taken at Pittsburgh (1889). Walther and others at the Free Lutheran Conferences * (1856—59) sought to establish general Lutheran fellowship on the basis of loyalty to the Augsburg Confession, holding that the other Lutheran confessions were not sufficiently known in America to serve as basis.

Doctrinal controversies among Lutherans during the second part of the 19th century focused doctrinal differences, alienated Lutherans, strengthened synodical walls, and occasioned some restatements of the boundaries of fellowship. The Missouri Synod instructed its delegates to the Synodical Conference not to deliberate with persons who had accused Missouri of Calvinism (*Synodalbericht*, 1881, 45). *Lehre u. Wehre* (LI:3 ff.) upheld the refusal of the Missouri delegates to pray with those of Iowa and Ohio at Detroit (the item quotes Rom. 16:17; Matt. 7:15; 2 Corinthians 6; 1 Tim. 6:3-5; Titus 3:10; 2 John 10:11; Jer. 23:31; Luke 21:17; etc.).

While the general trend in American Lutheranism at the end of the 19th century was to make confessional loyalty the basis of fellowship, there was no complete unanimity. Some, emphasizing the invisible Church, advocated general Christian fellowship (*e. g.*, Milton Valentine). This view was strenuously opposed, especially by those who emphasized the confessional nature of

altar fellowship (*e. g.*, Sigismund Fritschel; Missouri Synod; others).

The first half of the 20th century was marked by many efforts toward Lutheran unity and fellowship. Numerous statements were issued to show doctrinal positions as well as doctrinal agreement (or disagreement). Principles and methods varied. Some sought to adhere to the principles of Luther and Walther (at free conferences). Others demanded agreement on all formulated doctrines and such as are to be formulated (at times, exegetical agreement), holding that all joint work and worship is indicative of indifference toward, or agreement with, error. While selective fellowship has been advocated by some, others oppose it for the sake of order, and hold that the individual pastor or church has foregone the right of selective fellowship. Distinctions are also made between various types of fellowship (work, private and public prayer, pulpit, altar, etc.). Following the precedent set by Walther, the Missouri Synod College of Presidents called for free Lutheran conferences (1949). See *Lutheran Confessions; Unionism; Fundamental Doctrines; Union Movements;* related topics. EL

Patristic writings; standard church histories; Luther's works; V. Fern, *The Crisis in American Lutheran Theology,* Century, New York, 1927; F. Pieper, Conference Paper before the Oregon and Washington District, 1924; C. P. Krauth, *One Hundred and Five Theses;* Theses on the Galesburg Declaration on Pulpit and Altar Fellowship, prepared by Order of the General Council, 1876; F. Bente, *Was Steht der Vereinigung der Lutherischen Synoden im Wege?* CPH, 1917; M. Loy, M. Valentine, S. Fritschel, H. E. Jacobs, F. Pieper, E. T. Horn, F. A. Schmidt, *Distinctive Doctrines and Usages of the General Bodies of the Evangelical Lutheran Church in the United States,* Luth. Pub. House, Philadelphia; Th. Graebner, *The Problem of Lutheran Union and other Essays,* CPH, 1935; Pamphlets on Unionism (studies by various authors bound together in the Concordia Seminary, St. Louis, Library); T. F. Gullixson, *The Fellowship Question,* Augsburg Pub. House, Minneapolis, Minn., 1932; Th. Graebner-P. E. Kretzmann, *Toward Lutheran Union,* CPH, 1943; M. Reu, *In the Interest of Lutheran Unity,* 1940; H. E. Jacobs, "The Fellowship Question," *Luth. Church Review,* Oct., 1889;

G. W. Sandt, *Should Lutherans Get To-gether — or Unity Within the Lutheran Church*, General Council Pub. House, Philadelphia, 1915; Items in *Lutheran Cyclopedia* (Scribner, 1899) under *Altar Fellowship* and *Pulpit Fellowship;* Wm. Brenner, *Dangerous Alliances or Some Peace Snags*, published by Martin Luther Men's Society, Toledo, O., n. d.; J. H. C. Fritz, *Union or Unity? A Popular Presentation of a Timely Subject*, CPH, n. d.; C. A. Hardt, "Christian Fellowship," *CTM*, XVI: 433—66; W. A. Arndt, "Missouri's Condition of Church Fellowship," *CTM*, XVIII: 171—77; W. Arndt, "Selective Fellowship," *CTM*, XVII: 455—57; R. T. DuBrau, "New Testament Fellowship: A Study in Semantics," *CTM*, XXII: 334—42; Matthias Schulz, "The Question of Altar Fellowship According to Halle Resolutions," (translated and condensed by FEM) *CTM*, XVIII: 534—37; E. L. Lueker, "Walther and the Free Lutheran Conferences," *CTM*, XV:529ff.; W. G. Polack, "Lutheran Unity," *Luth. Witness*, June 14, 1949; *Theses on Fellowship* (submitted for discussion in accordance with resolution of Missouri Synod), 1949; E. C. Fendt (ed.), *What Lutherans Are Thinking*, Wartburg Press, Columbus, O., 1947; E. Rinderknecht, "Lutheran Union and the United Lutheran Church," *Luth. Ch. Quart.*, XIX:13—34; numerous items in Lutheran periodicals. *CTM*, VI:138—39 lists articles found in *CTM*, I—V (see also *CTM*, VI:53—64; 141 f.; 220—22; 778—80; 938—41; XV: 486—88; XVI:333—36; 338—39 and articles throughout). See references under *Church*. AHG, "Church Fellowship," *Abiding Word*, II (517—37) lists the following theses on the basis of some Missouri Synod essays: "1. The basis of true church fellowship is personal fellowship with Christ by faith. This saving faith, begotten by the Holy Ghost through the Word, and this faith alone, is the inward, invisible bond of fellowship truly uniting all believers in one spiritual body. 2. This inward, invisible fellowship should manifest itself according to God's will in outward, visible fellowship of believers in the local congregation and beyond the local congregation. We recognize fellow believers by their confession of a faith based on God's Word and expressed in the Confessions of the Lutheran Church. This confession of faith constitutes the outward bond of fellowship. 3. It is God's will that believers should always be intent to keep the outward bond of fellowship intact so that God's Word is

purely taught and the practice of the church is in harmony with that teaching. Believers who because of lack of knowledge do not comply with God's command to continue in His Word and as a result have fellowship with errorists, separate themselves from fellow believers that continue in all of God's Word and thus destroy the outward bond of fellowship (Now it is true, that when it comes to our 'doing according to the Word,' we will often fall short of the mark. Nor would we want to say that a church whose practice is not always in perfect harmony with the Word of God, thereby destroys the bond of fellowship between it and other fellow confessors). 4. The purpose of Christian fellowship is the mutual strengthening in faith, the preservation and promotion of the unity of faith, and the joint extension of God's kingdom throughout the world. The end purpose is the glory of God and the eternal welfare of men. Therefore we should diligently strive to preserve the true fellowship of faith that exists among us, avoid everything that hinders it, and strive to help remove all errors and difficulties that separate fellow believers from one another."

Fenelon (Francois de Salignac de la Mothe, 1651—1715). Archbishop of Cambrai; missionary to Huguenots; opponent of Jansenists; adopted ideas of Mme. Guyon *; wrote *Télémaque* and *De l' éducation des filles.*

Ferghil. See *Celtic Church*, 6.

Feria. Any weekday in distinction to Sunday. Thus, Good Friday is *feria sexta* in Holy Week.

Ferrara-Florence Council. See *Basel, Council of.*

Festivals. See *Church Year.*

Feth, John Henry Frederick. B. Feb. 10, 1861, at Cleveland, Ohio. Ed. Fort Wayne and St. Louis, grad. 1883. Asst. pastor at St. Matt., N. Y., 1883—85; pastor at New Haven, Conn., 1885—88; professor at Concordia Collegiate Institute, Bronxville, N. Y., 1888—1927; president from 1896 to 1918. Received D. D. from St. Louis, 1921. Died July 29, 1927.

Fetishism. A term derived from Portuguese *feitiço* (Lat., *factitius*), "charm, talisman," and now used by anthropologists in a great variety of senses, *e. g.*, denoting belief in charms or the personification and worship of sun, moon, stars, earth, mountains, rivers, springs, and other objects of nature, but generally understood to mean belief that a spirit may dwell temporarily or permanently in some material object, which thereby becomes an object of reverence or worship. It is thus connected with Animism. Such objects, or fetishes, are of the greatest variety — claws, teeth, horns, bones, or other parts of animals; shells, stones, leaves, pieces of wood or metal, rags, refuse, etc. Because of the indwelling spirit or magical powers, these fetishes, of which each has a special field of activity, are believed to be able to secure for the owner success in his undertakings, preservation from, and healing of, injuries and diseases, long life, courage, shrewdness, good weather, in fact, able to obtain for him anything he desires or to guard him against anything he fears. The savage will talk to it and entreat it, anoint it with oil, sprinkle it with blood. If he has great success with it, it may become the fetish of an entire tribe and the owner its priest. Fetishes may be found by some chance occurrence, or certain objects may become fetishes by incantation or by simple invitation extended to the spirit to dwell in the object.

Fetishism is found among all noncivilized races, but mainly among the Negro tribes of Africa. Traces have been discovered in ancient Greece, Egypt, Babylonia, India, China, also among modern civilized peoples. Idol worship is but one step removed from fetishism. The use of charms and amulets, though not identical with fetishism as above outlined, and the adoration Roman Catholics give to statues, pictures, and relics of saints, have a fetishistic basis. However, modern science of religion shows its hostility to Christianity when it asserts that the essential idea of fetishism is also found in the veneration of the Ark of the Covenant by Hebrews and of cross, baptismal water, and Eucharist by Christians; for no such notion was connected with the Ark by God's sanction.

Feuerbach, Ludwig (1804—72). Prominent representative of modern materialistic atheism; religion is mirror of man's ideas; God, heaven, eternal life, are merely human desires; propagated sensualism; wrote *Wesen des Christentums* (1841), *Grundsaetze der Philosophie der Zukunft* (1843); *Wesen der Religion* (1845); his materialism culminated in the formula: "Der Mensch ist, was er isst."

Fichte, Immanuel Hermann (1797 to 1879). Prof. at Bonn and Tuebingen; son of J. G. Fichte; held that philosophy must return to the view of personality in its conception of God; founded *Zeitschrift fuer Philosophie und Spekulative Theologie* (1837).

Fichte, Johann Gottlieb (1762 to 1814). Professor at Jena (1794) and later at Berlin; ardent patriot *(Reden an die deutsche Nation);* in his earlier writings he stressed the pure ego in individuality; later he held that individuality is of slight importance and sacrifices self in active striving for the highest good; the individual can become conscious of union with God through love in this life; rejected deity of Christ, atonement.

Fick, Hermann (1822—85). Studied at Goettingen; private tutor in Mecklenburg; came to America in 1846; pastor in New Melle, Mo., in Bremen north of St. Louis, in Detroit, in Collinsville, Ill., and in Boston, Mass.; not only a successful preacher, but also a man with pronounced literary ability, his *Lutherbuch* for schools being the classic of its day and his poems for special occasions, which appeared in the various periodicals of the Missouri Synod, characterized by warmth and power; wrote: "Gehe auf, du Trost der Heiden."

Fiducia Cordis. See *Certainty, Religious.*

Fifth Monarchy Men. A sect of English fanatical millenarians (1650 and after) who held that Christ would set up a fifth universal monarchy during the time of the Commonwealth.

Fiji Islands. A group in the South Pacific Ocean, belonging to Great Britain. Area, 7,083 sq. mi. Population, 293,764 (1950), of Melanesian stock; formerly cannibals. Missions were begun in 1834 by two English Wesleyan Methodists. After they had suffered much persecution, the Methodist Church became firmly established; whole tribes renounced idolatry in a day. The Roman Catholic Church began counter-missions in 1863. — Many Indian coolies are emigrating to the islands; the Methodist Mission Society of Australia is working among them. In 1902 the S. P. G. also entered the field. See *Melanesia.*

Filioque Controversy. One of the major disputes of the Early Church, which later became one of the chief points of difference between the Eastern and the Western Church. It concerns the fact of the procession of the Holy Ghost from the Father *and the Son* (*Filioque*). The Apostles' Creed begins the Third Article: "And in the Holy Ghost." To this the Constantinopolitan Creed added, "who proceedeth from the Father." The Latin Church added, "and the Son," mainly in the interest of the fight against Arianism.* The addition was used for more than two hundred years before it was formally accepted at the Council of Aachen (809). See *Ecumenical Creeds,* B 1c.

Fillmore, Charles. See *Unity School of Christianity.*

Final Judgment. See *Last Things.*

Final Perseverance of the Saints. Scripture teaches that God's elect saints will not be lost, but obtain everlasting salvation (Matt. 24: 22-24; 1 Cor. 1: 8, 9; 10: 13; etc.). This does not mean that the elect saints cannot fall from grace and so temporarily lose their faith (David; Peter); but it does mean that God's saving grace, without any merit on their part, will restore them to the state of faith, so that in Christ they finally die a blessed death. The doctrine of final perseverance of the saints is pure Gospel, designed to comfort anxious and doubting believers, and should not be misused in the interest of carnal security. Those inclined to fleshly security and sinning against grace should be warned by such earnest Law preaching as is found in Rom. 8: 21, 22 and 1 Cor. 10: 12. The doctrine of final perseverance glorifies divine grace, not human merit. The Reformed doctrine that the elect saints, once called, may lose the exercise of faith, but not faith itself, even if they commit enormous sins, is opposed to Scripture.

Finalism. The belief that ends or goals are present in all events. Hence it explains events, not on the basis of the past, but of the future.

Finances in the Church. 1. Christians must learn that the Word of God teaches that giving for the support of the Church is a Christian duty. The Apostle by the grace of Christ admonishes Christians to "abound in this grace also," and thereby "prove the sincerity of their love" to Christ and His Church (2 Cor. 8: 7-9). The Lord asks Christians to give financial support to their pastors (1 Cor. 9: 7-14; 1 Tim. 5: 17-18). The Lord took His children severely to task when they were remiss in the exercise of their duty to support the

Lord's work. (Mal. 3: 8-10; Hag. 1: 2-11.) The churches of Macedonia and the poor widow were praised because, in spite of their deep poverty, they gave liberally (2 Cor. 8: 1-4; Mark 12: 41-44). When the Tabernacle in the Old Testament was built, the people brought "much more than enough" and had to be "restrained from bringing" (Ex. 36: 5-7). The Lord in His Word promises to reward Christian giving (Mal. 3: 10; Luke 6: 38; Prov. 19: 17). Giving on the part of the Christian is an act of worship enjoined by the Lord. It is, therefore, quite proper that the giving of money be also made a part of the regular worship at the services of the church. In the Old Testament the Lord's injunction reads: "They shall not appear before the Lord empty; every man shall give as he is able, according to the blessing of the Lord, thy God, which He hath given thee" (Deut. 16: 16, 17). In the NT the Gospel says: "Upon the first day of the week let every one of you lay by him in store as God hath prospered him, that there be no gatherings when I come" (1 Cor. 16: 2).

2. Christians must be duly informed with reference to the needs of the Church. The average Christian knows little about these needs. The work of the Church, its opportunities and its needs, should be duly presented. This should be done not only in the pulpit, but also in the meetings of the voting members, the young people's society, and the ladies' society, as well as in the week day school and in the Sunday school. The members should also be urged to read the church papers and such special literature (folders with pictures) as may be issued by a church body from time to time. People will not give to anything in which they are not interested.

3. Christians should by a good financial system (every-member canvass and envelope system) be given an opportunity to contribute regularly and often. A congregational *budget* is a financial estimate of the moneys needed in the course of a year for salaries, light, fuel, repairs, printing expenses, synodical treasuries, etc. A synodical budget is an estimate of the moneys needed by a synod to carry on its work in the course of a year. The budget is desirable in order that the needs of the Church and the proportionate amounts needed by each treasury may be known. When a synodical organization, for instance, has many treasuries, some requiring much larger sums than others,

it is almost impossible for the individual Christian to determine the proportionate share which he is to give to supply the needs of each. Christians may, in addition to their regular contributions for the budget, give additional sums for specific purposes, which then must be used in accordance with the donor's wish. The pledging of certain moneys for the support of the Church is an old custom. Formerly *pledge cards* were not used, but so-called subscription lists *(Unterschriften)*. Such pledging is not contrary to the Scriptural method of freewill offerings; for it not only remains optional with the individual Christian to determine the amount of his pledge, but also to pay more if the Lord increases his income and to pay less if his decreased earnings prevent him from fulfilling his pledge.

4. The weekly *envelope system* is being successfully used by many congregations. It is essentially the same system that Paul suggested to the Corinthian congregation (1 Cor. 16:2), regular weekly giving. Some congregations use the single envelope system, the contributions being used both for the home church and for the church at large, the congregation deciding what percentage should be given to the church at large. Some congregations use the duplex envelope system, the one pocket being used for home purposes and the other for outside purposes. The duplex system is preferred by some because it keeps the needs of the church at large constantly in the minds of the members and gives better financial results. The Scripture enjoins Christians to support the Church by their freewill offerings, which should be given as the fruit of faith and in accordance with the ability of the individual Christian (Ex. 35:5; 1 Chron. 29:5; 1 Cor. 16:2; 2 Cor. 8:12).

5. It goes without saying that Christians should support their own church and not solicit contributions from people of other denominations or of the world. If, however, money is offered, provided that it is not money illegitimately gotten, it may be accepted. Raising money by means of bazaars and the like is not good practice: the buyer is not giving a freewill offering, but is paying for something which he gets in return. If an exorbitant price is charged, it is even more reprehensible. At that, less money is secured in this way than when Christians are trained to bring freewill offerings out of love to Christ and His Church.

6. *Tithing,* the giving of a tenth part of one's income, was commanded by God in the OT (Lev. 27:30). There were two (or three) sorts of tithes: the tithe paid to the Levites and priests (Num. 28:26, 27) and that paid for the Lord's feasts (Deut. 14:22 f. Perhaps a third tithe every third year for the poor, if this tithe has not already been included in the second, Deut. 14:28, 29). In times of religious depression the people neglected to pay tithes (Mal. 3:7-12). In the NT tithing is not enjoined; for this would be contrary to the Christian liberty which the child of God enjoys under the Christian dispensation. Thereby it is, however, not said that the Christians of the New Testament should not pay any tithes; but if they do so, it must be done voluntarily. Individual Christians even today pay tithes to the Lord. The average contribution of Christians today falls far short of the tenth part of their income.

7. A church extension fund provides a "rotary system of financing building projects," churches, schools, and parsonages. The money paid to this fund by congregations, through the budget, by direct gifts, loans, or legacies is lent without interest (or, perhaps, one-half or one per cent to pay operating expenses of the fund) to needy congregations, who, in turn, pay back certain sums annually until the whole amount has been paid.

8. Some church bodies have a pension system to provide funds for workers in the church when these are superannuated or by illness have been compelled to retire; also for the widows and orphans of such workers. Various relief systems are used. JHCF

Financing Education. See *Parish Education,* I.

Finbar. See *Celtic Church,* 6.

Finck, Heinrich (1445—1527). German composer of songs and choral music whom Martin Luther admired greatly.

Finland. Area: 136,054 sq. mi.; population: 4,032,538 (1952), mostly Lutheran, this having been the only recognized religion. Received Christianity from the English Henry, Bishop of Upsala, who came over with the crusade of Eric VIII of Sweden and was martyred in 1158. Thomas, an English Dominican, became the first bishop. In addition to Lutherans there are Greek Catholics and Raskolniks in Finland and a very small number of Roman Catholics, Baptists, Methodists, and Adventists.

Finland, Lutheranism in. 1. Swedish king Eric Jedvardson's crusade in 1155 established a Christian outpost in Finland with the English-born Henry, Bishop of Upsala, in charge. After his martyrdom in 1158, an English Dominican, Thomas of Upsala, became bishop of Finland about 1216. Under him Finland became a Catholic state in 1229. Finnish churchmen were educated in the universities of central Europe, and it is to their credit that corrupt conditions of those evil days did not exist in Finland during the pre-reformation era.

2. Pietari Särkilahti, a pastor and educator, converted to Lutheranism during his studies in central Europe, labored diligently (1516—22) to abolish evils of Catholicism and to establish the Lutheran faith. Bishop Martin Skytte, although a Catholic, favored the Lutheran Reformation and sent 8 Finnish students to study under Luther and Melanchthon in Wittenberg. Of these Michael Agricola is most prominent. Returning with a recommendation from Luther to the Swedish king, Agricola became assistant to Bishop Skytte. To teach the people in their own tongue, he prepared an ABC book in 1542, a prayer book of 770 pages in 1544, a translation of the NT in 1548, and an agenda in 1549. He is regarded as the father of Finnish literature. In 1554 Bishop Bothvid of Sweden ordained Agricola Bishop of Turku and his coworker Paavali Juusten as Bishop of Viipuri. In 1593 the Augsburg Confession was adopted by the Church of Sweden-Finland, and from then on only the Lutheran religion was tolerated.

3. In 1640 a university was established in Turku; it was moved to Helsinki in 1827. During the 17th century strict orthodoxy prevailed. Prof. Envald Svenonius (d. 1688) was its chief proponent. The entire Liber Concordiae was adopted as the confession of the Church in 1663. On that confessional basis, with its church polity already well established, a general Church Law was enacted in 1686.

4. Pietism, introduced by enthusiasts, soon took a conservative form known as the Earlier Awakening. Its noted representatives were John Wegelius, Sr. (d. 1725), John Wegelius, Jr. (d. 1764), and Abraham Achrenius (d. 1769). The leading men of the Church, however, during the first half of the 18th century were rationalists.

The Later Awakening after the turn of the century had several outstanding leaders. Many pastors joined the peasant leader Paavo Ruotsalainen (d. 1851). An "inner feeling" of grace, and hence a lack of assurance of salvation was characteristic of this pietism. Provost F. G. Hedgerb (d. 1893) broke away from the pietists and became the leader of the evangelical movement. Pastor J. T. Beck and other "evangelical" pastors represented the "Scriptural movement." Evangelicals, suffering persecution for opposing doctrinal indifference in the Church, organized the Gospel Association to carry on their work. The Association has translated and published the writings of Luther, now totaling about 12,000 pages. Pastor Henrik Renqvist (d. 1866), emphasizing prayer, became the leader of the "praying pietists." In northern Finland a new movement was begun by Pastor L. L. Laestadius (d. 1861) and developed by the lay preacher J. Raattamaa. They teach that the spoken word is the proper medium of the Holy Ghost and absolution by a believing Christian is necessary for conversion.

5. In 1870 a new Church Law was adopted, favorable to the liberals. Rationalistic criticism has prevailed in the theological dept. of the university of Helsinki, where pastors receive their education. In 1919—23 a few of the Evangelical (Gospel Association) pastors made contacts with the Lutheran free churches in Europe and with the Missouri Synod. (Pastor A. A. Uppala-Wegelius attended Concordia Seminary in St. Louis 1922—23). In 1921 they began to publish a theological magazine, *Paimen* (Shepherd), advocating purity of doctrine and the founding of a Lutheran free church. In conferences of Evangelical pastors a majority opposed the plan, and the Gospel Association urged its people to remain with the Church. But in 1923—24 seven pastors resigned from the state church and organized Lutheran free churches. Because of disagreement concerning Christ's active and passive obedience two of the pastors and one half of the congregations now have their own communion. Remaining pastors and congregations organized in 1928 the Luth. Free Church of Finland, which is affiliated with the Missouri Synod.

6. Sweden lost Finland to Russia in 1809. But the czars allowed Finland her own laws and religion. Gaining her independence in 1917, Finland became the most progressive and democratic

of European nations. Attacked by Russia in World War II, she was forced to make enormous sacrifices and then to pay exorbitant reparations. She is now under Communist surveillance.

7. Population of Finland is about four million (1948). Of these 96% are members of the Luth. State Church; 2% are Greek Orthodox; 2% are Reformed; 2,000 are Roman Catholics, and 2,000 are Jews. Foreign mission work is conducted in Africa, China, and Japan. First complete Finnish Bible was published in 1642, latest completely revised translation in 1938. First hymnbook for churches appeared in 1593, the latest in 1938. There are five bishoprics. The archbishop's seat, now occupied by Aleksi Lehtonen (1948), is in Turku. Each diocese is divided into provost-districts and is governed by a body consisting of bishop, chief provost, 2 assessors, secretary, and notary. Freedom of religion obtains, and continued pressure is exerted for the complete separation of Church and State.

8. A reflection of Lutheranism in Finland is seen in church organizations of Finnish origin in the United States and Canada. Laestadians, known here as Apostolic Lutherans, are the oldest and perhaps the largest Finnish religious group in America, but they are divided into several factions, as are their brethren in Finland, with whom they are in close contact. Suomi Synod, following the example of the State Church of Finland, is tolerant of all doctrinal movements and tendencies of the Mother Church. The National Church, organized by congregations that wanted to preserve a democratic form of church government and a right to call only doctrinally sound Evangelical pastors, maintained friendly relations with the Gospel Association, calling their pastors and supporting their foreign mission work. These relations ceased, however, when the Association took a hostile attitude toward the Free Church movement. Since then its interests have been with the Missouri Synod and the Synodical Conference.

GAA

Elis Bergroth, *Suomen Kirkko* ("The Church of Finland," 2 vols.); Lauri Takala, *Suomen Evankelisen Liikkeen Historia* ("The History of the Evangelical Movement in Finland," 2 vols.); A. A. Uppala-Wegelius, *Kirkkokysymys Raamatun ja luterilaisen tunnustuksen valossa* ("The Question of the Church in the Light of Scripture and the Lutheran Confessions").

Finney, Charles Grandison (1792 to 1875). Congregationalist; b. at Warren, Conn.; pastor of Broadway Tabernacle, New York City, revivalist, attaching importance to anxious seat; president of Oberlin College; d. at Oberlin, Ohio; author.

Finnian (d. ca. 550). Irish saint; founder of churches, monasteries, and schools; famous as educator.

Finnish Lutherans in America. 1. Finns started to come to America in the 1860's. The pioneer pastors were: A. E. Beckman (worked in Michigan, 1876—83); J. J. Hoikka (ordained 1883); J. K. Nikander (came to America in 1885; d. 1919); K. L. Tolonen (came to America in 1888); William Eloheimo (came to America in 1888).

2. Under the leadership of J. K. Nikander and other pastors named above *The Finnish Evangelical Lutheran Church (Suomi Synod)* was organized at Calumet, Mich. (March 25, 1890). Seventeen laymen participated in the meeting, and nine congregations were represented when the constitution was adopted. In 1896 this synod founded the Suomi College and Theological Seminary at Hancock, Mich. The official organ is the *Paimen Sanomia* (founded 1888). In 1920 it adopted a plan of cooperation with the United Lutheran Church. It supports the work of the Foreign Mission Society of Finland and stands close to the Finnish State Church theologically. Presidents: J. K. Nikander (1890—98), K. L. Tolonen (1898 to 1901), J. K. Nikander (1901—19), J. Wargelin (Jan. to June, 1919), Alvar Rautalahti (1919—22), A. Haapanen (1922—50), J. Wargelin (1950—). Statistics (1951): 86 pastors, 167 congregations, 21,948 communicant members.

3. The *National Evangelical Lutheran Church* was organized in 1898 under the leadership of W. A. Mandellöf. Its official publication, the *Auttaja,* is published at Ironwood, Mich. It carries on home mission work in several states and Canada.* Formerly it supported the Gospel Association of Finland, but its interests later were with the Missouri Synod and Synodical Conference. Presidents: J. W. Eloheimo (1898—1900), W. A. Mandellöf (1900—05), Wm. Williamson (1905—08), K. G. Rissanen (1908—13), P. Wuori (1913—18), A. Vasunta (1918—22), K. E. Salonen (1922—23), M. Wiskari (1923 to 1931), G. A. Aho (1931—53), J. E. Nopola (1953—). Statistics (1951): 28 pastors, 66 congregations, 5,489 communicant members.

4. The members of the *Finnish Apostolic Lutheran Church* are followers of Lars L. Laestadius.* They do not believe in an ordained ministry, insist on conversion through auricular confession, have no college or seminary, no mission fields, no publication house. The name was first adopted by a congregation in Calumet, Mich. (1879). A loose organization was formed in the late twenties, which conducts yearly meetings. Since that time the following have served as presidents: G. A. Marsh, John Oberg, Andrew Mickelsen. Statistics (1947): 20 ordained pastors, 60 congregations, 16,293 baptized members.

For additional information and historical background see *Finland, Lutheranism in.*

Neve-Albeck, *History of the Lutheran Church in America,* Luth. Lit. Bd., Burlington, Iowa, 1934 (pp. 330 to 334); John I. Kolehmainen, *The Finns in America,* Finnish Luth. Book Concern, Hancock, Mich., 1947.

Fioretti (It. "Little Flowers"). A collection of truth and legend concerning St. Francis.*

Fire Baptized Holiness Church of God of the Americas. See *Holiness Bodies, 2.*

Fire Worshipers. Name applied to Zoroastrians (see *Zoroastrianism*) and their modern representatives, the Parsees. Fire worship formed an element in many primitive religions, but in the old religion of Iran, especially as developed by Zoroaster, it is a very conspicuous characteristic. In Parsee temples a holy fire is perpetually burning, which is most carefully guarded, and protected from contamination. The modern Parsees, however, deny that they are fireworshipers and say that they regard fire merely as an emblem or manifestation of the Deity.

Firmelung. See *Confirmation.*

Firmilian. Bishop of Caesarea in Cappadocia; disciple of Origen; opponent of heretical baptism and of the supremacy of the Roman bishop; d. 269 in Tarsus.

First Book of Discipline. See *Presbyterian Bodies, 1.*

First Century Christian Fellowship. See *Buchmanism.*

First Dogmatic Constitution of the Church of Christ. See *Roman Catholic Confessions,* E 3.

First General Conference of Lutherans in America. See *Diets, Lutheran.*

Fischer, Albert F. W. (1829—96). Luth. pastor at Gross-Ottersleben near Magdeburg; edited *Kirchenlieder-Lexicon* (1878—79); founded *Blaetter fuer Hymnologie* (1883), a magazine devoted to hymnody.

Fischer, Christoph (Vischer) (1520 to 1597 or 1600). *Propst* (provost) at Jueterbogk; preacher at Schmalkalden, Meiningen, Celle, Halberstadt, and finally at Celle; wrote: "Wir danken dir, Herr Jesu Christ, dass du fuer uns gestorben bist."

Fischer, Ludwig Eberhard (1695 to 1773). Pastor of St. Leonhard in Stuttgart; finally chief court preacher and member of the consistory; wrote "Herr Jesu, der du selbst von Gott als Lehrer kommen."

Fish. Used extensively in early Christian symbolism. The letters of the Greek word *Ichthus* (fish) are the first letters of the Greek words for "Jesus Christ, God's Son (and) Savior."

Fisher, George Park (1827—1909). Congregationalist; b. at Wrentham, Mass.; professor of divinity and college preacher, Yale College, 1854—61; professor of ecclesiastical history, Yale Divinity School, 1861 (retired 1901); president of American Historical Association 1898; d. at Litchfield, Conn.; wrote: *History of the Reformation* (1873, new ed. 1906); *History of Christian Doctrine;* etc.

Fiske, John (1842—1901). Lecturer on philosophy and history, later assistant librarian at Harvard; conceived of evolution as caused by immanent God and tending toward the highest spirituality of man (human soul related to God); wrote *Outlines of Cosmic Philosophy* and other religio-philosophical works.

Fitch, Eleazer Thompson (1791 to 1871). Prof. at Yale; his *Two Discourses on the Nature of Sin* (1826) laid the groundwork for the New Haven Theology.

Five Articles of Deism. See *Deism,* III.

Five Mile Act. See *Presbyterian Bodies, 2.*

Five Points of Arminianism. See *Arminianism.*

Five Points of Calvinism. See *Calvinism*.

Fjellstedt, Peter (1802—81). Swedish pastor; missionary to India and Turkey (1828—40); in Sweden (1841—81); wrote a popular Bible commentary; friend of Augustana Synod in America.

Flabellum. In Roman Catholicism, a fan carried before the Pope; in Greek Catholicism, a fan waved to keep flies from the chalice.

Flacius (Vlacich), Matthias (1520 to 1575). Called *Illyricus* from the land of his birth; b. 1520. When at seventeen he wanted to study theology, his uncle, Baldo Lupetino, provincial of the Franciscans, pointed him to Luther as the restorer of the true Gospel. He came to Wittenberg in 1541. After intense spiritual struggles, made known to Bugenhagen and Luther, during which he was prayed for in church, he found peace of soul through justification by faith in Christ, and to this doctrine he dedicated his life. Professor of Hebrew in 1544. On bended knees and with tears he begged Melanchthon and the rest of his colleagues not to give in to the *Interim*, which he then attacked in writings. In 1549 he left Wittenberg and at Magdeburg earned his bread and continued his attacks on the *Interim* and the Adiaphorists (see the articles) and saved true Lutheranism. When George Major at Eisleben preached the necessity of good works for salvation, Flacius promptly sprang to the defense of salvation by grace alone; see *Majoristic Controversy*. When in 1552 Osiander came out with his Romanizing doctrine of justification and Duke Albrecht of Prussia tried to win the breadless and homeless Flaccius as an ally against Melanchthon, Flacius sided with Melanchthon against Osiander and thus proved that his fight was one of conscience, not personality. In a few months he wrote seventeen works to uphold the forensic doctrine of satisfaction and imputation in justification (see *Osiandrian Controversy*). In 1553 Caspar Schwenkfeld promulgated his "inner word" and his distinction between God's Word and Holy Scripture. Flacius defended the identity of the Word and Scripture and the efficacy of the means of grace from 1554 to 1557. In 1557 Flacius was called to the University of Jena. His efforts for peace with Melanchthon were futile, because Melanchthon would not condemn his error in the *Interim*. In 1558 Flacius attacked Pfeffinger's doctrine on Free Will and in the heat of debate with Victorin Strigel, in 1560, made the hasty statement that original sin belonged to the substance of human nature and was not merely a so-called "accident." Even such friends as Hesshusius and Wigand reproved him for this error. In 1571 he modified the statement. While Art. I of the Formula of Concord rejects this so-called Manicheism, it upholds the monergism of the Holy Ghost in the conversion of man as taught by Flacius. In the course of the controversy, 1561, Flacius was deposed, and escaped arrest by fleeing to Regensburg, where he continued his literary work. In 1566 he went to Antwerp, where William of Orange had granted religious liberty to the Calvinists and the Lutherans. The next year war drove him out, and he wandered about till he found an asylum in a cloister at Frankfurt, where the prioress, Catherine von Meersfeld, gallantly protected him until he died.

Alongside his polemics Flacius was also a great church historian. He projected the monumental *Magdeburg Centuries*, a general church history by centuries, with special reference to the rise and growth of Antichrist. In the *Catalogus Testium Veritatis* he gathered about 400 witnesses to the truth of the Gospel during the preceding ages. In his *Clavis* and *Glossa* he was a thorough reformer of the Biblical studies.

Flack, J. V. B. See *Christian Union*.

Flagellants. People who, inspired by religious zeal and fanaticism, whip themselves or inflict other severe corporal tortures upon themselves in the mistaken notion that they are thereby crucifying their own flesh, keeping their spirit in subjection, and earning some form of merit in the sight of God. Fanatics of this kind are found even in the early centuries, but the movement assumed the proportions of a religious epidemic in the thirteenth century, when a pilgrimage of these fanatics swept through northern Italy, crossed the Alps, and finally spent itself in Germany and the Slavic countries. In 1348—49 a similar epidemic occurred, which extended even to England. The flagellants usually founded fraternities, whose members bound themselves to observe a penitential season. At such times the deluded people wandered far and wide through the country, striking their bare backs with scourges and cudgels and inflicting worse tortures. Movements of this nature have been observed periodically up to the present time, the fanaticism of the flagellants often assuming alarming proportions. Thus the authorities of one of our southwestern States were compelled to stop the actions of some flagellants when it was found that they did not shrink even from crucifixion. It is practiced in the Philippines even today.

Flagon. See *Church Furniture,* 3.

Flatt, Johann Friedrich (1759 to 1821). B. at Tübingen, where he was professor of philosophy, 1785, and of theology, 1792, promoted, 1798. An enthusiastic Kantian, he was an exponent of the Biblical supranaturalism of the older Tübingen school, together with G. Chr. Storr, F. S. Sueskind, and K. C. Flatt.

Flattich, Johann Friedrich (1713 to 1797). Swabian preacher and pedagog, disciple of Bengel; chiefly known as a teacher; a striking personality, original humor, and a keen and accurate judgment, together with sincerity, uprightness, and courage, made him a remarkable character.

Fleischmann, Philipp. B. Jan. 22, 1815, in Regensburg, Bavaria; itinerant minister among the "separated Lutherans" in Pomerania and Hesse-Nassau; one of the founders and, temporarily, director of the Teachers' Seminary of the Missouri Synod; served several congregations; d. as pastor in Kendallville, Ind., Sept. 11, 1878.

Flesh. In Scripture, *flesh* stands for the material part of the human person, Ps. 16:9; 84:2; Rom. 13:14, especially when viewed in its weakness as compared with the divine essence, Ps. 78:39; 1 Pet. 1:24. In this sense the Incarnation was an assumption of the flesh. John 1:14. But the characteristic idea connected with *flesh* is an ethical one, denoting man's incapacity for good or, positively, the depravity and corruption of his entire nature (Rom. 6:19; 7:18; 8:3). This sinful flesh remains with the Christian even after conversion and hinders the efficacy of the divine Law, so that, although the Law gains the assent of the inner man, the spiritual, regenerated nature of man, it is not fulfilled because of this tendency of the flesh toward what is forbidden. See *Sanctification.* This fleshly (carnal) mind is enmity against God, Rom. 8: 4, 5, is the source and seat of all evil passions, and hence must result in death, Rom. 7:5; 8:8, 9. Hence, too, the

lusts and works of the flesh are opposed to holy, divine impulses and actions. Gal. 5:16; Eph. 2:3, 4. To crucify the flesh is the great object of the Christian life, attainable alone through the Spirit of Christ, who dwells in the regenerated. Gal. 5:25; Rom. 8:13.

Fletcher, John William (1729—85). Theologian; associate of John Wesley; author of many works on Arminianism.

Fliedner, Fritz (1845—1901). Son of Theodor Fliedner; studied at Halle, Tuebingen; while chaplain to legation of Germany in Spain he sought to evangelize that country; wrote life of Luther, Livingstone, and others, also hymnbook and other literature in the Spanish language.

Fliedner, Theodor (1800—64). B. in Epstein; studied theology at Giessen, Goettingen, and Herborn; pastor at Kaiserswerth, 1821—1849. Founded institution of deaconesses, Rhenish-Westphalian Prison Society, 1826; refuge home (10×10 feet) for discharged female prisoners; first infant school of Germany at Duesseldorf and Kaiserswerth, 1836; opened first Protestant deaconess house at Kaiserswerth, October 13, 1836; added a hospital and training school, 1846; an orphanage for girls, 1842; a retreat for female sufferers from mental diseases, 1847; personally established a deaconess house at Pittsburgh, Pa., 1849; hospitals at Jerusalem, Constantinople, and Alexandria; training schools at Smyrna, Jerusalem, and Beirut. When he died, there were 32 "mother houses" and 1,600 deaconesses. Issued a deaconess journal, *Armen- und Krankenfreund,* 1849. Established a deacons' house at Duisburg, 1849. Fliedner was weak in body, strong in spirit, sober in judgment, humble in character, untiring in service. See *Charities, Christian.*

A. R. Wentz, *Fliedner the Faithful,* Bd. of Pub. of the United Lutheran Church, Philadelphia, 1936.

Flitner, Johann (1618—78). Precentor, then diaconus at Grimmen, near Greifswald; town preacher near the end of his life; composed hymns during leisure years at Stralsund; wrote "Jesu, meines Herzens Freud'."

Flood, The. The deluge sent in the time of Noah as a judgment on the antedeluvians for their sins. The fountains of the deep were opened, and the rains poured down for forty days and nights. The waters covered all the high hills and prevailed for 150 days. All flesh (man, beast, bird, and creeping things) on the earth perished. Only Noah and the people and animals with him in the ark survived (Genesis 6 to 8).

The traditions of almost all primitive religions and. cultures speak of a catastrophe caused by a great flood. Especially the account of the Babylonians (Gilgamesh Epic) has been compared with the Genesis account. Extensive evidence has been sought by Christian apologists to substantiate the Biblical account.

A. M. Rehwinkel, *The Flood*, CPH, 1951.

Florence, Council of. A continuation of the Council of Basel. At this council the Eastern Church agreed to the *filioque* in the Creed and the act of union was drawn up.

Florida, Synod of. See *United Lutheran Church, Synods of,* 4.

Florilegia. Collections of choice sayings from the Fathers circulated especially during the Middle Ages to serve doctrinal, ethical, or homiletical purposes. See *Patristics.*

Flourney, Theodore (1854—1920). Prof. at Geneva; worked especially in the field of religious psychology.

Fluegel, Otto (1842—1921). German philosopher of the Herbartian school; opposed monism; held that God is finite.

Foertsch, Basilius (d. 1619). Wrote the devotional book *Geistliche Wasserquelle;* author of a number of hymns including "Heut triumphieret Gottes Sohn" and "Ich weisz, dass mein Erloeser lebt, obgleich der Feind," etc.

Font. A receptacle for the water used at baptism.

Foot Washing. A ceremony commonly performed in ancient times and particularly in the Orient as a duty of hospitality (Gen. 18: 4; Luke 7: 8) which was invested with a spiritual meaning by Christ when He washed the feet of His disciples (John 13: 4-20), thereby giving them a lesson in humility. Jesus, during the foot washing stresses inward purity (v. 10; cf. Luther, St. L. Ed., XIII: 1933). In early times the ceremony was legalistically observed. In the Middle Ages it was observed at the installation of bishops and princes. It was performed by the emperors of Austria annually to recent times. Sects in America (e. g., Mennonites) still

practice it. Luther held that the original act is repeated in our acts of humility, kindness, love, and service toward fellow men (St. L. Ed., XIII: 322 ff.).

Forbearance. See *Patience.*

Foreign Missions Conference of North America. See *Union Movements,* 13.

Foreign Missions, History of. See the various countries.

Foreign-Tongue Missions (*Fremdsprachige Missionen*). A term denoting mission work carried on among descendants of persons from European countries who have immigrated into the United States. It is a purely technical term. Slovaks, Hungarians, Italians, Serbs, Letts, Lithuanians, Persians, Poles, and members of other nationalities are ministered to spiritually in their own native tongue by the Missouri Synod and by other religious organizations, and in order to characterize this branch of home mission activity, the term was coined.

Foreknowledge, Divine. The attribute of God by which He through one simple and eternal act of His mind knows all things which have been, are, and shall be, or even in any way can be, that is, all things which are conditionally future or possible (1 Sam. 2: 3; 1 John 3: 20; 1 Kings 8: 39; Ps. 7: 9; 34: 15; 139: 1; Prov. 15: 3).

Foreordination. See *Predestination.*

Foreseen Faith. See *Intuitu Fidei.*

Forged Decretals. See *Pseudo-Isidorian Decretals.*

Forgeries. See *Apocrypha.*

Forgiveness of Sins. The act of divine grace by which, in virtue of the merits of Christ's atonement, appropriated by faith, God frees the sinner from the guilt and the penalties of his sins. The Law is vindicated by the atonement of Christ, and the penalty of sin is paid. God offers free and full forgiveness to all (2 Cor. 5: 18) and such forgiveness is received by all who believe in Christ as their Mediator and Redeemer (Acts 5: 31; 1 John 2: 12; Rom. 3: 24; Is. 1: 18; 55: 1, 2). Viewed from another angle, this transaction is called justification, not in the sense that the person justified is morally just, but just with respect to the Law and the Lawgiver. In other words, the person who has received pardon is justified in the sense that he is declared innocent, being placed in a position of not having broken the Law at all and not deserving of punishment. See *Justification*. Such forgiveness is granted believers as a free gift, not because of any merit or desert of their own. The whole scheme is one of mercy, to which the sinner makes his appeal and which has before the world was made provided a Redeemer who should reconcile men to God (John 3:16).

R. C. Rein, "Forgiveness of Sins," in *Abiding Word*, CPH, 1946, I, 146—167; District essays: Minnesota, 1915; Southern, 1904.

Form Criticism. See *Isagogics, 3*.

Formal Principle. The *principium cognoscendi* or formal principle of the Lutheran Church is that the Holy Scriptures are the source and norm of all doctrine. See *Grace, Means of*, I 4. W. H. T. Dau, "The Heritage of Lutheranism," *What Lutherans Are Thinking*, Wartburg Press, Columbus, 1947.

Formalism. A term applied to externalism, or undue emphasis placed upon external rules of morality or religion.

Formgeschichtliche Schule. See *Isagogics, 3*.

Formosa. Area, 13,890 square miles; population, 7,647,703 (1950). An island off the China coast, formerly belonging to China, taken by Japan, 1895; returned to China after World War II. Dutch missionaries, notably Junius and Candidius, worked here in the 17th century until expelled by the Chinese pirate Koxinga in 1661. The English Presbyterian Church began work in 1865 in Taifanfu, the Canadian Presbyterians in 1872 in Tanisui. After the closing of China to missions, many missions began work in Formosa. The Lutheran Church — Missouri Synod established work in 1952. Latest available statistics in 1952: approximately 18,000 communicants, 46 foreign workers; 72 ordained, 132 not ordained workers.

Forms, Book of. See *Agenda*.

Formula of Concord. See *Lutheran Confessions*, C 2.

Formula pii consensus. See *Lutheran Confessions*, A 5.

Fornication. See *Marriage*.

Forsander, Nils. B. Gladsax, Sweden, Sept. 11, 1846; grad. Augustana Coll.

and Theol. Sem., Paxton, Ill., 1872; D. D., 1894; professor Augustana Theol. Sem., 1899—1926; editor *Augustana Theological Quarterly*, 1900—12; contributed to *Korsbaneret* and other Swedish Lutheran periodicals; author: *Augsburgiska Bekännelsen; Life Pictures from Swedish Church History; Olavus Petri; The Marburg Colloquy; Lifsbilder ur Augustana Synodens historia*. D. Aug. 21, 1926.

Fortunatus, Venantius (530—609). B. in Italy; moved to Gaul (565); bishop of Poitiers (597); wrote hymns rich in romantic symbolism which mark the beginning of the medieval way of thought (*Vexilla Regis prodeunt, Agnosce omne saeculum, Salve, festa dies*). See *Hymnology*.

Fortunetelling. Under this heading are included all attempts, no matter how successful and no matter by what means obtained, to uncover the future, although revelations pertaining to the past are also commonly included in the term. On account of the unwarranted inquisitiveness of man and his desire to lift the veil of the future, attempts have ever been made to find ways and means of foretelling future events. Long lists of omens and portents were kept among various peoples, and certain individuals were regarded as having the special faculty of looking into the future and of prognosticating events. Sometimes fortunetellers made use of shrewd guesses, based upon a reading of the character and on the past history of the person concerned. In many cases the law of averages is applied. In still other cases the aid of the devil and of evil spirits is openly invoked. The future was alleged to be foretold from the flight of birds, from the position of the intestines in a slaughtered sacrificial animal, from the coincidence of minor happenings in a person's life, from the appearance of water or other liquids in sacred cups and other vessels, from the manner in which a deck of cards falls when dealt, from the configuration of the lines in a person's hands, from crystal globes, and from many other arbitrary factors. — The Lord condemns all attempts of this kind in unmistakable words, as when He forbids the use of divination, the observing of times and of the cry of birds, etc. (Lev. 19:26; Num 23:23; Deut. 18: 10, 11.) When Saul first became king, he cast out all those that had familiar spirits and the wizards out of the land, (1 Sam. 28:9), the witch at Endor being apparently the only person of that kind left in the country. But at a later date the Prophets of the Lord found it necessary to reprimand the people for their transgression of the Lord's command with regard to divination. Cp. Is. 44:25; Micah 3:7. Also 2 Kings 23:24; 21:6. As superstition has always existed in the world since the fall of man, so it has persisted also in our days. Interest in spiritualism and kindred subjects was stimulated by World War I, but was not much in evidence after World War II. Christianity takes an unequivocal stand against all such practices. See *Spiritualism.*

Forty-Hours Devotion. A service in the Roman Catholic Church in honor of the Eucharist which is performed while the host is on the altar and lasts forty hours.

Forty-Two Articles. See *Anglican Confessions,* 5.

Fossarians. 1. Grave diggers in the Early Church. 2. A hermit sect of the 15th century which observed its rites in ditches.

Fossum, Ludwig Olsen. B. June 5, 1879, at Wallingford, Iowa; studied at Ansgar Seminary and Luth. Seminary (United Norw. Church); ordained in 1902; organized Luth. Oriental Mission Society and became missionary at Soujbulak, Persia, 1910; District Commander of the Near East Relief at Erivan; reduced Kurdish language to writing and published a grammar, Lutheran Hymnbook, and Luther's Catechism in that language; published a work on Mohammedanism (in Norwegian); d. 1920.

Foster, Frank Hugh (1861—1935). Prof. at Pacific Theol. Sem., and Olivet College; leading scholar on New England Calvinism, of which he was an adherent in his earlier years.

Foster, George Burman (1858 to 1918). American Baptist theologian; prof. at Chicago University; important writings: *The Function of Religion in Man's Struggle for Existence; Christianity in Its Modern Expression.* While in his early years he held to a supernaturalistic theistic religion, he later championed naturalism.

Foundation of Faith. See *Fundamental Doctrines.*

Four Points. When the General Council was organized, all Lutheran bodies adopting its fundamental principles were asked to unite with it. The

Joint Synod of Ohio felt that un-Lutheran practices existed in the General Council and therefore asked the General Council at its Fort Wayne Convention (1867) to declare its position on four points: 1. Chiliasm; 2. Altar fellowship; 3. Pulpit fellowship; 4. Secret societies. The General Council was not prepared to answer at Fort Wayne (1867). In 1868 the Pittsburgh convention adopted answers drawn up under the leadership of C. P. Krauth. This *Pittsburgh Declaration* taught: "As regards Chiliasm . . . the General Council has neither had, nor would consent to have, fellowship with any synod which tolerated the 'Jewish opinions' or 'Chiliastic opinions' condemned in the XVII Article of the Augsburg Confession." "As regards secret societies . . . any and all societies for moral and religious ends which do not rest on the supreme authority of God's Holy Word, as contained in the Old and New Testaments — which do not recognize our Lord Jesus Christ as the true God and the only Mediator between God and man — which teach doctrines or have usages or forms of worship condemned in God's Word and the Confessions of His Church — which assume to themselves what God has given to His Church and its Ministers — which require undefined obligations to be assumed by oath, are un-Christian." "As regards the communion with those not of our Church we hold: That the principle of discriminating as over against an indiscriminate communion is to be firmly maintained. Heretics and fundamental errorists are to be excluded from the Lord's Table. The responsibility for an unworthy approach to the Lord's Table does not rest alone upon him who makes that approach, but also upon him who invites it." "As regards exchange of pulpits . . . no man should be admitted to our pulpits, whether of Lutheran name or any other, of whom there is just reason to doubt whether he will preach in pure truth of God's Word as taught in the Confessions of our Church. — Lutheran ministers may properly preach wherever there is an opening in the pulpit of other churches, unless the circumstances imply, or seem to imply, a fellowship with error or schism, or a restriction on the unreserved expression of the whole counsel of God."

Because the Declaration of the General Council regarding the "Four Points" was regarded unsatisfactory, the Ohio Synod refused to join, the

Iowa Synod withdrew after the first meeting, Wisconsin left in 1868, Minnesota and Illinois Synods in 1871, Michigan in 1887. Texas joined Iowa as a district in 1875. WGP

Four-Square Gospel, The. The International Church of the Four-Square Gospel was founded by the late Aimee Semple McPherson in Los Angeles, and organized in 1927. It is a typical Pentecostal sect. The four points which are said to constitute the Four-Square Gospel are: conversion, baptism of the Holy Ghost, including speaking in tongues,* divine healing,* the pre-millennial coming of Christ.

Fourier, Charles. See *Communistic Societies,* 5.

Fox, George. See *Friends, Society of.*

Fox Sisters. See *Spiritism.*

Foxe, John (1516—87). English martyrologist, who fled persecutions of Mary and wrote the famous *Acts and Monuments of These Latter and Perilous Days* while on the Continent.

Fra Angelico (Fra Giovanni de Fiesole; 1387—1455). The painter of mysticism over against the strong naturalism of the Florentine school; finest specimens of his art in the Monastery San Marco in Florence.

Fragment Hypothesis. See *Higher Criticism,* 13.

France (Gaul). Area: 212,659 sq. mi.; population: 42,400,000 (1950). 1. France was among the first of the European countries in which Christian churches were founded. At the beginning of the fourth century the entire province of Gaul had not only its Christian churches, but also regular bishoprics. Among the Franks, King Clovis, together with more than 3,000 of his men, embraced Christianity after the battle of Tolbiacum in 496. The Franks, who had embraced the Catholic faith, soon began to be regarded as the chief Catholic nation of Europe, although the establishment of the empire of Charlemagne for a while made France a part of the union of German nations. However, after the division of the empire in 843, France again became an independent state. As in Germany, so also in France, the kings were obliged to defend themselves against the encroachments of the Papal See. Louis IX, though so firmly attached to the Church as to be declared a saint after his death, nevertheless confirmed the right of the nation by the Pragmatic Sanction in 1269, the great paladium of the Gallican Church. In opposition to Pope Boniface VIII, who declared that everyone was a heretic who refused to believe that the king in temporal as well as spiritual matters was subject to papal power, the three estates of France convened in the General Diet (1302) and succeeded in maintaining the independence of the French kingdom. In 1303 the king of France succeeded in having a Pope elected who took up his residence at Avignon, where for more than a century (until 1408) the Papacy remained a tool in the hands of French kings. The Concordat, which Martin V proposed to France, was rejected in 1418 by the Parliament, which remained the steadfast defender of French liberty. France took a prominent part in all the great church movements of the Middle Ages, notably in the crusades, and within the French Church reformatory movements were time and again inaugurated for the purpose of restoring a purer form of Christianity or of overthrowing the Papacy. (Waldenses; Albigenses.)

2. Reformatory movements during the 16th and the following centuries were violently suppressed by long-continued and cruel persecutions. Nevertheless in many parts of France, especially in the South, the Reformation obtained a firm hold, and for many centuries the Huguenots maintained their religious independence. Henry IV, himself a Huguenot, on becoming king of France, changed his faith and became Catholic for political reasons. Under Louis XIV the Roman Church reached the zenith of its power and splendor. The French Revolution for a time seemed to sweep away the entire Church of France, the National Assembly, in 1790, decreeing that all ecclesiastical officers, under penalty of losing their office, should take an oath for the civil constitution of the clergy. Napoleon, on the contrary, regarded the establishment of the Roman Church as the religion of the State as necessary, and accordingly, in 1801, concluded a Concordat, by which, however, the Gallican liberties were preserved. In 1813 Napoleon, in a new Concordat, extorted some important concessions from the imprisoned Pope, and when the Pope revoked all he had done, Napoleon published a Concordat as the law of the empire on the very next day (March 25).

3. The kings of France who ascended the throne after the overthrow

of Napoleon, again recognized the Roman Church as the religion of the State, though they granted religious toleration to every form of public worship. The revolution of 1830 revealed the popular indignation against the Church, and although Louis Philippe made great concessions to the Church, Romanism lost the prerogative of being the religion of the State. The repeal of the Concordat and the Separation Law (December 11, 1905) radically changed the situation of the Church. This law, coming into force on Jan. 6, 1906, secured to the State the right of nominating bishops, repealed all State and municipal appropriations for public worship, abrogated all establishments of worship, the use of churches for divine service being permitted only by virtue of annual notifications to the civil authorities pending the time of their use. The Church, however, has complete freedom on the subject of its organization, its hierarchy, discipline, and liturgical arrangement.

4. The history of *French Protestantism* is a long record of conflicts with Romanism and of persecution at the hands of secular power controlled by it. In 1521 the University of Paris declared itself against the Reformation. In the same year, however, the first Protestant congregation was formed at Meaux, the bishop of the city, Briconnet, himself becoming a convert of Le Fevre and Farel, the most eminent of French preachers. In 1555 the first avowed French Reformed Church was established in Paris, and the First Synod of the First Protestant Church assembled privately in Paris, May 25, 1559. The Confession of Faith adopted at the First Synod consisted of 40 articles, which were strictly Calvinistic. In spite of the cruel persecution of the Calvinists, the Church continued to increase, so that Beza (who died in 1605) could count 2,150 churches in connection with the Protestant Church of France, some of which had 10,000 members.

5. The celebrated edict of January (1562) granted to the Huguenots provisionally the right to assemble for religious worship outside the towns. However, even against this trifling concession a number of parliaments, especially that of Paris, raised the strongest remonstrance. The Duke of Guise threatened to cut it with the edge of his sword and commenced hostilities the same night at Vassey, where a number of Huguenots were massacred. A bloody civil war followed, in which the Huguenots suffered heavy losses and which was ended by the Peace of St. Germaine (1570), in which the government gave to the Huguenots four fortified towns for the future. Upon this the Huguenots gained new hopes, especially since their chief defender, Henry of Navarre, was married to the king's sister. But, when all their chief men were assembled at Paris to celebrate the nuptials, the queen mother treacherously gave the sign for that bloody massacre known in history as the Night of St. Bartholomew, in which from 20,000 to 100,000 Protestants perished, among them the great Coligny. The Huguenots again rose in their despair and received new concessions in the Edict of Poitiers (1577). However, the Holy League, which had been organized by the Duke of Guise and his brother, compelled the king to revoke everything and take a pledge not to rest till the last heretic should be extirpated from France.

6. The assassination of the Duke of Guise and his brother by order of the king, led to the king's own assassination, upon which Henry of Navarre, who had been the head of the Protestants, ascended the throne; but only after he had joined the Roman Church (1593). By the Edict of Nantes (1598), which he declared irrevocable, freedom of faith and public worship, their rights as citizens, and great privileges as an organized political corporation, were granted to the Huguenots. After the assassination of this king (1610) the Protestants were again forced by persecution to take up arms in defense of their rights. Cardinal Richelieu disarmed them as a political party, though securing to them their former ecclesiastical privileges by the Act of Amnesty at Nimes (1629). About this time the number of the Huguenots had been reduced to only about half of what it was before the massacre of St. Bartholomew, and Louis XIV regarded it as his special mission to break the power of Protestantism in the State, and after protracted persecutions revoked the Edict of Nantes in 1685. During this time between thirty to forty thousand Protestants fled from France. Nevertheless, two million of the Reformed remained with no congregations except in the wilderness, and in 1744 they again had their first National Synod. Louis XV on May 14, 1724, issued the last great law against the Protestants, which enforced the most severe measures of Louis XIV. This attempt to

coerce the Huguenots into Catholicism only drove them farther away from it, and the provincial synods multiplied.

7. Antoine Court opened a school of theology at Lausanne, which continued to supply the Protestant Church with pastors till the time of Napoleon. After 1760 the principles of toleration began to prevail, and Louis XVI in November, 1788, published an edict of tolerance, which restored to the French Protestants their religious liberty. The Reformed French Church is divided into three groups: the Eglise Reformée Evangelique (orthodox), the Union d'Eglises Reformées de France (center), and the Eglises Reformées Unies (liberal).

8. In 1848 Frederick Monod (1794 to 1863) and others seceded from the State Church and in 1849 formed the Union des Eglises Evangéliques, generally called the Free Church. Lutheranism also found early adherents in France, some of whom suffered martyrdom for their faith; but the influence of Calvin soon prevailed. In 1648 Alsace and a number of other districts and towns in which the Lutheran Church was established either exclusively or partly, was ceded to France by the Peace of Westphalia. Religious liberty was guaranteed to the Lutherans and again confirmed by the Peace of Nymwegen in 1678. The congregations of the conquered German districts gradually coalesced into one Evangelical Lutheran Church of France. Since 1896 the Lutheran Church has maintained a mission in Madagascar.

Francis of Assisi, St.* (1182—1226). After a thoughtless youth, St. Francis dedicated himself to the imitation of Christ's voluntary poverty. Barefoot, in a coarse tunic, he preached repentance and brotherly love. A group of followers gathered around him, and he received papal approval of his methods. While Francis was in the Orient, his order was transformed by the hierarchy, and Francis afterwards gave himself over more and more to solitary life and imitation of Christ's suffering. Humble, gentle, and sincere, Francis is often regarded the most lovable figure in the history of the medieval church. See *Stigmatization; Franciscans.*

Popular legends concerning St. Francis are in *Fioretti* ("little flowers") which is extant in several translations. Best biographies are: L. Salvatorelli, *The Life of St. Francis of Assisi*, 1928; P. Sabatier, *Life of St. Francis of Assisi*

(tr. by Louise Seymour Houghton), Hedder & Stockton, London, 1924; J. Joergensen, *St. Francis of Assisi* (tr. by T. O'Conor Sloane), Longmans Green, London, 1912.

Francis, Benjamin (1734—1799). Studied at Bristol Baptist College; pastor at Horsley in Gloucestershire for forty-two years; author of many poetical compositions, among which: "In Loud, Exalted Strains the King of Glory Praise"; "Jesus, and Shall It Ever Be."

Francis de Sales (1567—1622). Bishop of Geneva, doctor of the Church, outstanding preacher. His *Introduction á la Vie Devote* is still popular among Roman Catholic laymen.

Franciscans. The followers of St. Francis, who, after receiving the papal blessing, were led to organize the first mendicant order. Their early years were marked by strict poverty, limited use of property, begging, humble service to all, and mission endeavors. Their intellectual activity did not equal that of the Dominicans, but they produced such theologians as Alexander of Hales, Bonaventura, Duns Scotus, and William of Occam. They rivaled the Jesuits in the Counter Reformation. For centuries the order was racked by disputes concerning the obligation of poverty; many of its members felt the arm of the Inquisition. In 1517, a split took place between the stricter faction (Friars Minor proper) and the moderate faction (Friars Minor Conventual). From the former went out the Friars Minor Capuchins. Today they are "united," but with "three distinct and independent branches." The female Franciscans are the Poor Clares. There is also a third order (Tertiaries).

Franck, Cesar (1822—90). Though of Belgian lineage, Franck is one of the great composers of France; his *Symphony in D Minor* is the only monumental symphony France has thus far produced. Franck taught organ at the Paris Conservatoire and devoted much of his life to teaching and composition; he served as organist of Ste. Clotilde in Paris for thirty-two years. Gounod was popular in Paris in Franck's day, and the genius of Franck was not recognized and appreciated. A mystical vein courses through much of his music, including his great organ compositions. His choral work "The Beatitudes" enjoys wide fame, though the work is not interesting throughout. Franck was a man of high ideals and profound religiosity, who never resorted to anything that was banal or in bad taste.

D. Ferguson, *A History of Musical Thought,* New York, 1948; P. H. Lang, *Music in Western Civilization,* New York, 1941; D. G. Mason, *From Grieg to Brahms,* New York, 1927.

Franck, Johann (1618—77). Studied at Koenigsberg, friend of Simon Dach and Heinrich Held, lawyer in 1645, burgomaster of Guben, his home town, in 1661; both secular and religious poetry, high rank as hymn writer, firm faith, deep earnestness, finished form, simplicity of expression; wrote: "Herr Jesu, Licht der Heiden"; "Schmuecke dich, o liebe Seele"; "Jesu, meine Freude."

Franck, Johann Wolfgang (1641 to after 1695). Perhaps the foremost composer of a pleasing and melodic type of Lutheran choral music known as the *cantiones sacrae.* Franck's compositions belonging to this category are well suited for the Lutheran church service and appeal to most classes of people. Franck was likewise a successful composer of operas. He died in Spain, where his operas had gained favor with Emperor Charles II. Some believe that he had been poisoned to death by a jealous rival composer.

S. Kuemmerle, *Enzyklopaedie der ev. Kirchenmusik,* Guetersloh, 1888.

Franck, Melchior (1573—1639). Believed to have written the hymn tune "Jerusalem, Thou City Fair and High"; prolific and highly talented composer of the Lutheran Church, who received much of his musical training from Hans Leo Hassler. He was a master of counterpoint, his music has strength of character and genuine musical worth, and he was among the first to write accompanied Lutheran church music. Outstanding also in the field of secular music, he towers above many of his well-known contemporaries. He was a court musician in Coburg from 1603 or 1604 until the end of his life.

G. Adler, *Handbuch der Musikgeschichte,* Frankfurt, 1924; F. Blume, *Die ev. Kirchenmusik,* Potsdam, 1931; P. H. Lang, *Music in Western Civilization,* New York, 1941.

Franck, Michael (1609—67). Studies interrupted by father's death, masterbaker at Schleusingen, then at Coburg; some of his hymns crude, but popular; wrote "Sei Gott getreu."

Franck, Salomo (1659—1725). B. at Weimar, March 6, 1659, probably educated at the University of Jena. He was secretary of Schwarzburg ducal administration, then of the consistory of Jena, and also of that in Weimar. He was a prolific poet. His hymns total 330. As a hymn writer he is distinguished for his ease, correctness, and adaptation to popular understanding and to congregational singing. He wrote texts for the cantatas of J. S. Bach. He died at Weimar, July 11, 1725.

Franck, Sebastian (1499—ca. 1542). At first a Lutheran, he later promulgated a mystical idealism, which attacked all systems bound by ecclesiastical rules. His *Chronica, Zeitbuch und Geschichtsbibel* was an attempt to show the vain presumption of the Catholic Church and all sects claiming to possess the right faith. Franck was opposed by Luther and Melanchthon.

Francke, A. G. G. B. Jan. 21, 1821, in Meinersen, Hannover, gained for service in America, ordained 1846, twice pastor at Concordia, Mo., pastor in Buffalo, 1856, in Addison, Ill., d. Jan. 3, 1879. Vice-President of Western District of Missouri Synod, president of the Board of the Addison Seminary, president of the Addison Orphan Asylum.

Francke, August Hermann (1663 to 1727). With Spener the foremost representative of Pietism; studied theology and ancient and modern languages, especially Hebrew, at Erfurt, Kiel, and Leipzig. Graduating 1685 at Leipzig, he lectured there for two years on Biblical Interpretation and with his friend Anton instituted the *collegium philobiblicum* for closer, devotional Bible study. Spending some time at Lueneberg as student and instructor, at Hamburg as teacher, and with Spener at Dresden, he returned 1689 to Leipzig, where his lectures aroused great interest, but also violent opposition as leading to pietistic self-complacency. Called as pastor to Hamburg in 1690, his sermons awakened deep interest, but after fifteen months his opponents brought about his banishment. Through Spener's influence he became pastor in Glaucha and professor at the University of Halle in 1692. Here he developed a most strenuous and successful activity as pastor, professor, educator, and organizer of charitable institutions; his orphanage, founded 1695, expanded into a cluster of educational and charitable institutions, sustained solely by faith. Under him Halle became the center of the Danish East Indian Mission; Ziegenbalg and Pluetschau, the first Lutheran missionaries in India, were trained there. Francke also carried on an enormous correspondence with individuals and societies throughout Germany and other countries on religious matters. His writings consist of hermeneutical, practical, exegetical, and polemical treatises; he also composed a small number of hymns. In him are exhibited great personal piety and marvelous zeal in philanthropical work; he appears in a less favorable light in his controversies with orthodox Lutheran theologians. See *Pietism*.

Francke, Gotthilf August (1696 to 1769). Son of A. H. Francke; educated at Halle; prof. at Halle (1726); cared for institutions of mercy established by his father; active in missions. American Lutheranism is indebted to him for supplying early Lutheran pastors, especially for the church in Pennsylvania.

Franckean Synod. Organized May 25, 1837, in Minden, N. Y., by a number of men of the Western Conference of the Hartwick Synod,* for whom the liberal position of that synod was not extreme enough. The Franckean Synod not only rejected the Augsburg Confession, but failed to declare its belief in some of the fundamental doctrines of the Bible, *e. g.*, the Trinity and the Deity of Christ. It held aloof from all other Lutheran synods until, in 1864, it was admitted to the General Synod. This led to the disruption of the General Synod and the founding of the General Council. Rev. Morris Officer of the Franckean Synod organized the Muhlenberg Mission in Africa in 1854. In 1908 the Franckean Synod, together with the Hartwick Synod and the N. Y. and N. J. Synod merged into the New York Synod of the General Synod. At the time of this merger it numbered 22 pastors, 31 congregations, and 2,329 communicants. See *United Lutheran Church, Synods of*, 18.

Constitution and Standing Ordinances of the Franckean Evangelic Lutheran Synod. Free Democrat Office, Norwich, N. Y., 1849.

Frank, Carl Adolf. Clergyman and editor; b. Feb. 28, 1846, Wimpfen, Germany; graduate of Concordia Seminary, St. Louis, Mo., 1868; pastor at Lancaster, Ohio, New Orleans, Zanesville, Ohio; professor at Columbus, Ohio, 1878—81; first editor of *Lutheran Witness*, 1881 to 1885; D. D., Concordia Seminary; d. as pastor in Evansville, Ind., Jan. 18, 1922.

Frank, Franz Hermann Reinhold von (1827—94). B. at Altenburg; d. at Erlangen. Studied at Leipzig, where under Harless he turned from rationalism to the Lutheran confessions and early Protestant theology; after 1857 professor of church history and systematic theology at Erlangen. He exercised a far-reaching influence as the dogmatician of the Erlangen theology.

Frank, John H. (1853—1915). Businessman of Milwaukee, member Grace Church; one of leading laymen of Wisconsin Synod. Helped found Milwaukee Lutheran High School, contributing liberally of his time and money.

Frankfort Recess. See *Lutheran Confessions*, C 1.

Franks, Saxons, and Other Germanic Nations, Conversion of. 1. Christianity may have been brought to Gaul, the present France, as early as the latter half of the first century, but there is no definite record of its establishment there until the second century. Noted men like Irenius Lugdunum (Lyons), Pothinus, and Benignus, friends and disciples of Polycarp, who, in turn, had been a disciple of John, spread the Gospel fairly well along the valley of the Rhone and into the interior. Somewhat later (316—400) came Martin, Bishop of Tours. His character, steeled by his experience as a soldier under Constantine, and his work were such that he succeeded in establishing Christianity among many of the Frankish tribes, also of northern and northwestern France, where it had hitherto been but imperfectly known and received. He was afterward made the patron saint of France, and St. Martin's Day was observed in other countries as well. In early days his tomb was a shrine, and his motto, *Non recuso laborem* (I will not draw back from the work), became a watchword for missionaries in all western Europe.

2. Mission work in what is now southern and western Germany was begun in the sixth century, when Fridolin, a missionary from Ireland, who had been in France, preached along the upper Rhine. Columban, also of Ireland, labored first in the valleys of the Vosges Mountains. When he became older, he moved still farther south and southeast, into Switzerland. He died at the monastery of Bobbio, in Italy, in 516. His work was continued by his disciple Gallus, who founded the village of St. Gall with its monastery and church.

3. Willibrord, known as the Apostle of Frisia, was a native of England, but he also studied in Ireland and started out from there to do his work. He labored in the extreme northwestern part of Germany and Holland. He died in 739. About Kilian, the Apostle of Wuerttemberg, very little is known outside the fact that he came from Ireland to preach the Gospel in southwestern Germany. This was in the eighth century. He died a martyr's death. Winfried (Winifred), or Boniface, often designated the Apostle of Germany, did his work between 716 and 755, chiefly in Thuringia, Hessia, and Franconia. His influence was very great, but, unfortunately, it rested largely upon the authority of the Pope, whom he visited several times. — The story of the conversion of Saxony is not altogether pleasant reading, for these people stubbornly resisted the invasion of the Christian religion, and Charlemagne * felt constrained to use force to subdue them, Wittekind, their king, finally accepting the Gospel. But their real conversion did not take place until they had received the poetical version of the New Testament, the so-called *Heliand,* by which the Gospel story was sung into their hearts. See also *Germany.*

Franzelin, John Baptist (1816—86). Jesuit, cardinal, outstanding Roman Catholic theologian; prof. at Roman college of Jesuits; papal theologian at Vatican Council; most noted work: *De Divine Traditione et Scriptura.*

Franzen, F. M. See *Sweden, Lutheran Church in,* 4.

Fraternities (Greek letter societies). Students' societies at universities, colleges, and high schools, the Greek letters designating different fraternities and standing for Greek words or phrases, often expressing a moral sentiment. They were nominally secret societies, having individual badges, coats of arms, flag, etc. They have rituals, which are usually based on Christian and pagan sources. Most fraternities are organized on a national basis with chapters at individual institutions. Chapter houses are often owned by the alumni.

The earliest fraternity, Phi Beta Kappa (organized at William and Mary, 1776) became purely honorary in 1826.

While the fraternities are influential at many institutions, they were never permitted at a few colleges and universities. Princeton has only local clubs, and local chapters are more influential at Harvard than the national organizations. See *Students, Spiritual Care of.*

Baird, *Manual of American Fraternities,* J. T. Brown, N.Y. (11th ed., 1927).

Frederick I. See *Norway, Lutheranism in,* 1; *Denmark, Lutheranism in,* 2.

Frederick III. See *Reformed Confessions,* D 2; *Frederick the Wise; Frederick the Pious.*

Frederick IV. King of Denmark (1699—1730); patron of missions; founded *East India Mission* at Tranquebar (1706) and *Collegium de promovendi cursu Evangelii* (1714).

Frederick August II, the Strong (1670—1733). Elector of Saxony, abjured Lutheran faith and joined the Roman Catholic Church to secure the Polish crown. His people, however, including the Electress herself, refused to follow their ruler and exacted of him a confirmation of all their rights and privileges, besides virtually depriving him of all ecclesiastical authority, as exercised by his Protestant ancestors.

Frederick Francis II (1823—83). Advanced cause of Lutheranism in Mecklenburg-Schwerin; made the Church independent of Ministerium (1849); aided Kliefoth in carrying out Lutheran ideals.

Frederick, J. See *Immanuel Synod.*

Frederick (III) the Pious (1515 to 1576). Elector of Palatinate; educated a Roman Catholic; won for Lutheranism by his wife; when controversies arose between strict Lutherans, Melanchthonians, and Calvinists in the Palatinate (1559), Frederick inclined more and more to the Reformed position; dismissed Lutheran pastors and made Heidelberg Catechism the norm of doctrine.

Frederick the Wise. Elector of Saxony since 1486, was a pious prince, who had his daily Mass even when hunting and traveling. In 1493 he went to the Holy Land as a plain pilgrim to obtain absolution from guilt and penalty. At the court church in Wittenberg he gathered the greatest number of relics in Germany, 19,013 in 1520. In 1502 he founded the University of Wittenberg. He saw the need of a reformation of the Church in head and members. He would not be a candidate for Germany's imperial crown, and his influence made young Charles the emperor. He would do nothing against God's Word and so did not interfere with Luther's work, though likely without real knowledge of its true nature; and he would not let Luther be punished without a fair hearing, though he risked his own electoral hat. Strange to say, he and his most famous subject never met. Just before his death he took the Holy Communion in both kinds (the first German prince to do so) — thus finally, professing the Lutheran faith. He died in the troublous times of the Peasant War in 1525.

Free Christian Zion Church. See *Evangelistic Associations*, 15.

Free Church. See *Presbyterian Bodies*, 1.

Free Church of England. See *England, Subsequent History of the Church of*, 5.

Free Lutheran Conferences. A series of conferences attended by pastors, candidates, and laymen held at Columbus, Ohio (Oct. 1—7, 1856), Pittsburgh, Pa. (Oct. 29—Nov. 4, 1857), Cleveland, Ohio (Aug. 5—11, 1858), Fort Wayne, Ind. (1859). The Augsburg Confession was discussed at the meetings. Invitations to attend the conferences were extended to all who subscribed to the Augsburg Confession without reservation. The formation of the Synodical Conference may be safely listed as a fruit of the discussions. After suggestions for free Lutheran conferences had been made by various Lutheran periodicals, the College of Presidents of the Missouri Synod followed the precedent set by Walther and called for free Lutheran conferences (1949).

E. L. Lueker, "Walther and the Free Lutheran Conferences," *CTM*, XV: 529 to 563; W. G. Polack, "Lutheran Unity," *Luth. Witness*, June 14, 1949.

Free Magyar Reformed Church in America. See *Reformed Church*, 4 d.

Free Methodist Church. See *Methodist Bodies*, 4 b.

Free Presbyterian Church of Scotland (1893). See *Presbyterian Bodies*, 1.

Free Protestants. See *Evangelical Protestant Church of North America*.

"Free Salvation." See *Methodist Bodies*, 2.

Free Spirit, Brothers and Sisters of the. A name given to various lay religious organizations of the Middle Ages which practiced personal piety and held that they were free from clerical authority. Their theology, quietistic and pantheistic mysticism, seems to have developed from the school of St. Victor.

H. Haupt, "Free Spirit, Brethren of the," *The New Schaff-Herzog Encyclopedia of Religious Knowledge*, 1909 (IV: 380).

Free Will. The Scriptural doctrine concerning the freedom of the human will stands in close connection with the doctrine concerning original sin, and it is from the viewpoint of original sin that the doctrine of the freedom of the human will after the Fall must be studied. While the Scripture emphatically declares that man, also after the Fall, continues to be a responsible moral agent, who in earthly matters, to some extent, may exercise freedom of will, it, nevertheless, asserts that "natural man receiveth not the things of the Spirit of God, neither can he know them" (1 Cor. 2: 14); that man, by nature, "is dead in trespasses and sins" (Eph. 2: 1); that "the carnal mind is enmity against God" (Rom. 8: 7); and that "no man can say that Jesus is the Lord but by the Holy Ghost" (1 Cor. 12: 3). Accordingly, the Scriptures deny to man, since the Fall and before his conversion, freedom of will in spiritual matters, and assert that his regeneration and conversion is accomplished entirely through the Holy Ghost by the Gospel. "God hath saved us, not according to our works, but according to His own purpose and grace" (2 Tim. 1: 9); "Turn Thou me, and I shall be turned" (Jer. 31: 18).

In accord with these words St. Augustine declares: "By the sin of Adam, in whom all men together sinned, sin and all the other positive punishments of Adam's sin came into the world. By it, human nature has been both physically and morally corrupted. Every man brings into the world with him a nature already so corrupt that he can do nothing but sin." As regards free will, he says: "By Adam's transgression the freedom of the human will has been entirely lost. In his present corrupt state, man can will and do only evil." This view of St. Augustine is in accord with the Scriptures, which declare that "it is God which worketh in you both to will and to do of His good pleasure" (Phil. 2: 13), and has been substantially adopted by the Lutheran Church, which, however, at the same time, rejects the postulates of fatalism. Cp. Formula of Concord, Art. II.

Opposed to the Scriptural doctrine, Pelagianism has held that by his transgression Adam injured only himself, not his posterity; that in respect to his moral nature every man is born in precisely the same condition in which Adam was created; that there is, therefore, no original sin; that man's will is free, every man having the power to will and to do good as well as the opposite; hence it depends upon himself whether he be good or evil. This extreme view of Pelagianism was modified by the Semi-Pelagianists and later on by the Arminians, who denied the total corruption and depravity of the human nature by the Fall, and admitted a partial corruption only. Thus their chief Confession says: "They, the Remonstrants [Arminians] do not regard original sin as sin properly so called, nor as an evil which, as a penalty in the strict sense of that word, passes over from Adam upon his posterity, but as an evil, infirmity, or vice, or whatever name it may be designated by, which is propagated from Adam, deprived of original righteousness, to his posterity." The Belgic Confession (Art. XV), which states the strictly *Reformed* doctrine, says: "Original sin is that corruption of the whole nature and that hereditary vice by which even infants themselves in their mothers' wombs are polluted, which, as a rule, produces every kind of sin in man and is therefore so base and execrable in the sight of God that it suffices to the condemnation of the human race." The Romanistic view is Semi-Pelagianistic. Cf. Bellarmin (*De Gratia Primi Hom.*): They [the Catholics] teach that through the sin of Adam the whole man was truly deteriorated, but that he has not lost free will nor any other of the *dona naturalia,* but only the *dona supernaturalia.* Opposed to Pelagianism, Semi-Pelagianism, Arminianism, and synergism, the Lutheran Confessions have always emphasized the total depravity of the human nature by the Fall and man's utter lack of freedom in spiritual matters since the Fall.

M. Luther, *Bondage of the Will* (translated by Henry Cole), Eerdmans, Grand Rapids, Mich., 1931.

Freedom, Christian. In general two theories of freedom obtain under this designation. The one seeks to express the rights of the individual, as defined and stimulated by the Renaissance * and 18th century liberal thought, in Christian terms. It describes the activity of man's self-expression and achievement of highest self-realization as a dynamic imparted by the Christian religion. The other concept adheres more closely to that of the New Testament. It regards man innately subject to the forces of death and the devil. His Christian freedom is that he has been liberated by Christ Jesus and freed to serve God. Parallel to this process is his freeing from the code of the Law as an obligation which he must fulfill in order to be godly, and his equipment with the Spirit of God to desire what God wills. This freedom does not imply the license to be ungodly, or unselfish, but is simply the will to concur with the will of God and to devote oneself completely to the welfare of man (Rom. 14:15; 1 Corinthians 8; Galatians 5). This concept was given a fresh and classic expression by Martin Luther, *The Freedom of the Christian Man.*

Freemasonry. 1. The Order of Ancient, Free, and Accepted Masons. Originally composed of honorary members (hence the Free and Accepted) of the guild of Masons during the Middle Ages — a privilege which was highly prized especially by those compelled to travel in foreign lands — the Masonic order was reorganized from a ritual with Christian elements to forms which eliminated what was specifically Christian and substituted the deism then current when the first lodge of "Speculative Freemasonry" was organized in London in 1717. The traditions which give the order a higher age than this are all legendary, if not pure invention. Knowledge of the order is obtained from its rituals, which have often been printed in the form of cypher codes for the convenience of Grand Masters instructing candidates in preparation for initiation. Public documents of Freemasonry are the annual Grand Lodge reports, various periodicals, the manuals published for the convenience of lodges, called Masonic Monitors or Ritualists, containing the charges, general regulations, and emblems, also much of the ceremonies of the order. A comparison of these public manuals with the printed rituals gives sufficient evidence for the character of the latter.

2. When Freemasonry became "speculative," it changed from trinitarian to deistic forms of worship and eliminated the name of Christ from Scripture passages and from its prayers, retaining the brotherhood of man and the father-

hood of God and the immortality of the soul, as religious doctrines, and offering these truths of religion, clothed in symbols, to those who come to its altars. The Bible is only one sacred book among many; the lodge rejects the notion that the religion of the Bible should possess a unique pre-eminence over the religion of other sacred books. Jesus Christ is not acknowledged as Savior, and the promise of eternal bliss is held out to all who follow the ethics of the Masonic Lodge. It is not possible to express the dependence on good works with greater definiteness than is done in the ritual of the Blue Lodge (the three degrees of Entered Apprentice, Fellow Craftsman, and Master Mason).

3. Due to the Wesleyan revival in England and the Great Awakening in the United States, with the influence of Protestantism still giving character to national life, Christianity, especially in the United States, was too strong to permit either Freemasonry or Oddfellowship to stress their deistic or anti-Church attitudes. While frankly anti-Christian in its French, German, and Italian branches, Freemasonry in England and the United States has always called itself a supporter of the morality and doctrines of Protestant Christianity. Very few candidates realize that they are joining an organization which is essentially antagonistic to the Christian belief in the inspiration of the Bible and the deity of Jesus Christ. Even in the more advanced degrees (of the American Rite, the Scottish Rite) and in the Mystic Shrine with its Mohammedan ritual, the anti-Christian features are only realized by those who make an independent study of the ritual and of the literature written by the spokesmen of the order. It is the pledge of a blissful hereafter coupled with the absence of all reference to repentance and to faith in Christ's atoning work, that has opened the eyes of many to the iniquity of Freemasonry.

4. The Order of DeMolay (organized 1919) has a ritual which in every sense reflects the anti-Christian elements of Masonry and which, in fact, is intended to serve as a training school for membership in the Masonic Order. The Rainbow Girls are a sorority of the same type. Freemasonry claims (1952) a membership of 3,726,744, and the Order of DeMolay approximately two million. See also *Eastern Star, Order of the.* See references under *Lodge.* TG

Freethinker. In general, one who, in questions of religion, recognizes no other authority than his own reason. In England, the term was applied to the deists of the 18th century, who still maintained a belief in a superior being, while the French freethinkers (Rousseau, Voltaire, Encyclopedists,* et al.) closely approached atheism. German free thought led to organization of *Freie Gemeinden.* See *Lichtfreunde.*

Freewill Baptists. See *Baptist Bodies,* 24.

Freie Gemeinde. See *Lichtfreunde.*

Frelinghuysen, T. J. See *Reformed Church,* 4 b.

French Catechism. See *Reformed Confessions,* A 7.

French Equatorial Africa, 959,256 sq. miles. Population, 4,406,520 (1952). A vast tract of land on the equator in Western Africa belonging to France, to which the former German Cameroons were added after World War I. A foreign staff of 360; 61,252 communicants. The Africa Inland Mission, and the Brethren (both British); the Erebro Missionsfoerening, Societe des Miss. Evangeliques de Paris (since 1892), Svenska Missionsfoerbundet, N. Am. Brethren, Adventists, Sudan Mission, United World Mission, Norske Misjonsforbund, Central Africa Pioneer Mission, Christian and Missionary Alliance, Church of Luth. Brethren, Co-operating Baptist Missions of N. America, Mid-Africa Mission, all carried on work. See *Missions, Bibliography.*

French Guiana. The Church of England carried on mission work since 1855. One foreign worker as of 1938. See *South America,* 14.

French Indo-China. A dependency of France in southeastern Asia, consisting of Annam, Cambodia, Cochin China, and Kwangchow, a total of 286,000 sq. mi. and some 27,030,000 (1949) people, mostly Malays and of Mongol stock. There were 109 foreign mission workers; 17,393 members; and 70 ordained and 126 not ordained native workers in 1952. The Christian and Missionary Alliance; the Adventists; Christian Missions in Many Lands; and C. I. M. Overseas Missionary Fellowship were active here. See *Missions, Bibliography.*

French Reformed Church. See *France,* 4.

French Revolution, The. See *France*, 2.

French Spirit. See *Norway, Lutheranism in*, 6.

French West Africa. In Central Africa, bordering on the Atlantic Ocean; 1,815,768 sq. mi., with a population of 16,535,000 (1949), mostly Mohammedan. It comprises: Senegal, with 1,764,000 people; French Guinea, with 2,180,000 people; Ivory Coast, with a population of 2,065,000; Dahomey, with 1,505,000 people; French Sudan, population of 3,177,000; Upper Volta; Mauritania, with a population of about 367,000; and Niger Territory, with a population of 2,029,000. It includes a large portion of the Sahara Desert. Among mission societies active here we find listed: Worldwide Evangelistic Crusade; Societe des Miss. Evangeliques de Paris; Church of England; Christian and Missionary Alliance; Gospel Missionary Union; Sudan Interior Mission; Methodist Missionary Society; Qua Iboe Mission; Paris Tabernacle Mission; the Adventists. Figures given are 226 foreign workers; total Christian community of 91,458. See *Missions, Bibliography*.

Frescobaldi, Girolamo (1583—1644) was organist of St. Peter's in Rome, and it is claimed that as many as twenty thousand people would attend his organ recitals. Frescobaldi was a contemporary of Sweelinck; with both of these men a new era began in organ history. Sweelinck was the father of the Lutheran North German School of Organists, while Frescobaldi became the father of the Roman Catholic South German School. His toccatas, ricercari, canzonas, fantasies, and fugues manifest his genius and a happy spirit of abandon not often found in the music of Roman Catholic composers. His *Fiori Musicali*, written for church services and played after the Credo and after Holy Communion, are, perhaps, his greatest and most famous works. G. Adler, *Handbuch der Musikgeschichte*, Frankfurt, 1924; G. Frotscher, *Geschichte des Orgelspiels und der Orgelkomposition*, Berlin, 1936; P. H. Lang, *Music in Western Civilization*, New York, 1941.

Fresenius, Johann Philip (1705—61). German pietist, loyal to Lutheran Confessions; pastor at Niederwiesen, Giessen, Darmstadt, Frankfort-on-the-Main; opposed Moravians; wrote *Sermons on the Epistles*, which were very popular; interested in American missions and aided the Stoevers in Virginia and Pennsylvania.

Freud, Sigmund (1856—1939). B. of Jewish parents in Moravia; studied at the University of Vienna; studied treatment of neuroses under Charcot in France; founder of psychoanalysis; developed techniques for treating hysteria and neuroses. In his *The Future of an Illusion* he describes religion as a neurosis of humanity in which the concept of God is a fictitious extension of the human father ideal as a refuge from fear. See *Psychology*, J 6.

Freund, Kornelius (1530—1591). Precentor in Borna near Leipzig, later in Zwickau; form of hymns rough, but contents full of depth; wrote: "Freut euch, ihr Menschenkinder all'."

Freylinghausen, Johann Anastasius. B. Dec. 2, 1670, at Gandersheim, Brunswick, Germany, was educated at Jena, Erfurt, and Halle. He became August Herman Francke's assistant at Glaucha, married his daughter, and later was his colleague at St. Ulrich's, in Halle, and eventually succeeded Francke to that pastorate and to the directorate of the Halle Institutions, which under him attained their highest development. He published *Neues Geistreiches Gesangbuch* (Halle) in 1704. He himself composed twenty-two hymn tunes. He died Feb. 12, 1739.

Freystein, Johann Burkhard (1671 to 1718), studied law at Leipzig and Jena, practiced principally at Dresden; influenced by Spener; wrote: "Mache dich, mein Geist, bereit." Edited *Choral Book* for England (1863).

Friar. A brother of a Roman Catholic mendicant order (Augustinian, Carmelite, Franciscan, Dominican).

Friars Minor. See *Franciscans*.

Frick, Wm. K. (1850—1918). Prominent in promoting General Council's English work in the Northwest, entered ministry 1783, professor at Gustavus Adolphus College 1883—89, pastor of Redeemer, Milwaukee, 1889—1918, president of the Synod of the Northwest 1894 to 1901, author of a life of Muhlenberg.

Fridolin. See *Germany*, 1.

Friedrich, Johannes (1836—1902). For a time, leader of the Old Catholics, priest, professor of theology at Munich, finally separated from the Old Catholics because he opposed the abolition of clerical celibacy. See *Old Catholics*.

Friend Societies. See *Child Care and Child-Placing Agencies.*

Friendly Islands. See *Tonga Islands.*

Friends of God. A name (cf. John 15:14, 15) applied chiefly to a group of mystics of the 14th century. It was used by mystics to express the freedom from servitude through Christ and elevation to true friendship with God. The Friends of God had no definite organization, but followed the teachings of Eckhardt, Tauler, Suso, Henry of Noerdlingen, Nicholas of Strassburg. Rulman Merswin (1307—72) was their chief author. The Benedictines gave him the cloister "Gruener Woerth," over which he ruled. His followers claim that Merswin obtained writings from the "Great Friend" whom they, however, failed to identify. Some of these writings, evidently falsely ascribed to a fictitious "Great Friend," are extant.

Friends, Society of. 1. Commonly called *Quakers,* a religious body founded by George Fox (1624—91) in the middle of the 17th century in England. Fox, who was a shoemaker by trade, was impressed by the lack of spirituality of both clergy and laity of his time and believed himself called to inaugurate a revival of primitive Christianity and to preach the doctrine of the "inner light," or the "Christ within." He began his ministry in 1647 and soon found followers, who first called themselves "Children of Truth," or "Children of Light," and finally adopted the name "Religious Society of Friends." Their number grew rapidly, including many of the higher classes, ministers of the Established Church, army officers, justices. The most noted converts were William Penn and Robert Barclay (1648 to 1690). During the first decades the Friends suffered much persecution, due not only to their holding public meetings, while other non-conformists met in secret, but also to their virulent polemics against existing churches and interruption of their services, refusal to take oaths, to pay tithes, and to take off their hats in court. In 1656 Quakerism was introduced into the New England States, but everywhere it met with persecution, especially by the Puritans in Massachusetts, who hanged a number of Quakers in Boston. Persecuted in England and New England, William Penn created an asylum for them in the colony of Pennsylvania, which he founded in 1682. Here they prospered and became known for their kind treatment of Indians and their efforts in behalf of the abolition of slavery.

2. *Doctrine.* Quakers deny that they are anti-Trinitarians. However, they reject such expressions as "person," "Trinity," etc., and use unbiblical modes of expression. Penn had a great admiration for Socinus, and though modern Quakers have expressed themselves more clearly, they still regard the writings of Penn and Barclay as authoritative. Other characteristic teachings are mainly the result of their doctrine of the "inner light." The outward redemption of Christ is not sufficient; there must also be present an inner redemption, which is imparted by the "inner light." Justification is not imputative, but is an inner change, followed by good works, which are necessary for salvation. God gives His Spirit without the means of His Word, and it is possible to be saved without having knowledge of the historic Christ. All those are members of the Church who are illuminated by the "inner light" and are obedient to it, be they Christians, Turks, Jews, or heathen. Baptism and the Lord's Supper, being "outward rites," are rejected. The services are completely non-liturgical. With covered heads they sit in their bare assembly rooms in silence, until someone, man or woman, is prompted to speak. If the Spirit prompts no one, the meeting ends in silence. God did not institute a special ministry. Anyone, man or woman, may teach, if called by the "inner light." By the middle of the 20th century, however, ministers have been employed, though they are not ordained and most of them do not receive any salary.

3. According to the theory of the "inner light," Quakers believe that each individual possesses a measure of the divine Spirit and is therefore entitled to deep reverence. Quakers believe in the brotherhood of man, the equality of all men, since they believe that every man, woman, and child has divine possibilities. Quakers have consistently advocated a broad humanitarianism and have been active in all phases of philanthropy, such as the abolition of slavery, prison reform, rehabilitation of the victims of war and other catastrophes. They are opposed in principle to any participation in war, capital punishment, litigation in court, and giving an oath. The church organization is simple, including monthly, quarterly, and yearly meetings. The term "monthly

meeting" designates a single congregation. Several congregations, or "monthly meetings," constitute the "quarterly meetings." The units of a larger district are known as "yearly meetings." See *Religious Bodies (U. S.), Bibliography.*

Fries, Jacob Friedrich (1773—1843). Prof. of philosophy at Heidelberg (1805), of physics at Jena (1816). Favored doctrines of Kant, but held that the mind can directly grasp transcendental truth through "Ahnung." Wrote: *System of Logic, System of Philosophy as an Evident Science,* and other works.

Frincke (Fricke), C. H. F. (1824 to 1905). B. at Bundheim, Brunswick; attended the teachers' seminary at that place; prepared for the ministry by Wyneken and Sihler; the first home missionary of the Missouri Synod, "without salary"; ordained 1847; pastor at White Creek, Ind., Indianapolis, Baltimore.

Fritsch, Ahasverus (1629—1701). Jurist in high positions at Rudolstadt, finally chancellor; full of enthusiasm for hymnology; wrote: "Der am Kreuz ist meine Liebe"; "Hoechster Koenig, Jesu Christ"; also arranged tunes.

Fritsche, Gotthold D. See *Australia, Lutheranism in.*

Fritschel, George John. B. May 24, 1867, at St. Sebald, Iowa; ed. Mendota school, Thiel College, Greenville, Pa.; bachelor's degree in 1886, master's in 1888; called as assistant to his father at Seminary in Mendota; studied at Univ. of Rostock, Erlangen, and Leipzig, 1889—92; pastor at Superior, Wis., 1892; professor in College of Texas Synod seminary at Brenham, Tex., 1892, for a number of years; also pastor at Galveston, Tex. Largely responsible for Texas Synod joining Iowa Synod. Pastor at Loganville and Fond du Lac, Wis. Professor at Wartburg Seminary, 1905—36. D. Oct. 5, 1941.

Fritschel, Gottfried. Prominent and scholarly theologian of the Iowa Synod; b. Dec. 19, 1836, at Nuremberg; studied under Loehe and J. T. Mueller, and at Erlangen, followed his brother Siegmund to America in 1857; became a leader in the Iowa Synod; professor of Exegesis and Dogmatics in Wartburg Seminary (St. Sebald, Iowa, and Mendota, Ill.); a prolific writer, a strong controversialist, and a regular contributor to the *Iowa-Kirchenblatt, Brobsts*

Monatshefte, and *Kirchliche Zeitschrift;* wrote: *Passionsbetrachtungen, Indian Mission in the 17th Century,* etc.; d. at Mendota, July 13, 1889.

Fritschel, Maximilian. B. 1868; son of Siegmund; educated at Thiel College, Wartburg Seminary, Rostock, Leipzig, and Erlangen; professor at Wartburg Seminary, 1891; pres., 1906; d. Jan. 1, 1940. He was a leading theologian of the Iowa Synod.

Fritschel, Siegmund. Brother of Gottfried F.; b. Dec. 3, 1833, at Nuremberg; d. at Dubuque, Iowa, 1900; studied under Loehe and was sent by him to America in 1853; took part in the organization of the Iowa Synod and assisted Grossmann in the work at the seminary; for a while had charge of a church in Wisconsin and also served the Buffalo Synod church at Detroit; returned to the seminary 1858 and labored side by side with his brother for more than thirty years, occupying the chair of Practical Theology. Dr. Krauth gives him much credit for his beneficial influence on the development of the General Council. He was a contributor to *Brobsts Monatshefte* and *Kirchliche Zeitschrift.*

A. Spaeth, *S. Fritschel, A Short Biography,* Wartburg Pub. House, Waverly, Iowa., 1901.

Fritz, John Henry Charles. B. July 30, 1874, at Martins Ferry, Ohio; graduated from Concordia College, Ft. Wayne, 1894; and from Concordia Seminary, St. Louis, 1897; pastor at Bismarck and Pilot Knob, Mo., 1897 to 1901; Brooklyn, N. Y., 1901—14; St. Louis, Mo. (Bethlehem), 1914—20; vice-president of the Western District, 1915—19; president, 1919—20; prof. of church history and pastoral theology, Concordia Seminary, St. Louis, 1920 to 1953; dean at Concordia Seminary, 1920—40; co-organizer of the St. Louis Noonday Lenten Services; co-founder of The Lutheran Church — Missouri Synod's radio and television mission. He frequently contributed to the *Lutheran Witness* and *Concordia Theological Monthly.* Editor of *Der Lutheraner,* 1949—53. Wrote *The Practical Missionary, Pastoral Theology, Essentials of Preaching, The Preacher's Manual.* Noted for his loyalty to the Word of God, his insistence that all the content and words of the Bible are inspired, and his interest in Bible class and pastoral work. D. April 12, 1953.

Fritzsche, Karl Friedrich August (1801—46). Prof. at Leipzig (1825), Rostock (1826), and Giessen (1841); chiefly interested in linguistic elements in exegesis and in textual criticism; wrote commentaries on Matthew, Mark, and Romans; author of *De nonnullis posterioris Pauli ad Corinthios epistolae locis dissertationes duae;* rationalistic theologian.

Fritzsche, Otto Fridolin (1812 to 1896). Brother of Karl Friedrich; prof. at Zurich (1837); wrote numerous works in the field of New Testament exegesis, church history, apocrypha and textual criticism.

Froberger, Johann Jakob (1616 to 1667). Pupil of Frescobaldi and Roman Catholic organist of south Germany. Bach regarded him with high esteem. Froberger became the creator of the clavier-suite, and the universally adopted suite sequence of *allemande, courante, sarabande,* and *gigue* was his invention. His music often lacks the freshness and spontaneity of the music written by Frescobaldi.

G. Adler, *Handbuch der Musikgeschichte,* Frankfurt, 1924; G. Frotscher, *Geschichte des Orgelspiels und der Orgelkomposition,* Berlin, 1936; P. H. Lang, *Music in Western Civilization,* New York, 1941.

Froebel, Friedrich (1782—1852). German educator. Founder of the kindergarten and exponent of a theory of education which holds that the work of the educator is primarily guidance, namely, that it permits, stimulates, leads, and directs self-activity and self-expression of the child's inner nature. The first duty of the teacher is to nurse the "divine nature" in the child, then correct aberrations and provide suitable self-activity. In 1837 Froebel opened a school for little children at Blankenburg, the first kindergarten. The central idea of the kindergarten is to use the self-activity of children for their education.

Froehlich, Bartholomaeus. Details of life not known. Pastor at Perleberg in Brandenburg, 1580—90. His hymn "Ein Wuermlein bin ich, arm und klein" appeared 1587 in Selnecker's *Christian Psalms.*

Froeschel, Sebastian (1497—1530). Intimate friend of Luther and Melanchthon; present at disputation between Luther and Eck; assistant of Bugenhagen at Wittenberg (1525); his writings are often interpretations of Melanchthon.

Frohnmeier, L. J. B. Dec. 12, 1850, at Ludwigsburg, Wuerttemberg, Germany; d. Mar.16, 1921, at Basel; missionary to Malabar Coast, India, 1876; recalled to be Inspector of Basel Mission, 1906.

Frohschammer, Jacob (1821—93). German philosopher and theologian; became priest (1847); his *Einleitung in die Philosophie und Grundriss der Metaphysik* attacked the teachings of Aquinas; his *Ueber die Freiheit der Wissenschaft* upheld the independence of philosophy; many of his writings were placed on the Index, and he was excommunicated (1871). He conceived the world as resulting from the imagination of God.

Frommel, Emil (1828—96). German prolific writer of popular books of healthy Christian character; pastor at Karlsruhe (1855) and Barmen (1862); military chaplain at Berlin (1869); court preacher (1871).

Frommel, Gaston (1862—1906). Prof. at Geneva; follower of Alexander Vinet; sought to construct doctrine by reference to the moral consciousness.

Frommel, Max (1830—90). Brother of Emil; through Harless a decided Lutheran; for a time in Breslau Synod; then general superintendent at Celle; also popular preacher and writer like his brother.

Frothingham, Nathaniel Langdon (1793—1870). Educated at Harvard; minister in the Unitarian Church at Boston for thirty-five years; published *Metrical Pieces;* among his hymns: "O Lord of Life and Truth and Grace."

Fry, Charles Luther. Son of Charles Livingston Fry; b. Mar. 16, 1894; studied at Muhlenberg College and Columbia U.; Ph.D., 1924; prof. at U. of Rochester, 1933—38; made numerous studies and surveys in the fields of sociology and religion; some of his publications are: *Diagnosing the Rural Churches,* 1924; *The U.S. Looks at Its Churches,* 1930; the summary of the Census of Religious Bodies, 1926; d. Apr. 12, 1938.

Fry, Elizabeth (nee Gurney), (1780 to 1845). A "female Howard" *; began to visit prisons in 1813. As a result societies for prison reform were organized in Great Britain and most countries of western Europe. Her reading of the

Scriptures in Newgate Prison is the subject of a famous picture.

Fry, Franklin Foster. B. Nov. 1, 1864, at Carlisle, Pa.; son of Jacob Fry; studied at Muhlenberg College and Philadelphia Seminary; ordained, 1888; acting pastor at Reading and Easton, Pa.; pastor at Bethlehem, Pa., 1890 to 1901; at Rochester, N. Y., 1901—27; Executive Secretary of the Board of American Missions, 1927; pres. of New York and New England Synod; leader in organizing ULCA; member of the Executive Board of the ULCA; delegate to the First World Convention of Lutherans at Eisenach; D. D., Muhlenberg College, 1913; d. Dec. 13, 1933.

Fry, Jacob. B. at Trappe, Pa., 1834; educated at Union College, Schenectady; licensed, 1854; professor of homiletics and pastoral theology in Philadelphia Seminary, 1891—1918; d. Feb. 19, 1920; author of *Elementary Homiletics* and *Pastor's Guide.*

Fuehrich, Joseph (1800—76). German painter of the idealist school; follows ancient style, thoughtful and expressive; fine composition work; among his paintings: "The Incarnation"; "The Prodigal Son."

Fuerbringer, Ludwig Ernst. B. March 29, 1864, at Frankenmuth, Mich.; graduated at St. Louis, 1885; pastor at Frankenmuth, Mich., 1885—93; professor at Concordia Seminary, St. Louis, 1893 to 1943 (retired); president, 1931—43; pres. em., 1943—47; d. May 6, 1947. D. D. Concordia College, Australia, 1924; Valparaiso Univ. Doctor of Letters, 1939. Editor of *Lutheraner* (1896 to 1947); *80 Eventful Years; Persons and Events;* former editor of *Statistical Year-Book;* editor of: *Synodical Handbook of the Ev. Luth. Synod of Missouri, Ohio, and Other States; Dr. Walthers Briefe; Men and Missions Series;* revised edition of Guenther's *Populaere Symbolik;* printed as manuscript: *Theologische Hermeneutik; Theological Hermeneutics; Liturgik; Einleitung in das Alte Testament; Einleiting in das Neue Testament; Introduction to the Old Testament; Book of Job.*

L. Fuerbringer, *80 Eventful Years,* CPH, 1944; L. Fuerbringer, *Persons and Events,* CPH, 1947; *The Eternal Why,* CPH, 1947.

Fuerbringer, Ottomar. B. June 30, 1810, in Gera, Thuringia; studied theology at Leipzig, 1828—30, together with Walther, Brohm, Buenger, and others of the circle led by Candidate Kuehn in their Biblical studies and devotional exercises. From 1831 to 1838 he was instructor in an institute for boys at Eichenberg, conducted by Pastor G. H. Loeber. He came to America as one of the Saxon pilgrims under the leadership of Martin Stephan, in 1839. Together with Brohm and Buenger he founded Concordia College in Perry Co., Mo., in which he was the first instructor in the classic languages and in history. In 1840 he became pastor in Venedy, Ill. He assisted in drawing up the constitution of the Missouri Synod, was present at the first meeting of the Synod, 1847; became a voting member at the second meeting, 1848. He became pastor of the congregations in Freistadt and Kirchhayn, Wis., 1851, and was thereby forced to take an active part in the controversy with Grabau; his articles appeared in *Der Lutheraner.* When the Missouri Synod was divided into Districts in 1854, he became president of the Northern District and retained this office until 1872. In 1858 he was called as pastor of St. Lorenz' Church in Frankenmuth, Mich. At the beginning of the Civil War he called together unmarried men in his parish and persuaded them voluntarily to fill the quota of men demanded from their county in order that the fathers of families might be exempted from military services. He was again prevailed upon to act as president of the Northern District, 1874—82. D. July 12, 1892. Pastoral wisdom combined with Lutheran soundness characterized his pastoral work; his deep learning and simple, popular style rendered him an effective preacher and catechist; his contributions to *Lutheraner* and *Lehre und Wehre* and his presidential addresses proved him to be, as Dr. A. L. Graebner says, "the profoundest thinker among the fathers of the Missouri Synod."

W. G. Polack, "Ottomar Fuerbringer," *CTM,* V: 211—17 (also in *CHIQ,* VII: 42—50).

Fugue. A musical composition in strict polyphonic style, in which, as the name indicates (from *fuga,* meaning flight), the theme introduced by one part or voice is repeated and imitated by the others in a more or less regular succession, Bach being the great master in this style.

Fulbert (ca. 960—1028). Bishop of Chartres; founder of the famous school there; propagated secular learning; upheld Church against nobles; distinguished between human knowledge and divine revelation.

Fulgentius Ferrandus (d. before 547). Deacon at Carthage; leader in North Africa among those who opposed condemnation of *Three Chapters.*

Fulgentius of Ruspe (468—533). Outstanding opponent of Arianism and Semi-Pelagianism; adherent of Augustinian doctrine.

Full Gospel. See *Pentecostalism.*

Full Gospel Assembly. See *Pentecostalism.*

"Full Salvation." See *Methodist Bodies,* 2.

Fuller, S. See *Congregational and Christian Churches,* A 2.

Fuller, Thomas (1608—61), a divine, antiquary, historian; a Royalist. Wrote *The History of the Holy Warre* (account of the Crusades). A *Pisgah-Sight of Palestine* (history and geography of the Holy Land); *The Church History of Britain.*

Funck, Johann (1518—66). Lutheran divine. B. in a suburb of Nuremberg. Studied at Wittenberg. Court preacher at Königsberg. He sided with Osiander and his son-in-law, Andreas Aurifaber, thereby focusing the wrath of Osiander's opponents upon himself. Accused of opposing the ecclesiastical and political measures of the government, he was beheaded at Königsberg.

Funcke, Friedrich (1642—99). Cantor at Perleberg, later at Lueneburg; pastor at Roemstedt; both hymn writer and musician; wrote: "Zeuch uns nach dir, so laufen wir."

Funcke, Otto (1836—1907). Pastor at Bremen, writer of devotional literature, some of his books being translated also into English.

Functionalism. See *Psychology,* J 3.

Fundamental Doctrines. In his book on the True Visible Church, Dr. C. F. W. Walther in proposition 18, C, says, "The Evangelical Lutheran Church strictly distinguishes between fundamental and non-fundamental articles of the Scriptures." The Bible passage that is adduced as basis for this distinction is 1 Cor. 3:11-15. Among the appended quotations from prominent theologians is one by Quenstedt which contains this definition of a fundamental article, "A fundamental article is a doctrine which

is of such a nature that it produces, and furnishes the foundation of faith and salvation." Continuing, Quenstedt quotes the famous theologian N. Hunnius and says that according to this scholar the foundation of faith is threefold, the essential or real, the instrumental, and the dogmatic foundation. It becomes apparent that Hunnius holds the essential or real foundation is the Triune God, who is to be apprehended in Christ by faith; that the instrumental foundation is the divine Word, and the dogmatic foundation is the sum of all fundamental articles. Quenstedt defines non-fundamental articles as articles which without injury to the foundation of faith may not only be unknown, but even denied. He takes for granted, of course, that such denial is not due to conscious opposition to Scripture teaching as such, but to ignorance of the meaning of the divine Word in a certain passage. He again refers to Hunnius and states that this Lutheran theologian lists as non-fundamental articles the teachings of the eternal rejection of certain angels, of the immortality of man before the fall, of the Antichrist, of the unpardonableness of the sin against the Holy Ghost, of Christian liberty in ecclesiastical usages, etc. The distinction must not be used to admit false liberalism into the Church, as though acceptance of certain teachings of the Word of God were a matter of indifference. It is made from the point of view of importance of teachings for the faith and life of a believer.

The question of fundamental and non-fundamental doctrines was much discussed after Walther had stated that he considered the taking of interest as forbidden in the Scriptures. He declared that he looked upon this teaching as a non-fundamental one. At that time he published the famous declaration (*Lutheraner,* vol. 27, p. 131): "Let everyone who so desires understand that we know to distinguish between articles of faith and Scripture doctrines which are not articles of faith. We insist indeed that no Scripture doctrine, may it appear great or small, may be regarded as an open question; but while we consider it necessary to contend most strenuously for every article of faith (on each one of which our faith and hope depend), to condemn the error that opposes it and to deny the hand of fellowship to those who stubbornly contradict the article in question, we by no means believe it necessary under all circumstances to contend to the utmost for other Scripture teachings that are not articles of faith, much less to pronounce a sentence of condemnation on the opposing error, although we reject it, and to deny fellowship to those who err in nothing but this point. If in a controversy the debate concerns itself with teachings that do not belong to the articles of faith, then it is of greatest concern to us to see whether the opponents indicate that they contradict because they refuse to obey the Word of God, that is, whether they, while apparently not attacking the fundamental doctrines of the Word of God, nevertheless destroy the foundation itself on which these teachings rest, the divine Word." Here Walther evidently uses the "articles of faith" in the sense of "fundamental doctrines." It should be noted that he does not declare the nonfundamental doctrines to be a matter of indifference, but he holds that an error in such doctrines does not necessarily lead to a separation. WA

C. F. Walther, "Die falschen Stuetzen der modernen Theorie von den offenen Fragen," *L. u. W.*, XIV:1868 (translated *CTM*, X:254 ff.); T. Graebner and P. Kretzmann, *Toward Lutheran Union,* CPH, 1943, 117 ff.

Fundamental Principles of Faith and Church Polity. See *General Council, 2.*

Fundamentalism. Title given to the religious position combating liberalism and Modernism * in twentieth century American Protestantism; name derived from *The Fundamentals* ("Compliments of Two Christian Laymen," Testimony Publishing Co., Chicago, 1910—1912). While adhering to the inspiration of the Bible and its cardinal doctrines, many protagonists of the movement have been associated with the Premillennialist Movement. The movement is essentially polemic, attacking liberalism in seminaries and church denominations, and causing sharp cleavages especially in Baptist and Presbyterian bodies. The movement is distinguished from Lutheranism by the latter's employment of the Bible not as code but source of faith, and by its emphasis on the culture of spiritual life by the means of grace rather than by controversy.

Future Reward and Punishment. See *Hereafter.*

Fux, Johann Joseph (1660—1741). Has been called "the Austrian Palestrina." Fux fought against the influence exerting upon church music in his day. He was a prolific composer of the Roman Catholic Church, whose music met with the strict standards set up by the Council of Trent. His *Gradus ad Parnassum* is an excellent manual on pure 16th century counterpoint.

G

Gabriel (lit., champion of God). Used as the proper name to designate the heavenly messenger who was sent to Daniel to interpret the vision of the ram and the he-goat (Dan. 8) and to communicate the prophecy of the seventy weeks (Dan. 9). In the opening pages of the New Testament he is employed to announce the birth of John the Baptist to Zacharias and that of the Savior to the Virgin Mary (Luke 1: 11, 26). Gabriel is ordinarily spoken of as one of the archangels, his superior dignity being deduced both from the august nature of his messages and from the phrase "that stand in the presence of God" (Luke 1:19). If it is permitted to generalize upon the incidents which are recorded in Scripture, Gabriel's special ministration is one of comfort and sympathy, as Michael's is that of contention against evil. See *Angels; Michael.*

Gabrieli, Andrea (ca. 1510—86). Venetian composer of the later Renaissance and the teacher of the Lutheran composer Hans Leo Hassler. In the music of Andrea Gabrieli and his nephew Giovanni, Venetian music of the 16th century arrived at its highest point of perfection. Both were active at St. Mark's Cathedral, succeeding Adrian Willaert. They wrote choral music for double, triple, and quadruple chorus; in these, low-voiced choirs were often contrasted with choirs of high voices and the music became at times pompous, festive, brilliant, and even rousing. Orchestral accompaniment played an important part in this music, often relegating the choral parts to the background. This music was the beginning of the Baroque Era, which produced Bach and Handel.

G. Adler, *Handbuch der Musikgeschichte,* Frankfurt, 1924; D. Ferguson, *A History of Musical Thought*, New York, 1948; P. H. Lang, *Music in Western Civilization*, New York, 1941; H. Leichtentritt, *Music, History and Ideas*, Cambridge, 1938; Karl von Winterfeld, *Johannes Gabrieli und sein Zeitalter*, Berlin, 1834.

Gabrieli, Giovanni (1557—1612). Nephew of Andrea Gabrieli and the teacher of Sweelinck and Schuetz. In several respects Giovanni overshadowed his uncle and developed further his ideas. His compositions often became emotional, rich and colorful, chromatic, and pictorial. His chromatic harmony betrays the influence of the Italian madrigal and his polychoral style the kindred spirit of the great Venetian painters Titian, Veronese, and Tintoretto, who are regarded as baroque painters.

Gaelic Society. See *Celtic Church*, 13.

Gaidheals, Church of. See *Celtic Church*, 12.

Galerius. See *Persecutions of Christians*, 4.

Galesburg Rule. A name given to a ruling of the General Council in regard to pulpit and altar fellowship at Galesburg, Ill., 1875. The declaration in regard to pulpit and altar fellowship, adopted by the General Council in 1868 (see *Four Points*), was explained in 1870 in answer to a question of the Minnesota Synod: "In employing the term 'fundamental errorists,' in the declarations made at Pittsburgh, it understands not those who are the victims of involuntary mistakes, but those who willfully, wickedly, and persistently desert, in whole or in part, the Christian faith, especially as embodied in the Confessions of the Church Catholic, in the purest form in which it now exists on earth, to wit, the Evangelical Lutheran Church, and thus overturn or destroy the foundation in them confessed." The Iowa Synod, asking a further explanation of this declaration, was given the answer by Dr. Krauth: "I. *The rule is:* Lutheran pulpits for Lutheran ministers only; Lutheran altars for Lutheran communicants only. II. The exceptions to the rule belong to the sphere of privilege, not of right. III. The determination of the exceptions is to be made in consonance with these principles by the conscientious judgment of pastors as the cases arise." (Akron Rule.) At Galesburg, in 1875,

the General Council declared: "The rule, which accords with the Word of God and with the Confessions of our Church is: 'Lutheran pulpits for Lutheran ministers only; Lutheran altars for Lutheran communicants only.' " However, this declaration is open to the interpretation that in certain cases Lutheran pulpits are open to non-Lutheran preachers and Lutheran altars to non-Lutheran communicants, as was virtually admitted by the General Council in answer to an appeal of the New York Ministerium against violations of the Galesburg Rule. The question whether the addition to the Akron Rule (1872) made at Galesburg (1875), *viz.*, "which accords with the Word of God and the Confessions of our Church," did not practically annul Points II and III, regarding the exceptions, was answered by the Council at Pittsburgh (1889) to the effect that "inasmuch as the General Council has never annulled, rescinded, or reconsidered the declarations made at Akron in 1872, they still remain, in all their parts and provisions, the action and rule of the Council."

S. E. Ochsenford, *Documentary History of the General Council of the Evangelical Lutheran Church in North America*, General Council Pub. House, Philadelphia, 1912; J. Deindoerfer, *Geschichte der Ev. Luth. Synode von Iowa und andern Staaten*, Wartburg, Chicago, 1897 (148—56).

Galileo (Galilei, 1564—1642). Italian astronomer and physicist. Because of his opposition to the Ptolemaic system he was twice brought before the Inquisition. He held that it was the duty of the theologian to harmonize Biblical phraseology with science. He made many discoveries in the fields of astronomy and physics.

Galleries *(Gemaeldegalerien)* **for Religious Art.** Although none of the great galleries of Europe may be said to be devoted entirely to religious art and some frankly favor secular art, there are a few collections in which the religious element predominates very decidedly, as in those of the Vatican at Rome, that of the Uffizi and that of the Pitti Palace, in Florence, that of the Royal Gallery of Dresden, that of the Royal Gallery of Madrid, that of the National Gallery in London, and those of smaller collections at Rome (Borghese), Naples, Munich, Brussels, Venice, Antwerp, and Milan. See *Architecture, Ecclesiastical*, 7.

Gallican Confession. See *Reformed Confessions,* B.

Gallicanism. The term applied to the polity of the Catholic Church of France until the rival theory of Ultramontanism gained the ascendancy. Gallicanism includes two primary principles: 1. The secular government is supreme in its own sphere. 2. The papal jurisdiction, even within the sphere of religion, is subordinate to the collective episcopate. These principles were generally maintained against papal absolutism from the thirteenth century to the days of Napoleon Bonaparte (Concordat, 1802). The foundation of these "Gallican Liberties," as they are called, was laid by Louis IX (1226—70) in the famous "Pragmatic Sanction," which overruled the arrogant pretensions of Clement IV by prohibiting all papal interference in the matter of ecclesiastical elections and all papal exactions and assessments without the king's consent. Wider in scope was the second "Pragmatic Sanction," issued, and incorporated with the laws of the kingdom, by Charles VII in 1438. It embodied twenty-three reformatory decrees of the Council of Basel directed against the extortionary and other arbitrary proceedings of the Papacy. In particular, it declared the supremacy of the national Church as against the papal ideal of universal rule. But the fullest expression of Gallicanism grew out of the quarrel between Louis XIV and Innocent X. In this quarrel the French clergy supported the king and issued the four famous propositions of Gallican liberty: 1. The authority of the Pope is limited to spiritual matters. 2. The authority of a council is above that of the Pope. 3. The authority of the Pope is restricted by the laws, institutions, and usages of the French Church. 4. The doctrinal pronouncements of the Pope are final and authoritative only with the concurrence of the whole Church.

Gallus, Jacob (1550—91). Latinized name of the German Roman Catholic composer Jakob Handl. Gallus was active largely in Vienna and Prague and helped to bring the chromatic Venetian style of Willaert and others into Germany. Together with Hassler and Gumpeltzhaimer he is representative of the finest German church music of the second half of the 16th century. G. Adler, *Handbuch der Musikgeschichte,* Frankfurt, 1924; F. Blume,

Ev. Kirchenmusik, Potsdam, 1931; P. H. Lang, *Music in Western Civilization,* New York, 1941.

Gallus, Nicolas (1516—70). Reformation leader in Regensburg; opposed Interim (1548); with Flacius opposed adiaphorism of Wittenberg theologians (wrote *Disputation von Mitteldingen,* 1550); with Flacius he also opposed Reformed leanings of Melanchthon; gave refuge to Flacius (1562—66).

Gambia. A British colony and protectorate in West Africa, of 4,005 square miles and a population of 272,713 (1950). Missions: Methodist Missionary Society; S. P. G.; West Indian African Mission. Christian community, about 2,300 members; a foreign staff of 9 ordained missionaries and 4 unordained men. See *Missions, Bibliography.*

Gambling (and **Lotteries**). Taking part in games of chance or hazard for money, the expectation being of a large return on the smallest possible stake — an obvious transgression of the Seventh Commandment. In the strictest sense of the word gambling refers to gaming in its worst form, implying professional play for a money stake by men who are unscrupulous adepts at so-called games of chance. Gambling is a vice which has been common among most savage and barbarian as well as among civilized nations. The ancient Germans were so addicted to it that they indulged in it regardless of the cost to themselves. In the Scandinavian countries, in England, and along the Mediterranean Sea the passion for gambling was just as pronounced. In Rome, particularly during the days of the empire, the practice was common, and various enactments were made against it. Legislation against the evil has, in Christian countries, become ever stricter, especially during the last four centuries, the statutes of Henry VIII, of Queen Anne, and of Queen Victoria being so stringent as finally to include all betting houses. In the United States statutes have been passed in practically all of the States, forbidding gambling for money at certain games, a number of jurisdictions including also betting in the category of gambling. In spite of this, however, gambling is almost universally practiced in most of our great cities, and with but a partial veil of secrecy thrown over the haunts where it is carried on.

In connection with gambling, *lot-*

teries ought to be considered, that is, schemes for the distribution of prizes by chance. Lotteries, like every other species of gambling, have a pernicious influence on the character of those concerned in them. As this kind of gambling can be carried on secretly and the temptations are thrown in the way of both sexes, all ages, and all classes of persons, it spreads widely in a community, and thus silently infects the sober, economical, and industrious habits of a people. The lotteries of countries and states, formerly more prevalent than now, have had a pernicious influence on the people.

F. E. Reinartz, "An Indictment of Gambling," *Luth. Ch. Quart.*, XI: 238—50; Wilhelm Stekel (trans. by James S. van Teslaar), "Gambling," *Peculiarities of Behavior*, Liveright, New York, 1943 (II: 233 ff.).

Gambold, John (1711—71). Ed. at Oxford; vicar at a small post in Oxfordshire; later joined Moravians and became one of their bishops; wrote: "Thee We Adore, Eternal God."

Gamma Delta. See *Students, Spiritual Care of, A.*

Gangra, Council of. (Against celibacy.) This synod, held at Gangra, in Paphlagonia (360), vindicated the sacredness of marriage and opposed clerical celibacy.

Ganse, Hervey Doddridge (1822 to 1891). Studied at Columbia College and New Brunswick Seminary; pastor in Reformed Dutch and in Presbyterian Church; recast the hymn "Nearer, My God, to Thee."

Gansfort, John Wessel (1420—89). Prominent member of the Brethren of the Common Life. His material principle was "faith in love."

Gardiner, Allen (1794—1851). B. in England; pursued missionary work in South Africa, later in South America; founded the Patagonian Missionary Society in 1844 and unsuccessfully attempted missions in Tierra del Fuego, perishing of hunger on its coast in 1851. The South American Missionary Society was immediately formed and is carrying on the work with much success.

Garve, Karl Bernhardt (1763—1841). Moravian; prof. at the Paedagogium in Niesky and seminary in Barby; pastor at Ebersdorf, Norden, Berlin, and Neusalz-on-the-Oder; his attempt to construct a philosophical basis for the Moravian theology beginning with

Kant's criticism proved a failure; his hymns have been freely received in Lutheran hymnbooks.

Gass, Friedrich Wilhelm Joachim Heinrich (1813—89). B. at Breslau; d. at Heidelberg. Studied at Breslau and Halle. Professor at Breslau, Greifswald, Giessen, and Heidelberg. He made valuable contributions to the study of the Greek Church, wrote on the history of Protestant dogmatics and on Christian ethics. He was a strong advocate of the Evangelical union.

Gassendi, Pierre (1592 to 1655). French philosopher; opposed philosophy of Descartes and Scholastic Aristotelianism and promulgated atomic materialism of Lucretius; emphasized importance of experimental research.

Gastfreundschaft. See *Hospitality.*

Gates, Theophilus (1787—1846). B. at Hartford, Conn.; experienced visions; 1810—35 he was in Philadelphia, where he criticized existing religions (published *Reformer*); unhappy home life caused him to become a perfectionist; in 1837 he launched his "Battle-Axe Experiment," which advocated free love based upon a "principle of holiness" (soul mate); his colony in "Free Love Valley" (near Philadelphia) soon disappeared after his withdrawal.

G. P. Albaugh, "Battle-Axe Experiment," V. Ferm, *An Encyclopedia of Religion*, Philosophical Library, New York, 1945.

Gaunilo (Count of Montigny, 11th c.). Criticized Anselm's ontological argument in his *Book in Behalf of the Fool.*

Gausewitz, Carl F. W. B. Aug. 29, 1861, at Reedsville, Wis.; ed. Northwestern College, 1875—79 (A. B.); Luth. Seminary, Milwaukee, 1879—82. Pastor: East Farmington, Minn. (Minn. Synod), 1882—85; St. Paul, Minn., 1885—1906; Milwaukee, Wis. (Wis. Synod), 1906—28; pres. of Minn. Synod, 1894—1906; helped organize Joint Synod of Wis., pres. of it, 1901—07; 1913—17. Chairman of Bd. of Trustees, Wis. Synod; member of many boards and commissions; pres. of Synodical Conference, 1912—27. Author of official catechism of Wis. Synod later adopted by Joint Wis. Synod. D. Sept. 4, 1928, at Milwaukee, Wis.

Gautama Buddha. See *Gotama.*

Gebhardt, Eduard von (1838—1925). Prominent modern German realist painter after the manner of Duerer; among his most noted paintings: seven mural paintings in Loccum, the Crucifixion, the Last Supper, and the Ascension.

Geddes, Alex. See *Higher Criticism*, 13.

Gehenna. See *Hereafter*, C 5.

Gehrke, G. See *Canada, Lutheranism in*, 19.

Geier, Martin (1614—80). B. at Leipzig. Prof. of Oriental languages there, also pastor and prof. of theology; later court preacher at Dresden. Wrote commentaries and hymns.

Geijer, Erik G. See *Sweden, Lutheran Church in*, 4.

Geiler von Kaisersberg, Johannes (1455—1510). German pulpit orator; chief work done as preacher in the cathedral of Strassburg.

Geistliche. See *Ministerial Office*.

Gellert, Christian Fuerchtegott. Born July 4, 1715, at Hainichen in the Saxon Harz; studied theology at Leipzig. After his graduation he became an assistant to his father; however, because of a poor memory he had to choose another profession. Gellert went back to Leipzig and graduated in the faculty of Belles Lettres. The following year he became lecturer in the faculty of Philosophy. As professor he was most popular with his students, among whom were Goethe and Lessing. His lectures were much favored because of their substance and high moral tone. Gellert's *Fables* won him fame and recognition as a German classicist. As professor extraordinary he lectured on philosophy, poetry, rhetoric, and moral philosophy. Gellert had a delicate constitution from childhood and after 1752 suffered greatly from hypochondria and d. at Leipzig, Dec. 13, 1769.

Gemara. See *Talmud*.

General Assembly. See *Polity, Ecclesiastical*, 7.

General Assembly of the Presbyterian Church in Ireland. See *Presbyterian Bodies*, 3.

General Association of Regular Baptist Churches in the U.S. See *Baptist Bodies*, 15.

General Baptists. See *Baptist Bodies*, 2, 18, 20.

General Church of the New Jerusalem. See *Swedenborgians*, 5.

General Conference. The First General Conference of Lutherans in Amer-

ica was held in Philadelphia, Dec. 27—29, 1898. The aim of the conference was "to afford a faithful presentation of how the living, urgent, doctrinal, and practical problems of the hour are being met within the several general bodies." Participating bodies were: General Council, General Synod, United Synod of the South.

H. E. Jacobs, *The First General Conference of Lutherans in America*, General Council Pub. Bd. & Luth. Pub. Soc., Philadelphia, 1899.

General Conference of Christian Churches. See *Congregational and Christian Churches*.

General Conference of Evangelical Lutheran Preachers in the State of Ohio and Adjacent States. See *Ohio and Other States, Ev. Lutheran Joint Synod of*, 2.

General Conference Mennonites. See *Mennonite Bodies*, 3.

General Confession. A public confession of sins made by the whole congregation with the pastor as distinguished from private confession by the individual. In Roman Catholic theology a general confession is a confession made by an individual in which he surveys his entire life, confessing even sins previously confessed.

General Convention. See *Protestant Episcopal Church*, 8.

General Convention of the Christian Church. See *Congregational and Christian Churches*, B.

General Convention of the New Jerusalem in U.S. See *Swedenborgians*, 4.

General Council. See *Holiness Bodies*, 2.

General Council of Congregational and Christian Churches. See *Congregational and Christian Churches*.

General Council of the Lutheran Church in North America, The. 1. This body owed its existence to the disruption within the General Synod in 1866. In the face of the rising tide of confessionalism within the Lutheran Church of America, which was principally due to the testimony borne by Walther and others, the General Synod * had received into membership the Melanchthon Synod, which stood committed to the "Definite Platform," * in 1859, and the un-Lutheran Franckean * Synod, at York, in 1864. The delegates of the

Pennsylvania Ministerium protested against the admission of the Franckean Synod and withdrew from the sessions of the General Synod. Immediately after the York convention the Ministerium founded the Philadelphia Seminary in opposition to the liberal Seminary at Gettysburg.

2. At the Fort Wayne convention, in 1866, the General Synod refused to seat the Pennsylvania delegates, whereupon this body severed its connection with the General Synod and a few weeks later issued a call, written by Dr. Charles Porterfield Krauth, "to all synods which confess the Unaltered Augsburg Confession, for the purpose of organizing a new general body upon distinctively Lutheran principles." In response to this call a convention was held at Reading, Pa., Dec. 12—14, 1866, at which delegates from the following thirteen synods were present: Pennsylvania Ministerium, New York Ministerium, Pittsburgh, Minnesota, English Ohio (former members of the General Synod), Joint Ohio, English District Synod of Ohio, Wisconsin, Michigan, Iowa (German), Canada, Norwegian, and Missouri. At this convention Krauth's *Fundamental Principles of Faith and Church Polity* were unanimously adopted and referred to the various synods for ratification. At the organization meeting at Fort Wayne, in November, 1867, it was found that the following synods had adopted the confessional basis of the Reading convention: Pennsylvania, New York, Pittsburgh, English Ohio, Wisconsin, English District of Ohio, Michigan, Swedish Augustana, Minnesota, Canada, Illinois, Iowa (German).

3. Ohio and Iowa desired a declaration on the part of the convention regarding the "Four Points": chiliasm, altar fellowship, pulpit fellowship, secret societies. The answer being unsatisfactory, these two synods refused to unite fully with the new body. For the same reason Wisconsin, Minnesota, and Illinois withdrew at subsequent conventions and helped to organize the Synodical Conference in 1872. Michigan also left the Council in 1887; and the greater part of the Texas Synod, admitted in 1868, joined Iowa in 1895 as a district. The English Synod of Ohio disbanded in 1871. The following synods afterwards united with the Council: Indiana (II), later called the Chicago Synod (1872), Holston (1874; left 1884), English Synod of the Northwest (1893), Manitoba (1897), Pacific (1901), New York and New England (1903), Nova Scotia (1903), Central Canada (1909). The leading men in the Council were Chas. Porterfield Krauth (president, 1870—79), Wm. J. Mann, W. A. Passavant, B. M. Schmucker, G. F. Krotel (president, 1869; 1889—91), J. A. Seiss (president, 1888), A. Spaeth (president, 1880—87), R. F. Weidner, G. H. Gerberding, J. A. W. Haas, H. E. Jacobs, C. A. Swensson (president, 1893), and T. E. Schmauck (president, 1907—18).

4. The doctrinal basis of the General Council was "the Unaltered Augsburg Confession, in its original sense, as throughout in conformity with the pure truth, of which God's Word is the only rule." The other Confessions "are, with the Unaltered Augsburg Confession, in the perfect harmony of one and the same Scriptural faith." Over against the congregations the General Council was a legislative body and considered conformity to its decision a moral obligation. In spite of its strictly Lutheran confessional basis, however, the General Council never issued a declaration satisfactory to the strict Lutherans in regard to the much-discussed "Four Points." According to the Akron-Galesburg * Rule, non-Lutherans were under certain circumstances to be admitted to the Lord's Supper, and there were exceptions to the rule: "Lutheran pulpits for Lutheran ministers." Its declaration against chiliasm leaves room for the finer kind, and, while its pronouncement on secret societies is in conformity with Lutheran principles, its practice has not conformed to its principles. The teachings of some of the leaders of the General Council on ordination, the ministerial office, conversion, predestination, the inspiration of the Scriptures, evolution, etc., were not always in harmony with the Bible and the Lutheran Confessions, and yet the General Council did not take such men to task.

5. The home mission work of the General Council was carried on chiefly in the Northwest and in Canada, the institution at Kropp, Germany, furnishing most of the German pastors.

6. The General Council conducted a mission among the Telugus in India and, jointly with the United Synod in the South, also in Japan. The Augustana Synod also had its independent mission in China. — The General Council maintained the following institutions: Seminaries: Philadelphia (Mount Airy, 1864), Maywood, Ill. (formerly in Chicago, 1891), Augustana (Rock Island, Ill., 1860), Waterloo, Ont. (1911); clas-

sical institutions: Muhlenberg College, Allentown, Pa. (1867), Wagner Memorial College, Staten Island, N. Y. (formerly in Rochester, 1883), Thiel College, Greenville, Pa. (Pittsburgh Synod, 1870), and the colleges of the Augustana Synod.* Within the General Council there were 18 orphans' homes and many other charitable institutions, maintained either by district synods or private associations. Many of these owe their existence to the labors of Dr. W. A. Passavant. The General Council also conducted an immigrant and seamen's mission and took the lead in deaconess work for many years. John D. Lankenau established the Mary J. Drexel Home in Philadelphia in 1888.

7. On Oct. 24, 1917, the General Council approved of the plan to merge with the General Synod and the United Synod in the South in the United Lutheran Church in America. In November, 1918, this merger was consummated in New York. The Swedish Augustana Synod, however, refused to enter the merger and has stood alone since that time. At the time of the merger the General Council numbered 13 synods, 1,059 pastors, 1,406 congregations, and 340,588 confirmed members. See also *United Lutheran Church.*

Church histories of Lutheranism in America; S. E. Ochsenford, *Documentary History of the General Council of the Ev. Luth. Church in North America,* General Council Pub. House, Philadelphia, 1912; Pamphlets: General Council (bound together in Concordia Seminary Library at St. Louis and containing the following: *Die Synode von Pennsylvanien und die letzte Versammlung der General-Synode zu Fort Wayne, Ind.,* Philadelphia, 1866; *Proceedings of the Convention Held by Representatives from Various Ev. Luth. Synods in the United States and Canada Accepting the Unaltered Augsburg Confession* at Reading, Pa., Dec. 12, 13, and 14, 1866, Bakewell and Martens, Pittsburgh, 1867; *Proposed Constitution of the General Council,* German edition of the Reading minutes); H. E. Jacobs, "The General Council," *Distinctive Doctrines and Usages of the General Bodies of the Ev. Luth. Church in the United States,* Luth. Pub. Soc., Philadelphia, 1902; A. Spaeth, "General Council of the Ev. Luth. Church in North America," *Luth. Ch. Review,* IV: 81—127.

General Eldership of the Church of God. See *Churches of God in North America.*

General School Board. See *Parish Education,* D 6.

General Six-Principle Baptists. See *Baptist Bodies,* 19.

General Synod of the Evangelical Lutheran Church in the United States of America, The. 1. Organized at Hagerstown, Md., Oct. 22, 1820. It was the first federation of Lutheran synods in America. The synods participating in the organization of the general body were the Pennsylvania Ministerium (founded 1748), the New York Ministerium (1786), the North Carolina Synod (1803), and the Synod of Maryland and Virginia (1820).

2. The idea of a general body was broached in 1811 by G. Shober and A. G. Stork of the North Carolina Synod and took definite shape in the *Planentwurf* adopted in 1819 in Baltimore by the mother synod and representatives of other synods. The Tennessee Synod objected to the organization on doctrinal grounds, and the Ohio Synod also refused to join in the movement. Nine pastors and four lay delegates attended the organization meeting. The New York Ministerium withdrew after the first meeting because of lack of interest.

3. In 1823 the Pennsylvania Ministerium severed its connection with the General Synod because the former feared centralized authority and also because some of its congregations feared infringement on their liberties. It was due chiefly to the exertions of S. S. Schmucker, for more than forty years a leading spirit in the General Synod, that that body survived its critical initial years. When the Pennsylvania Ministerium withdrew, a new synod was formed west of the Susquehanna River, the Synod of West Pennsylvania, which joined the General Synod in 1825. The Hartwick Synod (founded 1830) joined in 1831, the South Carolina Synod (founded 1824) entered in 1835, the New York Ministerium came back in 1837, the Synod of Virginia, which branched off from the Maryland Synod in 1829, was admitted in 1839. Other synods joined in the following order: Synod of the West in 1840 (was divided into Synod of the Southwest, the Illinois Synod, and the Synod of the West in 1846), East Ohio Synod in 1841, East Pennsylvania in 1842, Alleghany and Southwestern Virginia in 1843, Miami in 1845, Illinois and Wittenberg in 1848, Olive Branch in 1850, Pittsburgh, Texas, Northern Illi-

nois, and Pennsylvania Ministerium in 1853, Kentucky and Central Pennsylvania in 1855, Northern Indiana, Iowa (English), and Southern Illinois in 1857, the Melanchthon Synod in 1859, and the Franckean Synod and the Minnesota Synod in 1864.

4. In 1863, owing to the Civil War, the Southern synods, North Carolina, South Carolina, Virginia, and Southwestern Virginia, withdrew, and, with the Georgia Synod, organized the General Synod in the Confederate States. The admission of the Melanchthon Synod, which stood committed to the "Definite Platform," caused the withdrawal of the Scandinavians in 1860, and the reception of the un-Lutheran Franckean Synod in 1864 brought about the disruption of the General Synod in Fort Wayne, in 1866. The Pennsylvania Ministerium, the New York Ministerium, the synods of Illinois, Minnesota, Texas, and the English Synod of Ohio, together with the greater part of the Pittsburgh Synod, withdrew and organized the General Council. The Susquehanna Synod joined the General Synod in 1867, Kansas in 1869, Wartburg in 1877, German Nebraska and the Rocky Mountain Synod in 1891, California in 1892, and the New York Synod in 1908.

5. From its beginning the General Synod did not adhere to strict Lutheran confessionalism (see *Fellowship; Lutheran Confessions*). Neither the Confessions of the Lutheran Church were mentioned in its constitution nor even the Bible; and that the omission was intentional is evident from the fact that the General Synod maintained its silence in regard to its confession in spite of the vigorous protests of the Tennessee Synod and its refusal to join the general body on that account. Yet even the name Lutheran was not without some value. It kept many Lutherans from joining the sects, gave the Lutheran Church a standing among the sects and also in Europe, and diminished the danger of a merger with the Reformed churches in Pennsylvania and in the South. In opposition to the rationalism found in the New York Ministerium of that time it confessed "Jesus Christ as the Son of God and the Ground of our faith and hope," thus acting as a check on the inroads of Socinianism.

6. On the other hand, the platform of the General Synod was so broadly "evangelical" that some essentials of Lutheranism were lost sight of. Fraternizing with, and yielding to, the sects was looked upon as a matter of Christian duty. The Augsburg Confession was indeed recognized as a confession of the Lutheran Church, but a distinction was made between fundamental and non-fundamental doctrines, without defining what was meant by the terms. Schmucker, the theological leader of the General Synod for thirty-eight years, repeatedly declared: The Augsburg Confession was not to be followed unconditionally, its binding force was limited expressly to the fundamentals. The confessional deliverances of the General Synod until 1864 may be summarized as follows: The fundamental doctrines of the Bible, *i. e.*, the doctrines in which all evangelical (non-Socinian) Christians agree, are taught in a manner substantially correct in the doctrinal articles (I—XXI) of the Augsburg Confession. The doctrines concerning baptismal regeneration, the real presence of the body and blood of Christ in the Lord's Supper, for instance, were considered obsolete. The Reformed view of the "Sabbath" was generally adopted.

7. This modified Lutheranism was called "American Lutheranism." Those who defended the Confessions were decried as "Henkelites" and "Symbolists." In 1855 S. S. Schmucker prepared the "Definite Platform," * intended to be a substitute for the Augsburg Confession, and Benjamin Kurtz sponsored it most cordially in the *Lutheran Observer*. The confessional reaction, however, which had set in some ten years before, prevented the general adoption of this makeshift and even induced the General Synod to make the Augsburg Confession its doctrinal basis in 1864 (York Resolution). In course of time the official doctrinal basis of the General Synod conformed more and more to that of the Lutheran Church. In 1895, at Hagerstown, the General Synod defined "the Unaltered Augsburg Confession as throughout in perfect consistence" with the Word of God. In 1901, at Des Moines, the distinction between fundamental and so-called non-fundamental doctrines in the Augsburg Confession was dropped. In 1909, at Richmond, Va., the objection to "the secondary symbols of the Book of Concord" was withdrawn, and in 1913, at Atchison, Kans., all the Symbols of the Lutheran Church were formally and officially adopted, thus paving the way for the merger with the General Council. Still there remained a wide gap between the formal adoption and the actual recognition of the Confes-

sions, and teachings contrary to the Confessions, as enunciated by leading men in the General Synod, were tolerated without official censure; nor was un-Lutheran practice censured officially; neither did the General Synod ever take any action on the lodge question. Freemasons, not only among the laity, but also among the clergy, occupied positions of trust and honor in the General Synod. The leading men of the General Synod were S. S. Schmucker, J. G. Morris, Benj. Kurtz, Sam. Sprecher, J. A. Brown, J. G. Butler, C. Phil. Krauth, Wm. Reynolds, F. W. Conrad, L. A. Gotwald, E. J. Wolf, M. Valentine, J. W. Richard, D. H. Bauslin, G. U. Wenner, J. A. Singmaster.

8. Besides Home Mission work, carried on chiefly through the district synods, the General Synod conducted a mission at Guntur, India (begun by the Pennsylvania Ministerium in 1842), and another in Liberia, Africa (begun by the Franckean Synod). — Its educational institutions were: Seminaries: Hartwick (1815), Gettysburg (1826), Hamma Divinity School at Springfield, Ohio (1845), Susquehanna University at Selinsgrove, Pa. (1858), Western at Atchison, Kans. (1893), Martin Luther Seminary at Lincoln, Nebr. (1913); classical schools: Gettysburg (formerly Pennsylvania) College, Wittenberg at Springfield, Ohio, Hartwick in New York, Carthage College at Carthage, Ill., Midland at Atchison, Kans., and Watts Memorial College, India. Some of these institutions were the property of district synods. Of inner mission institutions the General Synod had orphanages at Loysville, Pa., Nachusa, Ill., Springfield, Ohio, and Lincoln, Nebr.; a home for the aged in Washington, D. C., and a deaconess institution in Baltimore.

9. In 1918 the General Synod entered the merger of various Lutheran bodies, which had its origin in the movement for a joint celebration of the Reformation Quadricentennial in 1917. At a meeting of the committee appointed to arrange a program for the celebration the laymen of the committee presented a plan, April 18, 1917, for a merger of the General Synod, the General Council, and the United Synod in the South. The General Synod approved of this plan in Chicago, June 20, 1917. The merger was consummated in New York in November, 1918. At the time of this merger the General Synod consisted of 24 district synods, 1,438 pastors, 1,846 congregations, and 364,072 confirmed

members. See also *United Lutheran Church.*

E. L. Hazelius, *History of the American Lutheran Church, from Its Commencement in the Year of Our Lord 1685 to the Year 1842,* E. C. Church, Zanesville, Ohio, 1846; S. S. Schmucker, *The American Church, Historically, Doctrinally, and Practically Delineated,* D. Harbaugh, Springfield, Ohio, 1852; J. L. Neve, *The Formulation of the General Synod's Confessional Basis,* German Lit. Bd., Burlington, Iowa, 1911; M. Valentine, "General Synod," *The Distinctive Doctrines and Usages of the General Bodies of the Ev. Luth. Church in the United States,* Luth. Pub. Soc., Philadelphia, 1902 (34—61); *Formula of Government and Discipline for Congregations and Synods,* Bell, Hagerstown, 1823; S. A. Ort, "Practical Work of the Lutheran Church of the General Synod," *Quart. Rev. of ELC,* VI:1—18; V. Ferm, *The Crisis in American Lutheran Theology,* Century, N. Y., 1927; A. R. Wentz, *History of the Gettysburg Theological Seminary,* United Luth. Pub. House, Philadelphia, 1926; E. J. Wolf, "Lutheranism in the General Synod," *Luth. Quart.,* XXI:285—303.

General Synod in Confederate States. See *General Synod,* 4; *United Synod of the Evangelical Lutheran Church in the South.*

General Synod South. See *United Synod of the Evangelical Lutheran Church in the South.*

Genesis, the Little. Another name for the Book of Jubilees. See *Apocrypha.*

Geneva Academy. See *Calvin, John,* 7.

Geneva Bible. See *Bible Versions,* K.

Geneva, Consensus of. See *Reformed Confessions,* A 9.

Geneva Theocracy. See *Calvin, John,* 5.

Genevieve, Ste. (422—512). Venerated (Jan. 3) by Roman Catholics as patron saint of Paris for her benevolence and alleged prophetic gift at the time of Attila's attack on Paris.

Gennadius, Confession of. See *Eastern Orthodox Confessions,* B 1.

Gentile. A term used in the LXX for non-Jews (compare "barbarian" in Greek usage). Non-Jews were admitted gradually into the Church (Acts 10:48). At Antioch mission work was first done among Gentiles (Acts 11:19, 20). Thereafter Gentile Christianity soon exceeded Jewish converts in numbers.

Gentile, Giovanni Valentino (d. 1567). Italian anti-Trinitarian; came to Geneva (1556—57) but left when all members of the colony were required to subscribe to an orthodox confession which emphasized the Trinity. Attacked John Calvin's doctrine of the Trinity in his *Antidota*. Charges against him of blaspheming the Holy Spirit and mocking the Reformed Church ended in his execution.

Genuflection. Bending the knee in humility and reverence, a custom dating from early Christian times.

Genus idiomaticum, maiestaticum, apotelesmaticum. See *Christ Jesus,* I C ff.

Geography, Christian. 1. Christian Geography concerns itself with the geography, life, and history of the Bible Lands, primarily of Palestine. It furnishes the historical setting of Scripture. Especially its archaeological aspect brings to life the domestic, social, political, and religious life of the past ages.

2. The chronology of Christian Geography may be divided into four periods. The first begins with Constantine's recognition of Christianity as a legal religion and continues through the eighteenth century. To satisfy the stream of pilgrims visiting holy sites and places in Palestine, legends and traditions were developed. The travel accounts of this period reflect these, a fact which further decreases their value.

3. In the fourth century the learned Eusebius in his *Onomasticon* alphabetically arranged Bible place names, of which he identified as many as possible and added data concerning distances and events. Jerome later translated this work into Latin.

4. The second period, the nineteenth century to 1890, continued the topographical interest. The journeys of Dr. Edward Robinson in 1838 and 1852 and his subsequent publications began the scientific approach. From 1871 to 1878 the Palestine Exploration Fund made the monumental survey of western Palestine for its authoritative map on a scale of one inch to a mile. Captains Conder and Kitchener were important participants. The achievements of Dr. Robinson and the Fund formed the basis of all later topographical work.

5. Various excavations were carried on during this period. Sir Charles Warren, Selah Merrill, Gottlieb Schumacher, Clermont-Ganneau, and Guthe were among those active in topographical and excavational exploration.

6. The third period extended from 1890 to 1914. It saw the beginning of the development of the two basic principles of modern scientific archaeology — "stratigraphy" and "typology." The former is the study of the physical relationship of man-made objects in the light of the strata in which they are found; the latter studies the relationship between these objects. In the excavation of Tell el-Hesi (Eglon), Sir Flinders Petrie developed and began to apply these principles by setting up a chronological scheme for dating objects and strata. Among the excavations of this period were those at Gezer (R. A. S. Macalister) and Samaria (G. A. Reisner and C. S. Fisher). F. J. Bliss, Duncan Mackenzie, C. Leonard Woolley, T. E. Lawrence, Ernst Sellin, Nathaniel Schmidt, Carl Watzinger, W. J. Moulton, and others explored and excavated during this period.

7. The fourth period began in 1920 and continues to the present. It saw the development to fine detail of the two principles of stratigraphy and typology. Significant was the organization of the Palestine Department of Antiquities and its control of archaeological activity. Aside from educational institutions, both the American and the British Schools of Oriental Research have contributed much to archaeological development.

8. Important excavations were carried on at Megiddo, Beth-shan, Tell Beit Mirsim, Jericho, Lachish, Mounts Ophel and Zion, and Jerash. An increasing number of minor excavations were made. Nelson Glueck completed an extensive survey of Biblical sites in eastern Palestine. Among the archaeologists of this period were John Garstang, W. J. Pythian-Adams, J. W. Crowfoot, J. L. Starkey, L. Harding, W. F. Albright, O. R. Sellers, Pére Abel, Pére Vincent, W. F. Badé, Millar Burrows, G. Ernest Wright, C. C. Mc-Cown, M. G. Kyle, C. S. Fisher, and Elihu Grant. EHK

The Westminster Historical Atlas to the Bible (Wright and Filson), pp. 9—14; pp. 103—106; *Archaeology and the Bible* (Barton), Part I, Chapter IV; *The Haverford Symposium on Archaeology and the Bible* (Elihu Grant ed.), Chapter I; *The Ladder of Progress in Palestine* (C. C. McCown).

George III of Anhalt (1507—53). Allied with the Reformers after 1530; coadjutor of the bishopric at Merseburg; did not join the Smalcald League, but favored Leipzig Interim; known for his piety, love of peace, and gentleness.

George the Bearded (1471—1539). Duke of Saxony; welcomed Luther's Ninety-five Theses and attacked the corruptions of the Church, but fiercely opposed Luther's doctrine of grace and rejection of the Council of Constance, though at Worms he opposed the breaking of Luther's safe-conduct; persecuted his Lutheran subjects and yet had to spread Luther's New Testament, with a few alterations; died relying solely on the merits of Christ.

George of Denmark (1653—1708). Consort of Queen Anne; consistent Lutheran; founded court chapel of St. James.

George, Duke of Saxony. See *George the Bearded.*

George Ernst of Henneberg-Schleusingen (1511—83). Active in framing of *Maulbronn Formula;* favored Reformed position in a church order instituted.

George, Margrave of Brandenburg (1484—1543); called the "Confessor"; helped his brother Albrecht Lutheranize Prussia; aided the Reformation in Silesia and in Ansbach; protested at Speyer; see *Lutheran Confessions.*

George, St. * Probably a Christian martyr of the third century; perhaps a victim of Diocletian's persecution. He is patron saint of England, the Order of the Garter, and many military orders. The czar's coat of arms bore his effigy. The legend of his combat with a dragon to liberate a princess arose about the 12th century, possibly founded on the myths of Perseus and Siegfried.

George Washington's Bodyguard. See *Veterans' Organizations.*

Georgia, Synod of. See *United Lutheran Church, Synods of,* 5.

Georgia-Alabama Synod. See *United Lutheran Church, Synods of,* 5.

Gerberding, G. H. B. Aug. 21, 1847, at Pittsburgh, Pa.; grad., Muhlenberg College in 1873 and Mt. Airy Sem. in 1876. Missionary pastorates at Chartiers, Pa.; Zion, Pittsburgh, N. S., Pa.; Pine Creek, McCandless Twp., Pa.; Butcher's Run (Memorial, Pittsburgh,

N. S.), Pa.; Jewett, Ohio; and St. Mark's, Fargo, N. Dak. Founder and first pres. of the Synod of the Northwest, U. L. C. A.; pres. of Chicago Synod, U. L. C. A.; professor in Chicago Luth. Sem., 1894—1920; professor in Northwestern Luth. Sem., 1920—26; retired to Hickory, N. C., 1926. D. D. from Muhlenberg College, 1892; LL. D. from Lenoir College, 1919; contributing editor of *The Workman* and of *The Lutheran.* Member Inner Mission Bd. U. L. C. A. Wrote: *The Way of Salvation in the Luth. Church; New Testament Conversions; Life and Letters of W. A. Passavant, D. D.; The Lutheran Pastor; The Lutheran Catechist; Problems and Possibilities; The Lutheran Church in the Country; The Priesthood of Believers; What's Wrong with the World? Lutheran Fundamentals.* Died March 27, 1927.

G. H. Gerberding, *Youthful Reflections,* Augsburg Pub. House, Minneapolis, Minn., 1928.

Gerbert of Aurillac. See *Popes,* 6.

Gerhard, Johann. B. Oct. 17, 1582, at Quedlinburg; d. Aug. 20, 1637, at Jena. The "arch-theologian," the standard dogmatician of the period of orthodoxy. Induced by Johann Arnd to study theology. Studied at Wittenberg, Jena, and Marburg. After passing through a severe sickness, he wrote *Meditationes Sacrae.* Highly recommended to Duke Casimir of Coburg, though only twenty-four years old, he was appointed superintendent at Heldburg and made Doctor of Divinity, having preached only four times. In 1615 the duke made him general superintendent at Coburg and entrusted him with the visitation of the realm and the drawing up of a new church order. Though eminently successful in these important duties, his inclination was toward a theological professorship. At last the duke's opposition was overcome, and Gerhard, especially through the remonstrances of the Elector of Saxony, George I, and the entreaties of the faculty of the university, in 1616 became professor at Jena. Here he remained to the end of his life, though called no less than twenty-four times to different universities, even to Upsala in Sweden. Though of delicate health, the amount of activity he developed as professor, author, adviser in theological, ecclesiastical, and even political matters — "the oracle of his times" — is truly prodigious. He was greatly beloved by the students, who on this account flocked to Jena. His most famous work is his *Loci Theologici* in nine volumes, begun at the age of twenty-seven and finished in 1622; other books: *Confessio Catholica*, his continuation of the *Harmonia Evangelistarum* of Chemnitz and Leyser, *Exercitium Pietatis*, various commentaries. The foremost champion of Lutheran orthodoxy, he was of a mild and irenic disposition.

E. R. Fischer, *Vita Joannes Gerhardi*, Christopher Coerner, Leipzig, 1723; C. J. Boettcher, *Das Leben Dr. Johann Gerhards*, Justus Naumann, 1858.

Gerhard, Johann Ernst (1621—68). Son of Johann Gerhard; prof. at Jena; edited his father's *Patrologia*.

Gerhardt, Paul (1607—76). The Asaph of the Lutheran Church; the greatest hymn writer after Luther, whom he exceeds in flexibility of form and in smoothness of language; b. at Graefenhainichen, near Wittenberg; at University of Wittenberg 1628—42; lived in Berlin as candidate of theology 1643 to 1651; *Propst* at Mittenwalde 1651; diaconus at Berlin 1657; deposed 1666; diaconus at Luebben 1668. The outward circumstances of his life are gloomy, but his hymns are full of cheerful trust, sincerely and unaffectedly pious, benign and amiable. Adhered loyally to Lutheran faith, even under persecution, refusing to sanction syncretism. His hymns reflect his feelings during this trying period; they show firm grasp of objective realities, but also transition to modern subjective tone of religious poetry; wrote, among others: "Froehlich soll mein Herze springen"; "O Jesu Christ, dein Kripplein ist"; "Nun lasst uns gehn und treten"; "Schaut, schaut, was ist fuer Wunder dar?" "Auf, auf, mein Herz, mit Freuden"; "O Haupt voll Blut und Wunden"; "Wie soll ich dich empfangen?" "Wir singen dir, Immanuel"; "Warum machet solche Schmerzen?" "Ein Laemmlein geht und traegt die Schuld"; "O Welt, sieh hier dein Leben"; "Sei mir tausendmal gegruesset"; "Sei froehlich alles weit und breit"; "Gott Vater, sende deinen Geist"; "Was alle Weisheit in der Welt"; "Du Volk, das du getaufet bist"; "Herr Jesu, meine Liebe"; "Der Herr, der aller Enden"; "O Jesu Christ, mein schoenstes Licht"; "Wie ist es moeglich, hoechstes Licht?" "Warum sollt' ich mich denn graemen?" "Befiehl du deine Wege."

A. Ebeling, *Die Gedichte von Paulus Gerhardt*, Hahnsche Buchhandlung, 1898; G. A. Wenzel, *Pictures from the Life of Paul Gerhardt*, Riegel, Easton, Pa., 1881; Wm. Dallmann, *Paul Gerhardt, His Life and His Hymns*, CPH, n. d.; K. Hesselbacher, *Paul Gerhardt, der Saenger froehlichen Glaubens*, Leipzig and Hamburg, 1936; N. Nelle, *Paul Gerhardts Lieder und Gedichte*, Hamburg, 1907.

Gericke, Christian William (1742 to 1803). Lutheran missionary; b. in Prussia; worked in Kudelore (1764), Negapatam (1783), and Madras (1787), India; traveled in Tamil Land.

Gerlach, Otto v. (1801—49). Pastor in Berlin; author of a three-volume commentary on the Bible, in which the Bible text is reprinted and brief introductions and explanatory remarks are added.

German Baptist Brethren. See *Brethren (German Baptist Brethren, Dunkers).*

German Catholics. The name of a sect which grew out of the reform movement within the Roman Catholic Church occasioned by the idolatrous veneration of the Holy Coat of Treves, against which Johannes Ronge (subsequently excommunicated) emphatically protested. Doctrinal differences weakened the power of the secessionists, and today only a remnant survives in Saxony.

German Evangelical Lutheran Synod of Maryland and the South. See *Maryland and the South, German Synod of.*

German Evangelical Ministers' Conference. See *Evangelical Protestant Church of North America.*

German Evangelical Protestant Ministers' Association. See *Evangelical Protestant Church of North America.*

(German) Evangelical Synod of North America. See *Evangelical and Reformed Church*, 2.

German Nebraska Synod. See *United Lutheran Church, Synods of*, 14.

German Reformed Churches. See *Reformed Church.*

German Seventh-Day Baptists. See *Brethren (German Baptist Brethren, Dunkers); Baptist Bodies*, 17.

German Southwest Africa. See *Southwest Africa.*

German Theology (Deutsche Theologie). A book containing a summary of the fundamentals of the Christian religion, "a noble booklet of the right understanding concerning Adam and Christ, and how Adam should die and Christ arise in us," as Luther puts it, who published the tract, first as a fragment, in 1516, and two years later in its complete form. It is a product of the best period of German mysticism and belongs to the school of Tauler,* who formerly was considered the author.

Germany. A. 1. *Early History*. Christianity had entered Germany as early as the third century, several flourishing congregations existing then in the Roman colonies of the Rhine and the Danube. During the Roman period these regions became Christian countries; during the Migration of Nations they became pagan or semipagan. Towards the end of the sixth century a great missionary activity set in on the part of the Franks (whose ruler Clovis had received Baptism 496) and of Britain. The first apostle of the Alemanni was Fridolin, a Celt (550); he was followed (610) by Columbanus, of the Celtic cloister Bangor, with twelve companions, one of them Gallus (d. 640) and Pirminius, a Frank (d. 753). To Bavaria with its scanty remnants of Christianity came the Frankish abbot Eustasius (615), later on Emmeran, at the end of the century Bishop Rupert of Worms, perhaps a Scot, who almost completed the Christianizing of the country, and the Frankish bishop Corbinianus. Kilian, a Celt, became the apostle of the Thuringians. The Frankish priest Amandus labored among the Frisians. The Anglo-Saxon Wilfred and the Anglo-Saxon Willibrord (657?—738?; "Apostle of the Frisians") were supported by Rome. Boniface performed splendid missionary work in Hesse and Thuringia; he was also instrumental in bringing the German Church into subjection to Rome.

2. The Saxons, after an earlier missionary attempt by two Anglo-Saxon monks, were compelled by Charlemagne, in the wars of 772—804, to profess Christianity and were won for Christianity through the patient labor of the Frankish priests in the eight bishoprics established by the ruler. Christianity was spread among the Wendish races in Holstein, Mecklenburg, Pomerania, and parts of Saxony and Lusatia from 919 to 973 by conquest, compulsion, German colonization, and more or less preaching; Mecklenburg, its depopulated districts peopled with German colonists, became Christian with the conversion of its ruler in 1161; Pomerania submitted to the Duke of Poland 1121, and Bishop Otto of Bamberg established the Church 1124—28. The Gospel was first brought to the Prussians (Letts) by Bishop Adalbert of Prague, martyred 997; in 1209 the monk Christian came to the Prussians, d. 1245 as bishop of the Prussians. The crusade of the Teutonic Knights and their allies ended 1283, with the greater part of the Prussians extirpated and Christianity established by a host of real missionaries.

B. *Germany and the Lutheran Church*. When Luther began his defense of the Gospel, he was followed by many monks of the Augustinians, Franciscans, Dominicans, Carmelites, and others. Strassburg was one of the first cities to declare for the Gospel (1523), followed by Magdeburg (1524), Bremen (1525), Brunswick (1526), Goslar, Eimbeck, Goettingen, Rostock, Hamburg. Electoral Saxony was the first country to introduce the Reformation (1525). Hesse followed the lead of Saxony (1528), as did Frankish-Brandenburg, joined by Nuernberg. Then came Brunswick-Lueneburg, East Frisia, Schleswig, Holstein, Silesia. On Luther's advice the Grand Master of the Order of Teutonic Knights, Albrecht von Brandenburg, became secular, the first Duke of Prussia (later a German state) (1525), and introduced the Reformation. Wuerttemberg came in 1534, followed by the city of Augsburg. Anhalt also came in 1534, as well as Pomerania and Westphalia. Luther's grim enemy, the bearded Duke George of Saxony, died in 1539, and just twenty years after the historic Leipzig Debate with Eck, Luther preached in Saint Thomas Church, and the Reformation was introduced. In the same year came Brandenburg; Kalenberg-Brunswick came, Mecklenburg, Quedlinburg, Naumburg, Brunswick, the Palatinate, and Cologne. At the Religious Peace of Augsburg of 1555 the Protestants were as strong as the Romanists. See *Reformation*.

C. 1. *Subsequent Developments*. The Catholics put forth strenuous efforts to halt the spread of Lutheranism and to reconquer lost ground. The activity of the Jesuits and of the courts of Austria and Bavaria, the virulent persecution and suppression of Protestantism (see *Counter Reformation*), and the Thirty Years' War saved a large portion of Germany, especially in South Germany, for Rome. Other portions were lost to Calvinism — the Palatinate in 1560, Bremen in 1595, Nassau in 1578 and 1586, Anhalt in 1596, Lippe-Detmold in 1602, Hesse-Cassel in 1605. In 1613 John Sigismund, Elector of Brandenburg, of the House of Hohenzollern, turned Reformed, the people, however, remaining true to the Lutheran Church.

2. The Union between the Lutherans and Calvinists, proposed by the king of Prussia in 1817 and approved by the great majority, was effected and sustained, partly by force, in Prussia; also in Nassau, Baden, the Palatinate, Anhalt, and to some extent in Hesse. The new Church thus brought into existence took the name Evangelical. The Separate Lutherans refused to have anything to do with it. See *Breslau* and *Free Churches*.

3. Prior to World War I the Lutheran, Reformed, and Evangelical Churches in Germany were organized as state churches, the government generally being in the hands of consistories and superintendents appointed by the secular governing body, which provided, in greater part, for the support of the congregations out of the national revenues and more or less controlled the affairs of the Church. Of these thirty-four Protestant church bodies before World War II, the Prussian (including the older provinces) is Evangelical, Hanover having a Lutheran as well as an Evangelical-Reformed organization; Schleswig-Holstein, Lutheran-Reformed-Evangelical; Nassau, Evangelical; Frankfort on the Main, Lutheran-Reformed. The other Evangelical Churches are the Palatinate, Baden, Hesse-Darmstadt, Sachsen-Weimar, Sachsen-Meiningen, Anhalt, Waldeck, and Bremen. Lippe-Detmold is Evangelical-Reformed. The Lutheran Churches are: Bavaria, Saxony, Wuerttemberg, Mecklenburg-Schwerin, Mecklenburg-Strelitz, Oldenburg, Braunschweig, Sachsen-Altenburg, Sachsen-Coburg-Gotha, Schwarzburg-Sondershausen, Schwarzburg-Rudolstadt, Reuss Older Line, Reuss Younger Line, Schaumburg, Luebeck, Hamburg. Alsace-Lorraine has a Lutheran and a Reformed organization. The constitution of the German Republic (1918) pronounced the separation of Church and State and complete equality among all religious denominations (religious freedom having been established already under the Empire by the several state constitutions and by imperial law). There is no longer a State Church,

theoretically. Neither is there, practically, a Free Church. The majority of the clergy and of the laity seem to desire some sort of state support and state control and a *Volkskirche* (People's Church, National Church), which the masses would regard as their Church without joining it individually.

4. During the days of the Weimar Republic, President von Hindenburg had protected the rights of the Church. When Hitler came to power, it was felt that the rights of churches would also be protected, especially in view of Hitler's speech at the Garrison Church of Potsdam (March 23, 1933). A wave of religious revival followed. The *Deutsche Christen* were organized, first as a nonparty organization, but the movement soon took on political significance and aligned itself with Nazism. Its leader, Ludwig Mueller, was elected Bishop of the Reich (Sept. 27, 1933). His attempt to unite the German Protestant churches in harmony with party principles (see *Barmen Theses*) led to the organization of the opposition pastors by Niemoeller *(Pfarrernotbund)*. Opposition to Mueller's church politics led to surveillance by police, arrests, and incarceration. Interference curtailed the activities of churches, schools, and military ministries during World War II. The Protestant churches emerged exhausted from the war.

5. The hardships endured during World War II drew the Protestant groups closer together. Efforts were made to unite all German Protestants into one group. In July, 1948, the EKiD *(Evangelische Kirche in Deutschland)* was organized as a federation of Lutheran, Reformed, and Evangelical churches. In the same year the VELKD *(Vereinigte Evangelische Lutherische Kirche Deutschlands)* was in the process of organization. Its purpose is to strengthen Lutheran consciousness through an organic union of all Lutherans. See *Union Movements*.

6. Free Conferences at Bad Boll, Germany, were arranged by representatives of the Missouri Synod and Lutheran churches in Germany (1948). These conferences were to be a *Begegnung* (meeting of minds). In 1949 representatives from other Lutheran bodies in Europe and America participated in the conferences.

7. In 1951 there were four free churches in Germany: *The Evangelical Lutheran Church of Old Prussia* (Breslau Synod); the *Evangelical Lutheran Free Church in Germany* (Saxon

Synod); the *Independent Evangelical Lutheran Church of Baden, Hessen and Niedersachsen;* and the *Evangelical Lutheran Refugee Mission.* These churches had also reached unity by that date.

For the more recent movements in Germany see references under *Barmen Theses;* F. E. Mayer, *The Story of Bad Boll,* CPH, 1949.

Germany, Catholic Church in. See *Roman Catholic Church.*

Gernler, Lucas. See *Reformed Confessions,* A 10.

Gerok, Karl von (1815—90). Ed. at Tuebingen; held positions in the State Church, since 1849 at Stuttgart, finally as chief court preacher and *Oberconsistorialrat;* eloquent preacher, but fame rests chiefly on his sacred poetry, especially his *Palmblaetter, Pfingstrosen,* and others; strictly speaking, he wrote only spiritual lyrics, not hymns for congregational use.

Gerson, Jean Charlier de (Johannes Arnaudi de Gersonio, 1363—1429). Theologian, philosopher, educator; educated under patronage of the Duke of Burgundy, first at Rheims, then at College of Navarre, in Paris; doctor of theology in 1392, chancellor of the University of Paris, 1395, prominent in the domain of ecclesiastical practice, preaching, and the cure of souls. He considered mysticism * as the soul of theology, but he opposed radical and absolute mysticism. Following his teacher, D'Ailly, in the field of church politics, he exerted a strong influence on the Council of Pisa, although he did not attend in person. His doctrine concerning the character of a church council as composed of hierarchical authorities, with every believer, nevertheless, having the right to voice his opinion, was accepted by the Council of Constance,* but his later influence at the meetings was insignificant, so that he finally withdrew in disgust, to wander into exile from fear of his former patron, the Duke of Burgundy. He spent his last years in Lyons. Among his writings: *Consolatio theologiae, Monotessaron* (a Gospel harmony), and others. He was later honored with the title *Doctor Christianissimus* (the most Christian doctor).

Walter Dresz, *Die Theologie Gersons,* Bertelsmann, Guetersloh, 1931.

Gesenius, Justus (1601—73). Studied at Helmstedt and Jena, pastor at Brunswick in 1629, court chaplain at Hildes-heim in 1636, chief court preacher and general superintendent at Hanover in 1642; an accomplished and influential theologian; edited Hanoverian hymnbooks from 1646 to 1659; aimed at correctness of style according to poetical canons; wrote: "Jesu, deine heil'gen Wunden"; "Wenn meine Suend' mich kraenken"; "O Tod, wo ist dein Stachel nun?" "O heiligste Dreifaltigkeit."

Gesenius, Wilh. (1786—1842). Renowned Hebraist, author of a Hebrew grammar and dictionary. He was a born teacher, extreme rationalist; was attacked by Hengstenberg in his *Evangelische Kirchenzeitung.* Wrote also *Der Prophet Jesaia.*

Gesius, Bartholomaeus (Gese; ca. 1560—ca. 1614). Lutheran choral composer who was active in Wittenberg prior to 1590. Gesius prepared many four- and five-part harmonizations which reveal his skill and spirit, but which likewise indicate that he took liberties with the chorale melodies which were unfortunate as well as confusing. In his *Passion According to St. John,* which Schoeberlein included in his *Schatz des liturgischen Chor- und Gemeindegesangs,* he departed from the recitative style of the Passion and, like Lechner, wrote figuratively, in polyphonic motet style. Spitta, in his work on Bach, claims he thus revealed the influence of Lassus.

E. E. Koch, *Geschichte des Kirchenlieds und Kirchengesangs,* Stuttgart, 1877 (vol. II); Karl von Winterfeld, *Der ev. Kirchengesang,* Leipzig, 1843 (vol. I).

Gess, Wolfgang Friedrich (1819—91). B. at Kirchheim; d. at Wernigerode. Studied at Tuebingen. After several pastorates he became professor of systematic theology and exegesis at Goettingen and Breslau, member of the Silesian consistory, then general superintendent of the province of Posen. Theologically he adhered to the modern kenotic school.

Gestalt School. See *Psychology,* J 5.

Gettysburg Seminary. See *Ministry, Education of,* VI C, XI B.

Geyer, Carl Ludwig. B. Mar. 16, 1812, at Zwickau, Saxony. Educated at *Gymnasium* at Zwickau, University of Leipzig. Passed theological examination in 1836. Became private tutor. Joined the Saxon Emigration in 1838. Taught school at Old Trinity, St. Louis, till 1840. Teacher at Johannesberg, Cape Girardeau Co., Mo., 1840—44. Ordained

Oct. 23, 1844. Pastor at Lebanon, Wis., 1844—60; at Carlinville, Ill., 1860—76; at Serbin, Tex., 1876—92. Married Johanna Maria Schwefel. Two sons entered the ministry. Wrote German primer which was widely used in Missouri Synod's schools. Died March 6, 1892.

A. C. Stellhorn, "Carl Ludwig Geyer," *CHIQ*, XII: 3—12.

Gezelius, Johann (1615—90). Prof. at Dorpat, Sweden; bishop of Abo, Finland. Labored to raise the intellectual standard of the Finnish clergy and the religious and secular knowledge of the people. Published many textbooks, an edition of the Greek New Testament, and other works. His exegetical work on the Bible was completed and published by his son, Johann Gezelius (1647—1718).

Ghiberti, Lorenzo (1378—1455). Italian painter and artist in bronze; received contract (in competition with Brunelleschi) for bronze doors of the Baptistery at Florence.

Ghirlandajo, Domenico Bigordi (1449—94). Italian painter, celebrated principally as teacher of Michelangelo; painted chiefly frescoes in his native city, Florence, but also in Sistine Chapel at Rome.

Ghost. A term applied to the immortal spirit in man (soul). It is also used of a phantom or apparition. See *Holy Ghost*.

Ghost, Holy. See *Holy Ghost*.

Gibbon, Edward (1737—94). English historian; Roman Catholic for a few years; wrote the monumental history *Decline and Fall of the Roman Empire*, characterized by vast erudition, but displaying at times hostility to the Christian Church.

Gibbons, Cardinal James (1834 to 1921). B. in Baltimore; educated in Baltimore and in Ireland; priest, 1861; bishop of North Carolina, 1868; "Primate of the United States," 1877; presided over third plenary council of Baltimore, 1884; created cardinal by Leo XIII; leader of Catholics in America; wrote: *Faith of Our Fathers*, a popular and skillful defense of Roman Catholicism.

Allen Sinclair Will, *Life of Cardinal Gibbons*, Dutton, 1922.

Gibbons, Orlando (1583—1625). One of England's foremost composers of church music. Though less prolific than William Byrd, he is regarded as his greatest rival. Gibbons has been called "the father of pure Anglican church music"; he consistently employed the English language in his choral works and was not influenced by the Roman masters as was Byrd. His style varies, and his compositions do not show the dry austerity so common in music of his day.

E. H. Fellowes, *Orlando Gibbons*, Oxford U. Press; J. Hawkins, *General History of the Science and Practice of Music*, London, 1875 (vol. II); W. H. Parry, *Thirteen Centuries of English Church Music*, London, 1946.

Gichtelians. Adherents of Johann Georg Gichtel; b. 1638, Regensburg; since 1667 in Amsterdam, where d. 1710; a German mystic and visionary and eccentric follower of Jakob Boehme,* who antagonized the Lutheran Church, especially its doctrine of justification. Because they rejected marriage and believed themselves as pure as angels, also called *Engelsbrueder*. Found in Holland, Hamburg, Berlin, and other places, and maintained themselves to nineteenth century.

Gideons. See *Bible Societies*, 5.

Gieseler, Joh. Karl Ludwig (1792 to 1854). Church historian; professor at Bonn; 1831 at Goettingen, where he displayed marked activity as professor of church history and dogmatics, and also in practical benevolences as curator of the Orphans' Home. His chief work is *Lehrbuch der Kirchengeschichte*, translated also into English.

Gifts, Spiritual. Any particular endowment of the believer, employed for the edification of the Church, 1 Cor. 7: 7; 12: 11; Rom. 12: 6. By the abundance and diversity of these gifts are revealed the riches of divine grace, 1 Pet. 4: 10. Several spiritual gifts, charisms, may be united in one individual. Among special gifts bestowed by the Holy Spirit upon the Early Church were some of a miraculous character — speaking in tongues, prophesying, healing the sick, and casting out demons. 1 Cor. 14; Matt. 10: 8; Mark 6: 13. These gifts particularly impose a heavy responsibility, hence the apostolic warning not to abuse them, and to retain the most excellent gift of all, which is love. 1 Cor. 13. In apostolic times these miraculous gifts were bestowed by the laying on of hands, Acts 8: 17; 19: 6, though occasionally they followed the simple preaching of the Gospel, Acts 10: 44, 46. As fast as the reigning power of heathenism was broken, the miraculous charisms became less frequent and seem to have disappeared after the fourth century, though not fully and forever, since phenomena like those of the first age have been observed in times of awakening. They have also accompanied the entrance of the Gospel into lands newly opened to the Christian message. See *Charismata*.

Gilbert Islands. See *Polynesia*.

Gildas (ca. 516—70). British monk and early British historian; wrote *Gildae Sapientis de excidio et conquestu Britanniae*, which gives a brief review of the history of Britain from the time of the Roman invasion to his own times.

Gilgamesh Epic. See *Babylonians, Religion of*, 6.

Gill, Thomas Hornblower (1819 to 1906). Owing to Unitarian tendencies led the life of an isolated student; belongs to small company of original British hymnists, noted for quaintness; wrote, among others: "O Mystery of Love Divine!"

Gillespie, Thomas. See *Presbyterian Bodies*, 1.

Gilman, Samuel. B. at Gloucester, Mass., Feb. 16, 1791. He attended the academy at Atkinson, N. H., and then Harvard College, graduating in 1811. After following a secular calling for several years, he returned to Harvard and served there as tutor for two years. He then was pastor of a Unitarian congregation at Charleston, S. C., until his death in 1858.

Gioberti, Vincenzo (1801—52). Italian; ordained priest (1825); later prof. at Turin, Italy; his philosophy held that God is true being *(ens);* all other things are the idea in God individualized and existent; attacked Jesuits; sought to liberalize the Papacy; reformer.

Giotto, properly *Ambrogiotto* or *Angiolotto Bondone* (1266—1336). Prevailed upon by Cimabue to study painting; his figures show life and freedom; noted paintings "Navicella" at Rome and frescoes at Florence.

Girard, Stephen (1750—1831). An American philanthropist, freethinker, and admirer of Voltaire and Rousseau; bequeathed large sums of money to hospitals, schools, and asylums, including $2,000,000 for a college for orphans in Philadelphia from which clergy were barred.

Girgensohn, Karl (1875 to 1925). German Lutheran theologian; prof. at Dorpat, Greifswald, and Leipzig; regarded as an outstanding representative of conservative Lutheranism; prolific writer.

Girl Scouts, Inc. There is no community of organization and administration between Girl Scouts and Boy Scouts of America. Like Scouting for boys, the Girl Scout movement has the following features: 1. a pledge and a law; 2. uniforms and insignia; 3. degrees of advancement; 4. church troops and non-church troops; 5. program of indoor and outdoor activities; 6. regular organization; 7. trained leaders. While headquarters exercise supervision in order to maintain uniform prescribed standards for advancement in the various degrees, it makes no attempt to encroach on the duties and prerogatives of the church and of the home. The meetings do not open with a religious ceremony. No religious topics are discussed.

Given, J. F. See *Christian Union*.

Giving, Christian. See *Finances in the Church*, 1.

Gjerset, Knut. B. Sept. 15, 1865, at Romsdal, Norway; came to America six years later; studied at Univ. of Minn.; Ph. D., Heidelberg, Germany; 1898; studied also at Berlin and Oslo; prof. at Ansgar Seminary (1893—95); Glenwood Academy (1900—02), Luther College (1902—36, except 1916—17, when pres. of Park Region Luther College); Litt. D. (St. Olaf College, 1925); knighted by the kings of Norway and of Denmark; founded Norwegian-American Historical Assn.; curator of Norwegian-American Historical Museum; vice-pres., later pres., of Iowa Historical Association; in addition to an English grammar, he wrote historical works on Scandinavian countries and Scandinavian people in America; d. Oct. 29, 1936.

Gjevre, Anders H. B. in Norway, June 9, 1852; came to America (1871); grad. from Luther College (1878) and Luther Seminary (1881); attended correspondence school of Harper at Chicago and Yale and Columbia Univ.; pastor at Wilmot, S. Dak. (1881—82), Appleton, Minn. (1882—84), Renville, Minn. (1885—86), Sawyer, Wis. (1886 to 1893), Fertile, Minn. (1893—1900), Graettinger, Iowa (1903—07), Grand Meadow, Minn. (1907—13); prof. of Hebrew, United Church Seminary (1897—98); Jewish Missionary, New

York (1900—03) and Minneapolis (1913 to 1930); outstanding linguist; wrote extensively, especially in the Semitic field; d. April 29, 1930.

Gladden, Washington (1836—1918). Congregational clergyman; pastor at Brooklyn (1860), Morrisania, N. Y. (1861), North Adams, Mass. (1866), Springfield, Mass. (1875), Columbus, Ohio (1882). Studied the writings of W. Robertson and H. Bushnell. While at North Adams he began his work of applying Christian principles to social problems. An early apostle of the social gospel.* He held that government should bring about social adjustments not by endorsing an economic program, but by inspiring individuals with ideals of justice, love, and service. Defended right of labor to organize. Organized *Christian League of Connecticut* (1883). Active in civic leagues. His poetry reveals mystical elements. E. T. Thompson, "Washington Gladden and the Development of 'New Theology,'" *Changing Emphases in American Preaching*, Westminster Press, Philadelphia, 1943; bibliography in *Who's Who in America* (1918—19).

Gladstone, William Ewart (1809 to 1898). "Grand Old Man." Prominent English statesman and noted author. Began career as High Churchman; disestablished Irish Church (Anglican); supported interests of Irish Catholic institutions; fought ritualism and ultramontanism (*The Vatican Decrees in Their Bearing on Civil Allegiance*, 1874; *Vaticanism*, and *Rome and the Newest Fashion in Religion*, 1875); held to the Bible as the Word of God.

Glasgow Bible Society. See *Bible Societies*, 4.

Glassites. See *Disciples of Christ*, 1.

Glassius, Solomon (1593—1656). He taught philosophy, Greek, and Hebrew since 1617 in Jena, became superintendent in 1625 at Sondershausen; in 1638 professor of theology at Jena as Gerhard's successor; from 1640 to the end of his life general superintendent and court preacher at Gotha. The greatest of his very numerous works is his *Philologia Sacra*.

Glaubensbekenntnis der wahren Inspirationsgemeinde. See *Amana Society*.

Glinka, Michael Ivanovich (1803 to 1857). Called by Franz Liszt the "Prophet-Patriarch of Russian Music." In his early life he acquainted himself intimately with Russian folk music and later studied the works of Haydn, Mozart, Beethoven; he studied in Milan, Rome, and Naples and became acquainted with Donizetti and Bellini. From 1836 to 1839 Glinka was choirmaster of the Imperial Chapel. His sacred choral music is of a pleasing character and is seldom purely Russian. He composed also operatic and orchestral music. Glinka died before he was able to carry out his plan of harmonizing the canticles of his Church in typical Russian harmonies.

Gloria in Excelsis. See *Canticles; Worship, Parts of*, 6.

Gloria Patri. See *Canticles; Worship, Parts of*, 4.

Glory. The Bible speaks 1) of the glory of God, the manifestation of His attributes, especially of His holiness and majesty (Ex. 33:18, 19; Is. 6:3; Ps. 63:2; 104; 31; 138:5; John 1:14; 2 Pet. 1:17); 2) of the glory of Christ*; 3) of the glory of the Church * Militant and Triumphant, which is also the glory of the individual believers, veiled and hidden to mortal eyes in this world, but to be fully revealed on the Last Day and culminating in the beatific vision (Ps. 17:15; 1 John 3:2; 1 Cor. 13:12; Rev. 22:4). The believers are participants of spiritual glory (John 17:22; 1 Cor. 2:7; 2 Cor. 3:18; 1 Pet. 1:8) and of eternal glory (Rom. 8:18; 1 Cor. 15:43; Phil. 3:21; 2 Thess. 2:14; 2 Tim. 2:10; 1 Pet. 5:10). In heaven they will have glorified bodies (Phil. 3:21). There are also degrees of glory in heaven (Dan. 12:3; Luke 19:12-26; 1 Cor. 15:41, 42). Christians are not to seek glory from men (Matt. 6:2; 1 Thess. 2:6), they are to seek only God's glory (1 Cor. 10:31; 2 Cor. 10:17). Cp. Luther, VIII:837; IX:1273; Laetsch, *The Abiding Word*, I:565 ff.; articles in Dogmatics on the Church Militant, State of Believers, Kingdom of Glory, Eternal Life. JMW

Glosses and Glossators. The practice of supplying manuscripts with glosses, *i. e.*, marginal notes to explain certain words in the text, dates back to classical times. Such glosses were also inserted in Bible manuscripts, both in the margin and between the lines. In the course of time they were extended to include a variety of explanatory material. Glossing was carried to the greatest length in the canon law by glossators, canonists living from the twelfth to the fifteenth century (especially in Bologna). By the successive additions of one master after another, a running comment was established, which explained, illustrated, and reconciled the various provisions. These glosses were held in high regard and enjoyed considerable authority.

Gluck, Christoph Willibald (1714 to 1787). Studied music in Prague, Vienna, and Milan; distinguished principally as operatic writer, spent his time between Paris and Vienna; wrote also *De Profundis* and an incomplete cantata, *"Das Juengste Gericht."*

Gnesio-Lutherans (Genuine Lutherans). A name given to those Lutherans who were led by Nicholas Amsdorf after the death of Luther (Flacius, Wigand, Gallus, Judex, Moerlin, Heshus, Timann, Westphal) and had their seat at Jena. Their opponents were called the Philippists (because they followed the synergism and other tendencies of Melanchthon — Camerarius, Bugenhagen, Eber, Crell, Major, Cruciger, Strigel, Pfeffinger, Peucer).

Gnosticism. 1. A movement the roots of which go into pre-Christian times (Hermetic Literature) and which had its *floreat* in the 2d and 3d Christian centuries. The name comes from a Greek word which means "knowledge" (*gnosis*). This "knowledge" consisted of occult lore and the possession of certain magical watchwords and secret names. All the sects claimed to be in possession of a secret divinely given message on which entrance into the higher life depended.

2. The beginnings of gnosticism must be sought in the fusion of religious beliefs and cultures which arose especially as a result of the rise of Persia and the conquests of Alexander. Even Judaism was not entirely free from this syncretism (Essenes, Therapeutae, Philo). Elements in gnosticism have been traced by various authors, each overemphasizing his investigation (Harnack: Hellenism; Anz: Babylonia; Bousset: Babylonia and Iran; Friedlaender: Pre-Christian Judaism; Reitzenstein: Egypt and Iran; Troje: India; Eisler: Orphic cults).

3. The basic idea of gnosticism was redemption, first, from the material world (matter considered evil) and then escape into a world of freedom, thus achieving the liberty implied in human spirit. The soul, escaping from matter is to be united with the *pleroma* or fullness of God.

4. While this redemption took place through initiations, rites, mysteries, magic (each sect having its own peculiarities), the more speculative adherents needed philosophical ideas. Hence the dualistic idea inherent in the redemption doctrine was expanded (supreme God — Demiurge; good — evil; light — darkness; heavenly fall — temporal fall; spirit — matter; *pleroma — hysterema*) and synthesized in the good God.

5. While many variations occur, the following gives an idea of theological systems in Christian times: God is pure abstraction, a fathomless abyss. From Him emanate divine potencies (*aeons*) which in their totality constitute the *pleroma* (fullness, ideal world of light opposed to *kenona*, or emptiness of matter). *Sophia* (wisdom) disturbed the harmony of the *pleroma* and fell into the formless chaos beyond (*hysterema*). Through matter she gave birth to *Demiurge* (identified with the Jehovah of OT). Redemption takes place through the restoring of the harmony of the *pleroma* and liberating sparks of light from matter. This is done by the most perfect aeon (*Soter*) who entered Jesus at Baptism and left Him before Calvary. Christ accomplishes His work by teaching *Wisdom*, which is received only by a select few (*pneumatikoi*, spirituals). The next class of men (*psychikoi*, psychics) must be content with faith, while the lowest (*hylics*, material) are doomed to destruction.

6. The ethical system aimed at overcoming flesh (matter) and developed both into strict asceticism and extreme libertinism.

7. Some of the more important gnostic leaders and movements are:

a. *Simon Magus* (Acts 8:9). Regarded as the originator of gnosticism in patristic literature (Samaria was an early bed of syncretism). Menander, another Samaritan, was his pupil.

b. *Cerinthus* (ca. 100). Active at Ephesus and reputed opponent of St. John (1 John). No writings survive; accounts in patristics vague and contradictory.

c. *Satornilus*, disciple of Menander, flourished in Antioch of Syria (Irenaeus, *Haer.* i, 24).

d. *Elkesai* promulgated his doctrine (all receive forgiveness of sins who accept his form of baptism and receive the doctrines of his books) in the trans-Jordanic regions (ca. 101). Teachings still influential in Arabia in 10th c.

e. *Basilides*. Disciple of Menander;

wrote Gospel of Alexandria, explained it in 24 books and wrote Gnostic hymns. Divergent accounts of his theories (Irenaeus, Hippolytus, Clement A., Origen, Eusebius) probably represent divergent views of his followers. Basic is a system of emanations terminating in matter. Jehovah created world; Jesus ended Jehovah's rule; salvation through knowledge; Jesus human only in appearance; Simon of Cyrene died in His stead on cross. His son, *Isidorus*, wrote *De anima, Ethica, Explanationes in prophetam Parchor*, of which fragments are extant in Irenaeus.

f. *Epiphanes*. Son of Alexandrian gnostic, Carpocrates; wrote *De iustitia* advocating communism (Clement A., *Strom.* 3, 2).

g. *Valentinus*. Egyptian; at Rome 135/160; wrote epistles, homilies, psalms; his gnosticism has threefold division of personality instead of two. More prominent of his pupils were Heracleon, Ptolemaeus, Florinus, Theotinus, Alexander, Axionicus, Marcus, and Theodotus (Epiphanius, *Haer.* 31, 7; Irenaeus, *Haer.* 13—21).

h. *Bardesanes* (Bar Daisan; 154 to 222). Born in Edessa, Syria; founder of Syriac Christian literature; author of ca. 150 Syriac hymns. Praised by Eusebius but blamed by Ephraem and others. Tried to remove responsibility for evil from God by ascribing to Him the planning but not creation of world. Hence association with gnostic ideas.

i. *Ophites* (Barbelo-Gnostici). Regarded the serpent as symbol of supreme emanation. The Fathers usually grouped anonymous and primitive groups under this name (Naassenes, Peratae, Sethians, Cainites, Archontics, Severians, Justinians, and many obscure sects).

j. Other Gnostic sects include: *Antitactae* (Clem., *Strom.* 3, 4); *Nicolaitans* (Rev. 2:6, 15. Irenaeus as well as Clement A. mention sect by this name which cultivated immorality as a way of asserting superiority over the flesh); *Prodiciani* (Clem., *Strom.* 3, 4).

k. *Marcion*. Born in Pontus (ca. 100); excommunicated by his father; repudiated by Polycarp as the firstborn of Satan; came to Rome (ca. 139) but soon rejected there also. Marcion's primary purpose was to free Christianity from "OT and Jewish influences." Jehovah was a just God (*Demiurge*), Jesus revealed the good God. He rejected the OT entirely and sought to purge the NT of all "Judaistic" elements. Three works are ascribed

to him: *Evangelium* (Luke mutilated); *Apostolicon* (10 Pauline Epistles); *Antitheses* (OT opposed to NT and self-contradictory). EL

Works of Harnack, Anz, Bousset, Friedlaender, Reitzenstein, Troje, Eisler; S. Angus, *The Mystery Religions and Christianity*, Scribner's, N. Y., 1925; A. Hilgenfeld, *Ketzergeschichte des Urchristentums*, Leipzig, 1884; E. F. Scott, "Gnosticism," in Hasting's *Encyclopedia of Religion and Ethics;* John Knox, *Marcion and the New Testament*, University of Chicago Press, 1942.

Gobat, Samuel. See *Abyssinia*.

God. The Being who has made the world and man and to whom man is responsible. Man's knowledge of God falls into two broad categories. God is apparent to man through the power and design in the natural world, through the pattern of the forces of history (Ps. 19; Rom. 1 and 2; Acts 17). Through these data man is able to construct a mental picture of a Force infinitely powerful, working out man's destiny with a heavy hand, confronting mankind with continuous challenge. Human reactions to this understanding of God result in reverence for nature and idolatry; or the attempt to rationalize God into abstract natural law and remove man's responsibility to Him (2 Pet. 3); or in despair and fear. This natural knowledge of God is basic to every human system of religion and most of its philosophy; it is insufficient for a satisfying and adequate faith in God as Father (*Deus incognitus*). — The functional insight into God is not a power within the range of human endowment (John 1:18). From behind the veil and mask of nature and history God speaks to man in an act of self-revelation through which His true nature and character are more completely clear. This act is the incarnation of Jesus Christ, the Son of God (*Deus revelatus*). The purpose of this incarnation was to remove the cleavage between God and man, to meet the problem of man's sin and rebellion against God, and to atone for that sin (2 Cor. 5:18-21). In this act God is revealed as a Being infinitely pained by man's deviation from His holiness, yet infinitely desirous to repair the breach, to the point of Himself assuming responsibility for this repair at the cost of His own sacrifice. Thus God is revealed as perfect and holy, as personal and driven by the will of love to bring man into conformity with Himself.

This revelation of God in His Son is communicated through the written Word, the secondary principle of revelation. The Word of God presents a few more data about His nature, which are intelligible and credible, however, only in the light of this central revelation in Christ Jesus, the Word of God. God is eternal, that is to say, not subject to time (Ps. 90; 2 Pet. 3). God is not confined to space. God is not limited as are creatures, in point of power, knowledge, or wisdom. All of the resources of the nature of God are at the disposal of the man in Christ, and by him are recognized to be at work for his good (Rom. 8). The insight into God and the power to grasp and to trust in God as his forgiving and enabling Father is the work of God Himself, the gift of His Spirit. The Christian Church has summarized the nature of God and the Christian's knowledge of God, therefore, in the concept of the Trinity, one Being expressing Himself toward men in the distinct personalities of Father, Son, and Spirit. RRC

R. R. Caemmerer, "The Nature and Attributes of God," *Abiding Word,* CPH, 1947 (II: 59—77).

God, Arguments for the Existence of (cf. *Apologetics*). Man knows that there is a God (cf. *God*) even without the special revelation in the Bible, because God Himself has inscribed this knowledge in his heart at the creation (Rom. 1: 19; Ps. 14: 1). Hence the existence of God need not be proved to anyone of morally sound mind. We thus gain the *natural,* or general argument for God's existence, *viz.,* God is acknowledged in man's universal moral consciousness. Closely related to this, is the *theological* argument for God's existence, *i. e.,* the Bible, without any explanation, encounters man with the fact of God's being and sovereignty, and this is at once understood and acknowledged. Further arguments for God's existence are reasonably deduced from His self-manifestation in the universe, human history, and man's conscience (Rom. 1: 20; Acts 14: 17; 17: 22 ff.). The *cosmological* argument reasons from the effect to the cause that this orderly world cannot be the effect of chance, but must have for its Creator an intelligent and omnipotent God. The *teleological* argument demonstrates God's existence from the evidences of design, purpose, and adaptation in the world. The *moral* argument for God's existence is based upon man's moral nature and the moral order which is everywhere traceable in the world. The *esthetic* argument is founded on the beauty and comeliness manifested in the universe, which must have as its Maker a loving God. The *ontological* argument reasons from the fact that the human mind has the necessary conception of a perfect and absolute divine Being, which conception must be founded on fact since it cannot exist in a vacuum. Though atheism denies the validity of these and other arguments for God's existence, unbiased reason, scrutinizing them objectively, must admit that they supply cumulative proof for God's existence. JTM

God-breathed. See *Theopneustia.*

God, Love of. See *Love; Lovingkindness; Lund, Theology of.*

Godet, Frederic Louis (1812—1900). Swiss Reformed; native of Neuchatel; tutor to crown prince of Prussia 1838 to 1844; pastor at Neuchatel; professor there in the theological school of the Established Church; then, 1873, in that of the Free Church; generally conservative in theology. *Commentaries on Gospels of John* and *Luke,* on *Romans, First Corinthians;* etc.

Godfather, Godmother. See *Sponsors.*

Godfrey of Fontaines (ca. 1260 to 1320). Bishop of Tournai; his *Quodlibeta* develops the thoughts of Thomas Aquinas.

Gods. See *Idolatry.*

Goenner, Johann Jakob (1807—64). Called, in 1843, as first full-time professor at Concordia College, then at Altenburg, Mo., he moved with the institution to St. Louis in 1849, retiring on account of illness 1861.

Goering, Jacob (1775—1807). Ed. by Helmuth; pastor at Carlisle and York, Pa.; published works against Anabaptists and Methodists.

Goerres, Joseph (1776—1848). Professor of history at Munich; in earlier years warm advocate of the ideas of the French Revolution; later a champion of ultramontanism; deplored the Reformation as a second fall and urged revival of medievalism.

Goethe, Johann Wolfgang von (1749 to 1832). B. in Frankfurt a. M.; d. at Weimar; greatest German poet. Although during his earlier life favorably disposed to Christianity, he later became impatient with Christian demands of self- and world-denial and inclined toward a pantheistic worship of nature as well as toward a worship of classical antiquity, fostered mainly by the fascination which the paganism of the ancient Greek and Roman world exerted upon him during his travels in Italy, 1786—88. As he had no true conception of the real character of sin, he had no appreciation of the Christian doctrine of redemption. Redemption to him was merely self-redemption, which, in accordance with the pantheistic aspect of his religion, is achieved by striving to comprehend the secrets of nature and to penetrate to the essence of things, as Faust tried to do. That is salvation by works, as he says in Faust, that "he may be redeemed who strives and labors" ("Wer immer strebend sich bemueht, den koennen wir erloesen"). Goethe was essentially a rationalist, as was Kant, and though he endeavored to penetrate into the realm of the eternal, he failed in the attempt.

Goethe, Matthias. See *Australia*, B 1.

Goetwasser, John Ernst. See *Gutwasser, John Ernst.*

Goeze, Johann Melchior (1717—86). B. at Halberstadt; d. at Hamburg. Studied at Jena and Halle. He held pastorates at Aschersleben, Magdeburg, and Hamburg. As defender of orthodox Lutheranism and foe of the Enlightenment, he engaged in a controversy with Lessing.

Gogarten, Friedrich (b. 1887). German Protestant theologian; pupil of Troeltsch; followed the theology of Kierkegaard, then Karl Barth, and finally became a champion of National Socialism (see *Barmen Theses*).

Gold Coast. 91,843 square miles; population: 4,111,680 (1948). A British colony in West Africa, on the Gulf of Guinea. Fetishism was rampant, of great cruelty. First missionary, Rev. Thomas Thompson, sent by the S. P. G. in 1751. Missions active there: the Ewe Church; Presbyterian Church of the Gold Coast; Methodist Church; Church of England; Church of Scotland; Basel Mission Society; Norddeutsche Missionsgesellschaft; African M. E. Church; African M. E. Zion Church; the Adventists. 241 ordained and 5,182 not ordained native workers; approximately 369,565 members, of them 117,542 given

as communicants (1952). See *Missions, Bibliography.*

Golden Rose. A costly ornament, blessed by the Pope every year on Laetare Sunday and often sent to Catholic sovereigns, churches, or communities as a token of esteem. The custom probably dates back to the eleventh century. The ornament, originally a single rose, now consists of a branch of roses, all of pure gold, sometimes worth several thousand dollars. Henry VIII received three golden roses, and in 1518 one was bestowed on Elector Frederick the Wise to make him proceed against Luther.

Good Friday. See *Church Year*, 8.

Good News. See *Associated Lutheran Charities*, D.

Good Shepherd, Sisters of. See *Sisterhoods.*

Good Works. 1. In the Biblical and proper usage of the term the outflow and fruit of faith, especially in the outward deeds of the believers, performed by them for love of Christ and God and in agreement with the Word and will of God. Every good thing that a Christian says and does, and every act by which he omits something evil, as an evidence of the divine life of faith in his heart, is a good work (Eph. 2:10; Titus 2:14; Heb. 13:20, 21). Good works, properly speaking, are not the believer's own performance, but the works of God in and through him; God gives both the incentive and the power for the performance of works that are well-pleasing in His sight (John 15:5; 2 Cor. 9:8; Phil. 2:12, 13; Matt. 5:16). It is true, of course, that owing to the presence of sin, of the natural depravity, the works of the believers are not in themselves perfect, neither in their inception nor in their fruition (Rom. 7:18, 19). But these flaws, imperfections, and frailties connected with the good works of the believers have been atoned for by Christ Jesus, for whose sake God looks upon these works, and upon those who perform them, as perfect (Rom. 8: 1, 10).

2. In direct contrast to the good works of believers (*iustitia spiritualis*) we have the fictitious good works of men who have no faith, but whose outward behavior in many instances resembles that of the Christians. If these works are an outflow of an attempt to merit righteousness before God, as in the penances of the Roman Church and in all other self-appointed forms of

religion, they defeat their own end. Such works are the basis of every false religion. The Formula of Concord says: "Without Christ, without faith, and without the Holy Ghost men are in the power of the devil, who drives men to manifold and open crimes" (II:29). It is true that we distinguish a certain form of civic righteousness (*iustitia civilis, opera externa*), with certain virtues connected with the outward maintenance of civic authority in the world, such as obedience to the laws, honesty in business, and similar desirable acts. It is true, also, that man has a free will to choose such outward manifestations and civic virtues and that they are often rewarded by a measure of wealth and honor in the world. But such exhibitions are not necessarily connected with a regenerated heart; they may be the outflow of natural altruism and even of the most extreme selfishness. They have nothing in common with the essence of good works as found in the lives of Christians.

3. That the good works of the believers, in themselves, merit no reward is evident from the passages adduced above. Where the Bible speaks of such rewards, it is evident that a reward of mercy is meant. God looks upon the imperfect good works of the believers, on account of the perfect obedience of Christ, as though they were in themselves good and perfect. In this sense, the good works will also serve as a criterion on the Last Day to prove the presence of faith. For, while good works are not necessary to salvation, as Georg Major * taught shortly after Luther's death, they are a necessary fruit and proof of faith, and the Lutheran Church has been unjustly accused of setting aside good works and a life of sanctification. See *Sanctification*.

Goodness. 1. The goodness of God is in Scripture exhibited in four aspects, as love, benevolence, grace, and mercy. "God is *Love* inasmuch as He longs for, and delights in, union and communion with the objects of His holy desire." (A. L. Graebner.) That world which is the object of His love was a lost world; yet God would not have His creatures perish, and He longs for reunion with them. John 3:16. He yearns in bitter anguish for the children which have gone astray. Is. 1:2-5; 49:15 f. Yet it is a holy desire; God cannot have communion with those who are separated from Him by sin.

To make them His own and unite them with Himself, He wrought a redemption. Is. 43:1. — The *benevolence* of God is that kindness by which He provides for the wants of His creatures. Ps. 104:27 f. Especially does He desire to promote the happiness of men, and hence He formed the plan of salvation. — "God is *gracious* inasmuch as He offers and confers His blessings regardless of the merits or demerits of the objects of His benevolence." Rom. 6:23; Eph. 2:8 f. That aspect of goodness by which He has compassion with the afflicted and bestows His benefits upon the miserable is called *mercy*. His mercy is plenteous and abundant and extends over all who suffer trouble and affliction, whether physical, mental, or spiritual, Ps. 68:5; Is. 49:13.

2. In a relative sense the creatures of God are also good (Gen. 1:31) even after the Fall (1 Tim. 4:4). But the goodness of the creature is not perfection (essential goodness) but is a dependent goodness, *i. e.*, the creatures are good only as God's handiwork.

Goodrich, Chauncey Allen (1790 to 1860). Congregational clergyman, educator and lexicographer; studied under Timothy Dwight; ordained pastor at Middletown, Conn.; prof. of rhetoric at Yale; supported Nathaniel Taylor and promulgated the ideas of the "New Haven Theology."

Gordon, George Angier (1853 to 1929). Congregationalist; lecturer at Yale; university preacher at Harvard and Yale. Opposed strict Calvinism but supported New England Theology. Wrote *Witness to Immortality; The Christ of Today; Through Man to God.*

Gore, Charles (1853—1932). Anglican bishop. The Oxford Movement, under his influence, underwent changes opposed by the old Tractarians. His *Lux Mundi* sought to bring the Christian creed into "relation with modern growth in knowledge" and caused the High Church to develop along modernistic lines.

Gosala (6th c.). Important Jewish atheistic leader; founder of Ajivikas.

Goeschel, Karl Friedrich (1784 to 1861). Jurist and philosopher. B. at Langensalza; d. at Naumburg. Studied at Gotha and Leipzig. Held judicial positions at Langensalza, Naumburg, Berlin, and Magdeburg. He endeavored to harmonize Christianity with modern culture.

Gospel. See *Grace, Means of.*

Gospel Association. See *Finland, Lutheranism in,* 4.

Gospel of Egyptians, Hebrews, Ebionites, Peter, James, etc. See *Apocrypha,* B 2.

Gossner, Johannes Evangelista (1773 to 1858). B. at Hausen; d. in Berlin. He renounced the Roman Catholic Church and took a pastoral charge in Berlin (1829). He is the founder of the great Mission Society that bears his name (Berlin II). For many years he was its head and directed its policy.

Gossner Missionary Society (*Gossnersche Missionsgesellschaft*), for short "Berlin II"; founded by Johannes Evangelista Gossner, 1836, at Berlin, Germany, influenced by Spittler and the Moravians. Gossner separated from the Berlin Missionary Society, believing that a different missionary policy at home and on the field should be observed, namely, that missionaries should, like Paul, support themselves by manual labor. Accordingly he sought and sent artisans, who were expected to witness for Christ by word and deed. Later he appears to have admitted that higher educational standards are also desirable. Work was begun in India and in Africa. Extraordinary successes were obtained in India among the Kols. Neither field could be worked during and since World War I by Germans. The Christians among the Kols in Bihar and Orissa, after some vicissitudes, succeeded in organizing an autonomous church, 1919, which was sponsored during the war by the United Lutheran Church in America. In 1949 the Gossner Ev. Luth. Church in India numbered 180,000. The Ganges Mission was split up between the English Baptist Missionary Society, the Regions Beyond Missionary Union, the Church Missionary Society for Africa and the East, and the Methodist Episcopal Church Foreign Missionary Society. The work in the Kamerun was discontinued.

Gotama (Sanskrit: *Gautama;* spelling *Gotama* comes from the Pali), family name of Siddhartha, son of the raja of the Sakya clan in the Ganges Valley, northeast of Benares; b. ca. 560 B. C. Founder of Buddhism. At twenty-nine, prompted by reflecting upon the frailty of human life, he renounced the succession to the throne and left wife and infant child (called by Buddhists "The Great Renunciation"), becoming a wandering mendicant. After the study of Brahmanic philosophy and six years of severe asceticism had failed to satisfy him, he received a vision whereby he became Buddha, *i. e.,* the "Enlightened One." In Buddhist terminology a Buddha is one who through knowledge of the truth and by overcoming all sin has escaped completely the burdens and pains of existence and then preaches the true doctrine to the world. The number of Buddhas is untold, the last historic one being Gotama. After his enlightenment, Gotama traveled about, preaching salvation, and organized a mendicant order for his followers. He died at eighty. For his teachings and their relation to Brahmanism see *Buddhism.*

Gotha Covenant. An agreement between John the Constant of Saxony and Philip the Magnanimous of Hesse to defend the evangelical faith (1526).

Gothic Bible Versions. See *Bible Versions,* I.

Gothic Style. See *Architecture, Ecclesiastical,* 5.

Goths, Conversion of. The Goths, an East-Germanic tribe, had originally lived along the lower Vistula, near the Baltic Sea. From here they moved to the north shore of the Black Sea, coming in conflict with the decaying power of the Roman Empire in the second half of the second century. Christian influence is noticeable among them after A. D. 276, but it was not till the time of Ulfilas,* or Wulfilas, that Christianity was formally established among them. This was between 341 and 380. The translation of the Bible into Gothic was an important factor in bringing about the conversion of the Goths. Unfortunately, Arianism got a foothold among the Goths, and their subsequent westward migration (Visigoths in France, Ostrogoths in Italy) spread the error far and wide. The end of the Visigothic power came in 711, when they were overwhelmed by the Arabs.

Gotter, Ludwig Andreas (1661 to 1735). Privy secretary, later *Hofrat* at Gotha; tendencies toward pietism; one of best hymn writers of the period; wrote "Herr Jesu, Gnadensonne."

Gotteskasten, Lutherischer. The name of a number of societies of professed Lutheran character in Germany, organized with the avowed intention of replacing the Gustav - Adolf - Verein, which had similar aims, but had become decidedly unionistic in tendency. The movement began in 1843; but the first society was not organized till 1851, in Hanover, this being followed by others in Mecklenburg, Saxony, Prussia, Bavaria, and elsewhere. The main object of the societies is to take care of Lutherans in the so-called *diaspora*, that is, those outside of Germany, chiefly by providing them with ministers, but also for related purposes, such as the training of pastors and the erection of churches.

Gottschalk. See *Predestinarian Controversy.*

Gottschick, Johann (1874—1907). Prof. of practical theology at Giessen and later Tuebingen; adherent of Ritschl.

Gottskalksson, Oddur. See *Iceland.*

Gotwald, L. A. (1833—1900). American Lutheran theologian and educator; ed. at Gettysburg; pastor till 1888, then prof. of practical theology in Wittenberg Seminary till 1895; on basis of charges brought against him by A. Gebhart, J. Gebhart, and E. E. Baker he was tried for his conservative position but acquitted by unanimous vote of the board of directors of his institution (1893).

Goudimel, Claude (ca. 1505—72). Foremost composer of the Reformed Church of the 16th century, often called "the high priest of Calvinistic music." He lived for a time in Rome, but was not as was formerly believed, the teacher of Palestrina. He was clearly a product of the Netherland School of composition. Goudimel was killed in the Massacre of St. Bartholomew's Night. His choral works are churchly and polyphonic in character, with the *cantus firmus* in the upper voice; in keeping with the tenets of Calvinism, they remain fairly simple and very sober. Goudimel was at his best in his motetlike compositions.

Guido Adler, *Handbuch der Musikgeschichte,* Frankfort, 1924; Friedrich Blume, *Evangelische Kirchenmusik,* Potsdam, 1931; Donald Ferguson, *A History of Musical Thought,* New York, 1948; P. H. Lang, *Music in Western Civilization,* New York, 1941.

Gounod, Charles Francois (1818 to 1893). Enjoyed popularity as a composer during his lifetime and in the first quarter of the 20th century. Particularly popular were his operas (*e. g.,* *Romeo et Juliette*) and his dramatico-religious music; he referred to the latter as "music treated in the style of fresco." His church music as well as his oratorios are too often operatic in character and spirit; the mystical as well as voluptuous and sensuous features found in them have helped disqualify his music for present-day use. Gounod was highly talented and a real master of orchestration; he will likely continue to enjoy wide fame as a composer of opera. He devoted two years of his eventful life to the study of theology and at one time had in mind to become a Roman Catholic priest.

Governmental Theory. See *Atonement, False Theories,* 5.

Grabau, John Andrew Augustus (1804—79). B. in Olvenstedt, near Magdeburg, Germany; studied theology at Halle; pastor of St. Andrew at Erfurt; because of his refusal to use the official Agenda (which he opposed for its Reformed tendencies) he was imprisoned twice; finally permitted to emigrate; members of his congregation in Erfurt and of the congregation at Magdeburg and other places emigrated with him; came to America (1839) and settled at Buffalo, N. Y., where Grabau served his people for 40 years. See *Buffalo Synod.*

J. A. Grabau, *Lebenslauf des Ehrwuerdigen J. An. A. Grabau,* Volksblatt Publishing Co., Buffalo, N. Y., 1879.

Grace. The good will and favor shown to one who can plead no merit but only his needs; particularly, the love of God in its relation to the sinner as such. There may be love, but not grace, between equals or between a judge and an innocent person. Between such there may be a relation of love or one of equity; but the quality of grace implies mercy or the feeling of compassion for one who has by every right forfeited his claim upon our love. Such is the grace of God to the sinner. It is called "free" grace because it is not grounded in any worthiness of man (Letter to the Romans). Any admixture of merit or deserts, as constituting a claim upon mercy, destroys the very idea of grace. Merit and grace are mutually exclusive.

Grace is universal. The entire world is its object. God became incarnate in Christ for the benefit of all men; He died for the atonement of the sins of all; all have been pronounced righteous through His resurrection; the invitation, or call, of grace is intended for all. No one is excluded from the salvation which grace has provided. (For the wrong view see *Calvinism*.)

The grace of God is revealed (1) in the sending of His Son into the flesh, (2) in the justification of the sinner who accepts Jesus Christ as his Substitute in the Judgment, and in the conversion of the sinner, and (3) in his glorification (resurrection, eternal life). It is this doctrine of grace that gives assurance to the faith of the Christian believer. Its promises are certain.

Grace is resistible, since it is offered to us through certain means. (See *Grace, Means of*.) Hence the constant warning of Scripture not to reject salvation; hence, also, in the experience of the Christian congregation the sad lapses from faith.

Saving grace, in Christian theology, has been distinguished in its various operations as "prevenient," inasmuch as by means of outward circumstances and associations, particularly through the outward hearing of the Word, the Holy Spirit would prepare the heart for conversion; as "operative," inasmuch as it generates faith; as "cooperative," inasmuch as it is active in the Christian, jointly with the regenerated will, unto the production of good works.

Scripture also employs the word "grace" in the sense of a gift possessed by man (1 Pet. 4:10). This, properly a result of divine grace and not, as in its original sense, a divine quality or attitude, has been called "infused grace." The Roman Church teaches justification by "infused grace" (*gratia infusa*) and by doing so destroys the essence of the Scriptural doctrine of grace (see *Infusion of Grace*).

See references under *Dogmatics*; Theo. Hoyer, "The Grace of God," *Abiding Word*, CPH, 1947 (II:200—34. See bibliography).

Grace, Means of. I. *The Doctrine in General.* 1. *Definition.* The term *means of grace* denotes the divinely instituted means by which God offers, bestows, and seals to men forgiveness of sins, life, and salvation. Properly speaking, there is but one means of grace, namely, the Gospel of Christ (Rom. 1:16 ff.), but since in the Sacraments

the Gospel appears as the *verbum visibile* (the visible Word) in contradistinction to the *verbum audibile* (the preached Word), it is rightly said that the means of grace are the Gospel and the Sacraments. The divine Law, though also a divine Word and used by the Holy Spirit in a preparatory way to work *contrition*, without which there can be no saving faith, is not, properly speaking, a means of grace, since it does not offer forgiveness of sins, life, and salvation, but merely demands, threatens, and condemns. It is thus the very opposite of a means of grace, namely, a "ministration of death" (2 Cor. 5:19-21). Prayer is not a means of grace, but faith in action and so a receiving means.

2. *The basis of the means of grace.* There are means of grace because there is, first, Christ's objective justification, or reconciliation (2 Cor. 5:19-21), and, second, Christ's direct institution. In other words, there is extant through Christ's active and passive obedience forgiveness for all (Rom. 5:12 ff.), and this forgiveness for all sinners Christ desires to have offered and conveyed to all men through the Gospel and the Sacraments (Mark 16:15, 16; Matt. 28:19, 20; AC, Art. V and VIII).

3. *The twofold power of the means of grace.* The means of grace have an offering or conferring power, by which God most earnestly offers to all men forgiveness of sins, life, and salvation (Luke 24:37; Acts 20:24; Acts 2:38; Matt. 26:28), and an operative or effective power, by which through them the Holy Spirit actually works faith and thus regeneration and sanctification in men (1 Thess. 2:13; Rom. 1:16; 1 Cor. 4:15; Rom. 10:17; 1 Pet. 1:23).

4. *The importance of the means of grace.* The doctrine of the means of grace is a fundamental doctrine, since it is a part of the doctrine of the divine Word, which is fundamental. Because God has willed to bestow His saving grace only through the means of grace (Sm. Art., III, viii, 3), the bestowal of the forgiveness of sins, life, and salvation is rendered impossible wherever the means of grace are rejected. For this reason Holy Scripture so earnestly inculcates faithful adherence to the Gospel and the administration of the Sacraments according to Christ's institution (Matt. 7:15; Rom. 16:17; 2 John 10, 11). Because of the strong emphasis laid upon the Word in the Confessions of the Lutheran

Church, the Holy Scriptures have rightly been called the Formal Principle of the Reformation, the divine Word being not only the norm of faith and life, but also the regenerative and sanctifying means by which the Holy Spirit operates.

5. *The means of grace and the Lutheran Church.* The doctrine of the means of grace is a distinctive feature of Lutheran theology. To this central teaching it owes its sanity and strong appeal, its freedom from sectarian tendencies and morbid fanaticism, its coherence and practicalness, and its adaptation to men of every race and every degree of culture. According to Lutheran doctrine, the means of grace are 1) unchangeable, since the Gospel is the means of grace till the end of time (Matt. 28:19, 20); 2) sufficient, for Christ instituted only the Gospel and the Sacraments to serve as means of grace; and 3) efficacious, the efficacy of the means of grace being objective, that is, not conditioned upon the personal faith of the administrator, upon his ordination, or upon his personal endowment, nor upon the intention of the priests "to do what the Church does" (Rome). While it is true that the hearers of the Word as well as the communicants and the subjects of Baptism derive no benefit from the means of grace unless they have faith (for faith is the receiving means or the hand reached out to obtain blessings offered in the conferring means), it does not follow that faith makes the means of grace effective. The Word is effective as the divine, living Word, and the Sacraments are true Sacraments (Christ's body and blood being really present in the Lord's Supper) by virtue of Christ's institution. It is therefore correctly said that faith does not belong to the essence of the means of grace, but merely receives its blessings, it being itself a blessed work through the means of grace by the power of the Holy Ghost (Eph. 1:19, 20). — While our Confessions generally speak of the *Word* and the Sacraments as being the means of grace (AC, V), they more specifically denote the Gospel as the means of grace (AC, V: . . . the *Word* and the Sacraments . . . that hear the Gospel). — Against the "enthusiasts" who teach that the Holy Spirit works in the hearts of men without the divine Word our Lutheran Confessions take a decisive stand (Sm. Art., III, 8; Large Catechism: Creed, III; F. of C., II, XI).

6. *The means of grace have the same effect.* The Sacraments have the same effect as the spoken or written Word, because they are nothing else than the visible Word or the Gospel, applied in sacred action in connection with the visible signs. For this reason the Sacraments offer, convey, and seal to the recipients forgiveness of sins, life, and salvation just as the Gospel does when it is spoken, contemplated, or read. It is therefore not in agreement with Scripture to ascribe to Baptism regeneration exclusively and to the Lord's Supper, as a special function, the implanting of the germ of the resurrection body. Also the Gospel regenerates when it is read, preached, or contemplated in the heart by men (1 Pet. 1:23).

7. *Calvinism and the means of grace.* Calvinism rejects the means of grace as unnecessary, for, as it avers, the Holy Spirit requires no escort or vehicle by which to enter into the hearts of men. The Reformed doctrine of Predestination excludes the idea of means which impart the Spirit and His gifts to men, the Holy Spirit working effectively only upon the elect. Hence even in its earliest days (Zwingli), Reformed theology substituted for the external word, as means of grace, an "inner word" through which alone the Spirit is said to work. Hence, too, the lack of emphasis, even in the best Reformed preaching, upon the divine Word as the vehicle of regenerating grace and upon the Sacraments. According to Reformed teaching, the office of the Word is merely to point out the way of life, without communicating that of which it conveys the idea. Reformed theology regards the Word and the Sacraments as necessary, since their office in the Church is a divine institution. But they are only symbols of what the Holy Spirit does within, the Holy Ghost working immediately and irresistibly. From these notions, already contained in Zwingli's *Method of Faith*, it was only another step to the so-called "enthusiast" (fanatical, *Schwaermer*) doctrine of the Anabaptists * and of the many sects since their day regarding the "inner light," generally identified with the "baptism of the Holy Spirit" and the "second conversion." The crudest extravagances of revivalism (Methodism, Pentecostalism, Holy Rollerism) have their root in this specifically Reformed doctrine of the immediate working of the Holy Spirit.

8. *Romanism and the means of grace.* Romanism, over against Calvinism, strongly insists upon the means of grace, especially the Sacraments, as absolutely necessary, since it is only by the Sacraments that divine grace is infused. But the doctrine of the Sacraments, as taught by Rome, is a perversion of the Scriptural doctrine of the means of grace, for Romanism has removed the doctrine of the Gospel, so that there is no comfort in its teaching for the alarmed sinner. It has, moreover, perverted the concept of grace, which does not mean forgiveness of sins in Roman theology, as this term is used by the Lutherans on the basis of Scripture, but infused divine power to earn salvation with the help of the Holy Spirit. Finally, Rome teaches a mechanical action (*ex opere operato*) of the Sacraments, that is, an efficacy without faith on the part of the communicant. With regard to Baptism, Rome teaches an absolute necessity, since it wipes out original sin in the baptized, which doctrine, too, is opposed to Scripture. The Catholic doctrine of the Sacraments is designed to uphold and strengthen its pernicious doctrine of work-righteousness, which is the fundamental error of antichristian Rome.

9. *The necessity of the means of grace.* The means of grace are necessary both because of Christ's command (divine institution) and their very function as means of grace. While God has not bound Himself to the means of grace (Luke 1:15, 41), He has bound His Church to them so that Christians dare not dispense with the preaching of the Word and the Sacraments (Matt. 28:19, 20), as some "enthusiasts" do (Quakers, Salvation Army). Nevertheless, Lutheran theology does not assert an absolute necessity of the Sacraments, since faith and regeneration can be worked by the Holy Spirit in the hearts of men through the divine Word without the Sacraments (this against Roman Catholic theology, which affirms their absolute necessity). But while lack of the Sacraments does not condemn in itself, contempt for them does (Luke 7:29, 30).

II. *Law and Gospel.* 1. *Distinction between Law and Gospel.* While the terms Law and Gospel at times are used for the entire Christian doctrine (Ps. 1:2; Mark 1:1), Law and Gospel in their meaning are contradictories or opposites, the one threatening and condemning, the other promising and forgiving (Rom. 3:19, 20; 3:24 ff.). The Law, in its proper sense, is the divine Word "that reproves sin" (F. of C., V). The Gospel is the joyous message of God's grace in Christ Jesus toward all sinners (John 3:16). This "distinction is to be maintained in the Church with great diligence as an especially brilliant light, by which, according to the admonition of St. Paul, the Word of God is rightly divided" (F. of C., V:2).

2. *The Moral Law and ceremonial laws.* While the ceremonial laws of the Old Testament have been abolished (Col. 2:16, 17), the Moral Law as God's "immutable will" is in force till the end of time (Matt. 5:17). But the Moral Law must not simply be identified with the Decalog, as given in the Old Testament (Exodus 20; Deuteronomy 5), since that contains ceremonial elements, meant only for the Jews (Deut. 5:15), but it is determined by the law of love (Matt. 22:35 ff.). The "Ten Commandments," therefore, must direct our conduct, inasmuch as they serve the principle of love (Rom. 13:8) and are restated in the New Testament (Rom. 13:9). The Third Commandment: "Remember the Sabbath day to keep it holy," is omitted in the New Testament, which shows that emphasis no longer rests upon the day, but upon the sanctifying through the divine Word (cf. Luther's explanation of the Third Commandment, Large Catechism).

3. *The use of the Law and the Gospel.* The use of God's holy Law is a threefold one. In the Formula of Concord our Church, in accordance with the Holy Scriptures, confesses in reference to this matter as follows: "The Law of God is useful 1) not only to the end that external discipline and decency are maintained by it against wild, disobedient men; 2) likewise that through it men are brought to a knowledge of their sins; 3) but also that when they have been born anew by the Spirit of God, converted to the Lord, and thus the veil of Moses has been lifted from them, they live and walk in the Law" (F. of C., VI). In the former Catechism of the Missouri Synod, under question 91: "What purpose does the Law, then, serve?" we find the following answers: "First, it checks in a measure, the coarse outbursts of sin and thereby helps to maintain outward decency in the world (a curb). Secondly, and chiefly, it teaches man the due knowledge of his sin

(a mirror). Thirdly, it leads the regenerate to know what are truly good works (a rule)." From that fatal hour when Adam fell into sin to the very last day of this present world's sin-cursed history, there never was, nor is, nor will be a single human being that could by his own efforts satisfy the demands of God's Law and thus stand in His holy presence by virtue of his own righteousness. They are all guilty, that is, they are all under condemnation, deserving of, and liable to, punishment at the hands of Him whose Law they have broken and whose sovereign majesty they have offended (Rom. 3:22 ff.). And that is the last word the Law has to say to the sinner. It leaves him with the threat of divine retribution upon his soul. — The Gospel of Jesus Christ, in its proper sense, is the glad tidings of forgiveness and peace, of life and joy, the eternal divine counsel of redemption, of which Christ Himself ever was, is, and will be, the living center, the very heart and soul. The Gospel, just as the divine Law, though in a different and opposite way, has a threefold use: 1) While the Law teaches the knowledge of sin, the Gospel teaches forgiveness of sin; 2) While the Law teaches what good works are, the Gospel produces true joy and zeal to do good works; 3) While the Law checks sin outwardly, but increases sin inwardly, the Gospel destroys sin both outwardly and inwardly. The difference between the Law and Gospel is well stated in the following axioms: "The Law prescribes, but the Gospel inscribes"; and "The Law kills the sinner, but not sin; the Gospel kills sin, but not the sinner."

III. *Holy Baptism as a Means of Grace.* 1. *Holy Baptism instituted by Christ.* Contrary to assertions of modern rationalists, who deny the divine institution of this Sacrament, Baptism has been instituted by our Lord (Matt. 28:18 ff.) and is to be used as a means of forgiveness of sins, life, and salvation till the end of time. Its visible element is water (1 Pet. 3:20 f.), and for this nothing else may be substituted. The mode of applying water, contrary to the affirmation of Anabaptist groups, is an adiaphoron, the Greek term *baptizein* signifying not merely immersing, but also washing, sprinkling, pouring, in fact, any application of water, and that not only in Biblical, but also in secular Greek (Mark 7:3 f.; Eph. 5:25, 26; Matt. 3:11; Acts 2:17;

Heb. 9:10, compared with Num. 19:13, 19; *Didache*). Anabaptist sects ignore the real purpose of Baptism, while stressing the form.

2. *The purpose of Holy Baptism.* The purpose of Holy Baptism is well stated in Luther's Small Catechism: "It works forgiveness of sins, delivers from death and the devil, and gives eternal salvation to all who believe this, as the words and promises of God declare." According to Holy Scripture, Christ sanctifies His Church by the washing of the water with the Word (Eph. 5:25, 26). Moreover, Baptism makes disciples of men (Matt. 28:19 f.). Again, Baptism saves (1 Pet. 3:21). Furthermore, Baptism is a washing of regeneration (Titus 3:5), by which men are born again (John 3:5, 6). Through Baptism we put on Christ (Gal. 3:26 f.), that is, His merits and righteousness, by the very faith, which, as an application of the Gospel, it creates in the heart (Gal. 3:26); for Baptism is pure Gospel, not Law, and hence it does not save mechanically (*ex opere operato*), but by faith, which receives the blessings it offers and which is worked by this very Sacrament. This is nothing unusual, for the Gospel is both the means of faith and the foundation of faith. Baptism also unites the baptized with the Triune God, for we are baptized into communion with the Father, Son, and Holy Ghost (Matt. 28:19 f.), as also into communion with Christ (Gal. 3:27). Lastly, through Baptism we are buried with Christ into death, that is, through Baptism we partake of the merits which Christ procured for the whole world by His vicarious suffering and death (Rom. 6:3 ff.). Baptism, as the application of the saving Gospel, is, therefore, a true means of grace. How Baptism saves, Luther in his Small Catechism shows by saying: "It is not the water indeed that does them, but the Word of God which is in and with the water, and faith, which trusts such Word of God in the water." What makes Baptism a means of grace, Luther explains thus: "Baptism is not simple water, but it is the water comprehended in God's command and connected with God's Word" (Gospel promise of salvation). Those who have fallen from baptismal grace should remember that God's promises of forgiveness, life, and salvation remain unshaken and that penitently they may at any time return to the Gospel

covenant, established by God with the baptized in and through Holy Baptism.

3. *The meaning of Holy Baptism.* In and through Baptism we are buried with Christ into death and arise with Him unto newness of life (Rom. 6:4). Luther in his Small Catechism thus points out the significance of Holy Baptism for the believer: "It signifies that the Old Adam in us should, by daily contrition and repentance, be drowned and die with all sins and evil lusts and, again, a new man daily come forth and arise, who shall live before God in righteousness and purity forever."

4. *Infant Baptism.* From the Apostolic age to the rise of Anabaptism in the sixteenth century the doctrine of infant Baptism (pedobaptism) was undisputed. As in the Old Testament, on the eighth day after their birth, male children were circumcised (Gen. 17:12; Lev. 12:3), so in the New Testament the Apostles baptized not only individual adults, but entire families (Acts 2:38, 39; 16:15, 33; 18:8; 1 Cor. 1:16). In addition to this, Baptism in the New Testament followed the Old Testament Sacrament of Circumcision (Col. 2:11, 12), and Christ's command to baptize all nations certainly also included infants (Matt. 28:19, 20). The need for infant regeneration is clear (Ps. 51:5; John 3:6; Eph. 2:3); and because Baptism is the washing of regeneration and renewing of the Holy Ghost (Titus 3:5; John 3:3-7), and Christ desires to have also little children brought to Him for the blessings of His grace (Mark 10:14), it is in agreement with Holy Scripture to insist upon pedobaptism. See *Baptism, Liturgical* and *Baptism, Roman Catholic Doctrine.*

IV. *The Lord's Supper as a Means of Grace.* 1. *The names of this Sacrament.* The names by which this Sacrament is known are derived partly from Scripture (1 Cor. 11:20; 10:21; Acts 2:42) and partly from church usage (the Sacrament of the Altar). The term *mass* should not be used in Lutheran or Protestant circles, since it designates the Roman Catholic perversion of the Lord's Supper and may thus cause confusion and offense.

2. *The institution of the Lord's Supper.* Of the institution of the Lord's Supper we have four accounts (Matt. 26:26-28; Mark 14:22-24; Luke 22:19,20; 1 Cor. 11:23-25). These accounts agree in all essentials, but supplement each other in details. All quote Christ's words: "This is My body." With re-

gard to the cup, Matthew and Mark emphasize the blood of the New Testament, which is given with the cup, while Luke and Paul stress the blessing given with the cup, the forgiveness of the new covenant, procured by the blood of Christ, which is offered to the communicant in the Sacrament.

3. *The Real Presence.* The words of institution: "Take, eat; this is My body," clearly state: "With this bread I give you My body." So these words are further explained in 1 Cor. 10:16, where the Apostle tells us that the bread is the communion of participation of the body and the cup is the communion of participation of the blood. Hence the bread is not transubstantiated into Christ's body (Roman Catholic doctrine), nor is there any consubstantiation or mixture of bread and body (a teaching of which the Reformed accused the Lutherans), nor is the body locally enclosed in the bread (which the Lutherans also were charged of teaching), but in, with, and under the bread and wine the communicant, even the unbelieving communicant (1 Cor. 11:27-29), receives Christ's true body, which was given into death, and His blood, which was shed for his sins. This is the point of controversy between Lutherans and Reformed. The question is not whether Christ is present according to His divine nature in the Sacrament, or whether the soul by faith is united with Christ (spiritual eating and drinking), or whether the believing communicant receives the merits of Christ's shed blood by faith (all of which is true and admitted by both Lutherans and Reformed), but what the Reformed deny is that the words of institution should be taken in a literal sense, or that in, with, and under the bread and wine the communicant receives Christ's true body and blood (Real Presence). This Real Presence the Reformed deny, teaching in its stead the real absence of Christ's body in the Sacrament, by resorting to a figurative, or symbolical, interpretation of the words. Carlstadt sought the figure in "this," Zwingli, in "is" (represents), Calvin and others in "body" (the sign of My body), others (Zanchi) in the entire statement. The multifarious attempts to pervert the true sense of the words are but so many evidences of the persistent refusal of the words to yield any other sense than the proper sense of the terms.

4. *The terrestrial elements in the*

Sacrament. While the heavenly elements in the Sacraments are the true body and the true blood of Christ, the terrestrial, or earthly, elements are true bread and true wine, for which no substitutes should be used, since the use of all substitutes make void, or at least render uncertain, the Sacrament (Matt. 26:29; Mark 14:25; Luke 22:18; 1 Cor. 11:21). What Jesus used was not unfermented juice of the grape (grape juice), but real wine, which was the beverage used in the Old Testament on all festive occasions. While the bread and wine are received in a natural manner, the body and blood, though received orally, or with the mouth, are received in an incomprehensible, supernatural manner, which reason cannot understand (no Capernaitic eating; the Real Presence a mystery). According to Christ's institution, the bread and wine should be received by all communicants (*sub utraque specie,* "under each kind"), not as the Romanists teach, *sub una specie,* by which the cup is denied to the laity. This is a violation of the Sacrament by which it becomes null and void.

5. *The purpose of the Lord's Supper.* The Lord's Supper is essentially the application of the Gospel, with all its spiritual blessings, in a sacred act. Hence, just like the Gospel in its proclamation, it, too, offers, conveys, and seals to the communicant forgiveness of sins, life, and salvation, strengthens his faith, promotes his sanctification through the strengthening of his faith, increases his love toward God and the neighbor, affords him patience in tribulation, confirms his hope of eternal life, and deepens his union with Christ and His mystical body, the Church (1 Cor. 10:17; Eph. 3:16; 1 Cor. 11:28). In addition, it also serves a confessional purpose (1 Cor. 10:20 f.; 11:26; Acts 2:42). All these blessings are mediated through the Gospel promise in the Sacrament ("Given and shed for you for the remission of sins") and are apprehended by faith in the divine promise. The words "This do in remembrance of Me" do not mean merely that the communicant is to remember the absent Christ, who atoned for his sins, but they invite the communicant to accept the gracious forgiveness offered in the Holy Supper (cf. *Apology:* " 'In remembrance of Christ' means to 'remember Christ' and receive Him by faith." XXIV, 72). The Lord's Supper differs from the preaching of the Gospel, which is addressed to all hearers, believers and unbelievers, and from Absolution, which is individually addressed to believers, or to believers as a penitent group, in this, that it offers the blessings of forgiveness of sins, life, and salvation individually to each communicant under the pledge of Christ's body and blood, received with the consecrated bread and wine. Since the Lord's Supper may be received unto damnation (1 Cor. 11:27-29), close, and not open, Communion should be observed, the pastor as the steward of the mysteries of God (1 Cor. 4:1) admitting only such as are able to examine themselves (1 Cor. 11:27). See *Grace, Sacrament, Lord's Supper, Roman Catholic Doctrine of.* JTM

J. T. Mueller, "The Means of Grace," *What Lutherans Are Thinking,* Wartburg Press, Columbus, Ohio, 1947; J. T. Mueller, *Christian Dogmatics,* CPH, 1934; F. Pieper, *Christliche Dogmatik,* CPH, 1917; C. F. W. Walther, *The Proper Distinction Between Law and Gospel* (tr. by W. H. T. Dau); M. Reu, *Die Gnadenmittellehre,* Wartburg Pub. House, 1917; M. Reu, *Can We Still Hold to the Lutheran Doctrine of the Lord's Supper?* Wartburg Press, Columbus, 1941; M. Luther, *Wider die himmlischen Propheten von den Bildern und Sakrament,* St. L. Ed., XX:133 ff.; Luther, *Dass diese Worte Christi: "Das ist mein Leib usw." noch fest stehen wider die Schwaermergeister,* St. L. Ed., XX: 762 ff.; D. *Martin Luthers Bekenntnis vom Abendmahl Christi,* XX:894 ff.; D. *Martin Luthers kurzes Bekenntnis vom heiligen Sakrament wider die Schwaermer,* XX:1765 ff.; F. R. Zucker, "Circumcision and Baptism," *CTM,* XV:245—59; Walter Geihsler, "The Law and the Gospel," *Abiding Word,* CPH, 1946 (I:105—23. See bibliography); Edwin E. Pieplow, "The Means of Grace," *Abiding Word,* CPH, 1947 (II: 322—46. See bibliography); S. W. Becker, "The Gospel," *Abiding Word,* CPH, 1947 (II:347—66. See bibliography); A. E. Neitzel, "The Sacraments," *Abiding Word,* CPH, 1947 (II:367—93. See bibliography); J. T. Mueller, "Holy Baptism," *Abiding Word,* CPH, 1947 (II:394—422. See bibliography); F. R. Zucker, "The Lord's Supper," *Abiding Word,* CPH, 1947 (II:423—46. See bibliography); O. Hallesby, *Infant Baptism and Adult Conversion,* Luth. Free Ch. Pub. Co., Minneapolis, 1924.

Gracián, Baltasar (1601—58). Spanish author; entered Jesuit order (1619); his *El Criticón* is a novel which evaluates civilization through its effects on savages; influenced Schopenhauer and Nietzsche.

Graded Sunday School Lessons. See *Parish Education,* E 5.

Grading. See *Christian Teaching,* M.

Gradual. The gradual was originally called the *responsorium graduale* because it was intoned by the precentor on the first step (*gradus*) of the ambo, from which the Epistle was read. Through the alleluias of the gradual the Church expresses its joy at the prospect of hearing the Word as proclaimed through the reading of the Gospel for the day. These alleluias are dropped during the season of Lent, and they are replaced by the liturgical tract. The gradual is a proper and varies from Sunday to Sunday. Its texts are from the Scriptures, usually from the Psalter. In Lutheran services of worship a fitting selection or a hymn by the congregation (usually a hymn to the Holy Spirit) may replace the gradual. In many churches only the alleluia represents the gradual.

W. E. Buszin, *The Graduals of the Church Year,* St. Louis, 1944; Gustave Reese, *Music in the Middle Ages,* New York, 1940.

Graebner, August Lawrence. Born July 10, 1849, at Frankentrost, Mich. D. at St. Louis, Mo., Dec. 7, 1904. Son of J. H. Philip Graebner. An eminent theologian of the Lutheran Church in America. He was early designated for the service in the Church. The plastic years of his youth were spent at Frankentrost and Roseville, Mich., and in St. Charles, Mo. A graduate of Concordia Seminary, Fort Wayne, and of Concordia Seminary, St. Louis, he became a teacher at the Lutheran High School (later called Walther College), St. Louis, in 1872. Three years later he accepted a professorship at Northwestern College, a Wisconsin Synod institution at Watertown. In 1878 that synod elected him to a chair at its newly founded seminary at Milwaukee. In 1887 he was called to the chair of Church History at Concordia Seminary, St. Louis, as successor to the sainted Prof. G. Schaller. After the death of Prof. R. Lange, head of the English Department, he lectured on Dogmatic Theology. Both as historian and dogmatician he rendered distinguished services to his Church. His *Luther-buechlein* and the more imposing *Dr. Martin Luther: Ein Lebensbild des Re-*

formators are works of high excellence, and his monumental *Geschichte der Lutherischen Kirche in Amerika,* the fruit of indefatigable investigation and research in Lutheran centers of the East, has stood the test of time. His thorough, though unique, *Doctrinal Theology,* a brief thetical compend of the outlines of Christian doctrine, is still highly esteemed. He was the founder of the *Theological Quarterly,* a publication attesting on every page his erudition, eloquence, and, above all, his strict fidelity to Scripture and the Lutheran Confessions. He contributed numerous articles for other synodical periodicals, frequently led the doctrinal discussions at synodical conventions, and was active as a member of the Board for Foreign Missions. He was generally recognized as a scholar of universal learning. In 1903 the theological seminary of the Norwegian Synod conferred upon him the honorary degree of Doctor of Divinity. In 1902 he visited the Lutheran churches in Australia and New Zealand.

Karl Kretzmann, "The Rev. Doctor August Lawrence Graebner," *CHIQ,* XX: 79—93.

Graebner, Carl Frederick. B. Oct. 8, 1862, at St. Charles, Mo.; grad. at St. Louis, 1885; pastor at Sedalia, Mo., 1885 to 1889; at Topeka, Kans., 1889—97; at Bay City, Mich., 1897—1903; pres. of College and Seminary at Adelaide, Australia, 1903—39; pres. of theological faculty until 1941; received D. D. from Concordia Seminary, St. Louis, Mo.; d. July 5, 1949.

Graebner, John Henry Philip. B. July 7, 1819; d. May 27, 1898. Under Loehe's direction he emigrated in 1847 with a company of Franconians, establishing a colony at Frankentrost, Mich. Pastor at Roseville, Mich., in 1853, also serving Mount Clemens. Called to St. Charles, Mo., in 1859, he labored faithfully there for many years.

Graebner, Theodore. B. Nov. 23, 1876, at Watertown, Wis., son of A. L. Graebner; grad., Concordia College, Ft. Wayne, Ind., 1894; Concordia Sem., St. Louis, Mo., 1897; instructor, Walther College, St. Louis, Mo., 1897 to 1900; instructor, Luth. Ladies' Sem., Red Wing, Minn., 1900—06; ordained 1902; ass't pastor, Trinity, Red Wing, Minn., 1902—06; missionary, Norwegian Synod, in Chicago area, and editor, *Illustrated Home Journal,* 1906—08; pastor, Jehovah Cong., Chicago, 1908 to

1913; prof., Conc. Sem., St. Louis, 1913 to 1950. Mem., Young People's Literature Bd., 1915—25; chrm., Bd. for Colored Missions, 1924—28; Bd. for Young People's Work, 1920—40; intersynodical com. on church union, 1923—26; chrm., commission on Fraternal Organizations, 1926—50; Director, Conc. Hist. Inst., 1927—50; mem., building com. of Conc. Sem., 1920—26; helped organize or fostered the organization of the Luth. Laymen's League, the Lutheran Hour, Luth. Women's League, and St. Louis Bach Soc.; mem., Philosophy Group of St. Louis; Missouri Academy of Science; Protestant mem. of Nat'l Com. of Civic Recovery; Civic Union of St. Louis; Victoria Inst., London; Philosophical Soc. of Great Britain; Council on Education in Gov't; lecturer, Bad Boll, Germany, 1948, 1949. Editor: *Lutheran Herald*, 1909—13; *Der Lutheraner*, 1913 to 1917; *Lutheran Witness*, 1913—49; departmental ed., *Lehre und Wehre* and *Homiletic Magazine*, 1913—18; *Bible Student Quarterly*, 1921—50; assoc. ed., *Concordia Hist. Inst. Quarterly*, 1928 to 1950; assoc. ed., *Cresset*, 1937—50; contributed to many other church papers and journals. Author: *Lessons for Sunday School; The Dark Ages; Prophecy and the War; The Expository Preacher; Spiritism; Evolution; The Pastor as Student and Literary Worker; Bible Dictionary; Essays on Evolution; The Secret Empire; Touring with God; A Handbook for Congregational Officers; The Story of the Catechism; The Story of the Augsburg Confession; The Pope and Temporal Power; Pastor and People; God and the Cosmos; Borderland of Right and Wrong; Problem of Lutheran Union*; trans., *Luther's Commentary on Galatians; War in the Light of Prophecy; The Business Man and the Church*; co-author, *Toward Lutheran Union; Annotated Pocket New Testament; Church Bells in the Forest; Prayer Fellowship; Is Masonry a Religion? Handbook of Organizations*; co-editor, *What Lutherans Are Thinking; The Historic Lutheran Position on Non-Fundamentals; A History of Concordia Seminary; Dr. Francis Pieper*, a biographical sketch. D. D., Luth. Seminary, Adelaide, Australia, 1930. D. Nov. 14, 1950. ARS

Graf, K. H. See *Higher Criticism*, 10.

Grail, Holy. See *Holy Grail*.

Gramann (Graumann), Johann (Poliander). B. July 15, 1487, in Neustadt, in the Bavarian Palatinate. After he finished his studies at Leipzig, he was appointed rector of the St. Thomas' School there. In spite of the fact that he was secretary to Dr. Eck at the Leipzig Debate, he espoused the cause of the Reformation because of Luther's strong appeal to Scripture and conscience. He openly joined Luther and Melanchthon and was appointed preacher at Wuerzburg and later at Nuernberg. From 1525 he was pastor at Koenigsberg until his death. He was a staunch confessor of the faith. He wrote a poetical version of Psalm 103, "My Soul, Now Praise Thy Maker," the oldest Lutheran hymn of praise. D. 1541.

Grand Army of the Republic. See *Veterans' Organizations*.

Grand View Theological Seminary. See *Ministry, Education of*, XI H.

Grant, Sir Robert (1779—1838). B. in Bengal, India. When he was six, the family moved to London. He was educated at Magdalen College, Cambridge, was admitted to the English bar in 1807, and in 1826 he became M. P. as his father had been. While in Parliament, he introduced a bill to remove restrictions imposed upon the Jews. The historian Macaulay made his maiden speech in Parliament in support of this measure. In 1831 Grant became privy councilor, in 1832 Judge Advocate General, and two years later was appointed Governor of Bombay, being knighted at the same time. Grant wrote twelve hymns, published posthumously under the title *Sacred Poems*. Well known are his hymns, "Oh, Worship the King," and "Savior, When in Dust to Thee."

Gratia Gratis Data; Gratia Gratum Faciens (grace given gratuitously; grace rendering acceptable). According to Roman Catholic theology, the supernatural grace of Christ, existing invisibly in the soul, tends either to the salvation of the person in whom it inheres or, through him, to the sanctification of others. In the former case it is called "ingratiating" (*gratia gratum faciens*), in the latter, gratuitously given (*gratia gratis data*), the term being based upon our Lord's words: "Freely ye have received, freely give" (Matt. 10:8). The *gratia gratum faciens* is intended for all men; the *gratia gratis data* is ordinarily the charism of the Prophets and Apostles and of the incumbents of the priesthood, though it occurs also in others.

Gratia Increata; Gratia Creata.

According to Roman Catholic theology, *gratia increata* (uncreated grace) is God Himself, inasmuch as He gives Himself to man. God is Love toward us, His creatures, so that from eternity He loves us, the Son of God became incarnate, and the Holy Ghost was poured out. *Gratia creata* is distinguished from God, who essentially is Grace, as the created gift of grace (*donum gratiae*), given to man as *actual grace* to aid toward his sanctification or as *habitual* or *sanctifying grace* to make his soul holy and righteous.

F. X. Schouppe, *Elementa Theologiae Dogmaticae*, Tom. II, ed. 21, Paris, Delhomme et Briguet, Editeurs.

Gratian (359—83).

Roman emperor (375—83); during his reign orthodox Christianity became dominant throughout the Roman Empire; severe in dealing with heathen and heretics.

Gratry, Alphonse (1805—72).

Noted Roman Catholic educator; in France; published four letters against the doctrine of Papal infallibility which he later retracted; in his philosophical system he sought God through feeling (entire personality) rather than through reason.

Grau, Rudolf Friedrich (1835—93).

German Lutheran theologian; prof. at Koenigsberg; wrote in the field of NT Introduction, Life of Christ; co-editor of *Beweis des Glaubens;* author of "Biblische Theologie des NT" in *Zoeckler's Handbuch.*

Graul, Karl.

B. Feb. 6, 1814, at Woerlitz; d. Nov. 10, 1864, at Erlangen. Lutheran theologian; called to the directorship of the Dresden-Leipzig Missionary Society in 1844, serving until 1860. From 1849 to 1853 he was in India, acquainting himself fully with mission problems and mastering the Tamil language. Much opposition was aroused by his treatment of the caste question.

Graun, Karl Heinrich (1701—59).

Native of Saxony; contemporary of J. S. Bach; received much of his training at the *Kreuzschule.* Influenced by Antonio Lotti, Graun decided to remain in Dresden after his graduation from the *Kreuzschule.* Wrote motets, church cantatas, and a passion, practically all of which were presented in the *Kreuzkirche.* Also began to write operas in Dresden. Frederick of Prussia engaged Graun for his *Kapelle* in Rheinsburg (1735) and later (1740) as his *Kapellmeister* at 2,000 *Taler* per annum. Graun now wrote operas almost exclusively, became an idol of the people and nobility, and enjoyed the esteem of his talented rival, Johann Adolf Hasse, and of Gotthold Ephraim Lessing. In 1755 he wrote his passion cantata *Der Tod Jesu* at the request of Princess Amalie, sister of Frederick the Great. This is his best-known work and crowded out Bach's monumental *Passion According to St. Matthew* in the second half of the 18th and the first half of the 19th centuries. In Germany *Der Tod Jesu* had the same hold on the people which Handel's *Messiah* had on the people of England and which Stainer's overestimated *Crucifixion* has today on many people in America. In 1756 Graun commemorated the Victory of Prague by composing a *Te Deum* which many believe excelled all his operas. Despite his ability, Graun may hardly be counted among the great composers of the Lutheran Church; he was influenced greatly by the Rationalistic movement, he neglected the chorale, too often strove for effects, and his so-called sacred choral music too often sinks down to the level of the sensuous and theatrical concert music.

Guido Adler, *Handbuch der Musikgeschichte*, Frankfurt, 1924; Friedrich Blume, *Evangelische Kirchenmusik*, Potsdam, 1931; Manfred Bukofzer, *Music in the Baroque Era*, New York, 1947; S. Kuemmerle, *Encyklopaedie der evangelischen Kirchenmusik* (I), Guetersloh, 1888; Paul Henry Lang, *Music in Western Civilization*, New York, 1941; P. Spitta, *Johann Sebastian Bach* (II), Leipzig, 1880 (p. 329); Karl von Winterfeld, *Der evangelische Kirchengesang* (III), Leipzig, 1847.

Great Awakening in England and America.

A religious revival almost in the nature of an epidemic, resulting chiefly from the work of the Wesleys in England and from that of George Whitefield and Jonathan Edwards in America. Due to the character of the preaching affected by these hortatory evangelists, great masses of people were aroused to a very high pitch of excitement, declaring their willingness to become members of the Church under circumstances of almost pathological intensity. The revivals in America started about 1725 and lasted until about 1775. After the death of the prime movers the excitement abated.

Great Bible. See *Bible Versions,* L 5.

Great Schism. A term applied to the separation of the Eastern Church from the Western in 1054. It is also used for the Papal Schism.

Greece. A peninsula in Southeastern Europe; divided by the Corinthian Gulf into two sections, Hellas, the northern, and Pelopennesus, the southern part, from about the fifth century B. C. till the second century A. D. the seat of an advanced classical civilization, but with all the attendant evils of an idolatrous heathenism, in which its foremost cities at the beginning of the Christian era, Athens and Corinth, together with the Macedonian cities Philippi and Thessalonica, excelled. In 1948 the area was estimated at 54,092 sq. mi., and the population at 7,108,814. Christianity was established here in exactly the middle of the first century, when the Apostle Paul began his work at Philippi. The country is still nominally Christian, the Greek Orthodox Church being the established religion. See *Eastern Orthodox Churches.*

Greek Church. See *Eastern Orthodox Churches.*

Greek Religion. The traditional Greek religion and the characteristics of the Greek gods were largely fixed by Homer. The chief deities of the pantheon were Zeus (Indo-European *Dyeus,* god of the sky; son of Cronus; ruler among the gods); Poseidon (son of Cronus; god of the sea); Hades (son of Cronus; god of the dead); Hera (sister and wife of Zeus); Athena (virgin goddess; personification of mind); Ares (god of war); Apollo (god of music and prophecy; shrine at Delphi); Aphrodite (goddess of love); Hephaestus (god of fire); Dionysus (Bacchus; god of vegetation and wine); Demeter (goddess of soil and fertility); Persephone (daughter of Demeter; wife of Hades); Hermes (god of herds, paths, roads, travelers; messenger); Artemis (moon-goddess; goddess of hunting and wild life); and others. In addition there were local cults, nymphs, and lesser deities in trees, fountains, and natural phenomena. Important deities were the Graces and Muses. Myths concerning the origin of the universe, man, animals, trees, and culture revolved around the deities. Some trends which had occurred in the Greek religion by the time of the Christian era were: 1) challenging of the anthropomorphic nature of Greek deities (Xenophanes and later writers); 2) attempts to remove deities from human experience (Epicureans and other materialists); 3) purification of traditional beliefs, and ethical and philosophical sublimations (Pindar and tragedians; Socratic school); emphasis on a future life and a mystic approach to deity (rites of Dionysus, Eleusinian mysteries; Orphism).

Green, Thomas Hill (1836—82). British Neo-Hegelian idealist; opposed the utilitarianism and agnosticism of his times; held that self-consciousness cannot be derived from material forces; consciousness of being a part of a larger whole he explained as evidence that the whole was created by an absolute mind.

Green, William Henry (1825 to 1900). Conservative Presbyterian; professor at Princeton (1851—96); chairman of American Old Testament Company of Anglo-American Bible Revision Committee; held verbal inspiration of the Bible; wrote: *Moses and the Prophets, Introduction to the Old Testament, Unity of the Book of Genesis.*

Greenland. The northernmost colony of Denmark. Area, 839,999 sq. mi. Population, 21,412 (1952). It was discovered by Norsemen in the 10th century; rediscovered by John Davis in 1585 and explored by William Baffin in 1616. In 1721 Hans Egede, a Danish Lutheran, established a mission there. Later the Moravians followed, but withdrew. Lutheranism is the dominant faith on the island. The Church in Greenland is in connection with the Danish Church. See *Missions, Bibliography.*

Greenwald, Emanuel (1811—85). Luth. pastor at New Philadelphia, Ohio, Christ Church, Easton, Pa., and at Holy Trinity, Lancaster, Pa.; first editor of the *Lutheran Standard* (1842); pres. of English District Synod of Ohio (1848 to 1850).

Gregorian Music. A. *Historical Sketch.* 1. Gregorian chant, also called plainsong, planesong, plainchant *(cantus planus),* choral *(cantus choralis),* is the unisonous, diatonic, worship music developed in the Christian Church for the Latin liturgy, named after Gregory I (d. 604), who with the help of his *schola cantorum* and with other church musicians, edited and collected the existing melodies of the formative period of the chant and issued these, together with new ones in the body of church music known as the *Antiphonale Missarum* (*antiphonarius cento*). The chant spread to England through Augustine (596), and in the empire of Charlemagne *scholae cantorum* were established, the *schola* at Metz achieving particular fame. St. Gall in Switzerland also became a Gregorian center. The golden era of the chant, the high point of Gregorian, dates from the time of Gregory to the year 1100. A period of decadence followed from about 1300. Mensurable music, polyphony, harmony, instrumental music, and the operatic style, all in their turn, contributed to the ruin of the chant. Changes in the method of chanting and the simplification of the melodies robbed the chant of its regular rhythm. A period of restoration began about 1850. The Benedictine monks at Solesmes, France, through scholarly research, have restored the original melodies and the method of chanting, and their findings have been embodied in the official Vatican edition of the chant.

2. The chant is used in varying degrees in the Lutheran and Anglican churches. Luther and contemporary composers adapted the Gregorian chant to the German language, in the German Mass of 1526, many of the German church orders in the ensuing years following suit and weathering the Pietistic and Rationalistic movements. In the nineteenth century, renewed interest in the chant was manifested in Germany and in America. Fr. Lochner offered his *Der Hauptgottesdienst* to restore the chant to the Church in America. At the turn of the century the first complete plainsong setting in English for the Lutheran Service of Holy Communion, Matins, and Vespers appeared in *The Choral Service Book* and the *Psalter* by Archer and Reed. A plainsong setting of the service appears in the *United Lutheran Service Book* and in the *American Lutheran Hymnal*. Other Lutheran bodies use plainsong for certain parts of the service or have issued special editions of Gregorian chant for the complete service. Scandinavian Lutheran Churches also adopted the Gregorian chant melodies for the vernacular. The Swedish plainsong service is especially noteworthy.

3. The Anglican Church and the Protestant Episcopal Church followed John Merbecke's example of *The Praier Book Noted* in 1549 and have adapted plainsong to the English language very extensively since 1850, primarily because of the work done by the Plainsong and Medieval Music Society and such individuals as Helmore, Hughes, and Douglas. CaB

B. *Character.* The present-day repertoire of Gregorian chant consists of about 3,000 melodies. Gregorian chant is unisonous and rhythmically free in character. It is based largely on prose texts taken from the Psalms. While some are simple and syllabic, other chants are melismatic and involved. The tonalities employed are modal, not major and minor. The claim formerly made that Gregorian chant is pure and absolute church music is today discarded; Gregorian chant is related not only to Jewish music of Old Testament times, but likewise to pagan Greek music and has a strong Oriental tinge. Gregorian chant is undoubtedly the finest chant music the world has ever known. WEB

Dom Gregory Sunel, *Textbook of Gregorian Chant*, McLaughlin & Reilly, Boston, Mass., 1929; Andrew F. Klarmann, *Gregorian Chant*, Gregorian Institute of America, Toledo, Ohio, 1945; Dom Dominic Johner, *A New School of Gregorian Chant*, Frederick Pustet, New York, N. Y., 1925; Dom Andre Mocquereau, *Le Nombre Musical Gregorian* (Volume I), Catholic Education Press, Washington, D. C.; Dom Andre Mocquereau, *The Art of Gregorian Music*, Washington, 1923.

Gregory I. See *Popes,* 4.

Gregory VII. See *Popes,* 7.

Gregory IX. See *Popes,* 12.

Gregory XI. See *Popes,* 14.

Gregory, Caspar Rene (1846—1917). B. at Philadelphia, Pa.; studied at Philadelphia, Princeton, and Leipzig; pastor of the American Chapel at the latter place; professor at the university; joined the German army during World War I and fell in France. Authority in isagogics and textual criticism.

Gregory the Illuminator (ca. 257 to 333). The reputed founder of the Armenian Church. Armenia had, however, accepted the Ebionite faith, and the work of Gregory consisted in converting the people to more orthodox faith. See *Armenia.*

Gregory Nazianzen. A leading theologian of the Eastern Church. B. near

Nazianzus, in Cappadocia, about A. D. 329; d. at Arianzus ca. 390. His mother was the pious Nonna, whose influence on his life was profound. He studied literature and rhetoric at Caesarea, in Cappadocia, and later spent some time at Alexandria and then at the University of Athens; also traveled in Palestine and Egypt; was a friend of Basil of Caesarea. Arian in his earlier days, he later became a champion of the Nicene orthodoxy, which he represented in Seleucia and especially in Constantinople, where he became bishop in 381; is said to have preached the first Christmas sermon in Constantinople, December 25, 379. Among his writings are 45 orations, 243 letters, and a large number of poems, the latter being written in the artificial style of the rhetorical school.

Gregory of Nyssa. Prominent theologian of the Eastern Church, younger brother of Basil the Great; was bishop of the small Cappadocian town of Nyssa; d. after A. D. 394. He was a contemporary of Gregory Nazianzen,* who expressed his sympathy to him at the death of his wife Theosebia. Gregory of Nyssa was a defender of orthodoxy and was prominent at various councils. Among his works are the *Hexaemeron* and the *Making of Man* (exegetical), the *Great Catechism* (dogmatic), *The Soul and the Resurrection*, in defense of the truth, and a number of minor writings.

Gregory of Rimini (14th century). General of Augustinian order; outstanding exponent of nominalism.

Gregory Thaumaturgus (Wonderworker). Bishop of Neo-Caesarea, in Pontus (244—270); pupil and admirer of Origen; zealous and successful missionary; attended the synod at Antioch (265) which condemned Paul of Samosata. His *Declaration of Faith* is the most unequivocal statement of Trinitarianism of the ante-Nicene age. The stupendous miracles attributed to him were not mentioned until a century after his death.

Gregory of Tours (538? — 594). Frankish bishop of Tours. In addition to his books of miracles and biographies, he wrote a *History of the Franks* which furnishes source material on the early Frankish Church and the Merovingians to 591.

Grell, Eduard August (1800—86). Studied at Berlin, under his father and others; organist and choirmaster, prin-

cipally at the court cathedral; teacher of composition; many musical compositions, among which arrangements of chorals for male chorus.

Grenfell, Bernard Pyne (1869 to 1926). Prof. at Oxford, England. Discovered and edited many Egyptian papyri (Oxyrhyncus, Amherst, etc.). Published (with Hunt) works on the sayings of Jesus.

Grenfell, George (1849—1906). B. at Sancreed, Cornwall. Sent out by the Baptist Missionary Society in 1875 to the Cameroons, West Africa, he explored rivers in the Congo Basin. In 1881 he, in company with others, established stations at Musuko, Vivi, Isangila, Manyanga. Later he violently protested to Leopold of Belgium against the maladministration.

Grenfell, Wilfred (1865—1940). B. at Parkgate, England; medical missionary in Labrador, 1887; founder and superintendent of the Royal National Mission to Deep-sea Fishermen.

Gretchaninoff, Alexander (b. 1864). Talented Russian composer whose sacred choral music has a beauty and an harmonic richness all its own, but whose texts are by no means of a confessional character.

Griesbach, Johann Jakob (1745 to 1812). New Testament scholar; issued an important critical work on the text of the New Testament, based on ancient manuscripts and the Church Fathers.

Grigg, Joseph (ca. 1720—68). Mechanic in earlier years, later minister, till his retirement in 1747; wrote and published many hymns, among them: "Behold, a Stranger at the Door."

Grimm, Karl Ludwig Willibald (1807—91). Professor at Jena and consistorial councilor; supranaturalist in theology; wrote *Lexicon Graeco-Latinum in Libros Novi Testamenti*, based on Wilke; in the English revision by Thayer, formerly the best general lexicon of the New Testament.

Groenning, Charles William. B. at Fredericia, Denmark, Nov. 22, 1813; entered Mission Institute, Hamburg, 1840; commissioned to Telugus, India, 1845; at Ellore, 1849; transferred to Lutheran General Synod, 1851; stationed at Guntur; returned to Europe, 1865; d. in Germany, 1898.

Gronau, Israel (d. 1745). Tutor at Orphan House in Halle, Germany; accompanied Bolzius to America as asst. pastor to Salzburgers.

Groningen School. A school of Dutch theologians which had its center at Groningen University and for a time dominated thinking in the Reformed Church of Holland. Though the number of adherents dwindled, its influence is still felt.

The movement originated at Utrecht University under the influence of Philip Willem van Heusde, a Platonist, who held that Christianity is essentially love, which, through fear of God, by its very nature tends to reconcile men with men as children of God (1804 to 1839). At Groningen there existed a similar group which met for study of the New Testament and was influenced by such men as Usteri, Twesten, Ullmann, Schleiermacher, Lessing, and Herder. The leading men in the movement were Hofstede de Groot, L. G. Pareau, van Oordt, and others.

The Groningen school was a reaction to the intellectual systems of theology. It centered its attention on personality, work, and example of Christ. In its Christology the Groningen school approached Arian and Apollinarian views. Christ is not God and man at the same time. His divine or spiritual nature is shared by God and man. It denied the doctrine of the Trinity. Christ did not die to atone for man's sin, but his death shows God's love and hence impels man to crucify his sensual life. While Christianity is the highest religion, it is not the only true religion. The school denied the infallibility of the Bible and ascribed higher authority to the New Testament than to the Old. Liberty in theological matters was emphasized.

Much of the literature of this school has not been translated from the Dutch. A. Koehler, *Die Niederlaendische Reformirte Kirche*, Deichert, Erlangen, 1856; Hofstede de Groot, *De Groninger Godgeleerden in hunne eigenaardigheid*, A. L. Scholtens, Groningen, 1855. Two periodicals, *Waarheid in Liefde* and *Geloof en Vrijheid* (still extant) were published by the school.

Groot, Gerhard (1340—84). Founder of the Brethren of the Common Life *; educated at the cathedral school of his native city, Deventer, Holland, and at the University of Paris; traveled in Germany and Austria; converted in

1374, after which he became a preacher of repentance, desiring to labor as a missionary preacher; made profound impression with his sermons. See *Brethren of the Common Life.*

Gross, C. B. Sept. 26, 1834, in Frankfurt-on-the-Main; entered Concordia Seminary at Altenburg 1847; graduated 1856; his first charge, Richmond, Va.; 1867 pastor of the congregation in Buffalo which had been formed by uniting those who withdrew from the Buffalo Synod, after the Buffalo Colloquy, with the Missouri Synod congregation; 1880 pastor of Immanuel Church, Fort Wayne, Ind.; president of the Eastern District; vice-president of the Missouri Synod; member of the Electoral College and of the General Relief Board; d. July 10, 1906.

Grosseteste, Robert (1175—1253). Lecturer and chancellor at Oxford; bishop of Lincoln; called "harbinger of the Reformation"; outstanding scholar. He emphasized the use of Scripture and preaching. Like Luther, he first sought help from the Pope to correct abuses but soon found that the Papacy was the cause of the abuses. He is known for his open rebukes of both the Pope and the king and for his reform efforts.

Grossmann, A. A. B. Feb. 18, 1890; ed. Concordia College, St. Paul, Minn.; Concordia Teachers College, Addison, Ill., grad. 1908; installed as teacher at Bethany, Milwaukee, 1908—20; first supt. of schools of South Wis. District 1920—24; asst. manager of C. P. H. 1924—31; recording sec'y of Walther League 1910; business manager of Walther League and managing editor of *Walther League Messenger* 1911; first ex.-sec'y W. L. 1918, president 1920 to 1928. Wrote, in collaboration with fellow superintendents, Vol. VIII of *Concordia Teachers Library.* Active in Lutheran Laymen's League. Married Myrtle L. Tenneson on July 3, 1915. D. Feb. 19, 1941.

Grossmann, C. G. L. (1783—1857). Prof. and pastor at Leipzig; defended confessional Lutheranism against the State Church and Romanism; founded the *Gustav-Adolf Verein.*

Grossmann, G. M. (1823—97). B. in Hesse; studied at Erlangen; was sent by Loehe to Michigan in 1852; inspector of teachers' seminary at Saginaw; removed to Iowa, 1853; president of Iowa Synod from its organization, 1854—1893; president of the seminary till 1875; founder of teachers' seminary at Waverly, Iowa, 1879; from 1885—95 pres. of Wartburg College at Waverly, Iowa; retired in 1894.

Grotius (de Groot), Hugo (1583 to 1645). Dutch scholar, lawyer, politician. Sided with Remonstrants, therefore sentenced to life imprisonment 1618; escaped to France 1621; Swedish ambassador to France 1635—45. Sought to unite all Christian denominations (*Way to Peace, Truth of Christian Religion*); used historico-philological method in Scripture interpretation (*Notes on Old and New Testament*); publicist (*Freedom of the Seas, Rights of War and Peace*); originator of the governmental theory of atonement.*

Gruber, Eberhard. See *Amana Society.*

Gruber, Franz Xaver. B. Nov. 25, 1787, in Hochburg, Upper Austria, served most of his life as Roman Catholic schoolmaster and parish organist in the town of Arnsdorf. He is known as the composer of the tune for "Silent Night, Holy Night," writing it while serving as organist and choir director in Hallein, where he died June 7, 1863.

Gruber, L. Franklin. B. May 13, 1870, at Reading, Pa.; grad. Muhlenberg College, 1898, and Philadelphia Sem. in 1901; pastor at Holy Communion, Utica, N. Y., 1902—08; St. Mark's, Minneapolis, Minn., 1908—14; Reformation, St. Paul, Minn., 1914—27. Pres. Chicago Sem., 1926—41; mem. of the Commission of Adjudication of U. L. C., 1936—42; mem. of Board of Education, U. L. C. A. Author of *The Truth About Tyndale's New Testament; The Wittenberg Originals of the Luther Bible; Whence Came the Universe? Is the Doctrine of an Infinite and Unchangeable Deity Tenable?* D. Dec. 6, 1941.

Grubermann, Barbara. See *Communistic Societies, 5.*

Gruendler, John Ernst (1677—1720). Missionary to India; taught in Francke's Paedagogium at Halle; went to Tranquebar (1709); founded station at Poreiar; Ziegenbalg's helper and friend.

Grueneisen, Karl (1802—78). Court chaplain, court preacher, prelate in Stuttgart; authority on art and hymnology; wrote *On Hymnbook Reform;*

editor of *Journal of Christian Art;* member of the committee which prepared the Wuerttemberg hymnbook (1842) and *Eisenach Entwurf.*

Gruenwald (Gruenewald), Matthias (ca. 1470—1525). Prominent German painter, the "German Corregio"; executed a great many church paintings, also religious woodcuts; chief work the altar at Isenheim.

Grundemann, Peter Reinhold. B. Jan. 9, 1836, at Buerwalde, near Berlin. Founder of Brandenburg Missionary Conference. Voluminous writer on missions. Foremost publication: *Allgemeiner Missionsatlas.* D. after 1904.

Grundschrift. See *Higher Criticism, 14.*

Grundtvig, Nicolai Frederik Severin (1783—1875). Danish bishop, poet, and hymnwriter; became his father's assistant in 1811; was suspended several times for using impassionate language against prevailing rationalism and against the clergy; in 1839 appointed pastor of a free church at Vartan; in 1861, at his fiftieth anniversary, the king conferred on him the title of bishop. He asserted that the Apostles' Creed is from the mouth of Christ Himself, and, as a living word, is above the Bible. He held a wrong position on the Scriptures. See *Denmark, Lutheranism in,* 8.

Grundtvigianism. See *Denmark, Lutheranism in,* 8.

Grynaus, Simon (1493—1541). Prof. of Greek and Latin at Heidelberg; succeeded Erasmus at Basel; entrusted by the Duke of Wuerttemberg with the establishment of the Reformation in Wuerttemberg and the organization of Tuebingen University; helped draw up the *First Helvetic Confession* (1540).

Gryphius, Andreas (*Greif*), 1616 to 1664. Studied at Leyden; was private tutor; settled in Fraustadt; appointed syndicus of the principality of Glogau 1650; one of principal poets of Silesia; wrote: "Erhalt uns deine Lehre."

Guaranty Theory. See *Atonement, Theories of,* 6.

Guardian Spirit. See *Angels.*

Guatemala. See *Central America,* 1.

Guenther, Martin. B. Dec. 4, 1831, in Dresden, Saxony. His parents being adherents of Martin Stephan, he came to America with the Saxon emigrants; studied at Altenburg and at St. Louis and assiduously applied himself to private study; ordained pastor at Cedarburg, Wis., in 1853; pastor in Saginaw, Mich., 1860; of St. Matthew's in Chicago 1872; in 1873 he became professor of Symbolics, Homiletics, Catechetics, and kindred branches in Concordia Seminary, St. Louis; while at the seminary, he founded the church at Kirkwood and served it for years. He was a master of the art of saying much in few words, particularly of bringing out the truth of the saving doctrine and of refuting error in terse and lucid language, as may be seen from his editorial writings in the *Lutheraner* and in *Lehre und Wehre*, from his contributions to the *Homiletisches Magazin*, and his *Populaere Symbolik*, a classic in its field; he also wrote a biography of Dr. C. F. W. Walther. D. May 22, 1893.

Guericke, Heinrich Ernst Ferdinand (1803—1878). Strict Lutheran theologian and opponent of Union in Prussia; studied at Halle; professor there in 1829; 1835 deposed from his professorship on account of his opposition to the Prussian Union*; served scattered Lutherans as pastor till forbidden in 1838; in 1840 reinstated as professor by Frederick William IV; in the same year he founded, with Rudelbach, the *Zeitschrift fuer die gesamte lutherische Theologie und Kirche*; wrote: *Neutestamentliche Isagogik* (1867) and *Handbuch der Kirchengeschichte* (9th ed., 1866), both of which are considered standards.

Guetzlaff, Karl Friedrich August ("Apostle to the Chinese," 1803—51). B. in Pomerania, Germany; studied at Halle and in the institute of Jaenicke; agent of the Netherlands Missionary Society to Batavia, 1831; then to Siam; resolved to penetrate China and became agent on coast vessel; interpreter of English consular service; distributed many Christian pamphlets to Chinese; trained native workers; translated Bible into Siamese; aided Robert Morrison with his Chinese translation; wrote various Chinese, English, and German books. See *China*.

Guidance. See *Christian Teaching*, B ff.; *Parish Education*, M 7.

Guidetti, Giovanni (1532 — 92). Pupil of Palestrina; chorister in papal choir; worked, with his teacher, on revised Gradual and Antiphonary; published a Passion based on a harmony of the gospels.

Guido of Arezzo (ca. 980—1050). Has been called the inventor of present-day music (*Beatus Guido, inventor musicae*). In order to enable the singer to sing unfamiliar melodies, he extended the system of notation invented one hundred years earlier. Guido introduced the use of four-staff lines and of clefs and first used a set of syllables to designate the individual tones of the scale; these he took from the first syllables of six lines of an ancient Sapphic hymn addressed to St. John the Baptist. Thus originated the sol-fa system, which is still used today.

Guild, Women's. See *Woman in Christian Society*.

Guilmant, Felix Alexandre (1837 to 1911). French organist who excelled as a performer, improviser, and pedagog. His compositions no longer enjoy the popularity they once enjoyed.

Guizot, Francois Pierre Guillaume (1787—1874). Prof. of history at the Sorbonne; filled highest political offices; leader of French Reformed Church, staunchly opposing liberal wing; prolific and brilliant writer.

Gumpeltzhaimer, Adam (1559 to 1625). Outstanding composer of the Lutheran Church. He was active in Wuerttemberg and Augsburg. His compositions show the influence the Venetian master Giovanni Gabrieli had exerted on him, but also that he was imbued with the spirit of Lutheranism. In his *Geschichte der Musik* (II, p. 559), Ambros states that the music of Gumpeltzhaimer is related in spirit to that of Gallus, but that his harmonies are richer and more colorful than those of this Roman Catholic master.

F. Blume, *Evangelische Kirchenmusik*, Frankfurt, 1924; S. Kuemmerle, *Encyklopaedie der evangelischen Kirchenmusik* (I), Guetersloh, 1888.

Gundert, Hermann (1814 — 93). Basel missionary to the Malabar Coast, India, 1839; active especially in a literary way; his Bible translations are still valuable.

Gundeson, J. G. See *Canada, Lutheranism in*, 22.

Gunkel, Hermann (1862—1932). German Protestant theologian; taught at Berlin, Giessen, and Halle; evolved the form-historical method of studying religious history.

Gunnerus, John Ernst (1718—73). Bishop of Trondheim; botanist; cultural leader of Norway.

Gunpowder Plot. A Catholic conspiracy to destroy the Protestant government of England by blowing up the Parliament buildings on Nov. 5, 1605, the opening day of the session, when the king, the Lords, and the Commons would all be present. Fortunately the plot was revealed, and the ringleaders were executed.

Gurney, Joseph John (1788—1847). English Quaker; well-educated and wealthy; Quaker minister (1818); advocated prison reform, removal of capital punishment, abolition of slavery; visited America, where his influence is still strong, some Quakers being called Gurneyites.

Gury, J. P. (1801—66). Jesuit; prof. of moral theology at the College of Rome and author of the *Compendium Theologiae Moralis*, essentially a reproduction of the ethical theories of the older Jesuits.

Gustav Adolf (*Gustavus Adolphus*, 1594—1632). King of Sweden, grandson of Gustav Vasa, champion of the Lutheran cause in Germany during the Thirty Years' War. Landing in Pomerania in 1630, he repeatedly defeated the imperial generals and conquered a large part of Germany, but was killed in the Battle of Luetzen, November 16, 1632.

Gustav Adolph Society (*Gustav-Adolf-Verein*). A Protestant society (unionistic), organized for the purpose of subsidizing evangelical churches in Roman Catholic countries; founded 1832 by Superintendent Grossmann in Leipzig; was united in 1842 with a society organized for similar purposes by Dr. Zimmermann in Darmstadt in 1841; enlarged by receiving Prussian missionary societies in 1844; was authorized to organize district societies in Bavaria (1849) and Austria (1861); soon extended to Hungary, Switzerland, France, Russia, Sweden, Romania, Italy, Holland, and Belgium. Prior to World War I the society had more than 3,000 local associations; the benefactions of the society amounted to some 40,000,000 marks; the working capital totaled 5,000,000 marks. See *Gotteskasten, Lutherischer.*

Gustav Vasa (1496—1560). Gained the first favorable impressions of Lu-theranism as an exile in Luebeck in 1519 and 1520. Freeing Sweden from the bloody tyranny of Christian II of Denmark, he was elected king of Sweden in 1523 and strengthened his throne by favoring Lutheranism and secularizing the wealth of the Romish Church. He corresponded with Luther, made Olaus Petri preacher at Stockholm and his brother Laurentius professor at Uppsala, and had Laurentius Andreae translate the New Testament. The Reichstag of Westeraes, in 1527, established the free preaching and teaching of the pure Word of God, while the Synod of Oerebro, in 1529, considered the best means of educating good preachers and teaching the true religion to the people. In 1559 Gustav sent the first Lutheran missionaries to the despised pagan Laplanders.

Gutenberg, Johannes (1400—68). German printer; either invented or perfected the modern art of printing and established the first printing press at Mainz; his first large production was a Latin Bible.

Guthrie, Thomas (1803—73). Presbyterian minister of Scotland; joined Free Church (1843); pulpit orator, philanthropist, and social reformer; founded "Ragged Schools"; edited Sunday magazine.

Gutwasser, John Ernst. The first Dutch Lutheran pastor in the City of New York. After receiving a promise of religious liberty for Lutherans in New Amsterdam (New York) from the West India Trading Co., Gutwasser was called (1657) and sent to America. The Reformed pastors protested and demanded his immediate return to Europe, which, however, his illness prevented. After Nov. 11, 1658, his name disappears from the records (see article in Jennson, *Lutheran Biographies*).

Guyau, Marie Jean (1854—88). French poet and philosopher; opposed the evolution theory of Herbert Spencer; he sought to build a religious system by harmonizing social ideals.

Guyon, Jeanne Marie (1648—1717). French mystic; her first work *Les Torrents Spirituels* describes souls tending to lose themselves in God; also wrote an exposition of Solomon's Song and of the Apocalypse, and *Moyen court et tres facile pour l'oraison.* She was persecuted as a leader of the Quietist movement.

H

Haas, J. A. W. Member of the General Council. B. 1862; ed. at the University of Pa., at the Lutheran Seminary at Philadelphia, and at Leipzig; ordained, 1888; pastor in New York; president of Muhlenberg College, Allentown, Pa. (1904). Wrote: *Trends of Thought* (1915); *In the Light of Faith* (1922); *Freedom and Christian Conduct* (1923); *The Unity of Faith and Knowledge* (1926); *The Truth of Faith* (1927); *What Ought I Believe* (1929); *The Christian Way of Liberty* (1930); *Christianity and Its Contrasts* (1932); *The Gospel of Mark; Bible Literature.* Co-editor of the *Lutheran Cyclopedia.*

Haas, Nicolas (1665—1715). Lutheran pastor in Saxony; voluminous ascetic writer; wrote: *Getreuer Seelenhirt, Biblischer Hauptschluessel,* Bible with interlinear notes, collections of sermons and other works.

Habermann (Avenarius), Johann. D. 1590 as superintendent at Zeitz; renowned Hebraist, but best known for his little book of prayers, a great favorite among devout Christians.

Habit. See *Christian Teaching,* G.

Hackett, Horatio Balch (1808—75). Baptist. B. at Salisbury, Mass.; professor at Brown, Newton, Rochester (New Testament Greek); d. at Rochester; wrote *Hebrew Grammar;* associate editor of *Smith's Bible Dictionary;* etc.

Hades. See *Hereafter,* C 4.

Hades Gospel. A term applied to the belief that heathen to whom the Gospel was not preached, those who heard the Gospel but did not accept it, and others will have another opportunity after death. 1 Pet. 3:18 f. is the *locus classicus* for adherents of the Hades Gospel. Other passages quoted: 2 Tim. 1:12; 1 John 3:8; Gen. 3:15; Matt. 5:26; Matt. 12:31, 32; Matt. 11:20; John 12:32; and passages proclaiming the universality of redemption. The Scriptural teaching is that Judgment follows death without a second chance.

T. Engelder, "The Hades Gospel," *CTM,* XVI: 293—300; 374—96; 593—615; XVII: 641—76.

Hadrian. See *Persecutions of Christians,* 3.

Haeckel, Ernst (1834—1919). German zoologist and philosopher; prof. at Jena, 1862. Popularized Darwinism in Germany, especially in *Natuerliche Schoepfungsgeschichte,* 1868, and expanded and developed it into a complete philosophical system. Made contribution to evolution in "biogenetic law," according to which development of the individual is a recapitulation of history of the race. In *Weltraetsel,* 1899, he took an uncompromising monistic standpoint. Organic life is evolved from the albuminoid compounds of carbon ("carbon theory") and human soul from "soul cell" of Protozoa. Denied existence of personal God and immortality. Exerted great influence, especially on freethinking masses. Also wrote *Der Monismus, Die Lebenswunder.* See *Monism.*

Haentzschel, Klemens Esaias. B. in Meissen, Saxony, Feb. 27, 1837; studied law in Leipzig; served in the Civil War; was parochial school teacher in Sheboygan and Fort Wayne; served sixteen years as professor in the Teachers' Seminary, Addison; d. Oct. 21, 1890.

Haering, Theodor (1848—1928). Prof. at Zuerich, Goettingen, and Tuebingen; modified Ritschlianism in the direction of conservative theology, ascribed strong ethical significance to life of Jesus.

Haerter, Franz Heinrich (1797 to 1873). Luth. pastor at Ittenheim and Strassburg; founder of Deaconess House in Strassburg (1842).

Haevernick, Heinrich Andreas Christoph (1811—45). B. and d. at Kroepelin. Studied at Leipzig, Halle, and Berlin. Taught at Geneva, Rostock, and Koenigsberg. Adopting Hengstenberg's Biblical approach, he defended the traditional views concerning the books of the OT.

Hafenreffer, Matthaeus (1561 to 1619). In 1590 court preacher at Stuttgart; later professor at Tuebingen; a man of very extensive learning in the Old Testament, the Church Fathers, and also in natural sciences and mathematics; teacher and friend of the astronomer Kepler; best-known works: *Loci Theologici* and *Templum Ezechielis.*

Hagen, Carl Frederick William. B. Sept. 30, 1859, at Sterley, Germany; graduated at St. Louis, 1885; pastor at Ludington (and Riverton), Mich., 1885 to 1898; at Detroit, Mich. (Immanuel), 1898—1938; chairman of Board of Directors of the Society of the Ev. Luth. Institute for the Deaf, Detroit, Mich., 1899—1914; chairman of General Board of Control, 1914—20; member of Board of Directors of Synod, 1920—35; d. Nov. 21, 1938.

Hagen, Peter (1569—1620). Rector of the Domschule in Koenigsberg; poems in ancient form; wrote: "Wir danken dir, Herr, insgemein"; "Freu dich, du werte Christenheit."

Hagenau Conference. Arranged by King Ferdinand in 1540 between the Roman Catholics (Morone, Eck, Faber, Cochlaeus) and the Evangelicals (Brenz, Capito, Osiander, Cruciger, and Myconius) for the purpose of establishing peace.

Hagenbach, Karl Rudolf (1801—74). German-Swiss church historian and theologian; prof. at Basel. Endeavored to reconcile culture and Christianity. Emphasized the imitation of Christ in life. Influenced by Luecke, Schleiermacher, and Neander, he, nevertheless, maintained an independent position. Published many works, including *Encyklopaedie und Methodologie, Lehrbuch der Dogmengeschichte, Grundzuege der Homiletik und Liturgik,* many articles in Herzog's *Realencyklopaedie.* Editor of *Kirchenblatt.*

Haggadah. See *Talmud.*

Hagia Sofia. See *Cathedrals.*

Hagiographa. Books of the Old Testament other than the "Law" and "Prophets" *(Kethubim).*

Hahn, August (1792—1863). Attacked Rationalism in 1827 at Leipzig; 1833 called to Breslau as professor and councilor of the consistory; there sought to win the "Old Lutherans" for the "Union"; edited Hebrew Old Testament.

Hahn, Hugo (1818—95). Rhenish missionary in Africa; worked among the Herero at New Barmen and Ovambo; founded the seminary "Augustineum" at Otjimbingue.

Hahn, Philipp Matthaeus (1739 to 1790). German pietist; the kingdom of Jesus is the center from which all is derived; theosophist views; Godhead is conscious only in Christ who was created from the essence of God before creation of the world; taught millennialism (unity of creature and Creator before eternity); denied eternal punishment.

Hail Mary. See *Ave Maria.*

Haiti. Western portion of Hispaniola Island in the West Indies. 10,714 sq. mi.; population, 3,111,973 (1950), most of them Negroes. Protestant community, approximately 75,000 communicant members; 75 ordained, 440 not ordained native workers; foreign staff: 514 (1952). The (British) Methodist Missionary Society; the African M. E. Church; the American Baptist Home Mission Society; the Lott Carey Baptist; the Protestant Episcopal Church; the Seventh-Day Adventists; Jacmel Baptist Church; Unevangelized Fields Mission; Church of God; Church of the Nazarene; East and West Indies Bible Mission; Wesleyan Methodist Missionary Society; West Indies Mission; World Evangelization Service; are listed as carrying on work. See *Missions, Bibliography.*

Halacha. See *Talmud.*

Haldaneans. See *Disciples of Christ,* 1.

Halevy, Joseph (1827—1917). Of Jewish parentage; French Orientalist and explorer; prof. at Paris; made researches in Abyssinia and Arabia; opposed to many conclusions reached by higher criticism of OT.

Half-Way Covenant, The. An expedient adopted by the New England churches (1662) according to which children of church members were entitled to Baptism, but if they appeared unregenerate as adults, they could not participate in altar and pulpit fellowship.

Halfdanarson, Helgi (1826—94). Icelandic Lutheran; prof. at Reykjavik; many of his hymns used in Icelandic Church; wrote a prominent catechism, *History of the Ancient Church, Christian Ethics,* and in the field of homiletics.

Hall, Granville Stanley (1846 to 1924). B. at Ashfield, Mass.; graduated from Williams College, spent several years in Germany studying philosophy and psychology; professor and lecturer on psychology at Antioch College, Harvard, Williams; in 1888 chosen president of Clark University; an important contributor to educational literature and a leading authority in that field; wrote: *Aspects of German Culture; Adolescence; Youth: Its Education and Regimen.*

Hall, Robert (1764—1831). Baptist; b. at Leicestershire, England; preacher at Bristol, Cambridge, Leicester, Bristol (d. there); occupied high rank as orator; grew somewhat conservative with age; wrote *Modern Infidelity.*

Hallel. The song of praise at the chief Jewish festivals, consisting, in its entirety, of Psalms 113—118.

Hallelujah. Taken directly from the Hebrew, from the Jewish Passover liturgy, its meaning, "Praise ye Jehovah," Rev. 19:1, 3, 6; sung after all antiphons, Psalms, verses, and responsories, also after the reading of the Epistle lesson; omitted in Lent.

Hallesche Nachrichten. A series of reports sent to Halle by early Lutheran pastors in America (Muhlenberg, Brunholtz, Handschuh, and others). These reports were printed with an introduction by J. L. Schulze. They offer much source material on the early history of Lutheranism in Pennsylvania.

Hamann, Johann Georg (1730—88). "Magus of the North"; studied all branches of human knowledge, but without any system; later on turned to the study of the Bible and Luther's writings and became a brilliant defender of the realities of the Christian faith in an age of rationalism and unbelief; was highly esteemed by Claudius, Jacobi, Herder, and even Goethe. F. Thoms, *Hamanns Bekehrung,* Bertelsmann, Guetersloh, rev. 1933.

Hamelmann, Hermann (1525—95). D. at Oldenburg. As priest he first opposed Luther, later was converted and labored zealously for the establishment of Lutheranism.

Hamestakan. See *Zoroastrianism.*

Hamilton, James (1819—96). Ed. at Cambridge; held various charges, the last at Bath and Wells; writer of unusual merit; among his hymns: "Across the Sky the Shades of Night."

Hamilton, Patrick. B. ca. 1504 of royal blood; abbot of Ferne when fourteen; studied at Paris; A. M. in 1520; professor at St. Andrew's University in 1523, when M. de la Tour vented Lutheran opinions. Lutheran books arrived in 1524. Hamilton was the first to preach the Lutheran teaching in 1526; fled to Wittenberg and Marburg in 1527; the first to defend theses at Marburg, *Patrick's Places,* which prove him a close student of Luther's *Freedom of a Christian Man;* returned to Scotland in 1527; married; preached; was tried and condemned for Lutheranism;

burned in 1528, twenty-four years old — the first Lutheran preacher and martyr of Scotland. See *Presbyterian Bodies,* 1.

Hamilton, Sir William. Scotch philosopher; b. 1788 at Glasgow; 1821 professor at Edinburgh; d. there, 1856; promulgated the doctrine of nescience; believed in existence of Absolute Being, the Source of the visible universe, but asserted that knowledge of this fact is impossible; faith is "organ by which we apprehend what is beyond our knowledge"; greatly influenced agnosticism of Mill and Spencer.

Hamma Divinity School. See *Ministry, Education of,* XI B.

Hamma, M. W. (1836—1913). Pastor of Lutheran General Synod; donated $200,000 to Wittenberg College, Springfield, Ohio, whose theological department is now called Hamma Divinity School.

Hammerschmidt, Andreas (ca. 1611 to 1675). B. at Bruex in Bohemia; received his early musical training at Schandau in Saxony from the cantor, Stephan Otto; was organist at Freiberg in 1635 and four years later at Zittau, in both instances successor to Christoph Schreiber, remaining 36 years at the latter place. Hammerschmidt was one of the most distinguished composers of music in the 17th century. His work is marked by great originality. He contributed largely to the choir and congregational music of his day in such works as his *Musikalische Andachten,* 1638, and *Fest-, Buss-, und Danklieder,* 1659.

Hammond, William. B. Jan. 6, 1719, in Battle, Sussex, England, was educated at St. John's College, Cambridge; joined the Calvinistic Methodists, but later the Moravian Brethren. Besides writing original hymns, he was among the first to publish translations of the old Latin hymns. He was a very learned scholar. He wrote, "Lord, We Come Before Thee Now." D. 1783.

Hammurabi, Code of. A legal code of Hammurabi, king of Babylon, written about 2000 B. C. and discovered in 1901. It contains 282 laws which the deity Shamash is claimed to have given to Hammurabi. R. F. Harper, *The Code of Hammurabi, King of Babylon,* Chicago University Press, 1904.

Hampton Court Conference. Meeting called by James I (1604) to discuss

differences between the Puritans and
the High Church Party. The Puritans'
hope for reform was disappointed, but
an important result was the publication
of the *King James Version.*

Handel, George Frederic (1685 to
1759). Though a native of Halle, Germany, Handel is commonly regarded as
an English composer; forty-five years
of his life were spent in England. Early
in life, the manifestation of his musical
genius as well as the counsel of the
Duke of Saxe-Weissenfels overcame
the opposition of his sixty-three-year-
old father, a surgeon, who regarded
music as an unworthy pursuit for his
talented son. George Frederic became
a pupil of Friedrich Wilhelm Zachow,*
whom he respected throughout life and
whose widow he later supported. After
three years of instruction, Zachow
claimed that his pupil knew more than
he did. At eleven years, Handel was
sent to Berlin, where he made the
acquaintance of the Italian composers
of opera Ariosti and Buononcini; the
latter later made life miserable for
Handel. In compliance with his father's
wish, Handel entered the University of
Halle in 1702 to study jurisprudence,
serving at the same time as organist
of the Schloss- und Domkirche. Later
he discontinued law studies and devoted himself entirely to music. In 1703
he went to Hamburg, where he became
a violinist in the orchestra of the German Opera House conducted by R.
Keiser; here he met Telemann and
Mattheson. The latter persuaded Handel to compose operas. In 1706 Handel
traveled in Italy, where his operas enjoyed popularity. He mastered the
Italian style of writing music and also
the style of Henry Purcell, whom he
soon surpassed. In 1710 Handel succeeded Abbé Steffani as *Kapellmeister*
of the Court of Hanover. In 1710 he
was granted a leave of absence to visit
London, where he enjoyed immediate
success. A second visit followed in
1712; Handel played truant and did
not again return to Hanover. Handel
wrote many operas and enjoyed a large
following. He was for a time chapel
master to the Duke of Chandos, during
which time he wrote his *Chandos Anthems* and two *Chandos Te Deums,* also
Esther, his first English oratorio. His
rivals in the operatic field made life
difficult for Handel so that he suffered
a nervous breakdown and became
bankrupt. As a result, Handel turned
to writing oratorios, a field in which
he is unexcelled to the present day.

Monumental works: *The Messiah, Saul,
Israel in Egypt, Samson,* and *Judas
Maccabaeus.* Handel did not turn to
writing oratorios for pious or religious
reasons, nor were his oratorios written
as church music. The confessional element, prominent in the cantatas and
passions of Bach, is absent in his music
based on sacred texts. With the possible exception of his *Messiah,* the style
of the music of his oratorios does not
differ from that of his operas. The texts
of his anthems and oratorios were
usually from the Old Testament. Although perhaps the greatest plagiarist
among the great composers, Handel
must, nevertheless, be counted among
the truly great. He was greatest when
writing choruses which depend for
their impressiveness on massiveness
and strength. His means are usually
simple and natural, not artificial or
forced. His solos, written in the bel
canto style, are more objective than
those of Bach; he expresses through
them not so much his own emotions,
but portrays the soul of the character
involved. His choral works are more
vocal, and his conception of melody
often differs radically from that of
Bach. Bukofzer remarks: "The worldly
grand manner of Handel and the spiritual attitude of Bach represent two
essential and at the same time complementary aspects of baroque music
which cause the curious paradox that
Bach and Handel are equals only when
they are incomparable." (*Music in the
Baroque Era,* 349.) Handel became
blind late in life; he lies buried in
Westminster Abbey. WEB

M. F. Bukofzer, *Music in the Baroque Era,* New York, 1947; D. Ferguson, *A History of Musical Thought,*
New York, 1948; N. G. F. Flower, *Handel, His Personality and His Times,*
London, 1929; Sir J. Hawkins, *A General History of the Science and Practice
of Music,* London, 1875; P. H. Lange,
Music in Western Civilization, New
York, 1941; H. Leichtentritt, *Music,
History, and Ideas,* Cambridge, Mass.,
1938.

Handmann, Richard (1840—1912).
Missionary; b. at Oschitz, Silesia; mis-
sionary in India, 1862—87; editor of
Leipziger Missionsblatt; wrote *Die Ev.-
Luth. Tamulenmission in der Zeit ihrer
Neubegruendung.*

Handschuh, John Fredrick (1714 to
1764). Pastor at Lancaster, Germantown, Philadelphia; one of the founders
of the Pennsylvania Ministerium.

Hanover, Evangelical Lutheran Free Church Mission Society. Separated from the Hermannsburg Mission in 1892. Worked especially in Africa.

Hanser, C. J. O. B. Sept. 7, 1832, at Schopflohe, Bavaria; studied at Concordia Seminary, St. Louis, pastor in Carondelet, Mo.; in Boston; Director of Concordia College, Ft. Wayne, 1872—79; pastor of Trinity Church, St. Louis; resigned, 1906, but served during two vacancies; d. Jan. 10, 1910; member of the Board for Colored Missions and Board for Foreign Missions; editor of *Missionstaube;* contributor to *Magazin fuer Ev. Luth. Homiletik;* autobiography: *Irrfahrten und Heimfahrten.*
C. J. O. Hanser, *Irrfahrten und Heimfahrten,* Luth. Pub. Co., Buffalo, N. Y., 1910.

Hanser, W. G. H. (1831—85). Brother of the above; pastor in Canada, Johannisburg, near Buffalo, and St. Paul's Church, Baltimore.

Hanson, Minnie. See *Evangelistic Associations,* 3.

Hanson, Osten. B. July 8, 1836, at Telemarken, Norway; came to America in 1855; lay preacher, ordained in 1861 by E. L. C. (since 1875 Hauge Synod); pastor in Goodhue County, Minn.; pres., Hauge Synod, 1875—76, 1887—93; helped revise Constitution of Hauge Synod, 1875; one of founders of Red Wing Sem. and the society which founded the Norw. Luth. Miss. in China. D. Aug. 4, 1898.

Harbaugh, Henry. B. Oct. 24, 1817, in Franklin County, Pa. His parents were Swiss. Ed. at Marshall College, Mercersburg, and ordained as a Reformed minister. He was pastor at Lewisburg, Lancaster, and Lebanon, Pa. In 1864 he became professor of theology at the Mercersburg Seminary and as such defended the Mercersburg theology. He was editor and also hymn writer. D. 1867.

Hard Shell Baptists. See *Baptist Bodies,* 11, 12.

Hardeland, August. B. Sept. 30, 1814, in Hanover; Rhenish missionary to Borneo, 1839; returned to Germany, 1848; in service of Netherland's Bible Society, 1849; returned to Borneo, 1850; superintendent of Hermannsburg Mission, 1857; in Africa, 1859—63; returned to Germany, 1864. Translated Bible into vernacular of Borneo; d. 1892.

Hardeland, Julius. Brother of the above; b. 1828 at Hanover; leader in

the mission work of the *Leipzig-Gesellschaft,* visiting the East Indian field twice.

Hardenberg, Albert Rizaeus (1510 to 1574). As a zealous exponent of the Reformation, he labored at Louvain, Aduard, Cologne, Einbeck, Bremen, Sengwarden, and Emden, where he died. At Bremen he became involved in a controversy over the Lord's Supper, holding un-Lutheran views.

Harders, Gust. A. (1863—1917). Sent by the "Rauhe Haus" to Riga, Russia, to serve in home for destitute children; educated at Springfield and Milwaukee seminaries; pastor in Milwaukee; resident superintendent of Arizona missions; poet, author of Indian mission novels: *Jaalahn, La Paloma, Wille wider Wille* (German).

Harless, Gottlieb Christoph Adolf von. B. at Nuremberg, 1806; d. at Munich, 1879; conservative Lutheran theologian; first studied philology, law, and philosophy, especially Spinoza and Hegel, at Erlangen, then theology at Halle under Tholuck's influence; then found in Luther's writings and the Confessions of the Lutheran Church the truth needed for his soul; in 1828 was called to Erlangen, where he exerted great influence and wrote his *Commentary on Ephesians* (1834), his *Theological Encyclopedia,* and his work on *Christian Ethics,* the last considered a classic; 1845 professor at Leipzig; 1850 court preacher at Dresden; 1852 president of the *Oberkonsistorialrat* at Munich, where he exerted great influence for sound Lutheranism.

Harmensen, James. See *Arminianism.*

Harmonists. See *Rappists.*

Harmonius. Son of the Syrian Gnostic Bardesanes, who, together with his father, published a "Gnostic Psalter" at the end of the second century. This hymnal contained 150 hymns. Ephraem Syrus composed his Syriac hymns to offset the dangers inflicted upon simple Christians who were being misled into false doctrine and moral corruption by the hymns of Bardesanes and Harmonius.

Harmony of the Gospels. 1. Works which combine into one continuous narrative the accounts of the four Gospels *(Diatessaron).* The earliest known work of this kind was that of Tatian. Later works: *De consensu evangeliorum* (Augustine); *Monotes-*

saron (John Gerson); *Harmoniae evangelicae libri quattuor* (A. Osiander); *Commentarii in harmoniam* (Calvin); *Harmonia quattuor evangelistarum* (Chemnitz); *Harmonia evangelica* (Lightfoot-Clericus).

2. A work exhibiting the text of the Gospels in parallel columns to show their agreement or differences. The earliest work of this type was that of Ammonius of Alexandria. This work induced Eusebius to work out his ten canons. Important parallel arrangements are: *Synopsis evangeliorum* (Griesbach); *Synopsis evangeliorum Matthaei, Marci, Lucae* (Anger); *Synopsis evangeliorum* (de Wette); *Synopsis evangelica* (Tischendorf), *Synopticon* (Rushbrooke), and modern harmonies by Robinson, Broadus, Burton, Goodspeed, and others.

Harms, Georg Ludwig Detlev Theodor (Louis, 1808—65). B. at Walsrode; d. at Hermannsburg. Studied at Goettingen. As his father's assistant and then as his successor, he began a great spiritual awakening in northern Germany and founded the Hermannsburg * Mission.

T. Harms, *Lebensbeschreibung des Pastors Louis Harms,* Hermannsburg, 1874.

Harms, Klaus (1778—1855). B. at Fahrstedt, Schleswig-Holstein; d. at Kiel, most influential Lutheran theologian in the first part of the 19th century; pastor and preacher. He grew up under rationalistic influences. At Kiel he passed from rationalism to positive Lutheranism. Influenced by Schleiermacher's *Reden ueber Religion,* the study of Scripture brought about his complete conversion. After several pastorates he was, in 1816, called as archdeacon to Kiel; later he was chief pastor and *Oberkonsistorialrat.* Being convinced that the Church had left the faith of the Reformation, he published for the tercentenary jubilee of 1817, together with Luther's Ninety-five Theses, 95 of his own against Rationalism and the attempted union between the Lutheran and Reformed Churches, which caused a tremendous sensation, calling forth no less than 200 answers. Author of several postils and a *Pastoral Theology.*

Klaus Harms, *Lebensbeschreibung verfasset von ihm selber,* Akadem. Buchhandl., Kiel, 1852; Klaus Harms, *Das sind die 95 Thesen oder Streitsaetze Dr. Luthers, theuren Andenkens — zum besondern Abdruck besorgt mit anderen 95 Saetzen als mit einer Uebersetzung aus A. 1517 in 1817 begleitet,* Akadem. Buchhandl., Kiel, 1817; Claus Harms, *Briefe zu einer naehern Verstaendigung ueber verschiedene meine Thesen betreffende Punkte, nebst einem namhaften Briefe, an den Herrn Dr. Schleiermacher,* Akadem. Buchhandl., Kiel, 1818; V. Ferm, *The Crisis in American Lutheran Theology,* Century, N. Y., 1927 (p. 117 ff.).

Harnack, Adolph (1851—1930). Son of Theodosius Harnack; educated at Dorpat; professor at Leipzig, Giessen, Marburg; 1889 at Berlin. He was a man of immense learning; theologically an exponent of Ritschlianism, the leader of that school. Teacher of Karl Barth.* Outstanding modern church historian. A consistent subjectivist, he altered specific Christian doctrines, the divinity of Jesus Christ, the Gospel of the forgiveness of sins, etc. Among his numerous writings his best-known work is his *Lehrbuch der Dogmengeschichte,* which is considered epoch-making, but is of a negative tendency. In 1881 he became one of the editors of the *Theologische Literaturzeitung;* other outstanding works: *Marcion; Apostles' Creed; Das Wesen des Christentums.*

W. Arndt, "Harnack's Theological Positions," *CTM,* XV:236—45; F. Pieper, "Adolf Harnack," *CTM,* I:651—59; Agnes von Zahn-Harnack, *Adolph von Harnack,* Tempelhof, Berlin, 1936.

Harnack, Theodosius (1817—89). B. at St. Petersburg; positive Lutheran theologian of modern type; 1848 professor at Dorpat; 1853 at Erlangen; returned to Dorpat, 1866; exerted great influence on the Lutheran Church in the Baltic provinces.

Harper, W. R. (1856—1906). First president of the University of Chicago; founder of the American Institute of Hebrew; author, editor, scholar, and a great organizer.

Harpster, John Henry. B. April 27, 1844, at Center Hall, Pa.; d. Feb. 1, 1911, at Mount Airy, Pa.; missionary of the Lutheran General Synod; sent, 1871, to Guntur, India; returned to United States, 1874; filled pastorates at Hays City, Kans., Trenton, N. J., Canton, Ohio; returned to India, 1893; took over Rajahmundry station, 1902; separated from General Synod, 1906, to continue with General Council; was a very successful missionary.

Harris, James Rendel (1852—1941). B. at Plymouth; English Friend; Biblical scholar; professor and lecturer in American and English universities and colleges; director of studies of Friends' Settlement, Birmingham; wrote: *Sidelights on New Testament Researches*, etc.

Harris, Samuel. 1. (1724—94.) "Apostle of Virginia"; Baptist, who after his conversion (1758) devoted his fortune to religious and charitable work. **2.** (1814—99.) Congregationalist; prof. of systematic theology in Bangor; pres. of Bowdoin; Dwight prof. at Yale; wrote numerous popular works.

Hart, Joseph (1712—68). B. in London, well educated, taught the classics for a number of years. From youthful piety he later lapsed into unbelief. However, at forty he had a change of heart, and under the influence of the Moravian Church he was converted. The desire to become a preacher grew in him despite his 48 years. He became pastor of an independent congregation in London and served this church for eight years. It is said that 20,000 people attended his funeral.

Hartmann, Karl Robert Edward von (1842—1906). German philosopher; b. in Berlin. Hartmann opposed Christianity, which he held had exhausted its potentialities in the Middle Ages. In his philosophical system the Absolute is the Unconscious. World process is the result of will and reason. The victory of reason over will is the purpose of the world — for the sake of the Absolute. The individual dare not seek happiness, since the reason for individual existence is only means for another. Attempts to find such happiness in this world (Greeks), in a future world (all who believe in immortality), or in evolution are illusions. Hartmann wrote his *Philosophy of the Unconscious* at the age of 27, and this work became the basis for his voluminous writings.

Hartmuth von Kronberg (d. 1549). German knight; sided with Luther in 1521; wrote to the Emperor to win him for Luther; relative of Franz von Sickingen and lost his castle for standing by him; received it back in 1541.

Hartwick, John C. (1714—96). Luth. clergyman, b. in Germany, d. in New York. Worked in New York, Pennsylvania, Maryland, Virginia, and New England. Left his estate for the founding of a seminary which has been named after him. See *Ministry, Education of*, VI B.

A. Steimle, "John Christopher Hart-

wick: His Missionary Career and the Founding of Hartwick Seminary," *Luth. Ch. Quart.*, X:174—75.

Hartwick Seminary. See *Ministry, Education of*, VI C, XI B.

Hartwick Synod. Organized Oct. 26, 1830, in Schoharie, N. Y., by the Western Conference of the New York Ministerium, the members of which wanted to satisfy their cravings for revivals more fully than they could in the mother synod with its increasing conservatism. Its territory covered fifteen counties in central New York. The Hartwick Synod acknowledged the Augustana as its confession and joined the General Synod in 1831. In 1908 it merged with the Franckean Synod, which had seceded from it in 1837, and with the New York and New Jersey Synod into the Synod of New York (General Synod). At the time of this merger the Hartwick Synod numbered 40 pastors, 44 congregations, and 5,686 communicants. See *United Lutheran Church, Synods of*, 18.

Harvest Home, Festival of. See *Church Year*, 15.

Hase, K. A. (1800—90). German theologian; held mediating position between rationalistic and orthodox theologians; sought to interpret the 17th-century orthodoxy in terms of idealism; prolific writer.

Hasse, Johann Adolf (1699—1783). Contemporary and personal friend of J. S. Bach; though active as an opera composer, also wrote some church music; pupil of Nicola Porpora and Alessandro Scarlatti. His masses have much in common with his operas; they are colorful and ornate, and hence he was idolized more than any other composer of his day. The Venetians admired him, and the Germans placed him high above Bach and Handel. Scheibe, who attacked Bach and his music very bitterly, was a great admirer of Hasse. Though still respected today, his fame is hardly to be compared with that of Bach and Handel.

Hasselquist, Tuve Nilson. B. Mar. 2, 1816, at Ousby, Skane, Sweden; grad. Univ. of Lund; ordained, June 23, 1839; served Church of Sweden until 1852, when he came to America. D. D. Muhlenberg College, 1870; pastor and home missionary, Galesburg, Ill., 1852—63; founded *Det Ratta Hemlandet*, first Swedish paper in America; pres. Augustana Synod, 1860; professor Augustana College and Sem., Paxton, Ill., 1863. Editor *Det Ratta Hemlandet,* now *Augustana,* 1855—91; author *Commentary on the Epistle to the Ephesians.* D. March, 1891.

E. Norlius, *Dr. T. N. Hasselquist,* Augustana Book Concern, Rock Island, Ill., 1900; O. F. Ander, *T. N. Hasselquist,* Augustana Book Concern, 1931.

Hassler, Hans Leo (1564—1612). Truly great Lutheran composer of the second half of the 16th century. Otto Kade (cf. *Allgemeine deutsche Biographie,* "Hassler") regards Hassler as the greatest German composer of his day. In his younger days he was a pupil of Andrea Gabrieli of Venice, at which time he was a fellow student of Giovanni Gabrieli and established an intimate and lasting friendship with this great teacher of Heinrich Schuetz. In the compositions of Hassler we find a happy fusion of Italian joy and German seriousness, a remarkable mastery of contrapuntal skill, and a sense of tonal and structural balance rarely found in music. About 400 of his compositions are today extant; due recognition was accorded him in the monumental series *Denkmaeler deutscher Tonkunst.*

References: G. Adler, *Handbuch der Musikgeschichte* (p. 391, Schering), Frankfurt, 1924; F. Blume, *Die evangelische Kirchenmusik,* Potsdam, 1931; E. E. Koch, *Geschichte des Kirchenlieds und Kirchengesangs,* Stuttgart, 1867; S. Kuemmerle, *Encyklopaedie der evangelischen Kirchenmusik;* P. H. Lang, *Music in West. Civ.* (cf. p. 3), Guetersloh, 1888; H. Leichtentritt, *Geschichte der Motette,* Leipzig, 1908; Idem, *Music, History, and Ideas,* Cambridge, Mass., 1938.

Hastings, Thomas (1784—1872). Grew up on frontier of New York State; teacher and editor; strong interest in church music; finally choirmaster in New York City; wrote, among others: "Delay Not."

Hatch, Edwin (1835—89). English theologian; spent some years as a professor in Canada (1859—66); his remaining years were spent at Oxford, England. He was a man of encyclopedic knowledge and broad scholarship, especially in the field of early Christian history.

Hattlestad, Ole J. (1823—92). Came to America from Norway (1846); served congregations at Leland, Ill., Milwaukee, Wis., and Decorah, Iowa;

co-editor of *Nordlyset;* pres. of Augustana Synod (1870—80; 88—90); editor of *Luthersk Kirketidende;* published *History of the Norwegian Augustana and Other Church Bodies in America.*

Hattstaedt, Otto F. B. Dec. 31, 1862, at Monroe, Mich.; ed. Concordia Col., Ft. Wayne, Ind., and Concordia Sem., St. Louis, grad., 1884; prof. at Concordia College, Milwaukee, Wis., 1884—1938; D. D. Con. Sem., 1930. Wrote: *Handbuch der Deutschen Nationalliteratur; Deutsche Grammatik; Geschichte des Sued-Wisconsin-Distrikts;* and devotional booklets. D. Nov. 29, 1950.

Hattstaedt, W. G. C. B. Aug. 29, 1811, at Langenzenn, Bavaria; sent to America by Loehe in 1844; located in Monroe, Mich.; founded congregations in southern Michigan; established connection with Wyneken and the "Saxon" pastors; charter member of the Missouri Synod; d. Mar. 22, 1884, as pastor in Monroe.

Hauck, Albert (1845—1918). Professor in Erlangen and Leipzig; historian of medieval German Church; co-editor with J. J. Herzog of volumes of second edition and sole editor of third edition of *Protestantische Realenzyklopaedie.*

Hauge, Hans Nielsen (1771—1824). Norwegian lay preacher and revivalist; converted to a living faith in Christ through reading Luther's works at the age of twenty-five; without any higher education began to preach the truth throughout the entire land; for this he was imprisoned, 1804—1814. His work and that of other lay preachers following him did much to counteract rationalism in Norway. He stood on the Lutheran Confessions, in the main, "emphasized, however, sanctification at the expense of justification"; a pietist. See *Norway, Lutheranism in,* 10; *Evangelical Lutheran Church,* 4.

A. C. Bang, *Hans Nielsen Hauge og hans Samtid,* Christiania, 1875; M. O. Wee, *Haugeanism: A Brief Sketch of the Movement and Some of Its Chief Exponents,* St. Paul, 1919; J. B. Bull, *Hans Nielsen Hauge, der Erwecker Norwegens,* Steinkopf, Stuttgart, 1926.

Hauge Norwegian Evangelical Lutheran Synod. See *Evangelical Lutheran Church,* 5 ff.

Hauge Synod. A Norwegian synod organized under the leadership of Elling Eielsen at Jefferson Prairie, Wis., April, 1846, with the name "Evangelical

Lutheran Church of America." In 1875 the organization was changed and the name "Hauge Norwegian Evangelical Lutheran Synod of America" adopted. In 1876 the followers of Eielsen * withdrew and formed the Eielsen Synod.

Haupt, Paul (1858—1926). Studied at Leipzig, Berlin, and the British Museum; prof. of Assyriology at Goettingen (1883—88); at Johns Hopkins, Baltimore, 1888; member of the Society of Friends; radical critic. Wrote: *The Sacred Books of the Old Testament* (*Polychrome Bible,* 1893 to 1894); *Biblical Love Ditties* (1902); *The Book of Canticles* (1902); *Koheleth* (1905); *The Book of Ecclesiastes* (1905); *Purim* (1906); *The Book of Nahum* (1907); *Biblische Liebeslieder* (1907); *Jonah's Whale* (1907); *The Book of Esther* (1908); *The Aryan Ancestry of Jesus* (1910); *Jesus* (1909); *The Burning Bush and the Origin of Judaism* (1910); *The Book of Micah* (1910).

Hausihl, Bernard M. See *Canada, Lutheranism in,* 1.

Hausrath, Adolf (1837—1910). B. at Karlsruhe; d. at Heidelberg; Reformed liberal theologian; a moderate adherent of the Tuebingen school; 1867 professor of church history at Heidelberg.

Haustafel. Translated, *table of duties;* a statement of morality for public and personal use; common in classic and folk literature. The most notable Lutheran example is that at the conclusion of Luther's Small Catechism; probably not altogether Luther's own, compiled from the ethical portions of the Epistles. While useful in reviewing the ethical teachings of the New Testament and potent in establishing habits of morality, it was sometimes separated from the motives of the life in Christ and served to create a legalistic cast to some Lutheran morality.

Havergal, Frances R. (1836—1897). The youngest child of William Henry Havergal, vicar of Astley, Worcestershire, was born there on Dec. 14, 1836. At the age of seven she began to write verses which gained some recognition. In spite of her frail health she mastered French, German, Italian, Latin, Greek, and Hebrew. In early life Miss Havergal entertained a morbid sense of the vanity of human life; however, this was changed, and the shadows were lifted. She was a diligent Bible reader, making that her first occupation in the morning. Miss Ha-

vergal was the most gifted and popular hymn writer that England produced in the last half of the 19th century.

F. R. Havergal, *Echoes from the Word,* Hand and Heart, London, 1879.

Hawaii (formerly the *Sandwich Islands*). Since 1898 a territory of the United States, 2,100 miles west of San Francisco, consisting of eight inhabited and a few very small uninhabited islands. Area, 6,441 sq. mi. Estimated population, 423,330, the races being thoroughly mixed. The natives belong to the Malayo-Polynesian stock. Capital city, Honolulu. The islands were discovered by Captain James Cook in 1778, the natives at that time practicing crude and sanguinary idolatry and human sacrifices with cannibalism. — *Missions.* A request for Christian teachers was sent to England by King Kamehameha in 1794, but without success. Missionary efforts began in 1820, when the American Board of Commissioners for Foreign Missions took hold of the work. The Christianization of the islands has since made great strides. In 1864 the American Board withdrew its supervision, having constituted a local church organization, the Hawaiian Evangelical Association. In 1861 the S. P. G. sent two missionaries to Hawaii; the first person to be baptized by them was the queen. This mission was later transferred to the American Protestant Episcopal Church. This Church has also entered upon mission work among the Chinese, Japanese, and Koreans. The Roman Catholic Church attempted to enter the islands in 1827, but her priests were banished in 1831. Another Roman Catholic mission was opened in 1839 and has operated since. At Molokai, a small island of the Hawaiian group, a leper colony was established in 1866. Missions: Assemblies of God, Methodist Church, Pentecostal Holiness Church, Protestant Episcopal Church, Seventh-Day Adventists. Missionary Church Assn. Southern Baptist Conv. Statistics: 126 ordained, 169 not-ordained native workers; 89 ordained, 66 not-ordained foreign staff; 30,302 communicants (1952). The Lutheran Church—Missouri Synod started a congregation there, after work by chaplains a few years earlier, in 1945. See *Missions, Bibliography.* OHS

Haweis, Hugh Reginald (1838 to 1901). Ed. at Cambridge, England; held several positions in the Established Church; wrote *The Picture of Paul, Story of the Four,* and others; hymn

"The Homeland, Oh, the Homeland" credited to him, but not on good authority.

Haweis, Thomas (1732—1820). B. at Cornwall, England, practiced medicine for a time but then turned to theology and became assistant chaplain at Lock Hospital, London. Later he was rector of All Saints, Aldwincle, and chaplain in Bath. He earned the distinction of being the most musical of the chaplains. He also was a prodigious writer in prose and poetry; however, his hymns have not more than ordinary value. Among his writings are a *Commentary on the Bible* and *A Translation of the New Testament.*

Hay, Charles Augustus (1821—93). Luth. clergyman of General Synod; b. at York, Pa.; grad. from Gettysburg; studied in Berlin and Halle; pastor at Middletown, Md.; prof. of Biblical literature and German at Gettysburg (1843); pastor at Hanover, Pa. (1848), and Harrisburg, Pa. (1849); withdrew his church from the Ministerium of Pennsylvania and joined Synod of East Pennsylvania (1857); prof. of Hebrew and Old Testament theology, pastoral theology, and German at Gettysburg (1865); pres. of East Pennsylvania Synod (1860, 1874), of General Synod (1881); trustee of Pennsylvania College. Translated Schmid's *Dogmatics,* some works of Luther, and wrote for periodicals and weekly papers.

Haydn, Franz Joseph (1732—1809). Austrian composer of German stock. In 1740 Joseph became a chorister at the Cathedral of St. Stephen in Vienna. Here he was under the influence of Karl Georg Reutter, choirmaster of the Cathedral, whose compositions were sparkling and rich in character. Most of Haydn's mature life was devoted to serving as *Kapellmeister* of the courts of Paul Anton Esterhazy at Eisenstadt or of the latter's brother, Nicolaus, at Esterhaz. In 1790 and 1794 Haydn visited London, where his work was received with loud acclaim. Haydn is at times referred to as "the Father of the Symphony," a misleading term, since the seed had been sown and had come to bloom already before his day. He is likewise referred to at times as "Papa Haydn," but this term, too, is misleading for Haydn's work as a composer reveals a spirit of independent fortitude which at times borders on revolution and iconoclasm. While his oratorios *The Creation* and *The Seasons* reveal the strong and wholesome influence of Handel, the homophonic character of his work in general betrays the reaction of his day against the polyphony of the Baroque Era. Haydn was a prolific composer; he wrote no fewer than 104 symphonies, much chamber music, many piano compositions, operettas, masses, smaller choral works, and compositions of various other types. His conception of church music was shaped largely by what he had heard in his youth in the Cathedral of St. Stephen in Vienna. Orchestral accompaniments were not unusual in this famous and beautiful cathedral, and the concerto idiom was not foreign to the Viennese service of worship. This largely explains the character of the masses by Haydn. The traditions of Vienna differed widely from those of Rome. Hence it is not surprising that the music of the Benedictus of a mass he wrote in 1782 is identical with the music of an aria found in his comic opera *Il mondo della luna (The World of the Moon),* written five years before. Haydn was a devout Roman Catholic, and, despite secular influences, there is a ring of sincerity and devotion in his sacred works which one must admire.
WEB

E. Buecken, *Musik des Rokoko und der Klassik. Handbuch der Musikwissenschaft,* Vol. V. Potsdam, 1927; K. Geiringer, *Haydn, A Creative Life in Music.* New York, 1946; idem, *Grove's Dictionary of Music and Musicians.* 4th edition. London, 1940; idem, *Thompson's International Cyclopedia of Music.* Article: Joseph Haydn. New York, 1939; P. H. Lang, *Music in Western Civilization.* New York, 1941; A. Schering, *Geschichte des Oratoriums.* Leipzig, 1911.

Haydn, Johann Michael (1737 to 1806), brother of Joseph, was preeminently a composer of church music; among his compositions may be found 20 masses, a number of offertories, and 114 graduals. From 1762 to 1806 he was *Konzertmeister* to the bishop of Salzburg. Though not as highly talented and versatile as his brother, Michael Haydn did excel his brother as a composer of music written in what is commonly regarded as ideal church music.

Hayes, Doremus Almy (1863—1936). B. at Russellville, Ohio; Methodist Episcopal; held various professorships; wrote *Synoptic Gospels and Book of Acts; Great Characters of the New*

Testament; and other works (listed in *Who's Who in America,* 1936—37).

Hayn, Henriette Louise von (1724 to 1782). Moravian; teacher and nurse at Herrnhut; gifted hymn writer; wrote "Seeing I Am Jesus' Lamb."

Hayunga, Herman. See *Canada, Lutheranism in,* 4.

Hazelius, Ernest Louis (1777—1853). B. at Neusalz, Silesia, Prussia; ed. in Moravian institutions; sent to teach Latin and Greek in Moravian school at Nazareth, Pa. (1800); joined Lutheran Church (1809); pastor in Hunterdon and Morris Counties; prof. at Hartwick Seminary (1815); wrote *Biography of Luther* (1813); *Materials for Catechization on Passages of Scripture* (1823); *The Augsburg Confession . . . with Notes and Observations* (1828); *The Life of John Henry Stilling; History of the Christian Church from the Earliest Ages to the Present Time* (vol. I); *History of American Lutheran Church* (1846). Life in works of Sprague, Morris, Jennson (see *Biographies*).

Heads of Agreement. A document which brought about a temporary union between Congregationalists and Presbyterians in England (1691).

Heart. In nearly all passages in which the Hebrew words *lebh (lebhabh)* and the Greek *kardia* occur they are used of a man's heart and usually in a psychological sense as the organ of feeling, thinking, and willing. The heart is the seat of life (Gen. 18:5; Judg. 19:5, 8; Luke 21:34). The heart is the center of life in all relations (Prov. 4:23) and sometimes used as a synonym with *psyche* and *pneuma* (compare Prov. 12:25 with Gen. 41:8; James 4:8 with 1 Pet. 1:22; Ps. 42:5 with Ps. 57:7). Man is said to lose his soul, but never his heart.

The spirit is the life principle of the heart and acts through it (spirit and heart paralleled: Ps. 34:18). With the heart man approaches God, through it Christ rests in him (Eph. 3:17; Gal. 2:20), and by it man is estranged from God (Eph. 4:18; Is. 1:5). The heart determines the character of man (Rom. 7; 1:21; 2:5; Acts 7:51; Luke 8:15). The heart is the treasury of good and evil (Matt. 12:34, 35), receives God's Word and the Holy Spirit (Matt. 13:19), is the organ of faith (Rom. 10:9), decision (Acts 5:4), and thought (Is. 10:7). It is the object of

Satan's activity (John 13:2; Acts 28:27). The works of the Law are written in the heart (Rom. 2:15) and in it is eternity (Eccl. 3:11).

H. Cremer, "Heart, Biblical Usage," *The New Schaff-Herzog Encyclopedia of Religious Knowledge,* Funk and Wagnalls, 1909 (V:177 ff.)

Heart of Mary Immaculate. A devotion, in the Roman Church, similar to that directed to the heart of Jesus (see *Sacred Heart*), but having for its object the physical heart of Mary. It was first propagated in the 17th century.

Heath, George (d. 1822). Facts of early life not known, Presbyterian pastor at Honiton, England, in 1770; contributed to hymnology and wrote, among others: "My Soul, Be on Thy Guard."

Heathenism. A general term designating all forms of religion exclusive of the Christian, Jewish, and Mohammedan. A heathen is originally a dweller on the heath, where the old idol worship managed to maintain itself even after Christianity had already become the religion of the inhabitants of the populous centers. Of special interest to Christians is the heathenism prevailing in the Roman Empire during the first centuries of our era. To give a full account of it in this article is, however, impossible. We can draw attention to only a few outstanding facts. At no time in history did heathenism seem to be more firmly entrenched than at the dawn of Christianity. There were "gods many and lords many," temples and shrines, cults and worships, in bewildering confusion. Religion was wrought into the very fabric of life. Besides, since the days of Augustus it had become an engine of state policy, such as it had never been before, culminating in the deification of the emperor as the incarnation of the state. Nevertheless there were evident signs of decay. The world was losing confidence in its gods. This appears above all in the syncretistic amalgam of gods and cults so characteristic of the religion of the empire. Literary testimonies tell the same tale. Greek philosophy had for centuries acted as a solvent of popular mythology. Xenophanes scoffed at man-made gods. Aristophanes ridiculed them in his comedies. Epicurus relegated them to a state of innocuous desuetude "amid the lucid interspace of world and worlds," while the Stoics reduced them to a pantheistic abstraction. Among the Romans, Lucretius proclaimed the gopsel of irreligion with burning passion and intense vehemence. The carpenter in Horace deliberates whether he should convert a rude log into a bench or a god (*Sat.*, I, 7, 1—3). Both Cicero and Juvenal treat the underworld as an old wives' fable. The naturalist Pliny is openly atheistic. But these and numerous other testimonies must not mislead us to the idea that paganism had spent its force. The religion of the cultured classes never reflects the religion of the crowd, nor were all the cultured irreligious. Tacitus wavered; Plutarch and others were devout pagan believers. Besides, there were many dual personalities among the most advanced thinkers, who out of deference to tradition or to the beliefs of the vulgar duly observed, and even championed, superstitious rites and ceremonies which they inwardly despised. And, as in all ages, there was not a little genuine superstition even among the most cultivated and enlightened circles. It need hardly be added that neither the wisdom of the philosophers nor the numerous forms of paganism satisfied the deeper cravings of the soul. On the vital questions of salvation and immortality the ancient world declared its own bankruptcy. It remained for Jesus of Nazareth to bring "life and immortality to light." — Turning to the moral side of pagan life, we may observe that the dark side of the picture has naturally been most emphasized, the monstrous crimes and hideous vices attracting the attention of satirists, moralists, and historians; that the virtues of which natural man is capable had not disappeared in this period; and that the moral tone of the second century, for example, was decidedly more elevated than under the early empire. Still the picture of the heathen world drawn by St. Paul is not overdrawn. Its vices and crimes, its unbounded luxury and shameless self-indulgence, have hardly been paralleled, certainly never exceeded, in the annals of history. We can here notice only in passing the extreme laxity of the conjugal tie, which elicited from Seneca the remark that women count their years, not by the consuls, but by the number of their husbands; the evils of the slave system (60,000,000 slaves in the empire!) with the consequent degradation of labor; the wild extravagances and luxuries of the rich and the abject misery of the poor; the coarse and inhuman brutalities of the amphitheater and the fierce passions of the circus, etc., etc. In short, the pagan world was in a state of moral decay, with no regenerative power to arrest its downward course. This was provided by that despised element of society which was deemed its greatest foe — the Christians.

Heaven. See *Hereafter*, A, C.

Heber, Reginald (1783—1826). B. in Malpas, Cheshire, England. His father was his first instructor. He was a very gifted child. At 7 he versified in English the Latin writer Phaedrus. At seventeen he entered Brasenose College, Oxford. His Newdigate prize poem, "Palestine," is probably the only one that has won a permanent place in poetical literature. After graduation and a tour of the continent, he was ordained Vicar of Hodnet. During this sixteen-year vicarage he wrote all of his hymns. In 1823 he received the degree of D. D. from the University of Oxford. He was called to India and was consecrated bishop by the Archbishop at Lambeth. In India he ordained the first native pastor of the Episcopal Church, Christian David, in his capacity as Bishop of Calcutta. He will ever be known by "From Greenland's Icy Mountains" and other hymns.

Hecker, Heinrich Kornelius (1699 to 1743). Pastor at Meuselwitz near Altenburg; neighbor of Christian Loeber; prolific poet, doctrinal hymns; wrote: "Gottlob, ein neues Kirchenjahr."

Hecker, Isaac Thomas (1819—88). Became a Roman Catholic (1844); joined Redemptorist Order; founded *Missionary Priests of St. Paul the Apostle* (Paulists *); active in Roman Catholic publicity work; founded *Catholic World* (1865) and *Young Catholic* (1871) publications.

Hedgerb, F. G. See *Finland, Lutheranism in*, 4.

Hedinger, Johann Reinhard (1644 to 1704). Fearless confessor of Eberhard Ludwig of Wuerttemberg; wrote a popular interpretation of the New Testament, books in the field of homiletics and pastoral theology, hymns. He caused a pietistic awakening which ended in separatism after his death.

Hedonism. The grossest form of eudemonism, which makes the pursuit and enjoyment of pleasure and the avoidance of pain the highest aim in life and consequently does not recognize any real ethical values. It was the moral principle of the Cyrenaics and some of the Epicureans. The hedonism of Hume, Bentham, and Mill, which makes happiness of all, or at least of the majority, the criterion, is properly utilitarianism.

Heerbrand, Jakob. B. 1521; studied at Wittenberg; diaconus at Tuebingen in 1544; deposed in 1548 for opposing the Interim; superintendent of Herrenberg in 1550; ambassador to Trent in 1552; helped Andreae reform Baden; chancellor of Tuebingen University; resigned in 1598 and died in 1600. His *Compend of Theology* is the best known of his writings, even translated into Greek.

Heermann, Johann (1585—1647). B. at Raudten, the son of a furrier; destined for the ministry; studied at Fraustadt, Breslau, and Brieg; tutor at Brieg and at Strassburg; returned to Raudten, his home, 1610; diaconus, later pastor, at Koeben; retired to Lissa, in Posen, 1638; distressing scenes and horrors of Thirty Years' War made deep impression upon him; several times lost all his personal effects; bore everything with great courage and patience; was well trained in the school of affliction and therefore well able to write his hymns of consolation; ranks with the best hymn writers of the century, some regarding him as second only to Gerhardt; wrote, among others: "Ach Jesu, dessen Treu'"; "Fruehmorgens, da die Sonn' aufgeht"; "Wir danken dir, Gott, fuer und fuer"; "O Jesu Christe, wahres Licht"; "O Jesu, du mein Braeutigam"; "Jetzt ist die Gnadenzeit"; "So wahr ich lebe, spricht dein Gott"; "O Gott, du frommer Gott"; "Gottlob, die Stund' ist kommen."

P. Wackernagel, *Johann Heermanns geistliche Lieder*, Liesching, Stuttgart, 1856; K. F. Ledderhose, "Das Leben Joh. Heermanns von Koeben," *Christliche Biographien*, Winter, Heidelberg 1857 (vol. 5).

Hefele, Karl Joseph von (1809—93). Eminent Catholic; priest, professor, author; his *Conciliengeschichte* (1873 to 1880) is a leading work on the history of councils; strenuous opponent of the Vatican decrees, though submitting later in the interest of peace. See *Old Catholics.*

Heffentraeger, Johann (1497—1542). First Reformation preacher at Waldeck; wrote a catechism and an agenda; Luth. pastor at Niederwildungen.

Hegel, Georg Wilhelm Friedrich (1770—1831). German philosopher; b. at Stuttgart; professor at Jena, Heidelberg and, after 1818, at Berlin; d. at Berlin. Main exponent of Absolute Idealism in modern philosophy. Everything that exists is the result, ultimately, of the development of one absolute thought or idea, or, expressed in terms of religion, the world, including nature and humanity, is only the self-manifestation of God. Though his philosophy claims to be in agreement with Christian doctrines and was hailed by many as the most rational explanation of Christianity, reconciling perfectly theology and philosophy, still, being in reality pantheism, it amounted to a complete negation of Christianity. Hegel did not believe in a concrete, historical Jesus, and in the Neo-Hegelian school his philosophy led to a destruction of the historical foundations of Christianity. Wrote: *Phaenomenologie des Geistes, Wissenschaft der Logik, Enzyklopaedie der philosophischen Wissenschaften.*

Hegesippus. A convert from Judaism; traveler and antiquarian; author of a collection of *Reminiscences* of the apostolic and postapostolic churches in five books, a work used by Eusebius, the historian, and designed, it would seem, to combat the Gnostic heresy. Hegesippus lived during the reigns of Hadrian, Antoninus, and Marcus Aurelius.

Heidegger, Henry. See *Reformed Confessions,* A 10.

Heidegger, Martin (1890—). Prof. at Freiburg, philosopher, laying foundations of existentialism, influenced by Kierkegaard.*

Heidelberg Catechism. See *Reformed Confessions,* D 2.

Heidelberg Polyglot. See *Polyglot Bible.*

Heiling, Peter. See *Abyssinia.*

Heim, Karl (1874—). Prof. at Muenster and Tuebingen, leader of new Protestant orthodoxy; competent in current philosophy, active in restating the essence and structure of the Christian's faith, in terms of practical experience and value.

Hein, Carl C. B. Wiesbaden, Germany, Aug. 31, 1868; ed. Gymnasium at Wiesbaden, and at Dillenburg; emigrated to America in 1884; Capital U. grad. class of 1885 after 3 yrs. sem. work; ordained on April 15, 1888; pastor at Marion, Wis., 1888—91; Detroit, Mich., 1891—1902; Trinity, Columbus, Ohio, 1902—25. D. D. in 1922. Offices held: 1912—20 pres. of Western District of Ohio Synod; 1919—24 first vice-pres. of Ohio Synod; 1930 until death first pres. of A. L. C.; commissioner of National Lutheran Council from 1918 until death; 1927—32 vice-pres.; 1933—37 pres.; member of various committees for unity; attended Lutheran World Conventions at Eisenach, Germany, 1923; Copenhagen, Denmark, 1929; Paris, France, 1935. D. April 30, 1937.

Heine, Heinrich. German poet; born 1799 at Duesseldorf, of Jewish parents; to promote his professional career, embraced Protestantism, 1825; after 1831 in Paris; died there, after many years of invalidism, 1856. One of the greatest lyric poets. Being a man of strange contrasts, there were in his character noble as well as ignoble traits. With bitter irony he attacked the religious, political, and social order of his time and preached "the gospel of the rehabilitation of the flesh." In later years his cynicism gave way to less ignoble sentiments, and it is even assumed by some that he returned to theistic beliefs.

Heinemann, Barbara. See *Amana Society.*

Heinrich Moller von Zuetphen (1488 to 1524). Augustinian monk; studied at Wittenberg; preached at Antwerp in 1522; imprisoned, but forcibly freed by the people, chiefly women; preached at Bremen in spite of the clergy, at Meldorp in 1524; burned by fanatic peasants.

Heinrici, Karl Friedrich (1844 to 1915). Prof. at Marburg and Leipzig; wrote a theological encyclopedia and extensive works on the NT, seeking especially to establish the relation of Hellenism to the NT.

Heintze, Richard William. B. Nov. 11, 1868, at Berlin, Germany; grad. St. Louis, 1890; pastor at West Hoboken, N. J., 1890—94; prof. at Concordia Collegiate Institute, Bronxville, N. Y., 1894—1926; librarian at Concordia Seminary, St. Louis, 1926—36. D. March 23, 1937.

Hejaz (Hedjaz), Kingdom of. Formerly part of the Turkish Empire; independent since June, 1916, included in Saudi-Arabia with the sultanate of Nejd. See also *Arabia.* Area, 150,000 sq. mi. Population (estimated), 2,000,000. Hejaz

contains the chief Islamic sacred cities, Mecca and Medina. Mohammedanism is the accepted religion. The capital is Mecca. Missions have found no footing there.

Held, Heinrich (1620—59). Studied at Koenigsberg, Frankfurt, and Leyden; lawyer at Guhrau, his native city; one of the best Silesian hymn writers; wrote: "Gott sei Dank durch alle Welt"; "Komm, o komm, du Geist des Lebens."

Helder, Bartholomaeus (?—1635). B. at Gotha. In 1607 he became schoolmaster at Freimar, near Gotha, and in 1616 pastor at Remstaedt, also near Gotha. Helder was a distinguished hymn writer and composer. His hymns were nearly all taken into the *Thuringian Hymnal.* His style marked the transition from the classical to the modern. He published *Cymbalum Genethliacum,* 1615, and *Cymbalum Davidicum,* 1620.

Helgason, Arni (1777—1869). Pastor at Gardar, Iceland; influential rationalist of the *Aufklaerung* movement.

Helgeson, Paul. See *Denmark, Lutheranism in,* 1.

Hell. See *Hereafter,* B.

Hellinck, Lupus (d. 1541). Referred to as "the Burgundian composer of the Rhau collection." Hellinck is represented in practically all German collections of sacred choral music published between 1520 and 1560. His settings are, in some respects, the most artistic of those compiled by George Rhau. His music has the polyphonic flow of the music of Despres, but it lacks the remarkable finesse of this great master, whom Luther admired so greatly.

Helmbold, Ludwig. German theologian and hymnist, "the German Asaph," was born at Muehlhausen, Thuringia, Jan. 13, 1532. He received his education at Leipzig and Erfurt, and served as lecturer at the University of Erfurt. In 1566 he was crowned poet-laureate by Emperor Maximilian II. He became deacon and later pastor of the Liebfrauenkirche in his home town. He wrote verse to the very last day of his life, April 8, 1598. He also wrote a complete metrical version of the Augsburg Confession.

Helmholtz, Herman von. See *Psychology,* G 3.

Helmuth, Justus Henry Christian.
B. May 16, 1745, at Helmstedt, Brunswick, Germany; ed. at Halle Orphanage and at Halle University (influenced by G. A. Francke); came to Philadelphia, Pa., 1769; pastor at Lancaster, 1769; St. Michael's and Zion, 1779; trained J. G. Butler, C. Endress, J. G. Lochmann, J. G. Schmucker, and S. S. Schmucker for the ministry; member of the American Philosophical Society. Wrote: *Empfindung des Herzens in einigen Liedern* (1781); *Denkmal der Liebe und Achtung, welche Seiner Hochwuerden, dem Herrn D. Heinrich Melchior Muehlenberg, gesetzt worden* (1788); *Betrachtung der ev. Lehre von der Heiligen Schrift und Taufe* (1793); *Kurze Nachricht von dem sogenannten gelben Fieber in Philadelphia* (1793); *Kurze Andachten einer Gott suchenden Seele* (1786); *Plan einer Anstalt zur Erziehung der jungen Prediger* (1805); *Etliche Kirchenlieder* (1809). D. 1825.

Helvetic Confessions. See *Reformed Confessions*, A 6.

Helvetic Consensus Formula. See *Reformed Confessions*, A 10.

Helwys, Thomas. See *Baptist Bodies*, 2.

Hemerobaptist (*Mandeans; Mendaeans*). The former, so called from their practice of daily ablution, are possibly identical with the Gnosticizing sect of the "Disciples of John" mentioned in the *Clementine Homilies*, where John is called a hemerobaptist. With these the Mandeans, to whom the name "Christians of John" is also sometimes applied, may have no historical connection. Their religious system is a wild conglomerate of pagan, Jewish, and Christian elements, which, according to Kessler, shows distinct traces of Babylonian mythology. A remnant of the Mandeans still exists in the marshy tracts of southern Babylonia.

Hemmeter, Henry Bernard. B. Dec. 24, 1869, at Baltimore, Md.; grad. at St. Louis, 1892; pastor at Baltimore, Md., 1892—95; Pittsburgh, Pa., 1895 to 1902; prof. at Concordia College, Conover, N. C., 1902—05; pastor at Pittsburgh, Pa., 1905—08; St. Louis, Mo., 1908—14; pres. of Concordia College, Conover, N. C., 1914—18; 1928—36; pastor at Rochester, N. Y., 1918—28; pres., Concordia Seminary, Springfield, Ill., 1936—45; editor of *Lutheran Witness;* chairman of Mission Board of English Synod; Publication Board of English Synod; Church Extension Board of Eastern District; received D. D. from Lenoir Rhyne College and Concordia Seminary, St. Louis, and LL. D. from Valparaiso Univ.; d. in Baltimore, July 22, 1948.

Hemming. See *Hemmingsen, Niels.*

Hemmingsen (Hemming), Niels (1511 or 1513—1600). B. at Erindlev, island of Lolland, Denmark; d. at Roskilde. Studied at Roskilde and Wittenberg, where he became a follower of Melanchthon. Regarded as the foremost theologian in Denmark, he held various positions at the University of Copenhagen. Later accused of crypto-Calvinistic leanings, he was dismissed from the university and went to Roskilde.

Hengstenberg, Ernst Wilhelm (1802 to 1869). Son of a Reformed clergyman, a moderate rationalist; first studied under the direction of his father, 1819, at Bonn; tutor in 1823; in 1824 *Privatdozent* (lecturer) in Berlin; 1825 licentiate of theology; 1826 professor extraordinary; 1828 full professor. Through private study of the Bible he had found in Christ his Savior, and in the Confessions of the Lutheran Church he saw the clearest expression of true Biblical theology. By his work of the interpretation and defense of the Old Testament he became the staunchest defender against rationalism, unionism, and the mediating theology of his day. As a mouthpiece of his testimony for the truth he founded in 1827 the *Evangelische Kirchenzeitung,* a most powerful organ in defense of the truth and in attacking error without fear. For forty-two years he was identified with this paper and was its chief contributor. Because of his orthodoxy he was disliked by the authorities in Berlin, who made attempts to transfer him to other places under the guise of promotion; but he refused all calls, looking upon his position in Berlin as the place assigned to him by God, and there he remained to the end of his life. He was subjected to violent slander and insult because of his defense of Bible doctrine and his attacks on error. — It must be said, however, that in the end he remained within the "Union" ("What God hath joined together let not man put asunder") and refused to break with the rationalists within the Church. Sternly opposed to rationalizing, he yet bespoke a certain measure of freedom

for theology. In his later years he adopted a Romanizing view of the doctrine of justification. — He was a very prolific writer. His chief works are: *Christologie des Alten Testaments, Beitraege zur Einleitung ins Alte Testament, Evangelium Johannis, Offenbarung Johannis, Die Psalmen* — all translated into English.
O. Zoeckler, "Ernst Wilhelm Hengstenberg," *Die Christliche Apologetik im 19. Jahrh.*, Bertelsmann, Guetersloh, 1904.

Henhoefer, Aloys (1789—1862). B. at Voelkersbach, Baden, of Catholic parents; through reading of Martin Boos and Scripture he began preaching justification by faith alone; was excommunicated for this and joined the Evangelical Church; exerted a great and beneficial influence in Baden.

Henke, Heinrich P. K. (1752—1809). Prof. of theology at Helmstedt. He approached theology from the humanistic, philosophical point of view. He saw divinity and deeds of God in the human history of Christ and felt that later doctrinal development was a perversion of the primitive faith.

Henkel, Wilhelm. B. July 2, 1868, in Brandenburg, graduate of Northwestern College and Milwaukee; Wisconsin Synod pastor, 1891—1912; prof. at Northwestern, Watertown, 1912—20; prof. at Wauwatosa, 1920—29; secretary of Joint Synod's Educational Commission; contributor to *Ev. Luth. Gemeindeblatt; Theologische Quartalschrift;* d. July 5, 1929.

Henkelites. See *General Synod*, 7.

Henkels, The. This family, which gave a large number of pastors and educators to the Lutheran Church in America, was descended from Anthony Jacob Henkel (1663—1728), who had been court chaplain to Duke Maurice of Saxony, but was exiled when the duke became a Roman Catholic. Anthony Jacob Henkel came to America in 1717 with his oldest son, Gerhard (with whom he is often confounded) and with his son-in-law, Valentine Geiger, settled at New Hanover, Pa. Dr. Kline assigns two terms of service to Anthony Jacob Henkel at New Hanover, 1717 to 1720 and 1723—28. He is regarded as the founder of the old Lutheran churches in Philadelphia and Germantown. On Aug. 12, 1728, he was killed by a fall from his horse; he lies buried in the shadow of the Germantown church.

2. *James Henkel,* the son of Gerhard Henkel, was the father of Moses (who became a Methodist minister), Paul, Isaac, John H., and two others. Of these, *Paul,* born in North Carolina in 1754, educated by J. A. Krug, ordained by the Pennsylvania Ministerium, 1792, was the most prominent. He was pastor at New Market, Va., Salisbury, N. C., and again at New Market, took part in the organization of the North Carolina Synod (1803), the Ohio Synod (1818), and the Tennessee Synod (1820). He was the great home missionary of the Lutheran Church in the early part of the 19th century. In New Market he established a printery, from which, in the course of time, many Lutheran books were issued, such as Luther's Catechism, the Augsburg Confession, a liturgy, hymnbooks, and, later, the complete *Book of Concord.* He died at New Market, Va., 1825.
3. Of the six sons of Paul Henkel — Solomon, Philip, Ambrose, Andrew, David, and Charles — all became Lutheran ministers except Solomon, who was a physician and manager of the printery at New Market. *Philip* was pastor in Greene Co., Va., and was the first to conceive the plan of organizing the Tennessee Synod as a protest against the colorless Lutheranism of the North Carolina Synod and other synods then forming the General Synod. He opened a union seminary in 1817, which, however, was of short duration. Two of his sons, Irenaeus and Eusebius, were Lutheran ministers, both locating in Western States. — *David,* "the most gifted of the Henkel family," a zealous defender of Lutheran truth in the days of Rationalism, was pastor in North Carolina, but his missionary journeys extended into Kentucky and Indiana. As early as 1817 he was requested by the North Carolina Synod to visit Lutherans in southeastern Missouri. D. in 1831, at the age of thirty-six years. — Andrew and Charles were pastors in Ohio. The latter translated the Augsburg Confession into English in 1834. — Ambrose was in charge of the publishing house at New Market, where he was pastor. — Of the two sons of David, Polycarp and Socrates, the latter was pastor for more than forty years in New Market, where he was of assistance in publishing the *Book of Concord,* while the former extended his missionary activities into Missouri. Solomon was a distinguished physician and much interested in the publication of good Lutheran books. Thus for almost two centuries the

Henkels made their influence felt for good in the Lutheran Church of America as earnest preachers, tireless missionaries, faithful educators, and zealous publicists.

Socrates Henkel, *History of the Ev. Luth. Tennessee Synod,* Henkel & Co., New Market, 1890; C. W. Cassell, W. J. Finck, E. O. Henkel, *History of the Lutheran Church in Virginia and East Tennessee,* Shenandoah Pub. House, Strasburg, Va., 1930; A. Stapleton (editor and publisher), *The Henkel Memorial,* York, Pa., 1910—17; B. H. Pershing, "Paul Henkel: Frontier Missionary, Organizer, and Author," *Luth. Ch. Quart.,* VII:125—51 (also in *CHIQ,* VII: 97—120); W. J. Finck, "Paul Henkel, the Lutheran Pioneer," *Luth. Quart.,* LVI:307—54; Th. Graebner, "Diary of Paul Henkel," *CHIQ,* I:16—21; 43—47; Th. Graebner, "Paul Henkel, an American Lutheran Pioneer in Missions, Organization, and Publicity," *CHIQ,* V:58—63.

Hennepin, Louis (1640 to 1702). French explorer and missionary; accompanied Laval to Quebec in 1675; traversed the region of the Great Lakes; explored the Upper Mississippi; returned to France in 1683 and published an account of his discoveries, in which he claimed credit unwarranted by the facts; d. in Holland.

Henotheism. A term coined by Max Mueller * to designate a sort of monotheistic polytheism which recognizes the existence of many gods, but emphasizes the worship of one of them as the chief god, or simply as *the* god. Examples of henotheism are found in ancient India and Babylonia. Evolutionistic science of religion * regards henotheism as an intermediate stage between polytheism and monotheism in the upward development of religion.

Henoticon. The "instrument of union" probably drawn up by Acacius and issued by Emperor Zeno (482) with a view to settling the Monophysite controversy.

Henry IV *(France).* See *Edict of Nantes.*

Henry IV *(Germany).* See *Popes,* 7.

Henry VIII. See *England, Reformation in,* 3; *Anglican Confessions.*

Henry, Duke of Saxony. B. 1473; won for the Reformation by his wife and brother-in-law, John the Constant; joined the Smalcald League in 1536.

His brother, George the Bearded, would make him successor on condition of becoming Catholic, which he spurned as a temptation similar to the one wherewith Satan tempted Christ. Matt. 4:9. On his accession in 1539 he introduced the Reformation in ducal Saxony with the help of Luther and others. Old age compelled him to transfer the government to his son Maurice, and death came soon after, in 1541.

Henry of Ghent ("Doctor Solemnis"; d. 1293). Scholastic philosopher; canon of Tournai, archdeacon of Bruges, master of theology at Paris. Wrote *Quodlibeta* and *Summa Theologica* (unfinished).

Henry of Langenstein (1340—97). Roman Catholic, celebrated, without justification, as a prophet of the Reformation. His chief work is *Epistola concilii pacis,* written with reference to the papal schism and called for conciliar reform.

Henry of Lausanne (12th century). Founder of the Henricians; fiery preacher against corruption of clergy and deviation from Apostolic teaching; arrested numerous times for attacking the teachings of the Church.

Henry, Matthew (1662—1714). Nonconformist; b. at Flintshire, Wales; Presbyterian pastor at Chester and Hackney; d. near Chester. *Exposition of the Old and New Testaments* (his work to *Acts* incl.), 6 volumes; has had many editions.

Hensman, J. G. See *Berean Bands.*

Heortology. The science of the festivals (*heorte,* Greek, meaning a festival) of the Christian Church, concerning itself with the origin, meaning, growth, and history of the festivals and periods, and their relation to one another.

Hephzibah Faith Missionary Association. See *Evangelistic Associations,* 8; *Holiness Bodies,* 2.

Heraclitus (ca. 536—ca. 470 B.C.). Ancient philosopher of Ephesus; called "the Obscure," "the Weeping Philosopher"; held that only change is real, everything is in a state of flux; the world was to him an ever-changing fire.

Herbaries. Books especially popular in the Middle Ages which dealt with medicine and magic as found in herbs.

Herbart, Johann Friedrich. B. at Oldenburg, 1776; d. at Goettingen, 1841.

Tutor at Interlaken; professor at Koenigsberg and Goettingen; prominent German educator and psychologist; was the first to perceive that education was thoroughly worthy of being considered an independent science. Developing and systematizing Pestalozzi's idea of "psychologizing" education, he became the first great scientific exponent of psychological education. According to Herbart the end and aim of eduation is to develop moral character. Character depends upon knowledge, ideas act as forces, so that the will, desire, interest, and feeling are all of them grounded in some sort of intellectual activity, thus the content of the mind largely regulates the behavior; hence the duty of the teacher "to fill the mind" with dominant thoughts and ideas, and the necessity of educative instruction, *erziehender Unterricht.*" Reflective thought makes the mind many-sided, and the necessary steps in producing this are clearness, association, system, method, from which were later developed the "Five Formal Steps," preparation, presentation, association, generalization, application, according to which the teacher first prepares the pupil by recalling such ideas as will put the mind in a receptive mood for the new material, which is then presented; this is then associated or compared with other ideas that may suggest themselves; then the central thought of the lesson is brought out and applied. These steps were to Herbart factors in the process of thinking rather than logical subdivisions of a lesson period, as was held by some of his followers. Works: *Allgemeine Paedagogik; Psychologie.*

Herberger, Valerius (1562—1627). B. April 21, 1562, ed. at Frankfurt and Leipzig; later became diaconus and eventually chief pastor of St. Mary's Church at Fraustadt, Posen, his native town. Herberger was an outstanding preacher in his day. The Romanists nicknamed him "The little Luther." Herberger was a man of prayer. A consecrated pastor, he led an exemplary life before his people and was known far and wide as a man with an apostolic spirit. He published many writings, especially sermon books. His outstanding hymn for the dying — and he had much experience with them — is 407 in the *Lutheran Hymnal*, "Farewell I Gladly Bid Thee."

Herbert of Cherbury. See *Deism,* III.

Herbert, George (1593—1633). Rector of Fuggelston St. Peter's at Bemerton. Marked by sane didacticism and devotional spirit. His main theme is the love and glorification of God. He is generally considered a member of the Metaphysical School. Chief works: *The Temple, Sacred Poems and Private Ejaculations; A Priest to the Temple.*

Herbert, Petrus. Native of Fulnek, in Moravia; member of the Moravian Brethren; died 1571 at Eibenschitz; one of the principal compilers of German hymnbooks; wrote: "Die Nacht ist kommen."

Herder, Johann Gottfried (1744 to 1803). General superintendent at Weimar; one of the great poets and writers of Germany; Lutheran by birth, early education, and office; his creed more humanitarian than Christian; together with Goethe, condemned the practice of Opitz, Klopstock, and others, who tried to "modernize" some of the old chorale texts, polish them, improve their texts and meters, etc. Herder and Goethe saw beauty as well as character in the ruggedness of the old chorales of the 16th century in particular; it was Goethe who spoke of Luther's German Sanctus, "Jesaja, dem Propheten, das geschah," as being "barbarisch gross." Herder was very much influenced by Percy's *"Reliquies of Ancient Poetry"* and helped initiate a much-needed reform in church music in Germany.

Schrade, Leo, *Herder's Conception of Church Music.* Valparaiso University Pamphlet Series, No. 10, The Musical Heritage of the Church, edited by Theodore Hoelty-Nickel.

Hereafter. A. *Heaven (Eternal Life).* 1. Eternal life, the gift of God through Jesus Christ, is the end of faith, the ultimate object of a Christian's hope and striving (Phil. 3:13 f.). The Bible describes eternal life as a kingdom (Luke 12:32), a paradise (Luke 23:43), an unfading inheritance (1 Pet. 1:4), a rest for the people of God (Heb. 4:9), Abraham's bosom (Luke 16:22), a marriage supper (Rev. 19:9), a crown of life (Rev. 2:10), to picture under earthly symbols the ineffable joys and pleasures of heaven.

2. While Scripture represents heaven as a place (John 14:2), a house with many mansions (John 14:2), everlasting habitations (Luke 16:9), a city (Heb. 11:10), a new heaven and a new earth (2 Pet. 3:13), it makes no at-

tempt to locate heaven. All human efforts to do so must fail and should be abandoned.

3. Essentially eternal life is immediate, uninterrupted fellowship with God. To be with God is to be in heaven (Luke 23:43; Ps. 16:11). The saints in light are with God and with His Son (John 17:24); they see God face to face, as He is, and know God even as they are known (1 Cor. 13:12; 1 John 3:2). Their knowledge of God and His wonderful works will no longer be partial, but perfect and complete (1 Cor. 13:9-12).

4. This blissful fellowship is unbroken by time, unmarred and undisturbed by sin or any of its disrupting consequences (John 3:16; Ps. 16:11). Pain and sorrow, tears and tribulation, hunger and thirst, even death will be no more (Rev. 7:16 f.; 21:4). In heaven the elect will behold the glory of Christ and in this vision will be unspeakably happy (1 Pet. 1:8), singing the praises of God and their exalted Redeemer (Rev. 5:11). The divine image will be fully restored (Ps. 17:15; Heb. 12:23). The glory which will be revealed surpasses human understanding (2 Cor. 12:4) and far outweighs the sufferings of this present time (Rom. 8:18). It is a blessedness beyond compare (2 Cor. 4:17).

5. The body of believers, too, will share in the glory of everlasting life. Transformed to resemble the glorified body of their Redeemer, it will be free from weakness, dishonor, and corruption (Phil. 3:21; 1 Cor. 15:42 ff.). The white robes mentioned in Rev. 7:9 f. are symbols of the sinlessness effected through the cleansing power of Christ's blood (Rev. 7:14). The institution of marriage will be abolished (Matt. 22:30). In glory the believers will be equal unto the angels of God (Luke 20:36). Whether the redeemed will recognize one another in heaven is not stated explicitly, but may be inferred from the story of the Transfiguration, where we are told that the disciples recognized Moses and Elijah (Matt. 17: 3, 4).

6. Although Scripture ascribes full salvation to all believers (John 3:16), there will be degrees of glory in accordance with the difference of the works which the believers performed while on earth (2 Cor. 9:6; Matt. 25: 14 ff.). Every man shall receive his reward according to his own labor (1 Cor. 3:8). It is futile and needless to speculate wherein this difference of glory consists. So much is certain:

a believer enjoying a greater measure of glory will not be envied by those who have less. It is inherent in eternal life with its absolute perfection that the difference in glory will not give rise to any evil thoughts.

B. *Hell (Eternal Punishment)*. 1. The doctrine of eternal punishment, repugnant to natural man, has been repudiated or explained away by errorists in ancient and modern times (cp. Origen, Universalists, Russellism, Restorationists), but it is clearly revealed in Scripture. To deny this doctrine is to reject the authority of Scripture.

2. According to the Bible the unbelievers will be damned (Mark 16:15). They will be punished with everlasting destruction (2 Thess. 1:9) to suffer the damnation of hell (Matt. 23:33). This punishment is variously described as unquenchable fire (Mark 9:44), outer darkness where there will be weeping and gnashing of teeth (Matt. 8:12), and a prison from which there is no escape (Matt. 5:26).

3. As regards the question whether the "fire of hell" (Matt. 25:41 *et al.*) is a material fire or not, restraint is in order. Since other expressions are used to depict the suffering of the lost (such as, "their worm shall not die," Mark 9:44; "they shall be cast into outer darkness," Matt. 8:12), all of them may well be understood figuratively. The description which the Bible gives of hell is to express in terms taken from human experience the unspeakable torments of body and soul visited upon the damned. Whatever has been said about the awful doom of the wicked is calculated to call sinners to repentance and warn them of the wrath to come (Luke 16:29-31). The reticence of Scripture is more impressive than the horrors of Dante's *Inferno*.

4. As the essence of heaven is fellowship with God, so the essence of hell is exclusion from this fellowship. Deprived of the blissful presence of God and the glory bestowed upon the believers (2 Thess. 1:9; Matt. 25:41), the unbelievers will languish in the company of the evil spirits to bemoan, in abject despair, their willful impenitence during the time of grace and their unalterable condemnation (Matt. 8:12). This punishment, which is never alleviated, will be eternal in the twofold sense that it suffers no interruption (Luke 16:24-26) and that it has no end (Mark 9:48). — Degrees of punishment are clearly taught in Matt. 11: 22-24 and Luke 12:47, 48. Those who

spurned the proffered grace and knew the Lord's will, will be punished more severely than those who never heard the Gospel. Hypocrites who devour widows' houses and for a pretense make long prayer shall receive the greater damnation (Matt. 23:14). Wherein this difference consists has not been revealed, and we should not presume to know.

5. To identify the destruction of the wicked with annihilation has no warrant in Scripture. If the punishment of the wicked consisted in their outright annihilation, the Bible could not speak of it as *everlasting* destruction (2 Thess. 1:9). This qualifying adjective precludes the possibility that the word "destruction" is equivalent to "annihilation." According to Rom. 2:8, 9 tribulation and anguish await those that obey not the truth; according to John 3:36 the wrath of God abides on those that believe not the Son. Neither could be predicated of men who cease to have a conscious existence. Destruction or perdition, when contrasted with life, denote not cessation of existence, but eternal misery, the loss of everlasting blessedness (Phil. 1:28).

6. The meaning of "eternal" has been called into question on the ground that the Greek word *aionios*, translated by "eternal" or "everlasting," does not denote "endlessness." While it is true that *aionios* (derived from the noun *aion*, meaning "age") is a relative term and may mean "age-long," "enduring for a time only," it must be conceded that this Greek word can also mean "everlasting," "endless," and it clearly has this meaning in all passages which speak of the destiny of men in the hereafter. In 2 Cor. 4:18 the *temporal* is contrasted with the *eternal (aionios)*. (Cp. also 1 Pet. 1:23 f.) After judgment is pronounced, the wicked will go into *everlasting* punishment, but the righteous into life *eternal* (Matt. 25:46). The same Greek word is used in both sentences. If *aionios* denotes endlessness in the one, it must necessarily have the same meaning in the other. The punishment of the wicked is unending misery and woe (Mark 3:29).

7. The same passages which unequivocally teach the eternity of punishment rule out as unscriptural the teaching of the ultimate salvation of all men. 1 Cor. 15:22, Eph. 1:10, and Rev. 21:5 cannot be adduced as proof for this contention, for when the Scriptures speak of the ultimate goal of the world's history, they refer only to the

blessed perfection of the faithful. 1 Cor. 15:28 and related passages teach the final victory of the kingdom of God, the subjugation of all the enemies of Christ, and do not state that all these enemies will be converted to God.

8. Regarding the location of hell it can be said that no physical location is intended by what Scripture says of the habitation of the wicked. Hell is where God reveals Himself in His vindictive justice to the finally impenitent.

9. One of the objections raised to the doctrine of eternal punishment is that it is inconsistent with the love of God to condemn men to unending perdition. It must be remembered, however, that while God is a God of love, His love is only one of His attributes. Justice is one of His attributes as truly as love. Since God is a perfect being, we find in Him the perfect and harmonious expression of all His attributes. It is significant, too, that the most solemn and explicit declarations of eternal punishment recorded in Scripture were spoken by the forgiving and compassionate Savior (Matt. 25:41; Mark 9:43, 44). Again it is argued that it is unworthy of a just God to punish men with everlasting condemnation. How can man presume to determine the justice of the infinite God according to human conceptions of justice? "As the heavens are higher than the earth, so are My ways higher than your ways, saith the Lord" (Is. 55:9). "His judgments are unsearchable and His ways past finding out" (Rom. 11:33), but they are "true and righteous altogether."

C. *Definition of Biblical Terms.* 1. *Heaven* is (1) the vaulted expanse of the sky with all the visible things in it (Heb. 1:10), the aerial heavens or sky where the clouds and tempests gather (Matt. 16:2), the starry heavens (Heb. 11:12). (2) Heaven is the dwelling place of God (Matt. 5:34; 23:22; Acts 7:49) and His holy angels (Matt. 18:10; 24:36), to which Christ ascended (Acts 1:10); the eternal home of all believers (Matt. 5:12; 1 Pet. 1:4).

2. *Paradise.* This word, commonly regarded to be of Persian origin, denotes (1) a garden or park, as the Garden of Eden (Gen. 2:8 ff.); (2) the heavenly Paradise, the home of the saints of God (Luke 23:43; 2 Cor. 12:4; Rev. 2:7).

3. *Sheol.* The etymology of this word, occurring sixty-five times in the Old Testament, is still obscure. Luther renders it *Hoelle* in all places except

four, Gen. 37:35; 42:38; 44:29,31, where he translates it with *Grube*. The Authorized Version renders Sheol by "grave" thirty-nine times, by "pit" three times, by "hell" thirty times, and by "deep" once. Since the derivation of this word is uncertain, the immediate and remote context must determine the exact meaning in each instance.

(1) One meaning of Sheol is "grave," the resting place of man's mortal remains. It is obviously so used Job 17:16 and Is. 38:10.

(2) Another meaning of Sheol is realm of the dead, *Totenreich*, into which all enter who depart this life, the righteous as well as the wicked (Gen. 37:35; Job 7:9; 14:13; Ps. 89:48; 31:17). Sheol is a general term used very much like our English "the hereafter" or "the beyond." The familiar phrase "to go down into Sheol" is equivalent to saying, "to die, to depart from the land of the living." It should be noted, however, that when the righteous are said to "descend into Sheol," their fate beyond is never taken into account (Gen. 37:35). The hope of the pious in the Old Testament is expressed differently. Cp. Ps. 73:24.

(3) In not a few passages Sheol is used to designate the place where the judgment of God overtakes the evildoer. Sheol receives such as are taken away in God's anger. Korah's rebel band went down to Sheol because they had provoked the Lord (Num. 16:30). Sheol is the place for harlots (Prov. 5:5). The anger of the Lord shall burn down to the lowest hell (Sheol) (Deut. 32:22). Ps. 49:14, 15 is particularly illuminating. According to this Psalm all men die physically, the righteous as well as the ungodly (v. 10), but there is a difference in their existence in the hereafter. The confidence of the Psalmist is expressed in the words "They (*i. e.*, the wicked) are laid in Sheol (A. V., grave), death shall feed on them, but God will redeem my soul from the power of Sheol (A. V., the grave); for He shall receive me." Clearly there is a sharp contrast between the doom of the ungodly and the glorious hope of the believer who hopes to rest securely in the hands of his God. Cp. Psalm 73.

4. *Hades*. In non-Biblical Greek this term denotes the unseen world, the realm of the dead. In the Old Testament Hades is used in almost every instance to translate the Hebrew Sheol. In the New Testaments it sig-

nifies "the grave" (Rev. 2:13, 14) or "death" (Acts 2:27,31). In Luke 16:23, Matt. 11:23, and other passages it denotes (like Gehenna, see below) the place of torment to which the unbelievers will be condemned. When the rich man found himself in Hades, he was not in an intermediate state, but "in torments." If Hades meant only the realm of the dead or a neutral state between heaven and hell, threats such as uttered in Matt. 11:23, "Thou, Capernaum, which art exalted unto heaven, shalt be brought down to hell (Hades)" would have no point.

5. *Gehenna* was originally the name of a deep, narrow glen southwest of Jerusalem which was so called from the cries of little children who were thrown into the fiery arms of Moloch. After these horrible sacrifices had been abolished by King Josiah (2 Kings 23:10), the Jews cast into it not only all manner of refuse, but even the dead bodies of animals and of unburied criminals to be burned. From this defilement and former desecration, Gehenna was applied to the abode of the wicked after death. It is so used in Matt. 5:22, 29; 10:28; Mark 9:43, 45; Luke 12:5, and James 3:6.

6. *Abyssos*, derived from an adjective meaning bottomless, unbounded, denotes (1) the deep (Gen. 1:2); (2) the depths of the sea as a symbol of great distress and anguish of soul (Ps. 71:20); (3) the abode of the dead, the grave (Rom. 10:7); (4) hell, as the abode of evil spirits presided over by Apollyon, the destroyer, Satan (Rev. 9:1,11; 17:8).

7. *Tartaros*. The word itself is not found in the Bible, but occurs only in a verb meaning to hold captive in Tartaros. Tartaros is the name of a dark subterranean region, regarded by the ancient Greeks as the abode of the wicked dead where they suffer punishment for their evil deeds; it answers to the Gehenna of the New Testament, which is a designation of hell (2 Pet. 2:4). CAH

Fr. Pieper, *Christliche Dogmatik*, CPH, 1917 (III:569—626); J. T. Mueller, *Christian Dogmatics*, CPH, 1934 (633 to 644); Joh. Gerhard, *Loci Theologici* (vols. 8, 9); H. Ebeling, *Der Menschheit Zukunft*, Hermann, Zwickau, 1913; Theodor Kliefoth, *Christliche Eschatologie*, Franke, Leipzig, 1886; C. E. Luthardt, *Die Lehre von den letzten Dingen*, Doerffling, Leipzig, 1870; R. Seeberg, *Ewiges Leben*, Deichert, Leipzig, 1915; August Althaus, *Die letzten*

Dinge, Steinhoefel, Verden, 1858; L. Fuerbringer, "Leading Thoughts on Eschatology in the Epistles to the Thessalonians," *CTM,* XIII:511—19; 591—603; 641—53; E. L. Valentin, *Sammlung der besten u. neueren Schriften vom Zustand der Seele nach dem Tode,* Dresden, 1735; P. Althaus, *Unsterblichkeit und ewiges Leben bei Luther,* 1930; J. A. Wist, *What the Bible Teaches About the World Beyond,* Luth. Lit. Bd., Burlington, Iowa, 1939; L. F. Gruber, *What after Death?* Luth. Lit. Bd., Burlington, Iowa; E. C. Pautsch, "Eternal Life," *Abiding Word,* CPH, 1947 (561—82. The bibliography gives references to District essays and *L. u. W.*); E. C. Fendt, "The Life Everlasting," *What Lutherans Are Thinking,* Wartburg Press, Columbus, 1947 (p. 307 ff.); George Beiderwieden, *Heaven,* CPH, 1937; *That Unknown Country, or What Living Men Believe Concerning Punishment after Death,* Nichols, Springfield, Mass., 1891 (gives historical synopsis and opinions of men then living, including H. E. Jacobs); M. Reu gives a select bibliography in *Christian Ethics,* pages 456—58.

For the Biblical terms see the commentaries. Some orthodox Lutheran exegetes (*e. g.,* G. Stoeckhardt, *I. Petribrief,* 153) define *Hades* and *Sheol* as "place and condition of the dead" or the realm of the dead.

Hereditary Sin. See *Sin, Original.*

Hereros. An African Bantu tribe in former German Southwest Africa, now under the dominion of the Union of South Africa. — The first missionaries were sent to the Hereros by the Rhenish Mission Society in 1829, followed by the Finnish Mission Society in 1870.

Heresimach. A heresy hunter; an opponent of heretics.

Heresiologist. A student of heresy; an opponent of heresy.

Heresy (G. "act of choosing," then "school" or "sect"). 1. Used in the LXX for choices which are either good or bad (Gen. 49:5; Lev. 22:18, 21, *et al.*). In Josephus it is used of either a party or a sect (cp. Acts 5:17; 15:5; 26:5; 24:5, 14). The term is used in the NT in a condemnatory sense; heretics are contentious (1 Cor. 11:16-19), deny the Lord, are pernicious, covetous, deceivers for gain, false teachers (2 Pet. 2: 1 ff.), subvert others, are sinners and self-condemned (Titus 3:10. Compare schism in 1 Cor. 1:10; 11:18; 12:25; Rom. 16:17).

2. Ignatius is the first to use the term among the Fathers (*ad Trall.,* 6; *ad Eph.,* 6). Justin terms heretics "godless," "impious," "blasphemous." The later Fathers frequently use the term. In earliest times Jewish sects and Greek schools were regarded heretics. In the 2d and 3d centuries the great heretics were the Gnostics.* Then came monarchianism,* montanism,* Paulicianism,* and Manichaeism.* Arianism,* Apollinarism,* Pelagianism,* Nestorianism,* monophysitism,* and monothelitism * were the outstanding heresies of the Nicene and post-Nicene era.

3. In early days already there was trafficking in heresy for personal gain (*e. g.,* to dislodge a rich bishop or draw away his followers). As church organization developed, heresy was suppressed because it threatened a political system. For almost twelve hundred years heresy was a capital crime. Hence in the Middle Ages, heresies became protests of individuals against an established order (speculative heresies: Cathari,* Bogomils,* Amalricians *; mystics *: John Tauler, Henry Suso, John Ruysbroek, Thomas à Kempis; enthusiasts: Joachimites,* Spiritual Franciscans *; anti-sacerdotalists: Peter de Bruys, Henry of Lausanne. From the viewpoint of the Catholic Church these were considered heretics as well as Wyclif and Hus).

4. Luther restored the term to its original meaning: Heresy is stubborn error in an article of faith in opposition to Scripture (St. L. XVII:1119; XIX: 960; XXII:1286); is an individually made doctrine and mode of living (XII:1459 f.); springs from pride (IV: 1500); cannot endure grace (III:1692) and substitutes works (VII:640); not evolved from Scripture, but from perverted minds (VIII:497; XVIII:1820 f.); pretends to be Scriptural (XI:1412); refuses to listen or be opposed (V:68); sins against Holy Ghost (V:68; XVIII: 723); errs in a fundamental doctrine (XVIII:307); errorists strive against recognized truth and their own conscience (XVI:2182). (See also the Confessions: AP, III:111, 121; XXIII: 37, 45; XXIV:67; Sm. Art. II:iv:7; III: viii:9; Treatise, 38, 72; F. of C., Introd., 3; Epit., XII:30; Sol. Decl., Introd., 17; VIII:17; XII:39).

5. Gerhard defines heresy: "In order to be properly called a heretic, it is required (1) that he be a person received by Baptism into the visible Church; (2) that he err in faith . . .; (3) that the error conflict directly with

the very foundation of the faith; (4) that malice and obstinacy be added to the error, so that, even though frequently admonished, he persistently defends his error; (5) that he excite dissensions and scandals in the Church, whereby he rends unity." (Tr., *Luth. Cyc.*) Walther summarized the teachings of Luther and the dogmaticians in three points: The heretic (1) errs in a fundamental article; (2) brings about divisions; (3) is convicted by truth and his own conscience. EL

G. Arnold, *Unparteiische Kirchen- und Ketzergeschichte*, Fritsch, Frankfurth, 1729; A. Hilgenfeld, *Ketzergeschichte des Urchristentums*, Leipzig, 1884; references under *Inquisition;* C. F. W. Walther, *Die Ev.-Luth. Kirche, die wahre sichtbare Kirche Gottes auf Erden*, ein Referat fuer die Verhandlung der Allg. Ev. Luth. Synode von Missouri, Ohio u. a. Staaten, 31. Okt., 1866 (thesis 5, 24); *Kirche und Amt* (part I, thesis 2).

Heresy (Roman Catholic Definition). Any doctrine contrary to the teaching of the Roman Catholic Church when held by one who professes Christianity. Various terms of censure are employed in condemning "heretical" propositions. If a proposition contradicts clearly defined teaching, it is simply "heretical"; if its logical consequences do so, it is "erroneous"; if it contradicts a doctrine not clearly defined, the proposition "approaches heresy"; if it contradicts a doctrine held as probably true, the proposition "approaches error"; if it is not clearly, but probably, heretical, it "savors of heresy." Propositions may also be "evil sounding," "offensive to pious ears," "rash," etc., etc. Pertinacious heresy, according to Roman principles, should be visited not only with spiritual, but also with physical punishments, including death.

Heretical Baptism. Baptism performed by heretics outside the pale of orthodox Christianity, was the subject of a heated controversy in the Church of the third century. The question was: Is heretical Baptism, even if administered in the right form, true Baptism, or is it merely a mock ceremony? Cyprian, the great African churchman, emphatically defended the latter position. "How can one," says he, "consecrate water who is himself unholy and has not the Holy Spirit?" Thus he made the virtue of the Sacrament dependent on the religious status of the administering agent. This view was shared by the African Church,

which rejected heretical Baptism in several synods at Carthage (255—56). The Church of Asia Minor took the same stand. On the other hand, the Roman bishop Stephen (253—57) vigorously defended the validity of heretical Baptism, provided it was administered in the name of the Trinity. This view ultimately prevailed. It was sanctioned by the Council of Nicaea in 325, adopted in North Africa in 348, and championed by the powerful voice of St. Augustine against the Donatists. The Augustinian view, which defends the validity of heretical Baptism as to form, but denies it any saving efficacy until the baptized heretic returns to the bosom of the true Church, is still held by the Roman Catholic Church, which "bases upon the validity of heretical and schismatical Baptism even a certain . . . claim on all baptized persons as virtually belonging to her communion."

Hering, Hermann Julius (1838 to 1920). Ed. at Halle, from 1878 till his retirement, 1908, prof. of practical theology at Halle; conservative theologian.

Herlitz, Herman. See *Australia, Lutheranism in*, B 1.

Herman, Nikolaus. Faithful friend of Johann Mathesius, pastor at Joachimstal, in Bohemia, and schoolteacher, at least after 1524; master in Latin school, also cantor, organist, and choirmaster; d. 1561; poet of the people, homely, earnest, and picturesque; very good musician; wrote: "Lobt Gott, ihr Christen allzugleich"; "Erschienen ist der herrlich' Tag"; "Die helle Sonn' leucht't jetzt herfuer"; "Hinunter ist der Sonnenschein"; and other hymns.

Herman, Rudolf (1887—). Prof. at Greifswald; studies in soteriology and Luther; opposed Hitler ideals.

Hermann von Wied (1477—1552). Archbishop and Elector of Cologne; first supported Papacy against Luther; advocated concessions to Lutherans at Augsburg (1530); sought to correct abuses in Cologne with the assistance of Erasmus; finally called in Lutherans, including Melanchthon; a book, *The Reformation of Cologne* (used by first Prayer Book of Edward VI), was prepared; the reformation work was stopped by Charles V (1545).

Hermann, Zacharias (1643—1716). Namslau, in Silesia, his home town; pastor and inspector at Lissa in Posen; lost several children in succession, which caused him to write "Wie kurz ist doch der Menschen Leben."

Hermannsburg Ev. Luth. Missionary Society. Founded by Pastor Louis Harms (b. 1808; d. 1865) at Hermannsburg, Germany; formerly connected with the unionistic North German Missionary Society. Candidates were given a religious and industrial training. The first eight missionaries and a colony of laymen were sent out in 1853 on the ship *Candace*. Louis Harms was succeeded by his brother Theodor Harms. Since World War I the field of this society in India was turned over to the American Lutheran Church.

Hermannus Contractus (1013—54). Wrote a number of tracts on music and is the author of several sequences, the most famous of which was his *Salve Regina*. He combined the sequence and the antiphon and thus helped pave the way for works of larger dimensions. As his name indicates, Hermannus was a hunchback; he studied at St. Gall and later became a Benedictine monk in the monastery of Reichenau.

Hermas, Shepherd of. See *Apostolic Fathers*, 5.

Hermeneutics. Hermeneutics is that branch of theology which concerns itself with the principles governing the interpretation of the Holy Scriptures. The term is taken from a Greek word which signifies to translate or to interpret *(hermeneuoo)*. While the Bible is a clear book, it must not be forgotten that it consists of 66 documents which were written in antiquity, in the period from about 1400 B. C. to A. D. 100, that their language is Hebrew or Greek or, in a few sections, Aramaic, and that therefore it is not surprising that theologians have found it necessary to speak of principles of interpretation for the Bible. Since it is given to us in human speech, the usual rules of human speech and thought have to be observed in its interpretation. In addition, the fact must not be overlooked that the Bible is an errorless book, being divine, and that the only attitude of the interpreter which is justified is that expressed in the words: Speak, Lord, Thy servant heareth. To some extent the Bible itself gives us the principles for its interpretation. It tells us, for instance, that Moses and the other Prophets spoke of Christ; hence we know that one of the rules of interpretation has to recognize that Christ

and His work are foretold in the Old Testament Scriptures. It states, furthermore, that no prophecy of Scripture dare be made the victim of interpreters' whims, 2 Pet. 1:20, that is, that no exegete or interpreter has the right to do with Scripture passages as he pleases, but that they must be sacred, inviolable to him, beyond criticism in their majesty, even if their content transcends his powers of comprehension. The New Testament in many instances interprets statements of the Old Testament, and its interpretations must be conclusive to us because they emanate from God Himself.

Speaking popularly, we may say that these are the chief principles of Biblical hermeneutics: 1. The Bible is the Word of God; 2. It comes to us in human speech, and in its interpretation the laws of human speech (grammar) and human thought (such as the differentiation between the affirmative and the negative and between the present, past, and future) must not be violated; 3. The Bible must be permitted to interpret itself as much as possible, which is especially true with respect to dark passages whose meaning we should seek in clear passages treating the same subject; 4. The Old Testament must be viewed as Christ-centered. The famous principle that no interpretation of the Scriptures is permissible which is contrary to the analogy of faith has reference to the explanation of dark or difficult passages. The analogy of faith, that is, the rule or norm of Scripture doctrine which no interpretation must offend against is the sum total of all the clear passages of Scripture which set forth a doctrine or doctrines. The principle simply means that the clear passages of the Scriptures must be our norm and not the dark or figurative passages. Speaking from another point of view, we say the interpretation of Scripture must be grammatical (no one has a right to twist its grammar in setting forth its meaning); it must be historical (it must recognize the Bible was written in ancient times and largely treats of historical matters); and it must be spiritual (it must recognize that we are dealing with a divine book of which Christ is the center). A vast literature on the subject is available. The Lutheran Church has always fostered Bible study, and the principles of interpretation have been given much consideration. On these principles and the literature cf. Dr. L.

Fuerbringer's booklet *The Chief Principles of Hermeneutics.* WA

Milton S. Terry, *Biblical Hermeneutics,* N. Y., 1884; F. W. Farrar, *History of Interpretation,* N. Y., 1886; G. H. Schodde, *Outlines of Biblical Hermeneutics,* Columbus, Ohio, 1917; V. E. Mennicke, "Bible Interpretation," *Abiding Word,* CPH, 1947 (II: 35—58. Popular treatment; references to Mo. Syn. literature); M. H. Franzmann, "Essays in Hermeneutics," *CTM,* XIX: 595 ff.

Hermits (Anchorites, Eremites). Religious orders whose members live in isolation from one another (Agonizants, Eremites of St. Augustine, Camaldolites, Carmelites, Carthusians, Celestines, Hieronymites, Servites, Order Vallombrosa and Williamites).

Hernaman, Claudia Frances (1838 to 1898). Composed more than 150 hymns, most of which are for children; also some translations from Latin and German; among her hymns: "Holy Jesus, We Adore Thee."

Herrnhut. See *Moravian Church,* 3.

Herrnschmidt, Johann Daniel (1675 to 1723). Studied at Altdorf and Halle; assistant to his father, then at the town church; later preacher at Idstein; then professor at Halle; wrote: "Lobe den Herren, o meine Seele."

Herzberger, F. W. B. Oct. 23, 1859, in Baltimore, Md.; pioneer missionary in Arkansas; pastor in Carson, Kans., Chicago, Ill., Hammond, Ind.; first city missionary (St. Louis) of Mo. Syn., 1898; prime mover and champion of many mission and charitable endeavors; wrote *The Family Altar;* d. Aug. 26, 1930.

Herzer, John Henry. B. Nov. 3, 1840, at Louisville, Ky.; grad. Con. Sem., St. Louis, 1865; pastor in Steele Co., Minn., 1865—68; at Minneapolis, Minn., 1868—79; Plymouth, Wis., 1879—1892; Athens, Ill., 1899—1922; prof. at Con. Sem., Springfield, Ill., 1892—1914; retired from professorship 1914; secretary of Synodical Conference 1875—76; Vice-President of Wisconsin District 1875—91; President 1891—92; wrote *Ev.-Luth. Katechetik;* Visitor, Wis. Dist., 1872; served colored congregation in Springfield 9 years; d. May 2, 1930.

Herzl, Theodor. See *Zionism.*

Herzog, Eduard (1841—1924). First bishop of the Old Catholic Church in Switzerland (1876); formerly priest in Bern. See *Old Catholics.*

Herzog, Johann Friedrich (1647 to 1699). Studied law at Wittenberg; tutor; practiced law at Dresden; played the lute; good musician; wrote: "Nun sich der Tag geendet hat."

Herzog, Johann Georg (1822—1909). An eminent German organist, he spent his earlier career at Munich, where he was organist in 1842, cantor in 1849, and professor at the Conservatorium in 1850. Removing to Erlangen, he became professor at the University and director of the *Singakademie.* He was a brilliant organ virtuoso, writing many standard works, including *Orgelschule, Choraele mit Vor-, Zwischen- und Nachspielen,* and *Chorgesaenge fuer den kirchlichen Gebrauch.*

Herzog, Johann Jakob (1805—82). Reformed theologian; b. at Basel; educated at Basel and Berlin; professor at Lausanne 1838, Halle 1847, Erlangen 1854 (died there); important works: *Oecolampadius; The Waldenses; Church History;* editor of a religious encyclopedia (22 vols., 1853—1868; 3d ed. by A. Hauck 1896—1909); last English *The New Schaff-Herzog* editions (1908; 1949—50): *Encyclopedia.*

Heshusius, Tilemann (1527—88). D. D. at Wittenberg, 1553; supt. of Goslar; deposed, 1556; driven out of Rostock for opposing worldliness; prof. at Heidelberg, but later deposed; supt. in Magdeburg; deposed for opposing an edict forbidding polemics; driven out of Wesel because of a work against the Antichrist; court preacher to Count Wolfgang of Pfalz-Neuburg, 1565; deposed and exiled by crypto-Calvinists, 1573; bishop of Samland in Koenigsberg until deposed in 1577; prof. at Helmstedt, where he helped to keep Brunswick from accepting the F. of C. Wrote commentaries, polemical works.

Hess, Johann (1490—1547). The Reformer of Silesia; b. in Nuernberg; upon hearing reports of events in Wittenberg he journeyed thither and became a friend of Luther and Melanchthon; pastor in Breslau (1523); known for his works of charity; founded hospital of All Saints at Breslau (1526).

Hesselius. Two early Swedish pastors in America; Andrew served at Christina (1713—23) and wrote *A Short Relation of the Present Condition of the Swedish Church in America* after his return to Sweden; Samuel served in America from 1719 to 1731.

Hessus, Eobanus (1488 to 1540, Humanist). Luther called him king of poets. He taught at Erfurt and Marburg, a fervent supporter of the Reformation.

Hesychius. An Egyptian bishop mentioned by Eusebius as the editor of a revised text of the Septuagint and of the New Testament. Hesychius would thus be an early textual critic. Of the character of his work nothing is known.

Heterodoxy. Teachings or beliefs which differ from a canon held to be orthodox.*

Heubner, Heinrich Leonhard (1780 to 1853). B. at Lauterbach. Studied at Wittenberg, where he later served as lecturer; superintendent and first director of the Wittenberg theological seminary. Loyal to the Lutheran Confessions, he opposed the Act of Union and the new liturgy.

Heune, Johann (1514—81). Pupil and friend of Justus Jonas; 1543—46 rector of court school at Pforta; later pastor at Schweidnitz; wrote: "Ach liebe Christen, seid getrost."

Hexaglot. See *Polyglot Bibles.*

Hexapla. See *Polyglot Bibles.*

Hexateuch. The name given to the first six books of the Bible. See *Higher Criticism,* 16.

Hey, Johann Wilhelm (1789—1854). Pastor at Toettelstaedt, court preacher at Gotha, superintendent at Ichtershausen, Germany; known for the songs he wrote for little children.

Heyer, John Christian Frederick. First missionary of the Lutheran General Synod to India; b. 1793 in Germany; studied in Philadelphia, Pa., and in Goettingen; home missionary in the Middle West 1819—39; appointed missionary of Pennsylvania Ministerium in 1840; sailing from Boston Oct. 14, 1841, and arriving in India in 1842, he immediately began work at Guntur, preaching his first sermon through an interpreter in August of that year. He was then nearly fifty years of age; 1846 to 1848 he spent in the United States, returning to India in the latter year; in 1850 the mission of the North German Missionary Society at Rajahmundry was taken over; in 1857 Heyer again returned to the United States to engage in home missions in Minnesota; in his seventy-seventh year he again went to India, remaining in Rajahmundry over a year; d. in America in November, 1873.

E. Theodore Bachmann, *They Called Him Father, The Life Story of John Christian Frederick Heyer,* Muhlenberg Press, 1942; A. R. Wentz, "Father Heyer Planted a Church," *Luth. Ch. Quart.,* XVI: 39—49; G. Drach, "Father Heyer the Pioneer," *Luth. Ch. Quart.,* XVI: 39—49.

Hicksites. Followers of Elias Hicks, liberalist and rationalist, who split from the Society of Friends in 1827. They number about 19,100.

Hierarchy. The word *hierarchy,* which may signify any body of officials arranged in gradation of rank, is most familiar as the title of the governing body of the Roman Church. The following canons of the Council of Trent apply here: "If any one saith that in the Catholic Church there is not a hierarchy by divine ordination instituted, consisting of bishops, priests, and ministers, let him be accursed." (Sess. XXIII, chap. IV, can. 6.) "If any one saith that besides the priesthood there are not in the Catholic Church other orders, both greater and minor, by which, as by certain steps, advance is made unto the priesthood, let him be accursed." (Can. 2.) "If any one saith that bishops are not superior to priests, . . . let him be accursed." (Can. 7.) A distinction is made between the hierarchy of order and the hierarchy of jurisdiction. The hierarchy of order, based on the "sacrament" of order and therefore really on the celebration of the Mass (see *Priesthood*), consists of the following ranks: bishop, priest, deacon, subdeacon (major orders; all, except last, claimed to be of divine institution), acolyte, exorcist, lector, doorkeeper (minor orders; admittedly of ecclesiastical institution). The bishop confers the power to celebrate Mass; the priest exercises this power; the deacon is the chief servant at Mass; the members of the other five orders are in various stages of candidacy. — As the hierarchy of order refers to the sacramental body of the Lord, so that of jurisdiction is said to refer to His mystic body, the Church. The hierarchy of jurisdiction is charged with the general guidance and control of the Roman Church and exercises legislative, judicial, coercive, and administrative functions. The most important dignitaries rank as follows: 1. the Pope; 2. cardinals*; 3. patriarchs (now only titular and honorary); 4. primates (having only a pre-eminence of honor over archbishops); 5. metropolitans or archbishops*; 6. bishops*, and suffragan bishops (assistants or substitutes). The Pope exercises his immediate jurisdiction at a distance through legates, nuncios, and apostolic delegates.* Divine institution is claimed, in this hierarchy, only for Pope and bishops. "Neither the consent nor vocation nor authority of the people is required" (Council of Trent, Sess. XXIII, chap. 4) for the ordination of any of these dignitaries, nor, indeed, for anything else. The hierarchy is supreme in the Roman Church and accountable only to itself; the prerogative of the laity is to listen, to submit, and to obey. They have abdicated the royal priesthood with which Scripture credits them, 1 Pet. 2:9; Rev. 1:6, as their "superiors" have forgotten the teaching of Christ and the Apostles, 2 Cor. 4:5; 1 Pet. 5:3; Matt. 20:25-27; 23:8-11.

Hieronymites. Four religious orders: 1) The Spanish Hieronymites established by Vasco (1370). The last convents fell in the Carlist struggles. 2) The Observantine Hieronymites founded by Lupus Olivetus (15th century) in Spain. 3) The Poor Hermits of St. Jerome established by Piethro Gambacorti near Montebello (1377). 4) The Congregation Fesulana established by Carlo de Montegranelli (1406).

High Church. See *Protestant Episcopal Church,* 4, 7; *England, Subsequent History of the Church of,* 2.

High Mass. See *Mass.*

High School, Lutheran. See *Parish Education,* G.

High School Teachers. See *Teachers,* B.

Higher Criticism. Historical sketch. Biblical higher criticism is an investigation of the origin of the books of the Bible. It is so called in distinction from lower criticism because it deals with the larger and more comprehensive questions in the writing of a given book, such as the authorship, historical background, authenticity, integrity, unity. (Cf. *Lower Criticism.*)

1. Higher criticism has been and may be pursued legitimately. Since, for example, several books of the Bible are anonymous, it is only natural for a student of the Bible to endeavor to determine the authorship of these books. And it will be a profitable study if the historical and literary data supplied by the Bible and secular sources are evaluated properly.

2. Today, however, the term higher criticism is usually not used in a neutral meaning. Most recent scholars who engage in this study ignore and directly deny the unequivocal statements of the Bible which bear on the questions of authorship and origin of the various books. Because of this negative approach to the Bible the term "higher criticism" today has a connotation of unbelief and denial of the truth as set down in Scripture.

3. Higher criticism in this negative aspect is not new. Already Origen,* 186—254/255 (*contra Celsum,* IV, 42) had to defend the Mosaic authorship and the unity of the Pentateuch against the pagan philosopher Celsus. During the Middle Ages sporadic doubts regarding the authorship of the Pentateuch are found in Jewish and Christian literature. More sweeping were the attacks on the Mosaic authorship of the Pentateuch by the English philosopher T. Hobbes * (1651) and the Jewish philosopher Baruch Spinoza * (d. 1677).

4. However, these views did not find general acceptance. Higher criticism as a systematic and general method with accepted criteria of investigation can be said to have begun in the latter part of the eighteenth century.

5. Since higher criticism was first connected with the study of the Pentateuch, a brief description of the manner in which the modern views of higher criticism on this book developed is in place. The Mosaic authorship is generally denied by the higher critical school of today. Its view of the origin of the Pentateuch rests on three widely accepted axioms: 1) The core of the book of Deuteronomy originated in the seventh century B. C. and was the Lawbook "planted" and "found" in the Temple at the time of King Josiah in the seventh century B. C. 2) The directions regarding worship and the Temple written by Ezekiel (chaps. 40—48) during the Exile were the germ idea from which the whole sacrificial system of the Pentateuch (the Priestly Code) developed. 3) This Priestly Code and its formal interpretation of the history of Israel received its final form and expression after the Exile during the time of Nehemiah.

6. These cardinal views regarding the origin of the Pentateuch rest upon the so-called source, or documentary, hypothesis. Higher critics almost without exception hold to the view that imbedded in our present Pentateuch there are four principal strata of ma-

terial of various ages. These sources in the order of their age are usually designated by the following capital letters: J (Jahwist), E (Elohist), D (Deuteronomist), and P (Priestly Code). While there is some disagreement as to the exact period of time required for the fusing of these individual documents into the present form of the Pentateuch, there is general agreement that the process began with the appearing of the J document about five centuries after Moses and that it was completed in the fourth century B. C., when the Priestly document was edited into and over the previous editions of the evolving Pentateuch.

7. Much detailed study has gone into the effort of isolating these documents. These four main strands have been separated on the basis of certain canons of literary research and on the basis of an accepted religious and historical philosophy. As literature the Pentateuch must be composite, it is maintained, because certain narratives (e. g., the creation story) and laws (e. g., the Decalog) appear more than once in a slightly different version. These so-called doublets appear in various stages of fusion. Some parallel accounts have been left almost unchanged and have merely been set down side by side; others have been woven together quite skillfully in the process so that only the seam and an occasional spot of color appears here and there to identify the original documentary material. A further proof in the field of language that the Pentateuch is the result of the work of many hands is sought in the vocabulary and style of the isolated sections. Thus, for example, the J-writer uses the term Jahweh (Jehovah) and the E-writer uses Elohim (God) as a designation of the Supreme Being. In addition, each author of the original documents has a considerable body of words which appear only in the designated strand. A distinct style is even predicated for each source. The J-writer is *volkstuemlich*, original; the Priestly writer is pedantic and statistically dry. The J-writer is often crassly anthropomorphic; the Priestly writer speaks of God in terms highly transcendental. Between this earliest and this latest writer there are various shadings and peculiarities of vocabulary and style to be noted.

8. As the last literary criterion already indicates, the documentary hypothesis also rests upon a philosophy of history. It is assumed that the religion of Israel developed from fetishism to polytheism to henotheism and finally into an ethical monotheism at the time of the eighth-century prophets. This monotheism found its noblest expression in a transcendental concept of God at the time of the Exile. Each of these sources therefore is found to reflect the religious views held at the time of the origin of these sources.

9. By and large the higher critic of today also has discarded all religious concepts which require faith in the miraculous origin and content of the Bible.

10. This view of the origin of the Pentateuch has been held in this general outline by the critical scholars since it was developed in its present form by K. H. Graf (1866) and Julius Wellhausen — 1844—1918; professor at Greifswald, Halle, Marburg, Goettingen — and hence has been called the Graf-Wellhausen theory. However, it had a long development and has undergone several transformations since the eighteenth century, which we shall trace very briefly.

11. Modern higher criticism did not have its origin in the workshop of the professional theologian. It was the Catholic physician Jean d'Astruc (1684 to 1766) who came forward with the theory that the Book of Genesis consisted of at least two primary documents. He identified these documents and traced them by the use of the divine names, Elohim and Jahweh. D'Astruc assumed that Moses had access to these sources as well as a number of lesser ones and incorporated them into the book as we have it.

12. The Mosaic authorship of the Pentateuch was at first also held by the man who can very well be called the father of modern higher criticism, Johann Gottfried Eichhorn, 1752—1827. He elaborated d'Astruc's documentary hypothesis by applying its principles to the whole Pentateuch. In the last edition of his *Einleitung in das Alte Testament* (1823—1826), he came to the conclusion that the Pentateuch was a compilation of sources later than Moses although he conceded that some of the sources may have been of Mosaic origin.

13. The development of the documentary theory, however, did not proceed in a straight line. Its line of descent from this origin made two main detours. A rival theory of the

origin of the Pentateuch was almost simultaneously introduced by the Scotch Catholic Alex Geddes (1737 to 1802) and later championed by Martin Leberecht De Wette (1780—1843). Since these scholars maintained that the Pentateuch is the result of the fusion of many independent strands and pieces, it has become known as the "fragment hypothesis." The redactor, or editor, of these many fragments was not Moses. The compiling took place at the time of the Exile although some of the material may be traced back to Moses' time. While the main thesis of this theory was later discarded, its defenders contributed one of the permanent features of the modern documentary theory: the origin of the core of the Book of Deuteronomy, now called the Deuteronomic code, as a part of the reform movement of King Josiah and attributed to Moses as a pious fraud.

14. A second rival theory which found favor for a time was the so-called "supplement hypothesis." In contrast to the previous theory, which begins with many pieces fused into a unit, this theory posits one substantial document (*Grundschrift*), which, however, was supplemented in the course of time by the additions of many writers. Since the core document first appeared in the eleventh or tenth century B. C., Mosaic authorship was considered impossible. The most influential sponsor of this theory was Heinrich Georg August Ewald (1803—75; German Orientalist, Hebraist, Biblical scholar).

15. Neither the fragmentary nor the supplement theory survived for many years. It was not long before the documentary theory was revived. Its rehabilitation began with the publication of H. Hupfeld's (1796—1866; professor at Marburg, Halle) *Die Quellen der Genesis*, in 1853, a century after d'Astruc's book had initiated the first documentary theory. It attracted the majority of Old Testament scholars. The form in which it was finally put by Graf and Wellhausen is today accepted in broad outline by almost all higher critics.

16. The other books of the Bible did not escape this critical approach. Already Geddes applied his theory also to the book of Joshua and accepted the same author for the first six books: the "Hexateuch" as it has been generally called since that time. Eichhorn in his introduction expressed the view that Isaiah 40—66, Daniel, Ecclesiastes, Esther, were written very late.

17. The same criteria are applied to the prophetic and poetic books. In addition, the meter of the poetic books has been set up as a criterion by many scholars. Another fundamental axiom accepted by almost all critics with respect to the Prophets is the view that the Prophets gave utterance only to messages of doom. All promises of salvation and restoration therefore are relegated to an author of a later period. There is almost universal agreement in the critical school of today on the fact that Isaiah 40—66 and the Book of Daniel are much later than the claims put forth by these two books.

18. From the very beginning the conclusions of higher criticism were vigorously contested by conservative scholars. The miraculous origin and content of the Bible have always been an axiom of faith with these Bible students and therefore carry their own verification. However, the conclusions of the critical school have also been attacked on their own ground. Proofs from literary and historical studies were marshaled to show that the Biblical view was just as plausible, to say the least, as the negative conclusions.

19. Investigations as detailed as those of the higher critics have been made to disprove the validity of the linguistic canons upon which rest the negative theories. On the basis of secular literature it was demonstrated that the application of the principles of the higher critic lead to absurd results. Why should not a Biblical writer be permitted to use synonyms, especially since synonyms do have their own connotation and are used deliberately by discriminating writers? O. T. Allis (b. 1880; professor at Princeton, and Westminster), *The Five Books of Moses*, even demonstrated that the literary criteria have not been consistently applied to the individual sources (J, E, etc.) and that when applied, they lead to decimation of the text.

20. It was also pointed out that the peculiar Hebrew style accounted for the repetitiousness of apparent doublets. Again often the purpose of a given section is abundant explanation for a difference in style. Deuteronomy, for example, is admonition and therefore hortatory; the laws of Leviticus must be couched in legal phraseology: both come from the same author.

21. It is also maintained that the

history and development of the Hebrew language is not sufficiently known to enable a student to limit the period of time exactly when a given word came into use and went out of use. If more literature of the Old Testament era in Hebrew were extant, a more reliable comparison could be made. Thus the shorter Hebrew form of the pronoun I (*'ani*) had been allotted to the latest of the Pentateuchal sources, that of the Priestly writer of the fourth century B. C. In the Ras Shamra (a closely related dialect) inscriptions from the sixteenth to the fourteenth century B. C., both forms of the pronoun, the shorter as well as the longer, are used side by side seemingly indiscriminately.

22. The opposing literature has also consistently pointed to the great divergence in the higher critical theories. In some areas there is indeed a general uniformity of viewpoint among critical scholars. However, there are no two critics that agree on a detailed analysis of the literature in question. Even in major issues, critics differ considerably. The same book or sections of a book are distributed by the various writers over many centuries and are allocated to many different hands. While this multiplicity of theories, often mutually contradictory, does not in itself preclude the possibility that one of the theories may be correct, it has been referred to as indicating the highly subjective character of this investigation and its lack of scientific checks and criteria.

23. The historical axiom of the higher critical school has also come in for review. The evolution of the religion of Israel as outlined by the negative view is attacked for lack of evidence and as a distortion of the data that are available.

24. The direction that higher criticism will take in the immediate future seems to be indicated by a growing respect for the value and authority of the Old Testament Scriptures. The higher critic looks at the Old Testament, which, according to his conclusions, is a jigsaw picture consisting of many little pieces. These little pieces were made at various times and by a host of writers and then put together gradually until the picture was finished. Now he asks himself, "What do these words put together thus by countless unknown hands mean to me?"

25. A rather pronounced trend in recent publications stresses the "relevance of the Old Testament." Using the term rather loosely, to be sure, this literature again speaks of the Old Testament as a revelation. In some mystic way it is often referred to as God's Word and authoritative in our lives. The new stress on synthesis rather than on analysis is also evident in the appearance of books entitled "Theology of the Old Testament."

26. This new emphasis is in some respects a complete about-face from the early rationalistic and purely intellectual approach to the Old Testament. The cause for it appears to be in the present world situation. All hope that man is climbing to a higher moral and ethical level has been shattered by the ominous and inhuman aftermath of the Second World War. With the optimism of the evolution of religion through human betterment shattered, men are forced to seek more abiding foundations.

27. Modern archaeology has also had a sobering effect on the course of higher criticism. The results of excavations have had a direct bearing on some of the strictly literary questions involved, as, for example, the Ras Shamra inscriptions. But it is, above all, in the historical field that archaeology has shown the theories of the earlier critics to be unreal fabrications of theory.

The literature on this subject is immense. The names of a few books are added. They are of recent date and give a complete bibliography. WR

Critical: Robert H. Pfeiffer, *Introduction to the Old Testament,* 1941; Harold R. Willoughby, editor, *The Study of the Bible, Today and Tomorrow,* 1947.

Conservative: James Orr, *The Problem of the Old Testament,* 1905; Oswald T. Allis, *The Five Books of Moses,* 1943; J. Coppens, *The Old Testament and the Critics,* 1942; John E. Steinmueller, *A Companion to Scripture Studies,* Vol. II, 1942; Wilhelm Moeller, *Einleitung in das alte Testament,* 1934.

Higher Education. 1. At the beginning of the Christian era the pagan world possessed numerous schools of advanced learning, the rhetorical and philosophical schools, the universities of Athens, of Rome, of Alexandria. Alexandria was for centuries the intellectual center of the world, where many of the early Church Fathers were educated. But as the danger of pagan learning and philosophy was more keenly realized, the catechumenal schools were developed into catechetical schools, which were designed to give a higher education to the leaders and ministers in the Church.

2. One of the first of these was the school at Alexandria, where Pantaenus (A. D. 179), Clement (216), and Origen (203) taught. Another school was established by Origen in Caesarea ca. 231; another about the same time by Calixtus at Rome, which rapidly developed into a flourishing school, was patronized by emperors, and possessed a large library. Though scholars of all classes came to these schools, where literature, history, and science were studied, they were planned especially for the training of the clergy under the direction of the bishop. These schools, later called episcopal or cathedral schools, spread over all Europe and continued throughout the Middle Ages; some of them persist to the present time. As promotion in the ranks of the clergy soon came to depend somewhat upon the studies pursued in these institutions, their importance increased.

3. During the 5th and the 6th century the Church Councils legislated that boys destined for the priesthood should be placed in these schools. As the attendance increased, appropriate buildings were erected, the teaching staff was augmented, the course of study regulated, and the life of teachers and pupils subjected to regular rules and canons. With the overthrow of Roman culture by the barbarians also higher education fell completely into the hands of the Church. From the 8th to the 12th century the monastic schools were of greater importance, but with the expansion of knowledge and the greater tolerance of inquiry the rigidity and narrowness of these schools resulted in the renewed growth and revived importance of the cathedral schools. The study of dialectics was emphasized, which stimulated an interest in intellectual activity and in the logical formulation and statement of religious beliefs. Plato and Aristotle dominated in these schools; the method was logical analysis of the subject, less observation and research; the knowledge was primarily of a theological and sophistical character.

4. Because of the scholastic movement and the new intellectual and educational interest, stimulated during the Crusades by the contact with Eastern and Saracen learning, a number of these cathedral schools developed into universities. The universities of Naples (1224), Bologna (1158), and Paris (1180) became prominent. During the 13th century 19 of these chartered institutions were created by Popes and monarchs; during the 14th century 25 more were added; during the 15th century, 30 more. These universities enjoyed certain privileges; students were exempt from military service and taxation, had their own internal jurisdiction, and were empowered to grant degrees, which meant a license to teach. Masters and students organized into groups, according to their national affiliation. The term *faculty* was, in the course of time, applied to the various departments of study, as, the faculty of theology, of law, etc., and finally to the instructors who had charge of a particular department. Method and content of study were dictated by scholasticism.* Education was still one of books, rather than of research and observation.

5. While these schools represent the intellectual and ecclesiastical education of the age, the institution of chivalry represents the education which secular society received, and the training in knightly ideals and activities formed the only education of the members of the nobility. This education was divided into two distinct periods: that of a page, which covered approximately the period from the seventh to the fourteenth year; and that of a squire, from the fourteenth to the twenty-first year, when, after going through some religious ceremonies, the squire was knighted. This education was rather a discipline both for the individual and for the social class to which he belonged; the intellectual element was very slight. Under chivalry the ideals constituting the character of a gentleman were more definitely formulated than in modern ages. The knight summed up his duties under his obligations to God, to his lord, and to his lady. Chivalry performed for the secular life a service similar to that performed by monasticism for the Church, inasmuch as both dignified the ideals of service and obedience.

6. The Renaissance * vitally affected the educational ideals of the age. The "new learning," the study of classical antiquity, wedged its way into all schools and universities. The most important phase of this revival was the restoration of the idea of a liberal education as formulated by the Greeks and adapted to the Romans by Cicero, Quintilian, Tacitus, and others. Paulus Ver-

gerius (died 1420) of Padua defines its aim thus: "We call those studies liberal which are worthy of a free man; those studies by which we attain and practice virtue and wisdom; that education which calls forth, trains, and develops those highest gifts of body and mind which ennoble men and are rightly judged to rank next in dignity to virtue only." The Renaissance education emphasized the physical element and endeavored to influence conduct and behavior.

It was practical and sought to train for effective citizenship and to produce practical judgment in everyday affairs. Its aesthetic element found expression in the study of literature and became the dominant feature in the work of the schools.

7. This broad content and scope of the Renaissance education was later restricted to the study of the languages and literatures of the ancients, which study, formerly but a means to the end, became the chief end in Humanistic education. The classics were studied chiefly for the sake of the language and less for the sake of their educational value. In Italian universities the "new learning" first found a permanent home; wandering "poets" brought it to the North. In 1494 a chair of "Poetry and Eloquence" was established at Erfurt, and by 1520 the "new learning" was at least represented in all the German universities. At Oxford it was introduced by a group of students from Italy, at Cambridge by Erasmus. The hostility of the Church led to the establishment of many schools embodying the new spirit under the patronage of monarchs and of the nobility, such as the court schools in Italy and the *Fuerstenschulen* in Germany. The *Gymnasium*, which has remained to this day, is the best type of Humanistic secondary schools in Teutonic countries. In many cases it developed from existing burgher and church schools. The *Gymnasium* at Strassburg, organized in 1537 by J. Sturm,* exerted the greatest influence of all of these schools. St. Paul's School of London, 1512, became the model for English advanced schools in curriculum, method, and purpose, and the narrow Humanistic training was continued in them almost up to 1860. The grammar schools of the American colonies, as to scope and method, were fashioned after the English schools. The Boston Latin School, founded 1635, has existed continuously to the present time.

But in America the Humanistic school gave place to a new type earlier than in any of the European countries.

8. The Reformation deeply affected educational ideas and aims. The interests of the Renaissance were chiefly literary and aesthetic; the Reformation again emphasized the religious and the moral interests. It made use of the "new learning," but the knowledge of languages and the culture they offered was to serve a higher purpose, the Word of God. Besides the vernacular, Latin, Greek, and Hebrew were studied; logic, mathematics, history, science, and music were added. The work of carrying out the ideas of Luther was largely left to his co-workers. Melanchthon became the *Praeceptor Germaniae;* he was to Germany as to educational reform what Luther was with respect to religious reform. Wittenberg, from which all these influences radiated, was remodeled along Humanistic-Protestant lines and became the model of many new universities.

9. At the death of Melanchthon there was scarcely a city in all Germany that had not modified its schools according to his direct advice or his general suggestions. Many of the universities and schools threw off their allegiance to the Pope and transferred it to princes and the state. But even under state control the dominant motive was a religious one, and the school plan was strongly Humanistic. These schools were early organized into a system, in Saxony in 1525, in Wuerttemberg in 1559. The effectiveness of the Protestant schools as a means of reforming social and ecclesiastical evils and of establishing churches induced the Roman Church to employ the same means. Teaching orders, especially Jesuits, adopting many of the ideas and methods of the Protestant schools, made education their chief aim and controlled the Roman Catholic institutions. While from a modern viewpoint their education was not broad, it was very thorough and effective.

10. All the colleges, with the exception of one, established in America before the end of the Colonial period, grew out of religious motives. The Puritans controlled Harvard University, established by act of the legislature of Massachusetts in 1636. William and Mary (established 1693) was a seminary for ministers of the Anglican Church; Yale (established 1701) was under Puritan auspices; Princeton (1746) was Presbyterian. The Academy

and College of Philadelphia (1753) owed its origin to Benjamin Franklin and was not under denominational control. King's College (Columbia), Brown (in R. I.), Rutgers (N. J.), and Dartmouth (N. H.), were established by the end of 1769.

11. After the Revolutionary War some States sought control of the colleges in their territory. The Dartmouth College Case decision of the Supreme Court (1819), however, protected educational corporations from political interference and thereby caused increased denominational interest in the erection of colleges. By 1900 there were almost 500 colleges in the U. S., and the number had more than tripled before the middle of the 20th century.

12. The development of public colleges and universities was slow. The University of Georgia was chartered in 1785 and opened in 1800; the University of North Carolina was chartered in 1789 and opened in 1795. Other early State universities were University of Vermont (1791, 1838), University of Virginia (opened 1825), University of Indiana (1820), University of Alabama (1831), University of Michigan (1841).

13. Technical higher education began with the establishment of Rensselaer Polytechnic Institute (Troy, N. Y., 1824). Emma Willard founded Troy Seminary (1821) for women. In 1837 Mary Lyon founded Mount Holyoke Seminary. Other early women's colleges were Rockford College, Elmira College, Vassar, and Wesleyan (Ga.). Oberlin College introduced coeducation in 1833. Johns Hopkins University became the first strictly graduate school in the U. S. (1876).

14. From the middle of the 19th century onward, efforts to broaden the curricular offerings became a prominent trend among colleges and universities. In the 20th century the financial support given universities by State appropriations, individuals, foundations, and organizations greatly increased.

15. Standards for colleges and universities have been set by State departments, colleges and universities, and voluntary organizations. The following are the regional or national accrediting associations: 1) the Association of American Universities (primarily graduate); 2) the American Association of Teachers Colleges; 3) New England Association of Colleges and Secondary Schools; 4) Middle States Association of Colleges and Secondary Schools; 5) the North

Central Association of Colleges and Secondary Schools; 6) Southern Association of Colleges and Secondary Schools; 7) Northwest Association of Secondary and Higher Schools.

16. The names of the American Association of Theological Schools and the American Association of Junior Colleges indicate their purpose. There are also professional associations (business, dental, journalism, nursing, pharmacy, social work, etc.).

17. In the 20th century enrollment rivalries and the greater demands for higher education caused new studies of standards, curricular offerings, and, to a lesser degree, teaching methods also on the college and university level.

Current information may be found in *American Universities and Colleges*, published by the American Council on Education, Washington, D. C.

For Lutheran colleges and universities see *Ministry, Education of*.

Hilary of Poitiers. "The Athanasius of the West"; of pagan parentage; bishop, though married, ca. 350; devoted himself to checking the spread of Arianism; banished; he withstood the Arians and their emperor in the East; returning, he purged Gaul, though not Italy, of the heresy; his chief work: *De Trinitate;* the first exegete among the Latin writers; composed hymns of great beauty and power; d. 366.

Hildebrand. See *Popes,* 7.

Hillel, I. Noted Jewish rabbi; b. ca. 75 B. C.; d. A. D. 10; Babylonian by birth; emigrated to Palestine; became president of Sanhedrin; in opposition to his colleague Shammai * advocated more lenient interpretation of the Law; claimed by Renan to have been Jesus' teacher, which, however, was disproved by Delitzsch.

Hillel Foundation. See *Students, Spiritual Care of,* A.

Hiller, Johann Adam (1728—1804). Studied at Goerlitz Gymnasium, in Dresden, and at University of Leipzig; conductor of Gewandhaus concerts; later *Musikdirektor* of Thomasschule; originator of *Singspiel;* among his compositions a Passion cantata.

Hiller, Philipp Friedrich (1699 to 1769). Pastor and hymn writer; wrote several books of devotion, such as *Kurze und erbauliche Andachten, Morgen- und Abendandachten nach dem Gebet des Herrn.*

Hilprecht, Hermann Vollrath (1859 to 1925). German-American Assyriologist; b. at Hohenerxleben, Germany; came to University of Pennsylvania, 1886; directed several of the university's expeditions to Nippur; wrote *Explorations in Bible Lands During 19th Century*.

Hinayana. See *Buddhism*, 6.

Hincmar (ca. 806—82). Archbishop of Rheims; adviser of Charles the Bald; strong in statesmanship and church government; upheld the rights of the national Church against Pope (Nicholas I) and Prince, and the assumed rights of the Metropolitan against the bishops. See also *Eucharistic Controversies*.

Hinduism. 1. Collective name for the religious and social systems of the Hindus. Hinduism is based on Brahmanism * and the old Vedic religion of India, but has strong admixtures of popular religious beliefs and practices. It developed since the rise of the "great heresies," Buddhism and Jainism,* and is today the religion of two thirds of the more than three hundred million inhabitants of India. Though the heretical systems of Buddhism and Jainism affected the native religion profoundly, the latter was able to survive, and this survival, with its later multiform developments, is designated by the term Hinduism. As Hinduism is a conglomeration of Brahmanism and popular beliefs and cults, particularly of the non-Aryan population, and as there are many degrees of this compromise, it presents a great variety of religious forms and an indefinite number of sectarian parties, which are on religious levels, varying from the metaphysical, monotheistic speculations of the cultured Brahmans down to the most degraded nature worship and demonology of the lowest classes.

2. Hinduism embraces the pantheism of the Upanishads, the speculations of the six orthodox systems of Brahmanic philosophy (see *Brahmanism*), asceticism and self-torture (see *Yoga* and *Fakir*), magic, a pantheon of innumerable male and female greater and lesser divinities, animism and fetishism, belief in innumerable evil spirits that must be propitiated or driven away, worship of celestial bodies, trees, rocks, of useful animals, particularly of the cow, and of harmful animals, as the snake, reverence for holy men, the saddhus, of whom there are at least five million, pilgrimages to sacred streams, as the Ganges, whose water is considered especially holy, to mountains, to Benares and other holy cities, pronounced phallicism, gross immorality, and prostitution in the temples.

3. Hinduism has in common with the older Brahmanism the fundamental doctrines of karma and transmigration * and the caste system, the latter in an extremely developed form. The division into castes is the basis of the whole social structure of India. Its beginning goes back to the time when the Aryan invaders, coming from the Punjab, pushed to the south and reduced the non-Aryan population to a position of servitude. Early in the Brahmanic period there developed four castes: the Brahman, or priestly, class, which is socially supreme; the Kshatriya, or warrior, class; the Vaisya, or agricultural, class; the Sudra, or servile, class. These four major castes are now subdivided into thousands of smaller groups, each of which is endogamous, that is, marriage is permitted only within the group. Even the Brahman caste is subdivided into many such endogamous groups, and in the lower classes subdivisions are especially numerous. The chief reason for the formation of these numerous castes is the difference in occupations and the mixture of races in varying degrees. Occupations are hereditary, and new castes are continually being formed, mainly because new occupations, hitherto unknown, arise. Besides the marriage restrictions all social intercourse, especially eating and drinking, with members of a lower caste is prohibited. Pariahs is the term applied to some of the lowest castes. They do not belong to the four original castes and, though not the lowest, are lower even than the Sudras.

4. During the early centuries of Hinduism the worship of two gods from out of the great pantheon of male and female deities, namely, of Vishnu and Siva, became prominent and divided the Hindu world into two great sects, the Vishnuites and the Sivaites. Vishnu was originally an old Vedic sun-god and now has become the most popular of the Hindu gods. He exerts his influence for the maintenance of the universe mainly through his *avatars*, *i. e.*, incarnations, in which he assumes animal, human, and superhuman forms. Siva is the old Vedic Rudra. His present worship includes many non-Aryan elements. His symbol is the phallus.

5. While Brahmanism emphasized knowledge and the performance of the ritual as the means of salvation, the Vishnuites and Sivaites lay great stress on the *bhakti*, *i. e.*, the personal faith in, and devotion to, their deity. However, this *bhakti* frequently leads to excesses. Prostitution is common in many Vishnuite temples, and certain Sivaite sects indulge in immoral orgies. The center of modern Hinduism is Benares, on the Ganges, with its more than two thousand temples. Thousands of other temples and innumerable shrines are found throughout India. Numerous priests, musicians, and temple-girls are associated with the larger temples. In Vishnuite temples there are images of Vishnu and minor deities, which every day are awakened, bathed, clothed, given food, as if they were human beings. In Sivaite temples the phallic stone is venerated with prayers and obeisances.

6. The most important sources of our knowledge of the earlier phases of Hinduism are the two great national epic poems, the *Mahabharata* (Great Bharata Story) and the *Ramayana* (Fortunes of Rama). The *Mahabharata*, the world's longest epic, consists of over 100,000 couplets, the oldest group of which dates back to ca. 400 B. C. In the course of centuries, historical, mythological, and didactic material was added to the original nucleus until the poem attained its present proportions. One of the heroes of the *Mahabharata* is Krishna, an *avatar* of Vishnu. The epic's most important part is an episode called *Bhagavad-Gita* (Song of the Blessed One), a frequently edited and popular book, which has exerted great influence on Hinduism. The *Ramayana*, also composed several centuries B. C., has for its subject another *avatar* of Vishnu. An important occurrence in the history of Hinduism is the rise of the sect of the Sikhs.* The introduction of Christianity and western civilization resulted in several reform movements, directed against polytheism, idolatry, and abuses of the old religion. In 1828 a theistic society, the Brahma-Samaj (Supreme Spirit Society) was founded by Ram Mohan Ray. He was succeeded, 1841, by Debendra Nath Tagore and, 1865, by Keshab Chandra Sen. The several branches into which the movement broke up attempted to combine the best elements of Hinduism with the monotheism and spiritual character of Christianity, one branch even asserting their

belief in a trinity, father, son, and spirit. The movement has ceased to be a force and now numbers only about 5,000 adherents. A similar monotheistic reform movement is the Arya-Samaj (Aryan Society), founded in 1875 by Dayananda Sarasvati. It regards the Vedas as divine revelation and is pronounced in its antagonism to Christianity. This movement is believed to have over half a million followers. The 1941 census of India (exclusive of Burma) gives the total population as 388,997,955. Of these, 255,030,506 are Hindus, 94,389,428 Muslims, 6,316,549 Christians, 5,691,447 Sikhs, 1,449,286 Jains, 114,890 Parsees, 232,007 Buddhists, 22,480 Jews. See *Religions, Comparative, Bibliography.* GVS

Hinkelmann, Abraham (1652—95). Preacher, professor, poet, and Orientalist. He labored at Luebeck, Hamburg, Darmstadt, and Giessen. He was suspected of Pietism.

Hippo Regius, Canon of. See *Carthage, Synods and Councils of; Carthage, Canon of.*

Hippolytus (ca. 160—235). Roman Christian; prolific writer (chief work: *Philosophumena*). By his opposition to lax discipline and Patripassian heresy of Pope Calixtus of Rome (217—222), he occasioned the *Schism of Hippolytus,* which lasted until the year 235, when, according to the chronological catalog of Popes from 354, a "presbyter" Hippolytus, together with the Roman bishop Pontianus, was banished to Sardinia. Thereupon both parties united in the election of a new Pope, thus ending the schism.

Hirschberger Bibel. The Bible reprinted with brief and pointed annotations and parallel references by Ehrenfried Liebich, pastor at Lomnitz, assisted by John Fr. Burg of Breslau. Printed at Hirschberg, 1756.

Hispaniola. Island of the West Indies; western third Haiti, remainder Dominican Republic. Discovered by Columbus; early called Espanola; Haiti perhaps aboriginal name. The Dominican Republic (Santo Domingo) has an area of about 19,330 sq. mi. and a population of about 2,167,000 (1951). The inhabitants are white, mulatto, and negro. There is no official state religion, but the inhabitants are predominantly Roman Catholic. Mission work is carried on by 12 Protestant societies with a total Christian community of about 26,000 (1952). See *Haiti.*

Historical Apologetics. See *Apologetics*, II.

Historical Criticism. See *Isagogics*.

Historical Materialism. See *Marx, Karl.*

Historical Societies. See *Archives*.

Historical Society of the Evangelical Lutheran Church. See *Archives*.

Historico-Religious School. See *Lutheran Theology after 1580*, 13.

History of Doctrine. See *Doctrine, Christian, History of; Dogmatics.*

History, Philosophy of. The pessimistic philosophy of history presumes that human events have no pattern and reveal no control or concern of God. The humanistic philosophy of history concerns itself with human events as reflections of human personality and/or groups (the hero dominant; sociological theories of history). The Christian philosophy of history views God as dominant in human affairs, controlling and moving all things for His purposes. On the material level, God is concerned with the preservation of the human race, with the dispersion of peoples over the globe, with their protection by government, commerce, and other human institutions. On the spiritual level, God employs history to keep man in awareness of his need for God, and its misfortunes and disasters as chastisements designed to turn man to God. Thus the Christian sees not only the pleasurable and beneficent events and trends of history, but also, in its disasters and horrors, the hand of God seeking out man that He might glorify him by humbling him. In this philosophy of history the greatest event is that in which God most directly has intervened to reveal His love to man, namely, the incarnation and redemption of Jesus Christ. All of the other events of history, in the economy of God's design, have but the one function of turning men to find Christ before He comes in Judgment to make an end of history and inaugurate the new heaven and the new earth. RRC

Otto Piper, *God in History*, Macm., 1939.

History of Susannah. See *Apocrypha*, A 3.

Hlavac-Kephalides, Matthew. See *Slovakia, Lutheran Theology in*, 1.

Hobbes, Thomas (1588—1679). English philosopher; b. at Malmesbury; d.

at Hardwick Hall. By the sensationalism of his philosophy ("only source of knowledge is sensation"), his denial of miracles and revelation, and, in general, by his critical, rationalistic attitude toward religious doctrines, he helped much to lay the foundations of English Deism.* The best statement of Hobbes' political and social philosophy is contained in his work *Leviathan* (1651).

Hochmann, E. C. See *Brethren* (*Dunkers*).

Hochstetter, C. B. Apr. 1, 1828, at Lorch, Wuerttemberg; studied theology in Tuebingen; pastor of St. John's, Fort Wayne; 1857 *Diakonus* of Pastor Grabau; joined the Missouri Synod in 1866, after the *Colloquium;* served in Pittsburgh, Indianapolis, Frohna, Mo., Stonebridge, Can., Wolcottsville, N. Y., Jordan, Can.; d. June 12, 1905; editor of *Luth. Volksblatt;* author of *Geschichte der Missouri-Synode.*

Hochstetter, John Andreas (1637 to 1720). A noted Pietist of South Germany; interested A. H. Francke in Jewish missions.

Hodge, Archibald Alexander (1823 to 1886). Presbyterian; son of Charles Hodge; b. at Princeton; missionary in India; professor of theology at Allegheny, Pa.; succeeded his father, at Princeton (d. there); one of the founders of the *Presbyterian Review.*

Hodge, Charles (1797—1878). Conservative Presbyterian theologian; b. at Philadelphia; began to teach in his alma mater, Princeton College, 1820, and was connected with its faculty until his death; founded the *Biblical Repository* (later called *Princeton Review*), 1825; wrote *Commentary on Romans* (among the best English commentaries on Romans); *Systematic Theology;* etc.

Hodza. M. M. See *Slovakia, Lutheran Theology in*, 2.

Hoe von Hoenegg, Matthias (1580 to 1645). B. at Vienna. Studied at Wittenberg. Third court preacher in Dresden; superintendent at Plauen; director of the Evangelical churches and schools at Prague; first court preacher in Dresden, where he remained until his death. He was politically active in the intrigues of the Thirty Years' War.

Hoeffding, Harald (1843 — 1931). Prof. at Copenhagen, Denmark; influenced by Kierkegaard; sought religious significance in the conservation of value; denied basic Christian tenets.

Hoefling, Johann Wilhelm Friedrich (1802—53). Conservative Lutheran theologian; educated at Erlangen; first pastor at several places, then professor of practical theology at Erlangen; in 1852 supreme consistorial councilor at Munich; one of the founders and editors of the *Zeitschrift fuer Protestantismus und Kirche;* wrote an extensive work on Baptism and *Kirchenverfassung;* originator of a peculiar theory of the holy office, denying its divine institution.

Hoelemann, Hermann Gustav (1809 to 1886). Prof. at Leipzig; conservative Lutheran theologian; most noted works: *Bibelstudien* and *Die Reden des Satans in der Heiligen Schrift;* held the orthodox Lutheran view of Inspiration.

Hoelscher, Gustav (b. 1877). Prof. at Halle, Giessen, Marburg, and Bonn; extensive writings on the Old Testament.

Hoen (Honius), Cornelius. Dutch theologian; d. at The Hague 1524; developed theory that *is* in words of institution of Eucharist means *signifies;* which Carlstadt, Zwingli, and Oecolampadius adopted; Luther rejected it.

Hoenecke, Adolf. B. Feb. 25, 1835, at Brandenburg; prepared himself for the university at Brandenburg Gymnasium; studied theology at Halle, where he was favored and influenced by Tholuck; was in Switzerland some years; then accepted offer of Berlin consistory to serve a number of years as pastor in America under an agreement which the Berlin Missionary Society had with the Wisconsin Synod. His American service was to count toward a later appointment in the Prussian Church. Once in America, Hoenecke found himself. A return to Germany and its confessional indifference was impossible to the man who had become immediately a fiery and devoted apostle of true Lutheranism. He did not hesitate to cast his lot with his new friends, sacrificing personal advancement. Pastor of the little rural parish of Farmington, 1863—66, he then came to the seminary at Watertown, teaching there until 1870. At this time an agreement with Missouri called for his service at St. Louis. The state of his health made acceptance impossible, and he followed a call to St. Matthew's, Milwaukee, which pastorate he retained until 1890, even after he had assumed

the directorate of the re-established seminary in 1878, filling the chair of Dogmatics and Homiletics. His learning made him the spiritual leader of the Wisconsin Synod to his dying day and left his imprint on every young pastor sent forth from the seminary. But it was more than scholarship that gave him influence; he was pre-eminently the expounder of the Gospel. His brilliant gifts, shining brightly even in controversies where they were unwillingly employed, made the Gospel stand out the more clearly. He was not so keenly concerned with matters of church government, though his sound judgment was ever sought, but rather found his task in fortifying the heart with the Truth; the rest, he reasoned, might then take care of itself. For many years he was editor in chief of the *Gemeindeblatt,* and under his directorate the *Theologische Quartalschrift* was founded, 1903. His many duties did not prevent his preparing numerous books, only one of which, *Wenn ich nur dich habe,* a volume of sermons, was published during his lifetime. Posthumously his lifework, the *Dogmatik,* was published, edited by his sons, Walter and Otto J. R. In the same manner a volume of *Entwuerfe* and a volume of Lenten sermons, *Ein Laemmlein geht,* were published. He was made D. D. by the faculties of Concordia, St. Louis, and of Northwestern Seminary, Watertown, Wis., 1903. He died at Wauwatosa, Jan. 3, 1908, generally acclaimed, within and without his synod, as one of the great men of the Lutheran Church of this country.

Aug. Pieper, "Dr. Hoeneckes Bedeutung fuer die Wisconsin-Synode und die amerikanisch-lutherische Kirche," *Theol. Quart.,* XXXII: 161—74; 225—44; XXXIII: 1—19; 81—101.

Hofacker, Ludwig (1798—1828) and **Wilhelm** (1805—48). Both born at Stuttgart; both very popular and influential preachers in Wuerttemberg at the time of the reawakening from rationalism to living faith in Christ. Ludwig's book of sermons has been sold in hundreds of thousands of copies and has exerted a very great influence in awakening sinners. Wilhelm's sermons were more polished, but less powerful.

Hofhaimer, Paul (1459—1537). Was perhaps the foremost organist of his day. Maximilian employed him as organist for his famous court at Innsbruck, as did also Elector Frederick the Wise of Saxony. Very little of his organ music is today available, and it is quite possible that he did much improvising at the organ. His music is more graceful and pleasing than the more archaic organ music of Konrad Paumann.

Hofmann, Heinrich (1824—1902). A very popular painter; free departure from strict classicism, with romantic tendency; among his well-known paintings: Christ in Gethsemane, Child Jesus in the Temple.

Hofmann, Johann Christian Konrad von. B. at Nuremberg 1810; d. at Erlangen 1877; considered the most influential Lutheran theologian of his type and time (see *Erlangen School*); educated at Erlangen and Berlin; first professor at Erlangen; 1842 at Rostock; recalled to Erlangen in 1845, where he remained to his end. Hofmann's theology is not that of the Lutheran Confessions, which is based entirely on the revealed Word of God. Hofmann, following Schleiermacher, tries to develop and unfold his theology from his own consciousness as a believer. "I, the Christian, am the proper material of my science as theologian," is his own confession. Christianity, according to him, is the communion of God and man as mediated by Christ, but Christ *in* us. He held that Christ suffered on our behalf, but not in our stead. His foremost writings are: *Weissagung und Erfuellung; Schriftbeweis, Die Heilige Schrift Neuen Testaments zusammenhaengend untersucht.*

Paul Wapler, *Johannes von Hofmann: ein Beitrag zur Geschichte der theologischen Grundprobleme der kirchlichen und der politischen Bewegungen im 19. Jahrh.,* Deichert, Leipzig, 1914.

Hoffman, Emil. B. March 1, 1862, at Oebisfelde, Saxony; ed. at Halle and at Kropp Seminary. Immediately after graduation he came to Canada; pastorates at: North Easthope-Wellesley-Gadshill parish, Canada; Hamilton (Canada), 1888—1904; Berlin, Ont., 1904 to 1912; Toronto, Ont., 1912—20; pres. of Canada Synod 16 yrs.; pres. of Waterloo Theol. Sem., 1920—26; mem., Ways and Means Com. that planned merger of general bodies in 1918. Instrumental in merging Canada Synod and Central Canada Synod. Delegate to Lutheran World Convention, Eisenach, 1923. D. D., Thiel Coll., 1911. D. April 11, 1926.

Hoffmann, Daniel (1538—1611). B. at Halle; d. at Wolfenbuettel. Studied at Jena. Prof. of ethics and dialectics and later of theology at Helmstedt; opposed the Philippists and Humanists there; kept Brunswick from joining the subscribers to the *Formula of Concord.*

Hoffmann von Fallersleben, August Heinrich (1798—1874). Hymnologist, poet, and philologist who did excellent research work particularly in the field of the pre-Reformation chorale and of the macaronic. His *Geschichte des deutschen Kirchenliedes* (Hanover, 1832 and 1854) still enjoys wide fame and use.

Hoffmann, Francis Arnold. B. June 5, 1822, at Kreis Minden, Westphalia, Prussia. Came to Chicago in 1840, taught school in Addison, prepared for the ministry under F. Schmid of Ann Arbor, pres. of Michigan Synod. Pastor at Addison until 1847; Schaumburg, Ill., 1847—51; active in organizing churches in northern Illinois. Ordained Elling Eilsen, first Norwegian pastor in America in 1843. Joined Missouri Synod in 1849. Resigned from ministry in 1851 because of illness. Became a lawyer, banker, statesman, co-founder of Republican party, Lt. Governor of Illinois, 1860—64. Retired from public life in 1875, and as "Hans Buschbauer" he devoted himself to writing on agricultural matters, editing *Haus- und Bauernfreund* for many years. He willed his library to Northwestern College, Watertown, Wis. D. Jan. 23, 1901.

K. Kretzmann, "Francis Arnold Hoffmann," *CHIQ*, XVIII: 37—54.

Hoffmann, Gottfried (1658—1712). Studied at Leipzig; conrector, then rector at Lauban, later at Zittau; most hymns written for his pupils; wrote: "Hilf, Jesu, dass ich meinen Naechsten liebe."

Hoffmann, John Martin Theodore Ernst (1823—87). B. at Treppeln, Prussia; studied in the seminary of the Berlin Mission Society; came to America (1850); served congregations in New York and Albany. Ardent supporter of the New York Ministerium.

Hoffmann (Hofmann), Melchior (ca. 1498—ca. 1544). Mystic and Anabaptist. He proclaimed the advent of the New Jerusalem, which was to be located at Strassburg, where he was later imprisoned. He has been regarded as the spiritual father of the Muenster tragedy. His followers became known as the Melchiorites.

Hoikka, J. J. See *Finnish Lutherans in America*, 1.

Hokanson, Magnus F. See *Augustana Lutheran Church*, 2.

Holbach, Paul Heinrich Dietrich, Baron d' (1723—89). French philosopher; b. at Edesheim, Palatinate, of German parents; lived in Paris, where his home became the meeting place of prominent freethinkers; was one of the Encyclopedists *; attacked Christian religion, as based on fraud and ignorance. His *Système de la Nature* teaches the crassest atheistical materialism. D. at Paris.

Holbein, Hans, the *father* (1460 to 1524) and the *son* (1497—1543). The former, with all the grace exhibited in his work, still deficient in grouping and coloring, although his altar of St. Sebastian in Munich shows independent art and a new German style. Hans the Younger soon excelled his father, who was his teacher, his work showing the culmination of the German Renaissance; rose to the zenith of honor and fortune at the court of Henry VIII of England, painting a great number of portraits which are still considered masterpieces of art, in spite of the fact that his style was somewhat hard and formal.

Holdemann, J. See *Mennonite Bodies*, 3.

Holiness. "Holiness is the absolute purity of God, according to which His affections, thoughts, will, and acts are in perfect consistency and harmony with His own nature and in energetic opposition to everything not in conformity therewith." (A. L. Graebner.) Cf. 1 Pet. 1:16; Ps. 145:17; Ex. 20:26. In this sense God alone is holy. His love is a holy love; His thoughts are holy thoughts; His will is a holy will; His acts are holy acts — inasmuch as they are divine, in perfect consistency and harmony with His divine nature. And thus God is the Source and Norm of all holiness, all things being sanctified as they are made His own and dedicated to His service. Since holiness is that purity which excludes everything that would defile, the holiness of God places Him in direct opposition to everything that is not in conformity with His nature. The wrath of God over sin is an exertion of His holiness (Rom. 1:18 ff.).

Holiness Bodies. 1. *History.* To counteract the wave of immorality and spiritual indifference which swept over the country at the close of the Civil War, a number of Methodists inaugurated the National Holiness Movement. It was their conviction that the churches had neglected Wesley's doctrine of Christian perfection and that the reintroduction of camp meetings, holiness meetings, the testimony technique, the class system, was essential to vital Christianity. The holiness movement gained momentum, and by 1890 bands of "sanctified believers" were organized as separate denominations in various parts of the country under such names as the Church of the Nazarene, the Pilgrim Holiness Church, the Holiness Church. Many of these groups were of the "Holy Roller" type. Between 1880 and 1900 a number of Evangelistic Associations were founded for the purpose of propagating the doctrine of entire sanctification and related views. The largest of these is the Christian and Missionary Alliance founded by A. B. Simpson, a Presbyterian. Almost simultaneously the Pentecostal Movement * gained a foothold, chiefly among the Baptists. Like the Holiness Bodies, these Pentecostals teach entire sanctification and are for that reason frequently classified with the Holiness Bodies. On the other hand, many of the Holiness Bodies subscribe to the four principles of the Pentecostals: Christ as Savior, Sanctifier, Healer, and coming King, also known as the "Full Gospel" or the "Four-Square Gospel." * Like the Pentecostals, many Holiness Bodies conduct "waiting meetings" with much groaning after the spirit, encourage speaking in tongues, seek faith healing.

2. It is rather difficult to make a clear distinction between the Holiness Bodies and the Pentecostals. The following churches are usually classified as Holiness Bodies: Apostolic Overcoming Holy Church of God (Colored), Assemblies of God, General Council, The Christian and Missionary Alliance, Christ's Sanctuary Holy Church (Colored), Church of Christ (Holiness) U. S. A. (Colored), Church of God, Church of God (Anderson, Ind.), The (Original) Church of God, Church of God (Salem, W. Va.), (Tomlinson) Church of God, Church of God and Saints of Christ (Colored), Church of God in Christ (Colored), Church of the Nazarene, Churches of God-Holiness, Church of Living God-Christian Workers for Fellowship (Colored), Church of Living God-"The Pillar and Ground of Truth" (Colored), Congregational

Holiness Church, Fire-Baptized Holiness Church of God of the Americas, Holiness Church, International Church of the Four-Square Gospel, Christian Nation Church, Church of the Full Gospel, Inc., House of the Lord, Kodesh Church of Immanuel (Colored), National David Spiritual Temple of Christ Church Union, Triumph the Church and Kingdom of God in Christ, Pentecostal Holiness Church, Pentecostal Assemblies of Jesus Christ, The Pentecostal Church, Inc., International Pentecostal Assemblies, Pentecostal Assemblies of the World, Pentecostal Church of God of America, Inc., Pentecostal Fire-Baptized Holiness Church, Calvary Pentecostal Church, Church of God in Christ (Colored), Pilgrim Holiness Church, United Holy Church of America, Inc. — The following Evangelistic Associations have all the marks of Holiness Bodies: Apostolic Christian Church, Apostolic Christian Church (Nazarene), Apostolic Faith Mission, Christian Congregation, Church of Daniel's Band, Church of God (Apostolic), Church of God as Organized by Christ, Hephzibah Faith Missionary Association, Metropolitan Church Association, Missionary Bands of the World, Missionary Church Association, Pillar of Fire. — For the typically Pentecostal Churches see the article *Pentecostalism.*

3. *Doctrine.* The Holiness Bodies subscribe to the fundamental doctrines of the Bible, but because of their literalistic and legalistic approach to the Bible there is great diversity among them concerning points of interpretation. Some believe that all forms of luxury are forbidden. Others hold that the charismatic gifts of the Apostolic Church must be present in the Church today. Still others believe that it is contrary to Christ's injunction to salary the ministry. All of them accept the theory of pre-millennialism.* Being committed to the Wesleyan Arminian theology, the Holiness Bodies believe in free will, human responsibility, and man's ability to reach entire satisfaction. They hold that Christ freed man not only from the curse and guilt of sin, but also from its power, for Christ is said to have prepared a "full salvation" for mankind. While Wesley believed that Christian perfection is obtained by a gradual process, the Holiness Bodies teach that the Holy Spirit bestows entire sanctification instantaneously. This is known as the "second blessing," the Holy Spirit's

work subsequent to, and different from, the work of conversion, in which after much tarrying and waiting the "Spirit-baptized" believer is freed completely from every inclination to sin. The theory of entire sanctification rests on the false premises that only conscious sins are truly sins; that God requires only a relative holiness, *i. e.*, a holiness according to the individual's ability; and that God would not command holiness if He did not also enable man to be holy. See *Religious Bodies (U. S.), Bibliography.* FEM

Holiness Methodist Church. See *Methodist Bodies,* 4 b.

Holl, Karl (1866—1926). B. at Tuebingen. Studied there. Assistant in the preparation of the edition of the Church Fathers by the Berlin Academy of Sciences; *privatdozent* at the University of Berlin, 1896; titular professor there, 1898; associate professor of church history at Tuebingen, 1900; professor of the same at Berlin, 1907. He was an eminent Luther scholar.

Holland. See *Netherlands.*

Hollaz, David (1648—1713). Pastor and provost in Jacobshagen, near Colberg, Pomerania; author of *Examen Theologicum Acroamaticum,* last of the great textbooks of Lutheran orthodoxy, excellent in arrangement and clearness of definitions.

J. Pelikan, "Natural Theology in David Hollaz," *CTM,* XVIII: 253—63.

Holmquist, Hjalmar. See *Sweden, Luth. Church in,* 6.

Holston Synod. See *United Lutheran Church, Synods of,* 11.

Holtzmann, Heinrich (1832—1910). Ed. at Heidelberg and Berlin; prof. of NT exegesis at Strassburg. A leading representative of the critical school. Among his works are: *Lehrbuch der historisch-kritischen Einleitung in das Neue Testament, Die synoptischen Evangelien, Lehrbuch der neutestamentlichen Theologie.*

Holy Alliance. An agreement signed by Alexander I of Russia, Francis I of Austria, and Frederick William III of Germany after the Congress of Vienna. It was an attempt to make Christianity basic in relations between states and between kings and subjects. Other nations of Europe joined the Alliance. Its idealism was used to defend the idea of the divine right of kings.

Holy Coat of Treves. This famous relic, preserved in the Cathedral of Treves (Trier), purports to be the seamless garment — *tunica inconsutilis* — woven by Mary for the Christ Child, miraculously extending as He grew, and worn by the Savior to the time of the crucifixion — the identical garment over which the Savior's executioners cast lots. Many legends concerning its preservation have been invented. It played a conspicuous part in the history of relics. In the days of Barbarossa it was the glory of Treves. On the eve of the Reformation it was solemnly displayed to the Emperor Maximilian and the assembled German princes. During the Reformation it was repeatedly produced as an antidote against heretical infection. The veneration accorded the relic in 1844, when its exhibition attracted one and a half million pilgrims to Treves, raised a loud protest among Protestants and some Catholics. In 1891 almost two million pilgrims passed through the cathedral to venerate and view the Holy Coat. Twenty other coats likewise claim to be the original.

Holy Days and Festivals. See *Church Year.*

Holy Ghost. The Holy Spirit (Spirit of God, Spirit of Christ, the Spirit is in Scripture identified with God (Ps. 139:7, 8; Acts 5:3, 4; Rom. 8:9; 1 Cor. 3:16; 2 Cor. 3:17). In part He is described as an independent personality contrasted with Father and Son and proceeding from them (Matt. 28:19; John 14:26; 15:26; Gal. 4:6). — The work of the Holy Ghost is described in Scripture as, in part, coinciding with the work of the Father (i. e., Creation, Job 33:41); and the functions which are frequently designated as "works of the Spirit" are likewise ascribed to Father and Son. In the Scriptures, acts are assigned to the Spirit specifically which bear upon the soul and thought of man, outside the creation and preservation of his body by the Father and his redemption by the Son. Thus the revealing of the truth and grace of God to man is such a work (1 Cor. 2:10, 11). It is the work of the Spirit to convert man and put the renewed life and spirit into him (John 3:5; 1 Cor. 12:3). The Holy Spirit preserves this power of saving faith (1 John 4:13). He enables the believer to resist the flesh and to produce the fruits of life in love (Eph. 4:22-24; Gal. 5:16 ff.; 1 Pet. 1:22). — In one sense the Holy Spirit is wholly beyond the reach of man; man makes no contribution to Him or to his grasp of Him (John 3:8). On the other hand, the Christian has received the power and presence of the Holy Spirit through the tool, administrated by another Christian, of Baptism (Titus 3:5), and can continually reinforce His presence through the Word of the Gospel (1 Pet. 1:22-25). He himself finally is equipped with the Holy Spirit to the specific end that he should communicate the grace of God in Christ Jesus, the forgiveness of sins, and the life of the Spirit to others (John 20:21-23; Matt. 28:19, 20; Luke 24:45-49). RRC

Holy Ghost and Us Society. A communistic sect founded 1893 by Frank W. Sandford, former Free Baptist pastor, with headquarters at "Shiloh," Durham Tp., Me. Community of goods, millenarianism, Baptism by immersion, belief in miraculous healing, are their main tenets.

Holy Ghost, Congregation of. A congregation of secular priests, formed to furnish missionaries for the most abandoned souls in both Christian and pagan lands. It chose Africa as its main field.

Holy Grail. A term properly applied to the legendary dish used at the Last Supper of the Lord, said to have been stolen by a servant of Pilate, used by him to wash his hands before the multitude, afterward given to Joseph of Arimathea as a memorial of Christ, and finally used by Joseph to collect the blood which flowed from Christ's body while He hung on the cross. The name was afterwards applied to the cup used at the Last Supper. Many men have gone in search of the Holy Grail, since it was said that Joseph of Arimathea had brought it to England, whence it was transported to India. The cup found by crusaders, at the capture of Caesarea, is now in Genoa. The legend was revived in 1925, after the finding of a very ancient sacramental cup in Antioch.

Holy Maid of Kent, or the *Nun of Canterbury* (Elizabeth Barton). Pretended to have heavenly visions, which were widely credited; she predicted dire calamity for England and a violent death for Henry VIII if he divorced Catherine of Aragon and married Anne Boleyn. She was tried for treason and beheaded (1534).

Holy Office of the Universal Church. See *Counter Reformation,* 1 c; *Inquisition.*

Holy Rollers. See *Holiness Bodies; Pentecostalism.*

Holy Roman Empire. An appellation applied to a territory which was co-extensive with the Latin Church. The crowning of Charlemagne as emperor (A. D. 800) by Leo III marks its formal beginning. When the Frankish state broke up, the Empire moved to Germany. After the interregnum the Empire became a German state, usually under a Hapsburg. Charles V, emperor at the time of the Reformation, joined the Empire to Spain. Napoleon brought about the dissolution of the Empire (1806).

Holy See. The jurisdiction of the Papacy.*

Holy Spirit. See *Holy Ghost.*

Holy Synod. 1) The board of the patriarchate of Constantinople; 2) the supreme council of the Greek National Church; 3) the governing body of the Russian Church; 4) the governing body of the Rumanian Church.

Holy Thursday. Maundy Thursday; formerly also Ascension Day.

Holy Water. In the Roman Catholic Church, water over which the prayer of consecration has been offered and which is used for Baptism and lustration.

Holy Week. See *Church Year,* 4, 8.

Homann, Ernst. See *Australia,* A 1.

Homburg, Ernst Christoph (1605 to 1681). Studied law; practiced at Naumburg; clerk of assizes and counselor; friend of Rist; great ability as poet; wrote: "Jesu, meines Lebens Leben"; "Ach wundergrosser Siegesheld."

Home-Finding Societies. See *Child Care and Child-Placing Agencies.*

Home Missions. See *Missions.*

Home Missions Council of North America. See *Union Movements,* 13.

Home Training. See *Christian Teaching,* O; *Parish Education,* A.

Homes for Convalescents and Chronically Ill. See *Hospitals, Sanatoria, and Homes for Convalescents and Chronically Ill.*

Homiletics. 1. Homiletics is the science of preaching. The term comes from the Greek for being together, as in a crowd or conversation. The term "homily" came to signify an address to a Christian congregation, in contrast to the evangelizing of non-Christians. The term has been applied either exclusively to the sermon in the parish service or more broadly to all preaching of the Christian religion. As a science, homiletics includes a formal theory: gathering preaching materials from the Word of God, from experience and observation, and from literature; arranging the materials in logical and psychological sequence; expressing the material in apt language; directing the material to the hearer by means of speech and bodily movement. Homiletics also includes a body of insights into the source and function of the Christian religion and its impact upon the human mind, and into human nature as it responds to the spoken word.

2. The Jewish synagog developed a standard form of worship which included a sermon (e. g., Luke 4:20). Any competent member of the congregation was eligible to deliver such a discourse, but, if possible, the task was assigned to itinerant religious teachers. They learned the science of their craft by simple conference with, or imitation of, other rabbis or through the great rabbinical schools.

3. The New Testament provides no homiletical theory. The Savior emphasized the content and purpose of the preaching message (e. g., Luke 24: 45-48). The Apostles stressed the sincerity and urgency of the message (e. g., 1 Thessalonians 4; 2 Corinthians 2—5; 2 Tim. 2:3; 1 Pet. 4:5). The early Christian Church soon developed a standard service in which teaching and preaching had a part (Acts 2:41-47; 6:4-8).

4. Under the influence of rhetorical theory, standards and principles of homiletics were crystallized. Augustine provided a summary of them in *De doctrina Christiana.* Under the influence of Aristotelian philosophy, principles of rhetoric and dialectic were applied to preaching. The influence of this method was curtailed, however, by the fact that most clerics were poorly trained and that the preaching which most stirred the people was the direct and popular message of the preaching friars.

5. The Protestant Reformation vitalized the message of the parish minister by enhancing the place of the sermon in the service, by making the pastor the shepherd responsible for the faith and life of his hearers, and by putting the Bible in the vernacular into the center of the sermon and the hearer's in-

terest. Luther himself was a direct and profuse preacher who employed a minimum of theoretical form in his approach to preaching. The Lutheran Church early put the emphasis, however, on a humanistically trained clergy. Thus principles of rhetoric and dialectic resumed a formal position in Lutheran preaching and in the training of Lutheran preachers. The theological disputes and the emphasis on doctrinal formulation of the sixteenth and seventeenth centuries gave more emphasis to the argumentative and polemical method in German Lutheran preaching than elsewhere. The prestige and position of theological faculties in Lutheranism produced a theoretical scaffolding for preaching which withstood the movements which might have worked adversely upon formal preaching, namely, Pietism,* Rationalism,* and the Enlightenment.*

6. In America homiletical theory was produced also by the dissenting communions, who here set up their strongest church organizations and seminaries. In the past, Protestant homiletical theory largely followed the patterns of the past, emphasizing the traditional forms and relating the sermon to the parish service. This process has been reinforced by the trend in much of Protestantism to a more adequate attention to the service as a whole (liturgical movement *).

7. At the present time the attempt is under way to review homiletical theory in the light of the psychology of the audience and of persuasion. The impetus for this emphasis has come in part from the new channels for evangelism in radio and publicity; in part from the effort to reach the public mind which is not habituated to the authority of the Word of God. This emphasis has begun with rethinking of the "delivery" of the message and of the speaker's total participation in his message. The principles of persuasion as applied to the intrinsic message of the Gospel and expressed to the audience by every means at the preacher's disposal are subjects of current scrutiny. The result is a homiletical theory which concerns itself not merely with the preacher's address to the Christian audience, but concentrates on the individual responding to analysis of his need and sympathy for his problem. See *Preaching, Christian.* RRC

J. H. C. Fritz, *The Preacher's Manual,* CPH, 1941; M. Reu, *Homiletics* (tr. A. Steinhaeuser), Columbus, Ohio, 1944

(5th ed.); R. W. Kirkpatrick, *The Creative Delivery of Sermons,* Macm., 1944. (Additional authors: Broadus, Luccock, Blackwood, Dargan.)

Homilius, Gottfried (1714 — 85). Pupil of J. S. Bach and later cantor of the *Kreuzschule* in Dresden; likewise given charge of the music of the three Lutheran churches of this city. Although Forkel, in his biography of Bach, subscribed to the statement that Homilius was the greatest Protestant church composer of his day, and although Homilius was, in more ways than one, an exemplary church musician and Christian character, his compositions reveal that he inherited very little of the great spirit of his teacher J. S. Bach. Instead he devitalized his music by emulating Graun and Hasse, Lotti and Leo. In addition, the rationalistic spirit of the age in which he lived did him far more harm as a composer than the pietistic era did Bach, who had the courage to ignore precepts, practices, and policies of the era of Pietism. It has been said that the motets of Homilius are in the field of Lutheran choral composition what the hymns of Gellert are in the field of the chorale. Homilius was, perhaps, more successful as a composer of chorale preludes for the organ.

Homme, Even Johannes. B. 1843 in Telemarken, Norway; came to America, 1854; studied at Luther College and Concordia Seminary, St. Louis; founded (1881) Wittenberg, Wis., where he also founded an academy, normal school, orphanage, and old people's home; active in the founding of the Bethany Indian Mission, Wittenberg, Wis.; established a printing concern (1881), also at Wittenberg, Wis., which published *For Old and Young, Sunday School Paper, Orphanage Calendar* (these in Norwegian), *Christian Youth, Sunday School Helper;* d. 1903.

Hommel, Friedrich (1813—92). Studied law at Munich, Bonn, and Erlangen; held various positions as assessor and counselor; through his acquaintance with Loehe, v. Tucher, and Layritz learned to know and appreciate the Lutheran music of the sixteenth and seventeenth centuries; as a result, *Liturgie fuer lutherische Gemeindegottesdienste, Psalter, fuer den Gesang eingerichtet, Geistliche Volkslieder,* his influence extending even to America. His son, Fritz Hommel (b. 1854), wrote numerous works on Assyriology and Arabic philology.

Homoios. See *Arianism*, 3.

Homoiousios. See *Arianism*, 3.

Homologoumena. See *Antilegomena*.

Homoousios. See *Arianism*, 2, 3.

Honduras. See *Central America, Missions in*.

Honesty. Christians are to be honest, upright, conscientious in all their dealings with men. This virtue is to manifest itself in their speech and actions. They believe in honesty, not merely as a policy that pays, but as a duty to God (*Concordia Bible Student*, 1940, No. 4, pp. 235, 240). Christians should be honest in business, make an honest living, render conscientious service for wages, pay their debts, remit their taxes, faithfully discharge the duties of their calling, be honest even in little things, manifest honesty in conduct and daily life (cp. Prov. 11:1; Luke 3:13; 16:10; 12:47, 48; Phil. 4:8; 1 Tim. 2:2; Heb. 13:18; 1 Pet. 2:12). See *Concordia Pulpit*, 1936, Vol. VII, p. 177.

Honorius I. See *Monothelitism*.

Honter, John (1498—1549). B. at Kronstadt; opened a printery and got out Luther's Small Catechism in 1545. Luther called him "the Lord's evangelist in Hungary."

Hooker, Richard (ca. 1553—1600). Anglican defender (moderate) of episcopacy; b. at Devonshire; graduated at Oxford; took orders 1581; received a living at Bucks; master of the Temple 1585; rector at Boscombe, then at Bishopsbourne (d. there); not eloquent preacher, but excellent writer; wrote *Laws of Ecclesiastical Polity*; 4 books 1594; 5th 1597; 3 books published posthumously (answer to Puritanism).

Hooper, John (ca. 1495—1555). "Father of the Puritans"; Zwinglian; b. at Somersetshire; on the Continent 1540 to 1549; refused to wear the vestments at his consecration as bishop of Gloucester 1550; suffered martyrdom at Gloucester.

Hope. The well-grounded expectation of things desired. The ground of Christian hope is the Word of divine promise. Christian hope is essentially faith concerning things to come; faith looks into the heart of God for a promised hope which is sure and final, the crowning glory of all faith. In heaven hope will be translated into joyous experience (Rom. 8:24, 25; 1 Cor. 13:13; Heb. 11:1; 13:14; 1 Pet. 1:3 f., 13; Tit. 3:7). The hope of the Christian is the fruit of justification (Rom. 5:4, 5), the anchor of his soul (Heb. 6:19); it is his helmet in battle against spiritual foes (Eph. 6:17), inspires to clean living, (1 John 3:3); makes glad in trials (Ps. 43:5; 146:5; Rom. 12:12; Heb. 3:6), and happy in death (Prov. 14:32; 2 Tim. 4:18). See Stalker's discourse on hope in *Theol. Monthly*, 1929, 361; Luther IX: 968; IV:475, 983; II:7; IX:627 ff., 1122; *Trigl.*, 207, 191; Laetsch, *The Abiding Word*, I:204, 208, 219; *Con. Pulpit*, 1936, Vol. VII, 178; Kretzmann, *Pop. Com.*, N. T., II, 662; Reu-Buehring, *Christian Ethics*, 152 ff. (relation to faith and love). JMW

Hopkins, Mark (1802—87). Congregationalist; educator; b. at Stockbridge, Mass.; physician; professor and president of Williams College 1830—87; president of American Board of Foreign Missions; d. at Williamstown; author.

Hopkins, Samuel (1721—1803). Congregationalist; b. at Waterbury, Conn.; pupil of Jonathan Edwards (elder); pastor at Newport, R. I. (d. there); founder of Hopkinsian theology (rejected doctrine of imputation of Christ's righteousness). See *New England Theology*, 2.

Hopkinsianism. See *New England Theology*, 2.

Hormisdas. Pope (514—23); brought about a reunion of the Eastern and Western churches (518).

Horn, E. T. (1850—1915). Liturgical scholar; b. at Easton, Pa.; educated at Gettysburg; pastor in Philadelphia, Charleston, S. C., and Reading, Pa.; professor at Philadelphia Seminary (Mount Airy), 1911—15; author of a number of liturgical works, also of a commentary on several Pauline epistles and of *Summer Sermons*.

Horrible Decree. See *Calvin, John*, 11.

Horst, Henry W. B. May 3, 1864, at Rendsburg, Germany; came to U. S. at age of 17; general contractor at Rock Island, Ill., 1892—1949; member of the Board of Directors of The Lutheran Church — Mo. Syn., 1917—44; honorary mem., 1944—49; co-founder of the Luth. Laymen's League; made comprehensive survey of mission activities in South America, 1928; LL. D., Concordia Seminary, St. Louis; d. Aug. 26, 1949.

Hosanna. Taken from the Hebrew (*hoshia-nah*), meaning: Save (O Lord), Ps. 118:25; a part of the great Hallel *;

also used by the people who went forth from Jerusalem to meet the Lord, Matt. 21:9; now applied to the second part of the Sanctus in the Communion service.

Hosius of Corduba (Cordova in Spain). Friend and counselor of Constantine. Prominent at the Council of Nicaea as a defender of orthodoxy; subscribed an Arian creed at Sirmium (357), which he abjured before his death (359).

Hoskins, Joseph (1745—88). Congregational minister at Bristol for ten years; during last three years of life wrote 384 hymns, among them: "Let Thoughtless Thousands Choose the Road."

Hospices, Christian Inns. These are homes in which fellow Christians who are strangers in a city may find food and lodging. The Christians of early times opened their own homes to such. While this, to a large extent, is still being done (guest room), yet, owing to the rapid increase of population in the cities and the changed housing conditions of our day, it has become almost impossible to accommodate the large number of fellow Christians coming to the cities, and therefore an increasingly large number of hospice homes are being established. These are under the supervision of the Church or some church society. These hospices also serve the purpose of keeping Christians, especially the young, from being lost to the Church.

Hospitalers. See *Military Religious Orders,* a.

Hospitality. In the Orient it has always been regarded a sacred duty to receive, feed, lodge, and protect any traveler who comes to a person's door. Strangers are treated as guests. In the Bible the importance of hospitality (Ger., *Gastfreundschaft*) is often stressed (*e. g.,* Gen. 14:18; 19:1-11; 43: 31-34; 45:16-20; 2 Sam. 9:7-13; 1 Kings 17:10-24; 2 Kings 4:8; Job 31:32; Luke 10:38; 19:1-10; Acts 10:6 ff.; 16:15; Rom. 16:1, 2; 2 Tim. 1:16; 3 John 5:8). It is enjoined (Lev. 19:34; Luke 14:12-14; Rom. 12:13; 1 Pet. 4:9; Heb. 13:2). Its violation was considered a great offense (Judg. 17:21; Luke 16:19-25; Matt. 25: 43 ff.). See Luther I:1133, 1706, 1721; P. Kretzmann, *Pop. Com.,* O. T., II, 727; N. T., II, 662; *Con. Pulpit,* 1936, Vol. VII, 179; Reu-Buehring, *Christian Ethics,* 368 ff.

Hospitals, Sanatoria, Homes for Convalescents and Chronically Ill (Affiliation is indicated as follows: ALC — American Luth. Church; Aug — Augustana Synod; Dan — Danish Lutheran; ELC — Ev. Luth. Church; Ex — Extrasynodical; Int — Intersynodical, *i. e.,* belonging to several synods; LB — Luth. Brethren; LF — Luth. Free Church; Mo — Mo. Synod; SC — Institutions within the Synodical Conference; ULC — United Luth. Church; UE — United Ev. Luth. Church).

California: California, 1414 S. Hope St., Los Angeles (Ex); Loamshire Rest, 1116 Princeton, Santa Monica (Ex); Santa Monica, 1250 16th St., Santa Monica (Ex).

Colorado: Alamosa Comm., 1st and Crestone, Alamosa (Ex); Even-Eber, Brush (Int); Lutheran, Sterling (Ex); Lutheran Sanatorium, 8300 W. 38 Ave., Wheat Ridge, Colo. (SC).

Illinois: Augustana, 411 W. Dickens, Chicago 14 (Aug); Lutheran Deaconess, 1138 N. Leavitt, Chicago (ELC); Walther Memorial, 1116 N. Kedzie, Chicago (SC); Lutheran Hospital, 506 5th Ave., Moline (Aug).

Indiana: Lutheran Hospital, Fort Wayne (Mo).

Iowa: Iowa Lutheran, 700 Parnell St., Des Moines (Aug); Lutheran, Fort Dodge (Ex); Lutheran, Hampton (SC); Lutheran, Sheldon (Ex); Lutheran General, 27th and Pierce, Sioux City (SC); Allen Memorial, Waterloo (Ex).

Michigan: St. Luke's, 1407 James St., Saginaw (Ex).

Minnesota: Bethesda, Crookston (Ex); St. Luke's, 715 S. Mill St., Fergus Falls (Ex); Immanuel, Mankato (Ex); Fairview, 2312 S. 6th St., Minneapolis (Ex); Lutheran Deaconess, 1412 E. 24th St., Minneapolis (LF); St. John's of Red Wing, 1407 4th St., Red Wing (Ex); Bethesda, 559 Capital Blvd., St. Paul (Aug); Bethesda Invalid, 249 E. Ninth St., St. Paul (Aug); St. John's, 390 Mounds Blvd., St. Paul (SC); St. John's, Springfield (ALC); Warren, 57 Wentzel St., Warren (Aug).

Missouri: Trinity Lutheran, 30th & Wyandotte, Kansas City (Aug); Lutheran Conval., 4359 Taft, St. Louis 16 (Mo); Lutheran, 2646 Potomac, Saint Louis 18 (Mo).

Montana: Stillwater Comm., Columbus (Ex); Rosebud Comm., Forsyth (Ex); Lutheran, Jordan (Ex); St. John's Luth., Libby (SC); Toole County, Shelby (Ex); Lutheran, Terry (Ex).

Nebraska: Bethpage, Axtell (Ex); Lutheran, Beatrice (SC); Lutheran, Columbus (Ex); Lutheran, Grand Island (Ex); Lutheran, Norfolk (Ex); Memorial, North Platte (Ex); Lutheran, Oakland (Ex); Immanuel Home, 34th & Fowler Ave., Omaha 11 (Aug); Immanuel Hospital, 34th & Fowler Ave., Omaha 11 (Aug); Lutheran, 24th Ave. & Harney St., Omaha (SC); Lutheran, York (SC).

New Jersey: Lutheran Memorial Hospital, Newark (Ex).

New York: Lutheran, 22 Junius St., Brooklyn 12 (SC); Norw. Luth. Deac., 4520 4th Ave., Brooklyn 20 (ELC); Luth. of Manhatn., 343 Convent Ave., New York 31 (Ex).

North Dakota: Good Samaritan, Ambrose (Ex); St. Luke's, Fargo (Ex); Grafton Deaconess, Grafton (Ex); Grand Forks Deaconess, Grand Forks (Ex); Lutheran, Hazen (Ex); Trinity, Minot (Ex); Northwood Deaconess, Northwood (Ex); Good Samaritan, Rugby (Ex); Wahpeton, 206 Montana Ave., Wahpeton (Ex).

Ohio: Lutheran, 2609 Franklin, Cleveland 13 (SC); Robinwood, 2517 Robinwood, Toledo (Ex); Luther Home, Williston (Ex).

Oregon: Columbia, Astoria (Aug); Emanuel, 2800 N. Commercial, Portland (Aug).

Pennsylvania: River Crest Prev., R. 29, Mont Clare (Ex); Children's, 2100 S. College Ave., Phila. 30 (ULC); Kensington Disp., 157 W. Susquehanna, Phila. 22 (Ex); Passavant Hospital, Reed & Roberts Sts., Pitts. (Ex); Passavant Mem., Rochester (Ex).

South Dakota: Lutheran Hospital, Canova (Ex); Britton, Britton (Ex); Lutheran, Hot Springs (Ex); Luther, Watertown (Ex); Peabody Mem., Webster (Ex).

Texas: Grace Lutheran, 701 S. Zarzamora, San Anton. 7 (ALC).

Wisconsin: Trinity, Ashland (Aug); Luth. Deaconess, Beaver Dam (Ex); Luther, Eau Claire (Ex); La Crosse, 1910 South Ave., La Crosse (SC); Layton Home, 2200 W. Kilbourn, Milwaukee (ALC); Milwaukee Hospital, 2200 W. Kilbourn, Milwaukee (ALC); St. Luke's, 230 W. Madison, Milwaukee, (Ex); Sheboygan Mem., 2633 N. 7th St., Sheboygan (SC); Bethesda Lutheran, Watertown (SC).

Wyoming: Memorial, Powell (Ex).

Virgin Islands: Queen Louise, St. Croix Christiansted (ULC). **HFW-CK**

Host. In the Greek, Roman Catholic, and Lutheran Churches, the consecrated wafers of Communion.

Hotman, Francois (1524—90). French Huguenot jurist; urged France to declare its independence of Rome; fled to Switzerland after the Massacre of St. Bartholomew; wrote *De Statu Ecclesiae, Jurisconsultus, Franco-Gallia,* and other works.

Hottentots. An African race allied to the Bushmen, originally dwelling as far south as the Cape of Good Hope, now hardly more than 50,000 strong. Most of the Hottentots are now semi-civilized. — *Missions.* Sporadic mission work was done by the Dutch in the 17th century. The first organized mission was that of the Moravian George Schmidt, in 1744 and again in 1792, followed by the London Missionary Society in 1799 and the Wesleyan Mission Society in 1816, the Anglican Church in 1847, the Rhenish Mission Society in 1829, and the Berlin Mission Society in 1838. Most of the Hottentots are now united with Christian churches.

Houghteling, James. See *Brotherhood of St. Andrew.*

Hours, Canonical. See *Canonical Hours.*

House of Bishops. See *Protestant Episcopal Church,* 8.

House of David. A small American communistic * sect. The founder, Benjamin Franklin Purnell (b. 1861, Maysville, Ky.), accepted the teachings of Joanna Southcott, 1890, and became a member of the Southcott Colony of Michael Mills in Detroit until its disruption by the police, 1892, because of immoral practices. Later Purnell brought a number of Mills's followers to Benton Harbor, Mich., where he established the Israelite House of David, 1903. He called himself the "Seventh-messenger Angel," "Son of Man," "Younger Brother of Jesus Christ," and taught a grossly materialistic doctrine. He and his followers considered themselves the offspring of the twelve lost tribes of Israel, who are now to be gathered and restored to their proper position as rulers and judges of God's kingdom to be established on this earth. While the bodies of "unbelievers" would not be resurrected and their spirits would be sexless, his converts would be resurrected both in body and soul and lead a blissful existence as men and women, as then all previous restrictions regarding the joys of life would be removed. Communism of goods, vegetarianism, and the wearing of long hair ("like Jesus") are strictly observed. Purnell's immoral practices were uncovered in 1923. Contrary to the society's teachings and belief, Purnell died in 1927. See *Religious Bodies (U. S.), Bibliography.*

House of Deputies. See *Protestant Episcopal Church,* 8.

House of God, the Holy Church of the Living God, The Pillar and Ground of the Truth, House of Prayer for All People. A small colored religious sect founded (1913) by R. A. Johnson in Washington, D. C., on the basis of claimed revelations.

House of the Lord. See *Holiness Bodies,* 2.

House of Prayer. See *Pentecostalism.*

Houtin, Albert (1867—1926). Leader in the Modernist movement in the Roman Catholic Church. Wrote *Histoire du Modernisme catholique.*

Hove, Elling. B. at Northwood, Iowa, March 25, 1863; grad. of Luther College and Concordia Seminary, St. Louis; ordained 1887; prof. at Luther College and at Luther Seminary, St. Paul; member of the Norwegian Lutheran Church. D. Dec. 17, 1927.

How, William Walsham (1823—97). Educated at Oxford; held a number of positions as clergyman, finally that of Bishop of Wakefield; wrote, among others: "O Word of God Incarnate."

Howard, John (1726—90). Prison reformer; studied nature and treatment of the plague; published: *The State of the Prisons in England and Wales, with Preliminary Observations and an Account of Some Foreign Prisons; An Account of the Principal Lazarettos in Europe;* d. of the plague.

Howe, John (1630—1705). "Platonic Puritan"; b. at Leicestershire; chaplain of Cromwell; in Ireland 1671; at Utrecht 1686; pastor in London 1687 (died there); wrote *The Living Temple,* etc.

Howison, George Holmes (1834 to 1916). American philosopher; instructor at Washington University, St. Louis; lectured at Harvard, Concord School, Michigan University; prof. at Massachusetts Institute of Technology and the University of California. Opposed monism; held a philosophical system which he called Personal Idealism.

Hoyer, Otto Daniel August (1849 to 1905). Ed. in Germany and graduated at Northwestern, Watertown, Wis., and in St. Louis; member of first class graduated at Northwestern; pastor at Neenah, Wis., Wisconsin Synod, and St. Paul, Minnesota Synod, 1872 to 1885; director of New Ulm (college and seminary) until 1893; director of Saginaw Seminary; inspector and professor at Northwestern 1905; editor of *Synodalbote* (Minnesota Synod) and *Synodalfreund* (Michigan Synod).

Hoyme, Gjermund. B. Oct. 8, 1847, at Valders, Norway; emigrated to America, 1851; grad. from Augsburg Seminary, 1873; pastor at Duluth, Minn., and Menomonie and Eau Claire, Wis.; pres. of the Norwegian-Danish Conference, 1886—90, and of the United Norwegian Lutheran Church in America, 1890—1902; author; d. June 9, 1902.

Hsin I Hui. "Hsin I" is the name adopted in China by many Lutheran bodies. The two words mean "faith, righteousness." The Missouri Synod and some others transliterate Lutheran with "Ludeh" and use this name. "Hsin I Hui" is the Chinese name for the United Lutheran Church in China. The mission of the U. L. C. is a part of this union. The Union was organized in 1920 by ten bodies on missions, the names of which and their headquarters are as follows: 1) The Board of Foreign Missions of the United Lutheran Church in America, New York; 2) The Augustana Synod Mission, Minneapolis; 3) Berliner Missionsgesellschaft, Berlin; 4) The Danish Lutheran Mission, Copenhagen; 5) The Finnish Mission, Helsingfors; 6) The Board of Foreign Missions of the Norwegian Lutheran Church of America (Evangelical Lutheran Church), Minneapolis; 7) The Norwegian Missionary Society, Norway; 8) Schleswig-Holsteinische Ev.-Luth. Missionsgesellschaft zu Breklum; 9) The Church of Sweden Mission; 10) Ostasien-Mission, Allgemeiner Evangelisch-Protestantischer Missionsverein (Weimar Mission), Berlin. (Max Zschiegner, *CTM,* VI:184.)

Huber Controversy. Samuel Huber, b. 1547 at Burgdorf, Switzerland, 1570 Reformed pastor in his native country, at the Colloquy of Moempelgard (Montbéliard), in 1586, opposed Calvin's doctrine on predestination, for which he was deposed from office. He subscribed to the Formula of Concord and became pastor at Derendingen. His theses on the sacrificial death of Christ for the whole human race, in 1592, brought him a call to the University of Wittenberg as colleague of Polycarp Leyser and Aegidius Hunnius, who hoped to find in him an aggressive opponent of Calvinists and Crypto-Calvinism. Here he taught and defended the universality of election to eternal life and accused his colleagues of Crypto-Calvinism. When various conferences and negotiations with him failed to convince him of his error, he was dismissed from his professorship. After wandering from place to place, an "embittered martyr of universalism," he died in 1624.

Hubert, Konrad (1507—77). Diaconus at St. Thomas in Strassburg; private secretary to the Reformed theologian Buzer; wrote "Allein zu dir, Herr Jesu Christ, mein' Hoffnung steht auf Erden."

Hucbald (ca. 840—930). Follower of Boethius; lived in Flanders; his *Harmonica Institutio* helped perpetuate the ideas and teachings of Boethius. In this treatise the proper sequence of the modes used in Gregorian chant was discussed, as was also their character and structure. The claims formerly made, namely, that in the organum of Hucbald we have the beginnings of counterpoint, have been discarded within the past few decades. Hucbald did not create the organum, but rather used the organum to codify systematically certain theoretical practices of the past. The treatise *Musica Enchiriadis,* the oldest known treatise on part and many-voiced music, once attributed to Hucbald, is today known to have been written by the German abbot Hoger von Werden (d. 902).

Huebmaier, Balthasar (ca. 1485 to 1528). B. at Friedberg. Studied at Freiburg. Held various pastorates, professing the Reformed faith; later adopted Anabaptist doctrines; established an Anabaptist community at Nikolsburg in Moravia. He was burned at Vienna.

Huebner, Johann (1668 — 1731). Studied at Leipzig; rector of the Gymnasium at Merseburg, Hamburg, and Johanneum; his *Zweimal 52 biblische Historien und Fragen* popularized the use of the Bible story in instruction; also wrote *Die ganze Historie der Reformation in fuenfzig Reden, nebst einem Schauspiele von Bekehrung der Sachsen zum Christentum,* rendered Thomas à Kempis' *Imitation of Christ* in German verse.

Huegel, Baron Friedrich (1852 to 1925). British Roman Catholic theologian; founded *London Society for the Study of Religion;* his works centered in mystical religion (*Mystical Element of Religion*).

Huegli, J. A. B. Jan. 23, 1831, in the Palatinate; studied theology in Saint Louis; was ordained 1856; served in Jonesborough, Ill., Pittsburgh, Frankenmuth (as assistant to Rev. Roebbelen), Saginaw; pastor of Trinity, Detroit, from 1860 to the day of his death, Apr. 12, 1904. Organized eight congregations in and near Detroit; one of the founders of the Deaf-mute Institute; contributor to *Lutheraner;* president of Northern District of Missouri Synod 1872—1875.

Huelsemann, Johann. Born 1602 at Esens, Ostfriesland; d. at Leipzig 1661; 1629 professor at Wittenberg; represented Lutheranism at the colloquy of Thorn 1645; went to Leipzig in 1646 as professor and pastor of Nicolai; a zealous Lutheran against Calvinism and Calixt; his best-known works: *Extensio Breviarii Theologici; Dialysis Apologetica* (against Calixt), *Calvinismus Irreconciliabilis.*

Hugo de Sancto Caro. B. end of 12th century; d. 1263; very active theological writer; division of Bible into chapters wrongly ascribed to him.

Hugo of St. Victor (monastery and school at Paris). Ca. 1097—1141. Founder of the medieval mysticism of France, combining mysticism and dialectics in the treatment of theology.

Huguenots. Originally a nickname applied to a party which had its beginning with the Reformation in Germany, a few adherents springing up in France. These French reformers received powerful support from Margaret of Valois, sister of the king, and Lutheran societies were organized by Gerhard Roussel and Jacob Lefèvre. The circulation of Lefèvre's New Testament by the thousands throughout France still further increased the number of reformers. In 1533 Calvin began to preach the new doctrine, and his efforts furthered the success of the French Protestants, who now began to be known by the name of Huguenots. Soon, however, persecution began, and the Huguenots, headed by Antoine de Bourbon, the king of Navarre, the Condés, and the Colignys, formed a strong opposition. When the Huguenots were prohibited from preaching, they took up arms to achieve religious liberty. With an occasional interval of peace or a hollow truce, the struggle went on for years. The most notable events were the Massacre of St. Bartholomew, Aug. 24, 1572, in which 5,000 Protestants were murdered in one night in Paris; and the Revocation of the Edict of Nantes, Oct. 22, 1685, which culminated in a systematic persecution lasting about twenty-four years. Public worship was prohibited; ministers were to leave France in fifteen days or embrace Roman Catholicism. Thousands, also some educated ministers, were sent to the galleys and died of hardship; thousands died in prison, and hundreds were cruelly executed. Some hundreds of thousands turned Catholic, while several hundred thousand left France despite the fact that emigration was forbidden. It has been estimated that about 100,000 found homes in Holland, 100,000 in England, Ireland, and America, 25,000 in Switzerland, and 75,000 in Germany. In many parts of France the persecuted people took all risks and met secretly for worship. The persecution continued till about 1787, when an edict of toleration was secured. See *France*, 5.

P. F. Willert, *Henry of Navarre and the Huguenots in France*, Putnam's, 1924; C. W. Baird, *History of the Huguenot Emigration to America*, Dodd, Mead & Co., N. Y., 1885.

Human Nature of Christ. See *Christ Jesus*, I.

Humanism. See *Renaissance; Reformation*, 3.

Humanism, the New. A philosophic process midway between mechanistic reduction of the human being to the animal level and supernaturalism. It seeks to emphasize the ethical nature of human experience and the freedom of man to be subject to that direction. Through Paul Elmer More it has been related to Christian concepts, but is essentially rational.

Humanism, Sixteenth-Century German. A movement among German schoolmen designed to correct decay of Latin and Greek style induced by Scholasticism.* In one sense the German humanists had some kinship with Erasmus * and the English humanists John Colet and Thomas More. Strictly speaking, the movement was confined to a specific area and to intellectual interests not strongly influenced by Italy and England. The movement coincided with a revival of interest in the literature of classical antiquity, which was fostered by editions of the classics and of the New Testament based on original manuscripts. Initiator of the movement was Rudolf Agricola, who promoted teaching by means of the gathering of material around common places, or *loci*, instead of the Scholastic method of disputation. Many humanists despised Scholastic studies and degrees and courted the favor of German princes through their verses. The movement coalesced through the dispute of John Reuchlin with the Dominican inquisitors on the validity of Hebrew studies, which resulted in the satirical *Letters of Obscure Men*. Humanism was attached to the Lutheran movement through Philip Melanchthon,* the *praeceptor Germaniae*, who was entrusted by Luther with the task of developing an educational system, under the patronage of the German princes, which would adequately implement the evangelical Reformation. Melanchthon founded the system of humanistic intermediate schools and of classical college studies which became traditional in German Lutheranism as basic for higher education in general and the training for the ministry in particular. Humanism emphasized graceful and apt style on the basis of classical models, and ethics reflecting the Natural Law common to classical as well as Christian thought. It provided linguistic tools for Scriptural studies. Its deference to philosophical method and natural ethics, however, curtailed, to some extent, the vitality of Luther's radical grasp of the Gospel. RRC

F. Paulsen, *Geschichte des gelehrten Unterrichts*, Leipzig, 1896; Peter Peterson, *Geschichte der arist. Philosophie im prot. Deutschland*, Leipzig, 1921; articles by Paul Joachimsen.

Humanitarianism. See *Social Work*.

Hume, David (1711—76). English philosopher and historian; a skeptic in philosophy and one of the leading English Deists. The antichristian movements of the 18th century were to a great extent based on his philosophy.

Humeral Veil (R. C.). A veil worn by the subdeacon at the Mass.

Humiliati. A Roman Catholic religious order probably founded by Johannes Oldratus (12th c.).

Humiliation of Christ. See *Christ Jesus,* II, 1.

Humility. Humility, "the gateway to Christianity," is lowliness of mind and is akin to meekness, modesty, self-abasement. It is the finest Christian virtue, the opposite of pride, a virtue "preached by many, liked by all, practiced by few." Praised in the Bible: Prov. 15:33; 18:12; 27:2; Col. 3:12; Eph. 4:2; enjoined Matt. 18:3, 4; James 4:6, 10, etc.; exemplified Gen. 18:27; 2 Sam. 7:18; Dan. 2:30; 1 Cor. 15:10; 2 Cor. 3:5; 12:7; Eph. 3:8; 1 Tim. 1:15; Luke 7:6, 7; John 1:27; 3:30. Christians should be humble a) before God, Gen. 32:10; Micah 6:8; Matt. 8:15, 17; Luke 5:8; 18:13; James 4:6, 10; 1 Pet. 5:5, 6; b) before men, Gen. 41:16; 1 Sam. 18:18; Luke 1:43; John 13:5-15; Rom. 12:3, 10, 16; Eph. 4:2; Phil. 2:3 ff. Cp. Luther, IX:1282, 1308 f.; VII:141, 1392 f.; XII:386, 686; *Trigl.,* 349, 27; 723, 90; *Concordia Pulpit,* 1936, Vol. VII, 180, 257, 271; Kretzmann, *Pop. Com.,* O.T., II, 727; N.T., II, 662; Reu-Buehring, *Christian Ethics,* pp. 210, 221 ff.

Humoral Doctrine. See *Psychology,* B 2.

Humphreys, Joseph (b. 1720). Associated first with the Wesleys, then with Whitefield, preaching at Bristol and elsewhere; wrote "Blessed Are the Sons of God."

Hungarian Confession. See *Reformed Confessions,* E 6.

Hungary. Originally an independent kingdom in the Danube basin, then united with Austria; since 1918 again independent, but greatly reduced in territory. It was occupied by the fierce Magyars, or Hungarians, toward the end of the 9th century and opened to Christianity under Stephen I (995—1038), called "the Saint," who overthrew heathenism by force and persuasion and attached the rising Church closely to Rome. During the Reformation period, Protestantism made such headway that toward the end of the 16th century the bulk of the population had accepted the new doctrines. Luther's writings were eagerly read among the German element of the population, Hungarian students went to Wittenberg and returned to spread the teachings of Luther among their people. On the other hand, the writings of Calvin found favor with the majority of the Hungarians proper, and in 1557 a Calvinistic creed was adopted. The Saxons of Transylvania adopted the Augsburg Confession. Thus the separation between the two churches was complete. The Counter Reformation, under the leadership of the Jesuits and abetted by the Hapsburg rulers, inaugurated a series of persecutions against the Hungarian Protestants, which, according to some authorities, were even more cruel and relentless than the persecutions of the French Huguenots in the days of Louis XIV. The famous Edict of Toleration, issued by Joseph II in 1791, granted the adherents of both the Helvetic Confession and the Augsburg Confession freedom of worship, although numerous annoying and humiliating restrictions were not removed until the 20th c.

Hunnius, Aegidius (1550—1603). B. at Winnenden; d. at Wittenberg. Studied at Tuebingen. As professor at Marburg, he labored to restore Lutheran orthodoxy. Called to Wittenberg, he opposed Calvinism in Saxony. He was called to other German territories for the same purpose. His writings are largely polemical.

Hunnius, Nikolas (1558—1643). Son of Aegidius. B. at Marburg; d. at Luebeck. Studied at Wittenberg. Joined the faculty there, 1609; superintendent of Eilenburg, 1612; professor at Wittenberg, 1617; pastor at Luebeck, 1623; then superintendent, 1624. Like his father, he was a defender of orthodox Lutheranism against Calvinism and Roman Catholicism.

Hunt, John (1812—1848). B. at Balderton, Nottinghamshire; d. on Fiji Islands; studied at Wesleyan Theological Institute, Hoxton; went as Wesleyan missionary to the cannibals of the Fiji Islands and had great success.

Hunt, Robert. See *Protestant Episcopal Church,* 1.

Hunt, William Holman (1827—1910). Belonged to the brotherhood of Preraffaelites and aimed at detailed and uncompromising truth to nature; among his paintings: "The Light of the World" ("Christ Teaching in the Temple").

Huntingdon, Countess of (1707—91). Founder of the Calvinistic Methodists. She attended meetings held by Wesley in Fetter Lane, and through her social position was able to bring Whitefield into contact with men of the upper classes. At the death of Whitefield she became trustee of his institutions in Georgia.

Hunton, William Lee. B. Feb. 16, 1864, Morrisburgh, Ont.; ed. Thiel Col-

lege 1886; A. M. from same 1889; Ph. D.
1899; D. D. 1920; grad. Phila. Theol.
Sem. 1889; ordained 1889; pastor at
Amanda, Ohio, 1889—91; Rochester,
N. Y., 1891—94; Buffalo 1894—98; Wilkes-Barre, Pa., 1898—1901; Chicago
1901—06; instructor Chicago Theol. Sem.
1902—06; Supt. Chicago Syn. Missions
1902—06; in 1901 he became assoc. editor
of *Luth. Graded S. S. Lessons* and *Luth.
Lesson Commentary;* assoc. editor of
The Lutheran, 1907—19, *Teacher Train-
ing Magazine,* 1914—21, *The Parish
School,* 1921—30; editor of *Luth. Mes-
senger,* 1908—18, *Luth. Young Folks,*
1908—30; literature mgr. of the Gen-
Council Pub. House, 1919—30; member
of the committee on common hymnal
for English Lutherans; secy. of the
Parish and Church School Bd. of the
U. L. C. A., 1920—30; Dir. of the Mt. Airy
Summer School, 1914—26. Author:
*Favorite Hymns; I Believe; Facts of
Our Faith;* co-editor *Parish School
Hymnal and Service Book.* D. Oct. 12,
1930.

Hunziger, August Wilhelm (1871 to
1920). B. at Dreiluetzow (Mecklenburg). Pastor in Mecklenburg; professor at Leipzig and Erlangen; pastor in
Hamburg. For a time he was an exponent of a more conservative Lutheranism; he changed to a more liberal position during the First World
War and the subsequent revolution in
Germany.

Hupfeld, Hermann. See *Higher
Criticism,* 15.

Hurban, Josef Miloslav. See *Slovakia, Lutheran Theology in,* 2.

Hus, John. 1. A forerunner of the
Reformation and martyr for the truth;
b. 1373 (?) at Husinec, Bohemia; studied
at the University of Prague; became
a priest in 1400 and in 1402 rector of
the university and preacher at Bethlehem Chapel, where the Czech language was used. A disciple of Wyclif,
he saw the more clearly the need of
purging the Church of popish errors
and corruption and began by denouncing the immorality of the laity and,
particularly, of the clergy. Wyclifism
spreading over the whole country, the
Pope ordered Wyclif's books burned
and Hus and his adherents banned.
Hus became the bolder in his accusations of the Church, and the interdict
was pronounced against Prague. Denouncing the crusade preached by Pope
John XXIII against the King of Naples,
a supporter of the antipope, and the

shameless traffic in indulgences incident
thereto as sinful, Hus was put under
the great church ban with all its curses,
1412. Appealing from the Pope to the
judgment of Jesus Christ, he left
Prague, king and people for him, and
wrote his book *On the Church,* a reproduction of Wyclif's *On the Church;*
and the movement spread beyond the
borders of Bohemia. Hus stood for
the supreme and only authority of
the Scriptures and held that the Church
is the body of the elect, consisting not
merely of Pope and clergy, that Christ
is its Head, not the fallible Pope; that
obedience to the Pope is not necessary
for salvation; that external membership
in the Church and ecclesiastical offices
are not infallible signs of election.

2. Unlike Wyclif he did not reject
transubstantiation nor, absolutely, the
invocation of saints and prayers for
the dead; and though he preached Christ
as the only Savior, he yet gave a place
to works in the justification of the sinner. Even so the Church of Rome could
not endure his testimony. He was cited
before the Council of Constance, speedily cast into loathsome prisons despite
the safe-conduct granted by Emperor
Sigismund and confirmed by Pope John
("no faith ought to be observed toward
a heretic"), and after three public hear-
ings, the only object of which was to
bully him into recanting, he was, on
July 6, 1415, condemned as a Wycliffian
heretic and, as the hypocritical formula runs, delivered into the hands of
the secular power. Protesting to the
last: "In the truth of the Gospel, which
I have written, taught, and preached,
I will die today with gladness," he was,
on the same day, burned alive at the
stake, and his ashes were cast into the
Rhine. "In John Hus the Holy Ghost
was very powerful," says Luther. *Jerome of Prague,* his devoted follower,
suffered the same death, May 30, 1416.
Hus wrote a number of Bohemian and
Latin treatises, numerous hymns, and
revised the old Bohemian version of the
Bible. His work could not effect a
Reformation, but did serve to bring out
the great need of it.

D. S. Schaff, *John Huss: His Life,
Teachings and Death — After Five
Hundred Years,* Scribner's, N. Y., 1915;
M. Spinka, *John Hus and the Czech
Reform,* 1941.

Huschke, Geo. Phil. Edw. (1801—86).
Prof. of jurisprudence at Rostock (1821)
and Breslau (1827); a leader among
the independent Lutherans of Breslau;
wrote *Wort und Sakrament die Fak-*

toren der Kirche, in which he advanced his belief that the Church is an organism formed by the Sacraments and hence should be kept independent of the state.

Husmann, F. W. B. Nov. 9, 1807, at Nordel, Hanover; teacher in Bremen; won through Wyneken's *Appeal;* his first colaborer in and near Fort Wayne; a zealous missionary; first secretary of the Missouri Synod; pastor of several parishes in Indiana; 1863 pastor in Euclid, Ohio; d. May 4, 1881.

Husserl, Edmund (1859—1938). German philosopher; gave to "phenomenology" the connotation which it generally has in the 20th century; most important work: *Logische Untersuchungen.*

Hussites. A general name for the followers of Hus. The fierce indignation aroused throughout Bohemia by the execution of Hus and Jerome, the refusal by the Council of Constance of the use of the cup — introduced during the imprisonment of Hus with his approval — as heretical, and the determination of the Hussites to defend their faith to the utmost, resulted in grave disorders and civil war; and the refusal of the estates to have Sigismund, "the word breaker," the brother of Wenzeslaus (d. 1419), for their king and the mobilizing of a crusade by the Pope against the "rebels and heretics" (1420) brought on the Hussite Wars. Both parties of the Hussites, the moderates, called Calixtines or Utraquists, who demanded freedom of preaching, Communion in both kinds, reduction of the clergy to apostolic poverty, and the repression of mortal sins (Prague Articles), and the radicals, the Taborites, who, in addition, rejected transubstantiation, the adoration of the saints, intercession for the dead, and, besides this, every custom not commanded in the Bible, demanded that the state regulate its affairs by the Bible, were given to the chiliastic and communistic vagaries, and set out to destroy the enemies of God with the sword; made common cause against the invaders, vanquished them again and again, and carried the war into the border states. The crushing defeat suffered by the fifth crusading army in 1431 blighted all hopes of both Emperor and Pope of subjecting the Bohemians by force. Negotiations between the Council of Basel and the Hussites resulted in the acceptance (1433) by the Utraquists of the *Compactata* of Prague, which

granted the administration of Holy Communion in both kinds, conceding the other points of the Articles in an illusory manner. The Taborites rejected the agreement and were wellnigh annihilated (1434). The majority of the Utraquists ultimately returned to the Catholic fold; a fraction merged with the Bohemian Brethren.

Huth, Carl Frederick Emil. B. Nov. 30, 1857, at Nieden, Germany; graduated at Concordia Seminary, St. Louis, 1881; professor at Concordia College, Milwaukee, Wis., 1881—1926; D. D. (St. Louis); d. April 23, 1926.

Huther, Joh. Edw. (1807—80). Pastor at Wittenfoerden, Germany; wrote exegesis of Pastoral and Catholic Epistles in *Meyer's Commentary.*

Hutten, Ulrich von (1488—1523). Prominent Humanist; made known in Germany Valla's work on the forged Donation of Constantine, which influenced Luther; wrote fiercely against Rome; offered his help to Luther in 1520, which was declined; entered the service of Charles V, but quit after the Edict of Worms became known; declined pay from Francis I of France and fled to Switzerland after Sickingen's death; d. miserably after his venereal disease had broken out anew.

Hutter, Elias (1553—1605 or 1609). Orientalist, Biblical scholar, professor at Leipzig. Produced the Hamburg and the Nuremberg polyglots; founded a school of languages at Nuremberg.

Hutter, Leonhard (1563—1616). B. near Ulm; professor at Wittenberg, 1596; one of the foremost representatives and defenders of sound Lutheranism, *"Lutherus redonatus";* his best-known works: *Compendium Locorum Theologicorum* (in numerous editions and translations), *Concordia Concors,* and *Loci Communes Theologici.*

Hutterian Brethren. See *Mennonite Bodies,* 3.

Huxley, Thomas Henry (1825—95). English biologist; b. near London; d. at Eastbourne; lectured on biology and related subjects at various London institutions and held several government positions; embraced Darwinism and became a skeptic, rejecting Christianity completely, and engaged in a warfare against Christian beliefs, a promoter of Agnosticism; wrote: *Man's Place in Nature* (1863); *Elementary Physiology* (1866).

Huyck, Jan. See *Reformed Church* 4 b.

Hyacinth, Father (Loyson Charles). Liberal Catholic theologian of France; b. at Orleans 1827; priest; professor of philosophy and dogmatics; joined successively the Dominican and Carmelite orders; eloquent preacher; highly esteemed by Pius IX; broke with Rome in 1869; condemned the papal syllabus of 1864 and the infallibility dogma; temporarily pastor of an old Catholic church at Geneva; established an independent "Gallican Church" in Paris; became a traveling lecturer in 1884; d. 1908.

Hyde, William Dewitt (1858—1917). Ed. at Harvard, Union Theological Seminary, Andover Seminary; president of Bowdoin College. He wrote extensively on ethics and practical idealism (*Practical Ethics; Practical Idealism; From Epicurus to Christ; Self-Measurement*); Congregationalist.

Hylomorphism. The theory in philosophy which holds that all material things are constituted of two principles. The one (G. *hyle*) remains the same and the other (G. *morphe*) is separated by change.

Hylozoism. A theory in philosophy which holds that life is a part of matter.

Hymnody, Christian. (*Historical.*) 1. From the evidence of the New Testament, psalms, hymns, and spiritual songs were in use in the Christian Church from the beginning (Eph. 5:19; Col. 3:16). But we have no evidence of the actual composition of hymns for use in public worship until the second century, when several writers refer to them. 2. The very earliest extant hymn seems to be that quoted by Duffield, a stanza to the Trinity: "My hope is God, my refuge is the Lord, My shelter is the Holy Ghost: be Thou, O Holy Three, adored!" Another very ancient hymn is that whose translation is now in common use: "Shepherd of Tender Youth." It was in the second and at the beginning of the third century that Bardesanes and his son Harmonius tried to spread their Gnostic speculations by means of hymns. To counteract the influence of this heretical move, Ephraem the Syrian, a little more than a century afterward, wrote many thousands of hymns, a fact which caused him to be called "Lyre of the Holy Ghost." A hymn by him which is still in use is one "On the Nativity of Our Lord." Other writers of the Orien-

tal Church whose hymns are still known and in use were Clement of Alexandria, Methodius, Gregory of Nazianzen, Synesius, later St. Andrew of Crete, St. John of Damascus, St. Cosmas, St. Theodore, and others. Greek hymnody is characterized by its objectiveness and by its faculty of sustained praise.

3. The Latin Church, from about the fifth century to the Reformation, produced a great number of singers, some of whose hymns are in common use to this day, also in translations and paraphrases. The choir is opened by Hilary of Poitiers, whose best-known hymn is *Lucis Largitor Splendide* ("Thou Splendid Giver of the Light"). Then follow Ambrosius, who wrote *O Lux Beata Trinitas* ("O Trinity of Blessed Light"); Ennodius, with his *Christe, Salvator Omnium* ("O Christ, the Savior of All"); Caelius Sedulius, whose *Hostis Herodes Impie* ("The Star Proclaims the King Is Here") is still a favorite; Fortunatus, by whom we have *Vexilla Regis Prodeunt* ("The Royal Banners Forward Go"); and Gregory the Great, whose best hymn seems to be *Rex Christe, Factor Omnium* ("O Christ, the Heaven's Eternal King").

4. In the Middle Ages at least a few names stand out prominently. Beda Venerabilis wrote *Hymnum Canamus Gloriae* ("A Hymn of Glory Let Us Sing"); some poet of the ninth century, possibly Rhabanus Maurus, *Veni, Creator Spiritus* ("Come, God, Creator, Holy Ghost"); the anonymous sequence hymn *Veni, Sancte Spiritus* ("Come, Holy Spirit"); to Bernard of Clairvaux a number of poems to the suffering Savior are ascribed; *Salve Caput Cruentatum*, of the 13th century, proved an inspiration to Paul Gerhardt for his "O Sacred Head, Now Wounded." Adam of St. Victor was the author of *Quem Pastores Laudavere* ("Whom the Shepherds Praised with Gladness"); Thomas of Celano, of the overwhelming *Dies Illa* ("Day of Wrath, O Day of Mourning"); Thomas Aquinas, of the well-known sequence *Lauda, Sion, Salvatorem* ("Zion, Lift Thy Voice and Sing"); an anonymous author wrote the appealing *Stabat Mater Dolorosa* ("At the Cross, Her Station Keeping"). Many hymns of the Middle Ages, translated or paraphrased at the time of the Reformation, are still used today.

5. Although the official language of the Church in the medieval period was Latin, hymns in the vernacular had been in use in Germany and the sur-

rounding countries for several centuries. Among such *Leisen*, as they were called, because they ended with *Kyrieleis* (Lord, have mercy), we have "Christ ist erstanden," "Gelobet seist du, Jesu Christ," and others. But the movement begun by Luther and his co-workers put hymns in the vernacular into the mouths of the entire congregation. Luther himself wrote thirty-six hymns and spiritual songs, helped to issue his first hymnal in 1524, encouraged others to write hymns, and fostered the cause of congregational singing in every possible way. The result was that thousands of hymns were written before the end of the century, many of them of extraordinary beauty and power, among the foremost singers being the Nuernberg school, with Spengler at their head, those of southern Germany, among whom were Huber and Schalling, those of central and northern Germany, among whom Decius and Ringwaldt take high rank. Other poets, such as Mathesius, N. Herman, Herberger, and Nicolai, followed.

6. The second great era of Lutheran hymn writing came in the seventeenth century, with Heermann, Rist, and Rinckart leading the van, and Paul Gerhardt reaching the highest stage since Luther. Later came men like Neumark, Homburg, and Albinus. Since the time of Pietism but few hymns in the real Lutheran objective style have been produced, some of the foremost authors being Scriver, Rodigast, Herrnschmidt, and Crasselius.

7. Protestant hymnody in England produced some veritable gems, especially at the time of the Wesleys, the most popular in common use being noted under the respective authors.

8. In America the sweet singers of Israel have also not been silent, the most prominent among them being Doane, Coxe, Muhlenberg, Phillips Brooks, Dwight, Alexander, Dexter, Wolcott, Harbaugh, Bethune, and a number of authors in the Lutheran Church, who have produced both original hymns and very acceptable translations, such as C. P. Krauth, Mrs. Spaeth, Schaeffer, Welden, Seiss, Loy, Schuette, Crull, and others. The lyre of Lutheran singers in America has but been tuned, but its songs are increasing at a creditable rate.

J. Julian, *Dictionary of Hymnology*, London, 1925 (former ed., 1882, 1907); Louis F. Benson, *The Hymnody of the Christian Church*, New York, 1927; W. Douglas, *Church Music in History and Practice*, New York, 1937; F. Blume, *Die Evangelische Kirchenmusik*, Potsdam, 1931; Clemens Blume with G. M. Dreves wrote *Analecta Hymnica Medii Aevi*, Leipzig, 1886—1922; E. Eckhardt, *Concordance to the Evangelical Lutheran Hymnbook*, CPH, 1929; H. v. Fallersleben, *Geschichte des deutschen Kirchenliedes bis auf Luthers Zeit*, Hannover, 1861; A. F. W. Fischer, *Das deutsche Ev. Kirchenlied des 17. Jahrhunderts*, Guetersloh, 1904—16 (also wrote *Kirchenlieder Lexicon*, Gotha, 1878—79); F. J. E. Raby, *History of Christian-Latin Poetry from the Beginning to the Close of the Middle Ages*, Oxford, 1927; F. Spitta, *Das deutsche Kirchenlied*, Gadow, 1912; E. Schmidt, *Fuehrer durch das neue Gesangbuch*, Erlangen, 1936; L. E. P. Wackernagel, *Der evangelische Kirchengesang*, Stuttgart, 1841; J. Westphal, *Das evangelische Kirchenlied nach seiner geschichtlichen Entwicklung*, Berlin, n. d.; C. v. Winterfeld, *Der evangelische Kirchengesang*, Leipzig, 1843—47.

Hymns of All Churches. See *Radio Evangelism*, 5.

Hypatia. Head of the Neoplatonic school at Alexandria; one of the most eloquent advocates of heathenism; mobbed and murdered by a band of Christian fanatics in 415.

Hyperdulia. See *Latria*.

Hypocrisy. In Greek the word "hypocrite" originally meant "playing the part of an actor on the stage"; the Bible has given it the meaning of dissimulating one's real character or belief, professing and pretending to be what one is not ("saints without and devil within"). Cp. Prov. 21:27; Is. 1:13-15; 29:13; Mal. 1:6-14; Matt. 6:1-5, 16; 7:5, 21; 15:7-9; 16:3; 23; Luke 11: 39-52; Rom. 2:2; 2 Tim. 3:5; Jas. 2: 14-26; Jude 12. Examples: Matt. 15:1-9; 22:18; 26:25; Luke 20:21 f.; John 18: 28-31; Acts 5:1-10. Hypocrites are found in the visible churches, but are not members of the Invisible Church. They are counterfeit Christians. Their punishment indicated Matt. 24:51. Cp. Luther IX:156, 1007, 1166; XXII:622; *Trigl.*, p. 1265; *Concordia Pulpit*, 1936, Vol. VII, 182; Walther, *Brosamen*, 195; F. Pieper, *Chr. Dog.*, III:484; P. Kretzmann, *Pop. Com.*, O. T., II, 333; N. T., II, 662.

Hypostatic (Hypostatical) Union. The term "hypostatic" is derived from the Greek noun *hypostasis,* which means person. The expression "hypostatic union" means "personal union" and denotes the union of Christ's two natures in His person (hypostasis). The expression stresses the fact that

the Son of God received into His divine person our human nature, so that by virtue of the personal union in His one and undivided person the divine and the human nature are most intimately and permanently united.

I

Icaria. See *Communistic Societies,* 5.

Iceland. Area, 39,809 sq. mi.; population, 144,293 (1951). Visited by Irish monks ca. 800, and Dicuil, in 825, speaks of "Thyle ultima." But Norwegians wiped out all traces of Christianity. About 980 Thorwalds Kodranson brought Bishop Friedrich from Saxony, who preached for five years and then had to return. Under King Olaf Trygvesson, 995—1000, many missionaries came by way of Norway, and in 1020 Christianity became the state religion under the Archbishop of Hamburg-Bremen, later under Lund, from 1152 under Nidaros. In 1261 Norway conquered all of Iceland, which fell to Denmark in 1387. Gizur Einarsson studied at Wittenberg and in 1540 was made Bishop of Slataholt and reformed the country according to Bugenhagen's Church Order for Denmark. Oddur Gottskalksson rendered the New Testament into Icelandic in 1540. Christian III of Denmark pushed the work with force. The Bishop at Reykjavik has under him nineteen provosts, and 180 pastors labor in 308 parishes. Observers tell us the Icelanders surpass all other European peoples in widely spread mental and moral education. — Home rule began 1874; independent republic since 1918. The national church is the Lutheran; complete religious liberty. The population is almost exclusively Lutheran.

Icelandic Congregation in New Iceland. See *Canada, Lutheranism in,* 13.

Icelandic Synod of America. See *Canada, Lutheranism in,* 13; *United Lutheran Church, Synods of,* 6.

Icon. A holy picture, usually in miniature, mosaic, statuette, or the like, in the Greek Church, representing Christ, the Virgin Mary, or some saint, and profusely ornamented with jewels; used in a superstitious manner.

Iconoclastic Controversy. A quarrel between members of the Eastern and the Western Church arising from the

fact that church images, especially statues, were used for purposes of adoration, pagan concepts, customs, and forms of worship being introduced. As a consequence the opposition to image worship became acute, particularly under Léo the Isaurian (emperor, 717 to 741), whose edicts of 726 and 730 attempted to put an end to the existing abuses by preventing all veneration of the icons and the superstition connected with them. When the emperor met with opposition, more severe measures were proposed. In the West the movement was emphatically opposed by Popes Gregory II and Gregory III. When parts of northern Italy broke with the emperor, Leo struck back by annexing Illyricum to the see of Constantinople and confiscating the papal revenues in southern Italy. A synod held at Constantinople, in 754, supported Emperor Constantine V, condemning all image worship. Under Leo IV a period of toleration ensued, and under Irene, the guardian of her infant son Constantine VI, the images, or icons, were practically restored. During the reign of Charlemagne the Caroline Books stated the objections to the reverence given to images. At the Council of Nicaea, in 787, iconoclasm was officially condemned, the resolution declaring that the images were to be regarded with respectful reverence, but that true worship was to be reserved for God alone. The controversy broke out once more in the ninth century, especially during the reign of Theophilus, but the early death of the emperor restored peace.

Id. See *Psychology,* J 7.

Idealism. The monistic system of philosophy which ascribes existence to ideas or thought perceptions rather than to material objects. The essence of the world as a whole and of its various parts does not consist in the phenomena that can be perceived with the senses, but in the "ideas" of these external perceptions. The philosophy of Plato was idealistic. The metaphysical idealism of Plato holds that there existed in the divine mind ideas, patterns, according to which individual things are formed. Reality proper does not belong to the individual tree, but to the archetype of the tree, the idea, of which the tree is but a perishable copy. The degree of reality attributed to any phenomenal form is to be measured on the scale in which it embodies the original idea. Modern psychological idealism endeavors to answer the question: Do things exist in themselves (realism), or do only the ideas we have of them exist? There is no reality independent of consciousness. A person cannot be sure of the reality of the tree in the yard, but only of his personal perception, mental picture, idea, of the tree. — Modern idealism was developed especially by German philosophers: Leibnitz,* Kant * (critical or transcendental idealism), Fichte * (subjective idealism), Schelling * (objective idealism), Hegel * (absolute idealism). It may also be a factor in shaping the philosophy of Christian Science. Idealism is opposed to realism, which asserts that objects exist independent of a conscious subject. One phase of realism is materialism.*

W. E. Hocking, *Types of Philosophy*, Scribner's, 1939; J. Royce, *The Religious Aspect of Philosophy*, Houghton-Mifflin, 1885.

Idiomatum (Idiomata). A term denoting an attribute or property, and used in Christology in the phrase *communicatio idiomatum*, or communication of attributes, resulting from the communion of natures *(communio naturarum)* in Christ by virtue of the personal union. When the Son of God assumed into His person true human nature, He assumed also the properties which belong to human nature (to be a creature, to be born, to suffer and die, to ascend and descend, to move about, etc.). All who deny the communication of attributes must deny also the personal union or the paramount mystery that the Logos was made flesh. The term *idiomata*, used in Christology, is understood in a wider sense, denoting not only the natural properties themselves, but also what they do and what they suffer *(actiones et passiones)*, by which the properties assert themselves (to create — to be created; to give life — to lose life; etc.).

Idolatry. 1. An act of false worship by which a person reveres and serves a strange god in place of, or in addition

to, the one true, Triune God, as revealed in the Bible. This idolatry may take various forms. It may consist in this, that a person believes in, worships, or fears, false gods, or idols, without ever having known anything about the one true God (Gal. 5:20). In this instance the heathen do not even try to follow the remnant of the natural knowledge of God in their hearts (Rom. 1:21), or they retain only a dim consciousness of one Supreme Being, who alone ought to be worshiped (cp. Acts 17:27). Others, like the Children of Israel, having known the true God, deliberately left Him and His worship for the sake of idols, making themselves molten images and worshiping the host of heaven (2 Kings 17:9-18). In this way they replaced the worship of the Lord by the service of false gods, thereby becoming guilty of gross idolatry.

2. A peculiar form of idolatry, closely connected with the gross variety, is that by which men presume to know and to worship the true God, but at the same time serve also other gods or creatures, which take the place of God in one way or another. We read of the people of Samaria, shortly after the king of Assyria had placed settlers from various Asiatic provinces there: "They feared the Lord and served their own gods, after the manner of the nations whom they carried away from thence" (2 Kings 17:33). The Lord plainly states: "I will not give My glory unto another" (Is. 48:11). He will suffer no other god beside Him, in His place and in addition to Him.

3. A further form of idolatry is the practice of having a picture, a statue, or some other representation which is intended to be a visible reminder of God and is honored with a worship more or less honestly having as its object God Himself. Of such a nature may have been the golden calf cast by Aaron. A similar idea may have attached to the two golden calves of Jeroboam (1 Kings 12:28-30). It may have been the idea which possessed the heart of Micah of Mount Ephraim when he had a graven image and a molten image cast for himself and caused a Levite of Bethlehem-Judah to become his priest (Judg. 17). It shows that a person may, with what seems to him a good intention, set up an image in the place of the true God and yet be fully guilty of gross idolatry in the sight of God. Thus the giving of divine honor to saints is a form of idolatry, also the substituting, in prayer, of some

imaginary deity, such as the "Supreme Architect of the Universe" and similar lodge idols.

4. The least apparent form of idolatry is that known as "fine" idolatry. It includes every form of behavior by which a creature is given the respect, the love, or the adoration which belong to God alone, as when people put their trust in wealth, in honor and advancement, when they think too highly of relatives, friends, and acquaintances, or in any other way transgress the requirement that we are to fear, love, and trust in God above all things.

Ignatius. See *Apostolic Fathers,* 2.

Ignorance. See *Knowledge,* 2.

I. H. C. See *Symbolism, Christian.*

Ihmels, Ludwig Heinrich (1858 to 1933). B. at Middels in East Frisia. Studied at Leipzig, Erlangen, Goettingen, and Berlin. Held various pastorates in East Frisia; director of studies at Loccum; professor of systematic theology at Erlangen and at Leipzig; bishop at Dresden. He inclined towards orthodox Lutheranism.

Ikhnaton (14th c. B. C.). Ruler of Egypt who sought to found a religion of mystical monotheism by substituting the worship of the sun for that of Amon.

Illinois, Evangelical Lutheran Synod of (1846—80). a) 1846—67. Organized when the Synod of the West was divided into three synods on June 4, 1846. The first convention was held in Hillsboro, Ill., on Oct. 15, 1846, with seven pastors, representing 15 congregations and 685 communicants. Decided to join the General Synod but did not send a delegate until 1848. The first president was Daniel Scherer, pioneer Lutheran missionary in Illinois. At the time of the first convention the Hillsboro Academy building was offered to the synod, and the offer was accepted. The institution founded by this synod was called "The Literary and Theological Institute of the Evangelical Lutheran Church of the Far West." From 1846 to 1852 the synod continued to operate the college in Hillsboro; then it was removed to Springfield, Ill., and the name was changed to "The Illinois State University."

b) 1867—80. When the Synod of Illinois decided to withdraw from the General Synod and join the General Council in 1867, a division took place. The synod was dissolved at Mount

Pulaski, Ill., on Aug. 24, 1867. The group joining the General Council adopted the name "Synod of Illinois and Adjacent States," and those remaining with the General Synod took the name "Synod of Central Illinois." The group remaining with the General Synod was given control of the Illinois State University, which soon closed because of the heavy indebtedness. The Missouri Synod purchased it from the Pennsylvania Ministerium in 1874. The practical department of Concordia Seminary was moved to this location.

Later the Synod of Illinois and Adjacent States withdrew from the General Council when the Council would take no definite stand on the "Four Points." In 1872 the Synod of Illinois helped to organize the Synodical Conference. It merged with the Missouri Synod on May 24, 1880, at Quincy, Ill., the pastors and congregations in Illinois joining the Illinois District, and those in Missouri, the Western District. At the time of the merging it had a membership of 23 pastors, 26 congregations, and 6,004 communicants. See *United Lutheran Church, Synods of,* 7.

HT

Illinois, Evangelical Lutheran Synod of Central (1867—1920). Organized Aug. 24, 1867, at Mount Pulaski, Ill., by the men who wished to remain with the General Synod after the Synod of Illinois I had joined the General Council. Rev. Ephraim Miller was its first president. In 1876 the German ministers (about one half of them) withdrew and organized the Wartburg Synod. The Synod of Central Illinois was unable to operate the Illinois State University at Springfield because of the heavy indebtedness. This group helped to found Carthage College, Carthage, Ill., in 1870. From 1897 to 1901 the Synod of Central Illinois was combined with the Synod of Southern Illinois and in 1918 entered the United Lutheran Church. On June 20, 1920, it merged with the Northern and the Southern Illinois Synods and part of the Chicago Synod into the Illinois Synod II of the U. L. C. At the time of this merger it numbered 25 pastors, 29 congregations, and 6,535 communicants. HT

Illinois, Evangelical Lutheran Synod of Central and Southern (1897—1901). Formed by a union of the Synod of Central and Southern Illinois at Hillsboro, Ill., Oct. 14, 1897. In 1901 the two synods resumed their separate existence. HT

Illinois, Evangelical Lutheran Synod of Northern (1851—1920). Organized Sept. 8, 1851, at Cedarville, Ill., by eight pastors and six laymen formerly belonging to the Franckean and the Illinois Synod I. The Rev. E. Miller was its first president. Its territory also covered parts of Iowa, Wisconsin, and Minnesota. It included a number of Scandinavians. This synod, together with the Synod of Illinois, controlled and operated the Illinois State University at Springfield, Ill. After 1867 it withdrew its support, and the institution was taken over by the Pennsylvania Ministerium by foreclosure of the mortgage (afterwards purchased by Missouri Synod for its practical seminary). In 1870 it helped to establish Carthage College, at Carthage, Ill. In 1860 the Scandinavians withdrew and formed a separate synod. In 1918 the Synod of Northern Illinois entered the United Lutheran Church and on June 10, 1920, with the Central and Southern Illinois Synods and a part of the Chicago Synod merged into the Illinois Synod II of the U. L. C. At the time of this merger it numbered 54 pastors, 60 congregations, and 6,575 communicants. HT

Illinois, Evangelical Lutheran Synod of Southern (1856—1920). Organized Nov. 7, 1856, at Jonesboro, Ill., by eight pastors formerly belonging to the Synod of the Southwest. They continued membership in the General Synod. The first president was Rev. D. Jenkins. Its territory also included parts of Missouri and Tennessee. In 1879 the pastors living in Tennessee formed the Middle Tennessee Synod. From 1897 to 1901 the Synod of Southern Illinois and the Synod of Central Illinois were combined. In 1918 the Synod of Southern Illinois affiliated with the U. L. C., and on June 10, 1920, it merged with the Central and Northern Illinois Synods and part of the Chicago Synod into the Illinois Synod II of the U. L. C. At the time of the merger it numbered ten pastors, 17 congregations, and 3,518 communicants. HT

Illinois Synods (bibliography for preceding synods). *Concordia Cyclopedia,* CPH, 1927; "Diamond Jubilee History of Carthage College," *CHIQ,* I, Nos. 2 and 3; *Proceedings of the Illinois Synod* (1852—80) in Pritzlaff Library, Concordia Seminary, St. Louis, Mo.; *Proceedings of the Illinois Synod* (1846 to 1867) in Carthage Library, Carthage, Ill.; *Proceedings of the Synod of Southern Illinois,* in Carthage Library; *Proceedings of the Synod of the Southwest,* Carthage Library; J. L. Neve, *A Brief History of the Lutheran Church in America.*

Illinois Synod of the United Lutheran Church. See *United Lutheran Church, Synods of,* 7.

Illuminati. Name of various religious societies in Europe from the 15th to the 18th century. Most noted of these is the *Illuminatenorden,* founded 1776 by Adam Weishaupt, ex-Jesuit and professor at Ingolstadt; a secret society, modeled after the Jesuit order and since 1780 connected with Freemasonry, aiming to propagate political and religious enlightenment. It soon spread to most European countries, with a membership of 2,000, including Goethe, Herder, Baron v. Knigge, and other noted men; but in 1784 it was expelled from Bavaria, and soon thereafter it collapsed.

Illumination. See *Conversion,* II, 1.

Image of God. 1. God created man in His own image (Gen. 1:27). Man, as all the creatures of God, was created good, "very good." Yet man was distinguished from and above all other creatures on the face of the earth by a manner of excellence peculiar to him alone. While plants and animals were made each after its kind, man was made after the image of God. By a creative process, God made man after His likeness. This image was not of the essence of man's nature, nor was it a gift bestowed upon man after his creation, but it was a concreated quality.

2. While Lutheran theologians generally hold that the image of God, which consists in the knowledge of God and holiness of the will, is lacking in man after the Fall (Col. 3:10; Eph. 4:24), some hold that such passages as Gen. 9:6 and James 3:9 still ascribe a divine image to man after the Fall. They hold that the intellect and will of man, possessed by man also after the Fall, constitute a similitude with God. Those who reject this view (Luther, Philippi, Hoffmann, Pieper) interpret Gen. 9:6 and James 3:9 as referring to the image that is to be restored again in Christ.

3. The latter hold that nothing that is in natural man can be the image of God. The upright body and the rational soul with its human understanding, affections, and will, while woefully corrupt in consequence of sin,

are still the constituent elements of the human nature and therefore must not be considered as being the divine image or parts thereof. Conscience,* too, and the Moral Law, inscribed in the human heart, whereby man is distinguished from brutes in his present state, cannot be subsumed under the image of God.

4. "In his original state, man was not only sound in body and soul, without a germ of disease or death, or a taint of sin, but endowed with concreated spiritual wisdom and knowledge, and with perfect natural righteousness, goodness, and holiness, in the image and likeness of the Triune God." (A. L. Graebner, *Outlines of Doctrinal Theology*, 57).

Images. The grossest form of idolatry consists in the worship of images. The human mind, when unenlightened by divine revelation, has always shown a strong tendency to represent the Deity in visible forms. To the ignorant mass of the people such images soon ceased to be representations and themselves became gods or, at least, habitations of gods. Israel was surrounded by idolatrous nations, against whose idols the Prophets found it necessary to wage unceasing, though not always successful, warfare. The primitive Christians were charged with atheism because they had no images. They gloried in their absence, and some of the early Fathers even condemned painting, and sculpture as wicked arts. With the decadence of the Church in the fourth century, however, images of Christ, the Virgin Mary, and the saints were brought into the churches and set up as objects of veneration. This practice has continued in the Roman and Greek Churches. Rome has been careful, in its official utterances, to avoid the charge of open idolatry, but it deliberately fosters the cult of images by solemnly consecrating them, by prescribing prayers to be used before them, by offering indulgences for their veneration, etc. The Council of Trent (Sess. XXV) decreed: "The honor which is shown them is referred to the prototypes which those images represent, in such wise that by (*per*) the images which we kiss, and before which we uncover the head and prostrate ourselves, we adore Christ; and we venerate the saints, whose similitude they bear." This definition finds a strange parallel in the defense of the heathen against the early Christians, as preserved by Lactantius: "We do not fear the images themselves, but those beings after whose likeness they were fashioned and by whose names they were consecrated." Prominent Roman theologians go far beyond the definition of Trent. Bonaventura says: "Since all veneration shown to the image of Christ is shown to Christ Himself, the image of Christ is also entitled to be prayed to." (*Cultus Latriae*, 1. III, dist. 9, art. 1, qu. 2.) Bellarmine teaches: "The images of Christ and the saints are to be adored not only in a figurative manner, but quite positively, so that the prayers are directly addressed to them, and not merely as the representatives of the original." (*De Imaginibus*, 1. II, c. 10.) See *Idolatry*.

Imagination. See *Christian Teaching*, B.

Imam ("he who is at the head"). A name applied to the Sultan and the most honored teachers of Mohammedanism. It is also applied to a class of the Mohammedan priestly body which is elected to office by the people and calls the people to prayer, performs religious ceremonies (marriage, burial, circumcision, etc.), and enjoys various privileges.

Imitation. See *Christian Teaching*, J ff.

Imitation of Christ. A book published by Thomas à Kempis under his name but which is taken chiefly from the diary of Gerard Groote. It has been the most popular of Christian devotional books.

Immaculate Conception. See *Mariolatry; Roman Catholic Confessions*, C.

Immanence of God. God is present in all creatures, yet he is never a part of them, but always remains the transmundane, transcendent God. The omnipresence of God must not be understood in the sense of pantheistic immanence. While it is true that God is so intimately joined to all creatures that in Him they live and move and have their being (Acts 17:28; Col. 1:17), nevertheless, the difference between God and His creatures always remains as great as that between the infinite and finite (Num. 23:19; 1 Sam. 15:29).

Immanuel Lutheran College. See *Ministry, Education of*, XI A 4.

Immanuel Synod of the Ev. Luth. Church in North America. Founded in Wall Rose, Pa., 1885, by "a number of Lutheran ministers and churches desiring to secure greater freedom in church life than was possible in some of the synods." "Liberal in regard to the secret society question." Territory: Ohio, Indiana, Illinois, Michigan, New Jersey, Pennsylvania, and District of Columbia. The movement never gained strength. In 1917 the Immanuel Synod dissolved by formal resolution. Rev. J. Frederick gathered a remnant about himself, which retained the name of Immanuel Synod and resolved to adopt the slogan, "Lutheran pulpits for Lutheran pastors, Lutheran altars for Lutheran communicants, and Lutheran cemeteries for departed Lutherans." It disbanded soon after Frederick's death, in 1921, some of the pastors joining other synods.

Immanuel Synod a. a. G. See *Australia,* B 1.

Immaterial Concepts. See *Psychology,* C.

Immediate Working of the Spirit. See *Grace, Means of,* I 7.

Immersion. One of the modes of applying water in Baptism, the individual baptized being entirely submerged in water. Particularly the Anabaptist churches hold that it is the only correct mode of baptizing. For a discussion see *Grace, Means of,* III, 1.

Immigrant and Emigrant Missions. The work of taking care of the physical and spiritual needs of the people who enter or leave a country, especially those of the same faith. Immigrant (emigrant) mission work played a prominent role in orientating the Lutherans during the mass immigrations of the 19th century. In 1862 the Pennsylvania Synod undertook immigrant work, and R. Neumann became their first immigrant missionary. He was soon joined in the work by W. Berkemeier, who became prominent. In 1867 a notice appeared in the *Lutheraner* (LXVIII: 1) stating that the New York City Conference had started an Emigrant Mission. Stephanus Keyl was called into the work. In 1869 the Missouri Synod took over the work. The *Lutherisches Pilgerhaus* was purchased opposite Castle Gardens in New York City (later sold). In the first twenty years of its existence the *Pilgerhaus* sheltered 79,843 Germans and 5,342 Scandinavians. Emigrant mission work was also conducted in Baltimore. The Augustana Synod likewise began immigrant mission work in the 19th century.

The work for the Missouri Synod is carried on by the Atlantic District under the supervision of the Metropolitan Lutheran Inner Mission Society, New York, N. Y.

Immortality. 1. The continued existence of the human personality after death. The OT does not so much teach the soul's immortality as take it for granted. God is called the God of Abraham, Isaac, and Jacob, thus implying their continual existence, since God could not be a God of the dead, but only of the living. Because Enoch lived a pious life, "God took him." Death as a state is referred to in terms that imply continual existence. The dead "go to their fathers," "are gathered to their people." Compare also Heb. 11:13-16 with reference to the patriarchs. In the NT, immortality is used in the sense of eternal life, the life of glory. That the believers after death are dwelling with Christ in bliss is the consonant doctrine of the NT. That immortality, however, is not a gift bestowed upon the believers, but a natural endowment of man is clear from the fact that also the wicked will, according to a like consonant teaching, continue to exist after death. (Matt 8:12; 11:23 f.; 2 Thess. 1:9; Rev. 20:10; 14:11; Matt. 25:41; Dan. 12:2.)

2. Of the passages quoted by annihilationists, Adventists, and others (see *Annihilationism*), some refer to eternal death, which is not the same as nonexistence. The teaching of the Scriptures is that, as one spiritually dead yet exists, so those swallowed up in the second death, eternal death, likewise exist, and exist forever. Other passages quoted by annihilationists refer to temporal death (Ps. 37:10, 20; 62:3; 16:10; 104:35). See *Hereafter; Immortality, Arguments for.*

See references under *Hereafter;* in addition: A. E. Taylor, *The Christian Hope of Immortality,* Macm., 1947.

Immortality, Arguments for (cf. *Apologetics*). There is hardly a tribe or people which does not believe in immortality, or life after death. While the concept of immortality is one innate in the soul, so that it naturally inheres in man's religious and moral consciousness, it may be argued and demonstrated on rational grounds. The *ethical* argument is founded upon the evident fact that evil is not adequately punished in this world, and yet the human sense of justice demands a vindication of God's perfect justice in some other world; in other words, the

guilty conscience demands a state after death for punishment. The *historical* argument proceeds from the fact that since all nations at all times have believed in immortality, the idea of immortality is a universal one, which must be founded on fact. The testimony of man's conscience to immortality is the witness of Him who gave man a conscience and a moral nature. Or, we may say, man's belief in immortality is a part of the divine Law written in the human heart. The *metaphysical* argument operates with the thought that since man's soul is absolutely simple, and not compounded, it cannot be destroyed by death, which essentially is the separation of parts, *i. e.*, of the body and soul of man. The soul being pure spirit, cannot be annihilated, as the body perishes, returning to dust. Hence the soul must live on in some other world. The *teleological* argument reasons from the fact that man, as a religious and moral being, does not attain the end of his existence on earth, his development here being imperfect. For this reason there must be a greater and better world, where man's religious and moral being may come into its own. We admit, of course, that these arguments alone do not convince an unbeliever, but they at least, by sound reasoning, support the probability of life after death. JTM
See references under *Apologetics.*

Immutability of God. Because in the divine essence or attributes there never has been, nor ever will be, nor can be, any increase or decrease, or development, or any change of whatever kind, God is declared to be *immutable.* This is already implied in His *indivisibility*, but is frequently stated in Scripture (*e. g.*, Ex. 3:14; Ps. 102:27). God is *infinite*, inasmuch as He is not limited by space or time, there being in Him no distinction of here or there, sooner or later. God must not be represented as diffused through space, since He is indivisible; He is not related to space at all, but is simply everywhere. And since His attributes are Himself, each of them — His power, His wisdom, His truth — is everywhere (Is. 57:15; Heb. 7:26; Ps. 139; 36:6, 7). God is likewise unlimited by time; He is *eternal.* There is in Him no sooner or later, neither past nor future, but a continual, unbroken, eternal present (Ps. 2:7; 90:2; 2 Pet. 3:8). "As He is present to all things regardless of space, He is also present to all things regardless of time. There is with Him

no difference of space and no difference of time, because there is with Him neither space nor time, all distances being *here* with Him and all durations being *now* with Him." (A. L. Graebner.) As God is infinite, His *life* also is infinite. God is Life in the highest sense of the term, being determined only from within Himself. All His works have all their cause or causes within Him (John 5:26).

Impanation. A term denoting doctrine concerning the mode of the Real Presence in the Sacrament. It was stated during the Middle Ages by Rupprecht of Deutz as follows: "The Word of the Father comes in between the flesh and the blood which He received from the womb of the Virgin, and the bread and wine received from the altar and of the altar, and of the two makes a joint offering. When the priest puts this into the mouth of the believer, bread and wine are received and are absorbed into the body, but the Son of the Virgin remains whole and unabsorbed in the received, united to the Word of the Father in heaven. Such as do not believe, receive, on the contrary, only the material bread and wine, but none of the offering." Accordingly, while the Roman Church taught transubstantiation, or a change of the substance of bread and wine (which retain only their accidental qualities) into the body and blood of Christ, the doctrine of Impanation regards the visible elements as retaining their substance and as including within that substance the body and blood of Christ. The error here is the assumption that there is in the Sacrament a local inclusion of the divine elements in the visible. The Formula of Concord declares that the "mode of union between the body of Christ and the bread and wine is a mystery" and does not decide positively what that mode is, but only negatively, what it is not. Thus quoting the Wittenberg Concord of 1536, it rejects transubstantiation, local inclusion and any durable joining together of the elements and the body and blood of Christ apart from the action of the Sacrament (*Thorough Declaration*, VII:14, 15). See also *Lord's Supper.*

Impediments of Marriage, Roman Catholic. Circumstances which render a marriage unlawful or invalid. To the impediments raised by Scripture and by nature the Roman Church has added a number of her own. Roman theologians distinguish two kinds of impediments: prohibitory, which render a marriage unlawful, but do not nullify it; and diriment, which make it null and void. Setting aside prohibitory impediments constitutes an ecclesiastical offense and requires that an expiation or reparation be made. Such prohibitory impediments are: 1) the prohibition against mixed marriage, that is, marriage of a Romanist to a baptized member of another Christian body (but see "clandestinity" below); 2) previous betrothal to another person; 3) the closed times, marriages being forbidden between the first Sunday in Advent and Epiphany and between Ash Wednesday and the Sunday after Easter. — Diriment impediments are: 1) defect of age (boys must be fourteen; girls, twelve); 2) impotency or insanity; 3) solemn vows (see *Vows*) and ordination; 4) certain crimes, e. g., adultery with promise of marriage when free; 5) blood relationship (Biblical, three degrees; Roman, four degrees); 6) affinity, the relationship to the kin of the spouse (also four degrees); 7) spiritual affinity, which is contracted in Baptism by the sponsors and the minister of the Sacrament (who may be a child, in emergency) with the baptized child and its parents; 8) disparity of worship: marriage of a baptized with an unbaptized person; 9) clandestinity: according to the decree *Ne Temere* (April 18, 1908), a marriage in which even one party is a Roman Catholic is null and void unless celebrated before a priest and two witnesses. — Dispensations * may be obtained from bishop or Pope when the impediments are admittedly of ecclesiastical origin. A dispensation for a mixed marriage is given only on condition that the Roman Catholic party is guaranteed free exercise of religion and promises to seek the conversion of the other, and that all offspring is reared in the Roman Church. See *Marriage*.

Impediments of Marriage, Scriptural and Natural. There are certain prohibitive degrees of marriage, those degrees of relationship either of *consanguinity*, or blood relationship, that of a common ancestry; or of *affinity*, that resulting from marriage, within which marriage is forbidden, either by direct prohibition in the Bible or by statute enacted by the government. The general rule is that one may not marry "flesh of one's flesh," that is, a person within, and up to, the second degree of relationship of either kind. See Lev. 18:6 ff. and related passages.

There are certain factors also which act as a hindrance to the consummation of marriage, as, impotency, an incurable disease, or other extremely unusual reasons. The Lutheran dogmaticians were not agreed on details of natural impediments. Gerhard held that lepers, epileptics, and persons afflicted with contagious diseases should not be allowed to marry. Chemnitz justified divorce in case of cruelty, poison, and plots on life.

Many of the States of the United States demand physical examinations and forbid marriage for certain causes.

Implicit Faith. See *Faith, Explicit and Implicit.*

Imprimatur. See *Index of Prohibited Books.*

Improperia. A section of the Roman ritual for Good Friday, the name "reproaches" referring to the fact that the text of this group of antiphons and responses is based upon Lam. 1:12.

Imputation. A term employed by some dogmaticians with reference to the sin of Adam and the righteousness of Christ. The sin of Adam is described as so attributed to every man as to be considered, in the divine counsels, his own and as rendering him guilty of it. Again, the righteousness of Christ is so attributed to man (a believer) as to be considered his own, and that he is therefore justified by it. See *Atonement, Christ, Faith, Forgiveness, Justification, Redemption; Sin, Original.*

In Coena Domini, Bull. Formerly issued by the Pope annually on Maundy Thursday, to be pronounced on that day and on Ascension Day and the Festival of Peter and Paul. It formulated the condemnation of numerous heresies, the Lutherans being included in 1524, and subsequent condemnations being added from time to time (1536, 1566, 1578 to 1583, 1609, 1627). The publication at Rome was discontinued by Clement XIV, in 1770, on account of the protest of secular powers, and the bull was finally withdrawn by Pius IX, in 1869, by the constitution *Apostolicae Sedis*, although this publication is, in some respects, a repetition of the original bull.

In Partibus Infidelium ("in the lands of the unbelievers"). Words formerly used to designate titular bishops (see *Bishop*), e. g., N., Bishop of Tyre, *in partibus infidelium* (or simply, *in partibus*). The term was abolished by the Congregation of the Propaganda in 1882.

In View of Faith. See *Intuitu fidei.*

Incarnation. 1. The incarnation of the Son of God, according to the Scriptures, consists in the assumption of a human body and soul by the Second Person of the Holy Trinity. The doctrine was stated in its simplest form by John (1:14). It is stated by Paul (Col. 2:9; 1 Tim. 3:16. Cf. Rom. 1:3; Phil. 2:7); by Luke (1:35); and the Lord Himself (Matt. 22:42 f. Cf. Ps. 110:1).

2. Prophecy points to this union of God with humanity in the Protevangel (Gen. 3:15) and in the *Immanuel* ("God with us") of Is. 7:14.

3. By this mysterious union, Jesus Christ was able to be the Mediator between God and man. "Thus it is that, though the two natures personally united in Christ are and remain essentially distinct, each retaining its own essential properties or attributes, its own intelligence and will, so that His divinity is not His humanity nor a part thereof, nor His humanity His divinity, that, while there is in Him no mixture or confusion of natures, there is in Christ a communion of natures, so that the divine nature is the nature of the Son of Man and the human nature is the nature of the Son of God." (ALG).

4. Inseparably connected with the doctrine of the Incarnation is the article of the Virgin Birth. The doctrine of the Virgin Birth is stated by Matthew (1:18, 25) and Luke (1:34 f.) and taught by Paul (Gal. 4:4. See Is. 7:14).

5. The testimony of the Early Church to the Virgin Birth is abundant. Apart from the Ebionites and some of the Gnostic sects, there were none who did not believe in the Virgin Birth. The greater Gnostic sects accepted it as a tenet. The Apostles' Creed (see *Ecumenical Creeds*) in its old form has the words: "who was born of the Holy Ghost of the Virgin Mary." The general belief in this as an article of faith is attested by Irenaeus, Ignatius, the Apologists, Justin Martyr, and many other Christian writers.

6. The Incarnation is a mystery beyond the understanding of human reason. Rationalists have maintained that incarnation involved a change which would have destroyed the Godhead. Christian apologists reply: In the Incarnation the divine nature is the active, as the human nature is the passive, factor; any change, therefore, which results from the act will affect the human nature, not the divine. The Logos did not cease to be God when He became flesh; for we are told that He was made man, not that He was changed into man, and the Scriptures continue to speak of the Logos incarnate in such a manner that each nature must be understood as retaining all its essential characteristics. In Christ two complete natures are united in the personality of one of them (the relation existing between body and soul is particularly weak as an analogy). The generation of the man Jesus and the union of the two natures were simultaneous. The human nature of Christ did not for a moment exist by itself. This human nature was not produced from the divine essence of the Holy Spirit, but, by His creative energy, from the body of Mary. When we say: "born of the Virgin Mary," the proposition denotes the material; when we say: "conceived by the Holy Ghost," it denotes the efficient energy.

The sinlessness of Jesus in itself is testimony for the miracle in His origin.

Athanasius, *The Incarnation of the Word of God* (tr. C. S. M. V. S. Th.), Macm., 1946; J. Gresham Machen, *The Virgin Birth of Christ*, Harper, 1932; D. M. Baillie, *God Was in Christ*, Scribner's, N. Y., 1948; A. Koeberle, "The Incarnation of Christ," *Journal of Theol. of ALC*, VII:1—13.

Incense, Significance of. In the Old Testament cultus the symbol of the worship and sacrifice of the people arising acceptably to God. Used in the Catholic (and in exceptional Lutheran) rites to solemnize certain worship functions.

Indefectibility. The Roman Catholic claim that the church (specifically, the see at Rome) can never become corrupt in faith and morals.

Independent Baptist Church of America. See *Baptist Bodies*, 28.

Independent Churches. Under this head are presented 1) those single churches which are not identified with any ecclesiastical body and have not even such affiliation as would entitle them to inclusion under a special name; 2) those churches, variously called union, federated, community, etc., which represent the movement toward denominational fellowship and the consolidation of church life for the purpose of securing more effective church work;

3) such churches as use a denominational name, but for one reason or another are not included in denominational lists and are not reported by the denominational officers. See *Community Churches.*

Independent Fundamental Churches of America. See *Fundamentalism.*

Indeterminism. A philosophical term meaning that certain decisions of the will are independent of preceding physiological or psychological causes. See *Free Will.*

Index of Prohibited Books. 1. A catalog of books which have been condemned by papal officials on religious or moral grounds and which members of the Roman Church are forbidden to read or possess. Before the invention of printing there was no established censorship; books that were adjudged dangerous were burned (*e. g.*, the writings of Hus by the Council of Constance). The papal bull *Exsurge Domine* (June 15, 1520) forbade the reading of all writings of Luther, even such as he would write in future, under pain of excommunication. The advent of the printing press and its great influence in spreading the Reformation led the Roman Church to establish a formal censorship. A committee of the Council of Trent considered the whole matter and submitted its findings to Pope Pius IV, who, in 1564, published his *Index Librorum Prohibitorum.* New titles were added to this list from time to time by the Congregation of the Index, and some extreme provisions were modified.

2. In 1897 Leo XIII established a new set of rules and defined the classes of prohibited books. Such are: all books defending "heresy" or attacking Roman doctrine or practice; the original text of Scripture when published by non-Catholics and all unapproved translations of Scripture, even by Catholics (except to those engaged in theological studies; see *Bible Reading*); obscene books, except expurgated classics; books of magic; unauthorized devotional books, etc. Leo XIII also published a new edition of the *Index.* The prohibitions are binding on all members of the Roman Church, including the learned. Whoever deliberately reads, keeps, or prints heretical books thereby (*ipso facto*) excommunicates himself; likewise, whoever prints books of Scripture or notes or commentaries on it, without the approbation of the ordinary (*Bull Officio-*

rum et Munerum, chap. V, 47—48). Permission to read prohibited books may be granted by special license. Romanists are bound to submit to the ordinary, before publication, all books concerned with religion and morality. These are examined by a censor, who approves them with the words *Nihil obstat* ("Nothing is in the way"), whereupon the ordinary gives license to print, with the word *Imprimatur* ("Let it be printed"). This license is inserted at the beginning of the book.

India. 1. Formerly a colonial empire of Great Britain; a sovereign republic since Jan. 26, 1950; divided into Hindustan and Pakistan, largely along the lines of religion. Area: 1,138,814 sq. mi. Population: 356,891,624 (1951), being a strange mixture of aboriginal Dravidian, Kolarian, Negrito, Aryan, Scythian, Mongolian, and Mongoloid peoples. Spanish, French, and English immigration since Vasco da Gama discovered a sea passage to India (1498) has increased the mixture. It is commonly accepted that 200 million, in 25 groups, speak the Aryan languages, 100 million speak the Dravidian language groups, and 15 million the Kolarian and other dialects. Specific Indian culture was introduced by the Aryans. Many hill tribes, possibly numbering 70,000,000, still cling to their aboriginal religion and customs. Their languages have not even been reduced to writing. Great educational strides have been made since 1854, but in spite of all efforts the rate of illiteracy is still very high.

2. 85 per cent of the people of India are Hindus. The chief religions of India are the Hindu; professed by 272,153,367 (est., 1951); the Mohammedan, professed by 41,568,797; the Sikh, professed by 3,973,916; and the Jain, professed by 1,427,000. Buddhists and Parsees form two additional religious groups. A 1947 estimate listed the Christian population at 5,634,000. The census of 1951 was expected to show several million more. Many of these Christians are without pastoral care.

3. The caste system separates and yet unites the people of India. It is both a religious and a social, civil institution, whose age is not known. The great Indian castes are the Brahman, or priestly class; the Kshatriya, or military class; the Vaisya, or farming and merchant class; the Sudra, or servile class. However, there are, in ad-

dition, many millions of people who have no membership in the foregoing castes, being of a still lower social order, who yet have caste laws among themselves and are bound by them with iron fetters. These are commonly called the Pariahs, or Panchamas. Each of the upper castes is again divided into a great number of sections, classified by their employment and even by geographical situation, evidenced by the fact that the Brahmanic caste alone is divided into some 2,000 separate families or trades, of whom many cannot intermarry or eat food cooked by the other; neither are they all of Aryan stock, some being colored and even black. Caste rules hermetically separate the members from other castes; being born into the caste, one cannot pass into another caste; neither can entrance into a caste be bought or conferred. Caste is lost by offending against caste rules of food or dress or observances. To be an "outcaste" is the worst punishment an Indian can imagine. The Hindu doctrine teaches the transmigration of souls and Karma, namely, that in a chain of rebirths a person inexorably receives rewards or punishments for good or evil deeds in earlier existences; the condition in life, whether one be of a high social station, or a Pariah, or an animal of some kind, or even a woman, being a result of Karma. Each caste is, in a sense, a trade guild, a mutual insurance society, and a religious sect. The caste exercises a very palpable supervision over its members from the close of childhood until death.

4. There are distinct traces that Christianity came to India very early, possibly already in the first century. Historical evidence that St. Thomas evangelized India is very tenuous. The "Thomas Christians" in southern India would appear to be traceable to Persia. They are divided into four sections: 1) Orthodox Syrians, or simply Syrians, who are Monophysites; they are subordinate to the Patriarch in Mardin, Chaldea. Frequently they are called Jacobites. 2) Romo-Syrians, who are in connection with the Roman Catholic Church. 3) Christians of St. Thomas, an independent Church, since 1880, in connection with the English Church Missionary Society. 4) The Syro-Chaldeans, who separated from the Romo-Syrians in 1880; they are Nestorians. Together these Syrian churches have some 700,000 members, largely in Travancore. It is unfortunate that they

are practically a part of the Indian caste system.

5. The opening of the sea passage to India by Vasco da Gama (1498) gave an impetus to Romish missions. The Portuguese merchant marine usually carried priests and monks in large numbers. In 1534 Goa was made a bishopric and the center for Roman Catholic missionary endeavor. Outstanding Roman Catholic missionaries were the Jesuits Francis Xavier (1542—1552) and Robert de Nobili (1605 to 1656), whose seemingly great missionary successes were owing to typically Jesuitic methods, which were even condemned by a papal bull (1744). In 1815 Abbé Dubois wrote that in spite of all earlier successes he could not say that during the twenty-five years of his activity in India he had found an upright and sincere Roman Catholic Christian.

6. *Protestant missions*, begun by Frederick IV of Denmark in 1706, are generally known as the Lutheran Danish-Halle missions in Tranquebar. The most prominent men were Bartholomew Ziegenbalg, H. Pluetschau, Philip Fabricius (1742—91), and Chr. Fr. Schwartz (1750—98), all of whom labored successfully. The rationalism of Germany wrought such havoc in the mission that it was discontinued in 1825. The mission came into the hands of the English S. P. G. Meanwhile William Carey, the great Baptist missionary, had come to India under the auspices of the Baptist Missionary Society, and finding the doors closed against missions by the powerful East India Company, he and his colleagues, Marshman and Ward, went to Danish Serampur. Here their Serampur Brotherhood began an unexcelled literary activity of Bible translation, producing some thirty translations of the whole Bible or of parts of the Bible in languages some of which they had to fix grammatically and lexicographically. Missionaries and agents were sent by them as far as Benares, Agra, Delhi, Bombay, Burma, the Moluccas, and Java. In 1816 the Brotherhood separated from the Baptist Mission Society, but most of their work ultimately was continued by that organization.

7. In 1797 W. J. Ringeltaube, a graduate of the Halle school, was sent to Calcutta by the Society for the Promotion of Christian Knowledge. Two years later he entered the service of the London Missionary Society in Travancore, where he worked with great success

until 1815. Chr. Fr. Schwartz had begun some work in Tinnevelly. This
was continued by Karl Rhenius (1814
to 1838), a product of Jaenicke's school
at Berlin, in the service of the Church
Missionary Society. This society has extended its work over all India, recently
having a Christian community of over
425,000.

8. In the early part of the nineteenth
century the American Board of Commissioners for Foreign Missions sent
Judson, Newell, Hall, and Rice to India,
who took hold of Madura and the Tamil
country. Judson joined the Baptists,
which brought the American Baptists to
India, beginning first in Burma, since
1837 to the Telugu district in the south,
and finally to Assam.

9. A second period of the mission
history of India begins with the coming of Dr. A. Duff, a missionary of the
Established Church of Scotland, who
pointed the way to missionary higher
institutions of learning, opening the
first high school at Calcutta. This plan
has been largely copied by other missionary societies, also by the government of India, which since 1854 has
evolved a very generous scheme of
national education, enlisting also the
missionary societies by what is termed
grants-in-aid.

10. The Leipzig Lutheran Missionary
Society, founded in 1836, took over
some of the remnants of the Danish-
Halle Mission after much had been
absorbed by the Church Missionary
Society. The Basel Missionary Society,
founded in 1815, entered India at Man-
galore. The Gossner Missionary Society
took over the work of Pastor Gossner of
Berlin, chiefly among the Kols at Chota
Nagpur, one of the most promising mission fields in India. Since the First
World War this mission has constituted
a native Lutheran Church. The United
Lutheran Church in the United States
has conducted missions in the Telugu
country in India since 1841 and 1874,
respectively. The Lutheran Church —
Missouri Synod has been working in
the North Arcot District since January,
1895, and in Travancore since 1907.
The American Lutheran Church took
over the Hermannsburg Mission in
1920.

11. In recent years the missionary
societies engaged in the various sections of India have increased rapidly,
and almost 150 organizations carry on
mission work there.

12. A distinct branch of mission
work is the Zenana and the medical

mission. Custom keeps the women
secluded to a great degree in the
zenanas (women's apartments), making
it very difficult for male missionaries
or doctors to bring them the Word of
God or minister to them in respect to
the needs of their bodily health. Women
workers are therefore trained and employed to a large extent in order to
reach the women in the zenanas, and
women doctors also find a rich field of
usefulness in India. See *Missions, Bibliography.*

Indian Philosophy. See *Brahmanism.*

**Indiana, the Evangelical Lutheran
Synod of (I).** The conflict between the
"Generalists" and the "Henkelites" was
carried beyond the Alleghanies in the
third decade of the nineteenth century,
and the Indiana Synod (I) was organized Aug. 15, 1835, at St. John's Church,
Johnson Co., Ind., by 6 pastors and
7 laymen, representing 10 congregations, in opposition to the "Generalists,"
who had banded together in Kentucky
in 1834. Three generations of the Henkels had visited Indiana on their missionary tours — Paul, his sons David
and Philip, and his grandson Eusebius
S., the last-named being one of the
founders of the Indiana Synod. This
synod adopted the same doctrinal basis
as the Tennessee Synod, but in the
course of time was strongly affected by
the waves of infidelity, Universalism,
revivalism, and annihilationism, which
carried away some of its leaders. A division came in 1849, the "Miller Faction," which the courts adjudged the
real Synod of Indiana, opposing the
liberalism of the leaders. This faction,
however, having exhausted its strength
in lawsuits, soon disbanded. The other
faction continued under the old name
until 1859, when it was dissolved by
demand of Rev. E. Rudisill. At the
time of its greatest strength the Indiana Synod had about 2,500 communicants.

M. L. Wagner, *The Chicago Synod
and Its Antecedents,* Wartburg Press,
Waverly, Iowa, 1909.

Indiana Synod (II). Was organized
Oct. 23, 1871, at East Germantown, Ind.,
by men formerly belonging to the
Union Synod and the English District
of the Joint Ohio Synod who desired
union with the General Council. It
consisted of 8 pastors and 23 congregations which adopted the doctrinal basis
of the General Council. When the
Illinois Synod (I) joined the Synod-

ical Conference, the Indiana Synod (II) branched out into Illinois and, since its interest centered about the Chicago Seminary, established by the General Council in 1891, adopted the name Chicago Synod in 1895. See *United Luth. Church, Synods of,* 8.

M. L. Wagner, *The Chicago Synod and Its Antecedents,* Wartburg Press, Waverly, Iowa, 1909.

Indiana, Synod of Northern. Organized Oct. 27, 1855, at Columbia City, Ind., by former members of the Olive Branch and Wittenberg Synods. Its territory included also Michigan. It united with the General Synod in 1857 and with it entered the United Lutheran Church in 1918. On June 10, 1920, it united with part of the Chicago Synod in forming the Michigan Synod (III) of the U. L. C. A. At the time of this merger it numbered 53 pastors, 77 congregations, and 7,128 communicants.

C. R. Defenderer, *Lutheranism at the Crossroads of America, A Story of the Indiana Synod of the U. L. C. A.* (commissioned by the Indiana Synod), n. p., n. d.

Indianapolis, the German Ev. Luth. Synod of. Formed in 1846 and formally organized in 1848 by a number of pastors who disagreed with the liberal tendencies of the Synod of the West. Rev. J. F. Isensee was president, Rev. J. G. Kunz, secretary, F. W. Wier, treasurer, Rev. Meissner, missionary at large. In 1848 it numbered five ordained and four licensed ministers, ten congregations, and 1,572 communicants. It was absorbed in the early 1850's by Ohio and Missouri.

H. Zorn, "Beginnings in Indianapolis," *CTM,* V:19—29.

Indifferentism. See *Adiaphora.*

Individual Differences. See *Christian Teaching,* C.

Individualism. *Philosophic,* holds that only individual things have independent existence and that the universe is but a collection of individuals, while Universalism holds that the universe exists as a compact organized whole and individual things are but dependent parts thereof. *Political* Individualism regards society and the state as an artificial device, whose value is gauged by its conduciveness to the good of individuals. *Economic* Individualism means free competition, resulting in the survival of the fittest, the state and other combines to keep

hands off the economic machinery. *Ethical* Individualism holds that each man's ideals are the measure of his morality, that everything is right that the individual believes to be right. According to this it is not a sin to transgress a law of God, but it is a sin to act contrary to one's own conviction and individual character.

Indo-China. See *French Indo-China.*

Indoctrination. See *Christian Teaching,* J.

Indra. See *Brahmanism,* 2.

Inductive Method. See *Christian Teaching,* K.

Indulgences. 1. The roots from which grew the Roman doctrine of indulgences are indicated in the article on Penitential Discipline.* As the penitential system changed its character and the sacrament of penance evolved, penance was no longer regarded as a mere expression of sorrow for sin or even as the discharge of church penalties, but as something that pleased God, had merit in His eyes, and was offered Him as a compensation for sin. As such it was held to remove, according to the degree of its merit, a portion of that temporal punishment of sin (chiefly purgatory) which could not be removed by absolution. Commutations of penance, or indulgences, therefore became commutations of divine punishment and were much sought after. By giving money to churches and monasteries, by pilgrimages, sometimes by direct payment to the priest, the account with God could be balanced. Contrition, or at least attrition,* was, in theory, necessary to gain an indulgence, but this condition was often held in the background.

2. The Crusades marked an epoch in the history of indulgences, for each Crusader received a plenary indulgence (see below). These are the first plenary indulgences on record, and they proved so attractive that they were later offered in the campaigns against the Waldenses and other "heretics" and even in the petty Italian squabbles of the Pope. Here again commutations were permitted; for one who could not fight in person might gain the precious indulgence for a cash equivalent. The Church's ability to grant indulgences in abundance became established when it was discovered that it had on hand an unlimited treasure of superfluous good works, which, for a consideration, could

be transferred to the account of those who had a shortage of their own (see *Opera Supererogationis*).

3. It remained for Boniface VIII, however, to discover the true financial possibilities of indulgences through the jubilee of the year 1300 (see *Jubilees*). The new vein was industriously worked till Boniface IX took another step forward and sold plenary indulgences outside of Rome. This Pope also seems to have been the first to give indulgences "from guilt and punishment" (*a poena et culpa*), or as a "full indulgence of all sins," terms which cause modern Roman scholars much embarrassment.

4. In the 15th century, indulgences began to be sold also for the dead in purgatory. Though the Pope was held to have the power, as custodian of the "treasure of the Church," to release all poor souls from purgatory at one stroke, no such wholesale delivery was undertaken, but only those souls were relieved whose friends or relatives bought indulgences for them. The purchase price was called "alms to the Church." The traffic in indulgences assumed ever greater proportions in which the Church sold freedom from purgatory for a fixed sum of money. Hus, Wyclif, and others raised their voices in vain.

5. Luther's exposure of indulgences convinced many of the corruption of the Roman Church and prepared them to welcome the restored Gospel; even sincere Romanists were filled with shame and horror. Yet Rome would not divorce itself from the practice. The Council of Trent made the questors of alms (preachers of indulgences) the scapegoats and "utterly abolished" their name and office (Sess. XXI, chap. 9), but enjoined "that the use of indulgences, for the Christian people most salutary, is to be retained in the Church," that, however, "moderation be observed," and "that all evil gains for the obtaining thereof be wholly abolished" (Sess. XXV, Decr. 4). Hence the Roman Church has to this day a bewildering profusion of indulgences. These may be plenary, remitting all the temporal punishment due to sin, or partial, *e. g.*, for forty days, for a year, etc., which means the equivalent of that period of canonical penance, not of that period of purgatory. Some indulgences can be gained only at particular places or at certain times; others are attached to objects, such as crosses, medals, scapulars. (*NB.* When such objects are sold or given away, the indulgence does not go along.) Cer-

tain prayers and devotional acts are heavily indulgenced (names of Jesus and Mary, 25 days; sign of the cross, 50 days; the same, with holy water, 100 days; "My Jesus, mercy!" 100 days; "Sweet Heart of Mary, be my rescue!" 300 days). Indulgences play an important part in the life of the children of Rome. Much of their zeal and charity flows from a desire to gain indulgences, more, if possible, than they need themselves, so that they may transfer the surplus. — Rome denies that God remits all punishment to those who trust in Christ (see 1 John 1:7; Titus 2:14; Rom. 8:33) and then bids her followers escape the punishment of God and gain indulgence of Him by kissing consecrated medals or wearing scapulars. Matt. 15:9.

H. C. Lea, *History of Auricular Confession and Indulgences in the Latin Church*, Lea Brothers, Philadelphia, 1896; T. Hoyer, "Indulgences," *CTM*, V:242—48.

Indult. A license from the Pope, permitting bishops and others to dispense from ecclesiastical laws, *e. g.*, fasting in Lent.

Industrial Homes. See *Rescue Homes*.

Industry and the Church. Twentieth-century industry has presented new problems to the Christian Church in the application of moral principles to a complex economic structure. With the rapid advance of industrialization and urbanization of life, the increase of large corporations and holding companies, impersonal control of industry, absentee ownership, and a managerial direction of the capitalist system, the problems of increasing concentration of wealth, use of natural resources, and their relation to the wage-earning public have awakened interest in the Church. The influence of the National Association of Manufacturers and the large steel, electrical, chemical, and food trusts on the work of the Church as well as its income has not been fully assessed. Areas of strain are to be found not only in labor-management relations, but also in the degree of interest and control by industry and its leaders of civic welfare, philanthropy, production and consumption of goods, and the ownership of property in the manufacturing and financial colossus which governs industry. These, as well as the benefactions of the industrial giants: Carnegie, Rockefeller, Du Pont, Morgan, and

Ford are to be viewed in the light of Lev. 19:13, Jer. 22:13, and James 5:1ff.

Papal encyclicals have given warning about the abuse of wealth and power as the most fertile ground for radical economic and political ideologies. The Protestants have been increasingly interested and active in Christian industrial reconstruction. The Church, which ministers to industrialist and laborer, applies the ethical teachings of Scripture impartially to both. See *Capital and Labor; Labor and the Church.* JD

A. W. Taylor: *Christianity and Industry in America*, N. Y., Friendship Press, 1933; R. H. Tawney: *Religion and the Rise of Capitalism*, N. Y., Brace, 1926; F. A. Knight and T. W. Merriam: *The Economic Order and Religion*, N. Y., Harper, 1945; T. Graebner: *The Business Man and the Church*, Clinton, S. C., Jacobs, 1942; E. B. Chaffee: *The Protestant Churches and the Industrial Crisis*, N. Y., Macmillan, 1933; A. I. Abell: *The Urban Impact on American Protestantism 1865—1900*, Cambridge, Harvard, 1943; S. Miller and J. F. Fletcher: *The Church and Industry*, N. Y., 1930; C. F. May: *Protestant Churches and Industrial America*, N. Y., Harper, 1949.

Ineffabilis Deus. See *Roman Catholic Confessions*, C.

Infallibility. See *Roman Catholic Confessions*, E 3.

Infant Salvation. The belief that infants are saved irrespective of Baptism. Calvin held that all elect infants were saved. Lutherans hold that with regard to infants of Christian believers who die without Baptism it is best to commend them to God's mercy, who has power to work faith also without the ordained means of grace (Luke 1:15, 44).

Infants, Faith of. See *Grace, Means of*, III, 4.

Infidelity. 1) The disavowal of a tenet of religion. 2) The lack of faithfulness to an obligation, especially marriage. (See *Orthodox; Marriage*.)

Infinite. *Divine infinity (infinitas)* is that attribute of God according to which He is contained within no bounds either of time (eternity) or of space (immensity). Scripture ascribes to God infinity a) as to His essence (Ps. 145:3) and b) as to His attributes (Ps. 147:5). Hence not only God in Himself is in-

finite, but also His knowledge, power, grace, etc.

Infralapsarians. See *Predestination*, 4.

Infusion of Grace. See *Grace, Means of*, I, 8.

Ingersoll, Robert Green. American lawyer and lecturer; b. 1833 at Dresden, N. Y.; d. 1899 at Dobbs Ferry, N. Y.; Union colonel in Civil War; as avowed agnostic he attacked Christian beliefs in his printed public lectures.

Inner Light. See *Grace, Means of*, I, 7; *Friends, Society of; Pentecostalism*.

Inner Mission. 1. Inner Mission (German, *Innere Mission*) designates a movement in the field of Christian social service which began in Germany with the tercentenary of the Reformation (1817). The founder and organizer of the movement was Johann Heinrich Wichern (1808—81). He established "Das Rauhe Haus" in Hamburg in 1833 as a rescue home for boys, later extending its program to include many other types of charitable and missionary work. Together with Theodore Fliedner he established the diaconate, concentrating his efforts primarily on the training of men.

2. The slogan of the Inner Mission movement is: "Die Seele der Barmherzigkeit ist die Barmherzigkeit mit der Seele." (The soul of charity is charity for the soul.) This slogan indicates clearly that the objectives of Inner Mission are both social and spiritual, that it is Christian social service in the fullest sense of the term.

3. Adolf Stoecker (1835—1909), a court preacher and member of the Christian Socialist Party, exerted much influence in the later development of the Inner Mission movement, providing the impetus to social reform and social action.

The Nazi regime and the Second World War combined to undo many of the social gains achieved by the Inner Mission in Germany. It may be said, however, that in its heyday Inner Mission was one of the greatest and most blessed movements in social work and in religious service to the whole personality of man.

The term Inner Mission was extensively used by Lutherans in America (although very little by Missouri Synod Lutherans, to whom "Inner Mission" stood for home mission) until about 1940, when the term "Social Missions" came into use. "Inner Mission" is still used, although with diminishing frequency, in some sections to designate Christian social service and Church-sponsored charitable enterprises. See also *Charities, Christian; Social Work; Social Reform; Social Action; Associated Lutheran Charities.* HFW

F. J. Ohl, *Inner Missions,* United Luth. Pub. House, Philadelphia, 1911.

Inner Word. See *Grace, Means of,* I, 7.

Innerlichkeit (inwardness). A word applied to Lutheran understanding of Christianity. It means that all concepts and acts arise from the inward fact of reconciliation and citizenship in God's kingdom.

Innocence. In the sense of sinlessness, the Bible uses this term only of Christ. Since man is by nature not holy, perfect, righteous, but a sinner, he is not innocent before God. See *Original Sin, Righteousness, Law.* (Cp. Job 9:28.) The Bible speaks of man's state of innocence before the Fall and of the believers serving God in "innocence and blessedness" (Luther to Second Article). We may otherwise speak of a man's innocence only relatively with respect to demands and judgments of civil laws, *e. g.,* not guilty of a gross moral offense (Ps. 18:26), without fault in the eyes of human judges and society in general (cp. Gen. 20:5; Job 33:9; Ps. 26:6; Jer. 2:35; Dan. 6:22). God regards the believers as innocent before Him when He sees them clothed in Christ's righteousness and cleansed by the Savior's blood. Cp. Luther IV:558; XII:1325; Kretzmann, *Pop. Com.,* N. T., II, 661 (sub Holiness); Reu-Buehring, *Christian Ethics,* p. 68. JMW

Innocent III. See *Popes,* 10.

Innocent VIII. See *Popes,* 17.

Innocent X. See *Popes,* 23.

Innocents, Feast of. See *Church Year,* 1.

Inquirant. See *Inquisition,* 2.

Inquisition, The. 1. Also called the *Holy Office* because of its supposedly sacred function in maintaining the integrity of the Roman Catholic faith, was an institution established for the detection and punishment of heresy, that is, all dissent from the accepted teachings and rites of the Church. It represents the culmination of the pernicious principle of applying the thumbscrew to the conscience, of resorting to force and violence to uphold religious uniformity and "orthodoxy." In carrying out this principle, the Inquisition has earned for itself the notorious distinction of being perhaps the most horrible engine of oppression that history knows of. Its record is a revolting chapter of fierce fanaticism and bigotry, of unspeakable atrocity and refined cruelty, of sovereign contempt and glaring defiance of the elementary canons of justice — all under the shield of Rome and in the sacred name of religion.

2. In outlining the history of the Inquisition, we shall say just a few words about its historical antecedents. Intolerance in the Christian Church began in the days of Constantine. It was embodied in the laws of, and energetically put into practice by, Emperors Theodosius and Justinian, who persecuted both heathen and heretics. The method of Charles the Great in "converting" the Saxons is a matter of familiar knowledge. Charles the Bald, in 844, enjoined upon the bishops *ut populi errata inquirant et corrigant* (that they should *inquire into* — hence the word *Inquisition* — the errors of the people and correct them). This is mentioned here because of the ill-omened term *inquirant.*

3. It was reserved, however, for the later Middle Ages to develop an organized inquisitorial system to guard the Church against the inroads of heresy. Synods and councils (Tours, 1163; the Third Lateran, 1179; Verona, 1184; and particularly Toulouse, 1229), seconded by secular rulers (Frederick Barbarossa and Frederick II), addressed themselves to the task of providing the legislative machinery and putting it into operation. This eventuated in the establishment of the *Episcopal Inquisition.* The Synod of Toulouse, 1229, which gave this stage of the institution its final form, enacted that the bishops should appoint a priest and one or two laymen to hunt out heretics in their sees and bring them to trial before the episcopal tribunal. Princes were ordered to destroy the homes of heretics, even if they were underground. Anyone giving aid and comfort to a heretic was liable to lose his office and his property. To escape the charge of heresy, all the inhabitants were bound to present themselves at least once a year at the confessional and to declare under oath, every two years, their allegiance to the Church.

4. Undue lenience on the part of

the bishops in enforcing these regulations induced Pope Gregory IX, in 1232, to take the trial and punishment of heresy out of the hands of the bishops and to entrust it to the Dominican friars, who had been replacing the bishops ever since they received papal sanction, in 1215. This marks the second stage in the history of the Inquisition. Inasmuch as the Dominicans were immediately responsible to no one but the Pope, with whom they communicated through the Inquisitors-General, the Inquisition may now be called the *papal* or the *Dominican*. Henceforth its activities were carried on on a wider scale and with greater stress and rigor. It was introduced into France against the protest of the Gallican Church, which resented it as a menace to its liberties. It was established in Spain, northern and central Italy, Germany, the Netherlands, and later (to combat the Wyclifite movement) in England.

5. To describe its work in anything like detail is, of course, impossible here. But a few facts must be noticed. The inquisitors were exempt from all jurisdiction, religious or secular, amenable only to the authority of the Pope. Thus there was nothing to check their activity (except lynch law, which in not a few cases was called into play). The inquisitor might be police, prosecutor, and judge at the same time. The slightest rumor, a vague suspicion, was deemed sufficient to warrant the arrest and trial of, perhaps, a wholly innocent person. At the trials the names of the accusers were never revealed. In short, the ordinary laws of justice did not seem to exist for the authorized guardians of the faith. As to the penalties inflicted, they ranged from fines, seizure of property, banishment, and imprisonment to hanging, drowning, or burning, according to the measure of adjudged guilt. Naturally, the confiscation of the heretic's property, a portion of which usually fell to the inquisitors became a powerful stimulus (Lea says the most powerful) in the heresy-hunting business. The exact number of victims, will, of course, never be known. Sufficient data, however, are preserved to enable us to form an idea of the extensive activities of the system. As early as 1243 the number of those sentenced to life imprisonment in France was so great that there were hardly stones enough to erect prison buildings. A single Inquisitor-General, Bernard de Caux,

sentenced from eight to ten thousand persons during his four years of office (1244—48). On May 12, 1234, six boys, twelve men, and eleven women were burned at Toulouse. In Germany the names of sixty-three Inquisitors-General have been preserved. Of these, Konrad of Marburg, called by Gregory IX the "Lord's watchdog," made himself so odious that after a short and bloody reign of terror he was murdered. Our limits forbid further details.

6. But a word must be said about the *Spanish Inquisition*, which represents the latest and most horrible stage of the institution. As to its origin and essential character the Spanish Inquisition was papal, but the control and administration were in the hands of the Spanish government. So far it was "Spanish." Attempts to exonerate the Papacy of the guilt and infamy incurred by the Spanish tribunals are vain. As the Spanish writer expresses it: "The Inquisition fused into one weapon the papal sword and the temporal power of kings." The Spanish Inquisition was established in 1480 and was not abolished until 1835. It was directed primarily against the *conversos*, sometimes called the new Christians, that is, such "converts" from the Jews and Moors as were suspected of secretly abiding by their ancestral faith. The motives which prompted Ferdinand and Isabella to introduce and maintain the Inquisition were threefold: They desired to purify their kingdom of heresy, to strengthen the compactness of their realm politically, and to share in the division of the spoils. During the first year of its activity the Inquisition, according to the Spanish historian Mariana, burned no fewer than 2,000 persons in the archbishopric of Seville and the bishopric of Cadiz. In 1483 Torquemada, whose name has become a byword for fierce and relentless fanaticism, gave the institution its full organization. Also, about this time a code of thirty-nine articles was drawn up to regulate the procedure of the Holy Office. By a flagrant perversion of justice the Inquisition proceeded on the presumption that the accused was guilty until he had proved his innocence. And since this was rarely possible, with the whole inquisitorial process, including the most refined and fiendish torture, against the defendant, it is no wonder that the lurid glare of the *auto da fé* was long a familiar spectacle in Spain. According to Llorente the first Inquisitor-

General Torquemada, during the eighteen years of his administration (1480 to 1498), burned 8,800 persons alive and 6,500 in effigy and sentenced 90,004 to other forms of punishment. Further statistics must be sought elsewhere. The Inquisition was introduced into the Spanish dependencies. It was abolished in Mexico in 1820 and in Peru in the same year. Prior to its abolition in Europe it had been losing its force. The number of burnings steadily diminished. In the eighteenth century, torture was abandoned. Napoleon struck off the heads of the hydra wherever he could. Though revived after his death, the Inquisition was in its last gasp. Its last victim was a schoolmaster in Spain, who was accused of deism and was hanged in 1826.

H. C. Lea, *A History of the Inquisition of Spain*, Macm., 1906—07; H. C. Lea, *The Inquisition in Spanish Dependencies*, Macm., 1908; H. C. Lea, *A History of the Inquisition in the Middle Ages*, 1887 (3 vols.); A. H. Verrill, *The Inquisition*, Appleton, 1931.

Insane Asylums. Governments have established institutions (state hospitals) to which insane people, after their case has been duly established, are committed for care, treatment, and safekeeping. Violent patients are placed in so-called maniac wards, while others are given more freedom and, if possible, are usefully employed in some way. When insane patients have sufficiently recovered, they are dismissed. The percentage of cures varies in different institutions in accordance with the classes of cases there treated, but, on the whole, excellent results are obtained. Insane asylums are also maintained by some church bodies. See *Hospitals*.

In-Service Training of Teachers. See *Teachers, A 8*.

Inspiration, Doctrine of. A. 1. By confessing the doctrine of inspiration, we declare our belief — based on the words of the Bible itself — that the Holy Spirit exercised a special influence by which He guided His chosen instruments to speak the things He desired them to speak, and to write the things He desired them to write, in the precise manner and in the very words in which He desired these things to be spoken or written. Inspiration differs from revelation inasmuch as revelation is a direct communication from God to man concerning things which it is necessary for man to know;

whereas inspiration is a special, potent activity of the Holy Spirit which He exercised upon those men whom He had chosen for His instruments to serve the purpose of spoken or written utterance. Revelations were already granted to the patriarchs; but they were not inspired to commit their revelations to writing. The prophets had revelations; but not all of them were inspired to communicate through the medium of writing the revelations they had received. Thus we possess no writings of the prophets Elijah and Elisha. St. Paul had revelations and was inspired to commit them to writing. Of St. Luke we do not read that he merely had revelations; but he was inspired to write his Gospel and the Book of Acts. Neither is inspiration the same as illumination, the latter being common to all Christians (Eph. 1:18; 3:9; 5:18), while the former was restricted to the holy men of God by whom the Holy Scriptures were given for our enlightenment. A Scripture based upon, or sprung from, revelation only or resulting from illumination would not be simply and in the Scriptural sense the "Word of God."

2. The fact of inspiration is taught in various passages of Holy Writ, both of the Old and of the New Testament. What is written in the Bible at one time attributed to "the Holy Spirit" or to "God" without mention of the divine Person, at other times to the human being, the instrument which God employed for the purpose of utterance. We read "God spake" or "the Holy Ghost spake"; but also "David spake" or "Isaiah spake" — the various terms being occasionally used in close textual connection. (Matt. 19:4, 5 and Gen. 2:24; 2 Sam. 23:1, 2; Matt. 22:43; 15:4, and Mark 7:10; Acts 28:25 and John 12:41; Acts 1:16 and other passages. Read also St. Paul's declaration Gal. 1:1, 12, where he reports the manner in which the Gospel was communicated to him.)

3. That the Holy Spirit suggested to the sacred penmen both the thoughts and the words (verbal and plenary inspiration) they uttered as they wrote, is a truth established by such texts as the following: 2 Tim. 3:16; Jer. 30:2; 1 Thess. 2:13; 2 Pet. 1:19-21; John 10:34, 35; Matt. 22:43, 44; Gal. 3:16; Heb. 12:27; 4:17.

4. To say that the Bible is the work of the Holy Spirit does not imply the suspension or extinction of the personality or individuality of the organs

employed by the Spirit of God. It is not without a peculiar purpose that God has given us the Old Testament by a variety of organs, Moses, David, Isaiah, and other Prophets, and the New Testament by four different Evangelists and several Apostles, and that Paul was not prompted to write all his Epistles in the same frame of mind and under the same circumstances. Even when Paul gives us his judgment or "opinion" (1 Cor. 7:25, 40), as distinguished from the commandments of God, it is because God would have him speak what he there speaks, and just as he speaks, "for our profit" (v. 35), and the Spirit of God did not in that moment withdraw His inspiring influence from the Apostle, who, as one who "has the Spirit of God," applied the general principle to an individual case by inspiration of God. "When Paul speaks of his expectation and hope and joy and desire, it is because God would tell us in His Word what was in the heart of His servant and Apostle, even as He inspired David to utter the joy and hope and anguish of his soul in words suggested by the Spirit of God, that such Scripture also should be profitable for consolation, for doctrine, for reproof, for correction, for instruction in righteousness, as truly as the Sermon on the Mount or the fifty-third chapter of Isaiah."

5. The relation between the Author proper and the penman whom He employed is expressed in the Nicene Creed by the phrase "*Who* spake *by* the Prophets.*" This phrase exactly summarizes not only the comparison between such texts as 1 Cor. 5:9 and 1 John 1:4 with that numerous group represented by Matt. 2:17 and 24:15; but is found as to its very terms in Rom. 1:2: "Which *He* had promised *by* His Prophets in the Holy Scriptures."

B. 1. *Luther and Inspiration.* It was through Luther that the Bible was again restored in the Church as the sole authority. In his lectures on the Psalms (1513—15) Luther has many statements in which he shows that he regards the Scriptures as the Word of God, regarding such expressions as "God speaks" and "Scripture speaks" as interchangeable. As late as 1516, however, he still surrendered his own right to understand and explain the Scriptures to the Fathers and the Church. In the controversies with Eck, Luther divorced himself from the authority of councils and by the time of the Diet at Worms had come to the conclusion that the infallible Scriptures are far above the authority of the entire human race. Thereafter the Scriptures remained Luther's sole authority. Although there were many things in the Bible which puzzled Luther, and even amazed him, he at no time admitted error in the Bible also in those parts which do not directly concern the fundamentals. (Luther's views on the *Antilegomena* do not affect this conclusion. See *Antilegomena.*) The above, however, applied only to the original manuscripts. At the same time he emphasized the human part in the writing of the Bible and avoided the dictation or mechanical theory.

2. The Confessions, although they do not give a separate systematic treatment of inspiration, show in many ways that they take for granted that the Bible is God's Word and the infallible guide and authority.

3. a. *Lutheran Dogmaticians* (early). Chemnitz not only sought to show the genuineness of Scripture as the inspired Word of God, but also to demonstrate historically that the writing of the Bible was a part of God's plan of revelation. Selnecker continued the investigation of Chemnitz under three divisions: 1) origin and necessity; 2) use; 3) evaluation (*Ansehen*). In regard to the last he held that since Scripture is throughout the Word of God, its content throughout is heavenly, divine, and spiritual. He maintained that the real meaning is not in the "dead letter," but comes through the enlightenment of the Spirit. Johann Gerhard emphasized that the Sacred Scriptures are *autopistos* (that is, they need no testimony except that of God, their Author) and held that the energy of Sacred Scripture which leads us to Christ also convinces us that God is the Author of the Bible.

b. Calixt differentiated between the articles of faith in the Bible and those parts of Scripture which serve only as introduction, means of presentation, etc. He regarded the articles of faith alone as strictly inspired, while in the rest there was an assistance or direction which preserved it from error. Over against this view, Calov held that the Bible forms a whole and formulated the phrase: *forma revelationis divinae est Theopneustia, per quam revelatio divina est, quod est.* He also distinguished between the "act of the revealing God" and the "form of the revealed Word." Feeling that Calov had gone too far toward a mechanical theory, Musaeus sought to elucidate human freedom in the act of inspiration and emphasized the divine direction first voiced by Calixt.

c. Quenstedt's presentation of inspiration is noteworthy because of the historical evidence which he marshals. He held that the Apostolic writing is the same as the preaching since both serve the purpose of awakening faith in Christ. He differentiated between the need of the whole Church and the immediate need of the writing. He distinguished an enlightenment (irradiatio) which preceded the impulse (impulsus) to write. Inspiration itself he characterized as the descension of the Holy Spirit to the capabilities of the agent. Evolving this still more, Dannhauer distinguished 1) aspiratio (the activity of the penman in obedience to divine will, such as study, comparison of OT, investigations, etc.); 2) postspiratio (the quiet influence of the Holy Spirit on the penman); 3) inspiratio (the culmination of inspiration); 4) respiratio (the working of the Holy Spirit in the hearts of those who read the Word).

d. Later dogmaticians of the classical period concerned themselves with problems given above and developed certain phases of them. One of the important problems which concerned earlier and later dogmaticians was the relation existing between revelation and inspiration.

4. Reformed. The early Reformed writers and confessions sought a strict view of inspiration which at times borders on legalism. A false spiritualism and the application of rational principles to the interpretation of Scripture (no contradiction between Scripture and "nature") modified their doctrinal and confessional conceptions of inspiration.

5. Roman Catholicism. Roman Catholicism sought to uphold the inspiration of the Scriptures. At the same time, however, it placed traditions of the Church alongside of the inspired Word (Council of Trent, IV:1). The addition of the latter necessarily modified the doctrine of the Bible inasmuch as the Sacred Scriptures are viewed as incomplete, insufficient, and difficult of interpretation. The final criterion of doctrine became, not an infallible Word, but an infallible pope.

6. Pietism and Rationalism influenced later conceptions of inspiration. The Rationalism of the eighteenth and nineteenth centuries led to a surrender of the Word of God. A popular theory in the first part of the twentieth century held that the Bible is a human account of divine revelation (Offenbarungsurkunde) and hence not without error. Others held that there were degrees of inspiration. Thoughts on inspiration in the middle of the 20th century ranged from a mechanical theory to total rejection of inspiration (see Dogmatics; Higher Criticism).

7. Lutheranism in America. The leading Lutheran bodies teach the inspiration of Scripture and regard the Bible as the only infallible guide of doctrine and life:

a. The Pittsburgh Agreement (adopted by the A. L. C. and the U. L. C. A., 1940) states: "The Bible consists of a number of separate books, written at various times, on various occasions, and for various purposes. Their authors were living, thinking personalities, each endowed by the Creator with an individuality of his own and each having his peculiar style, his own manner of presentation, even at times using such sources of information as were at hand. Nevertheless, by virtue of a unique operation of the Holy Ghost (2 Tim. 3:16; 2 Pet. 1:21) by which He supplied to the holy writers content and fitting word (2 Pet. 1:21; 1 Cor. 2:12, 13) the separate books of the Bible are related to one another and, taken together, constitute a complete, errorless unbreakable whole, of which Christ is the Center (John 10:35). They are rightly called the Word of God. This unique operation of the Holy Spirit upon the writers is named inspiration. We do not venture to define its mode or manner, but accept it as a fact."

b. The Common Confession (adopted by the Missouri Synod and the American Lutheran Church in 1950) has the following:

"Through the Holy Scriptures, which God caused to be written by men chosen and inspired by Him, God instructs and assures us regarding His will for us. The Holy Scriptures constitute His Word to men, centering in the revelation of Himself in the person and work of Jesus Christ for our salvation. Through the Holy Scriptures God continues to speak to men in all ages until the end of time. He speaks as the infallible and unchanging God, whose message to mankind never changes. Since the Holy Spirit by divine inspiration supplied to the holy writers content and fitting word, therefore we acknowledge the Holy Scriptures in their entirety as the inspired Word of God. His Holy Spirit testifies in our hearts that His Word is true, that He will keep all His promises to us, and that our faith in Him is not in vain.

"We therefore recognize the Holy Scriptures as God's inerrant Word, and this Word of God alone shall establish articles of faith (cf. Smalcald Articles, Part II, Art. II). We pledge ourselves to teach all things taught in the Holy Scriptures and nothing but that which is taught us by God in the Holy Scriptures" (Art. V). EL (B)

Standard Dogmatics *; references under Confessions (e. g., Reformed Confessions); M. Reu, Luther and the Scriptures, Wartburg Press, Columbus, Ohio, 1944; T. Engelder, Scripture Cannot Be Broken, CPH, 1944; P. E. Kretzmann, "The Christo-centric Theory of Inspiration," CTM, XV: 187—92; W. Dallmann, Why Do I Believe the Bible Is God's Word? CPH, 1937; W. Arndt, "Die Lehre von der Inspiration nach 1 Petr. 1, 10—12," CTM, V: 192—98; T. Engelder, "Verbal Inspiration—A Stumbling Block to Jews and Foolishness to Greeks," CTM, XIII: 8—39; 161—83; 240—64; 414—41; 481—510; 561—90; 731—57; 811—33; 888—926; W. Albrecht, "Holy Scripture the Word of God," Abiding Word, CPH, 1946 (II: 1—34); C. Eberhard, "Geography of the Bible in Relation to Inspiration," CTM, XV: 736—47; T. Engelder, "Haec Dixit Dominus," CTM, XVIII: 484—99; J. Urquhart, The Wonders of Prophecy, Christian Pub., Harrisburg, Pa., 1946; J. A. Dell, "The Word of God," What Lutherans Are Thinking, Wartburg Press, Columbus, Ohio, 1947 (p. 26 ff.); P. Schumm, "The Clearness and Sufficiency of Scripture," Abiding Word, CPH, 1946 (I: 58—66); W. Elert, Morphologie des Luthertums, Beck, Munich, 1931 (I: 158—76); W. Walther, "Das Erbe der Reformation," 1903 (Vol. I, Der Glaube an das Wort Gottes); W. Rohnert, Die Dogmatik der Ev. Lutherischen Kirche, Wollermann, Leipzig, 1902; Loraine Boettner, The Inspiration of the Scriptures, Eerdmans, 1940; M. G. Kyle, Mooring Masts of Inspiration, rev. 1933; The Infallible Word, A Symposium by Members of the Faculty of Westminster Theological Seminary, Presbyterian Guardian Pub. Co., Philadelphia, rev. 1946.

For difficulties of the Bible: W. Arndt, Bible Difficulties, An Examination of Passages of the Bible Alleged to Be Irreconcilable with Its Inspiration, CPH, 1932; W. Arndt, Does the Bible Contradict Itself? CPH, 1926.

Inspirationists. See Amana Society.

Inspirations-Gemeinden. See Amana Society.

Installation. See Ministerial Office, 5.

Institute of a Christian Man. See Anglican Confessions, 2.

Institutes of the Christian Religion. See Calvin, John.

Institutional Church, The. Name given at beginning of twentieth century to the American Protestant parish which undertook a program of recreational leadership and social service in addition to the functions of worship and cure of souls. It was the product theologically of the Social Gospel * with its emphasis on the tangible activities and expedient of religion, and socially of the shift in population of the American cities. As the older, wealthy parishes found their plants isolated from their own membership and surrounded by less privileged classes, the emphasis in church work shifted to an approach to physical need and a provision for leisure time. The designation is dying out, in part because of renewed doctrinal emphases in the ministry of the churches, in part because of more adequate social service to handicapped areas, in part because of the trend in all the churches toward a seven-day-a-week ministry and the recruitment of the total energies of the membership for church work. For literature see Joseph M. N. Gray, "The Institutional Church" in V. Ferm, Encyclopedia of Religion.

Instrumental Foundation. See Fundamental Doctrines.

Integrity. As applied to the books of the Bible, that attribute according to which no part of the original manuscript is wanting and all the parts now included in the Book belong to it as first drafted.

Intellectualism, Philosophical (modern). Teaches that we learn to know the essence of things not through the senses, sensationalism, but through the pure concepts inherent in the very nature of the mind. Learning is but a recollection of inborn ideas through suggestion of their imperfect copies in the phenomenal world. The intellect is the basis and the support of all existence (Idealism). Principles of ethics are grounded in reason, not in feeling. In theology the term is sometimes used over against mysticism, which unduly emphasizes the religious feeling, to point out the importance of a clear intellectual knowledge of revealed Scripture doctrines. However, such intellectual knowledge, though a prerequisite, is not yet faith.

Intemperance. Yielding to sinful desires, passions, sensual appetites; it is chiefly associated with the immoderate drinking of wine and other liquors, leading to intoxication. But it includes overindulgence in eating and all abuse of God's gifts. The temperate use of any divine gift is not forbidden, but everything is to be used with moderation (1 Cor. 7:31; 1 Tim. 4:4; 2 Pet. 1:6; Titus 2:12). Intemperate use of intoxicating drink, drunkenness, is a sin against the Fifth Commandment, Eph. 5:18; Prov. 20:1; 23:20, 29-33; Luke 21:34; Rom. 13:13; 1 Cor. 6:10; Gal. 5:21; 1 Tim. 3:8. Examples of drunkenness: Gen. 9:21; 19:33; 1 Sam. 25:36; Dan. 5:1-6. Cp. Luther XII:600; VI:150 ff.; Reu-Buehring, *Christian Ethics*, 212; indices in Kretzmann's *Pop. Com.* (sub *Drunkards, Drunkenness, Wine*).

Intention of Priest. See *Sacraments, Roman Catholic.*

Intentionalism. See *Jesuits and Jesuitism,* 5.

Intercession. See *Prayer.*

Interchurch World Movement. This was a movement, prior to World War I, for the purpose of Christianizing the world by heroic interdenominational efforts. Large sums of money were spent, but finally the effort proved a failure. See *Men and Religion Forward Movement.*

Interdenominational Co-operation. See *Federal Council of the Churches of Christ in America; National Association of Evangelicals; Union Movements; World Council of Churches.*

Interdict. A form of censure or punishment in the Roman Church by which people are debarred from public worship, the Sacraments, and Christian burial. General interdicts were pronounced, in the Middle Ages, against cities, provinces, and even nations (France in 1200; England, 1208—13), the innocent suffering with the guilty. The Papacy found the interdict a powerful weapon to bring public pressure to bear on refractory rulers. The original rigor of the provisions was gradually relaxed. General interdicts practically ceased several centuries ago because they could no longer be enforced, though as late as 1909 Pius X placed the town of Adria, northern Italy, under an interdict for fifteen days. Interdicts of individuals and smaller groups are still in vogue. Originally an interdict was considered equivalent to excommunication, but now those under its censure are not supposed to be given over to damnation. The practice, in all its forms, is a corruption of the Scriptural doctrine of excommunication (see *Keys, Office of*), in perfect keeping with the legalistic spirit of the Roman Church.

Interim. A temporary agreement in religious matters until the next General Council should make a permanent settlement. The *Augsburg Interim* was made at the Diet in 1548 after Charles V had crushed the Smalcald League at Muehlberg in 1546 and placed Elector John Frederick of Saxony and Landgrave Philip of Hesse in captivity. The authors were the bishops Julius von Pflug of Naumburg, Michael Helding of Mainz, and John Agricola, then court preacher of Elector Joachim II of Brandenburg at Berlin. Though the twenty-six articles compromised the Reformation truths all along the line, the document was accepted by Electors Joachim II of Brandenburg and Frederick II of the Palatinate, the Duke of Wuerttemberg, and Landgrave Philip of Hesse, if given his freedom; but the captive John Frederick of Saxony magnanimously rejected it, as did others, and most of the cities of the realm, especially Magdeburg, which became the asylum of true Lutherans. In southern Germany Charles V enforced it by the atrocities of his troops; Lutheran preachers were driven out, for instance, Wolfgang Musculus, who had to flee from his wife and eight children at Augsburg. The Interim was not to be binding on the Romanists, but only on the Lutherans. — Not satisfied with the Augsburg Interim, Maurice of Saxony had it modified in November, 1548, by Melanchthon, Bugenhagen, George of Anhalt, Paul Eber, Jerome Weller, Anton Lauterbach, George Major, and Joachim Cameraius, and it became the law of Saxony in December at Leipzig, hence *Leipzig Interim.* It compromised the article of justification by faith; it pledged the clergy to obey the Pope and the bishops; it brought back the Romish ceremonies at Baptism, confirmation, extreme unction, and Corpus Christi; the laws of fasting were placed into the hands of the emperor. Flacius and Amsdorf vigorously opposed Agricola and Melanchthon for betraying the truth (see *Adiaphoristic Controversy*). Maurice was to punish Magdeburg for its resistance. He gathered an army and then suddenly warred on the emperor at Innsbruck and forced from him the Treaty of Passau, which ended the Interim and gave religious liberty to the Lutheran governments. *Bekenntnis und Erklaerung aufs Interim durch Luebeck, Hamburg, Magdeburg, etc.*, Magdeburg, 1548; N. Amsdorf, *Antwort, Glaub und Bekenntnis auf das schoene und liebliche Interim*, n. p., 1548.

Interlude. A passage or interval for instruments only between stanzas of a hymn or between portions of the liturgy, offering a breathing pause to the singers or congregation; should conform to the character of the hymn or section of the liturgy.

Intermediate State. The interval of time which to human reckoning elapses between the decease of the believers of present and past ages and the revival of their bodies at the general Judgment has given rise to various speculations, all of which agree in the assumption of an intermediate state. Such are the theories of a state of sleep or insensibility (see *Psychopannychism*), the theory of a purgatory (see *Purgatory*), and the theory of a middle state or intermediate place. See also *Hereafter.* — The term "intermediate state" is also used by some synergists to designate an attitude of mind which is favorable to the acceptance of Christ, while conversion has not yet taken place. Scripture teaches clearly that conversion is a direct change from spiritual death to spiritual life, and the doctrine of an intermediate state finds no support in the Bible.

International Apostolic Holiness Union. Organized by M. W. Knapp in 1897 (Cincinnati, Ohio) for the purpose of uniting Holiness and Pentecostal groups. The movement developed into a denomination with the name Pilgrim Holiness Church.

International Association of Lutheran Students. See *Students, Spiritual Care of, A.*

International Bible Students' Association. See *Jehovah's Witnesses.*

International Conventions. See *International Council of Religious Education.*

International Church of the Four-Square Gospel. See *Four-Square Gospel.*

International Council of Religious Education. (This organization became the *Division of Christian Education* of the National Council of the Churches of Christ in the U. S. A., organized Nov. 29, 1950.) 1. *Origin.* The rapid spread of the Sunday school after the War of Independence led to the formation of many Sunday school unions. These unions were simply the expression of a deeply felt need for co-operative endeavor at a time when the movement was in its infancy, and neither an approved program nor standard study courses had appeared. Popular conventions were the rule, even prior to 1900, and a continuous and major problem dealt with at these conventions was the preparation of adequate courses for all age levels.

In 1905 the International Convention adopted the name "International Sunday School Association." In 1910 the officers of denominational boards were organized into "The Sunday School Council of Evangelical Denominations." In 1922 these two organizations united to form the "International Council of Religious Education." Doctrinal differences were recognized, but it was believed that these constituted no barrier to interdenominational co-operation.

2. *Organization.* The International Council of Religious Education became a complex organization utilizing the services of more than 2,000 persons, and representing 40 Protestant denominations of the United States and Canada. The Council was composed of 362 representatives (1949) elected by the denominational boards and state councils. The state councils were appointed to promote the policies and programs of the Council. The staff constituted the board of editors.

In the course of time the activities and services of the Council broadened to embrace almost every phase of Christian education. These departments were created: Children's Work, Young People's Work, Adult Work and Family Education, Leadership Education, Field Administration, Vacation Religious Education, Weekday Religious Education,

Research, Visual Education, Radio Education.

Membership in the Council was made voluntary and open to conservatives and liberals alike. Constituent groups were given a part in determining Council policies, procedures, and plans. The participating denominations were at liberty to make whatever use they chose of the materials prepared jointly by the members of the Council.

3. *Materials.* Through its lesson committees the Council provided outlines for all types of church schools and for all age levels from beginners to adults. Denominational editors and writers prepare the study materials on the basis of these outlines. The Council also publishes outlines of textbooks and of study units, such as the co-operative vacation and weekday church school texts and adult study guides. The Council outlines courses, recommends textbooks, and is the co-ordinating unit for interdenominational leadership training. It provides many services, mostly in pamphlet form, covering housing and equipment, records and reports, programs for special occasions, and numerous other phases of Christian education.

The *International Journal of Religious Education* was made the official publication of the Council of Religious Education. The Revised Standard Version of the Bible has been prepared under the direction of the Council. Summer camp conferences are another activity of the Council. Six regional conferences are held for the religious training of youth who are leaders. In 1940 the Council inaugurated similar conferences for the training of leaders in adult Christian education.

4. *Recent Developments.* The Department of Ecumenical Education was added to the many other departments. In 1943 the following action was taken: "That the International Council approve the recommendations for the creation of an 'inclusive co-operative agency' to continue and extend these agencies of the Church and to combine all their interests and functions, to be known as the North American Council of the Churches of Christ." The International Council of Religious Education had a working relationship with the Federal Council and with the Home Missions Council of North America and the Foreign Missions Conference of North America. The International Council of Religious Edu-

cation became a part of the National Council of Churches of Christ in America.

Conservatives are critical of these relationships. Many of them are deserting the Council on the ground that the liberals dominate it. They complain of the "trends in curriculum which are now definitely away from the old Bible-centered policy." They maintain that "liberalism and professionalism in the Council have destroyed lay interest in Sunday school co-operation"; that millions have been lost to the Sunday school because of progressive tendencies in the program of religious education projected by the Council. Conservatives have founded the National Sunday School Association, which is affiliated with the National Association of Evangelicals, organized in 1943. This group has already prepared a new series of outlines for Sunday school lessons and will probably parallel all the services of the International Council. ACM

International Graded Sunday School Lessons. See *International Council of Religious Education.*

International Journal of Religious Education. See *International Council of Religious Education.*

International Lutheran Hour. See *Radio Evangelism,* 6.

International Missionary Alliance. See *Evangelistic Organizations,* 5; *Missions,* B 15.

International New Thought Alliance. See *New Thought.*

International Pentecostal Assemblies. See *Holiness Bodies; Pentecostalism.*

International Sunday School Association. See *International Council of Religious Education.*

International Sunday School Convention. See *International Council of Religious Education.*

Internationale, Red. See *Marx, Karl.*

Internuncio. See *Legates.*

Interpretation, Biblical. See *Exegesis; Hermeneutics.*

Interstice. In Roman Catholicism, the time required to intervene between promotions.

Intersynodical Theses. See *Chicago Theses.*

Inter-Varsity Christian Fellowship. See *Students, Spiritual Care of,* A.

Intinction. One of the modes in which the Sacrament of the Altar is administered to the laity of the Eastern Church, *viz.,* by breaking the consecrated bread into the consecrated wine and giving to each communicant the two elements together in a spoon, "to prevent the possibility of a loss of either element." Intinction is now practiced also by some Protestant denominations in this way that the minister of the rite dips the wafer in the wine before giving it to the worshiper.

Intonation. In chanting, the notes leading up to the reciting tone and the act of intoning after such an introductory, indicating the proper pitch.

Introduction, Biblical. See *Isagogics.*

Introit. The initial Proper of the Order of Holy Communion (Morning Service; Common Service), so called because the officiating liturgist enters the sanctuary (*introitus:* entrance) while the choir chants the Introit. Its texts are usually from the Old Testament Scriptures; hence the Gloria Patri is added as its final division. The Introit consists of antiphon, Psalm, and Gloria Patri. In view of the fact that in the antiphon is expressed the thought of the day, it is usually repeated after the Gloria Patri. The Introit is believed to have been introduced by Pope Coelestine I (ca. A. D. 400) and consisted originally of an entire Psalm which was chanted antiphonally. It is traditionally sung in plain-song settings, and several Sundays of the church year have their name from the initial word of the Latin text of the Introit set aside for their Sunday.

W. E. Buszin, *Introits for the Church Year* (cf. Introduction), CPH, 1942.

Intuition of Right or Wrong. See *Conscience.*

Intuitionism. A term used in philosophy for the view that truth is immediate, *i. e.,* self-verifying in character. It is especially applied in the field of ethics to the school which holds that rightness or wrongness is known by direct intuition and without consideration of the results.

Intuitu fidei. The phrase means "in view of faith." It was used a great deal in the Predestinarian Controversy that burst upon the conservative Lu-theran Church around 1880. The expression was adopted by Lutheran theologians about 1600, chiefly through the influence of Aegidius Hunnius (1550—1603), professor at Wittenberg. In opposing the Calvinistic view that the election of God is an absolute one in which He is moved by His sovereign will, Hunnius and others taught that the divine election is not an absolute one, but that God chose people for eternal life "in view of faith." The term may have the meaning that God, in electing people to salvation, included faith in the decree of election, resolving to lead men to heaven by means of faith. A century after its adoption, however, it had come to have the significance that God, on account of the faith of certain people, that is, on account of the faith which He foresaw they would have, chose them to be heirs of eternal life. It is evident that in this presentation faith is viewed as a cause of our election and as the factor which "explains" the mystery of predestination. It is a view which contradicts the precious truth of complete and free grace. On the role given the term in the debates between Missouri and its opponents, see the article *Lutheran Church — Missouri Synod,* "Controversy on Election and Conversion." In the old days of the Missouri Synod many of its members had used the term, but through the Predestination Controversy it was eliminated. Since 1915 the tendency in the Lutheran Church of America has been to drop the expression. It is recognized that there is no Scripture warrant for it and that, while the phrase is capable of a correct interpretation, it can be misunderstood, to say the least. The so-called Chicago Theses of 1928 (drawn up by representatives of Ohio, Iowa, Buffalo, Wisconsin, and Missouri) take a stand against the use of the term, and so does the Declaration of the American Lutheran Church of 1938. The Missouri Synod reaffirmed its position in the Brief Statement of 1932, saying, paragraph 36: "Nor does Holy Scripture know of an election 'by foreseen faith,' or 'in view of faith,' as though the faith of the elect were to be placed before their election; but according to Scripture the faith which the elect have in time belongs to the spiritual blessings with which God has endowed them by His eternal election."

WA

F. Pieper, *Die Grunddifferenz* (The Fundamental Difference), paper read at the intersynodical conference at Watertown, Wis., 1903; Th. Graebner, "The Missouri Synod's Attitude Towards the Doctrine of Election 'Intuitu Fidei,'" *CTM*, XV: 616—21.

Investigative Judgment. See *Adventist Bodies*, 4.

Investiture, Struggle About. Investiture is the ceremony of inducting an abbot or a bishop into office. This rite became the subject of a long contention during the Medieval Age, with the Papacy on the one side and various secular rulers on the other. Before the fall of the Roman Empire the imperial influence was the stronger, and no important office was filled without the direct sanction of, often not without actual nomination by, the emperor. But when the power of the Papacy grew, the traditions respecting the rights of the emperors were often set aside. The struggle was especially severe in Germany, lasting there for about a century and a half (1050—1198). The matter was finally adjusted by means of the *Concordat of Worms*, which amounted to a compromise. See also *Concordat* and *Gregory VII*.

Invitatory. The phrase "Oh, come, let us worship the Lord, for He is our Maker" chanted responsively in the Matin service.

Invocation. 1) A prayer at the opening of a service or at any special occasion; 2) the words "in the name of the Father and of the Son and of the Holy Ghost" spoken at the opening of a service or at a special occasion.

Iowa and Other States, Ev. Luth. Synod of. A. *Early History.* 1. This synod was organized Aug. 24, 1854, at St. Sebald, Iowa, by the emissaries of Loehe in Neuendettelsau, Revs. G. M. Grossmann, John Deindoerfer, Candidate (later Dr.) S. Fritschel, and one lay member. In the forties Loehe had directed the men whom he sent to America to minister to the scattered Lutherans and to the Saxons in Missouri, thus promoting the founding of the Synod of Missouri, Ohio, and Other States. A breach between Loehe and the Missourians, caused by a difference in regard to the doctrine of the Church and the ministry, seemed to have been healed by the visit of Walther and Wyneken to Germany in 1851. However, Grabau's visit to Loehe two years later seems to have induced Loehe to found a new synod, which was to mediate between Grabau and the Missourians. It was with Loehe's consent that Grossmann and Deindoerfer, with a party of twenty Loehe adherents, left the Franconian colonies in Michigan, in the fall of 1853, and migrated to Dubuque, Iowa. Grossmann and five students of the seminary of which he had been the head in Saginaw, Mich., remained in Dubuque, while Deindoerfer and others went 60 miles farther northwest and founded St. Sebald, where, in 1854, also the Iowa Synod was founded. At the request of Grabau, who visited Dubuque in 1855, the young synod took charge of the Buffalo Synod congregations around Madison, Wis., Detroit, and Toledo. But the statement of Iowa's attitude to the Lutheran Confessions in the first number of the *Kirchenblatt* alienated Buffalo's affections. The Wartburg Seminary, founded in Dubuque in 1854, was transferred to St. Sebald in 1857. Prof. S. Fritschel raised enough money on a trip to Europe to pay the debt resting on it. In 1874 the seminary was moved to Mendota, Ill.; in 1889 back to Dubuque.

2. The Iowa Synod was in a strategic position for attending to the spiritual needs of the immigrants from Lutheran countries that poured into the Northwest, in the second half of the nineteenth century, and its home missionaries were scattered over the territory between the Alleghanies and the Pacific Coast. In its earlier days it also maintained a mission among the Indians in Idaho. In 1895, through the influence of G. J. Fritschel, the larger part of the Texas Synod (founded 1851) joined the Iowa Synod as a district. All the districts of the Iowa Synod: Iowa, Northern, Southern, Western, Wisconsin, South Dakota, North Dakota, and Texas (Synod), met annually, while the whole synod met as a convention of delegates every three years. Its foreign mission work was carried on in former years in connection with the General Council, Neuendettelsau, Hermannsburg, Leipzig, etc. After the First World War the Iowa Synod conducted the mission in former German New Guinea in conjunction with the United Ev. Luth. Church in Australia. Six missionaries were sent over in 1922. The synod also, since 1921, took care of the Tanganyika mission in former German East Africa.

3. Besides the Wartburg Seminary at Dubuque it maintained the Wartburg Normal School at Waverly, Iowa, Wartburg College at Clinton, Iowa, an

academy at Eureka, S. Dak., and Martin Luther Academy at Toledo, Ohio. It also had homes for the aged at Muscatine, Iowa, and Toledo. The Iowa Synod operated the Wartburg Publishing House, Chicago, published the *Kirchenblatt*, the *Lutheran Herald*, the *Kirchliche Zeitschrift*, and the *Wartburg Lesson Helps Series*.

4. The leading men of the Iowa Synod were the Fritschels (Gottfried, Sigmund, John, Max, and George J.), G. M. Grossmann, J. Deindoerfer, F. Richter, and J. M. Reu.

5. In 1925 the Iowa Synod numbered 587 pastors, 966 congregations, and 137,318 communicants, plus 5,600 in New Guinea. In 1930 the Iowa Synod merged with the Buffalo and Ohio Synods to form the American Lutheran Church (see B).

B. *Relation to Other Bodies.* 1. a. The controversy between the Missouri and Iowa Synods concerned (a) the Church and the ministry (Walther and Loehe, see A 1 above); (b) Antichrist and Chiliasm; (c) the Confessions and "open questions"; (d) Sunday; (e) usury; (f) justification; and (g) predestination and conversion. A brief synopsis follows:

b. While Iowa did not adopt a formal constitution at its organization, the first of its "guiding principles" reads: "Synod accepts all the Symbolical Books of the Evangelical Lutheran Church because it believes that all their symbolical decisions of disputable questions which had arisen before or during the time of the Reformation were made in accordance with the Word of God. But because within the Lutheran Church there are different tendencies, Synod declares itself in favor of that tendency which, by means of the Confessions and on the basis of the Word of God, strives toward a greater degree of perfection." In 1867 the Iowa Synod declared at Toledo: "There never has been absolute doctrinal unity in the Church, and it should not be made a condition of church fellowship." At the same convention, Iowa resolved to ask Missouri for a colloquium. The Missouri Synod gladly assented, and the colloquy was held at Milwaukee, Nov. 13—18, 1867, in view of the fact that some ministers of the Iowa Synod were favorably disposed toward Missouri. At this conference the attitude of both synods to the Confessions and to "open questions" and some points of eschatology were discussed. Time did not permit discussion of the doctrine of the Church and the ministerial office, on which the two synods had originally separated. No agreement was reached except in minor points. Iowa would not admit that the doctrine concerning Sunday, the first resurrection (Rev. 20), and Antichrist must be considered symbolically fixed by the Lutheran Church and classed as articles of faith. For the term "open questions" Iowa was willing to substitute that of "problems"; yet no agreement was reached as to what should be counted as problems. In 1879 Iowa stated its doctrinal position as follows: "Our Synod was from its very beginning persuaded to make a distinction between such articles in the Confessions of the Evangelical Lutheran Church as are necessary articles of faith and such other doctrines as are not doctrines necessary for salvation; and our Synod has considered it one of her duties very earnestly and emphatically as an important truth . . . that there are doctrines, even doctrines of the Bible, concerning which members of our Church may hold different views and convictions without thereby being compelled to refuse each other church fellowship. . . . In such matters unity should indeed be sought; but it is not absolutely required as in the doctrines of faith." In the controversy on election and conversion between Missouri and Ohio the Iowa Synod stated its position as follows: "The Lutheran Church has ever considered it Calvinistic error . . . to speak of election as having been made without reference to the conduct of man, merely in accordance with the pleasure of the divine will, and to denounce as an error that God made His election in respect to the faith which He foresaw, because, according to the doctrine of the Lutheran Church, God, in His eternal divine counsel, has decreed that He would save no one except those who would know Christ, His Son, and truly believe in Him." And Deindoerfer, in his *History of the Iowa Synod*, declared: "Although in former years the difference between us and the Missouri Synod did not stand in the way of church fellowship, the difference now existing in the doctrine of election is of such a nature that there can no longer be any church fellowship."

In the early part of the 20th century the Iowa Synod participated in the movement which led to the drafting of the Chicago Theses (see details under *Chicago Theses*). For its later relations to Missouri see articles on

American Lutheran Church and *Brief Statement.*

2. After the disruption of the General Synod in 1866, Iowa had participated in the meetings that led to the founding of the General Council and approved of that body's doctrinal basis. It did not join, because it regarded the General Council's answer on the Four Points unsatisfactory (see *Four Points; Galesburg Rule*). Still Iowa continued to maintain friendly relations with the Council and was represented in an advisory capacity at its meetings. In 1875 Pastor G. A. Schieferdecker, who had left the Missouri Synod in 1859 on account of his chiliastic teachings, returned to Missouri, and J. Klindworth led an exodus of twenty ministers into the Wisconsin Synod.

3. After the Ohio Synod withdrew from the Synodical Conference in 1881, a private conference was arranged between leaders of Iowa and Ohio. In 1887 arrangements were made for an official committee. The theses formulated by this committee were not accepted. In 1909 the Toledo Theses * were drawn up, on the basis of which fellowship was declared in 1918. Shortly thereafter a joint committee was named to discuss a merger of the two bodies. In 1925 the Buffalo Synod sent a delegation to the committee. On Aug. 10, 1930, the Iowa Synod, Ohio Synod, and Buffalo Synod merged to form the American Lutheran Church.

J. Deindoerfer, *Geschichte der Ev. Luth. Synode von Iowa u. anderen Staaten,* Wartburg Pub. House, Chicago, 1897; G. J. Fritschel, *Quellen und Dokumente zur Geschichte und Lehrstellung der Iowa Synode,* Chicago, Wartburg Pub. House, 1916; G. J. Fritschel, *Geschichte der lutherischen Kirche in Amerika, auf Grund von Dr. Jacobs Historie,* Guetersloh, 1896; G. A. Zeilinger, *A Missionary Synod with a Mission, A Memoir for the Seventy-fifth Anniversary of the Ev. Lutheran Synod of Iowa and Other States,* Wartburg Pub. House, Chicago, 1929; G. J. Fritschel, "The German Iowa Synod," *Distinctive Doctrines and Usages of the General Bodies of the Ev. Luth. Church in the United States,* Luth. Pub. Soc., Philadelphia, 1902.

Iowa, Synod of. See *United Luth. Church, Synods of, 9.*

Iran (Persia). Area 628,000 sq. mi.; population 19,139,568 (1951 est.), mostly Mohammedans, with some Armenians and Nestorians. Christianity found an early home in Persia, but was almost exterminated by Islam. The Moravians made unsuccessful mission attempts in the 18th century. Henry Martyn attempted mission work in 1811, spending ten months in Shiraz, where he translated the New Testament into the vernacular. In 1831 O. Dwight and E. Smith, sent out by the American Board (A. B. C. F. M.), essayed missions in Persia. The Basel Mission sent out C. G. Pfander in 1829, but no permanent result ensued. In 1871 the American Presbyterians took over the work of the American Board. In 1875 the C. M. S. entered the mission field, occupying Kerman in 1897, Yezd in 1898, Shiraz in 1900. Medical work has been a feature of modern missionary endeavor in Persia, hospitals for men and women being conducted in Espahan, Yezd, and Kerman.

Statistics: approximately 3,575 communicants; 11 ordained and 90 not ordained native workers; total foreign staff: 128. Active are: the Faraman Industrial School; Ev. Church of Iran; Iran Interior Mission; Bible Churchmen's Missionary Soc.; British Society for the Propagation of the Gospel Among the Jews; Church Missionary Soc.; Church Missions to Jews; Christliche Blindenmission im Orient; Assemblies of God; Seventh-Day Adventists.

Iraq. 116,600 sq. mi.; population, 4,799,500 (1947). 336 communicants; 8 ordained, twenty-five not ordained foreign workers. The Church of England, the Evangelical and Reformed Church, Near East and Arabian Mission, the Presbyterian Church, the Reformed Church, the Adventists, and the Lutheran Orient Mission and United Mission in Mesopotamia carry on work. See *Missions, Bibliography.*

Ireland (Eire), 26,592 sq. mi.; population, 2,958,878 (1951). 1. Has had a religious history differing from that of any other European country. Though in their early history the people of Ireland developed a peculiar type of Christianity, untouched by Roman influence, they have become the most devoted adherents of Roman Catholicism. Though they witnessed the destruction of their liberties by a conqueror (Henry II of England) acting under the warrant and sanction of a papal bull, they have bowed submissively under the yoke of papal supremacy. On the other hand, since the Reformation their attachment to Rome has involved them in a bitter conflict, reaching almost to our own day, against the glaring anomaly of a Protestant state church established in their midst and maintained at their expense.

2. In the light of available evidence the beginnings of Irish Christianity may be traced to about the end of the fourth century. In 431 Palladius was sent by Pope Coelestine V as "the first bishop to the Scots [*i. e.*, Irish] believing in Christ." Beyond this notice there is no record of any papal interference in the affairs of the Irish Church for several centuries. The mission of Palladius failed. The great missionary of early Ireland is St. Patrick, called "the Apostle of Ireland." We know little of his life. His death is placed between 465 and 493. In less than a century after Patrick's death, Ireland was covered with churches and with convents for men and women. When continental Europe was threatened with barbarism during the migrations, the Irish monasteries were centers of learning and missionary zeal. "Ireland dreamed of converting heathen Europe." Usually traveling in bands of twelve, with a thirteenth as leader, the missionary monks labored in Scotland, northern Britain, France, Italy, Switzerland, and Germany (doing here the pioneer work for St. Boniface).

3. This missionary period of Irish church history extended over centuries. It ceased with the loss of Irish independence through the Norman conquest and the establishment of Roman rule. With regard to the latter it must be added that already prior to the political subjugation the Papacy had been making notable progress in bringing the distant island under its jurisdiction. Pope Honorius, in 629, addressed a letter to the Irish clergy, urging them to adopt the Roman custom of keeping Easter. Before the end of the century the Roman practice was generally introduced. Gregory VII, as might be expected, boldly demanded of both clergy and laity of Ireland obedience to the blessed Vicar of St. Peter (*i. e.*, himself) and presented himself as the arbiter in all matters under dispute (1084). The archbishops of Canterbury, Lanfranc and Anselm, exercised a decisive influence in shaping the organization and ritual of the Irish Church in favor of Rome. The goal was reached when Pope Adrian IV — the only Englishman who ever sat on the papal throne — encouraged "his dearest son in Christ," King Henry II, to invade Ireland with

the laudable purpose of "enlarging the borders of the Church" and "extirpating the nurseries of iniquity from the field of the Lord."

4. Ireland came under British and papal rule in 1171 (and that was the beginning of woe). Adrian's successor, Alexander III, in three letters, addressed respectively to Henry, the Irish kings and nobles, and the hierarchy, enjoined obedience of Ireland to England and of both to the Holy See. Norman and Celt refused to mix, and for centuries after the conquest Ireland remained in a state of anarchic confusion. As has been said, the English power in Ireland has been "like a spear point embedded in a living body and inflaming all around it." This festering spear wound was rendered doubly poignant when in the Reformation period the English government endeavored to force Protestantism upon the staunch Irish Catholics by establishing the Anglican Church in their midst, with all the evils and iniquities that this policy entailed (surrender of church property, payment of tithes, deprivation of civil and political rights). The details of Irish history since the Reformation must be sought elsewhere. Our space will permit us to say but this, that it is a melancholy record of English tyranny (religious, political, and economic), oppression, violence, extortion, and exploitation, on the one hand, and of Irish degradation, suffering, and wretchedness, outbursts of fury, plots, uprisings, rebellions, agitations, etc., on the other — the logic of events, however, with the progress of more liberal ideas, leading to the gradual redress of accumulated wrongs in modern times. In 1829 the Catholic Emancipation Act was passed by the British Parliament. This measure restored civil rights to all the Catholics of the realm.

5. In 1869 the Episcopal State Church in Ireland was dissolved. This measure relieved the Irish Catholics of the odious obligation of contributing toward the maintenance of a religious establishment which they justly regarded as the symbol of their subjection and vassalage. Various other reforms designed to improve the condition of the Irish peasantry do not fall within the scope of this article. The Irish problem, not only as concerning the relation between Ireland and England, but also as relating to the antagonism between the North and South of Ireland itself, seems recently to have

reached what may prove to be a permanent solution. In 1922 a separate Parliament and executive government were established for northern Ireland (six counties, prevailingly Protestant), while in 1921 a treaty was signed by which the Irish Free State is to have the same constitutional status as any self-governing dominion of the empire. See *Celtic Church.*

J. L. Lanigan, *An Ecclesiastical History of Ireland,* Graisberry, Dublin, 1822; G. T. Stokes, *Ireland and the Anglo-Norman Church,* Hodder and Stoughton, London, 1897.

Ireland, John (1838—1918). American Roman Catholic prelate. B. in Ireland; at the age of eleven brought by his parents to St. Paul, Minn.; educated for the priesthood in France; ordained in St. Paul, 1861; archbishop in 1888; for many years a commanding figure in the Catholic Church of America. In 1891 the movement known as Cahenslyanism, which contemplated the appointment of other than English-speaking priests to minister to the needs of foreign-born Catholics ignorant of English, called forth Ireland's emphatic protest on the ground that such a plan tended to faction and division. Hence he is regarded as the typical representative of *Americanism* in the Catholic Church of the country. It must be added, however, that there are at present many parishes in the United States in which German, French, Polish, and Italian Catholics are served in their native tongues.

Irenaeus (the Peaceful). The most eminent teacher of the Church in the second half of the second century; b. probably at Smyrna between A. D. 115 and 125, pupil of Polycarp; taught for a time at Rome; sent as a missionary to southern Gaul, where, during the persecution under Marcus Aurelius (177), he was a presbyter in the church at Lyons. After the martyrdom of Bishop Pothinus, Irenaeus became his successor (178) and labored zealously for the spread of Christianity and the defense of its doctrines. Concerning the later facts of his life we have no authentic information. A doubtful tradition has it that he suffered martyrdom (202). — Irenaeus was an uncompromising foe of all heresy and schism, the great champion of orthodoxy against Gnostic speculation. Though mainly legalistic, his conception of Christianity is the soundest among the ante-Nicene fathers. Among his numerous writings

his *Refutation of Gnosticism (Adversus Haereses)* is the most important. See bibliography under *Patristics.*

Irenics. Also called Irenical Theology, a term used to designate the labors, attitude, or methods of the peacemakers of the Christian Church. Making peace implies a previous warfare. Hence irenics presupposes polemics (see *Polemics*), which in its true character should have no other aim than irenics, namely, to struggle for peace. The "bond of peace," Eph. 4:3, embraces all Christians, and "speaking the truth in love," v. 15, deserves to be emphasized at all times. However, he who truly seeks an ecclesiastical peace well-pleasing to God will find himself under necessity of carrying on controversies. True irenics, therefore, does not exclude polemics, but is another mode of gaining the same end. The conciliation of differences and the reunion of those who have been separated by schism and heresy (see *Heresy*) has in the Christian Church at all times walked side by side with polemics. As the danger of polemics lies in the direction of separatism and the magnifying of unessential differences, so irenical efforts are prone to degenerate into syncretism and unionism. Love of revealed Truth will ever guard against one as well as against the other.

Irish Articles. See *Anglican Confessions,* 8.

Irish Massacre. A terrible outburst of fury and fanaticism on the part of the Irish Catholics against the oppressive measures of the English government. Beginning in Ulster (1641), the revolt spread like wildfire over nearly the entire island, and the aim was complete extermination of Protestantism. It is needless to describe the atrocities committed (burning, drowning, even burying alive, etc.). The number of victims is estimated at from 40,000 to 400,000. A few years later (1649) Oliver Cromwell took fearful vengeance for the Irish massacre, executing what he thought "a righteous judgment of God" on the "barbarous wretches" who had shed so much innocent blood.

Iro-Pictish Church. See *Celtic Church,* 12.

Irons, Genevieve Mary. B. 1855; member of a family noted for poetical ability; contributed poems and hymns since 1876; her best hymn: "Drawn to the Cross, Which Thou Hast Blessed."

Irons, William Josiah (1812—83). Ed. at Oxford; held a number of charges in the Established Church, also noted lecturer; ranks with first of modern hymn writers; translation of *Dies Irae:* "Day of Wrath, That Day of Mourning."

Irregularity. In the Roman Catholic and Anglican Churches, impediments to holding office arising from defects or crimes.

Irresistible Grace. See *Common Grace.*

Irving, Edward (1792—1834). See *Catholic Apostolic Church.*

Isaac, Johann Levita. Eminent German-Jewish scholar; b. 1515 at Wetzlar; d. 1577 at Cologne; became rabbi, but forsook Judaism in 1546 and a few years later embraced Roman Catholicism; after 1551 professor of Hebrew at Cologne.

Isaak, Heinrich (ca. 1450—1517). Though a Fleming, Isaak was the first outstanding musician to give great impetus to the advancement of music in Germany. Isaak was a member of the Netherlands school of music composition. His music reveals a fondness for German and Italian folk song and, though he was an expert contrapuntist, is less involved than that of other eminent Netherlands composers. He is known to have written 23 masses, more than fifty short choral works, and ricercari and conzonas for the organ. He was active at the court of Maximilian at Innsbruck and of Duke Lorenzo de Medici (the Magnificent) at Florence.

G. Adler, *Handbuch der Musikgeschichte,* Frankfurt a. M., 1924. P. H. Lang, *Music in Western Civilization,* New York, 1941.

Isagogics. 1. This word is a term derived from the Greek which has the same meaning as the English word *introduction.* When used with reference to the Bible, it designates that study which pertains to everything that introduces a book of the Bible, so that we can understand its message all the better. It has to do with the author of a given book, the time and place of its composition, the people for whom it was written or to whom it was addressed, the occasion and the purpose of the work, its chief divisions, and the attacks made on its genuineness, and the reputation of those who attack it. It likewise treats of the assembling of the books into one collection and of the recognition given to the latter as inspired Scriptures called the canon, that is, the divinely given rule for our faith and life. The history of the sacred books during the centuries up to our time is included. Because the books of the Bible were composed in antiquity during a period covering about 1600 years, and because they were written in different languages from those used by the majority of the present-day readers, and because the conditions under which the first readers lived were markedly different from ours, it is highly desirable that an introduction to the various books be provided for the ordinary reader. The Scriptures are a clear book, but how much more readily will a person understand, for instance, the Epistle to the Galatians, if he becomes aware that it was written by St. Paul to oppose the false notion that the old Jewish Ceremonial Law is still binding for the children of God in the time of the New Testament! On the so-called disputed books see *Antilegomena.* On the whole field see John Schaller, *Book of Books.*

2. The study of Biblical introduction has been cultivated as long as there have been sacred writings which people can peruse. In the ancient Church, scholars like Eusebius and Jerome devoted much attention to it. In the days of the Reformation, Luther, ardent Bible student that he was, pursued it with diligence and deep insight. It began to flourish in an unprecedented way, however, in the eighteenth century, and ever since has been a favorite subject of study with theologians of all classes. In the eighteenth century, Rationalism arose, which treats the Scriptures as simply human books. Men like Semler (d. 1791) and Eichhorn (d. 1827) were influential in bringing about this attitude toward the Bible in many circles.

3. On OT Isagogics see *Higher Criticism.* In the field of the NT an extraordinary height of negative criticism was reached in the assumptions of the so-called Tuebingen school led by F. C. Baur (d. 1860), which held that there was a struggle between Petrinism and Paulinism in the first century, the latter defending the universality of the Gospel message, the former restricting it to the Jews, and that only those writings of the NT can be considered genuine which bear evidences of this alleged controversy. The result was that all of Paul's Epistles with the

exception of Romans, First and Second Corinthians, and Galatians were declared spurious, and that most of the NT books were dated as coming from the second century, which, of course, implied that they were not genuine. This school with its arbitrary assumptions, after several decades, lost its adherents. It was followed by the so-called school of liberal theology, which, though rationalizing, was more moderate in its critical pronouncements. Harnack and Juelicher are among its prominent exponents. After the First World War there arose the school of form criticism (formgeschichtliche Schule), which tries to determine the nature of the original documents which, so it is held, existed prior to the composition of our Gospels. Introductions written by English-speaking scholars that incline toward, or fully adopt, a negative attitude are those of Bacon, Moffatt, and the recent work of Goodspeed. The old conservative views accepting the genuineness of our NT books have been ably defended especially by Salmon and Th. Zahn. A popular work of value is Snowden, *The Making and the Meaning of the New Testament*. WA

Th. Zahn, *Einleitung in das N. T.*, Leipzig, 1924 (3d ed. This work has been translated into English); Geo. Salmon, *Historical Introduction to the Study of the Books of the NT*, London, 1884; J. Moffatt, *Introduction to the Literature of the NT*, N. Y., 1911; E. J. Goodspeed, *Introduction to the NT*, Chicago, 1937; S. A. Cartledge, *A Conservative Introduction to the NT*, Grand Rapids, 1938; H. C. Thiessen, *Introduction to the NT*, Grand Rapids, 1943.

Ishtar. See *Babylonians, Religion of*, 1.

Isidore of Seville. Archbishop of Seville, Spain, and encyclopedist; b. ca. 560, d. 636; of distinguished parentage and with a learning which embraced the entire range of the arts and sciences; wrote *Libri Sententiarum*, a book of dogmatics, and *Etymologiarum sive Originum Libri Viginti*, a great encyclopedia.

Isidorus. See *Gnosticism*, 7.

Isle of Pines. See *Cuba*.

Israelite House of David. See *House of David*.

Itala. See *Bible Versions*, J.

Italian Pentecostal Assemblies. Pentecostal * sect arising from a move-

ment in Chicago (1904). Headquarters: Newark, N. J.

Italy; Religious History to Reformation. At what time Christianity was first introduced into Italy is unknown, though there is abundant evidence that it was at an early date. In 49—50 Claudius expelled the Jews and Christians from Rome; in 57 the church at Rome was known "in the whole world," Rom. 1:8; in 64 the Christians in the capital were a "vast multitude" (*ingens multitudo*). At the time of Constantine, Christianity had taken firm root, and paganism was losing its hold. During this first stage the religious history of Italy did not differ essentially from that of the empire in general, though the commanding position and influence of the church of Rome and the germs of the Papacy, already manifest, lend it a somewhat distinctive character and indicate its subsequent trend. From the time that Constantine transferred the seat of empire to the Bosporus, and especially since the barbarian invasions, the religious history of Italy becomes virtually the history of the Papacy. It is the Papacy alone that gives a semblance of unity to the story of Italy during the Middle Ages. We can here only glance at a few outstanding facts. The Teutonic invaders, who professed Arianism, for the most part made no attempt to force their creed upon their new subjects. Odoacer and his conqueror, Theodoric, the Ostrogoth, were both tolerant, while the Lombards, who entered Italy as a nation in 568 and all but succeeded in establishing a permanent kingdom, though combining martial despotism with religious intolerance, not only eventually adopted the religion of Rome, but politically succumbed to the diplomacy of the Roman bishop and the weapons of his Frankish ally. The coronation of Charles the Great by Leo III in 800 formed the natural culmination of this alliance, while, at the same time, it resulted in a permanent separation between the East and the West. Unconsciously also the pope and the emperor prepared the ground for that fierce and protracted struggle between the spiritual and temporal powers which occupies so much space in the annals of the following centuries. Without giving details, suffice it to say that from the days of Otto I (crowned at Rome 962) to the age of Hildebrand, the emperors, generally speaking, had the upper hand in this conflict, while from the rise of Hildebrand (afterwards Gregory VII) to the overthrow of the Hohenstaufen house the popes asserted their supremacy. From the beginning of the fourteenth century the power of the Papacy began to decline, though it abated none of its pretensions. Its slavish dependence on the French kings during the "Babylonian captivity," the schism of forty years that followed, the authority assumed by the councils, show clearly that the palmy days of Gregory VII or of Innocent III were gone forever. It was left for the Reformation to proclaim full liberty to the captives.

Italy, Roman Catholic Church in. See *Roman Catholic Church* (history).

Itinerancy. A word expressing one of the most characteristic features of Methodism. The system of itinerancy was established by Wesley in England. It was designed to meet the need of pastoral service regularly in all districts which the limited number of pastors could not supply. Wesley's religious plans made it necessary for him to travel from town to town. He usu-ally stayed only a day or two in any place. Unable, as he thought, to win the ungodly and sinful from the church pulpit, he, with a few others, began field preaching. Seeing that with so small a number they could not do all the work necessary for carrying out their plans, Wesley openly approved lay preaching, and finally men called "helpers," who were not episcopally ordained, were permitted to preach and do pastoral work. This itinerancy has also been adopted in America. The length of time that each itinerant preacher may retain his charge has varied at different times and is now limited to three years.

Itinerarium. A prayer spoken before a journey by Roman Catholic monks and clergy.

Ius Naturale. See *Natural Law*.

Iustitia Originalis. Original righteousness, that is, the righteousness possessed by the primitive parents before their fall into sin.

J

J. A term used by Old Testament higher critics for the alleged oldest document (distinguished by preponderant use of *Jahveh* for God). See *Higher Criticism*, 6.

Jablonski, Peter (1618—70). Pastor in Danzig and Nassenhuben; joined *Unitas Fratrum;* consecrated bishop; pastor at Memel. His son *Daniel Ernst* (1660—1741) studied at various Dutch and English universities; preacher of Reformed congregation at Magdeburg; rector of Gymnasium at Lissa; court preacher at Koenigsberg and Berlin; sought to establish union between Lutherans and Reformed; ordained Nitschmann and Zinzendorf, first bishops of the Herrnhut group.

Jackson, Sheldon (1834—1909). Presbyterian missionary to Choctaw Indians, 1859—60; missionary superintendent in Iowa and Nebraska, 1879; superintendent of Alaska missions, 1882; editor of *Presbyterian Home Missionary*, 1882; superintendent of missions in Sitka, 1884; since 1877 in governmental employ in interest of schools in Alaska.

Jacobi, Friedrich Heinrich (1743 to 1819). German philosopher; opposed subjective idealism and dogmatic rationalism (Kant, Spinoza) and championed faith and feeling. We can know God only through faith, namely, through revelation in consciousness.

Jacobi, John Christian (1670—1750). Keeper of Royal German Chapel, St. James' Palace, London; published several collections of hymns; translated, among others: "God, Who Madest Earth and Heaven."

Jacobite Church. See *Monophysite Controversy.*

Jacobite Church in America. Since the Jacobites are an offshoot of the Syrian Monophysites, some adherents may be found among the Syrian emigrants to America. Their chief centers are New York and Chicago, and they are organized as the Jacobite Assyrian Apostolic Church.

Jacobs, Charles Michael. B. Dec. 5, 1875, Gettysburg, Pa.; grad. Luth. Theol. Sem. 1899; studied at U. of Pa. and U. of Leipzig; D. D. Muhlenberg Coll. 1913; LL. D. 1929; ordained 1899; pastor North Wales, Pa., 1899—1904; Allentown, Pa., 1904—13; prof. Luth. Theol. Sem. 1913 to 1938; vice-pres. Nat. Luth. Commission (see *Nat. Luth. Council*) 1917 to 1922; mem. Nat. Luth. Council from the time of its organization and served for a time on its Ex. Bd.; chm., Am. Com. for Luth. World Conv., 1920—23; co-editor Luther's Works in English, vols. I—VI. Wrote: *The Way — A Little Book of Christian Truth; The Story of the Church — An Outline of Its History; Helps on the Road; An Outline of Christian Doctrine.* Mem. bd. editors *Am. Ency. of Christianity; Luth. Ch. Quarterly.* D. Mar. 30, 1938.

Jacobs, David (1805—30). Started Gettysburg Gymnasium, 1827, from which Pennsylvania College grew.

Jacobs, Henry Eyster. B. at Gettysburg, Pa., Nov. 10, 1844; son of Dr. Michael Jacobs; ed. at Gettysburg Lutheran Coll. and Sem.; home missionary in Pittsburgh, 1868—70; principal of Thiel Coll., 1868—70; prof. of history and Latin at Gettysburg Coll., 1870—80; of ancient languages, 1880 to 1881; of Greek, 1881—83; prof. of systematic theology in the Luth. Sem. in Philadelphia, 1883; dean of the faculty, 1894—1920; president, 1920—28; d. July 7, 1932. He edited the *Lutheran Church Review,* 1882—96; supervised the editing of the *Lutheran Commentary,* 1895—98 and the *Lutheran Cyclopedia,* 1899. Among the many works from his prolific pen are the following: *The Lutheran Movement in England, History of the Lutheran Church in America, Elements of Religion, Commentary on Romans and First Corinthians, Life of Martin Luther, The German Immigration to Pennsylvania, 1709—1740, Summary of the Christian Faith,* and *A Translation of the Book of Concord, with an Introduction and Annotations.* He also wrote *The Doctrinal Basis of the United Lutheran Church in America.*

H. Offermann, "Henry Eyster Jacobs, the Theologian and His Theology," *Luth. Ch. Quart.,* VI:1—27 (list of Jacobs' works VI:220—24); B. Lotz, "Henry Eyster Jacobs (1844—1932) in Retrospect," *Luth. Ch. Quart.,* XVIII: 382—93; W. H. Cooper, "The Church's Opportunity in an Era of Theological Construction," *Luth. Ch. Quart.,* X:113—24.

Jacobs, Michael. B. Jan. 18, 1808, in Franklin Co., Pa.; assisted his older brother at Gettysburg *Gymnasium* 1829; prof. of mathematics at Gettysburg 1832; licensed by West Pennsylvania Synod 1832; conservative, opposed

Definite Platform *; pres. of West Pennsylvania Synod (three terms); wrote *Notes on the Rebel Invasion of Maryland and Pennsylvania and the Battle of Gettysburg.*

Jacopo da Voragine (ca. 1230 to ca. 1298). Dominican preacher; his *Golden Legends (Legendae Sanctorum;* a collection of traditions regarding saints) enjoyed great popularity during the Middle Ages.

Jacoponus da Todi *(Jacobus de Benedictus).* Noted hymn writer of the 13th century; b. in Umbria; after death of his wife withdrew from the world; lay brother in the Order of St. Francis till his death, 1306; fearless in his attacks on abuses of his day; among his hymns *Cur Mundus Militat* (Why Should This World of Ours Strive to Be Glorious), but especially the sequence, surcharged with the feelings of an anguished heart, *Stabat Mater Dolorosa.*

Jaebker, G. H. (1821—77). B. at Wimmern, Hannover; emigrated to America 1842; taught school; was prepared for the ministry by Wyneken and Sihler; served the church at Friedheim, Ind., from his ordination to his death, 1847—77; charter member of the Missouri Synod.

Jaeckel, Theo. (1829—1906). Pastor at Silesia, Wis., 1864, and at Winchester; Muehlhaeuser's successor at Grace, Milwaukee; secretary and treasurer of Wisconsin Synod; bequeathed substantial sums for his synod's work (endowments).

Jaenicke, Johann. B. at Berlin 1748; d. there July 21, 1827; pastor of Bethlehem Church, Berlin; founded mission seminary, 1800, from which 81 foreign missionaries were sent out.

Jahvists. See *Higher Criticism,* 6.

Jainism. A religious system of India founded in sixth century B. C. by *Mahavira,* "Great Hero" (also known as Jina, "Conqueror"), a contemporary of Gotama.* Jainism arose in opposition to Brahmanism,* as did Buddhism,* but, unlike the latter, prescribed asceticism as a means of attaining salvation, *i. e.,* the release of the soul from reincarnation. It regards the universe as eternal and denies the divine authority of the Vedas. Noteworthy is the Jain doctrine of *ahimsa,* avoidance of killing any living thing, even the smallest, including vermin. In the

first Christian century a schism brought
about a division into two sects: the
Svetambara (white-clad) and the Digambara (sky-clad, *i. e.*, nude). The
adherents may become members of
monastic orders or remain laymen.
Among the latter are found wealthy
and influential trades people, who have
built many costly and beautiful temples, such as the one at Mount Abu.
The late Mahatma Gandhi was influenced by the teachings of Jainism. The
census of 1941 lists 1,449,286 Jains in
India.

Jamaica. The largest of the British
West Indies, discovered by Columbus
in 1494. Area, 4,411 sq. mi.; population,
1,416,987 (1950 est.). Under the 150
years of Spanish rule more than
1,500,000 native Arawaks perished,
Negro slaves from Africa taking their
place. Emancipation was enacted in
1833. The English Slave Code of Jamaica (1696) required Christian instruction of the slaves. — *Missions.*
The Society for the Propagation of the
Gospel financed missionary endeavor
from 1703 to 1865. The Church Missionary Society began mission work in
1825. Moravians sent missionaries in
1754. The Wesleyan M. S. opened stations in 1789. American Baptists entered
in 1814, transferring their work to the
English Baptists in 1831. 23 organizations do mission work in Jamaica. Total
Christian community: 815,732 (1952).
219 ordained foreign workers; 279 not
ordained. See *Missions, Bibliography.*

James, William (1842—1910). American psychologist and philosopher; prof.
at Harvard for many years; wrote
Principles of Psychology (1890), *Pragmatism* (1907). See *Pragmatism; Psychology, G.*

Jamieson, Fausset and Brown. See
Commentaries.

Jane Francis de Chantel. See *Visitation Nuns.*

Jansenism. A reformatory movement within the Roman Catholic
Church of France, inaugurated by Cornelius Jansen (1585—1638, Dutch Roman Catholic theologian, bishop of
Ypres), and supported by many of the
most learned and earnest men of the
nation (among them Duvergier, Pascal,
Arnauld, Tillemont, Quesnel).

The movement was a serious attempt at reviving the Augustinian doctrine of sin and grace as a means of
counteracting the baneful influence of

Jesuitism and of quickening the spiritual life of the French Church. Jansen's
book *Augustinus* was immediately attacked by the Jesuits, who secured its
condemnation by Urban VIII in the
bull *In Eminenti* (1642). Anton Arnauld's attack upon the *opus operatum*
theory of the Sacrament and the lax
moral theology of the Jesuits was met
by the bull *Cum Occasione* of Innocent X (1653), which explicitly condemned five propositions from Jansen's
work. When the Jansenists protested
that the propositions in question were
not taught by Jansen in the sense in
which they were condemned, Alexander VII (Innocent's successor) boldly
declared that they contained the exact
meaning which Jansen intended to express. At the same time he demanded
of the Jansenists that they subscribe
to a formula of submission to Innocent's
bull. The refusal of the Jansenists to
yield to such willful proceedings
brought the combined powers of Pope
and king against them. The Pope abolished the convent of Port Royal. The
building was destroyed by order of "the
most Christian King" Louis XIV, the
church itself demolished, and even the
bones of the dead were torn from their
graves. Many of the Jansenists either
fled the country or were banished.
But the end was not yet. What may be
called the second stage of the Jansenist
movement was introduced by the publication of Quesnel's New Testament
with devotional comments, a work approved by Noailles, the Archbishop of
Paris, and recommended by the French
bishops. But the work provoked another outburst of Jesuit wrath and
another papal bull, the famous Constitution *Unigenitus* (1713) of Clement XI (characterized by Harnack as a
"*trauriges Machwerk*," a wretched performance), condemning one hundred
and one allegedly Jansenist propositions
in Quesnel's book. The quarrel that
ensued rent the French clergy into two
factions, the *Acceptants* and the *Ap-
pellants* (those who appealed from the
Pope to a general council). But the
papal ban (1718) and the secular power
ultimately crushed the spirit of Jansenism. Many Jansenists sacrificed their
convictions (among them Noailles),
others fell a prey to wild fanaticism,
still others found an asylum in Holland,
where a separatist community survives
to the present day.

L. Pastor, *History of the Popes,*
Herder, St. Louis, 1923—41 (vols. 28
to 34).

Janson, Eric. See *Sweden, Luth. Church in*, 5; *Communistic Societies*, 5.

Janzow, John Wm. Carl. B. March 7, 1875, Lewiston, Minn.; grad. Concordia Seminary, St. Louis, 1900; pastor, St. Ansgar, Iowa, 1900—07; pastor, Bethlehem Church, Adelaide, Australia, 1907—45; president, South Australian District, 1913—23; general president, Ev. Luth. Church of Australia, 1923 to 41. D.D., Concordia Seminary, St. Louis, 1934. D. July 20, 1949.

Japan. Area: 141,529 sq. mi.; population: 83,199,637 (1950). The major religions are Shinto, Buddhism, Confucianism, and Christianity. The earliest of these religions in Japan was Shinto. According to tradition Buddhism was introduced A. D. 552, and Confucianism somewhat earlier. Francis Xavier, Jesuit missionary, together with a Japanese convert introduced the Christian faith in 1549. By 1606 the number of Christians had reached several hundred thousands. Suspicion of the ultimate designs of the proponents of Christianity led to an edict (1606) which prohibited the profession or practice of Christianity. These prohibitions were not removed until 1872. A small number of Christians were still found in Japan when the edict was removed.

Hardly had the treaty of 1858 with the U. S. been ratified when Presbyterians, Episcopalians, and Dutch Reformed from the U. S. prepared to do mission work in Japan. J. C. Hepburn, S. R. Brown, G. F. Verbeck, and the native, J. H. Neesima, were outstanding missionaries of the early period. Their work contributed to social reform, education, and governmental policies. A spirit of nationalism dampened Christian interest in the 4th decade of the 20th century. After World War II, however, a new period of mission opportunity presented itself. 46 North American missionary organizations were active in Japan in 1952.

In 1892 the first Lutheran missionary from the United Synod of the South began mission work on the island of Kyushu. The United Ev. Luth. Church sent its first missionary in 1898, the General Council of the Luth. Church in the U. S. A. in 1908, the Icelandic Synod in 1916. After the formation of the United Luth. Church in America, the missionaries of the various Lutheran bodies in Japan formed the Japan Ev. Luth. Church. Pressure from the government caused the missionaries

from the Luth. Ev. Assn. of Finland (which entered the field in 1900) to co-operate with the Japan Ev. Luth. Church for a time beginning with 1940. The Luth. Church—Missouri Synod began work in Japan in 1948; the Ev. Luth. Church, Luth. Brethren, and Norwegian Luth. Church in 1949; the Augustana Synod and the Suomi Synod in 1950; the Luth. Free Church in 1951. The Lutheran bodies had a total of about 6,000 members (1952).

The number of full members of Christian churches in Japan was approximately 186,099 in 1952. See *Missions, Bibliography*.

Jatakas. See *Buddhism*, 2.

Java. An island in the Netherlands East Indies, area, 51,029, sq. mi.; population, 47,800,000, chiefly Malay stock. Ancient religion is Buddhism, supplanted to a great extent in the 15th century by Islam. Missions in the 17th century by the Dutch, who often used questionable methods to obtain converts. Modern missions are conducted by 20 societies. Approximately 600,000 communicants. See *Missions, Bibliography*.

Jealousy. The word is used both in a good and evil sense. God is rightly jealous of His divine honor (Ex. 20:5; 34:13, 14; Num. 25:11; Deut. 29:20; 32:16, 21; Isaiah 42:8; 48:11; 1 Cor. 10:22; Kretzmann, *Pop. Com.*, N. T., II, 137). It is God-pleasing when believers show a holy zeal for God's honor, are indignant over wickedness, or are moved by intense interest for the welfare of others (Ps. 79:5; Zech. 1:14; 8:2; 1 Cor. 10:22). In Rom. 10:19; 11:11 the word is used in the sense of emulation, and figuratively in 2 Cor. 11:2. All jealousy of men that is equivalent to suspicion and envy is sinful (Num. 5:14; Ps. 37:1; 73:3; Prov. 24:3, 19; Phil. 1:15. Examples: Gen. 4:5-8; 37:4-11, 18-28; 1 Sam. 18:8-30; Luke 15:25-32; Dan. 6:4; Matt. 27:18). Forbidden, Rom. 13:13; James 4:5; 1 Peter 2:1. (Cp. *Trigl.*, 633, 184). See indices in Kretzmann's *Pop. Com.* (sub Envy and Jealousy).

Jean Baptist de La Salle (1651 to 1719). See *Christian Brothers*.

Jean Paul (Friedrich Richter, 1763 to 1825). Studied at *Gymnasium* at Hof, became popular writer; advocated a religion of sentiment.

Jedvardson, Eric. See *Finland, Lutheranism in*, 1.

Jeep, Johann (1582—ca. 1650). Lutheran composer of church music who lived for some time in Nuremberg and who may have been a pupil of Hassler. His *Studentengärtlein*, which contained three-, four-, and five-part songs, was used widely in Germany in the 17th century and contained good music for students and young people; the collection was effectively used to divert the attention of Lutheran youth away from inferior Italian music of a degrading character.

Jehovah Conference. Founded 1893 by emissaries of the Lower Hessian Mission Association at Melsingen. Rev. Wm. Hartwig was the first to come over (1886) and was the president for many years. The Jehovah Conference rejected all Lutheran Confessions except the Augustana. It remained a small group. The last census listing the body (1926) gave 3 pastors and a total membership of 851. By the end of the 3d decade it had disappeared from statistical lists.

Jehovah's Witnesses. 1. A vehement adventistic group founded by "Pastor" C. T. Russell (1852—1916) and known first as Millennial Dawn, Watchtower Tract Society, International Bible Students' Society. "Pastor" Russell claimed to be the seventh messenger of Rev. 11:15. He gained a large following by ridiculing the Scriptural teaching on hell, the Trinity, the immortality of the soul, by denouncing the churches and our present social order, and by promising a "new world" of plenty for all downtrodden people. After his death in 1916 "Judge" Rutherford became his successor. Both men were prolific writers. Jehovah's Witnesses have sent their "messengers" into all parts of the world and have carried on a very active propaganda through their literature, the radio, and colporteurs.

2. The principles of the present Jehovah's Witnesses are virtually identical with the central thoughts presented by Russell. Under the guise of being Bible students they present their anti-Trinitarian, anti-Christian, and antisocial propaganda. The central idea is the belief in the complete reorganization of our present social order through the establishment of Jehovah's theocracy. The adherents consider themselves to be the faithful witnesses of Jehovah who must proclaim that the present "world" or social order is of the devil and will soon be destroyed in

the final war of Armageddon; that Jehovah is now gathering His faithful witnesses to establish His theocracy, which will be the only form of government in the "world to come," and will offer the only refuge for distressed humanity. According to Russell and Rutherford the "divine plan of the ages" is as follows: The history of the world falls into three great dispensations, in each of which man is given an opportunity to merit for himself the right to live in this world "for ages to come" by obedience to God's Law. The first dispensation was in charge of the angels, who, however, were unable to control the countergovernment which Satan had established. Satan misled Adam by teaching him the lie of the immortality of the soul. Through his disobedience to God's laws, Adam forfeited the right to live for himself and his posterity. In the second dispensation, beginning with Noah and ending with the Battle of Armageddon, Satan employed as his allies the capitalistic system, the human governments, and the churches to prevent man from being obedient to God's theocracy. Only a few men in the history of the world were able to withstand the onslaughts of Satan's allies and to merit the right to live in this world. The churches are singled out as the allies of Satan because the organized churches have undermined Jehovah's authority through the lie of the Trinity. Jehovah's Witnesses claim that only Jehovah is God and that the Logos, or Christ, dare not be worshiped as God. The statements in their literature concerning the deity of Jesus are very confusing. While they speak of Christ as God's Son, they deny the eternal pre-existence of the Second Person in the Trinity and speak of the Logos only as God's first creation, or as His chief administrator. Russell and Rutherford denied the deity of the God-Man Jesus and ridiculed the bodily resurrection of Christ. — The immortality of the soul is denounced as the lie of Satan. Hell is said to be a place of entire destruction or annihilation. In fact, they deny that man has a soul and claim that the word soul denotes only "the right to live." When man sinned he lost his right to life, and death is no more than the forfeiture of this right to live. — Their ransom theory is a complete perversion of the Scripture doctrine of Christ's reconciliation. Their claim is that by His perfect obedience the man Jesus earned the right to live in this world and to become the progenitor of a new human race. Jesus, however, voluntarily gave up His right to live (His lifeless body remained in the grave) and the right to live which He had earned He deposited with God, and thus Jesus has made it possible that God could restore the right to live to all men. In addition to Christ also the 144,000, Rev. 7:4, had been perfectly obedient to God's theocracy and thus had earned their right to live forever in this world. However, they, too, gave up their right to life, and with Jesus these 144,000 constitute "the Christ" who "gave their lives a ransom for many." Only the 144,001 will receive immortality. The rest of mankind will be resurrected, that is, new bodies will be created for all men who have lived before, and their right to life will be restored to them. They will be given an opportunity for one hundred years to be obedient to God's theocracy in the "new world." Those who at the end of the probationary period are not obedient will be annihilated. The obedient will live under God's theocracy for ages to come. — The whole system is based on work-righteousness and on the hope that a catastrophe will right the social and economic wrongs of mankind and prepare a world of material bliss. In 1952 there were 1,103 "companies" (congregations) in the U. S. See *Religious Bodies (U. S.), Bibliography.* FEM

Jellinek, Adolph (1821—93). Studied at Prague and Leipzig; rabbinical preacher in Leipzig and Vienna; prominent student of the Jewish Kabbala.

Jensen, Rasmus. See *Canada, Lutheranism in,* 1.

Jeremiah's Answer to Certain Lutheran Divines. See *Eastern Orthodox Confessions,* A 5.

Jeremias, Alfred. German Lutheran theologian; b. 1864 near Chemnitz; pastor of the Lutherkirche, Leipzig, and lecturer at the university; wrote on Assyriology and related subjects. D. 1935.

Jerome. One of the Fathers of the Church; b. 331 at Stridon, on the frontiers of Dacia; d. near Bethlehem, in 420; of Christian parentage, but was not baptized till 360, when he studied rhetoric and philosophy at Rome; lived in Gaul, then at Aquileia, on the Adriatic, till 373. After living at Antioch in Syria for a number of years, he devoted himself to the things of God, taught at Antioch, among the hermits of Chalcis, and studied at Constantinople and Rome. Becoming a close counselor of Pope Damasus, he undertook the revision of the Latin Bible then in use on the basis of the Greek New Testament and the Septuagint. This work occupied the scholar for many years, with some interruptions caused by other duties. He visited Antioch once more, also the various sections of the Holy Land and Egypt. In 386 he settled down in a hermit's cell near Bethlehem, where he spent the rest of his life in intense literary activity. To the last thirty-four years of his life belong the most important works of his career: his version of the Old Testament in Latin on the basis of the original text, the best of his Scriptural commentaries, his catalog of Christian authors, and the dialog against the Pelagians.* To this period belong also his passionate polemical writings, which distinguish him among the early Fathers. Jerome was buried at Bethlehem, but his remains were later removed, the church of Santa Maria Maggiore in Rome claiming the greater part of his relics. Among Jerome's works, besides the Bible translation noted above, now known as the Vulgate ("the common," since it was intended for the use of all men), are to be mentioned a book describing the chief places of interest in the Holy Land, several original commentaries on the Old Testament (chiefly Isaiah, Daniel, and Ezekiel), some New Testament commentaries, *De viris illustribus* (church history in biographies), books on hermits, and some treatises against Gnostic and Pelagian heresies. He also published some educational treatises. His theological position was not strong, since a clear exposition of doctrine caused him great difficulty, but his writings show much poetical skill. His great importance is due to the incalculable influence exerted through his Latin version of the Bible upon all subsequent theological development. See references under *Patristics.*

Migne's collection of Jerome's writings is still considered standard. For his life see F. W. Farrar, *Lives of the Fathers,* II:150—297. There are also lives by F. Z. Collombet, O. Zoeckler, and others.

Jerome of Prague (ca. 1379—1416). One of the closest friends of Hus. He visited Oxford and copied the *Dialogus* and *Trialogus* of Wyclif and thereafter championed Wyclifism. Burned at Constance.

Jerusalem, Synods of. During the Arian Controversy synods were held in Jerusalem in 335 and 349, during the Pelagian Controversy the meeting of 414, against the Severians that of 536, during the Monothelite Controversy that of 634, against iconoclasts that of 730. A very important one was that of 1672 which adopted decrees in favor of Eastern orthodoxy, some of which were directed against Calvinism. See *Eastern Orthodox Confessions,* A 2.

Jessup, Henry Harris. B. at Montrose, Pa., April 19, 1832; d. April 28, 1910, at Beirut, Syria. Was a graduate of Union Theological Seminary,.N.Y.; sent out by the American Board of Commissioners for Foreign Missions, 1855, first to Tripoli, then to Beirut; since 1870 he worked under the Presbyterian Board of Foreign Missions as professor in the Syrian Theological Seminary; author of note.

Jesuits and Jesuitism. 1. The Reformation was followed by the Counter Reformation. The latter was signalized by the appearance of new orders, chief among which is the Society of Jesus. Its founder, Ignatius Loyola (b. 1491), while a student of theology in Paris, gathered about him a few kindred spirits, and after taking the customary vows they volunteered their services to the pope. Paul III, after much hesitation, confirmed the new order (1540). Immediately Loyola's society was on the scene of action, and for two centuries and more (until its suppression in 1773) it was a potent force in European history.

2. Its character is described by Kurtz: "Never has a human society better understood to try the spirits and to assign to each individual member that position and to use it for that purpose for which it is best qualified. Never, on the other hand, has a system of mutual supervision been so thoroughly and so consistently carried out. Everything that is dear and sacred to man was merged in the interest of the society, in unconditional obedience to the superior. Country, relatives, inclination or aversion, even personal judgment and conscience, are nothing; the order is all. Besides, it made every means that the world affords, science, scholarship, art, secular learning, and (in connection with heathen missions) ,even colonization, commerce, and industry, subservient to its end. It gained control of the education of youth among the higher ranks and trained for itself

loyal and powerful patrons. By preaching, by the cure of souls, by the establishment of numerous brotherhoods and sisterhoods, it exercised its power over the people, took princes under tutelage in the confessional, forced itself into all relations, into all secrets. And all these manifold means, all the eminent forces and talents [with which it operated], united under a single will, served one purpose: positively, the promotion and expansion of Roman Catholicism; negatively, the suppression and extirpation of Protestantism."

3. All applicants for admission to the order must be at least fourteen years of age. A novitiate of two years' duration and of rigid disciplinary drill was followed by the promotion to the grade of "scholastics." Besides taking the three vows of poverty, chastity, and obedience, the novices now spent four or five years in liberal studies and then the same period of time as teachers of junior classes. Then followed a course in theology covering another four or five years, on the completion of which admission was given to the rank of "spiritual coadjutors." These constituted the bulk of the order. This class furnished the missionaries, the preachers, and the teachers; but they had no share in the government of the society. This was reserved for the "Professed of the Four Vows," who, in addition to the ordinary vows, took a vow of special allegiance to the pope. This group, always a small minority, were the *élite* of the society, closely associated with the general, who was clothed with absolute authority and controlled the entire machine. The general was represented in the various countries by the provincials, to whom the superiors of all houses and rectors of colleges were bound to report at stated intervals. To safeguard the powers of the general, reports were often sent to him directly, without the knowledge of the provincial. Indeed, a system of espionage and delation, to which even the general himself was subject to some extent, permeated the whole society.

4. Jesuit theology, while at first conforming to the Thomistic type of doctrine, which, in its turn, was modeled after that of St. Augustine, especially in the matter of sin and grace, soon shifted its position in the direction of Pelagianism in order to secure a leverage of attack upon the fundamental tenets of Protestantism. The hostility to Augustine became apparent in the *Ratio et Institutio Studiorum Societatis*

Jesu of Aquaviva, the fifth general of the order, in 1586, was especially fierce during the Jansenist controversy of the next century, and finally led to the dethronement of the ancient father in the days of Liguori (1699—1787). The latter, canonized in 1829, has, in the words of Harnack, taken the place of Augustine in modern Catholicism. On the other hand, the Jesuits were the most zealous advocates of papal absolutism. Only the papal power is derived from God, that of the secular government from the people, who therefore have the right to depose, banish, and even kill a tyrannical or *heretical* ruler.

5. Four points of the ethical teaching of Jesuits must be noted: *Probabilism, intentionalism,* or *expediency, mental reservation,* and *equivocation.* Probabilism has been described thus: *"Si est opinio probabilis, licitum est eam sequi, licet opposita sit probabilior."* That is to say, no guilt attaches to an action, though done contrary to one's own moral judgment, provided such action is supported by reasonable grounds (whatever these may be) or by the authority of some reputable teacher. Such "grounds" and such "authority" render the moral opinion *probabilis.* In short, conscience is replaced by other considerations, especially by obedience to external authority. *Intentionalism,* or the doctrine of expediency, is the maxim that the moral quality of an action is not determined by the action in itself, but by the end and aim which the action pursues. If the end is worthy and justifiable, the action employed to attain it is also worthy and justifiable, though it may be reprehensible and damnable in itself. Says Busenbaum (whose manual of moral theology went through more than fifty editions): *"Cum finis est licitus, etiam media sunt licita"* ("When the end is legitimate, the means are also legitimate"). Layman: *"Cui concessus est finis, concessa etiam sunt media ad finem ordinata"* ("To whom the end is permissible, to him are also permissible the means ordained to attain the end"). Very succinctly Wagemann: *"Finis determinat probitatem actus"* ("The end determines the probity of an action"). *Mental reservation* and *equivocation* may be illustrated by examples from Liguori, the founder of the Redemptorist Congregation, but an exponent of Jesuit casuistry and since 1871 an accepted Doctor of the Church. Says Liguori: "A confessor may affirm with an oath

that he is ignorant of a crime which he heard in confession, meaning thereby that he is ignorant of it as a mere man, though not as a minister of religion." An adulteress questioned by her husband may deny her guilt by declaring that she has not committed "adultery," meaning "idolatry," for which the term "adultery" is often employed in the Old Testament. In similar fashion, theft, fraud, breach of promise, perjury, may be whitewashed.

6. The educational system of the Jesuits was a marked advance upon anything previously known in the Catholic Church and became one of the most powerful factors in the Catholic reaction. It did not include primary education, but strove from the first to secure as many chairs as possible in the institutions of higher learning. In 1710 the Jesuits controlled the philosophical and theological studies in eighty universities, to say nothing of their influence in minor institutions. For about three hundred years they were accounted the best teachers in Europe, though the very nature of their society discouraged the habit of original and independent thought.

7. Immediately upon their confirmation by the pope the Jesuits opened their campaign against the Reformation. They were a controlling influence at the Council of Trent and determined the severely anti-Protestant position of that body. They were largely instrumental in suppressing the Reformation in Italy, indeed in all southern Europe. In Germany they worked with marked success from various centers, instigating Catholic princes to exterminate Protestantism by force. They were active in Austria (since 1551), Hungary, Tyrol, Silesia, Poland, Moravia, and even entered Russia in an attempt to convert the Czar. They were a powerful force in Spain and Portugal. Belgium was saved for Catholicism through their labors. Their entrance into France (1561), though exciting the jealousy and suspicion of the *Parliament* of Paris and the French clergy, was soon followed by a marked change of popular sentiment in favor of Catholicism. The horrors of St. Bartholomewtide and the assassination of Henry IV are laid to their charge. They denounced the Edict of Nantes, which granted a measure of toleration to the Huguenots, and they were in hearty accord with, if not actually responsible for, its revocation (1685) and all the horrors that followed. In England they kept up a secret

propaganda for more than a century. They made repeated attempts on the life of Queen Elizabeth and were implicated in the Gunpowder Plot. With the fall of the Stuarts their influence ceased. Even in Sweden a Jesuit won the confidence of Christina, the daughter of Gustavus Adolphus, and two Jesuit emissaries from Rome smoothed the way for her return to the Catholic fold. — The Jesuits not only endeavored to recover lost ground, but broke new ground in foreign mission fields. With a zeal, a courage, and a consecration unsurpassed they planted their mission stations in India, Japan, China, and Abyssinia, among the mines of Peru, on the Mexican plateau, in the wilds of the Rocky Mountains, and in the shades of Canadian forests. Their missionary methods (accommodations to heathen usage) were not as commendable as their devotion and even provoked papal censure.

8. The decline and (temporary) abolition of the Society of Jesus are traceable to its vicious ethical system, its constant intermeddling in politics, its increasing worldliness, and, above all, its extensive commercial activities. The Jesuits were banished from Portugal in 1759, from France in 1767, from Spain and all her dependencies in the same year. So strong was the pressure of public sentiment and of the Catholic courts of Europe that Clement XIV, in the famous bull *Dominus ac Redemptor* (July 21, 1773), suppressed the Jesuit Order. This did not mean permanent extinction. Many Jesuits changed their names, but not their principles, and joined other orders. Many more found an asylum in the territories of the freethinking sovereigns Frederick II of Prussia and Catherine II of Russia. The need of a new force to invigorate the Church after her severe trials during the French Revolution induced Pius VII to reverse the decree of Clement XIV, and by the bull *Sollicitudo Omnium Ecclesiarum* the Jesuits were reinstated (1814). Since then the order has been gradually gaining in power; it has practically controlled the Papacy and has succeeded in pushing ultramontanism to its logical conclusion, the proclamation of papal infallibility as a dogma of the Church. Naturally, it has again, since its restoration, frequently quarreled with the secular governments. It has not changed its character essentially. The Jesuit order numbered about 24,000 at the time of its suppression in

1773. In 1814 it numbered only a few hundred. The order grew rapidly in the first part of the 20th century, prior to World War II. From 1915—35 the order grew from 17,000 to 25,000 (including priests, scholastics, and lay brothers).

T. J. Campbell, *The Jesuits*, 1534 to 1921, N. Y., 1921; F. Parkman, *The Jesuits in North America*, Little & Brown, 1910; Paul and Dyke, *Ignatius Loyola*, Scribner's, 1927.

Jesus. See *Christ Jesus.*

Jesus, Lives of. See *Christ, Lives of.*

Jesus, Paintings of. Pictures of Jesus are found even in the catacombs, the frescoes showing the Good Shepherd, the Awakening of Lazarus, the Adoration of the Magi, and other scenes from His life. In the period after Constantine pictorial and plastic representations became more numerous, a statue being extant of the Good Shepherd, which is dated by scholars as of the third century. The representation of Christ is very common in mosaic work, as the Baptism of Christ in the cupola of the Dome at Ravenna, and Christ Before Pilate and Christ Blessing in St. Apollinare of Ravenna. During the Middle Ages the representation of Christ turned to strange ways, His character as Redeemer being relegated to the background, while all other considerations came to the front. Some of the subjects found at that time are Christ in the Glory of the New Jerusalem, Christ in His Majesty as Teacher, Christ on the Clouds of Heaven, Christ on the Globe of the World. The Renaissance paid more attention to the mother of Jesus than to the Savior Himself, although Mantegua painted a Crucifixion of Christ, da Vinci his immortal Last Supper, and Reni his Ecce Homo. Since the Reformation, Jesus is again receiving the attention to which His person and office entitle Him. With Duerer opening the line, and with Hofmann, Plockhorst, Thoma, Gebhard, Uhde, and Carolsfeld contributing during the last century, some notable work has been done in bringing the picture of Jesus, the Savior, before the eyes of men. The so-called portrait painting of Jesus according to Publius Lentulus is not authentic.

Jesus, Society of. See *Jesuits and Jesuitism.*

Jesus, the Son of Sirach. Author of *Ecclesiasticus.* See *Apocrypha.*

Jewish Calendar. See *Judaism, 4.*

Jewish Missions. The number of Jews in the world is usually placed at ca. 12,000,000, of whom more than 2,500,000 are in the U. S. and more than half of these in the city of New York. The Lutheran Church, from the days of the Reformation, attempted to call them to Christ, Luther making special efforts in this direction. Missionary societies for work among the Jews have been organized in large numbers, the first in modern times being the British Society for Propagation of the Gospel among the Jews, 1842. The first missionary appointed by the Lutheran Missouri Synod to work among the Jews in the United States was Daniel Landsmann. Then Rev. Friedmann served as a missionary in New York for many years, with occasional attempts in other cities by other men. See *Missions, Bibliography.*

Jews, Conversion of. The conversion of the Jews as a nation has been taught in connection with millenarian hopes. The claim is based upon Rom. 11:15-29, where, as the advocates of this theory declare, Paul both asserts and proves from the Old Testament prophecies that a final and universal conversion of the Jews to Christianity will take place. They maintain that such Old Testament prophecies as Isaiah 11:11, 12; 59:20; Jer. 3:17; 16:14, 15; 31:31; Ezek. 20:40 to 44; Hos. 3:4, 5; Amos 9:11-15; Zech. 10:6-10; 12:10; 14:1-20; Joel 3:1-17, must be taken in a literal sense. Moreover, they assert that the entire territory promised by God to Abraham has never been fully possessed by his descendants; hence the prophecies in Gen. 15:18-21; Num. 34:6-12; Ezek. 47:1-23, must refer to the millennial reign of Christ, in which the Jews will occupy the land described in these prophecies. Lastly they claim that the Jews, though scattered among the nations, have been preserved as a separate people for the very purpose of constituting a distinct people during the Savior's personal reign on earth.

The opponents of this theory assert that the literal interpretation of the Old Testament prophecies is untenable, since such an interpretation, in order to be consistent, must be literal in all its parts. This would imply that David himself, in person, will reign in Jerusalem (Ezek. 37:24); that the Levitical priesthood will be restored and bloody sacrifices offered to God (Jer. 17:25, 26); that Jerusalem must then be the center of government, and all worshipers must come monthly and from Sabbath to Sabbath, from the ends of the earth, to worship at the Holy City (Is. 2:3; Zech. 14:16-21). Thus the literal interpretation leads to the revival of the entire ritual system of the Jews, which was abrogated by Christ, and which is opposed to the clear teaching of the New Testament, which plainly teaches that in Christ all distinctions between Jew and Gentile have been abolished. Their main contention, however, is that both Isaiah and Paul, when speaking of the conversion of the Jews (Rom. 9:27, 28; Is. 10:22, 23; Rom. 11:5) refer to the elect saints in Israel, the Israel according to the spirit (Rom. 11:3-8, 25-32), the spiritual Israel. Their contention, based on Rom. 11:1-7, is that as in Israel, even in the time of the Old Testament, only those were saved who had been called by grace, so in New Testament times, while many are called, only few are chosen, and that these chosen ones will be brought in through the preaching of the Gospel (Rom. 11:5); hence such New Testament expressions as "Abraham's seed" (Gal. 3:29); "Israelites" (Gal. 6:16; Eph. 2:12-19); "citizens of the heavenly Jerusalem" (Gal. 4:26), etc., apply to all believers in Christ who have been gathered through the preaching of the Word, and not to reconverted Jews only.

Joachim, Friedrich (1546—1608). First evangelical archbishop of Magdeburg; disbanded cloisters; removed Roman Catholic ceremonies; unwillingly yielded to requests of the nobility of Magdeburg to introduce Formula of Concord; desired union between Lutherans and Reformed.

Joachim of Floris (ca. 1145 to ca. 1202). Italian mystic; joined Cistercian order; founded monastery in Fiore. Best known for his interpretation of history which he divided into three periods: 1) The Age of the Father (from the beginning to Christ); 2) The Age of the Son (from time of Christ to 1260); 3) Age of the Holy Ghost (from 1260 on). The last is the "Golden Age" of monasticism and the contemplative life. He opposed many of the abuses in the Church, the Crusades, indulgences, temporal power. His followers, the Joachimites, were condemned at Arles (1260).

Joan of Arc, or *Jeanne d'Arc,* the Maid of Orleans, a French peasant girl (1412—31). On the basis of visions which she claimed to have had, she donned a special military dress and placed herself at the head of an army of 6,000 French soldiers, her spirit causing the French to shake off the British oppression. Betrayed to the English, she was tried and burned at the stake. Joan of Arc was beatified in 1909 and canonized in 1920.

Joch, Johann Georg (ca. 1680—1731). Pietistic Lutheran; pastor and prof. at Erfurt; prof. at Wittenberg; his disputation *De desperatione salutari,* in which he set forth the wholesomeness of despair, caused a widespread controversy.

Jodl, Friedrich (1848—1914). German philosopher; sought to develop naturalistic ethics.

Johannitus. See *Arabic Philosophy.*

John XXII. See *Popes,* 13.

John XXIII *(Baltasare Cossa).* Pope 1410—15. A Neapolitan who was legate to Bologna and chamberlain to Boniface IX, became pope against considerable opposition. He promised to resign if Gregory XII and Benedict XIII would do likewise; when, however, his conditions were met, he reassumed the office of sovereign pontiff, but was soon deposed and imprisoned. John XXIII called the Council of Constance, which ended the papal schism involving three popes, John XXIII, Gregory XII, and Benedict XIII.

John Albrecht. Duke of Mecklenburg (1547—76); consolidatel the Lutheran Church in Mecklenburg; established the church order of 1552; reorganized the university of Rostock; favored *Formula of Concord.*

John Casimir (1564—1633). Duke of Saxe-Coburg; established the *Gymnasium* at Coburg; befriended John Gerhard.

John Chrysostom. See *Chrysostom, John.*

John the Constant. Elector of Saxony, b. 1468; educated at the court of his uncle, Emperor Frederick III; ruled with his brother, Frederick the Wise, since 1486, and alone since 1525. He remained constant to the Reformation against all attempts to draw him over to Rome. With Philip of Hesse he formed the *Torgau Bund* to defend the Reformation against the *Dessau Bund,* had the churches visited and reformed in 1528 and 1529, headed the historic Protest against the Romanists at Speyer in 1529, stood up courageously against the aggression of the papists at Augsburg in 1530, refusing to take part in the Corpus Christi procession requested by the Emperor, standing firm against the threats to depose him. When the theologians offered to present the Augsburg Confession without him, he replied: "I, too, will confess my Christ." When Emperor Charles asked for the reading of the Augsburg Confession in Latin, John objected: "We are Germans and on German soil, and so Your Imperial Majesty will also permit us to speak the German language" — which was done. While Philip of Hesse decamped, John boldly remained at Augsburg till the end. That was his own Augsburg Confession in actions; he took seriously his motto: *Verbum Dei manet in aeternum* ("The Word of God remains in eternity"), the initials of which he had put on the livery of his servants. He was the founder of the Smalcald League, but gladly granted the Nuernberg Religious Peace of 1532 to the Emperor, who was hard beset by France and the Turk. D. Aug. 16, 1532.

Theodor Kolde, "Johann der Bestaendige," in Albert Hauck, *Realenzyclopaedie fuer protestantische Theologie u. Kirche,* Hinrichs, Leipzig, 1901 (IX: 237—44).

John of the Cross, St. (1542—91). Spanish mystic; friend of St. Theresa, with whom he founded the Discalced Carmelites; wrote poems of lyrical and mystic beauty; his treatises on mysticism *(Dark Night of the Soul, Ascent of Mt. Carmel)* still widely read.

John of Damascus (called *Chrysorrhoas,* that is, the "Golden Speaker"). B. before 700, most likely in Damascus, d. 754 at Mar Saba, near Jerusalem. Although the country was even then Mohammedan, John grew up as a Christian, becoming a monk shortly after 730. He was ordained priest soon afterwards, but declined further honors and advancements. He spent most of his time in study, giving all his writings a careful revision before his death. Among his earliest writings are the three *Apologetic Treatises Against Those Decrying the Holy Images,* which brought upon him the wrath of Emperor Leo (see *Iconoclastic Controversy).* John did not brand the views of his opponents as heretical, but he defends his position with regard to the value of images on the basis of tradition and of inherent value. John's chief dogmatic work was his *Fount of Knowledge*, for centuries the standard of the Eastern Church. The third part of this work was by John himself divided into a hundred chapters and called an *Exposition of the Orthodox Faith*. John of Damascus was important also as a hymn writer, composing as a rule both words and music; among his best works in this field being sacred poems in iambic meter for Christmas, Epiphany, and Pentecost. He was also very skillful in acrostic work. Many of the minor writings formerly ascribed to John are now under dispute, the contention being that some of his contemporaries wrote in his style. See references under *Patristics*.

John Frederick the Magnanimous (1503—54). Son of John the Constant; Elector of Saxony. One of the first acts of his reign was to improve church affairs (1532). Desired peace with the Emperor, but when he realized that the Nuernberg Religious Peace would not be kept, he extended the Smalcald League for ten years and kept aloof from the diets. He pushed aside the legally elected Julius of Pflug and made Amsdorf bishop of Naumburg, thereby increasing the hostility of the Emperor. He ignored the rights of his cousin Maurice of Saxony when taxing and reforming the city of Wurzen. Philip of Hesse prevented war, but Maurice remained bitter and opposed the Smalcald League. When asked at the Diet of Regensburg (1546) why he was concentrating troops, he replied: "I wish to chastise disobedient princes." Thereupon the Smalcald League mobilized and was crushed by Alva in the battle of Muehlberg, the wounded Elector being taken prisoner. His electorate was given to Maurice of Saxony. He displayed great fortitude while a prisoner. He would not recognize the Council of Trent nor the Interim.* The Passau Treaty (1552) brought freedom to John Frederick. He died two years later.

John George I of Saxony. Elector 1611—56; valiant defender of Lutheranism, militantly opposed to Romanism and Calvinism; protested against the Edict of Restitution of 1629; his failure to promote the cause of the Swedish troops has been urged against him.

John of God (*Goth*), really *Juan Ciudad* (1495—1550). After an early life of dissipation founded an order in Granada called the Brothers of Charity, devoting himself chiefly to the nursing of the sick of the poorest classes and of the insane. The order was expanded after the death of John and still exists.

John of Jandun (d. 1328). Prof. of theology and philosophy at Paris; championed the king against the claims of the Papacy; wrote: *De potestate ecclesiastica;* collaborated with Marsilius of Padua in writing *Defensor Pacis*.

John Knox's Liturgy. See *Presbyterian Bodies, 1.*

John of Paris (d. 1306). French Dominican; sided with Philip the Fair in his conflict with Boniface VIII. In his *De regia potestate papali* he held that the priest was greater than the prince in spiritual things, but the prince greater than the priest in temporal things. His *Determinatio de modo existendi corporis Christi in Sacramento altaris* advocated the impanation view of the Lord's Supper.

John Pupper of Goch (d. 1475). Belgian adherent of the Brethren of the Common Life; followed Augustine's theology; opposed Scholasticism; his theological convictions have been summarized in the statement: "From God, through God, to God." Important works: *Concerning the Liberty of the Christian Religion; Treatise of the Four Errors Concerning Evangelical Law.*

John of Salisbury (d. 1180). Bishop of Chartres; taught that the prince received his power from the Church (*Policraticus*).

John Sigismund (1572—1619). Elector of Brandenburg. Ed. as a strict Lutheran, but embraced Reformed faith 1613 and became aggressively active in behalf of Calvinism; fell heir to Duchy of Prussia 1618. Since Sigismund the union of the Lutheran and Reformed Churches became a settled policy of the Berlin court.

John of Wesel. Reformer before the Reformation; studied at Erfurt, where he afterwards became rector; later canon at Worms, then professor at Basel, then again preacher at Worms, and finally at Mainz, where he was tried for heresy, for denying the authority of the Pope and of councils; he recanted; d. 1479 in the Augustinian monastery at Mainz.

Johnsen, Erik K. B. Sept. 20, 1863, at Stavanger, Norway; ed. at Stavanger Latin School, 1870—82; Christiania Univ., 1882—88 (Art., Philos., C. T.);

private instructor in theology, 1888 to 1891; immigrated, 1892; prof. of theology, Red Wing Sem., 1892—97; pastor, Hudson, Wis., 1897—1900; prof. theol., United Church Sem., 1900—17; Luther Theol. Sem., 1917—23; bd. of Publ., 1900—23; Union Com., 1905—12. Author: *En kort udredning; Paulus; Paul of Tarsus* (English edition by Peer O. Stromme), 1919; *Lykke i livet; I Kirke; Brevet til Hebraeerne, en Udredning; Guds rike i det gamle testamente* (edited by N. N. Ronning after Johnsen's death); Editor: *Folkekalender*, 1900 to 1922; *Julebok for barn*, 1902—17; *Hoymes efterladte skrifter*, two volumes, 1904; *Fredstanker* (sermons, 2d series); *Kors og krone* (sermons, 3d series), 1909; *Kristi lidelsehistorie*, 1909; *Andagtsstunder*, 1913. D. D. Augustana Sem., 1921. D. Jan. 21, 1923.

Johnson, Gisle. See *Norway, Lutheranism in*, 11.

Jommelli, Nicola (1714—74). Member of the "Neapolitan School"; lived as composer and director in several Italian cities; later for fifteen years *Kapellmeister* to the Duke of Wuerttemberg; his sacred music justly famous.

Jonas, Justus (1493—1555). Studied at Erfurt and Wittenberg; canon at Erfurt, later professor and then rector of the university; *Propst* at All Saints of Wittenberg 1521; professor of church law; one of the most active colaborers of Luther; later first evangelical superintendent in Halle, finally superintendent at Eisfeld, in Saxe-Meiningen; a learned theologian with sound views, noted also as hymn writer; wrote stanzas 4 and 5 of "Erhalt uns, Herr, bei deinem Wort"; "Wo Gott der Herr nicht bei uns haelt."

Jones, Abner. See *Congregational and Christian Churches.*

Jones, Samuel Porter (1847—1906). B. in Alabama; Methodist Episcopal; "Mountain Evangelist"; soldier in Civil War; lawyer, drunkard; converted, ordained 1872; pastor, agent of orphanage in Georgia; revivalist.

Jonsson, Finnur (1704—89). Bishop in Iceland; his *Historia ecclesiastica Islandiae* (4 vols.) is an outstanding work on the ecclesiastical and, in part, secular, history of Iceland.

Josenhans, Joseph. B. Feb. 9, 1812, at Stuttgart, Wuerttemberg; d. Dec. 25, 1884, at Leonberg. Inspector of the Basel Mission 1850; visited India in 1851 and reorganized all departments of the work; resigned 1879 and retired to Stuttgart.

Joseph, Sisters of St. A Roman Catholic female community founded by Jean Paul Medalle (1650), the members of which specialize in benevolent, educational, and mission efforts.

Joseph II and Josephinism. Joseph II of Austria (1780—90), imbued with the principle of the sovereignty of state rights, attempted a readjustment in the mutual relation of Church and State, so as to make the former subordinate and subservient to the latter. The scheme also included practical separation of the Church from the authority of Rome. The introduction of the new system was attended by incisive reforms, the most important of which was an Edict of Toleration (1781), granting to Lutherans and Reformed freedom of worship as well as access to civil offices. In addition, the following measures were enacted: 1. The language employed in the service of the church is to be the vernacular instead of Latin. 2. All religious orders not engaged in teaching or in spiritual work are to be suppressed. 3. All pilgrimages outside the national boundaries are prohibited. 4. All Austrian subjects are forbidden to study at Rome. 5. No bull or any papal communication, except as approved by the government, has any validity in the Austrian dominions. — These measures raised a storm of protest among the majority of the Austrian clergy. Pope Pius VI, in 1782, paid a personal visit to Joseph, but he was powerless to change the emperor's headstrong policy. But the disturbances that arose both in Austria and in her Netherlands possessions induced him to revoke part of his legislation, while after his death his successors did the rest, and the Josephine *régime*, established in hot haste and based on a wholly false theory, came to naught.

Joseph of the Studium (of Thessalonica). Among the foremost hymn writers of the Eastern Church; author of the Canons in the *Pentecostarion*, to which his name is prefixed; not to be confounded with St. Joseph the Hymnographer, who wrote "Stars of the Morning."

Josephus, Flavius (A. D. 37/38—100). B. in Jerusalem; of high-priestly descent; joined Pharisees; made a commander in Galilee during the Jewish rebellion; captured by Romans and given his freedom by Vespasian; went to Rome after the war and dedicated his life to the writing of the history of his people. Greatest Greek-writing Jewish historian. His works: *Jewish War; Antiquities; Autobiography; Against Apion.*

See works of Josephus in Loeb's Classical Library; G. Hoelscher in Pauly-Wissowa, IX.

Josquin de Pres (Despres; ca.1450 to 1521). Regarded by many as the first great composer since medieval times. Luther had a very high regard for him as a musician and as a master craftsman and remarked on one occasion: "Josquin is master of the notes, the others are mastered by them." Josquin was a direct predecessor of Palestrina; he was a pupil of Okeghem and shared much of his preceptor's contrapuntal skill. At times, however, the involved character of his music rendered its text rather unintelligible, thereby justifying the complaints of the Council of Trent, which insisted that the texts of sacred choral music be not obscured by their music and which, for this reason, pointed to the music of Palestrina as the ideal type of ecclesiastical choral music.

A. Guido, *Handbuch der Musik-Geschichte, Frankfurt* a. M., 1924; P. H. Lang, *Music in Western Civilization,* New York, 1941; D. Ferguson, *A History of Musical Thought,* New York, 1948; H. Leichtentritt, *Music, History and Ideas,* Cambridge, Mass., 1938; W. E. Buszin, "Luther on Music," *Musical Quart.,* Jan. 1946.

Jovinian (4th century). A "heretic" known only from the writings of his enemies; excommunicated by Siricius and Ambrose; all his teachings seem to have grown out of his opposition to Eastern monasticism (married people have equal merit with unmarried; fasting not better than enjoying food; denied perpetual virginity of Mary; denied sinlessness of the regenerates).

Jowett, Benjamin (1817—93). Master of Balliol College and Vice-Chancellor of Oxford. As an exponent of the Broad Church theology, he influenced the rise of critical interpretation. He was tried for the views expressed in his essay *On the Inspiration of Scripture.* Best known for his translation of Plato's *Dialogues.*

Jowett, John Henry (1864—1923). English Congregationalist; pastor at Fifth Ave. Presbyterian Church, N.Y., for seven years; returned to England (1918) and became pastor of Westminster Chapel, London. Wrote: *The High Calling, The Transfigured Church, Things that Matter Most, The Whole Armor of God.* Famous preacher.

Jox, J. H. B. Dec. 18, 1831, near Giessen, Hesse-Darmstadt; studied theology in the Practical Seminary at Fort Wayne; pastor at Freistadt, Wis., Logansport, Ind., 1865; vice-president of the Central District; founded numerous congregations in the vicinity of Logansport; d. March 21, 1893.

Jubilation. A special section, or coda, which was often sung on festival occasions at the end of the Gradual, carrying the final syllable of the Hallelujah with which the Gradual closed.

Jubilees. In 1300 Pope Boniface VIII announced in a bull that "not only full and copious, but the most full pardon of all their sins" should be granted all the faithful who would come to Rome that year, penitently confess their sins, and make a stated number of daily visits to the churches of St. Peter and St. Paul. A daily average of 200,000 pilgrims came to gain the precious indulgence. Two papal clerks were busy night and day raking in money. The people of Rome likewise reaped a golden harvest. Little wonder that the year of jubilee, which was intended for every hundredth year, was celebrated again in 1350, then in 1390 and since 1450 was set for every twenty-fifth year. Jubilees last from one Christmas to the next and begin with the ceremony of opening the "holy door." In the 15th century the popes, through various devices, realized enormous sums of money from the jubilees. All other indulgences were suspended; but those who could not come to Rome were enabled to gain the jubilee indulgence at home by fulfilling certain conditions and giving an "alms." Here, as elsewhere, the Reformation imposed changes, and later jubilees were no longer a source of revenue. The only jubilee in the last century was held in 1825. In the 20th century, jubilees were held in 1900, 1925, and 1950.

Jubilees, Book of. See *Apocrypha, A 4.*

Jubilus. A florid and melismatic rendition of the final syllable of the Alleluia of the Gradual which enjoyed widespread popularity in the Middle

Ages and of which Jerome said: "By the term *jubilus* we understand that which neither in words nor syllables nor letters nor speech it is possible to express or comprehend how much man ought to praise God." (Cf. *Music in the Middle Ages*, Gustav Reese, New York, 1940, p. 63.) The sequence *(sequentia)*, which originated in the eighth century, was an outgrowth of the jubilus.

Jud, Leo (1485—1542). One of the closest associates of Zwingli, supporting him with his humanistic erudition. Took part in formulating the Helvetic Confessions. Leader in Zurich Bible translation, and published catechisms.

Judaism. 1. The religion and religious practices of the Jews. The term is of Greek origin, occurring in the New Testament (Gal. 1:13, 14) and in the Apocryphal Books of the Old Testament (2 Macc. 2:21; 8:1; 14:8). The foundation of all forms of Judaism is the *Torah*, the Law, *i. e.*, the Five Books of Moses, which record how Jehovah by a covenant made the Jewish nation His people in a very special sense and how in His divine Law, revealed to Moses, He laid down His ordinances for the faith and life of His chosen people. Judaism was unique in the ancient heathen world through its doctrines that Jehovah is one God, the Creator and Ruler of the entire universe and all that is therein; that He is a spirit; that He is holy and demands holiness from His followers, yet ready to forgive the repentant sinner who seeks His mercy in faith; that He would in days to come provide a Messiah who would redeem His people and extend His kingdom over all the nations of the earth; and that after death follows life in the world to come where the righteous receive their blessed reward, but the wicked meet just retribution for their evil deeds. Unique was also the observance of the Sabbath as a day of rest. Characteristic rite of Judaism is circumcision as the sign of the covenant. Among its ceremonies, the several types of sacrifices at the national sanctuary held a central position prior to the destruction of the Temple.

2. During the centuries following the return from the Babylonian Exile, ca. 538 B. C., the voice of prophecy, which in days of religious decline kept reminding Israel of its obligations to Jehovah, became silent. But the loss of political independence, the trials of the Babylonian Captivity, and the difficulties encountered under successive foreign dominations, centered the nation's attention on its spiritual heritage as represented by the Torah. Much study was spent on it and on its interpretation in the light of the Prophets and of oral tradition. The sect of the Pharisees sprang up, which added its own regulations to those of the Torah and developed a system of obedience to the letter of the Law without true service of Jehovah. Another sect was the Sadducees, the liberals or freethinkers of their time. That many of the Jews, especially among the common people, adhered to the old, simple faith is obvious from the New Testament. With the conquest of Jerusalem by the Romans, A. D. 70, and the destruction of the Temple, the period of Judaism represented by the Talmud * set in. It is characterized by extreme legalism and ritualism, but no unified system of doctrine resulted until Moses Maimonides * in the 12th century codified the teachings of Judaism under thirteen principles: 1) The existence of the Creator and Ruler of all things; 2) His unity and oneness; 3) His spirituality; 4) His eternity; 5) the worship of Him alone; 6) the truth of the Prophets; 7) Moses the supreme Prophet for all time; 8) the revelation of the Torah to Moses; 9) the Torah the only and everlasting Law; 10) the Creator knows the thoughts and deeds of man; 11) the Creator rewards and punishes; 12) the coming of the Messiah; 13) the resurrection of the dead.

3. In modern times, Jews have gained a greater measure of freedom and the opportunity to play their part in the social, economic, and political life of the community in which they reside. This has had its effect on Judaism. Many still today adhere to orthodox Judaism in spite of the difficulty of adjusting their religious practices to prevailing conditions of modern life. Others, known as conservative, still regard the Torah and the traditional laws of Judaism as basic, but have made concessions by being less strict in observing the religious regulations. A third group adheres to Reform Judaism, which originated in Germany as a lay movement in the late 18th century with a view to adjusting Judaism to meet modern needs. Services are in the vernacular and are modernized. Reform Judaism aims to retain those elements of Jewish tradition which are regarded as permanent, but permits changes in all other respects. It stresses the prin-

ciple that the Jew has a mission in the modern world and must make his contribution towards enlightening mankind. Rabbi I. M. Weis says that Reform Judaism, like all forms of Judaism, "is built upon the immovable rock of an ethical God of universal justice, righteousness, and mercy; upon belief in the Fatherhood of God and the brotherhood of man; upon the doctrines of the sanctity of human life and equality of opportunity for the fulfillment of the individual and the enrichment of life. It believes, furthermore, that life is invaluable and that man, made in the image of God, must contribute not only to his own welfare, but to that of others." Thus the religious position of Reform Judaism is close to that of Unitarians.* Reform Judaism occupies a prominent position in the struggle against anti-Semitism (popular name for prejudice against Jews). According to Dr. Maurice E. N. Eisendrath, president of the Union of American Hebrew Congregations, Reform Judaism had in 1948 about 400 congregations with 100,000 families in the United States, its chief stronghold. In spite of the existing differences, orthodox, conservative, and reform Jews recognize each other as adherents of the family faith. Variations in belief and practice are viewed merely as expressions of different schools of Judaism.

4. Besides observing the Sabbaths, the new moons, several special fast days, and some minor festivals, Judaism keeps as major festivals: the Passover, celebrating the Exodus from Egypt, and Pentecost or Feast of Weeks *(Shabuoth)* in spring; the Feast of Trumpets or New Year *(Rosh Hashana)*, the Day of Atonement *(Yom Kippur)*, and the Feast of Tabernacles *(Sukkoth)* in fall. To these Mosaic festivals were added later *Purim*, or the Feast of Esther, celebrating the rescue of the Jews from Haman's plot, and *Chanukkah*, or Feast of Lights, commemorating the rededication of the Temple after its desecration by the Syrians. The latter falls near Christmas. In the era preceding A. D. 70 pilgrimages to the Temple were required in connection with observance of Passover, Pentecost, and the Feast of Tabernacles.

For the movement known as Zionism see the separate article. GVS

Judgment of Conscience. See *Conscience.*

Judgment, Final. See *Last Things.*

Judith. See *Apocrypha,* A 3.

Judson, Adoniram (1788—1850). American missionary; sent by the American Board of Commissioners for Foreign Missions to India; on his journey he was converted to Baptist views; became first American missionary to Burma; translated Bible into Burmese.

Juelicher, Gustav Adolf. B. 1857; 1889 prof. of New Testament Exegesis and History at Berlin and at Marburg; liberal theologian; wrote an *Introduction to the New Testament* and on the *Parables of the Lord.* D. 1938.

Julian the Apostate. Roman emperor (361—63), reared Christian; converted to theosophy and magic by Maximus, a Neoplatonist; initiated into the Greek mysteries; withdrew favors granted Christianity and at the same time sought to purify and enhance heathenism through ideals subconsciously borrowed from Christianity; reinstated at public expense the pagan cultus, rebuilt temples, recalled heathen priests, and was unweariedly active in promoting the cause of the "old faith."

Julian of Eclanum (d. ca. 454). Leader of the 18 Pelagian bishops who were deposed by the *Epistola tractatoria* of Zosimus (418). He held, in opposition to Augustine, that sin is a matter of the will and not a hereditary disease.

Julian, John (1839—1913). B. at Topcliffe, Yorkshire, eldest son of Thomas Julian of St. Agnes, Cornwall. He was vicar of Wincobank and of Topcliffe, also canon of York. He is noted for hymnological research work, resulting in A *Dictionary of Hymnology.* He composed a number of hymns and translations.

Julius II. See *Popes,* 19.

Julius Africanus (d. 240), author of a chronography, or universal history, beginning with the creation and carried down to 221. The work was much used by Eusebius and became the foundation of medieval historiography.

Julius of Brunswick (1528—89). Introduced the Reformation in Brunswick; did not put the Formula of Concord in his *Corpus Doctrinae.*

Jung, Carl G. (1875—). Pupil of Freud and developer of psychoanalysis, contrived introvert-extravert concept of personality; assigns importance to religious contribution to personality.

Jung, John H. S. (1740—1817). Prof. at Kaiserslautern, Heidelberg, and

Marburg; friend of Goethe and Herder; pietistic, mystic, theosophic.

Jurisdiction, Spiritual. See *Keys, Office of,* 8.

Jus Gentium. See *Natural Law.*

Jus Naturae, Naturale. See *Natural Law.*

Jus Novissimum. See *Canon Law.*

Justice, Divine. The justice of God is that quality in God by reason of which He legislates justly, His laws being the perfect expression of His holy will. He is true to His promises and will exact judgment in accordance with the principles of right. He is, indeed, Himself that principle; and being consistent with Himself, He is righteous (Deut. 32:4; Ps. 19:9). In His justice God has promulgated laws which are perfect. When they are transgressed, His justice demands punishment, and if vicarious atonement is made, it must consist of full satisfaction. The justice of God takes into account the manner and measure of sin committed (Matt. 11:21 ff.; Luke 12:47). The purpose of those punishments which justice inflicts is retribution (Heb. 2:2). But also the fulfillment of divine promises is exhibited as justice; what is in another respect credited to the grace of God, the Savior of sinners, is also referred to the righteousness of God, the Judge of the quick and the dead, to the justice of Him who will stand by His word and promise (Is. 54:10; 2 Tim. 4:8).

Justification. 1. That act of God by which He for Christ's sake declares the world innocent and acquitted.

2. The Lutheran Confessions (Ap. IV; Sm. Art., II:1) and the renowned teachers of the past (Luther, St. L. Ed., XIV:168; I:1441; VI:721; XVI:1664; Martin Chemnitz, *Loc. Theol.* II:200; Balthasar Meisner, *Anthropolog.* D. 3, disp. 24) call the doctrine of justification the most important teaching of divine revelation. The apprehension of this doctrine by Luther made him the Reformer of the Church, equipped by God for his great work.

3. The teaching of justification presupposes the doctrine that man both through his natural condition and his thoughts, words, and deeds is a transgressor of God's Law, subject to the divine wrath, and condemned to eternal death (Is. 64:6; Eccl. 7:20; Romans 1 to 3; Matt. 25:41. See *Sin*).

4. The doctrine includes as one of its chief elements the truth that God is moved to justify us by His grace. "Grace" is a particular kind of love. It is love directed toward those who are undeserving or unworthy (Rom. 3:23; 5:20).

5. God's grace carried out its benevolent design through the redemption of Christ. God sends His holy, innocent Son, lets Him become a human being and makes Him man's Substitute. This Substitute fulfills all the requirements of the Law in our place (active obedience). Besides, He suffers the pangs and woes which we had deserved (passive obedience). Thus divine justice is satisfied, and love triumphs too. Through Christ God reconciled the world unto Himself. This act of God in which He through Christ provided forgiveness of sins for the world is called objective justification (Rom. 5:12 ff.). Note that objective justification is not identical with the redemption, justification being a judicial act and redemption a sacrificial work).

6. The righteousness of Christ is given us by God in the Gospel and the Sacraments. These means of grace are a dynamic power which convey, present, and seal to us God's forgiveness (Rom. 1:16; John 15:3; Gal. 3:27). We appropriate this righteousness through faith (see *Faith*). The minute that we take the righteousness which Christ has won God pronounces us justified, free from sin, acquitted (subjective justification; Gen. 15:6; Luke 15). Regarding this doctrine the Apology states (IV: 84 f.): "Remission of sins is something promised for Christ's sake. Therefore it cannot be received except by faith alone. For a promise cannot be received except by faith alone. Rom. 4:16: 'Therefore it is of faith, that it might be by grace, to the end that the promise might be sure'; as though he were to say, If the matter were to depend upon our merits, the promise would be uncertain and useless, because we never could determine when we would have sufficient merit. And this, experienced consciences can easily understand. Accordingly, Paul says Gal. 3:22: 'But the Scripture hath concluded all under sin, that the promise by faith of Jesus Christ might be given to them that believe.' He takes merit away from us, because he says that all are guilty and concluded under sin; then he adds that the promise, namely, of the remission of sins and of justification, is given, and adds how the promise can be received, namely, by faith. This reasoning, derived from the nature of a

promise, is the chief reasoning in Paul and is often repeated. Nor can anything be devised or imagined whereby this argument of Paul can be overthrown. Wherefore let not good minds suffer themselves to be forced from the conviction that we receive remission of sins for Christ's sake, only through faith. In this they have sure and firm consolation against the terrors of sin and against eternal death and against all the gates of hell."

7. Since justification is brought about by God's grace through the sacrifice of Christ and we become possessors of it through faith, all human merit is excluded (Rom. 3:27 ff.). Faith is not merit, since we are not justified on account of our faith, but through faith (Johann Gerhard, *Loc. de Justif.,* 179). Justification takes place outside of us, at the tribunal of God (Rom. 8:33 ff.).

8. When the sinner has been justified, he has peace with God, enjoys Christian liberty, performs good works, and is filled with the hope of eternal life (Rom. 7:25; 8:1 ff.; John 8:36; Rom. 8:17).

9. Additional truths about justification are that it is not a long, drawn-out process, but occurs in a moment of time; that it is never partial, but always perfect and complete; that it is alike in all that are justified; that it puts us into a state of righteousness which continues as long as we are believers; that it can be lost; and that it can be obtained anew when it has been lost. C. f. WA, *The Abiding Word,* CPH, 1947 (II:235—57).

See standard Dogmatics * works; T. Engelder, "Objective Justification," *CTM,* IV:564ff.; W. Arndt, "The Doctrine of Justification," *Abiding Word,* CPH, 1947 (II:235—57. Gives select bibliography); Theo. Hoyer, "Through Justification unto Sanctification," *CTM,* XIII:81—111; E. W. A. Koehler, "Objective Justification," *CTM,* XVI:217—35; Werner Elert, *Morphologie des Luthertums,* Beck, Munich, 1931 (64—123); Adolf Koeberle, *The Quest for Holiness* (tr. J. C. Mattes), Augsburg Publishing House, Minneapolis, 1946; E. Preuss, *Rechtfertigung des Suenders vor Gott,* Schlawitz, Berlin, 1871; C. P. Krauth, *The Conservative Reformation and Its Theology,* Lippincott, 1871; Gustaf Aulen, *Christus Victor* (tr. A. G. Hebert), Macm., 1945.

Justification, Roman Catholic Doctrine of. See *Works, Merit of.*

Justin Martyr. Famous apologist and philosophical theologian; b. ca. 100 at Flavia Neapolis (now Nablus), in Samaria; suffered martyrdom at Rome under Marcus Aurelius 166. The son of heathen parents, he received a Hellenic education and earnestly sought for truth among the current systems of philosophy. After many disappointments he finally embraced Platonism, which seemed to bring him near the coveted goal — the vision of God and the eternal verities. At this juncture, however, while walking in silent meditation by the seashore, he encountered a venerable old Christian who, engaging him in conversation, shook his confidence in all human wisdom and directed him to the Prophets and Apostles as true teachers come from God. The ardent young Platonist became a Christian and, retaining his philosopher's mantle, devoted his life to the spread and vindication of Christianity. An unordained lay preacher, he traveled from place to place, combating heathen, Jews, and heretics. Besides, he wielded a vigorous, if unpolished, pen. His principal works are his two *Apologies,* the *Dialog with the Jew Trypho,* not to mention doubtful or spurious works under his name. The central idea in Justin's theology, strongly biased by Platonic and Stoic speculation, is his Logos doctrine. The Logos, or universal Reason, familiar to the thought of the Stoa and the Academy, Justin boldly identifies with the historic Christ, in whom the divine Reason became incarnate. He interprets Christ in terms of heathen philosophy. Indeed, Christianity is to Justin the true philosophy and the highest reason. Moreover, the preincarnate Logos scattered seeds of truth, not only among the Jews, but among Greeks and barbarians as well. "The footsteps of the Logos are to be traced throughout the ages, faintly luminous among the Greeks, brighter among the Hebrews, shining with full effulgence only at the advent of our Savior." Thus Socrates, Heraclitus, and others, according to Justin, were Christians in fact, if not in name. On the practical side, Christianity is to Justin essentially a new law. Justin had no proper conception of sin and grace. "His theology is legalistic and ascetic rather than evangelical and free."

Justinian I (*Flavius Anicius Julianus*), emperor of the East; b. 483 at Tauresium, in Macedonia; d. 565 at Constantinople; showed great military ability at an early age; consul in 521; emperor from 527; a man of unusual capacity for work; did much to restore empire to former glory; his religious policy governed by the conviction that the unity of the empire presupposed unity of faith; the code of Justinian aimed at the suppression of Hellenism and the strengthening of Christian

propaganda; missions were supported strongly; made the Niceno-Constanti-nopolitan Creed the sole symbol of the Church and accorded legal force to the canons of the first four Ecumenical Councils; in spite of all efforts he did not succeed in averting the growing estrangement between the Oriental and the Occidental Church.

K

Kaaba. Arabic for "cube." The an-cient heathen Arabic shrine, 36 ft. long, 30 ft. wide, and 45 ft. high, in the heart of Mecca. For practical reasons Mo-hammed retained it as the chief sanc-tuary of Islam, prescribed pilgrimages to it, and appointed it as *keblah*, the place towards which Moslems every-where must face when praying. Set in masonry in the southeast corner, at a height convenient for kissing by pil-grims, is the sacred Black Stone, the main object of veneration in the Kaaba. Every devout Moslem seeks to make at least one pilgrimage to the shrine in his lifetime.

Kabbala (neo-Hebraic, "reception," then, "received by tradition"). The eso-teric system or philosophy of the Jews, developed during the Middle Ages. Uniting the Bible with Hellenistic Ju-daism and Neoplatonic and Gnostic systems of emanation, it endeavored to solve the most profound problems con-cerning God and the universe, such as the nature of God (who is called *En Sof*, the "Infinite"), the origin of the visible universe (believed to be a pan-theistic emanation of the divine es-sence), the reconciliation of the im-perfection of the world with the perfection of God, the origin of evil, the atonement of sin. The Kabbalists based their doctrines on Scripture, not, however, by taking its literal or even its allegorical sense, but by ascribing deeply hidden meanings to figures, let-ters, and words. The names of God were believed to possess great magic powers, especially the *Tetragrammaton* (see *Shemhammephorash*). All this led to the most absurd jugglery of words and figures. The Kabbala spread widely during the twelfth century and gained friends even among Christian scholars in the fifteenth and sixteenth centuries (*e. g.*, John Picus and John Reuchlin). The most important kabbalistic works

are the *Sefer Yezirah* (6th century) and the book *Zohar* (Spain, 13th century).

Kaehler, Carl Martin August (1835 to 1912). B. at Neuhausen. Studied law at Koenigsberg and theology at Heidel-berg, Halle, and Tuebingen. *Privat-dozent* at Halle, 1860; associate profes-sor of theology at Bonn, 1864; then at Halle, 1867; professor of systematic theology and NT exegesis there, 1879. He founded no theological school, but exerted a powerful influence on theo-logical thought.

Kaeppel, George Christopher Al-bert. B. April 19, 1862, at Indianapolis, Ind.; graduated at Addison 1881; teacher at Wittenberg, Mo., 1881—83; at St. Louis (Trinity), 1883—97; professor at Teachers' Seminary, Addison (and River Forest), Ill., after 1897; former editor of *School Journal*; wrote: *Die Orgel im Gottesdienst; Orgelkomposi-tionen; Lieder fuer gemischte Choere; Lieder fuer Maennerchoere; Songs for Male Choir; Songs for Mixed Choir;* composer of several cantatas. D. Jan. 11, 1934.

Kaeppel, John Henry Christian. B. Sept. 15, 1853, Cleveland, Ohio; ed. Ft. Wayne and St. Louis (1875); taught parochial school in St. Louis, later in-structor at Walther College; ordained 1887; pastor at Jefferson City, Mo., 1887 to 1888; pres. of St. Paul's College, Con-cordia, Mo., 1888—1925. D. D., St. Louis, 1923. D. Feb. 3, 1925.

Kaffirs. The chief native race in southeastern Africa, a branch of the Bantu family. Missions were conducted by the Wesleyan Mission Society, the Berlin Mission Society I, and the Church of Scotland Mission.

Kaftan, Julius. B. at Loit, 1848, d. 1926; German Protestant theologian, ed. at Erlangen, Berlin, Kiel; prof. of the-ology at Basel, after 1883 at Berlin. A representative of Ritschlian theology, he emphasized the mystic element in Christianity, regarded the Christian religion as the revealed religion (*Offenbarungsreligion*), in which, whatever in other religious systems is found merely as impulse and want, is gratified. Wrote: *Truth of the Christian Religion; Christianity and Philosophy.*

Kaftan, Theodor (1847—1932). General superintendent of Schleswig-Holstein, 1886; retired, in Baden; conservative Lutheran theologian of the modern type; wrote: *Moderne Theologie des alten Glaubens.*

Kahnis, Karl Friedrich August (1814—88). One of the most prominent Lutheran theologians of the 19th century; *Privatdozent* at Berlin; professor extraordinary at Breslau, then professor at Leipzig. Kahnis was at first a staunch defender of confessional Lutheranism; later in life he adopted latitudinarian views in regard to the Trinity (subordinationism), Scripture, person of Christ, and the Lord's Supper. His chief works are: *Der innere Gang des deutschen Protestantismus* and *Die lutherische Dogmatik, historisch-genetisch dargestellt.*
A. Staehlin, "Die Theologie des Dr. Kahnis," *Ztschr. f. d. ges. luth. Theol. u. K.,* XXXIV: 93—120.

Kaiser (*Kaeser*), **Leonard.** Vicar at Waizenkirchen; publicly declared for Luther in 1524; imprisoned; recanted; troubled in conscience and went to Wittenberg in January, 1525; returned in 1527 on news of father's illness at Passau; fell ill; was imprisoned and tried under John Eck; burned at the stake Aug. 16, 1527.

Kaiserswerth. See *Charities, Christian,* 5.

Kalevala. A Finnish epic poem containing cosmological myths, legends, and some history.

Kalinnikoff, Basil Sergeivich (1866 to 1901). A Russian composer of sacred and secular music whose precarious health and untimely death prevented him, despite his great talents, from meeting with the success enjoyed by better-known Russian masters of his day.

Kalkar, Christian (1803—86). B. in Stockholm; son of Jewish rabbi; joined Christian Church in Denmark (1823); pastor of Seeland and Copenhagen; author.

Kalm, Peter (1715—79). Swedish naturalist; his account of travels in America furnishes material for early American Luth. history.

Kameroons. See *Cameroons.*

Kamphausen, Adolf Hermann Heinrich (1829—1909). Studied at Bonn; taught at Heidelberg, 1856—59, after which he returned to Bonn, becoming full prof. in 1868; member of the committee for the revision of Luther's translation of the Old Testament; published studies in the field of exegesis and Bible translation.

Kansas, Synod of. See *United Lutheran Church, Synods of,* 10.

Kansas City Platform. See *Congregational and Christian Churches,* A 3.

Kant, Immanuel (1724—1804). German philosopher; b. at Koenigsberg; after 1770 professor there. Exerted profound influence on modern philosophy. In *Kritik der reinen Vernunft,* which is of a critical, destructive nature, he attempted to show that the transcendent world, the existence of God, and the immortality of the soul are unknowable to pure reason. In *Kritik der praktischen Vernunft,* which has a constructive purpose, he endeavored to rebuild what he had destroyed. Freedom of man, immortality of the soul, existence of God (the three great principles of the "Enlightenment"*) are postulates of the practical reason, *i. e.,* of conscience. Prominent in his ethics is his "categorical imperative." In *Religion innerhalb der Grenzen der blossen Vernunft* he asserts that morality is the essence of religion. Saving faith is identical with a God-pleasing life.
G. H. Palmer, *Immanuel Kant, 1724 to 1804* (ed. by E. C. Wilm), Yale University Press, 1925; R. M. Wenley, *Kant and His Philosophical Revolution,* Scribner's, 1911; C. C. J. Webb, *Kant's Philosophy of Religion,* Oxford Press, 1926; G. T. Whitney and D. F. Bowers, *The Heritage of Kant,* Princeton University Press, 1939; H. S. Chamberlain, *Immanuel Kant: a Study and a Comparison with Goethe, Leonardo da Vinci, Bruno, Plato and Descartes* (tr., Lord Redesdale), John Lane, London, 1914.

Kantorei. Choral groups of the 15th and 16th centuries which furnished music for the churches and for the courts of the nobility. Their objectives and achievements had much in common with those of the *Schola Cantorum* of Gregory's day and of the school established in 1362 in Toulouse, France, by Pope Urban V. In Lutheran circles the *Kantorei* was employed to present, under the leadership of its cantor, the liturgical propers as well as the special choral music of the service, besides lending support to congregational singing and acquainting the congregation with new chorales. Johann Walther, Luther's musical collaborator, was the first cantor of the Lutheran Church (Torgau, Dresden). Through the activities of the Lutheran *Kantorei* the existence of the *Kalenden,* against whose degeneracy and corrupt practices Luther preached vehemently, soon came to its end.

Leo Schrade, "The Choral Music of the Lutheran *Kantorei,*" *The Musical Heritage of the Church,* Valparaiso University Pamphlet Series, No. 10 (Theo. Hoelty-Nickel, editor), pp. 70 to 83.

Kapff, Sixt Karl. Prominent Protestant pastor; b. at Gueglingen (Wuerttemberg), Oct. 22, 1805; d. in Stuttgart, Sept. 1, 1879; In 1833 he became pastor of the colony of Pietists at Kornthal, near Stuttgart; 1843 *Dekan* at Muensingen, 1847 at Herrenberg; in 1850 transferred to Reutlingen and in 1852 to Stuttgart, where he was *Praelat* and pastor of the Stiftskirche. Published sermons and devotional books.

Karaites. A Jewish sect which rejects rabbinical tradition and the Talmud, accepting the Old Testament as sole authority; founded by Anan ben David in the 8th century in Bagdad, from where it spread to Syria, Egypt, and Europe, flourishing especially in the 12th century. They now number 12,000 to 13,000, most of whom live in southern Russia.

Karg-Elert, Sigfrid (1877—1933). A composer of organ music whose compositions enjoyed wide use in the first half of the 20th century. On the whole, his compositions aim at external effects and lack depth as well as originality. His best-known works are his *Choral-Improvisations,* op. 65. Karg-Elert, however, outdid himself in such outstanding works as his *Fuge, Kanzone und Epilog* (op. 85, No. 3)), his *Symphonischer Choral, Jesu, meine Freude* (op. 87, No. 2), and his last work, the *Passacaglia, Variations, and Fugue on B-A-C-H.*

Karlstadt, Andreas Bodenstein von (1480—1541). Revolutionist of the Reformation. Supported Luther's theses 1517; participated in Leipzig Disputation; rushed reforms at Wittenberg; rejected the Real Presence at Orlamuende and encouraged incendiary methods of reformation; was expelled from Saxony and wandered from place to place; became professor at Basel and gave up political agitation.

Hermann Barge, *Andreas Bodenstein von Karlstadt,* Leipzig, 1905.

Karma. Sanskrit for "deed." The term for the Hindu doctrine of moral reward and punishment, based on the doctrine of reincarnation and designed to explain why there are such inequalities in human conditions — wealth and poverty, health and sickness, happiness and misery. It is Brahmanic in origin and found special development in Buddhism. Souls have been transmigrating for ages, and whatever happiness or sorrow an individual experiences is the unalterable recompense for good or evil deeds in former incarnations, and whatever good or evil deed an individual does will result in happiness or sorrow in future existences. Reincarnation continues until all acts of the present and previous existences have worked out their consequences. This may lead to an untold number of reincarnations. Salvation, *i. e.,* release from this continuous round of rebirths, can be attained only by being freed from the power of karma. The various Indian religions have each their own way in which this may be accomplished. See *Transmigration, Brahmanism, Buddhism,* 2, 3.

Karpocrates. Gnostic of the 2d century; founder of the antinomian Karpocratians.

Katharinus, Ambrosius (1487 to 1553). Teacher of law at Siena; became Dominican 1517; bishop of Minori; archbishop of Conza; opponent of Luther.

Kattenbusch, Ferdinand (1851 to 1936). Prof. at Giessen, Goettingen, Halle; follower of Ritschl; became prominent through his writings on the Confessions, history of the Apostolic Age, and Lutheran theology.

Kautzsch, Emil Friedrich (1841 to 1910). Prof. of Old Testament exegesis at Basel 1872, at Tuebingen 1880, at Halle 1888; noted Hebraist and grammarian.

Kavel, August L. C. See *Australia, Lutheranism in.*

Kawerau, Peter Gustav (1847 to 1918). Pastor and professor at Kiel and Breslau; provost at Berlin in 1907; one of the foremost writers on Luther; co-editor of Weimar Edition of Luther's works.

Keble, John (1792—1866). B. at Fairford, Gloucestershire; at the age of 15 won a scholarship at Corpus Christi College, Oxford; also the prize essay in both English and Latin, graduating *cum laude*. He took orders and held various positions as clergyman, the last, after his marriage in 1835, being that of priest at Hursley. He was the real author of the Oxford Movement; professor of poetry.

Keffer, Adam. See *Canada, Lutheranism in,* 5.

Keil, Johann Karl Friedrich (1807 to 1888). B. at Oelsnitz, Saxony; 1833 professor of Old and New Testament exegesis at Dorpat; removed to Leipzig 1859, and devoted himself to literary work and practical affairs of the Lutheran Church. In collaboration with Franz Delitzsch he wrote a commentary on the Old Testament. Among his other writings the most valuable is his *Introduction to the Old Testament*. Keil belonged to the orthodox conservative school of Hengstenberg and regarded modern development of so-called scientific theology as a passing phase of error.

Keim, Karl Theodor (1825—78). Modern critical theologian; studied at Tuebingen, influenced by F. C. Baur; 1860 professor of historical theology at Zuerich, 1873 at Giessen.

Keimann, Christian (1607 to 1662). Studied at Wittenberg; conrector, afterwards rector, at Zittau; distinguished teacher and scholar; hymns genuinely poetical and deeply spiritual; wrote: "Freuet euch, ihr Christen alle"; "Meinen Jesum lass' ich nicht."

Keinath, Herman O. A. B. Dec. 27, 1894, at Richville, Mich.; grad., Concordia Sem., St. Louis, 1918; asst. pastor, Immanuel, Grand Rapids, Mich., 1918 to 1926; prof., Concordia Teachers College, Seward, Nebr., 1926—42; Concordia Teachers College, River Forest, 1942 to 1952; attended Univ. of Nebr. and Univ. of Mich. (M. A.; Ph. D.); wrote *My Church, The History of the Missouri Synod for Young People* and many articles in *Concordia Theological Monthly, Lutheran Education,* and *Concordia Historical Quarterly;* mem., Synodical Bd. for Foreign Missions. D. June 13, 1952.

Keller, Benjamin (1794—1864). Ed. for ministry by G. H. E. Muhlenberg; helped establish the Lutheran Board of Publication; collected funds for the German professorship at Pennsylvania College.

Keller, Ezra (1812—48). Ed. at Pennsylvania College and Gettysburg; traveling missionary of the Pennsylvania Ministerium; first president of Wittenberg College, Springfield, Ohio.

Kelly, Thomas. B. July 13, 1769, at Kellyville, Athy, Queen's County, Ireland, educated at Portarlington and Kilkenny, also at Trinity College, Dublin University. Expecting to become a lawyer, he went to the Temple in London. While reading law, Kelly had to study Hutchinson's *Moses' Principia.* He also became interested in Romaine's teachings. As a result he developed a deep consciousness of sin. Becoming an ascetic, he took holy orders in the Established Church in 1792, and being in sympathy with the evangelical movement, he began to preach in Dublin. Having seceded from the Established Church, he built chapels with his own money at Athy, Portarlington, Wexford, Waterford, and elsewhere. He wrote more than 700 hymns, many of which are in use today. "Stricken, Smitten, and Afflicted" is one of his best-known hymns. D. May 14, 1854.

KELP. See *Radio Stations, Religious.*

Kelpius, Johann. See *Communistic Societies,* 4.

Kempis, Thomas à. See *Thomas à Kempis.*

Ken, Thomas (1637—1711). B. at Little Berkhamstead, orphaned at about four, he was brought up by a half sister and educated at Winchester and New College, Oxford. He possessed musical talents, particularly a fine voice. He held a number of positions as clergyman before becoming bishop of Bath and Wells. He was one of the seven bishops who refused to read, at the command of the king, "The Declaration of Indulgence." They were imprisoned for three years in the Tower and later deprived of office. He was a most eloquent preacher and was the author of the morning, evening, and midnight hymns, each of which concludes with the famous long-meter doxology, "Praise God, from Whom All Blessings Flow."

Kennicott, Benjamin (1718—83). Anglican Biblical scholar; b. at Totnes; canon of Christ Church, Oxford; died there; lifework: study of Hebrew manuscripts of Old Testament. *Hebrew Bible;* first volume, 1766; second, 1780.

Kenona. See *Gnosticism,* 5.

Kenosis. The doctrine, as taught by Orthodox Lutheranism, that Christ in His state of humiliation did not always and fully use the divine properties communicated to His human nature by virtue of the personal union, which took place when the Son of God, in His incarnation, assumed into His person our human nature. Scripture proof for this doctrine is given in Phil. 2:7: "But made Himself of no reputation," literally, "emptied Himself" (*ekenose*). Doing this, He "took upon Him the form of a servant and was made in the likeness of men." The doctrine of the *kenosis* must be distinguished from that of modern kenoticists (kenoticism), who teach that in His incarnation the Son of God (Logos) emptied Himself (according to His divine nature) either of His relative attributes only (omniscience, omnipotence, omnipresence; so Thomasius) or also of His immanent attributes (so Gess), so that the Logos became the human soul of Christ, a heresy, rendering the Son of God mutable and as such no longer God (so Dorner). Liberal kenoticism finally led to Modernism, which regards Christ as a mere man.

Kentigern. See *Celtic Church,* 6.

Kentucky Revival. See *Presbyterian Bodies,* 4 b.

Kentucky Synod. As early as 1821 Rev. Henry A. Kurtz petitioned the Tennessee Synod for aid in establishing a synod in Kentucky. A convention was held in Harrison Church, Nelson Co., Ky., Sept. 28, 1822, at which fourteen lay delegates from as many congregations in Kentucky and Indiana were present. A second convention was held in 1823. But the emissaries of the General Synod, Jenkins, Gerhart, and Yeager, counteracted the influence of the "Henkelites" and on Oct. 11, 1834, founded the Synod of the West,* which

was originally called the Kentucky Synod. — Another Kentucky Synod was formed out of the Synod of the Southwest in 1854. It joined the General Synod, but was absorbed, in October, 1865, by the Olive Branch Synod of Indiana.

Kentucky, Synod of. See *Synods, Extinct.*

Kentucky - Tennessee Synod. See *United Lutheran Church, Synods of,* 11.

Kenya Colony and Protectorate, formerly British East Africa. Area, 219,730 sq. mi. Population, 5,405,966 (1948), chiefly Arabs, Swahilis, Bantu, Somali, and allied tribes. Mombasa is the largest city. The prevailing religion is animistic. Islam has a great following. Mission work is conducted by 18 societies. Statistics: foreign staff of 288; 128,000 communicants. See *Missions, Bibliography.*

Kepler, Johann (1571—1630). German astronomer and mathematician; though he held the Copernican theory in general, he denied the existence of crystalline spheres; discovered important laws (3) of planetary motion. Kepler fixed the birth date of Christ at the time of the conjunction of Jupiter and Saturn in 747 a. u. c.; denied the Lutheran doctrine of ubiquity; opposed Calvinistic doctrine of predestination; held that God created the world in accordance with Pythagorean perfect numbers.

Ker, John (1819—86). Pastor in Glasgow; prof. of practical theology in United Presbyterian Theological Hall; wrote *History of Preaching; Memorial Discourses.*

Kerll, Johann Kaspar (1627—93). A famous Roman Catholic organist who received his musical training from Valentini, Carissimi, and Frescobaldi; he later served as organist in Munich and Vienna. In Munich he maintained high German standards which were soon discarded in favor of Italian standards after his death.

Keswick Conferences. Annual summer reunions, lasting one week, which have been held since 1875 at Keswick, England, chiefly to promote practical holiness by means of prayer, discussion, and personal intercourse. The meetings are held in a large tent and are attended by several thousand people, including representatives from foreign countries.

During his lifetime Canon Harford-Battersby presided over the conferences; after his death, Mr. Henry Rowker, and, after him, Mr. Robert Wilson. The Keswick movement is distinctly evangelical in character and is supported chiefly by the evangelical branch of the Church of England. The convention takes an active interest in missions and maintains a number of missionaries in foreign fields. The weekly organ of Keswick teaching is the *Life of Faith* (London, 1879 sqq.).

Ketteler, W. E. (1811—77). "The Fighting Bishop of Mainz," so called because of his conflict with the governments of the Upper Rhine (Baden, Hesse, Nassau, Wuerttemberg) in the endeavor to secure larger liberties for the Catholic Church. He was also a "fighter" against the dogma of papal infallibility, but after its formal promulgation he laid down his arms and came to terms.

Kettenbach, Heinrich von. A German Franciscan friar, who denounced the corruption of the Church and praised Luther, Melanchthon, and Karlstadt. He may have perished in the Peasant Revolt, 1525.

Kettler, Gotthard (d. 1587). Last grand master of the German Order; favored Reformation; organized churches, schools, and benevolences; gave Livland to Sigismund of Poland with the understanding that it have the Augsburg Confession.

Key Pastors. See *Armed Services Commission.*

Key to Theosophy. See *Theosophy.*

Keyl, Ernst Gerhard Wilhelm. B. at Leipzig, 1804; studied at the university there; pastor at Niederfrohna in 1829; an adherent of Stephan; emigrated with the Saxons and was their first pastor at Frohna, Mo., 1839—47; pastor at Freistadt and Milwaukee, Wis., 1847 to 1850; Baltimore, Md., 1850—69; Willshire, Van Wert Co., Ohio, 1869—71; an indefatigable student of Luther; wrote: *Katechismusauslegung, Predigt-Entwuerfe ueber die Sonn- und Fest-tags-Evangelien.* D. Aug. 4, 1872.

J. F. Koestering, *Ernst Gerhard Wilhelm Keyl,* CPH, 1882.

Keyl, Stephanus. B. June 27, 1838, in Niederfrohna, Saxony, Germany; came to America with the Saxon Fathers; graduated from Concordia College, Fort Wayne, 1857; Concordia Seminary, St. Louis, 1860; pastor in Philadelphia, 1862—67; immigrant missionary of the Mo. Syn., and caretaker of the "Lutherisches Pilgerhaus"; d. Dec. 15, 1905.

P. Roesener, *Stephanus Keyl,* CPH, 1908; Theo. Keyl, "Life and Activities of Pastor Stephanus Keyl," *CHIQ,* XXII: 65—77.

Keys, Office of. 1. The Office of the Keys (Matt. 18:19; Rev. 1:18) is a peculiar, special, unique, spiritual power given by the Lord to the Christian Church to distribute the blessings of the Gospel.

2. This power is received, not from a human source, but from Jesus Christ (Rev. 1:18; Matt. 18:15 ff.; Luke 7:48; Matt. 28:18, 19) through the medium of the Word (Eph. 6:17; Matt. 10:19, 20; Acts 10:44). From this it follows that Christ is the supreme Lord and Master to the exclusion of all others (Matt. 23:8; Col. 2:8) and the Word the supreme source of power in the Church on earth (1 Tim. 6:3-5; 1 Cor. 2:4, 5; Acts 20:32). Hence the Church should not permit any human authority to dictate its doctrine or creeds, nor itself go beyond the Word (Gal. 1:8; 3:10; Col. 2:8).

3. The power of the keys is exclusively a spiritual power including the possession and practice of all spiritual rights, duties, and privileges necessary for the welfare of the Church on earth (2 Cor. 10:4; Eph. 6: 10-17; Matt. 20:25-27; John 18:36). It does not include physical force and power. The power of the keys includes the conveying of grace to mankind through preaching, administering Baptism and the Lord's Supper, and through mutual conversation and consolation. In particular, the Office of the Keys gives power to remit and retain sins, that is, not merely to announce and to declare to men the remission or retention of sins, but actually to give forgiveness to penitent sinners and to deny forgiveness to impenitent sinners (2 Cor. 2:10; John 20:23. This follows from objective justification: 2 Cor. 5:19; Rom. 4:25; 5:18).

4. When the Church exercises its power of absolution, it makes a special application of the Gospel of Christ to individuals or to groups of individuals. The whole Gospel of Christ is an absolution, the latter not existing outside of the Gospel. Absolution, then, is the special form of administering the Gospel in which a minister or other Chris-

tian forgives the sins of others. It is not a better or more powerful absolution, but a special application which gives a person reassurance, renewal and repetition of forgiveness (Luke 7:47, 48).

5. The power of the keys comes from God, who alone can forgive sins (Is. 43:25; Mark 2:7). The original possessor of the keys is Jesus Christ (Mark 2:10). Christ transmitted the power to Peter (Matt. 16:19), to all the Apostles (John 20:23; Matt. 18:18) and to every believer in Christ (1 Cor. 3:22; 1 Pet. 2:9; Rev. 1:6; John 7:38, 39). Thus the whole Church of believers has the power of the keys (Matt. 18:19; 1 Cor. 5:4, 5; 2 Cor. 2:6-10), naturally including Christian women (Gal. 3: 26-28; 1 Pet. 3:1-6; 1 Tim. 5:4, 5). Believers, in accordance with the Word of God, delegate and transfer the public exercise of this office to called servants of the Word.

6. When the called ministers, or believers, employ the binding key or the loosing key, their act is as valid and effective in the sight of God as though Christ Himself had performed it (John 20:23). The validity is not dependent upon the faith, repentance, worthiness, good works, satisfaction, and so forth, of the individual pronouncing absolution. While the unbelief of man does not annul the validity of the forgiveness (Rom. 3:3), such forgiveness is received through faith (Acts 10:43).

7. The possession of the power of the keys obligates Christians to proclaim the Word publicly (by establishing and maintaining churches, doing mission work, etc.) and privately (Matt. 28:18 ff.), to adhere to the purity of the Word (Judg. 2:10; 1 Tim. 6:20; John 8:31 ff.), to express faith (Rom. 10:9), to forgive sins (Matt. 18:21 f., 23-35; Eph. 4:32), to practice discipline (Matt. 18:17; 1 Cor. 5:2-5; 1 Tim. 1:20; Titus 3:10, 11), to judge doctrine (Matt. 7:15; 1 John 4:1; Acts 17:10, 11), to observe all the duties inherent in the Office of the Keys. C.f. CCS, "The Office of the Keys," *Abiding Word*, I, 342 ff.

8. Roman Catholic Interpretation. a. According to the Roman interpretation, the power of the keys refers to the supremacy of jurisdiction vested in the pope, who has supreme dominion over the Church and all of its members. This includes: unqualified executive power; universal legislative power; supreme judicial power; infal-

libility *; primacy.* The pope holds that this supremacy originally belonged to Peter (a view contradicted by Luke 22:24-26; Matt. 18:1-4; Acts 15:7-30; Gal. 2:7-11; 1 Pet. 5:1; 2 Pet. 1:19; Eph. 2:20 as well as passages cited above), whose successor he claims to be.

b. Absolution. 1. Absolution from sin. The Roman Church teaches that only a priest can absolve (*Cat. Romanus*, II, 5, 23). A distinction is made between the power to absolve, which is conferred on the priest by ordination, and jurisdiction, which authorizes the priest to exercise this absolving power toward certain persons, though not for all cases (see *Reserved Cases*). Jurisdiction is ordinarily conferred by the bishop, and absolution given to a person over whom the priest has no jurisdiction is invalid, except in danger of death any priest has jurisdiction. The necessity for jurisdiction follows from the teaching that the priest, in confession, acts as a judge of the self-accused criminal who comes to him. In this judicial capacity he acts also when, after hearing the case, he pronounces absolution on the penitent. The Roman Ritual prescribes the following form of absolution: "I absolve thee from thy sins in the name of the Father and of the Son and of the Holy Ghost." The precatory form of absolution, such as, "May Jesus Christ absolve thee," etc., which was used in the Church during the first thousand years after Christ, is no longer permitted. Absolution to be valid, must be uttered by the priest in the presence of the person absolved. It is to be noted that, according to Roman doctrine, absolution absolves only from eternal punishment. Even after absolution the penitent is supposed to remain subject to temporal punishments for his sins at the hands of God. To escape these punishments, he must do the works of satisfaction enjoined by the priest, earn indulgences, etc. 2. Absolution from church penalties (excommunication, suspension, interdict) may be given either in the confessional or, apart from the so-called Sacrament of Penance, by any cleric having jurisdiction. The person absolved need not be present, or contrite, or even living.

C. C. Stephan, "The Office of the Keys," *Abiding Word*, CPH, 1946 (I: 342 ff. Extensive bibliography); W. H. Bouman, "The Practical Application of Matt. 18:15-18," *CTM*, XVIII:178—204;

The Catholic Encyclopedia, Appleton, N. Y., 1907—22 (later vols. by Encyclopedia Press).

Keyser, Leander S. A leading theologian in the General Synod; b. March 13, 1856; educated at Indiana University and Wittenberg Seminary; pastor at La Grange, Ind., 1879; Elkhart, Ind., 1883; Springfield, Ohio, 1889; Atchison, Kans., 1897; Dover, Ohio, 1903; professor of systematic theology in Hamma Divinity School, Springfield, Ohio, from 1911. Keyser is the author of a number of books, among these: *A System of Natural Theism* (tinged with evolutionism); *A System of Christian Evidences; In the Redeemer's Footsteps; In the Apostles' Footsteps; Contending for the Faith; The Problem of Origins;* also wrote many books on birds. D. Oct. 18, 1937.

KFGQ—KFSG—KFTW. See *Radio Stations, Religious.*

Kidd, Benjamin (1858—1916). English socialist; held that progress both in the animal and human realms comes only at great sacrifice in kind; wrote *Social Evolution, Principles of Western Civilization.*

Kieckhefer, Carl (1814—1901). Milwaukee businessman, member of St. John's; active layman during formative period of Wisconsin Synod; member of first board of control of Northwestern College.

Kieffer, George Linn (1883—1937). Studied at Gettysburg College and Luth. Theol. Seminary, Union Theol. Sem. (New York), Columbia Univ.; held several honorary doctorates; pastor at Rosedale, N. Y.; statistician and reference librarian of National Lutheran Council, 1919—37; associate editor *Lutheran Year Book* and *Lutheran World Almanac.*

Kierkegaard, Soeren Aaby. B. 1813 at Copenhagen; d. there 1855; Danish religious philosopher and author; inherited deep-seated melancholy from his father; a broken engagement left its marks on his writing; sought to adhere to the Lutheran Confessions; although he had studied theology, he never took office; attacked the Established Church, both clergy and lay members, for their worldliness; held that a Christian is an isolated individual, alone with God, and in contact with the world only through suffering; made important contributions to Christian psychology through his self-analyses. Though scarcely known beyond Denmark in his day, his works have since been widely studied and have influenced Karl Barth. See *Existentialism.*

The Augsburg Publishing House, Princeton University Press, and Oxford University Press have published English translations of Kierkegaard's works. Walter Lowrie, *A Short Life of Kierkegaard,* Princeton University Press, 1942; D. F. Swenson, *Something about Kierkegaard,* Augsburg Publishing House, 1941; J. T. Mueller, "Soeren Aaby Kierkegaard," *CTM,* XVI: 801—23.

Kiesling, Johann Tobias (1743 to 1824), a pious merchant in Nuremberg who supported many worthy projects in inner missions.

Kildahl, John Nathan (1857—1920). Graduate of Luther College and Luther Seminary; pastor; president of Red Wing Seminary, later of St. Olaf College; professor at United Norwegian Church Seminary and at Luther Theological Seminary; secretary and vice-president of the United Norwegian Church; vice-president of the Norwegian Lutheran Church; wrote a number of doctrinal monographs.

Kilian. See *Germany,* 1; *Celtic Church,* 9.

Kilian, Johann. B. of Wendish parents in Dahlen, Saxony, March 22, 1811; ed. at Bautzen, Leipzig, and Mission Institute at Basel; pastor in Kotitz, Saxony, 1837—48; translated Luther's Large Catechism into Wendish and also the Augsburg Confession; came to Texas with the Wendish Lutherans and served there as pastor 1854—84, the first colony being at Serbin; joined Missouri Synod in 1855. D. 1884.

Kilwardby, Robert (d. 1279). English Dominican; archbishop of Canterbury; took judicial records of Canterbury to Rome (not recovered); studied Aristotle and wrote commentaries on him; criticized doctrines of Aquinas; wrote *On the Origin and Divisions of Philosophy.*

Kimchi, David (ca. 1160—1235). Noted Jewish philologist and exegete; b. at Narbonne; wrote Hebrew grammar and lexicon, which were authorities for centuries; also Old Testament commentaries, some of which contained polemics against Christianity.

Kinderfrage. See *Christian Teaching, J.*

Kindergarten. See *Parish Education, B 5.*

Kindness. Kindness is a social virtue, manifesting love. Christians are to show kindness toward all men (Gal. 6:10; Eph. 4:32; 1 Cor. 13:4; 1 John 3:18; Prov. 19:22; 31:26; Luke 6:30, 34, 35; Col. 3:12, 14; 1 Pet. 3:8; 2 Pet. 1:7). Kindness means showing favors, benefits, compassion (Gen. 21:23; 2 Sam. 10:2; Job 6:14; Gal. 5:22. Examples: Ex. 2:6-10; Josh. 2:6-16; Ruth 1; 2; 2 Sam. 9:1-13; Job 29:11-16; Luke 7:2-5; 10:33-35; Acts 2:44-47; 9:36; 10:2-4; Rom. 15:26; 2 Cor. 1:1-5; 2 Tim. 1:16-18). See *Concordia Pulpit,* 1936, Vol. VII, p. 212; Kretzmann, *Pop. Com.,* O. T., I:447—50; II:242, 260. See also *Love, Lovingkindness.*

King, Christ as. In the hope of Israel in the Old Testament there lay the promise of a king (Ps. 110:1, 2; 2 Sam. 7:11-13; Pss. 8; 89; Dan. 7:13 f.). Christ was King even during the state of His humiliation, as is shown by His miracles and various Bible passages (Matt. 8:27; 11:27; John 5:17; 12:15). The powers of government which Jesus exercised in a hidden way during the State of Humiliation, He used fully and continually during the period between the Resurrection and Ascension (Matt. 28:18). The particular revelation of the divine powers became manifest with His ascension and His sitting down at the right hand of God.

The Scriptural teaching that Christ rules the world and His Church has given rise to the old distinctions of the Kingdom of Power, the Kingdom of Grace, and the Kingdom of Glory. These distinctions do not imply that Christ's kingdom is divided, but simply recognize a Scriptural fact that Christ rules the world in the interest of His Church. The Kingdom of Power is the term applied to Christ's rule of the entire world (Matt. 28:18, 19). The distinction between the Kingdom of Power and the Kingdom of Grace is simply that the adherents of the latter are "in the world but not of the world" (John 17:11, 15). Christ rules the world by exerting His power in the social structure; He rules the Church through the means of grace.* Christians participate in the affairs of the state (1 Tim. 2:1, 2) but require nothing of the state which demands the operation of the Holy Spirit (John

18:36. See *Kingdom of God; Church and State*). The Kingdom of Glory refers to Christ's rule in the world to come (1 John 3:1, 2) although the Kingdoms of Grace and Glory are a unit. C. f. OCH, *Abiding Word,* CPH, 1947 (II:140—44).

King, Henry Churchill (1858—1934). Professor and president of Oberlin; philosopher and writer on Christian personality.

King James Version. See *Bible Versions,* L 10.

Kingdom of God. The term was prominent in the proclamation of John the Baptist and of Jesus and the Apostles. It evidently is synonymous with the expression "kingdom of heaven." While formerly it was taken for granted that "kingdom of God" was simply another term for the Christian Church, scholars nowadays are quite unanimous in the view that kingdom here means dominion or rule, and that only in a derived way, by means of a figure of speech, does it in a number of passages designate the people who are the subjects in God's kingdom. When John preached that the kingdom of God had come near, he announced that God was now through the work of the Messiah laying the foundation for His gracious rule in human hearts. This rule presupposes that the forgiveness of sins has been procured for everybody and that people accept this forgiveness in true faith. Wherever there is such acceptance, God has entered the heart and governs the thoughts and the actions of man. The people who heard the message of John and of Christ were informed that God was preparing to do something special, that the fullness of the time had come, and that the plan of God for the salvation of the human race was now to be carried out. The term did not point to the establishment of an external kingdom like that of David or Solomon or the Roman Empire, but to something spiritual, the gentle rule of God through the Holy Spirit in the hearts of men. Passages which make it particularly evident that the rule of God is meant are, f. i., Matt. 12:28; Luke 11:20; Luke 9:27; Mark 4:11. Passages in which the kingdom, that is, the sum total of the subjects, is designated by the term, are, f. i., Matt. 13:41; 16:19; John 3:5. The kingdom is at times spoken of as a future blessing to which God's children look forward with longing anticipation. Cf. Matt. 7:21;

8:11. But it is likewise pictured as a present reality, f. i., Luke 16:16; 17:20. The rule of God here spoken of is mediated through the means of grace, the Word and the Sacraments, Mark 1:15; John 3:5. To be under the sway of this gracious rule of God must be our heart's desire. Cf. Matt. 13:4-46. WA

T. Zahn, *Grundriss der Neutestamentlichen Theologie*, p. 14 f.; commentaries on the passages cited.

Kingo, Thomas Hansen (1634 to 1703). Danish hymnist of Scotch descent; pastor in Slangerup; bishop of Fyen. His *Aandelige Sjunge Chor* was completed in 1681 and his *Den forordnede Kirkepsalmebog* in 1699. His choral tunes are often evolved from contemporary secular music. Among his hymns: "Like the Golden Sun Ascending," "The Sun Arises Now," "Over Kedron Jesus Treadeth." Called the "poet of Eastertide."

King's Book. See *Anglican Confessions*, 2.

King's Confession. See *Presbyterian Confessions*, 1.

King's Daughters. Founded Jan. 13, 1886, by Mrs. Margaret Bottome. Interdenominational in character. This society is found in North and South America; in Great Britain, Germany, France, and other countries of Europe; in China, Japan, India, Australia, etc. It seeks to influence "first the heart, next the home, then the church, and after that the great outside." The *Silver Cross* is the official weekly organ.

Kings, Divine Right of. The theory that a king holds his office by divine appointment and therefore is not responsible to his subjects. It was emphasized by the Stuarts in England during the 17th century.

Kingsley, Charles (1819—75). Anglican; b. in Devonshire; rector; professor of modern history at Cambridge; canon of Westminster; d. at Eversley. Versatile writer: sermons, novels, controversy with Newman, works on social questions, the novel *Hypatia*, etc.

Kinner, Samuel (1603—68). Studied at Breslau; later court physician at Brieg, in service of Duke of Liegnitz-Brieg; wrote fine Communion hymn "Herr Jesu Christ, du hast bereit't."

Kirchenbund. See *Australia, Lutheranism in*, B 1.

Kirchenordnungen. See *Church Orders*.

Kirchner, Timothy. B. 1533; deposed from his parish at Herbsleben in 1561, for opposing Strigel's false doctrine; professor at the new University of Helmstedt in 1576; assisted at the final revision of the Formula of Concord; was deposed in 1579 for criticizing his prince for consecrating his son as bishop of Halberstadt according to a Romanizing ritual; worked on the Apology of the Formula of Concord at Erfurt; professor at Heidelberg, deposed in 1583; d. in 1587 as superintendent at Weimar.

Kirk of Scotland. See *Presbyterian Bodies*, 1.

Kirkelig Sammler. See *Danish Lutherans in America*, 3.

Kirn, Otto (1857—1911). Professor at Basel and Leipzig. See *Atonement, Theories of*.

Kiss of Peace. An expression (or its equivalent) which occurs five times in the NT (Rom. 16:16; 1 Cor. 16:20; 2 Cor. 13:12; 1 Thess. 5:26; 1 Pet. 5:14). The kiss of peace soon found its way into the liturgy and was observed in connection with the Lord's Supper. The practice extended into the Middle Ages. Later kissing the altar, the hand, the vestment of the clergy, was substituted. Undoubtedly related is the kiss bestowed upon neophytes, the penitent, candidates for ordination, etc.

Kittel, Johann Christian (1732 to 1809). J. S. Bach's last pupil; organist in Langensalza, later in Erfurt, but with starvation salary; published *Neues Choralbuch* for Schleswig-Holstein and some chorals.

Kittel, Rudolf. B. 1853; from 1898 professor of Old Testament exegesis at Leipzig; modern theologian; critic; wrote extensively on Old Testament subjects, especially on the History of Israel; editor of an excellent edition of the Hebrew text. D. 1929.

Kitto, John (1804—54). Writer on Biblical subjects; b. at Plymouth; deaf at thirteen; trained as printer at missionary college, Islington (London); Malta 1827; traveled 1829—33; d. at Cannstatt, Wuerttemberg; *Pictorial Bible*, etc.

Kiwanis Club International. An organization somewhat similar to the Rotarians, organized in 1915 in Detroit, for the purpose of making practical application of the Golden Rule to modern life, especially to the conduct of business. Each local branch is limited to two men from each line of business.

Klein, Bernard (1793—1832). German composer of oratorios, motets, and other sacred music. He was musical director of the Cologne Cathedral and, later, teacher at the Royal Institute at Berlin, also director of music and teacher of singing at the University of Berlin. He wrote the oratorios *Job, Jephtha,* and *David.*

Klein, Henry Adam. B. Feb. 17, 1869, at Spring, Tex.; graduated Concordia Seminary, St. Louis, 1892; pastor at Chattanooga, Tenn., 1892—1902; missionary in Brazil, 1902—07; pastor at Wittenberg, Mo., 1907—10; St. Joseph, Mo., 1910—15; Collinsville, Ill., 1915 to 1922, also Vice-President of Southern Illinois District of Missouri Synod; president of Concordia Seminary, Springfield, 1922—35, when he died as the result of an accident, Dec. 21, 1935.

Kleine Gemeinde. See *Mennonite Bodies,* 3.

Kleutgen, Joseph (1811—83). Jesuit, rector of the Gregorian University. He reintroduced scholastic philosophy in the discussions of his times and thus influenced the rise of neo-scholasticism.

Kliefoth, Theodor F. D. (1810—95). Influential Lutheran theologian; 1840 pastor at Ludwigslust; 1844 superintendent at Schwerin; 1866 president of the superior ecclesiastical court. Kliefoth exerted a far-reaching beneficial influence in the Lutheran Church of Mecklenburg-Schwerin and beyond; wrote especially on church polity and liturgics, also exegetical works.

Klingmann, Stephan (1833—91). Educated at Basel; one of the organizers of the Michigan Synod; pastor at Adrian, Monroe, Scio; president of Michigan Synod, 1867—81, then vice-president; leader in synod at all times; standing delegate to General Council until his constantly unheeded protests led to separation.

Klopstock, Friedrich Gottlieb (1724 to 1803). One of the great German poets of the 18th century; author of the *Messiah,* in which, in an age of Rationalism and infidelity, he gives expression to his faith in Christ.

Klotsche, Ernest Heinrich (1875 to 1937). Studied at Mission College in Leipzig, Germany, Univ. of Nebr.

(Ph. D., 1918), Chicago Univ., Midland College, Atchison, Kans. (D. D., 1919); missionary to British India, then held pastorates in South Dakota and Nebraska; taught at Martin Luther Seminary (Lincoln, Nebr.) and Midland College; prof. of practical theology at Chicago Luth. Seminary (1930); author of *History of Doctrine; Christian Symbolics.*

Kluge, Joseph. Printer in Wittenberg at time of Luther; printed first Lutheran *Choralbuch, Geistliche Lieder zu Wittenberg,* 1543, containing practically all of Luther's hymns.

Knak, Gustav (1806—78). B. in Berlin, Germany; d. at Duennow, near Stolpmuende, Germany; successor to Gossner as pastor of the "Bohemian" Lutheran Church, Berlin; a warm friend of missions; author of "Lasst mich gehn," which became a favorite song all over the world.

Knapp, Albert (1798—1864). Educated at Maulbronn and Tuebingen; held a number of charges as clergyman, for almost thirty years at Stuttgart, where he was *Stadtpfarrer* at St. Leonhard's; as poet he was distinguished both by unusual talent and by striking originality; his spiritual lyrics have the cast of spiritual folk songs rather than hymns; wrote: "Eines wuensch' ich mir vor allem andern," "Wenn ich in stiller Fruehe," and others.

Knapp, Johann Georg (1705—71). B. at Oehringen. Professor at Halle, Pietist; after 1769 in charge of Francke's institutions there.

Knights of Columbus. A Roman Catholic fraternal order founded at New Haven, Conn., in 1882. The order was originally an insurance organization devoted to education, charities, and other benevolent purposes. Later membership was given to non-insurance members. In recent years the Knights of Columbus have taken an active part in Roman Catholic publicity efforts.

Knights Templars. See *Military Religious Orders.*

Knipperdolling, Bernhard (d. 1536). See *Mennonite Bodies.*

Knipstro, Johann Karl (1497—1556). Opposed Tetzel at Frankfurt 1518; preached Luther's doctrine and fled to Stettin; preacher in Stralsund; superintendent of Wolgast; professor at Greifswald; opposed the Interim and Osiander's false doctrine.

Knoepken, Andreas (ca. 1490 to 1539). Gained the city of Riga for the Reformation (1522) after a disputation with the Romanists in which he successfully defended 15 theses; in 1524 he published a commentary on Romans with an introduction by Bugenhagen; collaborated in the preparation of an Agenda based on Luther's *Formula missae;* wrote hymns (usually Low German) based on the Psalms.

Knoke, Karl (1841—1920). German Lutheran theologian and pedagog; president of normal school in Wunstorf; professor of theology in Goettingen 1885; wrote: *Outline of Practical Theology; Outline of Pedagogy and Its History; Luther's Small Catechism According to the Oldest Editions in High and Low German and in Latin.*

Knoll, Christoph (1563—1650). Studied at Frankfurt; assistant at Sprottau; then diaconus and finally archidiaconus; later pastor at Wittgendorf, where he died; wrote: "Herzlich tut mich verlangen."

Knoll, Michael Christian. Ordained by Lutheran pastors in London (1732); served Trinity Church, New York (1732 to 1750); it was a disturbed period in the history of the church, and Knoll resigned the year a division occurred in the church.

Knorr, Christian. Baron von Rosenroth (1636—89). Studied at Leipzig and Wittenberg; Orientalist; prime minister of Palsgrave Christian August of Sulzbach; wrote: "Morgenglanz der Ewigkeit."

Knowledge. 1. *Divine.* God is a God of knowledge (1 Sam. 2:3). His is an ever-present knowledge, one that directly knows things that exist and come to pass; not progressive knowledge, but ever total, perfect, and complete. As God had no beginning, His knowledge had no beginning; it was in this respect before time and created things and all temporal events (Eph. 1:4; Ps. 90:2). This foreknowledge includes a knowledge of the acts of men, both good and evil. But knowing all things as they are, God knows the acts of men as the acts of rational and responsible beings, who have a will of their own and act according to the counsels of their hearts.

2. *Human.* Man's knowledge is limited so that he does not understand the mysteries of life (Eccl. 11:5) and nature (Job 38 ff.). The brevity of his life further limits his knowledge (Job 8:9); Eccl. 9:12). As a result of the Fall, man's spiritual understanding is darkened so that he does not know the way of God (Eph. 4:18; Jer. 5:4; Is. 59:8; Jer. 8:7; 2 Pet. 3:5). Ignorance of God led to a self-centered way of salvation (Rom. 10:3; Eph. 4:18. Compare the *Eros* religion in Nygren, *Agape and Eros,* I:118—82), willful ignorance, and a reprobate mind (Rom. 1:28; 10:3; 2 Pet. 3:5; Matt. 13:15; Zech. 7:11) and sin (Rom. 1:28 ff.; John 15:21; 16:3). So great is the spiritual ignorance of men that they failed to recognize Jesus as God (John 14:9; 8:19; 1:5 ff.). Conversion is often called "enlightenment" in view of its effect on knowledge (for the change to true spiritual knowledge see *Conversion).* Man's ignorance has been divided into three types: a) *invincible ignorance,* in which the will has no part; b) *willful and obstinate ignorance;* c) a kind of *voluntary ignorance* which is neither altogether willful nor invincible.

Knowledge, Innate. See *Natural Law, 2.*

Knox, John (1505 or 1513—72). Founder of the Presbyterian Church in Scotland; b. at Giffordgate (?); attended university; priest ca. 1540; tutored; accompanied Wishart, a Scottish Evangelical clergyman on preaching tour; accepted call from Protestant congregation of St. Andrew's, 1546; upon the capitulation of St. Andrew's Castle to the French became a galley slave for nineteen months; acted as chaplain to Edward VI and had some influence on the English Reformation; served a refugee English congregation at Geneva for nearly three years and associated with Calvin; issued his famous *Blast Against the Monstrous Regiment of Women* and an elaborate treatise on predestination; returned to Scotland in 1559. Through his influence the free Parliament of 1560 adopted the *Confession of Faith* (compiled by Knox and his fellow preachers) and the *First Book of Discipline* and established the Reformed Kirk. In the struggle between Mary, Queen of Scots, and her Protestant subjects, Knox had frequent dramatic encounters with her. Exposed to many dangers, sometimes driven into privacy, again stepping forward and assailing wickedness, he attended to his duties as minister of the great parish church of Edinburgh and at the same time ordered the affairs of the national Church. In all his reformatory efforts politics and religion were closely intertwined. D. at Edinburgh. Chief work: *History of the Reformation in Scotland.*

Thos. McErie, *Life of John Knox,* Edinburgh, 1812; Wm. Taylor, *John Knox, A Biography,* New York, 1885; P. H. Brown, *John Knox, A Biography,* London, 1895.

Knubel, F. H. First president of the United Lutheran Church in America, 1918—44; b. May 22, 1870, in New York City; educated at Gettysburg and Leipzig; pastor in New York, 1896—1918; chairman of the National Lutheran Commission for Soldiers' and Sailors' Welfare during World War I, 1917—18; d. Oct. 16, 1945.

Knudsen, Hans (1813—86). B. in Copenhagen; sent as missionary to Tranquebar in 1838, where he did excellent work; returned to Europe in 1843; pastor there of two congregations and then of the Deaconesses' Home at Copenhagen; resigned this position in 1872 and founded the "Society for the Care and Education of Crippled Children," in which work he was a pioneer.

Koch, Eduard Emil (1809—71). Studied at Tuebingen; pastor in various cities, longest in Heilbronn; prominent in the field of hymnology, especially through his *Geschichte des Kirchenlieds und Kirchengesangs der christlichen, insbesondere der deutschen evangelischen Kirche.*

Kocherthal, Josua. "Der Hoch-Teutschen in Nord-America ihr Josua"; had been pastor in Eschelbroen, Bavaria, where he and his flock suffered much from the ravages of war. In 1704 he visited England with a view to finding a refuge for his people in America. With 53 souls he came to New York, Jan. 1, 1709, and settled them on land granted by Queen Anne in Newburg on the Hudson. Leaving his congregation in Falckner's care, he brought over several thousand immigrants more in June, 1710. These also made their home on the Hudson (East and West Camp). Kocherthal continued to minister to these Lutherans until his death, June 24, 1719. His remains are buried beneath his epitaph in the church at West Camp.

Kock, Peter (d. 1749). Swedish layman in Philadelphia; translated Luther's Catechism into English; his efforts in behalf of union between German and Swedish churches influenced

the organization of the Pennsylvania Ministerium.

Kodesh Church of Immanuel (colored). See *Holiness Bodies.*

Kodranson, Thorwalds. See *Iceland.*

Koegel, Rudolph (1829—96). Court preacher of William I; outstanding pulpit orator of Germany; many of his sermons printed.

Koehler, August (1835—97). In 1868 professor at Erlangen as successor of Delitzsch; his chief work: *Lehrbuch der biblischen Geschichte Alten Testaments;* his doctrine of inspiration not that of the Lutheran Church.

Koehler, Edward William August. B. Oct. 31, 1875, Wolfenbuettel, Braunschweig, Germany; ed. Concordia Coll., Ft. Wayne, Ind.; Concordia Seminary, St. Louis, grad. 1899; pastor: Billings, Mo., 1899—1902; Knoxville, Tenn., 1903 to 1909; prof., Mosheim Coll., Mosheim, Tenn., 1902—03; Concordia Teachers Coll., Addison and River Forest, Ill., 1909—51. Wrote: *The Annotated Catechism, A Christian Pedagogy, Summary of Christian Doctrine, Conscience,* and monographs. D. D. Concordia Sem., St. Louis, 1941. D. May 12, 1951.

Koehler, John Philip. B. 1859; grad. at Northwestern College, Watertown, Wis., and Concordia Sem., St. Louis; pastor at Two Rivers, Wis., 1882—88; inspector and prof. of Northwestern College, 1888—1900; prof. of N. T. exegesis, hermeneutics, liturgics, and music at Wauwatosa Seminary, 1900; pres., 1920 to his retirement (1930). His scholarship was a comprehensive and comprehending survey of life, thought, and emotion. Pre-eminently, however, he was a historian, who read the record of the Gospel in history in its widest sense, including the wide field of art, on which his views are illuminating. He stated his aim of teaching in these words: "The Gospel of Christ, the Savior of sinners, is that truth, that one truth, on which rests all true understanding in heaven and on earth." Author of *Paul to the Galatians,* 1910; *Church History,* 1917; *History of Joint Synod of Wisconsin,* 1925. D. Sept. 30, 1951.

Koehler, Philip (1828—96). Father of John Philip; ed. at Barmen; pastor in Wisconsin from 1855 on; leader in cause of sound Lutheranism; refused to sign petition for collection in *Landeskirche;* charter member of Northwestern board.

Koenig, Friedrich Eduard (1846 to 1936). *Privatdozent* and associate prof. of Old Testament exegesis at Leipzig; prof. at Rostock (same subject); later at Bonn; one of the leaders of conservative theology in opposition to extremes in higher criticism; wrote: *Historisch-kritisches Lehrgebaeude der hebraeischen Sprache, Hebraeisches und aramaeisches Woerterbuch*, and a number of exegetical and critical works.

Koenig, G. F. J. B. Sept. 23, 1825, at Haynholtz, Hanover; studied theology in Goettingen; sent to America by the "Stader Missionsverein" 1851; pastor in Cincinnati, Ohio, 1872; pastor of Trinity, New York; Visitor; member of Immigrant Mission and Jewish Mission boards and of Electoral College of Missouri Synod; d. Nov. 17, 1891.

Koenig, J. F. (1619—64). Prof. at Greifswald and Rostock; wrote *Theologia Positiva Acroamatica,* which formed the basis of most of the dogmatic lectures of the 17th century, especially of Quenstedt's *Theologia Didactico-Polemica.*

Koephl, Wolfgang. Printer in Strassburg at the time of the Reformation, also composer of several tunes now in use; published *Psalmen und geistliche Lieder,* 1537, *Ein neu auserlesen Gesangbuechlein,* 1545, and others.

Koerner, Christoph (1518—94). Prof. of theology at Frankfurt a. O.; worked on the Formula of Concord at Torgau in 1576 and at Bergen in 1577; "the Eye of the University"; wrote commentaries on the Psalms, Romans, Galatians, and on all the orations of Cicero; judged Major and Strigel mildly.

Koester, Henry Bernhard (1664 to 1749). German mystic; came to America (1695); founded Christ Church in Philadelphia; voluminous writer on mystical themes.

Koestering, J. F. B. Feb. 20, 1830, at Dahlinghausen, Hanover; graduate of Concordia Seminary, Ft. Wayne, 1853; pastor in Allen Co., Ind., Frankenthal, Iowa, Arcadia, Ind., Altenburg, Mo., St. Paul's in St. Louis; d. Jan. 1, 1908; wrote *Die Auswanderung der saechsischen Lutheraner.*

Koestlin, Heinrich Adolf (1846 to 1907). After completing his theological studies at Tuebingen, Koestlin held pastorates at Friedrichshafen, Stuttgart, Darmstadt, and a professorship at Friedberg. A penchant for conducting led the young theologian to organize the Wuerttemberg Evangelical *Kirchengesangverein* and to conduct its festivals. His *Die Geschichte der Musik im Umriss* and *Die Tonkunst* are rarely consulted today, largely because they are products of the Romantic Movement of the 19th century.

Koestlin, Julius (1826—1902). Ev. theologian; prof. at Goettingen, Breslau, and Halle; introduced features of Presbyterianism in German church government; he influenced especially the historical study of the Reformation and took an active part in the publication of the Weimar Edition of Luther's works. Wrote among others: *The Life of Luther; The Theology of Luther.*

Koethe, Friedrich (1781—1850). Prof. at Jena; superintendent at Allstaedt; early opponent of rationalism; published Lutheran Symbolical Books, Melanchthon's works.

Kohlbruegge, Hermann Friedrich (1803—75). Lutheran who later joined Reformed Church; pastor in Elberfeld (1848—75); published sermons, meditations on Matthew; defender of Calvinism.

Kohler, John (1820—98). Ed. at Pennsylvania College and Gettysburg; pastor at Williamsport, Pa. (1844), New Holland (1850), Trappe (1864), Stroudsburg (1873), Leacock (1884—93); principal at Muhlenberg College (1882 to 1884). Influential member of Pennsylvania Ministerium, holding various offices. Member of Church Book Committee of General Council. Advocated episcopal system.

Kohlhoff, John B. (1711—90). B. in Germany; served as missionary among the Tamils in India for 53 years.

Kohn, William C. B. June 2, 1865, at Chicago, Ill., graduated at St. Louis 1887; pastor at Chicago, Ill.: St. James', 1887—89; St. Andrew's, 1889—1912; chairman of Mission Board of Illinois District 1906—09; chairman of Church Extension Board of Northern Illinois District 1906—09; President of Northern Illinois District 1909—13; President of Concordia Teachers College, 1913 to 1939, resigned, but continued to teach; editor of *Lutheran School Journal* 1913; pres. of Army and Navy Board 1917—19; D. D. (St. Louis) 1929; d. March 13, 1943.

Kojiki. Oldest Japanese collection of source material on Shinto.

Kolde, Theodor Hermann Friedrich (1850—1913). From 1881 on prof. of church history at Erlangen; one of the most noted historians of the Reformation period and defender of Luther against Catholic attacks.

Kollar, Jan. See *Slovakia, Lutheran Theology in,* 2.

Kols. A collective name for aboriginal tribes in mountainous Chota Nagpur, Bengal, India. The language is a dialect of the Gond. Missions were begun by the Gossner Mission Society in 1845. In 1858 the Church Missionary Society granted £1,000 to this mission. In 1868 the Society for the Propagation of the Gospel entered the field. In 1891 the Dublin University Mission was established. The Roman Catholic Church came in 1880. Since the First World War the Gossner missions became autonomous.

Konfessionskunde. See *Symbolics.*

Koopmann, Wilhelm Heinrich (1814 to 1871). Opponent of rationalism and defender of confessionalism; studied under Klaus Harms; pastor at Heide, Lauenburg, Ottensen; general supt. at Altona; sermons published.

Koran. Arabic for "reading." The sacred book of Mohammedanism,* the source of Mohammedan doctrine and law. Its language is Arabic. The contents claim to be the "revelations" of Mohammed and consist largely of regulations, laws, promises to the faithful, warnings to the unbelieving, remonstrances, and legends. The text was collected after Mohammed's death by Abu Bekr and Omar from oral sources and from jottings, and ultimately edited by Caliph Othman (644—56). There are 114 *suras* (chapters), the first being the so-called *fatiha* (opening, *sc.,* the book), a short prayer in praise of God. The remaining *suras* are arranged on the basis of their length, the longest appearing at the beginning of the book. The Koran lays claim to divine origin, and tradition relates that its text from eternity has been extant in the seventh heaven and was revealed piecemeal to Mohammed by the angel Gabriel. The book contains, besides Mohammed's own material, old heathen Arabic tribal traditions and legends as well as Jewish and Christian elements, the latter often very much distorted.

Korea. 1. 1910—45 a part of Japan, under the name of Chosen. Area: 85,206 sq. mi.; population: 24,326,327. The country is mountainous, but has some broad, fertile plains. Keijo, or Seoul, is the capital. Since early times two languages have been in use; the spoken Korean vernacular, which belongs to the Mongol-Tatar family, and the written (ideographic) language of China. The early religion was animistic, with ancestor and nature worship. Buddhism entered from China, developing a strong hierarchy. Confucianism also has a large following. — Missions were begun by the Roman Catholic Church in the 18th century, which resulted in violent persecutions. However, the Roman Catholic Church now has obtained a firm footing. Protestant missions were attempted by Guetzlaff in 1832. The London Missionary Society sent Mr. Thomas in 1866, but he died before he was able to begin work. The United Free Church of Scotland made an attempt through J. Ross, who was missionary at Mukden. The New Testament was translated by him into Korean and spread in Korea clandestinely.

2. Korea was opened to foreigners by the United States in 1882, and foreign missionary societies immediately grasped the opportunity. In rapid succession the American Presbyterian and the Methodist Episcopal Missions in 1884 entered there. Dr. H. U. Allen of the Presbyterian Church in the U. S. A. was given charge of a hospital, where he did such successful work in allaying the suspicion and opposition of the Koreans that evangelistic work could be introduced already in 1885. The work increased so rapidly that strong self-supporting churches could be organized from Kang-Kei to Fusan. More than 50,000 converts have already been baptized by this mission. A theological school has been established at Pyengyang. The American Methodist Episcopal Mission has had such success that it was able to organize more than 115 churches in the Seoul and Chemalpo districts. Medical missions of the Presbyterians, Anglicans, and Methodists have done much to prepare the way for evangelistic work. Severance Hospital in Seoul, which is connected with the Presbyterian and the Society for the Propagation of the Gospel missions, has a flourishing medical training school, the students of which must be Christians. Missions are now being conducted by fifteen societies.

Statistics: 219,745 communicants, estimated on the basis of latest statistics available in 1952.

The Nevius method of doing mission work was developed and put into very successful practice in Korea. See *Nevius Method.*

Koren, Ulrik Vilhelm. B. in Norway Dec. 22, 1826; graduate of Kristiania University 1852; emigrated 1853; pastor at Washington Prairie, Iowa, 1853 to 1910; the first Norwegian pastor to settle west of the Mississippi; procured campus for Luther College, Decorah; taught there 1874—75; held many offices in the Norwegian Synod; secretary, Iowa District president, vice-president, president; author of poems, articles, and books; during the predestination controversy the chief champion of the true Lutheran doctrine of conversion and election; 1903 created D. D. by Concordia Seminary, St. Louis; d. Dec. 19, 1910.

Koreshanity. See *Communistic Societies,* 5.

Kottwitz, Baron Ernst v. Pietist; founder of an institution to provide work for the poor; rich philanthropist; the "patriarch" in Tholuck's *Die wahre Weihe des Zweiflers.*

KPOF. See *Radio Stations, Religious.*

KPPC. See *Radio Stations, Religious.*

Krafft, Johann (Crato von Crafftheim, 1519—85). German physician and defender of Protestantism. B. and d. at Breslau. Entered the university at Wittenberg, 1534, and spent six years as friend of Luther and Melanchthon, during which time he wrote down the table talks later published by Aurifaber. Physician in Breslau, 1550, and after 1560 to Emperors Ferdinand I, Maximilian II, and Rudolph II. He kept the Jesuits from embittering Maximilian to the point of actively joining the enemies of Protestantism. Favoring Melanchthonianism, he opposed Flacius and stricter Lutheranism.

Kraft, Adam (ca. 1450—1507). Rose from the position of stone mason to that of sculptor; simple, but effective work; noted for his Seven Stations on the way to the Cemetery of St. John in Nuernberg.

Kraft, Johann Christian (1784 to 1845). German Reformed; b. at Duisburg; tutor at Frankfurt; pastor at Weeze; professor at Erlangen 1818 (d. there); exercised vivifying influence on Bavarian Protestant Church.

Krakewitz, Berthold (1582—1642). Ed. at Wittenberg; superintendent and prof. at Greifswald; responsible for inclusion of the Formula of Concord among Confessions of Pomerania.

Krapf, Ludwig (1810—81). Studied in Tuebingen; made several attempts to Christianize Abyssinia; then settled on Mombasa and labored among the Suahelis and the Wanika tribe; explored large sections of East Africa; revised the Amharic Bible.

Krausert, Michael. See *Amana Society.*

Krauss, Elmer Frederick. B. Sept. 7, 1862, near East Greenville, Pa.; studied at Muhlenberg College (M. A., 1887; D. D., 1903); pastor in Pennsylvania, 1887—92; at Minneapolis, Minn., 1893 to 1894; at Leechburg, Pa., 1894—1900; prof. at Chicago Luth. Seminary, 1900; pres., 1915—20; dean extramural dept., 1921; author of *Galatians.* D. May 23, 1946.

Krauss, Eugen Adolf Wilhelm. B. June 4, 1851, at Noerdlingen, Bavaria; graduate of the Augsburg *Gymnasium;* studied theology at Erlangen and Leipzig 1869—73. A student of the Missourian writings, he severed, for confessional reasons, his connection with the State Church before he graduated; was received into the Missouri Synod and accepted a call to Cedarburg, Wis., 1874. In 1875 he returned to Germany to serve a congregation at Sperlingshof, Baden, which had withdrawn from the State Church. He proved himself a fearless and able champion of sound Lutheranism. In 1880 he was elected director of the Teachers' Seminary at Addison, Ill.; he was successful in impressing upon his students the great importance of the Lutheran day school and in deepening their love for it. In 1905 he was called to teach church history and propaedeutics at Concordia Seminary, St. Louis. "He possessed a commanding knowledge of the literature of the Lutheran Church and its opponents in the age of the Reformation and the centuries that followed, down to our times, and was not only an instructive, but also an entertaining speaker on any subject he chose to discuss." His articles in *Schulblatt, Lutheraner,* and *Lehre und Wehre,* his doctrinal essays in the Synodical Reports and his *Lebensbilder aus der Geschichte der christlichen Kirche* reveal his stupendous learning and are highly edifying to the lover of Lutheranism. Northwestern College, Watertown, Wis., conferred the title of Doctor of Theology on him. He died Oct. 9, 1924.

E. Krauss, *Meine Schuljahre*, CPH, 1920.

Kraussold, Lorenz. B. 1803; at the time of his death pastor and *Konsistorialrat* at Bayreuth; besides work in catechetics prominent in liturgics; published: *Zur Altarliturgie; Theorie des Kirchenliedes; Altaragende*, etc.

Krauth, Charles Philip. B. New Goshenhoppen, Pa., May 7, 1797. First studied medicine under Dr. Selden of Norfolk, Va., then, under influence of Rev. David F. Schaeffer at Frederick, Md., decided to study for the ministry. Studied theology under Schaeffer; assisted Rev. A. Reck at Winchester, Va.; licensed to preach by Pennsylvania Ministerium in 1819; pastor at Martinsburg and Shepherdstown, Va. Helped organize Synod of Maryland and Virginia 1820; ordained by it 1821; treas. and pres. of that synod; pastor of St. Matthew's, Philadelphia, 1827. Helped lay plans for Gettysburg Seminary; first sec'y of Seminary's Bd. of Directors; prof. at Seminary in 1833; pres. of Gettysburg College 1834—50; prof. at Seminary 1850—67. D. D. from Univ. of Pa. 1837. Helped edit *The Lutheran Intelligencer;* editor of the *Evangelical Review* 1850—61. D. May 30, 1867.

Krauth, Charles Porterfield. For twenty years one of the most prominent theologians of the General Synod and, after 1866, the leader and most conservative and influential theologian of the General Council. Krauth was "a star of the first magnitude in the Lutheran Church of America" (Dr. Bente), "the most eminent man in the English Lutheran Church of this country, a man of rare learning . . . wholeheartedly devoted to the pure doctrine of our Church as he had learned to understand it, a noble man and without guile" (Dr. Walther). He was the son of Charles Philip Krauth, b. March 17, 1823, while his father was pastor at Martinsburg, Va. He studied at Gettysburg College and Seminary, was licensed in 1841 and ordained in 1842. Till 1861 he served congregations in Canton (Baltimore), Shepherdstown and Martinsburg, Va., Winchester, Va., St. Thomas, W. I. (a Reformed congregation in the absence of its pastor), Pittsburgh, and Philadelphia. In 1861 he resigned in order to devote his time to editing the *Lutheran and Missionary*, which in his hand became a strong weapon against the excrescences of the "American Lutheranism" then rampant in the General Synod. At first

he, like his father, was in favor of peace and mutual toleration in the battle over the Lutheran Confessions. But later a study of these Confessions led him to a more soundly Biblical position. When the Philadelphia Seminary was established (1864), Krauth was appointed professor of Dogmatics. He was the leading spirit in the establishment of the General Council and the author of the *Fundamental Articles of Faith and Church Polity*, adopted at Reading in 1866, of the *Theses on Pulpit- and Altar-fellowship*, 1877, and of the constitution for congregations, 1880. He was president of the General Council 1870 to 1880. In 1868 he was appointed to the chair of Philosophy at the University of Pennsylvania, maintaining his chair at the seminary. Besides being editor of the *Lutheran*, the *Lutheran Church Review*, and Fleming's *Vocabulary of Philosophy* (1860), he was the author of many books. The most important of these is *The Conservative Reformation and Its Theology* (1872). D. in Philadelphia, Jan. 2, 1883.

A. Spaeth, *Dr. Charles Porterfield Krauth*, Christian Lit. Co., N. Y., 1898 (vol. 2 published by General Council Pub. House, Philadelphia, 1909).

Krebs, Johann Ludwig (1713—80). Pupil of J. S. Bach, upon whose name Bach loved to pun by saying that "he was the best crab (*Krebs*) in all the brook (*Bach*)." Although the chorale-preludes of the post-Bach era were too often musical bagatelles when compared with those of Bach and other masters, those of young Krebs were of a much higher caliber than those of his contemporaries. The same applies also to his absolute organ music. Krebs was a pre-eminent organ virtuoso of his day. He served as organist in Zwickau, Zeitz, and Altenburg (Germany).

Krebs, Johann Tobias (1690 to p. 1760). Father of Johann Ludwig Krebs and, like his son, a pupil of J. S. Bach. However, the younger Krebs excelled his father, who served as organist and composer in Buttelstaedt and Buttstaedt, Germany.

Kreinheder, Oscar Carl. B. Nov. 10, 1877, at Buffalo, N. Y.; grad. Concordia Seminary, St. Louis, 1901; pastor in East St. Louis, Ill., 1901—03; St. Paul, Minn., 1903—20; Detroit, Mich., 1920 to 1930; pres. of Valparaiso Univ., 1930 to 1940; d. 1946.

Kremmer, Karl Friedrich (1817 to 1887). B. at Schmalkalden, Germany;

d. at Tranquebar, India; attended Dresden Mission Institute 1843—46; Leipzig missionary to India 1846; Madras 1848 to 1858 and again 1865—75; excellent Tamil scholar; founded Cuddalore and Madura stations; senior of Leipzig Mission in India.

Kretzmann, Karl Gustave Henry (1877—1949); b. Dudleytown, Ind., Feb. 23, 1877; ed. Concordia College, Fort Wayne, and Concordia Seminary, St. Louis, Mo., grad. 1899. Pastor at Stamford, Conn., 1899—1905; Baltimore, Md., 1905—07; St. Paul's Church, New York City, 1907—22; Redeemer, Orange, N. J., 1922—43. First full-time curator of Concordia Historical Institute at St. Louis, 1943—48. Secretary of the Atlantic District and editor of the *Atlantic District Bulletin* for many years. Received honorary D. D., Hartwick Seminary, 1937. Wrote *Atlantic District and Its Antecedents* and *The Oldest Lutheran Church in America*. D. April 3, 1949, in St. Louis, Mo.

W. G. Polack, *Karl Kretzmann, D. D.*, CHIQ, XXII: 49—55.

Kretzschmar, Richard Th. B. May 7, 1868, at Mittweida, Saxony; graduated at Concordia Seminary, St. Louis, 1891; pastor of Emmaus Church, St. Louis, 1891—1940; President of Western District of Mo. Synod, 1921—38; editor of *Missionstaube* for a number of years; D. D. (St. Louis); member of Board of Control of Concordia Seminary and other important boards of Synod. D. March 5, 1940.

Krieger, Adam (1634—66). Pupil of Samuel Scheidt and Heinrich Schuetz, was a composer and poet whose arias helped popularize a new type of German *Lied* in the 17th century.

Krieger, Johann Philipp (1649 to 1725). Composer of operas who wrote also church music which, unfortunately, is no longer extant. His contributions to the development of the cantata are known to have been significant and likely influenced J. S. Bach as a composer of cantatas. Johann Rosenmueller was one of his teachers (Venice). Krieger spent forty years of his life as *Kapellmeister* and organist in Saxe-Weissenfels.

Krimmer Brueder-Gemeinde. See *Mennonite Bodies,* 3.

Krishna. An alleged incarnation of Vishnu, a god of Hinduism.*

Krispin, M. See *Reformed Confessions,* E 4.

Krist. An Old High German harmony of the Gospels composed by the Benedictine monk Otfrid of Weissenburg (ca. 790—875) in five books, in metrical, rhymed lines.

KRLW. See *Radio Stations, Religious.*

Krol, Jansen. See *Reformed Church,* 4 b.

Kromayer, Hieronymus (1610—70). B. at Zeitz, d. as professor at Leipzig; wrote *Theologia Positivo-Polemica* against Rome, Calvinism, and syncretism.

Kropatscheck, Friedrich (1875 to 1917). Prof. at Greifswald and Breslau; editor of *Biblische Zeit- und Streitfragen;* wrote *Das Schriftprinzip der lutherischen Kirche.*

Krotel, G. F. B. Ilsfeld, Wuerttemberg, Germany, Feb. 4, 1826; came to Philadelphia 1830; grad. Univ. of Pa. 1846 (D. D. 1865); LL. D. Muhlenberg College. One of influential men of General Council; pastor at Lebanon, Lancaster, and Philadelphia; pastor Evang. Luth. Church of the Holy Trinity, New York, 1868—95: Church of Advent, New York, from 1896; prof. Luth. Theol. Sem. 1864—68. Editor in chief *The Lutheran.* Pres. Luth. Ministerium of New York and of Luth. Ministerium of Pennsylvania 1866—68 and 1884—92. One of founders of General Council and its pres. 1869—70 and 1888—93. D. in New York 1907.

Krug, John Andrew (1732—96). One of Muhlenberg's co-workers; instructor at Halle; came to America (1763); pastor at Reading, Pa., and Frederick, Md.

Krummacher. Name of four prominent Reformed theologians of Germany. *Friedrich Adolf K.* (1767—1845). Taught in Hamm and Duisburg, made a special study of the parables of both the Old and the New Testament; became pastor in Kettwig, later in Bernburg, finally in Bremen; deeply religious, with strong poetical inclinations. — *Gottfried Daniel K.,* brother of the foregoing (1774—1837). Pastor at Baerl, Wuelfrat, and Elberfeld; a strong opponent of Rationalism and an equally vehement defender of Calvinistic predestination; opposed the Prussian union. — *Friedrich Wilhelm K.* (1796 to 1868). Son of F. A. K., studied at Halle and Jena; pastor at Ruhrort, Gemarke, Elberfeld, and Potsdam; strong opponent of Rationalism, but a friend of the Prussian union and of the Evangelical Alliance; author of many books. — *Emil Wilhelm K.* (1798 — 1886), another son of F. A. K. Studied at Jena and Tuebingen; pastor at Coswig, Baerl, Langenberg, and Duisburg; proponent of the union, although theologian of the positive persuasion; opposed Rationalism.

Kshatriya. See *Hinduism,* 3.

KTIS — KTW. See *Radio Stations, Religious.*

Kuder, Calvin F. Lutheran missionary to India; b. April 10, 1864, at Laurys, Pa.; commissioned to India by General Council 1891, arriving at Rajahmundry Nov. 14, 1891; given charge of seminary 1892; returned to the United States 1898; resigned 1899; sent out again 1908; returned to the United States April, 1913.

Kuebel, Robert Benjamin (1838 to 1894). D. as prof. of Systematic Theology at Tuebingen; claimed to be independent, but was influenced by Schleiermacher and Beck; had leanings to positive Lutheranism. Wrote: *Christliches Lehrsystem nach der Heiligen Schrift; Bibelkunde; Outline of Pastoral Theology;* commentaries on Matthew, Galatians, Philippians, Pastoral Epistles, James, Philemon.

Kuegele, F. B. April 16, 1846, at Columbiana, Ohio; studied theology at Concordia Seminary, St. Louis, graduating 1870; missionary in Nebraska; pastor at Cumberland, Md.; served the English church (Ohio Synod) at Coyners Store and Waynesboro, Va., 1879 to April 1, 1916, the date of his death. Charter member of Concordia Synod; first president of the English Missouri Synod; regular contributor to the *Lutheran Witness;* author of *Country Sermons* (5 vols.) and a devotional book.

Kuehl, Ernst Richard Theodor (1861 to 1918). Studied in Berlin; prof. of New Testament in Breslau, Marburg, and Koenigsberg; wrote *Die Briefe Petri und Judae* in Meyer's Commentary.

Kuenen, Abraham (1828—91). Dutch theologian, prof. at Leyden. In the struggle between orthodoxy and the liberal school he championed the cause of the liberals, although urging moderation. His most important work is *Historico-Critical Inquiry into the Origin and Composition of the Hexa-* *teuch,* a work of the Higher Critical School.

Kugler, Anna Sarah (d. 1930). Pioneer physician in the work of the General Synod; went to India (1883); founded hospital at Guntur.

Kuhn, Albert. B. 1835 in Switzerland; educated at St. Chrischona; came to Trinity, St. Paul, Minn., as assistant 1865; then pastor at Woodbury, Mankato, and Greenwood, all in Minnesota; president of Minnesota Synod 1876—83; champion of sound Lutheranism; active in the movement that led to affiliation with Synodical Conference and later to formation of the Joint Synod of Wisconsin and Other States; wrote: *History of Minnesota Synod,* 1910 (German); d. 1915.

Kuhnau, Johann (1660 — 1722). Predecessor of J. S. Bach in Leipzig, where he succeeded Johann Schelle as *Thomaskantor.* Kuhnau is at times referred to as the father of the piano sonata. In addition, he wrote 17 cantatas and a *Passion According to St. Mark.* In his cantatas he compromised between the old and the new cantata style; as a result, his cantatas often lack depth, solidity, and originality. The pietistic and sentimental spirit of his age found stronger expression in the choral works of Kuhnau than in the works of J. S. Bach, who, however, together with other prominent musicians of his day, held Kuhnau in high esteem.

A. Schweitzer, *J. S. Bach,* Leipzig, 1930; P. Spitta, *Johann Sebastian Bach,* Leipzig, 1930.

Kuinoel, Christian Gottlieb (1768 to 1841). Prof. at Leipzig and Giessen; philologist; wrote a number of commentaries.

Kulturkampf ("struggle for civilization," so called by R. Virchow). A violent quarrel between the Prussian government and the Roman Catholic Church; an outburst, under new conditions, of the long historic conflict between Church and State.

The star of Catholic Austria sank at Sadowa (1866) before the rising power of Prussia. Catholic France was humbled at Sedan (1870) by the same power. French help withdrawn, the last remnant of papal sovereignty was swept away in the same year. To crown all, the seat of empire was transferred to Berlin and a hereditary Protestant dynasty was created. The Roman Catholics immediately pursued a reactionary policy. William I, even before he was proclaimed Emperor, was requested to use his power for the Papacy and restore the papal states. The government's refusal to consider such a request, the consequent disappointment and agitation on the part of the Ultramontane Party, the open denunciation of the Protestant government from Roman Catholic pulpits created a situation which was bound to end in open conflict. This happened when the government espoused the cause of certain anti-infallibilists. A series of anticlerical enactments were passed to uphold the sovereignty of the state. The so-called "May Laws" (May 11—14, 1873; May 20, 21, 1874) were a vigorous assertion of German nationalism. Clerical education and clerical discipline were put under state control. As the struggle proceeded, the Church was reduc d to a state of helpless vassalage. These measures were met with stubborn resistance. Fines, banishments, imprisonment, deposition of refractory priests and bishops availed nothing. Nor could an understanding be reached during the Pontificate of Pius IX. When Leo XIII became pope, a more conciliatory policy was inaugurated, long negotiations followed, and the obnoxious laws were modified or repealed. The *Kulturkampf* ended in 1887.

Kunze, John Christopher. B. Aug. 5, 1744, at Artern on the Unstrut, Saxony; ed. at Halle (G. A. Francke), Rossleben, Merseburg, and the Univ. of Leipzig; called to Philadelphia in 1770 and became coadjutor of H. M. Muhlenberg at St. Michael's and Zion Congregations in Philadelphia; married Muhlenberg's second daughter, Margaretta Henrietta; succeeded Muhlenberg as chief pastor 1779; in 1784 he became pastor of Trinity and Christ Churches in New York; realizing that American Lutherans must train their own ministers, he started a *Seminarium* in Philadelphia in 1773, which, however, was closed by the Revolutionary War; prof. of Oriental languages in Columbia College 1784—87 and 1792—99; prof. of theology on the Hartwig Foundation 1797; official translator of Congress 1785; an outstanding scholar of his time, familiar with several sciences; d. July 24, 1807. His *A Hymn and Prayer Book for the Use of Such Lutheran Churches as Use the English Language* (1797) is the first Lutheran hymnbook in the English language and contains the earliest surviving translation of Luther's Cate-

chism in English in America. He trained the First English-Lutheran pastors in America. He grieved over the inroads of rationalism in his last years.

A. L. Graebner, *Geschichte der lutherischen Kirche in America*, CPH, 1892 (461—70 *et passim*); W. G. Mann, *Life and Times of Henry Melchior Muhlenberg*, Frederick, Philadelphia, 1887; *Hallesche Nachrichten;* C. F. Haussmann, *Kunze's Seminarium*, Am. Germania Press, Philadelphia, 1917.

Kurtz, Benjamin. B. at Harrisburg, Pa., Feb. 28, 1795; studied theology under George Lochman; assistant pastor to his uncle, J. Daniel Kurtz, at Baltimore in 1815; pastor at Hagerstown, Md., 1815—31, at Chambersburg, Pa., 1831—33; wielded great influence in General Synod as editor of *Lutheran Observer* 1833—61; visited Germany in 1826 in interest of the theological seminary at Gettysburg, and later in life founded Selinsgrove Missionary Institute; an advocate of English preaching, Sunday schools, protracted meetings, and temperance reform. His book, *Why Are You a Lutheran?* had wide circulation. Champion of "Definite Platform." D. Dec. 29, 1865.

E. W. Hutter, *Eulogy on the Life and Character of Rev. Benjamin Kurtz*, Private Printing, 1866; C. A. Hay, *Memoirs of J. Goering, G. Lochman, B. Kurtz*, Luth. Pub. Soc., Philadelphia, 1887.

Kurtz, Johann Heinrich (1809—90). Church historian and conservative Lutheran of modern type; studied at Halle and Bonn; from 1850 to 1870 professor at Dorpat; the rest of his life spent in literary labors; principal work: *Lehrbuch der Kirchengeschichte*. In his works on the Old Testament he makes too many concessions to modern higher criticism.

Kurtz, John Daniel (1763—1856). Son of John Nicolas; pastor in Baltimore, Md., 1786—1832; first president of General Synod 1820; re-elected 1823, 1827.

Kurtz, John Nicolas (d. 1794). Halle missionary; studied at Giessen and Halle; came to America 1745; ordained 1748; pastor at Tulpehocken and York, Pa.

Kurze, Guenther. B. Aug. 8, 1850; d. Jan. 21, 1918, at Bornsheim, Saxony; pastor at Bornsheim from 1889 to his death; *Kirchenrat;* voluminuous and well-informed author on missions; contributor to the *Allgemeine Missions-*

zeitschrift; founder of the *Thueringen-Missionskonferenz.*

Kusel, Daniel (1811—1905). Watertown, Wis., businessman; one of founders of St. Mark's, Watertown; member of first board of Northwestern College of Wisconsin Synod; was instrumental in securing present site of college; as treasurer was often called upon to furnish funds for professors' salaries.

Kuyper, Abraham (1837 — 1920). Dutch Calvinist; prime minister 1901; founder of the Free University; lectured extensively in the U. S.; founder of the Reformed Free Church 1886; many of his books were directed against Modernism and liberalism; an English translation of one of his important works is: *Encyclopedia of Theology.*

Kuzmány, Karol. See *Slovakia, Lutheran Theology in,* 2.

KVOB. See *Radio Stations, Religious.*

KWBU — KWLC. See *Radio Stations, Religious.*

Kwei. See *Confucianism,* 3.

Kyle, Melvin Grove (1858—1933). United Presbyterian; Egyptologist; b. in Ohio; minister 1886; president of Board of Foreign Missions; professor of Biblical Theology and Archaeology at Xenia Seminary; editor in chief of *Bibliotheca Sacra;* author especially of works dealing with OT criticism and archaeology.

Kyrie. See *Worship, Parts of,* 5.

L

Labadie, Jean de (1610—74). French mystic; b. at Bourg; Jesuit, priest, preacher; Protestant 1650; pastor at Montauban; founder of sect● in Amsterdam 1669; expelled; died at Altona, Germany. Some Labadists settled on the Hudson.

Labadists. See *Communistic Societies,* 4.

Labarum. The standard of the Emperor Constantine* in which was wrought the monogram of Jesus (IHC) as a result (according to tradition) of the vision seen before the battle of the Mulvian Bridge. See *Symbolism, Christian,* 6.

Laberthonniere, Lucien (1860—). French Roman Catholic theologian and philosopher; in his *Essais de Philosophie Religieuse* he developed a theory of divine immanence which was condemned by Pius X and placed on the Index.*

Labor and Capital. See *Capital and Labor; Industry and the Church; Labor and the Church; Social Gospel; Social Ethics; Socialism.*

Labor and the Church. The relations of the laborer and the Church have been much closer than the relations of organized labor and the Churches. Antipathy was aroused due to the early type of secret organization, violent strikes, and extralegal methods of operation by the Knights of Labor

in the 1880's and the I. W. W. With the organization of the A. F. L. in 1886 and the CIO in 1936, the Churches have increased interest in the problems and aspirations of workers. Labor demands often identified with Christian goals of justice and love, active arbitration of labor disputes by clergymen, and study of labor problems and publications have broken down the diffidence of labor and clergy toward each other. Labor institutes, youth studies of industrial problems, and the increasing activity of church members in union leadership have widened the areas of common Church-Labor interest. The Church has thus forestalled the inroads of socialism and Communism among the wage earners. Investigations of strikes, most notable of which was the 1919 Steel strike by Interchurch, has supplemented the social pronouncements on Labor. The U. L. C. in 1945 published a statement, "The Church Speaks on Labor," which is a model. But not only pronouncements are looked for. The proper application of 2 Thess. 3:10, 1 Tim. 5:18, Gal. 6:2, and Col. 3:22—4:1 to collective bargaining, co-operatives, working conditions, a just wage, and Sunday work has brought to the laboring groups greater interest in the Church. See *Capital and Labor; Industry and the Church.* JD

Liston Pope, *Labor's Relation to Church and Community,* Harper, N. Y., 1947; and *Millhands and Preachers,*

Yale, New Haven, 1942; Alexander Miller, *Christian Faith and My Job*, Ass'n Press, N. Y., 1946; Jerome Davis, *Labor Speaks for Itself on Religion*, Macm., N. Y., 1929; James Myers: *Do You Know Labor?* John Day, N. Y., 1943; W. H. Greever, *Human Relationships and the Church*, Revell, N. Y., 1939; C. Stelzle, *The Church and the Labor Movement*, Boston, 1910; John Daniel, *The Church and Labor-Management Problems of Our Day*, Bethlehem, 1948; G. B. Oxnam, *Labor and Tomorrow's World*, Abingdon-Cokesbury, N. Y., 1945.

Labrador. A dependency of Newfoundland, Dominion of Canada. Area, about 110,000 sq. mi. Population, 5,528 (1945), of whom about 1,300 are Eskimos. Missions were begun by the Moravians as early as 1752, but real footing was not found until 1771, when Nain was founded. Since 1884 more progress was made. Now nearly all of the natives are Christianized. Dr. Grenfell * established the Labrador Medical Mission.

Lachelier, Jules (1832—1918). French philosopher; teacher of E. Boutroux and H. Bergson; taught a system of modified Kantian idealism which he called spiritual realism.

Lachmann, Karl Konrad Friedrich Wilhelm (1793—1851). German philologist; applied textual criticism to the New Testament.

Lacordaire, Jean Baptiste Henri (1802—61). French Roman Catholic; first a follower of Rousseau, but moved by Lamennais' *Essai sur l'indifférence* to become a priest. He sought to interpret Catholicism according to principles of liberty and democracy while opposing free thought.

Lactantius. The "Christian Cicero"; an Italian by birth; pupil of Arnobius; professor of rhetoric at Nicomedia; converted to Christianity ca. 301. Principal works: *Divinae Institutiones*, an exposition and vindication of Christianity; *De Mortibus Persecutorum*, in which the punitive justice of God is shown to have overtaken the persecutors. D. ca. 330.

Ladies' Aid Societies. See *Woman in Christian Society.*

Ladrones Islands. See *Polynesia.*

Lady Chapel. Chapel to Mary in or with larger churches.

Lady Day. The Feast of the Annunciation, March 25.

Lady Huntingdon's Connection. See *Calvinistic Methodism.*

Laestadians. See *Finland, Lutheranism in*, 8.

Laestadius, L. L. See *Finland, Lutheranism in*, 4.

Lagarde, Paul Anton de (1827 to 1891). Prof. at Goettingen; philologist; considered Protestantism an obsolete phenomenon; desired a nationally controlled return to primitive faith; wrote: *The Four Gospels in Arabic; The Pentateuch in Coptic;* many monographs in the field of the Scriptures in Oriental languages.

Lainez, Diego (1512—65). Famous Jesuit, one of the original members who joined Ignatius Loyola in Paris; second general of the order, dominated the Council of Trent and determined, in large measure, its uncompromising anti-Protestant policy, besides advancing the cause of papal infallibility; in scholarship, adroitness, and worldly wisdom easily superior to Loyola.* See *Counter Reformation.*

Laity. The division of church members into clergy and laity is a valid one if the words simply stand for the distinction of those who have been called by the Church into the ministry of the Word from those who have not been so called. However, with the rise of the sacerdotal system, which culminated in the Papacy, the idea that the priesthood formed an intermediate class between God and the Christian congregation became prevalent, and both terms, clergy and laity, were thereby vitiated. — The doctrine of justification by faith alone abolished human mediation between man and God. Luther fully recognized the New Testament idea of the priesthood of all believers and proclaimed it with all the force of his eloquence. His language on this subject is very explicit: "Every Christian man is a priest and every Christian woman a priestess, whether they be young or old, master or servant, mistress or maidservant, scholar or illiterate. All Christians are, properly speaking, members of the ecclesiastical order, and there is no difference between them, except that they hold different offices." By the inculcation of this fundamental principle the laity recovered its position in the Church of Christ, and lay representation again became possible. "The restoration," says Litton, "in theory at least, of the laity to their proper place in the Church was an immediate consequence of the Reformation. By reasserting the two great Scriptural doctrines of the universal priesthood of Christians and of the indwelling of the Spirit, not in a priestly caste, but in the whole body of the faithful, Luther and his contemporaries shook the whole fabric of sacerdotal usurpation to its base and recovered for the Christian laity the rights of which they had been deprived. The lay members of the body of Christ emerged from the spiritual imbecility which they had been taught to regard as their natural state and became free, not from the yoke of Christ, but from that of the priest." See *Laymen's Activity in the Luth. Church; Priesthood.*

Lamaism. The form of Buddhism * of the Mahayana school first introduced into Tibet in the 7th century and still prevailing there today. From Tibet it spread northward into Mongolia and Manchuria. The term Lamaism is derived from *lama*, "superior one," designating originally Tibetan abbots and then extended to include all monks. At the head of this partly hierarchical and partly political religious system, which claims more than 10,000,000 adherents, are two lamas, the Dalai Lama at Lhasa, the capital of Tibet, and the Tashi Lama or Panchen Lama, residing at the monastery Tashilunpo near Shigatse. The former is also the ruler of the country. In Lamaism's highly developed ritual have often been noted many analogies to Roman Catholic rites, such as the choirs, processions, the worship of relics and saints, incense, holy water, and bells. Monasticism is developed to such an extent in Tibet that it is estimated that there is one monk to every three of the lay populaion. The use of prayer wheels is a widely known practice in Lamaism.

Lambert, Francis, of Avignon (1487 to 1530). Franciscan; his spiritual conflicts ended by reading Luther; one of the first French Protestants; translated writings of Luther into French and Italian; suffered want and persecution; finally, 1526, professor at the new University of Marburg; prominent in establishing the Reformation in Hesse; was at the Marburg Colloquium, but remained silent, for he had come to entertain the Zwinglian view.

Lambeth Articles. See *Anglican Confessions,* 7.

Lambeth Conferences *(Pan-Anglican Synod).* The first Pan-Anglican Synod, consisting of British, colonial, and American Anglican bishops met at Lambeth Palace (residence of the Archbishop of Canterbury) from September 24 to December 10, 1867, to discuss various questions affecting the organization and work of the Anglican communion as a whole. Similar conferences have been held at intervals of approximately a decade. The greatest general interest attaches to the Pan-Anglican Synod of 1888, since this synod sanctioned and adopted the definition of what is fundamental in the Christian system and might thus serve as a basis of a possible reunion of Christendom put forth by the General Convention of the Protestant Episcopal Church in Chicago in 1886. These articles were intended as an invitation to church union and a basis for it. The fundamentals of the articles (called the "Quadrilateral" because four in number) were: "The Holy Scripture of the Old and New Testaments as containing all things necessary to salvation and as being the rule and ultimate standard of faith; the Apostles' Creed as a baptismal symbol and the Nicene Creed as a sufficient statement of the Christian faith; the two Sacraments ordained by Christ Himself, Baptism and the Supper of the Lord, administered with unfailing use of Christ's words of institution and of the elements ordained by Him; the historic episcopate locally adapted in the methods of its administration to the varying needs of the nations and peoples called of God into the unity of His Church."

The Lambeth Conference is the central consultative body of the Anglican Communion. Its decisions, while not binding in conscience or in canon law on the separate churches of that communion, carry great moral authority.

Lambeth Quadrilateral on Church Unity (1888). See *Lambeth Conferences; Protestant Episcopal Church,* 4.

Lambillotte, Louis (1797—1855). Organist at Charleroi, then at Dinant; later member of the Jesuit order, residing at various monasteries; prolific composer of church music; also published the Gregorian *Antiphonary Lamennais.*

Lamennais, Hugues Felicité Robert de (1782—1854). French priest who in later life opposed Ultramontanism and defended freedom of conscience, assembly, and press.

Lamentabili, the Decree of 1907. See *Popes*, 30.

Lamentations. A section of the service for Good Friday in the Roman Church, that portion being introduced with the *Tenebrae factae sunt* ("And there was darkness"), the music being set to a text taken from the Lamentations of Jeremiah.

Lamettrie, Julien Offray de (1709 to 1751). Studied at Sorbonne in theology, especially that of Jansenism; rejected Christianity and entered the medical field; member of the Academy of Science of Prussia; published books defending materialism; denied God and immortality.

Lammers, Gustav A. (1802—78). Norwegian pastor; left State Church and organized the *Free Apostolic Christians* (Donatist and Baptist tendencies); rejoined State Church (1861).

Landsmann, Daniel. B. 1837 in Russia; d. May 13, 1896, in New York City. Landsmann was of Jewish extraction. Before his conversion and Baptism his name was Eliezer Bassin. Educated to be a teacher, he removed to Jerusalem, where he was converted to Christ by Missionary Stern. At Jerusalem, Landsmann suffered much for the sake of his faith; his wife divorced him, his children were taken from him, and he was persecuted even unto wounds. Later he went to Constantinople as a Christian missionary. Having come to the United States, he was brought into contact with the Missouri Synod, which had resolved to begin a Jewish mission. After spending nine months in the theological seminary at Springfield, Ill., he was appointed missionary to the Jews in New York City, beginning work among them in July, 1883. Here he labored unremittingly, faithfully, and successfully, encountering much opposition from the Jews, until he was called to the rest of his Lord.

Lanfranc (d. 1089). Archbishop of Canterbury. Banned and in peril of death, he vowed to become a monk and became a famous teacher and organizer at the monastery of Bec. Through diplomacies not always honest he managed to reach the height of power and aided William the Conqueror in unifying his rule and upheld the unity of the English Church.

Lang, Heinrich (1826—76). Studied at Tuebingen; pastor at Wartau (1848), Meilen (1863), and at St. Peter, Zurich (1871), Switzerland. A radical theologian, he rejected historical faith for the "modern" philosophical world view.

Lang, Johann Michael (1664—1731). Lutheran theologian of the Spener school; prof. at Altorf; chiliast; wrote in many fields of theology (important: *Kern des Wahren Christentums*).

Lang, Matthaeus (1469—1540). Studied at Ingolstadt and Wien; imperial secretary; bishop of Gurk; cardinal (1511); archbishop of Salzburg; at first favorably inclined to the evangelicals, he was won completely to the other side after receiving positions from the Pope; demanded of Staupitz the rejection of Lutheran heresy (1521); deposed Paul Speratus (1524); at Augsburg (1530) he declared himself a bitter foe of Luther.

Langbein, Bernhard Adolf (1815 to 1873). Deacon at Meissen; pastor at Chemnitz; court preacher at Dresden; consistorial councilor. Labored for confessional Lutheranism. Published many of his sermons.

Lange, C. H. R. B. Jan. 8, 1825, in Polish Wartenberg, Prussia; received a classical education; studied theology under guidance of private instructors; was induced by Pastor Loehe to come to America 1846; continued his studies in the Fort Wayne seminary and completed them in the Altenburg seminary; pastor in St. Charles, Mo., 1848; professor of English and philosophy in Concordia College and Seminary, in St. Louis 1858, in Fort Wayne 1861; pastor in Defiance, Ohio, 1872; of Immanuel's, Chicago, 1872—78; from 1878 to Oct. 2, 1892, the day of his death, professor of theology in Concordia Seminary, St. Louis. He was a profound thinker, thoroughly familiar with ancient and modern philosophy. He was in charge of the English work at the seminary, giving his lectures on philosophy, logic, exegetics, homiletics, etc., in the English language. He was the first one of the first generation of Missourians to pay special attention to the English language, wrote textbooks on English which were widely used at the time, and through his work at the Seminary at St. Louis wisely and successfully prepared the way for the transition period. Besides contributing as associate editor to the other periodicals of Synod, he edited the St. Louis *Theological Monthly*, published upon the outbreak of the controversy on election and conversion. In 1878 he was elected vice-president of Synod.

Lange, Frederick Albert (1828—75). B. in Wald, Germany; prof. at Zurich; neo-Kantian, he opposed materialistic metaphysics and held that materialism is valid only as a method; active in behalf of political freedom and the well-being of the working class. His important works: *Story of Materialism* (1866) and *The Labor Question* (1879).

Lange, Joachim (1670—1744). Prof. in Halle; a leader of the Pietists; violent controversialist; wrote against the orthodox Lutherans, especially against V. E. Loescher; also against the *Aufklaerer*, Thomasius, Wolff, and the *Wertheim-Bibel*. His voluminous works have no permanent value. He recommended Ziegenbalg and Pluetschau as missionaries to India.

Lange, Johann Peter (1802—84). Reformed theologian. B. in the parish of Sonnborn, near Elberfeld; d. at Bonn. Studied at the Gymnasium in Duesseldorf and the University of Bonn. Assistant minister at Langenberg, 1825; pastor of Wald, 1826; of Langenberg, 1828; of Duisberg, 1832; professor of theology at Zurich, 1841, a chair which had been refused to David Friedrich Strauss, whose life of Christ he refuted with his *Leben Jesu nach den Evangelien*, 1844—47; professor of dogmatic theology at Bonn, 1854; consistorial councilor, 1860. His *Theologisch-homiletisches Bibelwerk* is still highly esteemed.

Lange, Theodore. B. October 26, 1866, at St. Louis, Mo. Publisher, banker; manager of Louis Lange Publishing Co.; of *Abendschule* fame; served on Board for Young People's Work of Missouri Synod. D. 1934.

Langhans, Urban. A native of Schneeberg, Saxony, in the 16th century; *Diaconus* at Glauchau from 1546 to 1554, then at Schneeberg; wrote the delightful hymn "Lasst uns alle froehlich sein."

Langton, Stephen (d. 1228). Archbishop of Canterbury; his appointment by Pope Innocent III led to the humiliation of King John; to facilitate citation, he divided the Bible into chapters.

Language Question in the Lutheran Church (U. S.). The Lutheran

Church was transplanted on American soil mainly by Germans and Scandinavians. Since America became an English-speaking country, it was only natural that these Lutherans would not be able to hand down their own language to their progeny. In certain cases refusal on the part of some to use the English led to disastrous results. The Swedes along the Delaware, for instance, did not provide their young people with sufficient instruction in English; this was one reason why the group eventually was lost to the Lutheran Church. A few of the German groups, however, such as the New York Ministerium, made English their official language as early as 1807.

Many of the Lutheran fathers feared that a change from German to English would cause future generations to lose purity of doctrine. A transition was therefore strenuously opposed in many localities by the different leaders, frequently resulting in widespread loss to the Church. In some cases the problem was temporarily solved by organizing English synods. Over a period of years, however, the change to the English language was effected, and the great majority of Lutherans in the U. S. worship and transact synodical business in English. ARS

W. Baepler, *Century of Grace*, CPH, 1947; *Documentary History of the Ev. Luth. Ministerium of Pennsylvania and Adjacent States*, Bd. of Pub. of General Council, Philadelphia, 1898; V. Ferm, *Crisis in American Lutheran Theology*, Century, N. Y., 1927; Neve-Allbeck, *The Lutheran Church in America*, Luth. Lit. Bd., Burlington, Iowa, 1934; J. Nicum, *Geschichte des Ev. Luth. Ministeriums vom Staate New York*, Theodore Wischan, Reading, Pa., 1888; W. G. Polack, *The Building of a Great Church*, CPH, 1926; A. R. Wentz, *The Lutheran Church in American History*, United Luth. Pub. House, 1923 (new ed., 1933).

Lankenau, Francis James. B. Apr. 26, 1868, Fort Wayne, Ind.; studied at Concordia College (Fort Wayne, Ind.), Concordia Seminary (Springfield, Ill.); D. D. (St. Louis); pastor in New Orleans; pres. of Luther College (1902 to 1908); pastor, Napoleon, Ohio, 1908 to 1939; vice-president of Mo. Syn., 1926—39; author of *Church and Missions; The World Is Our Field;* d. July 16, 1939.

F. C. Lankenau, *Francis James Lankenau*, CPH, 1940; see also *CHIQ*, XII: 65—83.

Lao-Tse. See *Taoism.*

Laodicea, Synod of (ca. 364). Adopted 60 canons regarding church government and discipline which were confirmed by the Council of Chalcedon (451).

Lapland. An immense stretch of Arctic country in northern Europe, belonging to Russia, Denmark, Norway, and Sweden. Area, 150,000 sq. mi. The Laplanders (indigenous population) number about 30,000 (1950). In 1559 Gustav Wasa, King of Sweden, originated missionary work among them, which was continued by Karl IX and Gustavus Adolphus. From 1716 to 1722 Thomas von Westen (d. 1727) carried on earnest missionary work, which was resumed by Stockfleth (d. 1866) in the 19th century.

Lapsed (Lapsi). See *Persecutions of Christians,* 4.

Lardner, Nathaniel (1684—1768). Non-conformist; assistant minister (Presbyterian) in London 1729—51; became deaf; wrote: *Credibility of Gospel History.*

Larsen, Peter Laurentius. B. in Norway Aug. 10, 1833; graduated at Kristiania University; emigrated 1857; pastor; professor at Concordia Seminary, St. Louis; professor at Luther College, Decorah, Iowa, and its president; vice-president of the Norwegian Synod; president of the Synodical Conference; editor of *Maanedstidende* and *Kirketidende;* 1903 created D. D. by Concordia Seminary, St. Louis; knighted by King Haakon VII 1908; d. Mar. 1, 1915.

K. Larsen, *Laur. Larsen,* Norwegian-American Hist. Ass'n, Northfield, Minn., 1936.

La Salle, St. John Baptist de (1651 to 1719). See *Christian Brothers.*

Lasco, Johannes A. See *A Lasco, Johannes; Poland, Lutheranism in,* 2.

Lasius, Christoph. A Lutheran theologian. B. at Strassburg. Pastor at Spandau, Kottbus, and other places. Opposed Flacius. Wrote *Güldenes Kleinod; Grundveste der reinen evang. Wahrheit.* D. 1572.

Lassenius, Johann (1636—92). B. in Pomerania; d. at Copenhagen as court preacher; wrote against the Jesuits and is the author of several devotional books and some hymns.

Lasso, Orlando di (Roland de Lasso; ca. 1532—94). Composer of the Roman Catholic Church who is often referred to as the last great composer of the Netherland School. He was a contemporary of Palestrina and the teacher of Johann Eccard * and Leonhard Lechner.* His style was universal as well as versatile, and his motets are often thought to surpass those of Palestrina. Lassus was influenced by Josquin des Pres and Andrea Gabrieli; in his and Palestrina's music vocal polyphony reached its greatest height. Elegance and refinement, with (cf. his madrigals) depth and seriousness, distinguish his music. In his music we find a notable break from the past; music is no longer only a bearer, but also an interpreter of its texts. His settings of the Penitential Psalms are among his greatest works. He was active at the court of Albrecht V of Bavaria as composer for almost 40 years.

F. Blume, *Die evangelische Kirchenmusik,* Potsdam, 1931; H. Leichtentritt, *Geschichte der Motette,* Leipzig, 1908; O. Ursprung, *Die katholische Kirchenmusik,* Potsdam, 1931; Carl v. Winterfeld, *Zur Geschichte der Tonkunst,* Leipzig, 1850.

Last Things (Eschatology). Eschatology is that part of dogmatics, or doctrinal theology, which treats of the last things — immortality, the resurrection, life after death, the second coming of Christ, the final Judgment, and the end of the world. Immortality * and the life after death (see *Hereafter*) are treated in separate articles. Here matters centering around Christ's return to Judgment are treated.

1. *Signs of the Last Times.* In addition to His many direct promises to return (Matt. 25:31-32; Mark 13:26; Luke 21:27, 36), the Lord has placed a description of many signs into His Word by which believers are to recognize and be reminded that He shall come again. These signs are revealed in both the Old and the New Testament:

a. Signs of the last times in the physical world are those which are in the universe itself, signs in the sun, the moon, and the stars, in the planets and constellations (Joel 2:31; Matt. 24: 4-30; Luke 21:5-32). All decline and alteration in the manner in which the universe is made and runs is an indication that heaven and earth shall pass away (Heb. 8:13; St. L. Ed., VII:1840ff.).

b. The first of the signs in human history is the gross and fine materialism which rules the inhabitants of the world (Luke 17:26-30; 1 Thess. 5:1-3;

2 Tim. 3:1-5, 13; Jude 17—19; Matt. 7:13; 22:24).

c. Another sign is the preaching of the Gospel of the kingdom of God in all the world for a witness unto all nations (Matt. 24:14).

d. A third sign is the frequent appearance of unfaithful members within the Church, traitors to the truth of God, and antichrists without number (Matt. 24:11, 24-27; 1 Tim. 4:1 ff.; 2 Tim. 4:3, 4; 2 Thess. 2:3-11 — revelation of the Man of Lawlessness [or Sin]; 2 Pet. 2:1 ff.; 2 Pet. 3:1 ff.).

e. A fourth sign in history is the perilous times of which 2 Tim. 3:1 speaks (cf. 2 Pet. 3:3 ff.).

f. A fifth sign is the tragic lot of the Jews in the history of the world since the Crucifixion (Luke 21:32).

g. A sixth sign is the continual war cry (Matt. 24:6-8; Rev. 6:4).

h. Finally, the fact that men living in the very last times will not read the signs or, having read them, refuse to heed them is a sign of the last times (2 Peter 3). These and other signs point to the end of the world.

2. *Return of Christ.* It is a clear doctrine of Holy Scripture that the return of Christ will coincide with the end of the world (2 Pet. 3:7; 2 Tim. 4:1). The passages of Scripture do not permit separation in time of these two major events. The coming of Christ will be a visible coming (Acts 1:11; Matt. 24:27, 30; Luke 17:24) in the fullness of His divine glory and majesty and in the company of all His holy angels (Matt. 25:31; Luke 9:26). The return will be sudden and, despite all signs pointing to His return, almost completely unexpected (Luke 21:35; 17:24; 1 Thess. 5:2-4). The Lord's return will serve these purposes: a) to bring to life again all those who are in their graves (John 5:28, 29); b) to transform suddenly the bodies of the believers; c) to hold open and public Judgment over the human race; and d) to carry out the verdict of the Judgment. The end of the world and Christ's return will take place at a time set in eternity but unknown to men (Matt. 24:36, 42; Mark 13:32; Luke 12:40; Acts 1:7). The fact of Christ's return is emphasized by the Bible over against scoffers (2 Pet. 3:3, 4) and the forgetfulness of believers (Mark 13:37; Matt. 24:42). See *Millennium.*

3. *The end of the world* will coincide with Christ's coming. The world which God created (Gen. 1:1) shall "pass away" (Luke 21:33; Heb. 1:10-12;

Ps. 102:26-28. Cf. 1 Cor. 7:31; 1 John 2:17). The Bible says that the earth and the works therein "shall be burned up" (2 Pet. 3:10). Lutheran dogmaticians are divided with respect to the manner in which this is to occur. Some teach a total destruction of the world (annihilation; Gerhard, Quenstedt, Calov, and others), while others (Luther, Brenz) hold that only the form of this world as it appears now will pass (cf. Rom. 8:21).

4. *The Resurrection.* The resurrection of the body is an essential point in the creed of Christendom. This resurrection of all mankind is to take place immediately upon the return of our Lord Jesus Christ and the end of the world (Matt. 25:31, 32). Scripture knows of no lapse of time between Christ's return and the resurrection. Nor is the resurrection a long process, or even one including interruptions (cf. John 5:25; 6:40; 1 Thess. 4:16). The resurrection is to be universal (2 Cor. 5:10; Rev. 20:12), but there will be two distinct classes. Those who have done evil will arise to damnation (John 5:29; Matt. 25:41; Dan. 12:2). Those who fall asleep in Jesus will rise with a spiritual body (1 Cor. 15:44) fashioned like unto Christ's glorious body (Phil. 3:21; Luke 24:39; 1 Cor. 15:51, 52). While the body is sown in corruption, it will be raised in incorruption (1 Cor. 15:42); sown in dishonor, it will be raised in glory (1 Cor. 15:43); sown in weakness, it will be raised in power (1 Cor. 15:43); sown a natural body, it will be raised a spiritual body (1 Cor. 15:45).

5. *Final Judgment.* The Scriptures declare that there is to be a final Judgment (Matt. 25:31-33; 2 Cor. 5:10). This Judgment does not decide the question of eternal life or eternal death. That was determined already in the world (conversion or non-conversion, John 3:18). Christ at the final Judgment will pronounce sentence. There will be no need of questions of evidence or law, but the Judge, who knows all things, will proceed at once to pronounce sentence by judicial and final separation. Since faith and unbelief are invisible to created eyes, the outward fruits of both will be made to bear witness. "The works of love, by which the faith of the elect was active, will be brought forward, not by the righteous, to prove their righteousness, but by the Judge, to prove His righteousness, the righteousness of His Judgment. In like manner the failure of the unbelievers to bring the fruits of true faith, their

uncharitable conduct toward their fellow men, will also be called to witness to the unbelief which was in them and by which they not only failed to do good works, but also rejected the saving grace of God in Christ Jesus and are therefore justly condemned. Matthew 25." (ALG.) The Judge will award to the believers the Kingdom prepared for them by Himself, not as a remuneration, but as an inheritance (Gal. 3:26). The wicked works of the wicked will testify that, having done the works of their father, they are of their father, the devil (John 8:41, 44); and it is meet and right that they should share his abode. The condemned shall go away into everlasting punishment, and the righteous into eternal life (Matt. 25). C. f. WFW, "The Doctrine of Last Things," *Abiding Word* (I:544—60); JTM, *Dogmatics.*

Standard Dogmatics *; references under *Hereafter;* Paul Althaus, *Die Letzten Dinge,* Bertelsmann, Guetersloh, 1949 (5th ed.); L. Fuerbringer, "Leading Thoughts on Eschatology in the Epistles to the Thessalonians," *CTM,* XIII: 183—92; 265—73; 320—29; 401—14; 511—18; 591—603; 641—54; W. F. Wolbrecht, "The Doctrine of the Last Things," *Abiding Word,* CPH, 1946 (I:544—60. Gives extensive references to Mo. Syn. Essays); G. F. Hall, "Luther's Eschatology," *Aug. Theol. Quart.,* XXIII:1 ff.; Th. Kliefoth, *Christliche Eschatologie,* Leipzig, 1885; K. Stange, *Das Ende aller Dinge,* 1930; J. A. Seiss, *Last Times,* Philadelphia, 1878; W. F. Beck, "I Believe in the Resurrection of the Body," *CTM,* XVI:153—69.

Lateran Council IV *(Ecumenical).* The name Lateran is derived from the basilica of St. John Lateran in Rome, properly speaking, the cathedral of the Roman diocese, where the Pope is actually Bishop of Rome; St. Peter's is the seat of his alleged universal jurisdiction. The Fourth Lateran Council is the Twelfth Ecumenical, according to Roman Catholic reckoning; it was held in 1215, being attended by 412 bishops and 800 abbots and priors. Its resolutions are notable as containing the plans for the recovery of the Holy Land (see *Crusades)* and the general improvement of the Church; this included the condemnations of the Cathari * and Albigenses.* At this Lateran council the term *transubstantiation* was officially sanctioned, and the requirement of annual confession was codified.

Lateran Council V. (For derivation of the name "Lateran" see preceding article.) The Eighteenth Ecumenical Council, according to Roman Catholic reckoning, under Julius II and Leo X (1512—17), with an average attendance of 100—150 members. At this council the Pragmatic Sanction, according to which the emperor issued a rescript limiting the power of the Pope, especially with reference to the Gallican Church, was declared abolished, so that the Pope could not be bound by the resolutions of the Council of Basel, which declared the council's superiority to the Pope. This was done by the acceptance of the bull of Leo X known as *Pater Aeternus,* which declared that the Popes had always been superior to the councils. The council also ordered a strict censorship of books and confirmed the bull *Unam Sanctam.**

Latermann, Johann. B. 1620; professor at Koenigsberg, general superintendent at Derenburg; suspended because of immoral conduct; d. as an Austrian chaplain in 1662; a disciple of Calixt and originator of the modern type of synergism (Latermannianism): Man converts himself by making the right use of new spiritual powers communicated to him by God.

Latimer, Hugh (ca. 1490—1555). Martyr bishop; b. in Leicestershire; embraced Protestantism; bishop of Worcester 1535; lost King Henry's favor; Cranmer's *confidant* under King Edward; burned with Ridley, at Oxford, under Queen Mary.

Latin America. See *Central America; South America.*

Latin Bible Versions. See *Bible Versions,* J.

Latin Christianity. The beliefs and practices developed under the Papacy in Latin countries.

Latitudinarians. A name given to those churchmen in England who in the 17th century professed indifference to what they considered small matters in dispute between the Puritans and High Churchmen, laid more stress on classical philosophy than on Christian theology, and showed a spirit of tolerance toward dissenters. They at once took for their basis science and toleration. The general basis of Christian communion was to be found, they claimed, in a common recognition of the great realities of Christian thought and life, not in any outward adherence to a definite ecclesiastical system. Also called "Cambridge Arminians."

Latria, Dulia, Hyperdulia. Roman theologians distinguish three kinds of cultus: *latria*, the supreme honor due only to God; *dulia*, the honor given angels and saints; *hyperdulia*, the veneration accorded the Virgin Mary. They teach that these degrees of honor apply also to images and relics (therefore *latria* to the cross and images of Christ), the honor being, in each case, referred to the prototype. These distinctions do not alter the facts regarding the idolatrous practices of Rome (see *Saints, Worship of; Mariolatry; Images; Relics*); nor is anything gained by the sweeping assertion of the *Catholic Encyclopedia:* "Catholics, even the most unlearned, are in no peril of confounding the adoration due to God with the religious honor given to any finite creature, even when the word 'worship,' owing to the poverty of our language, is applied to both."

Latter Day Saints (Mormons). a. The Mormon Church was founded Apr. 6, 1830, by Joseph Smith (1805 to 1844). Being of an introspective nature and given to strong fantasies, Smith insisted that he was vouchsafed visions, during one of which his room was flooded with light and a heavenly messenger appeared to him, declaring that he was the angel Moroni sent by God and calling upon him to restore the Gospel in its fullness preparatory to the second coming of the Messiah. He was also informed that there was a written record on gold plates, giving an account of the former inhabitants of the North American continent. These plates Joseph Smith claimed to have interpreted by means of two stones in silver bows known as Urim and Thummin, which had also been buried in the hill Cumorah in northern New York in A. D. 420. Each plate of the record, according to Joseph Smith, was six inches wide and eight inches long and was filled with engraving in Egyptian characters, bound together in a volume, the book being something near six inches in thickness, a part of it being sealed. "The unsealed portion of the plates was translated, and the whole was again taken charge of by the angel." The part translated was published in 1830 as the *Book of Mormon* purporting to be an abridgment of the records of his forefathers made by the prophet Mormon, father of Moroni.

b. The Church was organized at Fayette, Seneca Co., N. Y., Smith himself having first been ordained to the Aaronic priesthood by John the Baptist and then to the apostleship by the Apostles Peter, James, and John. In 1831 the new church body numbered several hundred souls and moved to Kirkland, Ohio, while some of the members settled in Jackson Co., Mo., where they hoped to build the city of Zion with a magnificent temple. But they were driven out of Jackson Co., Mo., in 1833, and this persecution was one of the chief factors in directing the attention of fanatically inclined people to the new sect. Five years later Governor Boggs of Missouri issued an order against the Mormons in order to have them exterminated, and they were driven out of that State. They moved to Illinois, where, between 1838 and 1840, they had founded the city of Nauvoo, over which Smith had extraordinary civil and military authority. The city grew, soon numbering 2,100 houses, with a temple whose plans Smith claimed to have received from heaven. But there was some discontent, and the "prophet" was accused of immoralities and other misdeeds. Matters had reached such a state that civil war was imminent. Smith was induced to surrender and to go to Carthage, Ill. On June 27, 1844, a mob attacked the jail, overpowered the guard, killed Smith and his brother Hyrum, and wounded others of the prophet's party. — But the death of Smith did not mean the death of Mormonism. On the contrary, Brigham Young (1801—77), the man who now assumed the leadership of the sect, really made the Mormon Church the powerful organization which it is today. When the persecution once more became fierce, in 1846, the entire organization proceeded to move. Traveling by easy stages, they reached the Missouri River near the present site of Omaha and there went into winter quarters. An advance company of pioneers, under the leadership of Brigham Young, set out for the valley of the Great Salt Lake, in search of a new home far from the haunts of the "infidels." The result was the founding of Salt Lake City and the setting up of the provisional government of the State of Deseret. Other settlements were formed until they were scattered over the face of the entire region.

c. In 1850 the Territory of Utah was created and Brigham Young appointed governor, being reappointed in 1854, when Colonel Steptoe declined to accept the appointment for himself. Somewhat later, due to a misleading report, a detachment of 2,500 men under Alfred Cummings was sent to Utah, and matters assumed a threatening aspect, for the Mormons harassed and delayed the soldiers and prepared to lay waste their homes and lands rather than have them occupied by outsiders. But the difficulty was adjusted through the good offices of a peace commission. The army, under General Johnston, entered Salt Lake Valley in June, 1858, camping on the west side of the Jordan River, but subsequently marched to a point about forty miles south of Salt Lake City, where Camp Floyd was laid out. In 1877 Brigham Young died, and in 1880 John Taylor was elected president. He had been with Joseph Smith at Nauvoo and was shot and wounded when Smith was killed. He died in 1887, and in the same year was succeeded by Wilfred Woodruff, who, in 1890, issued his famous manifesto forbidding polygamy.

d. The Mormons have thirteen Articles of Faith:

1. We believe in God, the Eternal Father, and in His Son, Jesus Christ, and in the Holy Ghost. 2. We believe that men will be punished for their own sins and not for Adam's transgression. 3. We believe that through the atonement of Christ all mankind may be saved by obedience to the laws and ordinances of the Gospel. 4. We believe that these ordinances are: First, faith in the Lord Jesus Christ; second, repentance; third, baptism by immersion for the remission of sins; fourth, laying on of hands for the gift of the Holy Ghost. 5. We believe that a man must be called of God, by "prophecy and by the laying on of hands by those who are in authority, to preach the Gospel and administer the ordinances thereof." 6. We believe in the same organization that existed in the primitive Church, viz., apostles, prophets, pastors, teachers, evangelists, etc. 7. We believe in the gift of tongues, prophecy, revelation, visions, healing, interpretation of tongues, etc. 8. We believe the Bible to be the Word of God, as far as it is translated correctly; we also believe the Book of Mormon to be the Word of God. 9. We believe all that God has revealed, all that He does now reveal, and we believe that He will yet reveal many great and important things pertaining to the kingdom of God. 10. We believe in the literal gathering of Israel and in the restoration of the Ten Tribes; that Zion will be built upon this continent; that Christ will reign personally upon the earth; and that the earth will be renewed and receive its paradisiacal glory. 11. We claim the privilege of worshiping Almighty God according to the dictates of our conscience and allow all men the same privilege, let them worship how, where, or what they may. 12. We believe in being subject to kings, presidents, rulers, and magistrates, in obeying, honoring, and sustaining the law. 13. We believe in being honest, true, chaste, benevolent, virtuous, and in doing good to all men.

e. Concerning the origin of the Book of Mormon, Monson wrote: "One Solomon Spaulding (d. 1816) amused himself, after retiring from the ministry, by writing a book, in Biblical style, purporting to be the history of the peopling of America by the ten lost tribes of Israel. This manuscript Joseph Smith secured, and after altering it a little here and there (without, however, improving its style, for he was very poorly educated), he published it in 1830 under the name of the Book of Mormon and proclaimed it to be of equal authority with the Bible. . . . The plates are said to have been hidden in a hill about A. D. 420. Yet the inscriptions mention Calvinism, Universalism, Methodism, Millenarianism, and Roman Catholicism! Though polygamy is one of the main tenets of Mormonism, still it is condemned in the Book of Mormon. It was an afterthought and was revealed to the Church later, Jan. 12, 1843." (The Difference.)

f. The polygamy practiced by Mormons for about a half century was made more plausible by the claim that, as a result, many more faithful would get to heaven. It was stated that a woman could have the full benefit of hierarchal ordinance if she was "sealed" to one of the faithful, thereby becoming his "spiritual wife." The rites practiced in this connection as well as others of similar kind took place in the "temples" of the Mormons, to which no outsider could gain admittance. With regard to the so-called "baptism for the dead" a revelation of Joseph Smith stated that such as had been ordained for salvation, but had died without a knowledge of the Gospel should thus be prepared for eternal bliss.

g. The Latter Day Saints are divided into six denominations:

1. The Church of Jesus Christ of

Latter Day Saints (Salt Lake City group, 1,147,157 members in 1952).

2. *The Reorganized Church of Jesus Christ of Latter Day Saints* (Independence, Mo., group; opposed bigamy of Brigham Young; 126,453 members).

3. *Church of Christ* (hold the "Temple Lot" in Illinois which is to be the center of "the new land of Zion"; 2,225 members).

4. *Church of Jesus Christ* (founded by Wm. Bickerton at Greenock, Pa., 1862; opposed baptism for dead, polygamy; 1,550 members).

5. *Church of Jesus Christ* (founded by James J. Strang after Smith's death; claimed to have a book missed by Smith, "Book of the Law of the Lord"; about 120 members).

6. *Church of Jesus Christ* (founded by Alpheus Cutler; community of goods; 24 members). See *Religious Bodies (U. S.), Bibliography.*

Latvia. The land of the Letts, Indo-Germanic in blood and language, is the name now given to the former Russian provinces of Kurland and Livonia and parts of Vitebsk. Christianity came ca. 1180 with Meinhard, who built the first church at Uexkuell, or Ikeskola, and became the first bishop in 1186. Though he is called "the Apostle of Livonia," the country soon fell back into paganism. Berthold of Loccum followed, but fell in battle against the Livlanders in 1198. Ca. 1200 Albrecht of Bremen came with twenty-three shiploads of crusaders, founded Riga, became bishop, captured Dorpat in 1224, and made his brother Herman bishop. — Lutheranism was brought in early by Knoepken of Kuestrin, and Tegetmeier of Hamburg, helped by Albrecht of Brandenburg, Grandmaster of the German Order, who became a Lutheran in 1525 and made his country a secular duchy. Melchior Hoffmann preached Lutheranism at Dorpat. Gustavus Adolphus signed the charter of the University of Dorpat on June 30, 1632, in the camp at Nuernberg. Herman Samson labored much for the faith. Czar Paul I restored the "Sanctuary of Science" in 1802, and in 1817 the new curator, Count Karl Lieven, swept out Rationalism and restored a better Lutheranism. During the nineteenth century the Lutheran Church in the Baltic provinces was grievously oppressed by the Orthodox Church of Russia. — In 1919 Latvia became a republic. In the Bolshevik persecution of 1919 at least twenty-four Lutheran pastors of Latvia and Estonia were murdered. At the time of Latvia's annexation to Russia about two thirds of the total population (2,950,000) were Lutheran, one third Catholic, besides 200,000 Greek Orthodox Letts and a sprinkling of Baptists, Adventists, and others. The Lutheran Church was organized with two synods, one of the Germans and the other of the Letts, each having its bishop. The Catholics, through political intrigues, gained possession of the Lutheran St. Jacobi Church in Riga. The Russians occupied Latvia in June, 1940, and received it into the Soviet Union by decree on Aug. 5, 1940. See *Missions, Bibliography.*

Laud, William (1573—1645). Archbishop of Canterbury; b. at Reading; priest 1601; detested Puritanism and advocated High Churchmanship; rose rapidly by learning and ability; became primate 1633; failed to force Ritualism on the Scots; persecuted Non-conformists in England; was committed to the Tower 1641 and beheaded on Tower Hill 1645.

Lauds. A service of the canonical hours, usually combined with that of matins in both the Greek and the Roman Catholic churches, although sometimes given an independent position, just about at dawn.

Laurenti, Laurentius (1660—1722). B. at Husum, June 8, 1660, educated at Rostock, and in music at Kiel. He was appointed cantor and director of the music at the Lutheran Cathedral Church in Bremen. He is one of the best hymn writers of the Pietistic school. His hymns are based on the pericopes of the church year, in their application to the Christian's life. His 148 hymns were published in *Evangelia Melodica*, 1700.

Laurentius. Deacon of the church of Rome, suffered martyrdom under Valerian (253—60). Commanded by the greedy magistrate to show him the treasures of the church, he is said to have pointed to the sick and needy as constituting the congregation's wealth. For this he was slowly roasted to death. The story is first told by Ambrose, a hundred years after the event, and may therefore not be above suspicion.

Lauterbach, Richard (1502—69). Friend of Luther; deacon at Lessing, Wittenberg; superintendent at Pavia; prominent in Luther's *Table Talks.* *

Lauxmann, Richard (1834—90). German pastor and hymnologist; active in *Innere Mission;* edited Koch's *Geschichte des Kirchenlieds und Kirchengesangs* (added 8th volume); hymn writer.

Lavater, Johann Caspar (1741 to 1801). Swiss theologian, pioneer in personal counseling and pastoral ministry; contributed to decline of rationalism and reaction toward idealism.

Law, Canon. See *Canon Law.*

Law (eternal, divine, natural, human). See *Natural Law; Law and Gospel.*

Law, The Divine. See *Decalog; Grace, Means of,* II, 1 ff.; *Law and Gospel.*

Law and Gospel. The Formula of Concord (Art. V) defines the Law as follows: "The Law is properly a divine doctrine in which the righteous, immutable will of God is revealed, what is to be the quality of man in his nature, thoughts, words, and works, in order that he may be pleasing and acceptable to God; and it threatens its transgressors with God's wrath and temporal and eternal punishments. For as Luther writes against the Law stormers: 'Everything that reproves sin is and belongs to the Law, whose peculiar office it is to reprove sin and to lead to the knowledge of sins' (Rom. 3:20; 7:7); and as unbelief is the root and wellspring of all reprehensible sins, the Law reproves unbelief also."

The same document defines the Gospel: "The Gospel is properly such a doctrine as teaches what man who has not observed the Law, and therefore is condemned by it, is to believe, namely, that Christ has expiated and made satisfaction for all sins, and has obtained and acquired for him, without merit of his, forgiveness of sins, righteousness that avails before God, and eternal life.

"But since the term 'Gospel' is not used in one and the same sense in Holy Scriptures, we believe, teach, and confess that if by the term 'Gospel' is understood the entire doctrine of Christ which He proposed in His ministry, as also did His Apostles (in which sense it is employed Mark 1:15; Acts 20:21), it is correctly said and written that the Gospel is a preaching of repentance and of the forgiveness of sins." (Epitome, V:4 ff.). There is a difference between Law and Gospel only in the narrow sense.

Law and Gospel are alike in that both are God's Word, divine doctrines, to be applied to people everywhere (including Christians), and found in both the Old and the New Testament. Law and Gospel do not contradict each other.

Nevertheless, there is a difference between Law and Gospel (Rom. 10:4; Gal. 3:24; Zech. 11:7; Ezek. 13:9; Matt. 13:52; Luke 12:42). This distinction was put to use in the Bible (2 Sam. 12:13; Luke 7:36-50; Acts 2:37-39; 16:27-31; 1 Cor. 5:1-5; 2 Cor. 2:6-8).

Differences: a) While the Law was written into the heart of man (Rom. 2:14, 15), the Gospel is not known by nature but was revealed through Jesus and His Word. b) The Law contains commandments of what men are to do and not do; the Gospel reveals what God has done for our salvation. c) The Law promises eternal life conditionally; the Gospel promises it freely. d) The Law demands perfect fulfillment and pronounces curses and threats if there is no perfect fulfillment (Gal. 3:10); the Gospel has only promises and comforting assurances. e) The purpose of the Law is to serve as a curb (check coarse outbursts of sin), mirror (reveals sin — Rom. 3:20), rule (shows regenerate — who loves, and wants to serve, God and his fellow men — what good works are — F. of C., VI); the purpose of the Gospel is to forgive sins, give heaven and salvation as a free gift.

Law and Gospel are both operative in conversion (see *Contrition; Conversion*). The very nature of justification, however, excludes the Law and leaves the Gospel as the only means whereby God justifies the sinner (see *Justification*). The incentive power of the Gospel and the criterion of the Law are operative in sanctification (see *Sanctification; Good Works*).

The pastor must observe the use of Law and Gospel in his ministry and rightly divide the Word of Truth. C. f. WFG, *Abiding Word,* CPH, 1946 (I:105—23).

Standard Dogmatics *; C. F. W. Walther, *Gesetz und Evangelium,* 1897 (English edition by W. H. T. Dau. Pub. by CPH); W. Geihsler, "The Law and the Gospel," *Abiding Word,* CPH, 1946 (I:105—23. Extensive bibliography); W. Elert, "Gesetz und Zorn Gottes," *Morphologie des Luthertums,* Beck, Munich, 1931 (I:31—39); see references under *Decalog.*

Law, William (1686—1761). English theologian; because he refused the oath of allegiance to George I, he lost his position and lived an ascetic life devoted to charity. He was a genuine mystic. His *Serious Call to a Devout and Holy Life* has had wide influence.

Lay Abbot. A layman who, in recognition of services, has been given charge of an abbey.

Lay Baptism. Since the Office of the Keys is given to all Christians, the laymen have all rights and powers in the Church. By divine arrangement the pastor performs the ministry of the Word in the name of the congregation. In case of emergency, however, laymen perform such rites as Baptism (and other acts of the ministry). Water is applied to the subject, and the words "I baptize thee in the name of the Father and of the Son and of the Holy Ghost" are spoken.

Lay Brother (Sister). One who resides in a Roman Catholic monastery and obeys its rules but does not take holy orders.

Laying On of Hands. A ceremony of greatest antiquity, being mentioned frequently both in the Old Testament (for blessing, consecration, and healing) and in the New, where it is spoken of in the case of Christ and the Apostles in acts of blessing and of healing and in official acts of the public ministry, especially Baptism, confirmation, and ordination. The Roman Catholic doctrine makes the laying on of hands a sacrament by which the fitness for an office is conferred. Of the laying on of hands in ordination the AC states that if Holy Orders be understood as referring to the ministry of teaching the Gospel and administering the Sacraments, "we are not unwilling to call the laying on of hands a sacrament" (XIII:12, Triglot, p. 310).

Laymen's Activity in the Lutheran Church. The congregational polity of Lutheran churches directs the chief energies of men into channels of parish administration. Membership assemblies, boards of deacons, trustees, etc., provide outlet for time and capacity. Many parishes, in addition, organize groups of men for social and recreational purposes. These groups occasionally foster projects or direct service to the congregational budget or program of evangelism. They likewise become the nucleus for the organization of groups covering the entire church body. With the improvement in communications, these groups provide opportunity for the fellowship of their members on a national scale and for application to projects of church-wide significance. The national groups of the United Lutheran Church, American Lutheran Church, Augustana Synod, and Evangelical Lutheran Church of America are termed Brotherhoods. The United Danish Lutheran Church has an Association of Lutheran Brotherhoods. The Missouri Synod has the Lutheran Laymen's League. All groups are active in projects supporting youth endeavors, such as the Boy Scout program, scholarships at Lutheran colleges, and support of the parish youth program. They supply national directors with programs of stimulus for the parish group. The Missouri Synod organization promotes the Lutheran Hour, the most extensive broadcasting program in radio. The Brotherhoods have a national federation for mutual stimulus and co-ordination. Unofficial groups are at present supporting a program on intersynodical acquaintance and contact. RRC

Laymen's Missionary Movement. Organized in the chapel of the Fifth Avenue Presbyterian Church, New York City, Nov. 15, 1906, at a laymen's meeting held in commemoration of the centennial of the celebrated "Haystack Prayer Meeting," which inaugurated new interest in the whole work of foreign missions. The movement was heartily endorsed the next year by the annual conference of foreign mission boards of the United States and Canada. The plan of the movement is not to send out missionaries nor to administer missionary funds, but only to co-operate in the enlargement of the foreign mission work carried on by the various affiliated churches. Missionary campaigns were conducted and subcommittees appointed, and the results have been gratifying in stimulating giving for missionary purposes.

Laynez, Diego. See *Lainez, Diego.*

Layritz, Friedrich (1808—59). Studied theology at Erlangen; pastor at Hirschlach; greatly interested in hymnology and liturgics; published *Kern des deutschen Kirchengesangs,* in which he strongly advocated the restoration of the original form of the German rhythmical choral, his ideas being embodied in the *Choralbuch* named after him; published also *Liturgie eines vollstaendigen Hauptgottesdienstes nach lutherischem Typus* and instructions for Psalm chanting in the second edition of Loehe's *Agenda.*

Lazarists (*Congregation of the Mission*). A congregation of secular priests, founded by Vincent de Paul, 1625, to preach to the poor country people of France, who suffered from the ignorance and neglect of their pastors. Lazarists still prefer to be free to travel and accept parishes with regret. The congregation was hard hit by the French Revolution, many members being executed and many establishments destroyed. Their largest mission is in China. They have also been especially active in the American West, with headquarters at Perryville, Mo., and St. Louis (Kenrick Seminary).

Lea, Henry Charles (1825—1909). Ed. privately; member of the publishing house of Lea and Blanchard in Philadelphia; known for his studies of medieval history, especially those pertaining to the Inquisition. See references under *Inquisition*.

Leade, Jane (1623—1704). Founder of the *Philadelphia Society*, a group of religious mystics and enthusiasts; subject to mystical experiences, attacks, and visions.

League and Covenant, The Solemn. An agreement by Scotland and England aiming at the establishment of Presbyterianism in both countries. See *Presbyterian Confessions*, 1.

League, German Catholic (1609). A union of Catholic princes in Germany for the defense of Roman Catholicism against the Protestant Union (1608).

Learning, Types of. See *Christian Teaching*, D.

Lebanon. Area: 43,000 sq. mi.; population: 1,500,000. For church work see *Palestine*.

Lechler, Gotthard Victor (1811—88). Prof. at Leipzig; loyal to the Lutheran Confessions; especially interested in defending the Book of Acts; important works: *Die Geschichte des englischen Deismus; Apostolisches und nachapostolisches Zeitalter; Wiclif und die Vorgeschichte der Reformation.*

Lechner, Leonhard (1550—1606). A pupil of di Lasso and a composer of the Lutheran Church whose works are still quite unknown in America. His compositions reveal expert polyphonic craftsmanship, profound textual interpretation, and the vitalizing influence of the Italian madrigal. Lechner's *Passion According to St. John* as well as

his *Gespräche über Leben und Tod* are among his more noteworthy works.

Le Clerc. See *Arminianism.*

Lectern. See *Church Furniture*, 1.

Lection, Lectionary. See *Pericope.*

Lector. See *Hierarchy.*

Lee, Ann. See *Shakers.*

Leeson, Jane Eliza (1807—82). A prolific poetess, who published a number of collections of hymns, also paraphrases and translations; wrote: "Gracious Savior, Gentle Shepherd"; "Songs of Glory Fill the Sky," and others.

Legacies. See *Finances in the Church*, 7.

Legalism. a) Living according to laws; b) seeking salvation through works rather than grace; c) undue emphasis upon external form without proper realization of the inner spirit; d) insisting on strict application of church rules without proper regard to the specific circumstances in a given situation. See *Luther, Chief Writings of*, 3.

Legates. Emissaries representing the Pope. Legates *a latere* are the highest form of legation, being a cardinal sent on matters of international importance (representatives at Eucharistic Congresses are usually designated simply papal legate). Next in rank are *nuncios* who represent the Pope at foreign governments and handle affairs between Apostolic See and states (usually archbishops, titular or with a see). *Internuncios*, of lower rank than nuncios, represent the Pope at smaller states. *Apostolic delegates* are sent to countries which do not maintain diplomatic relations with the Vatican and watch over conditions of the Roman Church in such countries. *Vicar-apostolic*, usually a titular bishop, is appointed by the Pope for missionary regions where the ordinary hierarchy is not established.

Legion of Christ. See *Veterans' Organizations.*

Legislation on Christian Education. See *Christian Education*, J.

Lehmann, Wm. F. B. Oct. 16, 1820, in Markkraenigen, Wuerttemberg; came to America in 1824; prelim. ed. at Philadelphia; grad. at Theological Sem. at Columbus, Ohio, 1839; pastor, 1840—46; prof. at Capital University, Columbus, Ohio; its president for thirty-four years; several terms president of the

Synodical Conference, but opposed to "Missouri's" influence; "the most influential man in the Ohio Synod"; editor of *Luth. Kirchenzeitung*, 1859—80; also editor of *Lutheran Standard;* pastor of Trinity Church, Columbus; pres. of Ohio Synod. D. Nov. 28, 1880.

Lehr, Leopold Franz Friedrich, (1709—44). Studied at Jena and Halle, tutor at Orphanage in Halle; later at Koethen, where he became diaconus in 1740; wrote: "Mein Heiland nimmt die Suender an."

Leibniz (*Leibnitz*), **Gottfried Wilhelm von.** Noted German polyhistor; b. 1646 in Leipzig; many years official at Hanoverian court; d. 1716 in Hanover. Eminent as mathematician, philosopher, statesman, jurist, theologian. His system of philosophy purposes to be a Christian philosophy, uniting Christianity and a mechanical explanation of nature. The universe is made up of "monads," units endowed with physical and psychical properties, God being the Supreme Monad. He endeavored to unite Protestant and Roman, also Lutheran and Reformed churches. Main work, *Essais de Théodicée.*

Leighton, Robert (1611—84). Scottish prelate; Londoner; Presbyterian minister; divinity professor; Edinburgh; Archbishop (Anglican) of Glasgow 1670; resigned because unable to prevent harsh treatment of Presbyterians; author.

Leipzig, Colloquy at. See *Reformed Confessions*, D 3.

Leipzig Debate of 1519. A famous debate held at the instigation of Johann Eck, who issued a challenge to Karlstadt, but in reality attacked the position taken by Luther in his famous Ninety-five Theses. The disputants from June 27 to July 3 were Eck and Karlstadt, from July 4 to 13 Eck and Luther, the latter being driven into Scripture by the attacks of Eck, so that he even declared that councils could err, Holy Scripture alone being infallible. The debate marked the first climax in Luther's theological development. W. H. T. Dau, *The Leipzig Debate in 1519*, CPH, 1919.

Leipzig Interim. See *Lutheran Confessions*, C 1.

Leland, John (1754—1841). Preached at age of twenty; 1776—90 in Virginia, after that in Massachusetts; erratic disposition; of hymns ascribed to him

best-known is: "The Day Is Past and Gone."

Lemme, Ludwig (1847—1929). Ev. theologian; prof. in Breslau, Bonn, and Heidelberg. In theology he has held a positive position similar to that of Dorner and Rothe. He wrote extensively on doctrine, philosophy, and ethics.

Lenker, John N. B. Sunbury, Pa., Nov. 28, 1858; ed. Wittenberg College, Springfield, Ohio; Hamma Div. School; 1881 grad.; D. D. 1893; studied Univ. of Leipzig, Germany, 1882; ordained 1880; pastor Grand Island, Nebr., 1882—86; with Bd. of Christian Extension of Gen. Synod 1886—94; professor at Trinity Sem., Blair, Nebr., 1900—04; settled in Minneapolis, Minn., 1904; founder of Luther Press; founder and editor *Northern Review;* pres. Gen. Luth. Missionary Conf. Wrote: *Lutherans in All Lands; Lutherans in All Lands, Supplement; Die Lutherische Kirche der Welt; Three-Language Education.* Translator of Luther's works into English (20 vols.). D. May 16, 1929.

Lenski, Rich. C. H. Prominent theologian of Lutheran Ohio Synod; b. Greifenberg, Prussia, Sept. 14, 1864; graduated from Columbus Seminary 1887; held pastorates in Baltimore, Trenton, Springfield, and Anna, Ohio, 1887—1911; then became professor of Dogmatics and Homiletics at Columbus; author of homiletic expositions on the Eisenach Gospels and Epistles; *New Gospel Selections; St. Paul; The Active Church-member;* editor of the *Kirchenzeitung* till 1925. Wrote: *Interpretations* on books of New Testament; *Ancient Church Epistle Selections; St. Paul's Epistle to the Romans.* D. in 1936.

Lent. See *Church Year.*

Leo the Great. See *Popes*, 2.

Leo X. See *Popes*, 20.

Leo XIII. See *Popes*, 29.

Leonardo da Vinci (1452—1519). A universal genius in the plastic and pictorial arts; in painting he excelled in the disposition of light and shadow, founding new laws of composition and using also the hands as a psychological commentary; among his pictures are his "Baptism of Christ" and "The Resurrection of Christ," but above all his "Last Supper," which has been called "the grandest monument of religious art."

Leprosy. A bacterial disease, the chief characteristic of which is the replacement of normal tissue by diseased cells similar to those of tuberculosis.

The removal of leprosy is spoken of in the New Testament with one exception (Luke 17:15) as a cleansing. The fact that early Greek physicians used the word *lepra* (found in LXX and NT) for psoriasis caused discussion of the nature of the disease of the Old Testament. Leprosy was known in India in 1400 B.C. and is also undoubtedly referred to in the Egyptian papyrus Ebers (1550 B.C.). Some of the passages of the Old Testament which allude to the disease and give some symptoms are: Ex. 4:6; 7:10-13; Num. 12:10 ff.; Leviticus 13; 2 Kings 5:27; 15:5; 2 Chron. 26:23; 2 Sam. 3:29. The Old Testament also speaks of leprosy in garments (Lev. 13:47 ff.) and leprosy in houses (Lev. 14:34 ff.).

Leproseries were early established for those who suffered from this disease. Those who were not segregated were banished into desert and outlying districts. In the Early Church efforts were occasionally made to alleviate the condition of the victims. Also in the Middle Ages we find efforts in this direction.

It is estimated (1952) that there are between 2,000,000 and 7,000,000 lepers in the world, most of them being in India, China, and Central Africa. Much progress was made since the beginning of the 20th century in the treatment of leprosy (injections of sodium salts of chaulmoogra or sodium hydrocarpate and other treatments). Leprosy has been found less contagious than formerly believed, and segregation is considered necessary only during infective stages. This, together with the effectiveness of early treatment, has lessened the terribleness of the scourge.

Missions to lepers have been conducted by various societies, prominent among them being the American Missions to Lepers.

Lessing, Gotthold Ephraim. B. 1729 at Kamenz, Saxony, d. 1781 at Brunswick; since 1770 librarian at Wolfenbuettel; a German critic and dramatist, one of the most brilliant lights of the classical period of his country's literature; in theology, a prominent furtherer of the movement known as the *Enlightenment.** Though criticizing shallowness and philistinism of current rationalistic theology, he became one of the greatest promoters of rationalism in its worst form, especially by publishing the *Wolfenbuetteler Fragmente*. These were posthumous treatises by H. S. Reimarus of Hamburg, a freethinker, who subjected Bible and Christianity to a destructive criticism from the deistic standpoint, claiming that miracles are impossible and that Jesus and His Apostles were impostors. In the ensuing controversy, Lessing defended this vaunting irreligion, exerting himself to bring ridicule especially on Hauptpastor Goeze of Hamburg, the earnest and zealous upholder of Holy Scripture and the Lutheran Confessions. While residing at Hamburg, 1767—69, he had cultivated the clergyman's friendship, whose learning and courteous manners had attracted him and by whose valuable library he had profited. But now, a few years later, things had changed. Goeze was shocked by the *Fragmente* and Lessing's advocacy of them. What distress they would bring to Christian hearts, what doubting might they instill, how will the unbelieving multitude rejoice! It was from apprehensions like these that Goeze wrote his well-meaning protests, his admonitions dictated by love, desiring to win the man of whom he thought so much. The tone and style of Lessing's replies was 'diametrically opposite: trifling with holy matter, misusing his sparkling dialectics to cloak the weakness of his contentions, evading the point at issue, misrepresenting, insinuating, and even at times becoming grossly abusive. At last the Brunswick government stepped in, directing him to refrain from publishing further *Fragmente* of his series. He then resorted to his former "pulpit," the stage, and wrote *Nathan der Weise*, professedly to teach toleration; but it contained the same rationalistic views, and it was greeted with joy by enemies of the Christian truth. Lessing failed to grasp the essentials of Christianity: repentance, faith, vicarious atonement. He asserted that Christianity is merely a stage in the development of religion, which finds its culmination in a perfect natural religion. WS

See Lessing's *Erziehung des Menschengeschlechts;* the works mentioned above; alongside of Lessing's eleven *Anti-Goeze* one should read, in fairness to his admonisher: *Goezes Streitschriften gegen Lessing*, herausgegeben von Erich Schmidt, Goeschensche Verlagshandlung, Stuttgart, 1893.

Lessius, Leonard (1554—1623). Flemish Jesuit; ed. at Leyden; wrote extensively on morals; his *Theses Theologicae* (1586) caused a controversy on grace and inspiration in the Roman Catholic Church.

Lessons (Liturgical). See *Pericope*.

Letters of Obscure Men. See *Humanism, 16th Century German.*

Leusden, Johannes (1624—99). Dutch Hebraist; b. at Utrecht; highly esteemed professor of Oriental languages there; published, in collaboration with Athias, a Rabbi and printer, the Old Testament; author; d. at Utrecht.

Levellers, The. A faction with radical ideas on government and religion in Cromwell's army. They held there were two spheres of religion: 1) correct understanding of revelation (private); 2) works of love (subject to authorities).

Levirate Marriage. The arrangement of the OT whereby the widow of a man without male descendants was married by the brother and the first son of this union was reckoned as the son of the deceased (Deut. 25:5-10).

Levy-Bruhl, Lucien (1857—1939). French philosopher of the Comtian school; investigated primitive mentality.

Lex Naturalis. See *Natural Law.*

Lex talionis. The law of punishment in kind (Ex. 21:23).

Leyser, Polycarp (1552—1610). D. as pastor and professor at Wittenberg; was instrumental in restoring sound Lutheranism after crypto-Calvinism had been suppressed; after a short stay in Brunswick recalled to Wittenberg; 1594 court preacher at Dresden; joint author with Chemnitz and Gerhard of *Harmonia Evangelistarum.*

Libellatici. See *Persecutions of Christians,* 4.

Liber Pontificalis. A compilation of biographies with the alleged historical data concerning the bishops of Rome from St. Peter to the end of the seventh century. The first compilation of this name was made about the ninth century, and every edition of the *Pontifical Book* is based upon a list of Popes ending with Liberius (352—366) and an Index, which is kept up to date on the basis of history and tradition.

Liberal Catholic Church. This Church, historically related to the Dutch Jansenist Movement and the Old

Catholic Church,* was re-organized in 1915 on the syncretistic basis that all religions proceed from a common source and are of divine origin. The doctrinal system is patterned after theosophy, for this group teaches that man can develop his latent divine powers so that he will ultimately obtain mastery of the world. The Church is "Catholic" only inasmuch as it observes seven fundamental rites and the Episcopal Succession.

"Liberal" Jesus. See *Christ, Lives of.*

Liberal School of Interpretation. See *Isagogics,* 3; *Lutheran Theology after 1580,* 10.

Liberalism. Opposed to conservatism, liberalism denotes the principles and methods of those who in life, thought, politics, and religion endeavor to secure the largest measure of liberty for the individual regarding established custom and civil and divine authority. Political liberalism rapidly spread in those countries still having autocratic governments, and its fundamental idea is to secure for all citizens in a well-ordered commonwealth the greatest possible personal liberty, equal rights granted to all, special privileges to none. In theology, liberalism is the tendency which refuses to accept orthodox creeds and Scriptural teachings, but allows wide latitude with regard to religious beliefs. See *Modernism* and the references there given.

Liberia. A republic in West Africa; area, 43,000 sq. mi.; population (1952), 1,500,000. The colony was organized by the American Colonization Society (1818) for freed American Negroes. Missions by 11 societies; 29,169 communicants; 87 ordained, 392 not ordained native workers; foreign staff, 61 ordained, 167 not ordained workers.

Libertines. 1) Members of the synagog at Jerusalem; 2) an antinomian, pantheistic party existing at the time of the Reformation; 3) a political party which under the leadership of Ami Perrin opposed the moral reforms of Calvin; 4) men who indulge their appetites without restraint; 5) unrestrained freethinkers.

Liberty, Religious. See *Church and State.*

Libido. See *Lust; Psychology,* J 7.

Libri Carolini (*Carolinian Books*). A book of opinions given by theologians of Charles the Great concerning the resolutions of Nicea, 787, in matters of the Iconoclastic Controversy.*

Libya. See under Italy; about 679,358 sq. mi.; population, about 888,400 (1938). Mission work since 1889 by the North African Mission (British), with three foreign workers.

Licentiate. A term applied to ministerial candidates who were licensed but not ordained. In the early Lutheran churches of America it was common practice to license candidates and have them serve for a period of time before ordination. Ordination followed the receiving of a call. The Presbyterian Church observes the custom but regards the candidates as laymen until they are ordained.

Lichtenberg, Karl Wilhelm Franz (1816—83). Able leader of the Hannoverian Consistory; established synodical form of church government; furthered missions; introduced a new hymnbook.

Lichtenstein, Friedrich Wilhelm Jacob (1826—75). German Jewish Lutheran pastor; wrote *Lebensgeschichte des Herrn Jesu Christi.*

Lichtfreunde (or *freie Gemeinden*). German religious organizations with rationalistic tendencies, organized in opposition to the confessionalism of the Protestant state churches, under the leadership of Pastors Uhlich, Wislicenus, and others, in the forties of the 19th century, in Magdeburg, Koenigsberg, Halle, and other cities. After a decade of strenuous religious and later also political activity the movement declined, though *freie Gemeinden,* which more and more lost their religious character, maintained themselves in decreasing numbers to the 20th century.

Liddon, Henry Parry (1829—90). Anglican pulpit orator; b. at North Stoneham; priest 1853; educator; canon of St. Paul's 1870; High Churchman; biographer of Pusey; d. near Bristol; wrote: *On the Divinity of Our Lord and Savior Jesus Christ.*

Lidenius, John A. Early American-born Swedish Lutheran pastor who served at Raccoon (1756—63). See A. L. Graebner, *Gesch. der Luth. Kirche in America,* 123 ff.

Lidman, Jonas. Swedish pastor who served Lutherans on the Delaware for 11 years (1719—30). See A. L. Graebner, *Gesch. der Luth. Kirche in America,* 133 ff.

Lie. A statement or action made with the purpose of deceiving, often to the advantage of the deceiver. The Bible condemns lying in strong terms. Such as turn aside to lies (Ps. 40:4) are numbered with the wicked who go astray, speaking lies (Ps. 58:3); those who delight in lies are reckoned with the outcasts of Jehovah (Ps. 62:4); a false witness will utter lies (Prov. 14:5); a deceitful witness speaks lies (Prov. 14:25); he who speaks lies will not escape (Prov. 19:5); the wicked trust in vanity and speak lies (Is. 59:4). There are approximately fifty passages in the OT that denounce the telling of lies, and that with great emphasis and every show of loathing for him who is guilty of lying. The NT admonishes everyone to speak truth with his neighbor (Eph. 4:25).

On the basis of Scripture a lie may be defined as a conscious, deliberate falsehood, that is, one uttered in spite of better knowledge, with a cowardly, selfish, spiteful, or other evil motive, that is, with the intention of working harm to one's neighbor. This may be done in a positive manner, by making such statements as do not conform to the truth and of whose falseness the speaker is conscious. It may be done in a negative manner, by withholding such information in the possession of the person concerned as would clear up a situation and relieve someone under false suspicion. Nor is it always a matter of the mere form of words. "A person may tell the truth in such a way — with a shrug or a laugh or a peculiar emphasis — as to convey a false impression. It is a lie, however, because the purpose of the speaker is to deceive. We have known people to deceive in this way and then, when they were accused, to declare that they had spoken the precise truth. They were the worst kind of falsifiers, however, because they used the truth itself to coin a lie." (*Keyser.*)

Not every product of the imagination or every bit of fiction is a lie. No one would think of calling the fables of Aesop, the fairy tales of Grimm and Anderson, the parables of the Bible, allegories (Bunyan's *Pilgrim's Progress*), Luther's letters to Hans, lies. Doctors at times may withhold truth for the welfare of their patients. As all other sins, so lies also originate in the heart.

Truth speaking is necessary for social well-being and essential for the preservation of personal character and integrity.

Liebenzeller Mission, Wuerttemberg. Organized in Hamburg 1889; has stations in China; a branch of the China Inland Mission.

Liebestaetigkeit. See *Alms; Charities, Christian; Deaconesses; Inner Missions; Social Work.*

Liebich, Ehrenfried (1713—80). German pastor; outstanding hymn writer of the 18th century.

Liebig, George. See *Canada, Lutheranism in,* 5.

Liebner, Karl Theodor Albert (1806 to 1871). Lutheran mediating theologian. B. at Schkölen, near Naumburg; d. in Switzerland. Studied at Leipzig, Berlin, and Wittenberg (Theol. Seminary). Professor and university preacher at Göttingen, professor at Kiel; at Leipzig; court preacher and vice-president of the superior consistory of Saxony. His principal work is: *Die christliche Dogmatik aus dem christologischen Prinzip dargestellt,* 1849.

Life and Advent Union. See *Adventist Bodies,* 7.

Light and Darkness (symbolic). The Bible uses both terms not only in a physical sense (*e. g.,* Genesis 1), but many times metaphorically or symbolically. Thus it refers to God as Light, the Source of light, or as dwelling in light (Ps. 104:2; 27:1; 1 John 1:5; James 1:17; 1 Tim. 6:16; Rev. 21:23). Christ is called "the Light of the world" (John 1:4-9; 8:12; 9:5; 12:35 f.; *Trigl.* 1268). The Word of God, particularly the Gospel, is given to man to serve him as a light unto salvation (Psalm 119:105, 130; Prov. 6:23; Is. 8:20; Matt. 4:16; 2 Pet. 1:19). All believers are to function as lights in this world (Matt. 5:14-16; Luke 16:8; Eph. 5:8; Phil. 2:15; 1 Thess. 5:5; 1 Pet. 2:9). Furthermore, "light" is used figuratively to designate holiness and purity (Prov. 6:23; Is. 5:20; Rom. 13:12); spiritual illumination (2 Cor. 4:6; Eph. 5:14); the heavenly state (Is. 66:19, 20; Col. 1:12; Rev. 21:23; 22:5).

"Darkness" is used figuratively, as the direct opposite to "light" (John 3:19-21; 12:35, 36; Acts 26:18; Eph. 5:8), as a) symbolical of ignorance and spiritual blindness (Is. 9:2; John 1:5; 1 John 1:6; 2:8); b) characteristic of the powers of evil (Luke 22:58; Eph. 6:12; Col. 1:13; 1 Thess. 5:5; Rev. 16:10);

c) love of sin (Rom. 13:12, 13); d) sphere of evil deeds (Eph. 5:11); e) despair and misery of the lost, hell (Matt. 25:30); f) symbol of sorrow and distress (Joel 2:2); g) figurative of judgments (Matt. 8:12; 22:13). See Luther: (Light) VI:113 ff.; XII:299; XIII: 2461; (Darkness) IX:1187; XII:294, 1069; Indices in Kretzmann's *Pop. Com.*

JMW

Lightfoot, John (1602—75). English Hebraist; b. at Staffordshire; held various rectorates; vice-chancellor of Cambridge 1654; prebendary, 1668, at Ely (d. there); wrote: *Hours Hebrew and Talmudic* (ed. by Carpzov in Latin), etc.

Lightfoot, Joseph Barber (1828 to 1889), Anglican prelate; b. in Liverpool; priest 1858; divinity professor at Cambridge; New Testament reviser; canon of St. Paul's; bishop of Durham; d. at Hants; wrote: *Apostolic Fathers; Commentaries;* and other works.

F. W. Brooks, *Bishop Lightfoot,* Macm., 1894.

Liguori, Alfonso Maria de (1696 to 1787). One of the most influential Roman Catholic moralists; received an excellent education; became priest; founded the Redemptorist Order of mission-priests in 1732; was made bishop of Sant' Agata de' Goti in 1762, but retired in 1775; his most important work one on moral theology, in which the principles of the Jesuits are inculcated; used as the basis of moral instruction in many Roman Catholic institutions; also wrote books on pastoral and ascetic theology.

Liliencron, Rochus von (1820 to 1909). Studied jurisprudence and philology at Kiel, Berlin, and Copenhagen; professor at Jena; later editor of the Historical Commission of Munich, to collect and annotate the historical German folksongs of the Middle Ages, a task for which his studies and interest qualified him; published: *Deutsches Leben im Volkslied um 1530, Ueber Kirchenmusik und Kirchenkonzert,* etc.

Lilienthal, Theodor Christoph (1717 to 1782). Prof. and pastor at Koenigsberg; wrote a very valuable apologetic work: *Die gute Sache der in der Heiligen Schrift Alten und Neuen Testaments enhaltenen goettlichen Offenbarung,* against the Deists, the result of thirty years' labor, *Defensor Orthodoxiae Moderatissimus.*

Limbo. A name applied in Roman Catholic theology and tradition to a place where the souls of those unable, through no fault of their own, to enter heaven are supposed to be detained. The location assigned to it is the *limbus* (fringe) of hell. A distinction is made between the limbo of fathers and that of infants. In the limbo of the fathers "the souls of the saints before the coming of Christ were received, and there, without any sense of pain, upheld by the blessed hope of redemption, they enjoyed a quiet sojourn." (*Catechismus Romanus*, I: 6, 3.) In this limbo, as well as in purgatory, Christ is supposed to have appeared when He "went and preached unto the spirits in prison," (1 Pet. 3:19), and to have emptied it either at that time or when He ascended into heaven. The limbo of infants is apportioned to the souls of infants dying without Baptism. — The conditions in limbo have been much debated. One ingenious theory held that hell, purgatory, and limbo were superimposed, the fires burning with all fierceness in hell, the flames then passing through purgatory, their crests entering the limbo of infants, only the heat and smoke reaching the fathers. The accepted theory holds that there is perfect natural happiness in limbo, but no beatific vision. The *Catholic Encyclopedia* deplores the "absence of a clear, positive revelation on the subject." As a matter of fact, revelation shows both clearly and positively that limbo is pure fiction; for the Bible knows of only two places in the hereafter (Mark 16:16; Matt. 25:46).

Limborch, Philip van. See *Arminianism.*

Lindberg, Conrad Emil. B. at Jonkoping, Sweden, June 6, 1852; educated at Augustana College of the Swedish Augustana Synod and at Philadelphia; ordained, 1874; pastor in Philadelphia; 1876—79; in New York (Gustavus Adolphus), 1879—90; prof. of dogmatics at Augustana, 1890; vice-pres., 1901—10; dean, 1920—30; D. D., Muhlenberg College, Pa., 1893; LL. D., Muhlenberg College, 1910; wrote: *Apologetics; Christian Dogmatics and Notes on History of Dogma; Syllabus of Lutheran Church Polity;* chief editor *Augustana Theol. Quarterly.* D. Aug. 2, 1930.

Lindemann, Frederick. B. Jan. 12, 1851, in Baltimore, Md.; studied theology at Concordia Seminary, St. Louis; was pastor of congregations in Pittsburgh, Boston, Fort Wayne, and other cities; became professor at the Teachers'

Seminary in Addison in 1893; d. Dec. 13, 1907. Son of J. C. W. Lindemann.

Lindemann, Johann Christoph Wilhelm. B. Jan. 6, 1827, at Goettingen, Hanover. Circumstances preventing his entering college, he privately prepared for the teaching profession and in 1848 took charge of St. Paul's School at Baltimore. For a year he studied theology at the Practical Seminary, Fort Wayne, and in 1853 became assistant to President H. C. Schwan at Cleveland. In 1864 he was elected to the presidency of the Lutheran Normal at Addison, Ill. An excellent instructor and a deeply earnest man, he left his impress on his students. He was a prolific writer, edited the *Ev.-Luth. Schulblatt* (now *Lutheran Education*), and the *Lutherischer Kalender,* compiled various schoolbooks, and was the author of *Schulpraxis* (still held in high esteem), *Dr. Martin Luther als Erzieher der Jugend, Deutsche Grammatik,* and other books. D. Jan. 15, 1879.
A. C. Stellhorn, "J. C. W. Lindemann," *CHIQ*, XIV: 65—96.

Lindenau, Paul (1489—1544). Studied at Leipzig; entered Benedictine cloister; pastor at Zwickau, Werdau, Elsterberg, Neumark, and finally court preacher at Freiburg; furthered Reformation in Zwickau, Annaberg, and Meissen; opposed antinomian Schenk.

Lingard, J. (1771—1851). Distinguished Catholic historian and divine. His history of England, translated into various languages, traces the story from the Roman invasion to the year 1688. He is also the author of a translation of the New Testament.

Link, Georg (1829—1908). B. in Bavaria; studied at Concordia Seminary, Fort Wayne. A preacher of ability, he served congregations of the Missouri Synod at St. Louis, Mo., and Springfield, Ill. He wrote *Luthers Hausandacht.*

Link, John T. B. Nov. 23, 1873; grad. at Addison, Ill., 1895; prof. at Concordia Teachers College, Seward, Nebr., since 1908; Ph. D., Nebraska State Univ., 1932; wrote *Outlines in Geography; Short Course in Psysiology; Hints and Experiments in Teaching Physiology;* d. Dec. 20, 1936.

Link, Wenzeslaus (1483—1547). Studied at Wittenberg 1503; entered cloister at Waldheim 1506; on account of the farces and fables fed to the people by the drunken and lazy monks, he left for the cloister at Wittenberg; dean of the theological faculty in 1512; popular preacher at Nuernberg in 1517; zealous friend of Luther; succeeded Staupitz in 1520 as Vicar-General.

Lintner, George Ames (1796—1872). Luth. pastor in Schoharie and Cobleskill, N. Y.; opposed the New York Ministerium because he felt it to be disloyal to the Confessions, and led the movement for the founding of Hartwig Seminary.

Linus. Successor of Peter as Bishop of Rome, according to Roman Catholic lists of Popes.

Linzner, Georg. B. at Kamenz, Saxony; was private teacher in Breslau about 1680; wrote: "Meinen Jesum lass' ich nicht, denn er ist allein mein Leben."

Lions Clubs. The official name is the International Association of Lions Clubs. The organization is a civic club, founded 1918, similar in type to the noonday luncheon clubs like Rotarians and Kiwanis. Like these, the Lions Clubs seek to promote the theory and practice of good citizenship and of active interest in the moral welfare of the community, especially stressing high ethical standards in business and profession.

Lippi, Fra Filippo (1412—69). Italian painter, principally of frescoes; realistic to the point of not promoting edification, many of his characters being portraits of prominent men and women of Florence.

Lipsius, Richard Adelbert (1830 to 1892). Free-Protestant German theologian; extremely liberal; from 1871 to his death professor at Jena. Edited Apocrypha of the New Testament, etc.

Liquor, Use of. See *Intemperance.*

Liscow, Salomo (1640—89). Studied at Leipzig and Wittenberg; pastor at Otterwisch, near Lausick; later second pastor at Wurzen; prominent among hymn writers of his century; wrote: "Nun freue dich, o Christenheit"; "Schatz ueber alle Schaetze."

Liszt, Franz (1811—86). Piano virtuoso, conductor, and composer of the Romantic era. It was largely through his efforts, as through those of Paganini in the violin world, that piano virtuosity and the piano recital began to enjoy the favor they enjoy today. Liszt originated also the tone poem; he wrote twelve such works, the best-known being, perhaps, his *Les Preludes.* His

piano compositions, at one time very popular, betray an overindulgence in virtuosity, ornamentation, and sentimentalism. Likewise his masses and oratorios suffer from a conscious striving for effects and display.

Litany. From a Greek word meaning supplication, applied to the bidding prayers of the Church in general, especially the penitential hymns. Luther purified the chief litany and valued it very highly, giving it a prominent place in the liturgy.

Literal Interpretation. See *Exegesis,* 2, 4 ff.

Literary Criticism. See *Higher Criticism; Isagogics.*

Literature, Lutheran. 1. The Lutheran Reformation began as a distinctly literary movement. It was the first movement to capitalize on the invention of printing. Luther himself was the most widely read publicist of his time. His translation of the Bible standardized German expression for centuries to come. The Lutheran movement stirred both the intellectual classes and the vernacular group in Germany and the Scandinavian countries. Hence it produced a literature for professionals and a popular religious literature in the vernacular.

2. Luther's own utterance was concrete and deliberately idiomatic. His preaching was in the tradition of the folk preachers of the later fifteenth century; his polemic in the manner of current satire. The German Bible standardized a literary form which became basic in German literature, also after the interruption of the Thirty Years' War, and for the golden age of German literature thereafter.

3. Lutheran thought and expression had indirect influence on all German and Scandinavian literature. Some of the outstanding figures in German literature were sons of the Lutheran parsonage. A popular Lutheran literature developed, however, which was directly religious in content. *The Small Catechism,* and selected Bible stories, formed the primers of German and Scandinavian childhood. Standard devotional volumes were the nucleus of the average household's library. These volumes included: prayer books, some of huge scope and for every occasion in family and community; the hymnal, which was used for daily worship as well as group worship on Sundays; postils, or sermon collections, beginning

with Luther's and presenting collections of sermons of great preachers down to the present time; and devotional volumes written directly for family contemplation. Beginning with the seventeenth century, romances with religious content competed for the interest of Christian families with those of secular import. The nineteenth century developed, both in Europe and America, family magazines with religious emphasis, providing political comment, fiction, devotional material, and features of interest to individuals in the family. With the beginning of special activity in missions and charity, fostered by Pietism,* books and magazines for the people sought to stimulate interest and support for these projects.

4. Since Luther's own time the chief literature with direct religious content in the vernacular to achieve high literary excellence has been the hymn.* Vernacular worship, a unique Lutheran emphasis, made this a trend from the first.

5. The Lutheran Church has always been aggressive in the publication of professional literature. The doctrinal controversies climaxing in the Confessions * produced a huge literature in doctrine, interpretation of Scripture, and polemic. In keeping with the humanistic emphasis of earlier Lutheranism, the early literature was predominantly in Latin. The German and Scandinavian universities provided technical material in these fields for students and ministers in ever-mounting profusion. Each age of Lutheran thought — orthodoxy, Pietism, Rationalism, the Enlightenment, and the various trends of the nineteenth century — produced a huge bulk of exposition, propaganda, and debate. Technical journals, beginning with the late eighteenth century, provided special studies in the various disciplines of theology and were usually published under the auspices of theological faculties.

6. Significant in recent years is the rise of prestige of theological literature under Scandinavian auspices, in a field once dominated by German scholars.

7. A literature of critical review and restudy of Lutheran origins has emerged since the middle of the nineteenth century. Critical editions of the works of the reformers and scientific historical studies have stimulated this research. The result has been a heightened appreciation of the Lutheran Reformation, extending also through Reformed circles. This movement had not reached,

with its effects, into the masses before World War II. The stress and the questions of the war and its aftermath led to a reinterpreting of essential Lutheran thought, in Europe and America, also on the popular level. RRC

Lithuania. The last European land to be Christianized. Grand Duke Mindaug was baptized for political reasons in 1252, but soon made war on the Christians. Jagello was baptized in 1386, ended paganism, and brought the country under the influence of Poland, with which it was united in 1569; in 1795 and 1815 it fell to Russia. — When harsh measures were taken against the Protestants as early as 1524, Albrecht of Prussia did much for Lutheranism. Under Sigismund III the Jesuits caused fierce persecutions; in Schoeden almost all Lutherans were massacred by the Catholic Poles; even Peter the Great could do the Lutherans no lasting good. — In 1919 the country became a republic; capital, Vilna. At the time when Lithuania became a part of the U. S. S. R. its population was 2,900,000. Three fourths of the people were Roman Catholic, and Lutherans were a leading Protestant group. There were also some Reformed and a few Methodists and Baptists. It was admitted to the U. S. S. R. by Soviet decree, Aug. 3, 1940. The total Lutheran membership of Lithuania, Latvia, and Estonia numbers about 2,000,000 (1949).

Lithuanian National Catholic Church. A body of Old Catholics made up of emigrants from the Baltic provinces and organized by Rev. S. B. Mickiewicz.

Liturgics. The formal study of the liturgics, or liturgiology, that is, the study of the history and practice of public worship, the concept being originally connected with the celebration of the Eucharist in the public assembly of the congregation. The term "liturgy" is specifically applied to the formulary for the celebration of the Lord's Supper. In a wider sense the term denotes the whole system of formal worship, including texts, seasons, festivals of the church year, and so forth.

Two early types of worship may be distinguished in the New Testament. The Jerusalem type (Acts 2:42, 46; 5:42; 6:2-4) preserved certain Jewish forms with Christian additions. The Gentile-Christian form, with its emphasis on the Lord's Day and the Eucharist, developed in Asia Minor and Antioch (Acts 20:7;

1 Cor. 16:2). For the elements of worship see Col. 3:16; 1 Tim. 2:1. The *agape* usually preceded the Eucharist.

The second-century writings show a connection between the service of the Word and the Eucharistic service. The service of the Word included: readings from the Old Testament and writings of the Apostles, homily, common prayers, kiss of peace. The service of the Eucharist included a prayer of thanksgiving and consecration (including words of institution). The liturgy was congregational and included spontaneous responses. The *agape* and prophecy disappeared. At the beginning of the third century formal ritual patterns were recognized.

The Eastern liturgies, characterized by objectivity and repetition, are of two types: Syrian and Egyptian. The Coptic and Abyssinian liturgies belonged to the Egyptian. The Syrian Type (Antiochene) includes the Western Syrian (Antioch and Jerusalem), the Eastern Syrian (Persia and Mesoptamia), and the Cappadocian-Byzantine (Armenia and Byzantium). The Byzantine rite became the rite of the Eastern Orthodox Church.

In the West, Rome (Damasus, Gregory the Great, and others) and Carthage developed a liturgy which is called the Roman rite. Another form, influenced by Eastern liturgies, developed in parts of Spain, France, Germany, Britain, Sweden, and other countries. This is called the Gallican rite. The Roman rite, marked by simplicity and forcefulness, ultimately prevailed in the West.

During the Middle Ages the Eucharist became the most important part of worship. Its sacramental character faded into the background, and the Lord's Supper became an expiatory sacrifice.

Luther in 1516 stressed the importance of the Word in the service. In 1523 he published *Von Ordnung des Gottesdienstes in der Gemeine,* in which he criticized the silencing of God's Word, unscriptural material, the idea that a service was a meritorious work. In the same year he published his *Formula Missae* (approves Introit; Kyrie; Gloria in Excelsis; Collect; Epistle; Gradual, with limitations; Gospel; Nicene Creed; Sermon; Preface; Words of Institution; Sanctus and Hosanna; Elevation, for sake of the weak; Lord's Prayer; Pax and Collect; Benedicamus and Aaronic blessing). *The German Mass* (1526) approved the following:

Hymn or German Psalm; Kyrie; Collect; Epistle; German Hymn; Gospel; *Wir glauben all an einen Gott;* Sermon; Paraphrase of the Lord's Prayer; Exhortation to Communicants; Communion service (all prayers of Mass omitted; Agnus Dei or Sanctus sung during administration; Elevation retained).

The many liturgies which appeared in Germany between 1523 and 1555 have been classified as the Saxo-Lutheran (to which Luther's belonged), the ultraconservative, and the radical.

The Thirty Years' War, Pietism, and Rationalism affected liturgical development adversely. Later Frederick William III, Edelmann, Boechk, and Loehe worked for a return to historic types of liturgies.

The first American Lutheran liturgy of note was prepared by H. M. Muhlenberg and others and adopted by the Pennsylvania Ministerium in 1748. It was the historic Lutheran liturgy with Muhlenberg's changes and additions.

Close relations between Lutherans and Reformed, rationalism, and other factors influenced the liturgies after the death of the Patriarch Muhlenberg. In 1855 a liturgy by the General, New York, and Ohio Synods appeared, which in some measure returned to the old Lutheran forms. The Church Book of the General Synod (1868) made further improvements in the direction of Muhlenberg's liturgy.

In 1884 a joint committee of the General Council, General Synod, and General Synod South began work on a common liturgy. After each of the synods had published (1888; 1892) liturgies based on the work of this committee with variations, a standard text was finally agreed upon, and the liturgy became known as the Common Service. It represents the historic Lutheran liturgical tradition.

The Lutheran Church — Missouri Synod used the Saxon Agenda or Loehe's Agenda. In 1899 the English District, and in 1914 the Missouri Synod, adopted the Common Service.

The early development of the liturgy of the Ohio Synod was influenced by liturgies of the Pennsylvania Synod. The Augustana Synod used the 1811 liturgy of Sweden. Changes were made and a form ultimately adopted which returned to that of Olavus Petri (1531).

Though Calvin was more conservative than Zwingli, both Reformed leaders ultimately greatly modified the historic liturgy.

The Book of Common Prayer * benefited from Lutheran liturgies in Germany, and some of the former's translations were used in liturgies of American Lutherans. EL

L. D. Reed, *The Lutheran Liturgy,* Muhlenberg Press, Philadelphia, 1947; F. Lochner, *Der Hauptgottesdienst der evangelisch-lutherischen Kirche,* CPH, 1895; A. Wismar (ed.), *Pro Ecclesia Lutherana;* Y. T. Brilioth, *Eucharistic Faith and Practice, Evangelical and Catholic,* SPCK, London, 1934; G. Dix, *The Shape of Liturgy,* Dacre Press, Westminster, 1945; E. Underhill, *Worship,* Harper, 1937; W. D. Maxwell, *An Outline of Christian Worship,* Oxford, 1936; *Proceedings of the Valparaiso University Liturgical Institutes* (1950 and subsequently); J. A. Jungmann, *Missarum Solemnia,* Vienna, 1948; *Memoirs of the Lutheran Liturgical Assn.,* Pittsburgh, 1906; W. K. Lowther Clarke and Charles Harris (eds.), *Liturgy and Worship,* London, 1932; G. Rietschel, *Lehrbuch der Liturgik* (20th ed. by P. Graff), Goettingen, 1951; K. F. Mueller and W. Blankenburg (eds.), *Leiturgia,* Kassel, 1952; periodicals such as *Monatsschrift fuer Gottesdienst und Kirchliche Kunst, Una Sancta, Sursum Corda.*

Livingston, John Henry (1746 to 1825). Dutch Reformed; b. at Poughkeepsie, N. Y.; studied in Holland; held various pastorates; formed independent organization of Dutch Reformed Church of America 1771; d. as president of Rutgers College, N. J.

Livingstone, David. Scotch missionary and explorer; b. March 19, 1813, at Blantyre, Scotland; d. May 1, 1873, at Ilala, Africa. After taking his medical degree, he volunteered to the London Missionary Society and was sent to Bechuana Territory, laboring there nine years. From 1852 to 1873 he was missionary explorer, penetrating into the heart of Africa and making noteworthy discoveries. The record is found in his *Missionary Travels and Researches in South Africa.* After severing his connection with the L. M. S., he was appointed British consul, continuing his explorations. In 1857, while on a visit to England, he said in the Senate house at Cambridge: "I know that in a few years I shall be cut off in that country [Africa], which is now open; do not let it be shut again. I go back to Africa to try and make an open path for commerce and Christianity. Do you carry out the work which I have be-

gun." As a result of this address the Universities' Mission to Central Africa was organized. After his return to Africa he continued his explorations, and as no news came from him for nearly three years, Henry Stanley set out to find him, locating him at Lake Tanganyika. The next year Livingstone died. His body lies in Westminster Abbey.

Lobstein, Paul (1850—1922). German theologian; exponent of the school of Ritschl; wrote much on the theology and ethics of Calvin.

Lobwasser, Ambrosius (1515—1585). Professor of jurisprudence at the University of Koenigsberg, who, though a Lutheran, in 1573 prepared a German translation of the French metrical Psalms versified for the Reformed Church of the French-Swiss by Marot and Beza. Lobwasser adapted to his translations the musical settings prepared by Goudimel for the original French texts.

Lochman, George. B. Dec. 2, 1773, at Philadelphia; studied at the Univ. of Pa., and was tutored for the ministry by J. C. Helmuth; pastor in Pennsylvania Ministerium; member of committee to plan for a seminary of education; member of catechism committee; pres. of General Synod (1821); wrote *History, Doctrine and Discipline of the Lutheran Church* and *Evangelical Catechism;* d. July 10, 1826.

C. A. Hay, *Memoirs of J. Goering, G. Lochman, B. Kurtz,* Luth. Pub. Soc., Philadelphia, 1887.

Lochner, Friedrich. B. Sept. 23, 1822, at Nuernberg, Bavaria; studied liturgics under Hommel while in Neuendettelsau; sent to America by Loehe 1845; refused to remain with the United Lutheran and Reformed Salem Church of Toledo upon its refusal to constitute itself a Lutheran congregation; served at Pleasant Ridge and Collinsville, Ill.; pastor of Trinity, Milwaukee, 1850; one of the founders of the Teachers' Seminary; 1876—87 pastor at Springfield, Ill.; assistant pastor of Trinity, Milwaukee; d. Feb. 14, 1902; wrote *Passions- und Osterbuch, Liturgische Formulare,* and *Der Hauptgottesdienst der Ev.-Luth Kirche.*

Wm. Lochner (translator), "Friedrich Johann Carl Lochner, an Autobiography," *CHIQ,* VI: 110—17; O. F. Hattstaedt, "The Life and Works of Pastor Friedrich Lochner," *CHIQ,* XXI: 166—74.

Lochner, Karl Friedrich (1634—97). Vicar at Woehrd, later at Fuerth, where, in 1663, he became pastor, remaining there for the rest of his life; wrote: "Was gibst du denn, o meine Seele?"

Lochner, Louis. B. in Nuernberg, Bavaria, Apr. 7, 1842; graduated Concordia Seminary, St. Louis, 1864; pastor in Richmond, Va., and of Trinity Church, Chicago; d. Nov. 9, 1909; member of Board for Home Missions, directing also the work in South America, and for Deaf-Mute Missions.

Lochner, Stephan, middle of fifteenth century in Cologne, where he painted the Adoration of the Magi for the *Dom;* strong realism, but a fine use of perspective.

Loci. A technical term used in the classics to designate certain fundamental truths of some particular field of learning. Since the Reformation it has been applied in particular to books in the field of dogmatics. Melanchthon's book entitled *Loci communes* originated from his lectures on Romans, but was soon expanded to include also other doctrines of Holy Scriptures. The chief characteristics of the early collections in the field, also that of Gerhard, were the synthetic arrangement of the subject matter, the absence of prolegomena, the combination of the ethical with the doctrinal, the concluding sections not eschatological, but dogmatical. Later writers in this field called their monographs *loci theologici* and expanded their material as now commonly found in textbooks on dogmatics.

Paul Joachimsen, *"Loci Communes," Jahrbuch der Luther Gesellschaft,* 1926, 27—97.

Lock, Lars. Early Swedish Lutheran pastor in America (arrived ca. 1648); served Lutherans at Christina and Tinicum on the Delaware; d. 1688.

Locke, John. English philosopher; b. 1632 at Wrington; d. 1704 at Oates. Through his main work, *Essay Concerning Human Understanding,* he became the founder of psychological and philosophical empiricism. All knowledge is acquired by experience through the senses and through reflection on what the senses offer. Denied existence of innate ideas, even moral and religious, and believed mind to be *tabula rasa.* In *Reasonableness of Christianity* he asserted that true faith cannot be contrary to reason and aimed to establish "fundamental" truths, on the basis of which all Christians might unite. These are found in the Gospels and in Acts (in contradistinction to the Epistles) and are not mysteries (*e. g.,* Incarnation, Atonement), but the Messiahship of Jesus and the law of love. Thus, elevating reason above revelation, denying the doctrines of the natural depravity of man and the Atonement; and seeing in Jesus only the God-given Teacher and new Lawgiver, he promoted English deism and subsequent continental rationalism. In *Thoughts on Education* he distinguishes instruction, which develops the mental man and imparts knowledge, from education, which is concerned with the moral man, develops habits, and builds up character.

R. I. Aaron, *John Locke,* Oxford Press, 1937; James Gibson, *Locke's Theory of Knowledge,* Cambridge University Press, 1931; S. G. Hefelbower, *The Relation of John Locke to English Deism,* University of Chicago Press, 1918.

Lodges. Originally the hall or meeting place of the local branch of the Masonic and other secret societies; hence, the group of persons composing such a branch. The term is now commonly used as a synonym for a fraternal order or secret society.

Societies with a secret ritual were common among the ancient Greeks and Romans and are today found among most savage tribes. No modern lodge has any historic connection with either the secret societies of ancient times or the secret societies of the primitives. They are all patterned upon the model of the Masonic order, which had its first organized lodge in 1717 (see *Freemasonry*).

That which is common to all fraternal orders properly designated as "lodges" is 1) the ritual, made up of dialog, pantomime, and play acting to illustrate the importance and teachings of the order; 2) a ritualistic ceremony of initiation, always of a religious or semireligious character, with prayers, Scripture readings, and lessons inculcating some moral principle; 3) the aims of the lodge — moral and spiritual advancement and mutual aid in case of trouble, sometimes taking the form of payments of sick benefits and of a death benefit (insurance orders).

America has been the most fertile field for new lodges, several thousand being organized, each with its own ritual and usually some insurance feature, in the eighties and nineties of the last

century. Because organized on principles which ignored, for the sake of
quick growth and profits, the tables of
mortality, most of these organizations
defaulted on their payments of death
benefits and passed out of existence.
The loss to the membership ran into
billions of dollars, until the Mobile Law
prescribed insurance rates based upon
the tables of mortality, which had been
known and on which insurance was
based in other countries for several
centuries.

The ritualistic features of the lodge
have gradually lost drawing power
through new social factors, such as the
motion picture, the automobile, and the
radio. For this reason many orders have
made it possible to hold membership
without initiation and even without attending any meetings whatsoever. Such
organizations are not to be regarded as
"lodges" in the true sense. The insistence of the lodge upon a ritualistic
program for its meetings (although
often abbreviated or entirely omitted
in practice) is due to desire to retain
exemption from taxes which all States
in the USA have accorded the income
and funds of fraternal orders — a fraternal order being defined as one operating on a ritual.

For a discussion of the various secret
orders see *A Handbook of Organizations* by Theodore Graebner, Concordia
Publishing House, St. Louis, Mo., 1948.
TG

Some older works: T. Graebner, *Is
Masonry a Religion?* CPH, 1946; K.
Kurth, *The Lodge* (tract), CPH, n. d.;
A. Preuss, *A Dictionary of Secret and
Other Societies*, Herder, St. Louis, 1924;
C. A. Blanchard, *Modern Secret So-
cieties*, Nat. Christian Ass'n, Chicago,
1915; numerous tracts.

Loeber, C. H. Son of G. H. Loeber;
b. Oct. 11, 1829, in Kahla, Saxe-Altenburg; Saxon immigrant; studied theology at Concordia Seminary, Altenburg;
1850 pastor in Frohna, Mo., later in
Coopers Grove, Ill., and of St. Stephen's,
Milwaukee; 1885 director of Concordia
College, Milwaukee; 1894 chaplain of
Wartburg Hospital, Brooklyn; d. Mar.
18, 1897.

Loeber, Christian (1683—1747). General superintendent of Altenburg; collaborated on the 1736 edition of the
Weimarsche Bibel; author of a widely
used German textbook on dogmatics
(new edition with preface by Dr. C. F.
W. Walther).

Loeber, G. H. B. Jan. 5, 1797, at
Kahla, Saxe-Altenburg, graduate of
Jena; tutor, pastor in Eichenberg, Saxony; Saxon immigrant; pastor at Altenburg and Frohna; interested in the
founding of, afterwards instructor at,
the Altenburg Concordia; present at the
preliminary meetings for establishing
the Missouri Synod; with Dr. Sihler
Examinator of the theological candidates; respected and beloved for his
learning, modesty, and kindliness; d.
Aug. 19, 1849.

R. O. Rupprecht, "Gotthold Heinrich Loeber," *CHIQ*, XI: 48—54.

Loehe, Johannes Konrad Wilhelm.
B. Feb. 21, 1808, in Fuerth, near Nuernberg; d. Jan. 2, 1872. Studied at the
Gymnasium at Nuernberg; theology, at
Erlangen and Berlin. In 1837 he became pastor at Neuendettelsau, where
he married Helene Andreae-Heben-
streit, who died six years later. Loehe
never married again. He remained in
the State Church, although at different
times a break seemed inevitable. In
fact, he was suspended in 1860 for a
period of eight weeks because he refused to marry a man who according
to his conviction had been granted a
divorce contrary to the Scriptures. He
fearlessly bore testimony against the
rationalism of his time and against the
lax position of the State Church.

When Wyneken brought America's
spiritual need to the attention of the
German people, Loehe quickly responded. In the *Noerdlingen Sonntags-
blatt* he made an earnest plea for
workers and even went so far as to
publish, in 1843, a special paper in behalf of America's need, *Kirchliche Mitteilungen aus und ueber Nordamerika.*
At the suggestion of Dr. Sihler, Loehe
consented to have a theological school
established at Fort Wayne, Ind., in 1846,
under the leadership of Sihler. A seminary was opened in rented quarters,
with an enrollment of eleven students.
Soon thereafter land and buildings
were purchased with money which had
largely been collected by Loehe and
his friends.

When, in the following year, the
Missouri Synod was organized at Chicago, Loehe, upon its request, turned
over to it his *Nothelferseminar*, which
is still being continued as Concordia
Theological Seminary at Springfield,
Ill. As early as 1850 Loehe intimated
that the time had perhaps come when
he would be compelled to carry on his
work apart from the Missouri Synod, in

another territory of North America. The issue which finally separated Loehe and the Missouri Synod was the doctrine of the Church and the ministerial office. Loehe became the founder of the Iowa Synod, which was organized at St. Sebald, Iowa, Aug. 24, 1854.

In 1854 Loehe organized a deaconess society in Bavaria, and in the same year the Deaconess Home at Neuendettelsau was dedicated. A chapel was added in 1858, a *Rettungshaus* in 1862, a *Bloedenhaus* in 1864, a *Magdaleneum* in 1865, a hospital for men in 1867, a hospital for women in 1869.

Loehe also deserves mention as a writer. Among others he wrote the following books: *Einfaeltiger Beichtunterricht fuer Christen evangelisch-lutherischen Bekenntnisses* (1836), *Beicht- und Kommunionbuechlein fuer evangelische Christen* (1837), *Samenkoerner des Gebets* (1840), printed in about forty editions, *Handbuch an Kranken- und Sterbebetten* (1840), *Haus-, Schul- und Kirchenbuch* (1845), *Agende fuer christliche Gemeinden lutherischen Bekenntnisses* (1844), *Evangelienpostille* (1848), *Epistelpostille* (1858), and others.

J. Deinzer, *Wilhelm Loehe's Leben*, Nuernberg, 1873; T. Schaefer, *Wilhelm Loehe*, Bertelsmann, Guetersloh, 1909; Klaus Ganzert, *Loehes Gesammelte Werke*, Freimund Verlag, begun in 1951.

Loescher, Valentin Ernst (1673 to 1749). The staunchest defender of sound Lutheran doctrine during the Pietistic controversy at the beginning of the eighteenth century; versatile, and a man of sound learning; of ideal conduct in practical church service; b. 1673 at Sondershausen as the eldest son of J. Kaspar Loescher, superintendent of that district; received excellent preparatory training; studied theology at University of Wittenberg, then at Jena; after usual academic *Studienreise* settled at Wittenberg as *Dozent;* in 1698 pastor and superintendent at Jueterbock; soon forged to the front as a representative personality; 1701—07 superintendent at Delitzsch; opposed unionism * and every form of syncretism,* on which ground alone he condemned Pietism; fruit of controversy a notable historical work, *Historia Motuum;* professor at Wittenberg 1707 to 1709; superintendent of the consistory at Dresden, where he wrote *Timotheus Verinus,* his chief work against Pietism, also published first German magazine for theological articles, *Unschuldige Nachrichten von alten und neuen theologischen Sachen;*

in 1722, after a conference with the Halle theologians, published second part of *Timotheus Verinus,* in which the *malum pietisticum* was shown definitely and beyond defense; guarded the good confession of the Lutheran Church amidst all the disturbances of the times to his death; of his poetical efforts there remains "O unerhoerte Hoellenqual," the last stanza of "O Ewigkeit, du Donnerwort."

Loewenstern, Matthaeus Apelles von (1594—1648). Director of the prince's school at Bernstadt; later counselor at court; highly gifted hymn writer and musician; author of: "Nun preiset alle Gottes Barmherzigkeit"; among his tunes that of "Christe, du Beistand deiner Kreuzgemeine."

Loewenthal, Isidor (1829—64). B. 1829 in Posen, of Jewish extraction; came to United States 1846; converted to Christianity 1851; educated at Princeton 1852; commissioned Presbyterian Board missionary to Northern India 1856; translated Bible into Pushtu for the Afghans; assassinated in his home, Peshawur.

Loftis, Zenas Sanford. B. May 11, 1881, at Gainesboro, Tenn.; d. Aug. 12, 1908, at Batang, China; graduated from Vanderbilt University 1901; druggist at St. Louis, Mo., doing slum mission work among Chinese, equipped himself to be medical missionary, volunteering to go where no one else was willing to be sent; commissioned by Foreign Mission Society, Cincinnati, Ohio, to Tibet; died three months after his arrival.

Loggia. The first row of arcades in the second story of the Vatican Palace, in the arched cupolas of the first thirteen of which there are a total of 52 Biblical pictures after sketches made by Raffael.

Logia. See *Apocrypha*, B 2.

Logo-Tigiac. See *Celtic Church*, 2.

Logos. The opening sentence of John's Gospel reads, "In the beginning was the Word." The Greek term for word is *logos.* It is evident that the term designates the Second Person of the Trinity, who was in existence from eternity and in the fullness of time joined the human nature to His divine nature, John 1:14. It is not difficult to see why the Second Person of the Holy Trinity is called the "Word." When we speak a word, this word comes from us; it arises in us. Besides, it reveals what our thoughts are. The Second Person of the Trinity accordingly is called the Word because He is the Son of God, born of the Father in eternity. Besides, He reveals to us the thoughts of God about us, His love, His gracious plan of salvation. Concerning the question where John obtained the term we point to divine inspiration, the teaching of Christ Himself, and to the Old Testament, where, for instance, Wisdom is personified and said to have been before the earth was, Prov. 8: 28-32. Wisdom is a parallel term to "Word." *Logos*, it must be remembered, has the connotation of thought, understanding, principle. The assumption that John borrowed the term from the Egyptian Jewish philosopher Philo or that he took it over from the Stoic philosophy is a gratuitous one.

Lohmann, Rudolf (1825—79). Studied at Halle and Goettingen; successor of Theodore Harms; favored Immanuel Synod against Breslau in the church-government controversy; wrote *Lutherische und unierte Kirche, Von Luthers Tod bis zur Konkordienformel; Die kirchliche Krisis unserer Tage; Die lutherische Separation;* other works.

Lohmueller, Johann (d. 1560). Won for Lutheranism by Knoepken's sermons; Reformer of Livonia; Luther's *An die auserwaehlten lieben Freunde Gottes in Riga, Reval, Dorpat* is a reply to his letters.

Loisy, Alfred (1857—1940). See *Modernism.*

Lollards. A name applied chiefly to the followers of John Wyclif in England in the fourteenth and fifteenth centuries, due to the labors of Wyclif's "Poor Priests," by whose incentive evangelical preaching was once more introduced among the poorer people.

Lombard, Peter. See *Peter Lombard.*

London Missionary Society was founded 1795 at London, chiefly by Presbyterians and Episcopalians, but now supported mainly by Congregationalists. The fundamental principle of the society is to be interdenominational and "not to send Presbyterianism, Independency, Episcopacy, or any other form of church order or government (about which there may be a difference of opinion among serious persons), but the glorious Gospel of the blessed God to the heathen, and that it shall be left to the mind of the

persons whom God may call into the fellowship of His Son from among them to assume for themselves such form of church government as to them shall appear most agreeable to the Word of God." The centennial of the society was celebrated on Nov. 3, 1894, and Jan. 15, 1895. Missions were early established in Tahiti, South Africa, South India (Travancore, by Ringeltaube, 1804), Ceylon, China (1807), West Indies (1807), Mauritius (1814), Madagascar (1818), Malta (1816), Mongolia (1869), Africa (1879). Present fields: China, India, Africa, Oceania, and Australasia.*

London Polyglot. See *Polyglot Bibles.*

Long, Ralph H. B. Loudonville, Ohio, Dec. 3, 1882; ed. Capital Univ., college and seminary; served congregations at Newton Falls-Warren, Ohio, 1909—13; Zion, Coraopolis, Pa., 1913—21; St. Paul's, Pittsburgh, Pa., 1921—27; stewardship sec'y, Joint Synod of Ohio, 1927—30; 1930—48 exec. director of the National Lutheran Council. He received the degree of Doctor of Divinity from Capital Univ., 1931. Married Sarah Ellen Bachman, 1909, by whom he had three sons, the Revs. R. W. Long, J. R. Long, and E. Long. D. Feb. 19, 1948.

Long, Simon Peter. B. Oct. 7, 1860, at McZena, Ohio; educated at Capital Univ., Luth. Theological Sem., Mt. Airy, Shoemaker Oratorical School; pastor at Loudonville, Ohio (1886—90); Massillon, Ohio (1890—93); Columbus, Ohio (1893—98); Mansfield, Ohio (1903—18); Chicago, Ill. (1918—29); pres. of Lima College, Lima, Ohio (1898—1903); prof. at Chicago Luth. Bible School (1921—29); pres. of this Bible School (1926—28). Wrote *A Reply to R. G. Ingersoll-Bob's Bible, Prepare to Meet Thy God, The Wounded Word, The Great Gospel, The Eternal Epistle, The Way Made Plain, Prophetic Pearls, The Crime Against Christ.* D.D. from Wittenberg College (1909) and Susquehanna Univ. (1909). D. Jan. 3, 1929.

Longfellow, Henry Wadsworth (1807—82). The noted American poet; studied at Bowdoin College; held chair of modern languages there, later at Harvard; literary reputation great; poems known throughout English-speaking countries; wrote several hymns and translated Dach's "O wie selig seid ihr doch" ("Oh, How Blest Are Ye Whose Toils Are Ended!").

Long-suffering. See *Patience.*

Lope de Vega (Lope Felix de Vega Carpio, 1562—1635). Grad. of Alcola; first soldier, then took orders, became an officer of the Inquisition; d. a victim of hypochondria; most prolific poet of Spain, ballad writer; author of Christmas and Corpus Christi plays, also of mystical poems.

Lord's Day. See *Sabbath.*

Lord's Prayer *(Liturgical).* The use of the Lord's Prayer in the liturgy of the Church may be traced back to the times of Tertullian and Cyprian, if not to that of Justin, the joining in it being the privilege of all baptized members. It is used in the morning worship at the end of the General Prayer, as a summary of all petitions which Christians may tender to God. In the Communion service proper it combines the functions of the prayer of humble access and of consecration.

Lord's Prayer, The, is recorded Matt. 6:9-13 and in a somewhat different form Luke 11:2-4, which references point to two different occasions. It is usually divided into Invocation, Petitions, Doxology. The words "Our Father who art in heaven" are a summary of the whole Gospel; for no one can truly call God his Father unless he has by faith in Christ become a child of God. The Seven Petitions, brief in their wording, are so comprehensive in their meaning as to include all that man needs for his bodily and his spiritual welfare. The Doxology briefly states the reason why we address our supplications to our heavenly Father. "Amen" expresses the firm belief that our prayer will be heard.

Lord's Supper. See *Grace, Means of,* IV, 1 ff.

Lord's Supper, Controversies Regarding. See *Eucharistic Controversies.*

Lord's Supper (Liturgical). The liturgy of the Lord's Supper is included in the Morning Service; for, as a rule, the Sacrament should be celebrated in this service. A hymn serves as an introduction to this solemn service, an offertory often being selected for this purpose. The pastor having come to the altar during the singing of this hymn, the first part of the service of the Holy Communion follows, namely, the Preface. The Salutation and Response

are sung to indicate the opening of a new part of the service. The Prefatory Sentences (Sursum and Gratias) are held in an elevated tone, in conformity with the solemnity of the occasion. Then comes the impressive, beautiful Preface proper. Beginning in the fourth century Prefaces were composed for all the festivals and their seasons, these hymns now being known as Proper Prefaces. They are Eucharistic Prayers of singular beauty, seeming to gain, with every new sentence, in joyful cadence, until each one reaches its culmination in the burst of triumphant melody on the part of the congregation, in the response of the Hymnus Seraphicus, or Tersanctus (Is. 6:3; Ps. 118:26). The second part of the hymn, usually called the Benedictus, resolves the whole Sanctus into a hymn of praise to Christ as true God. John 12:41. — The second part of the Communion service proper is the Administration, which is opened with the chanting of the Lord's Prayer, here not so much a prayer of consecration as one of joyful access. By reciting this prayer, the communicants are made conscious of their adoption as children of God in Christ and feel that they may come to the Lord as fellow members of the same body. Immediately after the Lord's Prayer follow the Words of Institution, taken verbally from the Scriptures, without transcriptions and additions. These words teach the sacramental use, the sacramental presence, the sacramental benefit, and the sacramental institution, and are the formula of consecration. At the close of the consecration the pastor turns to the congregation with the Pax (Luke 24:30). As the pastor turns back to the altar, the congregation chants the Agnus Dei, during which the communicants begin to come forward. At this point the celebrant may administer the Blessed Sacrament to himself (AC, XXIV:34 [German]). In the words of distribution the word "true" is added on account of Reformed errors. — In the third part of the Communion service, the post-Communion, the Nunc Dimittis of the believers expresses the believing acceptance of the faithful; it is fitly closed with the Gloria Patri, a doxology to the Triune God for the manifestation of His glory, mercy, and power. Then the Thanksgiving Collect, expressing the gratitude of the believers for the benefits received, is chanted. The service closes with the Benedicamus (the Salutation and Response and the Versicle of Benediction) giving all glory to God alone. The congregation is dismissed with the Aaronic Blessing, Num. 6:24-26, to which the congregation responds with Amen.

Lord's Supper, Roman Catholic Doctrine of. The Roman Church usually refers to this Sacrament as the Eucharist and divides it into two parts: a Sacrament (Holy Communion) and a sacrifice (the Mass). This article will confine itself to the Sacrament, the Mass * being treated separately. The fundamental doctrine which governs the whole matter, including the Mass, is the doctrine of transubstantiation, defined as follows by the Council of Trent: "By the consecration of the bread and of the wine a conversion is made of the whole substance of the bread into the substance of the body of Christ, our Lord, and of the whole substance of the wine into the substance of His blood." (Sess. XIII, chap. 4.) Of the bread and wine only the outward appearance is said to remain, while St. Paul, 1 Cor. 11:27-29, speaks of bread and wine even after consecration. It is also to be noted that the consecration formula is said to bring about transubstantiation; this helps to lay the foundation for the idolatry of the Mass. Since the 13th century the Roman Church communes the laity only under one form, or kind, i. e., it gives them only the consecrated wafer, claiming that the body, of necessity, contains the blood. Only the officiating priest communicates himself under both forms; other priests are also limited to the wafer. Christ's word, Matt. 26:27: "Drink ye all of it," passes judgment on this practice. The worthy reception of the Sacrament is said to bring forgiveness only of "the lighter, so-called venial, sins" (*Catechismus Romanus*, II, 4.50), whereas greater benefits are ascribed to the Mass. The Christ-given Sacrament is robbed of its promise of full forgiveness in order that the man-made "sacrifice" may be exalted. Here, as in the other Romish sacraments, the benefits are, of course, *ex opere operato* (see *Opus Operatum*). "Sacramental confession, when a confessor may be had, is of necessity to be made beforehand by those whose conscience is burdened with mortal sin, how contrite even soever they may think themselves." (Council of Trent, Sess. XIII, can. 1.) The Roman Church requires its members to commune at least once a year, under pain of excommunication. Indulgences are offered for frequent,

especially daily, communion. A decree of Pius X, in 1910, declared that children should be admitted to Communion at about the age of seven, the ability to distinguish the eucharistic bread from common and material bread being made sufficient proof of fitness. Of minor importance is the insistence on wheat flour for the bread, the custom of adding to the wine some water, which is supposed to be changed into wine (*Catechismus Romanus*, II, 4.17), and the provision that communicants must fast from the midnight preceding Communion.

Lord's Table. See *Grace, Means of,* IV; *Church Furniture,* 1.

Loreto, Holy House of. A place of pilgrimage near Ancona, Italy. The "Holy House" is alleged to be the house in which Mary was born and in which she received the angel's message and is said to have been transported to Italy by angels.

Los von Rom (*Away from Rome Movement*). In a wider and more comprehensive sense this phrase is by some made to include all the anti-Roman tendencies within the last century in the various countries of Europe. Thus not only the numerous conversions to Protestantism, said to be about one million for Germany alone during the nineteenth century, but also the reorganization of governments on the principles of liberty (Italy, France, Austria, Belgium, even Spain and Portugal) come under the *Los von Rom* caption. But strictly speaking, the *Los von Rom* movement is Austrian in origin. Launched at first as a political slogan by Schoenerer, the leader of the German Nationalists, in 1898 as a protest against the anti-German attitude of the Vatican since the establishment of the German Empire, the phrase soon became the watchword of religious secessionists who severed their connection with Rome. Up to 1908 no fewer than 51,000 had become Protestants, while 16,000 joined the Old Catholics. For some years following, conversions took place at the rate of about 4,500 annually.

Lossius, Lukas (1508 or 1510—82). Assisted in introducing the Reformation in Lueneburg; later rector of school in Lueneburg; published *Psalmodia, hoc est, Cantica Sacra Veteris Ecclesiae Selecta*, 1553, with all liturgical chants.

Lotteries. See *Gambling*.

Lotti, Antonio (1667—1740). Pupil of Legrenzi and a member of the Neapolitan school of composers. Though perhaps the last representative of the old polyphonic school of composition, he helped introduce a new era with his new and more modern harmonies. Lotti wrote operas as well as church music and must be counted among the foremost composers of the Roman Catholic Church.

Lotze, Rudolph Hermann (1817 to 1881). German philosopher who held a system of teleological idealism. The ultimate substance is God, the good and personal, of whom all beings are parts without losing their selfhood.

Louis VI (1539—83). Son of Elector Frederick III, whom he succeeded (1576) as elector; friend of the Formula of Concord; sought to restore Lutheranism in the Palatinate.

Louis IX. See *France*, 1.

Louisville Resolution. A resolution adopted by the United Lutheran Church at Louisville, Ky. (Oct. 14—21, 1942) in reply to the Mendota Resolutions * of the American Lutheran Church: "Resolved, that we receive with appreciation and deep gratitude to God the resolution of the American Lutheran Church in convention assembled at Mendota, Ill., which recognized our fundamental agreement and proclaimed their readiness to establish full pulpit and altar fellowship with the United Lutheran Church in America. Resolved, that we instruct the president of our Church in conjunction with the president of the American Lutheran Church to consummate and declare at the earliest possible date the establishment of pulpit and altar fellowship."

Lourdes. A town in the French department of Hautes-Pyrénées, renowned in the Catholic world as a place of pilgrimage since the alleged Mariophanies (appearances of the Virgin) of the last century. In a grotto near the town, so the story goes, a beautiful lady in spendid white raiment appeared to a young peasant girl on the 11th of February, 1858. At a subsequent visit the lady identified herself with the words *"Je suis l'immaculée conception."* (I am the immaculate conception, *i. e.*, Mary). At a spot pointed out by "the Virgin" a spring of water with healing virtues miraculously burst forth. An investigation instituted about the middle of the year satisfied the Catholic authorities that the Mariophanies were indubitably authentic. Lourdes became a sacred spot, resorted to by multitudes of pilgrims from all quarters of the world. In 1876 a pilgrim church was erected. Miraculous cures are ascribed by Roman Catholics to the water.

Love. In the New Testament we have two significant Greek terms for "love": 1) *agapaoh (diligere)*, denoting a love founded in admiration, veneration, esteem, a kindly disposition to something; 2) *phileoh (amare)*, denoting an inclination prompted by sense and emotion. See a Bible concordance for the manifold use of "love" in the Bible. Cp. also *Concordia Pulpit*, 1936, Vol. VII, 237 ff. "Love" is used 1) to designate an attribute of God, showing particularly how He feels toward man (John 3:16; 15:9,13; Rom. 5:5; 1 John 4:8-10, 16, 19; Eph. 5:25. See also "Loving-kindness, Grace"; 2) to show what man owes to God (Matt. 22:37; Deut. 6:5; John 21:15-17; 1 John 4:19); 3) to describe the relationship that should bind man to all his fellow men (Matt. 22:39; John 13:34; 15:12; 1 John 3:11 ff.; 4:7 ff.; 1 Pet. 2:17; etc.). Love is the highest and foremost Christian virtue; true, God-pleasing love is the chief fruit of faith, worked by the Spirit through the Gospel (Gal. 5:22; 1 John 3:14); it manifests itself in willing, joyful obedience and service to God and in seeking always the true welfare of men in general (Gal. 6:10), for time and eternity (compassion, charity, evangelism). Cp. Reu-Buehring, *Christian Ethics*, pp. 148 ff.; 230 ff.; 273, 357. See *Charities, Christian*, 1 ff.; *Lund, Theology of.* JMW

Love Feast. See *Agape*.

Loving-kindness. Predominantly a Biblical word, used to express God's love to man, according to which He bestows the favors of His grace and mercy upon sinners, who are His enemies by nature and unworthy of His kindness (cp. Ps. 17:7; 26:3; 36:7, 10; 89:33; 103:4; 117:2; Jer. 31:3; Rom. 5:8; 1 Cor. 2:9; Eph. 1:3-5; 1 John 4:8-19). See Luther, XII:389. See *Grace, Love of God, Kindness, Mercy*.

Low Church. See *Protestant Episcopal Church*, 7; *England, Subsequent History of the Church of*, 2.

Low Sunday. Sunday after Easter (also named Quasimodogeniti). The name probably sprang from the contrast between this simple Sunday and the high festival preceding.

Lower Criticism. See *Textual Criticism.*

Loy, Matthias. B. Cumberland Co., Pa., Mar. 17, 1828; grad. Theol. Sem., Columbus, Ohio, 1849; hon. A. M. Capital U., 1853; ordained 1849; pastor Delaware, Ohio, 1849—65; prof. Capital U. 1865—1902; pres. Capital U. 1881—90; editor *Lutheran Standard* 1864—91; *Columbus Theol. Mag.* 1881—88; pres. Synod of Ohio 1860—78, 1880—94. Wrote: *Doctrine of Justification; Sermons on the Gospels; The Christian Church; Story of My Life; Sermon on the Mount; Sermons on the Epistles;* translated *Life and Deeds of Dr. Martin Luther,* by Rev. H. Fick. D. Jan. 26, 1915.

M. Loy, *Story of My Life,* Columbus Bk. Concern, 1908.

Loyalty Islands. See *New Caledonia* and *Polynesia.*

Loyola, Ignatius. Founder of the Society of Jesus; b. in the Spanish province of Guipuzcoa 1491; devoted his youth to the profession of arms; wounded during the siege of Pampeluna, 1521; read the lives of the saints during his convalescence; resolved, as a result, to dedicate his life to the service of God. After studying at various Spanish universities he went to Paris to take a course in theology, 1528. Here he associated himself with six kindred spirits, and together they formed the *Compania de Jesu* in order to combat the forces of evil, these being primarily the teachings of the Protestant reformers. The new order received the papal sanction in 1540. Loyola became its first general. D. 1556. Luther liberated millions from the shackles of the Papacy; Loyola invented a machine to rivet the fetters anew and to bind the Church irretrievably to the ideas of medievalism.

Paul v. Dyke, *Ignatius Loyola,* Scribner's, 1927.

Loyson, Fr. Hyacinthe (1827—1912). French independent; prof. at Avignon and at Nantes; excommunicated for his liberal views (1869), he joined the Old Catholics but left them because of his rationalistic views; founded Catholic Gallican Church; spent last years at Geneva seeking to establish joint worship for Christians, Jews, and Mohammedans.

Lucar, Cyril. See *Eastern Orthodox Confessions,* C.

Lucian the Martyr, presbyter of Antioch, teacher of Arius, whose main thought he anticipated; excommunicated according to Alexander of Alexandria, but reconciled with the Church before his martyrdom, 311; also known for his critical revision of the Septuagint and the Greek Testament. See *Arianism* (3).

Luciferians. Followers of Lucifer, bishop of Calaris in Sardinia (d. 371). They were a schismatic party, organized on strict Novatian principles; but in the beginning of the fifth century they returned to the Catholic Church. See *Novatian Schism.*

Lucretius (ca. 96—55 B.C.). A Roman poet who presented the atomic theory of Democritus and Epicurus in his poem: *De Rerum Natura.* He developed a thorough materialistic theory of evolution, holding that everything (including the soul) consists of fine particles of different shapes called atoms. Although he believed in the existence of gods, he did not fit them into his theory.

Ludaemilia, Elizabeth. Countess of Schwarzburg-Rudolstadt (1640—72). Well educated; lived for some years at castle of Friedensburg; wrote: "Jesus, Jesus, nichts als Jesus"; "Sorge, Vater, sorge du."

Ludolf of Saxony (ca. 1300—1377). Ascetic writer; wrote *Life of Christ* based on the Gospels and Church Fathers, considered one of the best books of the Middle Ages.

Luebeck, Vincent (1654—1740). Was a contemporary of J. S. Bach, who served as organist of the Nikolaikirche of Hamburg from 1702 to 1740. Bach repeatedly made it a point to hear Luebeck play and thought highly of him also as a composer. He was influenced by Buxtehude and Reincken; his music is virile and masculine in character and lacks the charm and grace of his French and Italian contemporaries.

Luecke, Gottfried Christian Friedrich (1791—1855). Prof. at Goettingen; mediating theologian of Schleiermacher's school; New Testament exegete.

Luecke, Martin. B. June 22, 1859, in Sheboygan Co., Wis.; ed. at Concordia College, Fort Wayne, and Concordia Seminary, St. Louis; grad. 1881; pastor at Bethalto, Ill., 1881—84; Troy, Ill., 1884—92; Springfield, Ill., 1892 to

1903; pres. of Concordia College, Fort Wayne, 1903—26; d. Apr. 13, 1926.

Luedemann, Hermann (1842—1933). Prof. in Bern; he held that the Christian faith is the normal reflex instilled in him by "his dependence on the endless Being who supports him." Wrote *Das Erkennen und die Werturteile; Christliche Dogmatik.*

Lufft, Hans (1495—1584). Printer at Wittenberg; known for first editions of Luther's works, especially the Bible translations.

Luger, Friedrich (1813—90). German Lutheran pastor whose sermons were popular; wrote: *Christus unser Leben; Der Brief Jacobus; Ueber Zweck, Inhalt, und Eigenthuemlichkeit der Reden Stephanus;* etc.

Lukas, Jan. See *Bohemia, Lutheran Theology in,* 2.

Lullus, Raimundus (1235—1316). First Christian missionary in Mohammedan countries; established schools for the training of missionaries and for the study of Oriental languages; went in person at the age of fifty-six; was martyred when he made his third attempt.

Lumber River Mission. See *Evangelistic Organizations,* 9.

Lund, Theology of. A term applied to theological thoughts emphasized and elucidated by theologians at the University of Lund, Sweden. Anders Theodore Samuel Nygren and Gustav Emanuel Hildebrand Aulén are the outstanding leaders. Aulén broke with Harnack's interpretation of church history and showed that Luther's Reformation went back to the Early Church. Rejecting phases of Harnack's interpretation of Christianity, the Lund theologians emphasize the *agape* (G., "love") of the Christian religion.

The *eros* (G., "love") of heathen writers (mystery religions, Plato, Aristotle, Plotinus) is a desire of good for self, man's effort to ascend to God, egocentric love, and primarily human love (also when applied to deity) which seeks to gain its own immortal life and recognizes value in its object on which it is dependent and by which it is determined. *Agape,* on the other hand, is self-giving, free, unselfish, uncaused, spontaneous love which comes down from above, being God's way to man. *Agape* is primarily God's own love; and when it appears in man, it takes its form from God's love. *Agape* does not depend on the merit of its object, but pours itself out freely and creates value in the object.

Nygren's work showed the continuity of *agape* in the Synoptic Gospels, Paul, and John. Paul emphasized especially the manifestation of the *agape* of God in the Cross.

The different conceptions of "love" (*agape, eros*) determine entirely different attitudes of life. Nygren's work shows the influence of *agape* and *eros* at various stages of Christian history (at times blended; *agape* prominent in the 1st and 16th century). These principles were applied to other areas and ultimately led to a scientific study of many areas of Christian belief. Aulén (*Faith of the Christian Church*) groups doctrines under four heads: I. Faith and Theology; II. The Living God; III. The Act of God in Christ; IV. The Church of God.

Anders Nygren, *Agape and Eros* (tr. by A. G. Hebert), Soc. for Promoting Christian Knowledge (U. S.: Macm.), 1932; Gustav Aulén, *Christus Victor* (tr. by A. G. Hebert), Soc. for Promoting Christian Knowledge (U. S.: Macm.), 1945 (see also Aulén's *Faith of the Christian Church,* tr. 1948). For a synopsis of some points of Lundensian theology see Ph. Watson, *Let God Be God* (Muhlenberg Press, 1948) and E. M. Carlson, *Reinterpretation of Luther.*

Lust. The Greek *epithymia* means desire, craving, longing, hankering for the forbidden (see Thayer, Lexicon; Fritz, *Preacher's Manual,* 314; F. Pieper, *Chr. Dog.* [Engl.] I: 559 f.). The word "lust" may denote any kind of desire: a) legitimate, intense longing (Ex. 15:9; Num. 11:34; Deut. 12:15); b) sinful, selfish craving for forbidden things, godless inclinations, yielding to sensual and immoral feelings and passions (concupiscence, Matt. 15:19; Gal. 5: 17-21; Eph. 2:1-5; 1 John 2:12-17; James 4:3 ff.). "Lust of the flesh," the evil desires have their seat in the sinful flesh (John 3:6; James 1:14, 15; Rom. 7:7 ff.). Every natural appetite may be perverted by sin unto lust (Rom. 13:14). Evil lusts war against the soul (Rom. 6:13; 1 Pet. 2:11). Christians are to keep body and mind under control (1 Cor. 5:27; 1 Pet. 4:7). They are to flee lusts (Eph. 4:22; 2 Tim. 2:22; Titus 2:12; 1 Pet. 2:11). See Luther IX: 684, 1194, 698; XII: 866, 577; Reu-Buehring, *Christian Ethics,* 97, 107, 198. See *Sin, Desires, Passions, Original Sin.*

Luthardt, Christoph Ernst (1823 to 1902). Positive modern Lutheran theologian; studied at Erlangen, Berlin; 1847 teacher at Gymnasium at Muenchen; in 1851 *Privatdozent* at Erlangen, 1854 professor extraordinary at Marburg; from 1856 to his end professor of systematic theology and New Testament exegesis at Leipzig. He belonged to the Erlangen school of Lutheran theology and was very active in practical church life and mission work. Since 1868 he edited the very influential *Allgemeine Evangelisch-Lutherische Kirchenzeitung.* Luthardt was a voluminous writer on dogmatics, apologetics, etc., but was not free from subjectivistic and synergistic tendencies in theology.

Luther, Bible Translations of. See *Bible Versions, M.*

Luther, Catechisms of. See *Catechetics; Catechisms, Luther's.*

Luther, Chief Writings of. 1. The loving care of Luther's contemporaries and followers and the industry of modern Luther research have made it possible for us to trace the development of Luther's thought in his chief writings.

2. Among Luther's very early writings, his lectures on Romans of 1515 to 1516 have attracted a great deal of attention, and properly so. For in these lectures, not discovered or published until the twentieth century, there is evident the Reformer's growing insight into the true meaning of the Gospel. Present, too, is testimony to his keen interest in the problems of individual and social ethics. Like the lectures on Romans, those on the Epistle to the Hebrews of 1517 show the eschatological bent of the theology of the young Luther and his intense effort to assert this prophetic faith within the context of the sacral Roman institution of salvation.

3. By 1519 Luther's thought had progressed considerably. That progress is reflected particularly in his commentary of that year on Galatians. From this charter of evangelical freedom against legalistic tyranny, Luther derived his incisive analysis of the distinction between the Law and the Gospel and his realization of the work of Christ as that of victorious liberation from Law and sin. The Galatians commentary was reworked in 1523, and a longer one appeared in 1535.

4. Perhaps the best-known of Luther's works are the trilogy that appeared in 1520 — *To the Christian Nobility, The Babylonian Captivity,* and *On Christian Liberty.* The first of these refutes three basic assumptions of the medieval Church: the supremacy of the spiritual over the secular arm; the absolute right of the Pope to interpret Holy Scripture; and the exclusive authority of the Pope to convoke a council. Closely associated with these assumptions is the sacramentalism and sacerdotalism of the Roman Church; this is subjected to serious scrutiny in the essay on the Babylonian Captivity. And against the entire authoritarian structure of the Church, Luther's treatise on Christian liberty asserted the freedom of the Christian from any heteronomous authority, but his bondage through the lordship of Christ to serve all men.

5. But the freedom of the Christian man can in no way be construed to prove the freedom of man as such in his relation to God. Luther made his position on this matter clear in his book *On the Bondage of the Will* of 1525, directed against Erasmus. This is certainly one of the most difficult of Luther's writings, and in the opinion of many students, his most profound. Not man, but God is the directing agent in the divine-human relationship; man does not choose, but is chosen. In later years, however, Luther warned that he had meant this treatise to be understood soteriologically, and not as an abstract philosophical discussion.

6. For the old Luther, probably no work is as revealing as his great commentary on Genesis, delivered from 1535 to 1545. Despite his insistence upon the literal meaning of the sacred text, Luther frequently goes far beyond either its explicit or implicit significance. Nevertheless — or, perhaps, therefore — the Genesis commentary contains some of his best theological work, combined with sections of deep devotion and much practical pastoral counsel. There are few theological problems left untouched in this, Luther's last great work.

7. During the time that he was lecturing on Genesis, the Reformer took time off to compose an essay *On the Councils and Churches* (1539). As recent studies have demonstrated, it is a work of profound historical and theological scholarship, written to overthrow the historical claims of the Papacy. The treatise is also revelatory of Luther's thought on the nature of the Church, a problem to which he

devotes the entire third section. Heie is the clearest and most systematic definition we have from his pen of the relationship between the empirical Church and the hidden, or as it was later called, "invisible" Church. Unfortunately, most of the above-mentioned writings are not available in English. Of the commentaries on Romans, Hebrews, and Galatians, only selections or abridgments have appeared. On the Bondage of the Will is to be had only in an antiquated and inaccurate translation, and the Genesis commentary is inaccessible to the English reader. JP

Luther and Civil Government. Luther's one great concern was: "When will I become righteous" and thus "get a gracious God?" He found a "gracious God" and thereby became "righteous," by justification by faith, in Rom. 1: 16, 17, without a priest and the visible organization of the Church. That discovery loosed the million ties binding together Church and State, making the Church a purely spiritual entity, a communion of believers. Arnold Berger calls this the greatest discovery that had ever come into the history of the Church and of world-transforming power. Ranke finds in the Reformation the breaking down of the political power of the ecclesiastical state, and in its stead "a completely autonomous state sovereignty, bound by no extraneous considerations and existing for itself alone." Luther said: "We give to the secular government all its rights and powers, which the Pope and all his have never done, nor ever will do." The state is the organized people, grown out of the family, "without a special commandment from heaven," and yet according to the clear will of God, grounded in human reason, and so an order of God. And so political activity is a duty, a service of God, that men devour not one another, like the wild beasts, but serve one another, each in his calling—master, servant, scholar, peasant, merchant, mechanic. Of course, inequality of position, yet equality of dignity and worth before God. Luther wanted neither autocracy nor mobocracy, but "lawocracy," book law, a constitution. He admired the ancient republics and Switzerland. If the Emperor broke the law, he was to be fought as a common robber. The government is to serve the people. It must be disobeyed when it commands matters contrary to God's Word. See Church and State.

Luther, Confessions of. See Lutheran Confessions.

Luther, Controversies of. a) With the Papacy. See Luther, Martin, 7 ff.

b) Leipzig Disputation with Eck. See Leipzig Debate.

c) With King Henry VIII of England. Luther's Babylonian Captivity encountered widespread opposition. Catharinus at Rome attacked it. Adrian of Utrecht, the future Pope Adrian VI, called Luther's Gospel freedom "a bondage of the devil." King Henry VIII wrote Emperor Charles V at Worms to make an end of Luther and in July, 1521, published An Assertion of the Seven Sacraments, Against Martin Luther. Luther denied the Pope's right of dispensation; but Henry VIII was married under papal dispensation. Five years later King Christian of Denmark induced Luther to try to win Henry VIII; but the King replied in the most insulting manner. Five years later Henry tried hard to win Luther for his divorce from Catherine, but Luther would not sanction it to please the King or even to win all England.

d) With the Anabaptists. While Luther was in the Wartburg, Zwilling (Didymus) and Carlstadt with their radical reforms caused a riot in Wittenberg. Luther secretly rode down and quieted the tumult. But the "Heavenly Prophets" from Zwickau came and stirred the dying embers into a blaze. The town council begged Luther to return and bring order out of chaos, which he did with eight sermons. The radicals went elsewhere, and the Diet of Speyer (1529) decreed drastic action against the Anabaptists, as they were called since 1525. In 1533 the Anabaptists made the city of Muenster in Westphalia their gathering place, proclaimed the millennium, endorsed communism and polygamy, and instituted a reign of terror and licentiousness. The city was captured in 1535, the leaders killed, and the radicals scattered.

e) With the Peasants. See Peasants' War.

f) With Erasmus. At first Erasmus, the greatest scholar of the age, favored Luther, but finally, under threat of losing his pension, wrote On Free Will against the Reformer (1524). Luther replied in his great work On the Bondage of the Will (1525), in which he showed from the New Testament that salvation does not depend on man's free will, but on God's free grace. This is regarded by many students as Luther's most profound work. Erasmus wrote a rejoinder, but Luther did not deign to reply. McGiffert says: "Luther was a genuine evangelical. And if Erasmus was not a thoroughgoing rationalist . . . his spirit was akin to that of the rationalists of all ages."

g) *With Zwingli.* As early as 1518 Zwingli began to read Luther and received religious power and moral depth from him. About 1523 Zwingli received his doctrine of the Lord's Supper from Cornelius Hoen of Holland and attacked Luther's position in 1524. As early as 1525 Zwingli said the Lutherans were "led by a different spirit" and used abusive language in his charges against them. It was natural that Luther should use sharp language in defending himself. When the Pope and Emperor united against the reformers, Philip of Hesse and Zwingli sought to build a political alliance with the Lutherans and endeavored to clear away the doctrinal differences at the Colloquy at Marburg, 1529 (see *Lutheran Confessions,* A 2). While Luther there gave Zwingli "the hand of peace and charity," he could not agree on the Lord's Supper with the Zwinglian view. "The text is too powerful for me and will not let itself be wrenched from the plain sense by argument." Luther "with splendid, dogged loyalty was faithful to the one great central matter on which he believed everything else depended" (Hough).

Luther and Councils. See *Councils and Synods.*

Luther, Descendants of. Lineal descendants of Luther (Lutherides) through his son Paul Luther and his daughter Margareta von Kunheim are listed at more than 1,300 in Otto Sartorius' *Luthers Nachkommenschaft in 400 Jahren* (and supplements). The first came to America in 1836. More than 150 are living in the U. S.

Luther, Doctrines of. References to Luther's teachings are found in many articles throughout this cyclopedia.

Luther and Education. See *Christian Education,* D.

Luther, Family Life of. Leonard Koppe of Torgau rescued a number of nuns from the cloister of Nimbschen and left them at Luther's door on Tuesday after Easter, 1523. Luther placed them in good families. One of the nuns, Katharina von Bora, he married on June 13, 1525, a crime punishable with death according to the canon law of those days. Kate was a good wife and a very capable manager, making both ends meet and saving a bit. They had six children: Hans, Elizabeth, Magdalene, Martin, Paul, Margaret. Little Elizabeth died in less than a year and Magdalene in her fourteenth year; the scene at her death is most touching. The letter Luther wrote from the Coburg to little Hans is unique in literature. Though Luther was an extremely fond father, he was not weak; especially would he brook no disobedience. On festivals he enjoyed a good dinner; but as a rule he fared frugally, sometimes working for days on dry bread and herring. He gave a home to Kate's aunt, Lena, and to no fewer than eleven of his orphaned nephews and nieces; and he had his table and house full of company all the time — quite a drain on the purse of the man generous to a fault. At table the famous "Table Talk" was noted down by various guests and later published. After supper, prayers, music, and singing. In the living room hung a picture of Mary with the boy Jesus; decorative and aromatic plants stood on the window sill; a huge tile stove radiated genial warmth. "Perhaps the cleanest and surely the most momentous of historic love affairs was that of Friar Martin and Sister Catherine," writes Preserved Smith, while the Catholic historian Jules Michelet says: "Among these joys Luther had those of the heart, of the man, the innocent happiness of the family and home. What family more holy, what home more pure? Holy, hospitable table, where I myself, for a long time a guest, have found so many divine fruits on which my heart yet lives."

Luther, Hymns of. At the time of Luther it was customary for the priests' choirs to do all the singing. It was in harmony with the doctrine of the spiritual priesthood, which Luther elucidated, that the laymen should take part in the service. Thus a practical need for hymns and tunes for congregational singing arose. The choral is Luther's very own gift to Christendom. Some of Luther's hymns are wholly original; some are original additions to some existing stanza; some are genial reproductions of Bible passages; some are translations or adaptations of extant material. For the hymns he composed melodies, *e. g.*, for the German *Sanctus*, Is. 6, and for "A Mighty Fortress Is Our God"; he adopted and adapted extant melodies; he had others compose melodies. In 1524 appeared the first Protestant hymnal, a booklet of eight hymns — four by Luther, three by Speratus, one by an unknown author. *Enchiridion, or Handbook,* was issued the same year, twenty-five hymns, eighteen by Luther. Also in the same year came out John Walther's *Spiritual Hymn Booklet* with thirty-two German hymns — twenty-four by Luther. In time twelve more were added. Luther loved art, and he would put all arts into the service of Him who had created and given them. In "A Mighty Fortress Is Our God" he is a consummate artist, poet, and composer — who is greater? Luther's hymnbook has influenced the hymnody of all Protestantism. One of the early complete collections is *The Hymns of Martin Luther* . . . with an English Version Edited by L. W. Bacon: 1. Dear Christians, One and All, Rejoice; 2. Look Down, O Lord, from Heaven, Behold; 3. The Mouth of Fools Doth God Confess; 4. Out of the Deep I Cry to Thee; 5. By Help of God I Fain Would Tell; 6. Savior of the Heathen, Come; 7. Now Praise We Christ, the Holy One; 8. All Praise to Jesus' Hallowed Name; 9. Christ Was Laid in Death's Strong Bands; 10. Come, God Creator, Holy Ghost; 11. Jesus Christ, Who Came to Save; 12. Come, Holy Spirit, Lord, Our God; 13. That Man a Godly Life Might Live; 14. Christ, Who Freed Our Souls from Danger; 15. May God be Praised Henceforth and Blest; 16. May God unto Us Gracious Be; 17. Happy the Man Who Feareth God; 18. Though in Midst of Life We Be; 19. Now Pray We God, the Comforter; 20. In Peace and Joy I Now Depart; 21. Wilt Thou, O Man, Live Happily; 22. God the Father, with Us Stay; 23. We All Believe in One True God; 24. Had God Not Come, May Israel Say; 25. These Things the Seer Isaiah Did Befall; 26. Strong Tower and Refuge Is Our God; 27. In These Our Days So Perilous; 28. Lord God, Thy Praise We Sing; 29. From Heaven Above to Earth I Come; 30. Dear Is to Me the Holy Maid; 31. Our Father, Thou in Heaven Above; 32. To Shepherds as They Watched by Night; 33. Lord, Keep Us in Thy Word and Work; 34. To Jordan Came Our Lord, the Christ; 35. Why, Herod, Unrelenting Foe; 36. Thou, Who Art Three in Unity.

L. E. P. Wackernagel, *Martin Luthers geistliche Lieder*, Stuttgart, 1848; Friedr. Spitta, *Die Lieder Luthers in ihrer Bedeutung fuer das evangelische Kirchenlied*, Goettingen, 1905; J. F. Lampert, *Luther's Hymns*, Gen. Counc. Publ. H., 1917; Paul Nettl, *Luther and Music*, Muhlenberg Pr., Philadelphia, 1948; Bacon-Allen, *The Hymns of Martin Luther*, New York, 1883; B. Pick, *Dr. Martin Luthers "Ein feste Burg ist unser Gott" in 21 Sprachen*, Severinghaus, Chicago, 1883; G. Wolfram, *Ein feste Burg ist unser Gott*, de Gruyter, Berlin-Leipzig, 1936.

Luther and Inspiration. See *Inspiration*, B 1.

Luther Leagues. See *Young People's Organizations, Christian.*

Luther Libels. As Bengel has pointed out: "No one after Christ had to bear as many calumnies as Luther, not even the Apostles." These calumnies may be divided into four classes: 1) Those intended to appeal to the superstitious (*e. g.*, Luther the son of the devil; Luther carried off by the devil); 2) attacks on Luther's moral character (*e. g.*, Luther left the Roman Catholic Church because of his love for wine, women, and song); 3) attacks which attempt to show a pernicious influence of Luther's work (*e. g.*, Luther's work occasioned the Peasants' Revolt, gave rise to Nazism, etc.); 4) attacks on Luther's temperament (irascible, hasty, stubborn, etc.). A large literature has grown up in which attacks are made and answered.

Luther, Liturgies of. In December, 1523, Luther published his *Formula Missae*, which omitted only the idolatrous sacrifice of the Mass. It had the Introit, Kyrie, Gloria in Excelsis, Collect, Epistle, either the Gradual or the Hallelujah, Gospel, Sequences, Creed, Sermon, Preface, Consecration, Sanctus, Benedictus with Elevation, Lord's Prayer, Pax, the pastor first communed himself and then the congregation — all in Latin but the sermon. Candles, incense, and vestments were matters wholly indifferent. Insistent calls came for an Order of Service in German. On Oct. 29, 1525, Luther's effort was tried in the City Church: Hymn, Kyrie, Collect, Epistle, Hymn, Gospel, Creed. Sermon, Preface, Lord's Prayer, Admonition, Consecration of

Bread and Distribution, Hymn, Consecration of Wine and Distribution, Collect. Benediction.

Luther, Martin (for Luther's Reformation see *Reformation*). B. Nov. 10, 1483, in Eisleben, Germany. D. Feb. 18, 1546, also at Eisleben. Father of Protestantism and founder of Lutheranism. Both Zwingli and Calvin were deeply influenced by him.

1. Information on ancestry is very scanty. The family name was variously spelled Chlotar, Luder, Ludher, and Lueder. The ancestral lands were at Moehra in Thuringia. Luther's grandparents, Heine and Margaretha (Lindemann) Luder, had four sons. The oldest, Big Hans, married Margaretha Ziegler and moved to the Harz Mountains to become a miner. Their eldest son was born in Eisleben and christened Martin on St. Martin's day in the near-by St. Peter and Paul's Church. The parents soon moved to Mansfeld, where their industry and thrift gradually improved their circumstances until by 1491 Hans Luther had become an influential citizen.

2. Martin's childhood was that of the normal Roman Catholic boy in the burgher home. His father wanted him to become a lawyer and sent him to three preparatory Latin schools, Mansfeld, Magdeburg, and Eisenach. In Mansfeld he received training in the first two "Haufen" preparatory to academy work. In Magdeburg, under the instruction of the Brethren of Common Life at the Cathedral School, he saw his first Latin Bible. In Eisenach he fortunately moved in the Schalbe-Cotta family circles, where he seems to have roomed at the Cottas and boarded at the Schalbes, whose son he tutored. Both families were very devout. A frequent guest was Vicar Braun from the neighboring Franciscan monastery at the foot of the Wartburg.

3. At age 18 Martin entered the University of Erfurt, one of about 2,000 students. After four years of closely supervised dormitory life he completed his A. B. and M. A. degrees in Liberal Arts and in May, 1505, entered the Erfurt Law School. He obtained a *Corpus Juris* to aid his studies. Then, quite unexpectedly, July 17, 1505, he entered the Black Cloister of the local Augustinian Hermits. Later he spoke of a severe thunderstorm and an accident while running with a knife which had wrung from him the vow: "Help, O Anne, I will become a monk." Doubtless, he had been contemplating

the step for some time, and these experiences merely brought out what was in his soul.

4. Luther did not find peace of mind and soul in the monastery, but he determined to keep his vows. By Apr. 3, 1507, he was ordained a priest and on May 2, 1507, celebrated his first Mass in the presence of his father and many friends. His superiors encouraged him to continue his studies leading to the degrees of *Biblicus, Sententiarius, Formatus*, and the final Doctor of Theology, which occupied the years from 1507 to 1512. The more he studied medieval theology and the more he became involved in the labyrinth of scholasticism, the more confused he became. The problem which disturbed him was: How may I render God gracious to my soul?

5. In 1508 Luther was called to Wittenberg to assist in the teaching of Moral Philosophy, but by 1509 had been recalled to Erfurt to assist Nathin by instructing the novitiates. In the late fall of 1510 Luther accompanied Anton Kress of Nuernberg to Rome in the interest of reorganizing the Augustinian Order. Erfurt was among the houses which disagreed with Vicar Staupitz as to the method of effecting the reforms. The two monks reached Rome in January of 1511. The Pope was in the Romagna. All of the cardinals but two were also absent. Few of the relic chambers were open. Luther was shocked by the worldliness of some of the Italian clergy. He climbed the *Scala Sancta* and prayed for his grandparents as a devout Catholic.

6. Shortly after his return to Germany he was recalled to the University of Wittenberg, where he was trained to succeed John Staupitz in the chair of *Lectura in Biblia* as soon as he had earned the doctorate, which was awarded Oct. 18—19, 1512. Between 1512 and 1518, while lecturing on Genesis, the Psalms, Romans, Galatians, and Hebrews, Luther evolved from a scholastic theologian to a Biblical humanist. In 1514, while lecturing on Psalm 71, he discovered his new key to the entire Bible in the principle of "justification by faith." Although he did not yet fully understand all of its implications, he did realize that he had found the "Gate to Paradise." As his New Theology began to develop, he gradually won the whole faculty of the university to his point of view, and by 1517 the school was becoming a center of Biblical humanism.

7. The New Theology, which was Christocentric and stressed *sola Scriptura*, was too dynamic to leave the Roman Church unaffected. A conflict with the traditional scholastic theology was unavoidable, and its first appearance was over the sale of indulgences. Luther first learned of the questionable practices of the local indulgence peddlers when his parishioners presented their indulgence purchases as a substitute for repentance and forgiveness of sins. On Oct. 31, 1517, Luther posted the notice of a debate on the school bulletin board (the north door of the Castle Church) and listed ninety-five points for discussion. He hoped that an academic debate would clarify the subject of indulgences and determine the position the university should adopt toward the practice. The timeliness of the subject was manifested by the unbelievable rapidity with which the Theses spread throughout Germany and the great numbers of people who agreed with Luther's stand. The financial returns from the sale of indulgences in Germany were severely affected.

8. The financial loss brought immediate reaction from John Tetzel, indulgence salesman in Luther's territory, from his brother Dominicans, and from Albert, Archbishop of Mainz, who was hoping thus to pay his "fee" to the Pope for his appointment to three simultaneous church offices. All of these forces brought pressure to bear upon the Pope to silence Luther and retain their lucrative concession.

9. The *Processus Inhibitorius* was accordingly set in motion. The Augustinian Order was instructed to discipline its recalcitrant member. Luther was summoned to the chapter meeting in Heidelberg in the spring of 1518. In the ensuing disputation his exposition of his position won many new converts and, instead of reprimanding their fellow monk, the Order asked Luther to write a further elaboration of his original *Ninety-five Theses*.

10. The Fiscal Procurator of Rome next opened formal case against Luther, charging "suspicion of heresy." Luther was summoned to Augsburg on Oct. 7, 1518, where the papal legate Cajetan was instructed to give him a "fatherly hearing." Honestly willing to be convinced on the basis of Scripture that indulgences were Biblical, Luther could not accept Cajetan's citation of Bull *Unigenitus*. Both were deeply disappointed at the failure to resolve their differences. Cajetan recommended to Luther's ruler, Elector Frederick the Wise of Saxony, that Luther either be banished or surrendered to Rome. Fully aware of the need for Frederick's vote if the coming Imperial elections were to be concluded satisfactorily, the Pope realized that the situation called for his utmost diplomacy.

11. The cautious Elector, conscientiously seeking to serve justice and truth, wrote to the faculty of his university at Wittenberg for an opinion on the case. Their reply of Nov. 28, 1518, has been discovered to have been written by Luther himself and signed by the faculty, further attesting their complete agreement with his views. Upon this statement of Luther's case and the advice of his court lawyers, the Elector refused to surrender Luther to Rome until he had been proved a heretic by some neutral tribunal. Luther officially appealed his case to a General Council.

12. Among the many opportunists seeking to serve their own interests by connection with the by now famous case were Miltitz and John Eck. The mission of Miltitz ended in ignominious failure, but John Eck gained more lasting fame. In order to gain evidence of heresy against Luther, a public debate was arranged between him and Eck to be held at Leipzig in 1518. Four secretaries recorded the minutes of the debate which were then to be judged by the universities of Erfurt and Paris. Erfurt refused to become involved in the issue, and Paris delayed its verdict until 1521, at which time they declared Luther guilty of 104 heresies. The widely publicized debate only served to widen the chasm between the opposing theologies and their respective followings. Until now hopeful of cleansing the Church of error, Luther began to realize that no reformation of the existing body was possible. From his first doubt of the Scriptural basis of indulgences, Luther began to question many other practices of the Church, such as saint worship, relics, Communion, and other sacraments.

13. After the election of Charles V as Emperor, Rome again turned its attention to the prosecution of the Luther case. The universities of Louvain and Cologne had issued condemnations of Luther's theology, and by June 15, 1520, the famous Bull *Exsurge, Domine* was drafted, which gave Luther

sixty days in which to recant. As the tension mounted, many Catholic schools burned Luther's books. At Wittenberg, Luther retaliated by burning the Canon Law and, as an afterthought, tossed the papal Bull into the flames. Rome's reply was the Bull of excommunication *Decet* announced on Jan. 3, 1521. Considerable pressure was exerted upon the young Emperor to condemn Luther likewise by the civil authorities. After much political maneuvering, Charles finally summoned Luther to the meeting of the Imperial Diet at Worms in 1521. Luther resisted all efforts to persuade him to recant and both privately and publicly reiterated his position that he could not recant unless convinced of his error on the basis of Scripture. Lacking the necessary support of the German princes to secure Luther's condemnation, Charles waited until the Diet had been dismissed, then in a rump session, called by the stragglers, declared Luther a heretic and an outlaw to be killed on sight. Luther's prince, who had left the Diet earlier because of illness, suspected what the outcome might be and arranged to have Luther placed in "protective custody" at the Wartburg Castle.

14. During these months of solitude, Luther re-examined his position and clearly realized that a reform of the existing Church was not possible, that the only solution was a return to the practices and tenets of early Christianity. He utilized his time in further writings and translations, chief of which was the translation of the New Testament into German from the original Greek.

15. In March, 1522, Luther returned to Wittenberg against the wishes of his prince to quiet the confused situation which had developed there under the ill-considered leadership of Carlstadt. He preached a series of eight sermons which were masterpieces of enlightenment and tolerance. He now began actively reorganizing the church services in conformity with early Christian practice, discarding all innovations instituted by men. Hymn singing was introduced, and the order of service was revised, providing greater participation by the congregation in the services. Of the many hymns attributed to him, Luther composed four, of which "A Mighty Fortress" is best known. He provided translations or lyrics for thirty-two others.

16. Other contributions to improve the standard of Christian understanding were the Large and Small Catechisms (1529) for instruction of both the youth and adults, the *Postillen* to provide sermon materials for the "emergency preachers" who filled the pulpits made vacant by the conversion of numerous congregations from Catholicism to Lutheranism, and his crowning achievement, the translation of the Bible (1534), which, begun at the Wartburg, in later editions was to occupy him continuously until his death. In addition to these labors, Luther wrote numerous tracts, letters, and treatises. More contributions flowed from his pen than from that of any writer of his own or other times.

17. The political situation which followed the Diet of Worms was even more confused. The Edict against Luther could not be enforced. New economic forces brought on other disturbances culminating in the Knights' Revolt (1523) and the Peasants' War (1524—1525). In both instances, Luther's writings were misconstrued. When he called upon the forces of law and order to quell the revolt, he was accused by his enemies of turning against the peasants.

18. When in 1529 the Second Diet of Speyer nullified an earlier pronouncement permitting a prince to control religious affairs in his realm, both factions prepared for violence. The rift which had developed among the followers of Luther and those of Zwingli divided the forces of the Protestants. An attempt to resolve their differences at the Marburg Colloquy late in 1529 ended in agreement on all points but that of Communion. Among other attempts at reconciliation between Catholics and Protestants was the Diet of Augsburg in 1530, which produced the Augsburg Confession, a declaration of the principles of Lutheranism as set forth by Melanchthon and others and accepted with reservations by Luther. He later produced his own articles of faith in the Smalcald Articles of 1537.

19. Never a robust man and beset by many attacks of illness, Luther led an amazingly active and productive life. Late in 1545 he was asked to mediate a bitter family quarrel among the Princes of Mansfeld. Although loath to undertake such an arduous journey in winter, Luther went to Eisleben, where many conferences were held and where he delivered several

sermons. The quarrel was settled on February 17, 1546, but that evening Luther experienced severe pains in the chest and, in spite of all treatment, died early the following morning in the presence of two of his sons, two doctors, members of the nobility, and several other friends.

20. Testimony of the love and esteem with which he was regarded by the German people was the homage given to his mortal remains as the funeral cortege returned to Wittenberg, where his body was laid to rest in the Castle Church on February 22, 1546.

EGS

Heinrich Boehmer, *Road to Reformation* (tr. by J. W. Doberstein and T. G. Tappert), Philadelphia, 1947; James Mackinnon, *Luther and the Reformation*, London and New York, 1925—30 (4 vols.); Heinrich Boehmer, *Luther in the Light of Recent Research* (tr. by Carl F. Huth, Jr.), New York, 1916; M. Reu, *Luther's German Bible*, Columbus, Ohio, 1934; *Martin Luther*, Atlantis Verlag, Berlin, 1933; Paul Nettl, *Luther and Music* (tr. by Frida Best and Ralph Wood), Philadelphia, 1948; E. Plass, *This Is Luther*, CPH, 1948; E. G. Schwiebert, *Luther and His Times*, CPH, 1950; R. H. Bainton, *Here I Stand — A Life of Martin Luther*, Abingdon-Cokesbury, 1950; Wm. Dallmann, *Martin Luther, His Life and His Labor*, CPH, 1951.

Luther Medals. See *Reformation Medals*.

Luther Monuments. Monuments of Luther are found especially in the German cities where Luther was active. Among the earliest is that at Wittenberg by Schadow. The one at Worms by Rietschel is the greatest. In it Luther rests his hand on the Bible. He is surrounded by the earlier reformers (Waldo, Wyclif, Hus, Savonarola), his protectors (Frederick the Wise, Philip of Hesse), Melanchthon, Reuchlin, and figures of the cities Speyer, Augsburg, Magdeburg.

There are six replicas of the original statue of Luther at Worms in the United States:

1) The first replica, dating from 1883, stands in front of Memorial Lutheran Church, Washington, D. C.

2) The statue on the grounds of Concordia Seminary, St. Louis, Mo., dating from 1903.

3) The statue at Luther College, Decorah, Iowa.

4) The statue in front of Wartburg Seminary, Dubuque, Iowa.

5) The statue on the campus of Concordia College, St. Paul, Minn.

6) The statue in Luther Memorial Park, Detroit, Mich.

Another large statue of Luther, but of independent design, is found in a park of Baltimore, Md. A seated statue of Luther is on the campus of the Lutheran Seminary at Gettysburg, Pa.

Two other important statues of Luther in Germany are those at Eisleben (Siemering) and the Luther-Melanchthon statue in Leipzig.

Luther, Music of. See *Music, Church*.

Luther Plays. See *Religious Drama.*

Luther and Psychology. See *Psychology, F.*

Luther, Reformation of. See *Reformation, Lutheran; Luther, Martin.*

Luther and the Reformation, Anniversaries of. In 1646 the centennial of Luther's death was observed particularly in Wittenberg and Erfurt but in succeeding centuries became more widespread. The anniversary of Luther's birth was not extensively celebrated until 1883, when, however, it became the greatest celebration in honor of Luther which had thus far occurred.

It took some time before there was agreement on a general date commemorating Luther's Reformation. Pomerania chose the anniversary of Luther's birth for this purpose. Other countries in Germany chose the date on which Lutheranism was introduced in their land. The celebration of the centennial of the publication of the 95 Theses began in 1617. John George II of Saxony was the first to introduce the yearly celebration. The anniversary of the 95 Theses is usually observed on Oct. 31 or the nearest Sunday. In America it is not only observed by Lutherans, but also often is the occasion for mass rallies by various Protestant bodies.

The anniversaries of other important events during the life of Luther are also observed (e. g., the centennial of the Augsburg Confession — first observed in 1630; centennial of the Catechism).

In addition to widespread celebrations, important literature is often published on the anniversaries, and, less frequently, attempts are made to have important events take place (*e. g.*, Prussian Union, 1817).

Luther Renaissance. The sterility of Rationalism * in Germany and the theological waywardness of Pietism * led, by the nineteenth century, to a reaction toward essential Lutheranism. The revived interest in Luther led to the publication of the Erlangen edition of the works of Luther and the advocacy of confessional Lutheranism. The controversies and theological currents engendered by these studies developed a huge literature on doctrinal and historical themes dealing with Luther and climaxed in the definitive critical edition of Luther's works (Weimar, 1883 ff.). A second period of the back-to-Luther movement begins with the twentieth century and the effort to discern the motives of the primitive Lutheran concepts introduced into the German Church by Luther's co-workers and successors. In Scandinavia reactions from the pessimism of Kierkegaard * and the scholarship of the Lund * group paralleled the Luther movement. In America the contributions to the movement were the primary scholarship of M. Reu, the St. Louis edition of Luther's works, the development of the Lutheran parish ideal, and in recent years studies in the heritage of the Lutheran liturgy. The Luther renaissance in its European phase has played a part in the neo-orthodoxy * particularly of Emil Brunner,* and thereby upon American neo-orthodoxy. The chief current area of discussion in the movement lies in the field of social ethics and the place of the Christian in government; this discussion has been emphasized by skepticism of Lutheran ethics induced by World War II. RCC

Werner Elert, *Die Morphologie des Luthertums*, Munich, 1931; O. A. Piper s. v. "Neo-Lutheranism" in Ferm, *Encyclopedia of Religion*, 1945, New York; Karl Holl, *Gesammelte Aufsaetze zur Kirchengeschichte*. Vol. 1, *Luther*. 6th ed. Tuebingen, 1932.

Luther, Sermons of. Luther's sermons generally can be classed as analytical homilies. They were richly illustrated. As a rule, Luther did not formulate his subject but used the text as theme and parts. His preaching has been characterized as of the "heroic" type. The following are noteworthy printed sermons: Latin sermons, 1512; exposition of the Lord's Prayer, 1517; sermon on the Ten Commandments, 1518; *Deutsche Kirchenpostille*, 1522—27, 1540; *Hauspostille*, 1544. Many more are in the works of Luther.

Luther Society (*Luther-Gesellschaft*). This is a society in Germany with headquarters at Wittenberg-Halle. It seeks to promote a better knowledge and understanding of Luther's works. For this purpose it issues a yearbook and scientific and popular serial publications.

Luther, Table Talk of. A collection of sayings by Luther at table made from memory by Veit Dietrich, Jerome Weller, von Platow, Roerer, John Matthesius (these occasionally), Anton Lauterbach (continuously, 1531—33 and 1537—39). John Aurifaber (boarder at Luther's home, 1537—40; 45—46) published *Table Talk* heard by himself and others, 1566. Lauterbach's *Diary* was published about the same time. Many editions have appeared since.

E. Plass, *This Is Luther*, CPH, 1948.

Luther Theological Seminary. See *Canada, Lutheranism in*, 20; *Ministry, Education of*, XI D.

Luther, Works of (editions). 1) Wittenberg edition, 1539—58 (19 vols.); 2) Jena edition, 1555—58 (13 vols., two supplementary vols., 1564—65, Eisleben); 3) Altenburg edition, 1661—64 (10 vols., additional vol., Halle, 1702); 4) Leipzig edition, 1729—40 (23 vols.); 5) Walch edition, Halle, 1740—53 (24 vols.); enlarged and reprinted as the St. Louis edition; 6) Erlangen-Frankfurt edition, 1826—98 (102 vols.); 7) Weimar edition, begun in 1883, the most complete and scholarly edition; 8) the Lenker edition, issued by the Lutherans in All Lands, Minneapolis (incomplete); 9) Holman edition (6 vols., offers select portions of Luther's writings). Individual books have been translated into English at an early date (*e. g.*, *Luther on Galatians; On the Bondage of the Will*) and have been re-edited and published. A recent edition issued in Germany is the Calwer Ausgabe (6 vols.), which gives selections in modern German. Luther's letters and his Table Talks have appeared in German and English editions.

Lutheran. The name applied to Luther and his followers first at the Leipzig Debate, July 4, 1519, and then by Pope Leo X in the bull of excommunication of Jan. 3, 1521, in order to stigmatize them as heretics and separatists from the Church. The insulting epithet was adopted as a badge of honor. In 1522 Luther wrote Hartmuth von Kronberg: "Christians do not believe in Luther, but in Christ Himself; the Word has them, and they have the Word. They let Luther go, be he scamp or saint. The devil take him if he can. But let him leave Christ in peace, then we shall also remain well." On the other hand: "If you think Luther's teaching is evangelical and the Pope's unevangelical, you must not throw down Luther altogether, or you will also throw down his teaching, which you admit is Christ's teaching, but you must say thus: Luther may be a scamp or a saint, I do not care; but his teaching is not his, but Christ's very own. For you see the tyrants are not concerned to do away with Luther only, but it is the teaching they wish to destroy, and it is for the teaching that they tackle you and ask you if you are Lutheran. Here you must verily not talk in reed words, but frankly confess Christ, no matter whether Luther, Nick, or George have preached Him; let go the person, but you must confess the teaching." Over against the unionists, who love to call themselves evangelical, we must also stress the word "Lutheran."

Lutheran Academy for Scholarship, The. Was officially organized on March 2, 1942, in Chicago, Ill. Membership is by invitation and is of three kinds: members, fellows, and award fellows.

The Academy meets annually for convention. Its officers are elected at these meetings.

The objectives of the Academy are the following:

"To preserve precious interests and corral reserve powers by giving impetus and pointed purpose to individuals in their life of study;

"To provide a richer soil for genuine research through the shared resources of an organization for Christian learning;

"To undertake joint projects which lie fallow for lack of concerted effort and mutual sacrifices of qualified men;

"To make available for use the work of the Church's best students.

"To give rich meaning to all learning by integrating under the lordship of Christ the truths of revelation and of nature for a power in the minds of men.

"To hold high the light of Christian culture in a civilization which by the increase of its pagan point of view has combined science with suicide."

The officers are a president, secretary, and treasurer. In addition, three trustees manage the financial affairs of the Academy.

The Academy publishes a quarterly journal, *The Lutheran Scholar.*

Lutheran Brethren. The Church of the Lutheran Brethren in America was organized at Milwaukee, Wis. (1900), with a nucleus of five congregations. Its first spiritual leader was K. O. Lundeberg, who sought to gain only true Christians for the church. This Norwegian group differs from others in accepting only those into membership who profess a personal experience of salvation.

The church has done extensive mission work (in proportion to its size) in China and African Sudan. The Lutheran Bible School, established at Wahpeton, N. Dak., and now located at Fergus Falls, N. Dak., is one of the first Lutheran Bible schools in America (1903). It has an Old People's Home at Sauk Center, Minn. Total membership (1952): 4,088. President (1953): C. E. Walstad.

Lutheran Bureau. See *National Lutheran Council.*

Lutheran Church. See *Luther, Martin; Lutheran Confessions; Reformation, Lutheran; Lutheran Theology after 1580;* under the names of various countries.

Lutheran Church in America. See under the names of the various countries and synods.

Lutheran Church—Missouri Synod, The. The name adopted in 1947 by that body of Lutherans in America which had previously named itself *The Evangelical Lutheran Synod of Missouri, Ohio, and Other States,* and generally known simply as "Missouri" or "Missouri Synod."

I. *Early History.* 1. The Synod, organized 1847, comprised the Saxon congregations in Missouri and the congregations served by the missioners of Pastor W. Loehe in Ohio and Michigan. Conspicuous among its founders were C. F. W. Walther, his associates, and W. Sihler. The Saxon pilgrims had come over in 1839. The "Emigration Regulations" thus state the reason: "All the undersigned acknowledge with sincerity of heart the pure Lutheran faith as contained in the Word of God, the Old and New Testaments, and set forth and confessed in the Symbolical Books of the Lutheran Church. After deliberate and mature counsel they can, humanly speaking, see no possibility of retaining in their present home this faith pure and undefiled, of confessing it and transmitting it to their posterity. Hence they feel in duty bound to emigrate and to look for a country where this Lutheran faith is not endangered and where they can serve God undisturbed in the way of grace revealed and ordained by Him, and where they can enjoy, without being interfered with, fully, without adulteration, the means of grace ordained by God for all men unto salvation, and can preserve them in their integrity and purity for themselves and their children. . . . Such a country as they are looking for is the United States of North America; for there, as nowhere else in the world, perfect religious and civil liberty prevails."

2. When Pastor M. Stephan of Dresden, a powerful preacher of the old Gospel, with whom they had established close relations, finally proposed emigration as the only solution, the oppression fast becoming unbearable, they finally agreed to it, some of them, however, only after much deliberation and severe conflicts of the soul. Six ministers: M. Stephan, E. G. W. Keyl, G. H. Loeber, O. H. and C. F. W. Walther, and E. M. Buerger, ten candidates of theology, among them Th. Brohm, O. Fuerbringer, J. F. Buenger, J. Goenner, G. A. Schieferdecker, four teachers, professional men, merchants, artisans, and peasants, most of them in good circumstances, in all about 750 persons, left their homes and friends in November, 1838, and arrived in St. Louis early in 1839. The congregation remaining in St. Louis, Trinity, worshiped for three years in the basement of Christ Episcopal Church; the rest settled on a tract of land in Perry Co., forming the congregations of Wittenberg, Altenburg, Frohna, etc. In the same year 95 emigrants from Prussia, under the leadership of M. Oertel. and 141 more from Saxe-Altenburg joined them.

3. To preserve their true Lutheran faith, however, the pilgrims had first to pass through a soul-trying testing. Clergy and laity, especially the leader, had fallen into doctrinal errors. They had gradually adopted the Romanizing conception of the Church and the ministry and developed a hierarchical tendency under Stephan. He had prevailed upon most of his followers to make him their bishop and to sign a document in which they vowed obedience to him in all religious matters and even in the business affairs of the community. Then, too, before the settlement in Perry Co. had advanced beyond its beginnings, in the season of Pentecost, 1839, charges of moral unfitness were brought against the leader. He was deposed from office and expelled from the settlement. Confusion resulted. The people felt that they had given their leader too much authority and that their confidence in him had been misplaced. They also blamed themselves for not recognizing his Romanizing views on the Church and the ministry.

4. Worst of all, these errors had begun to take root — the errors that the Lutheran Church, more particularly the adherents of Stephan, was *the* Church, without which there was no salvation; that the ministry was a mediatorship between God and man and entitled to unconditional obedience in all things not in conflict with the Word of God; that questions of doctrine were to be decided by the clergy alone, in whose hands also rested the power of the Keys, etc. The clergy "was troubled by the question whether the colonists constituted congregations with authority to call ministers, and many of the laymen entertained similar doubts concerning the right of the ministers to hold their office here after having left their charges beyond the sea. Walther, too, was for a time tossed about by doubts and fears." But it was Walther whose clear grasp and unfaltering presentation of the Scriptural principle involved placed the people on firm Lutheran ground. A public debate was arranged at Altenburg, Mo., in order that all might have an opportunity to unburden their hearts. Lawyer Marbach was the spokesman of the party which cast doubt upon the standing of the Saxon congregations as true churches. Walther proposed and defended eight theses, which clearly set forth what the Church really is; see *Altenburg Theses.* By the grace of God he prevailed, thereby not merely saving the settlements from disintegrating, but also establishing the congregations upon such a basis as to make them models for others.

5. The second contingent, outnumbering the first, was made up almost exclusively of the churches served or established by the missioners of Pastor W. Loehe of Neuendettelsau, who had been brought into the field chiefly through the influence of Rev. F. C. D. Wyneken, the pioneer missionary. Wyneken came over in 1838 to minister to the destitute Lutherans and was sent by the Mission Board of the Pennsylvania Synod to explore Ohio and Indiana, and his ringing appeals to friends in Germany for help in remedying the deplorable state of affairs enlisted the generous services of the Missionary Society of Stade, of Pastor Loehe, of Dr. L. A. Petri of Hanover, of the Society for North America in Dresden, and others in Bavaria, Hanover, and Saxony. Wyneken personally appeared in Germany to give more force to the appeal. The first to enlist were A. Ernst and G. Burger, whom Loehe instructed for a year and sent over in 1842. A year later Dr. W. Sihler consecrated himself to the work. He came highly recommended for his learning and ability by Dr. Rudelbach and Pastor Loehe and became pastor in Pomeroy, Ohio, later Wyneken's successor in Fort Wayne. Loehe further established, in the interest of the missions among the Indians, the mission colony of Frankenmuth, Mich., A. Craemer being the pastor-missionary. Others won for the work, some of them university graduates, others *Nothelfer:* W. Hattstaedt, F. Lochner, J. H. P. Graebner, F. Sievers, A. Wolter, F. A. W. Roebbelen, G. Schaller, E. A. Brauer, etc.

6. The chief factor in establishing connection between these various companies of staunch Lutherans was the *Lutheraner,* established September 7, 1844, by Walther. Wyneken and Loehe's men at once recognized in the Saxons true sons of the Lutheran Church. These men had been standing alone. Wyneken had been forced to leave the General Synod on account of its Zwinglianism, Methodism, and gross unionism; Sihler, Ernst, Selle, and others, the Ohio Synod on account of its un-Lutheran position with respect to unionism; Craemer, Lochner, Hattstaedt, and Trautmann, the Michigan Synod for the same reason. The Saxons, much to their sorrow, were prevented from establishing relations with Pastor Grabau in Buffalo and his adherents on account of the differences in the doctrine of the Church and the

Ministry. The best interests of the Lutheran Church required the organization of a synod which stood foursquare on the Lutheran Confessions. Pastor Loehe also advised his missioners to get into communication with the Saxons.

7. A meeting to discuss the organization of a new synod was held in Cleveland, 1845, by Wyneken, Sihler, and others; the Saxons, though heartily in favor of the step, were absent. The next meeting was held in St. Louis, 1846; in place of the Cleveland draft a new one, formulated by Walther and thoroughly discussed by his congregation, was signed by the Saxons and the three Eastern men present. In the same year this draft was approved by a conference of 16 pastors in Fort Wayne and submitted to the congregations.

8. The *organization* of the Missouri Synod took place on April 26, 1847, in St. Paul's, Chicago (Rev. C. A. T. Selle, pastor). The original framers signed the Fort Wayne draft, elected temporary officers, and then proceeded to receive others into membership. There were present 17 pastors, 1 professor (Wolter, Fort Wayne), 1 candidate for the ministry, 1 student of theology, and 4 lay delegates of congregations joining the organization. Four pastors who had not been able to be present were admitted to membership upon their written request. One pastor and 3 lay delegates attended to observe developments. A delegation of Watertown, Wis. (Pastor Geyer and his lay delegate), was present to protest against the organizing of a synod, there being no Scriptural authority for such an institution. It was pointed out to them that such an arrangement properly lies within the province of Christian congregations, belonging in the sphere of Christian liberty; that the general command, Eph. 4:3 and 1 Cor. 14:40, authorizes it; and that Acts 15 establishes a proper precedent. The amendment proposed by Trinity Church, St. Louis, declaring that Synod, in its relation to the individual congregation, is to be merely an advisory body, and that its resolutions have no binding effect until adopted by the congregation as not contrary to the Word of God and suited to its condition, was embodied in the constitution. 12 pastors became voting members, their congregations entering the organization; 9 pastors, 1 professor, and 2 candidates became advisory members. The

first officers, elected for a term of three years, were: Rev. C. F. W. Walther, president; Rev. W. Sihler, Ph. D., vice-president; Rev. F. W. Husmann, secretary; Mr. F. W. Barthel, treasurer. According to the first report of the treasurer the funds of the Synod amounted to $118.32¾. *Der Lutheraner* was offered by its founder and owner, Rev. C. F. W. Walther, as the official organ of Synod and was gladly accepted, Walther was retained as editor, and a special committee on publications was appointed. Synod further took steps to acquire full control of the log-cabin college and seminary near Altenburg, Perry Co., which the Saxons had established as early as 1839, and of the practical seminary in Fort Wayne, which Pastor Loehe and Dr. Sihler had founded in 1846, for the purpose of training pastors and teachers as quickly as possible. It was also resolved to ask Pastor Loehe and his mission board to give Synod full charge and control of the missions among the Indians in Michigan. A board was appointed to consider the matter of Foreign Missions, and a visitor, or home missionary at large, was appointed (Candidate C. Frincke) for the purpose of exploring new fields. Six conference districts were organized, with headquarters at St. Louis, Chicago, Fort Wayne, Monroe, Mich., Fairfield Co., Ohio, and New York City.

9. Of the voting congregations and pastors four were located in the State of Indiana: W. Sihler, Fort Wayne; F. W. Husmann and G. Jaebker, Adams Co.; G. K. Schuster, Mishawaka; two in Illinois: F. W. Poeschke, Peru, and W. Scholz, Minden; two in Ohio: A. Ernst, Neuendettelsau (Marysville), and G. Streckfuss, Willshire; one in Michigan: A. Craemer, Frankenmuth; one in New York: E. M. Buerger, Buffalo; and two in Missouri: C. F. W. Walther, St. Louis, and C. J. H. Fick, New Melle. Of the advisory pastors four were located in Ohio: F. W. Richmann, Lancaster; J. Trautmann, Danbury; J. E. Schneider, Marion; A. Detzer, Williams Co.; two in Illinois: A. Selle, Chicago; O. Fuerbringer, Elkhorn Prairie (Venedy); one in Michigan: Wm. Hattstaedt, Monroe; one in New York: Th. J. Brohm, New York City; one in Missouri: G. H. Loeber, Altenburg. When Synod held its second annual session, in 1848, it comprised 25 voting pastors and their congregations, among them F. Wyneken, Baltimore, 25 advisory pastors, and 5 teachers.

II. *Language.* 1. The original title of the Synod was *Deutsche evangelisch-lutherische Synode von Missouri, Ohio, und anderen Staaten.* The constitution provided for the exclusive use of German on the floor of Synod, making an exception only in the case of guests who were unable to use German. Most of the people in the congregations in the first decades had been born in Germany, and the pastors, professors, and teachers had, to a large extent, received their religious training in Germany. Only a few of them had come into intimate contact with English people (Professor Craemer, who had spent some years in England and had even formed connections with the University of Oxford; Professor Biewend, who had been teacher of Languages and Natural Sciences in Columbia College, Washington, D. C.; and Professor Lange, a graduate of the Altenburg Concordia, who devoted all his spare time to the study of English). Again, they found their field of labor among the German immigrants. They also felt that Luther's translation of the Bible was superior, loved the beauty and fervor of the German chorales, and knew the great value of the German devotional and theological books. They felt that more than a language would be lost if the German were discarded.

2. But from the very beginning Synod realized that its chief purpose was not to preserve a language, but to spread the Gospel. In 1855 the *Lutheraner* urged especially the younger generation to learn English. In 1850 Rev. G. Schaller confirmed a lady in the English language, who became a member of St. Peter's Lutheran Church in Baltimore, the first English congregation in the Missouri Synod (it also had the first parochial school among English congregations). In 1857 Synod declared: "We account it our sacred duty to found English churches as soon as it has become manifest that for the organization of a congregation there is a sufficient number of such as understand English better than German." The use of English gradually increased in the day schools. In 1872 Dietrich's Catechism was published in English. Of the 1881 class of graduates of the St. Louis Seminary one was assigned an English congregation and another established an English preaching station. In 1884 Synod advised the pastors of New Orleans to preach in the English language as often as possible and

organize English congregations. By the time the English Missouri Synod became a District (1911) there were more English congregations and preaching stations in the German than in the English Synod. The designation "German" was eliminated from the title of Synod by the adoption of a revised constitution in 1917. By 1925, 52 per cent of the whole Synod used German and 48 per cent English.

There was a French congregation among the original twelve parishes forming the Missouri Synod, the congregation on the Saminac River served by Rev. Poeschke, Peru, Ill. The Wendish language had been employed in Texas by Pastor Kilian and his son. After World War I the use of the English language in the service increased rapidly.

III. *Confessional Basis.* "Synod, and every member of Synod, accepts without reservation:

"1. The Scriptures of the Old and the New Testament as the written Word of God and the only rule and norm of faith and of practice;

"2. All the Symbolical Books of the Evangelical Lutheran Church as a true and unadulterated statement and exposition of the Word of God, to wit, the three Ecumenical Creeds (the Apostles' Creed, the Nicene Creed, the Athanasian Creed), the Unaltered Augsburg Confession, the Apology of the Augsburg Confession, the Smalcald Articles, the Large Catechism of Luther, the Small Catechism of Luther, and the Formula of Concord." (*Handbook,* CPH, 1949.)

IV. *Objects.* "The objects of Synod are:

"1. The conservation and promotion of the unity of the true faith (Eph. 4: 3-6; 1 Cor. 1:10) and a united defense against schism and sectarianism (Rom. 16:17);

"2. The joint extension of the Kingdom of God;

"3. The training of ministers and teachers for service in the Evangelical Lutheran Church;

"4. The publication and distribution of Bibles, church books, schoolbooks, religious periodicals, and other books and literature;

"5. The endeavor to bring about the largest possible uniformity in church practice, church customs, and, in general, in congregational affairs;

"6. The furtherance of Christian parochial schools and of a thorough instruction for confirmation;

"7. The supervision of the ministers and teachers of Synod with regard to the performance of their official duties;

"8. The protection of pastors, teachers, and congregations in the performance of their duties and the maintenance of their rights." (*Handbook,* CPH, 1949.)

V. *Doctrine.* From the beginning the Missouri Synod aimed at the ideal of strict adherence to the Scriptures and the Lutheran Confessions.

While the confessional basis of Synod is given above, various doctrinal statements by individuals, committees, and Synod form a prominent chapter in its doctrinal history. The *Altenburg Theses* * presented by Walther in the public debate at Altenburg, Mo. (1841), are the first. Early controversies with some members of his own church in St. Louis, with Pastor Wm. Loehe, and with the Buffalo Synod led Walther to make a thorough study of the doctrine of the Church and the Ministry. His position is elaborated in *The Voice of Our Church on the Question of Church and Office, The Correct Form of a Local Congregation Independent of the State,* and *The Evangelical Lutheran Church the True Visible Church on Earth* (see *Theses on the Church; Theses on the Ministry*). In May, 1881, Synod adopted theses on questions pertaining to election and conversion (see *Thirteen Theses*). Some years later F. Pieper published *Die Grunddifferenz* (1903), *Zur Einigung in der Lehre von Bekehrung und Gnadenwahl* (1913), and *Conversion and Election* (1913) on the same doctrines. For the jubilee year of 1922 F. Pieper wrote *What the Synod of Missouri, Ohio, and Other States During the Seventy-Five Years of Its Existence Has Taught and Still Teaches.* (Compare Pieper's *Ich glaube, darum rede ich* for the jubilee year 1897.) This document became the basis (often with only minor alterations) for the *Brief Statement* (see *Chicago Theses; Brief Statement*).

Important doctrinal statements are found in the *Lutheraner, Lehre u. Wehre, Lutheran Witness, Theological Quarterly, Theological Monthly,* and *Concordia Theological Monthly,* and also in Synodical and District Reports.

Missouri's interest in doctrine is evident from the dogmatical works published. Among the more prominent are: C. Loeber, *Ev. Luth. Dogmatik* (with foreword by Walther), 1872; Walther's edition of Baier's *Compen-*

dium, 1879; A. L. Graebner, *Doctrinal Theology,* 1910; F. Pieper, *Christliche Dogmatik,* 1924—28; J. T. Mueller, *Christian Dogmatics,* 1934; E. W. A. Koehler, *Summary of Christian Doctrine,* 1938; T. Engelder, *Scripture Cannot Be Broken,* 1944; T. Laetsch, *Abiding Word,* 1946/47.

Its loyalty to the Word of God has often been pointed to as a source of Missouri's strength. Dr. Walther and the other leading men of the Synod: Sihler, Fuerbringer, Craemer, Schaller, Lange, Guenther, and others, placed it squarely on the Word of God, on the Confessions of the Lutheran Church, and their successors, Dr. Stoeckhardt, Dr. Graebner, Dr. Pieper, his associates at St. Louis, and others, kept it there. The members of Synod have been thoroughly indoctrinated with the teachings of the Bible, the pastors and teachers in the seminaries, the lay members in the parochial school. This unique training of the clergy is continued by means of the pastoral and teachers' conferences and the study of the periodicals and publications of Synod. Missouri pastors are noted for their doctrinal sermons. Synod is also known for its efforts at thorough indoctrination of the laity (for details see *Parish Education*).

The Missouri Synod strives to keep its practice in harmony with its doctrine. Lodgery is regarded as a sin, chiefly against the First, Second, and Third Commandments, and treated as such. Worldliness in all its forms is unhesitatingly denounced as belonging to the works and ways of the devil. Unionism * in all its forms is opposed as unscriptural, wicked, insincere, and hypocritical. Missourians will not hold fraternal intercourse with hardened errorists (see *Heresy*). The doctrine of the Evangelical Lutheran Church, being the doctrine of the Bible, is to them holy and inviolable. They never understand how a distinction can be made between the doctrine of the Bible and the doctrine of the Church, for to their mind the Church has absolutely no business to teach anything but the doctrine of the Bible, and the Church attempting such a thing becomes a sect. Much might be said of the self-denial, aye, the self-sacrifice with which pastors, teachers, and also numerous laymen serve their Church and their Synod, but the real strength of the Missouri Synod is, as Hochstetter states in his *Geschichte* (p. 288), that its preachers and teachers and members

as a whole are poor and of a contrite spirit, and *tremble* at the Word of the Lord.

VI. *Church Polity.* 1. Synod has scrupulously guarded the rights of the local congregation. In its relation to its members, Synod is not a governing body, exercising legislative or coercive powers. In all matters involving the congregation's right of self-government Synod is but an advisory body. No resolution of Synod is binding upon the congregation which appears unsuited to its condition, and all resolutions of Synod become binding only through their acceptance by the congregations.

2. The majority of the Synodical Conference Interim Committee (1948) in an opinion held that synods and similar organizations "are an outgrowth of Christian love and Christian liberty. The work so done is both divinely appointed and God-pleasing (Matt. 28:19) so long as it does not violate the authority vested by God in the local congregation (*e. g.,* Matt. 18:17 f.; 1 Pet. 4:15). Synod is not a congregation . . . but an association of congregations. Synod, therefore, has and exercises only those rights which are delegated to it by the constituent congregations, which, in turn, possess these rights and powers by virtue of the believers in their midst (1 Cor. 3:21; 1 Pet. 2:9)." A minority report (one member) held that the name of "church" applies with equal propriety to the various groupings into which the Holy Spirit has gathered His believers, "local congregations as well as larger groups," and interpreted "ministry" in harmony with that view.

3. Synod receives into *membership* pastors, candidates for the ministry, professors, and teachers of parochial schools; but the unit of Synod is the congregation. Therefore only congregations have the right to vote in synodical matters. Every congregation has two votes, which are cast by the pastor and a lay delegate. In order to become a member, a congregation must send in its constitution for approval, and the first duly elected lay delegate of a congregation must sign the Constitution of Synod as the representative of his congregation. Pastors in charge of a congregation or without a charge, candidates, and teachers of parochial schools applying for membership, if not graduates from a seminary of the Synod, must submit to an examination (a *colloquium*), to prove their fitness and their orthodoxy. After they have

been found eligible, they sign the Constitution. Pastors whose congregations do not hold full or voting membership in Synod, assistant pastors, ministers of the Gospel without a charge, professors at the Synod's educational institutions, teachers of parochial schools, candidates for the ministry or for the office of teacher in a parochial school, are called advisory members. Barring the right to vote, they stand in the same relation to the Synod, and under the same supervision of the officers of Synod as the voting members. The congregations of advisory pastors are called upon to contribute for missionary and synodical purposes in the same manner as the congregations in full membership, and they, in turn, are entitled to the care and the advice of the officers of Synod.

VII. *Officers.* The President of Synod, besides performing the usual duties of such an officer, is charged with the supervision of the doctrine and official practice of all other officers of Synod, of the District Presidents, and of the Districts as such, attends the meeting of the Districts, visits annually all educational institutions, gives advice whenever requested, admonition whenever needed, and seeks to promote and maintain the unity of doctrine and practice among the Districts. The four Vice-Presidents act whenever requested to do so by the President, in his stead. The District Presidents are charged with the supervision of the doctrine, life, and administration of office of the pastors and teachers of their Districts and of the spiritual condition of the congregations, for which purpose they employ the institution of visitation, ordain and install, in person or by proxy, the candidates for the ministerial office and the pastors and teachers called to congregations in their Districts, and suspend from membership in Synod, until the next regular meeting of the District, such pastors, teachers, and professors as adhere to false doctrine or have given public offense by an ungodly life. They are assisted by the Visitors, who are charged with visiting each congregation and school of their circuit at least once in three years for the purpose of guarding the welfare of the congregation, fostering fraternal relations, and promoting the work of the Church. Besides, there are the other usual officers of such an organization; also the Board of Directors and the various other boards, charged with the execu-

tion of the multifarious business of Synod. — The Presidents of Synod were: C. F. W. Walther, D. D., 1847 to 1850 and 1864—78; F. C. D. Wyneken, 1850—64; H. C. Schwan, D. D., 1878 to 1899; F. Pieper, D. D., 1899—1911; F. Pfotenhauer, D. D., 1911—35; J. W. Behnken, D. D., 1935—.

VIII. *The Delegate Synod.* After Synod had been divided into four Districts, in 1854, all the pastors, professors, teachers, and a delegate from each congregation assembled every third year as Synod proper. But as this body soon became too large to be conveniently entertained by even a group of neighboring congregations, and as the proceedings were greatly impeded by the vastness of the assembly, the convention assembled in St. Louis in 1872 resolved that in the future groups of congregations composed of from two to seven should elect out of their midst one clerical and one lay delegate. Since 1917 the groups of congregations were made up of from five (larger) to ten (smaller) congregations. The electoral circuit was later changed to consist of from 10 to 15 congregations; the advisory groups of twenty.

IX. *The District Synods.* The rapid growth of Synod (after three years there were 75 pastors and 10 teachers; parishes: 23 in Missouri, 16 in Illinois, 12 in Indiana, 9 in Michigan, 9 in Ohio, 3 in New York, 2 in Wisconsin, 1 in Maryland) soon called for the division into Districts. The great distances, the poor facilities for traveling, and the great expense of the annual trip to Synod partly imposed too great a burden either upon the congregations or the pastors and teachers and partly interfered with a full attendance. The matter came up in 1849, but it was found advisable to defer it, as a division so soon after the founding of Synod might prejudice the accomplishment of some of the purposes for which Synod had been founded. Synod not yet being sufficiently knitted together, it was feared that the forming of branch synods would impair the unity of the Spirit and favor the growth of conflicting tendencies. But the division soon became imperative. The resolution was passed 1852 and 1853 that Synod be divided into four Districts, these to meet two years in succession separately and the third year in a general convention. The four Districts first met in 1855. They are:

1) The *Western District,* comprising the States of Missouri, Illinois, and

Louisiana: 22 voting and 25 advisory pastors and 11 teachers (Pres.: G. A. Schieferdecker, 1854—58; G. Schaller, 1858—63; J. F. Buenger, 1863—75; J. F. Biltz, 1875—91; C. C. Schmidt, 1891—98; P. Roesener, 1898—1901; J. J. Bernthal, 1901—19; J. H. C. Fritz, 1919—20; Fr. Brust, 1920—21; R. Kretzschmar, 1921 to 1939; P. Koenig, 1939—45; E. L. Roschke, 1945—51; T. A. Weinhold, 1951—).

2) The *Central District*, comprising Ohio and Indiana: 34 voting and 13 advisory pastors and 6 teachers (Pres.: Wm. Sihler, 1854—60; H. C. Schwan, 1860—78; W. S. Stubnatzi, 1878—80; J. H. Niemann, 1880—1909; J. H. Wefel, 1909—15; Wm. Moll, 1915—19; J. A. Schmidt, 1919—20; J. D. Matthius, 1920 to 1927; W. F. Lichtsinn, 1927—47; J. H. Meyer, 1947—51; Ottomar Krueger, 1951—).

3) The *Northern District*, comprising Michigan and Wisconsin: 12 voting and 7 advisory pastors and 6 teachers (Pres.: O. Fuerbringer, 1854—73; J. A. Huegli, 1873—75; O. Fuerbringer, 1875 to 1882; name changed to Michigan District in 1882).

4) The *Eastern District*, comprising New York, Pennsylvania, the District of Columbia, and Maryland: 10 voting pastors, 1 advisory pastor, 6 teachers (Pres.: E. G. W. Keyl, 1854—70; C. Gross, 1870—75; J. P. Beyer, 1875 to 1888; P. Brand, 1888—99; H. H. Walker, 1899—1915; F. C. Verwiebe, 1915—21; W. Broecker, 1921—28; J. K. E. Horst, 1928—31; Paul Fretthold, 1931—45; Chas. Behnke, 1945—).

5) Of these original Districts only the Central covers the same territory today; all the others have been divided or even redivided in the course of time, as they not merely grew in numbers, but also in territory. In 1874 the first Delegate Synod advised the congregations and pastors of Illinois to form a District in their State. The *Illinois District* had 139 pastors and 114 teachers (Pres.: H. Wunder, 1875—91; H. H. Succop, 1891—1903; H. Engelbrecht, 1903—07).

6) Pursuant to action by the same Delegate Synod the members residing in the States of Wisconsin and Minnesota formed the Northwestern District, and the members living in Michigan together with those in the Canadian province of Ontario continued as the *Northern District*. The reorganized Northern District met for the first time in Saginaw, 1875: 36 voting and 5 advisory pastors from Michigan; 5 voting

and 6 advisory pastors from Canada; 30 teachers from Michigan, 4 from Canada (Pres.: O. Fuerbringer, 1875 to 1882; see 3).

7) The *Northwestern District* organized 1875 in Watertown, Wis.: 32 voting and 13 advisory pastors and 27 teachers from Wisconsin, 6 voting, 13 advisory pastors, and 3 teachers from Minnesota. 15 pastors, 5 teachers, and 1 congregation were received into membership at this meeting (Pres.: K. J. A. Strasen, 1875—82).

8) Pursuant to a resolution passed by the synodical convention in 1876, the Delegate Synod of 1878 instructed the members of the Western District residing in Iowa to organize a District in their State. It numbered 44 pastors and 2 teachers (Pres.: J. Lorenz Craemer, 1879—88; Ph. Studt, 1888—91; Fr. Brust, 1891—94; E. Zuerrer, 1894—1900; O. Cloeter, 1900—06; E. Zuerrer, 1906 to 1909; A. D. Greif, 1909—14; Theo. Wolfram, 1914—27; H. Harms, 1927—36).

9) In the same year the pastors and congregations in the Canadian province of Ontario petitioned Synod to permit them to form a separate District, the *Canada* (now *Ontario*) District. Though their number was small, their wish was granted. 14 pastors, 1 teacher, 11 congregations (Pres.: A. Ernst, 1879—82; Chr. Hochstetter, 1882—83; F. Dubpernell, 1883—88; F. Bente, 1888—93; J. W. Weinbach, 1893—1906; G. Eifrig, 1906 to 1909; W. C. Boese, 1909—18; P. Graupner, 1918—21; F. Malinsky, 1921 to 1948; W. O. Rathke, 1948—).

10) The Northern District was now restricted to the Lower Peninsula of Michigan, the Upper Peninsula being attached to the Wisconsin District, and the name *Michigan District* was adopted (Pres.: Jos. Schmidt, 1882—91; G. Spiegel, 1891—1912; Theo. Engelder, 1912—14; E. A. Mayer, 1914—24; John Schinnerer, 1924—42; A. Zeile, 1942—).

11) In 1881 the Delegate Synod dissolved the Northwestern District, forming the Wisconsin and the Minnesota and Dakota Districts. The *Wisconsin District* met for the first time in Milwaukee in 1882. 72 pastors, 40 teachers, and 44 congregations were in full membership, and 30 congregations had not yet become members of the organization (Pres.: K. J. A. Strasen, 1882—85; H. F. Sprengeler, 1885—91; J. Herzer, 1891—92; B. Sievers, 1892—94; J. Strasen, 1894—1900; Cl. Seuel, 1900—06; H. Daib, 1906—16).

12) The new *Minnesota and Dakota District* met in St. Paul, Minn., in 1882;

49 pastors, 13 teachers, and 21 congregations in full membership (Pres.: O. Cloeter, Sr., 1882—85; Fr. Sievers, 1885—91; F. Pfotenhauer, 1891—1908; H. Schulz, 1908—10). Later this District was called the *Minnesota District* (see 22; 26. Pres. H. Schulz, 1910—12; R. Koehler, 1912—18; H. Meyer, 1918 to 1930; H. J. Bouman, 1930—33; J. C. Meyer, 1933—42; R. G. Heyne, 1942—48; H. A. Gamber, 1948—).

13) In 1881 the Delegate Synod also instructed the members of the Western District residing in the State of *Nebraska* to organize a new District; first meeting in 1882 at Logan: 32 pastors, 1 teacher, 19 congregations in full membership (Pres.: J. Hilgendorf, 1882 to 1900; C. H. Becker, 1900—15; C. F. Brommer, 1915—22).

14) Finally the same Delegate Synod authorized the members of the Western District residing in Texas, Louisiana, and the adjoining States to constitute a new District, to be known as the *Southern District;* first meeting in New Orleans, 1882: 20 pastors, 15 teachers, 13 congregations in full membership (Pres.: Tim. Stiemke, 1882—89; G. Birkmann, 1889—91; G. J. Wegener, 1891 to 1927; M. W. H. Holls, 1927—).

15) In 1887 two new Districts were detached from the former Western District, the Kansas and the California and Oregon Districts. The constituting meeting of the *Kansas District* (Kansas, Colorado, and Oklahoma) was held in Leavenworth in 1888: 42 pastors, 6 teachers, 30 congregations in full membership (Pres.: F. Pennekamp, 1888—94; C. Hafner, 1894—1906; F. Droegemueller, 1906—12; Theo. H. Juengel, 1912—19; Chas. F. Lehenbauer, 1919—32; W. Mahler, 1932—39; W. H. Meyer, 1939—).

16) The Pacific Coast had been a part of the Western District since 1860, when the first Lutheran minister settled at San Francisco, Rev. J. M. Buehler. The new District took the name *California and Oregon District;* first meeting in San Francisco, 1887; 12 pastors, 2 teachers, 7 congregations (Pres.: J. M. Buehler, 1887—99).

17) But before the close of the century all the pastors and congregations of this District came to the conclusion that it would be best to divide the Pacific Coast into two synodical Districts, the California and Nevada and the Washington and Oregon Districts. This project was sanctioned by the 1899 Delegate Synod. The *California and Nevada District* organized in Trinity Church, Los Angeles, 1900; 9 voting and 13 advisory pastors, 6 teachers (Pres.: J. M. Buehler, 1899—1903; G. Runkel, 1903—06; G. A. Bernthal, 1906—20; J. W. Theiss, 1920—24; A. Brohm, 1924—45; C. Fickenscher, 1945—).

18) The *Oregon and Washington District* (including Idaho), later called *Northwest District,* met for the first time in Portland, Oreg., in 1900: 7 voting and 2 advisory pastors, 1 teacher (Pres.: H. A. C. Paul, 1899—1903; W. Luessenhop, 1903—06; W. H. Behrens, 1906—09; L. Stuebe, 1909—18; J. A. Rimbach, 1918—21; W. Janssen, 1921—36; F. M. L. Nitz, 1936—48; C. H. Bensene, 1948—).

19) In 1904 the second foreign District was added, the *Brazil District* (Pres.: Wm. Mahler, 1904—10; Ad. Vogel, 1910—13; Aug. Heine, 1913—16; E. Mueller, 1916—21; J. Kunstmann, 1921—22; J. Busch, 1922—24; C. F. Lehenbauer, 1924—30; A. Heine, 1930 to 1942; R. Hasse, 1942—. See details under *Brazil*).

20) The Delegate Synod assembled in Detroit, 1905, granted a petition of the Southern District for a partition, by which the State of *Texas* became a separate District; first meeting in Houston, 1906: 42 pastors, 23 congregations, 11 teachers (Pres.: A. W. Kramer, 1906—09; C. A. Waech, 1909—12; G. Birkmann, 1912—20; H. Studtmann, 1920—26; J. W. Behnken, 1926—29; C. M. Beyer, 1929—42; E. A. Heckmann, 1942—48; O. R. Harms, 1948—50; R. Wiederaenders, 1950—).

21) In the same year Synod sanctioned also the division of the Eastern and of the Minnesota and Dakota Districts. The New England States, New Jersey, the eastern section of New York State, and London (England) constitute the *Atlantic District:* 95 pastors, 58 congregations, 27 teachers; first meeting in Boston, 1907 (Pres.: E. C. L. Schulze, 1906—18; H. Birkner, 1918—30; A. Brunn, 1930—41; G. Koenig, 1941 to 1942; H. J. Rippe, 1942—).

22) From the Minnesota and Dakota District the State of *South Dakota* was detached, and several parishes in the State of Nebraska were added to it: 39 pastors, 26 congregations, 3 teachers; first meeting in Freeman, S. Dak. (Pres.: A. F. Breihan, 1906—12; J. D. Ehlen, 1912—19; E. J. Jehn, 1919—21; F. W. Leyhe, 1921—36; Walter Nitschke, 1936—51; Phil. H. A. Mueller, 1951—).

23) In 1880 the Illinois Synod, formerly a part of the General Synod,

had united with the Illinois District of the Missouri Synod, bringing into the District 10 congregations, 22 pastors, and 2 teachers, which, with the increase the District had experienced in the six years of its existence, brought the numbers up to 96 congregations, 161 pastors, and 116 teachers. As the prospects for uniting all confessional Lutherans living in the various States into state synods had by this time about vanished, the District Synod in 1907 decided to divide the territory of the Illinois District into three parts, to be known as the Northern, Central, and Southern Illinois Districts. The *Northern Illinois District* met for the first time in Chicago in 1909; 108 voting pastors, 40 advisory pastors, 8 professors, 179 teachers, 108 congregations (Pres.: H. Engelbrecht, 1907—09; W. C. Kohn, 1909—13; Fr. Brunn, 1913—27; A. Ullrich, 1927—36; E. T. Lams, 1936—45; A. H. Werfelmann, 1945—).

24) The *Central Illinois District* met for its first session in Springfield, Ill., in 1909; 60 voting pastors, 26 advisory pastors and professors, 37 teachers, 62 parishes (Pres.: F. Brand, 1907—17; F. W. Brockmann, 1917—18; W. Heyne, 1918—28; P. Schulz, 1928—32; Ph. Wilhelm, 1932—33; W. E. Hohenstein, 1933 to 1935; J. C. Schuelke, 1935—42; Alb. C. Bernthal, 1942—48; E. F. Tonn, 1948—).

25) The *Southern Illinois District* met for its first session in Staunton, Ill., in 1909: 54 voting pastors, 9 advisory pastors, 30 teachers, 55 congregations (Pres.: F. W. Brockmann, 1907—09; U. Iben, 1909—12; J. G. F. Kleinhans, 1912—34; C. T. Spitz, 1934—45; E. H. Bohrer, 1945—46; P. Juergensen, 1946 to 1947; H. C. Welp, 1947—).

26) In 1910 North Dakota, together with the pastors and congregations in Montana, was organized as the *North Dakota and Montana District;* first meeting in Great Bend, N. Dak.: 20 voting pastors in North Dakota, 1 in Montana, 3 teachers; later a separate Montana District was organized, see 41 (Pres.: T. Hinck, 1910—24; J. P. Klausler, 1924—41; A. Jordan, 1941—42; A. H. Grumm, 1942—50; W. Cordts, 1950—).

27) Since 1911 the Missouri Synod has an exclusively *English District* (Pres.: H. P. Eckhardt, 1911—12; M. S. Sommer, 1912—15; J. A. Detzer, 1915 to 1918; O. C. Kreinheder, 1918—27; G. Schuessler, 1927—36; P. Lindemann, 1936—38; M. Walker, 1938—45; H. Bartels, 1945—51; Hugo Kleiner, 1951—.

For details see *Missouri and Other States, Synod of).*

28) In 1916 the Wisconsin District was divided into the *South* and *North Wisconsin Districts.* The *South Wisconsin District* had its first session in Watertown, Wis., in 1918; 100 pastors, 77 congregations, 74 teachers (Pres.: E. Albrecht, 1916—21; H. Grueber, 1921 to 1932; J. F. Boerger, 1932—36; F. A. Schwertfeger, 1936—48; A. H. Oswald, 1948—).

29) The *North Wisconsin District* had its first session in Clintonville in 1918; 105 pastors, 76 congregations, 20 teachers (Pres.: J. G. Schliepsiek, 1916 to 1918; H. Daib, 1918—36; W. L. Kohn, 1936—).

30) In 1921 the State of *Colorado* was detached from the Kansas District to form a District of its own, together with the congregation in Salt Lake City, Utah, and other preaching stations in that State; first meeting in Colorado Springs, 1921: 21 voting and 4 advisory pastors, 6 teachers (Pres.: O. Luessenhop, 1921—30; O. K. Hensel, 1930—34; F. W. Obermeier, 1934—42; E. J. Friedrich, 1942—50; H. G. Hartner, 1950—).

31) In the same year two of the western Canadian provinces organized as a separate District, the *Alberta and British Columbia District;* first meeting in Calgary, Alberta: 20 congregations, 18 voting and 10 advisory pastors, besides 22 congregations about to join the organization (Pres.: Aug. J. Mueller, 1921—30; W. C. Eifert, 1930—51; C. F. Baase, 1950—).

32) In 1922 the *Manitoba and Saskatchewan District* was organized at MacNutt, Saskatchewan; 32 voting and 8 advisory pastors (Pres.: P. Wiegner, 1922—24; C. T. Wetzstein, 1924—30; J. Lucht, 1930—51; L. W. Koehler, 1951—).

33) In 1922 two Districts formed in the territory of the Nebraska District. The *Southern Nebraska District* had 78 parishes in full membership, 18 advisory pastors, 45 teachers (Pres.: C. F. Brommer, 1922—24; W. Cholcher, 1924 to 1930; H. E. Meyer, 1930—36; A. J. C. Moeller, 1936—38; I. C. Heinicke, 1938 to 1949; A. F. Wegener, 1949—).

34) The *Northern Nebraska District,* including parts of Wyoming, had 66 parishes, 57 voting pastors, 31 teachers (Pres.: W. Harms, 1922—23; M. E. Mayer, 1923—39; W. E. Homann, 1939—).

35) The 32d convention of Synod, Ft. Wayne, 1923, granted the petition of the members of the Kansas District

living in the State of Oklahoma to organize the *Oklahoma District*, which takes rank as the 28th District; first meeting Okarche, 1924: 28 voting and 6 advisory pastors, 2 teachers, 29 congregations (Pres.: Hy. Mueller, 1924 to 1939; C. Matthies, 1939—40; E. Hauer, 1940—42; P. Hartenberger, 1942—43; O. Hoyer, 1943—).

36) The *Argentina District* was organized in 1927 (Pres.: A. T. Kramer, 1927—28; G. Huebner, 1928—41; A. C. Kroeger, 1941—42; S. Beckmann, 1942—).

37) The *Southern California District* was organized at Anaheim, Calif., in 1930: 36 pastors, 11 advisory pastors, 12 teachers, 42 congregations (Pres.: G. H. Smukal, 1930—42; W. F. Troeger, 1942—48; A. E. Mueller, 1948—).

38. 39) The Iowa District at its last joint meeting at Waterloo, Iowa, 1946, divided into the *Iowa East* (Pres.: H. Harms, 1936—38; C. Hesse, 1938—49; W. D. Oetting, 1949—) and the *Iowa West* (Pres.: A. Schwidder, 1936—45; H. Berner, 1945—47; Th. Hoemann, 1947 to 1948; G. W. Lobeck, 1948—) *District*. Both Districts elected their officers at Waterloo. The membership of the two *Iowa Districts* was nearly equally divided.

40) The *Southeastern District* was organized at Conover, N. C., in 1939. The *Statistical Yearbook* (1939) reports 54 pastors, 62 voting congregations (Pres.: G. J. Spilman, 1939—45; O. A. Sauer, 1945—48; R. S. Ressmeyer, 1948—).

41) The *Montana District* was organized at the Richland County Courthouse, N. Dak., at the session of the *North Dakota and Montana District* in 1945. The *Statistical Yearbook* (1945) reports 24 pastors and 36 voting congregations (Pres.: P. Freiburger, 1945—).

42) The *Florida-Georgia District* was organized at Orlando, Fla., in 1948; 34 voting delegates, 5 advisory pastors, 1 teacher, 8 advisory laymen present (Pres.: C. F. Kellermann, 1948—).

X. *Colleges and Seminaries.* See *Ministry, Education of*, VIII; XI.

XI. *Education.* See *Parish Education; Christian Education; Christian Teaching; Teachers;* and related topics.

XII. *Concordia Publishing House.* See *Publication Houses.*

XIII. *Magazines and Periodicals.* Important magazines and periodicals (some having been discontinued or combined with other publications): *Lutheraner* (1844), *Lehre und Wehre*

(1855), *Schulblatt* (1865; later *School Journal,* then expanded and called *Lutheran Education*), *Magazin fuer ev. luth. Homiletik and Pastoraltheologie* (1877), *Lutheran Witness* (1882), *Theological Quarterly* (1897; later *Theological Monthly*), *Missionstaube* (1879), *Pioneer* (1879), *Kinder- und Jugendblatt* (1889), *Young Lutherans' Magazine* (1902; continued *Concordia Magazine*), *Concordia Junior Messenger* (1922), *Lutheran Guide* (1892), *Fuer die Kleinen* (1895), *Concordia Theological Monthly* (1930), *Parish Education* (1948, continuing *News Service,* 1923), *Young World, Child's Companion, Tiny Tots, This Day* (1949). In addition there are publications by the Districts, in the interest of missions (*The Missionary Lutheran, The Deaf Lutheran, Noticiero de la Fe, The Good News*), benevolences (*The Lutheran Deaconess, The Bethesda Messenger, The Deaf Child's Advocate, The Lutheran Children's Friend, The Michigan Children's Friend, Bulletin, The Lutheran Herald for the Blind, Buenas Noticias para los Ciegos, The Lutheran Messenger for the Blind*) and by organizations within Synod (*The Nevada Lutheran, The Church Builder, The American Lutheran, Walther League Messenger, Concordia Historical Institute Quarterly, Lutheran Woman's Quarterly, The Lutheran Layman, Leader's Guide, Bible Student, The Cresset, Valparaiso University Bulletin, Gamma Delta Spectator,* and others).

XIV. *Sources of Strength.* See *Confessional Basis; Doctrine* (above).

XV. *Missions.* a. *Home Missions.* In the early history of American Lutheranism this term came to designate a sphere of activity peculiar to the American Church. The immigrations brought many people to America, including Lutherans, who left their pastors in Europe. *Home mission work* consisted in the efforts made to find the brethren of the faith and supply them with the ministry. The term, however, is now often extended to cover all mission work in the home country.

Home mission work has been the most important work of the Missouri Synod. Wyneken, Ernst, Sihler, Lochner, and others, the men sent over to America by Pastor Loehe, came here for the purpose of doing home mission work before Synod was founded. At the first convention of the Missouri Synod, Cand. Frincke was delegated as missionary at large for Wisconsin; but shortly after he became pastor in Indianapolis. In spite of lack of funds the early pastors and congregations carried on home mission work as best they could, establishing preaching stations or having a layman conduct "reading services." Thus F. Sievers * in 1856 on a missionary visit to the Chippewa Indians also looked up scattered Lutherans, preached, baptized, administered Holy Communion, and organized congregations in Minneapolis, Henderson, St. Peter, and Le Sueur, Minn. The following year Cloeter and Kahmeyer took up the work, and the places started by Sievers became bases for new mission work. In response to a letter addressed to Walther, J. M. Buehler was sent as missionary to the Pacific Coast (1860). Rev. J. Hilgendorf in Omaha, Nebr., made an exploratory trip to Colorado (1872) at the request of J. F. Buenger, pres. of the Western District. Although lacking funds, Hilgendorf reached Denver, Pueblo, and other points and managed to establish missions. In this manner work was carried on in newly settled wooded regions, on the prairies, and in the cities. Synod and every District had Boards for Home Missions, but financial means were sadly inadequate.

Synod has a Board for Missions in North and South America consisting of 9 members. It allocates funds to the respective Districts from a total budget submitted annually to the Board of Directors and the Fiscal Conference. Each District also has a board which supervises work in its territory.

In connection with, and in support of, this mission work a General Church Extension Fund was established in 1902, from which loans were and are granted through the Districts in order to assist mission congregations in erecting houses of worship. Annual repayments of at least 10 per cent are required. An operation fee of one per cent is charged.

b. See *Inner Missions.*

c. See *Immigrant and Seamen's Missions.*

d. See *Students, Spiritual Care of.*

e. *Indian Mission* was the first *Heidenmission* of the Missouri Synod. W. Hattstaedt (Monroe, Mich., 1844) had been charged by Pastor Loehe to look for opportunities for mission work among the American Indians, and he reported that the Michigan Synod was about to undertake the work, having already called Rev. F. Auch to Sebewaing for that purpose. Loehe proposed

to carry on the work along new lines, not by sending individual missionaries, but by establishing Lutheran colonies in the immediate vicinity of the Indian villages to serve as centers for the mission, the pastors of the congregations to act at the same time as missionaries. In pursuance of this plan, Frankenmuth, near Saginaw, was founded. The pastor, Rev. A. Craemer, undertook the work with wonted energy. He gained the confidence of Chief Bemasikeh, who brought two boys to him to be educated. Craemer visited the Indians along the Kawkawlin, Swan, Chippewa, Pine, and Bell rivers. In his school at Frankenmuth 30 Indian children, in 1846, received instruction in the Catechism and in Bible History. That same year 31 Indian children and young people were baptized.

At the request of Loehe the Mission House in Leipzig sent E. Baierlein, who was to settle among the Indians. He was installed as missionary Sept. 6, 1849, and was received into the tribe of Chief Bemasikeh. He erected a log church, with a belfry, and a log cabin for his home, cleared some land, setting aside a part of it as "God's acre," and named the place Bethany. In a remarkably short time he mastered the Chippewa language. The Roman Catholic missionary, afterward Bishop Baraga, permitted him to use his outlines of a Chippewa grammar and dictionary. In 1850 he had a book in the Chippewa language printed in Detroit, which contained a primer, appropriate reading lessons, Bible stories, a number of hymns, the Ten Commandments, the Apostles' Creed, the Lord's Prayer, both the morning and the evening prayer of Luther's Small Catechism, and a collect. He also translated the New Testament, some of the Psalms and parts of Isaiah into the Chippewa language. In 1849 four boys and a girl were baptized with the consent of their parents. The first adult baptized by him was a widowed daughter of Chief Bemasikeh, in 1849. The old chief, though dying unbaptized, admonished his people to follow the advice of the missionary. In 1853 the congregation had grown to 60 members.

In the missions at Sebewaing and Shabayonk (Missionaries Auch and Maier) prospects were also very bright. The whole mission came under the control of the Missouri Synod in 1849. Rev. C. J. H. Fick, Rev. A. Craemer, and Mr. F. W. Barthel constituted the first mission board. Most unfortunately the Leipzig Society transferred Rev. Baierlein to East India in 1853. The Indians sorrowfully took leave of him, even the heathen lamenting: "We shall be like a heap of dry leaves when the wind blows into it." The work was continued by Rev. Miessler, who had been Baierlein's assistant for eighteen months. But it no longer prospered. Whisky dealers, traders, and false prophets, white and Indian, filled the people with prejudice and distrust and persuaded many to leave the missions. In 1854 the whole congregation at Shabayonk turned back to heathendom. Sebewaing soon followed. In 1860, owing to the migratory habit of the Indians, also Bethany was abandoned. Only "God's acre," with 20 graves, remained to serve as a memorial of the good work done.

A new mission was begun in Isabella Co., Mich., where many of the Indians had settled temporarily; but the results were very unsatisfactory. In 1856 a mission post was established among the Chippewas in Minnesota at Mille Lacs or Rabbit Lake, Rev. O. Cloeter taking charge. But in the Indian war the Christian Indians were massacred, the missionary and his family driven away, and the station was laid waste. The Indian Mission was discontinued until 1899, when a mission was established in Shawano Co., Wis., among the Stockbridge Indians, "the last of the Mohicans." (The Mohicans were driven from the Upper Hudson in 1664 and found a new home in what is now Stockbridge, Mass. The remnants of the tribe, about a century later, moved to western New York, in 1833 to Green Bay, Wis.; amalgamated with the Munsees; settled on a reservation near Shawano in 1856. In 1909 they numbered 582 souls, all United States citizens. They had been ministered to by Congregationalist and Presbyterian missionaries; some time before 1899 this work had ceased.) Upon their request Rev. Th. Nickel of Shawano served them, 1898, and the next year Rev. J. D. Larson was ordained and installed as their first missionary, stationed in Red Springs. The church was built in 1901, the day school established in 1902, and a boarding school was built in 1920. There are 127 pupils enrolled, 30 of these from the Oneida Reservation; there are 2 woman teachers besides the missionary; 300 souls. In 1923 Candidate Cornelius Aaron, of the St. Louis Seminary, an Indian, was called to work among the Oneidas near Green Bay, but this work was discontinued.

f. *Foreign Missions.* For over four decades members of the Missouri Synod supported European Lutheran mission societies, principally the Leipzig and the Hermannsburg missions. As years passed, the desire for independent work grew stronger, and especially F. Sievers, Sr., of Frankenlust, Mich., urged Synod to send out its own foreign missionaries. In 1893 Synod created a Board for Foreign Missions and directed that work be undertaken in Japan. Unfavorable conditions there and the offer of an opportunity to begin in India caused the latter country to be chosen.

1. *India.* Missionaries Theo. Naether and F. Mohn, who had been dismissed by the Leipzig Mission for their stand on Verbal Inspiration, were received into the Missouri Synod and commissioned for work in India, Oct. 14, 1894, in St. Charles, Mo. Naether began his work in Krishnagiri, a town in the Salem District of Madras State. The work afterward was extended into the North Arcot District, where the stations of Ambur, Bargur, and Vaniyambadi were established and around them a number of outstations. In 1907 a young native Christian, G. Jesudason, a clerk in the office of the British Resident at Trivandrum, Travancore, sent an urgent appeal to the missionaries in behalf of seven heathen villages of the sambavar caste. As a result the mission extended its efforts to the area about Nagercoil near the southern tip of India. In 1912 missionary activities were also begun at Trivandrum, although here not the Tamil language is spoken, as in the other fields, but Malayalam. Missions to the Mohammedans were begun in 1923 when Dr. A. A. Brux established himself at Vaniyambadi. This project was suspended in 1936. A second approach was entered upon in 1950 but directed to the Moplahs in the Malabar District of the western coast of India. A year later the Vaniyambadi Moslem work was reopened.

Four missionary conferences have now developed in India. The Ambur Conference comprises stations at Ambur, Bangalore, Bargur, Kolar Gold Fields, Krishnagiri, Madras, Pernambut, and Vaniyambadi. The Nagercoil Conference includes that city and Collachel, Kodaikanal, Mathurai, Vadakangulam, Vallioor, and Colombo, Ceylon. The Trivandrum Conference along the southwestern coast is made up of missionaries stationed at Alleppey, Balaramapuram, Cherpalcheri, Ernakulam, Luthergiri, Nilamel, Ponvila, Shertalay,

Trivandrum, and in the Wynaad District. The Mohammedan Mission has stations at Vaniyambadi and Wandoor. Medical missions were begun in 1913, when Louise Ellermann, R. N., entered upon her work. Bethesda Hospital, Ambur, was organized by Dr. Theo. J. Doederlein, who had agreed to serve from 1921 to 1923. This has now grown to a hundred-bed institution with a strong out-patient department. Many lepers are treated with the help of a mobile clinic.

Schools have from the beginning been an important evangelistic agency. Besides the many elementary and four high schools, also three teacher-training institutes are maintained. Concordia Seminary of Nagercoil, since its founding in 1924, has lent much strength to the Church, enabling it to become ever more indigenous. Seventy-seven Indian pastors were listed in 1952. The first-to-be-ordained pastor was G. Jesudason, mentioned above, in 1921. Beginning in 1924, Sunday schools have played an increasing role in reaching youth.

Various experiments with industrial missions have met with indifferent success. A printing press, established at Vaniyambadi in 1928, continues to render much-needed service. The literature program of the mission receives continuous attention. The first novel written by one of our Christians was issued in 1951.

Efforts are increasing to create an indigenous Church. The Ambur District of the Evangelical Lutheran Church of India was organized in 1949, with the Rev. M. Philip as its first president. Special attention is being given to work among women. Bible women are trained for this work, and ladies' groups are organized with a mission objective. Young people's groups and men's clubs are also used to encourage the members in personal evangelism. Adult literacy training has netted good results in winning souls.

The mountain retreat at Kodaikanal, founded by the women of the Missouri Synod, provides a home and school for children of missionaries and is a retreat for them and their families in the hot season and a health resort in cases of sickness.

Statistics (1952): 41 male and 6 female missionaries; Indian workers: 552 (77 pastors, 4 evangelists, 130 catechists, 303 teachers, 27 Bible women, 11 industrial workers); schools: 95, with 10,370 enrolled; Sunday schools: 118, with 3,799 enrolled; Bethesda Hospital treated 55,234 cases during the 1952 period; members: 25,345 souls, of whom 8,609 are communicants. These are gathered in 409 congregations and preaching places. Church attendance totaled 861,093.

2. *China.* The father of the China Missions is Rev. E. L. Arndt. His glowing appeals aroused many hearts within the Synodical Conference to take a Christian interest in China and its 400,000,000 inhabitants. In 1912 the China Mission Society was organized. It sent out Rev. Arndt as the first missionary, in 1913. He selected the large city of Hankow for the field of his labors and took up the study of the extremely difficult Chinese language with such fervor and zeal that though no longer a young man, he began, after half a year, to preach and teach, to translate the Symbolical Books, to publish Lutheran literature and, in time, even to translate hymns into that language. On Sept. 27, 1914, he baptized his first converts. By 1921 there were 104 baptized members. In 1917 the Missouri Synod, upon request of the China Mission Society, took over the mission. The city of Enshih, 700 miles west-southwest of Hankow, a territory supplied by no other Protestant mission, was selected as the second main station, the third being Ichang, lying between the two points.

On the tenth anniversary of the mission, three additional stations were opened along the Yangtze River: Kweifu, Wanhsien, and Shasi. As a result of flood refugee work in 1931, the Han River area was opened to the Missouri Synod. Due to war pressures the mission moved westward to Chungking and south to Kunming. After World War II Shanghai became a center of activity.

Medical work and a school for blind and deaf were centered at Enshih, beginning in 1923. Services of the hospital were especially valuable during World War II. Considerable educational work was undertaken, although restrictive laws made this difficult. In 1922 a seminary was opened in Hankow. The first pastor, Mr. Pi, was ordained in 1934. The mission press served well until confiscated as a prize of war.

The internal political conditions of China and its wars have made mission work difficult. All workers except Rev. Arndt felt compelled to leave their stations for some seven months in 1927. At the beginning of World War II a party of 29 persons, representing five families, were interned and repatriated by the Japanese. After the war a large corps of workers was sent into China, but the rise of the People's Government made it seem necessary for the men to evacuate. The last to come out were the Rev. and Mrs. E. H. Thode in June, 1952.

For some time already an increasing voice had been given the Church in China, and as the missionaries were transferred to other fields (particularly the Philippines and Japan) the Chinese Christians assumed their responsibilities.

It is impossible to give any late statistics on China. The most recent ones, 1948, indicate about 2,000 members.

Work among the Chinese has shifted to the British Crown Colony of *Hong Kong* (1950) and to *Formosa* (1951), where the chief efforts have been directed to refugees, while the natives of these areas are also receiving attention. From Hong Kong work has extended to the Portuguese colony of *Macao* (1952). A Bible school at Rennie's Mill Camp has been effective in providing many who are ready to do evangelistic work. The training of theological students is carried on in Formosa. In 1953 the Rev. Paul Chang of the Hong Kong mission accepted a call to True Light Chinese Mission of the Missouri Synod in New York City.

Statistics for Hong Kong, Macao, and Formosa (1952): 2 male and 5 female missionaries; 3 additional male missionaries assigned to the field. 25 Chinese assistants. Members: 803, of whom 102 are communicants. 49,684 attended services during 1952. Sunday schools: 17, enrolling 1,076. Bible classes: 6, enrolling 172.

3. *The Philippine Republic.* Though Synod resolved in 1941 to begin work in the Philippines, World War II made this impossible until 1946, when the Rev. Alvaro Carino and the Rev. Herman Mayer were sent out. Manila was the point of entry, but from there fields have been established to the north in Binalonan, Candon, and La Trinidad. In late 1949 missionaries moved to the Island Mindanao, where centers were established at Davao City and Cagayan de Oro. The most recent penetration has been to the mountain tribes of Luzon in and about Guinzadan.

Two Filipino pastors assist in the work. The Rev. Guillermo Dionisio serves the Tagalog-speaking people of Manila, and the Rev. Simon Bilagot has been called by the Lutherans of the Philippines to be their missionary to the mountain tribes.

Young people's work receives special emphasis. In Manila considerable use is made of radio. Released-time classes enable the men to reach many children.

Statistics (1952): 8 male missionaries; 2 Filipino pastors. Souls: 1,007, of whom 236 are communicants. 30,325 attended services in 1952. Sunday schools: 22, enrolling 1,055. Bible classes: 18, enrolling 393. Released-time classes enroll 1,337.

4. *Japan.* In September, 1948, the pleas of many American soldiers of the Japan Occupation began to be answered. William J. Danker arrived in Tokyo as the first missionary of the Missouri Synod. Since it was possible to transfer seven missionaries from China and send out four others from the United States within the first year, the mission was able to establish itself quickly.

Three centers have been receiving special attention, Tokyo (Kanto area), Niigata Prefecture, and the northern island Hokkaido. Bible classes offered the best approach to the Japanese. Many children were reached through Sunday schools and later through kindergartens. A high school is maintained at Hanno. Church workers were trained in a Bible school, and since April, 1953, a theological seminary is being conducted. The radio is very much used. Because the Japanese are very literate, much attention has been given to the preparation and publication of literature.

To give the missionaries opportunity to study language without neglecting mission openings, ten theological students were sent from the States on two-year terms.

Statistics (1952): 29 male and 2 female missionaries; 31 Japanese teachers employed; souls: 567, of whom 458 are communicants; church attendance in 1952: 35,206. Schools: 5, enrolling 351. Sunday school: 25, enrolling 2,472. Bible classes: 62, enrolling 1,395.

5. *New Guinea.* Dr. Cl. Hoopmann, President of the Evangelical Lutheran Church in Australia, appealed to The Lutheran Church — Missouri Synod at its Centennial Convention in Chicago, Ill., 1947, to enter a field in the Central Highlands of New Guinea. This was done in late 1948 after another exploratory trip by a group of Australians.

This is the first effort of the Missouri Synod to work among primitive tribes. Though no Baptisms have taken place, large numbers have been reached in the four areas where missionaries are stationed: Chirunki (1952), Irelya (1949), Yaibos (1950), and Yaramanda (1948). Attendance in 1952 was 278,519. Generally these people are friendly and quite intelligent. Educational and medical work receive attention. The language of the tribes had to be reduced to writing. The Lutheran missions on the coast and on near-by islands have provided native teachers.

Being far removed from any commercial centers, the mission is compelled to have its own gardens and stores, prepare, its own lumber, and provide itself with other items. Since no roads are available from the coast to the highlands (average elevation about 5,000 ft.) air freight must be relied upon frequently.

Statistics (1952): 9 male and 2 female missionaries. Native teachers: 24. Stations: 31. Schools: 10, enrolling 265.

g. *Extraterritorial Missions:* The Missouri Synod established this classification at its Centennial Convention in 1947 to include missions in Central America, Mexico, and other areas beyond the continental United States. Up till that time these missions had been supervised by various District Mission Boards. They are now entrusted to the Board for Missions in North and South America.

1. *Mexico.* In 1922, C. Frieling began to explore mission possibilities among the German-speaking people in Mexico. The depression of the 1930's and the rise of nationalistic feeling forced the temporary suspension of the effort. Reopened in the 1940's, this work now reaches 192 souls, of whom 71 are communicants. In 1940 a mission among natives of Mexico City was undertaken by the Rev. C. A. Lazos. An institute for the training of native workers has been established at Monterrey.

Statistics for the native Church (1952): Pastors: 5. Souls: 261, of whom 204 are communicants. Attending the Institute: 12.

2. *Guatemala.* Attention was called to this field through the Lutheran Hour. The Rev. R. F. Gussick is the first missionary, having arrived in 1947. Eleven stations have been opened, and through laymen the Gospel has been brought to near-by countries. A hospital is maintained at Antigua.

Statistics (1952): Staff: 5 missionaries and 1 theological student. Souls: 507, including 149 communicants. Sunday schools enroll 330, and Bible classes enroll 67.

3. *Cuba-Isle of Pines* (1952). Two missionaries and two native workers are ministering to the spiritual needs of nine stations with 255 souls, of whom 136 are communicants. While the work in the Isle of Pines has been carried on for many years, it faces constant difficulties, important among them being the removal of our members. A school has been constructed in Cuba. One hundred are enrolled in Sunday school and 16 in Bible classes.

4. *Hawaii.* A survey in 1941 was to mark the opening of work in Hawaii, but Pearl Harbor interfered. During World War II the Armed Services Commission of The Lutheran Church — Missouri Synod maintained a service center in Honolulu. Provisions were made here for civilians as well as the military personnel. In 1945 the Rev. Adolph R. Meyer took over the work for the Mission Board. A parochial school was opened at an early date.

Statistics (1952): Staff: 2 American pastors and 3 lady teachers. Stations: 3. Souls: 420, including 204 communicants. School: 1, enrolling 59 children. Sunday schools enroll 279; Bible classes enroll 102.

5. *Venezuela.* This South American country was entered in 1951. At the close of 1952 it was served by two pastors and one lay worker. Membership totaled 277, of whom 81 were communicants. The school in Caracas enrolled 90 children. Four stations are being served.

6. *Panama* (1952). This country is being served at Balboa and Cristobal under the Armed Services Commission. Section f by HHK.

Other *Foreign Missions.* In 1926 H. Kuring of the Alberta and British Columbia District began mission work in *Alaska.*

See *Argentina; Brazil; Canada; Central America; Cuba; Japan; New Guinea; Nigeria.*

h. See *Deaf-Mute Missions.*

i. See *Jewish Missions.*

Foreign-Tongue Missions. The origin of these missions dates back to 1892, when under the supervision of Pastor A. Biewend work was begun among the Letts and Estonians in Boston. The Foreign-tongue Missions were taken over by Synod in 1899.

Pastor H. Rebane began work among the *Letts* in 1896 and organized congregations in Cleveland, Chicago, Wisconsin, South Dakota, Canada, the Western and the Pacific Coast territories being later assigned to other missionaries. At present there are more than 20 missionaries in the field. Work among the *Lithuanians* on the Atlantic Coast was begun in 1903. First pastor, Rev. H. S. Brustat, Boston. Later the work was taken up in Philadelphia, Scranton, Pa., Baltimore, Chicago, and in New York and Connecticut. At present there are 2 missionaries. In 1894, at the instance of Rev. F. Sattelmeier, pastor of an independent German-Polish congregation, the Eastern District began work among the *Poles* in various Eastern cities. Synod took it over in 1908. The *Finnish and Estonian* mission in Arizona was begun by the California and Nevada District and taken over by Synod in 1911; C. Klemmer, missionary. At present he is working among Estonians in Bogota, N. J., and New York. There are also some stations in Alberta. Rev. Joh. Pascha, working at eight stations in the East, among the *Persians*, called attention to great prospects there as well as in Pittsburgh and Chicago. Synod took over the mission in 1911, but expectations did not materialize; neither were later efforts to revive this mission of any avail. The work among the *Slovaks* was begun in 1912, in Detroit (now self-supporting), and taken over by Synod, with the sanction of the Slovak Synod, in 1914. There are also stations in Connecticut, Rhode Island, and New Jersey. In 1917 Synod took over the work among the *Italians*, Pastor A. Bongarzone, a converted priest, was in charge. There are 2 missionaries in the Eastern field (1945).

The Texas District started work among Spanish-speaking people in Texas in 1926, a mission which grew very rapidly. In 1940 the same District opened a mission among the natives of Mexico City through Pastor C. A. Lazos. A theological Seminary was opened in Mexico City. The official publication for Spanish work in Texas is: *Noticiero Luterano.*

XVI. *European Work and Connections.* The influence and work of Synod was not confined to America. When the state churches of Germany yielded to rationalism, the Missouri Synod broke fraternal relations with them, but received and treated the men of the Saxon Free Church as brethren. The relations established with Pastor F.

Brunn by Dr. Walther (1860) benefited both parties. Brunn's preparatory school provided Missouri with pastors and teachers, and Missouri sent over men to assist Brunn. The Missouri Synod was always in close connection with the Saxon Free Church. The Missouri Synod also has connections with Free Churches in Denmark and Finland. In 1896 a pastor of the Missouri Synod took charge of the Lutheran congregation established in London. After World War I, Dr. W. H. T. Dau visited Europe and strengthened old fraternal relations. After World War II the Missouri Synod helped the people of Germany financially and spiritually. It also participated in conferences *(Begegnungen)* held at Bad Boll. See Home Missions in Europe, Board for; *Australia; New Zealand.*

XVII. *Benevolences.* a. *Board of Support and Pensions.* Synod early realized its obligation to the aged servants of the Church and their widows and orphans. In 1872 Synod elected a Board of Support (1917, General Board of Support; now Board of Support and Pensions) which worked in conjunction with District Boards. The Support Fund derives its income from contributions by pastors and teachers and their employers, from legacies, and from the Three Million Dollar Fund raised by the Lutheran Laymen's League.* In 1938 Synod adopted a Pension Plan to which workers and their employers contribute and from which they then derive annuities upon disability or retirement (see *Handbook,* CPH, 1949, pp. 125—135).

b. *Indigent Students.* From the beginning congregations took up the matter of supporting needy students who were in training for service to the Church. J. F. Buenger founded a young men's society for this purpose. Many ladies' and young people's societies made it one of their aims. District boards control the disbursements.

c. The *General Relief Board* cares for sufferers from fire, flood, etc.

d. The *Board for Relief in Europe* was called into existence by the distress following World War I. It sent cash and foodstuffs to Europe and assisted in various ways in the rehabilitation of war sufferers.

e. In 1942 the President of Synod appointed the *National Advisory Emergency Planning Council* (executive committee: L. J. Sieck, L. Meyer, J. W. Behnken, R. R. Caemmerer, A. Doerffler, J. H. C. Fritz, F. C. Streufert, W. H.

Kroehnke). It dealt with such problems as shifting population, war workers, prisoners of war, postwar planning, distribution of Bibles, Christian literature, food and clothing to Europe; caring for children of Europe; preaching the Gospel to the stricken and providing facilities therefor; and many others (see *Proceedings,* 1947, pp. 647—63). See *Charities, Christian; Associated Lutheran Charities; Child Care and Child-Placing Agencies and Institutions; Aged and Infirm, Lutheran Homes for; Hospices, Christian Inns; Hospitals, Sanatoria, Homes for Convalescents and Chronically Ill; Deaconesses; Immigrant Mission.*

XVIII. *Doctrinal Discussions and Controversies.*

A. The *Lutheraner* early engaged in controversy with Dr. Wm. Nast, chief spokesman for the German Methodists and other Reformed churches which made efforts to bring German Lutherans into their church bodies. M. Oertel, who came over with the Saxons but later joined the Roman Catholics, ridiculed and reviled the Lutherans, and as a result there are polemics against him in the *Lutheraner.* In addition the *Lutheraner* met attacks of those in the *Turnerbund, Protestantenverein,* and in the lodges.

The Missouri Synod strove especially for a strict confessionalism in the Lutheran Church of America and thereby incurred the opposition of the so-called "American Lutherans" * and the support of the "Old Lutherans" * (see *Lutheran Confessions,* D 1; *American Lutheranism; Fellowship; Free Lutheran Conferences*).

B. *The Controversy on the Doctrine of the Church and the Ministry.* 1. The blind confidence placed in Stephan by the Saxon immigrants soon led to the belief that the Lutheran Church, more particularly, the adherents of Stephan, was the Church outside of which there was no salvation. Furthermore, the belief that the Power of the Keys * belong to the clergy alone began to take root. These beliefs and other factors caused Walther to study the doctrine of the Church and the Ministry for many years. The results of his study were printed in the works mentioned under *Doctrine* above. The Church in the real sense, he pointed out, is the communion of saints, *i. e.,* all who sincerely believe in Christ (the Invisible Church). This true Church is the possessor of spiritual treasures, rights, powers, and offices (for the full statement see *Theses on the Church.* See also *Church; Keys, Office of*).

2. This position of the Missouri Synod was tested and strengthened by the controversy with "the Synod of the Lutheran Church which Emigrated from Prussia," popularly known as the Buffalo Synod. Its leader, Rev. J. A. A. Grabau, who had been persecuted and imprisoned for his brave stand against the Prussian Union, held a doctrinal position similar to Stephan's. He and his associates maintained that the *one* holy Christian Church is a visible Church, "those who gather about the Word and Sacraments," and "these church gatherings are such as have the Word and Sacrament in purity in the ministry," there being thus no salvation outside of the Lutheran Church; regarding the Office of the Keys, that Christ did not give the keys of the kingdom of heaven to the Church and to each true believer, but solely and exclusively to the pastors; "it is therefore not for the congregation to judge and to command and to declare that the sinner is to be held as 'an heathen man and a publican' "; regarding the ministry, that "it is not the congregation which gives or conveys the holy ministry, but the Son of God," and if a congregation elects and calls a pastor without the assistance and presence of a representative of the ministry, "this has not the slightest validity before God and is vain arrogance"; ordination by other clergymen is by divine ordinance essential to the validity of the ministerial office; briefly, God would deal with us only through the ministerial office; "we also believe and confess that this office . . . forms a distinct and separate rank, or class"; regarding church government, that the congregation is not the supreme tribunal in the Church, but the synod as representing the church at large; "what is contrary to the Word of God or not is not decided by any one single church member, but by the Church itself in its symbols, church rituals, and synods"; at synodical meetings the laity may "listen, ask questions, and have them answered by the Word of God"; they are bound to obey their minister in all things not contrary to the Word of God; and the congregation has no right to judge the doctrine of its pastor. The doctrines defended by the "Missourians" (the name originated with Grabau) are summarized in the propositions forming the groundwork of *The Voice of the Church* (see *Theses on the Church*).

3. The controversy began before the organization of the synods. In 1840 Pastor Grabau issued a *Pastoral Letter,* a copy of which he sent to the Saxons, requesting their opinion on it. The opinion was written by Pastor Loeber in 1843. In a friendly spirit, dissent as to various points of doctrine was expressed in it. Grabau took the brotherly admonition amiss. Further correspondence brought out the divergence more clearly. Grabau and his three associates drew up a list of seventeen charges of error against the Missourians and declared that they could no longer consider them Lutheran ministers who adhered to the Word of God and the Lutheran Confessions. Congregations which had severed their connection with Buffalo and called Missourian pastors were branded as *Rotten* (heretical bodies), and the removal of their pastors was demanded by Grabau. Missouri held that these congregations had acted within their rights. The *Informatorium,* founded 1851, declared in its first issue: "Professor Walther and his adherents are surely heretics." Thereupon the *Lutheraner* also joined in the controversy.

4. In the same year Professor Walther and President Wyneken were sent to Germany to arrange for the printing of *The Voice of Our Church* and to confer with Loehe, who did not agree with Missouri. Many difficulties were overcome, but a complete understanding was not reached. Walther and Wyneken were well received by Dr. v. Harless and found themselves in full accord with Dr. Guericke and others. In 1853 Pastors Grabau and v. Rohr laid their case before the Church in Germany. The Leipzig Conference, the most important organization of Lutheran theologians of that period, issued an admonition to both parties, faulting Grabau for resorting too freely to excommunication and demanding of Missouri the removal of the so-called *Rottenprediger* (heretical pastors), which demand, however, upon being more fully informed, they later withdrew. As to the doctrine in controversy the Leipzig Conference demanded that it be treated as an "open question." The Conference of Fuerth took the same position. Missouri held that the only source and norm of doctrine is Scripture; it repudiated the modern doctrine that any matter, though it be clearly taught in the Bible, must be considered an open question till "the Church has spoken." They furthermore declared

that in the Lutheran sense "the Church had already spoken" — in its Confessions. The spokesmen of the General Synod also took a hand in the matter; but they did not fully understand the matter. Repeatedly efforts were made to bring the parties together in conference.

5. Already in 1846 the Saxons invited Grabau to a friendly conference to be held in Fort Wayne. St. Matthew's of Detroit asked him to confer with Craemer in its church. The Leipzig Conference and the Breslau Synod urged him to meet the Missourians in a "colloquium." Grabau refused, saying his conscience forbade it; and while Missouri as late as 1856, when the Ohio Synod again brought up the matter, stood ready to establish closer relations with Buffalo, Grabau, in 1859, prevailed upon his synod to renounce all fraternal intercourse with the Missouri Synod "as being heathenish and publican." In 1866 he excommunicated many of his own synod for "entertaining Missourian principles," in one instance an entire congregation. A split occurred in the Buffalo Synod. Grabau and a few adherents withdrew, and a "colloquium" was held in Buffalo (1866). Buffalo was represented by the pastors H. von Rohr, Chr. Hochstetter, and P. Brand and the laymen Chr. Krull, E. Schnorr, and H. A. Christiansen; Missouri by Professor Walther, Pastor H. C. Schwan, and Dr. Sihler, and the laymen J. C. D. Roemer, J. Keil, and J. C. Theiss. The representatives of Buffalo, with the exception of Pastor von Rohr, agreed with the Missourians on all points of doctrine. In 1867 a formal recognition of fraternal unity was sealed at a meeting between twelve ministers and five lay delegates of Buffalo and five Missourians, and eleven of the twelve ministers later joined the Missouri Synod.

C. *Controversy with the Iowa Synod.* The founding of the Iowa Synod (1854) was owing to the doctrinal disagreement between Pastor W. Loehe and the Missouri Synod. Loehe had taken a warm interest in the work of Wyneken and of the Missouri Synod. The disagreement first appeared when Loehe expressed his disapproval of that section of the constitution of the Missouri Synod which recognized the equality of the lay representatives with the clergy, "the American rule of the rabble in the Church." The efforts of Walther, Wyneken, and others to avert a break with the man to whom the Missouri Synod owed such an immense debt of gratitude proved unavailing. Other points of divergence developed and gave rise to the controversy with Iowa, the exponent of Loehe's theology.

1. As to the doctrine of the *Church and the Ministry*, Iowa rejected Thesis VI of the Ministry (see *Theses on the Ministry*). Rejecting Grabau's papistical doctrine of the absolute rule of the ministry, Loehe, like Grabau, did not believe that the Christians as spiritual priests transfer their rights to the pastor for public administration. Missouri taught that the office of the ministry is derived from the spiritual priesthood of believers, who possess all the rights of the Office of the Keys. "In the doctrine of the ministry," say the Davenport * Theses, "we cannot acknowledge that according to the Confessions of our Church the ministry through transference of the spiritual-priestly right comes to the individual Christian *(zustande komme)*. On the contrary we hold fast to this, that the public office of the ministry is transferred by God through the congregation in its entirety and essence by means of a regular call, because the *mandatum de constituendis ministris* (that is, the command to establish pastors) is given, not to the individual members, but to the Church as such." Again, ordination is simply a church ceremony, publicly attesting the validity of the call, said Missouri. Loehe was not ready to admit this. The Toledo Theses, agreed upon by the Ohio and Iowa synods in 1909, admit it. Finally, the disagreement on the doctrine of the Church is thus stated by the Davenport Theses: "We [Iowa] could not agree with the Synod of Missouri when it declared that the Church in its nature is invisible in the sense that all that belongs to its visibility must be excluded from the definition of its nature."

2. The synods differed also on the question of the basis of church unity, the completeness of the body of doctrine, and related topics. Iowa held: "Because within the Lutheran Church there are different tendencies *(verschiedene Richtungen)*, Synod declares itself in favor of that tendency which, by means of the Confessions and on the basis of the Word of God, strives toward a greater completeness." Missouri denied that there can be a true development of doctrine, "since all doctrines to be taught by the Church are once and for all set down in the Scriptures." This whole discussion concerned

itself with the definition of "open questions," regarding which Iowa said: "This expression self-evidently does not mean that the doctrines concerned are in themselves doubtful or uncertain, or even that they can arbitrarily be accepted or denied, but simply that they should not be treated as divisive of church fellowship. By open questions we have always understood, as distinguished from articles of faith, concerning which there must always be complete agreement in a church fellowship, such doctrines concerning which there may be a difference without breaking up the brotherhood of faith or church fellowship. Open questions in this sense cannot be such essential doctrines as are necessary for salvation and for the existence of the Church, but only such concerning which the Word of God contains either nothing at all or regarding which there is at least no completely clear expression of Scriptures, so that no complete consensus (no agreement) concerning them was formed in the Church, but always a difference of comprehension regarding them asserted itself even among the most orthodox teachers." (See *Davenport Theses*.) Missouri held that nothing taught in the Bible may be treated as an "open question"; that Christians should insist upon unity of the spirit; that persistent denial of any doctrine stands in the way of fellowship.

3. In regard to the Lutheran Symbols Iowa held: "In connection with the controversy regarding the Church and the Ministry the difference regarding the position toward the ecclesiastical symbols evolved. While from the side of Missouri the binding character thereof was extended without exception to all expressions of doctrine occurring therein, we confined it to that which the Confessions themselves wanted to establish, and for that reason differentiated between decisions of thesis and antithesis, as the conscience-binding substance of the Confessions, and extended explanations, proofs, etc., as constituent parts without immediate and independent symbolical significance." Missouri refused to accept the distinction and held that the Lutheran pastor is bound by all doctrine in the Confessions.

4. What of *Sunday?* Both synods were agreed that the observance of a particular day is not divinely commanded; but Iowa held that, even though the Augsburg Confession (Art. 28) rejects the contrary view, the con-

trary view, having been held by some Lutheran theologians, must be tolerated in the Church. — Missouri said: "The Pope is the very *Antichrist*." (Smalc. Art.; *Trigl.*, p. 475.) Iowa insisted that any Lutheran is at liberty to teach that Antichrist himself has not yet appeared. — As to the *millennium* (whether or not the "first resurrection," Rev. 20, is a bodily resurrection, which shall precede the general resurrection of the Last Day, and related questions), Missouri rejected Chiliasm in all its forms, as does the Augsburg Confession (Art. 17); Iowa, while not teaching Chiliasm as a synod, yet held that Chiliasm was legitimate Lutheran doctrine, a justifiable development of the Scripture teaching. (Rev. G. A. Schieferdecker, who had left Missouri on account of his Chiliastic teachings, was received into the Iowa Synod; later returned to Missouri. President Deindoerfer of the Iowa Synod himself was a Chiliast.) — A "colloquy" on these questions was held at Milwaukee in 1867. Iowa was represented by President G. Grossmann, Prof. S. Fritschel, Prof. G. Fritschel, and the lay delegate F. R. Becker; Missouri by President Walther, Dr. Sihler, Rev. J. A. Huegli, Rev. Chr. Hochstetter, and the lay delegates K. Koch, C. Wassermann, F. R. Stutz, and J. Bierlein. The attitude toward the Symbols, the subject of "open questions," and eschatological matters were discussed. Harmony was not attained. The controversy went on. True to its principle, Iowa was always ready to enter into church fellowship with Missouri in spite of doctrinal disagreement; Missouri, true to its principle, held that some of the differences involved such weighty matters of doctrine that church fellowship was impossible.

5. In the twentieth century, progress toward agreement was made, and the American Lutheran Church * adopted Missouri's *Brief Statement* together with the *Declaration* (see *Toledo Theses*, intersynodical; *Chicago Theses; Brief Statement*).

D. 1. *Controversy on Election and Conversion.* This controversy arose from a divergence on the question: Does a dissimilar conduct in natural men over against the converting and saving grace of God account for the fact that some are converted and saved while others remain unconverted and perish? The importance of the matter lies in the bearing it has on that other fundamental question: Does man's conversion and salvation depend solely upon God? (*Sola gratia.*) Dr. F. A. Schmidt correctly gauged the issue when he wrote: "This question (Does man's conversion depend upon God alone?) is, in a certain sense, the cardinal question of the whole controversy. The Missourians, of course, insist upon an unconditional affirmation of this question."

2. The controversy began in 1872, when Prof. G. Fritschel of the Iowa Synod insisted on the "dissimilar conduct," and Professor Walther answered with the article in *Lehre und Wehre:* "Is It Really Lutheran Doctrine that Man's Salvation, in the Last Analysis, Depends on His Free Self-determination?" The controversy became general when in 1880 Prof. F. A. Schmidt of the Norwegian Synod, at that time a member of the St. Louis faculty, repeated the charge of crypto-Calvinism against the Missouri Synod for rejecting the theory "that not the mercy of God and the most holy merit of Christ alone, but also in us there is a cause why God has elected us unto eternal life." (*Report of West. Dist.*, 1877.) Professor Stellhorn and others of the Missouri Synod sided with him; also the leaders of the Ohio Synod. A number of conferences and "colloquies" were held within the Missouri Synod and the Synodical Conference; but they failed to re-establish harmony.

3. In May, 1881, the Missouri Synod adopted the *Thirteen Theses.** In September, 1881, the Ohio Synod withdrew from the Synodical Conference. Those of its members who protested against this action of their synod formed the Concordia Synod. In 1883 the Norwegian Synod, reluctantly, also withdrew. The faculty of the General Council seminary sided with Ohio and Iowa; likewise the faculty of Rostock (Germany), in a formal opinion; in fact, most of the prominent Lutheran theologians throughout the world. The Synodical Conference stood pretty well alone. Led by Dr. Walther, Prof. F. Pieper, Rev. Stoeckhardt, Professors Hoenecke and A. L. Graebner, and others, for a time also by Prof. H. G. Stub and others of the Norwegian Synod, it unflinchingly maintained its position.

4. Concerning *Election*, Ohio (thus for the sake of brevity) taught that God did not elect "without having foreseen some difference in men"; that He elected "those of whom through His omniscience He foresaw that they would suffer themselves, by means of

His grace and power, to be brought unto faith in Christ and to be preserved therein," thus making election depend on the foreseen faith (intuitu fidei) or, as others put it, on the foreseen conduct, the foreseen non-resistance, of man. For Missouri's position see Thesis 10 and the Formula of Concord: "We reject the following errors: ... that not only the mercy of God and the most holy merit of Christ, but also in us there is a cause of God's election on account of which God has elected us to everlasting life." (Trigl., p. 837.) Whatever good God foresaw in any man could not have determined Him to elect this person; for whatever good is found in a man is entirely and solely the work of God's free grace. In other words, Ohio taught that election is the result of man's persevering faith, foreseen by God; the Synodical Conference, that faith is the result of the election of grace. Thesis 11. Form. of Conc.: "The eternal election of God not only foresees and foreknows the salvation of the elect, but is also, from the gracious will and pleasure of God in Christ Jesus, a cause which procures, works, helps, and promotes our salvation and what pertains thereto." (Trigl., p. 1065.) Again, the Synodical Conference repudiated the terminology which identified the general way of salvation for all men (according to which salvation is, of course, by faith) with election ("election in a wider sense") as contrary to the Scriptures and the Confessions.

5. As conversion is simply the execution of God's eternal election of grace and as faith would not, in this respect, constitute the "difference" required by the synergistic theory, unless conversion were the result, not of grace alone, but of grace and man's good conduct, the controversy at once took in, and soon centered in, the doctrine of conversion. The Missourians, as Dr. Schmidt correctly states, insisted upon an unconditional affirmation of the question: Does man's conversion and salvation depend upon God alone? Ohio would not give an unconditional affirmation. Rather, "it is undeniable that in a certain respect conversion and final salvation are dependent upon man and not upon God alone"; "according to the revealed order of salvation the actual final result of the means of grace depends not only on the sufficiency and efficacy of the means themselves, but also upon the conduct of man in regard to the necessary condition of passive-

ness and submissiveness under the Gospel call." And this submissiveness, the cessation of willful resistance, must be wrought by man himself, wrought, indeed, by the right use made of the "new powers imparted by grace," but wrought while man is still in the unconverted state, all of which the Synodical Conference opposed as a variety of Latermann's species of synergism ("the subtle synergism," as Dr. Schmauk of the General Council calls it, "which has infected nearly the whole of modern Evangelical Protestantism, and which is, or has been, taught in institutions bearing the name of our Church"), declaring that "the free will, from its innate, wicked, rebellious nature, resists God and His will hostilely, unless it be enlightened and controlled by God's Spirit." (Form. of Conc., Trigl., p. 888.) Ohio's insistence on the "right conduct of man over against converting grace" as explaining his conversion, salvation, and election, and the absolute rejection of it on the part of the Synodical Conference constituted the fundamental difference between the opposing bodies; it was, said Ohio, "the cardinal question of the entire controversy." Since grace is universal and all men are equally depraved and guilty, why are not all converted? The Synodical Conference left the question unanswered, as Scripture does. The other side solved the mystery by denying the equal guilt of men: "The dissimilar working of converting and saving grace is well explained on the ground of the dissimilar conduct of man over against grace." The Synodical Conference denied the "dissimilar conduct," identified it with the "dissimilar action" in Melanchthon's theory, pointed out that those who are dead in sins are equally, not dissimilarly, dead, and pointed to the Formula of Concord: "that when we are placed alongside of them and compared with them [and found to be most similar to them], we may learn the more diligently to recognize and praise God's pure, unmerited grace in the vessels of mercy." (Trigl., p. 1083.)

6. The Ohio Synod and others found the greater guilt in the willful resistance, and the right conduct, upon which, in the final analysis, all depends, in the suppression by man of his willful resistance, natural resistance being overcome by the Holy Spirit. The Synodical Conference denied, a) that Scripture and the Confessions make this distinction between natural and willful resistance, and b) that the un-

converted man can overcome his naturally willful, his willful natural resistance. In the later stages of the controversy the opponents taught 'that the
conversion of man is due, entirely and
solely, to grace, but his nonconversion
is due to the occurrence in him (such
occurrence being inexplicable, a psychological mystery) of a resistance
(willful resistance) which cannot be
overcome by the Holy Spirit, and that
he thus thwarts His converting grace,
while the resistance in others (natural
resistance) is of a kind which yields to
His converting grace. The Synodical
Conference objected, a) that "God, in
conversion, changes stubborn and unwilling into willing men through the
drawing of the Holy Ghost" (Form. of
Conc., *Trigl.*, p. 915) and b) that the
occurrence of a resistance of that sort
would again constitute the dissimilar
guilt. To sum up: The fundamental
difference lies, say the Ohioans, in the
Calvinistic leanings of the Synodical
Conference; according to Dr. Pieper
(*Conversion and Election*, p. 26): "The
fundamental difference consists in the
acknowledgment or rejection of an in-
soluble mystery in the fact that 'one is
hardened, blinded, given over to a
reprobate mind, while another, who is
indeed in the same guilt, is again converted.'" (Form. of Conc., *Trigl.*,
p. 1081.) — Another question arose:
Should a Christian be *sure of his salvation?* The Synodical Conference
affirmed it (Thesis 8); the opponents
denied it, as indeed their premises demanded.

7. The controversy also developed a
divergence on the *"analogy of faith."*
Ohio contended that the various doctrines of Holy Scripture must be modified according to inferences drawn
from the various doctrines, must be
harmonized with the *Lehrganzes* constructed by the theologian; the Synodical Conference, that all doctrines must
stand as they are revealed; that "human
reason must not be permitted to judge
whether there be any contradiction in
the articles of faith" and thus be made
the arbiter of faith; that, when two
doctrines seem to contradict each other,
the solution must be left to the light
of glory; and that the "analogy of faith"
is simply the sum and body of doctrines
revealed.

8. As to the charges of *Calvinism*
raised against the Synodical Conference,
the Synodical Conference always taught
that God desires the salvation of all
men; that there is no predestination to

damnation; that God seriously offers to
all his divine grace; that the election of
grace is not an arbitrary act of His
secret will, but the election of grace,
the grace in Christ, the grace of the
Gospel; that there are not two contradictory wills in God; that the sole cause
of a man's damnation is his wickedness,
his resistance to converting grace; that
grace is resistible, etc. See the first
division of the Thirteen Theses. The
charges were simply based on unwarranted inferences drawn from the rejection of the theory that man's conduct is the ground of explanation for
a person's conversion and final salvation. — As to the term *"intuitu fidei"*
(*election in view of faith*), this term
was coined by the ancient semi-Pelagians and, introduced by Aegidius Hunnius into Lutheran dogmatics, was used
by the later dogmaticians over against
the error of Huber (universal election)
and Calvinism (absolute election); but
as its employment in the doctrine of
election explains nothing with reference
to the mystery so long as faith is held
to be the work and gift of God, and
yields a good sense only when understood in an evil, synergistic sense, the
Synodical Conference would have none
of it. (For the Scripture proofs on the
various points see the doctrinal articles.)

9. The five Intersynodical Conferences held from 1903 (Watertown) to
1906 (Fort Wayne) hardly served to
bring the opposing bodies closer together. Since then good progress has
been made toward reaching an agreement on the basis of Scripture and the
Confessions. Since 1917 representatives
were appointed by the Missouri and
Wisconsin synods to confer with similar
committees of the synods of Ohio, Iowa,
and Buffalo. The theses proposed by
the Intersynodical Committee declare
that conversion is due solely to God's
grace and in no respect to man's conduct, and that the unconverted man can
in no way, neither by his natural
powers nor by his new powers granted
by grace, suppress or diminish his resistance. The agreement on the *sola
gratia* should carry with it the agreement on the "equal guilt" of man. See
Chicago Theses; Brief Statement. (Since
documents pertaining to doctrine drawn
up by the various synods are carefully
worded, they should be read and studied in their entirety. ED.)

XIX. *Statistics.* In 1847 the Missouri
Synod had 37 congregations, 4,099 souls,
and 764 parochial school children. Figures for 1883 give 1,054 congregations.

The *Statistical Yearbook* was published for the first time in 1884. The following table gives the statistics beginning with 1884.

Year	Congregations	Souls	Communicant Members	Parochial School Enrollment	Sunday School Enrollment
1884	1,198	348,182	197,284	62,772	3,272
1885	1,272	388,556	224,924	64,623	4,541
1886	1,346	436,353	245,773	68,546	5,329
1887	1,424	459,376	262,771	71,504	9,931
1888	1,465	482,467	276,444	72,825	10,504
1889	1,550	509,915	296,461	74,006	11,941
1890	1,622	531,357	303,183	78,061	13,891
1891	1,636	550,241	315,119	80,712	14,760
1892	1,729	580,014	330,082	83,514	16,656
1893	1,767	603,887	344,464	88,345	16,595
1894	1,825	627,689	357,186	85,679	20,824
1895	1,897	650,107	370,246	86,461	22,456
1896	2,015	662,048	380,006	87,908	22,707
1897	1,986	685,334	392,651	89,202	22,690
1898	2,041	696,791	400,169	89,775	22,588
1899	2,106	717,468	413,101	91,301	25,596
1900	2,147	728,240	422,565	92,042	24,717
1901	2,215	743,182	431,683	94,121	20,705
1902	2,267	755,149	440,431	95,967	22,326
1903	2,299	770,695	449,795	96,193	20,642
1904	2,367	790,505	461,867	96,888	23,447
1905	2,429	811,873	475,029	96,723	20,911
1906	2,475	819,049	481,242	96,964	20,888
1907	2,551	838,646	500,248	96,913	19,718
1908	2,599	855,725	510,502	96,035	20,514
1909	2,662	867,262	521,130	95,024	—
1910	2,736	878,654	529,287	93,890	53,343
1911	2,911	917,309	555,839	94,065	66,738
1912	2,917	934,199	565,129	94,167	71,966
1913	2,978	949,771	575,299	96,287	75,106
1914	—	—	—	—	—
1915	—	—	—	—	—
1916	3,094	972,138	598,777	96,737	85,910
1917	3,246	1,001,380	614,056	95,708	92,474
1918	3,244	1,010,092	621,886	84,832	92,316
1919	3,252	1,006,065	623,198	71,361	100,429
1920	3,283	1,009,982	623,228	73,063	108,133
1921	3,321	1,023,948	628,457	73,190	120,625
1922	3,450	1,041,514	638,951	76,317	127,236
1923	3,458	1,050,025	646,837	78,610	137,157
1924	3,497	1,069,922	658,671	79,326	146,684
1925	3,565	1,083,800	667,987	80,173	162,148
1926	3,645	1,086,955	675,956	81,082	170,722
1927	3,637	1,106,745	687,643	81,457	181,576
1928	3,687	1,122,174	703,059	81,049	189,820
1929	3,767	1,137,793	715,067	81,038	201,180
1930	3,843	1,163,666	731,119	79,956	210,988
1931	3,898	1,188,739	752,906	80,263	223,024
1932	3,939	1,210,206	772,734	79,204	233,279
1933	3,981	1,237,788	794,084	78,596	244,133
1934	4,059	1,267,958	814,916	78,681	252,487
1935	4,088	1,288,950	834,916	77,667	251,295
1936	4,163	1,305,500	853,524	76,811	249,229
1937	4,192	1,322,466	872,434	75,721	251,136
1938	4,228	1,348,833	894,785	73,284	273,265
1939	4,297	1,369,235	918,003	71,702	277,608
1940	4,358	1,392,337	941,292	71,151	281,572
1941	4,418	1,415,324	961,438	71,068	271,467
1942	4,447	1,423,954	980,095	70,647	262,276
1943	4,601	1,460,203	1,007,085	73,422	268,797
1944	4,564	1,501,314	1,033,875	76,277	279,411
1945	4,628	1,532,702	1,056,240	78,234	290,166
1946	4,688	1,581,486	1,086,592	82,029	310,501
1947	4,832	1,639,337	1,115,453	87,859	335,979
1948	4,906	1,694,024	1,145,414	92,487	364,065
1949	5,036	1,756,860	1,179,411	94,993	* 393,700
1950	5,137	1,810,953	1,211,254	98,136	* 425,499
1951	5,202	1,871,569	1,244,425	101,884	* 456,724
1952	5,316	1,936,370	1,282,584	106,309	* 493,477

* Statistics marked with an asterisk include North America only.

No statistics were gathered in 1914 and 1915. A special Sunday school listing was not placed on the questionnaire until 1910. Hence the abrupt increase for that year. Before 1919 many pastors included the pupils of part-time

schools in the parochial school enrollment. This was remedied with the introduction of a separate listing for
Saturday and summer schools in that
year. Notice the sharp decline in the
parochial school figures from 1917 to
1919. Statistics by AS

*Die Verfassung der deutschen evan-
gelisch-lutherischen Synode von Missouri, Ohio und anderen Staaten*, CPH,
1846; C. Hochstetter, *Geschichte der
evangelisch-lutherischen Missouri-Synode*, Naumann, Dresden, 1885; W. G.
Polack, *Building of a Great Church*,
CPH, 1926; W. H. T. Dau, *Ebenezer.
Reviews of the Work of the Missouri
Synod During the Three Quarters of
a Century*, CPH, 1922; W. A. Baepler,
A Century of Grace, CPH, 1947;
K. Kretzmann, *The Atlantic District
and Its Antecedents*, Atlantic Dist.,
1931; C. S. Mundinger, *Government in
the Missouri Synod*, CPH, 1947; G. Mez-
ger, *Denkstein*, CPH, 1922; F. Pieper,
"The Synodical Conference," *The Dis-
tinctive Doctrines and Usages of the
General Bodies of the Ev. Luth. Church
in the United States*, Luth. Pub. Soc.,
Philadelphia, 1902; Carl Mauelshagen,
*American Lutheranism Surrenders to
Forces of Conservatism*, University of
Georgia Division of Pub., 1936; Kraushaar, O., *Verfassungsformen der evangelisch-lutherischen Kirche Amerikas*,
Bertelsmann, Guetersloh, 1907; W. G.
Polack, *Fathers and Founders*, CPH,
1938. The archives of the Missouri
Synod are kept by the Concordia Historical Institute, St. Louis, its publication *Concordia Historical Institute
Quarterly* has valuable material with
references to the sources. Important
sources, in addition to those given
under XIII above, are the *Proceedings*
of the Delegate Synod, the *District Reports, Statistical Yearbook, Lutheran
Annual*. Consult also the bibliography
under the names of the men mentioned
in the article. For XVIII see references under doctrinal articles in this
volume.

Lutheran College and Seminary.
See *Canada, Lutheranism in*, 14.

**Lutheran Concordia College of
Texas.** See *Ministry, Education of*, IX.

Lutheran Confessions. The Reformation caused the confessional principle, which had been dead for many
centuries, to revive.

A. 1. *Birth and Early Years of
Lutheran Confessionalism* (1517—30).
During the early days of the Refor-
mation, Luther and his writings (95

Theses) served as unofficial confessions.
The first books to organize Lutheran
doctrines were the Catechisms of 1529,
published for the instruction of congregations.

2. *Historical Background of the
Augsburg Confession*. Three stages in
the historical background of the AC
may be distinguished: 1) The attempt
at *political federation* arose out of the
protest at the Diet of Spires which
made such a federation appear necessary for mutual defense. Landgrave
Philip of Hesse and Sturm of Strassburg succeeded in uniting Lutherans,
South Germans, and Swiss in a temporary federation whose details were
worked out in the so-called "Secret
agreement." To clear the way for
the federation, Philip of Hesse evolved
plans for settling the dispute between
Luther and Zwingli at a colloquy (Marburg). 2) The period of *political disintegration*. Melanchthon, after leaving Spires, had a change of heart and
sought to thwart the federation. Luther, especially, opposed a federation
without confessional unity. The representative of Elector John of Saxony
succeeded in postponing action on the
federation at Rotach June 7, 1529, and
in arranging a later meeting at Schwabach. At the meeting of Saalfeld, July 8,
Margrave George of Brandenburg-
Ansbach requested, as a prerequisite
for a federation, the adoption of a uniform confession, church order, and
other practical regulations. This request led to the presentation of the
Schwabach Articles October, 1529, prepared by Luther, Melanchthon, and
perhaps others between July 26 and
Sept. 14. In the meanwhile the Marburg Colloquy had been held Oct. 1—4,
1529, and had led to the publication of
the *Marburg Articles*, which, in the first
fourteen articles, enumerate the doctrines on which the Sacramentarians
and Lutherans agreed, and in the fifteenth, state the doctrine (Lord's Supper) on which they did not agree. The
Schwabach Articles finally defeated the
federation at the meeting of Smalcald
Nov. 29. 3) *The union of confession*.
When the Emperor's summons, Jan. 21,
1530, reached Elector John of Saxony,
he requested Luther, Melanchthon,
Jonas, and Bugenhagen to deliberate
concerning articles of faith and usage.
The results of their deliberations were
handed to Elector John at Torgau
March 27 and are known as the *Torgau
Articles* (manuscript discovered at
Weimar, 1830). Its ten articles treat

the following topics: of human doctrine and human order; of the marriage of priests; of both forms; concerning the Mass; of confession; of jurisdiction; of ordination; of vows; of the invocation of saints; of the German song. Luther, because he was under the ban, did not attend the Diet, but remained at Coburg. Since the summons had stated that "every man's opinions, thoughts, and notions" were to be heard, Melanchthon, using the *Torgau Articles* as a guide, prepared a statement of the Lutheran position and a preface. Eck's 404 abusive articles moved Melanchthon to include a summary of doctrine based on the seventeen *Schwabach Articles* and the *Marburg Articles*. Melanchthon changed the Confession repeatedly before the date of its presentation and also sent it to Luther for the latter's opinion. Various events (the ban on Evangelical preaching in Augsburg, the harsh message of Charles V to the Elector on May 27, the command to take part in the Corpus Christi procession, etc.), led to a rewriting of the preface so as to indicate that it was being submitted by others in addition to the Elector. The German draft of the Confession was read on June 25 "in the Palatinate, in the lower large room," by Dr. Christian Beyer, while the Latin copy was presented by Dr. Gregory Brueck. The so-called "Mainz manuscript" is a copy of the German original made at the time of the Diet for the archchancellery in Mainz. The AC was signed by Elector John and Duke John Frederick of Saxony, Margrave George of Brandenburg, Dukes Ernest and Francis of Lueneburg, Landgrave Philip of Hesse, Prince Wolfgang of Anhalt, and the representatives of Nuernberg and Reutlingen. (The signatories were feudal underlings of the Emperor who sought to assure and safeguard their feudal control of churches in their territories.) Before the close of the Diet, Weissenburg, Heilbronn, Kempten, and Windsheim also signed.

3. *Defense of the Confession.* At the meeting of the Papalist estates, June 26, the papal legate, Campanius, chose Dr. Eck (assisted by a score of theologians) to draft a reply. His *Responsio Catholica* attempted to show that the matters that were true in the AC were taken from Catholicism, that the AC was not in harmony with statements of Evangelical leaders, that the heresies in the AC had been condemned long ago, and that Luther was the

cause of the Anabaptist and Capernaitic heresies. Even the Papalist estates rejected this document because of its harshness July 15, and the *Confutatio Pontificia* was prepared and read to the Papalist estates Aug. 3. During the ensuing weeks Lutherans were subjected to tremendous pressure and intrigue. Although the *Confutatio* was not given the Lutherans, Melanchthon prepared an apology (*Prima Delineatio Apologiae;* not the one in the B. of C.) based on notes taken during the reading of the Confutation by Camerarius. When the recess Sept. 22 declared the AC "for good reasons answered and rejected by the Holy Scriptures and other writings," the Lutherans through Brueck presented the *Prima Delineatio,* which, however, was refused by the Emperor. After receiving a copy of the *Confutatio,* Melanchthon continued his work on the Apology and published the so-called *Apologia Confessionis* as a private document. It was signed with the AC at Smalcald in 1537. In mild and eloquent language the Apology defends the great Scriptural doctrine of salvation by faith alone. The Apology is, then, a refutation of the Confutation and a defense and amplification of the Augsburg Confession. The sequence of articles follows, in a general way, that of the Augsburg Confession and the Confutation. Articles, however, which were not disputed were treated briefly and those dealing with similar subject matter were combined. Like the Augsburg Confession, the Apology treats the fundamental Christian doctrines. The central theme, justification by grace through faith, is treated thoroughly in Art. IV and recurs frequently throughout the document. While the Apology is written with theological thoroughness, it still possesses the warmth of a living confession. Luther endorsed the Apology as well as the Augsburg Confession.

4. The outstanding characteristics of the Augsburg Confession are its objective universality, its emphasis on personal salvation through justification by faith, its air of reverent freedom, and its spirit of Catholic continuity. It claims to present nothing new, but only to re-emphasize the doctrines taught by the true Church through the ages. Building on the ecumenical creeds, it extends the confessional status to include the doctrine of man (Art. II), the unreborn will (XIX), the true doctrine of the salvation of man, justification by faith (IV), repentance

(XII), new obedience (VI), good works (XIX), daily life (XVI), Christ, the only Mediator (XX), true doctrine of the Word and the ministry (V), ordination (XIV), the Church (VII, VIII), confession and absolution (XI), the Sacraments (IX, X, XIII), and ecclesiastical rites (XV). It opposes Unitarians, Arians, Pelagians, Donatists, Anabaptists, Sacramentarians, and these abuses in the medieval Church: Holy Communion in one kind only, compulsory celibacy, the Mass as an expiatory sacrifice, obligatory auricular confession, obligatory feasts, ceremonies, fasts, monastic vows, the confusion of the spiritual and secular power of bishops.

5. *Subsequent History of the Augsburg Confession.* In Germany the AC became the confessional basis of the Smalcald League 1532 and was adopted by nearly all the Evangelicals within fifteen years after its presentation. In 1551 the Lutherans requested Melanchthon in the north and Brenz in the south to work out confessions supplementary to the AC for the Council of Trent (*Confessio Saxonica; Confessio Wuerttembergica*). In Austria the AC was early received by many; official toleration of its adherents was granted in 1568. In *Bohemia* many accepted the AC soon after the Diet, and it gained recognition among the *Unitas Fratrum* by way of the "Bohemian Confession." In *Silesia* official recognition for the AC was obtained through the Charter of Rudolf II 1609. In *Hungary* the AC was embodied in the *Confessio Pentapolitana* and won support until the reaction. In *Czechoslovakia* and *Yugoslavia* the two Lutheran groups adhere to the AC. In *Transylvania* the AC was accepted by Saxons. The Lutherans pledged themselves to it by oath 1572. In June of the same year, M. Lukas Ungleich presented a compilation of the AC (*Formula pii consensus inter pastores ecclesiarum Saxonicarum*) which was adopted. *Little Poland*, dominated by Wittenberg, adhered to the AC but with decided Reformed tendencies. Albrecht of Prussia had a translation made for *Greater Poland*; the first Lutheran synod 1565 pledged itself to the AC. In *Lithuania* about 2.5% of the population adheres to the AC. In *Latvia*, Lutherans have held the AC since the Diet of Augsburg. Fredrick II made the Bible, the ecumenical symbols, Luther's Catechism, and the AC the confessional basis for all *Danish* and *Norwegian* churches 1574. *Iceland*, connected with Denmark

and Norway, also accepted the AC. The AC was not formally received in Sweden until 1593, when it, together with the Bible, the ecumenical symbols, and the church order of 1571, became the confessional basis. In *Livonia* and *Estonia* the Diet of Reval 1524 decided for the Reformation, and the use of the AC was a matter of course. In *Russia* it became known through the Balkan States. The AC was translated into *English* at an early date. The 16 Articles (*Wittenberg Articles; Repetitio Augustanae*) agreed upon by a committee of Henry VIII and Lutherans (Luther, Melanchthon, Bugenhagen, Jonas Cruziger) in the year 1536 exerted (with the AC) a lasting influence on Anglican confessions and demonstrated what concessions the Lutherans were ready to make to win a country like England. Lutheranism came to the *Netherlands* at an early date, but years of persecution left only small remnants who adhered to the AC (Dutch ed. 1566). A *French* translation was made at the time of the Diet. Whether or not Charles V had the AC translated into *Spanish* is not known, but Spanish copies were available before W. War II. Charles V ordered an *Italian* copy prepared (best known of Italian translations is the one of 1562). The first Greek translation was published in 1559.

6. In *America* the AC is used from Alaska to Argentina, and the major Lutheran bodies in the U.S. are pledged to it. The Lutheran pastors who came in the 17th century were pledged to the AC and their congregations bound by it. The Ministerium of Pennsylvania and the Ministerium of York (which did not have the AC in their constitutions) required the pledge at ordination. In the 18th and 19th centuries the confessions became an empty form due to Pietism, Rationalism, and sectarianism. The reaction to the Prussian Union and the coming of the Old Lutherans brought renewed emphasis on the AC. S. S. Schmucker's "Definite Platform" * encountered decisive opposition. The Free Lutheran Conferences * (*CTM*, XV:529ff.) led to the formation of the Synodical Conference. The emphasis on confessionalism was also felt in the formation of the General Council 1867, which pledged itself to the whole Book of Concord. Schmauck, Jacobs, Krauth were especially active in the interest of confessionalism. In the General Synod there was also a trend toward

stricter confessionalism which made possible the formation of the U. L. C. A. (1918; pledged to all the Symbolical Books).

7. *Other Continents.* In *Africa* nearly all Lutherans use the AC (translated, for example, into Zulu, Twi, Shambala, Luhaya, Swahili). In *India* the Basel, Hermannsburg, Leipzig, Breklum, and Gossner missions used various Swedish and American editions (translated into Tamil by Cordes, 1853—54; Hermannsburg and the U. L. C. have a Telugu translation; Breklum Society translated it into Odiya; also translations in Hindi and Santali; Mo. Synod uses translation by N. Samuel). In *China* all missions use the AC (first translation, 1914, into Wenli; Mo. Synod uses translation by E. L. Arndt). In *Japan* the AC has been translated several times. The Ev. Luth. Syn. of *Australia* and the United Ev. Luth. Church pledge their pastors and people to the AC.

B. 1. *Second Period* (1530—46). While the AC was being established, Melanchthon was continually altering it and moving closer to the Reformed position. The *Variata* 1540 made great concessions in the article on the Lord's Supper. In 1536 a conference was held in the home of Luther between Lutherans and Reformed. As a result of the meeting the *Wittenberg Concord* was signed by the Reformed (Bucer, Capito, Albert) and the Lutherans (Luther, Melanchthon, Bugenhagen, et al.).

2. June 4, 1536, Pope Paul III finally called a general council to meet at Mantua on May 8, 1537, for "the utter extirpation of the . . . Lutheran heresy." In December, 1536, Elector John requested Luther to write a minimum statement to be considered at the Smalcald meeting in February. The work was completed in a short time and signed by a number of friends (Melanchthon with the reservation that the Pope might hold the primacy *jure humano*). Luther, because of illness, could not attend the meeting at Smalcald, which reaffirmed the AC and the Apology but did not act officially on Luther's Articles. Bugenhagen, however, succeeded in obtaining 44 signatures. Luther, perhaps in ignorance, published his Smalcald Articles as though officially signed. In lieu of Luther's articles, Melanchthon wrote a "Tract on the Power and the Primacy of the Pope," which was signed by the estates. Luther's articles

grew in esteem and were published in the Book of Concord 1580, with Melanchthon's Tract appended. Part I of the Smalcald Articles treats "the high articles of divine majesty"; Part II, the office and work of Christ, justification, the Mass, and the Papacy; Part III, sin, law, repentance, the Means of Grace, etc.

3. Eck was the first to point out the concessions made by Melanchthon in the *Variata* (at the discussions of Worms and Regensburg, which led to the Regensburg Interim). In the meanwhile, Agricola had jeopardized the doctrines of sin and grace, faith and justification, Law and Gospel. By 1543 Melanchthon had gone so far as to write articles for the Reformation of Cologne in a document in which Bucer prepared the items on Baptism and the Lord's Supper.

C. 1. *Third Period* (1546—80). After Luther's death the storm broke over the Evangelical Lutheran churches. South Germany and most of North Germany were conquered by the Emperor. The Augsburg Interim, 1548, which sacrificed the doctrine of justification by faith, recognized seven sacraments and transubstantiation, was accepted by most of the crushed Protestant princes. Melanchthon opposed the Augsburg Interim but soon became fearful and yielded in the Leipzig Interim (1548; compromised justification by faith; pledged the clergy to obey the pope; reintroduced Roman ceremonies at Baptism, confirmation, extreme unction, Corpus Christi; laws of fasting placed in the hands of the Emperor). Numerous controversies arose chiefly because of the Interim aberrations of Melanchthon's pupils, and the extremism of Flacius and others: Adiaphoristic, 1548; Osiandrian, 1550; Majoristic, 1551; Synergistic, 1555; Antinomistic, 1556; Flacian, 1560; Crypto-Calvinistic, 1571. The attempt to adjust controversies by academic disputations, to fix religion by dogmatic formulation, to restore peace by the Frankfort Recess 1558 and Naumburg Diet 1561, and the conflict regarding the *Variata* gave birth to at least 20 confessions between the death of Luther and the writing of the F. of C. The most important were: *Philippicum* (1560; all the writings of Melanchthon), *Brunswick* 1563, *Pomeranicum* 1565, *Prutenicum* 1567, *Thuringicum* 1570, *Brandenburgicum.*

2. In 1567 Jacob Andreae was ordered to draw up peace formulas. In

1574 Elector August ended the dishonest rule of the Philippists. The previous year Andreae had published "Six Christian Sermons," which, at the suggestion of Chemnitz, he revised into the *Swabian Concord* (11 articles). After being revised by Chytraeus and Chemnitz, they were known as the *Swabian-Saxon Concord*. A formula prepared by Lucas Osiander and Balthasar Bidembach was adopted at Maulbronn 1576. A meeting was called at Torgau May 6—June 7, 1576, attended by such leaders as Selnecker, Andreae, Chemnitz, Chytraeus, Musculus, and Koerner. This meeting formulated the *Torgau Book* on the basis of the *Swabian-Saxon Concord* and the *Maulbronn Formula*. After Elector August had received criticisms on the work, the final revision was made at Bergen by Chemnitz, Andreae, Selnecker, Musculus, Koerner, and Chytraeus. This *Bergen Book* (*Solid Declaration*), together with Andreae's *Epitome*, was finished by May 28, 1577. These two works were brought together in the *Book of Concord* (with Andreae's preface), which appeared officially at Dresden on June 25, 1580 (see *Book of Concord*). The *Epitome* 1) defines the state of controversy, 2) affirms the true doctrine, 3) rejects the false doctrines. The *Solid Declaration* omits this division and discusses matters at length. Both have introductions. The contents of the F. of C. may be summarized as follows: Introduction confesses the Scriptures as the only rule of faith and practice and also accepts Lutheran confessions previously adopted; Art. I rejects exaggerations of Flacius on original sin; (II) rejects synergism and upholds *sola gratia;* (III) emphasizes forensic character of justification; (IV) faith produces good works; (V) distinguishes Law and Gospel; (VI) explains the Christian use of the Law; (VII) the Real Presence; (VIII) personal union and attributes of Christ; (IX) the whole Christ descended to hell to proclaim His victory; (X) on Church ceremonies; (XI) rejects the doctrine of reprobation and teaches an election of grace; (XII) the rejection of heresies. The Book of Concord was signed by three electors, two bishops, eighteen princes, twenty-four counts, four barons, thirty-eight cities, and about eight thousand clergy in 1577 and 1578.

D. 1. *Subscription.* At the time of the departure from the Diet at Augsburg, Luther expressed the view that all who hold the AC, whether openly or secretly, must be regarded and treated as brothers. This view was re-emphasized by Walther (1855—1859; *Luth.* XII: 181 f.; *L. u. W.,* II: 84 f.), followed by such men as Krauth, Jacobs, Schmauck, and others. The acceptance of the Augsburg Confession indicates that the subscriber has the Lutheran attitude on the great fundamentals (*sola Scriptura, sola gratia, sola fide*) and by conscientious study will find himself in agreement with the doctrinal content of the other symbols (hereby is not implied that the individual reaches absolute and errorless perfection in exegesis, doctrine, life. Cf. *Luth.* I: 3, 83; XIII: 1; *West. Dist. Rep.,* 1867, 31).

2. In early American Lutheranism church conferences and synods did not emphasize confessional loyalty, and the confessions were often omitted in the constitutions. H. M. Muhlenberg sought to rally Lutherans around the Augsburg Confession "and other Lutheran Symbols." After Muhlenberg's death a trend away from the confessions was influenced by rationalism, and in the 19th century there were some who favored the abandonment of the confessions. The Tennessee Synod was probably the first to insist on a strict confessionalism. As the symbols came into prominence, distinctions between fundamental and non-fundamental doctrines were made. Schmucker's "Definite Platform" sought to eliminate certain doctrines which had been regarded as non-fundamental and rejected by some. The Iowa Synod gave up its attempt to establish boundaries between essentials and non-essentials but emphasized that the confessions must be historically interpreted (G. M. Grossmann).

3. The distinction between "articles of faith" by which the subscriber is bound and ordinary factual statements was prominently elaborated in America by C. F. Schaeffer (*Ev. Rev.,* 1850, 457 ff.). Some years later Walther sought to define the meaning of subscriptions: inasmuch as a confession is a statement of belief, the subscriber binds himself to all the doctrine therein contained but not to historical references, matters belonging to human sciences, logic, method of presentation, adiaphora, etc. (*Luth.* XIV: 201 ff.)

4. Because the Lutheran Church regards the confessions as a true declaration of Holy Scripture, it demands of

its teachers and pastors a *bona fide* subscription to the confessions as the pure and unadulterated declarations of the Word of God. Thus it demands a *quia* ("because" they are the Word of God) and not a *quatenus* ("in so far as" they are God's Word) subscription.
EL

Die Bekenntnisschriften der evangelisch-lutherischen Kirche. Herausgegeben vom deutschen evangelischen Kirchenausschuss im Gedenkjahr der Augsburgischen Konfession, Vandenhoeck u. Ruprecht, Goettingen, 1930 (1952 ed.); M. Reu, *The Augsburg Confession* (a collection of sources with an introduction), Wartburg, Chicago, 1930; *Concordia Triglotta,* CPH, 1921; J. T. Mueller, *Die Symbolischen Buecher der evangelisch-lutherischen Kirche,* Stuttgart, 1869; H. Heppe, *Bekenntnisschriften der altprotestantischen Kirche Deutschlands zur Zeit des Augsburgischen Religionsfriedens,* 1855; T. G. Tappert, "The Symbols of the Church," *What Lutherans Are Thinking,* Wartburg Press, Chicago, 1947; Hans von Schubert, *Der Reichstag von Augsburg im Zusammenhang der Reformationsgeschichte,* Hensius, Leipzig, 1930; M. Loy, *The Augsburg Confession,* Luth. Bk. Concern, Columbus, 1908; J. W. Richards, *The Confessional History of the Lutheran Church,* Luth. Pub. Soc., Philadelphia, 1909; T. Schmauk-C. Benze, *The Confessional Principle and the Confessions of the Lutheran Church as Embodying the Evangelical Confessions of the Christian Church,* Gen. Coun. Pub. Bd., Philadelphia, 1911; G. Fritschel, *The Formula of Concord — Its Origin and Contents,* Philadelphia, 1916; J. L. Neve, *The Augsburg Confession: A Brief Review of Its History and an Interpretation of Its Doctrinal Articles,* Philadelphia, 1914; C. Bergendoff, *Making and Meaning of the Augsburg Confession,* Rock Island, 1930; C. H. Little, *Lutheran Confessional Theology,* CPH, 1943; V. Ferm, *The Crisis in American Lutheran Theology,* Century Co., 1926; C. Mauelshagen, *American Lutheranism Surrenders to Forces of Conservatism,* University of Georgia Division of Pub., 1936; W. Arndt, "The Pertinency and Adequacy of the Lutheran Confessions," *CTM,* XX: 674 ff.

American Editions: Solomon D. Henkel & Bros., *The Book of Concord,* Newmarket, 1854; H. E. Jacobs, *The Book of Concord,* F. Smith, Philadelphia, 1882—83; *Concordia Triglotta,* CPH, 1921.

Lutheran Congregation. According to Lutheran teaching, the local congregation of believers has all spiritual powers, the powers summed up under the term Office of the Keys. Its sphere, as a church, is exclusively spiritual, being concerned solely with the building of Christ's kingdom on earth, and its governing principle is the Word of God. Accordingly, the government of the Lutheran Church is not hierarchical, as in the Roman Church, nor is it vested in an episcopate, as in the Anglican (Protestant Episcopal) and Methodist Episcopal churches, nor in an assembly of elders, as in the Presbyterian Church, nor in synods, or other more or less representative gatherings. Synodical resolutions within the Lutheran Church have no binding force in the administration of those affairs of the local congregation which are properly termed internal. The individual congregation is autonomous, has and discharges the supreme external authority, even as the Word of God is the only internal authority, in all matters of church life and work.

Lutheran Danish Halle Missions. See *Missions,* B 7.

Lutheran Deaconess Association. See *Deaconesses,* 9.

Lutheran Education Association. The Lutheran Education Association is an organization of Lutheran pastors, teachers, laymen and women who are particularly interested in promoting the cause of Christian education at all levels and by means of all the agencies which the Church has at her disposal.

It was felt that an organization of this type was needed in order to coordinate and fuse the educational thinking and efforts of individuals and smaller groups.

Furthermore, it was hoped that such an organization could stimulate the Church's teaching personnel so that its latent powers could be used to greater advantage or effectiveness. The need for unification of purpose and action was very definitely felt in this area.

Organized in 1942, the L. E. A. received Synod's endorsement at the 1944 Synodical Convention in Saginaw, together with the suggestion that the Executive Secretary of the Board for Parish Education be made an advisory member of the Executive Board of the Association.

Research, which is at the heart of educational progress and improvement, needed direction and stimulation in order that the best interests of the Church's educational program might be served. The organization hopes not only to give impetus and guidance to research projects, but also to disseminate the findings of research by means of its publications. A research council was created in 1946 and a director appointed. A continuous project of the council is the indexing of all research projects pertaining to Lutheran education. This is only one phase of the council's activity.

By establishing local chapters in areas where a concentration of Lutheran churches seems to warrant it, the LEA seeks to spread its influence and thus achieve those objectives for which it was called into being. This purpose can be accomplished by means of forums and meetings in which local matters pertaining to Christian education are discussed and impetus is given to appropriate action. Chapters have also been established in several of Synod's pastor- and teacher-training institutions.

The association uses several publication channels. These are:

1. Its annual yearbooks.

2. Monographs on various educational subjects.

3. Minutes and essays of its annual conventions.

4. Synod's official educational journal, *Lutheran Education*. (Besides articles on various topics, one section of this journal is devoted to news regarding the activities of the association and to a report of the monthly meetings of the Executive Board.)

Membership in 1952 totaled 1,173.

ALA

Lutheran Education Week. See *Parish Education*, M 5.

Lutheran Foreign Mission Societies in the United States, Early. In the early part of the 19th century, Lutherans in the United States showed their interest in foreign missions by supporting the various European and American foreign mission societies. At that time there was no distinctly Lutheran foreign mission enterprise in the United States.

2. In 1821 the Lutheran General Synod began to support Rhenius in India. The Central Missionary Society was formed at Mechanicsburg, Pa., in 1835, which was followed in 1837 by the German Foreign Missionary Society in the United States. This organization was to carry on work for both the Reformed and the Lutherans, but proved a failure. The name was then changed 1839 to the Foreign Mission Society of the Evangelical Lutheran Church in the United States of America.

3. When the confessional break came in the General Synod in 1867, the General Council organized its own foreign mission enterprise 1869.

4. The General Synod Foreign Missions were begun in co-operation with the American Board (ABCFM), the Rev. C. F. Heyer being called as the first missionary 1840. Fearing friction, Heyer resigned and was then called to the same field (India) by the foreign missionary organization in the Lutheran Ministerium of Pennsylvania, which had been in existence since 1836. He arrived in India in the spring of 1842, beginning work at Guntur. New stations were opened in the course of time. Rajahmundry was transferred to the Ministerium of Pennsylvania by the North German Missionary Society in 1845. Later this field was given over to the General Synod. The United Synod of the Evangelical Lutheran Church in the South began foreign mission work in Japan in 1892. By the merger of the General Synod, the General Council, and the United Synod, South, all foreign mission work was transferred to the new organization, the United Lutheran Church 1918. During and after World War I this organization gave extensive aid to the crippled German foreign missions.

5. The Iowa Synod (ALC) carried on its early mission work with the General Council, Neuendettelsau, Hermannsburg, Leipzig, and other societies. During World War I it conducted the mission in the former German New Guinea* in conjunction with the United Ev. Luth. Church in Australia. In 1921 it took over Tanganyika mission in former German East Africa.

6. The Ohio Synod (ALC) busied itself especially with home missions. In 1912 it took over part of the Hermannsburg field among the Telugus in India; the whole field was assigned to it after World War I.

7. The Norwegian Ev. Luth. Synod of America (Ev. Luth. Synod) supported missions in South Africa, India, China, Armenia, and other places.

8. The Augustana Synod early aided work in Africa, Australia, China, India, Madagascar, Palestine, Syria, and elsewhere. In connection with the General Council it co-operated in the

work among the Telugus in India. In 1882 it began work in Salt Lake City, Utah.

9. The Lutheran Church — Missouri Synod began its foreign mission work in 1893. In India Th. Naether and Franz Mohn had been dismissed by the Leipzig Mission because of their adherence to the inspiration of Scripture. These men were called as missionaries to India and commissioned in 1894. Work was begun in the Salem and North Arcot districts of the Madras Presidency. In 1913 a private organization within the Synodical Conference was formed for foreign mission work in China. The Rev. E. L. Arndt was sent out in 1914, locating at Hankow. The society's work was turned over to the Missouri Synod in 1917. Fields: India, China, New Guinea, Japan. The Missouri Synod began work in the Philippine Islands in 1946 at Manila, with Pastors A. A. Carino and H. Mayer as first regular missionaries.

10. For later developments see the articles on the respective synods and the National Lutheran Council.

Lutheran Free Church. The Lutheran Free Church was organized in Minneapolis, Minn., June, 1897, as the result of a dispute between the trustees of Augsburg Seminary, Minneapolis, Minn., and the United Norwegian Church. Before this formal organization, its churches and ministers were known as "Friends of Augsburg."

The Lutheran Free Church is a federated fellowship of Lutheran congregations, each one of which is regarded as sovereign "under the authority of the Word of God and the Spirit." The Annual Conference has advisory powers only. All members have a right to vote at this conference, as well as any other Lutherans who declare in writing their harmony with the principles of the Lutheran Free Church and willingness to work for the body. The common endeavors of the church, such as schools, missions, charities, and publications, are carried on by separate boards and corporations. It has a college, junior college, seminary, deaconess mother house, as well as charitable institutions. It is a member of the National Lutheran Council.

In 1951 it had 230 ordained ministers and a baptized membership of 59,860. Until 1923 presidents served as moderators of the Annual Conference only. In 1920 O. H. Sletten was elected for a three-year term. Presidents since

1923 are: E. E. Gynild, 1923—28; H. J. Urdahl, 1928—30; T. O. Burntvedt, 1928—.

Lutheran Free Church of Finland. See *Finland, Lutheranism in,* 5.

Lutheran Hospitals. See *Hospitals.*

Lutheran Hour. See *Radio Evangelism,* 6.

Lutheran Laymen's League. This laymen's organization within The Lutheran Church — Missouri Synod was organized June 22, 1917, while the Synod was in session at Milwaukee, Wis. The purpose and object of the League as stated by its founders is "to aid Synod by word and deed in its business and financial matters."

The immediate cause which led to the organization of the Lutheran Laymen's League was a synodical debt of $100,000. A meeting was called at the home of F. Pritzlaff, Milwaukee, with A. G. Brauer, Benj. Bosse, Edmund Seuel, Theo. Lamprecht, J. A. Leschen, A. H. Ahlbrand, Hy. W. Horst, H. Aug. Luedke, John W. Boehne, Wm. Schlake, and R. H. Leonhardt present besides Mr. Pritzlaff. Plans were discussed for removing the $100,000 deficit in the Synodical Treasury. The twelve men personally pledged themselves to $12,000, and before the close of the year the machinery which they had set in motion had produced $114,000 to cancel the synodical deficit.

On Nov. 11, 1919, when the country began to turn increased attention to the care and reward of its veterans, the Lutheran Laymen's League began collecting a Three Million Dollar Endowment Fund for the support of superannuated and infirm pastors, teachers, and professors, and their widows and orphans. When Synod met in 1920, the League turned over to Synod, as a first installment on this Endowment Fund, a sum amounting to over $2,000,000. In 1948 the fund amounted to $2,700,000.

In 1923, through contributions raised by members of the Walther League, and with the co-operation of the Lutheran Laymen's League, Radio Station KFUO was established at Concordia Seminary, St. Louis, Mo. With the removal of the Seminary to the new campus in Clayton, Mo., the League in 1926 appropriated $50,000 for the erection of a new building and the installation of modern equipment (see *Radio Stations, Religious*).

In 1930 the Lutheran Laymen's League undertook the sponsoring of the Lutheran Hour. For nine months this weekly program was carried on a nation-wide network of the Columbia Broadcasting System into the homes of America (for later expansion see *Radio Evangelism*).

By 1950 the League had enlarged its program and widened its activities. Its membership had been formed into local clubs, zones, and district organizations. A monthly program featuring administration, education, fellowship, and service is made available to all local units.

Opportunities are provided by the League to study and discuss in regional and city-wide seminars, under expert leadership, the problems which face the Church today. The League has also interested itself in visual education and has produced a number of full-length feature films, among them "Youth for the Kingdom" and "Messenger of Peace."

The League established a scholarship plan at the Lutheran University at Valparaiso, Ind. By 1948 two scholarships of $1,000 each were being awarded annually on the basis of a competitive examination open to all high school graduates who are members of The Lutheran Church — Missouri Synod. In 1948 also a financial effort was begun for the erection of a Memorial Building on the campus of Valparaiso University.

Thus the Lutheran Laymen's League strives to marshal the power of Christian manhood in a common brotherhood of service. TGE

Lutheran Literature. See *Literature, Lutheran.*

Lutheran Missionary Society for the Promotion of the Gospel. See *Bornholmers.*

Lutheran Outlook. See *American Lutheran Conference,* 10.

Lutheran Publishing House. See *Publication Houses.*

Lutheran School Club. See *Parish Education, J.*

Lutheran School Society. See *Parish Education, J.*

Lutheran Student Association of America. See *Students, Spiritual Care of, A.*

Lutheran Theological Seminary. *Ministry, Education of,* XI B.

Lutheran Theology after 1580. 1. The Book of Concord marked the beginning of a century of strict orthodoxy within the Lutheran Church. After a long

series of theological controversies, the Lutherans had finally achieved doctrinal unity in a collection of symbolical writings. A spiritual blessing which had been acquired with such great efforts had to be properly safeguarded against threats from within and from without. This determination accounts for the development of the large theological literature during that period.

2. The theological calm created by the signing of the Formula of Concord was first disturbed by two Christological Controversies, the Cryptist and Kenoticist Controversy between the Giessen and the Tuebingen theologians 1619—26 and the so-called Luetkemann Controversy (Luetkemann d. 1655). Of far greater danger to Lutheran orthodoxy, however, was the Syncretistic Controversy aroused by the unionistic efforts of G. Calixt (d. 1656) to reconcile the different religious bodies by differentiating between the exclusive and the inclusive aspects of truth. The consensus of the first five centuries of the Christian Church was to constitute the basis of union for all groups. Strict Lutherans opposed this as syncretism and crypto-Calvinism.

3. It has become a favorite habit with some writers to speak of dead orthodoxy. Dead bodies produce no useful work. The century of Lutheran orthodoxy contributed, among others, the following: the *Philologia Sacra* (1623) of S. Glassius, a classical work for more than two centuries; the *Officina Biblica* (1636) of Walther, the first historico-critical introduction to the Scriptures; the *Critica Sacra* (1680) and the *Hermeneutica* (1684) of Pfeiffer, a boon to the progress of exegesis; the Latin translation of the New Testament with notes and the *Tameion,* a concordance of the Greek New Testament, by Erasmus Schmidt (d. 1637); commentaries on several Old Testament books and on the Pauline Epistles by S. Schmidt; the *Biblia Illustrata* of Abr. Calov (d. 1686), a work of amazing research and learning; the *Loci Communes Theologici* and *Compendium Loc. Theol.* of Hutter (d. 1616); the *Loci Theologici* of J. Gerhard (d. 1637), the standard of Lutheran orthodoxy; the *Theol. Didactico-polemica* of J. A. Quenstedt (d. 1688).

4. Lest it be thought that this activity was merely one of the head and meant nothing to the heart, it is necessary to observe that this same period produced John Arndt's (d. 1621) *True Christianity,* J. Gerhard's *Meditationes*

Sacrae and *Schola Pietatis,* Chr. Scriver's devotional works. The heart, moreover, speaks in song. The century of Lutheran orthodoxy produced many of the Church's greatest hymns, as indicated by these names: J. Hermann (d. 1647), P. Fleming (d. 1640), M. Meyfart (d. 1642), M. Rinkart (d. 1648), T. Clausnitzer (d. 1648), J. Rist (d. 1667), S. Dach (d. 1659), H. Alberti (d. 1651), G. Weissel (d. 1655), and, after Luther, the greatest sacred poet of the Church, P. Gerhardt (d. 1676).

5. In spite of the demoralizing effect of the Thirty Years' War, the age of orthodoxy not only produced great hymn writers, also among the laity, but also devout rulers like Ernest the Pious of Saxe-Gotha (d. 1675), known in history as *Bet-Ernst,* who had published the famous Weimar exposition of the Bible, of which fourteen large editions appeared between the years 1641 and 1768. Gustavus Adolphus of Sweden encouraged the Lapp mission, which was also supported by Denmark. Various individuals went out to do mission work on their own account. The great work of A. H. Francke in the field of mercy and missions belongs to the period of Pietism.

6. Philipp Jacob Spener 1635—1705 is known as "the father of Pietism." At Frankfort-on-the-Main those who accepted his application of the Scriptures met with him in private for further instruction. Thus there originated in 1670 the *ecclesiolae,* which were to become one of the distinct characteristics of Pietism. His *Pia Desideria* 1675 gave Pietism a definite platform. From the University of Halle (founded in 1692) Pietism spread through Germany, Scandinavia, and Switzerland. By its unbalanced emphasis on Christian living at the expense of doctrine and believing, Pietism prepared the way for the era of Enlightenment or Rationalism.

7. Some notable works were produced in the period of Pietism, some by Pietists, others by their opponents in the orthodox camp. J. G. Walch (d. 1755) published his *Einleitung in die Religionsstreitigkeiten* and an edition of Luther's works. J. L. von Mosheim (d. 1755), "neither Pietist nor over-orthodox," by the publication of his *Institutes of Ecclesiastical History* became known as "the father of modern church history." J. Alb. Bengel (d. 1752), put out his *Gnomon N. T.* In the field of devotional literature Bogatzky (d. 1774) published his *Golden Treas-*

ury. The new spirituality of the time found expression in Francke's philanthropic institutions, the establishment of Protestant foreign missions (Ziegenbalg, Pluetschau, Schwartz, Egede), and in many of the Church's greatest hymns (Gerhardt) and music (Bach).

8. By the middle of the eighteenth century Rationalism had begun to spring up in the Protestant theology of Germany. Together with Deism in England and with Naturalism in France, it has become known as the "Enlightenment." G. W. Leibniz (d. 1716) and Chr. Wolff (d. 1754) had planted the seed. Frederick II of Prussia cultivated it in every way. Rationalism substitutes the dictates of human reason for the authority of God's Word. The chief Lutheran theologians in the development of Rationalism were J. A. Ernesti (d. 1781), New Testament exegesis; J. D. Michaelis (d. 1791), Old Testament exegesis; J. S. Semler (d. 1791), Biblical and historical criticism; J. G. Toellner (d. 1774), in the department of dogmatics. Rationalists made some noteworthy contributions to theological scholarship. W. Gesenius (d. 1842), for example, published a Hebrew-German dictionary (1810 ff.) and a Hebrew Grammar (1813) which are still being used, and K. G. Bretschneider (d. 1848) founded the monumental *Corpus Reformatorum.*

9. Rationalism suffered a serious blow at the hand of two of its most famous disciples. Immanuel Kant, though exalting human reason, also showed its limitations in spiritual matters, while K. A. von Hase (d. 1890), the brilliant church historian, is credited with having dealt the deathblow to vulgar rationalism with his *Hutterus Redivivus* (1828). F. D. E. Schleiermacher (d. 1834), sometimes styled the father of modern religious liberalism, made his contribution to the decline of the old Rationalism by identifying religious belief with religious feeling, thereby getting away from Rationalism's one-sided emphasis on reason. It must be remembered, however, that the old Lutheran theology had never been dead. This was forcefully demonstrated when Claus Harms (d. 1855) protested against religious indifference with his "Ninety-Five Theses." But neither did Rationalism die. Thus two streams of theological development can be traced in the Lutheran lands of Europe in the nine-

teenth and twentieth centuries, the liberalistic and the conservative.

10. Liberalistic theology derived the pattern of its development largely from the influence of Kant (d. 1804), G. F. W. Hegel (d. 1831), and Schleiermacher (d. 1834). For Kant not creeds, but moral precepts are the important factor in religion. Nevertheless he may be considered the founder of German Idealism by his emphasis on the idea of God, freedom, and immortality. Schleiermacher gave to theologians a new system of dogmatics which has served them as a guide irrespective of their attitude toward his anthropocentric emphasis in theology. Hegel converted historic religion into philosophical and rational ideas and stimulated the tendency to pantheism in theology. To the Hegelian radicals belonged D. F. Strauss (d. 1874), who with his *Leben Jesu* demonstrated the clash between Hegelian philosophy and Christianity. The new method of Biblical study introduced by J. Wellhausen and his school can be traced directly to the evolutionary ideas of Hegel. Another product of Hegel's philosophy in religion is F. C. Baur (d. 1862) and his school. Christianity is not a perfect religion, but an idea in the process of evolution. In the history of dogma Baur believed to see Hegel's scheme of thesis, antithesis, and synthesis in action. Other prominent representatives of Hegelian philosophy in theology were O. Pfleiderer (d. 1909), L. Feuerbach (d. 1872), and B. Bauer (d. 1882).

11. The first half of the nineteenth century experienced a revival of religion throughout Germany. Lutheran confessional theology appeared in a more conservative form as the "Theology of Repristination" and in a more liberal form as the *Erlangen Theology*. The former aimed to restore historic Lutheranism in the scientific form of the sixteenth and seventeenth centuries. To this group belonged A. Vilmar (d. 1868), E. W. Hengstenberg (d. 1869), C. P. Caspari (d. 1892), F. A. Philippi (d. 1882), Th. Kliefoth (d. 1895), and W. Loehe (d. 1872). The *Erlangen Theology* aimed to combine Lutheran theology with the new learning, differentiating between the Reformation and post-Reformation theologies in favor of the former. Confessional theology was not to be static but dynamic in the life of the Church, which was to the Erlangen theologians a purely religious fellowship. Outstanding theologians in this group were

J. C. K. von Hofmann (d. 1877), F. H. R. von Frank (d. 1894), G. Thomasius (d. 1875), and men of other universities like Theodosius Harnack (d. 1891), J. H. Kurtz (d. 1890), F. Delitzsch (d. 1890), F. A. Kahnis (d. 1888), and E. Luthardt (d. 1904).

12. A. B. Ritschl (d. 1889) broke with the theology of the Tuebingen school, eliminating the intellectual, emotional, and mystical from religion and emphasizing practical ethics. With his emphasis on the will, he set forth a moralizing religion after the fashion of Kant. Followers of Ritschl were W. Herrmann (d. 1922), A. von Harnack (d. 1930), and F. Loofs (d. 1928).

13. The Historico-Religious School of theologians stressed "the development of Christianity as seen in the light of its historical and geographical environment." Christianity, like other religions, is considered merely as a product of evolution. J. Wellhausen (d. 1918) applied this theory to the study of the Old Testament; W. Wrede (d. 1906) and others to that of the New Testament. The leading member of this school was E. Troeltsch (d. 1923), who attempted to solve the problems raised for both theology and philosophy by the development of historical science and the rise of historical relativism. Other prominent members were A. Deissmann (d. 1937), R. Otto (d. 1937), and A. Schweitzer. N. Soederblom (d. 1931) may be regarded as halfway between this group and the next.

14. More respectful of the creeds of Christianity were the following men of outstanding scholarship: in Biblical studies, Theodore Zahn (d. 1933), A. Schlatter (d. 1938), M. Kaehler (d. 1912), R. Kittel (d. 1929), and E. Koenig (d. 1936); in the field of Luther research, W. Walther (d. 1924), K. Holl (d. 1926), H. Boehmer (d. 1927), and H. Preuss; in systematic theology, L. Ihmels (d. 1933), O. Hallesby, Reinhold Seeberg (d. 1935), and Th. Kaftan (d. 1932). These men represent various shades of theological opinions and degrees of conservatism. Some, like Seeberg, interpreted orthodox Lutheranism in terms of Hegel's and Fichte's ethical idealism.

15. The term "Neo-Lutheranism" is used to designate the work of such scholars as W. Elert, P. Althaus, Jr., H. Sasse, K. Heim, G. Kittel, A. Koeberle, E. Sommerlath, W. Kuenneth, and J. Jeremias. These men have stimulated a new interest in Luther's work and in the New Testament. They attempt

to interpret Luther out of his own personal experience as contrasted with the theology of the Middle Ages and of later Lutheranism. The so-called Lundensian theology has received stimulation from, and given its support to, Neo-Lutheranism. The University of Lund has been the center of activity on the part of such eminent scholars as G. Aulén, A. Nygren, G. Ljungren, R. Bring, and H. Lindroth. The Third Reich actively interfered with the development of theology in Germany; its collapse has left the Protestant Church there in a state of confusion which is certain seriously to affect the fortunes of Lutheranism in Europe. Only time will tell in which manner and to what extent. LWS

Johann Heinrich Kurtz, *Church History*, Vol. III; J. L. Neve, *A History of Christian Thought*, Vol. II; E. H. Klotsche and J. Theodore Mueller, *The History of Christian Doctrine;* Vergilius Ferm, *Encyclopedia of Religion.*

Lutheran Women's Missionary League. The L. W. M. L. was organized July 8—9, 1942. It is the expansion of a number of organized women's groups that had been working, with singular success, in their respective Districts into a Synod-wide group.

Prior to the year 1928 a few pastors in some of the synodical Districts conceived the plan to enlist the great, unused talents of the women of their congregations in a type of mission crusade. An educational program was introduced. The women became aware of the needs for funds for special mission projects not provided for in the synodical budget.

During the intervening years (1928 to 1942) the directors of missions and pastors were watching the development and the achievements of these organized women's groups. They recognized the need for united effort throughout Synod. At the synodical convention in St. Louis, in 1938, the question of organized women's work was raised, and two proposals were submitted to that body. Synod took the plans under advisement and appointed a committee to study the situation and prepare recommendations for presentation at the next synodical convention. In 1941 the synodical convention gave its approval and encouragement to the creation of a Synod-wide organization of women within the Church.

The President of Synod appointed a committee of counselors, consisting of five pastors, to call a meeting of representatives of such Districts as had declared a willingness to take part in a general organization. The result was the Chicago conference of July 8—9, 1942, at which time and place the Lutheran Women's Missionary League was officially launched.

The L. W. M. L. is a delegate body, with the following officers: President, 1st vice-president, 2d vice-president, recording secretary, corresponding secretary, financial secretary, and treasurer. It meets in convention every two years. During the biennium the business of the League is administered by the Administrative Committee and the Executive Board.

The purpose of the organization is to promote missionary education, missionary inspiration, and missionary service. Its funds (freewill offerings only) are given for the support of mission projects for which no provision is made in the District or synodical budgets.

The official publication is the *Lutheran Woman's Quarterly.*

Headquarters: 3558 South Jefferson Ave., St. Louis 18, Mo. SFR

Lutheran World Federation. Conditions after the First World War, relief work by Lutherans of the United States and other countries, and in general the increased contact between Lutherans of the various parts of the world had created the desire for meetings in which the Lutherans of the globe would be represented and where issues of common interest could be discussed. The National Lutheran Council of the United States took a leading part in the organizational work that was required to make such meetings possible. The Allgemeine Evangelisch-Lutherische Konferenz, most of whose members lived in Germany, through its leading men, became another important factor in the movement. The name chosen for the assembly was "Lutherischer Weltkonvent," "World Convention of Lutherans." The first meeting (Lutheran World Convention) was held 1923 in Eisenach, near the Wartburg; Bishop L. H. Ihmels of Leipzig was chairman. A second meeting took place in Copenhagen in 1929. The convention assembled in Paris in 1935. The next meeting was to take place in Philadelphia, but on account of the Second World War all plans pertaining to this gathering had to be canceled. When after the cessation of hostilities negotiations could be resumed, it was resolved by the committee in charge to issue a call for a meeting to be held in Lund, Sweden, June 30 to July 6, 1947. The assembly convened as scheduled. Archbishop Eidem of Sweden presided. A constitution was adopted, and the name was changed to read "Lutheran World Federation." The confessional paragraph of the constitution reads, "The Lutheran World Federation acknowledges the Holy Scriptures of the Old and New Testaments as the only source and the infallible norm of all church doctrine and practice and sees in the Confessions of the Lutheran Church, especially in the Unaltered Augsburg Confession and Luther's Catechism, a pure exposition of the Word of God." On the nature and purposes of the Federation the constitution says: "The Lutheran World Federation shall be a free association of Lutheran churches. It shall have no power to legislate for the churches belonging to it or to interfere with their complete autonomy, but shall act as their agent in such matters as they assign to it. The purposes of the Lutheran World Federation are: a) To bear united witness before the world to the Gospel of Jesus Christ as the power of God for salvation; b) to cultivate unity of faith and confession among the Lutheran churches of the world; c) to promote fellowship and co-operation and study among Lutherans; d) to achieve a united Lutheran approach to ecumenical Christian movements and groups in need of spiritual or material aid." An assembly of the Federation is to be held every five years. The second meeting was in Hanover, Germany, 1952. WA

Proceedings of the Lutheran World Federation Assembly, Lund, Sweden, June 30—July 6, 1947, United Luth. Pub. House, Philadelphia, 1948.

Lutheran World Service. See *National Lutheran Council.*

Lutheranism, American. See *American Lutheranism.*

Lutheranism, Neo-. See *Luther Renaissance.*

Lutherischer Bund. An organization formed within the Synodical Conference in 1913 for the purpose of paying a certain sum of money upon the death of a member to his family or relatives.

Lutherischer Gotteskasten. A society in Germany similar to the Gustav-Adolf-Verein, differing from it, however, in this, that its purpose is to aid struggling Lutheran churches in countries outside Germany. The *Gotteskasten* was founded by Dr. Petri of Hanover, in 1853, assisted by Drs. Steinmetz and Muenchmeyer. Especially Hanover, Mecklenburg, and Bavaria show a large following. Lutheran churches in Holland, Switzerland, and America received financial aid. In addition, the society assists worthy theological students who pledge themselves later to serve Lutheran churches outside Germany. The annual income of the society amounted to some 90,000 marks before World War I.

Lutherischer Verein. Founded in Pomerania 1848 to champion the cause of Luther and Lutheran confessions. Similar societies were organized in other parts of Germany, and in 1849 a general association was formed at Wittenberg.

Lutherischer Weltkonvent. See *Lutheran World Federation.*

Luthersk Ugeblad. See *Danish Lutherans in America,* 3.

Lycanthropy. See *Transmigration of Souls.*

Lyons, Councils of. In addition to provincial councils: 1) The First Council of Lyons (considered by Roman Catholics the 13th Ecumenical) was called by Innocent IV in 1245; voted levies and aroused enthusiasm for the crusades; 2) The Second Council of Lyons (14th Ecumenical of Roman Catholics) was called by Gregory X 1274; concerned with the removal of schism between East and West; Greek representatives affixed their signatures to a confession embodying the *filioque,* but the union was dissolved eight years later.

Lyra, Justus William (1822—82). B. at Osnabrueck, Germany. Theologian and hymnologist. Devoted himself especially to the study of the liturgy; wrote scholarly treatises and composed many motets.

Lyra, Nicolaus de. French scholar and exegete; b. ca. 1270, d. at Paris 1340; member of the Franciscan order, provincial in Burgundy; later professor at the Sorbonne in Paris; his chief work a commentary on the Bible, noted for the rather good presentation of the literal sense, for which reason Luther repeatedly praised the work.

Lyte, Henry Francis (1793—1847). B. June 1, 1793, at Edham, Ireland, educated at Trinity College, Dublin, where three times he won the prize for the best English poem. He was led to the Gospel ministry and ordained in 1815. Early in his ministry he experienced a change of heart and found true peace in Christ. He was "jostled from one curacy to another" until he settled in 1823 at Lower Brixham, a fishing village. Being delicate and sensitive, he lost his health and eventually sought rest and restoration on the Continent. He died at Nice, Nov. 20, 1847. His last words were, "Peace and joy." He is best known to Christendom by "Abide with Me! Fast Falls the Eventide."

M

Mabillon, Jean (1632—1707). Historian of the Benedictine Order; spent over thirty years on his principal work, *Acta Sanctorum S. Benedicti*, in nine folio volumes, which shows extensive research as well as fearless criticism.

Maccabees, Books of. See *Apocrypha*, A 3.

Macedonian Controversy. See *Christological Controversies; Pneumatomachi.*

Macedonius. See *Pneumatomachi.*

Machen, J. Gresham (1881—1937). Professor at Princeton Theological Seminary, 1929 withdrew because of Fundamentalist-Modernist controversy and founded Westminster Seminary, Philadelphia; resisted further split resulting in Faith Seminary; helped form Independent Board of Presbyterian Foreign Missions, and therefore suspended from Presbyterian ministry; in 1936 became first moderator of new body called after 1939 the Orthodox Presbyterian Church. Wrote: *The Origin of Paul's Religion* (1921); *Christianity and Liberalism* (1923); *The Meaning of Faith* (1925); *The Virgin Birth of Christ* (1930).

Machiavelli, Niccolo (1469—1527). Italian statesman; deprived of his position by the Medici; wrote his *The Prince* to show how his country could become great if ruled by a prince without moral scruples.

Mack, Alexander. See *Brethren, Dunkers.*

Mackay, Alexander M. (1849—90). B. at Rhymie, Scotland; d. in Uganda, Africa. Founder of the Uganda Church. Moved by Henry Stanley's letter from Uganda to the *Daily Telegraph,* the Church Mission Society sent eight men, among whom was Mackay. In the face of great odds and much suffering Mackay held out, encouraging and comforting the Christians. He translated the Bible into the Swahili language.

Mackay, Margaret (1802—87). Married to an officer of the British army; d. at Cheltenham; published various prose works and *Thoughts Redeemed, or Lays of Leisure Hours;* among her 72 hymns: "Asleep in Jesus, Blessed Sleep."

Macleod, Norman (1812—72). Member of the Church of Scotland; one of the founders of the Christian Alliance; editor of the *Christian Magazine* and *Good Words.* He is known for his liberal theology, his mission zeal, and his social and educational accomplishments.

Madagascar. An island in the Indian Ocean, since 1896 a French colony. Area: 241,094 sq. mi.; population: 4,350,700 (1950), mostly Malagasy.

Prior to 1895 the native government was an absolute monarchy. The native religion is a crude form of idolatry, connected with ancestor worship. After unsuccessful attempts by the Roman Catholic Lazarists and Jesuits in the 17th century to gain a footing, the London Missionary Society succeeded in entering the island in 1818. Missionary work done by David Jones between 1820 and 1828 resulted in the founding of 32 schools. Queen Ranavalona began to persecute the Christians in 1835, and in 1849 the persecutions became more violent. The missionaries fled to Mauritius, and the mission stations were closed for twenty-six years; but secret intercourse was kept up, and the little band of faithful native confessors was strengthened. The severest persecutions were those of 1849 and 1857—60, in which thousands suffered shameful indignities by torture, and many were put to death. Ranavalona died in 1861. Radama II, on ascending the throne, immediately proclaimed religious liberty. Hundreds returned from banishment and places of hiding, where they had spent years of suffering. During the period of persecution the New Testament in the hands of the Malagasies had been the fruitful source of many conversions. The number of professed Christians after the persecutions ended was far greater than when the persecutions began. The queen and her prime minister were baptized in 1868, which served to make Christianity popular; many natives now professed the Christian faith. In 1870 the number of Christians was estimated at 250,000. How superficial, however, the Christianity of many was became manifest when in 1883 the French declared a protectorate over the island. In 1904 over 200,000 adherents of the London Missionary Society had forsaken this connection.

Statistics: Roman Catholics (1951): 699,000 members, 97 national and 303 foreign priests; Protestants (1951): 89 ordained, 12 unordained men, 172 women foreign workers; 819 ordained, 3,201 unordained national workers; 168,317 communicants. The S. P. G., *Norska Misjonsselskap*, Societé des Miss. Evangeliques de Paris, Ev. Luth. Church, Luth. Free Church, and Adventists carry on work in Madagascar.

OHS

Madison, James. See *Protestant Episcopal Church, 3.*

Madison Settlement (also referred to as "Madison Agreement"; Norwegian Lutheran Church, now Evangelical Lutheran Church; 1912). Already before 1890 the Norwegian Synod sought unity through free conferences. In 1905 the Hauge Synod, Norwegian Synod, and the United Church (Norwegian) elected committees which agreed on the doctrine of absolution (1906), lay activity (1906), and the call and conversion (1908). Disagreement occurred on the doctrine of election and predestination between the committees of the United Church and the Norwegian Synod. These two bodies elected new committees which adopted the "Settlement" at Madison, Wis. (Feb. 22, 1912). Content: "1. The union committees of the Synod and the United Church acknowledge unanimously and without reservation that doctrine of election which is presented in Article XI of the Formula of Concord and in Pontoppidan's *Sandhed til gudfrygtighed*, Question 548.

"2. Since both negotiating church bodies recognize that the Formula of Concord presents the pure and correct doctrine of the Word of God and the

Lutheran Confession concerning the election of the children of God to salvation, it is deemed unnecessary to church unity to draw up new and more extensive theses regarding this article of faith.

"3. Since, however, it is generally known that concerning the doctrine of election two forms of presentation have been used, both of which have gained prescriptive right and recognition within the orthodox Lutheran Church;

"While some, in agreement with the Formula of Concord, make the doctrine of election comprehend the entire salvation of the elect, from the calling to the glorification (Formula of Concord, Art. XI, 10—20), and teach an election 'to salvation through sanctification of the spirit and belief of the truth';

"Others, like Pontoppidan, in conformity with John Gerhard, Scriver, and other acknowledged teachers in the Church, define election rather as the decree of final glorification, with faith and perseverance wrought by the Spirit as its necessary presupposition, and teach that 'God has predestinated all those to eternal life who from eternity He has seen would accept the proffered grace, believe on Jesus Christ, and remain steadfast in this faith unto the end'; and since neither of these two forms of doctrine presented in this manner contradicts any doctrine revealed in the Word of God, but does full justice to the order of salvation as elsewhere presented in the Word of God and the Confession of the Church — we hold that this fact ought not to cause any division in the Church nor disturb that unity of Spirit in the bond of peace which God desires should prevail among us.

"4. Since, however, during the doctrinal controversy among us, words and expressions have been used — rightly or wrongly attributed to the one party or the other — which seemed to the other side a denial of the Confession of the Church or lead to such a denial, therefore we have agreed to reject all erroneous doctrines which seek to explain away the mystery of election (Formula of Concord, Art. XI, 51—64) either in a synergistic or Calvinizing manner. The Settlement rejected the doctrine: (5 a) that the mercy of God and merit of Christ is not the only cause of election, (b) that election takes into account anything that man is or may do or omit to do, (c) that faith is dependent on man's choosing or ability, (d) that faith is the result of an ability imparted to man by the call of grace (a power dwelling in the unregenerate heart); and (6 a) that God acts arbitrarily in election and without motive, (b) that God's will regarding salvation is of two different kinds, one revealed in Scripture and the other unknown and pertaining only to the elect, (c) that when resistance is removed in some who are saved and not in others who are finally lost, this difference in result has its cause in God, (d) that a believer can and ought to have an absolute certainty of his election and salvation instead of an assurance of faith, (e) all doctrines 'which directly or indirctly would conflict with the order of salvation and would not give to all a full and equally great opportunity of salvation.'"

The committee declared "that the essential unity now attained concerning these doctrines is sufficient for church union."

The *Austin Settlement* (1916—17) made three changes in the Madison Agreement: 1. omits paragraph 1 of the Madison Settlement; 2. substitutes in paragraph 3 *"Formula Concordiae*, Art. XI, 1—20" for Art. XI, 10—20; 3. in paragraph 4 substitutes "or on the other hand, weakens man's feeling of duty over against the acceptance of grace or of guilt for the rejection of grace" for "or, on the other hand, weakens man's feeling of responsibility over against the acceptance or rejection of grace."

Convention minutes of the Lutheran bodies mentioned; G. M. Bruce, *The Union Documents of the Evangelical Lutheran Church*, Augsburg Pub. House, Minneapolis, 1948; *Doctrinal Declarations*, CPH, n. d.; articles in various periodicals (e. g., *L. u. W.* LVIII: 222, 414, 511, 562, etc.).

Madison Theses (Iowa Synod, 1875). At the request of the Northern Iowa Conference of the Iowa Synod at Davenport, Iowa (1873), a number of theses were adopted explaining the relation of the Iowa Synod to the Missouri Synod. As a result two factions developed in the Iowa Synod. One held that the synod should follow the opinion of certain Neuendettelsau leaders and that the Davenport Theses modified the doctrinal position of Iowa. The Madison Theses of 1875 held: 1) the Iowa Synod does not follow any school, but declares itself loyal to the Confessions, permits differences in theological views only as long as the views are within bounds of the Confessions,

and repudiates doctrinal development (*Fortentwicklung*) which militates against the Confessions; 2) by making the doctrines of the Confessions binding it is not changing its position since it had formerly not excluded any particular doctrine; 3) since the form of the Davenport Theses is simpler and less ambiguous and offensive, the Synod adheres to them; 4) the Iowa Synod accepts the confessional statements regarding the ministry, but does not regard the Missouri position (without judging its correctness) as a doctrine of the Confessions; 5) the Iowa Synod accepts the confessional characterization of the Antichrist but does not regard the statement "the Pope is the Antichrist" (as the final and complete fulfillment) as an article of faith; 6) it acknowledges the doctrine of the Last Things as found in the Confessions, but does not reject details from prophecy as long as they are in harmony with the Confessions; 7) in the doctrine of Sunday the point concerning which the older dogmaticians disagreed (whether one day in a week must be selected in harmony with the order of creation) is not an article of faith; 8) "open questions" is synonymous with "nondivisive questions." (Full text in Deindoerfer, 141 ff.)

J. Deindoerfer, *Geschichte der Ev. Luth. Synode von Iowa u. anderen Staaten*, Wartburg, Chicago, 1897; G. J. Fritschel, *Quellen und Dokumente zur Geschichte und Lehrstellung der Iowa-Synode*, Wartburg, Chicago, 1916.

Madonna Paintings. The art of the Middle Ages chose the Madonna as one of its most favorite subjects, sometimes in a spirit of realism, oftener with the idealistic features introduced by Raphael. She is pictured on a throne, standing in contemplation with the Savior on her arm, sitting in a room with Jesus on her lap, out in the open in a bower of roses, often with animals to enliven the scene, such as a fish, a cat, a bird, a lamb; John is introduced in a number of instances as the companion of Jesus. Some of the most noted Madonnas are the Sistine Madonna of Raphael, now in the Dresden Gallery; the Beautiful Gardener, in the Louvre, similar ones in Vienna and in the gallery of the Uffizi; the Madonna with the Lamb, in Madrid; the Madonna with the Fan-palm, in London; the Madonna del Baldachino, in the Pitti Gallery, Florence; the Madonna della Sedia.

Madrigal. The madrigal is a type of secular choral music which flourished in the 16th, 17th, and 18th centuries, particularly in Italy, France, and England. Earlier madrigals were motetlike in character and employed the contrapuntal skills of the Netherland composers, which, however, did not prove to be ideal for a free and spontaneous type of secular choral music like the madrigal. The madrigal thus helped pave the way for music of a more homophonic and harmonic type and exerted a strong and even wholesome influence upon the development of the chorale and the Lutheran church cantata. Thus the chorale tune "In dir ist Freude" was originally an Italian madrigal. The madrigal also influenced compositions as Leonhard Schroeter's "Freut euch, ihr lieben Christen" and Bach's "Ach Gott vom Himmel, sieh darein." Madrigals were written by such Lutherans as Leonhard Lechner, Hans Leo Hassler, and Melchior Franck. The madrigals of the Lutheran masters of Germany lack the spontaneity, elasticity, charm, grace, and humor of those by the Italian and English composers.

Guido Adler, *Handbuch der Musik-Geschichte*, Frankfurt, 1924; Friedrich Blume, *Die evangelische Kirchenmusik*, Potsdam, 1931; Alfred Einstein, *The Italian Madrigal*, Princeton, 1949; P. H. Lang, *Music in Western Civilization*, New York, 1941.

Madsen, Peter (1843—1911). B. at Vinding, near Holsteboro, in Denmark, Professor of theology at Copenhagen, 1875; bishop of Zealand, 1909.

Magazines, Lutheran. See *Literature, Lutheran.*

Magdalen Homes and Orders. Magdalen Homes are homes for women who sinned grossly against the Sixth Commandment. At various times and places Magdalen orders have been established in the Roman Catholic Church for the reformation of such persons. Similar work in Evangelical circles was done by Theodore Fliedner at Kaiserswerth, 1833, and by such as since have emulated his example.

Magdeburg Centuries. See *Flacius, Matthias.*

Magdeburg, Joachim. B. ca. 1525; studied at Wittenberg; pastor at Dannenberg, Salzwedel, Magdeburg, and elsewhere; suffered much on account of Interim; wrote: "Wer Gott vertraut, hat wohl gebaut."

Magens, J. M. See *Danish Lutherans in America*, 1.

Magi. Originally one of the six tribes, or castes, into which, according to Herodotus, the ancient Medes were divided. They came into the ascendancy, first among the Medes, later among the Persians, by assuming priestly functions, a development similar to that of the Brahmans in India, and became a sacred caste, which under the Achaemenidae was invested with the functions of the Zoroastrian religion (see *Zoroastrianism*). The fact that Zoroaster was a Magian aided them in gaining this ascendency. Their priestly duties consisted mainly in guarding the sacred fire, reciting hymns, and sacrificing. They also practiced astrology and divination by means of dreams, and as early as at the time of Herodotus were noted for their "magic" arts. They exerted great influence in public and private affairs, especially at court.

Magic. The alleged art of bringing about supernatural results by means of occult agencies, conjurations, and incantations, usually malevolent, although they may also be benevolent, the former being designated demonistic. Among primitive races magic and superstition play a very important role, as in the case of voodooism of Africa. Magic has been practiced from ancient times in Babylonia, Persia, and Egypt, also in India. The Old Testament was definitely opposed to the use of magical arts as were also the Apostles (Acts 19:13-19). Magic is still prominent among some people today (*Sixth and Seventh Books of Moses*). Spiritists, clairvoyants, fortunetellers still prey upon the credulous.

Magister Sacri Palatii. An official of the Roman *Curia* who serves as chief chaplain and theological adviser of the Pope.

Magnificat. See *Canticles.*

Magnus, Duke of Mecklenburg (d. 1550). First evangelical bishop of Schwerin; present at the Diet of Augsburg.

Magnusson, Peter. Bishop of Westeras, Sweden; in 1531 he consecrated Laurentius Petri, the first archbishop of Upsala; important in the question of episcopal succession in Sweden.

Magyars. Mongolians, who originally lived along the Ural Mountains. In the ninth century they appeared at the Danube and eventually settled in Pannonia; they extended their campaigns to the North Sea and to Italy and Gaul. Christianized at the end of the tenth century and, although attempts were made to eradicate Christianity among them in the 11th century, it successfully maintained itself.

Mahabharata. See *Hinduism,* 6; *Sacred Literature.*

Mahatmas. See *Theosophy.*

Mahayana. See *Buddhism,* 6.

Mahu, Stephan. Composer of the Reformation era; Ambros regards his compositions as among the best of his day; one of his compositions based on "Ein' feste Burg ist unser Gott." W. Gosslau, *Die religioese Haltung in der Reformationsmusik,* Kassel, 1933.

Maier, Walter Arthur. Radio speaker, educator. B. Oct. 4, 1893, at Boston, Mass., son of Emil W. Maier. Ed. Concordia Institute, Bronxville, N. Y., grad. 1912; Boston U., B. A., 1913; Concordia Seminary, St. Louis, grad. 1916; Harvard U., M. A., 1920; Harvard U., Ph. D. in Semitics, 1929. Pastor of German internees, Gallup's Island, also at War Prison Camp No. 1 at Still River, Mass., 1917—19. Exec. sec'y, International Walther League, 1920—22; prof. of Semitic languages and Old Testament at Concordia Seminary, St. Louis, 1922—44, leave of absence 1944—50; speaker, International Lutheran Hour, 1930—31; 1935—50; editor, *Walther League Messenger,* 1920—44. Honorary D. D. Concordia College, Unley, South Australia, 1943; LL. D. Houghton College, 1945. Author of the following: *For Better, Not for Worse; The Lutheran Hour; Christ for Every Crisis; Christ for the Nation! Winged Words for Christ; The Cross from Coast to Coast; The Radio for Christ; Peace Through Christ; Courage in Christ; For Christ and Country; America, Turn to Christ! Christ, Set the World Aright! Jesus Christ, Our Hope; Rebuilding with Christ; Let Us Return unto the Lord; He will Abundantly Pardon; The Airwaves Proclaim Christ; Global Broadcasts of His Grace.* Died Jan. 11, 1950. *The Walter A. Maier Memorial Booklet,* Lutheran Laymen's League, St. Louis, Mo., 1950.

Maimonides (*Moses Ben Maimon*). Greatest medieval Jewish scholar and philosopher; b. 1135 at Cordoba; driven from Spain by persecution; lived in Fez, Palestine, Egypt; d. 1204, near Cairo. Exerted incalculable influence on development of Judaism, especially in his great attempt to reconcile Talmudic Judaism with Arabico-Aristotelian philosophy. His three great works (first two in Arabic, third in Hebrew): 1. *Commentary on the Mishna;* 2. *Guide of the Perplexed,* a philosophic interpretation of Judaism, valued also by Christian scholastics; 3. *The Strong Hand* (*Yad Hahazakah*), a compendium of Jewish law of monumental proportions.

Maistre, Joseph de (1754—1821). French Jesuit whose activities centered around political issues. Opponent of the philosophy of the Enlightenment, champion, especially in his *Du Pape,* of ultramontanism.

Maistre, Matthaeus le (Le Maitre; d. 1577). Composer of the Netherland School who succeeded Johann Walther as *Kapellmeister* in Dresden and wrote music for the Lutheran service of worship.

Major, Georg (1502—74). Lutheran theologian; studied at Wittenberg; later was made court preacher there; became professor in the theological faculty in 1545, afterwards superintendent at Eisleben for some time; he was suspected of being an *Interimist* (see *Interim*) and an *Adiaphorist* (see *Adiaphoristic Controversy*). The Majoristic Controversy * was brought on by the fact that Major stressed the "necessity" of good works in the wrong manner, namely, as being necessary for salvation, his emphasis being so strong that he seemed to hold that they were essential for salvation. He lived long enough to witness the overthrow of crypto-Calvinism.

Major, Johann (*Gross,* 1564—1654). B. at Reinstaedt near Orlamuende; diaconus at Weimar, pastor and superintendent at Jena in 1605, later also professor of theology; colaborer in editing the Weimar Bible; furnished the notes for Acts and for the Epistles of John; hymn "Ach Gott und Herr, wie gross und schwer," attached to a sermon he preached in Thuringia in 1613.

Majoristic Controversy. "Good works are necessary to salvation," wrote Melanchthon in 1535, but took it back on the earnest plea of Luther. But the Interim made similar concessions to Rome, and Georg Major was one of the authors. When he was made superintendent of Eisleben in 1550, the loyal

Lutherans, especially Amsdorf, objected. Justus Menius taught a like error and was attacked by Flacius and others. Major was willing to discontinue the phrase as ambiguous, but unwilling to condemn it as wrong. In the heat of battle Amsdorf also overshot the mark by saying: "Good works are harmful to salvation," for which he was attacked by Flacius and Wigand. The bitter controversy was settled in Art. IV of the Formula of Concord, which sharply differentiates between faith and good works and yet makes clear the intimate connection between the two as root and fruit.

Majus, Henry (1545—1607). Prof. at Wittenberg; one of the leading opponents of the Formula of Concord.

Majuscules. Uncial manuscripts. See *Manuscripts of the Bible.*

Malan, Henri Abraham Cesar (1787 to 1864). Studied at the Geneva Academy; first in accord with Unitarian tendency of Swiss Church at that time, later pastor in a separatist place of worship; originator of movement for better hymns in French Reformed Church; among his many hymns: "It Is Not Death to Die."

Malaya, British. Area: 50,690 sq. mi.; population: 5,420,738 (1951). Singapore is the foremost city, with a population of 679,659. The Straits Settlements are a crown colony. The population is Malaysian, with many Chinese and Eurasians. Missions by a number of churches and societies. The total Christian community numbered approximately 55,000 in 1952. See *Missions, Bibliography.*

Maldonatus, Johannes (1533—83). Roman Catholic exegete; Jesuit, 1562; professor at the Collegium Romanum, at the University of Paris; bitter opponent of the Huguenots (*maledicentissimus Maldonatus*). His commentaries on the Gospels and various Old Testament books evince great patristic scholarship and pointedly discuss the doctrinal differences between Romanism and Protestantism.

Malebranche, Nicole, French philosopher; b. 1638 in Paris; d. there 1715. His philosophy based on that of Descartes. Developed doctrine of "occasionalism," which, denying possibility of interaction of mind and body, assumes that on the occasion of each soul process, God produces the corresponding motion in the body.

Malta Bible Society. See *Bible Societies,* 4.

Malthus and Malthusianism. Thomas Robert Malthus (1766—1834), member of the Anglican clergy, professor at the East India College in Haileybury, promulgated the theory that the human population of the earth had the tendency to multiply by geometrical progression, while the increase in foodstuffs followed arithmetical progression, insisting that this was a law of nature. His claims, known as Malthusianism, led to the conclusion that the propagation of the human race should be controlled by legal means, in addition to the "positive" obstacles in the way of an increase in population. Malthusianism has influenced the practice of birth control.

Mamertine Prison. An ancient prison under the Church of St. Giuseppe, which tradition identifies with the place of imprisonment of Paul and Peter.

Man. Science divides the study of man into two branches: *physical anthropology,* which deals with the essence and origin of physical (animal) characteristics, and *cultural anthropology,* which deals with such branches as language, inventions, and customs of man.

Christian theology studies man's origin (see *Creation*), apostasy (see *Fall of Man*), sin (see *Sin; Original Sin*), and redemption (see *Justification; Grace; Conversion;* related topics).

Lutheran theology begins the study of man with the study of the infinite, gracious God, with whom man and the world stand in relationship. The proper understanding of man cannot be achieved through science, man's natural knowledge of God, or God apart from Christ (the Redeemer; God in Christ). For such an understanding is negative and accuses man of continual failure. Man is limited by his enslaved will and his incompetence to do anything good. Without Christ man is egocentric, and his behavior is directed to his own ends. Sin originates in the will, and concupiscence for evil in man is truly sin. The divine Law shows man what he really is, and his conscience, when it measures man by the divine standard, condemns him (see *Conscience; Contrition*). Thereupon conversion is the work of God by which He restores man to the proper relationship with Himself (see *Conversion*). The mercy of God to save sinners, to save His enemies, is contrary to reason. It is accepted by faith.

Since Christ lives in the believers (Christus in nobis), all that they say or do should be a "yes" to God's will. Man is once more the son of God and has thereby won perfect freedom.

E. Theodore Bachmann, "Man," What Lutherans Are Thinking, Wartburg Press, 1947 (148—72).

Mana. See Animatism.

Manasses, Prayer of. See Apocrypha, A 3.

Mandaeans. See Hemerobaptists.

Mandel, Herman. B. at Holzwickede in 1882. Privatdozent at Greifswald, 1906; professor there, 1911; professor of systematic theology at Rostock, 1912; at Kiel, 1918; at Kiel also teaching history of religion.

Manhart, Franklin Pierce. B. Catawissa, Pa., Aug. 30, 1852; grad. Missionary Inst., Selinsgrove, Pa., 1875; D. D. Gettysburg 1899; M. A. Univ. of Pa. 1896; LL. D. Wittenberg Coll., Springfield, Ohio, 1925; ordained 1878; pastor at Bloomsburg, Pa., 1881—89; Philadelphia 1889—93; supt. Missionary Inst. and pres. Susquehanna U. 1893 to 1895; head of Deaconess Motherhouse, Baltimore, 1896—1904; dean Theol. dept. Susquehanna U., 1904—; Sec. Gen. Synod, 1909—22 and 1926—; pres. 1922 to 1926; pres. Susquehanna Synod of Central Pa. 1923—24; pres. Susquehanna Summer Assembly, 1920—; Inner Mission Bd., 1913—18; dir. Luth. Publ. Board, 1892—1930; pres. Luth. Hist. Soc. of U. S. and Luth. Hist. Acad., 1911—; Snyder Co. Hist. Soc., 1913—; Del. to World Conv., Copenhagen, Denmark, 1929. Wrote: Present-Day Lutheranism; Lutheranism and Episcopacy; History of Susquehanna Synod. D. Sept. 13, 1933.

Manichaeism. 1. Religious system of Mani (A. D. 216—77), a Persian by birth, who claimed divine inspiration and the last and highest place in the long line of prophets. Persecuted at home, he traveled for many years, visiting China and India, and became acquainted with Buddhism. Returning to Persia ca. 270, he gained adherents at the court; but the hostility of the priestly caste brought about his ruin. He is said to have been crucified (or flayed alive) by order of King Behram, ca. 277.

2. His religious system is essentially heathen, though, like Gnosticism, it syncretistically incorporated Christian ideas. It is a sternly dualistic philosophy of nature. From all eternity there have been two antagonistic kingdoms, the Kingdom of Light and the Kingdom of Darkness, an idea based on the physical disharmony observable in the present world. An assault upon the world of light by Satan and his hosts ultimately results in the imprisonment of particles of light in the dark chaos of matter. From this union proceeds, at the behest of the good god, the visible world. The goal of the world process is the restoration of the imprisoned light (Jesus patibilis) to its original habitat. To thwart this design, Satan creates Adam and Eve and incites them to carnal lust with a view to multiplying the corporeal prisons of light, which he endeavors to hold in bondage. The Jesus impatibilis is sent from the sun in the semblance of a human body to teach men the way of salvation, that is, teach them to throw off the fetters of matter by the practice of ascetic virtues. The end of the long purgatorial process is the ultimate triumph of light and the destruction of the present world by a tremendous conflagration.

3. These wild speculations, given here only in broadest outline, were a serious menace to the Church. Manichaeism spread over the Roman Empire and gained many adherents, especially among the cultured and educated classes. In spite of persecution and proscription it showed remarkable vitality and reappeared under various modifications in numerous sects of medieval times (Catharists, Albigenses, etc.).

Maniple. See Vestments, Clerical.

Manitoba. See various articles on Canada.

Manitoba and Northwest Territories, Synod of. See Canada, Lutheranism in, 14.

Mann, Horace. B. at Franklin, Mass., 1796; graduated from Brown University 1819; admitted to the bar 1823; member of the Massachusetts House of Representatives and Senate; responsible for the enactment of an act creating the State Board of Education in Massachusetts, of which he was made secretary in 1837. To educate the public as to the needs and purposes of education, he and others lectured at hundreds of public meetings. He organized teachers' institutes and established state normal schools, collected and diffused information concerning the actual condition of public education, issued *Twelve Reports* on the condition of education in Massachusetts and elsewhere, which, together with his discussions on the aims, purposes, and means of education, occupy a commanding place in the history of American education. In 1843 he went to Europe to study its educational institutions. Member of Congress 1848; first president of Antioch College 1853; d. 1859.

Mann, W. J. Leading theologian of the General Council and one of its founders; b. May 29, 1819, at Stuttgart, Wuerttemberg; studied at Tuebingen; came to America at the urgent request of Dr. Schaff; first served a Reformed church; coeditor with Schaff of the *Deutsche Kirchenfreund* (from 1848); pastor of Zion Lutheran Church, Philadelphia, 1850; was among the leaders of the Pennsylvania Ministerium and a strong opponent of the "Definite Platform" theology. Mann was professor in the Philadelphia Seminary 1864—92 and a prolific writer. Author of *Life and Times of Henry Melchior Muhlenberg.* D. June 20, 1892.

Emma T. Mann, *Memoirs of the Life and Work of William Julius Mann,* Rodgers, Philadelphia, 1893; A. Spaeth, *Dr. W. J. Mann — In Memoriam,* Pilger Buchhandlung, Reading, Pa., 1895.

Manning, Henry Edward (1808—92). Cardinal; b. at Totteridge; studied at Oxford; priest (Anglican) 1832; rector; Tractarian; archdeacon of Chichester 1840; audience with Pius IX 1848; turned Catholic 1851; priest; Doctor of Theology in Rome 1854; archbishop of Westminster 1864; advocate of papal infallibility 1870; cardinal 1875; ultra of ultras among ultramontanes; prominent in educational, social, charitable activities; d. in London. Prolific writer. (See *Tractarianism; Ultramontanism.*)

Manning, James (1738—91). Baptist, founder of Brown U. at Providence, R. I.; organizer of the Warren Association (important in the struggle for religious liberty and mission work); influential in the adoption of the Federal Constitution.

Mansel, Henry Longueville (1820 to 1871). English theologian and philosopher of the Hamiltonian school; in his *The Limits of Religious Thought* he develops Hamilton's position "that the unconditioned is incognizable and inconceivable." Man cannot know God by reason or by an intuitive approach. Also wrote *The Philosophy of the Conditioned, Prolegomena Logica,* and other works.

Mansi, J. Dominicus (1692—1769). Learned Italian prelate; archbishop of Lucca; published *Sacrorum Conciliorum Nova et Amplissima Collectio,* a complete collection of the acts of the councils in thirty-one volumes; also a new edition of the *Annales* of Baronius with notes.

Mant, Richard (1776—1848). Educated at Oxford; Fellow of Oriel, tutor; then held positions as clergyman, also as bishop; Bampton lecturer in 1811; metrical version of Psalms; among his hymns: "For All Thy Saints, O Lord."

Mantova, Don Benedetto de. Author of the famous treatise *Del Beneficio di Giesu Cristo Crocifisso Verso i Christiani.* See also *Christ, Benefits of.*

Manuscripts of the Bible. 1. *Old Testament.* The original manuscripts of the inspired books of the Old Testament are lost, but copies (rolls or scrolls, Jer. 36:2; Luke 4:17), written by hand upon parchment derived from clean animals, were made for use by private individuals and in the religious services. Jewish tradition maintains that the canon of the Old Testament was established after the Exile in the days of Ezra, but even after that time only one book (Pentateuch) or a combination of several (Minor Prophets) was written on a single scroll. Prior to the Christian era the Hebrew of the Old Testament was written by means of consonants only, leaving it to the reader to suply the vowels required by the context. There were also no punctuation marks. Originally the individual words may not have been separated by spaces (*scriptio continua*) but the division of the text into paragraphs appears to be very ancient. The proper pronunciation of the consonantal text was handed down by word of mouth. In the synagogs trained lectors read the Scripture lessons on the Sabbath. The loss of Jerusalem as the religious center of the Jewish religion made it necessary to devise some system of fixing, so far as possible, the correct reading of the Old Testament Scriptures by means of the addition of vowel points to the consonants and the insertion of so-called accents which indicate the proper intonation. A mark was also devised to indicate the verse division. The gradual introduction of these symbols into the sacred text took place from the fourth to the tenth century after Christ under the guidance of Jewish scholars of the Old Testament known as the Masoretes. Extraordinary care was exercised in copying the Biblical books with the result that a comparison of the available Hebrew manuscripts which date from the tenth century onward shows practically no textual differences of any importance. Manuscripts prepared for use in the synagogs had to meet especially rigid standards of accuracy before being approved. Until recently the oldest extant dated Hebrew manuscript of the Old Testament was a copy of the Prophets bearing the date A. D. 916. In 1947, however, a complete copy of the Book of Isaiah and fragments of other books of the Old Testament were discovered in a cave west of the upper end of the Dead Sea. In the opinion of competent scholars these texts go back to the second century B. C. The fact that they do not differ materially from later copies of the Old Testament indicates the accuracy with which the Hebrew text was copied through succeeding centuries. The division of the Hebrew text into chapters as we find it in modern printed Hebrew Bibles was introduced from the Vulgate early in the fifteenth century. Luther, when translating the Hebrew Old Testament into German, used a printed edition of the entire Old Testament Scriptures which had appeared at Brescia, Italy, in 1494.

2. *New Testament.* a. The autographs of the New Testament, written in Hellenistic Greek upon papyrus or upon parchment (2 John 12; 2 Tim. 4:13), seem to have disappeared very early. As the churches, however, exchanged the Epistles and holy writings among one another (Col. 4:16; 2 Tim. 4:13) and were familiar with them (2 Pet. 3:15), it is evident that numerous copies of them were made. The writing was entirely in uncials (capitals), with no separation of words, except rarely, to indicate the beginning of a new paragraph, no breathings, accents, or distinction of initial letters, and with few, if any, marks of punctuation.

b. The New Testament canon was completed by the end of the first century; for the writings of the Apostolic Fathers, issued ca. 100—75, contain many allusions to, and quotations from, almost all the books of the New Testament. The Muratorian Canon or Fragments * show that the Church of Rome possessed an almost complete collection of the apostolic writings about the middle of the second century. Some churches wavered in the acceptance of certain books (Hebrews, Second Peter, Second and Third John, Jude, James, Revelation); these were called Antilegomena,* while the others, universally accepted, were called Homologoumena.

c. The external history of the New Testament text for a thousand years prior to the invention of printing can be traced by means of manuscripts. Of the 4,000 known manuscripts only about 30 include all the books; some of those of the fourth and fifth centuries contain also writings which, though not canonical, were read in the churches and studied by the catechumens. As papyrus disappeared from use, manuscripts were written on parchment (vellum), and the book form was substituted for the rolls. But as parchment was often very scarce, old manuscripts were sometimes reused, the old writing being erased or washed off. Unfortunately a Biblical manuscript was thus treated to make room for some patristic writing. Such manuscripts are termed *codices palimpsesti* (palimpsests) or *rescripti.* By use of chemicals the original text has often been recovered in modern times. In recent years the attempt to recover the original writing through ultraviolet rays on photographic plates has been successful.

3. a. The number of uncial manuscripts, ranging in date from the fourth to the tenth century, approaches now 200, though many of these are fragmentary. The most important are: Codex Sinaiticus, complete copy of the New Testament, 4th century, discovered (1844 to 1859), by Tischendorf in the Convent of St. Catherine at the foot of Mount Sinai, formerly in St. Petersburg (Leningrad), now in the British Museum, London; the Codex Vaticanus, 4th century, now in Vatican Library, Rome; the Codex Alexandrinus, 5th century, now in the British Museum, London; the Codex Ephraemi, palimpsest, 5th century, rewritten upon in the 12th century (original writing revived in 1835), now in National Library of Paris; Bezae (D), 6th century at Cambridge.

b. Beginning with the 10th century the uncial form of writing changed to the cursive. Of these manuscripts there is a great number. As might be expected, there are many variant readings, about 150,000 of the New Testament text, but in 95 per cent of these instances the correct reading is not difficult to establish, and in 95 per cent of the remainder the variants are of no importance as affecting the sense. "In the variety and fullness of the evidence on which it rests the text of the New Testament stands absolutely and unapproachably alone among ancient prose writings" (Westcott and Hort). While there were earlier divisions of the text, the present chapter division is attributed to Stephen Langton,* archbishop of Canterbury, and the present verse division was introduced by Robert Stephen (in his Greek edition, 1551).

c. The first printed copy of the Greek New Testament was the Greco-Latin New Testament edited by Erasmus and published by Froben of Basel in 1516. The Complutensian Polyglot, although printed sooner, appeared on the market later than that of Erasmus.

Marbach, John (1521—81). Ed. at Strassburg and Wittenberg; deacon at Jena (1540); pastor at Isny; pastor, later chief pastor at Strassburg. At Strassburg Marbach labored to replace Reformed teachings with Lutheran doctrines; present at the Council of Trent (1551); espoused the cause of the Formula of Concord. Although Melanchthon considered him of mediocre intellectual ability, Andreae and Brenz regarded him as an outstanding theologian.

Marburg Articles. See *Lutheran Confessions*, A 2.

Marburg Colloquy. See *Lutheran Confessions*, A 2.

Marcellus of Ancyra (d. ca. 374). Condemned by the Council of Constantinople (380) for holding Christological views resembling Sabellianism.

March, Daniel (1816—1909). Educated at Yale College and Divinity School; minister in the Congregational Church, later of a Presbyterian congregation at Philadelphia; wrote: "Hark, the Voice of Jesus Crying."

Marcion. See *Gnosticism*, 7 k.

Marcus Aurelius. See *Persecutions of Christians*, 3.

Marduk. See *Babylonians, Religion of*, 1.

Marenzio, Luca (ca. 1560—99). Composer of madrigals and of sacred choral music written for the Roman Catholic Church.

Margaret of Navarre (1492—1549). Sister of Francis I; patron of letters; shielded reformers.

Marheincke, Philipp Conrad (1780 to 1846). Prof. at Goettingen, Heidelberg, and Berlin; worked especially in the fields of dogmatics and symbolics; held the speculative view of Daub and Hegel, being equidistant from orthodox Lutheranism, Rationalism, and the old supranaturalism.

Maria, Queen of Hungary (1505 to 1558). Sister of Emperor Charles V; became Lutheran (probably later returned to Catholicism); Luther dedicated the interpretation of four of his Psalms to her.

Mariana, Juan (1536—1624). Spanish historian; Jesuit; taught theology at Rome and Paris, but retired to the Jesuits' house at Toledo, in Spain, in 1574, devoting the remainder of his life to literary pursuits. Besides his history of Spain he wrote also *De Rege et Regis Institutione*, a work in which tyrannicide is defended.

Mariolatry. 1. The worship accorded to the Virgin Mary particularly in the Roman Church. The *Catholic Dictionary* naively explains the fact that no such worship was known in the early centuries by saying: "There was the danger of scandal to the heathen, who, with their own inadequate notions of worship, might misconstrue the honor paid to Mary." (*Sic!*) (P. 562.) The scanty references to Mary in the New Testament, however, gave apocryphal writers a welcome opportunity to fill the empty spaces in her history with colorful legends. Monastics exalted her as the type and model of celibacy. And when the fourth century brought large numbers of half-Christianized pagans into the Church, who developed the worship of saints (see *Saints, Worship of*), Mary was speedily elevated above all others and hailed as queen of heaven. Churches and altars were raised in her honor, her pictures were venerated, and she was invoked for aid in every need.

2. This cult of Mary has flourished and grown in the Roman Church from that day to this, drawing ever-increasing strength from a variety of sources. It drew strength from medieval chivalry, which served Mary as the crown of womanhood, exalted above the angels; it was augmented by the custom of adding the Ave Maria to the Lord's Prayer, by the introduction of the rosary and the establishment of about

twenty feasts of Mary; it was aided by liberal papal indulgences and by a plethora of visions and miracles; Dominicans, Franciscans, Carmelites, and Jesuits vied with one another in advancing it. Through the efforts of the last named, the whole month of May was dedicated to the service of Mary, and the climax of the cult was reached when Pius IX decreed the dogma of the Immaculate Conception in 1854.

3. The decrees of the Council of Trent and the *Catechismus Romanus* employ moderate expressions concerning Mariolatry. What position she occupies in the Roman Church may, however, be gathered from the *Breviary:* "With what praises shall we crown thee, Mary? . . . You are the expiation of the curse of Adam, the payment of the debt of Eve. You are the most pure oblation of Abel, you are the ark of Noah. . . . You are the firm trust of Abraham. . . . Hail, holier than cherubim; hail, more glorious than seraphim! . . . Hail, cause of the salvation of all mortals; hail, mediatrix of all who are under heaven; hail, restoration of the whole world." (Office of Immaculate Conception.) She is called the gate of heaven, our hope, the joy of heaven, the star of the shipwrecked. (*Ibid.*) "You were afraid to approach the Father; He gave you Jesus as Mediator. But perhaps you fear also in Him the divine majesty because, though He became man, He nevertheless remained God. Would you have an advocate also with Him? Take refuge with Mary! . . . The Son will invariably hear His mother, and the Father will hear the Son. Children, she is the ladder of sinners, my highest confidence, the whole ground of my hope. . . . She will always find grace, and it is grace alone by which we are saved. Let us seek grace, and let us seek it through Mary." (*Ibid.*, April 26, B. M. V. *De Bono Consilio*.) It is only a step from such expressions to Peter Damian's apostrophe of Mary (*Serm. de Nativ. Mar.*): "All power is given to thee in heaven and on earth. Nothing is impossible to thee," and to the contention of other Romanists that the milk of Mary is present in the Eucharist. In practice, Rome has made a goddess of Mary. The doctrine of the Assumption of Mary was promulgated in 1950.

M. J. Scheeben, *Mariology,* Herder, St. Louis, rev. 1948 (Catholic).

Mariology. Teachings and opinions concerning Mary, mother of Jesus.

Marital Impediments. See *Impediments of Marriage.*

Marius Mercator. Ecclesiastical writer of the fifth century, very likely of North Africa; d. after 451; apparently a layman with a lively interest in theology; wrote against Pelagianism and Nestorianism.

Marnix, Philippe van (1538—98). B. at Brussels; studied under Calvin and Beza; statesman, soldier, theologian; played a major role in the advancement of Reformed theology in the Netherlands; resisted the Roman Catholic Inquisition; adviser of William of Orange in the fight with Spain for the independence of the Netherlands.

Maronites. A Syrian sect living chiefly in the Lebanon region, their name being derived from St. Maron, to whom a monastery was dedicated between Hamath and Emesa. They number about 200,000 adherents and are Monothelites in doctrine. See *Monothelite Controversy.*

Marot, Clement (1497—1544). Official poet of the Calvinists, wrote hymn versions of the Psalms which helped establish Calvinism in France particularly. Charles V and Catherine de Medici were among his admirers. Though he prepared his psalmodic hymns for austere John Calvin, Marot was a worldly-minded courtier. The grace and brilliance of his style made his poetry unique for his day.

Marperger, Leonhardt (1682—1746). Court preacher at Dresden; hymn writer and author of devotional books; edited the Dresden Hymnbook (1727, 1734, 1738).

Marprelate Tracts (1588—89). Attacked the Anglican Church and its officials; believed to have been written by John Perry (Puritan). Written in an offensive style, the tracts occasioned a great controversy.

Marpurg, Friedrich Wilhelm (1718 to 1795). Musicologist who exerted a great influence in the post-Bach days.

Marquesas Islands. See *Polynesia.*

Marquette, Jacques (Father). Famous Jesuit missionary and explorer; b. at Laon, France, 1637; sailed for Canada in 1666; established the mission of Sault Ste. Marie on Lake Superior in 1668; sailed down the Mississippi from the mouth of the Wisconsin River to the Arkansas in 1673; d. 1675.

Marriage, Biblical and Christian.

I. *History.* In the Old Testament the thought that marriage is an expression of the will of the Creator is implied. A lofty picture is repeatedly drawn of the family circle and the relationships existing in it (Gen. 23:1; 24:52; Judges 4, 5, and others). Worship is to be a distinctive feature of the home (Psalm 127 and others). The utterances of the Prophets of the Old Testament are full of statements in defense of purity, racial honor, and domestic virtue. The blessings of marriage and the evils of impurity are often used in a figurative way of spiritual relationships (as between God and His people).

In spite of this lofty idealism, and in spite of the fact that monogamy was considered ideal in the Old Testament (Gen. 2:24; Prov. 31:10-31), there is no general prohibition of polygamy in the Old Testament. Heroes of faith practiced it, and it persisted well into the Christian era. While polygamy is not specifically forbidden in the New Testament, it is contrary to the ideal of monogamy there upheld. The husband is to be "a one woman's man," and the wife is to be "a one man's woman" (1 Tim. 3:2, 12; Titus 1:6; cf. John 4:18). While Moses had prescribed procedures for divorce in the Old Testament (Deut. 24:1-4), Jesus recognized only adultery as cause for divorce (Matt. 19:7-9).

In the first centuries of the Christian era the view developed that virginity and celibacy were superior to marriage. Marriage had only a physical basis, and to marry was only to choose the lesser of two evils (wedlock—fornication). Influences from the East and the corruption of the heathen world undoubtedly influenced this type of asceticism. From earliest times, however, men opposed the ascetic ideal (Paphnutius, Julian of Eclanum). From the fourth century on asceticism became an established power. Ultimately celibacy was required of the clergy. In spite of vigorous protest and in spite of the fact that celibacy led to gross immorality, the Roman Catholic Church leaders (*e. g.*, Peter Damiani; Gregory VII), strove to maintain the celibacy of the clergy. This practice continued to occasion immorality which, in turn, was the constant target of reformers (William of Occam, John Wyclif, John Hus, Savonarola). Meanwhile secular marriage was raised to a sacrament under church supervision.

Luther's views on marriage, in opposition to Roman Catholic teaching, developed gradually and against varying backgrounds. Hence contradictory statements may be found in his writings. Generally speaking, Luther's earlier writings emphasize a strong naturalism in his approach to marriage, whereas his later and more mature writings emphasize a spiritual conception. His central teaching, salvation by faith and not works, was normative also here. In his approach to the subject Luther seeks to be Scriptural. The freedom of the individual, faith, and conscience are vital considerations. While Luther held that the normal sex urge is imperious and cannot be escaped, he, nevertheless, pleaded the cause of self-control. Luther had an abhorrence of divorce.

On the spiritual side Luther regarded marriage as an obedience of faith which lifts marriage above its gross naturalism. Luther wrote beautiful passages on marriage, and his own home life has been made an ideal.

While previously marriage had been under the control of the Church, Luther, while regarding it as an altogether sacred institution, held that it was *under the control of the State.* In his *Traubuechlein* (1529) he wrote: "Marriage and the married state are civil matters, in the management of which we priests and ministers of the church must not intermeddle. But when we are required, either before the church, or in the church, to bless the pair, or to pray over them, or even to marry them, then it is our bounden duty to do so." In accordance with his naturalism Luther also held that a Christian might marry an unbeliever, even a Turk.

These positions of Luther were developed in the Lutheran Confessions (see especially Augsburg Confession, XXIII, XXVII, and the Apology of the same). In the Apology of Melanchthon is the best formulation on marriage.

The Lutheran dogmaticians added little to what had been established in the Confessions. They fortified the position of Luther, sought to determine the Church's duty toward marriage (though granting that it was under State control), investigated impediments, causes for divorce, and other details.

Lutheranism in America was primarily concerned with doctrinal matters. Comparatively little attention was given to social problems. Evils such as immorality and divorce did not go unprotested, but there was no positive program until recent times. In the twentieth century, Lutherans became interested in the problems of marriage, and a vast literature is accumulating, and boards have been established to bring suggestions (e. g., *Committee on Family Life*).

In the course of time several steps developed in the process of marriage. These, in the Bible, often depended on social conditions and special circumstances (compare Gen. 2:23-25; 11:29; 24:65-67; and many other passages). The process soon came to consist of two steps: the agreement and the consummation with which a marriage feast was associated. The agreement was usually made by the fathers or other relatives, but also by the individual (Gen. 29:18), and even by a deputized servant (Genesis 24). After the Exile the custom of drawing up and sealing a contract came into vogue. (Tobit 7:14 ff.).

The Church in its early centuries, and in dealing with barbarians, did not concern itself with the control of matrimony or its process. Gradually the Roman Church took control, made marriage a sacrament, and demanded that marriage must take place under its auspices, restricted it, and also regulated the process in various ways. Luther and the Lutheran Confessions protested this and insisted on State control. This is still the position of the Lutheran Church (though it is immensely interested in marriage's spiritual and moral aspects). "Marriage is not a sacrament, but a civil status, of a civil character, entered upon by contract. It is therefore subject to the jurisdiction of the State. Since each one of the various States in our country has its own marriage laws, each State defines what constitutes marriage within that State. The legal maxim reads: Marriage valid where contracted is valid everywhere." (Fritz, *Pastoral Theology*, 161.) The acts of marriage are usually three: consent of two people to live in matrimony (the only step in common law marriage); obtaining a license (and meeting State requirements); the ceremony (by a person whom the State recognizes for this function).

II. *Definition and Principles.* "The state of marriage, or wedlock, is the joint status of one man and one woman, superinduced and sustained by their mutual consent, to be and remain to each other husband and wife in a lifelong union, for legitimate sexual inter-

course, the procreation of children, and cohabitation for mutual care and assistance" (A. L. Graebner).

The holiness of marriage, the sacredness of the marriage relationship, the fact that marriage is the normal state for the average adult, both from the social and from the hygienic standpoint, the fact that children are a gift of God, the fact that the family is the fundamental unit of the nation; all these truths must be kept before the Christian people of our country, lest the virus of antisocial and anti-Biblical poison enter their hearts and minds.

Lutherans hold that marriage must be entered into by mutual promise of contracting parties, given with the full knowledge and consent of the contracting parties' parents. Neither children nor parents may make exceptions to this rule, which is based upon Biblical example and ethical teaching. The promise must be given by the free will of the persons concerned, since duress or force invalidates a promise if the protest is registered in due time. That the contracting parties have reached the physical age and possess the maturity necessary for the successful carrying out of the prime object of marriage is not only self-evident, but is also specifically mentioned in the statutes of the several States and countries. The fact that parents give their children in marriage does not signify that the former have absolute power over their children, either in keeping them from getting married or in arbitrarily choosing spouses for them. Marriage is a natural right and therefore cannot be forbidden. The real affection of married people is a creation and gift of God, which cannot be set aside by absolute commands. In the twentieth century many States have set additional requirements for marriage which must be met (e. g., physical examination). Youth must be taught that the consent to live as husband and wife (engagement) has always been regarded as a most sacred promise which must not be made lightly or broken. Although the State does not, as a rule, acknowledge the force of a rightful betrothal according to Scriptural precedent, such broken promises or their equivalent are often brought up in socalled breach of promise suits. Of course, no person may enter into an actual marriage with a second person while still bound, before God and the State, to a previous spouse.

According to Scripture, marriage has

a threefold purpose: 1) companionship and mutual help; 2) procreation; and, 3) since the fall of man into sin, the avoidance of fornication (Gen. 2:18-24; 1:28; 1 Cor. 7:2). The refusal of sexual intercourse is the denial of a right and neglect of a duty assumed by marriage according to Gen. 2:24 and 1 Corinthians 7 and actually amounts to malicious desertion, for it militates against the purpose of marriage to propagate the human race and serve as a prophylactic against unchastity.

Marriage is intended by God to be a lifelong union, "until death do you part" (Rom. 7:2; 1 Cor. 7:39; Matt. 19:6; Mark 10:9). Here it makes no difference whether the one or the other spouse, according to the regular course of nature, later becomes impotent or, as the result of some disease, is no longer capable of performing the prime duties of marriage. The factor of mutual care and assistance becomes more prominent as the years go by, and Scripture emphasizes this phase of married life in words of great beauty (Gen. 2:18, 20; Eph. 5:28-33; 1 Cor. 7:12, 13; Col. 3:19; 1 Peter 3:7).

III. *Incidentals.* By *clandestine espousals* are meant engagements made without parental knowledge or consent. The *banns* of matrimony refer to a custom originating in medieval times and still practiced in some Lutheran churches, namely, announcing the intentions of persons to marry, praying for them, and giving anyone an opportunity to show just cause why the marriage should not take place. The *common law marriage* is the mere living together of a man and a woman as husband and wife, and with such intent, without legal marriage ceremony. The laws of our States now generally demand a marriage license and a legal marriage ceremony and even a physical examination. *Artificial insemination,* the impregnation of a woman with spermatozoa of a man who is not her husband, is contrary to the will of God (Gen. 2:24; Matt. 19:9). *Divorce.* According to the teaching of Christ there is only one cause for divorce, namely, fornication (Matt. 5:32; 19:9). *Malicious desertion* (1 Cor. 7:15) is not a cause for divorce, but divorce itself, which the innocent party suffers and is then free to procure a legal divorce and to enter upon another marriage. [Lutheran dogmaticians are not entirely agreed on some divorce grounds.]

Although mixed marriages, when a person of orthodox confession marries one of sectarian profession, are not forbidden in the Bible nor opposed by Luther, they are certainly discountenanced in the Bible and disapproved of by earnest Christians in view of the sad experiences with such marriages (1 Cor. 7:12-16). See also *Impediments of Marriage; Polygamy.*

J. H. C. Fritz, *Pastoral Theology,* CPH, 1932; G. E. Lenski, *Marriage in the Lutheran Church,* Lutheran Book Concern, Columbus, Ohio, 1936; references under pastoral theology; O. A. Geiseman, *Make Yours a Happy Marriage,* CPH, 1946; W. A. Maier, *For Better, Not for Worse,* CPH, 1939; E. Frenk, *Staying Married,* CPH (pamphlet); A. Hustad, *Strictly Confidential,* Bd. of Parish Ed., Minneapolis, 1944; E. W. Marquardt, *Why Was I Not Told?* CPH, 1939; F. E. Mayer, *To Sign or Not to Sign,* CPH (tract); W. F. Wolbrecht (ed.), *The Christian Family in the Modern World* (5th Yearbook), CPH, 1948. Books written by sociologists on marriage are numerous (*e. g.,* E. R. Groves, *The Family and Its Social Functions,* Lippincott, 1940; E. R. Groves & G. H. Groves, *The Contemporary American Family,* Lippincott, 1947).

Marriage Laws. There is no uniform marriage law. The following is a summary of laws as they obtain in the several States of the U. S.:

Marriage is often defined as a contract; but it is also more than a contract: it is a permanent change of status, or condition. It is the complete performance of a prior contract to marry. For a valid contract of this kind, also known as engagement, the parties must be competent, there must be agreement, the consent must be genuine, that is, free from fraud, duress, or mistake, and the agreement must be free from illegality. The express contract, or promise to marry, is proved, like other contracts, by the express words of the parties or by circumstantial evidence from their conduct, though explicit words have been spoken. If a man's conduct is such as to cause a woman to believe that he intends to marry, and she acts upon that belief, while the man permits her to go on trusting that he will carry his intention into effect, that will raise a promise upon which she may recover in some States.

The formal requisites of marriage are fixed by statute. They usually provide for marriage licenses, the performance of a ceremony of marriage by some magistrate or clergyman, and the return of the licenses with the attest that the marriage has been solemnized. Certain factors or conditions make a marriage voidable or void. When either party to a marriage is under seven years of age, the marriage is an absolute nullity. A marriage before the age of consent, as fixed by statute, is valid until voided. Persons who are below the legal age according to the statutes of the respective State are required to have the consent of their parents or guardians in a manner acknowledged by the law in order to make their marriage valid. This applies to both parties or either party. The marriage of insane persons is absolutely void. A number of States place incurable idiots and similar cases in the same category. Impotence in itself is no bar to marriage, but if marital intercourse is impossible on account of some incurable defect, the marriage will be annulled on application.

With regard to the relationship or consanguinity of parties, the subject is now generally regulated by statute in each State, the law stating definitely in which degrees of relationship marriage is prohibited. Most States expressly designate the second degree of consanguinity or affinity as the limit within which marriages may be contracted. The tendency in the last decades has been toward making the regulations stricter than before, to require a waiting period between the application for and issuance of licenses and to require blood tests and examinations.

It is essential for everyone dealing with matters pertaining to marriage and divorce to be acquainted with marriage laws as found on the statute books of his State. AJCM

R. V. Mackay, *Law of Marriage and Divorce* (brought up to date), Oceana Publications, New York. A summary of marriage laws is annually given in *The World Almanac.*

Marriage Liturgy. The parts of the marriage ceremony in the Roman Catholic Church in the 16th century were the questions with regard to possible obstacles and the act of marriage with ring ceremony and prayer at the doors of the church, and Mass with prayers and benediction over the wedded at the chancel railing.

This division Luther retained in his *Traubuechlein* of 1534. After the proclamation, the act of giving in marriage was performed "before the church," that is, at the doors, with the ring ceremony. In the church, before the altar, the Scripture passages referring to holy matrimony were read, and the service was closed with benediction and prayer over the wedded couple.

This order for the solemnization of matrimony, with its bipartite division, was generally accepted as fundamental. The text and the order of the several parts of the formula remained even after the external division was no longer observed, and the entire ceremony took place at the altar. In order to remove the apparent illogical procedure, many church orders placed the lessons first, then the giving in marriage, then the prayers and the benediction. The solution of the difficulty would be to use the original sequence in case of a marriage address, but the form in which the lessons precede the act of joining in matrimony when the address is omitted.

Lutherans in America employ many different marriage ceremonies, though basically similar. Service books, church books, agendas, etc., of the various Lutheran bodies contain forms for marriage.

Marsden, Samuel. B. July 28, 1764, at Horsforth, near Leeds; d. May 12, 1838, at Paramotta, Australia; second chaplain to settlement in New South Wales 1793; also colonial magistrate; returning to England, he enlisted interest in the Maoris on New Zealand and laid foundation for the Church of England Mission to them; returning from England in 1810 and hearing of disastrous conditions in the L. M. S. work among the Tahitians, he encouraged the missionaries to return to their fields, bought and equipped the *Active* in 1814, and sailed to New Zealand for extensive missionary operations, making no less than seven voyages in the interest of mission work. Few men have worked as successfully as Marsden.

Marsh, James (1794—1842). Congregationalist; pres. of and later prof. of philosophy at Univ. of Vermont; wrote *A Preliminary Essay to Coleridge's "Aids to Reflection"* (influenced Bushnell) and other works.

Marshall Islands. Polynesia, an archipelago in the West Pacific Ocean, formerly belonging to Germany; since World War I taken over by Japan; since 1945 under the U. S. A. Area: 60

sq. mi.; population: 10,350. Missions by the American Board (A. B. C. F. M.) and by the Hawaiian Evangelical Association among the native Micronesians. See *Missions, Bibliography.*

Marshman, Joshua (1768—1837). B. at Westbury-Leigh, England; d. at Serampore, India; originally a weaver until 1794; later studied Latin, Greek, Hebrew, Syriac; in 1799 was sent by the Baptist Missionary Society of England to join Carey in Bengal, India; opposition of East India Company forced withdrawal to Danish Serampore; engaged in almost unsurpassed literary activity. "The Serampore Trio" withdrew from the Baptist Missionary Society and carried on their work independently; translated the Bible into Chinese.

Marsilius of Padua. See *Councils and Synods,* 7.

Martensen, Hans Lassen (1808—84). D. at Copenhagen as bishop of Zealand, the highest ecclesiastical office of Denmark; prominent Lutheran theologian and dogmatician, with a speculative-mystic tendency. See *Denmark, Lutheranism in,* 9.

H. E. Jacobs, "Hans Lassen Martensen," *Luth. Ch. Rev.,* III:169—84.

Martianus Capella (5th century). Lived in northern Africa; his *Sartyricon,* or *Marriage of Philology and Mercury,* is an attempt to classify the culture of his day, and its description of the seven liberal arts gave the curriculum for medieval schools.

Martin, Adam (1835—1921). M. A., Hamilton College (Phi Beta Kappa); Hartwick Seminary; pastor at Middleburg, N. Y., 1861; first president of Northwestern College of Wisconsin Synod 1865—69; professor at Pennsylvania College, Gettysburg, until 1898; d. at New Haven.

Martin, John Nicholas (d. 1797). Early Luth. pastor in Georgia and South Carolina; fourth pastor of St. John's Church, Charleston.

Martin of Tours. See *Celtic Church,* 2; *Franks, Saxons, and Other Germanic Nations, Conversion of.*

Martineau, James (1805—1900). English Unitarian theologian; many years professor at Manchester New College; gifted preacher and apologist of theism against materialism, but rejected doctrines of Trinity, vicarious atonement, total depravity.

Martini, Olaus (1557—1609). Bishop of Upsala, Sweden; successfully opposed attempts of Charles IX to introduce Reformed teachings in Sweden and had a Lutheran constitution confirmed.

Martyn, Henry (1781—1812). B. at Truro, England; d. at Tokat, Asia Minor. He sailed for India 1805 as Anglican chaplain in the service of the East India Company, located in Dinapur, 1806, where he began missionary work among the natives. Stationed at Cawnpore in 1808, he translated the New Testament into Hindustani and Persian, the Psalms into Persian, and the *Prayer Book* into Hindustani. At Shiraz, in Persia, where he went in search of health, he translated the New Testament into Arabic. Returning to England via Asia Minor, he succumbed at Tokat.

Martyr. See *Persecutions of Christians.*

Martyr Theory. See *Atonement, Theories of,* 2.

Martyrdom of Isaiah. See *Apocrypha,* A 4.

Martyrium Clementis. See *Apostolic Fathers,* 1.

Martyrologia (*Martyrology*). See *Acta Martyrum.*

Marx, Heinrich Karl (1818—83). Son of a Jew; father had been baptized a Christian, but remained a liberal and rationalist; educated at the *Gymnasium* of Treves; studied law at Berlin, where he became acquainted with the "Young Hegelians" and was influenced by Hegel's dialectics; Ph.D. from Jena, 1841; the *Rheinische Zeitung* suppressed a year after he became editor; went to Paris and published one issue of the *Deutsch-Franzoesische Jahrbuecher;* in 1844 he prepared with Engels the *Holy Family,* an attack on Bruno Bauer; expelled from France for articles written for the radical German paper *Vorwaerts,* he went to Brussels; there he worked with a group of political exiles which made Brussels the center for Communistic propaganda; in 1847 he wrote *Misere de la Philosophie* and *Wage, Labor, and Capital;* in 1847 Marx and Engels were invited to join the Federation of the Just in London, by which they were later commissioned to draw up the *Communist Manifesto* (1847); expelled from Brussels after the February Revolution, later also from Paris, he went to London, where he took a leading part in organizing the International Working-men's Association (1864; the "Red International"); spent last days in poverty, misery, and illness. Marx was a political reformer rather than a philosopher. Important works: *Dissertation* (1841); *Kritik der Hegelschen Rechtsphilosophie* (1843); *Das kommunistische Manifest* (1847); *Das Kapital* (1867). His basic philosophy has been classified as historical materialism.

The *Communist Manifesto* is divided into four parts: 1) Bourgeois and Proletarians; 2) Proletarians and Communists; 3) Socialist and Communist Literature; 4) Position of the Communists in Relation to Various Existing Opposition Parties. Four basic suppositions are ordinarily regarded as underlying the *Manifesto:* 1) the application of Hegelian dialectic (thesis, antithesis, synthesis) to social theory; 2) the class struggle; 3) economic determinism; 4) labor theory of value and surplus value.

P. Bretscher, "The Communist Manifesto," *CTM*, XVII: 742—69 (gives select bibliography).

Mary, Bloody. Mary I, daughter of Henry VIII and Catherine of Aragon; queen of England 1553—58. Was educated a zealous Romanist; ordered execution of Jane Grey; married Philip II of Spain; restored papal power; burned Rogers, Latimer, Ridley, Cranmer, and 286 other Protestants, each martyrdom proving stronger than a hundred sermons against Popery. See *England, Reformation in,* 5.

Mary, Cult of. See *Mariolatry.*

Mary Festivals. A number of festival days in the Roman Catholic church year on which the special office dedicated to the Blessed Virgin is used. The great Mary festivals are the Feast of the Annunciation, on March 25, the Festival of the Purification of Mary, on February 2, the Festival of the Visitation of Mary, on July 2. Other festival days commemorate the conception of Mary, the day of her birth, of her marriage, of her seven agonies, of her assumption. The months of May and October are devoted to the commemoration of Mary, the emphasis being placed on the use of the rosary by the faithful.

Mary, Little Brothers of. See *Brothers Marists.*

Maryland and the South, German Synod of. Organized in 1874 by German pastors belonging to Maryland Synod for the purpose of uniting all German Lutheran pastors south of Philadelphia who were not affiliated with Missouri or Ohio. It was received into the General Synod in 1875, but disbanded within two years, many of its pastors and churches joining the Evangelical Synod of North America.

Maryland and the South, Synod of. See *Synods, Extinct.*

Maryland Synod. See *United Lutheran Church, Synods of,* 12.

Maryland Synod Question. A question debated in the Maryland Synod, beginning 1853. The question concerned the status of a pastor who severed synodical membership.

Maryland and Virginia, Synod of. See *Synods, Extinct.*

Mason, C. H. See *Church of God in Christ.*

Mason, Lowell (1792—1872). President of the Haendel and Haydn Society of Boston in 1827. He founded the Boston Academy of Music in 1832. He issued many popular collections of music, among them *Lyra Sacra* and *Cantica Laudis.*

Mason, William (1829—1908). Son of Lowell Mason, he studied piano in Boston and abroad under Liszt and others. He was for years a leading concert pianist.

Masorah (Massora) and the Masoretes. The tradition of the Jewish Church relative to the (consonantal) textual readings of the Pentateuch in particular and of the Old Testament in general. Masoretic studies were developed in the interest of accuracy in preserving the Old Testament text, so that the verses, words, and even the individual letters of the Old Testament text were counted, tradition declaring that there were 23,303 verses in the entire Old Testament canon. Certain peculiarities were noted and arranged in groups, and explanations of these difficulties were handed down by teachers from generation to generation. In connection with the work of the Masoretes, questions of spelling were discussed, and systems of vowel points were developed. The most celebrated of all Masoretes was Aaron ben Moses ben Asher (lived at Tiberias early in the tenth century). Thus the entire text-critical apparatus connected with the text of the Old Testament is included in the Masorah, as well as the division of the text into pericopes.

Masoretic Hebrew Text. See *Manuscripts of the Bible; Masorah.*

Mass. 1. The Roman Church teaches that the bread and wine "converted" in the Eucharist into the body and blood of Christ is not only to be received in Communion (see *Lord's Supper, Roman Catholic Doctrine of*), but is also to be offered up as a propitiatory sacrifice to God for the sins of the living and the dead. "In this divine sacrifice, which is celebrated in the Mass, that same Christ is contained and immolated in an unbloody manner who once offered Himself in a bloody manner on the cross: this sacrifice is truly propitiatory, and by means thereof this is effected, that we obtain mercy and find grace in seasonable aid if we draw nigh unto God, contrite and penitent, with a sincere heart and upright faith, with fear and reverence. For the Lord, appeased by the oblation thereof and granting the grace and gift of penitence, forgives even heinous crimes and sins. For the Victim is one and the same, the same now offering by the ministry of the priests who then offered Himself on the cross, the manner alone of offering being different." (Council of Trent, Sess. XXII, chap. 2.)

2. The officiating priest always communicates himself at the Mass; others may commune, but this is not required. The benefits of a mass are said to accrue to the whole church, but especially to the officiating priest, to those for whom it is particularly offered, and to all who devoutly attend it. During the ceremony the priest presents host and chalice to the worshipers for adoration (see *Elevation of Host*).

3. The ceremonies and words employed in the Mass are found in the missal (see *Missale Romanum*). Masses must be celebrated between dawn and midday, and only one mass a day can be said by a priest, except on Christmas and All Souls' Day or by special dispensation. Requiem masses are masses for the dead; low masses are without music; in high masses there is music, incense, etc.; pontifical masses are said by bishops. Throughout the Mass the "sacred" Latin tongue is employed; it is prescribed that some parts be spoken in a low tone. When a mass is requested by anyone, a tax or stipend, fixed by the bishop, is paid the celebrant.

4. The Mass is the center of the whole Roman system of worship; the Sacrament of Holy Communion has become its appendage and is overshadowed by it. As "a true propitiatory sacrifice, by which God is reconciled and made merciful to us" (*Catechismus Romanus*, II, 4. 76), a sacrifice "through which the richest fruits of that bloody sacrifice flow to us" (*ibid.*), it denies the all-sufficient power and merit of the sacrifice on Golgotha. If Christ won full remission of sins for men, there can be "no more offering for sin." Heb. 10:18. He established His holy Sacrament, as the words of institution and the writings of the Apostles show, that it should be received by penitent believers for the forgiveness of sins, not that they might idolatrously adore the consecrated elements and make a sacrifice of them. Scripture, in Heb. 7:27; 9:25-28; 10:11-18, clearly denies the need and the possibility of such a sacrifice.

Mass (*Liturgical*). The chief service of the Roman Church, embodying in it most of the dangerous doctrines which characterize this Church as a sect. The distinguishing and objectionable features of the Mass are the following: the *Confiteor,* with its confession of sins by the celebrating priest, the absolution being spoken by his assistants (for the false doctrine connected with this rite was that in donning his priestly vestments the priest became worthy of offering sacrifices for the sins of the living and of the dead); the *Secreta,* secret prayers murmured by the officiating priest, varying with the day and the occasion; the *Canon Missae* proper, in which the priest makes an offering of the unbloody sacrifice on the altar and adds the commemoration for the living and the dead.

Mass (*Music*). The Mass has been set to music by many Lutheran, Anglican, and Roman Catholic composers. In its musical setting, the Mass consists of the following five parts: Kyrie, Gloria in Excelsis, Credo, Sanctus, and Agnus Dei. While Gregorian (plainsong) settings were used during the Middle Ages, the polyphonic Mass began to ascend into prominence from 1200 to 1400. Within Roman Catholic circles the golden age for the polyphonic Mass began with Dufay (1400 to 1474) and reached its climax in Palestrina, Lassus, and de Monte. During this same era outstanding Masses were written by such Lutheran masters as Hans Leo Hassler, Antonio Scandello, Demantius, and others. Beginning with 1600 and extending down to the present day, the character of the Mass changed radically. The A Cappella Mass was replaced by the orchestrally accompanied Mass, which often became very theatrical, dramatic, bombastic, and secular in spirit and character. Steffano Bernardi (d. 1628) and Antonio Lotti continued to perpetuate the standards of former days, but the Masses of J. S. Bach, Cherubini, Mozart, Beethoven, Schubert, Liszt, Verdi, Franck, Gounod, Brahms, Bruckner, and of moderns like Zoltan, Kodaly, Roy Harris, and others, though by no means all in the same category or equally significant, are a far cry from the more conservative and churchly polyphonic Masses of former years.

Massacre of St. Bartholomew. See *Bartholomew, St., Massacre of.*

Massarelli, Angelo. See *Roman Catholic Confessions,* A 1.

Massie, Richard (1800—87). Noted as translator of Martin Luther's *Spiritual Songs* (1854); translated also other German hymns, including even the modern songs of Spitta; among his best translations: "All Praise to Jesus' Hallowed Name"; "Now Praise We Christ, the Holy One."

Massillon, J. B. (1663—1742). Perhaps the most famous of French preachers, of whom Louis XIV said that, while other preachers made him pleased with them, Massilon made him displeased with himself. He died as bishop of Clermont.

Material Principle. The material principle of the Lutheran Church is the doctrine of justification by faith alone *(sola fide).* See *Faith, Justification.*
W. H. T. Dau, "The Heritage of Lutheranism," *What Lutherans Are Thinking,* Wartburg, 1947.

Materialism. A philosophical theory which regards matter as the original cause of all, even psychic, phenomena. Asserting that all psychic processes are due to changes of material molecules, it in fact denies the existence of the soul. It reached its greatest development in the 18th century, in writings of French Encyclopedists * (see *Holbach*), and became prominent again in Germany in the middle of the 19th century (Vogt, Feuerbach,* Haeckel,* Buechner).

Mather Family. Congregationalists. Richard (1596—1669), came to America 1635; pastor at Dorchester, Mass. — Increase (1639—1723), Richard's son; pastor at Boston; president of Harvard;

studied sixteen hours daily; author. — Cotton (1663—1728), Increase's son; pastor of North Church, Boston, forty-three years; shared in witchcraft craze; published over 400 works: *Magnalia, Essays to Do Good,* etc.

Mathesius, Johann (1504—65). Studied at Ingolstadt; was attracted by some of Luther's writings; finished university work at Wittenberg; taught in school at Altenburg; rector of *Gymnasium* at Joachimstal; completed studies in theology, diaconus at Joachimstal in 1541; pastor in 1545; lovable and charitable spirit, model pastor, distinguished preacher; wrote: "Herr Gott, der du mein Vater bist"; also a biography of Luther, of whose Table Talk he had taken notes.

Mathews, Shailer (1863 — 1941). Baptist; b. at Portland, Maine; professor at Colby University, Maine; lecturer at Newton; professor of New Testament history and interpretation, systematic theology, historical and comparative theology at University of Chicago; dean of divinity school 1908; rejected divine origin of Bible and divinity and atoning death of Christ and held that religions, generally speaking, are mere products of the human mind. Wrote: *The Social Teachings of Jesus; The Church and the Changing Order; The Spiritual Interpretation of History; Dictionary of Religion and Ethics; The French Revolution; The Faith of Modernism; Creative Christianity.*

Matin. The early morning service; at the time of the Reformation one of the Canonical Hours and still observed as such by the Roman Church; rarely sung in the Lutheran Church, except on Sundays and holidays. See *Canonical Hours.*

Matrimony, Roman Catholic Doctrine of. The Roman Church counts marriage one of its seven sacraments, though it finds difficulty in providing for it, as to matter and form, a place under its own definition of a sacrament. The Council of Trent contents itself with claiming that Scripture "hints at," or "alludes to," matrimony as a vehicle of grace in Eph. 5:31, 32 (Sess. XXIV, *De Sacr. Matr.*). It nevertheless curses everyone who says "that matrimony is not truly and properly one of the seven sacraments of the evangelic law, instituted by Christ the Lord" (*ibid.,* can. 1). Rome insists on the sacramental character of marriage because it thereby draws this fundamental relation of life within the sphere of its power, under its claim of legislative authority in all matters falling under its spiritual jurisdiction. Consequently Rome asserts the right of regulating marriage and of adding new conditions to the Scriptural ones (see *Impediments of Marriage*). The Roman Church recognizes no legitimate cause for divorce, not even adultery, despite Matt. 19:9. Permanent separations are permitted, but no remarriage of either party during the lifetime of the other. In contrast to this apparent sacredness of the marriage tie stands the fact that many marriages which are valid by divine and civil law are declared null and void by the Roman Church because of impediments decreed by it. While loyal Romanists cannot be divorced, they may often secure a dissolution of marriage by instituting a careful search for impediments. See *Ne Temere*.

Mattes, John Casper (1876 to 1948). B. Nov. 8, 1876, at Easton, Pa.; educated at Philadelphia Luth. Sem.; D. D. from Muhlenberg College; served Church of the Savior, Trenton, N. J., 1901—15; St. John's, Scranton, Pa., 1915 to 1938; professor of theology, Wartburg Seminary, Dubuque, Iowa, 1939 to 1948; married Caroline Niedt, 1906, by whom he had six children; d. Jan. 27, 1948. He was a member of the General Council Church Book Committee; member of United Lutheran Common Service Book Committee; translated six hymns in the Common Service Book; member of Intersynodical Catechism Translation Committee and of the Parish Education Committee of the Iowa District of the American Lutheran Church. He was contributor to *The Lutheran, The Lutheran Church Review, The American Lutheran Survey, The Lutheran Church Quarterly, The Wartburg Seminary Quarterly,* the *Kirchliche Zeitschrift,* and numerous other periodicals. At the time of his death he was preparing a new translation of the *Book of Concord.*

Mattheson, Johann (1681—1764). Musician, critic, and writer, was a contemporary of Bach and Handel, who helped bring fame to Hamburg, where he induced young Handel to become a composer of operas. Mattheson infused the theatrical (operatic) style into church music and insisted that church music be theatrical and entertaining. It was through Mattheson, largely, that women began to take a more active part in the performance of church music. Before his day the music had been performed almost exclusively by men and boys.

Matthew of Janov (d. 1393). Outstanding Czech reformer; studied at Prague and Paris; wrote *Rules of the Old and New Testaments* (*Regulae Veteris et Novi Testamenti*).

Matthew's Bible. See *Bible Versions,* L 4.

Maude, Mary Fawler (nee Hooper, 1819—1913). Married clergyman of Church of England in 1841; distinguished for poetical ability; her best-known hymn: "Thine Forever, God of Love."

Maulbronn, Colloquy, Formula. See *Lutheran Confessions,* C 2.

Maundy Thursday. See *Church Year,* 8.

Maur, Saint, Congregation of. A famous French congregation of Benedictine monks, founded 1618. Its fame depends less on its restoration of Benedictine discipline than on its learning and scholarship, especially in patrology and history (Mabillon, Thierry). The Maurists, in their disputes with Trappists and Jesuits, showed calm moderation and intellectual superiority. The congregation was dispersed by the French Revolution.

Maurice, John Frederic Denison (1805—72). English clergyman; Unitarian by birth and education; entered the ministry of the Established Church (1828); sought to make Christianity palatable to the educated and liberal; held that the theologian must grapple with skeptical thought; emphasized the Fatherhood of God; sought to give a rational explanation of inspiration; emphasized the ethical and spiritual influence of the sacrifice of Christ; thus a leader of the Broad Church movement.

Maurice of Saxony (1521—53). Duke in 1541. Bribed by the promise of territory and the Electoral hat, he helped the Emperor crush the Lutheran Elector of Saxony, John Frederick, his cousin, and favored the Interim. Hated by the staunch Lutherans ("Judas"), fearing the growing power of the Emperor, incensed at the harsh treatment of his father-in-law, Philip of Hesse, he plotted against the Emperor, and having gathered an army to punish Magdeburg, he suddenly swept south, almost captured the aging Emperor at Innsbruck, and forced from him the Passau Treaty, so favorable to the Lutherans (1552). The next year he fell in the battle of Sievershausen.

Maurists. French Benedictines, famous for their critical editions of the Church Fathers.

Mauritius. An island near Madagascar, belonging to the British Empire. Area: 720 sq. mi.; population: 415,462. In 1598 it was uninhabited. Now it has a large East Indian population. In 1810 the island was nominally Roman Catholic. Missions by the Society for the Propagation of the Gospel, London Mission Society, Adventists. Total foreign staff: 22; baptized members: 6,794.

Maurus, Rhabanus (*Hrabanus,* ca. 776—856). Archbishop of Mainz; one of four authors to whom the hymn "Veni, Creator Spiritus" has been ascribed, as well as one or two others; prominent in both education and theology.

Maximian. See *Persecutions of Christians,* 4.

Maximus, the Confessor (580—622). Champion of orthodoxy in the Monothelite Controversy; abbot of the monastery of Chrysopolis near Constantinople; moved to North Africa; opposed the *Ecthesis* (639); helped induce the Pope to call the First Lateran Council (649) and probably originated the edict which condemned Monothelitism.

Maxwell, Mary Hamlin (1814—53). Published a volume of *Original Hymns* in 1849, with 107 poems, among which: "Saints of God, the Dawn Is Brightening."

Mayhew, Experience (1673—1758). A New England pastor and Indian missionary; had the oversight of six Indian Assemblies; translated parts of the Bible into the Indian language at the direction of the Society for the Propagation of the Gospel in New England.

Mayhew, Zachariah. Son of Experience Mayhew. Ministered to the Martha's Vineyard Indians from 1767 till his death, March 6, 1806.

Mazdeism. See *Zoroastrianism.*

McComb, William (1793—1863). For several years bookseller in Belfast; published several poetical works, which were later collected; wrote: "Chief of Sinners Though I Be."

McGiffert, Arthur Cushman (1861 to 1933). American theologian; b. at Sauquoit, N. Y.; Presbyterian minister; prof. at Lane and Union Seminaries; published *History of Christianity in Apostolic Age* (1897) and joined Congregationalists to avoid trial for heresy; president of Union Seminary. Wrote *Apostles' Creed, Church History of Eusebius, Martin Luther, the Man and His Work,* and others.

McGready, James. See *Presbyterian Bodies,* 4 b.

McKendree, William (1757—1835). Methodist Episcopal bishop; b. in Virginia; served in Revolutionary War; was converted 1787; bishop (first of American birth) 1808; traveled with Asbury; d. in Tennessee.

McKim, Randolph Harrison (1842 to 1921). Protestant Episcopal; b. at Baltimore; served in Confederate army; priest 1866; held various rectorates; wrote: *Leo XIII at the Bar of History,* etc.

McLaren, Alexander (1826—1910). English Baptist pulpit orator. He published many of his sermons and exegetical works.

McPherson, Aimee Semple. See *Foursquare Gospel.*

McTaggart, John Ellis (1866—1925). British philosopher; disciple of Hegel; held a theory of pluralistic idealism.

Mecca. See *Mohammedanism.*

Mechanism. A philosophy taught by the older French encyclopedists. An extreme materialism, which made the entire world as well as the individual human being and every other animate and inanimate creature, a machine driven by a blind fatalism.

Mechitarists. A religious order of Armenians organized by Mechitar for the purpose of uniting Armenians and Roman Catholics.

Mechthild of Magdeburg (1214—77). Religious mystic who was influential in introducing eschatological notions in the nunnery to which she retired and where she wrote *The Flowing Light of the Godhead.*

Medals, Devotional. See *Amulets.*

Median. See *Christian Teaching,* M.

Medici. A distinguished family of Florence from the middle of the 14th century till 1743, when the last of the line died, most of its members being patrons of literature and art: Cosmo (1389—1464), who formed the collection which became the Laurentian Library; Lorenzo the Magnificent (1449—92), who patronized scholars and artists, collected manuscripts at great expense, and made great additions to the Laurentian Library; Catherine (1519—89), who also fostered the arts and sciences.

Medici, Giovanni. See *Popes,* 20.

Medical Missions. 1. An important adjunct of late to religious missions. The term implies that medical science in all its various branches is put into the service of the propagation of the Gospel of Jesus Christ. Where the diffusion of medical knowledge or the application of medical science to physical ailment is an end in itself, it does not appear to belong legitimately to the domain of foreign missions, but is rather merely humanitarian work, being not based upon the charge of Christ to His Church found in Matt. 28:19.

2. Medical missions have a legitimate sphere as a forerunner of religious missionary effort and also supplementary to it. Their province is to break down natural native suspicion of, and opposition to, the foreign missionary and his message and to predispose the heathen favorably to both. They serve to point the divine love of the great Physician to the human race of all climes and all social conditions and should be used as an external means to demonstrate that He continues to bear the sorrows and diseases, physical and spiritual, of mankind. The helping, healing service of His followers and emissaries should exhibit the love of their Master, Jesus Christ, in whose name they forsake the comforts and temporal prospects of preferment in the homeland and come to distant and often dismal peoples and climes, frequently to expose themselves to suffering, persecution, and death. Medical missions are therefore chiefly a preparatory agency for foreign missions.

3. A second service rendered by medical missions consists in their conserving, as much as possible, the health of the religious missionary force. The history of foreign missions has demonstrated that health and life has frequently been sacrificed in primitive and unsanitary districts where medical skill under God's blessing might have been of incalcuable service. Because of want of medical attention for himself and for his family many a foreign missionary has been constrained to forsake his chosen lifework and to return to his native country, to the great injury of the mission field.

4. Woman's medical mission work has been recognized as a necessity in countries where the line of demarcation between the sexes is as sharply drawn as in India and China. As a rule, it is out of the question for male physicians to render medical service to a woman. Even in some of the long-established missionary hospitals in India no male physician is to this day permitted to cross the threshold. The condition of the female population of India, secluded in the zenanas, is therefore most pitiable. There is an almost unlimited sphere for female medical activity as a handmaid to the Gospel.

5. The history of medical missions shows that already the Danish-Halle Mission occasionally sent out missionaries who were qualified physicians, but who chiefly engaged in religious work. — On February 22, 1703, General Codrington bequeathed two plantations in Barbados to the S. P. G., conditioning that a number of professors and scholars be maintained there who should be "obliged to study and practice medicine and surgery as well as divinity" in order to enable them to "endear themselves to the people and have the better opportunities of doing good to men's souls whilst they are taking care of their bodies." The society accepted the bequest and sent out the Rev. J. Holt (1712). John Thomas, a ship's surgeon, who had already done independent work in India, was sent out with Carey in 1793 by the Baptist Missionary Society. The first Protestant medical missionary to China was the Rev. Peter Parker, M. D., who was sent out by the American Board of Commissioners for Foreign Missions in 1835. In 1839 the London Missionary Society sent out Drs. Lockhart and Hobson, who first labored in Macao, Shanghai, and Hong Kong. A well-known medical missionary was Dr. Hudson Taylor, the founder of the China Inland Mission. The first woman medical missionary to be sent to India was Dr. Clara Swain (1870), who has had a large succession of followers.

6. Well-nigh all the foreign missionary societies of Europe and America now recognize medical missions as a distinct department of their work.

Medina. See *Mohammed.*

Medler, Nicolaus (1502—51). B. at Hof; d. at Bernburg. Studied at Erfurt and Wittenberg. Teacher at Arnstadt and Hof; associate preacher there; private tutor and assistant preacher to

Luther in Wittenberg; chaplain to the exiled Electress Elizabeth of Brandenburg; pastor at Naumburg, where he introduced the Reformation; court preacher to Electress Elizabeth; superintendent at Brunswick; court preacher at Bernburg. Luther counted him among his three true disciples.

Medley, Samuel (1738—99). B. at Cheshunt, Hertfordshire, where he received a good education in his father's school. Dissatisfied with business, he entered the Royal Navy, but retired after being severely wounded in battle off Port Lagos, 1759. He was taken to the home of his grandfather, where he was converted and joined the Baptist Church in London. For several years he conducted a school, but later began to preach and received a call in 1769 to the Baptist Church at Watford. In 1772 he became pastor in Liverpool, where he labored successfully till his death, July 17, 1799. He is best known by his hymn "I Know that My Redeemer Lives."

Meekness. See *Humility.*

Mees, Theophilus (1848 — 1923). Prominent theologian of the Ohio Synod; b. in Columbus, Ohio; studied at Fort Wayne and St. Louis; ordained 1875; professor at Capital University, Columbus, Ohio, till 1888; president of Teachers' Seminary, Woodville, Ohio, 1888—1903; professor at Capital University and the Seminary since 1903. Editor of *Journal of Pedagogy,* 1900; *Theological Magazine,* 1912. Author of *Doctrinal History of Predestination, 1517—80.*

Megerle, Ulrich. See *Abraham a Sancta Clara.*

Megiddo Mission. A sect founded in Minnesota by L. T. Nichols; headquarters Rochester, N. Y.; strong Unitarian and Universalist tendencies, deny Trinity, Atonement, salvation by faith, eternal punishment of the wicked; emphasize non-worldly living.

Meinardus, Ludwig Siegfried (1827 to 1896). Composer, teacher, and writer on musical subjects. Destined to study theology by his parents, he persevered in the study of the cello, and on the advice of Schumann turned to composition. He spent his adult life as teacher at Dresden Conservatory and as composer and critic. He wrote numerous compositions, among them the oratorios *Simon Petrus, Gideon, Koenig Salomo, Luther in Worms,* and *Odrun.*

Meinhold, Johann (1861—1937). Son of Karl M.; professor at Greiswald and Bonn; exegete, collaborator in *Strack-Zoeckler Commentary.*

Meinhold, Johann Wilhelm (1797 to 1851). Educated at Greifswald; held various charges in the State Church; leaned toward Catholicism; his best-known hymn: "Guter Hirt, du hast gestillt."

Meinhold, Karl (1813—88). Prominent Lutheran theologian of Prussia; studied at Greifswald and Halle; secured the recognition of the Lutheran Church in Prussia.

Meisner, Balthasar (1587—1626). Studied at Wittenberg, where he became prof. of theology in 1613; author of the monograph *Philosophia Sobria,* which caused a good deal of discussion.

Meister, Christoph Georg Ludwig (1738—1811). Lutheran poet. B. at Halle. Rector and preacher at Ballenstedt; consistorial assessor and pastor at Bernburg-Waldau; at Altenburg; and at Duisburg, where he was also professor of theology at the same time; pastor and teacher of religion, later also rector at Bremen *Gymnasium.*

Meister Wilhelm. The name of several unknown masters of the 12th century, especially of one who apparently did much of the sculpture work on the façades of the cathedrals at Modena, Ferrara, and Verona.

Melanchthon, Philip. Born Feb. 16, 1497, at Bretten, Baden. Grammar school at Pforzheim. 1509—1511 completed B. A. at Heidelberg, influenced by Pallas Spangel, humanist. 1512—1516 completed M. A. at Tuebingen. Edited classics and served as corrector in printery of Anshelm at Tuebingen. Issued *Greek Grammar* 1518. Gained accolade of Erasmus 1515 for style, became noteworthy in circle of humanists.* Wrote preface to Grand-Uncle Reuchlin's *epistola clarorum virorum,* engaged in subsequent controversy, and was cited in *epistola obscurorum.* Recommended by Reuchlin for University of Wittenberg, arrived there Aug. 25, 1518. Here he was won temporarily by Luther for the cause of theology, gave up projected edition of Aristotle, studied and taught theology as well as classics. He lectured to an average of 400 students, sometimes outstripping Luther in popularity. The Peasant Revolt * and the movement of the fanatics * emphasized the need for an educational program to implement the Lutheran Reformation. Luther called on Melanchthon, the schoolman and educator, to devise the methods. Melanchthon now reverted to his Aristotelian training and planned an educational process incorporating classic languages and philosophy as basic for later specialized vocational studies. The princes were made the patrons of the organized program of instruction, and Melanchthon was the chief agent in preparing the visitation articles by which the government surveyed every parish in Electoral Saxony and supervised religious and moral life. In his plan of government the parish pastor not only led men to Christ through the Gospel, but served as the government's agent for the regulating of morality through the preaching of the Law. Melanchthon was even more hostile than Luther at Marburg * in 1529 against Zwingli. Guided by Luther, Melanchthon prepared the Augsburg Confession * for the Lutheran estates, who asserted their right to reform the Church within the feudal frame of the existing empire; he amplified its theology in the Apology. In 1521 Melanchthon issued his Loci Communes, in which he utilized the humanistic method of exposition to set forth the new doctrinal emphases of the Lutheran Reformation. In 1535 a revised edition, however, reflected the humanistic psychology, granting undue scope to the activity of the human mind in the conversion and faith; subsequent revisions only increased this emphasis. Melanchthon worked with Bucer on the Wittenberg Concord.* In 1540 an edition of the Augsburg Confession contained an ambiguous phrase concerning the Real Presence in the Sacrament, which became the issue of controversy between orthodox Lutherans and the mediating Philippist parties in subsequent years. Conferences in 1540 and 1541 between Evangelicals and Catholics, seeking to compose differences, had no result other than to reveal Melanchthon's trend to concession. This trend was evident in Melanchthon's approval of the Augsburg and Leipzig Interims of 1548; the subsequent controversies raged for half a century. Melanchthon joined with Flacius and Martin Chemnitz, however, against Andrew Osiander. The University of Jena became the spearhead of attack upon the Philippist party. The latter became involved with political leaders in de-

fending itself. Melanchthon died April 19, 1560. Lutherans regard his fame tarnished by his doctrinal compromises, particularly on free will and the Real Presence; but they are grateful for his Apology, and for his services in the establishing of humanistic education. Although not a creative theologian like Luther, he left lasting influence not only on educational institutions, but on the structure of the Church dominated by the government, and on the ethical attitudes of the German people which tended to confine religious impulses to the sphere of Church and heaven, away from participation in civil life. See Humanism. RRC

George Ellinger, Philipp Melanchthon, Berlin, 1902; Hans Engelland, Melanchthon, Glauben und Handeln, Munich, 1931; Karl Hartfelder, Philipp Melanchthon, in v. vii, of Monumenta Germaniae Paedagogica, Berlin, 1889; Paul Joachimsen, Sozialethik des Luthertums, Munich, 1927.

Melanchthon Synod. This was a schism, in 1857, in the ranks of the Maryland Synod, fostered by Benj. Kurtz and eleven other pastors, for the purposes of resisting the swelling tide of confessionalism in the Maryland Synod and encouraging the defenders of the "Definite Platform." * It repudiated baptismal regeneration, the denial of the divine obligation of the "Christian Sabbath," the doctrine of the real presence, etc. In spite of its un-Lutheran character this synod was received into the General Synod in 1859, thus furnishing one of the causes of the disruption of 1866. Four years after Dr. Kurtz's death the Melanchthon Synod reunited with the Maryland Synod (1869).

Melanesia. A group of islands in the Pacific, west of Polynesia, including about 250 islands, comprising chiefly the New Britain Archipelago, the Solomon Islands, the New Hebrides, the Fiji Islands, New Caledonia, also the Australian Territory and Australian Mandate in Papua, the Santa Cruz Islands, Loyalty Islands, Norfolk Islands, and others. The religion of the islands is largely animistic. The population is Negroid. 29 societies carry on mission work, among them The Luth. Church — Mo. Syn., the American Lutheran Church, the United Ev. Lutheran Church of Australia, and the Ev. Lutheran Church of Australia. Christian community, about 490,000 (1952). See Missions, Bibliography.

Melchites. The collective name of the orthodox Christians remaining in Roman provinces conquered by Arabs. Their name, from *melek*, king, signifies their loyalty to emperor and Pope and their distinction from Monophysites.

Meletian Schisms. Two. The Egyptian Schism (305—ca. 400) arose from the encroachments of Meletius of Lycopolis on the metropolitan rights of Peter of Alexandria. The Antiochian Schism (361—415) had its origin in the election of the Arian bishop Meletius, who immediately disappointed his party by his Nicene leanings, while he failed to satisfy the orthodox because of his Arian consecration.

Melin, Hans Magnus (1805—77). Prof. of theology at Lund, Sweden; published *Lectures on the Life of Jesus* (criticism of Strauss); *Greek Lexicon; Bible Translation with Commentary.*

Meliorism. In philosophy, a designation given to a view of the world which holds that at present the sum of the good exceeds the sum of the evil and that in the future the gain will be in favor of the good. The view attempts to mediate between optimism and pessimism and is favored by pragmatism.

Melito of Sardis. One of the great theologians of the second century. His reputed literary activity embraced the entire field of theology. Apart from fragments, his works are lost.

Melville, Andrew (1545—1622). Reformer in Scotland; defender of Presbyterianism; taught in France and Geneva; then principal of Glasgow, St. Mary's College, St. Andrew's; prof. of Biblical theology in Sedan, France. Reorganized Scotch universities and encouraged the study of Greek. Opposed the efforts of the kings to introduce Episcopalianism in Scotland, for which he was temporarily imprisoned. Participated in the writing of the *Second Book of Discipline.*

Memling, Hans (ca. 1430—94). Flemish painter, whose reputation extended to England and Italy; strong romantic tendency; among his sacred paintings: "The Last Judgment" (at Danzig), "Adoration."

Memory Work. *See Christian Teaching,* E.

Men and Religion Forward Movement. A movement begun in the early part of the 20th century for the purpose of enlisting all the men of all

Protestant churches in a combined effort to advance the cause of Christianity. A movement similar to the later Inter-Church World Movement, although not carried on on so large a scale as that.

Menander. See *Gnosticism,* 7 e.

Mencel, Hieronymus (1517—90). Supt. at Mansfeld, Prussia; published sermons on the Catechism; at first upheld the error that natural man is sin, but was led by Wigand to oppose it.

Mencius. See *Confucianism,* 2.

Mendelssohn-Bartholdy, Felix (1809 to 47). Christian (Lutheran) composer of Jewish lineage and the grandson of the philosopher Moses Mendelssohn. At the age of nine, Felix presented public performances and at the age of eleven produced musical compositions; his first symphony was written when he was fifteen years old, and his overture to *A Midsummer Night's Dream* was written at the age of seventeen. His journeys to Italy, England, Scotland, and Paris influenced his style and inspired much of his work. In 1829 Mendelssohn revived interest in the neglected works of J. S. Bach by performing Bach's *Passion According to St. Matthew* in grand concert style. His best-known choral works include his *Hymn of Praise* and his oratorios *Elijah* and *St. Paul.* His *Violin Concerto in E Minor* is often played, as are also his *Scotch, Italian,* and *Reformation* symphonies. While his organ works are not heard as often as the works of many other masters, his piano compositions enjoy widespread popularity. Mendelssohn founded the Leipzig Conservatory of Music and gave financial support to many talented but needy students of music. His compositions often lack depth and originality, but are usually brilliant, elegant, and interesting. He wielded a facile pen and the singability of his choral works is rivaled only by that of Handel, whom he dethroned as the dominant musical figure of England with his *Elijah* and other works. NG

Grove's *Dictionary of Music and Musicians,* Philadelphia, 1926. S. Hensel, *Die Familie Mendelssohn,* Berlin-Leipzig, 1921.

Mendicant Monks *(Begging Friars).* Members of monastic orders which originally carried the vow of poverty to extremes by renouncing every form of material proprietorship. The older orders, indeed, had always imposed the vow of poverty, which made the individual monastic incapable of holding property. No limit, however, was set to the possessions which a monastery might acquire and hold. The result was great corporate wealth, which, in turn, led to luxurious and loose living. To remedy this state of affairs, the mendicant orders were established in the Middle Ages. Their members were not to have any property, even in common, and were to rely for support on their own work and the charity of the faithful. The great mendicant orders are the Franciscans, Dominicans, Carmelites, Augustinians, and Servites. The mendicant principle was removed from these orders by the Council of Trent (Sess. XXV, ch. 3), which permitted all except the strict Franciscans to hold corporate possessions.

Mengs, Raphael (1728—79). One of the most distinguished artists of the 18th century; composition and groupings simple, drawings correct, coloring excellent; among his paintings: "Holy Night" and "Descent from the Cross."

Menius, Justus (1499—1558). Skeptic at Erfurt, converted at Wittenberg in 1519; 1529 superintendent at Eisenach, later also at Gotha; at Marburg disputation in 1529 and at Wittenberg Concord in 1536; wrote against the bigamy of Philip of Hesse; justified war on Emperor when he menaced the Gospel and opposed the Interim; against Osiander and for Major.

Menno Simons (1492—1559). See *Mennonite Bodies,* 1.

Mennonite Bodies (Anabaptists, *Taufgesinnte, Wehrlose, Waffenlose, Doopsgesind, Dooper,* etc.). 1. The origin of the Mennonite bodies is traced back to the Anabaptist fanatics, who at the time of Luther, under the leadership of Muenzer, Storch, etc., boasted of celestial revelations, rejected Baptism, subverted the existing forms of government, and caused general confusion for a number of years in Germany and other countries of Europe. In 1524 they incited the peasants of Germany to a ferocious uprising against their lords, who defeated them in 1525 and put to death their principal leader, Muenzer. In 1533 the Anabaptists made the city of Muenster, in Westphalia, their gathering place, ejecting the rulers of the city and all "infidels," proclaiming the advent of the millennium, endorsing Communism and polygamy, and instituting a reign of terror and licen-

tiousness. However, in 1535, the city was taken, the leaders of the Anabaptists killed, and the fanatics, seeking refuge, scattered over various countries of Europe, especially Holland and England, where some continued to preach their extravagant doctrines. Others disowned the wild fanaticism and coarse millennialism of Muenzer and Knipperdolling. They laid particular stress on the believer's Baptism as opposed to infant Baptism, the purity of the congregation by complete separation from the social order, and opposition to violence and war. In the course of time the members of these scattered communities found a leader in the person of Menno Simons (1492—1559), a former Roman Catholic priest, who was born in Witmarsun, Holland. He is regarded by the Mennonites, however, not so much as the founder of their sect as a prominent factor in its organization. The name "Mennonite" dates from 1550. In Holland, however, they were known by the name of *Doopsgesinde* and in Germany by that of *Taufgesinnte* or *Taeufer.* When William Penn acquired Pennsylvania from the English crown, he offered homes to the Mennonites, where they might enjoy the free exercise of their religious belief, and aided large numbers of Mennonites from Holland, Switzerland, and Germany to come to America. Individual families settled in New York and New Jersey as early as 1640; but the first Mennonite colony was formed in Germantown, Pa., in 1683. In the beginning of the 18th century the Mennonites spread northward and westward and have since spread to western Pennsylvania, Ohio, Indiana, Illinois, the Western States, and Canada.

2. *Doctrine.* While there is great doctrinal diversity among the various Mennonite bodies, they are all agreed on the following basic principles: The mystical union of the individual with Christ is manifested in the outward purity of the congregation. The *Brevis Confessio,* 1580, says that "Christ must be known and believed according to the spirit in His exaltation . . . so that the form and image of Christ is developed in us, that He manifests Himself to us, dwells in us, teaches us, completes the miracles in us according to the spirit which He performed while in the flesh, heals us of the sickness of our spirit, blindness, impurity, sin, and death, nourishes us with heavenly food, and makes us partakers of His divine nature, so that by His power the old

man in us is crucified and we arise to a new life, experiencing the power of His resurrection." In 1632 eighteen articles of faith were approved by a conference of Mennonites at Dort, Holland, and these articles are accepted by the great majority of the American Mennonites. A representative Mennonite summarizes the principles of these bodies as follows: "God the Creator of all things; the fall of man, through his disobedience; his restoration through the promise of the coming of Christ; the advent of Christ, the Son of God; redemption has been purchased by His death on the cross for all mankind, from the time of Adam to the end of the world, who shall have believed on and obeyed Christ. The law of Christ is contained in the Gospel, by obedience to which alone humanity is saved. Repentance and conversion, or complete change of life, without which no outward obedience to Gospel requirements will avail to please God, is necessary to salvation. All who have repented of their sins and believed on Christ as the Savior, and in heart and life accept His commandments, are born again. As such they obey the command to be baptized with water as a public testimony of their faith, are members of the Church of Jesus Christ, and are incorporated into the communion of the saints on earth. By partaking of the Lord's Supper the members express a common union with one another and a fellowship of love for, and faith in, Jesus Christ. The washing of the saints' feet is an ordinance instituted, and its perpetual observance commanded, by Christ. The state of matrimony is honorable between those spiritually kindred, and such alone can marry 'in the Lord.' The civil government is a part of God's ministry, and members are not permitted to despise, blaspheme, or resist the government, but must be subject to it in all things and obedient to all its commands that do not militate against the will and Law of God, and should pray earnestly for the government and its welfare and in behalf of their country. Christ has forbidden His followers the use of carnal force in resisting evil and the seeking of revenge for evil treatment. Love for enemies cannot be shown by acts of hatred and revenge, but by deeds of love and good will. The use of all oaths is forbidden as contrary to God's will, though simple affirmation is allowed. Those who willfully sin against God are to be excluded from the rights and privileges of the church, but are to be kindly exhorted to amend their ways, the object of expulsion being the amendment, not the destruction. of the offender, and for the benefit of the church. Those who, on account of their obstinacy, are finally reproved and expelled from the church, because separated from God, must also be shunned socially, 'that the openly obstinate and reprobate one may not defile others in the church,' though in case of need they are to be kindly cared for and admonished as those in need of spiritual help. At the end of earth and earthly existence, all those who have lived and shall then be living are to be changed in a moment at the sound of the last trump and are to appear before the judgment seat of Christ, where the good shall be separated from the evil; the good to enter into the heavenly joys prepared for them, the evil to depart forever from God's presence and mercy into the place prepared for the devil and his servants." (Census Report, Religious Bodies, 1937, p. 1003f.) — Baptism is administered by sprinkling or pouring. The celebration of the Lord's Supper twice a year is combined with the ceremony of footwashing.

3. The numerous schisms among the Mennonites were occasioned primarily by divergent views on discipline. In recent years, however, the seventeen separate bodies have taken steps toward closer co-operation, and the Mennonite bodies may now be classified in three groups: the conservative bodies, represented especially by the Amish party; the central wing, represented by the Mennonite Church; and the liberal wing, represented by the General Conference of Mennonites. — 1) *The Old Order Amish* and the *Conservative Amish Mennonites* represent the Amish Movement inaugurated by Jacob Amen in the latter half of the 17th century. These two bodies represent the most conservative Mennonites. Amen held that the excommunication of disobedient members implied the complete shunning of the banned person, including also his ostracism from all social relations, even within the circle of his own family. The Amish usually worship in houses; employ the German language; use hooks and eyes instead of buttons, which are said to be a sign of luxury or of the military. Other bodies which are opposed to such innovations as the Sunday school, the use of English, higher education, are

The Church of God in Christ (founded by J. Holdemann), The Old Order Mennonite Church, The Reformed Mennonite Church, The Stauffer Mennonite Church. Also the Mennonites of Russian extraction are usually very conservative. Many of the early Mennonites had found refuge in the Crimea of Russia, where they divided on such questions as immersion, experimental religion, entire sanctification. These divisions among the Russian groups are perpetuated in America by the following Mennonite bodies: The Mennonite Brethren Church of North America, Krimmer Brueder-Gemeinde, Mennonite Kleine Gemeinde, Evangelical Mennonite Brethren Conference, and the Hutterian Brethren (a communistic group). — 2) The Mennonite Church is the largest body and most closely identified with the history given above. Many of the Amish who in 1693 had seceded from the parent body have reunited with this group. The Mennonite Church represents the conservatively progressive element among the Mennonite bodies and in distinction from most of the strict Mennonites is organized to do educational, philanthropic, and missionary work. The Central Conference of Mennonites, represented chiefly in central Illinois, like the Mennonite Church, occupies a mediating position in theology and practice. The Conference of Defenseless Mennonites and the Mennonite Brethren in Christ belong to the central party, but differ from the Mennonite Church in their emphasis on entire sanctification, divine healing, and immersion. — 3) The General Conference, organized in 1860, comprises those Mennonite congregations which seek a more liberal interpretation of the Mennonite laws. They have relaxed the laws on such practical points as the women's prayer covering, footwashing, non-conformity to the world, and excommunication. They also employ the usual methods of the Protestant denominations in carrying on mission, education, and philanthropic work. See Religious Bodies (U. S.), Bibliography. FEM

Mennonite Brethren in Christ. See Mennonite Bodies, 3.

Mennonite Brethren Church of North America. See Mennonite Bodies, 3.

Menologion. 1) List of martyrs and saints in the Greek Church giving the festivals in their honor, Gospel selections, and legends; 2) service book of the Greek Church.

Mensa. See Church Furniture, 1.

Mensageiro Luterano. See Brazil, Lutheranism in, 6.

Mental Reservation. See Jesuits and Jesuitism, 5.

Mentzer, Balthasar. "Patriarch of true Lutheranism in Hesse"; b. 1565 at Allendorf; d. 1627; professor at Marburg, Giessen, and Marburg; earnest defender of Lutheran orthodoxy against efforts to introduce Reformed type of doctrine in Hesse. See Cryptist-Kenotist Controversy.

Mentzer, Johann (1658—1734). B. July 27, 1658, at Jahmen, near Rothenburg, Silesia, studied theology at Wittenberg, and held pastorates at Merzdorf, Hauswalde, and finally at Chemnitz. He was greatly interested in hymnology and was a good friend of J. C. Schwedler, Henriette Katharine von Gersdorf, and N. Ludwig von Zinzendorf, all hymn writers and close neighbors. He wrote a large number of hymns. Over thirty appeared in various hymnbooks of his time. He is known by "Oh, that I Had a Thousand Voices."

Merbecke, John (Marbeck; 1523 to ca. 1585). Organist, St. George's Chapel, Windsor, composer and editor of The Boke of Common Praier Noted, published in 1550 and an adaptation of early plain chant used in the rituals in the days of Edward VI. His liturgical music shares much of the simplicity employed in the early liturgical music of the Lutheran Church. Merbecke was persecuted for his faith and on one occasion (1544) barely escaped execution. After the death of Henry VIII he boldly testified regarding his faith. Oxford University granted him the degree of Mus. D. in the same year in which his Book of Common Prayer Noted appeared.

Mercadante, Francesco Saverio (1795—1870). Studied at Naples under Zingarelli; dramatic composer; lived in many cities of Italy, Spain, and Portugal; conductor of several large orchestras; wrote much sacred music.

Mercersburg Theology. A school of interpretation at Mercersburg, Pa., led by Philip Schaff and others who sought to vivify Calvinistic doctrine by introducing the Christocentric ideal. See Evangelical and Reformed Church, 1.

Mercier, Desire Joseph (1851—1926). Cardinal and archbishop in Belgium; as prof. of Thomist philosophy at Louvain he played an important part in evolving neo-Thomism; prominent opponent of German occupation during First World War; sought to unify Anglican, Protestant Episcopal, and Roman Catholic churches.

Mercy. That aspect of God's goodness by which He has compassion with the afflicted and bestows His benefits upon the miserable. God's mercy is plenteous and abundant and extends over all who suffer trouble and affliction, whether physical, mental, or spiritual (Ps. 68:5; Is. 49:13; Ps. 103:17; 108:4; Micah 7:18; Titus 3:5). As God is merciful, so men also should be merciful (Luke 6:36; Micah 6:8; Matt. 5:7).

Mercy, Sisters of. A name given to Roman Catholic congregations which devote most of their time to the destitute and education.

Merensky, Alexander. B. June 8, 1837, at Panten, Germany; d. March 22, 1918, at Berlin; sent as missionary of Berlin Missionary Society to Transvaal, Africa, 1858; returned to Germany 1882; founded mission station in Kondeland, Africa, 1891; inspector at Berlin 1892; a voluminous writer on missions.

Mergner, Adam Christoph Friedrich (1818—91). Studied theology at Erlangen; 1851 pastor in Ditterswind, 1870 superintendent in Muggendorf, 1874 in Erlangen, 1880 in Heilbronn; eminent musical gifts, which he used largely in the endeavor to restore the purity of the ancient Lutheran liturgy and hymnology; also composed tunes of striking originality and depth, especially for Gerhardt's hymns; edited *Choralbuch fuer die lutherische Kirche in Bayern*, containing some of his own compositions.

Merit. Roman theologians distinguish between merits of condignity *(de condigno)* and of congruity *(de congruo.)*. They define merits of condignity as merits to which, in justice, a reward is due; and merits of congruity as merits to which a reward is due only in propriety, especially in view of the nature of him who rewards. Applying this distinction to their doctrine of works, they teach that the good works of the regenerate, in so far as they proceed from free will, merit the grace of God and eternal life *de congruo;* while, in so far as they proceed from the working of the Holy Spirit, they merit

eternal life *de condigno.* The Apology of the Augsburg Confession (IV, 19) rejects this distinction as a screen for Pelagianism and a device which robs Christ of His honor to give it to men (III, 195—97) and nevertheless leads men into doubt and despair *(ibid.,* 200). See *Works, Merit of.*

Merkel, Paul Johann (1819—62). German prof. of jurisprudence; opponent of Prussian Union.

Merle d'Aubigne, Jean Henri (1794 to 1872). Celebrated Reformed Church historian; b. near Geneva; pastor (French) at Hamburg and Brussels; professor at Geneva 1831; helped to establish *église évangélique;* d. at Geneva; wrote *History of the Reformation* (not always reliable) and other works.

Merswin, Rulman. See *Friends of God.*

Mesrob (d. 440). Armenian bishop and scholar; allegedly invented Armenian and Georgian alphabet.

Messalians. Another name for Euchites.*

Messiah. One of the most significant names of the Savior on the basis of the prophetic sayings of the Old Testament, which pictured Him as the "Anointed of the Lord," one who should be endowed with the Holy Ghost without measure to be our Prophet, Priest, and King. The prototypes of the Messiah were the Old Testament patriarchs, prophets, priests, and kings, some of whom were designated as anointed, others being inducted into their office by means of anointing. Jesus repeatedly stated that He was the Messiah as foretold by the Prophets of old. John 4:26; 10:24, 25; Matt. 26:64. The corresponding Greek name is Christ. See *Judaism,* 1.

Metamorphosis. See *Transmigration of Souls.*

Metaphrastes, Simeon (10th century). Prominent theological writer at Eastern court; collected stories and legends of saints and martyrs which were later enlarged.

Metaphysical Argument. See *Immortality.*

Metaphysics. See *Psychology,* E; *Philosophy.*

Metempsychosis. See *Transmigration of Souls.*

Method of Faith. See *Grace, Means of,* I 7.

Methodist Bodies. 1. *History.* The Methodist churches owe their origin to the religious experiences of John Wesley (1703—91) and his co-workers during the third decade of the 18th century. In an age when spiritual indifference prevailed in the Anglican Church the Wesleys were concerned about furthering their own personal piety. At Oxford University Wesley and like-minded students organized the Holy Club, hoping that by following certain methods and rules they could attain greater piety in their personal life. However, in spite of carefully observing all the "methods" John Wesley could not gain assurance that he had attained the holiness which he thought was demanded of him in Heb. 12:14. On May 24, 1738, he attended a religious meeting in which Luther's preface to the Epistle to the Romans was read, and there he "felt his heart strangely warmed" and instantaneously gained the assurance that at last he had conquered sin and was now able to love God with all his heart. Shortly after this meeting Wesley and George Whitefield devoted themselves with tireless activity to "raise unto God a holy people and to convert sinners from the service of Satan to the service of God." The mission activity of Wesley and his co-workers resulted in one of the greatest revivals in the history of the Church. Wesley's unconventional methods, particularly his field preaching, the watch-night meetings, the employment of lay preachers, did not appeal to the Anglican clergy. Wesley, at first had no intention of founding a new church, but opposition within the Anglican Church, which excluded the "Methodists" from the Sacraments and closed its pulpits to their leaders, compelled Wesley to organize his followers in societies under the tutorship of lay preachers. Several such "congregations" were placed under the care of one lay preacher. This is known as the itinerancy. In 1744 Wesley organized the Annual Conference, in which all lay preachers were represented. Not until 1784 was the Methodist Church organized as a separate group in England. Methodism is represented chiefly in the English-speaking world in the British Isles, Australia, New Zealand, and especially in the United States (the Methodist Church of Canada lost its identity in the merger of several Reformed bodies, known as the United Church of Canada). In the United States, Methodism has experienced its greatest expansion. From the small beginnings in 1773, when the first Annual Conference was held, until the present time the Methodist Church has grown to become one of the largest Protestant denominations. The Methodist bodies number more than eight million members. The United Brethren Church,* the Evangelical Church,* and the large number of Holiness Bodies * are essentially Methodistic.

2. *Doctrine.* Wesley's theology was a modified Arminianism.* Because Wesley and his followers were interested more in "deeds than in creeds," Wesley granted great liberty in doctrine. The twenty-five articles prepared by Wesley as a doctrinal guide are patterned after the Thirty-nine Articles of the Anglican Church. It is significant, however, that the real standards of Methodist doctrine are Wesley's "preached sermons," in which great emphasis is laid on sanctification. Christian perfection may be viewed as the central doctrine of Methodism. Methodist theology is usually presented under four points: 1) universal salvation, 2) free salvation, 3) sure salvation, 4) full salvation. H. P. Sloan has summarized the four points as follows: Justification by faith alone; true freedom of human personality; the witness of the Spirit for assurance; and the doctrine of the pure heart. According to Wesley, salvation has not only been won for all men, but is also brought to all men, even those who do not hear the Gospel (universal salvation). Wesley held that all men who are obedient to the "Gospel" according to the measure of light given them are in the Kingdom. This implies, of course, that man is not totally depraved, but is free both to accept or reject the "Gospel" (free salvation). In line with the theory of human freedom, Wesley held that the Holy Spirit assures man of his salvation directly (sure salvation). The real heart of Wesley's theology was the doctrine of the pure heart (full salvation). Christian perfection in Methodist theology is the ability of man to overcome progressively the evil inclinations and to reach perfection. In recent years large sections of Methodism have become Modernist, and have re-defined Wesley's four points in accord with Liberal Theology. The transition from Wesley's individual perfection to Modernism's social perfection was comparatively simple. The Methodist Epis-

copal Church was the first denomination to adopt the Social Creed for the Churches. The Social Creed as adopted by the Methodist Church in 1907, restated in 1912, and greatly expanded in the "Discipline of 1944" makes it the duty of the church to help society in solving such economic, social, moral, political, and industrial problems as class tensions, racial inequality, agricultural problems, economic insecurity, industrial accidents, liquor traffic, child labor, international strife.

3. *Polity.* The church government may be defined as a government by conferences. The general lines laid down by Wesley developed in somewhat different directions in England and America. In England the conference remained supreme, while in America the superintendency became an episcopacy. When the episcopal form of government was adopted at the first Annual Conference in 1784, the government by conferences was not abrogated, but actually made an integral part of the episcopal system. The Methodist system operates under four types of conferences in close relation with the respective bishops: a) In the Quarterly Conference the class leaders, church officers, and the deacon or elder (pastor) of a congregation report on the spiritual condition to the district superintendent or presiding elder. b) At the District Conference the presiding elder, or district superintendent, hears reports from a number of neighboring parishes. c) The Annual Conference comprises the congregations and pastors of a district under the supervision of the bishop, who examines the work of the deacons and elders, supervises the work, and ordains the deacons. d) The General Conference, composed of an equal number of pastors and laymen, is the highest authority. In Methodist church polity the deacons and elders are pastors of local congregations, only the latter having the power to perform all the functions of the ministry and being eligible for the office of presiding elder (district superintendent). The bishops (general superintendents) are consecrated to preside at the Annual Conferences, examine the work of the deacons and elders, ordain and make the pastoral appointments, and have general oversight of the religious work. Methodist churches are often divided into the episcopal bodies (especially the Northern and the Southern Methodists) and the non-episcopal bodies. Since the merger of the Northern,

Southern, and Protestant Methodists in 1938 the episcopal system has been considerably relaxed, and this former division is hardly tenable today.

4. *The Separate Bodies.* a) *The Methodist Church.* This Methodist body came into being in 1938 by a merger of the Methodist Episcopal Church North, Methodist Episcopal Church South, and Methodist Protestant Church. In 1773 the first Annual Conference of Methodists was held at Philadelphia. And in 1784 Asbury and Coke, whom Wesley had commissioned as superintendents, were consecrated as bishops. The church government was therefore distinctly episcopal, and this caused a number of disagreements, notably the schism of 1792, when James O'Kelly and a large following organized the Republican Methodist Church. In 1830 the Methodist Protestant Church came into being as a revolt against the ecclesiastical rule of the clergy. Not until 1872 did the Methodist Church alter its constitution to admit lay delegates (men and women) to the General Conference. Wesley and his followers were among the early advocates of the abolition of slavery and permitted no slaveholder to occupy an official position in the Church. When Bishop Andrew of Georgia became a slaveholder through marriage and thus disqualified from his office, the Methodists of the Northern States insisted on his resignation, while the Southern Methodists preferred to separate peacefully from their Northern brethren. This was in 1846. This breach was healed in 1938.

b) *Non-Episcopal Methodist Bodies.* —*The Reformed Methodist Church* was founded in 1814 as a protest against the episcopacy and today lays great emphasis on entire sanctification and congregational supremacy. *The Wesleyan Methodist Church* was founded in 1843 as a protest against the refusal of the ecclesiastical authority to profess openly "Wesley's opposition to slavery." *The Primitive Methodist Church* traces its beginnings to the Kentucky Revival and particularly to the camp meetings conducted by the "Wilderness Evangelist," L. Dow. This body still strongly advocates the typical revival method. *The Congregational Methodist Church* was organized in 1850 in protest against ecclesiastical domination. In 1881 a split occurred, leading to the founding of the *New Congregational Methodist Church,* and in 1916 another split resulted in the founding of the *Reformed New*

Congregational Methodist Church. The *Free Methodist Church* was organized in 1860 as a protest against the alleged deviation of the parent body from the Wesleyan doctrine of entire sanctification. The *Holiness Methodist Church*, organized in 1900, holds the tenets of the Holiness Bodies.

c) *Colored churches.* The colored Methodist churches are episcopal. The majority of colored Methodists belong to three large colored bodies. In 1787 a separate Negro congregation was founded in Philadelphia under the discipline of the *Methodist Episcopal Church.* In 1816 an autonomous body was organized, and R. Allen was ordained as the first Negro bishop by Asbury. *African Methodist Episcopal Zion Church* was founded in Zion Church of New York in 1796 by the Negroes who had worshiped in the John Street Methodist Church (white). At first white "deacons" served them, but in 1821 it became an independent body. There is no doctrinal difference between the New York and the Philadelphia group of Negro Methodists. The *Colored Methodist Episcopal Church* came into being immediately after the Civil War and may be considered the colored parallel of the former Methodist Episcopal Church South. In addition to these three colored church bodies, comprising over one million members, there are the following smaller colored bodies: *Colored Methodist Protestant Church, Union American Methodist Episcopal Church, African Union Methodist Protestant Church, Reformed Zion Union Apostolic Church, Reformed Methodist Union Episcopal Church, Independent African Methodist Episcopal Church.* See *Religious Bodies (U. S.), Bibliography.* FEM

Methodist Episcopal Church. See *Methodist Bodies,* 4 c.

Methodist Fellowship. See *Students, Spiritual Care of,* A 3.

Methodist Protestant Church. See *Methodist Bodies,* 4.

Methodius (d. 311). Bishop of Olympus in Lycia; wrote *Symposium* in praise of virginity; *Aglaaphon* or *De Resurrectione* defending resurrection of the body against Origen; *De Libero Arbitrio* against Gnosticism on the origin of evil and free will; *Adversus Porphyrium.*

Methodius (d. 885). See *Cyrillus and Methodius.*

Methodology *(Theological).* That section of the preliminary work in the general study of theology which pertains to the form of study and the methods of attacking the problem of study.

Methods. See *Christian Teaching,* I.

Metropolitan. The title borne by the bishops of the capital (mother) cities of the Roman provinces. They presided at provincial synods and exercised general supervision over the other bishops of the province. The name occurs for the first time in the acts of the Council of Nicaea. See also *Archbishop; Polity, Ecclesiastical,* 3.

Metropolitan Church Organization. See *Evangelistic Associations,* 10.

Metz, Christian. See *Amana Society.*

Meumann, Theodore. Pastor in Prussia; came to America, 1861; pastor at Addison, Ill., and Platteville, Wis.; professor at Northwestern College of Wisconsin Synod, 1867—72; pastor at Fond du Lac, Wis.; returned to Hanover, Germany, 1876.

Meurer, Moritz (1806—77). Studied at Leipzig; private tutor, then pastor at Waldenburg, later at Callenberg, near Chemnitz; a diligent student of the Reformation era, on which he wrote extensively; also prominent as a writer in the field of ecclesiastical art, two valuable writings being: *Der Altarschmuck, ein Beitrag zur Paramentik,* and *Der Kirchenbau vom Standpunkt und nach dem Brauch der lutherischen Kirche.*

Meusel, Karl Heinrich (1837—89). B. in Niederau, Saxony; d. at Rochlitz. Vicar at Dresden, 1863; subdeacon at the Church of Holy Com., 1865; teacher at the *Gymnasium* at Bautzen, 1867; and in Dresden, 1871; pastor at Grosshennersdorf, 1873; superintendent at Rochlitz. He edited *Kirchliches Handlexikon.*

Meusslin, Wolfgang *(Meusel,* 1497 to 1563). Embraced Luther's views in 1527; chief pastor at Strassburg till the Interim; forced to flee; finally professor of theology at Bern; wrote: "Christ, Everlasting Source of Light."

Mexico, Lutheranism in. The Lutheran Church — Missouri Synod began work in Mexico in 1922. This work was directed primarily to German-speaking people. Since Mexican law demanded that the missionary be a native Mexican, the work came to a standstill after several years for lack of a missionary. It was revived in January, 1940, when Pastor C. A. Lazos, a native Mexican, who had been won for the Lutheran Church during his stay in Texas, returned to Mexico City. It was a slow and tedious struggle to win his first communicant members. In 1944 a well-situated piece of property was purchased in the colony of Santa Maria. In 1947 a school was begun. By 1952 there were 5 Mexican pastors serving 200 communicants in three places.

An English-speaking congregation has also been organized — the Lutheran Church of the Good Shepherd. Its church in the Lomas of Chapultepec was dedicated in December, 1948.

In 1941 the Rev. Felix Segovia was accepted into the Lutheran Church and in June of that year began mission work in Monterrey. To train a native ministry for Mexico the Instituto Concordia de Mexico was opened in Monterrey in September, 1947. The Lutheran Women's Missionary League contributed the funds for the erection of a church in Monterrey and the necessary quarters for the "Instituto."

HM

Mexico, Roman Catholic Church in. See *Roman Catholic Church.*

Meyer, Adolphus William. B. July 20, 1860, in New Zealand; graduated at Concordia Seminary, St. Louis, 1885; pastor at Rader, Mo., and Pittsburgh, Pa.; president of English Missouri Synod (two terms); president of St. John's College, Winfield, Kans., 1895 to 1927; pastor at Long Island City; editor of *Lutheran Guide* for some years. D. May 26, 1937.

Meyer, Heinrich August Wilhelm (1800—73). Pastor, later superintendent and consistorial councilor at Hanover; retired in 1865. His great work is a grammatico-critical commentary on the New Testament; after his death edited by various authors; this work is very valuable grammatically, but not free from the taint of liberalism.

Meyer, Herman E. E. (1881—1920). Educated at Northwestern College, New Ulm, Concordia (Milwaukee), Wauwatosa; pastor in Minnesota, 1904—13; principal of Milwaukee Lutheran High School two years; then professor at Wauwatosa Seminary of Wisconsin Synod; Secretary of Intersynodical Committee; managing editor of *Quartalschrift.*

Meyer, Johann Friedrich von (1772 to 1849). B. and d. at Frankfurt. Theologian, jurist, and statesman; president of the Bible Society in Frankfurt, 1816; wrote Bible commentaries. Influenced by rationalism in his earlier work, he later turned to mysticism and theosophy.

Meyer, J. Herman W. B. May 25, 1866, at Baltimore, Md.; grad. at Springfield, 1889; missionary at Fresno, Calif., 1889—90; pastor at Canistota, S. Dak., 1890—93; Waltham, Minn., 1893—1900; St. Paul, Minn., 1900—06; St. Louis, Mo., 1906—11; at Rost, Minn., since 1912; member of Board for Colored Missions; Pres. Minn. District, 1918—30; editor of *Missionstaube,* 1908—11; Wrote: *Dein Reich komme!* (2 vols.), 1909 and 1910; D. D., Concordia Seminary, Springfield, Ill., 1944; d. May 7, 1949.

Meyfart, Johann Matthias. B. Nov. 9, 1590, at Jena, where he studied and received several degrees. In 1616 he was made professor at Coburg, where he was a great oral force. After some time he left Jena and became thological professor at Erfurt, where he died Jan. 26, 1642. Meyfart is noted for his devotional works, in which he portrays a very earnest spirit. His outstanding hymn is "Jerusalem, Thou City Fair and High."

Mezger, George Leonard Peter. B. Dec. 28, 1857, at Braunschweig, Germany; graduated at St. Louis 1881; pastor at Waterloo, Iowa, 1881—85; near Okawville, Ill., 1885—95; at Decatur, Ill., 1895—96; prof. at Concordia Seminary, St. Louis, 1896—1923; professor at Theological Seminary, Zehlendorf, Berlin, Germany, 1923—31; D. D. (Northwestern College, Watertown, Wis.); editor of *Homiletisches Magazin;* wrote: *Entwuerfe zu Katechesen; Lessons in the Small Catechism; Bibelklasse,* Vols. 1 and 2; editor of *Denkstein zum 75jaehrigen Jubilaeum der Missouri-Synode.* D. Nov. 4, 1931.

Miami, Synod of. Organized Oct. 16, 1844, in Xenia, Ohio, under the leadership of Ezra Keller, first president of Wittenberg College. Its territory was southwestern Ohio. It joined the General Synod in 1845. It was one of the synods approving the "Definite Platform." In 1918 it joined the United Lutheran Church, and on Nov. 3, 1920, merged with the District Synod of Ohio (formerly of the General Council), the Synod of East Ohio, and the Wittenberg Synod (of the General

Synod) into the Ohio Synod of the U. L. C. At the time of this merger it numbered 45 pastors, 51 congregations, and 10,311 communicants. See *United Lutheran Church, Synods of,* 8, 22.

Michael. One of the archangels, or a member of the highest order of angels mentioned in Scripture. The name occurs in the Bible only four times, namely, in Dan. 10:13, 21; 12:1; Jude 9; Rev. 12:7. He is called a prince and one of the chief princes, a great prince, and he seems to have been one of the guardian angels of the Children of Israel at the time of the Exile. The New Testament pictures him as the special champion against the power of Satan, for he is represented as contending with the devil and as casting him out of heaven. In every instance the great power of the angel and his defense of the right are featured. — The passage Rev. 12:7 is by many Lutheran commentators *understood to refer to Jesus,* the Champion of His Church. See *Angels.*

Michael of Cesena (1270—1342). Franciscan monk; because the Pope had condemned aspects of the Franciscan ideals of poverty, he sought to organize opposition to papal claims and support the Emperor.

Michaelis, Christian Benedikt (1680 to 1764). B. at Elrich, near Nordhausen; d. at Halle. Studied at Halle. Associate, 1713—14, and full, 1714—31, professor there of philosophy; professor of theology, 1731—38; and of Greek and Oriental languages, 1738—64. Contributed to his uncle's (J. H. Michaelis') edition of the OT and put his own, with the Apocrypha in Greek and with the NT.

Michaelis, Johann David (1717 to 1791). Son of Christian Benedikt. B. at Halle; d. at Goettingen. Studied at Halle. Professor of philosophy, 1746—50, and of Oriental languages, 1750—91, at Goettingen. A prolific writer, he rendered outstanding services in the field of the Biblical auxiliary sciences, outwardly defending orthodoxy, which he inwardly did not accept. He is regarded as a founder of Syriac philology.

Michaelis, Johann Heinrich (1668 to 1734). Senior and inspector of the theological seminary at Halle; represented the critical school in Pietism; prepared an edition of the Hebrew Old Testament.

Michaelius, Jonas. See *Reformed Church,* 4 b.

Michaelmas. See *Church Year,* 16.

Michelangelo, Buonarroti (1475 to 1564). The most distinguished sculptor of the modern world, but also a master of painting and an architect of note; talent developed early; studied in the school of Lorenzo de Medici in Florence, after the death of his patron at Bologna; much work in sculpture in his earlier years, especially his "David," worthy counterpart of his "Moses" of later years; beginning with 1508, work on paintings of ceiling in Sistine Chapel of St. Peter's at Rome, nine paintings from Old Testament, series of Sibyls; last work in painting "The Last Judgment," from 1537—41, after which he devoted himself to the work of his appointment as architect of St. Peter's until his death.

Michelsen, Hans. Translated the New Testament into Danish (1524); secretary of Christian II, King of Denmark, Norway, and Sweden; accompanied the king into banishment (1523).

Michigan City, Ind., Theses. See *Toledo Theses* (Ohio and Iowa).

Michigan Synod (1920). See *United Lutheran Church, Synods of,* 13.

Michigan Synod. 1. In 1831 a number of Wuerttembergers immigrated and settled in Washtenaw Co., Mich. They wanted a pastor and sent to the Basel Missionary Society. As a result Pastor F. Schmid came to them in 1833. He founded twenty congregations and did much preaching here and there. With two others he founded the first Michigan Synod in 1840; it was called the Missionary Synod, for Indian missions seemed to be its first object. Three missionaries began work among the Indians at Sebewaing in 1845. Prospects appeared to be bright, for Pastor Loehe put his newly organized Indian Missions under the care of the Missionary Synod upon Schmid's pledge that confessional Lutheranism would be the unalterable program. Loehe's men, Hattstaedt, Trautmann, Lochner, and Craemer, joined the synod. In one year they realized that Schmid's pledge was merely a paper promise; the practice of the synod was quite otherwise. They left the synod in 1846. Schmid then joined the Ohio Synod. He had, after this, trained a few men himself and received a few from Basel to man the congregations he had organized and was ready for a second experiment.

2. In 1860 Stephan Klingmann and

Chr. Eberhardt came from Basel, and the second Michigan Synod was organized in Detroit with eight pastors and three delegates. The confessional declaration was soundly Lutheran, owing to the insistence of Klingmann and Eberhardt; but the battle was not nearly won. With splendid prospects before them through the work of Missionary Eberhardt, who extended his missionary travels as far as the mining regions of Lake Superior, there were never enough men to hold the fields, and too many of those who came were unionistic and often took their congregations to the other camp, as Basel indeed began to give this cause its whole support. Even those who remained in the synod often turned its slender resources over to the Basel missions, leaving little for their own work.

3. In 1867 the Michigan Synod joined the General Council, but unceasingly protested against the "Four Points." * Michigan, always represented by Klingmann, was put off from one meeting to the next, yet remained hopeful of better things. All hopes were shattered when the General Council met in Monroe, Mich., 1884. Two delegates preached in Presbyterian churches. The protest offered at once by Michigan delegates was tabled and evaded; protests in 1885 and 1886 met with a like fate. No delegates were sent in 1887, and in the following year Michigan formally resigned from membership.

4. Until this time Michigan drew its pastors from many sources, Basel (St. Crischona), Hermannsburg, Kropp; but it realized that it must have its own seminary. In 1885 A. Lange, formerly of the Buffalo Seminary, started work at Manchester with six students. A building was erected in Saginaw in 1887, and Lange remained for another year; but then doctrinal differences brought about his dismissal. Since then it had as directors F. Huber, O. Hoyer, W. Linsenmann, and F. Beer. It was closed as a seminary in 1907. Having left the General Council in 1888, the synod's intention was to join the Synodical Conference. This was done in 1892, when the *Allgemeine Synode von Wisconsin, Minnesota und Michigan (Ev. Luth. Joint Synod of Wisconsin and Other States)* was founded. The agreement with the other synods required that the seminary be discontinued; that was not kept, a faction developed which wanted to retain it. After a minority of ten had been suspended, who formed the Michigan District of the

Joint Synod, the majority severed relations with the Synodical Conference and with the Joint Synod in 1896. The leaders responsible for this were in an unnatural alliance with the Augsburg Synod until 1900.

5. After that things began to clear; new men (Bodamer, Krauss, Westendorf, Gauss), most of them graduates of Saginaw Seminary, took the helm. Conferences with Missouri, 1904, and the Michigan District of the Joint Synod, 1906, brought about a reconciliation. In 1909 the reunited synod resolved to return to the Joint Synod and did so at the Fort Atkinson session, 1909. Presidents to 1909: Schmid, 1860—67; Klingmann, to 1881; Eberhardt, to 1890; C. A. Lederer, to 1894; C. F. Boehner, to 1898; Bodamer, to 1903; Westendorf, to 1905; F. Krauss, since 1905.

Kurzgefasste Geschichte der Evangelisch-lutherischen Synode von Michigan und andern Staaten, Saginaw, Mich.; J. A. Russell, *The Germanic Influence in the Making of Michigan,* Detroit, Mich., 1927.

Micronesia. See *Polynesia.*

Midwest, Synod of. See *United Lutheran Church, Synods of,* 14.

Miessler, Ernst Gustav Hermann. B. Jan. 12, 1826, at Reichenbach, Silesia; d. March 1, 1916, at Chicago, Ill.; educated for missionary service at Dresden, Germany; came to the United States as a Leipzig missionary to the Chippewas near Saginaw, Mich., 1851; labored together with Baierlein and succeeded him at Bethanien (Bethany), 1853. The mission was nearly broken up by governmental transfer of the Indians to Isabella Co., Mich.; but Miessler continued to serve until 1869, when the station was closed by the Missouri Synod. Miessler then accepted a temporary supply position at Saginaw, retiring in 1871 from the ministry to engage in the study and practice of medicine at Chicago.

Migne, Jacques Paul (1800—75). Ed. as priest; held position at Puiseaux (Orleans); went to Paris after a quarrel with his bishop; established a great printery which published many valuable theological works, especially the *Cursus patrologiae completus.*

Milan, Edict of. The first edict of religious toleration, issued at Milan by Constantine in 313. It has been called "the great charter of the liberties of Christianity." After many persecutions had failed of their purpose, Constantine (and Licinius) thought it proper *"to give to Christians as well as to all others the right to follow that religion which to each of them appeared best."* Henceforth *"no man should be denied the privilege of choosing the worship of the Christians or any other religion."* Thus this famous edict recognizes the right of every man to worship God according to the dictates of his own conscience. Its advanced position, however, sprang from the exigencies of the political situation rather than from any appreciation, on the part of Constantine, of religious liberty as one of the original and inalienable rights of man. The "first Christian" emperor, as his subsequent conduct shows, considered the regulation of religious affairs as naturally belonging to his jurisdiction. Neither he nor, for that matter, the leaders of the Church themselves knew anything of the separation of Church and State, the great cornerstone of liberty.

Mildmay Institutions. A deaconess mother house, a nursing house, and a training house for home and foreign missionaries established by Rev. W. Pennefather at Barnet, later (1864) at Mildmay, near London, England, after the model of the Kaiserswerth institution in Germany, although in its details it has marked simplicity and adaptation to the work to which the British deaconesses have applied themselves. The influence of the Mildmay Home extends throughout England, as well as to the Continent and foreign countries.

Milic of Kremsier (d. 1374). Czech prelate; gave up his benefices and opposed papal abuses; imprisoned by Inquisition; often regarded as a reformer who prepared the way for John Hus.

Military Religious Orders. Associations of the Crusading period which combined military and monastic ideals. Originally established to protect and aid pilgrims to the Holy Land, they took prominent part in the Crusades and afterwards in fighting Mohammedans and heathen. Of about 20 orders three were important:

a. *Hospitalers* (Knights of St. John, ca. 1092). Founded for the purpose of caring for destitute and sick pilgrims at Jerusalem, they added the monastic (basically Augustinian rule) and knightly vows in 1118, with war against the infidels their chief aim, and added much to the military strength

of the Christians in the era of the Crusades; later they held the Island of Rhodes (1309—1523) and Malta as strongholds against the Mohammedans; Malta passing to England (1798), the old organization was dissolved.

b. *The Poor Knights of the Temple* (Templars). Founded by Hugue de Payens and Godeffroi de St. Omer (1119). Originally they were devoted to the protection of pilgrims. Their monastic vows were an adaptation of the Benedictine. Because their castles were located throughout the East and West, they soon came to function as international bankers. Desiring their wealth, Philip the Fair persuaded Pope Clement V to dissolve the order (1312).

c. *Teutonic Knights.* Originated as a brotherhood which cared for sick and poor German pilgrims at Acre (ca. 1189), converted to military order in 1198. Under its vigorous Grand Master Herman von Salza (1210—39) the order was engaged in the Christianization of Prussians along the Baltic. Later reverted to original duty of caring for sick. Dissolved by Napoleon (1809).

H. Prutz, *Die geistlichen Ritterorden*, Berlin, 1908.

Mill, John Stuart (1806—73). English philosopher and economist. Precocious child, educated by agnostic father. Many years in service of East India House. Coined name "utilitarianism" for ethical view held by him that actions are morally right if useful or beneficial to mankind; wrong, if harmful. Champion of women's rights. Main work, *System of Logic.*

Millais, Sir John Everett (1829 to 1896). English painter associated with the pre-Raffaellite movement; distinguished especially in the field of portraiture; painted "The Tribe of Benjamin Seizing the Daughters of Shiloh."

Millennial Church. See *Shakers.*

Millennial Dawn. See *Jehovah's Witnesses.*

Millennium (*Millenarianism, Chiliasm*). 1. The term *millennium* in theology signifies a period of one thousand years in duration, supposedly spoken of in Rev. 20:1-7. Millenarianism, or chiliasm, is accordingly the belief in the millennium and especially the tenet that Christ, at a time appointed by Him, will reappear on earth, where, with His saints, He will reign personally and in great glory for one thousand years or for an indefinitely long period; after this will occur the resurrection of the wicked, the final Judgment, and its eternal awards. — Millenarians, or chiliasts, have generally differed among themselves concerning the character of Christ's millennial kingdom, some viewing it as more and others as less spiritual in its nature, extension, duration, and joys; they differ also with regard to many other details and minor particulars. In general, however, they are agreed on Christ's personal advent and rulership on earth and a glorious period of peace and joy under the temporal reign of Christ. In consonance with the common doctrine of the Church, millenarians believe in the visible reappearance of Christ for the judgment of all men. They differ, however, from the common theological view by interposing a reign of one thousand years between the millennial coming of Christ and His coming unto Judgment.

2. Although not found in the OT, rightly understood, millenarianism is generally attributed to Jewish origin, being in accord with the grossly carnal conception of the Jews that Christ's kingdom would be earthly (see 2 Esdras 7:28 ff.). This apocalyptic teaching, however, was not the universal feeling of the Jews at the time of Christ. In the New Testament Christ indeed announces that the kingdom of God is at hand, but He does not speak of any provisory kingdom to be founded by Him (Mark 1:15). Christ's coming again is identical with the final Judgment (Matt. 19:28; cf. Mark 14:25). The Apostle Paul pictures the Church as enjoying the fruition of its faith, not upon earth, but in heaven (Phil. 3:20; 1 Cor. 15:25 ff.). The coming of Christ is a sudden coming to judgment (1 Thess. 4:15 ff.; 5:2 ff.). The New Testament teaches that the righteous and the wicked will be raised simultaneously, the former unto life, the latter unto damnation (John 5:28 f.; Matt. 25:31-46; Acts 24:15).

3. In the second century, chiliasm formed a constant, though not unquestioned, part of the church doctrine, until a radical change in external circumstances and in the attitude of many of its leaders towards the question forced it into the position of a heresy. The millennial theory is found more or less outlined in the Epistle of Barnabas (ca. 100), in the writings of Cerinthus, in the apocryphal books of Jews and Jewish Christians in the first age of the Gospel (the Book of Enoch, the Testament of the Twelve Patriarchs), in the writings of Papias, supposedly a disciple and friend of John the Apostle, in those of Irenaeus, Eusebius, Justin Martyr (ca. 150), Tertullian, etc. The first decided opponent of millenarianism was Caius, a Roman presbyter (ca. 200). The crass form in which chiliasm entered into the heresy of Montanism contributed to the strengthening of the antagonism to millenarian views. It was energetically opposed by the Alexandrian School, particularly by Origen. About the middle of the third century, Nepos, an Egyptian bishop, in defense of millenarianism wrote a work entitled A Confutation of the Allegorists, to wit, of those who explained the passages on which the theory of a millennium was based in an allegorical manner. This work was ably refuted by Dionysius of Alexandria. Among later theologians, Jerome was one of the ablest opponents of chiliasm. Gradually the tenet which had so widely prevailed became obnoxious and was proscribed, mainly because the condition and prospects of the Church had been altered. Whereas Christians at first had yearned for the reappearance of the Lord, Christians at a later time, perceiving the possibility and probability of a visible victory of the Christian Church over its adversaries by means of the Gospel, turned their attention to the restoration of the world by means of missionary endeavors.

4. During the Middle Ages the prevalent idea was that the Judgment and the end of the world would soon occur, since the dies irae was at hand. However, even in the Middle Ages "apocalyptic parties" — enthusiasts, whether individuals or in bands — were frequently to be found, and these looked for the miraculous advent of Jesus as the indispensable means of purifying and extending the Church. — The chief prooftext of millenarianism has always been Rev. 20:1-7, which they interpreted literally. Opposing this literal interpretation, their opponents have maintained that this passage does not treat of the second advent of Christ, and that, if the entire passage would be interpreted literally, the interpretation would result in hopeless confusion and absurdities.

5. At the time of the Reformation the traditional method of interpreting the Book of Revelation was abandoned. Luther and other leading reformers, regarding the Pope as the Antichrist, the appearance of whom was a direct

sign of the coming Judgment, were led to believe in the speedy coming of the Lord for the destruction of the world. However, millenarianism prevailed among mystical enthusiasts and sects and was espoused especially by the Anabaptists of Germany, who took possession of the city of Muenster and set up "the reign of the saints," which, however, ended in a speedy destruction of their own selves and their project. Yet even in the Lutheran Church, and even among conservative theologians, especially in later times, there have been adherents of the millennial doctrine. These views prevailed in spite of the condemnation of millenarianism in the Augsburg Confession (XVII) as well as in the Helvetic Confession (XI) of the Reformed Church, in which the doctrine was represented as mere visionary Judaism and rejected as a caricature of the true Gospel hope. Among those who espoused millenarianism was Jacob Boehme, and the mystics following Paracelsus. Millenarianism, however, gained its freest play in the 17th century, when the political commotions which distressed Europe, the revolutions in England, the religious wars in Germany, the maltreatment of the Protestants in France, spread millenarian teachings far beyond the walls of the conventicle. Toward the end of the 17th century the Lutheran Church was influenced in this direction especially by the Pietistic movement, particularly by Spener, who gave utterance to a refined millenarianism, and by Joachim Lange and the Berleburg Bible. Among the Lutheran theologians who defended the millenarian doctrine were Johann Albrecht Bengel, the author of the *Gnomon*, who expressed his chiliastic views in his commentary on the Apocalypse, published in 1740; he was followed by other divines of the Lutheran Church and has had followers down to the present time, though, in the main, conservative Lutheran exegetes maintain an antimillenarian stand. As in Germany, so in England and America, millenarianism continued to have devoted followers. In England millenarianism was strongly championed by the Plymouth Brethren, a sect which arose between 1820 and 1830. The Catholic Apostolic Church, founded by Edward Irving, maintained this tenet as one of its distinguishing features. According to Irving, Christ is to come and gather together His elect, the Jews are to be brought back to their ancient land, and through their instrumentality the Gospel is to be extended over the world. After a long period, during which the Lord will personally reign over the earth, will follow the Judgment and the end of the world.

6. In America, millenarianism was represented by the disciples of William Miller, the founder of an Adventist sect.

7. Millenarians may be divided into two groups, Pre- and Postmillenarians. *Premillenarians* hold that the millennium is a period of a world-wide righteousness, introduced by the sudden, unannounced visible advent of Christ; that before this coming of Christ takes place, the Gospel will be proclaimed throughout the world for a witness unto it; that the righteous will then rise and reign with Christ on earth; that the Lord and His saints will bring about a great tribulation, Rev. 2:22; that Israel will acknowledge the crucified Savior as the Messiah, Zech. 12:10; that through the outpouring of the Holy Ghost a vast number of sinners yet in the world will be converted, while Satan will be bound and locked in the abyss; that Satan, after a thousand years, will be unbound and make a final but vain effort to establish himself; that soon after this attempt he, his angels, and all lost souls that have been raised from the dead will be judged and hurled into the lake of fire, where they are doomed to everlasting torment; that the earth will be renewed by fire and become the eternal home of the redeemed. The *Postmillenarians* have, in the main, defended the following views: that through Christian agencies the Gospel will gradually permeate the entire world, becoming more effective than it is at present; that this condition will continue one thousand years; that the Jews will be converted either at the beginning or sometime during this period; that after this period of universal Gospel acceptance there will be a brief apostasy, followed by a dreadful conflict between Christian and evil forces; and that finally and simultaneously there will occur the advent of Christ, the general resurrection, the judgment of all men, after which the world will be destroyed by fire and new heavens and a new earth will be revealed.

8. Millenarians have differed as regards both the time and the place of the millennial reign. Some have attempted to fix a definite date, but others have refused to fix a definite period. The Montanists, Irvingites, and Mormons

selected the places in accordance with their sectarian belief. Many regarded Jerusalem as the center of Christ's reign (see *Jews, Conversion of, as a Nation*). The millennial joys have been variously described, ranging from intoxication of the senses to pure contemplation of Christ. While chiliasm presupposes the bodily reign of Christ, millennialism does not necessarily presuppose the personal presence of Christ on earth. See also *Dispensationalism.*

Miller, Charles Armand (1864 to 1917). Studied at Roanoke College, Luth. Theol. Sem. (Philadelphia), Chicago Theol. Sem.; pastor at Roanoke College Church, then in New York, in Charleston, S. C., then in Philadelphia; author: *The Way of the Cross; The Perfect Prayer.*

Miller, E. Clarence. Financier; b. 1867 in Philadelphia; member of Board of Publication and treasurer of United Lutheran Church from 1918 to his death, March 3, 1943.

Miller, George. See *Evangelical Church.*

Miller, George Benjamin. B. June 10, 1795; minister of New York Ministerium; prof. at Hartwick Seminary; d. April 5, 1869.

Miller, Jacob W. B. Sept. 16, 1860, at Cove, Md.; ed. St. Louis (1884); pastor at Clear Point, Ark., 1884—89; Little Rock, Ark., 1889—93; St. Paul, Minn., 1893—96; Ft. Wayne, Ind., 1896 to 1929; Vice-Pres. of Missouri Synod, 1908 to 1929. Sponsored purchase of Valparaiso University, Valparaiso, Ind., by members of Missouri Synod. Retired in 1929. D. May 11, 1933.

Miller, William. See *Adventist Bodies,* 1, 2.

Mills, Michael. See *House of David.*

Mills, Samuel John. B. April 21, 1783, at Torringford, Conn.; d. at sea, returning from Liberia, June 15, 1818. Father of foreign missionary movement in the United States. Organized as student, at Williams College, a foreign mission society and, together with Judson, was instrumental in spreading the thought through other colleges; gave incentive to the founding of the Board of Commissioners for Foreign Missions by overturing, in company with Adoniram Judson, Samuel Nott, Jr., and Samuel Newell, the General Assembly of the Church in 1810. As a result Judson

and others were sent out. Mills was not able to go, but continued his missionary efforts by exploratory work in the South and Central West; gave direct impulse to the organization of the American Bible Society, 1816, and to several missionary organizations, 1817; went to Africa with Ebenezer Burgess, arriving at Sierra Leone, 1818, and explored the country for the Liberia Colony.

Milman, Henry Hart ("The Great Dean," 1791—1868). B. at London; priest 1816; professor of poetry at Oxford; canon at Westminster; dean of St. Paul's 1849; d. near Ascot. Edited Gibbon, *Decline and Fall of the Roman Empire;* published *History of the Jews, History of Latin Christianity,* etc.; wrote also thirteen hymns, some of which are very popular (*e. g.,* "Ride On, Ride On, in Majesty").

Miltiades (2d century). Christian rhetorician; perhaps pupil of Justin; wrote against Montanists, Valentinians, Hellenes, and Jews; he gave Marcus Aurelius an *Apology of Christian Philosophy.* Excerpts of his work are in Eusebius.

Miltiades. Bishop of Rome (310/11 to 314); during his tenure the persecutions came to an end, and Christianity triumphed with Constantine.

Miltitz, Karl von (1490—1539). Saxon nobleman; nuncio of Leo X; dispatched by the latter to confer with Luther after Cajetan's defeat; but *apparent* diplomatic success availed nothing in settling a war of antagonistic principles.

Milton, John (1608—74). The son of John Milton, scrivener, was born in London. He entered Christ's College, Cambridge, at the age of seventeen; there he took his B. A. and his M. A. degrees. Leaving the university, he went to reside at Horton with his father, where he prepared himself for his future career by studying classical literature, philosophy, mathematics, and music. In 1638 he set out on a journey to the Continent, where he spent most of his time in Italy in the company of many of the great scholars. When rumors reached him of the impending break between the King and the Parliament, he returned home to offer himself to the cause of liberty. In 1642 he married Mary Powell, daughter of a Royalist family; the marriage was unhappy, and only after 1645, when the Cavalier cause was ruined, was a reconciliation effected between the two. In the meantime Milton wrote and published numerous tracts on political, social, and religious subjects. He became Foreign Secretary under the Commonwealth government in 1649. In 1652 he was afflicted with blindness. After the death of his first wife, he was married two more times, 1658 and 1663. His third wife survived him. With the Restoration in 1660, Milton was arrested, fined, and imprisoned. His last years were spent in literary seclusion.

John Milton ranks as a great pamphleteer, epic poet, and sonnet writer. To his first period belong such works as: *On the Morning of Christ's Nativity; L'Allegro; Il Penseroso; Lycidas.* The second period: *Of Reformation Touching Church-Discipline in England; Of Prelaticall Episcopacy; The Doctrine and Discipline of Divorce; Of Education; The Tenure of Kings; Areopagitica: for the Liberty of Unlicensed Printing; Treatise of Civil Power in Ecclesiastical Causes.* The third period: *Paradise Lost; Paradise Regained; Samson Agonistes; De Doctrina Christiana.* ECW

Minansa. See *Brahmanism,* 5.

Mind-Set. See *Christian Teaching,* D.

Miner, Alonzo Ames (1814—95). Universalist; pastor at Methuen, Lowell, Boston; editor of *Star of Bethlehem;* lectured on slavery and temperance.

Miniatures (in art), *Manuscripts, Gospels.* Miniatures, or small illustrations, included in so-called illuminated manuscripts, were extensively used in the Middle Ages, before the invention of the printing press, such calligraphic work being developed as an independent art; fine examples in Rome and in the monasteries of Bobbio, Monte Cassino, La Cava, Benevent.

Ministerial Office. (See also *Teachers.*)

1. The office of the ministry is a divine institution. The Scriptures clearly distinguish between the office of the ministry and the priesthood of all believers. While all Christians are priests before God and as such "should show forth the praises of Him who hath called them out of darkness into His marvelous light" (1 Pet. 2:9; Rev. 1:6), only some are incumbents of a special office in the Church, the office of the holy ministry. The Bible speaks of these incumbents in various terms (pastors, teachers, deacons, elders, *et al.*), indicating thereby the all-inclusive scope of the office (1 Cor. 12:29; Eph. 4:11, 12; 1 Cor. 4:1; Acts 20:28; Titus 1:5; 1 Tim. 3:1ff.). The office of a minister is not a continuation of the priesthood of the Old Testament (sacerdotal idea of Roman Catholic Church), nor does it consist in certain rights and powers vested in the Apostles which only they and their successors could and can confer upon others (apostolic succession of Episcopal Church), nor is it conferred indelibly upon any individual by the rite of ordination (*character indelebilis*), but through the work of the ministry Christ continues His prophetic office; those who have been called by Christian congregations or groups of congregations are Christ's undershepherds, Christ Himself being the one Lord and Master (Matt. 23:8). It is also not in accordance with Scriptural usage specifically to speak of ministers in terms which the Bible uses of all Christians, as, *e. g.,* divines (*Geistliche*) or priests (Gal. 6:1; 1 Pet. 2:5), as if a special *rank* (*Stand*) were given them; for the means of grace were given by God to the Christian congregation, which calls certain men to administer them for the Christian congregation, thus making them *ministrantes inter Cristianos.* (See Pieper, *Christliche Dogmatik,* III, p. 520f.) The Church has the obligation to carry out the Great Commission and may therefore create whatever offices are necessary. At present the Church calls pastors, teachers, missionaries, professors, synodical officials, and executive secretaries for missions, stewardship, welfare, and public relations, editors, counselors in education, and others.

2. If rightly understood, we may distinguish between the ministerial office *in abstracto* (*Predigtamt*) and the ministerial, office *in concreto* (*Pfarramt*). The Fifth Article of the Augsburg Confession speaks of the ministry of the Church *in abstracto* (*Predigtamt*): "That we may obtain this faith, *the ministry of teaching the Gospel and administering the Sacraments* was instituted. They condemn the Anabaptists and others, who imagine that the Holy Spirit is given to men without the outward Word, through their own preparation and works." The Fourteenth Article of the Augsburg Confession speaks of the ecclesiastical, or ministerial, office *in concreto* (*Pfarramt*): "Of ecclesiastical order they teach that no one should publicly teach in the Church or administer the Sacraments *unless he be regularly called.*"

3. The very fact that the local church is a divine institution goes to prove that the persons (bishops, ministers) of whom the Word of God speaks are the very men who are to serve the local churches as *their* teachers. At this fact, however, we do not arrive simply by way of deduction. Paul wrote to Titus: "For this cause left I thee in Crete, that thou shouldest *set in order the things that are wanting and ordain elders in every city,* as I had appointed thee" (Tit. 1:5). From these words we learn that every city, that is, each congregation in every city, should have its own elders, even as God has ordained; for the Apostle is not speaking in his own name, but in the name of the Lord. The Holy Ghost Himself, we are told, had made the bishops, or elders, at Ephesus overseers over the church of God at Ephesus, and they were not there simply because the church at Ephesus had for the time being considered it expedient or convenient to have them (Acts 20:28).

4. When the Lord called the twelve Apostles (Matt. 10:1 ff.; Luke 9:1 ff.), and later the Seventy (Luke 10:1 ff.), He made provision that the New Testament Church, beginning with the Day of Pentecost, should perform its work in this world through local churches (Acts 2:41, 42, 47; 4:4), each having its own servants of the Word (Acts 20:28). And while the Apostles were inspired teachers, which ministers are not, the Apostles themselves made no distinction between themselves and the elders *as far as the work of the ministry is concerned,* but spoke of these as having the same duties (2 Tim. 2:2; 1 Pet. 5:2), the same authority (Heb. 13:17), performing the same service (1 Cor. 3:5); and regarded them fully as their fellow ministers (Col. 1:7; 1 Cor. 3:22. Cf. 4:1; 1 Pet. 5:1). (Fritz, *Pastoral Theology.*)

5. Not the ordination, but the call received from a Christian congregation and accepted makes a man a public servant of the Word, and he ceases to be one when he no longer serves in or for a Christian congregation or group of congregations, e. g., Synod. Ordination is not a divine institution; the Lutheran Church in its Confessions has made it the public ratification of the acceptance of a call to a certain congregation or a certain field of Church work sponsored by a congregation or a group of congregations. Ordination and installation do not differ essentially. JHCF

See references under pastoral theology; C. F. W. Lindemann, *Ambassadors of Christ,* CPH, 1935; G. H. Gerberding, *The Lutheran Pastor;* C. F. Walther, *Die Stimme unserer Kirche in der Frage von Kirche und Amt,* Herrmann, Zwickau, 1894; C. C. Stoughton, *Set Apart for the Gospel,* Bd. of Pub. of ULCA; W. H. Greever, *The Minister and the Ministry,* Bd. of Pub. of ULCA, Philadelphia, 1946; P. F. Koehneke, "The Call into the Holy Ministry," *Abiding Word,* CPH, 1946 (I: 366—88); M. J. Steege, "The Lutheran Pastor," *Abiding Word* (I: 389—409); E. E. Foelber, "The Office of the Public Ministry," *Abiding Word,* 1947 (II: 474—92); T. F. Gullixon, "The Ministry," *What Lutherans Are Thinking,* Wartburg, Columbus, 1947.

Ministerium. The Pennsylvania Ministerium* and the New York Ministerium* are so called because these synods developed out of organizations composed exclusively of pastors. In 1792 laymen were admitted to certain sessions and given a vote.

Ministry, Education of. I. *Early History.* Christ, our Lord, personally instructed His disciples before commissioning them to preach. St. Paul and other Apostles, in like manner, trained their co-laborers for the work of the ministry by personal instruction. Giving "an answer to every man that asketh you a reason of the hope that is in you" (1 Peter 3:15) when facing Gnostics and heathen philosophers, demanded educated leaders in the Church. Gradually some of the catechetical schools, established for instruction in Christian doctrine preparatory to membership in the Church, extended their training to the preparation of men for the holy ministry. The most prominent were the schools at Alexandria and Rome. Information on the organization and curriculum of these schools is very meager.

II. *The Middle Ages* brought a decline in the standards. Students of theology were dependent upon the offerings of the cloister and episcopal schools (St. Gall and other monasteries); those in rural areas upon training by the local priest. This training became so deficient that bishops found it a burdensome task to preach a short sermon, and many priests had difficulty in reading the Scripture lessons for the Sunday. Charlemagne (742—814) gathered men of learning about him and encouraged the erection and maintenance of more and better schools for ministerial training. By the time of his death every cathedral was obliged to have its own school for the education and training of the clergy.

III. *The Pre-Reformation Period.* With the thirteenth century a great change was inaugurated. The theological schools were united with the universities. Paris and Oxford became famous for their course offerings (courses: Interpretation of Holy Scripture, Bible Doctrines, Morals, Church Law, Homiletics). At these universities both the lecture and disputation methods were used. Dormitories were provided for the students of theology. Then followed the impact upon ministerial training from the Renaissance (14th—16th centuries, in the revival of classical influence) and the Reformation (early 16th century).

IV. *Reformation Period.* Whenever the work of the Church must be reorganized under new environments, it faces new problems in the training of an efficient ministry. As the Reformation movement rapidly conquered the greater part of Central Europe, it was no easy matter to provide able ministers for the thousands of Evangelical congregations. The average education of the Roman Catholic priests was of a low standard. Luther, in his preface to the Small Catechism, states that "many pastors are quite unfit and incompetent to teach." The leaders of the Reformation were collected into a faculty at Wittenberg to train the future ministers, and every effort was made to remedy the deplorable situation as quickly as possible. However, this required time. During the first twenty-five years the majority of men ordained by Luther, Bugenhagen, and their assistants were without university or college education (of 1,750 men, 647 were "from the university"). Before the middle of the century men with a full university training had become the rule, and the standard of examinations prior to ordination was consistently raised. Scholastic Theology gave way to Bible Interpretation on the basis of the original languages (Hebrew, Greek) and commentaries on various books of the Bible appeared (Luther: Genesis, Prophets, Galatians). Next to the Exegetical Department was the Systematic, with the study of the doctrines of the Holy Scriptures. To these departments was added the Practical, emphasizing the teaching and preaching functions of the ministry. Thus the foundation was laid for present-day Lutheran theological seminaries, with their four departments (Exegetical, Systematic, Historical, Practical).

V. *Post-Reformation Period.* The beneficial influence of the Reformation on ministerial education was of rather brief duration. Within a century the training at the universities became primarily intellectual and philosophical. This brought a reaction in the Church in the form of Pietism (about 1700), which placed the emphasis on personal religious experience. A century later (1800) Rationalism gained control even in theological faculties, with the resultant devastating effect upon the ministry. In the nineteenth century scientific and liberal thinking dominated Protestant European theology, and the ideas and expressions of the European schools spread to other countries with the expected effect upon their ministers. While it is true that the European University offers its great treasures of knowledge to the student of theology, it is dangerous ground for him. The interest of such universities is "science." The interests of the Church of Christ, her confessions, her work, and her actual needs, are not sufficiently considered and protected. It has become a commonplace to see a theological faculty at a European university combine the most antagonistic theological views. Thus the school may undermine the very faith of the Church whose ministers it is to educate. This condition has called for the establishment of separate theological seminaries to counteract or prevent the evil effects of the university training and to supplement the defects of its instruction.

VI. *In the United States.* In the United States the Church is separate from the State. The Church, without any assistance or interference on the part of the State, organizes her congregations, builds her houses of worship, calls and supports her ministers, and also trains her ministers according to her own standards. Each denominational group formulates its plan of education, lays down its confessional basis, and establishes schools for its own communion. Protestant ministers who came with the early settlers or emigrated to the colonies before about A. D. 1700 were predominantly men educated in European universities. With the growth of an indigenous church came the need for educational institutions in which the ministry could be trained.

A. *Colleges,* patterned after European schools, were established. Harvard (1636), William and Mary (1693), Yale (1701), Princeton (1701) were all founded with the preparation of the ministry as one of the chief purposes. Today we are familiar with the distinction between college and seminary. In the early days the American college of liberal arts was a distinctively religious institution, and the education offered was centered in equipping men for the ministry. The Bible was taught in the original languages, and all students were obligated to acquaint themselves with its doctrines and precepts. Then followed special chairs of divinity in these schools. The first was the Hollis Professorship of Divinity at Harvard (1721), the next at Yale (1775). These few schools were inaccessible to candidates for the ministry living at a distance. These sought private instruction from a neighboring minister. This resulted in a lowering of standards and directed the churches to think of schools exclusively intended for ministerial training. Such were established at Harvard and Yale in 1819 and 1822 respectively. During this period other schools exclusively devoted to the training of ministers appeared. Some of these were church controlled, some were independent. The first separate seminary was established by the Dutch Reformed Church at Flatbush, Long Island, N. Y., in 1774.

B. At the beginning of the nineteenth century the Protestant churches had gained the conviction that each denomination could best train its own ministry by founding as many seminaries as it considered necessary under direct denominational control, setting its own educational standards and doctrinal position. Thus the American theological seminary, whether connected with a university or independent, came into existence. Many of these received a large percentage of students without college preparation. Problems incident to World War I (1918) gathered a group of theological educators. As a result a conference of seminaries was formed. This conference in 1936 became *The American Association of Theological Schools,* which adopted certain standards for accreditation and placed theological education at the graduate level, requiring an A. B. or its equivalent for admission to a three-year seminary course leading to the B. D., a faculty of at least four full-time professors, and other standards for library, equipment, finances, etc. Schools which do not conform to this pattern of four years' college and three years' seminary are not accredited. An analysis of the 1926 religious census figures for 17 of the largest white Protestant denominations in the United States had revealed that two out of five of all ministers in these denominations were not graduates of a college or theological seminary, while only one in three was a graduate of both. The highest proportion of ministers who were both college and seminary graduates was found in the Lutheran Church (Brown, *Ministerial Education in America,* page 25). Seminaries seeking accreditation of the American Association of Theological Schools are admitting only college graduates to a three-year course in theology.

C. *The Lutheran Church in America,* like the other churches, at first looked to Europe for its ministers. About the middle of the eighteenth century it became evident that this source of supply would be inadequate or cease entirely. A ministry would have to be trained by and in the Lutheran Church in her home on this continent. The beginning was made by appointing certain men as theological instructors, who were authorized to prepare young men for the ministry. These candidates were then examined by the clergy in convention. 1797 brought the establishment of the first school, when representatives of the estate of the Rev. John C. Hartwick (1714—96) resolved to establish a "theological and missionary seminary." In 1815 this seminary was located at Hartwick, N. Y. (incorporated, 1816). It was Lutheran in teaching and in the personnel of the trustees, but it was not an official seminary of the Church. Ten years later (1826) a school was opened at Gettysburg, Pa., the first official Lutheran theological seminary in the United States. 1830 marked the opening of the Evangelical Lutheran Seminary of Capital University at Columbus, Ohio, and the Lutheran Theological Southern Seminary at Columbia, S. C. In 1839 the Saxon immigrants to Missouri founded Concordia College as a classical college and school of theology (see XI, A, 1a). Since then sixteen Lutheran seminaries have been established in the United States (total 20) and three in Canada. (See also *Teachers, Education of.*)

VII. *Pre-Theological Training.* A. *General.* The first colleges in the United States were strictly religious institutions, and all students, irrespective of their future profession, were required to take the theological courses offered. The study made by William A. Brown (*op. cit.*, Vol. I, pp. 68, 69) revealed that in the last generation the attitude of the college toward religion has undergone a radical change. The colleges in the eastern part of the United States have gradually transferred their management from church control to independent and self-perpetuating bodies. Increasing emphasis has been placed upon the physical sciences. The classics and philosophy are no longer required subjects. These colleges are no longer schools of the humanities in which the prospective minister may find an adequate foundation for his theological studies. Religion is recognized, but only as one among many other competing interests, which must fight for its right to live. In the Western part of the United States the rise of the State universities affected ministerial training. In these schools the demand for practical courses, designed to fit men for their business or profession, has been crowding out the old type of liberal arts college. Religion can find no place in State-supported universities. By its omission from these institutions of higher learning many students are led to think that religion is not to be classed among the necessities of life. These changes in the American colleges are also reflected in the student body of the theological seminaries. During the last thirty years the number of students of theology coming from the large Eastern colleges has been steadily declining, and the number coming from State universities is comparatively small.

B. These trends have necessitated the establishment of many denominationally owned and controlled colleges. A listing of church-owned or controlled colleges may be found in the *Educational Directory of Colleges and Universities* issued by the Federal Security Agency.

C. *Lutheran Pre-theological Schools.* 1. The Lutheran Church in the United States has always emphasized the importance of Christian education on the elementary, secondary, and college level. In 1750 all churches but one in the Ministerium of Pennsylvania had flourishing schools. However, when the system of public schools became general a century later, the number of parochial schools diminished. A new impetus was given the parochial school by the Saxon colony of Lutherans and the organization of the Missouri Synod, which organized many Christian day schools. The churches in the Synodical Conference emphasize the importance of this early Christian training of the child (for statistics see *Parish Education,* D 7. See also *Teachers*).

2. At present the Lutheran churches are manifesting interest in Lutheran secondary schools to provide a continuation of the parochial school Christian atmosphere, instruction, and discipline. Lutheran High School Associations functioning in cities like Detroit, Mich., Cleveland, Ohio, Pittsburgh, Pa., Chicago, Ill., Milwaukee, Wis., St. Louis, Mo., Fort Wayne, Ind., Racine, Wis., and Minneapolis, Minn., have flourishing schools. (See *Parish Education,* G). Such schools are the proper link between the parochial school and the Christian college. The Lutheran Church has been deeply concerned to provide pre-theological education on the college level in schools under its own control, with Christian professors in a Christian atmosphere, and emphasizing their doctrinal position. Many of these offer the customary courses of a liberal arts college, some placing more emphasis on the classics. Many of these colleges are coeducational.

VIII. *Lutheran Colleges.* A. *Of the United Lutheran Church in America:*

1. Carthage, Carthage, Ill., founded 1870, coeducational

2. Gettysburg, Gettysburg, Pa., founded 1832, coeducational

3. Hartwick, Oneonta, N. Y., founded 1928, coeducational

4. Lenoir Rhyne, Hickory, N. C., founded 1891, coeducational

5. Marion, Marion, Va., founded 1873, women, Junior College

6. Midland, Fremont, Nebr., founded 1887, coeducational

7. Muhlenberg, Allentown, Pa., founded 1848, men

8. Newberry, Newberry, S. C., founded 1856, coeducational

9. Roanoke, Salem, Va., founded 1842, coeducational

10. Susquehanna University, Selinsgrove, Pa., founded 1858, coeducational
11. Thiel, Greenville, Pa., founded 1866, coeducational
12. Wagner Memorial Lutheran, Staten Island, N. Y., founded 1883, coeducational
13. Waterloo, Waterloo, Ontario, Canada, founded 1923, coeducational
14. Wittenberg, Springfield, Ohio, founded 1845, coeducational

B. *Of the Augustana Synod:*

1. Augustana, Rock Island, Ill., founded 1860, coeducational
2. Bethany, Lindsborg, Kans., founded 1881, coeducational
3. Gustavus Adolphus, St. Peter, Minn., founded 1862, coeducational
4. Upsala, East Orange, N. J., founded 1893, coeducational

C. *Of the Evangelical Lutheran Church:*

1. Augustana, Sioux Falls, S. Dak., founded 1860, coeducational
2. Concordia, Moorhead, Minn., founded 1891, coeducational
3. Luther, Decorah, Iowa, founded 1861, coeducational
4. St. Olaf, Northfield, Minn., founded 1874, coeducational

D. *Of the American Lutheran Church:*

1. Capital University, Columbus, Ohio, founded 1850, coeducational
2. Wartburg, Waverly, Iowa, founded 1868, coeducational

E. *Of the Lutheran Free Church:*
Augsburg, Minneapolis, Minn., founded 1869, coeducational

F. *Of the United Danish Church:*
Dana, Blair, Nebr., founded 1884, coeducational

G. *Intersynodical:*
Pacific Lutheran, Parkland, Wash., founded 1894

See also *Valparaiso University.*

IX. *Schools of the Missouri Synod.* The Lutheran Church—Missouri Synod has a number of schools which prepare students for admission to Concordia Seminary, St. Louis. The courses in these schools are those customary in high schools and junior colleges, with less emphasis on the sciences and more on the humanities. The language courses requisite for admission to Concordia Seminary are met (seminary admission requirements are given later). Through thorough integration and supervised study in dormitories over a period of six years, the schools are enabled to accomplish more toward proper preparation for theological studies than could be attainable by attendance at other schools on the secondary and higher level. Synod has resolved to establish a senior college, thus adding two years to the preparatory training and discontinuing the senior college work at Concordia Seminary. The preparatory schools are listed according to year of founding:

A. *In United States:*

1. Concordia College, Fort Wayne, Ind., founded 1846; deeded to Missouri Synod 1847; established as an academy and junior college 1861 (a resolution to close the school and to sell a major portion of this campus was adopted by the 1953 Synodical Convention. The same convention voted to construct a Senior College in Fort Wayne or its suburban area)
2. Concordia College, Milwaukee, Wis., founded 1881; Missouri Synod control 1887
3. Concordia Collegiate Institute, Bronxville, N. Y., founded 1881; Missouri Synod control 1896
4. St. Paul's College, Concordia, Mo., founded 1884; Missouri Synod control 1896
5. Concordia College, St. Paul. Minn., founded 1893
6. St. John's College, Winfield, Kans., founded 1893 by John Peter Baden; operated by the English Ev. Luth. Syn. of Mo., Ohio, and Other States until 1908; by the Kansas District until 1911; by The Luth. Church — Mo. Syn. since 1911.
7. Concordia College, Portland, Oreg., founded 1905
8. California Concordia College, Oakland, Calif., founded 1906
9. Lutheran Concordia College of Texas, Austin, Tex., founded 1926

B. *In Canada:*
Concordia College, Edmonton, Alberta, Canada, founded 1921

X. *Recruiting Students for Lutheran Theological Seminaries.* A. One of the larger Lutheran bodies (the U. L. C. A.) has a special department under its

General Board of Education for the purpose of recruiting suitable young men. This department is headed by a full-time general secretary. His work begins by reaching into the homes of the local churches, to influence parents toward dedicating their "choicest sons to the ministry." He secures lists of boys and young men from the pastors, continues contact with these by correspondence, pamphlets with general information about the ministry as a field of service, and personally or by representation addresses young people's groups.

B. In the *Missouri Synod* the constitution states as one of the objectives of the Synod: "The training of ministers and teachers for service in the Evangelical Lutheran Church." Every pastor and teacher, therefore, considers it as a part of his work to be on the alert for consecrated and intellectually qualified boys and young men who may become pastors and teachers. The nearest college of the Synod sends to each pastor application blanks to be handed to prospective students. A representative of the college, upon invitation, preaches a sermon on the service to be rendered by entering the ministry and then makes contact with prospective students and their parents. The parochial school (see above) offers opportunity to emphasize the ministry as a calling. The environment of such a school should cause more Christian boys to have the ministry in mind than would a less churchly environment during the elementary years. This probably accounts for the fact that the Missouri Synod has proportionately more students in its seminaries and teachers' colleges than have the other larger Lutheran bodies (cf. O. A. Winfield, *The Control of Lutheran Theological Education in America*).

C. *Entrance Requirements of Lutheran Theological Seminaries:* Most Lutheran seminaries require graduation from a recognized college, preferably Lutheran. College courses include the following languages: English, German, Latin, Greek. Some require two years of Hebrew in addition. Those preparing for the ministry in bilingual synods must be able to minister to their people in the respective foreign tongue (German, Swedish, Norwegian, Danish, Slovak, Finnish, Polish).

The minimum admission requirements at Concordia Seminary, St. Louis, Mo., are:

Course	High School Units	College Semester Hours
Religion	1.6	8
English	3	12
German	3	10
Latin	3	4
Greek	1	12
Social Studies (History)	2	9
Mathematics	2	—
Sciences	2	12
Humanities	—	5

The applicant must present a transcript of credits, an acceptable medical certificate, a brief autobiography, and a Christian character testimonial from his pastor. In 1949 Concordia Seminary had a four-year resident course. In the first two years the work toward the B. A. degree is completed. (When a senior college is established, the work for the B. A. will be completed there.)

D. *Control of Lutheran Seminaries:* Since they are established to train men for a distinctly confessional Lutheran ministry, the Synod or group of synods operating them writes the constitution by which the respective seminary is governed. The Synod elects the Board of Control and thus assures itself that its policies will be carried out. In most cases the membership of the board is divided between clergymen and laymen and thus the clerical view of the Synod is well represented.

The teachers at the seminary are selected either by the Synod in convention or by the Board of Control or by a Board of Electors, thus controlling the theological position of the teaching staff. (Many synods specify that a teacher at the seminary must have been in the active ministry for a number of years.) Teachers are pledged upon the Lutheran Confessions, which further assures the church body of the doctrinal purity of its seminary staff. Evidence that an instructor no longer holds the belief to which he has thus pledged himself makes him subject to discipline and eventual dismissal. Faithfulness to the doctrinal position of the Church is the *sine qua non*. In the event that a seminary should not conform to its wishes, the synodical body controlling the budget can withdraw financial support. Lutheran seminaries in the United States are, therefore, under the absolute control of the Church. (For further information consult O. A. Winfield, *ibid.*)

XI. *Theological Seminaries of the Lutheran Churches in America. A. Of the Synodical Conference:*
1. *The Lutheran Church — Missouri Synod:*

a. *Concordia Seminary,* St. Louis, Mo., was founded as a classical college and school of theology in 1839 by the Saxon immigrants. Its first home was in the forest of Perry County, Mo., near the village of Altenburg, and its first building was a log cabin erected by the members of its first faculty, all of whom were energetic young graduates of the great German universities of that time and candidates of theology, C. F. W. Walther, J. F. Buenger, O. Fuerbringer, and Theo. Brohm.

After the organization of the Evangelical Lutheran Synod of Missouri, Ohio, and Other States in 1847, ownership and control of this institution was assumed by the Synod. In 1849 the school was removed to St. Louis and relocated on South Jefferson Avenue. The Rev. C. F. W. Walther was elected its first professor of theology. He remained its leading teacher and president until his death in 1887. In 1861 the classical, or preparatory, department was removed to Fort Wayne, Ind.

In 1882 a new and imposing building supplanted the structure of 1850, which had been enlarged in 1858. In 1907 an additional building was added, increasing the capacity to three hundred resident students. In 1926 the seminary was removed once more, this time to the beautiful seventy-one-acre site on 801 De Mun, near Forest Park. An entirely new plant was erected, consisting of eighteen buildings and fifteen faculty homes (cost $3,000,000). A resident student population of four hundred can be accommodated.

The architecture is Tudor-Gothic. The complex of buildings includes the Pritzlaff Memorial Library, containing stacks for 70,000 books.

Radio Station KFUO, owned and operated by Synod through the Board of Control of the Seminary, is located on the western part of the campus and affords radio experience for students.

The seminary has an extensive *field work* program. A stipulated amount of diversified work in parishes, institutions, and mission fields is provided for each student, complementing classroom instruction and developing skills while rendering service to the Church.

For admission requirements cf. above, "Entrance Requirements of Lutheran Theological Seminaries."

The course of study extends over four years, with one additional year in a supervised internship, after completion of the third year in study. During the first two years the college courses, in addition to some theological courses, complete the requirements for a B. A. degree. (Integration of the courses offered at the eight preparatory schools through four years of high school and two years junior college, and the supervised study program of students in residence, results in progress in study which exceeds the average attainments of these six years of schooling.) The professional curriculum falls into the four traditional areas of exegetic, systematic, historical, and practical theology. The goal is to introduce each student to the essential knowledge and skills in these four areas, to outline to him the course that future growth and use of the material must take, and to implant the attitude that preparation for the ministry implies not merely knowing certain truths and acquiring certain skills, but putting the total man to work toward people for the building of Christ's kingdom.

The seminary has a Missions Department for the preparation of graduates and their wives, intending to serve in foreign fields and for specialized preparation, such as clinical training.

The seminary has a Post-graduate School, offering work for the S. T. M. and Th. D. degrees.

Concordia Seminary has had only five presidents: C. F. W. Walther to 1887; Francis Pieper to 1931; Ludwig Fuerbringer to 1943; Louis J. Sieck to 1952; Alfred O. Fuerbringer since 1953.

b. *Concordia Seminary,* Springfield, Ill., founded 1846; synodical control 1847. Pastor Wilhelm Loehe of Germany, in response to an appeal of Dr. Wm. Sihler, established a school for the training of Lutheran ministers at Fort Wayne, Ind. In 1861 the seminary was combined with the seminary at St. Louis, retaining its character as a "practical" seminary in contradistinction to the "theoretical" seminary. The purpose of the "practical" school was and is to train more mature men for the practical work of the ministry, by an abbreviated course of study. The college department of the St. Louis school was removed to Fort Wayne, Ind. The two seminaries were housed together for ten years. At that time the enrollment had outgrown dormitory facilities.

The "practical" seminary was offered a new home in the former privately owned Illinois State University, purchased by the congregation at Springfield, Ill. Removal was effected in 1874 to 1875.

The century-old seminary has had eight presidents: Dr. Wm. Sihler, Dr. C. F. W. Walther, Prof. Aug. Craemer, Prof. R. Pieper, Prof. R. D. Biedermann, Prof. H. A. Klein, Dr. H. B. Hemmeter, Dr. G. Chr. Barth, Dr. W. A. Baepler. Admission requirements: graduation from a standard high school; memberbership in a Synodical Conference congregation; minimum entrance age, twenty years.

Course of studies: Five years in residence, one year in supervised internship.

c. The Missouri Synod conducts the following seminaries in foreign lands:
North America: *Mexico*, Instituto Concordia de Mexico, Monterrey (1947)
South America: *Brazil*, Seminario Concordia, Porto Alegre (1907); *Argentina*, Seminario Concordia, Buenos Aires (1942)
Asia: *India*, Theological Seminary at Nagercoil (1924); *China*, Theological Seminary, Hankow (1922); *Japan:* On April 13, 1953, a theological training program was started at Tokyo; at Taipei, *Formosa* in 1952.

2. *Joint Synod of Wisconsin and Other States:*

a. *Evangelical Lutheran Theological Seminary, Thiensville, Wis.*, later known as "Northwestern University." Founded 1865, in conjunction with "Lutheran College" of the Wisconsin Synod at Watertown, Wis. 1870 theological students were transferred to Concordia Seminary, St. Louis, Mo., by arrangement with the Synod of Missouri, Ohio, and Other States. 1878 the Seminary was reopened by the Wisconsin Synod in Milwaukee, Wis. The federation and later amalgamation of the synods of Wisconsin, of Minnesota, and of Michigan resulted in an increased enrollment, necessitating a relocation. 1893 a new plant in Wauwatosa, Wis., became the home of the seminary. 1929 a new institution was built on an eighty-acre site at the village of Thiensville, Wis.

b. The seminary has had four presidents: Dr. E. Moldehnke, Prof. A. Hoenecke, Prof. A. Pieper, Prof. John P. Meyer. Faculty: six active members.

Admission requirements: graduation from Northwestern College, or B. A. from a recognized school, Christian character credentials. Courses of study: three years.

3. *Of the Norwegian Synod of the American Evangelical Lutheran Church: Bethany Lutheran Seminary*, Mankato, Minn. Founded 1946 as a theological department of Bethany Lutheran College. Ministerial students graduating from the Junior College at Bethany complete their preministerial training at Northwestern College, Watertown, Wis. Dean, Rev. Norman A. Madson.

Admission requirements: B. A. degree. A working knowledge of Latin, Greek, Hebrew, German, and Norwegian, if planning to enter the ministry in the Norwegian Synod. The customary credentials of Christian character and fitness for the work. Courses of study: 3 years.

4. *Of the Synodical Conference:*
Immanuel Lutheran College, Greensboro, N. C., founded 1902. Colored Theological Seminary, Junior College Normal and High School. Faculty: 9.

B. *Of the United Lutheran Church:*

1. Hartwick Seminary, est. 1797, New York City
2. Lutheran Theological Seminary, est. 1826, Gettysburg, Pa.
3. Lutheran Theological Southern Seminary, est. 1830, Columbia, S. C.
4. Hamma Divinity School, est. 1845, Springfield, Ohio
5. Lutheran Theological Seminary, est. 1864, Philadelphia, Pa.
6. Chicago Lutheran Theological Seminary, est. 1891, Maywood, Ill.
7. Central Theological Seminary, est. 1893, Fremont, Nebr.
8. Evangelical Lutheran Seminary of Canada, est. 1911, Waterloo, Ontario, Canada
9. Lutheran College and Seminary, est. 1919, Saskatoon, Saskatchewan, Canada
10. Northwestern Lutheran Theological Seminary, est. 1920, Minneapolis, Minn.
11. The ULCA opened a new theological seminary at Berkeley, Calif., in September, 1952, with 25 students and four professors.

C. *Of the American Lutheran Church:*

1. Evangelical Lutheran Theological Seminary, est. 1830, Columbus, Ohio
2. Wartburg Theological Seminary, est. 1853, Dubuque, Iowa

D. *Of the Evangelical Lutheran Church:*
1. Luther Theological Seminary, est. 1876, St. Paul, Minn.
2. Luther Theological Seminary, est. 1939, Saskatoon, Saskatchewan, Can.

E. *Of the Augustana Synod:*
Augustana Theological Seminary, est. 1860, Rock Island, Ill.

F. *Of the United Danish Church:*
Trinity Theological Seminary, est. 1884, Blair, Nebr.

G. *Of the Lutheran Free Church:*
Augsburg Seminary, est. 1869, Minneapolis, Minn.

H. *Of the Danish Church:*
Grand View Theological Seminary, est. 1896, Des Moines, Iowa

I. *Of the Suomi Synod:*
Suomi Theological Seminary, est. 1896, Hancock, Mich.

XII. *Some Leading Non-Lutheran Protestant Theological Seminaries in the U.S.*

(Listed according to States)

Berkeley Baptist Divinity School, Berkeley, Calif. (N. Bapt.)
San Francisco Theological Seminary, San Anselmo, Calif. (Presb.)
Columbia Theological Seminary, Decatur, Ga. (Presb.)
Gammon Theological Seminary, Atlanta, Ga. (Col. Meth.)
Bethany Biblical Seminary, Chicago, Ill. (Ch. of Breth.)
Chicago Theological Seminary, Chicago, Ill. (Cong.)
Evangelical Theological Seminary, Naperville, Ill. (Ev.)
McCormick Theological Seminary, Chicago, Ill. (Presb.)
Meadville Theological School, Chicago, Ill. (Unit.)
Northern Baptist Theological Seminary, Chicago, Ill. (Bapt.)
Seabury-Western Theological Seminary, Evanston, Ill. (P. E.)
Anderson College and Theological Seminary, Anderson, Ind. (Ch. of God)
Butler University, Indianapolis, Ind. (Disc. Christ)
Grace Theological Seminary, Winona Lake, Ind. (Breth.)
Central Baptist Theological Seminary, Kansas City, Kans. (Bapt.)
College of the Bible, Lexington, Ky. (Disc.)
Louisville Presbyterian Theological Seminary, Louisville, Ky. (Presb.)

Southern Baptist Theological Seminary, Louisville, Ky. (So. Bapt.)
New Orleans Baptist Theological Seminary, New Orleans, La. (Bapt.)
Bangor Theological Seminary, Bangor, Me. (Cong.)
Westminster Theological Seminary, Westminster, Md. (Meth.)
Andover Newton Theological School, Newton Centre, Mass. (Bapt.-Cong.)
Episcopal Theological School, Cambridge, Mass. (P. E.)
New England School of Theology, Brookline, Mass. (Ad. Christ.)
Calvin Theological Seminary, Grand Rapids, Mich. (Christ. Ref.)
Western Theological Seminary, Holland, Mich. (Ref.)
Eden Theological Seminary, Webster Groves, Mo. (Ev. Ref.)
Bloomfield Theological Seminary, Bloomfield, N. J. (Presb.)
New Brunswick Theological Seminary, New Brunswick, N. J. (Ref.)
Princeton Theological Seminary, Princeton, N. J. (Presb.)
Colgate-Rochester Divinity School, Rochester, N. Y. (Bapt.)
General Theological Seminary, New York, N. Y. (P. E.)
Moravian Theological Seminary, Bethlehem, Pa. (Morav.)
Crozer Theological Seminary, Chester, Pa. (Bapt.)
Divinity School of the Protestant Episcopal Church, Philadelphia, Pa. (P. E.)
Eastern Baptist Theological Seminary, Philadelphina, Pa. (Bapt.)
Pittsburgh-Xenia Theological Seminary, Pittsburgh, Pa. (U. Presb.)
Reformed Presbyterian Theological Seminary, Pittsburgh, Pa. (Ref. Presb.)
Theological Seminary of the Evangelical and Reformed Church, Lancaster, Pa. (Ev. and Ref.)
Theological Seminary of the Reformed Episcopal Church, Philadelphia, Pa. (Ref. E.)
Western Theological Seminary, Pittsburgh, Pa. (Presb.)
Austin Presbyterian Theological Seminary, Austin, Tex. (Presb.)
Southwestern Baptist Theological Seminary, Fort Worth, Tex. (Bapt.)
Protestant Episcopal Theological Seminary, Alexandria, Va. (P. E.)
Union Theological Seminary, Richmond, Va. (Presb.)

Virginia Theological Seminary, Lynchburg, Va. (Col. Bapt.)
Nashotah House Theological Seminary, Nashotah, Wis. (P. E.)
See *Roman Catholic Seminaries.*
LJS

W. A. Brown, M. May, *The Education of American Ministers,* Institute of Social and Religious Research, N. Y., 1934; R. L. Kelly, *Theological Education in America. A Study of One Hundred Sixty-One Theological Schools in the United States and Canada,* George H. Doran, N. Y., 1924; O. A. Winfield, *The Control of Lutheran Theological Education,* Aug. Bk. Concern, Rock Island, Ill., 1933; F. Gotwald, "Theological Education in the Lutheran Church Prior to the Founding of Wittenberg College and Seminary in 1845," *Luth. Quart.,* XLVI: 82—100; Bulletins of the American Association of Theological Schools; histories of individual theological schools (*e. g.,* A. R. Wentz, *History of Gettysburg Theological Seminary,* United Luth. Pub. House, Philadelphia, 1926; C. F. Haussman, *Kunze's Seminarium,* Americana Germanica Press, Philadelphia, 1917; T. Graebner, *Concordia Seminary,* CPH, 1927; C. V. Sheatsley, *History of the First Lutheran Seminary of the West,* Luth. Bk. Concern, Columbus, 1930; P. S. Vig, *Trinitatis Seminarium,* Danish Luth. Pub. House, Blair, Nebr., 1911; *Zum 50jaehrigen Jubilaeum des praktischen ev. luth. Concordia-Seminars zu Springfield, Ill., 1846—96*); T. Coates, *The Training of Ministers in the Missouri Synod; an Historical Study and Critical Evaluation,* doctor's dissertation in the library of Chicago Luth. Theol. Seminary.

Minneapolis Theses. Theses adopted by representatives of the Ohio, Iowa, and Buffalo Synods at Minneapolis, Minn., Nov. 18, 1925. The Theses became the basis for establishing pulpit and altar fellowship between the Ohio, Iowa, and Buffalo Synods in 1928. In 1928 they also became the basis for fellowship with the Norwegian Lutheran Church. On Aug. 11, 1930, the Ohio, Iowa, and Buffalo Synods formed the organic union called the American Lutheran Church. On Oct. 29—31, 1930, the newly formed American Lutheran Church federated with the Augustana Synod, United Danish Lutheran Church, Lutheran Free Church, and the Norwegian Lutheran Church (now Evangelical Lutheran Church) on the basis of the *Minneapolis Theses.* Contents:

I. Accept "without exception all the canonical books of the Old and the New Testament as a whole and in all their parts as the divinely inspired, revealed, and inerrant Word of God and submit to this as the only infallible authority in all matters of faith and life."

II. Accept the "symbolical books of the Evangelical Lutheran Church, not in so far as, but because, they are the presentation of the pure doctrine of the Word of God." (The Norw. Luth. Church in no way rejects any of the symbols, but subscribes only to the Ecumenical Creeds, Unaltered Augsburg Confession, and Luther's Small Catechism. It did not deem it necessary to subscribe the other symbols because they are unknown to her constituency.) Adherence pertains only to doctrinal content, but to doctrinal content without exception or limitation.

III. Church fellowship presupposes unanimity in the pure doctrine of the Gospel and the confession of the same in word and deed. Where Church fellowship ignores doctrinal differences or declares them a matter of indifference, there is unionism. The *Theses* endorse the rule "Lutheran pulpits for Lutheran pastors only, and Lutheran altars for Lutheran communicants only" as rejecting all unionism and syncretism.

IV. In points of doctrine the *Minneapolis Theses* endorse the *Chicago Theses* (1919) and reprint doctrinal parts under VI.

V. ". . . all organizations or societies, secret or open, as are either avowedly religious or practice the forms of religion without confessing as a matter of principle the Triune God and Jesus Christ as the Son of God, come into the flesh and our Savior from sin, or teach instead of the Gospel, salvation by human works or morality, are anti-Christian and destructive of the best interests of the Church and the individual soul and that therefore the Church of Christ and its congregations can have no fellowship with them." A Lutheran synod should not tolerate pastors who have affiliated with them, and pastors and congregations should constantly testify against the sin of lodgery and put forth efforts to enlighten and persuade people to sever their connection with such organizations. EL

The Theses are printed in *Journal of Theology,* Jan., 1941; *CTM,* I: 688 ff.;

XV: 193; *Doctrinal Declarations,* A Collection of Official Statements on the Doctrinal Position of Various Lutheran Synods in America, CPH, n. d.

Minnesota Synod. 1. The first work leading to the organization of the Minnesota Synod was done by pastors of the Pennsylvania and Pittsburgh synods. The man who gathered the first half dozen to form the synod was "Father" J. C. F. Heyer.* The founders were Heyer, Blumer, Wier, Brandt, Mallison, and Thompson; the latter two were English Lutherans and soon dropped out. Wier also soon left because of doctrinal differences. Heyer was pastor of the parent congregation, Trinity of St. Paul, but in 1863 resigned because of advanced age and was succeeded by G. Fachtmann from Wisconsin, who also guided the fortunes of the synod when Heyer returned to the East. At this time the missionary societies of the General Synod extended what aid they could with regard to men and money; but the sorely needed men came mostly from the Pilger Missionary Institute of St. Crischona, near Basel. Of the twenty who came in the earlier years of the synod's existence Emmel, A. Kuhn, F. Hoffmann, Seifert, C. J. Albrecht, Braun, and Hunziker may be mentioned. The struggling synod strove to free itself from the unionizing tendencies which flourished in spite of the Lutheran confessional declaration it had made. But Fachtmann sought to perpetuate this looseness. In 1867 J. H. Sieker, the first of Wisconsin's own pastors, was called to Trinity as Fachtmann's successor and became the leader. The uncompromising Lutherans rallied to his leadership. After causing much trouble, Fachtmann was finally expelled 1870.

2. In the meantime the Minnesota Synod had left the General Synod, pinning its hopes to the promise of confessional Lutheranism held out by the newly organized General Council. Sieker, as president, attended its meetings and demanded a declaration on the "Four Points." * As a satisfactory answer was not forthcoming, Minnesota severed connections with the Council in time to join the Synodical Conference at its organization in 1872. What induced it to take this step was the clarification of its relations with Wisconsin and Missouri. With Wisconsin, Minnesota had always had friendly relations. Delegates were exchanged at conventions; as early as 1864 there was an official request to share in the benefits of Northwestern College (and seminary), which was granted with the understanding that Father Heyer take up a collection for the institution in the East. In 1866 there had been the loan of Dr. Moldehnke for Minnesota's home missions. Formal recognition of doctrinal unity was reached 1869, when Hoenecke, after attending Minnesota's synod, reported to his brethren that complete harmony and agreement existed between the two bodies. This was made official the next year. An informal agreement, 1872, later ratified, permitted Minnesota to share in the expanded institution at Watertown, for which it offered to pay part of the salary of one professor. The *Gemeindeblatt* was made the official organ, and Sieker was added to its editorial committee.

3. This paved the way for friendly relations with Missouri, which had been in the field from the beginning. A Missouri delegation visited the synod of 1872 and after suitable preliminaries pronounced doctrinal agreement. The working arrangement with Wisconsin remained in force but a few years, when it was canceled and things drifted, Minnesota getting its ministers where it could, relying especially on Springfield, Ill., Seminary for its pastors. Meanwhile its missionaries had been active and were organizing congregations in the Dakotas, emphasizing the lack of suitable men to follow up their work. The question of "state synods" was a very live question in Minnesota and further delayed independent action in establishing a seminary, for it was hoped by many that a reorganization of that sort would secure for Minnesota's use some already existing schools. New "stipulations" with Wisconsin were adopted 1879 after a heated debate. Joint sessions were held in 1883 and 1886, after weathering the storm of the election controversy. At last, 1883, Dr. Martin Luther College, New Ulm, was founded (see *Albrecht, C. J.*); the building was erected the following year. It was a college together with a practical seminary, with O. Hoyer as its president. The *Synodalbote* was first published in 1886, but ceased publication in 1894. The relations begun with Wisconsin officially in 1864 resulted in an organic union between the two synods in 1892; the Joint Synod of Wisconsin, Minnesota, Michigan, and Other States was formed. The New Ulm institution became the teachers' semi-

nary of the Joint Synod in 1894; now also a preparatory institution for the office of pastor.

Home Missions were inaugurated with renewed energy, and Minnesota, with its adjacent western territories, since 1892 shows the greatest results and has the best prospects. The congregations in the Dakotas and in Montana have formed a separate District of the Joint Synod under the constitution of 1917. Presidents were: C. F. Heyer, 1860 to 1864; G. Fachtmann, J. H. Sieker, A. Kuhn, C. J. Albrecht, C. Gausewitz, A. Schroedel, A. T. Zich, E. Pankow, J. Naumann, J. R. Baumann, E. F. Albrecht.

E. A. Selke, *The Beginnings of the German Lutheran Churches in Minnesota*, CPH, 1929 (see also *CHIQ*, II: 75—81; 108:15); A. Kuhn, *Geschichte der Minnesota Synode und ihrer einzelnen Gemeinden, 1860—1910*, Louis Lang, CPH, 1910; J. P. Koehler, *Geschichte der Allgemeinen Evangelisch-lutherischen Synode von Wisconsin und anderen Staaten*, Northwestern Pub. House, Milwaukee, 1925.

Minor Orders. The four lower ranks of the Roman clergy: acolytes, exorcists, lectors, and ostiarii (porters). It is usually held that they do not receive the sacrament of Order. See *Hierarchy*.

Minorites. See *Franciscans*.

Minucius, Felix. Author of *Octavius*, an apology in the form of a dialog, in which the advocate of heathenism is convinced of his error and converted. He wrote before A. D. 200.

Miracle Plays. See *Religious Drama*.

Miracles. 1. A miracle is an event in the natural world differing from the ordinary course of nature and occurring in such a way as to call attention to the presence, power, and will of the living God. In the discussion we limit ourselves to the miracles recorded in Scripture, those special and exceptional acts of God, above and beyond nature, which are inseparable from Biblical history and revelation, treating the subject almost exclusively from the apologetic side.

2. A miracle is an event incomprehensible according to observed laws and produced by God independently of the natural order commonly observed. As Augustine has put it: "A miracle is not contrary to nature, but only [contrary] to what we know of nature." A miracle is a supernatural event; but all that is supernatural is not necessarily

miraculous. The angelic appearances so frequently recorded in the Scriptures were not the same thing, strictly speaking, as the miracles. They were, of course, real visitations from the unseen world; but they did not affect the course of nature; they were not events in the physical world. Nor is the work of divine grace in the human heart a miracle in this special sense. It is truly a supernatural work, a greater work indeed than any physical miracle. The power that lifts a soul from death to life, delivers it from the bondage and defilement of sin, and makes it meet for the fellowship of God is the mightiest power which has been manifested among men. All this is due to the supernatural energy of the Spirit of God. This work, however, is carried on in the spiritual realm and is now an established part of His Kingdom of Grace. A miracle, on the other hand, is a special event which took place in the physical realm. While it has a supernatural cause in the unseen world, it has a visible effect in the natural world and is wrought for a particular purpose.

3. A miracle is, first of all, a wonder. The miracles recorded in Holy Writ inspired amazement and were intended to startle men and arrest their attention. Thus it was that miracles so often took place in times of spiritual blindness and apostasy, as when Elijah came upon the scene. The wonder was intended to lead to its deeper meaning and to prepare the way for its real purpose or to call attention to a divine message which accompanied it. It is significant that, although this name frequently occurs, it is never used alone in the New Testament, but always in conjunction with one or both of the o'her names. A miracle was also a power or mighty work. It declared by the way it was done that God was present and was acting. The magicians of Egypt acknowledged this when they found themselves at length unable to repeat the miracles of Moses. "This is the finger of God," they said. Ex. 8:19. — The term by which miracles are most often described, both in the Old Testament and in the New, is the word *sign*. The value of a sign lies in what it points to. Miracles pointed to the divine authority of the agent by whom they were wrought. For while they were works of God, they were usually performed at the command or the prayer of some prophet or servant of the Lord. The miracles of Christ in the Bible are

called "signs," because, like finger posts, they point to some greater fact beyond them, namely, that the Son of God is indeed come down to dwell among men (Immanuel: God with us). They are called "powers" because the power of God is manifested in saving man from bearing the consequences of sin, from demon-possession, from disease, and from death; also, because the power of the Creator was present to do with His creatures — the water made wine, the sea calmed, the walking on the sea, the fish supplying the piece of money — as He would. They are "wonders" because all the people said: "We never saw it on this fashion," Mark 2:12. So many and so wonderful were the miracles that no enemy ever rose up in Christ's lifetime to contradict them; driven to bay, they tried to explain them blasphemously, saying that Satan was casting out Satan. Luke 11:15-20. It is true that the miracle is not the chief thing. It is but the scaffolding and not the building itself. We do not believe in Christ because we believe in miracles, but we believe in miracles because we believe in Christ, and we believe in Christ because we believe the written revelation concerning His Person and work. That is the pathway by which we have come to faith in Him. Christ performed miracles not of choice, but of necessity. "Except ye see signs and wonders, ye will not believe," John 4:48. "A wicked and adulterous generation seeketh after a sign," Matt. 16:4. But who will say that because we, who now read the inspired record of His life and works, do not see signs and wonders to convince us, therefore no signs and wonders ever occurred? You cannot thrust a dagger into the body without hurting the soul, and you cannot take your critical blade and cut off miracles from Gospel history without inflicting a mortal wound on that history. Miracles are so inevitably interwoven in the fabric of that history that the whole garment goes to pieces when you cut into it. The miracles of Christ were not isolated manifestations of supernatural power, put forth simply and solely to excite wonder and astonishment and, as it were, to compel belief. He refused, and very definitely, to work miracles of this kind. His miracles, rather, are the outcome of His wonderful and gracious character; they are integral portions of His teaching. Even the earliest Old Testament miracles display a marked superiority to many of the meaningless and lu-

dicrous "miracles" of the apocryphal gospels and medieval hagiologies.

4. In determining the credibility of miracles, we need to consider the occasion, the nature, and the worker of the miracle. The miracles of Jesus have a fit occasion, namely, a great human need. In estimating them, we are not to think about the possibility or credibility of a miracle in the abstract; we are rather to think of what we should reasonably expect on the part of a loving God in relation to men made in His image who are in the toils of sin and suffering. The occasion of Christ's miracles is no less an occasion than the need of redemption. The miracles of the Gospel are of a nature that fits this occasion. They reveal God's love; they bring God's love into touch with man's woes. Most of the miracles of Jesus were miracles of healing, not of nervous troubles only, but of leprosy, fevers, and various other diseases. Nor were they confined to healings; in three instances they were the raising of the dead to life. In every instance, save possibly the blighting of the fig tree, they came straight from the heart of God for the relief of human woe; and even the apparent exception of the fig tree is not a real exception; for it was a solemn warning, a parable in act, with a kindly purpose. Another characteristic of the Gospel miracles is that they fit the character of the worker. They are worthy of the divine Redeemer; they flow naturally from the Person of Christ. Christ Himself is the Supreme Miracle. His sinlessness; His freedom from any consciousness of sin; His superhuman knowledge; His universality; His freedom from errors that in the course of two thousand years would have been discovered and would have canceled His transcendency; His claims to be the Giver of eternal life, the Forgiver of sins, the Judge of the eternal destinies of men — these put Jesus in a class by Himself; and we are not surprised that in His redeeming love He did works that no man can do (John 1:14; 2:11; 20:31).

Miracles, Roman Catholic. The Christian fathers of the first three centuries very seldom report miracles, but rather speak of the age of miracles as past. With the fourth century, accounts of miraculous happenings increase. Degeneracy and credulity grew at an equal rate in the Church, and eventually new miracles were reported every day. There were miracles wrought by saints, by relics, by the Eucharist, by images, and by angels; there were visions, apparitions, and prodigies in fantastic variety. Many of these miracles were trifling, puerile, indecorous, or irreverent. Usually there was no proportion between the means and the end: amazing supernatural forces were employed on the silliest pretexts. Saints even matched miracles in mere trials of skill. The favorite object of miracles was to propagate rites, doctrines, and devotions that were without Biblical foundation or to emphasize the sanctity of some church, relic, or religious order. Thus it could occur that while St. Bridget had visions favoring the Franciscan view of the Immaculate Conception, her contemporary, St. Catherine of Siena, had visions establishing the contrary doctrine of the Dominicans. Ecclesiastical miracles have greatly decreased in modern times, but they have by no means become extinct, as witness the reported miracles at Lourdes, Treves, etc. How many of these miracles are imaginary or fraudulent it is impossible to determine; for the rest see Matt. 24:24; 2 Thess. 8:9; Rev. 16:14; Gal. 1:8.

Mirandola, Pico della (1463—94). Italian philosopher; studied philosophy and the humanities; tried to demonstrate the fundamental agreement of the heathen philosophers with each other and with Christian Scholasticism and mysticism; prepared 900 theses covering the domain of knowledge, some of which were declared heretical and the disputation forbidden by the Pope. The taint of heresy was later removed from Mirandola.

Miserere. Psalm 51 (Vulgate, Psalm 50). In the Roman Catholic Church the Miserere is chanted at the beginning of Lauds (Festivals excluded) and at the end of the Tenebrae service. The text of this Psalm has been set to music by many composers, notably of the Roman Catholic Church (e. g., Palestrina and Allegri).

Mishna. See *Talmud.*

Missa Brevis. A shortened Mass, in which the Greater Gloria and the Credo are omitted; it may also comprise only the Kyrie and the Gloria (e. g., Buxtehude's *Missa Brevis*). The Missa Brevis may be a complete Mass from the textual point of view, but its musical treatment is in that case as short as possible.

Missa Catechumenorum; Missa Fidelium. The chief parts of the ancient order of services, as used in all parts of the Church up to the fourth century, the Mass of the Catechumens, with the entire congregation, including also the applicants for membership and the penitents present, being the Office of the Word. With the dismissal of all noncommunicant members and visitors came the Mass of the Faithful, with the celebration of the Eucharist. See *Catechetics,* 3.

Missa Lecta. Low Mass; a mass in which everything is spoken.

Missa Solemnis. Solemn High Mass, the full ceremonial form of the Roman Mass. It is the same as the Missa Cantata, except that in the Missa Solemnis the Epistle and Gospel are chanted by the deacon and subdeacon. Fewer members of the clergy are required for the presentation of High Mass than for the performance of Solemn High Mass.

Missal. The chief service book of the Roman Catholic Church, combining all the various liturgical books formerly in use, giving the services for each day, but especially that of the Mass.

Missale Romanum. The book containing the complete service of the Roman Mass for the whole ecclesiastical year. Near the center of the volume are those portions which occur in every Mass, while the remainder of the book consists of the portions that vary according to feast or season. Prayers for the celebrants, rubrics, etc., are prefixed. The uniform edition was first published in 1570 and has been repeatedly revised.

Mission Covenant Church of America. See *Evangelical Mission Covenant Church of America.*

Mission Festivals. Observed, as a rule, once a year in Lutheran churches. The primary purpose of mission festivals is to arouse and further interest in foreign mission work. A secondary purpose is to gather funds for missions. The first mission festival was probably the one held in Berlin in 1831, although collections had been raised for foreign missions on special days before that date. The first such festival in the U. S. was reported from Edwardsville, Ill., 1855.

Mission, Inner. See *Inner Mission.*

Missionaries, Commissioning of. See *Ministerial Office,* 1.

Missionary Association of the Church. See *Danish Lutherans in America,* 3.

Missionary Bands of the World.
See *Evangelistic Associations*, 13; *Holiness Bodies*, 2.

Missionary Church Association. See *Evangelistic Associations*, 11; *Holiness Bodies*, 2.

Missionary Conferences are an effort jointly to study and solve problems arising in the mission fields and at the home base. They are either denominational or interdenominational and are constituted by voluntary participation of interested societies, administrators, and missionaries. Being altogether advisory, they have no legislative power. Almost all American, European, and Oriental countries now have conferences of this kind. International and world meetings have been held repeatedly, for instance, in Liverpool, 1860; London, 1878; London, 1888; New York, 1900; Edinburgh, 1910; Washington, D. C., 1925; Jerusalem, 1928; Tambaram, 1938; Willingen, 1952. The Conference Reports offer solutions to mission problems and are a treasury of missionary information, the most valuable being those of the Edinburgh meeting. The *International Review of Missions* is the official organ of the International Missionary Conferences.

Missionary Convention for Foreign Missions. See *Baptist Bodies*, 9.

Missionary Education Movement of the U. S. See *Union Movements*, 13.

Missionary Institutes. Usually organized and controlled by some mission society and connected with a mission home, they are schools for the training of workers in the foreign fields. They came into existence in 1702, when A. H. Francke opened his Oriental Seminary at Halle for this specific purpose. Jaenicke in Berlin (1800—1827) educated 80 young men for this work. The Basel Mission Society opened its seminary in 1816, the Barmen Society in 1828, the Gossner Society in 1836, the Leipzig Society in 1832 at Dresden and removed it to Leipzig in 1849, the Breklum Society in 1877. Neuendettelsau prepares some of its students for foreign missions since 1883. The Danish Mission School exists since 1862, the Swedish at Stockholm since 1855 and at Johanneslund since 1863. The Finnish Society has its own seminary at Helsingfors since 1866. As thoroughness is a Lutheran feature and principle, all these societies endeavor to give their future missionaries a solid training, the result of which is the efficiency of Lutheran missionaries, acknowledged by their colleagues everywhere. Several seminaries require a six-, others a five- or four-year course, according to circumstances, none less than three years of hard work. With some it is a college and a theological course combined; most of them study medicine; also manual training is practiced. The greatest care is taken in the choice of instructors as well as in the reception of applicants. Also non-Lutheran bodies have missionary institutes. In the Catholic Church the various orders, especially the Jesuits, are engaged in foreign missions. In America it has always been the rule to draw upon the theological seminaries for workers in the home and foreign mission fields; but in Europe, where the number of theological graduates who were ready to work in foreign fields was but small, mission societies had to open schools for the training of men for this particular work. Since about the middle of the past century, and to an ever-increasing extent, qualified physicians and unmarried women have been sent out, the latter principally to be active as teachers, nurses, and deaconesses among both heathen and converted women. The Missouri Synod conducts its Mission School as a department of the Post-Graduate School of Concordia Seminary, St. Louis, since 1940.

Missionary Societies. See *Lutheran Mission Societies; Missions*.

Missionary Synod. See *Michigan Synod*.

Missions. A. *Definition*. 1. The activity of the Church of Jesus Christ by which it sends and brings the Gospel of Jesus Christ to those who are, for the time being, deprived of it or are still pagan. The Scriptural foundation for this work is found in Gen. 22:18; Is. 49:6; Micah 4:1-5; Matt. 24:14; 28:18-20; Mark 16:15; Luke 24:46. 47; Ac s 1:8; 26:15-18; Rom. 1:16; Gal. 1:16; and many other passages. That the Apostles understood the command of the Lord (Matt. 28) to mean dissemination of the Gospel among Jews and Gentiles is evidenced by Gal. 2:9; Rom. 10:12-18; 1 John 1:1-4. And that the early Christians recognized their duty to propagate the Church of Christ by sending out missionaries can be gathered from Acts 13:1-5; 1 Thess. 1:8.

2. At the end of the first century A. D. there may have been some 200,000 professed Christians, and at the

time of Constantine, A. D. 325, the whole Roman Empire already was dotted with Christian churches, there being possibly some eight million Christians. The modern era of missions begins with the Reformation. Luther and his colaborers have often been accused of neglect of foreign missions and of a failure to appreciate their importance and their necessity. But Luther had to deal with conditions that made foreign missions for him and his followers an absolute impossibility. The visible Christian Church was almost entirely Roman Catholic, the wealth was concentrated in the hands of the priesthood and the monks, the Pope still governed the riches of the world, and, save for a small territory in Europe, was the absolute lord of the civilized world. As compared with his resources, kings and princes were in a wretched state of poverty; the seafaring nations were under Roman Catholic control; in fact, Alexander VI, in 1493, had presumed to parcel out the New World recently discovered between Spain and Portugal, conditioning this grant on the Christianizing of the natives. America, Africa, India, were thus open to none but Roman Catholic missions; the inquisition, with its *autos da fé* and other persecutions, was bent upon suppressing Protestantism in papal and other lands; and while Romish priests and monks accompanied all foreign expeditions, Protestants were *ipso facto* barred. But, above all, the Lutheran Reformers had their hands full with providing faithful ministers and teachers for the rapidly increasing Lutheran churches and countries. While foreign missions, then, were physically out of the question for the young Lutheran Church, home missions and the organization and staffing of the Lutheran churches was her specific task.

3. The term "mission" is variously employed. In Roman Catholic circles the word indicates special efforts put forth to deepen the religious life of the adherents of that Church. In Germany, missions are commonly divided into *Innere Mission* and *Heidenmission*. There *Innere Mission* signifies the care of the lapsed, forsaken, destitute, strayed, and needy in the home country; *Heidenmission*, of course, means missions to non-Christian peoples. In the United States the terms are frequently Home and World Missions (the term "World Mission" is replacing the term "Foreign Mission," though the latter is still used). Here the term Home

Missions points to the work done in the homeland, among the unchurched of all nations and peoples. World Missions are missions carried on in foreign countries, whether they be Christian or heathen countries.

B. *History of Protestant Foreign Missions.* 1. A succinct survey of Protestant World Missions shows us Adrianus Saravia, a Reformed minister of Antwerp (b. 1531, d. 1613 in England), as the first to issue a call for foreign missions. A colony of French Huguenots was led forth by the adventurer and renegade Durand de Villegaignon, 1555 and 1566, encouraged by Coligny, to Brazil, with a view to offering a haven of refuge against Romish persecution and with the added thought of evangelizing the American Indians. But the attempt proved abortive. In 1559 Gustavus Vasa of Sweden sent Lutheran pastors to the Laplanders in the far North for the purpose of bringing them nearer to the Lutheran Church; and Charles IX of Sweden and Gustavus Adolphus continued the work. In 1634 Peter Heiling, of Luebeck, made strenuous and withal not altogether defensible efforts to induce the Lutherans of Germany to engage in Foreign Missions, finally going to Abyssinia, where he translated the New Testament into the Amharic. But nothing further came of his efforts. Justinianus v. Weltz, a baron (b. in Saxony, 1621), wrote various papers in the interest of World Missions and finally went to Guiana as missionary, where he died soon after his arrival. In 1700 an Academy of Science was founded in Berlin under the leadership of the philosopher Leibniz, which, among other things, was to serve World Mission interests. Very little, however, resulted from all their efforts, except that the plea of Leibniz for Foreign Missions found lodgment in the heart of Aug. Herm. Francke, of Halle, who became a providential agent for extensive Foreign Mission endeavor.

2. The Netherlands, meanwhile, had freed themselves from the galling Spanish and Roman Catholic yoke and in the beginning of the 17th century succeeded to the overseas possessions of Spain in East India, the Moluccas, Ceylon, Formosa, and the Larger Sunda Islands. The East India Handelsmaatschappij was chartered in 1602 as a commercial company, but was also charged to carry on World Mission work among the natives in its larger Eastern dominions. Ministers of the Reformed faith were sent out by it, who

labored in the colonies, on an average, five years.

3. A *Seminarium Indicum* was organized in 1622 at the University of Leyden, which operated only twelve years, but not without good results. At the close of the 17th century the Dutch Reformed Church claimed in Ceylon some 350,000 converts; in Java, 100,000; in Amboina, 40,000. But after a few years the majority of these Christians had relapsed into heathenism, because the methods employed for conversion were in many instances questionable and not unlike those practiced by the Jesuit Xavier, who baptized thousands without Scriptural instruction.

4. The West India Company of the Netherlands, also a commercial organization, made an effort at World Missions in Brazil in 1621. Johann Moritz of Nassau-Siegen was appointed Governor-General at Pernambuco in 1636 and sent eight missionary pastors to that country, who translated the Catechism, organized a few schools, and baptized a small number of converted Indians. But the whole enterprise was abandoned in 1667; no lasting results had been obtained.

5. About this time Swedish Lutheran colonists had founded New Sweden on the eastern bank of the Delaware in America. Missionary work among the Indians was soon taken up, chiefly by such men as Campanius, who translated Luther's Small Catechism into the Indian tongue. Governor Stuyvesant of New Amsterdam, however, reduced the colony, and missionary effort soon ceased.

6. Meanwhile the missionary spirit began to take root in England. The persecuted Scotch and English Puritans went to North America and, though chiefly seeking refuge and peace for themselves, did not overlook the possibility of serving the native Indians in a religious way. Even Oliver Cromwell harbored plans for changing Chelsea College into a kind of missionary training-school. In 1649 the ordinance creating the "Corporation for the Propagation of the Gospel in New England" was passed, which was the earliest Reformed missionary body in England. This society exists under the name of "New England Company." The charter of the Massachusetts Colony (1628) provides that "the natives of the country may be won and mated to the knowledge and obedience of the only true God and Savior of mankind," and the original

seal of the colony represents an Indian uttering the words of the man of Macedonia, "Come over, and help us." It is true that the Indians soon received the most cruel and unjustifiable treatment on the part of the settlers. Nevertheless, such men as John Eliot of Roxbury, near Boston (d. May 20, 1690), and the Mayhew family on Martha's Vineyard (1646—1806), David Brainerd (d. October 9, 1747), and others did valiant and successful missionary work among them.

7. Systematic missionary labor, however, received its greatest impulse through the Lutheran Danish-Halle Missions in India. It received its first impulse from Frederick IV, a Lutheran king of Denmark. He had ascended the throne in 1699, already deeply impressed with the utterly hopeless spiritual condition of the heathen. Since 1621 Denmark had been in possession of a strip of land on the Coromandel Coast, southwest of Madras, in India, and the king now decided to send the Word of salvation to the natives. After consultation with his court chaplain Luetkens, who, in turn, got in touch with Spener, Joachim Lange, and Aug. Herm. Francke in Germany, two promising young men were secured, who declared their willingness to preach to the heathen in India: Bartholomaeus Ziegenbalg and Heinrich Pluetschau (1705). They reached Tranquebar in July, 1706. Thus the Lutherans made the first attempt at systematic missionary endeavor in India. August 7, 1707, the first Lutheran — in fact, the first Protestant — chapel for the natives in Asia was dedicated. Francke and his friends remained the chief religious support for this mission during the next century, no less than some sixty missionaries emanating from Halle, among whom Christian Friedrich Schwartz probably was the foremost. The fruits of this missionary enterprise, in the course of time, amounted to 20,000 converts.

8. Another Lutheran mission was fathered by Frederick IV, of Denmark, namely, that of Hans Egede, a Norwegian pastor. After much discouraging effort, Egede, in 1721, finally succeeded in being sent to Greenland, where he labored unremittingly for fifteen years. He died in Copenhagen in 1758. His son Paul succeeded him in the work. The Moravians meanwhile had entered the field, finally taking over the whole work, but quit it again in 1899.

9. The Moravians date back to the days of John Hus, who suffered death at the hands of the Roman Catholic Church in 1415. Roman Catholic persecution drove some of the followers of Hus to Saxony. Among these was a certain Count Zinzendorf, who settled in Berthelsdorf, near Dresden, Saxony. His grandson, Count Ludwig of Zinzendorf (1695—1760), became the founder of the religious society called *Unitas Fratrum,* or the Moravian Brethren. In 1722 many Moravians were expelled from Austria and were given a friendly asylum at Zinzendorf at Herrnhut, near Berthelsdorf. Through early contact with Francke in Halle, Zinzendorf had become deeply interested in Foreign Missions. The strictly Lutheran character was abandoned in the false interest of doctrinal unionism. World Missions, however, were recognized as the duty of every Christian community. On August 21, 1732, the first missionaries were sent to Danish St. Thomas, in the West Indies, to labor among the Negroes. These men were Leonhard Dobber and David Nitschmann. Since then the Moravians have sent out approximately 3,500 missionaries, who labored in the West Indies, Labrador, Dutch Guiana (Surinam), Georgia, Africa, Asia, and other areas.

10. Another society had been organized in England, which was destined materially to assist in the propagation of the Gospel in India through the Danish-Halle emissaries, namely, the Society for Promoting Christian Knowledge (1698), which owes its origin chiefly to the energetic activity of Dr. Thomas Bray. In addition to this the Society for the Propagation of the Gospel in Foreign Parts was founded (1701), which worked chiefly among the Indians and the Negroes of America, branching out into other foreign parts only in the succeeding century.

11. Scotland also entered into mission work by the organization of the Society in Scotland for Propagating Christian Knowledge (Edinburgh, 1709), whose missionaries first labored among the American Indians. David Brainerd was one of its missionaries.

12. England was destined to work far more extensively in the missionary field. After the loss of the Spanish Armada (1588) the star of Spanish colonial power in the Far East began to pale and that of England to glow. The charter given by Queen Elizabeth (1600) to the East India Company clothed it with well-nigh unlimited power. But for many years very little missionary work was done. The spirit of philosophical unbelief was rampant and deadened religious and therefore missionary life. Religious endeavor was a laughingstock and a byword. Christian teaching was almost extinct. However, through such men as Charles Wesley (1703—91) and George Whitefield (1714 to 1770), who had been influenced by Francke and the writings of Luther, a great religious awakening was brought about, which later led to a reformation of the Church, resulting in new and far-reaching missionary effort. One factor above others served to stimulate interest in Foreign Missions, namely, the epochal discoveries in the South Seas by James Cook (d. 1779) and the highly colored reports circulated in England and throughout Europe. New missionary societies were formed in rapid succession. Chiefly through the activity of William Carey, one-time cobbler and then Baptist minister, the "Baptist Missionary Society" was founded (October 2, 1792), and Carey himself was its first missionary to India. Then followed (1795) the organization of the London Missionary Society, whose early constituents were many Anglican and Presbyterian clergymen, but which latterly has been supported chiefly by Congregational or independent churches. Its best-known missionary was Robert Morrison, the pathfinder of modern missions in China. The Anglican Church Mission Society was founded April 12, 1799, and its first field was Africa. In 1813 the Wesleyan Methodist Missionary Society followed. Scotland also had a number of additional missionary societies, such as the Church of Scotland Foreign Missions Committee (1825), by which Dr. A. Duff was sent to India in 1829, the Foreign Missions Committee of the United Free Church (1843), the United Presbyterian Church of Scotland (1847), and others.

13. Among the later societies organized in Great Britain should be named the China Inland Mission, which came into being through the activity of Dr. Hudson Taylor and which meanwhile has found an associate constituency in other countries. This is an interdenominational organization, ignoring and obliterating all denominational differences.

14. North America also entered actively into Foreign Mission endeavor by the organization of the American

Board of Commissioners for Foreign Missions (1810), a society founded by the General Association of Congregational Churches of Massachusetts, by which Adoniram Judson was sent out. Through his defection to the Baptists the American Baptist Missionary Union came into being (1814). The Presbyterians first decided to support the American Board (1812); later they formed their own Presbyterian Board of Foreign Missions, North (1837).

15. Special mention must yet be made of the Students' Volunteer Movement, which is not a sending, but an enlisting society, and of the International Missionary Alliance (1887), which today is called the Christian and Missionary Alliances. Lutheran Foreign Missions were entered into in the course of the past century by nearly all Lutheran church bodies in the United States, among which special mention may be made of the United Luth. Church (formerly the General Synod, the General Council, the United Synod South), The Luth. Church — Missouri Synod, the American Luth. Church (formerly the Ohio, Iowa, and Buffalo Synods), the Ev. Luth. Church (formerly the Hauge Synod, Norwegian Synod, and United Church); Augustana Ev. Luth. Church; Luth. Free Church; Luth. Brethren; United Ev. Luth. Church.

16. In Germany, Rationalism had worked havoc during the 18th century, just as it had in England, and religion had sunk to a very low ebb. It was finally impossible to find men suited for Foreign Mission work. The Francke Institute had sadly degenerated. Only the Moravians continued to send men out into foreign fields. In 1800 a missionary training school was founded at Berlin by Pastor Jaenicke, in which some effective preparatory work was done. Its successor was the Berlin Missionary Society (Berliner Missionsgesellschaft), founded in 1824. For Southern Germany and Switzerland the Basel Evangelical Missionary Society (Evangelische Missionsgesellschaft zu Basel) was organized (1815). Berlin received a second society (1824) in the Society for Assisting Evangelical Missions among the Heathen (Gesellschaft zur Befoerderung der evangelischen Missionen unter den Heiden, Berlin I), in which such men as Wallmann and Wangemann were leaders. Another foreign missionary society was founded at Barmen (1819), the Rhenish Missionary Society (Die Rheinische Mis-

sionsgesellschaft), which sent out Hugo Hahn, Nommensen, and others. The Gossner Missionary Society (Die Gossnersche Missionsgesellschaft, Berlin II) was organized in 1836 by Joh. Ev. Gossner. The doctrinal position of these German missionary societies is unionistic, comprising both the Lutheran and the Reformed confessions.

17. Lutheran missionary societies are: 1. The Leipzig Ev. Luth. Missions (Die Ev.-Luth. Missionsgesellschaft zu Dresden, now Leipzig), founded in 1836, which has taken up some work of the old Danish-Halle Missions in India. Prominent in this society was Karl Graul. 2. The Hermannsburg Ev. Luth. Missionary Institute (Die Ev.-Luth. Missionsanstalt zu Hermannsburg), founded by Louis Harms in 1849. 3. The Society for Home and Foreign Missions According to the Principles of the Ev. Luth. Church (Die Gesellschaft fuer Innere und Aeussere Mission im Sinne der Ev.-Luth. Kirche), organized in 1886 in Neuendettelsau, Bavaria. 4. In 1887 the Schleswig-Holstein Ev. Luth. Missionary Society at Breklum (Die Schleswig-Holsteinisch Ev.-Luth. Missionsgesellschaft zu Breklum) was founded (see also Rhenish Missionary Society). — But on the Continent missionary zeal was not limited to Germany: Holland, France, Denmark, Norway, Sweden, Finland — all formed missionary societies for foreign work. A complete list of Foreign Mission Societies may be found in the World Missionary Atlas, edited by Harlan P. Beach and Charles H. Fahs, New York Institute of Social and Religious Research, 1925. A more recent list is found in E. J. Bingle and K. G. Grubb (editors), World Christian Handbook, World Dominion Press, 1952.

Missions, Bibliography. The literature pertaining to missions is immense. Bibliography is given in the International Review of Missions, organ of the International Missionary Conference. Current bibliographies are issued by the Missionary Research Library, 3041 Broadway, N. Y. This group is ready to render assistance to the student of missions.

General works on Missions (in which references to other works are found): E. M. Bliss, Encyclopedia of Missions, Funk & Wagnalls, 1904; Missionary Enterprise, Revell, 1908; A. Harnack, Missions and Expansion of Christianity in the First Three Centuries, Putnam, 1908; C. H. Robinson, History of Christian Missions, International Theol. Lib., 1915; W. O. Carver, *Course in Christian Missions*, Revell, 1932; A. D. Mason, *Outlines of Missionary History*, Doran, 1929 (expanded in Glover, *Program of World-Wide Missions*); G. Warneck, *History of Protestant Missions*, Revell, 1906; K. S. Latourette, *A History of the Expansion of Christianity*, Harper, 1937—45 (7 vols.); John Aberly, *An Outline of Missions*, Muhlenberg, Philadelphia, 1945; *World Missionary Atlas*, 1925; *Little Atlas of Catholic Missions*, Rome, 1925; E. J. Bingle and K. G. Grubb (editors), *World Christian Handbook*, World Dominion Press, 1952. See also references under *Statistics*.

Reports of missionary conferences: *e. g.*, *Report of the World Missionary Conference* (Edinburgh), 1910 (9 vols.); *Report of the Jerusalem Meeting of the International Missionary Council*, 1928 (8 vols.); *Madras Series Presenting Papers Based on the Meeting of the International Missionary Council at Madras*, India, 1939 (7 vols.).

References to books on specific fields of mission work, history of missionary societies, and work of denominations may be found in the general works above. General histories of societies and denominations also give mission work.

For missions of Lutherans in America see works listed under the various synods; works written on missions (W. G. Polack, *Into All the World;* George Drach, *Our Church Abroad;* F. J. Lankenau, *The World Is Our Field;* O. A. Buntrock, "The History of American Lutheran Missions in Asia, Africa, and Oceania since World War I," *CHIQ*, 1946 ff.; Rolf Syrdal, "Lutheran Missions," *What Lutherans Are Thinking;* W. H. T. Dau, *Ebenezer*); synodical reports, minutes, proceedings; reports of missionary organizations and conferences; books on missionaries (Fuerbringer, *Men and Missions;* Wolff, *Missionary Heroes of the Lutheran Church;* Bachman, *They Called Him Father*). Much space is devoted to missions in professional and popular journals and papers.

Missions, Foreign, of the Lutheran Church. See *Missions; Lutheran Foreign Mission Societies in the U. S., Early;* individual Lutheran bodies; countries.

Missions, Lutheran Negro (Synodical Conference). Negro missions are the chief practical work engaged in by the Synodical Conference (see *Synodi-*

cal Conference), and this joint work of the Conference also serves as a bond of union. The sixth convention (1877), upon motion of the Rev. H. A. Preus, for many years president of the Norwegian Synod, and also the third president of the Synodical Conference, resolved to begin mission work among the religiously neglected Negroes of the land (then numbering approximately six million, with about one million having church connections; today the Negro population of the United States numbers over fifteen million). Pastors J. F. Buenger, C. F. W. Sapper, and Mr. John Umbach, all of St. Louis, constituted the first Mission Board. The first missionary, the Rev. J. F. Doescher, began his work at New Wells, Mo., went south by way of Memphis, Tenn., to Little Rock, Ark., where he organized a Sunday school. From Little Rock, Ark., Pastor Doescher traveled through Tennessee, Georgia, Florida, Alabama, Mississippi, and Louisiana, preaching to groups of Negroes wherever he had an opportunity. In New Orleans, La., in the old, crumbling Sailor's Home, he conducted a Sunday school which at times had an enrollment of nearly 160 pupils.

After Missionary Doescher had left Little Rock, Ark., Candidate Frederick Berg, a graduate of Concordia Seminary, St. Louis, Mo., became his successor. In this city Pastor Berg organized the first colored Lutheran congregation of the Synodical Conference (St. Paul's) with three male members. The organization of this church took place on July 3, 1878. A month later the small congregation could dedicate its chapel (25×50 feet), the first chapel built for Negroes by the Synodical Conference. A Christian day school was opened in 1879 by Pastor Berg.

In November, 1880, the Rev. Nils J. Bakke, a graduate of Concordia Seminary, St. Louis, assumed charge of the work in the old Sailors' Home. The new mission station was named Mount Zion Lutheran Church. The Rev. Bakke served Mount Zion until August 10, 1891, when the Missionary Board requested him to begin work in the new promising mission field in the central South. He remained a faithful worker in the Negro Missions up to his death, May 8, 1921, serving in various fields and in many capacities, such as president of Immanuel Lutheran College, in Greensboro, N. C., Director of Missions, and General Publicity Secretary.

The request of the colored people themselves led to the establishment of stations at Meherrin, Va. (1883), Yonkers, N. Y. (1907), Springfield, Ill. (1881), and at a number of other places. Early in 1891 the Alpha Synod of North Carolina, which had been organized on May 8, 1889, appealed to President H. C. Schwan for assistance in its work. Before the Civil War, Lutheran planters provided somewhat for the spiritual needs of their slaves; but after the Emancipation even this ceased in most instances (see Alpha Synod). The appeal of the Alpha Synod was answered by the Missionary Board of the Synodical Conference. Missionary Bakke was transferred to North Carolina, arriving in Concord Sept. 18, 1891. The work soon took on large dimensions. It was extended to South Carolina in 1913, and late in December, 1915, following an appeal by Miss Rosa J. Young of Rosebud, Wilcox Co., Ala., into the Black Belt of Alabama. Pastor Bakke arrived at Rosebud on Jan. 13, 1916, to supervise the work. On Palm Sunday and Easter Sunday, 1916, there were baptized 58 persons, while 70 were confirmed. In less than a year the church had 187 members. The successor of Missionary Bakke in the "Black Belt" was the Rev. George A. Schmidt. Within six months he supervised the erection of five buildings, besides visiting all the existing schools and serving two congregations. In October, 1940, Supt. Schmidt went to Piney Woods Country Life School, conducted by Prof. L. C. Jones, to begin his work there among the students of that institution. Thereupon the Rev. E. A. Westcott took over the superintendency in the Alabama field. He served until 1945, when he accepted a call to a northern field of activity. On Oct. 2, 1945, the Rev. W. H. Ellwanger was installed as his successor, serving the field and the Selma Lutheran Academy as superintendent. The Piney Woods School was served until February, 1949, by the Rev. Wm. Wedig, Sr., and later by his son and the Rev. Brice Thompson. In 1949 there were in the Alabama mission field 34 congregations and two preaching stations, including congregations in the Pensacola area, under the supervision of the Rev. Wm. Kennell. The total number of souls in the Alabama field was listed as 3,523. There were 31 schools in this field with an enrollment of 1,227, taught by three pastors, three male and 28 female teachers. The contributions in

1948 amounted to $20,000 plus. However, not only in the South, below the Mason and Dixon line, but also in the Northern and Western States, from the Atlantic to the Pacific Coast, Negro congregations have been organized. Large numbers of mission congregations have become self-supporting. There were (1949) 19 such congregations, with 5,595 baptized and 3,643 communicant members. In addition, there were nine congregations which are supported by various synodical Districts of the Missouri Synod.

In 1947 the Negro congregations affiliated with the Synodical Conference contributed toward the work over $10,000 by school fees and more than $162,000 by Sunday school and church offerings. In order to prepare pastors and teachers for the work among the Negroes of the United States, the Synodical Conference in September, 1903, established Luther College in New Orleans, La., the Rev. F. J. Lankenau being the first teacher and president of the school. When the erection of essential new buildings became prohibitive because of high prices and the general depression throughout the country, the school was closed and the work of training pastors and teachers concentrated in Immanuel Lutheran College, Greensboro, N. C., a normal and theological school, which had been opened on March 2, 1903, in Concord, N. C., and moved to Greensboro on Sept. 12, 1905. It has three departments: a senior high school, a normal college, and a theological seminary. Prof. Wm. Kampschmidt, Ph. D., is the president and Prof. R. O. Lynn is the dean of the college. In 1948 about 135 students attended I. L. C., among them ten ministerial students. The chief objective of the institution is to train men for the ministry. At the same time provision is made to supply a general education for the Negro youth. The land on which the buildings of I. L. C. stand comprises somewhat more than 13 acres. Since the close of World War II I. L. C. has received various buildings from the Government, which were erected partly on the institution's land and used for military purposes. The physical properties embrace an administration building, erected in 1905, a girls' dormitory built in 1927, a science building, and three faculty houses. In May, 1947, the Missionary Board appointed a local Board of Control, with the Rev. G. E. Hageman as chairman and the Rev. M. S. Dickinson as secretary. The total valuation of property at I. L. C. is listed by a Real Estate Board as $257,000.

The rapid expansion of the Alabama field made it necessary for the Synodical Conference to open a school for training mission teachers and helpers in Alabama. On Nov. 13, 1922, Alabama Lutheran College was opened at Selma, Ala. In 1925 the Missionary Board purchased thirteen acres of land in the northeastern section of this city and erected suitable buildings, the entire project representing a cost of some $50,000. In 1948 a boys' dormitory was erected. The enrollment in the academy was listed in 1948 as 173, including ten students who have declared their intentions to enter the theological seminary at Greensboro, N. C. Here, too, a local Board of Control manages the institution. Another educational venture of the Synodical Conference is the Memphis Lutheran Cooperative School. While the Synodical Conference financed the erection of the building, the pupils by their payment of tuition make the school largely self-supporting. A local Board of Control, with the Rev. V. Bruegge, chairman, manages the affairs of this mission institution. For the better control of the vast mission field, superintendents were called to work together with the Missionary Board. Thus our Southern fields were (1949) in charge of superintendents. At its 39th convention at Milwaukee, Wis., in session from August 6 to 9, 1946, the Synodical Conference resolved that the synodical Districts receive into membership such Negro congregations as are located in their territorial area. Many Districts have favorably responded to this recommendation and have assumed the supervision and direction of churches in their field. Thus the services of Prof. W. H. Gehrke, who had served the Southeastern field as superintendent for many years, were no longer needed when the Southeastern District of the Missouri Synod integrated Negro congregations into its District.

In July, 1946, the Rev. Karl Kurth, St. Louis, Mo., succeeded Rev. L. A. Wisler (d. 1946) as Executive Secretary of the Missionary Board. The Missionary Board of the Synodical Conference is made up of members representing the four constituent Synods. The President of the Synodical Conference is ex officio a member of the Board. In 1878 the Synodical Conference resolved to publish a mission-

ary monthly in the interest of Negro Missions. The Rev. F. Lochner was elected editor in chief. The new periodical was known as Die Missionstaube ("The Mission Dove") and made its first appearance in 1879. The following editors were in charge of the magazine until its discontinuance in 1933: Pastors C. F. W. Sapper, C. J. Otto Hanser, Richard Kretzschmar, H. Meyer, C. F. Drewes (for many years mission director), and Dr. J. T. Mueller. Other publications: The Lutheran Pioneer, the Colored Lutheran, the Missionary Lutheran — since 1933. From the very beginning of Negro Missions the Christian day school has occupied a permanent part in the missionary program of the Synodical Conference. There were 45 such schools in operation in 1952, taught by 74 teachers. 2,857 children were enrolled according to the 1952 statistics. The combined totals of all fields in Negro Missions were listed (1952) as follows: Churches and preaching stations 113, souls 17,964, communicants 10,222, Sunday school enrollment 7,803. Contributions for the same year amounted to $313,000 plus. KK

Missions, Negro, in the U. S. The Negro question came to the United States when slaves were brought to Jamestown, Va., in 1619. The trade grew until it was abolished by the U. S. in 1807. By the end of the Civil War there were approximately 4,500,000 Negroes in the U. S. In the 20th century the Negroes have constituted approximately 10% of the population of this country.

Organized work among the Negroes was started in the American colonies by the Society for the Propagation of the Gospel in Foreign Parts in 1701. After the Revolutionary War the Protestant Episcopal Church continued the work, especially in South Carolina and Virginia. The Presbyterians began work among the Negroes at Hanover, Va., in 1747. The revivals of the Baptist Church in 1785 and 1790 gained many Negroes for the Church. The Baptist Church reported over two million colored members already early in the 20th century. The Methodists also began work early and reported a membership well over the 1½-million mark in 1906. The Roman Catholic Church ranks next to the Methodists in membership. The Church of God has a large colored membership. The Negro membership of the Episcopalian, Presbyterian, Congregational, and Lutheran

Churches was comparatively small in the first half of the 20th century.

The early Lutherans in America concerned themselves with the spiritual care of the Negro. In the *Halle Reports* there are entries showing the devout care which Muhlenberg and his co-workers gave also to the Negroes with whom they came into contact. The greater portion of Lutheran colored mission work has been done by the Synodical Conference (see *Missions, Lutheran Negro, Synodical Conference*). The American Lutheran Church colored mission work began in 1890. In 1950 the American Lutheran Church reported 13 missions plus two carried on co-operatively with the United Lutheran Church. It also voted in 1950 that this work be carried on through the National Lutheran Council. See *Missions, Bibliography.*

Missions, Roman Catholic Foreign. 1. The Roman Catholic theory of missions is set forth by von Tippe (quoted by Warneck, *Geschichte der protestantischen Mission,* 170): "If the one Church founded by Christ can be none other than the one Catholic Church which has continued from the times of the Apostles to the present day [note the identification of the invisible communion of saints with the visible Roman organization], it follows with inexorable logic that this Church, and this only, is charged with the task of missionizing the world (*Missionierung des Erdkreises*). Missionary activity among all the nations of the earth is dogmatically the exclusive and inalienable right of the Catholic Church." A higher authority, none other than Pope Leo XIII, in the encyclical *Sancta Dei Civitas* (Dec. 3, 1890), brands all Protestant missionaries as "disseminators of errors," who, while giving themselves "the appearance of being the apostles of Christ," are seeking "to extend the domain of the Prince of Darkness." In short, then, all Protestant mission work is an arbitrary invasion on Roman Catholic privilege. Again, it follows on these principles that the field of Roman Catholic missions is not the entire non-Christian, but the entire non-*Catholic* world. For the Roman Catholic Church all the countries of the earth fall into two divisions: 1. provinces of the Holy See, or *Catholicae regiones, i. e.,* such countries as acknowledge the Roman Catholic Church as the religion of the state or, at least, accord her a privileged position; 2. provinces of the Propaganda, or *acatholicorum et infidelium terrae* (countries of non-Catholics and unbelievers), or *omnes illae provinciae, civitates et terrae, quae magistratui infideli vel haeretico subiiciuntur, i. e.,* all those provinces, states, and lands which are subject to an unbelieving or heretical government. In short, all Protestant countries are included in this second division.

2. Catholic Foreign Missions begin with the era of geographical discovery and exploration. Portuguese and Spanish navigators embodied the crusading spirit and were animated at once by the lust of gold and zeal for the faith. The explorer and the friar came side by side, and the sword of the one was often used to enforce the argument of the other. Conquest implied the "conversion" of the natives. Thus the native populations of Mexico, the West Indies, and, in part, South America were "converted" to the Roman Catholic faith in an incredibly short time. The protest of Las Casas against all coercion and violence was a voice in the wilderness. The Portuguese at the mouth of the Congo and on the western coast of India adopted the same methods as the Spaniards in the New World. With the entrance of the Jesuits upon the field the second period of Catholic Foreign Missions may be said to begin. Their activities included India, Japan, China, Tonkin, the Philippines, Brazil, Paraguay, Canada, Abyssinia. Due recognition must be given to the self-denying devotion, zeal, and heroism of the Jesuit missionaries, while on the other hand their questionable missionary methods, dictated by motives of expediency and aiming more at the wholesale churching of multitudes than at genuine change of heart, not shrinking even from accommodation to heathen rites and ceremonies, have been severely condemned.

3. This second period of missionary activity was followed by a rapid decline. At the end of the eighteenth century the conditions in the Foreign Mission field were, in the words of a Catholic writer, "extremely dreary — almost everywhere nothing but ruins and desolation." The mechanical missionary methods, the decline of the Spanish and Portuguese powers, the abolition of the Jesuit order, and other causes combined to bring about this result. The restoration of the Jesuit order and, in no small degree, the stimulating effect of Protestant mission work, as well as the opening of new territories through colonial expansion, resulted in a revival

of Catholic missionary activity. What this revival means may be seen from the fact that at the beginning of the nineteenth century there were hardly 1,000 Catholic missionaries in the field, while in 1914 there were about 15,000. Catholic missions are established in nearly all parts of the world and are carried on by numerous religious orders (Jesuits, Franciscans, Lazarists, Dominicans, Carmelites, Capuchins, Benedictines), supported by various missionary societies (Lyons Missionary Society, founded in 1822, St. Boniface Society, St. Louis Society, etc.).

Mississippi Conference. See *Augustana Lutheran Church,* 8.

Mississippi Synod. See *United Lutheran Church, Synods of,* 15.

Missouri. The Lutheran Synod of Missouri, Ohio, and Other States. See *Lutheran Church — Missouri Synod.*

Missouri, Synod of, and Other States. Before the Revolution, Lutherans had settled in western North Carolina and eastern Tennessee, and later some of them moved to Missouri and Arkansas. They sought contact with the Missouri Synod, and in 1872 Professor Walther and others held a free conference with them at Gravelton, Mo., and organized "The English Evangelical Lutheran Conference of Missouri" — Pastors Andrew Rader, J. R. Moser, and Polycarp Henkel. New blood came into this body by the calling of Pastor A. W. Meyer in 1885 and Pastor William Dallmann in 1886, both of whom labored in Webster County. The Western District of the Missouri Synod appointed Pastor C. L. Janzow of St. Louis Visitor and promised to pay all missionary expenses. The conference asked the Missouri Synod to be received as a separate English Mission District, but were advised to organize an independent English Synod (1887).

A forward step was taken when the first English *city* mission was begun in Baltimore early in 1888; other cities followed. The fifteenth convention was the first one to be held in a city, St. Louis, October, 1888. "The Constitution of the General English Evangelical Lutheran Conference of Missouri and Other States," published before in the *Lutheran Witness,* was adopted, signed by twelve pastors and eight congregations, and Pastor F. Kuegele of Coyner's Store, Va., was elected president. Professor Crull's compilation of a hymnbook was gratefully accepted,

a Publication Board created, and a committee elected to prepare an Order of Service. It was also resolved to join the Synodical Conference. The next convention met in 1891 at St. Louis and changed the "conference" into a "synod." A revised and enlarged edition of the hymnbook was ordered and the "Common Service" secured.

Pastor C. A. Frank, who had started the *Lutheran Witness* on May 21, 1882, and presented it to Synod in 1888, now resigned as editor, and Pastor Dallmann was elected in his place, succeeded in 1895 by Professor Dau. The Publication Board at Baltimore got out the hymnbook, Dallmann's *The Ten Commandments,* the *Witness Tracts,* etc. Synod, in 1893, assumed control of Concordia College, Conover, N. C., and called Pastor Dau and Candidates Romoser and Buchheimer. At the same time Synod accepted Mr. John P. Baden's gift of St. John's College, Winfield, Kans., for which he promised $50,000; it was later turned over to The Lutheran Church — Missouri Synod. Pastor A. W. Meyer was elected editor of the *Lutheran Guide,* which had been started in January, 1893. In 1897 Synod resolved to get out a book of funeral sermons, a Sunday school hymnal, and a revised edition of the hymnbook, music and word editions. After much labor the books were placed on the market in 1912. Synod also resolved to ask The Lutheran Church — Missouri Synod whether the barriers which ten years ago had kept the English Synod from becoming an English District of the German Synod could not be removed. Negotiations were carried on till 1911. In that year the English Synod became an English District of The Lutheran Church—Missouri Synod, which event was celebrated at St. Louis, in Holy Cross Church, with the Te Deum. The first convention of the English District was held in Baltimore, 1912. Membership at that time: 60 congregations, 58 voting pastors, 14 professors and advisory pastors, 2 teachers; president, Rev. M. S. Sommer. See also *Lutheran Church — Missouri Synod.*

Miter (mitre). Headdress worn by bishops, patriarchs, and abbots to indicate their position.

Mizpah Benediction. The name given to the words of Laban in Gen. 31:49.

Moabite Stone. Discovered in 1868; written in characters akin to old

Hebrew letters; the inscription deals with the story in 2 Kings 3:4ff.

Modalistic Monarchianism. See *Monarchianism,* B.

Mode. The musical scales of the Middle Ages which, unfortunately, are at times called "church modes." There are two series, the Authentic and the Plagal. While the former cover an octave, the latter include an added half octave (tetrachord) from below. The authentic modes are called Dorian, Phrygian, Lydian, Mixolydian, Aeolian, and Ionian. Much early Lutheran church music was modal in character.

Moderates, The. A name applied to a group of theologians in the Church of Scotland who favored patronage, held that civil courts were supreme in ecclesiastical matters, and defended a "moderate" orthodoxy. The party became prominent under the Robertsonian administration (1752—82) and began to decline in 1832. At first it emphasized morals, but later held to a strict confessionalism.

Moderation. See *Intemperance.*

Moderator. The presiding officer of the General Assembly of the Presbyterian Church. See *Polity, Ecclesiastical.*

Modern Translations of the Bible. See *Bible Versions.*

Modernism. 1. The designation applied to the recent liberal movement in some quarters of the Roman Catholic Church. In the words of the *Catholic Encyclopedia,* Modernism "proclaims the inviolable sovereignty of the individual as against all external authorities." Father Tyrell, the leading exponent of Modernism in England, expresses himself thus: "The Truth of religion is in man implicitly, as surely as the truth of the whole physical universe is involved in every part of it. Could he but read the needs of his own conscience and spirit, he would need no teacher." (*Scylla and Charybdis.*) Under the leadership of Tyrell, Loisy, Houtain, and others, Modernism made considerable progress from 1888 to 1907. In the latter year it was suddenly and effectually curbed by the wrath of Pius X. The encyclical *Pascendi Gregis* condemns Modernism as "a synthesis of all heresies" springing from pride, curiosity, and ignorance of scholastic philosophy. The encyclical was reenforced by the decree *Sacrorum Antistitum* of 1910, which requires a formidable oath of all ranks of the clergy in favor of traditional Catholic belief and against every Modernist tenet. There were protests at the time, but Modernism is extinct in the Roman Church today.

2. Since approximately 1875 an increasing number of theologians in Reformed churches have challenged the old beliefs. Parading at first as liberal theology, this trend is now generally known as Modernism. Its premise is that there is no revealed and absolute truth and that man is constantly in search of religious truth. Modernism is a theological method rather than a system of beliefs, and follows the principles of the various schools of German liberal theology: Schleiermacher, who finds the source of truth in the "pious God-consciousness"; Ritschl, who made the theory of values the criterion of truth; Troeltsch, who sought truth in the comparative study of all religions. The modern scientific apparatus in the fields of philosophy, science, sociology, and psychology are considered the instruments to discover religious truth. Liberal theology claimed that the basic religious truths are: the fatherhood of God, the immanence of God, the brotherhood of man, the perfectibility of man.

3. On the basis of the foregoing principles, liberal theology held that the function of the Church was the establishment of the kingdom of God as an ethical and moral community of men. Since such a kingdom could not be established until the social ideals of Jesus had permeated the entire human society, liberal theology invented the social gospel. Modernism may, therefore, be summarized as follows: a) The religious experiences of the past and the present are the criterion and standard of truth. The Bible is viewed as a record of religious experiences of the Old Testament Prophets and particularly of Jesus. All religious concepts, such as sin, grace, redemption, heaven, must be reinterpreted in the light of our current religious experience. b) Its metaphysical assumption is that man's moral growth toward a unified personality is possible if man follows the biological and psychological laws of the universe. Such growth, however, presupposes that man has faith in a cosmic force which has been defined as the "personality evolving process." This is a redefinition of the term "God." Man must, furthermore, have faith in his own inherent capa-

bility for his development for a good life. c) The message of Modernism is the social gospel. FEM

J. G. Machen, *Christianity and Liberalism*, Eerdmans, Grand Rapids, Mich., 1923 (chief opponent of Modernism; see titles under *Machen)*; H. N. Wieman—B. E. Meland, *American Philosophies of Religion*, Willett, Clark & Co., 1936; for historical treatments see such works as Smith and others, *Religious Thought in the Last Quarter Century*; Roberts and Van Dusen, *Liberal Theology, an Appraisal*; L. Berkhof, *Recent Trends in Theology*.

Modesty. See *Humility*.

Moeckel, Johann Friedrich (1661 to 1729). Studied at Jena; private chaplain at Teisenort, then at Hayn; pastor at Neuhauss, Steppach, Limpach; wrote: "Nun sich die Nacht geendet hat."

Moehler, Johann Adam (1796—1838). The "Catholic Schleiermacher"; taught at Tuebingen, where, in 1828, he became prof. of theology; wrote a book on symbolics in which he attacked Protestantism and sought to idealize the decrees of the Council of Trent.

Moeller, Albert J. C. B. May 6, 1891, at Barnes, Nebr.; grad. from Concordia Sem., St. Louis, 1914; pastor at Champion (1914—16), Ainsworth (1916—21), Walton (1921—27), and Grand Island, Nebr.; pres. Nebraska Dist., 1936—38; pres. St. Paul's College, Concordia, Mo., 1938—50; held various synodical and District offices; d. Nov. 21, 1950.

Moeller, Henry. B. 1749 in Hamburg, Germany; pastor at various places in Virginia, Pennsylvania, and New York; chaplain in Revolutionary Army; one of founders of New York Ministerium; d. 1829 at Sharon, N. Y.

Moeller, Johann Joachim (1660 to 1733). B. at Sommerfeld; in last years of his life *Archidiaconus* at Krossen; wrote: "Ich habe g'nug"; "Das ist je gewisslich wahr."

Moempelgard *(Montbéliard)* **Colloquy.** Called in 1586 by the Lutheran Count William of Wuerttemberg to compose the differences between the Lutherans and the Calvinists. The Lutheran Jacob Andreae and the Calvinist Theodore de Beza discussed the Lord's Supper, the Person of Christ, Images, Ceremonies, Baptism, and Election. The deeper differences remained. Beza asked the Lutherans for brotherly love; Andreae would grant only general love.

Moenkemoeller, William. B. Nov. 9, 1867, in Westphalia, Germany; grad. at St. Louis, 1889; pastor at Cairo, Ill., 1889—92; Springfield, Mass., 1892—99; New Britain, Conn., 1899—1905; prof. Concordia College, St. Paul, Minn., 1905—33; wrote *Word Pictures of Bible Events* (a series); d. May 9, 1933.

Moerlin, Joachim (1514—71). Luther's chaplain in 1539; superintendent at Arnstadt; conscientious in office; deposed; opposed Interim* at Goettingen; fled for his life in 1550; admonished Osiander at Koenigsberg privately and then publicly; Duke Albrecht ordered silence; Moerlin refused and then was banished despite the petitions of the people; recalled in 1567; restored order as Bishop of Samland.

Moerlin, Maximilian (1516—84). Younger brother of Joachim; court preacher at Coburg; opposed Menius for siding with Major; first agreed with Flacius and then helped to depose him; was deposed himself.

Moffat, Robert (1795—1883). B. at Ormiston, Scotland. Sent by the London Missionary Society in 1816, he labored as missionary to Africa among Bushmen, Hottentots, and Bechuanas; won Africaner, a notorious and dreaded outlaw, for Christianity. In Kuruman, where he lived many years, he organized a school for native helpers. On a furlough to England he met David Livingstone and influenced him for African missions. Livingstone later became Moffat's son-in-law. In 1857 Moffat translated the Bible into the Bechuana language. He returned to England in 1870.

Moffatt, James (1870—1944). Presbyterian; Biblical scholar; b. at Glasgow; minister of Free Church; professor of Greek and New Testament exegesis at Oxford in 1911; translated Harnack's *Expansion of Christianity;* contributed to *The Expositor's Greek Testament;* wrote: *Introduction to the Literature of the New Testament*, 1911; new translation of *New Testament*, 1913; also *Old Testament*, 1924 ff.

Mogilas, Petrus (ca. 1597—1647). Influential theologian of the Greek Church; patriarch of Jerusalem, later metropolitan of Kief; wrote several liturgical works, but especially the Greek *Orthodox Confession of the Catholic and Apostolic Church of the East.* See *Eastern Orthodox Confessions*, A 1.

Mohammed (Mahomet, Muhammad). Founder of Mohammedanism (Islam) was born at Mecca in Arabia ca. A. D. 570. At the age of twenty-five he was married to the widow of a rich merchant. Now wealthy, he was in a position to indulge in religious contemplation. About fifteen years later, as a result of alleged visions and divine revelations, he began his religious reform movement at Mecca in a limited circle, his wife being his first convert. When he began to preach his doctrine in public, he met with determined opposition, which compelled him to flee from the city in 622, from which date the Mohammedan era is reckoned (*Hegira*). He was given a friendly reception at Medina, where he gained followers and organized a military force. After varying fortunes of war he finally, in 630, gained control of Mecca practically without resistance. This city then became the holy place of Islam. On June 7, 632, Mohammed died at Medina shortly after his return from the "Valedictory Pilgrimage" to Mecca. A mosque has been built over his tomb in Medina.

Mohammedanism (Islam). The religion founded by Mohammed. Its sacred book is the *Koran*, whose 114 suras (chapters) Mohammedans (Moslems) believe to have been divinely revealed to their prophet Mohammed. Considerable Jewish and some Christian influences, besides those of ancient paganism, can be traced in the Koran. Other major tenets of Mohammedanism are: the oneness of God, the existence of good and evil angels, the resurrection of the dead and the Final Judgment, the absolute decrees of God which predetermine man's actions. Prescribed religious practices are: purifications by washing, five daily prayers in the direction of Mecca, giving of alms, fasting during the month of Ramadan, the observance of Friday as a sacred day, and a pilgrimage (hajj) to Mecca at least once in the believer's lifetime to worship in the Kaaba, the chief sanctuary with the black rock believed to have fallen from heaven. Mohammedanism prohibits the use of alcoholic beverages, the eating of pork, usury, and the practice of sorcery. It holds that divine revelation was progressive through six prophets: Adam, Noah, Abraham, Moses, Jesus, and Mohammed, but the last named is the greatest, beyond whom there will be no other, hence the slogan: "There is no god except Allah, and Mohammed is his prophet."

Mohammedanism from its inception was a militant religion. During Mohammed's lifetime it conquered Arabia and under his immediate successors in less than a century swept over Persia, Syria, Palestine, the central regions of Asia, northern Africa, and Spain. It entered India ca. A. D. 1000 and through the westward march of the Mohammedan Seljuk and Ottoman Turks conquered the Balkan peninsula and parts of Hungary in the fifteenth century. At present Mohammedanism has largely been forced out of Europe except in Albania and European Turkey.

In the course of time some thirty sects have arisen within the pale of Mohammedanism. The Sunnites (ca. 150,000,000) regard Abu Bekr and the caliphs who followed him as the rightful successors of Mohammed, while the Shi'ites (ca. 20,000,000) favor Ali, the son-in-law of Mohammed. In addition there are some religious differences between these two sects which had their origin already in the early period of Islam. In the eighteenth century originated the Wahhabis, supporters of a reform movement aimed at restoring Islam to its early purity. The Ahmadiyya sect of India (1879) has introduced modifications into the teachings of Mohammedanism with a view to making the religion more attractive to minds influenced by Western culture.

While exact statistics are lacking, the total number of Mohammedans is estimated at ca. 316 million. Of these, ca. four million are found in Europe, 251 million in Asia, 60 million in Africa, and 75,000 in Oceania (1952).

GVS

Mohr, Joseph (1792—1848). Ordained priest in 1815; held various positions, all in the diocese of Salzburg; well-known carol: "Stille Nacht! Heilige Nacht!" written for Christmas, 1818, and immediately set to music by Franz Gruber.

Moibanus, Ambrosius (1494—1554). Studied at Krakau; rector in Breslau; left Breslau in 1521, studied under Reuchlin and joined the Reformation at Wittenberg; pastor of St. Elizabeth, Breslau (1525).

Molanus, Gerhard Walter (1633 to 1722). Studied at Helmstedt; professor of mathematics, later of theology, at Rinteln; still later superintendent of Brunswick-Lueneburg; wrote: "Ich trete frisch zu Gottes Tisch."

Moldehnke, E. E. (1835—1904). Amanuensis of Tholuck, Halle; rector of Lyck *Gymnasium;* field secretary of missions in Wisconsin, 1861; first professor at seminary and college at Watertown, Wisconsin Synod, 1863 to 1866; missionary in Minnesota, 1866; returned to Germany as pastor; back in America in eighties (with General Council).

Molinism. The name given to the views on grace and election taught by Louis Molina (Spanish Jesuit, 1535 to 1601). It sought to preserve the freedom of the will without denying the efficacy of grace. The doctrine was later changed with a view to special election. God gives grace to all, but to the elect He gives a grace so attuned to their disposition and opportunities that they inevitably, yet willingly, yield to it.

Molinos, Michael (1640—97). Spanish mystic; author of *Guida Spirituale;* persecuted by the Jesuits and, at their instigation, by Innocent XI. See *Quietism.*

Moller (Moeller, Mueller), Heinrich (1530—89). Professor of Hebrew at Wittenberg, 1560—74. D. in Hamburg as a result of imprisonment during the crypto-Calvinistic controversy.

Moller, Martin (1547—1606). Attended town school at Wittenberg and *Gymnasium* at Goerlitz; too poor to go to university; cantor at Loewenberg, then pastor at Kesselsdorf; 1572 *Diaconus* at Loewenberg; 1575 pastor at Sprottau; regarded initial letters of his name as a continual warning: *Memento mori;* wrote: "Nimm von us, Herr, du treuer Gott"; "O Jesu suesz"; "Ach Gott, wie manches Herzeleid"; "Hilf, Helfer, hilf in Angst und Not."

Monad. See *Arianism,* 1; *Monarchianism,* B 6.

Monadism. See *Leibniz, Gottfried Wilhelm von.*

Monarchianism. Attempts to harmonize the *unitas Dei* and the *trinitas* began in the 2d century. The Fathers accepted the oneness and Trinity of God, though not always with the clarity of the Nicene Creed. Two extreme parties arose in the effort to solve the Trinitarian mystery:

A. *Dynamic or Ebionite Monarchianism.* Christ is a pure man (though born in a wonderful way of the Virgin by the Holy Spirit) whom God endowed with His power (*dynamis*), thus adopting Him (adoptianism). Exponents of this theory were:

1. *Alogi* (Asia Minor). Denied that Jesus was the Logos, hence rejected the Johannine Gospel and Epistles; also rejected the Apocalypse because they considered it chiliastic; anti-Trinitarian (Epiphanius, *Haer.* 51).

2. *Theodotians.* Followers of Theodotus, a Byzantine tanner, who was excommunicated at Rome by Victor (192—202). Held that Jesus was a mere man, though preternaturally born and of higher piety than others. His disciples, Asclepiodotus and Theodotus II, tried to found their own church at Rome.

3. *Artemonites.* Followers of Artemon, who was excommunicated by Zephyrinus. Held that dynamistic monarchianism represented the original Apostolic doctrine and that the divinity of Christ was a relapse into heathenism.

4. *Paul of Samosata* (260—72). Most famous exponent of dynamic monarchianism; held that Jesus was "from below"; the Logos dwelt in Him not as a divine *hypostasis,* but as an operative power, gradually leading Him to a state of unique perfection and thus entitling Him to divine Sonship; Christ united with God by unity of will, but not of substance.

B. *Modalistic Monarchianism (Patripassianism).* The three divine persons are in some manner a manifestation of one and the same God; God revealed Himself as Father in the work of creation, as Son in the work of redemption, and as Holy Spirit in the work of sanctification. Important in the development of this branch of Monarchianism were:

1. *Noetus of Smyrna* (3d century). Held that Christ, being the Father, suffered for us.

2. *Calixtus I* ("Pope," 218—23).

3. *Beryllus* (3d century). Was drawn from patripassianism by Origen.

4. *Praxeas of Asia Minor* (2d century). Held that the Father became incarnate in the Son and took part in His suffering.

5. *Epigonus* (3d century). Disciple of Noetus, founded a church at Rome which was later headed by Cleomenes and Sabellius.

6. *Sabellius* (3d century). Modalistic monarchianism reached its full

development under him; God, the absolute Monad, reveals Himself in three *prosopa (personae)* each representing the entire Monad (Father — Creator and Lawgiver; Son — Redeemer; Holy Spirit — Giver of Life); condemned by Dionysius of Alexandria, who, however, fell into the opposite error of subordinationism.

See histories of dogma (especially Loofs, Seeberg, Harnack) listed under *Dogmatics; Doctrine, History of.*

Monarchical System. See *Polity, Ecclesiastical,* 5.

Monasticism. 1. *Definition.* The term monasticism covers a far-branching variety of phenomena and institutions which, however dissimilar, grow from the common root of asceticism. Underlying its formations is the consciousness of sin and the desire of a reunion with God. This reunion the monastic seeks to attain by renouncing self according to certain ascetic methods. Such methods are: renunciation a) of the everyday world: separation from ordinary life, more or less perfect seclusion; b) of family: the breaking of blood ties, celibacy; c) of property: a minimum of personal possessions or none at all; d) of pleasure and comfort: simple, poor, even insufficient food, clothing, and shelter; e) of will: humility, obedience to superiors; f) acts of self-mortification, partly to aid in subduing the flesh, partly to acquire merit before God: fasting, vigils, scourging, silence, sometimes torture and self-mutilation; g) frequent repetition of set prayers and acts of devotion; religious meditation. The three fundamental vows of the monastic are poverty, celibacy, and obedience. By employment of the methods enumerated monastics are supposed to gain a holiness and perfection unattainable by ordinary Christians.

2. *History.* Monasticism, in its essential features, was highly developed in India before the Christian era, presenting strange parallels to Western Monasticism. In Egypt, where the priests of Serapis lived a monastic life, Christian monasticism had its origin. Its first exponents, probably refugees from the persecution of Decius (ca. 250), lived in deserts as hermits.* Their numbers grew with the legal establishment of Christianity and the coincident decline of spirituality.

3. Late in the third century, Anthony (see *Anthony, St.*) began gathering hermits into colonies, while Pachomius founded the first monastery and drew up the first monastic rule. Thereafter the anchorite, or hermit, type of ascetic life rapidly yielded to the cenobite, or social, type. Basil of Cappadocia gave monasticism standing in the Greek Church and drew up regulations for its guidance. Through Athanasius, Augustine, Jerome, and others the monastic idea found acceptance in the West, many monasteries being founded under various rules. In the sixth century, Benedict of Nursia (see *Benedict, St.; Benedictines*) wrote the famous Benedictine Rule, which eventually superseded all others and regulated the monasticism of the West for many centuries. Its provisions are moderate and remarkable chiefly for insistence on permanent attachment to one monastery *(stabilitas loci)* and for emphasis on systematic labor. These features made the Benedictines pioneers and colonizers; but their operation also helped to give the order the corporate wealth and power which led to its decline.

4. The monks early became partisans of the Papacy against the secular clergy and the rulers. Boniface and Ansgar, the apostles of Germany and Sweden, were Benedictines and faithful agents of Rome. When the growing wealth of monasteries and abbeys led to relaxation of the Rule of Benedict, efforts at reform were made from time to time. In the 10th and 11th centuries the Cluniac movement (see *Cluniac Monks*), which Pope Gregory VII turned to good account for the Papacy, tried to reform monasticism and, at the same time, to infuse the monastic ideal into the church at large. The beginning of the 12th century saw a new effort at reform, the Cistercian (see *Cistercians*), led by the great Bernard of Clairvaux. In connection with it arose the military orders of the age of the Crusades, such as the Knights Templars and the Teutonic Knights, constituted, like the monastic orders of secular clergy, on the Augustine Rule.

5. Far more radical than earlier reforms was the establishment (ca. 1210), by Francis of Assisi (see *Francis, St.*) and Domingo (see *Dominic, St.*), of the Franciscan and Dominican orders, the mendicant friars, who were not to have any corporate property except necessary buildings, and who were to travel about as beggars, both as friends of the poor and as popular preachers. Ruled by "generals," unfettered by local at-

tachment, these orders became a useful militia of the Papacy. They were soon active throughout Europe, and their missionaries penetrated to the most distant lands; the Dominicans developed an unenviable skill as inquisitors. Gradually the discipline and the mendicant principle of these orders was relaxed, and by the time of the Reformation they, like other orders, had become degenerate.

6. The Reformation repudiated monasticism; but Rome continued to form new orders in large number. The Jesuits, founded 1534, and emphasizing a blind obedience to the Pope, became Rome's chief bulwark against Protestantism, and today they control the destinies of the Roman Church. It is instructive to observe the evolution of monastic principles. Many former rigors have been softened; the rules of poverty and seclusion have been greatly modified; the demand of celibacy has remained unaltered; but the vow of obedience, for obvious reasons, has been carried to its logical extreme. During the Dark Ages and later, monasteries were often centers of learning, and monks copied and preserved ancient manuscripts. There have been many pious and upright monks and nuns, who were benefactors of mankind. But monasticism itself is at variance with the principles of Christ and of nature, and much of the superstition, false doctrine, and corruption of the Church of Rome lies at its door. (For further information see *Nuns; Tertiaries; Profession of Monks and Nuns; Novice; Vows; Consilia Evangelica; School Brothers and Sisters; Orders in United States;* also individual orders: *Angelicals, Augustinians,* etc.) See *Asceticism.*

H. B. Workmann, *The Evolution of the Monastic Ideal,* Epworth, London, 1927; references under *Patristics; Doctrine, History of.*

Monergism in Conversion. In opposition to synergism,* the teaching that the grace of God is the only efficient cause in beginning and effecting the conversion* of men.

Mongols. Originally south of Lake Baikal, now in Mongolia and adjacent territory. (Area: 558,054 sq. mi.; population: 880,000, mostly nomadic Mongols and Kalmuks). In contact with Nestorian Christianity and with the Roman Catholic Church, especially in the 13th and 14th centuries; now almost entirely heathen, with missionaries of

several denominations, notably Danish Lutherans, trying to gain a foothold among them. See *Missions, Bibliography.*

Monica (or *Monnica*). Mother of Augustine,* the Latin Church Father; b. ca. 332, d. 387; a devoted and loyal Christian, even though she was married to Patricius of Tagaste, who was coarse and unfaithful; but such was the power of her Christian example that he was overpowered by its persuasion and became a Christian. Her famous son, whose early years justified the highest hopes of the parents with regard to a brilliant career, left the orthodox faith and was a heretic for many years. But such was the power of the prayers with which Monica attended his every step that Augustine was converted in 386, being baptized by Ambrose of Milan, Easter, 387. It was Ambrose who comforted Monica in her distress about her son, saying: "It is impossible that a son of so many prayers can be lost."

Monism. The metaphysical theory which reduces all phenomena, not to two principles, as does dualism, nor to more than two, as does pluralism, but to a single, material, or spiritual principle. While, for instance, dualism does not attempt to reduce such opposites as God and world, matter and spirit, body and soul, to one causal concept, asserting that they are inherently different and that the gulf between them cannot be bridged over, monism considers them merely modifications of one primal principle. Thus pantheism identifies God and the world, materialism regards matter, and spiritualism or idealism regards spiritual beings or ideas as the only basis of reality. However, metaphysical monism is not a tenable theory and, when brought into the realm of religion, generally becomes hostile to Christianity. Though the attempt to reduce varieties of phenomena in the world to a common causal principle is prompted by a desire implanted in our human nature, monism carries this process too far. The Biblical conception of the world is both dualistic and monistic, depending on the point of view. Over against pantheism it asserts the essential difference between the Creator and creation, while in regard to the question of origins it may be called monistic, since it traces all reality (except sin) to God. In recent years the term monism has especially been applied to the naturalistic philosophical movement based on biological evolution and fathered by Haeckel * and other materialists, according to which only the physical world has reality, the psychical being understood to be an essential element of the same and present in rudimentary form in matter from the beginning, a view differing only slightly from thoroughgoing materialism, which reduces the psychical to mere physical processes. On the basis of this philosophy an openly antichristian society was organized in Jena, Germany, 1906, called *Deutscher Monistenbund*, with Haeckel as its honorary president.

Monistenbund. See *Monism*.

Monk, William Henry (1823—89). B. in London, became organist at St. Matthias Church, Stoke Newington, where he conducted a daily choral service. He was also organist and choir director of King's College, London, and professor of music. From 1876 he was professor in the National Training School for Music and at Bedford College. His chief fame rests on his work as musical editor of *Hymns Ancient and Modern*, at which he was engaged practically until his death. "Coronae" and "Eventide" are melodies whereby he is remembered.

Monod, Wilfred (1867—). Professor of theology in Paris; revived principles of Gnosticism * and Manichaeanism.*

Monods, The. *Adolphe* (1802—56); French Protestant pulpit orator; pastor at Naples and Lyons; professor at Montauban 1836; pastor in Paris 1847; succeeded by his brother *Guillaume*. — *Frédéric*, another brother (1794—1863); founder of Eglise Libre de France 1849; believed in entire Bible. — *Jean Paul Frédéric* and *Théodore*, his sons, Reformed theologians.

Monograms of Christ. Abbreviations of names and designations referring to Christ, especially in the symbolism of ecclesiastical art, such as IHC (or S), which stands for the name Jesus; XP (Chi Rho), the first letters of the name Christ in Greek; Alpha and Omega, the name given to the Savior in the Book of Revelation, and many others, especially in the form of diagrams.

Monophysite Controversy. The Council of Chalcedon, in 451, declared that the Lord Jesus Christ is "of one substance with the Father . . . in two natures, without confusion, the dif-

ference of natures in no wise being abolished by the union which they possessed, but rather the properties of each nature being preserved and united in one person and one mode of being." Against this statement, which is strictly Biblical, opposition was voiced in several quarters, the contention being that there was only one nature (Greek: *mone physis*) in the person of Christ, namely, the divine nature, or a single compounded nature, but not two distinct natures.

The controversy was connected with that of Eutychianism. When Juvenal of Jerusalem supported the resolution of the council, a monk by the name of Theodosius was set up as a rival bishop, and Juvenal was forced to flee. In other places also bishops of the orthodox party were driven out, their places being filled by their opponents, of whom the strongest, intellectually, was Peter the Iberian. A large part of Palestine was carried away by the movement, which was not suppressed there till the year 453. In Egypt, matters took an even more serious turn, where Dioscurus, with his Eutychian leanings, wielded a powerful influence, so that his party even elected a patriarch with the same tendencies, namely, Timotheus Aelurus. When he was driven away, he returned with even greater prestige. It was only in 460, when Timotheus was banished, that the peace of the Church was restored in Egypt. Even in Antioch, otherwise generally orthodox, the Monophysite doctrine gained many adherents, and both Antioch and Jerusalem were for a while occupied by Monophysite bishops.

It was at this time that Acacius, who had followed Gennadius as patriarch of Constantinople, proposed a document, a formula of union, addressed to the bishops, clergy, monks, and people of Alexandria, Egypt, Libya, and Pentapolis. This was known as the *Henoticon* and was avowedly based on the faith confessed at the councils of Nicaea, Constantinople, and Ephesus. It asserted the consubstantiality of the Son of God with both the Father and with man, insisting that it was one and the same person who performed miracles and endured suffering. The document was so cleverly framed, as are most theological compromises, as to coax back all but the most radical into the fold of the Church. It is true that this solution resulted in a breach with the bishop of Roe, but matters were adjusted some thirty-five years later. The doctrine continued to be a bone of contention for almost another century, when the final schism of the Monophysite churches occurred, which has never been healed. At the present time the Coptic Church, the Abyssinian Church, the Syrian Jacobite Church, and the Armenian Church hold Monophysite errors. See *Coptic Church.*

Monotheism. The belief that there is only one God.

Monothelitism. The belief that Jesus acted as one, or (later) that Christ had one will. This movement was closely related to the subject of the Eutychian and the Monophysite controversies; for when the contention of a single nature in the person of Christ met with such determined opposition on the orthodox side, the attempt was first made, in Alexandria, to harmonize the opposing parties by using the terms "one energy" and "one will" (Greek: *monon thelema)* or at least "one state of will" as descriptive of the unorthodox views. Men who were inclined strongly toward a union at all costs, like the patriarch Sergius of Constantinople, rather supported the movement, so that a merger of Monophysites and Monothelites resulted in some parts of the Church. When Pope Honorius I was appealed to, he sided with those who regarded the insistence upon the resolutions of Chalcedon as overstrenuous, himself taking the position of confessing only one will of the Lord Jesus Christ. Sophronius, patriarch of Jerusalem, took exception to this stand, and the controversy continued till 681, when the Sixth Ecumenical Council met at Constantinople (called Trullan because it met in the domed hall, or *troullos,* of the imperial palace). This council, in the eighteenth session, accepted a decree acknowledging the teaching of two natural wills and two natural energies in Christ, but stating that the two natural wills are not opposed, but that rather the human will follows, and is subordinate to, the divine will. This position was later established by the second Trullan Council, in 692, and remained the doctrine of the Church, in agreement with John 1:43; 5:21; 17:24; Matt. 27:34. See *Christological Controversies.*

Monsell, John Samuel Bewley (1811 to 1875). Educated at Trinity College, Dublin; held various positions in the Anglican Church, last at Guildford; among his hymns: "Christ Is Risen, Hallelujah!"

Monstrance (Ostensorium). The vessel used in Roman churches to expose the consecrated wafer for adoration. It has a foot and stem like a chalice, while its upper part represents rays issuing from the host.

Montaigne, Michel (1533—92). Essayist, satirized the Church but did not leave it; graceful, pungent, witty author.

Montanism. In the Early Church an expectation of the immediate return of Christ was often current (2 Thess. 2: 2, 3). Fanciful hopes connected with that expected return led to chiliastic speculations (Pseudo-Barnabas, Papias, Justin, Irenaeus, Tertullian, Victorinus, Lactantius), especially among the followers of Montanus, called Montanists. Montanus founded this sect in the last half of the 2d century. Inveighing against increasing laxity and worldliness in the Church, he declared himself the instrument of the Paraclete promised by Christ (cf. John 14:16) and with two prophetesses (Prisca and Maximilla) announced the speedy establishment of the millennium centered at Pepuza in Phrygia. Disappointed in this prophecy, the movement turned to a rigorous legalism (marriage a necessary evil; fasts enjoined; women must avoid all ornaments; enjoyments are snares of Satan; those fallen into mortal sins cannot be restored to fellowship). The movement spread rapidly through Asia Minor, Gaul, Rome, and North Africa. Tertullian became its advocate in North Africa, where separate conventicles were established which were considered more spiritual congregations. The movement disappeared in the 6th century.

Monte Cassino. Monastery erected on Mons Cassinus in Campania by Benedict of Nursia in 529; considered a model for all other institutions of this type.

Montenegro. Formerly an independent principality of the Balkan States, now a part of Yugoslavia, forming its southwestern part, along the Adriatic Sea, with a population of about 225,000, the great majority of whom are members of the Greek Orthodox Church, although there are some Roman Catholics in the southern districts. See also *Greek Church.*

Monteverdi, Claudio (1567—1643). Composer of the early Baroque Era. Though active at St. Mark's Cathedral in Venice, Monteverdi is identified usually with the early development of the opera. Through his operas the *da capo aria* became prominent and found its way into Lutheran church music, particularly into its Passions and the Cantata. Through Monteverdi's music, too, accompanied music became more common in the churches, and homophony began to replace 15th- and 16th-century polyphony. Due to their obsolete character and style, Monteverdi's operas are rarely performed today.

Pruniers, H. *Monteverdi, His Life and Works.* London, 1926.

Montgomery, James (1771—1854). B. at Irvine, Ayrshire, Scotland, son of an Irish minister of the Moravian Church. At seven he was sent to Yorkshire to prepare for the ministry. While at school, his parents were sent to the West Indies as missionaries. Both parents died there. After the death of his parents he took work at Mirfield and later at Wath, but eventually set out for London with a copy of the poems he had written in the hope of finding a publisher for them. In this he failed. He now got in touch with the editor and owner of the *Sheffield Register.* He became co-editor. In 1794 Montgomery took over the paper and changed its name to the *Sheffield Iris.* At the age of forty-three he returned to the Moravian congregation at Fulneck. He was a zealous worker for missions and was an active member of the Bible Society. Besides contributing poetry and hymns to the world for a period of fifty years, Montgomery lectured on poetry and literature. In English hymnology he stands next to Isaac Watts and Chas. Wesley.

Moody, Dwight Lyman (1837—99). Independent evangelist; b. and d. at Northfield, Mass.; clerk in uncle's shoe-store at Boston; businessman, Sunday school worker, and lay preacher in Chicago; agent of Christian Commission during Civil War; preaching tours in England and America with Ira David Sankey, who had charge of the singing; published hymnal; founded Moody Bible Institute, Chicago, and other institutions; unordained; accepted Bible literally, preached powerfully, but with strong chiliastic tendency.

Moore, Thomas. Noted Irish poet. B. in Dublin, May 28, 1779; educated at Trinity College, Dublin; he later took up the study of law in London. In 1800 Moore published his *Anacreon* in Lon-

don, the following year his first volume of poems. In 1804 he received a government post at Bermuda, from which he returned to London, and in 1806 he published his *Odes* and *Epistles.* He was a writer of high merit. His association with Lord Byron was very cordial. Never in want, nevertheless the last days of his life were spent in sorrow. He had lost all his children. A downcast and grief-stricken man, he died, Feb. 26, 1852. His great hymn is "Come, Ye Disconsolate."

Moral Argument. See *Apologetics; God* (apologetics).

Moral Feeling. See *Conscience.*

Moral Influence Theory. See *Atonement, Theories of,* 4.

Moral Interpretation. See *Exegesis,* 3, 5.

Moral Law. See *Decalog; Grace, Means of,* II, 2.

Moral Obligation. See *Conscience.*

Moral Sense. 1) In 18th-century philosophy, an ability (marked by pleasure and displeasure) which developed in the mind as a result of the association of ideas; 2) in common usage it often includes some aspects of conscience.*

Moral Theology. A term used especially by Roman Catholics for Christian ethics.*

Morales, Christoforo (ca. 1500—53). Composer of the Roman Catholic Church. He was a contemporary of Palestrina, and was of Spanish descent. Much of his life was spent in Rome. Morales was a master of polyphony, and his music is noted for its purity and religious depth.

Moralities. See *Religious Drama.*

Morata, Fulvia Olympia (1526—55). Highly gifted Italian woman, devotee of humanistic culture; became acquainted with the reformatory movement at the court of the Duchess of Ferrara; studied the Scriptures and renounced Roman Catholicism; married a German physician and died at Heidelberg.

Moravia. Formerly a province or crownland of the Austrian Empire, now the west-central part of Czechoslovakia, belonging almost entirely to the basin of the March, or Morava; the home of the Moravian Brethren (*Maehrische Brueder*), or Unity of the Brethren.

Moravian Church. 1. The origin of the Moravian churches may be traced back to the work of John Hus, who in 1415 was burned at the stake at Constance, in Germany. For several years after the martyrdom of Hus and of his friend Jerome of Prague their followers had no special organization. At the beginning of the Reformation the "brethren" had more than 400 churches in Bohemia and Moravia and a membership of 150,000—200,000 souls. Cordial relations were established with Luther and Calvin, although no formal union with the German and Swiss churches was accomplished. In 1535 the Moravian *Confession of Faith* was adopted, which, with several exceptions, was approved by Luther.

2. In polity the Moravian Church was episcopal, having a supreme judge to preside in the assembly and a synod to decide matters of faith and discipline. The administration of the congregations was in the hands of elected elders, who had supervision over the church members. The promotion of the religious life of the women was in care of matrons. Priests, living at first in celibacy, were ordained after the Apostolic example and pursued trades for their support. From the time of the organization of the Moravian Church, churches pursued an aggressive policy, being active especially in the fields of education and literature. In nearly every large city they had schools and training houses. In 1593 they completed the translation of the Bible into both the Bohemian and the Moravian language.

3. The Moravian churches suffered severely during the Thirty Years' War, when their country was devastated. At its close, in 1648, the churches of Bohemia and Moravia were practically destroyed, large numbers of members having been put to death and others being compelled to flee to Hungary, Saxony, Holland, and Poland, where, as well as in Bohemia and Moravia, they continued in scattered communities. The last bishop of the United Moravian Church, the famous educator John Amos Comenius, died at Amsterdam in 1670. — In 1722 a small band of Moravians settled on the estate of Nicholas Louis, Count of Zinzendorf, in Saxony, where the village of Herrnhut arose. Other colonists came from various parts of Germany, and an association was formed in which the religious ideals of Zinzendorf and those of the

Moravians were combined. While the confessions of the existing Protestant Church were accepted, a distinct order and discipline in accord with the principles of the old Moravian Church was established under royal concessions. On August 13, 1727, the Moravian Brethren celebrated their first Communion as an organization in Germany; and this day is regarded by them as the beginning of their Church. In 1735 David Nitschmann was ordained as bishop, and in 1737 the episcopate was conferred upon Zinzendorf. Thus the *Unitas Fratrum,* or Church of Brethren, known at the present time in England and Germany as the Moravian Church, was established. With inimitable zeal, Zinzendorf devoted his time and energy to the congregation and promoted its interests until his death, in 1760. The chief purpose of the Church as conceived by him was to carry on evangelistic work in Christian and heathen lands.

4. The first Moravian missionary came to Pennsylvania in 1734. In 1741 Bishop Nitschmann and his associates founded the town of Bethlehem and a little later purchased the neighboring village of Nazareth, which had belonged to the evangelist George Whitefield. Here a co-operative union to develop the settlements and support missionary work was formed by the colonists and maintained until 1762. Missionary work was carried on also among the Indians. In 1749 an act of Parliament recognized the Moravian Church as "an Ancient Protestant Episcopal Church," by virtue of which it received standing and privileges in all British dominions. In spite of this the church remained a comparatively small body. Bethlehem, Nazareth, and Lititz, in Pennsylvania, and Salem, in North Carolina, were organized in colonial times as exclusive Moravian villages after the pattern of the Moravian communities in Germany, England, and Holland. Between 1844 and 1856 this exclusive system was abolished and the church reorganized to suit modern conditions.

5. *Doctrine.* The doctrines of the Moravian Church are stated mainly in Bishop Spangenberg's (1704—92), *Idea Fratrum* or *Kurzer Begriff der christlichen Lehre in der evangelischen Bruedergemeinde,* although this statement of doctrine was never received as a public confession. In Lutheran countries, such as Germany, the doctrines of

the Moravian Church were largely influenced by the Lutheran Confessions, while in England and America Reformed influence prevailed. In 1848 the Augsburg Confession, as such, was eliminated, and only Articles II, III, and IV were retained. Because Lutheran and Reformed elements largely predominated side by side in the Moravian Church, a strong unionistic tendency was developed and is maintained to this day. In the beginning of its history the Moravian Church was not free from fanaticism and fanatical excrescences. Thus the Trinity was conceived of in a grossly offending way, the first person of the Godhead being called Papa, Grandfather, or Father-in-law; the third person of the Godhead, Mama and the eternal Spouse of God the Father. The elimination of these extravagant and fanatic tendencies is largely due to Bishop Spangenberg. In general it may be said that the doctrine of the Moravian Church, in the main, represents the Calvinistic type of Protestantism. The whole Scriptures are accepted as an adequate rule of faith and practice, and the Apostles' Creed is regarded as formulating the prime articles of faith found in the Scriptures; but neither is consistently followed. Foot washing has been discontinued since 1818. Infant Baptism is practiced. On arriving at adult age, baptized members, after receiving religious instruction, are confirmed on application, and non-baptized applicants are received as members through Baptism, the usual method being by sprinkling. Holy Communion is open to communicant members of other churches.

6. *Polity.* The church government is presbyterian, for though each congregation has its own council, the general supervision rests with the provincial synod, comprised of an equal number of lay and cleric representatives, which deals with all matters of faith and practice. The Moravians believe that there are three orders of the ministry: deacons, presbyters, and bishops, the latter alone having the right to ordain. The Moravians have developed an elaborate liturgy.

7. *Work.* The Moravian Church has been very active in mission work. For many years their mission program was dedicated to the principle that the Moravian colonies should serve as a leaven within the respective communities in which the colonies were planted.

The early Moravians were not much concerned about gaining members for their own denomination and frequently recommended to the converts to join other existing Protestant denominations. They have been particularly active in the foreign mission field, and carry on work in thirteen fields, having some 140 stations and over 200 white and 2,500 native missionaries.

The Moravians are represented in ,the United States by the Moravian Church in America, whose history corresponds most closely with the one given above. The Evangelical Unity of Bohemian and Moravian Brethren are the descendants of the early Moravians who did not emigrate to Herrnhut in 1722, and are found primarily in Texas. There is also a small group of Bohemian Moravians in Iowa.

Moravian Missions. See *Moravian Church.*

More, Paul Elmer (1864—1937). American philosopher and literary critic; taught at Bryn Mawr, Harvard, and lectured at Princeton; editor of *Nation;* wrote *The Greek Tradition;* sought to defend Christianity on the basis of Greek dualism.

More, Thomas (1478—1535). English humanist; afterward Lord Chancellor of the kingdom; beheaded; studied law, was in field of politics; had a controversy with Tyndale and wrote against Luther in a bitter strain; his most famous book *Utopia.*

Morehead, John Alfred. B. Feb. 4, 1867; studied at Roanoke College, Luth. Theol. Seminary, Berlin and Leipzig universities; held several honorary doctorates; held two pastorates in Virginia; prof. and pres. of Southern Luth. Theol. Seminary, 1901—03; pres. of Roanoke College, 1903—19; held a number of executive positions, including that of pres. of the Lutheran World Convention; d. 1936.

S. Trexler, *Morehead, John A.,* Putnam's, N.Y., 1938.

Morison, John (1749—98). Studied at Aberdeen; parish minister at Canisbay, Caithness; member of committee to revise the *Translations and Paraphrases of 1745;* a book of Psalm versifications; wrote: "To Us a Child of Hope Is Born."

Morley, Thomas (1557—1604). Studied under Byrd, Bachelor of Music,

Oxford, 1588; Gentleman of the Chapel Royal, 1592; wrote many airs for popular songs, some of which are still in use; little sacred music.

Mormon, Book of. See *Latter Day Saints.*

Mormonism. See *Latter Day Saints.*

Morocco, Empire of. Area: 209,105 sq. mi.; population: Spanish Morocco, 795,000; French Morocco, 7,976,000, chiefly Berbers, Arabs, Jews. Dominant religion, Islam. Morocco is politically a French protectorate. Statistics of missions: 1,097 baptized members; 3 ordained, 2 not ordained native workers; a foreign staff of a total of 103; seven societies at work. See *Missions, Bibliography.*

Morris, J. G. B. Nov. 14, 1803, at York, Pa.; Lutheran theologian, member of General Synod; studied under S. S. Schmucker; pastor in Baltimore thirty-three years, then at Lutherville, Md.; noted as a pulpit orator; popular and prolific writer; d. at Lutherville, Md., Oct. 10, 1895.

J. G. Morris, *Fifty Years in the Lutheran Ministry,* J. Young, Baltimore, Md., 1878; J. G. Morris, *Life Reminiscences of an Old Lutheran Minister,* Luth. Pub. Soc., Philadelphia, 1896.

Morrison, Robert. B. Jan. 5, 1782, Morpeth, England; d. Aug. 1, 1834, Canton, China. Sent out as missionary by the London Missionary Society, he became the pioneer missionary to China. He landed at Macao, Sept. 7, 1807. In 1808 he accepted a position with the East India Company as interpreter. In 1813 the New Testament was published by him in Chinese. In 1834 he and Milne published the whole Bible translated into Chinese. His other great work is a dictionary of Chinese. For twenty-seven years he labored almost alone at Canton, holding out against well-nigh insurmountable odds.

Mortal and Venial Sin. See *Sins, Venial and Mortal.*

Mosaic Painting. The art of grouping and combining minute pieces of hard, colored substances, such as marble, glass, or natural stones, in a pattern or picture, the finished product resembling a painting.

Mosellanus, Peter (Peter Schade, 1493/4—1524). B. at Bruttig; d. at Leipzig. The "Melanchthon of Leipzig," humanist, he delivered the opening ad-

dress at the Leipzig debate (Carlstadt and Luther vs. Eck), 1519, and sent his friend Julius von Pflug an impartial account of it.

Moser, Johann Jacob (1701—85). Studied at Tuebingen; prof. at Tuebingen, and Frankfurt a. O.; counselor of Landgrave of Hesse-Homburg. Wrote extensively on political science; author of over 1,000 hymns.

Moses of Armenia (d. 487). Church father to whom the famous *History or Genealogical Account of Armenia Major* and *Geograhy of Armenia* are usually ascribed.

Moses, Assumption of. See *Apocalypticism; Apocrypha, A 4.*

Moses ibn-Ezra ben Jacob of Granada (ca 1070—ca. 1139). Jewish writer; b. in Spain; noted Talmudist, professor of Greek philosophy, and poet.

Mosheim, Johann Lorenz (1694 or 1695—1755). Describes himself as "neither Pietist nor overorthodox"; professor and chancellor at Helmstedt; 1747 in the same position at Goettingen; was considered the foremost theologian and scholar of the Lutheran Church of his days; wrote on all branches of theology, but especially on Church History.

L. Spitz, Jr., "Johann Lorenz Mosheim's Philosophy of History," *CTM,* XX: 321—39.

Mosque. A Mohammedan place of worship, with three essential parts: the Mihrab, or Hall of Prayer, the place of ablutions, and the assembly room for the reading of the Koran.

Mote, Edward (1797—1874). B. in London; after a wayward youth he joined the Baptist Church. Working as a cabinetmaker, he spent his spare time writing for the press. At the age of fifty-five he entered the Baptist ministry, and for the last twenty-six years of his life he was minister of the Baptist church at Horsham, Essex. He published *Hymns of Praise,* which contained about 100 of his own compositions. "My Hope Is Built on Nothing Less." D. at Horsham.

Motet (Motette). The motet was the most important type of sacred polyphonic choral music written through the course of five eventful centuries (ca. 1250—1750). It is usually an unaccompanied type of music based on a *cantus firmus.* While in the Roman Catholic Church the *cantus firmus* was Gregorian chant, in the Lutheran Church it was the chorale. In the 17th century the English began to call their motets "anthems," although today we usually think of the anthem as an accompanied sacred choral composition. The Lutheran masters excelled in writing motets. Bach's motets enjoy great fame today, though they were written when the motet was no longer in vogue and fully appreciated.

Willi Apel, *Harvard Dictionary of Music*, Cambridge, Mass., 1944. Hugo Leichtentritt, *Geschichte der Motette*, Leipzig, 1908.

Mother of God. A name applied to the Virgin Mary. See *Mariolatry*.

Mother Synod. See *United Lutheran Church, Synods of*, 24.

Motherhouse. See *Deaconesses*.

Mothers' Club. See *Parish Education, J.*

Motions (motus interni) in Conversion. See *Conversion*, II, 4.

Motivation. See *Christian Teaching, D.*

Motu Proprio. A decree issued by the pope himself and considered as absolutely authoritative by Roman Catholics. Particularly, Instruction on Sacred Music issued by Pius X.

Mourning Bench. A kneeler used in revivalistic Methodistic churches. After an exhortation by the evangelist those who feel sorrow over sins are invited to come to the bench and receive assurance of forgiveness.

Mozarabic Chant. The chant used in the churches of Spain during the Middle Ages.

Mozart, Wolfgang Amadeus (1756 to 1791). B. at Salzburg; educated by his father, a composer and violinist in the service of the Bishop of Salzburg, a musical center made famous by Johann Ernst Eberlin and Michael Haydn. As a child prodigy Wolfgang Mozart made concert tours to Vienna, Paris, London, and Italy.

While Mozart did much of his creative work in church music in Salzburg, his *Mass in C Minor* as well as his famous *Requiem* were written in Vienna. While his early church music is very conservative, in his later works he employed greater freedom; he had in the meantime been influenced by the Neapolitan masters Jommelli, Galuppi, Sammartini, and also by the more conservative Padre Martini. He was influenced in no small degree also by Handel, J. S. Bach, and by his personal friend Johann Christian Bach, the youngest son of Johann Sebastian. As a result, we find in the music of Mozart a fusion of many styles; like Lassus, he is one of the world's most universal composers, and even his church music was written in a style not at all typical of the Church for which it was written. The charm of his sacred music is so great that its texts recede into the background. It is claimed that his *Mass in C Minor* and his *Requiem* are sufficiently monumental to be put aside of his operas *Don Giovanni* and *Die Zauberflöte*. Particularly his choral works reveal a kinship with Bach and Handel and a blending of the baroque with the classical. Mozart's *Requiem Mass* is the greatest composition produced within the Roman Catholic Church in the 18th century. His works for orchestra, piano, and other instruments are among the great music of the world.

Alfred Einstein, *Mozart, His Character and His Work*, Oxford Press, 1945; Otto Jahn, *W. A. Mozart*, tr. by Townsend, London, 1891; W. J. Turner, *Mozart, the Man and His Works*, New York, 1938. WEB

Mozetta. A cape with a small hood worn by Roman Catholic dignitaries to show their office.

Muehlenberg, Heinrich Melchior, J. Peter G., Frederick, Henry, William Augustus, Henry Aug., Hiester, Fred Aug. See *Muhlenberg, H. M., and Family.*

Muhlenberg, W. See *Protestant Episcopal Church*, 4.

Muehlhaeuser, John. B. Aug. 9, 1804, in Wuerttemberg; studied in the Basel *Missionshaus;* colporteur in Austria; entered the Barmen *Missionshaus.* Was sent to America by the Langenberg Society. He came with Max Oertel, later turned Romanist, who assisted him in mission work in New York City. Ordained as pastor at Rochester, 1837, and joined New York Ministerium; in Wisconsin, 1846, as colporteur for American Tract Society; back at Rochester; returned to Wisconsin, 1848, with John Weinmann and W. Wrede, Langenberg missionaries; founded Grace Church, Milwaukee, long known as "Muehlhaeuser's." With his two friends he founded the Wisconsin Synod, 1849—50, for which he wrote the first constitution. President of the synod until 1860, when he was elected "Senior," an office created for him. D. Sept. 15, 1868.

Muehlmann, Johann (1573—1613). Studied at Leipzig and Jena; preacher in Leipzig; diaconus in Naumburg; pastor at Laucha; finally professor at Leipzig; staunch Lutheran; wrote: "Dank sei Gott in der Hoehe."

Mueller, George (1805—98). Studied at Halle, 1825; began to preach, 1826; prepared himself at London for missionary work, 1828; joined Plymouth Brethren; minister at Teignmouth, 1830; started Scriptural Knowledge Institution, 1834, and Bristol Orphanage, 1836. Relying upon prayer, he received nearly £1,000,000 ($4,860,000) for his orphanage and Christian charities without directly asking one single person for assistance, proving, as he said, that "Elijah's God still lives."

Mueller, Heinirch (1631—75). Among the foremost devotional writers of the Lutheran Church; in 1653 archdeacon of St. Mary's, in Rostock; 1662 professor of theology; 1671 superintendent. In Mueller orthodoxy and personal piety were most happily united. He was a very popular preacher. Chief works: *Der himmelische Liebeskuss* and *Geistliche Erquickstunden.*

Mueller, J. A. F. W. B. Oct. 22, 1825. Saxon immigrant; first graduate of log cabin college, Perry Co., Mo.; pastor in Manchester, Mo., 1847; of Immanuel, Chicago, of First Lutheran Church, Pittsburgh, in Johnsburg, Pa., in Chester, Ill.; vice-president of Eastern and of Illinois Districts, Missouri Synod. D. Dec. 26, 1900.

Mueller, Johann Georg (1759 to 1819). A Swiss educator and theological writer, also at times serving in political positions, a friend of Herder, who tried to simplify and "humanize" theology.

Mueller, Johann Georg (1800—75). Reformed teacher and student of comparative religion. Professor at Basel. Wrote: *Geschichte der amerikanischen Urreligionen;* studied the relation between the Semites and Hamites and published his conclusions in 1872.

Mueller, Julius (1801—78). Mediating theologian, defender of the Prussian Union; prof. in Goettingen, Marburg, Halle; wrote *Christliche Lehre von der Suende.*

Mueller, Karl (1852—1935). German theologian; prof. at Halle, Giessen,

Breslau, Tuebingen; wrote extensively in the field of church history.

Mueller, Max (1823—1900). German-English comparative philologist; many years prof. at Oxford; made researches into mythology and comparative religion; held that there are only two kinds of religions, salvation by works (all pagan religions) and by grace through faith (Christianity); edited *Sacred Books of the East,* 51 volumes of translations; wrote: *Science of Language, Chips from a German Workshop.*

Muenchmeyer, August Friedrich Otto (1807—82). Lutheran theologian. B. at Barskamp, Hanover; d. at Buer. Studied at Goettingen, Berlin, and at the Preachers' Seminary at Hanover. Pastor, 1840; superintendent at Cattenburg, 1851; member of the consistory, superintendent at Buer, and member of the ecclesiastical court of Osnabrueck. He advocated complete separation of Church and State.

Muenkel, Kornelius Karl (1809 to 1888). Lutheran preacher and theologian in Hanover; greatly influenceed Lutheran confessionalism in conjunction with Petri, Muenchmeyer, and others.

Muenster. A German cathedral church. The name is applied chiefly to cathedrals of a large and imposing type, such as those of Ulm, Strassburg, and Augsburg. The word *"Dom"* is a synonym for *Muenster.* See also *Cathedrals.*

Muenster, Sebastian (1489—1552). At first a Franciscan, he accepted the Reformation, became a pupil of Reuchlin, teacher of Hebrew in Basel; made a Latin translation of the Old Testament, very literal; later active in various sciences.

Muenzer, Thomas. B. 1489; preacher at Zwickau 1520; would surpass Luther as a reformer; ascetic fanatic and Anabaptist; depreciated the Bible and followed the "inner light" to kill the godless. Became a leader in the Peasants' War, was defeated at Frankenhausen, May 5, 1525, and beheaded.

Muffatt, Georg (ca. 1645—1704). Roman Catholic organist and composer; regarded as one of Frescobaldi's successors in South Germany.

Muhlenberg, Heinrich Melchior, and Family. 1. Heinrich Melchior M., "Patriarch of the Lutheran Church in America," was born September 6, 1711, at Eimbeck, Hanover, Germany. He entered the University of Goettingen as one of its first students in 1735. After his graduation he taught for one year at the Halle Orphanage and was pastor at Grosshennersdorf, Upper Silesia, 1739—41. Dr. Francke of Halle persuaded him, in September, 1741, to accept a call to the "United Lutheran Congregations" in Pennsylvania. After spending a few months with Dr. Ziegenhagen in London, he came to Philadelphia, via Charleston, S. C., November 25, 1742. He was recognized as the duly appointed pastor of the "United Congregations" in a service held in Gloria Dei Church, December 27. In 1743 the building of St. Michael's, Philadelphia, and Augustus Church, at The Trappe (still standing), was begun.

2. By preaching and faithful pastoral and missionary work Muhlenberg soon succeeded in establishing well-organized churches in eastern Pennsylvania and after the arrival of some helpers extended his work into other parts of Pennsylvania and into New Jersey. He organized the Pennsylvania Ministerium, the first Lutheran synod in the United States, in 1748. In 1750 he traveled with his father-in-law, John Conrad Weiser, via Kingston to the churches along the Hudson and in 1751 and 1752 served the old Dutch churches in New York and Hackensack, N. J. In 1758 and 1759 he spent several months in the churches on the Raritan in New Jersey. In the meantime he had placed an assistant who had arrived from Europe in parishes in Pennsylvania, Maryland, and Virginia. With the help of the Swedish Provost Wrangel the Ministerium was revived in 1760. From 1761 to 1776 Muhlenberg resided in Philadelphia, but his declining years (1776—87) were spent at The Trappe. In the winter of 1774—75 he visited the Lutherans in the South. Thus Muhlenberg's influence extended from Northern New York into Georgia and was felt in most of the original Thirteen Colonies for more than a century afterwards. He entered into rest October 7, 1787, and was buried in the shadow of the old church at The Trappe.

3. Muhlenberg was without a doubt a staunch Lutheran, loyal to the confessions of the Lutheran Church, fearless in his testimony to the truth, and filled with a burning desire to save souls. His Lutheranism, however, was tinged with pietism, as he was influenced by the Halle fathers, under whose supervision he had begun his work in America.

4. Muhlenberg married, in 1745, Anna Maria, daughter of Colonel Conrad Weiser, and thus became the founder of "a family illustrious in Church and State." His three sons, J. Peter G., Frederick A. C., and G. Henry E., were sent to Halle for their education, J. Peter G. (1746—1807) was ordained after his return to America (1768) and became the assistant to his father in the churches on the Raritan. After having been reordained by the Bishop of London (1772), an action which was necessary to become a licensed minister in Virginia, he took charge of the church at Woodstock, Va. In 1776 he exchanged his clerical robe for a colonel's uniform and served with distinction under Washington in the Revolutionary War, being a leader in the decisive battle at Yorktown. He afterwards became vice-president of Pennsylvania (with Franklin as president) and a member of Congress.

5. Frederick A. C. (1750—1801) became pastor of Christ Church, New York, fled at the approach of the British (1776), and assisted his father till 1779. Entering political life, he became a member of the Continental Congress and of the Pennsylvania Legislature. From 1789 to 1797 he was a member of Congress and speaker of the first and the third session.

6. G. Henry E. (1753—1815), "the American Linnaeus," ordained 1770, was assistant to his father in Philadelphia and on the Raritan and (1780 to 1815) pastor at Lancaster. His fame as a botanist rests on the discovery of more than 100 new plants. — Wm. Augustus M. (1796—1877). grandson of Frederick A. C. M., became an Episcopalian rector and the author of the well-known hymns "I Would Not Live Alway," "Savior, Who Thy Flock Art Feeding," and "Shout! the Glad Tidings."

7. Henry Aug. P. M., son of G. H. E., was pastor at Reading (1802—27), member of Congress for nine years, minister to Austria, 1838—40, nominated for governor of Pennsylvania, died before election (1844).

8. Hiester H. M., M. D. (1812—86), son of the foregoing and grandson of Governor Hiester of Pennsylvania, "one of the best-known and most esteemed laymen in the Lutheran Church of America," was the first treasurer of the General Council.

9. Frederick Aug. M., a second son

of G. H. E., was known as "the beloved physician of Lancaster."

10. His son, Frederick Augustus M., was the first president of Muhlenberg College at Allentown, 1867—77, and afterwards professor at Pennsylvania University.

11. The oldest daughter of the patriarch, Eva, married Rev. C. E. Schultze. Their son, John Andr. Schultze (1775—1852), was pastor 1796 to 1804, then member of the Pennsylvania Legislature and governor of Pennsylvania, 1823—29.

12. The second daughter of H. M. M., Margareta, married Dr. J. C. Kunze, the most learned emissary of Halle, pastor at Philadelphia, 1770—84, then pastor of the old Lutheran Church in New York till his death, 1807.

13. Mary Salome, H. M. M.'s fourth daughter, married Matthias Reichert, M. C. Their son, John W. Richards, was one of the most active pastors of the Pennsylvania Ministerium, 1824 to 1854. His son, M. H. Richards (1841 to 1898), was for many years professor at Muhlenberg College.

H. A. Muhlenberg, *The Life and Times of Major-General Peter Muhlenberg of the Revolutionary Army,* Carey and Hart, Philadelphia, 1849; M. L. Stoever, *Memoir of the Life and Times of Henry Melchior Muhlenberg, D. D., Patriarch of the Evangelical Lutheran Church in America,* Luth. Bd. of Pub., Philadelphia, 1856; W. Germann, *Heinrich Melchior Muhlenberg, Selbstbiographie,* Brobst, Diehl & Co., 1881; W. J. Mann, *Life and Times of Henry Melchior Muhlenberg,* Frederick, Philadelphia, 1887 (Gen. Counc. Pub. Bd., 1911); W. K. Frick, *Henry Melchior Muhlenberg, "Patriarch of the Lutheran Church in America,"* Luth. Pub. Soc., Philadelphia, 1902; T. G. Tappert & J. W. Doberstein, *The Journals of Henry Melchior Muhlenberg,* Ev. Luth. Ministerium of Pa., and Muhlenberg Press, Philadelphia, 1942; W. G. Polack, "Henry Melchior Muhlenberg," *CTM,* XIII: 673 to 683; M. E. Gladfelter, "Peter Muhlenberg, Statesman, Man of God." *Luth. Ch. Quart.,* XX: 205—12.

Muinntir. See *Celtic Church,* 3, 11.

Mullins, Edgar Y. (1860—1928). Pres. of Southern Baptist Theological Seminary; also pres. of the Baptist Young People's Union; wrote: *Why Is Christianity True? Axioms of Religion;* and other works.

Mumford, Stephen. See *Baptist Bodies,* 16.

Munger, Theodore Thornton (1830 to 1910). Congregationalist; wrote *On the Threshold; The Freedom of Faith; Lamps and Paths; Essays for the Day.* Sought to relate New Theology * to literature.

Mungo. See *Celtic Church,* 6.

Munk, Kaj. See *Denmark, Lutheranism in,* 12.

Munkacsy, Michael (real surname: Lieb, 1846—1900). Hungarian painter, studied chiefly at Munich and Duesseldorf; his work mainly genre (realistic) pictures; besides secular paintings: "Christ Before Pilate" and "The Crucifixion."

Muratorian Fragment (*Canon Muratori*) is a fragment (85 lines) of a Latin treatise on the Bible canon, giving a list of the books of the New Testament accepted as canonical in Italy about the latter half of the second century. It mentions the Gospel of Luke (which it calls the third) and of John, the Acts, Paul's Epistles to the Corinthians, Ephesians, Philippians, Colossians, Galatians, Thessalonians, Romans, Philemon, Titus, Timothy, Revelation, Jude, two Epistles of John, the Wisdom of Solomon, and as doubtful the Revelation of John and Peter. The Fragment was discovered in the Ambrosian Library at Milan (1740) by Muratori, its librarian.

Murillo, Bartolomeo Estaban (1618 to 1682). Greatest of all Spanish painters; noted especially for his exquisite coloring; among his numerous works: "Immaculate Conception" and "Holy Family."

Murray, Andrew. B. May 9, 1828, at Graaff-Reiner, South Africa; d. January 18, 1917, at Wellington, Africa; educated in Scotland and Holland; appointed to Dutch-Reformed pastorate, Bloemfontein, Africa, 1848; Worcester, Cape Town, 1860—1864; Cape Town, 1871; founded Huguenot Seminary; also Mission-training Institute, 1877; prominent in mission endeavor until 1906; traveled much in interest of missions; instrumental in opening up new fields in Bechuanaland, Nyasaland, and Mashonaland.

Murray, John (1741—1815). Founder of Universalist denomination in America; b. in England; left Established Church to join Methodists; later excommunicated for his universalistic views; came to America, 1770; since

1783 pastor of Universalist Society, Boston.

Murtoa College. See *Australia,* A 1.

Musaeus, Johann (1613—81). Great-grandson of Simon M.; prof. at Jena; defended Lutheranism against Catholics, Reformed, sectarians, deists, and pantheists; his syncretism and synergism combated by Calov.

Musaeus, Simon (1521—76 or 82). Prof. and superintendent in Jena; opposed, together with Flacius, the synergism of Pfeffinger and Strigel; exiled; superintendent at Bremen; took up the fight of Hesshusius against Hardenberg's Zwinglian doctrine of the Lord's Supper; exiled.

Musculus *(Meusel),* **Andreas** (1514 to 1581). A. M. at Wittenberg 1539; polemic against the Interim, Osiander, Stancarus, Melanchthon, Calvin; published an excerpt from Luther's works, the *Thesaurus;* active for the *Formula of Concord* at Torgau and Bergen; Superintendent-General of the whole Mark Brandenburg; used his influence with Joachim II for the confessional Lutheran position.

Music, Church. In keeping with Scriptural injunction (*e. g.,* Ps. 96; Col. 3:16) music is employed by the Christian Church to worship God and spiritualize man. Church music, therefore, is not an end in itself, but rather a vehicle employed by the Church for the purpose of helping to carry out the Great Commission imposed upon the Church by God Himself. That the means employed for worship should be worthy, fitting, and reverent seems self-evident.

Christ (Matt. 26:30) and the Apostles (Acts 16:25) employed music for worship purposes (cf. Paul's exhortations: Eph. 5:19; Col. 3:16). The report of Pliny to Emperor Trajan and the writings of the Church Fathers reveal the use of song by early Christians. Important advances were made liturgically and hymnologically by Bishop Ambrose.* Later Gregory the Great* sought to abolish the use of the Ambrosian Chant, claiming that it was secular and irreverent. The Gregorian Chant, prepared by Gregory's musicians and their successors, is related to Greek and Hebrew music. Its use was fostered by Charlemagne and schools established at Metz, Murbach, St. Gall, and other monasteries.

The Middle Ages were influenced by the teachings of Boethius, which held that music, as a branch of mathematics, was part of the quadrivium and possessed ethical potentialities and tendencies. Polyphony developed throughout the Gothic Period and ultimately led to the Renaissance. While the Renaissance rejected many teachings of Boethius and Cassiodorus, it continued to stress the scientific aspects of music. During this period music flourished at the courts, which caused music in the churches to suffer.

Music flourished early among Lutherans because of Luther's understanding of music and his enthusiasm for it. The doctrine of the universal priesthood of believers, together with other factors, shaped Luther's thinking along the lines of church music and liturgics, prompting him to encourage the singing of hymns (chorales) by the people. The people were not to be passive onlookers in the service of worship, but active participants. Luther did not favor discarding the choir, nor did he discard the music of the past. Youth should be exposed to good music not only for cultural reasons, but also that the great music of the Church might be understood by the people. Johann Walther * insisted that music is a part of theology. Hence in the 16th century, Lutheran students of theology were required to study liturgics, church music, and hymnology. Luther made knowledge and appreciation of music an important requirement for pastors and teachers. He thought of it as a means of worship which presents the Word and expresses the reactions of the Christian to blessings he receives in the service of worship. By 1525 Luther's *Formula Missae* had been published, hymns had been written by him and his followers, composers had begun to write choral music in which the chorale served as *cantus firmus,* and several *Gesangbuecher* had been published. Luther's many remarks concerning music eventually helped make of the Lutheran Church the "Singing Church" (see *Hymnody*) and provided for the same a rich musical heritage (see St. L. Ed., X:1424). Luther insisted that the youth of the Church be exposed to good and wholesome music. He maintained that "next to theology there is no art which is the equal of music, for she alone, after theology, can do what otherwise only theology can accomplish." (XXIa:1574.)

Moreover, other 16th-century Lutheran leaders like Melanchthon, Bugenhagen, Selneccer, Walther, Rhaw, concurred with Luther and adopted an evangelical attitude toward church music which allowed for progress and change and which later helped keep Lutheran music from becoming obsolete and archaic in character. Lutheran composers and hymn writers were encouraged to write in the idiom of their time and to use their talents in the service of the Church. Lutheran music naturally reflects the weaknesses of the era in which it was written, but the Lutheran Church has nevertheless acquired a large musical heritage. It is rich in all four areas of church music: chant, hymnody, choral music, organ music.

The Lutheran chorale has been regarded as best expressing the spirit of Lutheran worship. A great part of the Lutheran heritage in music, choral as well as instrumental, is based on the chorales of the Lutheran Church. The singing of hymns is an integral part of Lutheran corporate worship, and the Lutheran Church has and uses hymn versions of the various parts of the liturgy (e. g., Agnus Dei — O Christ, Thou Lamb of God; Gloria in Excelsis — All Glory Be to God on High; Nunc Dimittis — In Peace and Joy I Now Depart; Sanctus — Isaiah, Mighty Seer in Days of Old; etc.).

Distinctions between church music, concert, secular, and folk music were rarely, if ever, made until the 16th century, when the Reformed groups and the Council of Trent brought about the cleavage. Calvin and Zwingli held that the texts of Reformed hymnody be only the words of Scripture, notably the Psalter, though they granted that these could be versified, as was done by Marot and Beza. The Puritans and Pietists followed principles similar to those of Calvin and Zwingli. The Roman Catholic Church, the Eastern Orthodox Church, and the Anglican Church are other denominations which have established outstanding and distinctive schools of music.

While Pope Gregory the Great, Emperor Charlemagne, and others had established that the Gregorian plainchant * was the official chant music of the Roman Catholic Church, the Council of Trent resolved that Palestrina's music was to serve as the ideal type of ecclesiastical choral music and that composers of the Roman Catholic Church were to write their sacred choral music in the Palestrina style and idiom. Although the Motu Proprio (1903) of Pope Pius X hesitated to enforce this restriction, it nevertheless regarded Palestrina's style as the ideal type of churchly choral music, confirmed that the Gregorian plainchant, as edited by Solesmes monks, is the official chant music of the Church, and discouraged the use of instrumental music in the Roman Mass. While the Lutheran church choir is a part of the congregation, the choirs of the Roman Catholic Church are a lower clergy and point to the hierarchical character of Roman Catholicism. WEB

Guido Adler, Handbuch der Musikgeschichte, Frankfurt a. M., 1924; Heinrich Alt, Der christliche Cultus, Berlin, 1851; Friedrich Blume, Die evangelische Kirchenmusik, Potsdam, 1931; Manfred Bukofzer, Music in the Baroque Era, New York, 1947; Walter E. Buszin, "The Doctrine of the Universal Priesthood and Its Influence upon the Liturgies and Music of the Lutheran Church," Valparaiso University Pamphlet Series, No. 10, Valparaiso, Ind., 1946; Walter E. Buszin, "The Genius of Lutheran Corporate Worship," CTM, April, 1950; Edward Dickinson, Music in the History of the Western Church, New York, 1923; Winfred Douglas, Church Music in History and Practice, New York, 1937; Werner Gosslau, Die religioese Haltung in der Reformationsmusik, Kassel, 1933; Eduard E. Koch, Geschichte des Kirchenlieds und Kirchengesangs, Stuttgart, 1867—76; S. Kuemmerle, Encyklopaedie der evangelischen Kirchenmusik, Guetersloh, 1888; Paul Henry Lang, Music in Western Civilization, New York, 1941; Hugo Leichtentritt, Geschichte der Motette, Leipzig, 1908; Hugo Leichtentritt, Music, History and Ideas, Cambridge, Mass., 1938; R. Freiherr von Liliencron, Liturgisch-musikalische Geschichte der evangelischen Gottesdienste von 1523—1700, Schleswig, 1893; Emil Naumann, The History of Music, translated from German, London; Paul Nettl, Luther and Music, Philadelphia, 1948; Hans Preuss, Martin Luther der Kuenstler, Guetersloh, 1931; Johannes Rautenstrauch, Luther und die Pflege der kirchlichen Musik in Sachsen, Leipzig, 1907; Gustave Reese, Music in the Middle Ages, New York, 1940; Arnold Schering, "Die musikalische Ausgestaltung des evangelischen Gottesdienstes" in Eger-Ficker, Evangelischer Gottesdienst kirchliche Kunst, Halle, 1924; Ludwig Schoeberlein, Schatz des liturgischen Chor- und Gemeindegesangs, Goettingen, 1868—80; Theobald Schrems, Die Geschichte des Gregorianischen Gesanges in den protestantischen Got-

tesdiensten, Freiburg, 1930; Johannes Schuberth, *Das Wechselverhaeltnis von Choral und Orgelchoral im 16. und 17. Jahrhundert,* Kassel, 1931; G. Wauchope Stewart, *Music in the Church,* London, 1914; Arno Werner, *Vier Jahrhunderte im Dienste der Kirchenmusik,* Leipzig, 1933; Carl von Winterfeld, *Der evangelische Kirchengesang,* Leipzig, 1843 to 1847.

Mynster, Jakob Peter (1775—1854). Lutheran divine. B. and d. at Copenhagen. Studied there. Pastor on the island of Zealand, 1802; chaplain at the Church of Our Lady in Copenhagen, 1812; *Privatdozent* in the theological seminary there, 1813; court preacher, 1826; bishop of Zealand, 1834. He opposed Grundtvig and religious liberalism, publishing numerous sermons. Kierkegaard, at one time his student, later opposed his teaching.

Mysos, Demetrius (1519—70). Deacon of the Eastern Orthodox Church; sent to Wuerttemberg by his church for the purpose of becoming acquainted with Protestantism; became a close friend of Melanchthon.

Mysteries. Plays performed during the Middle Ages by guilds of laymen before the doors of cathedrals. Originally mysteries concentrated on the dramatic presentation of the life of Christ, but later the term was also applied to the dramatization of Old Testament stories and saints' lives.

Mystic Shrine. See *Freemasonry,* 3.

Mystical Interpretation. See *Exegesis,* 3, 5.

Mystical Union. The spiritual relationship established between the Christian and his Savior by the indwelling of the Triune God, specifically the Holy Ghost, in the heart of the believer, according to which the Spirit of adoption is sent into the hearts of the children of God (Gal. 4:6; Rom. 8:15), whereby they are sealed and have been given the earnest of their redemption (2 Cor. 1:22; Eph. 1:13 f.), also wisdom and revelation in the knowledge of their Savior (Eph. 1:17). This condition is established by the gift of faith in the heart, which should immediately be a living, fruitful agent in bringing about good works and in particular also consciousness of the power of God in the heart and life of each Christian. It is necessary that this consciousness be cultivated constantly, by an earnest study of the Word of God, by frequent attendance at the Lord's Table, by earnest participation in prayer both private and in the public assembly of the Christian congregation. The mystical union is to be distinguished from false mysticism.*

Mysticism. A. The goal of mysticism is the alleged intuitive and emotional contact with the Absolute ("that which is," "the Good," "God," and numerous other ultimate spiritual values). In its practical aspects it is the attempt to apperceive, utilize, and enjoy ultimate values.

The word "mysticism" (derived from the G. *mystikos,* "to be dumb," used in connection with the mystery religions) has been applied to a wide range of phenomena in modern times (demonology, magic, dreaminess, weird experiences, occultism, certain *Weltanschauungen,* etc.). Three types of mystics have been distinguished: 1) contemplative mystics; 2) personal mystics; 3) nature mystics.

When analyzed psychologically, certain steps in the mystic method may be distinguished, which, with variations, are found in Oriental and Occidental mysticism, Christian and non-Christian. These are: 1) freeing oneself from wrong; 2) freeing oneself of the *phantasmata* of the world; 3) departure into the realm of the pure through contemplation and yearning; 4) the mystic view or experience. Thus mysticism is not so much a doctrine as a method of thought — a reaching for the Infinite through methods of reasoning and attempted direct contemplation. The word "contemplation" is frequently used for mystic experience in pre-Renaissance Western writers.

While a relationship often exists in the methods of various mysticisms, the ultimate realities which mystics strove to realize differed. For St. Francis the absolute good was the incarnate Jesus, for Bernard the "Logos," in the mysticism evolved from Plato "the good Creator," "pattern of good," "reality," "that which gives truth to the objects of knowledge." Other realities are claimed by the mysticism of Taoism, Yoga, Sufism, and other Oriental cults.

Luther, in his early period, valued certain mystics, edited the *German Theology,* and commended the work of Tauler. John Staupitz, Luther's friend, was a mystic. Luther's system, however, centered in the external Word of God and its doctrine of justification. He condemned the mysticism of Carlstadt,

Anabaptists, Caspar Schwenkfeld, and others.

B. Considered historically, Christian mysticism is the cultivation of the consciousness of the presence of God, or the knowledge of God and intercourse with God, through internal light and the immediate operation of grace, in opposition to revealed faith, on the one hand, and speculative rational knowledge, on the other. A mystic is a person who claims to have, to a greater or less degree, such an experience of God, one not merely based and centered on an accepted belief and practice, but on what the person concerned regards as firsthand personal knowledge. Some writers insist that some of the outstanding teachers of the Church were mystics, such as Paul, John the Apostle, and Luther. That is true only in the sense that in these men, and in others, the mystical union* presented a vivid and powerful reality, according to which St. Paul could write: "I live, yet not I, but Christ liveth in me." Gal. 2:20. "I can do all things through Christ, which strengtheneth me." Phil. 4:13. — But the term mysticism, in its fantastic sense, is applied to that subjective state of mind according to which some people have been said to become spiritually, and even physically, united with the Godhead. It is in this sense that history speaks of great mystics. Dionysius the Areopagite was subject to such a fantastic form of mysticism; so also the German abbess and prophetess St. Hildegarde (1098—1179), the Scotch scholar Richard of St. Victor (d. about 1173), from whom all medieval mystics received their inspiration, and above all St. Bernard of Clairvaux (1091—1153), to whom a constructive or objective form of mysticism is generally ascribed. Among the Franciscan mystics there is St. Francis himself (1182—1226), as well as the poet Jacopone da Todi and the pious Angela of Foligno. In England there

were Richard Rolle (d. 1349), Walter Hilton (d. 1396), and Julian of Norwich (d. after 1413). In Germany and in the Low Countries we have Meister Eckhart (ca. 1250—1328), Heinrich Suso (ca. 1295 to 1365), Tauler (ca. 1300 to 1361), and Ruysbroeck (1293—1381), together with the author of German Theology, of which Luther thought very highly. Among woman mystics we have particularly Catherine of Siena (1347 to 1380), Catherine of Genoa (1447—1510), and Teresa (1515—82).

Leading mystics of the 19th and early 20th century were the Quaker John William Rowntree, (1868—1905), Lucie - Christine (1844 — 1908), and Charles de Foucauld (1858—1916).

In the 20th century interest in mysticism has been revived by authors like Friedrich von Huegel, Dean W. R. Inge, William James, Rufus M. Jones, and Evelyn Underhill. EL (A)

C. A. Bennet, A Philosophical Study of Mysticism, Yale University Press, 1923; W. K. Fleming, Mysticism in Christianity, Scott, London, 1913; E. C. Butler, Western Mysticism, Constable, London, 1922; E. Renan, Nouvelles etudes d'histoire religieuse, Colman Levy, Paris, 1884; Margaret Smith, An Introduction to the History of Mysticism, Macm., New York, 1930; A. Godferneaux, "Sur la psychologie du mysticisme," Revue Philosophique, L III: 156 ff. (the French were especially interested in the psychology of mysticism, cf. works of H. Delacroix); H. Hanse, "Gott Haben," in der Antike und im fruehen Christentum, Toepelmann, Berlin, 1939; Rufus Jones, New Studies in Mystical Religion, Macm., New York, 1927; W. R. Inge, Christian Mysticism, Methuen, London, 1899; The Philosophy of Plotinus, Longmans Green, 1929; E. Underhill, Mysticism, Matthew, London, 1911; The Essentials of Mysticism, Dutton, New York, 1920; writings of men mentioned above; R. Otto, Mysticism East and West.

N

Nabu. See Babylonians, Religion of, 1.

Nachtenhoefer, Kaspar Friedrich (1624—85). Studied at Leipzig; diaconus, later pastor at Meeder, near Coburg; pastor at Coburg in 1671; wrote: "Kommst du nun, Jesu, vom Himmel herunter auf Erden"; "Dies ist die Nacht, da mir erschienen."

Naegeli, Hans Georg (1773—1836). Swiss composer of folk songs and choral music and a music publisher (Zurich). He published works by Bach, Handel, Beethoven, and others; in 1828 appeared his Christliches Gesangbuch fuer oeffentlichen Gottesdienst und haeusliche Erbauung. Naegeli had little appreciation for the great music of the Church, and hence he and Justus Thibaut (1774—1840), the German champion of the Palestrina revival, attacked each other in violent controversy.

Naesman, Gabriel. Swedish Luth. pastor who served in America (1743 to 1751) and participated in the founding of the Pennsylvania Ministerium.

Naether, Karl Gustav Theodor. B. Sept. 14, 1866, at Bautzen, Germany; d. Feb. 13, 1904, at Krishnagiri, India; Leipzig missionary to India 1887; separated from Leipzig Mission for reasons of conscience in 1893; joined Lutheran Missouri Synod; visited the United States in company with F. Mohn and was commissioned as the first missionary to India of the Missouri Synod in 1894; organized Krishnagiri Station, Salem District, Madras State.

Nanino, Giovanni Maria (ca. 1545 to 1607). Composer of the Roman Catholic Church who sought to perpetuate the ideals established by Palestrina in church music. His work as a composer is important. He is not to be confused with his younger brother, Giovanni Bernardino (ca. 1560—1623), whose aims were similar to those of his older brother.

Nantes, Edict of. See *Edict of Nantes.*

Narses. See *Schools, Early Christian.*

Narthex. See *Architecture, Ecclesiastical,* 7.

Nasmith, David (1799—1839). Scottish philanthropist; founded the Glasgow City Mission in 1826 and established missions in the principal cities of England, Ireland, France, and the United States; the London City Mission in 1835.

Nast, William (1807—99). B. in Stuttgart, Wuerttemberg; came to America in 1828; Methodist minister in 1835; formed first German society of Methodist Episcopal Church; d. at Cincinnati; editor of *Christliche Apologete;* author.

Natal. A province in the Union of South Africa within the British Empire. Area: 35,284 sq. mi.; population: 2,052,000, inclusive of native Africans, chiefly of Zulu stock. Seat of the Norwegian Schreuder Mission.

National Association of Evangelicals for United Action. See *Union Movements,* 12; *Teachers,* E.

National Baptist Convention. See *Baptist Bodies,* 10.

National Baptist Evangelical Life and Soul Saving Assembly of the U. S. A. See *Baptist Bodies,* 29

National Bible Society of Scotland. See *Bible Societies,* 4.

National Christian Association. An organization which is opposed to secret societies. The movement for such an organization started in the City Hall, Aurora, Ill., in Oct., 1867. A national meeting was held at Pittsburgh, Pa., 1868, and representatives of seventeen denominations were enrolled. At this time the "National Association of Christians Opposed to Secret Societies" was formed as a non-sectarian organization. In 1874 it was incorporated as "The National Christian Association," articles having been filed with the Secretary of State of Illinois and a certificate of incorporation issued. Hon. Philo Carpenter of Chicago, one of the prime movers in this opposition to the lodge, who at that time had given more money to aid in the work than any other man, offered to the association a home, "so that its work of removing the obstacles to the coming of the kingdom of God might go on." Charles A. Blanchard, president of Wheaton College (d. 1925), was the first agent and lecturer (1870—72). The *Christian Cynosure* was started in 1868 and is the official organ. The office is in Chicago, Ill.

National Church. See *Finland, Lutheranism in,* 8; *Finnish Lutherans in America,* 3.

National Conference of Christians and Jews. Organized in 1928 to create closer relations between Christians and Jews. Headquarters: 381 Fourth Ave., New York, N.Y.

National Conference of Social Workers. See *American Association of Social Workers.*

National Council of the Churches of Christ in the United States. See *Union Movements,* 13.

National Council of Congregational Churches. See *Congregational and Christian Churches.*

National Councils. See *Councils and Synods,* 1, 5.

National Covenant. See *Presbyterian Confessions,* 1.

National David Spiritual Temple of Christ Church Union. See *Holiness Bodies, 2.*

National Grange. Like the Railroad Brotherhoods, the agricultural trades union known as the National Grange is a society based on occupational interests; and although working with an elaborate ritual it is not a lodge in the strict sense of the term. The two avowed purposes of the order are industrial benefits and the social improvement of its members. It has exercised considerable influence, especially in promoting co-operation among farmers. Politics are strictly kept out of the order. In its ritual of seven degrees there are the signs, passwords, and allegorical play acting characteristic of secret societies in America. The following is one of the typical obligations: "I hereby solemnly renew my obligation of secrecy and fidelity, taken in the first degree of this order; and further promise upon my sacred honor to keep the secrets, fulfill the obligations, and obey the injunctions of this second degree, and aid my brothers and sisters in doing the same." In all degrees pledges are made to observe the precepts and injunctions and not to reveal the secrets. As for participation in the ritual, the headquarters stated: "Through the earnest efforts of Brother Goss and others, the following amendment was placed in Grange Law: A member cannot be required to do anything in conflict with his religious convictions, and entire freedom of conscience is assured to all members in matters of prayer." Initiation on application only, without the ceremonial, has not been conceded by the order. Since the organization, however, is entirely devoted to the agricultural program of our country and contains no moral, religious, or spiritual goals, hence does not endeavor to establish a religious community based on ritualistic teaching, the Grange cannot be classified as a lodge in the exact sense of the term, nor its members as "lodge members." Membership (1952) was 850,000. TG

National Holiness Movement. See *Holiness Bodies, 1.*

National Intercollegiate Christian Council. See *Students, Spiritual Care of, A.*

National Lutheran Commission for Soldiers' and Sailors' Welfare. See *National Lutheran Council.*

National Lutheran Council. 1. The National Lutheran Council was formally organized as a common agency for nine Lutheran bodies in Chicago, Sept. 6, 1918. Co-operative efforts to promote and publicize the celebration of the 400th anniversary of the Reformation in 1917 gave incentive to its organization. The immediate result was to organize the Lutheran Bureau in November, 1917, as an agency to issue Lutheran publicity. During the same year the National Lutheran Commission for Soldiers' and Sailors' Welfare was organized to give spiritual ministration to the men in the Armed Forces. Thirteen Lutheran bodies co-operated in this ministry. As a result of their experiences in these emergency measures of co-operation some of the leaders were convinced that a permanent agency to represent common interests of Lutherans in America ought to be formed.

2. On July 17, 1918, fifteen representatives of various Lutheran bodies met in Harrisburg, Pa., to discuss the advisability and feasibility of organizing a national council of the Lutheran churches. A committee, which was appointed to formulate plans, met in Pittsburgh, Aug. 1, 1918, and reported to a group of representatives of eight Lutheran bodies at Chicago, Sept. 6, 1918, when the organization was effected. The groups represented were the General Synod, the General Council, the Joint Synod of Ohio, the Synod of Iowa and Other States, the Augustana Synod, the Norwegian Lutheran Church of America, the Norwegian Lutheran Free Church, and the Danish Lutheran Church. Delegates of the United Synod, South, were not present, but that body soon joined the original eight in the Council.

3. No formal constitution was adopted, but the purposes were set forth as follows:

"(1) True and uniform statistical information concerning the Lutheran Church in America.

"(2) Publicity in all matters that require common utterance by the Lutheran Church.

"(3) Representation of our Church in its relation to entities outside of itself, without prejudice to the confessional basis of any participating body, as well as bringing home to the Church a consciousness of general and specific needs for attention and action.

"(4) Activities dealing with, or the creation of agencies to deal with, the problems arising out of war and other emergencies where no such common Lutheran agencies now exist, and to co-ordinate, harmonize, and unify the activities of existing agencies.

"(5) The co-ordination of activities and agencies of the Lutheran Church in America for the solution of problems arising from social, economic, intellectual, or other conditions or changes affecting religious life and consciousness.

"(6) The fostering of true Christian loyalty and the maintenance of a righteous relation between Church and State as separate entities with correlated yet distinctly defined functions."

4. The termination of the war, Nov. 11, 1918, two months after the Council was organized, presented a new stupendous task — the reconstruction of prostrated Lutheran churches in Europe. Lutheran World Service, which was launched by the Council to meet this emergency in behalf of the co-operating churches, resulted in extraordinary success and was continued on a large scale until 1925. As a result of the fraternal contacts of this ministry of love, the Lutheran World Convention was organized in Eisenach, Germany, in 1923.

5. In 1926 revised regulations for the conduct of the Council were adopted.

6. For more than a decade the Council operated under these regulations. Its work was departmentalized into Administration, Publicity Bureau, and Reference Library and Statistics. In 1939 it was decided to establish a Department of Welfare to promote and assist Lutheran welfare agencies and organizations.

7. The emergency problems produced by World War II emphasized the necessity for enlarging the scope and activity of the Council. A new constitution went into effect January, 1945, after the approval by the co-operating bodies. No change was made in the basis which specifies the acceptance of the Holy Scriptures as the Word of God and the Unaltered Augsburg Confession and Luther's Catechism as a true exposition thereof. The purposes and objectives are the following:

a. To witness for the Lutheran Church on matters which require an expression of common faith, ideals, and program.

b. To bring to the attention of the participating bodies matters which in its judgment may require utterance or action on their part.

c. To represent Lutheran interests in America in matters which require common action, before

(1) National and State governments.

(2) Organized bodies and movements outside the Lutheran Church.

d. To emphasize the continuing importance of a right relation between Church and State.

e. To further the interests and the work of the Lutheran Churches in America.

f. To undertake and carry on such work as may be authorized by the participating bodies in fields where co-ordination or joint activity may be desirable and feasible, such as publicity, statistics, welfare work, missions, education, student work, and other fields.

g. To take the necessary steps to meet emergencies requiring common action, each participating body to determine the extent of its co-operation in emergency work.

h. To undertake additional work with the specific consent of the participating bodies.

8. The bodies which previously participated in the Council and approved the constitution are members. They are:

The United Lutheran Church in America, the Evangelical Lutheran Church, the American Lutheran Church, the Augustana Lutheran Church, the Lutheran Free Church, the United Evangelical Lutheran Church, the Danish Lutheran Church, and the Finnish Lutheran Church. Any other Lutheran body "may be admitted to participation in the work of the Council following the presentation in writing to the officers of the Council of its official declaration of its approval of the constitution, and its desire and purpose to participate." Representation is on the basis of one to each one hundred thousand confirmed members, provided, that each participating body shall be entitled to at least one representative.

9. The work of the Council is performed through divisions, departments, commissions, and bureaus. The following are functioning:

Division of Public Relations — Publicity, Statistics, Radio.

Division of Welfare, including a service to hospitalized veterans.

Division of American Missions — Ministry to war housing areas, rural church life, Christian approach to Jews.

Division of Student Service — Ministry to Lutheran students at State and secular universities.

Commission on Younger Churches and Orphaned Missions.

Bureau of Service to Military Personnel.

Lutheran Service Commission.

European Desk.

Lutheran Resettlement Service.

10. Arrangements to have the Council act as the national committee for the Lutheran World Federation were completed in 1947. RHL

National Lutheran Radio Week. See *Radio Stations, Religious,* 4.

National Red Cross. See *Red Cross.*

National School Association. See *Teachers,* E.

National Socialism. See *Socialism.*

National Union of Christian Schools. See *Teachers,* E.

National Youth Administration. See *Social Work,* D 1.

Nationalist Veterans of World War II. See *Veterans' Organizations.*

Natorp, Paul (1854—1924). German philosopher; prof. at Marburg; he implemented the social ideals of Pestalozzi from the philosophical side; neo-Kantian; also a composer.

Natura Naturans, Natura Naturata. Terms used by Averroes and later philosophers. The former designated the Creator, the latter the creature.

Natural History of the Bible. A study of the fauna and flora of the Bible, together with the climate conditions and other features which affect plant and animal life in Bible lands.

Natural Knowledge of God. See *Apologetics; God.*

Natural Law. 1. This term has been used in a variety of senses and more or less synonymously with "natural justice" *(ius naturae, ius naturale),* the "law of nations" *(ius gentium),* and "natural rights."

2. Although the concept of natural law was first developed by the early Stoics, the term itself *(lex naturae)* was originated by the later (Roman) Stoics. Over against those who held that all laws among men are but the product of utility and convention, the Stoics, following the lead of Socrates and Aristotle, asserted that behind all the changing laws of man is the changeless law of nature. They believed that nature has a rational basis and that human reason is a reflection

of this rationality. They concluded that, by thinking rationally, man can know not only what is but also what ought to be. The content of natural law, they believed, is deducible from those rules of conduct which are similar among widely separated peoples. This concept of natural law was further developed by the Roman jurists and was embodied in the Institutes of Justinian. Although Roman jurists considered natural law the basis of the civil law, they rarely put it into practice. To be sure, they called upon it to supplement the civil law where that was deficient, but they never invoked it to invalidate laws such as those governing property rights and slavery which were in conflict with natural law.

3. The Fathers of the Church, particularly the Latin Fathers, some of whom were deeply influenced by Roman law, shared this concept of natural law. But they identified it with the doctrine of the primitive natural revelation of God in the heart of man. They regarded the current conception of natural law as evidence of the truth of St. Paul's utterance on this subject in Romans 2. To the Fathers, then, natural law was the innate knowledge of right and wrong.

4. Although this concept was elaborated upon by medieval thinkers, especially by Thomas Aquinas, it was not fundamentally modified by them. Thomas divided all law into four classes: 1) eternal law, which exists only in the mind of God; 2) divine law, which is a part of eternal law and which has been directly revealed to men; 3) natural law, which is discernible by human reason and the knowledge of which has been moving from the imperfect to the perfect; 4) human law, which is the implementation of natural law within the changing situations of life. But in the Middle Ages, as in earlier, pagan times, such thinking remained essentially speculative; it had little or no practical effect upon the development of law and government.

5. It was not until modern times that the concept of natural law was implemented by political action. In fact, it was this concept more than any other which supplied the philosophical justification for the great revolutionary movements which have characterized Western civilization since the seventeenth century. The Protestant Reformation generally accepted the patristic view of natural law. Luther and Melanchthon were followers of Augustine

in this respect; they regarded the Decalog as the codification, given by direct revelation of the natural law. But the Renaissance, especially in its humanistic aspects, de-emphasized the divine and overemphasized the purely rational character of natural law. As a result, in the "Age of Reason" the concept of natural law was pressed into service as the ideological basis of "natural rights," the "social compact," constitutional government based on the consent of the governed, and the right of revolution. In one form or another this is the view of Locke, Rousseau, Paine, and Jefferson. The most typical and politically effective expressions of this view are the American Declaration of Independence and the French Declaration of Rights. Early nineteenth-century individualistic, liberal, democratic thought and action were largely the fruits of this concept.

6. In recent times the concept of natural law has been under increasing attack, especially from two quarters: 1) the historical school of jurisprudence conceives of law as nothing more than the product of historical development; 2) positivist social scientists regard law as nothing more than the result of personal and social relationships. Of late, however, the concept of natural law is being revived by writers who profess to have rediscovered the spiritual and teleological character of the universe.

7. In Lutheran theology natural law is a remnant of the knowledge with which man was created. Because man's awareness of natural law had become obscured by sin, God gave the Decalog to man and elaborated upon it in the Holy Scriptures. In accordance with the principle of *Sola Scriptura*, the law from within (subjective morality) must be interpreted in the light of the law from without (objective morality). WB

George Whitecross Paton, *A Textbook of Jurisprudence* (Oxford, 1946); R. W. Carlyle and A. J. Carlyle, *A History of Medieval Political Theory in the West*, Vols. I—III (New York, 1903); Georg Stoeckhardt, *Commentar ueber den Roemerbrief* (St. Louis, 1907).

Natural Rights. See *Natural Law.*

Naturalism. A term which has a variety of meanings, corresponding to the different senses in which "nature" and "natural" may be used. In its usual modern meaning, in theology and philosophy, it is the point of view according to which no consideration is given to anything "spiritual" or "supernatural," that is, to anything that goes beyond experience. It asserts that there is no reality except matter and that all, even psychical, phenomena may be explained through natural sciences, especially chemistry and physics, and that their ultimate basis is matter and motion. Such a view leads to materialism * and atheism * and hardly differs from positivism.* In theology, furthermore, naturalism asserts that only nature and not revelation can be the source of religious truth and denies everything miraculous and supernatural and consequently all fundamentals of Christianity. In ethics, naturalism is the doctrine that nature and natural impulses are the highest guide of man in moral conduct. Such a view has been variously developed in Stoicism, as well as by Rousseau, Tolstoy, Nietzsche, and is always hostile to Christianity, which finds the supreme rule of conduct in divine revelation, and may lead to such extremes as the elevation of every personal desire to a moral law, contempt of marriage, glorification of the nude. In art, naturalism denotes the decadent tendency which avoids all idealization and portrays only reality, whether beautiful or otherwise; in literature, a similar tendency which pictures men and circumstances true to reality, often emphasizing the immoral, as is done by Zola, Maupassant, Sudermann, Halbe.

Nat Worship. See *Burma.*

Naumann, Emil (1827—88). A pupil of F. Mendelssohn-Bartholdy, wrote in *Illustrierte Musikgeschichte* (1880 to 1885), which has been translated into English by F. Praeger and edited by Sir F. A. Gore Ouseley (London). This work has merit, but it is, nevertheless, a product of the Romantic era, which sought to interpret history on the basis of Romantic standards and practices and thus failed to understand the nature of music of preceding eras. Naumann was also a composer and editor; his *Psalmen auf alle Sonn- und Festtage des evang. Kirchenjahrs* were published by Bote & Bock as part of its *Musica Sacra* series and enjoyed wide use within the Lutheran Church of Germany.

Naumann, Justus H. (1865—1917). Pupil of Stoeckhardt (Planitz); graduated at Fort Wayne and St. Louis; Lutheran pastor in South Dakota; joined the Minnesota Synod in 1895;

nine years Superintendent of Missions; President of Minnesota Synod, 1912—17.

Naumburg, Convention of, 1561. Lutheran princes with their theologians reaffirmed the Augsburg Confession of 1530 in order to be able to enjoy also in the future the concessions of the Augsburg Religious Peace. The Preface declared the substantial agreement of the Augsburg Confession with the *Variata* (the changed edition) of 1540, and hence the Dukes Ulrich of Mecklenburg and John Frederick of Saxony withheld their signatures. The convention declined the invitation to the Council of Trent, since the Pope had no right to call a council, only the Emperor. See *Lutheran Confessions*, C 1.

Naval and Military Bible Society. See *Bible Society*, 3.

Nave. See *Architecture, Ecclesiastical*.

Navigator Islands. See *Samoa*.

Naville, Edouard Henri. Swiss Egyptologist; b. 1844 at Geneva; since 1891 professor there; for many years connected with Egypt Exploration Fund; wrote numerous works on Egyptology, also in relation to Old Testament problems. D. 1927.

Naylor, John (1838—97). Showed musical ability as choirboy; organist at Scarborough; later, organist and choirmaster at York Minster and conductor of York Musical Society; wrote four cantatas and many anthems and chants.

Nazarene, Church of. See *Church of the Nazarene*.

Nazarenes. A Judaizing Christian sect, which united the belief in the divinity and Messiahship of Jesus with the observance of the Mosaic Ceremonial Law (Sabbath, Circumcision, etc.), without, however, rejecting the authority of Paul and the validity of Gentile Christianity. According to Epiphanius (fourth century) they dated their settlement in Coele-Syria and the Decapolis from the flight of the Jewish Christians from Jerusalem to Pella immediately before the siege, A. D. 70. They are therefore in all probability the direct but degenerate representatives of the Jewish Christians of the first century. See *Ebionites*.

Nazarenes. An informal association of artists existing in Rome at the beginning of the 19th century, with Overbeck as their leader; prominent among them Philip Veit, 1793—1877 ("Simeon in the Temple"), noted for his fine line work, and E. Steinle, 1810 to 1886, with a tendency toward symbolism (frescoes in Cathedral of Cologne).

Ne Temere. The Council of Trent ruled that all marriages not performed by the parish priest were null and void. In 1908 the *Ne Temere* decree restricted this ruling to apply to Catholics only. Rome now teaches that the marriage of two non-Catholics performed by any authorized person is a valid marriage. However, Rome considers all baptized heretics who are "invincibly ignorant" as members of the "soul" of the church and therefore subject to Canon Law. According to the *Ne Temere* decree the marriage of such a baptized heretic to an unbaptized person is considered invalid. The Code of 1918, however, rules that all marriages, not only between nonbaptized persons, but also between a baptized heretic and a nonbaptized person, are valid. Mixed marriages, that is, marriages between a Catholic and a baptized Protestant, are still "gravely forbidden" and constitute a mortal sin. A dispensation from this "sin" can be obtained only if the non-Catholic party promises to adhere to the doctrine of the indissolubility of the marriage bond; not to interfere in the least with the Catholic party's religion; to have all children baptized and educated solely in the Roman Catholic Church; to observe the Church's teaching regarding birth control; and to submit to no other marriage ceremony besides that performed by the priest. The Catholic party must agree to endeavor to bring the non-Catholic into the Roman Catholic Church.

Neale, John Mason (1818—66). Translator of Latin and Greek hymns into English, served as warden of Sackville College, East Grinstead (England), during the last twenty years of his life; here he devoted much of his time to literary and scholarly pursuits. His translations, though not always true to the original, must be regarded as classic English masterpieces; many are paraphrases rather than translations. His *Essays on Liturgiology and Church History* (1863) still enjoys widespread use and esteem.

S. W. Duffield, *The Latin Hymn Writers and Their Hymns*, New York, 1889; *The Hymnal 1940 Companion*, Commission of the Protestant Episcopal Church, New York, 1949; Eleanor A. Towle, *John Mason Neale,* New York, 1906.

Neander, Joachim Neumann (1650 to 1680). A native of Bremen, regarded as the outstanding poet of the Reformed Church in Germany. Although profligate in his youth, he later became an ardent adherent of Phil. Jakob Spener. His collection *Glaub- und Liebes-Uebung* of 1679 contained his 57 hymns, a number of which were adopted readily by the Lutheran Church. The well-known hymn "Praise to the Lord, the Almighty" was written by him as was also "Wunderbarer Koenig." Neander wrote about twenty original hymn tunes.

Neander, Johann August Wilhelm (1789—1850). Of Hebrew descent; was strongly influenced by Schleiermacher's *Reden ueber die Religion;* 1812 professor at Berlin; his chief work: *Allgemeine Geschichte der christlichen Religion und Kirche.* Neander belongs to the school of pietistic re-awakening and exerted great personal influence in the Church. His influence upon the students of the university was especially marked.

Nebraska, German Synod of. See *United Lutheran Church, Synods of,* 14.

Nebraska Synod. John Hoeckendorf, formerly officer in the German army, member of P. Geyer's church, Lebanon, Wis., was a delegate to the meeting at which the Missouri Synod was organized. He took exception to a statement in the introduction to the proposed constitution and eventually, supported by some hundred families, divided his home church, becoming pastor of the seceders. 1865 to 1866, after the ground had been scouted, 50 to 60 families decided to establish new homes in Nebraska, taking their flocks and traveling in prairie schooners. They chose the region of which Norfolk later was the center, though then 75 miles from the nearest railroad. Hoeckendorf remained their pastor until his death, 1878. Having satisfied themselves on the doctrinal position of the Wisconsin Synod, the Norfolk church called Michael Pankow as their pastor on recommendation of Dr. A. F. Ernst. After three years Pankow joined the Wisconsin Synod, his church having by that time overcome its aversion to synodical connections. He soon organized other congregations and formed a conference, which was joined by a

number of other congregations founded in southern Nebraska by Jul. Kaiser. The Nebraska Conference had been organized as a District of the Wisconsin Synod for three years, when it received authority to establish a separate (District) synod of the Joint Synod, 1904, at Clatonia. As such it emerged from the reorganization of 1917 without any changes, territorial or otherwise, always having supported the institutions of the older synod.

Nebraska, Synod of. See *United Lutheran Church, Synods of,* 16.

Necrology. A list of the dead used in connection with prayers for the dead on All Souls' Day.

Necromancy. Consulting the spirits of departed persons (1 Sam. 28:3-19). Necromancers pretended to be able by incantations to call up the spirits of the dead and consult with them on the mysteries of the present and the future. This practice forbidden (Lev. 19:31; Deut. 18:11; Is. 8:19; 29:4. Cp. Luther IX:1603 ff.; *Trigl.,* p. 583, 12).

Nederlandsch Bijbelgenootschap. See *Bible Societies,* 4.

Negative Confession. See *Presbyterian Confessions,* 1.

Negro Missions. See *Missions, Lutheran Negro.*

Neitzel, Richard C. B. Sept. 8, 1875, in Pomerania, Germany; ed. Concordia Col., Milwaukee, Wis.; Concordia Seminary, St. Louis, grad. 1899; missionary in Oklahoma, 1899 to 1901; pastor: Kansas City, Kans., 1901—13; Summit, Ill., 1913—18; prof., Concordia Seminary, Springfield, Ill., 1918—51; secretary of Mo. Syn. Wartime Bureau, 1918; chairman of Mo. Synod's Catechism Committee. D. D. Concordia Sem., St. Louis, 1944. D. May 22, 1951.

Neo-Lutheranism. See *Luther Renaissance; Lutheran Theology after 1580,* 15.

Neo-Orthodoxy. A term applied to a movement in theology which opposes "modernism" or "liberalism" with its doctrine of an immanent God and the social gospel. The movement traces its origin to the thought of Kierkegaard,* Barth,* Brunner, and others. Niebuhr's dialectical concept of God (both transcendent and immanent), man, and history has aroused widespread interest in America. The term "neo" implies a new development of orthodoxy after a period of nationalism.

See references under *Barth, Karl; Kierkegaard; Switzerland, Contemporary Theology in;* Reinhold Niebuhr, *The Nature and Destiny of Man,* Scribner's (reviewed with evaluations of neo-orthodoxy in *CTM,* XIII: 156 ff.; XV: 640 ff.).

Neo-Platonism. A movement which sought to develop new thoughts from Platonic ideas. It was the last of the ancient schools of philosophy, set up as a rival to Christianity in the third century, attempting to adapt the ideas of Greek philosophy, together with Oriental conceptions, to the needs of the times. It teaches three successive grades of emanations from the Divine Being: intelligence, the world soul, and matter, the latter being evil, and lays stress upon asceticism as a means of liberating the individual soul from matter and restoring it to the Divinity. The best minds of the age shared in this movement. The traditional founder is Ammonius Saccas (d. 243) of Alexandria; but the chief expositor is his pupil Plotinus,* followed by Porphyry.* Though hostile to Christianity, it became, because of its asceticism and mystic character, a "bridge to Christianity" to some of its adherents, notably Origen and Augustine.

Neo-Scholasticism. A revival of the philosophical principles of Aristotle as developed by the Scholastics. This movement in the Roman Catholic Church was given impetus by the encyclical *Aeterni Patris.*

Neo-Thomism. A revival of the philosophy of Thomas Aquinas * and his followers, combining with certain doctrinal views a belief in the ultimate harmony of reason and faith and of the conclusions of philosophy with those of theology.

Nergal. See *Babylonians, Religion of,* 5.

Nero. See *Persecutions of Christians,* 3.

Nestle, Christopher Eberhard (1851 to 1913). Since 1898 prof. at the Evangelical seminary at Maulbronn, Wuerttemberg; belongs to the mediating school of theology; edited the *Greek New Testament* and wrote an *Introduction to the Greek New Testament.*

Nestorianism. 1. This movement takes its name from Nestorius,* whose false teaching in Christology, namely, that there was no communion of natures in the person of Christ and that Mary could not really be regarded as *theotokos* (mother of God), but *Christotokos* (mother of Christ), that Christ was the Son of God, the eternal Logos, in name only, stirred up a great deal of strife in the fifth century. The views of Nestorius were condemned by the Council of Ephesus, in 431, but his followers, known later as Nestorians, refused to accept the declaration of the council and set up an organization of their own. Breaking with the Monophysites, on the one hand, and with the Catholic churches of West Syria, on the other, they became a mighty church party, which was called after Nestorius and extended its missionary influence far into China.

2. The first extension of Nestorianism was from the eastern boundary of the Roman Empire into Persia. The movement was aided by the expulsion of the Nestorian teachers from the school at Edessa and by their settlement in Nisibis. From this school, as a center, the leaven spread throughout the Christian communities of the country. For some time afterwards the believers remained in outward connection with the Western churches, but the break with the Occidental Church came at the very end of the fifth century. This was done by Bebaeus II, and his successors followed his course also in this respect; for they placed Nestorians in all episcopal vacancies and eagerly sought to extend their domain in all directions. It was not long before Nestorianism was carried throughout Arabia and then toward the East; and there can be no doubt that not only China had many Christians of this type, but that India likewise was visited by the Nestorian missionaries. In spite of the persecutions of Turks and other enemies the Nestorians have managed to survive, their number in Kurdistan and Persia being about 150,000, in Chaldea (region in Asia on Euphrates River and Persian Gulf) 100,000, and in India 120,000.

Nestorius. 1. After 428 patriarch of Constantinople; objected to the term "mother of God" as applied to Mary and became a heretic in the doctrine of Christ.

2. The doctrine which Nestorius developed and to which he clung, although permitting himself an occasional lapse in the direction of a compromise with the orthodox party, stood out with peculiar force in the Christological con-

troversies of the fifth century. He taught that the incarnation did not consist in this, that the Son of God assumed true human nature in the womb of the Virgin Mary, but that through the meditation of the Holy Ghost Mary had given birth to a man who was in a peculiar and extraordianry sense an organ for the divinity, and that in this man the Logos had taken up His abode as in a temple. The union of the natures, therefore, was only moral. Nestorius conceded that Mary might be called a *Christotokos,* mother of Christ, but not a *theotokos,* mother of God.

Netherlands. 1. 12,868 sq. mi.; population, 10,200,280 (1952 est.). The conversion of Holland was begun under Dagobert I (628—638), continued by Willibrord, and completed by Charlemagne toward the end of the 8th century. The Reformation of the 16th century effected sweeping changes in this country, so that in the entire northwestern parts of the country Protestantism prevailed, Roman Catholicism having retained its foothold in the southern part. Among the Protestant churches the foremost is the *Reformed Church,* which took its rise at the beginning of the Reformation. Its doctrines and polity took form at the Synod of Dort (1619). It was not, however, until the Peace of Westphalia (1648) that the Reformed religion became the organized religion of the country, its adherents constituting the national Church. When William I became king in 1816, he called a general synod and offered to support the Church provided it would accept a constitution modified to suit his views. The Church complied, and the older strictly Presbyterian form of government was greatly modified. This constitution, accepted in 1816, is still the basis of the existing church order and the foundation of the "general regulations of the Reformed Church made in 1852." In 1857, under the influence of the Liberals and the Romanists, the government banished religious instruction from the schools, and in 1876 it changed the theological faculties in the universities into faculties of comparative religion. However, when rationalists secured these professorships, the orthodox party founded a Free Reformed University at Amsterdam in 1880. The same party has secured free schools all over Holland in which evangelical religion is taught. The public schools of Holland are non-confessional; but there are hundreds of private parochial schools supported by Protestants or Roman Catholics. Two considerable associations have been formed, one in 1860, another in 1877, to support and extend such schools.

2. *The Christian Reformed Church.* At the General Synod, 1816, a change in the subscription form for candidates aroused a great controversy. The question arose whether the standards of doctrine were authoritative *because* or *in so far as* they agreed with the Word of God. The Synod of 1835 wrote to every candidate to decide this for himself. In consequence of this change, as well as of oppressive measures, which interfered with the internal affairs of the Church, a secession was resolved upon by the evangelical party. The seceders organized the Christian Reformed Church, declaring that they did not wish to secede from the Church, but only from the bureaucratic administrative committee. Large multitudes soon joined them, and in 1836 their synodical meeting was held. These churches, which for a time suffered much persecution until they secured a legal standing, adhere to the doctrines and discipline of the Synod of Dort and thus are in agreement with the Reformed Church of America. In 1854 they established the Evangelical School at Kampen, and in 1879 higher education was provided for by the founding of the Free University of Amsterdam. In 1892 a union was effected between the Synod of the Christian Reformed Church and a certain provisional synod of Dutch Reformed churches which had originated in 1886. These united bodies style themselves "The Reformed Churches in the Netherlands" and have more than 700 churches.

3. *The Lutheran Church.* The Lutheran Church gained only minor importance in Holland. The first Lutheran congregation was established at Woerden; it adopted the Augsburg Confession in 1566. In 1605 a union was effected among seven Lutheran ministers, which in 1612 developed into the Lutheran Brotherhood. The last Lutheran synod under the Republic met in 1696. King William I, in 1818, gave the Evangelical Lutheran Church a new organization, which was modified in 1855 and 1859 so as to render the church independent of all state control. At first their ministers were all educated in Germany, but in 1816 a Lutheran seminary was founded in Amsterdam. Like other Protestant

bodies, also this Lutheran Church was affected by rationalism, and in 1791 a rupture occurred between the rationalists and those who insisted upon return to the old Confessions. This "old Lutheran Church" obtained legal standing in 1835 and legal confirmation in 1866. The sharp differences between the two bodies gradually subsided, and in 1874 they were reunited. The Evangelical Lutheran Church in Holland is divided into seven districts. Its seminary is connected with the University of Amsterdam. There are also churches styled the Evangelical Brotherhood at Zeist and Harlem, and German Evangelical churches at The Hague, Rotterdam, and Amsterdam.

4. *Baptists*. This body is often called "Mennonites," from Menno Simons. For a long time they had no central organization, but in 1650 an organization was effected. Afterwards, on account of doctrinal differences, a division occurred, the orthodox taking the name Zonists and the Liberals that of Lamists. In 1801 the two divisions reunited. This denomination has no common standard of doctrine, and Infant Baptism is rejected. In 1811 a general society was formed for the encouragement of theological education and for the support of the ministry among the poorer congregations. At the same time they enlarged the curriculum of their seminary, founded in 1731. All the congregations have perfect freedom in calling ministers and are independent as to government of their own affairs.

5. *Remonstrants*. This body dates from about 1618 and has for its aim the furtherance of the Gospel, while at the same time holding fast to freedom and toleration. The Church of Rotterdam is their principal church. The movement is not sound. See *Arminianism*.

6. *Roman Catholic Church*. Since the overthrow of the State Church in 1796, the Roman Church, with renewed interest, sought to regain the lost control. The hierarchy was established in 1853 with a great increase of priests. In the reconstituted hierarchy, Holland forms one province, divided into five dioceses.

7. *Missions*. Only very little missionary work was done by the Dutch in the 17th century among the natives of their extensive colonial possessions. Now and then a chaplain interested himself in the spiritual condition of the natives, but this cannot be said of most of them. As a rule, the trading companies exploited the people and opposed missions. In 1722 a colonial missionary seminary was organized at Leyden, but flourished only a short time. Not until the end of the 18th century was a missionary society organized. The oldest is "The Netherlands Missionary Society"(*Nederlandsch Zendelinggenootschap*), 1797. The first missionaries were sent to Ceylon, at that time a Dutch possession. Later, work was taken up in Java and the other Dutch dependencies. In 1826 Karl Friedrich Guetzlaff (b. July 8, 1803; d. Hong Kong, August 9, 1851) was sent to Batavia. Modern missions are listed under the names of countries.

Neudecker, Johann Christian Gotthold (1807—66). B. and d. at Gotha. Studied at Jena. Private scholar at Gotha, 1832; teacher, then rector at the Knabenbuergerschule there; second rector of the Garrison and Erfurt Vorstadtschule, 1855; director of the Gotha Buergerschule, 1860. Of his many writings those on the history of the Reformation are particularly noteworthy.

Neuendettelsau Missionary Society (*Gesellschaft fuer Innere und Aeussere Mission im Sinne der lutherischen Kirche*). Founded in 1849 in Neuendettelsau, Bavaria, by Pastor J. K. W. Loehe * with special reference to work among German immigrants in America and the American Indians. Later, work was begun in connection with the Lutheran Immanuel Synod in Australia among the natives in that country and in New Guinea, 1886. "The former work of the Mission in Australasia was transferred to the United Evangelical Lutheran Church of Australia by the Australian government in 1921, with the understanding that the Evangelical Lutheran Synod of Iowa and Other States (later American Lutheran Church) would assist in the work. The German missionaries in New Guinea remained at their stations after the society's administrative relationship ceased in 1914." Later Neuendettelsau took back the New Guinea mission.

When World War II broke out, 50 German missionaries and their families were removed from New Guinea and interned in Australia. The Lutheran World Federation, through the American Lutheran Council, sent a representative to confer with the government in Australia. The custody of the mission was given to the National Lutheran Council, which appointed the American

Lutheran Church to administer the field.

In addition to men supplied for New Guinea, the Neuendettelsau Society sent missionaries to Brazil, to the Ukraine, and for the diaspora (prior to World War II). It also developed an extensive inner missions program (deaconess home, mother houses, hospitals, etc.). See also under *Australia, New Guinea.*

Neukomm, Sigismund (1778—1858). Composer, organist, and concert pianist; toured in Sweden, France, Brazil, Russia, and England; wrote a prodigious number of compositions, including eight oratorios and numerous masses.

Neumann, Kaspar (1648—1715). Studied at Jena; chaplain of Prince Christian of Gotha; later held positions as pastor at Altenburg and Breslau; celebrated preacher; wrote: "Jesu, der du Tor' und Riegel"; "Gott, du hast in deinem Sohn."

Neumark, Georg (1621—81). Student of law at the University of Koenigsberg, and later secretary and librarian to the ducal court at Weimar, he is remembered today chiefly for his hymn "Wer nur den lieben Gott laesst walten."

Neumeister, Erdmann. B. May 12, 1671, at Uechteritz, ed. at Leipzig, entered the ministry, and held several pastorates and positions till in 1715 he accepted the appointment as pastor of St. James Church, Hamburg, where he died Aug. 18, 1756. Neumeister ranks high among the German hymn writers of the eighteenth century, not only for the number of his hymns, 650, but also for their abiding value. He was also an earnest and eloquent preacher, a staunch upholder of sound Lutheranism against Pietism and unionism. Not only a contemporary, but also an associate of J. S. Bach, he wrote the texts to some of the latter's cantatas. He also composed tunes for some of his hymns. It was his purpose to "preserve the simplicity of faith from the subjective novelties of this period."

Neve, J. L. (U. L. C.). B. 1865; ed. at Breklum and Kiel; ordained 1883; prof. in Chicago Seminary, 1887—92; Atchison Seminary, 1898—1909; since then at Springfield, O.; author of *Doctrinal Basis of General Synod; Free Church Compared with State Church; Brief History of the Lutheran Church in America; Church and Sects of Christendom,* 1940; 2d ed., 1944; *History of*

Christian Thought, Vol. I, 1943; Vol. II, 1946 (with Dr. O. W. Heick). D. Aug. 12, 1943.

Nevin, John Williamson (1803—86). Reformed; b. near Strassburg, Pa.; professor at Allegheny, Mercersburg, Lancaster; part founder of Mercersburg theology; d. at Lancaster, Pa.; editor of *Mercersburg Review;* author.

Nevius Method. A plan for mission work advocated by John Livingston Nevius and successfully applied for the first time in Korea.

Nevius was born March 4, 1829, near Ovid, N. Y.; studied at Princeton; Presbyterian missionary to China; while working at Chefoo (1871—93), he developed his plan for mission work and published it in the *Chinese Recorder;* missionaries in Korea read this report and invited him to Korea to present his plan; d. Oct. 19, 1893.

The method stresses Bible study. There are classes for men and separately for women in every church; station mass classes where all the people of a province gather; officers' and workers' classes; Bible institutes; theological seminaries and higher Bible classes for women; Bible correspondence courses.

The Nevius plan advocates self-support. The new Christians meet in homes and choose a member of their group as leader. As soon as they are able, they build their own church and pay their own pastor. The missionaries stress evangelism with a wide itineration. In Korea, however, churches were built in key centers with foreign funds, and parochial schools received small mission subsidies.

The plan aims at self-propagation. Every believer is to be a teacher of someone.

Self-government naturally develops in the method. Every group is under its unpaid leader; circuits under their paid helpers who later yield to pastors; circuit meetings train district, provincial, and national leaders.

Helen S. Coan Nevius (wife of the missionary), *The Life of John Livingston Nevius,* 1895; Charles Allen Clark, *The Nevius Plan of Mission Work in Korea,* Christian Lit. Soc., S. Minneapolis, 1937; F. E. Hamilton, "The Self-Support System in Korea," "*World Dominion,* July, 1930; R. Allen, *The Nevius Method in Korea.*

New Apostolic Church. See *Catholic Apostolic Church.*

New Birth. See *Conversion.*

New Britain Archipelago. See *Melanesia.*

New Caledonia, an island in the South Pacific Ocean belonging to France and containing a French penal colony. Dependencies: Isle of Pines, Wallis Archipelago, Loyalty Islands, Huon Islands, and Fortuna and Alofi. Area, 8,458 sq. mi. Population, 63,929 Melanesians, Polynesians, and of convict origin. Roman Catholic missions are conducted by the French Marists. Recently French Protestants have founded a station. The Loyalty Islands have been successfully taken hold of and Christianized by the L. M. S. in spite of Roman Catholic counterefforts.

New Church, The. See *Swedenborgians.*

New Congregational Methodist Church. See *Methodist Bodies,* 4 b.

New Divinity. See *New England Theology,* 2.

New England Primer. See *Catechetics,* 13.

New England Theology. 1. The theology of the early Puritans of New England was the so-called "covenant theology," according to which God dealt with man on the basis of two covenants (works and grace). The *Westminster Confession* had been formally adopted in 1648 by a synod convened at Cambridge, and it remained the standard of faith for all the New England churches until 1680, when the "leaders and messengers" of the churches in the Massachusetts Colony substituted the confession drawn up by the Congregationalists of the mother country known as the *Savoy Declaration.* The same change was made by the Connecticut churches in 1708.

2. Various factors (rise of Unitarianis,* planting of Methodism,* defection from orthodoxy at Harvard, end of compulsory support of religion by taxes, rise of transcendental philosophy, etc.) modified the traditional Calvinistic system of doctrine so as to make it more rational, more acceptable to believers, and more easily defensible. In their earliest development the more generally received of these new views were styled "New Light Divinity," "New Divinity," "Edwardian," "Hopkinsian," and "Berkshire" (because its prominent leaders resided in Berkshire County), "American Theology" (in England), and perhaps most frequently "New England Theology."

3. The most prominent leaders of the movement were the two Jonathan Edwards*; Joseph Bellamy (1719 to 1790; interpreter of Edwards; famous for such paradoxes as "God does as He would be done by when He punishes sinners to all eternity"; *True Religion Delineated, the Wisdom of God in the Permission of Sin);* Nathaniel Emmons (1745—1840; every human act dependent on First Cause); Samuel Hopkins (1721—1803; wrote *System of Doctrine* in which he developed the doctrine that holiness is "disinterested benevolence"); Nathaniel W. Taylor (1786—1858; sin is an unavoidable result in a moral universe of free agents; prepared way for Bushnell). The system began with Jonathan Edwards' sermon "Justification by Faith" (1734) and came to an end with Edward A. Park (1808—1900; editor of *Bibliotheca Sacra;* author, *Discourses of Some Theological Doctrines;* formulated New England Theology in rigid system). New England Theology spread rapidly in the orthodox Congregational churches in New England and the Western States and was favored by many in other Calvinistic bodies. The movement founded three theological seminaries (Andover, Yale, and Hartford School).

4. The specific principles of New England Theology led the adherents to deviate from the Old Calvinistic system on the following points: 1) Predestination secures the certainty of men's choices, but not the necessity; 2) Adam's guilt is not imputed to his descendants either in its mediate or immediate forms, but it constituted man so that he chooses wrong instead of right; 3) Christ suffered not the actual penalties of the Law but pains substituted for that penalty and designed to secure the moral government of the world; 4) Justification does not involve a transfer of guilt, but only a treatment of the believer as holy for Christ's sake; 5) Regeneration is a restoration of the life union lost in the Fall; 6) The elect can fall after regeneration but never will (perseverance).

F. H. Foster, *A Genetic History of New England Theology,* University of Chicago Press, 1907.

New Guinea. The largest island on the globe after the continent island of Australia. It belongs to the Melanesian group. Area, 93,000 sq. miles. Population. 1,007,000, about two thirds of these in the British portion. The southeastern section was formerly directly under British rule, transferred to Australia in 1906. After the First World War also the northeastern section, the former Kaiser-Wilhelmsland of German control, came under Australian rule. The western portion belongs to the Netherlands. The aborigines are Papuans, related to the Negro race.

Missions were conducted in Dutch New Guinea by the Berlin Gossner Mission Society since 1855, the first missionaries, Ottow and Geissler, doing valiant pioneer work. The Utrecht Mission Union (*Utrechtsche Zendingsvereeniging*) succeeded to their work. Good success was achieved, especially near the Geelvink Bay. — In British Papua the London Missionary Society began operations in 1871 with such outstanding men as Murray, Macfarlane, Chalmers, and Lawes. Than Lawes "no white man had ever had a more wide and varied knowledge of the mainland of New Guinea, or visited more tribes, or made more friends, or endured more hardships, or faced more perils." Since the Baptism of the first converts in 1881 steady progress has been made. A Wesleyan Methodist mission was begun 1881 off the southeastern coast. The Roman Church entered in 1889.

The Lutheran Church in New Guinea. In Kaiser-Wilhelmsland the Rhenish Missionary Society began work in 1887, waiting long for results. This mission came to be known as Lutheran Mission Madang. The Society for Home and Foreign Missions, According to the Principles of the Lutheran Church (Neuendettelsau, Bavaria) began to work in 1886. Its mission came to be known as Lutheran Mission Finschhafen. As a result of World War I the management of this mission was taken from the Germans by the government and surrendered to the United Evangelical Lutheran Church in Australia together with the American Lutheran Church in the U. S. On May 21, 1921, it was granted that the "Australian Lutheran Church supported by the Lutheran Organization in America be permitted to control the Lutheran Mission in New Guinea."

After February, 1927, it was possible for the German organizations to send new staff members of German nationality to New Guinea. This made possible a rather rapid advance of missionary work. In 1930 the Lutheran Mission Madang was given over completely to the American Lutheran Church. By 1939, when the war broke

out, the Lutheran Mission Finschhafen had about 40,000 baptized members and the Lutheran Mission Madang about 17,000. With the coming of the war a number of missionaries were taken prisoner, and eleven lost their lives. As a result of the war the mission was taken over by the National Lutheran Council as an orphaned mission. In 1953 these various groups formed one organization under the name "New Guinea Lutheran Mission." Membership (1953): 121,437.

In 1936 the Rooke-Siassi Island field was turned over to the Evangelical Lutheran Church of Australia, which is in affiliation with The Lutheran Church — Missouri Synod. In 1951 this work was expanded to the mainland where a station was opened at Menyamye among the Kuka Kuka tribe. Upon invitation of this church The Lutheran Church—Missouri Synod entered the Central Highland of New Guinea in 1948.

New Hampshire Confession. See *Baptist Bodies,* 5, 14.

New Haven Theology. New England Theology * as modified by a group of men, chiefly from Yale.

New Hebrides. An island group in the South Pacific under a commission of French and British officials. Area, 5,700 sq. mi. Population, 48,538 (1952). The natives belong to the Papuan race and are originally animists, head-hunters, and cannibals. Missions have been eminently difficult and successful. In 1839 John Williams of the London Missionary Society came to Erromanga and was at once killed. In less than twenty years fifty missionaries, white and colored, lost their lives. The Presbyterians of Scotland and Canada later entered the work. In 1848 J. Geddie came to Aneiteum, and in ten years the whole island was Christianized. In 1858 the United Presbyterians sent J. G. Paton (d. 1907), who won the whole island of Aniwa. In 1871 Bishop Patteson of the Society for the Propagation of the Gospel was killed on Nakapu Island. The islands are almost entirely Christianized. Only in a few the inhabitants are still pagan. The Roman Catholic Church also conducts missions on these islands.

New Humanists. See *Humanism, The New.*

New Jersey Synod. Organized Feb. 19, 1861, at German Valley, N. J., by 6 pastors and 4 laymen, who had received their dismissal in 1859 from the New York Ministerium. It consisted chiefly of the churches in the Raritan Valley, which had been founded more than a century before by Justus Falckner and had been fostered by Muhlenberg. In 1872 this body merged with the Synod of New York (founded 1867). See *United Lutheran Church, Synods of,* 17, 18.

New Jerusalem, Church of the. See *Swedenborgians.*

New Lights. The name given those among Congregationalists who favored revivals during the Great Awakening. The Old Lights were those who opposed such revivals.

New Measures. After rationalism had spent its force in American Lutheranism, some leaders, especially in the New York Ministerium (*e. g.,* Benj. Kurtz) held Methodistic revivals and certain other practices which were called "New Measures." The practices caused a controversy in the Lutheran Church and were rejected by the more conservative.

New School Presbyterians. In the controversies which led to a split in the Presbyterian Church in the U. S.* in 1837, the so-called "New School" strove for a liberal interpretation of the confessions and for union with Congregationalism and opposed slavery. Their opponents were called the "Old School." The two groups reunited in 1869.

New Side Presbyterians. See *Presbyterian Bodies,* 4.

New Theology. See *Liberalism; Modernism; New England Theology.*

New Thought. A movement which traces its origin to the activities of Phineas P. Quimby, whose technique and ideas are generally regarded as being reflected or present in the work of Mary Baker Eddy (see *Christian Science*). While the work of Quimby originally concerned itself chiefly with healing, the movement soon took on a philosophy of life which emphasized such ideas as the power of mind over body, autosuggestion, full life, and similar views. It also borrowed from movements in philosophy, psychology, theology, and psychical research.

While Quimby formed no organization, many were formed along the lines of "New Thought" (*Christian Science, Divine Science,* and others). National conventions were held, be-

ginning with 1894. An alliance was formed in 1908, being named the *International New Thought Alliance* in 1914.

New York, English Synod of. See *Synods, Extinct; United Lutheran Church, Synods of,* 18.

New York, German Synod of (*"Steimle Synod"*), founded March, 1866, by F. W. T. Steimle and a few others, for whom the New York Ministerium was not "German" enough and who were not satisfied with the "Ministerium's attitude to the Confessions of the Lutheran Church." After the New York Ministerium had taken its stand with the General Council, the members of the "Steimle Synod," with the exception of Steimle, reunited with the New York Ministerium (1872).

New York, Ministerium of. See *United Lutheran Church, Synods of,* 18.

New York and New England, Synod of. See *United Lutheran Church, Synods of,* 18.

New York and New Jersey, Synod of. See *United Lutheran Church, Synods of,* 18.

New York, Synod of (I). Organized October 22, 1867, by 17 pastors and 10 congregations, who under the leadership of Dr. H. N. Pohlman, the president of the New York Ministerium, seceded from that body because of its break with the General Synod in 1866. In 1872 it was merged with the Synod of New Jersey.

New York, United Synod of. See *United Lutheran Church, Synods of,* 18.

New Zealand. 1. An autonomous island colony of the British Empire in the South Pacific Ocean, 1,200 miles east of Australia. Area: 103,862 sq. mi.; population: 1,939,703 (1951). Through the efforts of Samuel Marsden mission work was started in 1809. On Christmas Day, 1814, the first religious service was held. The Wesleyan Society entered the field in 1822. The Presbyterians began work in 1844. The Roman Catholic Church came in 1836. Missions among Asiatics and aborigines are conducted by the Presbyterian Church of New Zealand, Church of England, Methodists, New Zealand Church Missionary Society, Presbyterians, Salvation Army. Statistics on missions: 23 Protestant groups are active. Total membership· 1,092,539 (1952).

2. New Zealand has no established Church, although the Anglican Church

is the most prominent, with a membership of about 650,000 (1952). The Presbyterian Church, reinforced by a large immigration from Scotland, numbers about 300,000 members. The Methodists, mainly Wesleyans, number about 90,000 and the Congregationalists about 4,000; the Baptists, about 27,000. Besides these denominations there are twelve or fifteen minor groups, such as the Plymouth Brethren, with about 18,000 members, and the Disciples, with about 11,000 members. The Roman Catholic Church numbers about 214,000 (1951). Of non-Christians there are Jews, Buddhists, and Confucianists, about 3,000. The Maoris are mostly reckoned among the Christian population.

3. Lutherans in New Zealand. The first German settlers came to Nelson in June, 1843. Four missionaries of the North German Mission Society were in their company. Others came in September, 1844. Because of difficulties with the Maoris about half of the emigrants went to Australia. The others founded the first Lutheran church in New Zealand in Nelson City. Missionary J. W. C. Heine became their pastor. They worshiped in a house presented to them by an Englishman, Mr. Sukelt, in 1848, until they were able to dedicate their church in 1876. Other settlements were begun at Waimea (1849) and Upper Moutere, the main colony (1850), both being served by Pastor Heine until 1865, when Pastor Christian Meyer began work at Waimea. In the same year a church costing £300 was dedicated at Upper Moutere. In 1882 Pastor Heine resigned, and Missionary Wm. Kowert became his successor. A little later Pastor Meyer went to North Island to serve some Germans in the province of Taranaki. After Pastor Kowert had left New Zealand, Pastor J. Thiel was sent there by the *Lutherischer Gotteskasten.* Lutheran churches were established at Norsewood (German and Swedish), Halcombe, Waitotara, Midhurst, Marton, Rongotea, and Wellington. Through two missionaries of the Hermannsburg Free Church, Pastors G. Blaess and J. Klitscher, the Missouri Synod was asked to interest itself in New Zealand. Dr. A. L. Graebner, in 1902, paid them a visit, as a result of which Pastor Martin Winkler, a graduate of St. Louis, was sent there in 1903. He was followed, in 1904, by Pastor F. Hassold. Through their efforts a native Maori, Hamuera Te Punga, was sent to the Springfield

Seminary of the Missouri Synod, graduated in 1912, and had begun work among the Maori in 1913. Since 1914 the New Zealand Lutherans, formerly affiliated with the Missouri Synod, have been a part of the Ev. Luth. Synod in Australia (see *Australia*). Lutherans number about 1,600 (1952). See *Missions, Bibliography.* OHS

Newcomer, Christian (1749—1830). Leader of the westward expansion in the U. S. of the United Brethren.*

Newfoundland. A British colony in North America, comprising the island known by this name and its dependency, Labrador. Area, 42,734 sq. mi. Population, 300,000, chiefly of English, Scotch, and Irish extraction and almost equally divided between Roman Catholics, Episcopalians, and Methodists. There is practically no native aboriginal representation.

Newman Club. See *Students, Spiritual Care of,* A.

Newman, John Henry (Cardinal, 1801—90). Author, theologian, a Founder of the Oxford Movement. Vigorously fought the infiltration of "Modernism" in the Church of England. Joined Roman Catholic Church and was made a Cardinal. Chief works: *Tracts for the Times; The Idea of a University;* *Apologia pro vita sua;* hymn, "Lead, Kindly Light."

Newton, John (1725—1807). After death of pious mother godless sailor, infidelity strengthened by reading of Shaftesbury; later he was converted and had intercourse with Whitefield, Wesley, and others; curate at Olney, where he published Olney's *Poems;* later rector of St. Mary Woolnoth, London; noted for warm heart, candor, tolerance, and piety; wrote, among others: "Glorious Things of Thee Are Spoken"; "How Sweet the Name of Jesus Sounds."

Newton, Sir Isaac (1642—1727). Mathematician, natural philosopher; prof. at Cambridge; most famous of his scientific works the *Principia,* 1687; was accused of entertaining Arian views, but theological works which he published do not justify the charge.

Nicaea, Council of. The first ecumenical council called at Nicaea in 325 to deal with the Arian controversy. The exact number of bishops assembled seems uncertain. The usual opinion that there were 318 rests on the authority of Athanasius; but Eusebius gives only 250. About one sixth of the entire number of bishops of the empire was present. The Latin Church was represented by only seven delegates. It is especially noteworthy that the bishop of Rome (who was not present in person) exercised no influence in the deliberations of the council. The sessions began about the middle of June (325) and continued for over one month. The opening address was delivered by Constantine, who advised the delegates to put away all strife and discord. Thereupon he yielded to the ecclesiastical presidents (who they were is doubtful) of the assembly, and the discussions began. On the importance of the council it is needless to dwell. It is "the most important event of the fourth century." "It forms an epoch in the history of doctrine, summing up the results of all previous discussions on the deity of Christ and the incarnation." On the other hand, it established a bad precedent in inflicting civil punishment on Arius and his followers and thus initiated the long train of evils resulting from the union of Church and State. See references under *Arianism; Doctrine, History; Ecumenical Creeds.*

Nicaragua. See *Central America, Missions in.*

Nicene Creed. See *Ecumenical Creeds,* B.

Nicholas, St. One of the most popular saints in East and West; bishop of Myra, Lycia, in the fourth century. He is the patron saint of Greece and Russia, of sailors, bakers, travelers, children — in general, of the common people, the poor and weak. On his festival (December 6) he brings secret gifts to German, Dutch, and Swiss children. In the United States he is identified with Santa Claus.

Nicholas I. See *Popes,* 5.

Nicholas of Clemanges *(Nicholas Poillevillain Clamanges),* French theological author and ecclesiastical statesman; b. ca. 1367, d. 1437 at Paris; studied at Paris under Gerson *; was active in the movement for healing the Great Schism *; was papal secretary, later canon at Langres; retired to Cistercian cloister to pursue Biblical studies; wrote treatises on the errors and corruptions of the Church of his time; a precursor of the "humanistic reformation."

Nicholites. Sect founded by Joseph Nichols in latter half of 18th century in Maryland, with religious beliefs much like those of Quakers, with whom they united after about twenty years of independent existence.

Nicolai, Christoph Friedrich (1733 to 1811). German rationalistic author and bookseller; edited, for many years, the *Allgemeine deutsche Bibliothek,* which became the organ of the crassest rationalism.

Nicolai, Philipp (1556—1608). Lutheran preacher and hymn writer of the early post-Reformation era. Unlike many others of his day, he helped perpetuate the spirit of virile heroism in the Lutheran Church during the trying days of the destructive Counter Reformation era. Nicolai is credited with having written the text and likely also the tune of two famous chorales of the Lutheran Church: "Wake, Awake, for Night Is Flying" ("the King of Chorales") and "How Lovely Shines the Morning Star" ("the Queen of Chorales"). The claims of former days that the latter was originally a secular love song have been disproved.

Nicolaitans. See *Gnosticism,* 7 j.

Nicolaus of Cusa (1401—64). B. at Kues on the Moselle; studied at Deventer, Heidelberg, and Padua; member of the council of Basel; supported first the conciliar, then the papal party; cardinal, 1448; bishop and reformer at Brixen; died at Todi in Umbria. A skeptic with reference to Scholastic proofs of theological truths, Cusa extolled "learned ignorance." However, a sudden intuition taught him that God is the coincidence of opposites and provided the key to positive truth. He strove to give intuition cognitive meaning in mathematical terms. Cusa advanced a theory of the rotation of the earth on its axis and the unmedieval conception of the infinity of the world in time and space. Chief works: *De docta ignorantia; De conjecturis; Apologia doctae ignorantiae; De visione Dei; De posset; De concordantia catholica; De auctoritate praesidendi in consilio generali; De pace fidei.*

The works of Nicolaus of Cusa were published by Jacob Faber Stapulensis, Paris, 1514; they were also published at Basel, 1565; the publication of a critical edition was undertaken by the Heidelberg academy in 1930; a German translation of the chief works published by F. A. Scharpff (Freiburg, 1862); E. Vansteenbergh, *Le Cardinal N. de C.,*

Paris, 1921; E. Cassirer, *Individuum und Kosmos in der Philosophie der Renaissance*, Leipzig, 1927; Henry Betts, *Nicolaus of Cusa*, London, 1932.   PR

Nicoll, William Robertson (1851 to 1925). Scottish divine; b. at Lumsden, Aberdeenshire; Free Church minister at Dufftown, Kelso; author; editor; originated and edited *The Expositor's Greek Testament*, 1897—1900; knighted, 1909.

Nicum, John. B. Winnenden, Wuerttemberg, Germany, Jan. 6, 1851. Ed. at Muhlenberg Col. and the Philadelphia Theol. Sem. Pastor at Frackville, Pa., 1876—78; Philadelphia, 1878—80; Syracuse, N. Y., 1880—87; Rochester, 1887 to 1894; pres. and prof., Wagner College, 1894—1902; sec., General Council, 1886 to 1897; sec. and pres., Home Mission Bd., General Council, 1887—97. Author: *History of New York Ministerium; Laws of the State of New York Relating to Churches*, 1886; *Confessional History of the Lutheran Church in the U.S.*, 1891, etc. D. 1909.

Niedner, Christian William (1797 to 1865). Lutheran church historian; prof. at Leipzig; lost his position as a result of his taking the part of the people in 1848; lived in poverty for a time at Wittenberg; then prof. at Berlin; chief work: *History of the Christian Church* (1846).

Nielsen, Rasmus (1809—1884). Prof. at Univ. of Copenhagen; successively a follower of Hegel, Kierkegaard, and Grundtvig; voluminous writer.

Niemann, J. H. B. 1848 at Melle, Hanover; graduated from Concordia Seminary, St. Louis, 1869; Pastor at Little Rock, Ark., Wyneken's successor in Cleveland, and President of the Central District of the Missouri Synod 1880 to 1909; d. March 15, 1910.

Niemeyer, August Hermann (1754 to 1828). B. and d. at Halle. Professor, chancellor of the university, and director of the Francke institutions in Halle. A great-grandson of A. H. Francke, he revived the universal esteem of the latter's foundations there. He composed the hymn "Ich weiss, an wen ich glaube."

Niemeyer, Herman Agathon (1802 to 1851). Son of A. H. Niemeyer; prof. in Jena; director of the Francke institute in Jena; wrote: *Collection of Confessions Published in the Reformed Church*.

Nietzsche, Friedrich. German philosopher; b. 1844 at Roecken, Province of Saxony; professor of classical philology at Basel, 1869—79; pronounced incurably insane, 1889; d. 1900 at Weimar. At first follower of Wagner and Schopenhauer; then, rejecting both, he developed an individualistic, anti-democratic, and bitterly anti-Christian, atheistic philosophy. Its fundamental idea is the "will to power" (*Wille zur Macht*), which underlies the "master morality" (*Herrenmoral*), by which certain highly endowed individuals rise above the common herd by ruthlessly developing their inherent power at the expense of the mass. It is opposed to the "herd or slave morality" (*Sklavenmoral*), represented by Christianity, which makes a virtue of piety and humility and tends to weakness. Christianity is a stain on the history of mankind, while the master morality produces the highest type of humanity, the "superman" (*Uebermensch*). Thus, by a process of self-apotheosis, Nietzsche found a substitute for God. Wrote: *Also sprach Zarathustra*, 1883—85; *Jenseits von Gut und Boese*, 1886; *Zur Genealogie der Moral*, 1887.

Nigeria (West Africa), Lutheran Missions in. The Synodical Conference was led into this field in 1935. An appeal was made to the Lutheran Church by a group of natives — known as the Ibibios — which had severed its connection with the Qua Iboe Mission, an Irish interdenominational mission society with headquarters at Belfast, Ireland, which began work in Nigeria in 1887.

The litte group was dissatisfied because leaders of the churches belonging to the Qua Iboe Mission were teaching doctrines contrary to the Scriptures. By searching their Bibles the perplexed natives became filled with a burning desire to have the Word taught to them as revealed by God Himself. They decided to send one of their native sons, Jonathan U. Ekong, to America with instructions that he find a church which would preach and teach the Word of God in its truth and purity. This young native was led into the Lutheran Church and was persuaded to prepare himself for the holy ministry. He enrolled in Immanuel Lutheran College at Greensboro, N. C. After his graduation Ekong returned to his people and urged them to join the Lutheran Church.

A petition was forwarded to the Synodical Conference. The Conference decided in 1934 to send a delegation of pastors — Henry Nau, Otto C. Boecler, and Immanuel Albrecht — to Nigeria in order to explore the possibilities of this field and to suggest and outline the future mission course of our Church. The delegation spent a few months in visitations and in consultations with British officials and returned to America with the recommendation that the Lutheran Church enter this field at once.

In 1936 Pres. Henry Nau of Greensboro, accompanied by his wife, sailed for Africa. Dr. Nau remained in Africa for 18 months and worked with great zeal and faithfulness for the establishment of a Church which would enhance the cause of true Biblical teaching. Prior to the departure of Dr. Nau for America, Pastors Wm. Schweppe and V. Koeper were commissioned as missionaries for the Nigerian Lutheran Church. In the following years other missionaries were sent from America to augment the force of workers. Thus in 1953 the staff consisted of 15 American pastors, 1 male and 2 female teachers, 10 native pastors, 2 American lay workers, and 3 doctors.

In 1948 there were in Nigeria 125 churches with a baptized membership of over 15,000, 93 schools with 6,000 children, taught by 250 Lutheran teachers. By 1952 there were 172 churches, over 26,000 baptized members, 98 schools with 12,151 pupils, and 501 teachers.

On Jan. 31, 1949, a Lutheran seminary was opened on the Obot Idim compound with an enrollment of ten native students. Wm. Schweppe was selected as the first president of the seminary, and Justus Kretzmann as dean. A secondary and normal school has been established. A hospital was dedicated in May, 1953.

The churches in Nigeria are organized as *The Evangelical Lutheran Church of Nigeria*.

Nigeria has a population of about 25,000,000. It is conservatively estimated that there are one million Christians in this land. KK

Nightingale, Florence. B. at Florence, Italy, May 15, 1820; d. at London August 13, 1910; philanthropist. Devoted her life to the care of the suffering and did pioneer work in the care of the wounded on the field of battle. She was trained at the Deaconess Institu-

tion at Kaiserswerth and later studied the nursing system of the Sisters of St. Vincent de Paul at Paris. With £50,000 which had been raised by subscription and given to her in recognition of her services in the Crimea, she established a Nightingale Home for the training of nurses at St. Thomas' and King's College Hospitals. Among others, she wrote and published the following works: *Notes on Matters Affecting the Health, Efficiency, and Hospital Administration of the British Army* (1859), *Notes on Nursing* (1860 and 1900), *Life or Death in India* (1874).

Nigrinus, Georg (1530—1602). Recommended by Melanchthon, he studied at Marburg; pastor at Homburg and Giessen; later became supt. of churches in Alsfeld and Nidda; championed the cause of the Formula of Concord.

Nigrinus, Theobald (d. 1566). Dominican monk; won for the Reformation and advanced it in Strassburg.

Nihil Obstat. See *Index of Prohibited Books.*

Nihilism. In philosophy, the doctrine that nothing exists and that knowledge, therefore, is impossible. In politics, the revolutionism of the Russian Nihilists, who, impelled by the despotic absolutism of the government, aimed to destroy social and political institutions. At first the movement, fostered by German materialism, manifested itself merely in revolutionary propaganda, but since the seventies of the past century terroristic methods were employed — assassination of Alexander II in 1881 and of high government officials before and since.

Nikander, J. K. See *Finnish Lutherans in America,* 1.

Nikon of Russia. Patriarch of Oriental Church; b. 1605, d. 1681; was priest, then monk, later metropolitan and patriarch of Novgorod; did much to improve the liturgical books and the order of worship; spent his last years in exile by the White Sea.

Nimbus. A halo which is represented in art as surrounding the heads of holy persons. Symbol is found in Greek, Roman, Brahmanic, Buddhist, as well as in Christian art.

Ninian. See *Celtic Church,* 3.

Nirvana (Sanskrit, "blowing out"). In Buddhism the highest goal of human endeavor, or salvation, which consists of a sinless, unconscious state (or, according to some texts, annihilation of individuality). In this state all passions and desires have been extinguished. It constitutes the final release from the continuous round of rebirths, with its concomitant sorrow and misery, to which, according to Indian doctrines of transmigration and karma, man is subject.

Nissen, R. Toender (1822—82). Prof. at the Univ. of Christiania, Norway; councilor of state and pres. of church department; wrote *Den Nordiske Kirkes Historie* (History of Church of the North) and a general church history.

Nitschmann, David. See *Moravian Church,* 3.

Nitzch, Friedrich (1832—1898). German Protestant; influenced by Ritschl; his work concerned itself chiefly with the history of dogma.

Nitzsch, Karl Immanuel (1789 to 1868). Mediating theologian and defender of the Prussian Union; greatly influenced by Schleiermacher; wrote *System der christlichen Lehre.*

Nocturn. See *Canonical Hours.*

Noesgen, Karl Friedrich. B. 1835. Positive Lutheran theologian of modern type; studied at Halle and Berlin; 1883 professor of New Testament Exegesis at Rostock; wrote on the synoptic gospels in commentary of Strack and Zoeckler; *Commentary on Acts* and other works.

Noetus of Smyrna. See *Monarchianism,* B 1.

Nohrborg, Anders. See *Sweden, Lutheran Church in,* 4.

Nominalism. As opposed to Realism and Idealism, it teaches that only individual objects have real existence, that so-called universals, general or abstract ideas, are but names, *nomina.* Thus the general idea "tree" does not really exist in itself, but only many individual trees exist. All trees resemble one another in some point, which point of resemblance the mind can consider apart from the points of difference. However, the idea we obtain by abstraction of all common points has no independent existence, no reality; it is merely a name. Roscelinus (1050) and Abelard (1079) were leading exponents of Nominalism.

Nommensen, L. See *Bataks.*

Non-Conformists. A name applied to the two thousand clergymen who, in 1662, rather than submit to the Act of Uniformity, left the Church of England. Later the name was applied in general to those Protestants who at any period in history have refused to conform to the doctrines and practices of the Established Church.

Non Expedit. A papal decree (1868) forbidding Roman Catholics to participate in certain Italian elections.

Non-Fundamental Doctrines. See *Fundamental Doctrines.*

Non-Installed Teachers. See *Teachers,* A 1 b.

Non-Jurors. English clergymen who refused to swear allegiance to William and Mary (1689) because they refused to break their oath to James II. The group separated from the Established Church.

Nones. See *Canonical Hours.*

Nordin, Robert. See *Bapt. Bodies,* 20.

Norelius, Eric. B. Oct. 26, 1833, at Hassela, Helsingland, Sweden. He heard of the work of L. P. Esbjoern and emigrated to America, 1850. Studied at Capital Univ. (1851—56). After his ordination (1856) he served as pastor at Red Wing and Vasa, Minn. He issued various publications and was made editor of the *Augustana.* Wrote extensively, especially in the field of biography and church history. His most important works are the biography of T. N. Hasselquist and his history of Swedish Lutherans in America. March 15, 1916.

E. Johnson, *Early Life of Eric Norelius,* Aug. Bk. Concern, Rock Island, Ill., 1934; Ira Nothstein, "Life and Work of Dr. Eric Norelius," *My Church,* Aug. Bk. Concern, n. d. (1:39 ff.); J. C. Jennson, *American Lutheran Biographies.*

Norma Normans (L. "the ruling rule"). A term applied to the Scriptures because they are the absolute norm of faith *(norma primaria, norma decisionis).* Holy Scripture as the decisive norm is absolutely necessary, being the norm which decides whether doctrines are true or false.

Norma Normata (L. "the rule having been ruled"). A term applied to the confessions as secondary norms *(norma secundum quid; norma secondaria; norma discretionis).* The confessions as distinguishing norms of the Church are only relatively necessary. They decide whether a person has clearly understood the true doctrines of the Bible.

Normal Schools. See *Teachers,* A 5.

North America, Ministerium of. See *United Lutheran Church, Synods of,* 24.

North American Council of the Churches of Christ. See *International Council of Religious Education.*

North American Old Roman Catholic Church. See *Old Catholics,* 2.

North American Phalanx. See *Communistic Societies,* 5.

North Carolina, Synod of. See *United Lutheran Church, Synods of,* 11, 19.

North Carolina, United Synod of. See *United Lutheran Church, Synods of,* 11, 19.

North German Missionary Society *(Norddeutsche Missionsgesellschaft).* Organized in 1836 by a merger of seven smaller missionary organizations in North Germany. A missionary institute was founded in 1837 at Hamburg. Since the society was unionistic in policy, stricter Lutheran elements withdrew in the course of time, forming their own organizations. Among its earliest missions were those begun in New Zealand, 1842; India, 1843 (later handed over to Lutherans in America); Gold Coast, Africa. (Information on the work of the society is given under the names of countries in which it was active.)

Northern Baptist Convention. See *Baptist Bodies,* 8.

Northern Presbyterians. See *Presbyterian Bodies,* 4.

Northwest, Synod of the. See *United Lutheran Church, Synods of,* 20.

Northwestern Lutheran Theological Seminary. See *Ministry, Education of,* XI B.

Northwestern Publishing House. See *Publication Houses.*

Norway, Early Christianity in. Norway heard of Christianity through the Vikings, who made piratical raids on England, Scotland, Ireland, and France. King Ivar "fell asleep in Jesus"; another was baptized with his family. King Haakon the Good (d. 961), brought up in the Christian religion by Athelstan, King of England, failed

to get his people to embrace Christianity. King Olaf Tryggvesson (d. 1000), with his priest Thangbrand, used violent methods in the attempt to introduce the Christian belief. When success seemed in Olaf's grasp, a coalition of his subjects and foreigners brought about the King's downfall. Olaf Haraldsson (d. 1030) continued the effort to introduce Christianity. He had the Englishman Grimkel for his missionary bishop. It was not until after Olaf's death, however, that political events helped Chistianity prevail. Grimkel had the body of Olaf Haraldsson exhumed and declared him a saint.

Norway, Lutheranism in. 1. The main stream of the Lutheran Reformation flowed into Norway through Denmark. It was a gradual process, with a few individuals, like the German monk Antonius, preaching the doctrines of the Reformation in Bergen in the face of hostile Roman priests and bishops as early as 1526. King Frederik I (1523 to 1533), in spite of his oath, was sympathetic to the Reformation and announced that men were free to preach either Roman or Lutheran doctrine. Bergen, center of commerce and shipping, helped spread the new teaching, which had come to them first. The Danish nobility, strongly inter-married into Norwegian families, saw in the Reformation a twofold opportunity: 1) to throw off the political and economic power of the Roman bishops; and 2) to get their hands on the wealth of the churches and monasteries. Many of them thus became "promoters" of the Reformation from selfish motives. Undoubtedly there were among the nobility others with higher motives who helped the cause.

2. King Christian III of Norway and Denmark, 1534—59; was won for Reformation while attending Diet of Worms; established the Reformation officially at the Diet of Copenhagen, 1536, the full effects of it reaching Norway in the following year. Catholic bishops were deposed, and Lutheran bishops gradually took their places. Priests, too, were removed. However, they were left until suitable successors could be found, thus dragging the process out toward the end of the century. The laity were, of course, lagging far behind. Only very slowly did the new teaching reach down to them, and their loyalty to the Roman priest caused frequent violence against the new Lu-

theran pastor. The ministers themselves were poorly trained. Both they and the people suffered under the handicap of having only the Danish Bible, hymnbook, and liturgy. Norwegian translations were slow in coming. The first great upswing in the progress of the Reformation came with Jorgen Erichsen, Bishop of Stavanger, 1571—1604. Known as "Norway's Luther," he had great influence on the spiritual life of clergy and people. His published sermons have been called the finest literature to come out of the Norwegian Reformation. By the end of the century it can be said that the Church of the Reformation was established and organized in Norway.

3. Lutheranism in Norway, as in Denmark, was closely bound to the Mother Church in Germany. Some of the earliest leaders in the Norwegian movement had been at Wittenberg. Torbjorn Bratt, first bishop of Trondheim, was there for two years, staying in Luther's home. Norwegian pastors in increasing numbers went to Germany for study. The "Ordinance," or Directory of Worship, of 1607, required theological candidates to spend some time at a foreign university. And an "ordinance" of 1629 demanded theological examination of every Norwegian candidate at the University of Copenhagen.

4. This connection with Germany necessarily brought the great theological movements from Germany to Norway. First came "Orthodoxy," the movement which characterized the Church's development in the 17th century.

5. This movement, which brought order and system into Lutheran theology and was Lutheranism's theological answer to Rome, had the same twofold effect in Norway as in Germany. It established the theology of the Church of Norway on a solid foundation. It rooted it in the Word of God. It built up a reverence for the Word among clergy and laity which later movements have never quite been able to erase. With it went an emphasis on catechetical instruction which produced a notable literature.

6. The movement, however, followed the pattern of its German development. Before the century had passed, the preaching had become stiffly correct in doctrinal content, but devoid of Gospel warmth. (The Law was overemphasized in many quarters, Christianity was intellectualized, and spiritual fervor in a life of Christian love was too often left out.) The Christian life was becoming cold and sterile in large sections of the Church. The ground was ripe for the initial appearance of the "French spirit" in Norway, with its culture, but also with its moral laxity and freethinking.

7. But the pendulum was due to swing back by the end of the 17th century. As Orthodoxy had risen to turn back the Counter Reformation and crypto-Calvinism, so Pietism came as an answer to dead orthodoxy and atheism. A new spirit of piety began to show itself. The devotional literature of the period of orthodoxy had trickled down to the laity, and there it held the fort against the movements that threatened the Church. Poets like Peter Dass were writing deeply spiritual hymns and songs, and people were singing them.

8. German Pietism came into Norway through Halle, where Francke was preaching the same message of spiritual awakening as Spener. However, it started in Norway as a fanatical and separatistic sectarianism which was hostile to the Church and the ministry, spiteful toward the Sacraments, and legalistic to an extreme. Nevertheless there was in the movement a stream of healthy piety which flowed into the Church. There was the so-called "syvstjernen," or seven-starred constellation in Romsdalen under the inspired leadership of Thomas von Westen (1682 to 1727). Their powerful preaching of repentance and the Cross, with a strong emphasis on catechization, influenced the whole spiritual life of the Norwegian Church. Confirmation was instituted in 1746. Eric Pontoppidan wrote an explanation to Luther's Catechism which has been a power in the Church ever since. By the end of the first half of the century, however, the Pietistic movement had run its course. It had dribbled off into subjectivism and fanaticism characterized by the same errors which its early Norwegian promoters had revealed.

9. Having been led through subjectivism into indifference to the means of grace, the Norwegian Church was now ripe for Rationalism and for the "French spirit" of Rousseau and Voltaire. Church leaders and clergy fell into the stream. Revelation gave way to reason. God, virtue, immortality were the passwords. Science, culture, and art became the main concern even of the clergy.

10. The strongest voice against Rationalism in Norway was that of Johan Nordal Brun (1745—1816), Bishop of Bergen at the beginning of the 19th century and the greatest preacher of his day. But now came the man who had the positive message and program that should bring revival to the Church of Norway. Hans Nielsen Hauge (1771 to 1824; "the Spener of Norway"), a layman, combined Orthodoxy's reverence for the Word with a deep personal piety. And preaching a ringing message of repentance, he set the whole Church on fire. A new impetus was given to lay preaching, which has continued to be a strong movement in the Church. Certain weaknesses were apparent, more in Hauge's followers than in the man himself. Sanctification overshadows justification. Hence considerable legalism has characterized the movement. The Sacraments are deemphasized, though Hauge never spoke against them. But on the whole Hauge wanted his movement to go forward within the established Church. He rejected the idea of schism and sectarianism. The theologians of the University faculty, Hersleb and Stenerson, helped bring Hauge and the ministry of the Church together.

11. Out of the same university came a new awakening led by Prof. Gisle Johnson (1822—1894) and Prof. Caspari. Their theology reflected the old healthy Orthodoxy, with the spiritual warmth of Hauge. Mission interest now took hold. Foreign, home, and inner mission societies were established. Some of these have been within the Church. Others have become schismatic groups, deeply subjective, "antichurchly," with laymen administering the Sacraments when they are used.

12. "Modernism," like the other movements, came to Norway from Germany, with its Higher Criticism. Since it came to dominate the university theological faculty, an independent theological seminary was established in Oslo, with a strongly conservative theology, in most instances even to this day. Most of the theological candidates come from this seminary at present. These bear the stamp of outstanding teachers like Moe and Hallesby, Aalen and Seierstad. The war, with its German occupation of Norway, purged the Norwegian Church with fires of persecution. The names of Bishops Berggrav, Fjellbu, and Smemo and of laymen like Ludvig Hope and Ronald Fangen exemplified the heroic stand of the Norwegian Church. Through the conflict the Church's relation to the State was redefined, but the Church continues to be a State Church.

13. Norwegian Lutheranism was transplanted to American soil in the middle of the 19th century, when the heavy immigration began. The two streams of religious thought which dominated Norway at that time still characterize Norwegian Lutheranism in America. There is the Haugean spirit of personal piety and lay activity. And, on the other hand, has persisted the emphasis on sound Bible doctrine and confessional Lutheran theology with which the students of Caspari and Johnson came out of the University of Oslo before being called to the American scene as pastors and teachers.

R. Tonder Nissen, *Den Nordiske Kirkes Historie;* A. Chr. Bang, *Den Norske Kirkes Historie;* P. G. Lindhardt, *Den Nordiske Kirkes Historie;* H. C. Christie, *Den Norske Kirke i Kamp;* Kristian Hansson, *Stat og Kirke.* HAP

Norwegian Church Mission by Schreuder (*Den Norske Kirkes Mission ved Schreuder*). Founded by Bishop Hans Schreuder through his *A Few Words to the Church of Norway,* 1842. Work was begun among the Zulus in Natal, Africa. The mission was much retarded by war between England and the Zulus. Work was also begun on Madagascar, which for some time was under the supervision of Schreuder. Schreuder remained in connection with the Norwegian Church Mission until 1873, when he separated. A special committee was then formed for the Church of Norway, headed by Bishop Tandberg.

Norwegian-Danish Augustana Synod. See *United Norwegian Lutheran Church.*

Norwegian-Danish Conference. See *Danish Lutherans in America,* 3.

Norwegian (European) Foreign Missions are being conducted by 1) the Norwegians among the Finns, since 1888. The work was originated by Bishop Skaar, of Tromsoe; 2) the Norwegian Mission Society (*Norske Missionsselskap*), Stavanger. The society is a union of various minor missionary societies which sprang up in Norway since 1814. These at first co-operated with the Basel Evangelical Missionary Society, later with the Rhenish Missionary Society, and ultimately founded the Norwegian Missionary Society, consisting chiefly of lay elements, 1843, the State Church and clergy as such holding a rather reserved position. The mission school at Stavanger was founded 1943.

Norwegian Evangelical Lutheran Synod of America. This synod was organized at Koshkonong, Rock Co., Wis. (where J. W. C. Dietrichson had been a Lutheran leader), in 1850. As originally formed, the synod was influenced by Grundtvigian* principles. Under the leadership of H. A. Preus the synod was dissolved in 1852 and reorganized in 1853 on the basis of a confessional constitution. In 1872 the Norwegian Synod participated in the formation of the Synodical Conference.* It withdrew from the Synodical Conference in 1883 because of difficulties arising from the predestination controversy but maintained fraternal relations with the Conference until 1912, when it adopted the Madison Settlement.* Together with the Hauge Synod and the United Norwegian Lutheran Church a majority of the Norwegian Evangelical Lutheran Synod formed the Norwegian Lutheran Church of America (now the Evangelical Lutheran Church*). A group which refused to accept the Madison Settlement organized the Norwegian Synod of the American Evangelical Lutheran Church.

J. L. Neve-W. D. Allbeck, *History of the Lutheran Church in America,* Luth. Lit. Bd., Burlington, Iowa, 1934; references under Evangelical Lutheran Church.

Norwegian Lutheran Church of Canada. See *Canada, Lutheranism in,* 20.

Norwegian Synod. See *Evangelical Lutheran Church,* 8; *Norwegian Synod of the American Evangelical Lutheran Church.*

Norwegian Synod of the American Evangelical Lutheran Church. 1. This Synod regards itself as the spiritual successor of that Norwegian Synod which was organized in the year 1853. Through years of solid growth, doctrinally and numerically, this original Synod maintained its conservative Lutheran position despite many an internal and external doctrinal controversy. The most serious of these controversies, the Schmidtian (see *Schmidt, Friedrich August)* controversy on Election in the '80's caused a

division and a serious loss in numbers. Repeated attempts to bring about unity and union among Norwegian Lutherans finally led to the adoption of the "Madison Settlement" in the year 1912 by the Hauge Synod, the United Lutheran Church (Norwegian), and the Norwegian Synod majority and to a union of these synods (1917) to form the Norwegian Lutheran Church in America (now Evangelical Lutheran Church*).

2. A minority group of the Norwegian Synod protested against this doctrinal "settlement" and the union which followed and instead formed the present Norwegian Synod of the AELC in the year 1918. This Synod joined the Synodical Conference in the year 1920 and has tried to maintain the doctrinal position of this Conference, of the original Norwegian Synod, and of such pioneer theologians as Walther, Pieper, Koren. The existence of this re-organized Synod is a testimony against the Madison Settlement (see *Madison Settlement).*

From a group which numbered ten voting pastors and an uncertain number of congregations and individual members, the Synod has grown to number (June, 1951) 66 ordained pastors and professors, 69 congregations, 10,663 souls, 7,191 communicants. Contributions to home purposes amounted (1951) to $228,644, and to synodical purposes (including missions) to $47,337. During the first ten years the young men of the Synod received their training for the ministry and for teaching in the church at institutions of the Missouri and Wisconsin Synods. Since 1926 the Norwegian Synod owns and conducts Bethany Lutheran Junior College and High School and Theological Seminary (1946) at Mankato, Minn. — with a property valuation of approximately $400,000 and an attendance of more than two hundred students. 13 Christian day schools are operated within the Synod. The publications appearing regularly are the *Lutheran Sentinel,* the annual report of the synodical convention, and a Lutheran annual in the Norwegian language (1951).

3. The Synod has, particularly during the first years of its existence, tried to reach as many as possible of those individuals and smaller groups who found themselves alone after the merger of 1917. Gradually the Synod's work has fallen into the normal groove of established home and foreign mission work. In the cause of foreign

missions the Norwegian Synod co-operates with the Synodical Conference in the Colored Mission in this country and Nigeria. SCY

Presidents: B. Harstad (pres. pro. tem., 1917; 1918—21); G. A. Gullixson (1921—26); Chr. Anderson (1926—30); H. M. Tjernagel (1930—34); N. A. Madson (1934—35); C. A. Moldstad (1935 to 1937); H. Ingebritson (1937—42); N. A. Madson (1942—46); A. Harstad (1946 to 1950); C. M. Gullerud (1950—).

Notker, Balbulus (the Stammerer; d. 912). Most illustrious musician connected with the famous Swiss monastery of St. Gall. Recent investigations made by J. Handschim, H. J. W. Tillyard, Egon Wellesz, and others have made it imperative to reject the long-accepted Notkerian hypothesis, according to which Notker was the inventor of the sequence.* Many sequences formerly attributed to the school of St. Gall are today known to have been written in other monasteries in German-speaking countries, which became centers of this new art of hymn writing. Documents older than those of St. Gall have been found also in central and southern France. Nevertheless, Notker remains an important person in the realms of church music and hymnology, and his sequences are still among the very best extant today.

Egon Wellesz, *Eastern Elements in Western Chant*, Bonton (Byzantine Institute), 1947.

Notre Dame (nuns). The name of several religious congregations of women, the most important being the School Sisters of Notre Dame and the Sisters of Notre Dame (of Cleveland, Ohio), both engaged in teaching.

Notz, Eugen. B. 1847; brother of Fredrich W. A. Notz; educated at Maulbronn and Concordia Seminary, St. Louis; pastor of Wisconsin Synod at Menomonie; professor at Milwaukee Seminary (Wauwatosa), 1878; d. 1903.

Notz, Friedrich W. A. B. Feb. 2, 1841, in Lehren-Steinsfeld, Wuerttemberg. Passed *Landesexamen* and entered Maulbronn; studied theology, philosophy, and philology at Tuebingen, 1859—64; Ph. D. in 1863 (degree was formally renewed by faculty of Tuebingen, 1913); came to Georgia as tutor, 1866; professor at Pennsylvania College, 1868; at Muhlenberg College, 1869, where he translated Dietrich's *Institutiones Catecheticae* (Latin) into German, a labor most useful to Lutheran

America. Attracted by the decided Lutheranism of Western synods, he got in touch with some Wisconsin leaders and came to Milwaukee for the Synodical Conference, 1872. Originally chosen to fill professorship at St. Louis, Walther suggested he help to build up Northwestern University, to which Wisconsin and Notz agreed. Professor, at first inspector, 1872—1912. Sec. German American Press Association, 1870; pres. German School Association of Pa., 1871; editor *Luth. Schulzeitung*, 1876 to 1894. Died Dec., 1922.

Nova Scotia. See *Canada*.

Nova Scotia, Synod of. See *Canada, Lutheranism in*, 3; *United Lutheran Church, Synods of*, 21.

Novatian (3rd century). Native of Phrygia (?); opposed Cornelius' elevation to bishop of Rome and had himself consecrated bishop (anti-bishop); his views differed from the views of Cornelius regarding the treatment of the lapsed (those who denied their faith under persecution; see *Novatian Schism*); opposed Monarchianism.*

Novatian, Schism of. Resulted from conflicting principles of church discipline represented, on the one hand, by Novatian and his party and, on the other, by the dominant Church. It broke out after the Decian persecution, when the treatment of the lapsed (see *Persecution of Christians*, 4) was a paramount question. Bishop Cornelius of Rome (251—53) favored a mild discipline, while Novatian, his defeated rival for the bishop's chair, advocated severest rigorism. The Novatianists, though admitting that God might pardon the lapsed, strenuously denied that the Church had any right to readmit them to its communion. They called themselves *Katharoi* (Puritans), contending that the Church, the visible Church, should be a communion of saints, and of saints only. They even rebaptized all who came to them from the Catholic Church. Against his will Novatian was chosen bishop by his partisans. Cornelius excommunicated him. In spite of opposition, especially by Cyprian of Carthage, the Novatians spread nearly over the entire empire. The Council of Nicea assumed, in the main, a friendly attitude toward them; but later on they were treated as heretics. Nevertheless traces of the sect are found as late as the sixth century. Novatian was a prolific writer. Jerome ascribes to him works *On the Passover;*

On Circumcision; On the Priest; etc. His most important work is his treatise *On the Trinity,* in which he refutes the Sabellians and Monarchians.

Novena. A nine-day period dedicated, in the Roman Church, to special prayer and devotion, either in mourning, in preparation for a festival, to gain petitions, or to win indulgences.

Novice. A person wearing the habit and living the life of a religious order or congregation during the period of probation, lasting from one to three years. Novices are still free to leave the order.

Noyes, John Humphrey (1811—86). B. at Brattleboro, Vt.; studied for ministry; advocated perfectionism, free love, and "Christian communism"; formed communist society at Putney, Vt., and later the Oneida Society in New York State; fled to Canada to escape arrest for adultery. See *Communistic Societies.*

Numinous. See *Otto, Rudolf.*

Nunc Dimittis. See *Canticles; Worship, Parts of,* 13.

Nuncios. See *Legates.*

Nuns. In the earliest period of the monastic movement there were female hermits. Monastic communities of women came into existence in the East during the third century, and by the end of the following century they had become established in the West. Augustine drew up a rule for a nunnery, and the sister of St. Benedict governed one under her brother's direction. The rule of enclosure was, at first, not strictly enforced, but more stringent provisions were made, until Boniface VIII made strict enclosure an inviolable law for all professed nuns. This law automatically precluded nuns from almost all works of charity, leaving to them only the education of girls. As a result, pious associations were formed which had no solemn vows (see *Vows*), but whose members led a common life and performed various works of charity (*e. g.,* the Daughters of Charity). Such associations, formed for missions, for teaching, for nursing, etc., have steadily multiplied.

Nuremberg Bible Society. See *Bible Societies,* 2.

Nuremberg, Diet of, 1522—23. Pope Adrian VI, through Chieregati, admitted the corruptions in the Church "from the head to the members,"

promised to reform, and asked that the Edict of Worms be carried out against Luther, "the second Mohammed." The Diet asked the Pope to reform the Church, otherwise they would do it themselves. Unless the "Hundred Grievances" were corrected, Luther could not be fought without great dangers. It was a nullification of the Edict of Worms and of the papal bull of excommunication.

Nuremberg, Diet of, 1524. Pope Clement VII, through Campegius (Campeggio), declared the "Hundred Grievances" the work of some evilminded persons and insisted the Edict of Worms be executed against Luther. The Estates, on April 18, said they would do so "as far as possible."

Nuremberg Normal Books. The name given to writings accepted as norms by pastors of Nuremberg and Brandenburg Ansbach (1573). They are *Ecumenical Creeds; Luther's Catechisms; Augsburg Confession; Apology, Loci, Examen, and Definitiones* of Melanchthon; *Saxon Confession; Answer to the Impious Bavarian Articles; Answer Concerning the Controversy of Stancarus; Brandenburg-Nuremberg Church Order.*

Nuremberg Religious Peace, July 23, 1532. Sultan Solyman was marching against Hungary and Austria, and so Emperor Charles had to stop his attack on the Lutherans and promise them friendship and Christian love till the next council. Charles sanctioned this at Regensburg, hence also *Regensburg Religious Peace.*

Nursery Class. See *Parish Education,* B 4.

Nursery Roll. See *Parish Education,* B 3.

Nussmann, Adolph (1739—94). B. in Germany; Franciscan monk was converted to Lutheranism; came to America (1773) as a result of the pleas of C. Laverly and C. Rintleman; a thorough scholar and devoted missionary, he laid the foundations for the Lutheran Church in North Carolina. J. B. Moose, "Adolph Nussmann, Pioneer Luth. Preacher in North Carolina," *Luth. Ch. Quart.,* XIII: 575—91.

Nyasaland. In southeastern Africa. British. Area: 37,596 sq. mi.; population: 2,407,000, mostly African natives. Missions by ten societies. Statistics: Christian community, 531,519, of whom 194,526 were classified as communicants.

78 ordained and 482 not ordained native workers; total foreign staff, 287.

Nyaya. See *Brahmanism, 5.*

Nyberg, Lorenz Thorstausen (1720 to 1792). A Lutheran pastor of Swedish descent who served the congregation at Lancaster, Pa.; together with some of his members he joined the Moravian Church (1746) and caused disturbances in Pennsylvania and Maryland.

Nygren, Anders Theodore Samuel. See *Lund, Theology of; Sweden, Luth. Church in, 6.*

O

Oaths. 1. An oath is a solemn declaration of truth-telling with an appeal to God or to a sacred or revered person or thing as witness. An oath is often inviting some form of evil or punishment upon the one making such asseveration in the event that he should be deliberately telling a falsehood. — Oaths are connected with vows, covenants, wagers, or ordeals as they have been found among people of every degree of civilization from very early times. Among primitive peoples, oaths were believed to alight on something or someone, the destruction of the person being invariably mentioned in connection with the asseveration. Often the oath was accompanied with a conditional curse, naming some members of the body. Thus the Romans swore by their eyes or by their head. Sometimes, among the more primitive nations, a person swore on another person as to his truthfulness or innocence, the oaths by near relatives, such as children or brothers and sisters, being considered particularly effective.

2. In the Old Testament oaths by false gods were most strictly prohibited, as being essentially idolatry (Jer. 5:7; Amos 8:14). But swearing by Jehovah, the true God, was regarded highly (Deut. 6:13; 10:20; Num. 30:2; Is. 65:16). Some formulas for the oath were: "as the Lord liveth" (Judg. 8:19; Hos. 4:15), "as God liveth" (2 Sam. 2:27), "as thy soul liveth" (1 Sam. 1:26). The phrase "as the Lord liveth" is expressly denoted as the introduction of a proper oath (Jer. 5:2). Oaths were often obtained by an adjuration, by which an oath was laid on a person or he was caused to swear (1 Kings 8:31; Ezek. 17:13). In the case of very solemn oaths and covenants the ceremony included a sacrifice, as in Genesis 15. Another ancient custom is that found in Gen. 24:2 and 47:29, where the one taking the oath was requested to place his hand under the thigh (the seat of generative power) of the one demanding the oath, the idea connected with the rite probably being that the descendants of the person concerned should be included in the obligation of the oath. The simplest gesture or ceremony of swearing was that according to which the right hand or both hands were lifted up to heaven (Gen. 14:22; Ex. 6:8; Num. 14:30; for latter two references see marginal notes).

3. In the New Testament the passage in Matt. 5:34,36 (cp. James 5:12) is often understood as an absolute prohibition of swearing in any form. But that the Lord was speaking relatively, with regard to the frivolous use of God's name, is evident from Matt. 23:16-22, where He explains the sin connected with this kind of oath. It is also clear that He permitted an adjuration to be addressed to Himself, and that He acted accordingly (Matt. 26:63, 64). And His emphatic "Amen, Amen" ("Verily, verily") has the practical force of an oath. — That the New Testament does not absolutely forbid the use of the oath is clear from Heb. 6:16: "For men verily swear by the greater; and an oath for confirmation is to them an end of all strife." In this connection the use of the oath in the writings of St. Paul cannot be overlooked, for we find such expressions in a number of passages (Rom. 1:9; Phil. 1:8; Gal. 1:20; 1 Thess. 2:5; 2 Cor. 1:23). Nevertheless, the ideal and proper situation is that pictured by Christ when He says: "Let your communication be, Yea, yea; Nay, nay; for whatsoever is more than these cometh of evil" (Matt. 5:37).

4. The attitude of the Church has, in general, been conformable to the position taken in the Scriptures. It is true that Chrysostom called the oath a snare of Satan and wanted by all means to avoid it, and that also Augustine disliked the oath, chiefly on account of the fear of perjury. But the majority of the teachers declare that, while trifling, frivolous, and profane swearing should undoubtedly be condemned and avoided, the serious use

of the oath is too clearly established in Scripture. This was the position taken especially by Athanasius. In later centuries the practice was fixed by the Canon Law, which required, for the validity of an oath: 1) *Veritas in mente* (truth in the mind), that is, that the words used must be an actual, straightforward expression of what the swearer means to state; 2) *iudicium in iurante* (judgment, or discretion, in the one who swears), that is, that the person concerned have attained to the age and to the understanding required to take an oath properly, the further requirement of a sound mind and sobriety being included, and that the person concerned have not been convicted of perjury; 3) *iustitia in obiecto* (justice in the object), that is, the object of the oath must be legitimate, for even an oath cannot bind a person to commit a sin.

5. At the present time, in order to surround the taking of oaths with the proper solemnity, certain formulas have come into use, the one most frequently employed being: "So help me God!" Writers on ethics also mention that solemn oaths should ordinarily be administered only in the proper surroundings, in rooms which are suitably furnished, where the associations are of a nature to make a deep impression and to discourage the notion of perjury. In view of the general disregard of the sacredness of the oath in our days it behooves all Christians to uphold the position of the Bible with respect to both the First and the Second Commandment.

Obedience. An obligation binding all men to respect and follow divine and human authority. God demands 1) perfect obedience to His Law (Micah 6:8; Deut. 27:26; Luke 10:28); 2) willing obedience of children to their parents (Eph. 6:1,2); 3) submission of servants to their masters (Col. 3:23; Eph. 6:6); 4) respect for, and obedience to, civil authority (Rom. 13:1-7; 1 Pet. 2:13ff.). Examples: Gen. 6:22; 12:1-4; Joshua 11:15; 2 Kings 18:6; Luke 2:39; Acts 26:19; Heb. 5:8. See *Concordia Pulpit,* 1936, Vol. VII, 283; Fritz, *Preacher's Manual,* 165 ff.; Luther IX:989; XIII: 639; XXII:122; *Trigl.* p. 1272; Kretzmann, *Pop. Com.,* N. T., II, 339, 663.

Oberammergau. A village in the Bavarian Alps which has become famous for the decennial performance of a passion play which had its origin in the community and is performed by members of the parish. It represents a continuance of the medieval passion plays.

Oberlin, John Frederick (1740 to 1826). Pastor in the Steintal (1767), a barren valley in the Vosges Mountains, inhabited by lazy and vicious people, half dullards and half brigands, among whom he spent his entire life and whom he transformed into thrifty and exemplary Christians. His wife, Magdalena Salome, was a great help to him in his work.

Oberlin Theology. View taught at Oberlin College by Charles G. Finney and his associates. It held that all responsible character pertains to the will in its attitude and action and that each moral agent determines for himself, in the exercise of his own freedom, under the motives which gather about him, whatever is morally trustworthy or blameworthy in his character and life; that sin is a voluntary failure to meet obligation; that righteousness is a voluntary conforming to obligation; neither sin nor holiness can thus be transmitted, inherited or imputed. The repentance required as a condition of salvation is the renunciation of sin, an obligation which presses upon every sinner and which is always within his power. The power to sin involves the power to renounce, and this voluntary renunciation of sin is the change required of every sinner in order to obtain acceptance with God. The work of the Holy Spirit in the sinner's conversion is a moral work, accomplished by the presentation of motives which induce repentance, and the subsequent work of sanctification and preservation is essentially of the same nature, a work accomplished by the Spirit through the truth. The sovereignty of God always works in harmony with the freedom and responsibility of the creature, so that one factor in man's salvation must always be his own voluntary co-operation.

Objectives of Christian Education. See *Christian Teaching,* P; *Parish Education,* D 2.

Oblate Fathers *(Oblates of Mary Immaculate).* A society of priests and laymen leading a common life, formed in 1816 to repair the havoc of the French Revolution. It seeks especially to influence rural and industrial populations through missions and retreats which inculcate devotion to the Sacred Heart and to Mary as a supernatural means of regeneration. The society also fosters young men's associations, Catholic clubs, etc., and has numerous institutions of learning, including industrial and reform schools.

Obligation, Feasts of. See *Saints' Days, Roman Catholic.*

Obrecht, Jacob (ca. 1430—1505). Flemish composer of the Netherland School. He was a pupil of Ockeghem and the musical mentor of Erasmus. A master of polyphony. His sacred compositions are profoundly religious in spirit, and his art is rooted in folk music.

Obscure Men, Letters of. In 1514 Reuchlin's partisans had published a collection of testimonial letters upholding Reuchlin's defense of Jewish literature: *Clarorum virorum ad Jo. Reuchlin Epistolae.* A few months later came this parodistic counterpart: the letters of *obscuri viri* to Ortuinus Gratius, satirizing this opponent of Reuchlin as well as scholasticism and its Dominican supporters. These letters in coarse Latin delivered a telling blow against scholasticism.* They were undoubtedly written by Crotus Rubianus, Ulrich von Hutten, Philip Melanchthon, and others.

Observantists. A branch of the Franciscans which observed the strict rule of St. Francis and existed as a separate body from the 15th to the 19th century.

Occam, William (1280—1349). A Franciscan schoolman (*Doctor Invincibilis*); b. near London, d. in Munich, studied at Oxford and at Paris, teaching for some years at the latter place; held the ideal of absolute poverty; imprisoned by the Pope at Avignon for four years; later excommunicated for opposition to the Pope; his chief book: *Quaestiones et Decisiones in Quattuor Libros Sententiarium* (Questions and Decisions on the Four Books of Sentences), and the two parts of a greater work: *De Sacramento Altaris* and *De Corpore Christi*, which Luther valued rather highly; considered one of the men whose works had some influence on events during the Reformation period.

Occasionalism. Descartes' view of the togetherness of soul and body in the pineal gland was unsatisfactory since the togetherness was contactual rather than rational. Two of his disciples, Arnold Geulincx and Nicholas Malebrance, sought to solve the difficulty by a theory called Occasionalism. Soul and body, it holds, cannot interact, but behind both is God, who produces in the mind ideas corresponding to the physical world, and the harmony which is evident is the result of the continual activity of God, who makes matter and mind interact.

Occom, Samson, a Mohican Indian. B. at Norwich, Conn., in 1732. At seventeen he was converted during one of Whitefield's revival meetings. He spent four years in diligent study of the Bible in the parsonage of the Rev. Eleazer Wheelock at Lebanon, Conn. In 1759 he was duly ordained and began work among the Montauck Indians of Long Island. In 1766 and '67 he visited England to raise funds to carry on educational work among the Indians of America. He was successful, raising nearly 15,000 pounds for a school which was later incorporated as Dartmouth College. The closing years of his life were spent in Oneida County, N. Y., where he died in 1792. He published *Choice Collection of Hymns and Spiritual Songs*, 1774. "Now the Shades of Night Are Gone" is his best-known hymn.

Occultism. See *Theosophy; Spiritism.*

Ochino, Bernardino (1487—1564). "One of the most striking and picturesque characters" of the Italian Protestants; the most powerful preacher since Savonarola; broke with Rome when he was past fifty, fled to escape the Roman Inquisition; spent three years at Geneva; fled from Augsburg, Germany, to escape the hands of Charles V; spent seven years in England as an evangelist among Italian merchants and refugees; returned to Switzerland 1553 and served a congregation at Zurich; published (under the influence of Socinus, it would seem) a catechism, which resulted in his deposition and expulsion, 1563. Driven out successively from Basel, Nuremberg, Cracow, he died at Schlackau, in Moravia, 1564, a victim of his skeptical speculations and the intolerance of his age.

Ochs, Carl Ernst Christoph. B. Feb. 10, 1812, at Greglineng, Wuerttemberg; d. Nov. 16, 1863; Leipzig missionary to India, 1842; furloughed 1855; returned to India 1856; separated from Leipzig Mission June 2, 1859, engaging in independent mission work; united with

Danish Lutheran Missionary Society 1863.

Ochsenford, Solomon E. B. Nov. 8, 1855, near New Hanover, Pa.; ed.: Mt. Pleasant Sem., Boyerstown, Pa.; Muhlenberg Coll., Allentown, Pa. (1876, B. A.; 1879, M. A.; 1896, D. D.); Luth. Theol. Sem., Philadelphia, Pa., grad. 1879; pastorates at: Selinsgrove, Pa., 1879—99; acting pastor, Rochester, N. Y., 1909—10; Bath, Pa., 1910—?; Eng. secretary, Ministerium of Pa., 1895—1902; sec., Bd. of Presidents, 1897—98; prof. at Muhlenberg Coll., 1899—1909; Eng. sec. of General Council, 1901—04; editor: *Lutheran Church Almanac*, 1883—1904; edit. staff of *The Lutheran*, 1883—1918. Author: *Lutheran Church in Selinsgrove, Pa.; The Passion Story; Muhlenberg College Quarter Centennial Memorial Volume; Luther's First Hymn Book; Danville Conference Jubilee Memorial Volume; Documentary History of the General Council; Lutheran Confirmation Book.* D. June 19, 1932.

Odd Fellows. Full name, Independent Order of Odd Fellows, organized in the latter part of the 18th century in England. The first grand lodge in the United States was established in 1825, with four degrees: the Initiatory, or White, degree; the degree of Friendship, or Pink degree; the degree of Love, or Blue degree; the degree of Truth, or Scarlet degree. The order is a secret organization, each member being obligated on his word of honor to secrecy and to obedience to all the laws and regulations of their lodges and the Grand Lodge. Originating out of the same deistic form of religion which called forth the Masonic Order, the Odd Fellows introduced into their ritual much moral and ("unsectarian") religious instruction. At each revision these principles were increased and deepened and strengthened until regenerative powers are claimed, as in the phrasing: "May your initiation and consequent practice aid in releasing you from all blindness of moral vision, set you free from the fetters of ignorance and error, and bring you from death in selfishness into a life of active benevolence and virtue!" There are in the prescribed prayers many Biblical allusions, but the God of Odd Fellowship is not the Triune God, but a "Supreme Being," salvation not by faith in Christ, but by works, *i. e.*, by a good, moral life, as taught in the lodge. The privilege of a burial ritual which asserts eternal rewards, is extended to every Odd Fellow. Membership (1952) about 1,530,000. See references under *Lodge*.

Oecolampadius (Grecized for Heussgen = *Hausschein* = candlestick), **Johannes** (1482—1531). B. in Wuerttemberg; assisted Erasmus in publication of Greek New Testament; was stirred by Luther's writings, but later came under Zwingli's influence; carried through reformation at Basel (since 1523); attended Marburg Colloquy; d. at Basel. Luther, always zealous for purity of doctrine, considered his early death "a retribution for his obstinately held errors."

Oehler, Gustav Friedrich (1812 to 1872). Prof. at Tuebingen, later at Breslau, then again at Tuebingen; opposed radical criticism.

Oertel, M. See *Lutheran Church — Missouri Synod*, I, 2.

Oetinger, Friedrich Christoph (1702 to 1782). B. in Goeppingen; d. in Murrhardt. Studied at Tuebingen. Private teacher there, 1731—38; held three pastorates, 1738—52; dean in Weinsberg, 1752—59, and Herrenberg, 1759 to 1766; prelate in Murrhardt, 1766—82. As Pietist, mystic, alchemist, and theosophist he occupies a rather unique position among the 18th-century theologians of Wuerttemberg.

Oettingen, Alexander von (1827 to 1905). Positive modern Lutheran theologian; professor of systematic theology at Dorpat; chief work: *Moralstatistik und die christliche Sittenlehre*.

Oettli, Samuel (1846—1911). Conservative evangelical; pastor, then prof. at Bern and Greifswald; contributor to Strack-Zoeckler's Commentary; also wrote *Der Kampf um Babel und Bibel; Die revidierte Lutherbibel*.

Offense. In the Biblical sense, anything whereby a person is led to sin or error or whereby he is encouraged to continue therein (G. *"skandalon,"* trigger stick of trap; trap, snare; impediment placed in the way to cause someone to stumble or fall; stumbling block). The seriousness of giving offense is evident from the fact that offense is an obstacle placed in the way of a person's eternal salvation (1 Cor. 8:11; Rom. 14:15).

Examples: Matt. 5:29,30; 18:6-10 (Mark 9:42-48); Matt. 16:23; 17:27; 24:10; 13:21 (Mark 4,17); Luke 17:1,2; John 16:1; Rom. 2:23,24; 14:1-23; 16:17; Rev. 2:14. Christ and the Gospel are an offense to some: Matt. 11:6 (Luke 7:23); Matt. 13:57 (Mark 6:3); Matt. 15:12; 26:31-33 (Mark 14:27, 29); John 6:61; Rom. 9:33; 1 Cor. 1:23; Gal. 5:11; 1 Peter 2:8. The Christian's conduct: Rom. 14:1, 3, 13-15, 19-21; 1 Cor. 10:23-33; 8:13; Matt. 17:27; 18:6; Rom. 16:17.

Offense is *given* by an uncharitable use of Christian liberty, without consideration for the weak Christian (1 Cor. 8:9, 10; Rom. 14:13-15), by false doctrine (Rom. 16:17), by unchristian life (Rom. 2:23, 24; Matt. 18:6), or by neglect of Christian duty (implied in foregoing references). Offense may be unjustly *taken* by a prejudiced, loveless judgment of a Christian's actions or words.

The Christian cannot avoid giving offense to the world by his Christian testimony, since the Gospel will always be a stumbling block to some who will not believe (Gal. 5:11; Rom. 9:33; 1 Peter 2:8). He must not avoid giving offense when such a course would involve denial or yielding of a truth of God's Word (Gal. 2:11-14). RGL

Theo. Graebner, *The Borderland of Right and Wrong*, (Ninth Printing), pp. 30—52; Edw. Koehler, *A Summary of Christian Doctrine*, p. 68; F. Pieper, *Christliche Dogmatik*, I: 672—74.

Offerings. See *Finances in the Church.*

Offertory. Originally the offertory was the first liturgical act of the *missa fidelium* — the Communion service proper, which followed the office of the Word. The offertory was thus the offering of one's self through prayer and supplication, which was then supplemented by placing upon the altar such gifts of the people which might be used as sacramental elements (bread and wine), or used in the *agape*, or given to the poor. During the Middle Ages the *offertorium* was taken away from people, and only the clergy offered oblations for eucharistic use. While various ceremonies accompanied this act, a choral group sang a Psalm with antiphon in a Gregorian chant setting. Each Sunday and feast day had its own offertory, which thus became a proper. Since these offertories were usually rather short, additional musical settings were added later; these included motets, songs, and organ compositions. In 1593 Palestrina thus published his *Offertoria per totum annum*. During the 18th century organ offertories were written by Le Begue, Grigny, and F. Couperin; in the 19th century, by such French composers as Batiste, Widor,

Saint-Saens, Guilmant, and others. In Italy such organ music was given the title *Elevazione;* cf. Frescobaldi's *Toccata avanti l'elevazione*. The Lutheran Church quite naturally refused to adopt the Roman Catholic conception of the offertory. Luther was willing to drop the offertory entirely and to begin the liturgy of the Holy Communion with the Preface. However, many did not follow him in this, and during the 17th century, congregations adopted the practice of using Pastor Georg Winer's (1583—1651) setting of *"Schaffe in mir, Gott, ein reines Herze."* While others used penitential hymns, hymns of praise, and Lenten hymns as the offertory of the service, still others inserted the Exhortation at this place in the service. However, using the Exhortation as well as penitential and Lenten hymns in the service of Holy Communion did not find ready acceptance among those who sought to bear in mind the joyful eucharistic nature of the service. While in our day "Create in Me a Clean Heart, O God" from Freylinghausen's *Gesangbuch* of the first part of the 18th century enjoys well-deserved wide use, some prefer to use plain chant settings of Psalm texts. WEB

Office of Christ. See *Christ Jesus.*

Office of the Dead. Service of the Divine Office used at funerals; originated in the 9th century and forms the basis of the Anglican burial ritual.

Office of the Keys. See *Keys, Office of.*

Office, Sacred Congregation of the Holy. A Roman Catholic office created in 1542 to supersede the Universal Roman Inquisition. Its duties are to judge heresies, dogmatics, and certain practical matters. See *Counter Reformation.*

Office of the Word (Liturgical). See *Worship, Parts of.*

Officiorum et Munerum. See *Index of Prohibited Books; Bible Reading.*

Ohio Conference of the Ministerium of Pennsylvania. See *United Lutheran Church, Synods of*, 22.

Ohio, District Synod of. See *United Lutheran Church, Synods of*, 22.

Ohio, English Synod of. See *United Lutheran Church, Synods of*, 22.

Ohio, Ev. Luth. District Synod of. See *United Lutheran Church, Synods of*, 22.

Ohio and Other States, Ev. Luth. Joint Synod of. 1. *History.* In the "Great Crossing" over the Allegheny Mountains at the close of the eighteenth century many Lutherans of the older settlements found their way into the Northwest Territory. The number increased when Ohio was made a State in 1802. These pioneers were soon followed by pastors, the first of these being John Stauch, who had been licensed by the Pennsylvania Ministerium in 1793 and ordained in 1804. He settled in Columbiana Co., Ohio, in October, 1806. He was followed by Wm. (Geo.) Foerster, who made his headquarters in Fairfield Co., in the same year (d. 1815). About the same time Paul Henkel, who had helped to organize the North Carolina Synod in 1803, began to make missionary journeys through the State. In October, 1812, the first conference of Lutheran ministers west of the Allegheny Mountains met at Stecher's Church, Westmoreland Co., Pa. Those present were Stauch, Foerster, John Reinhard, Jacob Leist, Henry Huet, A. Weyer. G. H. Weygandt and Heim attended as guests. Steck, Butler, Paul Henkel, and Simon were absent.

2. Yearly meetings of this "Special Conference" were held until permission was obtained from the mother synod (Pennsylvania Ministerium) to organize a separate ministerium. This was done on September 14, 1818, when at Somerset, Perry Co., Ohio, the first "General Conference of Ev. Luth. Preachers in the State of Ohio and Adjacent States" was formed, with John Stauch as its first president, Paul Henkel as secretary, and G. H. Weygandt as treasurer. Fifteen pastors and two catechists were enrolled, the largest number to constitute a Lutheran synod in America up to that time. Owing to the great distance and, partly, to the influence of the "Henkelites," the Ohio Synod declined to join the General Synod in 1820. During the earlier years fraternal relations were maintained with the Tennessee Synod. At the meeting of 1826, 16 pastors reported from four to eight congregations each, a total of 98, while 15 congregations were without a pastor.

3. The lack of ministers induced the newly organized synod (1818) to request Rev. Jacob Leist, with the help of Candidate David Schuh, to instruct young men for the ministry. A seminary was established in 1830 at Canton and, in 1831, transferred to Columbus. Candidate Wm. Schmidt became the first professor. In 1831, when Andrew Henkel was president, the synod was divided into an Eastern and a Western District. Other Districts were added in the course of time. Since 1833 it has been called the Joint Synod of Ohio. Since 1854 it met biennially as a delegate synod. Prof. W. F. Lehmann was president 1854 to 1859 and again in 1878, Dr. Matthias Loy from 1859 to 1894 (except in 1878), Dr. C. H. L. Schuette since 1894, Dr. C. C. Hein, 1925—30.

4. The first English District, founded 1836, left the mother synod and joined the General Synod in 1841 (East Ohio Synod). A second English District, formed in 1841, seceded in 1855, joined the General Synod and then the General Council (English Synod of Ohio). A third English District was organized in 1857, but without the consent of the mother synod it joined the General Council in 1867 (English District Synod of Ohio). The fourth English District dates from 1869. The other Districts added were the Southern (merged into the Western), the Northwestern (largely by secession from "Missouri" during the Predestinarian Controversy), the Northern (1851), Concordia (1876), Wisconsin (1890), Minnesota (1890), Kansas-Nebraska (1890), Texas (1890), Canada (1908), Australia (1908).

5. *Theology.* The doctrinal basis of the Joint Ohio Synod in its early days was nominally that of the Tennessee Synod; but still more than that synod it was affected by the unionism and the Methodistic measures of those days. The *Lutheran Standard* was established in 1842 and *Die Lutherische Kirchenzeitung* in 1860. Through Ernst and Burger, relations were established with Loehe, and the influx of German candidates strengthened the conservative party under the leadership of Dr. Wm. Sihler in the early forties. Though the conservatives withdrew in 1845, the synod, under the leadership of Lehmann and Loy, declared its unconditional acceptance of the Lutheran Confessions in 1848. Its contact with Missouri in the free conferences of 1856 to 1859 deepened the confessionalism of the Ohio Synod and caused it to take a determined stand against antichristian secret societies. It was the failure of the General Council to define its position on the "Four Points" * that caused the Ohio Synod to withdraw after having been present at the preliminary meetings in 1866 and 1867. In 1868 fraternal relations were established

with Missouri, and in 1872 the Joint Ohio Synod assisted in the organization of the Synodical Conference at Milwaukee. In January, 1878, the Ohio Synod conferred the degree of D. D. on Professor Walther. Only two years later Prof. F. A. Schmidt of the Norwegian Synod accused Walther of crypto-Calvinism. That was the beginning of the Predestinarian Controversy, which caused the Ohio Synod to withdraw from the Synodical Conference in September, 1881. The main controversialists in those days were Walther, Pieper, and Stoeckhardt on the side of the Missourians and Stellhorn, F. A. Schmidt, Allwardt, C. H. L. Schuette, and Ernst on the side of Ohio. At the intersynodical conferences, 1903 to 1906, efforts were made to heal the breach. The movement culminated in the drafting of the *Chicago Theses,** which, however, failed to bring about a rapprochement.

6. After the Ohio Synod withdrew from the Synodical Conference (1881), a private conference was arranged between leaders of Iowa and Ohio. In 1887 arrangements were made for an official committee. The theses formulated by this committee were not accepted. In 1909 the *Toledo Theses** were drawn up, on the basis of which fellowship was declared in 1918. Shortly thereafter, a joint committee was named to discuss a merger of the two bodies. In 1925 the Buffalo Synod sent a delegation to the committee. On Aug. 10, 1930, the Ohio Synod, Iowa Synod, and Buffalo Synod merged to form the American Lutheran Church.*

7. *Missions.* The Joint Synod of Ohio was active in the field of home missions, especially in the Northwest. It also conducted a mission among the colored in Baltimore and in the Black Belt of Alabama. In 1912 it took over part of the Hermannsburg field among the Telugus in India; after World War I the whole field was assigned to it. — Besides its theological seminary in Columbus it had the following educational institutions: Capital University, Columbus (1850), Luther Seminary, St. Paul, Minn. (1884), Hebron Academy, Hebron, Nebr. (1911), Luther Academy in Saskatchewan (1913), St. John's Academy, Petersburg, W. Va. (1921). The Woodville Normal School, established 1882, closed its doors in 1923. The Pacific Seminary, Spokane, Wash., was opened 1907, discontinued 1918. There was a practical seminary in Hickory, N. C., 1887—1912.

C. Spielmann, *Abrisz der Geschichte der evangelisch-lutherischen Synode von Ohio u. anderen Staaten . . . bis zum Jahre 1846,* Luth. Bk. Concern, Columbus, Ohio, 1880; R. A. Peter and Wm. Schmidt, *Geschichte der Allgemeinen evangelisch-lutherischen Synode von Ohio u. anderen Staaten,* Luth. Bk. Concern, Columbus, O., 1900; E. A. Boehme, *Manual of the Evangelical Lutheran Joint Synod of Ohio and Other States,* Luth. Bk. Concern, Columbus, O., 1910; C. V. Sheatsley, *History of the Evangelical Lutheran Joint Synod of Ohio and Other States,* Luth. Bk. Concern, Columbus, O., 1919; M. Loy, "Joint Synod of Ohio," *The Distinctive Doctrines and Usages of the General Bodies of the Evangelical Lutheran Church in the United States,* Luth. Pub. Soc., Philadelphia, 1902 (pp. 5—33); B. H. Pershing, "Synodical Organization in Ohio before 1850," *Luth. Ch. Quart.,* IX: 402—18.

Ohio, Synod of. See *United Lutheran Church, Synods of,* 22.

Ohio, Synod of East. See *United Lutheran Church, Synods of,* 22.

Ohl, Jeremiah Franklin. Clergyman. B. June 26, 1850; graduate of Lutheran Theological Seminary, Philadelphia, 1874; organizer and rector of Lutheran Deaconess Motherhouse, Milwaukee, and instructor at Lutheran Theological Seminary, Chicago, 1893 to 1898; city missionary in Philadelphia, 1899; superintendent of Philadelphia Lutheran City Mission, 1903; lecturer at Lutheran Theological Seminary, Philadelphia, 1910—11; engaged in prison reform; president of Inner Mission Society; author of a number of books; contributor to *Encyclopedia of Missions;* writer of hymn tunes and other church music. D. Jan. 21, 1941.

Ohly, Emil (1821—90). Positive theologian, although in the Prussian Union; pastor at Ginsheim; published *Vademecum pastorale,* edited a quarterly in the field of homiletics and pastoral theology, also a series of books containing occasional sermons, and some story books.

Oil, Holy. Three kinds of holy oil are consecrated by Roman bishops on Maundy Thursday and delivered to parish priests: 1) oil of catechumens (olive oil), used at Baptisms, ordination of priests, coronation of kings and queens, consecration of churches and altars; 2) chrism (olive oil mixed with balsam), used after Baptism, at confirmation, and consecration of bishops, Communion vessels and fonts; 3) oil of the sick (olive oil), used in extreme unction and the blessing of bells.

Okeghem (Ockeghem, Ockenheim), Jean d' (ca. 1430—ca. 95). B. at Dender, East Flanders; chaplain and composer of Charles VII of Paris; Louis XI appointed him treasurer of St. Martin's at Tours; wrote masses, motets, and chansons. He is often regarded as the founder of the second Netherland school which is distinguished from the first by the former's greater use of counterpoint and its facility in invention. Okeghem's pupils carried his art to all countries.

O'Kelly, James (ca. 1757—1826). First seceder from Methodist Church; b. in Ireland; itinerant preacher in America, 1778; elder of Methodist Episcopal Church, 1784; withdrew 1792 and formed the Republican Methodist Church; d. in Virginia. See *Congregational and Christian Churches*, B; *Methodist Bodies*, 4 a.

Olafsson, Stephan (1620—88). Ed. in Copenhagen; dean of Vallanes, Sweden; translated into Icelandic the hymns of Thomas Kingo and wrote many original hymns.

Old Catholic Church in America. See *Old Catholics*, 2.

Old Catholics. 1. Name applied to Catholics who reject the Vatican decree of papal infallibility and absolutism as an arbitrary dogmatic innovation and therefore have seceded from the Roman communion and established an independent organization. Foreshadowed by the anti-infallibilist literature which preceded the Vatican Council and by the stand of the eighty-eight bishops who voted against the new dogma at the council itself (all these bishops sacrificed conviction and conscience later on), the Old Catholic movement took its rise in the hostility of some of the leading scholars and divines of the Catholic Church, men who prior to the council had been esteemed as pillars and ornaments of the Church.

2. Leaders of the Old Catholics were von Schulte, professor at the University of Prague; Reinkens, professor of church history at the University of Breslau; Friedrich, who held the same chair at Munich; Reusch, professor of theology at Born; and, above all, John Joseph Ignatius von Doellinger, the noted scholar and historian, who, when called upon by the Archbishop of Munich to subscribe to the new dogma of papal infallibility, gave this classic answer March 28, 1871 (his words are well worth quoting in full): "As a Christian, as a theologian, as a historian, as a citizen, I cannot accept this dogma. Not as a Christian, because it is incompatible with the spirit of the Gospel and with the plain utterances of Christ and His Apostles. Not as a theologian, because the entire genuine tradition of the Church is irreconcilably opposed to it. Not as a historian can I accept it because as such I know that the persistent efforts to realize this theory of world dominion have cost Europe streams of blood, have ruined and thrown whole lands into confusion. . . . As a citizen, finally, I must reject it because by demanding the subjection of states and rulers and the whole political order to the papal power . . . it lays the foundation of endless discord between Church and State, between the clergy and the laity."

3. Doellinger was excommunicated, and all the adherents of the Old Catholic movement were branded by Pius IX in his encyclical of Nov. 21, 1873, as "miserable sons of perdition," who seek to undermine the foundations of the Catholic religion. In June of the same year the Old Catholics had effected a church organization at Constance in the very hall where, 360 years before, the Council of Constance had asserted its superiority over the Papacy. Reinkens was elected bishop, and a constitution was drawn up providing for clerical and lay representation in the government of the Church. Doctrinally the Old Catholics represent Tridentine Romanism as against Vatican Romanism, with a more friendly attitude, however, toward Protestant principles. They recognize as the rule of faith the Scriptures *and tradition*, but limit the latter to the Ecumenical Creeds held in common by orthodox Christianity, Catholic or Protestant. They also encourage Bible reading, admit the use of the vernacular instead of the Latin in public worship, and allow the clergy to marry. Still too close to Rome and, on the other hand, too far from Protestantism, the Old Catholics hold a position which has naturally failed to enlist much popular sympathy. Before World War II the Old Catholics numbered 500,000 in Europe.

4. In America the Old Catholics are represented by several groups which

have for one reason or another rejected the papal authority but retained the main doctrines and practices of the Roman Church. The four groups are: *American Catholic Church, American Old Catholic Church, North American Old Roman Catholic Church, Old Catholic Church in America.* While the *Liberal Catholic Church* and the *Polish National Church* have also rejected the papal supremacy and frequently are listed with the Old Catholics, their origin is different from that of the Old Catholics.

Old Fashion Revival Hour. See *Radio Evangelism, 5.*

Old German Baptist Brethren. See *Brethren, Dunkers, 3.*

Old High German Religious Poetry and Prose. In the 8th century there was a revival of learning and an introduction of Christianity into many parts of Germany. Some religious literature dates from this period, as the *Paternoster, Credo,* the Monsee-Vienna Fragments of a Gospel translation, the *Weissenburger Catechism,* versions of the Psalter, prayers, etc. Prominent Old High German literature are Otfrid's *Evangelienbuch,* the *Heliand,* and the eschatological poem *Muspilli.*

Old Lights. See *New Lights.*

Old Lutherans. Originally this term was applied to Lutherans in Prussia who refused to join in the Prussian Union of 1817 and 1830. Later applied to the confessional Lutherans who immigrated to America between 1838 and 1848 and who emphasized the fact that they were Lutherans of the old school, genuine, original Lutherans, because they had not accepted any innovation or modification of doctrine or practice. They pledged themselves unequivocally to all historic symbols of the Lutheran Church.

Frederick William III tried to unite the Lutherans and Reformed in Prussia by decrees. Naturally, many of the Lutherans found this impossible. The Rev. J. A. A. Grabau became the spiritual leader of the Prussian group. Their antipathy to this union resulted in mass emigration to America in 1839, they settled chiefly in New York and Wisconsin. Like-minded people followed in 1843 under the Rev. Adolph Kindermann. This group organized the Buffalo Synod in 1845.

A similar movement took place in Saxony when a unionistic *agenda* was introduced in 1812. The leader of the

Saxon group was the Rev. Martin Stephan of Dresden. With a large group of laymen as well as a number of pastors and theological candidates this group also came to America in 1839, settling in Missouri, and became instrumental in organizing the Missouri Synod in 1847. Smaller groups followed from time to time.

These groups believed in thorough education of their children and theological students. Seminaries were founded as soon as they arrived in America. Christian day schools also were established wherever their congregations existed. They showed a deep interest in the liturgical movement, and were consistently conscious of their Christian liberty.

The general trend in American Lutheranism a century ago was toward a more liberal theology. However, through the impact which the Old Lutherans made by their insistence on a confessional theology, the entire picture is changed today. ARS

V. Ferm, *Crisis in American Lutheran Theology,* New York, 1927; C. Mauelshagen, *American Lutheranism Surrenders to Forces of Conservatism,* Univ. of Georgia, 1936; Ralph D. Owen, "The Old Lutherans Come," *CHIQ,* April, 1947; F. Lichtenberger, *History of German Theoolgy in the 19th Century,* T. & T. Clark, Edinburgh, 1889.

Old Order Amish. See *Mennonite Bodies, 3.*

Old Order Mennonite Church. See *Mennonite Bodies, 3.*

Old Order or Yorker Brethren. See *Brethren, The River.*

Old People's Homes. See *Aged and Infirm, Homes for.*

Old Roman Catholic Church. See *Old Catholics.*

Old Roman Symbol. See *Ecumenical Creeds, A 4.*

Old School Baptists. See *Baptist Bodies, 11.*

Old School Presbyterian Church. See *New School Presbyterian Church.*

Old Side Presbyterians. See *Presbyterians, B 4.*

Old Syriac Version. See *Bible Versions, C.*

Olearius. The following are the most notable of this family of prominent theologians: 1. *Johann;* b. 1546 at

Wesel, d. as pastor and superintendent at Halle, 1623; son-in-law of Heshusius and strict Lutheran. 2. *Gottfried*, son of the former; b. 1604 and died at Halle 1685. 3. *Johann*, brother of preceding, b. 1611, d. 1684; hymn writer. 4. *Johann Gottfried*, son of No. 2; b. 1635; d. 1711 as consistorial councilor at Arnstadt; wrote: "Komm, du wertes Loesegeld." 5. *Johann*, brother of the former; b. 1639; d. 1713 as senior of the theological faculty at Leipzig. 6. *Johann Christian*, son of No. 3; b. 1646; d. 1699 as consistorial councilor at Halle; moderately pietistic. 7. *Johann Christophorus*, son of No. 4; b. 1668 at Halle; d. in 1747 as superintendent at Arnstadt; eminent hymnologist. 8. *Gottfried*, son of No. 5; b. 1672, d. 1715; professor of theology at Leipzig; had leanings toward Spener.

Olearius, Johann (1611—84). Lutheran hymnologist; studied at Wittenberg; adjunct of philosophical faculty; superintendent at Querfurt in 1637; court preacher and private chaplain at Halle in 1643; *Kirchenrat* in 1657; superintendent general in 1664; d. at Weissenfels; wrote commentary on the entire Bible and various devotional works; his *Geistliche Singekunst* is a collection of more than 1,200 hymns, 208 of them by himself; among his hymns: "Nun kommt das neue Kirchenjahr"; "Gelobet sei der Herr"; "O grosser Gott, du reines Wesen"; "Wenn dich Unglueck hat betreten"; "Lass mich, o treuer Gott, dein liebes Schaeflein bleiben."

Olevianus, Caspar (1536—87). German Reformed; b. at Treves; professor of theology at Heidelberg, 1561; Calvinized the Palatinate; prepared *Heidelberg Catechism* with Ursinus; one of judges who ordered Silvanus (anti-Trinitarian) beheaded; Berleburg; Herborn (d. there). See *Reformed Confessions*. D 2.

Olive Branch Synod. See *United Lutheran Church, Synods of, 8.*

Olivetans. A small Roman Catholic monastic order founded by Bernard Tolomei (14th century).

Olshausen, Hermann (1796—1839). B. at Oldeslohe, in Holstein; d. at Erlangen. Studied at Kiel and Berlin. *Privatdozent* at Berlin, 1820; extraordinary, 1821, and ordinary, 1827, professor at Koenigsberg; professor at Erlangen, 1834. He upheld the genuineness of the Gospels and published a commentary on the books of the NT.

Olshausen, Justus (1800—82). Professor of oriental languages at Kiel and Koenigsberg, wrote famous commentary on the Psalms (1853); Hebrew grammarian.

Olsson, Olaf (1841—1900). Swedish-born Lutheran; came to America, 1869; pres. of Augustana College and Seminary, Rock Island, Ill., 1891—1900; opposed the view of Waldenstrom of Sweden, who held that God, being Love, need not be reconciled, but that reconciliation is concerned with the removal of the sins of the world.

Oltramare, Paul (1854—1930). Swiss student of religions. He held that scientific and industrial progress had made religion obsolete. Religion, he held, is the result of ignorance and incapacity.

Oman, John Wood (1860—1939). Prof. at Westminster College, Cambridge; rejected inspiration, grace, faith, and emphasized a personal spiritualism.

Omnipotence. That attribute of God * by reason of which He can perform, and actually does perform, whatever He has purposed (Ps. 115:3; 135:6).

Omnipresence. The attribute of God according to which He is essentially everywhere. See *Immanence*.

Omniscience. See *Knowledge*.

Omoto-Kyo (Japanese, "fundamental faith"). It is an offshoot of Shinto; originated by a poor woman, O Nao Baasan, of the village of Ayabe, Province Tamba, Japan, in 1892, who asserted to have had divine revelations. The system is both imperialistic and socialistic. Its other characteristics are faith-healing, millenarianism, communism, perfectionism, mysticism, and the inculcation of patriotism. The writings of the founder form their sacred book and are known as *O Fude Saki*. The Japanese government declared the movement hostile to the state and its followers guilty of treason and took stringent measures to suppress it.

Onderdonk, Henry Ustic (1789 to 1858). Educated at Columbia College, New York; Episcopalian; rector in Brooklyn and in Philadelphia; later bishop of Philadelphia; leading member of committee of *American Prayer-book;* wrote: "The Spirit in Our Hearts."

Oneida Society. Also called *Perfectionists;* a communistic settlement, founded in 1847 at Oneida, N. Y., by John Humphreys Noyes, former Congregationalist minister and believer in perfectionism. Characteristic was their practice of "complex marriages," a kind of polyandry. Under certain restrictions any man could have intercourse with any woman, and permanent attachments were prohibited. Children were cared for by the community. Owing to public pressure this system was abolished in 1879 and the community reorganized into a stock company in 1881.

Onkelos. See *Bible Versions*, B.

Onomasticon. See *Geography, Christian*, 3.

Ontario. See *Canada*.

Ontological Argument. See *Apologetics; God*.

Ontology. A term applied to that phase of philosophy which concerns itself with the problem of being, or essence.

Oosterzee, Johannes Jacobus Van (1817—82). Dutch Reformed; b. at Rotterdam; preacher at Alkmaar, Rotterdam; professor of theology at Utrecht 1863; profound scholar; d. at Wiesbaden; wrote *Theology of the New Testament*, etc.

Open Questions. In the nineteenth century this term played an important role in the debates that agitated the Lutheran Church in America; the Iowa Synod opposed the Missouri Synod on this subject. Gradually clarity and a measure of understanding was reached. It was agreed that the term "open questions" should not be used to designate teachings not decided in the confessional writings of the Church. In the colloquy between Iowa and Missouri in 1867 the position was vindicated that the term should be looked upon as equivalent to theological problems, f. i., the question, on which day of the first week of the world the angels were created. According to this view, which the Missouri Synod has consistently championed, an open question is a point of theology which the Bible has not decided for us and where liberty of opinion must be permitted. In the *Lutheran Cyclopedia* Dr. Sigismund Fritschel deviates somewhat from this position and advocates the view which looks upon open questions as teachings in which a difference of opinion will not make church fellowship impossible,

because the teachings in question "are not articles of faith."

J. P. Beyer, *Stenographic Report of the Colloquy Between Iowa and Missouri; Davenport Theses* * of the Iowa Synod; C. F. Walther, "The False Arguments for the Modern Theory of Open Questions," *CTM*, X: 254—62; 351—57; 415—20; 507—13 (preceding tr. W. Arndt); 587—95; 656—66; 752—59; 827 to 834 (preceding tr. A. Guebert).

Opera Supererogationis ("works paid in addition"). The Roman Church teaches that the saints, by works of penance and charity, gained more merit than was needed to remove the temporal punishment of their own sins and that this excess, together with the merits of Christ, is in the keeping and at the disposal of the Church and can be applied by it to the needs of those who have not enough merit of their own to keep them out of purgatory. From this "treasury of the Church" Rome claims to impart in granting indulgences.* Concerning this horrible idea, that the just and holy God had nothing more to ask of the saints, but that, on the contrary, they made Him gifts of much that they did not owe Him, the Apology of the Augsburg Confession (VI, 45) says: "No one does as much as the Law requires; therefore it is ridiculous when they pretend that we can do more." (Cf. Luke 17:10.)

Ophites. See *Gnosticism*, 7 i.

Opitz, Martin (1597—1639). Studied at Frankfurt and Heidelberg; was employed in various political and diplomatic offices; poems noted for style, but lack depth; wrote: "Brich auf und werde lichte."

Optatus of Mileve (4th century). Theologian of North Africa known for the part he played in the Donatist Schism, on which his books are still the best source; also prominent as a church historian, emphasizing the unity of the Church under the primacy of Peter.

Optimism. In philosophy, the belief that this world is the best possible world or even absolutely good.

Opus Operatum. A term used by Roman Catholic theologians with reference to the Sacraments to express their doctrine that these Sacraments confer the grace of God by the working of the work (*opere operato*), that is, by the performance of the outward sacramental act, apart from the spiritual condition of the recipient (opere operantis). The Council of Trent says plainly: "If any one saith that by the said Sacraments of the New Law grace is not conferred through the act performed (ex opere operato), but that faith alone in the divine promise suffices for the obtaining of grace, let him be accursed." (Sess. VII, can. 8.) The Roman doctrine demands only that the recipient do not place an obstacle to grace (can. 6), e. g., by mortal sin or unbelief, and avers that if such obstacles do not intervene, grace is automatically conferred. The Apology of the Augsburg Confession (XIII, 18) says: "We condemn the whole race of scholastic doctors, who teach that on one who does not place an obstacle the Sacraments confer grace ex opere operato, without a good movement (sine bono motu) of the recipient. This is simply a Jewish notion, to think that we are justified by the ceremony, without the good movement of the heart, that is, without faith."

Opzoomer, Cornelis Willem (1821 to 1892). Dutch philosopher; prof. at Utrecht; held a pantheistic view; unnecessary to believe in immortality; man's highest desire should be that the will of God be done.

Orange Free State. Member of the Union of South Africa within the British Empire. Area: 49,647 sq. mi.; population: 879,071, mostly native Bantus. Official language, Dutch. The Dutch Reformed Church predominates. For missions see Africa.

Orange, Second Council of. See Pelagian Controversy.

Oratorians. A congregation of secular priests, founded 1550 at Rome by Philip Neri, who attracted the half-heathen Roman populace by simple preaching and good music (beginnings of the oratorio). Oratorians are restricted to prayer, the administration of the Sacraments, and preaching. They take no vows, retain their property, and may withdraw at any time.

Oratorio. It is difficult to give an adequate definition of oratorio, since there are different types of oratorios, secular and sacred. Some early oratorios were not very unlike an opera; scenery and costumes being used. Dialog, however, was not employed, and a narrator was not required. Since accompaniment, instrumental preludes and interludes, choruses, arias, and recitatives are employed in the oratorio and cantata, they are related to each other and the opera. Bach's Christmas Oratorio is in reality a series of six cantatas integrated into a unit. Basing our distinction on works like Handel's Messiah and the cantatas of Bach, one might say that while some oratorios employ the words of Scripture exclusively, the cantata includes also the subjective elements of reflection and contemplation. On the other hand, the latter elements of the Bach cantata found their way also into the oratorios of Felix Mendelssohn-Bartholdy and others. Although Passion oratorios exist, Passions, Masses, and other extensive compositions based on liturgical texts are usually not classified as oratorios.

The mysteries of the 14th and 15th centuries and the liturgical dramas of the late Middle Ages helped pave the way for the oratorio. The claims formerly made which insisted that the orationi of Filippo Neri (middle of the 16th century) helped substantially to give rise to the oratorio have been disputed by E. Selle (Neue Zeitschrift fuer Musik, 1864), Herman Kretzschmar, and others, since an oratory is hardly well suited for the performance of musical drama. People had grown weary of the diminutive madrigal and desired works of larger and more dramatic proportions. Neri's performances in the oratory included readings from the Scriptures, a sermon, and the singing of hymns. Hammerschmidt's Gespraeche zwischen Gott und einer glaeubigen Seele (1645) and works by other composers contributed to the early development of the oratorio. The operas of Monteverdi and the works of Anerio and Mazzochi influenced the development of the oratorio.

Oratorios in the more modern sense were written by Giacomo Carissimi (1605—74). Other 17th- and 18th-century composers of oratorios included Alessandro Scarlatti (1659—1725), Antonio Lotti (ca. 1665—1740), Antonio Caldara (1670—1736), Leonardo Leo (1694—1744), Johann Adolph Hasse (1699—1783), and Niccolo Jommelli (1714—74).

The Lutheran school of the 17th and 18th centuries included, first of all, Heinrich Schuetz,* whose oratorios deserve a place of honor, though they have as yet received little recognition in America. The oratorio was neglected by Lutherans between Schuetz and Bach. The oratorios of Bach's contemporaries, Georg Ph. Telemann and Johann Mattheson, are interesting, but often too dramatic, theatrical, and sensuous. Johann Christoph Friedrich Bach's (1732—95) *Die Kindheit Jesu* enjoyed popularity. Carl Philipp Emanuel Bach's oratorios are among his finest works.

Handel's * oratorios helped bring fame to England and developed among the English people a love for oratorio so genuine and intense that it has not abated since. Handel turned from the opera to the oratorio, and the style of his oratorios is essentially no different from the style of his operas. His oratorios were to be sung during the season of Lent, during which time the performance of theatrical performances was forbidden in England by law. Among the successors of Handel were John Christopher Smith (1712—95), Charles John Stanley (1713—86), Thomas Arne (1710—78).

That even Joseph Haydn came under the spell of Handel may be seen from his oratorios *The Creation* (1797) and the secular *The Seasons* (1801), not, however, from his *Seven Words on the Cross* (1797). Neither Beethoven (despite his *Mount of Olives*) nor Mozart play into the picture as writers of oratorios. Ludwig Spohr's (1784—1859) *Das letzte Gericht* and Mendelssohn-Bartholdy's *St. Paul* and *Elijah* were long popular.

Oratorios were written also by Wagner *(Das Liebesmahl der Apostel,* 1844), Liszt *(Christus,* 1866), Dvorak, Berlioz, Franck *(The Beatitudes,* 1879), Gounod *(The Redemption,* 1881; *Mors et Vita,* 1885), Saint Saens *(Christmas Oratorio; The Deluge),* J. Massenet *(Marie Magdeleine),* Hubert Parry *(Judith,* 1888; *Job,* 1892; *King Saul,* 1894), Horatio Parker *(Hora Novissima,* 1893), and Elgar *(Dream of Gerontius,* 1900).

In the 20th century great acclaim has been accorded Arthur Honegger's *King David* (1923), Igor Stravinsky's *Oedipus Rex* (1927), Paul Hindemith's *Das Unaufhoerliche* (1931), and William Walton's *Belshazzar's Feast* (1931).

WEB

Arnold Schering, *Geschichte des Oratoriums,* Leipzig, 1911; Annie Patterson, *The Story of the Oratorio,* London, 1915; Guido Adler, *Handbuch der Musik-Geschichte,* Frankfurt, 1924; *Harvard Dictionary of Music,* Cambridge, 1944; *Grove's Dictionary of Music and Musicians,* Philadelphia, 1926; Hermann Kretzschmar, *Fuehrer durch den Concertsaal* (II), Leipzig, 1899.

Oratory. In the Roman Church a structure, other than a parish church, in which Mass may be said. Oratories are either public, semipublic (as in seminaries, colleges, hospitals, etc.), or private (granted by papal indult to individuals or families).

Oratory of Divine Love. See *Counter Reformation,* 1 d.

Order of Ancient, Free, and Accepted Masons. See *Freemasonry,* 1.

Order of Worship. The chief service of the Lutheran Church may, in general, be divided into two large groups: I. The Word group, or homiletical part: a) Introit, Kyrie, Gloria; b) Salutation, Collect, Epistle, Gospel; c) Creed, Sermon, Hymn. II. The Eucharist, or sacramental part: a) Salutation, Preface, Sanctus, Exhortation; b) Lord's Prayer, Consecration, Distribution; c) Postcommunion. A more detailed division is the following: I. Service of the Word: a) Confession, b) Declaration of Grace. II. The Service Proper. Part One: The Word. Div. 1: a) Introit, b) Kyrie, c) Gloria in Excelsis; Div. 2: a) Salutation, b) Collect, c) Epistle, d) Hallelujah, e) Gospel, f) Glory Be to Thee, O Lord; Div. 3: a) Nicene Creed, b) Sermon, c) Offertory, d) General Prayer. Part Two: The Communion. Div. 1, Introduction: a) Salutation, b) Preface with Sursum, Gratias, Dignum, c) Sanctus with Hosanna, d) Exhortation; Div. 2, Consecration: a) Lord's Prayer, b) Words of Institution, c) Pax; Div. 3, Distribution: a) Agnus Dei, b) Distribution proper; Div. 4, Postcommunion: a) Nunc Dimittis, b) Versicle, c) Collect, d) Benedicamus and Benediction.

Orders in the United States. In 1494, when Luther was eleven years old, the first Christian chapel in America was consecrated by the first band of Roman Catholic missionaries. The Spanish conquerors found it possible to be, at the same time, brutal, inhuman fiends and pious promoters of the Roman faith. On their expeditions they were accompanied by monks, chiefly of the Franciscan, Dominican, Jesuit, and Carmelite orders, who established native missions. Dominicans, in 1547, made an unsuccessful attempt to missionize Florida; Franciscans, somewhat later, met with better success. Franciscans started missions in New Mexico (near Santa Fé, 1542), Texas (1546), and California (San Diego, 1769). While Mexico was the focal point of these Southern missions, the French possessions in Canada, particularly the city of Quebec, bore a like relation to the North. As early as 1615 Franciscans labored in Maine. The chief activity, however, was unfolded by the Jesuits, of whom Bancroft writes: "The history of their labors is connected with the origin of every celebrated town in the annals of French America: not a cape was turned, not a river entered, but a Jesuit led the way." Under incredible difficulties and privations they penetrated the wilderness and established missions from Pennsylvania to Missouri and from Michigan to Louisiana. Many suffered martyrdom under excruciating torture. As the number of Roman Catholics grew, the various monastic orders established themselves in America, until, at the present day, every important order is represented. Frequently communities which were expelled from European countries found an asylum here. The Paulists originated in America. Some of the orders lead an enclosed monastic life, but most of them are engaged in educational, missionary, and charitable undertakings.

Ordinance. See *Norway, Lutheranism in,* 3.

Ordinary, The. In the nomenclature of the Roman Church, one who has jurisdiction in his own right, as distinguished from one who has only delegated jurisdiction. The term is usually applied to diocesan bishops, who are held to exercise all functions of teaching, administration, and government in their dioceses in their own right, while parish priests and others perform their functions by virtue of power delegated to them by their bishops.

Ordination (R. C.). Ordination, or holy order, in the Roman Church, is held to be "truly and properly a sacrament, instituted by Christ the Lord" (Council of Trent, Sess. XXIII, can. 3). Though all ranks of the hierarchy of order (see *Hierarchy)* are ordained, only the ordination of bishops, priests, and deacons is commonly held to confer sacramental grace, consisting in spiritual power to discharge the duties of the office involved. In witness of this power an indelible mark is supposed to be impressed on the soul of the ordained (see *Character Indelebilis),* which forever distinguishes him from the laity and by virtue of which all his future official acts are valid and supernaturally efficacious, even should he be deposed. Order

is considered one sacrament, the deaconship conferring a part of its power (especially to assist at Mass), new powers being added by priesthood (especially that of offering the sacrifice of the Mass), and the fullness of power being reached in the bishop's consecration (administration of all sacraments, including order itself). Ordinarily only a bishop can ordain, and he does so by imposition of hands and invocation of the Holy Ghost. To a deacon he says: "Receive the power of reading the Gospel in the Church of God, both for the living and for the dead"; to a priest: "Receive power to offer sacrifice to God and to celebrate masses as well for the living as for the dead," and: "Receive the Holy Ghost; whose sins you will remit, they are remitted to them, and whose sins you will retain, they are retained." A bishop commissioned by the Pope, assisted by two other bishops, officiates at the ordination of a new bishop. See *Bishop;* also *Priesthood.*

Ordination and Installation. See *Ministerial Office,* 1, 5.

Ordo Romanus. A treatise describing Roman Catholic liturgies from the 8th to the 15th century.

Orelli, Hans Conrad von (1846 to 1912). Swiss Protestant; taught at Basel, becoming full prof. in 1881; pres. of the International Congress of Religions at Basel in 1907; among his writings: *The Old Testament Prophecy of the Consummation of God's Kingdom,* also expositions of Isaiah, Jeremiah, Ezekiel, and the Minor Prophets.

Organ. The most comprehensive and important of all wind instruments, the queen of all instruments and combination of instruments for use in churches. Its history goes back to earliest times, when a syrinx (a small pipe) and a collection of graduated pipes were first in use. The *ugab,* or organ, of Gen. 4:21 and Job 21:12 was probably a row of small pipes placed over a windbox, or sounding board, the wind being admitted to the individual pipe at the will of the player by means of a sliding strip of wood, this mechanism being the origin of our modern keyboard. The next step was to have more than one series of pipes; strips of wood passing lengthwise under the mouths, or openings, of each set enabled the player, by pulling a stop, to exercise a choice as to which he placed in use. The essential principles of organ construction having thus been discovered, the use of pipes of varying lengths, the use of series of pipes, and the use of stops, the expansion of the instrument, was possible, 1) by the placing of several sets of pipes or separate organs under the control of one player, with a separate manual for each organ; 2) by the use of keys, or pedals, to be played with the feet; 3) by the increase of the compass; 4) by the introduction of a great variety of tone; 5) by perfecting the bellows and wind supply and placing all the registers under the organist's control by means of mechanical appliances.

2. The organ in its more primitive form, known in that period as hydraulic organ, on account of the use of water for the purpose of graduating the passage of air from the air chamber to the pipes, was in use in the Church by the time of Augustine and Cassiodorus. Charlemagne introduced organs north of the Alps, and the art of building these instruments soon reached a comparatively high state of perfection, although they were unusually clumsy from the modern point of view. Wolstan gives an account of an organ which had 400 pipes and required the services of seventy men to pump sufficient air. The keys were connected with the valves of the pipes by means of heavy ropes and were usually three inches wide and one and one-half inches thick. Since the mere pressure of the fingers would have had little effect upon such ponderous keys, it was necessary to strike them with the clenched fist in order to produce a tone, and the length of the notes was correspondingly extended. In the course of time the improvements in the mechanism of the organ were of such a nature as practically to change the entire instrument.

3. In America the art of organ building has reached a very high degree of perfection, and one can hardly compare the modern instruments, having thousands of pipes, complete orchestration, and pneumatic and electrical control for every part of the mechanism, with the organs of the Middle Ages. Among the largest organs in the world at the present time are the following: that of Yale University; that of the Cathedral of the Incarnation, Garden City, N. Y.; of Royal Albert Hall, London; of the Town Hall, Sydney, Australia; of the Cathedral, Liverpool, England; of the Wanamaker Store, Philadelphia, the last-named instrument being a marvel of the organ builder's art. As far as the structure of the modern pipe organ is concerned, only the very small organs have one manual; four and even five rows of keys often being found, each representing a distinct instrument, the latter being named after its use or characteristics: as, the great organ, that used for grand effects, the principal manual; choir organ, that used for the accompaniment of voices; solo organ, that containing stops for solo use; swell organ, pipes placed in a distant box, with shutters opening and closing like Venetian blinds, by means of which the tone may gradually be increased or reduced; pedal organ, the pipes controlled by the pedals. The stops of a pipe organ control the passage of wind to the various sections, the mechanical stops being the coupler stops controlling the various sections, or separate organs, and the sounding, or speaking, stops controlling the quality of the tone produced or imitated; as, flute, violin, oboe, clarinet, etc. In reed organs the tone is produced by the passage of air under pressure through reeds of metal of the proper length to produce tones of the proper pitch and quality.

4. In the early years of the 20th century Albert Schweitzer of Strassbourg, Wilibald Gurlitt of Freiburg, and others of Southwest Germany, together with Christhard Mahrenholz of Hanover, instituted a movement which was directed against the usual organ of their day and of the present day, some of which were monstrous and unwieldy, their tone thick as well as sentimental. The new slogan was: "Back to Silbermann." Goottfried Silbermann was a famous organ builder of the 18th century who built organs of the so-called classical type. Erroneously these organs are often referred to as baroque organs. The classical organ does not seek to imitate an orchestra; its tone is a distinct organ tone. Many of the devices used in the romantic type of organ are rejected because they mechanize and sentimentalize the tonal qualities of the organ. Since the organ is intended largely for contrapuntal music in which each voice is of importance, each set of pipes possesses its own distinct quality that the individual voices of the composition may be heard with greater clarity. The fundamental laws which govern the use of the harmonics are taken into account, the organ is built in the open and not included largely in chambers, and it becomes unnecessary to build huge instruments

of more than three manuals. The classical organ is a straight organ and there is no borrowing of stops. The wind pressure is low and the console simple. The so-called slider chests are used. Building this type of organ was inaugurated in the U. S. by Walter Holtkamp, Cleveland, O. He was followed by G. Donald Harrison of the Aeolian-Skinner Organ Co., Boston, Mass., and others.

5. In the third decade of the 20th century the electronic organ began to come to the fore, which, however, musicians and organists usually consider inferior in quality to a good pipe organ.

Oriental Research, Schools of. See *Geography, Christian,* 7.

Orientation. The custom of placing a church in such a manner that in the axis of the structure the altar is given its place in the east end, while the main portal is on the west end. The symbolism of this feature, which goes back to early times, is readily seen. The Christian congregation faces the east, where the heavenly Sun, the Sun of Righteousness, arose.

Origen (185—254). 1. The most famous representative of the Alexandrian theology, which aimed at a reconciliation of Christianity and Hellenistic thought; a man of brilliant talents, vast erudition, prodigious industry, and, at the same time, of a highly speculative and mystical turn of mind. Born of Christian parents, he was placed under the tutelage of Pantaenus and Clement and, eighteen years old, became the leader of the catechetical school in Alexandria. He studied Hebrew, made journeys to Rome (211), Arabia, Palestine (215), and Greece. Ordained a presbyter by the bishops of Caesarea and Jersusalem, he was excommunicated by Demetrius of Alexandria on the ground of heresy and self-mutilation. Thereupon he opened a theological school at Caesarea and developed a remarkable literary activity. Under Decius he was captured and cruelly tortured, which caused his death (254). — Origen's theology is vitiated by his philosophy. He denied the physical resurrection and assumed the pre-existence and pretemporal fall of souls, an eternal creation, the final restoration of all men and fallen angels, etc. His commentaries, though useful and suggestive, are marred by allegorizing fancies. Works: *Hexapla,* the first polyglot Bible; commentaries; *Against Cel-*

sus; De Principiis, on the fundamentals of Christianity; *Stromata,* and a multitude of tracts, homilies, and letters.

2. The *Origenistic Controversy* arose over the question of Origen's orthodoxy and was carried on, at times with fierce personal rancor and bitterness, upwards of two centuries. Already attacked by Methodius of Tyre (d. 311), Origen was finally condemned as a heretic by the Fifth Ecumenical Council of Constantinople (553). The quarrel, however, was at its height between 394 and 438 and raged especially in Egypt, Palestine, and Constantinople. The monks of Egypt were divided into two bitterly hostile factions, the one slavishly following Origen in all his aberrations, the other, under the lead of Pachomius, condemning his mysticism and spiritualism. The leading men of the age, among them Jerome (who, at first an admirer, became a fierce opponent of Origen), Chrysostom, and Pope Anastasius, were drawn into the conflict. Anastasius condemned Origen at a Roman synod. The great leaders of the opposition were, however, Epiphanius of Salamis in Cyprus, who traveled over land and sea to purge the Church of Origenistic leaven, and Theophilus of Alexandria, who launched a great literary attack upon Origen. After 553 the authority of Origen was completely discredited.

The works on Origen are numerous. His works are found in the editions of Patristics (see *Patristics **). A good short study in A. C. McGiffert, *A History of Christian Thought,* Scribner's, 1932, and in Wace's *Dictionary * of Christian Biography.* Old, but still standard, is E. R. Redepenning, *Origines, Eine Darstellung seines Lebens und seiner Lehre,* 1841, 46. For his works see E. R. Redepenning, "Des Hieronymus wieder aufgefundenes Verzeichnis der Schriften des Origenes," *Zeit. f. d. hist. Theol.,* 1851, 66 ff.

(Original) Church of God, The. See *Holiness Bodies,* 2.

(Original) Church of God, The (Chattanooga, Tenn.) See *Church of God,* 4.

Original Sin. See *Sin, Original.*

Ormuzd. See *Zoroastrianism.*

Orosius, Paulus. A patristic writer at the beginning of the fifth century; d. ca. 418; was a presbyter in Africa; attacked Pelagius; his chief book a historical work: *Historiarum adversus Pa-*

ganos (a book of history, against the pagans).

Orphanages. See *Associated Lutheran Charities,* A 2; *Child Care and Child-Placing Agencies.*

Orr, James (1844—1913). United Presbyterian; native of Glasgow; pastor; professor of church history; promoter of union (1900) between United Presbyterian and free churches; repeatedly in America; wrote: *Problem of the Old Testament; The Virgin Birth.*

Ort, Samuel Alfred. B. Lewistown, Pa., Nov. 11, 1843; ed. Wittenberg Coll., 1863; ordained to Lutheran ministry 1865. Pastor at Louisville, Ky., 1874 to 1878; New York City, 1878—80. Prof. at Wittenberg Coll. and Sem., 1880—1910, pres., 1882—1900. Pres. of the General Synod, 1887. He was an orator of note and an inspiring teacher. D. 1911.

Orthodox. The term orthodoxy (opposite: heterodoxy) implies conformity with a certain standard of religious truth. Orthodoxy is soundness in doctrine, the confession of the doctrines revealed in the Word of God. Departure from the principles of Christianity is heterodoxy. The adherents of the Reformation were obliged to defend themselves against the accusation of heresy. By applying the only valid standard, Scripture, Lutherans proved their unity of doctrine with the true Church of Christ and in the *Formula of Concord* rejected from their association those who did not conform to that standard. See *Heresy; Creeds and Confessions.*

Orthodox Churches, Eastern. See *Eastern Orthodox Churches.*

Orthodox Confession of the Catholic and Apostolic Eastern Church. See *Eastern Orthodox Confessions,* A 1.

Orthodox Creed. See *Democratic Declarations,* 3.

Orthodox Lutheran Conference. The Orthodox Lutheran Conference was organized on Sept. 26, 1951, at Okabena, Minn., by ten pastors, who at that time or shortly thereafter withdrew from The Lutheran Church — Missouri Synod. Invitations to the organizational meeting were sent to all those who had previously signed the *Confession of Faith Professed and Practiced by All True Lutherans,* which had been adopted on Nov. 19, 1950, by the Lutheran Study Club of St. Louis and St. Louis County. Personal mem-

bership in the Orthodox Lutheran Conference is acquired by subscription to this Confession and corporate membership by subscription to Part I, with a statement that the congregation does not dissent from Part II.

The Orthodox Lutheran Conference accepts the Bible, the Lutheran Confessions as contained in the *Book of Concord* (1580), and the *Brief Statement.* It does not accept the Intersynodical *Chicago Theses, Doctrinal Declaration* (1938), *Doctrinal Affirmation* (1944), and the *Common Confession* (1950). In addition it has endorsed twelve points found in Part II of its *Confession.* The Conference holds that The Lutheran Church — Missouri Synod abandoned its historic position, especially by the adoption of the *Common Confession.*

The Orthodox Lutheran Theological Seminary, Minneapolis, Minn., began in Sept., 1952, with P. E. Kretzmann as president.

The Orthodox Lutheran Conference has two monthly publications: *The Orthodox Lutheran* and *The Orthodox Lutheran Theologian.* Statistics (1953): ten pastors, two professors, nine congregations. Officers elected at the organizational meeting were: President: Wallace H. McLaughlin; Vice-President: P. E. Kretzmann; Secretary: Albert Schupmann; Treasurer: Fred J. Niebruegge. C. f. WHM

Orthodox Presbyterian Church. See *Presbyterian Bodies,* 4.

Orthodoxism. Designation of a tendency and a condition which represents an extreme form of literal adherence to the system of orthodox doctrine as accepted by the Church, with a pedantic insistence on absolute uniformity in the use of terms, while at the same time neglecting the true piety of the heart and a corresponding behavior of the confessing Christian. It was undoubtedly due to this phenomenon in the seventeenth century that the movement of Pietism * arose as a kind of antidote against formalism in the outward presentation of Scriptural doctrines.

Orthodoxy, Age of. See *Lutheran Theology after 1580,* 3, 4, 5.

Orthodoxy, Neo-. See *Neo-Orthodoxy.*

Orzechowski, Stanislaus. A high ecclesiastic of Przemysl, Poland; married Magdalene Chelmicki in 1549; with fiery eloquence pilloried the clerical immorality in his *De Lege Coelibatus* in 1551; expelled, but returned to Romanism.

Osiander, Andreas. B. Dec. 19, 1498; a "homemade theologian"; priest at Nuremberg in 1520; introduced the Reformation; got acquainted with Luther in 1529; sided with him against Zwingli at Marburg; opposed the peasants and fanatics; at Augsburg, in 1530, courageous over against Melanchthon's concessions; worked on the Brandenburg-Nuremberg order of service 1530 to 1532, at Schmalkalden in 1537, at Hagenau and Worms in 1540 and 1541; reformed Pfalz-Neuburg in 1542—43. In 1537 he got out the first Protestant Gospel harmony in Greek and Latin; in 1539 he attacked Eck; in 1543 he published Copernicus' *Motion of the Heavenly Bodies;* in 1544 his *Conjectures on the Last Times,* in which he put the end of the world in 1656 and proved the papacy to be the Antichrist. In 1548 he opposed the Interim and in 1549 went to Koenigsberg and as professor taught falsely concerning justification. See *Osiandrian Controversy.* D. Oct. 17, 1552.

Osiander, Andreas, the Younger (b. 1562). Chancellor of Tuebingen Univ.; got out a new edition of the *Osiander Bible* and wrote *The Wuerttemberg Communicants' Booklet for Young and Plain People that Desire to Go to the Lord's Table,* the basis for the later *Wuerttemberg Confirmation Booklet.* His nephew, *Johann Adam* (d. 1697), chancellor of Tuebingen Univ., was a friend of Spener. The son of the latter, *Johann* (1657—1724), introduced confirmation.

Osiander, Lukas, the Elder (1534 to 1604). B at Nuremberg; d. at Stuttgart. Son of Andreas. Studied at Tuebingen. As a strict Lutheran pastor, theologian, and poet, he was active in many ways in both Church and State. He carried on polemics against Roman Catholics and Calvinists and labored for Lutheran union, also making a significant contribution to hymnology.

Osiander, Lukas, the Younger (1571 to 1638). B. at Stuttgart; d. at Tuebingen. Son of Lukas the Elder. Held various important ecclesiastical positions; professor of theology, 1619, and provost and chancellor of the university, 1620, at Tuebingen. He defended Lutheran orthodoxy and opposed Jesuits, Calvinists, and the Giessen Kenotists.

Osiandrian Controversy. Started by Andreas Osiander when he left Nuremberg to become professor at Koenigsberg and in 1550 published his longharbored error on justification by faith. He taught that God does not declare the sinner just, but makes him just; does not impute Christ's obedience and righteousness to the sinner, but has Christ Himself dwell in the sinner for his justification; does not act as a judge, but as a physician. The blessed assurance of salvation is not based on the objective work of Christ for the sinner, but on the pseudomystical union of Christ with the believer. Osiander's justification is not based on the atonement; it minimizes it; in fact, does not really require it. It is virtually the Romanist doctrine. He says himself good Romanists had found his teaching quite tolerable, and so it is no wonder Joachim Moerlin, Melanchthon, Chemnitz, and others vigorously attacked it. Osiander also held that Christ is our Righteousness only as to His divine nature. Francesco Stancaro, the Italian, opposed this with the equally erroneous statement that only the human nature of Christ is our Righteousness. Even Calvin and those of Zurich wrote against him. Art. III of the *Formula of Concord* settled the trouble by teaching that Christ is our Righteousness according to both of His natures.

Osler, Edward (1798—1863). Educated for the medical profession at Falmouth and London; later devoted himself to literary pursuits; prominent in hymnological work; wrote: "May We Thy Precepts, Lord, Fulfill," and others.

Ostensorium. See *Monstrance.*

Osusky, S. See *Slovakia, Lutheranism in,* 3.

Otfried von Weissenburg (ca. 790 to 875). Learned Benedictine, pupil of Rhabanus Maurus in Fulda, presbyter in Weissenburg and teacher at the monastery school; known in particular for his religious poem *Krist,* whose five books presenting the Gospel story in rhymed stanzas are notable for their lyrical beauty and depth and are still considered a source, not only for linguistic purposes, but also for an understanding of the theology of South Germany in the ninth century.

Other-World. See *Hereafter.*

Ott, John Henry. B. Jan. 4, 1861, at Tell City, Ind.; graduated at Northwestern College; attended Amherst, Berlin, and Halle universities; Ph. D.,

Halle, 1892; professor of English and History at Northwestern College of the Wisconsin Synod, 1885; librarian and bursar. Ott worked untiringly for Northwestern and was the father of its fine library. Retired, 1943; d. Oct. 31, 1945.

Otter, Jacob (ca. 1480—1547). Reformer in Kenzingen, Neckarsteinach, Solothurn, Aarau, and Esslingen; b. in Lauterburg, Alsace; published translation of Geiler's sermons 1510; converted to Lutheranism 1520; called to Esslingen 1532, where he directed the Reformation; wrote church constitution and catechism; influenced by Bucer; signed Wittenberg Concord.

Otterbein, Philip William. See *United Brethren,* 1.

Ottesen, Jacob Aall (1825—1904). Graduate of Christiania University 1849; came to the United States 1852; one of the founders of the Norwegian Synod, its secretary; the first to ally himself with the Missouri Synod (1857); co-editor of *Maanedstidende;* author.

Otto of Bamberg. See *Germany,* 2.

Otto of Freising (ca. 1111—58). Studied under Abelard; became Cistercian; elected bishop of Freising; exerted political influence; wrote a chronicle beginning with the creation of the world.

Otto, Rudolf (1869—1936). German Protestant; studied at Erlangen and Goettingen; taught at Goettingen, where he became extraordinary professor in 1906, finally at Marburg; coined the word "numinous" for the divine which is apprehended only by the religious faculty; belonged to historical and critical school; wrote, among others: *Das Leben und Wirken Jesu nach historisch-kritischer Auffassung; Darwinismus und Religion; The Idea of the Holy.*

Our Lady of Mercy, Sisters of. A congregation of women conducting schools, hospitals, etc., and engaged chiefly in educating the poor, visiting the sick, and protecting distressed women of good character.

Ouseley, Frederick Arthur Gore (1825—89). English composer and editor of church music. His music, though well written, is often rather uninteresting. He edited the sacred choral works of Orlando Gibbons, published theoretical works, and edited the

English edition of Emil Naumann's *Illustrierte Musikgeschichte.*

Overbeck, Franz (1837—1905). Professor at Jena and Basel, historian and philosopher, critical of current Christianity, skeptical of its relevance to modern life.

Overbeck, Fritz (1789—1869). Modern romantic idealist; one of a group of painters in Rome; excellent coloring, fresco work; among his paintings: "Joseph Sold by His Brethren."

Overture for Lutheran Unity. An overture of six paragraphs (with appended Minneapolis Theses *) adopted by the executive board of the American Lutheran Conference in Chicago, Ill., Jan. 7, 1944. Leading thoughts in the paragraphs are: 1) The Lutheran Church has always been rightly "jealous of the integrity of its doctrine and practice, rightly wary of indifferentism and latitudinarianism, no matter what emergencies may arise." 2) The Lutheran Church has always insisted upon genuine acceptance of its great historic standards. 3) Since some important points of doctrine were not issues in the 16th century but have more recently affected inner unity, Lutheran bodies in America have provided supplementary statements. 4) The Minneapolis Theses,* the Brief Statement,* and the Pittsburgh Agreement * "have made sufficiently clear the position of the three major groups within American Lutheranism." 5) "We, the constituent synods of the American Lutheran Conference, severally and collectively reaffirm our sincere and wholehearted adherence to our mutual pledge as to doctrine and practice in the Minneapolis Theses. We as earnestly expect of those with whom we seek complete fellowship that their doctrine and practice shall conform to their respective declarations." 6) "We submit the above statements to other Lutheran bodies with a view to the establishment of pulpit and altar fellowship."

Lutheran Outlook, Jan., 1944; "An Overture for Lutheran Unity," *CTM,* XV: 193—97; 274—76.

Owambo. A fertile strip of land in the western part of South Africa, with a population of industrious and successful natives. Discovered 1851 by Sir Francis Galton, opened for mission work in 1866, chiefly by German and Finnish societies, who translated

Luther's Catechism into the language of the Odongas.

Owen, John (1616—83). Learned Nonconformist; b. at Stadhampton; Presbyterian; Independent; preached before Parliament on day following execution of King Charles; vice-chancellor of Oxford 1652; pastor in London; d. at Ealing; prolific author.

Owen, Robert (1771—1858). English socialist and philanthropist; endeavored to improve social conditions of workingmen; founded numerous communistic societies in Great Britain, also one at New Harmony, Ind., all of which failed; sought to abolish religion, marriage, family, private property, because sources of all evil; was atheist, later spiritualist.

Oxford Group Movement. See *Buchmanism.*

Oxford Movement. See *Tractarianism.*

Oxford Tracts. See *Tractarianism.*

P

P. (*Priestly Code*). See *Higher Criticism,* 6.

Pacelli, Eugenio. See *Popes,* 33.

Pachelbel, Johann (1653—1706). Composer of the Lutheran Church. A native of Nuremberg, he later studied composition with Johann Kaspar Kerll while serving as organist of St. Stephen's Church in Vienna. Thereupon he served as organist in Eisenach, Erfurt, Stuttgart, Gotha, and Nuremberg. While active in Erfurt, he became acquainted with various members of the Bach family. Although he wrote also choral music, Pachelbel is known chiefly as a composer of organ music. Particularly his organ works based on the Lutheran chorale show a keen regard for the spirit of a sound liturgical service of worship. They are conservative, objective, clear, direct, and simple in expression, even when large in form and structure, and differ quite radically from the freer chorale preludes written by the masters of North Germany. His mastery of counterpoint is superb and his chorale fugues for the organ intrigued J. S. Bach to such an extent that he applied the techniques and style of Pachelbel to a number of his works.

F. Fratscher, *Geschichte des Orgelspiels und der Orgelkomposition,* Berlin-Schoeneberg, 1935; S. Kuemmerle, *Encyklopaedie der ev. Kirchenmusik,* Guetersloh, 1890; Johann Mattheson-M. Schneider, *Grundlage einer Ehren-Pforte,* Berlin, 1740, 1910.

Pachomius. See *Monasticism.*

Pacific-Northwest Synod. This district of the Joint Synod of Wisconsin had its beginning with the Tacoma independent congregation, which asked to be admitted to the Wisconsin Synod in 1895. It was received with its pastor, F. Wolf. Other congregations, such as Leavenworth, Mansfield, North Yakima, Ellensburg, Clarkston, were added from time to time through the efforts of home missionaries sent out by the Home Mission Board of the Wisconsin Synod. As a missionary district it remained part of the mother synod until the reorganization of 1917 authorized its independent status. The congregations met and organized as the Pacific-Northwest District of the Joint Synod in 1917 and elected F. Soll, Yakima, president.

Pacific Synod. See *United Lutheran Church, Synods of,* 23.

Pacifism. A. Pacifism may be defined as a way of life which is opposed to the use of force in the solution of social problems. More specifically, it means opposition to militarism and war.

The term pacifism is very wide and includes many shades of thought. On the extreme left are those who uphold the principle of absolute non-resistance, who regard it wrong to use physical force in any situation even in case of self-defense. On the right are the more moderate, but they, too, are uncompromisingly opposed to modern militarism and war.

Some pacifists include in their program the problem of race relations, class war, social injustice, and capital punishment; others confine themselves to active opposition to war and to the support of conscientious objectors.

What unites all shades of pacifists is the common belief that the use of force is an evil and offers no real solution to human problems; that a peaceful settlement of all controversies is possible and obligatory; that war is the greatest social evil and must be condemned.

Most pacifists base their position on the teachings of the New Testament, particularly on the Sermon on the Mount. They hold that modern war is incompatible with the religion of Jesus and that no true follower of the Savior can condone militarism or participate in modern war.

The non-Christian pacifists base their position on a purely humanitarian philosophy. The Oriental philosophies of Taoism, Confucianism, and Buddhism contain elements of pacifism. The most influential non-Christian pacifist in modern times has been the great Hindu "saint" Mahatma Gandhi. He consistently taught and lived non-violence and inspired millions of his countrymen to follow his example.

B. *History of Pacifism.* Christian pacifism turns to the New Testament for its foundation. But neither Jesus nor His Apostles give any specific directives regarding the Christian's attitude toward war. As in the case of slavery and other social evils, so here Jesus took for granted that His followers would apply the great principles of His religion to the social problems as they would arise in the course of human history.

In the Early Church pacifism seems to have been the accepted view. There is no evidence of Christians serving in the Roman Army from the time of the Apostles to about A.D. 170. The most noted of the ante-Nicene Fathers were very definitely opposed to military service and to war. Among them we find such writers as Athanagoras, ca. A.D. 176; Justin Martyr, ca. 150; Tertullian, ca. 200; Origen, ca. 225; Cyprian, ca. 250; Lactantius, ca. 300.

Celsus, ca. 176, the earliest literary opponent of the Christians, reproached them for being "un-Roman, unpatriotic, and unwilling to render military service" (Origen, *Contra Celsus,* VII, 68 to 73). Eusebius, the father of church history, ca. 325, relates how a high military officer left the Roman army after his conversion and suffered painful scourging, while others even suffered death, rather than continue their service in the army.

A noticeable change in the attitude of the leaders of the Church occurs after Constantine, when the Christian religion became the state religion of the Empire.

In the Middle Ages pacifism was represented by small groups of nonconformists like the Albigenses and Waldensians and the great churchman St. Francis.

At the time of the Reformation pacifism reappeared with the Bohemian Brethren, the Anabaptists, the Mennonites, the Schwenkfeldians, the Dunkards, the Dukhobors, the Shakers, the Quakers, and Erasmus.

Modern pacifism had its beginning in the period immediately following the Napoleonic wars. The first peace society in the world was organized in the summer of 1815 in the home of David Low Dodge, a merchant and devout Presbyterian of New York City. In December of the same year a second society was organized at Vienna, Ohio, which was chiefly composed of Friends. The third pacifist society was established on December 28, 1815, by Rev. Noah Worcester, aided by the Rev. William Ellery Channing. This was known as the Massachusetts Peace Society and was less radical than the others, sanctioning "defensive war." The American Peace Society was organized in 1828 to federate the various peace societies scattered from Maine to Ohio and South Carolina; the founder and leader was William Ladd, a radical pacifist.

During the Civil War pacifism suffered a great setback. The fact that the abolition of slavery was one of the great issues in the war brought confusion and division into the ranks of the pacifists. In 1866 the shattered forces were rallied and reorganized as the Universal Peace Union under the leadership of Alfred H. Love, a young Quaker merchant of Philadelphia.

During the First World War freedom of speech was more seriously curtailed than in any previous conflict, and for the first time in our history a universal draft was enforced. As a result, all opposition to war was driven underground. But after the war, pacifism emerged with renewed vigor, establishing fellowship with similar organizations in Europe and Asia and other countries.

The peace movement survived the Second World War. Thousands of pacifists suffered long years of imprisonment and the harsh and sometimes brutal treatment in concentration camps, rather than deny their conviction.

One of the most active peace societies in America today is the *Fellowship of Reconciliation.* It is international in scope and has affiliated societies in the leading countries of North and South America, Europe, Asia, and in New Zealand and Australia. The American headquarters are at 21 Audubon Ave., New York City 32, N.Y. It publishes a monthly magazine called *Fellowship* and issues many books and pamphlets.

There are two important collections of literature on pacifist movements in America. The one is *The Pacifist Research Bureau*, 1201 Chestnut St., Philadelphia, Pa. The other is *The Swarthmore College Peace Collection* at Swarthmore, Pa. These collections contain books, pamphlets, records, and documents concerning pacifism and the peace movements in the various countries of the world.

C. *Pacifism Today.* Pacifists hold that the futility and the evils of war were demonstrated by the two World Wars. The prospects of even greater horrors of atomic warfare in the future have greatly stimulated the growth of pacifism in nearly every country in the world today. AMR

Devere Allen, *The Fight for Peace*, Macm., 1930; Devere Allen, *Pacifism in the Modern World*, Doubleday Doran, New York, 1929; Cecil John Codoux, *The Early Church and the World*, T.T. Clark, Edinburgh, Scotland; G. J. Hering, *The Fall of Christianity*, Fellowship Pub., New York; Aldous Huxley, *Science, Liberty, and Peace*, Fellowship Pub., New York, 1946; Rufus M. Jones, *The Church, the Gospel, and War*, Harper, New York, 1948; Umphrey Lee, *The Historic Church and Modern Pacifism*, Abingdon-Cokesbury, Northville; Charles Clayton Morrison, *The Christian and the War*, Willett Clark, Chicago, 1942; A. J. Musti, *Not by Might*, Harper, New York, 1947; Walter W. Van Kirk, *Religion Renounces War*, Willett Clark, Chicago, 1934; Merle Curti, *Peace or War—The American Struggle, 1636—1936*, W. W. Norton, New York.

Pack, Otto von (ca. 1480—1537). Counselor and vice-chancellor of Duke George of Saxony, informed Philip, Landgrave of Hesse, 1527, of an alleged conspiracy of a number of Roman Catholic princes to conquer Hungary for Ferdinand I and then to suppress the Reformation in Germany. Philip and John, Elector of Saxony, thereupon formed an alliance for mutual defense. John's insistence that the alleged conspirators be questioned led to the exposure of a forgery supposedly perpetrated by Pack and admitted by him under torture. Pack was executed. Luther refused to admit a forgery and engaged in a controversy with Duke George regarding it. Philip profited by forcing the bishops of Bamberg and Wuerzburg to pay him an indemnity and the archbishop of Mayence to surrender his jurisdiction over Hesse.

Pagan (L. *paganus* fr. pagus, "village," "district"). A non-Christian. Since Christianity first came to the cities of the Roman Empire, those who lived in the country adhered longer to the Greek and Roman religion. Hence a "countryman" was often a heathen.

Paimen Sanomia. See *Finnish Lutherans in America, 2.*

Paine, John Knowles (1839—1906). American organist and composer, for twenty years professor of music at Harvard University, where he occupied the first chair of music in any American university.

Paine, Thomas (1737—1809). English-American author; b. at Thetford, England; d. in New York; took part in American Revolutionary War and French Revolution; was a freethinker and bitter enemy of Christianity; wrote *The Rights of Man* and *The Age of Reason*. In the latter he expounds Deism and states reason for rejecting Bible. Prophecy, miracles, mystery, are the three principal means of imposture. Rabidly attacked redemption and vicarious atonement. His language is satirical, often blasphemous.

Paix, Jakob (1550—after 1617). German composer whose *Tabulaturbuch* of 1583 illustrates particularly the use of coloratura and of figuration in 16th-century music.

Paleario, Antonio (ca. 1500—70). Italian Humanist; thrice accused of heresy, one charge, the last time, being that of teaching justification by faith; wavered temporarily, but at last attained martyr's courage and crown; wrote *Della Pienezza, Suffienza ed Efficacia della Morte di Christo*. See also *Christ, Benefits of.*

Palestine. The name originally applied to the coastal plain inhabited by the Philistines (Hebrew, *Pelishtim*) and lying along the southeastern Mediterranean. The Greeks, however, employed the name to denote the entire southern half of Syria, giving it the wider meaning with which we are familiar today. In its physical aspects Palestine may be roughly divided into four longitudinal sections running north and south. These are: The maritime plain bordering the Mediterranean, the central range of mountains, broken by the Plain of Esdraelon in the north, the eastern range beyond the Jordan, and the great gorge of the Jordan running from the foot of Lebanon to the Dead Sea. Though small in extent, its entire area being somewhat less than one fourth of the State of Illinois, Palestine was especially fitted to hold a chosen people destined to perform a peculiar mission. Separated by sea and desert from the surrounding nations, yet holding a central position among them, it was providentially appointed as the home of the people to whom were committed the oracles of God and from whom sprang the Messiah, the world's Redeemer.

2. The population of Palestine consists chiefly of Jews and Mohammedans. Next in number are the Christian denominations. Druses, Bahais, Hindus, Sikhs, and Metawihles are also represented.

3. Since World War I the Zionist hopes of the Jews greatly increased. The Balfour Declaration of the British government (Nov. 2, 1917) declared that the British government viewed "with favor the establishment in Palestine of a national home for the Jewish people." The General Assembly of the United Nations voted (Nov. 29, 1947) to partition Palestine into Jewish and Arab states. The Republic of Israel, which occupies the greater portion of Palestine, was proclaimed May 14—15, 1948. This republic was admitted to the United Nations May 11, 1949. See *Zionism.* The estimated population of Israel in 1952 was 1,602,000 (1,441,800 Jews; 160,200 Arabs).

4. *Missions.* The fanatic jealousy of the various religious adherents made Protestant missions almost impossible. In 1820 the American Board began operations by sending missionaries, chiefly to the Mohammedans and Jews, but without appreciable results. The Church Missionary Society entered early, but made no progress until, in connection with Frederick William IV of Prussia, it founded the Bishopric of Jerusalem (1840), of which Samuel Gobat (1846—79) was second bishop. Gobat succeeded in winning an opening among the Arabian orthodox population by Bible readers and by schools. German and English mission societies were called upon for assistance, and the Kaiserswerth deaconesses responded by founding a hospital and the girls' school Talithakumi. In 1853 the Berlin Jerusalem Society followed, taking over work in Bethlehem and the neighboring sections. Spittler sent a few missionaries to Jerusalem from the St. Chrischona School at Basel. After the Lebanon massacres in 1860 Ludwig Schneller gathered the orphans and founded the Syrian Orphanage near Jerusalem. The Church Missionary Society also continued its work, founding stations from Jaffa to Es Salt and Kerak. Later this society went deeper into medical and woman's work, doing especially good work among Mohammedans.

5. Missions are being carried on by the American Friends, the Christian and Missionary Alliance, British and Foreign Bible Society, Church Missionary Society, Jerusalem and the East Mission, Nile Mission Press, Trust Society, Furtherance of Gospel (Moravians).

Palestine Department of Antiquities. See *Geography, Christian,* 7.

Palestine Exploration Fund. See *Geography, Christian,* 4.

Palestrina, Giovanni Pierluigi da (1525—94). "The prince of music." Though a native of Palestrina, the ancient Praeneste, Palestrina spent his professional life in Rome, where he became *Maestro Compositore* of the Capella Juliana at St. Peter's. Despite hardships in Rome he declined offers to take up his work in Mantua and Venice. Palestrina showed consummate mastery of contrapuntal technique and artistic, devotional, and churchly character in his music. His compositions are vocal and choral. His individual voice parts rarely exceed an octave, his rhythms, though often subtle, are never too striking, his dissonances are carefully prepared and resolved, and, though at times dramatic, his music never jars or becomes too exciting. Despite its universal character, influence, ecumenicity, and wholesomeness, Palestrina's music is a true and typical expression of Roman Catholic piety and its spirit. Leichtentritt says: "Yet the astonishng fact remains that this music of Palestrina's, so full of the Renaissance spirit, was destined to become the most powerful musical ally of the Roman Catholic Church in its combat with Protestantism. To this very day Palestrina's music is justly admired as the most comprehensive, convincing, and successful interpretation of the true Catholic spirit, not only in music proper, but in all the world of art." (*Music, History and Ideas,* p. 86.) The various Palestrina legends spread largely by Baini (1775—1844) have been discredited. Thus the story told of the action taken by the Council of Trent with regard to Palestrina's music is largely legendary, and Baini's enthusiastic claim that Palestrina had prepared the Editio Medicea of the Graduale and Antiphonarium of the Roman Catholic Church, authorized by Gregory XIII and actually carried out by Felice Anerio and Francesco Suriano, is known to be fictitious. The Palestrina revival of the 19th century was started by Justus Thibaut (1774 to 1840), a jurist, and was given widespread support by the Cecilian Societies of Germany and by others. Like other great masters, Palestrina had no successors, though a number of Italian composers imitated him, at times with some success. WEB

P. H. Lang, *Music in Western Civilization*, New York, 1941; H. Leichtentritt, *Music, History and Ideas*, Cambridge, 1938; *The Oxford History of Music*, Vol. II, Oxford, 1905; Zoe Kendrick Pyne, *Palestrina, Life and Times*, London, 1922; Otto Ursprung, "Die katholische Kirchenmusik," *Handbuch der Musikwissenschaft* (Ernst Buecken), New York (reprint by Musurgia), 1931, 1949.

Paley, William (1743—1805). Anglican, apologist; b. at Peterborough; ordained 1767; rector of Bishopwearmouth 1795; d. at Lincoln. *Moral and Political Philosophy*, 1786 (essentially utilitarian); *Truth of Scripture History of St. Paul*, 1790 (Paley's most original work); *View of Evidence of Christianity*, 1794 (combats Deism); *Evidences of Existence and Attributes of the Deity*, 1802 (teleological argument popularized).

Palimpsests. See *Manuscripts of the Bible*, 2.

Palladius, Peter. See *Denmark, Lutheranism in*, 3; *Ireland*, 2.

Pallium. See *Vestments, Clerical.*

Palm Sunday. The Sunday of Holy Week, *i. e.*, the Sunday before Easter. The name is derived not only from the Gospel of the day (Matt. 21:1-9), but also from the fact that the blessing of the palms formerly took place on that day.

Palme, Rudolph (1834—1909). Musical director and organist at Madgeburg and composer of vocal and organ music, including *Orgelschule.*

Palmer, Christian David Friedrich (1811—75). B. at Winnenden, in Wuerttemberg; d. at Tuebingen. Studied at Schoenthal and Tuebingen. After holding important positions at Marbach and Tuebingen he was called to the chair of ethics and practical theology at Halle, 1852, where for almost twenty-two years he taught nearly every branch of practical theology. He was rector of the university in 1857 and 1858. He published works on homiletics, catechetics, pedagogy, hymnology, and pastoral theology. Palmer wrote the articles on church music in Herzog's *Real-Encyklopaedie*. He was influenced by Hanslick's aesthetic approach to music and had no appreciation for its confessional character.

Palmer, George Herbert (1842 to 1933). Prof. of Greek, then philosophy, finally, natural religion, moral philosophy, and civil polity at Harvard, upheld Christian theism; broad religious influence.

Palmer, Paul. See *Baptist Bodies*, 24.

Palmer, Ray (1808—87). A direct descendant of John Alden and his wife Priscilla, b. at Little Compton, R. I. He left home at thirteen because of poverty, securing a job in a Boston drygoods store. During this time he joined Park Street Congregational Church. Awakened to the ministry, he attended Phillips Academy, Andover, and also studied at Yale College. Palmer still continued his theological studies under pastoral supervision for one year at New York. Here he wrote "My Faith Looks Up to Thee." He held various positions in the Congregational Church. He is said to have written more hymns than any other American. His *Poetical Works* fill a volume of more than 350 pages.

Pamperrien, Karl Heinrich Ferdinand Ludwig (1845—1926). B. in Mecklenburg, Germany; educated at Berlin and Rostock; ordained at Rudolstadt April 22, 1877; Leipzig missionary to South India 1877; Tranquebar, 1878—80; Tanjore, 1880—84; instructor at Leipzig Mission Seminary, India, since 1885; returned permanently to Germany 1920, resided at Tostedt, Hanover.

Pamphilus. Presbyter at Caesarea in Palestine, friend of Eusebius (Eusebius Pamphili); founder of a theological school and of a famous library at Caesarea; d. a martyr, 309.

Panama. See *Central America, Missions in.*

Pancosmism. See *Pantheism*.

Panentheism. The view that God is immanent in all things (without, however, causing the individual things to lose their separate existence) and at the same time transcendent.

Pantaenus (d. ca. 202). First known teacher of the catechetical school of Alexandria, at the end of the second century; said to have made a missionary journey as far east as India (to southern Arabia); is credited with a number of works, his commentaries showing strong allegorizing tendencies; as teacher he employed scientific methods.

Pantheism. 1. The monistic religious and philosophical system according to which God and the universe are one. While theism * and deism * assume a personal, transcendent God, pantheism denies the personality of God, ascribes to Him merely an immanent existence in the world, and identifies the two, asserting that they are merely two names for the same reality. However, as there are two factors, either one may be considered as absorbing the other, and therefore two pantheistic views have developed. According to one view, proceeding from the unity of nature, God is merged in the world. This view, which is called pancosmism and which, by emphasizing nature, almost loses sight of God and consequently approaches atheism, was held by Spinoza,* Goethe,* the German and English Romanticists, Haeckel,* and other materialists. According to the other view, proceeding from the infinite and eternal God, the universe is merged in God. This view, which is called acosmism and which fundamentally denies the world or regards it as an illusion, is found in Brahmanism * and Neoplatonism.*

2. Though the term pantheism is modern, having been coined by John Toland,* 1705, the idea is quite old. It is the fundamental doctrine of the Greek Eleatic School. Neoplatonism looked upon the phenomena of the universe as emanations of the Deity. The Middle Ages produced only isolated cases of pantheism, as in the systems of Scotus Erigena and the mystic Meister Eckart. The most precise and consistent pantheist, not only of modern, but of all times, is Spinoza,' according to whom the All is *deus sive natura*, and the great multiplicity of phenomena in the universe are merely modes of the two attributes of God, thought and extension, and God has no reality except through his manifestations in nature. Spinoza's pantheism exerted a great influence on Herder and Goethe and the post-Kantian philosophers and theologians, Fichte, Schelling, Hegel, Schopenhauer, Schleiermacher.

3. Brahmanic philosophy created the conception of Brahma, the world-soul. Only he can obtain salvation, that is, release from transmigration,* who through profound contemplation has come to the realization of the illusion of phenomena and the identity of the *ego* with Brahma.

4. The great fallacy of pantheism is that, in addition to destroying the personality of God and reducing Him to a lower rather than to a higher object of worship, it also destroys the personality of man, who is merely one of the numberless parts that constitute the All. Thereby also individual responsibility and the moral world order are destroyed. Neither does it explain the existence of evil. Christ's redemptive work becomes an illusion. Pantheism is but a short step removed from atheism* and the latter term is sometimes used as embracing it. Mysticism, which endeavors to identify the thinker with the Deity, is often associated with pantheism.

Papacy. (See also *Roman Catholic Confessions*, E 3.) 1. The Papacy was of gradual growth, and its small beginnings are involved in obscurity. That Peter was the first bishop of Rome is legend, not history; in fact, it appears that there were no bishops, in the present sense of the word, till the second century.

2. Very early the church at Rome occupied a prominent place, for it was the oldest church in the West and was in the world's capital. Irenaeus, at the end of the second century, mentions the honorary pre-eminence of the church, not the bishop, of Rome. He even rebuked Bishop Victor as a troublemaker. A growing tendency appears in the history of the first three centuries to accord first the church, and then the bishop, of Rome a pre-eminence of honor in the Church. There also appears an increasing tendency of the Roman bishops to assert a supremacy of right, which was emphatically denied in all parts of the Church. The Christianization of the empire opened new opportunities. Still the First Ecumenical Council (Nicaea, 325) mentions the bishop of Rome only inci-

dentally, and the following councils * were neither convened by him, nor did he or his legates preside. In spite of his protests the Synod of Chalcedon (451) declared the patriarch of Constantinople his official equal.

3. The fall of the empire in the West (476) enabled the Roman bishops to increase their power and to subject one province after another to their spiritual sway. They soon proclaimed themselves the superiors of earthly rulers. (See Church and State.) Monasticism became a useful tool. With Gregory I (590—604) began the Papacy of the Middle Ages, and documents were forged to uphold all the papal pretensions. While the spread of Islam freed Rome from her Eastern rivals, her missionaries, as they converted the Germanic peoples to Christianity, simultaneously inculcated obedience to Rome. Pepin and Charlemagne, in return for papal favors, laid the foundation of the temporal power.

4. There followed nearly two centuries of eclipse and degradation for the Papacy, while the papal chair was stained with every form of crime and vice. Then Emperor Henry III made some attempts to reform the Church, and soon a new race of popes, supported by convenient forgeries, the False Decretals, aspired to greater power than any former pope had possessed. Through the genius of Gregory VII the Papacy rose to the meridian of its power, maintaining itself in the ascendancy for more than two centuries (1073—1303). The Crusades and the establishment of the mendicant orders were important factors. During this time the popes became lords of the earth. They triumphed over the imperial house of Hohenstaufen, humbled and deposed rulers, bestowed kingdoms, and wielded the scepters of both the spiritual and the political worlds. With the last years of Innocent III (d. 1303) a rapid decline of papal power began. France, England, and Germany revolted against political interference by Rome. For nearly seventy years (1309—76), the popes were practically captives at Avignon. Then two and even three popes simultaneously claimed the pontifical chair during the Great Schism (1378—1417).

5. The demand for a reform of the Church "in head and members" grew more and more insistent throughout Christendom; but though the Council of Constance (1414—18) healed the schism, it brought no actual reform, but burned Hus, the reformer. By the end of the 15th century the Papacy had regained much of its power, and the papal throne was occupied by some of the most degraded wretches on record. Through the Reformation, God definitely broke the power of the Papacy, and since then, despite all efforts of the Jesuits and others, papal power has been only an emaciated shadow of its former self. Even so-called Catholic countries have shown themselves less and less tractable to the political intrigues of the Roman Curia and have enacted laws to curb the power of the hierarchy and to protect their own sovereignty. The same year which saw the declaration of papal infallibility (1870) was also made memorable by the abolition of the last vestiges of the Pope's temporal power, which, however, was restored again by Mussolini in 1929.

For references to popes see under that entry; T. Hoyer, "The Papacy," Abiding Word, CPH, 1947 (II: 709—66); C. B. Gohdes, Does the Modern Papacy Require a New Evaluation? E. G. Behm, The Papacy Evaluated (for young people).

Papal Bull. See *Bulls.*

Papal Constitutions. See *Constitutions.*

Papal Legates. See *Legates.*

Papal Nuncio. See *Legates.*

Papal States. See *States of the Church.*

Papal Syllabus. See *Roman Catholic Confessions,* D.

Papias. See *Apostolic Fathers,* 4.

Papocaesarism. The theory that the Church, specifically the Roman pontiff, holds the supreme power, not only in matters pertaining to Church, but also to State. The theory was thus stated by Gregory VII: As the moon derives her light from the sun, so the emperor derives his authority and power from the pope.

Pappus, Johann (1549—1610). Lutheran theologian; prof. at Strassburg, then Muenster; succeeded Marbach as president of church convents; opposed Sturm and the Tetrapolitana; caused a Lutheran liturgy and the Formula of Concord to be adopted in Strassburg (1598).

Papua. See *New Guinea.*

Papyri. Reeds which grow on river banks, especially the Nile. Paper was made by laying layers of the pith crosswise. This paper was frequently used for making manuscripts * of the Bible.

G. Milligan, *Here and There Among the Papyri*, George H. Doran, N. Y., n. d.; W. Schubert, *Einfuehrung in die Papyruskunde*, Weidmann, Berlin, 1918; W. H. P. Hatch, *Principal Uncial Manuscripts of the New Testament*, 1939; E. C. Malte, "Light from Papyri on St. Paul's Terminology," *CTM*, XVIII: 499—517 (extensive bibliography).

Paracelsus von Hohenheim, Theophrastus Bombastus (1493—1541). B. at Einsiedeln, Switzerland; d. at Salzburg. Attempts to reform the medical guild and to establish the empirical principle in medicine earned Paracelsus bitter criticism and the unwanted appellation *Lutherus medicorum*. He was creative in his own right. An alchemist of a higher order, Paracelsus founded the study of iatrochemistry. His deep religiousness led him to conceive his medical calling as a divine mission of love. He developed a theology based on the Bible as interpreted through his nature philosophy rather than historically. His philosophy, which combines nature study with theosophy, established foundations for future Protestant nature mysticism. His name lived among German Pietists and his passion to unlock nature's secrets in Goethe's *Faust.*

Karl Sudhoff, *Paracelsus saemmtliche Werke*, Munich, 1921— (14 vols. printed, 1950) J. Strebel, *Paracelsus saemmtliche Werke in zeitgemaeszer Kuerzung*, St. Gall, 1944—; F. Gundolf, *Paracelsus*, Berlin, 1928; W. E. Peuckert, *Pansophie*, Stuttgart, 1936; F. Spunda, *Das Weltbild des Paracelsus*, Vienna, 1941; F. Oesterle, "Die Anthropologie des Paracelsus," in *Neue Deutsche Forschungen* (ed. Hans Guenther), Berlin, 1937 (vol. 5). PR

Paraclete. See *Holy Ghost.*

Paradise. See *Hereafter*, A, C 2.

Paraguay *(The Country).* Bounded on the north by Bolivia, on the east by Brazil, and on the south by Argentina — is about the size of Montana.

Since 1936 the Missouri Synod has a mission station at Hohenau in the midst of a large German colony. Three other mission stations were also established. In 1952 a total of 357 baptized members and 161 communicant members were served. See *South America*, 8.

Paramentics. 1. The study of paraments, or church vestments, coverings, and hangings, especially those pertaining to the furniture of the chancel, a distinction being observed between paramentics proper, as here defined, and paramentics in the wider sense, which includes the knowledge of the clerical vestments with the embroidery pertaining to them.

2. As far as the altar vestments and the Eucharistic cloths are concerned, the white linen paraments are used at all seasons of the church year, since they signify the unchanging doctrine of the Christian Church. There are mainly three white vestments to be considered in the first group of altar cloths: the white linen cloth covering of the altar, which should have no overhanging border of geometrical drawnwork, but which should have two layers of linen between it and the mensa; the Corporal, a square white linen cloth placed under the Eucharistic vessels, likewise without fringe or lace; the veil (if one is used), a square (30 by 30, 36 by 36 in.) of the finest linen procurable, its purpose being to cover the sacred vessels when they are on the altar and not in use. A veil of silk brocade is preferable to one of linen. A number of purificators (small squares of linen) will also be required. The pall, made of linen and folded or hemmed over a piece of cardboard, is used to cover the chalice when not in use.

3. The decorative vestments of the altar and of the reading desks (lectern, pulpit, and altar) are properly in the colors of the season. The frontal of the altar falls all the way to the floor. The purpose of the frontlet (or superfrontal) is to conceal the means by which the frontal is suspended. The antependium is the vestment hanging down from lectern and pulpit reading desk. There are altogether five liturgical colors: white, the color of the angels and of all saints, as Luther calls it, symbolizing innocence and holiness, majesty and glory; red, the majestic color of dominion, of joy, of light-giving doctrine, of the fire of the Holy Ghost, of blood and of martyrdom, symbolizing especially love, the love of the Bride, the Church, to Christ, the Bridegroom; green, the everyday color of the earth, the restful and refreshing color of hope, of peace, and of victory; violet, the solemn, earnest color of penitence and mourning, humility, concentration, and prayerful self-communion; and black, the color of the most profound humilia-

tion, sadness, and deepest mourning. It may be said, briefly, that white is used for Christmastide, Epiphanytide, Maundy Thursday, Eastertide, Ascensiontide, the Trinity octave, Michaelmas, and commemorations of saints, not martyrs (including the Blessed Virgin Mary); red, during Whitsuntide, the Reformation octave, and commemorations of martyred saints (including All Saints); green, from Septuagesima through Shrove Tuesday (if violet is not used) and during the after-Trinity season; violet, during the seasons of Advent and Lent, from Septuagesima through Shrove Tuesday, and on Days of Humiliation and Prayer; black only at ante-communion on Good Friday and when funeral services are held in the church.

C. C. Rolfe, *The Ancient Use of Liturgical Colours*, Parker, Oxford, 1879; F. R. Webber, "The Designs for Paraments," *Am. Luth.*, July, 1933; L. D. Reed, "Altar Vestments," *Am. Luth.*, Oct.-Nov., 1927; see also references under *Vestments; F. W.* Weidmann, "Eucharistic Vestments," *Pro Ecclesia Lutherana*, 1934, 70—86; P. Z. Strodach, "On Vestments for the Clergy," *Luth. Ch. Quart.*, XII: 312—16; General Rubrics of *The Lutheran Liturgy.*

Pardieck, E. B. at Indianapolis, April 29, 1867; graduated at St. Louis Seminary 1890; pastor in Chicago, Ill.; professor at St. Paul's College, Concordia, Mo., 1902—12; at Concordia Seminary, St. Louis, Mo., 1912—23; d. at Madison, Ind., March 21, 1926.

Pardons. See *Indulgences; Opera Supererogationis.*

Parents and Education. See *Christian Education*, D 3; *Parish Education*, B 1 ff.

Parents, Rights and Duties of. 1. Just as privileges are the correlate of obligations, so duties are the correlate of rights. To insist upon rights without paying proper attention to duties would amount to a most serious neglect of parental obligations. Children are gifts of God to the parents (Ps. 127: 3-5; 128: 3). In accordance with this fact, children ought to be regarded most highly and guarded most carefully. The sinfulness with which they are born into this world (John 3: 3, 6) makes it necessary that they be born again by the water and the Word (Eph. 2: 1, 5; 5: 26). Not only are parents to bring their children to the Lord in and by Holy Baptism, but they are also to instruct them, or

have them instructed, in the Holy Scriptures, which alone are able to make them wise unto salvation through faith which is in Christ Jesus (2 Tim. 3: 14-17). The fundamental passage laying this obligation upon parents is Eph. 6: 4. (Cp. Ps. 103: 13; Col. 3: 21.) To acknowledge a child as a gift of God, to accept it in the name of Jesus, to treat it as one of the redeemed of the Lord and as an heir of eternal life, that is the privilege of Christian parents.

2. The proper understanding of all these facts demands that parents feel the direct concern for the bringing up of their children in the instruction which is necessary for salvation. They are reminded of the example of Abraham (Gen. 18: 19; cp. Deut. 6: 6, 7; 11: 19, 20). This means that parents will acquaint their children with the one thing needful just as soon as possible. They will pray for them and over them even before the little ones are able to speak. They will teach them little prayers and tell them about their Savior just as soon as the first signs of response and understanding are evident. They will have regular home devotions, or family worship, making it a point to draw children into the circle of the wonderful facts presented. They will send them, if at all possible, to a Christian day school, to a Christian Sunday school, and to confirmation classes, showing their eager interest in the work of the children in every way. They will prayerfully and tactfully watch over the children of the adolescent age, to keep them with the Church and to lead them ever more deeply into the Book of books. Thus only will the end and aim of a complete education be reached, namely, that the man of God may be perfect, thoroughly furnished unto all good works.

Parent-Teacher Organizations. See *Parish Education*, J.

Pareto, Vilfredo (1848—1923). Italian economist and sociologist; prof. at Lausanne; considered religion wishful thinking; despised democracies and prepared the way for Fascism.

Pareus, David (1548—1622). Reformed theologian; held various pastorates; prof. at Heidelberg; issued the Neustaedter Bible; showed tendencies toward compromising with Lutherans but uncompromising toward Catholics; wrote several exegetical books.

Pariahs. See *Hinduism*, 3.

Paris Evangelical Mission Society.
Organized by French Reformed Protestants, 1822, through the merger of several already existing societies in France, which, however, remained auxiliaries. First general meeting 1824, when a training school for missionaries was established. During and since World War I the society fostered some of the former German missions in Africa. Fields: Africa and Australasia.

Paris Polyglot. See *Polyglot Bibles.*

Parish. The territory of a church in which its pastor exercises his office.

Parish Centers. See *Armed Services Commission.*

Parish Education. A. *Parish Education Defined.* 1. Christian education is a responsibility shared by the home and the Church. The divine obligation and prerogative of Christian parents to teach their children is clear from Scripture: Deut. 6:6, 7, Ps. 78:1-6, and Eph. 6:4. The responsibility of the Church to provide for the Christian education of its entire membership is evident from Matt. 28: 19, 20 and John 21:15-17. Since Christian education is thus a shared responsibility, the Church emphasizes the importance of Christian training in the home and organizes a comprehensive educational program that aims to reach all members of the congregation. God has not designated the agencies of Christian education that the Church is to set up in order to discharge its educational responsibility, but from Col. 1:10, 2 Pet. 3:18, Deut. 32:46, and Acts 20:28 it is clear that the parish education program is to be a lifelong program, a program that provides for the spiritual growth of the individual, a program that provides regular opportunities for Christian education, and a program that meets God's high standards of education.

2. *Parish education* includes all the educational activities carried on by the local parish. Though the agencies used to carry on these activities may vary from one congregation to another, all seek to achieve the threefold aim of Christian education: the glory of God, the temporal and eternal happiness of the individual, and the welfare of mankind in general. The program of parish education will vary somewhat from one church body to another. This article describes parish education in The Lutheran Church — Missouri Synod. References to parish education in other church bodies are specifically noted.

B. *Parish Education at the Preschool Level.* 1. Interest in the preschool age (children under six years of age) increased sharply after Froebel's * pioneer work with the kindergarten in 1837. The Church, however, was tardy in assuming its obligation to provide Christian education for the children who were too young to be enrolled in the formal agencies of the Church.

2. As the importance of the preschool years for education came to be more generally recognized, the Church began to give assistance in Christian preschool education. The preschool program of the Church includes four agencies: the Nursery Roll, the Nursery Class of the Sunday school, the Beginners' Department of the Sunday school, and the Kindergarten.

3. *The Nursery Roll.* — The names "Nursery Roll" and "Cradle Roll" are used somewhat interchangeably for the department giving attention to the infants and small children in the parish. The aims of the Nursery Roll are:

(1) To foster or awaken in parents a sense of responsibility for the religious instruction and training of their young children;

(2) To establish and maintain a bond of unity between the parents and the congregation;

(3) To give the church access to the homes of the unchurched.

The Nursery Roll commonly operates as a department of the Sunday school under the leadership of a Nursery Roll superintendent or secretary. Ordinarily and with the parents' consent, children are entered on the Nursery Roll either at birth or at Baptism. Nursery Roll workers also visit the homes of unchurched persons in the community and seek to enroll the small children. The Nursery Roll provides materials offering guidance to parents in Christian child training. These materials are distributed to the homes by the workers in this department.

4. *Preschool Classes in the Sunday School.* — The Sunday school gives special attention to children of preschool age. Three-year-olds who actually attend Sunday school comprise the *Nursery Class* as distinguished from the *Nursery Roll.* Children 4—5 years of age are enrolled in the Beginners' Department. Special materials are provided for these children so that instruction will be adapted to their level of understanding.

5. *The Kindergarten.* — Just as the Nursery Class and the Beginners' Department of the Sunday school provide an introduction to Sunday school for the small child, so the Lutheran kindergarten provides an introduction to the full-time parochial school. The kindergarten gives the young child the experience of working in a group and provides an interesting approach to school activities through the medium of play. In 1952 enrollment in 419 Lutheran kindergartens totaled 7,974.

C. *Parish Education at the Elementary Level.* For the history of Parish Education on the elementary level see *Christian Education.*

D. *The Parochial School.* 1. The parochial school, or Lutheran elementary school, is a school established, maintained, and controlled by a local congregation or by a group of congregations. All matters pertaining to the school are under the final jurisdiction of the congregation although immediate supervision is generally delegated to the pastor. In most instances a board of Christian education is elected by the congregation to exercise general supervision over the school.

2. What is the purpose of the congregation in maintaining a parochial school? This question is most readily answered by examining the "Distinctive Objectives of the Lutheran Elementary School" (*General Course of Study for Lutheran Elementary Schools,* 1943, p. 4).

"(1) Diligent teaching of God's Word in obedience to divine command. Deut. 6:6,7.

"(2) Provisions for both the temporal and eternal welfare of the child by means of an integrated Christian education in a single environment, which is substituted for the combination of the public school and part-time agencies of religious instruction.

"(3) Thorough indoctrination of the pupil in the fundamentals of Christianity.

"(4) Protection of the pupil against the dangers of a purely secular schooling.

"(5) Daily Christian pupil-fellowship as one of the most powerful factors in building character and training in Christian living.

"(6) Support of parenthood and home life for the purpose of strength-ening the very base of human society.

"(7) Stabilization and strengthening of the congregation and the Church generally through the training of a well-grounded, discerning laity and youth.

"(8) The maintenance of a single-minded, faithful ministry and teaching profession within the Church.

"(9) Christian citizenship grounded in obedience to God and His Word."

3. Since these objectives guide the conduct of the school, the school stresses the moral and religious education of its pupils, at the same time providing a complete education in the elementary school curriculum. This combination of a complete elementary education offered in a Christian environment and under the guidance of Christian teachers results in an educational product which is superior to the product of a purely secular educational system. In most instances Lutheran elementary schools have an enviable reputation in the community.

4. *Teachers.* See *Teachers.*

5. *The Curriculum.* — The curriculum may be defined as the sum total of the actual experiences the child has in school. In the Lutheran elementary school the teacher seeks to provide a truly Bible-centered curriculum. To accomplish this, the teacher sets the Word of God as the frame of reference to all the activities carried on in the school. It is God's Word that guides every activity and shapes every aspect of the program of the Lutheran elementary school.

6. To assist Lutheran teachers in thus sharing the school program, special materials of instruction have been produced. At first District boards of education and conferences of teachers promoted the production of such special materials. Since 1914, when the first General School Board was established, the production of such teaching materials has been taken care of by this board. Materials for the pupils have included textbooks in Bible History and Catechism and at one time or another textbooks for practically every school subject. Materials for the teacher have included a series of curriculum guides produced by the Curriculum Committee of the Board for Parish Education and the *General Course of Study for Lutheran Elementary Schools.*

7. *Statistics on Lutheran Elementary Schools.* — The following table presents

statistics on the parochial schools in The Lutheran Church — Missouri Synod:

Year	Congre-gations	Schools	Teachers	Pupils
1850	41	41	41	1,342
1860	155	129	129	6,843
1870	214	226	—	20,369
1880	851	784	—	43,368
1890	1,662	1,226	1,305	78,061
1900	2,147	*1,767	1,907	92,042
1910	2,736	*2,130	2,360	93,890
1920	3,283	*1,310	1,954	73,063
1930	3,843	1,339	2,335	79,956
1940	4,358	1,259	2,247	71,151
1950	5,871	1,271	3,161	98,136
1952	6,094	1,286	3,449	106,609

* See following paragraph for explanation (the statistics for congregations include preaching stations).

8. The growth of the elementary school system up to the year 1890 was consistent, although the early goal of having a school in every congregation was not attained. The figures for 1900 and 1910 take in many Saturday schools and summer schools, and the sharp loss of 800 schools in the period from 1910 to 1920 is largely a "paper loss." Some schools were closed during this period, but the loss was not nearly so great as the above statistics would seem to indicate. The loss in pupils between 1930 and 1940 can be largely attributed to the economic depression. Beginning with 1940, there developed an increasing interest in parochial schools and a willingness to support them.

9. *Parochial Schools in Other Lutheran Bodies.* — Although the Missouri Synod has the largest system of Protestant parochial schools, other Lutheran church bodies, particularly those within the Synodical Conference, are also fostering church schools. In 1952 the following statistics were reported:

Synodical Conference	Schools	Teachers	Pupils
Joint Synod of Wisconsin	193	510	17,281
Slovak Church	2	5	79
Norwegian Synod	13	13	262
Colored Missions	45	74	2,857

Other Lutheran Church Bodies			
American Lutheran Church	37	99	2,333

E. *The Sunday School.* 1. The Sunday school is a special school, meeting for approximately one hour on Sunday mornings. The institution has a two-fold purpose, education and missions. The Sunday school provides religious instruction for the children of the congregation and for the youth and adults enrolled in the Bible class department. In addition to serving the congregation as an educational agency, the Sunday school can make contact with unchurched persons in the community and win them for the church.

2. *History of the Sunday School.* See *Sunday School.*

3. *Sunday Schools in the Missouri Synod.* — Because of the strong emphasis on the parochial school, little attention was given to the Sunday school in the Missouri Synod in the early years of its history. Church leaders holding the ideal of a schoolhouse alongside every church could not be satisfied with duplicating the weak and inefficient sectarian Sunday schools. Also, they feared that by introducing the Sunday school they would supplant the parochial school.

4. As the Missouri Synod grew, many congregations were organized that did not or could not maintain parochial schools. Wanting to provide for the religious instruction of their children, they organized part-time agencies of religious instruction, including the Sunday school. Also congregations with parochial schools recognized that some of their own children were not enrolling in the parochial school and that the Sunday school could be used as a missionary agency. Thus many additional Sunday schools were established. The Sunday school has become the most widespread educational agency in the Missouri Synod, and there are few congregations without one.

5. *Sunday School Literature.* — The Concordia Sunday School Lessons were first produced in 1911. Before that time, Missouri Synod Sunday schools used a variety of materials. Some used the Catechism and Bible History, others introduced the courses of other church bodies. Within a few years the Concordia Series had supplanted most of this other Sunday school literature. At first, Sunday school materials were produced by part-time editors. Wm. H. Luke became the first full-time editor in 1927 and served until his death in 1932. A. C. Mueller assumed the position as editor of Sunday school materials in 1933.

6. Helps for teachers to accompany

the Sunday school lessons were also provided. The *Concordia Lesson Helps* were first produced in 1916; the *Concordia Sunday School Teachers' Quarterly* first appeared in 1923.

7. *Sunday School Teacher Training.* — As soon as pastors had to draw in untrained lay assistants for the important work of teaching in Sunday school, many of them began to hold regular teachers' meetings and to instruct their teachers in the lessons they were to present to their children. Others also included in their lectures, background material in the study of the Bible and suggestions as to methods of teaching.

8. Feeling that more effective and systematic work could be done through a pooling of efforts in Sunday school teacher training, some pastors provided leadership in establishing Sunday school associations. Associations were formed in St. Louis, Chicago, and Cleveland in the 1920's. By 1940 the number had probably grown to 75 associations in the United States. To bring the advantages of systematic study to teachers who could not attend Sunday school associations, a correspondence course was prepared by Paul E. Kretzmann.

9. In order to provide still more effectively for Sunday school teacher training, the Missouri Synod appointed a Sunday School Teacher Training Committee in 1938. This committee prepared a series of courses including textbooks and tests which are used in the training classes of the congregations. In the first nine years, 18,000 teachers were enrolled in this program for credit, and approximately 37,000 course cards were issued for completed courses. Additional thousands are taking the courses without working for credit.

10. *Statistics on Lutheran Sunday Schools.* — The following table presents statistics on Sunday schools in The Lutheran Church — Missouri Synod:

Year	Congregations	Sunday Schools	Enrollments	S. S. Teachers
1910	2,736	—	53,343	—
1920	3,283	1,587	108,133	9,553
1930	3,843	2,849	210,988	20,174
1940	4,358	3,635	281,572	29,531
1950	5,137	4,421	425,499	48,514
1952	5,316	4,618	493,477	54,617

Sunday schools in other Lutheran bodies (1951 statistics gathered by the National Lutheran Council):

Synodical Conference	Number	Teachers	Pupils
Joint Synod of Wisconsin	—	—	41,111
Slovak Church	46	371	3,070
Norwegian Synod	53	283	2,040
Negro Mission	64	—	3,574
Other Lutheran Church Bodies			
American Luth. Church	1,984	24,254	241,979
Augustana Synod	1,106	17,763	162,888
Evangelical Luth. Church	2,571	32,768	302,988
United Luth. Church	4,120	80,082	683,131
Luth. Free Church, 1949	356	2,729	19,457
United Evangelical	177	2,220	16,693
Suomi Synod	127	1,353	7,923
Danish Luth.	74	598	3,873
Finnish Apostolic, 1947	42	271	1,723
National Evangelical	47	294	2,186
Luth. Brethren	42	—	—
Eielsen Synod	7	25	210
Independent Congregations, 1948	—	—	465

F. *Other Agencies of Elementary Education.* 1. In addition to the religious instruction given in parochial schools and Sunday schools, congregations have established various other agencies for Christian education at the elementary level. These include confirmation instruction, vacation Bible schools, released-time classes, Saturday schools, and *Christenlehre.*

2. *Confirmation Instruction.* — Confirmation is a rite by which the individual confesses publicly his adherence to the teachings of the Lutheran Church and enters into communicant membership of the church. It is preceded by a course of instruction taught by the pastor, based chiefly on the Catechism. The instruction is a capstone to the elementary educational program of the church.

3. *Vacation Bible Schools or Summer Schools.* — Some congregations have used the summer school as an important part-time agency reaching all children of the congregation; other congregations have used it to give an intensive course in confirmation instruction. More recently the term "vacation Bible school" has come into use, and the vacation Bible school has been

recognized as a missionary agency as well as an effective educational agency. Congregations that have no parochial school find that the vacation Bible school provides much-needed time for more adequate instruction. Congregations with parochial schools are finding the vacation Bible school an effective feeder for their schools. Both types of congregations find that the vacation Bible school is helpful in winning the unchurched children of the community.

4. *Released-Time Classes.* — The public school authorities in many communities offer one hour of school time per week for religious instruction to be carried on by the churches that care to take advantage of the program. This instruction is usually conducted on the church premises. Parents must request the release of their children for the specified time, and the church must furnish the public school with enrollment and attendance reports. In 1952, 414 Missouri Synod congregations maintained such classes with a total enrollment of 18,156. In that year the total enrollment in released-time classes in the United States was estimated at 2,250,000.

The nation-wide program of released-time classes received a momentary setback by the decision of the Supreme Court in March, 1948, on the McCollum case. The Court ruled unconstitutional the use of public school systems to help any religious group spread its faith. Opponents of released time held the decision as a great victory. Many church leaders, however, felt that it was not only a great blow to weekday religious education but was a further step in the trend toward secularism.

Although the McCollum decision did wipe out the released-time program of some communities, most communities simply modify their programs to comply with the law which forbids the use of the public school buildings and public school machinery in aiding released-time programs. About 20 per cent of the communities which had conducted weekday religious programs discontinued them, and the number of pupils enrolled in such programs decreased by 10 per cent.

A second court case in New York, the Tessim Zorach and Esta Gluck case, tested the legality of the practice of releasing pupils from public schools to attend released-time classes. The United States Supreme Court upheld the decision of the Court of Appeals on the constitutionality of the New York released-time program. This decision of the Supreme Court opened the door for further extension of weekday religious education programs. Early in 1953, it was estimated that the enrollment in such weekday religious education classes was as high as any previous figure.

5. *Saturday Schools.* — Some congregations have made use of the Saturday school for religious instruction. The Saturday school is conducted usually for three hours, either in the morning or in the afternoon. It is sometimes used for confirmation instruction only, but many congregations conduct it for all elementary age groups. When used so, it becomes a year-round extension of the vacation Bible school. In 1952 the congregations of the Missouri Synod reported 764 Saturday schools with an enrollment of 16,272.

6. *Christenlehre.* — This was a type of catechetical instruction carried on either in a special service or in the regular church service. The instruction was intended for both young and old, although the children were asked the questions. Formerly *Christenlehre* was held on Sunday afternoons, but today most congregations that make use of *Christenlehre* allot 15 minutes or more of the morning service for this instruction. *Christenlehre* is usually conducted by congregations that do not maintain Sunday schools.

G. *Parish Education at the Secondary Level.* 1. Although Christian education at the secondary level was not given the same attention by Lutheran congregations as elementary education, the Church did seek to provide for the further Christian education of its newly confirmed. Three agencies were used for this purpose: Lutheran high schools, Bible classes, and young people's societies.

2. *Lutheran High Schools.* — The official position of Synod included from the beginning concern for schools of higher learning. In line with this policy a few Lutheran high schools were established in the period 1857—77. These schools lacked sufficient financial support, however, and they were eventually closed. Of existing Lutheran high schools the earliest dates from 1903. The great expansion of public secondary education in the years after the First World War was not paralleled by similar expansion of Lutheran high schools. Some schools were established, but there was no Synod-wide movement in

support of secondary education. Not until the 1944 convention was the area of Lutheran high schools assigned to an official synodical board for study and promotion. After 1944 there was an increase in the number of high school projects undertaken and a much more widespread interest in Lutheran high schools.

3. The following statistics on Lutheran high schools are reported for the year 1954:

Location and Name	Founded	Teachers	Students
Milwaukee, Wis., Lutheran H. S.*	1903	40	1,007
Chicago, Ill., Luther H. S. North	1909	26	575
Fort Wayne, Ind., Conc. Luth. H. S.	1916	21	432
Fond du Lac, Wis., Winnebago Luth. Academy **	1925	8	152
Racine, Wis., Lutheran H. S.*	1943	14	316
Detroit, Mich., Lutheran H. S.	1944	19	475
St. Louis, Mo., Lutheran H. S.	1946	32	632
Cleveland, Ohio, Lutheran H. S.	1948	26	445
Houston, Texas, Lutheran H. S.	1949	7	178
Chicago, Ill., Luther H. S. South	1951	22	437
Los Angeles, Calif., Dr. W. A. Maier Memorial	1953	7	108
Denver, Colo.. Lutheran H. S.	1954	—	—
Chicago, Ill., Walther H. S.	1954	—	—

* Joint project of Missouri and Wisconsin Synod congregations.

** Conducted by Wisconsin Synod congregations.

Note: To the total enrollment of 4,605 in Lutheran high schools should be added the 1,436 students in the high school departments of Missouri Synod colleges.

Some congregations have extended the parochial school to include the ninth grade. In 1952 there were 244 pupils in such ninth-grade classes.

4. *Bible Classes.* — Most congregations provide for additional Christian education at the youth level through the Bible class. In the typical congregation not more than 25 per cent of the youth of high school age are enrolled in Bible classes, but some congregations have been successful in achieving a much higher enrollment. An intensive Bible Study Program launched at the Centennial Convention in 1947 seeks to improve the Bible study situation in the Missouri Synod.

5. *Young People's Societies.* — In studying the parish educational program at the youth level, the important educational contribution of the youth organization must not be overlooked. Particularly important is the organized program of the Walther League. (See *Walther League.*)

H. *Parish Education at the Adult Level.* 1. From one point of view, adult education has always been emphasized in the Church. The Sunday service provided opportunity for worship; but it also provided opportunity for instruction, for the sermons preached in Lutheran churches are definitely didactic. From another point of view, adult education did not receive adequate attention, for the Sunday service did not provide sufficient time for it. To provide additional opportunity for adult instruction, many congregations established adult Bible classes, others established special classes, particularly for parent education, and many congregations used the topic studies of the Lutheran Laymen's League and the Lutheran Women's Missionary League in the meetings of their organizations. To give added impetus to the adult education program, Synod charged the Board for Parish Education with responsibility for this work and created the office of Secretary of Adult Education. After outlining a broad program of adult education the board has given special attention to expanding adult Bible classes.

2. *Adult Bible Classes.* — The need for special Bible classes for adults stems from the fact that the interests and the problems of young people and adults are markedly different. As long as a congregation maintains only one Bible class, it will attract chiefly the youth of the church. To increase interest in Bible classes a special Bible Study Program was inaugurated at the Centennial Convention in 1947. By 1952 enrollment in Bible classes had reached 148,279, which is approximately 12 per cent of the communicant membership.

3. *The Areas of Adult Education.* — The Board for Parish Education in setting up a program of adult education has emphasized the following eight areas:

a. *The Bible in Life:* Guidance in

using the Bible as the source of truth and the Book of life. 2 Tim. 3:16, 17.

b. *Christian Faith and Life:* Nurturing the Christian personality with Christian doctrine related to life. Col. 1:10.

c. *Christian Worship and the Arts:* Developing the devotional life of the Christian through a better knowledge and use of worship in personal life, in the family, and in the church. Ps. 29:2.

d. *The Adult and Christian Education:* Helping adults to appreciate a thoroughly Christian education and to participate in it; training them for Christian learning during all of life and for all of life. Matt. 28:19, 20.

e. *Christian Family Life:* Strengthening the Christian home and fostering Christian family living. Joshua 24:15.

f. *The Christian and the Church in the World:* Giving the individual Christian and the Church a sense of their primary importance as a leaven on earth and as bearers of the world's only regenerative force, the Gospel of Christ. Matt. 5:14-16.

g. *Personal Evangelism and Mission Study:* Training in the personal sharing of the Gospel and helping Christian adults understand and fulfill their tasks in home, foreign, and inner mission. John 4:38.

h. *The Stewardship of Self and Money:* Developing and using our abilities and possessions, spiritual, personal, and material, for greater service to Christ. 2 Cor. 8:5.

4. This program does not require new organizations, nor does it necessarily mean that special courses should be offered in each of the eight fields. These topics can be discussed in an informal way in the regular adult organizations of the parish. Such informal discussion is an important method in adult education.

I. *Financing the Program of Parish Education.* 1. The program of parish education maintained by the congregations of the Missouri Synod requires considerable effort on the part of the individual congregations. In addition to the time that is given to planning and carrying out the program, the congregation provides the necessary financial support. The amount of financial support needed will vary according to the type of program set up and the size of the congregation.

2. *Financing the Part-Time Program.* — The part-time program of Christian education is relatively inexpensive as long as the pastor is the only salaried person needed to conduct the program. The program of the Sunday school is self-supporting in most congregations, for the contributions of the members enrolled pay for the instructional materials needed. The other part-time agencies also involve comparatively little cost to the congregation. Some congregations engage a director of religious education to assist in conducting the part-time educational program. In addition to the cost of salaries and instructional materials, congregations must build and maintain a church plant adequate to house the part-time educational program. Congregations that maintain a parochial school use these facilities also for the part-time agencies. Other congregations find it necessary to provide special rooms for educational work.

3. *Financing Lutheran Elementary Schools.* — Lutheran elementary schools are typically financed completely by the congregation that maintains them. In beginning new schools, the mission boards may subsidize them in whole or in part, but as soon as possible the congregation assumes this responsibility. Costs vary greatly from one congregation to another due to several variable factors: the teacher-pupil ratio, the salaries paid to teachers, the type of building required, and the facilities provided for audio-visual aids, recreation, etc. Although the congregation finances the school, parents of children attending the school frequently make special contributions to the support of the school. These contributions may be either freewill offerings or payment of definite tuition charges.

4. *Financing Lutheran High Schools.* — The Lutheran high school is generally a joint project of several congregations. If the high school serves a number of congregations, the supporting organization may be an association of congregations or an association of individuals. The supporting organization provides the building and facilities, and the current expenses are provided for through tuition and congregational support. In 1953 it was estimated that the capital investment required in establishing a Lutheran high school was approximately $1,500 per pupil. At the same time the operating costs were estimated at $275 per pupil per year. These estimates are, of course, only a rough approximation, for just as with Lutheran elementary schools, the cost of a Lutheran high school will depend on several factors.

J. *Lutheran Parent-Teacher Organizations.* Since Christian education is a shared responsibility in which both home and school participate, there is the necessity for home and school to co-operate in the work of Christian education. Such co-operation implies that there will be opportunity for the parents and the teachers to discuss the Christian training of children. This matter may be discussed in general in the voters meeting, in Bible classes, or in men's and women's organizations of the church, but many congregations provide a special parents' organization for this purpose. Parents' organizations are known by a variety of names including the following: Parent-Teacher Association, Mothers' Club, Lutheran School Club, School Auxiliary, and Lutheran School Society. Monthly meetings are the rule in these organizations, and the program is usually planned jointly by parents and teachers. The aims of Lutheran parent-teacher organizations are 1) mutual home-school understanding; 2) home-school co-operation and unity; 3) providing for the school the necessary equipment and materials for effective teaching and training. In connection with the latter point the organization supplements the congregational budget and provides for instructional equipment. Lutheran high schools also sponsor parent-teacher organizations, with much the same purpose as the elementary school organization. In 1953 a National Lutheran Parent-Teacher League was formed as a department of the Lutheran Education Association.

K. *Educational Administration and Supervision in the Local Congregation.* 1. Since, in the Lutheran Church, the local congregation is the supreme authority in matters of organization and control of the parish program of Christian education, the local congregation may be said to be the most important unit of administration and supervision in Christian education. Authority and responsibility in this field are lodged in the pastor, the local board of Christian education, and the teacher and principal of the school, and the Sunday school superintendent.

2. *The Pastor and Educational Administration and Supervision.* — The ministry of the Word is committed to the Christians in the local congregation, individually and collectively. In the collective unit, the local congregation, God has provided for the public office of preaching and teaching (Eph. 4:11, 12).

In calling a pastor, the local congregation entrusts to him the feeding of the whole flock with the means of grace and expects him to give leadership in the development of an over-all program of Christian education for the entire membership of the congregation. Since he cannot discharge all of his educational responsibilities in person, it is necessary for the pastor to supervise the persons that are assisting him in the program. The pastor is the leader in the Sunday school, guiding the formation of policies, training the teachers and supervising them in their work, and often teaching the Bible class in person. The pastor is the superintendent of the parochial school. In this capacity he works together with the teachers in setting up policies that will make the school truly Christian; he promotes the school in sermons, in the congregation meetings, and in his official contacts in the community; and he supervises to some extent the educational program of the school. The pastor is also the leader in other part-time schools. He frequently teaches the released-time classes, and he often organizes and directs the vacation Bible school.

3. *The Local Board of Christian Education and Educational Administration and Supervision.* — The board of Christian education is elected by the congregation to exercise supervision over the educational program of the congregation and to assist the pastor and the teachers in discharging their responsibilities. The activities of the board will include the following:

(1) To provide a parish education program that meets the needs of the entire membership: child, youth, and adult.

(2) To study the participation of the children, youth, and adults of the congregation in the educational program of the church, and the extent to which each educational agency is utilized for mission purposes.

(3) To study the educational program of the congregation, to establish the needs, and to make plans to meet these needs.

(4) To provide lay leadership for the program of Christian education.

(5) To promote the various agencies of Christian education.

In some congregations the board of elders supervises educational activities, but most congregations find a separate board of education essential for giving adequate supervision to the educational program.

4. *Parochial School Teachers and Educational Administration and Supervision.* — Congregations that maintain parochial schools have in their teachers, persons professionally trained in education. It is common practice for congregations to lean heavily on the professional services of these teachers in the administration and supervision of the educational program. Besides their work in the parochial school, many teachers supervise the Sunday school and the vacation Bible school.

5. When two or more teachers are serving in the same school, the congregation ordinarily appoints one of them as principal. The principal takes the lead in faculty meetings, setting up the curriculum of the school, and evaluating the extent to which the objectives have been attained. The principal also is held responsible for carrying out school policies adopted by the board of Christian education, and he represents the school in the public relations field. Since Lutheran principals are always teaching principals (there was only one exception in 1947), they can exercise only indirect supervision. Teaching principals exercise leadership through faculty meetings and consultation with the teachers.

6. *The Sunday School Superintendent.* — The Sunday school superintendent holds an important position in the efficient administration of the Sunday school. Since the pastor has so many other responsibilities, the superintendent must give attention to the many details that are involved in the Sunday school program. He must provide leadership in setting a high standard for the Sunday school and in encouraging pupils and teachers to meet that standard. The superintendent supervises the business details of the Sunday school, such as enrollment, attendance, follow-up calls on absentees, and takes the lead in planning to meet local problems as they arise.

L. *Educational Administration and Supervision in the Synodical District.* 1. In 1914 the Missouri Synod appointed a General School Board to assist the congregations in carrying out a comprehensive and effective program of Christian education. During the following year or two the various synodical Districts appointed similar committees or boards. At first the District boards confined their attention to the parochial schools. As the responsibilities of the synodical board expanded, the District boards also expanded their activities

until they embraced all agencies of parish education from infancy through adulthood.

2. *The Activity of District Boards.* — The functions of the District Board for Parish Education are briefly defined in the synodical *Handbook:* "The District Board shall co-operate with Synod's Board for Parish Education and shall assist and advise the local congregation in the organization and maintenance of its parish schools and offer suggestions in furthering the work of parish education." Each of the Districts has set up detailed regulations for the work of its Board for Parish Education. These regulations usually specify that the board shall consider itself an advisory body in educational matters both to the District and its officials and to the congregations and their pastors and teachers. The scope of the District board's work includes supervision of all agencies of parish education. In carrying out this responsibility the board gathers accurate information on all phases of Christian education carried on in the District and in the individual congregation, and on the basis of such information makes recommendations to the District and its congregations. Recommendations to the individual congregation are made periodically, usually after personal visits either by the superintendent or some member of the board. Recommendations to the District are usually included in the report of the board to the annual District conventions.

3. *The Circuit Visitor.* — Educational supervision in the District is also carried on by Circuit Visitors. The synodical *Handbook* describes the Visitor as an assistant to the District President within the circuit. As a supervising pastor, the Visitor also supervises Christian education. The Visitor is thus co-responsible with the District Board of Education for supervising the educational work of congregations in his circuit. Besides providing leadership in the circuit for the entire work of the Church, including Christian education, the Visitor also visits the individual congregations, giving attention to all phases of parish education. Since the activities of the District Board of Education and the Circuit Visitor overlap, the District boards work closely with the Visitors in expanding and improving parish education.

4. *The District Superintendents.* — With the development of the program of the District Boards for Parish Edu-

cation the importance of supervision came to be recognized. It was manifestly impossible for District boards to deal adequately with their many problems on the basis of mere monthly meetings. Districts that were numerically strong and financially able appointed full-time functionaries to act as the executives of their Boards for Parish Education. These functionaries were given various titles, among them: Superintendent, Executive Secretary, Director of Christian Education, and Counselor in Parish Education.

5. The following list indicates the Districts that have instituted the office of Superintendent and the present and past incumbents of the office:

California-Nevada: (Rev.) Oscar H. Reinboth (1951—53).

Central District (Indiana, Kentucky, Ohio): A. C. Stellhorn (1918—21); O. E. Schroeter (1922—31); W. J. Gernand (1931—   ). Assistants: E. C. Sieving (1950—51); R. V. Schnabel (1952—   ).

Northern Illinois District: P. T. Buszin (1918—42); (Rev.) A. G. Merkens (1945—51); A. H. Kramer (1951 to   ). Assistant to the Director: A. H. Kramer (1947—51).

Michigan District: (Rev.) F. Meyer (1918—27); S. J. Roth (1927—   ); Assistant Superintendent: E. E. Hack (1945—   ); Assistant Superintendent: (Rev.) R. C. Rein (1947—52).

Iowa District: (Rev.) H. C. Seltz (1920—27); H. F. C. Mueller (1930—37), and in Iowa District West (1938—45).

South Wisconsin District: A. A. Grossmann (1920—24); B. Schumacher (1926—   ); (Rev.) Erich Brauer (1953 to   ).

Western District: Theo. Kuehnert (1921—26); H. F. Bade (1928—46); L. J. Dierker (1946—   ). Assistant: H. A. Leimer (1952—   ).

Kansas District: Wm. Nickel (1921 to 1933); (Rev.) A. F. Meyer (1948—52); A. C. Erxleben (1952—   ).

Nebraska District: H. Hillmann (1921 to 1924).

Northern Nebraska District: H. Hillmann (1924—41); E. Charles Mueller (1943—49).

Southern Nebraska District: H. Hillmann (1924—41); E. Charles Mueller (1943—   ).

Atlantic District: (Rev.) A. W. Brustat (1946—48); A. E. Wittmer (1951—   ).

Eastern District: (Rev.) E. E. Heuer (1946—53); H. G. Coiner (1953—).

North Dakota District: (Rev.) E. H. Bohrer (1946—53).

North Wisconsin District: A. L. Amt (1947—   ).

Central Illinois District: (Rev.) G. Albers (1949—51); (Rev.) R. C. Rein (1952—   ).

Colorado District: (Rev.) Arnold F. Meyer (1952—   ).

Minnesota District: (Rev.) H. J. Boettcher (1940—52); (Rev.) E. H. Bohrer (1953—   ).

Texas District: (Rev.) Martin L. Koehneke (1950—   ).

6. *Supervision in Districts That Have No Superintendents.* — Districts that lack the services of full-time functionaries have exercised supervision through members of the board and through the Circuit Visitors. Some Districts have appointed active teachers to act as school supervisors.

M. *Educational Administration and Supervision by the Board for Parish Education.* 1. The Missouri Synod appointed a General School Board at the 1914 synodical convention in order to give assistance in expanding and improving the system of parochial schools. In 1923 a Sunday School Board was established. These boards were joined in 1929 to form the present Board for Parish Education. The synodical *Handbook* outlines its functions as follows:

"a. assist in planning an effective program of parish education and especially seek to improve and extend the system of parochial schools in all congregations;

"b. watch for all movements and tendencies which might endanger the program of parish education and marshal all available resources to counteract such tendencies and movements;

"c. plan and direct the production of textbooks and other printed materials necessary for the carrying out of an effective program of parish education;

"d. assist in co-ordinating and integrating the various educational agencies and activities intended to promote parish education;

"e. assist the District Boards in supervising and directing all formal educational activities of the congregations of Synod, such as the Lutheran elementary and secondary schools, the Sunday school, summer school, vacation Bible school, the part-time religious school;

"f. initiate and direct research activities necessary to promote and improve parish education;

"g. advise Synod, its Districts, and congregations with respect to problems, needs, and possibilities in the field of parish education."

2. *The Staff of the Board for Parish Education.* — In carrying out its varied responsibilities the Board for Parish Education has delegated many activities to its staff. Synod created the office of Secretary of Schools in 1920, and A. C. Stellhorn was called to fill this position. At first the work of editing Sunday school literature was on a part-time basis, but a synodical resolution of 1926 created the office of editor of Sunday school materials. This position was held successively by Wm. H. Luke and Arnold C. Mueller.

3. As new responsibilities were assigned to this board, additional manpower was provided to cope with these responsibilities. Since 1940 the following persons have been added to the staff: Assistant Secretary of Schools, Wm. A. Kramer (1940—   ); editor of Bible class materials, J. M. Weidenschilling (1938—   ); editor of vacation Bible school materials, Arthur W. Gross (1946—   ); Secretary of Adult Education, Oscar E. Feucht (1946—   ); Executive Secretary, Arthur C. Repp (1943 to 1945), Arthur L. Miller (1946—   ); assistant editor of Sunday school materials, Allan H. Jahsmann (1948—   ); assistant editor of Sunday school materials for high school Bible classes, Walter Riess (1953—   ).

4. *Printed Materials for the Program of Parish Education.* — One of the major responsibilities of the Board for Parish Education has been the production of the textbooks and other printed materials for the program of parish education. Materials for the parochial school and the Sunday school have already been mentioned. In addition to these materials, lessons for Bible classes, vacation Bible school classes, released-time classes, and the cradle roll have been produced under the auspices of the Board for Parish Education. From 1923 to 1947 the *News Service* was published monthly in the interest of the parochial school. Beginning with 1948 this publication was renamed *Parish Education,* and was absorbed into a new journal of practical church work, *Advance* (1954).

5. *Promoting Parish Education.* — Another major responsibility of the Board for Parish Education is the promotion of Christian education. In a general sense many of its activities and publications are promotional. Members of the board and the staff promote parish education at conferences and other meetings in the interest of Christian education. They also write promotional articles on educational topics for the various church papers. Since 1944 the board has sponsored Lutheran Education Week as an annual occasion for the special promotion of the educational program of the Church. The general objectives of Lutheran Education Week are the following:

a. To acquaint the congregation and the community with the purposes and values of Christian education;

b. To stress the obligation of the home and the Church in training the young;

c. To emphasize the necessity of a congregational program of Christian education that reaches every age group: children, young people, and adults;

d. To encourage the congregation to study and evaluate its entire education program by means of an annual survey;

e. To work toward the improvement and expansion of the congregation's educational program;

f. To give recognition to the achievement of the educational agencies of the congregation and the educational system of the Church;

g. To invite and urge the congregation and the community to make use of the educational facilities of the Church.

6. *Co-operation with District Boards.* — Direct personal contact with the individual congregation in matters of Christian education is maintained by the District boards. The Board for Parish Education gives assistance to the District boards in supervising and directing the various educational agencies of the parish. Bulletins are issued regularly by the Board for Parish Education to provide information for the guidance of the District boards. Representatives of the District boards meet annually with the general board in an Educational Conference to discuss common problems. The staff of the Board for Parish Education also participates with the District directors of Christian education in an annual Superintendents' Conference. Co-operation with the District boards is a reciprocal process, for from the District boards and their superintendents, the Board for Parish Education receives both advice and assistance in discharging its responsibilities.

7. *Giving Guidance in Parish Education.* — The over-all activity of the Board for Parish Education is defined in its responsibility to advise Synod, its

Districts, and congregations with respect to problems, needs, and possibilities in the field of parish education. Advice to the individual congregations is provided through its publication *Parish Education* and through tracts and other materials made available for congregational use. Advice to the Districts is provided through special bulletins and through conferences and personal contacts with the District Boards of Education. Advice to Synod is included in such service to the congregations and the District boards. In addition the Board for Parish Education provides comprehensive reports to the triennial synodical conventions. These reports include a summary of the activities of the board and specific recommendations to Synod on educational matters. ALM

Walter H. Beck, *Lutheran Elementary Schools in the United States,* St. Louis: CPH, 1939; *Christian Preschool Education.* Second Yearbook of the Lutheran Education Association. River Forest, Ill.: Lutheran Education Association, 1945. *General Course of Study for Lutheran Elementary Schools.* St. Louis: CPH, 1943; H. H. Gross, "The Development of the Lutheran Parochial School System of the Missouri Synod." *Lutheran School Journal,* Vol. 71, 1935 to 1936; J. Arthur Koss, *The Lutheran Parent-Teacher Association.* River Forest, Ill.: Lutheran Education Association, 1944; Carl S. Meyer, *The Lutheran High School.* Published by the Lutheran Education Association and the Board for Parish Education, 1945; *One Hundred Years of Christian Education.* Fourth Yearbook of the Lutheran Education Association. River Forest, Ill.: Lutheran Education Association, 1947; *Proceedings of the Fortieth Regular Convention of the Ev. Lutheran Synod of Missouri, Ohio, and Other States.* CPH, 1947, 1950, 1953; A. L. Miller, *Educational Administration and Supervision of the Lutheran Schools of the Missouri Synod,* 1914—50. Eighth Yearbook of the Lutheran Education Association, 1951; *Parish-School-Home Relationships* (ed. by J. A. Koss). Ninth Yearbook of the Lutheran Education Association, 1952.

Park, Edward. See *New England Theology,* 3.

Parker, Daniel. See *Baptist Bodies,* 13.

Parker, Joseph (1830—1902). Eloquent Congregational clergyman; b. at Hexham; did not attend seminary;

pastor at Banbury, Manchester, London (City Temple); visited America; d. in London; wrote *The People's Bible,* and other works.

Parker, Theodore (1810—60). American Unitarian clergyman; pastor of Unitarian Church, West Roxbury, Mass., 1837; through study of German rationalists was led to deny authority of Bible and supernatural origin of Christianity, which older Unitarians still accepted, and saw that to base Unitarianism on Bible was untenable, thereby becoming leader of new school of Unitarians; repudiating all fundamentals of Christianity, he was ostracized by the Unitarian clergy, resigned pastorate in West Roxbury, and preached for fourteen years in a concert hall in Boston.

Parlin, Olaus (d. 1757). Swedish pastor at Wicaco, Philadelphia; successor to Acrelius * on the Delaware.

Parmenides (ca. 475 B. C.). Greek philosopher of the Eleatic school; reality is not becoming, but being, which P. considered pure extension and identified with pure thought. He denied creation and held that change is impossible.

Parochial Schools. See *Parish Education,* C, D; *Christian Education.*

Parousia (G. "presence" or "coming"). A word applied to Christ's return in glory on Judgment Day. See *Last Things.*

Parr, Samuel (1747—1825). Anglican; b. at Harrow-on-the-Hill; assistant master at Harrow; priest in 1776; vicar at Hatton (d. there) 1783; author; Ciceronian Latinist; famous for learning and dogmatism.

Parsees. Modern adherents of Zoroastrianism,* of whom a small number live in Iran but most of them in India, chiefly in the Bombay Presidency, where their Persian ancestors settled in the 8th century, when Moslems conquered Persia (Iran). They numbered approximately 124,000 in 1952. Because of their wealth and their social position they now form an important element of the population of India. They have tenaciously clung to their old religion, whose main tenets are the Zoroastrian dualism, belief in angels, demons, future life, sacredness of fire, veneration of the cow. Their dead are exposed on "towers of silence," to be devoured by vultures. See also *Fire-Worshipers.*

Parsimonius (Karge), George (1512 to 1576). Supt. of Bayreuth; denied doctrine of active obedience of Christ but later retracted.

Parsimonius, John. Pupil of Luther and Melanchthon; head of cloister school and abbot of Hirschau; denied Christ's descent to hell.

Part-Time Educational Agencies. See *Parish Education,* E, F.

Particular Baptist Bodies. See *Baptist Bodies,* 7.

Particular Church. See *Presbyterian Bodies,* 2.

Pascal, Blaise (1623—62). Celebrated French thinker, mathematician, and man of letters; known to the world as the author of *Provincial Letters* and *Thoughts.* Born at Clermont, he was educated at Paris and Rouen and showed remarkable genius and precocity. About the year 1655 he became associated with the Jansenists at the convent of Port Royal (near Paris) and soon championed their cause against the Jesuits. The *Provincial Letters* ("Letters written to a provincial . . . on the subject of morals and politics of the [Jesuit] fathers") appeared in 1656. Written with delicate irony and keen satire, these letters, the nearest modern approach to the Socratic dialog, constitute "the most fearful attack that any dominating party of the Church ever sustained" (Harnack). But Pascal as a Catholic and a Frenchman could not adopt the manner of Luther, and therefore his blows were less effective. The *Thoughts (Pensées)* are a series of detached fragments of composition, the unorganized material of a projected defense of Christianity, which the author did not live to complete.

Emilie Cailliot, *Pascal, Genius in the Light of Scripture,* Westminster Press, Philadelphia, 1945.

Pascha *(Passah).* The Feast of the Passover in the Old Testament, the word being widely applied to the Festival of Easter in the New Testament, in its Latinized form, paschal hymns, paschal offerings, and paschal candles being spoken of.

Paschal Candles (R. C.). Large candles lit from the day before Easter until Ascension.

Paschal Season. See *Church Year.*

Passavant, William Alfred (1821 to 1894). Lutheran; b. at Zelienople, Pa., 1821; d. at Pittsburgh; graduated 1842 from the Lutheran theological seminary at Gettysburg and ordained the same year; pastor in Baltimore 1842 to 1844, in Pittsburgh 1844—55; editor of the *Workman* 1880—87; introduced the Kaiserswerth system of deaconesses in America. Hospitals at Pittsburgh, Milwaukee, Chicago, and Jacksonville, Ill., were established through his efforts, orphanages at Rochester, N. Y., Zelienople, Pa., and Mount Vernon, N. Y., and Thiel College, Greenville, Pa. See *Charities, Christian.*

G. H. Gerberding, *W. A. Passavant,* Young Luth. Co., Greenville, Pa., 1906; O. N. Olson, "William Alfred Passavant and the Augustana Synod," *Aug. Quart.,* XXIV: 224—41.

Passion. A word applied to the suffering and death of Christ and thence also to that of martyrs.

Passion. Since the suffering and death of Jesus Christ are supremely important elements of His redemptive work, the Christian Church has for centuries observed not only Lent, Passion Week, and Holy Week, but it has also made diligent use of the Passion Story of our Lord. While in the Lutheran Church of the 16th century a Passion Harmony was read in Lenten services from Johann Bugenhagen's *Passionsbuechlein,* which was really a revision of the Passion Harmony used in Roman Catholic circles, and while, in keeping with this tradition, Lutherans in America are accustomed to hearing a Passion Harmony read during Lent (cf. *The Lutheran Lectionary,* p. 260 ff.), the Christian Church has also many musical settings of the Passion Story, some of which are centuries old.

Whereas the custom of reading the Passion Story in Holy Week has been traced back as far as the fifth century, the custom of presenting it as a kind of play, in which the words of the various individuals and of the mob were sung or chanted, has been traced back as far as the 12th century. A bass invariably sang the words of Christ very solemnly and impressively; the words of the Evangelist were sung by a baritone in a middle range, and the words of other individuals and of the mob *(turba)* were sung in a high range by a tenor. At first the parts were all sung by priests; later the parts of the mob were sung from the choir loft by a choral group. The purpose of dramatizing the performance was to help render the Latin text of the Passion Story intelligible to the audience. The text was monotoned in recitative style to a very great extent, though some parts, *e. g.*, the words of Christ, were at times sung to a chant of a more melodic character. Musical Passions became more dramatic at the time polyphony was introduced. Many are of the opinion that the words of the multitude *(turba)* helped encourage composers to write polyphonic Passions, since polyphony may readily be more effective than plain chant and recitative to accentuate the dramatic character of a text. Polyphonic Masses of a dramatic character were written by such early Roman Catholic masters as Lassus, Vittoria, and Byrd. In Lutheran circles, however, the dramatic element was at first conspicuously absent, as may be seen from the *Passion According to St. Matthew* by Johann Walter, Luther's musical consultant and "the Father of Lutheran Church Music," who was the first to use the German translation of the Bible prepared by Martin Luther in his setting of the Passion. Walter was of the opinion that church music is the bearer, not the interpreter, of the Word; hence, he employed the *stile famigliare*, which is homophonic and plain in character. Although they employed greater freedom in their Passions, the following Lutheran composers followed in the footsteps of Walter: Antonio Scandello (1517), Selneccer (1587), Vulpius, Mancinus. Demantius was among the first Lutheran masters to tear himself loose from the traditional plain-song type of Passion, as was also Joachim a Burck, who prepared settings also of Psalm 22 and of Isaiah 53 and who was clearly influenced by Lassus.

The motet type of Passion began to flourish with Obrecht (ca. 1500) and was perpetuated by de Rore (1557), Gallus (1587), and the Lutheran Lechner (1594). The Passions of a Burck may well be included in this category.

In the 17th century the Passion continued to become more dramatic; the baroque era made its influence felt also in this area. Not only the recitative, but also the aria and orchestral accompaniment were employed; greater liberties were taken with the text, and a close relationship soon began to make itself felt between the Passion and the oratorio. Thomas Selle's *Passion According to St. John* (1634) was among the first works to point to the baroque type of Passion. The old custom was perpetuated of presenting a St. Matthew Passion on Palm Sunday, St. Mark on the following Tuesday, St. Luke on Wednesday, and St. John on Friday. Parishes which were unable to present more elaborate settings of the Passion often substituted for these the hymn "O Mensch, bewein dein Suende gross," which was regarded as the chorale version of the Passion.

The most famous Lutheran Passions of the pre-Bach era were those written by Heinrich Schuetz. While his St. Mark Passion was written largely in the old recitative style, his Passions according to St. Luke and St. John were more polyphonic and are related to the style of Lassus. Schuetz's *St. Matthew Passion* is his most dramatic and hence most popular setting. Schuetz set also the *Seven Last Words* of Christ to music; in this composition he uses an instrumental accompaniment for the words of Christ. Schuetz's recitatives are of a new type and are not tempered by Gregorian influence. At times they are very closely related to the melodic aria. To some the Passions of Schuetz seem archaic, especially when compared with the Passions of Sebastiani (1672), Theile (1673), and J. S. Bach.

The Oratorio Passion was introduced by Johann Sebastiani; it is no longer a church Passion in the liturgical sense of the term. Bach's *Passions According to St. Matthew* and *St. John*, though monumental and superb, are of such large proportions that they are rarely performed in a church, as they were intended to be. The result is that they have been transferred largely to the concert stage, where it is difficult to create the atmosphere they need for their most effective performance. Bach was not the first to introduce the chorale into his Passions; Sebastiani had already done this. His librettos were those prepared by Brockes (St. John) and Picander (St. Matthew).

In and after Bach's day, Passions of a highly dramatic and at times of a highly sensuous and sentimental character were written by such composers as Telemann (St. John, 1741), Carl Phil. Em. Bach (1787 and 1788), and Karl Heinrich Graun. Graun's *Der Tod Jesu* (1755) was for several generations as popular in Germany as John Stainer's *The Crucifixion* was for many years in America; although superior to Stainer's opus, it was not an outstanding work, though it did help relegate the great Passions of Bach to oblivion for a century. Mention should yet be made of such outstanding works as Josef Haydn's *Die sieben Worte am*

Kreuz (1785), Beethoven's *Christus am Oelberg* (1803), and Pergolesi's *Stabat Mater*. During our 20th century the German composer Kurt Thomas wrote an a-cappella *Markus-Passion* which is as difficult as it is effective, and Hugo Distler's *Choralpassion* today enjoys widespread popularity in Germany. WEB

W. Apel, *Harvard Dictionary of Music*, Cambridge, Mass., 1944; F. Blume, "Die evangelische Kirchenmusik," *Handbuch der Musikwissenschaft* (Ernst Bucken), New York (reprint by Musurgia), 1931, 1949; J. A. Fuller-Maitland, *Grove's Dictionary of Music*, Vol. III, Philadelphia, 1926; O. Kade, *Die aelteren Passionskompositionen bis zum Jahre 1631*, Leipzig, 1893; H. Kretzschmar, *Fuehrer durch den Concertsaal*, Vol. II, Leipzig, 1899.

Passion Plays. See *Religious Drama*.

Passionists. A mendicant congregation under the immediate protection of the Pope, founded in Italy in 1737. Its members lead an austere life and, besides the usual vows, promise to practice and promote devotion to the Passion of Christ. They entered the United States in 1852 and are active in conducting missions and retreats.

Passions. See *Lust*.

Passiontide. See *Church Year*.

Pastor. See *Ministerial Office*, 1.

Pastor Aeternus. See *Roman Catholic Confessions*, E 3.

Pastor as Counselor. The pastor as counselor is concerned with that phase of the Christian ministry which aims to supply helpful advice and guidance to those who are confronted with perplexing problems and which is more familiarly known as the private cure of souls. Because of the ever-increasing complexity of modern living, this important pastoral activity is receiving ever greater recognition, especially by men with training in the field of psychology. And while it is doubtless true that many helpful contributions have been made by such research, enabling a consecrated pastor to analyze and treat the many problems of his people more effectively (see *Counseling*), it must not be overlooked that all pastoral counseling deserving of the name must be Biblical and Christian in character. A pastor may use every legitimate tool of modern psychology,* but he must never discard Scripture for mere tools. Essentially he is an assistant of the Great Physician whose foremost task is to deal with sin-sick souls and to lead them to walk more perfectly with God. Behind and beneath the counsel which he imparts there must be the aim to deepen repentance and faith and to strengthen and confirm men's reliance on the benign providence with which the heavenly Father watches over all His creatures, particularly His believing children.

Though there are many areas in which the conscientious pastor will want to make himself available to all who seek his counsel, the more vital aspects of this phase of the Christian ministry are his services to the physically and mentally ill as well as marriage and family-life counseling. OES

The literature in the field of pastoral counseling is large and constantly growing. At the present time the following are the more notable contributions to the general bibliography in this field. Anderson, *Every Pastor a Counselor*, Van Kampen Press; Bonnell, *Psychology for Pastor and People*, Harper; Hiltner, *Pastoral Counseling*, Abingdon-Cokesbury Press; Hiltner, *Religion and Health*, Macm.; Maves and Cedarleaf, *Older People and the Church*, Abingdon-Cokesbury Press; May, *Art of Counseling*, Abingdon-Cokesbury Press; Schindler, *The Pastor as Counselor*, Muhlenberg Press.

Pastor and Education. See *Parish Education*, K 2.

Pastor, Teaching. See *Teachers*, A 1.

Pastoral Office. See *Ministerial Office*.

Pastoral Theology. Pastoral Theology, or the doctrine of the knowledge of God and of divine things, *applied* by the *pastor*, the spiritual shepherd, to the *spiritual* needs of his flock. "Pastoral Theology is a God-given *(theosdotos)* practical aptitude *(habitus)* of the soul, acquired *(acquisitus)* by means of certain aids whereby a minister of the Church is enabled validly *(rato)* and legitimately *(legitime)*, for the glory of God and his own and his hearers' salvation, to perform all the functions incumbent upon him by virtue of his ministerial office." Walther's *Pastorale*, § 1. Pastoral Theology has been defined as "the art of applying truth." (Strictly speaking, Pastoral Theology includes homiletics and catechetics; in fact, neither of the two can be entirely ignored in a treatise on Pastoral Theology, and the only reason

for not according them more space in
such a treatise is that they are usually
treated as separate branches in the
theological curriculum."

Pastoral Theology is especially designed to be a guide to the *pastor*, or
minister, of the church in the faithful
performance of his official duties.

C. F. W. Walther, *Pastorale*, CPH, St.
Louis; J. H. C. Fritz, *Pastoral Theology*,
CPH, St. Louis, 1932; J. Schaller, *Pas-
torale Praxis in der Ev. Luth. Frei-
kirche Amerikas*, Northwestern Publ.
House, Milwaukee, 1913. C. F. W.
Walther, *Law and Gospel*, CPH; T.
Graebner, *The Borderland of Right and
Wrong*, CPH, St. Louis, 1938; T. Graeb-
ner, *Pastor and People*, CPH, 1932; T.
Laetsch (ed.), *Abiding Word*, CPH,
1946—47 (2 vols.); C. M. Zorn, *Ques-
tions on Christian Topics*, Milwaukee,
1921; A. W. Blackwood, *Pastoral Work*,
Westminster Press, Philadelphia, 1945;
A. Vinet, *Pastoral Theology*, T. & T.
Clark, Edinburgh, 1855; R. F. Weidner,
*Theological Encyclopedia and Meth-
odolgy*, Chicago, Wartburg, 1898;
F. Schulze, *A Manual of Pastoral The-
ology*, Herder, St. Louis, 1936; J. M.
Wilson, *Six Lectures on Pastoral Theology*, Macm., 1903.

Patarenes. A name indiscriminately
applied in the 13th century to sects
opposing the papal system. The name
may have originated with a dualistic
sect which originated in the Balkans.

Paten. See *Church Furniture,* 3.

Paternoster. Designation of the
Lord's Prayer according to its introductory words in Latin, like *Vaterunser*
in German.

Patience. Patience is a calm, un-
ruffled temper with which man bears
the evils of life, fortitude in presence of
duties and conflicts; it manifests itself
in humble submission to God's ruling
providence and to the varying attitudes
of men. Its supreme example are the
patience of God and Christ, Ex. 34: 6;
Rom. 2: 4; 15: 5; 1 Pet. 3: 20. Synonymous
expressions: endurance, constancy, forbearance, long-suffering, resignation.
Patience with respect 1) to persons
(*makrothymia,* 2 Sam. 16: 10-13; Col. 3:
12, 13; 1 Thess. 5: 14); 2) to things and
conditions (*hypomonae,* James 5: 11), to
results (James 5: 7; Luke 8: 15), to afflictions (Rom. 5: 3, 4; 12: 12; 2 Thess. 1: 4;
2 Tim. 3: 10, 11; 1 Pet. 2: 20; Rev. 1: 9. Examples: Ex. 16: 7, 8; Job 1: 21; 2 Tim.
2: 10; James 5: 11). A Christian virtue
of great value and often enjoined (*e. g.,*

James 1: 4). See *Concordia Pulpit*, 1936,
Vol. VII, 292; Luther IX: 850; XX: 12;
Trigl. 1274; Walther, *Law and Gospel,*
313; Kretzmann, *Pop. Com.,* O. T., II,
269, 335, 353; N. T., II, 663. JMW

Paton, John Gibson (1824—1907).
Presbyterian missionary; b. at Kirk-
mahoe, Scotland; d. at Canterbury,
Australia; served as city missionary in
Glasgow 1847—57; began work in
Tanna, New Hebrides, 1857, in the
service of the United Presbyterian
Church; after extensive journeys lo-
cated on Aniwa, where he was
eminently successful; translated and
published parts of the Bible into the
Aniwan language.

Patriarch. The title of the highest
dignitary in the ecclesiastical hierarchy
as the latter developed after the days of
Constantine. A patriarch's jurisdiction
corresponded, in the main, with a civil
diocese, which since the reorganization
of the Roman Empire under Diocletian
included various provinces. Thus he
ranked above the metropolitan, or provincial, bishop. This tendency toward
centralizing ecclesiastical authority issued ultimately in the four great patriarchates of Constantinople, Alexandria,
Antioch, and Jerusalem. In the West,
the bishop of Rome, claiming the primacy, refused the patriarchal title, and
the name archbishop was commonly
applied to the highest representatives of
the episcopal order. In modern times
the heads of the Armenian, Coptic, and
Jacobite churches are called patriarchs,
as also the archbishops of Venice and
Lisbon. The Russian patriarchate,
which since 1589 had become independent of Constantinople, was abolished by Peter the Great (1721) and
was replaced by the Holy Synod, the
highest executive tribunal in the
Eastern Church.

Patriarchal Council. See *Councils
and Synods,* 1.

Patrick, St. Reputed to have been
the apostle of Ireland, winning it to
Christianity from 432 on. But it is
probable that Ireland was Christianized before that date from England and
that Patrick merely played a prominent
role in the Irish Church. His name
was really Sucat, and he seems to have
called himself Patricius because he
hailed from a patrician family. He was
probably born ca. 380 in Banaventa,
Scotland, and was rather loose in
morals in his early youth, though, as
some say, he was the son of a deacon

and the nephew of a presbyter. In his sixteenth year he was kidnaped by pirates and compelled to herd swine in Ireland. He escaped to the Continent, where he received the training that enabled him to return to Ireland as missionary, not under papal jurisdiction. Some say that he was sent from England to Ireland; others, from Gaul. D. ca. 460. We have an autobiography of him, entitled *Confessio*. Patrick has become almost entirely a legendary figure. See *Celtic Church,* 5.

W. M. Letts, *St. Patrick, the Traveling Man,* Edinburgh, England, 1932.

Patrimony of St. Peter. 1) Revenues from the lands of the Roman See; 2) the Papal States (up to 1870).

Patripassianism. See *Monarchianism,* B.

Patristics. 1. Patristics is the branch of theological knowledge which deals with the lives and writings of the Church Fathers. The term *patrology* is often applied to the historical side of the study and *patristics* to the formal study of the writings of the Fathers. The patristic era is often divided into the ante-Nicene and post-Nicene periods. These larger periods are again subdivided.

2. Much of the patristic literature, especially of the first three centuries, survives only in fragmentary form. The *Ecclesiastical History* of Eusebius preserves important quotations and biographical facts. Later, Photius wrote his *Bibliotheca* to acquaint readers with the patristic literature accessible to him. The *Hiera* of Leontinus and John combines quotations from the Fathers with Biblical passages for didactic purposes (still extant in *Sacra Parallela*). Beginning with the sixth century, expositions were compiled *(catena)* as an aid to exegetical study. Patristic quotations are also preserved in heretical writings.

3. The earliest writings were grouped under the title *Apostolic Fathers,** that is, those of subapostolic teachers, some of whom had enjoyed personal intercourse with the Apostles.

4. During the second and third centuries, Christianity was defended against Judaism, paganism, and false teachings in the Church. In opposition to Judaism, Christian writers showed that Christians had all the prerogatives of the people elect or true Israel. The attacks of heathenism were chiefly philosophical attempts to blot out Christianity and attacks of the populace

on Christians. Justin,* Aristides,* Ariston,* Apollinaris,* Miltiades,* Tertullian,* Quadratus,* Justin,* Tatian,* Athenagoras,* Melito of Sardis,* and Theophilus * were outstanding writers of this period.

5. During the third century the patristic writings show a trend toward giving systematized expression to convictions. From these formulations, controversies in this and later centuries originated. During the early part of the third century Gnosticism reached its zenith, and later Arianism developed.

6. The fourth and fifth centuries are often called the golden age of patristic literature. Literature of the Church flourished at this time for various reasons. Constantine gave liberty to the Christian Church (313), thus making it possible for authors to write without fear. The various problems of the Trinity gave writers a great theme and led to erroneous (the heresies of Arius, Apollinaris, Origen; Monophysitism; Antiochianism; Nestorianism) as well as orthodox works also on Christology. In addition, Donatism * and Pelagianism * vexed the Western Church, and Manichaeism * was present in both East and West. These heresies * were opposed by orthodox writers. Outstanding fathers of the period were Athanasius,* Augustine,* Eustathius of Antioch,* Eusebius of Caesarea,* Basil of Caesarea,* Gregory Nazianzus,* Diodorus,* Chrysostom,* Aphraates,* Ephraem,* Jerome,* Ambrose,* Wulfila,* Hilary,* John Cassian,* and others.

7. The fifth century ushered in a decline in patristic literature. Controversies had devastated the Church and were still present, but interest in theological polemics had waned. The Western Church was disturbed by barbarian invasions, which spread ruin in their wake. The centralization of power in the Church with its emphasis on system tended to stifle independent investigation. Furthermore, as ages of productive writing are often followed by ages of synthesis and collection, so the golden age of patristic literature was followed by the age of the *Catena, Florilegia,* and *Compendia (i.e.,* of collecting).

8. Although in the narrower sense the term "Fathers" is usually applied to those who wrote before the Dark Ages, the patristic era is at times extended to the 14th century. Often all respected

theologians who lived and wrote in the past are referred to as "Fathers."

9. The Lutheran Church regards the writings of the Fathers with respect. It does not claim to be a new church started in the 16th century, but the continuation of the Apostolic Church, which existed down through the ages as a spiritual body which embraced all those who believed in Christ. Thus the members of the true Church study the writings of those who have gone before, realizing, however, that even the greatest among them was not infallible, but subject to sin and error, and hence must be judged by the Bible.
EL

Johannes Quasten, *Patrology*, Newman, Westminster, Md., 1952— ; C. W. Farrar, *Lives of the Fathers*, A. & C. Black, Edinburgh, 1889; F. Cayre, *Manual of Patrology and History of Theology*, Desclee and Co., 1936, 1940; A. C. McGiffert, *A History of Christian Thought*, 1932—33 (2 vols.); Joseph Defarrari (Editorial Director) and others, *The Fathers of the Church*, Fathers of the Church, Inc., N. Y. (six volumes published in 1949; the entire set is to contain 72 volumes); *Early Christian Writers*, Newman, Westminster, Md.; G. Krueger, *History of Early Christian Literature in the First Three Centuries* (tr. by C. R. Gillett), Macm., 1898; Ernest Leigh Bennet, *Handbook of the Early Christian Fathers*, Williams and Norgate, 1920; E. J. Goodspeed, *A History of Early Christian Literature*, U. of Chicago Press, 1942; Basilio Steidle, *Patrologia, seu Historia antiquae Litteraturae Ecclesiasticae*, Friburgi Brisgoviae, 1937; see also references under *Apocrypha* and *Apostolic Fathers*. The references to editions of the Fathers are given in works cited above. An old, but still useful, translation is found in the well-known *Ante-Nicene Fathers* and *Post-Nicene Fathers*.

Patron Saints. As patrons are persons who protect and promote the interests of others, so patron saints, in the Roman Church, are supposed to be the special protectors and celestial advocates of those by whom they are elected or to whom they are assigned. They are honored by their clients with a special veneration. Only canonized saints are eligible. Every church has its patron saint, who is usually also the titular, after whom the church is named. His festival is celebrated with particular solemnity. Countries have patron saints; *e. g.*, England, St. George; Germany, St. Michael; France, St. Denis;

Ireland, St. Patrick; Scotland, St. Andrew; Canada, St. Anne and St. George; the United States, Our Lady of the Immaculate Conception. Among the patron saints of trades and professions are: Andrew (fishermen); Cosmas and Damian (doctors); Christopher (porters); Cecilia (musicians); Crispin (shoemakers); Hubert (hunters); Stephen (stonemasons); Vitus (comedians and dancers). For illnesses: Claire and Lucy (eye trouble); Agatha (diseases of the breast); Apollonia (toothache); Blasius (sore throat); Benedict (poison); Hubert (dog bite). Persons, too, may have patron saints, usually those on or near whose festival they were born or whose name they bear.

Patronage. The right of presenting a fit person to an ecclesiastical office. In the Early Church the right of placing a priest in a parish belonged to the bishop. Later, when lords built churches, the rights of patronage were gradually yielded to them. Thus the rights of patronage in many instances devolved upon temporal rulers. In the 12th century the Pope through mandates or expectatives and other means sought to regain the rights of patronage, but England took the lead in organized resistance to the encroachment in the 14th century. The rights of patronage include, in addition to presentation, distinctions and pecuniary support. The patron has the duty of maintaining the benefice. The rights of patronage exist in Roman Catholic churches, England, Scotland, and, to a lesser degree, in Germany, Sweden, and Denmark. The system has been repeatedly modified.

Patteson, John Coleridge (1827 to 1871). English missionary bishop; b. in London; d. at Nukapu, Melanesia. He succeeded Bishop Selwyn of the Melanesian Mission, being ordained a bishop in 1861. In the *Southern Cross* he cruised much in the interest of spreading the Gospel among the Melanesians. On a missionary tour to Nukapu he was slain by the natives. Max Mueller wrote of him: "To have known such a man is one of life's greatest blessings." His name "will live in every cottage, in every school and church in Melanesia." Besides outstanding gifts for mission work, Patteson had a special gift as a linguist, controlling no less than forty languages and dialects.

Patton, Francis Landey. B. Warwick, Bermuda, Jan. 22, 1843; ed. at U. of Toronto, Princeton Theol. Sem., 1865.

Ordained to Presbyterian ministry, 1865; held pastorates in New York, Nyack, and Brooklyn; prof. of theology, McCormick Sem., Chicago, 1872—81; also pastor of Jefferson Park Church, Chicago, 1874—81; prof. at Princeton Theol. Sem., 1881—88. Author: The *Inspiration of the Scriptures; Summary of Christian Doctrine; Fundamental Christianity*, 1926. D. Nov. 25, 1932.

Paul, Lives of. The numerous books on the life of the Apostle of the Gentiles can be divided into two classes, conservative and negatively critical works, with many occupying a middle position. Prominent conservative works are those of Conybeare and Howson, F. W. Farrar, A. T. Robertson, William Dallmann and Olaf Moe. Of the negatively critical works there are some that say Paul derived his message not from Christ, but from Judaism, and especially from the so-called Jewish apocalyptic writings like the Book of Enoch (Wrede and others). Another group holds that Paul derived his distinctive religious teachings from the mystery religions of his time (Bousset, Loisy, and K. Lake). By some it is held that Paul was strongly influenced by Stoicism (Clemen). The attempt is made in some works to destroy the divine character of Paul's conversion by holding that lightning struck near him when he approached Damascus or that he suffered a sunstroke (the old Rationalists). Some say that he had an epileptic seizure and in that condition had hallucinations (Klausner and others). Some believe that the conversion of Paul must be explained psychologically, as an event that took place in his mind as a result of deep brooding (Baur, Holsten). In a masterful way the views of unbelieving critics as to the conversion of Paul and the source of his message are refuted by J. G. Machen in *The Origin of Paul's Religion*.

Paul III. See *Roman Catholic Confessions*, A 1.

Paul of Samosata. See *Monarchianism*, A 4.

Paul of Tella. See *Bible Versions*, C 2.

Paulicians. A Gnostic-Manichaean-Marcionite sect to be traced in Armenia since the middle of the seventh century, where they remained, in spite of persecutions, until their removal to Thrace ca. 970. In the eleventh century

they, in part, returned to the Church, while others identified themselves with various other sects. They taught a kind of dualism. A demiurge made the material world and man's body, while a good god made heaven and man's soul. Christ saves humanity from the former for the latter. They reject the Old Testament and some books of the New, adhering chiefly to the Pauline Epistles and the Gospel according to St. Luke. See *Dualism, Gnosticism.*

Paulinism. See *Isagogics.*

Paulists. "The Congregation of Missionary Priests of St. Paul the Apostle" (Paulist Fathers) is of American origin, having been founded in New York in 1858 by five native priests, all converts from Protestantism. Its primary object is to make converts to Catholicism. This object is pursued through lecturing and preaching and through a systematic literary propaganda. "The Paulist Fathers also consider it part of their vocation to influence the secular press in the interests of Catholic truth" (*Catholic Encyclopedia*).

Paulus Diaconus (son of) **Warnefried** (720?—795?). A Longobard historian and very distinguished scholar at the court of Charlemagne; also a poet, was the author of a Roman and of a Longobard history and compiler of a postil. See *Preaching, Christian, History of*, 7.

Paulus, H. E. Gottlob (1761—1851). Prof. at Jena, Wuerzburg, and Heidelberg; representative of extreme rationalism.

Paumann, Konrad (1410—73). Known as "the Father of German Organ Music." Though blind, Paumann was the most famous instrumentalist of Germany of the second half of the 15th century. He was active at Nuremberg. His *Fundamentum Organisandi*, devoted to the science and art of improvising, exerted a great influence. Since the Germans were not able to sing the French texts of the Burgundian chansons, Paumann arranged these for instruments and thus helped develop the instrumental style in Germany.

Pax Romana. See *Students, Spiritual Care of*, A.

Pax Vobiscum. A special benediction spoken or chanted by the pastor after the consecration of the elements in the Eucharist, just before the Agnus Dei: The peace of the Lord be with you always!

Peace Movements and Congresses. See *Pacifism.*

Peasants' War. An uprising of German peasants in 1525, brought on by the oppression exerted upon them by the wealthy and powerful landowners who were still operating under the feudal system. The rights of the peasants had been dependent on custom rather than on law, and the establishment of the codified Roman Law in the courts of Germany enabled the powerful lords to deprive the peasants of many claims. Luther at first took the side of the peasants as being the downtrodden class; but when they did not heed his warning to abstain from the use of violence and murder, he called upon the constituted authorities to make use of governmental power. The noblemen crushed the revolt with ruthless cruelty, executed Thomas Muenzer,* one of the leaders, and slaughtered thousands. Luther's admonitions to be merciful to peasants innocently involved were disregarded by most of the lords.

Paul Althaus, "Luthers Haltung im Bauernkriege," *Luther-Jahrbuch,* VII; W. Zimmermann, *Allgemeine Geschichte des groszen Bauernkrieges — nach handschriftl. u. gedruckten Quellen,* Koehler, Stuttgart, 1841; H. J. Grimm, "Luther, Luther's Critics and the Peasant Revolt," *Luth. Ch. Quart.,* XIX: 115—32; C. M. Jacobs, "John Brenz on the Moderation of the Princes Toward the Rebellious Peasants, 1525," *Luth. Ch. Quart.,* I: 182—90.

Pecaut, Felix (1827—98). One of the founders of the free church in Neuchatel, Switzerland. He held that the source of religion should be the Bible divested of its supernatural elements.

Pecci, Vincenzo Gioachino. See *Popes,* 29.

Peck, John Mason (1789—1858). Baptist itinerant missionary in Illinois and Missouri; established a school at Rock Spring, Ill., which later merged with Shurtleff College; founded the "American Baptist Home Mission Society" with J. Going.

Pedagogy. See *Christian Teaching.*

Pedersen, Christian (1480—1554). B. at Svendborg, Denmark; studied in Sweden and Paris; became chancellor of Hans Weze, archbishop of Lund; fled to his fugitive king, Christian II, in the Netherlands, where he advocated the Reformation; after the imprisonment of Christian II, Pedersen returned to Malmö, where he became a printer; founder of modern Danish literature; published a Danish New Testament and Psalms (1529); chief worker on the Bible of Christian III (1550); wrote other works based on Luther's writings.

Pedobaptism. See *Grace, Means of,* III, 4.

Peirce, Charles Sanders (1839 to 1914). Founder of pragmatism; b. in Cambridge, Mass.; his father, Benj. Peirce, supervised his education and trained him especially in concentration; grad. from Harvard, 1859; joined U. S. Coast Survey; studied with Agassiz; lectured at Harvard in philosophy; influenced by George Boole's *The Mathematical Analysis of Logic* and *An Investigation of the Laws of Thought;* laid foundation in logic of relations; dealt with foundations of logic; coined the word "pragmatism" in 1905. The pragmatism of Peirce differed from that of James inasmuch as Peirce's pragmatism had room for a conception of the Absolute.

Pelagian Controversy. 1. This controversy takes its name from Pelagius, who, to combat those who made the doctrines of free grace and of the total depravity of the human heart a license for sinning and to create a motive for monkish asceticism, insisted much more strongly than other teachers of the Church before him on the existence of natural moral powers in fallen man. He therefore chiefly concerned himself with anthropology, the doctrine of man, and soteriology, the doctrine of salvation, conversion.

2. While, of course, the Apostolic churches had the full light on these as on all other doctrinal questions and believed in salvation by grace alone (*sola gratia*), according to 1 Cor. 2:14, Eph. 2:1-9, Rom. 8:7, 1 Cor. 12:3, James 1:14, 15, there had not been full agreement herein among the Church Fathers of the following centuries. In general they agreed that man's nature has been depraved by the Fall and that man therefore needs God's grace and a rebirth; but while some taught a *total* depravity and stressed grace alone, such as Tertullian, Cyprian, Hilary of Poitiers, especially Ambrose, others, like Clement of Alexandria and the Alexandrians of the third century in general, and the Greeks Basil, Gregory Nazianzen, Gregory of Nyssa, Didymus, and Chrysostom, contended that man has retained a remnant of free will, which is active toward the good independently

of the operation of grace. The fifth century was to bring out this moot question into full discussion between Augustine and Pelagius and their respective followers.

3. In his earlier writings Augustine, too, did not fully exclude the "free will" from participating in conversion, but in the course of his spiritual development he came to exclude it more emphatically than any Church Father before him. On the other hand, however, rationalistic speculation led him on to the false doctrine of absolute election. Guericke describes his theory as follows: All men since Adam's fall (which ruined human nature both physically and morally) are essentially in the same state of estrangement from God and of condemnation, in which they can do only what is displeasing to God. From this state they may be rescued solely by the grace of God in Christ. This grace of God attracts the depraved will of man with inner conquering necessity (*gratia irresistibilis*), and whoever receives it is saved. However, not all men receive it; but out of mankind, equally depraved in all its individuals (*massa perditionis*), God, according to His compassion in Christ, elects some unto salvation, fitting them thereto by kindling faith in them by His grace (*gratia praeveniens, operans et cooperans*); all the remainder of mankind God, according to His justice, leaves in its depraved state and consigns to merited damnation. The reason why grace is accorded only to a part of humanity can be sought solely in an eternal, holy, inexplicable, absolutely free decree (*decretum absolutum*) of God.

4. Over against this, Pelagius taught: Man's nature is not depraved since Adam's fall, but, on the contrary, is still in its original state, a state of indifference morally, without virtue or vice and capable of both, and it depends solely on the will of the individual to develop the moral germs of his nature and to be saved. Of course, an irresistible grace and an absolute predestination did not fit into his system; but, on the other hand, real grace, according to Pelagius, was not needed to save man, and salvation by Christ was rather a superfluous exertion on the part of God. The very essence of the Christian religion was destroyed by this system and naturalism substituted, though probably the author was not aware of the fact.

5. The Church very quickly sided with Augustine in this controversy. Pelagius first taught his wrong views in his commentary on the Pauline Epistles; then he spread them personally at Rome, ca. 409. Later he went to Carthage with his disciple and friend the monk Coelestius. When the latter applied for the office of a presbyter, he was accused of heresy and had to defend himself before a synod at Carthage, 412. Two fundamental statements of Coelestius were here discussed: 1) that Adam's sin affected only himself and not his progeny, and 2) that children were born in the state in which Adam was before the Fall. Since Coelestius refused to retract these statements and a number of conclusions drawn therefrom, he was excommunicated.

6. Meanwhile Pelagius had gone to Palestine, where there was less accurate definition of doctrine than in the Occident, and he managed to escape blame at two Oriental synods, when he, too, had been accused of heresy. But Augustine wrote a book setting forth how the Orientals had been duped by the duplicity of Pelagius, and the African bishops at the synods of Mileve and of Carthage, 416, condemned Pelagianism and induced Bishop Innocent I of Rome to agree to this condemnation. It was shown from the writings of Pelagius and Coelestius that they defended the free will, caused man to become proud of himself, and denied grace in the specifically Christian sense, because they called the natural powers of man grace, or gave God's Law or also His providence that name. However, Pelagius and Coelestius succeeded in cajoling Zosimus, the next bishop of Rome, into pronouncing them orthodox once more. But the Africans insisted at the synods at Carthage, 417 and 418, that Pelagianism be condemned, adopting eight or nine canons against the heresy. Emperor Honorius also took a stand against Pelagianism, and finally Zosimus, too, was persuaded to side with the Africans. The Occidental bishops signed this verdict, and the eighteen who refused were deposed from office.

7. Especially through the influence of the layman Marius Mercator also the Orient agreed to condemn Pelagianism at the ecumenical synod at Ephesus, 431, because it was found to be closely allied to Nestorianism. Yet the Orient never fully accepted the Augustinian theology. Men like Theodore of Mopsuestia and Isidore of Pelusium taught a system that might be called a mean between it and Pelagianism.

8. In the Occident, too, the Scriptural doctrine that after the Fall man is altogether corrupt and can be saved only by divine grace, that those who are saved are saved without merit of any kind, and that those who are lost are lost by their own fault alone, had to be defended against new foes, who at once took the place of the vanquished Pelagians — the semi-Pelagians. While the Pelagians held that the power of natural man for good, "free will," is not at all impaired, the semi-Pelagians held that "free will" is only partially impaired, needing the assistance of Grace, — salvation thus depending on grace *and* the right use of the natural powers. In the controversy also this problem was debated — which Scripture leaves, and Christian theology must leave, unsolved — why not all men are saved, since grace alone saves, universal grace, and since all men are in equal corruption and guilt. In this discussion both parties erred. Augustine had recourse to the explanation that the reason was to be found in God, who does not treat all men alike, does not offer effective grace to all — a virtual denial of the universality of grace. His followers ordinarily refrained from this rationalizing deduction; they did not blame God for the damnation of any man; yet at times they gave voice to the explanation mentioned. The semi-Pelagians rationalized along the opposite lines, explaining the fact that some are saved while others are not by an alleged inner condition and receptiveness in man, some making the right use of their natural powers, others not. Augustine himself had to refute certain monks of Adrumetum, who misconstrued his doctrine of absolute predestination by concluding therefrom that all moral exertion was superfluous and all punishment of sin unjust.

9. The first real semi-Pelagians whom Augustine had to oppose were called Massilians and were a Gallican party, their leader being the abbot John Cassianus of Massilia (d. 432). He taught that man, in spite of an inclination to evil in him after the Fall, could by free choice accept the good when it was offered him, but needed God's grace to increase in sanctification. According to him there would be a constant co-operation of grace and free will to save man. Though Augustine wrote a book to justify his system against the attacks of these Gauls, and though after his death his friend Prosper Aquitanus wrote more, yet the semi-Pelagian party in Gaul increased. The Roman bishop Coelestinus, induced by Prosper, made a statement condemning the Gauls for their opposition to Augustine, which, however, did not give any clear doctrinal decision. Vincentius of Lerins, also a monk and by the Catholics considered extremely orthodox, belonged to the semi-Pelagian party. In fact, monkdom needed this doctrine to support its contention of its own special meritoriousness.

10. After the death of Augustine some of his followers, *e.g.*, Prosper and Leo the Great, sought to tone down the harshness of Augustine's absolute predestinarian doctrine. They distinguished a general and a special grace; only reception of the latter would save. But they stated that it was an unexplained mystery why not all men received the special grace. Others of Augustine's disciples, however, clumsily stressed the harsh features of their master's predestinarian doctrine. Their statements were really nothing new; but the semi-Pelagians represented them as going beyond Augustine and succeeded in having the presbyter Lucidus condemned and forced to recant the strict Augustinian system at the synods of Arelate and Lugdunum, 472 and 475, and having semi-Pelagianism, as set forth, by the order of synod, by Bishop Faustus of Rhegium, sanctioned. In his treatise Faustus says that free will and grace are as co-operative for man's salvation as the divine and human natures were co-operative in the person of Christ. He held that free will was not entirely destroyed by Adam's fall, but that an indestructible germ of good remained.

11. But this was a victory of semi-Pelagianism only in the Gallican Church. Again the African bishops, chiefly Fulgentius of Ruspe, in Numidia, objected. Fulgentius wrote two volumes in refutation of Faustus' book. Also the Gallican archbishop Caesarius of Arelate (d. 542) again spoke up for Augustine's doctrine, and many others in Gaul. Through the influence of Caesarius it came about that, at the Council of Orange, 529, the Augustinian doctrine was restated, not only over against Pelagianism, but also over against semi-Pelagianism. However, the harsh portions of Augustine's doctrine were not accepted. A predestination unto damnation was again denied, and semi-Pelagianism was condemned in clear terms, yet without mentioning of names. These decrees were ratified in the same year

by the synod at Valence and 530 by the Roman bishop Boniface II.

12. The Occident had therefore taken a decided stand for the essential anti-Pelagian features of Augustine's doctrine, his doctrine of sin and grace. But the speculative dialectic predestinarian feature was not clearly settled and continued to cause confusion in church doctrine; that was to be removed only a thousand years later by Luther. Semi-Pelagianism itself also soon arose again and became the recognized doctrine of the Church during the Middle Ages. Despite its clear and full refutation by Luther, the Church of Rome has retained it.

See references under *Doctrine, History of;* Franz Klasen, *Die Innere Entwicklung des Pelagianismus,* Herder, Freib. u. Bri., 1882.

Pelagius. The chief exponent of Pelagianism, a British monk, lived in the beginning of the fifth century; had considerable philological learning, but was a shallow thinker and had little spiritual experience, believing that monkish outward probity was the true spiritual life. He spread his heretical views in Rome, North Africa, and Palestine. See *Pelagian Controversy.*

Pellican (Kuerschner), **Konrad** (1478—1556). Cofounder of the study of Hebrew in Germany and prominent worker for the Reformation in Basel and Zurich; studied at Heidelberg and at the Franciscan cloister in Ruffach, later at Tuebingen; made a specialty of Hebrew, which he taught in various cities; joined the movement of the Reformation on the Swiss side; wrote *Commentaria bibliorum.*

Penance. The fourth of the seven sacraments of the Church of Rome. With it are connected so many unscriptural doctrines and practices that it is not surprising that the Reformation began with a protest against one of its offshoots (see *Indulgences*). The sacrament of Penance was molded from the Office of the Keys, as conferred by Christ, and the ancient Church's practice of requiring public penance for grave offenses (see *Penitential Discipline*), under the influence of the Roman doctrine of the merit of works and with the aid of the monastic spirit. The following doctrine is decreed by the Council of Trent (Sess. VI., chap. 14, and Sess. XIV): Penance is a sacrament instituted by Christ for reconciling the faithful to God as often as they fall into sin after Baptism. It is necessary to their salvation and constitutes "a second plank after shipwreck" (Baptism being the first). The essential parts of the sacrament are contrition, confession, and satisfaction by the penitent, and absolution dispensed by the priest. Contrition is sorrow of mind and a detestation of sin committed, with the purpose of not sinning in the future. (But see also *Attrition.*) The contrite sinner must confess to a priest (see *Confession*), at least once a year, every mortal sin (see *Sins, Venial and Mortal*), of which he becomes conscious after examining all the folds and recesses of his conscience, together with the circumstances under which it was committed. A sin knowingly kept back is not forgiven. After confession the priest pronounces absolution, which is not "a bare declaration of the Gospel," but a judicial act (see *Absolution*), by which the penitent is reconciled to God and freed from eternal, though not from temporal, punishment (see *Purgatory*). To remove temporal punishment, the priest imposes works of satisfaction (such as fasting, prayer, alms), the doing of which renders satisfaction to God (see *Works, Merit of*) and removes temporal punishment, which, however, may further be removed by other means (see *Indulgences*).

2. This sacrament the Roman Church sets before the gate of heaven, teaching that no one who sins after Baptism can be saved without it, that though repentance be ever so sincere and faith in Christ's merit ever so lively, yet without confession, satisfaction, and absolution by the priest (or, at least, the desire for them), they avail nothing. "If any one saith that there are two parts only of penance, to wit, the terrors with which the conscience is smitten upon being convinced of sin, and the faith generated by the Gospel or by the absolution, whereby one believes that his sins are forgiven him through Christ: let him be accursed." (Council of Trent, Sess. XIV, can. 4.) "If any one saith that God always remits the whole punishment together with the guilt and that the satisfaction of penitents is no other than the faith whereby they apprehend that Christ has satisfied for them: let him be accursed." (Can. 12.) Faith is presupposed, but is distinctly ruled out as in any sense a part of penance. (*Catechismus Romanus,* II, 5, 5.) — The *Augsburg Confession* states the Scriptural doctrine as follows (Art.

XII): "Those who fall after baptism may obtain forgiveness of sins at any time when they come to repentance, and the Church ought to grant absolution to such as return to repentance. Repentance, however, consists properly of these two parts: the one is contrition, or the terrors injected into the conscience by the knowledge of sin; the other is faith, which arises from the Gospel or from absolution, believes that the sins are forgiven for Christ's sake, comforts the conscience, and frees it from terrors. Then good works must follow, which are fruits of repentance."

Penington, Isaac (1616—79). An outstanding preacher of the Society of Friends; son of lord mayor of London; married Mary Springett, who, by previous marriage, was mother of the wife of William Penn; frequently imprisoned; his writings amounting to more than eighty are considered of high authority by Quakers.

Penitence, Day of *(Busstag).* The annual day of humiliation and prayer is commonly celebrated either on the last Sunday of the church year or on Sunday Quinquagesima, the Sunday preceding Lent; in some congregations, which celebrate a special Harvest Home Festival, the last Thursday in November has been set aside for a day of penitence. A feature of the services is usually the reading or chanting of the Litany.

Penitential Discipline. The procedure in use in the early Christian Church by which a person who had become guilty of a transgression of the Moral Law or of the decrees of the Church, or both, was given a form of punishment which was intended, at the same time, to restore him as a member of the respective congregation, usually by a series of steps in the discipline. When, even in the first century, a worldly spirit in the form of voluptuousness, selfishness, pride, and other sins became apparent, it was rooted out by Apostolic exhortation and discipline. If a person, at that time, caused public scandal by serious departure from the true doctrine or Christian conduct and in spite of sincere and repeated admonition persisted in error, he was excommunicated; but the penitent was received again after his sincerity had been proved. 1 Cor. 5:1; 2 Cor. 2:5; Matthew 18. In later times stages of penance were observed. During the first stage, the *fletio,* the penitents stood

at the door of the church in mourning dress, making supplication to the congregation to be restored to membership. During the second stage, *auditio,* they were again admitted to the reading of the Scriptures and to the sermon, but were obliged to occupy a place near the doors, that of the *lugentes* or *hiemantes.* During the third stage, *substratio,* they were once more permitted to kneel at prayer. And finally, in the fourth stage, *consistentia,* they took part again in the whole worship, with the exception of the Lord's Supper, during the celebration of which they were merely allowed to look on. It was only after they had been received into full membership once more by absolution and reconciliation and by the laying on of hands on the part of the bishop and the entire clergy, together with the kiss of brotherly love, that they were again accounted full members of the congregation.

Penitentiaria. See *Curia, Roman.*

Penn, William (1644—1718). Son of English admiral; turned Quaker at university and was disowned by his father; anti-Trinitarian; several times arrested for preaching; received grant of lands now constituting the States of Delaware and Pennsylvania in satisfaction of his father's claims against the Crown; founded Philadelphia 1681; went to America, 1682, to escape persecution; made the colony a refuge for Quakers; treated Indians with exemplary fairness and concluded Great Treaty with them in 1683; revisited Pennsylvania 1699 to 1701. Toleration was practiced in his colony from the very first; advocated complete freedom of religion and conscience.

For Lutherans associated with Penn see J. W. Richards, *Penn's Lutheran Forerunners and Friends,* Bk. Concern, Columbus, O., 1926.

Pennsylvania, Ministerium of. See *United Lutheran Church, Synods of,* 24.

Pennsylvania, Synod of. See *United Lutheran Church, Synods of,* 24.

Pennsylvania, Synod of Central. See *United Lutheran Church, Synods of,* 24, 25.

Pennsylvania, Synod of East. See *United Lutheran Church, Synods of,* 24, 25.

Pennsylvania, Synod of West. See *United Lutheran Church, Synods of,* 24, 25.

Pensions, Ministerial. A system under which minister and congregation alike pay a certain percentage of the pastor's salary into a pension fund, which provides an income for him when he retires from active duty. See *Lutheran Church — Missouri Synod,* XVII a; *Finances in the Church,* 7; *Lutheran Laymen's League.*

Pentapolitana, Confessio. See *Lutheran Confessions,* A 5.

Pentateuch, Unity of. See *Higher Criticism.*

Pentecost. See *Church Year,* 10.

Pentecostal Assemblies of Jesus Christ. See *Holiness Bodies,* 2; *Pentecostalism.*

Pentecostal Assemblies of the World. See *Holiness Bodies,* 2; *Pentecostalism.*

Pentecostal Church, Inc. See *Holiness Bodies,* 2; *Pentecostalism.*

Pentecostal Church of God in America, Inc. See *Holiness Bodies,* 2; *Pentecostalism.*

Pentecostal Church of the Nazarene. See *Church of the Nazarene.*

Pentecostal Fire-Baptized Holiness Church. See *Holiness Bodies,* 2; *Pentecostalism.*

Pentecostal Holiness Bodies. See *Holiness Bodies,* 2; *Pentecostalism.*

Pentecostalism. Modern Pentecostalism originated about 1900 in Kansas and spread rapidly to Texas, California, and to many other parts of the world. Pentecostalists believe that the Pentecostal miracles (speaking in tongues, the gift of healing, prophecy) are the normal experience of every truly converted believer. The "spirit-baptized" Pentecostals are the typical "Holy Rollers," and their meetings are accompanied by much shouting, testifying, speaking in tongues, and similar emotional exhibitions, which are said to be visible evidence of the Holy Spirit's immediate presence. The psychological phenomena of Pentecostalism resemble the ecstatic experiences of Montanism, the frenzied orgies of the French prophets or Camisards, the tongues movement under Irving, the emotional excitement of the Wesleyan and Whitefield revivals, and the jerking exercises of the Kentucky revival. The theology of modern Pentecostalism may be designated as a fusion of the "inner light" theory of Baptist theology and perfectionism of Arminian theology. Pentecostals usually claim to proclaim the "Full Gospel" or the "Four-Square Gospel," and their local churches frequently are called Full Gospel Assembly, or the Four-Square Church, to indicate that the doctrines of conversion, entire sanctification, divine healing,* and the premillennial coming of Christ receive special emphasis. The center of their preaching revolves about the necessity of being baptized with the Holy Ghost, and some even classify statistically their membership as converted, saved, and spirit-baptized members. The Pentecostal Holiness Church, a representative group of Pentecostalism, believes "that Jesus Christ shed His blood for the remission of sins that are past, for the regeneration of penitent sinners, and for salvation from sin and sinning. It also teaches and firmly maintains the Scriptural doctrine of justification by faith alone; that Jesus Christ shed His blood for the complete cleansing of the justified believer from all indwelling sin and from its pollution, subsequent to regeneration; and that entire sanctification is an instantaneous, definite second work of grace, obtainable by faith on the part of the fully justified believer. It also teaches that the Pentecostal baptism of the Holy Ghost and fire is obtainable by a definite act of appropriating faith on the part of the fully cleansed believer, and that the initial evidence of the reception of this experience is speaking with other tongues as the Spirit gives utterance." (Census Report, 1936, p. 1321.) The following groups are Pentecostal: Pentecostal Holiness Church, Pentecostal Assemblies of Jesus Christ, The Pentecostal Church, Inc., International Pentecostal Assemblies, Pentecostal Assemblies of the World, Pentecostal Church of God of America, Inc., Pentecostal Fire-Baptized Holiness Church, Calvary Pentecostal Church, Church of God in Christ (Pentecostal), Pilgrim Holiness Church, House of Prayer. — Several of the groups known as "Church of God," The International Church of the Four-Square Gospel, and some of the churches listed as Holiness Bodies are typically Pentecostal. See *Religious Bodies (U. S.),* Bibliography.   FEM

Percept. See *Christian Teaching,* B.

Perceptual Learning. See *Christian Teaching,* D.

Perdition. See *Hereafter,* B.

Peretti, Felice. See *Popes,* 22.

Perfectionism. 1. Under this term is understood the doctrine according to which freedom from sin is possible in this life. That such perfection is attainable in this life was maintained in the Catholic Church by the Franciscans, Jesuits, and Molinists. They taught that in some cases one who is justified may, by special grace of God, attain to such perfection as to avoid all sins and even to offer an obedience beyond the demands of the Law. This claim was denied by the Dominicans and Jansenists. However, in maintaining the doctrine, its supporters usually based many of their claims on the distinctions between mortal and venial sins.

2. In the Protestant churches while perfectionism was denied by Luther and Calvin, "Christian perfection" is permanently a doctrine of all Methodists * and bodies in accord with Methodistic teachings and tendencies. This "Christian perfection," which Methodist theologians have advocated, is not a perfection of justification, but of sanctification. In teaching this doctrine, John Wesley, in a sermon on Christian perfection, based upon Heb. 6:1: "Let us go on unto perfection," founded his arguments chiefly on the commandments and promises of Scripture concerning sanctification. However, he guarded his doctrine by saying that it is neither an *angelic* nor an *Adamic* perfection and hence does not exclude ignorance and error of judgment, with consequent wrong affections. Perfection, as defined by Wesley, is not, then, perfection according to the absolute Moral Law, but perfection according to the special remedial economy introduced by that attainment in which the heart, being sanctified, fulfills the Law by love. Its involuntary imperfections are provided for by that economy, without the imputation of guilt, as in the case of infancy and of irresponsible persons.

3. The doctrine of perfectionism has also been found in the writings of Clemens Alexandrinus, Kempis, Fénelon, and other writers, Roman Catholic and Protestant. It is also maintained by the "Converts," who teach that in the case of the justified the body of death and sin comes to be crucified and removed, and other parts subjected to the truth, so as not to obey any suggestion or temptation of the Evil One, but to be free from actual sinning and transgressing the Law of God and in that respect perfect. "Yet doth this perfection still permit of a growth; there remaineth a possibility of sinning, where the mind doth not most diligently and watchfully attend unto the Lord." (Cf. the Society of Friends, Eighth Prop.) The Oberlin School of Theology (Boston, 1839), C. G. Finney (*Syst. Theol.*, Oberlin, 1878), teaches that it is impossible for sin and virtue to coexist in the human heart at the same time, "as virtue and sin belong only to voluntary actions"; and that the soul is either wholly consecrated to Christ or it has none of His Spirit. These two states may alternate, and this man may be a Christian at one moment and a sinner the next; however, he cannot be at one moment a sinful or imperfect Christian. "Every lapse into sin involves, for the time, an entire interruption of obedience, which is the beginning of the Christian life. The promises of God and the provisions of the Gospel are such that when fully and continually embraced, they enable the believer to live a life of uninterrupted obedience — an attainment which may be truly encouraged and expected in the present life." The advocates of this view, however, deny that anyone may claim to be a perfect Christian under this theory because he does not remember any conscious failure, "since even present failure is not always a matter of distinct consciousness, and the past belongs to memory and not to consciousness." In addition to these advocates of perfectionism, there are dispersed groups of Christians, usually in doctrinal accord with the Methodist or Arminian teachings, who advocate entire holiness, or sanctification, or perfection, in this life. To these belong the advocates of the "victorious life," who maintain that "so long as a fully surrendered believer simply trusts the Lord Jesus to keep him and to conquer his temptations for him, he need not commit willful sin." (*How to Live the Victorious Life.* By an Unknown Christian.)

4. In a general way, the doctrine of perfectionism implies that since Jesus is a present Savior from sin, He is able to keep those who trust in Him from falling into any sin whatever. Hence, if the soul would trust Him completely, it would be preserved from all deliberate sin, and its unintentional wrongdoings, which are errors rather than sins, would not be imputed to it. Some of the advocates of this theory claim to have so lived in the presence of Christ as to have been unconscious of any sin for weeks and months. More

generally, however, those who hold this view, while insisting upon the possibility of the life "without sin," also confess that they occasionally fail to keep a complete and undeviating trust in Christ and so temporarily fall away from the condition of "perfect sanctification," or "the higher life," in which they maintain it to be their privilege to walk. The opponents of perfectionism maintain that this doctrine is based upon the misinterpretation of the Scriptural ideas of sanctification and justification as well as upon defective ethical standards and upon an unscriptural antinomianism, quoting such prooftexts as 1 Pet. 5:8; Matt. 26:41; 1 John 1:8.

W. E. Sangster, *The Path to Perfection*, Abingdon-Cokesbury, N. Y., r. 1944 (*CTM*, XV:430); Newton Flew, *The Idea of Perfection in Christian Theology*, London, 1934; H. Lindstroem, *Wesley and Perfection*, Aktiebolaget, Stockholm, 1946; E. T. Clark, *The Small Sects in America*, Abingdon-Cokesbury, 1937.

Pergolesi, Giovanni (1710—36). Italian composer whose early death may have been due to his profligacy. He was keenly aware of the distinctive character of the various orchestral instruments used in his day, an awareness which made itself felt also in the clear counterpoint of his compositions. His works reveal warmth and profound emotional affection, as may be seen in his *Stabat Mater*.

Perichoresis (G., "surrounding"). A term used in theology for the most intimate union, communion, and interpenetration. It was used by John of Damascus to describe the human and the divine nature in Christ. This usage as well as an application to the Trinity is found in Lutheran dogmaticians.

Pericope. 1. A word taken from the Greek, meaning a section, and applied to the fixed portions of the Scripture read as lessons on the Sundays and festivals of the church year. Such a division of the Scripture text was in use even in the ancient synagog, the Law and the Prophets being divided into 54 such lessons each. There are indications that the early Christians made a similar division of the Bible text for their use as early as the first century, the reading of the Apostles (that is, of the Epistle lessons) being added to that of the Law and of the Prophets, as the ancient liturgies show.

2. The system of the Western Church, which differs from that of the Oriental denominations and also from the Gallican, Mozarabic, and Ambrosian lectionaries, is commonly, and doubtless correctly, ascribed to Jerome, who founded it upon customs obtaining in his time. His *Comes*, that is, companion for the reading of the Bible, was variously modified till the time of Charlemagne, since when it has been fixed in the so-called ancient pericopal system, as in use in the Lutheran Church to this day. Many church orders of the 16th century prescribed the duty of preaching at the principal service on the Gospel for the day. It became the custom for devout persons to read the Gospel and Epistle lessons before coming to church and to expect to hear the pericope expounded and applied. The richness, order, relations, and completeness of the pericopes raise the service of the church above the individual peculiarities of the preacher and the tone of the world and insure a systematic and complete instruction of the people. At the same time the general lack of information on other parts of the Bible suggested the advisability of using other series of pericopes from time to time, in alternate years or less often, and therefore other lists of pericopes have been arranged — twenty-five or more, such as the Eisenach, Thomasius, Wuerttemberg, Nitzsch, Nassau, and Synodical Conference Systems.

3. The term "lectionary" is applied to the lists of such lessons, and "lection" to the passage from Scripture.

Perrinists. See *Libertines*.

Perronet, Edward (1726—92). Of French descent, baptized and reared in the Church of England, yet at an early age he joined the Wesleys and became an itinerant preacher for them. However, he had a temporary falling out with them and became a minister of a small independent chapel at Canterbury. This church he served until his death. He is known by his "All Hail the Power of Jesus' Name."

Persecution by the Catholic Church. 1. Persecution, or the infliction of penalties for deviation from an acknowledged standard of religious belief, is an invasion upon man's original rights as an individual personally accountable to God. Wrong in principle, it is foolish as a policy, since, as Luther said, "belief is a free thing, which cannot be compelled." Persecution has its roots in mistaken religious zeal, in ignorant fanaticism, in the natural malice of the human heart, and sometimes also in the pagan notion (bequeathed *mutatis mutandis* to the Christianized Roman Empire) that uniformity in religion is essential to the welfare of the State. This latter aspect of the matter brings us face to face with the beginnings of persecution in the Christian Church. Constantine, who issued an edict of toleration in favor of the Christians, banished, now Arius, then Athanasius, according to his own changing religious opinions. Emperor Theodosius, in his code of laws, made the slightest deviation from the orthodox Trinitarian faith subject to heavy penalties, including capital punishment. In 385 the Spanish bishop Priscillian, with six of his adherents, was tortured and beheaded at Treves. This was the first instance of the infliction of the death penalty on the basis of heresy in the Church.

2. The leading divines of the Church, such as Jerome and Augustine, advocated physical coercion against schismatics and heretics. Augustine justified the theory of persecution by referring to the Mosaic legislation and to a single New Testament text, *Compelle intrare* (Luke 14:23), which he misinterpreted. Leo the Great, the first representative of a universal Papacy, expressly declared his approval of the execution of the Priscillianists. Thomas Aquinas, one of the highest authorities in the Roman Catholic Church, expresses himself as follows: *Si falsarii pecuniae vel alii malefactores statim per saeculares principes iuste morti traduntur, multo magis haeretici, statim ex quo de haeresi convincuntur, possunt non solum excommunicari, sed et iuste occidi.* ("If counterfeiters and other criminals are immediately and justly delivered unto death by the civil authorities, much more may heretics, immediately upon their conviction, not only be excommunicated, but justly put to death.") The Canon Law laid down the same principles. Among the forty-three "heresies" of Luther condemned by the bull of Leo X the thirty-third runs as follows: *Haereticos comburi est contra voluntatem Spiritus* ("To burn heretics is against the will of the [Holy] Spirit") — a papal approval of the burning of heretics from the year 1520.

3. Such, then, was the legal and theological basis of the relentless attitude of the Roman Catholic Church toward heretical belief. Acting on these principles, she has stained her annals with the blood of an army of heretics much larger than the host of Christian martyrs under heathen Rome. We can only mention, in passing, the crusades against the Albigenses under Innocent III, the *autos da fé* of the Spanish Inquisition, the frightful atrocities of the Duke of Alva in the Netherlands, the massacre of St. Bartholomew, the persecution of the Huguenots after the revocation of the Edict of Nantes (1685), the fires of Smithfield under Bloody Mary, the slaughter of the Waldenses in the valleys of Piedmont; in general, the dreadful work of the Catholic reaction to check the Reformation.

4. The Roman Catholic Church has never officially disowned the theory of persecution and intolerance, nor has she raised her voice in favor of religious freedom. Pius IX, in 1864, expressly condemned the doctrine of religious liberty as a pestilential error, and his successor, Leo XIII, endorsed this position, besides condemning as among the evil consequences of the "revolution" (*i. e.*, the Reformation) of the sixteenth century the separation of Church and State and the equality of all religions before the law. On the other hand, Cardinal Gibbons frankly disavows the principle of persecution. "From my heart," says he, "I abhor and denounce every species of violence and injustice and persecution of which the Spanish Inquisition may have been guilty. And in raising my voice against coercion for conscience' sake, I am expressing not only my own sentiments, but those of every Catholic priest and layman in the land." (*The Faith of Our Fathers.*) These liberal sentiments of the American prelate, however, present a strange and glaring contrast to the authoritative utterances of the Pope and to the notorious fact that "no public worship except the Roman Catholic was tolerated in the city of Rome before 1870," when the Papacy was shorn of its temporal power. See references under *Inquisition.*

Persecutions of Christians. 1. Persecution may spring from blind zeal for an accepted standard of truth, from motives of worldly policy, or from sheer malice and cruelty. In every case it is a gross violation of the sacred rights of conscience, unwarranted alike by reason and Christianity. Yet the history of persecution forms a large and lurid chapter in the annals of mankind. In the early Christian Church, persecution was almost inevitable. Never were two powers more diametrically opposed in their innermost spirit and genius than the Roman Empire and the Christian Church. The one was carnal, the other spiritual. The one was an earthly political fabric, fondly believed to be the handiwork of the national gods and to represent the highest and eternal idea of human society; the other openly avowed its belief in the transitory character of all earthly kingdoms and the ultimate triumph of the Kingdom of God. The one worshiped the emperor as the incarnation of Roman greatness; the other bowed the knee to none other save the King of Kings and the Lord of Lords. Here no compromise was possible. It was a question of to be or not to be for both antagonists. The wide cleavage manifested itself in various ways. The Christians were charged with arrogance and presumption because they claimed to possess the only true and universal religion, a notion utterly incomprehensible to the heathen world. They were accused — with entire justification from the Roman viewpoint — of treason and disloyalty for refusing divine honors to the emperor. Their close union and frequent meetings in like manner aroused the suspicion of treasonable tendencies against the state. The absence of all visible objects, images, altars, etc., in their worship laid them open to the charge of atheism. Their aversion to the idolatrous ceremonies attending public festivals and public affairs in general stamped them as misanthropes and haters of society. All public calamities, such as floods, earthquakes, etc., were interpreted as the undoubted signs of the wrath of the gods against the inroads of Christianity. Then, too, heathen priests, artisans, and tradesmen, whose living depended on the maintenance of the traditional faith, constantly stirred up the fury and fanaticism of the populace against the innovators (Christians). Finally, the common people readily believed the foulest calumnies designed to stigmatize the Christians; for example, that they were guilty of Oedipean weddings and Thyestian feasts (i. e., of incest and cannibalism).

2. Fortunately, the Roman government did not at once recognize the inherent antagonism of principles involved. Christianity was at first regarded as a sect of Judaism, and as such it shared with Judaism the protection (and contempt) of the state; cf. Acts 18:12 ff. As soon, however, as it became clear that Christianity was independent of any locality (Jerusalem), that it was an organization held together by a community of distinctive beliefs and practices, it was looked upon as a menace to the integrity of the empire and to the social order and was accordingly proscribed. This change in the imperial policy came about possibly under the Flavian emperors (69—96). The Neronian persecution, we know, was based on the vague charge that the Christians were haters of society, not that the religion itself was a crime. In the days of Trajan (112) the mere profession of Christianity entailed condemnation. A closer study of Trajan's rescript to Pliny seems to make it evident that this emperor did not, as is commonly supposed, initiate a new policy against the Christians, but rather that he modified an already established precedent by instructing his governor not to "seek out" the Christians for trial, but to condemn and punish them if formally denounced and convicted. In other words, he advocated a policy of wise moderation, though he could not blink the fact that Christianity as such was already under the ban of the empire. Regarding the subsequent attitude of the state, it must suffice to say that the more Christianity spread, the more stringent were the measures adopted to suppress it.

3. Passing on to the persecutions themselves, it is noteworthy that the first imperial persecution, that under Nero (64), was not due to any settled policy, but was accidental, so to speak. Suspected of burning Rome, the imperial monster incriminated the Christians to shield his own head. The gruesome tale, told by Tacitus, how a "vast multitude" of Christians were crucified or sewed in the skins of wild beasts and exposed to savage dogs in the arena or covered with pitch and nailed to posts of pine, and then lighted to illuminate the imperial gardens by night, is familiar to all. During the Flavian period the persecution of the Christians as disturbers of the public peace was, in the words of Mommsen, "a standing matter, as was that of robbers." Domitian, in particular, who called himself "Lord and God," condemned many to death on the charge of atheism. The persecution under Trajan (98—117) extended over Asia Minor, Syria, and Palestine. Among noted martyrs of his reign are Ignatius, bishop of Antioch, who was carried to Rome and thrown to the wild beasts in the Colosseum, and Symeon, bishop of Jerusalem, who

was crucified at the age of one hundred and twenty. Hadrian (117 to 138) protected the Christians against popular outbursts of fury, but continued the policy of punishing all who were convicted by an orderly legal procedure. Antoninus Pius (138—161) adopted a similar course in forbidding mob violence and demanding regular proceedings. In the case of Polycarp, however, whose martyrdom is to be assigned to this reign rather than to the following, the will of the authorities was overruled by the vehement fury of the crowd. "Away with the atheists! Give us Polycarp!" The aged bishop of Smyrna was burned at the stake. He had been a disciple of the Apostle John. Marcus Aurelius (161—180), the stoic philosopher, abandoned the more liberal policy of his predecesors and sought out the Christians for trial (prohibited by Trajan). An unprecedented storm of persecution swept over the Church, particularly in Vienne and Lugdunum (Lyons) in Southern Gaul, where the bodies of the martyrs lay in heaps upon the streets, until they were burned and the ashes cast into the Rhone. At the beginning of the third century the rigid law of Septimius Severus, which forbade the further spread of Christianity and Judaism, produced a violent persecution in Egypt and North Africa, which yielded some of the most illustrious examples of Christian constancy and fortitude.

4. Passing over the minor persecutions of the following decades, we next mention the great tribulation under Decius (249—260), who with characteristic energy determined to destroy the Church as an atheistic and seditious sect. This persecution extended over the whole empire, was conducted with more relentless vigor, and produced a larger number of martyrs than any which had preceded it. It also sifted the chaff from the wheat. The numerous apostates *(lapsi)* were classified as *Thurificati, i.e.,* such as offered incense to the national gods; as *Libellatici, i. e.,* such as procured from the civil authorities a false certificate that they had done so; as *Acta Facientes, i. e.,* such as made false depositions concerning their Christianity. Decius' successor, Valerian, sought to undermine the new faith by banishing, and later inflicting the death penalty upon, the bishops and leaders of the Church. The calm of forty years which followed was succeeded by the last and most violent persecution of all, that under Dio-

cletian and his coregents and successors. Under the incessant goadings of his son-in-law Galerius, Diocletian, in 303, issued three edicts against the Christians, to which Maximian (a coregent) added a fourth in 304. All Christian churches were to be destroyed, all Bibles burned, all Christians deprived of civil rights, and all, without exception, were to sacrifice to the gods on pain of death. A fifth edict by Galerius, in 308, in order to force heathen defilement upon the Christians, required that all provisions in the markets should be sprinkled with sacrificial wine. The historian Eusebius, dwelling on the horrors of this persecution, tells us that he saw with his own eyes how churches were razed, the Scriptures burned, Christians hunted, tortured, and torn to pieces in the amphitheater. The executioners grew weary, their swords dull. But the end of it all was the complete victory of the Cross. Constantine's edict, in 313, which granted *et Christianis et omnibus liberam potestatem sequendi religionem, quam quisque voluisset* (in a word, religious liberty), marks the downfall of heathenism and the beginning of a new era.

E. Gibbon, *Decline and Fall of the Roman Empire;* G. Uhlhorn, *The Conflict of Christianity with Heathenism* (tr. E. C. Smith), Scribner's N. Y., c. 1879 (later editions); Antonio Gallonio, *Torture: Torments of the Christian Martyrs,* Walden Publ., N. Y., 1939.

Perseverance. See *Final Perseverance.*

Persia. See *Iran.*

Personal Union in Christ. See *Christ Jesus.*

Personalism (and Personalistic Psychology). Designation of a school of philosophy which emphasizes the differentiation between the personal, on the one hand, and the impersonal, or mechanical, on the other. Personalism in the generic sense, therefore, connotes all the data of self-conscious life. According to this view, the characteristic personal values and experiences constitute the final tests of truth and reality, and in the metaphysics of the personalistic psychology conscious personality is the ultimate nature of all reality. Religious personalism regards the real framework of reality as spiritual and makes the active, living God both the immanent reason and the power of the life of the world and all beings in the world. One could conceivably bring this into full harmony with Acts 17:28.

Perspicuity of Scripture. See *Inspiration.*

Persuasion. See *Homiletics, 7.*

Peru. See *South America, 9.*

Peshitta. See *Bible Versions,* C.

Pessimism. The philosophical view which considers the world the worst possible world and man's lot in the world as negative; evil is always triumphant, and good is always defeated. Notes of extreme pessimism are already found in the writings of the early Greeks (*e. g.,* Hesiod), or even before that in some of the statements in Job. Schopenhauer sought to expound pessimism philosophically. Pessimism may result from the frustration of ideals.

Pestalozzi, Johann Heinrich (1746 to 1827). One of the world's greatest pioneer educators and a Swiss patriot who did much for his country by his work for social regeneration through educational reform. Because of incapacity for business his life was full of failures, while his educational endeavors were crowned with signal success. His educational institution at Burgdorf became a center of educational experiments, investigation, and training such as the world had not hitherto seen. His purpose was to "psychologize" education. All educational processes must start from "nature," *i. e.,* the child's own interest and activities. Education must be essentially religious, must develop man as a whole, must stimulate and guide self-activity, and be based upon intuition *(Anschauung)* and exercise. Works: *Lienhard and Gertrude; How Gertrude Teaches Her Children.*

Petau, Dennis (1583—1652). French Jesuit; emphasized historical rather than speculative theology.

Peter, Acts of. See *Apocrypha.*

Peter de Bruys. See *Pierre de Bruys.*

Peter (St.), Chair of. See *Papacy.*

Peter of Chelczich (ca. 1390—ca. 1460). Founder, with Gregor of Chelczich, of the Bohemian-Moravian Brethren *; his *The Net of Faith* advocated complete separation of Church and State.

Peter Damian (1007—72). Friend of Popes, especially Gregory VII; fought corruption of clergy.

Peter the Hermit (ca. 1050—1115). Although not the instigator of the First Crusade,* he supported it with full enthusiasm, especially after the Council of Clermont. After the destruction of his own unorganized group he waited for the main army at Constantinople, returned to Europe after Jerusalem was taken, and died there.

Peter Lombard (d. 1164). One of the foremost Schoolmen, a pupil of Abélard, but greatly influenced by St. Bernard and Hugo of St. Victor, was teacher of theology at, and bishop of, Paris. His dogmatic treatise *Sententiarum Libri Quattuor* was for centuries the textbook in theological seminaries and won for him the title of *Magister Sententiarum.* His book is the first real system of dogmatics in the Occidental Church; it is a collection of the doctrinal utterances of the Fathers systematized and contradictions resolved dialectically. By him the Church was entirely won over to the speculative system of the Scholastics. The Lateran Council of 1215 officially authorized his *Sentences* as the theological textbook. He also effectively helped to blend Mysticism with Scholasticism.

Peter Martyr (*Vermigli,* 1500—62). The ablest and most learned among the Italian Protestants of the sixteenth century and an inflexible champion of Calvinism; b. in Florence; visitor-general of Augustinians; taught at Strassburg, Oxford, Zurich (d. there); wrote: *Tractatus de Sacra Eucharistia, Disputatio de Eodem Sacramento,* etc.

Peter of Ravenna (406—450). "Doctor of the Church"; famous as orator (called "Chrysologus"); opponent of Monophysitism.

Peter's Pence. A tax levied by the Pope on English householders. The tax was extended to the Scandinavian countries and Poland. The Pope tried unsuccessfully to impose it on Spain. It ceased with the Reformation. Since then voluntary Peter's Pence have been gathered, especially in France.

Petersen, Johann Wilhelm (1649 to 1727). Lutheran theologian, poet, mystic, and chiliast. B. at Osnabrueck; d. near Zerbst. Studied at Giessen and Rostock; visited the universities of Leipzig, Jena, and Wittenberg. He held various pastorates and professorships; wrote commentaries and hundreds of hymns in German and Latin. With his theories of chiliasm he departed from orthodox Lutheranism.

811

Petrarch (1304—74). Italian poet; "father of humanism"; studied at Montpellier and Bologna; made extensive journeys and became highly interested in classical antiquity, which he sponsored especially at Arqua, near Padua.

Petri, Carl J. B. June 16, 1856, Rockford, Ill.; one of six in the first class graduated from Augustana College, Rock Island, Ill., 1877. Pastor, Philadelphia, Pa., 1880—84; prof., Gustavus Adolphus College, St. Peter, Minn., 1884—88; pastor, Minneapolis, Minn., 1888—1926. Vice-pres., Bd. of Directors, Gustavus Adolphus College; vice-pres., Bd. Managers, Immanuel Deaconess Institution, Omaha, Nebr.; pres. of Augustana Children's Home and of Augustana Mission Cottage. Home for the Aged. In 1926 presented with gold altar cloth by Crown Prince Gustav Adolph for his work among the Swedish people in America; A. M., 1899, D. D., 1901; both degrees conferred by Augustana College and Theological Seminary. Influential member of various other boards within the Augustana Synod during his entire ministry of 46 years. D. Oct. 24, 1926.

Petri, Laurentius (1499—1573). Brother of Olavus Petri,* studied in Wittenberg. joined his brother upon his return, 1527 in reformation of Sweden, after 1531 Protestant archbishop, active in establishing church polity and liturgy; led fight on Calvinistic doctrine and polity under Erik XIV; 1571 introduced distinctively Lutheran church order.

Petri, Ludwig Adolf (1803—73). Senior pastor at the Kreuzkirche at Hanover; considered the most influential Lutheran theologian of his time in Hanover; staunch opponent of rationalism and the Union.

Petri, Olavus (1497—1573). Studied under Luther in 1516; furthered the Reformation in Sweden after 1520; routed Romanism at the Diet of Vesteras in 1527; published the Swedish New Testament in 1526, the whole Bible in 1541, the hymnal in 1530, a postil, short catechism, and Communion service in 1531. Condemned to death in 1540 by Gustavus Vasa; pardoned.

Petrinism. See *Isagogics,* 3.

Petrobrusians. Followers of Pierre de Bruys.*

Petrock, St. See *Celtic Church,* 6.

Petrucci, Ottaviano (1466—1539). Father of type music printing and regarded the greatest master of music printing as an art. He discovered a method of printing with a press, the *Patronendruck* (pattern printing), which the Germans had done by hand. He printed individual masses, motets, lamentations, frottolas, and lute tablatures. He acquainted the world with the works of Despres, Obrecht, Isaak, Obreghem, de la Rue, and others. Georg Rhaw learned from him and printed music in the early stages of the Reformation.

Petursson, Hallgrimur (1614—74). Icelandic hymnist; studied at Holar, later at Copenhagen; made use of secular subjects first, later religious; the Icelandic Paul Gerhardt, his Passion hymns especially notable.

Petursson, Petur (1808—91). Pastor in Iceland (1838), pres. of the seminary of Reykjavik (1847); bishop of Iceland (1866); continued Finnur Jonsson's *Ecclesiastical History of Iceland* from 1740 to 1840.

Peucer, Caspar (1525—1602). Studied (chiefly medicine and mathematics) at Wittenberg; lived in Melanchthon's home and married his youngest daughter; instructor at Wittenberg (1554) and prof. of medicine (1560); appointed general supt. of Latin schools by Elector Augustus and the Elector's physician; used his position to further the cause of the Philippists and crypto-Calvinism; the *Corpus Doctrinae* was authorized in Saxony, and the Wittenberg Catechism was published; in 1574 Peucer was arrested by the Elector and for twelve years (beginning 1576) was kept in close confinement; the last sixteen years of his life he served as physician and councilor at Dessau. Peucer is regarded as chief exponent of Melanchthonianism and crypto-Calvinism.

Peutinger, Konrad (1465—1547). German humanist; studied at universities in Italy; interested particularly in history and in German antiquities, doing much work in sources; although sympathetic to the cause of the Reformation, he never formally broke with Rome.

Pezel, Christoph (1539—1604). B. at Plauen; d. at Bremen. Studied at Jena and Wittenberg. Professor in the Philosophical faculty (1557), preacher at the Schlosskirche and member of the theological faculty (1569), at Wittenberg; banished for his crypto-Calvinism, 1576; received a position from Count John of Nassau, 1577; openly accepted Calvinism; succeeded Glanaeus in Bremen, 1581. He is the chief author of the Wittenberg catechism, 1571, and of the Bremen catechism, which he substituted for Luther's.

Pfaff, Christoph Matthaeus (1686 to 1760). Chancellor of the University of Tuebingen, at seventy years chancellor of Giessen; wrote on almost every department of theology; lived in the transition period from Pietism to Rationalism; was inclined to Pietism; advocate of unionism; originator of the *Kollegial-System* of Church government. See *Collegiate System.*

Pfaff's Bible. Christoph Matthaeus Pfaff directed the German translation of the Bible which appeared at Tuebingen, 1727, also known as *the Bible of Tuebingen.* Pfaff's erudition was immense, but he was of a doubtful moral character. He made several unsuccessful attempts to unite the Lutheran and the Calvinistic churches.

Pfarramt. See *Ministerial Office.*

Pfarrernotbund. See *Germany,* C 4.

Pfeffer, Paul (1651—1710). B. at Neustadt, in the principality of Glogau; at the time of his death mayor of Bautzen; wrote: "Ach, jawohl bin ich nunmehr entgangen."

Pfefferkorn, Georg Michael (1645 to 1732). Studied at Jena and Leipzig; private tutor at Altenburg; last position: *Konsistorialrat* and superintendent at Graefentonna; wrote "What Is the World to Me."

Pfeffinger, Johann (1493—1573). Became subdeacon in Salzburg, then preacher in Passau, where he became acquainted with Luther's Scriptural teaching; studied at Wittenberg, was pastor at Sonnenwalde, Eicha, Belgern, finally pastor of St. Nicolai in Leipzig, assisted in introducing the Reformation in Schoenburg; was connected with the developments which led to the Leipzig Interim, showed leanings toward synergism by emphasizing the liberty of the human will; his writings chiefly in the field of moral theology and polemics.

Pfeiffer, August, Orientalist (1640 to 1698). Prof. of theology at Leipzig; d. as superintendent in Luebeck. His chief fame rests on his exegetical and hermeneutical works: *Dubia Vexata, Critica Sacra, Thesaurus Hermeneuticus.*

Pfeiffer, Edward. B. Nov. 23, 1857,

at Columbus, O.; grad. Ohio Coll. of Agriculture & Mechanic Arts, 1876; Capital Univ., Columbus, 1878 (M. A., 1881); Columbus Sem., 18881; pastorates at Allegheny (now Pittsburgh), Pa., 1881—85; Delaware, O., 1885—90; Fremont, O., 1890—1899; prof. at Columbus Sem., 1899—1925; pres. of various Ohio Synod boards; edited *The Little Missionary,* 1886—91; editor of missionary dept. of *Lutheran Standard,* 1891—1925; author: *Mission Studies;* trans. *Anti-Calvinism.* D. Dec. 19, 1926.

Pfleiderer, Otto. B. 1839, d. 1908; 1870 professor at Jena; 1875 till his death professor of systematic theology at Berlin; an extreme liberal; denied the divine origin of Christianity.

Pfotenhauer, Frederick. B. April 22, 1859, at Altencelle, Hanover; graduated at St. Louis 1880; traveling missionary in Minnesota and the territories of Dakota and Montana (stationed at Odessa, Minn.) 1880—87; pastor at Lewiston, Minn., 1887—94; at Hamburg, Minn., 1894—1911; D. D. (St. Louis); President of Minnesota and Dakota District 1891—1908; Vice-President of Missouri Synod 1908—11; President 1911—35; Honorary Pres. 1935 until his death, Oct. 19, 1939.

E. A. Mayer, "Dr. Friedrich Pfotenhauer," *CHIQ,* III:1—22; H. A. Grueber, "F. Pfotenhauer: The Man and the Leader," *ibid.,* 22—25.

Phallicism or Phallism. A type of nature worship showing the rapid degeneration of the original conception of God, inasmuch as the generative powers of the earth are worshiped, as symbolized in the male organ or phallus. The custom is widely spread, even among races of some advancement, and in many instances the ceremonies of the cult are wildly orgiastic.

Pharisees. See *Judaism.*

Phelps, Sylvanus Dryden (1816 to 1895). Educated at Brown University; pastor in Baptist denomination; number of publications; among his hymns: "Savior, Thy Dying Love."

Philadelphia Association. See *Baptist Bodies,* 4.

Philadelphia Confession. See *Baptist Bodies,* 4; *Democratic Declarations,* 3.

Philanthropinism. A humanitario-educational movement which derived its name from Basedow's Philanthropinum at Dessau, 1774. It drew attention to existing defects in education and led to salutary reforms. Aiming to educate men who recognized the community of interest among all human beings, it respected distinction neither of class nor of creed. Manual work was introduced for social and educational reasons; the vernacular was emphasized; object teaching; language was taught by improved methods. Everything was done to make learning attractive and experience as broad as possible. Special attention was given to physical exercises, health, and diet. Suitable textbooks for children were written, and juvenile literature was published. Basedow, Campe, and Salzmann were the chief promoters of the movement.

Philaret's Catechism. See *Eastern Orthodox Confessions*, A 4.

Philip of Hesse (1504—67). Met Luther at Worms in 1521 and opposed the breaking of the safe conduct; studied the New Testament and Luther's works; made war upon Sickingen and the peasants; introduced reforms and founded the University of Marburg. After the Protest at Speyer, in 1529, he tried to unite all Evangelicals, the German Highlanders, and the Swiss, and had Luther and Zwingli meet at Marburg. He signed the Augsburg Confession, though not satisfied with the article on the Lord's Supper. He formed a league with the Swiss, but could not help them at Kappel, in 1531; however, he became the soul of the Smalcald League. In 1534 he reinstated Duke Ulrich of Wuerttemberg, and the Reformation was introduced, and the Anabaptists at Muenster were crushed; he sought to win England, France, and Denmark for the Smalcald League against the threatening Emperor. Philip was in danger of losing his lands and his head because he had transgressed imperial law by his bigamy; he saved himself by promising to favor at all times the house of Hapsburg, to break off with foreign powers, and to draw the sword for the Emperor. At the outbreak of the Smalcald War he was put under the ban. He gathered a considerable army; but lack of unity in the command of the Protestant army kept it from scoring a decisive victory, and the Emperor won the victory at Muehlberg, in 1546, and the Landgrave made an unconditional surrender. Contrary to the imperial promise, he was kept a close prisoner in the Netherlands. He was broken and accepted the Interim, though his clergy did not. The Treaty of Passau, in 1552, gave him

freedom, and he returned home and devoted himself to his people.

Philippi, Ferdinand (1840—90). Son of F. A. Philippi; wrote on the Antichrist, the Book of Enoch, and contributed to Meusel's *Handlexikon*.

Philippi, Friedrich Adolf (1809 to 1882). Son of a Jewish banker; early in life came under Christian influences; was induced by Hengstenberg to study theology; found in the Lutheran Confessions the truth that satisfied the longings of his heart and defended them to the end of his life with all the means of his great learning. He became *Privatdozent* in Berlin 1837, professor at Dorpat 1841, at Rostock 1851 (to his end). He exerted a great influence both at Dorpat and at Rostock. His chief works are his *Commentary on Romans* and *Kirchliche Glaubenslehre*. Upheld the doctrine of inspiration.

Philippicum, Confessions of. See *Lutheran Confessions*, C 1.

Philippine Islands. Area: 115,600 sq. mi.; population: 21,000,000 (1951); embraces some 7,083 islands. In 1898 the Islands became a possession of the United States, but became an independent country on July 4, 1946. Discovered by Magellan in 1521, conquered by Spain in 1542, ceded to the United States by the Treaty of Paris, December 10, 1898, following the Spanish-American War. The native inhabitants are Malay. Manila is the capital. In some sections a high type of civilization obtains; in others, coarse savagery. Spanish was the official language until 1930; English is quite generally spoken; at present the Tagalog dialect is officially called the national language. The Spaniards introduced Roman Catholicism. An Independent Catholic Church was organized since American occupation. It received consecration of several of its bishops from the Episcopal Church. Protestant missions are conducted by a number of American societies. The Lutheran Church — Missouri Synod entered the Philippine Islands in 1946, beginning at Manila. Total foreign staff (of the missions of various church bodies) 536 (1952); 1,314,000 communicants. See *Missions, Bibliography*.

Philippists. Followers of Philip Melanchthon, who toned down Luther's doctrine of monergism, *sola gratia*, and, like Erasmus, attributed to man a faculty of applying himself to grace. Melanchthon also toned down the Lutheran doctrine of the Lord's Supper in order to open the doors to the Calvinists. When he compromised the truth by accepting the Interim, he was opposed by the true Lutherans, e. g., Flacius. At first the Philippists gained ground, and true Lutheranism seemed doomed; but their duplicity became known, and they were suppressed in 1574, and the *Formula of Concord* brought peace to the torn Church.

Phillimore, Greville (1821—84). Educated at Westminster and Oxford; vicar of Downe-Ampney; later rector of Henley-on-Thames, finally at Ewelme; published sermons; wrote "Ev'ry Morning Mercies New."

Philo Judaeus (ca. 30 B. C. to A. D. 50). Prominent Hellenistic-Jewish philosopher; lived in Alexandria. He sought to fuse Judaism and Greek thought by showing that the latter was contained in the Old Testament. He regarded the world as imperfect and held that God's contact with it was through the Logos. By extreme allegorizing he gives persons and events of the Old Testament an idealized meaning.

Philology, Biblical. That branch of theological science which deals with the study of the original languages in which the Bible was written, the Hebrew and Aramaic in the Old Testament and the Greek of the New Testament.

Philosophical Apologetics. See *Apologetics*, III.

Philosophy. Philosophy, according to its etymology, signifying the love of wisdom, has almost from the beginning been identified with the search for this wisdom, and the resulting body of knowledge of general principles explaining facts and existences, elements, powers or causes, and laws, has engaged some of the most brilliant minds in the history of the world.

Philosophy is the science of the principles which underlie all knowledge and existence. It tries to think methodically and clearly about notions which come up in our thinking but are not solved by the special sciences. It endeavors to unite all human experience, knowledge, and the results of sciences and to present a harmonious and comprehensive view of the world. While the separate sciences have to do with the various fields of knowledge, philosophy investigates knowledge itself, its principles and methods.

The main divisions of philosophy are 1) epistemology, or theory of knowledge, dealing with the limitations and grounds of knowledge; 2) metaphysics, dealing with the principles at the basis of all phenomena; 3) natural philosophy, dealing with the nature and origin of the world; 4) psychology; 5) logic; 6) ethics; 7) aesthetics. In popular usage, the word *philosophy* is used for wisdom and comfort. Philosophy is related to religion in so far as it, too, is concerned with the nature of God and His relation to the world. Philosophy of history seeks to find the meaning of the course of history (Tertullian, Origen, Augustine, Giovanni Battista Vico, Lessing, Herder, Kant, Fichte, Schelling, Hegel). Philosophy of religion aims to investigate religions generally and impartially.

Philosophy is naturally divided into two groups: formal philosophy, which is the science of knowledge; and material philosophy, which tries to grasp the truth and the essence of the universe. Formal philosophy is divided into logic and metaphysics, the former dealing with the science of the intellect or the mind, the latter with reason and the domain of ideas. After formal philosophy has laid the foundations of all scientific procedure, the material or real philosophy attempts an understanding and an explanation of the universe, that is, of nature, of spirit, of God. The philosophy of nature deals with matter and energy as expressed in the organism. The philosophy of spirit treats of the individual spirit in the science of psychology, of organized community life in political science, of beauty in its various forms in the science of art. And the Philosophy of God, finally, takes up the idea and the reality of religion in the philosophy of religion, morality in the science of ethics, and the development and progress or retrogression of humanity in the philosophy of history.

It is evident, then, that a religious encyclopedia is concerned with philosophy chiefly as it appears in the philosophy of religion, in ethics, and in the philosophy of history. We are anxious to know just how near the intellect and reason of man has come to the understanding of God and of things divine and to the explanation of the relation which obtains between Deity and the mundane sphere, or the universe as such.

That the human mind, by careful reasoning, is able to arrive at some knowledge of God (Rom. 1:18-25) is evident from the writings of various philosophers, even before the time of Christ. It is true that it is hard to distinguish between pure philosophical reasoning and traditional material which has been elaborated to some extent. Nevertheless, it is amazing to find that the ancient philosophers were able to draw a picture of the Supreme Being which shows Him as the one Ruler of the Universe, one in essence, though He may have many names; the Father of men and of all created things, omnipotent, omnipresent, omniscient, eternal, holy, just, wise, and truthful. The statement of Paul (Rom. 1:18) is in thorough agreement with the facts presented in the writings of many tribes and nations, namely, that "they know God, but worship Him not."

If the science of philosophy, especially that of the philosophy of religion, had continued along the lines of the last remnant of the natural knowledge of God, as shown by Paul in both Romans 1 and 2, there would have been no need of debates and encounters between himself and the Epicureans and the Stoics in Athens (Acts 17:18). Nor would it have been necessary for him to warn the Colossians to "beware lest any man spoil you through philosophy and vain deceit, after the tradition of men, after the rudiments of the world, and not after Christ" (Col. 2:8). Although he undoubtedly had in mind chiefly the Judaizing, Gnosticizing errorists who were at that time infesting Asia Minor, the tenor of his words is such as to carry with them the condemnation of every form of philosophy which is not in agreement with revealed Truth.

The pre-Christian Greek philosophers performed a propaedeutic service to Christianity. Greek philosophers sought the one permanent element (Thales, Anaximenes, Diogenes of Apollonia, Democritus, Anaxamander, Anaxagoras), the Being (Xenophanes, Parmenides, Zeno), the law of change (Heraclitus), the mathematics of the universe (Pythagoras), without arriving at satisfaction. The Sophists made man the measure of all things, gave language precision, and brought in skepticism. Socrates and Plato (see *Socrates*) brought in inductive reasoning and general definition. They developed the doctrines of Ideas and Recollections (which played such a prominent part in the later struggles between realists and nominalists), and turned philosophy into a study of ethics. After Aristotle (for his contributions see *Aris-*

totle) the Pyrrhonists once more turned to skepticism. In a period of corruption the Epicureans and Stoics made happiness the goal of philosophy, the one on a materialistic, the other on a dualistic (matter—God or fate) basis. This stream of philosophy had run its course before the time of Christianity.

The Jew Philo of Alexandria sought to harmonize Greek philosophy with the Old Testament. He sought, especially to reconcile the Supreme Good of Plato with the Jehovah of the Old Testament. His thoughts seem to have exercised a great influence on the intellectuals among Western Jews.

The Apostolic Church, on the whole, took a very uncompromising stand over against all philosophy, whether it was outspokenly heathenish in character or paraded with the mask of truth. The injunction not to conform to this world (Rom. 12:2) was literally followed, especially since the great majority of Christians expected the return of the Lord at an early date. While the doctrines of the Scriptures and the heavenly mysteries were taught with much love and devotion, the wisdom of this world was largely ignored. The Christians considered themselves strangers and pilgrims, who had no continuing city here (for Eastern speculation in the primitive Church see such articles as *Gnosticism*). But see, in this connection, *Justin Martyr, Dial.* 2—4, and the Clementine *Homilies* and *Constitutions*.

Matters were changed with the establishment of the first catechetical schools. While Irenaeus and Tertullian were successfully combating the influence of Gnostic philosophy in the West, the Christian Stoic Pantaenus founded the catechetical school of Alexandria. At the beginning of the third century his pupil and assistant, Titus Flavius Clemens, took up his work. The object which he had in mind is apparent from his books *Admonition to the Greeks* and *Paidagogos (Concerning True Philosophy)*. His idea was an amalgamation of traditional Christianity with the philosophical culture of his day to gain a Christianity of a higher order. His ideas were carried out by Origen and Plotinus. The doctrines of the latter, as published by his disciple, Porphyry, contain a merger of Christianity and heathenish philosophy in the form of Neoplatonism. By this move, philosophy had ceased to be a rival and an enemy of Christianity, and the ideas of Plotinus as popularized by

Porphyry had their influence upon the Christian Church for centuries. The school of Neoplatonism in Athens, in which Proclus taught the system after the manner of the later Scholastics, was not closed until 529.

In the Dark Ages much of Greek philosophy disappeared in wide areas of the Western World (Boethius * was the last true philosopher before the time of the nominalists and realists, with the exception of John Scotus Erigena). During the Medieval Age the theology of the Church was governed by the philosophy of Aristotle (see *Arabic Philosophy* for its spread). Scholasticism * was a controlling movement among the leaders of the Church, and this was governed by Aristotelian logic and Neoplatonism. This is evident from the writings of the Scholastics, such as John Scotus Erigena of the 9th century, Lanfranc, Roscellinus, and Anselm of the 11th century, Abélard, Gilbert of Poitiers, Peter Lombard, and John of Salisbury in the 12th century, and Alexander of Hales, Albertus Magnus, Thomas Aquinas, and Duns Scotus in the 13th century. Because of this fact, theology degenerated to a point where it could hardly be designated as such, and decay of the Church's life is largely attributable to this fact.

Luther in his youth was influenced by nominalist philosophy. He thought highly of William of Occam because he saw traces of the influence of the Gospel in him. Nevertheless, he often repudiated systems of medieval philosophy because of what they had done to free grace. He spoke of Aristotle in harsh terms. His position over against philosophy may be summarized as follows: Luther "maintained an ambivalent attitude toward the place of philosophy in the Church and the Church's teaching. In general he regarded philosophy as dangerous; and yet, when the occasion seemed to demand it, he was not at all averse to philosophical speculation. . . . Luther saw that philosophy and theology differ as to method, content, purpose and result. . . . The work of the theologian is to describe the workings of faith, and do so in faith's own terms. . . . Nevertheless, the Reformer was competent in the use of Aristotelian logic and . . . acknowledged it as valid." (J. Pelikan, *From Luther to Kierkegaard.*)

Through Melanchthon the influence of ancient philosophies came to bear on the construction of Lutheran thought. Melanchthon brought about the influence of classic philosophy in the schools, in ethics and in theology. His description of faith in intellectual terms has been designated the "Melanchthonian blight." This influence never entirely disappeared. Traces of Scholastic influence are noticable, even in the literature of the 17th century.

For the influence of philosophy in theology in the 18th, 19th, and 20th centuries see *Rationalism; Deism;* the philosophers (Leibniz, Wolff, Semler, Kant, Fichte, Schelling, Hegel, and others); theologians (*e. g.*, Schleiermacher), *Doctrine, Christian, History of; Dogmatics; Existentialism;* and similar topics.

All movements opposed to the pure and complete doctrine of the Bible are in reality efforts of human philosophy to replace the revealed truth of the Word. Philosophy may be the handmaid of Christianity, of Christian theology, but the reverse must not take place. Though theology has often been despised by philosophers who did not appreciate its fundamental importance, it is not elated over the decay of philosophical studies. If philosophy will serve theology in the proper way, both will be able to serve the Church.

T. Gomperz, *Greek Thinkers* (4 vols.), Scribner's, 1901—11; H. O. Taylor, *The Classical Heritage of the Middle Ages,* Macm., 1911; T. Whittaker, *The Neo-Platonists,* Cambridge University Press, 1901; Maurice de Wulf, *History of Medieval Philosophy* (2 vols.), Macm., 1926 (see also his other works); J. Pelikan, *From Luther to Kierkegaard,* CPH, 1950; for philosophical problems generally see such works as D. D. Runes, *The Dictionary of Philosophy,* Philosophical Library, New York, 1942; V. Ferm, *An Encyclopedia of Religion,* Philosophical Library, New York, 1945.

Philosophy of Lutheran Education. See *Christian Education, G.*

Philosophy of Religion, The. A department of learning which tries to bring religion into the domain of subjects which may be analyzed on the basis of a reasonable approach, chiefly from the angle of regarding it as a normal and permanent function in human life. The chief approach of this branch of learning consists in using the data of knowledge, or "the knowledge of acquaintance" which religion supplies, in an attempt to criticize, organize, and interpret this information by combining it with all the "knowledge about" religion that it can obtain. Very much of the work done in this field has been along the lines of Christian ethics rather than with regard to revealed truths of doctrine. In many instances the results have been to read Scripture in the light of this philosophy rather than to have Holy Writ speak for itself first.

Philoxenus. See *Bible Versions*, C 2.

Photinianism. The Christology of Photinus, bishop of Sirmium, in Pannonia. Denying the separate personality of the Logos, Photinus, like Paul of Samosata, held that Christ was merely a supernaturally begotten man, who became the Son of God by adoption.

Photius (ca. 820—891). One of the most learned men of his days; twice appointed — though not a cleric, but statesman and soldier — patriarch of Constantinople and twice deposed by succeeding rulers and twice banned by the Pope; played a prominent part in the events connected with the schism between East and West; his chief polemic work: *Treatise on the Mystagogy of the Holy Spirit.* See also *Filioque Controversy.*

Piccolomini, Aeneas Sylvius. See *Popes*, 15.

Pick, Bernhard. B. Kempen, Prussia, December 19, 1842; ed. at Breslau and Berlin; grad. Union Theol. Sem., 1868. Ordained Presbyn. ministry, 1868; pastor, New York, 1868—69; N. Buffalo, N. Y., 1869—70; Syracuse, 1870 to 1874; Rochester, 1874—81; pastor Luth. chs., Allegheny, Pa., 1881—95, Albany, N. Y., 1895—1903; occasional supply, New York, 1903—05; pastor, Newark, N. J., 1905— . Author: *Luther as a Hymnist*, 1875; *Jewish Life in the Time of Jesus* (in German), 1880; *Life of Jesus According to Extra- Canonical Sources*, 1887; *Hymns and Poetry of the Eastern Church*, 1908; *Jesus in the Talmud*, 1913. Editor: *Luther's "Ein' feste Burg,"* in 21 Languages 1883; *Luther's Hymn of the Reformation, in English*, 1892; *Lyra Gerhardti*, 1906. D. April 10, 1917.

Pico dello Mirandola, Giovanni, Count (1463—94). Scholar of the Renaissance who sought a synthesis of truth also in the field of religion.

Pieper, August. B. at Carwitz, Pomerania, Sept. 27, 1857. He was a graduate of Northwestern College and Concordia, St. Louis, when he accepted his first pastoral charge at Kewaunee, Wis., 1879—85. Was compelled to leave his next parish, Menomonie, Wis., 1890,

because of broken health. After regaining strength, he became pastor of St. Mark's, Milwaukee, 1891. His rare gifts as a preacher and organizer made him a central figure in the development of the Wisconsin Synod, supported as these qualities were by a keen mind and sound scholarship. He left St. Mark's 1902 and filled the chair of Isagogics and Old Testament Exegesis at Wauwatosa Seminary after that. A close observer of contemporary Lutheranism and a fearless critic of the sins of the times within and without his Church, he impressed his students with the Gospel as an intensely practical force. His opinions commanded respect because they were the result of painstaking, accurate scholarship, as his *Commentary on Isaiah* (German) and his contributions to *Quartalschrift* show. A volume of *Hausandachten* testifies to his pastoral interests. D. Dec. 23, 1947.

Pieper, Franz August Otto. B. June 27, 1852, at Carwitz, Pomerania; graduated at St. Louis, 1875; pastor at Centerville, Wis., 1875—76; Manitowoc, Wis., 1876—78; prof. at Concordia Seminary, St. Louis, Mo., 1878—87; D. D. (Northwestern College, Watertown, Wis.; Luther College, Decorah, Iowa); President of Concordia Seminary, St. Louis, Mo., 1887—1931; President of Missouri Synod, 1899—1911; d. June 3, 1931.

Pieper's outstanding theological contributions were in the field of dogmatics. True to his conviction that the person who himself clearly understands a doctrine can and should present it clearly, Pieper always strove to present Biblical doctrine clearly. His scholarly treatment of textual criticism, exegesis, history, etc., may be seen in the footnotes of his *Christian Dogmatics.* Pieper kept the practical purpose of theology in the foreground, so that the doctrines presented appeal not only to the mind but also to the heart.

Pieper gave special attention to the doctrines of grace and inspiration. "It is, to be sure, to his (Pieper's) and Walther's credit that the *sola gratia*, the lifeblood of the Lutheran Church in all ages and the core of her message, was more and more effectively worked out as a dogma (*theoretisch*) among Lutheran churches of our land and that clarity and purity (*Sauberkeit*) of theological thought was furthered." (M. Reu.) Pieper's many articles on inspiration attest his lifelong interest in the *sola Scriptura.*

As President of Synod, he practiced his conviction that "in the Church nothing is mere theory." He was the optimistic and enthusiastic leader of Synod during a period of intensified activity along every line of church work. His knowledge was put to work for the Church with the conviction that true "Christianity . . . represents a life, not a system of creedal formulas or a compend of religious teaching" (Dau). His manner of preaching was clear and enlightening, and the language of his sermons simple and noble.

Pieper wrote able polemics against rationalistic tendencies in the Lutheran Church (Kahnis, Hofmann, Luthardt). He was editor of *Lehre und Wehre;* wrote *Christliche Dogmatik; Conversion and Election; Zur Einigung; Das Wesen des Christentums; Die Grunddifferenz in der Lehre von der Bekehrung und Gnadenwahl; A Brief Statement of the Missouri Synod's Doctrinal Position; Ich glaube, darum rede ich; Unsere Stellung in Lehre und Praxis; Das Fundament des christlichen Glaubens; Die rechte Weltanschauung; Der offene Himmel.* EL

L. Fuerbringer, "F. Pieper als Theolog," *CTM,* II: 721 ff., 801 ff.; W. H. T. Dau, "Dr. Francis Pieper the Churchman," *CTM,* II: 729 ff.; T. Laetsch, "Dr. Pieper als Prediger," *CTM,* II: 761 ff.

Pieper, Reinhold. B. March 2, 1850, at Carwitz, Pomerania; graduate of Watertown and, 1876, of Concordia Seminary, St. Louis; pastor at Wrightstown, Wis., and Manitowoc (Wisconsin Synod); 1891 president and professor of Exegetics, Homiletics, and Church History at Concordia Seminary, Springfield (successor to Prof. F. A. Craemer) and pastor at Chatham and Riverton, Ill., retired 1914, retaining charge of his congregations up to his death, April 3, 1920. Contributor to *Lehre und Wehre;* published five volumes of sermons, a textbook on homiletics, and three volumes of lectures on Luther's Catechism.

Pierre de Bruys (d. ca. 1126). Pupil of Abélard; exponent of evangelical poverty; opposed church buildings, prayers for dead, Infant Baptism, veneration of the cross, and additional ceremonies of the Roman Church; burned as heretic.

Pierson, Allard (1831—96). Pastor of a Walloon Church in Holland; resigned because of unbelief; humanist; denied that Jesus and Paul ever lived.

Pierson, Arthur Tappan (1837 to 1911). Graduated at Hamilton College in 1857, Union Presbyterian Seminary, N. Y., 1860; filled pastorates at Binghamton, N. Y.; Norwalk, Conn.; Waterford, N. Y.; Detroit, Mich.; Indianapolis, Ind.; Philadelphia, Pa.; London, England; editor of the *Missionary Review of the World* since 1888; an authority on missions and a voluminous and forceful writer; d. immediately after return from a trip to the Orient.

Piers Plowman (The Vision of William Concerning Piers the Plowman). A didactic poem commonly attributed to William Langland (ca. 1332—1400), offering some criticism of the corruption and the shams in the Church and attempting to create a love of truth and an appreciation of the dignity of labor.

Pieta. The technical term for a representation of the lament of Mary, the mother of Jesus, after His death, a favorite subject during the Middle Ages, both painters and sculptors using it freely.

Pietism. A movement of the late 17th and early 18th centuries against the prevailing orthodoxism, in spite of the fact that men like Arndt, Herberger, and Nicolai tried to combine full orthodoxy with spiritual life. The main causes are undoubtedly to be found in the conditions following the Thirty Years' War, when a generation of people which had become estranged from an orderly church life had to be trained in the faith and in the ordinances of the Church. Men like Grossgebauer felt that the doctrine of justification had been stressed in a onesided way, at the expense of sanctification, so that the fruits of faith were often not apparent and the congregational life was characterized by a dead formalism. In combating this situation a Reformed leaven was added to the Lutheran mass, so that the final result was an emotionalism which deprecated the power of the means of grace as such and stressed spiritual exercises as being more important. Philip Jacob Spener in Frankfurt became a leader in the Pietistic movements, especially by establishing his conventicles or *ecclesiolae in ecclesia,* groups in which the piously inclined could exercise themselves in forms of Christian conduct, especially by an emotional reflecting on inner experiences. Pietism sponsored chiefly three fundamental errors: 1. The concept *piety* is separated from the means of grace and thus placed in a false relation to religion and salvation; 2. The concept *orthodoxy* is misunderstood and misapplied, so that indifferentism with regard to normative information from Holy Writ is underestimated; 3. There is erroneous teaching on the concepts *spirit* and *letter*, *spirit* and *flesh*. Out of these errors grew a contempt for the means of grace, an underestimation of the office of the Christian ministry, mixture of sanctification and justification, chiliasm, a false mysticism, and a general schismatic attitude. Men like Loescher opposed Pietism, especially in his *Unschuldige Nachrichten* and his *Timotheus verinus*. Nevertheless the movement spread to Leipzig and Halle, where August Hermann Francke, otherwise a very earnest and devout Christian theologian, took over the stress on the *feeling* of contrition and the *feeling* of grace. One of the consequences of the Pietistic movement, which placed pious desires and emotions before the pure doctrine, was an increased amount of rationalizing that finally opened the way to Rationalism. See *Lutheran Theology after 1580*, 6, 7.

T. Hoyer, "Der Pietismus," *CTM*, VI: 496—501, 816—22; N. C. Carlsen, "Lutheran Piety," *What Lutherans Are Thinking*, Wartburg Press, 1947.

Pighius, Albert. See *Reformed Confessions*, A 9.

Pilate, Acts of. See *Apocrypha.*

Pilgrim Fathers. See *Congregational and Christian Churches*, A 1.

Pilgrim Holiness Church. See *Holiness Bodies; International Apostolic Holiness Union.*

Pilgrimages. 1. From the earliest times Christians visited the places associated with the Savior's earthly life. Increasing numbers journeyed to the Holy Land after Helena, the mother of Constantine, had at an advanced age devoutly explored the Bible scenes. Soon the notion developed that special virtue dwelt in such "holy places" and that prayer offered there was of unusual efficacy. When a special boon was desired of God, a pilgrimage was undertaken, or a vow of pilgrimage was made if the favor should be granted in advance. In course of time new places of pilgrimage were added, particularly Rome and the graves of martyrs. Reports of miraculous cures at certain shrines found eager believers and multiplied the number of pilgrims. They began to travel in organized companies, under armed protection. Hospices were built for them, notably in the Alps, and their feet wore new roads. Gradually the pilgrimages changed their character: they appeared as actions inherently pleasing to God, as works of merit, which would either avail toward salvation or counterbalance sin. Under the latter aspect they were prescribed as works of penance, the penitents traveling barefoot, in coarse garb, often fasting and sometimes bearing chains. Pilgrimages became a part of the normal life of the times, of which the law took cognizance. Even in war a kind of sacrosanct character was accorded the pilgrims.

2. The outrages committed against pilgrims by the Moslems were one of the reasons which caused the Crusades, and the military orders were formed for their protection. Some became professional pilgrims and wandered all their lives from one shrine to another. Domestic duties were neglected, and vices and gross superstitions of every description were bred. The *Imitation of Christ* might well say: "Who wander much are but little hallowed." Since pilgrims did not come empty-handed, there was lively competition between the guardians of the various shrines. The shrine which could boast the most astonishing relics and the most stunning miracles reaped the largest revenue. New inducements were added by the development of indulgences: during the jubilee of 1300, the daily average of pilgrims in Rome was estimated at 200,000. The Reformation dealt pilgrimages a hard blow, even among Romanists. In the 19th century, however, there began a revival of the practice, which, in some instances, gathered crowds that compare with medieval figures. Centers of modern pilgrimage are Loreto (Italy), Einsiedeln (Switzerland), Fatima (Portugal), and especially Lourdes (France). Even the United States has places of pilgrimage, one of them at Auriesville, N. Y., where three priests were killed by Indians.

See references under *Crusades;* M. M. C. Calthrop, *The Crusades*, T. C. & E. C. Jack, London, n. d.; H. Lamb, *The Crusades — Iron Men and Saints*, Garden City Publ. Co., N. Y., 1930.

Pilgrim's Hour. See *Radio Evangelism*, 5.

Pillar of Fire. See *Evangelistic Associations*, 14.

Pious Society of St. Jerome. See *Bible Societies,* 6.

Piran. See *Celtic Church,* 4.

Pirkheimer, Willibald (1470—1530). Studied at Padua and Pavia; became official of the empire; patron of humanism; favored the Reformation from the humanistic angle, but was never identified with its real purpose; was most likely connected with the *Letters of Obscure Men* and similar movements.

Pirmin. Theologian of the eighth century, reformer of the monastic orders in Southern Germany; missionary in the country of the Alemanians, established the rule of St. Benedict over against that of Columba, as this had been brought to Western Europe by Irish missionaries; later active in Alsace, finally establishing the monastery Hornbach in the Palatinate. D. 753.

Pisa, Council of, 1409. The first of the three so-called reforming councils, was called through, and dominated by, the influence of the French theologian Gerson, who taught that the authority of a council was greater than that of a Pope and that such a council should convene to reform the corrupt Church in head and members. The Council of Pisa was especially to make an end of the papal schism (1378 to 1417). It declared both the Pope at Rome, Gregory XII, and the one at Avignon, Benedict XIII, deposed because they would not appear before the council and in their stead elected Alexander V. Since the other two still retained a large following, there were now three Popes, who anathematized each other, and the council was dissolved without effecting any reform whatever.

Piscator (Fischer), **Johannes** (1546 to 1625). Studied under Andreae and Heerbrand; held pastorates at Heidelberg, Siegen, Neustadt, and Moers; became professor at Herborn and writer of many exegetical, dogmatic, and polemical works; issued the Herborner or Berner Bible; known in particular for his denial of the redeeming power of the active obedience of Christ.

Pistis Sophia. See *Apocrypha,* B 5.

Pistorius, Herman A. (1811—77). Lutheran pastor at Suepplingen; upheld confessional Lutheranism and opposed the Prussian Union *; joined the Breslauers. (See *Breslau Synod.*)

Pistorius, Johannes (d. 1583). Hessian theologian of the Reformation period; supt. at Alsfeld (1541); opposed Interim; defended Lutheranism at Naumburg and Frankfurt; later opposed the *Formula of Concord* on account of its doctrine of ubiquity.

Pittsburgh Agreement, The. Agreement adopted in 1940 by the A. L. C. and the U. L. C. A. Text: "I. That all persons affiliated with any of the societies or organizations designated in the Washington Declaration of the U. L. C. A. as 'organizations injurious to the Christian faith,' should sever their connections with such society or organization and shall be so admonished; and members of our churches not now affiliated with such organizations shall be warned against such affiliation. Especially shall the shepherds of the flocks be admonished to refuse adherence and support to such organizations. II. That pastors and congregations shall not practice indiscriminate pulpit and altar fellowship with pastors and churches of other denominations, whereby doctrinal differences are ignored or virtually made matters of indifference. Especially shall no religious fellowship whatsoever be practiced with such individuals and groups not basically evangelical. III. 1. The Bible (that is, the canonical books of the Old and New Testaments) is primarily not a code of doctrines, still less a code of morals, but the history of God's revelation for the salvation of mankind and of man's reaction to it. It preserves for all generations and presents, ever anew, this revelation of God, which culminated and centers in Christ, the Crucified and Risen One. It is itself the Word of God, His permanent revelation, aside from which, until Christ's return in glory, no other is to be expected. 2. The Bible consists of a number of separate books, written at various times, on various occasions, and for various purposes. Their authors were living, thinking personalities, each endowed by the Creator with an individuality of his own, and each having his peculiar style, his own manner of presentation, even at times using such sources of information as were at hand. Nevertheless, by virtue of the unique operation of the Holy Spirit (II Timothy 3:16; II Peter 1:21) by which He supplied to the Holy Writers content and fitting Word (II Peter 1:21; I Corinthians 2:12,13) the separate books of the Bible are related to one another, and taken together, constitute

a complete, errorless, unbreakable whole of which Christ is the center (John 10:35). They are rightly called the Word of God. This unique operation of the Holy Spirit upon the writers is named inspiration. We do not venture to define its mode, or manner, but accept it as a fact. 3. Believing, therefore, that the Bible came into existence by this unique co-operation of the Holy Spirit and the human writers, we accept it (as a whole and in all its parts) as the permanent divine revelation, as the Word of God, the only source, rule, and norm for faith and life, and as the ever fresh and inexhaustible fountain of all comfort, strength, wisdom, and guidance for mankind."
Doctrinal Declarations, CPH, n. d.; Luth. Ch. Quart., XIII: 346.

Pittsburgh Declaration. See *Four Points; Galesburg Rule.*

Pittsburgh Infirmary. See *Deaconesses.*

Pittsburgh Synod (I and II). See *United Lutheran Church, Synods of*, 26; *Synods, Extinct.*

Pius II. See *Popes,* 15.

Pius V. See *Popes,* 21.

Pius VI. See *Popes,* 26.

Pius VII. See *Popes,* 27.

Pius IX. See *Popes,* 28.

Pius X. See *Popes,* 30.

Pius XI. See *Popes,* 32.

Pius XII. See *Popes,* 33.

Placement of Teachers. See *Teachers,* A 6.

Plainchant. See *Gregorian Music.*

Plainsong. See *Gregorian Music.*

Plan of Union. See *Congregational and Christian Churches,* A 3.

Planck, Gottlieb Jakob (1751—1833). Prof. at Goettingen; church historian; rational supernaturalist in theology; his works are marred by a subjectivistic interpretation of historical facts.

Planentwurf. See *General Synod,* 2.

Planus. See *Gregorian Music.*

Plath, Karl (1829—1901). Filled positions in seminary at Wittenberg and at the Francke institutions in Halle, 1856—63; inspector of Berlin I Missionary Society, 1863—71; of Gossner Missionary Society, 1871—77; first

inspection visit to India, 1877—78; second to India and Palestine, 1887—88; third to India, 1895—96.

Platner, Tileman (1490—1551). Intimate friend of Luther, Melanchthon, and Justus Jonas; as supt. of Stolberg he introduced the Reformation there.

Plato (*Platonism*). This philosopher (428—347 B. C.), the most important among the pupils of Socrates, opened a school of his own in Athens after the death of his teacher. His teaching may be briefly summarized as follows: The world is dual, consisting of the transient, phenomenal world, known to us through the medium of our senses, and the permanent, invisible world, which we can know only through our reason. Everywhere we find behind the things of sense, which we can comprehend by actual contact, and behind qualities and relations no less permanent ideas, which represent reality. The highest of all is the idea of the Good, which is also the Beautiful, God. Plato believed in the transmigration of souls, with a thousand years between rebirths. The state is to him an institution for the education of society; his concept of the state was somewhat modified in later years. After Plato's death the academy continued as a philosophic school until all schools of this type were closed by the edict of Justinian in A. D. 529. See also *Neoplatonism.*

Platon's Catechism. See *Eastern Orthodox Confessions,* A 4.

Pledge Card. See *Finances of the Church,* 3.

Pledging. See *Finances of the Church,* 3.

Plenary Council. A meeting of all bishops and archbishops in a territory presided over by a papal legate.

Plenitudo Potestatis. Leo I's declaration of the full power of the Pope over a metropolitan bishop.

Pleroma. *Gnosticism,* 3 ff.

Plethon, George Gemisthus (1355 to 1450). A Byzantine who migrated to Italy; leading popularizer of Plato at the time of the Italian Renaissance.

Plitt, Gustav Leopold (1836—80). Prof. at Erlangen; wrote on the *Augsburg Confession* and its *Apology* and began a life of Luther (completed by E. F. Petersen). Together with Herzog he was engaged, at the time of his death, in preparing the second edition of the *Realenzyklopaedie fuer prote-stantische Theologie und Kirche.*

Plockhorst, Bernhard (1825—95). Idealist, but influenced by the historical school; known for his excellent coloring; among his paintings: "Christ Taking Leave of His Mother" and "The Consoling Christ."

Plotinus (ca. 205—70). Most prominent Neoplatonic philosopher; b. in Egypt; taught in Rome since 244; d. in Campania. His philosophy is the last important attempt of the Greeks to solve the riddle of the universe. See *Neoplatonism.*

Pluetschau, Heinrich ((1678—1747). With Bartholomaeus Ziegenbalg, the pioneer Lutheran missionary to India. B. at Wesenberg, Mecklenburg-Strelitz; d. near Itzehoe, Schleswig-Holstein. Educated in Halle, he was sent out with Ziegenbalg as missionary from Denmark on the *Sophie Hedwig,* arriving at Tranquebar, July 9, 1706. Much opposition was encountered from the Danish East India Company; but undaunted by opposition and affliction, he soon mastered the native Tamil language and began to preach and minister to the natives. His chief work consisted in superintending the educational activities of the Portuguese and Danish schools. Returning to Germany and Denmark in 1711, he reported on the work at Tranquebar and pleaded for understanding and support. Later he accepted a pastorate at Itzehoe (Beidenfleth). Thus Ziegenbalg and Pluetschau became the founders of the Danish-Halle mission in India.

Pluralism. The belief that there are many ultimate substances and not one (monism) or two (dualism). Empedocles (470 B. C.) held that there were four original substances; Montaigne felt that diversity is the rule of nature; Leibnitz advocated a pluralism in his system of monads; in America Charles Peirce,* William James,* and John Dewey * rejected monism in favor of pluralism; ideas of diversity are also found in the General Semantic movement.

Plymouth Brethren. See *Brethren, Plymouth.*

Plymouth Separatists. See *Congregational and Christian Churches,* A 1.

Pneumatomachi. The term means "adversaries of the Holy Spirit" and may properly be applied to all who entertain false views of the doctrine of the Holy Spirit. The name originated subsequently to the Arian controversy. When the controversy regarding Christ's divinity ceased, the denial of the divinity of the Holy Spirit became the distinguishing doctrine of the Semi-Arians, some of them denying His divinity, others also His personality. The term Pneumatomachi dates from A. D. 360, when it was applied by Athanasius to the Macedonians (after Macedonius, their leader), who declared the Holy Ghost to be a mere creature and inferior to the Son. The heresy was condemned by the Council of Constantinople (381).

Poach, Andreas (1516—85). Exponent of strictest Lutheranism. Pastor at Halle, 1541; at Nordhausen, 1547; at Erfurt, 1550, where he became involved in the antinomian controversy and was deposed; pastor at Uttenbach, near Jena. He published Luther's sermons.

Pococke, Edward (1604—91). Anglican Orientalist; Oxonian; chaplain at Aleppo, 1630; prof. of Arabic at Oxford, 1636, of Hebrew, 1648; wrote commentaries and other works; assisted in preparation of Walton's *Polyglot Bible.*

Pohlmann, Henry Newman. B. March 8, 1800, in Albany, N. Y.; served as pastor at Saddle River and Ramapo, New Germantown, German Valley, Spruce Run, First Lutheran Church in Albany; pres. of New York Ministerium (21 yrs.), New York Synod (5 yrs.), New York and New Jersey Synod (7 yrs.), General Synod (3 terms). D. Jan. 20, 1874.

Polack, William Gustave. B. Dec. 7, 1890, at Wausau, Wis., son of Teacher H. A. Polack; grad. of Concordia College, Fort Wayne, Ind., 1910; Concordia Seminary, 1914; ordained and installed Aug. 16, 1914, as asst. pastor, Trinity, Evansville, Ind.; chief pastor 1921—25; prof. of Church History, Hymnology, and Liturgics, Concordia Seminary, St. Louis, 1925—50; minister of Clear Lake Chapel, Clear Lake, Ind., 1938—50; chrm. Intersynodical Committee on Hymnology and Liturgics, 1929—49; chrm. Young People's Literature Bd., 1926—29; charter member Concordia Historical Institute, sec'y 1927—37, pres. 1945—49; mem. Editorial Com., *Lutheran Witness,* 1925—50; chrm. 1949—50; editor: *Concordia Historical Institute Quarterly,* 1928—50; *Concordia Junior Messenger,* 1928—39; *Concordia Historical Series;* associate editor: *Cresset,* 1937—50; contributor to many other church papers. Editor in chief: *Lutheran Hymnal.* Author: *Choice Morsels; John Eliot; David Livingston; Into All the World; Story of Luther; Day by Day with Jesus; Story of C. F. W. Walther; Beauty for Ashes; The Lord Is My Shepherd; Fathers and Founders; Martin Luther in English Poetry; Story of Our Favorite Hymns; Hymns from the Harps of God; The Building of a Great Church; Handbook to the Lutheran Hymnal; Rainbow over Calvary; Seven Ways of Sorrow,* coauthor; *How the Missouri Synod Was Born; Beside Still Waters.* Litt. D. from Valparaiso Univ. in 1942. D. June 5, 1950.

Poland. 1. At the time of the Reformation a mighty kingdom, extending from the Baltic to the Black Sea. It received its Christianity both from the Greek Church (through Bohemia) and from the Roman Catholic, coming under the authority of the latter during the 10th century. Never specially devoted to Rome and affording hospitable reception to anti-Roman movements (Waldenses, Hussites, Beghards, etc.) before the Reformation, Poland was prepared to receive the new ideas emanating from Wittenberg and Geneva. Luther's writings were from the first eagerly and widely read. Polish students resorted to Wittenberg and returned home filled with enthusiasm for the Reformer and his teachings. As early as 1524 there were five Lutheran churches in the city of Danzig. In the same year we find Luther in correspondence with professors of the evangelical doctrine in Riga, Reval, and Dorpat. Concurrently with Lutheranism the Reformed type of doctrine found acceptance. The reform movement was strengthened by the Bohemian Brethren, who sought refuge in Poland from the persecutions in their own land. The accession of Sigismund Augustus (1548—1572), a friend of reform, augured well for further progress. Unfortunately he lacked the qualities necessary for independent and decisive action.

2. To present a united front against their enemies, the three main branches of Protestantism effected an organic union (a rather mechanical one, to be sure) at the general synod of Sandomierz (1570). This was followed, in 1572 (when the monarchy became elective), by the so-called *Pax Dissidentium* (Peace of the Dissidents), an agreement among the nobility opposed, of course, by the Catholics, which required every new sovereign to declare under oath his willingness to extend equal protection to the Protestants and Catholics of the kingdom. But the forces of reaction were in operation. The first king, Henry of Anjou, took the oath reluctantly and left Poland in 1574 to occupy the throne of France. Stephen Bathori (1575—86) took the same oath, but later joined the Roman Church and opened the door to the Jesuits. Sigismund III (1587—1632) was educated and converted by the Jesuits, and open persecution began, including the burning of Bibles and Protestant literature.

3. The Colloquy of Thorn (1645), designed to restore unity between Catholics and Protestants, not only failed in this, but severed the bond between the Lutherans and Calvinists. In 1717 the Protestants were denied the right to build churches; in 1734 they were barred from the diet and from civil offices. Nor was Protestant liberty regained until the downfall of Poland toward the end of the century. This also meant a loss of over two million Roman Catholics to the Russian Church. Polish insurrections against Russian rule in the 19th century (1830 and 1861) cost the Romish Church severe retrenchments of her liberties. All immediate intercourse with Rome was prohibited, all episcopal authority in the schools withdrawn, and all mixed marriages made subject to the Russian law (1832). In 1867 the affairs of the Catholic Church were put in the hands of a special commission in St. Petersburg. The introduction of the Russian language in the services of the Church (1870) was strongly resisted, but the trouble was finally settled by means of a compromise. Czarism and Vaticanism could, of course, never live peaceably under one roof. — In the republic of Poland (since 1918) the Roman Catholic Church was by the constitution declared to be the dominant religion, though freedom of conscience was granted to all. Poland was devastated by World War II, which also brought chaos in the field of religion.

Poland, Lutheranism in. 1. One of the earliest points of contact between Poland and Luther's Reformation was the association of Philip Melanchthon with Polish humanists. Partly through Melanchthon's correspondence and partly through Polish students at the University of Wittenberg, Luther's doctrines spread into Poland, gaining support chiefly among two groups: the scattered settlements of Germans and the adherents of the Unity of Bohemian Brethren.

2. But nascent Polish Lutheranism was forced to compete for supremacy with other anti-Roman parties, especially with Socinianism and with the Polish Reformed. Leader of the latter was John a Lasco or Laski (d. 1560), probably Poland's outstanding theologian in the sixteenth century. Though he held Luther in high regard and regarded himself as loyal to the Augsburg Confession, Laski's doctrine of the Lord's Supper and of the person of Christ is Reformed. This became abundantly clear in his controversy with Joachim Westphal.

3. The high-water mark of Lutheran prestige in Polish theology was attained by the Consensus of Sandomierz in 1570. Poles of Lutheran and Reformed persuasion joined with the Bohemian Brethren in acknowledging each other's position as orthodox. Included in this Consensus was a more or less Lutheran statement of the controverted doctrines of the Lord's Supper and of Christology.

4. Subsequent events indicated, however, that the Reformed element in Polish Protestantism would not agree to such a statement. Within a generation after the Consensus, Polish Protestantism had virtually disappeared, and only in much later years did Lutheranism begin to assert itself in Poland again. JP

Theodor Wotschke, *Geschichte der Reformation in Polen*, Leipzig, 1911; Jaroslav Pelikan, "The Consensus of Sandomierz," *Concordia Theological Monthly*, XVIII (1947), pp. 825—837.

Polemics. The controversial side of theology; in a narrower sense, the principles and methods of argument as applied to controversy within the Christian Church. In this sense polemics is distinguished from apologetics, which is concerned with the defense of Christianity against those who attack it from without. See *Apologetics*.

Policraticus. See *John of Salisbury*.

Polish National Church. See *Old Catholics*.

Polish National Church of America. An organization of Polish Catholic churches which owes its origin to the resentment of Polish parishioners against the autocratic religious, political, and social power exercised by the priests in various American cities — Chicago, Buffalo, Cleveland, Scranton,

and others. In 1904 an organization was effected at Scranton, Pa., where a convention was held, attended by 147 clerical and lay members from various States. This organization rejects papal infallibility and the exclusive claims of Romanism. Its doctrinal position may be judged by the following thesis: "Faith is helpful to man toward his salvation, though not absolutely necessary." In polity the synod is the highest authority. The congregations are governed by a board of trustees, elected by the members. The movement, initiated in Chicago by Rev. Anthony Kozlowski, was finally merged in the Polish National Church.

Polity, Ecclesiastical. 1. That branch of theology which treats the principles of church government. As a visible society the church must preserve external form and order for the efficient administration of the Word and Sacraments. The exercise of discipline in the case of sinning or lapsed members (Matt. 18) is a fundamental part of this administration, intimately bound up with the power of the Keys. (See *Keys, Office of.*) Where our Lord instructs His disciples in the right use of the keys, He says: "Tell it unto the church," v. 17. This cannot mean the Church Universal, which no man's voice can reach; but the brother who would gain a brother is directed to the church before which they can both appear, which in its assembly may hear the complaint and admonish the offender. It is immaterial whether this church, or assembly, be large or small. "For where two or three are gathered together in My name, there am I in the midst of them," says Christ in the context, v. 20. "To the church of God which is at Corinth" (1 Cor. 1:2) Paul, as an Apostle of Jesus Christ, says: "Put away from among yourselves that wicked person" (1 Cor. 5:13). The Apostle himself judges concerning the offender as present in spirit where this congregation is gathered together (v. 3). He considers it the business of the congregation at Colossae to provide for ample preaching of the Word in its midst and to admonish Archippus to the faithful performance of the duties of his office (Col. 4:17). All the admonitions of Rev. 2 and 3 to watch over, and maintain, purity of doctrine and holiness of life are addressed to local churches by the Spirit of Christ. The various churches in Macedonia, Achaia, and Galatia were severally called upon to contribute toward the collection for the needy brethren in Judea (1 Cor. 16:1; 2 Cor. 8 and 9). All the tasks of the Church and the powers requisite for their valid performance are thus seen to be allotted to local congregations. Accordingly, the local church, the congregation of believers locally circumscribed, is the seat of authority in the Church of Christ. That form of government will be pleasing to its Lord which recognizes in the fullest degree the authority of the local congregation.

2. In the early Christian Church we find the institution of elders or bishops for the administration and guidance of the churches. Locally the officers of the churches were designated by the concurrent action of the membership. At the election of Matthias (Acts 1) the entire congregation selected the candidates, and choice was made by lot. In Acts 6 the congregation elected the seven deacons. Thus in the regulation of its internal affairs the congregation is supreme. Ecclesiastical polity, however, is concerned specifically with the relation of congregation to congregation. Such relations existed from the earliest days of Christianity. At first the Apostles formed the main external bond, since it was a characteristic of the Apostolate that it was undivided, and every Apostle belonged to each Christian congregation. The results of Apostolic work were communicated to the several congregations and became the subject of their deliberations. The church at Jerusalem sent its deputies to Antioch to learn the result of the preaching of the Word in that region (Acts 11:19-26); and that at Antioch provided for the temporal relief of the church at Jerusalem (Acts 11:29, 30). Letters of commendation are given from one church to another (Acts 18:27; Rom. 16:5; 2 Cor. 3:1). Churches in a province united in appointing a common representative (2 Cor. 8:19, 23). In the synod at Jerusalem (Acts 15), we find delegates from the churches at Antioch and Jerusalem, a full report of the discussion, the record of the resolution passed, and the letter formulated to be sent to the church at Antioch.

3. It was at a later time that the outward organization of the Church was gradually effected. The congregations united into dioceses and the dioceses into larger aggregates under a metropolitan bishop. This process of centralization was at last accompanied by the claim that the organization was of itself of divine origin and authority and that obedience was to be unconditionally rendered it under the penalty of the loss of salvation. Yet there is also another extreme — that of absolute detachment of the congregational units. Undoubtedly there is not only a right, but also a duty of external fellowship among congregations. Every local church has its share in the work of the Church Universal. Because there is only "one body and one Spirit, one hope, one Lord, one faith, one Baptism, one God and Father of all," therefore not only every individual Christian, but also every local church, or congregation, should be "giving diligence to keep the unity of the Spirit in the bond of peace" (Eph. 4:3 ff.). The natural result is the organization of churches into larger assemblies, or synods, in which their representatives meet on an equal footing. Such synods are consociations of sister churches, not judicatories whose enactments must be respected as binding upon the several churches thus united in a common cause. "In their relation to the several congregations, synods are advisory bodies only, as far as the internal affairs of the congregations are concerned." (A. L. Graebner.) Civil governments, being endowed with legislative authority, can enact laws which the subjects are bound to obey "for conscience' sake." But churches are not endowed with such power, and in the Church there are no subjects but unto Christ. The Church shall use those powers which Christ has delegated to it; and when one church exercises such powers according to Christ's instructions, such action should be respected by all other churches. Thus, when a sinner, after due admonition, has been excommunicated by a congregation, he should be held excommunicate by all other congregations. Of course, the right to use does not imply the right to abuse, and when one congregation finds that another congregation has abused the power of the keys, it is not bound by such tyrannous action any more than one is held to honor the unlawful acts of an agent who openly disregards the will and instructions of his principal. But when a church thus sets aside the judgment of a sister church, it does not exercise a superiority over it, but carries out the command of the common Head of the Church, whose will the sister church has not performed, but violated. Thus, also, every congregation is charged to

preach the Gospel and to administer the Sacraments. But no church, no Apostle, no angel from heaven, is empowered to alter the Gospel or a Sacrament; and when a church harbors or disseminates false doctrine, it becomes the duty of every other church to reprimand the erring church by correction and reproof, not because of any superior dignity or authority of its own, but because of the superior dignity and authority of Christ and His Word.

4. The above system is sometimes called the Congregational System as distinguished from the Papal, the Presbyterian, the Episcopal, and others. (See articles on various denominations; also *Territorial System*.) Most of the Lutheran synods of America are organized on strictly congregational lines, although some, notably the United Lutheran Church, yield more judicial functions to the synod assembled in convention and otherwise in its relation to the congregations than others. In the congregational system the congregation as a body has the highest power in the management of all its internal and external ecclesiastical and congregational affairs. No arrangement or decision for the congregation or for a church member as such has any validity, whether it proceed from an individual or from a body in the congregation, if it is not made in the name of, and according to the general or particular authority given by, the congregation; and that which is arranged or decided by individuals or smaller bodies in the name and by authority of the congregation may at any time be brought before the congregation, as the highest tribunal, for final decision. Hence the right to call, to elect, and to install the minister, or ministers, teacher, or teachers of the parochial schools and all other officers of the congregation rests entirely with this local church.

5. *The Monarchical, or Papal, System.* Here the government is vested in the Pope, to whose infallible commands the people are subjected. The Papal System may also be termed the Hierarchical. In the post-Apostolic age an error crept into the Church regarding the function of bishops. Whereas this title had been synonymous with elders (and equivalent to the more modern *pastor* or *minister*) in Biblical and Apostolic usage, it gradually was restricted to the heads of dioceses. Moreover, a priestly function was attributed to the ministry. From this time date the various orders of the clergy, grad-

uated in rank from archbishops, metropolitans, and bishops down to the lower ranks of deacons, lectors, catechists, notaries, etc. At the head of the entire system is the universal episcopate, or papacy. See *Papacy.*

6. *The Episcopal System.* According to this view of the constitution of the Church, the bishops are the successors of the Apostles, who have a perpetual governing power in the Church. Apostolic Succession is a doctrine of the Anglican Church, particularly of the High Church party in that denomination. (See *Apostolic Succession.*) The strict Anglican does not acknowledge the validity of any other ordination but that conferred by the laying on of hands by some bishop in Apostolic Succession. He acknowledges the true ministry only in the Roman Catholic, Greek Catholic, Anglican, Protestant Episcopal, and Swedish Lutheran Church, the assumption being that episcopal consecration can be traced in the ministry of these denominations clear back to the Twelve. As a matter of fact, the notion of the divine right of the historic episcopate and the hypothesis of an apostolic succession of manually consecrated bishops are without warrant in either the Scriptures or the earlier monuments of Christian antiquity. The Lutheran Church of certain parts of Germany and of the Scandinavian countries has retained the title of bishop for its chief regional heads or superintendents. But the Lutheran Confessions constantly emphasize the inherent right of every congregation to set apart its own pastor and the absolute equality of all pastors. The early Lutheran instructions and constitutions nowhere regard the episcopate as the exclusive form of church government and never reserved confirmation for it. As the *Wittenberg Reformation* (1545) was careful to state: "When our Lord Jesus Christ says: 'Tell it to the church,' and with these words commands that the church should be the highest judge, it follows that not only one class, namely, bishops, but also other God-fearing learned men from all classes are to be set as judges and to have decisive votes, as it was yet in the council of Ephesus, where priests and deacons had decisive votes *(voces decisivas)*."

7. *The Presbyterian System.* In this system the government "is exercised by the people through representatives whom they elect and who are called presbyters, or elders." Of these there

are two kinds, the teaching elders, or ministers, and the ruling elders, or laymen. "They hold to the unity of the Church, and the government is administered through a series of ascending courts: The General Assembly, covering the nation; the Synod, covering the State; the Presbytery, covering the country or territory corresponding thereto; and the session, which deals with the local congregation." In the Presbyterian Church of the United States "the General Assembly is the highest judicatory. It shall represent, in one body, all the particular churches of this denomination." "To the General Assembly belongs the power of deciding in all controversies respecting doctrine and discipline, of reproving, warning, or bearing testimony against error in doctrine or immorality in practice." Accordingly, the General Assembly is the supreme court of the Presbyterian Church. Its interpretations are therefore final and mandatory as the interpretation of the Church. Locally, all ministers and an elder from each congregation "within a certain district" constitute the Presbytery, and all are under the care of, and required to report to, the Presbytery. The Assembly is given the authority "of superintending the concerns of the whole Church." It has charge of the work of the Church in such matters as education and missions. It may also systematize the plans of, and regulate the aid secured for, missions within the bounds of the presbyteries. Throughout the Presbyterian System the elders have the rest of legislative, executive, and judicial power.

Werner Elert, "Kirchenverfassung," *Morphologie des Luthertums*, Beck, Munich, 1931 (I: 320—35); C. S. Mundinger, *Government in the Missouri Synod*, CPH, 1947; J. L. Neve, *The Free Church System Compared with the German State Church* (tr., C. E. Hay), German Lit. Bd., Burlington, Iowa., 1903; J. L. Shaver. *The Polity of the Church*, Church Polity Press, Chicago, 1947; C. Jenkins, *Episcopacy Ancient and Modern*, Soc. for Promoting Christian Knowledge, London, 1930; A. Brunn, *The Polity of a Lutheran Congregation*, CPH, 1940. See references under *Church*.

Pollich, Martin von Mellrichstadt (Dr. Mellerstadt d. 1513). Physician of Frederick the Wise, distinguished for his learning, took part in establishing the University of Wittenberg, where he also taught Scholastic theology and medicine; had presentiment of coming importance of Luther as Reformer of the Church.

Polyandry. See *Polygamy*.

Polycarp. See *Apostolic Fathers, 3*.

Polygamy. A peculiar perversion of the original order of God, amounting almost to a subversion of the real object of the married estate, according to which one person enters into marital union with two (bigamy) or more persons of the opposite sex. Polygamy is commonly divided into *Polygyny*, or the marriage of two or more women to the same man, and *polyandry*, the state in which one woman has two or more "husbands." Polygyny has been practiced in many parts of the world, but the usual situation is this, that only the powerful and wealthy are in a position to support a harem of two or more women. The different wives may live together in one establishment, or the individual women may be granted their own houses or apartments. In many cases there is a favorite wife, who, with her children, occupies a superior position in the household of the harem. This condition is still more pronounced in the case of concubinage, in which usually only one wife is regarded as the true consort of the husband, the others occupying inferior positions little better than those of kept women. Polygamy was practiced very extensively in the Orient and among many uncivilized and semibarbarous peoples in all parts of the world. It is prevalent in Africa. The polyandrous form of polygamy is far less frequent than polygyny. Its chief home is in India and in the central and southeastern part of Asia, in the Marquesas Islands, and among certain tribes of Southern Africa. Where it is generally accepted, the family relation is established and traced through the mother.

The fact that polygamy is not in agreement with the original plan and order of God is apparent even from its early history; for it was Lamech, a member of the Cainite division of the human race, who first took unto him two wives, Adah and Zillah (Gen. 4:19). The story of the patriarchs of the OT (Abraham, Jacob) offers unusual circumstances and cannot be included outright in the history of polygamy. King David had a number of wives, and Solomon had seven hundred wives and three hundred concubines (I Kings 11:3). The custom of polygamy was continued throughout the period of kings, the fact of their having many wives being stated in some instances.

The advent of the Christian era changed conditions for the better. Christianity had a very decided influence upon the status of women, and it discouraged polygamy from the start. The rule which was laid down from the beginning, when God made one man and one woman to live together in holy wedlock, was emphatically upheld by Jesus when He referred to the words of Genesis that "they twain shall be one flesh" (Gen. 2:24; cf. Matt. 19:4-6; Mark 10:2-12). The same thought is basic in the entire New Testament (Eph. 5:22-33; 1 Thess. 4:4; 1 Pet. 3:1-7; 1 Tim. 3:2,12; 5:9).

The situation in the so-called Christian countries is, in general, in keeping with the New Testament teaching, which, in turn, agrees with the original order of God. Even as womanhood has in every way been elevated, owing to the influence of Christianity, so polygamy, as one phase of the degradation of women, has been eliminated by law.

Polyglot Bibles. The *Hexapla* of Origen is the earliest polyglot and the greatest endeavor undertaken by a single scholar. The earliest attempt at a printed polyglot was a projected work of the celebrated printer Aldus Manutius; but only one page of this was published. The first printed polyglot Bible was the *Biblia Sacra Polyglotta* (Hebrew, Chaldee, Greek, Latin), published in Complutum, Spain, by Cardinal Francis Ximenes de Cismeros in 1522 at his own expense, 50,000 ducats. Only six hundred copies were printed. Other editions of a polyglot Bible are: the *Antwerp Polyglot*, 8 vols, folio, 1509 to 1572, printed at the expense of Philip II of Spain, whence also called *Biblia Regia*. It contains in addition to the Complutensian texts, a Chaldee paraphrase and the Syriac version. The *Paris Polyglot*, 10 vols., large folio, 1645. In addition to the contents of the former works, this has a Syriac and Arabic version of both Testaments together with the Samaritan Pentateuch. The *London Polyglot*, 6 vols., folio, 1657. More comprehensive than any of the former. Edited by Brian Walton. The *Leipzig* (or Reineccius') *Polyglot (Biblia Sacra Quadrilinguica)*, 3 vols, folio, 1713—57. In this edition also Luther's German translation is given. The *Heidelberg* (or Bertram's) *Polyglot*, 3 vols., folio, 1586; the *Hamburg* (or Wolder's) *Polyglot*, 1596; *Bagster's Polyglot*, 1831.

The last-named contains in one volume the Hebrew text, the Samaritan Pentateuch, the Septuagint, the Vulgate, and the Syriac version, the Greek text of Mill in the New Testament, together with Luther's German, Diodati's Italian, Ostervald's French, Scio's Spanish, and the English Authorized Version of the Bible. *Polyglottenbibel zum praktischen Handgebrauch*, edited by Stier and Theile. It contains the Hebrew, the Septuagint, the Vulgate, and German in the Old Testament and the Greek, the Vulgate, and German in the New Testament. The *Hexaglot Bible*, 6 vols., royal 4to, 1876. It contains the Holy Scriptures of the Old and New Testaments in the original tongues, together with the Septuagint, the Syriac (of the New Testament), the Vulgate, the Authorized English and German, and the most approved French versions.

Polygyny. See *Polygamy*.

Polynesia. A name often applied to the three island groups of Melanesia,* Micronesia, and Polynesia. In the narrow sense Polynesia includes the following principal groups: Hawaiian Islands, Samoa, Tonga, and the islands of the French Establishment in Oceania. Australasian societies, London Missionary Society, Assemblies of God, Société des Missions Evangéliques de Paris, Seventh-Day Adventists, The Lutheran Church — Missouri Synod, Methodist Church, Missionary Church Association, Pentecostal Holiness Church, and the Southern Baptist Convention carry on work in Polynesia. Statistics (1952): 65,547 communicant members. The natives of Polynesia are of the Caucasoid-Mongoloid and Negroid-Mongoloid type.

Micronesia includes the Pelew, Ladrones, Caroline, Marshall, Gilbert, Mariana, Guam, Fiji, and other islands. The people are Malayan. Missions are carried on by the Methodist Church of Australasia, Christian Missions in Many Lands, Assemblies of God, Seventh-Day Adventists, London Missionary Society, and the American Board of Commissioners for Foreign Missions. Statistics (1952): 48,914 communicants. See also *Melanesia*.

Polytheism. The belief that there are many gods, a manifestation of heathenism, frequently consisting in deification of natural forces and phenomena, and of man (as the anthropomorphism of classical and Germanic mythology). In a wider sense it includes East Asiatic religions, Buddhsm, Hinduism, Confucianism,

Shinto, etc., as well as animism (ca. 780,000,000); in a narrower sense, only animism (ca. 123,000,000). The question whether polytheism is a stage in the upward development of religion, from fetishism to monotheism, or a degeneration of the pure God-given religion of original man, is answered by the Bible in the latter sense in Rom. 1.

Pomeranicum. See *Lutheran Confessions,* C 1.

Pomponazzi, Pietro (1462—1525). Italian Renaissance philosopher; wrote *On the Immortality of the Soul,* which opposed ideas of Thomas Aquinas; held that immortality, miracles, etc., could not be logically proved but are accepted by faith.

Pond, Enoch (1791—1882). Congregationalist; b. in Massachusetts; pastor at Auburn, Mass.; orthodox in Unitarian controversy; professor, president, of Bangor Theological Seminary; d. at Bangor; wrote: *The Mather Family; Lectures on Christian Theology;* and others.

Pontifical College. Originally the religious advisers of the Roman emperor; in the Roman Church it originally designated any college or seminary directly established by the Papacy; soon thereafter it came to be applied to institutions for training missionaries and then to all academic schools granting degrees.

Pontificalia. 1) Rights and privileges of a bishop; 2) ceremonies at which the bishop must wear crosier and mitre.

Pontoppidan, Erick (1698—1764). B. at Aarhus, Jutland; Danish bishop, the "Spener of Denmark"; court preacher and professor extraordinary at Copenhagen; a prolific writer on pastoral and practical subjects. His *Explanation of Luther's Catechism* has been in use for almost two hundred years.

Pope *(Election, Rites, Dress, Officers).* 1. The Pope is elected by the College of Cardinals. Nine days are given to the funeral rites of the dead Pope and to preparations for the election; on the tenth day the cardinals enter the conclave to be stringently secluded from the world until they have made their choice. This may be either by acclamation, scrutiny (ballot), or compromise (entrusting the election to a small committee). A majority of two thirds is required for election. The successful candidate announces what name he will bear as Pope, is given the fisherman's ring, and robed in the papal vestments, and the cardinals adore him. The news is proclaimed to the people. If the newly elected Pope is not already a bishop, he must be consecrated such.

2. The ceremony of coronation with the tiara takes place on a balcony of St. Peter's amid great pomp. From that day a Pope reckons his pontificate. Popes carry such titles as Pontifex Maximus (high priest), Vicar of Christ, Servant of the Servants of God, and are addressed as Your Holiness and Most Holy Father. They are adored with genuflections, and as a special privilege they permit the faithful to kiss their feet. In solemn ceremonies they are carried on a portable chair, preceded by the papal cross and accompanied by two large fans of peacock feathers.

3. A Pope's ordinary costume resembles that of a bishop, but is white; he wears low red shoes. On special occasions his vestments are very elaborate and costly. His insignia are a straight crosier, the pallium, and the tiara, or triple crown. The latter, shaped like a beehive and ornamented with priceless jewels, is worn only on state occasions. It is an emblem of princely authority and has been variously explained as signifying rule over the Church Militant, Expectant, and Triumphant, or authority in heaven, earth, and purgatory. The Pope's *famiglia,* or civil court, consists of a number of cardinals, who live in the papal palaces (palatine cardinals), domestic prelates, such as the superintendent of the household, the master of the chamber, the master of the sacred palaces (a theological adviser); various clerical and lay chamberlains (some paid and some honorary), secretaries, and other officials. The Swiss Guard (100 men, in sixteenth-century uniforms) act as papal bodyguard; there are also gendarmes to do police duty and two other military companies, the Palatine Guard and the Noble Guard. For spiritual officials see *Curia; Roman Congregations;* see also *Vatican.*

Pope, Alexander (1688—1744). B. in London, received only a desultory education with priestly instruction; however, his genius was evident quite early. After his father's death he removed to the villa at Twickenham, which with its gardens and grotto is so intimately associated with his memory. Pope became the typical man of letters and the great representative English poet of the first half of the 18th century. Among his works are his translations of Homer's *Illiad* and *Odyssey*, etc. He wrote no hymns for distinct public use, but several have been so introduced, and among them, "Rise, Crowned with Light, Imperial Salem, Rise."

Pope, Primacy of. See *Roman Catholic Confessions*, E 3.

Popes. The following are listed among the more prominent Popes:

1. *Sylvester I* (314—35). Bishop of Rome during the reign of Constantine and the Council of Nicaea (which he did not attend); consecrated famous Roman churches.

2. *Leo the Great* (440—61). Opposed Pelagians, Manichaeans, etc.; strengthened papal authority in Spain, Gaul, and the East; persuaded Attila to spare Rome; first bishop of Rome to insist on recognition of his claim to supremacy as Peter's successor and hence often regarded as the first Pope; definition of person of Christ at Chalcedon (451).

3. *Vigilius* (538—55). Protégé of Empress Theodora; influenced by threats of Justinian, he condemned the "Three Chapters" *(judicatum Constitutum)*.

4. *Gregory I* ("the Great," 590—604). "Father of Medieval Papacy"; educated in the Latin Fathers, especially Augustine; writings emphasize superstitious and traditional elements (miracles, ecclesiastical practices, demonology, merit, etc.) and excelled especially in the field of homiletics, liturgics, hymnody; wrote *Regula Pastoralis, Antiphonarium, Sacramentarium, Benedictionale;* elected Pope unanimously in 590 and exercised the temporal power of an absent exarch, thus extending the papal power into the temporal realm (defended separation of Church and State in theory); rejected title of *Papa Universalis* but nevertheless interfered in various dioceses; opposed secularization of clergy; sent Augustine to England.

5. *Nicholas I* (857—67). Championed primacy of the Pope; intervened in marital affairs of Lothaire II; deposed Photius and reinstated Ignatius, an act which became important in the *"filioque"* controversy.

6. *Sylvester II* (Gerbert of Aurillac; 999—1003); outstanding scholar of the 10th century; studied at Auvergne, Barcelona, Rome, Reims; distinguished as teacher of philosophy, dialectic, and mathematics.

7. *Gregory VII* (Hildebrand; 1073 to 1085). Raised the papal glory to its highest peak; adviser to five Popes, beginning with Leo IX; instituted reforms against concubinage of clergy, simony, and investiture by secular rulers; opposed by Henry IV of Germany, whom, however, he forced to cross the Alps in winter and stand in penitential garb at Canossa; Henry IV finally defeated Rudolph (protégé of Gregory), set up a rival Pope, and besieged Gregory in Rome; died in exile.

8. *Adrian IV* (1154—59). The only Englishman to become Pope; known for his vigorous insistence on the spiritual and temporal primacy of the Pope over emperor (Frederick I).

9. *Alexander III* (1159—81). Continued the struggle of Adrian IV with Frederick I; canonized Thomas à Becket; successful in his struggle with Henry II of England; opposed by the Antipopes Victor IV, Paschal III, Callixtus III, and Innocent III.

10. *Innocent III* (1196—1216). Studied at Rome, Paris, Bologna; raised secular power of Papacy to its highest development; interfered successfully in political affairs in Germany (elected Otto IV as emperor); received England, Portugal, Denmark, Aragon, and other countries as fiefs; zealous in the promotion of the first crusades; wrote numerous books *(e. g., De contemptu mundi)*.

11. *Gregory IX* (1227—41). Resisted Frederick II's attempts to extend power of emperor over Pope; excommunicated him for relinquishing the idea of a crusade against the Saracens; gave Dominicans almost exclusive control of the Inquisition; published the famous collection of Decretals.

12. *Boniface VIII* (1294—1303). Patron of learning; practiced nepotism; sought to establish supremacy of the Papacy as claimed by Innocent III; issued the bull *Unam Sanctam;* conflict with Philip the Fair, who taxed the clergy during the war with England; captured by Philip's agents, died soon after being rescued.

13. *John XXII* (1316—34). Struggled with Emperor Louis of Bavaria; opposed Franciscan interpretation of poverty; remodeled curia.

14. *Gregory XI* (Pierre de Beaufort; 1370—78). Condemned 18 Theses of Wyclif; placed Florence under interdict and squelched the rebellion; ended *Babylonian Exile* by returning to Rome (last of the French Popes).

15. *Pius II* (Aeneas Sylvius Piccolomini; 1458—64). Upheld the superiority of the ecumenical council over the

Pope (Basel); later denounced this view in the bull *Execrabilis*.

16. *Sixtus IV* (1471—84). Erected splendid buildings in Rome (*e. g.*, Sistine Chapel); enlarged Vatican library; promoted Immaculate Conception; promoted religious communities; vigorously opposed Waldensians; introduced the Inquisition in Spain (1478); addicted to avarice, nepotism, and simony.

17. *Innocent VIII* (1484—92). Interfered in political matters of several countries (declared Henry VII king and confirmed Maximilian as king of the Romans); strengthened the Inquisition and preached crusade against the Waldensians.

18. *Alexander VI* (1492—1503). Known for his mental gifts and moral defects; through his adulterous relations with Vanozza de Cataneis four children were born; his nepotism (especially in the case of Cesare Borgia) and his immoralities greatly influenced the preaching of Savonarola, who was martyred during his papacy (1498).

19. *Julius II* (Giuliano Rovere; 1504 to 1514). Made league with Germany and France and defeated the Venetians; later joined the Venetians against France; called the Fifth Lateran Council at Rome (1512); founded the Holy League; patron of art; Pope at the time of Luther's visit (1510, 1511).

20. *Leo X* (Giovanni de Medici; 1513 to 1521). Sought to advance the political fortunes of the Papacy and his own family; established a Concordat with Francis I of France (1516); displayed gross misunderstanding in his treatment of the Lutheran Reformation.

21. *Pius V* (Michael Ghilieri; 1566 to 1572). Sought to carry out the reforms of the Council of Trent; published *Catechismus Romanus*, breviary, and Roman missal; fought "heresies"; excommunicated Elizabeth of England.

22. *Sixtus V* (Felice Peretti; 1585 to 1590). Sought to enforce the regulations of the Council of Trent; ordered bishops to report to Rome at stated intervals; fixed the number of cardinals (bull *Postquam verus*, 1586); collaborated with Philip of Spain in the war against England; published Sixtine edition of the *Vulgata* (bull *Aeternus ille;* later repealed).

23. *Innocent X* (Giambattista Pamfili; 1644—55). As cardinal participated in the deliberations at Trent; rejected articles of the Westphalian Treaty unfriendly to Rome (bull *Zelo Domus Dei,* 1648); precipitated the Jansenist contro-

versies by condemning five propositions from the *Augustinus* of Jansenius; interfered in political matters.

24. *Benedict XIV* (Prospero Lambertini; 1740—58). A scholar and famous author himself, he furthered education, literature, and science; his friendly character made it possible for him to conciliate European powers and win friends beyond Romanism; condemned Jesuit accommodation * to heathen rites in India and China; Voltaire dedicated his work on Mohammed to him.

25. *Clement XIV* (Giovanni Lorenzo Ganganelli; 1769—74). A scholarly Pope, he furthered the arts and sciences as well as commerce and industry; sought to live in peace with the ruling powers of his day; at the instigation of the Bourbons, he suppressed the Jesuit order (brief *Dominus et Redemptor,* July 21, 1773).

26. *Pius VI* (Giovanni Angelico Braschi; 1775—99). Fought Febronianism (Febronius pseudonym for N. von Hontheim, 1701—1790; held Papacy limited by General Councils in doctrine, by national churches in discipline) in Germany; Josephinism in Austria; Gallicanism in France; joined the powers against the French Republic (1792); Bonaparte occupied papal states, Pope captured (1799) and died in exile.

27. *Pius VII* (Luigi Barmola Charamonti; 1800—23). Saw Papacy reach its lowest ebb; struggles with Napoleon (Concordat of 1801; Napoleon's 77 articles subjecting every public act of the Church to the approval of the secular government; Napoleon selected bishops); Congress of Vienna (1815) restored much of the papal power.

28. *Pius IX* (Giovanni Maria Mastei Ferretti; 1846—78). Lost papal states (1870), thus creating the "Roman Question"; declared the dogma of Immaculate Conception (1854); held Vatican Council, which declared papal infallibility (1870); created many new dioceses, especially in the U. S.

29. *Leo XIII* (Vincenzo Gioachino Pacci; 1878—1903). Known for his cultural, social, and scholarly activities; sought to bring the Catholic Church into harmony with governments stressing personal liberty; active in worldwide promulgation of Catholicism; influenced revival of Thomistic Scholasticism; founded Catholic University, Washington, D. C.

30. *Pius X* (Giuseppe Melchiore Sarto; 1903—14). Issued the decree *Lamentabili* and encyclical *Pascendi*

against Modernism; reorganized Roman Curial Congregation; established Biblical Institute at Rome; created the periodical *Acta Apostolicae Sedis.*

31. *Benedict XV* (Giacomo Paolo Giacomo della Chiesa; 1914—22). Known especially for his efforts toward peace in World War I (a plaque describing these efforts is on his tomb); opposed Modernism; published new Code of Canon Law, 1918.

32. *Pius XI* (Ambrosio Damiano Achille Ratti; 1922—29). Known for his many encyclicals *(Casti Connubii* on birth control; *Deus Scientiarum Dominus* on higher education); played an important role in Catholic Action and Lay Apostolate; concordat with Italy (1929) placing the Vatican City under papal sovereignty; established Russian, Ruthenian, Romanian and Ethiopian colleges; founded Institute for Christian archaeology; well educated.

33. *Pius XII* (Eugenio Pacelli, 1939 to). Active in field of diplomacy (established concordat with Prussia in 1929; papal Secretary of State in 1930); traveled widely (in U. S. in 1936); early papal utterances emphasized peace and opposition to Communism. EL

Horace K. Mann, *Lives of the Popes in the Early Middle Ages,* Herder, St. Louis, 1925—32 (18 vols.); L. Pastor, *History of the Popes,* Herder, St. Louis, 1923—41 (34 vols.); Leopold von Ranke, *History of the Popes,* Colonial Press, N. Y., 1901. The list of Popes by Roman Catholics is usually given in Roman Catholic cyclopedias * and at the end of histories of the Roman Catholic Church.

Popes, Captivity of. See *Avignon.*

Pornocracy (904—63). The control of the Papacy by depraved women and its consequent deep moral debasement. Theodora, the mistress of the powerful Margrave Adalbert of Tuscany, a well-born and beautiful, ambitious, and voluptuous Roman, wife of a Roman senator, as well as her likeminded daughters Marozia and Theodora, filled for half a century the papal chair with their paramours, sons, and grandsons. Sergius III (904—11), Marozia's paramour, starts the disgraceful line. Archbishop John of Ravenna was made Pope John X (914—28), to be near his mistress Theodora. Later, when he tried to cast her off, he was cast into prison and smothered with a pillow by order of Marozia. John XI was the son of Marozia and Pope Sergius III; Octavianus, grandson of Marozia, was Pope John XII (956—63) and the first Pope

to change his name. He was made Pope when only sixteen years old. He was an archprofligate and a blasphemer. He would sell anything for money. He made a boy of ten years a bishop; he consecrated a deacon in a stable; in hunting and dice playing he would invoke the favor of Jupiter and Venus; in his orgies he would drink the health of Satan. He was deposed by Otto I at a synod at Rome, 963, because of incest, perjury, blasphemy, murder, and other sins.

Porphyry (233—ca. 304). Neoplatonic philosopher; b. in Syria; disciple of Plotinus in Rome; ablest expounder of Neoplatonism; wrote polemics against Christianity, which were destroyed by Theodosius.

Porst, Johann (1668—1728). Studied at Leipzig; held positions of tutor, later pastor in Berlin, chaplain to the queen, and provost of Berlin; strongly addicted to Pietism, all his literary work breathing its spirit; best known for his preparation of hymnal *Geistliche liebliche Lieder,* some of which are objectionable on account of their chiliastic tendency or their subjectivism.

Port Royal. Famous Cistercian convent near Paris, established at the beginning of the 13th century; prominent in the 17th century as the mainstay of Jansenism *; abolished in 1709, the building and church being destroyed by order of Louis XIV.

Porta, Conrad (1541—85). B. at Halberstadt. Pastor in Eisleben. Published *Pastorale Lutheri,* a selection of passages from Luther's works on pastoral theology.

Portico. See *Architecture, Ecclesiastical,* 3.

Portugal, Catholic Church in. See *Roman Catholic Church.*

Positivism, the philosophical system of Auguste Comte, French philosopher (1798—1857), as laid down in his *Cours de Philosophie Positive,* 1830—42, *Système de Politique Positive,* 1851—54, *Catéchisme Positiviste,* 1852, and called so because it deals only with "positive" knowledge, *i. e.,* knowledge arrived at not by philosophical theorizing, but by experience and observation. It assumes three stages through which human knowledge passes, theological, metaphysical, positivist. Human thought had to pass through the two former to arrive at the last; but now that the stage of positivism has come, theology and metaphysics must be rejected. Positivism does not look for causes, as do theology and metaphysics, but only for laws, namely, those laws which govern the coexistence and sequence of the phenomena, the ordered organism of the world. Accordingly, the world is explained on the basis of natural sciences, which Comte reduced to six and classified, beginning with the most general and proceeding to the more complex, each succeeding science depending upon the foregoing, *viz.*, mathematics, astronomy, physics, chemistry, biology, sociology, laying special stress on the last-named, as whose founder he is generally recognized. In his later years Comte endeavored to construct a new positivist "religion" on the basis of this philosophy, a "Religion of Humanity," in which a cult of the human race or veneration of men of genius takes the place of worship of God. This religion (called by Huxley "Catholicism minus Christianity") which rejects belief in God, soul, and immortality and has nine sacraments, a special priesthood and ritual, a new calendar with thirteen months, each dedicated to a great benefactor of mankind, and 84 festivals, found adherents for a time in France, but particularly in England, where a few Positivist societies are still extant.

Postlude (Postludium; Nachspiel). An organ composition played at the conclusion of a service of worship. In view of the fact that the postlude has been regarded as a part of the service of worship ever since the close of the 18th century, it is incumbent upon the organist to play postludes which bespeak the spirit of the service of worship which they bring to a close.

Postmillenarians. See *Millennium*, 7.

Post-Nicene Fathers. Patristic writers after the Council of Nicaea (325). See *Patristics*.

Postulant. 1) R. C., applicant for admission to an order; 2) Episcopalian, applicant for ordination.

Postulators. See *Canonization*.

Powell, Thomas Edward (1823 to 1901). Educated at Oxford; held various charges in the Established Church; published a book of *Hymns, Anthems, etc., for Public Worship;* wrote: "Bow Down Thine Ear, Almighty Lord."

Practical Theology. A term applied, especially in America, to those departments of theological training which concern the practical work of the ministry. Although applied to a variety of subjects, it usually includes the following: 1) the gathering and introducing of individuals into true church fellowship (evangelistics, diaconics, catechetics); 2) the guidance and promotion of the Christian life (liturgics, homiletics, various phases of pastoral theology); 3) the organization of the church (polity).

Praemunire, Statute of. Statutes (the first enacted in 1353 and continuing to Henry VIII) preventing the encroachment of papal jurisdiction and upholding the independence of the royal courts.

Praetorius, Benjamin (1636—74). Studied theology, probably at Leipzig; was made poet laureate in 1661; pastor at Gross-Lissa in Saxony; wrote: "Sei getreu bis an das Ende."

Praetorius, Hieronymus (1560 to 1629). Cantor at Erfurt and later organist of the Church of St. James at Hamburg, he was one of the German followers of the Venetian school of church music, his music often exhibiting a multiplicity of parts. Most of his works, chiefly motets, are contained in a five-volume edition of *Opus Musicum.* He also had a share in editing the *Hamburger Melodeyen-Gesangbuch* of 1604.

Praetorius, Jakob (ca. 1580—1651). The older son of Hieronymus, was a pupil of Sweelinck at Amsterdam and, later, organist of the Lutheran Church of St. Peter in Hamburg. Sweelinck thought so highly of him that he dedicated a five-part *Canticum nuptiale* to his pupil at the time of his marriage in 1608. Mattheson refers to Jakob Praetorius as a great organist, and Johann Rist not only penned his epitaph, but also referred to him as the Jubal of Hamburg. His compositions reveal artistic freedom and inventiveness.

Praetorius, Michael (1571—1621). "One of chief founders of German baroque music" (Lang) and important in history of Lutheran church music. Son of a Lutheran pastor and throughout his life a loyal Lutheran. He received his early training at the *Torgauer Lateinschule.* In 1612 he succeeded Thomas Mancinus at Wolfenbuettel as *Hofkapellmeister* and held a political office. Through his efforts and research, Praetorius preserved many Lutheran chorales. In 1613 he became acquainted with Venetian music; from this time on his music began to reflect the influence of the Italians. However, he did not succeed in appropriating the Italian style and spirit thoroughly, and he is often not at his best, as was Hassler, when merging the Italian style and spirit with the German. He was greater as editor and arranger than as an original composer. His *Musae Sioniae* was, together with Bodenschatz's *Florilegium Portense,* the most outstanding German collection of choral music of early baroque times. It contained no less than 1,248 settings of 537 chorales gathered from many parts of Germany. The collection is a complete record of the hymns and chorales used and extant in his day. Of importance are likewise his collections *Leiturgodiae Sioniae, Urania, Polyhymnia,* and *Puericinium.* As a composer and editor he was too prolific, succumbing at times to carelessness and superficiality. However, Praetorius was also a great scholar and one of the first musicologists of the Lutheran Church. His *Syntagma Musicum* includes ecclesiastical music in all its phases, a discussion of the secular music of the ancients and of musical instruments, notably the organ, of secular music of the 17th century, notation, and terminology. WEB

F. Blume, "Die evangelische Kirchenmusik," *Handbuch der Musikwissenschaft* (Ernst Bucken), New York (Reprint by Musurgia), 1931, 1949; S. Kuemmerle, *Encyklopaedie der ev. Kirchenmusik,* Guetersloh, 1890; P. H. Lang, *Music in Western Civilization,* New York, 1941; E. Naumann, *The History of Music* (Vol. 1), London; Carl von Winterfeld, *Der ev. Kirchengesang.* Leipzig, 1943—47.

Pragmatic Ethics. See *Social Ethics; Pragmatism.*

Pragmatic Sanction. See *France,* 1; *Gallicanism.*

Pragmatism. In philosophy, a logical process intended to aid in making ideas clear. This process proposes that the meaning of an idea should be determined by the practical or pragmatic difference it would make if it were assumed to be true. As between two ideas, if there were no difference in effect, it could be concluded that either the difference was purely verbal or the two ideas meant the same thing. This point of view, emphasized first by Charles Peirce, was extended by William James, who proposed the pragmatic test for the nature of truth itself.

Ideas were to be held true if they worked. That is, if the practical consequences of acting on an idea brought to the individual concerned personal satisfaction, the idea was to be regarded as acceptable or true "in so far forth." James wanted to confine the application of pragmatism to problems not otherwise verifiable, while others felt that the test might be made in any instance. Dewey is sometimes considered a pragmatist, but he himself preferred the designation instrumentalism for his philosophy, and, later, experimentalism. That is, if a conception is offered as to how an adaptation might be made, man acts upon this theory experimentally to learn whether the consequences which flow from the action indicated will bear out his anticipation. Pragmatism has emphasized the employment of interest in learning, because the pragmatic test of truth is affected by the interest of the learner. Pragmatism may have some value in education as influencing method, e. g., in a modified progressivism, but it must not be permitted to apply its ideas in the field of the transcendental, since in the religious the divine revelation is the deciding factor.

Prague Articles. See *Hussites.*

Praxeas. See *Monarchianism,* B 4.

Prayer. 1. Prayer, in the narrower sense, is a request, or petition, for benefits or mercies; in the wider sense, any communion of the soul with God. It has been divided into adoration, by which we express our sense of the goodness and greatness of God; confession, by which we acknowledge our unworthiness; supplication, by which we pray for pardon, grace, or any blessing we want; intercession, by which we pray for others; and thanksgiving, by which we express our gratitude to God. Private prayer is either an ejaculation, a short wish, or an appeal addressed to God spontaneously springing from the mind; or it is secret or "closet" (Matt. 6:6) prayer, as when the Christian communes with God upon entering into any important engagement, or when calamities threaten. From private prayer, family prayer (the family altar), and social prayer, as part of the public worship, are distinguished. Only that is true prayer which is made with an honest soul to the only true God. All other prayer is idolatry.

2. Prayer is commanded by God (1 Chron. 16:11; Ps. 50:15; Matt. 7:7; Phil. 4:6), is endowed with His promises

(John 16:23; Ps. 91:15, 16; James 5:16b; Heb. 10:23b; Is. 54:10; Rom. 8:32; Eph. 3:20), and hence is a vital part of Christian life. Prayer, to be valid, must be offered to the Triune God (1 Sam. 7:3; Is. 42:8) and not to idols (e. g., Supreme Being, Great Spirit, Architect of the Universe, etc.: John 5:23; John 14:6; Acts 4:12. 1 Tim. 2:5 excludes the mediation of saints); must proceed from faith (Matt. 21:22; James 1:6,7) which is created by the Holy Spirit (1 Cor. 12:3; Rom. 8:26) and by its very nature excludes willful sin (Is. 59:2; Prov. 1:28; Ps. 66:18; Is. 1:15; John 9:31); must be conditioned by the will of God (1 John 5:14; cf. Rom. 8:28) and must be as broad as *living* mankind (1 Tim. 2:1; Heb. 9:27).

3. In the life of the individual, prayer must be more than an emergency measure, a way of escape from troubles and difficulties that distress. It must be a working force that reaches out for the more abundant life promised by the Savior (1 Thess. 5:17; Rom. 12:12; Is. 1:18; Ps. 32:5). Prayer must be an integral part of the home if it is to function according to God's plan and is essential to the Church in its life and functions (Luke 11:13; Matt. 18:19, 20). Congregational prayer unites hearts and minds. The congregation prays that the Lord give its pastor "utterance" and open doors to him. The pastor prays that God may strengthen his congregation "with might by His Spirit in the inner man." Pastor and people present the special needs of the individual members and families to the Throne of Grace. C. f. CAB, *Abiding Word*, CPH, 1946 (247—66).

4. There are many kinds and forms of prayer. In the Old Testament the word *tephillah* is used very frequently, chiefly in the sense of calling upon God, but also in that of making intercession for someone. It occurs in the heading of the following Psalms: 17, 86, 90, 102, 142, also in Hab. 3:1. The word *sheelah* is used for prayer in general; the word *todeh* is employed for the special prayer of thanksgiving. But there are many other divisions and subdivisions of prayers, as the headings of the various Psalms clearly show. In the New Testament the classic passage is 1 Tim. 2:1: "I exhort, therefore, that, first of all, supplications, prayers, intercessions, and giving of thanks be made for all men." This clearly indicates that the Christians, the children of God, in observing the requirements of the Second Commandment, are required to bring their needs and their desires to the attention of their heavenly Father, that they are to be in constant communication with Him with regard to the sum total of human misery and with respect to all the individual and sundry needs of the various stations of life, that they are to keep in mind also the needs of others, and that they must never forget to offer to the Lord the sacrifice of their lips.

5. It is most interesting and instructive to note that Jesus was in constant communication by prayer with His heavenly Father. Not only do we find Him pronouncing the blessing upon the food at the two great feedings narrated in the Gospels, but His prayers in the Garden of Gethsemane and on Calvary testify to the fact that His relation with His God and Father was of a very intimate kind. This appears also from the fact that He repeatedly retired for solitary prayer. Cp. Mark 1:35, 45; John 6:15. It is proved particularly by the great sacerdotal prayer of the Savior on the evening before His death, John 17, and by the incomparable Lord's Prayer, which, in but seven petitions, embraces all the needs of men over against their God. Matt. 6:9-13; Luke 11:2-4.

The Bible clearly expects the believers to pray, and the reasons are correctly stated in our Catechism, when it is said that the incentives to prayer are, first, God's command and promise and, secondly, our own and our neighbor's needs (Ps. 122:6; Jer. 29:7; Matt. 5:44; Luke 6:28; Matt. 6:6; 9:38; 24:20; 26:41; 1 Thess. 5:17, 25; 1 Tim. 2:8; James 5:13; Rom. 8:26; Luke 18:1-7).

6. We have many excellent examples of men and women of prayer, both in the Scriptures and in history. Thus the example of Abraham, both in his own home and in his intercessory prayer for the cities of Sodom and Gomorrah, has ever been held up for emulation. Other men of prayer were Moses, David, Asaph, Solomon, Hezekiah, Ezra, Daniel, Zacharias, Paul, John, and, in later history, Chrysostom, Augustine, some of the saner mystics of the Medieval Age, Luther, Starck, George Mueller of Bristol, Seiss, Walther, and a host of others. See *Worship*.

C. A. Behnke, "Prayer," *Abiding Word*, CPH, 1946 (extensive references); W. A. Arndt, *Christian Prayer*, CPH, 1937.

Prayer Books. The name given by some liturgical churches to their service books. The *Roman Breviary and Missal* contains the liturgy of the Mass and other material for services and devotions. The *Book of Common Prayer* * is the service book of the Anglican Church, also of the Protestant Episcopal Church of America. The *Presbyterian Book of Common Prayer* was written by Knox (1562) on the basis of that of Edward VI. It is used in the United States as emended in 1661. The *Sunday Service of the Methodists* was prepared by John Wesley on the basis of the *Book of Common Prayer* (liturgy shortened; twenty-five articles instead of thirty-nine). See *Liturgics*.

Prayer Fellowship. See *Fellowship*.

Prayer, Liturgical. The sacrificial part of public worship, including principally the hymns, collects, and the general prayer in the morning service, the entire preface with its prayers and the Trisagion, as well as the Agnus Dei in the Communion service, and all the canticles in use, whether in the chief service or in the minor services. Antiphonal chanting is commonly considered sacrificial in nature, though these parts should be considered sacramental if they include a proclamation of the Word. For ordinary worship in the Lutheran Church only set or fixed prayers are ordinarily permissible, since the prayers in public worship are the expression of the entire congregation, and not of any individual, speaking on the spur of the moment, however appropriate his prayer may be considered otherwise. As far as the attitude during prayer is concerned, it may be said that the ancient posture was that of standing, with eyes directed upward, and often with outstretched hands. The practice of kneeling in worship was developed in the West. In the Lutheran Church the practice of kneeling is still observed in many congregations by having the communicants kneel during the confession and the absolution following. In many churches the communicants kneel also when they receive the Lord's Supper, the gesture of adoration, in this case, being directed not to the elements, but to the Lord, whose body and blood are received. The prayers for the dead, as in use in the Roman Church, have naturally been discontinued in the Lutheran Church. See *Worship*.

Prayer Meetings. Special stated services, common in Reformed circles, usually held on an evening about the middle of the week, the chief features of such meetings being the singing of evangelistic or hortatory hymns, extemporaneous prayers by worshipers called upon without discrimination for that purpose, and the relation of religious experiences by individuals either with or without special invitation. These meetings are based upon the notion that prayer is a means of grace, the use of the Word of God for the purpose of instruction being omitted entirely or almost so. In this form prayer meetings are not Lutheran in character.

Prayers for the Dead. See *Dead, Prayers for*.

Preaching. See *Homiletics*.

Preaching, Christian, History of. 1. Christian preaching, properly so called, has as its content the Word of God, 2 Tim. 4:2, especially the Gospel of Jesus Christ, 1 Cor. 2:2. Every sermon should be Christ-centered. The purpose of Christian preaching is to bring the sinner to a knowledge of his sins, Rom. 3:20; to repentance and faith in Christ, Mark 1:14,15; 16:15,16; to strengthen the Christian's faith, 2 Pet. 3:18; to encourage him to lead a Christian life, Rom. 12:1f.; and to comfort him in his trials and tribulations, Rom. 15:4; and all this to the glory of God.

2. While the sermon in its technique does not differ from any other speech or address, yet because of its content (Law and Gospel) and its purpose (the salvation of men) it far transcends in grandeur any oral discourse and is in a class by itself. The great preachers of Old Testament times were the Prophets, among whom Isaiah excels. Isaiah was a highly educated man; Amos was merely a shepherd and a gardener, not trained in the school of the prophets, Amos 7:14,15. Ezekiel and Jeremiah were mighty Prophets. Jonah, not to mention others, preached to the people of Nineveh, a heathen nation.

3. The great preacher was Jesus Christ Himself, Mark 1:14,15; Luke 4: 43, 44; Matt. 4:17. From Jesus we should learn what and how to preach.

4. Christian preaching by men in New Testament times dates back to the time when Jesus "ordained twelve that they should be with Him and that He might send them forth to preach," Mark 3:14, and when He gave to His Church the commission to preach, Mark 16:15; also Luke 24:47; Acts 1:8.

5. Of the disciples we are told that "they went everywhere preaching the Word," Acts 8:4. Thus preaching in the course of time was heard throughout

the Roman Empire (Paul's far-flung ministry).

6. We know little of the preaching of the first two centuries. Preaching was informal. It was by men who had no special training for their work, but whose heart was aflame with the love of Christ. Origen, 186—253, injured preaching by allegorizing, much of which was done until the time of the Reformation, and even since. Beginning with Origen, we hear of theological schools, religious libraries, and sermons taken down in shorthand, but no sermons of that period are in existence. From Constantine, 272—337, and ending with Chrysostom, 347—407, and Augustine, 354—430, preaching blazed forth in new splendor; young men could attend theological schools, churchgoing became fashionable, but with many Christianity was nothing more than a mere name. Augustine's fourth book of *De Doctrina Christiana* has been called the first book on homiletics. This influenced preaching from Leo the Great, 390—461, to Gregory the Great, 540—604.

7. During the period from 600 to 1100 increasing attention was given to Ceremonialism and the Mass much overshadowed preaching. The entire history of the Church shows that, as soon as the Word of God was not given its due place and importance in preaching in the church services, ceremonialism and formalism became the outstanding feature of "worship." When sermons were preached at all, they were in Latin, which the people did not understand. Most of the lower clergy were ignorant and irreligious. Charlemagne, 742—814, ordered Paulus Diakonus to compile a book of sermons (*Homiliarium*) according to the pericopic system, which book was to serve as a model for the preachers in preparing their sermons, or at least to persuade them to translate the sermons and read them to their audiences.

8. Beginning with the twelfth century, preaching was of a better kind, although it did not reach the height to which it attained during the time of the Reformation and which it has held since. Peter the Hermit, d. 1115, fanatical but eloquent; Bernard of Clairvaux, 1091—1153, whose sermons showed some orderly arrangement, and who prior to his death preached eighty-six sermons on the Song of Solomon and at his death had only begun with the third chapter; the Dominican preachers, an order founded to counteract the

preaching of the Waldenses; Anthony of Padua, d. 1231, who preached to crowds of twenty to thirty thousand, divided his sermons into several heads (something new in sermonizing at that time), used illustrations, and went to the extreme in allegorizing; Thomas Aquinas, d. 1274, who combined profound studies with practical preaching: these are outstanding preachers of that period, the twelfth and thirteenth centuries. Other preachers were Eckhart, Tauler, Suso, Albertus Magnus, Nikolaus von Landau, Heinrich Friemar. The outstanding German preacher of this period was Berthold von Regensburg, 1220—72. He was called "the Chrysostom of the Middle Ages." He was a born orator. Since he preached in the German language, the people flocked to him in great numbers, as a rule under the open sky, as many as sixty thousand (some say even two hundred thousand). He did not hesitate to speak to the people of their sin, preached against indulgences and against depending on the intercessory prayers of the saints and Mother Mary.

9. Other preachers prior to the Reformation were the so-called "reformers before the Reformation," Wyclif, Hus, Savonarola, all three of them powerful preachers, but men who, after all, did not strike at the root of the trouble, the false doctrine of the Papacy.

10. The Reformation ushered in a new era in preaching in a threefold aspect which had been somewhat forgotten: The purpose of Christian preaching is to proclaim to a sinful world the grace of God in Christ Jesus; the source of the Christian sermon is Holy Scripture, the inspired Word of God; in the church service and in the life of the church, preaching, or the sacramental part of the worship, must be given first place, the sacrificial part of the worship, second place. Names of preachers which deserve mention in this period are, in Germany: Luther, Bugenhagen, Brenz, Valerius Herberger, Christian Scriver, Heinrich Mueller, Val. Ernst Loescher; in pietistic circles: Spener, Aug. Herm. Francke; on the British Isles: Colet, John Knox, Tillotson, Baxter, Whitefield, Wesley, Rob. Hall, Chalmers; in France: Bossuet, Bordaloue, Massillon, of the Church of Rome, and Jean Claude and Pierre du Bosc of the Reformed Churches; in Holland: Jaques Sourin. For a later period such deserve mention as Bengel, 1687—1752, famous

for his *Gnomon;* Zinzendorf, 1700—60; J. L. Mosheim, 1694—1755, the church historian who by his preaching attracted large audiences especially from the middle and upper ranks.

11. The period of Illuminism (Aufklaerung) and that of Rationalism, which have their counterpart in present-day Modernism, had a dire effect on preaching. The deism of England and the materialism of France found a ready acceptance in Germany. "Some preachers, unable to find in the Bible, as they read it, topics of sufficient interest, gave lectures upon economical or social subjects, such as agriculture, vaccination, and the making of wills — or upon subjects taken from the natural sciences, such as the structure of fishes and birds. Most of this school, however, a very numerous one, took to 'moral preaching.' Sometimes they changed the language of the Bible, in order to make it, as they said, more rational. For conversion or regeneration, they spoke of amendment of life; for justification, of forgiveness on condition of repentance; for the Holy Spirit, of the exercise of the higher reason; for the atonement of Christ, of the spirit of sacrifice which He has taught us by His example, and so on. Sermons in our day preached and published with blast of trumpet as being new and up to the coming time, may find their parallel in volumes on which the dust of a hundred years has gathered." (Ker, *History of Preaching,* p. 247.) Preachers of that stripe were Spalding and Zollikofer. They preached the churches empty. Over against these, such men as Oetinger, d. 1782, Jung-Stilling, d. 1817, and Lavater of Zurich, d. 1801, exerted a good influence.

12. Friedrich Schleiermacher, 1768 to 1834, attacked rationalism, but himself remained a rationalist and ushered in modernism. The inner consciousness of the individual heart, not Scripture, was his source of doctrine. The purpose of preaching, he said, is to awaken religious feeling, not to instruct or to incite to action. His preaching was topical. He did not write his sermons, but carefully prepared them. Over against the rationalism of Schleiermacher such men arose as Hofacker and Claus Harms. Hofacker, 1798—1828, said: "I have but one sermon. I preach the Lamb that was slain." Claus Harms, 1778—1855, grew up under rationalistic influences, but was aroused by Schleiermacher's negative theology to strike out for positive theology by diligently studying the Bible. By ninety-five theses, written by him against rationalism, he issued a call to the Church to return to the Reformation. He was a forceful preacher, using the topical method. Rudolf Stier, 1800—62, said the sermon should be Scriptural and be applied to the hearer. Friedrich W. Krummacher, 1796—1868, was the most popular German preacher of his day. Theremin, 1780—1846, was for a long time the most popular preacher in Berlin. Ludwig Harms, 1808—65, exerted a tremendous influence by his preaching and other labors. R. Koegel, a most brilliant preacher, said that the sermon must be a battle. Other preachers of those days were Julius Mueller, Beck of Tuebingen, Luthardt, Steinmeyer, Gerok, Uhlhorn.

13. Of English and other preachers there should be mentioned Melvin, Frederick Robertson, Canon Liddon, Alford, Newman Hall, Wilberforce, Magee, Guthrie, Caird, Cumming, Ker, Maclaren, Spurgeon, J. H. Jowett, James Stewart, A. J. Gossip, Leslie Weatherhead.

14. In the Lutheran Church of America we have had such outstanding preachers as Walther, 1811—87, Seiss, 1823—1904, and others. Walther was an eminent doctrinal preacher, who prepared his sermons with great care, well outlining his thought material and speaking in simple and beautiful language. Seiss's sermons are outstanding for their textuality, good homiletical make-up, and richness of thought. In recent years W. A. Maier was a favorite radio preacher.

15. Of the preachers in non-Lutheran Protestant churches in America such names may be mentioned as Henry Ward Beecher, Phillips Brooks, Charles G. Finney, William S. Rainsford, Dwight L. Moody, H. E. Fosdick, C. E. Macartney, and others.

16. The first part of the present century has produced many good pulpit orators. The large number of books on homiletics published in recent years is evidence of the fact that the importance of preaching is still being emphasized. JHCF

J. A. Broadus, *Lectures on the History of Preaching,* Armstrong, N. Y., 1893; E. C. Dargan, *The Art of Preaching in the Light of History,* Doran, N. Y., 1922; J. H. C. Fritz, *The Preacher's Manual,* CPH, 1941; H. C. Howard, *Princes of the Christian Pulpit and Pastorate,* Cokesbury Press, Nashville,

1927, 1928; A. W. Blackwood, *The Protestant Pulpit*, Abingdon-Cokesbury Press, N. Y., 1947.

Preadamites. The term, signifying a race of men older than Adam, was first employed in the title of a book published in 1655 in Paris by Isaac Peyrerius. A considerable number of treatises were written in opposition and others in defense, those who defended the existence of the Preadamite race, basing their mistaken argument mainly on Rom. 5:12-14. Adam is presumed to be referred to as ancestor to the Jews only while the Gentiles are held to be descended from the Preadamites.

Predestinarian Controversy (847 to 868). This was a rediscussion of the stricter and the laxer view of the Augustinian doctrine of predestination. (See *Pelagian Controversy*.) Gottschalk, a Saxon monk at Fulda, compelled to remain monk against his will by the influence of his superior, Rhabanus Maurus, was a close student of Augustine's works and became an enthusiastic adherent of his doctrine of absolute predestination. He accused the greater part of his contemporaries as semi-Pelagians because they had forgotten this doctrine or circumvented it. Gottschalk, however, went farther than Augustinianism, teaching a twofold predestination, to salvation and to condemnation (not, however, as his opponents accused him, unto evil). In 840 and 847 Gottschalk spread his doctrine in Italy. He was opposed first chiefly by Rhabanus Maurus, who, however, misrepresented his teachings. A synod of Mainz, 848, excommunicated Gottschalk as a heretic, and Hincmar of Reims, his metropolitan, was instructed to deal with him. He was again condemned by a synod at Quiersy, 849, and, refusing to recant, was whipped and imprisoned for twenty years, until his death, in the monastery of Hautvilliers. Remaining true to his convictions, he was refused Communion and burial in consecrated ground.

His doctrine did not fare so badly as himself. His hasty condemnation and the rather startling fact that two high church dignitaries condemned Augustine's doctrine aroused general attention, and soon a number of notable men entered the lists for Gottschalk. An appeal of Gottschalk to Pope Nicholas I at first promised to be successful, but was finally outmaneuvered by Hincmar. Public opinion on the question was swung around to favor Gottschalk chiefly by Bishop Prudentius of Troyes, by the learned monk Ratramnus at Corbie, and by the scholarly abbot Servatus Lupus at Ferrieres. Hincmar, hard pressed, now sought the alliance of other men, among them the learned Scotus Erigena, whose heretical views, however, brought increased suspicion on Hincmar. Nevertheless Hincmar succeeded in getting another synod of Quiersy, 853, to adopt four propositions against the system of Gottschalk. This synod did not essentially deviate from the Augustinian system, but, on the one hand, denied only a twofold predestination and, on the other hand, expressly stated that God wills the salvation of all men, although not all are saved. But many pertinent questions were passed over in silence. By the influence of Archbishop Remigius of Lyons a synod at Valence, 855, accepted six theses of strict Augustinianism against the four of the former synod to vindicate the friends of Gottschalk. Here a duplex predestination was asserted and salvation by Christ restricted to the baptized members of the Church, all others being excluded. Hincmar and Remigius intended to get together on this matter at a new synod, but the synod was never held, and the controversy ended with several lengthy books of Hincmar's against Gottschalk, leaving the debated subject as unclear as it had been before the controversy began. After seven centuries the divergent opinions on the mooted subject had fully developed into the two extremes of Roman Catholic semi-Pelagianism and Calvin's predestinarianism, between which the Lutheran Church found the right mean. For Predestinarian Controversy in the American Lutheran Church see *Ohio Synod, Luth. Ch. — Mo. Synod*.

Predestination. 1. According to Holy Scripture all that God does in time for our conversion, justification, and final glorification is based on, and flows from, an eternal decree of election or predestination, according to which God before the foundation of the world chose us in His Son Jesus Christ out of the mass of sinful mankind unto faith, the adoption of sons, and everlasting life. Holy Scripture teaches that this election is not based on any good quality or act of the elect, nor on "faith unto the end which God foresaw in the elect" (*intuitu fidei finalis*), but solely on God's grace, the good pleasure of His will in Christ Jesus. Scripture does not teach that there is an election of wrath for those who are lost, but consistently declares that God earnestly desires the salvation of all men and that those who are lost are lost by their own fault. Holy Scripture does not solve the discrepancy which exists for the human mind between the doctrine of universal grace and the doctrines of election and salvation by grace alone. The doctrine of the election of grace, properly used, will not foster carnal security, but will make the believer conscious of the matchless glory of the grace of God, serve as a constant incentive to sanctification, comfort him in the ills and tribulations of this life, and give him the blessed assurance of his final salvation. Since the doctrine of election by grace is so clearly taught in Holy Writ, it is written for the learning of all Christians. C. f. FK, *Abiding Word*, I: 522—43.

2. The decree of predestination has been defined as "an eternal act of God (Eph. 1:4; 2 Thess. 2:13; 2 Tim. 1:9), who, for His goodness' sake (2 Tim. 1:9; Rom. 9:11; 11:15) and because of the merit of the foreordained Redeemer of all mankind (2 Tim. 1:9; Eph. 1:4; 3:11), purposed to lead into everlasting life (Acts 13:48; 2 Tim. 1:9; 2:10; Rom. 8:28,29), by way and means of salvation designated for all mankind (Eph. 1:4,5; Rom. 8:29,30; 1 Pet. 1:2), a certain number (Acts 13:48; Matt. 20:16; 22:14) of certain persons (2 Tim. 2:19; 1 Pet. 1:2; John 13:18), and to procure, work, and promote what would pertain to their final salvation (Rom. 8:30; Eph. 1:11; 3:10,11; Mark 13:20-22)." (A. L. Graebner.)

3. The Lutheran Church teaches: "The predestination or eternal election of God extends only over the godly, beloved children of God, being a cause of their salvation, which He also provides, as well as disposes what belongs thereto. Upon this [predestination of God] our salvation is founded so firmly that the gates of hell cannot overcome it (John 10:28; Matt. 16:18). This [predestination of God] is not to be investigated in the secret counsel of God, but to be sought in the Word of God, where it is also revealed. But the Word of God leads us to Christ, who is the Book of Life, in whom all are written and elected that are to be saved in eternity, as it is written Eph. 1:4: 'He hath chosen us in Him [Christ] before the foundation of the world.' . . . Thus far a Christian should occupy himself [in meditation] with the article concerning the eternal election of God as it has been revealed in God's Word, which presents to us Christ as the Book of Life, which He opens and reveals to us by the preaching of the holy Gospel, as it is written Rom. 8:30: 'Whom He did predestinate, them He also called.' In Him we are to seek the eternal election of the Father, who has determined in His eternal divine counsel that He would save no one except those who know His Son Christ and truly believe on Him. Other thoughts are to be [entirely] banished [from the minds of the godly], as they proceed not from God, but from the suggestion of the evil Foe, whereby he attempts to weaken or entirely to remove from us the glorious consolation which we have in this salutary doctrine, namely, that we know [assuredly] that out of pure grace, without any merit of our own, we have been elected in Christ to eternal life and that no one can pluck us out of His hand." (*Formula of Concord*, Epitome, XI. *Trigl.*, pp. 833, 835.)

4. While the Lutheran Church thus upholds the doctrine that God has elected those who shall be saved, it maintains that grace is universal, that God has not predestined any to damnation; that the Gospel is seriously and effectively offered to all men; that, if any are lost, it is their own fault. Calvinism, on the other hand, claimed that the eternal decree of predestination was altogether arbitrary in God and that "the rest of mankind God was pleased, according to the unsearchable counsel of His own will, whereby He extendeth or withholdeth mercy as He pleaseth for the glory of His sovereign power over His creatures, to pass by and to retain them to dishonor and wrath for their sins, to the praise of His glorious justice." (*Westminster Confession of Faith*, chap. 3, § 7.) Calvinists are divided into two groups: Supralapsarians (who teach that God has created some to salvation and others unto damnation) and Infralapsarians (who maintain that God has merely permitted man to fall). The Supralapsarians' scheme that makes the decree of election motivate the decree of the Fall itself and conceives the decree of the Fall as a means for carrying out the decree of the double election, while the Infralapsarian scheme makes the decree of election come after the decree to create and permit to fall. In addition to this, we have the Arminian scheme, according to which the decree of redemption precedes the decree of election which is conditioned

upon the foreseen faith of the individual, man possessing free will and having the power to accept grace or to reject it. The Infralapsarians, then, teach that God decreed to withhold faith from the reprobate, to pass them by. Thus, according to the Calvinistic view, predestination includes reprobation, God reprobating the non-elect by His sovereign act for the manifestation of His own glory. The non-elect are thus retained to dishonor and wrath for their sins to the praise of God's glory and justice. (*Confession of Faith*, chap. 3, secs. 3—7.) In contradistinction to this view Lutheran theologians have always maintained that Scripture, in spite of all its emphasis on foreordination, never speaks of a foreordination to death or of a reprobation of human beings apart from their sins. See *Thirteen Theses*.

Lutheran Confessions; Dogmatics *; A. Hunnius, *Articulus de Providentia Dei et Aeterna Praedestinatione*, 1603; Werner Elert, *Morphologie des Luthertums*, Beck, Munich, 1931 (103—23); *Missourische Abhandlungen ueber die Gnadenwahl und Bekehrung*, CPH, 1890 and later dates; A. H. Allwardt, *Zeugnis wider die neue, falsche Gnadenwahlslehre der Missouri Synode*, Loewenbach, Milwaukee, 1882; G. J. Fritschel, *Die Schriftlehre von der Gnadenwahl*, Wartburg Publ. House, 1914; G. J. Fritschel, *Zur Einigung der amerikanisch-lutherischen Kirche in der Lehre von der Bekehrung und Gnadenwahl*, Wartburg Publ. House, 1914; C. W. Schaeffer, W. J. Mann, A. Spaeth, H. E. Jacobs, "Concerning the Dogma of Predestination," *Luth. Ch. Rev.*, III: 223—36. During the time of the Predestination Controversy in America a voluminous literature arose, some of the more important is given in J. L. Neve, *Brief History of the Lutheran Church in America;* much material is found in contemporary church periodicals and tracts; thus Concordia Seminary, St. Louis, has collections under the titles: C. F. W. Walther, *Tracts on Predestination Essays in Lutheran Polemics;* F. Pieper, *Conversion and Election, A Plea for a United Lutheranism in America*, CPH, 1913; L. S. Keyser, *Election and Conversion, A Frank Discussion of Dr. Pieper's Book on Conversion and Election, with Suggestions for Lutheran Concord and Union on Another Basis*, German Lit. Bd., Burlington, Iowa, 1914; A. L. Graebner, "The Doctrine of Predestination as Taught in Eph. 1:3-6,"

Theol. Quart., 5:25—46; T. Engelder, "Let's Get Together on the Doctrine of Conversion and Election," *CTM*, VI:539—43; T. Graebner, "Predestination and Human Responsibility," *CTM*, V:164—71; J. T. Mueller, "Die Gnadenwahl nach Zeit und Ewigkeit," *CTM*, V:748—57; F. Kramer, "The Doctrine of Election or Conversion," *Abiding Word*, CPH (I:522—43); articles in Jacobs-Haas, *Lutheran Encyclopedia*. These articles give the various positions held at the time when the work was published. The bibliography above also gives titles representative of various positions.

Predigtamt. See *Ministerial Office.*

Pre-existence of Christ. See *Christ Jesus.*

Pre-existence of the Soul. See *Transmigration of Souls.*

Preface. The beginning of the Communion Service proper. It includes the *Salutation* ("The Lord be with you"), the *Sursum Corda* ("Lift up your hearts"), *Eucharistia* ("Let us give thanks unto the Lord, our God"), *Contestation* ("It is truly meet, right, and salutary," etc.) and the Proper Prefaces. The Preface is a very early part of worship, being mentioned in the 103d canon of the African code (418).

Prefect, Apostolic. In the Roman Catholic Church, a dignitary who is in charge of a territory which does not have a residing bishop.

Preger, John William (1827—98). German theologian; wrote a biography of Matthias Flacius, history of German Mysticism, and edited Luther's *Table Talks.*

Prelate. In Roman Catholicism, an ecclesiastic who has jurisdiction over other ecclesiastics and rights of precedence.

Prelude (Praeludium; Vorspiel). The church prelude is a composition which is part of the liturgical service of worship, in which it is used to introduce either the service itself or one of its hymns. Its performance, therefore, is not an end in itself, nor is it to introduce a foreign, inappropriate, and subjective element into the church service. Since the prelude is introductory in character and, in addition, a part of the service of worship, its very nature, style, and spirit should be thoroughly in keeping with the service in which it is used; if it is used to introduce a hymn, its mood, key, tempo, and spirit should be related to the hymn as closely as possible that both might constitute a unit and help unify and integrate the worship service. While fitting free preludes, which are not based directly on thematic materials taken from a hymn, may be used, the Lutheran Church, in particular, urges that hymn preludes be used. These are based directly on hymns of the Church. The chorale preludes of the Lutheran masters of the 17th and 18th centuries are among the finest organ music extant; they constitute a large and important segment of the great musical heritage of the Lutheran Church, are heard often in concerts and recitals, but are best suited for use in a decorous and dignified service of worship.

Premillenarians. See *Millennium*, 7.

Premonstratensians. An order of canons * regular, founded by Norbert, at Prémontré, France, in 1120, to preach and to achieve personal holiness. Inner decay, the Reformation, and secularization have left its membership small, but it has numerous tertiaries in England and America.

Pre-Raffaelites. Members of a brotherhood of artists, including Dante Gabriel Rossetti, W. Holman Hunt, John Millais, Thomas Woolner, and William Michael Rossetti, whose chief aim was to return to the truth and earnestness which distinguished the Italian painters before Raffael.

Presanctified, Mass of. In the Roman Catholic Church a celebration of the Mass in which there is no consecration of the wafer, but the priest uses and consumes a wafer which was previously consecrated or sanctified. This Mass is celebrated on Good Friday only.

Presbyter. See *Elders; Polity, Ecclesiastical*, 7.

Presbyterian Bodies. The Presbyterian and Reformed Churches perpetuated the doctrinal and governmental features (see *Polity, Ecclesiastical*) which were emphasized by John Calvin and perpetuated in Switzerland, Holland, France, western Germany (by the Reformed Church*), and in Scotland, Ireland, England, and America.

1. *Presbyterianism in Scotland.* Calvin's doctrinal and ecclesiastical system was transferred to Scotland by John Knox * and established there in 1620.

In order to understand the history of Scotch Presbyterianism, we must bear in mind the political, social, and religious condition prevailing at the time wnen Knox became influential. In Scotland the Reformation had found root at a very early date, and the efforts to put down by force the growing spirit of inquiry and the return to primitive Christianity proved utterly ineffectual. The protomartyr of the Scottish Reformation was Patrick Hamilton, who was burned at the stake February 29, 1528. The martyrdom of George Wishart was dreadfully avenged by the murder of Cardinal Beaton. The assassination caused a certain reaction in favor of Rome, for the cardinal had been ardently patriotic. The Romanist party sought help from France; the Protestants, from England. The assassins of the cardinal and many who were not in sympathy with them were compelled to take refuge in the castle of St. Andrews, which, after a protracted siege, surrendered to the attacks of the royal army and of a French fleet. Among the defenders of St. Andrews was John Knox, the founder of the Scotch Presbyterian Church. Having toiled as a galley slave for nineteen months, Knox was released and became one of the chaplains of Edward VI. As such he took part in the preparation of the English prayer book of 1552 and became one of the most potent factors in introducing Reformed principles and doctrines.

The year 1560 witnessed the consolidation, national recognition, and establishment of the Reformed Church. In this year the first general assembly was held, and the *Scotch Confession of Faith* and the *First Book of Discipline* were issued. The government of the Church was vested in superintendents, ministers, doctors, elders, and deacons. The Lord's Supper was to be celebrated four times a year. In towns there was to be daily service. Marriages were to be performed "in open face and public audience of the Kirk." The *Book of Common Order*, often called "John Knox's Liturgy," originally prepared by the English congregation at Geneva for its own use, was recommended in 1564 and was generally, though not exclusively, used in public worship for eighty years. The Reformation in Scotland took a form different from that of the Reformation in England, partly because in England the king and the bishops were in favor of the Reformation, while in Scotland they were against it. The

Reformation in Scotland was effected by Presbyterians, and the government of the Church naturally became Presbyterian. The present Kirk of Scotland has been established in its essential features, both in doctrine and polity, since 1567, when its presbyterian form of government was acknowledged by Parliament and it became the state church.

The relation of Church and State caused a number of divisions. The first formal division arose in 1688, when the Cameronians, dissatisfied with the compromising spirit of the Church, refused to concur in the Revolution settlement. The separatists remained an isolated body until 1876, when they joined the Free Church. Next came two secessions, which eventually coalesced in the United Presbyterian Church. The first, the Associate Synod, originated through the deposition in 1733 of Ebenezer Erskine (1680—1754) for preaching a sermon claiming for Christ the headship of the Church and declaring the "Church the freest society in the world." This was aimed especially at an Act of Assembly (1732), which had placed the election of ministers in the hands, not of the congregation, but of the majority of elders and heritors. In 1747 the body of seceders had 45 congregations, when the great "breach" took place on the question of the lawfulness of taking a certain burgess oath. This breach led to complete separation, which was not healed until 1820, when the United Secession Church was formed. This Church was distinguished for its foreign missionary enthusiasm and grew and prospered until the union of 1847. The second secession, which later led to the formation of the United Presbyterian Church, was the Relief Church, which originated with Thomas Gillespie, who stood almost alone until 1761, when a presbytery was formed "for the relief of Christians oppressed in their Christian privileges." This Church was distinguished for its liberal spirit. The union of the Associate Synod and Relief Churches was accomplished in 1847, when the United Presbyterian Church was organized.

Latest in origin, but largest and most influential, came the Free Church, in 1843. The Free Church sprang into being on a national scale. Those who came out of the Established Church claimed to be the true Church of Scotland and at once set about making its whole organization independent of the the State. The contention of the Free Church party was that the spiritual liberties of the Church were being challenged by the State and that the whole principle of spiritual independence was involved. The year 1900 is a historic date in Scottish history, when, amid a scene of great enthusiasm, the union of Free and United Presbyterian Churches in Scotland was consummated in Edinburgh, the new body adopting the name of United Free Church of Scotland. The doctrinal position of Scottish Presbyterianism has never been defined anew since the *Westminster Confession* approved it in 1646. The statement of the present position of the United Free Church is contained in the Acts of 1905 regarding the spiritual independence and of 1900 effecting the Union. With the exception of minor modifications the theology of the United Free Church is the Calvinistic doctrine of the *Westminster Confession.* — Other independent churches are: The *Free Presbyterian Church of Scotland* (1893), the *Reformed Presbyterian Church,* which is the legitimate descendant and representative of the Covenanted Church of Scotland in its period of greatest purity (1638—49), and the *United Original Secession Church,* which dates from 1733, when Ebenezer Erskine was deposed. Presbyterian Church in the United States: see below.

2. *Presbyterian Church of England.* Also in England the Presbyterian Church, especially the presbyterial polity, met with much hostility. As a result of Queen Elizabeth's oppression a considerable number of persons in 1556 had separated themselves from the Established Church and maintained religious services according to the Presbyterian order. Their sufferings did not deter others who still remained in the Church from going still farther and holding conferences, or ministers' meetings, one of which, in London, deputed in 1572 two of its members to visit Wandsworth, a village near that city, where they formally organized a "Particular Church," in accordance with Presbyterian order. This was the first open formation in England of a church different from that which had been established. Under Charles I, Laud, who said he regarded Presbytery as worse than Romanism, promoted those Star Chamber prosecutions of the Nonconformists which have always been regarded as a stain in English history. The king's own conduct drove the great mass of the Presbyterian Church into the ranks of the Parlia-

mentarians, while the subsequent alliance of the Parliament with the Scottish army, together with the decisions of the Westminster Assembly in 1647, resulted in the overthrow of the Episcopal Church and its replacement in the establishment by that of the Presbytery. By this Assembly the Calvinistic system of doctrine was expressed in the *Westminster Confession* and its system of polity in the *Directory of Church Government*.

The establishment was now Presbyterian, yet the Presbyterian polity was accepted largely only in London and Lancashire. Cromwell replaced Presbytery by Independency. But in 1662, by the Act of Uniformity, every minister not episcopally ordained was obliged to be reordained; adherence to everything in the *Book of Common Prayer* was made obligatory; obedience to the bishop and abjuration of the Solemn League and Covenant, with an additional oath declaring that it was not lawful under any circumstances to take up arms against the king, was insisted upon. More than 2,000 parish ministers refused obedience to the Act and on August 24 resigned their congregations, walking out of their manses and leaving their pulpits empty. By the Conventicle Act these men were forbidden to preach to their former congregations and by the Five-mile Act could not live within five miles of their former parishes. In 1688 came the Revolution, and under the "Happy Union" arrangement of 1691 all branches of Nonconformity were consolidated into a single community, though no authority existed to enforce the *Westminster Confession* or the *Directory of Church Government*. In order to distinguish between the enemies of the parties opposing the episcopacy, the following facts must be borne in mind. While the Puritans agreed with the Established Church of England as to doctrine and polity, they insisted upon "purity" with regard to elimination of every ceremony and rite which they looked on as remnants of popery. When the Established Church insisted upon "conformity," the Puritans, not willing to yield, were called "Nonconformists." The Puritans were strict Calvinists, but opposed the episcopacy. Those who desired that the presbyterial polity of Geneva be adopted were called Presbyterians; such as rejected the presbyterial form of government and demanded that each congregation remain independent were called "Independ-

ents" or "Congregationalists." From this last party, later on, the Baptist Church was largely recruited.

Not a few of the congregations had left the parish churches in 1662 and provided themselves with small chapels for their religious services. These survived for a time, but later on they joined the Scotch Presbyterians, who had been gathered into small congregations in London. By 1772 these London congregations, 7 in number, formed themselves into "the Scots Presbytery of London." This "presbytery," while claiming communion with the Church of Scotland, had no ecclesiastical connection with it and was really little more than a "ministers' meeting." In 1836 the presbytery changed its title to that of "The London Presbytery in Communion with the Church of Scotland." In 1839 the Scottish Assembly counseled these members to organize themselves as "The Presbyterian Synod in England." In 1843 came the fateful disruption of the Scottish Establishment, when the Presbyterian Synod in England divided. The majority cast its lot with the Scottish Free Church and retained the name of Presbyterian Synod in England, while the minority remained in connection with the Scottish National Church and formed itself into the "Scottish Presbytery in London in Connection with the Church of Scotland." In 1850 this presbytery, like the two others that had been formed, was organized as "The Synod of the Church of Scotland in England." The Free Church "Presbyterian Synod in England" remained in friendly relations with the Old Presbyterian and the United Secession Congregations, so that, in 1863, the United Presbyterian Church in Scotland formed its congregations in England into the English Synod. In 1876 the English Synod united with the Presbyterian Synod in England, the uniting churches taking the name of "The Presbyterian Church of England."

3. *Presbyterian Church in Ireland.* At the time of the Ulster Plantation, under James I (1603—25), Presbyterians gained a permanent footing in Ireland. The settlers, most of whom were Scottish Presbyterians, began to arrive in 1610. Presbyterian ministers began to come from Scotland in 1613, and for a time they were appointed, without reordination, to vacant churches in the Established Church. In 1641 there was a rebellion in Ireland, in the course of which thousands of Protestants were massacred. In 1642

the Scottish army was sent to quell the rebellion, each Scottish regiment having a chaplain and a regular kirk session selected from the officers. These, on June 10, 1642, at Carrickfergus, Ireland, formed the first presbytery, consisting of five chaplains and four elders. Other ministers were sent over from Scotland, and new presbyteries were formed. At the time of Cromwell there was a General Synod, with 80 congregations and 70 ministers. In 1661, 64 ministers were rejected for refusing to conform to the Established Church, and many Presbyterians emigrated to America. King William III authorized a payment of 1,200 pounds per annum to the Presbyterian ministers of Ireland in recognition of the loyal support of Presbyterians on his arrival in Ireland in 1690. This was the beginning of the *Regium Donum*, which subsequently was increased and continued to be given to ministers until 1871. Toward the end of the first half of the 18th century some of the ministers came under the influence of Modernism. The Congregation of Seceders was formed in 1741, and in time there came to be a Secession Synod as well as a Synod of Ulster. The ministers of secession congregations also received a *Regium Donum* from the government. In 1825 some of the ministers of the Synod of Ulster were charged with spreading Arian views; so under the leadership of Rev. Henry Cooke the Synod of Ulster declared in favor of the doctrine of the Trinity. Seventeen ministers in 1829 withdrew from the synod and subsequently formed the Remonstrant Synod of Ulster. In consequence of this the two orthodox synods, the Synod of Ulster and the Secession Synod, were united in 1840 and formed the General Assembly of the Presbyterian Church in Ireland. Even before the Ulster Plantation there were Presbyterians in the south of Ireland. Gradually increasing in number, the Southern Association, in 1809, became the Synod of Munster. In 1840 the orthodox members of this synod withdrew and formed themselves into the Presbytery of Munster, which in 1854 joined the General Assembly of the Presbyterian Church in Ireland. — Besides these synods, another Presbyterian Church flourished, *viz.*, the Reformed Presbyterian, or Covenanting, Church of Ireland, which traces its origin to the Covenanters of Scotland. Covenanters who had fled from persecution in Scotland and had settled in the north-

eastern part of the island became the founders of the Covenanting Church in Ireland, called the Society People. The presbytery was organized in 1792 and in 1811 a synod of 12 ministers. In 1840 a number of congregations and ministers withdrew on account of a controversy regarding the power of a civil ruler. Some of these congregations later joined the Presbyterian Church of Ireland. Standards of the Church are the *Westminster Confession* and *Catechisms*, together with the *Testimony*, in which the Church's distinctive position is clearly defined. — *The Secession Church in Ireland.* The Secession movement in Scotland, spreading to Ireland, established itself widely in the north of that country. The Secession Church in Ireland, at present numbering only a few congregations, is organized under the name of the Associate Synod of Ireland or the Presbyterian Synod of Ireland.

4. *Presbyterianism in America.* The Presbyterians in the United States are primarily of English extraction, totaling about 3,100,000 (1950). Those of Scottish descent number only about 200,000 (1950). a. The *Presbyterian Church in the United States of America* (Northern Presbyterians). While Anglican ministers with Presbyterian views were among the early American colonists, the first presbytery was organized in 1706. The Presbyterian Church was unable to establish itself in the New England States, which was the stronghold of Congregationalism, but gained its largest following in Pennsylvania. The Great Awakening, during the first half of the eighteenth century, deeply affected Presbyterian church life. The Tennents, father and son, endorsed the revival system of Whitefield and demanded that only such candidates should be admitted to the ministry as had "experienced" conversion, and founded the Log College, later Princeton, to train candidates whose chief requisite was "a religious experience." Tennent and his followers were known as the New Side, while the Old Side believed that Calvinism was theologically opposed to revivalism and that only college-bred men should be admitted to the ministry. This controversy was settled in 1788. During the first part of the nineteenth century the Presbyterian and Congregational Churches operated under the Plan of Union which allowed Congregational ministers to serve Presbyterian congregations and vice versa. This plan was

abandoned in 1837. However, the aftermaths led to the division into old- and new-school Presbyterians, in which Albert Barnes of the new school was brought to trial for heresy. As a result of the Kentucky Revival the Cumberland Presbyterian Church seceded from the Kentucky presbytery in 1810. In 1858 the Presbyterian Church, United States (Southern Presbyterian) came into being as a result of the slavery question. Toward the close of the nineteenth century liberal theology began to make inroads into the Presbyterian Church. The Charles A. Briggs * heresy trial, and especially the revision of the confession indicated a drifting away from the old Calvinistic position. Liberal theology was openly advocated in the Auburn Affirmation of 1923.* The Welsh Presbyterians united with the Northern Presbyterians in 1920. The union endeavors between the Presbyterian Church and the Episcopalian Church have been unsuccessful until now (1950). b. The *Cumberland Presbyterian Church*, like the Christian Churches * and the Disciples,* grew out of the Kentucky Revival under the leadership of James McGready. Many Presbyterians frowned on the revival technique, the employment of untrained preachers, revision of the *Westminister Confession* in the interest of Arminian theology and the principles of revivalism, and especially upon the "bodily exercises" of the Kentucky Revival. The Synod of Kentucky dissolved the Cumberland Presbytery because it had sanctioned and encouraged the unpresbyterian principles of the Kentucky Revival. In 1810 the disenfranchised Presbyterians organized the Cumberland Presbytery, and later the Cumberland Presbyterian Church. Several attempts at reunion with the parent body have miscarried as well as union endeavors with the Methodist Church. Doctrinally, the Cumberland Presbyterians hold a position between Calvinism and Arminianism, maintaining the sovereignty of God and the perseverance of saints, but also the doctrine of universal salvation. There is also a colored Cumberland Presbyterian Church. c. The *Presbyterian Church in the United States* (Southern Presbyterian) is virtually identical in theology and polity with the Northern Presbyterian Church. The schism which separated the two was occasioned by the slavery question in 1858. The Southern Presbyterians have remained more conservative in theology than the Northern Presbyterians, though in 1938 the Southern Presbyterians revised the *Westminster Confession* along the same lines as the Northern Presbyterians. d. The *Orthodox Presbyterian Church* was founded by J. Gresham Machen in 1936 when he and a number of followers in opposition to Modernism in the Northern Presbyterian Church were suspended from the ministry on the ground of insubordination. e. The *Bible Presbyterian Church* was founded by a number of men who with Machen had been suspended, but who differed with Machen on abstinence and eschatology. f. The Scotch Presbyterians are frequently known as Covenanters.* Many of the Covenanters interpreted covenanting not only as a political, but also as a religious function. Covenanting was viewed as a public testimony to one's belief that the Bible must be literally followed not only in the realm of religion, but in the realm of the social relations as well. For that reason some Covenanters were opposed to the singing of hymns not contained in the Bible. They observe Sunday as the New Testament Sabbath and practice close Communion. Covenanting also forbids them to participate in the affairs of a government which does not recognize the Triune God. Nor will they permit membership in secret societies. The Scotch Presbyterians have remained very conservative in their Calvinistic theology and have been strong advocates of the inerrancy of Scripture. In America these views are held by the following groups: The *Synod of the Reformed Presbyterian Church of North America, The General Synod of the Associate Reformed Presbyterian Church, The Synod of the Associate Presbyterian Church of North America. Reformed Presbyterian Church in North America — General Synod.* g. The *United Presbyterian Church in the United States* is the union of several groups of Covenanters and Secession Scotch Presbyterians effected in Pittsburgh in 1858. It professes the doctrine of verbal inspiration and the *Westminster Confession.* This group, however, now teaches universal grace, unconditional universal infant salvation, open Communion. It is no longer opposed to the singing of hymns and permits membership in secret orders. See *Religious Bodies (U. S.), Bibliography.*

Presbyterian Church in the United States of America. See *Presbyterian Bodies,* 4 a.

Presbyterian Confessions. 1. Early Protestant statements in Scotland took the form of *Covenants* by which the signers agreed to defend to the death "the true Church" (1556, 1557, 1559). The earlier Covenants were safeguards against Roman Catholicism, the later, against episcopacy. The *National Covenant* (subscribed by James VI in 1581; also called *King's Confession* and *Negative Confession)* endorsed the Confession of 1560 and contains a strong statement against the Papacy. The renewal of the Covenant (1638) included statements against bishops and measures of Charles I. The *Solemn League and Covenant* (adopted by the English Parliament 1644) was used by Puritans in their attempt to force Presbyterianism on the Established Church of England as a reward to the Scots for their assistance in the struggle against Charles I.

2. The *Scotch Confession of Faith* was hastily drawn up by Knox and his associates and ratified by the three estates (1560). It is decidedly Calvinistic. In it the Church is stated to be one from the beginning to the end of the world and to exist where the Gospel is preached, the Sacraments are administered, and discipline is exercised.

3. The *Westminster Confession.* a) The Long Parliament made it possible for the Puritans to seek a reformation of the English Church and a system of doctrine harmonious with the Church in Scotland and on the Continent. Parliament issued an ordinance (June 12, 1643) ordering an assembly of divines to meet at Westminster on July 1, 1643, and draw up articles for the national Church. The Assembly consisted of 121 members (9 Episcopalians, who seldom attended; Presbyterians in the majority; a small but influential number of Independents; a few Erastians). Ten Lords and 20 Commoners also attended. Six Scottish representatives came in after the Assembly and Parliament had bound themselves by the Solemn League and Covenant. The Assembly drew up seven documents: 1. Form of church government which forced Presbyterianism on the Anglican Church; 2. *Book of Discipline;* 3. Directory for ordination; 4. *Larger Catechism;* 5. *Smaller Catechism.* (The Apostles' Creed is omitted from the Larger and annexed to the Smaller with the note: "Not . . . composed by the Apostles . . . or to be esteemed canonical

Scripture." The Descent to Hell is described as continuing "in the state of the dead and under the power of death until the third day." The Shorter Catechism begins: "What is the chief end of man? To glorify God and to enjoy Him forever"); 6. Directory for worship; 7. *Westminster Confession of Faith.* b) The *Westminster Confession* presents Calvinism in its maturity. It starts from God's sovereignty and justice, rather than from His love and mercy, and makes the predestinarian scheme control the historical and Christological scheme. Noteworthy tenets are: 1. "By the decree of God, for the manifestation of His glory, some men and angels are predestinated unto everlasting life, and others foreordained to everlasting death . . . to the praise of His glorious justice." 2. Perseverance of the saints. 3. The spiritual reception of Christ's body and blood by "worthy receivers" and the reception of the outward elements (without "the thing signified thereby") by "ignorant and wicked men." 4. *Covenant theology (i. e.,* God offered salvation to man on two covenants: works and grace. The first came to an end through the sin of Adam. The second is divided into a period of the Law in the Old Testament and of Grace in the New). 5. The Sabbath is kept holy when men are taken up "the whole time in the public and private exercise of His worship." 6. Civil magistrates may not assume "the administration of the Word and Sacraments or the power of the keys," but are to aid the Church and suppress heretics.

4. In England the Confession was set aside when the *Thirty-Nine Articles* were reinstated by Charles II (1660). The General Assembly of Scotland approved the *Westminster Confession* (1647) and required ministers and elders to subscribe it (1690, 1699, etc.). This remained law until the *Declaratory Act* (1879) modified some of the extreme Calvinistic statements. In 1890 the English Presbyterian Church had adopted *Twenty-Four Articles of Faith* and later (1892) declared that the *Westminster Confession* must be understood in the light of these. The *Savoy Declaration* (1658) and London Confession of English Baptists incorporated large sections of it. The American Presbyterian churches early adopted it, the Synod of Philadelphia approving it in its Adopting Act (1729). Later, chapters on government and religious liberty were modified. It was the standard confession of New England Congregational-

ist churches until the 19th century. Today it is authoritative in most Presbyterian churches though often modified in content. EL

P. Schaff, *Creeds of Christendom*, Harpers, New York, 1899—1905 (3 vols.); T. Hoyer, "The Historical Background of the Westminster Assembly," *CTM*, VIII:573—91 (good bibliography listed).

Presbyterian Synod in England. See *Presbyterian Bodies*, 2.

Presbyterian System. See *Polity, Ecclesiastical*, 7.

Presbytery. 1 Tim. 4:14, a body of individuals responsible for the teaching of the Church. In modern Presbyterian polity the ministers and elders of the churches of a given area organized to adjudicate and to administer authority over churches and ministers.

See *Elders; Polity, Ecclesiastical*, 7.

Preschool Education. See *Parish Education*, B.

Prescience, Divine. Prescience is an attribute of God sometimes called foreknowledge. It is difficult to conceive of God's prescience because man has no analogous faculty. We can make certain inferences about the future, but God beholds all things as if present. The prescience of God comprehends all events, however contingent on human activity or freedom. It comprehends all temporal events (Ps. 90:2; Matt. 24:36). That God has foreknowledge also of the acts of man, both good and evil, is the plain teaching of Scripture (Is. 48:8). But knowing all things as they are, God knows the acts of men as the acts of rational and responsible beings, who have a will of their own and act according to the counsels of their hearts (Jer. 7:24); and thus the foreknowledge of God does not exclude, but rather includes, the agency of the human will and the causality of human counsels. — Again, "God's foreknowledge of His own acts, especially of the rulings of His providence, does not exclude, but includes, the prayers of His children, which He in His counsel has answered before they were uttered, permitting them to enter as a powerful factor into the government of the universe (Is. 65:24; James 5:16f.; Ps. 33:10ff.)." A. L. Graebner.

Presence, Divine. See *Holy Ghost*.

Presiding Elders (now called District Superintendents). In the Methodist communion, elders who are appointed for limited terms by the bishops to represent them in the care of the interests of the Church in particular districts. Their duty is to visit churches, preside at quarterly and district conferences, and supervise traveling and local preachers.

Press, Religious. See *Publication Houses; Religious Press*.

Pressius, Paul. See *Reformed Confessions*, E 4.

Preterition. A doctrine of election held by Calvinists, according to which God passed by a portion of mankind and retained it to dishonor and wrath (*Westminster Confession of Faith*, 3:7). See *Predestination*.

Pre-Theological Schools. See *Ministry, Education of*, VII.

Preus, A. C. See *Evangelical Lutheran Church*.

Preus, Christian Keyser (1852 to 1921). Graduate of Luther College, Decorah, Iowa, and Concordia Seminary, St. Louis, Mo.; pastor; professor at Luther College and its president 1902 to 1921; vice-president of Norwegian Synod.

Preus, Herman Amberg. B. in Norway, June 16, 1825; graduate of Christiania University 1848; emigrated 1851; one of the organizers of the Norwegian Synod and its second president; coeditor of *Maanedstidende* 1859—68; author of articles and pamphlets; president of Synodical Conference; proposed Negro Missions 1877; d. July 2, 1894.

Prevenient Grace. See *Grace*.

Pride. The opposite of humility. Pride is always represented in the Bible as sin and vice. Cp. Prov. 21:4; 16:18; 29:23; 26:12; Is. 3:18ff.; 1 Cor. 4:7; 1 Pet. 5:5; James 4:16; 1 John 2:16. Pride may manifest itself 1) with respect to God, as spiritual arrogance and self-assertion (self-righteousness), Matt. 23:6ff.; Luke 18:11; Rev. 3:17,18, etc.; 2) with respect to other people, as haughtiness, feeling of superiority, boasting, vainglory, Prov. 14:21; Job 12:2; Ps. 101:5; Jer. 9:23. God will punish the proud, Deut. 8:11ff.; Prov. 8:13; Is. 2:11ff.; John 5:44; James 4:6. See *Concordia Pulpit*, 1936, Vol. VII, 320ff.; Fritz, *Preacher's Manual*, 168, 316; Luther IV:2071; I:985; XIII:1213, 2307; *Trigl.*, p. 683, 21; Kretzmann, *Pop. Com.*, O. T., I, 455; II, 222, 237, 616.

Prierias (*Silvester Mazzolini*, called Prierias from his birthplace Prierio).

Magister Sacri Palatii (Master of the Sacred Palace) and professor of theology; undertook a refutation of Luther's theses in his *Dialogus,* etc., "a dialog against the presumptuous conclusions of Martin Luther." Luther's brief and pointed answer called forth a reply from Prierias (1518), which the Reformer published with the necessary comment and sent to the author with the advice to stop writing books and making himself ridiculous.

Priest, Christ as. The priestly office of Christ is the heart of the Christian faith. This topic takes us back to the climax of Old Testament worship and the silence of the multitude in the moment of the reconciliation with God through the hands of a mediator.

While in Hebrew conceptions the prophet was the representative of God, the priest was the representative of the people (Heb. 5:1). Thus Christ was given by God to be man's Representative (Heb. 2:14-17).

The priestly work of Christ was foretold in Old Testament prophecy and foreshadowed in types prefiguring Christ (Ps. 110:1, 4; entirely priestly office). The priests and sacrifices of the Old Testament were imperfect, but Christ, His work, and His sacrifice were perfect (1 Pet. 1:19, 20; Heb. 9:12-14).

Later dogmaticians distinguish in Christ's performance of His priestly office between the active and passive obedience. The active obedience consists in His substitutionary work of freeing us from the demands of the Law and obtaining for us a perfect righteousness by perfectly fulfilling, as our Substitute, the entire Law in all its demands so that His righteousness may be made our own by faith (Matt. 5:17; Gal. 4:4, 5; Rom. 10:4). His passive obedience consists in His substitutionary work of freeing men from the penalties provided by the Law of God for all sinners. He did this by taking our sins upon Himself and suffering in our stead our punishment (Is. 53; Gal. 3:13; Eph. 5:2; Col. 1:14; 1 John 1:7; 1 Pet. 2:21-24).

Christ's priesthood continued after His ascension to heaven (Heb. 7:23, 24). He continues to intercede for us as our High Priest (Heb. 7:25; Rom. 8:34; 1 John 2:1, 2). C. f. OCH, "Office or Work of Christ," *Abiding Word,* CPH, 1947 (II:135—44).

Priesthood. 1. In the New Testament there is no need of a priesthood to offer sacrifice for sin as did the priesthood of the Old Testament (Heb. 7:22-28; 10:9-14). Instead, all believers constitute a spiritual priesthood (1 Pet. 2:9; Rev. 5:10), which is to offer itself to God (Rom. 12:1; Heb. 13:15) and into whose charge Christ has given all the rights and powers of His kingdom (Matt. 18:18-20; 1 Cor. 3:21-23). To all believers belongs the right of selecting and calling ministers (Acts 1:15-26; 6:2-6), whom God has chosen and appointed (Acts 13:2, 4; 1 Cor. 12:28), and of setting them apart through ordination (Acts 14:23; 6:6), to act as servants of Christ and His Church (2 Cor. 4:5) in preaching the Word and administering the Sacraments (Titus 1:9; 1 Cor. 4:1).

2. Opposed to this Scriptural position stands the Roman doctrine of the priesthood. 1) Rome teaches that "there is in the New Testament a visible and external priesthood" (Council of Trent, Sess. XXIII, can. 1), whose "proper and especial functions" are the offering of sacrifice in the Mass and the forgiving and retaining of sins. (*Catechismus Romanus,* II, 7. 24.) This is brought out clearly at the ordination of a priest (see *Ordination*). As the propitiatory sacrifice of the Mass is the center of Roman worship, so it is also the foundation and the keystone of the priesthood. A subordinate place is assigned to the preaching of the Word; it is not even held an essential of the priestly office. (Council of Trent, *l. c.*) Since the Mass as a propitiatory sacrifice is purely a human figment, the whole theory of the Roman priesthood collapses with it. 2) Rome denies the laity every right in connection with the ordination and calling of the clergy. "In the ordination of bishops, priests, and of the other orders neither the consent nor vocation nor authority of the people ... is required." (Council of Trent, Sess. XXIII, chap. 4.) A curse is pronounced on anyone claiming such rights for the laity. (*Ibid.,* can. 7.) The bishop inquires into the fitness of candidates, decides who shall be ordained, ordains them, assigns them to churches, transfers them, and deposes them, as he sees fit. The congregations have nothing whatever to say in the matter. 3) Rome claims that in ordination an indelible sign is impressed (see *Character Indelebilis; Ordination*) and that those who have this sign, therefore the clergy, by divine right form an order essentially distinct from those who have not that sign, the laity. (Council of Trent, Sess. XIII, can. 4.) It is asserted that this

clerical order, or hierarchy, is superior to the laity, is the sole depositary of all spiritual or sacred authority, and is therefore vested with the right of ruling and governing the Church. It decides all questions relating to doctrine, policy, and government, while the laity is frankly declared to be neither competent nor authorized to speak in the name of God or the Church in such matters. Its only function is respectfully to accept and obey the decisions and orders of the hierarchy. Not even the property of the congregation is under the laity's control. If laymen are commissioned to share in the administration of such property, this is granted them not as a right, but as a privilege. Even then they can act only under the control of the ordinary,* with whom the final decision rests.

3. There are few doctrines in which the Roman Church has so obviously turned the plans of God upside down as in its doctrine of the priesthood. Christ instituted a ministry of the Word, and Sacraments, which is to impart to men the reconciliation with God accomplished through His own all-availing, ever-sufficient sacrifice (1 Cor. 2:2); Rome established a priesthood to reconcile men to God through its own sacrifices in a man-made ceremony. Christ, the Head, gave to His Church, the body, consisting of all believers, all the rights, powers, and privileges which He conferred (vide supra); Rome vested these rights, powers, and privileges in her priesthood, robbing the laity, the larger part of the Church, of nearly its whole heritage. Christ bade His followers practice humility, acknowledge one another as equals, and serve one another (Matt. 20:25-28; 23:8; 1 Pet. 5:3; 2 Cor. 4:5); Rome denies this equality and demands that her priesthood be acknowledged and respected as a superior class, to whom unquestioning submission and obedience are due. (For obligations of priesthood see Celibacy; Breviary; for gradations of rank, Hierarchy; Ordination; Bishops.)

Priesthood, Universal. The New Testament recognizes in Christ the Representative of the true primeval priesthood after the order of Melchizedek (Heb. 7 and 8); but there is nothing corresponding to the priests of the Old Covenant in the Christian Church. The idea which pervades the New Testament teaching is that of a universal priesthood. All true believers are made kings and priests (Rev. 1:6; 1 Pet. 2:9), bring spiritual sacrifices (Rom. 12:1), and, having received a true priestly consecration, may draw near and enter the Holy of Holies (Heb. 10:19-22). As priests the Christians possess all the treasures won for mankind by the suffering of Christ. They have God, Christ, pardon, the means of grace, the keys of heaven (1 Cor. 3:21). They have the privilege of free access to God without human mediators (Eph. 2:14, 18). As possessor of the priesthood, the Church teaches, administers the Sacraments, judges doctrine, absolves and excommunicates, calls ministers and teachers, etc. If a congregation or a union of congregations does missionary work, trains ministers, and publishes literature in defense of the truth, it is by virtue of the universal priesthood. See also preceding article. See Keys, Office of.

L. W. Spitz, "The Universal Priesthood of Believers," Abiding Word, CPH, 1946 (I:321 ff., lists references to essays by E. Pardieck, G. Stoeckhardt, and others); R. C. H. Lenski, Kings and Priests, The Universal Priesthood of Believers Presented on the Basis of Holy Writ, Luth. Lit. Bd., Burlington, Iowa, 1927.

Priestley, Joseph (1733—1804). English theologian and famous chemist and physicist; became dissenting minister; later waged bitter controversy against all positive Christian doctrines; emigrated to America, 1794, where he organized several Unitarian congregations.

Priestly Code. See Higher Criticism, 6.

Prima Delinatio Apologiae. See Lutheran Confessions, A 3.

Primacy of the Pope. See Roman Catholic Confessions, E 3.

Primate. See Hierarchy; Roman Catholic Confessions.

Prime. See Canonical Hours.

Primer. See Anglican Confessions, 9.

Primitive Baptists. See Baptist Bodies, 11.

Primitive Colored Baptists. See Baptist Bodies, 12.

Primitive Methodist Church. See Methodist Bodies, 4 b.

Principal. See Parish Education, K 5.

Prior. A monastic official ranking next below an abbot and acting either as assistant to an abbot or as superior of a monastic house which has no abbot.

Priscillianists. A sect of Gnostic-Manichaean tendencies in Spain and Gaul. Their religious system was dualistic and emanationistic. They forbade not only carnal pleasures, but also marriage; and yet they seem to have indulged occasionally in impure orgies. Their leader was a layman, Priscillianus, later bishop of Avila. A synod at Saragossa, 380, excommunicated them, and Bishop Ithacius, a man of evil fame, persuaded Emperor Gratian to banish all Priscillianists. Emperor Maximus was induced to put them to the torture, and Priscillianus and some others were beheaded at Treves, 385. This was the first instance of the death sentence being applied to heretics. Nevertheless the sect was still numerous in the second half of the 6th century.

Prison Gate Mission. This mission looks after the spiritual care of convicts and discharged prisoners. See *Elizabeth Fry*. The American Prison Association, incorporated 1871, provides employment for discharged convicts. The Society for the Friendless is engaged in prisoners' aid work and prison reform.

Prithivi Matar. See *Brahmanism, 2.*

Private Confession. See *Confession.*

Private Judgment. The right of the individual Christian to decide matters pertaining to faith and morals for himself on the basis of divine revelation, to search Scripture and judge doctrine for himself, is a right which God Himself has given and which the Christian is required to exercise. The right to judge and pronounce on matters of faith, morals, and doctrine belongs to every Christian (1 Thess. 5:21; 1 Cor. 10:15; 1 John 4:1; Matt. 7:15; Luther, XIX:241—349; X:1540—43). This right does not place the individual in the seat of authority, since the norm must always be the Word of God (Is. 8:20; 2 Tim. 3:15-17; 1 Tim. 6:3ff.; Acts 17:11; Luther, XVIII:1294; XV:1565; III:503; IX:1236f.; XV:1549), to which the individual Christian has the right and duty to go for himself and which he is to study for himself (Acts 17:11).

Those who remove the right of private judgment (Romanists, who emphasize the voice of the Church as though it were the final criterion) prevent Christians from performing a duty imposed on them by God and enslave conscience and faith.

The right of private judgment is abused when a departure from Scripture as norm occurs or when the human mind is made a judge over Scripture (Ps. 19:7; 2 Tim. 3:16; Eph. 2:20; 1 Thess. 2:13; Deut. 4:2; Rev. 22:18, 19; 1 Tim. 6:3ff.; 2 Pet. 1:20, 21; 2 Cor. 2:17; 10:5).

T. Engelder, "The Right and Wrong of Private Judgment," *CTM*, XV:217 to 236; 289—314; 385—402; 433—59. This article brings many quotations from Luther and also from the writings of those who prohibit private judgment or uphold an unscriptural and antiscriptural view of it. RGL

Privilegium Canonis. The law of the Roman Church according to which anyone who maliciously injures, strikes, or slaps any cleric, lay brother, or novice is excommunicated *latae sententiae* (see *Excommunication*), except in case of self-defense and the like. To mark the heinousness of the offense, the culprit must be avoided by the faithful. If the injury is slight, the bishop can absolve from the excommunication, otherwise only the Pope. The higher the injured cleric's rank, the graver the offense.

Probabilism. See *Jesuits and Jesuitism, 5.*

Problem Solving. See *Christian Teaching, H, K.*

Probst. See *Provost.*

Probst, Jacob (1486—1562). B. in Ypers, Flanders; pupil of Luther; preached at Ypers; condemned; escaped to Wittenberg; through the influence of Luther he came to Bremen and organized the Lutheran Church; vainly opposed Calvinism there.

Procession of the Holy Spirit. The relation of the Holy Spirit to the other Persons of the Trinity is called *procession*. The Holy Ghost proceeds from the Father and the Son (John 14:26; 15:26; Gal. 4:6; John 20:22). This doctrine is emphasized in the Confessions of the Western Church. Into the Niceno-Constantinopolitan Creed the Council of Toledo, Spain (A. D. 589), inserted the word *Filioque* ("and from the Son"), an addition which the Greek Church never sanctioned and which later contributed toward bringing about the great Eastern Schism. Through the resolution of 589 the word *Filioque* entered into the Nicene Creed. The essential nature of the Holy Ghost's procession is as little understood by the human intellect as is the "generation" of the Son.

Processional. Hymn sung during a procession, usually by clergy and choir; also collections of hymns, etc., for such processions.

Processions. Processions, though not peculiar to the Roman Church, are commonly associated with it. The Roman clergy form a procession when they approach the altar for Mass and other services, and again when they return to the sacristy. Solemn public processions are held in certain places on Palm Sunday, Corpus Christi* and other festivals or as an expression of thanksgiving, of penitence, or of honor to a dignitary. They are also held in times of calamity, or to plead for rain or fair weather, to drive away storms, etc. There may be music, candles, statues of saints, and relics. Those lowest in rank march first; those highest in dignity, last. The greatest magnificence in processions was reached during the Middle Ages.

Procopius of Gaza (ca. 465—538). Celebrated Oriental Church Father, sophist and rhetorician; wrote *catena* on Old Testament.

Procurator. A person authorized to manage the affairs of another; especially, the procurator fiscal, an official who represents a diocese in trials and court proceedings. This refers to the Roman Church. — The procurator of Judea, like Pontius Pilate, was a Roman official under the legate of Syria.

Prodiciani. See *Gnosticism,* 7 j.

Professed of Four Vows. See *Jesuits and Jesuitism,* 3.

Profession of Monks and Nuns. The ceremony by which a novice,* having completed the novitiate, enters a religious order or congregation. The essential part is the taking of the three vows of poverty, chastity, and obedience, the last of which binds the novice to the rule of the order. There may also be special vows, e. g., to shun ambition, to nurse the sick. Profession may be solemn or simple (see *Vows*). Solemn profession is found only in religious orders properly so called and must be preceded by at least three years of simple profession. It is always perpetual. The property of the professed passes to the convent or monastery, and he is rendered incapable of subsequently acquiring or holding any. Simple profession is sometimes perpetual. When it is temporary, the professed may, at its expiration, return to the world. Those bound by simple profession may retain

and acquire property, but not administer it or dispose of it. Candidates for profession must be at least sixteen years old.

Profession of the Tridentine Faith. See *Roman Catholic Confessions,* A 2.

Professional Literature, Lutheran. See *Literature, Lutheran,* 5.

Progressive Education. See *Christian Teaching,* J.

Progressive Orthodoxy. The name originally given to the Andover theology, which sought to keep the tenets of Calvinism in a modernized form.

Prohibited Degrees. Those degrees of relationship, either of consanguinity or blood relationship, that of a common ancestry or of affinity, that resulting from marriage, within which marriage is forbidden, either by a direct prohibition in the Bible or by a statute enacted by the government. The general rule is that one may not marry "flesh of one's flesh," that is, a person within, and up to, the second degree of relationship of either kind. See *Impediments of Marriage, Scriptural and Natural.*

Prohibition. See *Temperance Movements and the Lutheran Church.*

Promotor Fidei. See *Canonization.*

Propaedeutics, Theological. The entire body of rules and principles pertaining to the study of theology as a whole, including encyclopedia, methodology, bibliography, and related subjects.

Propaganda, Congregation of the, *Congregatio de Propaganda Fide* (the Congregation for the Propagation of the Faith). Commonly called simply *The Propaganda,* is a permanent commission of cardinals charged by the Pope with the management and direction of the entire mission work of the Roman Catholic Church. It was established by Gregory XV in 1622, comprising at the time thirteen cardinals with some subordinate officials. At present the number is much higher. The field of the Propaganda is the world, as far as it is not officially Roman Catholic. Only those territories which are hierarchically constituted are exempt from its jurisdiction. A new mission is placed under the direction of a prefect (not a bishop) and is called an *apostolic prefecture.* As the work advances, the prefecture is raised to the dignity of an *apostolic vicariate,* with an acting bishop at its head as the vicar of the

Pope (who is the actual bishop). Finally, if conditions warrant, the vicariate, in turn, is superseded by the *diocese* under the control of a missionary bishop, who holds the same rank as ordinary bishops, with the exception that he is subject to the Propaganda. Organized on the principle of authority and provided with ample means for exercising it, the Propaganda is in full control of a smoothly running missionary machine.

Propagation of the Gospel. See *Evangelism.*

Prophet, Christ as. The office of a prophet might be simply described: God spoke to the prophet, and the prophet reported to the people (cf. Ex. 7:1; 4:15,16; Micah 3:8; Ezek. 11:5; especially, Heb. 1:1,2).

In the Old Testament, Christ in many instances performed His prophetic work personally. Thus the Angel of the Lord * is frequently mentioned as the Messenger sent by the Lord to reveal His will, a Messenger in whom was the name of the Lord (Ex. 23:20, 21); who is called Lord (Gen. 16:13; 22:14); and speaks of Himself as God (Gen. 31:11-13); as the Lord (Gen. 22: 15, 16; Ex. 3:2, 13-15). This Angel of the Lord brought messages of the Lord to Hagar (Gen. 16:7-10; 21:17-19); to Abraham (Gen. 22:11-19); to Jacob (Gen. 28:11-22; cp. 31:11-13); to Moses (Ex. 3:1-22); and others.

Christ frequently mentioned His prophetic mission during the years of His public ministry (Luke 4:16-29; John 18:37). He was anointed to be a Prophet (Acts 10:38). Some people of New Testament times recognized Jesus as the Prophet who was to come (John 6:14; 7:40,41; 4:19 ff.; Matt. 21:46; Luke 7:16; 24:19). That the holy writers were constantly aware of Christ's prophetic office is evident from the terms they apply to Him: Teacher (John 3:2); Witness (Rev. 1:5); Word (John 1:1); Truth (John 14:6); Light of the World (John 1:8,9); Servant of God (Is. 42:1; 49:6); Angel of the Lord (Gen. 22:1); Angel of the Covenant (Mal. 3:1); Apostle (Heb. 3:1); Good Shepherd (John 10:11); Bishop (1 Pet. 2:25).

In His state of humiliation, Christ regularly referred His interrogators to the Old Testament Scriptures (Luke 10:26; Matt. 22:29,31; John 5:39; Luke 24:27). Though He also preached Law (Matt. 5—7; 23), Christ's chief and proper function was to preach the

Gospel (John 1:17). Even His miracles, signs, and wonders had as object to make it easier for people to believe His message (Mark 1:27; 9:24). The theme of His prophecy was the proclamation of Himself as the long-promised Messiah (John 4:25 f.).

When Christ ascended into heaven, He entrusted His prophetic office to the Church — the community of those anointed through Him to be priests and prophets (1 Pet. 2:9; John 20:21; Matt. 28:20). C. f. OCH, "Office or Work of Christ," *Abiding Word,* CPH, 1947 (II:127—35).

Prophetic Religion. See *Switzerland, Contemporary Theology in,* 3.

Propitiation. The Greek equivalent is also translated "mercy seat" (Heb. 9:5), and is itself equivalent to a Hebrew word meaning a covering, properly the cover, or lid, of the Ark of the Covenant, where the Lord communed with the representative of His people (Ex. 25 and 37). On the lid of the sacred Ark the high priest once a year sprinkled the blood of sacrifice in order to make propitiation for the sins of the people. All of this furniture and action was typical. Christ is the propitiatory Sacrifice for the sins of the world. His blood covers our guilt, and we obtain the benefits of this propitiation by putting our confidence in His atoning blood. It is true that God requires no outside motive to induce Him to pity the sinner. In this sense nothing is needed to render Him propitious. But He has Himself determined the manner in which mercy can be obtained for the sinner. The change which takes place in the individual sinner's status is that brought about by the application of Christ's merits to the individual through faith, particularly of Christ's sufferings and death. See *Atonement, Reconciliation, Faith, Conversion.*

Propria (*Liturgical*). The two chief parts of the Roman missal, the first being the Proper of the Masses of the Season (*Proprium Missarum de Tempore*), giving the services for each day from the First Sunday in Advent to Holy Saturday, as well as the Ordinary of the Mass, the *Canon Missae,* and the prefaces for the entire year; the second, the Proper of the Masses of the Saints (*Proprium Missarum de Sanctis*), with the services for saints' days and other important mystery festivals.

Proselytes. In its original connotation "strangers," "outsiders," specifically such as lived in the midst of a people and enjoyed its hospitality; later, such as were gained from among the Gentiles for the Jewish religion, either by accepting its doctrines without formally joining (proselytes of the gate) or by accepting even the distinguishing sacrament of circumcision (proselytes of righteousness). The term has since gained the meaning of persons who are won for the convictions of a religious group to which they did not originally belong.

Prosopa. See *Monarchianism,* B 6.

Prosper of Aquitania (Aquitanicus). A disciple of Augustine and defender of the orthodox truth against the Semi-Pelagianism as found in Gaul about the third decade of the fourth century; one of his best-known writings is *De gratia Dei at de libero arbitrio;* a stronger defender of the Roman see.

Prosper Tiro (5th century). Pupil of Augustine; opposed Pelagians and wrote apologies of St. Augustine; his *Epitoma Chronicon* is a valuable historical source.

Protestant Education in the United States. Education in the Colonial period of America was basically Christian. While the major task of Christian education was assumed by the home, schools were also instruments of religion. In New England, Church and State combined to administer the schools. The heterogeneous population of the middle colonies established different types of schools, most of them, however, under some religious sponsorship. The Anglican influence dominated education among the southern colonies. The churches' influence continued until about 1750, when a more secular spirit began to show itself because of the growing economic and political interests. With the possible exception of the University of Pennsylvania the nine universities founded before the Revolution were established under the direct control of the churches.

While in a number of instances a form of catechetical instruction was given by pastors to the children of the congregation on Sunday morning during early colonial times, Sunday schools following the pattern of Robert Raikes appeared soon after the Revolution (1785) chiefly in the middle States. From the start these Sunday schools were more closely associated with the Church than in England, where they were distinctly part of a lay movement. With the growth of the public

school system in the United States, general education was gradually eliminated from the Sunday school curriculum. Though the curriculum of the public schools was at first strongly influenced by religious thought, it thinned out in time. The churches were forced to depend more and more upon the Sunday schools to teach religion outside of the home.

The early hold of the Sunday schools on the American scene can be seen in the fact that on December 26, 1790, the First Day or Sunday School Society was organized in Philadelphia as an interdenominational effort to bring elementary and religious education to the underprivileged. In 1824 it merged with similar groups to form the American Sunday School Union. This new group had the ambitious purpose to establish a Sunday school in every village of the country, especially in the pioneer areas. The Union was instrumental in producing a vast amount of literature for pupils and teachers. 1832 marked the beginning of the convention movement in Sunday schools when the first national convention was held in New York. With the sixth convention in 1872 it became international in scope. This convention made history when it adopted the International Sunday School Lessons and thus introduced uniform lesson plans to serve all denominations.

With the years the scope of the Sunday school was increased upward to include the young people and adults and downward to reach the preschool child.

The Sunday School Council of Evangelical Denominations was organized in 1910 because of differences of opinions which had arisen on principles governing the curriculum. The newly organized group represented chiefly the denominational editors and publishers and tended to stress newer trends in education rather than the Bible content. By 1922 differences between the major groups were no longer evident so that they united in the formation of the International Sunday School Council of Religious Education. This Council, which in time dropped the name Sunday School, became the most influential group in Protestant religious education. In November, 1950, it became an integral part of the National Council of the Churches of Christ in the United States of America, constituting the Division of Christian Education.

Various attempts have been made to supplement the work of the Sunday school. Notable among these was the establishment of the vacation Bible school in 1901. In 1905 Dr. George U. Wenner read a paper proposing a plan whereby religion could be taught in co-operation with the public schools under a released-time plan. His suggestions were adopted with some modifications in Gary, Ind., in 1914. Such weekday schools, usually conducted under the auspices of the local churches or council, became popular in various parts of the country. The decision rendered in the Champaign Case (1948) has placed such schools in jeopardy because in many instances they were conducted in public school buildings under the auspices of the administration.

By and large Protestant churches have not accepted the parochial-school idea because they have feared that such schools tended to atomize American society. Outside of the Lutheran and Roman Catholic Churches only a few denominations have seriously considered conducting parochial schools (Reformed, Mennonite, and Seventh-Day Adventist).

With the growing criticism of the inadequacy of the Sunday school and the legal difficulties associated with the released-time program, serious thought has been given to induce the public schools to introduce into their curriculum some form of religious education chiefly of an historic nature which would be satisfactory to Christians and non-Christians alike. Others have resolved that the chief emphasis must return to the home and that the Sunday school curriculum must emphasize greater co-operation between parent, child, and teacher. ACR

A. A. Brown, *A History of Religious Education in Recent Times*, Abingdon, N.Y., 1923; Marianna Brown, *Sunday School Movement in America*, Revell, N.Y., 1901; E. M. Fergusson, *Historic Chapters in Christian Education in America*, Revell, N.Y., 1935; C. L. Hay, *The Blind Spot in America's Public Education*, Macm., N.Y., 1950; M. Reu, *Catechetics*, Wartburg, Chicago, 1927; E. H. Rian, *Christianity and American Education*, Naylor, San Antonio, 1949; P. H. Vieth (ed.), *The Church and Christian Education*, Bethany, St. Louis, 1947.

Protestant Episcopal Church. 1. This denomination as a separate organization dates back to the year 1789, when it secured Episcopal independence of the Church of England, and the Rev. William White of Pennsylvania and the Rev. Samuel Provoost of New York were ordained bishops of the Episcopal Church in America.

a. Permanent worship on this side of the Atlantic was begun in 1607, when the Rev. Robert Hunt celebrated the Eucharist for the first time at Jamestown in the Virginia Colony. Church work, however, was attended with many difficulties. This resulted in unfortunate conditions, which the Bishop of London tried to remedy by sending the Rev. James Blair as missionary to the colonies. He accomplished much, securing pastors for many churches and obtaining, in 1693, a charter for William and Mary College, which had been founded at Williamsburg, Va. The harsh tone prevalent in the Church of England manifested itself also in Virginia after the colony had passed under the immediate control of the crown; and rigid laws in regard to Puritans and Quakers were enforced.

b. In New England the Puritans applied to the Anglicans the same proscriptions from which they themselves had fled. Accordingly, in New England, only isolated attempts at church organization could be made. In 1698 an Episcopal church was established at Newport, R. I., and in the same year Trinity Church, New York City, was dedicated. In Maryland the growth of the Church was equally slow. However, the arrival, in 1700, of the Rev. Thomas Bray, the commissary of the Bishop of London, gave it new life. Under his leadership the Society for the Propagation of the Gospel was organized in England, and it was largely owing to the influence of this society that the Episcopal Church in America was established on a firm foundation. This society, in 1702, sent a delegation to visit the churches in America. Through the work of the delegation the number of churches was greatly increased, and a better grade of ministers was secured for them. Thus this mission was the beginning of a new era in the history of the Episcopal Church of America.

c. One of the men whose influence was largely felt in the early colonial Church was Dean Berkeley, later Bishop of Cloyne in Ireland, who came to Newport, R. I., in January, 1729, with the purpose of founding a university in the colonies. This purpose remained unaccomplished, since the financial support which had been promised was not given him. However, Dean Berkeley became one of the earliest and most munificent benefactors of Yale College and after his return to Europe aided largely in forming the charters and in directing the course of King's College at New York, now Columbia University, and of the academy and college of Philadelphia, now the University of Pennsylvania.

2. As a result of the Revolutionary War the Anglican churches in America lost their organization. The first move towards an organization was made in 1782 by the Rev. Wm. White of Philadelphia, who published anonymously a pamphlet entitled *The Case of the Episcopal Churches in the United States Considered*. In this he urged that, without waiting for a bishop, the churches should unite in some form of association and common government, and he outlined a plan which embodied most of the essential characteristics of the diocesan and general conventions as adopted later. Even before this time the Maryland Legislature had, in 1779, passed an act committing to certain vestries as trustees the property of the parishes, but also prohibiting general assessments. The following year a conference was called, and a petition was sent to the Legislature, asking that the vestries be empowered to use the money obtained from pew rents and other sources for parish purposes. Since it was essential that the organization should have a title, the name Protestant Episcopal Church was used. This name was formally approved by a conference at Annapolis in 1783 and was definitely adopted by the General Convention of 1789. When it became evident that the Episcopal churches of the different States were organizing independently, a movement to constitute an Episcopal Church for the whole United States was inaugurated largely by the initiative of Dr. William White at an informal meeting at New Brunswick, N. J., in May, 1784. Three States — New York, New Jersey, and Pennsylvania — were represented. Correspondence with other States resulted in a convention in New York in October of the same year, attended by delegates from eight States. In September, 1785, a convention was held at Philadelphia; seven of the thirteen States were represented. New England was not represented at all, and there were numerous protests from many quarters against the proposed plan of organization. In spite of this the convention adopted the principles recommended in the previous year and drew up a constitution and a liturgy under the general oversight of Drs. Wm. Smith and Wm. White.

3. As the matter of organization progressed, there was a general desire to be connected with the Church of England. Accordingly, an appeal was made to the archbishop and bishops of the Church of England, and having obtained favorable replies, Drs. White and Provoost went to England, where they were consecrated in February, 1787. As Dr. Seabury had already been consecrated bishop by the nonjuring Scottish bishops in 1784, there were now three bishops. This number was essential to the constitution of the House of Bishops. But subsequently Dr. James Madison was elected Bishop of Virginia and consecrated in England, so that any objection to the Scottish office was obviated. In 1789 Bishop Seabury joined the other bishops. Two houses were now constituted in the General Convention, and the constitution and the *Book of Common Prayer* were adopted. For twenty years and more the Church had to combat various hostile influences, since it was widely distrusted, being regarded as an English institution. The loss of the Methodist element, in consequence of the Revival movement, deprived it of some strength, and growth was slow.

4. a. A change came about in the second decade of the 19th century, when new bishops were elected and consecrated and sent to the newly settled sections in the West. In 1821 the Domestic and Foreign Missionary Society was organized, and work was begun both in the foreign field and in the remoter regions of the States. As in England, so also in America, two parties, or rather tendencies, developed in the course of time, styled, for convenience' sake, Evangelical and High Church. The High Church party emphasized the Church as a comprehensive, ecclesiastical, authoritative unity, and the Evangelical party, while not denying the authority of the Church, emphasized the spiritual freedom of the individual.

b. About 1845 W. Muhlenberg, one of the most remarkable men in the history of the Church, came into prominence. He founded the system of church schools, organized the first free church of any importance in New York City, introduced the male choir, sisterhoods, and the fresh-air movements. In a memorial drawn up by him, signed by a number of prominent clergymen and addressed to the College of Bishops, he raised the question whether the church with "her fixed and invariable modes of worship and her traditional customs and usages" was competent for the great and catholic work before it. In reply to this query the memorial suggested that "a wider door might be opened for admission into the Gospel ministry of all men who could not bring themselves to conform in all particulars to our prescriptions and customs, yet are sound in the faith." This memorial prepared the way for the issuance of the famous *Lambeth Quadrilateral on Church Unity* in 1888 and for the movement in favor of the revision of the *Book of Common Prayer,* completed in 1892.

c. The outbreak of the Civil War caused a temporary division in the Church, in consequence of which the Protestant Episcopal Church in the Federal States was organized. However, at the close of the war the breach was immediately healed. After the war the old controversy between the Evangelical and High Church parties was renewed, and in 1873 some of the extreme evangelicals, under the leadership of Bishop George D. Cummins of Kentucky withdrew, organizing the Reformed Episcopal Church. In 1886 the Brotherhood of St. Andrew was organized for the purpose of fostering more active mission work. For the work of social service and community welfare central, provincial, and diocesan boards and commissions have been formed from one end of the country to the other. The Episcopal Church has played a prominent part in the interfaith movements designed to bring all churches into close fellowship. The proposed merger between the Northern Presbyterian Church and the Episcopal Church had not been consummated by 1950.

5. *Doctrine.* Whereas the Church of England emphatically acknowledged the three doctrinal symbols of the Church, the Apostles', Nicene, and Athanasian creeds, the adoption of these confessions had caused more or less disturbance in the Protestant Episcopal Church. When the liturgy for the American Episcopal Church was prepared at the convention of 1785, the Nicene and Athanasian creeds, including the words of the Apostles' Creed "descended into hell," were discarded. Since the English archbishop insisted

upon the acceptation of the ecumenical symbols, the General Convention of 1786 restored the Nicene Creed and left it optional with the individual congregation whether or not to retain the words of the Apostles' Creed "descended into hell." The Athanasian Creed, one of the symbols of the Anglican Church, was unanimously rejected by the convention of 1789, chiefly because of its damnatory clauses. The *Thirty-nine Articles* of the Church of England, with the exception of the twenty-first, which relates to the authority of the General Council, and with some modifications of the eighth, thirty-fifth, and thirty-sixth articles, were accepted by the convention of 1801 as a general statement of doctrine, and they are appended to the prayer book. Adherence to them as a creed, however, is not generally required, either for confirmation or ordination, although this rests with the bishop.

6. The Episcopal Church, while expecting of all its members loyalty to the doctrine, discipline, and worship of the one holy Apostolic Church in all essentials, on the other hand, from its own standpoint, allows great liberty in non-essentials. For the unity of Christendom and also as a basis of general confession the following articles, known as the *Lambeth Articles,* were formulated in England in 1888, which may be regarded as the general doctrinal standards of the Protestant Episcopal Church: a) the Holy Scriptures of the Old and New Testaments, as "containing all things necessary to salvation" and as being the rule and standard of faith; b) the Apostles' Creed as the baptismal symbol and the Nicene Creed as a sufficient statement of the Christian faith; c) the two Sacraments ordained by Christ Himself — Baptism and the Supper of the Lord — ministered with unfailing use of Christ's words of institution and of the elements ordained by Him; d) the historic episcopate, locally adapted in its methods of administration to the varying needs of people and nations called of God into the unity of His Church. In the Baptism of children either immersion or pouring is allowed. Participation in the Sacrament of the Lord's Supper is limited to those who have been confirmed, although the custom is growing of regarding all baptized persons as virtually members of the Church and as such permitted to commune if they so desire.

7. The Episcopal Church, like its parent, the Anglican Church, allows

great latitude in doctrine. Contradictory views on fundamental doctrines are tolerated. According as churchmen follow certain theological or liturgical views, the Episcopal Church is usually grouped under three trends or tendencies: the *High Church*, Romanizing in its cultus and theology, some Episcopalians accepting the Roman Catholic doctrine of purgatory, transubstantiation, and Mary-worship; the *Low Church*, which includes the Evangelical party; and the *Broad Church*, which represents the liberal trend inaugurated in the Anglican Church by Coleridge.* A large section of the Anglican Church has accepted the liberal viewpoint of Modernism.*

8. *Polity.* a. The system of ecclesiastical government includes the parish, or congregation, the diocese, the province, and the General Convention. A congregation, when organized, is "required, in its constitution, or plan, or articles of organization, to recognize and accede to the constitution, canons, doctrine, discipline, and the worship of the Church and to agree to submit to, and obey, such directions as may be from time to time received from the bishop in charge and council of advice." Officers of the parish are the rector, who must be a priest; wardens, usually two in number, representing the body of the parish and usually having charge of the records, the collection of alms, and the repairs of the church; and vestrymen, who are the trustees and hold the property for the corporation.

b. The direction of spiritual affairs is exclusively in the hands of the rector. The government of the diocese is vested in the bishop and the diocesan convention, the latter consisting of all the ordained clergy and of at least one lay delegate from each parish or congregation. This convention meets annually, and election of delegates to it is governed by the specific canons of each diocese. Sections of States and territories not organized into dioceses are established by the House of Bishops and the General Convention as missionary districts. The dioceses and missionary districts are assembled into eight provinces to procure unity and cooperation in dealing with regional interests, especially in the fields of missions, religious education, social service, and judicial proceedings.

c. The General Convention, the highest ecclesiastical authority in the Church, consists of two houses, the House of Bishops and the House of Deputies. The House of Bishops includes every bishop having jurisdiction, every bishop coadjutor, and every bishop who by reason of advanced age or bodily infirmity or other disability has resigned his jurisdiction. The House of Deputies is composed of delegates elected from the dioceses, including for each diocese not more than four presbyters canonically resident in the diocese and not more than four laymen, communicants of the Church, resident in the diocese. The two houses sit and deliberate separately. The General Convention meets every three years, usually on the first Wednesday in October. In the House of Bishops the senior bishop in the order of consecration, having jurisdiction within the United States, is the presiding bishop. Next to him stands the bishop next in seniority by consecration. Three orders are recognized in the ministry — bishops, priests, and deacons. A bishop must be consecrated by not fewer than three bishops. He is the administrative head and spiritual leader of his diocese, presiding over the diocesan convention, ordaining deacons and priests, instituting rectors, etc. In case of the inability of a bishop to perform all the duties of his office, a bishop coadjutor or a suffragan bishop may be elected. The election of the rector is according to diocesan law, and notice of the election is sent to the ecclesiastical authority of the diocese. Lay readers and deaconesses are appointed by the bishop or ecclesiastical authority of a diocese or missionary district to assist in public services or in the care of the poor and sick, and in religious training. The support of the rector and the general expenditures of each local church are in the care of the vestry, and the salary of the bishop is fixed by the diocesan convention, and the amount is apportioned among the churches of his diocese.

9. *Work.* The Episcopal Church carries on so-called "domestic" mission work. This includes work among the Indians, Negroes, and in Alaska, Hawaii, the Panama Canal Zone, Virgin Islands, and Puerto Rico. Foreign mission work is carried on in ten countries. In its educational work the Episcopal Church supports thirteen theological institutions and a number of church colleges and academies. The Episcopal Church has a relatively large number of male and female orders, and in addition fosters the organization of men

and boys in so-called "brotherhoods." See *Religious Bodies (U. S.), Bibliography.*

Protestant Seminaries. See *Ministry, Education of.*

Protestant War Veterans. See *Veterans' Organizations.*

Protestantism. The term is derived from the Protestation submitted by the Evangelical party at the Diet of Speyer, in 1529. The Lutheran states in this Protestation declared their readiness to obey the emperor and the diet in all "dutiful and possible matters," not, however, any order considered by them repugnant to God and His holy Word, to their soul's salvation, and to their good conscience. The essential principles involved in their agreement were, first, the authority of Scripture, to be explained by itself; secondly, freedom of conscience. Protestantism, then, is essentially the doctrine of religious liberty, but a liberty on the basis of obedience to God and His holy Word. Regarding faith and works it is in complete opposition to Romanism. Rome says: Where good works are, there are faith and justification; Protestantism says: Where faith is, there are justification and good works. Accordingly, there has been, on the basis of the Aristotelian distinction of matter and form, the distinction of the material and the formal principle of the Reformation. The material principle is justification by faith in Christ; the formal principle, the authority of the Scriptures as the rule of faith. The whole character of Protestantism is favorable to civil and religious freedom, to the rights of the individual, and to the development of those inventive capacities which have given rise to the achievements which are summed up in the word civilization. The spirit of Protestantism favors universal education, since every Christian is required to read the Scriptures and to take part in the government of the Church. Liberty of thought and freedom of speech and of the press, these foundations of modern life, are all involved in the emphasis placed by Protestantism upon the freedom and responsibility of the individual.

Prothonotarius Apostolicus. A member of the highest college of prelates in the Roman Curia, whose duty it is to register records of unusual importance, such as papal acts, canonization proceedings, and the like.

Providence. Divine providence is that activity of God whereby He uninterruptedly upholds, governs, and directs the world which He has made (Heb. 1:3; Ps. 104; Acts 17:25ff.; Matt. 4:4; Col. 1:1). Divine providence extends over the entire creation. It provides for the continued existence of all individual creatures, directs their actions, and controls their destinies (Col. 1:16,17). This includes lifeless creation (Job 9:5,6; 28:25; Ps. 89:10; 148:8), plant life (Ps. 147:9; 104:13,14), animal life (Ps. 145:15; 104:10-25; Jonah 4:11), the world of men (Matt. 6:26-28; 5:45; 18:14; Ps. 139:13,15,16; Jer. 1:5) and all that concerns men (Prov. 21:1; Luke 12:7; Ps. 31:15; Jer. 10:23; Prov. 20:24; Ps. 139; Ps. 91:1, 3; Ps. 121), heaven, hell, in fact, everything (Luke 12:6,7; Heb. 1:3).

Divine providence normally expresses itself in definite laws (Gen. 8:22) which represent inner urges and drives implanted by God in His creatures. These laws proclaim the benignity of the Creator (Acts 14:17).

Divine providence is ordinarily exercised through secondary causes, which, however, are operative only so long as God works through them. Scripture teaches that both God and the means are operative (Ps. 65:9-11; Is. 55:10; Ps. 127:1; 1 Cor. 12:6), a fact which cannot be completely explained by the human mind.

Divine providence deprives men neither of their liberty nor of their responsibility; it neither reduces men to automata nor makes God responsible for sin (Rom. 1:19-28). Thus while God is operative in men and acts through men also when their deeds are evil (Acts 17:28; see 2 Sam. 24:1; 16:10), He is not the author of sin (Ps. 50:16-21).

From the viewpoint of God all is predetermined and immutably fixed (Acts 4:27,28; Job 14:5), yet from the human viewpoint things happen contingently, events can be modified and depend on circumstances and decisions which men make and for which they are responsible (Is. 38:1-5; Ps. 55:23).

The ultimate goals of divine providence are (1) the temporal and eternal welfare of men, particularly the salvation of the elect; (2) the spreading of the Gospel; (3) the promotion of the glory of God (Rom. 8:28). C. f. PFB, "The Providence of God," *Abiding Word,* CPH, 1947 (II:78—111).

References are given in article condensed above; E. W. Hinrichs, "God's Direction in Our Lives and the Element of Chance," *CTM*, XVII: 425—39.

Provident Associations *(Armenpflege)*. These are voluntary organizations for the relief of destitute individuals and families. Their final purpose, however, is not simply to provide food and clothing, but to investigate the causes of poverty (unemployment, drunkenness, illness, bad home conditions, etc.) and apply such remedial agencies as may be at their disposal. Provident associations advise citizens not to give indiscriminately to beggars and to the needy, but to contribute toward the relief of poverty through organized agencies.

Province. See *Protestant Episcopal Church*, 8.

Provincial Council. See *Councils and Synods*, 1, 3.

Provincial Letters. See *Pascal, Blaise*.

Provincial. The head of a province in monastic government, ranking next to the general.

Provoost, Samuel. See *Protestant Episcopal Church*.

Provost. Ecclesiastical dignitary; head of cathedral chapter, or second to dean of the chapter; Protestant equivalent in a German district *(Probst)*; head of a Catholic religious order.

Prudentius, Aurelius Clemens (348 to ca. 413). B. in the north of Spain, received a good education befitting his social standing. For a number of years Prudentius was engaged in the practice of law, at first as pleader and afterwards as judge. He probably rose to a Roman governorship. At 57 he determined to quit all his secular employments and devote the remainder of his life to advancing the interests of Christ's Church by the power of his pen. He retired to a monastery and there wrote those sacred poems upon which his fame now rests. He wrote about 28 hymns in all. Bently calls him "the Horace and Virgil of the Christians." Luther desired that Prudentius be studied in the schools, and Rudelbach was of the opinion that "the poetry of Prudentius is like gold set with precious stones."

Prussian Bible Society. See *Bible Societies*, 2.

Prussian Union. Attempts to unite the Lutheran and Reformed churches date from the days of the Reformers. During the 16th and 17th centuries, when pure doctrine was emphasized, union attempts resulted in emphasizing doctrinal differences. Pietism,* with its emphasis on the intensity of piety, tended to minimize doctrinal differences although it did seek to adhere to the facts of revealed truth. The so-called Enlightenment * was not interested in confessional loyalty and saw in union movements only a tendency toward tolerance.

In the 19th century a movement toward Biblical Christianity manifested itself. In Europe and America Lutheran and Reformed often labored together in opposition to rationalism. This awakening did not emphasize confessional loyalty and contributed toward union movements.

Since the time of John Sigismund the Hohenzollern had favored a union of Lutheran and Reformed churches. Friedrich William III felt that the time was ripe for the union in Prussia and on Sept. 27, 1817, proclaimed that he would celebrate the 300th anniversary of the Reformation by uniting the Reformed and Lutheran churches of Potsdam. Other churches were urged to follow this example, and the union was to be voluntary. Compulsory measures, however, were soon adopted: in 1821 candidates at their examination were required to pledge loyalty to the union; in 1823 ministers were pledged to the confessional writings of the United Evangelical Church to the extent that such confessions were in harmony; in 1830 it was decreed that the names "Lutheran" and "Reformed" be no longer used; in 1832 the union became compulsory for the army and the faculty at Bonn was unionized; in 1834 the use of the new Agenda (at first voluntary) was prescribed. While enactments of 1834 and 1852 showed some leniency to confessional positions, those of 1853 and later by Friedrich William IV became more stringent in support of the Prussian Union.

Prutenicum. See *Lutheran Confessions*, C 1.

Psalms as Hymns. Many of the hymns contained in the Book of Psalms were written expressly for use in public worship, as their superscriptions and dedications show. The regular Psalms for the week's services were: Psalms 24, 48, 82, 94, 81, 93, and 92; those of the Festival of Trumpets, Psalms 81 and 29; at the Passover the great Hallel, Psalms 113—118; and the other great festivals had similar provisions. The so-called Psalms of Degrees, Psalms 120—134, were probably chanted by the pilgrims on their way to Jerusalem for one of the high festivals. In the Christian Church the hymns of the Psalter were in use from the beginning, the practice often being to take them over in their entirety, without any attempt at metrical paraphrase. Some of the Reformed denominations were formerly very insistent upon the use of Psalms only in public worship; but the custom of using metrical versions has gradually made headway.

Psalms, Musical *(Psalmentoene).* Psalmody occupies an intermediate position between liturgical recitative and the elaborated singing of the chorus or of the congregation (between *accentus* and *concentus*). There are eight Psalmtones, corresponding to the eight divisions of the octave in ancient music, augmented, in the course of time, by a ninth or foreign tone, usually treated as a separate tone, the usual tone, in the Lutheran Church, for the Magnificat and the Aaronic benediction. Each Psalmtone is characterized, first, by the tone to be followed in the intonation of the Psalm text, always the dominant of the given key; secondly, by the melodic caesura, which ends the first half of the verse. The conclusion of the Psalm tone does not determine the church tone to which it belongs. The ferial form of Psalm tone is used during the week and on ordinary Sundays, the festal form on festivals, especially the high festivals, and in the chanting of the Magnificat and the Benedictus.

Psalms of Solomon, The. See *Apocrypha,* A 4.

Psalter, English. The use of the customary metrical hymns, even if paraphrased from the Psalms, being frowned upon by some Reformed denominations, especially in Great Britain, the result was that the Psalms themselves were often rendered into a form of English verse, even in hexameter and in blank verse. One of the first complete versions after the Reformation was that by Crowley, in common meter, set to harmonized chant in 1549. Ten years later permission to use Psalms publicly in worship was granted, and partial and complete versions became very numerous in England and Scotland. The Puritans of New England lost no time in making versions for use in public worship, the first book

published by them in America being the so-called *New England* (or *Bay*) *Psalter,* characterized by its rigorous literalism. It appeared in 1640, the same year in which steps were taken in England to issue more correct versions of the English Psalter. In 1696 there appeared *A New Version of the Psalms of David, Fitted to the Tunes Used in Churches,* by N. Tate and N. Brady. The work, of course, is of unequal merit, but there are examples of very sweet and simple verse, with true poetical fire. In the last two centuries, versions of Psalms by Addison, Watts, Dwight, Montgomery, Lyte, Keble, and others appeared, in which some specimens were of very high merit and have been very widely accepted. The Psalms may be expected to inspire many more poets to express the thoughts of God in the deepest, tenderest, and most intense form.

Pseudepigrapha. See *Apocrypha.*

Pseudo-Christs. See *Christs, False.*

Pseudo-Dionysius. See *Dionysius the Areopagite.*

Pseudo-Isidorian Decretals. 1. a. A collection of ecclesiastical laws made either in Franconia or Rome ca. 850, containing, besides many genuine decretals, also many forged ones. An earlier, but honest collection had been made in Spain and erroneously attributed to Bishop Isidore of Seville. This Frankish fraud also went out under that respected name. Pseudo-Isidore begins with the fifty Canones Apostolici; then follow fifty-nine forged decretals, which are assigned to the thirty oldest Popes, from Clement to Melchiades (d. 314). The second part embraces, besides the purported original document of the Donation of Constantine, genuine synodal decrees, falsified apparently only in one passage. The third part, again, contains decretals of Sylvester, the successor of Melchiades, down to Gregory II (d. 731), of which thirty-five are not genuine.

b. The non-genuine decretals are for the most part not altogether forgeries, but are rather based upon the literature of theology and canon law then existing, amplified or altered, and wrought up to serve the purposes of the compiler or compilers. The fraudulent nature of the collection cannot be doubted. Earlier collections begin with the decretals of Siricius, 384. Here we have such from the very first bishops of

Rome of which nothing was ever heard before. Purporting to be written by Roman bishops of the first century, they are yet couched in Franconian Latin of the 8th and 9th centuries, and they represent state and church affairs after the Franconian pattern of the early Middle Ages and quote Scripture from post-Jeromean translations. In them the Roman Bishop Victor (ca. 200) is made to write to the Alexandrian Bishop Theophilus (ca. 400) concerning the celebration of Easter, etc.

c. The forgery was made to further the new conception of the Church which had come into vogue. It stressed, on the one hand, the independence of the Church from the State and the exalted and inviolate nature of the spiritual priestly power. On the other hand, it sought to limit the power of the metropolitans by constantly claiming that they were subordinate to the patriarchs and the Pope, and it was untiring in the praises of the Roman Church above all others, which exalted position was claimed to be due, not to later arrangements, but to Christ's own direction, and therefore it was necessary that the last control of all church affairs, and especially the last word in all affairs of the bishops, whether they appealed or not, should be with the Roman Church, with the Pope as the supreme bishop of the entire Church. It was, in fine, a fraud intended to authorize the arrogated power of an inviolate priest caste, especially of the bishops, and, chief of all, of the Pope. In the non-critical age in which they originated they were readily accepted as genuine and quoted right and left. Even such as refused to submit to their directions nevertheless did not doubt their genuineness. The Magdeburg Centuriators were the first conclusively to prove them spurious. The Jesuit Turrianus tried to vindicate them; but the Reformed theologian David Blondel refuted him so thoroughly that even in the Roman Catholic Church their non-genuineness has since been admitted.

2. The so-called *Donatio Constantini* rests chiefly upon the authority of this fraudulent collection of decretals, and it, too, is evidently spurious. In the first part of it, the so-called *Confessio*, Constantine makes a confession of his faith and relates in detail in what wonderful way he was converted to Christianity by Pope Sylvester and cured of leprosy. In the second part, the so-called *Donatio*, he confers upon the chair of Peter, with recognition of its absolute

primacy over all patriarchates of the empire, imperial power, rank, honor, and insignia, as well as all privileges and claims of imperial senators upon its clergy. In order that the possessor of this gift might be able at all times to maintain the dignity of his position, he gives him the Lateran Palace, transfers to him independent dominion over "the city of Rome and all the provinces, towns, and commonwealths of Italy, as well as of the Occident" (*i. e.*, the whole West Roman Empire). He removes his own imperial residence to Byzantium, "because it is not just that the emperor should have temporal power at the same place where the chief seat of the priests and the head of the Christian religion has been established by the heavenly Emperor." This was something never heard of before. Pope Hadrian I had indeed mentioned to Charlemagne, in 788, a donation of Constantine augmented by other princes; however, that did not include the whole of the Western Empire, but only Italy, or rather, a part of Italy, the *patrimonium Petri;* nor did it give the Pope sovereign territorial authority. But this bold forgery intended to show that it was legitimate for the Pope to lord it over the princes and that these should receive their dominion from his hand.

Pseudo-Messiahs. See *Christs, False.*

Psyche. See *Psychology,* B f.

Psychiana. This religious cult was founded by Frank Robinson in Moscow, Idaho. It denies all Christian truths, such as the reality of sin and punishment, the personality of God, the vicarious atonement, the deity of Christ, and ridicules Christianity as "a senseless and untrue statement, and originated in pagan superstition," and states that when man studies himself he will "realize the amazing fact that everyone is definitely and inseparably joined to the great living God-law of the universe; and that this mighty invisible dynamic force can and will give man whatsoever things he desires," even complete freedom from physical death.

Psychiatry. See *Psychotherapy.*

Psychical Research. The investigation of such phenomena as clairvoyance, telepathy, and mediums. The first society for such investigation was founded in England (*Society for Psychical Research*) in 1882. A similar organization was formed in America through the influence of William James in 1885. The latter is now called the *American Society for Psychical Research*. Both the British and American societies publish *Proceedings* and a *Journal*.

Psychoanalysis. See *Psychology*, J 6 f.

Psychology. A. *Definition.* The word *psychology* is derived from the Greek words *psyche*, meaning soul or mind, and *logos*, meaning discourse, theory, or science. The word *psyche* was from early times also used in other senses, such as spirit, breath, and principle of life. The tendency today is to define psychology broadly as the science of experience and behavior. More specifically it attempts to understand, predict, and control human behavior. Current psychology generally omits or avoids the study of the soul as such and gives its attention to behavioral elements. Understanding human behavior may be, and usually is, the ultimate object of psychological research, but the study of animal behavior may be given considerable attention in the process of investigation.

The term "psychology" apparently was first used by German scholars of the sixteenth century. Its first form appears to have been "psychologia." It is said that Melanchthon used the term as a title of a prelection. Its further use appears in some medical writings. *Psychologia* and *somatomia* were spoken of as the two principal parts of *anthropologia*. The term appeared in technical literature from time to time, but it did not come into a more general use in the modern languages before the nineteenth century. (See *Oxford English Dictionary*, VIII, 1552.)

B. *Early Developments.* 1. The roots of naturalistic psychology may be traced to early forms of mythology, not as a separate system of thought, but combined with, and woven into, a primitive culture. Attempts were made to explain life, including mental life, in a world which to the primitive mind often appeared as more chaos than cosmos. Natural man soon observed that human life was more than body, bone, muscle, and tissue. His dreams and imaginary flights, while the body was asleep or at rest, called for explanation. But concepts involving immaterial and incorporeal forms and substances are difficult to understand. Thus a double materialism developed. Soul or mind was thought of as vapor, air, blood, or some other material substance.

2. Likewise, as in mythology, mental powers and forces came to be closely associated with the elements, air, fire, earth, water. The early form of the temperament theory serves as an illustration. Air was thought to be related to the sanguinary temperament, earth to the melancholic, fire to the choleric, and water to the phlegmatic. Later the temperaments were thought to be based on the body fluids or humors (Galen, ca. A.D. 131—210). The elemental basis as well as the "humoral doctrine" was gradually abandoned, but the fourfold classification of temperaments has been retained in the psychologies until the present century.

3. The relation of psychology to mythology is indicated by the personification of the soul as a princess named Psyche, so beautiful that even Venus became jealous of her and imposed many hardships on her.

C. *Approach to Immaterial Concepts.* 1. In Greek philosophical writings the explanation of soul, mind, reason, intelligence, and will was approached with a new vigor and placed on a higher intellectual level. In this period the penetrating philosophies of Plato and Aristotle were epochal. Here too, however, soul, mind, intellective powers, and will were discussed as aspects of a broader philosophy which took in a wide range of cosmological factors and human experiences.

2. Both Plato and Aristotle placed psychical forces and forms on an immaterial basis, at least, in part. Plato elevated consciousness into the realm of the spiritual. He considered the soul immortal and incapable of dissolution. To him the idea in its purest form was the ultimate in mental life, and matter was of secondary importance. God was the supreme mind. Apparently, man's soul was closely attached to, or a part of, an immortal god or gods.

3. Aristotle, a pupil of Plato, likewise sought the ultimate of man's existence. He disagreed with Plato that ideas were the ultimate. He considered soul the actuality of the body and made a distinction between souls of plants and animals and that of man, the chief difference being man's intellective capacity. Besides the five senses he spoke of a common sense which is conscious of and classifies and co-ordinates the sensory experiences. He distinguished between passive reason, which acts as a receptor for the senses, and active reason, which provides forms of thought,

may exist apart from soul and body, and is immortal and eternal.

4. Plato and Aristotle lifted mental life from the material to the immaterial and systematized psychological thought in a cosmological frame. The influence of their philosophies on later movements of thought is little short of phenomenal.

D. *The Relationship to Christianity.* 1. The basis for the Christian approach to psychology is laid in Genesis and in the historical unfolding of the Genesis account as recorded in the Scriptures. According to Genesis, man was created a being consisting of body and soul (Gen. 2:7). Man was created in the image of God with the command and potentiality to be fruitful and to have dominion over every living thing (Gen. 1:27, 28). Thus man's pre-eminent position in the order of creation of the world and all things therein had been established. Although created in the image of God, man is not a god, not even a lesser god, nor a part of God, but a separate being from God, a creature. That Adam was an intellective being is evident from his ability to name every creature that passed before him (Gen. 2:19, 20). Man had a free will, subject only to the will of God. An innate knowledge of right and wrong was implanted in him that he might subdue the earth and enjoy its fruits, but he was forbidden to eat of the "tree of knowledge of good and evil." With the fall into sin came a stricken conscience, conflicts, a sense of guilt, even a projection of guilt, and with the promise of a Savior from sin came faith and hope. Thus the basic concepts soul, intellect, knowledge, free will, conscience, sense of guilt, conflicts, heredity, environment, and emotion were fully established in man's creation and early history.

2. Psychology is not treated as a separate subject in the Bible. It is no more than an essential part of the total framework of the Scriptures. Psychology as a separate and distinct field of systematic activity is a development of the last hundred years, more particularly of the twentieth century. Yet as we examine the Scriptural account, we note many words and expressions having a psychological meaning and connotation. Thus we find the powerful effects of emotions on man referred to, as, for example, in the Psalms. Solomon directed attention to the great need of divine wisdom in a godly personality. The Savior Himself frequently pointed out the need of translating knowledge into action (transfer). Paul speaks of the Christian's need to devote his entire being to the Lord's work, and he recognized individual differences (cf. Romans 12). The very essence of Christianity, man's possessing a soul, the immortality of the soul, the inspiration of the Scriptures, sin, forgiveness of sin and eternal life by grace through faith, regeneration and the miraculous work of the Holy Spirit in and through Word and Sacrament, all have been great stumbling blocks to philosophies, systems of logic, and psychologies if and when these were based solely on naturalistic thought and effort.

3. It has been the determined and conscious purpose of Christians of all ages to guard these and other values against all encroachments, no matter from which source the attack came. With that not every effort of psychological thought and experimentation was condemned. On the contrary, many Christians became intensely interested in the study and explanation of mental phenomena.

E. *The Confluence of Theology and Philosophy During the Middle Ages.* 1. Following the Apostolic age the central movement of thought was influenced by (1) the religion of the Christian Church; (2) the heritage of philosophy and the classics; (3) the current thought as represented by sects, cults, and ethnic groups. These were not the only factors, of course, but all three take a dominant position in the writings of the ante-Nicene period. Out of this complex, theology gradually assumed the ascendancy and maintained its position of pre-eminence throughout the post-Nicene period and during the Middle Ages. The great intellectual minds of the Middle Ages were theologians. In addition they were philosophers, poets, psychologists, and logicians.

2. St. Augustine (354—430) has been called the greatest metaphysical mind of his age. He influenced later thought to a marked degree. His writings cover many areas of theology and human thought and experience. In Book X of his *Confessions* he discusses his psychological ideas in some detail. He considered soul the life-giving force. It seems that he separated soul and mind, the latter being a functional power. Both soul and mind were immaterial. Because of his reason and understanding, man was superior to the animals. St. Augustine's psychological terminology revolved around such concepts as sensation, reason, memory (or the

act of remembering), learning, thinking, conscience, free will, dreams, and others. He recognized four "perturbations of the mind": desire, joy, fear, and sorrow. In this he came close to the emotional theory of the modern behaviorists. To memory he devoted much space. He exalts its function and usefulness and called it "the belly of the mind."

3. St. Augustine was well acquainted with the philosophies of Plato and Aristotle and classical literature. He learned much from them, but he rejects them all as valid sources of information in spiritual matters. In matters concerning God, faith, salvation, and holy life he gradually learned to depend on Scripture and Scripture alone. Astrology and similar practices he rejected completely.

4. Of the many sources and writings during the Middle Ages, a brief reference to the work of Thomas Aquinas (1225—79) is necessary. Aquinas was first of all a theologian and a churchman; but he was also a philosopher, a psychologist, and above all, a logician. He followed Aristotle in his ideas of mind, soul, and body. In fact, he has been called the Christian Aristotle. His explanations of soul, mind, and emotions are systematic, encyclopedic, and metaphysical. His rigid logic and his ideological conclusions have been characterized as more metalogical (beyond or outside the scope of logic) than metaphysical.

5. Nevertheless, with all of the energy he devoted to logic and inference, Aquinas held that in spiritual matters revelation was the only reliable source. Natural reason could not fathom the mysteries of spiritual life. But the line between revelation and reason had been obscured. And, of course, Scripture no longer stood alone as the accepted authority. Ecclesiastical pronouncements, traditions, and legends had by this time made deep inroads into all matters religious.

F. *The Reformation and Psychology.* 1. Luther, the central figure of the Reformation, had been educated in the traditional materials and schools of thought of his era. Luther's writings give ample evidence that he was acquainted with the Greek philosophers, the poetry and literature of the classics, the mixture of religion and human reason of the Church Fathers, the systematized and fine-spun logic of the Scholastics, the creative efforts of the Renaissance, and the secular interests of the Humanists. While he had a deep interest in the dignity and welfare of man and in establishing the rights of the individual, he was not concerned with the development of a new system of philosophy or psychology. His energies were spent in a return to Scripture as the sole basis for Christian faith and life. All human knowledge and activity was judged in the light of God's Word. The simplest statement of God's natural gifts to man was summarized in his *Small Catechism* in the explanation of the First Article of the Creed: "I believe that God has given me my body and soul, eyes, ears, and all my members, my reason and all my senses, and still preserves them."

2. Speculative philosophies, ecclesiastical fiats and legends, the black arts, horoscopy, and superstitions were critically examined and denounced in rugged terms as so much nonsense or the work of the devil. Adiaphorous materials were left open and placed in the may-or-may-not category. Reasonable and sensible laws, decrees, and explanations were evaluated properly and given support.

3. Not all of the contemporary reformers or those who supported the Reformation followed the exact pattern of Luther. Some fell under the spell of humanistic philosophies or other schools of thought, from which Luther himself remained remarkably free.

G. *The Philosophical-Experimental Approach to Modern Psychology.* 1. If it can be said that the mind of the Middle Ages was largely conditioned by a confluence of theology and philosophy, following the Reformation the trend of thought more and more came under the spell of a confluence of philosophy and science. In time the worship of *nous* (mind, intellect) became a dominating influence at the expense of Christian theology. In such an atmosphere it was inevitable that philosophy and philosophies would flourish and luxuriate. Even a casual examination of the philosophical materials makes it clear that modern psychology draws heavily on the speculations of the seventeenth, eighteenth, and nineteenth centuries. Different forms of dualism, materialism, idealism, innate intelligence, psychophysical parallelism, the influence of the environment (*tabula rasa*), associationism, sensation, perception, phrenology, biological determinism, all were proposed and defended by one or the other philosophy.

2. While psychology received much

of its materials from the philosophical thought preceding the modern period, in due time it was influenced by the scientific developments and experimental techniques to an even greater extent. Yet philosophy also held its ground, for a scientific experiment is often preceded and followed by speculative recitals.

3. The earlier experiments of the last century drew heavily on physics and physiology and are more properly designated as psycho-physics than psychology. In this period the experiments in sensation by Ernst Heinrich Weber (1795—1878), the work of Herman von Helmholtz (1821—94) in vision, and the pressure experiments of Gustav Theodor Fechner (1801—87) serve as illustrious examples.

4. The work of Wilhelm Wundt (1832—1920), who established the first psychological laboratory in Leipzig, 1879, was somewhat more directly in the field of pure psychology. Wundt drew students from many countries, including the United States. Many of his American students became recognized leaders in experimental psychology. Analysis of conscious processes, memory experiments (Ebbinghaus), experiments in reaction time, introspection, analysis of the learning process, systematic observation of child development (Preyer in Germany and G. Stanley Hall in America), are all part and parcel of modern psychology.

H. *Nature and Scope of Modern Psychology.* By the end of the nineteenth century psychology had emerged as a separate branch of learning. The contributions of William James (1842 to 1910) had broken the close attachment to philosophy and given psychological thought a wide scope of materials. Since 1900 a large number of scientific students have led to a further clarification of psychological materials, methods, and principles. By 1940 large universities were offering as many as fifty or more courses in different aspects of psychology. Individuals and so-called "schools of psychology" contributed their own particular theories and frames of reference and thus crosscurrents of thought resulting in "psychologies" have become common. Generally, however, the attempt to establish facts by rigid experimentation remained uppermost.

I. *Sources from Which Psychology Draws Material.* An examination of standard texts shows that psychology is drawing materials from sources other than philosophy and scientific investigation *per se.* Biology, physiology, anatomy, and roentgenology are contributory sciences. Observations of growth during the prenatal and postnatal periods and the entire life span are correlated with growth in emotion, learning, and personality as a whole. The extensive use of statistics has become necessary to attain accuracy and precision in experimental work. The refinements of psychometrics have given a more precise concept of individual differences, intelligence, achievement, aptitude, special ability, interests, emotions, and other aspects of human behavior. Natural history, including biological evolution, and the attempt to analyze the simplest forms of behavior, more particularly learning, have led to animal experimentation, brain extirpation, and most recently, to the induction of abnormal behavior under controlled conditions. From the early ontological and phylogenetic surmises have come specific experiments and observations in the relative influence of heredity and environment. Cell twins, fraternal twins, siblings, foster children, and parent-child relationships in similar and different environments have become the object of minute study. The observation of abnormal behavior has become an integral part of general psychological thought. Further study of perception, thinking, imagination, and the growth of language has been undertaken. The study of the learning process was shifted from an introspective approach to objective observation covering the entire life span.

J. *Schools and Systems.* 1. "The quest for certainty," to borrow an expression from John Dewey, is not satisfied with mere atomistic experimentation. A theoretical description of the phenomena of experience and behavior is a natural by-product of experimental efforts. The points of departure which have grown up with experimentation and observation have come to be known as systems or schools of psychology. But the grouping of fellow workers holding a somewhat similar point of view as a school is not entirely accurate. In each school are subcurrents and divergent positions, as marked as the differences between so-called schools. The schools to which reference is frequently made are

(1) Structuralism
(2) Functionalism
(3) Behaviorism
(4) Gestalt or Configuration

(5) Psychoanalysis or dynamic psychology

2. Structuralism flourished at the beginning of the present century. It attempted to analyze sensation, images, and affections as elements of consciousness. Its chief method was introspection. Structuralism sought to find the pure elements of the mind. It did not concern itself with meaning directly because meaning was more than an elementary mental process. Emphasis was thus placed on the elements rather than on the reaction of the organism as a whole.

3. The functionalists are more concerned with the activities of the mind than its structure. Mind and behavior are considered inseparable. Functionalism therefore dealt with feelings, impulses, behavior, and habits. It makes controlled observation a major part of its investigative technique. Its chief contributions are in the field of learning and education.

4. Behaviorism has little faith in the analysis of consciousness by introspection or any other method. It operates chiefly with the stimulus response theory of simple behavior situations, because it believes that only in that way observation is accurate and objective. Reflexes and mechanistic responses are described in great detail, little attention is given to motivation by thought and reason. The conditioned response, or substitute stimulus, is accorded the place of honor in the method of investigation. While behaviorism has been helpful in making psychological investigation more objective, it may be criticized for not giving sufficient attention to motivation of behavior and for making inferences from outward behavior without taking the individual's inner thoughts into consideration, which might possibly be arrived at by introspection or some form of projection.

5. The Gestalt school (known in America as Configuration) emphasizes the total pattern of the learning act and takes issue with the piecemeal theories of the behaviorists. It operates with the concept of insight as a basis for an intelligent response and does not accept the trial-and-error pattern of learning proposed by the Functionalists. It supports its position by experimentation in both human and animal learning. Gestalt theories have exercised a wide influence on recent psychological and educational thought in America.

6. The well-known Psychoanalytic school (or Freudianism, named after Sigmund Freud, its founder) has recently been a prolific source of psychological thought and stimulation. Analysis of its tenets is difficult because its literature is vast and the crosscurrents within the school are strong.

7. Much is made of the libido, which is defined as a sex instinct or the urge to life. The id, defined as a reservoir of pleasure-seeking human impulses, the ego, that is, the recognition of reality principles, and the superego, or conscience, are basic terms which Psychoanalysis employs to describe the stream of life resulting from the trauma and frustrations that interfere with the natural impulses of the libido. The school is principally interested in the behavioral disorders and the forms the disorders may take in psychic life. Its therapeutic technique through abreaction or mental catharsis finds widespread use in psychiatry, literature, the arts, including motion picture entertainment.

8. Adherence to any single school or system by current psychologies is infrequent. It is probably correct to say that the majority of modern psychologists lean toward eclecticism.

K. *Influence of Psychology.* 1. It may be said, then, that psychology has developed a field of materials of its own even if the method of investigation is largely that of the natural sciences. In fact, psychology has been so broadened in scope that specialization within the field has become necessary. A modern psychological society may classify its membership under as many as fifteen or twenty different specialties.

2. Having developed materials and principles to which psychology has a priority, it has in turn invaded many fields of human endeavor, education, medicine, industrial management, art, advertising, salesmanship, vocational guidance, and others.

L. *Contribution of Christianity to Psychology.* 1. The position of Christianity toward psychology has been referred to in sections 4, 5, and 6 above. The question still remains: What influence shall Christianity exercise on psychology, present and future? It is not a mere excursion in forensics to say that psychology could hardly have reached its present state of development without the contributions which Christianity has made. True Christianity has persistently held certain sacred values and has thereby forced psychology into a field of its own in the study of psychic phenomena. Psychology has been driven into the open, as it were, and thus has applied itself to psychic materials that are amenable to the methods of natural science.

2. It is furthermore questionable whether modern psychology would have attained its rigid technique in experimental work if Christian theology had not been so intent on seeking the truth in all matters. In cultures where Christianity has had little influence we have a strange mixture of cultism, animism, and practical psychology even today. Even in Western culture the so-called rackets, such as phrenology, physiognomy, astrology, and crystal gazing, are on the fringe of scientific psychology. Modern psychology might still be bounded by superstition and soothsaying but for the rejection and condemnation of such and similar practices by Christianity long before the modern era.

3. The problem of dualism is sometimes thought of as interfering with progressive psychological thought. Christianity has from Bible times held that the individual has a body and a soul. While man is a dichotomous being structurally, for all practical ends here on earth he acts as one being, as a single self, at least under normal circumstances. Functionally, man is a monistic being. The study of man's functional mental life is as important as the study of his bodily functions. It is true, of course, that the structure of the body, unlike the structure of the soul, is subject to investigation by natural science. Science has little to offer about the structure of the soul. Naturalistic speculation about the soul, when it goes beyond or contrary to revelation, is patently futile.

4. Christianity cannot serve itself or psychology to the best advantage by a wholesale acceptance or condemnation of psychological theories and findings. Its judgment and attitude must be guided by the explicit and particularized findings in each instance. Al S

Psychology and Education. See *Educational Psychology*.

Psychology of Religion. The application of psychology to the field of religion, especially that of religious consciousness in anti-Christian religions. It is a "science" that attempts to collect available facts of the religious consciousness as found in various races and countries, to systematize them under some scientific description, to establish the interrelation between them, and, if possible, to explain them on the basis of general psychological principles. While some branches of this science, especially as found in Scripture, have their value also in revealed religion, the only function of the psychology of religion in the field of conservative theology is to explain the phenomena which are connected with the remnant of the natural knowledge of God and of the written Law in the hearts of all men.

Psychopannychism. See *Soul Sleep*.

Psychotherapy. A general method of treating mental and physical illness, principally through the means of suggestion, to be distinguished from psychiatry, which is concerned with mental diseases only. Psychotherapy has been used by many cults, both religious and mystical, through the ages, but gained new prominence especially on account of the treatments introduced by Mesmer, the school of Salpetriere in Paris, the Freudian movement (which Jung and Adler have attempted to modify), and the Emmanuel Movement of Boston. Within certain limitations, and barring all charlatanry, the value of certain principles of psychotherapy may well be recognized.

Ptolemies. The common or family name of a series of Egyptian kings: Ptolemaeus Lagus, the founder of the dynasty (d. 283 B.C.); Ptolemaeus Philadelphus, the alleged initiator of the Greek translation of the Old Testament, known as the Septuagint (d. 247); Ptolemaeus Euergetes (d. 221); Ptolemaeus Philopator, who is said to have persecuted the Jews (d. 204); Ptolemaeus Epiphanes (d. 181); Ptolemaeus Philometor, whose campaigns are described in the Books of the Maccabees (d. 146); Ptolemaeus Physkon or Euergetes II (d. 117). Other Ptolemies had no relation to sacred history. The prophecies concerning the Ptolemies are found in Daniel 11.

Public Schools, Bible Reading in. See *Christian Education*, J 5.

Public Schools, Religion in. See *Christian Education*, J 5.

Public Worship. See *Worship, Order of; Worship, Parts of*.

Publication Houses, Lutheran. The invention of the printing press has been termed one of the most important factors in the development of democracy and in religious thought. It is significant that the first book to be produced from movable type was the Bible, printed by Johann Gutenberg in the year 1455. About the time Luther posted his Ninety-five Theses on the door of a small church at Wittenberg the concept of free thought and free speech had begun to germinate and take root. Luther himself used the printing press to the fullest possible advantage.

The first press in the United States was set up in the English Colonies at Cambridge, Mass., in 1638, as part of an institution of learning which later became Harvard University. The first book produced on this press was *The Whole Book of Psalms*, now generally referred to as the *Bay Psalm Book*. In the year 1663 Harvard College ordered a Bible printed in the Indian language on its presses. Sermon books and other religious materials also were produced, in addition to many other materials for the college. The art of printing advanced and spread throughout the country as more areas were settled.

The various Lutheran immigrants settling in different parts of the country promptly made use of the printing press. In a number of cases periodicals, later adopted as official, had their beginning prior to the actual formation of the church body.

In the United States the Lutheran publishing houses which have made their impact upon the religious life of the people are: Augsburg Publishing House, Minneapolis, Minn., serving The Evangelical Lutheran Church; the Augustana Book Concern, Rock Island, Ill., serving the Evangelical Lutheran Augustana Synod; Concordia Publishing House, St. Louis, Mo., serving The Lutheran Church — Missouri Synod; the Lutheran Publishing House, Blair, Nebr., serving the United Evangelical Lutheran Church; the Messenger Press, Minneapolis, Minn., serving the Lutheran Free Church; Northwestern Publishing House, Milwaukee, Wis., serving the Evangelical Lutheran Joint Synod of Wisconsin and Other States; the United Lutheran Publication House, Philadelphia, Pa., serving the United Lutheran Church in America; and the Wartburg Press, serving the American Lutheran Church.

Augsburg Publishing House. Augsburg Publishing House, Minneapolis, Minn., owned and operated by the Evangelical Lutheran Church, traces its history back to July 16, 1873, when a periodical committee was elected by the Conference. On June 13, 1890, the Conference, the Anti-Missourian Brotherhood, and the Norwegian Augustana Synod merged into one synod called the United Norwegian Lutheran Church of America. The publishing concern of the former Conference then became the property of the new United Church, and the name Augsburg Publishing House was adopted.

The business changed quarters several times until in 1908 it moved into the new building at the present location.

On June 9, 1917, a new merger took place when the United Church, the Hauge Synod, and the Norwegian Synod united to form the Norwegian Lutheran Church of America. The publication business of the two latter synods was consolidated with Augsburg Publishing House. On June 14, 1946, the Church changed its official name to Evangelical Lutheran Church.

Since 1890 the general managers have been: Lars Swenson (1890—1904), Erik Waldeland (1904—17), A. M. Sundheim (1917—28), and R. E. Haugan since January 1, 1929. In 1952 the firm employed over 200 workers.

Augustana Book Concern. The publication activities of the Augustana Synod began in 1851, when L. P. Esbjörn issued a tract for immigrants. Four years later T. N. Hasselquist set up a printing press in his home in Galesburg and issued various books, pamphlets, and periodicals.

In 1858 the Swedish Lutheran Publication Society was organized to take over the periodicals and conduct a printing business in the basement of Immanuel Church in Chicago. The Synod took over this business in 1860. When the entire establishment was lost in the fire of 1871, Augustana College was asked to carry on the publishing work. Needing funds, the school sold the business in 1874 to Engberg-Hohnberg & Lindell in Chicago. This firm served the Synod for fifteen years, when a new publication society, "Ungdomunens Vänner," was started at Augustana College. — Various items were published by this society. It was reorganized as the Augustana Tract Society and secured interest in the printing plant of Thulin and Anderson, Moline, Ill. This venture was not successful, and in 1884 reorganization again took place, and the Augustana Book Concern was formed "for the benefit of Augustana College" at Rock Island, Ill. It was a printing venture without synodical sanction. In addition there were other publishing ventures, and general confusion developed.

In 1889 the Augustana Synod voted to establish a Board of Publication, which took over the affairs of the Augustana Book Concern and formed a new corporation known as the Lutheran Augustana Book Concern. This organization gathered all the other publishing ventures under its roof. The net worth of the publishing plant has grown from $6,000 in 1889 to over $750,000 in 1952. The institution is governed by an elected board. A. G. Anderson was the first manager. He was succeeded by J. G. Youngquist in 1927. Birger Swenson, the present manager, has served since 1945. The organization employed somewhat over a hundred workers in 1952.

Concordia Publishing House. In 1844 members of Trinity Lutheran Church in St. Louis felt that the doctrines as taught by their leaders should reach more people. Rev. Carl Ferdinand Wilhelm Walther, who was called from Perry County, Mo., to succeed his brother, Otto Walther, as pastor of Trinity Church, was editor and manager of the printing activities. The congregation obtained funds through individual contributions or made appropriations from the treasury. In 1849 the activity was recognized as a Publication Society. In the early days printing and binding was done in various job shops. One of the major projects was a periodical named *Der Lutheraner.* The first issue bears the date September 7, 1844. When Synod was organized in 1847, it adopted this periodical as its official organ. It is still being published every two weeks and has an English parallel, the *Lutheran Witness.*

In 1857 Synod appointed a Publication Committee consisting of E. W. Leonhardt, C. Roemer, and T. Schuricht. These men, together with Louis Lange and E. F. W. Meier, in 1867 advanced $3,000 for the establishment of a modest printing plant in one of the rooms connected with Concordia Seminary. In 1869 a plan was submitted to the synodical convention held in Fort Wayne, Ind., for the establishment of an official printing plant to be owned and operated by Synod. The plan was adopted, and the first building was erected on the Seminary grounds in 1870. The earlier printing activity, known as the *Synodaldruckerei,* now was given the official name of *Concordia-Verlag,* or Concordia Publishing House.

Publishing activities grew so rapidly that additional property was acquired at the corner of Miami and Indiana Avenue for the erection of a new building. The project was completed in 1874. At that time M. C. Barthel was placed in charge of manufacturing and selling and was known as General Agent. The business continued to flourish so that additional buildings were added in 1887 and 1892 along Jefferson Avenue. In 1891 Martin Tirmenstein succeeded M. Barthel as manager. Other buildings were added in 1911, 1925, and 1941 under the management of E. Seuel, who succeeded Tirmenstein in 1907. In 1944 O. A. Dorn was appointed manager upon Seuel's retirement. The publishing activity continued to flourish with the growth of the Church so that another large factory building was added in 1952.

One of the earlier publishing projects was a journal of education originally known as *Das Schulblatt,* which now bears the title *Lutheran Education.* This periodical has been issued regularly for over a hundred years. Among the major productions was the printing of the complete works of Martin Luther, published in German, the first one appearing in 1882, and the publication of the *Triglot* in 1921. The *Concordia Theological Monthly* was begun in 1855 as a German periodical under the title *Lehre und Wehre.* Many other theological and devotional books are part of the printing and publishing record of Concordia Publishing House.

The establishment employed over four hundred people in 1952 and occupied 250,000 square feet of floor space. It is one of the largest religious printing plants in the world.

Lutheran Publishing House. The publishing activities of the United Evangelical Lutheran Church actually began in 1877 by a group of Danish Lutheran pastors when they founded the periodical *Danish Luthersk Kirkeblad,* which later became the official periodical of the church body.

A special committee was appointed by the Church in 1884 to prepare plans for the establishment of a publishing plant. The committee carried on until 1891, when the activity was taken over officially by the Church, to be directed by a publication committee. In 1893 the Church voted to establish the Danish Lutheran Publishing House at Blair, Nebr.

In its early years the language used in the books and periodicals issued by the plant was almost exclusively Danish. The rise of a new generation brought a demand for the use of the English language in church and school work.

The organization is controlled by a board of seven members elected by the annual convention of the church body. The present manager is P. A. Magnussen.

The Messenger Press, formerly known as the Lutheran Free Church Publishing Company, is the publishing house of the Lutheran Free Church. It was organized in 1896 by friends of Augsburg College and Theological Seminary, and it was operated in Minneapolis, Minn., in the interests of that school and the newly organized Lutheran Free Church. In 1923 it was reorganized and was made the official publishing house of the Lutheran Free Church.

The Messenger Press is a nonprofit corporation, the earnings of which have to be used for the advancement of the Lutheran Free Church. Its corporation is responsible to the Lutheran Free Church, so it becomes the publishing agent of the Church.

At the present time it has a manufacturing plant at one location in Minneapolis and a retail store at another. From these two divisions come the publications of the Lutheran Free Church and the books and supplies that are provided for the convenience of the congregations in this church body.

A. B. Batalden is the present manager of the Messenger Press.

Northwestern Publishing House. The Evangelical Lutheran Joint Synod of Wisconsin and Other States resolved in 1876 to establish a synodical bookstore. A committee engaged F. Werner to operate the bookstore in connection with his own bookstore, F. Werner & Son, for a nominal remuneration in Milwaukee, Wis.

On June 23, 1891, the Synod resolved to establish a combined bookstore and printing shop. The committee elected for this purpose carried out this resolution, and on August 28, 1891, the business was opened in a rented building in Milwaukee. Leo Benson became the first manager. This business was incorporated as Northwestern Publishing House on October 8, 1891.

After only a few months Benson resigned, and Teacher H. Gruel was appointed manager. When he accepted a call, Adelbert Schaller succeeded him and served until 1898. On May 16, 1898,

Julius Luening assumed the duties as manager and continued to conduct the affairs of Northwestern Publishing House until 1945. The Board appointed Herbert Schaefer to succeed him.

Among the more important publishing projects was the establishment in 1865 of an official synodical periodical, the *Gemeindeblatt,* with Prof. Mohldenke as editor. An English companion periodical, the *Northwestern Lutheran,* made its appearance in 1914. At this time an English hymnbook also was published.

The plant was housed in various buildings in Milwaukee, but in 1914 Northwestern Publishing House finally moved into its own building. However, in 1947 the Board was notified that the city desired to purchase for public purposes the entire block in which the Publishing House was located, and a new home had to be found. On April 24, 1949, the present plant, located at West North Avenue and North 37th Street, was dedicated. The organization employs 42 persons.

The United Lutheran Publication House. The Board of Publication of the United Lutheran Church in America (United Lutheran Publication House), chartered January 28, 1919, is the merged board of the Lutheran Publication Society (General Synod), the Board of Publication of the General Council of the Evangelical Lutheran Church in North America, and the Board of Publication of the United Evangelical Lutheran Synod (South). It dates its organization from the year 1855, in which the Lutheran Publication Society was organized.

The need for catechisms and hymnals for use in the congregations of the Evangelical Lutheran Church led to the organization in 1855 of a Lutheran Publication Society in the General Synod. This was not officially recognized by that body until its meeting in 1857, when it was given official recognition as a Board of Publication by the election of two members of the General Synod to the Board of Directors. In view of subsequent Lutheran history the action of that body at the same session is significant: "That it be recommended to the Board of Publication to issue no books devoted to the existing controversies of the Church."

The need for the organization of a Board of Publication by the General Council was accepted without comment by the congregations withdrawing from the General Synod to form the General Council in 1867.

The organization of the Board of Publication of the United Synod South followed in due course when the southern synods withdrew from the General Synod because of sectional differences. The United Lutheran Publication House publishes and circulates the official organ of the United Lutheran Church in America, *The Lutheran*, but the control of editorial policies is in the hands of the "Church-Papers Committee" of the United Lutheran Church. Church-school curricular material prepared by the Parish and Church School Board of the United Lutheran Church is also published.

The other publications are hymnals and catechisms. Books of devotion and on religious themes are also published under the name of "Muhlenberg Press."

The Board of Publication operated eight branches in key cities in 1952.

The first business manager of the Board of Publication was Grant Hultberg, D. C. L., who assumed office in 1919 and who held the office till his death in 1938. The present executive secretary and business manager of the Board, Col. H. Torrey Walker, assumed his duties in 1939.

The Wartburg Press. 1. In Ohio the Joint Synod of Ohio began its printing activities through synodical committees as synodical agent. When the activity grew, it was felt that a more effective publication program would result through the establishment of the Church's own printing plant. The combined printing and publishing office began its operations on April 1, 1881, under the name of Lutheran Book Concern located in Columbus, Ohio.

2. After using rented property for almost twelve years, a building was purchased at 55 East Main Street into which the concern was moved January 18, 1893. As the business grew, the buildings were enlarged and remodeled to accommodate the increased activities.

3. When the American Lutheran Church was formed in 1930, the three constituent bodies merged their publication interests, with the Columbus plant as headquarters.

4. The former Iowa Synod's publishing plant, the Wartburg Publishing House in Chicago, was continued as a branch office until 1944, when conditions resulting from the war forced its closing. However, to serve the Church's constituency in the Northwest, a branch store and office was opened in Omaha, Nebr., in 1947. In 1944 the organization

was given the official title the Wartburg Press.

5. Since its establishment in 1881 there have been four managers: J. L. Tranger from 1881 to 1899; F. J. Heer from 1899 to 1906; A. H. Dornbirer from 1907 to 1940; D. M. Shonting from 1940 to 1949; and Elmer Dornbirer since 1949.

OAD

Publicity, Church. Christ's missionary command to His Church, as the guardian of His truth, demands that every means be utilized to bring the glad tidings of salvation to the attention of all men (Matt. 28:18). The great spiritual treasures that Christians enjoy are not to be selfishly guarded for personal use only, but are to be proclaimed far and wide to a fast-moving world. The Church is to employ every opportunity to go out into the world and by insistent presentation of the cause of the Lord compel the spiritually diffident bystander to come into the fold (Luke 14:23). A policy of aggressive publicity as to its stand and what it has to offer is, on the part of the Church, not only in harmony with the missionary precepts of Jesus Christ, but a necessity if the Gospel is to exert the greatest possible influence.

Publicity was part of the church program in the early New Testament era. The faith of the early established churches was spoken of as far as civilization reached (Rom. 1:8). On the day of Pentecost the Gospel was preached in many languages to many different people (Acts 2:1-11). The Apostle Paul was untiring in his preaching campaigns and making known everywhere the Gospel of Jesus.

Through the New Testament centuries until the invention of the printing press the Church publicized not so much through the printed word as through the spoken word. Beginning with Luther and the Reformation, however, the printed word established itself more and more as a competent means for bringing the life-giving message to the attention of the world.

When Lutheranism moved to the shores of America, it was quickly mindful of this fact. So, for example, a group of Saxon immigrants (the forebears of the Missouri Synod) were in this country no more than five years when they issued a paper called *Der Lutheraner*. In the formative period of early American Lutheranism this paper proved not only a great publicity agent, but also a power in uniting the widely scattered Lutherans on a firm confessional basis.

As one Protestant denomination after the other established itself in this country, publications in the form of such official organs became a part of their publicity setup. Today there is hardly a sizable church body in America which is not represented by some periodical exercising a policy of aggressive publicity. See *Religious Journalism.* In the course of time local and sectional periodicals have appeared in denominational circles, representing their specific interest in circumscribed localities. Besides this, various ins'itutions and organizations with benevolent or missionary purposes have found it expedient to issue periodicals in the interest of their respective causes. And since missionary endeavors and works of Christian benevolence are but the natural expression of Christian faith, these numerous papers have a special value as a means of presenting the Church's claims also to the outsider.

In general the character of pioneer publicity work which Protestantism exerted in this country did not call for extensive use of publicity methods in the modern sense of the term. It was not until about 1915 that various denominations began to realize the value of arousing and systematically organizing the latent publicity possibilities within the Church.

Soon after the beginning of the twentieth century Protestant bodies added to their already organized departments of missions, stewardship, finance, evangelism, etc., a bureau of publicity. Since that time publicity has become a valuable factor and art in the business world of our day. The Church, which has in its possession the pure Gospel, has the duty to use every means to bring and keep its soul-winning truth before the eyes of men.

The past 35 years have shown the wisdom of establishing such publicity departments. For out of well-organized church publicity there has resulted a more extensive use of the public press and local advertising material. By means of tracts, brochures, pamphlets, posters, and other promotional material church publicity departments have brought about stimulation for the working programs of their respective denominations. Furthermore, it is principally through the publicity departments of the various denominations that local circles and congregations have been aroused to publicize the precious wares they have to offer the souls of men.

The well-organized and effective congregation of today, therefore, considers publicity an indispensable part of its program. It will employ bulletin boards, local parish papers, daily or weekly newspapers, Sunday bulletins, tract racks, leaflets, and any other feasible means to bring the verities of Scripture before the eyes of men.

However, church publicity, regardless of what phase of work it may be, must keep clear of cheap sensationalism by which commercial advertising so largely is characterized. All of its endeavors in behalf of the Gospel should be in harmony with the dignity of its message. EWG

Manual of Practical Church Work, Luth. Press, n. p., n. d.; Paul J. Hoh, *Parish Practice, A Manual of Church Administration,* Muhlenberg Press, Philadelphia, c. 1944 (pp. 102—17).

Puerto Rico. An island in the West Indies. Since July 25, 1952, a commonwealth, wholly autonomous in all matters regarding its local government. It is voluntarily associated with the U. S. Area: 3,435 sq. mi.; population: 2,210,703 (1950). The island belongs to the greater Antilles. Discovered by Columbus in 1493. Dominant religion, Roman Catholic. Missions by a number of American churches. Statistics: Foreign staff, total of 116. Protestant community, 137,185, of which 44,575 are communicants (1952).

Pullus, Robert (d. 1150). Medieval theologian; wrote especially on repentance; held that the forgiveness of sins depends on the sacramental system.

Pulpit. See *Church Furniture,* 1.

Pulpit Fellowship. See *Altar Fellowship; Fellowship.*

Punishment, Eternal. See *Hereafter; Last Things.*

Puranas. See *Sacred Literature.*

Purcell, Henry (1658 or 1659—95). Still regarded by many as the foremost composer of music England has thus far produced. With Purcell began a new era in English music. While very little is known of his early life, his activities as Master of the Choristers of Westminster Abbey (1680—95) and as a member of the King's Band are better known. Purcell was a versatile composer who composed masterpieces in every branch of music used in his day. There is much justification for the criticism that there is no essential difference between the character of his sacred and secular works; this criticism applies also to Handel, who was strongly influenced by Purcell's style and much of whose music might easily be mistaken for music by Purcell. However, the music of Handel is less segmentary than much of the music written by Purcell; it is likewise better suited for larger choral groups. The instrumental music of Purcell is better known in America than his choral works.

G. Adler, *Handbuch der Musikgeschichte*, Frankfurt, 1924; M. F. Bukofzer, *Music in the Baroque Era*, New York, 1947; P. Lang, *Music in Western Civilization*, New York, 1941; J. F. Runciman, *Purcell*, London, 1909; E. Walker, *A History of Music in England*, London, 1907.

Purgatory. The *Catechismus Romanus* treats of purgatory very briefly. It says (I, 6.3): "Besides [hell] there is a fire of purification, where the souls of the pious, after having been tortured for a set time, are purified, so that the entry into the eternal fatherland, into which nothing impure enters, can be opened to them." The Council of Trent decrees "that there is a purgatory and that the souls there detained are helped by the suffrages of the faithful, but principally by the acceptable sacrifice of the altar" (the Mass). (Sess. XXV.) It requires that "the more difficult and subtle questions . . . be excluded from popular discourses before the uneducated multitude. In like manner such things as are uncertain, or which labor under an appearance of error, let them not allow to be made public and treated of." *(Ibid.)* The doctrine is briefly this: Those who die in a state of grace, but have not fully absolved, in this life, the temporal punishments remaining after absolution, must suffer for them after death in the fires of purgatory before they can go to heaven. The length of suffering depends on the amount of unexpiated sin. The time can, however, be shortened through the assistance of the living (by prayers, masses, indulgences). When it is considered that a large portion of Roman doctrine is colored by the conception of purgatory, the basis of this doctrine becomes of surpassing importance. Romanists have referred to such passages as Matt. 5:26; 1 Cor. 3:13-15; but Addis and Arnold's *Catholic Dictionary* (p. 704) frankly admits: "We doubt if they [the Scriptures] contain an ex-

plicit and direct reference to it." That is quite true. The Bible knows no purgatory, and the doctrine has not grown from the inspired Word, but seeped into the Church, in early times, from the speculations of Plato and other heathen and from Jewish superstitions. 2 Macc. 12:42-46. From small beginnings it grew into a cancer that poisoned the lifeblood of the Church and brought forth numerous morbid excrescences. It led to a denial of the all-sufficient satisfaction of Christ and to the substitution of man-invented works as a means of satisfying the justice of God. (See *Indulgences.*) Many of the popular notions regarding purgatory current among Romanists are not so much based on direct teaching of the Church as on purported visions and revelations.

Purificators. In liturgical churches a piece of fine linen or lawn used during the celebration of the Lord's Supper to wipe out chalice and paten and to remove any impurities in the course of the celebration.

Puritans. The term "Puritans," in use since about 1563, designates a faction in the Anglican Church which aimed at carrying on the work of reformation in the English Church to what they regarded as perfection. The movement began when John Hooper was appointed to the See of Gloucester and, under the influence of Zwingli and Bullinger, refused to wear the required clerical vestments. This "Vestiarian Controversy," strengthened by priests who had been exiled by Mary Tudor, had spent the years of her reign in Frankfurt and Geneva, and returned under Elizabeth, thoroughly imbued with the spirit of Calvin, represents the first phase of Puritanism: Opposition to the rites and vestments inherited from the Old Church as remnants of the Papacy. When the Anglican Church government tried to enforce the church regulations, Puritanism entered the second stage: Objection to the Episcopacy. They found no warrant in Scripture for church government by bishops, but demanded greater lay influence, extremists working toward introduction of Presbyterianism after the model of the Scottish Church. All along the line, almost from the beginning of the movement, runs the emphasis on better preaching by the clergy. When the repressive acts of Elizabeth drove Puritans underground, private, often secret meetings of clergymen were held for mutual edification and instruction.

But gradually these conventicles ("prophecies," "prophesyings," 1 Cor. 14: 22-24) became the centers of a movement to undermine the State Church establishment; because the State government supported the bishops, Puritans turned against the royal supremacy in the Church; and with this Puritanism enters the last stage. Puritan representatives were elected to the House of Commons, and their opposition to royal demands grew as the Stuarts in their church policy became extremely "high church." With their policy of the "divine right of kings" the Stuarts made many political enemies; and these joined the already strong Puritan, anti-royal party in Parliament, though they often did not share their religious and ecclesiastical convictions. So Puritanism became practically a political party which for a time held the majority in the House of Commons, with the help of Scottish Presbyterians defeated the king and the Anglican party, and even, in the Westminister Assembly and the Parliament of 1660, made the Presbyterian "Westminster Confession" the "Public Confession of the Church of England" — a resolution, however, which was forgotten in the following restoration. Puritans did not want to separate from the established Church, but work as a leaven within. But when, under James I and Charles I, persecution of dissenters became too severe, many of them left England, going chiefly to Holland, to Amsterdam and Leyden (whence, in 1620, the Pilgrim Fathers came to America). Others organized separate churches (Independents, Congregationalists). TH

W. Haller, *The Rise of Puritanism,* 1938; M. M. Knappen, *Tudor Puritanism,* 1939; D. Neal, *The History of Puritans;* R. G. Usher, *The Presbyterian Movement in the Reign of Queen Elizabeth,* 1905; R. G. Usher, *The Reconstruction of the English Church,* 1910 (Vol. I); T. Hoyer, "The Historical Background of the Westminster Assembly," *CTM,* XVIII: 572 ff.

Purnell, Franklin. See *House of David.*

Pusey, Edward Bouverie (1800 to 1882). Tractarian *; b. at Pusey, Berkshire; as Fellow in Oriel, Oxford, intimate with Keble and Newman; studied in Germany; professor (Hebrew) and canon at Oxford; made it task of his life to reform Anglican Church and unite England with Rome; took part in Oxford Movement, becoming its head after Newman's defection to Catholicism; composed seven *Tracts for Times;* expressed Romanizing views on efficacy of Eucharist; was suspended from preaching, 1843—46; d. near Oxford. After Pusey's sermon on the Eucharist approaching Roman idea (1843), the tenets of Tractarianism were often called *Puseyism.* Wrote *Eirenicon;* editor of *Library of the Fathers.* Remark attributed to Pius IX: "Pusey rang in the Roman Church in England, but failed to follow the sound of the bell himself."

Puseyism. See *Pusey, E. B.*

Pye, Henry John (1825—1903). Educated at Cambridge; rector at Clifton-Campville; joined Roman Church in 1868; compiled book of hymns, in which "In His Temple Now Behold Him."

Pythagoreanism. A system of ideas reputedly originated by Pythagoras, a partially legendary figure. Pythagoras (6th century) was born in Samos and founded a school at Crotona.

The Pythagoreans introduced the system of opposites (Light/Darkness; One/Many; etc.) into Greek philosophy. They held that reality consists of mystical numbers and geometric figures, being a dual existence in the form of unlimited space and numbers. They taught a system of reincarnation according to which the soul is timeless and is imprisoned in bodies without becoming a part of them. The Pythagoreans applied numbers to music, medicine, and other sciences.

Q

Q. The first letter of the German word Quelle (source). Higher critics of the NT hold that the authors of the Gospel of Matthew and Luke used Mark and Q as sources. While at one time scholars referred to the "logia" mentioned by Papias as Q, this view is being discarded and the "logia" spoken of by Papias identified with the Gospel of Matthew.

Quadragesima. A name applied to the Lenten Season (see *Church Year*), or more properly to the first Sunday of Lent.

Quadratus (2d century). Christian apologist who presented an apology to Emperor Hadrian.

Quadrilateral. See *Lambeth Conferences; Protestant Episcopal Church,* 4.

Quakers. See *Friends, Society of.*

Quartodeciman Controversy. A discussion of the ante-Nicaean period concerning the date of the Easter celebration, one part maintaining that it ought to be celebrated on the 14th of Nisan (hence the name), that being the date of the Jewish Passover and, according to many, also the date of Christ's resurrection. The quarrel was intensified by a false understanding of John 18:28. The matter was finally settled by the Council of Nicaea (325), which fixed the first Sunday after the first full moon after the beginning of spring as the day for the celebration of Easter.

C. J. Hefele, *Decision of the Easter Question* (trans. by W. R. Clark), Edinburgh, 1894 (I: 298 ff.); T. Zahn, *Geschichte des neutestamentlichen Canons,* Leipzig, 1889 (I: 180 ff.).

Quatember. A popular abbreviation of *quatuor tempora,* the designation of the four principal seasons of fasting in the Roman Church, fixed by Urban II in 1095 as being the weeks in which fasting should be practiced not only on Fridays, but also on Wednesdays (and Saturdays); they are the weeks following Ash Wednesday, Pentecost, the Festival of the Elevation of the Cross (September 14), and the day of St. Lucia (December 13). The corresponding English name is Ember Days.

Quatenus and Quia Subscriptions. See *Lutheran Confessions,* D 2.

Queensland, Evangelical Lutheran Synod of. See *Australia,* B 1.

Quellen. See *Higher Criticism,* 6; Q.

Quenstedt, Johann Andreas (1617 to 1685). Nephew of Johann Gerhard; studied at Helmstedt and at Wittenberg, where he became professor, first of geography, logic, and metaphysics, and in 1660 full professor of theology, occupying after Calov's death first place in the faculty. Though educated as a student under Calixt, he afterward, at Wittenberg, refuted the syncretistic tendencies of the former. Quenstedt has been called the "Bookkeeper of Lutheran orthodoxy." His most noted work is *Theologia Didactico-Polemica sive Systema Theologicum,* a standard of Lutheran orthodoxy, its definitions and theses based upon J. F. Koenig. Quenstedt was noted for his quiet, mild, and irenic disposition.

Quesnel, Pasquier (1634—1719). Member of the oratory of Jesus in 1657; wrote his renowned book of Christian reflections on the Four Gospels, a devotional commentary on the Gospels; condemned by papal decree, at the instigation of the Jesuits, in 1708, the book was placed on the list of prohibited publications by the bull *Unigenitus* in 1713; the author was forced to flee to Amsterdam, where he died in the Roman faith.

Quetzalcoatl. See *Aztecs, Religion of.*

Qui Pluribus. See *Bible Reading.*

Quicunque. See *Ecum. Creeds,* C.

Quidditas. A term used by the Scholastics for "essence."

Quietism. A form of mysticism which declares that spiritual exaltation is reached by self-abnegation and by with-drawing the soul from all outward activities, thereby fixing it in passive religious contemplation. Quietism was fostered in Spain by Michael Molinos (1627—96) and his followers and in France by Madame Guyon (1648 to 1717), who caused a controversy between Bossuet and Fenelon.

Quimby, Phineas P. See *Church of Christ, Scientist; New Thought.*

Quinquagesima Sunday. See *Church Year,* 3.

Quistorp. Name of several prominent Lutheran theologians. Johann (1584—1648). Studied at Frankfurt and Rostock; professor of theology at Rostock, later also superintendent; wrote: *Articuli Formulae Concordiae illustrati,* and others; firm in his confession, practical in his preaching, zealous for the education of the young, indefatigable in his ministerial activity. — Johann Nicolaus (1651—1715). Superintendent and professor of theology at Rostock, notable as teacher and writer in the field of exegesis and systematic theology.

R

Rabbi. A term meaning "master" (H. "great man," "chief"), used of Christ and others in the New Testament *(e. g.,* Matt. 26:25; John 3:10). The word came to be a title of authoritative teachers of Judaism.

Rabbinism. A designation applied to the scholastic Judaism which developed from the fourth century before Christ, in connection with the academies which were then established, till the completion of the *Talmud* in Babylon and in Palestine.

Rabelais, Francois (1494—1553). Literary genius, diligent student of languages, including Hebrew and Greek; "a priest upon whom his vows sat lightly." Wrote *Gargantua* and *Pantagruel* against evils of his time, sparing neither clergy nor Pope.

Rabinowitsch, Joseph. Originator of the Jewish-Christian movement in Kishine; born in 1837, reared in strict Judaism; turned to Christian views after a visit to Palestine; studied New Testament, established congregation; baptized in 1885; issued a number of apologetic tracts.

Rabbula of Edessa. See *Bible Versions,* C 4.

Race Relations. See *Social Action.*

Rachmaninoff, Sergei (1873—1943). Russian composer, pianist, and conductor, who, after the fall of the Czarist regime, became a citizen of the U. S. Though regarded chiefly as a romantically inclined composer of secular instrumental music, Rachmaninoff also composed much church music which is thoroughly Russian. Despite its excellent properties, the characteristic Russian moodiness and nostalgia of much of this music renders it unsuitable for use in a genuinely Lutheran service.

Racovian Catechism. See *Socinianism.*

Radbertus, Paschasius (ca. 786 to ca. 865). French abbot; distinguished writer of the age of Charles the Great; studied at Corbie; distinguished for learning and piety; was instructor, later abbot, at Corbie; his views on the Eucharist prepared the way for the doctrine of transubstantiation (see *Lord's Supper);* he was opposed by Rhabanus Maurus and others. See also *Eucharistic Controversies.*

Radio Evangelism, Network. 1. The history of religious broadcasting began on Jan. 2, 1921, when Edwin Van Etten, rector of Calvary Episcopal Church of Pittsburgh, Pa., conducted an Epiphany service over Station KDKA, Pittsburgh. Other broadcasts of individual stations followed. It was not long after this that chain broadcasting was perfected and that religious programs on the network were introduced.

2. Religious broadcasting over nation-wide networks became an established part of American radio by the middle of the 20th century. Each network recognized the obligation, in the public interest, convenience, and necessity, of devoting at least some time to the transmission of religious programs.

3. The attitudes and policies of the various networks toward religious broadcasting differed substantially. The National Broadcasting Company and the American Broadcasting Company made it a policy to grant free time for the broadcasting of religious programs to the three major faiths: Protestant, Catholic, Jewish. The time allotted to Protestantism was not granted to individual denominations. The Columbia Broadcasting System established its Columbia Church of the Air, giving time on successive Sundays to representatives of various denominations in proportion approximately equal to the numerical strength of the denomination within our country.

4. The Mutual Broadcasting System, on the other hand, while also donating considerable time for religious programs, is the only network to sell time for religious purposes (1947). At the same time, however, this network established several rigid limits on religious programs:

a. No programs shall exceed one-half hour in duration;

b. No program shall extend beyond 1:00 P. M., Eastern Standard Time;

c. No program shall feature any appeal for funds.

5. Among the paid network broadcasts which became prominent before 1950 are the following: the Old-Fashioned Revival Hour and the Pilgrims' Hour (Charles Fuller); the Young People's Church of the Air

(Percy Crawford); the Voice of Prophecy (representing the Seventh-Day Adventist Church). Among the sustaining religious broadcasts are the following: Hymns of All Churches; Wings over Jordan; Religion in the News; Sunday Evening Vespers; the Columbia Church of the Air.

6. The International Lutheran Hour (Bringing Christ to the Nations) became the most prominent Lutheran network program on the air. Beginning with two stations in 1935 (WXYZ, Detroit; WLW, Cincinnati), the Lutheran Hour was broadcasting over more than 1,100 stations in 1953. In 1953 the Lutheran Hour was broadcast in 58 countries (Alaska, Angola, Australia, Austria, Bahamas, Barbados, Bermuda, Bolivia, Brazil, British Guiana, Canada, Ceylon, Chile, Colombia, Costa Rica, Cuba, the Dominican Republic, Dutch Guiana, Ecuador, El Salvador, Ethiopia, Fiji Islands, Formosa, Germany, Guatemala, Haiti, Hawaii, Honduras, Hong Kong, Jamaica, Japan, Lebanon, Liberia, Luxembourg, Madagascar, Malaya, Mexico, Monaco, Mozambique, Newfoundland, New Zealand, Nicaragua, Panama, Paraguay, Peru, Philippine Islands, Portuguese India, Puerto Rico, Saar, Spanish Morocco, Tangiers, Tasmania, Trieste, Trinidad, United States, Uruguay, Venezuela, Virgin Islands). In the same year it was heard in 56 languages (Afrikaans, Albanian, Amharic, Arabic, Armenian, Bengali, Bulgarian, Burmese, Chinese, Czech, Danish, Dutch, English, Estonian, Finnish, Flemish, French, German, Greek, Gujarathi, Hebrew, Hindustani, Hungarian, Icelandic, Indonesian, Italian, Japanese, Javanese, Kanarese, Korean, Latvian, Lithuanian, Malayalam, Malayan, Marathi, Misri, Norwegian, Persian, Polish, Portuguese, Punjabi, Pushti, Romanian, Russian, Siamese, Slovak, Spanish, Swedish, Taiwanese, Tamil, Telegu, Turkish, Ukrainian, Urdu, Yiddish, Yugoslavian).

7. The speaker of Bringing Christ to the Nations from its beginning until the end of 1949 was Walter A. Maier,* professor of Old Testament Interpretation at Concordia Theological Seminary, St. Louis. His Scripture-founded, Christ-exalting messages enjoyed the acclaim of millions of men and women in all denominations. Lawrence Acker was the speaker during the 18th season and Armin C. Oldsen during the 19th and 20th season. It was planned to have guest speakers during 1954.

8. The mail response, representing communications from all over the world and from various types and groups of listeners averaged twelve to fifteen thousand letters per week. ERB

Radio Stations, Religious. *Brief Historical Sketch of the Rise of Christian Radio Stations.*

1. Christian churches in general were slow to realize the vast potentialities of owning and operating a radio station. In the early days of radio, facilities were available in abundance for the various denominations, and the Federal Government would have gladly assigned desirable frequencies to them. The commercial interests, however, soon came into possession of practically all radio frequencies. Here and there a denomination or an individual congregation had the vision and courage to make application with the Federal Communications Commission (originally called the Federal Radio Commission) for authorization to construct a radio station. Some of the successful applicants dropped by the way after a few years of operation or sold out completely to the commercial interests or inserted a clause into the sales contract reserving a small amount of time for the continuation of their religious broadcasts.

The opportunity to get more AM (amplitude modulation) stations with a good frequency and considerable power and time became remote. FM (frequency modulation) offers the Church a second chance. FM, a new system of broadcasting, different from the conventional system of AM, made available a host of new frequencies to accommodate not only a few more hundred, but a few more thousand stations.

2. The religious radio stations and their operators in the U. S. are (1953):

Arkansas: KRLW — Southern Baptist College, Walnut Ridge.

California: KFSG (FM: KKLA) — Echo Park Evangelistic Assn., Los Angeles; Maranatha B/cg. Co., Inc., Los Angeles; KPPC — Pasadena Presbyterian Church, Pasadena.

Colorado: KPOF — Pillar of Fire, Inc., Denver.

Illinois: WMBI (FM: WMBI-FM) — Moody Bible Institute of Chicago, Chicago; WCBD — Christian Catholic Church, Chicago; WCFL, Chicago.

Indiana: WGRE (FM) — DePauw University, Greencastle.

Iowa: KFGQ (FM: KFGQ-FM) —

Boon Biblical College, Boone; KWLC — Luther College, Decorah.

Kentucky: WMTC — Kentucky Mountain Holiness Assn., Van Cleve; WSDX (FM) — So. Baptist Theological Seminary, Louisville.

Louisiana: KVOB (FM: KVOB-FM) — Central La. B/cg. Corp. (Louisiana Baptist Assn.), Alexandria; WWL (FM: WWLH) — Loyola University, New Orleans.

Michigan: WMRP—Methodist Radio Parish, Inc., Flint; WMPC — Liberty Street Gospel Church of Lapeer, Lapeer.

Minnesota: KTIS (FM: KTIS-FM) — Northwestern Theological Seminary and Bible Training School, Minneapolis; WCAL (FM: WCAL-FM) — St. Olaf College, Northfield.

Missouri: KFUO (FM: KFUO-FM) — The Lutheran Church — Missouri Synod, Clayton.

New Jersey: WSOU (FM) — Seton Hall College, South Orange; WAWZ — Pillar of Fire, Zarephath.

New York: WKBW — WKBW, Inc. (Churchill Tabernacle), Buffalo; WBBR — Watch Tower Bible and Tract Soc., Inc., New York.

Rhode Island: WPTL — Providence Bible Institute, Providence.

Texas: KMHB (FM) — Mary Hardin-Baylor College, Belton; KWBU — Baylor University (Baptist General Convention of Texas), Corpus Christi; KYBS (FM) — Baptist General Convention of Texas, Dallas; KSMU (FM) — Southern Methodist University, Dallas; KELP — Paso B/cg. Co., Inc. (Richey Evangelistic Assn.), El Paso; KHBL (FM) — Wayland Baptist College, Plainview; KFTW — S. W. Baptist Theological Seminary, Fort Worth.

Virginia: WBBL — Grace Covenant Presbyterian Church, Richmond.

Washington: KTW — First Presbyterian Church, Seattle; KGA — Gonzaga University, Spokane.

3. KFUO, "The Gospel Voice," was founded Dec. 14, 1924, when a 500-watt transmitter with other necessary equipment, also a control room and a studio, were dedicated to the glory of God in the attic of the old Concordia Seminary on S. Jefferson Ave., St. Louis, at the cost of $14,000 contributed by members of the Lutheran Laymen's League, the students of the Seminary, the Walther League, and individuals. J. H. C. Fritz and Walter A. Maier constituted the first Radio Committee. The St. Louis Lutheran Publicity Organization appropriated an annual sum toward the

maintenance of the station. When the station was founded, only two hours a week were utilized. In 1925 Herman H. Hohenstein was called as full-time director of the station. The station was moved to the campus of the new Seminary (801 De Mun Ave., St. Louis) and rebuilt in 1927 at a cost of $50,000, contributed by the Lutheran Laymen's League. On the day of dedication, May 29, 1927, the Lutheran Laymen's League presented the new building, the new towers and antenna system, and the new 1,000-watt transmitter to The Lutheran Church — Missouri Synod as an outright gift. After the removal of the station to the new Seminary the hours of operation were increased to approximately 30 hours a week. In 1940 the Federal Communications Commission granted KFUO a new frequency, with full day-time broadcasting privileges, from 80½ to 102½ hours a week. This grant from the Government necessitated the erection of a new tower and antenna system and the enlarging and renovation of the radio building. A new 5,000-watt transmitter, too, was installed, which made KFUO a greater missionary agency than before. These improvements entailed an expenditure of over $100,000 and made KFUO one of the leading religious radio stations in the world.

Subsequently KFUO installed an FM transmitter and enlarged the radio building.

The KFUO Radio Committee consists of 13 members (1953) and Radio Director. The Board of Control of Concordia Seminary has been given charge of the station by The Lutheran Church — Missouri Synod.

KFUO is dedicated to the preaching of the Gospel of Jesus Christ. It has therefore always placed its religious programs first in importance. The Gospel is presented in various ways, such as sermons, sermonets, devotions, meditations, Bible hours, dramas, dialogs, interviews, round-table discussions, and poems. However, the station does not broadcast religious programs exclusively. Its schedule of programs includes an abundance of good music and news releases covering world news, civic affairs, sports, agriculture, etc. KFUO is supported solely by voluntary contributions from larger and smaller Lutheran congregations, organizations, societies, and from many individuals.

4. The KFUO Radio Committee also serves as the National Radio and Tele-

vision Committee of the Missouri Synod. One of the activities of this committee is the annual promotion of National Lutheran Radio and Television Week. The purpose of this week is to encourage individual congregations or groups of congregations to avail themselves to the fullest possible extent of the radio and television facilities in their communities. Radio committees in the various Districts of The Lutheran Church — Missouri Synod throughout the United States and Canada co-operate with the National Board in sponsoring this annual movement. The sectional committees arrange for Lutheran broadcasts in many localities where a radio station is available. HHH

Raffael Santi (1483—1520). Among the greatest Italian painters; noted for charm and nobility of drawing, for unit composition, for moderate characterization, and for rich coloring, under the influence of classicism, but combining with it an almost ethereal romanticism; his madonnas with much womanly charm, especially the Sistine Madonna, now at Dresden; his "Burial of Christ" full of emotion and contrast; in his later years paintings for the Camera della segnatura of the Pope (in the Vatican); also the "Liberation of Peter" and several large altar paintings; the canons of his art continued by his many pupils.

Raikes, Robert (1735—1811). B. at Gloucester, England; editor and printer of the *Gloucester Journal;* was much interested in social and philanthropic questions, especially in prison reform; saw the chief cause of degradation in the neglect of adequate training of children. In 1780 he engaged a woman to take charge of a Sunday school for depraved and vicious children. Accounts of the work in his *Journal* attracted much attention. Though Raikes is not the founder and "father" of the Sunday school, he became its first great propagandist and promoter. See *Sunday School.*

Railroad Brotherhoods. The labor unions in which railway engineers, firemen, conductors, carmen, trainmen, clerks, telegraphers, and others hold membership have the name "Brotherhood" in their titles. Usually the activities of the societies are conducted under a ritual, and initiation is under an obligation which has the form of an oath. While these ceremonials are very similar to those of the lodge, so that we are dealing with labor unions which partake of the character of a secret order,

one cannot fail to recognize that in purpose the brotherhoods and the fraternal orders differ essentially. The railroad brotherhoods are not organized to establish a brotherhood along fraternal, but along industrial lines, and religious principles, teachings, and practices are not of the essence of the order or among the declared purposes. The railroad brotherhoods do not belong to the organizations which derive their essence from "fraternal" relations or from purposes directed toward character building or preparation for the life to come. The purpose of the organization, even if it has religious ceremonies, is not religious or social, but is for the improvement of the laboring man's condition, hence is economic and directly related to the calling of those organized. If a man wants to work on the railroad, he must be a member of the union. The religious features are an *accidens,* not the essence or purpose of the order, a difference which must be kept in mind in passing judgment on the affiliation of Christian church members with these brotherhoods. See Bibliography under *Lodges.* TG

Rainbow Girls. See *Freemasonry,* 4.

Rainy, Robert (1826—1906). Pastor of Free Church of Scotland; prof. of history (1863) and principal (1874) of New College, Edinburgh; influential in the Union of the Free Church and United Presbyterian Church in Scotland; outstanding orator; author.

Rakau Catechism. Book of instruction of the Polish Unitarians, work on which was begun by Faustus Socinus, completed by Schmalz, Moscorow, and Voelkel; issued in Polish in 1605, German in 1608, Latin in 1609; the name taken from the city where it was first printed.

Ram Mohan Roy (1772—1833). Founder of the Brahma Samaj, which took much of its ethics from the Christian religion; regarded as the founder of the study of comparative religion.

Ramadan. The ninth month of the Mohammedan year, during which the adherents of Islam commemorate the giving of the Koran by fasting.

Ramayana. See *Hinduism,* 6; *Sacred Literature.*

Rambach, August Jakob (1777 to 1851). B. at Quedlinburg; d. at Ottensen. Studied theology at Halle. Deacon at St. Jacobi Church, 1802; chief pastor at St. Michaelis, 1818; and senior of the ministerium, at Hamburg, 1834. He is noted as a hymnologist, possessing a hymnological library of two thousand volumes, later presented by his widow to the city library of Hamburg.

Rambach, Johann Jakob (1693 to 1735). Studied at Halle; was interested by Michaelis in the study of the Old Testament and assisted him in the preparation of his Hebrew Bible; 1719 at Jena, under Franz Buddeus; in 1727, after Francke's death, his successor as ordinary professor, also preacher at the *Schulkirche,* being popular in both fields; in 1731 superintendent and first professor at Giessen, later also director of the *Paedagogium;* a voluminous writer, known for the thoroughness of his research work; wrote: "Gesetz und Evangelium sind beide Gottesgaben"; "Baptized into Thy Name Most Holy"; "My Maker, Be Thou Nigh."

Ramsay, Sir William Mitchell (1851 to 1916). Scottish classical scholar and church historian; b. at Glasgow, professor at Oxford and Aberdeen; traveled extensively in Asiatic Turkey in the course of his researches in the history of early Christianity; lectured at Baltimore, etc.; knighted; wrote: *The Church in the Roman Empire; St. Paul the Traveler and the Roman Citizen;* etc.

Ramus, Petrus (*Pierre de la Ramée,* 1515—72). French philosopher; b. near Soissons; d. in Paris; vigorous opponent of Aristotelian scholastic philosophy; converted to Calvinism by Beza; fled from Paris to Germany and Switzerland; returned 1571 and perished in Massacre of St. Bartholomew.

Randall, John. See *Baptist Bodies,* 24.

Ranke, Leopold von (1795—1886). Celebrated historian and founder of a school of historians; professor at Berlin; wrote: *Die roemischen Paepste, ihre Kirche und ihr Staat im 16. und 17. Jahrhundert; Deutsche Geschichte im Zeitalter der Reformation.*

Ransom. See *Atonement; Justification.*

Ranters. A name given by Presbyterians to mystical and antinomian radicals of the Cromwellian period. They were frequently accused of lewdness and irreligious actions and utterances.

Rappites (Harmonists). Followers of Georg Rapp (1757—1847). In 1805 he founded a communistic community at Harmony, Pa.; emigrated to Indiana 1814, founding New Harmony; returned to Pennsylvania 1824, founding Economy, near Pittsburgh. The community gradually died out because it had adopted celibacy.

Ras Shamra. See *Higher Criticism,* 21.

Raselius, Andreas (ca. 1563—1602). Composer of Lutheran church music who was active in Regensburg and Heidelberg. Like some of his contemporaries, Raselius tried to write contrapuntal arrangements of chorales in such a manner that the congregation could sing the simple chorale as *cantus firmus,* while the choir sang the remaining parts contrapuntally. His settings differed from those of his contemporaries in this, that the counterpoint he employed was not of a simple *nota con.ra notam* type.

Rashdall, Hastings (1858—1924). English theologian and philosopher; sought to combine features of idealism and utilitarianism; wrote *Theory of Good and Evil.*

Raskolniki. See *Russian Sects.*

Rasmussen, Peter Andreas (1829 to 1898). B. in Norway; came to America, 1850; teacher; attended the Practical Seminary, Fort Wayne, 1853 to 1854; pastor, editor, publisher, author; member of Eielsen Synod, Norwegian Synod, of the church organization known as "Anti-Missouri," and United Norwegian Lutheran Church.

Rathmann, Herman (1585—1628). Pastor in Danzig. In a controversy with his colleague Corvinus on the efficacy of the words of Scripture he asserted that they had not in themselves the power to convert.

Ratichius, Wolfgang (1571—1635). Studied at Hamburg and Rostock; concentrated on the field of education and compiled his educational principles in his *Nova didactica,* became educational adviser in various parts of Germany, but was considered a practical failure except for his insistence on the use of the vernacular and on psychological principles.

Ratio Studiorum. Educational code of Jesuits * inaugurated in 1599.

Rational School. See *Isagogics,* 3.

Rationalism. The term "rationalism" has been used in many different ways, and care must be exercised to avoid misrepresentation.

Lucretius, the Roman poet-philosopher, ascribed to the Greeks the leadership in investigating the essence of things on the basis of reason. As used in philosophy, the origin of rationalism is usually traced to the Eleatic School (Parmenides, Xenophanes), Pythagoreans, and Plato. It is applied to systems which are deductive; which hold that reason, apart from sense, is the highest criterion; which apply mathematical methods; or which make coherence a criterion of truth. As contrasted with empiricism, rationalism has been described as having the following marks: abstract, supernatural, absolute, certain, peaceful, authoritative, eternal, and religious (H. Martin, *The Inquiring Mind*).

The religious usage of the term does not correspond completely to the philosophic usage. As applied to scholasticism, rationalism implied the application of dialectics to theology. When applied to the theology of Zwingli or Calvin, the term is often meant to imply that these theologians interpreted revelation in such a way as to render it harmonious with deductive reasoning, logic, and/or phenomena.

In the 17th century attempts were made to show that Christianity is a reasonable faith (Joseph Glanvill: *Anti-Fanatical Religion and Free Philosophy;* John Tillotson; John Locke: *Reasonableness of Christianity;* Samuel Clarke: *The Truth and Certainty of the Christian Revelation*). Revelation was not rejected, but the contention held that revelation is in harmony with reason (rational supranaturalism).

When reason gained the upper hand, the transition to deism followed. A step in this transition may be seen in the work of John Toland *(Christianity Not Mysterious),* which held that revelation could offer nothing above reason. The rationalism of deism rejected revelation, but was tempered by the assumption of five doctrines of "universal religion."

The next stage was the rejection of all dogmatic assertions, thus leading to the rationalism of skepticism. Leaders in this phase of rationalism were Thomas Hobbes, David Hume, Bernard de Fontenelle, Pierre Bayle, Francois Marie Arouet de Voltaire, Denis Diderot, Michel Eyquem Montaigne, Claude Adrien Helvetius, Frederick the Great, Ethan Allen, Elihu Palmer, Gouverneur Morris, and others.

Rationalistic skepticism led to atheism and mechanistic philosophies (early modern exponents: Lucilio Vanini; Julien de la Mettrie, Baron d' Holbach).

Four types of attitudes toward rationalism in the religious realm are: 1) Revelation is above reason; 2) Revelation and reason are in harmony; 3) Revelation and reason are in conflict, but may be held in compartments; 4) Revelation is to be discarded in favor of reason. Rationalists who are anti-authoritarians must be distinguished from those who are anti-supranaturalists. EL

W. E. H. Lecky, *History of the Rise and Influence of the Spirit of Rationalism in Europe,* Longmans, Green, 1904; J. M. Robertson, *Short History of Free Thought,* Watts & Co., 1906; H. Martin, *The Inquiring Mind,* Barnes & Noble, 1947; J. F. Hurst, *History of Rationalism,* Carlton & Porter, N. Y., 1866; H. R. Mackintosh, *Types of Modern Theology,* Scribner's, N. Y., 1939; T. Engelder, *Reason or Revelation,* CPH, 1941.

Ratisbon Book. The formula of agreement upon which the Regensburg Conference * was held.

Ratisbon Conference. Sometimes erroneously called *Interim,* at Regensburg, in April, 1541, between Gropper, Pflug, and Eck on the one side, and Melanchthon, Bucer, and Pistorius on the other. Here was the nearest approach to a reunion between the Lutherans and the Papists. And yet, despite the earnest efforts of Contarini and Karl, the conference came to naught. The Papists, with growing concern, viewed the spread of Lutheranism and mistrusted their emperor more than did the Lutherans, and the political difficulties kept Charles from taking harsh measures against the Lutherans. In great disgust Charles left on July 29, saying he would now, like all the rest, work only for his own interests.

Ratramnus. See *Eucharistic* and *Predestinarian Controversies.*

Ratzeberger, Matthias (1501—59). Became acquainted with Luther at Wittenberg; physician to Elector John Frederick; lay student of the Bible, who often came to Luther and Melanchthon in religious matters and attended the diets of Frankfurt and Speyer.

Rauh, Frederic (1861—1909). French philosopher; advocate of materialistic and experimental morality.

Rauhes Haus. See *Inner Mission*, 1.

Raumer, Karl Georg von (1783 to 1865). B. at Woerlitz; German mineralogist and historian (history of education). Studied mineralogy and geology at Paris, but influenced by Fichte and the work of Pestalozzi, he turned to education. In 1823 he became teacher and later principal of a private school at Nuremberg, where he also founded an institution for delinquent boys. In 1827 he re-entered the public service; was appointed professor of mineralogy in the University of Erlangen. *History of Education from the Revival of Classical Learning Down to Our Time.*

Rausch, Emil Friedrich (1807—84). Studied at Marburg, Halle, and Berlin; truly awakened to the truth of the Lutheran Confessions as pastor in Kassel, where he testified against rationalism; persecuted and driven out of Kassel, he continued to testify at Rengshausen, where he also founded a home for neglected boys, likewise a printing establishment; issued several series of sermons.

Rauschenbusch, Walter (1861—1918). Leader of social gospel movement in early twentieth century with Washington Gladden and Shailer Mathews. Professor of church history at Rochester Theological Seminary 1903—18, after teaching at German Baptist Seminary 1897—1902 and pastorate at Second German Baptist Church, New York City, 1886—97. His father, Augustus, who came to the U.S. as a Lutheran missionary and joined the Baptists in 1858, had also taught church history at Rochester Seminary. Walter Rauschenbusch identified the kingdom of God with social evolution and economic-political reformism as part of Christian life, stressing personal regeneration in combination with politico-social change for this world in preference to apocalyptic and spiritual views of the kingdom of God. His social gospel was an application of ethical "Kingdom" principles to the economic and social order. Became a member of the Christian Socialist Fellowship as an "academic socialist." Organized the Brotherhood of the Kingdom with Samuel Z. Batten and others in 1892. The Rauschenbusch Memorial Lectureship, founded in his memory at Colgate-Rochester Divinity School in 1929, pre-sents lectures on social Christianity. The first four annual lectures were given in 1931. Author of: *The Kingdom of God* (1895); *Christianity and the Social Crisis* (1907); *Prayers of the Social Awakening* (1910); *Christianizing the Social Order* (1912); *Dare We Be Christians* and *Social Principles of Jesus* (1916); *A Theology for the Social Gospel* (1917). See *Social Gospel.* JD

A. E. Burckhardt, *Walter Rauschenbusch as a Representative of American Humanism,* unpublished S. T. M. thesis at Union Theol. Seminary, New York, 1925; A. M. Singer, *Walter Rauschenbusch and His Contribution to Social Christianity,* Boston, Badger, 1927; Dores R. Sharpe, *Walter Rauschenbusch,* New York, Macm., 1942; Vernon P. Bodein, *The Social Gospel of Walter Rauschenbusch and Its Relation to Religious Education,* New Haven, Yale Press, 1944.

Raymond of Sabunde. A fifteenth-century Spanish savant; ca. 1430 taught medicine, philosophy, later also theology at Toulouse, wrote book *Liber naturae sive creaturarum,* thereby becoming founder of natural theology, claiming a virtual agreement between faith and understanding and placing the book of nature next to the book of God's revelation, the Bible; tried to prove practically every truth of Christianity by logical deduction.

Real Presence. See *Grace, Means of,* IV, 3.

Realism, practical, as opposed to idealism, is the attitude to take things as they really are in life and to make the best of them. The realist deals with facts and is seldom swayed by high ideals; he seeks less to improve the world than to make use of it. Philosophical Realism is the theory that general abstract ideas have real existence, independent of individual objects. Thus the idea of a circle exists apart from round things (Nominalism, Idealism). Psychological Realism teaches that things have real existence, independent of our conscious experience. The tree I see exists not merely in my consciousness, as a concept of my mind, but there really is a tree in the yard. Common sense is realistic as it assumes that objects we perceive really exist. Still, in hallucinations we see things which are not real. In literature, realism as opposed to romanticism and idealism, pictures life, not as it should be, but as it is, setting forth details of life, based upon observation of social and physiological phenomena.

Realism, Biblical. See *Switzerland, Contemporary Theology in*, 7.

Realschule. A secondary school of Germany, which offers a six-year course in modern subjects, as distinguished from the *Gymnasium*, which emphasizes classical studies. In 1859 it was organized as a school for general culture rather than for vocational training. The *Real-Gymnasium* offers a nine-year course in science, mathematics, drawing, two modern languages, and Latin.

Reason and Faith. See *Rationalism*.

Rebling, Gustav (1821—1902). Organist and composer who helped bring musical fame to Magdeburg. The style of his compositions was typical of German organists of the 19th century: it is usually churchly and objective, but often also dry and pedantic, especially when compared with the works of the masters of the 17th and 18th centuries.

Recall. See *Christian Teaching*, E.

Recapitulation. In theology the theory, first advanced by Irenaeus, that the Logos, in His state of humiliation, went through all the experiences of the life of a sinner in order to purge man's sinfulness by His sinlessness. In pedagogy the theory that a human being must grow through all the biological and social experiences of the human race, according to the theory of evolution, in order to reach maturity.

Recessus Jenensis. A compromise offered to the vicar general of the Augustinian order by Staupitz in 1511, in which he stated that he would not relinquish his position as provincial of Saxony. His compromise suggestions seemed so acceptable that the opponents promised to submit them to the convent. However, this led to a bitter discussion, with the majority of the fathers refusing to sanction the agreement. Since Luther and his friend Johann Lang voted in favor of the suggestion of Staupitz, they were dismissed from the Erfurt institution.

Rechlin, Friedrich. B. Feb. 16, 1851, on the Island of Ruegen in the Baltic; came to America, 1867; grad. from the Teachers Seminary at Addison, Ill., 1869; teacher at Davenport, Iowa, Albany, N. Y., Trinity Church, Cleveland, Ohio; prof. at the Teachers Semi-

nary in Addison, 1893 (later also at River Forest, Ill.). D. Dec. 9, 1915.

Recluses. Hermits immured in their cells (or caves; even tombs), as a special service to God. Some were monastics, their cells being near monasteries and churches; others, especially lay persons, dwelt in isolation, in forest or wilderness. They were admired and fed by the ignorant populace, among whom they enjoyed an odor of special sanctity and often a reputation for miraculous powers. Some of them were evidently demented. There were recluses as late as the 17th century.

Recollects. One of the reform parties within the Franciscan order named after the "recollection houses" founded by them to give opportunity for prayer and penance. Their separate existence ceased in 1897.

Reconciliation. The act of making those friends again who were at variance, or restoring to favor those who had fallen under displeasure. The enmity between God and the world has been removed by the death of Christ, and this gift is appropriated by the sinner through faith (Acts 10:43; 2 Cor. 5:19; Eph. 2:16). Man is spoken of as becoming reconciled to God, but never as reconciling himself to God. Christ reconciles both Jews and Gentiles to God "by His cross." Peace is made between God and man, not in the first instance, by subduing the enmity of man's heart, but by removing the enmity of "the Law," "Christ having abolished in His flesh the enmity, even the Law of Commandments." The reconciliation of man with God, which has been prepared for all men by the atonement of Christ, becomes effective in the individual when he, by the power of the Spirit in the Word, accepts the meritorious sacrifice of Christ through "faith in His blood." (Cp. 2 Cor. 5:18, 19.) See also *Atonement*.

Records. See *Christian Teaching*, V.

Recreation. Refreshment of body and mind through natural expression of human interests during leisure time, by diversion, agreeable exercise, play, and the like.

Play activities date from ancient times (*e. g.*, wrestling, tag games, ball games). The Greek educational theory and practice emphasized adequate training of the young in mind, spirit, and body.

That the body as well as the soul

should be cherished and nurtured is in accordance with the importance assigned by the Bible to the human body (body specially formed by God, Gen. 2:7; body is temple of God, 1 Cor. 3:17; 6:19; body assumed by Christ in incarnation, John 1:14; body shares in resurrection, Phil. 3:21; 1 Cor. 15:12).

Among the types of recreation mentioned in the OT are: racing (Ps. 19:5; Eccl. 10:11), "mirth making" (Neh. 8:12), feasting (Amos 8:10), storytelling and riddles (Judg. 15:12; Ezek. 17:2), children playing (Zech. 8:5), and dancing * (Job 21:11), archery (1 Sam. 20:36 ff.). Attempts to introduce national games similar to those of the Greeks were made during the reigns of Antiochus Epiphanes and Herod the Great, but met with severe criticism (1 Macc. 1:10-14; Josephus, *Antiq.,* 15:8:1). Some recreations mentioned in the NT are: feasting and merrymaking (Luke 15:25; cf. John 2:1 ff.), music and dancing * (Luke 15:25), children making music and dancing (Matt. 11:17). Allusions to Greek games are frequent in the NT (*e.g.,* 1 Cor. 9:24 ff.; 2 Tim. 4:7 ff.; Heb. 12:1). There are also instances in the Bible in which entertainment took place under sinful circumstances (*e.g.,* Ex. 32:6; Judg. 16:25; 1 Sam. 25:36; Amos 6:5 ff.; Matt. 14:6 ff.).

During the Dark and Middle Ages the Teutonic influence caused interest in physical and military games. The monastic view that the body should be degraded to glorify the soul caused a negative attitude toward pleasurable bodily recreation. During the Renaissance movement humanistic interests fostered ideals in opposition to those of monastic asceticism.

Luther restored a positive attitude toward recreation. His view is summarized in the words: "God has indeed created body and soul and desires both to be allowed and given recreation (*Erquickung*), but with proper measure and purpose" (*Masz und Ziel*). (St. L. Ed. I:1711.) Luther emphasizes the importance of the body (VIII:851; VIII: 1248). Not to take care of the body, or abuse it, as was done in the monastery, he considered a mortal sin (XIII:785). The pleasing things at hand should be enjoyed (V:1566—70), but also recreation should be sanctified by prayer (V:1111).

Although sports developed comparatively early in England, it was Puritanism with its emphasis upon a harsh and joyless existence which was brought to New England and fostered the idea that recreation and leisure were idleness and sin.

The earliest form of recreation to appear in America were "bees," and community celebrations (*e.g.,* husking bees, church socials, etc.). The centralization of population in the larger cities and shortened working hours led to the development of systems of parks and playgrounds, camps, and other forms of planned recreation. The early offerings for recreation were confined generally to sports, games, and physical activities for the young. Then there followed arts, crafts, hobbies, music, dramatics, and finally all leisure interests of all people were included — interests which give a natural expression and satisfaction during leisure time.

The Lutheran Church — Missouri Synod from earliest times (C. F. W. Walther, J. F. Buenger, *Luth.* VII:170) stressed the need of a youth organization among the primary purposes of which were entertainment, social contacts, and recreation (*e. g.,* music, entertaining games, good reading. Cf. *Luth.* LXII:387 ff.). In the course of time churches gave increased attention to recreation for all age groups. LFW

E. Eckhardt, "Jugend," "Jugendverein," *Reallexikon,* Success Printing Co., St. Louis, 1910; G. B. Fitzgerald, *Community Organization for Recreation,* Barnes, N. Y., 1948; Gardner, *Handbook for Recreation Leaders,* U. S. Dep't of Labor, 231, U. S. Printing Office, 1936; J. Hastings, *Dictionary of the Bible,* N. Y., 1898; Nixon and Cozens, *Introduction to Physical Education,* Saunders, Philadelphia, 1941; C. Peters, "Achieving Witness in Christian Recreation," *CTM,* XXI:37—43.

Rector. An academic title, given in some countries to the chief executive officer of a university and to principals of Catholic colleges and seminaries the world over. In the Anglican Church it is the ecclesiastical title of a clergyman who has charge of a parish and full possession of all consequent rights and privileges. In the Protestant Episcopal Church in America the title is also used, though the ecclesiastical status of the rector differs from that of the Anglican rector.

Recusant. A term applied to those who refused to acknowledge the king's supremacy or refused or neglected to attend church and worship after the manner and customs of the Anglican Church. This term differs from Nonconformist in that it includes also recusants in the Roman Catholic Church.

Red Cross. Organized as the American Association of the Red Cross in 1881 by special efforts of Miss Clara Barton, who was its first president. In 1905 the name was changed to National Red Cross, the President of the Uni'ed States becoming its president and the War Department its auditor. The cornerstone to a memorial building in Washington was laid in 1915, and the building became the national headquarters in 1917. The Red Cross not only cares for wounded and sick soldiers during the time of a war, but also provides so-called disaster relief in times of peace.

Redemption. To "redeem," literally, means to "buy back." Redeem as well as redemption are used both in the classical Greek writers and in the New Testament for the act of setting free a captive by paying a ransom, or redemption price. In Christian theology the terms stand for our recovery from sin and death by the obedience and sacrifice of Christ, who on this account is called the Redeemer (Rom. 3:24; Gal. 3:13; Eph. 1:7; 1 Pet. 1:18 f.; 1 Cor. 6: 19 f.; Matt. 20:28; 1 Tim. 2:6; Is. 59:20; Job 19:25). The subjects in the case are sinful men; they are under guilt, under the curse of the Law, the servants of sin, under the power and dominion of the devil, liable to the death of the body and to eternal punishment. To the whole of this class the redemption applies itself. There is a deliverance from sin, its mastership, and all evils that follow transgression. Yet it was not a gratuitous deliverance; the ransom, the redemption price, was exacted and paid. The precious blood of Christ was given for captive and condemned men. According to Eph. 1: 7-10 the Gospel of Christ and the redemption in Him, whereby we are made abundantly wise unto salvation, is a manifestation of the mystery of the divine will, the revelation of a divine decree, which but for that revelation would have remained hidden in the heart of God, who, according to His good pleasure, which He has purposed in Himself, executed His counsel in the fullness of time (Gal. 4:4, 5). The singling out of Abraham, Isaac, Jacob, Judah, and David as ancestors of the promised Messiah, the setting apart of His peculiar people, and the wondrous ways by which He led that people through the centuries before the fullness of time were preparatory measures to the great series of events extending from the Annunciation to the death and burial of Christ and the completion of His work, upon which the seal of divine authority was stamped by the glorious resurrection of the Savior of mankind.

Redemptorists. An order of missionary priests, founded by Alphonsus Liguori at Scala, Italy, in 1732, mainly to "preach the Word of God to the poor." In addition to the three usual vows its members promise to refuse all ecclesiastical dignities outside of the order and to persevere in the order till death. The Redemptorists, in spite of some fundamental distinctions, closely resemble the Jesuits in purpose and methods and have repeatedly taken their place when the latter were expelled from a country. In the United States the order does both parish and mission work. It has convents in most large cities, serves chiefly German and Bohemian congregations, and makes a specialty of preaching missions.

Redenbacher, Wilhelm (1800—76). Lutheran divine. B. at Pappenheim; d. at Dornhausen. Studied at Erlangen. Held pastorates in Bavaria and Saxony. He opposed rationalism and, as pastor at Sulzkirchen, the order of the Bavarian ministry of war requiring all soldiers, also Protestants, to genuflect to the host when carried in procession. He was suspended and condemned to a year in prison; Protestant pressure, however, induced the king to remit the latter penalty. After a pastorate in Saxony he returned to Bavaria. He published sermons, devotional books, and history.

Redpath, Henry Adeney (1848 to 1908). Anglican; Biblical scholar; b. and d. at Sydenham; priest, 1874; rector; lecturer at Oxford; completed Hatch's *Concordance to the Septuagint* (Oxford, 3 vols.); other works.

Reed, Andrew (1788—1862). An English philanthropist of renown; one of the most successful and popular preachers (Congregationalist) of his day; founded Hackney Grammar School, London Orphan Asylum, Infant Orphan Asylum at Wanstead, the Asylum for Fatherless Children at Reedham, the Idiot Asylum at Earlswood (with a branch at Colchester), and the Hospital for Incurables; established schools for children and founded the first pennybank for savings; refused remuneration for his services, contributed a large part of his yearly income to charity, and lived in a simple way; visited the United States in 1835; wrote many works on practical theology and was the author of many hymns, among them "Holy Ghost, with Light Divine."

Reform Judaism. See *Judaism*.

Reformation, Anglican. See *England, Reformation in; Anglican Confessions*.

Reformation, Lutheran. 1. A reformation is a change back to a former normal condition. It presupposes formation and deformation.

2. *The Reformation* in church history designates the movement in the 16th century which aimed to restore the Church, founded by Jesus Christ, deformed in the course of centuries, chiefly by the Papacy, to its early normal condition, and which resulted in the separation of a great part of the Western Church from the medieval Church of Rome.

3. There were movements preparatory to the Reformation. *Humanism* provided freedom of thought and learning; but in Italy it absorbed the pagan philosophy of the ancient classics; in Germany and Italy it fostered study of the Scriptures, but promoted only a moral and ethical reformation. The *universities* took the lead in demanding reform, but beyond furnishing the intellectual centers for the spread of criticism they could not go. *Mysticism* insisted on inwardness of religion and a personal relationship between creature and Creator against the externalism and institutionalism of the Church, but lost all objectivity and became totally subjective. The growing *nationalism* had its place in the preparation for a successful reformation in arousing violent criticism of the arrogant claims and opposition to the demands of a "foreign prince," and as a result the willingness to protect a fellow citizen against attacks from abroad.

4. None of these, however, could accomplish a true reformation of the Church, chiefly because the real root of corruption was not recognized; this was the doctrine of the meritoriousness of good works in the way of salvation. This is a direct denial of the central truth of the Gospel. This fact points out not only that a thorough reformation of the Church was needed, but that a reformation involving separation

from the old Church was justified. It was hopeless to expect such a reformation from the Church itself. Since the days of the Cluniac revival this had been attempted by individuals and associations within the Church; outstanding among these were the Waldenses, first to call attention to the fact that the Church had obscured the source of religion — a "back-to-the-Bible" movement; they were driven underground by persecution. — Wycliffe * and Hus,* who saw and proclaimed the basic fault in the Church, were cut off in the beginning of their real reform work, and the whole movement, being linked closely with a nationalistic endeavor, was stifled by changes in the political world. (For men commonly called "Reformers before the Reformation," see, in addition to those mentioned in this paragraph, *Savonarola; Jerome of Prague; Wessel, Johann;* and the *Brethren of the Common Life*.)

5. The never-failing weapon of the Church by which every reform effort, in fact, all opposition to the hierarchy was killed, was the Interdict (a papal decree by which the priests of a land were kept from functioning, totally or partially); the power of this weapon again lay in the universal belief in the divine primacy of the Pope, giving him right and power arbitrarily to stop administration of sacraments by ordained priests (the only ordinary means of grace) and so virtually to close heaven to all who were affected by the Interdict. All popular or official support of a reformer was always effectively quashed by this weapon.

6. Even the greatest reform effort instigated by a part of the Church, the Reform Councils, backed by lay influence, failed because no one in their midst seems to have recognized the root of corruption in the Church; they were concerned only with reform of abuses; furthermore, the history of the Councils shows that Papacy and hierarchy were opposed to reform. How completely the Councils failed even to produce a moral reform is evident from this, that, despite the fact that the Papacy had almost lost its authority by action of the Councils, yet the moral level of its incumbents sank to lowest ebb in the Renaissance Popes. Add the example of Savonarola to show the hopelessness of accomplishing a reform from within the Church.

7. The man of the Reformation was Martin Luther. The beginning of the

Reformation is the moment when Luther, moved by an increasingly bitter soul struggle, seeking the answer to the question: How do I obtain a gracious God? found it in the words of St. Paul, Rom. 1:17. The Church could not give him assurance of God's grace; the requirement of good works as, at least, a partial price of grace left the matter doubtful: Had he done enough? Was what he had done good enough? The Church would not give another answer; doubt kept souls in bondage and willing to pay for priestly service. St. Paul told him that in the justification of a sinner before God his own works, whether good or evil, do not enter in at all; the sinner is justified solely and only by God's grace by imputation of the righteousness of Jesus Christ through faith.

8. What he had found he preached and taught. When he found that through indulgences the people were taught a false way of salvation, he attacked that unsavory traffic, Oct. 31, 1517. When the specters of excommunication and interdict began to loom in the distance, he attacked the Pope's primacy jure divino, both on Scriptural and historic grounds (Leipzig Debate, 1519). He taught Christians (in the Letter to the Christian Nobility of the German Nation and On the Babylonian Captivity of the Church, 1520) that religion is a personal matter between the sinner and his God, without mediation of a special priesthood; if he has found God's grace through faith in Christ, neither priest nor Pope can separate him from God and heaven — thus robbing the Interdict of its power and insuring the success and permanency of his reformation. Before Emperor and the representatives of the Church he upheld the sola Scriptura as source of doctrine, and every Christian's right of private judgment against dictation of Church and secular power (Worms, 1521). The same Scriptural standard he maintained against the radicals in Wittenberg, 1522: While all that is forbidden by Scripture must be abolished, all rites and customs of the old Church which embody nothing that is prohibited may be retained.

9. Action against Luther by papal authorities was begun at once after the posting of the 95 Theses on Oct. 31, 1517. It reached its culmination in two papal bulls, the Exsurge, Domine of June 15, 1520, threatening Luther with excommunication if he did not recant within 60 days, and the actual Bull of Ex-

communication, the Decet Romanum of Jan. 3, 1521, which excluded Luther from the Roman Church. The separation was accepted by Luther and his co-laborers in Wittenberg by the public burning of the papal bull Exsurge, Domine on Dec. 10, 1520. It was officially endorsed by the Emperor in the Edict of Worms, which outlawed Luther and his followers. The Edict was published as a resolution of the German Diet; in fact, it was presented to, but not accepted by the Diet; after the Diet had adjourned, it was discussed and adopted by the Emperor and a few of his electors and princes, antedated and published as an edict adopted by the Diet. The question of its validity, it seems, never arose, perhaps because it was not enforced (except sporadically in Hapsburg territories) for political reasons. The papal interdict was threatened, but not imposed, since by that time it was evident that the German people, instructed by Luther, would simply have ignored it.

10. The Reformation spread rapidly, entering the various lands chiefly through Luther's writings; these were read by earnest priests, and, convinced, they began to preach Luther's teaching. So the Reformation always grew, as it were, from the bottom up; never was it imposed by governments. That was tried by Christian II of Denmark for political reasons; he was deposed and exiled, 1523. But through preaching the sentiment among Danish people by 1527 had changed so greatly that their representatives in the Diet granted toleration. By 1530 a Lutheran confession was prepared.

11. Not all government officials who adopted Lutheranism were perfect; political and personal reasons at times played a motivating role in their efforts to introduce the Reformation in their lands. But this can be said: The occasional use of force on the part of Protestants was almost always due to one or two reasons: Roman attacks in persecution of the Reformation had to be met in defense of life and property; Romans were always the aggressors, Protestants always on the defense. — Or government officials had to use police power to quash plots instigated by Roman agents against those who permitted introduction of the Reformation. Protestant governments were officially deposed by the Pope, making every consistent Catholic a traitor; resulting rebellious moves had to be met by force.

12. By 1540 the Roman Church had lost all of northern, most of middle Germany; all of the Scandinavian countries; in the buffer states (Poland, Bohemia, Moravia, Hungary, Transylvania) nine-tenths of the population was said to be Lutheran; even in South Germany Lutheran influence was strong. England had separated from Rome, and, though still Catholic, was beginning to lean toward Protestantism. That was the reason why the Roman Counter Reformation was turned from a policy favoring compromise to open and violent attack, led by the newly organized Jesuit Order, in the end involving most of western Europe in the religious wars. At about the same time Calvinism began to supplant Lutheranism in some of the German states; one of the reasons for this no doubt was that, facing the Counter Reformation and its Inquisition the people of these lands found Calvinism more attractive since it was more aggressive, favoring the use of force not only in defense, but in attacking Romanism.

13. The Lutheran Reformation is the mother of all the reform efforts of that and the succeeding periods. Others reaped, at least in part, where Luther had sown. The division in the Protestant Church is not a result of the Reformation, but a misdevelopment of Reformation principles; it resulted when certain leaders departed from the authoritative Word and followed either their human reason or their own subjective opinions.

14. If the Reformation needed a justification, the history of the following centuries has certainly furnished it in the higher moral life and the greater culture of the people adopting it. Even the higher moral tone in the old medieval Church is a result of the Reformation, which changed public opinion and constrained that church to cater to it. See also *Denmark, Germany, Norway, Sweden, Luther, Martin.* TH

J. Mackinnon, *The Age of the Reformation,* Henry Holt, N.Y., 1929; P. Smith, *The Age of the Reformation,* Henry Holt, N.Y., 1920; P. Smith, *Life and Letters of Martin Luther,* Houghton, Boston, 1911; F. M. Lindsay, *History of the Reformation,* Scribner's, 1906; J. Koestlin, *The Theology of Luther in Its Historical Development and Inner Harmony* (tr. C. E. Hay), Luth. Pub. Soc., Philadelphia, 1897; J. Koestlin, *Life of Luther,* Scribner's,

N.Y.; Th. Kolde, *Martin Luther,* Perthes, Gotha, 1884; Monographs of *Verein fuer Reformationsgeschichte;* A. C. McGiffert, *Martin Luther, the Man and His Work,* Century, N.Y., 1910; H. Boehmer, *Road to Reformation,* Muhlenberg P., Phila., 1946; B. K. Kuiper, *Martin Luther, The Formative Years,* Eerdmans, Grand Rapids, Mich., 1943; *Cambridge Modern History,* II—IV; see references under *Luther, Martin;* popular works: H. E. Jacobs, *Martin Luther,* Putnam's; W. Dallmann, *Martin Luther* (CPH); W. G. Polack, *The Story of Luther* (CPH); S. N. Carpenter, *The Reformation in Principle and Action,* Luth. Publ. Soc., 1917; E. Schwiebert, *Luther and His Times* (CPH), 1950.

Reformation Medals. Few fields of modern numismatics attracted the attention of collectors so early or have been studied and published so carefully as the medals and coins relating to Luther and the Reformation. A monograph on the subject in Latin, *Vita Mart. Lutheri et Historia Reformationis numis illustrata* appeared as early as 1699. One of the most important collections of engravings of Luther medals, containing plates of 145 medals with explanations is that of Christian Juncker, *Vita D. Martini Lutheri et successuum Evangelicae Reformationis Jubilaeorumque Evangelicorum,* Frankfurt and Leipzig, 1699. A work based on Juncker appeared in 1739 by F. C. Lesser, under the title of *Besondere Muenzen,* Frankfurt and Leipzig. Another authoritative and standard work was published by H. G. Kreussler, *Luthers Andenken in Muenzen* (Leipzig, 1818). Recently Max Bernhart gave a thorough analysis of the contemporary Luther medals in his article "Reformatorenbildnisse auf Medaillen der Renaissance," published in the periodical *Numismatik,* December, 1933. A comprehensive collection of Luther and Reformation coins and medals is deposited in Concordia Historical Institute, St. Louis, Mo.

Reformation, Reformed. See *Calvin, John; Zwingli, Ulrich; Reformed Church; Reformed Confessions; Presbyterian Confessions.*

Reformation, Roman Catholic. See *Counter Reformation.*

Reformed Churches. 1. The original home of the Reformed Churches is chiefly in Switzerland, France, Holland, Scotland, and England. The name "Reformed" was applied especially to the followers of Zwingli and Calvin, who hoped to reform the church by abolishing the papal ceremonies and to establish the church government according to their interpretation of the Bible. Since the Arminian Controversy in 1610 the Reformed are divided into the Calvinistic and Arminian Reformed. The term "Reformed" is rarely used when speaking of the adherents of Arminian theology, while the term is used to denote Calvinists. In Scotland and England the followers of Calvin's principles in theology and polity are today generally known as Presbyterians, while the adherents of Calvin on the Continent, especially in Switzerland, Holland, France, and parts of Germany, adopted as their official designation the term "Reformed." In its restricted sense, therefore, the term "Reformed" is used to denote those continental Calvinistic Churches whose theology is Calvinistic and church polity Presbyterian. The difference between Presbyterian and Reformed Churches is chiefly in the different nomenclature: the Reformed Churches use the terms consistory, classis, synod for the Presbyterian terminology of session, presbytery, assembly.

2. *Reformed Church in Holland.* The Reformed Church of the Netherlands was an outgrowth of the Zwinglian Reformation of the 16th century. In Holland the labors of the "reformers before the Reformation," John Wesel Gansevoort (1420—89), Johann Wessel (1419 or 1420—98), and Rudolf Agricola prepared the way for the conflicts of civil and religious liberty which later on took place in the Low Countries. Gansevoort was an eminent teacher at Heidelberg, Louvain, Paris, Rome, and at last head of the celebrated school in his native city of Groningen, where he died in 1489. Agricola was professor in the University at Heidelberg and was noted for his classical and scientific attainments, especially for his skill in the use of the Greek New Testament. The work of these two men prepared the way for the civil and religious conflict which followed under Charles V and his son, Philip II of Spain. However, especially after Martin Luther had proclaimed the great doctrines of the Scriptures which shook the world, evangelical truth struck its roots deep down into the hearts of the people. Though the Evangelicals were violently persecuted by the papists, confessors and martyrs for Christ were never wanting for the persecutions of the

government and the Inquisition. Because of their manifold afflictions the Evangelicals in Holland called their churches "the churches of the Netherlands under the cross." For many years they worshiped privately in scattered little assemblies, until they finally crystallized into a regular ecclesiastical organization. Nor could the ban of the empire or the curse of Rome keep down the rising spirit of these heroic believers in Christ. The hymns of Beza and Clement Marot, which have been translated from the French, rang out the pious enthusiasm of the multitudes, who were stirred by the eloquence of their preachers. In 1563 the Synod of Antwerp was held, which adopted the Belgic Confession and laid the foundations of the Church, to which subsequent synods only gave more permanent shape, especially the Synod of Dort,* which in 1610 adopted the five points of Calvinism.* Her scholars and theologians, her schools and universities, her zeal and martyr spirit, gave the Reformed Church of Holland the leading position among the sister churches of the continent, while her religious liberty made her a refuge for the persecuted of other lands; the Waldenses, Huguenots, Scotch Covenanters, and the English Puritans found a welcome at her altars. It was in Holland also that John Robinson and his followers, who later became the voyagers of the *Mayflower,* found a refuge for eleven years, and this explains the large influence which the Reformed Church of Holland has exercised not only over its direct adherents who emigrated to America, but also over other American churches of the Reformed type.

3. *Reformed Church in Germany.* The Reformed Church was established in Germany largely as a result of the controversy concerning the Lord's Supper. During the Crypto-Calvinistic Controversy the Palatinate under Elector Frederick III in 1563 officially accepted the Calvinistic doctrine of the Lord's Supper. The members of the German Reformed Churches profess a Lutheranism which is dominated by Melanchthonianism with its rationalistic and unionistic principles. The Heidelberg Catechism, adopted in 1563, is a compromise between Melanchthon's and Calvin's theology and is unsatisfactory to both genuine Lutherans and strict Calvinists. In 1614 Brandenburg under Sigismund became Reformed. Until 1817 the Reformed and the Lu-

theran Churches existed side by side as the two Protestant parties in many German provinces. The Prussian Union * of 1817 was designed to erase the doctrinal differences, but only added another church body to the existing two, namely, the *United Evangelical Church*, and until the present time Germany has this tripartite division of churches.

4. *Reformed Churches in America*. a) The *Reformed Church in the United States* was organized by German Reformed. It is now united with the former Evangelical Synod, the merger known as the *Evangelical and Reformed Church*.* b) The *Reformed Church in America*. The Reformed Church in America was founded by emigrants from Holland, who formed the colony of the New Netherlands, under the authority of the States-General and under the auspices of the Du'ch East India Company. With Governor Minuit, in 1626, came two *krank-besoeckers*, or *zieken-troosters*, that is, comforters of the sick, namely, Jansen Krol and Jan Huyck. The first minister, Jonas Michaelius, graduate of the University of Leyden and afterwards a missionary in San Salvador and Guinea, arrived in 1628, and a church was organized with at least 50 communicants, consisting both of Walloons and Dutch. The first church building was erected in New Amsterdam in 1633. At first the work was in charge of the Synod of Holland, but the American colonists sought greater freedom from the mother church, and under the leadership of T. J. Frelinghuysen arranged for the training of its own clergy by founding in 1766 Rutgers College at New Brunswick, N. J. The Reformed Dutch Church in the United States, as it was known in 1792, expanded especially in New York and New Jersey. In 1850 large numbers of Hollanders, in some instances entire congregations, with their pastors, emigrated to America, especially to Michigan and Iowa. "The doctrinal standards of the Reformed Church in America are the Belgic Confession, the Heidelberg Catechism, and the Canons of the Synod of Dort. The church is thus a distinctively Calvinistic body. It has a liturgy for optional use in public worship, with forms of prayer. Some parts of the liturgy, as those for the administration of Baptism and the Lord's Supper and for the ordination of ministers, elders, and deacons, are obligatory; the forms of prayer, the marriage

service, etc., are not obligatory. Children are "baptized as heirs of the Kingdom of God and of His Covenant"; adults are baptized (by sprinkling or immersion, as preferred) on profession of repentance for sin and faith in Christ. All baptized persons are considered members of the church, are under its care, and are subject to its government and discipline. No subscription to a specific form of words being required, admission to Communion and full membership is on confession of faith before the elders and minister." (Census Report, II, p. 1506.) c) The *Christian Reformed Church* was organized in 1857 by such Dutch emigrants to Michigan and Iowa as did not approve of the doctrinal and disciplinary position of the older Dutch Reformed groups. This body has remained conservative, and adheres strictly to the Calvinistic theology as laid down in the Belgic Confession, the Canons of Dort, and the Heidelberg Catechism. It follows the custom of the Reformed Presbyterian Church in using Psalms in the public service, although in recent years this rule has been relaxed. In addition to its college and seminary at Grand Rapids, it supports a flourishing system of Christian elementary schools. d) The *Free Magyar Reformed Church in America* is a small body of Hungarian Reformed who did not agree to the "Tiffin Agreement" whereby they were transferred from the mother church in Hungary to the Reformed Church in the United States. It accepts the Reformed confessions, and in church polity occupies middle ground between episcopacy and Presbyterianism. See *Religious Bodies (U. S.), Bibliography*. FEM

Reformed Church in the United States. See *Evangelical and Reformed Church, 1*.

Reformed Confessions. A. 1. *Swiss Reformed*. The *Sixty-Seven Articles* (1523) of Zwingli are similar to the 95 Theses of Luther inasmuch as they were prepared for public discussion at Zurich. They emphasize salvation for all who believe the Gospel (XV); Christ the only high priest (XVII); Mass not a sacrifice, but a commemoration (XVIII); oppose purgatory (LVII) and celibacy (LIX).

2. *Ten Theses of Bern* (1528) were prepared by Zwingli for a discussion at Bern and emphasize that the Christian is born of God's Word. They oppose the corporeal and essential

presence (IV), invocation of mediators (VI), purgatory and offices for the dead (VII), worship of images (VIII), imposed celibacy (IX).

3. Zwingli submitted his own *Confession of Faith to Emperor Charles V* at Augsburg, which differed from the Lutheran Confession chiefly on the Lord's Supper and original sin.

4. The *Exposition of the Christian Faith to King Francis I* (1531) embodies Zwingli's beliefs concerning God, Sacraments, saint worship, Mariolatry, incarnation, justification, Christ's person, the Church, magistrates, faith and works, remission of sins, eternity, and less important doctrines.

5. *First Confession of Basel (Confessio Fidei Basileensis;* 1531; 22 articles) was prepared by Oecolampadius and is essentially in agreement with confessions of Zwingli.

6. The *Helvetic Confessions* are the most important documents of the Swiss Protestant churches. The *First* (1536; 27 articles) was drawn up because of efforts to unite Lutherans and Reformed (Bucer, Capito) and the prospects of another general Council by Bullinger, Myconius, Grynaeus, and others. It treats Holy Scripture (I—V); the doctrine of salvation (VI—XIII); the Church, Word, Sacraments, and church ordinances (XIV—XXVII). This proved too short and too Lutheran and was displaced by the *Second Helvetic Confession* (adopted 1566; 30 articles), which was originally prepared by Bullinger as his private confession. It treats the Scriptures and traditions (I, II); God (III); idols and worship through Christ (IV, V); Providence (VI); creation (VII); sin (VIII); free will (IX); predestination and election (X); Christ (XI); Law and Gospel (XII, XIII); repentance and justification by faith (XIV, XVI); Church, ministry, and Sacraments (XVII to XXII), and less important matters of doctrine and polity. The Helvetic Confession was adopted in Switzerland, Scotland, Hungary, France, and Poland.

7. Calvin, during his first stay at Geneva, prepared a *French* Catechism (1536; 58 articles) treating man, true and false religions, knowledge of God, sin and death, way of salvation, the Law, predestination, faith, justification, sanctification, regeneration, good works, creed, Sacraments, Church, traditions, excommunication, and civil magistrates.

Reworked and printed (1541), it became the basis for other catechisms.

8. Continued debates between Lutherans and Reformed regarding the Sacrament led to the writing of the *Consensus of Zurich* (final form, 1549; 26 articles). The first draft (by Calvin with notes by Bullinger) was called the *Consensus Tigurinus.* It was adopted by various Swiss centers, thus creating unity. It contains Calvinistic doctrine adjusted to Zwinglian expression asserting that we receive Christ's body in the Sacrament by the power of the Spirit and the lifting of our souls to heaven (restricted to the elect).

9. The *Consensus of Geneva* (1552) is an elaborate argument by Calvin defending absolute predestination. It was occasioned by the fierce attacks of Albert Pighius (d. 1542; Catholic; wrote *De libero hominis arbitrio et divina gratia* against Luther and Calvin) and Jerome Bolsec (Carmelite monk, then Protestant, then Catholic again; wrote notorious libels against Calvin).

10. *The Helvetic Consensus Formula* (1675). After the adoption of the Canons of Dort (1619) a relatively liberal school arose at Saumur. Louis Cappel (1585—1658) demonstrated the recentness of vowel points and errors in the sacred text (*Critica Sacra*); Moses Amyraut (1596—1664) developed conditional universalism in election; Josue de la Place (1585—1658) denied immediate imputation of Adam's sin. In opposition to these, John Henry Heidegger (1633—98), with the collaboration of Lucas Gernler (d. 1675) and Francis Turretin (1623—87), wrote the *Consensus Formula.* It defended, in 26 articles, inspiration (even of vowel points), absolute predestination, immediate imputation of Adam's guilt, and other doctrines.

B. *Reformed Confessions in France.* The *Gallican Confession (Confession of Rochelle)* was drawn up by Calvin, adopted by the Synod of Paris (1559), revised by Beza, and adopted by the Seventh National Synod at La Rochelle (1571). Its 40 articles are a summary of the doctrine and discipline of Calvin. It was superseded by the *Declaration of Faith of the Reformed Church in France* (1872).

C. 1. *The Reformed Confessions in the Netherlands.* The *Belgic Confession* (1561; with the *Heidelberg Catechism* the recognized symbol of Holland, Belgium, and Dutch Reformed in America) was prepared by Guido de Bres (ca.

1523—67; Reformed evangelist and martyr of the Netherlands) and adopted at Dort (1619). Its 37 articles follow the Gallican Confession but are more on Trinity, incarnation, Church, Sacraments.

2. The opposition of the Arminians to the Calvinistic doctrines on predestination led the states general of the Netherlands to convene the Synod of Dort (Nov. 13, 1618—May 9, 1619), which was attended by deputies from the states (62) and 24 foreign divines (Great Britain, Switzerland, Palatinate, Hesse, Bremen; Lutherans not represented). In the 125th session the Five Articles of the Arminians * were rejected and Remonstrants * expelled. Thereafter the Canons on the five articles upholding Calvinism were adopted: I. Predestination (18 articles); II. Redemption (9); III, IV. Man's Corruption and Conversion (17); V. Perseverance (15).

D. 1. Reformed Confessions in Germany. The Tetrapolitan Confession (Confessio Suevica or Argentinensis; 23 articles; oldest Reformed symbol in Germany) was hastily prepared by Bucer (with Capito and Hedio) at Augsburg (1530) for Constance, Lindau, Memmingen, and Strassburg and sought to effect a compromise between Lutherans and Reformed on the Sacraments.

2. The Heidelberg Catechism (Palatinate Catechism) was drawn up by Zacharias Ursinus (1534—83; disciple of Melanchthon; professor at Heidelberg) and Caspar Olevianus (1536—87; professor at Heidelberg; Calvinized Palatinate) by order of Frederick III ("the Pious"; 1559—76; favored Calvinistic view on the Lord's Supper in the Lutheran-Reformed controversy in Palatinate) for use in the schools in order to Calvinize his Lutheran territories (1562). It is reticent on predestination, firm on the Lord's Supper, and polemic on the Mass. Its 129 questions are divided into three parts: I. Misery of man; II. Redemption of man; III. Gratitude due from man.

3. Brandenburg Confessions. a. John Sigismund (Elector of Saxony, 1608 to 1619), although pledged to Lutheranism by his father, prepared his own Confession (1614) in which he endorsed Reformed doctrine, but with the reservation that God is not the cause of damnation.

b. During the Thirty Years' War efforts were made (William of Branden-

burg and William of Hesse) to unite Lutherans and Reformed in order to present a common front against the enemy. A colloquy was arranged at Leipzig (1631), but differences on communication of attributes, Eucharist, and election were especially noticeable. Protocols of the meeting were published.

c. The Declaration of Thorn is a very careful statement of the Reformed Creed drawn up for the Conference of Thorn (1645; called by Ladislaus IV of Poland to prevent strife between Catholics, Lutherans, and Reformed). It is divided into a general part and special declaration. Clergy from Poland, Lithuania, and Brandenburg signed it.

d. Less important Reformed confessions are: Confession of Elector Frederick III (1577); Confession of Anhalt (1581); Confession of Nassau (1578); Bremen Confession (1598); Hessian Confession (1608); Confession of Heidelberg Theologians (1607); Catechism of Emden (1554).

E. 1. Reformed Confessions of Bohemia, Poland, and Hungary. Before the Reformation the catechism The Smaller Questions (1489; 51 questions in three divisions: faith — Creed; hope — Lord's Prayer; love — Ten Commandments) served confessional purposes among Waldensians in Bohemia.

2. The Bohemian Catechism (1521; 75 questions) follows the Smaller Questions, but also treats the Beatitudes, and has more on idolatry, worship of Mary, saints, and martyrs, and the Lord's Supper.

3. After the Reformation the Bohemians wrote 34 confessions. The first (Bohemian Confession, 1535) was presented to Ferdinand at Vienna. It adhered closely to the Augsburg Confession, and Luther published it with favorable comment.

4. Emperor Maximilian II (1564—76) permitted the Protestants to send their own confession to a diet of Prague. Utraquists, Lutherans, Calvinists, and Bohemian Brethren agreed upon a moderate statement prepared by Paul Pressius and M. Krispin (1575). It followed the Augsburg Confession, but agreed with Melanchthon's later views on the Lord's Supper.

5. The Consensus of Sandomierz (1570) is the only important confessional document of Poland. It states that the three evangelical churches (Lutherans, Zwinglians, and Moravians)

agree on the doctrines of God, Trinity, Christ, justification, and other important dogmas. In the Lord's Supper it distinguishes between the visible elements and the heavenly substance.

6. The *Hungarian Confession* was prepared at the Synod of Czenger (1557—58) and is strongly Calvinistic. See *Presbyterian Confessions.* EL

E. F. K. Mueller, *Die Bekenntnisschriften der Reformierten Kirche,* Deichert, Leipzig, 1903; H. Heppe, *Bekenntnisschriften der Reformierten Kirchen Deutschlands,* Fridrichs, 1860; *Bekenntnisschriften und Formulare der niederlaendisch-reformierten Kirche,* Kaufmann, Elberfeld, 1901; P. Schaff, *Creeds of Christendom,* Harpers, 1899—1905.

Reformed Ecumenical Synod, First. Convened at Grand Rapids, Mich., Aug. 14—30, 1946. Such a synod was first suggested by H. H. Kuyper (1924) to the Reformed Church in South Africa. In 1927 this group made overtures for synods to the Reformed Church of the Netherlands. These two groups, together with the Christian Reformed Church in America, arranged the synod. It adopted the following bases for future synods: The Holy Scriptures of the OT and NT (in their entirety regarded as infallible) as interpreted in Reformed Confessions (Helvetica Prior, Heidelberg Catechism, Confessio Gallicana, Confessio Belgica, Confessio Scotica, Westminster Confession, Canons of Dort, Thirty-Nine Articles). Church polity was not made a criterion of membership.

Calvin Berkhof, "First Reformed Ecumenical Synod," *Calvin Forum,* Nov., 1946; Calvinistic Action Committee, *Calvinism in Times of Crisis,* Baker Book House, Grand Rapids, 1947.

Reformed Episcopal Church. This denomination owes its origin to Bishop George David Cummins * of Kentucky, a former member of the Protestant Episcopal Church and a representative of the evangelical element in that Church, which was strongly opposed to High Church, or ritualistic, tendencies. For some time he had been much disturbed by the decidedly ritualistic tendencies of his Church and by the loss of true catholicity, and he now felt the criticisms uttered against him as new evidence of these tendencies. In consequence of this he withdrew on November 10, 1873. A number of other clergymen of his faith shared his opinions, and on a call from him 7 clergymen and 20 laymen met in New York City on December 2 and organized the Reformed Episcopal Church. — In doctrine the Reformed Episcopal Church accepts the evangelical doctrines as set forth in the Thirty-nine Articles of the Protestant Episcopal Church, the Nicene Creed, and the Apostles' Creed, with the omission of the words, "descended into hell." It rejects the doctrine that the presence of Christ in the Lord's Supper is a presence in the elements of bread and wine and that regeneration is wrought by and through Baptism. Instead of the words "priest" and "altar" the terms "ministers" and "Lord's Table" are substituted. — The polity agrees with that of the Protestant Episcopal Church. For public worship the Church accepts the *Book of Common Prayer* as revised by the General Convention of the Protestant Episcopal Church in 1785; but it holds that no liturgy should be imperative and reserves full liberty to alter, abridge, enlarge, and amend the same as may seem best, provided "that the substance of the faith be kept entire."

Reformed Mennonite Church. See *Mennonite Bodies,* 3.

Reformed Methodist Church. See *Methodist Bodies,* 4 b.

Reformed New Congregational Methodist Church. See *Methodist Bodies,* 4 b.

Reformed Presbyterian Church. See *Presbyterian Bodies,* 1.

Reformed Presbyterian Church of North America. See *Presbyterian Bodies,* 4.

Reformers Before the Reformation. See *Reformation, Lutheran,* 4.

Regalia Petri. "The various rights and high prerogatives which, according to Romanists, belong to the Pope as a kind of universal sovereign and king of kings." The term "regalia" is also applied to certain ecclesiastical privileges regarding which various sovereigns clashed with the Roman See. See *Investiture.*

Regeneration. See *Conversion,* II, 1.

Regensburg Conference. See *Ratisbon Conference.*

Reger, Max (1873—1916). Roman Catholic composer of organ music who based many of his compositions on the Lutheran chorale. He was the son of a Bavarian teacher and received much of his training from Hugo Riemann. He was a great admirer of Bach and, like Brahms, excelled as a composer of chamber music. While his choral works, in some instances, are monumental (*e. g.*, Psalm 100), Reger is largely thought of as a composer of organ works. Althouh his small compositions (*e. g.*, *Thirty Short Chorale Preludes; Orgelwerke*, op. 67) are excellent, his larger works for organ are too often extremely difficult, pompous, complex, and adventurous. Reger wrote largely for the virtuoso organist, and his harmony and counterpoint often become an end in themselves.

Guido Adler, *Handbuch der Musikgeschichte*, Frankfurt, 1924; D. N. Ferguson, *A History of Musical Thought*, N. Y., 1948; G. Frotscher, *Geschichte des Orgelspiels und der Orgelkomposition*, Schoeneberg, Berlin, 1935; H. Pappen, *Max Reger*, Leipzig, 1921; B. Weigl, *Handbuch der Orgelliteratur*, Leipzig, 1931.

Regula Chrodegangi. A rule drawn up in 760 by Chrodegang, bishop of Metz, member of the order of Benedictines. Intended first of all for the clergy of his diocese, and numbering 34 chapters, it was later expanded into 80 chapters. The purpose of the *regula* was to raise the moral and spiritual level of the clergy. It found such great favor that, in 817, it was made obligatory for the whole empire.

Regular Baptists. See *Baptist Bodies*, 21.

Regular Clergy. See *Secular Clergy.*

Regular Veterans' Association. See *Veterans' Organizations.*

Rehmcke, Johannes (1848—1930). Prof. of philosophy at St. Gall, Berlin, Greifswald; sought a philosophy outside of materialism and idealism; sought especially to determine the essence of consciousness; God is the real.

Reichert, G. A. (1795—1877). Luth. missionary in western Pennsylvania until 1837.

Reimann, Georg (1570—1615). B. at Leobschuetz, upper Silesia; at time of his death professor of rhetoric at Koenigsberg; wrote: "Wir singen all' mit Freudenschall"; "Aus Lieb' laesst Gott der Christenheit."

Reimarus, Hermann Samuel (1694 to 1768). Prominent German rationalist; taught at Wittenberg, rector in Wismar, in 1727 professor of Hebrew and Oriental languages at the *Gymnasium* in Hamburg; wrote *Apologie oder Schutzschrift fuer vernuenftige Verehrer Gottes*, from which Lessing culled the so-called *Wolfenbuettler Fragmente*, which established the negative deistic criticism in Germany, chiefly because they were influenced by the German philosopher Wolf. The *Fragmente* are a vicious attack, even on the morality of the writers of the Bible. (See *Lessing, Gotthold Ephraim*).

Reincarnation. The doctrine of the transmigration of souls (*metempsychosis*), as taught in various non-Christian religions. The theory appears in various forms, all of which hold that the soul may re-enter some body or succession of bodies, thus leading a continued existence. See *Transmigration of Souls.*

Reineccius, Jakob (1572—1613). B. at Salzwedel; d. at Hamburg. Studied at Wittenberg. Pastor at Tangermuende; pastor and provost at St. Peter's, Berlin, 1601; pastor of *Katharinenkirche*, Hamburg, 1609; inspector of the Gymnasium there, 1612. He published collections of sermons and other theological works.

Reinhard, Franz Volkmar (1753 to 1812). German theologian; prof. at Wittenberg; outstanding preacher and author. Belonged to the Lutheran school of supranaturalists who held to revelation but explained away much of the miraculous content of the Bible. Issued 35 volumes of sermons and wrote extensively in the field of ethics and dogmatics.

Reinke, A. B. Sept. 29, 1841, at Winsen, Hanover; graduate of Concordia Seminary, St. Louis, 1864; pastor in Blue Island, Ill., and of Bethlehem, Chicago; founded the Deaf-mute Mission of the Missouri Synod; main founder of the Old Folks' Home in Arlington Heights; member of Board for Deaf-mute Missions; d. Nov. 18, 1899.

Reinken, Johann Adam (1623 to 1722). Outstanding representative of the famous Lutheran North German School of Organists of the 17th and 18th centuries. Reinken was a native of Holland; he was a pupil of Heinrich Scheidemann,* whom he succeeded (1654) as organist of the *Katharinenkirche* in Hamburg, where he served for 68 years. He was one of the founders of the German opera in Hamburg, and J. S. Bach made several journeys to Hamburg to consult the aged Reinken and to hear him play. It was Reinken who remarked to Bach: "I had thought that the art of improvisation had died, but I see it will continue to live on through you." Reinken was a great organist and improviser. His compositions too often stress his desire to display thorough passage work; as a result, their form and structure is often weak. His *Hortus Musicus* is played occasionally by performers of chamber music.

G. Frotscher, *Geschichte des Orgelspiels und der Orgelkomposition*, Berlin-Schoeneberg, 1935; H. C. Lahee, *The Organ and Its Masters*, Boston, 1902; C. F. Abdy Williams, *The Story of Organ Music*, London-New York, 1905.

Reiterated Conversions. See *Conversion*, II, 8.

Relativism. While the term *relativity* is applied to Einstein's mathematical theory of space-time, which makes direction and distance, rest and motion, measurement, duration and related matters relative to a frame of reference, the term *relativism* is applied to the view which holds that truth may vary from individual to individual (knowledge is relative to the mind which knows it; the content of which the mind is aware is relative to past experiences; moral codes are relative to culture and experience).

Released-Time Classes. See *Christian Education*, E 9 ff.; *Parish Education*, F 4.

Relevance of Old Testament. See *Higher Criticism*, 25.

Relics. The Roman Catholic position on relics is given as follows by the Council of Trent (Sess. XXV, *De Invoc.)*: "The holy bodies of holy martyrs and of others now living with Christ . . . are to be venerated by the faithful; through which [bodies] many benefits are bestowed by God on men, so that they who affirm that veneration and honor are not due to the relics of saints or that these and other sacred monuments are uselessly honored by the faithful and that the places dedicated to the memories of the saints are in vain visited with the view of obtaining their aid, are wholly to be condemned." This unscriptural and superstitious veneration of relics is one of the most striking contributions of the semipaganism that invaded the Church in the fourth century.

2. Both the Old and the New Testament instill respect for the mortal remains of the godly dead, but they know only one way of showing this respect — decent burial. So the early Christians honored the remains of the martyrs, risking their own lives to give them a Christian burial. They assembled at the tombs of the martyrs to keep alive their memory, to exhort one another to like faithfulness, and to praise God, who had kept the martyrs steadfast to the end.

3. In the fourth century this respect and honor turned to a worship of relics, which assumed increasingly fantastic forms. Relics came to be regarded as having inherent supernatural properties. Churches were built over the tombs of martyrs; the graves of others were rifled, so that unprovided churches might deposit the relics under their altars or permit the faithful to touch and kiss them. A definite traffic in relics developed; and when the visible store proved inadequate, dreams, visions, and apparitions disclosed new supplies of astonishing variety, ranging from the feathers of angels to some hairs of the beard of Noah, the son of Lamech. Such objects commanded staggering sums; and, indeed, had they possessed only a portion of the miraculous virtues ascribed to them, they would have been cheap at any price. Prayer and worship in their presence were supposed to carry uncommon sanctity and virtue in the eyes of God. They were held to have the power of healing disorders of body and mind, of defending against the wiles of the devil, of giving peculiar sanction to oaths, and of bringing about miraculous happenings. Since the division of a relic was claimed to leave its efficacy unimpaired, fragments of relics were worn as charms or amulets.

4. The veneration shown to relics was accounted a meritorious work, pleasing to God, and rewarded by Him with temporal and eternal benefits. Nor are these the superstitions of a past age. They are teachings and practices current in the Roman Church today, and if, for reasons of expediency, they are kept in the background in enlightened countries, they come to the front all the more frankly in Pope-ridden lands. Even now no Roman church is dedicated without having relics in its altar. The chapter on fraudulent and duplicate relics cannot be opened here, diverting as it is. The unblushing frankness of the *Catholic Encyclopedia* is refreshing. It admits (see *Relics)* that "many of the more ancient relics duly exhibited for veneration in the great sanctuaries of Christendom or

even at Rome itself must now be pronounced to be either certainly spurious or open to grave suspicion." Yet it calls those "presumptuous" who blame the Church for continuing to dupe the people, because, forsooth — the fraud is so old. That is bad enough. But far more serious is the fact that by the cult of relics, as by so many other practices of the Roman Church which have neither command nor promise in Scripture, men are drawn away from the living God, in whom alone there is help. Instead, they are taught to put trust in men, living men and dead men — even in the bones and ashes of men.

Relief Church. See *Presbyterian Bodies*, 1.

Relief Work. This is work done by the Church for the relief of people visited by such calamities as fire, flood, tornado, pestilence, and the like. Some churches have a special fund out of which such relief can be granted as soon as needed. See *Benevolence*.

Religion, Comparative. The study of the various religions and religious systems of the world in a comparative way. In the strict sense, comparative religion aims to examine all aspects of religions according to scientific principles and on the basis of the results of such investigations to construct histories, psychologies, and philosophies of religion. Comparative religion has also been used to show the superiority of one religion over other religions.

Whereas comparative symbolics deals particularly with the creeds of Christian bodies, comparative religion deals with Christian and non-Christian religions.

L. H. Jordan, *Comparative Religion, Its Genesis and Growth*, Edinburgh, 1905; V. Ferm, *Encyclopedia of Religion*, Philosophical Library, N. Y., 1945 (gives extensive bibliography on the various religious systems); *Religion in the Twentieth Century*, Philosophical Library, N. Y., 1948; F. Max Mueller, *Sacred Books of the East*, 1879—1910 (first published in 51 volumes); E. Hershey Sneath, *The Evolution of Ethics as Revealed in the Great Religions*, Yale U. Press, 1927; J. G. Frazer, *The Golden Bough*, 1911 (later editions; abridged ed. by Macm., 1947); Florence M. Fitch, *Their Search for God*, Lothrop, N. Y., 1947; S. H. Kellogg, *A Handbook of Comparative Religion*, Eerdmans, Grand Rapids, 1951; Selwyn G. Champion and Dorothy Short, *Read-*

ings from World Religions, Beacon Press, 1951; E. D. Scoper, *The Religions of Mankind*, Abingdon-Cokesbury, 1951. W. Bertelsmann, *Christentum und nichtchristliche Religion nach der Auffassung Luthers*, Bertelsmann, Guetersloh, 1932; P. E. Kretzmann, *The God of the Bible and Other Gods*, CPH, 1943.

Religion and Higher Education. See *Students, Spiritual Care of.*

Religion in the News. See *Radio Evangelism*, 5.

Religion, Philosophy of. Since philosophy aims to find the ultimate principles underlying all phenomena and their relation to one another, philosophy of religion is the science which investigates the essence, content, significance, and value of religion, the psychological laws underlying it, the reasons for its varied historical manifestations, and its relation to the nature of man and his position in the universe and to all other experiences of the human soul. See *Apologetics*, III, B; *History, Philosophy of.*

Religion, Psychology of. See *Apologetics*, III, D; *Psychology; History, Philosophy of.*

Religion, Science of. The science which, based on the evolutionary hypothesis, aims to investigate the psychological, physiological, and ethnological bases of religion, the primitive popular ideas which underlie all historical religions, and the alleged development of religion from that of primitive man upward. As it aims to present a history of the development of the forms of religious thinking and concerns itself especially also with the genesis of Christianity, which it regards, not as an absolute religion, but merely as a stage in an evolutionary process, it is opposed to the Biblical conception of revealed religion.

Religious Bodies (U. S.), Bibliography. See references under *Anglican Confessions; Christian Church, History of; Creeds and Confessions; Doctrine, Christian, History of; Dogmatics; Encyclopedias; Lutheran Confessions; Presbyterian Confessions; Reformed Confessions.*

For membership see references under *Statistics.*

T. Engelder, W. Arndt, T. Graebner, F. E. Mayer, *Popular Symbolics*, CPH, 1934; F. E. Mayer, *Religious Bodies in America*, CPH; J. L. Neve, *Churches and Sects of Christendom,* Lutheran Literary Board, Burlington, Iowa, 1940; E. H. Klotsche, *Christian Symbolics,* Lutheran Literary Board, 1940, Burlington, Iowa; F. S. Mead, *Handbook of Denominations,* Abingdon-Cokesbury, 1951.

H. K. Rowe, *The History of Religion in the United States,* Macm., N. Y., 1928; W. W. Sweet, *Religion in Colonial America,* Scribner's, N. Y., 1940; W. W. Sweet, *The Story of Religion in America,* Harpers, N. Y., 1930. *American Church History Series* (12 vols.; Scribner's); M. Phelan, *New Handbook of All Denominations,* Cokesbury, Nashville, Tenn., 1933; R. S. Howell, *His Many Mansions,* Greystone, N. Y., 1940; J. K. Van Baalen, *Chaos of Cults,* Eerdmans, Grand Rapids, Mich., 1938; E. T. Clark, *The Small Sects in America,* Cokesbury Press, N. Y., 1949 (revised ed.); H. C. Weber, *Yearbook of American Churches,* Round Table Press, N. Y., 1933; C. S. Braden, *These Also Believed,* Macm., N. Y., 1949.

E. E. Aubrey, *Present Theological Tendencies,* Harpers, N. Y., 1936; H. R. Mackintosh, *Types of Modern Theology,* Scribner's, N. Y., 1939; Wieman and Meland, *American Philosophies of Religion,* Willet, Clark, Chicago, 1936.

Religious Census. The Federal Government gathered statistics for religious bodies for the first time in 1850. Previously it had been feared that the State might dominate the Church if it were permitted to gather census material or that such a census endangered the separation of Church and State. The government census reports not only give statistics, but also extensive information on the history and positions of the various bodies.

Religious Drama. The word "drama" comes from the Greek and means "deed," "act." Already in ancient times it was used for imitation or play worked up according to rules of art. The term is also used in a wider sense for any demonstration in action as opposed to abstraction. There are many examples of dramatic action in the Bible (see, for example, Jeremiah 19; 27; 28; Ezekiel 4).

Natural instincts for imitation and rhythm in man originally led to imitative action. Hence dramatic action played a prominent part in primitive worship. Various actions, often including dancing and pantomime, accompanied prayers and incantations in heathen religions. Funerals often furnished the occasion for dramatic action.

1. *Classical Religious Drama.* The great dramas of the Greek writers of tragedy (Aeschylus, Sophocles, Euripides, and others) were given at the feast of Dionysius. The dramas of Aeschylus were deeply religious and dealt with such problems as the power of the gods and their relation to men, nemesis, and future life. The plays of Sophocles dealt with faith and moral issues, especially as the latter concerned human relationships. Euripides is often regarded as the "liberal" in this trio. He was interested in showing psychological reasons for action. Under Roman influence the drama lost its religious character. Early Christians opposed the theater because of its idolatry and obscenity and crushed classical drama for a thousand years.

2. *Medieval Drama.* The spiritual dramas of the Middle Ages originated with the Church. The first were written in Latin by churchmen and presented at the chief church festivals (Christmas, Lent, Easter, Corpus Christi). Plays and pageants became parts of elaborate processions (*e. g.,* Corpus Christi) in which guilds, nobility, city fathers, and common folk took part (into these processions secular and diverting features were introduced). For when the liturgy of the Church became elaborate, it offered opportunity for dramatic action. Symbolic acts soon led to Passion Plays (*i. e.,* religious dramas which were developed from the responses and readings of Holy Week and of the Lenten season and eventually portraying the events of Holy Week). The Saints' Plays developed out of processions and festivals in honor of saints. From the Saints' Play developed the Miracle Play, using chiefly the material connected with the legends of the saints and their intercession for those who venerate them. The Mystery Plays, on the other hand, originally were enactments of scenes from the life of Christ and, later, of the entire Bible. The distinction between Mysteries and Miracle Plays disappeared, and the terms were used interchangeably (as in England). The Morality Play was another type of religious drama of the Medieval Period which sought to present a moral lesson through the personification of vices and virtues (*e. g., Everyman*).

In the course of time the dramas were presented by guildmen. In their hands they were secularized and finally banished from the churches. Other factors also led to the disappearance of the religious drama. Buffooneries and fools' plays directed against ethical weaknesses and immoralities, especially of the clergy, were performed at Shrovetide (*Fastnachtspiele;* 73 titles between 1430 and 1515 are extant). In the meanwhile the revival of classicism brought renewed interest in the dramas of Seneca, Plautus, and Terence. These factors led to the disappearance of the religious play and the gradual rise of the secular.

3. *The Lutheran Reformers.* Luther and his co-workers took a positive attitude toward secular drama (see *Theater)* and encouraged religious drama. The publication of Luther's Bible in 1534 and Luther's praise of religious drama contained in it evoked the thought of using the stage for the Reformation. Hundreds of dramas were written, and for three generations thousands produced and watched religious plays. Drama took a place alongside preaching as a means of indoctrination. At no other time in the subsequent history of drama has there been such singleness of purpose and universal participation.

Valten Voith and Bartholomaeus Krueger dramatized the entire story of the Bible. Other authors concerned themselves with sections of the Old and New Testaments or the Apocrypha (*e. g.,* Hans Sachs, Hans Tirolf, Georg Major, Joachim Greff, Cornelius Crocus, Sebastian Wild, Johann Bertesius, Leonhard Culmann, Johannes Chryseus, Sixt Birck, Hans Ackermann, Paul Rebhun, Joerg Wickram, Nikodemus Frischlin, C. Lasius, Johannes Krueginger, Wilhelm Gnapheus). The *Prodigal Son* of Burkard Waldis is the outstanding German drama of the 16th century. In the field of Moralities the allegorical material of the English drama *Everyman* was frequently treated.

Drama was also used for polemical purposes by the Evangelicals. Pamphilus Gengenbach of Switzerland wrote tendential *Fastnachtspiele* (some before the Reformation; his *Nollhart,* 1517, designated the Pope the Antichrist). Others in this category are: Niklaus Manuel, Wilibald Pirkheimer, Thomas Naogeorg (*Pammachius, Mercator, Incendia),* and the drama *Das Concilium Zutrent.* The opposition replied with such dramas as those of Simon Lemnius (usually directed

against Luther's marriage). Among the dramas dealing after the death of Luther with doctrinal quarrels and other matters are: *Phasma* (N. Frischlin), *Lutherus Redivivus* (Z. Rivander) and *Papista Conversus* (Z. Rivander). A. Hartmann, Martin Rinckart, and H. Kielmann (*Tetzelocramia,* 1617) are among the many who dramatized Luther's life.

Often borrowing from classical material, dramatists of the 16th century also wrote historical-novelistic and didactic-satirical dramas, often for the purpose of praising virtue.

4. The Jesuits, noticing the influence of Evangelical dramas, soon became active in the production of plays and continued until the dissolution of their order (1773). Their dramas of fixed form were presented with great pomp for pedagogical purposes.

5. *Modern Religious Drama.* The Passion Play of Oberammergau is performed by the inhabitants of that village in the Bavarian Alps every tenth year. About 700 people participate in its production. The play, which presents the Passion of Christ with tableaux from the Old Testament and appropriate music, originated in 1633 as a result of a vow by the villagers made in gratitude for deliverance from a pestilence.

At the beginning of the twentieth century interest (long dormant) in religious drama revived. Pageants used to teach children Bible stories soon led to dramatized stories. Dramas and pageants are widely used to promote interest in missions and church history. The radio and motion pictures are increasingly used for the dramatic presentation of religious truth (*e. g., Martin Luther* film). As soon as television became established, churches sought ways of using this medium for their programs (*e. g.,* "This Is the Life" Series). Programs containing pageants or dramas are increasingly used on anniversaries and important church festivals (*e. g.,* Luther's anniversary; Easter).

Novelistic dramas based on Biblical narrative became prominent in the 20th century (*e. g.,* Maxwell Anderson, *Journey to Jerusalem;* John Masefield, *The Trial of Jesus;* C. R. Kennedy, *The Terrible Meek).* Dramas with religious themes are numerous (*e. g.,* Marc Connelly, *The Green Pastures).* EL

References to primitive and Greek dramas are given in E. L. Lueker, *The Origin of the Greek Tragic Drama* (unpublished thesis), Washington University, St. Louis, 1940; Karl Young, *The Drama of the Medieval Church*, Clarendon Press, Oxford, 1933; Neil C. Brooks, "Processional Drama and Dramatic Procession in Germany in the Late Middle Ages," *The Journal of English and Germanic Philology*, XXXII:141—71; Hugo Holstein, *Die Reformation im Spiegelbilde der dramatischen Literatur*, Halle, 1886; Harold Ehrensperger, *Conscience on Stage*, Abingdon-Cokesbury, 1947; H. E. Luccock & F. Brentano, *The Questing Spirit*, Coward-McCann, New York, 1947.

Religious Education. See *Christian Education*.

Religious Education Association. The Religious Education Association was organized in 1903, chiefly through the influence of William R. Harper. Its headquarters are in Chicago. Management and control have been entrusted to a board of directors, consisting of the elected officers of the Association, of one representative from each of the regularly constituted local or regional groups, and forty-five members elected for a three-year period. The by-laws governing the Association have been reprinted at various times in *Religious Education*, the official publication of the Religious Education Association. *Religious Education* and the regional groups are the means through which the Association seeks to implement its views and exert its influence.

The Religious Education Association is "a voluntary organization of persons interested in furthering religious idealism through education." It is a "pioneering, inter-faith fellowship" which welcomes liberal Protestants, Catholics, and Jews. Anyone may apply for membership, but "the Board of Directors has the right to accept or to reject any and all applications for membership" (Art. II, By-Laws). This clause betrays the determination of the Association to restrict membership to liberals. At any rate, it has not adopted an "inclusive policy" which would align conservatives and liberals on equal terms. It works independently, "free from any institutional alliances"; the members may speak and write as they choose, unhampered by any authority from above.

According to the By-Laws, the purpose of the Association is "the promotion of fellowship in the study of the aims, the processes and the emerging issues of moral and religious education." Another purpose, going beyond that of mutual study, is "to inspire the *educational* forces of our country with the *religious* ideal; to inspire the *religious* forces of our country with the *educational* ideal, and to keep before the public mind the ideal of religious education, and the sense of its need and value." In keeping with its purpose, the Religious Education Association has taken a profound interest in any movement promising to bring about the realization of the religious ideal in state-supported educational institutions. It has been equally concerned to see the educational method pursued and achieved in the Church and its instructional agencies.

The Association has espoused the cause of *religious* education, not *Christian* education as such, "religious" being taken in a broad sense so as to include the "spiritual values" in the public school, and concepts which conservative Christians do not accept as falling within the sphere of religion. The members of the Association, on the whole, are protagonists of progressive religious education with its emphasis on experience and growth, as opposed to the so-called "authoritarian approach" of Fundamentalists and others. *Religious Education*, a scholarly publication, bears the stamp of liberalism. The contributors are, chiefly, liberal scholars who do not leave their readers in doubt as to where they stand. Many of the articles which have appeared in this publication are valuable as objective studies of problems which concern the religious teacher and leader. Sometimes conservative and liberal views have been printed side by side.

The Religious Education Association encountered distrust and opposition from the very beginning because of its liberalism. Since progressive religious educators are usually liberal in their theology, conservatives looked upon progressive religious education as an instrumentality calculated to rob the church of its doctrinal heritage and threatening its very existence. In view of the waning influence of liberalism, it is difficult to forecast the course the Religious Education Association will follow in the years that lie ahead.

ACM

Religious Humanism. A movement, chiefly of left-wing Unitarians, which holds that scientific advance has removed the distinctions between the secular and the sacred and man must seek his salvation through control of the physical and social world. The doctrines of the religious humanists were published in 1933 in the *Humanist Manifesto*. For humanism and its relation to religion in general see *Renaissance; Reformation, Lutheran,* 3.

Religious Journalism. See *Religious Press; Publication Houses; Religious Tract Movement.*

Religious Liberty. Religious liberty is the freedom of religious profession and worship. It is based upon the assumption that conscience must be permitted to act without constraint or hindrance. Conscience acknowledges the laws of God and human responsibility. Hence no human government has a right to hinder any form of religion or to support any to the injury of others. This implies that all churches and persons are equal before the law in the matter of protection or restraint. This separation of spiritual and civil affairs is emphatically taught by Jesus Christ in John 18:36 f. See *Church and State.*

In the United States the Government acknowledges religious liberty as an absolute personal right. Church and State as such are entirely divorced. All denominations are equal and free in the eye of the law. The Constitution of the United States provides that "no religious test shall ever be required as a qualification to any office or public trust under the United States"; and "Congress shall make no law respecting an establishment of religion or prohibiting the free exercise thereof." How far these limitations of the powers of Congress affect the legislation of individual States was a mooted question until the Nebraska Language Case and the Oregon School Case were decided by the Supreme Court of the United States. During and after World War I a number of States passed laws prohibiting the use of foreign languages in all graded schools, public, private, and parochial. Among these were Iowa, Nebraska, and Ohio. No attempt was made to deny that the legislation was aimed particularly at the use in such schools of the German language. In 1923 various cases growing out of this legislation were appealed to the Supreme Court. The Iowa case was brought by August Bartels, a teacher in St. John's Evangelical Lutheran Parochial School at Maxfield, those from Nebraska, by the Nebraska District of the Evangelical Lutheran Synod of Missouri, Ohio, and Other States, by Dietrich Siefken and John Siedlik of Platte County and by Robert T. Meyer, who was a teacher in Zion Parochial School in Hamilton County, and those from Ohio by Emil Pohl, teacher, and H. H. Bohning, trustee of St. John's Evangelical Congregational School at Garfield Heights. In all these cases the State courts had sustained the validity of the law.

The statutes were held invalid by the Supreme Court. The "Nebraska" decision is one of the most important ever handed down by the Supreme Court of the United States, inasmuch as it not only permitted the teaching of foreign languages in private schools and thus vindicated the rights of parents to determine the education of their children, but gave guarantees of religious liberty which the American people had never before possessed. It has been noted that the Constitution only prohibits Congress from restricting religious freedom; it says nothing of the obligations of the individual States under this clause, and the question has often been debated whether the States are under the same restrictions in this respect as Congress. This question was now settled. The decision declared these various language laws as in direct opposition to the Fourteenth Amendment of the Federal Constitution, which declares: "No State shall deprive any person of life, liberty, or property without due process of law." The opinion said that the liberty thus guaranteed "without doubt denotes not only freedom from bodily restraint, but also the right of the individual to contract, to engage in any one of the common occupations of life, to acquire useful knowledge, to marry, establish a home, and bring up children" — note the following — "to worship God according to the dictates of his own conscience, and, generally, to enjoy those privileges long recognized by common law as essential to the orderly pursuit of happiness by free man." By this clause was added the keystone to the American doctrine of religious freedom. The decision was quoted by the Supreme Court when in 1925 it declared unconstitutional the Oregon Law, which compelled all children under sixteen years to attend the public schools. That decision said: "Under the doctrine of Meyer *vs.* Nebraska, 262 U.S. 390, we think it entirely plain that the Act of 1922 unreasonably interferes with the liberty of parents and guardians to direct the upbringing and education of children under their control. As often heretofore pointed out, rights guaranteed by the Constitution may not be abridged by legislation which has no reasonable relation to some purpose within the competency of the State."

Religious Orders. See *Orders in the United States.*

Religious Press. About 1,200 periodicals serve as purveyors of religious news and views in America. Not included in this number are the general and specialized journals that concern themselves with the advancement of religious purposes without bearing on the news.

The first exclusively religious periodical was the weekly *Christian History* (Boston, 1743), an octavo news magazine devoted to promoting the Great Revival. It lasted two years. From 1745 to 1772 three religious papers were attempted at New York and two magazines at Philadelphia, but only one survived its first year.

Religious journalism came into its own after the Revolutionary War. From 1789 to 1830 upwards of 500 religious periodicals were founded. One third survived. Circulation figures of 5,000 to 10,000 were common. The *Christian Advocate* (Methodist) in 1829 had the world's record circulation — 25,000 copies.

The next half century was a golden age for the religious press. By 1880 the number of journals had increased to 550, with each inhabitant averaging three subscriptions. The religious newspaper was the favored journal of the American people.

Toward the end of the century religious journalism declined with the rise of the secular press and dwindled in influence as religious journals tended to become mouthpieces of denominations and media of sectarian promotion. Only journals of broader interest, such as the *Independent* (New York, 1848), maintained their standing.

Most active in the field of religious journalism is the Roman Catholic Church. Practically every diocese has its weekly newspaper. These papers carry local, national, and foreign news, editorials, columns, sports, women's news, pictures, cartoon strips, etc. National and foreign news, special features and columns are syndicated by the National Catholic Welfare Conference.

Weeklies for 32 dioceses in the Midwest and Far West are prepared by the *Denver Register* for 681,364 subscribers, according to the June, 1950, Standard Rate and Data Service. *Our Sunday Visitor* (Huntington, Ind.), the national edition of the Fort Wayne diocesan weekly, has a circulation of 687,514. It is quick to reply to attacks on the Church.

Two Catholic weeklies, *America* (circulation 35,000), published by the Jesuits, and *Commonweal* (circulation 11,124), published by a group of Catholic laymen, have an influence much greater than their circulation figures would suggest. *Commonweal* presents the most enlightened Catholic view on national issues.

The *Christian Science Monitor* is often regarded as an outstanding example of non-Catholic journalism. A daily, edited with Christian Science views in mind, it cannot classify as a religious journal.

Protestant journalism is continuing on a denominational basis. While the Catholic press is on a weekly schedule, the Protestant press is predominantly biweekly. An exception is the weekly *Christian Advocate*, a Methodist publication. Established in 1826, it now has a circulation of 316,867. Other prominent Protestant periodicals are the *Baptist Leader*, circulation 52,791; *Presbyterian Life*, circulation 77,753. All denominational publications recorded large increases in circulation in the wake of World War II. Protestant journalism is increasingly availing itself of *Religious News Service*, a news-gathering service out of New York City.

Most influential among Protestant journals of a non-denominational character are the *Christian Century* (weekly, established 1884, circulation figures unavailable) and the *Christian Herald* (monthly, established 1878, circulation 376.099). *Christian Century* editorials are widely quoted for their factual incisiveness.

The *Protestant World*, "a newspaper dedicated to the common causes of Protestantism throughout the world" and sponsored by a corporation that includes the names of many distinguished Protestant leaders, appeared in 1950. The major design of the weekly is "to present fairly, comprehensively, concisely, and accurately the news of what Protestant churches, denominations, leaders, boards, and agencies are doing and saying, together with digests of such other news as may bear upon the religious life and thought of the nation" (quoted from May 31, 1950, sample copy).

Lutheran journalism, too, is showing signs of greater activity. Official organs of the Lutheran bodies record circulation advances. Leading Lutheran Journals in America are: the *Lutheran*, United Lutheran Church; the *Lutheran Standard*, American Lutheran Church; the *Lutheran Herald*, Evangelical Lutheran Church; the *Lutheran Companion*, Augustana Synod; the *Lutheran Witness*, The Lutheran Church — Missouri Synod.

By 1950 a number of Lutheran centers in the Missouri Synod had founded local newspapers, which serve their areas with more complete coverage of news than is possible through synodical organs. These Lutheran centers are St. Louis, Mo.; Detroit, Mich.; Milwaukee, Wis.; Cleveland, Ohio; Washington, D. C.; New Orleans, La.; Houston, Tex.; Saginaw, Mich. See also *Theological Journals; Publication Houses.* GM

Religious Society of Friends. In 1827 Elias Hicks withdrew from the Society of Friends * and organized the Religious Society of Friends (Hicksites; General Conference), which was more liberal in theology than the parent body. In 1845 another group under the leadership of John Wilbur withdrew from the Society of Friends to organize a conservative Religious Society of Friends (Wilburites).

Religious Tract Movement. Publication and distribution of tracts has exerted an impressive influence upon public opinion and upon the history of the world ever since the advent of writing. The religious tract movement received its greatest impetus from the invention of movable type and from the Reformation of Martin Luther.

Employing the printing press for the first time in history to influence the masses, Martin Luther wrote numerous tracts on religious and educational issues. Copies were sold on the streets of practically every country in Europe by publishers and their agents. Everyone profited from the sales except Luther himself.

The Methodist movement in England made extensive use of religious tracts to propagate its views. John Wesley wrote, printed, and circulated many of the tracts himself.

The Society for Promoting Christian Knowledge, established in 1701, was a pre-Wesley development. The Society for Promoting Religious Knowledge Among the Poor, organized in 1750, and similar societies organized in Edinburgh and Glasgow in 1756, were tract-producing agencies which owed their existence to Wesley's influence. The first tract-distributing society was another creation of Wesley, the Society for the Distribution of Religious Tracts Among the Poor.

Wesley said: "Men wholly unawakened will not take the pains to read the Bible. They have no relish for it. But a small tract may engage their attention for half an hour and may, by the blessing of God, prepare them for going forward." Such tracts were published by this society as *Ten Short Sermons, Tokens for Children, A Word to a Swearer, A Word to a Drunkard,* etc. About 1790 Hannah More appeared as a writer of popular tracts, such as that entitled *William Chip.* During the first year of her work she distributed two million tracts. These attempts paved the way for tract societies along broader and better-organized lines.

In 1799 the Religious Tract Society of London was organized by the Rev. George Burder, Joseph Hughes, and others. As a result of the work of this organization the Brititsh and Foreign Bible Society came into existence. Other tract societies of Great Britain are the Religious Tract and Book Society of Scotland, dating back to 1793; the Stirling Tract Enterprise, founded in 1848; the Dublin Tract Society; and the Monthly Tract Society of London, organized 1837. — Many tract societies are found in other countries of Europe, India, China, Australia, New Zealand, South Africa, West Indies, and Canada.

In the United States such tract societies as the following were organized: Massachusetts Society for the Promotion of Christian Knowledge, 1803; Connecticut Religious Tract Society, 1807; Vermont Religious Tract Society, 1808; the Protestant Episcopal Tract Society, 1809; New York Religious Tract Society, 1812; Evangelical Tract Society, Boston, 1813; Albany Religious Tract Society, 1813; New England Tract Society, 1814; Religious Tract Society of Philadelphia, 1815; Religious Tract Society of Baltimore, 1816; New York Methodist Tract Society, 1817; Baptist General Tract Society, 1824; American Tract Society, Boston, 1823; American Tract Society, New York, 1825; New York Tract Society, 1827; New York City Mission and Tract Society, 1864; Willard Tract Society, Boston, 1866; Monthly

Tract Society of the United States, New York, 1874. The New England Tract Society, organized in 1814, became in 1823 the American Tract Society, with headquarters in Boston.

In 1878 the American Tract Society of Boston merged with the society of the same name in New York, eliminating the confusion resulting from the existence of two societies with the same name.

The Baptist General Tract Society, organized in Washington in 1824, was transferred to Philadelphia and in 1840 became the American Baptist Publication Society. The New York Methodist Tract Society, organized in 1817, later became incorporated as the Tract Society of the Methodist Episcopal Church.

One of the largest distributors of religious tracts in the United States is Good News Publishers, with its subsidiary Tract Club of America, both organized in 1938. The Tract Club numbers 10,000 members and carries on a tract program supported by subscription and sales, with an annual budget of approximately $150,000. Average distribution of tracts by Good News during the years 1944—48 was 24,000,000 a year.

Le Tourneau Foundation, founded, organized, and supported by an American industrialist, Robert Le Tourneau, regularly distributes approximately 12,000,000 free tracts a year. In 1947 alone, the Foundation published and distributed 47,000,000 tracts.

The oldest American tract publisher, the American Tract Society, is supported (1950) by 1,350 members and 6,000 contributors. Annual budget of the organization is $60,000, with a yearly distribution during 1944 and 1945 of approximately 3,000,000 tracts.

Largest Lutheran producer of tracts in the United States is the American Lutheran Publicity Bureau of New York. Organized in 1914, the bureau has been supported by memberships and freewill contributions. Like the Le Tourneau Foundation, the A. L. P. B. has distributed the great bulk of its 50,000,000 tracts free to those who "will prayerfully and carefully use them."

Other tract distribution agencies in the United States are the Moody Press, of Chicago, Ill.; Gospel Tract Distributors, Portland, Oreg.; Loizeaux Bros., New York City, N. Y.; and Pilgrim Tract Society, Randleman, N. C.

By 1950 developments included the entry of church denominations together with official church boards and agencies into the field of tract production and distribution. There has been some indication of the growth of tract missions for the organized distribution of tracts, although most tract agencies have depended on individual and otherwise unrelated organizations to act as distributing agents. OCH

Relly, James. See *Universalists.*

Remanence. In the doctrine of the Lord's Supper, Lutherans teach that the bread remains bread and the wine remains wine (*i. e.,* remanence). See *Grace, Means of,* IV.

Rembrandt, van Ryn, Paul Harmens (1607 or 1616—69). Dutch painter living in Leyden and Amsterdam; became famous through his portrait of his mother, after which he continued as a celebrity; master of effects of light and shade in both paintings and etchings, but did not cultivate ideal beauty; among his most noted pictures: "The Sacrifice of Abraham"; "The Woman Taken in Adultery"; "The Descent from the Cross."

Remensnyder, Junius Benjamin. Theologian and author; b. Feb. 24, 1841, Staunton, Va.; served during Civil War with 131st Pa. Volunteers 1862—63; grad. Gettysburg Lutheran Seminary 1865; pastor, Lewiston, Pa., 1865—67; Philadelphia, Pa., 1867—74; Savannah, Ga., 1874—80; St. James Church, New York, 1880—1924; pres. of General Synod 1911—13; D. D. from Newberry College; LL. D. New York Univ., 1902. Wrote: *Lutheran Manual; What the World Owes Luther;* etc.; d. Jan. 2, 1927.

Remigius of Rheims (ca. 437—533). Became bishop in his twenty-second year; his fame rests on the record testified to by Gregory of Tours that he converted the Frankish king Clovis to Christianity, in 496; was active in mission work and made every effort to raise the moral level of the clergy.

Remonstrant Synod of Ulster. See *Presbyterian Bodies,* 3.

Remonstrants. See *Arminianism.*

Renaissance. Literally "rebirth," a movement of the later Middle Ages, which began with the revival of learning along the lines of the ancient languages and Oriental culture, caused the age of Humanism in Italy, France, England, Germany, and Spain, gave a new impetus to the various forms of art along ancient classical lines (particularly painting, sculpture, and architecture), and was a powerful factor in preparing the way for the Reformation, chiefly by arousing men's minds and by causing Greek and Hebrew to be studied extensively in western Europe. — In ecclesiastical art, that period which brought about a decided modification in classical forms, the final strange result being the later development of fantastic forms for solid construction, resulting in the Baroque and Rococo.

Renan, Joseph Ernest (1823—92). French Orientalist and author; prepared for priesthood, but renounced orders and studied Semitic philology; professor at College de France, 1862. His notorious *Vie de Jésus*, first volume of *Origines du Christianisme*, appeared 1863. His Jesus is ambitious, vain, sensuous, half-consciously deceiving himself and the people. Suspended from college same year, but reinstated 1871. Member of Academy, 1879. Other works: *Les Apôtres, Saint Paul, L'Antechrist, Histoire du Peuple d'Israel.*

Renata (or *Renee* 1511—75). Duchess of Ferrara, distinguished alike for piety and learning; patron of the Reformation; temporarily imprisoned by her husband and threatened with banishment by her own son; went to France and died a Huguenot.

Rendtorff, Franz (1860—1937). German theologian; prof. at Kiel and Leipzig; pres. Gustav Adolf-Verein; authority on liturgics of early Christianity and religious instruction.

Reni, Guido (1575—1642). Italian painter of the Bolognese School; refined and ideal style, modified by his own personality; master of coloring; besides his "Aurora" a fine "Ecce Homo" and a "Crucifixion."

Renouvier, Charles Bernard (1815 to 1903). French idealistic philosopher; influenced by Kant and Leibnitz; neocritic; held that reality consists of subjects as experienced.

Renqvist, Henrik. See *Finland, Lutheranism in,* 4.

Reorganized Church of Jesus Christ. See *Latter Day Saints,* g 2.

Repass, Stephan A. B. Nov. 25, 1838, at Wytheville, Va.; grad. Roanoke Coll., Salem, Va., 1866, and Philadelphia Sem., Mt. Airy, Pa., 1869; pastorates at: Salem, Va., 1869—72; Staunton, Va., 1884—85; Allentown, Pa., 1885—1906; served in Army during Civil War; pres., theol. sem., Salem, Va., 1873—84; pres., General Synod South, 1871—72; mem., Common Service Com., same

synod; pres., Muhlenberg Coll. Bd., 1886—1906; editor: *The Church Messenger;* D.D., Hampton-Sidney Coll. and Roanoke Coll., 1876. Died June 2, 1906.

Repentance. The change of the mind from a rebellious state to one of harmony with the will of God, from trusting in human merit to trusting in the merit of Christ. It embraces contrition, consciousness and conviction of sin, accompanied by sorrow for it, and above all, faith, which is followed by renunciation of the former walks and habits of life and sanctification. Repentance is a total change of heart and life, its author being God Himself (Jer. 31:18 f.; Acts 26:29; 5:31). The means to repentance is the Word of God. See *Contrition, Conversion, Faith, Sanctification.*

In addition to references given under cross references above see K. H. Ehlers, "Repentance," *Abiding Word,* CPH, 1947 (II:258—74).

Repetitio Augustanae. See *Lutheran Confessions,* A 5.

Reports. See *Christian Teaching,* V.

Repristination, Theology of. See *Lutheran Theology after 1580,* 11.

Reprobation. See *Predestination,* 4.

Republican Methodist Church. See *Methodist Bodies,* 4.

Requiem *(missa pro defunctis; Totenmesse):* The Roman Catholic mass for the dead. In the Requiem Mass the *Gloria* and the *Credo* are omitted; its component parts are: *The Introit* (which always includes the words: Requiem aeternam dona eis, Domine — Grant them rest eternal, Lord, the *Kyrie,* the *Dies Irae,* the *Offertory,* the *Sanctus* including the *Benedictus* and *Osanna)* and the *Agnus Dei* (each stanza closing with *dona eis pacem).* While the Lutheran Church does not pray for the souls of the dead, and hence does not use the Requiem Mass, the *German Requiem* of Johannes Brahms, which is based on Scripture passages only, is Lutheranism's only outstanding requiem mass.

Requiescat (in pace). Prayer for the rest of the dead. See *Requiem.*

Reredos. See *Church Furniture,* 1.

Rescript. A written reply by the Papacy on matters pertaining to favors or judicial controversies.

Rescue Homes (*Houses of Correction*). These are institutions established and maintained by the state or by a church body to which wayward boys and girls are committed for correction. Also called Industrial Homes.

Reservations of the Eucharist. The practice of keeping, for various purposes, portions of the elements consecrated in Holy Communion. In early times the deacons carried the Sacrament to the sick and others who could not be present at the celebration. Later, superstitious practices arose: Wafers were buried with the dead, seated in altars, or carried by travelers as protective charms; important documents were signed with a pen dipped in consecrated wine. The doctrine of transubstantiation introduced other abuses, such as the festival of Corpus Christi and the practice of exposing the host for adoration or of keeping it in a tabernacle * above the altar, that the faithful might visit it and pray before it.

Reserved Cases. The power to absolve from certain particularly grave (?) sins is reserved by bishops and Popes to themselves. Since, therefore, ordinary priests have not been given jurisdiction (see *Absolution*) in such cases, their absolution, even if given, is declared "of no weight whatever," "not merely in external polity, but also in God's sight" (Council of Trent, Sess. XIV, ch. 7). At the point of death, reservations are waived, and any priest may absolve from any sin. This practice, for which there is no Scripture warrant, evidently serves to emphasize the claim that the Pope is the source of the absolving power. See also *Excommunication.*

Resettlement Administration. See *Social Work*, D 1.

Resinarius, Balthasar. Choral composer of the Reformation era. His German name was Balthasar Harzer. In his early years he was a pupil of Heinrich Isaac and a member of the *Hofkapelle* of Maximilian I at Innsbruck. Later in his life he became a Lutheran bishop at Lippa; his music was used in Austria as well as in Germany.

Resistible Grace. See *Common Grace.*

Responses. Words or short sentences by the people in a service in answer to the officiating minister. The responses "Amen," "Hallelujah," and "Hosanna" are taken from the Old Testament. The response "Kyrie eleison" ("Lord have mercy") was ordained to be used by the Council of Vaison (492). "Glory, glory in the highest" was used in the 5th century. Responsaries containing sentences for the minister and congregation have been compiled.

Responsio Catholica. See *Lutheran Confessions*, A 3.

Responsory. Either a Psalm (entire or in sections) sung or chanted between readings or the response of the people in an antiphonal section of the liturgy, as in the second part of a versicle.

Restitution (*Apocatastasis*). The doctrine of the final restoration or salvation of all mankind, or, in a wider application, also of all evil spirits. The doctrine was taught by Origen (d. 254) on the basis of God's omnipotence and the indestructibility of human freedom. Others have sought to defend it by misapplying Acts 3:21: "Whom the heaven must receive until the times of restitution of all things," which refers to Christ's second coming to judge the quick and the dead, receive His saints into glory, and condemn the wicked to everlasting punishment (Matt. 25: 41-46). The doctrine of restitution has been peculiar to Unitarians and Universalists, but it plainly contradicts Holy Scripture and is at variance with God's holiness and righteousness.

Restoration of Israel. See *Jews, Conversion of; Millennium.*

Restorationism. See *Restitution; Universalists.*

Results of Christian Education. See *Christian Education*, K.

Resurrection of the Body. See *Last Things*, 4.

Retention. See *Christian Teaching*, E.

Retention of Sins. See *Keys, Office of.*

Reu, J. M. Noted theologian of the Iowa Synod; b. 1869 in Bavaria, educated at Oettingen and Neuendettelsau; came to America 1889, pastor at Rock Falls, Ill., 1890—99, professor of theology at Dubuque Seminary from 1899. After 1905 he was also editor of the *Kirchliche Zeitschrift.* Author of *Old Testament Pericopes, Catechetics, Katechismusauslegung, Homiletics*, and, especially, of *Quellen zur Geschichte des kirchlichen Unterrichts*, at which he had been working since 1904 and for which the University of Erlangen conferred on him the title of Th. D. He was a contributor to *Archiv fuer Reformationsgeschichte und Zeitschrift fuer Geschichte der Erziehung und des Unterrichtswesens in Deutschland.* He also wrote: *Life of Luther for Young People, Thirty-five Years of Luther Research,* and a number of catechetical and pedagogical works. Member of Union Committee of the Am. Luth. Ch.; d. at Rochester, Minn., Oct. 14, 1943.

Kirchliche Zeitschrift, 1876—1943. Reu Memorial Number, Wartburg Press, 1945 (contains articles by A. Pilger, J. Becker, J. C. Mattes, H. L. Fritschel, H. L. Lutz, W. Arndt, T. G. Tappert, H. A. Preus, R. H. Long, C. Bergendoff).

Reubke, Julius (1834—58). Pupil of Liszt and a composer, whose tensely dramatic *Ninety-fourth Psalm* is often played in concerts by virtuoso organists. This is the only work we have from Reubke, who died an early death.

Reuchlin, Johannes (1455—1522). German Humanist; studied at Freiburg, later at Paris and at Basel, where he specialized in Greek; studied jurisprudence at Orleans and Poitiers; counselor of Count Eberhard im Bart; court judge in Stuttgart; studied Hebrew and did special research work; published a grammar, *De Rudimentis Hebraeicis (Of the Rudiments of Hebrew),* and other writings of a similar nature; became involved in a controversy with the Jews, the matter, after some years, being twice decided in his favor, the judgment being reversed by the Pope when he believed Reuchlin to be in sympathy with Luther. Reuchlin took an active interest in the Humanist movement, also by publishing the *Clarorum Virorum Epistolae (Letters of Well-known Men)* and *Epistolae Obscurorum Virorum (Letters of Obscure Men).* During the last years of his life he was professor of Greek and Hebrew at Ingolstadt and then at Tuebingen. He was a granduncle of Melanchthon, whom he recommended for the chair of Greek at Wittenberg.

Reusner, Adam (1496—1575). Studied at Wittenberg; private secretary of Georg Frundsberg, later adherent of Schwenkfeld; wrote: "In Thee, Lord, Have I Put My Trust."

Reuss, Eduard Guillaume Eugene (1804—91). Alsatian-French theologian; prof. at Strasbourg; used historical method in Bible interpretation; wrote: *History of Theology in the Age of the Apostles; The Bible, a New Translation with Introductions and Commentaries.*

Reuter, Friedrich Otto. B. Oct. 11, 1864, at Erzgebirge, Germany; studied at Braeunsdorf and Waldenburg, Saxony; held several positions as teacher and cantor in Germany; called to Winnipeg in 1905, to Chicago in 1906; professor of music at the Teachers' Seminary, New Ulm, Minn., from 1908; prolific writer of church music along classical lines. D. June 9, 1924.

Reuterdahl, Henrik (1795—1870). B. at Malmö; d. at Upsala. Studied at Lund. Docent at the theological seminary there, 1817; associate adjunct in the theological faculty, 1824; prefect in the seminary, 1826; later chief adjunct and chief librarian of the university, 1838; full professor of theology, 1844; deputy to the diet, 1844; provost of the cathedral at Lund, 1845; minister of religion, 1852—55; bishop of Lund, 1855; archbishop, 1856. As a church dignitary he discouraged defections from the Lutheran Church. He helped to found the *Theologisk Quartalskrift* and published his *Svenska Kyrkans historia* in three volumes, giving critical attention to his source materials.

Reval, Diet of. See *Lutheran Confessions,* A 5.

Revelation. A direct communication of truth before unknown from God to men. Revelation is not to be confused with inspiration. Revelation was that operation of the Holy Spirit by which truths before unknown were communicated to men; inspiration implied more than this — it included also that operation of the Holy Spirit by which the Prophets and Apostles were excited to write truths for the instruction of others and were guarded from all error in doing it. Every part of the Bible is given by inspiration, though not every part was the result of immediate revelation. Much of it is the record of eyewitnesses. — In a narrower sense, revelation is used to express the manifestation of Jesus both to Jews and Gentiles as Savior of the world (Luke 2:32) and particularly the manifestation of divine glory at the last Judgment (Rom. 8:19).

Revenue, Church. See *Finances in the Church.*

Revers. A term used by Lutherans to indicate a written (often in the presence of witnesses) acceptance of doctrine and policy.

Revesz, Imre (1826—81). Hungarian Reformed; native of Debreczen; pastor there from 1856; stubbornly resisted Austrian invasions of rights of Hungarian Protestants; wrote *Basal Principles of Protestant Church Organization,* and other works, in Hungarian.

Revised Standard Version. See *Bible Versions,* L 14.

Revised Version. See *Bible Versions,* L 12.

Revival of Confessional Lutheranism. See *Lutheran Confessions,* D.

Revival of Learning. See *Renaissance.*

Revivals. 1. The phrase "revivals of religion" is commonly employed to indicate renewed interest in religious subjects or, more generally, a period of religious awakening, the word "revival" being derived from the Latin *revivo,* to live again. In its best sense it may be applied to the work of Christ and the Apostles, to the Reformation of the 16th century, etc. However, frequently the word is applied to excitements which can hardly be called religious because they do not truly revive the real spiritual life of the soul by the preaching of the Word of God, but consist in bare enthusiastic outbursts of emotion, brought on by various means. Generally the term *revival* is confined to a certain increase of spiritual activity within the Protestant churches of the English-speaking peoples.

2. There were revivals in Scotland at Stewarton, 1625—30, at Strotts, 1630, and at Combuslang and Kilsyth, 1742. The enterprises of Wesley and of Whitefield in England, from 1738 onward, were thoroughly revivalistic. In 1734 there were revivals at Northampton, Mass., and throughout New England in 1740 to 1741, the Rev. Jonathan Edwards being the chief instrument in their production. From the close of the Great Awakening, as the revival just mentioned was called, there were no general revivals in America until ca. 1800, when Dwight and especially Lyman Beecher began their remarkable work. At the same time revivals broke out in Kentucky, which spread to Pennsylvania and Ohio and were attended by violent physical phenomena called the "jerks." Other revivals that have become well known were those aroused by Asahel Nettleton in Massachusetts, New York, and in the South; by Charles Grandison Finney in New York; by Dwight Lyman Moody, who was followed by Benjamin

Fay Mills in 1886; Reuben Archer Torrey, especially since 1893; and J. Wilbur Chapman, the foremost of the three. In 1911 Chapman returned from an evangelistic journey around the world, during which he visited eleven countries and spoke in sixteen cities in Australia, China, Japan, and England. Other famous revivalists were Gipsy Smith and Billy Sunday. The great revival in America in 1857 spread to Ulster in 1859 and to Scotland and parts of England in 1864. Of especial note is the Welsh revival of 1904—06, which is known as the Great Welsh Revival. During that time it is estimated that 100,000 professed conversions took place.

3. Besides these, other revivals have from time to time occurred, and nearly all denominations have aimed at their production. The means adopted are prayer for the Holy Spirit, meetings continued night after night, even to a late hour, stirring addresses, chiefly by revivalist laymen, and "after-meetings" to deal with those impressed. Ultimately it is found that some of those apparently converted have been steadfast, very many have fallen back, while spiritual apathy proportioned to the previous excitement temporarily prevails. Thorough religious instruction, attended by sanity and wise management of church work, has at present largely taken the place of the old-type revival excitement.

F. G. Beardsley, *History of American Revivals,* Am. Tract Soc., N. Y., 1904; W. W. Sweet, *Revivalism in America: Its Origin, Growth and Decline,* Scribner's, N. Y., 1944.

Reynolds, William Morton (1812 to 1876). Studied at Jefferson College and Gettysburg Seminary; prof. at Pennsylvania College; pres. of Capital University, Columbus; pres. of Illinois State University; entered Protestant Episcopal Church (1864); founded *Evangelical Review;* translated Acrelius' *History of New Sweden.*

Rhabanus Maurus. A prominent churchman of the time of Charles the Great; b. ca. 776 or 784, d. 856; educated at Fulda, member of the Benedictine order; was ordained priest; became abbot at Fulda, later archbishop of Mainz; a leading authority on the Bible, on later ecclesiastical literature, and on canon law; wrote commentaries covering most of the books of the Bible, also two books of homilies and various books on doctrine and ecclesiastical discipline. See *Predestinarian Controversy.*

Rhaetic Confession. A document drawn up after several conferences in the autumn of the year 1552. The document resulted from theological discussions occasioned by the position taken by Renato Kamillo on questions concerning the Trinity, conversion, and the Sacraments. Johann Komander and Philipp Gallicius sent it to Bullinger for his criticism. This being favorable, the confession was signed by the great majority of pastors involved in the controversies.

Rhau (Rhaw), Georg (1488—1548). The first cantor of St. Thomas Church in Leipzig and the official printer of the Reformation movement. He served as cantor for only one year (1519—20); when Duke Georg opposed Luther and his adherents, Rhau and Poliander (rector of St. Thomas) sacrificed their positions. After serving as schoolmaster in Eisleben, Rhau took up his duties as printer in Wittenberg (1525). He published many of Luther's tracts as well as books on musical theory and books for the church, school, and home. The early Lutheran Church took an interest in church music and printed it through Rhau (the art of printing music had been invented by Petrucci * a few years previously). Some (*e. g.,* Rost, Eitner) believe that Rhau composed the twelve-part mass he conducted at the time of the Leipzig Debate (1519; it is believed that this debate persuaded Rhau to become a Lutheran). Rhau's most outstanding musical publication was his *Newe deudsche Geistliche Gesenge — fur die gemeinen Schulen-Wittenberg, 1544.* The volume contains 123 compositions, many of which had before been unknown and unavailable. The quality of the music is high (*e. g.,* that of Senfl, Ducis, Dietrich, Mahu, Isaac, Stoltzar, Hellinck, Agricola). Thirty compositions were based on chorales by Luther. Rhau helped perpetuate the influence and ideals of Walther and Luther's music. He took the church year into consideration and helped bring certain outstanding composers of the Lutheran Church to the fore.

F. Blume, *Die evangelische Kirchenmusik,* Potsdam, 1931; E. E. Koch, *Geschichte des Kirchenlieds und Kirchengesangs,* Stuttgart, 1866—67; S. Kuemmerle, *Encyklopaedie der evangelischen Kirchenmusik,* Guetersloh, 1894; J. D. Vonder Heidt, *Geschichte der evangelischen Kirchenmusik in* *Deutschland,* Berlin, 1926; Carl von Winterfeld, *Der evangelische Kirchengesang,* Leipzig, 1843.

Rhegius (Rieger), Urbanus (1489 to 1541). Popular preacher at Augsburg; sided with Luther against Rome; after hesitating, he sided with Luther against Zwingli. When Charles V prohibited preaching in 1530, Rhegius left, met Luther at Coburg, and became a good Lutheran reformer in Lueneburg. He opposed the Anabaptists and took part in the Wittenberg Concord of 1536 and the Hagenau convention. Died sincerely mourned by Luther.

Rheims Version. See *Bible Versions,* L 9.

Rheinberger, Josef (1839—1901). Organist and composer, spent the most productive years of his life in Munich. In his earlier years Joh. Georg Herzog and Franz Lachner were his most influential teachers. He was eminently successful as a teacher, and his works may be found in various areas of musical composition. In his twenty sonatas for organ he made no attempts to write in the classical sonata form: he was aware of the unsuitability of this form for music written for the organ and thus avoided making the mistakes made by his contemporaries. Though dry and uninspiring at times, his works were written carefully as well as skillfully.

Rhenius, C. T. E. (1790—1838). Educated in Jaenicke's Institute for Missions, Berlin; commissioned as missionary to India by the Church Missionary Society, England, 1814, going first to Tranquebar, then to Madura; translated parts of the Bible; engaged in extensive missionary operations; removed to Palamcottah, 1820; severed connection with C. M. S., 1835, for reasons of conscience. Urged to return to his former people, he organized the German Evangelical Mission. His work was eminently successful.

Rhenish Missionary Society (*Rheinische Missionsgesellschaft zu Barmen*). Organized at Elberfeld, 1799; founded the Bergische Bible Society and the Tract Society of the Wuppertal. In 1819 a similar society, which co-operated with the Basel Missionary Institute, was formed at Barmen. The two were merged into the Rhenish Mission Society, with offices at Barmen, in 1828. Missionaries were sent to South Africa (1829), Borneo (1834), Sumatra (1826), Nias (1863), China (1846), New Guinea

(1887). The tendency of the society is unionistic. The World War did not affect its work very seriously. The New Guinea field has been given over to the American Lutheran Iowa Synod. Fields: China, Borneo, Sumatra, Nias, Southwest Africa, New Guinea. See *Missions,* B 16.

Rhetoric. See *Homiletics,* 4.

Ricci, Matteo (1552—1610). Italian Jesuit; missionary to India (1578); went to China (1583); friendship of the emperor made it possible for him to do extensive mission work; wrote histories, geographies, and Christian works in Chinese; most famous *On the Nature of God.*

Ricercare. The early ricercari of the 16th and 17th centuries, written for the lute, clavichord, and organ, were of various types, often serving as the instrumental counterpart of the motet. On the other hand, the ricercari of Cavazzoni published in 1542—43 have more of the character of a fantasia or canzona, in which each theme is allowed more room for a fuller treatment than was the case in the instrumental motets, in which imitation was a prime feature. The ricercari of Andrea Gabrieli (ca. 1550) concentrated more on a monothematic treatment and thus helped pave the way for the fugue. Buxtehude, Kerll, and Froberger were eminently successful in writing ricercari of this type, as was also Bach, who, in 1748, included one in his *Musikalische Opfer.* Because of its various uses, the term *ricercare* (from Italian ricercare, to search out diligently) is still difficult to define. The ricercari of Hassler and Palestrina (published by Boosey and Hawkes) as well as those of Frescobaldi are excellent for use in the church service.

Richard, J. W. B. Feb. 14, 1843; education at Roanoke College, Pennsylvania College, and Gettysburg; prof. at Carthage College, 1873; sec'y of the Bd. of Church Extension, 1883; prof. at Wittenberg Seminary, 1885; prof. at Gettysburg, 1889; wrote a biography of Melanchthon; contributed to *Lutheran Quarterly;* wrote *Confessional History of the Lutheran Church;* inclined to Melanchthonianism; d. March 7, 1909.

Richard of St. Victor (d. 1173). French Augustinian monk; pupil of Hugo of St. Victor at Paris; prominent figure in the struggle of Thomas à Becket with Henry II of England; his theology strangely tinged with

mysticism, by which he hoped to save it from atrophy; much of his expository work along allegorical lines.

Richards, John (1803—54). Grandson of Muhlenberg; held pastorates at New Holland, Trappe, Germantown, Easton, and Reading; published sermons and contributed to *Evangelical Review.*

Richards, Matthias Henry (1841 to 1898). Son of John W.; prof. at Muhlenberg College (1868—98); editor of *Sunday School Lessons,* the *Helper,* and on the staff of the *Lutheran.*

Richelieu, Cardinal Armand Jean Duplessis (1585—1642). French ecclesiastic, chief minister, and virtual ruler of France during the last eighteen years of his life; wily diplomat, sagacious statesman, ruthless warrior-priest; his policy, in brief: The exaltation of the French monarchy to a dominant position in Europe. To this end he supported the *Protestants* in the Thirty Years' War against the power of Hapsburg, while at home he crushed the power of the Huguenots as a political party in the interest of monarchical absolutism.

Richmond, Mary. See *Social Work,* B 5.

Richmond Theses. Theses adopted at Richmond, Ind., by representatives of Iowa and Ohio shortly after the latter had withdrawn from the Synodical Conference. These theses were not considered as being on a par with theses like the Toledo or Davenport Theses of the Iowa Synod. They, however, have an official character inasmuch as they were presented by official representatives (though not officially adopted at a session of the synodical body).

J. L. Neve, *A Brief History of the Lutheran Church in America,* German Lit. Bd., Burlington, Ia., 1916 (p. 373); G. J. Fritschel, *Quellen u. Dokumente zur Geschichte und Lehrstellung der ev. luth. Synode von Iowa u. a. Staaten,* Wartburg Pub. House, Chicago, Ill., n. d. (theses printed pp. 364—68).

Richmond Resolutions. Resolutions adopted by the General Synod in 1909 after the General Council had pointed out discrepancies in the confessional statements of the General Synod. In these resolutions the General Synod held that it had never subscribed to "any edition of the confession save the 'unaltered' form . . . known as the *Editio Princeps* of 1530—31," and hence the identical one subscribed by the General Council, United Synod of the South, and the Joint Synod of Ohio. "When the General Synod says in her formula of confessional subscription that she accepts 'the Augsburg Confession as a correct exhibition of the fundamental doctrines of the Divine Word,' she means . . . that the fundamental doctrines of God's Word are correctly set forth in the Confession. She does not mean that some of the doctrines . . . are non-fundamental and therefore may be accepted or rejected; she means that they are all fundamental." The Resolutions classify the other symbols as "Secondary Symbols," which are to be held in high esteem because they explain and unfold "the doctrines of the Augsburg Confession." Regarding the statement "the Word of God as *contained* in the Canonical Scriptures . . ." in the General Synod's formula of confessional subscription, the Resolutions explain that the difference between "*is* the Word of God" and "*contains* the Word of God" had not been made ("or at least in vogue") when the formula was written. The Resolutions reject the view ascribed to the statement "contained in" and adopt "is the Word of God."

J. L. Neve, *A Brief History of the Lutheran Church in America*, German Lit. Bd., Burlington, Ia. (pp. 451—53). The references to primary sources are given).

Richter, Aemilius Ludwig (1808 to 1864). B. at Stolpen, near Dresden, Saxony; prof. at Universities of Leipzig, Marburg, Berlin; an authority on Protestant church polity; wrote: *Lehrbuch des katholischen und evangelischen Kirchenrechts mit besonderer Ruecksicht auf deutsche Zustaende, Die Geschichte der evangelischen Kirchenverfassung in Deutschland, Die evangelischen Kirchenordnungen des 16. Jahrhunderts;* coeditor of an edition of *The Canons and Decrees of the Council of Trent.*

Richter, Christian Friedrich (1676 to 1711). Studied at Halle; inspector of the *Paedagogium;* later physician to all the Franckean institutions; important hymn writer of the Pietists; wrote: "Es glaenzet der Christen inwendiges Leben."

Richter, F. B. 1852 in Saxony; pres. of Iowa Synod 1904—26; educated at Erlangen, Leipzig, and St. Sebald, Iowa; pastor at Mendota, Ill., and professor at the seminary 1876—94; president of

Clinton College, 1894—1902; then became editor of the *Kirchenblatt.* At the 50th anniversary of the Iowa Synod he was elected its (third) president. D. Oct. 18, 1934.

Richter, Ludwig (1803—84). German painter; very sympathetic, popular touch; appeals to a wide audience, especially by means of his woodcut series and cycles, among them "The Lord's Prayer," one of the most beautiful spiritual songs; among his etchings: "Christmas Night"; "Psalm 65"; "House Blessing."

Ridley, Nicholas (ca. 1500—55). Martyr bishop; espoused Protestantism ca. 1536; bishop of Rochester, later of London; influential under Edward VI; supported Jane Grey; suffered martyrdom with Latimer at Oxford.

Riedel, Karl (1827—88). Organizer and conductor of the famous Riedelsche Verein of Leipzig, which in 1859 attracted widespread attention to itself by performing Bach's *Mass in B Minor* and which revived many other choral works by masters of earlier centuries. Riedel edited much music written by such masters as Eccard and Schuetz.

Riegel, Friedrich Samuel (b. 1825). Edited the music found in Schoeberlein's *Schatz des liturgischen Chorund Gemeindegesangs.* Like Schoeberlein and Winterfeld, he was influenced by the church music philosophy of Justus Thibaut and regarded the choral music of the 16th century as representing the ideals of ecclesiastical choral music. His own arrangements and harmonizations, as found in Schoeberlein's *Schatz,* were prepared in the style and spirit of the 16th-century music.

Rieger, Georg Konrad (1687—1743). D. as first preacher of *Hospitalkirche* at Stuttgart, Wuerttemberg; a most gifted preacher of the Wuerttemberg Pietistic school; wrote *Herzpostille.*

Rietschel, Christian Georg (1842 to 1914). Studied at Erlangen, Berlin, and Leipzig; held various positions as pastor, especially at Ruedigsdorf, Wittenberg, and Leipzig; later professor of practical theology at Leipzig; greatly interested in liturgics and church music; wrote: *Die Aufgabe der Orgel im Gottesdienst; Der evangelische Gottesdienst, Lehrbuch der Liturgik,* etc.

Rietschel, Ernst Friedrich August (1804—61). German sculptor, studied at Dresden and under Rauch in Berlin, later at Rome; elected to professorship of sculpture at Dresden; produced many works imbued with much religious feeling, with an appealing realism; among his works: a life-sized Pietà, executed for the king of Prussia, and the monument of Luther at Worms, completed by his pupils.

Riggenbach, Christoph Johannes (1818—90). Reformed theologian; 1851 professor at Basel; at first radical in theology, later more moderate; collaborator on *Lange's Commentary;* hymnologist.

Righteousness. The righteousness of God is the essential perfection of His nature (see *God*). The term "righteousness" is applied to Christ not only in view of His essential righteousness, but also in view of the righteousness which He gained for mankind (see *Atonement; Christ Jesus; Justification*). The righteousness of the Law is that righteousness which obedience to the Law requires (see *Decalog; Law and Gospel*). The righteousness of the Christian is the righteousness of faith (see *Conversion; Faith; Justification*).

Rig-Veda. See *Veda.*

Rinck, Christian Heinrich (1770 to 1846). Composer and organist, was a pupil of Kittel, a pupil of Bach, who engendered in young Rinck a profound respect for the illustrious *Thomaskantor.* In his humility and honesty Rinck resented it bitterly when well-meaning people referred to him as a second Bach. His organ music was at one time played a great deal, also in America; however, it is rapidly passing out of use today.

Rinckart, Martin (1586—1640). Studied in Latin school of his home town, Eilenburg, then at University of Leipzig; *Cantor,* then *Diakonus* at Eisleben; later pastor at Erdeborn and Lyttichendorf; finally *Archidiaconus* at Eilenburg, where he passed through the horrors of the Thirty Years' War; a voluminous writer, also of poetry; wrote: "Nun danket alle Gott."

Rincker, Leroy C. B. Aug. 20, 1896; graduated from Concordia College, Milwaukee, and Concordia Seminary, St. Louis (1922); member of the faculty of Concordia College, Milwaukee (1923); president, 1936; D. D., Concordia Seminary, St. Louis, 1952; d. Jan. 28, 1953.

Ring (*Marriage*). Used of old as a symbol of faithfulness. The ring, preferably gold, which was always associated with enduring fidelity and worth, is properly used by both bride and groom as a wedding pledge, preferably at the time of betrothal, but certainly in one form of the marriage ceremony (exchanging rings; "with this ring I thee endow"). To confine the ring to the bride alone is to hint at a double standard, which would be at absolute variance with the standpoint of the Bible.

Ringeltaube, Wilhelm Tobias. B. 1770 at Scheidelwitz, Silesia; educated at Halle; sent to India under the auspices of the London Missionary Society, 1804; landed at Tranquebar, December 5, 1804; called to Travancore by the Christian Vedamanickam, 1806, and became founder of Protestant missions in that native state, introducing Lutheran Catechism and doctrine; labored with much success until 1816, when he departed for Ceylon, via Madras. His end is shrouded in mystery.

Ringwaldt, Bartholomaeus (1532 to ca. 1600). B. at Frankfurt a. O., ordained in 1557. He held the office in two pastorates before settling at Langenfeld, Brandenburg, where he spent the greater part of his life. He was a popular poet and exerted considerable influence. A stanch Lutheran, he was fearless in his denunciation of the morals of his day. He was one of the most prolific hymn writers of the 16th century. Wackernagel gives 208 items under his name.

Rippon, John (1751—1836). Ed. at Baptist College, Bristol; pastor in London from 1773 till his death; one of the most popular and influential men of his denomination; wrote "The Day Has Dawned, Jehovah Comes."

Rist, Johann (1607—67). B. at Ottensen, near Hamburg; attended school in Hamburg; at twenty he graduated from the Gymnasium Illustri at Bremen; then he studied at the University of Rinteln, where, under the influence of Josua Stegmann, he began to take an interest in hymnology. Then he studied Hebrew, mathematics, and medicine at Rostock. In 1635 he settled down at Wedel, near Hamburg, and there devoted his time to pastoral duties and to poetry. In 1644 he was created Poet Laureate. Rist was a voluminous and many-sided writer. His secular works are of great interest to the student of history. He wrote about 680 hymns and spiritual songs. He takes high rank as a hymn writer, possessing a noble, classical style, and objective in character.

Ritschl, Albrecht (1822—89). Studied at Bonn, Halle, Heidelberg, and Tuebingen (Baur); first professor at Bonn; 1864 at Goettingen; 1874 also consistorial councilor. Originally a pupil of Nitsch, Tholuck, Julius Mueller, and Rothe, then a Hegelian and a pupil of the Tuebingen School of Baur. Since 1857 he became more and more the founder of a school of his own, influenced by Kant, Schleiermacher, and Lotze. Ritschl claimed to be evangelical, even Lutheran, and to preach Christ. But actually he undermined Biblical Lutheranism everywhere, founding his theology not on the infallible, inspired, and revealed Word of God, but on the consciousness of the believer as presented to us especially in the New Testament writings, which, in turn, the theologian makes his own by actual experience of the power of Christ working in His Church. Religion, according to Ritschl, is the faith in high spiritual powers, which elevated man to a higher sphere. Christ is called God, though His pre-existence before the world is denied. There is no original sin. Sin is mistrust in God, and its true punishment is the feeling of guilt; God looks upon it as ignorance. There is no wrath of God over sin and no vicarious atonement of Christ. God is Love, and as soon as man realizes this, he is redeemed and justified. From this follows the new life of love toward God, faith, prayer, humility, and patience. This Ritschlian School has representatives in many of the German universities and is, in fact, what in this country was called "German theology" — a subversion of Christianity. Ritschl's main work is *Die christliche Lehre von der Rechtfertigung und Versoehnung*.

A life of Ritschl was written by his son, Otto Ritschl (*Albrecht Ritschls Leben*, Freiburg, 1892—96); outstanding work: *Die christliche Lehre von der Rechtfertigung und Versoehnung*, Goettingen, 1870—74 (1st ed.); F. E. Mayer, "Ritschl's Theology," *CTM*, XV: 145—57; H. R. Mackintosch, *Types of Modern Theology*, Scribner's, N. Y., 1939 (138—80).

Ritual. See *Liturgics; Worship, Parts of.*

Rituale Romanum. In the early centuries of the Church, and in fact up to the time of the Reformation, there had been a diversity of liturgies in various parts of Christendom. Naturally the Eastern liturgies maintained themselves even after the great schism. And the Ambrosian Liturgy, the Mozarabic Liturgy, the Gallican Liturgy, and even the English Liturgy, were retained in spite of the superior power of the Roman See. But the decisions of the Council of Trent made the use of the Roman Liturgy obliga'ory in all parts of the Church, and hence the *Rituale Romanum* is fundamental for all modern breviaries and missals. A complete missal includes also the office for the dead, or the *Totenmesse.*

River Brethren. See *Brethren, The River.*

Robbia, Luca della (and the Robbia family), ca. 1400—82; Italian sculptor; celebrated as the creator of one of the bronzes for the sacristy of the cathedral at Florence. His work in enameled terra cotta, known as "della Robbia" work, was continued by members of his family, especially his nephew Andrea and his grandnephew Giovanni; work shows great charm and grace.

Robert of Sorbonne (1201—74). Founder of the Sorbonne, the theological college of the University of Paris.

Robertson, Archibald Thomas (1863 to 1934). B. at Chatham, Va.; professor of New Testament interpretation at Baptist Seminary, Louisville, since 1888. Monumental *Grammar of the Greek New Testament* (3d ed. 1919), and other works on the New Testament.

E. Gill, *A. T. Robertson, A Biography*, Macm., 1943.

Robertson, Frederick William (1816 to 1853). Ed. at the Edinburgh Academy and University and Oxford; pastor at Cheltenham, Oxford, Brighton; famous as a preacher who emphasized the relation of the Church to the world, but is unorthodox in his views on Inspiration and Atonement.

Robertus, Galliae Rex (970—1031). Surnamed Le Devot on account of his piety and simplicity of character; fame as hymn writer not well established, although the sequence "Veni, Sancte Spiritus" ("Come, Holy Spirit") is attributed to him.

Robinson, Charles Seymore (1829 to 1899). B. at Bennington, Vt.; educated at Williams College. He studied theology at Union Seminary in New York and at Princeton and became a Presbyterian minister. He was also very successful as editor of hymnbooks. He is known by his hymn "Savior, I Follow On."

Robinson, Edward (1794—1863). Biblical scholar; b. at Southington, Conn.; professor at Andover Seminary and Union Seminary; twice in the Orient; d. in New York City; translated Buttmann's *Greek Grammar*, Winer's *Grammar of New Testament Greek*, Gesenius' *Hebrew Lexicon*, etc.; established *Bibliotheca Sacra* 1843; wrote important works on Palestine, etc.

Robinson, Frank. See *Psychiana*.

Robinson, John (ca. 1576—1625). Minister of the Pilgrim Fathers; b. in Lincolnshire; ordained; officer of Separatists at Scrooby; pastor in Amsterdam (1608) and Leyden (with Brewster as ruling elder, 1609; died there); author.

Rochelle, Confession of. See *Reformed Confessions*, B.

Rochet. A white linen vestment, decorated with lace or embroidery, distinctive of Roman prelates. It resembles the surplice, but has tight sleeves and reaches only to the knees. Bishops wear it at confirmation.

Rock, Johann. See *Amana Society*.

Rocky Mountain Synod. See *United Lutheran Church, Synods of*, 27.

Rococo. See *Architecture, Ecclesiastical*, 6.

Rodigast, Samuel (1649—1708). Studied at Jena, where he was appointed adjunct of the philosophical faculty in 1676; corrector of the Gray Friars' *Gymnasium* in Berlin 1680; later rector, holding this position till his death; wrote poems in the style of Gerhardt, his best hymn being that written for a sick friend in Jena: "What God Ordains Is Always Good."

Roehr, Johann Friedrich (1777 to 1848). Violent defender of rationalism; chief court preacher, supreme councilor, and general superintendent at Weimar.

Roerer, Georg. A corrector in Wittenberg, member of what Luther jokingly termed his Sanhedrin, the group that met with him in the strenuous work of translating the Bible into German, 1522—34; prepared one edition of Luther's *House Postil* and was a prominent factor in shaping the text of the Luther translation.

Rogation Days. The three days before Ascension Day, which have been kept since ancient times as days of prayer and supplication. They are still observed by many Protestants and by the Roman Church. In the latter a procession is held, and the Litany of the Saints is chanted on each day. A similar ceremony takes place on April 25 (St. Mark's Day). The Sunday before the Rogation days is called Rogation Sunday.

Roger Williams Club. See *Students, Spiritual Care of*, A.

Rogers, John (1500?—1555). Lutheran through Tyndale; in 1537 prepared the whole Bible with notes; published, under the name of Thomas Matthew, the first English Lutheran commentary on the Bible, having "the character of a Lutheran manifesto . . . chiefly remarkable for the excessive Lutheranism of its annotations," says Hoare. He was the first martyr under Bloody Mary, Feb. 4, 1555, his wife and children cheering him to remain faithful till death. "He was burned alive for being a Lutheran."

Rohmer, Friedrich (1814—56). German philosopher; by regarding the universe as the body of God he sought to harmonize theism and pantheism.

Rohr, Heinrich K. G. von (1797 to 1874). Captain in the Prussian army; resigned as a protest against the "Union"; organized Grabau's emigration; farmer at Freistadt, Wis.; taught school, studied, and took a parish 1843; separated from Grabau with a group 1866; president of group till death.

Rohr, Philipp Andreas von. Son of H. K. G. von Rohr; b. Feb. 13, 1843, at Buffalo; graduate of Buffalo Synod Seminary, 1863; pastor at Toledo; 1866 to 1908 pastor at Winona, Minn., which parish grew to be the largest in Minnesota; joined Wisconsin Synod, 1877; its president from 1889 until his death, December 22, 1908. Left Buffalo Synod 1866 to form separate body, which, as its last president, he dissolved peacefully, 1875. Forceful, practical, endowed with sound judgment and keen and ready understanding, he is largely responsible for the development of the synod and its missions and institutions during his term of office.

Rohrlack, August (1835—1909). B. in Prussia; sent to America by Loehe; served as missionary in Wisconsin and later became pastor at Reedsburg;

served many years as Secretary of the Missouri Synod.

Rolf, E. See *Canada, Lutheranism in,* 11.

Rolle, Johann Heinrich (1718 to 1785). A composer whose church music at one time enjoyed wide use in Lutheran churches. His ideal preceptor was Karl Heinrich Graun. Rolle's church music was sentimental and vapid and has fallen into disuse.

Roman Catechism. See *Catechetics,* 8; *Roman Catholic Confessions,* A 3.

Roman Catholic Church and the Bible. See *Bible Reading.*

Roman Catholic Church, History of, since the Reformation. 1. The history of the Roman Catholic Church since the Reformation is a many-sided subject. It is, first of all, a long and bitter conflict between Romanism and Protestantism, a conflict waged on both sides, at times with great bitterness, though with this important distinction, that in the case of the Protestants such methods violated one of the principles for which the Reformation contended, namely, the sacred rights of conscience, while in the other the use of force had the sanction of Catholic tradition, which has never been revoked.

2. At the threshold of our period the outstanding fact is that after various futile attempts at reconciliation the Roman Catholic Church put forth all her energies to stem the tide of the Reformation. To this end it was necessary, first of all, to standardize Catholic theology as it had been developed by the medieval theologians. This was done at the famous Council of Trent (convened with interruptions from 1545 to 1563), which threw a brazen wall around Catholic dogma. The distinctive doctrines of the Reformation, notably that of justification by faith alone, were declared anathema, and the gulf between Protestantism and Romanism became fixed and impassable. The council also introduced some wholesome disciplinary reforms concerning the traffic in indulgences, the morals of the clergy, the monastic orders, and other matters, the Reformation thus proving itself a blessing to the Church which attacked and condemned it.

3. Doctrine and discipline settled at Trent, the Church was ready for vigorous action against all heretics. Two mighty engines were soon in action, the one the Inquisition which "con-

vinced" the gainsayers with the gallows and the galleys, the rack and the fagot; the other, the newly founded order of the Jesuits, a powerful organization, instinct with one spirit, obedient to one will, listening at the doors of every cabinet in Europe, shaping the policies of kings, largely controlling education, and, above all, sticking at no means, however damnable, to accomplish its end — and that end the extinction of Protestantism and the exaltation of the Papacy.

4. In *Italy* the Inquisition, already established by Paul III in 1542, carried on its work with such relentless severity that by the end of the century every trace of Protestantism had vanished. Venice alone witnessed some three thousand heresy trials, with smaller numbers in other cities. Persecution was accompanied by a crusade against all heretical literature, the first index of prohibited books being published in 1559.

5. In *Spain* the mild light of the Reformation faded away in about two decades before the lurid glare of the *auto da fé.*

6. In *France* the Reformed Church (Huguenots) had to live in the face of severe persecution and repressive legislation. . . . The Inquisition was a more pitiless foe than heathenism could have bred. *(Cambridge Modern History.)* A book dedicated to Henry III in 1581 places the number of those who had fallen within the few preceding years for their religion at 200,000. The Edict of Nantes issued by Henry IV in 1589 granted the Huguenots, numbering at that time about 1,250,000 souls, full liberty of private conscience, with restrictions, however, as to liberty of public worship. Pope Clement VIII, successor of Gregory XIII, who glorified the Massacre of St. Bartholomew's Day, denounced the edict in unmeasured terms "as the most accursed thing that can be imagined, whereby liberty of conscience is granted to everybody, which is the worst thing in the world." When Henry IV fell by the assassin's knife (1610), Paul V saw in the tragic fate of the king the avenging finger of God. The publication of the edict was followed by a period of remarkable growth and development of French Protestantism, which numbered among its adherents some of the most useful, intelligent, and patriotic citizens of France. The supreme folly and bigotry of Louis XIV (1643—1715) inaugurated a "reign of terror" for his Protestant

subjects. Louis, the embodiment of absolutism, galled by the thought that any of his subjects should hold religious convictions at variance with those of their monarch and instigated by his Jesuit advisers, in 1865 declared the "perpetual *and irrevocable*" (so Henry IV had called it) Edict of Nantes revoked. The savage character of the Edict of Revocation will appear from a few of its provisions. "It pleases us," says the king, "that all the temples of the said R. P. R. [Reformed Pretended Religion] situated within our kingdom . . . shall be immediately destroyed." "We command all ministers of said R. P. R. who will not be converted to the Catholic, Apostolic, and Roman religion to leave our kingdom within fifteen days after the publication of our present edict." "We forbid private schools for the instruction of the children of said R. P. R." Under penalty of a heavy fine "all children of persons of the said R. P. R. shall for the future be baptized by the parish priest" and "educated in the Catholic, Roman, and Apostolic religion." "We make very express and repeated prohibitions to all our subjects of the said R. P. R. from departing . . . from our said kingdom," etc., etc. Despite this latter prohibition the publication of the edict was followed by an exodus of from three hundred thousand to one million Huguenots, who on peril of their lives quit the land of their birth and found homes in England, Denmark, Holland, Sweden, and Germany, the Elector of Brandenburg receiving twenty thousand refugees and declaring that he would sell his silver plate rather than see them suffer want. This act of Louis XIV was hailed with delight by nearly all the dignitaries of the Catholic Church, including Pope Innocent XI, who celebrated the event with a Te Deum; but it was unanimously condemned by the voice of Protestant Europe. Nor did the Edict of Revocation achieve its purpose. In spite of repressive legislation the Huguenots, half of whom remained in the country, continued their worship in secret as the so-called "Church of the Desert," adopting the fitting device: *Flagror, non consumor* ("I burn, but am not consumed").

7. On the other hand, the age of Louis XIV with the religious tyranny, the profligacy, hypocrisy, and Jesuitical morals of the court prepared the soil for the abundant crop of French infidelity and radicalism, which led to the temporary abolition of Roman Ca-

tholicism, and indeed of all religion, during the French Revolution. Voltaire, the leading spokesman of the new thought, gave out the slogan: *Ecrasez l'infame* ("Crush the wretch"), by which he meant the Roman Catholic Church as a tyrannical, intolerant, and persecuting institution. At the same time he rendered signal service to the cause of freedom by his fearless advocacy of religious toleration, which gave the deathblow to persecution in France. In 1787 the ill-fated Louis XVI issued the Edict of Versailles, which gave to non-Catholics full civil rights. The Constituent Assembly in 1789 confiscated all the property of the Church and in the following year decreed the Civil Constitution of the clergy, that is, it nationalized the Church by making the priests the salaried officers of the state. It also declared that religious freedom was one of man's inalienable rights. These measures were, of course, condemned by the Pope, who forbade the clergy to take the oath of conformity to the Civil Constitution. As a result the French clergy was split into two factions, and religious chaos and anarchy ensued. In 1793 the atheistic party of the revolutionists took summary measures in dealing with the religious situation by abolishing not only Roman Catholicism, but Christianity itself. All the churches in Paris were closed, sacred images torn down, the symbol of the cross replaced by that of "the Holy Guillotine," and to crown all, a famous actress, representing the "Goddess of Reason," received the homage of the atheists in the Cathedral of Notre Dame. This wild orgy of religious nihilism was soon followed by the theatrical mummeries attending the inauguration of a new cult, that of the "worship of the Supreme Being." This was sponsored by the dictator Robespierre, who declared that "if there were no God, men would have to invent one," and therefore, though abolishing Christianity as an old superstition, he wished to retain a bald deism and the belief in the immortality of the soul as the religious foundation of the new order. A few months after the spectacular ceremonies of the "Festival of the Supreme Being" the head of Robespierre fell under the guillotine. Thus did the Revolution officially annihilate the Gallican Church.

8. Needless to say, however, a reaction set in. The Directory (1795—99) had permitted Christian worship, and though it, too, exacted the "civic oath"

from the priests, many thousands of the clergy who had emigrated returned to their parishes and swore allegiance to the state. Meanwhile a new power appeared on the scene — Napoleon Bonaparte. One of the objects of his Italian campaign was to chastise the Pope for his inflexible hostility to the French republic. Napoleon entered Rome and quickly compelled Pius VI, who later died in a French prison, to sign the humiliating Peace of Tolentino. On his return from Egypt, Napoleon calmly pushed aside the futile Directory and proceeded to the business of reorganizing the government and laying plans for universal sovereignty. Wiser than a Robespierre and other revolutionary fanatics, he realized the importance of reaching a *modus vivendi* (an understanding) with the Papacy. Accordingly he entered into negotiations with Pius VII and concluded with him a solemn treaty, called a concordat, by which the affairs of the French Church were adjusted. The Concordat provided: The Catholic religion is recognized as the religion of the majority of the French people; all church property remains in the hands of the secular government; the government pledges itself to support the clergy; the state appoints the bishops, while the Pope confirms the appointments; the bishops nominate the priests, the validity of the nomination to be approved by the government. While thus the Church was apparently placed almost wholly under state control, the Papacy, possessing the right to confirm *(or reject)* the state's nominees for the office of bishop, was the real gainer in the transaction. The Napoleonic system, with some later modifications, remained in force until 1905. In the year previous the French president Loubet paid an official visit to the king of Italy at Rome. Pope Pius X regarded this as an affront to his dignity, for the Papacy has never become reconciled to the seizure of the Papal States in 1870, which it considers an act of ruthless usurpation. Pius, accordingly, sent a note of complaint to the French government, whereupon the latter, by a majority of 386 against 111 votes, declared "that the attitude of the Vatican rendered necessary the separation of Church and State" (December 9, 1905). The majority of the French clergy were willing to accept the new law, but the Vatican pronounced against it. In language worthy of a Hildebrand, Pius X fulminated his condemnation of the separation law in the encyclical *Vehementer nos,* which, among other things, declares that the measure is opposed to "the divine institution, the essential principles, and the liberties of the Church" and that "it is a grave offense against the dignity of the Apostolic See and Our own person, and against the episcopal and clerical orders and the Catholics of France." The refusal of the clergy to conform to the new system has resulted in the rather anomalous situation that at present the Catholic Church of France is continuing its services in churches to which it is not legally entitled, a state of affairs which can hardly be permanent.

9. In *Germany* the history of the Roman Catholic Church since the Reformation presents, particularly in its earlier stages, a determined onslaught against the principles of freedom so heroically championed by Luther. The Roman Catholic Emperor Charles V put Luther and his followers under the ban and endeavored to check the Reformation movement with the edge of the sword. His defeat by the Elector Maurice of Saxony was followed by the Peace of Augsburg (1555). This was a compromise which invested the territorial princes with the authority to determine the religion of their subjects *(cuius regio, eius religio),* thus placing Lutherans and Catholics on a basis of equality before the law. The territorial system, an advantage at first for the cause of the Reformation, eventually proved highly detrimental. Instigated by the Jesuits, who worked with marked success from various centers (Ingolstadt, Vienna, Cologne, Prague), the Catholic princes exerted severe pressure upon their Protestant subjects by excluding them from civil offices, expelling evangelical preachers, compelling obdurate Protestants to leave their territory, and requiring all officers to swear by the Tridentine Confession.

10. In *Bohemia* the Letter of Majesty, wrung from the reluctant hands of Rudolf II in 1609 and granting the inhabitants freedom of choice between Romanism and Lutheranism, was flagrantly disregarded by Matthias (1612 to 1619) and torn to pieces by Ferdinand II (1619—37).

11. The Thirty Years' War (1618 to 1648), with its frightful sacrifice of life and property, was the bursting of the storm which had been brewing. When, after long years of bloody strife, the Peace of Westphalia (1648) guaranteed the liberties of Protestantism, both Lutheran and Calvinistic, and, as the Ro-

man Catholic Lord Acton says, became "the basis of public law and political order of modern Europe." It is the first public document of our period to use the word *toleration* in settling religious dissension. It placed Romanism, Lutheranism, and Calvinism (minor sects are expressly excluded) on the same legal basis and thus created an era in modern history. The Catholic party had failed to exterminate Protestantism and to re-establish its waning authority in the land of Luther. As might be expected, Pope Innocent X, "by the fullness of his power, utterly condemned, rejected, declared invalid, unjust, and iniquitous," etc., the principles of freedom enunciated by the treaty. But papal bulls had lost their effect. A generation later the Elector Frederick William of Brandenburg welcomed twenty thousand Huguenot refugees within his dominions, while Frederick the Great declared that in his kingdom "everybody can be saved according to his own fashion." True, this was only the tolerant policy of a progressive monarch, who still had the control of religious affairs in his hands. Full religious liberty as a fundamental and inalienable right of the individual subsequently became a law of the German Empire. What is still wanted is the complete separation of Church and State, which is the natural corollary of religious liberty. Since World War II, the political and ideological tensions in Germany make any prediction as to the fulfillment of this desire impossible.

12. In *Austria*, where the Reformation was nearly extinguished by the Jesuitical Counter Reformation, Protestant principles ultimately prevailed. In 1781 Emperor Joseph II issued an edict of toleration, while the Constitution of 1868 grants freedom of conscience. It might be mentioned that Hungary, which toward the end of the 16th century numbered two thousand Protestant churches, had only one hundred and five at the time of the emperor's edict. Catholic reaction also attained a full measure of success in Bohemia, Silesia, Livonia (though checked here by Gustavus Adolphus), Carniola, and elsewhere.

13. Passing on now to a survey of Roman Catholicism in *England,* we note that its history took an entirely different course from what it did on the Continent. In France the Roman Catholic Church always remained in a dominant position. In Germany her ambitions to regain her lost supremacy were

decisively curbed by the Thirty Years' War; but the treaty which ended that struggle guaranteed her a legal place. In England, on the contrary, her position until comparatively recent times was, apart from periods of insolent triumphs, one of subjection, degradation, civil disability, even outlawry. As late as the middle of the 18th century an English court decided that the existence of Roman Catholics within the realm was made possible only by the lax enforcement of the law. Even John Locke, the philosopher of English toleration, excluded the Catholics from the free exercise of religion on the ground that they were a menace to the state. To explain the English attitude, it is only necessary to bear in mind a few facts, such as the horrors of the persecution under Queen Mary, the attempted subjugation of England by Philip II of Spain, the numerous popish conspiracies against the life of Queen Elizabeth, the Gunpowder Plot of Guy Fawkes, and the Roman Catholic doctrine of the authority of the Popes over civil rulers. These facts will not justify, but, as remarked, they will explain, the severe laws enacted against the Catholics by Queen Elizabeth and her successors. Another factor working in the same direction was the conviction of the English rulers that the safety and stability of their government depended in large measure on absolute religious uniformity. Hence the penal legislation against all dissenters.

14. The Reformation, it has been said, "entered England by a side door," when Henry VIII (1509—47) broke with the Pope and nationalized the English Church. The Supremacy Act of 1534 declared that Henry was "on earth the Supreme Head of the Church of England." In other words, England was to remain Catholic without the Pope. Henry burned, beheaded, or hanged both Protestant and Roman Catholic dissenters, the one for denying transubstantiation, the other for denying the royal supremacy in religious affairs. It must be said, however, that Henry's quarrel with the Papacy saved the Protestants from the keener edge of persecution.

15. Under Edward VI (1547—53) Protestantism, amid much civil disorder and bloodshed, was established by law. The Act of Uniformity (1549) prescribed the use of the *Book of Common Prayer,* compiled by Archbishop Cranmer, while the *Forty-two Articles of Religion* (later reduced to thirty-

nine) provided a Protestant confession of faith. To enforce these changes, a new code of ecclesiastical law was drawn up, which, though milder than the Roman Catholic canon law in shrinking from the death penalty, was formidable enough.

16. The accession of Queen Mary (1553—58) was the signal for a vigorous Catholic reaction. Resolved to restore Catholicism, the queen opened up negotiations with Rome, and an obsequious Parliament "decided by a formal vote to return to the obedience of the Papal See, receiving on their knees the absolution, which freed the realm from the guilt incurred by its schism and heresy." Rome rejoiced that the prodigal had returned to his father's house. Three hundred Protestants fell victim to the bigotry of Queen Mary; but every heretic who was burned produced at least a hundred more.

17. The work of Mary was undone by her sister Queen Elizabeth (1558 to 1603), who, with little religious conviction of her own, favored Protestantism for two reasons: first, she was determined to uphold the royal supremacy against all papal interference; secondly, all the Catholics of her realm who remained loyal to the Pope denied her right to the crown, especially since Paul V, in 1570, had excommunicated and deposed her as a heretic. The Act of Supremacy of 1559 declared the queen to be the "Supreme Governor" of the English Church. The Uniformity Act of the same year prohibited, on penalty of imprisonment, even death in case of repeated offenses, the use of any but the Anglican liturgy, besides enforcing church attendance by the imposition of a fine. It is estimated that about two hundred Catholic priests and Jesuits suffered death during the reign of Queen Elizabeth, but, as Green says, "if Elizabeth was a persecutor, she was the first English ruler who felt the charge of persecution to be a stigma on her rule." "She rested her system of repression on purely political grounds." In 1582 the Jesuits were banished from the country on pain of death, though many remained and continued their work in secret. Constant plottings on the part of the Catholics to place Mary, Queen of Scots, on the English throne determined Elizabeth to order her cousin to the block (1587). This was followed by a gigantic effort on the part of Philip II of Spain to avenge the death of Mary and to strike a decisive blow at Protestantism. The "Invincible

Armada," consisting of one hundred and sixty ships, set sail from Lisbon with the papal blessing in 1588, but — "God blew with His winds, and they were scattered." This signal rebuff destroyed forever the hopes of regaining England for Catholicism and of rolling back the tide of the Reformation.

18. James I (1603—25), the inflexible advocate of the divine right of kings, persecuted all dissenters, Puritan and Catholic. The latter, who questioned his right to the crown, he sought at first to conciliate by relaxing the penal laws against them. This indulgence was followed at once by an increase of avowed Catholics, to the great alarm of Parliament, which confirmed the statutes of Elizabeth. The king, to vindicate himself from the suspicion of undue lenience toward his Catholic subjects, rigorously executed the anti-Catholic statutes, denying Catholics even the right to educate their children in their own faith. Catholic disappointment and resentment took concrete form in an attempt to blow up the House of Parliament on the day the king was to open the session (November 5, 1605), the ultimate aim being to rally the English Catholics to open revolt and establish a Catholic government. This Gunpowder Plot failed, and the conspirators, Robert Catesby, Guy Fawkes, and others, were executed. Henceforth the Catholics were practically deprived of the protection of the law and were subject to terrible oppression.

19. Under Charles I (1625—49), whose wife was a Roman Catholic and whose ecclesiastical adviser was Archbishop Laud, a man of Catholic leanings, the laws against the Catholics were rarely enforced. The short-lived dominance of Puritanism during the Commonwealth (1649—60) was followed by the re-establishment of Episcopal worship and the enactment of more laws against dissenters. It would carry us beyond the scope of this article to give the details of this legislation. Suffice it to say that it is repugnant to every sense of humanity and justice and condemned thousands to languish and die in filthy English prisons or drove them for refuge beyond the borders of the country. One such enactment must be specifically mentioned as being directed against the Roman Catholics, with whom we are now concerned. The secret treaty of Charles II (1660—85) with Louis XIV of France for the restoration of Catholicism in

England led the English Parliament to the passage of the Test Act, which required all persons holding office under the crown, civil or military, to declare against transubstantiation and to receive the Sacrament within three months after admittance to office. A similar measure, the Disabling Act of 1678, excluded all Catholics from sitting in the English Parliament and required of all members a declaration against the sacrifice of the Mass and the invocation of saints.

20. James II (1685—88), the last of the Stuarts, had openly joined the Roman Catholic Church in 1669. Like all the Stuarts, who learned and forgot nothing, he proceeded in the business of government on the theory that he was the State — *and the Church.* Nevertheless he took the oath on the constitution and promised "to preserve this [English] government, both in Church and State, as it is now established." After taking this oath, he treated all the laws against the papists as null and void, received a papal nuncio at court, sent an agent to Rome to promote the restoration of Catholicism, and forbade the English clergy to preach against "the king's religion." Deaf to all counsels of moderation, he was determined "to lose all or to win all." And he lost all. "To his policy," says Macaulay, "the English Roman Catholics owed three years of lawless and insolent triumph and a hundred and forty years of subjection and degradation." The English nation deposed him and gave the crown to his son-in-law, William of Orange, who had been reared a Protestant. The spirit of the new king showed itself in the Act of Toleration of 1689, which is a milestone in the progress of religious liberty in England. Officially the document is called "An Act for Exempting Their Majesties' [William and Mary] Protestant Subjects Dissenting from the Church of England from the Penalties of Certain Laws." That is to say, the ban was finally lifted from *non-Catholic* dissenters, Catholics being excluded. Nay, in 1700 Parliament passed an act which offered a reward of a hundred pounds for the discovery of any Romish priest performing the offices of his Church, incapacitated every Roman Catholic from inheriting or purchasing land, etc., etc. The Catholics of Ireland fared even worse than those of England. More than a century was to elapse before public opinion in England was ready to grant civil and religious franchise to the downtrodden

Catholics of the kingdom. The Catholic Emancipation Act was passed in 1829.

21. Besides its conflict with Protestantism the Roman Catholic Church has had trouble within its own camp. As a protest against Jesuitism the movement begun by Cornelius Jansen, bishop of Ypres, and ably supported by the learning and genius of many of the noblest minds of France, among them Blaise Pascal, the historian Tillemont, and the poet Racine, agitated the Gallican Church for over a century, and it required the combined powers of king and Pope to hold it in check (see *Jansenism*). Also in matters of ecclesiastical polity the French clergy caused the Papacy concern. From the days of the Tridentine Council, but especially since the end of the 16th century, the French bishops, actuated by national pride and by a desire for personal independence in the management of their affairs, maintained an unfriendly attitude toward the claims of papal absolutism and autocracy. These sentiments took definite form in four propositions, published in 1682 (Gallican Liberties), which declared the absolute sovereignty of secular princes in temporal affairs and conceded only a limited primacy of the Pope in spiritual matters, all papal deliverances depending for their validity on the ratification of a general council. In other words, an ecumenical council is the highest court of appeal. These propositions were condemned by several Popes as null and void, and Louis XIV, who in occasional moments felt some concern for his soul, practically retracted them, though there was no formal revocation. It remained for Napoleon I, who, to realize his ambition of absolute control of Church and State, endeavored to use the Papacy as his willing tool, unwittingly to drive the French bishops into the arms of Rome. Since the days of Napoleon, as Harnack says, the French have been the mainstay of Ultramontanism (see *Gallicanism*).

22. A movement in Germany, akin to Gallicanism, is associated with the name Hontheim, who in 1763 published his work on the reunion of Christendom and the legitimate power of the Papacy. In discussing the latter, he advocated the episcopal theory of church government and declared the Papacy guilty of usurpation in the course of its history. The book was declared "pestilential" by the Pope in 1764 and placed on the index. Its author was compelled to recant. But

this failed to check Febronianism, as the movement is called. In 1769 the archbishops of Mainz, Cologne, and Trier, who, being at the same time secular princes, favored Febronianism, drew up a series of thirty articles in the form of complaints against the Roman Curia and defended episcopacy. These they submitted to the Emperor Joseph II, who, however, declined to favor the petitioners.

23. Equally unsuccessful was the attempt to sever connections with Rome in 1786. In that year the above-mentioned dignitaries assembled at Ems and in a series of twenty-three articles laid down their grievances against the Papacy. The aim was to establish a German Catholic National Church, completely independent of papal jurisdiction. But the German bishops found it more to their liking to obey the Pope in distant Rome than to accept the rule of the archbishops at their own gates. The secular princes also opposed the plan, and the whole movement came to naught. Nevertheless, as Harnack says, "since the days of the Council of Constance the sovereignty of the bishops and the insignificance of the Pope have never been more boldly asserted than by the German bishops at Ems a hundred years ago." What promised to become a more serious menace to the papal power were the reforms of Joseph II of Austria. We have already referred to his Edict of Toleration published in 1781. This was only part of a wider plan of reform designed to sever the Catholic Church of Austria from Rome and make it immediately dependent on the state. To this end all ecclesiastic intercourse with Rome was made strictly subject to state control, and all the institutions of the Church, as far as they did not serve the cause of education, were abolished. Of two thousand monasteries six hundred went down before these measures. The protest of the bishops and the Pope, even a personal visit of the latter, proved unavailing against the impetuous zeal of the emperor. In the end, however, these reforms failed. Undertaken in hot haste and unsupported by public sentiment, they were followed by an inevitable reaction at the emperor's death (1790). At the Congress of Vienna (1815) Freiherr von Wessenberg warmly advocated the establishment of the Catholic Church of Germany under a German primate; but in the war of conflicting opinions regarding the constitution of the proposed Church the plan

failed. Rome has always succeeded in overcoming the antipapal tendencies within her own pale. Indeed, the Vatican Council put the capstone on the hierarchical pyramid.

24. Rome has not been so successful in holding her power in the secular sphere. The modern state, acknowledging no sovereignty save its own will, has risen over the protest of the Roman Catholic Church, and that even in countries where the Church's spiritual authority is unchallenged. As early as 1606 the Doge of Venice defied the interdict of Paul V by threatening with death any one who paid any attention to it. In 1870 the national tendencies toward a united Italy swept away the Papal States as a separate political unit and deprived the Pope of the last remnant of political power. Similarly, Spain and Portugal have, since the first half of the last century, resented papal interference in their politics. The same is true of France, Austria, and Belgium. This modern trend toward the separation of Church and State has been met with the unqualified hostility of the Papacy. It was condemned by Pope Pius IX in the syllabus of 1864, while Leo XIII, in the encyclical *Libertas Praestantissimum Naturae Donum* of 1888 calls the separation of Church and State a "pernicious maxim" *(perniciosa sententia)*, thus implicitly condemning the American Constitution. On the other hand, the removal of anti-Catholic barriers by Protestant governments during the 19th century has opened the door to renewed Catholic activity in Protestant countries. Thus the Church is endeavoring to rebuild the waste places even in Norway, Sweden, and Denmark, where Catholicism had become almost extinct. Holland proclaimed toleration in 1848. The Jesuits returned, and shortly after the hierarchy was re-established. In England the hierarchy had been extinct since 1585; it was restored in 1858, in Scotland in 1878. The revival of English Catholicism was strengthened by the strongly Romanizing Oxford, or Tractarian, Movement under the leadership of Newman and Pusey, which carried hundreds of the Anglican clergy and thousands of the laity back into the folds of Rome.

25. If the Roman Catholic Church has lost her political power, she has fastened her hold all the more securely on the individual conscience. By a striking coincidence the total extinction of her temporal power and the acme

of her spiritual authority fell in the same year, 1870, when the dogma of papal infallibility was promulgated. Since then the authority of the Church resides in a single individual, the Pope at Rome. According to Roman Catholic doctrine the Pope is the vicegerent of God on earth, the supreme judge in matters of faith and morals, the sole guide and director of the consciences of men.

26. The Papacy was moving toward this goal through its entire history, though it remained for a modern Pope to "put across" the claim of infallibility as a dogma of the Church. Various causes conspired toward this end. In the first place, the turn of political affairs in the early 19th century favored papalism. When Napoleon concluded his Concordat with Pius VII in 1802, his aim was to establish a national Church completely under his own control, but what he actually did was to deliver the Gallican Church into the hands of the Pope. True, the Concordat provided that the appointment of bishops should belong to the state, but the Pope was granted the authority to institute the appointees. Thus the real head of the French episcopate was not the emperor, but the Pope. Napoleon had been clearly outwitted in the transaction, and he soon realized this, when Pius VII refused to institute some of the episcopal nominees. As has been said, "Pius established in France for the first time a hierarchy of which the Pope was the ruling chief." The diplomacy of Pius was ably supported by such writers as the Savoyard de Maistre, who advocated as the one and only panacea for the ills of society absolute submission to the Papal See. Needless to say that the Jesuits were active in the same cause. Also in Germany the danger of episcopalism (Febronianism) passed away when in 1803 the three powerful ecclesiastics, the archbishops of Trier, Mainz, and Cologne, were shorn of their temporal power and reduced to mere officials of the state. But the real builders of the modern Papacy are the Jesuits. Their labors in the field of ecclesiastical history, in dogmatic and moral theology, all looked toward the dogma of papal infallibility as the logical and necessary result. They undermined all authorities in order to erect a single one at Rome. They impaired the authority of the Scriptures by filing away at the doctrine of inspiration almost to the vanishing point. They overthrew the accepted notion of

tradition by insisting that true tradition is what the Church (*i. e.*, the Pope) in any period of its history has decreed, thus making it possible for Pius IX to declare: "I am the tradition." They ignored the witness of history, impugned the authority of the Fathers, discovered innumerable heresies in the most venerated teachers of the Church, declared the acts of councils (as far as they did not favor papal pretensions) pure forgery — and amid falsification and error one solid immovable rock, the chair of St. Peter is witnessing to the infallibility of the successor of St. Peter. In its struggle against Jansenism, which was a vigorous protest against the moral laxity of the Jesuit confessional, Jesuitism was compelled to train its guns against the authority of St. Augustine. Liguori (1699—1787), the champion of probabilism,* Liguori, the saint (1829), the doctor of the Church (1871), has usurped the place of St. Augustine in modern Catholicism. And Liguori declared that the individual conscience can find no peace except in the absolute authority of the confessor and that the latter must apply the divine Law according to the principles of probabilism.

27. In view of these developments the dogma of papal infallibility would appear to be a very natural result. When all authorities are torn down, the authority of bishops, the authority of councils, the authority of tradition, the authority even of conscience and of the Scriptures, then a new authority must arise in a Church that is built on authority. Nor could this destructive process have been carried on so successfully had not the new authority been all along in contemplation and ready to replace the old when conditions were ripe for the change. In the history of the Papacy the fullness of time had come when the obstacles that stood in the way of its ambition were removed. It remained only that the Bishop of Rome be solemnly declared the universal bishop, the incarnate tradition, the absolute confessor, the living oracle of truth, the infallible teacher of faith and morals, the representative of God on earth. All this happened with some dissenting voices — soon all but drowned in the general clamor of approval — in 1870.

28. As an aftermath of this new dogma we may at this point mention the so-called *Kulturkampf*, which for two decades embroiled the Prussian government with the Church of Rome.

The conflict was brought about by the attitude of Prussia in supporting "some teachers in state-aided Catholic schools whom the bishops wanted to dismiss because of their anti-infallibilist opinions." During the quarrel that ensued the "May Laws" were passed, which were an attempt, on the part of the state, to control the education, discipline, appointment, and excommunication of the clergy, in other words, to deprive the Roman Catholic Church of practically all liberty. Fines, imprisonment, deposition, coercion, availed nothing against the clerical opposition encountered by this drastic legislation. Conditions became intolerable, there being in Prussia, when the conflict was at its height, no fewer than 1,400 Roman Catholic churches without a spiritual head. Nor was there any improvement in the situation during the pontificate of Pius IX, whose inflexible obstinacy precluded any amicable adjustment of difficulties. His successor, however, Leo XIII, pursued a wiser and more conciliatory policy. He immediately opened up long negotiations with Bismarck with the result that the obnoxious "May Laws" were virtually repealed. Vatican diplomacy had scored a victory, and Bismarck, who at the outset had proudly declared, "We shall not go to Canossa," went at least half the distance, if not a little farther.

29. In more recent times the Papacy has had some trouble with the wayward children of its own household. The movement known as "Modernism," a term invented by the Jesuits of Rome to denote various liberal trends of theological thought at variance with Catholic belief, drew from Pius X, in 1907, the encyclical *Pascendi Dominici Gregis* against what he termed "the synthesis of all heresies." And to safeguard the Church and the papal authority still more effectively, he sent out a circular letter to the Catholic clergy of Europe and America requiring all priests to take the anti-Modernist oath, the beginning and conclusion of which is as follows: "I accept everything which has been defined by the unerring magisterium of the Church . . . founded on Peter, the prince of the apostolic hierarchy. . . . So I promise, so I swear." In France, as a result of this, about fifteen hundred Catholic priests have rejected the Papacy, while numerous others took the oath under protest, declaring that, while giving formal, outward assent, they reserved the right of entertaining their own personal convic-

tions. Among the representatives of Modernism are men who hold extremely radical views, such as Loisy (1857—1940), onetime leader of French Modernism, as well as those who stand on more conservative ground. Loisy's critical position was subversive not only of Roman Catholicism, but also of Protestantism, indeed of Christianity itself. Father George Tyrrelt in England, attacked Medievalism and Ultramontanism, refused to recant, and was buried in unconsecrated ground. In Italy, too, Modernism found defenders, among them some of the most eminent scholars, such as Giovanni Luzzi of Florence, who protested against the Medieval ecclesiasticism of the Vatican. Scherr, Schnitzer (*Hat Jesus das Papsttum gestiftet?*), Koch, and others in Germany raised their voices against the religious tyranny of Rome, and many of the clergy simply refused to take the anti-Modernist oath.

At the end of the 19th and during the first half of the 20th century the Roman Pontiffs have taken a lively interest in all social questions, such as labor and capital, education, the family. Leo XIII in 1891 published the encyclical on the condition of labor. This social encyclical was followed by the encyclicals of Pius XI on Christian education, Christian marriage, reconstructing the social order, atheistic Communism. Pius XI furthered Catholic Action, a laymen's movement under priestly supervision. The purpose is twofold: first, to indoctrinate the Roman Catholics in the Church's position on social and moral issues, and, second, to employ these indoctrinated Catholics as a "lay apostolate" to disseminate Catholic principles on moral philosophy. Through the National Catholic Welfare Conference, an agency of the archbishops and bishops of the United States, the Roman Catholic Church is endeavoring to exert its influence in American social, educational, political, industrial, recreational, and rural life.

Statistics. According to the latest available sources the Roman Catholic population of the world is about 421,341,000 (1952). See *Religious Bodies (U. S.), Bibliography.*

The Catholic Encyclopedia, R. Appleton, N. Y., 1907—22 (later Encyclopedia Press); D. Attwater, *Catholic Encyclopaedic Dictionary*, Macm., 1939; *Official Catholic Directory*, P. J. Kennedy and Sons, N. Y.

Roman Catholic Confessions. In addition to the Ecumenical Creeds * (in which the Roman Church differs from the Eastern * in the *filioque* *), the Roman Church accepts the pronouncements of its councils * and decrees of its Popes.

A. 1. The principal source and highest standard of the R. C. Church are the *Decrees of the Council of Trent*. The Council (counted among the ecumenical by R. Catholics) was convened by Paul III (Dec. 13, 1545—Dec. 4, 1563; interruptions of 3 and 10 years) as a reaction against Protestantism and for the purpose of settling doctrinal disputes and instituting reforms. 25 public sessions were held, but most of the work was done in committees controlled by papal legates. It avoided doctrinal questions disputed in Catholic schools and confined its decisions to refutations of Protestant tenets. The doctrinal sessions concern: symbols of faith (III); Scriptural canon (Apocrypha * included) (IV); original sin, including rejection of intrinsic corruption of man (V); justification by faith alone rejected (VI); Eucharist (XIII); penance and extreme unction (XIV); aspects of communion (XXI); sacrifice of the Mass (XXII); ordination (XXIII); sacrament of marriage (XXIV); purgatory, veneration of relics and images, indulgences, fasting, index, etc. (XXV). The disciplinary measures included residence of bishops and priests, training of clerics, reformation of religious orders and of finances. The decrees were signed by 255 fathers. The original acts (prepared by Angelo Massarelli) are deposited in the Vatican. The Pope reserved for himself exclusive right of interpretation.

2. The Council of Trent declared the need for a binding formula of faith, which was prepared by the College of Cardinals (1564) by order of Pius IV. This *Profession of the Tridentine Faith* consists of 12 articles, the first giving the Nicene Creed and the other 11 embodying the doctrines of the Council of Trent. It was made binding on all priests and teachers and contains the oath of allegiance to the Pope.

3. The Council of Trent also proposed a catechism which was prepared by Leonardo Marini, Egidio Foscarari, Muzio Calini, and Francesco Fureiro by command of Pius IV. The *Roman Catechism (Catechismus Romanus)*, prepared for teachers not pupils, is divided into four parts: Apostles' Creed; Sacraments; Decalogue; Lord's Prayer. Important catechisms were prepared by Canisius, Bellarmine, Bossuet, and others, especially after the Jesuits devoted themselves to this work. That of Canisius (1556) was the chief catechism of Catholics for two centuries.

B. *Papal bulls against the Jansenists.* *

C. *Papal definition of the Immaculate Conception.* Pius IX in an open letter (1849) invited opinions concerning definitions of the Immaculate Conception. 600 bishops replied; all except four assented, but 52 considered the time inopportune. In 1854 Pius read the bull *Ineffabilis Deus:* "the Blessed Virgin Mary in the first instant of her conception was by a singular grace and privilege of Almighty God, in view of the merits of Christ Jesus, the Savior of mankind, preserved free from all stain of original sin. . . ." All were held to believe it on pain of excommunication. See also *Mariolatry.*

D. *Papal Syllabus.* The first was issued by Pius IX (1864) against 80 theses, including pantheism, materialism, rationalism, indifferentism, socialism, secret societies, Bible societies, matters pertaining to Church and State (condemns religious liberty, separation of Church and State. Romanism alone has right to state recognition and to control education, science, and literature), "errors" in civil society, ethics, matrimony, and the views concerning the Pope. The second list by Pius X (*Lamentabili sane exitu*, 1907) condemns Modernism in 65 theses directed especially against Loisy.

E. 1. *Vatican Council* (Dec. 8, 1869, to Oct. 20, 1870; considered by Catholics the 20th Ecumenical Council) was convened by Pius IX in the bull *Aeterni Patris Unigenitus Filius* (1868), which even invited Protestants and Greeks. Even before the council was convened an anti-infallibility campaign was led by Doellinger.* 719 prelates were present at the opening session, which was a gorgeous ritualistic ceremony. The second session was a profession of faith by all the fathers before the Pope, followed by the episcopal oath of feudal submission to the Papacy. Three matters were laid before the Council: on rationalism, on the Church of Christ, on matrimony. The last was postponed indefinitely. Two were adopted:

2. *Constitution on the Catholic Faith* (*Dei Filius*, April 24, 1870) contains four chapters: God as Creator (I); Revelation (II); Faith (III); Faith and Reason (IV). 18 canons condemn pantheism, rationalism, and naturalism.

3. *First Dogmatic Constitution of the*

Church of Christ (Constitutio Dogmatica Prima de Ecclesia Christi; July 18, 1870; called Pastor aeternus) treats in four chapters: the institution of the Apostolic Primacy in Peter; the perpetuity of St. Peter's Primacy in the Roman Pontiff; the power and nature of the Primacy of the Pope (holding that the Pope is, by the ordinance of God, entitled to a complete and immediate jurisdiction in faith, morals, discipline, and government over all pastors and peoples, jointly and severally, throughout the whole world); the infallibility of the Roman Pontiff. The last dogma states: "We teach and define that it is a dogma divinely revealed that the Roman Pontiff, when he speaks *ex cathedra* — that is, when, in discharge of the office of pastor and doctor of all Christians, by virtue of his supreme apostolic authority, he defines a doctrine regarding faith or morals to be held by the universal Church, by the divine assistance promised to him in blessed Peter (Luke 22:32) — is possessed of that infallibility with which the divine Redeemer willed that His Church should be endowed for defining doctrines regarding faith and morals, and that therefore such definitions of the Roman Pontiff are irreformable of themselves and not from the consent of the Church."

4. The debate on papal authority was long and lively, lasting from May to July. Petitions signed by 137 prelates urged the inopportunity of the dogma. Before the last vote, 56 bishops returned to their flocks because they did not care to vote openly against the Pope. EL

See references under *Councils and Synods;* P. Schaff, *Creeds of Christendom,* Harpers, 1899—1905; Martin Chemnitz, *Examen Concilii Tridentini,* Schlawitz, Berlin, 1861.

Roman Catholic Education in the United States. Roman Catholic parochial schools are an outgrowth of the mission schools. The earliest mission schools, founded in Florida and New Mexico, were in existence by 1629. The special quality of parish support now associated with the parish school system was found only in English-speaking settlements. The year 1640 saw the establishment in Maryland of the first Roman Catholic elementary school in the English colonies.

Financial support came from state subsidies, public taxation, church contributions, and tuition. State support was withdrawn after 1800, when the secularized public school was born.

During pre-Revolutionary days Catholic elementary education had a gradual but persistent growth. The tolerant attitude of the Quakers was favorable to rapid expansion in Pennsylvania, where the first Roman Catholic parish was established in 1730. The foundation of schools as a regular and permanent feature of parish work may be said to have begun at that time.

Between 1800 and 1840 the system of schools followed the Church in its western expansion, and Roman Catholic textbooks began to appear. The aid of public educational funds was lost, but five teaching communities made it possible to carry on the work of the schools and to extend the educational system.

The great immigration that began about 1840 helped to spread the Roman Catholic schools. Between 1833 and 1860 from twenty-two to twenty-five religious orders were introduced from Europe to teach in the schools, and their membership was rapidly augmented. After the financial support of public educational funds had been withdrawn and the public schools had become secularized (ca. 1850), the Roman Catholics realized more keenly than ever before that it was a matter of religious necessity for them to erect and maintain their own schools and that, as Bishop Hughes (1797—1864) declared, "In this age and country the school is more necessary than the church." The 200 parish schools of 1840 were multiplied several times during the ensuing decade. Academies for girls were founded by the Ladies of the Sacred Heart and other sisterhoods, and the Christian Brothers took the lead in the field of secondary education for boys.

Religious instruction has always been of special interest to the Roman Catholic people from Colonial times. The First Plenary Council at Baltimore in 1852 begged the Bishops to see to it that church schools be established, and, if necessary, to use church funds for the purpose. The Second Plenary Council in 1866 added a plea to the parents to co-operate with the pastors who founded such schools. In 1875 the Second Congregation on Propaganda in Rome in special instructions to the bishops of the United States classified the non-sectarian public schools as dangerous unless safeguards to the faith of the children were added and urged the founding and fostering of

Catholic schools. The Third Plenary Council in Baltimore in 1884, while admitting that many Roman Catholic children must attend the public schools, ordered that a school be established within two years near each church unless the bishop allowed a postponement. The Council insisted on the obligation of Catholic parents to provide Roman Catholic education for their children.

At the present time instruction in Roman Catholic parochial schools ordinarily is carried on by religious communities especially devoted to such work or by the clergy, assisted as circumstances require by lay persons. The supervision of the parochial schools is usually in the hands of the pastors. Parish schools of a diocese are under the supervision of a diocesan superintendent or diocesan examiner appointed by the bishop. Some of the parochial schools, especially the high schools, are supported and directed by several parishes acting together or under the supervision of the bishop. Private academies and colleges are usually directed and owned by religious communities, but the seminaries devoted to the education of the secular clergy and some other diocesan institutions are directly under the episcopal supervision. The Catholic University of America is a pontifical institution, with a director appointed by the Pope, but is under the general supervision of the hierarchy of the United States "according to a divine constitution."

National Catholic Welfare Conference statistics, gathered in 1952:

Elementary schools, 8,589; instructors, 66,525; pupils, 2,560,815. (Gain in the last decade of 572 schools, 5,779 instructors, 546,033 pupils.)

Secondary schools, 2,189; instructors, 27,770; students, 505,572. (Gain in last decade of 70 schools, 5,255 instructors, 120,446 students.)

Teachers' colleges and normal training schools, 25; instructors, 695; students, 6,779. (Loss in last decade of 7 schools, 181 instructors, 1,297 students.)

Junior colleges — coed., 2; for men, 4; for women, 20.

Senior colleges — coed., 13; for men, 41; for women, 110.

Universities, 30.

Universities and colleges (junior and senior), 220; instructors, 17,998; students, 292,881. (Gain in last decade of 24 schools, 4,987 instructors, 132,512 students.)

Seminaries — major, 156; instructors, 1,251; students, 9,426.

Seminaries — minor, 197; instructors, 1,804; students, 16,896.

Totals: Schools of all classifications, 11,376; instructors, 116,043; students, 3,392,369. New institutions established, 823. Faculty increase, 16,555. Student increase, 547,959. AWG

Catholic Colleges and Schools in the United States, 1944, Department of Education of the National Catholic Welfare Conference, Washington, D. C.; *Catholic School Journal,* Vol. 47, No. 10, December, 1947, Bruce Publishing Co., Milwaukee, Wis.; *Catholic School Journal,* 1953, p. 15; Roy J. Deferrari, *Essays on Catholic Education in the United States,* Catholic University of America Press, District of Columbia, 1942; James A. Burns, "Growth and Development of the Catholic School System in the United States," in *National Catholic Education Association Bulletin,* 1912; *National Catholic Almanac for 1953,* St. Anthony Guild, Paterson, N. J.

Roman Catholic Lay Societies. In addition to many organizations in the field of history, the sciences, and medicine, the Roman Catholics have the Knights of Columbus, a powerful and aggressive group of men, the Queen's Daughters, a society of women, and various sodalities in the field of religion, economics, and sociology.

Roman Catholic Modernism. See *Modernism,* 1.

Roman Catholic Reformation. See *Counter Reformation.*

Roman Catholic Seminaries. Institutions devoted to the training of the Roman Catholic clergy. There are 156 major seminaries and 197 minor. See *Roman Catholic Education in the U. S.; Jesuits and Jesuitism;* various orders; *Ministry, Education of; Roman Catholic Church; Ministerial Office.*

Roman Congregations. The most important organizations of the Roman Curia, which transact most of the papal business. The membership consists of cardinals, who alone have votes, but most of the detailed work is done by expert subordinates. The decisions of the Congregations are final and are rated as decisions of the Pope himself. The Congregations are: 1) The Congregation of the Holy Office, or Inquisition, of which the Pope himself is prefect, deals with all questions, of doctrine, with the repression of heresy, and with indulgences. One of its departments examines and condemns books that are considered dangerous (see *Index of Prohibited Books*). 2) The Congregation of the Consistory (Pope also prefect) prepares the business to be laid before the consistory * and governs the dioceses not under Propaganda (see 7 below). 3) The Congregation for the Oriental Church has charge of all matters pertaining to relations with the Eastern Church. 4) The Congregation of the Sacraments deals with matters relating to matrimony, ordination, and the other "sacraments." 5) The Congregation of the Council has supervision of the secular clergy and the laity and of the observance of ecclesiastical law (fasting, tithes, etc.). 6) The Congregation of Religious Orders looks after all that pertains to religious orders and organizations. 7) The Congregation of Propaganda regulates ecclesiastical affairs in so-called "missionary" countries. 8) The Congregation of Rites has jurisdiction over rites, ceremonies, cases of beatification and canonization, and relics. 9) The Congregation of Ceremonies directs the ceremonial of the papal court. 10) The Congregation of Extraordinary Ecclesiastical Affairs, whose head is the Secretary of State, has no fixed scope. 11) The Congregation of Seminaries and Universities supervises the curriculum at Roman Catholic institutions of learning. 12) The Congregation of the Basilica of St. Peter.

Roman Question. See *Popes*, 28.

Romanesque Style. See *Architecture, Ecclesiastical*, 4.

Romania. A country of Southeastern Europe, enlarged, since the First World War, to include Transylvania, the Bukovina, and Bessarabia, with a population of almost 16,000,000 (1951) and an area of 91,671 sq. mi. The inhabitants for the most part are desecendants of the ancient Roman Moesians and Dacians, the great majority of whom are members of the Orthodox Greek Church, which is the state church, although the other churches are permitted to exist. The Russian sect of the Lipovanians numbers about 150,000 and the Roman Catholics, 1,500,000 (1952). Evangelical Christians, especially those of the Lutheran confession, are much scattered, except in Bessarabia, while Methodists, Anglicans, and Presbyterians are also represented. Jews and Armenians together number about 300,000.

Romoser, George August. B. Sept. 14, 1870, at Baltimore, Md.; graduated at Concordia Seminary (St. Louis) 1892; professor at Concordia College, Conover, N. C., 1892—99; president 1900—11; pastor at Cleveland, Ohio (Grace), 1912 to 1914; professor at Concordia Collegiate Institute, Bronxville, N. Y., 1915 to 1918, president 1918—36; Vice-President of English District of Missouri Synod 1912—15; editor of the *Lutheran Witness* 1900—14. D. D., St. Louis, 1930; d. July 9, 1936.

Ronsdorf Sect. See *Ellerians*.

Rood. Cross or crucifix, especially applied to the cross over the entrance to the chancel in Roman Catholic churches.

Rood Screen. A screen used especially in the Middle Ages, to separate the chancel or choir from the nave.

Roos, Magnus Friedrich (1727 to 1803). B. at Sulz; d. at Anhausen. Studied at Tuebingen. Pastor at Lustnau and dean of the diocese of Bebenhausen, 1767; lectured on theology at Tuebingen; later went to Anhausen. A moderate Pietist, he occupied the theological position of Johann Albrecht Bengel, also with respect to his eschatology. He wrote commentaries and other theological works, particularly devotional.

Rorate Masses. A name derived from the Introit for the Wednesday of the third Sunday in Advent, in the Roman calendar, which, in its Latin form, began with the word "rorate." Rorate Masses are read daily from the Wednesday of the third Sunday in Advent until Christmas Eve. They are celebrated in honor of the Virgin Mary.

Rore, Cipriano de (1516—65?). Pupil and successor of Adrian Willaert, chapelmaster of St. Mark's Cathedral in Venice. While de Rore followed in the footsteps of his mentor, he at the same time contributed toward the further advancement of music. His use of chromatics was extraordinary, his harmonies were more complex and colorful than those of Willaert, and his treatment of texts was intense as well as pithy. De Rore wrote motets, madrigals, and eight-voiced antiphonal choruses.

Rosary. A mode of prayer used in the Roman Church in connection with a string of 165 beads, 150 smaller beads being divided into 15 groups of 10 (decades) by the insertion of 15 larger beads. The rosary is begun by making the sign of the cross and reciting the Creed, the Lord's Prayer once, Ave Maria * three times, and the Gloria once, while holding the small cross attached to the string. For each small bead an Ave Maria is said; for each larger one, the Lord's Prayer. During the recital of each decade a "mystery" is to be contemplated, there being five joyful mysteries (the Annunciation, Visitation, Birth of Jesus, Presentation, and Finding of Jesus in the Temple), five sorrowful mysteries (Agony at Gethsemane, Scourging, Crowning with Thorns, Carrying the Cross, Crucifixion), and five glorious mysteries (Resurrection, Ascension, Descent of the Holy Ghost, Assumption of Mary, Coronation of Mary). Rosaries are blessed by Popes, bishops, etc., and then convey indulgences. Members of confraternities of the rosary recite the rosary at least once a week; "living rosaries" (15 members) divide the decades for daily recitation. The idea of counting prayers was probably introduced by the early monks. The fact that Buddhists and Mohammedans have contrivances resembling the rosary makes Matt. 6:7 apply all the more strikingly.

Roscelin of Compiegne (12th century). A monk known for his defense of nominalism and opposition to realism.

Roscelinus, Johannes. A false teacher of the last part of the 11th and the first decades of the 12th century; d. some time after 1120; chiefly known for his doctrine of tritheism, of three separate, self-existent beings instead of a trinity of persons in the divine essence, although he tried to avoid heresy by speaking of a union of the persons in power and will. He was opposed especially by Abelard in his book *De Trinitate* ("Of the Trinity").

Roseland, Jens C. (J. C. Jensson). B. March 25, 1859, at Sandnaes, Jaederen, Norway; came to America in 1861; ed.: Augustana Sem., Springfield, Ia.; Marshall Classical Academy, Wis.; Mt. Airy Sem., Pa.; North Dak. Univ.; Williamette Univ.; pastorates at: Wiota, Ia., 1880; Leland, Ill., 1881—85; Milwaukee, Wis., 1885—90; Jefferson Prairie, Wis., 1884—99; Austin, Minn., 1899 to 1907; Hayfield, Minn., 1899—1906; Chicago, Ill., 1907—12; Crookston, Minn., 1912—14; Silverton, Oreg., 1914—. Changed his name from Jensson to Roseland in 1890; served as sec. of Norw. Augustana Synod, 1885—90, of United Norw. Ch., 1894—1917, and of Pacific Dist. of Norw. Luth. Ch., 1917—. Author: *Et Varsko; American Lutheran Biographies; The Free Will Tithe; Kvindens Stemmeret.* D. Dec. 17, 1930.

Rosenius, Karl Olof (1816—68). Lutheran lay preacher and revivalist in Sweden; preached the Gospel of the grace of God unceasingly, but did not sufficiently distinguish between objective and subjective justification and stressed the "life within" more than the objective means of grace. His writings, originally appearing in the *Pietist,* were and are widely read. See *Bornholmers.*

Rosenmueller, Johann (ca. 1620 to 1684). A significant composer of the Lutheran Church whose sacred and instrumental works are beginning to enjoy the recognition and use they so well deserve. His style betrays Italian influence. Because of false and evil gossip, Rosenmueller fled from Germany and lived for many years in Venice, where he enjoyed the personal friendship of Legrenzi and other Italian masters and where he likewise was the teacher of his compatriot, Johann Philipp Krieger. Rosenmueller wrote also in larger forms, and his orchestral works are heard occasionally in America. Several are ascribed to him with some uncertainty, and his *Welt, ade, ich bin dein muede* (World, Farewell, Of Thee I'm Weary) was used often at funerals by J. S. Bach.

Rosicrucians. Members of a mythical society said to have been founded in the 15th century by Christian Rosenkreuz and kept secret until the 17th century. The first notice of this society appeared in *Fama Fraternitatis des loeblichen Ordens des Rosenkreuzes,* 1614, now regarded as fiction, the work of Johann Val. Andreae, a Lutheran theologian, whose motives in writing this satire were to combat alchemy, astrology, and Roman Catholicism. However, the publication was exploited by many interested in alchemy who claimed membership in the order and formed branches in varous parts of Europe, which existed to the middle of the 18th century. A Rosicrucian Society has been established in San Jose, Calif., commonly known as Amorc. This order claims to be an age-old fraternity of thinking men and women. It advertises that it is not a religious sect, but the underlying principles are not only unChristian, but actually anti-Christian. The theory is that at one time man was in possession of all knowledge, and men and women "attained the highest degree of mental, physical, and spiritual development, and possessed all of the wealth of happiness, material blessings, and mystical powers ever dreamed of in the hearts of human beings." Rosicrucianism claims to have means of developing the latent clairvoyant and mystical powers which reside in every human being. These latent powers are the means whereby man can contact the great cosmic intelligence (the Rosicrucian concept of God). When properly guided in exploiting his own inner self, man will find "the law of personal evolution," and by co-operation with this law man can "make out of his individual life the greatest success and the greatest power that is humanly possible," for "all of the powers and all of the creative abilities expressed in the universe are also within man's own body. The inner part of man is a greater kingdom than any kingdom that exists on the face of the earth." Christ is said to have been "the highest consciousness of God in man and represented the powers of the cosmic universe." In short, Rosicrucianism is a system which considers man to be a divine fragment and master of his own destiny. FEM

Rossetti, Dante Gabriel (1828—82). British painter and poet; chief guiding spirit in the pre-Raffaelite movement; influential in bringing about a revival of Gothic art in England.

Rota Romana. See *Curia, Roman.*

Rotach, Meeting of. See *Lutheran Confessions,* A2.

Rotary International. Founded at Chicago in 1905, the organization derives its name from the rotation of meetings at the business offices of the members. It is founded on a code of ethics by which business standards are raised to conform to the principle of duty toward human society. "Service is the basis of all business." Fair dealings and honest methods are held forth as ideal. Local Rotary Clubs consist of one representative from each distinct line of business or profession.

Roth, Karl Johann Friedrich (1780 to 1852). Lutheran jurist and statesman. B. at Vaikingen, Wuerttemberg; d. at Munich. Studied law at Tuebingen. Held various important positions in the Bavarian government, including the presidency of the supreme consistory, 1828—48. He enjoyed the respect and confidence of the clergy, though some considered him remiss in his support of

the Protestants in the genuflection controversy (cf. Redenbacher). Besides other works, he published selections from Luther's writings.

Rothe, Johann Andreas (1688 to 1758). Studied at Leipzig; Zinzendorf's pastor in Berthelsdorf; later pastor at Hermsdorf and finally at Thommendorf; wrote: "Now I Have Found the Firm Foundation."

Rothe, Richard (1799—1867). Mediating theologian and defender of Union; holding, at bottom, Schleiermacher's principles; joined the *Protestantenverein,* an organization "for evangelical freedom," with strong liberal tendencies, denying the binding power of the Lutheran Confessions; an original thinker and prolific writer; professor at Wittenberg, Heidelberg, Bonn, Heidelberg.

Rous, Francis (1579—1659). Born at Halton, Cornwall, educated at Oxford in law, he was member of Parliament during the reign of James I and of Charles I and member of Westminster Assembly, of the High Commission, and of Triers for examining and licensing candidates for the ministry. He also held appointments under Cromwell. In 1643 the Westminster Assembly was called to deal with the Uniformity of Worship between England and Scotland. Rous' version of the *Psalms Translated into English Metre* was approved by the Assembly and authorized by the House of Commons for general use. His best-known Psalm is "The Lord's My Shepherd, I'll Not Want."

Rousseau, Jean Jacques (1712—78). Influential French author; b. at Geneva; apprenticed to engraver, then lackey, music teacher, clerk, tutor, private secretary, playwright, composer; lived mainly in France until exiled because of his *Emile;* fled to Russia and England; returned to Paris; d. at Ermenonville. His three great works are based on the principle that man is good by nature and that modern forms of society, being unnatural, cause evil. In *La Nouvelle Heloise,* an emotional love story, passion disregards barriers of "man-made" morality. *Contrat social* teaches that all men are born free and that sovereignty is vested in the people. *Emile* (called by Goethe *das Naturevangelium der Erziehung*) claims to show that if a child is kept from error and vice and its inherently good nature developed, it can by itself attain to art, morality, and sense of God. While Rousseau antagonized some real abuses and stimulated some reformers constructively (e. g., Pestalozzi), his influence on the whole has been detrimental, as he denied original sin and asserted that man has good moral impulses by nature. Not only did his theories bear fruit in the excesses of the French Revolution, but as apostle of naturalism his influence continues to the present day. His autobiography, Confessions.

Rovere, Giuliano. See Popes, 19.

Royce, Josiah (1855—1916). Harvard philosopher, advocate of idealism. Influenced in part by James, but retained absolute nature of idealism; influenced W. E. Hocking.

Rubens, Peter Paul. Greatest of Flemish painters (1577—1640). Did much portrait work; a master of technique, both in modeling and drawing, but strongly sensual; among his paintings: "The Crucifixion of Christ."

Rubric. Directions in liturgical books showing the usage of prayers and the performance of ceremonies.

Rudbeck, John (ca. 1580—1646). Bishop of Vesteras; chaplain of Gustavus Adolphus.

Rudelbach, Andreas Gottlob (1792 to 1862). B. at Copenhagen, d. at Slagelse, Denmark; heroic defender of sound Lutheranism; received his education in his native city; in 1829 accepted a call to Glauchau, Saxony, where, as pastor and superintendent, he exerted great and beneficial influence in promoting uncompromising Lutheranism, founding and editing, with Guericke, the Zeitschrift fuer die gesamte lutherische Theologie und Kirche. In 1845 the gross unionism of the State Church forced him to resign his pastorate, and he returned to Denmark as pastor at Slagelse. Rudelbach was a man of profound learning and deep spirituality and a decided opponent of the Union. Among his many writings the most important is perhaps Reformation, Luthertum und Union.

Rudman, Andrew (d. 1708). Studied under Jasper Svedberg at the University of Upsala, came to America in 1797, and served as first provost of the Swedish churches along the Delaware; pastor at Wicaco, where he built Gloria Dei Church (now owned by the Episcopalians); preached in English as well as Swedish; served as pastor of the Dutch Lutheran church in New York; ordained Justus Falckner in Gloria Dei Church, 1703, to become his successor in New York; served English Episcopal churches at Frankfort and Oxford.

Rudolph II. See Lutheran Confessions, A 5.

Rudra. See Brahmanism, 2.

Rueckpositiv. A detached division of the organ located behind the back of the organist and concealing him thus from the view of those present in the nave of the church. The main function of the Rueckpositiv is to accompany chant and choral music. While the choir manual of the organ usually replaces the Rueckpositiv, Walter Holtkamp and others, in their effort to restore the baroque type of organ of the 16th to the 18th centuries to the churches of America, have met with some success in restoring also the Rueckpositiv to the organs of our day.

Rufinus, Tyrannius (ca. 345—ca. 410). Latin church writer; b. in northern Italy; d. in Sicily; friend of Jerome; of a strong ascetic tendency; settled on Mount Olivet to minister to pilgrims; made presbyter; translated many works of the earlier Church, also church history of Eusebius, which he continued; in later life in controversy with Jerome.

Ruhland, Friedrich Carl Theodor. B. April 26, 1836, at Grohnde, Hanover; studied at Loccum; graduated from Concordia Seminary (Practical Dept.); pastor in Oshkosh, Wis. (1859), in Wolcottsville and Buffalo, N. Y., in Pleasant Ridge, Ill.; in 1872 he accepted a call to the churches in Dresden and Niederplanitz, Saxony, which had left the State Church for the sake of confessional Lutheranism. His and Pastor Brunn's testimony bore much fruit, and in 1876 the Saxon Free Church was organized, Ruhland being elected president. On a visit to this country he lost his life in an accident June 3, 1879.

H. Ruhland, "Friedrich Carl Theodor Ruhland," CHIQ, VIII: 25—31, 57 to 62 (tr. R. W. Heintze).

Rule of Faith (Regula Fidei). See Ecumenical Creeds.

Rumania. See Romania.

Runkel, G. Originally affiliated with the Buffalo Synod, he joined Missouri in 1867, ministering to churches at Aurora, Ind., and Los Angeles, Calif.; at his death President of the California and Nevada District; d. 1905.

Ruotsalainen, Paavo. See *Finland, Lutheranism in,* 4.

Rupert of Worms. See *Germany,* A1.

Ruperti, Hans Heinrich Justus Philipp. B. Dec. 21, 1833, near Stade, Hanover; pastor, Emigrant House in Bremerhaven, 1856—72; at St. Matthew's, New York, 1873—76; member of the New York Ministerium. Died as Superintendent General of Holstein May 16, 1899. Published several collections of sermons.

Rupff (Rupsch), Konrad (d. ca. 1525). *Kapellmeister* for Frederick the Wise in Torgau. In 1524 Luther asked Rupff and Johann Walther to come to Wittenberg to assist him in preparing his *Deutsche Messe.* Three solid weeks were devoted to this task. How much was contributed by Rupff is not known.

Rupprecht, Philip Martin Ferdinand. B. Nov. 10, 1861, at North Dover, Ohio; graduated at Concordia Seminary (St. Louis), 1884; pastor near Cole Camp, Mo., 1884—89; at Detroit, Mich., 1889—96; assistant editor and proofreader at Louis Lange Publ. Co., 1896 to 1900; chief proofreader and house editor at Concordia Publishing House, St. Louis, Mo., 1900 to 1942; (D. D., St. Louis, 1936); editor of *Concordia Lesson Helps,* 1916—20; wrote *Bible History References* (2 vols.). D. July 5, 1942.

Russell, Arthur Tozer (1806—74). B. at Northampton, March 20, 1806, ed. at St. John's College, Cambridge. In 1829 he was ordained by the Bishop of Lincoln. Russell held a number of pastorates, the last near Brighton. Russell started his ecclesiastical career as an extreme high churchman, but through the study of St. Augustine his views were changed. He was a prolific writer in both prose and poetry. He wrote 140 hymns; they are characterized as gracious and tender, thoughtful and devout. His translations are vigorous and strong. He died Nov. 18, 1874.

Russell, Charles Taze. See *Jehovah's Witnesses.*

Russellism. See *Jehovah's Witnesses.*

Russia. 1. The story of how the Gospel came to Russia is similar to that of the conversion of the Franks at the time of Chlodwig; for the Eastern Slavs accepted Christianity in a body when their Prince Vladimir was baptized. The foundation of the Russian Empire had been laid by the Norman or Va-rangian Rurik in 862. A century later Olga, a princess of his house, was baptized while on a visit to Constantinople. After personally studying the representations of Mohammedans, Jews, and missionaries of the Latin and Greek churches, Olga's grandson Vladimir sent envoys to other lands to report to him on the different religions. Constantinople and Justinian's Church of Saint Sophia made such a deep impression on the envoys that they reported to the king in favor of Olga's religion. Married to Anna, sister of the Emperor Basil, Vladimir and his twelve sons were baptized at Kieff in 988, the idol Peroun was sunk in the Dnieper, and the whole population immersed themselves in its waters, while Greek priests read the baptismal service from the banks. The books of Cyrillus and Methodius * were read in their own tongue. Thus arose, in full stature, the Church of Russia, soon to become the strongest representative of the Greek Orthodox Church.

2. Vladimir and his successors sought to make provision for schools and the training of the clergy, a certain degree of culture being in evidence in their ranks at that time; but conditions were unfavorable for a true religious awakening, and the masses were openly pagan and utterly ignorant. The Mongol invasion was a blow to the Church, weak as it was in true spiritual life, and the fact that natives became religious leaders shortly after was not conducive to a strengthening of religious consciousness. Gennadius, Patriarch of Constantinople during the middle of the 16th century, granted the Russian Church the right to choose and consecrate its own metropolitans. This resulted in delivering the Church to the power of the grand dukes, Ivan the Terrible dominating affairs with willful caprice.

3. Moscow became a third Rome, and the Church became a powerful agency in the country, with four archdioceses and seven dioceses. Monasteries multiplied, and the wealth of the Church grew to amazing proportions. In 1589 Job was consecrated independent Patriarch of Russia, as one of the four of the Orthodox Greek Church. But the Russian clergy, on the whole, remained ignorant, even the bishops being included in this category, so that Protestant travelers in the land reported that Christianity was practically nonexistent. It was not till the 17th century that the influence of Western learning made itself felt in Russia, the

college at Kieff, founded by Peter Mogilas in 1631, being a center of learning for over a century.

4. For a while the movement known as the Enlightenment was on the verge of entering Russia, but during the latter part of the reign of Alexander I a reaction set in, and during the greater part of the 19th century the more conservative church leaders were in power, with the theological seminaries in Petrograd, Moscow, Kieff, and Kazan as the centers of learning and influence. Up to the time of the establishment of the Soviet Republic (1922) the Orthodox Greek Church was the State Church of Russia, almost 100,000,000 of the inhabitants being, at least nominally, members of this body. The reign of terror following the Bolshevist *régime* in Russia overthrew the Church as a ruling factor and, in most cases, produced chaos. It would be difficult to overemphasize the blasphemous manner in which sacred things were regarded and the diabolical methods with which they were treated. The Church seems to exist at the present time only on a plane of sufferance, with millions of former adherents openly blaspheming everything that is holy.

5. Of other churches that have entered the domain of Russia the Roman Catholic Church was fairly strong in Russian Poland. The Reformed churches of Russia enjoyed a measure of freedom before World War I, but their total number was well under a hundred thousand. See *Russian Sects.*

6. Soon after the Reformation, Lutherans from western Europe began to migrate to Russia. Already during the reign of Ivan the Terrible (1547—84) Lutheran colonists and prisoners of war settled along the Volga. The first Lutheran church was erected in a suburb of Moscow in 1576, but was frequently destroyed and rebuilt. Peter the Great (1682—1725) ended the persecution of Lutherans and encouraged the immigration of Lutherans, a policy continued by his successor. The Lutheran Church was formally organized in 1832, when the state recognized the Lutherans as a "privileged Church." After the Bolshevists came to power, the organized Lutheran Church ceased to exist, many Lutherans undoubtedly joining Baptist churches, toward which the Kremlin took a more lenient attitude. The Lutheran population of Russia was given as 1,000,000 (1937), of which about seven tenths were German Lutherans.

Russian Bible Society. See *Bible Societies,* 4.

Russian Orthodox Church. See *Eastern Orthodox Churches.*

Russian Sects. Are divided into two groups. 1. The Raskolniki ("schismatics"), who dissent from the hierarchy and ritual of the Orthodox Church, but not from its dogma. Their origin dates back to the revision of the liturgy in the 17th century, which they opposed. There are two branches, the Popovtsy, who have priests, and the Bezpopovtsy, who do not. 2. Those who dissent also from the dogma. These sects arose mainly through foreign influence and number more than 200. The more important are the mystic Khlysty, who are anti-Trinitarian, and the Skoptsy, who practice castration, the rationalistic Doukhobors and Molokani, and the numerous pietistic-evangelical Stundists, who arose through Baptist influence ca. 1864. Russian sects have at all times been persecuted more or less by the Russian Church and were not given complete religious freedom until the revolution of 1917. Their adherents have been variously estimated up to 20 million. See also *Russia.*

Ruthenian Rite. The Byzantine rite as modified for use in the Gallican Church.

Rutherford, J. F. See *Jehovah's Witnesses.*

Rutilius, Martin (1550—1618). Studied at Wittenberg and Jena; held charges at Teutleben and Weimar; the hymn usually ascribed to him: "Ach Gott und Herr, wie gross und schwer."

Ruysbroeck, Jan van (1294—1381). Dutch mystic; studied at Brussels, where he also became priest and vicar; retired to a monastery at Groenendael, giving himself to a life of contemplation; influenced largely by Meister Eckart, he developed a mystical system which he presented in a number of books, one not in agreement with the clear presentation of the doctrine of God in Holy Writ and which borders on pantheism; his pupil Groote was the founder of the Brethren of the Common Life.

Rygh, George Alfred Taylor. B. March 21, 1860, at Chicago, Ill., of Andreas Rygh and Andrine (Holter). Attended Luther College, 1876—81 (A. B.); Luther Sem., 1882—83; Capital Univ., 1881—82, 1883—84 (C. T.). Teacher, Luther College, 1883. Pastor, Portland, Me., 1884—89. Teacher, Wittenberg Acad., 1889—90. Pastor, Grand Forks, N. Dak., 1890—91. Teacher, Scandinavian languages, North Dakota Univ., 1891—95. Pastor, Mt. Horeb, Wis. (and pres., Mt. Horeb Acad.), 1895—98; Chicago, Ill. (Bethlehem), 1899—1910. Teacher, St. Olaf College, 1910—11, 1912 to 1913. Editor, *United Lutheran*, 1909 to 1914; assoc. editor, *American Lutheran Survey*, 1914—21; *Lutheran Church Herald*, from 1925 on; pastor, Minneapolis, Minn. (Faith Cong.), from 1920 on; Board of Home Missions, 1906—09; Com.

on English Hymnbook (translated hymns into English), 1902—13; Centennial Com., 1923—25. Translated Grossner's *Treasury*, 1906; Rosenius' *A Faithful Guide to Peace with God*, 1923; and other books; author *Morgenroedens Vinger*, 1908; *The Shadow of a Wrong*, 1908; *The Pioneers*, 1909; *Sangkor*, 1909; *John Harding*, 1910. Litt. D. from Newberry Coll., Newberry, S. C., 1917. National Lutheran Council Commissioner to Baltic States, 1919 to 1920. He was ordained in 1884. Married Clara Louise Aaker, 1895. D. 1942.

S

Saadia ben Joseph. See *Bible Versions*, F.

Sabaism. See *Sabianism*.

Sabatier, Louis Auguste (1839 to 1901). French Protestant; b. at Vallon; professor of Reformed dogmatics at Strassburg 1868; expelled 1873 because of his animosity to German régime; professor of dogmatics (1877) in newly founded Protestant theological faculty of the Sorbonne; dean of the theological faculty 1895; conservative at first, absolutely liberal at last; d. in Paris.

Sabbatarianism. In a special sense this term denotes the tenets of all those who hold that the Christian Sabbath should be kept on the seventh day (Saturday), especially the Adventists, Seventh-Day Baptists, and some scattered communistic societies. In a wider sense the term also signifies those who hold that the Lord's day should be observed among Christians exactly in the same manner as the Jews were enjoined to keep the Sabbath, or those who entertain rigid views regarding Sabbath observation. Thus in the Presbyterian *Shorter Catechism* we read: "The Sabbath is to be sanctified by holy rest all that day, even from such worldly employments and recreations as are lawful on other days, and spending the whole time in public and private exercise of God's worship, except so much as should be taken up in the works of necessity and mercy." In the 17th century the recurrence of the Puritanical Sabbath interpretation led to a controversy regarding the manner in which Sunday should be kept. This arose out of the publication of King James' *Book of Sports*, published in 1618. A controversy was carried on between the

High-churchmen, who were generally in favor of the king's views, and the Puritans, who were strongly opposed to them.

Sabbath. 1. The seventh day of the week established as a day of rest for the Jews in commemoration of the seventh day of Creation week and the release of the Jews from their bondage in Egypt. Although God rested from His work on the seventh day and sanctified it, the Bible does not say that He commanded Adam and Eve to keep that day (Gen. 2:2,3). It is nowhere stated that Adam and Eve, Noah, Abraham, Isaac, or Jacob observed the seventh day as the Sabbath.

2. The Israelites knew nothing of the Sabbath day when they left Egypt, for when God gave them manna in double portion on the sixth day, they were surprised and asked Moses what it meant. Moses told them, and the next day was the Sabbath (Ex. 16:22-30). This has been regarded as the time of the institution of Sabbath observance (cf. Deut. 5:15).

3. God gave the Israelites very strict laws regarding the Sabbath. Cessation from work, however, was only a means to an end. The Sabbath day was a memorial of God's love and kindness which He manifested in the work of creation, and it was to incite the Israelites to give thanks and praise unto God (Ex. 20:8,11; Deut. 5:15).

4. The Sabbath day of the Jews is not a law binding on Christians. The fact that nobody today observes the Sabbath day as God had commanded that it should be observed in the Old Testament goes far to show that some universal change in this matter must have taken place. At least on one occa-

sion Jesus did not only overlook, but even defended, a breach by His Apostles of the Sabbath commandment (Mark 2:23-28). The Pharisees thought that the plucking of ears of grain on the Sabbath was a breaking of the law (Ex. 20:10). Jesus defends the disciples by three arguments: 1) David broke a ceremonial law by eating the showbread (1 Sam. 21:1-6); 2) by announcing the principle: "The Sabbath was made for man and not man for the Sabbath"; 3) by stating: "The Son of Man is Lord also of the Sabbath." Thus the Lord shows that as far as a specific day is concerned, it is of a ceremonial and transient character, which in itself should be respected as long as that ceremonial law is in force, but may as readily be omitted when the law would be abolished. If the Sabbath was "made for man," on account of man's needs and for his benefit, then, the conditions being changed, the law will change. Jesus shows that this is to happen. For, as indicated in the third argument, the Son of Man has the power to abolish even the Sabbath.

5. God had given the Jews certain laws which did not concern any one else; for example, the laws governing circumcision, the Passover, the Day of Atonement, the sacrifice of lambs, etc. The purpose of these laws was for one thing to be a heavy burden on the Children of Israel and so to keep awake in them the desire for a Messiah, who would redeem them from the curse of the Law. Then, again, these laws were to foreshadow the work and the sacrifice of the Messiah. Now the Messiah has come, and hence all these ceremonies of the Old Testament have served their purpose and are revoked. The Lord Jesus expressly places the Sabbath law in the same class with the laws concerning sacrifices, as does Paul (Col. 2:16, 17).

6. While Jewish Christians continued to observe the Sabbath, Gentile Christians soon chose the first day of the week as a day of worship because the Lord had risen on that day (cf. Acts 20:7; Rev. 1:10). Characteristics of the Jewish Sabbath were added to the Lord's day, as when it was made a day of rest (Constantine, 321). In England in the 17th century Christians gradually assumed the view that Sunday is the New Testament Sabbath. However, neither Scripture nor the ancient fathers placed the first day of the week instead of the Old Testament Sabbath. The fact that the early Christians chose

Sunday as a day of public worship is no proof that the Church Universal is in duty bound to do the same (Col. 2:16, 17; Gal. 4:10, 11; 5:4).

7. Although there is no divinely appointed day of rest or worship in the New Testament, God has told us how to worship Him. His Word shall be preached. The Sacraments are to be administered. Public prayer and praise shall be in vogue. If this is to be done, it is evident that a certain time and place must be fixed for public worship. While in the Old Testament God prescribed time and place of public worship, He has in the New Testament left these things entirely to the discretion and choice of His people.

8. The Augsburg Confession discusses the Sabbath and Sunday in Article XXVIII under the general topic of Ecclesiastical Power. The Lutheran confessors say (Concordia Triglot, pp. 91, 92, §§ 55—66): "It is proper that the churches should keep such ordinances for the sake of love and tranquillity, so far that one do not offend another, that all things be done in the churches in order and without confusion (1 Cor. 14:40; cp. Phil. 2:14); but so that consciences be not burdened to think that they are necessary to salvation, or to judge that they sin when they break them without offense to others; as no one will say that a woman sins who goes out in public with her head uncovered, provided only that no offense be given. Of this kind is the observance of the Lord's day, Easter, Pentecost, and like holy-days and rites. For those who judge that by the authority of the Church the observance of the Lord's day instead of the Sabbath day was ordained as a thing necessary do greatly err. Scripture has abrogated the Sabbath day; for it teaches that, since the Gospel has been revealed, all the ceremonies of Moses can be omitted. And yet, because it was necessary to appoint a certain day, that the people might know when they ought to come together, it appears that the Church designated the Lord's day for this purpose; and this day seems to have been chosen all the more for this additional reason, that men might have an example of Christian liberty and might know that the keeping neither of the Sabbath nor of any other day is necessary. There are monstrous disputations concerning the changing of the law, the ceremonies of the new law, the changing of the Sabbath day, which all have sprung from the false belief that there must

needs be in the Church a service like to the Levitical and that Christ had given commission to the Apostles and bishops to devise new ceremonies as necessary to salvation. These errors crept into the Church when the righteousness of faith was not taught clearly enough. Some dispute that the keeping of the Lord's day is not indeed of divine right, but in a manner so. They prescribe concerning holy days how far it is lawful to work. What else are such disputations than snares of consciences? For although they endeavor to modify the traditions, yet the mitigation can never be perceived as long as the opinion remains that they are necessary, which must needs remain where the righteousness of faith and Christian liberty are not known. The Apostles commanded, Acts 15:20, to abstain from blood. Who does now observe it? And yet they that do it not sin not; for not even the Apostles themselves wanted to burden consciences with such bondage; but they forbade it for a time, to avoid offense. For in this decree we must perpetually consider what the aim of the Gospel is."

Sabbatine Privilege. The Roman Catholic belief that Mary releases from purgatory those who have revered her especially (Saturday is Mary's day).

Sabellianism. See *Monarchianism*, B 6.

Sabianism. The religion of the Sabians, an ancient, syncretistic, Mesopotamian sect, which worships the sun, moon, and stars. It rejects Jesus as the Messiah and claims to follow John the Baptist.

Sabina. A martyr of the second century, a widow of Rome, who was gained for the Christian faith by her slave Serapia of Antioch and therefore condemned to death with her. A special chapel was built in Rome for their relics.

Sacer, Gottfried Wilhelm (1635 to 1699). B. in Naumburg, Saxony, where his father was senior burgomaster. He studied philosophy and law at Jena. In 1665 he entered military service. After two years he toured Holland and Denmark. After this he followed his profession as lawyer in Brunswick and later in Wolfenbuettel, where he was appointed counselor of the exchequer. He earned a fine reputation as lawyer and statesman, being unselfish and conscientious, particularly in handling the cases of the poor. He was crowned poet

laureate by the Emperor of Austria. He is judged by many to be one of the greatest German hymnists immediately following the Gerhardt period. He wrote 65 hymns. They are characterized as having poetic glow, dramatic force, Scriptural content, and excellent style.

Sacerdotalism. A term denoting the usage of certain religions, also sections of the Christian Church, by which the priests are given a special station over against the laity, as an order through whom alone the relation with the deity can be established. Thus the hierarchy of the Roman Catholic Church and of the Eastern Orthodox Church is properly discussed under sacerdotalism.

Sachs, Hans (1494—1576). Famous German shoemaker and poet; one of the first singers of the Reformation in Germany; lived all his life in Nuremberg, except during his wanderings as journeyman; many of his poetical works pertain to the daily life of the German burghers, bringing home truths in a homely fashion; he wrote few poems which may fittingly be called hymns; one of his most celebrated poems: "Die Wittenbergisch Nachtigall" (meaning Luther).

Sack, Friedrich Samuel Gottfried (1738—1817). Prussian theologian; court preacher of Frederick II; bishop of Ev. Church; leader in the Prussian Union Movement.

Sack, Karl Heinrich (1790—1875). German theologian; prof. at Berlin and Bonn; wrote in the field of apologetics, polemics, and history of preaching.

Sacrament of the Altar. See *Grace, Means of*, IV, 1 ff.

Sacramentalism. A designation applied to the tendency found in the Roman Catholic Church and in other bodies with a strong hierarchical trend to give to the Sacraments, specifically the Eucharist, a relatively higher inherent saving power than the Word. The tendency usually accompanies externalism in some form or other.

Sacramentals. In the terminology of the Roman Church certain rites and actions, admittedly of ecclesiastical institution, but having some outward resemblance to Sacraments. Such are prayer (especially the Lord's Prayer) and alms, when said or given in the name of the Church or in a consecrated place; confession; the blessing of bishops and abbots; holy water, blessed candles, medals, etc. The pious use of sacramentals is supposed to remit venial sins.

Sacramentary. In Roman Catholicism, books containing prayers for Mass, ordination, and other Roman Catholic sacraments.

Sacramentarian. A term originally applied to Zwingli, Calvin, and their followers because of their insistent denial of the Real Presence. The term has also been applied to those who uphold the efficacy of the Sacrament.

Sacraments, The. 1. The Sacraments are sacred acts of divine institution, by which, wherever they are properly performed by the prescribed use of the prescribed external elements in conjunction with the divine words of institution, God, being, in a manner peculiar to each Sacrament, present with the word and elements, earnestly offers to all who partake of such Sacraments forgiveness of sins, life, and salvation and operates toward the acceptance of such blessings or toward greater assurance of their possession.

2. This definition, though not found in Scripture in the same terms, is Scriptural inasmuch as it states the marks common to two peculiar institutions described in Holy Writ which in the Christian Church are designated as Sacraments, Baptism and the Lord's Supper. As these institutions are not termed Sacraments in the Holy Scriptures, there is no cogent necessity of restricting the term to these institutions. Any sacred rite or performance or institution, e. g., the act of absolution, the administration of an oath, the rite of confirmation or ordination, might be called a sacrament. But when Lutheran theologians maintain that there are but two Sacraments and shape their definition as above, they mean that the Scriptures know of but these two institutions admitting of this definition, Baptism and the Lord's Supper, as institutions intended for the Church of the New Testament, and that, whatever else may be called a sacrament, is not of the same nature as these institutions to which we apply and restrict this term in theology.

3. The proper performance of these sacred acts, in order that they may be sacramental acts, requires the prescribed use of prescribed external elements in conjunction with the words of institution. These elements — water in Baptism, bread and wine in the Eucharist — are essential to the respective

Sacrament, and so is their prescribed use. In Baptism and in the Lord's Supper, when these Sacraments are administered, the divine Author of these institutions is, in a peculiar way, present in and with the word and elements in their sacramental use. The spiritual blessing dispensed in the Sacraments is the benefit of Christ's redemption, forgiveness of sins, the salvation which Christ, the Mediator, has merited for all mankind. And this appropriation of such benefits to the individual sinner is all the more apparent as, in the Sacraments, God takes each candidate for Baptism and each communicant, separately and individually assuring him to whose body the sacramental water is applied, or him who eats and drinks his Savior's body and blood, that his sins are forgiven unto him. And here, again, the full pardon thus freely and unconditionally offered and extended to the sinner can be, and often is, rejected, its acceptance refused. The Sacrament is not a charm, a magic lotion or potion, but a means of grace. Being but another form of the Gospel, it, too, is the power of God unto salvation to every one that believeth. ALG

Sacraments, Roman Catholic. 1. The *Catechismus Romanus* (II, 1. 6) defines Sacraments as follows: "The Sacraments of the New Law are signs instituted by God, not invented by men, of which we believe with certainty that they contain in themselves the power to effect whatever sacred thing they declare." The "sacred thing" which they declare and effect is said to be "the grace of God, which makes us holy and provides us with capacity for all divine virtues" (*Ibid.*, 7). It is further taught that every sacrament requires a material element in conjunction with words (10. 11).

2. The Roman Church asserts that seven observances satisfy these conditions and that therefore the number of sacraments in the New Testament is seven. This number was fixed in comparatively recent times. Till late in the Middle Ages theological writers assigned numbers varying from two to thirty. Bernard of Clairvaux named ten sacraments. Gradually the number seven established itself in favor; but it was authoritatively sanctioned only at the Council of Florence, in 1439. The Council of Trent (Sess. VII, can. 1) binds the Roman Church to seven sacraments in these words: "If any one saith that the sacraments of the New

Law were not all instituted by Jesus Christ, our Lord, or that they are more or less than seven, to wit, Baptism, Confirmation, the Eucharist, Penance, Extreme Unction, Order [ordination], and Matrimony; or even, that any one of these seven is not truly and properly a sacrament: let him be accursed." The bold assertion that these seven "sacraments" rest on the institution of Christ, cannot look to the Bible for verification. No refinement of exegesis can extract from the story of Pentecost a sacrament of confirmation or show a sacrament of extreme unction established in James 5. Even the voice of tradition fails. The Romanist is reduced to what, after all, is his real and only refuge, namely, to the fact that the Church has so decreed. Hence the Catholic Encyclopedia must content itself with claiming that for some sacraments Jesus "determined only in a general way that there should be an external ceremony, by which special graces were to be conferred, leaving to the Apostles or to the Church the power to determine whatever He had not determined, e. g., to prescribe the matter and form of the sacraments of Confirmation and Holy Orders." No Scripture passages are offered in which Jesus leaves to the Apostles or to the Church this remarkable power of determining what He has not determined.

3. Among its sacraments the Roman Church names three as being more necessary than the others: Baptism, Penance, and Holy Orders. The Eucharist is said to be the most sacred and glorious of the sacraments. Three sacraments — Baptism, Confirmation, and Holy Orders — are never repeated because they are supposed to impress an indelible mark on the recipient (see Character Indelebilis). Baptism prepares for the reception of the other sacraments, which can be conferred only on the baptized. Confirmation and Holy Orders are administered only by bishops, while only those who have received holy orders can validly administer the other sacraments (excepting Baptism in case of necessity).

4. The validity of a sacrament is not made dependent on the personal worthiness of the officiating priest; though the priest be a hypocrite, the sacrament is valid if properly administered. But the comfort contained in this assurance is limited by the peculiar doctrine of "priestly intention," a doctrine of which the Scripture knows nothing and which was unheard of till the idle speculations of the scholastics gave birth to it. According to this doctrine the priest must have the intention of doing, in the sacrament, what the Church does, that is, he must intend to administer the rites which he is conducting, as a sacrament; if he lacks this intention or has another intention, the sacrament is not valid. "If any one saith that, in ministers, when they effect and confer the sacraments, there is not required the intention at least of doing what the Church does: let him be accursed." (Council of Trent, Sess. VII, can. 11.) Roman writers vie with one another in minimizing the likelihood that even a bad priest would act without intention; but the fact remains that by this doctrine they undermine the certainty of grace in the Sacraments and make the mental attitude of the priest an essential factor in their efficacy. Oddly enough, the Roman Church, under the same doctrine of intention, admits the validity of Protestant Baptism and therefore does not rebaptize Protestant converts.

5. In the doctrine of the Sacraments, as elsewhere, the insistence of the Roman Church on works as against faith is manifested, for it denies that the grace of God which is offered in the Sacraments is appropriated through faith alone and teaches instead that this grace is conferred by the performance of the sacramental act on all those who merely place no obstacle in its way. See Opus Operatum; see also Baptism, Roman Catholic Doctrine of; Confirmation; Lord's Supper; Matrimony; Ordination; Penance; Priesthood; Unction, Extreme.

Sacred Heart (nuns). A congregation which aims to spread devotion to the physical heart of Jesus by practicing spirituality and doing works of mercy.

Sacred Heart of Jesus, Devotion to. The devotion paid in the Roman Church to the physical heart of Jesus. A French nun, Margaret Mary Alacoque, claimed that on June 16, 1675, Jesus in a vision, declared to her that special devotion should be offered to His sacred heart. Rome was long unfavorable to the devotion, but the Jesuits pushed it vigorously, confraternities practicing it multiplied, and step by step Rome yielded to the increasing pressure, first conceding the devotion and then a festival. The devotion steadily increased its hold on the Roman Church. Groups, congregations, and states consecrated themselves to the Sacred Heart. In 1875 this consecration took place throughout the Catholic world; on June 11, 1899, Leo XIII, as the "great act" of his pontificate, consecrated all mankind to the Sacred Heart. The object of the devotion is defined by the *Catholic Encyclopedia* as "a devotion to the love of Jesus Christ in so far as this love is recalled and symbolically represented to us by His heart of flesh." The most important confraternity of the devotion is the League of the Sacred Heart, or Apostleship of Prayer. The devotion to the Immaculate Heart of Mary is analogous.

Sacred Literatures. In the more influential religions of the world we find the following books or collections of books which are accorded a place of veneration as the source of truth: The Hinayana school of Buddhism has its sacred canon in the Pali language, chiefly in the *Tripitaka*, or Three Baskets. The Mahayana school of Buddhism has its sacred literature in the Sanskrit language, which includes a *Tripitaka*, accounts of the life of Buddha, and the *Saddharmapundarika*, the Lotus of the True Law, with a number of lesser books. In the earlier stages of Confucianism the ancient classics played a great role, and they are still regarded with reverence by the educated Chinese. These classics are: 1) the *Yi-King*, or Book of Changes, 2) the *Shu-King*, or Book of History, 3) the *Shi-King*, or Book of Poetry, 4) the *Li-Ki*, or Book of Ceremonial Usages, 5) the *Ch'un Ch'iu*, the annals of the state of Lu, attributed to Confucius himself. In addition to these five classics there are four books: 1) *Lun Yu*, or the Analects, chiefly on ethics and government, 2) *Ta-Hsueh*, the Great Learning, or the methods of Confucious, 3) *Chung Yung*, the Doctrine of the Mean, on the moral responsibility of man, 4) the writings of Menicus on ethics and politics. Earlier Hinduism grew up under the influence of the Vedas, the *Rig-veda* alone consisting of 1,017 hymns in connection with the ritualistic services of the religion. The later, popular religious literature of India centers about two great epic poems, the *Ramayana* and the *Mahabharata*. A section of the latter, the *Bhagavad-gita*, was particularly influential in shaping religious ideas of India. The eighteen *Puranas* form another division of popular sacred literature in Hinduism; they deal with cosmology,

history, and religious philosophy. The sacred book of Mohammedanism is the *Koran*, a collection of 114 sections known as Suras, made more than fifteen years after Mohammed's death and intended chiefly for ritual prayer. Of religious organizations that have a more or less tenuous relation to Christianity we might mention Christian Science, with its strange scripture *Science and Health with Key to the Scriptures*, and the Latter-Day Saints, with their *Book of Mormon*. Judaism recognizes the Old Testament, but only with a veil drawn over the Messianic sections, and the *Talmud*. The only true, God-inspired book in use among men is the Bible of the Christian religion.

Sacrifice for Sin. See *Atonement*.

Sacrilege. All profanation, making profane, of holy things, by despising, polluting, desecrating, misusing things consecrated to God. Examples: Gen. 25:33; Lev. 10:1-7; Num. 3:4; 2 Sam. 6:6,7; 2 Chron. 26:16 ff.; Matt. 21:12,13; Luke 19:45; 1 Cor. 11:29; John 2:14-16; Rom. 2:22; 2 Kings 21:4-7. Forbidden: Lev. 19:8; 21:9; 1 Cor. 3:17; Titus 1:11; 1 Peter 5:2.

Sacristan. A person having charge of the sacristy and its contents (vestments, etc.). This office, more responsible than that of sexton, was formerly held by clerics, but is now usually filled by laymen.

Sacristy. A room, usually near the altar, where objects used in the service are stored and where clergy and others gather to prepare for the service.

Saddharmapundarika. See *Sacred Literatures*.

Saeculum Obscurum. A designation very commonly applied to the tenth century of the Christian era, on account of the practically total absence of theological productions, the similar retrogression in the domain of all other divisions of knowledge, and the demoralization and increasing worldliness of the clergy.

Saggitarius (Schuetze), Kaspar (1643—94). B. at Lueneburg; d. at Jena. Studied at Helmstdt; traveled; finished his studies at Leipzig, Wittenberg, Jena, and Altdorf. Rector at Saalfeld, 1668; professor at Jena, 1671; transferred to the chair of history, 1674. He specialized in the history of early Christianity in Germany. His *Disser-*

tatio de praecipuis scriptoribus historiae Germanicae, 1675, marks the first efforts toward a history of German historiography.

Sahidic Bible Version. See *Bible Versions*, D.

St. Andrew, Brotherhood of. See *Brotherhood of St. Andrew*.

St. Elisabeth. See *Elisabeth, St.*

St. George Church. See *Canada, Lutheranism in*, 1.

St. John's College. See *Ministry, Education of*, IX.

St. Paul Theses. See *Chicago Theses*.

St. Paul's College. See *Ministry, Education of*, IX.

Saint-Maur, Congregation of. See *Maur, Saint, Congregation of*.

Saint Saens, Camille (1835—1921). French composer, musician, painter, poet, philosopher, and astronomer. He was influenced by Berlioz and Liszt, and his music reveals expert workmanship and elegance rather than depth and solidity. Saint Saens' *Christmas Oratorio* is heard occasionally, as are also many of his instrumental works.

St. Simon, Claude Henri de Rouvray, Comte de (1760—1825). French philosopher; fought with French troops in American Revolution; social reformer; his views distorted by his followers.

Saints. See *Brethren, Plymouth*.

Saints, Communion of. See *Church*.

Saints' Days, Roman Catholic. The Roman Church, in addition to the feasts of the church year, such as Christmas, Epiphany, and Easter, observes numerous saints' days, *i. e.*, days assigned in its calendar to the memory and veneration of particular saints. Every new saint, as he is canonized, is allotted his day. Most of these days are observed only in the Mass and the office (see *Breviary*) of the day, and no general obligation regarding them rests on the laity. Others are "feasts of obligation," on which all are bound to hear Mass and abstain from servile work. During the Middle Ages, and even later, the great number of feasts of obligation was a serious nuisance, which kept the poor from earning a livelihood and encouraged others in laziness. In some places the workless days of the year, including Sundays, reached and even exceeded a hundred. This condition no longer obtains, though there are still large variations in different countries. In the United States there are only six days of obligation that may fall in the week: Christmas, New Year, Ascension, Assumption, All Saints, and Immaculate Conception. The Council of Baltimore, in 1852, would even have reduced the number to four, had not the Pope demurred.

Saints, Worship of. 1. This form of idolatry, which is practiced in the Roman Catholic and the Eastern Churches, is lineally descended from the heathen cults that were uprooted by Christianity. Unsound tendencies appeared as early as the third century, but the real development of saint worship came after Christianity had been fully established. The masses which then flooded the Church were not thoroughly Christianized, but retained various heathen concepts and customs, which, in course of time, established themselves in the Church in more or less modified forms. The claim of some writers that the gods, demigods, and heroes of heathen mythology were deliberately replaced by Christian equivalents may lack foundation, but the parallels between heathen cults and the adoration of saints are numerous and striking.

2. Gradually the reverence which the Early Church had shown to the memory of the martyrs and to their tombs was perverted into an adoration of these martyrs. On the supposition that they and other saints had special influence with God because of their merits and that in some way they received information of the needs of the faithful on earth and interceded for them with God, it was held very profitable to ask their intercession and to conciliate their favor by calling on them and giving them honor. In time these ideas became general, overrode all opposition, were adopted by church councils, and became a prolific source of other superstitions and heathenish usages. The saints practically developed into minor deities, to whom prayers and oblations were offered for aid. Each nation, city, profession, and trade was assigned its tutelary saint, and each individual had a guardian saint. One saint protected against hail, another against fire, a third against poison. St. Appollonia cured toothache, St. Othilia, eye trouble; St. Gallus looked after geese, St. Eulogius after horses, and St. Anthony after pigs.

3. All this the Roman Church ac-

cepted expressly or tacitly and so accepts it to this day. The Council of Trent enjoins on the ministers of Rome that "they especially instruct the faithful diligently concerning the intercession and invocation of saints," "teaching them that the saints, who reign together with Christ, offer up their own prayers to God for men; that it is good and useful suppliantly to invoke them and to have recourse to their prayers, aid, and help, for obtaining benefits from God, through His Son, Jesus Christ, our Lord." (Sess. XXV.) The *Catechismus Romanus* (III, 2.12) answers in the affirmative the question: "Will they [the saints], if prayed to, not gain the forgiveness of sins for us and procure for us the grace of God?"

4. Thus Rome makes the saints intercessors and mediators between God and men, in the face of such passages as 1 Tim. 2:5; 1 John 2:1; Heb. 4:14-16; 7:25. It robs Christ of His honor to confer it on creatures; it does this, however much it may insist that He is the one, or chief, Mediator; for it does not accept Him as the sole Mediator. Again, Rome commits idolatry in addressing prayers to any but God. It cannot escape this charge by making a distinction between *latria*, offered to God, and *dulia*, offered to creatures. Even if the distinction were observed by the average Romanist, there would remain the fact that Scripture contains not a single command, not a single promise, and not a single example on which such invocations can be founded, but, demands, on the contrary, that prayer be addressed to God alone (*e. g.*, Ps. 50:15; Matt. 4:10). Thus the invocation of saints, as practiced in the Roman Catholic Church, is not only superfluous and useless (Is. 63:16; Job 14:21), but sinful and wrong. It is evident, also, that a popular saint would require something approaching omnipresence and omniscience.

5. Roman writers frequently try to gloss over the facts in this matter. Cardinal Gibbons writes: "There are expressions addressed to the saints in some popular books of devotion, which, to critical readers, may seem extravagant" (*Faith of Our Fathers*, p. 148). He excuses such expressions as enthusiastic hyperboles of affection. This excuse will certainly not be urged regarding the prayers in the Roman *Breviary*. Two such prayers are therefore offered here, each bearing a papal indulgence of 100 days. The following prayer, sanctioned by Leo XIII, is to be used by priests before saying Mass in honor of a saint: "O Saint N., behold, I, a miserable sinner, trusting in your merits, offer now the most sacred Sacrament of the Body and Blood of our Lord Jesus Christ for your honor and glory. I pray you humbly and devotedly to intercede for me today that I may be able to offer so great a sacrifice worthily and acceptably, that I may be able, with you and all His elect, to praise Him eternally and to reign with Him, who lives and reigns forever. Amen." After Mass the priest may say the following prayer, approved by Pius IX: "Guardian of virgins, holy Father Joseph, to whose faithful care Innocence itself, Christ Jesus and Mary, virgin of virgins, has been committed: I beseech and implore you by both these dearest pledges, Jesus and Mary, that you will make me, preserved from all uncleanness, always serve Jesus and Mary most chastely, with an unspotted mind, a pure heart, and a chaste body. Amen." While the first of these prayers is an appeal for intercession, it will be noted that the second is much more: a direct appeal to St. Joseph to grant spiritual gifts — and that is plain, undisguised idolatry.

St. Victore, Adam de. Prominent hymn writer of the 12th century (died 1192); very prolific; most of the seasons of the church year having been supplied with sequences by him, among which *Quem Pastores Laudavere* ("Whom the Shepherds Praised with Gladness").

Salesian Nuns. See *Visitation Nuns.*

Salesians. A society of Roman priests, founded 1859, having for its chief purpose the teaching and training of neglected boys. Support is furnished chiefly by the society's tertiaries, called "co-operators."

Salig, Christian August (1692 to 1738). D. as rector at Wolfenbuettel; wrote history of the *Augsburg Confession* and of the Reformation; pietistic, yet very valuable.

Salmeron, Alphonsus (1515—85). Spanish Jesuit, whose influence was great at the Council of Trent. See *Counter Reformation.*

Salutation. See *Worship, Parts of*, 10.

Salvador. See *Central America.*

Salvation. See *Absolution; Atonement; Christ Jesus; Conversion; Pre-*

destination; Faith; Gospel; Grace, Means of; Incarnation; Propitiation; Redemption.

A treatment under this title (with references): W. Arndt, "Salvation," *What Lutherans Are Thinking*, Wartburg Press, Columbus, 1947.

Salvation Army. 1. The Salvation Army owes its origin to William Booth (1829—1912), a minister of the English body known as the New Connection Methodists. From his earliest preaching, which began when he was sixteen years of age, he was deeply impressed with the fact that an important percentage of the crowds which fill the towns and cities of England lay outside the influence of the Christian churches. In an effort to reach these people, he inaugurated a series of open-air meetings in London, the first of which was held July 5, 1865. As the attendance increased, the meetings were held in a tent and afterwards in a theater. Evangelists were soon sent out in different directions to preach and teach. At first General Booth, with whom his wife, Mrs. Catharine Booth, was always intimately associated, regarded the Army as primarily supplementary to the churches. However, as it enlarged, it developed into a distinctive movement, with a people of its own. Although the movement was English in origin, it rapidly extended into other countries. Converts from England, finding homes in the United States, Canada, and other lands, began working according to the methods of the Army and followed their efforts by urging the general to send them trained leaders from the International Headquarters in London. The first country thus entered was France, in 1880, followed by the United States, in 1881.

2. *Doctrine.* The Salvation Army has no formal creed and gives little attention to the discussion of doctrinal differences. However, in general, it is strongly Arminian (Methodistic) rather than Calvinistic. It does not lay stress upon the Sacraments of Baptism and the Lord's Supper, regarding them as unessential. Admission to its membership is not founded upon any acceptance of creed, but is based upon the most solemn pledges to Christian and humane conduct. This includes total abstinence from intoxicating liquors and all harmful drugs. These pledges are known as the "Articles of War" and must be signed by every soldier. The form of worship is elastic, and no pre-scribed regulation is given for the conduct of services. These services include open-air meetings, a characteristic being the preaching of women, salvation meetings for the conversion of the impenitent, holiness meetings for the deepening of the spiritual life among the soldiers and adherents, junior meetings, and Sunday schools for the conversion and training of children.

3. *Polity.* The actual government of the Army is practically autocratic, though the commanding officer is assisted in decisions by officers of every grade and rank. The officers are commissioned to pass through training schools or give other evidence of abilities sufficient to qualify them for their work. Educational tests are not emphasized, although mental qualifications are taken into consideration, and the applicant is urged to improve himself mentally, socially, and religiously. The International Headquarters of the Army are in London, but each country has its own organization, under the direction of the commander, who is assisted by a responsible officer for provinces.

4. *Work.* The work carried on by the Army is divided into two important branches, called, respectively, field and social work. The field work includes the societies or corps organizations, for religious meetings which aim at the conversion of sections of the community not reached by the Church, especially the vicious and criminal classes.

In World Wars I and II the Salvation Army was active in work among the Armed Forces (although in World War II it was banned or curtailed in Axis countries). In the United States the Army has an extensive social service program (family welfare, missing persons bureau, care of unmarried mothers, settlements, children's homes, "Harbor Light" for alcoholics, USO, employment bureaus, clinics, emergency services, rural welfare, etc.).

The Salvation Army had centers in 94 countries and territories at the beginning of 1950.

Salza, Herman von. See *Military Religious Orders*, c.·

Salzburgers, Banishment of. The history of Protestantism in the Austrian crownland of Salzburg (ruled by an archbishop) is largely a history of oppression and persecution, culminating at various points in the expulsion of the Protestants. Introduced at an early period, the doctrines of Luther, in the face of repressive measures, made such progress that in 1588 Archbishop Dietrich, after a personal consultation with the Pope, gave the Protestants the choice either to return to the Church of Rome or to leave the country, the latter alternative including forfeiture of property. Numerous exiles found an asylum in Austria, Swabia, and elsewhere. These were followed by others 1613—15. Protestantism was thought to be exterminated, but it lived in secret, even among many who had outwardly returned to Catholicism, and nurtured itself on Lutheran books, carefully hidden from Catholic eyes. But the Jesuits sniffed out the heresy. Schaitberger, the leader of the Protestants, showed by a written confession that he and his associates were Lutherans and as such entitled to legal recognition under the provisions of the Treaty of Westphalia (1648). But this did not alter the intolerant course of the reigning archbishop. In the midst of winter (1685) a decree of banishment was issued, and groups of exiles, torn from their children, to say nothing of the loss of their property, wandered over the snow-clad mountains to Ulm, Augsburg, and other cities. The last edict of banishment was issued in 1731 on the pretext that the Protestants were fomenting sedition and rebellion. William I of Prussia received 20,000 fugitives, while a small number found refuge in the Colony of Georgia, in the New World. The Salzburg Colony in Georgia, for whom Samuel Urlsperger served as financial agent, was established in 1734 and became known for its evangelical fervor.

G. G. Goecking, *Vollkommene Emigrationsgeschichte von denen aus dem Erzbistum Salzburg vertriebenen Lutheranern*, Wagner, Frankfurt u. Leipzig, 1734—37; W. J. Finck, *Lutheran Landmarks and Pioneers in America*, Gen. Counc. Pub. H., 1913; A. R. Wentz, "The Salt that Kept Its Savor," *Luth. Ch. Quart.*, VIII: 13—39; N. D. Kretzmann, "The Salzburgers and Their Descendants," *CHIQ*, XVII: 33 ff.; S. Urlsperger, *Sammlung ausfuehrlicher Nachrichten von Salzburg Emigranten*, Halle, 1735—46; P. A. Strobel, *The Salzburgers and Their Descendants*, Kurtz, Baltimore, 1855.

Samoa (Samoan Islands). Formerly called the Navigator Islands, a group of islands in the South Pacific Ocean. A part belongs to the United States of America; area: 76 sq. mi.; population: 12,908; capital: Pago Pago. Western Samoa belongs to New Zealand. Area:

1,133 sq. mi.; population: 59,306. Polynesian stock.

John Williams, the Apostle of the South Seas, sent out by the London Missionary Society, worked in Samoa. In 1830 he left behind 8 Tahitian teachers. The Wesleyan Methodist Missionary Society followed in 1835. The islands are now rated as Christian. The men trained in the London Missionary Society school at Manua have done mission work in the neighboring islands, going as far as the Gilbert Islands. French Roman Catholic missionaries came in 1845.

Sanatoria. See *Hospitals, Sanatoria, Homes for Convalescents and Chronically Ill.*

Sanchez, Thomas (1550—1610). Jesuit of Spain; author of *De Matrimonio*, a work which, because of its shameless discussion of sexual immorality, belongs among the most notorious products of Jesuit casuistry.

Sanctification. In its wider sense the term *sanctification* includes all those effects of God's Word produced in the heart and life of man, beginning with his rebirth from spiritual death to spiritual life and culminating in spiritual perfection in life eternal. When used in this wide sense, sanctification includes the call, conversion, regeneration, illumination, justification, the renewing of the image of God in man (Eph. 5:26; Acts 26:18; Heb. 10:14; 2 Thess. 2:13). See *Conversion; Justification.*

When used in the narrower sense, sanctification refers to the spiritual growth which follows upon justification. The Christian by the grace of God cooperates in this work, and daily through the Holy Spirit's work faith is increased, love toward the brethren is strengthened, confidence in God and His promises is confirmed and established, the image of God is renewed, the Christian becomes more and more righteous, more and more holy, more and more blessed, and more firm in faith and godliness. It is used in this narrow sense in the Bible when it is pointed out as a consequence of justification and is thus distinguished from justification (Rom. 6:22; 2 Peter 3:18; Rom. 6:15-23).

This sanctification is the work of the Holy Spirit alone; it is the work of His grace and mercy (Phil. 2:13; Gal. 5:22f.). Sanctification, like redemption and creation, is a work of God. The Holy

Spirit teaches the believers (John 14:26), guides them into truth (John 16:13), glorifies Christ (John 16:14), fills them with His gifts (1 Cor. 12: 7-11), teaches prayer (Rom. 8:15, 26), strengthens their conviction that they are the children of God (Rom. 8:16), gives strength in the battle against the flesh (Gal. 5:16-18, 22), works righteousness, peace, joy (Rom. 14:17), and hope (Rom. 15:13).

Sanctification in the narrower sense is carried on only in the Christian, the believer, not in the unbeliever (John 3:6; Eph. 2:10; Matt. 7:16-18; Luther, St. L. Ed., I:1577). The believer's good works are not in themselves perfect, but because of the Christian's faith in the forgiveness of God, these sins of weakness found even in their best good works are forgiven (John 15:3; cf. Matt. 25:21 ff.; Luther, XIV:88; Apology, III:4; Heb. 11:4). After conversion the Christian becomes a willing co-worker with the Holy Spirit in the work of sanctification (2 Cor. 6:1; 2 Peter 3:18; 2 Cor. 7:1; Phil. 2:12, 13; 1 Tim. 4:14; F. of C. Thor. Dec., II:65, 66).

The very purpose of Jesus' work of redemption is the sanctification of man. The Christian is not only to have the righteousness of Christ, by which he covers himself and by which he is accepted before God, but the Christian is also to have his own righteousness, his own innocence (Luke 1:68, 69, 74, 75; 2 Cor. 5:15; John 15:5, 8; Eph. 2:10; 1 Peter 2:24; Matt. 7:21).

In this life sanctification remains imperfect, is a matter of growth (Eph. 4:15; 1 Cor. 3:9; Phil. 3:12; 1 Cor. 9:24), and differs in the same Christian at different times (Gal. 2:11; Gal. 5:11; Rom. 7:14-19; 1 John 1:8).

The only means through which God performs His work of sanctification is the Gospel and the Sacraments. (See *Grace, Means of*.)

The most comforting part of this doctrine is that which speaks of the completion of sanctification in heaven (1 Cor. 15:19; 13:12; Rev. 21:4; Ps. 17:15; Rev. 7:9-14). C. f. RLS, *The Abiding Word*, CPH, 1947 (II:275—98).

Extensive bibliography listed in work cited above; A. Koeberle, *The Quest for Holiness*, Augsburg Publishing Co. (c. Harper, 1936; tr. by J. C. Mattes); C. G. Carlfelt, "The Work of the Holy Spirit," *What Lutherans Are Thinking*, Wartburg Press, 1947; L. M. Eystrom, *Christ Our Sanctification*, Aug. Bk. Concern, Rock Island, Ill., 1928; C. Bergendoff, *The Secular Idea*

of Progress and the Christian Doctrine of Sanctification, Aug. Book Concern, Rock Island, 1933; F. Pieper, *Christian Dogmatics*, Vol. 3; works listed under *Dogmatics*.

Sanctified Believers. See *Holiness Bodies*, 1.

Sanctifying Grace. See *Gratia Increata*.

Sanctorum Communio. See *Church*.

Sanctus. See *Worship, Parts of*, 11.

Sanday, William (1843—1918). Anglican; b. at Holme Pierrepont, Nottingham; priest 1869; professor of exegesis at Exeter; divinity professor and canon of Christ Church, Oxford. *Authorship and Historical Character of the Fourth Gospel*, 1872; contributions to *Ellicott's Handy Commentary*, 1878; joint editor of *Variorum Bible*, 1880; *Examination of Harnack's "What Is Christianity?"* 1901, etc.

Sandel, Andrew. Luth. pastor; came to America at the request of Rudman; returned to Sweden (1719) after serving in the neighborhood of Philadelphia.

Sandemanians. See *Disciples of Christ*, 1.

Sandin, John (d. 1748). B. in Sweden; pastor in Racoon, N. Y.; one of the founders of the Pennsylvania Ministerium.

Sandomierz, Consensus of. See *Reformed Confessions*, E 5.

Sandt, G. W. B. Feb. 22, 1854, Belfast, Pa.; grad. Mt. Airy Luth. Seminary, 1881; D. D. from Thiel College, 1905; LL. D., 1922; prof. Augustana College, Rock Island, Ill., 1884—89; pastor, Weissport, Pa., 1889—91, Wilkes-Barre, Pa., 1891—96; managing editor, *The Lutheran*, 1896—1907; editor in chief 1907 to 1930; wrote: *Luther's 95 Theses*, *Christian Science Weighed and Tested*, *American Lutheran Union and Church Unity*, *Biography of Th. E. Schmauk*. D. Jan. 8, 1931.

Sandusky Resolutions. Resolutions adopted by the American Lutheran Church, Oct. 14—20, 1938, at Sandusky, Ohio. The Resolutions state that "the *Brief Statement* * of the Missouri Synod together with the *Declaration* * of our Commission be regarded as sufficient doctrinal basis between the Missouri Synod and the American Lutheran Church ... we believe the *Brief Statement* of the Missouri Synod viewed in the light of the *Declaration* of our

Commission is not in contradiction to the *Minneapolis Theses.*" * The resolutions declared willingness to continue discussion of the articles termed "nondivisive of church fellowship" in the *Declaration.* They also stated that the American Lutheran Church expected no erection of opposition altars even though fellowship were not immediately declared, and reported "marked progress" in negotiations with the U. L. C. A.

See *Minutes* of the American Lutheran Church, 1938; the resolutions are printed in the *Luth. Wit.* (Nov., 1938, p. 373) and the *CTM* (X: 59, 60), "The Fellowship Convention: Sandusky, Ohio, Oct. 14—20, 1938," *Luth. Standard,* Nov. 12, 1938, pp. 3—13.

Sangstad, Christian. See *Canada, Lutheranism in,* 24.

Sankey, Ira David (1840—1908). Methodist lay evangelist, active as choir leader and Sunday school superintendent; joined D. L. Moody in Chicago and was for years associated with him in evangelistic work; compiled *Gospel Hymns,* also *Sacred Songs and Solos,* of which millions of copies were sold.

Sankhya. See *Brahmanism,* 5.

Sansovino, Andrea (1460—1529). Tuscan sculptor and architect; appointed by Pope Julius II to build the tombs of Cardinals Rovere and Sforza; among his other works: "Baptism of Christ"; "Madonna and Child."

Santo Domingo. See *Hispaniola.*

Sapper, Karl F. W. (1833—1911). Studied at Hermannsburg and was sent to America by Pastor Louis Harms 1866; pastor at Carondelet (St. Louis), Mo., and Bloomington, Ill.; member of the Board for Colored Missions.

Saravia, Adrianus. See *Missions,* B 1.

Sarcerius (Sorck), Erasmus (1501 to 1559). B. at Annaberg, near Chemnitz; d. at Magdeburg. Taught at Luebeck, 1531—36; rector of the Latin school at Siegen, 1536; superintendent and chaplain to Count Wilhelm of Nassau, 1537, directing his efforts to the reformation of Nassau; court chaplain and preacher at Dillenburg, 1541, also superintendent of the country. The *Interim* compelled him to leave Nassau and accept a pastorate at Leipzig, 1548. He was superintendent at Eisleben as Georg Major's successor, 1554, and took a pastorate in Magdeburg in 1559. He opposed the teachings of Melanchthon

where they departed from orthodox Lutheranism. He published a catechism, commentaries, sermons, and other theological works.

Sarcophagus (in art). A stone coffin or chestlike tomb, bearing elaborate carvings and inscriptions. Many sarcophagi have been preserved from the early period of the Church, and the sculpture work on them is as elaborate as that of the paintings in the catacombs, pictures from both the Old and the New Testament being used freely; some fine specimens in Ravenna and in the Lateran Museum.

Sarkilathi, Pietari. See *Finland, Lutheranism in,* 2.

Sarpi, Paolo (1552—1623). Italian monk and historian; stern foe of the Papacy and the Jesuits; championed the cause of the Republic of Venice in its quarrel with Paul V. Sarpi's history of the Council of Trent is strongly antipapal. Sarpi has been called a semi-Protestant. He was suspected of heresy by the Inquisition. "I wear a mask," says he, "but only of necessity, because without it no one can live in Italy."

Sartorius, Ernst Wilhelm Christian (1797—1859). Confessional Lutheran theologian; ed. at Goettingen; prof. at Marburg and Dorpat; 1835—59 superintendent at Koenigsberg.

Saskatchewan Lutheran Bible Institute. See *Canada, Lutheranism in,* 20.

Satan. See *Devil.*

Satisfaction for Sin. See *Justification.*

Satornilus. See *Gnosticism,* 7 c.

Saturday School. See *Christian Education,* E 9 ff.; *Parish Education,* F 5.

Saubert, Johann (1638—88). B. at Nuremberg; at time of his death professor of theology and superintendent at Altdorf; published the *Nuernbergisches Gesangbuch* (Nuremberg Hymnal) in 1677; wrote: "Es donnert sehr, o lieber Gott."

Saupert, A. (1822—93). B. at Altdorf, Germany; a Loehe missionary; completed theological training at seminary of Ohio Synod, Columbus, Ohio; directed by Professor Winkler of Columbus, Ohio, to Evansville, Ind., 1845; pastor there to his death; joined Missouri Synod, 1848; founded all the older congregations in Evansville and vicinity.

Saurin, Jacques. Greatest French Protestant pulpit orator; b. at Nimes, 1677; pastor in London, The Hague (d. there, 1730). *Discourses upon the More Memorable Events in the Bible; Sermons.*

Savannah Resolution. A resolution adopted by the U. L. C. A. at Savannah, Ga., 1934. After citing reasons which made it desirable to have closer relationship with other Lutheran bodies, the resolution gave the following as a basis for fellowship: "We recognize as Evangelical Lutheran all Christian groups which accept the Holy Scriptures as the only rule and standard for faith and life, by which all doctrines are to be judged, and who sincerely receive the historic Confessions of the Lutheran Church (especially the Unaltered Augsburg Confession) 'as a witness of the truth and a presentation of the correct understanding of our predecessors' (Formula of Concord, Part II, Introd.; ed. Jacobs, p. 538); and we set up no other standards or tests of Lutheranism apart from them or alongside of them. We believe that these Confessions are to be interpreted in their historical context, not as a law or as a system of theology, but as a 'witness and declaration of faith as to how the Holy Scriptures were understood and explained on the matters of controversy within the Church of God by those who then lived'" (Formula of Concord, Part I, Introd.; ed. Jacobs, p. 492).

The U. L. C. reiterated this position at Minneapolis, 1944, declared that in addition to the historic Confessions "we will impose no tests of Lutheranism and beyond which we will submit to no tests of Lutheranism," and stated that it regarded itself "as in full fellowship with all those other Lutheran church bodies in America which with us accept the established Confessions."

Convention Minutes; *Doctrinal Declarations*, CPH, n. d.; E. Rinderknecht, "Lutheran Union and the United Lutheran Church," *Luth. Ch. Quart.*, XIX: 21.

Saving Faith. See *Faith.*

Savior. See *Christ Jesus.*

Savonarola, Jerome (1452—98). Dominican monk; an Italian reformer of considerable note, very properly put in line with Wyclif, Hus, and Jerome of Prague. His success, however, was only temporary, chiefly because of his confusing Church and State. He had attained to a purer knowledge of the saving truth through diligent study of Augustine and Holy Writ and, since 1489, came into the light as an eloquent, passionate, even recklessly bold preacher of repentance at Florence. Though he scathingly rebuked the sins of the rulers of his time, not even sparing the Pope, and of the people and insisted on clean living, yet he did not hold that men could be saved by their own works or by indulgences, but that the grace of God, through Christ Jesus, was the only means to this end and that really good works could be expected only where the heart had been regenerated by faith. But Savonarola also set himself up as a divinely inspired prophet and believed himself chosen to reform, not only the Church, but also the State. In many instances his predictions, both political and such as pertained to the private life of individuals, proved to be true. He became the idol of the people of Florence and vicinity, who now began to put into practice not only his moral and religious, but also his political ideals of a democratic theocracy. The Pope's attempt to dissuade him from his reformatory endeavors by the offer of the red hat was futile. He preferred the red hat of martyrdom. Meanwhile political affairs grew unfavorable for him and thwarted some of his predictions. There also ensued a famine, which pressed heavily upon the people. Popular favor began to waver, the nobles and the libertine youth had long been filled with rage against him, and now, in 1497, the papal ban was hurled at him, and the interdict was pronounced over the city. A fanatical mob took him prisoner, his bitterest enemies became his judges, and they condemned him to be hanged and burned at the stake as a demagog and heretic. He died (May 23, 1498) in pious submission to, and cheerful trust in, Him who died for him. His chief work, *Trionfo della Croce* (Triumph of the Cross), is an able apology of Christianity. Luther republished an exposition of the 51st Psalm, written by Savonarola in prison, because he considered it an example of evangelical doctrine and Christian piety.

W. H. Crawford, *Girolamo Savonarola*, Jenning & Graham, Cincinnati, 1907; P. Misciatteli, *Savonarola* (tr. by M. Peters-Roberts), Appleton, N. Y., 1930; A. G. Rudelbach, *H. Savonarola und seine Zeit*, aus den Quellen dargestellt, Perthes, Hamburg, 1835; P. Villari,

The History of Girolamo Savonarola, Longman, Green, 1863.

Savoy Declaration. See *Democratic Declarations,* 2; *Congregational and Christian Churches,* A 2.

Saxon Confession. See *Lutheran Confessions,* A 5.

Saxon Immigration. See *Lutheran Church — Missouri Synod.*

Saxons, Conversion of. See *Franks, Saxons and other Germanic Nations, Conversion of.*

Saxony, Lutheran Free Church of Saxony and Other States. 1. The spirit of indifference and unionism, which, in 1817 and later, had brought about the "Union" in Prussia between the Lutheran and Reformed Churches, had also produced in the other Lutheran State Churches a practical union between truth and error. Notorious unbelievers were not merely retained in office, but were advanced to the most important positions, while faithful preachers of the Gospel were frequently frowned upon and in some instances forced out of office. The forming of free churches, standing on the confessional basis, offered the only escape from this intolerable condition. Thus the Saxon Free Church came into existence. This body was organized by Lutherans in Saxony and Hesse-Nassau. In 1846 Pastor F. Brunn, with 28 families, withdrew from the State Church on account of the "Union" and formed the independent congregation at Steeden. (See *Brunn.*) In 1853 Pastor Hein withdrew and became pastor of two other "free" congregations. Pastor Brunn, through the study of the Bible and of Luther, of the Lutheran dogmaticians and Walther, had learned to know and love true Lutheranism and labored incessantly to spread it at home and abroad.

2. In Dresden, Saxony, an association of awakened Lutheran laymen was formed about the middle of the 19th century, which had for its object the study and spread of Lutheranism. They held private devotional meetings, in which they read the Bible, Luther's writings, the Lutheran Confessions, Brunn's *Ev. Luth. Kirche und Mission;* and through Dr. C. F. W. Walther, in 1860, these men, both at Dresden and Zwickau, became earnest readers of the *Lutheraner* and even of *Lehre und Wehre.* By these means and through their connection with Pastor Brunn they became well grounded in the

teachings of the Lutheran Church, so that, when in 1868 the abolition of the rigid pledge to the Lutheran Confessions * was agitated in Saxony, to be replaced by a vaguely worded vow, they vigorously protested to the church authorities. When, in 1871, the change went into effect, they, for conscience' sake, withdrew from the State Church as being no longer truly Lutheran and formed independent congregations. A number of the clergy had joined in the protest, but not one of them had the courage to cast his lot with these faithful Lutheran laymen. Pastors Brunn and Hein were unable, because of distance and stress of work, to minister to their fellow confessors. From the Breslau Synod they differed in the doctrine of the Church and the ministerial office. Dr. Walther, to whom they applied, recommended Pastor F. C. T. Ruhland of Pleasant Ridge, Ill., to them, who was known to them by his forty theses on the State Churches. In 1872 he was installed as pastor of Trinity Church of Dresden and St. John's Church of Planitz. In 1873 Dresden called Pastor E. Lenk, and Pastor Ruhland remained in Planitz till 1879. (See *Ruhland.*)

3. In August, 1876, a preliminary meeting was held for the purpose of organizing a synod. The draft of a constitution was laid before the congregations for approval, those in Nassau and five in Saxony, and on November 6, 1876, the Synod of the Ev. Luth. Free Church of Saxony and Other States was organized. Pastor Ruhland was the first president. At the first annual meeting at Planitz, in 1877, nine pastors (among them Lic. G. Stoeckhardt and O. Willkomm, later president), one teacher, and six lay delegates were present. The Free Church, with its official organ *Die Ev.-Luth. Freikirche* (H. J. Naumann in Dresden, publisher), bravely fought the battle of true Lutheranism and despite much opposition and many obstacles had a steady and healthy growth. A number of pastors and congregations from the State Churches joined it in the course of time. In 1892 its membership was 12 congregations, 12 pastors, and ca. 3,000 souls, in 130 localities in Saxony, Nassau, the grand duchy of Hesse, Rhenish Prussia, Hanover, and Pomerania. In 1908 the *Hermannsburger Freikirche,* seven pastors with their congregations, merged with the Saxon synod, which has (1948) 45 pastors and 15,184 baptized souls.

4. In 1922 a seminary was established in Berlin-Zehlendorf, which ob-

viated the necessity of sending students to America, which, however, is in the Russian occupation zone. On June 13, 1948, a new seminary was dedicated at Oberursel, Germany.

5. Since the revolution of 1918 the growth of the Free Church has been more rapid. A number of pastors of the *Volkskirche* joined it.

6. In 1855 Pastor N. P. Grunnet withdrew, for the same confessional reasons, from the State Church of Denmark and organized the *Ev. Luth. Free Church in Denmark*. His preaching attracted thousands. He was later assisted by his son, who had studied theology at the seminary of the Missouri Synod. The results of employing lay preachers proving disastrous in the extreme, the Missouri Synod sent over two pastors who, after Pastor Grunnet's death, took charge of the remnants of his flock. In 1911 the Danish Free Church united with the Saxon Synod.

7. In January, 1948, a union with the Ev. Luth. Church in former Old Prussia (Breslau Synod) was established on the basis of the following declaration: "The Ev. Luth. Church in former Old Prussia and the Ev. Luth. Free Church, after a series of colloquies, have reached complete agreement in faith and doctrine on the basis of unconditional submission to the Holy Scriptures and to the Lutheran Confessions, including the Formula of Concord. Both Churches recognize the concept of the Church contained in Article VII of the Augsburg Confession as decisive, in which agreement (*consentire*) concerning the doctrine of the Gospel and concerning the administration of the Sacraments is demanded. On this basis they jointly erect church fellowship in the sense of pulpit and altar fellowship." The Breslau Synod has (1948) 53 pastors and 42,897 baptized members.

Saybrook Platform. One of the platforms of Congregationalism adopted in 1705 in Connecticut, which was formally abrogated in 1784, although it remained in more or less active use for many years longer. The framers of this platform accepted the Westminster and Savoy Confessions with respect to doctrine, but not as to church government.

Sayce, Archibald Henry (1846 to 1933). Anglican, Orientalist; b. at Shirehampton; priest 1871; professor of Assyriology, Oxford, 1891; member of Old Testament Revision Company. *Mon-*

uments of the Hittites; Higher Criticism and the Verdict of the Monuments; etc.

Sayings of Jesus. See *Apocrypha,* B 2.

Scaer, Charles. B. Oct. 11, 1857, Van Wert, Ohio; ed. at Ohio Northern Univ., Ada, Ohio, and Tri-State College, Angola, Ind.; admitted to the ministry in 1900 after private study in theology; prof. at St. John's College, Winfield, Kans., 1894—1927; wrote *Treatise on Conscience;* d. June 9, 1928.

Scala Sancta (holy steps). 28 steps near the Lateran, alleged by Roman Catholics to be those ascended by Christ to the pretorium of Pilate.

Scaliger, Joseph Justus (1540 to 1609). Illustrious French classical scholar; b. at Agen, France; joined Reformed Church 1562; professor at Geneva 1572; Leyden 1593; founder of modern chronology; d. at Leyden. *De Emendatione Temporum,* etc.

Scandello, Antonio (1517—80). Composer who, though originally an Italian and a Roman Catholic, became a Lutheran and succeeded Matthaeus Le Maistre as *Kapellmeister* in Dresden. Scandelli helped introduce refreshing elements of Italian music into Lutheran church music. His *Passion According to St. John* (1561) was more dramatic and artistic than the Passions written by Johann Walther, and his setting of the Resurrection (1573?) helped pave the way for the *Historia der Auferstehung Jesu Christi* by Heinrich Schuetz (1623). Scandello's music enjoyed popularity in the 16th century.

F. Blume, *Ev. Kirchenmusik,* Potsdam, 1931; S. Kuemmerle, *Encyklopaedie der ev. Kirchenmusik,* Guetersloh, 1894; P. H. Lang, *Music in Western Civilization,* New York, 1941; H. Leichtentritt, *Geschichte der Motette,* Leipzig, 1908; C. von Winterfield, *Der ev. Kirchengesang,* Leipzig, 1941.

Scapular. Two little pieces of woolen cloth, joined by cords, worn under the clothing by devout Roman Catholics, one segment on the breast, the other on the shoulders. Scapulars were introduced by the Carmelites, to whose general, Simon Stock (d. 1265), the Virgin Mary is said to have handed a scapular with the promise, "No one dying in this scapular will suffer eternal burning." Pope John XXII (1316—34), in his *Sabbatine Bull,* relates that Mary appeared to him and informed him that she goes to purgatory every Saturday to free those who wear the scapular.

Some Romanists accept this bull as genuine, others reject it. Scapulars must be properly blessed and worn constantly to be effective. There are now about a score of different kinds, and as many of these as desired may be worn, one over the other. Since the wearing of numerous pieces of wool is very irksome in summer, a papal provision of 1910 provided that a medal may be worn instead of a scapular or any number of scapulars. This scapular medal must be separately blessed for each scapular represented, and when a scapular or medal is found, stolen, sold (except commercially), or given away, it is just so much wool or metal, the blessing having departed.

Scarlatti, Alessandro (1660—1725). Italian master of the Baroque Era, leader of the Neapolitan school of opera who excelled also as a composer of church music. Orchestral accompaniment developed a strong individuality of its own in his operas, the arias of his operas are outstanding. His church music reveals his mastery of polyphonic techniques, and his cantatas and oratorios are among the best works of his day. As was the case also with other masters of the 17th and 18th centuries (e. g., Antonio Lotti), the influence of the opera made itself felt to such an extent in Scarlatti's cantatas and oratorios that the operatic overshadowed the religious. It was through him that the A-B-A pattern of the da capo aria received its stereotyped character and general adoption.

E. J. Dent, Alessandro Scarlatti, His Life and Works, London, 1905; D. Ferguson, A History of Musical Thought, New York, 1948; D. J. Grout, A Short History of Opera, New York, 1947; R. Haas, Die Musik des Baroks, Potsdam, 1927.

Scepticism. See Skepticism.

Schade, John Caspar (1666—98). Studied at Leipzig and Wittenberg; Diaconus at Berlin, with Spener as Probst; earnest and faithful pastor; wrote "Meine Seel', ermuntre dich"; "Meine Seel' ist stille."

Schadow, Friedrich Wilhelm (1789 to 1862). Painter of historical scenes; joined with Cornelius, Overbeck, Veit, and others in the revival of the Italian renaissance; joined the Roman Church, became prof. at the Academy of Art in Berlin, then at Duesseldorf; among his paintings: The Wise and the Foolish Virgins; Christ on the Mount of Olives; Christ at Emmaus.

Schaefer, Theodore (b. 1846). Chief expositor of work of Inner Missions; since 1872 president of Deaconess Home at Altona; wrote: Die weibliche Diakonie, 3 vols.; Leitfaden der Inneren Mission; Praktisches Christentum, 4 vols.

Schaeffer, Charles Frederich. B. Sept. 3, 1807, Germantown, Pa.; ed., Univ. of Pa.; studied theology under his father; pastor, New York, 1829; Carlisle, Pa., 1829—31; and other places; Luth. prof. of theology in the Columbus sem., 1840—46; at Gettysburg, 1857 to 1864; at Philadelphia, 1864—79. In addition to translating German theological works, he wrote a commentary on Matthew and contributed to the Evangelical Review. D. Nov. 23, 1879.

Schaeffer, Charles William. B. 1813, Hagerstown, Md.; ed. Univ. of Pa. and Gettysburg Th. Sem.; pastor at Barren Hill, Pa., 1834—40; Harrisburg, Pa., 1840—49; Germantown, Pa., 1849—64; pres., General Synod, 1859; pres., General Council, 1868. Wrote : Early History of the Lutheran Church in America, 1857; contributor to Evangelical Review; translator of hymns from the German. He died in 1898.

Schaff, Philip (1819—93). Reformed theologian; b. at Chur, Switzerland; studied in Germany; traveled extensively; tutored in Berlin; professor of theology at Mercersburg, Pa., 1844; part founder of the Mercersburg theology; secretary of Sabbath Committee, New York City, 1863; professor in Union Seminary 1870, holding various chairs; prominent in the Evangelical Alliance and in the revision of the Evangelical Bible; d. in New York City. History of the Christian Church; edited translation of Lange's Bibelwerk; edited Schaff-Herzog Encyclopedia, The Nicene and Post-Nicene Fathers, etc.

Schaitberger, Joseph (1658—1733). Leader of the Salzburgers at the time of the expulsion decree in 1685. After a vain endeavor to secure legal recognition for himself and his followers by proving that they adhered to the Augsburg Confession (recognized with Calvinism and Catholicism by the Peace of Westphalia 1648), he settled at Nuremberg, supporting himself with hard labor and writing tracts for the encouragement of his oppressed associates at home.

Schaller, Johannes. B. Dec. 10, 1859, in St. Louis; d. Feb. 7, 1920, at Wauwatosa; son of Prof. G. Schaller; graduate of Northwestern College and St. Louis Seminary; pastor at Little Rock, 1881; Cape Girardeau, 1885; professor at New Ulm (then a theological seminary), 1889. When this institution was converted into a teachers' seminary, 1893, he became its president and as such exerted wide and wholesome influence in the cause of parish schools, of which he was an ardent and convincing advocate. On Hoenecke's death he was made president of Wauwatosa Seminary, 1908, taking the vacant chair of dogmatics. His scholarship was supported by a most winning personality, which reached out far beyond the classroom. His *Bibelkunde,* translated by himself and entitled *Book of Books,* was used as textbook in many Lutheran institutions. His *Pastorale Praxis* (1913) deals more fully with the problems of the Lutheran pastor in the United States. Valuable, and the best index to Schaller as theologian and man, is *Biblical Christology* (1918). His death when in his prime was a serious loss to Lutheran America.

Schaller, Johann Michael Gottlieb. B. Feb. 12, 1819, at Kirchenlamitz, Bavaria; confirmed and instructed in Latin, etc., by Pastor Wm. Loehe; attended the *Gymnasium* at Nuremberg; studied theology at Erlangen, where he graduated, 1842. After serving as vicar at Windsbach and at Kattenhochstadt, Bavaria, he came to America in 1848, at the insistence of Pastor Loehe, who was anxious to have the American Church profit by the splendid gifts of "his Timothy" and hoped to have him assume the direction of affairs in Michigan. However, Schaller became pastor of the congregation in Philadephia in 1849. He joined the Missouri Synod the same year. In 1850 he acted as vicar during the vacancy in Baltimore. At the session of the Missouri Synod of 1850 he was convinced by Walther's arguments that Loehe had fallen into error, and his love of the truth was greater than his respect and great love for his spiritual father. The same year he became pastor of the church in Detroit and later vice-president of the Northern District. From 1854 to 1872 he served as vicar (of President Wyneken), and later as pastor, of Trinity Church, St. Louis. In 1857 he was elected president of the Western District. From 1872 to 1886 he was professor of church history and other branches in Concordia Seminary, St. Louis. D. Nov. 19, 1887. Wm. Schaller, "Gottlieb Schaller," *CHIQ,* XVI: 34—48; 65—96.

Schalling, Martin (1532—1608). B. at Strassburg; attended the University at Wittenberg; was a favorite pupil of Melanchthon and a friend of Nicolaus Selnecker. He became diaconus at Regensburg, and later on at Amberg, Bavaria. He then served as preacher at Heidelberg; eventually he was appointed pastor at Nuernberg, where he remained until blindness compelled him to retire. D. at Nuernberg. His hymn "Lord, Thee I Love with All My Heart" is still a favorite.

Schartauans. A name given to the followers of Henric Schartau (1757 to 1825) of Sweden. Schartau was active chiefly at Lund and gave a new emphasis to churchmanship. See *Sweden, Lutheran Church in,* 4.

Scheele, Kurt Henning Gezelius von (1838—1918). B. at Stockholm; Swedish Lutheran theologian; professor at Upsala; bishop of Wisby; wrote on catechetics and symbolics; collaborator on Zoeckler's *Handbuch.*

Scheffler, Johann (Angelus Silesius) (1624—77). B. of Lutheran parents in Breslau, Silesia. In youth he became interested in the mystics, especially in the teachings of a Spaniard, John ab Angelis, thenceforth assuming the name Angelus. The name Silesius is derived from his native state. The cobbler Jacob Boehme, another mystic, became his preceptor. Later on he studied medicine at Breslau and also at Strassburg. He became the private physician to the Duke of Wuerttemberg-Oels, Sylvius Nimrod. Later on he was Imperial court physician to Emperor Ferdinand III. However, he soon gave up his profession and became a Catholic priest in Neisse. He ended his checkered career in a monastery. He published *Heilige Seelenlust.* He is probably best known by his hymn "Thee Will I Love, My Strength, My Tower."

Scheibel, Johann Gottfried. B. 1783 at Breslau; a fearless champion of Lutheranism; at first pastor, in 1818 also professor of theology, in his native city; wrote against Rationalism, and when Frederick William III introduced the Union of the Lutheran and Reformed Churches, he opposed it and was suspended in 1830; in 1832 he moved to Dresden, but was compelled to leave the city because of a polemical Reformation sermon; 1836 at Glauchau, 1839 at Nuremberg; d. there in 1843.

Scheidemann, Heinrich (ca. 1596 to 1663). 17th century organist of the

Katherinenkirche in Hamburg, pupil of Sweelinck, who, together with Jacob Praetorius, brought the Sweelinck style of organ playing to northern Germany. This style was later perpetuated through his pupil Johann Adam Reinken, who, in turn, helped pass it on to J. S. Bach. Scheidemann is reputed to have been a brilliant organist; his compositions reveal his solid and masterful musicianship.

G. Frotscher, *Geschichte des Orgelspiels und der Orgelkomposition*, Berlin, 1935—36.

Scheidt, Christian Ludwig (1709 to 1761). B. at Waldenburg; at time of his death *Hofrat* and librarian in Hanover; wrote "By Grace I'm Saved."

Scheidt, Samuel (1587—1654). "The most talented pupil of Sweelinck" (Eitner), and "the real founder of the German Protestant organ composition" (Leichtentritt). Scheidt was a friend of Heinrich Schuetz and Johann Hermann Schein. As organist at Halle he became the founder of the conservative and Lutheran Central German School of Organists. A prolific composer, Scheidt wrote choral as well as organ music. He was a master of form and invention, whose *Tabulatura Nova* "bids farewell to the old Nordic style and definitely associates music with the new Italo-German baroque" (Lang). Like the compositions of Sweelinck, Scheidt's music is pure, clear, and expertly contrapuntal. His rather difficult and rugged choral music bespeaks the spirit of 16th (not 17th)-century Lutheranism, and his *Goerlitzer Tabulaturbuch* was among the first *Choralbuecher* of Germany; with it is said to have begun the practice of accompanying congregational singing at the organ.

W. Apel, *Masters of the Keyboard*, Cambridge (Mass.), 1947; F. Blume, *Ev. Kirchenmusik*, Potsdam, 1931; F. Dietrich, *Geschichte des deutschen Orgelchorals im siebzehnten Jahrhundert*, Kassel, 1932; G. Frotscher, *Geschichte des Orgelspiels und der Orgelkomposition*, Berlin, 1935—36; H. Leichtentritt, *Music, History and Ideas*, Cambridge (Mass.), 1938; C. Mahrenholz, *Samuel Scheidt, sein Leben und sein Werk*, Leipzig, 1924; R. Haas, *Die Musik des Barocks*, Potsdam, 1927.

Schein, Johann Hermann (1586 to 1630). Succeeded Seth Calvisius as cantor of St. Thomas in Leipzig. His compositions reveal the influence of the Venetian masters (*e. g.*, Gabrieli) and are often highly subjective and dramatic. Though excelled by Schuetz and Scheidt, Schein wielded a great influence in his day, was an able representative of the baroque spirit in Germany, and was one of the most colorful characters in the history of Lutheran church music. Like Schuetz, he became more dramatic as he grew older.

Scheler, Max Ferdinand (1874 to 1928). German prof. of philosophy at Cologne and Frankfurt; influenced by Eucken, but later joined the followers of Husserl at Munich and investigated psychological and sociological aspects of phenomenology.

Schellenecker. See *Selnecker, Nikolaus.*

Schelling, Friedrich Wilhelm Joseph von (1775—1854). German philosopher. Prof. at Jena, Wuerzburg, Munich; since 1841 at Berlin. His philosophy underwent several changes. At first he developed his *Identitaetsphilosophie* (the ideal and the real are absolutely identical) and a pantheistic system of nature philosophy which was opposed to current rationalistic theology and greatly influenced his contemporaries. Later he became theist, influenced by the theosophist Boehme.* Still later he approached Biblical Christianity more closely.

Schelwig, Samuel (1643—1715). Lutheran theologian, violent opponent of Pietism; studied at Wittenberg; taught at Thorn, later professor of philosophy at Danzig; also pastor at the Trinitatis Church; in his quarrel with Spener and others he was joined by Loescher; wrote a number of books, particularly with regard to his controversies. See *Pietism.*

Schemelli, Georg Christian (born 1676). Cantor at Zeitz, was the editor of the *Musicalisches Gesangbuch* of 1736, which J. S. Bach helped him prepare and for which Bach wrote a number of melodies which are arias rather than hymn tunes. Though Schemelli enlisted the services of Bach in order to gain wider acceptance of his Gesangbuch, his book did not meet with general approval.

Schenk, Hartmann (1634—81). B. at Ruhla, near Eisenach, at time of his death pastor in Ostheim; wrote hymn for the close of service: "Nun, Gott Lob, es ist vollbracht."

Schenkel, Daniel (1813—85). Protestant prof. at Heidelberg; influential in the organization of the German Protestant Union.

Scherer, M. G. G. B. Mar. 16, 1861; educated at Roanoke, ordained 1883; pres. of North Carolina College, 1896 to 1899; prof. there, 1901—04; pres. United Synod in the South, 1914—18; sec. of United Lutheran Church, 1918 to 1932; wrote, with Knubel, *Our Church;* author of *Christian Liberty and Christian Unity;* d. March 9, 1932.

Schernberg, Theoderich. Lived at end of fifteenth century, was clergyman at Muehlhausen, known especially for his mystery play based on the life of the female Pope Johanna, a play published a century later by Tilesius of Hirschberg.

Schertzer, Johann Adam (1628 to 1683). Prof. of theology at Leipzig; author of an excellent Hebrew grammar and of a number of dogmatic and polemic works: *Breviarium Theologiae; Systema Theologiae; Collegium Anticalvinianum.*

Scheurl, Christoph Gottlieb Adolf (1811—93). Studied in Erlangen and Muenchen; prof. in Erlangen, chiefly in the fields of Roman law and canon law; coeditor of *Protestantismus und Kirche;* wrote *Ueber die lutherische Kirche in Bayern* and other monographs showing a sound Lutheran background.

Schicht, Johann Gottfried (1753 to 1823). Early training as organist and pianist; law student at Leipzig; pianist at *Gewandhauskonzerte;* afterward conductor; *Kantor* of Thomaskirche; three oratorios and other sacred music.

Schick, Georg. B. Feb. 25, 1831, attended the *Gymnasium* at Frankfort on the Main; studied theology and philosophy at Erlangen, Berlin, Heidelberg, graduated 1851; studied at the Sorbonne (Paris); private tutor; refused to enter the service of the unionistic State Church as assistant pastor in Frankfort; joined Missouri Synod as pastor in Chicago 1854; professor of ancient languages at Concordia College (St. Louis, Fort Wayne) 1856, with title of Conrector, later Rector; made Doctor of Philosophy 1906 by St. Louis Seminary; retired 1914; d. Jan. 3, 1915. He was a master of the science of philology and of the art of teaching the classical languages.

L. Fuerbringer, "Rector George Schick," *80 Eventful Years,* CPH, 1944.

Schieferdecker, Georg Albert. Born Mar. 12, 1815, in Leipzig, Saxony; graduate of University of Leipzig; came over with M. Stephan; ordained 1841 as pastor in Monroe Co., Ill.; pastor in Altenburg, Mo.; President of Western District, 1854. Divested of the pastorate by his congregation and of his membership in Missouri Synod for his chiliasm, he joined the Iowa Synod. Renouncing his chiliasm, he again joined Missouri and became pastor in Hillsdale and Coldwater, Mich., and (1876) in New Gehlenbeck, Ill.; d. Nov. 23, 1891. Author of devotional books.

A. R. Suelflow, *Georg Albert Schieferdecker and His Relation to Chiliasm in the Iowa Synod* (unpublished B. D. thesis in Concordia Seminary, St. Louis, library), 1946.

Schilling, Johann. One of the rebellious spirits in the Peasants' War, appearing on the scene between 1520 and 1525; was guilty of promulgating rebellion against the constituted authorities, especially in Augsburg, where he had a strong following; he disappeared during the war against the nobles.

Schinkel, Karl Friedrich (1781 to 1841). German architect; studied drawing and design at Berlin; professor at Berlin Royal Academy; erected many public buildings and churches; books on architecture.

Schirmer, Michael (1606—73). Studied at Leipzig; taught at the Gray Friars' *Gymnasium* in Berlin; had many domestic and personal afflictions; wrote: "Nun jauchzet, all' ihr Frommen"; "O Heil'ger Geist, kehr' bei uns ein."

Schism. See *Heresy, Fellowship.*

Schism Between East and West. The complete and permanent separation of the Greek and Roman churches was long a-preparing. The first tangible beginning may be said to have lain in the formal adoption of the *Filioque* * from the Athanasian into the Nicene Creed by the Council of Toledo, 589. The Greeks called this a falsifying of that symbol. The second Trullan Council of Constantinople (*Quinisextum*), 692, decided a number of differences between the two churches in favor of the Greeks. (Certain Latin council decrees and papal decretals were ruled out as sources of canon law, while certain Greek documents were added, some rulings of the Roman Church concerning celibacy, fastings, images, etc., were condemned, and the Patriarch of Constantinople once again was declared equal to the Bishop of Rome). But the matter became really acute when Photius, Patriarch of Constantinople, whom Pope Nicholas I would not recognize, called the Eastern bishops to a council at Constantinople in 867, at the same time charging the Pope with divers heresies (falsifying of a symbol, false doctrine of the Holy Ghost, of fasting, etc.). This gave the threatening schism a doctrinal basis and made of a personal quarrel a quarrel of the churches. The council took sides with Photius and pronounced the ban upon Nicholas. Although a later council at Constantinople, 869, condemned Photius and favored the Pope, yet a politico-ecclesiastical question concerning Bulgaria prevented a real cementing of the two churches. Later Photius again came into power, and because he would not agree to give up his claims to Bulgaria at another synod at Constantinople, 879, he was afterward put under the ban by the Pope. The quarrel, after resting for two hundred years, broke out again when Michael Cerularius, Patriarch of Constantinople, in 1053, renewed the accusations of Photius, adding as a new indictment the Roman practice of using unleavened bread in the Lord's Supper. In 1054 each party put the other under the ban, and thus the rupture became complete, and has never again really been healed, though various attempts were made, the last and most energetic, and for a brief time seemingly successful, under Joannes VII Palaeologus at Florence, 1439. The doctrinal differences named were probably not the most vital reasons for the schism, but rather the unwillingness of the East to submit to the Pope.

Schism, Papal (*Great Schism*). The great division in the ranks of the Church at the end of the fourteenth and the beginning of the fifteenth century, agitating and shattering the Church as no other schism had done before. After the death of Pope Gregory XI, in 1378, sixteen cardinals residing at Rome elected Archbishop Bartholomew of Bari as Pope Urban VI, while thirteen other cardinals, dissatisfied with their choice, went to Avignon, in southern France and elected Cardinal Robert of Geneva as Pope Clement VII, alleging that coercion had been brought to bear upon the College of Cardinals at the election in Rome. Sentiment in Italy and also in Germany, England, Denmark, and Sweden favored Urban VI, while France acknowledged Clement VII, later drawing also Scot-

land, Savoy, Castile, Aragon, and Navarre to his cause. Thus two Popes, each with his College of Cardinals, were arrayed against each other, the controversy occasionally assuming alarming proportions and being carried on with great bitterness. Urban VI was followed by Boniface IX (1389—1404), Innocent VIII (1404—06), and Gregory XII (1406—15). Clement VII (died 1394) was followed by Benedict XIII. In order to remove the schism, the Council of Pisa (1408) deposed both Gregory XII and Benedict XIII, electing in their place Alexander VI, who was succeeded in 1410 by John XXIII. But the two deposed Popes refused to acknowledge the action of the council, with the result that three men now claimed to be the successors of Peter. The Council of Constance (1414—18) in 1415 declared that it possessed the supreme ecclesiastical authority. It deposed John XXIII and once more declared Benedict XIII as a schismatic, the latter, however, defying the sentence of deposition till his death in 1424. The council, on November 11, 1417, elected Martin V, and this election gradually received the approval of the majority of church dignitaries. The last opposition came to an end in 1429, when Clement VIII, nominal successor of Benedict XIII, relinquished his dignity.

Schlatter, Adolf von (1852—1938). Reformed theologian; studied at Basel and Tuebingen; professor at Greifswald, 1888; Berlin, 1893; Tuebingen, 1898; his theology of the modern type; wrote on Biblical theology, historical and exegetical subjects.

Schlatter, Michael (1716—90). German Reformed pioneer; b. in Switzerland; ordained in Holland; sent by the Holland synods as missionary to German Reformed people of America 1746; pastor in Philadelphia and Germantown 1747; organized German Reformed Synod same year; resigned his charge 1755; chaplain of Royal American Regiment 1757—59; thereafter in retirement; d. near Philadelphia.

Schlegel, Johann Adolf (1721—93). Lutheran theologian. B. at Meissen. Deacon at Schulpforta, near Naumburg, 1751; first pastor and professor of religion at Zerbst, 1754; at Hanover, 1759; superintendent and member of the consistory there, 1775; superintendent of the county of Hoyerswerda, 1782. Wrote seventy-five original hymns; rewrote eighty-seven.

Schleiermacher, Friedrich Daniel Ernst (1768—1834). 1. B. in Breslau; d. in Berlin; founder of modern Protestant theology; the son of a Reformed army chaplain; entered the Moravian Seminary at Barby in 1785; dissatisfied, he left in 1787 for Halle, where he studied Kant and Greek philosophy; for a time private tutor; in 1796 Reformed preacher at the Charité in Berlin. Against the then prevailing "enlightenment" he wrote, in 1799, his *Reden ueber die Religion*, in which he gave his conception of religion and the Church. Religion is to him "the taste and feeling for the infinite." Of this work it is said that it has influenced modern theology more than any other work; but it utterly failed to do justice to the Christian religion. Schleiermacher here lays the foundation for the entirely subjectivistic character of present-day theology. According to him, Christianity does not even claim to be the final form of all religion. Traces of the philosophy of Kant, Leibniz, and Spinoza may be found in this work.

2. In 1802 Schleiermacher had himself transferred to Stolpe; in 1804 he was appointed professor at Halle, 1807 in Berlin; 1809 he became preacher at the *Dreifaltigkeitskirche* and in 1810 dean of the theological faculty of the new university. In this double capacity he remained to the end of his life. In 1811 he issued his *Kurze Darstellung des theologischen Studiums*, in which he showed theology as an organic whole and practical theology as its fruit. His chief work is *Christlicher Glaube, nach den Grundsaetzen der evangelischen Kirche im Zusammenhang dargestellt* (1821—22). Here religion is defined as the feeling of absolute dependence upon God, who is the highest Causality, manifesting Himself in His attributes of omnipotence, eternity, omnipresence, and omniscience. In Christ was the highest consciousness of God; redemption through Him is the communication of His consciousness of God to the believer. The result in the faithful is regeneration. Christ's supernatural birth, resurrection, ascension, and second advent are discarded. The Holy Spirit is regarded as a spirit proceeding from Christ and pervading the Church, the community of the regenerate. — Schleiermacher, though attacking Rationalism, did not teach Biblical Christianity. He was both a rationalist and a pantheist. His pernicious influence upon modern Protestant theology is clearly traceable, having led

it into the paths of developing its doctrines from the inner consciousness of the individual heart instead of founding it upon the impregnable rock of Holy Scriptures.

R. B. Brandt, *The Philosophy of Schleiermacher*, Harpers, 1941; R. Munro, *Schleiermacher*, Paisley: Alexander Gardner, 1903; Frederica Rowan, *The Life of Schleiermacher* (Autobiography and Letters), Smith, Eldor and Co., London, 1860; the collected works were published by Reimer in Berlin; J. T. Mueller, "Schleiermacher, His Theology and Influence," *CTM*, XV:73—93.

Schleininger, G. J. Nikolaus. Prominent Jesuit and homiletician of the last century, his most imporatnt work being a monograph on the ministerial office according to the example and the teaching of the saints and the greatest church orators, on the basis of which he published a shorter summary.

Schleswig-Holstein Ev. Luth. Missionary Society at Breklum. See *Missions,* B 17.

Schletterer, Hans Michel (1824—93). Founder of the Augsburg School of Music. He wrote several cantatas and 17 books of choruses.

Schleupner, Dominicus. Evangelical theologian of the Reformation period; was canonicus in Breslau, when he decided to continue his theological studies in Wittenberg; became preacher in Nuernberg in 1522 at Luther's recommendation, where he was active in establishing sound Lutheranism.

Schlick, Arnold (ca. 1460—1527). Though blind, he became famous as an organist and lutanist and was the author of the first German tablature book. From his *Spiegel der Orgelmacher und Organisten* of 1511 we can ascertain the character and structure of German organs of the Reformation era. Schlick was instrumental in improving the organ, increasing its compass to three octaves in the manuals and to one and one-half in the pedals. Many of his compositions were based on liturgical texts. Like Paumann, he was fond of having the *cantus firmus* in the bass.

W. Apel, *Masters of the Keyboard,* Cambridge (Mass.), 1947; G. Frotscher, *Geschichte des Orgelspiels und der Orgelkomposition*, Berlin, 1935—36.

Schmalkaldic League. A defensive league of Evangelical princes organized at Schmalkalden, in Hesse-Nassau,

Germany. When after the second Diet of Speier, 1529, the future looked very dark for the Protestants, a meeting was called by Philip of Hesse, Nov. 25, 1529, to consider what could be done if the resolution of the Diet (to enforce the Edict of Worms) was carried out. On Dec. 22, 1530, they again met to protest to the Emperor against the recess of the Diet of Augsburg which gave the Protestants six months of grace, after which force would be used to bring them back into the old Church. When the Emperor did not react, the League was organized, March 29, 1531, by nine princes and eleven cities, for six years. It was purely a defensive alliance, against attack threatened by the Emperor and the Diet, and especially by the two Catholic Leagues, the League of Regensburg and the League of Dessau, formed in 1524 and 1525, resp. Therefore Luther hesitantly gave his consent (he had refused to sanction the League of Torgau in 1526); he was persuaded that the Emperor, in attacking a principality for the sake of the people's faith, was overstepping his constitutional rights; princes therefore had the right to defend their land against such an attack without being guilty of rebellion. Action did not immediately result, because the Emperor needed the aid of the Protestant princes against the Turk; hence a truce was declared in the Peace of Nuernberg, 1532. Denmark and a number of German princes and cities joined, strengthening the League; even Catholic countries offered aid against the growing power of the Hapsburgs. 1535 the League was prolonged for another ten years. After 1540 the League disintegrated and was defeated in the Schmalkaldic War.* TH

Schmalkaldic War. Until ca. 1540 the policy of Charles V toward the Evangelicals was one of reconciliation; for this purpose he wanted a council called. But time and again the Pope frustrated his desires. When in 1542 Charles practically forced him to call the Council of Trent, the Pope issued a program for this council which made it impossible for Protestants to take part; and Charles saw his last hope of reuniting the two parties in the Church by negotiation defeated. He now decided to use force of arms. The League was craftily undermined, the scandalous bigamy of Landgrave Philip of Hesse and the jealousy of Duke Maurice of Saxony offering welcome opportunity. In June, 1546, the two leaders of the League, Philip of Hesse and

Elector John Frederick of Saxony, were put under the ban of the Empire. The forces of the Protestants were split when Maurice betrayed his allies and invaded Electoral Saxony; and the Emperor decisively defeated the League at Muehlberg, April 24, 1547. The League was dissolved; the Emperor imposed the Augsburg and Leipzig Interim on Protestant Germany. The purpose of the League, however, was attained when in 1552 Maurice turned against the Emperor and, with the help of France, forced him to agree to the Treaty of Passau, 1552, and finally to the Religious Peace of Augsburg, 1555, which granted to princes the free exercise of the faith of their choice in their lands (*cuius regio eius religio*). The princes' choice was only between Lutherans and Roman Catholics; Calvinists were not included. This action became one of the causes of the Thirty Years' War. TH

Schmauck, Theodore Emmanuel. The leading spirit in the Lutheran General Council at the beginning of the 20th century and its last president, who "cast the great influence of his personality into the balance for the advancement of conservative Lutheranism"; the son of Pastor Benj. Wm. Schmauck; b. in Lancaster, Pa., May 30, 1860; entered Pennsylvania University 1876; graduating with high honors in 1880, he entered the Philadelphia Seminary. Upon his graduation in 1883 he became the associate of his father in "Old Salem" Church in Lebanon, Pa. He continued to serve this church after his father's death till his own end came. In 1889 Schmauck became the literary editor of the *Lutheran* and took over the editorship of the *Lutheran Church Review* in 1895. In 1896 he began the publication of the *Lutheran Graded Series and Commentaries for Sunday Schools*. He was pre-eminently the Lutheran pioneer in this field. His qualifications for leadership caused him to be elected, in 1903, to the presidency of the General Council, an office which he held until this body was merged into the United Lutheran Church (1918). Under his able leadership the General Council reached its confessional high-water mark in 1907. In 1911, in addition to his many duties as pastor, preacher, editor, president, and member of many boards, he became professor of Apologetics and Ethics at Mount Airy. When the prospects of a merger between the General Council, the General Synod, and the United Synod in the South began to materialize, Schmauck's conservatism at first caused him to look with disfavor upon such a union. But his influence was on the wane. He yielded and became one of the chief promoters of the merger movement and also of the organization of the National Lutheran Council, 1918. With all his other activities he found time to write a large number of books; outstanding among them: *A History of the Lutheran Church in Pennsylvania, 1638—1820; The Confessional Principle and the Confessions of the Lutheran Church* (with Dr. Benze), "an epoch-making work" (Jacobs); *How to Teach in Sunday School*, the ripe fruit of many years of study in this field. Died March 23, 1920.

G. W. Sandt, *Theodore Emmanuel Schmauck, D. D., LL. D., A Biographical Sketch with Liberal Quotations from His Letters and Other Writings*, United Luth. Publishing House, Philadelphia, 1921.

Schmelen, Heinrich (1777—1848). Founder of the Nama mission; forced to flee to London before the French; studied in Berlin, but returned to London; did mission work among the Hottentots, then went to Namaland; translated four Gospels with the help of his wife, a native; his work taken over by the Rhenish Society.

Schmid, Christian Friedrich (1794 to 1852). B. at Bickelsberg, Wuerttemberg; d. at Tuebingen. Studied at Maulbronn and Tuebingen. Lecturer in practical theology at Tuebingen, 1819; associate professor, 1821, and full professor there, 1826. His influence was chiefly due to his strong Christian character and successful teaching. Inclined to Bengel's Lutheranism, he opposed Hegelian philosophy and the Biblical criticism of F. Chr. Baur.

Schmid, Frederick. B. at Walddorf, Wuerttemberg, Germany, Sept. 6, 1807; came to America, 1833; preached in Detroit, Mich., Aug. 18, 1833; organized *First German Society of Scio*, first German parish in Michigan; also began first Lutheran mission among Chippewa Indians; first Lutheran pastor in Michigan; d. Aug. 30, 1883.

Schmid, Heinrich (1811—85). Prof. at Erlangen 1848—81; best known for his *Dogmatik der ev. luth. Kirche*, a presentation of Lutheran dogmatics from orthodox Lutheran theologians; translated into English by Hay and Jacobs; *Church History* and other historical writings.

Schmidt, Carl Christoph. B. Nov. 8, 1843, at Bonfeld, Wuerttemberg; graduate of St. Louis Seminary 1868; pastor in New York City, Elyria, O., Indianapolis, Ind., St. Louis, Mo.; Vice-President of Western District of Missouri Synod 1889—91; President, 1891—98; Vice-President of Missouri Synod 1899 to 1908; Doctor of Divinity *honoris causa*; wrote: *Erkenntnis des Heils; Glaube und Liebe; Katechismuspredigten; Lasset euch versoehnen mit Gott; Leichenreden; Weg des Lebens*. D. Oct. 25, 1925.

Schmidt, Christian (1683—1754). B. at Stolberg, at time of his death pastor of the *Bergkirche* near Eilenburg; wrote: "Frohlocket, jung und alt."

Schmidt, Erasmus (1560—1637). Adjunct of philosophy at Wittenberg, professor of Greek and mathematics; author of a Latin translation of the New Testament with notes, an improvement on Beza's work; also editor of a concordance of the New Testament, which was the basis of K. G. Bruder's *Concordance*.

Schmidt, Friedrich August. B. in Germany Jan. 3, 1837; graduate of Concordia College 1853 and of Concordia Seminary 1857; pastor at Eden, N. Y., and Baltimore (Missouri Synod 1857 to 1861); teacher at Luther College 1861—72; Norwegian Synod professor at Concordia Seminary 1872—86, Luther Seminary 1876—86, Anti-Missouri Seminary 1886—90, Augsburg Seminary 1890—93, United Norwegian Church Seminary 1893—1912; edited *Lutheran Watchman* 1866—67, *Altes und Neues* 1880—85, *Luthersk Vidnesbyrd* 1882 to 1890, *Luthersk Kirkeblad* 1890—95; author of *Naadevalgsstriden* 1881; *Sandhed og Fred* 1914; created D. D. by Capital University 1883. D. May 15, 1928.

Schmidt, Hans Christian. B. May 25, 1840, at Flensburg, Schleswig; d. March 6, 1911, in India; trained by Groenning for missionary work; commissioned by the American Lutheran General Synod 1870; arrived at Rajahmundry, India, 1870; first home furlough in 1883; second, 1894; declined recall to America 1901, removing to the Nilgiris 1903, where he died. Was a successful missionary.

Schmidt, Johann Eusebius (1670 to 1745). Studied at Jena and Erfurt; curate, then pastor at Siebleben, near Gotha; popular hymn writer; wrote: "Fahre fort, fahre fort, Zion."

Schmidt, Martin Joseph. B. Mar. 25, 1846, at Altenburg, Mo.; graduated at Concordia Seminary (St. Louis) 1868; pastor in Platte Co., Mo., then in Clinton Co., Mich., finally at Saginaw, Mich., 1872—94; President of Michigan District 1882—91; president of Concordia College, Fort Wayne, Ind., 1894 to 1903, then professor till 1917; D. D. (St. Louis). D. May 1, 1931.
W. F. Kruse, "Prof. Martin Joseph Schmidt, D. D.," *CHIQ,* V: 35—46.

Schmidt, Sebastian (1617—96). Rector and minister at Lindau; professor of theology in Strassburg during the Thirty Years' War; wrote works on exegetical and Biblical theology, *Collegium Biblicum;* edited a Latin translation of the Bible, published at Strassburg after his death.

Schmidt, Wilhelm (1839—1912). German Protestant theologian; pastor at Schoenstedt, Henschleben, and Cuertow; professor at Breslau; author of: *Zur Inspirationsfrage; Der alte Glaube und die Wahrheit des Christentums,* and others.

Schmidt, William. B. Dec. 11, 1803, at Dunsbach, Wuerttemberg, Germany; studied at Halle Univ.; tutor in family of British Consul, 1826; came to America 1826; pastor at Weinsberg, O. (1827 to 1828); Canton, O. (1828—30); prof. and pres. of Capital Univ. (1830—37). D. Nov. 3, 1839.

Schmidt, William. B. July 26, 1855, at Hermannsburg, Hanover, Germany; came to America (1871); studied at Capital Univ. (1872—75, B. A.; 1875 to 1876, M. A.; 1877—78, D. C. T.); pastor, Mercer Co., O. (1878—81); Pomeroy, O. (1881—86); prof. at Luther Seminary, Afton, Minn., and St. Paul, Minn. (1886 to 1927); Member Intersynodical Committee of the Ohio Synod (1917—31), of the Board of Foreign Missions of ALC (1930—31); vice-pres. of Minn. Dist. of Ohio Synod. Wrote *Sighard the Centurion, Aethelburga, Geschichte der Ohio Synode, Ramuldu, Sternenauge, Die goldene Quelle, Landolf, Durch Luther befreit, Der Herr ist Gott, Gedenkschrift der Ohio Synode, Friedensklaenge, Christ Conquers, Ben Juda the Shepherd, Pantherleap.* Associate editor of *Lutherische Kirchenzeitung;* editor, *Lutherischer Kalender.* D. May 31, 1931.

Schmieder, Heinrich C. See *Canada, Lutheranism in,* 14.

Schmieder, Heinrich Eduard (1794 to 1893). Theologian of the Evangeli-

cal Church; studied in Schulpforta and Leipzig; embassy preacher in Rome, then taught at Schulpforta; after 1839 at the Wittenberg Theological Seminary, with which he was connected for the rest of his life; showed strong tendency toward theosophy and was attracted by the mysticism of Jacob Boehme; contributor to the Gerlach Bible, also wrote a devotional exposition of John 17.

Schmolck, Benjamin (1672—1737). B. at Brauchitzchdorf. Studied at Leipzig and became assistant to his father at Brauchitzchdorf. After a year he was called to the Friedenskirche at Schweidnitz, Silesia, where he remained till his death. He wrote a number of devotional books, in which his hymns were included, a total of 1183. He was the most popular German hymn writer in his day. He was called "the second Gerhardt" and "the Silesian Rist."

Schmucker, Beale M. B. Aug. 26, 1827, in Gettysburg, Pa.; son of S. S. Schmucker; a great Lutheran liturgical scholar; educated at Gettysburg; held pastorates at Martinsburg, Va., Allentown, Easton, Reading, and Pottstown, Pa., where he died in 1888. Always more conservative than his father, he became a member of the General Council through the influence of Dr. Krauth. Coeditor of *Hallesche Nachrichten.*
A. Spaeth, *Memorial of B. M. Schmucker,* Gen. Counc. Pub. H., Philadelphia, 1889.

Schmucker, John George. B. Aug. 18, 1771, in Michaelstadt, Germany; emigrated 1785; noted pastor and author in Lutheran General Synod; studied under Paul Henkel and in University of Pennsylvania; joined Pennsylvania Ministerium in 1792; pastor at Hagerstown and York. D. Oct. 7, 1854.

Schmucker, Samuel Sprecher. Son of John G., b. Feb. 28, 1799, Hagerstown, Md.; ed., U. of Pa. and Princeton Theol. Seminary; D. D., U. of Pa. and Rutgers College; pastor, York, Pa,; New Market, Va. In 1823 began privately preparing students for the ministry; founder, Gettysburg College; prof. there 1826 to 1864; one of the authors of the *Definite Platform.** Author: *Lutheran Manual on Scriptural Principles; Retrospect of Lutheranism in the U. S.; Vindication of American Lutheranism;* etc. He was the most influential man in the Lutheran General Synod between 1826 and 1864. D. July 26, 1873.
P. Anstadt, *Life and Times of S. S. Schmucker,* P. Anstadt & Sons, York,

Pa., 1896; V. Ferm, *The Crisis in American Lutheran Theology*, Century, N. Y., 1927; A. R. Wentz, "The Work of Samuel Simon Schmucker," *Luth. Quart.*, LVII: 61—89; L. Schmucker, *The Schmucker Family and the Lutheran Church in America*, 1937.

Schnedermann, Georg Hermann (1852—1917). Luth. theologian; studied at Leipzig and Erlangen; taught in Switzerland, continued studies at seminary in Leipzig; taught at Basel, later again at Leipzig; interested in particular in Bible exposition and the background of the life of Jesus; wrote: exposition of Corinthians and the Captivity Letters in *Strack's Commentary* and monographs in the field of systematic theology.

Schneegasz, Cyriacus (1546—97). Studied at Jena; pastor at Friedrichroda, at the same time adjunct to the superintendent at Weimar; diligent pastor, mighty in Scriptures; wrote: "Das neugeborne Kindelein"; "Herr Gott Vater, wir preisen dich."

Schneider, Johann Christian Friedrich (1786—1853). Attended Zittau *Gymnasium* and Leipzig University; studied music under Unger at Zittau; organist and musical director in Leipzig; many oratorios, cantatas, and choruses.

Schneider, Johannes (1857—1930). German theologian; studied at Greifswald, Leipzig, Bonn, and Muenster; pastor at Wartburg, Lichtenau, and Elberfeld; statistician of Ev. High Consistory (1918—23); honorary prof. at Berlin Univ. (1923—31); Executive Director of German Ev. Church Council (1924—27); emeritus (1927—30); wrote: *Die Saekularisation von 1810 und die Dotationsansprueche der Kirche, Die Kant-Laplacesche Weltentstehungstheorie und die Schoepfungsgeschichte der Bibel*, and others. He continued the publication of *Kirchliches Jahrbuch fuer die Ev. Landeskirchen Deutschlands* begun by his father. The American Lutheran Statistical Assn. provided money for one edition.

Schneller, Johann Ludwig (1820 to 1896). B. at Erpfingen, Wuerttemberg; d. in Jerusalem; school teacher at Bergfelden, 1838; Klein-Eisslingen, 1839—40; Gansslosen, 1840—42; Vaihingen, 1843 to 1847; St. Chrischona, near Basel, 1847—54; transferred to Jerusalem, 1854 to 1860, where he founded large orphanage after massacre in Syria by Mohammedans, teaching various branches of handicraft; also organized a teachers' seminary and an asylum for the blind. His work was continued in Jerusalem by his son Ludwig.

Schnepf, Erhard (1495—1558). Influenced by Luther's Disputation at Heidelberg in 1518; reformed Nassau; reformed Wuerttemberg on the return of Duke Ulrich; driven from his chair at Tuebingen for opposing the Interim in 1548; helped to organize the University of Jena; opposed the Philippists.

Schnorr von Carolsfeld, Baron Julius (1794—1872). German painter; trained principally at Vienna and Rome; earlier work shows influence of Duerer; later joined the classicists; became associated with Cornelius, Overbeck, Schadow, and Veit; later work in style of Renaissance; distinguished especially for his *Bible in Pictures*, full of creative power.

Schober, Gottlieb. B. 1756; trained in the Moravian faith; successful lawyer; late in life entered the ministry and became pastor at Salem, N. C.; he drew up the "Proposed Plan" for the General Synod; prominent in organizational work of the General Synod; pres. of General Synod, 1825; member of the Board of Directors of Gettysburg Seminary; d. 1838.

Schodde, George Henry. B. April 15, 1854; Allegheny, Pa.; ed. Theol. Seminary, Columbus, O., and Universities of Tuebingen and Leipzig; specialist in Hebrew and Semitic languages; pastor, Winchester and Martin's Ferry, O., 1877—80; prof. at Columbus, O., seminary from 1880 on; editor, *Lutheran Standard*, 1880—1901; of *Theological Magazine* since 1897; translator and writer: *Outline of Biblical Hermeneutics* and *The Protestant Church in Germany*. D. Sept. 15, 1917.

Schoeberlein, Ludwig (1813—81). A Lutheran theologian who enjoys wide fame as a liturgiologist, helped prepare the liturgy used in the Castle Church in Hanover. His greatest accomplishment was his *Schatz des liturgischen Chor- und Gemeindegesangs*, in which much material suitable for use in Lutheran liturgical services was made available. This work influenced liturgiologists of the Lutheran Church, including Friedrich Lochner. In 1875 Schoeberlein began to edit and publish *Siona*, a periodical devoted to church music and liturgics.

Schoenherr, Johann Heinrich (1770 to 1826). German theosophist. His theology, which claimed to harmonize revelation and natural sciences, is dualistic. Fire and water are principles of all reality. The universe and God are the result of their union and interaction.

Schoenherr, Karl Gottlob (1824 to 1912). Painter of historical subjects; prof. at the academy in Dresden; many Biblical pictures, among them "Christ at the Door."

Schola Cantorum. See *Gregorian Music.*

Scholasticism. 1. The name of the dominant Occidental theology, chiefly dogmatics, of the later Middle Ages, so called from its being taught in the schools. It did not aim at creating new doctrines, but generally took for granted that the then existing *corpus doctrinae* of the Church, both Scriptural and man-made doctrines, was the embodiment of the truths of religion, and by dialectics (examining and dissecting the concepts) and speculation (investigating the nature of transcendental matters) it attempted to discuss these doctrines, to comprehend, harmonize, and prove them, not from the Bible, but from reason. The manner of this reasoning was largely patterned after that of Aristotle, whose philosophical works became known to Western thinkers in the thirteenth century.

2. A mooted philosophical question gave rise to opposing factions in Scholasticism during the whole time of its domination; *viz.,* whether the general concepts are themselves real, whether one knows the essence of things by their means, or whether these concepts are merely a method of thinking required by the peculiarities of our reason, without guarantee that our thinking really grasps the nature of things. On this question philosophers were divided into three schools: two diverging schools of Realism and a school of Nominalism. Nominalism held, with the Stoics, that the general concepts (*universalia*), which designate the common characteristics of a class of things, are mere abstractions made by human reason from the existing objects (*nomina*) and having no reality outside of the human mind (*universalia* POST *res*); but Realism, with Plato and Aristotle, contended for the reality of the general concepts, for their objective existence before, and outside of, the human mind. But the one school of Realism, following Plato, taught that the general concepts were actually and really present as prototypes in the divine reason, before the things themselves came into being, and then also in the human mind before the contemplation of the empirical things (*universalia* ANTE *res*), while the other school, with Aristotle, considered the general concepts to lie in the things themselves and thence to get into the human mind only by means of experience (*universalia* IN *rebus*). Since Augustine, Realism had dominated in philosophical theology, until, toward the end of the 11th century, Roscelinus advocated Nominalism, applying it chiefly to the doctrine of the Trinity. He was chiefly opposed by Anselm of Canterbury, the true father of Scholasticism.

3. Other celebrated exponents of Scholasticism were Abélard, Peter Lombard, Alexander of Hales, Albertus Magnus, Thomas Aquinas, Duns Scotus (the former a Dominican, the latter a Franciscan; after them are named the Thomist and Scotist factions, the former given to Aristotelian Realism, the latter to Platonic, Occam (Nominalist), and Biel.*

4. In the 12th century Scholasticism was fighting for recognition; in the 13th it reached its zenith; in the 14th and 15th it declined and degenerated altogether into a petty wrangling over words. Though, as thinkers, some of the Scholastics ranked high, they were not really theologians, since they lacked the one essential of a theologian, the purpose and ability of setting forth nothing more or less than the truths of the Bible.

5. The *mystics* of the Middle Ages, in part, stood out as opponents of dialectic Scholasticism, as Bernard of Clairvaux,* Rupert (the former also a champion of Biblical theology); in part they blended Mysticism and Scholasticism, as especially Bonaventura.* Roger Bacon was another of the few learned men of those days who contended for the sole authority of the Scriptures; also Nicolaus de Lyra, Gerson,* and some others.

Schongauer, Martin (ca. 1445—91). German painter, himself a pupil of Isenmann; teacher of Holbein the Elder and Deurer; delicacy combined with monumental effects; painted Madonna of the Rose Bower.

School Auxiliary. See *Parish Education, J.*

Schools, Early Christian. The term "school" is here used not only for actual places of instruction, but also for theological tendencies. In some instances, adherents of a school imitated pagans (Tertullian, *De Pallio*) and spoke of Christianity as a "philosophy" and Christ as a "philosopher." Six schools became especially prominent in the early ages:

1. *Alexandrian.* At Alexander a university developed out of the catechumenate school. It flourished under Pantaenus (d. 202; teacher of Clement; made missionary journey to India), Clement,* and Origen.* Its chief characteristics were allegorical exegesis * and speculative theology, influenced by Philo.

2. *Roman.* The term "Roman School" is used for a tendency which flourished under Hippolytus.* Although Hippolytus used typology, he did not go to the extremes of the Alexandrian School.

3. The *Caesarean School* was started by Origen,* whose books formed the nucleus of the library of Pamphilus (d. 309; ardent defender of Origen; wrote *Apology for Origen* with Eusebius; martyr under Maximus). The Caesarean School influenced the Three Cappadocians.*

4. *Antiochene.* The tendency of this "school" is generally regarded as having originated with Lucian.* It employed the grammatico-historical method and opposed the allegorical method of the Alexandrian school. After the condemnation of Nestorius the school shifted to Nisibus and Edessa.

5. The School of *Nisibus* flourished under Narses (d. 502).

6. The School of *Edessa* flourished under Ephraem.* Another famous teacher was Marius. See *Exegesis.*

Schools, Elementary — Central — Consolidated — Secondary — Sunday. See *Parish Education; Christian Education,* D 5, E.

Schools, Non-Lutheran. See *Protestant Education in the U. S.; Roman Catholic Education in the U. S.; Teachers,* E.

Schop, Johann. Prominent musician in Hamburg ca. 1640; noted violinist; wrote tunes to several of Rist's hymns, also for his *Hausmusik.*

Schopenhauer, Arthur (1788—1860). German philosopher, whose egotism and individualism caused his life to be an unhappy one. He rejected the moralism, philosophy of religion, and

idealism of his contemporaries for aesthetics. He emphasized the Transcendental Aesthetic in the first section of Kant's *The Critique of Pure Reason* An examination of the sensuous experience of man reveals that he is driven by a will to live, an inner urge for sensations. This Schopenhauer regarded as a part of the Universal Will, the process of becoming, which is a blind and irrational force and brings suffering to humanity. Man may overcome his slavery to this Universal Will by conquering his own desires. Schopenhauer regarded compassion as the highest moral principle.

M. W. Boyer, *Highways of Philosophy,* Muhlenberg Press, 1949 (bibliography given).

Schott, Heinrich Augustus (1780 to 1835). Theologian; prof. at Wittenberg and Jena; supernaturalist; wrote an epitome of Christian theology, a work on eloquence, an historical critical introduction to the New Testament, and other works.

Schreuder, Hans Palladan Smith (1817—82). B. at Sogndal, Norway; d. at Untunjambili, Natal, Africa; consecrated bishop of the cathedral of Bergen 1866; founder of the Schreuder Mission in South Africa.

Schreuder Mission. See *Norwegian Church Mission by Schreuder.*

Schroeckh, Johann Matthias (1733 to 1808). Prof. at Leipzig and Wittenberg; rationalistic church historian; his chief work, *Christliche Kirchengeschichte,* in 45 volumes; the two last edited by Tzschirner.

Schroedel, Andrew. B. Jan. 29, 1851, at Neustadtren, Kulm, Bavaria; came to America, 1853; grad. from Northwestern College, Watertown, Wis., 1873; from Concordia Seminary, St. Louis, Mo., 1876; pastor in Wis.; prof. at Northwestern College, Watertown, 1889—93; pres. of Minnesota Synod, 1906—09.

Schroedel, George Carl. B. August 21, 1878, in Wood County, Wis.; graduated at St. Louis 1902; pastor at Hurley, Wis., 1902—05; Manawa, Wis., 1905—11; Wausau, Wis., 1911—23; prof. at St. John's College, Winfield, Kans., 1924—39. D. May 28, 1939.

Schroeder, Johann Heinrich (1667 to 1699). Studied at Leipzig, under influence of Francke; pastor at Meseberg; Pietistic tendency; wrote: "Eins ist not, ach Herr, dies eine."

Schroeter, Leonhard (ca. 1540—95). Became the leader of the Magdeburg School, where he succeeded his personal friend and fellow Philippist. Schroeter wrote much excellent music for the Lutheran service of worship and still enjoys a very good reputation as a composer.

Schubert, Gotthilf Heinrich von (1780—1860). Lutheran; a firm believer in the Bible; first studied theology, but because of rationalism turned to medicine and natural sciences; prof. at Erlangen and Munich; his chief scientific work, *Die Geschichte der Seele*. He found in nature the footprints of God. Brilliant author of Christian tales.

Schuelke, August. B. May 7, 1866, at Berlin (now Kitchener), Ont., Can.; graduated at St. Louis 1888; assistant prof. and inspector at Concordia College, Fort Wayne, Ind., 1888—90; pastor at Crown Point, Ind., 1890—1906; prof. at Concordia Teachers College, Seward, Nebr., since 1906; Treasurer of Nebraska District 1912—23; of Southern Nebraska District 1923—32. D. March 21, 1932.

Schuerer, Emil. B. 1844, d. at Goettingen 1910; theologian of the Ritschlian School; professor at Leipzig, Giessen, Kiel, 1895 at Goettingen; chief work: *Geschichte des juedischen Volks im Zeitalter Jesu Christi* (done into English).

Schuette, Conrad Hermann Louis. B. June 17, 1843, at Vorrel, Hanover; emigrated 1854; ed. Columbus, O., theol. seminary; pastor, Delaware, O., 1865 to 1872; prof. Capital Univ., Columbus, 1872; pres., 1890, also professor of Symbolics at the Seminary; elected general president of the Joint Synod of Ohio and Other States in 1894; became president of the National Lutheran Council in 1923; contributed five original hymns and several translations from the German to the hymnal of 1880, among the latter: "O Holy, Blessed Trinity"; "Now Christ, the Very Son of God"; author of *Church-members Manual Before the Altar, Testimonies unto Church Union.* D. Aug. 11, 1924.

Schuetz, Heinrich (Sagittarius; 1585 to 1672). Great composer of the Lutheran Church. Leichtentritt calls him "the greatest composer of German church music before Bach" (p. 127), while Lang regards him as "one of the outstanding creative geniuses in musical history" (p. 397). In addition to being a great composer, Schuetz was a devout orthodox Lutheran and a strong character. In his compositions he expressed a strong Biblical faith and manifested a mastery of the various contrapuntal techniques. His music expresses a happy fusion of the subjective and the objective, of the melodic and the dramatic, of the German idiom and the Italian. The profound sincerity of his religious spirit found an ideal vehicle of expression in his music. His *History of the Resurrection* helped prepare the way for the oratorio, while his *Biblical Scenes* served as precursors for the cantatas of Buxtehude, Bach, and others. Schuetz's three Passions are among his most famous works and, though written while he was an old man, reveal his mastery of the dramatic element; each is, however, different from the other in style and expression. Schuetz was the first to introduce opera into Germany. He rarely included the chorale in his works and stressed the *cantiones sacrae* rather than the chorale. Many have sought to imitate Schuetz but have failed. As a composer he was prolific.

H. J. Moser, *Heinrich Schuetz, Sein Leben und sein Werk*, Kassel, 1936; E. H. Mueller, *Heinrich Schuetz*, Leipzig, 1925; F. Spitta, *Heinrich Schuetz und seine Bedeutung fuer die Kirchenchoere*, Goettingen, 1914; general references found under *Music, Church.*

Schuetz, Johann Jakob (1640—90). Studied law at Tuebingen, practiced at Frankfurt; intimate friend of Spener, later a separatist; wrote: "Sei Lob und Ehr' dem hoechsten Gut."

Schuh, Lewis Herman. B. July 7, 1858, at Galion, Ohio; studied at Capital Univ. (D. D.), Puget Sound Univ. (Ph. D.); held pastorates at Canal Winchester, O., Tacoma, Wash., Columbus, O.; president Capital Univ., 1901—12; pastor at Grove City, O., 1912—14; at Toledo, O., 1914, till his death, in 1935; held various positions in the Joint Synod of Ohio; author of *Enjoying Church Work; Occasional Sermons; Funeral Sermons;* etc.

Schultens, Albert (1686—1750). Dutch Orientalist; b. at Groningen; professor of Oriental languages at Franeker and Leyden (d. there); father of modern Hebrew grammar, pioneer of Comparative Semitics; wrote *Hebrew Origins,* etc.

Schultze, Viktor. B. 1851. Since 1883 professor of church history and Christian archaeology at Greifswald;

has written many monographs in his field: *Das evangelische Kirchengebaeude; Archaeologie der altchristlichen Kunst; Die altchristlichen Bildwerke und die wissenschaftliche Forschung;* and others. D. 1937.

Schulz, Johann Abraham Peter (1747—1800). A composer of German folk song whose simple religious music is used to some extent also in America. In his compositions we often find a fusion of art- and folksong.

Schulz, Paul. B. Mar. 23, 1879, at Lindenau, West Prussia; graduated from Fort Wayne (1897) and Concordia Seminary, St. Louis (1900); pastor at Bradford, Ind., New Albany, Ind., Brownstown, Ind., Cincinnati, Ohio, and Springfield, Ill.; pres. of Central Illinois District (1927—32); member of the Board of Directors of The Luth. Church — Missouri Synod (1932—50); D. D. from Concordia Seminary, St. Louis; d. Jan. 30, 1950.

Schulze, Ludwig Theodor (1833 to 1918). Studied at Berlin, where he also entered the faculty, his chief fields being New Testament exegesis and Biblical theology; became professor at Univ. of Koenigsberg, then at the Theological Seminary in Magdeburg; professor of systematic theology at Rostock; published sermons, an *Introduction into the New Testament,* several biographies, and books in other fields.

Schumann, Robert (1810—56). Composer of the Romantic era, achieved fame also through his writings and through his hearty support of such endeavors as founded the *Leipzig Conservatory of Music* by Mendelssohn and the organization of the *Bach Gesellschaft* of Germany. Through his literary activities Schumann called the attention of the music world to geniuses like Brahms and Chopin; this he did notably in his *Neue Zeitschrift fuer Musik.* Despite the fact that Schumann never mastered the art of orchestration, proved to be a poor teacher and a poor conductor, and, too, despite the fact that he was a leading spirit in the Romantic movement of the 19th century, Schumann will likely always be remembered as a great composer. Notwithstanding their defects of form, his symphonies hold their own and are often played. As a writer of music for the piano and of songs he ranks with the best; though seldom heard, his choral music is indeed worthy of notice and use. He was among the most

beautiful and unselfish characters of the music world and was inspired to produce much of his greatest work through his devoted and highly talented wife, Clara.

G. Adler, *Handbuch der Musikgeschichte,* Frankfurt, 1924; E. Dannreuther, *The Oxford History of Music* (vol. 6), London, 1932; A. Einstein, *Music in the Romantic Era,* New York, 1947; D. Ferguson, *A History of Musical Thought,* New York, 1948.

Schupp (Schuppius), Johann Balthasar (1610—61). B. at Giessen; d. at Hamburg. Studied philosophy and theology at Marburg; master's degree at Rostock. Professor of history and oratory at Marburg and preacher at the Elizabethkirche; court preacher and counselor of the consistory for Landgrave Johannes von Hesse-Braubach, 1646; pastor of the Jakobikirche at Hamburg, 1649. His satirical writings displeased his fellow pastors.

Schwabach Articles. See *Lutheran Confessions,* A 2.

Schwaermer. See *Grace, Means of,* I, 7.

Schwan, Heinrich Christian. Born April 5, 1819, at Horneburg, Hanover; studied at the *Gymnasium* of Stade and at the universities of Goettingen and Jena; graduated 1842; after tutoring for a short time, was ordained September 13, 1843, taking charge of a mission in Leopoldina, Bahia, Brazil. Having promised his uncle Wyneken to keep the need of the Lutherans in the United States in mind, he came over in 1850, was installed as pastor of the small congregation at Black Jack (New Bielefeld), Mo., and received as member of the Missouri Synod at its fourth annual meeting (1850). In 1851 he was called to Zion Church, Cleveland, O., serving it till 1899, during the last decades as associate pastor. He popularized the use of a Christmas tree in American church services by placing one in Zion Church in 1851 (there are records of an earlier use by J. Muehlhaeuser at Rochester, N. Y., 1840; another, but not in church, 1847. See *CHIQ,* XVII:4ff.). From 1852 to 1878 he served as Vice-President of the Central District, Vice-President of the General Body, and President of the Central District; from 1878 to 1899 as President of the General Body. On the fiftieth anniversary of his ordination, 1893, Luther Seminary of the Norwegian Lutheran Synod conferred upon him the honorary degree of Doctor of Divinity. D. May 29, 1905.

Dr. Schwan is counted among the fathers of the Missouri Synod. An earnest disciple and able exponent of confessional Lutheranism, he was one of the chief builders of the faithful and flourishing Lutheran church of the city of Cleveland and a trusty counselor and teacher of the whole Synod, his influence extending even beyond its confines. His unwavering fidelity to the Lutheran Confessions, combined with a fine Christian tact, a well-poised mind, and sound judgment concerning men and the times, together with his modesty and refinement, fitted him for the position of President, especially during the trying days of the controversy on election and the stirring times of the period of expansion then setting in. A lifelong student and expert teacher of the Catechism, he ably supervised the writing of the Synodical Catechism, published in 1896. The synodical sermons printed in the *Lutheraner* reveal his mastery in unfolding the meaning of the text and in presenting and aptly applying the most sublime truths in simple, popular language.

E. W. Meier, "Life and Work of Henry C. Schwan," *CHIQ*, XXIV: 132—39, 145—72; XXV:72—85, 97—121.

Schwartz, Christian Friedrich (1726 to 1798). One of the foremost Lutheran missionaries to India; b. at Sonnenburg, Prussia; d. at Tanjore, India. Through A. H. Francke's influence, Schwartz was prevailed upon to enter the service of the Danish-Halle Mission in Tranquebar, arriving there July 30, 1750. Four months after his arrival he delivered his first Tamil sermon from Ziegenbalg's pulpit. He moved from Tranquebar to Trichinopoly, where he labored from 1762 to 1778. In 1767 he became an English chaplain, severing his connection with the Danish-Halle Mission. In 1778, at the request of the Rajah, he settled at Tanjore and later was made guardian to the heir apparent. His political and religious influence was far-reaching, his probity universally acknowledged.

Schwarz, Bishop. See *Catholic Apostolic Church*, 2.

Schwarz, Johann Michael Nikolaus (1813—87). B. at Hagenbuechach, Bavaria; missionary to India 1843; director of seminary 1845—49; Trichinopoly, 1852—59; Mayaveram, 1859—69; d. 1887 at Tranquebar; an author of repute; revised Tamil Bible.

Schweigger, Solomon (1551—1622). Attached to the German embassy at Constantinople, Schweigger continued efforts to unite the Eastern Orthodox Church and the Lutheran Church. See *Eastern Orthodox Confessions*.

Schweitzer, Albert (1875—). Clergyman, philosopher, physician, and music critic; prof. at Strassburg; medical missionary in Africa. As a theologian, Schweitzer emphasizes the apocalyptic element in the teaching of Jesus Christ.* He does not adhere to fundamental doctrines, *e. g.*, deity of Christ. In his *Philosophy of Civilization*, Schweitzer holds that all world views based on nature are pessimistic, since nature is ultimately life-denying. Man must affirm his will to live over against a negating nature, thus leading to a philosophy of love. He wrote a life of Johann S. Bach and with Widor published Bach's organ works.

George Seaver, *Albert Schweitzer, The Man and His Mind*, Harper, 1947.

Schweizer, Alexander (1808—88). Prof. and pastor in Zurich; eminent Reformed theologian and dogmatician; greatly influenced by Schleiermacher; chief representative of the left wing of this school.

Schwenkfelders. 1. This body traces its origin back to the work of Kaspar Schwenkfeld, a counselor at the court of the Duke of Liegnitz, in Silesia. When Luther entered upon his work of reforming the Church, Schwenkfeld, at the age of twenty-five, threw himself into the new movement with great energy. Although he was not an ordained clergyman, he took a prominent part in the religious work and especially in the reformation of the Church in Silesia. However, as he was independent in his thinking, he soon began to preach doctrines which brought him in opposition to the Reformation. Thus he rejected the doctrine of justification by faith, took exception to Luther's adherence to Scripture as the only source and norm of faith, and inveighed against the Lutheran doctrine of the efficacy of the Sacraments as means of grace. He also rejected pedobaptism and in 1531 declared himself at variance with all the articles of the *Augsburg Confession*, claiming that he would rather be a papist than a Lutheran. Strongly opposed to the formation of a Church, he did no more than gather congregations, in consequence of which he was compelled to flee from one place to another in order to escape persecution. He died in Ulm in 1561.

2. After Schwenkfeld's death his followers, although not organized into an independent church body, assembled for occasional meetings and conferences in Silesia, Switzerland, and Italy. In order to escape persecutions, these followers, early in the 18th century, decided to emigrate to America; and in September, 1734, about 200 persons landed at Philadelphia. They obtained homes in Montgomery, Bucks, Berks, and Lehigh Counties, Pa., where the greater number of their descendants are now to be found. Toward the close of the Revolutionary War a closer church organization was formed, and in 1782 a constitution was adopted. In common with the Quakers, Mennonites, and kindred bodies they voiced their opposition to wars, secret societies, and the taking of oaths.

3. The doctrinal standards of the Schwenkfelders are set forth in the following books: *The Confession of Faith of Schwenkfelders in Goerlitz,* 1726; *Catechism of Schwenkfelders in America,* 1855. Christ's divinity, they hold, was progressive, and His human nature partook more and more of the divine nature, without losing its identity. The Lord's Supper, a symbol of both Christ's humanity and divinity, is regarded as a means of spiritual nourishment, however, without any change of the elements, such as is asserted in transubstantiation. They regard Infant Baptism as not Apostolic and the mode of Baptism as of no consequence. The only officers are ministers, deacons, and trustees, who are elected and ordained by the local churches. Though numbering only about two thousand members, this body maintains a liberal arts college at Perkiomen, Pa., and is planning to publish the voluminous writings of Schwenkfeld. The Schwenkfelders have relaxed their opposition to wars and secret societies.

Schwerdtfeger, Samuel. See *Canada, Lutheranism in,* 4.

Science. Originally designating all knowledge or learning, the term science has come to be limited to the systematized knowledge and study of the physical world. Two important tools employed in this study — logic and mathematics — are sometimes referred to as the abstract sciences. The concrete sciences fall into either of two main categories — physical science (astronomy, physics, chemistry, geology) and biological science (zoology, botany, bacteriology, paleontology), or cut across both (biochemistry, biophysics).

The distinguishing characteristic of the sciences compared to other fields of accurate knowledge is emphasis on the method employed, namely, the scientific method. In the early history of science, authority was considered supreme, and for centuries the supreme authority was Aristotle.* The type of reasoning followed was almost without an exception deduction. The generalized principle was cited, based upon authority, and the specific point in question was settled by application of this general principle.

Revolting against this often unfruitful and inaccurate method, Francis Bacon * by his writings gave impetus to the already growing and functioning inductive method which had been ably applied by Galileo * in his demonstration of the laws governing falling bodies. Bacon's extreme view that only the inductive method should be allowed has been supplanted by a compromise. The scientific method in modern science involves these basic steps — observation, formulation of a hypothesis, directed and controlled experimentation, drawing of conclusions. Conclusions thus reached are to be considered tentative, subject to revision or changes upon the discovery of new facts. The deductive method is employed in visualizing the possible results to be expected from experimentation after a hypothesis has been formulated.

Science strives to arrive at a complete understanding of the ultimate nature of matter and of the laws relating to its various forms and manifestations. It assumes the principle of causality which was first formally stated by Leucippus: "Nothing happens without a cause, everything has a cause and is necessary." Although denied by Hume * and others, this principle unlerlies all science, the aim of which is to trace this relationship between cause and effect through all of the mass of natural phenomena.

Lord Kelvin has been credited with the statement that we can fully know only what we can measure. This represents substantially the viewpoint of modern science. Since observation underlies the entire scientific method, great emphasis is placed on accurate observation and measurement, and there is a general reluctance to allow or consider non-physical or non-material evidence. There is, for instance, a great reluctance on the part of organized science to accept the conclusions of reputable scientists based on experiments claiming the existence of extrasensory perception. It is perhaps partly because of this hesitancy to allow nonmaterial evidence that the so-called conflicts between science and religion exist. The Christian religion, concerning itself with the soul and its relationship to God, is based upon the premise of divine authority and inspiration, three quantities which are out of the realm of physical measurement. By the very nature of the case, then, it is not surprising that certain conclusions reached by science appear to conflict with Scriptural truth. OTW

Science and Health. See *Church of Christ, Scientist.*

Science, Philosophy, and Religion, the Conference on. Organized 1939 to integrate the contributions of various fields for the preserving of democracy and world peace.

Scotch Confession of Faith. See *Presbyterian Bodies,* 1; *Presbyterian Confessions,* 2.

Scotists. See *Scholasticism.*

Scotland, Reformation in. 1. Strict Calvinism was speedily and successfully established in Scotland through the vigorous measures of John Knox. The struggle between Presbyterianism and Episcopalianism lasted over a century, but since 1688 Scotland has been overwhelmingly Presbyterian. The first presentation of Scotch Presbyterian doctrine was the confession composed by John Knox in 1560. This, however, was replaced by the *Westminster Standards* in 1647. The union with England (1707) brought Scotland no political or industrial prosperity. Both the landed aristocracy and the crown claimed the right of appointing clericals to office, which was incompatible with the unity and independence of the system of Scotch Presbyterian organization. In 1743 the Covenanters, who had already separated, organized as Reformed Presbyterians. In 1752 a new body separated and called itself the "Relief." In the course of a century the number of separatist organizations had grown to about 500 congregations; in 1847 they were combined as the United Presbyterian Church.

2. At the beginning of the 19th century a re-awakening under Thomas Chalmers took place in the Church of Scotland. However, the patronage struggle was resumed, which finally led to the "Disruption" and the organization of the Free Church of Scotland. The Free Church doubled its membership in the next sixty years, until in 1874 the Right of Patronage was removed by Parliament, when the Established Church again gained in popularity. The close of the last century, therefore, witnessed three great Presbyterian churches in Scotland: the Established Church, the Free Church, and the United Presbyterian Church. The difference between them was principally their various attitudes as to the relation of Church and State. Negotiations for union between the Free and United churches, opened in 1863, resulted in the organization of the United Free Church of Scotland, October 31, 1900. A small minority of 27, who opposed the union, now declared itself to be the only true, legitimate Free Church and laid claim to all the property of the organization. A settlement was finally accomplished after a long-continued struggle. Besides the bodies mentioned, there are three other small Presbyterian churches in Scotland: 1) the Free Presbyterian Church, 2) the Reformed Presbyterian, 3) and the original secession, properly called the Old Light.

3. *The Scotch Episcopal Church.* The Scotch Episcopal Church was in former times the great rival of the Presbyterian Church, but after the downfall of the Stuarts that Church was almost eliminated from the country. In 1792 it was granted full toleration.

4. *Congregationalists.* The Congregational Church in Scotland was founded in 1728 by John Glas, a minister of the Established Church. Other Congregational churches were organized later; they joined the Congregational union organized in 1863. A division in the Secession Church in 1841 resulted in the founding of the Evangelical Union. In 1896 the Congregationalist Church and the Evangelical Union were united to form the present Congregational Union of Scotland. The number of Baptists in Scotland is comparatively small. Their doctrine is Calvinistic, their worship simple, and their organization strictly Congregational, for which reason they are enumerated under this heading.

5. Among the other Protestant bodies the Methodists, both Wesleyan

and primitive, are most important. There are also small bodies of Quakers, Irvingites, Unitarians, and Swedenborgians. The Roman Catholic Church is represented in Scotland by about half a million members, most of whom are of Irish descent, although 30,000 of them are Scotch. This element is found among the Highlanders of Gaelic tongue, who have remained loyal to the Roman Catholic hierarchy. Institutions such as Bible and tract societies, city missions, schools for morally neglected children, temperance societies, and others have been created by the Church. Extensive bibliography on the Scottish Church given by F. R. Webber, "Some Famous Scottish Preachers of Post-Reformation Times," *CTM*, XVII: 583—616.

Scott, Thomas (1705—75). Teacher; belonged to Independents; minister at Ipswich; sole pastor of congregation after 1740; several collections of hymns, in which: "Return, O Wanderer, Return."

Scott, Sir Walter (1771—1832). Received very broad education; holds very high rank as novelist and historian; very successful also as poet; no direct contributions to hymnody, but lines: "When Israel of the Lord Beloved," from *Ivanhoe*, and paraphrase of *Dies Irae*: "That Day of Wrath, That Dreadful Day," have come into use.

Scott, Walter. See *Disciples of Christ*, 2 d.

Scott's Bible. A family Bible, with original notes, practical observations, and marginal references, published in 1796, 4 vols., and in the 9th edition, in 1825, 6 vols., by Thomas Scott, a clergyman of the Church of England (b. 1747, d. 1821).

Scottish Presbytery in London in Connection with the Church of Scotland. See *Presbyterian Bodies*, 2.

Scottish Rite. See *Freemasonry*, 3.

Scotus Erigena, John. See *Erigena, John Scotus*.

Scotus, John Duns (*Doctor Subtilis*). See *Duns Scotus, John; Scholasticism*.

Scouting. See *Boy Scouts of America; Camp Fire Girls; Girl Scouts, Inc.*

Scriptorium. In monastic establishment a large room set aside for the copying of manuscripts and books. Sometimes this was done by dictation, especially when many copies were required for school use; but in the case

of rare copies a single copyist would often toil over the work for weeks and months.

Scriven, Joseph (1820—86). Educated at Trinity College, Dublin; went to Canada in 1845, living last at Port Hope, on Lake Ontario; his hymn "What a Friend We Have in Jesus" a great favorite.

Scrivener, Frederick Henry Ambrose (1813—91). Church of England theologian and New Testament scholar; wrote many books on New Testament criticism; edited a Greek text of the New Testament.

Scriver, Christian (1629—93). His father died in 1629; boy able to get education with help of rich relative; studied at Rostock; tutor at Segeberg; *Archdiaconus* at Stendal 1653; pastor at Magdeburg 1667; later also assessor at the consistory; then scholarch and finally senior; in 1690, *Konsistorialrat* and private chaplain at Quedlinburg. Very popular and influential preacher; author of *Seelenschatz* and of *Zufaellige Andachten* (devotional books); hymns full of devotion and with power of Gerhardt; wrote: "Der lieben Sonne Licht und Pracht"; "Auf, Seel', und danke deinem Herrn."

Scrutiny (L. "examination"). In the Early Church, an examination of the faith and life of candidates for baptism, often held on Ash Wednesdays. In the Roman Catholic Church, a mode of election (especially of the pope by the ballot of cardinals); also the examination of candidates for religious orders.

Scudder, John (1793—1855). Missionary of the Reformed (Dutch) Church; b. at Wynberg, South Africa; sent to Ceylon by the American Board; transferred, in 1836, to Madras for literary work. The Arcot Mission grew up under his direction. Eight sons, two granddaughters, and two grandsons have been in the service of that mission. Ill health drove him to Africa, where he died.

Sculpture. See *Art, Ecclesiastical and Religious*.

Seabury, Bishop. See *Protestant Episcopal Church*, 3.

Seal, Sacramental. See *Character Indelebilis*.

Seal of Confession. A term used especially by Roman Catholics to designate the obligation of the priest to reveal nothing (without permission) said at confession.

Seamen's Homes. Owing to the fact that the life of a seaman takes him away from the home and exposes him to many temptations, institutions have been established which seek to provide a home for seafaring men while they are on shore. Homes have also been established for disabled seamen (e. g., Sailors' Snug Harbor, Staten Island, N. Y., founded 1801). The American Seamen's Friend Society, editing the *Sailors' Magazine*, cares for seamen in New York, sends chaplains to other ports, and places libraries on vessels. — Mission work among the seamen is carried on by various Lutheran church bodies at various ports.

Sebastian, St. Martyr who, according to tradition, concealed his religion and entered the army of Diocletian in order to protect Christians. When discovered, he was condemned to be shot by archers. Christians found him pierced by arrows but living, and he survived. Thereupon he was condemned to be beaten to death (A. D. 288).

Sebastian's Society. See *Veterans' Organizations.*

Sebastiani, Johann (1622—83). Native of Weimar, helped contribute to the musical fame of Koenigsberg. His fame rests largely on his *Matthaeuspassion* (1672). Though not monumental from the artistic point of view, two features are responsible for its distinction: 1) the parts of individuals are not assigned to soloists in the traditional manner, and the historical narrative is presented by means of an accompanied ariośorecitativ; 2) to incite to greater devotion, pertinent chorale stanzas were introduced.

Secession Church in Ireland. See *Presbyterian Bodies, 3.*

Seckendorf, Veit Ludwig von (1629 to 1692). B. at Herzogenaurach; d. at Halle. Studied at Strassburg. Page to Duke Ernest the Pious and supervisor of the library; gentleman of the bedchamber, 1648; court councilor and councilor of justice, 1652; privy court councilor and councilor of the Board of Domains; chancellor, 1664; chancellor and president of the consistory under Maurice, duke of Saxony-Zeitz, 1664; chancellor of the newly founded University of Halle, 1692. A friend of Spener, he reconciled the Pietists and the orthodox clergy of Halle, 1692. His

fame rests chiefly on his *Commentarius historicus et apologeticus de Lutheranismo*, 1692, for which he had access to a wealth of material not available to any other scholar then or since. It constitutes a refutation of the Jesuit L. Maimbourg's *Histoire du Lutheranism*. A German version by E. Frick was abridged by C. F. Junius and once more by J. F. Roos, who also prepared a German abridged version directly from the original.

L. W. Spitz, "Veit Ludwig von Seckendorf: Statesman and Scholar," *CTM*, XVI: 672—84.

Second Advent of Christ. See *Last Things.*

Second Birth. A term used of Conversion.*

Second Blessing. See *Holiness Bodies, 3.*

Secondary Education. See *Parish Education, G.*

Secret Agreement. See *Lutheran Confessions, A 2.*

Secret Societies (Mysteries of Primitive Religions). In many heathen religions the degeneration which followed the repudiation of the transmitted monotheism quickly led to customs and rites which made secrecy a chief consideration. The leading men of a tribe or nation invested certain religious exercises with a veil of mystery which could not be lifted except to the initiates. The proceedings of most of these societies are carried out with much mummery, show of disguise, and the use of various devices to awe and terrify outsiders. The functions may be of an initiatory type, and in that case are often connected with the rites of puberty, or they may be of a politico-judicial or of a magico-religious form. The appeal of the mysterious is so great that secret societies are found not only among so-called primitive races, but also among those who claim a greater degree of enlightenment, as is the case in many of the lodges or secret orders in America and elsewhere. See *Mystery Religions; Lodges.*

Sect. The word as used in the Latin classics seems derived from *sequor* "to follow" and denoted the following of some leader. Later the word came to mean "to separate from" as though derived from *seco.* The word, which often has a negative connotation, was frequently applied to those who separated from state churches. It has been applied to groups which separated from the parent body, which were schismatic in doctrine and practice, or to bodies because they are small.

Secular Clergy. Parish priests, bishops, and other members of the Roman clergy who live in the everyday world (*saeculum*) without being bound by a monastic rule are called secular clergy, in distinction from the members of religious orders, who have withdrawn from the world, are bound by a rule (*regula*), and are therefore known as regular clergy. The secular clergy essentially contains the hierarchy and holds precedence.

Secularism. A system of ethics based on natural morality independent of supernaturalism. It traces its origin to George Jacob Holyoake (1817–1906; Owenite minister who turned to rationalism; wrote *A History of Co-operation* and other works; edited *Oracle of Reason, Reasoner*). Secularism champions freedom of thought, the freedom to differ, and the right to question any principle or premise. It emphasizes a non-religious approach to the good of the present life and social welfare.

Sedulius, Coelius (ca. 450). Probably born at Rome. His early life was devoted to heathen literature, of which he probably was a teacher. Converted rather late in life to Christianity, he yearned to attract the heathen by telling them of the wonders of the Gospel. This moved him to write. His works include *Carmen Paschale*, a poem on the whole Gospel story, and *Hymnus de Christo*.

See. The seat of a bishop or his jurisdiction; the *Apostolic See* is applied to the jurisdiction of the pope.

Seeberg, Reinhold (1859–1935). B. in Livonia; studied at Dorpat and Erlangen; at first associate professor at Dorpat; in 1889 professor of church history and New Testament exegesis at Erlangen; 1898 professor systematic theology at Berlin; influential Lutheran theologian of modern type; author of an extensive *History of Dogma* and other works.

Seehofer, Arsacius (d. 1545). B. in Muenchen; became Magister in Ingolstadt, used Melanchthon's notes on the Pauline letters, whereupon he was incarcerated and excluded from the university. After Argula von Staufen and others had protested and Luther had written a sharp condemnation of the

procedure, Seehofer escaped from prison and went to Wittenberg, was active for the Reformation in Prussia, taught in Augsburg, became pastor in Wuerttemberg, where he was active in introducing the Reformation; wrote a number of books, which were promptly placed on the Index of Prohibited Books by the Roman Church.

Seelsorge. "The care of souls," a German word applied to the pastoral work of the minister.

Segnatura. See *Curia, Roman.*

Seiffert, Max (1868–1948). Musicologist of Germany, who received much of his training from Philipp Spitta and who later prepared editions of music, much of which is part of the distinctive musical heritage of the Lutheran Church, e. g., the works of Scheidt, Tunder, Weckmann, Bernhard, Joh. Gottfr. Walther, and Zachow. Seiffert made available, too, the works of Sweelinck, and he was the foremost authority of our day on the *Generalbasspraxis* of the 17th and 18th centuries. Several volumes of the monumental *Denkmaeler deutscher Tonkunst* were prepared by Seiffert; for some years he served as editor in chief of the *Internationale Musikgesellschaft*, and his *Organum* series, published by Kistner and Siegel of Leipzig, is known and used widely also in America. Because of Seiffert's outstanding musicological accomplishments the University at Kiel conferred upon him the degree of Doctor of Divinity.

Seiss, Jos. A. Noted pulpit orator and author; b. March 19, 1823 at Graceham, Md.; son of a Maryland miner; grew up under Moravian influences; educated at Gettysburg; licensed by the Lutheran Virginia Synod 1842; held pastorates in Maryland, including Baltimore, 1842–58; 1858 pastor of old St. John's, Philadelphia; from 1874 till his death, 1904, he served the Church of the Holy Communion. Seiss exerted a strong influence in the Pennsylvania Ministerium and the General Council, serving a number of terms as president of both bodies. He is the author of *Ecclesia Lutherana, Lectures on the Gospels, On the Epistles.* His works *On the Last Times* and *On the Apocalypse* are pervaded with chiliasm. His pulpit style was stately, dignified, and artistic rather than churchly.

Self-Abasement. See *Humility.*

Self-Denial. To have fellowship with

Christ involves denying oneself, crucifying the flesh, taking up the cross, and following Jesus in complete self-surrender (Luke 9:23; 14:27; Gal. 5:24; Rom. 8:13). It means, not to follow one's own will, but to do the will of Christ (1 Cor. 6:20), give up everything that is sinful, forego one's own comfort and pleasure in order to serve God and promote the welfare of others. It is the opposite of self-will and self-indulgence. Paul calls it a "gymnastic unto godliness" (Phil. 4:11-13; 3:7, 8). Examples: Gen. 13:9; 17:8; Heb. 11:25; Num. 16:15; 1 Sam. 12:3, 4; Matt. 4:20; 9:9; Luke 5:11; 21:4; Acts 2:44f.; 4:34; 20:32; 1 Cor. 4:9-12; 10:33; Gal. 5:24; 1 Pet. 4:1, 2. See *Concordia Pulpit*, 1936, Vol. VII, 376; Kretzmann, *Pop. Com.*, O. T., II, 247, 465; N. T., II, 664; Reu-Buehring, *Christian Ethics*, 212. See *Asceticism*.

Self-Righteousness. See *Pride*.

Selfishness. The root of all unholy desires and impulses (*e. g.*, avarice, greed, lust). The essence of sin is selfishness; forbidden in the Ninth and Tenth Commandments (Luke 6:32; Phil. 2:4; 1 John 3:17; Prov. 11:26; Hag. 1:4; Zech. 7:6; 2 Tim. 3:2; James 2:15, 16). Examples: Gen. 4:9; 1 Sam. 25:11; Esther 6:6; Mark 10:37; Luke 10:31, 32. Cp. *Concordia Pulpit*, 1936, Vol. VII, 378; Luther, VIII, 1595f. Selfishness is a primary evil in the world and in the visible churches. See Reu-Buehring, *Christian Ethics*, pp. 7, 93ff.; E. W. Koehler, *Christian Pedagogy*, 198.

Selle, Christian August Thomas. B. Feb. 21, 1819, in Gelting, Schleswig; subteacher at fifteen; emigrated to America 1837; printer's apprentice and factory worker, he privately studied theology and was licensed to preach by Ohio Synod; continued his studies under the guidance of Dr. Sihler; pastor of First St. Paul's Church, Chicago, 1846; charter member of the Missouri Synod; at Crete, Ill., 1851; Rock Island, Ill., 1858; second professor at the Teachers' Seminary (Fort Wayne, Addison), 1861, and editor of the *Schulblatt;* retired, 1893; d. April 3, 1898.

Selle, Thomas (1599—1663). Played an important part in making Hamburg the musical Mecca of Germany. As cantor of the *Johanneum* of Hamburg, Selle had charge of the music in five large churches, including the famous St. *Katharinenkirche*. The musical vespers conducted on Saturdays through five weeks of each year in each of these churches enjoyed widespread popularity; music played a very important part also in the regular Sunday morning services. In 1641 Selle began also to take charge of the music in the Hamburg Cathedral, where he thus became a *canonicus minor*. Selle was an assiduous worker. Though little known today, his compositions attracted much attention his own day; he wrote secular as well as sacred works, his church music reveals the influence of the early baroque, and he helped pave the way for Buxtehude, J. S. Bach, and others of the late baroque.

Sellin, Ernst Friedrich Max. B. 1867; d. April 3, 1898. Prof. of Old Testament exegesis at Rostock; wrote on Old Testament subjects; critic; editor in chief of a comprehensive modern commentary on the Old Testament; wrote volume on Minor Prophets.

Selnecker (Selneccer, Schellenecker), Nikolaus (1530—92). B. at Hersbrueck; was organist in the chapel at Nuernberg at twelve. Matriculating at Wittenberg, he was a favorite of Melanchthon. He held successively the positions of lecturer at the University of Wittenberg, court preacher at Dresden, professor of theology at Jena, professor at Leipzig, and likewise pastor of St. Thomas Church at that place, court preacher at Wolfenbuettel; co-worker on the Formula of Concord; later spent some time at Halle, Magdeburg, and Hildesheim. His frequent movements from one part of the country to another were largely due to the atmosphere of acute theological controversy in which he lived. He helped to develop the famous Motet Choir of St. Thomas Church, Leipzig, later conducted by J. S. Bach. He wrote much Latin verse and many German hymns, and published *Christliche Psalmen*. He was a very prominent figure in the church history of the latter part of the 16th century, one of the great champions of pure Lutheran doctrine.

Selwyn, George Augustus (1809 to 1878). Studied at Eton and Cambridge; appointed the first bishop of the Anglican Church in New Zealand; became the founder of Melanesian mission, using his own vessel, the *Southern Cross*, to make his trips; work was further built up under Patteson; finally bishop of Litchfield, England.

Semantics, General. A discipline intended to train men in efficient methods of evaluation formulated by Alfred

Korzybski and publicized under the name *General Semantics* in his book *Science and Sanity* (1933).

Although the system is described as non-Aristotelian, it preserves the aims of Aristotle, but seeks to bring up to date the scientific methods of 350 B. C., which it claims have been unknowingly reflected in the structure of the Indo-European languages and have thus been retained in human evaluations to the present day, leading to serious results, many of which are said to be derived from an absolutistic, two-valued, either-or orientation. Hence it strenuously opposes ethical statements which classify behavior as only *either* good *or* bad, *either* right *or* wrong. General Semantics evaluates behavior on the basis of a scale of many degrees between the two opposite extremes by considering the particular time, space, and context of actions. With its judgment based upon time, space, and context, this morality (which would then be a matter of self-control) is aimed at accumulating knowledge and making progress in civilization. Co-operation and freedom in the use of the language medium for these purposes would demand the elimination of conscious or unconscious assumptions, premises, creeds, prejudices, etc., that do not correspond to the scientific facts known about men and the physical world, that cause, in the estimation of the General Semanticists, inadequate evaluations and lead to insanity, and that otherwise impede the progress of men.

Hence they reject a belief in beings, events, or places whose reality or existence cannot be, or has not been, scientifically observed or determined. Statements involving a divinity or a "hereafter" are therefore considered non-sense statements, which cannot be checked to determine their correspondence to, or conflict with, scientific facts.

General Semantics with all its implications is based upon Korzybski's distinction between the chemistry-binding class of life (or plants, which can take in and use the energies of sun, soil, water, and air), the space-binding class of life (or animals, which can appropriate the basic energies and also move about in space), and the time-binding class of life (or man, who can bind energies and space, and, through the mechanism of recorded and spoken symbols, can also start where the previous generation left off and continue accumulating knowledge for proper evaluation and guidance of his actions).

General Semanticists apply the "scientific method" to all areas of human endeavor because it is considered to be the most accurate of all the evaluative and predictive systems which have been employed. Its use is regarded as essential to sane living in the present stage of man's development.

The methodology is being spread by two international organizations, courses in numerous universities, and is being applied by several thousand people in their personal and professional lives (1948). AHN

Alfred Korzybski, *Science and Sanity*, International Non-Aristotelian Library, Lakeville, Conn., 1948 (3d ed.); Korzybski, *Manhood of Humanity*, E. P. Dutton, N. Y., 1921; Samuel Hayakawa, "The Non-Aristotelian Revision of Morality," *ETC.: A Review of General Semantics*, III, 3 (Spring, 1946), pp. 161 to 173; Hayakawa, "Ethics of Time-Binding," *Papers from the Second American Congress on General Semantics*, M. Kendig, editor, Institute of General Semantics, Chicago, 1943, pp. 28 to 32; Cassius Keyser, *Mathematical Philosophy*, Dutton, N. Y., 1922, Chapter XX, "Korzybski's Concept of Man," pp. 422—451; Brock Chisholm, "Can Man Survive?" *ETC.: A Review of General Semantics*, IV, 2 (Winter, 1947), pp. 106—111; Chisholm, "Changing Sources of Security," *ETC.: A Review of General Semantics*, V, 1 (Autumn, 1947), pp. 1—7; Wendell Johnson, *People in Quandaries: The Semantics of Personal Adjustment*, Harper, N. Y., 1946; Irving J. Lee, *Language Habits in Human Affairs: An Introduction to General Semantics*, Harper, N. Y., 1941; S. I. Hayakawa, *Language and Thought in Action*, Harcourt Brace, N. Y., 1949; George Lundberg, *Can Science Save Us?* Longmans, Green, N. Y., 1947; John Seeley, "Can Man-in-Society Survive?" *ETC.: A Review of General Semantics*, V, 1 (Autumn, 1947), pp. 38—42; Edward Thorndike, "Science and Values," *ETC.: A Review of General Semantics*, I, 1 (August, 1943), pp. 1 to 11; Rudolf Carnap, "Probability as a Guide in Life," *ETC.: A Review of General Semantics*, V, 4 (Summer, 1948), pp. 263—267; Anatol Rapoport, *Science and the Goals of Man*, Harper, 1950.

Seminaries. See *Ministry, Education of.*

Seminarium Indicum. See *Missions, B 3.*

Semi-Arianism. See *Arianism*, 3.

Semi-Pelagianism. See *Pelagian Controversy*, 7—10.

Semler, Johann Salomo (1725—91). Father of modern Biblical criticism; was raised in Pietistic surroundings, but soon drifted into Rationalism. In 1752, at the instance of Baumgarten, he was called as professor of theology to Halle, where with his rationalism, by word and letters, he undermined almost all the doctrines of the Church. Miracles and prophecies are explained as deceptions and accommodation to prevailing ideas of time and surroundings. At the end he realized the destructive influence of Rationalism; he had sown the wind and was reaping the storm. He died of a broken heart.

Senegal. A colony in French West Africa. Area: 77,730 sq. mi.; population: 1,764,000 (1949). The inhabitants in Senegal are chiefly Mandingoes, Foolahs, Sarakoles, and other Negro tribes. Animism prevails. Islam has large following. Mission work by the *Societe des Miss. Evangeliques* and Worldwide Evangelization Crusade. Foreign staff, 13; Christian community, 300 (1952).

Senegambia. See *Senegal*.

Senfl, Ludwig (ca. 1492—ca. 1555). A favorite composer of Martin Luther. Senfl was a favorite pupil of Heinrich Isaak and his successor at the famous court of Maximilian the Great in Innsbruck. Later he was active in Munich at the court of Duke William of Bavaria, a rabid foe of Lutheranism. Luther's letters to Senfl were delivered through an intermediary; it is believed by some that Senfl was a Lutheran at heart. Georg Rhau's collection *Neue deudsche Geistliche Gesaenge*, published in Wittenberg in 1544, contained eleven compositions by Senfl based on chorales. Not one, however, is based on a Lutheran chorale; Senfl dared base compositions only on pre-Reformation chorales. Senfl's music reveals a superb mastery of the linear polyphonic style of the Netherlanders. He was clearly influenced by Despres, his style often refuses to cling to tradition, and he helped prepare the way for Lassus, who was to become one of his successors in Munich.

W. Gosslau, *Die religioese Haltung in der Reformationsmusik*, Kassel, 1933; H. Leichtentritt, *Geschichte der Motette*, Leipzig, 1908; E. Naumann, *History of Music*, London; J. D. von der

Heydt, *Geschichte der ev. Kirchenmusik in Deutschland*, Berlin, 1926; C. von Winterfeld, *Der ev. Kirchengesang* (I), Leipzig, 1843.

Sensation. See *Christian Teaching*, B.

Sensationalism, or *Sensualism*. The theory that all knowledge or ideas originate in sense perceptions. Philosophically it leads to empiricism*; ethically, to hedonism.*

Sensori-Motor Learning. See *Christian Teaching*, G.

Sensualism. See *Sensationalism*.

Sensuality. See *Lust*.

Separate Baptists. See *Baptist Bodies*, 22.

Separatists. See *Congregational and Christian Churches*, A 1.

Sepp, Johannes Nepomuk (1816 to 1909). Studied at Muenchen; made extensive journeys; became professor at Muenchen and wrote a reply to Strauss's *Life of Jesus*, adding to his work the account of the Book of Acts; after 1870 opposed the doctrine of Infallibility and joined the Old Catholic group; made several trips to Palestine in the interest of Christian archaeology, which he presented in monographs; also studied German, specifically Bavarian, antiquities.

Septuagesima Sunday. See *Church Year*, 3.

Septuagint. See *Bible Versions*, A.

Sequence. Viewed simply as a musical term, the word "sequence" refers to the immediate repetition of a short musical phrase at another pitch. When used liturgically, however, the term refers to additions which follow immediately after the Alleluia, hence "sequence." Sequence texts are lengthy poems whose musical setting is usually syllabic. Each stanza has two lines which are alike as far as syllabic accentuation and number of syllables are concerned. C. Blume, E. Wellesz, and others insist that sequences originated before the days of Notker of St. Gall (d. 912), but admit that Notker established the sequence. Among the most famous sequences of the Middle Ages we find: *Media vita in morte sumus* (Notker), *Veni Sancte Spiritus, Dies Irae*, and *Victimae paschali*. Polyphonic settings of sequences were written by Willaert, Jommelli, and other masters of the Roman Catholic Church.

W. Apel, *Harvard Dictionary of Mu-*

sic, Cambridge (Mass.), 1944; G. Reese, *Music in the Middle Ages,* New York, 1940; E. Wellesz, *Eastern Elements in Western Chant,* Boston, 1947.

Serampur Brotherhood. See *India,* 6.

Seraphim. Heavenly beings described Is. 6:2,3 as an order of angels who stand around the heavenly throne, having each six wings, also hands and feet, and praising God with their voices. They are commonly classified with the cherubim as archangels. See *Angels; Cherubim.*

Serapion (4th century). Friend and supporter of Athanasius.

Serbia. Now a part of Yugoslavia (language, Slavic). Adopted Christianity in the 8th century. It has a small number of Evangelical, Roman Catholic, Jewish, and Mohammedan inhabitants, but the leading church is the Serbian Orthodox Church (approximately six million members), affiliated with, and holding the same views as, the other Eastern Orthodox churches. Highest authority: the National Synod, consisting of the Patriarch and three other bishops. All religions are recognized and enjoy equal rights (1949).

Serbian Orthodox Church in the United States. See *Eastern Orthodox Churches,* 6.

Sergius. See *Monothelitism.*

Serle, Ambrose (1742—1812). Commissioner in the English government transport office; author of several prose works, one of which includes hymns; wrote: "Thy Ways, O Lord, with Wise Design."

Sermon. See *Homiletics; Preaching, Christian, History of.*

Servetus, Michael (1511—53). Noted Spanish physician and anti-Trinitarian; b. at Tudela; studied at Toulouse; at coronation of Charles V came to Germany, where, in 1531, he published his anti-Trinitarian doctrines in *De Trinitatis Erroribus;* returned to France, where his main work, *Christianismi Restitutio,* appeared, 1553. After he had escaped the Catholic inquisition, he was arrested while passing through Geneva and through Calvin's influence condemned to death as heretic and burned alive, October 27, 1553. See *Calvin, John,* 6; *Unitarians.*

Service Books. General designation for the liturgical books used in conducting church services. In the time

before the Reformation the number of such books was very great, including not only Sacramentaries, but also Missals, Breviaries, Troparia, Cantionalia, also smaller directives for various occasions and for the separate parts of the services. In the Lutheran Church the number of service books is considerably smaller, the Agenda for public worship containing practically everything that is required for that purpose, the smaller pocket Agendas offering the material needed for pastoral acts of a more private nature, such as house Communions and emergency Baptisms, also funerals, and the Lectionaries (if any) giving the pericopes prescribed by church usage. In some cases Antiphonaria and other books with musical settings complete the equipment required for worship.

Service Centers. See *Armed Services Commission.*

Service Commission. See *National Lutheran Council.*

Service Pastors. See *Armed Services Commission.*

Servites. See *Annunciation, Orders of.*

Settlements. In modern social work, special rooms or houses (settlement houses, neighborhood houses, etc.) devoted chiefly to social welfare work. A settlement house usually includes meeting rooms, soup kitchens, day nurseries, gymnasiums, and sometimes dispensaries. A notable example is Hull House in Chicago.

Seuel, Edmund. B. April 21, 1865, Vincennes, Ind.; ed. Concordia Col., Fort Wayne, Ind., and Concordia Sem., St. Louis, Mo., grad., 1886; pastor and missionary at large at Ogallala, Nebr., 1886 to 1888; prof., Walther Col., St. Louis, Mo., 1888—1907; manager, Conc. Publ. House, St. Louis, Mo., 1907—44; mem., Bd. of Directors, Luth. Ch. — Mo. Synod, 1917—41; treas. of same synod, 1914—42; cofounder of Luth. Laymen's League; Litt. D., Concordia Sem., St. Louis, 1936; Mus. D., Valparaiso Univ., Valparaiso, Ind., 1936. D. May 9, 1951.

Seven Deadly Sins. See *Sins, Venial and Mortal.*

Seven Gifts of the Holy Spirit. A term often applied to the list of virtues in Is. 11:2.

Seven Sleepers of Ephesus. Christian youths who, according to a legend, having been walled up in a cave during the Decian persecution, fell asleep and awoke after ca. 200 years to find the Christian Church everywhere established.

Seven Sorrows of Our Lady. Roman Catholic devotions used by the Servites during Lent and September 15.

Seven Virtues. See *Cardinal Virtues.*

Seventh-Day Adventists. See *Adventist Bodies,* 4.

Seventh-Day Baptists. See *Baptist Bodies,* 16, 17.

Severinghaus, J. D. (1834—1905). Leader among the Germans in the Lutheran General Synod; graduated from Wittenberg Seminary, 1861; founder of the *Lutherische Kirchenfreund,* 1869; established connections with Breklum in 1878; founded a seminary in Chicago, 1883, which was afterwards transferred to Atchison, Kans.

Severus, Sulpicius (ca. 363—410). Latin church father who spent much of his time in a monastery at Aquitaine; wrote *Sacred History* (to A. D. 400), *Life of St. Martin of Tours, Three Dialogs.*

Sext. See *Canonical Hours.*

Sexton. Originally an attendant on the clergy, the term is now generally used of one who cares for church property, rings the bell, and performs other related functions.

Sexual Life. See *Marriage.*

Seyffarth, Gustav. B. July 13, 1769, in Uebigow, Prov. of Saxony; attended St. Afra's School, Meissen; studied theology, philosophy, and philology at Leipzig for four years; received the degree of Ph. D.; continued his studies, especially the languages of the ancient Bible versions; published a work on the pronunciation of Greek; was in charge of the continuation of Spohn's work on the Egyptian language — one of the most learned Egyptologists of his day. Since 1823 professor of archaeology at Leipzig; resigned because of the intrigues of the Freemasons, drawing a full professor's pension. Meeting Walther and Wyneken in 1851, he came to America and filled gratuitously, for three years, a professorship at Concordia College and Seminary, St. Louis. Returned to his archaeological studies in New York, 1859. The titles of his works cover 13 octavo pages. D. Nov. 17, 1885.

The Literary Life of Gustav Seyffarth, an Autobiographical Sketch, Steiger, N. Y., 1886; biography in Jennsson, *American Lutheran Biographies.*

Shakers. 1. Popular name of oldest American communistic sect, the "United Society of Believers in Christ's Second Appearing," or "Millennial Church," founded about the middle of the 18th century in England by Ann Lee (1736 to 1784). In 1747 a number of Quakers, incited by the fanatic preaching and ecstasies of the "French Prophets," formed a small society, the members of which, because of their movements during religious excitement, were derisively called "Shaking Quakers." These were joined, 1858, by Ann Lee, who became the real founder of the sect and a "prophetess," claiming to be an incarnation of Christ and enjoining celibacy upon her followers. Because of persecution and imprisonment, she emigrated to America, 1774, with eight adherents. They first settled at Watervliet, N. Y., gaining followers in spite of persecution. The first society was organized, 1787, at Mount Lebanon, N. Y. Its missionary activity reached its height 1805—35, when new societies were organized in Eastern States, in Kentucky, Ohio, and Indiana, with a membership of 5,000. But since 1860 it suffered a steady numerical decline.

2. Their teachings were as follows: God has a dual nature, partly male, partly female. Adam, created in God's image, also was dual. His fall consisted in transgressing the law of chastity. Christ, like all other spirits, also is dual and was incarnated in Jesus and Ann Lee, representing male and female elements of God. However, neither Jesus nor Ann Lee are to be worshiped, only loved and honored. Consequently the Shakers rejected the Holy Trinity and atonement, also physical resurrection, Last Judgment, and eternal damnation. Other tenets were their pronounced communism, celibacy, non-resistance, and non-participation in war, perfectionism, spiritism, insistence upon public confession. The government of each community was vested in four elders, two men and two women. Their services consisted of hymns, addresses, and especially of a rhythmical marching, in which men and women were grouped separately.

Shamanism. Name of animistic cult of Uralo-Altaic peoples of northern Asia, applied also to that of Eskimo and American Indian tribes. It is practiced by the *shaman,* or medicine man, who, combining the functions of exorcist, sorcerer, priest, and doctor, claims to be able to command supernatural forces, divine, heal, drive out evil spirits, and, in general, avert evil and accomplish good for those who employ him, and plays a leading role in ceremonial dances and feasts. The trance, induced by self-hypnotism, and the use of drums are common characteristics of his performances.

Shamash. See *Babylonians, Religion of,* 1.

Shammai. Jewish Rabbi of first century B.C., contemporary of Hillel and with him member of Sanhedrin. In opposition to the liberal-minded Hillel he favored a strict, even severe, interpretation of the Law.

Shang-ti. See *Confucianism,* 3.

Shastras, or *Shasters,* strictly, the law books of the Hindus, but in common usage, any of their sacred writings, including the *Vedas,* their commentaries, and the six orthodox systems of Indian philosophy. See *Brahmanism.*

Shedd, William G. T. (1820—94). Presbyterian; b. at Acton, Mass.; pastor; professor, last in Union Theological Seminary, New York City (d. there); wrote: *History of Christian Doctrine; Dogmatic Theology;* etc.

Sheeleigh, Matthias. B. Dec. 29, 1821, at Charleston, Pa.; ed. Pa. Coll., Gettysburg, Pa. (M. A., 1861); Theol. Sem., Gettysburg, Pa., 1852; pastorates at Valatie, N. Y., 1853—57; Minersville, Pa., 1857—59; Philadelphia, Pa., 1859 to 1864; Stewardtsville, N. J., 1864—69; Whitemarsh and Upper Dublin, Pa., 1869—98; sec., Gen. Synod, 1866—1900; sec., East. Pa. Synod, 1861, pres., 1871; director of Theol. Sem., Gettysburg, Pa., 34 years until his death; author of many hymns and poems; translator; editor: *Lutheran Sunday School Herald,* 1860—1900; *Luth. Almanac and Year Book,* 1871—1900; co-editor, *Luth. Home Journal,* 1859—60; D.D. Newberry Coll., Newberry, S. C., 1885. D. July 15, 1900.

Sheldon, Charles Monroe (1857 to 1946). Congregationalist; b. at Wellsville, N. Y.; pastor in Waterbury, Vt., and Topeka, Kans.; minister at large; aim: to advance practical Christianity; prolific miscellaneous writer. Wrote *In His Steps.*

Shem-hammephorash, שֵׁם הַמְּפֹרָשׁ, term used by Jews of Middle Ages to designate the Tetragrammaton, יהוה, the Old Testament divine name, commonly pronounced "Jehovah" by Christians. The Jews avoided its pronunciation. Magic powers were attributed to it by the Kabbala, and he who knew its secret could perform miracles. Meaning of term not assured; perhaps "the distinctive name." Also a designation of ridicule used by Luther in writing against the Jews.

Shen. See *Confucianism,* 3.

Sheol. See *Hereafter,* C 3.

Shepherd of Hermas. See *Apostolic Fathers,* 5.

Shiites (from Arabic *shiʻa,* "party"). Name of one of the two main divisions of Mohammedanism. The principal difference between them and the other great division, the Sunnites, is their belief that the caliphate is hereditary and not elective, that consequently it belonged to Ali, Mohammed's son-in-law, and his descendants, and that the first three caliphs, Abu-Bekr, Omar, and Othman, who were elected to the office, were usurpers. They are found scattered over the whole Moslem world, but especially in Persia, where their confession was made the state religion in 1512, and among the common people of India. Of the total Mohammedan population of the world of 221,000,000, the Shiites number about 15,000,000. They are divided into many sects. The religious systems of the Assassins, Druses, and Babists are derivative of the Shiite religion.

Shinto. 1. The ancient native religion of Japan. The primitive Japanese cult was a crude polytheistic nature worship. It included the worship of all those beings that excite admiration, awe, or terror. To these was applied the name *kami,* the Japanese name for the deity; literally, "above, superior." Such *kami* were, besides human beings, the sun, the heavens; rain, thunder, winds; animals, such as the tiger, wolf, fox, serpent, also birds; plants, trees, mountains, seas, etc. In time these crude beliefs developed mythological aspects. The chief source of our knowledge of ancient Japanese cosmogony and mythology are two old semihistorical records, the *Kojiki,* compiled A. D. 712, and the *Nihongi,* compiled A. D. 720. They relate that a male *kami,* Izanagi, and a female *kami,* Izanami, together brought the islands of Japan into existence and also gave birth to many of the gods and goddesses in the

Shinto pantheon. The most eminent of these is Amaterasu, the sun goddess, who now holds the highest rank and is worshiped at Ise, the center of Shinto.

2. This crude nature worship had no name until the 6th century, when Buddhism was introduced into Japan and the name Shinto, a Chinese expression meaning "the way or doctrine of the gods" and the equivalent of the Japanese *Kami-no-michi*, was applied to the native religion to distinguish it from its new rival. From that time on Shinto developed other features, which were partly due to Chinese influence. Ancestor worship * crept in, and the dead, especially deceased emperors, famous men, scholars, warriors, began to be regarded as *kami*. New *kami* were continually added to the pantheon, until they became innumerable.

3. The gods are, as a rule, considered to be beneficent, though they may cause illness and misfortune if their worship is neglected. On the other hand, the aid of the gods is sought as a protection against plagues and disasters.

4. Important is the fact that reverence for the emperor became a part of Shinto and the native religion was made to serve the interests of his house. This cult of the mikado was given a quasihistorical basis by attributing divine descent to him. He was said to be the direct descendant of the sun goddess.

5. The Shinto shrines are simple, unpainted, wooden structures. Before them are the *torii*, gateways, consisting of two uprights, with two cross-beams at the top, the upper slightly curved and projecting beyond the lower. The interior of the temples is almost bare. There are no idols, unless the *shintai*, or "god-bodies," are regarded as such. These *Shintai* are mirrors, swords, precious stones, and other objects, in which the *mitama*, or spirit of the deity, is believed to reside. However, these *shintai* are contained in boxes and are seldom exposed to public view. The *shintai* of the chief diety, the sun goddess, is the mirror, a symbol of the brilliancy of sunlight.

6. The Shinto cult has a ritual and a hereditary priesthood, the emperor being the chief priest. Celibacy is not enjoined upon the priests, neither do they wear any distinctive dress except when they officiate. Public worship in the ordinary sense is not held, the priests worshiping by themselves. The laity, however, also come to the shrines to worship. A bell or gong is rung to call the attention of the god or goddess to the worshiper. The worship consists of obeisances and clapping of hands. Offerings of food, drink, and fabrics were formerly made, but these have in modern times been replaced by the *gohei*, sticks, to which strips of white paper are attached. These, of course, are merely representations or imitations of the fabrics formerly offered.

7. Shinto has no code of ethics for its followers. It considers man to be inherently good, and everything is well if he follows his own good impulses. Any impurities caused by contact with things that defile can be easily cleansed away, and bathing is one of the principal means of purification. There is no sense of sin, and consequently the ideas of forgiveness of sins and of redemption are entirely lacking. The teachings regarding the soul and the life beyond the grave are vague. Belief in life after death is expressed, but there is no teaching regarding heaven and hell. To sum up, Shinto is a mixture of nature, ancestor, and hero worship, a cult that has neither sacred books nor dogmas nor a code of ethics.

8. After the introduction of Buddhism into Japan Shinto remained an independent cult for some time, but about the 9th century it was absorbed by the alien religion. The two religions formed one system under the name of Ryobu-Shinto, in which Buddhism, however, exerted the greater influence. This state of affairs continued until the 18th century, when a strong reaction in favor of Shinto set in. This revival of the ancient faith, with its mikado cult, led to the restoration of the imperial power in 1868, which had for centuries been eclipsed by the *shoguns*, the Japanese feudal lords. However, a cult so barren in ethical teachings as Shinto is, compared with Buddhism, could exert only little influence on the people. It became a vehicle for the expression of patriotism and loyalty to the emperor and was kept alive by pilgrimages and festivals.

After the close of World War II, Shinto was deprived of its favored position as the state religion of Japan. It was no longer permitted to teach Shinto in regular school hours nor to draw support for it from state funds. The declaration of the emperor disavowing any divine status for himself also helped to break the hold which

Shinto had exercised over the people of Japan.

As it is practically impossible to differentiate between Shintoists and Buddhists in Japan, no statistics regarding the adherents of each can be given. See *Religion, Comparative* (bibliography).

Shrovetide. A name for the Tuesday before Ash Wednesday, or the three days preceding Lent. It is derived from the Latin word *scribo*, to write, and gained the notation to confess, or to shrive. The idea was that the days before Lent were to be devoted to an acknowledgment and confession of sins in order to have the heart conditioned for the proper observance of the holy season.

Shrubsole, William (1759—1829). B. at Sheerness, in the isle of Shippey, Kent, England. He was the son of a master mastmaker, who was also a lay preacher. William was engaged as a shipwright in the dockyard. At 26 he moved to London. During the last twenty years of his life he was a member of the Congregational Church, active in benevolence and reformatory institutions. He contributed hymns to various religious magazines. Seven of his hymns are in common use. He is probably best known by "When, Streaming from the Eastern Skies."

Shu. See *Confucianism*, 2; *Sacred Literature.*

Shu-King. See *Sacred Literature.*

Shulchan aruch. One of the great law compendiums of Judaism, based on a great commentary of Joseph Karo (1488—1575), which covered all the decisions since the completion of the Talmud. *Shulchan aruch* (the prepared table) offers a summary of the greater work, as it drew on the authority of the great teachers of Judaism. It became a great unifying agent among the conservative Jews.

Siam. See *Thailand.*

Sibel, Kaspar (1590—1658). Dutch Reformed; b. at Unterbarmen, Germany; pastor; last charge Deventer, Holland (d. there); arranged for Synod of Dort; revised Dutch Bible; manuscript autobiography.

Sibylline Books. A collection of apocryphal prophecies, partly of Jewish, partly of Christian origin, containing polemics against polytheism, visions of a Golden Age, the coming of Christ, the final Judgment, etc. The mass of material accumulated from the second century B. C. to about the fourth or fifth after Christ. Some of the Christian Fathers unhesitatingly appealed to these oracles in defense of Christianity. Others used them with caution or ignored them entirely.

Sicarii. Name applied to the organization of the extreme zealots among the Jews from the days of the Maccabees to the destruction of Jerusalem. They carried a knife or stiletto under their outer garment (hence the name) and bound themselves by the most terrible oaths to work toward the destruction of the Roman masters of the land. Their activity, especially during the Jewish War, became one of ruthlessness and terrorism, many of them being criminals of the lowest type. After the fall of Jerusalem the last remnant of the *Sicarii*, under the leadership of Eleazar, fled to the fortress Masada near the Dead Sea, where the last 960 committed suicide.

Sichardus, Johannes (ca. 1499 to 1552). Humanist and jurist; studied in Erfurt and Ingolstadt, taught at Muenchen and Basel; made extensive journeys, studied at Freiburg, became professor at Tuebingen and occupied various positions of importance, especially as counselor of Duke Christoph of Wuerttemberg; an adherent of the Reformation, but in an irenic spirit; published an edition of the *Recognitiones Clementis.*

Sickingen, Franz von (1481—1523). Champion of the knights against the princes; wrote for the Reformation and would gladly have given most of his income to translate Luther into French to win the Emperor; twice invited Luther to his castles, "inns of righteousness" for the persecuted reformers; killed in fight against Elector of Treves at Landstuhl.

Sidgwick, Henry (1838—1900). Prof. at Cambridge, England; active in psychical research; wrote *Methods of Ethics* and other works; advocated a utilitarianism tempered by intuitionism.

Sidonius Apollinaris (430—87). Excelled as poet and orator; became bishop of Clermont in Gaul; a man of many-sided interests; lacking somewhat in depth, but upheld ecclesiastical organization; helped to defend his city against the Goths, but was taken captive; after his liberation he reassumed his office as bishop; nine books of letters form his most notable writings.

Sieck, Henry. B. July 1, 1850, at Mannheim, Baden, graduate of Concordia Seminary 1873; pastor in Memphis, Tenn., South Bend, Ind., Zion Church, St. Louis, and elsewhere in the Missouri Synod; president of St. John's College, Winfield, Kans., 1893; pastor of Mount Olive Church, Milwaukee; published several volumes of English sermons; d. Sept. 7, 1916.

Sieck, Louis J. B. Mar. 11, 1884, at Erie, Pa.; graduated from Concordia College, Milwaukee (1901), and Concordia Seminary, St. Louis, 1904; asst. pastor to F. Pfotenhauer, Hamburg, Minn., 1904; asst. pastor at Zion, Saint Louis, 1905; pastor, 1914—43; teacher, public speaking, Walther College, Saint Louis, 1909—10; pres., Concordia Seminary, St. Louis, 1943—52; member. Bd. of Directors, Valparaiso, 11 yrs.; chrm., National Advisory Emergency Planning Council of The Luth. Church — Missouri Synod; pres., St. Louis Pastoral Conference, 24 yrs.; member, Bd. of Control, Concordia Seminary, Saint Louis, 1923—52; organizer and pres., Luth. Publicity Organization, 21 yrs.; pres., St. Louis City Mission Society, 10 yrs.; charter member, Concordia Historical Institute; vice-pres., State Historical Society of Missouri; co-author, *The Glory of Golgotha;* contributed to theological publications; D. D., Concordia Seminary, St. Louis, 1939. His sermons were simple, straightforward, practical, and at all times Christ-centered. He was a theologian in his own right. Studied under Pieper and Stoeckhardt. He excelled as an administrator and organizer. D. Sept. 17, 1953.

Sieffert, Friedrich Anton Emil (1843 to 1911). German Protestant theologian; studied at Koenigsberg, Halle, and Berlin; taught at Bonn, became professor at Erlangen, then at Bonn; wrote a monograph on the Galatian question, also a commentary on Galatians for Meyer's *Commentary.*

Siegler, Richard. B. July 20, 1859, at Wallin in Pomerania; emigrated in 1863; trained at Northwestern College, Watertown, Wis., and the Lutheran Theol. Seminary at Milwaukee (now at Thiensville), Wis. Pastor at Ellington and Barre Mills, Wis.; from 1910 on for 25 years he served as field representative of educational institutions and

missions of the Joint Synod of Wisconsin. D. Nov. 6, 1941.

Sieker, Johann Heinrich. B. Oct. 23, 1838, at Schweinfurth, Bavaria; emigrated to Wisconsin, 1847; studied at Gettysburg (Wisconsin Synod had no seminary of its own); ordained as Lutheran pastor of Granville, Wis., 1861; in full accord with the leaders of Wisconsin Synod in its withdrawal from the General Synod; pastor of Trinity, St. Paul, 1867, becoming a member of the Minnesota Synod and its president; induced it to withdraw from the General Council and to join the Synodical Conference; pastor of St. Matthew's, New York, the oldest Lutheran congregation in the United States, 1876; joined Missouri in 1881, the congregation in 1885; founder of Concordia Collegiate Institute, Bronxville, developed from the academy of St. Matthew's, the congregation becoming a most generous supporter of the college, Inner Mission, and charitable institutions. D. Dec. 30, 1904.

P. Roesener, *Johann Heinrich Sieker,* Waisenhaur, W. Roxbury, Mass., 1905.

Sierra Leone. A British colony and protectorate on the west coast of Africa, between Liberia and French Guiana. Area, 27,925 sq. mi. Population, 1,975,000 (1950 est.), mostly Negroes. Missions by a number of Reformed churches and societies. Statistics: Foreign staff, 155; Christian community, 54,449; communicants, 23,130 (1952).

Sieveking, Amalie (1794—1859). Gave her services to the hospitals in Hamburg during the cholera epidemic of 1831; formed a Protestant sisterhood, 1832, for the care of the sick and the poor.

Sievers, G. E. C. Ferdinand. B. May 18, 1816, at Lueneburg, Hanover; graduate of Goettingen; studied at Berlin and Halle. Won through Wyneken's appeal, he headed the Lutheran colonists sent by Loehe, who founded Frankenlust, Mich., 1847, remaining their pastor till his death, September 9, 1893. An energetic missionary, he traveled in Michigan, Ohio, Wisconsin, and Minnesota, founding congregations in Bay City and vicinity, and in Minneapolis and other parts of Minnesota. As chairman of the Board for Missions among the Heathen he frequently visited the stations of the Indian Mission. His incessant appeals in behalf of Foreign Missions resulted in the founding of the Missouri Synod's Foreign Missions, 1893.

A. R. Suelflow, "The Life and Work of Georg Ernst Christian Ferdinand Sievers," *CHIQ*, XX, 135—41; 180—87; XXI, 36—41; 75—87; 100—14; 175—80; XXII, 43—48; 77—84.

Siger of Brabant (ca. 1235—ca. 80). French philosopher; influenced by Averroes; opponent of Thomas Aquinas and Albertus Magnus.

Sigismund, John. See *John Sigismund.*

Signorelli, Luca (ca. 1441—1523). Italian painter; applied anatomical knowledge to painting; frescoes in Cathedral of Orvieto, including "Resurrection of the Dead"; "Madonna Enthroned," in the Cathedral of Perugia.

Sigtuna Stiftelsen. See *Sweden, Lutheran Church in,* 6.

Sihler, Wilhelm. 1. B. Nov. 12, 1801, at Bernstadt, Silesia; entered college at ten, the military school at fifteen, lieutenant at eighteen. Taking his discharge, he entered, 1826, the University of Berlin, where he heard philosophical, philological, and a few theological lectures; a great admirer of Schleiermacher. Graduating as Ph. D., he tutored for a year and in 1830 became instructor at a private college in Dresden. A rationalist till now, the grace of God here led him to know his sinfulness and his Savior and, greatly through his intercourse with such pronounced Lutherans as Professor Scheibel, Dr. Rudelbach, and Pastor Wermelskirch, to study and love the Bible and the Lutheran Confessions. Forced to relinquish his position at Dresden on this account, he became a private tutor in Livonia, 1838, on the island of Oesel, 1840, at Riga.

2. Desirous of entering the ministry, Wyneken's *Appeal*, together with the advice of his pastoral friends and the Dresden Mission Society, won him for the work in America. Recommended by Dr. Rudelbach and by Pastor Loehe, the professors at Columbus, Ohio, directed him to Pomeroy, Ohio, where he preached his inaugural sermon January 1, 1844. Here he contributed articles to the *Lutherische Kirchenzeitung* and wrote *A Dialog of Two Lutherans on Methodism.*

3. Through the *Lutheraner* he became acquainted with Walther and the other confessional Lutherans. In 1845 he, with others, withdrew from the Ohio Synod because of its unionistic position. In July of the same year he became Wyneken's successor at Fort Wayne, having charge of three preaching stations besides and laboring with great success for the planting of the Church in the surrounding counties. A thoroughly Scriptural preacher (he published three volumes of sermons) and conscientious pastor, insisting on purity of doctrine, holiness of life, and the old-fashioned Lutheran Church discipline, and, particularly, laying great stress on the training of the children in school and *Christenlehre*, as well as on the training of children and adults in the Catechism, he left behind him, at his death, "a congregation thoroughly indoctrinated, full of living faith, and rich in good works."

4. The Missouri Synod owes its character and growth, under God, particularly to three men — Walther, Sihler, and Wyneken. Sihler took a prominent part in the work of the conferences leading to the organization of the Synod. He was its first Vice-President, overseeing the eastern part of the Synod, and the first President of the Central District, zealous in preserving pure Lutheranism and ever alive to its missionary opportunities. Taking up the work begun by Wyneken, of training men for the ministry, he established, with the help of Loehe, the Practical Seminary at Fort Wayne (1846) and served as its president and professor till 1861. In 1857 he founded, with others, the Teachers' Seminary at the Fort Wayne College; he was president of Concordia College, Fort Wayne, and repeatedly served as instructor. A zealous champion of confessional Lutheranism and a keen-eyed, warmhearted promoter of Synod's practical work, advocating these things with all the force of his sturdy Christian character (at conventions and colloquies) and of his blunt and vigorous pen (he wrote a number of pamphlets and over 100 articles for Synod's periodicals), he put a lasting mark upon Synod. D. Oct. 27, 1885.

W. Sihler, *Lebenslauf*, CPH, 1879 (vol. 1); Lutherischer Verlagsverein, N. Y. (vol. 2); W. Sihler, *Autobiographie,* CPH, 1880; E. G. Sihler, "Memorial of Dr. William Sihler (1801—85)," *CHIQ*, V: 50—57.

Sikhs. Originally an Indian sect, now grown into a nation, principally found in the Punjab. Founded by Nanak (b. 1469), who endeavored to unite Mohammedanism with Hinduism, rejecting the social and ceremonial restrictions of the latter. Their chief religious tenet is strict monotheism. The doctrines of reincarnation,* karma,* and nirvana * were retained, while the Hindu caste system and pilgrimages were rejected. Their sacred book is the Grantha, preserved in the capital, Amritsar. In the middle of the 19th century they came into conflict with the British, who defeated them in two campaigns and in 1849 annexed the Punjab. They number about 5,500,000 (1950 est.).

Silent Reading. See *Christian Teaching,* K.

Siloam Inscription. An inscription found near the Pool of Siloam; written in Old Hebrew alphabet.

Simon. See *Christs, False.*

Simon Magus. See *Gnosticism,* 7 a.

Simon, Richard (1638—1712). Roman Catholic scholar and critic; one of the pioneers of the historico-critical method in its application to the books of the Bible. His *Histoire Critique* ("Critical History of the Old Testament"), published in 1678, was condemned as heretical, but was republished by the author in Rotterdam in 1685. Simon also made respectable contributions to the study of the Biblical text and of ancient versions.

Simony (for derivation of word see Acts 8:18-20). The purchase or sale of anything spiritual for money or other temporal consideration. Many of the earlier church councils found it necessary to condemn simony, and Justinian (533) caused an imperial decree against it, engraved in marble, to be placed in St. Peter's Church at Rome because simony had been used in papal elections. Pope Gregory I (599) urged various bishops to purge their churches of simony; the practice had evidently become general. It rose to still greater heights in the 11th century. In 1033 a twelve-year-old boy became Pope as Benedict IX, his father having bought the papal dignity for him. Benedict, in turn, sold the office to Gregory VI. A resolute opponent of simony arose in Gregory VII (1073 to 1085), who was determined to put an end to lay investiture as then practiced, which he termed simony. Kings and other rulers claimed the right of nominating candidates to ecclesiastical dignities that fell vacant in their territories and of investing them with the material possessions that went with the office. During the vacancy of a benefice the ruler appropriated the income. He also took the personal property of the deceased prelate and received a fee from the new incumbent at his investiture. Under such conditions, benefices were often practically sold to the highest bidder regardless of his fitness. Gregory's efforts led to a long struggle, which was ended by later popes through a compromise, in which the Church gained most of her points. But if Gregory had driven the devils of simony out of the temporal princes, they appear to have made their lodging thereafter in the hierarchy, particularly at Rome. Popes became the worst offenders. It is illuminating to find that some of the later canonists taught that what was simony in others was not simony in the popes, because everything in the Church was theirs. Dante's *Inferno* makes Nicholas III the mouthpiece of the simoniacs in hell and refers to the simony of Boniface VIII and Clement V. On the eve of the Reformation the venality of Rome reached its height. Everything spiritual was frankly for sale, and the most shameless methods were employed to increase the profits, the same preferment being sold to as many as possible, though only one could hold it, and old men being preferably appointed, so that a new vacancy might occur soon. From this curse, as from some others, the Roman Church was delivered by the Reformation.

Simpson, A. B. See *Evangelistic Associations,* 5.

Sin. Sin is Scripturally defined as the transgression of the divine Law (1 John 3:4). Sin always has its root in the will of the individual. Irrational beings cannot sin. Yet this does not mean that every sin is connected with a direct act of the will; it may be involuntary, or it may be a state or condition. There are different kinds and different degrees of sin: original sin (see *Sin, Original*); actual sin — every act, thought, emotion, conflicting with the Law of God. Actual sins may be involuntary or may be sins of ignorance (Acts 17:30). There is the sin of omission, which is a neglect of duty or a failure to measure up to full responsibility. But there is also voluntary or presumptuous sin, committed against the warnings of conscience and with the consent of the will, a violation of known duty. The necessary consequence of sin is guilt; on the part of God, it is righteous wrath and punishment. Willful sins grieve the Spirit and sear the sinner's conscience until he can no longer feel the point of the Spirit's sword (Heb. 4:12). The heart becomes too hard to be softened or pricked and the sinner too blind to see and too deaf to hear. He no longer desires salvation; he has sinned away his day of grace. The Lord in love had pleaded with him, but he refused to hear and repent; and when, in the day of reckoning, he cries for mercy, his cries are unheard. The day of salvation has ended, and the door of mercy is closed. The Lord declares: "My Spirit shall not always strive with man" (Gen. 6:3). There is a limit to God's long-suffering and patience (Acts 7: 51-53). This state of hardening of the heart is not identical with the unpardonable sin. The hardened state of the soul may be reached by omitting to do what the Holy Ghost wants, namely, to accept Christ. The unpardonable sin, on the other hand, while a true hardening (self-hardening) of the heart, always implies the rejection and repudiation of truths which had once been accepted by intellect and conscience. See *Sin, Unpardonable.*

Sin, Original *(Inherited).* 1. This term, in its ordinary acceptation, does not refer to the origin of sin in the beginning, but it signifies both the guilt of Adam's sin imputed to his offspring (hereditary guilt, Rom. 5:12; see Formula of Concord, I, Art. 1; Sol. Decl., § 9), and the corruption of man's nature, which took place when sin entered and which ever thereafter has inhered in the human will and inclinations. The texts which particularly refer to original sin are Gen. 5:3; John 3:6; Ps. 51:5; Gen. 6:5; Job 15:14; Rom. 14:23. Original sin is not an activity, but a quality, a state, an inherent condition. It exists, even though there be no conscious, voluntary act of the internal or external powers, of the mind or the body. Yet it is "a root and fountainhead of all actual sins." It is their parent, and they are its offspring. It is the silent, unseen cause; they are the effects.

2. The description of original sin given in the Augsburg Confession, Art. II, contemplates it not in the abstract, as though it were something which subsists in itself and were capable of being viewed apart, but as inhering in the nature of man and inseparable from it even in thought, so long as it continues to exist. It has no existence apart from human nature and hence cannot be described as something

that is "essential and self-subsisting." (See Formula of Concord, Epitome, chapter I.) The Second Article, therefore, speaks of men with sin, the sin with which they are born, and declares that this sin consists in this, that they are "without the fear of God, without trust in God, and with concupiscence." It sets forth their natural disability from birth with reference to that which is good in the eyes of God, and their positive inclination toward all that is evil. When it says that they are "without the fear of God, without trust in God," the meaning is, not only that they do not, but that they cannot and can never, by their own reason or strength, truly fear God, or trust in Him and love Him as He would have them fear, trust, and love. In order that they may do this, a work of divine grace is necessary in them. And when the article says that they are "with concupiscence," the meaning is that they are, in all the powers of their being, in those of the understanding, reason, heart, and will, as well as in those of the body, full of evil desire and evil inclination, according to Gen. 8:21 and 6:5: "The imagination of man's heart is evil from his youth," "only evil continually."

3. The reality of original sin is denied by all forms of Pelagianism (see *Pelagianism*), which includes the Modernistic error and Christian Science. Against all these errors our Confession affirms that "this disease, or vice of origin, is truly sin." The Formula of Concord says: Original sin "is an entire want or lack of concreated original righteousness in Paradise, or of God's image, according to which man was originally created in truth, holiness, and righteousness, and at the same time an inability and unfitness for all the things of God." And further: "Original sin (in human nature) is not only such an entire absence of all good in spiritual, divine things, but instead of the lost image of God in man it is at the same time also a deep, wicked, horrible, fathomless, inscrutable, and unspeakable corruption of the entire nature and all its powers, especially of the highest, principal powers of the soul in understanding, heart and will; that now, since the Fall, man inherits an inborn wicked disposition and inward impurity of heart, evil lust and propensity. We all, by disposition and nature, inherit from Adam such a heart, feeling, and thought as are, according to their highest powers and the light

of reason, naturally inclined and disposed directly, contrary to God and His chief commandments; yea, they are enmity against God, especially as regards divine and spiritual things. For in other respects, as regards natural, external things which are subject to reason, man still has, to a certain degree, understanding, power, and ability, although very much weakened, all of which, nevertheless, has been so infected and contaminated by original sin that before God it is of no use." (*Concordia Triglotta*, p. 863.) And, again, the same confession says: "We believe, teach, and confess that original sin is not a slight, but so deep a corruption of human nature that nothing healthy or uncorrupt has remained in man's body or soul, in his inner or outward powers." (*Ibid.*, p. 781.)

4. In order that human nature may be delivered from this horrible evil and healed, the Holy Spirit's work of regeneration and sanctification is necessary; and as a means to this end He uses Baptism; for original sin condemns and brings eternal death "upon those not born again through Baptism and the Holy Ghost. (Augsb. Conf., Art. II. *Conc. Trigl.*, 43.) It is covered and forgiven before God for Christ's sake "in the baptized and believing." (Form. of Con. *Conc. Trigl.*, *l. c.*) "He that believeth and is baptized shall be saved." Mark 16:16. — The final separation of the human nature and the corruption inhering in it, which separation God alone can effect, will come to pass "through death, in the resurrection, where our nature which we now bear will rise and live eternally, without original sin, and separated and sundered from it." (Form. of Con. *Conc. Trigl.*, 873.)

Sin, The Unpardonable. 1. To this sin the following passages refer: Matt. 12:31; Mark 3:29; Luke 12:10; Heb. 6:4-6; 1 John 5:16. If we compare these passages with one another, it becomes plain that the sin against the Holy Ghost, or the unpardonable sin, consists in a knowing, conscious, stubborn, and malicious opposition to divine truth once recognized as such, and in blasphemous hostility against it. J. Gerhard defines it as "an intentional denial of evangelical truth, which was acknowledged and approved by conscience, connected with a bold attack upon it, and voluntary blasphemy against it." Quenstedt sets it forth in three points somewhat more elaborately. "The sin against the Holy Ghost consists 1) in a denial of

evangelical truth, which was evidently and sufficiently acknowledged and approved and which denial was effected by a full, free, and unimpeded exercise of the will; 2) in a hostile attack upon the same; 3) in a voluntary and atrocious blasphemy." — The stubborn and malicious opposition, which is the essence of the unpardonable sin, may be further distinguished as follows: 1) Some not only have internally experienced the truth, given their assent to it, but have also externally received it and have nevertheless set themselves against it, to which class all apostates belong, and to whom Heb. 6:4 applies. 2) Others have not outwardly confessed themselves to it, but are at the same time convinced in their minds of its reality, yet, notwithstanding, obstinately and wickedly oppose it, as the Pharisees and scribes did, who did not believe in the doctrines of Christ, but were convinced from the works of Jesus and the Scriptures of the Old Testament that Christ was true God and revealed divine truths. From this it is easily perceived that the Apostle Peter, though he denied his Master and the truth, as also Paul, who was a reviler, a blasphemer, and a persecutor of divine truth previous to his conversion, are not to be classed among those who have committed the sin against the Holy Ghost, in that the first transgressed hastily, through fear of men, and the second did so through ignorance, as he says 1 Tim. 1:13.

2. The unpardonable sin is called the sin against the Holy Ghost not with reference to the person of the Holy Spirit, who then would appear to have precedence of the Father and the Son, but must be understood of His office, in that He reveals and testifies to the heavenly truths. It is a conscious resistance to the special work of the Holy Ghost to call, enlighten (Eph. 1:17,18), convert, renew (Eph. 5:9; Titus 3:5), and sanctify man (2 Thess. 2:13; Eph. 4:30; 1 Cor. 6:11).

3. This sin is unpardonable, not because of any unwillingness in God, but because of the condition of him who commits it. It cannot be forgiven, not because the mercy of God and the merits of Christ are not sufficiently great, but because in consequence of his obdurate rejection of the Word of the Holy Spirit, the judgment of final obduration is pronounced against him. The Holy Spirit has forsaken him utterly, and repentance has become impossible.

Sinaiticus, Codex. See *Manuscripts of the Bible,* 3.

Singmaster, J. A. B. 1852; educated at Gettysburg; held Lutheran pastorates in Pennsylvania and in Brooklyn, N. Y., 1876—1900; then became professor of Systematic Theology in Gettysburg Seminary; president of the seminary from 1906; president of General Synod 1915—17; editor of *Lutheran Quarterly* and author of *Systematic Theology, Reformers Before the Reformation,* etc.; outlined the mode of procedure for the "Merger" of 1918; d. Feb. 27, 1926.

Sinlessness. See *Innocence.*

Sins, Venial and Mortal. 1. The Roman Church teaches that sins, in their own nature, vary in degree of gravity, the weightier ones meriting eternal death (mortal sins: pride, envy, anger, dejection, avarice, gluttony, lust), while the lighter ones only weaken grace and can be satisfied by temporal punishment (venial sins). The character of a sin is held to be determined by the amount of deliberation involved and the degree of wrong committed (theft, *e. g.,* being mortal or venial according as the amount stolen is large or small). Only mortal sins require the sacrament of penance (see *Confession*). The guilt of venial sins can be removed by good works. (*Catechismus Romanus,* II, 5. 46.)

2. This philosophical distinction conflicts with the Scriptures, which teach that every sin as such merits the wrath of God (James 2:10; Gal. 3:10; Matt. 5:18,19) and is therefore mortal (Rom. 6:23; Ezek. 18:4); but that every sin ceases to be mortal when faith in Christ intervenes (Rom. 8:1; 1 John 1:7). The relative deadliness of sin, accordingly, is not dependent on intrinsic differences in sins, but solely on the sinner's relation to Christ.

Sisterhoods. Of the Roman Catholic sisterhoods, or religious organizations for women, which are not treated in separate articles (as are *Angelicals, Benedictines,* etc.), the following may be briefly mentioned: 1) Sisters of the Good Shepherd. An institute to shelter fallen women and girls who come voluntarily or are sent by civil or parental authority (called penitents); also neglected children (called preservates). Penitents may remain for life as quasi-members of the society (magdalens). — 2) Little Sisters of the Poor. An institute to provide for home-

less old men and women. As there is no fixed income, funds are usually procured by begging from door to door. — 3) Sisters of the Holy Child Jesus. Founded by Mrs. Connelly, an American convert. The principal object is the education and instruction of females of all classes and ages, either individually (as prospective converts) or in schools and colleges. — 4) Sisters of St. Joseph. A name borne by various communities, some educational, others conducting homes, hospitals, asylums, etc. — 5) Felician Sisters. An educational sisterhood, founded in Poland, teaching in Polish parish schools. — 6) Sisters of the Immaculate Heart of Mary. An educational sisterhood. See also *Brotherhoods.*

Sisters of Charity. Popular name for the order of nuns founded by St. Vincent de Paul, Louise Merilla, and Mlle. le Gras.

Sisters of the Good Shepherd. See *Sisterhoods.*

Sisters of Mercy. Founded by Catherine McAuley (1827, Dublin) for the performance of all the works of mercy.

Sisters of St. Joseph. See *Sisterhoods.*

Siva. See *Hinduism,* 4.

Six Articles. See *Anglican Confessions,* 4.

Sixtus IV. See *Popes,* 16.

Sixtus V. See *Popes,* 22.

Sixty-Seven Articles. See *Reformed Confessions,* A 1.

Skarga, Peter (1536—1612). Jesuit active in rehabilitating Catholicism in Poland and bringing the Ruthenians to the fold of Rome.

Skepticism. That phase of philosophic thought which, in opposition to dogmatism, holds that the attainment of truth is impossible. Its principal exponent among the ancient philosophers was Pyrrho of Elis (b. ca. 365 B. C.). Like the Stoics and Epicureans, Pyrrho pursues the practical aim of finding mental peace and quiet. To obtain this, however, all metaphysical speculation is futile, resulting rather in perplexity and disquiet. No two schools of philosophy agree on first principles, because the essence of things is incomprehensible. The attitude of the sage is therefore a suspension of judgment. He neither denies nor affirms categorically, since in every case the *pro* and the *con* may be defended with equal force and plausibility.

Skoptsy. See *Russian Sects.*

Skytte, Martin. See *Finland, Lutheranism in, 2.*

Slander. A sin against the Eighth Commandment, its particular features being a form of defamation by which another person (or persons) is held up to ridicule, disgrace, contempt, and hatred, chiefly in speech, signs, and gestures, to which we may add the written or printed defamation known as libel. While a libel may be produced without being communicated, slander can hardly be said to have any existence unless it is communicated to the mind of another. Black (*Law Dictionary*) defines slander as the speaking of false and malicious words concerning another whereby injury results to his reputation, and a slanderer as one who maliciously and without reason imputes a crime or fault to another of which the latter is innocent.

The Bible is very emphatic in its denunciation of slander (Ps. 31:13; Prov. 10:18; Jer. 6:28; 9:4; Ps. 50:20; Ps. 101:5; 1 Tim. 3:11).

Slavery, Biblical Reference to. Want and war were the chief causes of slavery in the ancient world. Reduced to servitude by want, war, or capture, the slave took the place of modern machinery in ancient times, and the achievements of early civilizations were, in many respects, made possible by slavery.

Though slavery was practiced among the Jews from the time of Abraham, consciousness of caste is hardly noticeable in the days of the patriarchs, and master and slave lived together in early Israel as members of a household (Gen. 15:2, 3; Gen. 24; 1 Sam. 9:5-10; 1 Sam. 25:14 ff.; Prov. 29:19-21; and others). During the period of the kings the condition of slaves became more intolerable (2 Kings 4:1; Amos 2:6; 8:6). Nehemiah made efforts to rectify conditions which fostered slavery after the exile.

The servitude of Hebrew slaves was regulated by benevolent laws which regarded the Hebrew slave rather as a hired servant (Ex. 21:1 ff.; Lev. 25:39-55; Deut. 15:12-18). The lot of foreign slaves (cf. Deut. 20:10 ff.) was less tolerable (Judg. 1:28 ff.), but they, too, lived as members of a religious community (Deut. 12:12 ff.; 16:11 ff.; 21:10 ff.). The nations which sold Israelites into slavery were denounced (Amos 1:6; Joel 3:6). The number of slaves in Israel was never as large as among the Greeks and Romans.

While Christianity did not demand that masters release their servants (see Eph. 6:5 ff.), it did invite all men to become the children of God and, hence, brethren among whom social distinctions were non-existent (Gal. 3:26-28; Col. 3:10 f.; Philemon; 1 Cor. 7:21 ff.; Eph. 6:5 ff.). As a result, slavery gradually disappeared in Christian countries.

Slavery and Lutheranism in America. While generally the Lutherans in America were opposed to slavery in the early nineteenth century, there are a number of instances of Lutheran clergy and laymen owning a few slaves. During this period no official action, either for or against slavery, was taken by any Lutheran church body. The first synod to come out with an antislavery resolution was the Frankean in 1838. Others were slow to follow. In 1846 the Pittsburgh Synod followed with similar resolutions. The General Synod, hoping to avoid a split in its own midst, postponed its convention scheduled for 1861. The inevitable break between the Lutherans in the General Synod, however, came in June, 1861, although the Southern synods did not organize a separate body until 1863, naming their body the "Ev. Luth. Synod of the Confederate States of America." Oddly enough, the division in the Lutheran Church occured before any of the synodical bodies took legislative action. After actual hostilities broke out between the North and the South, both groups of Lutherans pledged their loyalty to their respective governments.

The Missouri Synod, although it also had a number of congregations south of the Mason-Dixon line, was not affected in the same degree as the General Synod. The disagreement over the slavery question in this synod was very slight. Under the leadership of Dr. C. F. W. Walther it steered its course through these troublesome days without shipwreck. The remaining synods, though generally opposed to slavery, were not affected to any extent, since their congregations were concentrated in the Northern States.

The break caused by the Civil War in the General Synod was eventually healed. After the southern group changed its name a number of times and the General Council had been formed, the three groups merged on Nov. 15, 1918, to form the "United Lutheran Church in America." ARS

Der Lutheraner; C. W. Heathcote, The Lutheran Church and the Civil War, Burlington, Iowa, 1919; H. E. Jacobs, History of the Ev. Lutheran Church in the United States, New York, 1893; A. R. Wentz, Lutheran Church in American History, Philadelphia, 1925; J. L. Neve, History of the Lutheran Church in America, Burlington, Iowa, 1934.

Slavic Religion. According to the best information obtainable, both the Elbe Slavs and the Russians had a chief deity, one so high that even the name could not be uttered. Yet tradition speaks of Perun, the thunder god (developing into a sky god), as a name which was known to all the Slavic races, although the Elbe Slavs also referred to Svantovit as one worthy of the highest worship. Other Slavic gods were Rugievit or Rinvit, Gerovit (the war god), Triglav (three heads), and others. The Elbe Slavs also worshiped several goddesses. The Russian Slavs (also the Czechs and Poles) had other gods besides Perun, such as Veles (the god of flocks), Chors (apparently a sun god), and others, some of whom have survived in folklore to this day. Where the Slavic religion deteriorated in the direction of fetishism, it included the worship of water, fire, mountains, and trees. Necessary concomitants of idol worship were temples and sacrifices, together with feasts of the gods.

Slavonic Bible Versions. See Bible Versions, H.

Sleidanus (Philippi), Johann (1506 to 1556). German statesman and historian. B. at Schleidan; d. at Strassburg. Studied languages and literatures at Liége and Cologne, and law at Paris and Orleans. His political appointments made it possible for him to collect the materials for his history: De statu religionis et rei publicae Carolo V Imperatore commentarii, 1555. By virtue of this work he may justly be called the annalist of the Reformation.

Slovak Evangelical Lutheran Church (Slovenská Evanjelická Luteránska Cirkev). 1. The founding fathers of the SELC emigrated to this country from Slovakia, the eastern part of the present Czechoslovakian Republic. They came as early as 1875, but mostly in the years 1890—95, and settled in the eastern part of Pennsylvania. Many of them came westward to Illinois and Minnesota.

2. In their native land they had been members of the Evangelical Lutheran Church, which had a distinguished history behind it. Within a short time after their arrival, congregations were organized, among the first being those at Streator, Ill., Freeland, Pa., Nanticoke, Pa., Minneapolis, Minn. At first the congregations were much neglected, owing to the lack of regular and properly indoctrinated pastors and teachers. To no small degree the General Ev. Church of the Augsburg Confession in Hungary was responsible for this sad state of affairs, as it did nothing whatsoever for the spiritual welfare of its former members. In their spiritual need the Slovaks turned to other Lutheran congregations and pastors, mostly German Lutheran, who served them and allowed them the use of their churches and schools for divine services.

3. The first steps to organize the Slovak Lutherans into a church body were made June 4, 1894, at Mahanoy City, Pa. Five pastors and seven lay members were present. A "Slovenský Evanjelický Seniorát" (Slovak Evangelical Seniorate) was organized. The official organ of this first church body was Cirkevné listy (Church Letters). This association was of short duration, for it showed little progress and not much activity.

4. The real beginning to organize a Slovak Lutheran synod was made at three pastoral conferences held in Wilkes-Barre, Pa., June 9, 1899, in Braddock, Pa., Jan. 16—17, 1900, and again in Braddock, Pa., June 4, 1902. Here at St. Paul's Church (nine pastors, four of these affiliated with the Missouri Synod) a mutual understanding was reached, and it was decided to organize the Slovak Evangelical Lutheran Synod. But because of the fact that only pastors were present at this conference, another meeting was held in Connellsville, Pa., attended not only by pastors, but by lay delegates from the respective congregations. Thus the Slovak Evangelical Lutheran Synod was actually organized at St. Peter's Ev. Lutheran Church, Connellsville, Pa., Sept. 2—4, 1902. Its official organ was the Luterán (The Lutheran), published in Cleveland, Ohio, by John Pankuch. Rev. Daniel Z. Lauček served as the Synod's first president, Rev. Drahotín Kvačala as secretary. The original

charter was granted to the Synod in 1903, at Wilkes-Barre, Luzerne County, Pa., under the name "The Slovak Ev. Synod of the Augsburg Confession in Pennsylvania." The Synod professed its adherence to the Confessions of the Evangelical Lutheran Church and declared itself in full accord with the Missouri Synod in doctrine and practice. In 1908 the Synod joined the Synodical Conference of the Evangelical Lutheran Church of North America.

5. All pastors and congregations were elated over the success of their first synodical convention and pledged themselves to work in the spirit of brotherly love and unity. Nevertheless, the first years of the organization were marked by strife and struggle. Some pastors severed their connection with the Synod because of its true Lutheran practice, as in its firm stand against open Communion, and some pastors were suspended for this cause. It seemed that the Synod would disband. But with the help of God it has remained true to the Word of God and the Lutheran Confessions to this present day.

6. On Jan. 24, 1945, the original charter was amended and changed in accordance with the new constitution at the Luzerne County Court House, Wilkes-Barre, Pa. The Synod's present official name is "Slovak Evangelical Lutheran Church" (Slovenská Evanjelická Luteránska Cirkev).

7. The doctrinal position of the SELC is as follows: The Slovak Evangelical Lutheran Church, and every member thereof, accepts without reservation:

1) The Scriptures of the Old and the New Testament as the revealed and inspired Word of God and the only rule and norm of faith and practice.

2) All the Symbolical Books as a true presentation and exposition of the Word of God, to wit: the three Ecumenical Creeds; the Unaltered Augsburg Confession of 1530; the Apology of the Augsburg Confession; the Smalcald Articles; the Large and the Small Catechism of Luther; and the Formula of Concord.

8. The SELC has neither a theological seminary nor any institution of higher learning. Its pastors and teachers are educated in the colleges and seminaries of the Missouri Synod. To prepare the young men for the ministry in the Slovak churches the SELC has a duly called professor of Slovak at the St. Louis Seminary.

9. The SELC is governed by its duly elected officers and a Board of Directors. The Church holds regular conventions every second year in the month of October. A complete report is published in book form. The Church has six visitors and is divided into three Districts, the Eastern, Central, and Western. Pastoral conferences are held at appropriate times in each District.

10. For the purpose of carrying out mission work at home and abroad the SELC has a Mission Board consisting of four members. To collect the necessary funds for mission purposes and administration the Church has a budget system in effect. Funds for Foreign, Negro, and Jewish missions are sent through the channels of the Missouri Synod and Synodical Conference respectively. The missions in Canada and Argentina are being carried on and administered by the Church itself.

11. The official organs of the SELC are the *Svedok* (The Witness), published in the Slovak language, and the *Lutheran Beacon,* published exclusively in English. The *Svedok* has a number of subscribers in Czechoslovakia, Yugoslavia, and Hungary.

12. The youth of the SELC is organized in the Slovak Luther League, founded in St. Paul's Ev. Lutheran Church, Whiting, Ind., Sept. 5, 1927. The League works in close co-operation and fellowship with the International Walther League. The official organ of the Slovak Luther League is *The Courier.*

13. For the dissemination of Christian literature, books, and pamphlets the Church has a Publication Department which is in close business association with Concordia Publishing House in St. Louis, Mo. The Church has published various books for church and school use, most important among them being the *Book of Concord (Symbolické knihy),* and the *Slovak Hymnal,* the so-called *Tranoscius,* which is over 300 years old.

14. Divine services are held in both languages, English and Slovak. The *Lutheran Hymnal* has been introduced in all congregations of the SELC.

15. In recent years the SELC accepted the offer of members of St. Luke's Congregation, Slavia (Oviedo), Fla., Mr. Andrew Duda and family, of 40 acres of land and $90,000 for the purpose of establishing, building, and maintaining a haven of mercy to care for orphans, the aged, and superannu-

ated pastors and teachers. The Lutheran Haven, as it is officially called, is administered as a non-profit corporation set up and established according to the laws of the State of Florida.

16. During World War II the SELC served its men and women in the Armed Forces of our country through its Army and Navy Board in conjunction with the Armed Services Commission of the Missouri Synod.

17. For the benefit of retired and disabled pastors and teachers and their families an Annuity Fund went into effect Jan. 1, 1944.

18. The SELC numbered (1951) 59 ordained ministers and 6 teachers; 63 organized congregations and 4 preaching places; 20,808 baptized members; 15,250 communicant members; 46 Sunday schools with 3,070 children; valuation of property: $3,604,292; congregational income: $606,176 for local expenses, $78,713 for work at large. JSB

The following have been the presidents of the Slovak Ev. Luth Church: Daniel Z. Lauček, 1902—05; John Pelikán, 1905—13; Stephen Tuhý, 1913—19; John Pelikán, 1919—21 (during 1920, when President Pelikán made an official visit to Czechoslovakia, the Rev. John Somora was president *pro tem.*); John Somora, 1921—22; John S. Bradáč, 1922—39; Andrew Daniel, 1939—49; Paul Rafaj, 1949— .

Slovak Zion Synod. See *United Lutheran Church, Synods of,* 28.

Slovakia. The Slovaks, a Slavic race, have been living in their present habitation from time immemorial. The great Moravian kingdom was in existence long before the Huns and Magyars came to Europe. King Rastislav, a Christian, called German monks to Christianize the Slovaks; but it was only after Cyrillus and Methodius,* whom the Greek Emperor Michael sent at the request of the king in 863, preached in the Slavic tongue, that the nation was won for the Gospel.

Slovakia, Lutheran Theology in.
1. Although the Lutheran Reformation had spread to Slovakia during Luther's lifetime, political and social conditions there, especially the domination of Hungary, prevented the development of an indigenous Lutheran theology such as had sprung up in the Scandinavian lands. What theological work there was in the 16th and 17th centuries largely mirrored the thought that was prevalent at the time in

Germany. One of the theologians whose work has been preserved, Matthew Hlaváč-Kephalides (*floruit* 1670) is an excellent example of this fact.

2. It was not until the time of the Enlightenment that Slovak Lutheranism began to produce some independent theological work. Ján Kollar (1793 to 1852), M. M. Hodža (1811—70), and Karol Kuzmány (1806—66), professor of practical theology at Vienna, were all more or less strongly influenced by Hegelian idealism. But the most significant theological figure in the 19th-century Slovak Lutheranism was Jozef Miloslav Hurban (1817—88), founder of the journal *Církevní Listy*. His treatise *Unia* of 1846 was directed against the proposed union of the (Slovak) Lutherans and the (Hungarian) Reformed. In it he clearly defines the distinctive character of Lutheranism over against Calvinism. For his theological and ecclesiastical labors, Hurban was awarded the doctorate by the University of Leipzig.

3. Among our contemporaries, perhaps the outstanding Slovak Lutheran theologian is Samuel Š. Osuský (b. 1888), formerly bishop of western Slovakia and now professor at Bratislava. He is chiefly concerned with the philosophy of religion and has produced significant studies on apologetics and on the problem of evil. JP

J. Borbis, *Die evangelisch-lutherische Kirche Ungarns* (Leipzig, 1861); S. S. Osusky, *Filozofia Sturovcov* (3 vols.; Bratislava, 1926—32).

Smalcald Articles. See *Lutheran Confessions,* B 2.

Smalcald League. See *Schmalkaldic League.*

Smalcald War. See *Schmalkaldic War.*

Smaller Questions. See *Reformed Confessions,* E 1.

Smend, Julius (b. 1857). Studied at Bonn, Halle, and Goettingen; held various positions as pastor at Paderborn, Bonn, Siegen, and Seelscheid; professor at seminary in Friedberg, later at University of Strassburg, now at Muenster; prominent in liturgiology and hymnology; associate editor, with F. Spitta, of *Monatsschrift fuer Gottesdienst und kirchliche Kunst;* also published books on liturgics and related subjects, especially *Der evangelische Gottesdienst.*

Smith, Eli (1801—57). B. at Northfield, Conn; d. at Beirut; American Board missionary to the Near East, especially Syria; translated the Bible into Arabic.

Smith, Gerald Birney (1868 to 1929). Professor of theology at Chicago; leader in movement modernizing and socializing theology; influenced by Ritschl.*

Smith, John (ca. 1570—1612). English clergyman; left Anglican Church; influenced by Mennonites, he joined Baptist Church. See *Baptist Bodies, 2.*

Smith, Joseph. See *Latter Day Saints.*

Smith, Preserved (1880—1941). Author, translator, editor; son of Henry Preserved Smith; b. in Cincinnati; librarian at Union Seminary in New York; wrote: *Critical Study of Luther's Table Talk; Life and Letters of Martin Luther* (1911, 1914); etc.

Smith, Rodney (b. 1860). English Methodist, revivalist; b. at Wanstead; gypsy; converted, 1876; Salvationist; founder of Gypsy Gospel Wagon Mission; missioner of National Free Church Council 1897; made visits to America.

Smith, Samuel Francis (1808—95). B. under the sound of the Old North Church chimes in Boston, ed. at Harvard and Andover. He held several charges as Baptist minister in New England; was prof. of modern languages in Waterville College; also active in Christian journalism. His publications include several biographical works and various missionary writings. Author of "My Country, 'Tis of Thee," "The Morning Light Is Breaking," and others.

Smith, William Robertson (1846 to 1894). Prof. of Oriental languages and Old Testament exegesis at Free Church College, Aberdeen, Scotland; editor, *Encyclopedia Britannica;* prof. at Cambridge; higher critic and student of comparative religion.

Smith, William. See *Protestant Episcopal Church, 2.*

Smyth, John. See *Baptist Bodies, 2.*

Social Action. (See *Social Reform, Social Work*). This term is used to describe an organized effort by individuals or groups who are attempting to change existing economic or social institutions. It differs from social work (social service), which is concerned with the alleviation of distress and the creation of socially adequate personalities rather than with changes in existing institutions. It is akin to social reform and social engineering, which aid social action in working out the solutions of social problems and provide it with plans and specifications for desirable changes in the economic or social order. Movements to reform politics, employer-employee relations, interracial relations, etc., come under the head of social action. It operates through propaganda, legislative lobbies, and similar devices.

Social Compact. See *Natural Law, 5.*

Social Creed. See *Methodist Bodies, 2.*

Social Ethics. Social ethics concerns the standards of good behavior of people toward one another, individually or in groups; and the motives for this behavior. Jesus Christ outlined the foundations of Christian social ethics by interpreting the standards laid down in the Old Testament in such a way that their reference to the inner and total life of man would be unmistakable; and by describing Himself and the Christian man's relation to Him as basic for this behavior. Thus the Old Testament materials on social ethics — family relations, responsibility in community and nation, behavior of employer or employee — are not superseded, but woven into the Christian ethics of the New Testament. The Apostles make application of the Savior's work as well as point of view in their ethical materials. They describe the Christian and the Christian Church surrounded by, and in contact with, the unbelieving world. They schedule the attitudes and resources of Christian parents, children, citizens, employers, and employees in their various spheres of activity, as life lived in Christ and through the power of His redemption.

Historically, social ethics has suffered from distortion of the ideal in actual practice. With the development of the episcopacy and sacerdotalism the pressure upon the Christian and his good conduct began to be, not his inner contact with Jesus Christ, but the discipline of the Church. Hence a faulty authoritarianism disfigured the institutionalized Church throughout the Middle Ages, which only in exceptional instances was abridged by the piety of special devotion or closer insight into the genuine source of good conduct.

The sacrament of penance and the system of indulgences completed the spectacle of individual ethical behavior completely at the mercy of the priesthood. As an institution, however, the Church served to set standards of morality and decency within the community; it became the censor of morals and summoned high and low alike to meet its standards upon pain of churchly penalty.

The Lutheran Reformation began with the promise of a revived Christian social ethics. The doctrine of grace and the redemption of Christ were made basic for the new life of the Christian man. Martin Luther, in addition, by teaching and example made the calling of the Christian man, in family, community, and occupation, the proving ground of the spiritual vitality engendered by Christ. Thus the stage was set for a renascence of the primitive social ethics of the New Testament. This promise failed, however, to come true. The Lutheran churches took over the established task of moral direction of the community, irrespective of the spiritual stature of the members of the congregation. The Fanatic and Enthusiast excesses demonstrated the need for discipline in addition to doctrine. The dynamic for good conduct, by Luther expressed as love, was diverted to the natural law and subservience to authority, ecclesiastical or civil. Thus Lutheran orthodoxy very early developed a social ethics which was not genuinely Christian in its basis and presuppositions, and restricted and authoritarian in its scope. The charge has been made without satisfactory rebuttal that its ethics robbed the individual of the critical discernment of the social institutions in which he lived.

Reformed Protestantism began parallel to Luther in developing its social ethics. However, its adherents lived chiefly in the cities and were swayed by the mercantilistic and capitalistic objectives of citizens. Also this trend tended to weaken the criticism to which Christians subjected their institutions. Whereas the Lutheran criticism became defective toward political institutions, Reformed came short toward the economic. In more recent centuries this has been evident in the easy complacence with which the Church has acquiesced in the unsatisfactory relations between capital and labor, and in the manner in which it has embraced the pragmatic philosophy, that that which produces good results is good, regardless of the desire for those results.

The fact that Lutheran social ethics has not in practice been put to work does not curtail its significance. No system of social ethics in actual practice at the present time has proved vital and workable. Furthermore, new interest has emerged, in view of the moral collapse of social institutions, in primitive Christian and in essential Lutheran social ethics.

A complete social ethics, on the basis of the Word of God and the redemption of Jesus Christ, distinguishes between, and operates with, three problems: (1) What is the motive which leads man to do the will of God? It is his restoration to God through Christ Jesus. (2) What is the form which his participation in life with people takes? It is love, his total will and self directed to undertake, alone and with others, the responsibility for the welfare of other people. (3) What are the areas in which this love asserts itself? Every area of life that concerns people involves and supplies occasion for the putting to work of the Christian dynamic and the Christian directive.

The problems of social ethics have frequently been isolated to concern questions of social legislation, moral pressure, and the expression of social justice. The Church rightly plays its part in social ethics, not as it invades the function of other agencies, but as it equips individuals and groups to play their part in other agencies, as citizens, or members of professions, or members of families. The Church does not supplant the family, but it energizes children and parents to be God's people and to love one another. The Church does not supplant the State for social ends, but it actuates the citizens who are its members to undertake the burdens and responsibilities which citizenship affords. RRC

Paul Joachimsen, *Sozialethik des Luthertums*, Munich, 1927; Emil Brunner, *The Divine Imperative* (tr., Olive Wyon), Philadelphia, 1931; Martin Luther, *On the Freedom of the Christian Man*, 1520; A. D. Mattson, *The Church and Society*, Wartburg Press, Columbus, 1947; A. Koeberle, *Luthertum und Sociale Frage*, Doerffling und Franke, Leipzig, 1931.

Social Gospel. The teaching of a social salvation which has as its objective the rebirth of society through change of the social order by mass or group action. Although directed mainly toward social classes, it is subjectivistic in its attempt to persuade individuals to adopt and practice the social ethics of Christ. Thus the conception has applicability of the teachings of Christ to social and individual morality. Among extreme exponents of the Social Gospel there is no prerequirement of reconciliation of the individual to God through grace, by faith in Christ Jesus, the divine Redeemer, and little reference to the regenerative work of the Holy Spirit in the individual. For many adherents the Social Gospel is essentially a this-worldly gospel of works and not a Gospel of grace for this life and heaven. The term is inadequate, since it is difficult to separate "social" from "individual" gospel when applied to Christian life.

The Social Gospel movement may be traced to the early nineteenth century in the United States, stemming from the views of Schleiermacher and Ritschl, and to the reform political movements of the eighteen thirties in Europe and England, which were the outgrowth of industrialization, human dislocation, social injustice, and labor turmoil which accompanied the great migration of peoples and an expanding American and world frontier. It grew amazingly in the late nineteenth and early twentieth centuries, but began to decline already before World War II, according to some of its earlier proclaimers, having proved inadequate in the serious testing of the First World War and the world-wide depression.

Formulated largely by academic theologians, its philosophical principles were laid down and expounded by Richard Ely (Economic Formulator), George T. Herron (Legislative Advocate), Washington Gladden (Social Gospelite), Shailer Mathews (Theological Reformist), Walter Rauschenbusch (Kingdom Socialist), Charles A. Ellwood (Christian Sociologist), Graham Taylor (Social Activist), Charles Stelzle (Practical Labor Service), Harry F. Ward (Christian Marxist), F. J. McConnell (Democratic Reformist), Kirby Page (Pacifistic Socialist), E. Stanley Jones (Idealistic Socialist), and John C. Bennett. The Federal Council of Churches in its Social Creed of 1912, following the Methodist form of 1908, which was revised in 1919 and 1932, has a summary of the Social Gospel aims. Reinhold Niebuhr (Theological Socialist) has largely repudiated the extremes of his precursors and, like

C. Neal Hughley, who supports Niebuhr, has critically scrutinized and rejected most of the Social Gospel. The abovementioned leaders sought to make their systems of ethics, based, it must be noted, largely on particular precepts of the Prophets and Jesus, applicable to social, economic, and international ills through concerted church, legislative, and community action.

The Social Gospel flourished especially among the Methodists, Baptists, Congregationalists, Unitarians, and the Episcopalians. These groups have their Social Service commissions, sometimes organic, sometimes quasi-official, in line with those of the Federal Council of Churches, on race relations, housing, industrial and labor or economic conditions, family life, and international peace. They issue literature and undertake instruction in these and other social problems within the churches.

Critics of the Social Gospel have seen in it an idealistic, purely humanitarian, falsely optimistic, utopian and pacifistic, social reformist movement not essentially Christian, because it bypassed the essential elements of Christian doctrine and life, or because it has not fulfilled the expectations of its advocates. It is admitted by most observers that a new social consciousness, attitudes, and sense of responsibility has been awakened in many Christian denominations. Constructive activity in social fields has been engendered by deeper thinking on the practical aspects of the Christian vocation.

The Lutheran Church, although quietistic in attitude toward some social questions, motivated by the thought that the Gospel of Christ for mankind is charity for the soul, which is the soul of charity, has carried on extensive welfare and social activities through such agencies as the Associated Lutheran Charities, a Board of Social Missions in the U. L. C., and the National Lutheran Council.

Roman Catholics developed Social Action concomitantly with the Social Gospel through the impulse and sanctions of the papal encyclicals *Rerum Novarum* (Leo XII in 1891) and *Quadragesimo Anno* (Pius XI in 1931). The activity of the Social Action Department of the National Catholic Welfare Conference has been fostered by the Bishop's Program for Social Reconstruction of 1919, under such leaders as John A. Ryan and Joseph Husslein.

The Jewish communities and leaders have espoused a similar interest in social problems through the Central Conference of American Rabbis and the Social Justice Commission. Based largely on the precepts of the Old Testament Law and Prophets, they have developed their program outside the forms of the old orthodoxy. JD

Ernest Troeltsch, *The Social Teachings of the Christian Churches* (Engl. tr., Olive Wyon, 2 vols., N. Y.), Macm., 1949; C. H. Hopkins, *Rise of the Social Gospel in American Protestantism 1865 to 1915*, New Haven, Yale, 1940; W. A. Visser 'tHooft, *Background of the Social Gospel in America*, London, Oxford, 1928; F. E. Johnson, *The Social Gospel Re-examined*, N. Y., Harper, 1940; H. P. Douglass, *The Protestant Church as a Social Institution*, N. Y., Harper, 1935; H. R. Niebuhr, *The Social Sources of Denominationalism*, N. Y., Holt, 1929; C. Neal Hughley, *Social Trends in Protestantism*, N. Y., Kings Crown Press, 1948; *Hartwick Seminary Conference on the Social Mission of the Lutheran Church*, Princeton, N. J., 1944; C. C. Morrison, *The Social Gospel and the Christian Cultus*, N. Y., Harper, 1933; E. E. Fischer, *Social Problems, The Christian Solution*, Philadelphia, U. L. P. H., 1927; Abraham Cronbach, *The Bible and Our Social Outlook*, Cincinnati, Union of Hebrew Congregations, 1941. Also see volumes by authors mentioned under *Capital and Labor*, W. Rauschenbusch, *Industry and the Church, Labor and the Church.*

Social Reform. (See *Social Action, Social Work.*) Social reform is not revolutionary, *i. e.*, aiming at complete change of the social order, as social action may be on occasion. It accepts the existing fundamental social and economic structure of society, but seeks to eliminate the evils which result from improper or faulty functioning of the social system. While its motivation derives from the individual and group distress which social work seeks to alleviate, it proceeds beyond the point of alleviation and attempts to remedy the causes of distress, insofar as they may seem to result from maladjustments in the social order. Temperance movements and anti-vice crusades are examples of social reform movements.

Social Service. See *Social Work.*

Social Work. (See *Charities, Christian; Associated Lutheran Charities; Inner Mission; Social Action; Social*

Reform; American Association of Social Workers; Sociology.)

A. *Definition.* — Social work (from Latin *socialis; socius*, an associate), also called Social Service, may be defined in simplest terms as "any activity to promote social welfare" (Webster) or, more poetically, *The Art of Helping People Out of Trouble* (title of book by Karl de Schweinitz, Houghton-Mifflin, 1924). The Dictionary of Sociology (Philosophical Library, 1944) defines social work as "the processes involved in adjusting an individual's relationships with other persons and with his wider social and economic development." These definitions are true to the facts as stated, but fail utterly to describe the full scope, the aims, and the significance of social work. As a matter of fact, social work is not a well-defined and circumscribed activity which remains static long enough to be fully analyzed and described; nor can it ever be that, since it deals with human personalities, developed not only by heredity, but by many continually changing environmental factors, and with society in its many and ever-changing phases of social and economic organization. Social work can be defined and understood only through a study of its history, its goals, and its present development. The following facts may serve as a background:

B. *History.* — 1. The genesis of social work lies in the concept of the responsibility of one man for the welfare of another, already indicated in Cain's question "Am I my brother's keeper?" (Gen. 4:9.) The pre-Christian world did not lack humanitarian impulses, and the literature of all the nations of antiquity tells of their efforts to alleviate the sorry lot of the poor and the sick. With the advent of Christianity the Christian ideal of love of God and love for fellow men became the motive (John 13:34), and the resultant charitable service to those in need was regarded as the fruit of Christian faith (Gal. 5:6; 1 John 3:17).

2. This service was given by the personal ministrations of individual Christians or the labors of the deacons (Acts 6:1-6) in the simple economy of early Christendom. For a brief period of time a form of voluntary Christian communism seems to have been practiced (Acts 2:44, 45). In later centuries, as the Church grew and spread throughout the world, it was inevitable that she should exercise almost complete control over the activities and in-

stitutions of charity. Institutional care of certain types of the needy, such as the sick, the infirm, the crippled, was fostered by religious orders, while the relief of individuals and families was supervised by the parish priests. Since indiscriminate almsgiving, however, was fostered by the Church as an expression of Christian charity and as a meritorious service to God, the number of mendicants, encouraged in leading lives of idleness, gradually grew to such proportions that mass relief (soup kitchens, etc.) had to be resorted to in all larger centers of population. At the close of the Middle Ages the question of poor relief had become one of the chief issues of the day.

3. The Reformation and the accompanying changes in the economic, social, and spiritual areas of life swept away many of the old concepts of charity as well as the old system of poor relief. Dawning recognition of poverty as a social rather than an individual problem brought about the gradual inauguration and development of the English poor-law system. This established the responsibility of government for the alleviation of social ills and constituted the real beginning of our social legislation and of the system of modern social work.

4. It must not be supposed, however, that as one system of relief failed, another was speedily put into its place. Actually progress came slowly and haphazardly. In the middle of the 19th century there still was much indiscriminate giving to the poor; hospitals and charitable foundations still operated without a definite plan of selective charity, so-called "outdoor relief" still provided inadequate benefits unequally administered. It was out of a recognition of this intolerable confusion and its sorry consequences that the London Charity Organization Society was born in 1869. This society represented the first real attempt at co-ordination of welfare activities under a definite plan of community organization and the first approach to case-work service as we understand it today. Transplanted to the United States in 1877, this movement was the direct ancestor of the present system of social service. Important milestones in progress should be noted. In the 1890's the age-old concept of character deficiency in individuals as the primary cause of poverty gave way to a recognition of environmental causes of mass poverty. This naturally resulted in the growth of so-

cial action movements designed to abolish the social inequalities and the economic and political ills which seemed to produce poverty and its attendant evils.

5. The end of the First World War marked the definite beginning of the modern social case-work system. Mary Richmond wrote her epochal book *Social Diagnosis* in 1917 and *What Is Social Case Work?* in 1922 (Russell Sage Foundation, New York). Thorough investigation, an accurate diagnosis, and specific treatment of each case were recognized as indispensable elements in the process of case work. Gradually the emphasis on self-help grew stronger. "Help the client to help himself." The family was recognized as a basic unit in society, and the relationships of the family to the complex structure of the social order were given much attention. It was inevitable that these emphases should develop the "psychological approach" in social case work. Problems of personality are recognized as a potent cause of social maladjustments, particularly since the beginning of the Second World War, and continually enlarging knowledge of the "dynamics of social behavior" provides social case workers with new tools with which they may aid individuals and families to make happy and satisfying adjustments to everyday living in our present social order.

C. *Types of Social Work.* — 1. Social work may be classified according to its fields of activity as case work, group work, and community service. Case work may be loosely defined as work with individuals or closely knit small groups, as families, while the term group work obviously defines the function of social workers in assisting groups or committees in achieving more satisfactory experiences through social co-operative activity. Community organization also is concerned with groups and attempts to assist groups (communities) in achieving a certain unification of purpose and action in the field of social welfare. (See "Social Case Work," "Social Group Work," and "Community Organization" in *Social Work Year Book for 1954*, American Association of Social Workers, New York, for complete analyses.)

2. Social case work attempts to make highly specialized services available in certain areas of need. Among these are child welfare, family service, service to transients, medical social service, psychiatric social service, and others more

or less clearly defined. Recognized graduate schools of social work are providing an increasing number of courses of study for the training of professional workers in specialized services.

D. *Organization of Social Work Agencies.* — 1. Social work organizations may be classified according to sources of support, areas of responsibility, and methods of control and administration, as public or private agencies. Public agencies are generally administered as a function of local, State, or national governments. They are created by legal enactment and supported by funds raised by taxation. The increasing concern of the Federal Government for social welfare is evidenced by recent events, such as the establishment of the Federal Emergency Relief Administration, the Works Progress Administration, the National Youth Administration, the Resettlement Administration, and, above all, the adoption of the Federal Social Security Act of 1935. The Second World War and its aftermath added many new functions to the program of governmental assistance, and especially the extension of this assistance to the international field through the operation of the United Nations Relief and Rehabilitation Administration (UNRRA). Continued development of Federal concern for public welfare resulted in the establishment of a Department of Health, Education, and Welfare in 1953.

2. In general, the concentration of welfare services in governmental agencies, local, State, and Federal, has progressed to the extent that the services offered by public agencies now completely overshadow the efforts of private agencies, measured in terms of funds expended, number of clients served or variety of services rendered.

3. Private Social Agencies are agencies founded by private initiative, governed by boards or committees of privately chosen individuals and supported by funds gathered through voluntary subscriptions. Many private agencies have combined in Community Chests and similar co-operative movements for better control and more equitable distribution of funds made available through public subscriptions. Other private social agencies have been established by church groups according to denominational preference and are, in general, supported by these groups either through voluntary gifts by members or assessments levied upon local churches.

E. *Christian Social Service.* — 1. The Christian social service generally has adopted the methods and techniques of secular social service as well as its classifications of types of service. It is sponsored by Christian groups in its agency development and governed by Christian principles in the execution of its work, although the governing principles naturally vary according to the religious tenets of the sponsoring groups.

2. Christian social service is distinguished from secular social work, first of all, by its motivation. While secular social service may be motivated by humanitarian principles, a sense of justice and fair play, or just plain expediency, Christian social work has retained the motivation of Christian love (charity), which is enjoined in the Scriptures and which characterized the charitable labors of the early Christians. This Christian love is a product of the Christian faith in Christ as Lord and Redeemer and is indissolubly linked with it in its expression in Christian life (Gal. 5:6).

3. A further distinction between secular and Christian social service is found in the areas in which it operates in human life. Secular social work commonly recognizes three basic types of human needs: biological, psychological, and social. It ignores the spiritual aspects of life and therefore falls short of a service to the whole personality of man. Christian social service is built upon the premise that man's right relationship to his God is just as vital to his happiness and well-being as his right relationship to his fellow men. While secular social service may at best regard religion and church membership as a "resource," which may have considerable value in certain cases, Christian social service fosters religion and church membership as a vital and indispensable force in the lives of its clients.

4. It is apparent that the distinctive philosophy of Christian social service will also cause it to extend its goals beyond the limits of man's life on earth. While it is desirous of achieving, as is all social work, a better world for the greater happiness of men, it looks beyond the limits of time and place and seeks to aid men in achieving eternal life.

F. *Lutheran Social Work.* — 1. Lutheran social service is rooted in the Cross-centered theology of Lutheranism, which exalts the love and mercy of God. The theology of Calvinism, centered in the doctrine of the justice and majesty of God, exalting the ideal of the Kingdom of God on earth, is inclined to stimulate men to engage in social action and social reform rather than in service to individuals through the medium of case work.

2. Early efforts of Lutherans in America were carried on under the name of Charity. (See *Charities, Christian.*) Today the term social service has almost displaced the earlier appelation in the terminology of the Church.

HFW

Socialism and Communism. Socialism is the form of social organization in which property is controlled for the common good rather than for the profit of the individual. It is thus in contrast with capitalism, in which property is controlled for the benefit of the individual or of a group of individuals. Socialism does not deny that in theory capitalism can contribute to the welfare of all; but it is pessimistic concerning the power of the altruistic motives of the capitalistic individual to surmount his selfishness. Socialism does not presume to operate with motives less selfish than those of capitalism; but it does seek to supplant capitalism by a form of organization which checks the selfish impulses of the individual and regulates the supply of the physical and economic resources for the advantage of all the people. Historically socialism has appeared in several forms.

1. Socialization of resources in an originally capitalistic state. That is the process demonstrated to a slight degree in the New Deal in the United States of America and more signally in postwar England. This is a result of the industrialization of a community or nation and of the effort by the people through their government to prevent the exploitation for private gain of natural resources, such as coal or electric power, or economic resources, such as the control of public utilities and the sale of securities. It is an inevitable stage in the government of a nation which confronts simultaneously the falling level of resources and the perfected organization of private business.

2. Social security for capitalistic purposes. The illustration of this trend is Germany under Bismarck. The purpose of the institution of social security, medical and unemployment insurance, etc., is to thwart the rise of the workers against capitalistic control. Some observers put this construction upon the American New Deal.

3. Fascism. This name is derived from the socialist party in pre-war Italy, which gave its name to the program developed by Mussolini and to an even more thorough degree by Hitler in Germany. Viewed historically, this and the communistic phase of socialism described below are symptoms of a world revolution paralleling the industrial revolution and marking the effort of the workers to gain control of economic forces which had been utilized to their disadvantage. They are in reaction to the presumption of the industrial operator that his skill at industrial organization, financing, and scientific research entitle him to more profit than the worker; that it is he and not the worker who actually "produces" the goods. Fascism and Communism operate through an indoctrination of the masses that the people's state is the complete orbit of the individual's life and the safeguard of his well-being; hence they are called totalitarian. Fascism is even more explicit than Communism in making the state supreme in the mind of each citizen. Unlike Communism, it did not adopt a totally hostile attitude to religion, but sought to assign it a purely ideological sphere. Fascism claimed the support of the industrialists who sought in it a barrier to Communism. American symptoms of Fascism have occurred chiefly in politically motivated programs of exaggerated old-age security and "share the wealth" devices. Fascism is in principle only partial in its socialism in that it always operates with hostility toward, and exploitation of, "inferior" races or groups within the state.

4. Communism. Whereas other forms of socialism are attempts, at least in part, to achieve social welfare of the masses by means of existing political and economic processes, Communism is revolutionary. It proceeds from the premise that capitalism and democratic forms of government permitting capitalism are decadent and antisocial. Karl Marx was dominated by the Hegelian assumption that the struggle of the classes can result only in higher form of society which is classless and in which production is owned and operated by the worker class. In practice the Communistic revolution is in charge of the Communistic party. These individuals regard themselves as immune to the motives of bourgeois and cap-

italistic society. They set themselves to achieve their design through the overthrow of existing states, the removal of religious institutions (or their confinement to an impotent sphere), the indoctrination of the masses, and the collectivization of agriculture and industries. The program has been carried out most thoroughly in the Union of Soviet Socialistic Republics, the Russian state, of which but a tiny minority are members of the Socialist party. The Russian revolution of 1917 wavered between a number of alternatives. The first decision was that of adhering to the program of Bolshevism, the overthrow of the provisional government of Kerensky on the basis that it was too bourgeois and hostile to the interests of the masses. The second concerned the goal of communizing Russia only, or the world. The ascendancy of Joseph Stalin after the death of Lenin and the banishment and murder of Leon Trotzky signaled the design to sovietize Russia first and make it a base for world revolution. The mechanisms of international Communism involve espionage, sabotage, the control of labor unions, the infiltration of government agencies, and the conversion of the intelligentsia. These experiments operated successfully in Russia with its heritage of group life and its cultural tensions. To what degree they can be generally successful in a less idealistic society such as American and Britain is the most fateful question today.

In the nineteenth century socialism and Communism were promoted largely by agnostic and antiecclesiastical thinkers. Hence the churches took a stand against them. The Roman Catholic Church has maintained its hostility most consistently. While the social encyclicals of Pope Leo XIII pioneered in demanding justice for the workers, they at the same time sought to maintain the supremacy of the Church in human relations and repudiated socialism as anti-Biblical and as destroying the natural impulses for personal improvement. The social gospel of nineteenth-century Protestantism found many of its aims paralleled by socialism, although it differed from its motives. Current social thought in liberal Protestantism, therefore, repeats socialistic criticisms of the profit motive in capitalism. The World Council of Churches at Amsterdam in 1948 found it difficult to express this criticism without slighting its hostility to Communism or its friendship for American capital. Some

Fundamentalist theorists parallel the Roman Catholic defense of the profit motive, prompted by their controversy with Protestant liberalism. The chief problem of socialism for the Church in America lies in the growing significance of the labor union as a source of social thought among the masses and in the recognition of what is essential to Christian faith in social organization and what is destructive for the Christian Gospel. RRC

Karl Marx and Friedrich Engels, *The Communist Manifesto,* 1849; N. Lenin, *State and Revolution,* 1917; Nikolai Berdyev, *The Origin of Russian Communism,* 1937; William Temple, *Christianity and Social Order,* 1942; Eduard Heimann, *Communism, Fascism, or Democracy?* 1938; Encyclicals of Leo XIII (see, *e. g.,* Joseph Husslein, *Social Wellsprings,* 1940); Reinhold Niebuhr, *An Interpretation of Christian Ethics,* 1935; Emil Brunner, *Justice and the Social Order,* 1945; John Bennett, *Christianity and Communism,* 1951.

Society for Assisting Evangelical Missions Among Heathen. See *Missions,* B 16.

Society of Cardinal Ferrari. See *Bible Societies,* 6.

Society of Friends. See *Friends, Society of.*

Society for Home and Foreign Missions According to the Principles of the Evangelical Lutheran Church. See *Missions,* B 17.

Society Islands, *Tahiti Islands.* A group of islands in the South Pacific Ocean, formerly called *Georgian Islands,* belonging to France since 1880. Area, 600 sq. mi. Population 24,820 (1946), of Polynesian stock. Discovered by Spain 1606. Captain Cook visited the islands in 1777. In 1797 the London Missionary Society began operations, the *Duff* arriving in March of that year. After many mistakes and disappointments the victory was finally won. In 1826 eight thousand Tahitians had been baptized. The whole Bible had been translated into the vernacular in 1835. French Roman Catholics forced their way into the islands and caused great affliction. The L. M. S. was expelled, but the French Evangelical Missionary Society took its place and organized the scattered congregations into a church. The western islands in this group were temporarily protected against French Catholic aggression by

England. Raiatea, where John Williams worked since 1819, was the seat of much missionary success. It is the policy of France to oppose Protestant missionary endeavor. See *Polynesia*.

Society of Jesus. See *Jesuits and Jesuitism*.

Society People. See *Presbyterian Bodies*, 3.

Society for the Promotion of Christian Knowledge. See *Bible Societies*, 3; *Missions*, B 10.

Society for the Promotion of the Gospel Among the Danes in North America. See *Danish Lutherans in America*, 3.

Society for the Propagation of the Gospel in Foreign Parts. See *Bible Societies*, 3; *Missions*, B 10.

Society for Reformation Research, American. Group of American scholars, in process of being expanded to Europe, organized to foster historical research, translation, and publication in the field of the Reformation; annual meeting synchronized with American Society of Church History and American Historical Society; president, Prof. Harold J. Grimm; secretary-treasurer, Prof. George W. Forell.

Society in Scotland for Propagating Christian Knowledge. See *Missions*, B 11.

Society of the Woman in the Wilderness. See *Communistic Societies*, 4.

Socinianism. The theological system of Faustus and his followers. 1. During the Reformation there arose a number of anti-Trinitarians in Europe, mainly in Italy. They found refuge for a time in Switzerland, then, expelled from there, in Transylvania and Poland, where anti-Trinitarians became numerous, especially among the Polish nobility. These scattered elements were united by Faustus Socinus, who came to Transylvania, 1578, and Racow, Poland, became the center of the movement and seat of a flourishing school. The confession around which the Socinians rallied is the Racovian Catechism. (*Catechesis Ecclesiarum Polonicarum*. Pol., 1605; Lat., 1609.) For a half century after the death of Socinus, Socinianism, under the leadership of distinguished theologians, Crell, Schlichting, Wolzogen, Wissiwatius, *et al.*, experienced a remarkable growth; but then the Roman Catholic reaction set in. Their school was destroyed, their

churches closed, and in 1658 they were expelled from Poland. While anti-Trinitarians have maintained themselves in Transylvania to the present day (ca. 60,000), the Polish Socinians fled to Prussia and other parts of Germany and to the Netherlands, but found little toleration. Even in England they were persecuted, until the rise of Deism afforded them protection. English anti-Trinitarianism, which found a fuller development in America, is, however, really an independent movement; for which see *Unitarians*.

2. The Socinian theological system, in spite of its supernaturalism (which American Unitarians have rejected completely), is essentially rationalistic. The Bible is the only source of religious truth, but can contain nothing contrary to reason. The doctrines of the Trinity, original sin, predestination, especially are rejected. Christ is a human being, who, however, because of His supernatural birth and translation to heaven, was empowered to show men the way to God through His teaching and life. Whosoever enters on this way is given forgiveness of sins and eternal life. The death of Christ is not a vicarious atonement, but merely testifies to the truth of His teachings and earned for Him divine honor. Baptism and Communion are useful, but not necessary ceremonies.

Socinus. Latinized name (Sozzini) of two Italian anti-Trinitarians, founders of Socinianism. *Laelius Socinus* (1525—62), b. at Siena, devoted himself to theological studies, which led him to doubt the divinity of Christ. Since 1547 he traveled widely and associated with Protestant reformers, but for fear of persecution never openly expressed his true convictions. These he embodied in his writings, which he willed to his nephew Faustus. D. at Zurich. — *Faustus Socinus* (1539—1604), b at Siena; since 1562 at Zurich, where he studied the literary legacy of his uncle and became firmly established in his anti-Trinitarian views. After twelve years at Florence and four at Basel he went to Transylvania, then to Poland, where he found various scattered Unitarian elements, especially among the upper classes. These he freed from anabaptistic and chiliastic admixtures and unified and organized them. Lived mainly in Cracow, but spent last years in retirement.

Sociology. (See *Social Work*). Sociology is defined as the scientific study of the phenomena which develop out of the group relations of human beings. It indicates an organized and ever-increasing body of knowledge which is usable in the understanding, control, and correction of social relations. Sociology is subdivided into an increasing number of categories indicative of the widening field of inquiry in environmental science. Thus we have Rural and Urban Sociology, Biological and Historical Sociology, Political and Cultural Sociology, and many other divisions. The term "sociologist" and "social worker" are sometimes used interchangeably, but the distinction between the science of sociology and the profession of social work is being drawn with increasing clarity.

Socrates (ca. 470—399 B. C.). The first Athenian-born philosopher. The son of a sculptor and a midwife, Socrates forsook his father's profession to pursue one which he compared to that of his mother, yielding his time, under the guidance of a *daimon*, or familiar spirit, to "brown studies," or trances, and to engaging in philosophic discussion with those whom he buttonholed in public and private places in Athens. Socrates distinguished himself as a soldier in two periods of military service, but twice at the risk of his own life defied rulings of the government in power. Most exasperating to the Athenian people was Socrates' "gadfly" criticism of the follies and vices of their form of democratic government and of the inanities of the popular theology. Accused at last "of not believing in the gods of the state, of proclaiming other gods, and of corrupting the youth," Socrates was condemned to death and drank the hemlock as a martyr to his cause in 399 B. C.

Socrates himself wrote nothing and is remembered through widely diverging contemporary accounts. Aristophanes has caricatured him, probably playfully, in the *Clouds* as petty, bourgeoise, and antidemocratic. Xenophon has described him in the *Memorabilia* as a practical man of action. Plato's dialogs have idealized him as a hero of dialectic. Aristotle credits him with being the first to seek natural definitions or universal principles — though only in moral matters. The dispute is long-standing to what extent Socrates stood in the Sophist tradition as a skeptic and humanistic moralist, disdaining metaphysics, as the *Memorabilia* suggest, and to what extent the metaphysical doctrines which Plato puts into

his mouth are Socrates' own. The opinion is gaining favor that the earlier dialogs, including also the *Phaedo*, the *Symposium*, and the *Republic*, are a faithful account of Socrates' own teaching and that he was a metaphysician as well as a moralist.

Of philosophic importance is the "Socratic method," for which both Xenophon and Plato credit Socrates. This is a method of teaching in which the master imparts no information ("Socratic irony" — thus the Delphic oracle's pronouncement that there was no man wiser than Socrates was interpreted by him to mean that he alone knew his own ignorance), but by question and answer elicits more and more adequate explanations or inclusive definitions from the learner. A presupposition of this method is the theory of *anamnesis*, or recollection, *i. e.*, the assumption of innate factors which determine a convergence in human thought toward ultimate agreement or universal standards. The method begins with a critical demolition of unexamined opinions; hence the celebrated inscription at Delphi, "Know thyself," is declared by Socrates the beginning of wisdom. Results of this method applied to ethical problems are the ultimate union of the theoretic and the practical, the notion that virtue is teachable and evil the result of ignorance, and the conviction that the virtues are one.

Among the disciples of Socrates, some (notably Aristippus and Antisthenes) developed his ethical doctrines in opposition to the older metaphysical speculations, while others (especially Euclid and Plato) united the Socratic notion of the Good with the Eleatic concept of being, thereby re-establishing the union, dissolved in skepticism, between the philosophy of morals and the philosophy of nature. RL

Socrates. Greek church historian at Constantinople; b. ca. 380; in 439 wrote a church history of seven books, continuing that of Eusebius and covering the time from 306 to 439; but not fully reliable.

Sodality. See *Confraternity.*

Soden, Hans Karl Hermann von (1852—1914). B. at Cincinnati, Ohio; studied at Tuebingen; since 1893 prof. of New Testament exegesis at Berlin; belonged to liberal Ritschlian school; prepared a critical edition of the New Testament.

Soederblom, Nathan (1866—1931). Swedish Lutheran theologian; studied at Upsala Univ., Ecole des Hautes Etudes, Paris, Univ. of Paris; prof. at Upsala (1901—14), Univ. of Leipzig (1912—14), archbishop and prochancellor at Upsala (1914—31); received honorary degrees from many leading universities; member of the Swedish Academy (1921), honorary member and official in numerous honorary societies; received Nobel Peace Prize (1930). Soederblom sought freedom of research but at the same time advocated respect for tradition. He was a leader in peace and ecumenical movements. His works cover a wide area, including studies on Mazdaism, philosophy of religion, and Luther. Among others he wrote *The Religions of the World, Introduction to the History of Religion, Christian Fellowship.*

T. Graebner, "Nathan Soederblom," *CTM*, XV: 314—28.

Soedermann, August Johan (1832 to 1876). Received his musical training in Germany, was a Swedish composer whose works express the virile and staunch character of their composer. Soedermann is highly thought of among Scandinavians; his works bespeak the spirit of the Swedish people.

Sohm, Rudolf (1841—1917). Church historian and teacher of ecclesiastical law; studied at Rostock, Berlin, Heidelberg, and Muenchen; professor in Goettingen, then at Freiburg, Strassburg, and Leipzig; wrote on various topics in the field of the relation of Church and State, also a short church history, many articles on church polity.

Sola Fide (L. "by faith alone"). The Scriptural doctrine that the believer is justified by faith alone without the deeds of the Law (Rom. 3: 28; Phil. 3: 9). This is called the material principle * of the Lutheran Church. "Men cannot be justified before God by their own strength, merits, or works, but are freely justified for Christ's sake, through faith, when they believe that they are received into favor and that their sins are forgiven for Christ's sake, who by His death has made satisfaction for our sins." (AC, Art. IV). See *Faith.*

Sola Gratia (L. "by grace alone"). The Scriptural doctrine emphasized by the Lutheran Church, namely, that salvation is not by works (which, however, are fruits of faith), but by grace. See *Atonement, Conversion, Faith, Grace, Predestination, Redemption, Material Principle,* and related topics.

Sola Scriptura (L. "Scripture alone"). The formal principle * of the Lutheran Church, that the Bible is the only norm of doctrine and life *(norma normans).* Formula of Concord: "First [then we receive and embrace with our whole heart] the Prophetic and Apostolic Scriptures of the Old and New Testaments as the pure, clear fountain of Israel, which is the only true standard by which all teachers and doctrines are to be judged." See *Grace, Means of; Bible; Inspiration.*

J. T. Mueller, "The Sola Scriptura and Its Modern Antithesis," *CTM*, XVI: 5—24.

Solemn League and Covenant. See *Presbyterian Confessions,* 1.

Solid Declaration. See *Lutheran Confessions,* C 2.

Solomon Islands. Melanesia, a group of islands in the South Pacific Ocean, partly under Great Britain, 3,400 sq. mi., with a population of 44,122, and Lae on New Guinea as headquarters; partly under Australian care, with 11,458 sq. mi. and a population of 95,248, with Tulagi as headquarters. Most of this territory belonged to Germany until the First World War. The inhabitants are Melanesians, most of them until recently savage and cannibalistic and uncivilized according to Western standards. Considerable mission work has been done in that area, especially by the Anglican Melanesian Mission. The Roman Catholic Church began work in 1898. See *Melanesia.*

Soma. See *Brahmanism,* 2.

Somaliland. An area of 264,248 sq. mi., with a population of 1,601,159, in Africa, partly under British, French, and Italian control, the latter section bordering on Abyssinia, enlarged by Jubuland, which was taken from German East Africa after the First World War. Missions by the Evangeliska Fosterlands Stiftelsen. Total Christian community, 335; foreign staff, 12, of them four ordained.

Sommer, Martin Samuel. B. Mar. 31, 1869, Blenheim, near Baltimore, Md., son of the Rev. Wm. Sommer and Emilie, nee Fritzsche; studied at Baltimore City College and Concordia Seminary, St. Louis; served as pastor, Grace Church, St. Louis, 1891 to 1920; pres., English District, Missouri Synod, 1914—19; prof. of homiletics at Concordia Seminary, St. Louis, 1920 to 1947; co-editor of *Lutheran Witness*

1914—49; Doctor of Letters from Valparaiso Univ., 1937; d. at St. Louis Dec. 16, 1949.

R. L. Sommer, "Martin Samuel Sommer," *CHIQ*, XXIII: 123 ff.

Sommer, Peter Nicholas. B. Jan. 9, 1709, in Hamburg, Germany; received his theological education in Germany; became Luth. pastor in Schoharie Co., N. Y. (1743), where he worked for nearly fifty years; served a wide area of Lutheran settlements; d. Oct. 27, 1795.

Song Service. A form of worship in public assembly of the congregation, in which the feature of song predominates, the hymns and anthems rendered usually following some progressive line of thought in order to present some fundamental Christian truth or express Christian thought and feeling.

Song of the Three Children. See *Apocrypha*, A 3.

Sons of Robert E. Lee. See *Veterans' Organizations*.

Sophronius. See *Monothelitism*.

Sorley, William Ritchie (1885 to 1935). British philosopher; prof. at Cambridge; wrote *The Moral Life; A History of English Philosophy;* and others; exponent of the Moral Argument (see *Apologetics*).

Soteriology. That part of dogmatics, or doctrinal theology, which treats of the work of salvation as wrought by the Second Person of the Trinity. In Lutheran circles, more specifically the doctrine of Holy Scripture concerning the application of the merits of Christ to the individual sinner, whereby the sinner is led to the actual possession and enjoyment of the blessings which Christ has procured for all mankind. See *Redemption, Atonement*.

Soul, The. The vital principle in man, whereby he perceives, reasons, and learns. The rational soul is simple and immaterial (not composed of matter and form). All languages apparently distinguish between soul and spirit. However, psychologists by no means agree in their definitions of the two; some give to the spirit the higher potency, others, to the soul. From mind, soul is commonly distinguished by referring mind to the various powers which the soul possesses. Spirit, when considered separately, may signify the principle of life; mind, the principle of intelligence; whereas soul always refers to the essential nature, the essence of man's being. See *Angels, Flesh, Immortality, Image of God*.

Soul Sleep. The doctrine of soul sleep (psychopannychism) implies that the souls of the departed sleep as long as the body lies in the grave. Scripture, however, does not refer to the soul's sleep, but simply to the soul's rest, as Rev. 14:13. Naturally, we may say that the dead sleep; but this refers to the body, not to the soul; cp. Heb. 4:9-11. Since with death all experiences of time and space come to an end, the interval between death and the resurrection does not exist for the soul. See *Death, Annihilationism, Eternal Life*.

Source Hypothesis. See *Higher Criticism*, 6.

Souter, Alexander (b. 1873). Presbyterian; classical scholar; b. at Perth, Scotland; professor at Aberdeen 1897; of New Testament Greek, Oxford, 1903; wrote: *Text and Canon of New Testament*, 1913; *Pocket Lexicon of Greek New Testament*, 1916; and others.

South Africa. See *Africa*.

South America. The southern continent on the Western Hemisphere. Area, 6,894,000 sq. mi. Population, 109,500,000. The South American countries are Argentina, Bolivia, Brazil, Chile, Colombia, Ecuador, Paraguay, Peru, Uruguay, and Venezuela. Dependencies of European states are British Guiana, Dutch Guiana, and French Guiana. The Falkland Islands off the southeast coast belong to Great Britain.

1. *Argentina,* or the Argentine Republic, second largest state in South America. Area, 1,153,418 sq. mi. Population, 15,893,827, of whom about 2,000,000 are foreign-born. Capital, Buenos Aires; population, 3,000,371. Greatest length of Argentina, 2,300 miles; greatest width, 930 miles. First declaration of independence, July 8, 1816. Promulgation of present constitution, 1949. Native population, descendants of early Spanish settlers, mixed with aboriginal Guarani and Quichua stock. The Roman Catholic religion is supported by the state, but religious liberty is recognized. The president of the republic must be a Roman Catholic and an Argentinean by birth. Spanish is the official language. Missions by a large number of churches and societies, among them The Lutheran Church — Missouri Synod and United Lutheran Church in America. Statistics: Prot-

estant Christian communicants, 89,000 (1952).

2. *Tierra del Fuego,* south of Argentina. Area: 18,530 sq. mi.; east part belongs to Argentina, west part to Chile. Was entered for missionary purposes by Captain Allen Gardiner in 1822. In 1844 he founded the Patagonian Missionary Society, which later adopted the name of South American Missionary Society. In 1850 he and his companions met death by starvation. The message of the party to the world was: "My soul, wait thou only upon God, for my expectation is from Him." Ps. 62:5. Very successful work has since been done by the South American Missionary Society.

3. *Bolivia,* an inland republic of South America. Area, 416,404 sq. mi. Population, 3,019,031 (1950), fully 50 per cent being native Indians. Capital, La Paz, with a population of 319,600. Spanish is the official language, although many natives speak only their own language. The present constitution was adopted 1880. The Roman Catholic religion is recognized by the state, but toleration is practiced. — Missions by a number of churches and societies. Statistics: Protestant Christian communicants, 6,770 (1952).

4. *Brazil, United States of,* a federal republic of South America, consisting of 20 federated states and the Territory of Acre. Area, 3,286,169 sq. mi. Population, 52,645,479 (1950), including native-born, Italians, Portuguese, Spanish, Germans, Japanese, and Americans (U. S.). Capital, Rio de Janeiro; population, 2,335,931. Brazil is the largest state in South America, exceeding in size the United States (exclusive of Alaska) by some 250,000 sq. mi. Its length is 2,691 and its width 2,500 miles. It was discovered in 1500 by Cabral, a Portuguese. Brazil was declared a republic 1889. Portuguese is the official language. The Roman Catholic Church is dominant. All but 100,000 inhabitants, excepting also the Indian tribes in the interior, are said to be of that faith. Religious liberty is guaranteed. The native inhabitants are of Portuguese, native Indian, Negro, and mixed descent. Since the First World War there has been a very strong European immigration. Missions by a number of churches and societies, among them The Lutheran Church — Missouri Synod. Statistics: Protestant Christian communicants, 651,655 (1952).

5. *Chile, Republic of,* a state on the west coast of South America. Area, 286,322 sq. mi. Population, 5,866,189 (1951 est.), almost exclusively of European extraction with some 100,000 native Araucans and other natives. Total length, 2,800 miles. Average breadth, ca. 100 miles. Santiago, the capital, has a population of 1,120,000. The Spanish yoke was thrown off 1810—18. The present constitution was adopted in 1833. The language is Spanish. The Roman Catholic Church dominates, being supported by the state; but religious liberty is assured by the constitution. Missions conducted by a number of organizations. Statistics: Protestant Christian communicants, 95,315 (1952).

6. *Colombia, Republic of,* in the extreme northwest of South America. Area, 439,825 sq. mi. Population, approximately 11,259,700 (1950 est.), mainly whites and half-castes, with several hundred thousand Indians. Bogota, the capital, has a population of 503,000. The republic was established by Simon Bolivar in 1819, who revolted against Spain. Spanish is the official language. Roman Catholicism is the state religion. Toleration, though not constitutionally guaranteed, is actually practiced. Missions by the Gospel Missionary Union, Presbyterian Church in U. S. A., Seventh-Day Adventists. Statistics: Protestant Christian communicants, 11,325 (1952).

7. *Ecuador, Republic of,* on the Pacific coast of South America. Area, 101,481 sq. mi. Population, 3,324,000 (1948), of Spanish descent, Indians, and mixed races. Quito, the capital, has a population of 212,873. Spanish is the official language. Roman Catholicism is the state religion, with no toleration of other religions. The present constitution dates from 1906. Missions by the Christian and Missionary Alliance, Gospel Missionary Union, Seventh-Day Adventists. Statistics: Protestant Christian communicants, 1,862 (1952).

8. *Paraguay, Republic of,* an inland republic of South America, comprising Paraguay proper and the Paraguayan Chaco. Area, 150,515 sq. mi. Population, 1,405,627 (1950), the majority a mixed race, descended from Spaniards and Guarani Indians. The common language is a corrupt form of Guarani; but Spanish is spoken in the chief centers. Asuncion, the capital, has a population of 205,605. The present constitution was adopted in 1870. The Roman Catholic Church is dominant, but toleration is practiced. Missions by a number of churches and societies. Statistics:

1,985 (1952) Protestant Christian communicants.

9. *Peru, Republic of,* on the Pacific coast, between Ecuador and Chile. Area, 482,257 sq. mi. Population, 8,492,873 (1950 est.), chiefly Peruvians of Spanish descent and Indians. Lima, the capital, has a population of 520,528. Independence from Spain was declared in 1821. The present constitution was accepted in 1920. Spanish is the prevailing language. The Roman Catholic religion is the state religion, but toleration exists. Missions by a number of churches and societies. Statistics: Protestant Christian communicants, 25,260 (1952).

10. *Uruguay, Republic of,* the smallest republic in South America. Area, 72,172 sq. mi. Population, 2,353,000 (1949 est.), chiefly native Uruguayans, with many Spaniards and Italians and mixtures. Montevideo, the capital, has a population of 850,000. Independence from Spain was declared in 1825. The present constitution came in force in 1919. The majority of the people are Roman Catholics. Church and State are separate, and there is complete religious tolerance. Missions by a number of churches, including The Luth. Church — Missouri Synod. Statistics: Protestant Christian communicants, 8,047 (1952).

11. *Venezuela, Republic of.* The northernmost state of South America, comprising twenty federated states, one federal district, and two territories. Area, 352,141 sq. mi. Population, 4,985,716 (1950). The country was discovered by Columbus in 1498. Venezuela was the first of the South American countries to declare independence from the Spanish yoke, July 5, 1811. Caracas, the capital, has a population of 487,903. The inhabitants of Venezuela are a mixture of Spanish and Indian blood; but there are many Negro and aboriginal Indian tribes. Spanish is the official language. The prevailing religion is Roman Catholic. Religious liberty is constitutionally guaranteed. The wealth of the country consists in its large oil deposits which are being developed by U. S. and Dutch oil companies. Missions by a number of churches: Assemblies of God, Baptists, Brethren, Ev. Free Church of America, New Tribes Mission, Pentecostal, Orinoco River Mission, Presbyterian, Scandinavian Alliance, Venezuelan Christian Mission, Seventh-Day Adventist, The Luth. Church — Mis-

souri Synod. Statistics: 5,943 communicants (1952).

12. *British Guiana,* a British colony in northeastern South America. First settled by the Dutch in 1580; ceded to Great Britain in 1814. Area, 89,480 sq. mi. Population, 425,156 (1950), most of whom are Negroes and East Indian coolies (Hindus), with some aboriginal Indian tribes. The capital, Georgetown, has a population of 73,509. Liberty of conscience prevails. The Moravians began work among the Negroes in 1735 and later among the Arawaks, but it was finally discontinued. Later other societies followed. Missions by a number of churches, among them the United Lutheran Church in America. Statistics: Protestant Christian communicants, 39,173 (1952).

13. *Dutch Guiana,* or *Surinam,* belonging to the Netherlands since 1667, on the northeast coast of South America. Area, 54,291 sq. mi. Population, 221,000 (1950), exclusive of Negroes and bush Indians. Paramaribo, the capital, has a population of 67,381. Liberty of conscience prevails. Missions were begun by the Moravians in 1738 among the bush Negroes. Statistics: Protestant Christian communicants, 43,381.

14. *French Guiana,* or *Cayenne,* a French colony in northeastern South America. Settled by the French in 1626. Area, 34,740 sq. mi.; population, 28,537 (1946). Cayenne, the capital, has a population of 10,961. France has a penal colony in French Guiana. The climate is very unhealthful. The Roman Catholic Church prevails. See *Missions, Bibliography.*

South America, Roman Catholic Church in. See *Roman Catholic Church.*

South Australia, Evangelical Lutheran Synod of. See *Australia.*

South Carolina, Synod of. See *United Lutheran Church, Synods of,* 29.

Southcottians. Followers of Joanna Southcott (1750—1814) of England, an uneducated woman who claimed to possess supernatural gifts and to be the woman of Revelation 12. At the age of sixty-four she declared that she, as "bride of the Lamb," would give birth to the Messiah, but died the same year. She obligated her followers to observe Mosaic laws regarding the Sabbath and clean and unclean meats. Once numerous, the sect gradually dwindled, becoming extinct at the end of the 19th century. The movement has had several offshoots, among them the House of David.*

Southern Baptist Convention. See *Baptist Bodies,* 9.

Southern Defenders of America. See *Veterans' Organizations.*

Southern Presbyterians. See *Presbyterian Bodies,* 4.

Southern Rhodesia. See *Africa.*

Southern Seminary. See *Ministry, Education of,* XI B.

Southwest Africa. Formerly German Southwest Africa, a protectorate mandated to the Union of Southwest Africa. Area: 328,393 sq. mi.; population: 288,000, mostly Ovambas, Hereros, Bergamaras, and Hottentots. Missions by the Church of England, *Rheinische Missionsgesellschaft, Suomen Laehetysseura,* Church of the Province of South America of Damaraland. Total foreign staff of 119, 45 of them ordained; 71,097 Protestant communicants (1952); 28,000 Roman Catholics.

Southwest, Synod of the. See *Synods, Extinct.*

Sovereignty of God. See *Calvin, John,* 10.

Sozomenos, Hermias Salamanes. Of Constantinople, in 439, wrote a church history in nine books for the years 323 to 423, based on Socrates' contemporary work.

Spaeth, Adolph. A leader in the Lutheran General Council; b. Dec. 29, 1839, in Wuerttemberg; educated at Tuebingen; private tutor in Italy, France, and Scotland till 1864, when he accepted a call as associate pastor (with Dr. W. J. Mann) of Zion Church, Philadelphia. In 1867 he took charge of St. Johannis. In 1873 he became professor in the Philadelphia Seminary, was president of the General Council 1880—88 and of the Pennsylvania Ministerium 1892—95. He wrote the biographies of Dr. Mann and of Dr. C. P. Krauth (whose son-in-law he was). Besides being a historian he was a liturgical scholar, a gifted pulpit orator, and wrote a number of homiletical works. D. June 25, 1910.

Mrs. A. Spaeth, *Life of Adolph Spaeth Told in His Own Reminiscences,* Philadelphia, 1916.

Spain. Religious history to the Reformation. Apart from the legend that James the Elder brought Christianity to Spain, the statement of Paul concerning his intended visit there (Rom. 15:24), and the mere notices of Tertullian and Irenaeus that there were Christians also in Spain, we know nothing of the origin and early history of the Spanish Church. But the letters of Cyprian in the third century and, particularly, the canons of the Synod of Elvira at the opening of the fourth bear clear testimony to the general spread of Christianity and, it must be added, to an extraordinary laxity in morals and discipline. Of the Teutonic invaders who settled in Spain at the beginning of the fifth century, the Suevians, veering unsteadily between Arianism and Catholicism, surrendered to the Arian Visigothic king Leovigild and disappeared as an independent nation (585). The Goths, on the other hand, after vainly attempting to establish Arianism as the dominant religion, adopted Catholicism at the Synod of Toledo (589), and thus religious unity was preserved. The Saracenic invasion (711) gave rise to that age-long struggle between the Cross and the Crescent, which finally resulted in the capture of Granada, the last stronghold of Islam in Spain (1492).

Spain, Roman Catholic Church in. See *Roman Catholic Church.*

Spalatinus (1484—1545). The name given to *George Burkhardt,* who was born at Spalt. He became a priest in 1508 and bought a Bible at a high price; tutored John Frederick, son of the Elector of Saxony; private secretary to Frederick the Wise in 1514 and as such of very great service to Luther, who wrote him more than 400 letters. After Frederick's death in 1525 Spalatin went to Altenburg and visited the churches; wrote an account of the great *Reichstag* of Augsburg in 1530; took the sick Luther home from Smalcald in 1537; helped reform Ducal Saxony and consecrate Amsdorf bishop of Naumburg in 1542.

Spangenberg, August Gottlieb (1704 to 1792). Studied and lectured at Jena; joined Moravian Church, 1733; capable organizer and administrator for his church in England, West Indies, Pennsylvania, and North Carolina; in addition to hymns, he wrote *Idea fidei fratrum* and a life of Zinzendorf.

Spangenberg, Cyriakus (1528 to 1604). Son of Johann Spangenberg. B. at Nordhausen; d. at Strassburg. Studied at Wittenberg. Pastor at Mansfeld, 1550; general dean of the county and assessor of the Eisleben consistory, 1559; defending Flacius' doctrine of original sin, he was excommunicated and fled into the district of Sangerhausen, where he wrote historical works and polemical treatises; expelled from there, 1578, he came to Strassburg; preacher at Schlitzee-on-the-Fulda, 1581; deprived of office, 1591; again to Strassburg, 1595. He also published commentaries, sermons, and spiritual comedies.

Spangenberg, Johann (1484—1550). A faithful supporter of Luther, became a pastor at Nordhausen in 1524, where he established Lutheranism and founded a *Gymnasium*. In Nordhausen he wrote his *Cantiones ecclesiasticae* of 1545, taking the church year into consideration. This collection contained music for the worship services of the Lutheran Church and became one of the foremost music publications of the Reformation era. Upon the recommendation of Martin Luther, Spangenberg became a pastor in Eisleben in 1546.

Spanish Inquisition. See *Inquisition*, 6.

Sparre, Aage. See *Denmark, Lutheranism in*, 1.

Speaking in Tongues. See *Pentecostalism; Tongues, Gift of.*

Special Conference. See *Ohio and Other States, Evangelical Joint Synod of*, 2.

Speckhard, Hermann. B. Aug. 5, 1859, at Friedberg, Hesse; graduate of Concordia College, Fort Wayne, and Concordia Seminary, St. Louis; pastor in Hillsdale (1882), Ionia, and (1894) Saginaw, Mich.; d. there; contributed to *Lehre und Wehre* and *Homiletic Magazine;* vice-president of the Missouri Synod and of the Synodical Conference. D. Dec. 28, 1916.

Spee, Friedrich von (1591—1635). Roman Catholic religious poet; b. at Kaiserswerth; d. at Treves; was professor of grammar, philosophy, and ethics in the Jesuit college at Cologne after 1621; then cathedral preacher at Paderborn; later at Wuerzburg and at Peine, near Hildesheim; prominent as a leader in the Roman Catholic Counter Reformation; issued two collections of religious poems.

Speer, Robert Elliott (b. 1867). Presbyterian layman; b. at Huntingdon, Pa.; educated at Princeton; secretary of Presbyterian Board of Foreign Missions since 1891; made three great tours of visitation, two carrying him to Asia (1896—97 and 1914—15), one to South America (1909); wrote *Presbyterian Foreign Missions* (1901); *South American Problems* (1912); *Studies in Missionary Leadership* (1914); and others.

Spegel, Haquin (1645—1714). Third archbishop of Upsala; great traveler, having visited Denmark, Germany, Holland, and England; among his hymns: "The Death of Jesus Christ, Our Lord."

Spencer, Herbert (1820—1903). English philosopher; b. at Derby; lived in London; d. at Brighton. In his philosophy, which is a materialistic monism and influenced by Comte's positivism, he distinguishes between the knowable and the unknowable. It is futile to investigate the unknowable (agnosticism). To explain the knowable, he developed a system of philosophy based on the theory of evolution. Unlike Darwin, who was interested mainly in the origin of species, Spencer applied the theory of evolution not only to all forms of organic life, but also to mental and social phenomena. His attempt to show that the same law of development is at the basis of all phenomena is contained in a series entitled *Synthetic Philosophy*, of which the following appeared: *First Principles, Principles of Biology, Psychology, Sociology, Ethics.* He held that all religion has its origin in ancestor worship.* Evolution precludes the desire for redemption and reunion of the creature with his Creator.

H. Spencer, *Synthetic Philosophy,* Appleton, 1901.

Spener, Philipp Jakob (1635—1705). B. in Upper Alsace. Generally regarded as the father of Pietism; he is at least "the most influential center of this movement." He received a devout education from his parents and additional spiritual nourishment from Johann Arndt; later, from writings of Richard Baxter. He entered the University of Strassburg and studied under Dannhauer and Johann and Sebastian Schmidt. In 1663 assistant preacher at the cathedral; in 1666 called as senior pastor to Frankfort on the Main. Here, in 1670, he introduced his *collegia pietatis,* or private devotional gatherings, twice a week, in his house. In 1675 he published his *Pia Desideria,* which attracted wide attention. In the first part are pictured the deplorable conditions in the Church as he saw them, and, secondly, helpful measures were proposed for their improvement, stress being laid especially on personal piety by means of private devotional gatherings. These recommendations aroused both hearty acceptance and violent opposition and ushered in the Pietistic Controversy. In 1686 Spener accepted a call as court preacher to Dresden, at that time a most influential position in the Lutheran Church. From here he influenced greatly A. H. Francke and Paul Anton at Leipzig in organizing the so-called *Collegia Biblica*. In 1691 he was called as provost of St. Nicolai to Berlin, where he was instrumental in placing his friends, Francke and Anton, as professors in Halle. Spener wanted to be an orthodox Lutheran, but had evidently imbibed many ideas from Reformed sources. He stood for a mild form of Chiliasm. See *Pietism*.

Spengler, Lazarus (1479—1534). Studied at Leipzig; held position in town clerk's office at Nuremberg; later himself town clerk, then *Ratsherr;* met Luther in 1518 and espoused cause of Reformation; leader of the work in Nuremberg and vicinity; included in Bull of Excommunication of 1520; instrumental in opening a *Gymnasium* in his city; upheld strict Lutheranism at Augsburg in 1530; wrote: "Durch Adams Fall ist ganz verderbt."

Spengler, Oswald (1880—1936). Influenced by Nietzsche; his *Decline of the West*, in which he held that the West had begun to decline in 1800, influenced some German and American thinkers.

O. Spengler, *The Decline of the West*, Knopf, 1932.

Speratus, Paul (1484—1551). B. in Swabia. He studied at various universities, probably even in Paris and Italy, receiving a D. D. degree from the University of Vienna. He became preacher at Wuerzburg and Salzburg, but was forced to leave both places for expressing his evangelical views openly. He was one of the first priests to marry and was condemned therefor by the theological faculty of Vienna and imprisoned for a time by King Ludwig at Olmuetz. After that he came to Wittenberg, where he worked with Luther, assisting him in the preparation of the first Lutheran hymnbook. Then he was appointed court preacher at Koenigsberg, and he seems to have had a great deal to do with drawing up the Liturgy and Canons for the Prussian

Church. He died as Lutheran bishop of Pomerania, while living at Marienwerder.

Spiecker, Johannes (1856—1920). Educated at Tuebingen and Bonn; pastor at Herchen 1883—85; instructor at Barmen Missionary Institute 1885; director of Rhenish Missions 1908; visited Africa twice and Dutch East Indies once in the interest of missions.

Spieker, G. F. (1844—1913). Historian; educated at Gettysburg and Philadelphia; Lutheran pastor 1867—83; taught Hebrew at Muhlenberg College 1883—94; professor of church history in Philadelphia Seminary 1894—1913.

Spinoza, Baruch (Benedict de, 1632—77). Philosopher; b. at Amsterdam of Jewish parents, who, persecuted in Portugal, had sought refuge in the Netherlands; excommunicated by synagog because of his religious views; spent uneventful life in the Netherlands, gaining livelihood by grinding lenses. One of most influential philosophers of modern times. In his *Tractatus Theologico-Politicus*, 1670, he attacked the Christian view of revelation and the authenticity of the Old Testament. Religiously his *Tractatus* contained principles of rationalism which appeared a century later. Politically it anticipated Rousseau's ideas in the latter's *Contrat Social*. In his main work, *Ethica*, 1677, he developed, in contradistinction to Descartes' dualism, a pantheistic monism. There is only one infinite substance, God (or nature), with an infinite number of "attributes," of which man can comprehend only two, thought and extension. Ideas and physical objects are "modes" of these attributes. See *Pantheism*.

E. J. Wild, *Selections*, Scribner's, 1930.

Spires, Diet of, 1526. The Peace of Madrid gave Charles V a free hand, and he would now have enforced the fierce Edict of Worms of 1521 and crushed the Lutherans; but the newly formed Holy League of Cognac and the invading Turk stayed his hand. The Diet unanimously resolved: "Each one is to rule and act for himself as he hopes and trusts to answer to God and the Imperial Majesty." That opened the door for the spread of Lutheranism; it gave independence from Rome, at least to the Lutheran territorial princes; it divided Germany religiously. The most important diet since Worms.

Spires, Diet of, 1529. Victorious over the Holy League of Cognac, an alliance of France, England, the Pope, Venice, and Milan, Charles V, conscious of his power, most autocratically canceled the perfectly legally passed laws of the Diet of Spires of 1526 and also most autocratically commanded the Estates forthwith to execute the fierce Edict of Worms of 1521. This unconstitutional act gave pause even to some of the Catholic Estates; but the stalwart reactionary papistic majority enacted into law the wishes of the Emperor. On April 19 the Lutherans protested against this act of tyranny — "In matters concerning God's honor and the salvation of souls each one must for himself stand before God and give account, so that herein no one can excuse himself by the action or resolution of others, either more or less." The Emperor rejected the protest and even imprisoned the bearers. Luther's heroic stand at Worms in 1521 made possible this glorious Protest at Spires in 1529, from which all Protestants take their title. In 1542 the Emperor had to make concessions to get Lutheran help against the invading Turk, and in 1544 more concessions to get Lutheran help against France to win the Peace of Crespy, Sept. 14, 1544, which gave him a free and strong hand to crush the Lutherans at Muehlberg.

Spirit. See *Holy Ghost.*

Spirit Baptized. See *Pentecostalism.*

Spiritism (Spiritualism). An unchristian, antichristian cult, based on an alleged intercourse with the souls of the dead. The founding of this cult, in its present form, is ascribed to the Fox Sisters of Hydeville, N. Y. Spiritist mediums come under the condemnation of the Word of God (Deut. 18:10, 11).

Spiritists are given to the study of psychic phenomena and explain them in terms of discarnate spirits who may be contacted by the living. They believe in a continuous development here and hereafter. Those who are here are to seek the counsel of and communion with those who are beyond. Man is to enjoy love and freedom. Spiritism denies the deity of Jesus Christ, the existence of devil, demons, and angels. The New Testament "is made up of traditions and theological speculations by unknown persons" (*Outlines of Spiritualism for the Young*, 13, 14). In the Spiritualistic book *Whatever Is, Is Right* we find the following assertions: "What is evil? Evil does not exist; evil is good. What is a lie? A lie is the truth intrinsically; it holds a lawful place in creation; it is a necessity. What is vice? Vice, and virtue, too, are beautiful in the eyes of the soul. What is murder? Murder is good. Murder is a perfectly natural act." According to Spiritist doctrine, marriage is not a divine institution, in which in reality God joins together one man and one woman, but it is based on the laws of human nature and is the result of "natural and spiritual affinities." The two parties united are not so much united into one flesh as virtually into one spirit and one soul. Divorces are to be freely given when desired by one or both parties. Dr. Day, of Montville, Conn., quotes a prominent Spiritist as saying: "Free love is the central doctrine of Spiritualism. The new social order is a social harmony based upon passional attractions. . . . Attraction is our only law." Statements regarding God and the Bible are often blasphemous in nature. By testimony of its leading exponents, Spiritism is a Christless cult, opposed alike to Christian doctrine and morals.

Spiritism was formally introduced in the United States in 1848. The National Spiritualists' Association was organized in 1893 (headquarters in Washington). The best-known Spiritist seminary is the Morris Pratt Institute, Whitewater, Wis. A noted camp is the Lily Dale, N. Y.

George Lawton, *The Drama of Life after Death*, 1932; F. E. Mayer, *The Religious Bodies of America*, Bibliography, Part XII, Sec. II. CPH.

Spirits. See *Angels.*

Spiritual Coadjutors. See *Jesuits and Jesuitism, 3.*

Spiritual Exercises. A book by Ignatius Loyola * (first printed, 1548) which became a chief instrument of the Jesuits. It consists of meditations in four divisions: 1. man and sin; 2. kingdom of Christ; 3. suffering and death of Christ; 4. resurrection and ascension of Christ.

Spiritual Life. See *Conversion; Justification; Sanctification.*

Spiritus Gladius. See *Symbolism, Christian.*

Spitta, Friedrich (1852—1924). Pastor and professor in Strassburg and later in Goettingen. He wrote several volumes on liturgics, church music, and exegetical subjects, among them: *Liturgische Andacht zum Luther-Jubilaeum, 1883; Ein' feste Burg; Der Chorgesang im evangelischen Gottes-*

dienst; Drei kirchliche Festspiele, Weihnachten, Ostern und Pfingsten; Zur Reformation des evangelischen Kultus; Das Johannesevangelium.

Spitta, Johann August Philipp (1841 to 1894). Like his brother Friedrich, was active in the Schuetz revival; his *Johann Sebastian Bach* is still the most monumental work on Bach, and his edition of the organ works of Dietrich Buxtehude (Breitkopf and Haertel) is still the most complete and authoritative edition available. The first volume of his work on Bach was published when Spitta was only thirty-two years old and established the fame he never lost. He helped organize the *Bach-Gesellschaft* and taught for many years at the University of Berlin. His second volume on Bach was published in 1880.

Spitta, Karl Johann Philipp (1801 to 1859). B. in Hannover. The Spitta family were Huguenots who suffered during the Roman Catholic persecutions in France. To his mother's fostering care he wrote the finest hymn ever written on the Christian home, "O Happy Home Where Thou Art Loved Most Dearly." Spitta started to write verse when he was eight. He became the greatest German hymn writer of the 19th century. He studied at the Lyceum in Hannover and at Goettingen, largely under Rationalistic influence. After graduating he was engaged in a private family as tutor; but from 1828 till his death he was a popular preacher and successful pastor of several Lutheran churches. However, his reputation rests principally upon his hymns, which are deeply spiritual. His *Psalter und Harfe* was translated by Richard Massie in 1860. His hymn collections passed through many editions.

Spittler, Christian Friedrich (1782 to 1867). B. at Wimsheim (Wuerttemberg); distinguished for his services in behalf of missions; was called 1801 to Basel as assistant in the *Christentumgesellschaft;* in 1812 he founded a publishing house at Basel, in 1834, a lending library; but in 1841 he limited his establishment to Bibles, tracts, and the publication of the literature of the *Christentumgesellschaft;* in 1840 he esablished the missionary institution at St. Chrischona, near Basel.

Spittler, Louis Timotheus (1752 to 1810). Studied at Stuttgart and Tuebingen Univ.; prof. at Goettingen; as long as he was associated with Walch, he specialized in church history; after

Walch's death, in political history; his *Grundriss der Geschichte der christlichen Kirche* emphasizes governmental and constitutional history.

Spohr, Ludwig (1784—1859). German composer, violinist, and conductor who enjoyed a world-wide reputation in his day, but whose compositions are rarely heard today. At times his music is suave and sensuous, at other times pedantic and severe. This applies also to his oratorio *The Last Judgment.* Two or three of his violin concertos are heard occasionally, and a fair amount of his music reveals excellent symmetry of form and mastery of technical workmanship.

Sponsors. The persons making the required professions and promises in the name of the infants presented for Baptism in the Christian Church. It was an ancient custom to have such persons present at Baptism, and the Lutheran Church has upheld the custom, principally on account of the Anabaptists, some of whom contended that an adult could never know whether he were truly baptized or not. Not only are the sponsors to bear witness of the performance of the act, but they are also to act as spiritual guardians for the child, if this becomes necessary and is possible for them to do. Sponsors should be chosen only from the number of those who are in communion with the Church of the true faith, that is, of the orthodox Lutheran Church. It is understood that the sponsors make the promises not in their own name, but in that of the child whom they represent, the latter becoming subsequently responsible. In the case of witnesses not members of the faith to which the congregation concerned belongs, the questions ordinarily addressed to the sponsors are omitted.

Sprague, William Buell (1795 to 1876). Compiler, biographer; b. at Andover, Conn.; pastor at West Springfield, Mass. (Congregational), Albany (Presbyterian); d. at Flushing; wrote *Annals of the American Pulpit,* and others.

Sprecher, Samuel. B. 1810 at Williamsport, Md.; pastor at Williamsport, Md.; at Harrisburg, Martinsburg, and Chambersburg, Pa.; brother-in-law and supporter of S. S. Schmucker; pres. of Wittenberg College (1849—84); pres. of Lutheran General Synod at the time of the secession of the General Council; in his earlier days a strong advocate of the Definite Platform,* but in his later life said: "I now regard all such modifications of our Creed as hopeless . . . an increased knowledge of the spirit, methods, and literature of the Missouri Synod has convinced me that such alterations are undesirable; that the elements of true Pietism — that a sense of the necessity of personal religion and the importance of personal assurance of salvation — can be maintained in connection with a Lutheranism unmodified by the Puritan element." D. Jan. 10, 1906.

Spurgeon, Charles Haddon (1834 to 1892). Celebrated English preacher; b. at Kelvedon; son of Independent minister; joined Baptists 1851; pastor in London 1854; trained young preachers at his pastors' college; preached in Metropolitan Tabernacle (seating 6,000) from 1861; opposed baptismal regeneration; withdrew from Baptist Union 1887, although remaining a Baptist; d. at Menton, France. Annual volumes of sermons from 1856; *The Treasury of David, Lectures to My Students*, etc.

Staake, W. H. (1846—1924). Lawyer, prominent member of Lutheran General Council; member of various boards and treasurer of the General Council 1876 to 1918.

Stabat Mater. The musical form or setting of the well-known Latin hymn by Jacoponus da Todi (d. 1306), the subject being the crucifixion of Christ, sung during Passion Week in the Roman Church; ancient setting is still in use, but many composers have since written music, especially Palestrina, Pergolesi, and Rossini, the compositions now being in use not only on the Feast of Seven Dolors, but also, in the form of a cantata, in Protestant circles.

Staden, Johann (1581—1634). Composer and organist of Nuremberg who came under the spell of the early Baroque, departed from the old traditional style of Lutheran Church music, and helped produce accompanied vocal and choral music for the church, school, and home. While his works often lack depth and solidity, they nevertheless exerted a rather wholesome effect in Germany during the 17th century.

Stainer, Sir John (1840—1901). English organist and choirmaster at St. Paul's Cathedral, Oxford University, and other places. Best remembered for the popular oratorio *The Crucifixion*. He also wrote other oratorios and an-

thems, and two manuals entitled *Harmony* and *The Organ*.

Stall, Sylvanus (1847—1915). Lutheran preacher, author, publisher; educated at Gettysburg, Union, and General Theological seminaries; pastor 1874 to 1879; associate editor of *Lutheran Observer* 1890—1901; of *Stall's Lutheran Yearbook and Historical Quarterly*; author of devotional works and books on sexual hygiene (Purity Series).

Stancarus, Franciscus (ca. 1501 to 1574). Italian monk with training in scholastic theology. B. at Mantua; d. at Stobniz, Poland. Opposed Osiander at Königsberg. He taught that Christ is our Mediator with God only in His human nature. He labored in Italy, Switzerland, Germany, Poland, Hungary, and Transylvania.

Stanford, Charles Villiers (1852 to 1924). A native of Dublin and a leading spirit in the musical circles of England in the 19th century, received his advanced musical training in Germany (Reinecke) and was later (1904) elected a member of the Royal Academy of Arts in Berlin. His Irish background helped inject into his music an individuality which was quite uncommon among his colleagues in England. Stanford was versatile as well as prolific. Although he wrote symphonies and large choral works (*Mass in G, Te Deum, Requiem*), he was at his best in his smaller works. His choral works are heard quite often, particularly in Anglican services of worship.

Stanley, Arthur Penrhyn (1815—81). Anglican; b. in Cheshire; ordained 1839; canon of Canterbury 1851; professor of church history, Oxford, 1856—64; dean of Westminster 1864; favored union of Church and State; liberal in religious matter and leader of Broad Church party; traveled and wrote much; d. in London. *Life of Thomas Arnold; Memorials of Westminster Abbey*; and others.

Stanley, Sir Henry Morton (1841 to 1904). American explorer; b. near Denbigh, Wales. Stanley, who was a newspaper correspondent in later life, was sent by the *New York Herald* in 1869 to find Livingstone in Africa, which he accomplished on Nov. 10, 1871, at Ujiji, on Lake Tanganyika. He explored the Congo 1872—77, opening the way for the establishment of the Congo Free State and thus for religious missions. He was also instrumental in calling missionaries to Uganda (1875).

A. H. Godbey, *Henry M. Stanley,* Globe, Chicago, 1890.

Staphylus, Friedrich (1512—64). B. at Osnabrueck; d. at Munich. Studied at Cracow and Padua. Professor, 1545, and rector, 1547, at the university at Koenigsberg; councilor of Duke Albrecht of Prussia, 1548. He became involved in controversies with Wilhelm Gnapheus and A. Osiander. Disgusted with Protestant dissensions, he joined the Roman Church and helped to restore Roman Catholicism in Austria and Bavaria.

Stapulensis, Jacobus Faber (1455 to 1536). Prominent Protestant of France; his education comprehended a thorough training in the classics; he promoted Aristotelian philosophy, advocated a better exegesis of the Scriptures, translated the Bible, and prepared the way for Calvin and Farel; edited the Church Fathers; wrote commentaries on Holy Scripture.

Starck, Johann Friedrich (1680 to 1756). Pastor at Frankfort on the Main; was a mild, practical Pietist after Spener's model; his chief work is his *Daily Handbook,* perhaps the most widely used prayer book in the Lutheran Church.

Starck's Synopsis. See *Commentaries.*

Starke, Christoph (1684—1744). Student at Halle; pastor and teacher at Neunhausen; chief pastor at Driesen; chiefly known for his *Synopsis,* a theologico-homiletic commentary upon the Bible of great homiletic value.

State Church. The established church of a realm which enjoys certain privileges, usually including state financial support.

In medieval Catholicism and in early Protestantism little tolerance was granted dissenting minorities. Especially in England and Scotland intolerance toward those who did not adhere to the State Church was practiced. The Peace of Augsburg (1555) allowed princes to choose the religion (Protestant or Catholic) for a realm.

The Peace of Westphalia introduced a more tolerant attitude. Gradually dissenting groups were permitted to worship unmolested. In realms where the system of State Churches continued, dissenting groups were usually permitted, but did not enjoy the privileges of the established Church. A wide divergence of practice exists in modern State Churches.

States Bible. See *Bible Versions,* K.

States of the Church, The, or *The Papal States.* 1. Formerly a territory in Central Italy, running, roughly, from the mouth of the Po to the mouth of the Tiber, under the immediate sovereignty of the Pope; since 1870 annexed to the kingdom of Italy. The origin of the temporal power of the Pope dates back to the transaction between Stephen III (sometimes called Stephen II, since his predecessor Stephen died three days after his election) and Pepin the Short of France, by which the Pope conferred upon Pepin the coveted crown of the Franks, and Pepin, in turn, beat back the assaults of the Lombards, who threatened the city of Rome and bestowed the conquered territory upon the Pope (754).

2. This "Donation of Pepin" marks the beginning of the temporal sovereignty of the Roman Pontiffs. It was an event big with historical consequences. The history of the Papal States forms an intricate and highly diversified chapter in the religious and political development of Europe. We can note here only a few of its salient features. During the moral degeneracy of the Papacy in the 9th and 10th centuries the papal possessions, indeed the papal office itself, became a prey of warring factions, which forgot all dignity and decency in the mad scramble for power and position. By the middle of the 11th century the papal jurisdiction was not recognized beyond the city of Rome and its immediate vicinity. During its conflict with the empire the Papacy did not succeed in greatly strengthening or extending its temporal power.

3. The "Babylonian Captivity" at Avignon in France meant a practical surrender of temporal rule in Italy. During this period the States of the Church were seized by petty tyrants, who ruled in their own name. On their return to Rome the Popes were obliged to re-establish their temporal authority, a task not completed until the end of the 16th century. Temporarily destroyed by Napoleon, the Papal States were restored by the Congress of Vienna (1815). The odious clerical administration with its oppressive taxation, its discrimination against the laity (excluded from all higher offices), and other grievances led to an insurrection in 1831 and 1832, promptly crushed, however, by Austrian troops. The policy of Pius IX seemed at first to augur

better times, but his concessions did not satisfy the radical party. A revolution broke out in Rome in 1849. Pius was compelled to flee, but returned in the following year under the protection of the French.

4. The last stage in the history of the Papal States is connected with the unification of Italy under a single ruler. As early as 1860 all of the Pope's dominions, with the exception of Rome and adjacent territory, had been incorporated into the new kingdom. When the troops of Napoleon III were removed in 1870, Victor Emmanuel entered Rome, made it the capital of united Italy, and the States of the Church became a part of a united Italy. Feb. 11, 1929, Cardinal Pietro Gasparri (representing the Pope) and Benito Mussolini signed the Lateran Treaty, which created the Vatican City ruled by the Pope (110 acres and adjoining properties).

Stations of the Cross. A series of 14 images, or pictures, representing incidents (some legendary) of the Passion, usually ranged at intervals around the walls of Roman Catholic churches. One of the most popular Roman devotions consists in passing from station to station with certain prayers and meditations. The indulgences thus gained are not specified, but are understood to be remarkably great.

Statistics, Ecclesiastical. That branch of theological science which comprehends the entire Kingdom of God in its earthly manifestation. It includes: geographical statistics — the extent of Christendom in its expansion throughout the world; numerical statistics — an account of its numerical strength; social statistics — its moral statistics and the agencies and techniques through which it expresses itself; and comparative statistics — picturing the comparative strength of the various sections of Christendom and its progress over non-Christian religions.

General. Harry Hansen (ed.), *The World Almanac and Book of Facts,* New York World Telegraph and the Sun, New York 15, N. Y. Information, statistics, and the addresses of all religious denominations where statistical material is available; *The Statesman's Year-Book,* Macm.

Census of Religious Bodies, Government Printing Office, Washington, D. C.

George Ketcham, *Yearbook of American Churches,* Federal Council of Churches, New York 10, N. Y.

Frank S. Mead, *Handbook of Denominations in the United States,* Abingdon-Cokesbury, Nashville, Tenn., 1951.

Missions. Directory of World Missions, International Missionary Council, New York, N. Y.

Denominational. Lutheran World Almanac and Encyclopedia, National Lutheran Council, New York 16, N. Y.

Armin Schroeder (ed.), *Statistical Yearbook,* The Lutheran Church — Missouri Synod, St. Louis, Mo. (CPH). Statistical publications may be obtained from the headquarters of other Lutheran bodies and from the National Lutheran Council, New York, N. Y.

Official Catholic Directory (World), P. J. Kenedy and Sons, New York 8, N. Y.

The National Catholic Almanac (U. S. only), published by St. Anthony's Guild, Paterson, N. J.   EJS

Statistics, Educational. See *Christian Education,* F; *Parish Education.*

Stauch, John. B. Jan. 25, 1767, in York Co., Pa.; preached in western Maryland, western Virginia, western Pennsylvania, and Ohio (1787—93); ordained a catechist at Philadelphia and licensed to preach for one year in Washington Co., Pa.; first Lutheran preacher in Ohio (1799) and Kentucky (1800); came to Columbiana Co., Ohio (1808), to organize congregations and conduct revivals; moved to Crawford Co., Ohio (1829); pres. of the General Conference of the Joint Synod of Ohio (1818—20; 1822; 1824); traveled 100,000 miles preaching in five States; d. July, 1845.

Stauffer Mennonite Church. See *Mennonite Bodies,* 3.

Staupitz, Johann von. Led in founding the University of Wittenberg in 1502; as head of the Augustinians he urged Bible study; discovered Luther, comforted him, made him his successor at Wittenberg in 1512; left Luther's cause in 1519; abbot of the Benedictine cloister of St. Peter at Salzburg in 1522; d. 1524.

Stearns, S. See *Baptist Bodies,* 22.

Stedingers. Frisians of the lower Weser, who, because they revolted against the oppression of nobles and priests, were nearly extirpated by a crusade sanctioned by Pope Gregory IX in 1234.

Steele, Anne (1716—78). Daughter of a Baptist clergyman; published

Poems on Subjects Chiefly Devotional; a leading hymn writer; wrote, among others: "Lord of My Life"; "To Jesus, Our Exalted Lord."

Steffani, Agostino (1653—1728). Roman Catholic clergyman, influential in music during the Baroque Era. Steffani exerted a great influence on Handel and recommended Handel for the position of *Kapellmeister* at the court of the Elector of Hanover. His influence kept German music from becoming too serious and ponderous. One of his outstanding compositions is *Stabat Mater.*

Stegmann, Josua (1588—1632). B. Suelzfeld, Germany; studied at Leipzig and after having received his degree was an adjunct of the philosophical faculty. Later on he became pastor at Stadthagen and was also first professor of the *Gymnasium* there. In 1617 he received his degree of D. D. from Wittenberg, and when the *Gymnasium* at Stadthagen was changed into a university and transferred to Rinteln, he became a professor of theology there. He later became the victim of persecution at the hands of Benedictine monks and also suffered greatly during the Thirty Years' War. He has bequeathed to us the beautiful hymn "Abide, O Dearest Jesus." All his worry and trouble shortened his life.

Steimle, F. W. T. See *New York, German Synod of.*

Steimle Synod. See *United Lutheran Church, Synods of,* 18.

Stein, Henry Fred Andrew. B. Aug. 29, 1867, at Baltimore, Md.; graduated at St. Louis, 1889; pastor at Springfield, Mass., 1889—92; prof. at Concordia Institute, now at Bronxville, N. Y., 1892 to 1948; M. A., Ph. D., New York, University; d. May 10, 1948.

Steinbach, Ch. F. A pioneer pastor of the Missouri Synod; held pastorates at Liverpool, Ohio, Sheboygan and Milwaukee, Wis., and Fairfield Center, Ind.; d. Jan. 11, 1883.

Steinbart, Gotthilf Samuel (1816 to 1888). Prof. at Basel; his philosophy centered in a religious hedonism.

Steiner, Rudolf (1861—1925). Hungarian by birth; for a while associated with Annie Besant and theosophy; father of anthroposophy, an outstanding characteristic of which is the attempt to attain higher knowledge through a system of meditation.

Steinhausen, Wilhelm (1854—1925). German painter; exponent of realism, but with a sympathetic touch; his use of prints from stones paved the way for a new popular art in Germany; much of his work in series, such as "The Birth of Christ," but also individual paintings: "Emmaus"; "John the Baptist"; "The Sermon on the Mount."

Steinle, Eduard (1810—86). German painter, one of the so-called "Nazarenes" school of Overbeck; rich imagination, tendency toward the symbolical; much work in sepia and crayon; frescoes in Cathedral of Cologne.

Stellhorn, F. W. "Pre-eminently the scholar of the Ohio Synod"; b. Oct. 2, 1841, in Hanover, was educated at Fort Wayne and St. Louis; Lutheran pastor in St. Louis 1865—67, in De Kalb Co., Ind., 1867—69; professor at Northwestern College, Watertown, 1869 to 1874, at Fort Wayne 1874—81. In 1881, as a result of the Predestination Controversy, he severed his connection with the Missouri Synod and accepted a position in the college and seminary of the Ohio Synod at Columbus. He was the president of the seminary 1894 to 1900 and dean after 1903. Stellhorn was editor, for a number of years, of the *Lutherische Kirchenzeitung,* and of the *Theologische Zeitblaetter* since 1881. Author of commentaries on the historical books of the New Testament, Romans, and the Pastoral Epistles; Greek Lexicon. D. March 17, 1919.

Stephan, Martin. B. Aug. 13, 1777, in Stramberg, Silesia; studied theology at Halle and Leipzig; pastor of the church at Haber, Bohemia; a year later, of the Bohemian St. John's Congregation, Dresden, preaching also in German. While Rationalism dominated the pulpits of Dresden, "he preached the Gospel, having experienced its power in his own soul," and multitudes flocked to hear him. By reason of his understanding of the genuine Gospel and of his psychological insight he also excelled as a spiritual adviser, able to comfort and strengthen the stricken conscience and doubting heart. His activity thus transcended the limits of his parish. He it was who through his straight Lutheran Gospel advice brought peace to the soul of C. F. W. Walther in his student days. He became the counselor of a number of pastors who clung to the old Lutheran faith, and in the course of time he became their spiritual leader. His long-cherished plan of emigrating to a land of freedom was finally, in 1836, when the oppression was growing unbearable, accepted by them and their people. In 1838 came his suspension from office (the charges against him, however, had not been proved) and the emigration. The doctrinal errors, which had gradually, at first imperceptibly, been vitiating his theology and his fall from grace, in consequence of which he was deposed from office in Perry County, Mo., in 1839, have been set forth elsewhere. (See *Missouri Synod*.) He was transported to Illinois, where some time afterward he served as pastor of the Lutheran congregation at Horse Prairie near Red Bud, where he died Feb. 22, 1846. See Forster, W. O., *Zion on the Mississippi*.

Stephan, M. Son of the preceding; b. July 23, 1823, in Dresden, Saxony; studied at Concordia College, Altenburg, Mo.; studied architecture in Dresden; was encouraged by Dr. Walther and others to prepare for the ministry; graduate of Concordia Seminary, St. Louis, 1853; first charge, Theresa, Wis.; at one time assistant pastor to Dr. Sihler and instructor in secular branches in the Fort Wayne seminary; last charge in Bremer County, Iowa; d. Jan. 16, 1884. He furnished the plans for a number of churches and for the St. Louis Seminary, 1849.

Stephen I. See *Hungary*.

Stephen I of Rome (253—57). Was the great opponent of Cyprian * in the question of heretical Baptism, maintaining that the validity of the Sacrament depended not on the officiating person, but solely on the institution of Christ and on the administration in conformity therewith.

Stephen, Robert. See *Manuscripts of the Bible*, 3.

Steuerlein, Johann (1546—1613). Son of Caspar Steuerlein, the first Lutheran pastor of Schmalkalden; studied law; became town clerk of Wasungen, later secretary in chancery at Meiningen, and finally mayor of that place; here he also died. He was crowned as poet by Emperor Rudolf II in recognition of his work of rhyming the Old and New Testaments in German. He also wrote a metrical version of Ecclesiasticus. He was an excellent musician and published his own melodies and four-part settings.

Stewardship. A Scriptural term used to describe man's divinely appointed relationship to God. A steward in ancient times was a trusted servant, under whose administration the master placed his property and interests for their enlargement and advancement (*e. g.*, Gen. 39: 4-6). The Bible usually employs the term in this secular sense, although it also applies the term to pastors (1 Cor. 4: 1; Titus 1: 7), and to Christians in general (1 Peter 4: 10).

Stewardship is the recognition and fulfillment of the personal privilege and responsibility to administer all the material, physical, mental, and spiritual endowments of life according to the will of God and for the best interests of His kingdom. Although stewardship is sometimes identified with sanctification, it could be more properly described as a narrower term, included in sanctification.

Christian stewardship proceeds from the acknowledgment of the basic truths that God is the true Owner of all that we are and have (Ps. 24: 1; 100: 3; 1 Chron. 29: 14; 1 Chron. 4: 7; 6: 19), that we ourselves belong to God by virtue of our creation, preservation, redemption, and sanctification and have as our chief purpose to glorify Him (Rom. 14: 7, 8; 1 Cor. 10: 31; 1 Peter 4: 11), that all talents and endowments of every kind are temporarily placed in our charge (Luke 12: 20; 16: 2), and that we must render to God an account of their use (2 Cor. 5: 10).

Every Christian is a steward under God, whether many or few talents have been entrusted to him. The motivation for Christian stewardship is supplied by the Gospel. To motivate stewardship with the Law (merit, reward, social gospel) is to invalidate its Christian character and eventually to destroy Christian faith. RGL

W. Arndt, "Justification, Sanctification, and Stewardship," *CTM*, VIII: 98—110; P. Lindemann, *My God and I* (a new edition of *Christian Stewardship and Its Modern Implications*), CPH, 1949; Karl Kretzschmar, *The Stewardship Life*, CPH, 1929; W. C. Birkner, "Christian Stewardship," *Abiding Word*, 1946 (I: 457-81. This gives references to District essays and summarizes Christian stewardship thus: God, the Creator and Preserver, is also the owner of all things. . . . "Our" possessions come to us undeservedly through the mercies of God, the Owner, who distributes them according to HIS gracious will and gives directions regarding their use. This stewardship relation to God is not a degrading experience but a privilege. Our possessions are to be used according to the will of the Owner. . . . While stewardship is also a matter of obedience to God's command, the prime motive which dominates us as we discharge our stewardship obligations is gratitude to God and love for our fellow men); J. E. Herrmann, *The Chief Steward*, CPH, 1951.

Stewardship of Money. That the Church needs money to carry on its work is a self-evident fact. It is also a fact that the work of the Church is often hindered by lack of funds; the church deficit has frequently become proverbial. The average Christian does not contribute in accordance with his means. Is the Church itself not largely responsible for this condition? An improvement in church finances ought to be worked out according to the following lines: 1. Christians must learn that the Word of God teaches that giving is a Christian duty. Christians should abound also in the grace of giving and thereby prove the sincerity of their love. 2 Cor. 8:7, 8. 2. Christians must be duly informed with reference to the needs of the Church. The work of the Church, its opportunities and its needs, should be duly presented. This should be done not only in the pulpit, but also in the meetings of the voting members, the young people's society, and the ladies' society, as well as in the weekday school and in the Sunday school. The members should also be urged to read the church papers and such special literature (folders with pictures) as may be issued by a church body from time to time. People will not give to anything in which they are not interested. 3. Christians must by a good financial system (every-member canvass and envelope system) be given an opportunity to contribute regularly and often.

Stier, Ewald Rudolf (1800—62). Studied at Berlin and Halle; pastor and superintendent at various places, last at Eisleben; deeply interested in Biblical study; edited polyglot Bible together with Theile; wrote: "Wir sind vereint, Herr Jesu Christ." Stier is known especially for his commentaries (Hebrews, James, Ephesians, Jude, Isaiah, and, above all, his *Reden Jesu*).

Stigmatization. The appearance, on the bodies of certain persons, of wounds resembling those received by Jesus from the crown of thorns, the nails, and the spear. The first person reported to have been so marked was Francis of Assisi (see *Francis, St.*), who, in 1224, is supposed to have received the marks, or *stigmata*, in hands, feet, and side from a seraph while keeping a forty-day fast on Mount Alvernus, in the Apennines. Since then 80 or more cases of stigmatization have been reported, some only partial, others complete. Those affected were usually monastics of hyperascetic tendencies, and about five sixths were women. The stigmata are supposed to be accompanied with intense suffering. The presence of these marks has, in some cases, been attested by large numbers of reputable witnesses. The question of their causation is another matter. Many Roman Catholics consider them miraculous. In some instances deliberate fraud has been proved, while in others there is no evidence of dishonesty. Among the various theories that have been advanced, two may be mentioned: the one holding that the mind, under abnormal conditions (as in hypnosis) can bring about such phenomena on the body; the other, that the stigmatics, in a state of ecstasy or hysteria, unconsciously or half-consciously inflicted the stigmata on themselves.

Stillingfleet, Edward (1635—99). Anglican prelate; b. at Cranborne; rector; dean of St. Paul's; bishop of Worcester; d. at Westminster. Apologetic (*Rational Account of the Grounds of the Protestant Religion*), controversial, and metaphysical writings.

Stobaeus, Johann (1580—1646). Studied under Eccard at Koenigsberg; also attended university; cantor at the cathedral school; later *Kapellmeister;* important composer of church music; published *Cantiones Sacrae.*

Stocker, John. Nothing definite known of his life; contributed nine hymns to the *Gospel Magazine* during 1776 and 1777, among which: "Gracious Spirit, Dove Divine."

Stockflett, Niels J. Christian (1787 to 1866). "Apostle of the Laplanders"; after military career studied theology at Upsala and Christiania; after ordination (1825) studied language of Laplanders; translated the NT for the Lapps.

Stockmann, Ernst (1634—1712). B. at Luetzen; at time of his death *Oberkonsistorialrat* and *Kirchenrat* at Eisenach; wrote: "Gott, der wird's wohlmachen."

Stoddard, Solomon (1643—1729). Grandfather of Jonathan Edwards,* pioneer Congregationalist minister, developed practice called *Stoddardeanism* of admitting to full membership also those who could not relate an experience of regeneration, contrary to stricter practice in New England; active in political movements.

Stoecker, Adolf (1835—1909). Court preacher at Berlin 1874—90; organizer of city mission work in Berlin 1877; of the Christian Socialist Party 1878, demanding government protection for the workingman; of the Evangelical Socialist Congress 1890; of the Free Ecclesiastical Socialist Conference 1897; encountered considerable opposition; harmed his cause by anti-Semitic propaganda. See *Inner Mission,* 3.

Stoeckhardt, George. 1. B. Feb. 17, 1842, at Chemnitz, Saxony; received his preparatory education in the *Lateinschule* at Tharandt and the *Fuerstenschule* at Meissen; studied theology at Erlangen and Leipzig 1862—66; tutor at a ladies' seminary, Tharandt, 1866—70; assistant pastor of a German Lutheran church at Paris; for three months at the Sedan hospital 1870—71; private tutor in Old and New Testament Exegesis at Erlangen and, at the same time, teacher of religion in the *Gymnasium* of that city 1871—73; took the degree of Lic. Theol. (Leipzig); pastor of the church at Planitz, Saxony, 1873—76, making the acquaintance of Pastor Ruhland of the Free Church congregation and of the theological literature of the Missouri Synod. As his protest against the indifferentism and unscriptural practice of the State Church (the pastors were refused the right, for instance, of suspending impenitent sinners from Communion; gross errorists were retained in office) remained unheeded, he renounced his connection with the consistory (of the 181 pastors who had begun the fight only Stoeckhardt and Pastor Schneider fought to the end) and, on being suspended, resigned from his office. With a part of his congregation he joined the Saxon Free Church, becoming second pastor of the church at Niederplanitz 1876 to 1878, together with Pastor Ruhland founded the *Freikirche,* the organ of the Free Church (for his articles on apostasy in the State Church he was, in 1879, sentenced to eight [four] months' imprisonment), and prepared a number of boys for college. In 1878 he became pastor of Holy Cross Church, St. Louis, and, having since 1879 lectured on Old and New Testament Exe-

gesis at **Concordia Seminary,** was elected professor in 1887. In 1903 Luther Seminary, Hamline, Minn., created him a Doctor of Divinity. D. January 9, 1913.

2. Stoeckhardt was an exegete of the first rank. Coupled with his great learning, his familiarity with the original languages, etc., and his logical mind was his firm belief in the verbal inspiration of the Scriptures and his childlike acceptance of all the teachings of Scripture, his great love of the revealed truth. He permitted nothing but the text to influence his thought. Concentrating all the powers of his believing heart and mind on the written Word, he obtained a wonderful grasp of the deep thoughts of the Spirit, and he had the rare gift of unfolding them in concise, clear, convincing language. Besides his exegetical articles in *Lehre und Wehre* he wrote commentaries on Romans, Ephesians, First Peter, Isaiah 1—12, *Ausgewaehlte Psalmen,* and *Biblische Geschichte.* His mastery in exegesis made him the forceful preacher he was. "His sermons are full of the marrow and substance of Scripture, meaty, solid, well compacted." He wrote *Passionspredigten, Adventspredigten, Gnade um Gnade* (on the Gospel pericopes), and contributed most valuable material, such as the *Studies on the Pericopes,* to the *Homiletic Magazine.*

3. The Missouri Synod owes much to Stoeckhardt; his exegetical ability and love of the truth of Scripture made him one of the leaders, with Walther, in the controversy on election and conversion and in the other battles the Church was, and is, engaged in, such as Verbal Inspiration. In line with the article written on his accession to the chair of Exegesis: "How Can and Should Each Individual Lutheran Lend His Aid Toward the Preservation of the Pure Doctrine by the Church?" he labored, by word and pen (his doctrinal articles in *Lehre und Wehre,* in *Lutheraner,* and in the synodical reports) to conserve this most precious treasure of the Missouri Synod; and he admirably succeeded in impressing upon both his students and his readers his exegetical method, his loving reverence for the written Word.

O. Willkomm, *Georg Stoeckhardt, Lebensbild,* Herrmann, Zwickau, 1914; E. Biegener, "Karl Georg Stoeckhardt, D. Theol., 1842—1913," *CHIQ,* XXI: 154—66.

Stoeppelwerth, Henry John. Born Oct. 11, 1869, at Washington, Mo.;

graduated at St. Louis, 1893; professor at St. John's College, Winfield, Kans., 1893—1934. D. Oct. 16, 1934.

Stoicism. Greek school of philosophy, founded ca. 300 B. C. by Zeno of Cyprus, who taught in a *stoa, i. e.,* portico, at Athens. It holds a materialistic view of the universe and a pantheistic conception of God. Its chief characteristic, however, lies in the field of ethics. In opposition to contemporaneous Epicureanism it maintained that the supreme aim in life is not pleasure, but virtue, or living in harmony with nature. The greatest virtues are practical wisdom, bravery, temperance, justice. In consequence it teaches self-control, a complete suppression of all passions. Though Stoicism resembles certain Christian elements, it is fundamentally different. Its ethics, like Pharisaism, is based on egoism and self-sufficiency; it boasts of its own merits and is without knowledge and need of grace. It has no compassion for the oppressed and weak and, if obstacles prove insurmountable, advocates, as the final resort, suicide. Moreover, as susceptibility to the contrast between the pleasant and unpleasant is a part of our true human nature, the Christian ideal is not sublime indifference to pain and pleasure, not the repression of all emotions and impulses, but rather their sanctification.

Stolberg, Friedrich Leopold (1750 to 1819). German poet, statesman, and theological writer; friend of Klopstock, Goethe, and other literary men; originally Lutheran, the current rationalism moved him to join the Roman Catholic Church, which he contacted at Muenster, where Roman Catholics stressed the Bible and Christian mystics. In addition to poetic works, he wrote a *History of the Religion of Christ, Considerations and Reflections of the Sacred Scripture, Book of Love,* and others.

Stole. See *Vestments, Clerical.*

Stolee, Michael Olaf J. B. 1871 in Norway; emigrated to America 1886; graduate of St. Olaf College and United Norwegian Church Seminary (1900); studied in Paris and at the University of Christiania; missionary in Madagascar 1901; professor at United Norwegian Church Seminary 1911, Luther Theological Seminary 1917.

Stoltzer, Thomas (ca. 1480—1526). German composer of the Reformation era, was among the composers represented in Georg Rhaw's *Neue deudsche Geistliche Gesenge* of 1544. In his *Music in Western Civilization* (New York, 1941), Lang puts him aside of men like Duerer, Cranach, and the Holbeins (p. 201). While his counterpoint is at times similar to that of Okeghem, it has, at the same time, more energy and warmth.

Stone, Barton. See *Churches of Christ; Congregational and Christian Churches; Disciples of Christ.*

Stone, Samuel John (1839—1900). B. in Whitemore, Staffordshire, educated at Charterhouse and Pembroke College, Oxford; curate, first of Windsor, then of St. Paul's, Haggerstonn, London; succeeded his father as vicar in 1874, and in 1890 accepted the rectorship of All-Hallows-on-the-Wall, London. During his life he published four volumes of poetry. He was a member of the committee for *Hymns Ancient and Modern* in the latter stages of that work. He published many hymns attaining a wide popularity, among them, "The Church's One Foundation."

Storch, Nicholas. See *Mennonite Bodies,* 1.

Stork, Charles August G. Early Lutheran pastor in North Carolina; b. June 16, 1764, in Germany; came to America 1788; served Salisbury, Organ, and Pine churches in North Carolina, and established numerous other churches; visited churches in Tennessee, Virginia, and South Carolina; eloquent preacher; frequently presided at synods. D. March 29, 1831.

Storr, Gottlob Christian (1746 to 1805). B. at Stuttgart, d. there as court preacher and consistorial councilor; founder of the so-called Older Tuebingen School of Theology; Biblical supranaturalist; opponent of Semler's theory of accommodation, by which divine revelation is to be explained, according to modern critics.

Storr, Johann Christian (1712 to 1773). B. at Heilbronn. After various pastorates he was court chaplain and preacher at Stuttgart; counselor of the consistory and prelate at Alpirsbach. He was a disciple of Bengel; inclined to Pietism. His *Christliches Hausbuch* was popular.

Stoss, Veit (ca. 1440—1533). German wood carver; figures known for their grace; but they lacked naturalness; his entire style affected; among his more pretentious creations: altar of Mary in the church at Cracow.

Strack, Hermann Lebrecht (1848 to 1922). Prof. in Berlin; positive theologian of the Prussian Union; wrote *Einleitung in das Alte Testament;* with O. Zoeckler editor of *Kurzgefasster Kommentar zu den heiligen Schriften.*

Strasen, Karl J. A. B. May 30, 1827, at Juergenshagen, Mecklenburg-Schwerin, Germany. Graduate of Practical Seminary, Fort Wayne (now at Springfield, Ill.); served a congregation at Collinsville, Ill., till 1859; then called to Watertown, Wis., where he was pastor over forty years; favorably known throughout the Missouri Synod as president of the Northwestern District (now North and South Wisconsin Districts). D. Feb. 26, 1909.

Strauss, David Friedrich (1808—74). B. at Ludwigslust, Wuerttemberg; Rationalist, who applied Hegel's pantheistic and materialistic philosophy to religion and theology; studied at Tuebingen under F. C. Baur; for a while vicar, then *repetent* at Tuebingen. His *Leben Jesu* appeared in 1835, written when he was twenty-seven. In this work he advanced the so-called "mythical" theory of the Gospel narrative of the life of Christ, in which he assumed a gradual development of the Christian religion, analogous to heathen mythology, without any intentional fabrication on the part of the Apostles. This work created an immense sensation. In later life he put forth even more advanced radical views, especially in *Der alte und der neue Glaube.*

Streckfuss, Friedrich. B. Sept. 7, 1852, in Van Wert Co., Ohio.; graduate of Concordia College, Fort Wayne, and Concordia Seminary, St. Louis (1874); pastor at Young America, Minn.; 1892 professor of Latin in the Proseminary and of Symbolics in the Seminary at Springfield; d. there April 14, 1924.

Streeter, Burnett Hillman (1874 to 1937). Outstanding scholar of the Anglican Church; prof. at Oxford; his work on NT introduction received wide acclaim; investigated NT teachings on the ministry; sought to show that there is no contradiction between science and religion; outstanding work: *The Four Gospels.*

Streissguth, W. (1827—1915). Educated at Basel; pastor of Swiss colony, Green Co., Wis.; joined Wisconsin Synod 1854; pastor at Milwaukee, Fond

du Lac, St. Paul, Kenosha; president of Wisconsin Synod 1864—67.

Streit, Christian. B. June 7, 1749, near New Germantown, N. J.; grad. Univ. of Pa., 1768 (M. A., 1771); studied theology under Muhlenberg and Wrangel; pastorates at Easton, Pa., chapl. of Eighth Virginia Regiment, 1769—78; Charleston, S. C., 1778—80; New Holland, Pa., 1782—85; Winchester, Va., 1785—1812. While here he instructed a number of men for ministry, among them Paul Henkel. D. March 10, 1812.

Streufert, Frank Carl. B. Apr. 30, 1874; graduated from Concordia College, Fort Wayne and Concordia Seminary, St. Louis (1895); traveling missionary for northern California, 1895; served various parishes in California, 1895 to 1902; pastor at Chicago, Ill., 1902—32; secy. of Missions for The Luth. Church—Missouri Synod, 1932—53; held various offices in the Northern Illinois Dist.; member of the Bd. of Directors, The Luth. Church—Missouri Synod; Bd. for Army and Navy (1917—19); secy. of the Campaign for the Collection for Veterans of the Cross (1919 to 1920) and of the L. L. L. Endowment Campaign (after World War I); edited *Northern Illinois Messenger* (1915—32) and *Soldier and Sailor Bulletin* (World War I) and prepared various materials; D. D., Concordia Seminary, St. Louis, 1943; d. Sept. 17, 1953.

Strieter, John August Fred. B. Dec. 26, 1854, at Cleveland, Ohio; graduated at Fort Wayne, Ind., 1878; teacher at Dubuque, Iowa, 1878—80; Akron, Ohio, 1880—84; Frankenmuth, Mich., 1884 to 1897; Cleveland, Ohio, 1897—1903; prof. at Concordia Teachers College, Seward, Nebr., 1903—27; d. Dec. 15, 1927. J. Strieter, *Lebenslauf,* F. M. Leutner, Cleveland, 1904.

Strigel, Victorinus (1524—69). One of the foremost representatives of the Melanchthonian school of Protestantism; studied at Freiburg, in 1542 at Wittenberg, where he absorbed the spirit of Melanchthon; taught at Wittenberg, Erfurt, and Jena; engaged in a debate at Weimar with Flacius on questions of synergism; moved to Leipzig, later to Heidelberg; like Melanchthon, he never distinguished clearly between philosophy and theology, and his teaching on free will and on original sin was condemned in the Formula of Concord.

Strong, Augustus Hopkins (1836 to 1922). Baptist; b. at Rochester, N. Y.;

pastor; professor of theology; president of Rochester Theological Seminary 1872—1912; d. at Pasadena, Calif.; wrote *Systematic Theology; Great Poets and Theology;* and others.

Strong, Nathan (1748—1816). B. at Coventry, Conn., graduated from Yale with high honors, studied law, but later turned to theology. In 1773 he was ordained pastor of the First Congregational Church, Hartford, and remained there until his death. He founded the *Connecticut Evangelical Magazine* and also took part in establishing the Connecticut Home Mission Society. He was the principal editor of the Hartford *Selection,* 1799. He wrote the hymn "Swell the Anthem, Raise the Song."

Stuart, Janet Erskine (1857—1914). English nun; known for her writings on asceticism and educational topics.

Stub, Hans Gerhard. B. Feb. 23, 1849, at Muskego, Wis.; studied at Cathedral School, Bergen, Norway; Luther College; Concordia College, Fort Wayne; graduated at Concordia Seminary, St. Louis, 1872; pastor in Minneapolis; professor of Luther Seminary 1878 (studied two years at Leipzig), at Luther College (and pastor at Decorah, Iowa) 1896, at Luther Seminary 1900 to 1917; vice-president of Norwegian Synod 1905; president 1910; of the Norwegian Lutheran Church of America 1917. First president of the National Lutheran Council; preached opening sermon at the Eisenach World Conference 1923. Editor of *Evangelisk Luthersk Kirketidende, Teologisk Tidsskrift;* author of *Naadevalget, Mod Frimureriet, Udvalgelsen,* etc. In the election and conversion controversy he took a leading part on the side of the Synodical Conference. Subsequently he upheld the Madison Theses. Knighted by King Haakon VII. Received the title of LL.D. from Luther College 1924; of D.D. from Concordia Seminary, St. Louis, 1903. D. Aug. 1, 1931.

Life in O. M. Norlie, *Prominent Personalities* (see *Biography*).

Stubnatzi, Wolfgang Simon. B. 1829 at Fuerth, Bavaria; sent over by Pastor Loehe 1847; studied in the Fort Wayne Seminary (now at Springfield, Ill.); pastor at Coopers Grove, Ill., 1849—62; assistant of Dr. Sihler 1862; pastor of Immanuel Church, Fort Wayne, 1868; visitor, vice-president, and president of the Central District; d. Sept. 13, 1880.

Stuckenberg, John Henry Wilburn (1835—1903). Studied at Wittenberg College (Springfield, Ohio), then at universities of Halle, Goettingen, Tuebingen, Berlin; held pastorates in the ULCA in Ohio, Indiana, and Pennsylvania; professor at Wittenberg Seminary (Hamma Divinity School); pastor of the American Church in Berlin, 1880—94; liberal in theology; wrote: *History of the Augsburg Confession; Christian Sociology; The Social Problem;* and others.

Student Service Commission. See *Students, Spiritual Care of,* C.

Student Volunteer Movement for Foreign Missions (S.V.M.F.M.). 1. The S.V.M.F.M. goes back to the first International Conference of Christian college students held at Mount Hermon, Mass., 1886. At the adjournment of the conference about 100 of the participants had declared themselves "willing and desirous, God permitting, to become foreign missionaries." This was owing, to a great extent, to the earnest efforts of R. P. Wilder. Wilder and J. S. Forman were sent on a tour to the colleges of the United States with a view to interesting the student bodies in the new movement. In December, 1888, a society was formed for the purpose of doing more efficient work in this direction, which adopted the above name.

2. The purpose of the movement is expressed in the following sentences: "a. To awaken and maintain among all Christian students of the United States and Canada intelligent and active interest in foreign missions; b. to enroll a sufficient number of properly qualified student volunteers to meet the successive demands of the various missionary boards of North America; c. to help all such intending missionaries to prepare for their lifework and to enlist their co-operation in developing the missionary life of the home churches; d. to lay an equal burden of responsibility on all students who are to remain as ministers and lay workers at home, that they may actively promote the missionary enterprise by their intelligent advocacy, by their gifts, and by their prayers." The declaration of the movement for all members is: "It is my purpose, if God permit, to become a foreign missionary." The declaration, however, is not a binding promise, but an expression of earnest intention to serve if the Lord does not interpose insurmountable obstacles.

3. The slogan of the Volunteer Movement is: "The evangelization of the world in this generation." Its members are solicited from the colleges and universities of the United States and Canada. This marks the movement as interdenominational in character. Its activities are directed toward the students in and out of educational institutions. Secretaries visit colleges and universities, lecture on missions and give instructions regarding them, form foreign mission student classes and direct their work, always seeking contact with the individuals. Intimate relations with the Y. M. C. A. and Y. W. C. A. in colleges and cities are maintained. The *Intercollegian* constantly keeps the movement before the student bodies and the Christian churches. Also much other literature for the purpose of giving information bearing on foreign missions is published.

4. At stated times district conventions are held, in which specially prepared programs are followed, the meetings lasting as long as ten days. Quadrennially national gatherings are conducted, in which outstanding and peculiarly fitted men deliver addresses. Missionaries from all over the world participate in these meetings with prepared addresses and reports. The propaganda work of the society has been eminently successful, more than six thousand members, male and female, having gone into the foreign field, serving their respective churches.

5. The S. V. M. is a recruiting and not a sending society. The movement spread to England (1892), to the Continent, and to Asia. A World's Student Christian Federation was formed. The official organs are the *Student Volunteer* and the *Student Movement*. The office of the S. V. M. F. M. is at 156 Fifth Ave., New York City.

Students, Spiritual Care of. A. *General.* 1. Prominent in the beginning of American higher education was the determination to integrate religion with higher education in church-controlled colleges. Education was one of the great interests of the Church, which created hundreds of the denominational colleges that are located all over the land. Harvard, for example, owes its existence to the Puritans; Princeton to the Presbyterians; the University of Chicago to the Baptists; Yale to the Congregationalists; Northwestern University to the Methodists; Gettysburg and Concordia (Ft. Wayne) colleges to

the Lutherans. The steady rise of State universities, inaugurated by Thomas Jefferson when in 1819 he founded the publicly controlled University of Virginia, and the progressive secularization of higher education gradually induced the churches to follow their students to State and privately controlled colleges and universities in order to keep them with the Church.

2. While a few local churches and voluntary agencies assumed the responsibility for initiating church-centered student programs before 1900, general denominational support of student work did not come until shortly after the turn of the century.

3. Principal religious student organizations include the Canterbury Club (Episcopal); the Congregational Christian Student Fellowship (Congregational-Christian); Roger Williams Club (Northern Baptist); Baptist Student Union (Southern Baptist); Methodist Student Movement (Wesley Foundation in State institutions and Methodist Fellowship in Methodist and independent colleges); Westminster Foundation (Presbyterian); Gamma Delta, the International Association of Lutheran Students (Synodical Conference); Lutheran Student Association of America (this intersynodical student association grew out of a national student conference called together by the Lutheran Brotherhood at the time of their biennial conference in Toledo, Ohio, in May, 1922); Beta Sigma Psi, a social fraternity controlled by Synodical Conference Lutheran students, which fosters spiritual welfare, provides opportunity for Christian fellowship, and encourages high scholarship; the Newman Club (Roman Catholic); Pax Romana (the Roman Catholic international student body); and the Hillel Foundation (Jewish, sponsored by B'nai B'rith, a national order nearly 100 years old).

4. Before the denominations accepted their new responsibility, early State college presidents, many of whom were clergymen, endeavored to meet the religious needs of students by providing daily chapel services and by encouraging the work of Christian student societies and of the local churches. The first student Y. M. C. A.'s were organized in State universities, namely, at the University of Michigan and at the University of Virginia, during the academic year 1858—59.

5. Major interdenominational student movements are: the National In-

tercollegiate Christian Council (formed in 1935 "to provide a national center through which united responses could be given to the needs of the changing local and regional situation"); the World's Student Christian Federation (a world-wide fellowship of Christian students founded in Sweden in 1895 by representatives of American and European Student Christian movements); the United Student Christian Council (the U.S.A. section of the World's Student Christian Federation, organized in 1944); and the Inter-Varsity Christian Fellowship (an international, interdenominational, and evangelical student movement which had its origin at Cambridge University, England, in 1877).

B. *Lutheran in America.* 1. Lutheran student work had its beginning in 1907, when the Board of Home Missions of the General Council placed a pastor in Madison, Wis., to explore opportunities for student work at the University of Wisconsin. The 19th annual convention of the English Evangelical Lutheran Synod of the Northwest, in the year 1909, appointed a Committee on College and University Student Work and memorialized the General Council, at the convention in the same year in Minneapolis, to take definite steps toward a proper and adequate solution of the problems of Christian instruction at State and non-Lutheran institutions of learning in the United States and Canada.

2. With the formation of the United Lutheran Church, in 1918, the responsibility for student work, hitherto directed by the Committee on Student Life of the General Council, was taken over by the newly constituted Board of Education. In co-operation with the Women's Missionary Society, which had voted to assume the support of a woman secretary, the Board, in 1919, elected Miss Mary Markley as secretary of the Board for work among women students. At the same time it elected Rev. Paul H. Krauss as secretary for student work at non-Lutheran colleges and universities. Rev. Krauss, who resigned after serving one year, was succeeded in 1921 by Rev. C. P. Harry.

3. When various Lutheran bodies organized the American Lutheran Conference, a Student Service Commission was created to which each of the five constituent bodies contributed one member. Rev. Frederick Schiotz was the first executive secretary of that commission.

4. The affiliation of the American Lutheran Conference with the National Lutheran Council led to a suspension of independent student work by the United Lutheran Church and the American Lutheran Conference and brought the student work of these two bodies under the joint direction of the Student Service Commission of the National Lutheran Council, whose first executive secretary was Rev. Morris Wee.

C. *Missouri Synod.* 1. Prior to 1923, when "Synod instructed President Pfotenhauer to appoint a committee to consider the spiritual needs of our students in non-synodical institutions of higher learning," the initiative for student work was wholly dependent on farsighted, campus-conscious men within their respective synodical Districts. It was such aggressive leadership which induced the South Wisconsin District to launch student work at the University of Wisconsin in the year 1920, with Rev. Ad. Haentzschel as the first student pastor. Six years later, in conjunction with the North Wisconsin District of the Missouri Synod and the entire Wisconsin Synod, a student chapel, with conjoined parsonage, was erected on a site facing the campus in Madison.

2. With impetus provided by the Student Welfare Committee (later called the Student Service Commission) other Districts recognized their obligations to serve the Church's college youth and appropriated moneys commensurate with existing needs and opportunities. The total cost of student chapels and centers, authorized by various synodical Districts during the years 1945—46, exceeded one million dollars.

3. Synod, in 1926, approved the calling of "a general student pastor who shall devote his full time to general work under the direction of the Student Welfare Committee." Financial limitations, however, necessitated postponement of action until 1939, when the Student Service Commission was enabled to call an executive secretary. This position was filled in 1940 by Rev. R. W. Hahn, who had served as student pastor at the University of Alabama from 1929 to 1940.

4. The four-point program of the Church's work on the campus is: soul conservation, soul reclamation, soul

winning, and training for Christian service.

5. It is the obligation of the synodical Student Service Commission to co-operate with District Mission Boards in intensifying the Church's campus ministry.

6. While in most places student work is carried on by pastors of college community congregations, full-time student pastors are called to conduct this phase of the Church's work where conditions warrant intensified student work. The formation of student "congregations," a new development in student work, enables students to participate in the work of the Kingdom and thus prepare them for service in the congregations which will claim their membership.

7. Through the joint efforts of Attorney Eugene Wengert of Milwaukee and the Student Service Commission, an organization of Synodical Conference Lutheran men and women with college training was effected in 1946 for the purpose of enlisting the talents of the educated laity for greater service to the Church. RWH

Stump, Jos. Educator; b. Oct. 6, 1866, at Marietta, Pa.; educated at Columbus and Philadelphia; professor at Chicago Lutheran Seminary 1915—20; at Fargo, N.Dak., since 1921, then at Minneapolis; author of an explanation of Luther's Catechism, a *Life of Melanchthon;* a *Handbook of Christian Ethics;* a *System of Christian Dogmatics;* etc. D. May 24, 1935.

Stundists. See *Russian Sects.*

Sturm, Beata (1682—1730). Alias Tabea, Acts 9:36; b. at Stuttgart. In her youth she was blind for about two years. Although her eyes were weak, she read the Bible through thirty times. She had a good memory and could repeat a sermon almost word for word. She studied the writings of Luther and confessed that no one had so beautifully preached Christ to her and made so much of Him as Luther had .done. She visited widows and orphans, the poor, sick, and needy, and especially such as were in spiritual trouble. She would deprive herself of necessities in order to give to others.

Sturm, Jakob (1489—1553). B. and d. at Strassburg, where he performed his lifework as reformer, statesman, and educator. He aided the Protestants at the diets of Speyer, 1526 and 1529, and of Augsburg, 1530, where he had a part in drawing up the *Confessio tetrapolitana.* He founded a *Gymnasium* at Strassburg, which became a pattern for many similar schools.

Sturm, Johannes (1507—89). German educator. Impressions received while attending the school of the Brethren of the Common Life at Liége, influenced him in his organization of the *Gymnasium* at Strassburg, 1537, which he conducted for nearly forty years. His aim of education was piety, knowledge, eloquence. The curriculum of the school was entirely classical and therefore somewhat narrow. Cicero and Demosthenes were especially imitated. Sturm's strength lay in his ability to organize and in his mastery of rhetoric and style. His ideas concerning organization and subject matter were influential in shaping the school system of the German states; his course of study, slightly amplified, was adopted in the higher schools, the *Gymnasien.* Through his relation with Bucer he embraced the Protestant faith.

Sturm, Julius Karl Reinhold (1816 to 1896). Studied theology at Jena; held various positions as tutor, later as pastor, for many years at Koestritz; d. at Leipzig; one of the most important of modern German sacred poets; from his many collections of poems a number have passed into hymnals as hymns of the Church, but most of them belong to the category of sacred lyrics.

Sturm, Leonhard Christoph (1669 to 1729). German architect, whose ideas, as brought out in his writings on architecture, were of deciding influence in the art of church building in Protestant circles of Germany.

Stylites *(Pillar Saints).* Hermits who withdrew from the world by taking up their abode on the top of a pillar. The first and most famous was Simeon Stylites, who lived on a pillar near Antioch for thirty years (430—59). He found many imitators, especially in Syria and Palestine, among them several women. A railing kept the hermits from falling from their lofty perches, and food was brought up a ladder; sometimes a tiny hut protected them. The practice never found favor in the West, but there were Stylites among the Ruthenian monks as late as 1526.

Suarez, Francis (1548—1617). Spanish Jesuit; author of *Defensio Fidei Catholicae,* etc., directed against James I of England and vindicating the right of the Pope to depose kings.

He also published an elaborate commentary on the works of Thomas Aquinas and numerous other works.

Sub una specie; sub utraque specie. See *Grace, Means of,* IV 4.

Sublapsarians (or *Infralapsarians*). A name given to those of the moderate Calvinists who held the view that God did not decree to create a part of mankind unto damnation, as the Supralapsarians hold, but, viewing mankind as fallen, decreed to withhold His grace from the greater number, the reprobate *(Decrees of Synod of Dort; Westminster Confession).*

Subordinationism. The doctrine that the Son of God, because He is begotten of the Father, is subordinate to the Father in essence and majesty, He being God in a second or lesser sense of the term. Subordinationism varies from its extreme form (Arianism, Ritschlianism, Modernism) to more subtle expressions of the heresy, based upon misinterpretation of Christ's words: "My Father is greater than I" (John 4:28). These, however, do not refer to His divine nature, but to His human nature, and that in His state of humiliation, as the context shows.

Subscription to Confessions. See *Lutheran Confessions,* D.

Subscription Lists. See *Finances in the Church,* 3.

Succop, H. H. B. July 13, 1845, in Pittsburgh, Pa.; graduate of Concordia College, Fort Wayne, and Concordia Seminary, St. Louis; pastor at Wallace, Ont., Can., 1869—72; at Sebringville, Ont., Can., 1872—75; of St. John's Church, Chicago, 1875—1919; president of the Illinois District, vice-president of the Missouri Synod; a forceful preacher, a wise pastor; he stood high in the councils of Synod; Concordia Seminary, St. Louis, conferred on him the title of D. D.; d. Dec. 24, 1919.

Sudan. A vast country south of Egypt, controlled partly by France, partly by England. *Anglo-Egyptian:* 969,600 sq. mi.; population: 6,000,000. Foreign staff of 113, of whom 30 are ordained, in the British part; 1,066 communicants. *French Sudan:* 591,054 sq. mi.; population: 3,794,270. The Sudan Interior Mission and the Christian and Missionary Alliance are active in this area. Foreign staff of 93, of whom 38 ordained; 798 communicants. See *Missions, Bibliography.*

Sudra. See *Hinduism,* 3.

Suffragan. A diocesan bishop is called a suffragan (elector) of his archbishop or metropolitan. The title is also applied to a titular bishop who assists a diocesan bishop.

Suffrages. A short intercessory prayer, petition, or call, particularly one introduced into the Litany, as the Response of the people: "We beseech Thee to hear us, O Lord," in the Major Litany.

Sufism. Name of mystic-theosophical movement in Islam, whose oldest adherents wore garments of wool (Arabian, *suf*). From ascetic beginnings in the 8th century it gradually developed into pantheism. Produced extensive literature. Found chiefly in Persia. Its propaganda spread to England and America.

Suicide. "Suicide is the willful and voluntary act of a person who understands the physical nature of the act and intends by it to accomplish the result of self-destruction" (Black, *Law Dictionary*). Suicide is a transgression of the Fifth Commandment, for no person is the absolute owner of his body and life in the sight of God. Many heathen have either been indifferent to the problem of suicide or openly advocate its use. Thus suicide was treated as venial by the Romans, and it was esteemed a virtue, in certain cases, by the Stoic and Epicurean philosophers. To this day certain forms of suicide are regarded as highly virtuous in heathen countries.

Sullivan, Arthur Seymour (1842 to 1900). A product of the Leipzig Conservatory of Music, was the most popular English composer of the 19th century. Mendelssohn and Schubert influenced him greatly, and his light operas, written to the libretti of W. S. Gilbert, enjoy widespread popularity to this day. His choral works *The Light of the World* and *The Golden Legend* are sung occasionally by choral groups; many know him only as the composer of "The Lost Chord" and "Onward, Christian Soldiers," products of 19th-century Victorian music.

Sulpicians. A congregation of secular priests, not bound by vows, founded in 1642. They conduct theological seminaries, among them several in the United States. Sulpicians have spiritual direction of the students at the Catholic University at Washington.

Sumatra. Island of the Dutch (Netherlands) East Indies, Sunda group. Area, 164,148 sq. mi. Population, 12,000,000 (1951 est.); Malays, Hindus, Chinese. Aboriginal natives still exist in the interior; they are animists. Buddhism is outranked by Islam. The island was first visited by Europeans in 1449. 246,810 Protestant communicants (1952). For missions and statistics, see *Java*.

Summa. A term used frequently in the Middle Ages to apply to an elaborate, detailed, and all-embracing system of science and philosophy, with its moral and ethical principles derived partly from the ancient philosophers, especially Aristotle, partly from the Bible as in the *Summa Theologica* of Aquinas.

Summer Schools. See *Parish Education*, F 3.

Sunday Evening Vespers. See *Radio Evangelism*, 5.

Sunday School. 1. Although Roxbury, Mass., is often credited with having established the first Sunday school in America (1674), the Sunday school movement did not become widespread until Sunday schools were organized in England in the last half of the 18th century to provide instruction for destitute and neglected children whose education was otherwise neglected. Robert Raikes (1735—1811), editor of a newspaper in England, popularized the Sunday school in the 1780's. The children attended Raikes' school from ten to twelve o'clock in the morning and from one to five o'clock in the afternoon. Instruction was given in reading and in the church catechism. Many similar schools were established, and by 1800 there were many Sunday schools in all parts of England. Since these Sunday schools were designed to give the rudiments of a general education, they were non-denominational and were usually conducted independently of the churches.

2. In the United States Sunday schools followed a different pattern. In the first place, the purpose of Sunday schools in America was soon restricted to the teaching of religion. Then, too, each denomination established its own Sunday schools and recruited teachers for them. Since the public schools do not teach religion, the Sunday schools have become for many church bodies the only means of providing formal religious instruction for the young. Church bodies that maintain parochial schools have been

somewhat slower than others in establishing Sunday schools, but the Sunday school has experienced a remarkable growth.

Sunday School Council of Evangelical Denominations. See *International Council of Religious Education*.

Sunday School Literature. See *Parish Education*, E 5.

Sunday, William Ashley ("Billy"; 1863—1925). B. at Ames, Iowa; professional baseball player; revivalist 1896 and Presbyterian minister 1903; sometimes religious buffoon, again impressive Christian preacher.

Sunnites (from Arabian *sunna*, "tradition"). Name of the larger of the two main divisions of Mohammedanism. They are the orthodox branch, holding to the Koran and to tradition, while the Shiites are considered the heterodox.

Suomi Synod. See *Finnish Lutherans in America*, 2; *Finland, Lutheranism in*, 8.

Suomi Theological Seminary. See *Ministry, Education of*, XI.

Superego. See *Psychology*, J 7.

Supererogation, Works of. In Roman Catholic theology, works which are performed by the faithful, particularly by members of holy orders, over and above those that are required, according to their supposition, for salvation. Such works may then be credited to others, by an ingenious arrangement transferring their merits.

Superintendents, Sunday School. See *Parish Education*, K 6.

Superiors. See *Abbot*.

Supernaturalism. A term which received its meaning in the narrower sense during the Age of Enlightenment. Deists and others claimed that reason, operating with a "natural theology," was a sufficient norm for religious truth, whereas their opponents held that religious truths were supernatural and made known to man by divine revelation. The authenticity of this revelation was attested, in part, by supernatural prophecies and miracles. After Kant and Hegel the term supernaturalist was applied to those who held the absolute transcendence of God and later to numerous systems within Christianity which rejected reason as an absolute norm and held authoritarian, inner, emotional, or other criteria. See *Doctrine, History of; Deism; Rationalism* (and the references given).

Supervision, Educational. See *Parish Education,* K; *Teachers,* A.

Supplement Hypothesis. See *Higher Criticism,* 14.

Supralapsarians. See *Predestination,* 4.

Supremacy of the Pope. See *Luther, Chief Writings of,* 4, 7; *Roman Catholic Confessions; Papacy.*

"Sure Salvation." See *Methodist Bodies,* 2.

Surinam. See *South America,* 13.

Surplice. See *Vestments, Clerical.*

Susannah, History of. See *Apocrypha,* A 3.

Susquehanna Synod. See *United Lutheran Church, Synods of,* 25.

Susquehanna Synod of Central Pennsylvania. See *United Lutheran Church, Synods of,* 25.

Suso, Henry (1300—66). Because of his poetic language and symbolism called the Minnesinger of Mysticism; was a representative of ethical or practical mysticism, like Tauler and Rusbroek, but not a pantheist like his teacher Eckhart.

Suttee (Sanskrit, *Sati*, "virtuous"). Name given in India to a widow who voluntarily sacrifices herself on the funeral pyre of her deceased husband; also to the rite itself. Forbidden in British territory since 1829 and now extinct.

Svebilius, Olof. Archbishop of Sweden at the end of the 18th century; sent Rudman and Biorck to America; the original letter written by him to Swedes in America was preserved by the Swedish Church in Philadelphia.

Sveinsson, Brynjolf. Icelandic bishop (17th century); discovered the poetic Edda.

Svenonius, Envald. See *Finland, Lutheranism in,* 3.

Sverdrup, Georg. B. Dec. 16, 1848, at Balestrand, Norway; graduate of Christiania University 1871; studied at the universities of Erlangen and Paris; professor at Augsburg Seminary, Minneapolis, 1874—1907; president 1876 to 1907; president of the Lutheran Free Church 1894—97; editor of several papers; author of many books and articles; not ordained as pastor. D. May 3, 1907.

Swabian-Saxon Concord. See *Lutheran Confessions,* C 2.

Swedberg, Jesper (1653—1735). Professor at Upsala, bishop of Skara, interested in practical evidences of religious faith, friendly to Church of England in Britain and America.

Sweden. *Conversion to Christianity.* In 829 Swedes came to Charles the Great and begged for missionaries. Anskar, a Frank, was sent; he was successful at Birka and after two winters returned to report. Made Archbishop of Hamburg, he sent Ardgar and returned himself, 848—50. Sigurd of England brought Christianity to the northern part of Sweden. After 1150 King Erik led a crusade to bring Christianity to Finland, and in 1164 an archbishopric was erected at Upsala, and a crusade was made to Estland, another once more to Finland, and still another to Karelia. Against much opposition clerical celibacy was now introduced. The famous Brigitta did much good (d. in 1373). The University of Upsala was founded in 1477.

Sweden, Lutheran Church in. 1. The pattern of religious thought which emerged out of the Swedish Reformation followed in the main German models. Olavus Petri (1493—1552) more than any other teacher gave the clergy in his doctrinal, liturgical, polemical, and homiletical writings a statement of faith which established the Swedish Church as Lutheran for centuries. His brother Laurentius Petri (1499—1573) preserved an episcopal church structure and an order of worship which saved the best elements of the past for the new order. The result of their labors is evident in the ability of the evangelical Church to defend itself against a romanizing liturgy of John III (1592—99), against the Counter Reformation in the reign of Sigismund, so that at Upsala in 1593 the Church definitely declared itself as Lutheran. Calvinism as a doctrine had also been rejected, but something of Calvin's theocratic spirit was in the program of Charles IX, whose son Gustavus Adolphus considered it a worthy thing to give his life for his country and the Church of God within it.

2. Between the Swedish Church and the State a remarkable unity prevailed in the 17th century, which made pos-

sible a program of education and discipline unrivaled in any other evangelical country. But the State influenced the administration of the Church no more than the Church guided the policies of government. A rigorous system of instruction in the Catechism laid the foundation of obedience to the Church, and a strict observance of liturgical days and forms inculcated in the people a religious culture. The ecclesiastical authority was able to maintain itself against a variable royal power, and a line of strong bishops (Rudbeck, Svebilius, the Benzelius family, Jesper Swedberg, Spegel) left its impress on the national life. The century of the great kings, Gustavus Adolphus, Charles X, XI, XII, and of the great bishops saw a centralization of church government in the Church Law of 1686, the founding of schools for training both clergy and laity, a new Bible translation, a new catechism, hymnbook, and handbook (of worship), and a system of church registers. The doctrinal constitution of the Church was clearly defined in the Law of 1686: "all shall confess, jointly and severally, their belief in the Christian doctrine and faith as it is founded in God's holy Word, the prophetical and apostolic writings of the Old and New Testaments, and set forth in the three chief creeds — the Apostolic, Nicene, and Athanasian, as well as in the Unaltered Augsburg Confession of the year 1530, accepted in the Council of Upsala of 1593, and explained in the whole, so-called, Book of Concord."

3. A strict orthodoxy characterized the Church of the 17th century, and the faith tended to be stated in intellectual terms. The absolute power of the monarch as well as the interests of the bishops favored a uniformity of doctrine and of discipline, which resulted in severe discipline. But underneath, a more popular mysticism nourished itself on the writings of Arndt and Scriver, and some of the earliest influences of Pietism came with returning soldiers of the wars of Charles XII. The more conservative Pietism of Spener found ingress through the higher classes in Stockholm and had its noblest exponent in the work of Eric Tolstadius (d. 1759), a Stockholm pastor. Against a tendency of the Estates to take over a suzerainty in the Church formerly exercised by the King, the Church fought to retain its independence. At the same time as it faced in the political

realm a new democratic spirit, it was challenged by a Pietistic movement which was less interested in institutional uniformity than in individual experience. In 1721 conventicles were anew forbidden, but this could not exclude the radical Pietism of Dippel and his followers, who preached a freedom in doctrine and life opposed to both the orthodox and the older Pietists. For the time being the orthodox retained control, but a later development under Zinzendorf's disciples caused Herrnhut ideas to permeate wide areas, especially in middle and southern Sweden. The writings and songs of the movement left abiding traces. Meanwhile the ideas of the Enlightenment further undermined an orthodoxy which was unpopular with a tolerant and increasingly secular generation. Emanuel Swedenborg and Linné were children of this era when old and new currents met in a bewildering swirl. In the broad masses the ground was being prepared for later revivals. The period of Gustav III (1772—92) had witnessed a great influx of foreign ideas and customs, especially French, and religious life was at a low ebb. Rationalism weakened further the ranks of the orthodox. A new handbook and catechism were characterized by the prevailing neology.

4. In protest against the liberalism of the Church, groups of "Readers," especially in Northern provinces, criticized the clergy and the "new book." The postils of Anders Nohrborg (1725 to 1767), together with Luther's and Arndt's writings, were the daily bread of these Pietists. Following the Napoleonic wars, a reaction against the excesses of revolutionary freedom set in, and a list of brilliant teachers and thinkers adorned the Church and university of the first half of the 19th century. Geijer (d. 1847) and Tegner (1782—1846) set a Christian pattern in the writing of history and poetry, while Franzén (d. 1847) and Wallin (d. 1839) gave the Church a new hymnbook of high quality. A new emphasis on the Church was given by Henric Schartau (d. 1825), and Lund became a center of conscious churchmanship. When in 1865 the Estates were organized into a bicameral Diet, the Church received its own Convocation, meeting each five years and with decisive power in ecclesiastical matters.

5. But the revivalist groups also became stronger and more powerful. The followers of Eric Janson emi-

grated in 1845. As long as Rosenius lived (d. 1868), the revivalist groups, which had been stimulated by the work of George Scott in Stockholm (around 1840), remained within the Church, but under Waldenstroem the Swedish Mission Covenant, in 1878, began a separate existence. Its doctrine of the atonement went back through men like Anders Knoes to Moravian ideas of a century earlier. The old conventicle laws had held until the persistent witness of the Baptists in the middle of the century led a more tolerant age to repeal them, in 1860. Dissenters were more apt to seek freedom, however, in emigration, which in the last half of the century drained a country of five million people of almost one fifth of its population. Social conditions were as responsible as ecclesiastical, and the Church began to take an interest in current ills. In temperance reform Peter Wieselgren (1800 to 1877) took a commanding part.

6. Since the beginning of the present century strong currents have been set in motion within the Church in the fields of theology, missions, church art and music, the diaconate, and ecumenicity. Einar Billing led the way in a deeper study of the original message of the Church and inspired others to renewed study of the Lutheran sources. Archbishop Nathan Soederblom (b. 1866) not only became an authority on the comparative study of world religions, but emphasized the uniqueness of revelation in Christianity and sought to unite the Churches of Christendom in combating evils of the age which undermined all religion. The Stockholm meeting of 1925 is a landmark in progress toward church unity. Out of a renewed study of Luther and the early Christian Church has come a group of teachers, especially at Lund, who have challenged Harnack's interpretation and given a new conception of the self-authenticating Gospel of the love of God in Jesus Christ. Gustav Aulén (*Christus Victor*) and Anders Nygren (*Eros and Agape*) have had international influence. *Svensk Theologisk Kvartalskrift* begun 1925, is an unusually strong theological organ. Manfred Björkquist has made Sigtuna Stiftelsen [Sigtuna Foundation] a power in interpreting the Gospel to the new conditions of social and cultural life. A conscious attempt to bring the Church closer to contemporary needs also has produced a new Bible translation, a revised handbook, a new hymnbook and *Koralbok*. A widespread interest in liturgy and art has found expression in new forms of church architecture, in vestments, even in a Book of Hours. In the ecumenical movement Sigtuna has provided a center. Bishop Yngve Brilioth is the head of the Faith and Order Movement, Anders Nygren has succeeded Archbishop Erling Eidem as president of the Lutheran World Federation. Hjalmar Holmquist has brought the study of church history to a new peak in the *Svenska Kyrkans Historia*, now being produced by various scholars.

7. The Augustana Synod, organized 1860, gathered the largest number of Swedish immigrants in America and preserved here the forms and spirit of the Mother Church, using the same Order of Service, devotional literature, and a modified church organization (without bishops). In the 19th century the revival spirit of the home parishes characterized the immigrants; in recent times the Synod has come to a more sympathetic understanding of the treasures it has received from the ancient Church of Sweden. CB

Swedenborgians. Followers of the doctrines of Emmanuel Swedenborg (1688—1772), Swedish scientist and theosophist. He was born at Stockholm, son of a Lutheran court chaplain, and reared amid pious influences. He studied at the University of Upsala, devoted himself to scientific, especially mineralogical, engineering, and physiological, research.

1. His scientific achievements were extraordinary. He proposed theories and worked on inventions which were far in advance of his time. His important scientific works are: *Opera Philosophica et Mineralia,* 1734; *Oeconomia Regni Animalis,* 1740—41; *Regnum Animale,* 1744. In middle age, as the result of alleged visions, he discontinued his scientific endeavors and devoted himself to theology, resigning his government position in 1747. He asserted that in 1743 God had opened his sight to the view of the spiritual world and that from that time on he was given the privilege of conversing with spirits and angels and to receive revelations of divine mysteries. The result of these revelations was a new theological system. He taught that God is one divine person, namely, Jesus Christ, who is the incarnation of Jehovah and in whom there is a trinity of essence, called Father, Son, and Holy Spirit, and that these stand for divine

love, divine wisdom, by which love manifested itself, and divine operation and are related to one another in God as soul, body, and action in man. Redemption consists in this, that Jehovah became incarnate and by vanquishing temptations and by His suffering subjugated eternally the "hells," the enemies of the human race, thereby liberating mankind, and now holds these enemies in subjection in the heart of every man who will co-operate with Him by faith and obedience. Justification means applying this redeeming work to those who believe in, and are obedient to, Him. Another fundamental doctrine is that regarding Scripture and its interpretation. Certain Biblical books have a twofold sense, literal and spiritual, and are written according to a uniform law, called that of "correspondences," or analogy between spiritual and natural things. Swedenborg was chosen by God to reveal this spiritual, inner, symbolical sense to the world. This revelation of the spiritual sense by him constitutes Christ's second coming, the "clouds" (Matt. 24:30) being the literal, the "power and great glory" the internal sense. Through his revelations also was established the "New Church," prophesied in Rev. 21, and dating from 1757. In that year the old Apostolic Church, founded by Christ, came to an end, the final Judgment took place, and the holy city, New Jerusalem, descended from heaven. Swedenborg denied original sin. Man's freedom enables him to choose and follow the good. At death man goes to an intermediate realm, from which he either ascends to heaven and becomes an angel or sinks to hell to become an evil spirit.

2. Swedenborg's theosophical writings are numerous, the most important being *Arcana Coelestia,* an exposition of the spiritual sense of Genesis and Exodus (1748—56), and the *Vera Christiana religio* (1771), in which his theology is systematically presented.

3. Swedenborg's followers met for the first time in London in 1783 and organized the first society in 1788. A General Conference met in 1789. In 1821 the "General Conference of ministers and other members of the new Church signified by the New Jerusalem in the Apocalypse" was organized.

4. The first Swedenborgian society in America was founded in Baltimore, 1792, and in 1817 the *General Convention of the New Jerusalem in the* U. S. A. was organized. In 1951 it numbered 4,621 members. Its headquarters: Boston, Mass.

5. In 1890 a considerable number withdrew from the General Convention and organized the *General Church of the New Jerusalem* (regards Swedenborg's writings as divinely inspired and emphasizes life and work). In 1951 it reported 1,496 members. Headquarters: Bryn Athyn, Pa.

Swedish Evangelical Mission Covenant Church. See *Evangelical Mission Covenant Church.*

Swedish Lutheran Ansgarius Synod. See *Evangelical Mission Covenant Church.*

Swedish Lutheran Mission Synod. See *Evangelical Mission Covenant Church.*

Swedish Mission Covenant. See *Sweden, Lutheran Church in,* 5.

Swedish Missionary Societies (*European*). 1. Swedish Missionary Society (*Svenska Missionssälskapet*) founded January 6, 1835. Works chiefly among Finns and was united with the 2) Evangelical National Missionary Society (*Den Evangeliska Fosterlandstiftelse*), founded 1856, which consists of a large number of minor societies. Headquarters at Stockholm. In 1863 a seminary was established at Johannelund, near Stockholm. Missions in India and Africa. 3) The Swedish Church Mission (*Svenska Kyrkans Mission*), Stockholm, founded 1874, a state institution, headed by the Archbishop of Upsala. During the First World War and afterwards this mission administered the Leipzig Missions in India. Fields: China, India, Africa. There are many additional missionary societies in Sweden.

Sweelinck, Jan Pieterszoon (1562 to 1621). The Father of the North German School of Organists. Considered by some the greatest of all Dutch organists and the last of the Netherland composers, created a new era for organ music and made of the organ a real church instrument. Like Frescobaldi, his eminent Italian contemporary, he was also a great teacher and taught such illustrious organists as Scheidt, Scheidemann, Jacob Praetorius, Strunck, and others, who contributed substantially to the great musical heritage of the Lutheran Church. Sweelinck was a Calvinist and wrote notably choral music for the worship services of the Reformed. It is only in recent years that his real greatness as a choral composer has been recognized. In his works one finds the old polyphony blended with the homophony of his day. Many of the traits found in the music of Scheidt may be traced back to Sweelinck.

W. Apel, *Masters of the Keyboard*, Cambridge (Mass.), 1947; H. Besseler, *Die Musik des Mittelalters und der Renaissance*, Potsdam, 1931; M. Bukofzer, *Music in the Baroque Era*, New York, 1947; G. Frotscher, *Geschichte des Orgelspiels und der Orgelkomposition*, Berlin, 1935; R. Haas, *Die Musik des Barocks*, Potsdam, 1927; P. H. Lang, *Music in Western Civilization*, New York, 1941.

Swensson, Carl A. B. June 25, 1857, at Sugar Grove, Pa.; educator, author, political leader, the outstanding figure among Swedish-Americans in the 19th century; educated at Augustana Seminary; pastor at Lindsborg, Kans., and founder of the Lutheran Bethany College there in 1881; organized educational work among the Swedes and gave tone and direction to their spiritual thought; educated the Middle West in music through the institution of the Messiah Festival in 1882; president of the General Council 1893—95; also active in politics, member of the Kansas Legislature; d. at Los Angeles, Calif., Feb. 16, 1904.

R. Segerhammar, "The Preaching of Dr. Carl Aaron Swensson," *Aug. Quart.*, XXVI: 143—54; P. H. Pearson, "Carl Swensson, Churchman, Educator, Patriot," *Aug. Quart.*, XVIII: 249—65.

Swetambra. See *Jainism.*

Swete, Henry Barclay (1835—1917). Anglican; textual critic; b. at Bristol; priest 1859; rector; professor at King's College, London, 1882; Cambridge 1890; d. at Hitchin; author of *The Old Testament in Greek;* edited the Septuagint, etc.

Swift, Jonathan (1667—1745). Dean (Anglican; St. Patrick's, Dublin, 1713); greatest English satirist. His *Tale of a Tub* (1704), story of three brothers (Peter = Romanists, Martin = Anglicans, Jack = Dissenters), making alterations in three new coats (Christian truth) bequeathed to them by their father in his will (Bible), with instructions for wearing them.

Switzerland. 1. Christianity was first introduced into Switzerland by St. Gall, a native of Ireland and a pupil of Columban, ca. A. D. 610. Induced by the persecution which consequently arose, the colaborers of St. Gall left Switzerland for Italy. St. Gall alone remained, he being too ill to be removed. Retiring to a sequestered spot with a few adherents, he built the monastery of St. Gall in the canton called by the same name. After his death his scholars, together with other monks of Ireland, carried on his work until the whole country was subjected to Romanism.

2. The Reformation secured a hold in Switzerland in 1516, and from that time till 1526 Zurich, which was entirely German, was the center of reformational activity. From 1526 to 1532 the Reformation movement was communicated from Bern, which was both German and French, and extended to the center of Switzerland. In 1532 Geneva became the focal point of the reformational propaganda.

3. The reform movement in Switzerland owes its beginning and success mainly to the work of Ulrich Zwingli. Beginning in 1516, after having been greatly influenced by Humanism, he began to expound the Gospel as preacher in the Abbey of Einsiedeln. The influence of his enthusiastic teaching was soon extensively felt, so that already in 1522 Erasmus estimated "those who no longer adhered to the See of Rome" in the cantons at about 200,000 persons. As the Reformation spread, changes in the mode of worship were introduced. In 1523 the Council of Zurich required that "the pastors of Zurich should rest their discourses on the words of Scripture alone." Soon the abolition of images in churches followed; the clergy was no longer prohibited from marrying, and in 1525 the Mass was superseded by the simple ordinance of the Lord's Supper. Meanwhile the Reformation had spread to Appenzell and Schaffhausen and other parts of the near-by cantons. In 1530, at the Diet of Augsburg, when the *Augsburg Confession* was presented, the Swiss theologians presented their own confession, drawn up by Bucer, known as the *Tetrapolitan Confession* (from the four towns it represented, *viz.*, Constance, Strassburg, Lindau, and Memmingen). The two confessions differed mainly with regard to the real presence of Christ in the Lord's Supper, which the Lutheran theologians affirmed and Zwingli denied.

4. Meanwhile the five Romish cantons determined to check the further

progress of the Reformation by force of arms. The Protestant cantons formed a confederacy and by resolution, adopted at Aargau May 12, 1531, instituted a strict blockade of the five Romanist cantons. Hereupon, goaded on by the consequent famine and its attendant miseries, these cantons determined on war and entered the field on October 6, 1531. The first engagement, which took place at Kappel, October 11, 1531, proved most disastrous to Zurich and fatal to Zwingli, who was slain in the battle.

5. After the death of Zwingli the Swiss Reformation centered at Geneva, where William Farel at first proclaimed its tenets about 1532. Banished from the city, he was soon recalled, and in 1535 the council of the city proclaimed its adherence to the Reformed doctrines. In 1536 John Calvin arrived in the city, and on July 20, 1539, the citizens permanently abjured popery and professed Protestantism, after a struggle in which Calvin and Farel had been banished. In 1541, however, Calvin returned, making Geneva the center of his activity. He framed a civil code for Geneva, and under him Geneva became a republic, firmly established, governed by an oligarchy, pervaded by an ecclesiastical spirit, and renowned in the history of the world. Thus Geneva became the center of the Reformed Church. After the death of Calvin (1564) the Catholic reaction was felt also in Switzerland. For many years the Roman Catholic power seemed to predominate in the country. Toward the close of the 17th century the struggle between the two religious parties assumed an open character, and in 1703 the Catholic and the Protestant cantons took up arms against each other. For several years a civil war was carried on, until at last, in 1712, the Protestants gained a decisive victory at Villmergen, completely routing the Catholics.

6. Since that time the majority of the inhabitants of Switzerland are Protestants. The present constitution of Switzerland grants complete and absolute liberty of conscience and of creed, free worship is guaranteed, civil marriage is compulsory, and subsequent religious services are optional. The cantons have the right to maintain peace and order among the different religious communities and to prevent encroachment of ecclesiastical authorities upon the rights of citizens. All bishops must receive the approval of the federal government, and the liberty of press, petition, and association is guaranteed, although Jesuits and all religious orders and associations which are affiliated with them are prohibited. In the last century much work has been done by the Presbyterians, Baptists, and Methodists. Of these bodies the Methodists and Baptists are the most numerous. Besides the Reformed State Church, the Free churches of French Switzerland, constituting the three bodies of Geneva, Voud, and Neuchatel, deserve notice. Theological instruction is given by the theological faculties of Zurich, Bern, Basel, Lausanne, and Geneva, and by the academy of Neuchatel. As in Germany, so also in Switzerland, Modernism, or Liberalism, has gained a firm foothold in most of the institutions of learning.

Switzerland, Contemporary Theology in (*Theology of Crisis; Dialectical Theology*). 1. By the second decade of the 20th century it seemed to many observers that the type of theological liberalism inaugurated by F. D. Schleiermacher (d. 1834) and reworked by Albrecht Ritschl (d. 1889) was inadequate. That it was by no means dead can be seen from the work of some outstanding Ritschlians, notably Adolf Harnack (d. 1930) and Ernst Troeltsch (d. 1923).

2. Significant is the fact that, like Ritschl, both Harnack and Troeltsch were intensely concerned with the relevance of Christian history for the modern Church. Though they believed that the history of Christianity must result in the repudiation of classical Christian theology, their interest in the history of Christian thought nevertheless stimulated the study and publication of many of the monuments of Christian history, notably the New Testament and the writings of Luther and the other Reformers. Under the influence of Harnack's *History of Dogma* and Troeltsch's *Social Teachings* the history of Christian thought assumed an important place in theological scholarship and education.

3. But this very influence was to destroy much of the liberalism it was intended to buttress. For one of Adolf Harnack's pupils at Berlin was Karl Barth (b. 1886). The historical study of the New Testament, seen in such a movement as the *Formgeschichte* school and in Albert Schweitzer's works on New Testament eschatology, had begun to stress the dynamic and prophetic character of New Testament

religion as well as its essential unity in the acknowledgment of Jesus as Messiah. Similarly, the renewed interest in Luther's writings and thought, which had been intensified since the quadricentennial of the Reformer's birth in 1883, had helped to make Barth and many of his contemporaries dissatisfied with the moralism and optimism of the Ritschlian school. In addition, Barth's thought had been molded by the pessimism and Christian skepticism of Sören Kierkegaard (d. 1855) and the profound religious and psychological insights of Fyodor Dostoevsky (d. 1881). World War I, which came while Barth was pastor in Safenwil, Switzerland, provided the occasion for his final break with Ritschlian idealism and for the publication of his epoch-making *Roemerbrief* in 1919.

4. "Paul, as a child of his age, addressed his contemporaries. It is, however, far more important that, as Prophet and Apostle of the Kingdom of God, he veritably speaks to all men of every age." With this first sentence of the *Roemerbrief* Barth indicated his new departure: Paul — and Luther and Calvin and Kierkegaard — were to be interpreted in terms of how they speak to our contemporary situation, not merely in terms of their own historical environment. Speaking from this presupposition, Barth proceeded to denounce the Church and the world, theology and philosophy, in the name of the "wholly Other," who renders all things of earth fundamentally questionable. It was "a religious criticism of religion" (W. Pauck).

5. Karl Barth's rediscovery of the Christian doctrine of the sovereignty of God and his repudiation of Ritschlian immanentism was bound to draw the support of some and the fire of others. Among those who associated themselves with him were both Lutheran and Reformed theologians. Because of his dependence upon Luther, Barth's theology was far more Lutheran than that of many so-called Lutherans in the 1920's; his increasing study of Calvin, especially after 1925, made Barth congenial to large sections of the Reformed Church in Switzerland, Germany, France, the Netherlands, England, and eventually the United States.

6. Probably the best-known of Barth's theological associates is Emil Brunner of Zurich (b. 1889). More systematic and scientific than Barth,

Brunner has been instrumental in relating many of Barth's insights to the problems of the modern mind and the modern Church. For that reason, however, Barth and Brunner have parted company. As mentioned above, Barth has inclined more and more in recent years to Calvin and to orthodox Calvinism; this trend in his thought, coupled with the extreme Biblicism evident in the volumes of his *Kirchliche Dogmatik* that have appeared thus far, has caused him to deny all validity to "natural" theology and to ascribe not only pre-eminence, but also absolute uniqueness to all parts of the Biblical revelation. Brunner, on the other hand, has just as violently asserted the Pauline doctrine of the revelation of God in the Creation, though often making unfortunate concessions to modern, especially scientific, thought.

7. Common to both Barth and Brunner is an insistence upon Biblical realism. This is seen very clearly in Brunner's *The Divine Imperative*, a study of Christian ethics that seeks to restate the reformatory doctrine of "orders" and "vocation" for modern life. They also share a certain arbitrariness in their theology which has frequently embarrassed their followers on both sides of the Atlantic.

8. The theology of Karl Barth and Emil Brunner is subject to the same criticisms that can validly be made of all Reformed theologians on the means of grace, the Church, the distinction between the Law and the Gospel, etc. In addition, as has already been mentioned, the theology of crisis has frequently conceded too much to the modern temper. From a Lutheran point of view several observations are nevertheless in place. No one can deny that by their work Barth and Brunner have done much to bring modern Protestantism closer to true Christianity. Their work has also encouraged Lutherans of all lands to consider more carefully their own heritage. It is for Lutherans to begin to restate the Lutheran faith as vigorously as Barth and Brunner have voiced many of the basic tenets of Calvinism. For without too much fear of contradiction it can be asserted that theirs has probably been the most important theological work since Schleiermacher. JP

Many of the writings of both Barth and Brunner have been translated into English. An adequate and critical monograph is sadly lacking. Wilhelm

Pauck's *Karl Barth: Prophet of a New Christianity?* though still useful, is out of date. Cornelius van Til's *The New Modernism* is as unreliable as it is unsympathetic. Among Lutheran writings, Herman Sasse's *Here We Stand* deals some telling blows, but one of the best Lutheran answers is that of Adolf Koeberle of Switzerland, tr. as *The Quest for Holiness.*

Syllabus and Encyclical of Pius IX. See *Roman Catholic Confessions,* D.

Syllabus of Errors, Papal. See *Roman Catholic Confessions,* D.

Sylvester I. See *Popes,* 1.

Sylvester II. See *Popes,* 6.

Symbola Catholica *(Oecumenica).* See *Ecumenical Creeds.*

Symbolical Books. See *Creeds and Confessions* (and references at the end of the article).

Symbolics. That branch of theological knowledge which treats of the origin, rise, nature, and contents of those public confessions of the Church in which a summary of her doctrines is presented. *Comparative Symbolics* is the study of the various creeds, particuarly of Christian bodies, in comparison with the confessions of the several churches.

Symbolism, Christian. 1. A symbol may be defined as a familiar object used to express an idea. Thus a Latin cross is used to express the idea of the Crucifixion, or as an expression of the idea of Christianity. It is supposed by some that such signs or devices were used in the early days of Christianity. A Latin cross might be inscribed upon the tomb of a true believer to signify that he had died in the Christian faith. Early tombs sometimes bear such devices.

2. Symbolism as it is known today, came into use in the days of the great architects, painters, and sculptors. It was used by these men as an identifying label. For example, an altar might contain the figure of the Lord Jesus and the Four Evangelists. Obviously the simplest identifying label might have been the names of the Lord and the Evangelists. However, in medieval days, the ordinary peasant was often unable to read or write, and in order to distinguish the five figures in the altar or its reredos, the sculptor placed some familiar object in the hand of each of the figures; usually the instru-

ment of his martyrdom, if any. Thus our Lord was shown holding a small Latin cross in His hand. St. Matthew held a copy of his Gospel and a battle-ax, the supposed instrument of his martyrdom. St. Mark, in addition to a copy of his Gospel, held a club, the traditional weapon with which he was slain. St. Luke held his Gospel and a short-handled ax. Since St. John died a natural death, he was made to hold his Gospel, as well as a chalice out of which a serpent was rising. Later, St. Matthew was shown with a small angel back of him; St. Mark with a lion at his feet; St. Luke with an ox; St. John with an eagle, a reference to Rev. 4:7.

3. Where the Twelve Apostles were shown in the reredos, in the form of paintings or sculpture, here again each one carried some familiar object in order to identify him. Simon Peter usually carried two great keys, St. Andrew rested one arm upon a saltire cross, St. James carried a pilgrim's staff and a shell, etc. As time went on, other objects became associated with each Apostle. For example, the Apostle Paul was usually shown holding a large book and a sword, with the words *Spiritus Gladius* upon the pages of the book; but in other examples one finds him holding a shield of faith, or a scourge, or casting a serpent into a fire.

4. As time went on, other great Christian leaders were shown by means of sculpture, painting, or stained glass. Symbols were invented in order to identify them. Stephen was pictured with several stones lying at his feet; St. Columba, the missionary, was shown with a coracle; Boniface with a fallen oak at his feet or else a Bible transfixed with a sword; St. Agnes carried a lamb; and St. Lawrence leaned upon a gridiron, the instrument of his death.

5. It will be observed that all these were identifying labels and were not used apart from the paintings or sculptures that they identified. In the days when the peasantry could not read, such signs had their value; and in our own day several church architects have used such things where there are a number of persons shown in a painting, stained glass, or sculpture.

6. The IHC abbreviation is not a symbol at all, but merely the ancient form of the name "Jesus." In early manuscript this was given *IHCOYC,* and often merely *IHC.* This has become so well known that it has been used frequently even where there

is no painting or sculpture of the Lord accompanying it. The form IHS, either with or without periods is sheer ignorance, for the Greek Sigma was "C" and later "Σ" and certainly never "S." Attempts to make a fanciful acrostic out of it are the invention of an eccentric monk of the 15th century. FRW

E. Geldart, *Manual of Church Decoration and Symbolism*, London, 1897.

Symbolists. A name applied by the adherents of "American Lutheranism" * to confessional Lutherans ("Old Lutherans" *).

Symeon Metaphrastes. Byzantine scholar of the 10th century whose most important work was *Lives of the Saints (Menologion)*.

Synagog. The Jewish place of worship and the only place of religious assembly since the destruction of the Temple; a large assembly room with the ark and the platform, or pulpit, and usually a special gallery for women.

Syncretism. Both a tendency and a movement, according to its etymology *(synkretizein)* meaning "to be strong together," "to stand united," although it was later derived from *synkerannymi*, "to mix up." Syncretism is practically a synonym of unionism, for it signifies the perverse attempts to combine unlike and irreconcilable elements in the interest of a false union. The term is applied chiefly to three syncretistic controversies: 1) that of 1645—56, during which years Georg Calixt * proposed an amalgamation of strict Bible doctrine, or sound Lutheranism, with Reformed doctrine; 2) that of 1661—69, when Elector Friedrich Wilhelm of Brandenburg tried to silence the Lutheran clergy in their attack on Reformed errors, one of those losing their positions on account of his refusal to accept the pledge being Paul Gerhardt *; 3) that of 1675—86, when Abraham Calov made his final stand against the syncretism of Calixt and his colleagues. The syncretistic notions of the 17th century gained in power, the practical result of the movement being seen in the United Evangelical Church of Germany and America and in the wave of malignant unionism which is sweeping through not only Reformed circles, but also some Lutheran church bodies.

Syneidesis. See *Conscience.*

Synergism (G. "to work with"). Synergism developed out of an attempt to solve an apparent contradiction. Holy Writ teaches the native corruption of man (John 3:6). It also teaches with equal clarity that God's love perfected a redemption from the penalty of eternal death, which His holiness and justice had to pronounce over the world of sinners. This redemption is all-inclusive (John 3:16; 1 Tim. 2:4; Ezek. 33:11; 2 Cor. 5:19). But the precious comfort of this truth accrues to the individual only if and when he personalizes it by faith (Gal. 3:11; Mark 16:16).

Three propositions have been held regarding the "how" of this personalizing: 1) God alone is active in bringing man to faith; 2) man weighs the evidence for and against acceptance of God's overture of love and thereupon decides by the strength of spiritual powers that are natural to him to become a Christian; 3) God begins and man completes the conversion; or man begins and God completes it. Synergism, generally speaking, holds that men are not altogether spiritually dead and that, in consequence, the reaction of men to the offer of God's grace is different, some less violently and stubbornly resisting the converting efforts of the Spirit than others.

Synergism is defended by arguments like the following: 1) if the individual can do nothing regarding his conversion, he will become careless and fatalistic; 2) sinners are called upon to repent in the Bible; hence it is implied that man has the power to heed the command (Mark 1:15; Acts 2:38; command does not imply power to obey, cp. command to keep God's Law); 3) if man is entirely passive in the moment of conversion, then the change is a mechanical one (but man is conscious of conversion, and his soul is active in it; cp. man's physical creation. Eph. 1:19, 20; 2 Cor. 4:6; John 1:12, 13); 4) though God must be said to make conversion a possibility, man makes it a reality; 5) passages such as Luke 7:30 and Matt. 23:37 teach that man can hinder, whence it may be deduced that man can also co-operate; 6) man has the ability to cease resistance (Acts 7:51). In regard to 4—6 it may be said that the man who *can* accept the Gospel *has* accepted it (1 Cor. 2:14; Phil. 2:3).

Scripture teaches that man is spiritually dead (John 5:24; Eph. 2:1) and antagonistic to spiritual things (Rom.

8:7,8; 1 Cor. 2:14), and it emphatically teaches that the working of God's grace is active in the act of conversion. Whatever synergism there is *follows* upon conversion and is itself the effect of God's monergism (Eph. 2:8-10; John 6:44,64,65; Rom. 9:16; 2 Cor. 4:6; Col. 1:13; Eph. 4:24 — "created"; 2 Cor. 5:17). For historical matters see *Synergistic Controversy*. C. f. EMP, "Synergism," *Abiding Word*, CPH, 1947, 299—321 (bibliography listed).

Synergistic Controversy. In the second edition of his *Loci*, in 1535, Melanchthon, in conversion, taught three co-operating causes: 1) God's Word, 2) the Holy Ghost, 3) man's will not resisting the Word of God. Following Erasmus, he ascribed to man a faculty to apply himself to the grace of God (working together with God — *synergein*) and put the statement into the Interim in 1548. It did not cause much alarm at this time; but when Pfeffinger, in 1555, taught the same, only more boldly, and was upheld by Major, Eber, and Crell, then Stolz, Amsdorf, Flacius, and others publicly opposed the error. The error was condemned in the *Weimar Confutation Book* of 1558—59, which Prof. Viktorin Strigel and Pastor Huegel condemned, for which they were jailed by Duke John Frederick of Saxony. The matter was debated at Weimar August 2—8, 1560, when Strigel held that in the will of the unregenerate there was a latent power co-operating toward conversion; which, of course, all loyal Lutherans promptly condemn. The *Book of Confutation* was now carried out so rigorously that the autocratic Duke John Frederick, by a Consistorial Order of July 8, 1561, deprived the ministers of the right to excommunicate and vested it in a consistory at Weimar. Flacius protested in the name of liberty of conscience and the Church, where only Christ and His Word may decide, whereupon followed, December 10, 1561, the prompt expulsion of Flacius, Wigand, Musaeus, and Judex from Jena. Strigel was reinstated after signing a rather ambiguous declaration. Forty pastors would not sign the document and were promptly exiled. In 1567 Duke John William became the ruler, and he dismissed the Philippists (the followers of Philip Melanchthon) and recalled the loyal Lutherans, all but Flacius, who in the heat of debate at Weimar had asserted original sin was not an "accident," but of the "substance" of man. This controversy was formally

ended in Ducal Saxony by the Final Report and Declaration of the Theologians of both universities of Leipzig and Wittenberg (1571). Here Luther's monergism was upheld and Philippian synergism condemned. The *Formula of Concord*, in Articles I and II, rejects the extremes of Strigel and Flacius, and teaches that man is purely passive in the instant of conversion and after that, of course, co-operates with the Holy Ghost. If man spurns the means of grace, he is lost through his own fault.

Synod of Dort. 1. A synod convened by the States General of the Netherlands at Dort, Nov. 13, 1618, and adjourned May 9, 1619. *Origin.* The opposition of Arminius to the Augustinian and Calvinistic doctrines on predestination gave rise to a bitter controversy. In 1610, in Five Articles, the Arminians presented a petition to the States of Holland and West Friesland, which was called a Remonstrance, in consequence of which they were called Remonstrants. This synod met to discuss these views, which they condemned.

2. *Organization.* The synod, when organized, consisted, first, of the deputies from the States, who properly constituted the national synod, numbering 39 ministers, 5 professors, and 18 ruling elders; secondly, of 24 foreign divines. The States General were represented by lay commissioners. The only Protestant kingdom in Europe that sent deputies was Great Britain. Besides these and the divines of the United Provinces there were delegates from Switzerland, the Palatinate, Hessen, and Bremen. The Lutheran churches were not represented, and no delegates from France were present.

3. *Proceedings.* During the 22d session the Remonstrants were told that they could merely express their opinions, and the synod would pronounce judgment. Episcopius, in an elegant speech, defended the Arminian doctrine, and the Remonstrants then successively submitted written statements in defense of each of the Five Articles. When asked to put their objections to the confession in writing, they at first refused, but finally complied. At the 57th session the Remonstrants were expelled from the Synod.

4. *Decisions.* In the 125th session it was voted that the Five Articles of the Remonstrants were contrary to the doctrine of the Reformed Church and that their objections to the confession

and the catechism were not supported by the authority of Scripture. The final decision was expressed in the form of canons, which were adopted and signed by all at the 136th session. The doctrine of absolute predestination was maintained. For about two centuries the decisions of the Synod of Dort were the basis of the Reformed Church in Holland.

Synod of the Reformed Presbyterian Church in America. See *Presbyterian Bodies,* 4 f.

Synod of the West. See *Kentucky Synod; United Lutheran Church, Synods of,* 8; *Synods, Extinct.*

Synodical Conference of North America, The Ev. Luth. 1. A federation of synods comprising The Lutheran Church — Missouri Synod, the Joint Synod of Wisconsin and Other States, the Slovak Ev. Luth. Church of America, and the Norwegian Synod of the American Ev. Luth. Church. The Synodical Conference is the second largest body of Lutherans in America. It acknowledges the canonical books of the Bible as the Word of God and stands on the Confessions of the Lutheran Church, membership in it depending on the full and honest adherence to them in doctrine and practice. Its purpose is: to express and confess the unity of the Spirit existing in the constituent synods; to give mutual aid and assistance toward the strengthening of their faith and confession; to promote, and preserve over against all disturbances, the unity in doctrine and practice; to bring about concerted action in the common cause; to work toward the geographical delimitation of the synods wherever feasible; and to unite all Lutheran synods of America into one orthodox American Lutheran Church.

2. The Synodical Conference is a federation, not a merger, of synods, being, in the main, merely an advisory body; the synods retain their full sovereignty, have full control of their educational, benevolent, and missionary activities, the Colored Mission (see *Missions, Lutheran Negro; Nigeria*) alone being conducted by the Synodical Conference as such, and pass finally on the admission of new members and the alliance with other bodies on the part of any of the constituent synods.

3. Voting members are all pastors and lay delegates elected by their respective synods as their representatives; advisory members, all present standing members of the synods and all those who have served in the previous meeting of their synods as delegates of a congregation. Each synod is entitled to at least four representatives, further representation being determined by the size of the voting membership. There is an equal number of clerical and lay representatives. The stated meetings were formerly held annually. In 1879 it was resolved to hold the meetings biennially.

4. *History.* A federation of synods on the basis of a straight acceptance of the Lutheran Confessions had always been aimed at by the lovers of the American Lutheran Church. Dr. Walther proposed in 1856 that free conferences be held "with a view toward the final realization of one united Ev. Luth. Church of North America." Representatives from the Ohio, New York, Pennsylvania, and Missouri Synods met for this purpose in the years 1856 to 1859 (54 clerical and 19 lay representatives being present at the first conference); but no permanent organization was effected. The General Council, organized in 1866 (1867) as a protest against the un-Lutheran position of the General Synod, proving to be lacking in consistent Lutheranism (its attitude regarding altar and pulpit fellowship, the lodge question, and chiliasm revealing its laxity and unionistic spirit; see *Four Points*), Missouri, Ohio, and the Norwegian Synod refused to join, and shortly Wisconsin, Minnesota, Illinois, and, later, Michigan withdrew. At conferences, held in 1867 and after, between representatives of Missouri and Ohio, in 1868 between Missouri and Wisconsin, in 1869 between Missouri and Illinois, and repeatedly between Missouri and the Norwegians, the various synods found themselves in harmony. In 1870 the Joint Synod of Ohio, at the instance of its Eastern District, appointed a committee to confer with similar committees of synods occupying the same confessional position for the purpose of effecting a closer union. Representatives of the synods of Ohio, Missouri, Wisconsin, Illinois, and the Norwegian Synod met twice in 1871 and adopted a draft for the proposed union, declaring that the organization of a new general body along strictly confessional lines, free from all unionistic and lax practices, was necessary for the preservation and spread of Lutheran unity; and July 10—16, 1872, at Milwaukee,

the Synodical Conference was organized and held its first convention, the synods represented at the conferences of 1871, together with Minnesota, forming the federation. Officers: Prof. C. F. W. Walther (Missouri), president; Prof. W. F. Lehmann (Ohio), vice-president; Rev. P. Beyer (Missouri), secretary; Mr. J. Schmidt (Ohio), treasurer.

5. In the interest of the preservation of the unity of the Spirit the convention of 1876 ordered that the reports of the proceedings of the various synods and districts be exchanged, passed upon by committees, and laid before the Synodical Conference at the next convention. The same convention advised that all the synods without delay take the necessary steps toward organizing State synods, uniting in one organization all congregations of the Synodical Conference within the respective state or territory. It also advised its synods to establish one common pastors' seminary, to take the place of all existing seminaries, the same with regard to the teachers' seminaries. As a result of these overtures the Concordia Synod of Virginia, which had joined in 1876, became a district of the Ohio Synod in 1877, the Illinois Synod was consolidated with the Illinois District of the Missouri Synod in 1879 (1880), and the Missouri Synod organized the districts of Illinois, Iowa, Nebraska, and Kansas to become, eventually, State synods. This project, as well as that relative to the common seminaries, was later abandoned. The situation arising from the overlapping of the territory of the synods, however, still calls for a closer amalgamation.

6. The controversy on election and conversion brought on in 1881 (1882) the withdrawal of the Ohio Synod. Those refusing to go with Ohio formed the Concordia Synod, which belonged to the Synodical Conference from 1882 to 1886, when it merged with the Missouri Synod. In 1883 the Norwegian Synod withdrew, hoping thereby the sooner to adjust the difficulties in its midst arising from the controversy, but maintained fraternal relations with the Synodical Conference until 1912, when it adopted the Madison Theses of union. The Norwegian Synod of the American Ev. Luth. Church, formed by those who disagreed with the Madison Theses, joined the Synodical Conference in 1920. The English Synod of Missouri joined in 1888, merging with the Missouri Synod in 1911. The Michigan Synod, formerly of the General Council, joined in 1892 and the Nebraska District Synod in 1906 (see *Wisconsin, Synod of*). The Slovak Ev. Luth. Church joined in 1908.

7. Originally the Synodical Conference was overwhelmingly German, but the use of the English language became preponderant. The presidency of the Conference has been held by Prof. C. F. W. Walther (Missouri; 1872—73), Prof. W. F. Lehmann (Ohio; 1873—76; 1877—80), Rev. H. A. Preus (Norwegian; 1876—77), Prof. P. L. Larsen (Norwegian; 1880—82), Rev. J. Bading (Wisconsin; 1882—1912), Prof. L. Gausewitz (Wisconsin; 1912—27), Prof. L. Fuerbringer (Missouri; 1927—44), Rev. E. Benj. Schlueter (Wisconsin; 1944—50), Prof. G. Chr. Barth (Missouri; 1950—52), Prof. W. A. Baepler (1952—   ).

8. *Doctrinal Position.* The chief mark of distinction of the Synodical Conference is its adherence to God's Word and the Lutheran Confessions and its earnest desire to live up to them in practice (see the articles on the member synods). Its orthodoxy, a matter of faith and conscience, of living and loving obedience to God's Word, determines its attitude toward other churches. It regards the spreading of false doctrine as a sin of disobedience to God and abhors unionism.* As it will not tolerate false doctrine in its own midst, so it does not maintain fraternal relations with those who tolerate persistent upholders of unscriptural and un-Lutheran doctrine and practice. Loving God's Word and the Lutheran Confessions, it is anxious to establish fraternal relations with all who are of the same mind and seeks to remove doctrinal differences by coming to an agreement in the truth. That was the purpose of the Free Conference of 1856 and later, of the offer of the founders of the Synodical Conferences in 1903—06, of the conferences held since 1917 between committees appointed by the synods of Missouri and Wisconsin, on the one hand, and of Ohio, Iowa, and Buffalo, on the other, and by willingness officially expressed by member synods to discuss doctrinal matters with other Lutheran bodies.

The Synodical Conference opposes anti-Christian and anti-Scriptural lodges and bears testimony over against ecclesiastical organizations which tolerate them. It opposes membership in such lodges as the Masons, which practice crass unionism by bringing together for religious exercises professed followers and outspoken enemies of Christ.

Proceedings of the Ev. Luth. Synodical Conference of North America; minutes of constituent synods; references given under articles on the synods mentioned above; F. Bente, *American Lutheranism,* CPH, 1919; J. L. Neve, *The Lutheran Church in America,* Luth. Lit. Bd., Burlington, Iowa, 1934; A. R. Wentz, *The Lutheran Church in American History,* United Luth. Pub. House, Philadelphia, 1932; J. T. Mueller, *History of the Synodical Conference,* CPH.

Synods. See *Councils and Synods; Polity, Ecclesiastical,* 3.

Synods, Extinct (see also *sub voce;* cross references to fuller treatments are also given under the separate listings). (NOTE: "Extinct Synods" does not mean that the synods so designated have in every case gone out of existence, but simply that they no longer exist under that name. A number of smaller bodies, which in most cases were only temporary organizations pending the formation of permanent bodies, have not been listed.) Allegheny Synod (General Synod; ULCA), 1842—1938; Alpha Synod of the Ev. Luth. Church of Freedmen in America (United Synod, South), 1889—92; Augsburg Synod (Independent), 1876—1902; Buffalo Synod (Independent), 1845 to 1930; Canada, Synod of Central (General Council), 1908—25; Chicago Synod (General Council), 1895—1920; Concordia Synod (of Virginia, Joint Ohio), 1865—1920; Concordia Synod (of Pennsylvania, Synodical Conference, 1882 to 1886; Concordia Synod (of the West), 1862—64; Franckean Synod (New York, General Synod), 1837—1908; Georgia Synod (General Synod; United Synod in the South), 1860—1930; Hartwick Synod (New York, General Synod), 1830—1908; Hauge Synod (merged with other Norwegian synods in 1917); Holston Synod (Tennessee and Virginia), 1860—1922; Illinois Synod I (General Synod and Synodical Conference), 1846 to 1875; Illinois, German Synod of (see Wartburg Synod); Illinois, Synod of Central (General Synod), 1867—97, 1901—20; Illinois, Synod of Central and Southern (General Synod), 1897—1901; Illinois, Synod of Northern (General Synod), 1851—1920; Illinois, Synod of Southern (General Synod), 1856—1920; Indiana Synod I (Independent), 1835 to 1859; Indiana Synod II (General Council), 1871—75; Indiana, Synod of

Northern (General Synod), 1855—1920; Indianapolis Synod (Independent), 1846 to 1852; Immanuel Synod (Independent), 1885—1921; Iowa and Other States, Ev. Luth. Synod of (Independent), 1854—1930; Kentucky Synod (General Synod), 1854—65; Manitoba Synod (General Council), 1897—1947; Maryland and Virginia, Synod of (General Synod), 1820—29; Maryland and the South, German Synod of (General Synod), 1874—76; Melanchthon Synod (General Synod), 1857—69; Miami Synod (in Ohio; General Synod), 1847 to 1920; Michigan Synod I (Independent), 1840—46; Michigan Synod II (Independent), 1860—1919; New Jersey, Synod of (General Synod), 1859—72; New York Ministerium (General Synod; General Council), 1786—1929; New York, Synod of, I (General Synod), 1867—72; New York, Synod of, II (General Synod), 1908—29; New York, German Synod of (Steimle Synod), 1866—72; New York and New England, Synod of (General Council), 1902—29; New York and New Jersey, Synod of (General Synod), 1872—1908; North Carolina, Synod of (General Synod; United Synod in the South), 1803—1921; Norwegian Synod (Independent; member of Synodical Conference, 1872—83; merged with other Norwegian Synods in 1917); Ohio, The Synod and Ministerium of English (General Synod), 1836—58; Ohio, Synod of East (continuing the Synod and Ministerium of English Ohio), 1858 to 1920; Ohio and Other States, The German Synod of (see Augsburg); Ohio, English District Synod of (General Council), 1857—1920; Ohio and Other States, Joint Synod of (Independent; member of Synodical Conference, 1872 to 1881, 1882), 1918—1930; Pennsylvania, Synod of Central (General Synod), 1855—1923; Pennsylvania, Synod of East (General Synod), 1841—1938; Pennsylvania, Synod of West (General Synod), 1823—1938; Pittsburgh Synod I (General Council), 1845—1919; Pittsburgh Synod II (General Synod), 1867 to 1919; Southwest, Synod of the (General Synod), 1846—56; Steimle Synod (see New York, German Synod of); Susquehanna Synod (General Synod), 1867—1924; Susquehanna Synod of Central Pennsylvania (ULCA), 1924 to 1938; Tennessee Synod (Independent; United Synod South; ULCA), 1820—21; Tennessee, Synod of Middle (General Synod), 1879—1904; Union Synod (in Indiana; General Council), 1859—71; Virginia, Ev. Luth. Synod of (General

Synod; United Synod in the South), 1829—1922; Virginia, Synod of East (General Synod), 1826—50; Virginia, Synod of Central, 1847— ; Virginia, Synod of Southwestern (General Synod), 1842—1922; West, Synod of the (General Synod), 1835—52; West, Mission Synod of the (Franckean), 1866; Wittenberg Synod (in Ohio; General Synod), 1847—1920.

Syriac Bible Versions. See *Bible Versions,* C.

Syrian Jacobite Church. See *Monophysite Controversy.*

Syrian Orthodox Church in the U. S. A. See *Eastern Orthodox Churches,* 6.

Syvstjernen. See *Norway, Lutheranism in,* 8.

T

Ta Hsueh. See *Sacred Literatures.*

Tabernacle. The receptacle, or shrine, often richly ornamented, in which the pyx, monstrance, etc., are kept in Roman churches. It is usually placed on the high altar or above it. A red lamp is kept burning before it.

Table of Duties. See *Haustafel.*

Table of the Lord. See *Grace, Means of,* IV.

Taborites. See *Bohemian-Moravian Brethren.*

Tabula rasa. Literally, a blank waxed tablet; a term used by Stoics (see *Stoicism*) and later by Locke and other sensationalists (see *Sensationalism*) for the soul, which at birth is a blank, without innate ideas, upon which in the course of time, ideas are imprinted by experience. Opposed to doctrine of original sin. See *Empiricism.*

Taeufer. See *Brethren, Dunkers.*

Tahiti Islands. See *Society Islands.*

Tallis, Thomas (ca. 1510—85). Was a master composer of English church music. He was an excellent contrapuntist, his music is churchly, and his versatility, together with his other gifts, put him among the most outstanding composers of church music. Like Handel, he is often at his best in music of a massive character, though he wrote also beautiful music of a delicate nature. *Tallis' Canon* (*Lutheran Hymnal,* No. 558, first tune) is rightly considered one of the most famous hymn tunes of the Christian Church.

W. A. Barrett, *English Church Composers,* New York, 1911; Sir John Hawkins, *A General History of the Science and Practice of Music,* London, 1875; E. Walker, *A History of Music in England,* London, 1924.

Talmage, Thomas De Witt (1832 to 1902). Pulpit orator; b. at Bound Brook, N. J.; Dutch Reformed pastor; Presbyterian pastor in Brooklyn, N. Y., 1869 to 1894; Washington (d. there). Author.

Talmud (Hebrew, "instruction"). A collection of Jewish law, consisting of two main parts, the Mishna, and its commentary, the Gemara. The basis of Jewish law is the Pentateuch; but as this was definitely fixed and the continually changing conditions, especially during the postexilic period, called for new decisions and laws, a rabbinical supplement to the Pentateuch, orally transmitted, grew up. This material, called Mishna (neo-Heb., "repetition"), was sorted and reduced to writing about the beginning of the third century after Christ by Rabbi Judah, "the Prince." It is written in post-Biblical Hebrew and has six parts, which contain laws on 1) agriculture, 2) Sabbaths and festivals, 3) marriage and divorce, 4) civil and criminal cases, 5) sacrifices, 6) Levitical purity. During the following centuries the development of the traditional law continued, and the Mishna, in turn, became the text of a still more extended commentary in the Jewish academies of Palestine and Babylonia. This exposition, called Gemara (Aramaic, "completion"), contains, besides the subjects treated in the Mishna, a heterogeneous collection of information on philosophy, history, natural sciences, geography, archaeology, astronomy, medicine, art, commerce, etc., in short, an encyclopedia of the knowledge of those centuries. Accordingly, the Talmud is not a lawbook in the modern sense, in which laws are definitely and concisely stated, but rather a legal source book, an archive, which contains untold opinions and happenings, more or less closely connected with Jewish law. There are two recensions of the Talmud, the Palestinian, "Talmud Yerushalmi," written in West Aramaic and completed ca. A. D. 370, and the much more important Babylonian, "Talmud Babli," written mainly in East Aramaic and completed a century later. The discussions in the Talmud, which, in so far as they are interpretations of the Pentateuch, belong to the Midrash (exposition of the Old Testament) literature of the Jews, may be classified into two main elements, the *halacha,* which deals exclusively with the Law, and the *haggadah,* the illustrative, ethical, historical, biographical, legendary, material. See *Jews.*

I. Epstein, *The Talmud* (unabridged English translation), Soncino Press, Bournemouth, England (34 vols.).

Tanganyika Territory. Formerly German East Africa. Taken by the British during World War I. The Ruanda and Urundi districts were mandated to Belgium, the Kionga Triangle to Mozambique (Portuguese East Africa), and the remainder to the British Empire. Headquarters of the British section are at Dar-es-Salaam. Total area of the British mandate, 362,000 sq. mi. Population, 7,600,000 (1950). Missions by the Augustana Lutheran Church (former work of Leipzig Mission, taken over 1922) and other bodies. 225,500 Protestant communicants; a total Protestant community of 373,300 (1952). Roman Catholics: 710,000 (1952).

Taoism. 1. One of the three great religions of China, traditionally founded by Lao-tse (Latinized, Laocius), Chinese sage and elder contemporary of Confucius (ca. 600—ca. 520 B. C.). Lao-tse is the reputed author of a small book of 5,000 characters, called *Tao-Teh-King,* which is the chief source of our knowledge of early Taoism.

2. This system was at first merely philosophical, and only after six or seven centuries did it develop into a religion. It is mystical and quietistic and based on the idea of the *tao,* a term practically untranslatable, but variously rendered "way, truth, doctrine, word." Tao is the highest being, the primary cause of the physical as well as of the moral world. All true virtue consists in being one with the Tao. Hence it is the highest goal of human development. He who in self-effacement, lack of desire, and in meditation strives to understand the Tao will not perish in death, but find salvation. In sharp contrast to the conservative Confucius, who up-

held the principles of filial piety and obedience to authority and whose chief aim was the welfare of the state, Lao-tse's system had to do with the individual and aimed to achieve the happiness and improvement of man-kind, not through civil and social rules of conduct, but by making the individual pure and sincere.' While Confucius demanded fulfillment of those duties upon which the structures of the state, society, and family rest, Lao-tse advocated gentleness, moderation, modesty, and love for one's fellow men. Characteristic are his maxims: "He who overcomes other men has force, but he who overcomes himself is mighty"; "recompense injury with kindness."

3. Taoism experienced further development at the hands of Lao-tse's disciples, of whom the most noted was Chwang-tse, who lived in the fourth century B. C. After Chwang-tse the system began to degenerate, especially through the influence of Chang-tao-ling of the first century after Christ, who is recognized as the founder of modern Taoism. It also was strongly influenced by Buddhism, which was introduced into China in the first century after Christ.

4. Modern Taoism is characterized by a mass of superstitions, magic, occult practices, and a quest for the elixir of immortality. Besides the metaphysical Buddhism and the ethical Confucianism * it has become the naturalistic religious system of China. The highest god in its pantheon is San-Ching, "The Three Pure Ones," a triplicate form of Lao-tse, corresponding to the triplicate representation of Buddha as past, present, and future. The second highest god is Yü Hwang Shang Ti, who rules over the affairs of the world. Other gods are the stars, especially the five planets, the dragon-king, who is a personification of water, gods of the various professions and callings, and innumerable evil spirits that keep the superstitious people in a continuous state of terror. Imitating Buddhism, Taoism introduced temples, a priesthood, and a monastic system. Its head is a descendant of Chang-tao-ling, who by Europeans is called the "Taoist pope" and by the natives "Master of Heaven." He resides in the province Kwangsi. While the educated classes despise Taoism for its superstitions, it has a great hold on the masses. However, all uneducated Chinese are syncretists and follow whatever appeals to them in the three religions. See *Religion, Comparative* (bibliography).

Tappan, William Bingham (1794 to 1849). B. in Beverly, Mass. In early manhood he taught school in Philadelphia. From 1826 until his death he was in the employ of the American Sunday School Union as manager and superintendent at Cincinnati, at Philadelphia, and at Boston. In 1841 he obtained license to preach as a Congregational minister, but having no pastoral charge, he was never ordained. From 1819 to 1849 he continued to write and publish poetry, amounting in all to eight or ten volumes. He died at West Needham, Mass. "There Is an Hour of Peaceful Rest" and " 'Tis Midnight; and on Olive's Brow" are two of his hymns still in use.

Targums. See *Bible Versions,* B.

Tarnow, Paul (1562—1633). Prof. at Rostock. Wrote *On the Holy Ministry,* against Rome; *On the Holy Trinity,* against Socinus; a commentary on the Gospel of St. John. His contention that the absolution must not be spoken categorically, but hypothetically ("If thou believest"), was generally repudiated as conflicting with the doctrine of justification, making faith the cause of forgiveness. — *John Tarnow* (1586 to 1629), nephew of Paul; prof. at Rostock; exponent of the grammatico-historical method of exegesis over against the dogmatic method; wrote a number of commentaries on the Old Testament; championed religious toleration by the state.

Tartaros. See *Hereafter,* D 7.

Tasmania. The smallest state in the commonwealth of Australia. Area, 26,215 sq. mi. Population, 257,078. The aboriginal population died out, mostly through wars with English immigrants, before any mission work was done among them.

Tatian (110—172). Apologist and Christian philosopher; pupil of Justin Martyr, whom he met at Rome ca. 150. His *To the Greeks* is a mordant and scathing denunciation of Greek mythology and philosophy. His *Diatessaron* (harmony of the four Gospels) proves that the four canonical Gospels were in use in the middle of the second century. Toward the end of his life he became involved in Gnostic aberrations besides demanding ascetic abstinence in Christian life. See references under *Patristics.*

Taufgesinnte. See *Mennonite Bodies.*

Tauler, Johann (ca. 1300—61). German mystic; b. in Strassburg. When fifteen years old, he entered the order of the Dominicans, studying theology at Cologne. As a result of the controversy between Emperor Louis IV and Pope John XXII, Tauler, with his order, was banished from Strassburg; but he returned three and a half years later. He was reputed to be the greatest preacher of his time, his sermons exhibiting his piety, sincerity, and warmth of feeling, having a marked influence on his contemporaries and winning the commendation and regard of Luther. He wrote *The Book of Spiritual Poverty.* See also *Mysticism.*

Tausen, Hans (1494—1561). Danish reformer; vice in cloister drove him to Wittenberg (1519); prof. and pastor at Copenhagen; twice exiled. Bishop of Ribe in 1541. Tausen gave Denmark the Lutheran Confession, the Danish Bible, the Danish language in the church service, the Lutheran hymnal, and the Lutheran school.

Taverner, Richard (1505—75). Translated the Augsburg Confession and the Apology into English in 1536; published the first English Lutheran dogmatics in 1538, before there was one in German; two editions of the Bible and two editions of the New Testament; the first English Lutheran postil, a translation of the sermons of Sarcerius or Corvinus; in 1552 Edward VI licensed him to preach.

Taylor, James Hudson (1832—1905). Founder of China Inland Mission; b. at Barnsley, England; d. at Changsha, China. After studying medicine for some years, he offered his services to the China Evangelization Society. Worked in China with various missions 1854—60. Returning to England 1860 for five years, he published *China; Its Spiritual Need and Claim.* In 1866 he left for China with sixteen other men. Taylor accomplished a great deal of work as director of the Mission, traveling extensively and lecturing. Later he returned to Switzerland. On a last visit to China he unexpectedly passed away.

Taylor, Jeremy (1613—67). Author, schoolteacher, renowned preacher of his day, chaplain to Archbishop Laud. Main works: *A Discourse of the Liberty of Prophesying; The Rule of Exercises of Holy Living; A Course of Sermons for All Sundays of the Year* (earned for him the surname of "Chrysostom," *i. e.*, the "golden-mouthed"); *The Golden Grove* (a book of devotions).

Taylor, John. See *Latter Day Saints.*

Taylor, Nathaniel. See *New England Theology*, 3.

Taylor, Thomas Rawson (1807—35). An English Congregational minister, b. at Osset near Wakefield. After serving as apprentice to a merchant and also in a print shop, through the example of the piety of the printer and his guidance, he prepared himself for the Congregational ministry at Airedale Independent College. Soon after he became pastor of an independent church in Sheffield; but after six months he was obliged to give up his charge because of ill health. He then became classical tutor in his alma mater. His career was again interrupted, and he died of consumption, when only twenty-eight years old. He is remembered by his hymn "I'm But a Stranger Here; Heaven Is My Home," for which Arthur S. Sullivan supplied the tune.

Taylor, William (1821—1902). American Methodist Episcopal missionary; b. in Rockbridge Co., Va.; d. at Palo Alto, Calif.; for many years an itinerant missionary and evangelist in Australia (1862), India, Africa, and Central and South America. Having been ordained "Bishop of Africa" at the age of sixty (1884), he attempted to found a self-supporting industrial mission in Africa (Liberia, Angola, Kongo) with a large following of male and female evangelists, most of whom were unfit for the work. The project was visionary and proved a distinct failure. Later his missions were taken over by the Methodist Episcopal Church, which placed Bishop Hartzell in charge of the Taylor fields.

Tchaikovsky, Peter Illyitch (1840 to 1893). Is still, many believe, the most popular and the most widely known composer Russia has produced. His music is a typical expression of the Russian temperament. It is interesting to note that Tchaikovsky did not study musical theory until he was twenty-one years of age — that, in his youth, he knew nothing of Bach or Beethoven and very little of Russian folk music. He admired Mozart greatly. Nicholas Rubinstein later helped make his works popular in Russia; in America he gained widespread fame and conducted an orchestra at the time Carnegie Hall was dedicated. He wrote six symphonies, three piano concertos, a violin concerto, chamber music, songs, and much other music. Tchaikovsky was thoroughly despised by Brahms because of his lack of moderation and self-control; his church music often lacks the reserve we expect to find in worship music and is frequently quite moody and uneven, though very vocal, singable, and effective.

Calvocoressi-Abraham, *Masters of Russian Music*, New York, 1936; G. Adler, *Handbuch der Musikgeschichte*, Frankfurt, 1924; D. Ferguson, *A History of Musical Thought*, New York, 1948; P. H. Lang, *Music in Western Civilization*, New York, 1931.

Teachers. A. *Lutheran Elementary School Teachers.* 1. *Types and Number.* The elementary schools of The Lutheran Church — Missouri Synod in 1953 were in charge of the types and numbers of teachers shown in the following statistics:

	North America	South America	Total
No. of Schools	1,161	141	1,302
Enrollment	107,319	6,110	113,429
Men Teachers	1,743	127	1,870
Women Teachers	1,759	64	1,823
Total Teachers	3,502	191	3,693

North America Only

Number of Schools	1,161
Enrollment	107,319
Installed Men Teachers	1,553
Men Students, Teachers' Colleges	80
Other Luth. Students and Other Men	73
Pastors Teaching	21
Men Emergency Teachers	16
Total Men Teachers, North America	1,743
Women Graduates, Teachers' Colleges	232
Women Students, Teachers' Colleges	265
Students, Graduates, Other Luth. Colleges	308
Other Regular Women Teachers	738
Women Emergency Teachers	216
Total Women Teachers, North America	1,759
Total Men and Women Teachers, North America	3,502

a. *The installed male teacher* is the regulation teacher of the Missouri Synod school system. He is a graduate of one of the two teachers' colleges of Synod, which provide for a four-year college course, aimed at the teacher's calling; or if he is a graduate of another Lutheran institution, he must be officially approved as a regular male teacher. Such a teacher is eligible for a formal (written) call, for installation, and for advisory membership in Synod. He is counted among the clergy, though not a pastor, and his official status is permanent. He is ordinarily a married man and devotes his entire life and time to his calling. Minimum graduation requirements for a diploma are three years of college; but most students complete a fourth year and receive a Bachelor of Science in Education degree. Both teachers' colleges are accredited by the North Central Association of Colleges and Secondary Schools.

b. *The non-installed male teacher* is a teacher doing supply work, or a young graduate teacher who prefers not to be formally called for the time being, or a teacher not yet officially approved, or, as in the case of Brazil, a lay male teacher.

c. *The teaching pastor* is usually the pastor of a small congregation who teaches his own full-time parochial school because the congregation may not as yet be able or willing to engage a teacher. During the first three quarters of a century of Synod's history, teaching pastors exceeded the number of regular male teachers, owing mostly to a constant teacher shortage and a universal insistence on parochial schools.

d. *The woman teacher* may or may not be a graduate of Synod's teachers' colleges. If she is a graduate, she has the same training as the men; if not, she may belong to one of several classes: a Lutheran public school teacher with the necessary professional training who has decided to be a teacher in a Lutheran school; a graduate of a teachers' college of another Lutheran synod, especially one affiliated with the Synodical Conference of North America; a capable girl selected from the congregation and given the necessary in-service training; or, in emergency, any capable and suitable woman, married or unmarried, who assists temporarily. The woman teacher, because of her sex, is not regarded eligible for a formal and permanent call, or for advisory membership in Synod, just as women are not regarded eligible for the voting membership or church boards in the local congregation. Her "call" is in the form of a solemn written agreement, which may

be either temporary or permanent, subject to dissolution if intended marriage or other personal affairs make this necessary. Her installation is rare, but optional. The limitations of her official status do not affect the divinity of her commission or calling. In a minority of cases, women teachers serve a lifetime; yet, the general average tenure for woman teachers was only 4.098 years in 1938, according to a rather thorough survey then made by Edwin J. Wibracht. (For Synod's pronouncement on "The Status of the Woman Teacher," see *Proceedings*, 1941, p. 156; and for a theological study of the subject, see "Von dem Beruf der Lehrerinnen," by Dr. G. Stoeckhardt, *Concordia Theological Monthly*, October, 1934, p. 764. A reprint of an earlier article in *Lehre und Wehre*.)

e. *Male or Female Student Teachers.* The men in this classification are either students at the teachers' colleges or theological students sent out to do supply teaching, ordinarily after a summer course at the teachers' colleges. The women in this category are students at the teachers' colleges. The rule is that men students teach for only one year, while women students, in time of emergency, often continue teaching indefinitely.

2. *The Status of the Installed Male Teacher.* During both World War I and World War II the regular male teacher was classified by the Government as "a minister of religion" and exempted from military service. In the official Diploma of Vocation, or formal call, for such a teacher it is stated that he is called "to the sacred office of a servant of the Word" and "in the name of the Triune God and by His authority is asked to assume this office as part of the public ministry at this place." The duties of his office are then particularized as those of a Christian educator, who is usually asked also to take over the local ministry of music and to perform educational duties that extend beyond the elementary school, such as directing youth organizations, teaching Bible classes of adults, and conducting a divine service in the absence of the pastor. In some cases, congregations have authorized such a teacher to assist the pastor at the Communion table or to perform other pastoral acts in an emergency.

3. *The Lutheran Teacher's Call.* All classes of Lutheran teachers have a divine call, in the Scriptural sense that they are active "in the Word and doc-

trine" and by virtue of the fact that they are regarded called by the Lord through the Christian congregation to perform a part of the public ministry by publicly teaching and training either children alone, as in the case of the woman teacher, or also adults, as in the case of the male teacher. But only the office of the regular male teacher, like that of the pastor, professor, and other full-time male servants of the Church, is dignified by a formal, permanent call; the rest are informally and temporarily engaged, though some women teachers continue to serve the same school indefinitely. The teacher's call is issued by a local congregation, or by a group of congregations in the case of a joint school, and the teacher is salaried by such congregation or congregations. By virtue of his call and placement, the teacher and his family automatically become members of the congregation that has engaged him, of the Visiting Circuit and District of the Synod in which the congregation is located, of local conferences, and, by his *first* call and placement, also of Synod itself. A transfer to another congregation is effected only when such other congregation extends a formal call to him and, after prayerful consideration and consultation with his present congregation, he becomes firmly convinced that the Lord is indicating the change and thus calling him away from his present charge. Reasons for removing a teacher from office are the same as those for pastors and other called servants, namely, a manifestly offensive life, adherence to false doctrine, unfaithfulness in performance of official duties, and incapacity or inefficiency.

4. *The Supervision of Teachers.* The Lutheran teacher is under the supervision of both the congregation he serves and Synod, to which he belongs. The congregation exercises its supervision through its pastor and board of education. Synod supervises the teacher, along with the pastor and congregation, through a local Circuit Visitor and the President of the synodical District, and in a special manner through a District Board of Education and a District Superintendent or Secretary of Education, where this office has been established. A form of supervision is also exercised by local conferences.

5. *Teacher Training.* Even before The Lutheran Church—Missouri Synod was organized in 1847, its founders

made provision for the training of Lutheran male teachers. The earliest steps were taken in 1843, in connection with the rehabilitation of the Perry County, Missouri, College; but more definite attempts were made in 1846, when a Lutheran seminary for pastors and teachers was founded at Fort Wayne, Ind. This was followed by a private seminary for teachers in Milwaukee, 1855, which Synod transferred to the Fort Wayne seminary in 1857; and then, in 1864, Synod opened a special Lutheran teachers' seminary at Addison, Ill. A preparatory department for this seminary was founded at Seward, Nebr., in 1894, its graduates finishing their course at Addison, until the Seward institution was made a full seminary in 1906. In 1913 the Addison institution was relocated at River Forest, Ill., a western suburb of Chicago. Both institutions go by the name of Concordia Teachers College, each providing for four years of college. Besides a thorough course in religion and the common branches of learning, both general and professional, these schools also prepare their students as organists and choir directors.

In the fall of 1953, River Forest had a total of 638 college students, 353 men and 285 women; Seward, 298 (including 12 general students), 158 men and 140 women. In its high school department Seward had 150 students, 82 boys and 68 girls (including 20 pastoral and 13 general students). Total in high school and college, 448; total in teacher training, 403. Total teacher-training students for River Forest and Seward, 1,041.

In addition, Synod's preparatory colleges for pastors, most of them with four years of high school and two years of college, had the following number of teacher-training students in the fall of 1953:

A. COLLEGES WITH NO SPECIAL TEACHER-TRAINING COURSE

Location	High Sch. Dept.		College Dept.		
	Boys	Girls	Men	Women	Total
Bronxville, N.Y.	8	—	5	16	29
Concordia, Mo.	17	—	—	—	17
Milwaukee, Wis.	15	—	—	—	15
Portland, Oreg.	11	—	4	—	15

B. COLLEGES WITH A SPECIAL TEACHER-TRAINING COURSE

Location	Boys	Girls	Men	Women	Total
Austin, Tex.	34	—	10	—	44
Edmonton, Alta.	4	6	1	—	11
Ft. Wayne, Ind.	2	—	16	37	55
Oakland, Calif.	13	28	12	11	64
St. Paul, Minn.	15	—	25	65	105
Winfield, Kans.	10	25	17	119	171
Totals	129	59	90	248	526

Austin and Edmonton were added by Synod to the latter group in 1953. Fort Wayne, with a teacher-training course in the college department since 1950, gradually eliminated its high school department, and had only the senior class left in the fall of 1953. It will be supplanted by a senior college for pastors in a few years. Winfield has a two-year terminal college course for women during an emergency which had not been relieved by 1953. Except for those from Winfield and Edmonton (which trains teachers mainly for Canada), the students from all preparatory colleges will continue their studies at River Forest or Seward for a diploma or a degree; but after two years of college, those in Group B may be assigned for supply teaching after taking a special summer course at the teachers' colleges.

All the preparatory colleges are to provide a high school course for men and women which will lead to entrance at the teachers' colleges, except the preparatory colleges named in the previous paragraphs, which are to provide for a two-year pre-teacher-training college course, and may or may not have a full high school department.

Valparaiso University is to be explored as an additional source of women teachers.

6. *Placement of Teacher Graduates and Students.* Men graduates are honored with a formal call; women graduates and students are secured through a written application. All graduates and students are looked upon as equally available to any congregation of Synod. Hence, they are not called or applied for by name, but by means of a blanket call for a candidate (male graduate) or a blanket application for a woman graduate or a student of either sex, which is then assigned by the synodical Assignment Board. This Board is made up of the President, the Vice-Presidents, and the District Presidents of Synod, with the representatives of the institutions which train teachers, the Secretary of Schools, and the representatives of boards present in an advisory capacity.

The mode of procedure in the placement of graduates and students is as follows: The time for the issuance of calls and applications is announced in the church papers. Congregations send their calls and applications to their respective District Presidents, who forward all teacher calls and applications to the Secretary of Schools for registration, summarization, and report to the Assignment Board. The teachers' colleges and Concordia Seminary, St. Louis, Mo., send to the Secretary of Schools a characterization of all available graduate teachers and teacher students. The Secretary of Schools prepares two assignment manuals, one for calls and one for applications, which contain all necessary information for the Assignment Board. According to the needs of the congregations and the gifts of available persons, calls and applications are then assigned. The institutions fill in the names of persons assigned and hand the documents to these persons. Unsupplied calls or applications are returned to the congregations by the respective Presidents.

7. *The Teachers' Bureau.* After the first placement of graduates, the latter are considered under the jurisdiction of Synod and its officials, chiefly the District Presidents. When congregations call "from the field," that is, teachers already in service, the custom is to select a slate of suitable candidates, and from that slate to elect and call a teacher. According to synodical regulations, "Congregations shall seek the advice of the respective District officials when calling pastors or teachers." (Synodical *Handbook*, 1947, Art. 4.01.) It is usually the District President or Superintendent of Education who is consulted. These officials know their field. But when it is a matter of calling from another District, they often lack the necessary information or acquaintance with persons. Hence, the College of Presidents in 1944 recommended the establishment of a Teachers' Bureau under the management of the Secretary of Schools. This Bureau has a complete record of elementary and high school teachers, of all the schools and their facilities. District officials or schools may obtain lists of suggested candidates for a given school position, or information on names submitted.

8. *In-Service Training of Teachers.* Men or women who graduated years ago with only two years of college training, or who otherwise lack the necessary scholastic credits, or desire to increase their credits, resort to in-service training of one kind or another. Quite generally they attend the summer schools of River Forest, Seward, Valparaiso University, or any other college or university; or they take extension or correspondence courses during the school year. The aim is to secure at least a bachelor's degree, and,

if possible, also a master's degree. Some male teachers are also working for a doctor's degree. Outside of such formal schooling, however, there is a continuous in-service training on the part of all teachers by means of the very act of teaching, serving as organist and choir director, and a wide professional experience otherwise; there is reading, private research, writing, and speaking; there are conferences and special study clubs of teachers. Many a girl or other woman teacher, especially during an emergency, has to receive her training in the schoolroom, with the help of experienced teachers.

9. *Educational Journals for Teachers.* Since 1865, a year after the establishment of a Lutheran teachers' seminary at Addison, Ill., the teachers have had a professional journal, successively known as the *Evangelisch-Lutherisches Schulblatt* (1865—1920), *Lutheran School Journal* (1921—47), and *Lutheran Education* (1947 forward). Since 1923 the teachers also had access to the *News Service,* a monthly paper devoted to the promotion of parochial schools, published by Synod's General Board of Education. By order of Synod this paper was sent free of charge to all pastors, teachers, professors, and other servants of the Church during the years 1945—47 and then expanded by another order of Synod into a promotional paper of the Board of Education under the name *Parish Education,* which began publication on Jan. 1, 1948. *Parish Education* is now to be absorbed by a general journal of practical church work. Many teachers also subscribe for the technical or practical journals of non-Lutheran schools.

10. *Teachers' Conferences.* The synodical *Handbook,* adopted in 1947, states the following: "Purposes of Conferences — The official conferences of pastors and teachers shall be conducted for the spiritual and professional growth of their members. Attendance shall be obligatory. Matters pertaining to Christian doctrine and practice, to professional problems, to the proper conduct in office, to private study, to the welfare of the respective congregations and schools, to the work of the District and of Synod at large, or to any other professional matter, shall at all times receive due and sympathetic attention. The members of the conference shall aim to cultivate brotherly fellowship, be mutually helpful in every way possible, and encourage, instruct, and admonish one another in a spirit of sincerity and Christian love. Professional conferences have no administrative functions." (Art. 4.111.) "Every District shall encourage joint conferences of pastors and teachers." (Art. 4.105.) "Every District of Synod shall arrange conferences for its teachers. The minutes and essays, or a reasonably comprehensive summary of the essays of such conferences, shall be submitted to the District convention in like manner as those of pastoral conferences." (Art. 4.103.) "Pastors and teachers are encouraged to organize smaller conferences in addition to their regular conferences, and to meet for the purpose of discussing doctrinal, professional, and practical matters." (Art. 4.107.) The teachers' conferences, or joint conferences of pastors and teachers, are usually also attended by women and various supply teachers. Essays and practical demonstrations of methods make up the programs.

B. *Lutheran High School Teachers.* Private high schools are maintained at Milwaukee, Wis., Racine, Wis. (both of these jointly with Wisconsin Synod churches); Fort Wayne, Ind., Chicago, Ill. (3), Los Angeles, Calif., Detroit, Mich., St. Louis, Mo., Cleveland, Ohio, Denver, Colo., and Houston, Tex.

The teachers in these high school departments or private high schools are selected from among the pastors and teachers of Synod, and in the private high schools also from among the laity, both men and women. The Teachers' Bureau keeps a record of them and also aids in securing such teachers. High school teachers are required to have a bachelor's or a master's degree and to have specialized in the subjects they are to teach. The high schools have united in the Association of Lutheran Secondary Schools. In 1952 the private high schools alone had an enrollment of over 4,000.

C. *Teachers in Missions. The Foreign Missions* of The Lutheran Church — Missouri Synod in India, Japan, New Guinea, and the Philippine Islands in 1952 maintained 112 parochial schools. The majority of these, 95, are in India. *The Colored Missions* of the Synodical Conference, the same year, reported 45 schools in North America, and 111 schools with 368 teachers in Africa.

D. *Teachers of Other Lutheran Synods. The Joint Synod of Wisconsin,* in 1953, had 195 parochial schools, 238 male and 304 female teachers. It maintained a teachers' college, Dr. Martin Luther College, at New Ulm, Minn., and the

Winnebago Lutheran Academy, Fond du Lac, Wis., as a private high school, with high school departments at the teachers' college, at Northwestern College, Watertown, Wis.; Michigan Lutheran Seminary, Saginaw, Mich.; and Northwestern Lutheran Academy, Mobridge, S. Dak. *The Slovak Church,* 1953, reported two elementary schools and two male teachers and three women teachers. It trains its pastors and teachers in the Missouri Synod or other Synodical Conference institutions. *The Norwegian Synod* had 13 schools in 1953, with four male and 15 female teachers. It maintains Bethany Lutheran College at Mankato, Minn., for general educational purposes and the training of its pastors and teachers. The foregoing synods belong to the Synodical Conference.*

The American Lutheran Church reported for 1953 that it maintained 44 parochial schools in North America, taught by 104 teachers. In India it has 111 village schools, taught by 307 teachers; two high schools and one industrial school (for girls), taught by 60 teachers.

E. *Teachers of Non-Lutheran Denominations.* The National Union of Christian Schools (non-denominational, but basically Christian Reformed and Dutch Reformed) in 1952 reported 158 schools. — Teachers receive their training at Calvin College, Grand Rapids, Mich. *The Mennonites* reported 59 parochial schools in 1952, all but two of them established since 1938. The number of teachers was not given. *The Orthodox Presbyterians,* during the same year, had three full-time elementary schools in operation. One school, opened during 1947, began with 97 pupils at Oostburg, Wis.

In 1953, churches of various Protestant denominations in America, including Baptists, Episcopalians, Christian, and others, had already established schools, and the National Association of Evangelicals (including 30 Protestant denominations) had formed a National School Association, and called Mark Fakkema, formerly Executive Secretary of the National Union of Christian Schools, to devote his whole time to the establishment of elementary schools. The Association has 83 schools, and all Protestant denominations several hundred. See also *Roman Catholic Education in the United States.* ACS

General works on Christian Education; *Hundred Years of Christian Education* (fourth Yearbook), Luth. Ed.

Assn., River Forest, Ill.; Edwin H. Rian, *Christianity and American Education;* Frank E. Gaebelein, *Christian Education in a Democracy.*

Teachers' Bureau. See *Teachers,* A 7.

Teachers' Seminaries. See *Teachers,* A 5.

Teachers' Training, Sunday School. See *Parish Education,* E 7.

Teaching. See *Christian Teaching.*

Te Deum Laudamus. One of the great canticles of the Christian Church; it has a fixed place in the Order of Matins and, in keeping with Lutheran tradition, should be sung often on Sundays and the great festivals of the church year. Its authorship cannot be determined with certainty. Many excellent musical setting of the Te Deum have been written. Luther's setting, formerly often heard in Lutheran churches, is based on Gregorian chant and is one of his great creations.

Tegner, Esaias. See *Sweden, Lutheran Church in, 4.*

Teichmueller, Gustav (1832—88). B. at Braunschweig; prof. at Dorpat; wrote *Philosophy of Religion,* in which he opposed developmental theories of religion, and positivism; he sought to base his religious views on a new metaphysics based on the Ego and consciousness of the divine; rejected the idea of a new life in Christ.

Telemann, Georg Philipp (1681 to 1767). Composer of the Lutheran Church who interested himself also in philosophy (Descartes), statesmanship, musical criticism, and musicology. Telemann was a leading spirit in German music activities of the late Baroque era; he was active particularly in Hamburg, where he helped guide the affairs of the Hamburg Opera and induced young Handel to become a composer and conductor of operas.

R. Haas, *Die Musik des Barocks,* Potsdam, 1927.

Teleological Argument. See *Apologetics; God, Arguments for Existence of; Immortality, Arguments for.*

Television. After World War II television became an important means of communication. By 1950, 105 television stations were operating in the United States. Religious organizations soon used television facilities, and the stations themselves sponsored religious programs. The Lutheran Television

Productions Committee of The Lutheran Church — Missouri Synod was organized June 28, 1951, and distributed the film "This Is the Life" in 1952—53. See *Radio Stations, Religious; Religious Drama.*

Teller, Wilhelm Abraham (1734 to 1804). Leading theologian of the Enlightenment in Germany; prof. at Helmstedt; provost of the high consistory at Berlin; sought to surmount orthodoxy and pietism with a mild rationalism; wrote *Lehrbuch des Christlichen Glaubens, Woerterbuch des Neuen Testaments, Die Religion der Vollkommenen* (Christian perfectibility).

Temperance Movements and the Lutheran Church. The temperance movement, advocating abstinence from the use of intoxicants, deals with an age-old problem in the United States. Legislation on the State and local level has been repeatedly tried throughout the 19th century, culminating in the 18th Amendment to the Federal Constitution in 1919, going into effect a year later. The amendment forbade the "manufacture, sale, or transportation of intoxicating liquors" in the United States and its territories, only to be repealed in the 21st Amendment to the Constitution in 1933.

The attitude of the Lutheran Church in America towards temperance movements has not always been uniform. The General and Northern Illinois Synods in 1853 expressed "great pleasure" over the passage of the "Maine Law" in 1844 forbidding the sale of intoxicating drinks in that State except by licensed agents. When in June, 1889, the State of Pennsylvania voted on a prohibitory amendment to the State Constitution, a large majority of the voters of the State did not favor it, even though the General Synod in convention assembled that year passed the following resolution: "The General Synod, in accord with previous deliverances of the Synod, bids the prohibitory Constitutional Amendment in Pennsylvania Godspeed and hopes her members, in the exercise of their Christian liberty as citizens, will all vote for it." The Augustana Synod in its convention of 1889 also expressed itself in favor of the amendment in a resolution. The same body urged the Nebraska voters in 1890 to adopt a prohibition amendment. In 1893 the United Norwegian Synod expressed the conviction "that it is the duty of every church member and citizen, by word and example, to take an active part in doing away with the godless and ruinous traffic."

In the present century various synods of the Lutheran Church have also been active in the temperance and prohibition movements. The General Synod in 1918 adopted the report of the Committee on Temperance, stating: "For this and all the great victories over organized and nefarious liquor traffic we give devout thanks to the great Head of the Church, who has beyond question providentially led and helped us in this great contest. Our Church of the General Synod has ever been found on the right side and by her ministers and laymen has actively and practically assisted in achieving this most significant victory of moral reform of all time."

The Augustana Synod resolved at its convention in 1930 "that we reaffirm our steadfast purpose to oppose any and all measures looking to the repeal of the Eighteenth Amendment." Other synods, especially the Scandinavian groups, have followed similar programs.

The Missouri Synod has followed the Scriptural principle expressed by St. Paul (Rom. 14:3, 15-21) that it is not in its sphere to pass any resolutions either for or against the manufacture or sale of intoxicating liquors. However, it has always held that excessive drinking is sinful and that reform can be achieved only through the Gospel of Christ. ARS

See minutes of the bodies mentioned above; *Lutheran Cyclopedia;* for general information E. H. Cherrington, *The Evolution of Prohibition in the United States,* 1920.

Templars, Knights. See *Military Religious Orders.*

Temporal Power. See *Papacy; States of the Church; Church and State.*

Temptation. The act of putting a quality of man to the test, specifically his life with and toward God. The Word of God describes this process of testing as carried out for the sake of two ultimate aims. This one is the aim of God to make man's need of God clear and thus drive him to God as source of spiritual life (1 Corinthians 10). The other purpose in the act of temptation is to loosen man's grasp on God and to plunge him into thoughts and acts contrary to his life in God and for God. World, flesh, and devil co-operate in activities toward that goal

(James 1 and 4). God Himself, in His great purpose, can employ also these tests for His great ends (Job 1 and 2). The alert Christian will recognize the struggle in his own life between the forces of God and of sin and will value every reminder to strengthen his own spiritual life and grow in grace; this quality of alertness composes the Christian's soberness and patience (Philippians 2 and 3; 1 Peter 5; 1 Thessalonians 5).

Tempus Clausum. See *Closed Season.*

Ten Articles. See *Anglican Confessions,* 1.

Ten Theses of Bern. See *Reformed Confessions,* A 2.

Tenebrae. The service of Matins and Lauds observed in the Roman Catholic Church on the nights of Wednesday, Thursday, and Friday of Holy Week. The service is dramatic, and the lessons are from the Lamentations of Jeremiah. While the responsory *Tenebrae factae sunt* has been used in the Lutheran Church ever since the 16th century, especially on Good Friday, the *Tenebrae* service as such has been used but rarely, since the theatrical character of the Roman *Tenebrae* was frowned upon by Lutherans.

Tennent, William. See *Presbyterian Bodies,* 4.

Tennessee Synod. See *Henkels; United Lutheran Church, Synods of,* 11.

Tennessee, Synod of Middle. Came out of the Kentucky and the Southern Illinois synods in 1878, consisted of about twenty small congregations, and belonged to the General Synod. Its pastors joined the Olive Branch Synod in 1894. See *United Lutheran Church, Synods of,* 19.

Tennyson, Alfred, Lord (1809—92). The most representative poet of the Victorian Age, was born the fourth in a family of twelve children in the rectory of Somersby in Lincolnshire. Tutored by his father, he later proceeded to Trinity College, Cambridge, where he won recognition by his poem *Timbuctoo.* His literary career dates from 1830, when he published a volume of lyrical poems. Among his better-known poems are *Palace of Art, Oenone, The Lady of Shalott, Locksley Hall, The Princess, Ode on the Death of the Duke of Wellington, Charge of the Light Brigade, Maud and Other Poems, Idylls of the King, Enoch Arden, The Holy Grail, Crossing the Bar.* In memory of his bosom friend Sir Arthur Hallam, Tennyson wrote the long elegy *In Memoriam.* In this work Tennyson offered a solution for the conflicts between science and religion which became popular.

Teresa, St. (1515—82). Spanish saint; mystic and visionary reformer; Carmelite; wrote her own life and *The Way of Perfection.*

Terminism. The teaching of a limited term of grace accorded to man as an individual. The doctrine is not identical with that of hardening of the heart (see *Sin*) or with that of the unpardonable sin (see *Sin, Unpardonable*); it assumes that God has from eternity fixed a day beyond which the individual will not respond to the operations of the Holy Spirit, or that every person has a special day of visitation. The Terministic Controversy involved the entire Lutheran Church early in the 18th century. Terminism was defended by the Pietists, who claimed such texts as Matt. 3:7 ff.; 7:21; 20:1-16; 2 Peter 2:20; Heb. 6:4 ff. The orthodox dogmaticians emphasized that God desires the salvation of every man during his entire life and that an abbreviated day of grace is due to the self-hardening of the heart against the means of grace. They based their opposition to Terminism on Luke 23:40 ff.; Rom. 5:20; Is. 65:2. Terminism has also been taught by the Quakers.

Territorial System. The theory of church government which assumes that temporal rulers have by virtue of their office the right to govern the Church, to regulate its affairs, to banish persons guilty of heresy and forbid the introduction of new creeds. The territorial system was formulated at the close of the 17th century, but even in the minds of its most ardent defenders never included the sovereign's right to impose his own belief upon his subjects, to dictate in matters of religion. See *Polity, Ecclesiastical; Collegiate System.*

Terry, Milton Spenser (1840—1914). Methodist Episcopal; b. at Coeymans, N. Y.; pastor near New York City; professor of Hebrew and Old Testament exegesis at Garrett Biblical Institute 1884. Author.

Tersanctus. See *Canticles.*

Tersteegen, Gerhard (1697—1769). B. at Moers (Muers) in Rhenish Prussia. He received a classical training in Latin at Moers. He then was apprenticed to his older brother, a shopkeeper at Muehlheim on the Ruhr. Later he started in business for himself, taking up the more lucrative occupation of weaving silk ribbons. He was religiously inclined from his youth and secured a cottage near Muehlheim, where he led a life of seclusion and self-denial for many years. In the course of time he began to exhort and preach in private, later in public, gatherings. His influence became very great. He wrote 111 hymns, most of which appeared in his *Spiritual Flower Garden.*

Tertiaries. Several Roman religious orders, besides having rules for monks and nuns, have a so-called Third Rule (hence tertiaries), under which the laity can join these orders. Tertiaries may be a) regular, living in convents, under simple vows, or b) secular, living in the world, bound only by a solemn promise. Some tertiaries wear the habit, the majority only the scapular of their order and, possibly, a girdle. They are bound to definite prayers and observances, to which certain indulgences are attached. Any Romanist may join a third order, but not more than one. The number of tertiaries cannot be given, but the Franciscans, the most numerous, number probably two and a half million throughout the world. Tertiaries contribute greatly to the power and prestige of the Roman Church.

Tertullian. The father of Latin theology and one of the greatest teachers of the early Church; b. at Carthage ca. 150; received a thorough training in ancient literature and philosophy; distinguished as an advocate and rhetorician; embraced Christianity between his thirtieth and fortieth year; some time later joined the Montanists, whose principles appealed to his rigid austerity and asceticism; d. between 220 and 240. Tertullian was a man of rare genius and originality, keen, witty, sarcastic and always intensely in earnest. A man of strong convictions and violent temper, he wields a vigorous pen. The determined foe of all worldly wisdom, he is the antithesis of Origen and asks scornfully: "What has Christ to do with Plato, Jerusalem with Athens?" His theology centers about the Pauline doctrine of sin and grace. His numerous writings fall into three classes: apologetic, polemic, and ethical. Among his apologetic works the *Apologeticus*

against the heathen is pre-eminent, a great plea for religious liberty. Supplementary to it is *De Testimonio Animae.* His polemics are directed chiefly against the Gnostics, besides including various tracts against particular errors (*Against Praxeas, On the Resurrection,* etc.). Ascetic writings: *On Prayer, On Penance, On Patience, De Spectaculis,* etc. Finally, Tertullian wrote various treatises in vindication of Montanism.

James Morgan, *The Importance of Tertullian in the Development of Christian Dogma,* Kegan Padel Trench, Trubner, London, 1928; see references under *Patristics.*

Test Act. An act passed in England in 1673 requiring a person to renounce the doctrine of transubstantiation to be eligible for public office. Its purpose was to exclude Roman Catholics from office.

Testament of Job. See *Apocrypha,* A 4.

Tests. See *Christian Teaching,* L 4.

Tetragrammaton. See *Shem-hammephorash.*

Tetrapolitan Confession. See *Reformed Confessions,* D 1.

Tetzel (Diez), Johann (ca. 1450 to 1519). The well-known Dominican friar and hawker of indulgences, whose unscrupulous effrontery in recommending the merits of his wares called forth Luther's protest and challenge and thus became the immediate occasion (not cause) of the Reformation.

Teutonic Knights. See *Military Religious Orders,* c.

Texas Synod. See *United Lutheran Church, Synods of,* 30.

Textual Criticism. That branch of theological study which aims to determine the incorruptness or integrity of the text in its individual parts, thereby laying the basis for actual interpretation. See *Manuscripts of the Bible.*

Westcott and Hort, *The New Testament in the Original Greek* (Introduction and Appendix), New York, 1882; F. G. Kenyon, *Handbook to the Textual Criticism of the New Testament,* London, 1912; Nestle-v. Dobschuetz, *Einfuehrung in das Griech. N. T.,* Goettingen, 1923 (4th ed.); A. T. Robertson, *Introduction to the Textual Criticism of the New Testament,* New York, 1925; W. Arndt, "The Chief Principles of New Testament Textual Criticism," *CTM,* V:

577—84; E. E. Flack, "The Sacred Text, the Lutheran Evaluation of Biblical Criticism," *What Lutherans Are Thinking*, Wartburg Press, Columbus, Ohio, 1947.

Tezcatlipoca. See *Aztecs, Religion of.*

Thailand. The name given to Siam on May 11, 1949. Country in eastern Asia. Area, 514,000 sq. mi.; population, 18,836,000 (1951), of Mongolian and Indonesian stock. Buddhism is the state religion. Animism prevails throughout the country. Islam has many followers. Nestorianism had a footing in the 19th century. Missions were begun by Karl Guetzlaff under the Netherlands Missionary Society in 1828. Persecutions have done much to hinder the work. The Church of Christ in Siam, American Baptists, Presbyterians, and Adventists carry on work. Statistics: 14,612 communicants; 40 ordained and 83 not-ordained native workers; a total of 172 in the foreign staff, 37 of them ordained. Roman Catholics, 53,000; 63 national and 57 foreign priests (1952). See *Missions, Bibliography.*

Thanksgiving Day. A festival celebrated in the United States, pursuant to a proclamation of the President and of the governors of the several States, on the fourth Thursday in November. It was first celebrated by the Pilgrims out of gratitude for their remarkable deliverance when famine seemed to stare them in the face (1621). After 1630 Thanksgiving was celebrated by the Pilgrims after each harvest. The first State to establish an annual Thanksgiving was New York (1830). The custom of setting the day aside for the purpose of worship became fixed when Abraham Lincoln issued a proclamation (1864) calling upon the nation to thank God and made the fourth Thursday in November the date for Thanksgiving.

Thayer, Joseph Henry (1828—1901). Congregational Biblical scholar; b. in Boston; professor at Andover and Harvard; d. at Cambridge. Translated Winer's and Buttmann's New Testament grammars and Wilke-Grimm *Clavis.*

Theater. Some ancient heathen authors (*e. g.*, Xenophon, Plato, Plutarch, Ovid, Seneca, and Tacitus) already pointed to the dangers of the theater. The early church fathers opposed the theater of their day on the grounds that it taught idolatry and was immoral. After the Christian Church had crushed the ancient drama, the latter did not revive for a thousand years. It was the Church which again brought the drama to the foreground, using it for religious instruction *(Passion Plays, Saints' Plays, Miracle Plays, Moralities).* These plays gradually lost their religious significance and were banned from the churches (where they had been performed), but in the meanwhile they had led to the revival of the secular theater. Humanism with its emphasis on the classics brought about renewed interest in the Greek and Roman dramas.

Luther shared the interest of contemporary scholars in Greek and Latin tragedies and comedies (XXII:1826). He felt that the comedies, in spite of their obscenity, should be read by youths in order that they might learn Latin and because the comedies urged youth to marry and taught the duties of various stations in life (XXII:1559). Though opposed to their immorality, idolatry, and anti-Scriptural thought, Luther at times quoted the ancient dramatists for the purpose of illustration or elucidation (*e. g.*, St. L. Ed., I:857, 895; III:1651; V:839, 1312, 1489). While he opposed the buffoonish (*schauspielerartig*) religious dramas as presented under the Papacy, Luther encouraged the use of drama for spreading the Word. He points out that when the preaching of the Word was forbidden in the Netherlands, many were converted through religious plays (XXIb:2856).

The Lutheran dogmaticians (*e. g.*, Leonard Hutter, Dannhauer, Buddeus) included comedies among the plays as evils which aroused passions and lusts. Lutheran theologians in America (*e. g.*, Walther, A. L. Graebner, C. C. Schmidt, Louis Fuerbringer) continued to warn against the evils of the theater of their day. An example of the warnings in the third decade of the twentieth century may be found in the *Concordia Cyclopedia* (1927 edition).

In the fourth decade the immorality of the theater called forth the following resolutions of the National Lutheran Council against the moving picture menace: "Motion pictures might be at all times and often are legitimate entertainment as well as an important educational factor. . . . But at the present time many pictures stand charged with serious offenses against decency and morality. . . . We appeal to our Lutheran people to withhold their patronage from all motion pictures which have a degrading influence and are a menace to home, church, and country." Lutheran people were called upon to make their influence felt in creating a public opinion opposed to such motion pictures and to bring pressure for legislation against immoral pictures.

The fifth decade witnessed an improvement in the type of pictures shown in response to an aroused public opinion, as outlined above, and pressure of such groups as the Roman Catholic League for Decency. There were indications that movies and theaters were at times being used for cultural and educational purposes. See *Religious Drama*. EM

C. F. W. Walther, "Etwas den Theaterbesuch betreffend," *Luth*. 25:92 to 94; A. L. Graebner, "Das heutige Theater," *Luth*. 56:17—20; C. C. S. (Schmidt?), "Das Theater im Gegensatz zum Christentum," *Luth*. 48:72; L. Fuerbringer, "Das heutige Theater," *Luth*. 60:18—20; T. Graebner, "Das heutige Theater," *Luth*. 70:154—157; *CTM*, VI:306 f.

Theatines. Founded by G. P. Carafa (later, Paul IV) in 1529 for the purpose of elevating the lives of the clergy and laity; became known for mission activity.

Thebesius, Adam (1596—1652). B. at Seifersdorf, studied at Wittenberg; at time of his death pastor in Liegnitz; known for his gift of fervent prayer; wrote: "O grosser Schmerzensmann."

Theism. In opposition to atheism, general term for any kind of belief in God, embracing the various forms of monotheism and polytheism. In a more restricted sense, in opposition to deism and pantheism, a monotheistic belief in a personal God, who is not only the Creator, but also the Preserver and Ruler of the world.

T. Graebner, *God and the Cosmos*; L. S. Keyser, *A System of Natural Theism*.

Theiss, John William. B. Sept. 20, 1863, at Zelienople, Pa.; grad. Concordia Seminary, St. Louis, 1886; pastor, Madisonville, Ohio, 1886—89; Portland, Oreg., 1889—93; Santa Rosa, Calif., 1894 to 1904; Los Angeles, Calif., 1904—28. Poet. Wrote: *Gepflueckt am Wege*, etc.; d. March 3, 1932.

Theocracy. A form of government, as that of ancient Israel, in which God is directly recognized as the civil Ruler

and gives laws in the political as well as moral realm.

Theodicy. The vindication of God's justice in dealing with mankind and of His wisdom in governing the world. The word dates back to the celebrated essay by this name, published by Leibniz in 1710, but has since been used as a more general term for the rational argument in defense of divine love, wisdom, and justice. Its particular purpose is to demonstrate the righteousness of God with reference to sin and to physical evil (suffering) existing in the world and to show that, in spite of sin and other evils, God appears in the creation and government of the world as the highest Wisdom and Goodness. See *Leibniz*.

Theodore of Mopsuestia (ca. 350 to 428). An exegete of the Antiochian school; made bishop of Mopsuestia, in Cilicia, ca. 392; wrote commentaries on almost all the books of Scripture; but his rationalistic mode of interpretation and the odium his pupil Nestorius brought upon his name later led to his condemnation in the *Tria Capitula*, a judgment confirmed by the Council of Constantinople in 553. The Three Chapters condemned the writings of Theodore of Mopsuestia, of Theodoret of Cyprus, and a letter of Ibas. See *Three Chapters, Controversy of*.

Theodore of Studion (759?—826). B. in Constantinople; became a monk, 781; through his ability for organization he revived the monastery of Studion in Constantinople through adaptation of the rule of St. Basil; championed the worship of images; his charges of adultery against Constantine VI and position on image worship brought him frequent persecutions and banishment.

Theodore of Tarsus (602—90). B. at Tarsus; ed. at Athens; monk in Tarsus and Rome; made archbishop of Canterbury (667) and united the English Church with Rome and established papal supremacy in England.

Theodoret (ca. 386—ca. 457). Bishop of Cyrus in Syria; a disciple of Theodore of Mopsuestia, but avoided the rationalistic tendencies of his teacher; besides commentaries on the Old Testament he wrote an *Ecclesiastical History*, a continuation of that of Eusebius. Becoming involved in the Nestorian and Eutychian controversies of his time, he was deposed by the Robber Synod of Ephesus in 449, but reinstated by the Council of Chalcedon in 451.

Theodosius I (ca. 346—95). Surnamed the Great. Elevated to the purple by Gratian he became Emperor of the East, repelling the Gothic invasion along the Danube. Baptized in 380 as a Trinitarian, he promulgated various edicts against Arianism and other heresies and summoned the second General Council (381) to supplement the labors of Nicaea. Living for some years at Milan, he enjoyed the friendship of its bishop, St. Ambrose. When, in 390, he ordered the masacre of Thessalonica, Ambrose refused him permission to enter the church at Milan, readmitting him to the Sacrament only after the performance of public penance. Theodosius was sole emperor for four months before his death in 395.

Theodotians. See *Monarchianism,* A 2.

Theodulf of Orleans (d. 821). Influential theologian at the time of Charlemagne; bishop of Orleans; advanced education and culture among clergy and lay people; accused of conspiracy, he was banished under Louis the Pious to Angers, where he died.

Theological Argument. See *Apologetics; God* (Apologetics).

Theological Education. See *Ministry, Education of.*

Theological Education, Lutheran Postgraduate. There are six Lutheran theological seminaries in America offering work in theology beyond the B. D. degree. These are Concordia Seminary in St. Louis, Mo.; Augustana Theological Seminary, Rock Island, Ill.; Chicago Lutheran Seminary, Maywood, Ill.; Hamma Divinity School, Springfield, Ohio; Lutheran Theological Seminary of Philadelphia (Mount Airy), Pa.; and Lutheran Theological Seminary, Gettysburg, Pa.

The Graduate School of Concordia Seminary, St. Louis, Mo. — History. The Graduate School of Concordia Seminary was established by resolution of Synod in 1920. The first graduate courses were offered in 1922, six students enrolling. Owing to the peculiar conditions of the 1930's (the nationwide economic depression, teaching staff undermanned, large undergraduate classes), the graduate work was discontinued from 1931 to 1938. In the fall of 1938 graduate courses were resumed and the activities of the school were expanded to include pastors' institutes and extension work. In 1941 the Mis-

sion Department was included in the Graduate School. In the summer of 1951, Summer School on the graduate level was inaugurated. In the same year Graduate Hall was erected to provide more adequate room and other facilities for the growing Graduate School.

Courses Offered. The Graduate School of Concordia Seminary offers advanced courses in all departments of theology, including philosophy. The Mission Department offers a variety of courses preparatory for service in foreign mission fields and for work among the deaf and foreign-language groups.

Requirements for Admission. To be admitted to the Graduate School of Concordia Seminary, the applicant must hold the degrees of Bachelor of Arts and Bachelor of Divinity or their equivalents and must have maintained a high scholarly record for previous work done in theology.

Degrees Conferred. The Graduate School of Concordia Seminary offers work toward the S. T. M. and since 1944 also toward the Th. D. degree.

The Graduate School of Concordia Seminary has as its background the traditions of theological scholarship transplanted to American soil from the great German universities of the early 19th century. It has a faculty of specialists for every department and an expanding library for graduate work.

Augustana Theological Seminary, Rock Island, Ill. Augustana Theological Seminary began to offer graduate work as early as 1892. The degree to which the course led was called C. S. T., which was a prerequisite for the degree of Doctor of Sacred Theology. No specific residence requirements were made, but the candidate was guided in his pursuit of advanced studies in all departments of theology by a system of supervised home study and personal consultation. A thesis and comprehensive examinations completed the requirements for the degree.

In 1935 this plan was discontinued. Since then the graduate department has been reorganized, and Augustana offers postgraduate work leading to the Master's degree, for which 24 hours of credits plus a thesis and comprehensive examinations are required.

Chicago Lutheran Seminary, Maywood, Ill. Chicago Lutheran Seminary was one of the first among Lutheran seminaries in America to offer postgraduate courses in theology. Like

Augustana, it began this work in the early 90's of the last century. The postgraduate work offered was designed to lead to the degree of Doctor of Divinity. This original program of graduate studies was discontinued some years ago and replaced by a graduate school which aims to meet the requirements of contemporary graduate standards.

The seminary offers to pastors courses leading to the graduate degrees of Master of Sacred Theology and Doctor of Sacred Theology. The S. T. M. is considered chiefly an aid to the pastors of superior initiative and intelligence who wish further to enrich their pastoral service. The Doctor's degree is, in a particular sense, reserved to the student giving promise of developing unusual ability in, and of making original contributions to, a specialized field of theological learning.

Graduates of approved institutions holding the Bachelor of Divinity degree or its equivalent are eligible for admission to graduate studies.

Hamma Divinity School, Springfield, Ohio. Graduate work at Hamma Divinity School was introduced in 1924. Only the Master's degree is conferred. Requirements are 24 semester hours beyond the B. D. plus a thesis. Greek and Hebrew are the specific language requirements. The degree must be earned within five years.

Lutheran Theological Seminary of Philadelphia (Mount Airy), Pa. Graduate work in theology was first offered at Lutheran Theological Seminary at Philadelphia in 1913. Work is offered for the Master's degree. The requirements for this degree are 24 semester hours. No specific language requirements, unless necessary in the particular area in which the candidate is concentrating his studies, are demanded.

Lutheran Theological Seminary, Gettysburg, Pa. Graduate work at Gettysburg was started in the mid-20's. Work is offered toward the Master's degree only. Requirements for this degree, 24 semester hours plus thesis and comprehensive examination. Language requirements are one additional language besides English.

The Needs for Graduate Studies in the Lutheran Church of America. At the beginning of the 20th century the pastor was still the best and frequently the only educated man in his community. Even as late as 1910 there were few high school students to be found in the average parish of the Lutheran Church, and college graduates were exceedingly rare. There has been a tremendous progress in education in America since that time. In 1949 to 1950 the colleges and universities of the United States conferred a total of 433,734 Bachelor and first professional degrees. There are 324 colleges and universities in the United States offering graduate work. In 1949—50 a total of 58,219 Master degrees and 6,633 Doctor degrees were conferred. The six graduate schools in the Lutheran Church of America have, compared with these figures, an insignificant enrollment, and there are only a few graduate schools of theology in other church bodies which could be compared with the graduate schools of our secular colleges and universities.

In the past, American Lutheranism could look to the great Lutheran universities of Europe for leadership in theological research and scholarship. But as a result of World War II, many of these schools were lost to unhampered Lutheran theology or have been so seriously crippled in financial support and personnel that it will require considerable time before they can possibly regain their former eminence. This situation placed a new responsibility upon the Lutheran Church in America and its theological schools.

AMR

Theological Encyclopedia. See *Encyclopedia, Theological.*

Theological Journal. See *American Lutheran Conference,* 10.

Theological Journals. A partial listing of the more important current theological and religious journals with denominational background, if known. This listing is not intended to be exhaustive.

SCHOLARLY

(Unless otherwise indicated, these appear quarterly)

American Ecclesiastical Review, monthly (Roman Catholic) — Catholic University of America Press, Washington 17, D. C.

Anglican Theological Review (Episcopalian) — 600 Haven St., Evanston, Ill.

Australasian Theological Review (Lutheran) — 70 Pirie St., Adelaide, South Australia

Bible League Quarterly (Non-denominational) — Bible League, Drayton House, Gordon St., London W. C. 1, England

Bible Translator (Non-denominational)

— United Bible Societies, 146 Queen Victoria St., London E. C. 4, England

Bibliotheca Sacra (Baptist) — Dallas Theological Seminary, 3909 Swiss Ave., Dallas 4, Tex.

Catholic Biblical Quarterly (R. C.) — Catholic University of America Washington 17, D. C.

Catholic Historical Review (R. C.) — Catholic University of America Washington 17, D. C.

Christian Scholar (Non-denominational) — Commission on Higher Education N. C. C. A., 257 4th Ave., New York 10, N. Y.

Church History (Non-denominational) — American Society of Church History, Witherspoon Bldg., Philadelphia 7, Pa.

Church Quarterly Review (Anglican) — Welbeck St., London W. 1, England

Concordia Theological Monthly (Lutheran) — 3558 S. Jefferson, Saint Louis 18, Mo.

Cross Currents (Non-denominational) — 3111 Broadway, New York 27, N. Y.

Deutsches Pfarrerblatt — Essener Druckerei, Gemeinwohl, G. m. b. H. Kaninenbergstr. 41, Essen, Germany

Ecumenical Review (Non-denominational) — World Council of Churches, 156 Fifth Ave., New York 10, N. Y.

Erevna (Swedish Lutheran) — Prof. H. Odeberg, Box 91, Lund, Sweden

Evangelical Quarterly (Reformed) — James Clarke & Co., Ltd., 5 Wardrobe Pl., London E. C. 4, England

Evangelische Theologie, monthly — Christian Kaiser Verlag, Muenchen, Germany

Expositor and Homiletic Review, monthly — The Expositor East Aurora, N. Y.

Fuer Arbeit und Besinnung, semimonthly (Protestant) — Buchhandlung der Evang. Gesellschaft, Stuttgart S, Faeberstrasse 2, Germany

Harvard Theological Review (Non-denominational) — Harvard University Press, Cambridge 38, Mass.

Hibbert Journal (Reformed) — George Allen & Unwin, Ltd., 40 Museum St., London W. C. 1, England

Iliff Review, 3 issues annually (Methodist) — The Criterion Press, 2201 S. University Blvd., Denver 10, Colo.

International Journal of Religious Education, monthly — 79 East Adams St., Chicago 3, Ill.

International Review of Missions — Edinburgh House, 2 Eaton Gate London S. W. 1, England

Interpretation (Non-denominational) — 3401 Brook Rd., Richmond 27, Va.

Journal of Bible and Religion (Non-denominational) — National Association of Biblical Instructors 73 Main St., Brattleboro, Vt.

Journal of Biblical Literature (Non-denominational) — Society of Biblical Literature and Exegesis, 222 N. 15th St., Philadelphia 2, Pa.

Journal of Religion (Non-denominational) — University of Chicago Press, 5750 Ellis Ave., Chicago 37, Ill.

Lutheran Education, monthly — 3558 S. Jefferson Ave., St. Louis 18, Mo.

Lutheran Quarterly — 18 Carlisle St., Gettysburg, Pa.

Moslem World (or Muslim World) — Hartford Seminary Foundation Hartford 5, Conn.

Pastoral Psychology, monthly — 159 Northern Blvd. Great Neck, New York

Quartalschrift — Theological Quarterly (Lutheran) — Northwestern Publishing House, Milwaukee 8, Wis.

Reformation Review (Non-denominational) — International Council of Christian Churches, 15 Park Row, New York 38, N. Y.

Reformed Journal, monthly — 255 Jefferson Ave., S. E., Grand Rapids, Mich.

Religion in Life (Non-denominational) — Abingdon-Cokesbury Press, 150 Fifth Ave., New York 11, N. Y.

Religious Education, semimonthly — 545 W. 111th St., New York 25, N. Y.

Review and Expositor (Baptist) — 2825 Lexington Rd., Louisville 6, Ky.

Review of Religion, semiannually (Non-denominational) — Columbia University Press, 2960 Broadway, New York 27, N. Y.

Student World (Non-denominational) — Student Christian Movement 156 Fifth Ave., New York 10, N. Y.

Theological Studies (Jesuit) — Woodstock College, Woodstock, Md.

Theologische Literaturzeitung, monthly — J. C. Hinrichs Verlag, Scherlstr. 2, Leipzig, Germany

Theologische Zeitschrift (Reformed) — Verlag Friedrich Reinhardt, A. G., Basel 12, Switzerland

Theology Today (Presbyterian) — P. O. Box 29, Princeton, N. J.

Union Seminary Quarterly Review (Non-denominational) — Union Theological Seminary, 3041 Broadway, New York 7, N. Y.

Westminster Theological Journal (Orthodox Presbyterian) — Chestnut Hill, Philadelphia 18, Pa.

Zeitschrift fuer die Alttestamentliche Wissenschaft — Verlag Alfred Toepelmann, Berlin W 35, Germany

Zeitschrift fuer die Neutestamentliche Wissenschaft — Verlag Alfred Toepelmann, Berlin W 35, Germany

Zeitwende, monthly — Evangelisches Verlagswerk, Stafflenbergstr. 28, Stuttgart O, Germany

POPULAR

(Unless otherwise indicated, these are weekly)

America (Roman Catholic) —
329 W. 108th St., New York 25, N. Y.

American Lutheran, monthly —
1819 Broadway, New York 23, N. Y.

Ansgar Lutheran (United Evangelical Lutheran Church) — Lutheran Publishing House, Blair, Nebraska

Augustinian, quarterly (North American Old Roman Catholic Church) — P. O. Box 1002, Lansing, Michigan.

Australian Lutheran, biweekly (Evangelical Lutheran Church) — Lutheran Publishing House, 70 Pirie St., Adelaide, South Australia

Bible Banner, monthly — 1619 Portland Ave., Minneapolis 4, Minn.

Bible Society Record, monthly —
450 Park Ave., New York 22, N. Y.

Biblical Archaeologist, quarterly —
Drawer A, Yale Station
New Haven, Conn.

Biblical Missions, monthly (Presbyterian) — 246 West Walnut Lane Philadelphia 44, Pa.

Catholic Digest, monthly —
41 E. Eighth St., St. Paul 2, Minn.

Catholic World, monthly —
411 W. 59th St., New York 19, N. Y.

Christian Advocate (Methodist) —
740 Rush St., Chicago 11, Ill.

Christian Beacon (Bible Presbyterian) — Hadder and Frazer Aves., Collingswood, N. J.

Christian Century (Non-denominational) — 407 S. Dearborn, Chicago 5, Ill.

Christian Evangelist (Disciples of Christ) — Christian Board of Publication, St. Louis 3, Mo.

Christian Herald, monthly —
419 Fourth Ave., New York, N. Y.

Christian Life, monthly (Non-denominational) — 434 S. Wabash, Chicago 5, Ill.

Christian Register, monthly —
25 Beacon St., Boston 8, Mass.

Church Management, monthly —
1900 Euclid Ave., Cleveland 15, Ohio

Churchman, biweekly (Anglican) —
Churchman Co., New York 16, N. Y.

Commonweal (Roman Catholic) —
386 Fourth Ave., New York 16, N. Y.

Confessional Lutheran, monthly —
310 S. Cherry St., Morrison, Ill.

Converted Catholic, monthly —
27 E. 22nd St., New York 10, N. Y.

Current Religious Thought, bimonthly — Current Religious Thought Press, Oberlin, Ohio

Evangelisch-Lutherische Kirchenzeitung, biweekly — Evangelische Presseverband fuer Bayern, Himmelreichstrasse 4, Muenchen 22, Germany

Evangelisch-Lutherisches Kirchenblatt, bimonthly — Prof. H. Rottman, Caixa Postal 911, Porto Alegre, R. G. S.

Faith-Life, monthly (Protes'tant Group — Wisconsin) — Mosinee, Wisconsin

Friends-Intelligencer (Friends) —
1515 Cherry St., Philadelphia 2, Pa.

King's Business (Episcopal) — 558 S. Hope St., Los Angeles 13, Calif.

Living Church (Episcopal) — Church Literature Foundation, 407 E. Michigan St., Milwaukee 2, Wis.

Lutheran (United Lutheran Church) — United Lutheran Publishing House, 1228 Spruce St., Philadelphia 7, Pa.

Lutheran Beacon, monthly (Slovak Ev. Lutheran Church) — Pioneer Globe Printers, 420 S. Sixth St., Minneapolis 15, Minn.

Lutheran Companion (Augustana Synod) — Augustana Book Concern, 639 38th St., Rock Island, Ill.

Lutheran Herald (Evangelical Lutheran Church) — Augsburg Publishing House, Minneapolis 15, Minn.

Lutheran Sentinel, biweekly (Norwegian Synod) — Lake Mills, Iowa

Lutheran Standard (American Lutheran Church) — Wartburg Press, 55 E. Main St., Columbus 15, Ohio

Lutheran Witness, biweekly (The Lutheran Church — Missouri Synod) — Concordia Publishing House, 3558 S. Jefferson Ave., St. Louis 18, Mo.

Lutheran World, quarterly (National Lutheran Council) —
50 Madison Ave., New York 10, N. Y.

Lutheraner, biweekly (The Lutheran Church — Missouri Synod) — Concordia Publishing House, 3558 S. Jefferson Ave., St. Louis 18, Mo.

Moody Bible Institute, monthly — 820 S. La Salle St., Chicago 10, Ill.

National Council Outlook, monthly (N. C. C. A.) — 297 Fourth Ave., New York 10, N. Y.

National Lutheran (National Lutheran Council) — 50 Madison Ave., New York 10, N. Y.

Northwestern Lutheran, biweekly (Wisconsin Synod) — Northwestern Publishing House, 3616-32 West North Ave., Milwaukee 8, Wis.

Orthodox Lutheran, monthly (Orthodox Lutheran Conference) — The Orthodox Lutheran, Okabena, Minn.

Pastor, The, monthly (Methodist) — Methodist Publishing House 810 Broadway, Nashville 2, Tenn.

Presbyterian Guardian, monthly — 728 Schaff Building, 1505 Race St., Philadelphia 2, Pa.

Presbyterian Life, semimonthly (North Presbyterian) — 321 S. Fourth St., Philadelphia 6, Pa.

Presbyterian Outlook — 1 N. Sixth St., Richmond 19, Va.

Pulpit Digest, monthly — 159 Northern Blvd., Great Neck, N. Y.

Revelation, now *Eternity* (Presbyterian) — P. O. Box 2000, Philadelphia 3, Pa.

Shepherds (Methodist) — 1908 Grand Ave., Nashville 4, Tenn.

Watchman-Examiner (Baptist) — 23 E. 26th St., New York 10, N. Y.

EJS

Theological Problems. See *Open Questions.*

Theological Schools. See *Ministry, Education of.*

Theological Society, American. Association organized 1912 for fostering "the interests of present-day constructive theology" by providing discussion, fellowship, and joint projects; confined to theological experts in the vicinity of New York City.

Theology. In the abstract or narrow, that is, proper, sense a practical, God-given quality, by which a person may understand, accept, expound, impart to others, and defend, the truth of Scriptures as containing the way of salvation. In its wider, concrete sense the entire body of knowledge pertaining to the understanding and exposition of the Bible. This knowledge is commonly divided into four groups: 1) exegetical theology, which includes Biblical isagogics and the history of the canon and translations, hermeneutics and textual criticism, exegesis of the Old and the New Testament, and a study of modern translations; 2) systematic theology, which embraces dogmatics or doctrinal theology, the study of the Symbolical Books, moral philosophy and Christian ethics, and often also apologetics and polemics; 3) historical theology, which includes church history and archaeology and its various periods, the history of dogma and confessions, and pa-

tristics; 4) practical theology, with subdivision of pastoral theology and church polity, catechetics, homiletics, diaconics and missions, liturgics and hymnology, and Christian art and architecture.

Theology, Natural. Man has a natural knowledge of God (Rom. 1:19 ff.; Acts 14:16 f.; 17:26 ff.). This is not contradicted by texts which declare that natural man does not "know" God (Eph. 2:12; Gal. 4:8). Saving faith through knowledge and acceptance of Christ is created by the Holy Spirit through the Word. Yet the light of reason is sufficient to establish not only the existence but also such attributes as the power, the wisdom, and the justice of God, by induction and deduction, to the satisfaction of the human mind, which bears the idea of God within itself and naturally demands of, and dictates to, itself and other rational minds some recognition of the first fundamental truths of natural theology. Of course the religions of the heathen world and the books of ancient and modern philosophers also bear witness to the truth that human reason in its present natural state is woefully depraved. The Apostle teaches that the mind of natural man is vain, his understanding darkened, his heart hardened, insensible to impressions, that the god of this world has blinded the minds of them which believe not (Eph. 4:17 f.; 2 Cor. 4:4). God's handwriting in nature bears with it a natural conviction, while the power of Scripture is supernatural, effecting in the heart of the reader a spiritual discernment and divine assurance of the truths therein set forth (1 Cor. 2:7 ff.). See *Apologetics.*

Theopaschites. Believers in the doctrine of Theopaschitism, or Patripassianism, the doctrine, defended especially by Monophysites, that when Christ suffered and died, the entire Godhead suffered and died, especially the Father. The doctrine was rejected by orthodox Christianity on the basis of the fact that Scripture teaches that only the Son of God became incarnate, suffered, and died, and not the Father and the Holy Ghost.

Theophany. A designation applied in general to all manifestations or visible appearances of a supreme being or a deity, so that there is a possibility of a direct communication between God and man, especially in a direct impartation of His will and Word. In the Old Testament, theophanies occurred in particular when God revealed Himself in some kind of visible form, as in Isaiah 6, or when the Second Person of the Godhead manifested Himself as the Angel of the Lord or the Angel of the Presence in numerous instances. It would seem that the Lord never showed Himself in the fullness of His majesty, for in Ex. 33:18 ff. the direct vision of the glory is denied to Moses, and only an afterglimpse is permitted when the Lord has passed by.

Theophylact (d. ca. 1107). Archbishop of Achrida and metropolitan of Bulgaria in 1078; wrote commentaries on the Minor Prophets and on the greater part of the New Testament.

Theopneustia. A term denoting the fact that Holy Scripture was given by the process of "God-breathing," by which the Holy Spirit "in-breathed" or inspired into the holy writers the very thoughts and words which He wished them to write. The doctrine is based upon 2 Tim. 3:16: "All Scripture is God-breathed," which the Authorized Version renders: ". . . is given by the inspiration of God." On the basis of Scripture orthodox theology teaches both the verbal and the plenary inspiration of the Scriptures, both of which the term *Theopneustia* implies.

Theosophy. 1. This term is employed rather loosely to denote those philosophical systems which claim to enable man to know God and divine things by direct inspiration and direct contact with deity. In the Orient it is represented chiefly by Buddhistic mysticism. The Neo-Platonic philosophy of Plotinus is another form of theosophy. In the Middle Ages the mysticism of Meister Eckhardt and Jacob Boehme is correctly termed "Theosophy."

2. In modern times theosophy is represented in the teachings of the Theosophical Society. This society was organized in New York in 1875 by Mme. Helena Petrovna Blavatsky (1831—91), Russian, who traveled extensively in America and India, where she is alleged to have contacted Mahatmas, or "Great One," the chief idea apparently being an amalgamation of Christianity and Buddhism, to which end she and her followers studied Arian, occult, cabalistic, and Indian writings and also spiritism, unexplained laws of nature, and physical powers of man.

3. The promoters of the cult promise a clear insight into the immaterial, spiritual world and power to perform miracles, one of their aims also being the universal brotherhood of humanity without distinction of race, creed, or color. That the cult is blasphemous is evident even from this summary, and we may summarize its antagonism to Christianity under three points. First, theosophy is pantheistic. Its founder, Madame Blavatsky, says: "We believe in a universal divine principle, the root All." Theosophy rejects a personal God. It believes that God is made up of everything. Horse and star and tree and man are parts of the theosophist's god. Secondly, theosophy teaches reincarnation. It says that we have three souls, an animal soul, a human soul, and a spiritual soul. The animal soul becomes, after a while, a wandering thing, passing into other human beings. The soul keeps wandering on and on and may have innumerable different forms. It is simply the old Hindu doctrine of the transmigration of souls, slightly refined to suit European and American tastes. In a country where lizards and cows are not worshiped it would hardly do to try to proselyte people to the Hindu faith that they or their children may be reborn as lizards, cats, or cows! Hence, theosophy confines reincarnation to the human race. The third main point of theosophy in its antagonism to the Christian religion is the doctrine of the so-called "karma," or the "doctrine of consequences." It was the doctrine of Buddha and of Robert Ingersoll. It is the old heathen fatalism in its crudest form. According to the "karma," men are under the merciless law of cause and effect to the extent that it is useless to repent; for there is no one to forgive. It is all a question of consequence, that's all. Hence there is no place for prayer, repentance, and forgiveness in the theosophic system.

4. The Yoga * system looms large in modern theosophy. Yoga is a short cut to human perfection by observing certain bodily and mental exercises. The bodily exercises include correct breathing, proper posture, contortions, and total abstinence to weaken the body. The mental exercises include absolute concentration and ultimate union of the mind with the cosmic soul.

5. In Madame Blavatsky's *Key to Theosophy*, a kind of catechism, written evidently for simple-minded Christian people, she makes use of the following dialog: "Do you believe in God?" Answer: "That depends on what you mean

by the term." "I mean," says the inquirer, "the God of the Christians, the Father of Jesus, and the Creator, the Biblical God of Moses, in short." Answer: "In such a God we do not believe." Question: "Do you believe in prayer, and do you ever pray?" Answer: "We do not. We act instead of talking." Question: "Then you also reject resurrection in the flesh?" Answer: "Most decidedly we do." According to the same textbook theosophists profess to believe "in a universal divine principle." Theosophy denies that there is eternal reward or eternal punishment. It rejects the vicarious atonement of Jesus and the remission of sin.

Therapeutae. A group of ascetics in Egypt which existed at the time of Philo of Alexandria and are described by him in his *Concerning the Contemplative Life.*

Therapeutic. See *Psychology,* J 7.

Thesaurus Meritorum. A treasury of merits which the Roman Catholic Church claims to possess and from which it grants indulgences.* The treasury is supposedly filled by merits of Christ and superabundant work of saints.

Theses, Altenburg. See *Altenburg Debate and Theses.*

Theses, Ninety-Five, of Harms. Claus Harms at Kiel in 1817 published Luther's Ninety-five Theses together with ninety-five of his own against Rationalism and the union of the Lutheran and Reformed Churches; a great stir resulted.

Claus Harms, *Das sind die 95 Thesen oder Streitsaetze Dr. Luthers, theuren Andenkens, — zum besondern Abdruck besorgt und mit andern 95 Saetzen als mit einer Uebersetzung aus A. 1517 in 1817 begleitet,* Academ. Buchhandl., Kiel, 1817; Claus Harms, *Briefe zu einer naehern Verstaendigung ueber verschiedene meine Thesen betreffende Puncte, nebst einem namhaften Briefe, an den Herrn Dr. Schleiermacher,* Academ. Buchhandl., Kiel, 1818.

Theses, Ninety-Five, of Luther. 1. Our Lord and Master Jesus Christ, in saying: "Repent ye," etc., intended that the whole life of believers should be penitence. 2. This word cannot be understood of sacramental penance, that is, of the confession and satisfaction which are performed under the ministry of priests. 3. It does not, however, refer solely to inward penitence; nay, such inward penitence is naught unless it outwardly produces various mortifications of the flesh. 4. The penalty thus continues as long as the hatred of self — that is, true inward penitence — continues, namely, till our entrance into the kingdom of heaven. 5. The Pope has neither the will nor the power to remit any penalties, except those which he has imposed by his own authority or by that of the canons. 6. The Pope has no power to remit any guilt except by declaring or warranting it to have been remitted by God or, at most, by remitting cases reserved for himself; in which cases, if his power were despised, guilt would certainly remain. 7. God never remits any man's guilt without at the same time subjecting him, humbled in all things, to the authority of His representative, the priest. 8. The penitential canons are imposed only on the living, and according to them no burden ought to be imposed on the dying. 9. Hence the Holy Spirit acting in the Pope does well for us, in that, in his decrees, he always makes exception of the article of death and of necessity. 10. Those priests act wrongly and unlearnedly who, in the case of the dying, reserve the canonical penances for purgatory. 11. Those tares about changing the canonical penalties into the penalty of purgatory surely seem to have been sown while the bishops were asleep. 12. Formerly the canonical penalties were imposed not after, but before absolution, as tests of true contrition. 13. The dying pay all penalties by death and are already dead to the canon laws and are by right relieved from them. 14. The imperfect soundness or charity of a dying person necessarily brings with it great fear, and the less it is, the greater the fear it brings. 15. This fear and horror are sufficient by themselves, to say nothing of other things, to constitute the pains of purgatory, since it is very near to the horror of despair. 16. Hell, purgatory, and heaven appear to differ as despair, near-despair, and peace of mind differ. 17. With souls in purgatory, seemingly, it must needs be so, that, as horror diminishes, charity increases. 18. Nor does it seem to be proved, by any reasoning or any Scriptures, that they are outside of the state of merit or of the increase of charity. 19. Nor does this appear to be proved that they are sure and confident of their own blessedness, at least not all of them, though we may be very sure of it. 20. Therefore the Pope, when he speaks of the plenary remissions of all penalties, does not mean simply of all, but only of those imposed by himself. 21. Thus those preachers of indulgences are in error who say that by the indulgences of the Pope a man is loosed and saved from all punishment. 22. For in fact he remits to souls in purgatory no penalty which, according to the canons, they would have had to pay in this life. 23. If any entire remission of all penalties can be granted to anyone, it is certain that it is granted to none but the most perfect, that is, to very few. 24. Hence the greater part of the people must needs be deceived by this indiscriminate and high-sounding promise of release from penalties. 25. The same powers which the Pope has over purgatory in general, every bishop has in his own diocese, and, in particular, every curate in his own parish. 26. The Pope acts most rightly in granting remission to souls, not by the power of the keys (which is of no avail in this case), but by way of suffrage. 27. They preach human doctrine who say that the soul flies out of purgatory as soon as the money thrown into the chest rattles. 28. It is certain that, when the money rattles in the chest, avarice and gain may be increased, but the suffrage of the Church depends on the will of God alone. 29. Who knows whether all the souls in purgatory desire to be redeemed from it, according to the story told of Saints Severinus and Paschal? 30. No man is sure of the reality of his own contrition, much less of the attainment of plenary remission. 31. Rare as is a true penitent, so rare is one who truly buys indulgences, that is to say, most rare. 32. Those who believe that through letters of pardon they are made sure of their own salvation will be eternally damned along with their teachers. 33. We must especially beware of those who say that these pardons from the Pope are that inestimable gift of God by which man is reconciled to God. 34. For the grace conveyed by these pardons has respect only to the penalties of sacramental satisfaction, which are of human appointment. 35. They preach no Christian doctrine who teach that contrition is not necessary for those who buy souls out of purgatory or buy confessional licenses. 36. Every Christian who feels true compunction over his sins has plenary remission of pain and guilt, even without letters of indulgence. 37. Every true Christian, whether living or dead, has a share in

all the benefits of Christ and of the Church, given him by God, even without letters of indulgence. 38. The remission, however, imparted by the Pope is by no means to be despised, since it is, as I have said, a declaration of divine remission. 39. It is a most difficult thing, even for the most learned theologians, to exalt before the people the great riches of indulgences and, at the same time, the necessity of true contrition. 40. True contrition seeks and loves punishment, while the ampleness of pardon relaxes it and causes men to hate it or at least gives them occasion to do so. 41. Apostolic pardons ought to be purchased with caution, lest the people falsely suppose that they are to be preferred to other good works of charity. 42. Christians should be taught that it is not the mind of the Pope that the buying of indulgences is to be in any way compared with works of mercy. 43. Christians should be taught that he who gives to a poor man or lends to a needy man does better than if he buys indulgences. 44. For by a work of charity, charity increases, and man becomes better, while by means of indulgences he does not become better, but only freer from punishment. 45. Christians should be taught that he who sees anyone in need and, passing him by, gives money for indulgences is not purchasing the indulgence of the Pope, but calls down upon himself the wrath of God. 46. Christians should be taught that unless they have superfluous wealth, they are bound to keep what is necessary for the use of their own households and by no means to lavish it on indulgences. 47. Christians should be taught that while they are free to buy indulgences, they are not commanded to do so. 48. Christians should be taught that the Pope, in granting indulgences, has both more need and more desire that devout prayer should be made for him than that money should be freely paid. 49. Christians should be taught that the Pope's indulgences are useful if they do not put their trust in them, but most hurtful if through them they lose the fear of God. 50. Christians should be taught that, if the Pope knew of the exactions of the preachers of indulgences, he would rather see the Basilica of St. Peter burned to ashes than that it should be built up with the skin, flesh, and bones of his sheep. 51. Christians should be taught that the Pope, as is his duty, would rather, if necessary, sell the Basilica of St. Peter and give of his own money to those from whom the preachers of indulgences extract money. 52. Vain is the hope of salvation through letters of indulgence, even if a commissary — nay, the Pope himself — were to pledge his own soul for them. 53. They are enemies of Christ and of the Pope who, in order that indulgences may be preached, condemn the Word of God to utter silence in their churches. 54. Wrong is done to the Word of God when in a sermon as much time is spent on indulgences as on God's Word, or even more. 55. The mind of the Pope cannot but be that, if indulgences, which are a very small matter, are celebrated with single bells, single processions, and single ceremonies, the Gospel, which is a very great matter, should be preached with a hundred bells, a hundred processions, and a hundred ceremonies. 56. The treasures of the Church, whence the Pope grants indulgences, are neither sufficiently named or known among the people of Christ. 57. It is clear that they are at least not temporal treasures; for these are not so readily lavished, but only accumulated by many of the preachers. 58. Nor are they the merits of Christ and of the saints; for these, independently of the Pope, are always working grace to the inner man and the cross, death, and hell to the outer man. 59. St. Lawrence said that the treasures of the Church are the poor of the Church; but he spoke according to the use of the word in his time. 60. We are not speaking rashly when we say that the keys of the Church, bestowed through the merits of Christ, are that treasure. 61. For it is clear that the power of the Pope alone is sufficient for the remission of penalties and of reserved cases. 62. The true treasure of the Church is the holy Gospel of the glory and grace of God. 63. This treasure, however, is deservedly most hateful because it causes the first to be the last. 64. But the treasure of indulgences is deservedly the most acceptable because it causes the last to be the first. 65. Hence the treasures of the Gospel are nets wherewith of old they have fished for men of means. 66. The treasures of indulgences are nets wherewith they now fish for the means of men. 67. Those indulgences which the preachers loudly proclaim to be the greatest graces are seen to be truly such as regard the promotion of gain. 68. Yet they are in reality in no degree to be compared with the grace of God and the piety of the Cross. 69. Bishops and curates ought to receive the commissaries of apostolic pardons with all reverence. 70. But they are still more bound to open their eyes and ears lest these men preach their own dreams in place of the Pope's commission. 71. He who speaks against the truth of apostolic pardons, let him be anathema and accursed. 72. But he, on the other hand, who is seriously concerned about the wantonness and licenses of speech of the preachers of pardons, let him be blessed. 73. As the Pope justly thunders against those who use any kind of contrivance to the injury of the traffic in pardons. 74. Thus, indeed, much more, it is his intention to thunder against those who, under the pretext of granting indulgences, use contrivances to the injury of holy charity and of truth. 75. To think that papal indulgences have such power that they could absolve a man even if — to mention an impossibility — he had violated the Mother of God, is madness. 76. We affirm, on the contrary, that papal indulgences cannot take away even the least of venial sins as regards its guilt. 77. The saying that, even if St. Peter were now Pope, he could grant no greater graces, is blasphemy against St. Peter and the Pope. 78. We affirm, on the contrary, that both he and any other Pope has greater graces to grant, namely, the Gospel, powers, gifts of healing, etc. 1 Cor. 12:6, 9. 79. To say that the cross set up among the insignia of the papal arms is of equal power with the Cross of Christ is blasphemy. 80. Those bishops, curates, and theologians who allow such discourses to have currency among the people will have to render an account for this. 81. This license in the preaching of pardons makes it no easy thing, even for learned men, to protect the reverence due to the Pope against the calumnies or, at all events, the keen questioning of the laity. 82. For instance: Why does not the Pope empty purgatory for the sake of most holy charity and of the supreme necessity of souls — this being the most just of all reasons — if he redeems an infinite number of souls for the sake of that most perishable thing, money, to be spent on building a basilica — this being a very slight reason? 83. Again: Why do funeral masses and anniversary masses for the deceased continue, and why does not the Pope return, or permit the withdrawal of, funds bequeathed for this purpose, since it is wrong to pray for those who are already redeemed?   84. Again:

What new kind of holiness of God and the Pope is it to permit an impious man and an enemy of God, for money's sake, to redeem a pious soul, which is loved by God, and not rather to redeem this pious soul, which is loved by God, out of free charity, for the sake of its own need? 85. Again: Why is it that the penitential canons, long since abrogated and dead in themselves, in very fact and because of non-use, are still redeemed with money, through the granting of indulgences, as if they were still valid? 86. Again: Why does not the Pope, whose riches are at this day more ample than those of the wealthiest of the wealthy, build the one Basilica of St. Peter with his own money rather than with that of poor believers? 87. Again: Why does the Pope grant indulgences to those who, through perfect contrition, have a right to plenary remissions and indulgences? 88. Again: How much greater would be the benefit accruing to the Church if the Pope, instead of once, as he does now, would bestow these remissions and indulgences a hundred times a day on any one of the faithful? 89. Since it is the salvation of souls, rather than money, that the Pope seeks by granting indulgences, why does he suspend the letters and indulgences granted long ago, since they are equally efficacious? 90. Repressing these scruples and arguments of the laity by force alone and not solving them by giving reasons for so doing is to expose the Church and the Pope to ridicule of their enemies and to make Christian men unhappy. 91. If, then, indulgences were preached according to the spirit and mind of the Pope, all these questions would be resolved with ease; nay, they would not exist. 92. Away, then, with all those prophets who say to the people of Christ, "Peace, peace!" though there is no peace. 93. Blessed be all those prophets who say to the people of Christ, "The cross, the cross," and there is no cross. 94. Christians should be exhorted to strive to follow Christ, their Head, through pain, death, and hell; 95. And thus to enter heaven through many tribulations rather than in the security of peace.

Theses on the Church. Theses from Walther's *The Voice of the Church* (an elaboration of the Altenburg Theses * which the Missouri Synod held in its controversies on the Church, especially against Grabau). The text reads: "1. The Church, in the proper sense of the word, is the communion of saints, *i. e.*, the totality of all who are called out of the lost and condemned human race by the Holy Ghost, through the Gospel, sincerely believe in Christ, and by this their faith have been sanctified and made members of the spiritual body of Christ. 2. No infidel, hypocrite, unregenerate man nor heretic belongs to the Church in the proper sense of the word. 3. The Church, in the proper sense of the word, is invisible. 4. To this true Church of the believers and saints Christ has given the keys of the kingdom of heaven, and she, therefore, is the proper and sole possessor and bearer of all the spiritual, divine, and heavenly treasures, rights, and powers, and offices, etc., which Christ has gained and which are to be found in the Church. 5. Although the true Church, in the proper sense of the word, is essentially invisible, her presence may nevertheless be definitely known, her unfailing marks being the pure preaching of the Word of God and the administration of the holy Sacraments according to the institution of Christ. 6. In a tropical sense also the visible totality of the called, *i. e.*, the totality of all those who hold and profess the preached Word of God and use the holy Sacraments, good and bad together, according to Holy Scripture is termed the Church (the universal catholic Church), and the various divisions of it, *i. e.*, the congregations found in different places, in whose midst the Word of God is preached and the Sacraments are administered, are called churches (particular churches), and this for the reason that the true and properly called Church of the believers, saints, and children of God is contained in the visible congregations; and the elect must not be sought outside of the society of the called. 7. As those visible congregations which essentially retain the Word and the Sacraments according to the Scriptures bear the name of churches in view of the fact that the true invisible Church of believers is found in their midst, these visible congregations also, by reason of the presence among them of members of the invisible Church, even though there were but two or three of them, possess the power which Christ has given to His whole Church. 8. Although God gathers for Himself a church of the elect also there where the Word of God is not preached in its purity and the Sacraments are not administered entirely in accord with the institution of

Christ, provided the Word of God and the Sacraments are not rejected altogether, but essentially remain, nevertheless everyone is bound for the sake of his own salvation to shun all false teachers and to avoid all heterodox associations, or sects, and, on the other hand, to adhere to, and to profess, the faith of orthodox congregations and their orthodox preachers where he finds such. 9. It is only the communion with the invisible Church, to which originally all those glorious promises concerning the Church were given, which is indispensably necessary for salvation."

Theses on the Ministry. Theses from Walther's *The Voice of the Church* (an elaboration of the Altenburg Theses * which the Missouri Synod held in its controversies on the Ministry, especially against Grabau). The text reads: "1, The holy office of preaching (*Predigtamt*) or the ministry (*Pfarramt*) is not identical with the priesthood of all believers. 2. The office of preaching, or the holy ministry, is not a human institution, but an office instituted by God Himself. 3. The establishment of the office of the ministry is not optional, but is divinely enjoined upon the Church, and until the end of days the Church may not, ordinarily, dispense with it. 4. The ministry is not a separate holy estate like the Levitical priesthood, standing out as more holy than the common estate of all Christians, but it is an office of service. 5. The ministry has the power to preach the Gospel and to administer the Sacraments and the power of spiritual jurisdiction. 6. The office of the ministry is delegated (*uebertragen*) by God through the congregation, the possessor of all church power, or the Keys, by means of the divinely prescribed call of the congregation. The ordination, with laying on of hands on those called, is not a divine institution, but an apostolic, ecclesiastical rite and merely a public solemn attestation of such call. 7. The holy ministry is the power conveyed by God through the congregation, the possessor of the priesthood and all church power, to administer on behalf of the congregation (*von Gemeinschafts wegen*) in public office the rights of the spiritual priesthood. 8. The office of the ministry is the highest office in the Church, from which all other offices in the Church are derived as from their source. . . . 9. The ministry has indeed the divine

right to judge doctrine; the laity, however, also has this right; for which reason laymen have also seat and voice with the ministers in church courts and councils."

Theudas. See *Christs, False*.

Thibaut, Anton Friedrich Justus (1774—1840). A jurist; helped instigate the Palestrina renaissance in the 19th century and insisted that music, in order to be churchly, must be sung a cappella and modeled after the style of Palestrina. He set forth his theories in his *Ueber Reinheit der Tonkunst*, which influenced Winterfeld, Schoeberlein, Friedrich Lochner, and others who have insisted that the Palestrina idiom should be the ideal also of the Lutheran Church.

Thiele, Gottlieb A. B. 1834; educated at Halle; missionary of Wisconsin Synod, 1864; pastor in Wisconsin until elected professor at Milwaukee Seminary, 1887; resigned, 1900; pastor in West Allis, Wis.; d. 1919.

Thieme, Karl (1862—1932). Prof. at Leipzig; wrote: *Die sittliche Triebkraft des Glaubens; Die christliche Demut; Jesus und seine Predigt; Von der Gottheit Christi; Die Augsburger Konfession und Luthers Katechismen*.

Thirteen Articles. See *Anglican Confessions*, 3.

Thirteen Theses. Theses adopted by the Missouri Synod in 1881 on the questions of election and conversion. The text reads: "1. We believe, teach, and confess that God has loved the whole world from eternity, has created all men for salvation and none for damnation, and earnestly desires the salvation of all men; and hence we heartily reject and condemn the contrary Calvinistic doctrine. 2. We believe, teach, and confess that the Son of God has come into the world for all men, has borne, and atoned for, the sins of all men, has perfectly redeemed all men, none excepted; and hence we heartily reject and condemn the contrary Calvinistic doctrine. 3. We believe, teach, and confess that God earnestly calls all men through the means of grace, *i. e.*, with the intention of bringing them through these means unto repentance and unto faith and of preserving them therein to the end and of thus finally saving them, wherefore God offers them through these means of grace the salvation purchased by Christ's atonement and the power of accepting this salvation by faith; and hence we heartily reject and condemn the contrary Calvinistic doctrine. 4. We believe, teach, and confess that no man is lost because God would not save him, or because God with His grace passed him by, or because He did not offer the grace of perseverance to him also and would not bestow it upon him; but that all men who are lost perish by their own fault, namely, on account of their unbelief, and because they have obstinately resisted the Word and grace of God to the end; . . . and hence we heartily reject and condemn the contrary Calvinistic doctrine. 5. We believe, teach, and confess that the *persons concerned* in election or predestination are only the true *believers,* who *believe to the end* or who *come to faith at the end of their lives;* and hence we reject and condemn the error of Huber that election is not particular, but universal, and concerns all men. 6. We believe, teach, and confess that divine election is *immutable,* and hence, that not one of the elect can become reprobate and be lost, but that every one of the elect is surely saved; and hence we heartily reject and condemn the contrary Huberian error. 7. We believe, teach, and confess that it is folly and dangerous to souls, leading either to carnal security or to despair, when men attempt to become or to be certain of their election or their future salvation by *searching out the eternal mysterious decree of God;* and hence we heartily reject and condemn the contrary doctrine as a piece of pernicious fanaticism. 8. We believe, teach, and confess that a believing Christian should endeavor from the revealed Word of God to become sure of his election; and hence we heartily reject and condemn the contrary papistic error that a man can become and be certain of his election and salvation only through a new, immediate revelation. 9. We believe, teach, and confess, a) that election does *not* consist of the *mere foreknowledge of God* as to which men will be saved; b) also, that election is *not* the *mere purpose of God* to redeem and save mankind, for which reason it might be termed *universal,* embracing *all men* generally; c) that election does *not* concern *temporary believers,* Luke 8:13; d) that election is *not* the *mere decree* of God to save all those who believe to the end; and hence we heartily reject and condemn the contrary errors of the rationalists, Huberians, and Arminians. 10. We be-

lieve, teach, and confess that the *cause* which moved God to choose the elect is solely His grace and the merit of Jesus Christ, and *not any good thing* which God has foreseen in the elect, even *not the faith foreseen* by God in them; and hence we reject and condemn the contrary doctrines of the Pelagians, Semi-Pelagians, and synergists as blasphemous, frightful, subversive of the Gospel and therefore of the entire Christian religion. 11. We believe, teach, and confess that election is not the mere foresight or foreknowledge of the salvation of the elect, but also a *cause* of their salvation and what pertains thereto; and hence we heartily reject and condemn the contrary doctrines of the Arminians, the Socinians, and of all synergists. 12. We believe, teach, and confess that God has "still kept secret and concealed much concerning this mystery and reserved it alone for His wisdom and knowledge," which no man can or should search out; and hence we reject the attempt to penetrate into what is not revealed and to harmonize with reason those things that seem to contradict our reason, whether this is done in the Calvinistic or in the Pelagian-synergistic theories. 13. We believe, teach, and confess that it is not only neither useless nor even dangerous, but rather necessary and wholesome to present publicly also to our Christian people the mysterious doctrine of predestination, as far as it is clearly revealed in God's Word; and hence we do not agree with those who think that this doctrine must either be entirely concealed or must be reserved only for the disputations of the learned."

Thirty-Nine Articles. See *Anglican Confessions,* 6.

Thirty Years' War. A European war lasting from 1618 to 1648, with its chief campaigns on German soil. Though usually called a religious war and exhibiting some of the aspects of such a conflict, it was influenced to a large extent by power politics and greed. The chief religious features are the following. When in 1617, Ferdinand of Styria, a fanatical enemy of Protestantism, was crowned king of Bohemia, he immediately instituted proceedings against the Protestants. But the Protestant leaders penetrated into the castle of Prague, threw the imperial commissioners out of the window and organized a general uprising throughout the country. The Protestant army was completely defeated on Nov. 8, 1620, and more than 30,000 Protestant families were driven out of the country. Five years later the Protestant princes of Germany rallied under the head of Christian IV of Denmark, but he was also defeated on Aug. 27, 1626, the commander of the imperial army, Tilly, again being the victor. Denmark was eliminated by the separate peace of Luebeck on May 22, 1629. In June of the next year Gustav Adolf of Sweden landed in Germany, in defense of his homeland and church against Wallenstein and Sigismund III of Poland, as a champion of the Protestant cause. Tilly was twice defeated by the Swedish armies, at Breitenfeld and on the Lech, and was killed in the latter battle. Ferdinand charged Wallenstein with the formation of a new army, which met the Swedish invaders at Luetzen. Wallenstein was defeated, but Gustav Adolf fell, and the emperor took new courage. Wallenstein was assassinated in 1634, but the Protestant armies had lost their champion and were badly defeated at Noerdlingen on Sept. 6, 1634, the result being that the electors of Brandenburg and Saxony deserted the Protestant cause and made peace with the emperor. At this time the French statesman Richelieu, anxious to bring about a humiliation of Austria, took the army of Duke Bernhardt of Saxe-Weimar into the French service, and the war was revived with extreme fierceness and cruelty. Bavaria was ravaged, and two Austrian armies defeated by the Swedish general Torstenson. It was at a time of general exhaustion that the peace of Westphalia (at Osnabrueck and Muenster) was concluded on Oct. 24, 1648.

Tholuck, Friedrich August Gotttreu (1799—1877). Studied at Breslau and under Neander in Berlin; converted to faith in Christ as his personal Savior especially through his intercourse with Baron von Kottwitz; professor at Berlin; professor at Halle and preacher to the university; wrote commentaries on John, Romans, and Hebrews, also a number of historical works, and was a contributor to Hengstenberg's *Kirchenzeitung*. He favored the Prussian "Union," fought the *rationalismus vulgaris* in rationalistic Halle, but was bitter against the Lutheran *Orthodoxie*. He won many students over from Gesenius and Wegscheider for Christ — the "Students' Father."

Thoma, Hans (1839—1924). With Gebhardt and Steinhausen exponent of modern German realism, but with a great deal of charm and feeling; one of his earlier paintings "Christ and Nicodemus"; two of his latest paintings "The Sinking Peter" and "The Risen Christ and Mary Magdalene," notable for exquisite detail work and fine coloring.

Thomas à Kempis (1379—1471). A German mystic; b. in Kempen, near Cologne. His true name was Haemmerken (Malleolus). A member of the order of the Brethren of the Common Life, he entered the monastery of Mount St. Agnes near Zwolle, where he spent seventy-one years in cloistral seclusion. Often ascribed to his pen is *De Imitatione Christi*, which, in general a product of Mysticism, has won the approval of the Roman Catholic Church and from a somewhat different viewpoint has appealed to a large number of Protestants. It has four chapters: "Admonitions Useful for a Spiritual Life," "Admonitions Concerning the Interior Life," "Concerning the Holy Communion," "Of Interior Consolation." The apparent sincerity and singleness of heart of the author, the admonitions to a holy life, always striking a responsive chord in the Christian heart, the fact that the book is saturated with the Scriptures, and the undoubted tendency of many Protestant readers to understand what they read in the light of their better Christian knowledge — all this serves to explain the evident popularity of this book during more than four centuries. But it is, after all, a product of medieval scholastic theology; for Thomas à Kempis was under the influence of Thomas Aquinas, the recognized dogmatician of the medieval Western Church. He stresses sanctification without directing the sinner to the doctrine of justification, demands the practice of complete self-denial for the purpose of meriting salvation, and, though speaking of Christ's sacrifice for the sins of the world, fails to point out that by faith alone Christ's merits are appropriated by the sinner.

Thomas Aquinas. See *Aquinas, Thomas.*

Thomas Christians. See *India,* 4.

Thomas, John (1805—71). English physician and founder of Christadelphians *; b. in London; came to America 1832; joined Disciples of Christ, but believing that all churches taught false doctrines, left that denomination, published his own views, and organized his followers, whom he called Christadelphians.

Thomas, W. H. Griffith (1861—1924). Anglican; b. in England; priest 1885; vicar of St. Paul's; principal of Wycliff Hall, Oxford; professor of Old Testament, Wycliff College, Toronto, 1910; author; conservative theologian.

Thomasius, Christian (1655—1728). Studied philosophy and jurisprudence; at first *Privatdozent* at Leipzig; because of satirical criticism of theologians and scholars banished from the university; through Elector Frederick III of Brandenburg called to Halle in 1690; external contact with the pietism of Spener and Francke did not influence him internally; one of the foremost pioneers of Enlightenment and the exponent and advocate of Territorialism in church polity; opposed punishment for witchcraft and the application of torture. See also *Territorial System*.

Thomasius, Gottfried (1802—75). Positive Lutheran theologian; studied at Erlangen, Halle, and Berlin; spent seventeen years as pastor at different places; in 1842 called to Erlangen as professor of dogmatics, where he exerted great influence also as university preacher; his chief work, *Christi Person und Werk*, marred by his kenotic error. See *Kenosis*.

Thomists. See *Scholasticism*.

Thorlaksson, Paul. See *Canada, Lutheranism in*, 13.

Thorn, Conference of; Declaration of. See *Reformed Confessions*, D 3.

Thorn, Massacre of. The judicial murder of ten of the leading citizens of the Protestant city of Thorn, in Poland, in 1724. Enraged by the insolent bearing of the Jesuit students on the occasion of a religious procession, a Protestant mob stormed and destroyed the Jesuit college of the town, though without endangering human life. The responsibility for the act was charged by the Jesuits upon the city authorities, and the legal proceedings that followed issued in the death penalty against the accused.

Thornwell, James Henley (1812 to 1862). B. in Marlborough District, S. C.; prof., later pres., South Carolina College; various pastorates, and prof. at Theological Sem., Columbia; outstanding logician and scholar; leading organizer in Presbyterian Church.

Thorwaldsen, Albert Bartholomew (1770—1845). Danish sculptor; studied at Copenhagen, where he gained the first gold medal in sculpture; then in Rome, where he came under the influence of Canova; many subjects from classical mythology, but also "Christ and the Twelve Apostles," "Come unto Me," "St. John Preaching in the Wilderness," and "The Angel of Baptism."

Three Chapters, Controversy of. A political move of Emperor Justinian I, which was intended to keep the powerful Monophysite party with the Church by certain concessions or resolutions approaching compromises. Since the school of Antioch had been particularly emphatic in opposing Monophysitism, it was necessary, in Justinian's opinion, to neutralize the effect of its standpoint in the matter. About 544 Justinian issued an edict in which he condemned the so-called Three Chapters, that is, the statements of Theodore of Mopsuestia, Theodoret of Cyrus, and Ibas of Edessa concerning the doctrine at issue, namely, whether there is one or whether there are two natures in the person of Christ. At a synod held at Constantinople in 548 the bishops were prevailed upon to give written verdicts for the condemnation of the Three Chapters. In order to avoid the appearance of opposing the resolutions of the Council of Chalcedon, it was said that only individual members of that council, and not the entire body, had approved of the strong anti-Monophysitic statements passed in 381. The result was that the Fifth Ecumenic Council, assembled at Constantinople in 553, resolved to "anathematize the Three Chapters before mentioned, that is, the impious Theodore of Mopsuestia with his execrable writings, and those things which Theodoret impiously wrote, and the impious letter which is said to be by Ibas, together with their defenders and those who have written, and do write, in defense of them, or who dare to say that they are correct, and who have defended, or do attempt to defend, their impiety with the names of the holy Fathers or of the holy Council of Chalcedon." See *Christological Controversies*.

Thring, Godfrey (1823—1903). B. at Alford, Somerset, and was educated at Shrewsbury School and at Balliol College, Oxford. He served different charges as curate and rector. He has written many hymns, about 25 of which are contained in different church hymnals in England and America. "His hymns," says Dr. Julian, "are mainly objective and are all of them of a strong and decided character. In some of his finer hymns his tone is high and his structure massive; in several others his plaintiveness is very tender, whilst very varied, and his rhythm is almost always perfect. The prominent features throughout are a clear vision, a firm faith, a positive reality, and an exulting hopefulness."

Thrupp, Adelaide (19th century). She was either the daughter or the wife of Joseph Francis Thrupp (1827—67). Some of her verse appeared in *Psalms and Hymns*, 1853. Her hymn, at least stanzas 1 and 3, "Lord, Who at Cana's Wedding Feast," in several collections.

Thurificati. See *Persecutions of Christians*, 4.

Tibet (Thibet). Country in Central Asia, under Chinese sovereignty. Area, estimated 469,413 sq. mi. Population, 2,000,000 (1951 est.), of Mongolian stock. Buddhism, in the form of Lamaism, is the dominating religion. Missions have been repeatedly tried, *e. g.*, by Moravians, Scandinavian Alliance, Christian and Missionary Alliance, but all without appreciable success.

T'ien. See *Confucianism*, 3.

Tiepolo, Giovanni Batista (1692 to 1769). Italian painter, last of Venetian school; modeled himself after Paul Veronese; very productive, rich in color, clear in drawing; noted for his Old Testament pictures.

Tierce. See *Canonical Hours*.

Tierra del Fuego. See *South America*, 2.

Tietze, Christoph (1641—1703). Studied at Altdorf and Jena; pastor at Laubenzedel, then at Henfenfeld, finally chief pastor at Hersbruck; wrote: "Ich armer Mensch, ich armer Suender"; "Was ist unser Leben."

Tigurinus, Consensus of. See *Reformed Confessions*, A 8.

Tillotson, John (1630—94). Anglican prelate; b. at Sowerby; rector; dean of St. Paul's; archbishop of Canterbury; d. in London. Famous preacher; combatted deism and Catholicism without much success because himself a latitudinarian. See *Deism* III, 2.

Time. Eras of time in the Old Testament were based on the reign of kings and other important events (Ex-

odus: 1 Kings 6:1; reformation: Ezek. 1:1; erection of Solomon's Temple: 1 Kings 9:10; Babylonian Exile: Ezek. 33:21; earthquake: Amos 1:1; and others). The Seleucidan era, which began 312 B. C., was widely used among Jews and continued at Alexandria until the 16th century. When under foreign rule, the Jews often figured their eras according to the system of their conquerors. Shortly after the time of Christ, Jews began to figure from the time of creation, which they regarded as being about 4,000 years before the destruction of the Temple.

The Christian era is reckoned from the birth of Christ on the basis of the writings of a monk, Dionysius Exiguus.*

James Ussher * propounded a system of chronology which was later printed in the margin of the King James Version. The system is still widely quoted, although scholars have frequently challenged its accuracy. Some of the dates according to this chronology are (B. C.):

4004 — The Fall
2348 — The Flood
2234 — The Confusion of Tongues at Babel
1921 — The Call of Abraham
1706 — Jacob's Family Enters Egypt
1491 — The Exodus
1451 — Beginning of the Conquest of Canaan
1394 — Othniel Becomes Judge of Israel
1095 — Saul Becomes King of Israel
1004 — Dedication of the Temple of Solomon
975 — Division of the Kingdom
721 — Captivity of Israel
587 — Captivity of Judah
535 — Return of Jews under Zerubbabel
4 — Birth of Christ

By projections into the past based upon calculations of cause and effect a much more extensive time span has been evolved, especially in connection with theories of evolution.* According to this there was a vast period of astronomical time before the earth existed. A vast period of the "earth," or geological time, passed before living structures appeared. The period of living structures is divided into the Archaeozoic, Palaeozoic, Mesozoic, and Cenozoic, the last being the age of animals and man. The Cenozoic period is divided into the Tertiary (age of mammals) and Quartenary (age of man) periods. The age of man is again divided into Eolithic (early Stone Age),

Paleolithic (old Stone Age), Mesolithic (middle Stone Age), Neolithic (new Stone Age), Chalcolithic (Stone-Copper Age), Bronze Age, Iron Age, and subsequent periods. See *Evolution*.

Common observation has led to the conclusion that time is something which has moved out of the past and moves into the future. There has been no agreement among philosophers regarding the nature of time. Among the ancients, Parmenides regarded appearances (such as becoming, change, time) as illusions, whereas Heraclitus regarded change as being characteristic of all. Newton and his followers regarded time as being independent of events, whereas the school of Leibniz held time to be the relationship between events and as dependent on events.

According to Einstein's theory of relativity, time is relative to the point or system of observation. Royce's theory of time takes the consciousness into consideration. Thus the "before" and the "after," as fixed by the conscious time span of the observer, are a part of the series within the present. St. Augustine regarded time as a psychological phenomenon (the remembered; the anticipated). Bergson, Whitehead, and others regarded time as modal, or the manner in which the determined ("past") is related to the potential ("future"). EL

Tindal, Matthew. See *Deism*, III, 5.

Tintoretto, real name *Jacopo Robusti*, (1518—94). Devoted student of antique sculpture and anatomy; rose to high fame; very productive; most of his compositions at Venice, among them "The Crucifixion"; produced some outstanding paintings.

Tiro, Prosper. See *Prosper Tiro*.

Tischendorf, Konstantin (1815—74). Most noted for his researches of the Greek New Testament text; found, Feb. 4, 1859, the *Codex Sinaiticus*, a manuscript of the New Testament of the middle or end of the 4th century, in the convent at Sinai (now in Stalingrad); became more and more conservative toward the end of his life, as seen especially in his pamphlet *When Were Our Gospels Written?*

Titian, or *Tiziano Vecellio* (1477 to 1576). Distinguished Italian painter and head of the Venetian school; equally notable in landscape and in figure painting, in sacred and in profane subjects, in ideal heads and in portraits, in frescoes and in oils; among his paintings "Assumption of the Virgin"; "The Death of St. Peter the Martyr"; "Christ in the Garden."

Titius, Christoph. See *Tietze*.

Tithing. See *Finances in the Church*, 6.

Tittmann, Johann August Heinrich (1773—1831). B. in Langensalza; d. in Leipzig. Studied at Wittenberg and Leipzig. Lectured at Leipzig, where he became professor extraordinary in philosophy in 1796, in theology in 1800, and professor primarius in 1818. An eloquent preacher. He represented a rationalistic supernaturalism.

Tobit. See *Apocrypha*, A 3.

Toccata. A composition for organ or some other keyboard instrument which is free and often brilliant in character. The early toccatas by A. Gabrieli, Claudio Merulo, and Frescobaldi were far more than mere display pieces; while the toccatas of the North German masters, including Buxtehude and Bach, are at times quite rhapsodic, they still manifest a spirit of restraint which permits them to be regarded as lively preludes, especially when followed by a sedate fugue.

Togoland. A former German colony in West Africa. Area, 13,040 sq. mi. Population, approximately 971,824 (1949). After the First World War mandated to France and Great Britain. Protestants, 35,000; Roman Catholics, 120,000 (1952).

Tokens of Remembrance. Small leaflets, folders, or booklets, also plaques finished in an artistic manner, such as tokens of confirmation, given by pastors or sponsors in remembrance of the day of confirmation.

Toland, John. See *Deism*, III, 4.

Toledo, Council of. Of the various synods and councils held at Toledo, in Spain, which was a prominent ecclesiastical city in the early centuries, that of the year 447, with its first pronouncement of the doctrine of the Trinity and the emphasis of the procession of the Holy Spirit from the Father and the Son (see *Filioque Controversy*), and that of 859, when Recared I went over to the orthodox Church and induced a considerable number of his people to deny Arianism, and when Arianism was condemned in thirteen canons, are the most important.

Toledo Theses (Iowa Synod, 1867). In 1856 the Iowa Synod adopted theses in which it stated that it bound its pastors to the Lutheran Confessions, but made a distinction between essentials and non-essentials (the theses and antitheses were essential; proof, elucidations, etc., were *accidens*) and held that the Confessions must be interpreted historically rather than dogmatically. Criticisms of this position by the Buffalo and Missouri Synods caused doubt within the Iowa Synod itself, and S. Fritschel was sent to Germany to secure opinions from recognized faculties on the basis of publications of Iowa. Such opinions were given by the faculty at Dorpat and by Luthardt, v. Harless, Christiani (Riga), Muenkel, and Guerike. The faculty at Dorpat and Dr. Muenkel criticized the differentiation between essentials and unessentials as made in 1856. At Toledo, Ohio (1867), the Iowa Synod formulated nine theses on the question: "What is necessary for church unity?" Summary of theses: "Unity in the preaching of the Gospel" applies to the confession of the Church, which must hold all articles of faith without error. The doctrine of the Gospel is the doctrine of justification through faith. Nevertheless, the unity of the Church is a fundamental and never absolute unity. Essential, or fundamental, doctrines are those which the Church has fixed in her Confessions. Thereby is not said that this must apply to all unessential and incidental teachings in the Confessions, but only to the articles of faith established by the Church.

Kirchenblatt, Jan., 1858; J. Deindoerfer, *Geschichte der Ev. Luth. Synode von Iowa u. anderen Staaten,* Wartburg, 1897; G. J. Fritschel, *Quellen und Dokumente zur Geschichte und Lehrstellung der Iowa Synode,* Wartburg, Chicago, 1916.

Toledo Theses (Ohio and Iowa). After the Ohio Synod withdrew from the Synodical Conference (1881), a closer relationship developed between the Ohio and Iowa Synods. An informal conference was held at Richmond,* Ind., 1883. In July, 1893, a colloquy was held in Michigan City, Ind., by representatives of the Ohio Synod (M. Loy, F. W. Stellhorn, H. Ernst, H. A. Allwardt, G. F. H. Meiser, H. Doermann, and others) and of the Iowa Synod (S. Fritschel, W. Proehl, R. Richter, Th. Meier, P. Bredow, F. Lutz, C. H. Caselmann, and others). Six theses were drawn up as a result of this colloquy, which, however, were not adopted by the synods because of some minority prejudices. Another colloquy was held at Toledo, Ohio, in 1909, at which the Michigan Theses were revised and adopted by both synods (thereafter known as the *Toledo Theses*). Fellowship, however, was not declared until 1918 after the Iowa Synod had separated from the General Council (1917).

Content. Theses I. "The Church, in the proper sense of the term, is the communion of true believers as it is begotten through the means of grace and as by their use it edifies itself. . . . According to its real essence the Church is . . . invisible. . . . Common participation in the means of grace is the necessary form of the Church's appearance and the infallible mark of its existence." II. "The Office of the Ministry rests upon a special command of the Lord, valid throughout all time, and consists in the right and power conferred by special call to administer the means of grace publicly and by commission of the congregation. The call (to the pastorate) is a right of the congregation within whose bounds the minister is to discharge the office." III. "A binding subscription to the Confessions (of the Church) pertains only to the doctrines of faith therein set forth, and to these without exception . . . the doctrine of Sunday . . . is not to be excluded. . . ." IV. "All doctrines revealed clearly and plainly in the Word of God are . . . dogmatically fixed as true and binding upon the conscience, whether they have been symbolically settled or not. . . . There is . . . no authority whatever of departing from any truths clearly revealed by the Scriptures, be their contents considered fundamental or non-fundamental. . . . Full agreement in all articles of faith constitutes the irremissible condition of church fellowship. Persistent error in an article of faith must under all circumstances lead to separation. Perfect agreement in all fundamental doctrines, though not attainable on earth, is nevertheless an end desirable and one we should labor to attain. Those who knowingly, obdurately, and persistently contradict the divine Word in any of its utterances whatsoever thereby overthrow the organic foundation (of the faith) and are therefore to be excluded from church fellowship." V. "Any chiliasm which conceives the kingdom of Christ to be something external, earthly, and after the manner of the kingdoms of the world, and which teaches a resurrection of all believers before the Day of Judgment shall come, is a doctrine directly contrary to the analogy of faith and is to be rejected as such. . . . The belief . . . that the reign of Christ and His saints referred to in Revelation 20 is an event belonging to the future, as also that the resurrection there spoken of is to be understood as a bodily resurrection of some believers unto life everlasting, is an opinion which, though not incompatible with the analogy of faith, cannot be strictly proved from Scripture, no more than the spiritual interpretation of said passages can be shown to be the true one." VI. "The error of Missouri on predestination we find to consist in this, that thereby the universal gracious will of God and His decree of election are so separated as to exclude one another and that thus two contradictory wills are affirmed of God. . . . Concerning conversion . . . we confess that, viewed as the placing or planting of a new spiritual life, conversion does not depend to any extent whatsoever on any co-operation . . . but that it is wholly and solely the work of the Holy Ghost. . . . We deny that the Holy Ghost works conversion according to a mere pleasure of His elective will or despite the most willful resistance . . . but we hold that by such stubborn resistance both conversion and eternal election are hindered." EL

Minutes of the Ohio and Iowa Synods; G. J. Fritschel, *Quellen und Dokumente zur Geschichte und Lehrstellung der ev. luth. Synode von Iowa u. a. Staaten,* Wartburg Pub. House, Chicago, Ill., n. d.; S. Fritschel, "Die Thesen des Kolloquiums von Michigan City," *Kirchliche Zeitschrift,* XVII:161 to 170; XVIII:33—48; the Michigan City Theses are quoted from the *Kirchenzeitung* by F. Pieper, "Das Colloquium der Synoden von Ohio und Iowa," *L. u. W.,* XXXIX:257—64; the Toledo Theses are reprinted in *Doctrinal Declarations,* CPH, n. d.

Toleration Edict of Joseph II. An edict promulgated in 1781 and granting (with certain restrictions) freedom of worship to the Lutheran and Reformed churches of Austria. See *Joseph II and Josephinism; Roman Catholic Church, History of.*

Tolstadius, Eric. See *Sweden, Lutheran Church in,* 3.

Tolstoy, Count Leo (1828—1910). Russian author; b. near Tula, central Russia; 1851—56 army officer, taking part in Crimean War; after that lived on family estate; during last part of life renounced use of his wealth and lived as peasant; excommunicated by Holy Synod 1901. After writing a series of novels among them *War and Peace* and *Anna Karenina,* he devoted himself to theological studies. He rejected the doctrines of the Trinity, deity of Christ, atonement, original sin, as well as all claims of Orthodox, Roman, and Protestant churches and found the essence of Christianity in the Sermon on the Mount, laying special emphasis on "resist not evil." Matt. 5:39. Institutions of civilization based on force, *e. g.,* prisons, police, army, navy, are immoral. Though he loved his people passionately, his views are a curious mixture of truth and error, mysticism, fatalism, pessimism, Socialism. Main religious works: *Critique of Dogmatic Theology,* 1882; *Four Gospels Harmonized and Translated,* 1882; *What I Believe,* 1884; *The Kingdom of God Is Within You,* 1893.

(Tomlinson) Church of God. See *Church of God,* 6; *Holiness Bodies,* 2.

Tonga Islands. Otherwise *Friendly Islands,* under the protectorate of Great Britain. Consist of some 150 small islands southwest of Samoa. Area, 385 sq. mi. Population, 45,558 (1948). Missions were attempted as early as 1797 by the London Missionary Society. The Wesleyans gained a footing in 1882. After the acceptance of Christianity by Chief Taufaahan the evangelization of the islands made rapid progress. Friction between the king and the Wesleyans led to the establishment of the Free Church of Tonga. The king (George) died in 1893, generally respected. The natives are now Christians. They have been very active in mission work in the South Pacific.

Tongues, Gift of. 1. The New Testament contains references to the appearance of the gift of tongues, not only at Pentecost, but in connection with the conversion of Cornelius, in connection with the advent of the Holy Ghost at Ephesus, and in connection with the church at Corinth. It has been a much-discussed question whether the speaking in tongues of Acts 2:4 ff.; 10:46; and 1 Cor. 14 were the same phenomenon. At any rate, both the gift of speaking in tongues which the speaker had never learned and the gift of speaking in unknown tongues (unknown to the audiences) were given for a purpose in the days of the early Christian Church, being, like the miracles of

Apostolic days, witness to the supernatural origin of Christianity.

2. As that first age came to its close, the extraordinary gifts disappeared, one by one, from common use. With the barriers of paganism broken down, it was sufficient that the Spirit of God should bear witness with the spirits of those who were saved by faith in that One who was lifted between the heavens and the earth (John 16:13; Eph. 4:21). He "shall bring all things to your remembrance" that Christ has spoken (John 14:26). He testifies of Jesus and His power to save. He convicts of sin. He witnesses to the fact of a new birth. He gives power and strength. He affords leadership and guidance. He cleanses and purifies.

3. The gift of tongues has been claimed by religious groups of every age: the Shakers, the Irvingites, the Mormons, the Pentecostal Church, the Assembly of God, Holy Rollers, Full Gospel Mission. The gift is generally manifested in a crowd and in a scene of confusion and tumult. In no case is there substantial evidence of any sort that the persons who claimed to speak by inspiration in other languages actually used other languages. The testimony is universally that of the person who claimed to have spoken in "other tongues" or of interested witnesses. Whenever men of any linguistic knowledge have investigated the phenomena, they have united in testifying that the language spoken was indeed unknown. These tongues are (in every case that has come under critical observation) a jargon language, composed of sounds an exact classification of which it is impossible to make.

Tonsure (Latin, *tondere,* "to shear"). A round shaven spot on top of the head, which distinguishes the Roman clergy from the laity. It may be conferred on boys as early as the eighth year as a preparation for receiving holy orders. The tonsure increases in size as the cleric advances in dignity, the simple tonsure having a diameter of about one and a fourth inches, that of priests somewhat over three inches. Monastic tonsures are larger and sometimes leave only a circle of hair. Tonsures must be renewed monthly.

Toplady, Augustus Montague (1740 to 1778). B. at Farnham, England, educated at Westminster School and at Trinity College, Dublin; ordained to the ministry of the Church of England, 1762, he was some time afterwards appointed vicar of Broadhembury, Devonshire. In 1775 he was a preacher in the chapel of French Calvinists in Leicester Fields, London. He was a powerful and popular preacher. He wrote a series of vituperative tracts in a long and bitter controversy with John Wesley, but is now remembered only for one hymn, "Rock of Ages."

Torgau Articles. See *Lutheran Confessions,* A 2.

Torkillus, Reorus. Holds the distinction of being the first Lutheran pastor to labor within the present limits of the United States; b. in Sweden, 1599; came to New Sweden on the Delaware with the second expedition in 1639 (according to Johnson, in 1640); ministered to the colonists at Fort Christina (Wilmington) until his death, Sept. 7, 1643, leaving his congregation in charge of Campanius *; lies buried under the "Old Swedes' Church" at Wilmington, the oldest Protestant church building in the United States.

Torquemada. See *Inquisition,* 6.

Torrey, Joseph (1797—1867). Congregational theologian; prof. of Greek and Latin, then of intellectual and moral philosophy, at the U. of Vermont; pres., 1863—65; translated Neander's church history, wrote on the theory of art, and other works.

Torrey, Reuben Archer (1856 to 1928). Congregationalist; b. at Hoboken, N. J.; pastor in Ohio and Minnesota; superintendent of Moody Bible Institute 1889 to 1908 and pastor in Chicago; evangelistic tour of the world, especially of Great Britain and America; dean of Bible Institute, Los Angeles, 1912; believed in the inerrancy of Scripture, divinity and atonement of Christ, etc.; prolific writer, but with chiliastic tendencies.

Totemism. From *totem,* an Ojibway Indian word. An ethnological phenomenon found in its fullest development among North American Indians and aborigines of Australia. Also found among Bantus of Africa, Dravidian peoples of India, and in Melanesia, with isolated cases elsewhere. Its characteristic features are as follows: Tribes are subdivided into clans. Each clan has assumed as an emblem a totem, which may be a species of animal, as bear, wolf, kangaroo, tortoise, or, less frequently, of plants, or, rarely, of an inanimate object, as sun, moon, cloud, rain, wind. Each member of the clan believes himself intimately related to the species or object which gives the clan its name, and in some cases the totem is considered the ancestor of the clan. The totem is an object of respect and as every animal or plant of the particular species is considered a kinsman, friend, and ally of the clan and the clan members identify themselves with the totem, it must not be injured or killed, except in self-defense, nor, as a rule, eaten. The clan members owe one another mutual protection. In some instances exogamy is a concomitant feature of totemism, that is, men are not permitted to marry women of the same clan. No satisfactory explanation of the origin of totemism has as yet been given. The totem poles of the Indians along the northwestern American coast are posts into which heads of animals and men are carved, with the totem at the top.

Totenfest (*Commemoration of the Dead*). A special Sunday, usually the last Sunday of the church year, devoted to the remembrance of those who have died in the course of the year. In the time of Augustine the special offerings and acts of charity done in the name of the dead on that day were thought to be of value to the deceased. Much of the superstitious belief concerning this festival has been concentrated on All Souls' Day. The Lutheran Church, where it has retained a day for the commemoration of the dead, has eliminated all superstitious features. Still, its observance is not proper, its establishment being due to sentimental reasons. It is contrary to the spirit of the church year.

Toulouse, Synod of (1229). See *Inquisition*, 3.

Tract. A tract is a Psalm, or a portion of a Psalm, which is sung to an elaborate and ornate (melismatic) chant. It is used as part of the Gradual from Septuagesima until Easter, at times also in Advent, notably in the Roman Catholic Church. Luther inclined to the view that Graduals containing a tract have a tendency to burden the service of worship liturgically.

Tractarianism. Sometimes called the *Oxford Movement,* the name given to the Catholic revival in the Church of England which began at Oxford in 1833 with the publication of *Tracts for the Times.* The leaders of the movement were John Keble and John Henry Newman. At a meeting of several of the

clergy of the Church of England, Rev. Newman suggested the idea of the *Tracts for the Times,* which was adopted. During the following eight years ninety tracts were published. The general teaching of the Tractarians included Apostolic Succession, baptismal regeneration, confession, the Real Presence, the authority of the Church, and the value of tradition. In 1843 Newman resigned his incumbency in the State Church of England and was received into the Roman Church in September, 1845. The effects of the movement were 1) a revival and strengthening of the High Church section of the Established Church; 2) increase of learning, piety, and devoutness among the clergy; 3) establishment of sisterhoods and other religious and charitable institutions; 4) development of ritual, as symbolic of Catholic doctrine; 5) a large secession of English clergy and laity to Rome. See *Pusey, Edward B.*

Tracts for the Times. See *Tractarianism.*

Tradition. In the ancient Christian Church the word *traditio* (G. *paradosis*) was used of instruction given by one person to another. This tradition was divided into oral and written tradition. Gradually the word "tradition" was assigned to all oral and sacred teachings not found in the Sacred Canon.

Emphasis on tradition antedates New Testament times. The Jews held that God gave Moses, in addition to the written Word, oral traditions which were handed down by word of mouth. The decisions of their doctors and priests became the source of their traditions, which are gathered chiefly in the Mishna and Gemara (see Matt. 15: 2, 3; Mark 7:3-13; 2 Thess. 2:15; 3:6).

Early Church Fathers (*e. g.,* Irenaeus, Tertullian, Clement of Alexandria) frequently appealed to oral traditions. Augustine, however, held that a tradition could not be relied upon unless it were consistent and universal. In the Dark Ages extensive compilations of patristic writings (with more or less pagan learning included) were continued (*e. g.,* Cassiodorus, Isidore of Seville, Rhabanus Maurus, Walafrid Strabo, Alcuin of York). Reliance on this tradition thereafter increased, but it was given a telling blow by Peter Abelard's *Yea and Nay,* which showed the fathers to be contradictory and ambiguous.

As Luther rejected "enthusiasm," so he also rejected the extravagant claims for tradition of the Roman Church. On the other hand, he opposed the spirit of radicals who sought to overthrow everything ("It is dangerous and terrible to hear or believe something contrary to the unanimous witness, faith, and teaching of the one holy Christian Church"). Luther preserved the traditional parts of the Catechism and the Creed. His treatment of the Canon shows that Luther felt free to investigate· traditional decisions even in the most important matters. As decisions of councils and individual Christians must be measured by the Word of God, so writings of ancient and modern teachers must be subjected to the Holy Scriptures (*norma normans*). The Augsburg Confession speaks of its contents as "the sum of our doctrine in which, as can be seen, there is nothing that varies from the Scriptures, or from the Church Catholic, or from the Church of Rome as known from its writers." It, however, opposes abuses which had crept into the Church.

The Council of Trent placed traditions of the Church alongside the inspired Word as a norm and thus prepared the way for the doctrine of the infallibility of the popes.

The position of Lutherans in America is that Scripture is the ultimate norm (*norma normans*) by which all writings, ancient and modern, are to be judged. EL

Traditions of Matthias. See *Apocrypha,* B 2.

Traducianism. The teaching that the soul of the individual is not a new creation, but is derived from the parents. While not distinctly stated in Scripture, it is preferred to the doctrine of Creationism, as on the latter supposition it is difficult to account for the transmission of sin (natural depravity, original sin) from parents to offspring.

Traherne, Thomas (1637?—74). English clergyman; wrote *Roman Forgeries, Christian Ethics, Centuries of Meditation,* and numerous religious poems.

Training of Child. See *Christian Teaching.*

Training School for Teachers. See *Teachers.*

Trajan. See *Persecutions of Christians,* 3.

Trandberg, P. L. See *Bornholmers.*

Transcendence. The teaching that God is supermundane, that is, absolutely free and absolutely superior to all earthly, material things. God is the Absolute One whom the heaven of heavens cannot contain (1 Kings 8:27; Job 11:8-10). This does not mean that God has His position outside the earth as a mere onlooker or judge (see *Deism*). God is transcendent and immanent at the same time. Since He is the supramundane Ruler, there can be no world outside Him. The world is a place created by Him for His own free activity (Acts 17:28; Jer. 23:23).

Transcendentalism. Term applied to the idealistic philosophy of Kant, which attempts to explain the possibility of having knowledge of principles that transcend human experience. Applied also to certain religious, philosophical, and social teachings current in New England in the thirties and forties of the 19th century and centering in Ralph Waldo Emerson, who with several others organized the Transcendental Club (1836).

Transept. See *Architecture, Ecclesiastical,* 7.

Transfer of Training. See *Christian Teaching,* L.

Translations, Bible. See *Bible Versions.*

Transmigration of Souls, or *Metempsychosis.* 1. The doctrine that the soul at death passes into another body, that of a human being, animal, or plant. This widely prevalent belief is based on an animistic conception of nature (see *Animism*). If not only human beings, but also animals, plants, and inanimate objects have souls, these various forms of existence must be on the same plane and therefore may be interchangeable.

2. Metempsychosis is one of the most prominent features of the religions of India, where it has a distinctly ethical and religious character. They teach that a man is reborn to expiate sins committed in previous lives. Thereby the soul is purified until it finally returns to God, its Source. This doctrine is not found in the *Rig-Veda,* but made its appearance in India with the rise of Brahmanism.* The latter teaches that at death the soul is reincarnated immediately either in a higher or lower state than it previously had, depending upon the deeds, whether good or evil, committed in previous existences. The six orthodox systems of Brahmanic philosophy have each their own doctrine as to how salvation, *i. e.,* release from the continuous round of rebirths

with its concomitant suffering, may be obtained.

3. As Buddhism denies the existence of the soul, it also theoretically denies metempsychosis, but teaches what practically is the same thing, namely, that man's *karma*, *i. e.*, his character entities, or the ethical consequences of his deeds, migrate and determine the state of future existences and finally end in nirvana.*

4. It is not definitely known whether or not the Egyptians believed in transmigration. Herodotus asserts that they did, but no text has thus far been found to support the assertion, though the belief in metamorphosis, that is, the magical change from human to animal form, was quite prevalent in Egypt and forms the subject of several chapters of the Book of the Dead.

5. In Greece, metempsychosis was taught by the Orphics, Pythagoras and his school, Empedocles, and also by Plato, according to whom the soul must migrate through human and animal bodies for 10,000 years until it returns to the Deity, its Source. Aristotle rejected the doctrine, but it is found again in Neoplatonism, in the teachings of several Gnostic sects and of the Manicheans, and in the Talmud and the Kabbala. The Talmudists taught that, as God had created only a certain number of Jewish souls, these had to be reincarnated again and again, sometimes even in the bodies of animals. The doctrine was also held by the Celtic Druids and early Teutons and is found today among savage and barbarian peoples in many parts of the earth. It is a fundamental doctrine in modern Theosophy.

6. As this belief is totally at variance with divine revelation, it has always been rejected by the Christian Church. Not identical with metempsychosis, but related to it, is totemism * as well as the belief in metamorphosis. That human beings can be changed to animals is a widely current belief (*e. g.*, Circe turning men into swine) and was found especially among the old Germanic peoples. Numerous evidences of this belief are found in German and Scandinavian folklore (*e. g.*, in Grimm's *Maerchen*). The old Germanic peoples called a man turned into a wolf a werewolf and one changed into a bear or other wild beast a berserker. *Lycanthropy* is the term applied to this form of metamorphosis.

Transubstantiation. See *Grace, Means of*, IV 3.

Transvaal, formerly the *South African Republic*. A province in the Union of South Africa within the British Commonwealth of Nations. The country was taken from the Boers and annexed by the British in 1902. Missions by the Hermannsburg Mission (1857); the Berlin Mission (1859); Wesleyan Methodists (1871); Anglicans (1877).

Trappists (Order of Reformed Cistercians). A monastic order, stricter than even the Carthusians, originating in a Cistercian reform by Abbot de Rancé at the monastery of La Trappe in Normandy (ca. 1664). The monks rise at two o'clock and devote eleven hours to prayer and masses and five hours to manual labor. From their two daily meals, meat, fish, and eggs are rigidly excluded. They may speak to superiors, but never among themselves except by signs. At night unbroken silence must reign. Gethsemane Abbey, in Kentucky, is the best known of three abbeys in this country.

Trautmann, Philipp Jakob (1815 to 1900). B. in Rhenish Bavaria; sent to America by Pastor Loehe 1845; pastor in Danbury, Ohio; became a member of the Missouri Synod at its first convention; pastor in Adrian, Mich., 1850; retired 1882, repeatedly supplying vacancies.

Tre Ore. In the Catholic Church the three hours from 12 noon to 3 in the afternoon on Good Friday, during which the deepest silence is observed in commemoration of Christ's suffering on the cross. A procession is usually held, especially in large churches.

Treasury of Merits. See *Thesaurus Meritorum*.

Trench, Richard Chenevix (1807 to 1886). Archbishop of Dublin (Anglican); b. at Dublin; educated in England; professor of New Testament exegesis at Cambridge; dean of Westminster; archbishop; d. in London; poet and scholar; wrote: *New Testament Synonyms*, etc.

Trent, The Council of. See *Roman Catholic Confessions*, A.

Tressler, V. G. A. B. April 10, 1865, Somerfield, Pa.; ed. at Gettysburg College (Pa.), Chicago Univ.; McCormick Theol. Sem., Leipzig Univ., Univ. of Berlin, and Univ. of Paris; Lutheran pastor, San Jose, Calif., 1891—98; lecturer, San Jose Academy, 1896—98; dean and prof., Ansgar College, Hutchinson, Minn., 1901—02; prof. Wittenberg Coll., 1903—05; Hamma Divinity School, 1905—; pres. General Synod, 1917—18; d. Sept., 1923.

Treves, Holy Coat of. See *Holy Coat of Treves.*

Tridentine Creed. See *Roman Catholic Confessions.*

Trinidad (and *Tobago*), an island in the West Indies, forming with Tobago a British crown colony. Discovered and named by Columbus 1498. Area, 1,976 sq. mi. Population, 635,843 (1950), mostly of Spanish and Negro mixture. Missions by a number of churches. Statistics: 38,443 Protestant communicants (1952).

Trinitarians. A monastic order founded by St. John of Matha in 1198. The first objective of the order was to secure release of slaves. It afterwards expanded its activities to social service.

Trinity. 1. The eternal, infinite Spirit, subsisting in three Persons, Father, Son, and Holy Ghost. God is one (Is. 44:6; 48:12; Deut. 6:4; 1 Tim. 2:5). God is also three. The one statement does not contradict the other. The divine plurality is indicated in the Hebrew word for God, *Elohim,* which is the plural form of the noun, yet expressing not a plurality of gods, but a plurality in God, as indicated by the singular form of the predicate, *e. g., created* (Gen. 1:1). Although a Trinity, the divine Unity is one undivided and indivisible divine Essence, and the divine Trinity is not a Trinity of parts, but of persons, each of whom is in the same sense God. There is no God but the First Person; there is no God but the Second Person; there is no God beside the Third Person; and yet each Person is God, the same God, the only God. And again, the First Person is not the Second nor the Third; the Second is not the First nor the Third; the Third is not the First nor the Second. "There is one Divine Essence which is called, and truly is, God. In this one Divine Essence there are three Persons, equally powerful, equally eternal, God the Father, God the Son, and God the Holy Ghost, all three *one* Essence, eternal, undivided, without parts, of infinite power, wisdom, and goodness, the Creator and Preserver of all things, visible and invisible." (Augsburg Confession, Art. I.)

2. All similes, comparisons, images, or illustrations by which men have tried to represent the doctrine of three Persons in one Godhead fail to illustrate; much less do they explain. The Trinity has been compared to fire, which is said to possess the three "attributes" of flame, light, and heat; but this division is highly artificial, and the comparison is altogether faulty, because Father, Son, and Holy Ghost are not so many attributes of God, but are, each of them, God Himself. The Trinity has been compared to the division of the human being into body, soul, and mind; but each of these constituents is not separately a human being, while each of the divine Persons, separately considered, is truly God (as when it is said that "in Him [Christ] dwelleth all the fullness of the Godhead bodily").

3. The doctrine of the Trinity is, like all the rest, entirely beyond our powers of comprehension. By this we do not say that there is here a contradiction with human reason; it would be so if we taught: "There is only one God"; and: "There are three Gods." But such is not the doctrine of Scripture. There is one God — there are three Persons — these three are one God. There is here not, properly speaking, a mathematical difficulty; in other words, the matter that is incomprehensible is not the numeral terms: one — three, but it is the relation of the three Persons to one another, the manner in which they are united in one Godhead, one divine Being, without being only parts of that Being. In the words of the Augsburg Confession: "By this word 'person' is not meant a part or an attribute of another." And this is the mystery of the Trinity.

4. That the Father, the Son, and the Spirit are three distinct Persons is evident from the narrative of the Baptism of Christ. Matt. 3:13-17. The Father proclaims Himself in the voice from heaven: "This is My beloved Son, in whom I am well pleased." The Son is visibly present as He stands in the River Jordan. The Holy Ghost descends upon Him from above in the likeness of a dove. The three Persons are mentioned in the Great Commission. Matt. 28:19. They are clearly distinguished in Is. 48:16, where mention is made of one who sends (the Father), of one who is sent (the Messiah), and of the "Spirit of the Lord God." In another passage, Is. 63:9, 10, there is a reference to the Lord who sends the "Angel of His presence" (cf. Gen. 48:16) and to the "Holy Spirit." Gen. 1:1-3 and Ps. 33:6 also refer to the Lord, the Word

(cf. John 1:1), and the Spirit, or Breath, of God, as Maker of heaven and earth.

5. These three Persons are in many passages, both of the Old and the New Testament, declared equally powerful, equally eternal (Eph. 1:10; 3:14-16; John 8:58; Job 33:4). Of each of the three Persons, acts of divine power are predicated. All receive, in an equal degree, that honor and adoration which is due only to the Creator of all things, the Lord of heaven and earth. The entire and absolute equality (in rank) of the Father and the Son cannot be stated more succinctly than in John 5:23 (cf. Heb. 1:6; or the omnipotence of the Son than in Is. 9:6; or the omniscience of the Spirit than in 1 Cor. 2:10 (cp. vv. 11, 13, 14). Hence the Athanasian Creed is right when it asserts: "Of these three Persons none is the first, none the last, none the greatest, none the smallest, but all three Persons are equally eternal, equally great. . . . Yet there are not three Gods, but one God."

Trinity Theological Seminary. See *Ministry, Education of,* XI F.

Tripitaka. See *Sacred Literatures.*

Trisagion, or Seraphic Hymn. The hymn of the Communion liturgy following the Preface, based upon the song of the seraphim, Is. 6:3, but enlarged by the greeting of the great Hallel, Ps. 118: 25, 26.

Tritheism. The heretical doctrine that Father, Son, and Holy Ghost are not three distinct Persons in the one and undivided divine Essence, but three distinct essences, or gods. While Monarchianism denies the three Persons in the Godhead, teaching that there is but one divine person, Tritheism denies the unity of God, teaching in its place three numerically distinct natures, or essences, and so a modified form of polytheism. Tritheism was defended as late as the 6th century by groups of Monophysites in Asia Minor. In the Middle Ages the heresy was revived by Roscellin. It has found defenders even in modern times.

Triumph the Church and Kingdom of God in Christ. See *Holiness Bodies,* 2.

Triumphal Arch. See *Architecture, Ecclesiastical,* 7.

Troeltsch, Ernst (1865—1925). German Protestant theologian; b. at Augsburg, taught at universities of Goettingen, Bonn, Heidelberg, and since 1908 professor of Systematic Theology, Berlin, successor to Pfleiderer; one of the founders of the *religionsgeschichtliche* school.

Trope. A textual addition to the official authorized texts of the Roman Mass. Such additions were, for example, inserted into the Kyrie. The chorale "Kyrie, God Father in Heaven Above" (*L. H.,* No. 6) is such a trope.

Trotzendorf (Friedland), Valentin (1490—1556). One of the great Protestant schoolmen of the Reformation period; studied under Luther and Melanchthon; became rector of the Latin school at Goldberg, Silesia, 1531. Under his direction the school became famous and attracted hundreds of students. It was purely humanistic; Latin, Greek, and Religion were the only subjects of instruction; the use of any language but Latin in conversation was prohibited. A series of calamities broke up the school in 1554.

Truber, Primus (1508—86). Preached in German and Wendish, or Slovenian, at Laibach; had Wendish catechisms and commentaries printed in Germany and thus founded Protestantism in Krain; twice exiled.

Trullan Councils. See *Monothelitism.*

Trumbull, Henry Clay (1830—1903). American author and clergyman in the Congregational Church; army chaplain during the Civil War; 1875 editor of the *Sunday School Times;* wrote: *War Memories of an Army Chaplain; The Knightly Soldier; Principles and Practice;* and others.

Truth, God as. God is *Truth* inasmuch as what He does is in agreement with what He says or promises. There is in Him no discrepancy between His will and His words. There is no change of will in God which might put Him at variance with His promises. Human promises often fail of fulfillment, whereas in God there is no such shortcoming or discrepancy, and therefore hope based upon His promises is never vain. Thus, as God is at all times and everywhere Himself, His words are at all times and in every instance the words of God, who cannot lie.

Tryggvesson, Olaf. See *Norway, Early Christianity in.*

Trzanowski (Tranousky), G. (1592 to 1637). The "Slavonic Luther."

B. at Cieszyn, Silesia. Studied at Cieszyn; Guben, Saxony; Kolberg, Pomerania; Wittenberg. Teacher at St. Nicholas in Prague; tutor in the home of a Bohemian noble; headmaster at a school in Holesnov, Moravia; pastor in Valasske Mezirici, Moravia. In 1624 the Evangelical clergy were ordered to leave Moravia, and Trzanowski went to Cieszyn and from there to Bielsko, where he found protection under Baron John Sunegh, who sheltered him during the Counter Reformation. In 1631 he was called to a congregation at Liptovsky Svaty Mikulas, Slovakia, where he stayed until his death. Trzanowski translated the Augsburg Confession into Czech in 1620. His most characteristic publication was his hymnbook, *Cithara Sanctorum*, which has appeared in 150 editions and has been extensively used by Slovak Lutherans in the United States, Canada, and South America.

Andrew Wantula, "The Slavonic Luther," *CTM*, XVII: 728—37.

Tschackert, Paul Moritz Robert (1848—1911). Followed Tholuck in theology; 1899 professor of church history at Goettingen; prolific writer; together with Bonwetsch edited Kurtz's church history (13th and 14th editions).

Tuch, Johann Christian Friedrich (1806—67). B. at Quedlinburg; d. at Leipzig. Studied at Halle. *Privatdozent*, 1830, then associate professor there; associate professor at Leipzig, 1841; full professor, 1843; also canon of Zeitz, 1853. His chief work was his *Kommentar ueber die Genesis*.

Tucher, Gottlieb von (1798—1877). Judge of Supreme Court at Munich, 1856—68; greatly interested in liturgics; published *Kirchengesaenge der beruehmtesten aelteren italienischen Meister* and *Schatz des evangelischen Kirchengesangs*.

Tucker, Abraham (1705—74). British moralist and metaphysical writer; advocated utilitarianism; wrote *Free Will, Foreknowledge, and Fate; Man in Quest of Himself; Light of Nature Pursued*.

Tucker, Charlotte Maria (1821 to 1893). B. at Barnet, England; d. at Amritsar, India. After having been a successful writer of stories, she went to India at the age of fifty-four as a missionary (1875), defraying her own expenses, laboring first at Amritsar, later at Batala, among the Mohammedans. She was one of the pioneer workers in the zenana mission. Already before going to India, she had acquired the Urdu (Hindustani dialect) and used it like an Oriental. Also in India she was a prolific author. Her *Pearls of Wisdom*, explanatory of the Lord's Parables, was circulated throughout India.

Tucker, William Jowett (1839—1926). Presbyterian clergyman; prof. at Andover Theological Seminary; pres. of Dartmouth College; active in the field of social ethics.

Tuebingen School. See *Isagogics*, 4; *Lutheran Theology after 1580*, 12.

Tuition. See *Parish Education*, I.

Tunder, Franz (1614 or 1615—67). An eminent Lutheran composer of the Baroque Era and the father-in-law of Dietrich Buxtehude, his successor at the *St. Marienkirche* in Luebeck, may have received his training from Frescobaldi (Mattheson) and thus established a relationship between the North and South German schools of organists. It is believed that Tunder instituted the *Abendmusiken* in Luebeck, which later became famous under Buxtehude's direction and which induced young J. S. Bach to journey to Luebeck to hear them and become personally acquainted with Buxtehude.

Tunic. A sacklike vestment with slits for head and arms (sometimes with sleeves), worn by bishops and subdeacons. The dalmatic is just like it.

Tunisia (Tunis). A French protectorate in North Africa; one of the former Barbary States under the sovereignty of Turkey. Capital, Tunis. Area, ca. 48,195 sq. mi. Population, 3,143,498 (1946), among them 1,937,834 Arabs and Bedouins, the remainder being Europeans and Jews. Islam is the dominant religion. Protestant missions, as in all French possessions, are greatly hampered. Algeria borders on Tunis to the west and is also a French protectorate. In Algeria and Tunis missions are conducted by a number of churches and societies. Statistics: about 300 Protestant Christians.

Turkey, the Republic of. Formerly the *Ottoman Empire*. Since World War I stripped of much of its former territory. Turkey embraces Asia Minor, southeastern Europe, Constantinople, and much of Arabia and Anatolia. Area in Europe, 9,256 sq. mi. Population, 1,626,299 (1952). Of these 5,213 are Protestants. The Christian churches consist mostly of foreign residents and people belonging to families which were never Moslem, but whose fathers belonged to the ancient Christian churches. Turkey in Asia has an area of 285,246 sq. mi. Population 19,308,441. The American Board and Seventh-Day Adventists are active here with about 3,000 members and adherents in 1952. The Greek Orthodox Church, under the Ecumenical Patriarchate of Constantinople, numbers 103,000 members, and the Roman Catholics 11,000. Since World War I, under the Republic, the various patriarchs of the branches of the Greek Orthodox Church are regarded as performing functions purely ecclesiastical. See *Eastern Orthodox Churches.*

Turretin, Francis. See *Reformed Confessions,* A 10.

Tuttiett, Lawrence (1825 to 1897). A clergyman of the Church of England, born at Colyton, Devonshire, educated at King's College, London, entered the ministry in 1848 and later became vicar of Lea Marston, Warwickshire. From 1870 to 1880 he was incumbent of the Church of St. Andrew's, Scotland, where he became, he said, "quite a Scotchman at heart." His last charge was that of prebend at St. Nimians Cathedral, Perth. Among his published volumes are *Hymns for Churchmen* and *Hymns for the Children of the Church.* His hymns are characterized by smoothness of rhythm, directness of aim, simplicity of language, and deep earnestness. "Father, Let Me Dedicate All This Year to Thee."

Twenty-Eight Theses. See *Barmen Theses.*

Twenty-Five Articles of Religion. See *Democratic Declarations,* 6.

Twenty-Four Articles. See *Presbyterian Confessions,* 4.

Two-Seed-in-the-Spirit Predestinarian Baptists. See *Baptist Bodies,* 13.

Tychonius (4th century). Pelagian and Biblical scholar; opposed rebaptism of those who entered the Pelagian sect; held that there were unholy men in the Church and its ministry; his book on hermeneutics is an early attempt at rules of interpretation, some of its principles still being used by some interpreters.

Tye, Christopher (ca. 1510—72). Was one of England's great composers of church music. Though his style is a bit archaic and stiff, especially when based on Latin texts, his compositions based on English texts are fresher and more appealing.

Tyler, Bennet (1783—1857). Congregational clergyman; pres. of Dartmouth College; pastor at Second Church, Portland, Md.; chief opponent of the New Haven Theology of Nathaniel W. Taylor; when the Theological Institute of Connecticut was founded to offset the influence of the New Haven theology, Tyler became its pres. and prof. of theology.

Tyndale, William (ca. 1485—1536). Unable to translate the New Testament in all England, he probably went to Wittenberg. He "reproduced in English Luther's German Testament," which was smuggled into England early in 1526; in the same year he printed his *Prolog to the Epistle to the Romans,* a paraphrase of Luther's famous work; in 1528 *The Parable of the Wicked Mammon* and *The Obedience of a Christian Man;* in 1532 *The Exposition of the Sermon on the Mount.* Held Reformed doctrine concerning the Lord's Supper. Burned at Vilvorde.

Tyndall, John (1820—93). British physicist; b. in County Carlow, Ireland; professor at Royal Institute, London, since 1853; made many visits to Switzerland to study glaciers; retired 1887. Together with Darwin and Huxley a noted exponent of the evolutionary theory. Popularized Spencer's materialistic and agnostic views on religion.

Typological Interpretation. See *Exegesis,* 7.

Typology. See *Geography, Christian,* 6.

Tyrrell, George (1861—1909). Left the Anglican Church and became a member of the Jesuits. Denied inerrancy of Roman Catholic theology. Wrote, among others, *Christianity at the Crossroads.*

Tzschirner, Heinrich Gottlieb (1778 to 1828). B. at Mittweida, near Chemnitz; d. at Leipzig. Studied at Leipzig. *Privatdozent* at Wittenberg, 1800; soon adjunct of the philosophical faculty there; then deacon of his native town; prof. of theology at Wittenberg, 1805; at Leipzig, 1809. His lectures inspired Leopold von Ranke and Karl Hase to write objective history.

U

Ubiquity. This term means "every-whereness" and was used by Lutheran theologians in the sense of "omnipresence," especially the omnipresence of Christ according to His human nature (Matt. 28:20). The Reformed theologians charged the Lutherans with teaching a local ubiquity or a local extension of the human nature of Christ, which, however, the Lutherans denied. The term originated in the scholastic schools of the Middle Ages.

Uganda Protectorate. In East Africa, north of Lake Victoria Nyanza, a British protectorate since 1894. Area, 94,204 sq. mi. Population, about 5,000,000 (1948). Christian missions were introduced through Henry Stanley, by whom the Church Missionary Society was called in 1875. Alexander Mackay was the real founder of the mission. Violent persecutions were encountered under King Mwanga, fostered by French Roman Catholic priests. An Anglican bishopric has been established. Missions by the British and Foreign Bible Society, Church Missionary Society, Africa Inland Mission. Statistics: 104,833 Protestants; the Roman Church claims 986,000 (1952).

Uhde, Fritz von (1848—1924). German painter, exponent of radical realism, with a tendency toward Socialistic interpretation; very original in the conception of his paintings, making the Biblical characters, especially Christ, appear in the conditions and circumstances of the present; among his paintings: "Suffer the Children"; "Holy Night"; "Come, Lord Jesus, Be Our Guest."

Uhlhorn, Johann Gerhard Wilhelm (1826—91). Lutheran preacher and theologian; court preacher at Hanover 1855; member of consistory 1866; abbot of Loccum 1878; published *Geschichte der christlichen Liebestaetigkeit*, 3 vols., 1882 to 1890; *Kampf des Christentums mit dem Heidentum* 1874.

Uitzilopochtli. See *Aztecs, Religion of.*

Ulfilas (*Wulfilas*) (ca. 310—83). The first bishop of the Goths, a Germanic tribe, at that time having its home along the northwestern shore of the Black Sea, near the mouth of the Danube. A Christian from his youth, since his mother was a member of the Church, he was trained for the ministry in Constantinople, being made bishop in 341, and did yeoman's service in the conversion of the Gothic people; at first an adherent of the Nicene Creed, he turned Arian in 360; his most noted work that of the translation of the Bible (with the exception of the Four Books of the Kings) into Gothic, the first translation of the Bible into any Germanic tongue, his work following the original quite slavishly. See *Bible Versions.*

Ullmann, Karl (1796—1865). Prof. at Halle and Heidelberg; prelate or representative of the Evangelical Church in the upper chamber; favored union between Lutheran and Reformed churches in Baden; opposed Rationalism; editor of *Theologische Studien und Kritiken.*

Ulrich von Hutten (1488—1523). Humanist, writer, friend of Luther in the early days of the Reformation; descendant of a noble Frankish family; eager for education and culture; studied at the University of Cologne and became a prominent classical scholar; wrote early satirical pamphlets against Ulrich von Wuerttemberg; after 1517 active in the interest of freeing Germany from the incubus of the Roman Curia, the humanistic side being most prominent in his efforts; after the disputation at Leipzig he openly espoused the side of Luther, but his zeal was often of the fleshly kind, and he was inclined to carry out his designs by force of arms; obliged to flee under the ban of the emperor, he sought various places of refuge, finally at Zurich, where Zwingli befriended him till his early death.

Ulrici, Hermann (1806—84). Prof. at Halle; philosopher, opponent of Hegel; theistic; wrote *Ueber Prinzip und Methode der Hegelschen Philosophie; Glauben und Wissen.*

Ulster Plantation. See *Presbyterian Bodies,* 3.

Ultramontanism. 1. The theory of the Italian party (*ultra montes,* beyond the mountains, *i. e.,* the Alps) in the Roman Catholic Church which favored papal supremacy as opposed to Gallicanism, or the theory that the final authority resides in the collective episcopate. It contemplates, in its widest reach, a politico-ecclesiastical government under the immediate and irresponsible control of the Papacy, a universal Christian (*i. e.*, Catholic) society under the Pope's sovereign dominion. Ultramontanism is, therefore, the implacable foe of all individualism, freedom, and tolerance, of all separatism and independence, and particularly of the Protestant Reformation.

2. The theory has never been realized, not even in the Vatican Council of 1870. It has a long history. Its roots may be traced to the imperial idea in pagan Rome, the emperor being world priest and world monarch in one person. When Rome became Christian and the Church was modeling her organization on that of the empire, the bishops of Rome, as the metropolis, were not slow to recognize, to their own advantage, an analogy between their position and that of the civil ruler. With the abolition of the imperial office (A. D. 470) they fell heir to much of the emperor's power. The scheme of ultramontanism (if we may use the term at this stage) was fully worked out in the notorious forgery known as the Donation of Constantine (see *Pseudo-Isidorian Decretals*).

3. The restoration of the empire under Charlemagne (crowned by the Pope in 800) proved to be the source of endless complications and conflicts between the rival claims of Pope and emperor, resulting, in the end, in the triumph of the Papacy, that is to say, of the ultramontane theory. Such Popes as Gregory VII, Innocent III, and others were virtually world rulers, who wielded both the civil and the spiritual sword as their legitimate right. Boniface VIII, arrayed with sword, crown, and scepter and greeting the thronging pilgrims in Rome with the words: "I, I am emperor" (*Ego, ego sum imperator*), represents the pinnacle of medieval ultramontanism. But these claims were persistently contested and never fully realized. The rise of modern states with a pronounced national consciousness curtailed the Pope's temporal power. On the other hand, in its spiritual aspect, ultramontanism, after many ups and downs (Febronianism,* Jansenism,* Gallicanism,* Josephinism *), has been pushed forward to its logical conclusion in the dogma of papal supremacy and infallibility of the year 1870. But in the light of modern papal utterances the comprehensive ideal of a theocratic *régime,* including civil and religious sovereignty, is by no means abandoned.

Umbreit, Friedrich Wilhelm Karl (1795—1860). Prof. at Heidelberg; mediating theologian with supernatural tendencies; wrote a number of commentaries on Old Testament books and on Romans.

Unam Sanctam. A papal bull issued in 1302 by Boniface VIII from the Lateran, in defiance of Philip the Fair of France, who with his people had set himself against the secular pretensions of the Papal See. The bull lays down dogmatic propositions on the unity of the Church, the position of the Pope as supreme head of the Church, and the duty of "every creature" to submit to the Pope in order to belong to the Church and to obtain salvation. Boniface asserted that both swords, spiritual and secular, are under the control of the Church, the spiritual wielded by the clergy *in* the Church, the secular employed by the hand of civil authority *for* the Church, but under the direction of the spiritual power. That the temporal power is independent was called a Manichean heresy. This bull met with violent opposition on the part of the king and Parliament of France, but the principles it advocated have never been renounced by the papal court.

Unamuno y Jugo, Miguel de (1864 to 1936). Outstanding Spanish poet, philosopher, essayist, and literary man; prof. at Salamanca; influenced by Kierkegaard, the importance of whose work he stressed at a very early date.

Uncials. See *Manuscripts of the Bible.*

Uncreated Grace. See *Gratia Increata.*

Unction, Extreme. 1. The seventh sacrament of the Roman Church, extreme unction, is administered to those who are dangerously ill and are expected to die, usually after they have received Communion. The officiating priest anoints the sick person with holy oil on the eyes, ears, nostrils, mouth, hands, feet, and reins (the last omitted with women), saying: "By this holy unction and by His most tender mercy may the Lord forgive thee whatsoever thou hast committed by sight" ("by hearing," etc.). If the patient recovers, the rite may be repeated when he is again critically ill. Extreme unction is said to "confer grace, remit sin, and comfort the sick" (Council of Trent, Sess. XIV, can. 2); especially, to give strength to resist the devil (*Catechismus Romanus*, II: 6, 14, 3).

2. Romanists quote James 5:14, 15 as the institution of this sacrament — a passage that gives no token of having so solemn a mission, does not speak of preparation for death, lays all emphasis on the prayer of faith, and refers to the anointing with oil, as does Mark 6:13, for bodily healing. Rome remains true to itself to the last and ushers its adherents out of the world bidding them trust in a human figment, working *ex opere operato* (see *Opus Operatum*), instead of directing them to the all-sufficient and all-comforting merits of Christ.

Underhill, Evelyn (1875—1941). English mystic poet and author; wrote *A Barlamb's Ballad Book*, *Mysticism* (passed through many editions), *Immanence*, *Man and the Supernatural*, *Concerning the Inner Life*, *The Rhythm of Sacrifice*, *the Golden Sequence*.

Unfederated Malay States. See *Malaya, British*.

Ungleich, M. Lukas. See *Lutheran Confessions*, A 5.

Uniate Churches. See *Union Movements*, 2.

Uniates. Several bodies of Eastern Christians, both in Europe and Asia, who, while in communion with Rome, are permitted to retain certain traditional local peculiarities in discipline and worship. As a rule, they employ their native language in their liturgies, celebrate the Eucharist under both kinds, allow their priests to marry once, and have a body of canon law of their own.

Unierten. See *Evangelical and Reformed Church*, 2.

Uniform Sunday School Lessons. See *Union Movements*, 11.

Unigenitus. Bull issued by Clement XI in 1713 against the Jansenist Pasquier Quesnel, whose commentary on the New Testament, though warmly approved by the French clergy, did not meet with the favor of the Jesuits. From this work are extracted one hundred and one propositions, which the bull condemns as "false, captious, ill-sounding, offensive, scandalous," etc., etc. The propositions are not verbal citations from Quesnel's book, but doctrinal theses purporting to represent his theological standpoint. Some of these sentences are put in an exaggerated form, others are clearly patristic, and still others are thoroughly Biblical. The bull pronounces a general condemnation upon all. A few are here inserted: *Jesu Christi gratia, principium efficax boni cuiuscumque generis, necessaria est ad omne opus bonum* (The grace of Jesus Christ, the efficacious principle of every kind of good, is necessary for every good work). *Fides est prima gratia et fons omnium aliarum* (Faith is the first gift of grace and the source of all the others). *Interdicere Christianis lectionem sacrae Scripturae, praesertim Evangelii, est interdicere usum luminis filiis lucis et facere, ut patiantur speciem quandam excommunicationis* (To forbid Christians to read Holy Scriptures, especially the Gospel, is to forbid the children of light the use of the lamp and to make them suffer a species of excommunication). Many of the French clergy, including the archbishop of Paris, protested against the bull and appealed to the decision of a general council. But: *Roma locuta, causa finita* (Rome has spoken, the matter is settled).

Unio Mystica. See *Mystical Union*.

Union Movements. 1. Union movements in the Christian Church vary in character. (1) Some groups seek to bring about union through strict doctrinal agreement, the only God-pleasing basis for church union and fellowship. (2) Advocates of unionism favor union by compromise, according to the slogan *In necessariis unitas, in non-necessariis libertas, in utrisque caritas, i. e.,* union without doctrinal unity and in spite of doctrinal differences. (3) The purpose of some union movements is simply to draw Christians closer together with a view to co-operation in certain areas of activity and to present a united front against atheism and other foes.

2. Since Apostolic times heresy has disrupted the outward unity of Christendom. Many of the heresies of the early centuries were incorporated with the Papistic system and are maintained by the Roman Catholic Church to this day. The arrogant claims of the bishop of Rome split the Church into East and West and have been the major cause of schism for centuries. Unsuccessful attempts were made to unite the Eastern and Western Churches (Lyons, 1274, and Florence, 1439). Rome has succeeded in bringing groups of Christians under her jurisdiction as *uniate churches*, that is, groups in fellowship

with Rome, but granted certain concessions, such as marriage of the clergy.

3. Through the Reformation, Luther restored the Church to its Apostolic purity, but Protestantism split into two branches, the Lutheran and the Reformed. Efforts to unite the two churches proved futile. At Marburg (1529) Luther took a firm stand in favor of union based on unity of doctrine, while Zwingli was willing to compromise in unionistic fashion. The Wittenberg Concord (1536) failed to unite the Swiss and the Lutherans. Melanchthon, a thoroughgoing unionist, urged acceptance of the *Augsburg* and *Leipzig* interims, although they compromised the precious truths so dearly purchased through the Reformation and had no other purpose than to force the Lutherans back into the Catholic fold. Melanchthon altered the Augsburg Confession (*Variata*), thus making a concession to the Reformed in the doctrine of the Lord's Supper, and played into the hands of Calvin, who hoped to unite the Lutherans and the Reformed. Melanchthon's betrayal of the truth occasioned the crypto-Calvinistic controversy, undermined the unity of the Lutheran Church, and jeopardized its doctrinal foundation. The aim of the Philippists was to unite Lutherans and Calvinists on the basis of the *Variata*, to which Calvin could readily subscribe. The strife was settled through the adoption of the Formula of Concord (1577), and thus Lutheranism was saved.

4. A conference between Anglicans and Lutherans (1538) bore no fruit. Negotiations of Protestant churches with the Eastern Church (1575) failed to bring the two churches closer together. Efforts to unite English Protestants and Catholics were made without success. Such efforts have always failed because union as understood by the Papists means a return to the Catholic Church and a surrender of those Christian truths which Protestants hold dear. For some time after the adoption of the Formula of Concord it was a generally accepted principle among Lutherans that union with dissident groups cannot be achieved except on a confessional basis. This principle began to give way under the impact of Pietism and Rationalism, for both Pietism and Rationalism with their emphasis on life and their indifference to pure doctrine encouraged the unionistic spirit. Lutherans and Reformed were urged to disregard doctrinal differences. What separates the churches must not be considered divisive of fellowship. Union, it was said, should express itself in joint participation in the Lord's Supper and in church government. Frederick William III called upon the two churches to unite and form the Evangelical Church (Unierte Kirche). This Prussian Union (1817) was purely unionistic, for all distinctive doctrines were to be treated as nonessential. It was the hope of the King of Prussia that the two churches would in the course of time forget their differences and become one church under the more generic name of Evangelical; but his meddling brought another church into existence.

5. During the nineteenth century interest in church union on a unionistic platform was not very strong throughout the Christian world. Uniting bodies, as a rule, were basically one in confession, and therefore doctrinal compromise was not required. Thus a number of groups of Evangelical persuasion organized in the United States and formed the Evangelical Synod of North America. Various Presbyterian groups united into one body. Reformed churches of the United States, holding the Presbyterian system, united in 1907 to form the Council of Reformed Churches. The Methodists in Canada united in 1874 and 1883 to form the Methodist Church of Canada. The Presbyterian Church united with the Cumberland Presbyterian Church in 1906. The United Evangelical Church was organized in 1894. The Synodical Conference was organized in 1872. The Lutheran Church — Missouri Synod, the Joint Synod of Wisconsin and Other States, the Slovak Evangelical Lutheran Church of America, and the Norwegian Synod of the American Evangelical Lutheran Church are now united in the Synodical Conference.

6. The first half of the twentieth century will go down in history as an era of union and unionism. The seed of rationalism inherent in Reformed theology continues to germinate and produce new sects. Modernism, the ultimate expression of rationalism, is responsible for division and for the rise of Fundamentalism, which clings to the saving truths of the Word but has, in many of its sectors, embraced chiliasm and other errors. While modernistic churchmen seek to bring the churches together on a unionistic basis, Fundamentalists, aware of the apostasy, are drawing closer together and organizing

to defend the Christian heritage. It would be beyond the scope of this article to list all present-day sects that are seeking to unite with others and the threescore cases in which mergers have been discussed, attempted, or achieved. Only some of the more prominent can be mentioned.

7. Northern Baptists and Free Baptists (1911); merger of three Lutheran bodies to form the Norwegian Lutheran Church (1917); merger of 45 synods to form the United Lutheran Church (1918); Presbyterian Church in the U. S. A. and the Welsh Calvinistic Church (1920); the Evangelical Association and the United Evangelical Church (1922); Reformed Church in the United States and Hungarian Reformed Church (1924); Methodist, Congregational, and Presbyterian Churches of Canada united to form the United Church of Canada (1925); Congregational and Christian Churches united to form the General Council of Congregational and Christian Churches (1931); merger of Ohio, Iowa, and Buffalo Synods to form the American Lutheran Church (1930); merger of Evangelical Synod and Reformed Church in the United States to form the Evangelical and Reformed Church (1934); merger of Northern Methodist, Southern Methodist, and Protestant Methodist Churches (1939); merger of the Evangelical Church with the United Brethren to form the Evangelical United Brethren Church (1947). Northern Baptists favor union with the Disciples. Negotiations between the Presbyterians and Episcopalians have not resulted in union. As late as 1948 the conservative Southern Baptists refused to negotiate for co-operation with the modernistically inclined Northern Baptist communion. For many years efforts have been made through intersynodical conferences to unite the Lutheran bodies of the United States.

8. Two distinct union movements are going forward in Europe, the EKID (*Evangelische Kirche in Deutschland*) and the VELKD (*Vereinigte Evangelische Lutherische Kirche Deutschlands*). As early as 1900 an appeal was made urging all Lutheran territorial churches to unite on the basis of the Lutheran Confessions and thus form a *Corpus Lutheranorum*. The appeal went unheeded. At the close of World War I hopes of union were frustrated because liberalism had weakened the confessional consciousness. The spirit of the Prussian Union was still strong.

After the church struggle in 1933 attempts were made to unite the various territorial churches for the purpose of protecting the Church against the assaults of the neo-pagan philosophy of Hitler and Rosenberg. The war arrested the union movement, but the hardships entailed by the war had drawn the Protestant groups closer together. After the collapse in 1945 plans were made to unite all the churches in one large German Church (EKID). If EKID became a church, it would unite Lutherans, Reformed, and Evangelicals (United) on a grossly unionistic basis.

9. A number of territorial Lutheran churches were opposed to such unionism. Since the close of World War II confessional Lutherans have been trying to effect a union of all Lutheran territorial churches on the basis of the Lutheran Confessions, principally the Unaltered Augsburg Confession and Luther's Small Catechism. The constitution was presented at a meeting held July, 1948, in Eisenach. As soon as three territorial churches approve the constitution, the VELKD will be a reality. It is hoped that in the course of time all Lutheran territorial churches will unite with VELKD and thus help to preserve the heritage of the Reformation. Steps have also been taken toward a union of the Free Churches of Germany. Leaders of the Breslau Free Church and the Saxon Free Church have been in conference and have declared their doctrinal unity. Five other Free Lutheran Churches have united to form the Independent Lutheran Church, which also has entered into fellowship with the other two Free Churches.

Although the confessional Lutherans were opposed to any strategy that would have as its aim the union of all German Protestants on a non-confessional basis, they were willing to consent to a federation of all Protestant groups which would enable all the churches to co-operate in the interest of the general welfare of German Protestantism. Representatives of the three Protestant church bodies met July, 1948, in Eisenach, for the purpose of discussing the organization of EKID. They sought an understanding on two problems: Should EKID be a church or a federation? Should the constituent churches distribute the Lord's Supper to members of the other churches? The constitution of EKID now declares that body to be a federation, not a church, of Lutherans, Reformed, and Evangelical (United) Churches. Members of one of the constituent churches will not necessarily be admitted to Holy Communion in another. The Free Churches protested against the organization of EKID and, on confessional grounds, declined to enter the federation.

10. Alliances, federations, associations, and councils are a part of the union movement, and they are legion. Only the larger groups will be listed. The Evangelical Alliance was formed in London (1846) for the purpose of bringing about a closer fellowship among the believers of the various Protestant communions. Eligible for membership are all who accept the doctrine of inspiration, the doctrine of the Trinity, the deity of Christ, the vicarious atonement, and other fundamentals. The Federal Council of the Churches of Christ in America was organized in Philadelphia (1908) and has represented 25 denominations. Modernists dominated the FCCCA. The Baptist World Alliance was organized to further universal Baptist fellowship and co-ordinate Baptist missionary enterprise. The Lutheran World Federation, formerly known as Lutheran World Convention, held its first meeting in Eisenach (1923). Its purpose is to bring about closer fellowship and co-operation between Lutherans of all nations.

11. Although Fundamentalists and modernists held membership in the FCCCA, the Modernists controlled the Council. Fundamentalists, unable to make their influence felt through the Council, have founded two rival organizations. The American Council of Christian Churches was organized in 1941 by Fundamentalists who maintain that the modernistic Federal Council does not speak officially for the millions of Fundamentalists in the denominations affiliated with the Council. Its purpose is "to enable evangelical Christians to accomplish tasks that can be better done in co-operation than separately, including joint witness to the glorious grace of Christ the Savior." A second purpose is to challenge the claim of the Federal Council that it speaks for all Protestant churches, particularly in the field of religious broadcasting, and in making contacts with the various government offices. Taking the position that the Bible demands "separation from apostasy," the ACCC accepts as constituent members only

such individuals and groups as have withdrawn from the FCCCA. It militantly opposes the FCCCA, rejects "tongues," "sinless perfection," and "healing," and, like the Evangelical Alliance, confesses the fundamentals of Scripture. Fifteen communions are listed as holding membership in the American Council. The ACCC publishes its own series of Uniform Sunday School Lessons. Its official organ is the *Christian Beacon.*

12. The National Association of Evangelicals for United Action was organized in Chicago (1943) on a doctrinal basis similar to that of the ACCC, but it favors communions which believe in "tongues," "sinless perfection," and "healing." In distinction from the ACCC, which demands "separation from apostasy," the NAE leaves it to the discretion of the individual whether or not he will co-operate with a church body identified with the FCCCA. In its official organ, *United Evangelical Action,* the NAE attacks the FCCCA and has said that the "Federal Council has forfeited the right to represent American Protestantism." The growth of the NAE from a handful of forward-looking leaders to a membership of 4,000,000 has been called "a modern miracle." This aggressive group has set up ten commissions which operate in such fields as Radio, Christian Relief, Foreign Missions, Christian Schools, Evangelism, Home Missions, Sunday Schools, Youth, etc. In keeping with one of its major purposes, to revitalize the Sunday school, it has founded the National Sunday School Association and publishes outlines for uniform lessons. A committee has published a philosophy of Christian education entitled *Christian Education in a Democracy.* Affiliated with the NAE are a number of Holiness communions whose peculiar views the ACCC rejects. There is no indication at the present time that a union of the ACCC and the NAE will be consummated.

13. A number of interdenominational agencies have been created for the purpose of co-ordinating and integrating specific types of work. These agencies, eight in number, were operating in 1948—49 with offices and staffs on a budget of almost $800,000. They are the Federal Council of the Churches of Christ in America, the Foreign Missions Conference of North America, the Home Missions Council of North America, the International Council of Religious Education, the

Missionary Education Movement of the U. S. and Canada, the National Protestant Council on Higher Education, the United Council of Church Women, and the United Stewardship Council. Plans for the merger of these agencies were completed in the early part of 1950, and the National Council of the Churches of Christ in the United States was formed at the constituting cónvention in Cleveland, Ohio, Nov. 29, 1950, when the merger of the eight agencies was consummated. The original proposal of the Joint Study Committee was for "the creation of a single corporate agency to succeed all of the existing agencies." The consolidation of these eight agencies does not constitute an organic union of denominations, but it is a merger of agencies for the purpose of co-operation. Nevertheless, some conservatives regard the merger as a thoroughly unionistic endeavor to establish a superchurch with coercive and dictatorial powers.

14. Unionists have long envisioned a global union of all Christian communions on a unionistic basis. Plans for a World Council of Churches were taking shape in the thirties. But the movement for the organization of such a council may be traced back to the World Conference of Missions which met in Edinburgh (1910), for the idea of bringing the Christians of the world together originated at this conference.

15. The immediate antecedents of the World Council were the meeting of the Committee on Life and Work of the Churches (Stockholm, 1925; Oxford, 1937), the World Conference of Faith and Order (Lausanne, 1927; Edinburgh, 1937), and the World Missionary Council (Jerusalem, 1928; India, 1938—39). The meeting for the official formation of the World Council of Churches, scheduled for Utrecht (1938), could not be held because of wartime conditions. Nevertheless, much work was done during the ensuing years, and after the cessation of hostilities Amsterdam was chosen as the place for a meeting which has been designated "the most important Christian gathering in centuries."

The World Council of Churches became a reality when on August 3, 1948, 450 delegates from 42 countries, representing 150 churches, unanimously adopted the following resolution: "That the First Assembly of the World Council of Churches be declared to be and hereby is constituted in accordance with the constitution drafted at Utrecht in 1938 and approved by the churches; that the Assembly consist of those persons who have been appointed as official delegates of churches adhering to the Council; and that formation of the World Council of Churches be declared to be, and hereby is, completed." All leading Christian communions, except the Roman Catholics, are represented in the Council. ACM

Union and Unity Movements, Lutheran, in the United States. Until about the middle of the 18th century no attempt was made to form an organization of Lutheran churches in the United States, except among the Swedes, who were closely connected with their mother country. The outstanding task was to gather Lutherans into congregations. An attempt to form a Swedish-German Lutheran synod failed chiefly because of the efforts of some to include Zinzendorf in the organization.

The Pennsylvania Synod (United Pastors; United Congregations) was organized on Aug. 26, 1748, under the leadership of H. M. Muhlenberg. This organization was active until 1754, when a lull in its activities occurred. Through the efforts of Muhlenberg and Provost Wrangel a pastoral conference was organized (1760), known successively as "the Annual Ministerial Conference of the United Swedish and German Lutheran Ministers," "an Ev. Luth. Ministerium in North America," "the German Ev. Luth. Ministerium of Pennsylvania and Adjoining States." Other early synods were: New York (1786), North Carolina (1803), Joint Synod of Ohio (preachers' conference, 1818; title "Synod" added, 1825); Maryland and Virginia Synod (1820); Tennessee Synod (1820). As the wave of migration moved toward the Pacific Ocean, many synods were organized.

Already in 1807 J. H. C. Helmuth urged that synods be organized into a larger body. The General Synod * was organized at Hagerstown, Md., Oct. 22, 1820. 26 synods belonged to the General Synod in 1860.

At the time of the Civil War the Southern synods withdrew from the General Synod and organized the Ev. Luth. Church in the Confederate States of America (1864; see *United Synod of the Ev. Luth. Church in the South*).

Differences between the "American Lutherans" * and conservatives led to division in the General Synod. The reception of the Melanchthon Synod

(1857) caused the withdrawal of the Swedes (see *Augustana Synod*). Discussions regarding the admission of the Franckean Synod caused the Pennsylvania Ministerium to sever its connection with the General Synod (1866) and take the initiative in the organization of the General Council.*

In the course of time the General Synod, the United Synod, and the General Council began exchanging delegates and published a Common Service. Free conferences were held in 1877, 1878, 1898, 1902, and 1904. The proposal to unite the three synods was made in the Joint Quadricentennial Committee for the Celebration of the Reformation in 1917. The merger convention was held in New York, Nov. 14 to 18, 1918 (see *United Lutheran Church*).

The Missouri Synod was organized April 26, 1847, in St. Paul's Church Chicago. The Free Lutheran Conferences (1855—58) inaugurated a movement to unite Lutherans who were loyal to the Augsburg Confession. The Synodical Conference * was organized at Milwaukee, Wis., July 10—16, 1872. The Lutheran Church—Missouri Synod and other members of the Synodical Conference made efforts to achieve doctrinal unity with other Lutheran bodies. The *St. Paul Theses, Chicago Theses, Brief Statement,* and *Common Confession* are some of the documents resulting from such efforts (for details read, in order: *Chicago Theses, Brief Statement, Common Confession*).

The Ohio Synod * withdrew from the Synodical Conference (1881) and was approached for conferences by the Iowa Synod.* On the basis of the Toledo Theses * the Ohio Synod, Iowa Synod, and Buffalo Synod * merged to form the American Lutheran Church (1930).

In 1870 there were four Norwegian * Synods in America: Eielsen's Synod, Norwegian Synod, Augustana, and Conference. Later there were six, the Hauge Synod having been formed from the Eielsen and the Anti-Missouri Brotherhood from the Norwegian. The Norwegian Synod early sought to unite Norwegians through free conferences. The first was held at Decorah, Iowa. Others followed (1881, 1882, 1883, 1885, 1886, 1887). The secession of the Anti-Missouri Brotherhood halted union efforts (1888). The Augustana, the Conference, and the Anti-Missouri Brotherhood united in 1890 to form the United Church. Committees of the Hauge

Synod, Norwegian Church, and Free Church began negotiating in 1906. The Madison Agreement * was adopted in 1912, and the merger took place in 1917 (see *Evangelical Lutheran Church*).

Swedish Lutherans had originally been affiliated with the Northern Illinois Synod. In 1860 the Swedes withdrew and formed the Scandinavian Augustana Synod with the Norwegians. The Norwegians and Swedes separated peaceably in 1870. The Augustana Synod joined the General Council (1867) and remained in it until 1918 (see *Augustana Synod*).

The Danish Ev. Luth. Church in America was organized in 1872 ("Missionary Association of the Church"), the Danish Ev. Luth. Church in North America in 1894 (22 pastors who did not approve the Grundtvigian constitution of the older church), the Danish Ev. Luth. Church Association in 1884. The last two joined to form the United Danish Ev. Luth. Church in America in 1896.

The Finnish Ev. Luth. Church of America (Suomi Synod) was organized in 1890, the Finnish National Luth. Church in 1898, and the Finnish Apostolic Luth. Church about 1928.

In 1930 the Augustana Synod, United (Danish) Lutheran Church, Lutheran Free Church, Norwegian Lutheran Church (Evangelical Lutheran Church), and the American Lutheran Church formed the American Lutheran Conference * on the basis of the Minneapolis Theses.*

By the end of 1950, the American Lutheran Church, the Ev. Lutheran Church (Norwegian), and the United (Danish) Ev. Lutheran Church had sanctioned a merger of these bodies. The Augustana Synod and the Lutheran Free Church were invited to participate in negotiations toward organic union.

In the last part of the fifth decade of the 20th century union and unity efforts were intensified. The National Lutheran Editors Association in 1948, the American Lutheran Conference in 1948, the Ev. Lutheran Church in 1949, the Executive Committee of the American Lutheran Conference in 1949, and the College of Presidents of The Lutheran Church — Missouri Synod in 1949 favored the calling of free Lutheran conferences.

Thirty-four church leaders met in Minneapolis, Jan. 4, 1949, and urged a closer organizational affiliation of the participating bodies in the National Lutheran Council.* Representatives of the American Lutheran Conference endorsed this plan the following day. On April 26 and 27, 1949, representatives of the bodies participating in the National Lutheran Council met and resolved to place before said bodies the question of an organic union of the bodies participating in the National Lutheran Council. This move failed to obtain the necessary support (1950).

EL

See references under *United States, Lutheranism in.*

Union of South Africa. A Dominion within the British Commonwealth of Nations, composed of the provinces Cape of Good Hope, Natal, Transvaal, and the Orange Free State. Area, 473,089 sq. mi. Population in 1951, 10,500,000. Some mission work was done by the Dutch in the seventeenth century. The Moravians sent George Schmidt in 1737, but his stay was short. In 1792 the Moravians again took up operations and with more success. The S. P. G. came in 1819, gradually enlarging its work. The South African Society for Promoting the Extension of Christ's Kingdom was formed in 1799. The London Missionary Society took up the work in 1811. In 1816 Robert Moffatt came. Quite a number of American, British, and Continental missions are now operating in the Union and in the neighboring British Protectorates Bechuanaland (area 275,000 sq. mi., population 289,000 — 1950), Basutoland (area 11,716 sq. mi., population 574,000—1950), and Swaziland (area 6,700 sq. mi., population 197,000 — 1950); sixteen Lutheran groups are active including the E. L. C. from the U. S. A. The statistics: About 1,500,000 Protestant communicants and 500,000 Roman Catholics (1952).

Union Synod of the Evangelic (sic) Lutheran Church. Organized in November, 1859, by former members of the defunct Indiana Synod (I). Its purpose was to unite all Lutherans in Indiana into one synod. Fraternal relations were at first maintained with the Joint Synod of Ohio, under the leadership of E. S. Henkel, president; but later efforts to unite with it failed because of the laxity of the Union Synod. In 1859 it was a member of the General Synod. In 1869 it resolved to join the General Council, but dissolved in 1871. Its pastors helped to form the Indiana Synod (II) of the General Council, which in 1895 became the Chicago Synod. At one time or other 17 pastors and 27 congregations were connected with the Union Synod.

Unionism (union churches, unionist). A non-Biblical term applied to varying degrees of co-organization, coworship, or collaboration between religious groups irrespective of creeds or spiritual convictions.

The term came into prominence as a result of the Prussian Union,* which sought to unite Lutherans and Reformed on a basis which compromised confessions ("Unionists, the adherents of the union between Lutherans and Reformed established in 1817," Meyers *Konversationslexikon*). This usage of the word influenced the American usage (thus already in *Ohio Gazette,* 1837) and especially the usage of conservative Lutherans in the 19th century (for Walther's position see *CTM,* XV: 538, footnote 19).

Some prominent definitions are: "The union of parties adhering to varying religions or confessions into one congregation or Church" (Meyers *Konversationslexikon*); the union of Reformed and Lutherans into one body *(Die Religion in Geschichte und Gegenwart);* "mingling of truth and error; church fellowship between true believers *(Rechtglaeubigen)* and errorists *(Falschglaeubigen)* or the union of both into an external church organization. It includes all ecclesiastical collaboration in which error is tolerated and the Lutheran Confession is not given proper consideration [*zu kurz kommt*]" (Eckhardt, *Reallexikon*); "Religious unionism consists in joint worship and work of those not united in doctrine. Its essence is an agreement to disagree. In effect, it denies the doctrine of the clearness of Scripture." *See Fellowship.*

See references under *Fellowship;* see references under *Union Movements;* in addition the following: J. H. C. Fritz, *Religious Unionism,* CPH, 1930; J. W. Schillinger, *Why Lutherans Do Not Participate in Union Services,* Luth. Book Concern, Columbus, Ohio, n. d.; W. A. Poovey, *Questions That Trouble Lutherans,* Wartburg Press, 1946; C. Bergendoff, "Lutheran Unity," *What Lutherans Are Thinking,* Wartburg Press, 1947; N. Soederblom, *Christian Fellowship or United Life and Work of Christendom,* Fleming-Revell, N. Y., 1923; J. S. Stowell, *The Utopia of Unity,* Fleming-Revell, N. Y., 1930; M. Bach, *Report to Protestants,* Bobbs-Merrill, N. Y., 1948.

Unitarians. Unitarianism is the belief that God is unipersonal. This view was held in the early Christian Church by the Monarchians * but condemned at Nicaea in 325. Not until the Renaissance did Unitarianism seriously disturb the Church. A number of Anabaptists, and especially independent thinkers in Italy and in Poland, were outspoken Unitarians or Anti-Trinitarians, known as Socinians,* especially Michael Servetus, Faustus Socinus, and Francis David. In England, owing to Socinian influences, Unitarian views were adopted by individuals, and at the beginning of the 19th century Unitarianism was organized as a distinct denomination under the leadership of Priestley, Lindsey, and Martineau. In America, Unitarianism developed at first within the New England Congregational churches. One of the principles of early Congregationalism was that every individual congregation must be granted ultimate liberty in fixing its own doctrinal statement and the right "to seek more light." Thus these Congregational churches became a haven for all "religious seekers." Unitarian principles crept into the Congregational churches of eastern Massachusetts though originally they were strictly Calvinistic and Trinitarian, and by 1785 the majority of these Congregational churches had accepted the Unitarian principles. In 1805 Henry Ware was called as professor of theology at Harvard University, the center of training for Congregational ministers, though he was an avowed Unitarian. The protest of many Trinitarian Congregationalists compelled the Unitarian Congregationalists to separate from the Congregational churches and organize themselves as a Unitarian body. In 1819 W. E. Channing, in the ordination sermon of Jared Sparks, set forth his Unitarian views, which were accepted as the platform of American Unitarianism. In 1825 the American Unitarian Association was organized to do missionary work. However, the organization is so loosely welded together that for decades the denomination made no progress.

Doctrine. Unitarianism can hardly be said to have a creed. Unitarians believe that the individual must be free to form his religious beliefs as his reason dictates. They are agreed in denying the Trinity, the deity of Jesus, the sinfulness of mankind, the authority of Scripture, in fact, all specifically Christian doctrines. Unitarians are outspoken humanists and believe in the essential dignity and perfectibility of human nature. For this reason their religious interests have been primarily this-worldly, and they have been active in works of philanthropy and in education. Unitarianism has indirectly been a factor in the spreading of liberal theology in the Protestant churches. In recent years the Unitarians have joined the Universalists,* since the modern Universalists believe in the unipersonality of God and the Unitarians in the salvation of all men. The distinction between the two systems has been stated epigrammatically: The Universalists believe that God is too good to damn man, and Unitarians believe that man is too good to be damned. See *Religious Bodies (U. S.), Bibliography.* FEM

Unitas Fratrum. See *Bohemian-Moravian Brethren.*

United American Free Will Baptist Church (Colored). See *Baptist Bodies,* 25.

United Baptists. See *Baptist Bodies,* 26.

United Brethren. 1. The Church of the United Brethren in Christ must not be confused with the Moravian Church, which is also known as the *Unitas Fratrum.* The United Brethren are Methodistic in theology and church polity. Their founder and leading theologian, Philipp William Otterbein (1726—1813), had been trained for the Reformed ministry in Germany and came to America in 1752 to minister to the spiritually neglected and scattered Germans of Reformed antecedents, settling first at Lancaster, Pa. About 1754 Otterbein claimed to have had a deep religious experience, and he strenuously opposed the "educational religion" of his denomination. Later he came into personal relations with Martin Boehm (1725—1812), a member of the Mennonite community, who had passed through a similar religious experience, and together they conducted evangelistic work among the scattered settlers in Pennsylvania. They were joined by men of every creed — Lutherans, Reformed, Mennonites, Dunkers, etc. Otterbein aroused the opposition of his co-religionists when he introduced revival meetings, protracted prayer meetings, love feasts, and the class system. As Otterbein had offended his fellow ministers to such a degree as to arouse opposition, he, in

1774, accepted a call to Baltimore, Md., where he served the congregation on an independent basis. For the next fifteen years he continued his evangelistic labors among the German Reformed communities. In 1789 a meeting of these revivalist preachers was held in Baltimore, and a confession of faith and rules of discipline were adopted, based upon the rules adopted four years before for the government of Otterbein's independent church in Baltimore. During the following decade similar councils were called at irregular intervals, and these culminated at the conferences held in Frederick County, Maryland, in 1800, in the formation of a distinctly ecclesiastical body under the name of "United Brethren in Christ." Thirteen preachers were in attendance, and Otterbein and Boehm were elected bishops, in which office they both remained until their death. Bishop Otterbein came into close relations with Bishop Asbury of the Methodist Church. However, as the Methodist Church was unwilling to accept German-speaking churches into the Methodist Church, the two bodies remained distinct. Asbury had taken the same attitude toward the former Lutheran Jacob Albrecht, the founder of the Evangelical Church.* During the first years of the 19th century the movement continued to grow, and preaching places were established in Ohio, Indiana, and Kentucky. The first general conference was held in 1815, four conferences being represented by fourteen delegates. This conference arranged and adopted a book of discipline, accepting in general the system agreed upon in the conference of 1789. This same conference was also significant for its recognition of a change that had taken place in the churches regarding the use of the English language. This change was recognized by the conference held in 1817, which ordered the confession of faith and the book of discipline to be printed in both German and English. The United Brethren merged with the Evangelical Church (1947) to form the Evangelical United Brethren Church.

2. *Doctrine.* The doctrine of the United Brethren is Arminian, and the brief thirteen articles of the "Confession of Faith" are but modifications of the Methodist Confessions. Pietism, legalism, and emotionalism are characteristic of this church body. Concerning the Sacraments the United Brethren in Christ hold that Baptism and the Lord's Supper should be observed by all Christians, but that the manner of celebrating the Lord's Supper, the mode of Baptism, and the practice of foot washing should be left to the judgment of each individual. The question of baptizing children is left to the parents' choice.

3. The *United Brethren in Christ (Old Constitution).* In 1889 a division occurred over the proposed revision of the constitution. The old constitution of 1844 proscribed slaveholding, membership in secret societies, and "conformity to the world." After the Civil War the majority believed that the time had come to revise the constitution, not only because the question of slaveholding was no longer a vital issue, but also because they believed the time had come to liberalize the Church's position on many matters of life. The minority was opposed to many amendments which would make it possible for the members "to be conformed to the world." Under the name of United Brethren (Old Constitution) they claimed to be the rightful owners of the church property, and a number of lawsuits for possession of property took place. At present a fraternal spirit has been established between the two groups.

4. The *United Christian Church.* This denomination was organized in 1864 by members of the United Brethren who believed that the Church was permitting its members to be conformed to the world in such questions as membership in secret societies and following "worldly" styles and fashions in dress. See *Religious Bodies (U.S.), Bibliography.* FEM

United Brethren in Christ. See *United Brethren, 3.*

United Christian Church. See *United Brethren, 4.*

United Church in Canada. In 1925 the Methodist, Congregational, and Presbyterian Churches of Canada formed the United Church of Canada on a broad doctrinal basis, each denomination giving up its distinctive character. The Baptist churches refused to join this merger because they are opposed in principle to every form of ecclesiastical organization. The Anglican Church did not join the union because of its adherence to the theory of the Apostolic Succession. The United Church of Canada is not the national church of Canada, nor has it succeeded in uniting the three denominations, for many of the Presbyterian and Congregational churches, especially in the larger cities, have continued their separate existence. See *Canada, Protestantism in; Union Movements*, 7.

United Congregations. A name given to the three early congregations at Philadelphia, New Hanover, and Trappe, who sent a commission to London and Halle to appeal for help. Later the name was applied to all the congregations which joined them. See *United Lutheran Church, Synods of*, 24.

United Danish Church. See *Danish Lutherans in America.*

United Evangelical Action. See *Union Movements*, 12.

United Evangelical Church. This denomination reunited with the Evangelical Church in 1922, from which it had separated in 1891. See *Evangelical Church* and *Evangelical Congregational Church.*

United Evangelical Church (German). See *Reformed Church*, 3.

United Evangelical Lutheran Church of Germany. See *Union Movements*, 8 f.

United (Danish) Evangelical Lutheran Church in North America. See *Danish Lutherans in America.*

United Free Church of Scotland. See *Presbyterian Bodies*, 1.

United Holy Church of America, Inc. See *Holiness Bodies*, 2.

United Lutheran Church in America, The. Organized Nov. 14, 1918, at Trinity Lutheran Church, New York City. Headquarters: The Lutheran Church House, 231 Madison Ave., New York City. Presidents: F. H. Knubel, 1918—44; Franklin Clark Fry, 1944—.

I. *Formation.* — Three general bodies merged to form the ULCA. They were the *General Synod of the Ev. Luth. Church in the U.S. of America*,* organized at Frederick, Md., 1821, whose oldest constituent synod was organized Aug. 15, 1748; the *General Council of the Ev. Luth. Church in North America*,* organized at Fort Wayne, Ind., Nov. 20—26, 1867, by synods which had separated themselves from the General Synod as protagonists of a more conservative Lutheranism and of synodical subscription to the Unaltered Augsburg Confession after the Fort Wayne convention of the Gen-

eral Synod in 1866; and the *United Synod of the Ev. Luth. Church in the South*,* organized 1886 at Roanoke, Va., as a merger of the Tennessee Synod (1820) with a portion of the General Synod which had seceded in 1863 and had organized at Concord, N. C., as the General Synod of the Ev. Luth. Church in the Confederate States of America.

Several Free Lutheran Diets, beginning with that in Philadelphia (1877), led to the conclusion of those taking part from these three bodies that they were not so far apart as they had supposed. It strengthened this conclusion to have members from these bodies work together on a joint commission to prepare a common service, an undertaking proposed by the southern Synod in 1876. This work was completed in 1887 and emphasized the common bond. A series of general conferences among the bodies, beginning in 1898, and an agreement to prevent frictions in the establishment of missions furthered the feeling of oneness. Doctrinal discussions, beginning in 1907, brought about the removal of separating doctrinal barriers by 1911. The immediate impetus for the merger was given by the work of the representative committee appointed with delegates from each body in 1914 to plan a fitting Reformation Quadricentennial for 1917. A spirit favoring merger was developed in the rank and file of the different bodies by the co-operation fostered in the work of the National Lutheran Commission for Soldiers' and Sailors' Welfare, a work which, after the merger, was taken over by the newly established National Lutheran Council (Sept. 6, 1918); and also by co-operative undertakings in the field of youth and Brotherhood work. All constituent synods of the three bodies except the Augustana accepted the merger. The newly constituted body did not, however, think of its organization as a final and satisfying answer to the problem of Lutheran unity in this country, but preambled its constitution with the words: "We invite, and till such end be attained, continue to invite all Evangelical Lutheran congregations and synods in America, one with us in the faith, to unite with us."

II. *Doctrinal Basis.* — According to the second article of its constitution, the ULCA receives and holds the canonical Scriptures of the Old and New Testaments as the inspired Word of God and as the only infallible rule and standard of faith and practice, according to which all doctrines and teachers are to be judged. It accepts the three ecumenical creeds as important testimonies drawn from the Holy Scriptures and rejects all errors which they condemn. It receives and holds the Unaltered Augsburg Confession as a correct exhibition of the faith and doctrine of the Evangelical Lutheran Church, founded upon the Word of God; and acknowledges all churches that sincerely hold and faithfully confess the doctrines of the Unaltered Augsburg Confession to be entitled to the name of Evangelical Lutheran. It recognizes the Apology of the Augsburg Confession, the Smalcald Articles, the Large and Small Catechisms of Luther, and the Formula of Concord as in the harmony of one and the same Scriptural faith.

III. *Statistics.* — In 1952 the ULCA was constituted of 34 synods (see *United Lutheran Church, Synods of*) and 5 Affiliated Churches. In 1952 it had on its roll 4,253 congregations and 4,032 pastors. Its baptized membership (1952) numbered 2,087,945, confirmed 1,448,422, and communing 1,018,793. Its net gain of adult members in 1952 over 1951 was 24,830. The synods listed 4,171 Sunday schools, with 701,084 pupils and 82,195 staff members. Its increase in pupils in 1952 over 1951 was 20,424. Weekday schools (inclusive of vacation Bible school, and "Children of the Church" program) numbered 5,913, with 23,467 teachers and 213,915 pupils, an increase in pupils in 1952 over 1951 of 11,540. Catechumens under instruction for the year numbered 69,684. The total valuation of congregational properties including church buildings, parsonages, schools, parish houses, and other property (but not endowments, which totalled $10,692,094) was $349,132,799, with an indebtedness against it of $25,437,435, noting an increase in valuation in 1952 over 1951 of $39,838,172 and of indebtedness of $4,492,828. Congregational current expenses were $28,822,079, special projects, $21,385,245, for a total of $50,207,324 and marking an increase in 1952 over 1951 of $5,614,273. Total unapportioned benevolence was $5,361,608; apportioned, $7,444,459; a total of $12,806,067. The above totals concern only the constituent synods. They do not include the Affiliated Churches.

IV. *Affiliations.* — The ULCA has consistently adhered to the principle of non-participation in groups in which co-opted individuals have the same standing as official representatives of participating churches, and of co-operation with inter-church bodies only where its own confessional standards are safeguarded and unimpaired. In accordance with these principles the United Lutheran Church has membership in the Lutheran World Federation, the National Lutheran Council, and Lutheran World Relief. Through the last named it is associated with CRALOG, LARA, CROP, the American Council of Voluntary Agencies for Foreign Service. The ULCA also participates in the work of the American Bible Society and the British and Foreign Bible Society. In the interdenominational field it has held consultative membership in the Federal Council of the Churches of Christ in America, and in 1949 it became a charter member of the National Council of the Churches of Christ in the U.S.A. Prior to the formation of the NCCCUSA, boards and agencies of the ULCA held membership as follows in agencies now merged in the NCCCUSA: the Board of Foreign Missions was a member of the Foreign Missions Conference of North America; the Board of American Missions was a member of the Home Missions Council; the Women's Missionary Society and the Board of Foreign Missions participated in the Missionary Education Movement, Student Volunteer Movement, Boards of Union Christian Colleges in the Orient; the Laymen's Movement for Stewardship had membership in the United Stewardship Council; the Board of Parish Education and the Board of Publication had consultative membership in the International Council of Religious Education. The ULCA also had a consultative relationship with the Protestant Radio Commission. From its inception the United Lutheran Church has taken a leading part in the organization of the World Council of Churches, of which it is a member.

V. *Affiliated Churches.* — Amendments to the Constitution of the ULCA in 1950 and 1952 provided that an Ev. Luth. church, fostered by its Board of Foreign Missions, "and which has accepted ARTICLE II (Doctrinal Basis) and ARTICLE XV (Affiliated Churches) of the ULCA Constitution, and whose constitution has been approved by the Executive Board, may be received into relationship with the ULCA as an Affiliated Church by a majority vote at any regular convention." Such churches are entitled to two representatives with seat and voice but no vote at conventions. Five of the six ULCA missions (the mission in China was the exception) were thus received at the Des Moines, Iowa, convention, Oct. 4, 1950, as follows:

The Andhra Evangelical Lutheran Church, India. Organized April, 1927. Headquarters: Andhra Church Office, Guntur, Andhra State, India. This church consists of five district synods: East Godavari, West Godavari, Central Guntur, East Guntur, and West Guntur. These have (1952) 2,133 congregations, 819 schools, 72,368 pupils, 8 hospitals, 43 hostels. Enrolled are 239,868 baptized and 123,208 confirmed members. Pastors number 129, other evangelical workers 666, schoolteachers 2,759, other workers 887. In addition a missionary staff of 24 pastors, 27 wives, 5 unordained men, and 32 single women are active in this church. Its property valuation is $1,680,000.

The Evangelical Lutheran Church in Japan. Organized April, 1927. Headquarters: Luth. Theol. Seminary, 921 Chome, Saginomiya, Nakano Ku, Tokyo, Japan. This church counted (1952) 42 congregations, 5,999 baptized and 3,417 communing members; it has enrolled 44 national pastors, 3 evangelistic workers, 238 national schoolteachers, 16 ordained and 15 unordained missionaries. It supports 35 schools, a theological seminary, 2 children's homes, 1 old people's home, and 1 widows' home. No figures on property valuation are available since the war.

The Evangelical Lutheran Church in British Guiana. Organized July 15, 1943. Headquarters: Lutheran Courts, New Amsterdam, British Guiana. This church counted (1952) 41 congregations, 5,670 baptized and 2,550 communing members, and has on its roll 4 ordained missionaries, 3 ordained nationals, 2 unordained missionaries, and 75 other national workers. It supports 12 schools and has a property value of $159,700.

The United Evangelical Lutheran Church, Argentina. Organized Jan. 7, 1948. Headquarters: Cuenca 3285, Buenos Aires, Argentina. This church consists of 15 congregations with 4,350 baptized and 2,455 communicant members. It does work in Spanish, German, English, Slovak, and Hungarian, with Lithuanian and Estonian work in prospect. It numbered (1952) 14 pastors and 8 additional missionary workers. It supports 5 day schools, an institute, a theological seminary, a girls' hostel,

a women's Bible training school, and a home for the aged. The property value is conservatively estimated at $270,000.

The Evangelical Lutheran Church in Liberia. Organized May 20, 1948. Headquarters: Lutheran Mission, Monrovia, Liberia, Africa. The church numbered (1952) 27 congregations with 15 additional preaching points, 1,987 baptized and 983 confirmed members, and has on its rolls 6 ordained nationals, 39 unordained workers, 13 ordained missionaries, 16 missionaries' wives, 3 unordained men, and 13 single women. It supports 32 mission schools, 1 hospital, and 7 dispensaries. Its property evaluation is $83,500. WT

See references in the article *United Lutheran Church, Synods of; United States, Lutheranism in.*

United Lutheran Church, Synods of. 1. *California, Synod of.* In 1886 Samuel B. Barnitz, the General Synod's secretary of Home Missions, sent Oliver C. Miller to California. Together with four other General Synod missionaries, Miller organized the Synod of California on April 2, 1891. As a part of the General Synod, the Synod of California joined the United Lutheran Church in 1918. In 1952 the synod numbered 112 pastors, 83 congregations, 17,943 communicants. John E. Hoick, *The Fruitage of Fifty Years in California: A History of the . . . Synod of California* (1941).

2. *Canada, Synod of.* Missionary efforts were undertaken in Ontario by the Pittsburgh Synod, and these resulted in the formation of the Canada Conference of the Pittsburgh Synod in 1853. On July 21, 1861, this conference resolved itself into the Synod of Canada, which was originally a part of the General Synod, but in 1867 joined in the formation of the General Council. In 1908 the Synod of Central Canada was organized as a result of English missionary activity in Ontario on the part of the General Council, and on June 12, 1925, this synod merged with the older Synod of Canada after both synods, in 1918, had become a part of the United Lutheran Church. The older synod founded the Evangelical Lutheran Seminary of Canada at Waterloo, Ont., in 1911, and four years later Waterloo College was established in connection with it. Until the merger of 1925 the Synod of Central Canada cooperated with the Synod of Canada in the maintenance of these institutions. In 1952 the synod numbered 93 pastors,

118 congregations, 24,590 communicants. Emil Hoffmann, *Festschrift zur Feier des 50jaehrigen Jubilaeums der ev-luth. Synode von Canada* (1911); V. J. Eylands, *Lutherans in Canada* (1945).

3. *Caribbean Evangelical Lutheran Synod.* The Caribbean Ev. Lutheran Church was organized in the spring of 1952 and was admitted to the United Lutheran Church as a synod in October of the same year. At the time of its organization the synod included 14 congregations in Puerto Rico and 5 congregations in the Virgin Islands. It had 2,051 communing members. The Rev. Eduardo Roig was the first president.

4. *Florida, Synod of.* On Sept. 24, 1928, the thirteen congregations and their pastors in Florida, formerly constituting the Florida Conference of the Georgia Synod, formed the Synod of Florida. In the same year this new synod was received into the United Lutheran Church, of which the parent body was a part. In 1952 the Synod numbered 25 pastors, 22 congregations, 3,775 communicants.

5. *Georgia-Alabama Synod.* Organized July 20, 1860, as the Synod of Georgia, the territory of this body included congregations in Florida and Alabama as well as Georgia. In 1928 the congregations in Florida withdrew to form the separate Synod of Florida. In 1930 the Synod of Georgia changed its name to Georgia-Alabama Synod. The original Synod of Georgia participated in the organization of the General Synod in the Confederate States, in the United Synod of the South, and, in 1918, in the United Lutheran Church. In 1952 the synod numbered 33 pastors, 40 congregations, 5,552 communicants.

6. *Icelandic Synod.* From 1873 to World War I about 75,000 Icelanders emigrated from their native country to settle in the Western Hemisphere. The largest concentrations of these immigrants occurred in Manitoba, Minnesota, and the Dakotas. The first Icelandic Lutheran service was held in Milwaukee on Aug. 2, 1874, the Rev. Jon Bjarnason officiating. Congregations were soon formed under the leadership of clergymen from Iceland. In 1884 the Rev. Hans Thorgrimssen proposed a union of these congregations, and on June 25, 1885, the Icelandic Evangelical Lutheran Synod of America (now abbreviated into Icelandic Synod) was organized in Winnipeg. Notable in the constitution was provision for female suffrage; the Icelandic Synod was

the first Lutheran body in America to grant women the right to vote and hold office. During the first decade of the twentieth century the synod was torn by strife over Biblical inspiration and confessional subscription, and some Icelanders, together with their pastors, became Unitarians. Meanwhile the small synod felt the need of association with other Lutheran bodies, and it was drawn especially to the United Lutheran Church by common missionary and educational interests. As a result the Icelandic Synod was received into the United Lutheran Church in 1940. In 1952 the synod numbered 14 pastors, 37 congregations, 2,001 communicants. K. K. Olafsen, *The Icelandic Synod* (1935); B. B. Jonsson, *Minningarrit, 1885—1910* (1910).

7. *Illinois Synod of the United Lutheran Church.* A merger (June 10, 1920) of the Northern Illinois, Southern Illinois, and Central Illinois Synods (formerly of the General Synod), and portions of the Chicago Synod (formerly of the General Council). The history of this body goes back to 1835, when the Synod of the West was organized to embrace congregations in Kentucky, Indiana, Illinois, and Missouri. When the Synod of the West dissolved in 1846, the congregations in central and southern Illinois formed the Illinois Synod. With the establishment of congregations in the northern part of the State, the Northern Illinois Synod was organized Sept. 8, 1851. Five years later the Synod of Southern Illinois was formed by pastors who formerly belonged to the Synod of the Southwest. When the original Illinois Synod joined the General Council in 1867, some of the pastors withdrew to organize the Synod of Central Illinois and retain their connection with the General Synod. In 1897 this Synod of Central Illinois merged with the Synod of Southern Illinois to form the Synod of Central and Southern Illinois, and after the formation of the United Lutheran Church, the Synod of Central and Southern Illinois united with the Synod of Northern Illinois and portions of the Chicago Synod to form the new Illinois Synod. Carthage College, in Carthage, Ill. (founded 1870), and the Chicago Theological Seminary, in Maywood, Ill. (founded 1891), are in the territory of this synod. In 1952 the synod included 188 pastors, 152 congregations, 43,338 communicants. Lee M. Heilman, *Historic Sketch of the . . .*

Synod of Northern Illinois (1892); Martin L. Wagner, *The Chicago Synod and Its Antecedents* (1909).

8. *Indiana, Synod of.* This synod traces its origin to two major roots. The first of these is the Synod of the West, organized in 1835. Some of the pastors and congregations of this body joined with others to form the Miami Synod in 1844. Four years later the Indiana congregations and pastors of the Miami Synod helped to form the Olive Branch Synod, which was associated with the General Synod and had a continuous existence down to the year 1920. The second major root of the present Synod of Indiana resulted from the activity of Tennessee Synod missionaries, who, in 1835, organized the Synod of Indiana. This body, which was later in connection with the General Council, had a variety of names and after 1871 was known as the Chicago Synod. After the formation of the United Lutheran Church, on June 24, 1920, the Olive Branch Synod merged with a portion of the Chicago Synod to form the present Synod of Indiana. By 1934 all congregations beyond the geographical limits of the State of Indiana were dismissed to other synods, and so the Synod of Indiana is today a body limited to the State whose name it bears. In 1952 the synod numbered 94 pastors, 117 congregations, 19,019 communicants. Oct. 28, 1848, is the official founding date of this synod. C. R. Defenderfer, *Lutheranism at the Crossroads of America: a Story of the Indiana Synod* (1946).

9. *Iowa, Synod of.* Seven pastors with a variety of former synodical affiliations organized the Synod of Iowa on Feb. 10, 1854. In 1857 the synod joined the General Synod, and in 1918 it became a part of the United Lutheran Church. In 1952 it numbered 46 pastors, 34 congregations, 15,420 communicants.

10. *Kansas, Synod of.* Organized Nov. 5, 1868, the Synod of Kansas joined the General Synod the following year. In 1918 it entered the United Lutheran Church. Two educational institutions, Midland College and Western (now Central) Theological Seminary, were established on the territory of the Synod of Kansas with the aid of other neighboring synods. In 1952 the synod numbered 38 pastors, 44 congregations, 7,553 communicants. H. A. Ott, *A History of the . . . Synod of Kansas* (1907).

11. *Kentucky-Tennessee Synod.* At the end of the eighteenth and beginning of the nineteenth centuries Lutherans migrated westward across the mountains from Virginia and the Carolinas into the territory of the present States of Kentucky and Tennessee. Especially active on this frontier were the men who, on July 17, 1820, founded the Tennessee Synod, which distinguished itself in its early history by zeal for the Lutheran Confessions. In 1860 the congregations in Tennessee withdrew to form the Holston Synod. Both the Holston and the Tennessee Synods joined the United Synod in the South in 1886, and in 1918 they became a part of the United Lutheran Church. In 1921 the Tennessee Synod merged with the Synod of North Carolina to form the United Synod of North Carolina, and in 1922 the Holston Synod merged with the Synods of Southwestern Virginia and Virginia to form the present Synod of Virginia. Meanwhile other congregations in western Tennessee and in Kentucky were affiliated with the Synod of Indiana, the Synod of Ohio, and other bodies which merged into these. By a realignment of synods in 1934, these congregations were released to form the new Kentucky-Tennessee Synod, which was organized June 6, 1934, and received into the United Lutheran Church the same year. In 1952 the synod numbered 30 pastors, 31 congregations, 5,416 communicants.

12. *Maryland Synod.* Organized as the Maryland and Virginia Synod Oct. 11, 1820, by a conference of the Ministerium of Pennsylvania, this body became the Synod of Maryland after the organization of a separate Synod of Virginia in 1829. Immediately after its organization the synod participated in the formation of the General Synod and remained prominent in the affairs of the General Synod until this body dissolved with the formation of the United Lutheran Church in 1918. It was among the sons of the Maryland Synod that "American Lutheranism" * found its warmest advocates. S. S. Schmucker was the author of the "Definite Synodical Platform," * and Benjamin Kurtz, editor of *The Lutheran Observer,* was its champion. But when the synod refused to sanction the "Definite Synodical Platform," Kurtz and his friends withdrew in protest to organize the Melanchthon Synod in 1857. This breach was healed after Kurtz's death. The Maryland Synod was active in the establishment of the theological seminary at Gettysburg (1826) and of

Pennsylvania (now Gettysburg) College (1832). In 1952 the synod numbered 163 pastors, 142 congregations, 44,107 communicants. Abdel Ross Wentz, *History of the . . . Synod of Maryland* (1920).

13. *Michigan, Synod of.* Merger (June 10, 1920) of a portion of the Synod of Northern Indiana (formerly a part of the General Synod) and a portion of the Chicago Synod (formerly associated with the General Council). In 1934 the congregations in the State of Indiana were dismissed to the Synod of Indiana in the attempt to limit Michigan Synod congregations to the State of Michigan. In 1952 the synod numbered 42 pastors, 32 congregations, 8,337 communicants. The official founding date (as determined by the oldest of the merging bodies) is Oct. 27, 1855. Eugene Poppen, *Century of Lutheranism in Michigan* (1934).

14. *Midwest, Synod of the.* Organized July 24, 1890, by German-speaking pastors of the Nebraska Synod, under the original name of the German Synod of Nebraska, this body changed its name on June 14, 1937, to the Synod of the Midwest. From 1913 to 1934 the synod maintained a theological seminary, Martin Luther Seminary, at Lincoln, Nebr. The synod joined the General Synod in 1891 and became part of the United Lutheran Church in 1918. In 1952 the synod numbered 90 pastors, 76 congregations, 14,168 communicants. H. Wellhausen, *Geschichte der Deutschen Ev.-Luth. Nebraska-Synode* (1916).

15. *Mississippi Synod.* Organized July 25, 1855, by pastors of the Synod of South Carolina who had undertaken work in Mississippi about ten years earlier. It entered the United Synod in the South in 1886, and with it became a part of the United Lutheran Church in 1918. In 1952 the synod numbered 8 pastors, 11 congregations, 503 communicants.

16. *Nebraska, Synod of.* In 1858 the Rev. H. W. Kuhns was sent out by the Allegheny Synod in Pennsylvania to serve as a missionary in Nebraska. Out of his labors developed the Synod of Nebraska, which was organized in Omaha Sept. 1, 1871. Four years later the synod joined the General Synod, and in 1918 it became part of the United Lutheran Church. In 1952 the synod numbered 61 pastors, 58 congregations, 16,479 communicants.

17. *New Jersey, Synod of.* Congre-

gations in the State of New Jersey which were members of the United Synod of New York, the Ministerium of Pennsylvania, and the Central Pennsylvania Synod were released from these bodies in order to form a new Synod of New Jersey, which was organized June 20, 1950. According to statistics for the year 1952, the new synod comprised 140 pastors, 132 congregations, 32,920 communicants. Alfred Hiller, "History of the Lutheran Church in New Jersey," in the *Lutheran Quarterly*, XXVIII, p. 98 ff.; Theodore G. Tappert, "Early Lutheranism in Southern New Jersey," in the *Lutheran Church Quarterly*, XIX, p. 305 ff.

18. *New York and New England, Synod of.* The beginning of synodical history on the territory of New York and New England was made when the Ministerium of New York was organized in Albany on Oct. 23, 1786, under the leadership of John C. Kunze. Its constitution was based on that of the Ministerium of Pennsylvania, but differed from the latter in that laymen were for the first time given voice and vote in the deliberations of the body. The Ministerium of New York participated in the founding of the General Synod but withdrew immediately, not to return until 1837. Meanwhile the Ministerium had begun to be harassed by internal contention and division. In 1830 some congregations and pastors in central New York withdrew to form the Hartwick Synod, which joined the General Synod the following year. In 1837 some congregations and pastors withdrew from the Hartwick Synod on the ground that its position was not sufficiently liberal and founded the Franckean Synod, which in 1864 was admitted to the General Synod. In 1859 the Ministerium's congregations in New Jersey were dismissed in order to permit them to organize the New Jersey Synod. In protest against the reception of the Franckean Synod into the General Synod, the Ministerium withdrew from the General Synod in 1867 and participated in the formation of the General Council. This in turn precipitated further internal dissension, and two fifths of the congregations and pastors withdrew from the Ministerium to form the English Synod of New York in the same year, 1867. This synod retained connection with the General Synod, and in 1872 it merged with the New Jersey Synod to form the Synod of New York

and New Jersey. Meanwhile, in 1866, several pastors, under the leadership of F. W. T. Steimle, withdrew from the Ministerium on the ground that it had ceased to be German and truly Lutheran and formed the German Synod of New York, popularly called the "Steimle Synod." This defection was healed in 1872. The language question led to another and a more friendly division in 1902, when the English-speaking pastors and congregations withdrew from the Ministerium to form the New York and New England Synod, which, like the parent body, retained its connection with the General Council. In 1908 the three General Synod bodies on the territory of New York and New England (Hartwick Synod, Franckean Synod, and Synod of New York and New Jersey) merged to form the New York Synod (II). After the formation of the United Lutheran Church in 1918, the New York Synod (II), the New York Ministerium, and the New York and New England Synod merged on June 5, 1929, to form the United Synod of New York (later Synod of New York and New England). Wagner College, on Staten Island, N. Y. (founded 1883), and Hartwick College, Oneonta, N. Y. (founded 1928), are on the territory of the Synod of New York and New England. In 1952 this synod comprised 408 pastors, 350 congregations, 96,821 communicants. J. Nicum, *Geschichte des Ev.-Luth. Ministeriums vom Staate New York* (1888); Harry J. Kreider, *Lutheranism in Colonial New York* (1934); P. A. Strobel, *Memorial Volume . . . of the Hartwick Lutheran Synod* (1881); W. van Alstine, *Historical Review of the Franckean Synod* (1893); Samuel Trexler, *Crusaders of the Twentieth Century; a Lutheran Story in the Empire State* (1926).

19. *North Carolina, United Synod of.* Lutheran congregations appeared in North Carolina after the middle of the eighteenth century and were served especially by pastors supplied by the Helmstedt Missionary Society in Germany. On May 2, 1803, these congregations organized the Synod of North Carolina. Its territory was extended to include congregations in South Carolina and Virginia and, after the westward migration set in, in Tennessee. The Synod of North Carolina participated in the founding of the General Synod in 1820 and 1821, and this was one of the reasons for the withdrawal of the Henkels and the organization

of the Tennessee Synod in 1820. The territory of the Synod of North Carolina was further reduced by the organization of the South Carolina Synod in 1824, the Southwestern Virginia Synod in 1841, and the Mississippi Synod in 1855. During the Civil War the Synod of North Carolina withdrew from the General Synod and helped to organize the General Synod in the Confederate States (1864), which later became the United Synod in the South. After the formation of the United Lutheran Church the Tennessee Synod was reunited with the Synod of North Carolina on March 2, 1921, to form the United Synod of North Carolina. On the territory of the synod is located Lenoir Rhyne College, at Hickory, N. C., founded 1891. In 1952 the synod numbered 183 pastors, 173 congregations, 31,407 communicants. G. D. Bernheim and G. H. Cox, *The History of the . . . Synod and Ministerium of North Carolina* (1902).

20. *Northwest, Synod of the.* Organized Sept. 23, 1891, at St. Paul, Minn., this synod was the fruit of intensive missionary work undertaken by the English Home Mission Board of the General Council. On account of some misunderstandings which caused offense to the Augustana Synod, the Synod of the Northwest was not received into the General Council until 1893. From that time until 1918 it remained in the General Council and then became a part of the United Lutheran Church. The territory of the synod embraces Minnesota, Wisconsin, the Dakotas, Montana. In 1952 the synod included 169 pastors, 141 congregations, 60,422 communicants. George H. Trabert, *English Lutheranism in the Northwest* (1914); Paul H. Roth, *Story of the English . . . Synod of the Northwest* (1941).

21. *Nova Scotia Synod.* There were Lutherans among the earliest colonists in Nova Scotia, and the first Lutheran Church was built in Halifax in 1761. But since the Lutherans in Nova Scotia were so remote from the major Lutheran settlements in North America, they were largely neglected in the early years. In 1874 the congregations were affiliated with the Pittsburgh Synod, and on July 10, 1903, they formed the independent Nova Scotia Synod. From 1903 until 1918 the synod was connected with the General Council, and since 1918 it has been a part of the United Lutheran Church. In 1952 the synod embraced 14 pastors, 32 con-

gregations, 2,865 communicants. D. L. Roth, *Acadie and the Acadians* (1891); V. J. Eylands, *Lutherans in Canada* (1945).

22. *Ohio, Synod of.* The history of the present Synod of Ohio goes back to the migration of Lutherans to the region west of the Allegheny Mountains and the formation, in 1812, of the Ohio Conference of the Ministerium of Pennsylvania. This conference became an independent synod Sept. 14, 1818, and refused to join the General Synod when this was organized three years later. In 1831 the synod was divided into districts, and after 1833 it was called the Joint Synod of Ohio. One of the Joint Synod's districts was the English Synod of Ohio, which was organized Nov. 7, 1836, became independent of the Joint Synod in 1840, when it entered into connection with the General Synod, and in 1858 took the name Synod of East Ohio. Some of the pastors of this synod who were laboring in the northwestern part of the State withdrew from the English Synod of Ohio and organized the Wittenberg Synod on June 8, 1847. Earlier than this, on Oct. 16, 1844, a few other pastors of the English Synod of Ohio, together with some pastors from the East who were laboring in the southern part of the State, organized the Synod of Miami, which joined the General Synod in the following year. In 1867, ten years after a new English District of the Joint Synod of Ohio was formed, on Aug. 26, 1857, this district joined the General Council, severed its relations with the Joint Synod, and became known as the District Synod of Ohio. In this way four new synods appeared in Ohio in addition to the Joint Synod, three of them connected with General Synod (East Ohio, Wittenberg, Miami) and one connected with the General Council (District Synod of Ohio). When the United Lutheran Church was organized in 1918 and these four synods became parts of it, steps were quickly taken to merge them into one body, and this was accomplished on Nov. 3, 1920, with the formation of the Synod of Ohio. On the territory of this synod are located Wittenberg College and Hamma Divinity School, founded in Springfield, Ohio, 1845. In 1952 the synod comprised 279 pastors, 279 congregations, 72,599 communicants. Arthur H. Smith, *A History of the East Ohio Synod* (1924); A. J. Imhoff, *History of the . . . Synod of Miami* (1894); George W. Mechling, *History of the . . . District Synod of Ohio* (1911); C. S. Ernsberger, *A History of the Wittenberg Synod* (1917).

23. *Pacific Synod.* Ten pastors of the Synod of the Northwest who lived west of the Missouri River organized the Pacific Synod on Sept. 26, 1901. The territory of the synod includes Washington, Oregon, British Columbia, and Alaska. In 1910 a theological seminary was established, first in Portland and then in Seattle, but it suspended operation in 1932. The synod became a part of the United Lutheran Church in 1918. In 1952 it numbered 58 pastors, 42 congregations, 6,986 communicants.

24. *Pennsylvania, Ministerium of.* The appellation "mother synod of the Lutheran Church in America" is often applied to the Ministerium of Pennsylvania because it was the first permanent Lutheran synod in North America and because many of the later synods grew out of it. Organized in Philadelphia Aug. 15, 1748, it was an outgrowth from the "United Congregations" which had called Henry Melchior Muhlenberg to America in 1742. It existed at first without constitution or formal name. An early designation was the Ministerium of North America, and only later, after the organization of a second synod (the Ministerium of New York), was the present name adopted (1792). The body was originally called a ministerium rather than a synod because only pastors were accorded a voice and a vote. After laymen were seated as regular delegates in 1792, the body was officially designated the Synod of Pennsylvania. Before the middle of the nineteenth century, however, the name Ministerium of Pennsylvania and Adjacent States was restored although it was no longer precisely appropriate. In 1818 the Ministerium proposed the formation of a union of Lutheran synods, which resulted in the organization, in 1821, of the General Synod. The Ministerium was especially interested in preserving contact with the new synods which were developing as a result of its missionary activity, but in 1823 the Ministerium withdrew from the General Synod, which it had helped to create. Fear of centralized authority, which played a part in this withdrawal, was not shared by most of the congregations west of the Susquehanna River which, in 1825, separated from the mother synod to form the Synod of West Pennsylvania and remain in connection with the General Synod. Sympathy with

the position of the General Synod caused another exodus among congregations in the eastern part of the State which, in 1841, formed the Synod of East Pennsylvania. These defections and the extensive use of the German language largely isolated the Ministerium from influences which caused other synods to introduce "new measures." In spite of the pietistic inheritance from the Muhlenberg era, therefore, the Ministerium remained comparatively conservative. In 1853 it joined the General Synod again. But when the great controversy over the "Definite Synodical Platform" broke out, some leaders of the Ministerium (notably William J. Mann) rose to the defense of the Augsburg Confession; and when, in 1864, the liberal Franckean Synod was admitted to the General Synod, the Ministerium withdrew once again. Under the leadership of Charles Porterfield Krauth the Lutheran Theological Seminary at Philadelphia (Mount Airy) was founded in 1864, and the Ministerium took a leading part in the formation of the General Council (1867). In the same year Muhlenberg College was founded, and in the years which followed an intensive inner mission program was inaugurated, which was marked by the establishment of a mother house of deaconesses (1855), homes for orphans and aged people, hospices, dispensaries, summer camps, and institutional chaplaincies. In 1916 the first full-time president of synod was elected. Two years later the Ministerium became a part of the United Lutheran Church, in which it remains, numerically, the largest synod. In 1950 its congregations in the State of New Jersey were dismissed to the newly organized Synod of New Jersey. In 1952 the Ministerium included 509 pastors, 568 congregations, 176,166 communicants. *Documentary History of the Ministerium of Pennsylvania, 1748 to 1821* (1898); Helen E. Pfatteicher, *The Ministerium of Pennsylvania* (1938); Theodore E. Schmauk, *History of the Lutherans in Pennsylvania* (1903); Theodore G. Tappert, "Two Hundred Years of the Ministerium of Pennsylvania," in *Minutes* of the Ministerium of Pennsylvania, 1948.

25. *Pennsylvania Synod, Central.* This body is the result of a merger of those synods in central and eastern Pennsylvania which were formerly associated with the General Synod. The earliest of these to be organized was the Synod of West Pennsylvania, which

seceded from the Ministerium of Pennsylvania in protest against the latter's withdrawal from the General Synod in 1823. With its territory west of the Susquehanna River, the Synod of West Pennsylvania was founded Sept. 5, 1825. With the growth of this synod, the congregations farthest west withdrew to form the Allegheny Synod on Sept. 9, 1842. Still another synod was formed out of the Synod of West Pennsylvania when a number of pastors and congregations withdrew to organize the Synod of Central Pennsylvania on Feb. 21, 1855. Meanwhile there was a second split from the Ministerium of Pennsylvania on the part of pastors and congregations in the eastern part of the State who advocated "new measures," the introduction of the English language, and connection with the General Synod. This group organized the Synod of East Pennsylvania on May 2, 1842. Twenty-five years later, with the growth of this synod, the Susquehanna Conference of the Synod of East Pennsylvania organized itself as the independent Susquehanna Synod on Nov. 5, 1867. Since this separation was on practical and administrative grounds, the new Susquehanna Synod retained its connection with the General Synod. After all five of these synods had become parts of the United Lutheran Church in 1918, steps were taken looking toward consolidation. On May 22, 1924, the Synod of Central Pennsylvania merged with the Susquehanna Synod to form the Susquehanna Synod of Central Pennsylvania, which abbreviated its name into Susquehanna Synod on April 11, 1932. After proposals to merge the Ministerium of Pennsylvania with other synods in eastern and central Pennsylvania had failed, the present Central Pennsylvania Synod was organized on June 8, 1938, by a merger of the Synod of West Pennsylvania, the Synod of East Pennsylvania, the Allegheny Synod, and the Susquehanna Synod. The Lutheran Theological Seminary at Gettysburg (founded 1826) and Gettysburg College (1832) proved to be a focus of unity. Susquehanna University (1858), in Selinsgrove, Pa., is also located on the territory of the synod. Congregations of the synod located in the State of New Jersey were transferred to the new Synod of New Jersey in 1950. In 1952 the Central Pennsylvania Synod included 469 pastors, 604 congregations, 144,126 communicants. A. Stump & H. Anstadt, eds., *History of the . . . Synod of West Pennsylvania* (1925); W. H. Bruce Carney, *History of the Allegheny . . . Synod of Pennsylvania,* 2 vols. (1918); M. Coover *et al., History of the . . . Synod of East Pennsylvania* (1893); F. P. Manhart, ed., *The Susquehanna Synod* (1917).

26. *Pittsburgh Synod.* Before the close of the eighteenth century the first congregations were established west of the Allegheny Mountains in Pennsylvania by missionaries sent out by the Ministerium of Pennsylvania. Other missionaries continued to be sent into this territory in the early decades of the nineteenth century. Some congregations attached themselves to the Ohio Synod, others to the Synod of West Pennsylvania and (after 1842) to the Allegheny Synod. But it was felt that a new synod in western Pennsylvania would best serve the needs of this territory. Accordingly eight pastors and twenty-six congregations organized the Pittsburgh Synod on Jan. 15, 1845. The original territory in western Pennsylvania was extended by the inclusion of a district in eastern Ohio. Later, especially as a result of the missionary zeal of William A. Passavant, the synod developed missionary interests in Nova Scotia, Ontario, Texas, and the Virgin Islands. After the disruption of the General Synod, to which it had belonged since 1853, the synod was divided. The majority voted in 1867 to join the General Council. A minority withdrew in protest and organized the Pittsburgh Synod of the General Synod. After these two synods became a part of the United Lutheran Church in 1918, a reunion was promptly effected on Nov. 18, 1919, under the full name of the Pittsburgh Synod of the Evangelical Lutheran Church. In 1952 the synod included 290 pastors, 310 congregations, 73,694 communicants. Ellis B. Burgess, *Memorial History of the Pittsburgh Synod* (1925).

27. *Rocky Mountain Synod.* The territory of the Rocky Mountain Synod comprises the States of Wyoming, Colorado, New Mexico, and a part of adjacent Texas. Missionary work had been undertaken in this territory by the Nebraska and Kansas Synods, but it was believed that the organization of an independent synod was desirable. Accordingly nine pastors and two laymen met in Manitou, Colo., on May 6, 1891, to organize the Rocky Mountain Synod, which immediately joined the General Synod. In 1918 it became a part of the United Lutheran Church.

In 1952 the synod included 39 pastors, 20 congregations, 4,921 communicants. Robert B. Wolf, *History of the Rocky Mountain Synod* (1941).

28. *Slovak Zion Synod.* As a result of immigration from the Austro-Hungarian Empire and later from Czechoslovakia, Slovak-speaking congregations began to appear toward the close of the nineteenth century in some of the northern States from Minnesota to Connecticut. Some of the Slovak pastors and their congregations met in Braddock, Pa., on June 10, 1919, to organize the Slovak Lutheran Zion Synod, which was received into the United Lutheran Church the following year. In geographical extent this is by far the largest synod in the United Lutheran Church, but most of its congregations are located in Pennsylvania, New Jersey, and New York. In 1952 it numbered 42 pastors, 48 congregations, 11,769 communicants.

29. *South Carolina, Synod of.* Before the middle of the eighteenth century a few Lutheran congregations made their appearance in the State of South Carolina. In 1788 seven Lutheran pastors and nine Lutheran congregations, together with several German Reformed pastors and congregations, organized an ecclesiastical body known as the *Corpus Evangelicum.* This organization soon disappeared, but in their isolation the Lutheran pastors continued to seek some form of external union. Finally, on Jan. 14, 1824, six pastors and five laymen organized the Synod of South Carolina. This synod helped to organize the General Synod of the Confederate States in 1864, the United Synod in the South in 1886, and the United Lutheran Church in 1918. Two educational institutions are on its territory: the Lutheran Theological Southern Seminary, in Columbia, S. C. (founded 1830), and Newberry College, in Newberry, S. C. (founded 1856). In 1952 the synod numbered 102 pastors, 127 congregations, 22,298 communicants. S. T. Hallman, *History of the . . . Synod of South Carolina* (1924).

30. *Texas Synod.* In 1850 the first missionaries were sent to Texas by C. F. Spittler, the head of St. Chrischona, famous missionary institute in Basel. Five of these Chrischona missionaries met with C. Braun, who had been sent to Texas by William A. Passavant of the Pittsburgh Synod, and on Nov. 10, 1851, they organized the First Evangelical Lutheran Synod of Texas. This

synod was at first connected with the General Synod and then, from 1868 to 1895, with the General Council. In 1895 the majority voted to join the Synod of Iowa and other States, with which it became a part of the American Lutheran Church in 1930. The minority continued under the name Texas Synod, in 1915 joined the General Council, and in 1918 became a part of the United Lutheran Church. In 1952 the synod included 32 pastors, 33 congregations, 6,127 communicants. J. Mgebroff, *Geschichte der Ersten Synode von Texas* (1902); M. Heinrich, *History of the First . . . Synod of Texas* (1927); F. F. Eberhardt, *History of the . . . Texas Synod* (1926).

31. *Virginia, Synod of.* The Lutheran pastors and congregations in Virginia participated in the organization of the Synod of Maryland and Virginia in 1820. Nine years later, on Aug. 10, 1829, the pastors and congregations in Virginia withdrew from this synod to organize the Synod and Ministerium of Virginia. On Sept. 20, 1842, six pastors left this body to form the Synod and Ministerium of Southwestern Virginia. A third synod was organized on the territory of the State when on Sept. 29, 1860, the Holston Synod was organized by pastors and congregations in western Virginia and in Tennessee who withdrew from the Tennessee Synod. The Synod of Virginia and the Synod of Southwestern Virginia were members of the General Synod, and both withdrew to participate in the formation of the General Synod in the South in 1864 and in the United Synod of the South in 1886. The Holston Synod, on the other hand, was not a member of the General Synod, belonged to the General Synod in the South from 1867 to 1872, to the General Council from 1874 to 1886, and to the United Synod in the South from 1886 to 1918. All three synods in Virginia (Virginia, Southwestern Virginia, and Holston) became parts of the United Lutheran Church in 1918, and on March 17, 1922, the three synods merged into the Synod of Virginia. Roanoke College, in Salem, Va. (founded 1842), and Marion Junior College, in Marion, Va. (founded 1873), are on the territory of this synod. In 1952 the synod had 104 pastors, 180 congregations, 18,636 communicants. C. W. Cassell *et al., History of the Lutheran Church in Virginia and East Tennessee* (1930).

32. *Wartburg Synod.* While the ma-

jority of German-speaking pastors and congregations withdrew from the General Synod upon the formation of the General Council in 1867, a minority remained loyal to the General Synod. Among these were pastors and congregations of the Central Illinois Synod, who, in 1873, formed the German Conference of that synod and then, in 1876, organized as the Wartburg Synod. In the early years the synod secured its pastors from the seminary in Breklum, Schleswig-Holstein, Germany. The Synod became a part of the United Lutheran Church in 1918. In 1952 the synod included 62 pastors, 44 congregations, 13,461 communicants. (The official date for founding is 1875.) Walter E. Kaitschuk, *History of the Wartburg Synod* (1940).

33. *West Virginia, Synod of.* In 1903 the Allegheny Conference of the Maryland Synod called the attention of the synod to the urgent need for missionary work in the State of West Virginia. The matter was referred to the General Synod Board of Home Missions, but in the meantime the Maryland Synod itself sent a missionary and supported his work. A number of congregations were quickly formed, and on April 17, 1912, these congregations united with several congregations of the Allegheny Conference of the Maryland Synod to organize the Synod of West Virginia. The new synod belonged to the General Synod from the beginning, and in 1918 it became a part of the United Lutheran Church. In 1952 the synod included 21 pastors, 33 congregations, 4,296 communicants.

34. *Western Canada, Synod of.* The earliest German Lutheran congregation to be organized in western Canada was Trinity Church in Winnipeg, Manitoba, founded 1888. Under the direction of the General Council's German Home Mission Board, and with the help of pastors trained in the seminary at Kropp, Schleswig-Holstein, Germany, other congregations soon formed among immigrants in the provinces of Manitoba, Saskatchewan, Alberta, and British Columbia. On July 16, 1897, these congregations with their pastors organized the Synod of Manitoba and the Northwest Territories. On June 22, 1947, the name of the synod was changed to the Synod of Western Canada. Since 1913 the Lutheran College and Seminary at Saskatoon, Sask., has been training native pastors. In 1952 the synod included 60 pastors, 121 congregations, 9,027 communicants. *Denk-*

*schrift zum Silberjubilaeum der ev.-
luth. Synode von Manitoba u. a. Pro-
vinzen* (1922); V. J. Eylands, *Lutherans
in Canada* (1945). TGT

United Lutheran Publishing House.
See *Publication Houses.*

**United Nations Relief and Rehabil-
itation Administration.** See *Social
Work,* D 1.

**United Norwegian Lutheran
Church.** This body was organized in
June, 1890, by the Norwegian-Danish
Augustana Synod, the Norwegian Lu-
theran Conference, and the Anti-Mis-
souri Brotherhood.

In 1860 Scandinavians withdrew
from the Northern Illinois Synod of
the General Synod and formed the
Scandinavian Augustana Synod. By a
peaceful separation from this Augustana Synod the Norwegian Lutheran
Conference and the Norwegian-Danish
Augustana Synod were organized in
1870.

The election controversy occasioned
a secession of a body from the Norwegian Synod * in 1887. This body
organized the Anti-Missouri Brotherhood.

This Anti-Missouri Brotherhood
took the initiative in negotiating union
with the Hauge Synod, the Norwegian
Lutheran Conference, and the Norwegian-Danish Augustana Synod. In 1888
articles of union were adopted at Eau
Claire, Wis., which accepted Pontoppidan's Catechism on the doctrine of
predestination. The articles were
adopted by all the synods except the
Hauge in 1889, and the merger took
place in 1890, thus forming the United
Norwegian Lutheran Church.

In 1917 the United Norwegian Lu-
theran Church united with the Hauge
Synod and a large part of the Norwe-
gian to form the Norwegian Lutheran
Church of America (now called the
Evangelical Lutheran Church*).

J. L. Neve-W. D. Allbeck, *History of
the Lutheran Church in America,* Luth.
Lit. Bd., Burlington, Iowa, 1934; A. R.
Wentz, *The Lutheran Church in Amer-
ican History,* United Luth. Pub. House,
Philadelphia, 1933; references under
Evangelical Lutheran Church.

United Original Secession Church.
See *Presbyterian Bodies,* 1.

United Presbyterian Church. See
Presbyterian Bodies, 1.

United Secession Church. See *Presbyterian Bodies,* 1.

**United Society of Believers in
Christ's Second Appearing.** See
Shakers.

**United States, Lutheran (Confes-
sional) Theology in.** The early Lutherans in America came from Sweden,
Holland, and Germany. They brought
with them a determination to adhere
to the Lutheran Confessions. The instructions given by the Swedish government to Gov. John Printz of New
Sweden (1642) read in part: "Above
all things shall the Governor consider
and see to it that . . . proper care be
taken that divine services are jealously
performed according to the Unaltered
Augsburg Confession, the Council of
Upsala, and the ceremonies of the
Swedish Church." Pastors and congregations of Dutch extraction subscribed
to the Amsterdam Church Order, which
pledged them to the Unaltered Augsburg Confession. The doctrinal position
of the German Lutherans is indicated
in the title of Joshua Kocherthal's
church book, which is, *A Church Book
of the Church of the Germans Who
Embrace the Augsburg Confession.*

Henry Melchior Muehlenberg, who
arrived in America in 1742, and his
fellow workers from Halle pledged
themselves at their ordination to all the
Symbolical Books and were sent to
America with instructions to "teach the
Word of God . . . according to the rule
and guidance of the Holy Scriptures
and also the Symbolical Books of the
Lutheran Church." But these men had
the pietistic conception of the Lutheran Confessions, with many of its
implications.

When the Pennsylvania Ministerium
was organized by Muehlenberg (1748),
it had no constitution, nor did it formally declare its relation to the Book
of Concord. However, at the time of its
organization it obligated John Kurtz
at his ordination to teach only that
"which harmonizes with the Word of
God and the Confessions of the Lutheran Church," and at the dedication
of St. Michael's Church, Philadelphia,
it reminded the congregation that "in
this church the Ev. Luth. doctrine according to the foundation of the Prophets and the Apostles and the Unaltered
Augsburg Confession and all the other
Symbolical Books should be taught."

After the death of Muehlenberg
(1787) a general deterioration of Confessional Lutheranism followed. The
rationalistic and unionistic influence of
Halle found its way into American Lu-

theranism. The revised constitution of the Pennsylvania Ministerium (1792) omitted all confessional tests. The second president of the New York Ministerium, Dr. F. H. Quitmann, was frankly an exponent of rationalism. His evangelical catechism, published with the approbation of his synod (1814), has no relation with Luther's Catechism.

To bolster up Lutheranism and to counteract the dangers confronting it, the General Synod was organized in 1820. In its constitution no reference. is made to the Lutheran Confessions, although it pledged the professors at its seminary at Gettysburg (est. 1826) to the "Scriptures of the Old and New Testaments as the inspired Word of God and to the Augsburg Confession and the Catechism of Luther as a summary and just exhibition of the fundamental doctrines of the Word of God." In the constitution prepared for the governing of district synods (1829), candidates for ordination were required to declare that they believed that the fundamental doctrines of the Word of God are taught in a manner substantially correct in the doctrinal articles of the Augsburg Confession." However, these confessional obligations lacked the necessary clearness and definiteness and opened the door to latitudinarianism. In a letter addressed to the Evangelical Churches of Germany (1845) the General Synod stated regarding its doctrinal position: "In most of our church principles we stand on common grounds with the Union Church in Germany. The distinctive views which separate the Old Lutherans and the Reformed Church we do not consider essential." In addition to unionism, doctrinal indifferentism, and rationalism, the influence of Puritanism was apparent. Emphasis was placed upon works, external conduct, and the performance of certain religious duties called "new measures," like Sabbath observance, abstaining from alcoholic drinks, revivals, etc.

One of the first in the East to protest against the non-confessional trends in the American Lutheran Church was Paul Henkel of New Market, Va. In 1820 he withdrew from the North Carolina Synod, which was advocating the establishing of the General Synod, and organized the Tennessee Synod on a strong Lutheran confessional basis. The Henkels translated the Book of Concord into English. Another influential spokesman for confessional Lutheranism was the *Lutheraner*, issued by C. F. W. Walther (1844). It was relentless in its criticism of the Puritan and Methodistic doctrines and practices of the General Synod and caused many to realize that the historic platform of Lutheranism had been abandoned. The organization of the Missouri Synod (1847) and its rapid growth was a boon for Lutheran orthodoxy. A number of young theologians trained in the Old Lutheran School of Rudelbach, Guericke, Harless, and others arrived from Germany and assumed leadership in their Lutheran bodies. A strong immigration of Old Lutherans from Germany and Scandinavia made its influence felt. All these factors contributed toward creating and strengthening conservative Lutheranism.

"The Definite Synodical Platform" (1855), published anonymously but fathered by S. S. Schmucker, B. Kurtz, and S. Sprecher, leaders in the General Synod, was intended to counteract the growing confessional Lutheranism in America. It was an American recension of the Augsburg Confession, charging the basic Lutheran Symbol with a number of errors, and endeavored to represent "American Lutheranism." The document found little sympathetic response and was never adopted by the General Synod, although this body in 1859 admitted as a constituent member the Melanchthon Synod, which charged the Augustana with teaching the alleged errors of regeneration by Baptism, of the Real Presence, private confession and absolution, and the denial of the divine institution of the Sunday. The public reaction to the "Definite Platform" induced C. F. W. Walther to invite all Lutheran clergymen who subscribed to the Augsburg Confession to meet in free conferences * for doctrinal discussions. Four conferences were held (1856—59).

When the Franckean Synod, which had never adopted the Augsburg Confession, but had an independent declaration of faith excluding several features of Lutheranism, was accepted as a member of the General Synod (1864), the delegates of the Pennsylvania Ministerium, in which the confessional trend had been growing, in protest left the convention and formed the General Council. Its confessional basis was the Holy Scriptures and all the Confessional Books of the Lutheran Church. Still not all conservative bodies joined, charging the General Council that it was not definite on the "Four

Points" *: chiliasm, mixed Communion, exchange of pulpits with sectarians, and secret or anti-Christian societies. In 1869 the General Council set forth a declaration condemning the lodge and gross chiliasm. In 1875 it adopted the Galesburg Rule,* which, as Dr. Jacobs pointed out, really was the Akron Rule of 1872, stipulating Lutheran altars for Lutheran communicants and Lutheran pulpits for Lutheran pastors, the exceptions to this rule belonging to the sphere of privilege, not of right.

After the formation of the General Council the doctrinal position of the General Synod became progressively more conservative, until at the convention at Atchison, Kans. (1913), the secretary reported that all the district synods had approved the revised articles of the constitution, which subscribed to the canonical Scriptures of the Old and New Testaments as the Word of God and the only infallible rule of faith and practice and to the Unaltered Augsburg Confession as a correct exhibition of the faith and doctrine of our Church as founded upon the Word. It recognized the secondary symbols as "expositions of Lutheran doctrine of great historical and interpretative value and especially recommended the Small Catechism as a book of instruction."

During the Civil War five Southern synods seceded from the General Synod and in 1863 organized the General Synod of the Ev. Luth. Church in the Confederate States of America. In 1886 this group, together with other Southern Lutheran bodies, created the United Synod of the Ev. Luth. Church in the South. In its doctrinal statement the Scriptures were accepted as the only rule of faith and life and the ecumenical symbols, together with the Unaltered Augsburg Confession, as a correct and faithful exhibition of the doctrines of Holy Scriptures in matters of faith and practice. The other Confessions of the *Book of Concord* were declared to be a correct and Scriptural interpretation of the doctrines taught by the Augsburg Confession and in full harmony with one and the same Scriptural faith.

In 1918 the General Synod, the General Council, and the United Synod of the South merged into the United Lutheran Church in America. The doctrinal platform (see *United Lutheran Church in America*) includes subscription to the canonical Scriptures of the Old and New Testaments and to all Lutheran Confessions. In 1940 this body adopted the Pittsburgh * Agreement, which formally places it on record as opposed to fellowshiping pastors and churches of other denominations, whereby doctrinal differences are ignored or virtually made matters of indifference, and as opposed to secret anti-Christian societies. A number of leaders refused, however, to accept the statements on the Scriptures in the Pittsburgh Agreement, because in their opinion it taught the verbal inspiration of the Holy Scriptures.

The Missouri Synod, which since its organization undauntedly adhered to the infallible Scriptures and all Confessional Books of the Lutheran Church, was consistently opposed to all forms of unionism and syncretism, drew into its orbit like-minded synods, and established with them in 1872 the Synodical Conference. The charter members were Missouri, Wisconsin, Ohio, Norwegian, Minnesota, and Illinois. During the Predestination Controversy (see *The Lutheran Church — Missouri Synod*) the Ohio Synod withdrew (1881). In order to prevent a split in its own body, the Norwegian Synod left the Synodical Conference (1883), although it maintained fraternal relations until the adoption of the Madison Theses * in 1912. At the present time the Synodical Conference embraces The Lutheran Church — Missouri Synod, the Ev. Luth. Joint Synod of Wisconsin and Other States, the Slovak Ev. Luth. Church, and the Norwegian Synod of the American Ev. Luth. Church. The National Ev. Luth. Church (Finnish) is in fellowship with this group. The Synodical Conference holds a very strict confessional position and maintains strict discipline in this respect. In view of the controversies in the Lutheran Church in America in the past, the Missouri Synod stated its doctrinal position in the *Brief Statement* * of 1932. Although this document has not been formally adopted by all members of the Synodical Conference, all subscribe to its doctrinal statements.

The Ohio Synod, Iowa, and Buffalo merged into the American Lutheran Church in 1930. Its confession of faith includes the Holy Scriptures as the inspired Word of God and all Confessional Books of the Lutheran Church. The American Lutheran Church in 1930, together with the Augustana Synod, the United Danish Lutheran Church, the Lutheran Free Church, and the Norwegian Lutheran Church, organized the American Lutheran Conference on the basis of the Minneapolis Theses.* This body accepts without exception all the canonical books of the Old and New Testaments, as a whole and in all their parts, as the divinely inspired, revealed, and inerrant Word of God and without reservations the Symbolical Books of the Lutheran Church. The Norwegian Lutheran Church, in agreement with the Lutheran Church of Norway and Denmark, has officially accepted only the three ecumenical creeds, the Unaltered Augsburg Confession, and Luther's Small Catechism. This position does not imply that the Norwegian Lutheran Church rejects the remaining Symbolical Books of the Lutheran Church. These other Symbolical Books are not known to her constituency generally, so it has not deemed it necessary to require formal subscription to the entire *Book of Concord*. The American Lutheran Conference is formally opposed to all syncretism and unionism and to anti-Christian lodges.

Thus an examination of the doctrinal statements in the constitutions of the Lutheran bodies in America reveals a common acceptance of the Holy Scriptures as the inspired Word of God and those formulations of faith known as the Symbolical Books of the Lutheran Church.

"Such differences as exist between Lutheran groups arise over the question of the extent and authority admitted to the Confessions. The protagonists for an authoritative theology, rendering an undisputed decision on every point of doctrine, are to be found in the Synodical Conference. The other Lutheran bodies in America, equally vigorous in their adherence to the Augsburg Confession, maintain that certain doctrines, not essential to salvation, must be considered 'open questions.'" (Neve-Allbeck, *The History of the Lutheran Church in America*, p. 366.)

"The principal features of practice in which there is lack of unanimity are those of pulpit and altar fellowship with non-Lutherans and membership, especially on the part of pastors, in secret societies. Both practices are interpreted to have relation to the doctrinal problems of syncretism and Socinianism." (Neve-Allbeck, *op. cit.*, p. 369.) WAB   •

For bibliography see references under *American Lutheranism; Definite Platform; Diets, Luth., in America; Free Conferences; Lutheran Confessions; Old Lutherans; United States, Lutheranism in;* and the items, doctrinal statements, and Lutheran bodies mentioned in this article.

United States of America, Religious History.

1. The purpose of this article is not so much to give anything like a detailed account of the numerous religious groups pursuing their several ends within the broad limits and the untrammeled liberties of our country as to draw attention to some of the outstanding principles which have guided the religious development and determined the religious life of the nation. For over one hundred years after the discovery of America the religious history of the country was the history of the Roman Church * in this country.

2. Some Protestant churches, such as those of Massachusetts, Pennsylvania, and Maryland, owe their origin to European intolerance and persecution. Fugitives for conscience' sake laid the foundations of these commonwealths and contributed large numbers to the population of the other colonies. Puritans, Quakers, Huguenots, Presbyterians, Lutherans, Roman Catholics, and others, seeking that freedom of faith and worship which was denied them in their native land, emigrated to America to breathe the air of liberty. Puritanism was dominant in New England, Quakerism in Pennsylvania, and Episcopalianism in Virginia and the South.

3. That the American colonists, though in large part fugitives from persecution in Europe, had not — with some noteworthy exceptions — grasped the meaning of religious freedom is written in plain and indelible letters over the chapter of colonial history. Protesting against intolerance in Europe, they practiced it in America. Advocating the sovereignty of conscience when under oppression, they ignored its authority when in power. Non-conformists in the Old World, they insisted on rigid conformity in the new. Thus the Puritans of New England established a theocratic government, which was deemed the "best form of government in a Christian commonwealth," in that it made "the Lord God our Governor," gave "unto Christ His due *pre-eminence*," and was the form "received and established among the people of Israel." No one could hold a political office who was not a member of the Church, that is to say, of the Puritan establishment. Membership in a private religious association

was treason against the State and "high presumption against the Lord." Romanists, Prelatists, Baptists, Quakers, were not tolerated. Blasphemy, perjury, adultery, witchcraft, abuse of parents (if the child was over sixteen years of age), were punishable by death. Fines, imprisonment, the scourge, the stocks, ear slitting, nose boring, etc., were the approved methods of enforcing discipline and religious uniformity. The foregoing applies in a general way to the Puritan colonies of Massachusetts, Connecticut, and New Haven, although the penal codes of the several colonies were not strictly identical.

4. The colony of New Amsterdam restricted religious liberty, and after passing under the power of England, the Episcopal Church was established by law and supported by taxation, while severe laws were passed against the Catholics.

5. Pennsylvania also started with the principle of freedom of conscience, but from 1693 to 1775 no one could hold office who did not profess the orthodox doctrine of the Trinity and reject the Roman Catholic doctrine of transubstantiation and the Mass as idolatrous. Even a man like Benjamin Franklin submitted to this test when he entered upon the duties of the various offices which he held.

6. The first and only colony established by Catholics was Maryland and religious freedom was granted to all "who believe in Christ," whether Romanist or Protestant. This enlightened policy, enacted into a law of the State in 1649, was reversed in 1691, when Episcopalianism was forcibly introduced and the Catholics were completely disfranchised.

7. In Virginia the Episcopal Church was supported by the State. A law of 1643 expressly prohibited any person dissenting from the doctrines and usages of the established Church from preaching and teaching the Gospel within the limits of the colony.

8. In the Carolinas and in Georgia full civil and religious liberty was granted to all Christians except the Roman Catholics. There was no established church.

9. The colony of Rhode Island, founded by Roger Williams, who was banished from Massachusetts, deserves special mention, inasmuch as here the spheres of Church and State were cleanly separated, thus anticipating the principle embodied in the Federal Constitution. (See *Church and State*.)

10. In Virginia the efforts of dissenting denominations (Presbyterians, Baptists, Quakers), combined with the powerful advocacy of Thomas Jefferson, resulted in the disestablishment of the Episcopal Church before the Declaration of Independence. The framers of the Constitution had learned from history the folly and the mischief of religious coercion and persecution, and therefore they wisely held aloof from any legislation for the control of faith and worship. Nor could they, under the circumstances, have very well done anything else. When the colonies, after achieving their independence, coalesced into a nation, they could not grant liberty to one church, or sect, to the exclusion of the rest. "The liberty of all was the best guarantee of the liberty of each." Thus has the American Constitution solved a problem of the ages. It cut the Gordian knot by which State and Church had been intertwined and thus inaugurated an epoch in the history of legislation.

11. The separation of Church and State involves the voluntary principle for the maintenance of the former. That is to say, no church or sect may appeal to the State for special patronage or financial support. All expenses necessary for running the church's machinery, such as the erection of seminaries for the training of the clergy, the payment of ministers' salaries, etc., must be met by voluntary contributions. So far from being a disadvantage, this system tends rather to promote liberality and stimulate personal interest in the work of the church. The experience of a century and a half has fully justified the American principle of separation of Church and State. Says the late James Bryce: "So far from suffering from the want of State support, religion seems in the United States to stand all the firmer, because, standing alone, she is seen to stand by her own strength." And again: "Christianity influences conduct not indeed half as much as in theory it ought, but probably more than it does in any other modern country." (*The American Commonwealth.*) Separation of Church and State also means the secularization of public instruction. This, again, has led some church bodies, Catholics and Lutherans, to maintain their own parochial schools in order to provide for the religious education of their children. Otherwise the Sunday school is made to supply this need as well as it may.

12. When the colonial period came to an end (1783), there were about 3,000,000 inhabitants, made up of almost every branch of Protestantism. There were few Catholics. Up to 1840 the total immigration did not exceed half a million. After that immigrants came in numbers, the Germans and the Irish forming the largest contingents. The Roman Catholic Church constitutes about one third of the Christian population, the principal divisions of Protestantism about one half. The remainder consists of minor sects, of which there is a bewildering variety. Besides, there are numerous smaller bodies which reject the ecumenical creeds, such as the Unitarians, Universalists, Swedenborgians, Christian Scientists, and others. Protestantism is the dominant religious force of the country.

13. Unlike other countries, in which usually one particular form of confession prevailed, the United States of North America has become the home of practically every denomination and sect in existence. The Pilgrim Fathers, who landed on Plymouth Rock on Dec. 25, 1620, and founded a colony, which became the germ of the New England States, were the first to seek a place of refuge on the hospitable shores of the Western Continent. They were followed by the Puritans, who, for reasons similar to those of the Pilgrim Fathers, came to America and formed the various Puritan settlements in Massachusetts. In both these colonies Church and State were more or less mingled, the only relation to which these immigrants were accustomed. The peculiarities of the Puritans of New England have come down to us in the Congregationalists, though in the course of time these have greatly deviated from the doctrinal tenets and customs of their forefathers. The early settlers of Virginia brought with them an episcopal form of service, and out of this settlement grew the Protestant Episcopal Church of this country. The Reformed (Dutch) Church was the outgrowth of the Dutch settlement in New York and New Jersey. The Presbyterian churches of this country originated from parties and immigrants from England, Ireland, and Scotland who settled within the limits of various colonies. The Baptists originated among the Puritans and were banished from their midst. Methodism in this country was propagated by the followers of Whitefield and Wesley, and their

growth was rapid, since their zeal was great. The Roman Catholics of Maryland were from England, those of Florida from Spain, and those of the Great Lakes region and the Mississippi Valley from France. The Quakers originated in England and found their way among the American colonists. The Lutherans emigrated from all parts of Germany and the Scandinavian countries, as also from Russia and Austria. See details under the names of the individual denominations. See also *Religious Bodies (U. S.), Bibliography; Statistics; Union Movements.*

United States, Lutheranism in. The Lutheran Church in the United States, like many other groups, was transplanted on American soil by early immigrants. Traces of these plantings date back more than 300 years. The earliest Lutheran churches within the present boundaries of the U. S. came into being on Manhattan Island (Dutch, Scandinavian, and German, 1623), later served by Pastors J. E. Gutwasser, J. Fabricius, and B. Arensius, and along the Delaware River (Swedish settlements, 1638) served by Pastors R. Torkillus, J. Companius, L. Lock, and others. Pastor Justus Falckner, the first Lutheran pastor ordained on American soil (Nov. 24, 1703, at Gloria Dei, Wicaco [Philadelphia], Pa.), served the far-flung parish along the Hudson and on Manhattan Island. Later settlements were made in the State of New York in the Schoharie Valley (1710) under Pastor J. Kocherthal. In the South the Salzburgers, under Pastors J. M. Bolzius and I. C. Gronau, settled near Savannah, Ga., in 1734. During these pre-Revolutionary days, New York, Pennsylvania, Delaware, and Maryland became very popular as settlements for European Lutherans. Pastors active during this time were the Falckners, A. J. Henkel, W. C. Berkenmeyer, and the Stoevers. Up to the latter part of the 18th century the history of Lutheranism is not only the history of immigration, but also of individual congregations being organized in almost all Lutheran settlements. At the same time it was a period of confusion. The congregations were widely scattered and poor. The lack of pastors was a serious hindrance. Some of them were adventurers and impostors.

The period of larger organizations or synods was inaugurated by Pastor H. M. Muehlenberg when he organized the Pennsylvania Ministerium in 1748.

He was the true builder of the Lutheran Church in America, bringing order out of chaos. His liturgy also was instrumental in unifying those early congregations. Synodical organizations coming into being during this time were the New York Ministerium (1876) and the Synod of North Carolina (1803).

The contributions which Muhlenberg made toward confessional Lutheranism were counteracted by the rationalism and indifferentism which gripped the Lutheran Church from 1787 to 1817. Dr. F. H. Quitman of the N. Y. Ministerium edited an entirely rationalistic hymnal and catechism in 1814. Fraternization among Moravians and Episcopalians was common. This same laxness had also crept into the Synod of North Carolina under Pastor G. Schober.

Then, however, new life came into the un-Lutheran Lutheranism. Immigration from Lutheran countries reached the peak during this next period (1817—1860), bringing with it strong confessional tendencies and new synodical organizations (Ohio Synod, 1818; Synod of Maryland and Virginia, 1820; Buffalo Synod, 1845; Missouri Synod, 1847). Besides a reaction to unionism had set in among the Lutherans in America. The Tennessee Synod was organized in 1820 as a protest against the unionism of the Synod of North Carolina. Under these circumstances the General Synod was organized in 1820 without a confessional basis by J. G. Schmucker, J. D. Kurtz, and G. Schober. It was only a loose organization, without which, however, the Lutheran Church would not have fared too well, since it opposed Socinianizing elements. Gettysburg Seminary was also organized under its auspices. Until shortly before the Civil War, the General Synod took in almost two thirds of all Lutheranism in the country.

This period is characterized also by its lack of pastors. Individual pastors trained a few students in their homes; some attended the seminaries of other denominations. A number of attempts were made to establish theological seminaries. However, these did not materially change the picture. Another serious problem affecting the church at this time was the language question. Stubborn adherence to the mother tongue drove many of the young English-speaking people into the hands of the English denominations.

Mission and eleemosynary work was carried on. For many years the General Synod tried to follow the settlers into the West through its Home Missionary Society. Active in the work were C. F. Heyer, Jesse Hoover, and Ezra Keller. The first foreign missionary, C. F. Heyer, was sent to India by the Pennsylvania Ministerium in 1841. Dr. W. A. Passavant became very active in establishing hospitals and orphanages in the East and Middle West. He also introduced deaconess work there.

Naturally, with such divergent backgrounds, training, and nationalities, doctrinal disagreement was bound to follow. The next period is typified by great doctrinal conflicts. The attempt by S. S. Schmucker, Samuel Sprecher, and Ben. Kurtz to introduce the "Definite Platform" in 1855, which proposed a modification of the Augsburg Confession, conforming it to Reformed theology, was met with strong opposition from almost all synods. Other controversial points at this time were Antichrist, Church and Ministry, "Open Questions," Sunday, and Predestination.

Lutheranism was in a turmoil. Reaction against indifference and confessional laxity set in. This, as well as the Southern synods leaving the General Synod (General Synod South, 1863) during the Civil War, all but disrupted it. In 1866 the General Council was organized under the auspices of the Pennsylvania Ministerium, with the ambitious program of uniting all confessional Lutherans into one body. This was not achieved because strong confessional groups like the Missouri Synod did not participate. Others, which had joined, left it again when the Council did not clarify its position on chiliasm, altar and pulpit fellowship, and secret societies. The Scandinavian groups which had immigrated in such large numbers during this period organized their own synods, of which one affiliated with the General Synod, but withdrew in 1860.

The field was now open for the remaining independent confessional bodies to organize the Synodical Conference in 1872, which was another attempt to unite the Lutheran Church in America. The Missouri, Ohio, Norwegian, Wisconsin, and Minnesota Synods formed this federation under the leadership of C. F. W. Walther. The period of intersynodical mergers was begun in 1917. The quadricentennial of the Reformation, through the impetus of laymen, was instrumental in uniting the General Synod, the United Synod South, and the General Council in the United Lutheran Church. The Rev. F. H. Knubel was elected its first president. The Norwegian groups, excluding a minority, merged to organize the present Evangelical Lutheran Church in 1917. Three independent German synods, the Ohio, Iowa, and Buffalo Synods, united to form the American Lutheran Church in 1930, with the Rev. C. C. Hein as president. That same year this church body joined with the Augustana Synod, the United Danish Luth. Church, the Lutheran Free Church, and the Evangelical Lutheran Church in a federation called the American Lutheran Conference. Its first president was Pastor Otto Mees. Formal organization of the National Lutheran Council, an agency serving the Lutheran Church of America, was effected in 1918. The United Luth. Church, the Synods of the American Luth. Conference, and the Icelandic Synod were represented at its organizational meeting. Dr. H. G. Stub was chosen president. A free association of world Lutheranism was begun in 1923, called the Lutheran World Convention, a name since changed to the Lutheran World Federation.

The Lutheran Church of America has shown a definite trend toward confessionalism during the last one hundred years. Then there was doctrinal and confessional laxity, fraternization and fellowship with non-Lutherans. Today every Lutheran group accepts the Augsburg Confession as being in agreement with the inspired Word of God. Lutheran altars for Lutheran communicants only, and Lutheran pulpits for Lutheran ministers only, is the generally accepted principle today. All this augurs a new period in the history of Lutheranism, that is, the merger and union of larger bodies. ARS

Israel Acrelius, *History of New Sweden,* Historical Soc. of Pa., 1874; E. L. Hazelius, *History of the American Lutheran Church, from Its Commencement in 1685 to the Year 1842,* Zanesville, Ohio, 1846; C. W. Schaeffer, *Early History of the Lutheran Church in America,* Luth. Lit. Bd., Philadelphia, 1857; A. L. Graebner, *Geschichte der Lutherischen Kirche in Amerika,* CPH, 1892; H. E. Jacobs, *History of the Evangelical Lutheran Church in the United States,* Christian Lit., New York, 1893;

G. J. Fritschel, *Geschichte der Lutherischen Kirche in Amerika, auf Grund von Dr. Jacobs Historie,* Guetersloh, Germany, 1896; O. Kraushaar, *Verfassungsformen der evangelisch-lutherischen Kirche Amerikas,* Bertelsmann, Guetersloh, 1907; W. J. Finck, *Lutheran Landmarks and Pioneers in America,* United Luth. Pub. House, Philadelphia, 1913; J. L. Neve, *A Brief History of the Lutheran Church in America,* German Lit. Bd., Burlington, Iowa, 1916 (later ed., 1934); F. Bente. *American Lutheranism,* CPH, 1919; A. B. Faust, *The German Element in the United States,* Steuben Soc., New York, 1927; A. R. Wentz, *The Lutheran Church in American History,* United Luth. Pub. House, Philadelphia, 1923 (later ed., 1933); V. Ferm, *The Crisis in American Lutheran Theology,* Century, New York, 1927; Carl Mauelshagen, *American Lutheranism Surrenders to Forces of Conservatism,* Univ. of Georgia, 1936.

United States, Roman Catholic Church in. See *Roman Catholic Church.*

United Stewardship Council of the United States and Canada. See *Union Movements,* 13.

United Student Christian Council. See *Students, Spiritual Care of,* A.

United Synod of the Ev. Luth. Church in the South. 1. During the Civil War the Southern synods took umbrage at certain resolutions passed by the General Synod in regard to the war and withdrew in 1863. In 1864, at Concord, N. C., these synods, North Carolina, South Carolina, Virginia, and Southwestern Virginia, together with the small Georgia Synod, organized the Ev. Luth. Synod of the Confederate States of America. After the war (1866) the name was changed to The General Synod of the Ev. Luth. Church of the South. When the confessionalism of this synod had reached a point satisfactory to the Tennessee Synod, which had never joined any general body, and the Holston Synod, which for some time had been connected with the General Council, they entered into an agreement with the General Synod of the South and on June 23, 1886, organized the United Synod of the South on the doctrinal basis adopted in Salisbury, N. C., in 1884. This doctrinal basis was practically that of the Tennessee Synod since 1866 — all the Confessions of the Lutheran Church.

2. The adoption of this basis was a

triumph for the confessional fidelity of the Tennessee Synod, and also for the unflinching testimony of the Missouri Synod, over the liberalism of Dr. J. Bachmann, who had for years opposed the confessionalism of the Tennessee Synod. Yet the actual conditions prevailing even after the adoption of this sound Lutheran basis betokened a certain indifferentism, and the practice in regard to lodge and pulpit and altar fellowship did not always agree with the principles, in spite of the efforts of the Tennessee Synod to induce the United Synod to take a determined stand. The North Carolina Synod, especially, refused to yield, so that finally Tennessee felt obliged to compromise. The official organ of the United Synod was the *Lutheran Church Visitor.*

3. After the United Synod in the South had co-operated with other Lutheran general bodies for some time, notably in the preparation of the Common Service, for which the United Synod justly claims to be entitled to special credit, it was but natural that this body should gladly enter into the Merger of 1918, which resulted in the United Lutheran Church in America. The resolution to do so was passed Nov. 6, 1917, at Salisbury, N.C.

4. The leading men in the United Synod were the Henkels, E. T. Horn, A. G. Voigt, W. H. Greever, M. G. G. Scherer. — The theological seminary of the synod (founded 1830) is located at Columbia, S.C. Its colleges are: Newberry, S.C. (founded by the S.C. Synod 1832), Roanoke College, Roanoke, Va. (founded by the Va. Synod 1842), Lenoir-Rhyne (founded by the Tennessee Synod in 1891 and richly endowed by Daniel Rhyne in 1922), Hickory, N.C. — Besides the Home Mission work the United Synod conducted a mission, jointly with the General Council, in Japan. At the time of the merger in 1918 the United Synod in the South consisted of eight synods, 262 pastors, 494 congregations, and 55,473 confirmed members. See also *United Lutheran Church.*

C. W. Heathcote, *The Lutheran Church and the Civil War,* Luth. Lit. Bd., Burlington, Iowa; F. Bente, *American Lutheranism,* CPH, 1919; A. R. Wentz, *The Lutheran Church in American History,* United Luth. Pub. House, Philadelphia, 1932; J. L. Neve, *History of the Lutheran Church in America,* Luth. Lit. Bd., 1934; H. E. Jacobs, *A History of the Ev. Luth. Church in America,* Scribner's, 1912.

United Zion's Children. See *Brethren, The River.*

Unity of Bohemian Brethren. See *Bohemia, Lutheran Theology in; Bohemian-Moravian Brethren.*

Unity School of Christianity. Organized (1889) by Charles and Myrtle Fillmore in Kansas City, the school claims two million followers. Its theology is in line with the New Thought * movement though of a less radical nature. It emphasizes healing (especially mental), prayer, and related activities. It teaches that God is the original spiritual Being. Man has being in God's being and exists in God's man as a perfect idea of man. The atonement is the union of man with God the Father in Christ, or the at-one-ment, or agreement, or reconciliation, of man's mind with Divine Mind through the superconsciousness, or Christ mind. Redemption means the unification and spiritualization of soul and body consciousness in Spirit.

Universal Education. See *Christian Education,* D.

"Universal Salvation." See *Methodist Bodies,* 2.

Universalists. 1. Adherents of Universalism, the belief that God ultimately will destroy all sin and save the whole human race. Universalists find the doctrine of endless punishment incompatible with the belief that Truth and Good will finally be victorious. While Universalism is almost as old as Christianity and has found many adherents, especially since the Reformation, the Universalist denomination is an American organization of comparatively modern origin. Its founder is John Murray, b. 1741 at Alton, England, d. 1815 in Boston. At first a Methodist, he was induced by James Relly, a former Methodist preacher in London, to accept Universalism. He came to America in 1770, which year is regarded by the denomination as the year of its origin. His preaching resulted in the formation of societies in New York, Pennsylvania, and Massachusetts, and denominational organization was effected 1785.

2. In the nineties Hosea Ballou (1771 to 1852), who held more radical views than Murray, became the recognized leader. In 1803 an anti-Trinitarian creed, the Winchester Profession, consisting of three short articles, was adopted. In 1899 a still shorter statement of Universalist principles was

adopted, which asserted belief in "the universal fatherhood of God; the spiritual authority and leadership of His Son, Jesus Christ; the trustworthiness of the Bible as containing a revelation from God; the certainty of just retribution for sins; the final harmony of all souls with God."

3. Universalists hold that punishment for sin is the inevitable consequence of sin, "the wounds, the damage, the shame" in man's soul, that its purpose is beneficent, namely, to deter from further sin, that the period of probation for the sinners — and that means all men — does not end with this life, but everyone after death will be subject to disciplinary processes and given an opportunity forever to develop upward and Godward. This continual upward progress of mankind toward holiness and perfection is the fundamental doctrine of Universalism today. With regard to Christ's person, work, and redemption, Universalists are practically Unitarians, and their position has been stated thus: "that Jesus had the same essential spiritual and human nature as other men; but that He was chosen of God to sustain a certain unique relation on the one hand toward God and on the other toward men, by virtue of which He was a revelation of the divine will and character and a sample of the perfected or full-grown man." Consequently the doctrines of vicarious atonement and justification through imputation of Christ's righteousness are rejected. Sins are pardoned when the sinner ceases from sin and becomes obedient. With regard to other doctrines there is a great variety of belief; but all Universalists practically agree on denying original sin, the existence of the devil, the resurrection of the body, Christ's second coming, the final Judgment, the efficacy of the Sacraments, and the real presence in Communion.

4. The denomination numbers 62,000 members (1953). Its greatest strength is in Massachusetts and New York. The Universalist Publishing House is at Boston, where the *Universalist Leader* is published. They have three theological seminaries, at Canton, N. Y., Tufts College, Mass., and Chicago. There are also a number of societies in Canada, and a mission is carried on in Japan. In 1831 a number seceded from the denomination and organized under the name of Universal Restorationists. While the majority held with Ballou that sinners are punished for their sins only in this life, the Restorationists believed that the wicked are punished for a time also after death. They disbanded 1841. Mention must also be made of the fact that there are many adherents of Universalism outside the denomination. Unitarians generally hold Universalist views, as do some members of the Reformed churches, particularly among the liberal Congregationalists. See *Religious Bodies (U. S.), Bibliography*.

Universities. See *Higher Education*.

Unorganized Italian Christian Churches of North America. Pentecostal * sect arising from a movement in Chicago in 1904. 9,500 members.

Unpardonable Sin. See *Sin, the Unpardonable*.

Unterschriften. See *Finances in the Church*, 3.

Upanishads. See *Brahmanism*, 4; *Hinduism*, 2.

Upsala, Diet of. See *Sweden, Lutheran Church in*, 1, 2.

Urlsperger, Johann August (1728 to 1806). German theologian and controversialist; a man of great learning and an earnest thinker; defended the evangelical truth against philosophical and rationalizing theories; founded the *Deutsche Christentumsgesellschaft* in Basel for the advocacy and defense of the pure doctrine; but the society, to his disappointment, devoted its efforts rather to the promotion of true piety as understood in those days.

Urlsperger, Samuel (1685—1772). German Lutheran theologian; father of preceding, influenced by Francke; pastor at Augsburg; confidential agent for Salzburg * Colony in Georgia.

Ursinus, Zacharias (1534—83). German Reformed; b. in Breslau; disciple of Melanchthon; professor of theology at Heidelberg; together with Olevianus (disciple of Calvin) wrote *Heidelberg Catechism* (publ. 1563); d. at Neustadt.

Ursula, St. A mythical character around which fantastic legends were woven in the Middle Ages, the favorite one representing her as a Christian princess from Britain, who was massacred at Cologne by the Huns with 11,000 maidens. Intelligent Romanists have discarded the legend. It has, however, enabled the city of Cologne to send an abundance of relics throughout Christendom and even to India and China.

Ursulines. A religious order of women, having the sole purpose of educating young girls.

Uruguay. The smallest of the South American republics. Area about 72,000 sq. mi. Population 2,600,000 (1951), largely of Latin origin. There is perfect separation of Church and State. Uruguay has been a pioneer in education. It is the only country in the world to offer free graduate courses in medicine, engineering, architecture, and other professions. The Lutheran Church — Missouri Synod began its work in Montevideo in 1935. The first congregation was organized ten years later. Statistics: 7,000 Protestant communicants, 1,833,000 Roman Catholics (1952). See also *South America.*

Ussher (Usher), James (1581 to 1656). Luminary of Irish Church; b. in Dublin; archbishop of Armagh 1625 to 1640; preacher in England (d. there); scholarly writer. His chronology of the Bible appeared for a long time in the Authorized Version.

Usury. 1. According to general usage, the taking of interest in excess of the rate permitted by law; more strictly, in agreement with the law of love, the indiscriminate taking of interest and, in the strictest interpretation of the term, the taking of interest in any form. — The Old Testament clearly distinguishes between the taking of interest from a fellow believer and from one who was not a member of the chosen people of God. It was forbidden to an Israelite to take from a fellow Israelite interest of any kind in return for a loan (Ex. 22:25-27; Lev. 25:35-37; Deut. 23:20), whether of money or food; but from one who was not an Israelite it was permitted to take interest (Deut. 23:20; cp. 15:6; 28:12).

2. In the New Testament the question is taken up from the viewpoint of brotherly love. Taking interest is not specifically forbidden, yet gratuitous lending is commended, and where the need of the neighbor requires it, donating is urged outright (cp. Luke 6:34, 35).

3. In the early days of the Church the taking of interest, especially in an indiscriminate manner, was reproved. It was only from the enemy that interest could rightfully be taken. As a general rule, the practice of the indiscriminate taking of interest was prohibited to all Christians, without distinction of persons.

4. Among Lutherans in America, Walther especially opposed the taking of interest. The controversy which resulted occasioned statements by Walther which differentiated between agreement on *Schriftlehren* and *Glaubensartikel* as a prerequisite for fellowship.

Utilitarianism. See *Pragmatism.*

Ultraquists. See *Bohemian-Moravian Brethren; Bohemia, Lutheran Theology* in, 4; *Hussites.*

V

Vacation Bible School. See *Christian Education,* E 9 ff.; *Parish Education,* F 3.

Vacherot, Etienne (1809—97). Prof. of philosophy at Sorbonne, France; held that God arises in human thought through ideas of perfection, which, however, cannot exist in reality.

Vaiçeshika. See *Brahmanism,* 5.

Vaihinger, Hans (1852—1933). German philosopher; prof. at Halle; his *Die Philosophie des Als Ob* holds that religion, though fictitious, has ethical value.

Vaisya. See *Hinduism,* 3.

Valdez, Juan and Alfonso De. Reformers within the Roman Church, twins; b. ca. the end of the 15th century in Spain, the former dying at Naples in 1541, the latter at Vienna in 1532. Both had an opportunity to observe and study the Lutheran Reformation, but they never rightly and fully entered into its spirit. Although Juan, especially, had an understanding of many points of the truth, as his foremost work, *Alfabeto Christiano* (Christian Alphabet), shows, he did not comprehend the real mystery of iniquity at the papal court, and his books were forbidden a few years after his death. To his school belonged Aonio Paleario * and Don Benedetto de Mantova.*

Valentine, Milton. B. Jan. 1, 1825, near Uniontown, Md. Leading exponent of the confessional trend in the

Lutheran General Synod; educated at Gettysburg; pastor till 1866, then professor at Gettysburg Seminary, president of the college for sixteen years; from 1884 professor of Systematic Theology in the Seminary. His *Christian Theology* (1906) makes concessions to evolutionism, Puritanism, and Reformed theology. D. Feb. 7, 1906.

Valentinus. Gnostic philosopher. Taught at Rome ca. the middle of the second century; several times excommunicated; retired to Cyprus, where he died ca. 160. His system, reared on a Platonic background, is a dark, illimitable ocean, in which Oriental and Greek speculation together with Christian ideas, grotesquely perverted and misused, are strangely commingled. The Primal Being unfolds by emanation into thirty eons, among them the ideal Man, the ideal Church, and the heavenly Christ (a Platonic conception). These constitute the Pleroma, or heavenly universe, as against the Kenoma, emptiness, the chaotic world of matter. A disturbance in the cosmic equilibrium necessitated a restoration. Redemption is therefore a cosmic process, performed by a redeemer who has nothing in common with Jesus of Nazareth. See *Gnosticism.*

Valerian. See *Persecutions of Christians,* 4.

Valla, Laurentius (1407—57). Italian humanist. In his *Forgery of the Donation of Constantine* he demolished a fraud imposed upon Christendom for centuries. This, together with his attacks upon the Vulgate's Latinity, the apostolic origin of the Apostles' Creed, and of Christ's letter to Abgarus, led to his citation before the Inquisition. Under the liberal Pope Nicholas V he rose to prominence at the papal court.

Valparaiso University. A Lutheran university owned and operated (since 1925) by the Lutheran University Association and located at Valparaiso, Ind., 50 miles southeast of Chicago.

The history of Valparaiso University begins, as an ideal, in 1850, when the "Statuten fuer das Concordia Collegium" of the Missouri Synod defined "Concordia College" as "Concordia University," with the intention of including other curricula along with theology. Synod's unexpected growth and accompanying financial limitations, however, made it necessary to concentrate on the founding of a seminary.

In the meantime, Sept. 21, 1859, saw the opening of the Valparaiso Male and Female College, a secular institution, at Valparaiso, Ind. The effects of the Civil War caused classes to be suspended in 1869, but four years later Prof. Henry Baker Brown, a former instructor at Northwestern Normal School of Republic, Ohio, reopened it as the Northern Indiana Normal School and Business Institute. In 1881 he was joined by Prof. Oliver Perry Kinsey, and together, on their philosophy of educational opportunity for everyone, they provided amazingly inexpensive schooling on any level. In 1907 the Normal School was renamed Valparaiso University. Between 1859 and 1925, when effects of World War I again threatened to close its doors, nearly 79,000 students are reported to have attended its classes.

The vision of Lutheran higher education had not been lost, and when the Rev. George F. Schutes of Immanuel Church, Valparaiso, informed a group of pastors and laymen at Fort Wayne that the university could be purchased, action was immediately taken. The Lutheran University Association took over Valparaiso University on Sept. 8, 1925. Through a Synod-wide canvass funds were provided, and W. H. T. Dau became the first president. Within the next four years accreditation as a university was obtained.

The original 46-acre campus was groomed, its buildings modernized, and in 1939 a new Health and Physical Education Building was opened. In 1944, 90 acres of additional property were purchased. Continued growth and expansion of the physical plant marked later years.

Valparaiso University's accreditation includes ranking by such agencies as the North Central Association of Colleges and Secondary Schools, the Association of American Law Schools, the American Bar Association, the Board of Regents of the University of the State of New York, the Council of Medical Education and Hospitals of the American Medical Association for Pre-Medical Education, the Teacher Training and Licensing Commission of the Indiana State Board of Education, the Committee on Admissions from Higher Institutions of the University of Illinois as class "A" in all departments of the College of Arts and Sciences, the National Association of Schools of Social Administration.

The enrollment (about 2,000 at the middle of the 20th century) represents a nation-wide geographic spread. For courses and degrees offered the current catalog should be consulted.

The presidency of Valparaiso University has been held by W. H. T. Dau (1925—29); O. C. Kreinheder (1930 to 1939), O. P. Kretzmann (1940—).

Vanderkamp, John T. (1747—1811). B. at Rotterdam, Holland; d. in South Africa; doctor and pioneer missionary in South Africa; ordained by London Missionary Society 1798; sailed to South Africa in missionary interest on convict ship; arrived at Cape Town in March, 1799; labored at Great Fish River, chiefly among Hottentots and Kaffirs; removed his adherents to Algoa Bay 1802; redeemed many slaves with his private funds from cruel Boer masters; broke down much opposition of Europeans in Africa to missionary labors among the natives and was an eminently successful missionary.

Vardhamana. See *Jainism.*

Variata. See *Lutheran Confessions,* B 1; *Union Movements,* 3.

Varuna. See *Brahmanism,* 2.

Vatican. The palace of the Pope at Rome, situated on Vatican Hill, on the right bank of the Tiber. While the Vatican was a papal residence since the ninth century, it has been the Pope's chief palace only since about 1370. Pope after Pope has added to the buildings, and to the treasures which they contain, with marvelous results. The Vatican buildings cover about thirteen and a half acres and contain twenty courtyards, eight grand staircases, a large number of chapels, and some thousand rooms, among them many splendid apartments, designed and decorated by Michelangelo, Raffael, and other masters. The Sistine Chapel, with its frescoes by Michelangelo, is world-famed. Only about two hundred rooms are occupied for residential purposes by the Pope, his secretary of state, and his chief officials and closest attendants. The rest are used in carrying on the administration of the Church of Rome and in housing the Vatican Library, the papal archives, and various extensive and valuable collections of antiquities, relics, papyri, inscriptions, paintings, and statuary. Within the precincts of the Vatican is also the famous Church of St. Peter, one of the world's finest structures. In its crypt are the tombs of Popes and royalties and the reputed tomb of St. Peter.

Negotiations begun in 1926 led to the Treaty of Conciliation and Concordat (signed Feb. 11, 1929), which established the independent State of Vatican City. The Lateran Agreement was later put into the constitution of Italy (Mar. 26, 1947). The Vatican City State includes 13 extraterritorial buildings in Rome. Pius XII is its sovereign (1954). Area: 108.7 acres. Population: 1,010 (1952).

Vatican Council. See *Roman Catholic Confessions,* E.

Vaticanus, Codex. See *Manuscripts of the Bible,* 3.

Vatke, Wilhelm (1806—82). Prof. at Berlin; liberal theologian; opponent of Hengstenberg.

Veda (Sanskrit, "knowledge"). Name of earliest Indo-Germanic literary records and sacred scriptures of ancient India, consisting of four collections of hymns, of which the oldest is the *Rig-Veda,* antedating 1000 B. C.

Vedanta. See *Brahmanism,* 5.

Vedanta Society. A movement, resulting from lectures on Vedanta philosophy, one of the six orthodox systems of Brahmanic philosophy (see *Brahmanism*), delivered, 1894, in New York, by Swami Vivekananda (b. 1863 in Calcutta; attended Parliament of Religions, Chicago, 1893; returned to India 1900; d. 1902). Organized and incorporated 1898. Grew slowly, with headquarters in New York and other centers in Boston, Pittsburgh, San Francisco, Los Angeles, St. Louis, and other places. It had 11 societies and over a thousand members in 1950. Claims to have no purpose of forming new sect or creed, but to expound Vedanta philosophy, which is explained as "end of all wisdom," how it may be attained, and to give philosophic and scientific basis to religion.

Vedic Religion. See *Hinduism.*

Vehicle, Word as. See *Grace, Means of,* I, 5, 7.

Velasquez, Diego Rodriguez de Silva y (1599—1660). Greatest of Spanish painters and one of the greatest of all nations; superb colorist, excellent draughtsman, unity of impression; painted chiefly secular, but also religious subjects.

Velthusen, John Caspar (1740 to 1814). Prof. at Kiel, Helmstedt, and Rostock; general superintendent of the duchies of Bremen and Verden; his voluminous writings cover almost all fields of theology; influenced by the Enlightenment. While Velthusen was professor at Helmstedt, Pastor Nussmann of North Carolina requested him to send help to the Lutherans there. Help was furnished through the printing and selling of books.

Venantius Prudentius Clementianus Fortunatus. See *Fortunatus, Venantius.*

Veneration of Relics. See *Relics.*

Veneration of Saints. See *Saints, Worship of.*

Venezuela. See *South America, 11.*

Veni, Creator Spiritus. The author of this stately hymn of the Middle Ages is not definitely known, Charlemagne and Rhabanus Maurus being mentioned oftenest; translated by Luther, from whose version it came into English ("Come, God Creator, Holy Ghost").

Venial Sins. See *Sins, Venial and Mortal.*

Venite. The liturgical name for the first Psalm (Ps. 95:1-7) of Matins; the name is derived from the first words of the Vulgate version: *Venite exultemus Domino.*

Vera Christiana Religio. See *Swedenborgians, 2.*

Verbeck, Guido Fridolin (1830—97). B. at Zeist, Holland; d. at Tokyo, Japan; joined Moravians 1846; in America 1852; appointed missionary to Japan by Reformed Church of America 1857; instructor at Nagasaki; the Imperial University a result of his work; adviser to Japanese government until 1877; ban against Christianity in Japan lifted through his influence; instructor in Union Theological Seminary, Japan.

Verbum Audibile. See *Grace, Means of,* I, 1.

Verbum Visibile. See *Grace, Means of,* I, 1.

Verdi, Giuseppe (1813—1901). Regarded by many as the most representative and most popular composer of operas Italy has produced. His operas are colorful and theatrical. Verdi's *Requiem* is as exciting and dramatic as are many of his operas and should not be regarded as church music. He based also other compositions on sacred texts, *e. g., Stabat Mater, Te Deum,* and *Laudi alla Virgine Maria.*

Vergerius, Petrus Paulus (or *Vergerio Pierpaolo,* 1498—1565). Italian reformer; began his career as a prominent lawyer in Venice; devoted himself to the service of the Church after the death of his wife; rose rapidly to influential positions; was delegated to Diet of Augsburg 1530; sent to Germany 1535 in the matter of the Council at Mantua; conferred with Luther, whom he called a "beast," possibly possessed of a demon; bishop of Capo d'Istria 1540; excited suspicion by his conciliatory conduct at Worms 1540; studied the writings of Luther; broke with Rome in 1545; labored for some years after his excommunication, 1549, in southern Switzerland; spent the last twelve years of his life in the service of Duke Christopher of Wuerttemberg; maintained an extensive correspondence; wrote numerous inflammatory and polemical tracts against the Papacy.

Verigin, Peter. See *Doukhobors.*

Veronica, St. A legendary matron of Jerusalem, who is said to have given her headcloth to Jesus as He passed her on the way to Golgotha that He might wipe the blood and sweat from His face. The cloth is supposed to have retained the imprint of His features. Roman churches at Rome, Milan, and Jaen (Spain) each have this miraculous cloth.

Verse. In the Bible, the smallest division of a chapter, consisting usually of a sentence or phrase or, in poetry, of two or more parallel lines; in hymnody, a single metrical line, made up of a number of accented feet according to a certain rule.

Versicle. A sentence chanted or spoken in a service by a pastor to which the choir or congregation responds.

Versions, Bible. See *Bible Versions.*

Vespers. A liturgical service which may be conducted late in the afternoon or in the evening. The *Magnificat* is the great liturgical chant of Vespers. While many use the *Nunc Dimittis* instead, this Song of Simeon as well as the *Kyrie* and the *Lord's Prayer* have really been drawn into Vespers from Compline, the last office hour of the day, whose brief liturgy is suitable for later hours of the evening.

Vestiarian Controversy. A controversy which began in England when John Hooper * refused to wear vestments at his consecration as bishop of

Gloucester, 1550. It again burst forth in 1564, when an attempt was made to secure uniformity of vestments in England.

Vestments, Clerical or Priestly. 1. In use in the Christian Church since the earliest days, the *tunica talaris*, fashioned after the common tunic of the period, being represented as the bishop's or presbyter's dress in the second century. The *dalmatica* was practically an ungirdled tunic, richly ornamented and worn over the first. It soon became the distinctive garment of the deacons, its color being white and its material linen. The *paenula* or *casula* (chasuble) was originally a storm cloak of heavy woolen cloth, with a hole in the center, through which the head was thrust. Its later form was circular or elliptical and its color usually a chestnut brown. The pallium scarf was derived from the pallium mantle. It was made of white wool and ornamented with crosses. In the Orient, as the *omophorion*, it was the badge common to all bishops. In the Occident the wearing of the pallium was soon restricted to metropolitan bishops upon whom the Pope conferred the distinction. The stole, or *orarium*, was of white or colored cloth, properly a neckcloth. The maniple, originally a napkin or towel used by deacons, later became a kind of handkerchief for general use by the clergy. The amice was a linen collar worn during Mass; it is now the priest's shoulder cloth. The alb was a robe of white linen or silk, with brightly tinted silken or golden border. It is now simply a long, white garment. The cope is worn by bishops, priests, and laymen for such ceremonies as processions. The girdle, whose purpose is obvious, was in general use almost from the first. There were many other articles of vesting and adornment in the Middle Ages, but these are the principal ones. To this day the amice, the alb, the girdle, the maniple, the stole, and the chasuble are used by Roman Catholic priests during Mass. They have been widely restored in the Anglican Church during the celebration of the Eucharist.

2. The following vestments are worn by a priest at Mass: 1) amice, an oblong linen cloth about the shoulders; 2) alb, a white linen vestment with sleeves, reaching from head to foot; 3) cincture, a belt, usually of linen; 4) maniple, an ornamental band over the left forearm; 5) stole, a narrow strip of fabric, worn about the neck and crossed over the breast; 6) chasuble, the outer and chief vestment, elaborately embroidered, covering front and back and having an opening for the head. — The cope, a long cloak open in front, is worn at processions, vespers, etc.; the dalmatic is worn by deacons and bishops; the tunicle is worn by subdeacons and bishops; the surplice, or cotta (of white linen), is the most common outer vestment, used, *e. g.*, in choir or at the administration of the Sacraments; similar to it is the rochet, which, however, has close-fitting sleeves or no sleeves at all.

3. Luther's position regarding the use of vestments was a very conservative one, and the Lutheran Church has never declared against their use. The chasuble has never gone out of use in the Scandinavian Churches, although it was finally abolished in Germany in the first quarter of the nineteenth century. The alb, assimilated in form to the surplice, has persisted in the Scandinavian countries, in Slovakia, and to a limited degree in Germany and Hungary. The girdle has survived in Sweden, where also the amice has become the collar of the alb. The stole and the maniple disappeared from use in the Lutheran Church in the seventeenth century. The mitre fell into desuetude in the sixteenth century, but the cope has continued in use in Scandinavia as an episcopal vestment. All the vestments named have been widely restored in many parts of the Lutheran Church, especially in Scandinavia and America. The widespread use of surplice-and-stole in American Lutheranism, a combination which has no warrant in historic Lutheran practice as normal service garb in the church, is traceable to Anglican influence. The widely used black gown is, properly considered, an academic vestment and should adhere closely to this style. The bands worn by the clergyman, as well as the ruffed collar in use among Scandinavian Lutherans, are part of the old domestic and street dress of the learned professions on the continent and, like the gown, have no liturgical significance.

J. Braun, *Die Liturgische Gewandung im Occident und Orient, nach Ursprung und Entwicklung, Verwendung und Symbolik*, Herder, Freiburg im Breisgau, 1907; J. O'Brien, *History of the Mass and Its Ceremonies in the Eastern and Western Church*, Cath.

Pub. Soc., N. Y., 1882; P. Severinsen, *De rette Messeklaeder* (tr. J. Madsen), Church Historical Soc. of Denmark, 1924; F. W. Weidmann, "Eucharistic Vestments," *Pro Ecclesia Lutherana*, 1934, 70—86.

Vestry. See *Elders*.

Veterans' Organizations. Veterans' organizations have played a large part in American history. After the War of the States there was organized the Grand Army of the Republic, "an organization for Union soldiers and sailors of the Civil War." Its obligation, its religious funeral ceremonies, its religious ceremonial for Memorial Day (with prayers and Scripture readings) mark the G. A. R. as a typical lodge. After the war with Spain came the United Spanish War Veterans and the Veterans of Foreign Wars. Veterans' organizations which came into being since World War I are: the American Legion (founded 1919); Disabled American Veterans (founded 1921); Allied American Veterans of All Wars (founded 1922); American Veterans' Association (founded 1932); Regular Veterans' Association (founded 1934). After the Second World War other groups were formed, such as the Nationalist Veterans of World War II; the Protestant War Veterans; American Order of Patriots; Southern Defenders of America; the Christian Brotherhood of War Veterans; George Washington's Bodyguards; the Legion of Christ; the Sons of Robert E. Lee; and the Sebastian's Society. For relatives of service men and women we have the American War Dads and the Navy Mothers Club.

While the G. A. R. was marked by its completely religious ritual as a typical lodge, the same does not hold good regarding the orders which grew out of World Wars I and II. Some have a ritual with a religious ceremonial and obligations but do not make the use of the ritual for initiation obligatory upon candidates. In others prayers are omitted when a member objects on grounds of conscience. So in the American Legion, which also has a short form for initiation, not involving religious teachings or goals. Others, like the Veterans of Foreign Wars, have also noted the trend away from ritualism and use only a brief form which includes little but the membership obligation. TG

T. Graebner, *A Handbook of Organizations*, pp. 290—315; Bureau of Information of Luth. Ch. — Mo. Syn., *Report on Veterans Organizations*, CPH, 1946; Committee of the Luth. Joint Synod of Wisconsin, *Veterans Organizations Examined in the Light of Scripture*, Northwestern Pub. House, Milwaukee, 1947.

Vetter, Daniel (d. 1721). Organist of the *Nikolaikirche* in Leipzig while Joh. Kuhnau was cantor at St. Thomas. Vetter died in Leipzig two years before the arrival of J. S. Bach. His compositions for the organ are used today and are part of the musical heritage of the Lutheran Church.

Viaticum. According to Roman Catholic doctrine, the final food for the way, namely, in preparation for death, that is, the celebration of the Eucharist, according to the Roman rite, where the probability of recovery is practically excluded. The celebration is usually made with great pomp and ceremony, especially as to conveying the consecrated host to the sickbed. If time will at all permit, the sprinkling of the sickroom with holy water is prescribed before the patient receives the wafer at the priest's hand. The *viaticum* is not to be identified with extreme unction. See *Unction, Extreme*.

Vicar. One who supplies the place of another, a term used in the early Church for a secular clerk who officiated in a church owned by a religious order. The term is used in England of a priest who officiates in a parish, the revenues of which belong to another. In the Episcopal Church in America a clergyman who is the incumbent of a parish under a rector is so designated. In the Lutheran Church the word is often applied to an unordained student of theology who serves as an assistant in church or school.

Vicar Apostolic. See *Legates*.

Vicar of Christ. A term assumed by the Pope and based on the Roman Catholic belief that the Pope is the representative of Christ.

Vicar-General. A cleric who occupies the highest office in a diocese after the bishop, being empowered to exercise the episcopal jurisdiction in the bishop's name and stead.

Vicarious Suffering. See *Atonement; Justification*.

Victor of Rome. Bishop of Rome 190—202. Staunch opponent of the Quartodeciman practice in the Easter controversy and probably the author of a tract against the playing of dice and all games of chance (*De Aleatoribus*). "It is written in the tone of a papal encyclical and in rustic Latin." See *Quartodeciman Controversy.*

Victoria, Evangelical Lutheran Synod of. See *Australia,* B 1.

Victorious Life (*Perfectionism*). That a Christian who has fully and continually embraced the Gospel of Christ can lead a victorious life, that is, a life actually free from sin, has been taught by various persons and parties within the Christian Church. Thus Roman Catholics have taught that in some cases, by special provision of God, particular saints may become so sanctified as to avoid all sins, offering an obedience even beyond the demands of the Law. Likewise Arminians (Methodist Churches and Evangelical Association) have taught a relative perfection, which consists in the suppression of unholy thoughts and desires. Similarly the Oberlin School taught that "the beginning of the Christian life is entire obedience" and that "the promises of God and the provisions of the Gospel are such that, when fully and continually embraced, they enable the believer to live a life of uninterrupted obedience." Above all, however, the doctrine of the victorious life, or perfection, has been accepted by scattered groups of Christian denominations (Pentecostal Churches, Holiness Churches) connected more or less with Methodism, which zealously advocate entire holiness or sanctification, or perfection in this life, their theory of perfection being based upon misunderstanding of Scriptural passages.

Vig, Peter S. B. Nov. 7, 1854, near Kolding, Denmark; tutored privately in Denmark; studied in Chicago; grad., Missionary Inst. at Copenhagen, 1884; immigrated in 1879; instructor, Danish High School, Elkhorn, Iowa, 1884—85; pastor, Jacksonville, Iowa, 1885—88; prof., theol. sem., West Denmark, Wis., 1888—93, and pastor at Luck, Wis. (again 1905—09); prof., theol. sem., Elkhorn, Iowa, 1894—96; pres., Trinity Sem., Blair, Nebr., 1896—99; 1902—05; 1909—; pastor at Elkhorn, Iowa, 1899 to 1902. Author: *Danske i Amerika; Elk Horn i Iowa; Nordboerne finder vei til Amerika, Trinitatis Seminarium; Den forenede danske Ev. Luth. Kirke i Amerika; The Danish Ev. Luth. Church in America; Den Danske Udvandring til Amerika; Den Aarsager og Veie; Danske i Kamp i og for Amerika.* D. D., Luther Theol. Sem., St. Paul, 1921. Died March 21, 1929.

Vigilius. See *Popes,* 3.

Vigils. See *Canonical Hours.*

Vigness, Lauritz Andreas. B. Jan. 14, 1864. Studied at Augustana College and Dixon College (A. B.); professor at Augustana College 1886, Highland Park College 1890, Jewell Lutheran College 1894; principal of Pleasant View Lutheran College 1895; president of St. Olaf College 1914—18; secretary of the Board of Education of the Norwegian Lutheran Church of America 1918. D. Sept. 21, 1947.

Vignola, Giacomo Barozzi di (1507 to 1573). Italian architect; one of the builders of St. Peter's in Rome, especially in the construction of the cupolas; published a book on the orders of pillars.

Villegaignon, Durand de. See *Missions,* B 1.

Vilmar, August Friedrich Christian (1800—68). Most prominent Hessian theologian of the 19th century; studied at Marburg; passed from doubt and rationalism to a firm faith in Christ and the Scripturalness of the Lutheran Confessions; exerted great influence in the education of the Hessian clergy as director of the *Gymnasium* at Marburg, superintendent at Kassel, and theological professor at Marburg; his doctrine of the Church is Romanizing; wrote: *Collegium Biblicum.*

Wilhelm Hopf, *August Vilmar,* Marburg, 1913.

Vincent, John Heyl (1832—1920). Methodist Episcopal; b. at Tuscaloosa, Ala.; pastor in New Jersey and Illinois (Joliet, Chicago, etc.); established Sunday school papers; editor of Sunday school publications of Sunday School Union; chief organizer of Chautauqua Assembly, 1874; chancellor of Chautauqua Literary and Scientific Circle, 1878; bishop, 1888; resident bishop in Europe, 1900; retired, 1904; author.

Vincent of Lerins (d. ca. 450). The most famous disciple of the semi-Pelagian Johannes Cassianus; b. in Gaul; became a monk of the monastery of Lerinum; author of *Commonitorium pro Catholicae Fidei Antiquitate et Universitate*, in which he laid down the proposition that the Catholic faith is, *quod semper, quod ubique, quod ab omnibus est creditum* (what always, what everywhere, what by all has been believed), a principle upheld by the Catholic churches today.

Vincent, Marvin Richardson (1834 to 1920). B. at Poughkeepsie, N. Y.; Methodist Episcopal minister; pastor (Presbyterian) at Troy and New York City; professor at Union Seminary, 1883; translated Bengel's *Gnomon;* published *Word Studies in the N. T.*

Vincent de Paul (1576—1660). Roman priest; at one time a Moslem slave; devoted his later life to the poor, especially to French galley slaves and the Christian slaves in Barbary; founded the Lazarist order and the Sisters of Mercy.

Vinci, Leonardo da. See *Leonardo da Vinci*.

Vinet, Alexander Rodolphe (1797 to 1847). Swiss Reformed, second Pascal; b. at Auchy, Vaud; professor of French literature at Basel; professor of theology at Lausanne; led Free Church movement in Vaud; d. at Clarens; *Homiletics,* etc.; hymns.

Virgin Birth. See *Incarnation.*

Virgin Islands of the United States, formerly Danish West Indies, bought by the United States from Denmark for $25,000,000 in 1917. Discovered by Columbus in 1494. Area, 133 sq. mi. Population, 26,654 (1950), chiefly blacks. Education is compulsory. Missions by several American Churches, among them United Lutheran Church in America. Statistics: total foreign staff, 30; 7,399 communicants.

Virginia, Synod of. See *United Lutheran Church, Synods of,* 31.

Virginia, Synod of Central. See *Synods, Extinct.*

Virginia, Synod of East. See *Synods, Extinct.*

Virginia, Synod and Ministerium of Southwestern. See *United Lutheran Church, Synods of,* 31.

Virginia, Synod of Southwestern. See *Synods, Extinct.*

Vischer. See *Fischer, Christoph.*

Vischer, Peter (1455—1529). German sculptor, son of a worker in bronze; his work shows the transition from the Gothic to the Renaissance forms; attained great fame beyond Nuremberg and even beyond Germany; his most celebrated work the tomb of St. Sebaldus in Nuremberg, which contains seventy-two figures besides those of the Apostles and Prophets.

Vishnu. See *Brahmanism*, 2; *Hinduism,* 4.

Visible Church. See *Church.*

Visions. Appearances, or revelations, of God or a representative of the Godhead, either at night, in realistic dreams, or by day, in manifestations during which the person or persons concerned may be in full possession of their senses. During Biblical times the Lord frequently availed Himself of such manifestations in order to make His will known to prophets and others, as the Scripture accounts show. However, the idea of visions has been abused by false prophets, who claimed to have had revelations of God's will outside of the truth set forth in Holy Writ. Several false religions as well as many falsifications of the true religion have been connected with alleged visions of the supernatural, as in the case of many Roman Catholic legends.

Visitation Articles. See *Melanchthon, Philip.*

Visitation Nuns (*Salesian Nuns*). An order founded by Mme. de Chantal, in 1610, under the guidance of Francis of Sales. The rule is moderate, but all property is held in common, even beds, beads, etc., being changed every year. The chief activity is the education of girls, especially of higher Roman Catholic society.

Vitringa, Campegius (1659—1722). Dutch Reformed Old Testament scholar; b. at Leenwarden; professor of Oriental languages at Franeker 1681 (d. there); founder of historical exegesis; wrote *Commentary on Isaiah* (valuable), etc.

Vittoria, Francisco de (1480—1546). Spanish Jesuit; joined the Dominican order; laid the foundation for international law with his principle that such law rests on the agreement of the majority of nations.

Vittoria, Tomas Luis de (ca. 1540 to 1611). Roman Catholic composer of church music. Though a Spaniard, he spent much of his life in Rome, where he lived as a contemporary of Palestrina. In his compositions may be found an intimacy of expression which adds to their interest and in no way detracts from their intrinsic worth.

Vivekananda, Swami. See *Vedanta Society.*

Voes, Heinrich. See *Esch, Johann, and Voes, Heinrich.*

Voetius, Gisbert (1588—1676). Most important Dutch Reformed theologian of 17th century; b. at Heusden; preacher at Ulymen; delegate to Dort; professor at Utrecht, 1634; combated Arminianism, Cocceianism, Descartes' philosophy (see *Cocceius* and *Descartes*); d. at Utrecht.

Vogt, Karl (1817—95). German naturalist; b. at Giessen; prof. there, 1847; dismissed because of political activities; from 1852, professor of geology, later also of zoology, at Geneva. Was one of the most zealous champions of materialism and Darwinism, with all their logical consequences. Wrote: *Koehlerglaube und Wissenschaft,* 1855; *Vorlesungen ueber den Menschen,* 1863.

Voice of Prophecy. See *Radio Evangelism,* 5.

Voigt, Andrew George. Theologian and educator of the Lutheran United Synod South. B. Jan. 22, 1859, at Philadelphia, Pa.; studied in Gettysburg, Philadelphia, and Erlangen; pastor at Hainesport and Riverside, N. J. (1883 to 1885); Wilmington, N. C., (1898—1903); prof. at Newberry College (1885—89), Southern Seminary (1892—98); pres. of Thiel College (1889—91); dean of Southern Seminary (1903—33); pres. United Synod South (1906—10); served on important boards and commissions. Wrote *Why We Are Lutherans, Commentary on Ephesians, Biblical Dogmatics.* Contributed to various journals. Editor of *Lutheran Visitor.* D. Jan. 2, 1933.

J. W. Horine, "In Memoriam: Andrew George Voigt, D. D., LL. D.," *Luth. Ch. Quart.,* VI: 345—52; G. P. Voigt, "Andrew George Voigt," *Luth. Ch. Quart.,* XVII: 199—203.

Volckmar, Tobias (1678—1756). Lutheran composer of church music whose compositions at times show the influence of Johann Krieger, his teacher. His chorale preludes are today played also by American church organists.

Volckmar, Wilhelm Valentin (1812 to 1887). Studied at Marburg; music teacher at Homberg Seminary after 1835; gifted organ virtuoso; composed many works, also sacred; published *Orgelschule* and *Schule der Gelaeufigkeit.*

Voliva, Wilbur Glenn. B. March 10, 1870, near Newton, Ind.; studied at Hiram College, Union Christian College; minister in Christian Church (Disciples of Christ); held a number of pastorates; joined Christian Catholic Church in 1899; overseer of that church in Australia, 1901—06; general overseer of mother church in Zion City, Ill., from 1907. D. Oct. 11, 1942.

Voltaire (1694—1778). Assumed name of *François Marie Arouet,* noted French author, historian, philosopher; b. in Paris; educated by Jesuits; 1726—29 in London, where he came under the sway of Deism; 1750—53 at court of Frederick the Great, Berlin; since 1758 on his estate near Geneva; d. in Paris. Voltaire exerted a great but pernicious influence. Though not an atheist, but rather a Deist, he did not appreciate the truths of the Gospel. Antagonized by the persecuting and privileged Jesuitism, which dominated France and against which he directed his *"Ecrasez l'infâme!"* ("Crush the infamous one!"), he was led to a bitter hatred against every form of Christianity, which became more and more satirical and blasphemous. By his hostility against absolutism in State and Church he helped much to bring about the French Revolution. Wrote numerous tragedies, novels, epic poems, historical and philosophical works. Among the latter, *Dictionnaire Philosophique, Les Moeurs et l'Esprit des Nations.*

J. Morley, *Voltaire,* Macm., 1871; N. L. Torrey, *The Spirit of Voltaire,* Columbia University Press, 1938.

Voluntarism. Voluntarism is the opposite of intellectualism. In philosophy, the attempt to interpret ultimate reality in terms of will rather than intellect. In theology, the basing of moral and logical distinctions on the will of God rather than on reason, i. e., whatever God wills to be so is on that basis right, true, and good.

Volunteers of America. This organization, a secession from the Salvation Army, was formed in the spring of

1896 by Mr. and Mrs. Ballington Booth. From the beginning the organization has been declared to be an auxiliary of the Church, and converts have been advised to unite with churches of their preference. In doctrine the Volunteers of America are in harmony with all essential points of doctrine as held by the evangelical churches. Their principles are stated in the Book of Rules issued by order of the Grand Field Council. — The government of the Volunteers of America is democratic, and the term "military," which appears in their Manual, is applied only in the bestowing of titles, the wearing of uniforms, and the movement of officers. A post consists of an officer in charge, assistants, secretary, treasurer, trustees, sergeants, corporals, and soldiers. The Commander in Chief, or General, is elected for a term of five years. His cabinet, or staff, consists of the vice-president, with title of Major General, the secretary, with title of Colonel, the treasurer, with title of Colonel, and the regimental officers. — The different departments of work carried on by the Volunteers of America are rescue and prison work, industrial, girls', and children's homes, hospital and dispensary work, and "restoration work" among men and women whose misfortunes or misdeeds have placed them beyond the pale of good society. The organization has 24,976 members as compared with 232,631 in the parent body (1953).

Voodooism. Name of certain practices and beliefs current among Negroes of the West Indies and southern United States, brought originally from Africa; consisting of snake and devil worship, fetishism, dances, incantations, charms, and, formerly, occasional sacrifice of girl children, performed by priests or "doctors," whose services were often employed to wreak vengeance on some enemy.

Vopelius, Gottfried (1635—1715). For thirty-eight years a cantor of the *St. Nikolaikirche* in Leipzig, is today remembered chiefly as the editor of the well-known *Neu Leipziger Gesangbuch* of 1682.

Voskamp, Karl Johannes. B. Sept. 18, 1859, at Antwerp, Belgium; educated at Duisburg and Berlin; in 1884 sent to Canton, China, by the Berlin Missionary Society; labored in the Fa Yuen district; home furlough in 1898; transferred to Shantung 1898; since 1925 connected with the United Lutheran Church in America. Voskamp is a well-known and eminently successful missionary and an author of renown. He resided last at Tsingtao, China.

Voters, Congregational. See *Polity, Ecclesiastical.*

Votive Mass. A Roman Catholic Mass not liturgically prescribed, the form of celebration being left to the officiating priest.

Votive Offering. In Roman Catholic usage, prescribed to a shrine or saint in fulfillment of a vow or as an expression of thankfulness.

Vows. Rome's position on religious vows follows from its teaching on the subject of "evangelical counsels." If God counsels voluntary poverty, obedience, and celibacy as exceptionally meritorious, then, it is argued, He will also be pleased if men vow, or promise, to Him to observe these counsels. Such vows are made by those entering the various religious orders. These vows are sometimes only temporary, but usually perpetual. They are also classified as either solemn or simple, the former implying that an absolute and irrevocable surrender has been made and accepted, while the latter are less sweeping (see *Profession of Monks and Nuns*). Solemn vows must always be preceded by simple. The Pope can dispense from all vows. The Roman Church attempts to compel observance of monastic and other vows, using force if necessary. Luther strongly and justly condemned the fact that Rome considers the vow of celibacy binding even if those who have taken it find, in more mature years, that they have not received the gift of continence (1 Cor. 7:7).

Vulgate. See *Bible Versions,* J 2.

Vulpius, Melchior (d. 1615). One of the foremost Lutheran composers of church music of his day. While very little is known of his life, it is known that he was cantor in Weimar ca. 1600. He was an industrious and prolific composer, his compositions are churchly and virile, and many of his works, including his *Matthaeus-Passion,* are available in modern editions. Vulpius wrote the chorale melodies *Christus, der ist mein Leben, Jesu Kreuz, Leiden und Pein,* and *Gelobt sei Gott* (*Lutheran Hymnal,* Nos. 53, 140, 208).

W

Wacker, Emil (1839—?). B. Kotzenbuell; Lutheran pastor; studied at Copenhagen, Kiel, and Berlin; called as pastor and rector of the Deaconess Home at Flensburg 1876; wrote: *Diakonissenspiegel, Die Laienpredigt und der Pietismus in der lutherischen Kirche, Der Diakonissenberuf, Eins ist not,* etc.

Wackernagel, Karl Eduard Philipp (1800—77). Educated at University of Berlin; master of a school in Berlin, then at Stettin; professor in *Realgymnasium* at Wiesbaden, then at Elberfeld; last years of life spent in Leipzig; successful teacher, especially noteworthy for hymnological research embodied in *Das deutsche Kirchenlied, von der aeltesten Zeit bis zu Anfang des 17. Jahrhunderts,* indispensable to students of early German hymnody.

Wadeland, Martin Enoch. B. Sept. 18, 1876; studied at St. Olaf College and United Church Seminary; pastor at Fertile, Iowa; St. Ansgar, Iowa; taught at St. Ansgar Seminary; secy., Young People's Luther League of the United Norwegian Church (now Evangelical Lutheran Church); literary editor, Augsburg Publishing House; member of various boards; author of many stories; D. D., 1928, Bethany College; d. Dec. 30, 1933.

Wafer. See *Altar Bread.*

Waffenlose. See *Mennonite Bodies.*

Wagner, Anton. B. Jan. 20, 1830, at Allendorf an der Lumda, Hessen; came to America 1849; graduate of Fort Wayne Seminary; pastor in Watertown, Wis., 1855, Freistadt, Wis., Pleasant Ridge, Ill., of Zion Church, Chicago, Ill., 1867 to 1909; pioneer of Missouri Synod in Chicago; d. Jan. 10, 1914.

Wagner, Charles (1851—1918). B. in Alsace; founded several popular universities under the auspices of the Society for the Promotion of Morality.

Wagner, Georg Gottfried (1698 to 1759). Pupil of Kuhnau and J. S. Bach who wrote church music, oratorios, overtures, concertos, trios, and compositions for the violin. His motet *Blessing, Glory, Wisdom, and Thanks* was formerly attributed by many to Bach.

Wagner, Tobias (1598—1680). Lutheran theologian; pastor at Esslingen; prof. at Tuebingen; confessional opponent of skepticism, atheism, and Cartesian philosophy.

Wakamba Mission, East Africa, founded by the *Bayerische Gesellschaft fuer Ev.-Luth. Mission in Ostafrika* (Bavarian Ev. Luth. Missionary Society) in 1886; taken over by the *Ev.-Luth. Mission zu Leipzig* (Leipzig Mission) in 1893.

Walch, Christian Wilhelm Franz (1726—84). German theologian; prof. at Jena and Goettingen. An exponent in his writings of supranaturalism, he personally shared the orthodoxy of his father. He wrote on Lutheran symbols and Lutheran dogmatics, but most of his works are in the field of history (history of Catharina von Bora, history of the Popes, history of the New Testament, history of heresies, church history of the 18th century, and others).

Walch, Johann Ernst Immanuel (1725—78). Prof. of philosophy, logic, metaphysics, and other subjects at Jena. His works concern themselves chiefly with the history of early Christianity.

Walch, Johann Georg (1693—1775). B. at Meiningen; d. at Jena. Studied at Leipzig. Associate professor at Jena for philosophy and antiquities, 1718; full professor of oratory, 1719; of poetry, 1721; associate professor of theology, 1724; full professor, 1728; senior professor, 1750; ecclesiastical councilor for Saxe-Weimar, 1754. Besides publishing many works of his own, he edited the works of Luther (Latin works translated into German; new edition published by CPH, St. Louis, 1880). His *Historische und theologische Einleitung in die Religionsstreitigkeiten,* etc., is still useful.

Waldenses (*Waldensians, Vaudois*). A religious group which grew out of movements started by Arnold of Brescia, Peter de Bruys, Henry of Cluny, and, especially Peter Waldo (d. ca. 1217). Peter Waldo gave away his wealth, had a translation made of portions of the Bible into the French Provence vernacular, preached, and founded a society (Poor Men of Lyons) for the spreading of the Gospel, which soon gained many followers, particularly in valleys of Piedmont and the adjacent French territory. Being under the papal ban, they were, for centuries, driven from their homes or were ruthlessly massacred. In 1848 King Charles of Sardinia granted them civil and religious liberty. They rejected purgatory, masses for the dead, indulgences, worship of saints, relics, and images, most church holidays, dedications and consecrations, and the authority of the hierarchy, including that of the Pope, whom they declared to be the Antichrist, and believed the Church to be the congregation of the elect, that an unbelieving priest could not validly administer the Sacraments. At first those joining the Waldensian "fraternity" had to take the threefold oath of poverty, celibacy, and obedience to superiors. The "friends," or "the faithful," did not take the vows of the "brethren" and "sisters," but merely accepted the Waldensian doctrine. The outstanding characteristics of the Waldenses were their preaching, their missionary zeal, and their knowledge of the Bible, especially of the New Testament. In early times they had bishops, presbyters, and deacons; but their church government as well as their doctrine and practice were modified in the course of time. Since the Reformation, when they joined the Reformed party, the Waldenses closely resemble the Presbyterians in doctrine and polity. Their *Brief Confession of Faith of the Reformed Churches of Piedmont* (1655) is based on the French Reformed *Confessio Gallicana*.

Critical studies of the Waldenses begin with J. J. Doellinger, *Beitraege zur Sektengeschichte des Mittelalters*, Muenchen, 1890; Philip Schaff, *Creeds of Christendom*, Harpers, 1899—1905; H. C. Lea, *A History of the Inquisition in the Middle Ages*, Macm., 1908—11 (3 vols.).

Waldenstroem, Paul Peter (1838 to 1917). Swedish theologian and educator and one of the foremost leaders of the Free Church movement in Sweden; in 1872 he advanced the idea that the reconciliation through Christ is not of God to us (denying the wrath of God), but of us to God. Waldenstroem has exerted great influence both in Sweden and in America.

Wales. In Wales the ancient Celtic Church, having been founded at a very early period, was entirely independent of the Church of Rome. In consequence Christians there were obliged to seek refuge in the mountainous district of Wales, where they gradually diminished in numbers, ignorance and superstition overspreading the entire country. The Reformation of the 16th century reached Wales through England. Gospel truth spread rapidly among the mountaineers,

and a simple Scriptural piety developed among them. Later on ignorance and vice again prevailed, and both clergy and laity became ignorant and immoral. The Rev. Griffith Jones established among them a system of education now known as the Welsh Circuiting Schools, by which he accomplished great good, establishing 3,495 schools, in which 158,237 pupils were educated. The majority of the Welsh people are Methodists. See *Celtic Church.*

Walker, Herman Henry. B. Sept. 28, 1842, at Brockhausen, Germany; grad. at St. Louis 1865; pastor at Paterson, N. J., 1866—74; York, Pa., 1874—?; vice-pres. of Eastern District 1885—99; pres. of Eastern District 1899—1915; D. D. (St. Louis). D. July 4, 1927.

Walker, Jesse (d. 1835). Methodist Episcopal; b. in North Carolina; traveling preacher in Tennessee and Kentucky 1802, Illinois 1806; planted Methodism in St. Louis 1820; among the Indians 1823; d. in Cook County, Ill.

Walker, Williston (1860—1922). Congregationalist; b. at Portland, Maine; taught in Bryn Mawr College and Hartford Seminary; professor of ecclesiastical history, Yale; wrote: *History of Congregational Churches in the United States; The Reformation;* and other works.

Wallin, Johan Olaf (1779—1839). The greatest Swedish hymnist of the last century; held charges in various cities of Sweden; contributed some 150 hymns; recast the hymn by Spegel "The Death of Jesus Christ, Our Lord."

Walliser, Christoph Thomas (1568 to 1648). Composer of the Lutheran Church who based his motets on Lutheran chorales and presented them in the churches of Strassburg. His style reflects Italian influence. Though little known in America, Walliser was highly regarded by his contemporaries.

Walter of Mortagne (d. 1174). Theologian; taught at Ste. Genevieve, Paris; espoused indifferentism in the battle over universals.

Walter of St. Victor (d. 1180). Pupil of Hugo of St. Victor; polemicist. He opposed scholasticism, holding that dialectics can reveal formal but not material truth.

Walther, Carl Ferdinand Wilhelm. 1. "The most commanding figure in the Lutheran Church of America during the nineteenth century" was born Oct. 25, 1811, at Langenchursdorf, Saxony. His father, grandfather, and great-grand-father had been Lutheran ministers be-fore him. He received his preparatory training at home, in the village school, and in the city school at Hohenstein, graduated from the *Gymnasium* at Schneeberg in 1829, and took up the study of theology at the University of Leipzig. The teachers at the *Gymnasium* were rationalists. Walther did not lose his faith in the Holy Scriptures as being God's revealed Word (taught him by his father), but he did count the years spent there as years in which he was not truly converted. "I was eight-een years old when I left the *Gymnasium*, and I had never heard a sentence taken from the Word of God out of the mouth of a genuine believer. I had never had a Bible nor a catechism but merely a miserable *Leitfaden,* which contained heathen morality." Rational-ism held sway also at Leipzig. Walther was led to believe in Jesus Christ through an elderly candidate, Kuehn, who led the studies and spiritual exer-cises of a group of earnest students, but whose theology was of a pronounced pietistic type; through the wife of *Steuerrevisor* Barthel, who, when Wal-ther was on the verge of spiritual despair, pointed him direct to the grace of God in Christ; and through Pastor Stephan, who advised him to lay hold of the full, free, and unconditional promises of the Gospel ("a man who, by God's grace, saved my soul").

2. Leaving the university for one semester on account of severe illness, he took up the study of Luther's writings in his father's library, and later on em-ploying a second period of ill health in Perry County, Mo., in the same manner, he acquired a thorough familiarity with the works of the Reformer. He gradu-ated in 1833, became a private tutor, and was ordained in 1837 to the ministry at Braeunsdorf, Saxony.

3. The local church and the church authorities were steeped in rationalism, and since Walther's firm stand for the Lutheran Confessions and Lutheran practice was met by opposition and even persecution, he resigned his pastorate and joined the Saxon emigrants. He arrived at St. Louis in February, 1839, and shortly afterwards he took charge of the pastorate at Dresden and Jo-hannisberg in Perry County, Mo. He gave his active support to the founding of the log-cabin college at Altenburg and for a time served as instructor. The

sad task of unmasking the leader of the Saxon emigrants, M. Stephan, fell to his lot, and it was he who, in the ensuing confusion, brought light and peace to the disturbed consciences of the people. In eight theses he established (April, 1841) the Scriptural doctrine of the Church (see *Luth. Ch.— Mo. Syn.; Altenburg Theses),* the principles there laid down being later elaborated by him in the books *The Voice of Our Church on the Questions of Church and Office* (1852), *The Correct Form of a Local Congregation Independent of the State* (1863), and *The Evangelical Lu-theran Church the True Visible Church on Earth* (1867).

4. In April, 1841, C. F. W. Walther became the successor of his older brother, Otto Hermann, in the pastorate of the St. Louis congregation and there successfully applied the principles set forth in the three books mentioned. In 1844 he began, with the financial back-ing of his congregation, the publication of the *Lutheraner,* which served to bring together faithful Lutherans in various sections of the country. In the conferences of 1845 and 1846, in which the question of organizing a confessional Lutheran synod was discussed by a number of pastors and a draft for the constitution drawn up, Walther took a leading part. When the Missouri Synod was organized in 1847, he was elected its first president, serving as such until 1850 and again from 1864 to 1878. On the removal of the Altenburg college to St. Louis, Walther was elected professor of theology, serving in Concordia Semi-nary from 1850 until his death and re-taining general supervision over the congregations.

5. As theological professor and pres-ident and leader of Synod he labored indefatigably and succeeded in firmly grounding it on the Word of God and on the Lutheran Confessions; nor could he, being a lover of peace and loving Zion as he did, refuse to take a leading part in the controversies thrust upon Synod. (See *Luth. Church—Mo. Synod,* XVIII.) It was a mission of peace which took him and Wyneken to Ger-many in 1851—52. Pastor Loehe was beginning to deviate from the Lutheran doctrine of the Church and the Ministry. The mission ultimately failed of its pur-pose. In 1853 Walther and his congrega-tion founded a Bible Society, which imported the genuine *Luther-Bibel* and published the *Altenburger Bibelwerk* and several editions of the Bible. Con-cordia Publishing House, St. Louis,

which later took over its work, itself owes its origin largely to Walther's efforts. At Walther's suggestion the Missouri Synod, in 1855, founded *Lehre und Wehre*, a theological monthly, edited at first by Walther, later by the faculty of Concordia Seminary. At his suggestion, too, free conferences were held by members of various Lutheran bodies in 1856, 1857, 1858, and 1859, "with a view toward the final realization of one united Evangelical Lutheran Church of North America." He was one of the representatives of his synod at the colloquy with members of the Buffalo Synod in 1866 and at the colloquy with the Iowa Synod in 1867. He attended, as a matter of course, the three conferences held in 1868—69 between representatives of the Missouri Synod and of the Ohio, Wisconsin, and Illinois Synods, respectively, the convention held by these bodies in 1871, and the meeting in 1872, which organized the Synodical Conference, whose first president he was.

6. In 1871 his *Gospel Postil* was published, in 1876 *Brosamen*, in 1882 the *Epistle Postil;* later, *Festklaenge, Gnadenjahr, Licht des Lebens, Casual-Predigten und Reden,* etc. ("Walther is a model preacher in the Lutheran Church. How different the position of the Lutheran Church would be in Germany if many such sermons were delivered!" — *Dr. A. Broemel.*) In 1872 Walther attended, and furnished the theses for, a free conference of English Lutherans at Gravelton, Mo., which developed into the English Synod of Missouri and Other States (now English District of the Missouri Synod). In the same year his *Pastoral Theology* was published. In 1878 Capital University (Ohio Synod) conferred upon him the title of Doctor of Divinity. (He had refused, in 1855, to accept this title at the hands of the University of Goettingen, for confessional reasons.) From 1879 on much of his time was taken up by the controversy on Election and Conversion. He spent these latter years of his life, as indeed all the years of his service in the Church, in inculcating the doctrines of *sola gratia* and *gratia universalis.* His ministry and his life ended on May 7, 1887.

7. His ministry is not ended; in his writings, comprising, besides the books mentioned, his amplified edition of Baier's *Compendium Theologiae Positivae,* two books on the *Law and the Gospel* and others, two volumes of *Letters,* and innumerable pamphlets, articles in the periodicals, and essays published in the Synodical Reports — enough to make a full-sized "five-foot bookshelf" — he has left the Church an inexhaustible store of Scriptural theology.

8. The following evaluations of Walther may be quoted. The *Allg. Ev.-Luth. Kirchenzeitung* of Leipzig: "His activities were felt as a mighty inspiration by the Lutheran Church of all continents." *Lutheran Observer:* "The principles of pure Lutheranism were from the first insisted upon by Walther and his *confrères,* and to this day the Missouri Synod stands for the most conservative type of Lutheranism to be found in the United States." Dr. F. Pieper: "Walther, as respects spiritual experience, theological learning, logical acumen, and the gift of presentation, certainly does not stand behind the majority of our theologians, and, in our judgment, he surpasses many of them in these things." Walther himself says: "A pupil of Luther, and, as I hope to God, a faithful pupil, I have only stammered after this prophet of the last world all that I have hitherto published and written." And he succeeded in implanting the Lutheran loyalty to God's Word in the hearts of many.

M. Guenther, *Ein Lebensbild von Dr. Walther,* CPH, 1890; D. H. Steffens, *Carl Ferdinand Wilhelm Walther,* Luth. Pub. Soc., Philadelphia, 1917; C. L. Janzow, *Life of Rev. Prof. C. F. W. Walther, D. D.,* American Luth. Pub. Bd., Pittsburgh, 1899; L. Fuerbringer, *Briefe Dr. Walthers* (2 vols.), CPH, 1915; W. G. Polack, *The Story of C. F. W. Walther,* CPH, 1947; E. Engelder, "Walther, a Christian Theologian," *CTM,* VII: 731 ff.; 801 ff.

Walther, Johann (1496 to 1570). Served as Martin Luther's musical counselor, and is commonly referred to as "the father of Lutheran church music." His professional life was spent at the *Torgauer Lateinschule* and at the Dresden *Hofkapelle* of Elector Maurice of Saxony. Walther spent three weeks in Luther's home in 1524, helping him to prepare the music for his *Deutsche Messe.* On the basis of Walther's report, it is known that Luther was well qualified to compose music. In his *Matthaeus-Passion,* Walther was the first composer to base a Passion on the text of Luther's translation of the Bible; he was the first Lutheran to write a Passion and in this recitative Passion adhered to his principle that church music is only the bearer, not the interpreter of the Word. His *Geistliches Gesangbuechlein* of 1524, for which Luther wrote the foreword, is famous to this day; it is not a hymnal, but a collection of five-part music for choirs. Five editions were published, also Latin texts were used, and many selections were based on Luther's hymns. The chorale served as *cantus firmus*. Walther, a layman, fought Philippism and Crypto-Calvinism and likewise opposed the fanaticism of those who sought to oversimplify church music. Despite the claims of some, it cannot be proved with certainty that Walther composed hymn tunes. The text of "Der Braeut'gam wird bald rufen" (*Lutheran Hymnal,* No. 67) is attributed to Walther.

Walter E. Buszin, *Johann Walther, Composer, Pioneer, and Luther's Musical Consultant.* Valparaiso Church Music Series, No. 3, 1946.

Walther, Johann Gottfried (1684 to 1748). Cousin of J. S. Bach and a court musician at Weimar, where he and Bach enjoyed each other's friendship and contributed to each other's musical growth. His *Musikalisches Lexikon* was the first musical lexicon published in Germany. His organ works based on the chorale are excellent church music and enjoy widespread use today.

Walter E. Buszin, *Johann Gottfried Walther.* Valparaiso Church Music Series, No. 4, 1947; Walter E. Buszin, Foreword — *Memorial Collection of Organ Preludes and Variations by Johann Gottfried Walther.* St. Louis (Concordia), 1948.

Walther League. See *Young People's Organizations, Christian,* III.

Walther, Michael (1593—1662). Superintendent-General in Celle; author of an excellent exposition of the catechism, of the *Officina Biblica* (isagogics), and the *Harmonia Biblica.*

Walther, Otto Hermann. Older brother of Carl Ferdinand Wilhelm Walther; b. Sept. 23, 1809, at Langenchursdorf, Saxony; became assistant of his father; joined the Saxon emigrants; talented poet and a deeply spiritual nature; became pastor of the "Saxon" congregation in St. Louis, which three years later adopted the name "Trinity." Died Jan. 21, 1841.

Paul Walther, "Otto Hermann Walther," *CHIQ,* XVIII: 110—19.

Walther, Wilhelm Markus (1846 to 1925). Positive Lutheran theologian; pastor at Cuxhaven; professor of church history at Rostock; wrote very extensively on the Reformation. Luther, German medieval translation of the Bible, etc.; also against A. Harnack's *Wesen des Christentums; Lehrbuch der Symbolik.*

Walton, Brian (1600—61). Anglican; Biblical scholar; b. in Yorkshire; rector; bishop of Chester 1660; d. in London. Editor of *London Polyglot,* 6 folio vols., 1654—57 (most complete and scholarly polyglot).

Wangemann, Hermann Theodor (1818—94). B. at Wilsnack, Germany; rector and assistant pastor at Wollin 1845; director of seminary at Kammin 1849; director of Berlin Missionary Society 1865; visited Africa 1866—67 and again 1884—85. A voluminous writer on mission topics.

War. 1. A contest between nations and states (international war) or between parties in the same nation or state (civil war), carried on by force of arms.

2. Wars are spoken of very frequently in the Bible; in fact, the entire history of the Children of Israel, from the time of the conquest of Canaan until the Exile, is chiefly an account of battles and wars, the reign of Solomon being the only period of relief of any length during all those centuries. With regard to the Canaanitish nations, which occupied the territory promised to Abraham and his descendants by the Lord, He Himself decreed a war of extermination upon them. It was also the Lord who commanded the Children of Israel to punish the idolatry of the nations east of the Jordan by a war of extermination, the tribes under the leadership of Sihon and Og thus being wiped out. During the centuries that Israel and Judah were independent nations, both as a united people and as a divided kingdom, they were obliged to wage war against, or to defend themselves against invasions from, practically every nation in that part of the world, the Egyptians, the Ethiopians, the Libyans, the tribes of the deserts toward the south, the Edomites, the Moabites, the Ammonites, the Syrians, the Philistines, the Assyrians, the Chaldeans, and others being named as enemies who sought the destruction of the people of the Lord.

3. That many of these wars were just wars, undertaken with the full consent of the Lord, appears from His consent or His direct command, as when David time and again inquired of the Lord whether he ought to attack his enemies. That some of the wars were

such as were sent by the Lord as a form of punishment upon a reprobate and disobedient nation is clear from Deut. 28:49 ff. and from the many examples in the history of the people of the Lord when He permitted their enemies to harass them. Reasons for such wars are the contempt of the Word of God (Lev. 26:25; 1 Kings 8:33; 2 Kings 3:3); the shedding of innocent blood (Judg. 9:1; 2 Sam. 12:9, 10); avarice and unrighteousness (Amos 9:1; Micah 2:1); false ambition and pride (Is. 13:1 ff.). From the New Testament it appears that wars are a scourge of the Lord, whether they are justified or unjustified; for wars and rumors of wars are spoken of in such a connection (Matt. 24:6).

4. The attitude of the Christian with regard to the subject of war is given in the Scriptures, especially in the Fourth Commandment and the passages which pertain thereto. The entire matter is well expressed in Article XVI of the Augsburg Confession, which states: "Of civil affairs they [our churches] teach that lawful civil ordinances are good works of God and that it is right for Christians to bear civil office, to sit as judges, to judge matters by the imperial and other existing laws, to award just punishments, *to engage in just wars,*" etc. (*Conc. Trigl.,* 51.) See *Pacifism.*

War and Prophecy. Those who believe in the supernatural origin of the Bible hold the possibility of prophetic foreknowledge of political events. In Matt. 24:6, 7 the Lord spoke of wars as a sign of the end of all things.

Wars often cause a large volume of prophetic literature, especially chiliastic, to appear. Writers of this literature seek materialistic contemporary evidence for their view regarding the meaning of prophetic passages. They endeavor to show that certain contemporary wars and nations involved in such wars were specifically mentioned, also in matters of detail; and emphasize such matters as the return of Israel, the Antichrist, the battle of Armageddon, and the millennium. Attempts have also been made to set dates for the beginning of the millennium.

Investigations have led to the following conclusions: ". . . the method of interpretation employed leads to contradictory results; . . . this method of reading prophecy has failed in the past whenever predictions have been based upon it; . . . only by misstating historical facts (1518 for 1517, 666 for 663, etc.) even a semblance of fulfillment can be

asserted with reference to past history; . . . there is an utter absence of Scriptural warrant for this method of interpreting prophecy."

Th. Graebner, *War in the Light of Prophecy,* CPH, 1942.

Ward, James (1843—1925). British philosopher and psychologist; held that the world is a realm of psychic entities approaching ends.

Warfield, Benjamin Breckenridge (1851—1921). Conservative Presbyterian theologian; b. at Lexington, Ky.; prof. of New Testament Literature and Exegesis at Allegheny, Pa., 1878; professor of Didactic and Polemic Theology at Princeton, 1887; d. at Princeton. Edited *Presbyterian and Reformed Review;* published: *Divine Origin of Bible,* 1882; *Inspiration,* 1882; *Introduction to the Textual Criticism of the New Testament,* 1886; and others.

Warneck, Gustav Adolf (1834 to 1910). B. at Naumburg, near Halle; d. at Halle. Served pastorates at Raitzsch, Dommitsch, Rothenschirmbach; was inspector of missions at Barmen; retired in 1896 and was made honorary professor of missions at Halle. He founded the Saxon Provincial Missionary Conference in 1879, was secretary of the committee of German missions 1885—1901, and founded the *Allgemeine Missionszeitschrift* (1874), being its editor many years. He was a voluminous writer on mission topics. His chief books are *Abriss einer Geschichte der protestantischen Missionen von der Reformation bis auf die Gegenwart* (Leipzig) and *Evangelische Missionslehre* (3 vols.).

Warner, D. W. See *Church of God,* 3.

Wars of Religion. See *Huguenots.*

Wartburg Press. See *Publication Houses.*

Wartburg Synod. See *United Lutheran Church, Synods of,* 32.

Wartburg Theological Seminary. See *Ministry, Education of,* XI C.

Wasa, Gustav. See *Gustav Wasa.*

Washington, Booker Taliaferro (1858—1915). B. near Hales Ford, Va.; son of a mulatto slave and a white man; studied at Hampton Normal and Agricultural School, Va., and other schools; later appointed instructor at Hampton; organized Tuskegee (Ala.) Normal School 1881, where he did much work for the elevation of the Negro race.

Washington Declaration (Declaration of Principles Concerning the Church and Its External Relationships). After the United Lutheran Church was organized, its Executive Board was frequently asked to define its attitude toward co-operative movements looking toward church union, and toward other organizations, tendencies, and movements. At its Second Convention (Washington, D. C., 1920) the U. L. C. A. adopted the Washington Declaration. The declaration has five major sections:

A. *Concerning the Catholic Spirit in the Church.* This, the longest section, declares and explains the belief in the one, holy, catholic, and apostolic Church, the existence of which is not capable of demonstration, but rests "upon our belief in the continued life of Christ in all his Christians." This Church "performs its earthly functions and makes its presence known among men through groups of men who profess to be believers in Jesus Christ. In these groups the Word of God is preached and the Sacraments administered." "Every group of professing Christians calling itself a church will seek to express in its own life the attributes of the one. holy, catholic, and apostolic Church. . . . 1. By professing faith in Jesus Christ . . .; 2. By preaching the Word and administering the Sacraments . . .; 3. By works of serving love . . .; 4. By attempts to secure universal acceptance of the truth which it holds and confesses." Every such group, even if partial and imperfect, is an expression of the one holy Church. That body, however, in which the Word of God is most purely preached and confessed and the Sacraments administered in the closest conformity to the institution of Christ "will be the most complete expression of the one holy Church. For this reason it is necessary that, when occasion arises, any such group of Christians shall define its relationship to other groups and organizations which do not bear that name." Hence each church should be ready "to declare unequivocally what it believes . . . approach others without hostility, jealousy, suspicion, or pride . . . grant cordial recognition to all agreements which are discovered between its own interpretation of the Gospel and that which others hold . . . co-operate with other Christians in works of serving love . . . in so far as this can be done without surrender of the Gospel, without denial of conviction, and without suppression of its testimony as to what it holds to be the truth."

B. *Concerning the Relation of the Evangelical Lutheran Church Bodies to One Another.* The U. L. C. A. "recognizes no doctrinal reasons against complete co-operation and organic union" with church bodies calling themselves Evangelical Lutheran and subscribing the Lutheran Confessions.

C. *Concerning the Organic Union of Protestant Churches.* The Declaration states: ". . . we hold the union of Christians in a single organization to be of less importance than the agreement of Christians in the proclamation of the Gospel. . . . We believe that a permanent and valid union of churches must be based upon positive agreements concerning the truth for which the united church body is to stand."

D. *Concerning Co-operative Movements Among the Protestant Churches.* This section states the earnest desire to co-operate "in works of serving love . . . provided that such co-operation does not involve surrender of our interpretation of the Gospel, the denial of conviction, or the suppression of our interpretation of the Gospel." The purpose, underlying principles, and effect "upon the independent position of our Church as a witness to the truth of the Gospel" must determine co-operation. Nine paragraphs list fundamental doctrines (including the Real Presence) which a movement or organization must hold before the U. L. C. A. enters into co-operation with it. The U. L. C. A. cannot enter organizations or movements "whose purposes lie outside the proper sphere of church activity," and there are organizations (e. g., for social or political reform) which the Church as such cannot enter, but commends to its pastors and members. No synod, conference, or board has the power of independent affiliation with "general organizations and movements."

E. *Concerning Movements and Organizations Injurious to Christian Faith.* This section warns against these.

The U. L. C. A., at Buffalo, N. Y. (1922), did not become a regular member of the Federal Council of Churches, but resolved that the "relationship shall be of a consultative character by which the United Lutheran Church may have a voice but no vote, thus securing to it entire autonomy . . . in regard to the decisions and actions of the Federal Council of Churches but at the same time the privilege of co-operating in such tasks and problems as it may elect." EL

See the minutes of the U. L. C. A. conventions (1920, 1922); "Declaration of Principles Concerning the Church and Its External Relationships," *CTM*, VI: 46—53; *Doctrinal Declarations*, CPH, St. Louis, n. d. The Washington Declaration is a lengthy document and should be studied in its entirety for a thorough understanding of its principles.

Watchtower Tract Society. See *Jehovah's Witnesses.*

Water, Holy. In the early Middle Ages, people took home baptismal water for various superstitious purposes. This led, in both the Greek and the Roman Churches, to the blessing of water outside of Baptism. In Roman churches the ceremony takes place every Sunday. The priest exorcises salt and water, prays over them, and mingles them in the name of the Trinity. The water is then used for a variety of purposes. It is placed in a font at the church door, sprinkled over the audience before High Mass, used to bless candles, etc., taken home by the people. Miraculous virtues are ascribed to it. It is supposed to cure diseases of body and mind, remit venial sin, deliver from infestations of the devil, make fields fertile, chase the plague, break up storms, etc. The superstitious ceremony of blessing the water, since it has neither divine command nor promise, is an infraction of the Second Commandment and, essentially, a form of witchcraft.

Waterloo Seminary. See *Canada, Lutheranism in*, 9.

Watson, Richard (1737—1816). Anglican; b. at Haversham, Westmoreland; professor of chemistry; rector; bishop of Llandaff; d. at Calgarth Park; wrote: *Apology for Christianity* (against Gibbon); *Apology for the Bible* (against Paine); and others.

Watts, Isaac (1674—1748). B. at Southampton, oldest son of a respected Nonconformist, was offered an education at one of the universities with a view to ordination in the Church of England, but refused and entered an independent academy. After tutoring for six years he became pastor of the distinguished Independent Church at Mark Lane, London. Not long afterward his health failed, and Mr. Samuel Price was appointed his assistant and later his co-pastor. For the last 36 years of his life he lived the quiet life of a semi-invalid as the guest of Sir Thomas Abney and afterwards of his widow, devoting his time to the production of theological and lyrical works. His *Logic*

was for long a textbook at Oxford. Watts wrote about 600 hymns. He published his chief work, *Psalms of David Imitated*, in 1719.

WAWZ. See *Radio Stations, Religious*, 2.

WBBL. See *Radio Stations, Religious*, 2.

WBBR. See *Radio Stations, Religious*, 2.

WCAL. See *Radio Stations, Religious*, 2.

WCBD. See *Radio Stations, Religious*, 2.

WCFL. See *Radio Stations, Religious*, 2.

Webb, Thomas (1724—96). Methodist; b. in England; soldier in America; joined the Methodists 1765; lay preacher in New York City, etc., and Portland, England, at outbreak of Revolution; d. in Portland; pioneer of Methodism in America.

Weber, Ferdinand Wilhelm (1836 to 1879). Studied at Nuernberg and Erlangen; vicar to Loehe; instructor at the mission school in Neuendettelsau; Loehe's successor. His outstanding scholarly work is *System der altsynagogalen palaestinischen Theologie*, the first successful attempt to systematize the religious thought of early Judaism on the basis of original sources.

Weber, Karl Maria von (1786—1826). Inherited musical talent developed very early; studied under Heuschkel and Michael Haydn; noted concert pianist; typical representative of the Romantic era. He was, first and foremost, a composer of operas (*Freischuetz, Euryanthe, Oberon*), in which field he excelled and exerted a beneficial influence. He leaned heavily towards brilliancy and theatrical effectiveness. His songs are among the best in song literature. His works for the piano (e. g., his *Konzertstueck*) are Romantic to the core; in his sonatas he ignores the classical pattern and again reveals his strong Romantic bent. Abbé Vogler helped develop von Weber's musical proclivities without making of him a charlatan. Von Weber wrote two Masses which can hardly be regarded as ideal or typical church music.

Weber, Max (1865—1920). German economist whose chief work, *Gesammelte Aufsaetze zur Religionssoziologie*, seeks to show the relation existing between religion and economics.

Weckmann, Matthias (1621—74). Pupil of Heinrich Schuetz, regarded as one of the noteworthy composers of the Lutheran Church. He studied with Jakob Praetorius and learned from Heinrich Scheidemann. Active in Dresden, Denmark, and Hamburg, Weckmann excelled as a composer of choral and organ music. Excellent editions of his music have been published in recent time.

Wee, Mons Olsen. B. May 13, 1871, near Bergen, Norway; studied at Red Wing Seminary, Univ. of Minnesota, Univ. of Edinburgh (Scotland); Lutheran missionary in Persia; held pastorates in South Dakota and Minnesota; prof. at Red Wing Seminary, 1908—17; prof. at Luther Theol. Sem. (St. Paul, Minn.), 1917—42; author of: *Absolution; Who Is Jesus? Men Who Knew God.* D. April 16, 1942.

Wegelin (Wegelein), Josua (1604 to 1640). B. in Augsburg, studied at Tuebingen, was for a short time pastor at Budweiler; later appointed fourth diaconus of the Franciscan Church at Augsburg. In 1629 he was compelled to leave Augsburg at the instigation of the Benedictine monks. He was recalled as archdiaconus of the Franciscan Church, when Gustavus Adolphus took over the city. He was again forced to flee for refuge in Pressburg, Hungary, where he became pastor senior and later Doctor of Theology. He lived through more than 20 years of the Thirty Years' War. He wrote "On Christ's Ascension I Now Build."

Wegelius, John. See *Finland, Lutheranism in,* 4.

Wegs, Michael. See *Weisze, Michael.*

Wegscheider, Julius August Ludwig (1771—1849). Prof. at Halle. His *Institutiones Theologiae Christianae Dogmaticae* is considered the standard dogmatic work of Rationalism. According to him a supernatural revelation was impossible.

Wehrlose. See *Mennonite Bodies.*

Weidenheim, Johann. Circumstances of his life not known, except that he lived at the end of the 17th century; hymn "Herr, deine Treue ist so gross" commonly ascribed to him.

Weidner, Revere Franklin. Leading educator and author in the Lutheran General Council; b. Nov. 22, 1851, in Pennsylvania; educated at Muhlenberg College and Philadelphia; pastor at Phillipsburg, N. J., at the same time teaching English and logic at Muhlenberg until 1877; pastor of St. Luke's, Philadelphia, 1878—82; then professor of Dogmatics and Exegesis at Rock Island, till 1891. His main work was done as professor of Dogmatics and Hebrew Exegesis and as president of Chicago Seminary, 1891—1915. He did much to develop the Chicago Seminary and was a prolific writer, not only reproducing German theological works in English, but also writing various exegetical and dogmatic works himself. D. Jan. 5, 1915.

Weigel, Valentin (1533—88). German mystic; b. at Grossenhain, Saxony; since 1567 Lutheran pastor at Zschopau. Though apparently irreproachable in ministerial office, he was at heart completely at variance with the teachings of his Church, as was discovered after his death. His theosophic, pantheistic system, according to which the church dogmas are merely an external allegorical cloak for deeper truths, had adherents for several centuries (*Weigelianer*).

Weimar, Colloquies and Conventions of. Weimar was a stronghold of Gnesio-Lutherans in the 16th century. Among important conventions and colloquies held there were: convention regarding the Interim, 1548; Flacian Synod against Philippists, 1556; colloquies concerning the *Weimar Confutation Book,* 1558—60; colloquy between Wittenberg theologians and those of Jena, 1568—69; synod which discussed original sin, 1571.

Weimarisches Bibelwerk (*Ernestinische Bibel, Nuernberger Bibel, Kurfuerstenbibel*). Annotated Bible by John Gerhard, Glassius, Dilherr, and other theologians. Not critical or controversial, but very good popular commentary. Has instructions how to read and understand the Scriptures, table to read the Bible in one year, chronology, topical index, and "helps." New edition prefaced by Dr. C. F. W. Walther. First published in 1640.

Weinbrenner, Johann (1797—1860). B. at Glade Valley, Md.; pastor (German Reformed); left Reformed Church 1825; organized Church of God 1830 (revivals, washing of feet, immersion); d. at Harrisburg, Pa.

Weingaertner, Sigismund. Preacher said to have lived near Heilbronn or at Basel, beginning of 17th century; hymn "Auf meinen lieben Gott" ascribed to him; but there are still doubts concerning authorship.

Weise, Christian (1642—1708). B. at Zittau; 1676 prof. of rhetoric and politics at Weissenfels; 1678 rector of the *Gymnasium* at Zittau; poems show simplicity and depth; wrote "Ach seht, was ich fuer Recht und Licht."

Weiser, John Conrad, Jr. Son of John Conrad, Sr. (d. 1746; prominent early Lutheran colonist); b. Nov. 2, 1696, at Afstaedt, Germany; came to America in 1710; learned Indian language and lore after he was given to Quagnaut, Maquas chief; traveled extensively among Indians and served as interpreter; during the struggle between British and French in America he kept the friendship of Indians on the British side; later he gained the friendship of the Indians for the revolutionists; for many years he arranged treaties with Indians. Weiser was a lay leader among Lutherans at Tulpehocken; instrumental in mission work among Indians; wrote some Lutheran hymns; d. July 30, 1760; his daughter married H. M. Muhlenberg.

Weismann, Anders Christian. B. in Denmark, March 8, 1863; came to America in 1888; studied at Chicago Theological Seminary and Trinity Seminary, Blair, Nebr.; pastor at Jacksonville, Iowa, Lincoln, Nebr., Denver, Colo., Coulter, Iowa, Warren, Pa., Webster Groves, Mo., McNabb, Ill.; held several offices for the Pension Fund of the United Danish Church; pres., Bd. of Publication; pres., Illinois Dist.; d. May 24, 1936.

Weiss, Johannes (1863—1914). Prof. of New Testament Exegesis at Marburg; theologian of the left wing of the Ritschlian school; applied Wellhausen's theory to the New Testament.

Weiss, Karl Philipp Bernhard (1827 to 1918). Father of the preceding; prof. at Koenigsberg, Kiel, Berlin; also consistorial councilor; theologian of the Prussian Union; prolific writer on the New Testament, especially commentaries, notably in Meyer's *Commentary;* his writings reveal the influence of higher criticism.

Weisse, Christian Herman (1801 to 1866). Philosopher and prof. at Leipzig; formulated a system of Christian theism; opposed pantheism of Hegel.

Weisze (Weisse, Wiss, Wegs, Weys, Weyys), Michael (ca. 1480—1534). B. in Neisse, Silesia, became a priest, and for a time was a monk at Breslau. Moved by Luther's writings, he and two other monks left the convent and took refuge in the Bohemian Brethren's House at Leutomische, Bohemia. He joined the Brethren and became their pastor at Landskron, Bohemia, and at Fulneck, Moravia. He was a man of great influence among them, a member of their council, and editor of their first hymn-book in German. This book contained 155 hymns, most, if not all, of which were either translations by him from Bohemian into German or originals by himself. Wrote "Christ, the Lord, Is Risen Again."

Weiszel (Weissel), Georg (1590 to 1635). B. in Domnau, near Koenigsberg, studied at the University at Koenigsberg and later at Wittenberg, Leipzig, Jena, Strassburg, Basel, and Marburg. In 1614 he became rector of a school in Friedland, near his native city, and returned three years later to Koenigsberg to resume his theological studies. In 1623 he became pastor of the church in Koenigsberg and served there until his death. Weissel has written about twenty hymns. They are chiefly designated for the festivals of the church year; all "good in style, moderate in length, and varied in meter." He has given us the Advent hymn "Lift Up Your Heads, Ye Mighty Gates."

Weiszes Kreuz. A society organized in 1882 for the purpose of caring for wounded or sick soldiers of the army of Austria-Hungary and for the purpose of placing, and caring for, officers or their widows or orphans in proper institutions. Different from White Cross League.

Weizsaecker, Karl Heinrich von (1822—99). B. at Oehringen; d. at Tuebingen. Studied at Schoental and Tuebingen. Prof. at Tuebingen, 1861, as successor to F. Chr. Baur in church history; chancellor of the university in 1890. He considered himself a disciple of Baur, writing particularly on early Christianity.

Weller, Geo. B. Jan. 8, 1860, at New Orleans, La.; graduated at St. Louis, 1882; pastor at Marysville, Nebr.; director and prof. at Concordia Teachers College, Seward, Nebr., 1894—1924; d. Dec. 17, 1924, at Seward.

Weller, Hieronymus (1499—1572). Studied at Wittenberg; converted by one of Luther's sermons; became inmate of the Reformer's house for eight years; 1536 rector of schools in Freiberg; staunch Lutheran in the Adiaphoristic and Majoristic controversies; wrote commentaries, a postil, on propaedeutics, ethics, homiletics.

Weller, Jakob (1602—64). Studied at Wittenberg and was made *professor extraordinarius* 1634; superintendent in Brunswick and in 1646 court preacher in Dresden, successor of Hoe von Hoenegg; wrote against Calixt and a fearless witness against the sins of court life, especially drunkenness.

Wellhausen, Julius. See *Higher Criticism,* 10.

Welsh Presbyterians. See *Presbyterian Bodies,* 4.

Weltanschauung. See *History, Philosophy of.*

Weltz, Justinian Ernst, Freiherr (Baron) von (1621—68). B. at Chemnitz, Saxony, of Austrian extraction; Lutheran by profession; published five mission treatises (1663, 1664); ordained "Apostle to the Heathen" in Holland; went to Dutch Guiana (Surinam), where he soon died.

Wendt, Hans Hinrich (1853—1928). German theologian; starting with the Ritschlianism system of doctrine, he developed an independent one.

Wenner, George Unangst. B. near Bethlehem, Pa., May 17, 1844; studied at Gettysburg College, Yale College (B. A.; M. A.), Union Theological Seminary (B. D.); founded German Lutheran Christ Church, N. Y. (1869), and served this church until his death; organized Southern Conference of the New York Synod; pres., New York and New Jersey Synod (1904—08); pres., second Synod of New York (1908—10); chairman, Liturgical Committee (General Syn.); chairman, Committee of Deaconess Work, 1885—99 (instrumental in founding Deaconess Motherhouse, Baltimore); founder of several organizations for pastors; chairman, Committee on Weekday Instruction in Religion, Federal Council of Churches of Christ in America; one of the founders of the Federal Council; and vice-chairman of its Administrative Committee; delivered many important lectures and addresses; author of the order of worship adopted by the General Synod; author of the "Germanicus" in *Lutheran Observer;* published *Der Sonntagsgast* (1872—1932); D. D. (Gettysburg College, 1888); L. H. D. (Susquehanna University, 1917); LL. D. (Gettysburg College, 1924); d. Nov. 1, 1934.

Werner, Georg (1589—1643). B. near Koenigsberg; at time of his death diaconus in Koenigsberg; wrote: "Nun treten wir ins neue Jahr"; "Der Tod hat zwar verschlungen"; "Freuet euch, ihr Christen alle."

Wertheim Bible. A German version of the Pentateuch, published in 1735. It was a product of vulgar rationalism by J. L. Schmidt (d. 1750); printed in secret and published anonymously. An imperial mandate in 1737 ordered its confiscation and the apprehension of its author.

Wesel, John of. See *John of Wesel.*

Weseloh, Henry. B. Nov. 1, 1851, in Hanover, Germany; graduated at St. Louis, 1876; served Immanuel Luth. Church, Cleveland, Ohio, for 49 years; editor of *Kalender fuer deutsche Lutheraner,* 1909—22; wrote: *Das Buch des Herrn und seine Feinde; Gottes Wort eine Gotteskraft; Die Herrlichkeit Gottes in der Natur;* d. Aug. 30, 1925, at Cleveland, Ohio.

Wesley, Charles (1708—88). The youngest, eighteenth, child of Samuel and Susanna Wesley; b. at Epworth, England; d. in London; studied at Westminster School, then at Oxford; college tutor, one of first band of "Oxford Methodists"; ordained 1735; secretary to General Oglethorpe in Georgia; returned to England 1736; under influence of Zinzendorf and Moravians; shortly afterward itinerant and field preacher to the end of his life; co-worker of his brother John; rank as English hymnwriter very high; of 6,500 hymns credited to him, many of high excellence; published most of his hymn collections together with his brother John, the first collection appearing in 1739, the last in 1786; a great many of his hymns appear in most English collections, *e. g.,* "Oh, for a Thousand Tongues to Sing," "Jesus, Lover of My Soul." Many of them are pre-eminently evangelical, though of a very subjective character.

Wesley Foundation. See *Students, Spiritual Care of,* A.

Wesley, John (1703—91). Founder of Methodism; b. at Epworth, England; graduated at Oxford; priest 1728; fellow at Oxford; director there of Holy Club, whose members, because of their methodical habits and exercises, came to be called Methodists; missionary in Georgia 1733; fell in with some Moravian brethren; received assurance of his salvation May 24, 1738, ca. 8:45 P. M., at Moravian meeting in London while listening to the reading of Luther's Preface to Romans; repaired to Herrnhut to visit the Moravian leaders; found most parish churches closed to him on his return; commenced field preaching, sent out lay preachers, and began to provide chapels in 1739; formed first society of followers 1740; held first Methodist conference in London 1744; never withdrew from the Church of England, yet suffered unending vexations; d. in London. Though Wesley sneered at Luther's doctrine of justification as expounded in *Commentary on Galatians*, he repeatedly said when dying: "How necessary it is for everyone to be on the right foundation!" "I the chief of sinners am, But Jesus died for me." Wesley is supposed to have traveled over 200,000 miles, to have preached over 40,000 times (two to four times daily), and to have written over 200 works (*Notes, Sermons*, etc.). He also published hymns, almost wholly translations from German, such as "Jesus, Thy Blood and Righteousness," "Commit Thou All Thy Griefs," "Jesus, Thy Boundless Love to Me," and others.

The literature on Wesley is voluminous; standard life: J. S. Simon, *John Wesley, the Master Builder*, 1927; the standard edition of Wesley's *Journal* is that of N. Curnock in 8 vols. (1909—16); H. Lindstroem, *Wesley and Sanctification*, Epworth Press, London, 1946; John Telford, *The Life of John Wesley*, Eaton and Manis, N. Y., n. d.

Wesley, Samuel (1766—1837). Son of the famous hymn writer and the nephew of the founder of Methodism, was the leading English organist of his day and the dominating figure in English church music in the early part of the 19th century. Wesley revived interest in Bach in England before Mendelssohn's revival took place in Germany. While it is not known definitely whether he left the Church of England, he did write four Masses and many short works for the services of the Roman Catholic Church. Owing to an accident, he was often afflicted by a serious mental malady which proved to be a serious handicap in his musical activities.

Wesley, Samuel Sebastian (1810 to 1876). Son of Samuel Wesley, served as organist of Hereford Cathedral, Leeds Parish Church, and Winchester and Gloucester Cathedrals. He was the leading spirit among English church musicians of early Victorian times. While some of his compositions are inferior for worship purposes, others are tolerably good and are still heard today.

Wesleyan Methodist Church. See *Methodist Bodies*, 4 b.

Wesleyan Methodist Church in America. This body withdrew from the Methodist Episcopal Church (1843) because of the slavery question and dislike of the episcopacy. Doctrinally, the Wesleyan Methodists were in harmony with the other Methodists. They preserved the conference system, but clergy and laymen were equally represented at Annual Conferences. Membership: 34,200 (1953).

Wesleyan Methodist Missionary Society. See *Missions*, B 12.

Wessel, Johann (*Wessel Harmenss Gansfort*, 1419—89). Pre-Lutheran Reformer belonging to the Brethren of the Common Life; studied at Zwolle and Cologne; taught at Paris, lived at Rome, then at Basel, finally at and near Groningen; a strong Humanist, but deepened and enriched by a theology which was remarkably pure, although he was nearer to Augustine and Bernard than to Luther.

Wessel, Louis. B. July 14, 1864, at St. Louis, Mo.; graduated at St. Louis 1886; pastor at Nokomis, Ill., 1886—92; professor at Concordia Seminary, Springfield, Ill., 1892—1933; D. D. (St. Louis); wrote: *Sermons and Addresses on Fundamentals; Prooftexts of the Catechism, with a Practical Commentary; Festival and Occasional Sermons.* D. Jan. 31, 1933.

West Indies. See *Cuba, Jamaica, Haiti, Puerto Rico, Antilles.*

West, Mission Synod of the. See *Synods, Extinct.*

West, Synod of the. Was organized Oct. 11, 1834, by emissaries of the General Synod, in opposition to Tennessee influence, at Jeffersontown, Ky. It was originally called the Kentucky Synod. Rev. Jacob Crigler was its first president. The name Synod of the West was adopted at the second convention, in Louisville, 1835, by five pastors and four laymen. The Synod of the West was admitted to the General Synod in 1841. In 1846 it was divided into three parts — the Illinois Synod, the Synod of the Southwest, and the Synod of the West, this latter part consisting of the members in Indiana. The congregation at Fort Wayne which Wyneken had served until 1845 and of which Dr. Sih-

ler was then the pastor, suspecting that this division was a move to attach the Synod of the West more closely to the General Synod, withdrew and helped in the organization of the Missouri Synod, while a number of German pastors organized the Indianapolis Synod. The remaining members of the Synod of the West were absorbed by the Olive Branch and the Miami Synod in the early fifties. See *United Lutheran Church, Synods of,* 8.

West Virginia, Synod of. See *United Lutheran Church, Synods of,* 33.

Westcott, Brooke Foss (1825—1901). Prof. at Cambridge, England; published with J. A. Hort a critical edition of the New Testament (1881).

Westen, Thomas von (1682—1727). Apostle of the Norwegian Lapps; b. at Drontheim; instructor at Mission Institute, Drontheim, 1716; visited the Lapps for mission purposes in company with Kjeld Stab and Jens Bloch, whom he ordained as missionaries; founded Finnish Seminary 1717; second visit to Lapps 1718; third missionary journey 1722; educator of missionaries to Lapps.

Western Canada, Synod of. See *United Lutheran Church, Synods of,* 34.

Westminster Catechisms. There are two of them, the Larger Catechism being designed for ministers and for use in public worship and the Shorter Catechism for instruction of the young. Both were approved by Parliament in 1647. The Scotch Kirk adopted them in July, 1648, and again, after they had temporarily been repealed under Charles II, in 1690. Next to the *Heidelberg Catechism* the *Westminster Catechisms* are the most widely circulated of Reformed Catechisms. However, they differ from the *Heidelberg Catechism* in being more decidedly Calvinistic. Back of these two catechisms were John Craig's *Scotch Catechism* and especially Calvin's Catechism. The Shorter Catechism, which is simply an abridgment of the Larger, is noted for its terse brevity and precision of questions and answers. It differs from most catechisms in having the following peculiarities: 1) The substance of the questions is repeated in the answers, and the use of the third person is maintained throughout. 2) It follows a new order of topics for the old order of the Apostles' Creed. 3) Dealing with dogmas, it addresses itself to the intellect rather than to the heart. The *Westminster Shorter Catechism* has never

been revised, although in 1908 the General Assembly of the Presbyterian Church in the United States of America (North) appointed a committee to prepare a catechism "to be simpler in nature than the Shorter Catechism." However, this new catechism was not to become "one of the standards of the Church."

Westminster Confession. See *Presbyterian Confessions,* 3.

Westminster Foundation. See *Students, Spiritual Care of,* A.

Westphal, Joachim (1510—74). Born and died at Hamburg. Studied at Hamburg, Lueneburg, and Wittenberg, as pupil of Luther and Melanchthon. Teacher at Hamburg; lectured at Wittenberg; preacher at St. Catharine's in Hamburg, 1541; superintendent, 1571. He engaged in various theological controversies, on the side of Aepinus; of Flacius (*Interim*); against Melanchthon and Georg Major; and defended Luther's doctrine of the Lord's Supper against Calvin, Bullinger, and others.

Westphalia, Peace of. The treaty which brought to a close the Thirty Years' War (1648) was drawn up in Muenster and Osnabrueck, Westphalia. Among the results in the religious realm may be noted: 1) the medieval idea of centralized power under Pope and Emperor came to an end; 2) the reaffirmation of the Peace of Augsburg with the recognition of the Reformed as "related to the Augsburg Confession"; 3) the dispensation of properties and conducting of services was to be judged by the "norm year" (Jan. 1, 1624); 4) where this "norm year" could not be applied, the ruler had the *ius reformandi;* 5) certain rights were given to people who lived in a state where the government held a religious position different from theirs; 6) the regulation of the right of rulers to determine reformation in their territory; 7) territorial adjustments brought changed ecclesiastical jurisdiction.

Wetstein, Johann Jakob. See *Arminianism.*

Weyermueller, Friedrich (1810—77). Layman; educated in his native town, Niederbronn, in Alsace; excellent knowledge of German poetry, which stimulated him to write verses at an early age, mainly of a sacred character; in 1852 associate of the consistory at Niederbronn; aided cause of Lutheranism by his poetry; his poems not hymns,

in the strict sense, but many have been adapted for use in worship.

Weys, M. See *Weisze, Michael.*

Weyys, Michael. See *Weisze, Michael.*

WGRE. See *Radio Stations, Religious.*

Whately, Richard (1787 to 1863). Educated at Oxford; fellow; then professor of political economy at Oxford; later archbishop of Dublin (d. there); wrote: *Historic Doubts About Napoleon Bonaparte; Elements of Logic;* etc.; also the hymn "Guard Us Waking, Guard Us Sleeping."

Whitby, Synod of. An assembly convened by Oswy, king of Northumbria, in 664 in order to settle the differences between the Irish ecclesiastics, who had come in from the north, by way of Scotland and Lindisfarne, and the Roman ecclesiastics, who were moving up from the south. The chief points under discussion were the date of Easter, the shape of the tonsure, and certain problems of jurisdiction. Colman was the head of the Irish group, while Wilfrid spoke for the Roman party. The southern view having prevailed at the meeting, Colman and the Irish monks left Northumbria.

White Cross League. A society organized 1883 by Bishop Lightfoot against immorality. In 1885 a branch was also organized in North America and later in Switzerland, France, and Germany.

White, Ellen G. See *Adventist Bodies,* 3, 4.

White Friars. Another name for Carmelites, given them because of the white wool garment adopted in 1287.

White, Henry Kirke (1785—1806). Early development of genius; followed literary pursuits in his early teens, but died while at the University of Cambridge, England; among his most popular hymns: "Oft in Sorrow, Oft in Woe."

White, Thomas. See *Baptist Bodies,* 20.

White, William. See *Protestant Episcopal Church,* 1.

Whitefield, George (1714 to 1770). Founder of Calvinistic Methodism; b. at Gloucester; alternated in youth between deplorable escapades and spells of religious enthusiasm; joined Holy Club of Oxford; deacon 1736; in Georgia 1738; back to raise funds for orphanage and to be ordained priest; began open-air preaching Feb. 17, 1739; never surpassed as field preacher, holding spellbound audiences of every kind and size, occasionally of from 25,000 to 30,000 people and often preaching forty to sixty hours a week; clashed with Wesley (Arminian) on predestination question 1741; presided at first conference of Calvinistic Methodists 1743; visited Wales, Scotland, Ireland; seven times in America; died, and lies buried, at Newburyport, Mass.

Fullest account of Whitefield's life in Luke Tyerman, *The Life of the Rev. George Whitefield,* 1876—77 (2 vols.); his works were collected 1771—72 in seven volumes.

Whitehead, Alfred North (1861 to 1949). British philosopher and mathematician; taught at Trinity College, Cambridge, University of London, Harvard University (retired, 1938). The only reality for Whitehead is that which is perceived by subjects; reality consists in "prehensive occasions" based upon the pattern of events and having feeling for other "occasions." These entities themselves are dependent upon eternal objects (similar to Plato's ideas) from which they are a selection. God as the dwelling of forms is "unchanged." The movement toward selection is God's consequent nature which is influenced by the pattern of events.

Whitsunday. See *Church Year,* 10.

Wichern, Johann Heinrich. See *Inner Mission,* 1.

Wiclif, John. See *Wyclif, John.*

Widor, Charles Marie (1845—1937). Pupils of Lemmens and Fetis, was organist in Lyons, later in Paris. He was eminently successful as a teacher of organ and also as composer, though his organ compositions no longer enjoy their former popularity. Widor and Albert Schweitzer prepared an edition of the absolute organ works of Bach which was published by G. Schirmer of New York.

Wiek, Amund Larson. B. Jan. 19, 1861, at Rio, Wis.; pastor at Minneapolis, Cokato, French Lake, Minn., and Sisseton, S. Dak.; Secy., Eielsen Synod; editor, *Den Kristelige Laegmand.* D. Sept. 30, 1922.

Wieseler, Karl (1813—83). Prof. at Kiel and Greifswald; Luth. theologian; worked and wrote in the fields of Old and New Testament exegesis, isagogics, New Testament criticism, Biblical and early ecclesiastical history. His chief contribution to theology was his

fruitful opposition to the conception of ancient Christendom advanced by Strauss and Baur.

Wieselgren, Peter. See *Sweden, Lutheran Church in,* 5.

Wiesenmeyer, Burkhard. B. at Helmstedt; ca. 1640 teacher at the Gray Monastery in Berlin; assisted with first Lutheran hymnal in Berlin; wrote "Wie schoen leucht't uns der Morgenstern."

Wigand, John (1523—87). Staunch Lutheran in the Adiaphoristic, Majoristic, Osiandrian, Synergistic, and Flacian controversies; wrote ten volumes of the great *Magdeburg Centuries* (see *Centuries, Magdeburg*); professor at Jena in 1560; twice banished; professor at Koenigsberg; bishop of Pomerania and Samland.

Wilberforce, William (1759—1833). English philanthropist; one of the most powerful antislavery agitators in England; instrumental in having bill against importation of Negroes into British territory passed in 1807. His influence also helped to curb the powerful East India Company, which opposed all mission work in India, and finally was instrumental in having its charter revoked (1813, 1833, 1859). He also was the leader in the organization of the Clapham Missionary Society.

Wilburites. See *Religious Society of Friends.*

Wilfred. See *Germany,* 1.

Wilkinson, Sir John Gardner (1797 to 1875). English traveler, Egyptologist; b. at Hardendale; four times in Egypt; d. in Wales; wrote: *Manners and Customs of the Ancient Egyptians,* etc.

Will, Enslaved, Free. See *Conversion,* I; *Free Will; Luther, Chief Writings of,* 5.

Willaert, Adrian (ca. 1485—1562). Regarded as the founder of the Venetian school of church music; some regard him also as the father of the madrigal. Zarlino and Cyprian de Rore were two of his most outstanding pupils. Willaert's church music is less archaic than that of his predecessors; with his double-chorus music, thus written to overcome acoustical problems presented by St. Mark's Cathedral, a type of choral music developed which soon became distinctive among the Venetian masters. Willaert was a true master of Netherland polyphony.

Willard, Frances Elizabeth (1839 to 1898). Graduated 1859 from North-western Female College, Evanston, Ill.; president and professor of esthetics of the Woman's College at Evanston 1871 to 1874; became corresponding secretary in 1874 and in 1879 president of the National Woman's Christian Temperance Union; and in 1887 also president of the World's Woman's Christian Temperance Union; was in favor of a woman's suffrage as early as 1877; a member, in 1844, of the executive committee of the Prohibition Party.

Willbye, John (1574—1638). Composer of English madrigals; lived in London. While it is said (Walker) that his Latin motets are by no means extraordinary, his sacred choral works based on English texts are more successful. His sixty-five madrigals are among the finest music of their type.

William of Auvergne (d. 1248). Bishop of Paris; active in political affairs of Louis X; his writings influenced the rise of Scholasticism.

William of Auxerre (d. 1230). Prof. of theology at Paris; wrote a *Summa Theologica.* He gave the minimum formula for the intention of priests (to will to do what the Church does).

William of Brandenburg. See *Reformed Confessions,* D 3.

William of Champeaux (ca. 1070 to 1121). French scholar; archdeacon of Notre Dame and instructor in dialectics; founded Abbey of St. Victor; bishop of Chalons-sur-Marne; Abelard one of his pupils; defender of realism of universals.

William of Hesse. See *Reformed Confessions,* D 3.

William of Malmesbury (ca. 1096 to ca. 1148). English historian; wrote *Deeds of the English Kings* (from Saxon invasion to 1128), an important source work.

William the Silent. Count of Nassau, Prince of Orange (1533—84). Founder of the Dutch Republic; educated in Lutheran faith at home of his parents until fifteenth year, then in Catholic faith at the Spanish court; penetrated designs of Spanish and French rulers against Protestantism and ever afterwards curbed his tongue, though he spoke seven languages and was naturally eloquent; became leader of revolt of Netherlands against Spain; fought with varying success against the Spaniards under Alva, John of Austria, and the Duke of Parma; openly professed himself a Calvinist 1573; received hereditary stadholdership of United Provinces 1581; Philip II could vanquish him only by assassination.

William of St. Thierry (d. 1150). Friend of Bernard; wrote against Abelard; wrote doctrinal, exegetical, practical, and historical works.

Williams, John (1796—1839). Missionary to Polynesia. Sent to the Society Islands 1816 by the London Missionary Society; finally settled on Raiatea; discovered the island of Rarotonga 1823, where he later translated parts of the Bible into the native language; after spending 1838 to 1844 in England, he returned to the islands in the company of sixteen new missionaries. Williams was among the very foremost of South Sea missionaries. He found a violent death at the hands of natives.

Williams, Roger (ca. 1604 to 1683). Founder of Rhode Island; b. probably in London; pastor at Salem, Mass., 1635; advocated liberty of conscience; banished; founded Providence 1636 (obedience required "only in civil things"); for a few months a Baptist, then a comeouter, holding that no church had all marks of the true Church; d. at Providence; wrote *Bloody Tenent,* and other works.

Williams, Sir George (1821—1905). B. in Somerset, England; converted at a Congregational service; founded Young Men's Christian Organization; knighted by Queen Victoria; worked for social reform.

Williams, William (1717—91). The chief hymn writer of Wales, b. at Cefny-Coed in the parish of Llanfair-y-bryn, near Llandovery. He was ordained deacon of the Established Church in 1740 and for three years served the curacies of two small congregations. Being denied ordination to the priesthood because of overzealousness in preaching, he joined the Calvinist Methodists and adopted Wales as his parish, becoming a flaming evangelist. In the progress of his ministry his itinerations averaged 3,000 miles a year for fifty years. He has been called the "Sweet Singer of Wales" and the "Watts of Wales." "He did for Wales what Wesley and Watts did for England or what Luther did for Germany." He knew the power of sacred song in reaching the hearts of men and wrote 800 Welsh hymns and more than 100 in English. He is probably best known for "Guide Me, O Thou Great Jehovah."

Willibrord. See *Germany,* 1; *Franks, Saxons, and Other Germanic Nations,* 3.

Willkomm, Martin. B. in India, Jan. 23, 1876; son of Otto Willkomm; studied in *Gymnasium* at Niederplanitz, Germany, and at Concordia Seminary, St. Louis; served as pastor in Muehlhausen, Alsace, and at Planitz; pres. of the Free Church of Saxony; director of Theological Seminary, Berlin-Zehlendorf (1923); prof. of Dogmatics and Church History there for 22 years; editor of *Die Ev. Luth. Freikirche* and *Schrift und Bekenntnis;* wrote especially on Luth. Confessions; D. D. (Concordia Seminary, 1934); d. June 1, 1946.

Willkomm, Otto Heinrich Theodor. B. Nov. 30, 1847, at Ebersbach, Lausitz; studied theology at Leipzig and served in the Leipzig Mission in India 1873 to 1876. Severing his connection with the Saxon State Church for confessional reasons, he was called to Crimmitschau, Saxony, 1876 and to Niederplanitz 1879, congregations belonging to the Saxon Free Church, and served as president of this body 1879—1907; pastor emeritus since 1917. Concordia Seminary, St. Louis, conferred the title of Doctor of Divinity on him in 1921. He wrote a number of valuable treatises, edited the *Ev.-Luth. Freikirche* 1879—1919, and published the *Hausfreund-Kalender* 1885—1924. D. 1933.

Wilson, Robert Dick (b. 1856). Presbyterian, Orientalist; b. in Indiana, Pa.; professor in Old Testament department of Western Theological Seminary, of Semitic Philology and Old Testament Introduction at Princeton 1900. Syriac and Hebrew textbooks, etc. *Studies in the Book of Daniel.*

Winchester Profession. See *Universalists.*

Winckler, Hugo (1863—1913). German orientalist; b. at Graefenhainichen, near Wittenberg; from 1904 on professor at Berlin; d. at Wilmersdorf. Wrote numerous works on Assyriology and related subjects.

Winckler, Johann (1642—1705). Lutheran pastor. B. at Goelzern, near Grimma; d. at Hamburg. The son of poor peasants, he studied at the school in Grimma, at St. Thomas' in Leipzig, and at the university there. His first pastorate was in Homburg vor der Hoehe, 1671. After becoming superintendent in Braubach, 1672, court preacher in Darmstadt, 1676, pastor in Mannheim, 1678, and superintendent in

Wertheim, 1679, he was appointed chief preacher of St. Michael's in Hamburg, 1684, where he became senior minister in 1699. He was an intimate friend of Spener, whose conventicles he defended.

Windelband, Wilhelm (1848—1915). Prof. at Strassburg and Heidelberg; wrote *History of Modern Philosophy* and other works; held that science may ascertain facts but values must be supplied by philosophy; differentiated method in natural and historical science.

Windows, Art. See *Art, Ecclesiastical,* 3.

Winebrennerians. A Baptist denomination founded by John Weinbrenner (1797—1860) in 1830; its character is strongly Arminian and premillenarian; it insists on immersion in Baptism, observes the Lord's Supper in the evening, and has the washing of feet; its polity is presbyterial.

Winer, Johann Georg Benedikt (1789—1858). B. and d. at Leipzig; Rationalist, but later approached orthodox position; prof. at Leipzig, Erlangen, Leipzig; noted for his *Grammatik des neutestamentlichen Sprachidioms,* a standard work for nearly 75 years and repeatedly translated into English.

Winfrid. See *Boniface.*

Wings over Jordan. See *Radio Evangelism,* 5.

Winifred. See *Franks, Saxons, and Other Germanic Nations,* 3.

Winkworth, Catherine (1829—78). B. in London, a woman of a high degree of culture and a devoted member of the Church of England. She was an active and ardent supporter of societies for the education and uplift of women. Her lifework, however, was the translation into English of the best of the German hymns. This work is embodied in her published *Lyra Germanica* and her *Christian Singers of Germany.* Of her hymnological work Dr. Julian justly says: "Miss Winkworth, although not the earliest of modern translators from the German into English, is certainly the foremost in rank and popularity. Her translations are the most widely used of any from that language and have had more to do with the modern revival of the English use of the German hymns than the versions of any other writer."

Winterfeld, Karl von (1786—1852). A jurist, among the foremost musicologists of the 19th century. His *Johannes Gabrieli und sein Zeitalter* (1834) and his *Der evangelische Kirchengesang* (3 vols.; 1843—47) are still regarded as monumental works despite their deficiencies. Winterfeld underestimated the music of J. S. Bach and of other composers of the Baroque Era because he had come under the spell of Justus Thibaut and others, who insisted that only a-cappella music may be regarded as ideal choral music for the church.

Wischan, F. B. 1845 in Germany, Lutheran pastor in Philadelphia 1870 till his death, 1905; "the soul of the Board of German Missions" of the General Council; editor of *Luth. Kirchenblatt.*

Wisconsin, Ev. Luth. Joint Synod of. 1. The Joint Synod of Wisconsin and Other States is a consolidation of several separate and independent Lutheran synods, *viz.:* Wisconsin,* Minnesota,* and Michigan.* Organically this body has passed through two distinct stages in its development, an earlier one in which the constituent synods retained their individuality and independence, being associated with one another only in certain phases of their work, and the present one in which they dissolved their existing organizations (at least as functioning bodies) and reconstituted themselves as one Joint Synod with a number of districts. The first association was formed in 1892, the amalgamation took place in 1917.

2. The *Allgemeine Ev. Luth. Synode von Wisconsin u. a. St.* was organized Oct. 11, 1892, in Milwaukee. It united into one body the afore-mentioned neighboring synods without destroying their identity, but provided for joint use of their several educational institutions. Wisconsin was at that time replacing its old Milwaukee Seminary with a new building in Wauwatosa, Wis. This new Theological Seminary now became the property of the Joint Synod, with Dr. A. Hoenecke as Director. Minnesota's Dr. Martin Luther College at New Ulm, Minn., was converted into a teachers' seminary under the directorship of J. Schaller. Michigan's Theological Seminary was supposed to be discontinued and reorganized as a preparatory school (*Progymnasium*). Northwestern College, Watertown, Wis. (Aug. F. Ernst, pres.), was relieved of its normal department, but provided the pre-Seminary course for the ministerial students of the entire body. Home missions were

co-ordinated, but remained under the jurisdiction of the constituent synods. As a new venture the Joint Synod undertook the evangelization of the Apache Indians of Arizona, first planned by Wisconsin alone. Wisconsin and Minnesota had both taken part in the founding of the Synodical Conference, 1872. Michigan had joined in 1890. Their doctrinal position and confessional declarations were and are those of the Synodical Conference. — In 1904 the Nebraska Conference of the Wisconsin Synod was given the status of a District Synod. In the meantime the Joint Synod had also suffered a loss. A majority of the congregations and pastors of the Michigan Synod had not taken kindly to the thought of closing their Theological Seminary. Other internal difficulties led to a split within this body, and in 1896 the majority left not only the Joint Synod, but also the Synodical Conference. A minority remained with the Joint Synod as one of its districts. Ten years later the two groups reconciled their differences, with the result that since 1909 Michigan resumed its old place as a member of the Joint Synod and also the Synodical Conference. In the following year Michigan Lutheran Seminary at Saginaw, which had been closed for some time, was reorganized under the leadership of Director O. J. R. Hoenecke as a preparatory school in the growing educational system of the Joint Synod.

3. By this time the need for redistricting was becoming more and more obvious. As a result a new constitution was presented in 1915, approved by the several constituent synods and districts in the following year, and put into operation in 1917. The complete amalgamation which this new constitution provided was a fruit of the ever closer co-operation which had been practiced by the member synods, and the mutual understanding which grew out of their joint work. In the new body the old Wisconsin Synod accounted for four districts: Northern, Southeastern, and Western Wisconsin, and the Pacific Northwest District (formerly a Wisconsin mission). Minnesota was made into two: Minnesota, and Dakota and Montana, Michigan, and Nebraska each represent one district. The special needs of the Dakota and Montana Districts were recognized by the founding in 1928 of Northwestern Lutheran Academy at Mobridge, S. Dak. In the following year the Theological Seminary was trans-

ferred from Wauwatosa to a new set of buildings near Thiensville, Wis., its present location. The educational institutions of the Joint Synod now represent a well-integrated system: academies and preparatory departments (on the high school level) at Saginaw, Mobridge, New Ulm, and Watertown; a teachers' college at New Ulm and a full four-year college at Watertown; a theological seminary at Thiensville. — During the middle twenties a serious controversy occurred which grew out of some cases of discipline. As a result a considerable number of pastors and congregations severed their connection with the Synod.

4. Presidents during the first phase of the Joint Synod's existence were: Dr. A. F. Ernst, 1892—1901; C. Gausewitz, 1901—07 and 1913—17; F. Soll, 1907 to 1913. Since the reorganization of 1917: G. E. Bergemann, 1917—33; John Brenner, 1933—53; Oscar Naumann, 1953—. Statistics (1952): Stations, 837; active pastors, 650; baptized members, 316,839; communicant members, 218,520. Contributions (1950): For home purposes, $6,012,130; work at large, $1,061,933 (for statistics on education see *Parish Education*, D 9, E 10; *Teachers*, D). Official publications: *Ev.-Luth. Gemeindeblatt* (established by Wisconsin Synod 1865); *Northwestern Lutheran* (established by Joint Synod 1913); *Theological Quarterly* (established in 1903 as *Theologische Quartalschrift*). The Synod also owns and operates Northwestern Publishing House, Milwaukee, and a Home for Old People at Belle Plaine, Minn. ER

John P. Koehler, *The History of the Wisconsin Synod* (published serially in *Faith-Life*, 1938—44); A. P. Sitz and G. A. Westerhaus, "Brief History of the Wisconsin Synod," *Northwestern Lutheran*, May 5, 1940; Martin Lehninger, *Continuing in His Word*, 1951.

Wisconsin Synod. 1. The Ev. Luth. Ministerium of Wisconsin was founded by Pastors John Muehlhaeuser,* J. Weinmann (perished at sea, 1858), and W. Wrede (soon returned to Germany) at Milwaukee, Dec. 8, 1849. It was formally organized in May, 1850, at Granville, a village near Milwaukee, where two other pastors were present, the five serving 18 congregations. The three founders were graduates of the Barmen Training School for Missionaries and were sent to America by the Langenberg Society, for some years the chief source from which pastors were drawn. Muehlhaeuser and his associates were Lutherans and upheld the Lutheran Confessions, as their first constitution shows; but there was too much dependence on the uncertain Lutheran East, where the founder had spent his first ten years in America, and on the indeterminate Lutheranism of Germany. Congregational delegates constituted the "synod" together with the pastors, but the "ministerium" reserved for itself certain privileges, for example, in the licensing and ordaining of ministers. The great problem was to secure suitable pastors. Muehlhaeuser established connections with the Pennsylvania Synod and with individual pastors of the East and also kept in close touch with the Langenberg Society, which was soon reenforced in its American undertakings by the Berlin Society. The Barmen school furnished many of the early ministers. Others came from Basel. Among these pioneers were C. F. Goldammer, J. Bading, Ph. Koehler. W. Streissguth, E. Mayerhoff, G. Reim, Ph. Sprengling, G. Fachtmann, Dr. E. Moldehnke, Dr. Th. Meumann.

2. As the tide of immigration spread and congregations were established as far north as Green Bay and west as La Crosse, the need for trained men became increasingly acute. The synod, which had already shown a trend toward greater confessionalism, decided in 1863 to establish its own seminary and college. Bading was sent to Europe to collect funds and a library. Though his mission was successful, the synod did not reap the results; the money was retained by the German authorities because the Wisconsin Synod had clarified its confessional position to a positive and uncompromising Lutheranism which was distasteful to its former patrons, who, though Lutheran in intent, belonged to the Prussian State Church. In the meantime the seminary had been opened in September 1863 in a dwelling in Watertown, with two students and Dr. E. Moldehnke as professor. In the following year 11 were enrolled, and ground was broken for the first building of Northwestern University, as the combined seminary and college was now called. Prof. Adam Martin was its first president. Adolf Hoenecke was called as professor of theology in 1866. After Wisconsin had definitely broken with its unionistic friends in Germany by its declaration of 1867 and at the same time taken a decisive stand against the newly organized General Council because of its

lack of a definite position on altar and pulpit fellowship with the heterodox, it readily came to full agreement in doctrine and practice with Missouri in a meeting of representatives of the two bodies in 1868. At this time a plan was worked out to simplify and strengthen the educational system. Missouri was to furnish a professor and send some of its students to Watertown. Wisconsin was to discontinue its seminary and send its students and a professor to St. Louis. Under this arrangement Prof. F. W. Stellhorn represented Missouri at Watertown from 1869 to 1874. Professor Hoenecke was called to Saint Louis, eventually declined, however, when the agreement to exchange professors was suspended by common consent. In 1878 the arrangement was terminated, when Wisconsin reopened its own seminary under Hoenecke, this time in Milwaukee.

3. Having now settled its doctrinal position and found its place in the Lutheran Church of America, Wisconsin co-operated in the founding of the Synodical Conference in 1872. While not entering upon Walther's plan for the forming of state synods (see article on Synodical Conference), Wisconsin did lend its wholehearted and active support in the controversy on election which in 1881 led to the secession of Ohio and a division in the Norwegian Synod of that time. This controversy did not materially weaken Wisconsin; it lost a few congregations and pastors, but gained internal strength and also added a few pastors to its ranks who shared its position.

4. Since the early sixties relations with the Minnesota Synod had been friendly. Delegations at synodical meetings were exchanged. A working arrangement was established whereby the Minnesota students were sent to Northwestern College. At the same time the *Gemeindeblatt* (founded in 1865 by Wisconsin) was made the official publication of Minnesota as well. When Michigan severed its connection with the General Council in 1888, a closer approach became possible in that direction also and was sponsored particularly by Minnesota. As a result Michigan first became a member of the Synodical Conference and then in 1892 joined the other two bodies in forming the Joint Synod of Wisconsin, Minnesota, Michigan, and Other States, an association in which the constituent synods retained their individuality and independence, but pooled their re-

sources in the field of higher education. In 1904 Nebraska, previously a conference of Wisconsin, attained District status in the Joint Synod. This rather loose type of organization was eventually replaced by a complete amalgamation of these several bodies. A new constitution was drafted in 1915 and put into operation in 1917. In this new body (Ev. Luth. Joint Synod of Wisconsin and Other States,*) the old Wisconsin Synod loses its identity, accounting for three of the eight districts which now make up the larger organization. Its presidents until 1917 were: Muehlhaeuser, 1850—60; Bading, 1860 to 1864; Streissguth, 1864—67; Bading, to 1889; Ph. von Rohr, to 1908; G. E. Bergemann, to 1917. Statistics: pastors, 290; congregations, 400; communicants, 100,000. ER

John P. Koehler, *Geschichte der Wisconsin-Synode,* Northwestern Publishing House, 1925; "History of the Wisconsin Synod," *Faith-Life,* 1938 to 1944; A. P. Sitz and G. A. Westerhaus, "Brief History of the Wisconsin Synod," *Northwestern Lutheran,* May 5, 1940.

Wisdom of God. Wisdom is the attribute of God by which He chooses, disposes, and directs the proper means to the proper ends (Job 12:13; 1 Tim. 1:14; Is. 55:8, 9). The greatest exhibitions of the wisdom of God are the plan of creation and the plan of salvation. But though these counsels have been in a measure revealed to us, there are many things which God has reserved, in His wisdom, to Himself (Rom. 11:33 ff.).

Wisdom of Sirach. See *Apocrypha,* A 3.

Wisdom of Solomon. See *Apocrypha,* A 3.

Wise, John (1652—1725). Congregational pastor at Ipswich, Mass.; upheld democratic church government in his *The Churches' Quarrel Espoused;* opposed a condemnation in a witchcraft trial.

Wishart, George. See *Presbyterian Bodies,* 1.

Wiss, Michael. See *Weisze, Michael.*

Witchcraft. 1. The practice of occult arts by witches, or wizards, who perform their work with the aid of the devil. That witchcraft has been practiced in the past and therefore is possible is a fact, as appears from a number of Scripture passages (Deut. 18:10 f.;

Lev. 20:27; 1 Samuel 28; Acts 8:9; Gal. 5:20; Acts 13:8; 19:19).

2. In the early Christian Church witchcraft of every kind was forbidden, either on the ground of the emptiness of the practice or that of its positive godlessness and commerce with the devil. In the Church of the early Middle Ages special rules of penance were made for women convicted of witchcraft. But at the beginning of the 13th century, when the abomination of the Inquisition * was introduced, the use of magic and witchcraft was everywhere suspected and immediately branded as a desertion of God for the service of evil spirits. In 1231 a bull of Pope Gregory IX invoked the use of civil punishment against every form of heresy connected with sorcery. Toward the end of the 15th century the provisions which brought witches under the power of the Inquisition were enlarged, so that trials for witchcraft became very common. "While the ordinary tribunals were regarded as competent, the union of heresy and witchcraft made the duty of the inquisitors plain, and there was no need to wait for an accuser; the witnesses did not even need to be named; a counsel for defense was not necessary, indeed, if such a one were too zealous, he might be suspected of complicity in the offense; instruments of torture were suggested." (*Standard Encyclopedia.*)

3. After the Reformation the crime of witchcraft was again the subject of legal enactments, also under the influence of the Church. Thus Elector August of Saxony supported a decree against sorcery, making it a capital offense with the words: "that any one should forget his Christian faith and make an agreement with the devil." A perfect epidemic of witch prosecution broke out in Germany at the end of the 15th century, spreading into France, Italy, Spain, the Netherlands, and England and continuing through the 16th, 17th, and 18th centuries. The number of its unfortunate victims, members of both the Catholic and Protestant churches, is estimated at many thousands. Some of the tortures and ordeals resorted to in the examination of persons suspected of witchcraft were almost of a diabolical nature.

4. In America the first witchcraft persecution broke out in 1692, in Salem, Mass., the occasion being some meetings in the family of a minister by the name of Parrish. A company of girls had been in the habit of meeting a West Indian slave in order to study the "Black Art."

Suddenly they began to act mysteriously, bark like dogs, and scream at things unseen. An old Indian servant was accused of bewitching them. The excitement spread, and impeachments multiplied. A special court was formed to try the accused, as a result of which the jails filled rapidly, many persons being found guilty and condemned to death. It was unsafe to express any doubt as to a prisoner's guilt. Fifty-five persons suffered torture, and twenty were executed. In spite of all efforts to the contrary, witchcraft trials on the basis of church law in Catholic countries have survived almost to the present day, individual cases having been recorded as late as toward the end of the past century.

5. The Bible strongly opposes and condemns witchcraft and all related magic works (see passages in 1 above).

H. C. Lea, *Materials Toward a History of Witchcraft*, U. of Pennsylvania Press, Philadelphia, 1939 (3 vols.); C. W. Olliver, *An Analysis of Magic and Witchcraft*, Rider & Company, 1928; G. L. Kittredge, *Witchcraft in Old and New England*, Harvard U. Press, 1929.

Witt, Christian Friedrich (1665 to 1716). The author of the *Psalmodia Sacra* of Gotha (1715); wrote a number of hymn tunes which are still used today. Some attribute the tune "Es ist genug" (*Lutheran Hymnal*, No. 196) to Witt.

Wittenberg Articles of 1536. Dr. Robert Barnes, Bishop Edward Fox of Hereford, and Archdeacon Richard Heath came to Wittenberg on Jan. 1, 1536, and till April discussed the Augsburg Confession and agreed to its teachings. July 11 there was laid before the Convocation *The Book of Articles of Faith and Ceremonies*, which was greatly influenced by the *Wittenberg Articles*. In part it went over into *The Institution of a Christian Man*, or *The Bishops' Book*, of 1537. This, in turn, influenced *The Thirty-nine Articles* of the Episcopal Church, and these are also, substantially, the articles of the Methodists. See *Anglican Confessions; Lutheran Confessions.*

Wittenberg Concord. When Philip of Hesse could not get the Swiss at Marburg, in 1529, nor the German highland cities at Augsburg, in 1530, to accept the Biblical doctrine of the Lord's Supper, Bucer persisted till he got some of the highlanders to accept the Lutheran teaching and to sign the *Wittenberg Concord* on May 26, 1536. Though they sent friendly greetings, the Swiss would not accept this offer of peace and charged Bucer with trying to smuggle Lutheranism into their country.

Wittenberg Synod. Organized June 8, 1847, by eight pastors ("bishops") formerly belonging to the English Synod of Ohio (East Ohio). Territory: Northwestern Ohio. Among the prominent men of the synod were Ezra Keller and Sam. Sprecher. It joined the General Synod in 1848. It was one of the synods approving of the "Definite Platform." * In 1918 it entered the United Lutheran Church and, on Nov. 3, 1920, merged with the East Ohio, the Miami Synod, and the District Synod of Ohio into the Ohio Synod of the U. L. C. At the time of this merger it numbered 55 pastors, 74 congregations, and 12,590 communicants. See *United Lutheran Church, Synods of,* 22.

C. S. Ernsberger, *A History of the Wittenberg Synod of the General Synod of the Evangelical Lutheran Church,* Luth. Book Concern, Columbus, Ohio, 1917.

Witzel, Georg (1501—73). Roman Catholic reformer at the time of the Reformation; b. in Bacha; studied a semester at Wittenberg and came under the influence of Luther and Melanchthon; pastor in Wenigen-Lubnitz, Thueringen; preacher against abuses in the Roman Church and also oppression of lower classes; the Peasants' Revolt brought him under suspicion; he appealed to Luther for help and through him obtained a position near Wittenberg. He felt there was a lack of piety and good works among the Evangelicals and concluded that their doctrine hindered works. He favored the Anabaptists and became a friend of John Campanus. After the latter became an anti-Trinitarian, Witzel through patristic study and the influence of Erasmus returned to Catholicism, which he sought to advance through reform. His previous marriage brought him under suspicion of Roman Catholics. Throughout the remainder of his wandering life he sought to gain adherence for his reform program which, however, was rejected at the Council of Trent.

Wizenmann, Thomas (1759—87). Swabian theologian and philosopher; shared the views of Lavater, Hamann, and Claudius; joined Collenbusch circle; wrote *Geschichte Jesu nach Matthaeus, Goettliche Entwicklung des Satans.*

WKBW. See *Radio Stations, Religious,* 2.

WMBI. See *Radio Stations, Religious,* 2.

WMPC. See *Radio Stations, Religious,* 2.

WMRP. See *Radio Stations, Religious,* 2.

WMTC. See *Radio Stations, Religious,* 2.

Wohlgemuth, Michel (1434—1519). German painter, under influence of the art of the Netherlands, but with an awkward style and flat modeling; his shop produced many altars, but few of intrinsic value.

Wohltaetigkeitskonferenz. See *Deaconesses,* 8.

Wold, Oscar Rudolph. B. Aug. 11, 1874; studied at Red Wing Seminary, Concordia College, Moorhead, Minn., Chicago Luth. Seminary; missionary to China, 1898—1905; prof. at Red Wing Seminary (on furlough); missionary in China, 1910—29; pres. Central China Union Luth. Sem., 1913—29; pres. Chinese Luth. Church, 1920—29; d. Oct. 11, 1929.

Wolf, Edmund Jacob. Historian; b. Dec. 8, 1840, in Pennsylvania; educated at Gettysburg; Lutheran pastor in Baltimore; from 1873 prof. of Church History and New Testament Exegesis at Gettysburg Lutheran Seminary; perhaps the most conservative of the influential members of the General Synod after the Fort Wayne disruption of 1866; author of *The Lutherans in America* (1891). D. Jan. 10, 1905.

Wolfenbuetteler Fragments. See *Lessing.*

Wolff, Christian, Freiherr von (1679 to 1754). German philosopher; 1707 professor of mathematics and natural philosophy at Halle; deposed 1723 and banished from Prussia through influence of Halle Pietists; went to Marburg; later recalled to Halle. Though he accepted revelation, reason was his final authority. Logical consequence of his method was rationalism, which through his system gained increasingly strong foothold in Germany.

Wolfgang von Anhalt (1492—1566). Met Luther at Worms 1521 and favored the Reformation; signed the Augsburg Confession 1530; joined the Smalcald League; exiled by the Emperor; present at Luther's death; opposed the Interim.*

Wollaeger, Herman William Frank. B. Dec. 7, 1872, at Milwaukee, Wis.; graduated at St. Louis, 1895; pastor at Hartford, Conn., 1900—04; Ph. D. (Heidelberg); professor at Concordia College, St. Paul, Minn., 1904—41. Died July 14, 1941.

Wolsey, Thomas (ca. 1475—1530). "I and my King"; received cardinal's hat 1515; became real ruler of England; instigated Henry VIII's controversy with Luther; burned Luther's books and "Tyndale's Lutheran translation"; was overthrown on failing to obtain the divorce Henry VIII was seeking; remarked on deathbed: "If I had served God as diligently as I have done the king, He would not have given me over in my gray hairs."

Woltersdorf, Ernst Gottlieb (1725 to 1761). German poet, educator, preacher, and author; studied at Halle 1742, but in 1744 was compelled by illness to discontinue and to travel; called as second pastor to Bunzlau 1748; became identified with an orphan asylum in 1754.

Woman as Teacher. See *Teachers,* A 1 d.

Woman in Christian Society. The New Testament, in common with the revelation of the Old Testament, places woman on a high level and creates the basis for a noble concept of ethical equality with man. It does so by making woman equal to man as a shareholder in the gifts of the Holy Spirit, by removing sex as a factor in the reception and exercise of the life of God, and by presenting noble illustrations of Christian womanhood. This ideal is further implemented in the New Testament by the definition of woman's sphere of service as one unique to her and essential to the world. The ascetic ideal, however, exalted celibacy as a state of virtue superior to that of marriage and thereby cast a taint upon woman as an agent defacing the ideal state. The New Testament knows of no such taint, but rather puts the responsibility for lust upon human nature itself and upon the unregenerate flesh of the Christian; and it stoutly rebukes the incipient strains of asceticism and deprecation of marriage which time brought with it. The "inferiority" which St. Paul allegedly assumes for woman is such through the point of view of asceticism and puritanism. In his original intention Paul emphasized the need for the Spirit, both in man and in woman, and outlined the sphere of woman's service. Already in the Apostolic Age special spheres of labor in the Church were devised for women without families. Under the influence of the ascetic ideal these spheres of service were broadened into the work of welfare, which, despite the disfiguring factor of celibacy, remains one of the most worthy aspects of Roman Catholicism. The factor of service and sacrifice, however, was so buried under the ascetic ideal and faulty religious motivation that the Protestant Reformation had no recourse other than to attack the system directly. In riper years, Luther himself, the ex-monk, married an ex-nun as a symbol and testimony of this revolt. Thereby he sought not to afford himself or others a license for lust, but he sought to establish an object lesson in the concept of the Christian calling. This concept, basic to Lutheran ethics, views man as living in the vocations of family, state, and occupation, and woman as likewise fulfilling her vocation as wife, mother, friend, and citizen; and the fulfilling of this vocation with the help and for the glory of God constitutes a Christian service higher in meaning than all celibate or contemplative artificial expedients.

The New Testament ideal brought about vast changes in the attitude toward woman in its world. Whereas woman had been regarded as a chattel or object of lust, she was enabled to assume the regard and worth due her in God's plan. Likewise the Protestant Reformation served to restore the family ideal, not only in its communions, but also in Roman Catholicism.

Women have been particularly active in the Lutheran program of the Church and of welfare. The Deaconess * program originated in the attempt to utilize the New Testament method of providing definite areas of service for women not in families. With the progress of the industrial revolution and the expanded leisure of women of the middle classes, Lutheran women have found more and more opportunity for rendering service to objectives of the Church, also when they were wives and mothers. American Lutheran church life has imitated the custom of other churches of organizing the women of the parish in specific groupings (ladies' aid, women's guild, businesswomen's church groups, young women's groups) and for specific services. The parish groups thus foster fellowship between the women of the church, occupy themselves with study or mission enterprises, engage in fundraising pursuits, and otherwise are at the disposal of specific parish programs. In more recent years the added leisure time away from housework has made possible the organizing of women's groups on a national scale. In the Lutheran churches of America these are: ULCA: Women's Missionary Society; ALC: Women's Missionary Federation; ELC: The Women's Missionary Federation; LFC: Women's Missionary Federation; Danish ELC: Women's Mission Society; United Danish Lutheran Church: Women's Missionary Society; Missouri Synod: Lutheran Women's Missionary League. The contributions for all purposes, and the membership, for 1946—47:

Group	Membership	1946 Contributions
ULCA	75,329	$706,383.68
ALC	37,360	197,021.64
ELC	130,000	427,457.78
LFC	10,000	17,526.65
DELC	4,000	3,271.00
UDLC	9,000	4,912.90
Mo. Synod	100,000	55,830.26

RRC

Woman's Christian Temperance Union. Organized in Cleveland, Ohio, during the great temperance crusade of 1874. Those who would become members must sign the total abstinence pledge. The badge of the society is a bow of white ribbon. The motto reads: "For God and Home and Native Land." Mrs. Annie Wittenmeyer was the first president. Miss Frances E. Willard succeeded her in 1879 and remained president until her death, in 1898. The W. C. T. U. is the largest organization in the world managed and controlled by women. The organization carries on its work by means of the following departments: organization, preventive, educational, evangelistic, legal, and social. In addition, there are two branches: the Young Woman's Branch and the Loyal Temperance Legion Branch. The W. C. T. U. also stands for a single standard of purity for men and women, or, using the words of Miss Willard, for "a white life for two," as also for woman's equality in the home, the church, and the State. It is largely due to the W. C. T. U. that in the textbooks of our public schools special reference is made to the effects of alcohol and narcotics, and its Sunday school department secured the teaching of quarterly temperance lessons in the International Sunday School Series.

Women's Mission Society. See *Woman in Christian Society.*

Women's Missionary Federation. See *Woman in Christian Society.*

Women's Missionary League. See *Woman in Christian Society; Lutheran Women's Missionary League.*

Women's Missionary Society. See *Woman in Christian Society.*

Woodd, Basil (1760—1831). B. at Richmond in Surrey. His widowed mother's influence and upbringing were most salutary. At 17 he entered Trinity College, Oxford. Taking holy orders in 1783, he was chosen lecturer of Saint Peter's, Cornhill, the following year. He became morning preacher at Bentinck Chapel and purchased the lease of the chapel (it being a proprietary chapel) in 1793 and held the incumbency together with the rectory of Drayton from 1808 to his death. He took a great interest in the religious societies and in the antislavery movement. His outstanding hymn is "Hail, Thou Source of Every Blessing."

Woodruff, Wilfred. See *Latter Day Saints,* c.

Woolman, John (1720—72). American Quaker; his efforts to remove social ills are given in his *Journal;* known especially for his opposition to slavery.

Woolston, Thomas. See *Deism,* III 5.

Word of God. See *Bible; Inspiration; Logos; Revelation; Grace, Means of.*

Wordsworth, Christopher (1807—85). Educated at Cambridge; brilliant scholar; held positions as master and lecturer, then parish priest, finally bishop of Lincoln; very voluminous writer, among his works *The Holy Year,* containing "Songs of Thankfulness and Praise" and others.

Works. See *Good Works; Sanctification.*

Works, Merit of. 1. Since the central purpose of the Christian religion is to restore men to the blissful and intimate fellowship with God which Adam's sin forfeited for our race, the central doctrine of the whole Christian system must be the doctrine which teaches by what means men may obtain forgiveness of sins, reconciliation with God, and eternal life. All other doctrines will be in various states of dependence on this one; and if serious error creeps in at this point, many other doctrines will be affected; in fact, the whole system of doctrine will be vitiated. This very condition is found in the teaching of the Roman Catholic Church; for almost all the doctrines and practices which in that Church obscure the light of the

Gospel grow from its unscriptural teaching regarding the merit of works as a cause of man's salvation.

2. The Roman Church denies that men are justified before God only through faith in the merit of Christ. "If any one says that men are justified, either by the sole imputation of the justice of Christ or by the sole remission of sins, to the exclusion of the grace and the charity which is poured forth in their hearts by the Holy Ghost and is inherent in them; or even that the grace whereby we are justified is only the favor of God: let him be accursed." "If any one saith that justifying faith is nothing else but confidence in the divine mercy, which remits sins for Christ's sake, or that this confidence alone is that whereby we are justified: let him be accursed." (Council of Trent, Sess. VI, can. 11. 12.)

3. Rome denies that the justification of the sinner before God is a judicial act, in which God declares the sinner just by imputing to him the righteousness of Christ, which he has apprehended by faith. Instead, it teaches that justification consists of the following process: The unmerited grace of God touches the sinner's heart and calls him to repentance and faith. The sinner may, of his own power, accept or reject this grace. If he accepts it and turns to God, he receives, through Baptism, full forgiveness of his past sins. That forgiveness is the one part of justification. The other part consists in this, that the sinner, by the renewal of his inner nature, is himself transformed into an intrinsically just man. As a just man he is able to do good and perfect works, which fulfill the demands of God's Law, render satisfaction for sin, and merit rewards of God, including eternal life. The Council of Trent teaches: "If any one saith that the justified, by the good works which he performs through the grace of God and the merit of Jesus Christ, whose living member he is, does not truly merit increase of grace, eternal life, and the attainment of that eternal life — if so be, however, that he depart in grace — and also an increase of glory: let him be accursed." (Sess. VI, can. 32.) "Life eternal is to be proposed to those working well unto the end and hoping in God, both as a grace promised to the sons of God through Jesus Christ and as a reward which is, according to the promise of God Himself, to be faithfully rendered to their good works and merits." (*Ibid.,* chap. XVI.)

4. This teaching means, then, that Jesus does not really save men, but en-

ables them to save themselves. Grace and works cannot divide the field. St. Paul, as though he referred to the last quotation, argues: "If by grace, then is it no more of works; otherwise grace is no more grace. But if it be of works, then is it no more grace; otherwise work is no more work." Rom. 11:6. The Scripture, with one voice, testifies that alone through faith in Christ's merit can sinners be reconciled to God, while their own imperfect works can claim no merit before Him. Luke 17:10. This is the argument of the entire Epistle to the Romans (see especially chap. 4) and to the Galatians (see chap. 3).

5. This doctrine was restored to the Church by Luther, and it became the cornerstone of the Reformation. Rome, however, can make no concessions to it, no matter how clearly it is revealed in the Bible, without yielding its whole position. It has arranged its entire household on the basis of the merit of works. Nor are the works to which it ascribes merit only those commanded by God; in large part they are self-elected, man-made works (see *Consilia Evangelica*), such as fasting, vigils, celibacy, praying by rote, and similar ascetic and devotional contrivances. And while Rome refuses to let its adherents trust in the all-sufficient merits of Christ alone, it teaches them not only that they themselves can merit eternal life of God, but that they can have recourse to the merits of the saints (see *Saints, Worship of*) and even can themselves earn greater merit of works than they need, which superfluous merit may be applied to the needs of others. See also *Opera Supererogationis; Merit*.

Works of Spirit. See *Holy Ghost*.

Works Progress Administration. See *Social Work*, D 1.

World Alliance for International Friendship Through Religion (founded 1916). Its purpose is to unite all Christians and churches by means of international friendship, to prevent war through a League of Nations, to increase our friendship with such foreign countries as Japan, China, Mexico, and Latin America, and, by the enactment of good laws, to protect aliens. International world conferences are held and magazines published. Headquarters: 170 E. 64th St., New York City.

World Conference of Faith and Order. See *Union Movements*, 15.

World Conference of Missions. See *Union Movements*, 14.

World Council of Churches. Movements which led to the organization of the World Council of Churches were: movements that aimed at co-ordination of existing church work; movements that aimed at focusing the attention of Christians on practical and contemporary world problems; movements that aimed at discussing doctrinal agreements underlying the disunion of Christendom. The modern ecumenical movement was initiated at Geneva in 1920, when largely at the suggestion of the Federal Council of Churches plans were formulated for a conference of all Protestant churches to meet at Stockholm in 1925. The aims of this conference were primarily to unite the churches of the world for social work, such as rehabilitation after the First World War. Almost simultaneously the Protestant Episcopal Church, which at that time was not a member of the Federal Council, issued an invitation to the churches of the world to unite on a broad doctrinal basis. The Anglican and the Eastern Orthodox Churches readily lent their support to this union endeavor. In 1937 the two movements converged when the majority of Protestant churches met at Oxford and Edinburgh to discuss the possibilities of church union. The delegation at Oxford concerned itself primarily with the life and work of the Church, while the topic for discussion at Edinburgh was chiefly faith and order. In 1937 the two groups agreed to appoint continuation committees which were to lay the foundation for the proposed World Council of Churches and to prepare a draft for a constitution. Specific steps leading to the formation of the World Council were: (1) The meeting of the Committee of Thirty-five under Wm. Temple's chairmanship at Westfield, Onson, England, in 1937; and the meeting of the Committee of Fourteen at Utrecht in 1938. The organizational meeting was scheduled for 1941 but had to be postponed until 1948 at Amsterdam. The constitution lists the following functions of the World Council of Churches:

1. To carry on the work of the Faith and Order and the Life and Work movements;

2. To facilitate common action by the Churches;

3. To promote co-operation in study;

4. To promote the growth of ecu-

menical consciousness in the members of all Churches;

5. To establish relations with denominational federations of world-wide scope and with other ecumenical movements;

6. To call world conferences on specific subjects as occasion may require, such conferences being empowered to publish their own findings. See *Union Movements*, 14 f.

F. E. Mayer and R. C. Meyer, "The World Council of Churches: A Theological Appraisal," *CTM*, XXIV: 161 ff.; references under *Religious Bodies (U. S.)*, *Bibliography*.

World Missionary Council. See *Union Movements*, 15.

World's Student Christian Federation. See *Students, Spiritual Care of*, A.

Worldview, Christian. See *History, Philosophy of*.

Worms, Conference of. A meeting held in November, 1540, and in January, 1541, the object being to promote some understanding between the Roman and the Lutheran theologians. There were eleven men on the Roman side, with Granvella as the representative of Charles V and the legate Campegius as the chief spokesman, while Melanchthon was the leader of the Lutherans. But a few days after the real opening, when a discussion between Eck and Melanchthon was well under way, the conference was adjourned to the Diet of Regensburg, without having accomplished anything.

Worms, Consultation of. A meeting of Lutheran and Roman Catholic theologians held in Worms in 1557. The men on the Evangelical side were themselves at odds, because the Flacian party had refused to acknowledge the Wittenberg party unless the men in this group would cleanse themselves "of synergism and Zwinglianism." Other designations used were Interimists, Adiaphorists, Majorists, Osiandrists. The preliminary efforts at effecting a united front having failed, the meeting was nevertheless called, Bishop Julius von Pflug acting as chairman. The greatest difficulty arose when the Romanists refused to accept the Bible as the only and final norm of doctrine. It became evident that the Augsburg Confession alone would not be accepted as the common confession, and the meeting was adjourned in December.

Worms, Diet of, 1521. The first one of young Emperor Charles V, where on April 18 Luther made his world-changing speech, making the Reformation a purely religious affair. He stood upon Scripture, in which his conscience was bound, and stood alone against Pope, prelates, and Emperor. His private interpretation of Scripture was put above the interpretation of the world; councils had erred and contradicted one another. At the same time the Diet presented the famous *Centum Gravamina*, the "Hundred Grievances," which the German nation had against the scandalous abuses of the Papacy. Former Diets had made similar protests against abuses. This time, as previously, no real reforms were effected.

A. R. Wentz, *When Two Worlds Met, The Diet of Worms, 1521*, Luth. Pub. House, Philadelphia, 1921.

Worship, Divine. A public or private service expressing a person's or congregation's reverence to the revealed Triune God; according to the Lutheran view not merely an approach to God in prayer, praise, and thanksgiving (commonly known as the sacrificial elements of worship), but chiefly an acceptance of God's gift of grace to men, through the means of grace (the sacramental element). Worship is spiritual, but the spirit of devotion is strengthened by outward forms and ceremonies.

Worms, Edict of. The condemnation of Luther issued by the Diet of Worms.*

Worship Hour, Family. The Family Worship Hour is a fifteen-minute radio program dedicated to the revival of the family altar. The idea of visiting by radio in the homes with prayers, hymns, and meditations originated in the Pittsburgh, Pa., area in 1943. Many consultations with religious leaders and radio people took place before definite plans could be made. Through the zeal and interest of a number of men and women an organization was formed and incorporated under the laws of the State of Illinois for non-profit corporations in November, 1947.

The Family Worship Hour prepares electrical transcriptions and offers them to the radio stations gratis on a sustaining basis. The first broadcast was made Sept. 27, 1948, over eleven stations. In less than a year over one hundred stations carried the transcriptions in thirty-two States and Canada. TDM

Worship, Order of. There are a few of the church orders of Canono-Catholic times which have either remained practically unchanged to the present time or have influenced present orders to a great extent.

1. The liturgy of the Roman Church was established in the basic features of its present form by Gregory the Great (590—604). Not only did the Roman rite, as fixed by him, tend to emphasize the difference between Rome and Constantinople, but it also brought out the sacerdotal idea as it gained ground in the West under the influence of Gregory. In spite of Gregory's conservative position, the Roman rite began to supersede other rites which had been in use in the West. In the German Empire, which at that time included Gaul, Pepin and Charlemagne virtually succeeded in abolishing the Gallican Liturgy, the Roman Ordinary of the Mass being introduced by main force.

2. In England the Council of Clovesho prescribed the Roman rite for the entire country (747), although it never fully succeeded in replacing the ancient forms.

3. In Ireland, the synods of Tara (692), of Kells (1152), and of Cashel (1172) passed resolutions favoring the Roman rite alone.

4. In Spain, the Synod of Burgos (1085) declared the Roman Liturgy valid for the entire country. Thus, by the 12th century, the Roman forms had superseded, or supplanted, the rites previously in use in Spain, France, Germany, England, Scotland, Ireland, and Italy, with the exception of the archbishopric of Milan and individual dioceses at Seville, Toledo, Salamanca, and Valladolid, in Spain.

5. There was a revision of the Roman Liturgy in the 16th century, the Breviary of Quignon appearing in 1539 and the Breviary of Pius V in 1568. Since these efforts, however, did not meet with general satisfaction, Clement VIII, in 1604, issued a new Roman service book, which was finally revised under Urban VIII and appeared in 1634. It may be said to be a recast of the Gregorian Liturgy, the framework and much of the liturgical material having been retained.

6. The order of service in the celebration of Mass in the Roman Church at present contains the following parts: the solemn beginning of Mass, with the Introibo (Psalm 43) and the Gloria Patri; the Confiteor, or confession of sins by the priest; the Introit of the day with the Gloria Patri; the Kyrie, followed by the Gloria in Excelsis; the Collect, introduced with the Salutation

and Response; the reading of the Epistle; the Gradual, or Hallelujah; the Gospel, preceded by the Benediction and Salutation, with Response by the priest's assistants; the Nicene Creed; the Offertory, or the Oblation, with the Invocation and the Lavabo; the secret prayers, murmured by the priest; the Preface, including everything from the Salutation to the Sanctus; the Canon of the Mass, including the offering of the unbloody sacrifice, the consecration, the Elevation and Adoration, and the Commemoration for the living and the dead; the preparation for Communion; the prayers preceding the distribution (Agnus Dei and several collects); the distribution, the priest first taking bread and wine himself and then administering the bread, if there are communicants; the Communion Psalm, the Postcommunion; the end of Mass; the Benediction, the reading of John 1:1-14.

7. The Liturgy of the Church of England and also of the Protestant Episcopal Church in America was derived from Ephesine or Gallican sources, reaching England in the last part of the second century or in the third century by way of Lyons. It was afterward modified by Augustine of Canterbury and by Theodore of Tarsus. A revision by Osmund of Salisbury (1087) resulted in a compromise between the Roman and the Gallican rite. In 1516 the ancient Use of Salisbury was amended and revised, a second revision being undertaken in 1541. Eight years later, under the influence of the Reformation, the First Prayer Book of Edward VI, with the order for the chief service, appeared. It showed strong Lutheran influence. The Second Book of Common Prayer, of 1552, was compiled after Calvinistic influences were becoming apparent in England. It was suppressed in 1553, at the accession of Mary. The Book of Common Prayer, containing slight concessions to the non-conformist element, was authorized in 1662. The Parliament in England refused to accept alternatives by the Church Assembly (1927—28). The Prayer Book was twice revised in America (the latest revision in 1928).

8. The order of the chief service in the Anglican Church is the following: Lord's Prayer; Collect for Purity; Ten Commandments, with the response Kyrie, Collect of the day; Epistle, the congregation seated; Gospel, the congregation standing; Nicene Creed; announcements, Psalm; Sermon; sen-

tences relating to offering; General Prayer, Exhortation and Invitation; Confession and Absolution; Comfortable Words; the Communion service.

9. The order of worship in the Lutheran Church of America is based largely upon the work of Luther, whose *Formulae Missae* of 1523 and *Deutsche Messe* of 1526 exerted a wide influence. An abbreviated form of the Saxon and Prussian orders has been in use in many German congregations, while English congregations use the Common Service, or the Order of Holy Communion, as compiled from the best orders of the 16th century.

10. In the Liturgy of the Reformed Churches in America the sacrificial idea preponderates. In most denominations a number of hymns, alternating with prayers and readings, precede the sermon, and the services close with prayer and benediction. Great emphasis is placed upon the prayers in public worship, and the hymns and music are usually made an outstanding feature of the services. There is a certain tendency, also, to make the services more beautiful by introducing liturgical material, though the execution of liturgical parts is commonly left to a choir. See also *Worship, Parts of.*

Worship, Parts of. In following the sequence of parts in the order of worship, their significance should be noted.

1. Versicles are short passages of Scripture intended to incite the worshipers to devotion and to suggest the central thought of the part following.

2. The Confession of Sins is properly made as a preparatory step, to obtain the first assurance of the forgiveness of God, at the very beginning of worship. It has taken the place of the ancient Confiteor, in use after the poison of false doctrine had entered the Church. In the Confiteor the priest knelt and made confession of his sins to "Almighty God, to the blessed Virgin Mary, the blessed archangel Michael, the blessed John the Baptist, the holy Apostles Peter and Paul," etc. The meaning of this confession was that the priest, having doffed his usual clothing and having donned his priestly vestments, was worthy of offering the sacrifice for the living and for the dead. In this sense the Confiteor was to be condemned. The Confession of Lutheran worship is made for the entire congregation.

3. The Introit (entrance) is the opening of the Psalm of the day, spoken or chanted after the preparation, to indicate the character of the day and the nature of the spiritual food offered to the congregation. It is a remnant of the primitive psalmody, which was probably taken over into the early Church from the services of the synagog. Originally the entire Psalm was chanted or sung antiphonally between the officiating clergy and the choir at the great entrance of the officiating priest and his assistants. Luther favored the use of the entire introductory Psalm, but the abbreviated form remained, chiefly on account of lack of time.

4. The Introit is followed by the Gloria Patri or the Small Doxology to the Holy Trinity, by which the use of the Psalter as used in New Testament times is distinguished from its use in the synagog worship.

5. The Kyrie is a plea for the removal of misery and suffering, a confession of the wretchedness to be borne as a consequence of sins now forgiven. It is addressed to the Lord of mercy, in whom we not only have forgiveness of sins, but also help and assistance in every need.

6. The Gloria in Excelsis fittingly follows as a hymn of adoration, celebrating God's glory as manifested in the merciful gift of His Son, who bore all our sins and infirmities.

7. The Collects are prayers in which the wants and perils, or the wishes and desires, of the people or the entire Church are together presented to God.

8. The reading of the Epistle is followed by the Hallelujah on the part of the congregation, which praises the Lord for the unspeakable gift of His Word. At this point may be sung the Graduale (sequence, prose, tract, trope), originally merely an extension of the last syllable of the Hallelujah, in order to permit the lector to proceed from the Epistle to the Gospel ambo, but later developed into a special hymn or a series of responses and versicles, from which the liturgical plays were developed. The announcement of the Gospel is hailed with the sentence "Glory be to Thee, O Lord," and the "Praise be to Thee, O Christ," at the close signifies the grateful acceptance of the Word by the congregation. Then the Creed is said or chanted.

9. In the Offertory following the sermon the congregation confesses its grateful and humble acceptance of the

Word which has just been proclaimed, all the faithful offering themselves, their substance, and the sacrifices of prayer, praise, and thanksgiving to the Lord. This act has nothing in common with the oblation of the Mass which is practiced by the Roman Church at this point.

10. The Salutation, with its Response, is sung at the opening of the Communion service to indicate the beginning of a new part of the service.

11. The Preface is preceded by the prefatory sentences (Sursum and Gratias) and is distinguished for impressiveness and beauty, setting forth the reason for the hymn of praise which follows the chanting of the Preface (whether common, for ordinary Sundays, or proper, for festival seasons). This hymn of praise is known as the Sanctus, in which the combination of heaven's and earth's chorus results in an exalted strain of glorification and thanksgiving.

12. After the consecration of the elements the pastor chants the Pax, to which the congregation responds with the Agnus Dei ("O Christ, Thou Lamb of God"), during which the communicants move forward to the altar.

13. The Nunc Dimittis opens the Postcommunion. The believer, having received the fullness of God's grace and mercy, feels that he may now depart in peace to his home.

14. In the Benedicamus the congregation is called upon to give all honor to God alone, in order to receive from Him the final blessing.

15. The Canticles, among which the Benedictus (the song of Zacharias) and the Magnificat (the hymn of Mary) are best known, are, as a rule, used only in the minor services.

H. Asmussen, *Die Lehre vom Gottesdienst*, Munich, 1937; A. W. Blackwood, *The Fine Art of Public Worship*, Cokesbury, 1939; S. F. Brenner, *The Way of Worship*, Macm., 1944; L. Fendt, *Der Lutherische Gottesdienst des 16. Jahrhunderts*, Munich, 1923; see additional references under *Liturgics*.

Worship, Private. 1. That the worship of God in the midst of the congregation, in the assembly of those who confess the true God together, is required of all believers, appears from various parts of the Bible. As the Old Testament speaks of blessing the Lord in the congregations (Ps. 26:12) and of desiring to go to the house of the Lord with the multitude that kept the holyday (Ps. 42:4) so the New Testament admonishes us not to forsake the assembling of ourselves together (Heb. 10:25).

2. Just as important, however, for the nurture of the Christian's spiritual life is the daily communication with the Lord by way of private worship, by prayer, by reading the Word of God and meditating upon it, and by discussing its truths with others. David writes that he prayed and cried aloud evening and morning and at noon (Ps. 55:17). It is said of the godly man that he meditates in the Word of God day and night (Ps. 1:2). Again and again the value of direct communication with the Lord by means of prayer is emphasized in the Bible (Ps. 109:4; 141:5; Matt. 6:6). And we have the examples of consecrated men and women who remained in such communication with the Lord always, as Cornelius (Acts 10:2, 30); Daniel (chap. 6:10; 9:3, 4); David (2 Sam. 7:27; 1 Chron. 18:25); Elisha (2 Kings 4:33; 6:17); Ezra (chap. 10:1); Hannah (1 Sam 1:10); Anna the prophetess (Luke 2:37); Paul (Acts 20:36); Peter (Acts 10:9); and others. Examples of such as studied the Word of God and meditated upon it in private worship are Mary, the mother of Jesus (Luke 2:19, 51); the Ethiopian eunuch (Acts 8:28 ff.); the Bereans (Acts 17:11); the prophets of old (1 Pet. 1:10, 11).

3. Home devotions may easily be arranged, either in the morning or in the evening, preferably right after meals, when all the members of the family are together. A few stanzas of a hymn may be sung, or the head of the house may at once read a chapter or a passage from the Bible or from some good book of exposition or devotion based on a Bible passage. This will be followed by one or more prayers suitable to the time or occasion and, possibly, by a recital of a part of the Small Catechism. The home service may close with the Lord's Prayer and the Benediction. The liturgical orders of Matins, Vespers, and Compline may well be used.

Wortman, Denis, D. D., L. H. D. (1835—1922). B. in Hopewell, N. Y. He was a graduate of Amherst College, 1857, and of New Brunswick Theological Seminary in 1860, in which he was ordained a minister of the Gospel in the Reformed Church in America. He held pastorates in Brooklyn, Philadelphia, and Schenectady, N. Y. He served his denomination as secretary of Ministerial Relief and was president of its General Synod. Wrote: "God of the Prophets, Bless the Prophets' Sons."

Wounds, Five Sacred. The wounds of Jesus, which became an object of veneration by Roman Catholics during the Middle Ages.

WPTL. See *Radio Stations, Religious,* 2.

Wreford, John Reynell (1800—81). Educated at Manchester College, York; nonconformist minister; later withdrew from ministry and opened a school; among his hymns: "Lord, While for All Mankind We Pray."

Wright, Andreas. B. in Norway, Sept. 13, 1835; pastor, Coon Prairie, Rushford, and Highland, Wis.; one of the founders of Norwegian Augustana Synod, United Norwegian Lutheran Church; served as secy. and later pres. of the Norwegian Augustana Synod; promoter of colleges and seminaries (Augustana, Salem); editor of *Luthersk Kirketidende* and *Børnebudet;* author of numerous books; member of many committees and boards; d. Nov. 15, 1917.

Wright, George Frederick (1838 to 1921). Congregationalist; b. at Whitehall, N. Y.; graduate of Oberlin; pastor; professor at Oberlin, first of New Testament Language and Literature, then of Harmony and Science and Religion, 1881—1907; served on United States Geological Survey; editor of *Bibliotheca Sacra,* 1884—1921; *Scientific Confirmations of Old Testament History;* and other works.

WSDX. See *Radio Stations, Religious,* 2.

WSOU. See *Radio Stations, Religious,* 2.

Wucherer, John Frederick (1803 to 1881). Friend of Loehe and cofounder with him of inner mission work in Bavaria. During the early years of his ministry he fought rationalism; in his later years he championed the cause of the Lutheran Confessions; throughout his life he was active in inner missions.

Wuerttemberg Bible Society. See *Bible Societies,* 2.

Wuerttemberg Confession. See *Lutheran Confessions,* A 5.

Wuerttemberger Summarien. Eberhard III, Duke of Wuerttemberg, ordered these *Summarien* printed to take the place of the *Summarien* by Veit Dietrich, which through the plundering of the churches in time of war had become scarce. They were written by Johann Jakob Heinlin (d. 1660), Jeremias Rebstock, and Johann Konrad Zeller (d. 1683) and were published in 1669. To the second edition explanatory remarks were added by members of the Tuebingen faculty: Johann Wolfgang Jaeger, Johann Christian Pfaff, and Andreas Adam Hochstetter. An edition was published as late as 1878 and later. The books contain no translation of the Bible, but only *summaries* of the contents of the various books of the Old and New Testaments and, at the end of each chapter, useful applications.

Wulfila. See *Ulfilas.*

Wunder, Heinrich. B. March 12, 1830, at Mueggendorf, Bavaria; studied at the *Missionshaus* in Neuendettelsau at the age of fourteen; later at Fort Wayne and Altenburg; ordained at Millstadt, Ill., 1849; came to Chicago 1851, serving St. Paul's for sixty years and contributing a great deal to the firm founding and rapid growth of the Missouri Lutheran Synod in Chicago and vicinity; first president of the Illinois District, 1874—91 (the financial assistance his congregation received after the Chicago fire was applied to the rebuilding, not of the homes of members, but of the church and school); St. Louis conferred on him the title of D. D.; d. Dec. 22, 1913.

O. H. Schmidt, "Heinrich Wunder, D. D.," *CHIQ,* V: 53—59.

Wundt, Wilhelm Max. See *Psychology,* G 4.

Wuttke, Karl F. A. (1819—70). Prof. at Berlin and Halle; advocate of the Lutheran Confessions within the Prussian Union; wrote on the history of heathendom, contemporary superstitions of the German people, and an outstanding work on Christian ethics.

WWL. See *Radio Stations, Religious,* 2.

Wyclif, John (ca. 1324—84). 1. "The Morning Star of the Reformation"; b. of noble parentage near Richmond, in Yorkshire, England. He was connected with Oxford University as student or teacher the greater part of his life. He was also a parish priest, last at Lutterworth, a small market town in Leicestershire, near Birmingham.

2. Wyclif's repeated opposition to the Pope's meddling in English affairs of State and Church and his other anti-Romish activities caused his citation before ecclesiastical tribunals, which, however, failed to silence him. Besides preaching himself, Wyclif trained and sent out itinerant preachers. He also issued numerous Latin treatises and many English tracts against Romish

errors. With the aid of Nicholas of Hereford, one of his pupils, he translated the Bible from the Latin Vulgate and in 1382 issued this first complete English Bible.

3. His attack upon the dogma of transubstantiation aroused a bitter controversy between him and the mendicant friars. At times he seems to teach the Lutheran doctrine of the Lord's Supper, and then again he speaks of the bread and wine as being "Christ's body and blood figuratively and spiritually." The two Sacraments he considered real means of grace; but he seemed to believe that an unbelieving priest could not administer them effectively. Confirmation and extreme unction are to him mere human institutions. Enforced auricular confession he termed "a sacrament of the devil" and denounced purgatory as a blasphemous swindle. Although he taught that Christ is the only Mediator between God and man, and though he delighted to dwell on the love of Christ, he ascribed a certain degree of meritoriousness to the good works of a Christian. He upheld the separation of Church and State and taught that the Church is the congregation of the elect. Enforced celibacy he considered immoral and apparently also thought it unscriptural "that ecclesiastical men should have temporal possessions." He maintained that the only Head of the Church is Christ and that the Pope is Antichrist; and yet he never left the Romish Church. But after his death, the Council of Constance, in 1415, excommunicated him, and thirteen years later his bones were burned and their ashes thrown into the Swift.

Cambridge Medieval History (vol. VII); R. Vaughan, *Life and Opinions of John de Wycliffe*, London, 1831; R. Buddensieg, J. *Wiclif*, Halle, 1865.

Wyneken, Friedrich Konrad Dietrich. "Father of Home Missions in The Lutheran Church — Missouri Synod," and one of the triumvirate (Walther, Wyneken, Sihler) associated in the founding and building of The Lutheran Church — Missouri Synod, was born May 13, 1810, at Verden, Province of Hanover, Germany. His father was the Lutheran pastor of the local church, and Wyneken was the youngest of six sons, and he had five sisters. His pre-theological training began in his home *Gymnasium,* and his theological training was completed at Goettingen and Halle. As private tutor of a young nobleman he traveled in France and Italy and was also rector of the Latin school at Bremerford.

Rev. Hanfstengel of Leesum, near Bremen, gave the first impetus to Wyneken's acceptance of the Bible as the full Word of God and Jesus Christ as his Savior from sin. Added influence came later from the younger Tholuck in Halle and from his own private study of the Bible. As a linguist he had a ready command of his native German, French, and English. Having heard much of the great spiritual distress existing among his countrymen in North America, his love of Christ compelled him to become a missionary among them.

He landed in Baltimore in midsummer 1838, friendless, finally met the Rev. J. Haesbert, assisted him for a short time in congregational work, and then was sent west by the executive board of the Mission Society of the Pennsylvania Synod. The congregations at Friedheim and Fort Wayne, Ind., being vacant owing to the death of Rev. Jesse Hoover, Wyneken accepted their call as pastor, but also performed the duties of traveling missionary in northwestern Ohio, southern Michigan, and northern Indiana with undaunted courage in the face of many hardships.

Failing health and an earnest desire to obtain help, both men and money, for the cause of the Lutheran Church in America took him to Germany in 1841. His celebrated *"Notruf"* — titled "The Distress of the German Lutherans in North America," and his lectures in Nuernberg, Erlangen, Dresden, Leipzig, and other places gained the support of such influential personages as Wilhelm Loehe, Karl von Raumer, William Sihler, Paul Baumgart, all of which stimulated not only such men as Sihler, Lochner, Craemer, and others to come to America, but also caused smaller colonies of people to emigrate with them. Added to this was the generous work of the Missionary Society of Stade, the Loehe *Nothelfer,* L. A. Petri of Hanover, the Society for North America in Dresden, which resulted in such developments as the Franconian settlements in Michigan and its missions among the native Indians, the training of young men for work in the Midwest with the subsequent establishment of a practical seminary at Fort Wayne, all of which is directly accountable to the energetic and enthusiastic efforts of Wyneken. To him The Lutheran Church — Missouri

Synod owes a considerable portion of its original stock.

His mission work continued until 1845, when he was called to become Haesbert's successor at St. Paul's in Baltimore. Taking a firm stand against unionism, indifference, and the lodge (perhaps the first pastor in America to publicly condemn secret orders), he built his congregation on truly Lutheran confessional principles. Not long after he severed his connections with the General Synod for confessional reasons and, having in Fort Wayne made the acquaintance of the Saxons in Missouri through the *Lutheraner,* he took a keen interest in the early deliberations which resulted in the organization of the Missouri Synod, being present at the Cleveland meeting where preliminary plans were drawn up. He joined Synod at its second convention and was elected its second president in 1850, having previously been called to serve Old Trinity Congregation in Saint Louis. The year following his election as president, he and Walther were sent to Germany for the purpose of adjusting the doctrinal differences which had arisen between Loehe and the Missouri Synod. During his early presidency, Synod, because of rapid growth, was divided into four Districts, the heated Buffalo-Missouri controversy came to a head, and finally, with the added burdens of office, his health became impaired, and he was granted a leave of absence by his congregation. Thus in 1859 he settled near Fort Wayne, devoting his full time to the presidency. He discharged his duties with vigor and enthusiasm, visiting as many as sixty congregations in one year, stressing at conventions and visitations the necessity of doctrinal purity and a sound program of Christian education, the importance of a sanctified Christian life, and the need for ceaseless warfare against sectarianism, lodges, worldliness, and indifference. His wise leadership in this direction supple-

mented that of Walther and Sihler, and resulted in a group of congregations firmly grounded and knit together by the Word of God. The evangelical character of the Missouri Synod, is, to a high degree, the result of his influence.

On Aug. 31, 1841, Wyneken was married to Marie Sophie Wilhelmine Buuck, the second oldest daughter of "Father Buuck" of Adams County; she bore him thirteen children. In 1864, owing to increasing age and bodily infirmities, he was relieved of the presidency, took charge of Trinity Church in Cleveland, latterly as assistant to his son, retired 1875, and died at the home of his son-in-law in San Francisco, May 4, 1876. EJS

J. C. W. Lindemann, article on Wyneken in *Amerikanischer Kalender fuer Deutsche Lutheraner,* 1877; W. H. T. Dau (ed.), *Ebenezer,* reviews of the work of the Missouri Synod during three quarters of a century, 1847—1922, CPH, 1922; Carl Mauelshagen, *American Lutheranism Surrenders to Forces of Conservatism,* Athens, Ga., 1936; *The Effects of German Immigration upon the Lutheran Church in America,* Athens, Ga., 1936; G. E. Hageman, "Friedrich Konrad Dietrich Wyneken," *Men and Missions* (L. Fuerbringer, ed.), Vol. III, CPH, 1926.

Wyneken, Henry C. Son of Friedrich K. D. Wyneken; b. in Fort Wayne, Ind., Dec. 13, 1844; ed. at Concordia College and Seminary; instructor in the institute of Pastor Brunn in Steeden, Germany; assistant to his father (later, first pastor) and principal of Trinity Lutheran School, Cleveland, Ohio; 1876 prof. of Exegesis, Homiletics, Catechetics, and other branches in Concordia Seminary, Springfield, Ill.; retired 1890 on account of ill health; served two small churches in the vicinity of Springfield; founder of the colored mission in Springfield; revised the *Altenburger Bibelwerk;* d. Jan. 21, 1899.

X

Xaverian Brothers. A religious teaching institute of laymen, founded in Belgium in 1839, primarily for American work. It entered the United States in 1854.

Xavier, Francis (1506—52). Famous Jesuit missionary and a man of ex-

traordinary earnestness, energy, and devotion; one of the original number who, with Loyola, formed the Society of Jesus; ordained to the priesthood in 1537; began his missionary labors in India (later in Japan) in 1542 and achieved astonishing results, at least *numerically.*

Xenophanes (6th century B. C.). Greek philosopher; regarded as founder of the Eleatic school; opposed anthropomorphic conceptions of God; regarded God as one.

Ximenes (Jimenes), Francisco (1436 to 1517). Spanish provincial of the Franciscan order, confessor to Queen Isabella, archbishop of Toledo and primate of Spain, cardinal, inquisitor general of Spain, soldier, and statesman; founded the University of Alcala de Henares (Complutum) and planned the *Complutensian Polyglot Bible,* the first Bible with various languages in parallel columns. Made regent in 1516; dismissed by Charles V.

XPI. The first three Greek capital letters of the word *Christos* (chi, rho, iota).

Y

Yang. See *Confucianism, 3.*

Yi-King. See *Sacred Literatures.*

Yin. See *Confucianism, 3.*

Ylvisaker, Ivar D. B. at Trondhjem, Norway, May 26, 1868; brought to America as child; studied at Luther College, Decorah, Iowa, Luther Seminary, St. Paul, Minn.; held pastorates at Great Falls and Helena, Mont., Mayville, N. Dak.; pres. of the North Dakota District of the Norwegian Lutheran Church (since 1917); pres. of the ministerium of the same church; member of several committees and boards, including the one which brought about the merger called the Norwegian Lutheran Church of America (now the Evangelical Lutheran Church). D. 1926.

Ylvisaker, Johannes Thorbjoernsen. B. in Norway, April 24, 1845; emigrated 1871, graduate of Luther College, Decorah, Iowa, and Concordia Seminary, St. Louis; studied at Christiania and Leipzig; pastor at Zumbrota, Minn., 1877; prof. at Luther Seminary 1879; coeditor of *Kirketidende;* author of many books and articles; 1904 created D. D. by Concordia Seminary and Wauwatosa Lutheran Seminary; knighted by King Haakon VII; member of the Norwegian Synod 1871—1917; member of the Norwegian Lutheran Church of America 1917; d. Oct., 1917.

Yoga. One of the six systems of Indian philosophy. Teaches how, by ascetic discipline, concentration of thought, suppression of breath, and sitting immovably, to unite the soul with the Supreme Spirit and thereby to obtain complete control over the body (culminating sometimes in ecstasy and catalepsy), miraculous powers, and finally release from rebirth, *i. e.,* salvation.

York Resolution. An amendment to the constitution of the General Synod, drawn up by H. N. Pohlman for the convention at York, Pa., 1864, after the delegates of the Pennsylvania Ministerium had withdrawn. It was favorably acted upon by the General Synod and adopted by a majority of eighteen District Synods (the four synods which rejected it, however, remained in the General Synod). The amendment reads: "All regularly constituted Lutheran Synods not now in connection with the General Synod, receiving and holding with the Evangelical Lutheran Church of our fathers, the Word of God as contained in the Old and New Testaments, as the only infallible rule of faith and practice, and the Augsburg Confession as a correct exhibition of the fundamental doctrines of the Divine Word, may, at any time, become associated with the General Synod by complying with the requirement of this constitution, according to the ratio specified in Art. 2 d." The same convention adopted essentially the action of the Pittsburgh Synod, framed by C. P. Krauth (1856), defending the Augsburg Confession against charges of error.

See reference under *General Synod;* A. Spaeth, *Charles Porterfield Krauth,* Gen. Council Pub. House, Philadelphia, 1909 (II: 127—39).

Yorker Brethren. See *Brethren, the River.*

Young, Brigham (1801—77). B. at Whitingham, Vt.; converted to Mormonism, 1832; at death of Joseph Smith, 1844, became president; when, under pressure of hostile public sentiment, Mormons determined to leave Illinois, he led his followers successfully to Utah and founded Salt Lake City, 1847; was appointed governor of Utah, 1850; he ruled despotically, violently opposing the United States Government at times, and promulgated the doctrine of polygamy; but through his organizing talent contributed much to the industrial and material development of the community; d. at Salt Lake City.

Young Men's Christian Association. The beginning of the Y. M. C. A. was made in London, June 6, 1844. The original purpose was "to seek to win over young men to the faith and love of Jesus Christ." George Williams was the parent of this movement. Soon the association widened its scope of work by defining its object as being "improvement of the spiritual and mental condition of young men." As a result of the London association two associations were established in 1851, in Montreal and in Boston. When the New York association was founded in 1852, it extended its object to include "the spiritual, mental, and social welfare of young men" and but a few years later amended its fundamental article to read: "The object of this association shall be the improvement of the spiritual, mental, social, and physical condition of young men." "This last broad definition of the aim of the Y. M. C. A. became characteristic of the North American association as a whole . . . and it is from that definition that the entire variety of departments into which the work of the brotherhood is divided has taken its rise." In its earlier years the Y. M. C. A. claimed to be "an essentially religious, pronouncedly religious, an aggressively evangelistic and missionary movement." "The spiritual is the fundamental feature of its fourfold work." While never claiming to be a church, it stressed its purpose of existing and serving the Church; and while these ideas prevailed, the movement was strongly unionistic, members being solicited on the basis of such statements as "Men of all creeds and no creed mingle freely here," "Religious belief or church membership is not an essential." Since 1922 the various branches were permitted to elect or appoint not to exceed ten per cent of its managing board from members of the Association not identified with churches defined as evangelical. As far as the members are concerned, the Y. M. C. A. long since abandoned the evangelical test, except as to officers, its purpose being stated in terms so broad as to eliminate religious convictions as a condition of membership.

The Y. M. C. A. distinguishes between active and associate members, the latter being made up of those who cannot, or do not desire to, pledge their assent to the religious platform of the Y. M. C. A. The organization does not exact any religious pledge or confession from those who simply desire to have access to its colleges, business and vocational schools, gymnasia, reading rooms, etc. Hence it cannot be maintained that by paying for these club, etc., privileges a person enters into spiritual union with the Y. M. C. A. as such. Also, holding a position in the educational program, the athletic departments, libraries, could not be considered a denial of the faith. The program of the association is now almost exclusively on the social side, offering club features at low rates to the young men of the community. Membership (1953) about 4,000,000. TG

Young People's Church of the Air. See *Radio Evangelism*, 5.

Young People's Organizations, Christian. I. 1. *Development of Youth Work in America.* Young people's work in Protestant churches did not begin in individual denominations, but began with the interdenominational program known as the Young Men's Christian Association in 1845, the first boys' department being established in this organization in 1866.

2. Another contribution to the youth movement in Protestant churches was made by the International Society of Christian Endeavor started by Francis E. Clark in 1881, and the young people's societies which were brought into existence as a result of this program.

3. There were other movements which gave impetus to youth work in Protestant churches, such as the Sunday school movement fostered especially in England by Robert Raikes; the Knights of King Arthur, started in 1892 by William Byron Forbush; the Woodcraft Indians, founded in 1902 by Ernest Thompson Seton, a program which may be called a forerunner of the Boy Scout movement in England, coming to the United States in 1910; the International Sunday School Association, beginning to be recognized in 1906.

4. Protestant denominations at first used and adopted youth programs developed outside the Church. Gradually they began to publish their own materials.

5. Boston University set up a Department of Religious Education in 1918. In 1920 this university set up a Department of Young People's work.

Since that time other colleges and universities have established courses dealing with youth work.

6. The trend in Protestant denominations in later years has been toward co-operation and interdenominational activities. This trend is evident also in the Protestant youth programs, especially in the United Christian Youth Movement, "a co-operative effort on the North American continent of Protestant denominations and state and national interdenominational youth agencies to unite young people in a program of action." Purposes are "to give to young people a sense of comradeship with all other Christian youth," and "to express the basic unity in Christ of that mighty company dedicated to the building of a Christian world." Other co-operative efforts include the United Student Christian Council, a federation on the national level of twelve church student movements, the Student Y. M. C. A. and Y. W. C. A., the student volunteer movement, and the interseminary movement; the World Student Christian Federation, seeking to unite internationally the efforts of Protestant students; the Youth for Christ movement, sponsored not by denominations, but independently.

II. *Lutheran Organizations Outside Synodical Conference.* 1. *The Luther League of the American Lutheran Church.* The Luther League was organized in 1930 and includes the youth groups of the American Lutheran Church, formed in 1930, when the Buffalo Synod, the Iowa Synod, and the Joint Synod of Ohio and Other States merged. National headquarters are in the Wartburg Press Building, 57 East Main St., Columbus 15, Ohio. Its membership is 37,000 in 1,665 leagues (1954). There are 165 young adult groups with 3,300 members. Conventions are held biennially. The program is under a youth director, nominated by the general board of the Luther League and elected by the youth board of the American Lutheran Church. Financial support is obtained through the Good Faith offerings of the Luther Leaguers and an apportionment in the budget of the Church.

A youth magazine, *One,* is published by the Luther Leagues of the American Lutheran Church, the Evangelical Lutheran Church, the Lutheran Free Church and the United Evangelical Lutheran Church.

2. *The Youth Program of the Au-gustana Evangelical Lutheran Church.* Many societies and a number of Conference Leagues were in existence in the Augustana Evangelical Lutheran Church before the organization of the Synodical Luther League December 2—4, 1910. The League was followed by the Synodical Luther League Council in 1924. In 1927 the Church provided for an executive secretary, now termed Youth Director, and appropriated funds for this office. In 1945 the Church provided for a Board of Youth Activities to supervise the youth program of the entire Church, including the Augustana Luther League. The Luther League is the youth organization in the Augustana Evangelical Lutheran Church. It numbers 40,000 Leaguers, of whom 35,000 are Hi-Leaguers and Senior Leaguers and 5,000 Confirmation Leaguers. There are 1,250 societies (1954). The governing body of the Luther League is the Augustana Luther League Council, consisting of the elected executive committee and the presidents of the thirteen Conference Luther Leagues. The Council meets biennially. The Augustana Luther League sponsors biennial international youth conferences, which have no business meetings, but have a program that is educational and inspirational. The program of the Luther League is financed through offerings of the Leaguers; the Board of Youth Activities receives funds from the Church, which also salaries the Youth Director. The Luther League is intergrated with the Church as follows: The Youth Director, in addition to carrying out the program outlined by the Board of Youth Activities of the Church, guides the program and activities of the Augustana Luther League. The President of the Luther League is a member of the Board of Youth Activities. National offices are at 2445 Park Ave., Minneapolis 4, Minn.

3. *The Young People's Luther League of the Evangelical Lutheran Church.* When in 1917 the Hauge Synod, the Norwegian Synod, and the United Norwegian Church joined to form the Norwegian Lutheran Church of America, renamed in 1946 the Evangelical Lutheran Church, the Young People's Luther League was formed as the youth organization of this new body. Conventions are held biennially. The Luther League elects and salaries its executive secretary. Its program is financed through the Youth in Action

offering. National offices are at 422 S. 5th St., Minneapolis 15, Minn. This League numbered (1950) 2,500 societies and 80,000 members.

4. *The Luther League Federation of the Lutheran Free Church.* The Luther League Federation was organized at a meeting held Nov. 12—14, 1920. The Federation since 1944 employs a part-time youth director. Funds are provided by the offerings of the Leaguers. The national office is at 2122 Riverside Ave., Minneapolis 4, Minn. The membership of the Federation is about 8,000 young people in 300 societies (1954).

5. *The Luther League of the United Evangelical Lutheran Church.* Youth work in societies and districts has been carried on since 1896. The Luther League was organized in 1935. There is a part-time youth director. Funds for the program are gathered through Good Faith offerings from the local leagues, through budget allotments of the Church and synodical districts, through other agencies of the Church, and through other sources. Membership: 2,758 members in 153 societies (1954).

6. *The Luther League of America of the United Lutheran Church in America.* The first national convention of young people from those congregations which in 1918 organized the United Lutheran Church in America convened Oct. 30—31, 1895. Oct. 31, 1895, is regarded as the organization date of the Luther League of America. In 1918 the Luther League became the official youth organization of the United Lutheran Church. Conventions are held biennially. Funds are gathered through the contributions from the Luther League societies, an appropriation of the Church, and special gifts of friends. There is a full-time executive secretary. Publication: *Luther Life.* The national office is at 405 Muhlenberg Building, 1228 Spruce St., Philadelphia 7, Pa. Membership: 31,560 in 1,950 societies (1954).

7. *The American Evangelical Lutheran Youth Fellowship of the American Evangelical Lutheran Church.* It was with the idea of enjoying the life described by Bishop Grundtvig that the young people of the American Evangelical Lutheran Church organized youth societies with a program consisting of Danish folk music and sacred music, folk games and folk dances of Denmark, a program of lectures on religious, cultural, and historical subjects, and current events. The church-wide

League was organized in 1900. The League has always defended its right to remain a separate organization in the Church. There are annual conventions. Funds are gathered through national dues, a grant from the Church, and the Youth Sunday offerings. Membership is 925 (1952) in 50 societies.

8. *The Luther League of the Suomi Synod.* Youth work in the Suomi Synod began in organized form in 1894, when a seaman mission pastor formed a young people's Christian association in San Francisco. The present synodical Luther League was organized in 1944. A field secretary is elected by the synod. Biennial conventions are held. Financial support is received from the Luther League Conferences. The membership is 1,651 in 94 societies.

III. *Youth Organizations in the Synodical Conference.* 1. *The Walther League.* Youth organization of the Lutheran Synodical Conference; organized May 23, 1893, Trinity Church, Buffalo, N. Y.; national office: 875 North Dearborn St., Chicago 10, Ill.

Membership: Young people, approximately ages 13—24, 80,000 membership in United States and Canada; 3,656 societies, 1,121 Junior, 2,535 Senior and Combined (1953).

Objects: To assist in keeping the young people in the Church; to promote systematic study of the Bible and constant growth in Christian knowledge; to assist in training the young people for a life of Christian service; to assist the pastors in serving fellow Lutherans who are traveling and who are away from home; to further love for, and to assist in, increasing active participation in the mission work of the Church both at home and abroad; to foster Christian love and fellowship and to provide material for wholesome recreation; to encourage the support of charitable endeavors in the Lutheran Church; to promote loyalty to the Christian home; to help organize and maintain societies; to unite all young people's societies in the Synodical Conference in one body and thus establish a closer outward union between them.

Program: The program functions under the guidance of the Executive Secretary called by the Executive Board, who serves as head of the Christian Growth department. Assistants responsible to the Executive Board through the Executive Secretary are called or appointed as needed. In 1954 there are: the Managing Director, who supervises all business affairs; the Managing Editor, and the Promotion Manager. The program includes Bible study, worship, missions, topics, parish help, recreation, charity, special projects, quest for talent, talent festival, choral union, Lutheran Service Volunteer schools, conferences, camps, conventions, rallies, financial contributions, publications, Wheat Ridge Foundation. The League trains regional youth workers who work under the direction of the executive board.

The League supports the Wheat Ridge Foundation maintaining the Lutheran Sanatorium at Wheat Ridge, Colo., serving Lutherans afflicted with tuberculosis. The League has developed a program of medical social work with social workers in a number of cities. Scholarships are given for graduate study of medical social work. This program is supported through the annual Christmas seal effort.

Another major effort in the League program is leadership training. The League and the Board for Young People's Work of The Lutheran Church — Missouri Synod since 1944 have conducted Lutheran Service Volunteer schools for the youth of the Church to help them develop in worship, working with groups, community singing, recreation, drama. Youth workers' conferences are conducted for pastors, teachers, and other youth workers since 1948.

Publications: *Walther League Messenger*, Alfred P. Klausler, editor; *Workers Quarterly*, Alfred P. Klausler, editor; O. P. Kretzmann, *The Pilgrim* and *The Road Back to God;* Andrew Schulze, *My Neighbor of Another Color;* A. R. Kretzmann, *Symbols;* W. G. Polack, *How the Missouri Synod Was Born; Walther League Manual; ABC of Youth Work.*

Staff: Executive secretary; managing director; assistants; 25 to 30 full-time paid employees.

Finances: The League owns its own building in Chicago; supports its program through freewill offerings and other projects; budget about $89,000 a year.

The Lutheran Church — Missouri Synod in 1920 elected a Board for Young People's Work, composed of two pastors, two teachers, and one layman. Synod has charged this board to promote and guide work among young people in all Districts and congregations of Synod; to effect full co-operation between the Board and the Wal-ther League Executive Board by means of representatives and reports between these two boards; to encourage all congregations to organize youth societies and to affiliate them with the Walther League; to make suggestions to the seminaries and teachers' colleges for courses in youth work; to provide suitable materials for official periodicals of Synod; to arrange youth conferences; to encourage the formation of youth committees in the Districts; to provide leadership training schools for young people and also for pastors, teachers, and lay counselors.

2. *The Luther League of the Slovak Evangelical Lutheran Church.* The Luther League was organized Sept. 5, 1927. Conventions are held annually. National dues are gathered in the societies. In addition to materials prepared by the League, some of the materials of the Walther League are used. The membership is approximately 850. Expenditures are about $1,500 annually.

Inter-Church Activities of Lutheran Youth Groups. For a number of years some of the Lutheran youth organizations have planned and worked together in discussing youth problems, sharing experiences and materials, and taking joint actions on some projects. Luther Leagues of the denominations represented in the American Lutheran Conference, the United Lutheran Church in America, and the Suomi Synod prepare topics jointly. In 1937 the youth groups of the Churches composing the American Lutheran Conference held simultaneous conventions and some joint sessions. Since 1946 the All-Lutheran Youth Leaders Council, composed of youth leaders of ten Lutheran youth groups, have met in January. Their purpose is to get acquainted with each other and to learn from one another. In 1948, young people and leaders of Lutheran youth groups met for an All-Lutheran Youth Conference. Some training schools and camps are operated jointly. Four youth groups jointly publish a youth magazine, *One.*

IV. *Other Official Protestant Youth Organizations* (the statistics, unless otherwise stated, are for 1949):

1. *The Baptist Training Union* (Southern Baptist Convention). Organized 1934; successor to Baptist Young People's Union, 1896—1934; under guidance of Sunday School Board of Southern Baptist Convention, 161 Eighth Ave., North, Nashville 3, Tenn.; aim: training of the individual

in church membership. Young people served: 224,757 (1952).

2. *The Baptist Youth Fellowship* (American Baptist Convention, formerly Northern Baptist Convention). Organized 1941; designed to serve the 400,000 young people in the Church; aim: to build Christ-centered lives, encourage world understanding, missionary effort, study and adjustment of political, social, and economic issues; five standing committees: personal Christian living, evangelism, world service, Christian citizenship, leadership; national office: 1703 Chestnut St., Philadelphia 3, Pa.

3. *The Baptist Young People's Union* (Baptist Convention of Ontario and Quebec, official since 1936). Organized 1891; first national convention 1936; 10,261 young people; aim: win other youth to Christ and Church; Bible study; deepen personal religious experience; support missionary program; office: 223 Church St., Toronto 2, Ontario, Canada.

4. *Christian Youth Fellowship* (Disciples of Christ). Organized 1938; office: 222 Downey Ave., Indianapolis 7, Ind.; first national meeting 1943; 250,000 young people; opportunity for missionary activities offered through the United Christian Missionary Society; aim: develop consciousness of God and sense of personal relationship to Him; an understanding and appreciation of Jesus' life and teachings, the Bible, Christian interpretation of life.

5. *Westminster Fellowship* (Presbyterian Church, U. S. A.). Organized 1943; first national meeting 1944; 309,312 young people; aim: acquire dynamic faith through Christian experience, worship, study, join with others to build Christian world; office: 1105 Witherspoon Building, Philadelphia 7, Pa.; four commissions: faith and life, stewardship, Christian fellowship, Christian outreach.

6. *The Presbyterian Youth Fellowship* (Presbyterian Church, U. S.). Organized 1895; first national meeting 1903; 125,000 young people; aim: develop Christian fellowship, train for Christian service, bring way of Christ to bear on society; national office: Box 1178, 8 North 6th St., Richmond 9, Va.; special projects: missions, finance, Negro fellowships, Youth Sunday.

7. *Cumberland Youth Fellowship* (Cumberland Presbyterian Church). Young people, 15,000; aim: lead youth to Christ as Savior, Friend, Companion, Lord, and follow Him, to develop in

participation in life and work of Church, Christian fellowship, through Christ build better community and world; national office: McKenzie, Tenn.

8. *The Young People's Christian Union* (General Synod of the Associate Reformed Presbyterian Church). Organized 1884; first national meeting 1895; membership in Union: 1,200; three commissions: Christian faith and life, Christian missions and service, Christian comradeship; national office: Winnsboro, S. C.

9. *Youth Fellowship* (United Presbyterian Church). Organized 1874; first national meeting 1889; aim: to develop leadership; foster spiritual growth; provide opportunity for Christian service, fellowship, recreation; four commissions: worship, study, service, recreation; national office: 209 9th St., Pittsburgh 22, Pa.

10. *The Youth Fellowship* (Evangelical and Reformed Church). Organized 1937; first national meeting 1937; 200,000 young people; aim: to know God better, worship, study His Word, do His will, know Jesus and His way and follow Him, know their Church, take part in work, develop love to Church, join others in fellowship and work, serve needy and good causes; national office: 1505 Race St., Philadelphia 2, Pa.

11. *Reformed Church Youth Fellowship* (the Reformed Church in America). Organized 1946: first annual conference 1950; estimated number of young people, 30,000—40,000; aim: bring activities of youth into unity of purpose and action; encourage Christian attitudes; promote world mission of Church; national office: 156 Fifth Ave., New York 10, N. Y.

12. *Methodist Youth Fellowship* (the Methodist Church). Organized 1939; first national meeting 1940; successor to the Epworth League, including the youth of the former Methodist Episcopal Church, the Methodist Episcopal Church, South, the Methodist Protestant Church; 2,000,000 youth; aim: develop meaningful friendships; build Christian character; provide youth a chance for self-expression; build Christian social order; national office: Box 871, Nashville, Tenn.

13. *The Young People's Missionary Society* (Free Methodist Church of North America). Organized 1919; first national meeting 1931; 6,141 young people; aim: assist youth in church and prepare them for efficient leadership in church, encourage Christian

stewardship, direct Christian activities, encourage Christian growth in grace, and to become intelligent supporters of the missionary program; national office: Winona Lake, Ind.

14. *The Nazarene Young People's Society* (Church of the Nazarene). Organized 1923; first national meeting 1923; 70,000 in the organization in the U.S., 7,000 in other countries; aim: build Christian experience and holy character, save others; national office: Box 527, 2923 Troost Ave., Kansas City 10, Mo.

15. *The American Moravian Youth Fellowship* (Moravian Church in America). Planning to organize in 1950; 5,600 youth; aim: strengthen bonds between youth to serve Jesus Christ; national office: 69 West Church St., Bethlehem, Pa.

16. *Church of the Brethren Youth Fellowship* (Church of the Brethren). Organized 1904; first national meeting 1919; aim: to demonstrate that God is Owner of all things, to develop loyalty to Jesus Christ and His way of life, study New Testament and follow it, work and worship with youth of other denominations, races, nations, live moderately, eat temperately, dress simply, stress home and rural heritage, devote time to private devotion, family worship group meditation; national office: 22 South State St., Elgin, Ill.

17. *The Anglican Young People's Association* (Church of England in Canada). Organized 1902; first national meeting 1931; aim: for Christ and the Church, promote religious, social, intellectual welfare; principles: worship, work, fellowship, edification; national office: 604 Jarvis St., Toronto 5, Ontario, Canada.

18. *Pilgrim Fellowship* (Congregational Christian Churches). Organized 1936; first national meeting 1938; aim: practice Christian patriotism which recognizes the authority of God in conscience as supreme, achieve Christian personality patterned after Jesus, work for a united church, practice Christian freedom, promote program of Jesus, work for international peace and security, secure equal rights and opportunities for all, strive for justice in the social order; four commissions: personal action, social action and service, missionary action, interdenominational action; national office: 19 South La Salle St., Chicago 3, Ill.

19. *The Youth Fellowship of the Evangelical United Brethren Church* (Evangelical United Brethren Church).

Organized 1946; first national meeting 1946; 140,000 young people; aim: to lead youth to an understanding and appreciation of Jesus Christ and acceptance of Him as Savior and Lord in all of life and conduct, to provide opportunity for service, to unite youth for Christ and the Church, encourage to faithfulness, unity activities, train youth for Christian work; national office: 1900 U. B. Building, Dayton 2, Ohio.

20. *Friends Youth Fellowship* (Five Years Meeting of Friends). Organized 1935; aim: to help young Friends to know through experience the love of God, to help youth understand that basic teachings of Jesus are meant for this world without diminution, to help youth carry out these principles of Jesus Christ; national office: 101 South 8th St., Richmond, Ind.

21. *Seventh-Day Baptist Youth Fellowship* (Seventh-Day Baptist Church). Organized 1940; aim: Christian fellowship, education in Christian beliefs, learning to worship and lead in worship; national office: Alfred Station, New York.

V. *Roman Catholic Youth Organizations. The National Catholic Youth Council* was initiated in 1937 and operates under the Youth Department of the National Catholic Welfare Conference. There are two sections: the diocesan and the college and university sections. The primary purpose of the diocesan section is to place youth's forces under the sponsorship of the ordinary. The college and university section is divided into two sections: one serving students in Roman Catholic colleges, the other to serve Roman Catholic students in other colleges; the National Federation of Catholic College Students and the Newman Club Federation, respectively. The National Catholic Youth Council provides on a national scale a device by which all existing youth councils and organizations of the Roman Catholic Church are unified. National offices are at 1312 Massachusetts Ave., N. W., Washington, D. C.

The Sodality of Our Lady was founded in the Roman College of the Society of Jesus in 1563 by a young Jesuit teacher, John Leunis, who wanted to band together in a lay religious order young men in colleges. The order aims to strengthen Catholic life in parish and school; to promote Catholic social action; to foster devotion, reverence, and love to the Virgin

Mary and thereby develop the religious and spiritual life of its members. Sodalists are promised various indulgences. Annual summer schools of Catholic Action are conducted in St. Louis as well as in regional schools. National offices: 1315 South Grand Blvd., St. Louis, Mo. CP

A Classified Bibliography of Youth Publications, United Christian Youth Movement, Chicago, 1948; M. M. Chambers, Youth Serving Organizations, American Council on Education, Washington, D. C., 1948; M. M. Chambers and Elaine Exton, Youth, Key to America's Future. An Annotated Bibliography, American Council on Education, Washington, D. C.; Harner, Youth Work in the Church, Abingdon-Cokesbury, 1942; current program materials of the youth organizations.

Gerald Jenny, The Youth Movement in the American Lutheran Church, Augsburg Pub. House, Minneapolis, 1928; C. Peters, Developments in the Youth Program of the Lutheran Churches in America, unpublished thesis, Concordia Seminary, St. Louis, 1951; ABC of Youth Work, Walther League, Chicago, 1949; T. C. Coates, "A Century of Youth Work," Walther League Messenger, LIII: 334—35; 363—65; W. F. Weiherman (ed.), Fifty Years, Walther League, Chicago, 1943; H. E. Simon, Background and Beginnings of Organized Youth Work in the Missouri Synod, unpublished thesis, Concordia Seminary, St. Louis, 1944; O. H. Theiss, "The Way of the Years," Walther League Messenger, LI: 480—83; 508—10; 512; Walther League Manual, Chicago, 1935.

Daniel A. Lord, The New ABC of Sodality Organization, The Queen's Work, St. Louis, 1947; National Catholic Welfare Conference, Washington, D. C.; Proceedings, National Conference on Catholic Youth Work, 1947, Youth Dept., N. C. W. C., Washington, D. C. (also the agenda of the second conference, 1949); Youth Series, The Youth Dept., N. C. W. C., Washington, D. C.

Young Women's Christian Association of the United States of America. This society originated as a Union Prayer Circle, formed in New York by Mrs. Marshall O. Roberts. The name was changed in the same year to Ladies' Christian Association. Its purpose was "to labor for the temporal, moral, and religious welfare of young self-supporting women." In 1866 the name was changed to Ladies' Christian Union, and in the same year the Young Women's Christian Association of Boston was organized. In the course of years similar organizations were founded, which then developed into the present Young Women's Christian Association. Its purpose is to look after the mental, physical, social, and spiritual interests of young women. Any young woman of good moral character may become a member. In character, work, and methods the organization closely resembles the Young Men's Christian Association. A Young Women's Christian Association of Great Britain and Ireland was organized in 1855.

Youth Work. Youth work in the Church is the training of youth in Christian growth during the post-confirmation period. Through such training, young people are taught the truths of the revealed Word of God. Having been brought to faith in Jesus Christ as their personal Savior through the work of the Holy Spirit, youth work aims to help the young people grow in faith, in understanding of the will and purpose of God, in Christian living. Thus young people are helped to grow up that they are "the salt of the earth" and "the light of the world" in their life in the home and family, in the Church, in the State, in economic relationships, and in society at large.

Youth is often dissatisfied with education, with living conditions, with their elders. Youth wants to learn, wants to obtain the right kind of knowledge, and youth wants counsel and help.

Seeking to learn, youth finds itself in an age in which man thinks that he is able to develop himself to perfection, that he is not by nature sinful, that the machine age is hastening this progress to perfection. Today's youth is living in an age in which the Church is losing its influence among many. Youth sees many church people confess one thing and often do the opposite. Many people are unable to understand what personal religion may mean in their lives. Wavering between two opposites, the revealed religion of the Triune God and the notion that man does not need God, modern man experiences an uncertainty and fear which is reflected in modern youth. Thus modern youth is heir to the split personality of the twentieth century which plagues this generation.

The problems of youth are many: sex, morals, their economic future, a vocation, unemployment, war and peace, problems of personal faith and religion, social adjustments, community life, life in the Church, education, and others.

Youth is idealistic. The Church seeks to meet this idealism by providing a satisfying youth program through the Board for Young People's Work and the International Walther League, a program which encourages and guides in Christian growth, centered in the conquering Christ (see *Young People's Organizations*, III, 1).

Through Bible study, mission study and activities, topics, parish help, recreation, charity, quest for talent, serving as officers, committee and board members, and other activities, young people participate in a youth program in the home societies and congregations.

Uniting in a program of fellowship and inspiration and recreation at zone rallies, young people share with one another their experiences, study together, discuss matters of importance to their faith and living, play together, worship together, and thus strengthen and encourage one another.

In international and district endeavors, such as the Talent Festival, Choral Union concerts, Lutheran Service Volunteer schools, conferences, camps, conventions, rallies, Christian giving, publications, Wheat Ridge Foundation, etc., young people experience the larger fellowship with others who with them are enjoying their fellowship in Christ.

The Church, through the Walther League and the Board for Young People's Work, conducts youth workers' conferences for pastors, teachers, youth leaders, Walther League officers, to help them in carrying out the program with ever greater effectiveness. The program includes worship, group work technique, community singing, recreation, drama, Bible study, and provides for actual participation in working out the activities.

Utilizing the program for youth, working usually through pastors, parochial school teachers, youth counselors, the Church offers guidance and help to its youth. Especially effective is the experience of young people to work and play with a group of other young people. If the youth leader will refrain from being too censorious and negative, but will be one of the group, will plan and work and play with them, he becomes an important person to the young people to help them solve their own problems. Young people then realize that their leader understands them, is interested in them, wants to be helpful where he can. Having established rapport between himself and the group, the youth worker will find that young people will seek him out to talk about their problems. The successful youth leader will develop the art of listening and of helping the youth to see several possible solutions, and thus he will help young people to find their own solution.

Providing a Christ-centered youth program (see *Young People's Organizations*, III, 1), guiding the youth in using this program toward realizing Christian growth, thus also bringing about a more integrated personality, a greater ability to meet the problems of life by deepening the Christian faith and trust in God, the Church seeks to prepare its youth for this life and for life eternal. CP-LCW

See references under *Young People's Organizations* and *Recreation;* American Youth Commission, *Youth and the Future*, American Council on Education, Washington, D. C.; *Christian Growth*, Walther League, Chicago, 1948; S. Hiltner, *Pastoral Counseling*, Abingdon-Cokesbury, Nashville, 1949; A. B. Hollingshead, *Elmtown's Youth*, J. Wiley & Sons, New York, 1949; A. R. Kretzmann, "What Young People Do for the Church," *Today*, Feb.-March, 1948, 84—96; *Worship, A Christian Outline*, Walther League, Chicago, 1944 and 1948 (mimeographed); P. H. Landis, *Adolescence and Youth*, McGraw-Hill, New York, 1947; H. M. Bell, *Youth Tell Their Story*, American Council on Education, Washington, D. C., 1938; Georgine Theiss, *Drama*, Christian Growth Pamphlet XI, Walther League, Chicago, 1949; O. H. Theiss, *Group Work*, Walther League, Chicago (mimeographed); *Walther League Messenger*, monthly publication of the Walther League, Chicago; R. C. Wick, *Toward Understanding Youth*, Bd. of Youth Activities, Augustana Ev. Luth. Church, Minneapolis, 1948; R. M. Wittenberg, *So You Want to Help People*, Association Press, New York, 1947; *Workers Quarterly*, Walther League, Chicago.

Yugoslavia. Area, 99,044 sq. mi; population, 16,545,000 (1952 est.). As a result of World War I the old kingdoms of Serbia and Montenegro and parts of the Empire of Austria-Hungary were constituted a new kingdom. Added treaty awards were made in 1947. On Nov. 29, 1945, the country was declared a republic. The areas formerly known as Croatia and Slovenia are almost wholly Roman Catholic, the remainder of the country Serbian Orthodox. Some ten per cent of the population is Mohammedan. In 1952 some 35,000 Protestants were registered, of whom 5,000 are Lutheran.

Yukon. See *Canada.*

Z

Zahn, Franz (1833—1900). B. Moerss, Germany; inspector of North German Missionary Society 1862; founder of Continental Missions Conference 1866; voluminous author.

Zahn, Gottfried (1705—58). Founder of the orphanage at Bunzlau, which, however, was closed by his enemies in 1753, while he and the teacher were imprisoned. He, however, won Woltersdorf for his cause, and the king granted him a permit to open another orphanage in 1754.

Zahn, Johannes (1817—95). Studied theology at Erlangen and Berlin; teacher at *Lehrerseminar* in Altdorf, lived in Neuendettelsau after retirement; prominent hymnologist and church musician; edited *Bavarian Choralbuch,* also *Die Melodien der deutsch-evangelischen Kirchenlieder.*

Zahn, Theodor (1838—1933). Prof. at Goettingen, Kiel, Erlangen, Leipzig; 1892 at Erlangen as professor of New Testament Exegesis as successor to von Hofmann. He is considered the leader of conservatives in New Testament criticism, in opposition to the radicalism of Adolf Harnack. Zahn's leading works of New Testament studies are the monumental *Einleitung in das Neue Testament* (Engl. trans.) and *Kommentar zum Neuen Testament* (1903 ff.).

Zarathustra. See *Zoroaster.*

Zehner, Samuel (1594—1635). B. at Suhl, south of the Thuringian Forest; at time of his death superintendent at Schleusingen; wrote: "Ach Gott, gib du uns deine Gnad'" while a suburb was being sacked.

Zeisberger, David (1721—1808). Moravian missionary among the Indians; b. at Zanchtenthal, Moravia; d. at Goshen, Ohio. Having emigrated from Saxony to Georgia 1738, he removed to Pennsylvania 1740, founding the towns of Bethlehem and Nazareth. 1743 he entered upon missionary work among the Indians, laboring among the Delawares, Iroquois, and others. But his work suffered grievously through the wars. Zeisberger, at various times, founded towns for his Indian flocks, such as Friedenstadt, Schoenbrunn, Gnadenhuetten (in Ohio), New Salem, Ohio, Goshen, Ohio; but almost all were destroyed. He labored among the Indians from 1743 to 1808, loved and honored as a father.

Zell, Matthaeus (1477—1548). Pastor of the Cathedral in Strassburg (1518); through the influence of the Bible, Luther, and John Geyler, he was won for the evangelical cause; began his reformation activity in 1521 with a series of sermons on Romans; the citizens were won for his cause; his *Christian Vindication,* a reply to attacks of monks, became the basis for the reformation in Strassburg; refrained from participation in theological quarrels; sheltered those persecuted because of their religion (including Caspar Schwenkfeld); excommunicated by Rome in 1524 because of his marriage to Catharina, a highly gifted woman who supported the Reformation through letters and other writings.

Zeller, Christian Henry (1779—1860). B. in Castle Hohen-Entringen, near Tuebingen; studied law at Tuebingen 1797—1801; later made instructor and school superintendent at Zofingen; helped establish a seminary and a home for poor children at Beuggen 1820, which he conducted according to the ideas of Pestalozzi and in a somewhat pietistic manner; wrote: *Lehren der Erfahrung, Seelenlehre.*

Zenana Mission. Name applied to the mission work done in the zenanas (women's apartments) in India, since the status of women in that great country is one which excludes them from social intercourse and confines them to the interior of the home, in a state of complete dependence upon the whims of the men of the house.

Mission work is possible in part through the fact that women may listen behind curtains to the discourses of missionaries, and in part through the faithful work of Bible women, who may visit the inmates of the zenanas and teach them directly. These Bible women are chiefly natives, but there are also many white women engaged in the work.

Zend-Avesta. I. e., Avesta with commentaries (Zend), sacred scriptures of Zoroastrianism and the Parsees, consisting of three parts: Yasna (liturgical texts), Venidad (ritual laws), and Yashts (poems containing mythology and legends of ancient Iran). The most important and oldest part of the Yasna are the Gathas, hymns, most of which are attributed to Zoroaster.

Zeno of Citium (ca. 336—264 B. C.). Greek philosopher; founder of Stoicism.*

Zeno of Elea (b. ca. 490 B. C.). Greek Eleatic philosopher; known for his paradoxes on motion; father of dialectics.

Zezschwitz, Gerhard von (1825—86). Conservative Lutheran theologian; professor of theology at Leipzig, Giessen, Erlangen; a prolific writer, chiefly on practical theology and catechetics; exerted great personal influence as teacher and preacher.

Ziegenbalg, Bartholomaeus (1683 to 1719). The first German Lutheran missionary to India. Educated by August Hermann Francke at Halle, Ziegenbalg and Heinrich Pluetschau were sent by Frederick IV of Denmark as missionaries to India, arriving at Tranquebar, India, July, 1706. Surmounting much opposition on the part both of the Danish governor in India and of the Hindus, he learned the vernacular in a year, did great missionary work, founded a school for native helpers, built a church, still in use today, engaged in much literary work, and translated the New Testament and the Old Testament as far as the Book of Ruth into Tamil. With the assistance of B. Schultze (Madras) and J. E. Gruendler the translation of the whole Bible was completed and published in 1728, being the first translation of the Bible into one of the languages of India. In 1715 Ziegenbalg returned to Germany because of ill health, calling forth much enthusiasm by his addresses and reports. King George I of England, to whom Ziegenbalg had been presented,

wrote him, expressing satisfaction, "not only because the work undertaken by you of converting the heathen to the Christian faith doth, by the grace of God, prosper, but also because that in this our kingdom such a laudable zeal for promotion of the Gospel prevails." In 1716 Ziegenbalg again set out for Tranquebar, but passed away at the age of thirty-six years. The influence of Ziegenbalg and Pluetschau is still felt in India.

Ziegler, Kaspar (1621—90). Studied law, also theology; practiced with great success; friend of Abraham Calov; at time of his death prof. of law at Wittenberg; wrote: "Ich freue mich in dir."

Ziegler, Theobald (1846—1918). German philosopher; prof. at Strassburg; wrote on education and ethics; sought to separate ethics from the supranatural.

Ziethe, Wilhelm (1824—1901). Noted preacher of the positive type of the Prussian Union; pastor in Berlin 1861 to 1895; very popular.

Zikkurat. See *Babylonians, Religion of,* 4.

Ziller, Tuiskon (1817—82). B. at Wasungen; educated at Meiningen and Leipzig; lectured at Leipzig; opened his pedagogical seminary in 1864; founded the Association for Scientific Pedagogy in 1869. Ziller developed and applied to public schools Herbart's ideas, emphasized the moral end of education, demanded that the different parts of study be graded, associated, and unified, history and religion forming the core around which all other subjects are grouped; theory of "concentration." All instruction to contribute to the training of a strong moral character. Works: *Foundation of the Doctrine of Educative Instruction; General Pedagogy.*

Zillerthaler Emigration. An emigration of about four hundred persons who, to escape the persecution following their secession from the Roman Catholic Church, left their native valley (Zillerthal) in Tyrol and found a domicile in Silesia. The emigration took place in 1837, and the exiles united with the Protestant Church of Prussia.

Zimmermann, Ernst Christoph Philipp (1786—1832). German rationalistic theologian; active exponent of the Union in Baden; published sermons; founded *Allgemeine Kirchenzeitung* (Darmstadt) and *Allgemeine Schulzeitung.*

Zimmerman, John L. Prominent layman in Lutheran General Synod; b. March 18, 1956, in Mahoning Co., Ohio; graduated from Wittenberg College 1878; author of the "Merger" resolution in 1918; home in Springfield, Ohio; d. Sept. 17, 1941.

Zinzendorf, Nicolano Ludwig, Count (1700—60). Founder of reorganized Moravian Church, or Unity of Brethren; b. at Dresden; grew up in Pietistic surroundings; made friends with Catholic and Reformed notables on his travels; purchased Berthelsdorf, where he wished to build up a community of heart-and-soul Christians; settled body of Moravians on part of his estate, colony being called Herrnhut, 1722; expelled from Saxony; made Moravian bishop in Berlin 1737; traveled extensively in Europe and America, establishing Moravian colonies (Bethlehem, Pa.); passed his latter days in somewhat depressing circumstances at Herrnhut; wrote many hymns strongly subjective in character, e. g., "Jesus, Thy Blood and Righteousness" (see J. *Wesley*), and many not in keeping with the dignity of the Church. See *Moravian Church.*

Zion City. See *Dowieites.*

Zionism. A modern Jewish movement whose objects are to create an asylum for oppressed and persecuted Jews and to preserve Judaism from becoming submerged in the culture of other peoples. Throughout the centuries Jews have yearned for a Jewish homeland, and this yearning always became intense during persecutions. The anti-Semitism in Europe in the second half of the 19th century resulted in attempts to settle Jews in Palestine; but no organization was effected until Theodor Herzl, a Viennese physician (1860—1904), wrote *Der Judenstaat,* 1896, which resulted in the first Zionist Congress at Basel, 1897, where the Zionist organization was formed and the program formulated "to establish for the Jewish people a publicly recognized, legally secured home in Palestine." Numerous congresses have been held since. However, nothing was achieved until World War I, when Zionism entered a new phase. England and the United States became the centers of Zionist propaganda. In 1917 Balfour expressed the British government's approval of the movement, and proposals intended to "ultimately render possible the creation of an autonomous commonwealth" for the Jews, were adopted at the San Remo peace conference, 1920, which later became a part of the Palestine Mandate given the English Government by the League of Nations.

The Jewish population in Palestine increased rapidly after 1917 (65,000 in 1917; 1,440,000 in 1952). Agricultural settlements were formed; the Hebrew University established on Mt. Scopus; schools and high schools established; Tel Aviv, an all-Jewish city, established; commerce and manufacture promoted.

On May 14, 1948, the independent state of Israel was established, and on February 14, 1949, a constitution setting up a republican form of government was adopted.

Zoar Separatists. See *Communistic Societies,* 5.

Zoeckler, Otto (1833—1906). Prominent Lutheran theologian of the Prussian Union influenced by the Erlangen school; *Privatdozent* at Giessen; professor at Greifswald to the end of his life. Zoeckler was a prolific writer, chiefly on apologetic subjects regarding the inner harmony of revealed religion and true science. The best book on these is perhaps his *Gotteszeugen im Reich der Natur.* He wrote commentaries in *Lange's Commentary,* with H. L. Strack edited a commentary on the Bible; editor of *Handbuch der theologischen Wissenschaften* and of the *Evangelische Kirchenzeitung* (founded by Hengstenberg).

Zorn, Carl Manthey. B. March 18, 1846, at Sterup, Schleswig; graduated at Leipzig, 1870; missionary of the Leipzig Mission Society in India, 1871 to 1876; pastor at Sheboygan, Wis., 1876 to 1881; Cleveland, Ohio (Zion), 1881 to 1911, when he retired; D. D. (St. Louis); a voluminous writer. Among his books are many popular expositions of Bible books, the most comprehensive being that on Colossians; *Bekehrung und Gnadenwahl; Eunike; Crumbs; Food on the Way; Handbook for Home Study; Questions on Christian Topics,* and others; d. July 12, 1928.

C. M. Zorn, *Dies und das aus dem Leben eines ostindischen Missionars,* CPH, 1907; *Dies und das aus fruehem Amtsleben,* CPH, 1912; *Abwaerts, Aufwaerts,* Northwestern Pub. House, Milwaukee, 1910.

Zoroaster. Grecized name of Zarathustra, founder of Zoroastrianism * and alleged author of Zend-Avesta.*

Exact time and place of birth and place of activity unknown; but it seems assured that he lived a considerable time before the 6th century B.C. in Iran. Details of his life also shrouded in obscurity, but tradition tells the following: B. 660 B.C. At age of thirty he received revelations from Ahura Mazdah regarding new monotheism which he was to preach in opposition to contemporary polytheism. For eleven years he went from court to court in Iran without success, until he converted King Vishtaspa, 618 B.C., through whose influence the new religion spread widely. Was slain at the age of seventy-seven in a religious war.

Zoroastrianism. 1. The religion of Persia prior to the Mohammedan conquest. Its traditional founder is Zoroaster,* its sacred book the Avesta.* Other sources are texts written in Pahlavi, the medieval Persian, collected from the third to the ninth century, of which the most important is the *Bundahishn,* a work containing cosmogony, mythology, and legend.

2. Before Zoroaster the religion of the Persians was a polytheistic nature worship (see *Brahmanism*). Among their deities were Mithra, the sun god, Ahura Mazdah, or "Wise Lord," the sky god, a fire spirit, numerous evil spirits, called daevas. This nature worship was reformed by Zoroaster in the direction of a practical monotheism. Of the old gods he chose Ahura Mazdah (later Persian, Ormuzd) and ascribed to him absolute supremacy, rejecting all other gods. The name Mazdeism, therefore, is also applied to the Avestan religion. Zoroaster also taught an ethical dualism, which, as Zoroastrianism developed during the following centuries, became more and more pronounced and the most characteristic doctrine of the system.

3. Beside Ahura Mazdah, who is the creator of the universe, the guardian of mankind, the source of all that is good, and who demands righteousness of his people, there existed from eternity a powerful evil spirit, Angra Mainyu, or Ahriman, who is the source of all evil and the implacable opponent of Ahura Mazdah and who endeavors to lead men from the path of virtue. Between these two spirits is man, who has a free will to choose between good and evil and will be rewarded or punished accordingly. Characteristic of the system also is a well-developed angelology and eschatology.

4. Associated with Ahura Mazdah are a large number of good spirits, presided over by six archangels, the Amesha Spentas, or "Immortal Holy Ones," who are personified attributes of the supreme deity and regarded as his main agencies. They are: Good Thought, Best Righteousness, Wished-for Kingdom, Harmony on Earth, Salvation, Immortality.

5. Opposed to the good spirits and associated with Ahriman is a hierarchy of evil spirits. The conflict between these two forces will continue until the end of the world cycle, which consists of 12,000 years, when Ahura Mazdah will finally triumph and Ahriman be overthrown. The last period of 3,000 years of this cycle begins with Zoroaster's prophetic career.

6. Zoroaster's ethical code lays great stress on "good thoughts, good words, good deeds." To be good, however, means chiefly to abstain from demon worship and to worship Ahura Mazdah and follow his precepts. Body and soul must be kept pure. It is also man's religious duty to foster agriculture, cattle raising, and irrigation, to protect especially the cow and the dog, to abstain from lying and robbery. The elements of earth, fire, and water must be kept from defilement. Because of the last injunction Zoroastrians neither bury nor cremate their dead, as thereby earth and fire would be defiled, but expose them to vultures on "towers of silence." Forgiveness of sins has no place in the system; sins must be counterbalanced by good works. Three days after death the souls cross the Cinvat bridge to be judged, the righteous passing on to heaven, the wicked to the tortures of hell. If good and evil deeds balance exactly, the soul passes to an intermediate place, called Hamestakan, where it experiences neither bliss nor torture.

7. At the Last Day all men will be raised from the dead and subjected to another ordeal. They must pass through molten metal, which causes joy to the good, but extreme pain to the wicked. After that all souls, even of the wicked, being purified, will be taken to heaven and a new world established, which shall endure to eternity.

8. Zoroaster's teachings did not involve a ritual. Later, however, a complete ceremonial worship and a priesthood developed (see *Magi*). Important rites were the preparation of the *haoma,* a sacred drink, and in later

centuries fire ceremonies (see *Fire Worshipers*). Marriage was a religious duty, and intermarriage of those closely related, even of brother and sister, was permitted. Zoroastrianism made considerable progress under the Achaemenian kings (558 to 331 B. C.); but whether it was universally accepted during that period is not known. It received a setback through the conquest of Persia by Alexander the Great and under Greek and Parthian rule had difficulty in maintaining itself. In the Neo-Persian empire (A. D. 226 to 637), under the Sassanid dynasty, it again became the dominant religion; but after the Moslem conquest it began to decline rapidly, yielding to Shiite * Mohammedanism. Due to Moslem persecution many Zoroastrians emigrated to India, where they settled chiefly in the Bombay presidency. These are the Parsees.* See *Religion, Comparative, Bibliography.*

Zschiegner, Max Henry. B. Sept. 9, 1897, in New York State; graduated from Concordia Seminary, St. Louis, 1921; served as missionary to China from 1921 till his sudden death, Jan. 23, 1940; married Helen Marie Rathert, 1922, in China; four sons born to this union. President of Concordia Seminary, Hankow, from 1929; member of *Chinese Lutheran Witness* editorial staff; translator, writer of a number of books in the Chinese language; gifted artist.

Zuccheto. The cap worn by the Roman Catholic hierarchy.

Zucker, John Frederick. B. Sept. 2, 1842, at Breitenau, Bavaria; graduated at Erlangen 1865; missionary of the Leipzig Mission Society in India 1870 to 1876; pastor at Brooklyn, N. Y., 1876 to 1879; professor at Concordia College, Fort Wayne, Ind., 1881—1921; D. D. (St. Louis); President of Concordia College, Fort Wayne, Ind., 1879—81; d. Sept. 13, 1927.

Zuetphen. See *Heinrich Moeller von Zuetphen.*

Zurich, Consensus of. See *Reformed Confessions,* A 8.

Zwick, Johannes (ca. 1496—1542). Studied at various universities; priest in 1518, at Riedlingen in 1522; evangelical preacher at Constance, finally at Bischofszell, where he died of the pestilence; wrote: "Auf diesen Tag gedenken wir."

Zwingli, Confessions of. See *Reformed Confessions,* A 1—5.

Zwingli, Ulrich (1484 to 1531). 1. Founder of Swiss Reformed Church; b. at Wildhaus; received humanistic education; became parish priest, exhibiting lively papal, patriotic, and political interest, at Glarus, 1506—16 (began to study Greek, 1513, and was field chaplain of Swiss forces at battles of Novara and Marignano), at Einsiedeln (ridiculed indulgences as a comedy, but sought and received appointment as papal acolyte), and at Zurich, 1519. Only in 1520, under the influence of Luther's writings, which he had read and spread, did Zwingli begin real reformatory work, preaching against fasting and monasticism, maintaining that the Gospel alone should be the rule of faith and practice, and giving up the papal pension. He contracted a secret marriage, 1522; adopted Hoen's doctrine of the Eucharist, 1524; abolished the Mass, 1525; declared (1526) that the truth of his opinion on the Eucharist had been revealed to him in a dream, and called Luther's interpretation of the words of institution "not only uncultivated, but wicked and frivolous"; attended Marburg Colloquy, 1529 (the only meeting with Luther); published (1530) his *Ratio Fidei,* an exposition of the Christian faith, which shows that he had indeed a spirit very different from that of Luther; set on foot far-reaching politico-religious schemes; humiliated the Catholic cantons, 1529, but fell at Cappel, 1531.

2. Like Luther, he was a born musician and fond of company; unlike Luther, he defended the death penalty for unbelievers. Both recognized Scripture as the only authority in religion, but Zwingli interpreted it to satisfy his reason.

Jean Grob, *Life of Ulric Zwingli,* Funk and Wagnalls, 1883; S. M. Jackson, *Huldreich Zwingli,* Putnam's, 1900; S. M. Jackson, *Selected Works of Huldreich Zwingli,* U. of Pennsylvania Press, 1901; J. P. Whitney, "The Helvetic Reformation," *Cambridge Modern History,* II: 305—41 (voluminous bibliography of material published to the time of the printing of this work on pp. 773—78).

Zygomalas, John (1498—1578). Secretary to the Eastern Orthodox * patriarchs Joasaph and Jeremiah II; favored cause of Protestants. See *Eastern Orthodox Confessions.*